The College Sourcebook

for Students with Learning and Developmental Differences

Midge Lipkin, Ph.D.

Cover art and design: Erik Ledder

Database and programming: Don Beattie, Mary MacDonald Murray

Editors; Wintergreen Orchard House:
Meghan Dalesandro, Jillian Locke, Tammy Lynn Lucke, Erika Schieck

Copyright Notice

Wintergreen Orchard House is a division of Alloy Education,
an Alloy Media + Marketing company.

Printed in The United States of America

ISBN 1-933119-30-6 College Sourcebook for Students with Learning and Developmental Differences

All inquiries and order requests should be addressed to:
Wintergreen Orchard House
2 Lan Drive, Suite 100
Westford, MA 01886
P: 978 692-9708
F: 978 692-2304
www.WintergreenOrchardHouse.com

ABOUT THE AUTHOR

The information in this book was compiled by Dr. Midge Lipkin to fill a critical information gap she encountered in the course of her educational consulting practice. In assisting clients with the school placement process, she found they needed access to an easily understood, accessible source of data that enabled them to assess, on statistically comparable bases, the merits and possibilities of attending various colleges and universities that accept students with a variety of disabilities.

Dr. Lipkin's current practice focuses on neuropsychological evaluation, college placement, elementary and secondary school counseling, and therapeutic and emotional growth placement. Through Schoolsearch, she provides direct assistance with all phases of the elementary, secondary school, and college selection and placement process. Starting with a detailed analysis of students' objectives, needs, and credentials, she helps them evaluate potential schools and then guides them through the application and follow-up stages.

Dr. Lipkin has many years of experience in the field of education. Some of her professional assignments have been:

- Psychoeducational Advisor, Learning Impairment Training Program, Division of Child Psychiatry, New England Medical Center
- Director of Dorchester Children's Mini School (private day school for emotionally disturbed and learning disabled children)
- Educational Administrator, Dorchester Mental Health, Children's Clinic
- Instructor/Lecturer on teaching students with Learning Disabilities
  - Assumption College
  - Boston College
  - Boston University
  - Lesley College
  - Perkins School for the Blind

In addition to her Ph.D. in School Administration and Special Education, Dr. Lipkin has earned a Certificate for Specific Language Disability from the Massachusetts General Hospital. She also holds an M.A. in Education from Boston University, a B.S. from Lesley College, and is a certified educational planner.

Dr. Lipkin is the author and publisher of *The Schoolsearch Guide to Private Schools in the Northeast*, *The Schoolsearch Guide to Private Schools for Students with Learning Disabilities*, and *The Schoolsearch Guide to Colleges with Programs or Services for Students with Learning Disabilities*.

ACKNOWLEDGEMENTS

I would like to thank my husband, Alton; my children, Stephen, Deborah, and Amy, and their spouses Janet, Peter, and David; and my grandchildren, Todd, Michelle, Margo, Robyn, Heather, Jodi, and Jason for their understanding of this important project. A special thank you to my friend Laurie Nash for her continual suggestions and edits, Cristina Woods for her support as well as her edits, and Lucky Melanson, my dedicated office manager.

A special thank you and my appreciation for all the professionals who contributed articles to make this source book more informative:

Ivy West: *How University of Puget Sound Differentiates High School from College*
David Luker and Ted May: *Learning Disabilities on the College Campus*
David Keevil, Psy.D.: *Attention Deficit-With or Without Hyperactivity*
Marcia Rubinstien: *Nonverbal Learning Disabilities-NLD*
Diane Adreon and Jennifer Drocher: *Asperger's and Higher Functioning Autism*
Kathleen Trainer, MSW, Psy. D.: *Obsessive Compulsive Disorder*
Ann Helmus, Ph.D.: *Neuropsychological Evaluation*
Mark Greenstein: *ACT vs. SAT for Students with Learning Differences*

TABLE OF CONTENTS

Table of Contents: College Profiles by State

INTRODUCTION

Radical changes in the post-secondary school education of students with learning disabilities (LD) have occurred over the last 30 years. Today, thousands of LD students, as well as students with other developmental differences, are earning high grades in U.S. colleges by using a variety of compensatory skills, classroom aids, and special services. When they graduate, they will enter and succeed in business, industry, and the professions. Yet only a few decades ago, most of these students were unable to matriculate because they could not meet college entrance criteria. If admitted, the majority received poor grades or dropped out because they could not handle the academic work. Educators labeled special needs students as dull, lazy, or uninterested and made no effort to discover why they didn't succeed.

This revolution in status was triggered by a chain of events: psychological research, Federal law regarding the public schools, and the rapid development of responsive college-level resources. First, scientists gained a clearer and more compassionate understanding of learning disabilities and how they affect students' performance in the classroom and in life. Diagnostic testing methods were developed to pinpoint students' deficits, and experts evolved teaching techniques to address different learning styles. These advances were reinforced by the passage of Public Law 94–142, the Handicapped Children Act of 1975, which mandated all states to provide compensatory education for LD students through high school.

In 1970, under the guidance of Dr. Gertrude Webb, Curry College (Milton, Massachusetts) became the first college to offer a comprehensive program for students with learning disabilities. Then the rapid growth in the number of LD high school graduates with compensatory training (and shrinking college enrollments) put pressure on the academic community to develop LD-responsive resources. Thus, during the 1980s many other U.S. colleges and universities followed Curry's lead by creating LD programs or offering support services.

Students with special needs who are applying for post secondary education today must understand that in order to qualify for admission, they are required to meet the college and university requirements. Colleges are more aware of these students' needs for accommodations and are often willing to assist them in their quest so they will find success. Diagnostic Criteria DSM-IV includes such diagnoses as OCD (Obsessive Compulsive Disorder), NVLD (Nonverbal Learning Disabilities), Autism Disorder, and Asperger's Disorder; students with these disabilities are enrolled in colleges today. Often these students are high functioning and will be able to adjust to college life and the academic curriculum.

We live in a wonderful time. Students who have learning disabilities are understood. Accommodations and services help these students adjust to campus life. With these resources, students have had successful college experiences. Today, students with developmental differences are also attending college. Many of the same services and accommodations that have assisted students with learning differences are also helping this population to feel confident in college.

A number of articles addressing these differences focus on the services and accommodations students will need to be successful in college. Since many parents and students often ask how a high school education differs from a college education, Ivy West from the University of Puget Sound has drawn specific analogies so students will have a better understanding of these differences.

How University of Puget Sound (UPS) Differentiates High School from College

Personal Freedom in High School	Personal Freedom at UPS
High school is mandatory and probably free.	College is voluntary and very expensive.
Other people structure your time.	You structure your time.
Parents and others guide moral decisions.	You guide your own moral decisions.
Others guide appropriate behavior.	You guide your own behavior.
You are a minor.	You are an adult.

High School Classes	UPS Classes
You go from one class directly to another.	You may have hours between classes.
You spend 30 hours a week in class.	You spend about 15 hours a week in class.
A class lasts for 5 to 10 months.	A class lasts 16 weeks.
Your school day looks full.	Your day looks like you have lots of free time.
Doing homework is the last part of your day.	Homework is an all-day activity.
Homework is highly structured.	Homework is largely self-directed reading.
Homework is collected and graded.	Homework is often not collected or corrected.

High School Teachers	UPS Instructors
Carefully monitor attendance.	Probably notice if you are absent.
Remind you of incomplete work.	Assume you know what you need to do.
Approach you if you seem to need help.	Wait for you to ask for help.
Often available to talk before and after class.	Are available during office hours.
Provide you with what you miss if absent.	Assume you will get what you missed.
Follow a textbook.	Might follow textbook. Lectures are important.
Write key info on board or give hand-outs.	Expect you to figure out what is important.
Teach to the intellectual middle of the class.	Teach to the intellectual top of the class.

Studying in High School	Studying in College
Study an hour or so before a test.	Study 2 or 3 hours per day for each class hour.
Readings are thoroughly discussed in class.	Readings may not be discussed at all in class.
You know what to expect on a test.	Professors say, "Know everything."

Tests in High School	Tests in College
Testing is frequent and covers one section.	Tests occur every 4–6 weeks and cover a lot.
Makeup tests are easily available.	Make-up tests are seldom an option.
The teacher reminds you to make up a test.	You must take initiative for possible make-up.
Review sessions are routine.	Review sessions are rare.
Tests ask you to give back facts.	Exams require analysis and synthesis.

Grades in High School	Grades in College
Everything you do contributes to your grade.	Papers and exams determine grades.
Good homework grades can save you.	Homework carries little or no weight.
Extra credit can help raise a grade.	Extra credit does not exist.
If grades improve, you get the better grade.	Your grades are an average of all exams.
You graduate if you pass required courses.	You graduate if your GPA meets requirements.
Effort Counts	**Results Count**

Chapter I: SCOPE AND PURPOSE

The College Sourcebook for Students with Learning and Developmental Differences provides, in an easy-comparison format, detailed information for the 2005-2006 academic year on colleges and universities as well as some community colleges. This source book covers:

- programs, services, and accommodations for students with specific learning disabilities (LD) and/or attention deficit disorder/attention deficit hyperactivity disorder (ADD/ADHD) as well as developmental differences including nonverbal learning disabilities (NLD), Asperger's Disorder, and obsessive compulsive disorders (OCD);
- related key data, such as:
  - admissions procedures and requirements
  - academic curricula and graduation criteria
  - class size, diversity, and campus facilities

At first glance, the task of finding a suitable college for a student with special needs might seem relatively easy: every university, college, junior college, and community college that receives Federal funds is barred from discriminating against applicants with learning disabilities by Section 504 of the Rehabilitation Act of 1973. (Almost all colleges rely directly or indirectly to some extent on Federal funds for research, scholarships, student aid, and/or other functions.) This Federal requirement holds true only if the LD applicants meet the particular admissions criteria the college has set for all new entrants. No school is required to lower its entrance standards so candidates with learning disabilities and/or developmental disorders can compete successfully against other high school graduates for admission. Even more importantly, no college has to modify its curriculum or provide the support services that many special needs students require to handle academic work.

For any student, the college application process can be time-consuming and challenging because it involves matching his/her academic gifts, interests, and goals with different schools' criteria. For special needs students and their parents, educators, and social services consultants, the task can be particularly tedious, frustrating, and confusing because their range of options is even more complicated.

DEFINING THE APPLICANT'S EDUCATIONAL GOALS AND NEEDS

The Key Questions

Before beginning the college search process, the student, parent, or college counselor needs to assess the potential applicant's strengths and weaknesses and define related academic and life goals. Each of the colleges listed in this directory offers some unique advantages for the special needs students. But none of these schools is right for every student. These colleges vary widely in terms of curriculum, campus location, social atmosphere, sports, and recreation programs, as well as in the remedial programs or support services/accommodations they offer. Therefore, it is important to define the applicant's goals and needs before investigating and comparing the advantages of the various colleges' programs and services.

The key questions that need to be answered are:

- What is the type and the severity of the student's disability?
- What special education factors need to be considered in selecting a college?
- What other educational and social services does the student need to obtain from the college to meet his/her life goals?

Defining The Disability

In order to better understand specific learning disabilities and other developmental differences, professionals around the country have been asked to:

- define the disability;
- explain how each disability is diagnosed;
- discuss the various treatments, both medical and environmental that are effective with these students;
- address the accommodation these students might need when attending college; and
- reveal what students report back, regarding their adjustment to college life

To qualify for participation in any college-level special needs program or to receive related services and accommodations, the student must have a professional evaluation that proves he/she has special needs. Such an evaluation can be obtained through a public school system or from a private evaluator. The specific tests required differ from college to college. A number of the colleges have listed their test requirements. (In some instances, testing may also be conducted by the college or university itself.)

Learning Disability

Public Law (PL) 94-142, the Handicapped Children Act of 1975, mandates that all states provide a free and adequate education for all children, regardless of handicap, through the secondary level. The official legal definition of "learning disability" states:

> *Specific learning disability means a disorder in one or more of the basic psychological processes involved in understanding or using language, spoken or written, which may manifest itself in an imperfect ability to listen, think, speak, read, write, spell, or to do mathematical calculations. The term includes such conditions as perceptual handicaps, brain injury, minimal brain dysfunction, dyslexia, and developmental aphasia. The term does not include children who have learning problems that are primarily the result of visual, hearing, or motor handicaps, mental retardation, emotional disturbance, or environmental, cultural, or economic disadvantage.*

Some colleges with programs or services for students with learning disabilities use a broader definition of "learning disabity" than specified in PL 94-142. But, simply stated, a student is generally deemed to have a learning disability if there is a significant discrepancy between his or her innate cognitive ability and his or her ability to perform in school. The LD student consistently exhibits difficulties in study skills and/or underachieves, performing below the level expected in view of his/her apparent intelligence, health, and life circumstances.

To be eligible for special needs services in the public school system and to qualify for college programs, the student must first undergo a professional evaluation. Field observations, interviews with parents and teachers, and a test battery are correlated to develop a profile of the special needs student. (The test battery usually includes a WISC-IV or a WAIS-III, various tests that pinpoint specific learning disabilities, and social/emotional assessment instruments.) The evaluation culminates in an Individual Education Plan (IEP), which specifies long-term educational goals for the student, annual teaching objectives, and the resources to be executed in working to achieve these goals. PL 94-142 requires public school systems to provide this service for adults as well as school-aged children, but does not require colleges to do so or authorize funding at the college level. (For more detailed information, please refer to Chapter II: Learning Disabilities.)

ADD/ADHD

Until October 1991, all students having an attention deficit disorder (ADD) or an attention deficit hyperactivity disorder (ADHD) were classified as learning disabled. At that time, the Federal government accepted a new classification under the umbrella of Special Needs which covers the more than 300,000 students known to have ADD/ADHD without LD.

ADD is characterized by inattention and impulsivity; in addition, ADHD also includes hyperactivity. The diagnostic criteria required includes onset before age 7, as well as a history of more than six months. Those students classified as ADD/ADHD do not meet the criteria for pervasive developmental disorder, schizophrenia, affective disorder, severe or profound mental retardation, or response to unusual circumstances, (i.e., abuse at home). (Please refer to Chapter III, ADD/ADHD.)

Special Educational Considerations

Most students with special needs have IEPs that specify ongoing guidance and academic counseling throughout high school. To ensure the continuation of special services, it is important that students become aware of their strengths and weaknesses to effectively self-advocate in college. They should have access to a profile of their disabilities, in terms of scope and severity, and reports of the progress made in developing compensatory skills and strategies.

It is crucial to review the student's IEP carefully before selecting a college and not rely solely on the student's relative success in high school as the basis for choice. Even high I.Q. students without any disabilities can find the move from high school to college academically and socially challenging. Most colleges expect students to be self-motivated with self-directed study habits. The level of the academic work in college is much higher than in high school, and the social environment, particularly for students who live on campus, is more sophisticated and thus, can be quite demanding.

Two factors that are critical for success at the college level are good study habits and a sense of self-worth. These attributes seem to pose problems for most special needs students. Strategies learned in high school can prove inadequate for the special needs student in college without the support of a formal program or special services. It is easy to overlook or take for granted the special accommodations (for example, untimed testing or use of a tape recorder for note taking) that the student was permitted in high school and that are necessary if he/she is to keep up with classmates. The applicant needs to find a college(s) that specifically sanctions those accommodations (or equivalents) or offers a full-scale LD program for support, with a faculty advocate to help with special problems.

College Search Criteria

Students with special needs are succeeding in every subject area from anthropology to zoology at colleges and universities across the country. They are participating fully in all other aspects of college life: on and off-campus sports, drama companies, sororities and fraternities, and the myriad other activities that make the college experience memorable. It would be a mistake to focus solely on the availability of programs and services. After all, one cannot become a member of a ski team in most Florida schools or find an esoteric course in archaeology at the local community college that would lead to a high-prestige field work assignment with a world-renowned scientist.

HOW TO SELECT AND APPLY TO AN APPROPRIATE COLLEGE

Special Needs Admissions: Some Reality Checks

For any student with special needs, the college selection and application process can be a reality test of his/her compensatory skills and strategy training. The keys to a successful college placement are research, analysis, planning, and systematic follow-through, the very skills that are difficult for many special needs students. Furthermore, the admissions procedures for college special needs programs are often more time-consuming and more complex than for the standard college applicant. For example, many schools require special needs applicants to take additional tests, submit statements of deficit, or provide other evidence demonstrating the extent and nature of their disabilities.

Unfortunately, many special needs students assume they can attend any college or university that has a special needs program or offers special needs services. Unlike the public school system, colleges do not have to accept students who don't play by their rules. A student who relies on misconceptions about ease of entry is likely to fail to be admitted to the college of his/her choice. In fact, he/she is unlikely to get into any college if paperwork is incomplete or not submitted on time. It is important to check out the specific admissions policy of each college rather than make any assumptions.

These cautions apply whether or not the college has an "open" rather than a "selective" admissions policy or a "rolling" rather than a "fixed" deadline for application submission. In colleges with an open admissions policy, any student with a high school diploma or its equivalent is theoretically eligible to enroll. Many junior colleges and community colleges have open admissions. But keep in mind that some of these schools have a limited number of special needs places, and others are not staffed to handle all types of disabilities.

Selective admission simply means that a school uses a set of criteria to evaluate each applicant for admission. The criteria may include standardized test scores above a certain percentile or a specific high school grade point average (GPA). However, students with lower scores and GPAs should still apply. Most selective admissions schools evaluate each applicant on a variety of factors; therefore, a student whose standardized test scores are below the school's stated cut-off point might still be considered for admission if he or she has strong credentials in other areas.

A rolling application deadline does not mean that the school welcomes last-minute application filing, but simply that the admissions office makes decisions about applications as they arrive. The earlier a student applies, the better the chance for acceptance. Schools with rolling admissions can have either a selective or an open admissions policy.

The division between colleges that offer full LD programs and those that offer services and/or accommodations is fuzzy. One school's program may be another's services. Programs usually have staff specially trained to remediate deficits and to assist students in developing compensatory skills. Some programs require students to attend a pre-freshman orientation to acclimate themselves to the rigorous pace of college. An advocate often assists students in course selection and meets with individual professors to help them understand each student's needs. Programs are often diagnostic and prescribe an educational plan for each student. Tutoring is often a key component of special needs programs.

Some colleges and universities require special needs students to apply a number of months in advance of the regular application deadline. Many schools require the special needs applicant to apply first to the admissions office which will refer the applicant to the special needs program if a disability is suspected or if a statement verifying a disability is included in the application package. The special needs department then determines if the student qualifies for its program and if his/her deficits can be served. Other colleges require special needs applicants to apply directly to the school's special program. (In this case, students may be judged by different standards from those used for students without disabilities.)

In some colleges, services are simply academic assistance, such as tutoring and counseling that are offered to the entire student population, not just special needs students. Other colleges offer services for special needs students that focus on compensating for deficits. Some of the schools with special needs services also have learning centers staffed by trained specialists. (There is sometimes a charge for using these services.) A student who applies to a school with special needs services will generally be judged by the same standards as all other applicants. Once accepted and enrolled, however, he/she may take advantage of these services to succeed in the mainstream academic curriculum.

Many schools with special needs programs or services offer certain accommodations designed to help students with special needs succeed. Academic adjustments may include schedule modifications or special concessions like take-home tests, oral exams, or note takers, as well as special aids, such as tape recorders and word processors. Each school's general policy regarding accommodations is listed in its profile, found in Chapter III. However, the student should be reminded that individual instructors and departments may have different policies.

The Application Process

At the beginning of the senior year of high school, when students determine their final choices and application forms are in hand, they should:

- confirm the suitability of the choices
- obtain advice on filling out college applications
- review the essay for content and grammatical errors
- ask teachers to write recommendations
- request that official high school transcripts are sent to the colleges
- request that official score reports from ACT/SAT be forwarded to the schools
- discuss financial aid resources, if necessary
- confirm that recommendations were mailed

Recently, many colleges have stated that they prefer an electronic application; therefore, it is important to determine this preference before too much time is spent filling out a printed application. Save a copy of the final version for the student's own records. Timely submission is essential.

A word about financial aid: the cost of higher education is indeed high–and it continues to rise. Financial aid, however, is available from a variety of sources. Access depends on one's need and one's willingness to search. High school and private guidance counselors are also a good source of information. Federal funding of compensatory education does not exist at the college level.

Interviewing

Although a number of colleges require or recommend individual interviews, more and more schools do not. Formal college interviews can usually be scheduled during the summer after the student's junior year of high school. When visiting a college, the applicant should ask questions that demonstrate his/her interest in attending that particular school.

Interviews with the special needs department, especially those with programs, are particularly important. Directors of special needs departments are looking for motivated students who can self-advocate. The interviewer wants to determine if the student understands his/her strengths and weaknesses and learn about the accommodations the student successfully used in the past. The colleges want to accept students who will succeed in their environment.

It is also essential at this time for the student to determine if the college can meet his or her needs. It is vital to feel comfortable with the personnel and with the services that will be offered. Both the student and the special needs department should determine if there is a fit.

The following are typical questions students should be prepared to answer:

- Describe your learning or developmental difference.
- When was your disability first diagnosed?
- Describe your academic strengths and weaknesses.
- Were you enrolled in a special needs program in high school?
- Have you had private tutoring?
- If you have been tutored, describe your most successful experience.
- How much time did you spend studying each day for each subject?
- What accommodations do you feel you would need in college?
- How much individual or group tutoring do you feel you will need in college?

At the same time, the student should also ask a number of questions to clarify his/her needs:

- Who determines the services and accommodations that I will receive?
- Will I have individual or group tutoring?
- How often can I have a tutor?
- Will I have an advocate?
- Who is responsible for contacting my professors for accommodations?
- Will I be allowed to carry a lighter course load?
- What are the hours that the center is open for help?

Chapter II: LEARNING DISABILITIES

LD Defined

Chances are most people have met someone who has a learning disability. Current statistics from numerous studies indicate that between 6% and 8% of the school age population have learning disabilities. Learning disabilities can impact a person throughout their lives, however it is in the formal educational environments where the majority of people with LD are impacted.

The perception of the term "learning disability" by the general public spans a gamut of views. The most negative belief is that learning disabilities are just an excuse for poor school performance. Students may struggle to maintain a positive self esteem since they are often perceived as being academically lazy, unmotivated, or not that bright.

People who have educated themselves about learning disabilities realize that people with learning disabilities have many notable attributes, including:

- To have an LD, a person must have an average to above average I.Q,
- People with LD often benefit from having instructors use pedagogical practices that incorporate a variety of teaching modalities,
- There are adjustments, modifications, or accommodations that can help level the academic playing field for individuals with LD, and
- People with LD lead successful and productive lives!

The Individuals with Disabilities Educational Act (IDEA) is federal legislation that protects students in the primary and secondary grades (pre-school through high school graduation). Section 504, The Rehabilitation Act of 1973 (Section 504) and the Americans with Disabilities Act, 1990 (ADA) protects all students regardless of academic placement (secondary or post-secondary). However, ADA and Section 504 both have distinctly different provisions for post-secondary students. Know what your responsibilities and the institutional responsibilities are as a student at the post-secondary level.

Diagnosing LD

The diagnostic process for determining whether or not a student has a learning disability can be lengthy and involve a number of different steps. Diagnostic assessment is approached differently by each school district and often by individual local school. In public education, the assessment procedure is usually initiated by a teacher, a parent, or the student themselves. A referral to assessment is often made when there is a concern about difficulties in a specific academic area, with a specific academic skill or with the person's content mastery. The first step in the process is to intervene in the least intrusive manner possible. This includes teachers gathering information about a student's academic performance and then a team of educators, along with the student and parent, developing strategies to be used in the classroom. If these classroom interventions prove unsuccessful, a teacher, parent, or student can request that a special education evaluation be conducted.

Many schools and clinicians, until recently, diagnosed learning disabilities using standardized tests of cognitive ability, as well as achievement tests in the areas of reading, math, and writing. The diagnosis of a learning disability is attained by detecting a numeric discrepancy (usually a formula) between the student's actual performance scores when compared to expected achievement test scores.

However, the recent reauthorization of IDEA in late 2004 brought about significant changes to the diagnostic process for learning disabilities. I.Q./achievement discrepancy is no longer the primary method used to identify students as having a learning disability. According to this new view, the discrepancy models work against students by postponing instructional support services for struggling students. If services could be provided when the student experiences academic difficulty, the new argument states, then academic problems may/could be prevented. The reauthorization discussion did bring into question whether or not learning disabilities were real or just differences.

The new approach to identification and assessment of students with learning disabilities allows the classroom teacher to intercede and hopefully result in the student's academic difficulty being resolved without having to identify the student as having a disability. This approach proposes that by using the best educational practices available, such as, practices with recognized effectiveness, practices that are scientifically-based and researched instructional approaches, a student's academic difficulties can be corrected without needing to use special education services.

Various Treatments

People don't outgrow their learning disability but do learn to compensate and go on to live very fulfilling lives. Even though a learning disability does not disappear, given the right types of educational experiences and the right compensatory strategies, a student's ability to learn is comparable to his non-LD peers. The brain's flexibility to learn is enormous, and research continues to reinforce that human beings retain this ability to learn throughout life.

Even though learning disabilities cannot be cured, there is hope. Because certain learning problems reflect delayed development, many students do eventually catch up. An individualized, skill-based approach often succeeds in helping, as do learning activities which engage several skills and senses. What is often seen by LD professionals at the University of Denver is that graduating students find a work environment which is very compatible with the way they learn, find the work environment more hospitable to their learning needs, and as a result, find this work environment easier to succeed in.

Any well-researched treatment recommended by a qualified professional is likely to have some value. There is rarely just "one" intervention that will have a positive impact on a child with a learning disability. Often, a multidimensional educational approach works best. "Cure" therapies-including computer software, one-size-fits-all reading programs, restricted diets, special glasses, etc.-must be viewed with caution. We encourage students not to view their LD as a form of illness or deficit; it doesn't need to be cured.

Successful college students have either developed their own compensatory skill system including using the resources available to help meet the academic demands. Any student entering college needs to consider many factors, but a student with LD entering college must think about:

- strategies for managing large amounts of reading;
- developing competence in class content;
- consider testing history and techniques;
- being objective about their writing ability and their willingness to access support to improve their writing;
- and finally; course load demands.

Academic Accommodations

At the college level, students with learning disabilities are expected to be responsible for disclosing that they have a learning disability and to know and be responsible for requesting accommodations. This responsibility actually begins with the admission process to college. The question becomes, when should a student disclose? Should disclosure come before or after acceptance to the institution? We suggest that students discuss this question with the disability services staff of the institution they are considering attending. Colleges that have an open enrollment admissions policy means that disclosure of a disability may be unnecessary. Schools that use a competitive admissions process may discourage disclosure except to the appropriate institutional staff. Students should research if there are any special consideration(s) made on status, including disability at the institution they are applying. A student with a disability must remember that post-secondary institutions cannot demand that a student disclose their disability before, during, or after being admitted to the institution. However, every student should research the campus climate regarding disability and talk to the people "in the know" on campus. Remember, once you're admitted and you decide you need accommodations, you will have to disclose. For your consideration: disclosure of a disability during the admissions process can actually be helpful at some institutions. However, there is the right and wrong way to disclose during the admissions process. Calling the institution, talking to disability services staff and, if possible, to students with disabilities currently enrolled in the school can be a good way of testing the college climate. In a few words: check the school out before your decide whether or not to disclose.

A college student needs to be able to document that he or she has a disability, including learning disabilities, before qualifying for academic and physical accommodations. Together, the student and the college staff will explore what accommodations would allow the student to more fully participate in the college's programs and activities. While colleges that receive federal funding must provide reasonable accommodations, not all colleges offer academic support services to students with learning disabilities. Prospective college students, their parents, and high school college counselors need to evaluate and research the level of support services that a college provides past the level of reasonable accommodation.

Adjustment to College Life

University of Denver students with learning disabilities say: "High school students with learning disabilities who are considering going to college should follow their goal!" More than ever before students with learning disabilities are applying to, enrolling in, and graduating from America's colleges and universities.

College students with learning disabilities, when asked about what makes them successful in college, usually talk about strategies in the area of personal strengths and self-awareness, and in the area of awareness of college resources. The research seems to support the idea that these strategies predict academic success, more than I.Q., academic achievement, or standardized testing. Self-advocacy is also key; the more comfortable a student is with self-advocating, the better they do academically.

Advice from current college students to prospective college students includes being aware of strengths, being able to advocate for oneself, and being persistent. The prospective college student needs to be able to discuss their academic strengths and weaknesses. A frank discussion of the psycho-educational testing with the testing clinician is an excellent place to start. Students that have learned to accept their learning disability also have a leg up in the college admission process. A student who can refer to themselves as a student with a learning disability is more likely to seek out support for that learning disability. Students who can compartmentalize their learning disability, recognize areas where the learning disability does and does not impact their life, and be willing to do what's necessary to be academically successful have a good chance of succeeding at college.

Students who have made the transition from high school to college often discuss how important it is to be grounded in knowing one's own behavior patterns, and knowing one's hot buttons. Students who sought out support from day one reported being more emotionally able to deal with all the changes happening around them. College, at times, can demand that students with LD make sacrifices to be successful, which can bring stress and frustration. Students report that the college experience offers new, but sometimes dangerous, channels for this frustration. They emphasize that it is important to find safe and healthy ways to use this emotional energy. Bottom line: students with LDs do have to work harder, don't fight it.

Successful college students with learning disabilities are united in their determination and perseverance to be academically successful. These are students who know they work very hard to get their well-deserved grades. Many college students with learning disabilities have the experience of embracing their learning disability at some point in their college career. Students often graduate with the knowledge that their character, values and personality has been shaped by their learning disability and come to realize that their LD has given them the tools to be successful during and after college in fact, for the rest of their life.

Students report that while "mentors" are very important part of the successful college experience, other support systems are also necessary in college. The habit of studying together in small groups outside of class proves to be invaluable to many students, not just those with learning disabilities. Students who use these collaborative groups report that they learn more than by studying alone. Another support system to access is good advising. Good advising is critical for the successful student because it helps focus and define a student's academic program. Support systems that are not frequently considered support systems are extracurricular activities and jobs. Rather than detracting from academic performance, being active on campus and/or working actually can increase students' overall satisfaction, can provide positive structure, and great learning opportunities.

Students who recognize their own need for support in the areas of time management, organization, tutoring, and written expression development come to college with a valuable tool: self-knowledge.

Finally, college students at the University of Denver openly discuss the value of diversity. Students with disabilities recognize that they too bring diversity to the campus in terms of their learning styles and the manner in how they think about and experience the world.

David Luker
The Learning Effectiveness Program
The Center, University of Denver
Denver, CO 80208-2372

Ted May, Director
University Disability Services
University of Denver
Denver, CO 80208-2372

CHAPTER III: COLLEGE STUDENTS AND ADD: THINKING AHEAD

ADD/ADHD Defined

First, a quick note: for this brief article, we'll refer to all diagnosed "attention deficits" with or without hyperactivity and impulsivity as "ADD."

What is ADD? These days it can be an excuse, a catch phrase, a punch line. "Everyone has ADD," don't they. It's true that in an increasingly fast-paced, competitive, clamorous world, even people without ADD can feel distracted, impulsive, forgetful, inattentive, and fidgety. These are all common symptoms of ADD. However, overwhelming as these feelings can be, experiencing them doesn't necessarily mean you have ADD. You may just have a very busy, stressful life.

ADD is a neurological syndrome. That means its "hard wired" from birth, part of the way you're made. As it's currently understood, the symptoms of ADD are partly the result of lower levels of certain neurotransmitters in certain parts of the brain. And while being the parent of a person with ADD can be a heck of a lot of work, ADD is not "caused" by bad parenting. And you can't get ADD from copying your older brother, either.

Most people with ADD are distractible, impulsive, and physically and/or mentally restless. They have been this way since childhood, and their symptoms have been more prevalent and intense than in the average person. In fact, the diagnosis of ADD indicates that a person's distractibility, impulsivity, and restlessness have been so intense that it has interfered with his/her everyday functioning–at home, at school, with friends and family, on the soccer field, and so forth.

Diagnosing ADD

There is no foolproof test for ADD. The "gold standard" of diagnosis is still the clinical history–a careful review of behavior, health, experience, and performance from birth to the present. Diagnosis should be done by qualified, experienced clinicians. Whenever possible, the diagnosing clinician should interview parents and teachers, and should review school information. Check-lists or questionnaires can be helpful, but they should never be used alone to make a diagnosis.

In addition to the clinical interview and review of history, various forms of testing can be helpful. Neuropsychological testing can provide insight not only into whether a person may have ADD, but into how that person perceives, thinks, and performs. It can indicate the presence of a learning disability or developmental disorder. A qEEG (quantitative electroencephalogram) can indicate the likelihood of ADD with a high degree of accuracy in many cases. SPECT scans are used to demonstrate blood flow in an individual's brain; researchers have found that certain patterns may indicate the presence of ADD.

Careful diagnosis is important because many things can look like ADD. Disorders of development, learning, mood, or anxiety can all have "ADD-like" symptoms. Head injury, endocrine imbalances, the effects of toxic substances, family stress, and trauma add further complexity to the diagnostic picture. And these diagnoses aren't mutually exclusive: a person can have two, or three, or little inconclusive bits of all of them. This is why diagnosis is still an art, as well as a science. We're all complicated, so really understanding ourselves is usually a complicated process, too.

Treatments for ADD

The essential first step in treatment is accurate information. People with ADD (and the family, friends, teachers, and coworkers of people with ADD) need a clear, pragmatic understanding of what ADD is, and what it isn't. Luckily, there are all sorts of sources for really good information: books, websites, support groups, and so forth. (We like starting with Ned Hallowell and John Ratey's latest *Delivered from Distraction*, but we're biased.)

Many treatments for ADD are available, some with proven efficacy, others with more anecdotal support. There is no "one-size-fits-all" approach to treating ADD. However, for students, the treatment of choice often includes medication, counseling/coaching, and academic accommodations.

Treatment usually includes medication because medication has a good track record and strong empirical support. Stimulants such a Ritalin, Concerta, Adderall, and others work to change neurotransmitter levels in the prefrontal cortex, allowing a person with ADD to "put on the brakes," improve attention, concentration and memory, and reduce impulsivity and hyperactivity. There is now at least one non-stimulant medication on the market that does essentially the same thing. If these medications don't work for an individual, a variety of other kinds of medications are available.

However, medication alone is rarely the answer. Habits of mind are learned from birth. If you've never been able to reliably attend, concentrate, and problem-solve, if you have always procrastinated, and always been disorganized, just taking a pill won't make you an academic star. It may make such stardom possible, but it won't guarantee consistent success.

To ensure success, people with ADD need structure-consistent, reliable strategies; an environment conducive to success' and continued, regular support from knowledgeable, helpful, likeable people. That last category is particularly important. Many people with ADD benefit from working on a regular basis with a coach, psychotherapist, or counselor who is specifically trained and experienced at working with ADD. This relationship, and the skills and strategies learned and sustained, can be central to academic and career success.

ADD at College

College can be overwhelming for students with ADD. At college, students are faced with far more responsibility than they have had before. They need to balance their social life and academic life. They must take responsibility for basic daily routines-when they wake, eat, work, play, do chores, and sleep. And they must cope with piles of academic work, spread out over broad spans of time.

Many intelligent, talented, and optimistic students with ADD hit college for the first time and flounder. They no longer have reminders from parents and oversight from teachers. Their academic schedule is varied and flexible, with long periods of "free" time. Entertaining distractions are endless and appealing. And when a student with ADD misses class, hands papers in late, and forgets to attend office hours, professors often assume the student lacks motivation, doesn't like the class, and doesn't care. Falling behind is easy, and disastrous.

Without careful preparation, effective strategies, and consistent support, it's all too easy for students with ADD to run into serious trouble at college. This can be true even for those students who sailed through high school without particular difficulty: the demands of college can be particularly daunting for those who got through high school on natural intelligence and the ability to "wing it." And unfortunately, the determination to work hard is necessary but not sufficient to success; many students with ADD enter college determined to study hard and remain focused. But as fall changes to winter, and the college year grinds on, determination wanes and distractions rise. It's very difficult to remain sufficiently determined. And determination alone doesn't necessarily equal attention, concentration, and good time management. College is a huge challenge for people with ADD. That's why it's so important to prepare for success ahead of time.

ADD and College Success

How do students with ADD succeed in college? They plan ahead! And they include in their planning three essential things: the right college, the right coach, and the right accommodations. Let's look briefly at each.

The Right College

When it comes to ADD, not all colleges are created equal. Some provide a broad range of accommodations and services for students with ADD, others pat you on the back and throw you into the deep end. Most are somewhere in between. It's enormously important to do your homework before applying to (and accepting an offer from) a college. You need to know what the college offers students with ADD, how you qualify for services and accommodations, whom you will work with on campus, and so forth. You need to think about campus size, class size, housing, and social distractions. Does the college have course requirements? There are numerous questions to consider, and ADD makes the answers particularly important.

There are a number of good books that can help you with your search (including this one). Find someone who understands ADD to help you as well-a counselor, an understanding parent, a dedicated teacher. Visit the campus, the learning center, inquire about coaching specifically for students with ADD, talk with students with ADD who go to the college. Give yourself time as this is a really important decision.

The Right Coach

A pronouncement: every college student with ADD should work with a coach. The coach must be experienced at working with students with ADD (not just LD). The student and coach should meet three or four times a week. If you have ADD, your coach may be the most important person you know at a college.

Why a coach? Any student with ADD can tell you what it takes to succeed at college. You have to work hard, keep your eye on the ball, make it to class on time, and so forth. However, with ADD, even if you know what you have to do, that doesn't mean you're going to do it. If you have ADD, consistency and dependability can be elusive goals, even with the best intentions. Regular meetings with a coach who understands ADD can help you keep track of your obligations, and meet those obligations.

Academic strategies that worked in high school may not work for college. A coach can teach you college strategies, but equally as important, a coach can help make sure you use those strategies consistently. It's important not to fall behind, and consistency is key.

Expect to spend some time finding the right coach. You can start by asking the college learning center for recommendations or referrals, either on or off campus.

The Right Accommodations

Colleges generally offer accommodations to students with learning differences. Accommodations ensure that students with ADD have the best chance to learn, and, to demonstrate what they've learned. Common accommodations include untimed tests, waiver of foreign-language requirements, detailed lecture notes, regular tutoring at the Learning Center, and so forth.

Accommodations are not "one-size-fits-all" and different students need different sorts of accommodations. For example, will you be less distracted if you live in a single room? Or will you feel socially isolated, and spend all your study time Instant Messaging your friends? Do you learn more effectively by listening to lectures (sitting in the front row and taking notes), or do you need small classes with lots of discussion? Do you need a smaller course load your first year? Do you need extra time to check your exams for silly mistakes? Do you need help breaking long assignments into brief tasks? The list of possible accommodations is potentially endless, but many of them will not apply to you. It is important that you know ahead of time which accommodations will be most helpful.

It's also important that you have documentation supporting your request for accommodations. For legal and ethical reasons, colleges will not give you accommodations simply because you think it's a good idea. While a letter from your physician may be sufficient, many colleges and universities now require full neuropsychological testing to support a request for accommodations. This kind of testing is usually time-consuming and expensive. You may have to schedule it months in advance. So, if you think you will be requesting accommodations from your college of choice, you should check early to see what kind of documentation you will need to support your request.

After you have been tested, talk with the neuropsychologist about the implications of your results. Discuss which accommodations will be most helpful for you, given your particular strengths, weaknesses, and learning style. The neuropsychologist's report should include those recommendations in writing, so that you can give them to the college, refer to them when necessary, and share them with your coach.

Good Luck!

College can be a lot of fun, and it can be a lot of hard work. Enjoy your independence and freedom, but don't try to get through college alone. Get lots of assistance and support: from family, friends, fellow students, professors, librarians, tutors, and your coach. In fact, become an expert at finding the right kind of assistance and support; this expertise will be invaluable throughout your life. Get to know and respect the way you think, work, and play. And then do the very best you can at all three. Good luck!

David Keevil, Psy.D.
The Hallowell Center
Sudbury, MA

CHAPTER IV: NONVERBAL LEARNING DISORDER (NLD)

NLD Defined

Nonverbal learning disorder is a category used to describe a diverse group of learners whose ability with language-related tasks is significantly better than their abilities to process and integrate nonverbal knowledge, including tactile, visuo-spatial, affective, or experiential information. NLD is considered a learning disability because the reliance on verbal skills over nonverbal creates a condition of intellectual disparity within the same brain. Although many people with this diagnosis have a pattern of assets, such as early speech and vocabulary development, remarkable rote memory skills, attention to detail, highly developed verbal ability, and strong auditory retention, they also suffer (in varying degrees) from deficits in the following three categories:

Motor: lack of coordination, problems with balance, and graphomotor skills;
Visual-spatial: lack of image, poor visual recall, faulty spatial perception, difficulty with spatial relations; and
Social: inability to comprehend nonverbal communication, difficulty adjusting to transitions and novel situations, and deficits in social judgment.

People with NLD rely almost entirely on information which they receive through the auditory mode and view the world in a unilateral, rigid manner. Almost all experience is processed through the analytical scrutiny of the left brain, the rational hemisphere designed to respond to verbal instructions, to solve problems by logically and sequentially analyzing parts of the whole, to control feelings, and to operate in a consistent, planned, and structured manner. Most people with NLD have difficulty with functions usually associated with the right brain, such as relying on intuition, exhibiting fluidity and spontaneity, dealing with open-ended questions, and expressing feelings.

Although intellectually capable, the diagnostic categories range from average to superior. Most people with NLD have trouble understanding such nonverbal communication as facial expression, body language, tone of voice, and choice of words. As a result, they are easily confused in social situations, where much of the communication and interaction is nonverbal. Most children with NLD feel confused and anxious in social situations. As they become adolescents and adults, managing this characteristic anxiety becomes a primary need. Without appropriate intervention, the frustration that results from the inability to understand and emulate demands of the neurotypical world can lead to depression and isolation.

Diagnosing Nonverbal Learning Disorder

The syndrome of Nonverbal Learning Disorders was first described by Dr. Byron Rourke (Rourke 1989), who states that individuals who qualify for the actual diagnosis must show a pattern of primary neuropsychological deficits in tactile perception, visual perception, and motor coordination which combine to create secondary deficits that affect the way children pay attention to and explore their environment. The secondary deficits engender tertiary deficits in nonverbal memory, abstract reasoning, executive functions, and specific aspects of speech and language. This cascade of deficits ultimately causes varying, but measurable levels of impairment in academic performance, social functioning, and emotional well-being.

NLD is defined not only by its deficits, but also by the presence of a number of assets. In order to meet the diagnostic criteria, individuals must display relatively intact simple motor skills, good auditory perception and attention, and rote memory for simple verbal material (Rourke 1995). In fact, it is often the presence of the assets that makes the diagnosis so complicated, since people with NLD regularly use their assets to compensate for the deficits until issues become too overwhelming.

In order to accurately assess any learning style, it is important to take a comprehensive medical, developmental, and educational history. If there are indications that a difference in learning style might be causing educational, social, or emotional difficulties, a testing psychologist with expertise in learning disabilities should be engaged to conduct a psycho-educational assessment. Further testing should be done by a neuropsychologist if any of the following concerns are revealed by the results of the initial battery:

a) a discrepancy between one set of skills and another;
b) a discrepancy between assessed potential and actual productivity;
c) a serious emotional consequence related to academic settings; and/or
d) a significant amount of scatter in the accomplishment of tasks.

A neuropsychologist, who is trained to assess brain function, is often the ultimate diagnostician for people with NLD. Neuropsychological testing can show differences in the execution of commands controlled by the different hemispheres of the brain and can also describe the operating levels of executive function. In some cases, however, it is important to have projective testing and a psychiatric evaluation to rule out a thought disorder and to assess anxiety and mood. When all professionals agree that testing results indicate disparate function and ability between the two hemispheres of the brain, it is generally appropriate to diagnose NLD.

Treating NLD

Unfortunately, there is no single medication or group of medications known to be effective in remediating NLD. Professionals who prescribe medication for people with NLD should be guided by the presentation of somatic and emotional symptoms which result from situations tangential to the cognitive profile of the syndrome. For example, people who are consistently frustrated by their inability to apply a certain concept, or by their inability to read and interpret social cue, can develop dysthymia or depression. For them, anti-depressants can help re-establish efficacy and optimism. Others react to cognitive frustration and social/emotional difficulties with extreme anxiety. In many cases, an appropriate dosage of anti-anxiety medication can help an individual develop the confidence to initiate productive thoughts and deeds. Medication can reduce acute symptoms related to NLD, but there is no treatment for the syndrome itself.

The best medication for NLD is the consistent provision of beneficial interventions from the time of diagnosis. There are many ways that parents, educators, and professionals can help people with NLD develop to their optimal level of cognitive and emotional achievement. Interventions should be directly related to the problems they address, with special consideration to the unique personality of the person with NLD. For example, NLDers who have trouble with executive functions need to learn about long-term strategies which can help them take control of the things that affect their lives.

People with NLD construct the reality of their worlds through language. NLDers can learn to help themselves through anxieties which interfere with task completion by simply learning to talk themselves through confusing situations. Once they "hear" themselves describe the challenges, they are often able to develop a plan to address them. For many people with NLD, it is comforting to have a reservoir of social scripts for use until certain responses become automatic. Students entering new schools should reconsider situations which are likely to occur. They can then meet a professor or roommate, attend a social function, or even ask questions in the library without becoming flustered. For NLDers, it is critical to plan ahead and to remember that successful life plans don't happen by default.

People with NLD feel most comfortable in situations where they can maximize their assets and minimize their deficits. Some NLDers derive great benefit from working with an organizational management coach to identify that they can choose a life style, course schedule, or social activity which helps them acquire the energy and enthusiasm they need, at the pace they need, and with the awareness they need.

College Accommodation

The most important thing that students with NLD should do before attending college is learn about and acknowledge their individual strengths and weaknesses. Students who have trouble waking early should try to schedule classes that take place during their peak awareness times. NLDers with direction problems should arrive on campus early enough to learn what happens where, and how to get from one place to another. Students with a disorder of sensory integration, a common companion to NLD, should identify residential settings which offer the maximum physical and emotional comfort. It can be helpful to request a single room or housing in a quiet or wellness dorm. Many NLDers prefer to live off-campus to minimize the stress of constant social interaction. An educational consultant who is familiar with ramifications of this syndrome can be an effective helper in selecting a productive post-secondary environment.

Although the syndrome of NLD is technically considered a learning disability, it has ramifications that extend far beyond the boundaries of the classroom. In order to make sure they remain on solid emotional ground, students with NLD who have never lived away from home should develop a strategy for student-family communication. They should also develop basic competencies in time and money management.

People with NLD have great verbal skills, but most have great difficulty reading emotional states, body language, facial expression, and tone of voice. For students whose pattern of difficulties suggests that they might struggle to negotiate life beyond the classroom, it is appropriate that parents ask the learning resource director, the dean, older students, residence assistants, or heads of campus activity groups to reach out. Students who feel personally welcomed at activities or events will experience diminished anxiety.

Accommodations that were successfully implemented in high school should continue in the college setting. Because each person with NLD has a unique configuration of assets and deficits, no two NLDers will need the same supports and accommodations. However, depending on individual need, suggestions from the IEP, or recommendations made by the diagnostician, some or all of the following options might be beneficial:

- Testing and exams administered on computer
- Testing administered privately in a distraction-reduced environment
- Test questions read aloud
- Note-takers
- Oral exams
- Assistive technology
- Extended time or untimed accommodation for testing
- Extended time for papers and assignments
- Access to writing center and subject tours
- Scaffolding for long-term assignments
- Peer and professional tutoring
- Professional awareness of NLD and its ramifications
- Regularly scheduled meetings to monitor academic, medical, and emotional wellness

Adjustment to College Life

For many students with NLD, college is the highlight of their academic career. Their newfound academic and social independence gives them more control to identify the cognitive and emotional situations which feel comfortable. Many students with NLD are relieved to learn that colleges which are larger and more diverse than previous educational institutions offer wider social possibility and acceptance. Others prefer a smaller campus where class size is limited and the campus is easier to negotiate. Nevertheless, like all people with NLD, college students are primarily affected by the two most disabling characteristics of the syndrome-anxiety and difficulty adapting to transitions or novel experiences. For each student, of course, the situations which cause these problems vary, but they are always best served by an environment which provides consistency and safety.

One student, who acknowledges a lack of control over executive functions, noted that she was always losing things-from her favorite sweater to the course syllabus. This is a common problem for NLDers which can create additional expense and anxiety for the student who loses clothing, books, and computers. Learning to take note of things around them before moving from one space to another is a skill which becomes critically important for NLDers in college.

Many report that it is very difficult to learn to live with a roommate. Although NLDers are generally quite interested in forming social relationships, they are often extremely vulnerable and defenseless against deception and mockery. Their fragile sense of self-esteem can be destroyed by bullies or interactions with unscrupulous individuals. An unfortunate rooming match, who might be merely annoying to a neurotypical student, could be devastating to a student with NLD. For some NLDers, in fact, establishing the intricate balance of a roommate relationship while adjusting to a major transition in all other areas of life, could be overwhelming. Most college housing offices are responsive to a letter from a physician stating why a single room is recommended.

There are several areas regarding academic requirements which can be troublesome for students with NLD. Those who have specific waivers for foreign language or certain types of higher level math must make certain that avoiding such classes will not have an adverse effect on their graduation requirements. Sometimes, simply choosing the right mix of classes can be arduous. For students with NLD, who traditionally fear new things, it can be difficult to take the leap of faith required for studying a topic they have never approached. Combined with their inability to decipher the campus buzz about which courses are interesting and which are deadly, NLDers often have difficulty selecting a properly balanced course of study.

One student reports failing miserably at course selection until he made peace with the realization that, for students with NLD, it is critical to preview all course choices with the learning disability coordinator, academic advisors, and even the instructors themselves. Indicating that a well-developed strategy is critical to functional success, he advises students with NLD to be scrupulous about collecting information on where to go for help. Although neurotypical students can usually develop spontaneous compensations, students with NLD need to know exactly where to go for help, when and where each professor holds office hours, and the availability of supports such as writing workshops, tutoring, math labs, and counseling. Accessibility of professors is another important concern for students with NLD, who like to clarify information by asking questions. Learning formats which discourage such behavior will probably not feel supportive.

Sometimes, students with NLD find themselves on a campus which is governed by a social style they neither like nor understand. At some schools, NLDers who don't want to become part of the athletic scene or fraternity world can have difficulty finding activities they enjoy or meeting people they like. They need to learn that it can take more time and effort to fine-tune a social style that is somewhat atypical. Counseling beforehand and continuing confirmation of self-esteem can make this task easier.

Students with NLD represent a broad range of intellectual capabilities, social acumen, and emotional strength. Nevertheless, all must pay scrupulous attention to the fundamental aspects of college life long before each semester begins. For students with NLD, it is important to have both Plan A and Plan B in place before leaving for college so that reasonable contingencies exist for all possibilities. In order to facilitate a successful transition to a post-secondary setting, NLDers should pay careful attention to the following:

- Course selection
- Housing
- Accessibility of professors
- Availability of support services
- Awareness and acceptance of diverse learners
- Extracurricular offerings
- Health and counseling facilities
- Student diversity
- Campus safety

The final requirement in promoting college success for a student with NLD is something that every student needs–a loving community of family, friends, and advisers. A support system that is informed, proactive, and optimistic can make the difference between success and failure.

Marcia Rubinstien
Certified Educational Planner
West Hartford, CT

CHAPTER V: ASPERGER'S DISORDER

Asperger's Disorder Defined

The term autism spectrum disorders (ASDs) refers to a group of neurodevelopmental disorders which affect development in the areas of social interaction, communication, and behavior. ASDs affect each individual differently and to varying degrees of severity, so symptoms can occur in any combination and can range from the very mild to the severe. Those individuals who fall within the "average" range or higher on intelligence tests are often referred to as having either "high-functioning autism" (HFA) or "Asperger's Syndrome" (AS), or both.

Social Skills: Some individuals with HFA and AS are not very interested in social interactions. Many students, however, very much want to develop friendships and romantic relationships, but they often have difficulty making and keeping friends; understanding others' feelings; taking others' perspectives; using and understanding nonverbal communication (such as eye contact, gestures, and body language); and may not pick up on subtle social cues or follow accepted social conventions.

Speech, Language, and Communication: Individuals with HFA and AS are frequently described as having advanced vocabularies and may speak in an overly formal and/or stilted-sounding manner. Additionally, they may speak in a monotone; they are unaware of the volume of their voice; and they may stand too close to others when speaking. Individuals with ASD also frequently have difficulty engaging in reciprocal (back-and-forth) conversations and in taking the listener's needs into account by talking at length about a topic of high interest, resisting others' attempts to change the topic, and failing to provide relevant background information when introducing a topic or telling a story. Individuals with HFA and AS may have problems with comprehension, resulting in difficulties in following multi-step directions and long discussions. Students with ASDs also tend to interpret language in an overly literal way, and often have difficulty understanding figures of speech, humor, sarcasm, or slang.

Repetitive and Restricted Activities, Interests or Behaviors: Individuals with severe ASDs may exhibit body mannerisms, such as rocking or moving their hands in unusual ways. These body mannerisms may also manifest themselves in high-functioning individuals, although in a subtler way. Students with ASDs also frequently display an intense interest in one or two topics or activities which they pursue to the exclusion of many other activities. These interests may be quite typical for others their age (e.g., video games, computers, science, math), but they often prevent the student from engaging in other social activities and may result in a lack of motivation for activities or courses not involving these areas. Some students with ASDs tend to exhibit a need for "sameness" or predictability in their environments, which may result in inflexible behavior when their environment or an established routine is altered. For example, some individuals will have difficulty if their dorm room furniture is rearranged, while others may become anxious when a class is cancelled, they oversleep and do not have time for breakfast, or the semester schedule changes to a reading days/exam schedule. Some individuals with ASD may also have difficulty being flexible about following rules, becoming so agitated when other students break an established rule that they may attempt to "enforce" the rules on their own. Such students may benefit from having a peer mentor who can help them negotiate these situations.

Diagnosing ASD

At the current time, there are no medical tests that can diagnose ASDs. Instead, diagnosis is based on observed behaviors as provided by specific criteria. Typically, a psychologist makes the diagnosis; however, other medical professionals, such as pediatric neurologists, psychiatrists, or developmental pediatricians can make a diagnosis of an ASD.

The diagnosis distinction between HFA and AS is unclear at this time. It should be noted, however, that the diagnostic criteria for AS and ASD are identical with respect to symptoms of social impairment and restricted and repetitive behaviors. Students with AS, unlike ASD, must speak before the age of two, and their cognitive development must be in the average range or higher. Even though the criteria for AS do not include impairments in communication, most individuals with AS do have difficulty in this area.

Treatments and Interventions

While there are currently no medical interventions that "cure" the ASDs, medical and educational strategies can be effective in helping individuals manage some of their symptoms and improve quality of life.

Individuals with ASD are sometimes given prescription medications to help them manage certain ASD symptoms, including rigid, inflexible behavior or co-occurring symptoms, such as ADHD, anxiety, and depression. These medications should be used cautiously in individuals with ASD because the medications and their side effects have not been thoroughly studied. Limited research suggests that individuals with ASDs may respond to lower doses than generally used and may exhibit unusual side effects.

Education goals and accommodations for students with ASDs tend to focus on addressing social skills, communication, and sensory and organizational needs. Students with ASD are often eligible to receive special education services under the Individuals with Disabilities Education Act (IDEA) and/or Section 504 of the Americans with Disabilities Act (ADA). Students with more severe presentations of ASD are often identified under the IDEA category of "Autism," while higher-functioning students, such as those with AS, receive accommodations through Section 504 plans. When these higher-functioning students are eligible for special education, they may receive services under a number of IDEA eligibility categories, such as "Gifted," "Other Health Impaired," "Specific Learning Disabilities," and/or "Emotionally Disturbed."

These categorizations often create difficulties in transition planning as the unique needs of these students may not be taken into account. Nonetheless, college student disability offices should review each student's IEP to determine what specific supports were provided for the student in his/her high school.

Issues in Transition

Individuals with higher functioning ASD are likely to face difficulties with academic content, organization, time management, and study skills. These difficulties are exacerbated by a number of issues in college settings, including proper identification of students in need of services, the hidden nature of the disability, students' reluctance to disclose their disability, larger class sizes, and limited teacher-student contact.

When planning for the transition to college, the major issues to consider are: (1) deciding what type and size of college to attend and where the student is going to live; (2) assessing and teaching independent living skills; (3) discussing when and how to disclose one's disability; (4) identifying appropriate academic supports and accommodations; (5) identifying necessary social supports; and (6) developing strategies to assist the student in adjusting to the college environment.

Choosing a College: A number of considerations should be taken into account with respect to this issue, including: the type of college, the number of students, the average class size, the campus layout, and the proximity of the campus to home.

For some students with ASDs, serious consideration should be given to starting at a community college which may offer more individual attention. Many students with ASDs have difficulty navigating large campuses and may find smaller college campuses easier to learn and less overwhelming. At the same time, a smaller school may increase the visibility of "being different," while a larger school may offer more diversity and more opportunities to meet individuals with similar interests.

Technical or trade schools may allow more concentrated focus in one's area of interest, and specialized schools may not require students to take as many required "general" courses. These aspects may be advantageous for students with AS who are highly skilled in specific areas and have difficulties in other areas.

Living arrangements also require serious consideration, for example whether the student should live on or off campus, whether the student should live at home, and whether the student should have roommates. It may be helpful for students with ASDs to consider living at home their first year of college so they can get used to the academic and organizational demands of college before having to deal with the additional social and living challenges. Some students who do not like to drive or use public transportation, however, may find commuting to school too difficult.

For many students with ASDs, sharing a dorm room is extremely difficult, given their difficulty with the sensory and social demands of sharing a small living space. A single room should therefore be considered. Even with a single room, however, there are still the same challenges that result from dorm living including sharing communal bathrooms and crowded and noisy quarters. An option for parents is to provide their student with an open-ended bus, train, or plane ticket so the student can stay in close touch with family and visit when the need arises. Pre-paid phone cards or cell phones can also provide a sense of security for the student.

Independent Living Skills: In evaluating the pros and cons of living away from home, it is important to consider the individual's sensory issues, daily living skills, problem-solving skills, and decision-making skills. Common problems that arise include sensitivity to noises and smells, physical comfort in furniture, personal hygiene, waking up to an alarm clock, getting to class on time, understanding meal plans, using a campus ID, handling fire drills in the middle of the night, and finding public rest rooms. Parents may want to post information in the student's room and/or create a resource guide of helpful information such as rules and safety guidelines, insurance information, emergency phone numbers, bank account information, and campus health care information. Students with ASDs and their families should carefully consider the supports needed to handle those and any other issues that may arise. Additionally, for individuals with ASD who need more assistance and supervision of daily living skills, living at home–at least initially–may be more appropriate.

Self-Advocacy: Disclosure of one's disability is necessary to receive accommodations based on ADA, as IDEA no longer applies once students exit the public school system. In most college settings, students are responsible for advocating for themselves, meaning that students must initiate contact with the school's disabilities office to disclose their disability and must approach their professors regarding the accommodations they will need to be successful. Ideally, the student will have been taught this self-advocacy while in high school. If not, some families may wish to address this issue by hiring a liaison between the student and school personnel.

Academic Support and Accommodations: Individuals with ASD require such accommodations as preferential seating, tape recorded lectures, exam administration in quiet and less-distracting environments, and extra time on exams. Although ADA provides some specific types of accommodations, many students with ASD may benefit from additional accommodations, including the following: assistance with course selection, avoidance of group projects and group discussions, flexible class schedules, flexible assignment due dates, oral exams, and the ability to attend other sections of the same course. Still other accommodations include assistance in developing study skills and organizational skills, assistance with long-term projects, and tutoring in specific areas. As individuals with ASD have problems seeking out available tutoring, an outside tutor or life coach may be required.

Social Supports: Students with ASD may suffer from social isolation because of their difficulties forming relationships, therefore adjusting to the social demands of a college setting may be the most challenging area for students with ASD. Establishing a "point person" to go to when confused or stressed may be helpful. College students themselves can also serve as peer mentors, providing social assistance on a volunteer basis. Other roles include serving as a liaison for communication between the student and his/her parents, assisting the student in navigating through various aspects of college life such as understanding the unwritten social rules of classroom, dorm, and campus behavior. It is important to teach students with ASD about hazing and exploitation, and to provide them with a list of people to contact in the event such hazing or exploitation occurs.

Adjusting to the Transition

There are numerous strategies that can ease the transition from high school to college. Such strategies include taking a college course while attending high school, taking a summer course on campus the summer before beginning college, and planning to take more time than the average four years to complete college with a reduced course load.

Students should become familiar with the campus before starting school by visiting the college's website, studying the college maps, and walking through their schedule prior to the first day of class. Students may also benefit from specific information regarding orientation activities, procedures for checking into the dorm, and registering for classes.

The scheduling of an ASD student's classes can also make the transition to college easier. Students should not schedule classes back-to-back unless they are in the same building, and students should never sign up for classes that meet earlier than they wake up.

Conclusion

There is tremendous variation in how individuals with ASDs describe their college experiences. Some find college to be an extremely positive experience, a place where they are appreciated for themselves and not singled out for their differences. Still others find that the physical environment and social demands of universities conflict with the needs of ASDs students. The development of coping strategies, in addition to taking advantage of the available accommodations, is essential to success. Students will be most successful when all services are coordinated before the commencement of the school year. This will give the parents reassurance that colleges are cognizant of their student's needs.

Diane Adreon, Associate Director and Jennifer S. Durocher, Assistant Director
University of Miami Center for Autism & Related Disabilities

CHAPTER VI: OBSESSIVE COMPULSIVE DISORDER

OCD Defined

Obsessive Compulsive Disorder (OCD) is characterized by recurrent obsessions and compulsions. Obsessions are intrusive, irrational thoughts. Compulsions are repetitive behaviors done to reduce the anxiety caused by the obsessions. To meet the criteria for this disorder, the obsessions and compulsions need to take up a total of at least one hour a day. Like all psychiatric disorders there are mild, moderate, and severe cases of OCD.

There are many different obsessions and compulsions. The most common obsession is a fear of contamination or a fear of germs. Individuals with this obsession worry excessively about germs and getting "dirty" or contaminated by others. They often compulsively wash and avoid touching things that they perceive as filled with dangerous germs. Sometimes particular people are avoided due to a concern that these individuals are a source of contamination. Once an individual with OCD experiences the feeling of being contaminated, rituals are done to reduce that uncomfortable feeling. These rituals may include washing excessively, mental rituals (counting or saying certain phrases), or touching or walking rituals. Washing rituals are the most common and they often lead to very long showers, red chapped hands from excessive washing, and even clogged toilets from excessive wiping with too much toilet tissue. These individuals also may have trouble using public rest rooms, touching doorknobs, and being around crowds.

Another common OCD symptom that many young people have involves an obsession about writing and/or reading. They worry that their reading and/or writing is not perfect enough. As a result they may re-write or write over letters, and they may re-read things over and over again a certain number of times. These symptoms usually impact reading and writing, making school performance painstakingly slow.

Other common OCD symptoms involve verbal rituals including repeating phrases or getting others to repeat phrases a certain number of times. It can also include socially impairing symptoms of checking and asking questions for reassurance. This can include asking friends, "Are you mad at me?" repeatedly or saying, "I am sorry" again and again for no rational reason. Checking can involve checking locks a certain number of times, checking closets and under the bed, and other rituals often done at night before going to sleep or when leaving a room. Switching lights on and off a certain number of times is also common.

OCD symptoms may vary but the intrusive and disturbing nature of obsessions and the burden of the compulsions plague people with this disorder. People with OCD are well aware of how irrational the obsessions and compulsions are but feel trapped by them. This disorder takes up a lot of time and energy and without effective treatment may lead to depression due to how impairing these symptoms can become.

Treating OCD

Effective treatment for OCD involves Cognitive Behavioral Therapy (CBT). This therapy focuses on establishing goals of exposure and response prevention. The individual with OCD works to become exposed to the obsession and to resist the compulsion. With practice, this extinguishes the urge to do the compulsion and reduces the obsessions. CBT is a particular form of therapy that is specific to symptom reduction and very different from common "talk therapy." A therapist needs specific training in cognitive behavior therapy, specific to OCD, to guide the patient and family in doing exposure response prevention in a structured manner that is challenging but not overwhelming.

When OCD is severe, CBT treatment cannot be as effective because the level of anxiety is too high to be able to do the exposure prevention exercises. When this is the case, medications are used to reduce the anxiety caused by OCD. A psychiatrist is usually consulted to determine the type of medication needed to help reduce the OCD symptoms. Sometimes this is an easy process, with the first medicine tried found to be effective. In other cases, medication becomes a complicated process of trial and error until the right medication or combination of medications is found to reduce the OCD symptoms and provide relief.

Going to College

Young high school students with OCD are in most ways like any other student, except for their OCD symptoms. If their symptoms do not interfere with their school functioning, people at school may not be aware of the OCD. For example, an individual with contamination fears may spend a long time taking showers at home or hand washing but this does not interfere with academic functioning. Some students may have symptoms that directly impact their school functioning and may have had accommodations made at school to help them. For example, a student who re-reads may have needed books on tape to get through assignments and/or extra time to complete assignments in high school. Students with OCD that slows down their production at school often are given untimed tests or extended time to complete assignments.

College life represents a new challenge for a young person with OCD because it blends home and school. Living in a dorm can be challenging for a student with OCD, especially if there are contamination issues. Evaluating what a student with OCD needs when choosing a college situation is a very individual process.

Some aspects to consider involve the living situation. Depending on the severity of the OCD and the motivation of the student, a dorm situation may or may not work. In an ideal situation, a dorm with other students living in close quarters can provide the ultimate exposure. Some students find their contamination and checking behaviors dramatically decrease in these situations. Many report they could not do their rituals in these settings, and that provided the "response prevention" that decreased their symptoms. Some say their OCD disappeared in the dorm because of this. Others with more severe symptoms become highly anxious with the idea of sharing a room and someone touching their things and/or sharing a bathroom with others who might "contaminate" the bathroom. In addition, students with OCD generally need a regular amount of sleep. When they are sleep deprived, their symptoms can dramatically worsen. Dorm living is not always conducive to regular sleep patterns.

For individuals with severe OCD who are unable to tolerate regular dorm living, several options exist. One is a request for a single room. Some students can handle sharing the bathroom as long as they have their own room. Having their own room helps with the sleep issue and allows them to feel more in control of their things, reducing their anxiety about contamination concerns. Others may need off-campus housing in the form of an apartment close to school, if they feel they really cannot tolerate sharing bathrooms and living with others in the unstructured dorm setting. Students with the most severe OCD symptoms may need to live at home and commute to school. These students benefit, at least initially, from family support and the familiar surroundings of their home.

It is hoped that all college students with OCD continue to work in therapy to challenge their OCD and increase their level of independent functioning. Often students start out in a more restrictive setting of home or single room and, as they recover from OCD, they are able to transition into a more traditional dorm setting.

It is important to balance the need to challenge the OCD symptoms through college life with the need to make the student comfortable enough to be successful. This is a balance best achieved through the advice of the treatment team and of course the input of the student with OCD. Transitioning to college is often an anxiety provoking situation for students and parents without OCD; anxiety is a normal reaction when a child is reaching this milestone. For the student with severe OCD, a step-by-step plan could be put into place with the first step being a more protected living situation and gradually increasing the goals to full on-campus living when ready.

College Academics

Some students with OCD may need extra academic support due to the manner in which the OCD affects schoolwork. Extra time on tests and assignments may be needed. Books on tape may be helpful to reduce re-reading. A tutor may be helpful to break assignments down into manageable pieces. A tutor can also help the student to set limits and to avoid over-protection due to an obsessive need for everything to be too complete or perfect.

Most students with OCD are like other students who want to do well in college and enjoy their college years. College can represent an opportunity for personal growth and mastery in many areas, including in the area of overcoming OCD. A plan for college needs to be individualized for a student with OCD in a way that provides an opportunity to challenge the OCD symptoms but not overwhelm the student. A team approach working closely with the student, parents, and professionals, as well as the college, can serve to develop a setting that fosters learning, reduces OCD symptoms, and leads to a successful college experience.

Dr. Kathleen B. Trainer, MSW, Psy.D.
Child Psychiatry
Massachusetts General Hospital
Boston, MA

CHAPTER VII: NEUROPSYCHOLOGICAL EVALUATION

Introduction

A neuropsychological evaluation is a comprehensive assessment of an individual's cognitive, emotional, and behavioral functioning. The results of this evaluation aid in the process of identifying educational programs that are well-suited to a student's learning style. In addition, a comprehensive evaluation is required by colleges and testing services as documentation that a student has a disability and will need specific accommodations.

A neuropsychologist is a clinical psychologist who has undergone additional post-doctoral specialization training in neuropsychology, the study of the relationship between brain organization and behavioral/cognitive functioning. In the course of a neuropsychological evaluation, the clinician assesses the individual's overall cognitive capacity, academic skills, language processing, visual-spatial skills, efficiency of learning and recalling various types of information, concentration, approach to tasks (i.e., "executive functioning"), fine motor control, and social/emotional functioning. Each of these areas potentially influences a student's ability to manage academic demands. Determining the profile of strengths and weaknesses allows the neuropsychologist to anticipate the types of challenges that a student is likely to confront academically and to formulate recommendations for necessary accommodations as well as compensatory strategies.

The Neuropsychological Assessment Process

In order to assess the student's functioning, the neuropsychologist integrates information obtained from three sources: standardized testing, history, and observations. Although standardized testing scores provide critical information regarding a student's learning profile, it is the interpretation of these results in light of the student's history and clinical observations that is critical to understanding the learning style of a student. In order to accurately interpret testing results, the neuropsychologist needs to obtain information about many aspects of the student's history, including family history of neurological, learning, or emotional disorders; early development of language, motor, social, attentional, and pre-academic skills; medical history, particularly neurological issues; and educational history. This information about the student's history is typically gathered through a clinical interview with the student and/or parents, questionnaire data, and review of previous testing reports, educational plans, or medical records.

Clinical observation is crucial to understanding what the test results convey about the learning style of the student. The neuropsychologist needs to assess whether the student's performance on the tests is being adversely affected by factors such as fatigue, inattention, or anxiety. Observation of the process by which the student approaches tasks is necessary to understand the scores obtained. For example, two students could achieve the same score on a test for different reasons: one student's performance might have been undermined by lack of conceptual knowledge while the other student's score was compromised only by a careless error in the context of intact conceptual understanding. The evaluator typically provides information in the report about the specific difficulties that diminished the student's performance on certain tests. Finally, the neuropsychologist looks for patterns of behavior during the evaluation process; for example, students with language processing issues will often show signs of increased anxiety during tests that make significant expressive language demands such as repeating complex stories.

A neuropsychological evaluation involves the administration of a battery of standardized tests which allow for assessment of the functional domains that are listed below. Many of these tests are interactive in nature; there are very few "pencil and paper" tasks. While all neuropsychological evaluations involve assessment of the core areas of functioning, the specific battery of tests may vary somewhat depending upon the nature of the referral question.

Cognitive Capacity

Administration of a standardized intellectual battery, such as the Wechsler Adult Intelligence Scales, Stanford-Binet Intelligence Scale, or the Woodcock-Johnson Psychoeducational Battery: Tests of Cognitive Ability, allows the clinician to have an overview of the level of overall intellectual functioning relative to peers as well as the pattern of skills (e.g. whether the scores cluster in the same range or show wide variability).

Academic Skills

Assessment of the level of development of basic academic skills is typically done using a battery of tests such as the Wechsler Individual Achievement Tests or the Woodcock Johnson Psycho-educational Battery: Tests of Achievement. Subtests of these batteries allow for assessment of reading skills (sight word recognition, decoding, comprehension, and reading rate), spelling, written expression, and mathematical ability (conceptual knowledge and calculation skills). For students who are known or suspected to have a slow reading rate, additional tests of reading fluency are typically used, such as the Test of Word Reading Efficiency, Nelson-Denny, and the Gray Oral Reading Test. It is often useful to compare the student's reading comprehension on an untimed test, such as the Gray Silent Reading Test, and a timed test, such as the Gray Oral Reading Test, to determine the extent to which time demands interfere with comprehension.

Language Processing

In addition to assessing written language skills (i.e., reading, written expression), it is important to understand the student's capacity for understanding verbally presented information and expressing thoughts verbally. Standardized assessment of vocabulary knowledge, efficiency of word retrieval, comprehension of complex language, and the ability to organize language output involve the use of instruments such as the Boston Naming Test, Peabody Picture Vocabulary Test, Clinical Evaluation of Language Fundamentals, and the Wide Range Assessment of Memory and Learning Battery.

Learning and Memory

Neuropsychologists typically assess whether there is a difference in the ability to learn and recall information depending on the modality in which it is presented; specifically, the assessment determines whether there is a difference between verbal and visual material. Similarly, there is typically an assessment of whether a student has relative strengths or weaknesses in rote learning versus conceptual learning. With regard to memory, the neuropsychologist needs to determine the integrity of the abilities to encode, store, and retrieve information. Batteries such as the Wide Range Assessment of Memory and Learning are useful in this aspect.

Attention and Concentration

Information about the student's ability to sustain concentration is obtained through both formal testing and questionnaire data. Formal assessment tools require the student to sustain concentration over an extended period of time on stimuli that are not intellectually engaging. For example, the Conners' Continuous Performance Test is a computer based test that requires the student to stay focused on letters that come on the screen over a period of 14 minutes. Tests of "working memory" (i.e., the capacity for holding and mentally manipulating information) are also relevant to the assessment of the attentional system and are measured by some subtests of the Wechsler Intelligence Scales (Working Memory Index subtests).

Test results need to be combined with other sources of information such as responses to the Brown Adolescent ADD Scales, which is a semi-structured interview administered by the neuropsychologist. The student is asked to rate the frequency of occurrence of difficulties that are associated with attentional difficulties (e.g., "forget to bring books to class" and "have trouble focusing on the speaker").

Executive Functioning

Executive functioning refers to the ability to independently organize complex information and includes skills such as the ability to appreciate the structural framework of text, develop an organizational structure for written expression, and sequence the steps necessary to carry out a multi-step task. These skills are difficult to evaluate formally, but some of the underlying cognitive skills can be assessed using instruments such as the Delis-Kaplan Executive Function System, Trail Making Test, Stroop Test of Color Word Interference, and the Wisconsin Card Sorting Test. Another important aspect of executive functioning is processing speed, which involves the speed of response to stimuli and is measured with some of the subtests of the Wechsler Scales (Processing Speed Index subtests) and of the Woodcock-Johnson batteries. In addition, there is a standardized questionnaire assessing executive functioning skills in the home and school environment, the Behavior Rating Inventory of Executive Functioning (BRIEF), that has normative data for students through age 18 years.

Motor Control

In terms of academic functioning, the most relevant aspect of motor functioning is graphomotor control, which refers to the fine motor control necessary for handwriting. The neuropsychologist assesses both the legibility of the handwriting and the rate of output. Rate of graphomotor output can be formally assessed by tests of copying speed such as the Coding subtest of the Wechsler Intelligence Scales.

Social-Emotional Functioning

In addition to clinical interview, there are standardized questionnaires that can be used to assess emotional well-being, including the Minnesota Multiphasic Personality Inventory (MMPI) and the Personality Assessment Inventory. These instruments provide information regarding the significance of symptoms of emotional disorders such as anxiety or depression as well as underlying personality traits.

Uses of Neuropsychological Evaluations for Adolescents

College Selection

The neuropsychological evaluation provides important information about a student's strengths and weaknesses, which can be used in determining the type of college that would be most appropriate in terms of class size, instructional approach, strength of the program in potential major subjects, and level of support available on campus. Educational consultants and other professionals who work with students in choosing colleges will often use information about the student's learning style to determine the best match with a student's needs. For example, the adolescent's learning profile will determine whether a college program designed specifically for students with learning disabilities would be more desirable than a more traditional college that offers learning center support.

Standardized Testing Accommodations

In order to obtain accommodations on standardized tests (e.g., Scholastic Aptitude Test), a student has to provide documentation of a learning disability or attentional disorder in addition to evidence that the accommodation has been necessary in the high school environment, which generally involves a current special education plan (e.g., Individualized Educational Plan or 504 plan). A comprehensive evaluation testing must be completed within three years of the testing date.

According to the policy statement of the Educational Testing Service (ETS), the evaluation needs to include assessment of the following domains at a minimum: Cognitive Ability, Academic Achievement, and Information Processing (which includes memory, linguistic and visual processing, processing speed, executive functioning, and motor skills). The ETS emphasizes the need for a "well-written diagnostic summary," cautioning that, "assessment instruments and the data they provide do not diagnose; rather they provide important elements that must be integrated by the evaluator with background information, observations of the client during the testing situation and the current context."

"Professional judgment (must) be used in the interpretive summary." The report of the evaluation must contain all standardized scores, a specific diagnosis of a learning disability, an explanation of how the learning disability affects the student's functioning, and a rationale for recommended accommodations. A copy of the "Policy Statement for Documentation of a Learning Disability in Adolescent and Adults" is available through www.ets.org/disability.html.

The College Board, which is responsible for the administration of the SAT, is enforcing the standards for documentation much more stringently now that the examinations are not "flagged" as having been administered under non-standard conditions. Therefore, it is particularly important for students to be evaluated by neuropsychologists who are experienced in providing the appropriate documentation and who can assist in the appeals process if the initial application for accommodations is denied.

Typical accommodations for standardized testing include: extended time, administration in a separate room, provision of a reader, bypass of writing disability (e.g., scribe, word processing), and recording answers directly on the test booklet rather than a separate answer sheet.

Accommodations in College

A current neuropsychological evaluation (no more than three years old) typically provides the documentation required by colleges to provide accommodations. The evaluation is generally submitted to the dean in the office of student services or disability services once a student has been accepted to the program. The most common accommodations available at the college level include extended time on tests, waiver of foreign language requirements, a reader for examinations, and the use of strategies to bypass handwriting difficulties on examinations (e.g., scribe, word processing).

Self-awareness

Adolescents who undergo the process of neuropsychological evaluation should be encouraged to meet with the evaluator upon completion of the assessment in order to obtain feedback about their learning style. It is important for adolescents to understand their strengths and how to use them to their best advantage in college. In addition, adolescents should be given information regarding ongoing areas of challenge and how to bypass or compensate for these weaknesses. Students should also be provided with a clear way of explaining their learning difference to a professor or employer and encouraged to self-advocate for what they need.

Conclusion

A thoughtful, well-written neuropsychological evaluation is a very useful document for students with learning issues. When the results are properly diagnosed, the student will obtain accommodations to which they are legally entitled, but, more importantly, this will help the student better understand his/her own strengths and challenges. The college years mark an important transition for students with learning differences because there is a much wider range of options for post-secondary education, providing the opportunity for choosing a program that is better tailored to the student's needs. That allows the student to become increasingly familiar within his/her learning strengths rather than weaknesses.

Ann Helmus, Ph.D.
Children's Evaluation Center
Newton, MA

CHAPTER VIII: ACT VS. SAT

The revised ACT and SAT present both obstacles and opportunities for special needs students. This chapter compares and contrasts these two college entrance exams.

The ACT

The ACT, a three hour and 25 minute multiple choice test, is divided into four main sections: English, Math, Reading Comprehension, and Science Reasoning. A fifth section, a written essay, is offered, but not required by every college. At the time that a student registers for the ACT, he/she will decide whether or not to sign up for the 30 minute optional essay.

The first and longest section, English, predominantly comprises multiple choice grammar questions. Students are asked to identify errors in punctuation, subject/verb agreement, pronoun usage, parallelism, tenses, modifiers, and word choice. They are also required to evaluate suggested sentence changes, marking those that result in effective improvements.

The 60 minute Math section covers arithmetic, geometry, algebra, data interpretation, and trigonometry. Most students have covered all of these topics with the exception of trigonometry by the middle of their sophomore year of high school. By learning two equations, the three or four trigonometry questions are easily answered.

The Reading Comprehension section comprises four 700–900 word passages, each of which is followed by 10 questions. The passages, excerpts from previously published articles, cover the categories of fiction, social science, humanities, and natural science. All answers can be arrived at by using material and inferences from the text. For many students, Reading Comprehension is the section where they are most pressed for time. Answer choices require scrutiny; the difference between a right and wrong answer often rests on one word.

The Science Reasoning section contains seven passages that describe an experiment or set of experiments and the resulting data. The 40 questions involve data interpretation and reasoning; they do not test the student's knowledge of biology, chemistry, or physics. Thus, to successfully complete this section, prior knowledge is not required. Indeed, the ACT goes out of its way not to present experiments that might have been presented in a science textbook. Nonetheless, students familiar with basic terminology, such as "degrees Centigrade" or "joules/second" have a comfort level that is lacking in students not previously exposed to this terminology.

While the experiments can be complex, most of the questions are relatively simple. The well-coached student learns where to quickly find answers and how to avoid distractions. Students coached in □what to look for and what is likely to be irrelevant□ usually find they can complete all seven passages with a high rate of success.

The optional Essay section was added to the ACT in 2005. In 30 minutes, students are asked to respond to one open-ended question. Through June 2005, prompts have been related to the school experience:

- Should teenagers be required to maintain a C average in school before receiving a driver's license?
- Should high schools require students to complete a certain number of hours of community service?
- Should school start early in the morning?
- Are high school sports generally beneficial?

Two professional readers score the essays on a range of 0-6. Should the readers' grades differ by two or more points, a third reader evaluates the essay. Since there are no specific attributes for which readers give or deny points, the essays are scored holistically. Logically supporting a position, writing with clarity, and using grammar correctly are the ostensible criteria. Readers are not supposed to evaluate spelling and length of essay. It remains to be seen, however, whether readers would ever give a perfect score to a short essay filled with spelling errors.

The New SAT

The new SAT, inaugurated in March 2005, is divided into 10 sections and lasts three hours and 45 minutes. Three sections focus on Math skills, three are devoted to Critical Reading, and three comprise Writing. The last section, Equating, falls into one of the aforementioned categories, but is not included in the student's score.

The Math sections rely upon a student's coursework in arithmetic, algebra I, and geometry. Unlike the ACT, the SAT does not test trigonometry. Since the new SAT does not include questions relating to Algebra II, it is suitable for most students who have completed the sophomore year of high school. The Math sections also include questions on data interpretation and logical reasoning. About 1/3 of the questions come from outside traditional high school curricula. SAT Math requires resourcefulness; in a single problem, students may be required to use both geometry and algebra.

The Critical Reading sections include sentence completion and reading comprehension questions. Sentence completion relies upon a student's vocabulary and reasoning skills. Although success on the reading comprehension section is enhanced by a student's strong vocabulary, the questions following the passage usually enable the student to infer the meaning of difficult words.

As in the ACT, the SAT reading passages are selected from published works, but on this test, the passages are more obscure. Answers to the questions require a higher degree of scrutiny than is found on the ACT.

Writing sections combine an essay and multiple choice questions where students are asked to identify errors or improve sentence structure. The essays are scored on a scale of 0-6 by two trained readers. The March 2005 topics included:

- Is the opinion of the majority (in government or in any other circumstances) a poor guide?
- Is creativity needed more than ever in the world today?
- Are people better at making observations, discoveries, and decisions if they remain impartial?
- Is a person responsible, through the example he or she sets, for the behavior of other people?

ACT	SAT
English: Essay, 30 minutes (optional) Grammar, 45 minutes	Writing: Essay, 25 minutes Grammar, 35 minutes
Math: 60 minutes; includes trigonometry	Math: 70 minutes; no trigonometry
Reading: 4 passages, 35 minutes	Critical Reading: 4 passages & 19 sentence completions, 70 mins
Science Reasoning: 35 minutes	No Science
No Equating Section	Equating Section, 25 minutes
205 minutes (Including 30 minutes optional) 3.5 hrs or 3.75 hrs + 40 minutes extra time	225 minutes
$28 (+ $14 for optional writing section)	$41.50
Score choice	No score choice

The tests have become similar, but ACT remains a bit broader in content.

ACT and SAT Accommodations for Students with Special Needs

The form requesting special accommodations can be filled out by the high school or the neuropsych evaluator. Not everyone who seeks consideration is approved. Of the 50,000 who sought ACT accommodations in 2004, 88% of the requests were honored, according to ACT spokesman Charles Parmalee. SAT approval rates are similar, but the specific percentage is unavailable.

Students who receive extended time no longer have their scores "flagged." Until 2003, colleges were aware of which applicants had taken the test under non-standard conditions. Although most colleges did not discriminate against those granted extended time, some did. In 2002, the College Board settled a lawsuit brought by a Berkeley-based disability rights group and in June 2003, scores were no longer differentiated. The ACT followed suit in October 2003. At that time, just under 5% of SAT testers had been granted special accommodations; as expected, that percentage has risen since then.

With the SAT, students granted extend time will be allotted time and a half; on the ACT, students can receive up to 100% additional time for testing. For both tests, other accommodations might include: tests written in Braille, use of computers for writing the essay, or the assistance of a reader.

Which Test Is Better For My Student?
Students requiring extended time might find the SAT lengthy. The ACT permits a student to take the exam during the regular school day.

Which test is best for me?	ACT	SAT
Strong vocabulary		✓
Strong math	✓	
Difficulty interpreting data and charts		✓
Trouble focusing on details	✓	

While the SAT subtracts 25% of incorrect answers from the total number of correct answers, the ACT does not penalize for incorrect answers.

A Suggestion On Test Choice
When a student is attempting to determine which test would be most appropriate, I suggest taking two diagnostic tests in The Real ACT Prep Guide and two exams found in The Official SAT Study Guide. After equating the scores, the student will be able to determine which test is preferred. Appropriate tutoring should follow.

Students who are starting at a community college almost certainly do not need to present SAT or ACT scores. Even among four-year colleges, quite a few have dropped the SAT/ACT requirement. At these schools, emphasis is placed on three years of grades and recommendations.

Mark Greenstein, J.D.
President of Ivy Bound Test Preparation
New Britain, CT

Below is a table that includes the old ACT Composite scores with corresponding SAT I scores.

ACT COMPOSITE	SAT I SCORE
15	1060
17	1210
19	1350
20	1410
21	1500
22	1530
23	1590
24	1650
25	1700
26	1760
28	1820
28	1860
29	1920
30	1980
31	2040
32	2130
33	2190
34	2260
35	2340
36	2400

Source: College Board, Data Extrapolated

CHAPTER IX: THE COLLEGE PROFILE FORMAT

School profiles have been organized alphabetically by state and then alphabetically by name. Below are the categories that were considered in preparing the college summaries. For each individual college report, we included only the respondent's affirmative answers. That is, in response to our multi-part query about accommodations, a school might only offer untimed exams: in that case, we left the other items unchecked.

RATINGS

For most schools, at the very top of the page, two aspects are headlined: selectivity and service level. This notation makes it easier for students to select suitable colleges.

SELECTIVITY

All colleges were asked to rate their relative selectivity. To help them determine an appropriate rating, they were given the following guidelines:

Secondary School

	Class Rank	Grades	SAT	ACT	% Accepted
Most Selective	Top 10-20%	A/B+	1250-1600	Above 29	40% or less
Highly Selective	Top 20-35%	B+/B	1100-1250	28 or better	40-60%
Very Selective	Top 35-50%	B/B-	950-1100	26 or better	60-75%
Selective	Top 50-65%	B-/C+	750-900	24 or better	75-90%
Less Selective	Below 65%	C or below	Below 800	21 or better	Over 90%

SERVICE LEVEL

This rating will be the single most important factor for many students using this book. Colleges were asked to identify the level of service provided for special needs students: accommodations, services, or comprehensive program. They based their assessments on the following sets of definitions, with each category providing increasingly more services.

ACCOMMODATIONS

Least Amount of Service

- Services and accommodations offered conform to Federal laws.
- There is no specific department responsible for special needs students.
- Students must seek out and arrange any special programs or accommodations they require.
- Services are available to all students, not only documented special need students.
- Students are fully mainstreamed.
- Tutoring may be available, but not by special needs specialists.

SERVICES

Standard Amount of Services

- The college has a structure for providing services to special needs students.
- A student service office is in charge of arrangements for special needs students.
- There is no special needs student advocate.
- Documentation of disability is required.
- Students are mainstreamed, but with support services offered.
- Tutoring may be available, including special needs specialists and readers.
- Personal tutoring may be at additional cost.
- Students may be referred to private services in the community.

PROGRAMS

Most Comprehensive Program

- The college provides intense support in a special needs specific program.
- Staff includes trained learning specialist.
- The program has a director.
- Students are required to spend a specific amount of time each week in learning centers.
- The documentation of disability is required.
- LD assessment is offered.
- There is communication between the special needs staff and regular faculty.
- A fee is often charged in addition to tuition.
- Counseling is available, as well as tutoring.
- A separate application to the special needs program is required.
- Special arrangements are often made for course selection.

NAMES, TITLES, ADDRESSES, AND SIZE

Wherever possible, to encourage contact with both the admissions office and the special needs program, this book lists two pairs of officials with their addresses and telephone numbers. This general information section also presents data on undergraduate and LD enrollment.

ADMISSIONS INFORMATION

The application information section indicates the proportion of applicants who eventually become students, together with key information on regular and special application deadlines. Under admissions process, each college was asked to describe briefly the application and documentation flow to the point of applicant notification of acceptance/rejection.

The most important criteria for admission are rated. Among the factors considered are SAT/ACT scores, class rank, interview, GPA, I.Q. tests, application, course selection, extracurricular activities, school transcript, personal statement, psychoeducational tests, and recommendations. The relative weight of these factors varies with each school.

The respondents were asked whether:

- standardized tests were waived
- SAT subject tests were required
- WAIS-IV was required and the acceptable score range
- documentation of special needs was required. If so, how current the diagnostic testing had to be and what tests are recommended

High school course requirements (English, math, science, foreign language, and history) are also specified, together with waivers for standard high school courses (such as foreign language and math).

SPECIAL NEEDS PROGRAMS AND SERVICES

The colleges were asked to describe: special orientation for special needs students, syllabus during orientation, special needs program (remedial or course reinforcement), student mainstreaming, recommended course credits per semester, time required (or recommended) in learning center, services offered to special needs students or to all students, counseling offered on a group or individual basis, as well as availability of vocational counseling, and support groups.

Graduation Requirements: course credits, GPA, years to complete degree, math waiver options, foreign language waiver options, and other requirements.

Staff: director, number of staff members (part or full time), availability and responsibility of faculty advocate.

Scope of Diagnostic Testing: ADD, ADHD, I.Q., math, personality, organization, handwriting, social skills, perceptual skills, fine motor skills, spoken language, written language, spelling, reading, and study skills.

Tutoring: individual or group tutoring offered by graduates, peers, faculty, LD staff, or teacher trainees, in math skills, study skills, language arts, written expression, word processing, time management, learning strategies, and/or organizational skills.

Academic Accommodations: availability of priority registration; lighter course load; exam accommodations including oral, untimed, take-home, on computer, with extended time, on-tape, modified exam, or in a separate room.

Program Strengths: Each college provided a brief description of its unique program. The statement sums up the school's philosophy and character, while providing prospective students, parents, and guidance counselors with a sense of the school's commitment to students with special needs.

GENERAL INFORMATION

The General Information section of each college or university profile begins with an overview of campus life at the school, ratio of men to women, percentage of foreign students, campus milieu and environs, and availability of student housing.

The colleges provided the verbal and math SAT/ACT scores for incoming freshmen, as well as the students' standing in their high school class.

The Expenses section includes the cost of tuition, room and board, books (when applicable), and the learning disabilities program for the most recent calendar year. These numbers are subject to change by the schools without notice. Note that at some schools, students enrolled in the special needs program may have additional expenses above and beyond the standard tuition costs.

We trust that you will find this information helpful. Remember the most valuable resource of all is yourself. Organizing information, meeting deadlines, asking questions when confused all require your investment of effort. We wish you the best of luck in this demanding, yet rewarding process!

College Sourcebook for Students with Learning and Developmental Differences

Descriptions of Colleges and Universities

Alabama State University

Montgomery, AL

Address: 915 S. Jackson Street, Montgomery, AL, 36101
Admissions telephone: 800 253-5037
Admissions FAX: 334 229-4984
Director of Admissions: Danielle Kennedy-Lamar
Admissions e-mail: dlamar@asunet.alasu.edu
Web site: http://www.alasu.edu
SAT Code: 1006

Director, University Services: Jessyca Darrington
LD program telephone: 334 229-4382
LD program e-mail: jdarrington@asunet.alasu.edu
Total campus enrollment: 4,689

GENERAL

Alabama State University is a public, coed, four-year institution. 168-acre, urban campus in Montgomery (population: 201,568), 91 miles from Birmingham; branch campuses in Birmingham and Mobile. Served by air and bus; train serves Birmingham. Public transportation serves campus. Semester system.

LD ADMISSIONS

A personal interview is not required. Essay is not required.

SECONDARY SCHOOL REQUIREMENTS

Graduation from secondary school required; GED accepted.

TESTING

All enrolled freshmen(fall 2004):

Average SAT I Scores:	Verbal: 390	Math: 380
Average ACT Scores:	Composite: 16	

Child Study Team report is not required. Tests required as part of this documentation:

- [ ] WAIS-IV
- [ ] WISC-IV
- [ ] SATA
- [ ] Woodcock-Johnson
- [ ] Nelson-Denny Reading Test
- [ ] Other

UNDERGRADUATE STUDENT BODY

Total undergraduate student enrollment: 1,967 Men, 2,744 Women.

Composition of student body (fall 2004):

	Undergraduate	Freshmen
International	0.1	0.3
Black	96.2	95.4
American Indian	0.1	0.1
Asian-American	0.2	0.1
Hispanic	0.3	0.2
White	1.5	2.8
Unreported	1.6	1.1
	100.0%	100.0%

26% are from out of state. 8% join a fraternity and 6% join a sorority.

STUDENT HOUSING

Freshmen are not required to live on campus. Housing is guaranteed for all undergraduates. Campus can house 2,107 undergraduates.

EXPENSES

Tuition (2005-06): $4,008 per year (in-state), $8,036 (out-of-state).
Room & Board: $3,800.

There is no additional cost for LD program/services.

LD SERVICES

LD program size is not limited.

LD services available to:

- [ ] Freshmen
- [ ] Sophomores
- [ ] Juniors
- [ ] Seniors

Academic Accommodations

Curriculum		In class	
Foreign language waiver	[ ]	Early syllabus	[ ]
Lighter course load	[x]	Note takers in class	[x]
Math waiver	[ ]	Priority seating	[ ]
Other special classes	[ ]	Tape recorders	[x]
Priority registrations	[ ]	Videotaped classes	[ ]
Substitution of courses	[ ]	Text on tape	[ ]
Exams		**Services**	
Extended time	[x]	Diagnostic tests	[ ]
Oral exams	[x]	Learning centers	[x]
Take home exams	[ ]	Proofreaders	[ ]
Exams on tape or computer	[ ]	Readers	[ ]
Untimed exams	[x]	Reading Machines/Kurzweil	[ ]
Other accommodations	[ ]	Special bookstore section	[ ]
		Typists	[ ]

Credit toward degree is not given for remedial courses taken.

Counseling Services

- [ ] Academic
- [ ] Psychological
- [ ] Student Support groups
- [ ] Vocational

Tutoring

	Individual	Group
Time management	[ ]	[ ]
Organizational skills	[ ]	[ ]
Learning strategies	[ ]	[ ]
Study skills	[ ]	[ ]
Content area	[ ]	[ ]
Writing lab	[ ]	[ ]
Math lab	[ ]	[ ]

LD PROGRAM STAFF

Total number of LD Program staff (including director):

Full Time: 1 Part Time: 1

Auburn University

Auburn University, AL

Address: 202 Martin Hall, Auburn University, AL, 36849
Admissions telephone: 334 844-4080
Admissions FAX: 334 844-6436
Registrar/Assistant Vice President, Enrollment Management: Doyle Bickers
Admissions e-mail: admissions@auburn.edu
Web site: http://www.auburn.edu
SAT Code: 1005 ACT Code: 11

LD program name: Program for Students with Disabilities
LD program address: 1244 Haley Center
Director: Dr. Kelly Haynes
LD program telephone: 334 844-2096
LD program e-mail: psd@auburn.edu
LD program enrollment: 290
Total campus enrollment: 18,896

GENERAL

Auburn University is a public, coed, four-year institution. 1,871-acre campus in Auburn (population: 42,987), 35 miles from Columbus GA and 60 miles from Montgomery. Served by bus; major airport serves Atlanta GA (118 miles); smaller airport serves Columbus GA; train serves Montgomery. School operates transportation around campus and to student residential areas. Semester system.

LD ADMISSIONS

Students do not complete a separate application and are not simultaneously accepted to the LD program. A personal interview is not required. Essay is not required.

SECONDARY SCHOOL REQUIREMENTS

Graduation from secondary school required; GED accepted. The following course distribution required: 4 units of English, 3 units of math, 2 units of science, 3 units of social studies.

TESTING

SAT Reasoning or ACT required. SAT Subject recommended.

All enrolled freshmen(fall 2004):

Average SAT I Scores:	Verbal: 553	Math: 569
Average ACT Scores:	Composite: 24	

Child Study Team report is not required. A neuropsychological or comprehensive psycho-educational evaluation is required for admission. Must be dated within 24 months of application. Tests required as part of this documentation:

- [x] WAIS-IV
- [ ] WISC-IV
- [ ] SATA
- [x] Woodcock-Johnson
- [x] Nelson-Denny Reading Test
- [ ] Other

UNDERGRADUATE STUDENT BODY

Total undergraduate student enrollment: 9,842 Men, 9,080 Women.

Composition of student body (fall 2004):

	Undergraduate	Freshmen
International	0.4	0.8
Black	9.7	7.5
American Indian	0.6	0.5
Asian-American	1.5	1.5
Hispanic	2.0	1.3
White	84.7	87.2
Unreported	1.1	1.2
	100.0%	100.0%

30% are from out of state. 18% join a fraternity and 31% join a sorority. Average age of full-time undergraduates is 20. 28% of classes have fewer than 20 students, 59% have between 20 and 50 students, 13% have more than 50 students.

STUDENT HOUSING

52% of freshmen live in college housing. Freshmen are not required to live on campus. Housing is not guaranteed for all undergraduates. Campus housing is available as per space availability. Sorority housing is provided within women's housing. Campus can house 3,117 undergraduates. Single rooms are available for students with medical or special needs. A medical note is required.

EXPENSES

Tuition (2005-06): $4,800 per year (in-state), $14,400 (out-of-state). Tuition is higher for architecture and veterinary science programs.
Room & Board: $6,952.
There is no additional cost for LD program/services.

LD SERVICES

LD program size is not limited.

LD services available to:

- [x] Freshmen
- [x] Sophomores
- [x] Juniors
- [x] Seniors

Academic Accommodations

Curriculum		In class	
Foreign language waiver	[ ]	Early syllabus	[ ]
Lighter course load	[x]	Note takers in class	[ ]
Math waiver	[ ]	Priority seating	[ ]
Other special classes	[ ]	Tape recorders	[x]
Priority registrations	[x]	Videotaped classes	[ ]
Substitution of courses	[ ]	Text on tape	[ ]
Exams		**Services**	
Extended time	[x]	Diagnostic tests	[ ]
Oral exams	[ ]	Learning centers	[ ]
Take home exams	[ ]	Proofreaders	[ ]
Exams on tape or computer	[ ]	Readers	[ ]
Untimed exams	[ ]	Reading Machines/Kurzweil	[x]
Other accommodations	[ ]	Special bookstore section	[ ]
		Typists	[ ]

Credit toward degree is not given for remedial courses taken.

Counseling Services

- [x] Academic
- [x] Psychological
- [x] Student Support groups
- [x] Vocational

UNIQUE LD PROGRAM FEATURES

We have over 1,000 students with Attention Deficit Disorder, health conditions, psychological disorders, mobility impairment, and hearing/visual impairment. Our programs and services make classes and exams accessible and usable by students with all types of disabilities, giving them the opportunity to pursue higher education. We have a full-time professional staff interpreter in our program for students who are deaf. We contract with interpreters if more services are needed. All of the University transportation buses are accessible; they each have a lift for wheelchairs, carts, etc., and large print signage, as well as audible announcements of stops by the drivers.

LD PROGRAM STAFF

Total number of LD Program staff (including director):

Full Time: 3 Part Time: 3

There is an advisor/advocate from the LD program available to students.

Key staff person available to work with LD students: Dr. Kelly Haynes, Director.

LD Program web site: http://www.auburn.edu/academic/disabilities/

Auburn University Montgomery

Montgomery, AL

Address: P.O. Box 244023, Montgomery, AL, 36124
Admissions telephone: 800 227-2649
Admissions FAX: 334 244-3795
Associate Director of Admissions and Records: Valerie Crawford
Admissions e-mail: mmoore@mail.aum.edu
Web site: http://www.aum.edu
SAT Code: 1036 ACT Code: 57

Student Services Coordinator: Tamara Massey-Garrett
LD program telephone: 334 244-3631
LD program e-mail: tmassey2@mail.aum.edu
Total campus enrollment: 4,340

GENERAL

Auburn University Montgomery is a public, coed, four-year institution. 500-acre campus in Montgomery (population: 201,568). Served by airport and bus; train serves Birmingham (100 miles). Public transportation serves campus. Semester system.

LD ADMISSIONS

A personal interview is recommended. Essay is not required.

SECONDARY SCHOOL REQUIREMENTS

Graduation from secondary school required; GED accepted. The following course distribution required: 4 units of English, 4 units of math, 3 units of science, 2 units of foreign language, 2 units of social studies, 2 units of history, 2 units of academic electives.

TESTING

SAT Reasoning or ACT required. SAT Subject recommended.

All enrolled freshmen(fall 2004):

Average ACT Scores: Composite: 20

Child Study Team report is not required. Tests required as part of this documentation:

- ☐ WAIS-IV
- ☐ WISC-IV
- ☐ SATA
- ☐ Woodcock-Johnson
- ☐ Nelson-Denny Reading Test
- ☐ Other

UNDERGRADUATE STUDENT BODY

Total undergraduate student enrollment: 1,485 Men, 2,681 Women.

Composition of student body (fall 2004):

	Undergraduate	Freshmen
International	0.0	0.9
Black	39.2	33.7
American Indian	0.4	0.5
Asian-American	1.8	1.7
Hispanic	0.7	1.1
White	54.6	59.8
Unreported	3.3	2.3
	100.0%	100.0%

3% are from out of state. 6% join a fraternity and 4% join a sorority. Average age of full-time undergraduates is 22. 47% of classes have fewer than 20 students, 51% have between 20 and 50 students, 2% have more than 50 students.

STUDENT HOUSING

22% of freshmen live in college housing. Freshmen are not required to live on campus. Housing is guaranteed for all undergraduates. Campus can house 934 undergraduates.

EXPENSES

Tuition (2005-06): $4,800 per year (in-state), $14,400 (out-of-state). Room: $3,060. Board: $4,172.

There is no additional cost for LD program/services.

LD SERVICES

LD program size is not limited.

LD services available to:

☐ Freshmen ☐ Sophomores ☐ Juniors ☐ Seniors

Academic Accommodations

Curriculum		**In class**	
Foreign language waiver	☐	Early syllabus	☐
Lighter course load	■	Note takers in class	■
Math waiver	☐	Priority seating	☐
Other special classes	☐	Tape recorders	■
Priority registrations	☐	Videotaped classes	■
Substitution of courses	☐	Text on tape	☐
Exams		**Services**	
Extended time	■	Diagnostic tests	☐
Oral exams	■	Learning centers	■
Take home exams	☐	Proofreaders	☐
Exams on tape or computer	☐	Readers	■
Untimed exams	■	Reading Machines/Kurzweil	■
Other accommodations	☐	Special bookstore section	☐
		Typists	☐

Credit toward degree is not given for remedial courses taken.

Counseling Services

- ☐ Academic
- ☐ Psychological
- ☐ Student Support groups
- ☐ Vocational

Tutoring

	Individual	Group
Time management	☐	☐
Organizational skills	☐	☐
Learning strategies	☐	☐
Study skills	☐	☐
Content area	☐	☐
Writing lab	☐	☐
Math lab	☐	☐

LD PROGRAM STAFF

Total number of LD Program staff (including director):

Full Time: 4 Part Time: 4

Birmingham-Southern College

Birmingham, AL

Address: 900 Arkadelphia Road, Birmingham, AL, 35254
Admissions telephone: 205 226-4696
Admissions FAX: 205 226-3074
Vice President for Admission and Financial Aid: Sheri Salmon
Admissions e-mail: admission@bsc.edu
Web site: http://www.bsc.edu
SAT Code: 1064 ACT Code: 12

LD program name: Couseling and Health Services
LD program address: Box 549010
LD program contact: Jane S. Seigel
LD program e-mail: jseigel@bsc.edu
Total campus enrollment: 1356

GENERAL

Birmingham-Southern College is a private, coed, four-year institution. 198-acre, urban campus in Birmingham (population: 242,820), three miles west of business district. Served by airport, bus, and train. School operates transportation to entertainment district on weekends. Public transportation serves campus. 4-1-4 system.

LD ADMISSIONS

Students do not complete a separate application and are not simultaneously accepted to the LD program. A member of the LD program does sit on the admissions committee. A personal interview is recommended. Essay is required and may be typed.

For fall 2004, 20 completed self-identified LD applications were received.

SECONDARY SCHOOL REQUIREMENTS

Graduation from secondary school required; GED accepted. The following course distribution required: 4 units of English.

TESTING

SAT Reasoning or ACT required. SAT Subject recommended.

All enrolled freshmen(fall 2004):

Average SAT I Scores:	Verbal: 608	Math: 589
Average ACT Scores:	Composite: 26	

Child Study Team report is not required. A neuropsychological or comprehensive psycho-educational evaluation is required for admission. Tests required as part of this documentation:

- [x] WAIS-IV
- [x] WISC-IV
- [x] SATA
- [x] Woodcock-Johnson
- [x] Nelson-Denny Reading Test
- [ ] Other

UNDERGRADUATE STUDENT BODY

Total undergraduate student enrollment: 541 Men, 806 Women.

Composition of student body (fall 2004):

	Undergraduate	Freshmen
International	0.0	0.1
Black	4.1	5.8
American Indian	0.0	0.1
Asian-American	3.5	2.7
Hispanic	1.4	0.9
White	90.2	90.0
Unreported	0.8	0.4
	100.0%	100.0%

23% are from out of state. 48% join a fraternity and 65% join a sorority. Average age of full-time undergraduates is 20. 61% of classes have fewer than 20 students, 38% have between 20 and 50 students, 1% have more than 50 students.

STUDENT HOUSING

93% of freshmen live in college housing. Freshmen are not required to live on campus. Housing is guaranteed for all undergraduates. Campus can house 1,390 undergraduates. Single rooms are available for students with medical or special needs. A medical note is required.

EXPENSES

Tuition (2005-06): $20,425 per year.
Room: $5,000. Board: $2,080.
There is no additional cost for LD program/services.

LD SERVICES

LD program size is not limited.

LD services available to:

- [ ] Freshmen
- [ ] Sophomores
- [ ] Juniors
- [ ] Seniors

Academic Accommodations

Curriculum

- [ ] Foreign language waiver
- [ ] Lighter course load
- [ ] Math waiver
- [ ] Other special classes
- [ ] Priority registrations
- [ ] Substitution of courses

Exams

- [x] Extended time
- [x] Oral exams
- [ ] Take home exams
- [ ] Exams on tape or computer
- [x] Untimed exams
- [x] Other accommodations

In class

- [ ] Early syllabus
- [ ] Note takers in class
- [x] Priority seating
- [x] Tape recorders
- [ ] Videotaped classes
- [ ] Text on tape

Services

- [ ] Diagnostic tests
- [ ] Learning centers
- [ ] Proofreaders
- [ ] Readers
- [ ] Reading Machines/Kurzweil
- [ ] Special bookstore section
- [ ] Typists

Credit toward degree is not given for remedial courses taken.

Counseling Services

- [x] Academic
- [x] Psychological
- [ ] Student Support groups
- [x] Vocational

Tutoring

Individual tutoring is available.

	Individual	Group
Time management	[x]	[ ]
Organizational skills	[x]	[ ]
Learning strategies	[x]	[ ]
Study skills	[x]	[ ]
Content area	[x]	[ ]
Writing lab	[x]	[ ]
Math lab	[x]	[ ]

LD PROGRAM STAFF

Total number of LD Program staff (including director):

Full Time: 1 Part Time: 1

There is an advisor/advocate from the LD program available to students.

Key staff person available to work with LD students: Jane S. Seigel, Personal Counselor/Coordinator of Academic Accommodations

Faulkner University

Montgomery, AL

Address: 5345 Atlanta Highway, Montgomery, AL, 36109
Admissions telephone: 334 386-7200
Admissions FAX: 334 386-7137
Director of Admissions: Keith Mock
Admissions e-mail: kmock@faulkner.edu
Web site: http://www.faulkner.edu
SAT Code: 1034 ACT Code: 3

LD program name: Project Key
LD program address: 5345 Atlanta Hwy
Director, Project Key: Pat Morrow
LD program telephone: 334 386-7185
LD program e-mail: pmorrow@faulkner.edu
LD program enrollment: 31
Total campus enrollment: 2,274

GENERAL

Faulkner University is a private, coed, four-year institution. 78-acre, suburban campus in Montgomery (population: 201,568), 109 miles from Birmingham; branch campuses in Birmingham, Huntsville, and Mobile. Served by airport, bus, and train. Public transportation serves campus. Semester system.

LD ADMISSIONS

Students complete a separate application and are not simultaneously accepted to the LD program. A member of the LD program does not sit on the admissions committee. A personal interview is required. Essay is not required.

SECONDARY SCHOOL REQUIREMENTS

Graduation from secondary school required; GED accepted. The following course distribution required: 3 units of English, 3 units of math, 3 units of science, 3 units of history.

TESTING

ACT required; SAT Reasoning may be substituted. SAT Subject recommended.

All enrolled freshmen(fall 2004):

Average SAT I Scores: Verbal: 508 Math: 508
Average ACT Scores: Composite: 20

Child Study Team report is not required. A neuropsychological or comprehensive psycho-educational evaluation is required for admission. Tests required as part of this documentation:

- ■ WAIS-IV
- ☐ WISC-IV
- ☐ SATA
- ■ Woodcock-Johnson
- ☐ Nelson-Denny Reading Test
- ☐ Other

UNDERGRADUATE STUDENT BODY

Total undergraduate student enrollment: 923 Men, 1,415 Women.

Composition of student body (fall 2004):

	Undergraduate	Freshmen
International	0.0	0.2
Black	15.4	22.2
American Indian	1.1	0.7
Asian-American	1.1	0.5
Hispanic	3.3	1.9
White	78.0	72.8
Unreported	1.1	1.7
	100.0%	100.0%

10% are from out of state. 50% join a fraternity and 50% join a sorority. Average age of full-time undergraduates is 21.

STUDENT HOUSING

63% of freshmen live in college housing. Freshmen are required to live on campus. Housing is guaranteed for all undergraduates. Campus can house 460 undergraduates. Single rooms are available for students with medical or special needs. A medical note is required.

EXPENSES

Tuition (2005-06): $10,500 per year.
Room: $2,500. Board: $2,700.
There is no additional cost for LD program/services.

LD SERVICES

LD program size is not limited.

LD services available to:

■ Freshmen ■ Sophomores ■ Juniors ■ Seniors

Academic Accommodations

Curriculum		In class	
Foreign language waiver	■	Early syllabus	■
Lighter course load	■	Note takers in class	■
Math waiver	■	Priority seating	■
Other special classes	☐	Tape recorders	■
Priority registrations	■	Videotaped classes	☐
Substitution of courses	■	Text on tape	■
Exams		**Services**	
Extended time	■	Diagnostic tests	☐
Oral exams	■	Learning centers	■
Take home exams	☐	Proofreaders	☐
Exams on tape or computer	■	Readers	■
Untimed exams	■	Reading Machines/Kurzweil	■
Other accommodations	■	Special bookstore section	☐
		Typists	■

Credit toward degree is not given for remedial courses taken.

Counseling Services

- ■ Academic
- ☐ Psychological
- ☐ Student Support groups
- ☐ Vocational

Tutoring

Individual tutoring is available weekly.

Average size of tutoring groups: 1

	Individual	Group
Time management	■	☐
Organizational skills	■	☐
Learning strategies	■	☐
Study skills	■	☐
Content area	■	☐
Writing lab	■	☐
Math lab	■	☐

LD PROGRAM STAFF

Total number of LD Program staff (including director):

Full Time: 2 Part Time: 2

There is an advisor/advocate from the LD program available to students. 30 peer tutors are available to work with LD students.

Key staff person available to work with LD students: Pat Morrow, Director, Project Key

Huntingdon College

Montgomery, AL

Address: 1500 East Fairview Avenue, Montgomery, AL, 36106-2148
Admissions telephone: 800 763-0313
Admissions FAX: 334 833-4347
Director of Admission: Christy Mehaffey
Admissions e-mail: admis@huntingdon.edu
Web site: http://www.huntingdon.edu
SAT Code: 1303 ACT Code: 18

LD program name: College Services
LD program address: 1500 East Fairview Avenue
Dir of Student Activities & Career Resources: Jennifer Ishler
LD program telephone: 334 833-4556
LD program e-mail: jishler@huntingdon.edu
LD program enrollment: 15
Total campus enrollment: 731

GENERAL

Huntingdon College is a private, coed, four-year institution. 58-acre, suburban campus in Montgomery (population: 201,568), 90 miles from Birmingham. Served by airport and bus; major airport and train serve Birmingham. School operates transportation to organized events. Semester system.

LD ADMISSIONS

Application Deadline: 08/01. Students do not complete a separate application and are not simultaneously accepted to the LD program. A member of the LD program does not sit on the admissions committee. A personal interview is recommended. Essay is not required. Students must present documentation for physical or mental impairment so that access to reasonable accommodations can be determined.

SECONDARY SCHOOL REQUIREMENTS

Graduation from secondary school required; GED accepted. The following course distribution required: 4 units of English, 3 units of math, 2 units of science, 2 units of foreign language, 2 units of history.

TESTING

SAT Reasoning or ACT required. SAT Subject recommended.

All enrolled freshmen(fall 2004):

Average SAT I Scores:	Verbal: 529	Math: 519
Average ACT Scores:	Composite: 23	

Child Study Team report is not required. A neuropsychological or comprehensive psycho-education evaluation is not required for admission. Tests required as part of this documentation:

- [ ] WAIS-IV
- [ ] WISC-IV
- [ ] SATA
- [ ] Woodcock-Johnson
- [ ] Nelson-Denny Reading Test
- [ ] Other

UNDERGRADUATE STUDENT BODY

Total undergraduate student enrollment: 218 Men, 397 Women.

Composition of student body (fall 2004):

	Undergraduate	Freshmen
International	1.0	2.5
Black	12.8	12.0
American Indian	0.5	1.0
Asian-American	0.5	0.5
Hispanic	0.5	0.5
White	83.7	79.3
Unreported	1.0	4.2
	100.0%	100.0%

19% are from out of state. 23% join a fraternity and 24% join a sorority. Average age of full-time undergraduates is 20. 70% of classes have fewer than 20 students, 30% have between 20 and 50 students.

STUDENT HOUSING

83% of freshmen live in college housing. Freshmen are required to live on campus. Housing is guaranteed for all undergraduates. Campus can house 616 undergraduates. Single rooms are available for students with medical or special needs. A medical note is required.

EXPENSES

Tuition (2005-06): $15,250 per year.
Room & Board: $6,100.
There is no additional cost for LD program/services.

LD SERVICES

LD program size is not limited.

LD services available to:

- [x] Freshmen
- [x] Sophomores
- [x] Juniors
- [x] Seniors

Academic Accommodations

Curriculum		In class	
Foreign language waiver	[ ]	Early syllabus	[ ]
Lighter course load	[x]	Note takers in class	[x]
Math waiver	[ ]	Priority seating	[ ]
Other special classes	[ ]	Tape recorders	[ ]
Priority registrations	[ ]	Videotaped classes	[ ]
Substitution of courses	[ ]	Text on tape	[ ]
Exams		**Services**	
Extended time	[x]	Diagnostic tests	[ ]
Oral exams	[x]	Learning centers	[ ]
Take home exams	[ ]	Proofreaders	[ ]
Exams on tape or computer	[x]	Readers	[x]
Untimed exams	[x]	Reading Machines/Kurzweil	[ ]
Other accommodations	[x]	Special bookstore section	[ ]
		Typists	[ ]

Credit toward degree is not given for remedial courses taken.

Counseling Services

- [x] Academic — Meets 4 times per academic year
- [ ] Psychological
- [ ] Student Support groups
- [ ] Vocational

Tutoring

Individual tutoring is available weekly.

Average size of tutoring groups: 4

	Individual	Group
Time management	[x]	[x]
Organizational skills	[x]	[x]
Learning strategies	[x]	[x]
Study skills	[x]	[x]
Content area	[x]	[x]
Writing lab	[ ]	[x]
Math lab	[ ]	[x]

LD PROGRAM STAFF

Total number of LD Program staff (including director):

There is no advisor/advocate from the LD program available to students. 10 peer tutors are available to work with LD students.

Key staff person available to work with LD students: Dr. Sidney J. Stubbs, Associate Dean for College Services/Registrar.

Jacksonville State University

Jacksonville, AL

Address: 700 Pelham Road, Jacksonville, AL, 36265-1602
Admissions telephone: 256 782-5268
Admissions FAX: 256 782-5291
Admissions Officer: Martha Mitchell
Admissions e-mail: info@jsu.edu
Web site: http://www.jsu.edu
SAT Code: 1736 ACT Code: 20

LD program name: Disability Support Services
LD program address: 700 Pelham Road North
Director of Disability Support Services: Dan L. Miller
LD program telephone: 256 782-5093
LD program e-mail: dss@jsu.edu
LD program enrollment: 79
Total campus enrollment: 7138

GENERAL

Jacksonville State University is a public, coed, four-year institution. 325-acre campus in Jacksonville (population: 8,404), 75 miles from Birmingham; branch campuses in Ft. Payne, Guntersville, Oxford, and Snead. Major airport serves Birmingham; bus and train serve Anniston (10 miles). Semester system.

LD ADMISSIONS

Students do not complete a separate application and are not simultaneously accepted to the LD program. A member of the LD program does sit on the admissions committee. A personal interview is not required. Essay is not required.

For fall 2004, 24 completed self-identified LD applications were received. 24 applications were offered admission, and 24 enrolled.

SECONDARY SCHOOL REQUIREMENTS

Graduation from secondary school required; GED accepted. The following course distribution required: 3 units of English, 4 units of academic electives.

TESTING

SAT Subject recommended.

All enrolled freshmen(fall 2004):

Average SAT I Scores:	Verbal: 473	Math: 470
Average ACT Scores:	Composite: 20	

Child Study Team report is required if student is classified. A neuropsychological or comprehensive psycho-educational evaluation is required for admission. Must be dated within 36 months of application. Tests required as part of this documentation:

- [x] WAIS-IV
- [x] WISC-IV
- [ ] SATA
- [x] Woodcock-Johnson
- [ ] Nelson-Denny Reading Test
- [ ] Other

UNDERGRADUATE STUDENT BODY

Total undergraduate student enrollment: 2,875 Men, 3,994 Women.

Composition of student body (fall 2004):

	Undergraduate	Freshmen
International	0.9	1.0
Black	27.4	22.2
American Indian	0.8	0.7
Asian-American	0.9	1.0
Hispanic	0.7	1.0
White	64.9	71.6
Unreported	4.4	2.5
	100.0%	100.0%

13% are from out of state. 3% join a fraternity and 3% join a sorority. Average age of full-time undergraduates is 23. 41% of classes have fewer than 20 students, 44% have between 20 and 50 students, 15% have more than 50 students.

STUDENT HOUSING

20% of freshmen live in college housing. Freshmen are not required to live on campus. Housing is guaranteed for all undergraduates. Campus can house 1,737 undergraduates. Single rooms are available for students with medical or special needs. A medical note is required.

EXPENSES

There is no additional cost for LD program/services.

LD SERVICES

LD program size is not limited.

LD services available to:

- [x] Freshmen
- [x] Sophomores
- [x] Juniors
- [x] Seniors

Academic Accommodations

Curriculum		In class	
Foreign language waiver	[ ]	Early syllabus	[x]
Lighter course load	[ ]	Note takers in class	[x]
Math waiver	[ ]	Priority seating	[x]
Other special classes	[x]	Tape recorders	[x]
Priority registrations	[x]	Videotaped classes	[ ]
Substitution of courses	[ ]	Text on tape	[ ]
Exams		**Services**	
Extended time	[x]	Diagnostic tests	[ ]
Oral exams	[x]	Learning centers	[x]
Take home exams	[ ]	Proofreaders	[ ]
Exams on tape or computer	[x]	Readers	[x]
Untimed exams	[x]	Reading Machines/Kurzweil	[x]
Other accommodations	[x]	Special bookstore section	[ ]
		Typists	[ ]

Credit toward degree is not given for remedial courses taken.

Counseling Services

- [x] Academic — Meets 6 times per academic year
- [x] Psychological
- [x] Student Support groups
- [x] Vocational

Tutoring

Individual tutoring is available daily.

Average size of tutoring groups: 4

	Individual	Group
Time management	[x]	[x]
Organizational skills	[x]	[x]
Learning strategies	[x]	[x]
Study skills	[x]	[x]
Content area	[x]	[x]
Writing lab	[ ]	[ ]
Math lab	[ ]	[ ]

UNIQUE LD PROGRAM FEATURES

DSS has a proactive philosophy that endorses Academic Coaching. DSS seeks to enhance student persistence that leads to satisfactory placement in field of study. DSS works closely with various agencies, especially the Alabama Department of Rehabilitation Services.

LD PROGRAM STAFF

Total number of LD Program staff (including director):

Full Time: 1 Part Time: 1

There is an advisor/advocate from the LD program available to students.

Key staff person available to work with LD students: Dan L. Miller, Director of Disability Support Services.

LD Program web site: www.jsu.edu/depart/dss

Judson College

Marion, AL

Address: P.O. Box 120, Marion, AL, 36756
Admissions telephone: 800 447-9472
Admissions FAX: 334 683-5282
Assistant Vice President for Enrollment Management: Michael Scotto
Admissions e-mail: admissions@future.judson.edu
Web site: http://home.judson.edu
SAT Code: 1349 ACT Code: 22

Senior Vice President/Interim Dean of Faculty: Dr. Mark Tew
LD program telephone: 334 683-5104
LD program e-mail: mtew@judson.edu
Total campus enrollment: 345

GENERAL

Judson College is a private, women's, four-year institution. 80-acre, rural campus in Marion (population: 3,511), 27 miles from Selma and 75 miles from Birmingham. Served by bus; major airport and train serve Birmingham. Semester system.

LD ADMISSIONS

A personal interview is required. Essay is not required.

SECONDARY SCHOOL REQUIREMENTS

Graduation from secondary school required; GED accepted. The following course distribution required: 4 units of English, 2 units of math, 2 units of science, 3 units of social studies, 5 units of academic electives.

TESTING

SAT Reasoning or ACT required.

Child Study Team report is not required. Tests required as part of this documentation:

- ☐ WAIS-IV
- ☐ WISC-IV
- ☐ SATA
- ☐ Woodcock-Johnson
- ☐ Nelson-Denny Reading Test
- ☐ Other

UNDERGRADUATE STUDENT BODY

Total undergraduate student enrollment: 19 Men, 326 Women.

17% are from out of state.

STUDENT HOUSING

Housing is guaranteed for all undergraduates. Campus can house 269 undergraduates.

EXPENSES

Tuition (2005-06): $9,434 per year.

Room & Board: $6,318.

There is no additional cost for LD program/services.

LD SERVICES

LD program size is not limited.

LD services available to:

☐ Freshmen ☐ Sophomores ☐ Juniors ☐ Seniors

Academic Accommodations

Curriculum		**In class**	
Foreign language waiver	☐	Early syllabus	☐
Lighter course load	☐	Note takers in class	☐
Math waiver	☐	Priority seating	☐
Other special classes	☐	Tape recorders	■
Priority registrations	☐	Videotaped classes	☐
Substitution of courses	☐	Text on tape	☐
Exams		**Services**	
Extended time	■	Diagnostic tests	☐
Oral exams	■	Learning centers	☐
Take home exams	☐	Proofreaders	☐
Exams on tape or computer	☐	Readers	☐
Untimed exams	■	Reading Machines/Kurzweil	☐
Other accommodations	☐	Special bookstore section	☐
		Typists	☐

Credit toward degree is not given for remedial courses taken.

Counseling Services

- ☐ Academic
- ☐ Psychological
- ☐ Student Support groups
- ☐ Vocational

Tutoring

	Individual	Group
Time management	☐	☐
Organizational skills	☐	☐
Learning strategies	☐	☐
Study skills	☐	☐
Content area	☐	☐
Writing lab	☐	☐
Math lab	☐	☐

Miles College

Birmingham, AL

Address: P.O. Box 3800, Birmingham, AL, 35208
Admissions telephone: 800 445-0708
Admissions FAX: 205 929-1627
Director of Admissions: Christopher Robertson
Admissions e-mail: admissions@mail.miles.edu
Web site: http://www.miles.edu
SAT Code: 1468 ACT Code: 28

Coordinator of Disability: Leon Jones
LD program telephone: 205 929-1447
LD program e-mail: ljone@miles.edu
Total campus enrollment: 1,716

GENERAL

Miles College is a private, coed, four-year institution. 35-acre, suburban campus in Fairfield (population: 12,381), five miles west of Birmingham. Major airport, bus, and train serve Birmingham. Public transportation serves campus. Semester system.

LD ADMISSIONS

A personal interview is not required. Essay is not required.

SECONDARY SCHOOL REQUIREMENTS

Graduation from secondary school required; GED accepted. The following course distribution required: 20 units of English, 20 units of math, 20 units of science, 20 units of social studies, 20 units of history.

TESTING

All enrolled freshmen(fall 2004):

Average ACT Scores: Composite: 17

Child Study Team report is not required. Tests required as part of this documentation:

- ❑ WAIS-IV
- ❑ WISC-IV
- ❑ SATA
- ❑ Woodcock-Johnson
- ❑ Nelson-Denny Reading Test
- ❑ Other

UNDERGRADUATE STUDENT BODY

Total undergraduate student enrollment: 1,716.

Composition of student body (fall 2004):

	Freshmen
International	0.0
Black	97.5
American Indian	0.0
Asian-American	0.0
Hispanic	0.0
White	0.6
Unreported	1.9
	100.0%

90% are from out of state. 2% join a fraternity and 6% join a sorority. Average age of full-time undergraduates is 20.

STUDENT HOUSING

Freshmen are not required to live on campus. Housing is guaranteed for all undergraduates. Campus can house 804 undergraduates.

EXPENSES

Tuition (2005-06): $5,408 per year.

Room & Board: $5,136.

There is no additional cost for LD program/services.

LD SERVICES

LD program size is not limited.

LD services available to:

❑ Freshmen ❑ Sophomores ❑ Juniors ❑ Seniors

Academic Accommodations

Curriculum		**In class**	
Foreign language waiver	❑	Early syllabus	❑
Lighter course load	❑	Note takers in class	❑
Math waiver	❑	Priority seating	❑
Other special classes	❑	Tape recorders	❑
Priority registrations	❑	Videotaped classes	❑
Substitution of courses	❑	Text on tape	❑
Exams		**Services**	
Extended time	❑	Diagnostic tests	❑
Oral exams	❑	Learning centers	❑
Take home exams	❑	Proofreaders	❑
Exams on tape or computer	❑	Readers	❑
Untimed exams	❑	Reading Machines/Kurzweil	❑
Other accommodations	❑	Special bookstore section	❑
		Typists	❑

Credit toward degree is not given for remedial courses taken.

Counseling Services

- ❑ Academic
- ❑ Psychological
- ❑ Student Support groups
- ❑ Vocational

Tutoring

Individual tutoring is available daily.

Average size of tutoring groups: 2

	Individual	Group
Time management	❑	❑
Organizational skills	❑	❑
Learning strategies	❑	❑
Study skills	❑	❑
Content area	❑	❑
Writing lab	❑	❑
Math lab	❑	❑

UNIQUE LD PROGRAM FEATURES

In order that these services are available either the student has been recognized with said problem(s) or the student asks for help on his/her own.

LD PROGRAM STAFF

Total number of LD Program staff (including director):

Full Time: 3 Part Time: 3

Key staff person available to work with LD students: Dean Hattie Lamar, Dean of Academics.

Samford University

Birmingham, AL

Address: 800 Lakeshore Drive, Birmingham, AL, 35229
Admissions telephone: 800 888-7218
Admissions FAX: 205 726-2171
Dean of Admission and Financial Aid: Phil Kimrey
Admissions e-mail: admiss@samford.edu
Web site: http://www.samford.edu
SAT Code: 1302 ACT Code: 16

LD program name: Disability Support Services
Counselor/Disability Suport Services: Anne R. Sherman, MS
LD program telephone: 205 726-4078
LD program e-mail: arsherma@samford.edu
LD program enrollment: 31, Total campus enrollment: 2,856

GENERAL

Samford University is a private, coed, four-year institution. 180-acre, suburban campus in Birmingham (population: 265,968); study center abroad in London, England. Served by air, bus, and train. 4-1-4 system.

LD ADMISSIONS

Students do not complete a separate application and are not simultaneously accepted to the LD program. A member of the LD program does not sit on the admissions committee. A personal interview is recommended. Essay is required and may be typed.

SECONDARY SCHOOL REQUIREMENTS

Graduation from secondary school required; GED accepted. The following course distribution required: 4 units of English, 3 units of math, 3 units of science, 2 units of social studies, 2 units of history.

TESTING

SAT Reasoning or ACT required. SAT Subject recommended.

All enrolled freshmen(fall 2004):

Average SAT I Scores:	Verbal: 578	Math: 572
Average ACT Scores:	Composite: 25	

Child Study Team report is not required. A neuropsychological or comprehensive psycho-education evaluation is not required for admission. Tests required as part of this documentation:

☐ WAIS-IV	☐ Woodcock-Johnson
☐ WISC-IV	☐ Nelson-Denny Reading Test
☐ SATA	☐ Other

UNDERGRADUATE STUDENT BODY

Total undergraduate student enrollment: 1,061 Men, 1,829 Women.

Composition of student body (fall 2004):

	Undergraduate	Freshmen
International	0.6	0.5
Black	3.3	6.3
American Indian	0.0	0.3
Asian-American	0.3	0.7
Hispanic	1.6	0.8
White	93.2	89.2
Unreported	1.0	2.2
	100.0%	100.0%

53% are from out of state. 29% join a fraternity and 34% join a sorority. Average age of full-time undergraduates is 21. 58% of classes have fewer than 20 students, 40% have between 20 and 50 students, 2% have more than 50 students.

STUDENT HOUSING

93% of freshmen live in college housing. Freshmen are required to live on campus. Housing is not guaranteed for all undergraduates. Housing is provided only to single unmarried undergraduates. Campus can house 1,860 undergraduates. Single rooms are available for students with medical or special needs. A medical note is required.

EXPENSES

Tuition (2005-06): $14,642 per year.
Room: $2,736. Board: $2,880.
There is no additional cost for LD program/services.

LD SERVICES

LD program size is not limited.

LD services available to:

■ Freshmen ■ Sophomores ■ Juniors ■ Seniors

Academic Accommodations

Curriculum		**In class**	
Foreign language waiver	☐	Early syllabus	■
Lighter course load	☐	Note takers in class	■
Math waiver	☐	Priority seating	■
Other special classes	☐	Tape recorders	■
Priority registrations	■	Videotaped classes	■
Substitution of courses	■	Text on tape	■
Exams		**Services**	
Extended time	■	Diagnostic tests	☐
Oral exams	■	Learning centers	■
Take home exams	☐	Proofreaders	☐
Exams on tape or computer	■	Readers	■
Untimed exams	■	Reading Machines/Kurzweil	■
Other accommodations	■	Special bookstore section	☐
		Typists	■

Credit toward degree is not given for remedial courses taken.

Counseling Services

■ Academic
■ Psychological
■ Student Support groups
■ Vocational

Tutoring

Individual tutoring is available.

	Individual	Group
Time management	■	☐
Organizational skills	■	☐
Learning strategies	■	☐
Study skills	■	☐
Content area	■	☐
Writing lab	☐	■
Math lab	☐	■

LD PROGRAM STAFF

Total number of LD Program staff (including director):

Full Time: 3 Part Time: 3

There is an advisor/advocate from the LD program available to students. 1 graduate student is available to work with LD students.

Key staff person available to work with LD students: Anne Sherman, Counselor/Disability Support Services.

Spring Hill College

Mobile, AL

Address: 4000 Dauphin Street, Mobile, AL, 36608
Admissions telephone: 800 742-6704
Admissions FAX: 251 460-2186
Dean of Enrollment Management: Florence W. Hines
Admissions e-mail: admit@shc.edu
Web site: http://www.shc.edu
SAT Code: 1733 ACT Code: 42

LD program name: Student Academic Services
Coordinator, Academic Advising & Support Services: Ashley Dunklin
LD program telephone: 251 380-3470
LD program e-mail: adunklin@shc.edu
LD program enrollment: 45, Total campus enrollment: 1,212

GENERAL

Spring Hill College is a private, coed, four-year institution. 450-acre, suburban campus in Mobile (population: 198,915). Served by air, bus, and train. Public transportation serves campus. Semester system.

LD ADMISSIONS

Students do not complete a separate application and are not simultaneously accepted to the LD program. A member of the LD program does not sit on the admissions committee. High school waivers are accepted for foreign language. A personal interview is recommended. Essay is required and may be typed.

SECONDARY SCHOOL REQUIREMENTS

Graduation from secondary school required; GED accepted. The following course distribution required: 4 units of English, 3 units of math, 3 units of science, 2 units of social studies, 1 unit of history, 3 units of academic electives.

TESTING

ACT required; SAT Reasoning may be substituted. SAT Subject recommended.

All enrolled freshmen(fall 2004):

Average SAT I Scores:	Verbal: 568	Math: 548
Average ACT Scores:	Composite: 24	

Child Study Team report is not required. A neuropsychological or comprehensive psycho-educational evaluation is required for admission. Must be dated within 36 months of application. Tests required as part of this documentation:

- [x] WAIS-IV
- [x] WISC-IV
- [x] SATA
- [x] Woodcock-Johnson
- [x] Nelson-Denny Reading Test
- [ ] Other

UNDERGRADUATE STUDENT BODY

Total undergraduate student enrollment: 476 Men, 768 Women.

Composition of student body (fall 2004):

	Undergraduate	Freshmen
International	0.3	1.4
Black	12.9	14.4
American Indian	0.6	0.8
Asian-American	1.0	1.3
Hispanic	7.1	6.0
White	72.0	73.6
Unreported	6.1	2.5
	100.0%	100.0%

49% are from out of state. 24% join a fraternity and 27% join a sorority. Average age of full-time undergraduates is 20. 53% of classes have fewer than 20 students, 46% have between 20 and 50 students, 1% have more than 50 students.

STUDENT HOUSING

90% of freshmen live in college housing. Freshmen are required to live on campus. Housing is guaranteed for all undergraduates. Campus can house 866 undergraduates. Single rooms are available for students with medical or special needs. A medical note is required.

EXPENSES

Tuition (2005-06): $19,658 per year.
Room: $4,000. Board: $3,730.
There is no additional cost for LD program/services.

LD SERVICES

LD program size is not limited.

LD services available to:

- [x] Freshmen
- [x] Sophomores
- [x] Juniors
- [x] Seniors

Academic Accommodations

Curriculum		In class	
Foreign language waiver	[x]	Early syllabus	[ ]
Lighter course load	[ ]	Note takers in class	[ ]
Math waiver	[ ]	Priority seating	[x]
Other special classes	[ ]	Tape recorders	[x]
Priority registrations	[ ]	Videotaped classes	[ ]
Substitution of courses	[ ]	Text on tape	[ ]
Exams		**Services**	
Extended time	[x]	Diagnostic tests	[ ]
Oral exams	[ ]	Learning centers	[ ]
Take home exams	[ ]	Proofreaders	[ ]
Exams on tape or computer	[x]	Readers	[x]
Untimed exams	[ ]	Reading Machines/Kurzweil	[ ]
Other accommodations	[x]	Special bookstore section	[ ]
		Typists	[ ]

Credit toward degree is given for remedial courses taken.

Counseling Services

- [ ] Academic
- [ ] Psychological
- [ ] Student Support groups
- [ ] Vocational

Tutoring

Individual tutoring is available daily.

	Individual	Group
Time management	[ ]	[ ]
Organizational skills	[ ]	[ ]
Learning strategies	[ ]	[ ]
Study skills	[ ]	[ ]
Content area	[ ]	[ ]
Writing lab	[ ]	[ ]
Math lab	[ ]	[ ]

LD PROGRAM STAFF

There is an advisor/advocate from the LD program available to students. 49 peer tutors are available to work with LD students.

Key staff person available to work with LD students: Ashley Dunklin, Coordinator, Academic Advising & Support Services.

LD Program web site: http://camellia.shc.edu/sas/acsupport/support.htm

Stillman College

Tuscaloosa, AL

Address: P.O. Box 1430, 3600 Stillman Boulevard, Tuscaloosa, AL, 35403
Admissions telephone: 205 366-8837
Admissions FAX: 205 247-8106
Director of Admissions: LaTanya Hatter
Admissions e-mail: admissions@stillman.edu
Web site: http://www.stillman.edu
SAT Code: 1739 ACT Code: 44

LD program name: Student Development Center
Director of Student Development: Jacqueline Currie
LD program telephone: 205 366-8894
LD program e-mail: jcurrie@stilllman.edu
Total campus enrollment: 1,116

GENERAL

Stillman College is a private, coed, four-year institution. 100-acre, urban campus in Tuscaloosa (population: 77,906), 60 miles from Birmingham. Served by bus and train; major airport serves Birmingham. School operates transportation to airport, medical facilities, and U of Alabama. Semester system.

LD ADMISSIONS

Students do not complete a separate application and are not simultaneously accepted to the LD program. A member of the LD program does not sit on the admissions committee. A personal interview is recommended. Essay is required and may be typed. Totality of LD student record will be reviewed by an admissions committee.

For fall 2004, 1 completed self-identified LD application was received. 1 application was offered admission, and 1 enrolled.

SECONDARY SCHOOL REQUIREMENTS

Graduation from secondary school required; GED accepted. The following course distribution required: 4 units of English, 1 unit of math, 1 unit of science, 1 unit of history, 16 units of academic electives.

TESTING

SAT Reasoning recommended. ACT recommended. SAT Subject recommended.

Child Study Team report is not required. A neuropsychological or comprehensive psycho-educational evaluation is required for admission. Tests required as part of this documentation:

- ☐ WAIS-IV
- ☐ WISC-IV
- ☐ SATA
- ☐ Woodcock-Johnson
- ☐ Nelson-Denny Reading Test
- ☐ Other

UNDERGRADUATE STUDENT BODY

Total undergraduate student enrollment: 679 Men, 779 Women.

Composition of student body (fall 2004):

	Undergraduate	Freshmen
International	0.0	0.5
Black	99.4	96.8
American Indian	0.0	0.0
Asian-American	0.0	0.1
Hispanic	0.0	0.7
White	0.6	1.2
Unreported	0.0	0.7
	100.0%	100.0%

27% are from out of state. 8% join a fraternity and 17% join a sorority. Average age of full-time undergraduates is 21. 65% of classes have fewer than 20 students, 30% have between 20 and 50 students, 5% have more than 50 students.

STUDENT HOUSING

96% of freshmen live in college housing. Freshmen are required to live on campus. Housing is guaranteed for all undergraduates. Single rooms are available for students with medical or special needs. A medical note is required.

EXPENSES

Tuition (2005-06): $9,550 per year.

Room: $2,400. Board: $2,550.

There is no additional cost for LD program/services.

LD SERVICES

LD program size is not limited.

LD services available to:

☑ Freshmen ☑ Sophomores ☑ Juniors ☑ Seniors

Academic Accommodations

Curriculum
- Foreign language waiver ☐
- Lighter course load ☐
- Math waiver ☐
- Other special classes ☐
- Priority registrations ☐
- Substitution of courses ☑

Exams
- Extended time ☑
- Oral exams ☑
- Take home exams ☑
- Exams on tape or computer ☑
- Untimed exams ☑
- Other accommodations ☐

In class
- Early syllabus ☐
- Note takers in class ☐
- Priority seating ☑
- Tape recorders ☑
- Videotaped classes ☐
- Text on tape ☐

Services
- Diagnostic tests ☐
- Learning centers ☐
- Proofreaders ☐
- Readers ☑
- Reading Machines/Kurzweil ☑
- Special bookstore section ☐
- Typists ☐

Credit toward degree is not given for remedial courses taken.

Counseling Services

- ☑ Academic
- ☐ Psychological
- ☐ Student Support groups
- ☐ Vocational

Meets 2 times per academic year

Tutoring

Individual tutoring is available weekly.

Average size of tutoring groups: 8

	Individual	Group
Time management	☑	☑
Organizational skills	☑	☑
Learning strategies	☑	☑
Study skills	☑	☑
Content area	☑	☑
Writing lab	☑	☑
Math lab	☑	☑

LD PROGRAM STAFF

Total number of LD Program staff (including director):

Full Time: 2 Part Time: 2

There is an advisor/advocate from the LD program available to students. The advisor/advocate meets with faculty 1 time per month and students1 time per month. 5 peer tutors are available to work with LD students.

Key staff person available to work with LD students: Jacqueline Currie, Director of Student Development.

Troy State University

Troy, AL

Address: University Avenue, Troy, AL, 36082
Admissions telephone: 800 551-9716
Admissions FAX: 334 670-3733
Dean of Enrollment Services: Buddy Starling
Admissions e-mail: admit@troy.edu
Web site: http://troy.troy.edu
SAT Code: 1738 ACT Code: 48

LD program name: Adaptive Needs Program
LD program address: 215 Trojan Center
Director, Adaptive Needs Program: Deborah G. Sellers
LD program telephone: 334 670-3220
LD program e-mail: dsellers@troy.edu
LD program enrollment: 48, Total campus enrollment: 5,487

GENERAL

Troy State University is a public, coed, four-year institution. 577-acre campus in Troy (population: 13,935), 50 miles from Montgomery; branch campus in Phenix City. Served by bus; airport serves Montgomery; train serves Birmingham (180 miles). Semester system.

LD ADMISSIONS

Students do not complete a separate application and are not simultaneously accepted to the LD program. A member of the LD program does not sit on the admissions committee. A personal interview is required. Essay is not required. There is a "special admission" policy dependant upon ACT/SAT scores and high school GPA.

For fall 2004, 17 completed self-identified LD applications were received. 17 applications were offered admission, and 17 enrolled.

SECONDARY SCHOOL REQUIREMENTS

Graduation from secondary school required; GED accepted. The following course distribution required: 4 units of English, 4 units of math, 4 units of science, 2 units of foreign language, 4 units of social studies.

TESTING

SAT Reasoning or ACT required. SAT Subject recommended.

All enrolled freshmen(fall 2004):

Average ACT Scores: Composite: 20

Child Study Team report is not required. A neuropsychological or comprehensive psycho-educational evaluation is required for admission. Must be dated within 36 months of application. Tests required as part of this documentation:

- [x] WAIS-IV
- [x] WISC-IV
- [ ] SATA
- [x] Woodcock-Johnson
- [x] Nelson-Denny Reading Test
- [ ] Other

UNDERGRADUATE STUDENT BODY

Total undergraduate student enrollment: 1,857 Men, 2,750 Women.

Composition of student body (fall 2004):

	Undergraduate	Freshmen
International	10.6	3.9
Black	23.8	28.9
American Indian	0.4	0.5
Asian-American	0.0	0.5
Hispanic	0.6	0.9
White	60.2	62.5
Unreported	4.4	2.8
	100.0%	100.0%

14% are from out of state. 23% join a fraternity and 18% join a sorority. Average age of full-time undergraduates is 23. 44% of classes have fewer than 20 students, 50% have between 20 and 50 students, 6% have more than 50 students.

STUDENT HOUSING

Freshmen are not required to live on campus. Housing is guaranteed for all undergraduates. Campus can house 1,573 undergraduates. Single rooms are available for students with medical or special needs. A medical note is required.

EXPENSES

Tuition (2005-06): $4,004 per year (in-state), $8,008 (out-of-state).
Room: $2,300. Board: $2,512.
There is no additional cost for LD program/services.

LD SERVICES

LD program size is not limited.

LD services available to:

- [x] Freshmen
- [x] Sophomores
- [x] Juniors
- [x] Seniors

Academic Accommodations

Curriculum		In class	
Foreign language waiver	[ ]	Early syllabus	[ ]
Lighter course load	[x]	Note takers in class	[x]
Math waiver	[ ]	Priority seating	[x]
Other special classes	[ ]	Tape recorders	[x]
Priority registrations	[ ]	Videotaped classes	[ ]
Substitution of courses	[ ]	Text on tape	[x]
Exams		**Services**	
Extended time	[x]	Diagnostic tests	[ ]
Oral exams	[x]	Learning centers	[ ]
Take home exams	[ ]	Proofreaders	[x]
Exams on tape or computer	[ ]	Readers	[x]
Untimed exams	[ ]	Reading Machines/Kurzweil	[ ]
Other accommodations	[ ]	Special bookstore section	[ ]
		Typists	[ ]

Credit toward degree is not given for remedial courses taken.

Counseling Services

[x]	Academic	Meets 4 times per academic year
[x]	Psychological	
[x]	Student Support groups	Meets 24 times per academic year
[ ]	Vocational	

Tutoring

Individual tutoring is available daily.

Average size of tutoring groups: 1

	Individual	Group
Time management	[x]	[ ]
Organizational skills	[x]	[ ]
Learning strategies	[x]	[ ]
Study skills	[ ]	[x]
Content area	[ ]	[x]
Writing lab	[ ]	[x]
Math lab	[ ]	[x]

LD PROGRAM STAFF

Total number of LD Program staff (including director):

Full Time: 1 Part Time: 1

There is an advisor/advocate from the LD program available to students. 1 graduate student and 2 peer tutors are available to work with LD students.

Key staff person available to work with LD students: Deborah G. Sellers, Director, Adaptive Needs Program.

Troy State University Dothan

Dothan, AL

Address: P.O. Box 8368, Dothan, AL, 36304
Admissions telephone: 334 983-6556, extension 231
Admissions FAX: 334 556-1040
Coordinator for Admissions: Reta Cordell/Andrew Rivers
Web site: http://dothan.troy.edu
SAT Code: 346 ACT Code: 15

Director, Counseling and Career Services: Keith Seagle
LD program telephone: 334 983-6556, extension 221
LD program e-mail: kseagle@troyst.edu
LD program enrollment: 24, Total campus enrollment: 1,538

GENERAL

Troy State University Dothan is a public, coed, four-year institution. 260-acre campus in Dothan (population: 57,737); branch campus in Ft. Rucker. Served by air and bus. Public transportation serves campus. Semester system.

LD ADMISSIONS

Students do not complete a separate application and are not simultaneously accepted to the LD program. A member of the LD program does sit on the admissions committee. A personal interview is not required. Essay is not required.

SECONDARY SCHOOL REQUIREMENTS

Graduation from secondary school required; GED accepted. The following course distribution required: 4 units of English, 4 units of math, 4 units of science, 4 units of social studies, 6 units of academic electives.

TESTING

SAT Reasoning required. ACT required; SAT Reasoning may be substituted. SAT Subject recommended.

All enrolled freshmen(fall 2004):

Average ACT Scores: Composite: 22

Child Study Team report is not required. A neuropsychological or comprehensive psycho-educational evaluation is required for admission. Must be dated within 36 months of application. Tests required as part of this documentation:

- ■ WAIS-IV
- ■ WISC-IV
- ☐ SATA
- ■ Woodcock-Johnson
- ☐ Nelson-Denny Reading Test
- ■ Other

UNDERGRADUATE STUDENT BODY

Total undergraduate student enrollment: 536 Men, 963 Women.

Composition of student body (fall 2004):

	Undergraduate	Freshmen
International	0.0	0.0
Black	23.2	22.4
American Indian	1.2	1.1
Asian-American	0.0	1.4
Hispanic	2.4	2.2
White	73.2	70.5
Unreported	0.0	2.4
	100.0%	100.0%

7% are from out of state. Average age of full-time undergraduates is 27. 64% of classes have fewer than 20 students, 36% have between 20 and 50 students.

STUDENT HOUSING

Single rooms are not available for students with medical or special needs.

EXPENSES

Tuition (2005-06): $4,004 per year (in-state), $8,008 (out-of-state).

There is no additional cost for LD program/services.

LD SERVICES

LD program size is not limited.

LD services available to:

■ Freshmen ■ Sophomores ■ Juniors ■ Seniors

Academic Accommodations

Curriculum		In class	
Foreign language waiver	☐	Early syllabus	☐
Lighter course load	■	Note takers in class	☐
Math waiver	☐	Priority seating	☐
Other special classes	☐	Tape recorders	■
Priority registrations	☐	Videotaped classes	☐
Substitution of courses	☐	Text on tape	☐
Exams		**Services**	
Extended time	■	Diagnostic tests	■
Oral exams	■	Learning centers	☐
Take home exams	☐	Proofreaders	☐
Exams on tape or computer	☐	Readers	■
Untimed exams	■	Reading Machines/Kurzweil	■
Other accommodations	☐	Special bookstore section	☐
		Typists	☐

Credit toward degree is not given for remedial courses taken.

Counseling Services

- ☐ Academic
- ☐ Psychological
- ☐ Student Support groups
- ☐ Vocational

Tutoring

Individual tutoring is available daily.

Average size of tutoring groups: 1

	Individual	Group
Time management	■	☐
Organizational skills	■	☐
Learning strategies	■	☐
Study skills	■	☐
Content area	■	☐
Writing lab	☐	☐
Math lab	☐	☐

LD PROGRAM STAFF

Total number of LD Program staff (including director):

Full Time: 4 Part Time: 4

There are no advisor/advocate from the LD program available to students. 30 peer tutors are available to work with LD students.

Key staff person available to work with LD students: Keith Seagle, Director, Counseling and Career Services.

Tuskegee University

Tuskegee, AL

Address: P.O. Box 1239, Tuskegee, AL, 36088
Admissions telephone: 800 622-6531
Admissions FAX: 334 724-4402
Director of Admissions: Vinette Ashford
Admissions e-mail: admiweb@tusk.edu
Web site: http://www.tuskegee.edu
SAT Code: 1813 ACT Code: 50

Director, Student Life and Development: Minnie R. Austin
LD program telephone: 334 727-8837
LD program e-mail: maustin@tuskegee.edu
Total campus enrollment: 2,480

GENERAL

Tuskegee University is a private, coed, four-year institution. 5,000-acre campus in Tuskegee (population: 11,846), 30 miles east of Montgomery and 135 miles south of Atlanta. Airport, bus, and train serve both Montgomery and Atlanta. Semester system.

LD ADMISSIONS

SECONDARY SCHOOL REQUIREMENTS

Graduation from secondary school required; GED accepted. The following course distribution required: 4 units of English, 3 units of math, 2 units of science, 3 units of social studies, 4 units of academic electives.

TESTING

SAT Reasoning required; ACT may be substituted.

All enrolled freshmen(fall 2004):

Average SAT I Scores:	Verbal: 450	Math: 440
Average ACT Scores:	Composite: 19	

Child Study Team report is not required. Tests required as part of this documentation:

- ❑ WAIS-IV
- ❑ WISC-IV
- ❑ SATA
- ❑ Woodcock-Johnson
- ❑ Nelson-Denny Reading Test
- ❑ Other

UNDERGRADUATE STUDENT BODY

Total undergraduate student enrollment: 1,046 Men, 1,464 Women.

Composition of student body (fall 2004):

	Undergraduate	Freshmen
International	0.1	0.6
Black	76.1	74.0
American Indian	0.0	0.1
Asian-American	0.0	0.1
Hispanic	0.0	0.0
White	0.4	0.2
Unreported	23.4	25.0
	100.0%	100.0%

64% are from out of state. 6% join a fraternity and 5% join a sorority. Average age of full-time undergraduates is 20. 54% of classes have fewer than 20 students, 35% have between 20 and 50 students, 11% have more than 50 students.

STUDENT HOUSING

98% of freshmen live in college housing. Freshmen are required to live on campus. Housing is guaranteed for all undergraduates. Campus can house 2,020 undergraduates.

EXPENSES

Tuition (2005-06): $11,690 per year.

Room & Board: $6,150.

LD SERVICES

LD services available to:

❑ Freshmen ❑ Sophomores ❑ Juniors ❑ Seniors

Academic Accommodations

Curriculum		In class	
Foreign language waiver	❑	Early syllabus	❑
Lighter course load	❑	Note takers in class	❑
Math waiver	❑	Priority seating	❑
Other special classes	❑	Tape recorders	❑
Priority registrations	❑	Videotaped classes	❑
Substitution of courses	❑	Text on tape	❑
Exams		**Services**	
Extended time	❑	Diagnostic tests	■
Oral exams	❑	Learning centers	■
Take home exams	❑	Proofreaders	❑
Exams on tape or computer	❑	Readers	❑
Untimed exams	❑	Reading Machines/Kurzweil	❑
Other accommodations	❑	Special bookstore section	❑
		Typists	❑

Credit toward degree is not given for remedial courses taken.

Counseling Services

- ❑ Academic
- ❑ Psychological
- ❑ Student Support groups
- ❑ Vocational

Tutoring

	Individual	Group
Time management	❑	❑
Organizational skills	❑	❑
Learning strategies	❑	❑
Study skills	❑	❑
Content area	❑	❑
Writing lab	❑	❑
Math lab	❑	❑

University of Alabama

Tuscaloosa, AL

Address: Box 870100, Tuscaloosa, AL, 35487-0100
Admissions telephone: 800 933-BAMA
Admissions FAX: 205 348-9046
Assistant Vice President for Undergraduate Admissions/Financial Aid: Mary K. Spiegel
Admissions e-mail: admissions@ua.edu
Web site: http://www.ua.edu
SAT Code: 1830 ACT Code: 52

LD program name: Office of Disability Services
LD program address: Box 870185
Director Office of Disabiltiy Services: Judy Thorpe
LD program telephone: 205 348-4285
LD program e-mail: jthorpe@aalan.ua.edu
LD program enrollment: 468, Total campus enrollment: 16,568

GENERAL

The University of Alabama is a public, coed, four-year institution. 1,000-acre campus in Tuscaloosa (population: 77,906), 50 miles from Birmingham; branch campuses at Maxwell Air Force Base and in Gadsden. Served by bus and train; major airport serves Birmingham. Public transportation serves campus. Semester system.

LD ADMISSIONS

Students complete a separate application and are not simultaneously accepted to the LD program. A member of the LD program does not sit on the admissions committee. A personal interview is recommended. Essay is not required.

SECONDARY SCHOOL REQUIREMENTS

Graduation from secondary school required; GED accepted. The following course distribution required: 4 units of English, 3 units of math, 3 units of science, 1 unit of foreign language, 3 units of social studies, 1 unit of history, 5 units of academic electives.

TESTING

SAT Reasoning or ACT required. SAT Subject recommended.

All enrolled freshmen(fall 2004):

Average SAT I Scores:	Verbal: 557	Math: 558
Average ACT Scores:	Composite: 24	

Child Study Team report is not required. A neuropsychological or comprehensive psycho-educational evaluation is required for admission. Must be dated within 36 months of application. Tests required as part of this documentation:

- ■ WAIS-IV
- ☐ WISC-IV
- ■ SATA
- ■ Woodcock-Johnson
- ☐ Nelson-Denny Reading Test
- ■ Other

UNDERGRADUATE STUDENT BODY

Total undergraduate student enrollment: 7,170 Men, 8,031 Women.

Composition of student body (fall 2004):

	Undergraduate	Freshmen
International	0.5	1.1
Black	8.9	12.6
American Indian	0.4	0.6
Asian-American	1.0	0.9
Hispanic	1.7	1.1
White	87.5	83.7
Unreported	0.0	0.0
	100.0%	100.0%

21% are from out of state. 20% join a fraternity and 26% join a sorority. Average age of full-time undergraduates is 20.42% of classes have fewer than 20 students, 44% have between 20 and 50 students, 14% have more than 50 students.

STUDENT HOUSING

71% of freshmen live in college housing. Housing is guaranteed for all undergraduates. Campus can house 4,500 undergraduates. Single rooms are available for students with medical or special needs. A medical note is required.

EXPENSES

Tuition (2005-06): $4,864 per year (in-state), $13,516 (out-of-state). Room: $3,120. Board: $1,904.
There is no additional cost for LD program/services.

LD SERVICES

LD program size is not limited.

LD services available to:

■ Freshmen ■ Sophomores ■ Juniors ■ Seniors

Academic Accommodations

Curriculum		In class	
Foreign language waiver	☐	Early syllabus	☐
Lighter course load	■	Note takers in class	■
Math waiver	☐	Priority seating	■
Other special classes	☐	Tape recorders	☐
Priority registrations	■	Videotaped classes	☐
Substitution of courses	■	Text on tape	■
Exams		**Services**	
Extended time	■	Diagnostic tests	☐
Oral exams	■	Learning centers	■
Take home exams	☐	Proofreaders	☐
Exams on tape or computer	■	Readers	☐
Untimed exams	☐	Reading Machines/Kurzweil	■
Other accommodations	■	Special bookstore section	☐
		Typists	■

Credit toward degree is not given for remedial courses taken.

Counseling Services

- ■ Academic
- ■ Psychological
- ■ Student Support groups
- ■ Vocational

Tutoring

Individual tutoring is available weekly.

	Individual	Group
Time management	■	☐
Organizational skills	■	☐
Learning strategies	■	☐
Study skills	■	☐
Content area	■	☐
Writing lab	■	☐
Math lab	■	☐

LD PROGRAM STAFF

Total number of LD Program staff (including director):

Full Time: 3 Part Time: 3

There is an advisor/advocate from the LD program available to students.

Key staff person available to work with LD students: Judy Thorpe, Director; Office of Disabiltiy Services.

LD Program web site: www.ods.ua.edu

University of Alabama at Birmingham

Birmingham, AL

Address: 1530 Third Avenue S, Birmingham, AL, 35294
Admissions telephone: 800 421-8743
Admissions FAX: 205 975-7114
Director of Admissions: Chenise Ryan
Admissions e-mail: undergradadmit@uab.edu
Web site: http://www.uab.edu
SAT Code: 1856 ACT Code: 56

LD program name: Disability Support Services
Director, Disability Support Services: Dr. Angela M. Stowe
LD program telephone: 205 934-4205
LD program e-mail: dss@uab.edu
LD program enrollment: 62, Total campus enrollment: 11,441

GENERAL

University of Alabama at Birmingham is a public, coed, four-year institution. 265-acre campus in Birmingham (population: 242,820). Served by airport, bus, and train. Public transportation serves campus. Semester system.

LD ADMISSIONS

Students do not complete a separate application and are not simultaneously accepted to the LD program. A member of the LD program does not sit on the admissions committee. A personal interview is not required. Essay is not required.

For fall 2004, 9 completed self-identified LD applications were received. 9 applications were offered admission, and 7 enrolled.

SECONDARY SCHOOL REQUIREMENTS

Graduation from secondary school required; GED accepted. The following course distribution required: 4 units of English, 2 units of math, 2 units of science, 2 units of social studies.

TESTING

SAT Reasoning or ACT required. SAT Subject recommended.

All enrolled freshmen(fall 2004):

Average SAT I Scores:	Verbal:	Math:
Average ACT Scores:	Composite: 23	

Child Study Team report is not required. A neuropsychological or comprehensive psycho-educational evaluation is required for admission. Must be dated within 36 months of application. Tests required as part of this documentation:

- [x] WAIS-IV
- [x] WISC-IV
- [ ] SATA
- [x] Woodcock-Johnson
- [ ] Nelson-Denny Reading Test
- [x] Other

UNDERGRADUATE STUDENT BODY

Total undergraduate student enrollment: 4,107 Men, 5,847 Women.

Composition of student body (fall 2004):

	Undergraduate	Freshmen
International	1.9	3.0
Black	36.2	32.7
American Indian	0.1	0.4
Asian-American	3.6	3.2
Hispanic	1.4	1.1
White	55.0	57.5
Unreported	1.8	2.1
	100.0%	100.0%

5% are from out of state. 6% join a fraternity and 6% join a sorority. Average age of full-time undergraduates is 22. 34% of classes have fewer than 20 students, 48% have between 20 and 50 students, 18% have more than 50 students.

STUDENT HOUSING

37% of freshmen live in college housing. Freshmen are not required to live on campus. Housing is not guaranteed for all undergraduates. Must be a full-time student. Campus can house 1,700 undergraduates. Single rooms are available for students with medical or special needs. A medical note is required.

EXPENSES

Tuition (2005-06): $3,840 per year (in-state), $9,600 (out-of-state). Tuition is higher for Schools of Health-Related Professions and Nursing.
Room: $3,390.
There is no additional cost for LD program/services.

LD SERVICES

LD program size is not limited.

LD services available to:

- [x] Freshmen
- [x] Sophomores
- [x] Juniors
- [x] Seniors

Academic Accommodations

Curriculum		In class	
Foreign language waiver	[ ]	Early syllabus	[x]
Lighter course load	[ ]	Note takers in class	[x]
Math waiver	[ ]	Priority seating	[x]
Other special classes	[ ]	Tape recorders	[x]
Priority registrations	[x]	Videotaped classes	[ ]
Substitution of courses	[ ]	Text on tape	[x]
Exams		**Services**	
Extended time	[x]	Diagnostic tests	[ ]
Oral exams	[x]	Learning centers	[ ]
Take home exams	[ ]	Proofreaders	[ ]
Exams on tape or computer	[x]	Readers	[x]
Untimed exams	[ ]	Reading Machines/Kurzweil	[x]
Other accommodations	[x]	Special bookstore section	[ ]
		Typists	[ ]

Credit toward degree is not given for remedial courses taken.

Counseling Services

- [ ] Academic
- [ ] Psychological
- [ ] Student Support groups
- [ ] Vocational

Tutoring

Individual tutoring is not available.

	Individual	Group
Time management	[ ]	[ ]
Organizational skills	[ ]	[ ]
Learning strategies	[ ]	[ ]
Study skills	[ ]	[ ]
Content area	[ ]	[ ]
Writing lab	[ ]	[ ]
Math lab	[ ]	[ ]

LD PROGRAM STAFF

Total number of LD Program staff (including director):

Full Time: 3 Part Time: 3

There is an advisor/advocate from the LD program available to students.

Key staff person available to work with LD students: Dr. Angela M. Stowe, Director, Disability Support Services.

University of Alabama at Huntsville

Huntsville, AL

Address: 301 Sparkman Drive, Huntsville, AL, 35899
Admissions telephone: 800 UAH-CALL
Admissions FAX: 256 824-6073
Associate Vice President for Student Administrative Services/Registrar: Ms. Ginger Reed
Admissions e-mail: admitme@email.uah.edu
Web site: http://www.uah.edu
SAT Code: 1854 ACT Code: 53

LD program name: Disability Support Services
504 Coordinator: Rosemary Robinson
LD program telephone: 256 824-6203
LD program e-mail: robinsonr@email.uah.edu
LD program enrollment: 132, Total campus enrollment: 5,523

GENERAL

University of Alabama in Huntsville is a public, coed, four-year institution. 376-acre campus in Huntsville (population: 158,216), 100 miles from both Birmingham and Nashville. Served by air and bus. Public transportation serves campus. Semester system.

LD ADMISSIONS

Students complete a separate application and are simultaneously accepted to the LD program. A member of the LD program does not sit on the admissions committee. A personal interview is recommended. Essay is not required.

For fall 2004, 37 completed self-identified LD applications were received. 37 applications were offered admission, and 37 enrolled.

SECONDARY SCHOOL REQUIREMENTS

Graduation from secondary school required; GED accepted. The following course distribution required: 4 units of English, 3 units of math, 3 units of science, 4 units of social studies, 6 units of academic electives.

TESTING

SAT Reasoning or ACT required.

All enrolled freshmen (fall 2004):

Average SAT I Scores: Verbal: 574 Math: 583
Average ACT Scores: Composite: 25

Child Study Team report is not required. A neuropsychological or comprehensive psycho-educational evaluation is required for admission. Must be dated within 60 months of application. Tests required as part of this documentation:

- ■ WAIS-IV
- ■ WISC-IV
- □ SATA
- ■ Woodcock-Johnson
- □ Nelson-Denny Reading Test
- ■ Other

UNDERGRADUATE STUDENT BODY

Total undergraduate student enrollment: 2,715 Men, 2,751 Women.

Composition of student body (fall 2004):

	Undergraduate	Freshmen
International	2.6	3.2
Black	13.1	14.7
American Indian	1.3	1.5
Asian-American	2.9	3.5
Hispanic	1.9	1.8
White	78.1	75.1
Unreported	0.1	0.2
	100.0%	100.0%

11% are from out of state. 7% join a fraternity and 7% join a sorority. 41% of classes have fewer than 20 students, 51% have between 20 and 50 students, 8% have more than 50 students.

STUDENT HOUSING

40% of freshmen live in college housing. Freshmen are not required to live on campus. Housing is guaranteed for all undergraduates. Campus can house 1,028 undergraduates. Single rooms are available for students with medical or special needs. A medical note is required.

EXPENSES

Tuition (2005-06): $4,688 per year (in-state), $9,886 (out-of-state).
Room: $3,720. Board: $1,600.
There is no additional cost for LD program/services.

LD SERVICES

LD program size is not limited.

LD services available to:

■ Freshmen ■ Sophomores ■ Juniors ■ Seniors

Academic Accommodations

Curriculum		In class	
Foreign language waiver	□	Early syllabus	■
Lighter course load	■	Note takers in class	■
Math waiver	□	Priority seating	■
Other special classes	□	Tape recorders	■
Priority registrations	□	Videotaped classes	■
Substitution of courses	□	Text on tape	■
Exams		**Services**	
Extended time	■	Diagnostic tests	□
Oral exams	■	Learning centers	□
Take home exams	□	Proofreaders	□
Exams on tape or computer	□	Readers	■
Untimed exams	■	Reading Machines/Kurzweil	■
Other accommodations	■	Special bookstore section	□
		Typists	■

Credit toward degree is not given for remedial courses taken.

Counseling Services

- ■ Academic
- ■ Psychological — Meets 16 times per academic year
- □ Student Support groups
- □ Vocational

Tutoring

Individual tutoring is available daily.

	Individual	Group
Time management	■	■
Organizational skills	■	■
Learning strategies	■	■
Study skills	■	■
Content area	□	□
Writing lab	■	□
Math lab	■	■

LD PROGRAM STAFF

12 peer tutors are available to work with LD students.

Key staff person available to work with LD students: Rosemary Robinson, 504 coordinator.

LD Program web site: www.uah.edu/disability

University of Mobile

Mobile, AL

Address: P.O. Box 13220, Mobile, AL, 36663-0220
Admissions telephone: 251 442-2273
Admissions FAX: 251 442-2498
Director of Admissions: Kris Nelson
Admissions e-mail: adminfo@umobile.edu
Web site: http://www.umobile.edu
SAT Code: 1515 ACT Code: 29

Director of Audie Services: Barbara Smith
LD program telephone: 251 442-2276
LD program enrollment: 10, Total campus enrollment: 1,628

GENERAL

University of Mobile is a private, coed, four-year institution. 800-acre, urban campus in Mobile (population: 198,915). Served by air, bus, and train; major airport serves New Orleans (170 miles). Semester system.

LD ADMISSIONS

Students do not complete a separate application and are not simultaneously accepted to the LD program. A member of the LD program does not sit on the admissions committee. Essay is not required.

For fall 2004, 6 completed self-identified LD applications were received. 5 applications were offered admission, and 4 enrolled.

SECONDARY SCHOOL REQUIREMENTS

Graduation from secondary school required; GED accepted.

TESTING

ACT recommended.

Child Study Team report is not required. A neuropsychological or comprehensive psycho-education evaluation is not required for admission. Tests required as part of this documentation:

- [ ] WAIS-IV
- [ ] WISC-IV
- [ ] SATA
- [ ] Woodcock-Johnson
- [ ] Nelson-Denny Reading Test
- [ ] Other

UNDERGRADUATE STUDENT BODY

Total undergraduate student enrollment: 575 Men, 1,228 Women.

Composition of student body (fall 2004):

	Undergraduate	Freshmen
International	6.8	3.0
Black	10.4	22.4
American Indian	1.6	1.9
Asian-American	0.0	0.0
Hispanic	0.4	0.3
White	79.2	64.3
Unreported	1.6	8.1
	100.0%	100.0%

53% of classes have fewer than 20 students, 46% have between 20 and 50 students, 1% have more than 50 students.

STUDENT HOUSING

Freshmen are not required to live on campus. Housing is guaranteed for all undergraduates. Campus can house 501 undergraduates. Single rooms are available for students with medical or special needs. A medical note is required.

EXPENSES

Tuition (2005-06): $10,230 per year.

Room: $3,710. Board: $2,680.
There is no additional cost for LD program/services.

LD SERVICES

LD program size is not limited.

LD services available to:

- [x] Freshmen
- [x] Sophomores
- [x] Juniors
- [x] Seniors

Academic Accommodations

Curriculum

- [ ] Foreign language waiver
- [ ] Lighter course load
- [ ] Math waiver
- [ ] Other special classes
- [ ] Priority registrations
- [ ] Substitution of courses

Exams

- [x] Extended time
- [ ] Oral exams
- [ ] Take home exams
- [x] Exams on tape or computer
- [x] Untimed exams
- [ ] Other accommodations

In class

- [ ] Early syllabus
- [ ] Note takers in class
- [ ] Priority seating
- [x] Tape recorders
- [ ] Videotaped classes
- [ ] Text on tape

Services

- [ ] Diagnostic tests
- [x] Learning centers
- [ ] Proofreaders
- [ ] Readers
- [ ] Reading Machines/Kurzweil
- [ ] Special bookstore section
- [ ] Typists

Credit toward degree is not given for remedial courses taken.

Counseling Services

- [x] Academic
- [ ] Psychological
- [ ] Student Support groups
- [ ] Vocational

Tutoring

Individual tutoring is available daily.

Average size of tutoring groups: 2

	Individual	Group
Time management	[ ]	[ ]
Organizational skills	[ ]	[ ]
Learning strategies	[ ]	[ ]
Study skills	[x]	[ ]
Content area	[ ]	[ ]
Writing lab	[x]	[ ]
Math lab	[x]	[ ]

LD PROGRAM STAFF

There is an advisor/advocate from the LD program available to students.

University of Montevallo

Montevallo, AL

Address: Station 6030, Montevallo, AL, 35115
Admissions telephone: 800 292-4349
Admissions FAX: 205 665-6032
Director of Admissions: Lynn Gurganus
Admissions e-mail: admissions@um.montevallo.edu
Web site: http://www.montevallo.edu
SAT Code: 1004 ACT Code: 4

LD program name: Services for Students with Disabilities
LD program address: Station 6250, Montevallo
Coordinator of Services for Students with Disabilities: Deborah McCune
LD program telephone: 205 665-6250
LD program e-mail: mccuned@montevallo.edu
LD program enrollment: 75, Total campus enrollment: 2,614

GENERAL

University of Montevallo is a public, coed, four-year institution. 160-acre campus in Montevallo (population: 4,825), 30 miles from Birmingham. Major airport and train serve Birmingham; bus serves Calera (eight miles). Semester system.

LD ADMISSIONS

Students do not complete a separate application and are not simultaneously accepted to the LD program. A member of the LD program does not sit on the admissions committee. A personal interview is not required. Essay is not required.

SECONDARY SCHOOL REQUIREMENTS

Graduation from secondary school required; GED accepted. The following course distribution required: 4 units of English, 2 units of math, 2 units of science, 2 units of social studies, 2 units of history, 4 units of academic electives.

TESTING

SAT Reasoning or ACT required. SAT Subject recommended.

All enrolled freshmen(fall 2004):

Average ACT Scores: Composite: 23

Child Study Team report is not required. A neuropsychological or comprehensive psycho-educational evaluation is required for admission. Must be dated within 36 months of application. Tests required as part of this documentation:

- ■ WAIS-IV
- ■ WISC-IV
- ■ SATA
- ■ Woodcock-Johnson
- ■ Nelson-Denny Reading Test
- ☐ Other

UNDERGRADUATE STUDENT BODY

Total undergraduate student enrollment: 818 Men, 1,739 Women.

Composition of student body (fall 2004):

	Undergraduate	Freshmen
International	2.2	1.8
Black	13.5	13.1
American Indian	0.8	0.6
Asian-American	0.6	0.8
Hispanic	1.2	1.3
White	81.5	81.3
Unreported	0.2	1.1
	100.0%	100.0%

5% are from out of state. 17% join a fraternity and 17% join a sorority. Average age of full-time undergraduates is 21. 38% of classes have fewer than 20 students, 60% have between 20 and 50 students, 2% have more than 50 students.

STUDENT HOUSING

64% of freshmen live in college housing. Freshmen are required to live on campus. Housing is guaranteed for all undergraduates. Campus can house 1,252 undergraduates. Single rooms are available for students with medical or special needs. A medical note is required.

EXPENSES

Tuition (2005-06): $5,460 per year (in-state), $10,920 (out-of-state).
Room & Board: $3,966.
There is no additional cost for LD program/services.

LD SERVICES

LD program size is not limited.

LD services available to:

■ Freshmen ■ Sophomores ■ Juniors ■ Seniors

Academic Accommodations

Curriculum		In class	
Foreign language waiver	☐	Early syllabus	☐
Lighter course load	■	Note takers in class	■
Math waiver	☐	Priority seating	■
Other special classes	☐	Tape recorders	■
Priority registrations	■	Videotaped classes	☐
Substitution of courses	☐	Text on tape	■
Exams		**Services**	
Extended time	■	Diagnostic tests	☐
Oral exams	☐	Learning centers	☐
Take home exams	☐	Proofreaders	☐
Exams on tape or computer	■	Readers	■
Untimed exams	☐	Reading Machines/Kurzweil	☐
Other accommodations	☐	Special bookstore section	☐
		Typists	☐

Credit toward degree is not given for remedial courses taken.

Counseling Services

- ☐ Academic
- ☐ Psychological
- ☐ Student Support groups
- ☐ Vocational

Tutoring

Individual tutoring is available weekly.

Average size of tutoring groups: 2

	Individual	Group
Time management	■	☐
Organizational skills	■	☐
Learning strategies	■	☐
Study skills	■	☐
Content area	☐	☐
Writing lab	☐	■
Math lab	■	■

LD PROGRAM STAFF

Total number of LD Program staff (including director):

Full Time: 1 Part Time: 1

There is an advisor/advocate from the LD program available to students.

Key staff person available to work with LD students: Deborah McCune, Coordinator of Services for Students with Disabilities.

University of North Alabama

Florence, AL

Address: UNA Box 5121, Florence, AL, 35632
Admissions telephone: 800 TALKUNA
Admissions FAX: 256 765-4349
Dean of Enrollment Management: Kim Mauldin
Admissions e-mail: admissions@una.edu
Web site: http://www.una.edu
SAT Code: 1735 ACT Code: 14

LD program name: Student Life/Developmental Services
LD program address: UNA Box 5008
Associate Director, Student Life-Developmental Service: Jennifer Adams
LD program telephone: 256 765-4214
LD program e-mail: jsadams@una.edu
Total campus enrollment: 5,112

GENERAL

University of North Alabama is a public, coed, four-year institution. 125-acre campus in Florence (population: 36,234), 125 miles from Birmingham. Served by bus; airport and train serve Birmingham; major airport serves Huntsville (60 miles). Semester system.

LD ADMISSIONS

A personal interview is required. Essay is not required.

SECONDARY SCHOOL REQUIREMENTS

Graduation from secondary school required; GED accepted. The following course distribution required: 4 units of English, 2 units of math, 2 units of science, 3 units of social studies.

TESTING

SAT Subject recommended.

All enrolled freshmen(fall 2004):

Average SAT I Scores:	Verbal: 483	Math: 492
Average ACT Scores:	Composite: 21	

Child Study Team report is not required. Tests required as part of this documentation:

☐ WAIS-IV	☐ Woodcock-Johnson
☐ WISC-IV	☐ Nelson-Denny Reading Test
☐ SATA	☐ Other

UNDERGRADUATE STUDENT BODY

Total undergraduate student enrollment: 2,011 Men, 2,841 Women.

Composition of student body (fall 2004):

	Undergraduate	Freshmen
International	4.8	4.1
Black	8.3	9.7
American Indian	1.8	1.6
Asian-American	0.8	0.7
Hispanic	0.8	0.8
White	78.7	75.7
Unreported	4.8	7.4
	100.0%	100.0%

17% are from out of state. 4% join a fraternity and 5% join a sorority. Average age of full-time undergraduates is 22. 46% of classes have fewer than 20 students, 50% have between 20 and 50 students, 4% have more than 50 students.

STUDENT HOUSING

Freshmen are not required to live on campus. Housing is guaranteed for all undergraduates. Campus can house 1,281 undergraduates.

EXPENSES

Tuition (2005-06): $3,528 per year (in-state), $7,056 (out-of-state).
Room: $1,960. Board: $2,180.

There is no additional cost for LD program/services.

LD SERVICES

LD program size is not limited.

LD services available to:

■ Freshmen ■ Sophomores ■ Juniors ■ Seniors

Academic Accommodations

Curriculum		**In class**	
Foreign language waiver	☐	Early syllabus	☐
Lighter course load	☐	Note takers in class	■
Math waiver	☐	Priority seating	☐
Other special classes	☐	Tape recorders	■
Priority registrations	☐	Videotaped classes	☐
Substitution of courses	☐	Text on tape	☐
Exams		**Services**	
Extended time	■	Diagnostic tests	☐
Oral exams	■	Learning centers	■
Take home exams	☐	Proofreaders	☐
Exams on tape or computer	☐	Readers	■
Untimed exams	■	Reading Machines/Kurzweil	☐
Other accommodations	☐	Special bookstore section	☐
		Typists	☐

Credit toward degree is not given for remedial courses taken.

Counseling Services

■ Academic
☐ Psychological
■ Student Support groups
☐ Vocational

Tutoring

Individual tutoring is available.

	Individual	Group
Time management	■	■
Organizational skills	■	■
Learning strategies	■	■
Study skills	■	■
Content area	■	■
Writing lab	■	■
Math lab	■	■

LD PROGRAM STAFF

Total number of LD Program staff (including director):

Full Time: 3 Part Time: 3

There is an advisor/advocate from the LD program available to students.

Key staff person available to work with LD students: Jennifer Adams, Assoc Director, Student Life-Developmental Service.

LD Program web site: http://www2.una.edu/devservices/services.htm

University of South Alabama

Mobile, AL

Address: 307 University Boulevard, Mobile, AL, 36688-0002
Admissions telephone: 800 872-5247
Admissions FAX: 251 460-7876
Director of Admissions: Melissa Haab
Admissions e-mail: admiss@usouthal.edu
Web site: http://www.southalabama.edu
SAT Code: 1880 ACT Code: 59

LD program telephone: 251 460-7212
Total campus enrollment: 10,350

GENERAL

University of South Alabama is a public, coed, four-year institution. 1,215-acre campus in Mobile (population: 198,915); branch campus in Fairhope. Served by air, bus, and train. Public transportation serves campus. Semester system.

LD ADMISSIONS

A personal interview is required.

SECONDARY SCHOOL REQUIREMENTS

Graduation from secondary school required; GED accepted.

TESTING

SAT Reasoning or ACT required.

All enrolled freshmen(fall 2004):

Average ACT Scores: Composite: 22

Child Study Team report is not required. Tests required as part of this documentation:

- ☐ WAIS-IV
- ☐ WISC-IV
- ☐ SATA
- ☐ Woodcock-Johnson
- ☐ Nelson-Denny Reading Test
- ☐ Other

UNDERGRADUATE STUDENT BODY

Total undergraduate student enrollment: 4,018 Men, 5,554 Women.

Composition of student body (fall 2004):

	Undergraduate	Freshmen
International	5.2	4.5
Black	15.5	18.2
American Indian	0.7	0.9
Asian-American	2.5	2.8
Hispanic	1.6	1.6
White	69.6	67.6
Unreported	4.9	4.4
	100.0%	100.0%

14% are from out of state.

STUDENT HOUSING

Housing is guaranteed for all undergraduates. Campus can house 2,000 undergraduates.

EXPENSES

Tuition (2005-06): $3,310 per year (in-state), $6,620 (out-of-state).
Room: $2,856. Board: $3,016.

There is no additional cost for LD program/services.

LD SERVICES

LD program size is not limited.

LD services available to:

■ Freshmen ■ Sophomores ■ Juniors ■ Seniors

Academic Accommodations

Curriculum		In class	
Foreign language waiver	☐	Early syllabus	☐
Lighter course load	■	Note takers in class	■
Math waiver	☐	Priority seating	☐
Other special classes	☐	Tape recorders	■
Priority registrations	☐	Videotaped classes	☐
Substitution of courses	☐	Text on tape	☐
Exams		**Services**	
Extended time	■	Diagnostic tests	■
Oral exams	■	Learning centers	■
Take home exams	☐	Proofreaders	☐
Exams on tape or computer	☐	Readers	■
Untimed exams	■	Reading Machines/Kurzweil	■
Other accommodations	☐	Special bookstore section	☐
		Typists	☐

Credit toward degree is not given for remedial courses taken.

Counseling Services

- ☐ Academic
- ☐ Psychological
- ☐ Student Support groups
- ☐ Vocational

Tutoring

	Individual	Group
Time management	☐	☐
Organizational skills	☐	☐
Learning strategies	☐	☐
Study skills	☐	☐
Content area	☐	☐
Writing lab	☐	☐
Math lab	☐	☐

LD PROGRAM STAFF

Total number of LD Program staff (including director):

Full Time: 2 Part Time: 2

University of West Alabama

Livingston, AL

Address: Station 4, Livingston, AL, 35470
Admissions telephone: 205 652-3578
Admissions FAX: 205 652-3522
Director of Admissions: Richard Hester
Admissions e-mail: admissions@uwa.edu
Web site: http://www.uwa.edu
SAT Code: 1737 ACT Code: 24

Vice President of Student Affairs: Danny Buckalew
LD program telephone: 205 652-3581
LD program e-mail: db@uwa.edu
Total campus enrollment: 1,637

GENERAL

University of West Alabama is a public, coed, four-year institution. 600-acre campus in Livingston (population: 3,297), 60 miles from Tuscaloosa. Served by bus; major airport serves Birmingham (116 miles); other airport and train serve Meridian, MS (40 miles). Semester system.

LD ADMISSIONS

A personal interview is required. Essay is not required.

SECONDARY SCHOOL REQUIREMENTS

Graduation from secondary school required; GED accepted. The following course distribution required: 3 units of English, 3 units of math, 3 units of science, 3 units of social studies, 3 units of academic electives.

TESTING

ACT required. SAT Subject recommended.

Child Study Team report is not required. Tests required as part of this documentation:

☐ WAIS-IV ☐ Woodcock-Johnson
☐ WISC-IV ☐ Nelson-Denny Reading Test
☐ SATA ☐ Other

UNDERGRADUATE STUDENT BODY

Total undergraduate student enrollment: 747 Men, 878 Women.

Composition of student body (fall 2004):

	Undergraduate	Freshmen
International	0.0	1.0
Black	42.4	41.8
American Indian	0.0	0.2
Asian-American	0.0	0.6
Hispanic	1.5	0.9
White	56.1	55.5
Unreported	0.0	0.0
	100.0%	100.0%

15% are from out of state.

STUDENT HOUSING

Freshmen are not required to live on campus. Housing is guaranteed for all undergraduates. Campus can house 833 undergraduates.

EXPENSES

Tuition (2005-06): $3,838 per year (in-state), $7,676 (out-of-state).
Room: $1,460. Board: $1,612.
There is no additional cost for LD program/services.

LD SERVICES

LD program size is not limited.

LD services available to:

☐ Freshmen ☐ Sophomores ☐ Juniors ☐ Seniors

Academic Accommodations

Curriculum		**In class**	
Foreign language waiver	☐	Early syllabus	☐
Lighter course load	■	Note takers in class	■
Math waiver	☐	Priority seating	☐
Other special classes	☐	Tape recorders	■
Priority registrations	☐	Videotaped classes	☐
Substitution of courses	☐	Text on tape	☐
Exams		**Services**	
Extended time	■	Diagnostic tests	■
Oral exams	■	Learning centers	■
Take home exams	☐	Proofreaders	☐
Exams on tape or computer	☐	Readers	■
Untimed exams	■	Reading Machines/Kurzweil	☐
Other accommodations	☐	Special bookstore section	☐
		Typists	☐

Credit toward degree is not given for remedial courses taken.

Counseling Services

☐ Academic
☐ Psychological
☐ Student Support groups
☐ Vocational

Tutoring

Individual tutoring is available.

	Individual	Group
Time management	☐	☐
Organizational skills	☐	☐
Learning strategies	☐	☐
Study skills	☐	☐
Content area	☐	☐
Writing lab	☐	☐
Math lab	☐	☐

LD PROGRAM STAFF

Key staff person available to work with LD students: Danny Buckalew, Vice President of Student Affairs.

University of Alaska Anchorage

Anchorage, AK

Address: 3211 Providence Drive, Anchorage, AK, 99508
Admissions telephone: 907 786-1480
Admissions FAX: 907 786-4888
Admissions Supervisor: Cecile Mitchell
Admissions e-mail: enroll@uaa.alaska.edu
Web site: http://www.uaa.alaska.edu
SAT Code: 4896 ACT Code: 137

LD program name: Disability Support Services
LD program address: UAA Business Educ. Bldg. Rm. 105
Director: Kaela Parks
LD program telephone: 907 786-4535
LD program e-mail: ankmk4@uaa.alaska.edu
LD program enrollment: 450
Total campus enrollment: 15,481

GENERAL

University of Alaska Anchorage is a public, coed, four-year institution. 428-acre, urban campus in Anchorage (population: 260,283); extension sites in Chugiak-Eagle River and at local military bases. Served by air, bus, and train. Public transportation serves campus. Semester system.

LD ADMISSIONS

Students do not complete a separate application and are not simultaneously accepted to the LD program. A member of the LD program does not sit on the admissions committee. A personal interview is not required. Essay is not required.

SECONDARY SCHOOL REQUIREMENTS

Graduation from secondary school required; GED accepted.

TESTING

SAT Reasoning considered if submitted. ACT considered if submitted. SAT Reasoning or ACT required. SAT Subject recommended.

All enrolled freshmen (fall 2004):

Average SAT I Scores: Verbal: Math:
Average ACT Scores: Composite:

Child Study Team report is not required. A neuropsychological or comprehensive psycho-educational evaluation is required for admission. Must be dated within 36 months of application. Tests required as part of this documentation:

- ■ WAIS-IV
- ■ WISC-IV
- ■ SATA
- ■ Woodcock-Johnson
- ■ Nelson-Denny Reading Test
- ■ Other

UNDERGRADUATE STUDENT BODY

Total undergraduate student enrollment: 5,539 Men, 8,622 Women.

Composition of student body (fall 2004):

	Undergraduate	Freshmen
International	2.5	2.4
Black	4.1	4.2
American Indian	13.5	9.8
Asian-American	8.0	6.0
Hispanic	3.9	4.2
White	63.6	69.5
Unreported	4.4	3.9
	100.0%	100.0%

5% are from out of state. Average age of full-time undergraduates is 31. 57% of classes have fewer than 20 students, 39% have between 20 and 50 students, 4% have more than 50 students.

STUDENT HOUSING

23% of freshmen live in college housing. Freshmen are not required to live on campus. Housing is not guaranteed for all undergraduates. Subject to space availability. Campus can house 950 undergraduates. Single rooms are available for students with medical or special needs. A medical note is required.

EXPENSES

Tuition (2005-06): $2,952 per year (in-state), $9,048 (out-of-state). $2,370 per year (state residents, lower division), $2,700 per year (state residents, upper division), $7,440 (out-of-state, lower division), $7,770 (out-of-state, upper division). Residents of the Canadian Northwest and Yukon Territories are considered state residents for tuition purposes.

Room: $4,710. Board: $3,100.
There is no additional cost for LD program/services.

LD SERVICES

LD program size is not limited.

LD services available to:

■ Freshmen ■ Sophomores ■ Juniors ■ Seniors

Academic Accommodations

Curriculum		In class	
Foreign language waiver	☐	Early syllabus	■
Lighter course load	■	Note takers in class	■
Math waiver	☐	Priority seating	☐
Other special classes	☐	Tape recorders	■
Priority registrations	■	Videotaped classes	☐
Substitution of courses	■	Texts on tape	■
Exams		**Services**	
Extended time	■	Diagnostic tests	☐
Oral exams	■	Learning centers	■
Take home exams	☐	Proofreaders	☐
Exams on tape or computer	■	Readers	■
Untimed exams	☐	Reading Machines/Kurzweil	■
Other accommodations	■	Special bookstore section	☐
		Typists	☐

Credit toward degree is not given for remedial courses taken.

Counseling Services

- ■ Academic
- ■ Psychological
- ■ Student Support groups
- ■ Vocational

Tutoring

Individual tutoring is available weekly.

	Individual	Group
Time management	■	☐
Organizational skills	■	☐
Learning strategies	■	☐
Study skills	■	☐
Content area	■	☐
Writing lab	■	■
Math lab	■	■

UNIQUE LD PROGRAM FEATURES

DSS provides a full-range of services on a service-provision level, but less than those offered at a programatic level.

LD PROGRAM STAFF

Total number of LD Program staff (including director):

Full Time: 3 Part Time: 3

There is an advisor/advocate from the LD program available to students.

Key staff person available to work with LD students: Kaela Parks, Director.

LD Program web site: www.uaa.alaska.edu/dss

University of Alaska Fairbanks

Fairbanks, AK

Address: PO Box 757500, Fairbanks, AK, 99775-7500
Admissions Telephone: 800 478-1823
Admissions FAX: 907 474-5379
Director of Admissions: Nancy Dix
Admissions e-mail: fyapply@uaf.edu
Web site: http://www.uaf.edu
SAT Code: 4866 ACT Code: 64

Disability Services Coordinator: Mary Matthews
LD program e-mail: fnmkm@uaf.edu
LD program telephone: 907 474-7043
Total campus enrollment: 7,610

GENERAL

University of Alaska Fairbanks is a public, coed, four-year institution. 2,250-acre campus in Fairbanks (population: 30,224), 350 miles from Anchorage; branch campuses in Bethel, Dillingham, Kotzebue, and Nome. Served by air, bus, and train. Public transportation serves campus. Semester system.

LD ADMISSIONS

A personal interview is not required. Essay is not required.

SECONDARY SCHOOL REQUIREMENTS

Graduation from secondary school required; GED accepted. The following course distribution required: 4 units of English, 3 units of math, 3 units of science, 3 units of social studies, 3 units of academic electives.

TESTING

All enrolled freshmen (fall 2004):

Average SAT I Scores:	Verbal: 528	Math: 518
Average ACT Scores:	Composite: 21	

Child Study Team report is not required. Tests required as part of this documentation:

- ☐ WAIS-IV
- ☐ WISC-IV
- ☐ SATA
- ☐ Woodcock-Johnson
- ☐ Nelson-Denny Reading Test
- ☐ Other

UNDERGRADUATE STUDENT BODY

Total undergraduate student enrollment: 2,611 Men, 3,698 Women.

Composition of student body (fall 2004):

	Undergraduate	Freshmen
International	1.9	1.9
Black	3.6	3.3
American Indian	20.2	17.4
Asian-American	2.5	2.9
Hispanic	3.1	2.6
White	58.8	65.8
Unreported	9.9	6.1
	100.0%	100.0%

15% are from out of state. Average age of full-time undergraduates is 23. 67% of classes have fewer than 20 students, 30% have between 20 and 50 students, 3% have more than 50 students.

STUDENT HOUSING

47% of freshmen live in college housing. Freshmen are not required to live on campus. Housing is guaranteed for all undergraduates. Campus can house 1,554 undergraduates.

EXPENSES

Tuition (2005-06): $3,270 per year (in-state), $10,890 (out-of-state).

Room: $2,990. Board: $2,590.

There is no additional cost for LD program/services.

LD SERVICES

LD program size is not limited.

LD services available to:

☑ Freshmen ☑ Sophomores ☑ Juniors ☑ Seniors

Academic Accommodations

Curriculum		In class	
Foreign language waiver	☐	Early syllabus	☐
Lighter course load	☐	Note takers in class	☑
Math waiver	☐	Priority seating	☐
Other special classes	☐	Tape recorders	☑
Priority registrations	☐	Videotaped classes	☐
Substitution of courses	☐	Texts on tape	☐
Exams		**Services**	
Extended time	☑	Diagnostic tests	☑
Oral exams	☑	Learning centers	☐
Take home exams	☐	Proofreaders	☑
Exams on tape or computer	☐	Readers	☑
Untimed exams	☑	Reading Machines/Kurzweil	☑
Other accommodations	☐	Special bookstore section	☐
		Typists	☐

Credit toward degree is not given for remedial courses taken.

Counseling Services

- ☐ Academic
- ☐ Psychological
- ☐ Student Support groups
- ☐ Vocational

Tutoring

Individual tutoring is available.

	Individual	Group
Time management	☐	☐
Organizational skills	☐	☐
Learning strategies	☐	☐
Study skills	☐	☐
Content area	☐	☐
Writing lab	☐	☐
Math lab	☐	☐

LD PROGRAM STAFF

Key staff person available to work with LD students: Mary Matthews, Disability Services Coordinator.

Alaska Pacific University

Anchorage, AK

Address: 4101 University Drive, Anchorage, AK, 99508-3051
Admissions telephone: 800 252-7528
Admissions FAX: 907 564-8317
Director of Admissions: Michael Warner
Admissions e-mail: admissions@alaskapacific.edu
Web site: http://www.alaskapacific.edu
SAT Code: 4201 ACT Code: 62

Coordinator, Disability Support Services: Tamera Randolph
LD program telephone: 907 564-8345
LD program e-mail: tamera@alaskapacific.edu
Total campus enrollment: 588

GENERAL

Alaska Pacific University is a private, coed, four-year institution. 170-acre, suburban campus in Anchorage (population: 260,283). Served by air. Semester system.

LD ADMISSIONS

A personal interview is recommended. Essay is not required.

SECONDARY SCHOOL REQUIREMENTS

Graduation from secondary school required; GED accepted.

TESTING

SAT Reasoning or ACT required. SAT Subject recommended.

All enrolled freshmen (fall 2004):

Average SAT I Scores:	Verbal: 522	Math: 495
Average ACT Scores:	Composite: 21	

Child Study Team report is not required. Tests required as part of this documentation:

- [ ] WAIS-IV
- [ ] WISC-IV
- [ ] SATA
- [ ] Woodcock-Johnson
- [ ] Nelson-Denny Reading Test
- [ ] Other

UNDERGRADUATE STUDENT BODY

Total undergraduate student enrollment: 122 Men, 311 Women.

Composition of student body (fall 2004):

	Undergraduate	Freshmen
International	1.9	0.5
Black	5.8	6.3
American Indian	3.8	12.3
Asian-American	5.8	2.9
Hispanic	1.9	2.7
White	77.0	71.0
Unreported	3.8	4.3
	100.0%	100.0%

25% are from out of state. Average age of full-time undergraduates is 25. 94% of classes have fewer than 20 students, 6% have between 20 and 50 students.

STUDENT HOUSING

82% of freshmen live in college housing. Freshmen are required to live on campus. Housing is not guaranteed for all undergraduates. Availability of space varies from term to term, first time freshmen are required to live on campus during their freshman year. Campus can house 126 undergraduates.

EXPENSES

Tuition (2005-06): $18,232 per year.
Room: $3,300. Board: $3,500.

There is no additional cost for LD program/services.

LD SERVICES

LD program size is not limited.

LD services available to:

- [x] Freshmen
- [x] Sophomores
- [x] Juniors
- [x] Seniors

Academic Accommodations

Curriculum		**In class**	
Foreign language waiver	[ ]	Early syllabus	[ ]
Lighter course load	[x]	Note takers in class	[x]
Math waiver	[ ]	Priority seating	[ ]
Other special classes	[ ]	Tape recorders	[x]
Priority registrations	[ ]	Videotaped classes	[ ]
Substitution of courses	[ ]	Texts on tape	[ ]
Exams		**Services**	
Extended time	[ ]	Diagnostic tests	[ ]
Oral exams	[ ]	Learning centers	[ ]
Take home exams	[ ]	Proofreaders	[ ]
Exams on tape or computer	[ ]	Readers	[ ]
Untimed exams	[x]	Reading Machines/Kurzweil	[ ]
Other accommodations	[ ]	Special bookstore section	[ ]
		Typists	[ ]

Credit toward degree is not given for remedial courses taken.

Counseling Services

- [ ] Academic
- [ ] Psychological
- [ ] Student Support groups
- [ ] Vocational

Tutoring

Individual tutoring is available.

	Individual	Group
Time management	[ ]	[ ]
Organizational skills	[ ]	[ ]
Learning strategies	[ ]	[ ]
Study skills	[ ]	[ ]
Content area	[ ]	[ ]
Writing lab	[ ]	[ ]
Math lab	[ ]	[ ]

LD PROGRAM STAFF

Total number of LD Program staff (including director):

Full Time: 1 Part Time: 1

Key staff person available to work with LD students: Tamera Randolph, Coordinator, Disability Support Services.

University of Arizona

Tucson, AZ

Address: P.O. Box 210066, Tucson, AZ, 85721-0066
Admissions telephone: 520 621-3237
Admissions FAX: 520 621-9799
Director of Admissions: Lori Goldman
Admissions e-mail: appinfo@arizona.edu
Web site: http://www.arizona.edu
SAT Code: 4832 ACT Code: 96

Coordinator, Learning Disabilities Program: Christine Salvesen
LD program telephone: 520 626-9234
Total campus enrollment: 28,368

GENERAL

University of Arizona is a public, coed, four-year institution. 353-acre, suburban campus in Tucson (population: 486,699); branch campus in outskirts of Tucson. Served by air, bus, and train. Public transportation serves campus. Semester system.

LD ADMISSIONS

A personal interview is not required.

SECONDARY SCHOOL REQUIREMENTS

Graduation from secondary school required; GED accepted. The following course distribution required: 4 units of English, 4 units of math, 3 units of science, 2 units of foreign language, 1 unit of social studies, 1 unit of history.

TESTING

SAT Reasoning or ACT required. SAT Subject recommended.

All enrolled freshmen (fall 2004):

Average SAT I Scores: Verbal: 552 Math: 563
Average ACT Scores: Composite: 24

Child Study Team report is not required. Tests required as part of this documentation:

- ☐ WAIS-IV
- ☐ WISC-IV
- ☐ SATA
- ☐ Woodcock-Johnson
- ☐ Nelson-Denny Reading Test
- ☐ Other

UNDERGRADUATE STUDENT BODY

Total undergraduate student enrollment: 13,029 Men, 14,503 Women.

Composition of student body (fall 2004):

	Undergraduate	Freshmen
International	1.0	3.0
Black	3.2	3.1
American Indian	2.1	1.9
Asian-American	6.5	5.6
Hispanic	14.3	15.2
White	66.4	65.5
Unreported	6.5	5.7
	100.0%	100.0%

24% are from out of state. 7% join a fraternity and 11% join a sorority. Average age of full-time undergraduates is 21. 31% of classes have fewer than 20 students, 53% have between 20 and 50 students, 16% have more than 50 students.

STUDENT HOUSING

65% of freshmen live in college housing. Freshmen are not required to live on campus. Housing is not guaranteed for all undergraduates. Priority is given to freshmen and sophomores. Campus can house 6,317 undergraduates.

EXPENSES

Tuition (2005-06): $4,394 per year (in-state), $13,578 (out-of-state). Room: $4,100. Board: $3,360.

There is no additional cost for LD program/services.

LD SERVICES

LD program size is not limited.

LD services available to:

☐ Freshmen ☐ Sophomores ☐ Juniors ☐ Seniors

Academic Accommodations

Curriculum		**In class**	
Foreign language waiver	☐	Early syllabus	☐
Lighter course load	■	Note takers in class	■
Math waiver	☐	Priority seating	☐
Other special classes	☐	Tape recorders	☐
Priority registrations	☐	Videotaped classes	☐
Substitution of courses	☐	Text on tape	☐
Exams		**Services**	
Extended time	■	Diagnostic tests	☐
Oral exams	☐	Learning centers	■
Take home exams	☐	Proofreaders	☐
Exams on tape or computer	☐	Readers	☐
Untimed exams	☐	Reading Machines/Kurzweil	■
Other accommodations	☐	Special bookstore section	☐
		Typists	☐

Credit toward degree is not given for remedial courses taken.

Counseling Services

- ☐ Academic
- ☐ Psychological
- ☐ Student Support groups
- ☐ Vocational

Tutoring

	Individual	Group
Time management	☐	☐
Organizational skills	☐	☐
Learning strategies	☐	☐
Study skills	☐	☐
Content area	☐	☐
Writing lab	☐	☐
Math lab	☐	☐

UNIQUE LD PROGRAM FEATURES

A specific program for LD/ADD students is available. The fee-for-service program is in addition to the support services office.

LD PROGRAM STAFF

Total number of LD Program staff (including director):

Full Time: 4 Part Time: 4

Key staff person available to work with LD students: Christine Salvesen, Coordinator, Learning Disabilities Program.

Arizona State University - Main Campus

Tempe, AZ

Address: Tempe, AZ, 85287
Admissions telephone: 480 965-7788
Admissions FAX: 480 965-3610
Director of Undergraduate Admissions: Tim Desch
Admissions e-mail: information@asu.edu
Web site: http://www.asu.edu
SAT Code: 4007 ACT Code: 88

Disability Specialist: Phyllis Jones
LD program telephone: (480) 965-9469
LD program e-mail: phyllis.jones@asu.edu
Total campus enrollment: 39, 377

GENERAL

Arizona State University - Main Campus is a public, coed, four-year institution. 722-acre, suburban campus in Tempe, seven miles from Phoenix (population: 1,321,045); branch campuses in east Mesa and west Phoenix. Served by air, bus, and train. School operates on-campus shuttle and transportation to east Mesa, downtown Phoenix, and west Phoenix. Public transportation serves campus. Semester system.

LD ADMISSIONS

A personal interview is not required. Essay is not required.

SECONDARY SCHOOL REQUIREMENTS

Graduation from secondary school required; GED accepted. The following course distribution required: 4 units of English, 4 units of math, 3 units of science, 2 units of foreign language, 1 unit of social studies, 1 unit of history.

TESTING

SAT Reasoning or ACT required. SAT Subject required.

All enrolled freshmen (fall 2004):

Average SAT I Scores: Verbal: 547 Math: 559
Average ACT Scores: Composite: 23

Child Study Team report is not required. Tests required as part of this documentation:

- ☐ WAIS-IV
- ☐ WISC-IV
- ☐ SATA
- ☐ Woodcock-Johnson
- ☐ Nelson-Denny Reading Test
- ☐ Other

UNDERGRADUATE STUDENT BODY

Total undergraduate student enrollment: 16,979 Men, 18,212 Women.

Composition of student body (fall 2004):

	Undergraduate	Freshmen
International	1.6	2.9
Black	3.3	3.6
American Indian	2.0	2.3
Asian-American	5.1	5.2
Hispanic	12.7	12.2
White	70.4	69.7
Unreported	4.9	4.1
	100.0%	100.0%

23% are from out of state. 10% join a fraternity and 9% join a sorority. Average age of full-time undergraduates is 21. 40% of classes have fewer than 20 students, 44% have between 20 and 50 students, 16% have more than 50 students.

STUDENT HOUSING

52% of freshmen live in college housing. Freshmen are not required to live on campus. Housing is guaranteed for all undergraduates. Campus can house 5,913 undergraduates.

EXPENSES

Tuition (2005-06): $4,311 per year (in-state), $15,000 (out-of-state). Room: $4,275. Board: $2,493.

There is no additional cost for LD program/services.

LD SERVICES

LD program size is not limited.

LD services available to:

☐ Freshmen ☐ Sophomores ☐ Juniors ☐ Seniors

Academic Accommodations

Curriculum		In class	
Foreign language waiver	☐	Early syllabus	☐
Lighter course load	■	Note takers in class	☐
Math waiver	☐	Priority seating	☐
Other special classes	☐	Tape recorders	☐
Priority registrations	☐	Videotaped classes	☐
Substitution of courses	☐	Text on tape	☐
Exams		**Services**	
Extended time	☐	Diagnostic tests	☐
Oral exams	☐	Learning centers	☐
Take home exams	☐	Proofreaders	☐
Exams on tape or computer	☐	Readers	☐
Untimed exams	☐	Reading Machines/Kurzweil	☐
Other accommodations	☐	Special bookstore section	☐
		Typists	☐

Credit toward degree is not given for remedial courses taken.

Counseling Services

- ☐ Academic
- ☐ Psychological
- ☐ Student Support groups
- ☐ Vocational

Tutoring

	Individual	Group
Time management	☐	☐
Organizational skills	☐	☐
Learning strategies	☐	☐
Study skills	☐	☐
Content area	☐	☐
Writing lab	☐	☐
Math lab	☐	☐

UNIQUE LD PROGRAM FEATURES

The ASU Disability Resources for Students Office (DRS) is the recipient of a Department of Education Student Support Services TRIO Grant. This grant supports the provision of limited enhancement (non-mandated) services for 270 at-risk students with disabilities, including students with learning disabilities.

LD PROGRAM STAFF

Total number of LD Program staff (including director):

Full Time: 3 Part Time: 3

Key staff person available to work with LD students: Susan DeFrank-Wingate, Student Support Coordinator.

Arizona State University West

Phoenix, AZ

Address: P.O. Box 37100, Phoenix, AZ, 85069-7100
Admissions telephone: 602 543-8203
Admissions FAX: 602 543-8312
Registrar: Thomas Cabot
Admissions e-mail: west-admissions@asu.edu
Web site: http://www.west.asu.edu/

Disability Outreach and Ed. Coordinator: Denise Labrecque
LD program telephone: 602 543-8145
LD program e-mail: denise.labrecque@asu.edu
LD program enrollment: 60, Total campus enrollment: 6,317

GENERAL

Arizona State University West is a public, coed, four-year institution. 300-acre, urban campus in Phoenix (population: 1,321,045); main campus in Tempe. Served by air, bus, and train. School operates transportation to main campus. Public transportation serves campus. Semester system.

LD ADMISSIONS

Students do not complete a separate application and are not simultaneously accepted to the LD program. A member of the LD program does not sit on the admissions committee. A personal interview is not required. Essay is not required.

SECONDARY SCHOOL REQUIREMENTS

Graduation from secondary school required; GED accepted. The following course distribution required: 4 units of English, 4 units of math, 3 units of science, 2 units of foreign language, 1 unit of social studies, 1 unit of history.

TESTING

SAT Reasoning required of some applicants. ACT required of some applicants. SAT Subject recommended.

All enrolled freshmen (fall 2004):

Average SAT I Scores:	Verbal: 508	Math: 507
Average ACT Scores:	Composite: 21	

Child Study Team report is not required. A neuropsychological or comprehensive psycho-educational evaluation is required for admission. Must be dated within 36 months of application. Tests required as part of this documentation:

- ☑ WAIS-IV
- ☑ WISC-IV
- ☐ SATA
- ☑ Woodcock-Johnson
- ☐ Nelson-Denny Reading Test
- ☑ Other

UNDERGRADUATE STUDENT BODY

Total undergraduate student enrollment: 1,236 Men, 2,990 Women.

Composition of student body (fall 2004):

	Undergraduate	Freshmen
International	0.3	0.8
Black	5.6	5.3
American Indian	1.8	2.0
Asian-American	4.5	3.9
Hispanic	18.2	17.6
White	64.8	67.1
Unreported	4.8	3.3
	100.0%	100.0%

1% are from out of state. Average age of full-time undergraduates is 24. 31% of classes have fewer than 20 students, 64% have between 20 and 50 students, 5% have more than 50 students.

STUDENT HOUSING

15% of freshmen live in college housing. Freshmen are not required to live on campus. Housing is guaranteed for all undergraduates. Campus can house 414 undergraduates. Single rooms are available for students with medical or special needs. A medical note is required.

EXPENSES

Tuition (2005-06): $3,973 per year (in-state), $12,828 (out-of-state). There is no additional cost for LD program/services.

LD SERVICES

LD program size is not limited.

LD services available to:

☑ Freshmen ☑ Sophomores ☑ Juniors ☑ Seniors

Academic Accommodations

Curriculum		**In class**	
Foreign language waiver	☐	Early syllabus	☑
Lighter course load	☑	Note takers in class	☑
Math waiver	☐	Priority seating	☑
Other special classes	☐	Tape recorders	☑
Priority registrations	☑	Videotaped classes	☐
Substitution of courses	☑	Text on tape	☑
Exams		**Services**	
Extended time	☑	Diagnostic tests	☐
Oral exams	☑	Learning centers	☑
Take home exams	☐	Proofreaders	☐
Exams on tape or computer	☑	Readers	☑
Untimed exams	☐	Reading Machines/Kurzweil	☑
Other accommodations	☑	Special bookstore section	☐
		Typists	☑

Credit toward degree is not given for remedial courses taken.

Counseling Services

- ☑ Academic
- ☑ Psychological — Meets 6 times per academic year
- ☑ Student Support groups
- ☑ Vocational

Tutoring

Individual tutoring is available daily.

Average size of tutoring groups: 3

	Individual	Group
Time management	☑	☑
Organizational skills	☑	☑
Learning strategies	☑	☑
Study skills	☑	☑
Content area	☑	☑
Writing lab	☑	☑
Math lab	☑	☑

LD PROGRAM STAFF

Total number of LD Program staff (including director):

Full Time: 3 Part Time: 3

There is an advisor/advocate from the LD program available to students.

Key staff person available to work with LD students: Denise Labrecque, Disability Outreach and Ed. Coordinator.

LD Program web site: http://www.west.asu.edu/sa/drc/

Embry-Riddle Aeronautical University

Prescott, AZ

Address: 3700 Willow Creek Road, Prescott, AZ,
Admissions telephone: 800 888-3728
Admissions FAX: 928 777-6606
Director of Admissions and Enrollment Management: Bill Thompson
Web site: www.pr.erau.edu
SAT Code: 4305 ACT Code: 149

Director, Health Services: Sandra Palmer
LD program telephone: 928 777-6653
LD program e-mail: palmers@erau.edu
Total campus enrollment: 1, 637

GENERAL

Embry-Riddle Aeronautical University is a private, coed, four-year institution. 565-acre campus in Prescott (population: 33,938), 100 miles from Phoenix. Served by air and bus; major airport serves Phoenix. School operates campus shuttle service. Semester system.

LD ADMISSIONS

Students do not complete a separate application and are not simultaneously accepted to the LD program. A member of the LD program does not sit on the admissions committee. A personal interview is not required. Essay is not required.

SECONDARY SCHOOL REQUIREMENTS

Graduation from secondary school required; GED accepted. The following course distribution required: 4 units of English, 3 units of math, 2 units of science, 2 units of social studies, 1 unit of history.

TESTING

SAT Subject recommended.

All enrolled freshmen (fall 2004):

Average SAT I Scores:	Verbal: 553	Math: 579
Average ACT Scores:	Composite: 24	

Child Study Team report is not required. A neuropsychological or comprehensive psycho-education evaluation is not required for admission. Tests required as part of this documentation:

- ☐ WAIS-IV
- ☐ WISC-IV
- ☐ SATA
- ☐ Woodcock-Johnson
- ☐ Nelson-Denny Reading Test
- ☐ Other

UNDERGRADUATE STUDENT BODY

Total undergraduate student enrollment: 1,446 Men, 278 Women.

Composition of student body (fall 2004):

	Undergraduate	Freshmen
International	3.0	3.1
Black	4.1	2.3
American Indian	0.5	0.9
Asian-American	7.3	6.5
Hispanic	8.1	6.6
White	61.6	69.4
Unreported	15.4	11.2
	100.0%	100.0%

78% are from out of state. 9% join a fraternity and 17% join a sorority. Average age of full-time undergraduates is 20. 44% of classes have fewer than 20 students, 54% have between 20 and 50 students, 2% have more than 50 students.

STUDENT HOUSING

97% of freshmen live in college housing. Freshmen are required to live on campus. Housing is not guaranteed for all undergraduates. Assignments made on a space available basis. Campus can house 802 undergraduates. Single rooms are not available for students with medical or special needs.

EXPENSES

Tuition (2005-06): $23,550 per year.
Room & Board: $6,730.
There is no additional cost for LD program/services.

LD SERVICES

LD services available to:

■ Freshmen ■ Sophomores ■ Juniors ■ Seniors

Academic Accommodations

Curriculum		In class	
Foreign language waiver	☐	Early syllabus	☐
Lighter course load	■	Note takers in class	■
Math waiver	☐	Priority seating	☐
Other special classes	☐	Tape recorders	■
Priority registrations	☐	Videotaped classes	☐
Substitution of courses	☐	Text on tape	☐
Exams		**Services**	
Extended time	☐	Diagnostic tests	☐
Oral exams	☐	Learning centers	☐
Take home exams	☐	Proofreaders	☐
Exams on tape or computer	☐	Readers	☐
Untimed exams	■	Reading Machines/Kurzweil	■
Other accommodations	☐	Special bookstore section	☐
		Typists	☐

Credit toward degree is not given for remedial courses taken.

Counseling Services

- ☐ Academic
- ☐ Psychological
- ☐ Student Support groups
- ☐ Vocational

Tutoring

Individual tutoring is available.

	Individual	Group
Time management	☐	☐
Organizational skills	☐	☐
Learning strategies	☐	☐
Study skills	☐	☐
Content area	☐	☐
Writing lab	☐	☐
Math lab	☐	☐

LD PROGRAM STAFF

There is an advisor/advocate from the LD program available to students.

Key staff person available to work with LD students: Sandra Palmer, Director, Health Services.

Northern Arizona University

Flagstaff, AZ

Address: P.O. Box 4084, Flagstaff, AZ, 86011-4084
Admissions telephone: 888 MORE-NAU
Admissions FAX: 928 523-0226
Director of Admissions: David Bousquet
Admissions e-mail: undergraduate.admissions@nau.edu
Web site: http://www.nau.edu
SAT Code: 4006 ACT Code: 86

LD program name: Disability Support Services
LD program address: Box 5633, Flagstaff, AZ, 86011-5633
Interim Director: Jane Mulrooney
LD program telephone: 928 523-8773
LD program e-mail: Jane.Mulrooney@nau.edu
LD program enrollment: 117, Total campus enrollment: 13,333

GENERAL

Northern Arizona University is a public, coed, four-year institution. 730-acre campus in Flagstaff (population: 52,894), 140 miles from Phoenix; branch campus in Yuma. Served by air, bus, and train. School operates transportation on campus. Public transportation serves campus. Semester system.

LD ADMISSIONS

Students do not complete a separate application and are not simultaneously accepted to the LD program. A member of the LD program does not sit on the admissions committee. A personal interview is not required. Essay is not required.

For fall 2004, 69 completed self-identified LD applications were received.

SECONDARY SCHOOL REQUIREMENTS

Graduation from secondary school required; GED accepted. The following course distribution required: 4 units of English, 4 units of math, 3 units of science, 2 units of foreign language, 1 unit of social studies, 1 unit of history.

TESTING

SAT Reasoning considered if submitted. ACT considered if submitted.

All enrolled freshmen (fall 2004):

Average SAT I Scores:	Verbal: 531	Math: 529
Average ACT Scores:	Composite: 22	

Child Study Team report is not required. A neuropsychological or comprehensive psycho-educational evaluation is required for admission. Tests required as part of this documentation:

- [x] WAIS-IV
- [ ] WISC-IV
- [ ] SATA
- [x] Woodcock-Johnson
- [ ] Nelson-Denny Reading Test
- [ ] Other

UNDERGRADUATE STUDENT BODY

Total undergraduate student enrollment: 5,561 Men, 8,179 Women.

Composition of student body (fall 2004):

	Undergraduate	Freshmen
International	2.3	1.8
Black	2.3	2.1
American Indian	5.1	7.5
Asian-American	2.4	2.1
Hispanic	10.1	10.8
White	74.8	73.8
Unreported	3.0	1.9
	100.0%	100.0%

15% are from out of state. 8% join a fraternity and 5% join a sorority. Average age of full-time undergraduates is 22. 37% of classes have fewer than 20 students, 54% have between 20 and 50 students, 9% have more than 50 students.

STUDENT HOUSING

80% of freshmen live in college housing. Freshmen are not required to live on campus. Housing is guaranteed for all undergraduates. Campus can house 5,602 undergraduates. Single rooms are not available for students with medical or special needs.

EXPENSES

Tuition (2005-06): $4,223 per year (in-state), $12,853 (out-of-state). Room: $3,256. Board: $2,704.
There is no additional cost for LD program/services.

LD SERVICES

LD program size is not limited.

LD services available to:

- [x] Freshmen
- [x] Sophomores
- [x] Juniors
- [x] Seniors

Academic Accommodations

Curriculum

- [ ] Foreign language waiver
- [ ] Lighter course load
- [ ] Math waiver
- [ ] Other special classes
- [ ] Priority registrations
- [ ] Substitution of courses

Exams

- [x] Extended time
- [ ] Oral exams
- [ ] Take home exams
- [ ] Exams on tape or computer
- [ ] Untimed exams
- [ ] Other accommodations

In class

- [ ] Early syllabus
- [ ] Note takers in class
- [ ] Priority seating
- [ ] Tape recorders
- [ ] Videotaped classes
- [ ] Text on tape

Services

- [ ] Diagnostic tests
- [ ] Learning centers
- [ ] Proofreaders
- [ ] Readers
- [ ] Reading Machines/Kurzweil
- [ ] Special bookstore section
- [ ] Typists

Credit toward degree is not given for remedial courses taken.

Counseling Services

- [x] Academic
- [x] Psychological
- [x] Student Support groups — Meets 12 times per academic year
- [x] Vocational — Meets 12 times per academic year

Tutoring

Individual tutoring is available weekly.

	Individual	Group
Time management	[ ]	[ ]
Organizational skills	[ ]	[ ]
Learning strategies	[ ]	[ ]
Study skills	[ ]	[ ]
Content area	[ ]	[ ]
Writing lab	[ ]	[ ]
Math lab	[ ]	[ ]

LD PROGRAM STAFF

Total number of LD Program staff (including director):

Full Time: 2 Part Time: 2

100 peer tutors are available to work with LD students.

Key staff person available to work with LD students: Jane Mulrooney, Interim Director.

LD Program web site: www.nau.edu/dss

University of Phoenix

Phoenix, AZ

Address: 4615 East Elwood Street, Phoenix, AZ, 85040-1958
Admissions telephone: 480 317-6200
Admissions FAX: 480 643-1479
Director of Admissions: Beth Barilla
Web site: http://www.phoenix.edu
SAT Code: 1024

LD program contact: Beth Barilla
LD program e-mail: beth.barilla@phoenix.edu
LD program telephone: 480 317-6200
Total campus enrollment: 159,987

GENERAL

University of Phoenix is a private, coed, four-year institution. Main campus and four other campuses in Phoenix (population: 1,321,045); branch campuses and centers in California, Colorado, Florida, Georgia, Hawaii, Idaho, Illinois, Kansas, Louisiana, Maryland, Michigan, Nevada, New Mexico, Ohio, Oklahoma, Oregon, Pennsylvania, Texas, Utah, Washington, and Wisconsin and in British Columbia and Puerto Rico; distance education provided by Online Campus. Public transportation serves all campuses.

LD ADMISSIONS

A personal interview is not required. Essay is not required.

SECONDARY SCHOOL REQUIREMENTS

Graduation from secondary school required; GED accepted.

TESTING

Child Study Team report is not required. Tests required as part of this documentation:

- ❑ WAIS-IV
- ❑ WISC-IV
- ❑ SATA
- ❑ Woodcock-Johnson
- ❑ Nelson-Denny Reading Test
- ❑ Other

UNDERGRADUATE STUDENT BODY

Total undergraduate student enrollment: 32,133 Men, 40,161 Women.

Composition of student body (fall 2004):

	Undergraduate	Freshmen
International	15.3	14.7
Black	10.3	10.6
American Indian	0.8	0.7
Asian-American	1.3	2.5
Hispanic	6.0	7.4
White	25.3	36.0
Unreported	41.0	28.1
	100.0%	100.0%

STUDENT HOUSING

Housing is not guaranteed for all undergraduates.

EXPENSES

There is no additional cost for LD program/services.

LD SERVICES

LD program size is not limited.

LD services available to:

❑ Freshmen ❑ Sophomores ❑ Juniors ❑ Seniors

Academic Accommodations

Curriculum		In class	
Foreign language waiver	❑	Early syllabus	❑
Lighter course load	❑	Note takers in class	❑
Math waiver	❑	Priority seating	❑
Other special classes	❑	Tape recorders	❑
Priority registrations	❑	Videotaped classes	❑
Substitution of courses	❑	Text on tape	❑
Exams		**Services**	
Extended time	❑	Diagnostic tests	❑
Oral exams	❑	Learning centers	❑
Take home exams	❑	Proofreaders	❑
Exams on tape or computer	❑	Readers	❑
Untimed exams	❑	Reading Machines/Kurzweil	❑
Other accommodations	❑	Special bookstore section	❑
		Typists	❑

Counseling Services

- ❑ Academic
- ❑ Psychological
- ❑ Student Support groups
- ❑ Vocational

Tutoring

	Individual	Group
Time management	❑	❑
Organizational skills	❑	❑
Learning strategies	❑	❑
Study skills	❑	❑
Content area	❑	❑
Writing lab	❑	❑
Math lab	❑	❑

Prescott College

Prescott, AZ

Address: 220 Grove Avenue, Prescott, AZ, 86301
Admissions telephone: 800 628-6364
Admissions FAX: 928 776-5242
Director of Admissions: Timothy Robison
Admissions e-mail: admissions@prescott.edu
Web site: http://www.prescott.edu/
SAT Code: 484 ACT Code: 5022

LD program name: LD Program/Student Services
Learning specialist: Patricia Quinn-Kane
LD program telephone: 928 350-1009
LD program e-mail: pquinn-kane@prescott.edu
LD program enrollment: 50, Total campus enrollment: 805

GENERAL

Prescott College is a private, coed, four-year institution. One-acre campus in Prescott (population: 33,938), 100 miles from Phoenix. Served by air and bus; major airport serves Phoenix. Semester system.

LD ADMISSIONS

Students do not complete a separate application and are simultaneously accepted to the LD program. A member of the LD program does not sit on the admissions committee. A personal interview is recommended. Essay is required and may be typed.

SECONDARY SCHOOL REQUIREMENTS

Graduation from secondary school required; GED accepted.

TESTING

SAT Reasoning or ACT required. SAT Subject recommended.

All enrolled freshmen (fall 2004):

Average SAT I Scores:	Verbal: 573	Math: 513
Average ACT Scores:	Composite: 24	

Child Study Team report is not required. Tests required as part of this documentation:

- [ ] WAIS-IV
- [ ] WISC-IV
- [ ] SATA
- [ ] Woodcock-Johnson
- [ ] Nelson-Denny Reading Test
- [ ] Other

UNDERGRADUATE STUDENT BODY

Total undergraduate student enrollment: 314 Men, 443 Women.

Composition of student body (fall 2004):

	Undergraduate	Freshmen
International	0.0	0.1
Black	0.0	1.6
American Indian	0.0	1.8
Asian-American	0.0	1.6
Hispanic	0.0	4.2
White	87.8	86.9
Unreported	12.2	3.8
	100.0%	100.0%

87% are from out of state. Average age of full-time undergraduates is 26. 100% of classes have fewer than 20 students.

STUDENT HOUSING

Freshmen are not required to live on campus. Housing is not guaranteed for all undergraduates. Single rooms are not available for students with medical or special needs.

EXPENSES

Tuition (2005-06): $17,280 per year.
There is no additional cost for LD program/services.

LD SERVICES

LD program size is not limited.

LD services available to:

- [x] Freshmen
- [x] Sophomores
- [x] Juniors
- [x] Seniors

Academic Accommodations

Curriculum		In class	
Foreign language waiver	[ ]	Early syllabus	[ ]
Lighter course load	[ ]	Note takers in class	[x]
Math waiver	[ ]	Priority seating	[ ]
Other special classes	[ ]	Tape recorders	[x]
Priority registrations	[ ]	Videotaped classes	[ ]
Substitution of courses	[ ]	Text on tape	[ ]
Exams		**Services**	
Extended time	[x]	Diagnostic tests	[ ]
Oral exams	[ ]	Learning centers	[ ]
Take home exams	[ ]	Proofreaders	[ ]
Exams on tape or computer	[ ]	Readers	[x]
Untimed exams	[ ]	Reading Machines/Kurzweil	[ ]
Other accommodations	[ ]	Special bookstore section	[ ]
		Typists	[ ]

Credit toward degree is not given for remedial courses taken.

Counseling Services

- [x] Academic
- [x] Psychological
- [ ] Student Support groups
- [ ] Vocational

Tutoring

Individual tutoring is available daily.

Average size of tutoring groups: 1

	Individual	Group
Time management	[x]	[ ]
Organizational skills	[x]	[ ]
Learning strategies	[x]	[ ]
Study skills	[x]	[ ]
Content area	[x]	[ ]
Writing lab	[ ]	[ ]
Math lab	[ ]	[ ]

LD PROGRAM STAFF

There is an advisor/advocate from the LD program available to students. The advisor/advocate meets with faculty 10 times per month and student 3 times per month.

Key staff person available to work with LD students: Patricia Quinn-Kane, Learning Specialist.

University of Arkansas

Fayetteville, AR

Address: 232 Silas Hunt Hall, Fayetteville, AR, 72701
Admissions telephone: 800 377-8632
Admissions FAX: 479 575-7515
Interim Director of Undergraduate Recruitment: Dawn Medley
Admissions e-mail: uofa@uark.edu
Web site: http://www.uark.edu
SAT Code: 6866 ACT Code: 144

Director, Center for Students w/ Disabilities: Dr. Linda Watts
LD program telephone: 479 575-3104
LD program e-mail: lwatts@uark.edu
LD program enrollment: 95 Total campus enrollment: 13,817

GENERAL

University of Arkansas is a public, coed, four-year institution. 345-acre campus in Fayetteville (population: 58,047), 110 miles from Tulsa. Served by bus; major airport serves Tulsa; smaller airport serves Highfill (25 miles); train serves Little Rock (194 miles). School operates transportation around campus and to local apartment complexes, downtown, and shopping malls. Public transportation serves campus. Semester system.

LD ADMISSIONS

Students do not complete a separate application and are not simultaneously accepted to the LD program. A member of the LD program does not sit on the admissions committee. A personal interview is recommended. Essay is not required.

For fall 2004, 125 completed self-identified LD applications were received. 100 applications were offered admission, and 97 enrolled.

SECONDARY SCHOOL REQUIREMENTS

Graduation from secondary school required; GED accepted. The following course distribution required: 4 units of English, 4 units of math, 3 units of science, 3 units of social studies, 2 units of academic electives.

TESTING

SAT Reasoning or ACT required. SAT Subject recommended.

All enrolled freshmen (fall 2004):

Average SAT I Scores:	Verbal: 579	Math: 581
Average ACT Scores:	Composite: 25	

Child Study Team report is not required. A neuropsychological or comprehensive psycho-educational evaluation is required for admission. Must be dated within 36 months of application. Tests required as part of this documentation:

- ■ WAIS-IV
- ☐ WISC-IV
- ☐ SATA
- ■ Woodcock-Johnson
- ☐ Nelson-Denny Reading Test
- ■ Other

UNDERGRADUATE STUDENT BODY

Total undergraduate student enrollment: 6,609 Men, 6,209 Women.

Composition of student body (fall 2004):

	Undergraduate	Freshmen
International	1.4	2.1
Black	4.6	5.3
American Indian	2.5	2.1
Asian-American	2.7	2.7
Hispanic	2.2	1.8
White	84.7	83.8
Unreported	1.9	2.2
	100.0%	100.0%

9% are from out of state. 13% join a fraternity and 16% join a sorority. Average age of full-time undergraduates is 21. 41% of classes have fewer than 20 students, 45% have between 20 and 50 students, 14% have more than 50 students.

STUDENT HOUSING

83% of freshmen live in college housing. Freshmen are required to live on campus. Housing is guaranteed for all undergraduates. Campus can house 5,141 undergraduates. Single rooms are available for students with medical or special needs. A medical note is required.

EXPENSES

Tuition (2005-06): $4,361 per year (in-state), $12,089 (out-of-state). Tuition is higher for College of Business Administration.

Room: $3,782. Board: $2,583.

There is no additional cost for LD program/services.

LD SERVICES

LD program size is not limited.

LD services available to:

■ Freshmen ■ Sophomores ■ Juniors ■ Seniors

Academic Accommodations

Curriculum		In class	
Foreign language waiver	☐	Early syllabus	☐
Lighter course load	☐	Note takers in class	■
Math waiver	☐	Priority seating	■
Other special classes	■	Tape recorders	■
Priority registrations	■	Videotaped classes	☐
Substitution of courses	☐	Text on tape	☐
Exams		**Services**	
Extended time	■	Diagnostic tests	■
Oral exams	■	Learning centers	■
Take home exams	☐	Proofreaders	☐
Exams on tape or computer	■	Readers	■
Untimed exams	☐	Reading Machines/Kurzweil	■
Other accommodations	☐	Special bookstore section	☐
		Typists	■

Credit toward degree is not given for remedial courses taken.

Counseling Services

- ☐ Academic
- ☐ Psychological
- ☐ Student Support groups
- ☐ Vocational

Tutoring

Individual tutoring is not available.

	Individual	Group
Time management	☐	☐
Organizational skills	☐	☐
Learning strategies	☐	☐
Study skills	☐	☐
Content area	☐	☐
Writing lab	☐	☐
Math lab	☐	☐

LD PROGRAM STAFF

Total number of LD Program staff (including director):

Full Time: 4 Part Time: 4

There is not an advisor/advocate from the LD program available to students. 1 graduate student is available to work with LD students.

Key staff person available to work with LD students: Dr. Linda Watts, Associate Director.

University of Arkansas at Little Rock

Little Rock, AR

Address: 2801 South University Avenue, Little Rock, AR, 72204-1099
Admissions telephone: 501 569-3035
Admissions FAX: 501 569-8956
Director of Admissions: John Noah
Admissions e-mail: adminfo@ualr.edu
Web site: http://www.ualr.edu
SAT Code: 6368   ACT Code: 132

Director of Disability Support Services: Susan Queller
LD program telephone: 501 569-3143
LD program e-mail: slqueller@ualr.edu
Total campus enrollment: 8,383

GENERAL

University of Arkansas at Little Rock is a public, coed, four-year institution. 150-acre, urban campus in Little Rock (population: 183,133). Served by airport, bus, and train. Public transportation serves campus. Semester system.

LD ADMISSIONS

A personal interview is not required. Essay is not required.

SECONDARY SCHOOL REQUIREMENTS

Graduation from secondary school required; GED accepted.

TESTING

Child Study Team report is not required. Tests required as part of this documentation:

- [ ] WAIS-IV
- [ ] WISC-IV
- [ ] SATA
- [ ] Woodcock-Johnson
- [ ] Nelson-Denny Reading Test
- [ ] Other

UNDERGRADUATE STUDENT BODY

Total undergraduate student enrollment: 3,295 Men, 5,088 Women.

7% are from out of state.

STUDENT HOUSING

Housing is not guaranteed for all undergraduates. Commuter campus. Campus can house 306 undergraduates.

EXPENSES

There is no additional cost for LD program/services.

LD SERVICES

LD program size is not limited.

LD services available to:

- [ ] Freshmen
- [ ] Sophomores
- [ ] Juniors
- [ ] Seniors

Academic Accommodations

Curriculum		**In class**	
Foreign language waiver	[ ]	Early syllabus	[ ]
Lighter course load	[x]	Note takers in class	[x]
Math waiver	[ ]	Priority seating	[ ]
Other special classes	[ ]	Tape recorders	[ ]
Priority registrations	[ ]	Videotaped classes	[ ]
Substitution of courses	[ ]	Text on tape	[ ]
Exams		**Services**	
Extended time	[x]	Diagnostic tests	[ ]
Oral exams	[x]	Learning centers	[ ]
Take home exams	[ ]	Proofreaders	[ ]
Exams on tape or computer	[ ]	Readers	[x]
Untimed exams	[ ]	Reading Machines/Kurzweil	[x]
Other accommodations	[ ]	Special bookstore section	[ ]
		Typists	[ ]

Credit toward degree is not given for remedial courses taken.

Counseling Services

- [ ] Academic
- [ ] Psychological
- [ ] Student Support groups
- [ ] Vocational

Tutoring

Time management	[ ]	[ ]
Organizational skills	[ ]	[ ]
Learning strategies	[ ]	[ ]
Study skills	[ ]	[ ]
Content area	[ ]	[ ]
Writing lab	[ ]	[ ]
Math lab	[ ]	[ ]

LD PROGRAM STAFF

Total number of LD Program staff (including director):

Full Time: 1   Part Time: 1

Key staff person available to work with LD students: Katy Evans, Student Development Specialist.

Arkansas State University

State University, AR

Address: P.O. Box 10, State University, AR, 72467
Admissions telephone: 800 382-3030
Admissions FAX: 870 910-8094
Director of Admissions: Paula James Lynn
Admissions e-mail: admissions@astate.edu
Web site: http://www.astate.edu
SAT Code: 6011 ACT Code: 116

LD program name: Office of Disability Services
LD program address: P.O. Box 360
Director of Disability Services: Dr. Jennifer Rice-Mason
LD program telephone: 870 972-3964
LD program e-mail: jrmason@astate.edu
LD program enrollment: 161, Total campus enrollment: 9,262

GENERAL

Arkansas State University is a public, coed, four-year institution. 941-acre campus in Jonesboro (population: 55,515), 70 miles from Memphis, TN; branch campuses in Beebe, Mountain Home, and Newport. Served by airport and bus; major airport serves Memphis, TN; train serves Walnut Ridge (30 miles). Semester system.

LD ADMISSIONS

Students complete a separate application and are not simultaneously accepted to the LD program. A member of the LD program does not sit on the admissions committee. A personal interview is not required. Essay is not required. They require that students seeking assistance contact their office one semester before they enroll.

For fall 2004, 225 completed self-identified LD applications were received. 207 applications were offered admission, and 207 enrolled.

SECONDARY SCHOOL REQUIREMENTS

Graduation from secondary school required; GED accepted.

TESTING

ACT required; SAT Reasoning may be substituted. SAT Subject recommended.

All enrolled freshmen (fall 2004):

Average ACT Scores: Composite: 21

Child Study Team report is not required. A neuropsychological or comprehensive psycho-educational evaluation is required for admission. Tests required as part of this documentation:

- [ ] WAIS-IV
- [ ] WISC-IV
- [ ] SATA
- [ ] Woodcock-Johnson
- [ ] Nelson-Denny Reading Test
- [x] Other

UNDERGRADUATE STUDENT BODY

Total undergraduate student enrollment: 3,960 Men, 5,466 Women.

Composition of student body (fall 2004):

	Undergraduate	Freshmen
International	0.7	1.3
Black	23.9	15.7
American Indian	0.6	0.4
Asian-American	0.4	0.7
Hispanic	1.5	0.9
White	69.9	79.6
Unreported	3.0	1.4
	100.0%	100.0%

10% are from out of state. 15% join a fraternity and 11% join a sorority. Average age of full-time undergraduates is 23. 44% of classes have fewer than 20 students, 50% have between 20 and 50 students, 6% have more than 50 students.

STUDENT HOUSING

42% of freshmen live in college housing. Freshmen are required to live on campus. Housing is guaranteed for all undergraduates. Campus can house 2,315 undergraduates. Single rooms are available for students with medical or special needs. A medical note is required.

EXPENSES

Tuition (2005-06): $4,260 per year (In-state), $10,965 (out-of-state).

Room: $2,150. Board: $2,040.

There is no additional cost for LD program/services.

LD SERVICES

LD program size is not limited.

LD services available to:

- [x] Freshmen
- [x] Sophomores
- [x] Juniors
- [x] Seniors

Academic Accommodations

Curriculum

- [ ] Foreign language waiver
- [ ] Lighter course load
- [ ] Math waiver
- [ ] Other special classes
- [ ] Priority registrations
- [ ] Substitution of courses

Exams

- [x] Extended time
- [ ] Oral exams
- [ ] Take home exams
- [ ] Exams on tape or computer
- [ ] Untimed exams
- [ ] Other accommodations

In class

- [ ] Early syllabus
- [x] Note takers in class
- [ ] Priority seating
- [x] Tape recorders
- [ ] Videotaped classes
- [ ] Text on tape

Services

- [ ] Diagnostic tests
- [ ] Learning centers
- [ ] Proofreaders
- [x] Readers
- [ ] Reading Machines/Kurzweil
- [ ] Special bookstore section
- [ ] Typists

Credit toward degree is not given for remedial courses taken.

Counseling Services

- [x] Academic
- [x] Psychological
- [x] Student Support groups
- [x] Vocational

Tutoring

Individual tutoring is available daily.

	Individual	Group
Time management	[x]	[ ]
Organizational skills	[x]	[ ]
Learning strategies	[x]	[ ]
Study skills	[x]	[ ]
Content area	[x]	[ ]
Writing lab	[x]	[ ]
Math lab	[x]	[ ]

UNIQUE LD PROGRAM FEATURES

Assistance and accommodations are provided on an individual basis and are determined by a students disability documentation. Appropriate accommodations should be requested by the student after verification of his or her disability is received. Support services provided by the Office of Disability Services include: Orientation and Registration, Intake and Assessment, Note taking, Test Administration with Accommodations, Reader Services, Computer and Technology Demonstrations for all Students, Physical Adaptations inside and outside of the classroom, Guidance and Counseling, Adaptive Physical Education Course, Priority Registration, and Interpreter Services.

LD PROGRAM STAFF

Total number of LD Program staff (including director):

Full Time: 5 Part Time: 5

There is an advisor/advocate from the LD program available to students. The advisor/advocate meets with faculty 1 time per month. 1 graduate student is available to work with LD students. Key staff person available to work with LD students: Leonardo Glover, Learning Disability Specialist. LD Program web site: http://disability.astate.edu.

Arkansas Tech University

Russellville, AR

Address: 1509 North Boulder Avenue, Russellville, AR, 72801-2222
Admissions telephone: 800 582-6953
Admissions FAX: 479 964-0522
Director of Enrollment Management: Ms. Shauna Donnell
Admissions e-mail: tech.enroll@atu.edu
Web site: http://www.atu.edu
SAT Code: 6010 ACT Code: 114

LD program name: Jackie Nichols
LD program address: ATU, Tomlinson
Coordinator of Disability Services: Jackie Nichols
LD program telephone: 479 964-3230
LD program e-mail: jackie.nichols@atu.edu
LD program enrollment: 80, Total campus enrollment: 6,091

GENERAL

Arkansas Tech University is a public, coed, four-year institution. 516-acre campus in Russellville (population: 23,682), 78 miles from Little Rock; branch campuses in Ft. Smith and abroad in Vancouver, Canada. Served by bus; major airport and train serve Little Rock; smaller airport serves Ft. Smith. Semester system.

LD ADMISSIONS

Students do not complete a separate application and are simultaneously accepted to the LD program. A personal interview is required. Essay is not required.

SECONDARY SCHOOL REQUIREMENTS

Graduation from secondary school required; GED accepted. The following course distribution required: 4 units of English, 4 units of math, 3 units of science, 1 unit of social studies, 2 units of history, 4 units of academic electives.

TESTING

SAT Subject recommended.

All enrolled freshmen (fall 2004):

Average SAT I Scores: Verbal: 467 Math: 472
Average ACT Scores: Composite: 22

Child Study Team report is not required. A neuropsychological or comprehensive psycho-education evaluation is not required for admission. Tests required as part of this documentation:

- [ ] WAIS-IV
- [ ] WISC-IV
- [ ] SATA
- [ ] Woodcock-Johnson
- [ ] Nelson-Denny Reading Test
- [ ] Other

UNDERGRADUATE STUDENT BODY

Total undergraduate student enrollment: 2,509 Men, 2,696 Women.

Composition of student body (fall 2004):

	Undergraduate	Freshmen
International	2.0	1.1
Black	5.3	4.3
American Indian	2.0	1.6
Asian-American	1.0	1.0
Hispanic	2.0	1.8
White	87.7	90.3
Unreported	0.0	0.0
	100.0%	100.0%

4% are from out of state. Average age of full-time undergraduates is 22. 34% of classes have fewer than 20 students, 57% have between 20 and 50 students, 9% have more than 50 students.

STUDENT HOUSING

55% of freshmen live in college housing. Freshmen are required to live on campus. Housing is guaranteed for all undergraduates. Campus can house 1,727 undergraduates. Single rooms are available for students with medical or special needs. A medical note is required.

EXPENSES

Tuition (2005-06): $4,290 per year (in-state), $8,580 (out-of-state).
Room: $1,996. Board: $1,758.
There is no additional cost for LD program/services.

LD SERVICES

LD program size is not limited.

LD services available to:

- [x] Freshmen
- [x] Sophomores
- [x] Juniors
- [x] Seniors

Academic Accommodations

Curriculum		In class	
Foreign language waiver	[ ]	Early syllabus	[ ]
Lighter course load	[ ]	Note takers in class	[x]
Math waiver	[ ]	Priority seating	[ ]
Other special classes	[ ]	Tape recorders	[x]
Priority registrations	[ ]	Videotaped classes	[ ]
Substitution of courses	[ ]	Text on tape	[ ]
Exams		**Services**	
Extended time	[x]	Diagnostic tests	[ ]
Oral exams	[x]	Learning centers	[ ]
Take home exams	[ ]	Proofreaders	[ ]
Exams on tape or computer	[ ]	Readers	[x]
Untimed exams	[x]	Reading Machines/Kurzweil	[x]
Other accommodations	[x]	Special bookstore section	[ ]
		Typists	[ ]

Credit toward degree is not given for remedial courses taken.

Counseling Services

- [x] Academic
- [x] Psychological
- [x] Student Support groups
- [x] Vocational

Tutoring

Individual tutoring is available daily.

	Individual	Group
Time management	[x]	[x]
Organizational skills	[x]	[x]
Learning strategies	[x]	[x]
Study skills	[x]	[x]
Content area	[x]	[x]
Writing lab	[x]	[x]
Math lab	[x]	[x]

LD PROGRAM STAFF

Total number of LD Program staff (including director):

Full Time: 2 Part Time: 2

There is an advisor/advocate from the LD program available to students.

Key staff person available to work with LD students: Jackie Nichols, Coordinator of Disability Services.

University of Central Arkansas

Conway, AR

Address: 201 Donaghey Avenue, Conway, AR, 72035
Admissions telephone: 800 243-8245
Admissions FAX: 501 450-5228
Director of Admissions: Penny Hatfield
Admissions e-mail: admissions@uca.edu
Web site: http://www.uca.edu
SAT Code: 6012

LD program name: UCA Disability Support
LD program address: 201 Donaghey Avenue SC01A
LD program telephone: 501 450-3135
LD program e-mail: crystalh@uca.edu
LD program enrollment: 30, Total campus enrollment: 9,047

GENERAL

University of Central Arkansas is a public, coed, four-year institution. 365-acre campus in Conway (population: 43,167), 30 miles from Little Rock. Served by bus; major airport and train serve Little Rock. Semester system.

LD ADMISSIONS

Students do not complete a separate application and are not simultaneously accepted to the LD program. A member of the LD program does not sit on the admissions committee. A personal interview is required. Essay is not required.

For fall 2004, 30 completed self-identified LD applications were received.

SECONDARY SCHOOL REQUIREMENTS

Graduation from secondary school required; GED accepted. The following course distribution required: 4 units of English, 3 units of math, 3 units of science, 3 units of social studies, 6 units of academic electives.

TESTING

SAT Subject recommended.

All enrolled freshmen (fall 2004):

Average ACT Scores: Composite: 23

Child Study Team report is not required. A neuropsychological or comprehensive psycho-educational evaluation is required for admission. Must be dated within 36 months of application. Tests required as part of this documentation:

- ■ WAIS-IV
- ☐ WISC-IV
- ☐ SATA
- ■ Woodcock-Johnson
- ■ Nelson-Denny Reading Test
- ☐ Other

UNDERGRADUATE STUDENT BODY

Total undergraduate student enrollment: 3,027 Men, 4,697 Women.

Composition of student body (fall 2004):

	Undergraduate	Freshmen
International	1.3	1.8
Black	16.6	16.6
American Indian	0.4	0.8
Asian-American	1.8	1.5
Hispanic	1.8	1.3
White	74.7	75.1
Unreported	3.4	2.9
	100.0%	100.0%

3% are from out of state. Average age of full-time undergraduates is 21. 39% of classes have fewer than 20 students, 58% have between 20 and 50 students, 3% have more than 50 students.

STUDENT HOUSING

90% of freshmen live in college housing. Freshmen are required to live on campus. Housing is guaranteed for all undergraduates. Single rooms are available for students with medical or special needs. A medical note is required.

EXPENSES

Tuition (2005-06): $4,500 per year (in-state), $9,000 (out-of-state).
Room: $2,380. Board: $1,800.

LD SERVICES

LD program size is not limited.

LD services available to:

■ Freshmen ■ Sophomores ■ Juniors ■ Seniors

Academic Accommodations

Curriculum		In class	
Foreign language waiver	☐	Early syllabus	☐
Lighter course load	☐	Note takers in class	■
Math waiver	☐	Priority seating	■
Other special classes	☐	Tape recorders	■
Priority registrations	■	Videotaped classes	☐
Substitution of courses	☐	Text on tape	■
Exams		**Services**	
Extended time	■	Diagnostic tests	☐
Oral exams	☐	Learning centers	☐
Take home exams	☐	Proofreaders	☐
Exams on tape or computer	☐	Readers	■
Untimed exams	☐	Reading Machines/Kurzweil	☐
Other accommodations	☐	Special bookstore section	☐
		Typists	■

Counseling Services

- ☐ Academic
- ☐ Psychological
- ☐ Student Support groups
- ☐ Vocational

Tutoring

Individual tutoring is not available.

	Individual	Group
Time management	☐	☐
Organizational skills	☐	☐
Learning strategies	☐	☐
Study skills	☐	☐
Content area	☐	☐
Writing lab	☐	☐
Math lab	☐	☐

LD PROGRAM STAFF

Key staff person available to work with LD students: Crystal Hill, Director.

LD Program web site: http://www.uca.edu/divisions/student/disability/

Harding University

Searcy, AR

Address: 900 East Center Street, Searcy, AR, 72149
Admissions telephone: 800 477-4407
Admissions FAX: 501 279-4129
Assistant Vice President for Admissions: Glenn Dillard
Admissions e-mail: admissions@harding.edu
Web site: http://www.harding.edu
SAT Code: 6267 ACT Code: 1240

LD program name: Student Support Services
LD program address: Box 12235
Disabilities Specialist/Counselor: Teresa McLeod
LD program telephone: 501 279-4019
LD program e-mail: tmcleod@harding.edu
LD program enrollment: 130, Total campus enrollment: 4,037

GENERAL

Harding University is a private, coed, four-year institution. 200-acre campus in Searcy (population: 18,928), 50 miles from Little Rock; branch campuses in Memphis and abroad in Brisbane, Australia; Vina del Mar, Chile; London, England; Athens, Greece; and Florence, Italy. Served by bus; airport and train serve Little Rock. Semester system.

LD ADMISSIONS

Students do not complete a separate application and are not simultaneously accepted to the LD program. A member of the LD program does not sit on the admissions committee. A personal interview is required. Essay is not required.

For fall 2004, 52 completed self-identified LD applications were received. 52 applications were offered admission, and 52 enrolled.

SECONDARY SCHOOL REQUIREMENTS

Graduation from secondary school required; GED not accepted. The following course distribution required: 4 units of English, 3 units of math, 2 units of science, 3 units of social studies, 3 units of academic electives.

TESTING

SAT Reasoning or ACT required. SAT Subject recommended.

All enrolled freshmen (fall 2004):

Average SAT I Scores:	Verbal: 562	Math: 547
Average ACT Scores:	Composite: 24	

Child Study Team report is not required. A neuropsychological or comprehensive psycho-educational evaluation is required for admission. Must be dated within 12 months of application. Tests required as part of this documentation:

- [x] WAIS-IV
- [x] WISC-IV
- [ ] SATA
- [x] Woodcock-Johnson
- [ ] Nelson-Denny Reading Test
- [ ] Other

UNDERGRADUATE STUDENT BODY

Total undergraduate student enrollment: 1,860 Men, 2,218 Women.

Composition of student body (fall 2004):

	Undergraduate	Freshmen
International	3.4	3.7
Black	3.1	3.9
American Indian	0.9	0.9
Asian-American	0.6	0.7
Hispanic	1.1	1.2
White	88.3	87.5
Unreported	2.6	2.1
	100.0%	100.0%

69% are from out of state. 45% join a fraternity and 47% join a sorority. Average age of full-time undergraduates is 20. 52% of classes have fewer than 20 students, 36% have between 20 and 50 students, 12% have more than 50 students.

STUDENT HOUSING

97% of freshmen live in college housing. Freshmen are not required to live on campus. Housing is guaranteed for all undergraduates. Campus can house 2,990 undergraduates. Single rooms are available for students with medical or special needs. A medical note is required.

EXPENSES

Tuition (2005-06): $10,800 per year.
Room: $2,636. Board: $2,676.
There is no additional cost for LD program/services.

LD SERVICES

LD program size is not limited.

LD services available to:

- [x] Freshmen
- [x] Sophomores
- [x] Juniors
- [x] Seniors

Academic Accommodations

Curriculum

- [ ] Foreign language waiver
- [x] Lighter course load
- [ ] Math waiver
- [x] Other special classes
- [x] Priority registrations
- [ ] Substitution of courses

Exams

- [x] Extended time
- [x] Oral exams
- [ ] Take home exams
- [ ] Exams on tape or computer
- [ ] Untimed exams
- [ ] Other accommodations

In class

- [ ] Early syllabus
- [x] Note takers in class
- [x] Priority seating
- [x] Tape recorders
- [ ] Videotaped classes
- [x] Text on tape

Services

- [ ] Diagnostic tests
- [ ] Learning centers
- [x] Proofreaders
- [x] Readers
- [x] Reading Machines/Kurzweil
- [ ] Special bookstore section
- [ ] Typists

Credit toward degree is not given for remedial courses taken.

Counseling Services

- [x] Academic
- [x] Psychological
- [ ] Student Support groups
- [x] Vocational

Tutoring

Individual tutoring is available daily.

	Individual	Group
Time management	[x]	[x]
Organizational skills	[x]	[x]
Learning strategies	[x]	[x]
Study skills	[x]	[x]
Content area	[x]	[ ]
Writing lab	[x]	[ ]
Math lab	[x]	[ ]

UNIQUE LD PROGRAM FEATURES

Staff count below does not include student workers who provide a significant amount of the tutoring service.

LD PROGRAM STAFF

Total number of LD Program staff (including director):

Full Time: 1 Part Time: 1

There is an advisor/advocate from the LD program available to students. The advisor/advocate meets with students 1 time per month. 1 graduate student and 29 peer tutors are available to work with LD students.

Key staff person available to work with LD students: Teresa McLeod, Coordinator Student Support Services.

Henderson State University

Arkadelphia, AR

Address: 1100 Henderson Street, Arkadelphia, AR, 71999-0001
Admissions telephone: 800 228-7333
Admissions FAX: 870 230-5066
Director of Admissions/University Relations: Vikita Hardwrick
Admissions e-mail: admissions@hsu.edu
Web site: http://www.getreddie.com
SAT Code: 6272 ACT Code: 126

LD program name: Vickie Faust
LD program address: Box 7594
LD program telephone: 870 230-5475
LD program e-mail: faustv@hsu.edu
Total campus enrollment: 3,036

GENERAL

Henderson State University is a public, coed, four-year institution. 147-acre campus in Arkadelphia (population: 10,912), 68 miles from Little Rock. Served by bus and train; airport serves Little Rock. Semester system.

LD ADMISSIONS

Students do not complete a separate application and are not simultaneously accepted to the LD program. A member of the LD program does not sit on the admissions committee. A personal interview is required. Essay is not required.

SECONDARY SCHOOL REQUIREMENTS

Graduation from secondary school required; GED accepted. The following course distribution required: 4 units of English, 4 units of math, 3 units of science, 2 units of social studies, 1 unit of history.

TESTING

SAT Subject recommended.

All enrolled freshmen (fall 2004):

Average SAT I Scores: Verbal: 504 Math: 526
Average ACT Scores: Composite: 22

Child Study Team report is not required. A neuropsychological or comprehensive psycho-education evaluation is not required for admission. Tests required as part of this documentation:

- ☐ WAIS-IV
- ☐ WISC-IV
- ☐ SATA
- ☐ Woodcock-Johnson
- ☐ Nelson-Denny Reading Test
- ☐ Other

UNDERGRADUATE STUDENT BODY

Total undergraduate student enrollment: 1,350 Men, 1,765 Women.

Composition of student body (fall 2004):

	Undergraduate	Freshmen
International	2.6	2.4
Black	18.0	16.9
American Indian	1.3	0.7
Asian-American	0.9	0.5
Hispanic	1.1	1.2
White	75.2	77.5
Unreported	0.9	0.8
	100.0%	100.0%

10% are from out of state. Average age of full-time undergraduates is 22. 56% of classes have fewer than 20 students, 43% have between 20 and 50 students, 1% have more than 50 students.

STUDENT HOUSING

67% of freshmen live in college housing. Housing is guaranteed for all undergraduates. Single rooms are available for students with medical or special needs. A medical note is required.

EXPENSES

Tuition (2005-06): $4,050 per year (in-state), $8,100 (out-of-state).
Room: $2,104. Board: $1,784.
There is no additional cost for LD program/services.

LD SERVICES

LD program size is not limited.

LD services available to:

■ Freshmen ■ Sophomores ■ Juniors ■ Seniors

Academic Accommodations

Curriculum		In class	
Foreign language waiver	☐	Early syllabus	☐
Lighter course load	☐	Note takers in class	■
Math waiver	☐	Priority seating	☐
Other special classes	☐	Tape recorders	■
Priority registrations	☐	Videotaped classes	☐
Substitution of courses	☐	Text on tape	■
Exams		**Services**	
Extended time	☐	Diagnostic tests	☐
Oral exams	☐	Learning centers	☐
Take home exams	☐	Proofreaders	☐
Exams on tape or computer	■	Readers	☐
Untimed exams	■	Reading Machines/Kurzweil	☐
Other accommodations	☐	Special bookstore section	☐
		Typists	■

Credit toward degree is not given for remedial courses taken.

Counseling Services

- ☐ Academic
- ☐ Psychological
- ☐ Student Support groups
- ☐ Vocational

Tutoring

Individual tutoring is available weekly.

	Individual	Group
Time management	☐	☐
Organizational skills	☐	☐
Learning strategies	☐	☐
Study skills	☐	☐
Content area	☐	☐
Writing lab	☐	☐
Math lab	☐	☐

LD PROGRAM STAFF

There is an advisor/advocate from the LD program available to students.

Key staff person available to work with LD students: Vickie Faust, Assistant Director.

Hendrix College

Conway, AR

Address: 1600 Washington Avenue, Conway, AR, 72032
Admissions telephone: 800 277-9017
Admissions FAX: 501 450-3843
Vice President for Enrollment: Kevin C. Kropf
Admissions e-mail: adm@hendrix.edu
Web site: http://www.hendrix.edu
SAT Code: 6273 ACT Code: 128

LD program name: Hendrix College Counseling Center
Coordinator of Academic Support: Dionne Jackson
LD program telephone: 501 450-1482
LD program e-mail: jackson@hendrix.edu
LD program enrollment: 11, Total campus enrollment: 1,042

GENERAL

Hendrix College is a private, coed, four-year institution. 160-acre campus in Conway (population: 43,167), 25 miles north of Little Rock. School operates transportation to Little Rock. Served by bus; major airport and train serve Little Rock. Semester system.

SECONDARY SCHOOL REQUIREMENTS

Graduation from secondary school required; GED accepted. The following course distribution required: 4 units of English, 3 units of math, 2 units of science, 2 units of foreign language, 3 units of social studies.

TESTING

SAT Reasoning or ACT required. SAT Subject recommended.

All enrolled freshmen (fall 2004):

Average SAT I Scores:	Verbal: 642	Math: 609
Average ACT Scores:	Composite: 27	

Child Study Team report is not required. Tests required as part of this documentation:

- [ ] WAIS-IV
- [ ] WISC-IV
- [ ] SATA
- [ ] Woodcock-Johnson
- [ ] Nelson-Denny Reading Test
- [ ] Other

UNDERGRADUATE STUDENT BODY

Total undergraduate student enrollment: 500 Men, 579 Women.

Composition of student body (fall 2004):

	Undergraduate	Freshmen
International	0.3	1.1
Black	3.1	4.1
American Indian	1.4	1.6
Asian-American	3.7	3.1
Hispanic	0.7	2.8
White	75.5	70.2
Unreported	15.3	17.1
	100.0%	100.0%

37% are from out of state. Average age of full-time undergraduates is 20. 62% of classes have fewer than 20 students, 37% have between 20 and 50 students.

STUDENT HOUSING

97% of freshmen live in college housing. Freshmen are required to live on campus. Housing is guaranteed for all undergraduates. Campus can house 920 undergraduates. Single rooms are available for students with medical or special needs. A medical note is required.

EXPENSES

Tuition (2005-06): $21,336 per year.

Room: $2,760. Board: $3,550.
There is no additional cost for LD program/services.

LD SERVICES

LD program size is not limited.

LD services available to:

- [x] Freshmen
- [x] Sophomores
- [x] Juniors
- [x] Seniors

Academic Accommodations

Curriculum

- [ ] Foreign language waiver
- [ ] Lighter course load
- [ ] Math waiver
- [ ] Other special classes
- [x] Priority registrations
- [ ] Substitution of courses

Exams

- [x] Extended time
- [ ] Oral exams
- [ ] Take home exams
- [ ] Exams on tape or computer
- [ ] Untimed exams
- [x] Other accommodations

In class

- [ ] Early syllabus
- [ ] Note takers in class
- [ ] Priority seating
- [x] Tape recorders
- [ ] Videotaped classes
- [x] Text on tape

Services

- [ ] Diagnostic tests
- [ ] Learning centers
- [ ] Proofreaders
- [ ] Readers
- [ ] Reading Machines/Kurzweil
- [ ] Special bookstore section
- [ ] Typists

Counseling Services

- [x] Academic
- [ ] Psychological
- [ ] Student Support groups
- [ ] Vocational

Tutoring

	Individual	Group
Time management	[x]	[ ]
Organizational skills	[x]	[ ]
Learning strategies	[x]	[ ]
Study skills	[x]	[ ]
Content area	[ ]	[x]
Writing lab	[x]	[ ]
Math lab	[ ]	[x]

LD PROGRAM STAFF

Total number of LD Program staff (including director):

Full Time: 1 Part Time: 1

Key staff person available to work with LD students: Mary Anne Siebert, Ph.D., Director of Counseling Services.

John Brown University

Siloam Springs, AR

Address: 2000 West University Street, Siloam Springs, AR, 72761
Admissions telephone: 877 JBU-INFO
Admissions FAX: 479 524-4196
Vice President for Enrollment Management: Don Crandall
Admissions e-mail: jbuinfo@jbu.edu
Web site: http://www.jbu.edu
SAT Code: 6321 ACT Code: 130

LD program name: Office of Disability Services
Director: Becky Lambert
LD program telephone: 479 524-7217
LD program e-mail: blambert@jbu.edu
LD program enrollment: 22, Total campus enrollment: 1,712

GENERAL

John Brown University is a private, coed, four-year institution. 200-acre campus in Siloam Springs (population: 10,843), 70 miles from Tulsa and 30 miles from Fayetteville. Major airport and train serve Tulsa; smaller airport and bus serve Fayetteville. School operates transportation to airports. Semester system.

LD ADMISSIONS

Students do not complete a separate application and are not simultaneously accepted to the LD program. A member of the LD program does sit on the admissions committee. A personal interview is not required. Essay is not required.

SECONDARY SCHOOL REQUIREMENTS

Graduation from secondary school required; GED accepted. The following course distribution required: 4 units of English, 4 units of math, 3 units of science, 2 units of social studies, 1 unit of history.

TESTING

SAT Reasoning or ACT required. SAT Subject recommended.

All enrolled freshmen (fall 2004):

Average SAT I Scores:	Verbal: 573	Math: 558
Average ACT Scores:	Composite: 24	

Child Study Team report is not required. A neuropsychological or comprehensive psycho-educational evaluation is required for admission. Must be dated within 60 months of application. Tests required as part of this documentation:

- ■ WAIS-IV
- ■ WISC-IV
- ■ SATA
- ■ Woodcock-Johnson
- ■ Nelson-Denny Reading Test
- ☐ Other

UNDERGRADUATE STUDENT BODY

Total undergraduate student enrollment: 1,712.

Composition of student body (fall 2004):

	Undergraduate	Freshmen
International	9.8	6.9
Black	2.4	2.8
American Indian	2.7	2.3
Asian-American	1.7	1.7
Hispanic	1.4	2.0
White	81.0	83.1
Unreported	1.0	1.2
	100.0%	100.0%

65% are from out of state. Average age of full-time undergraduates is 20. 56% of classes have fewer than 20 students, 43% have between 20 and 50 students, 1% have more than 50 students.

STUDENT HOUSING

93% of freshmen live in college housing. Freshmen are required to live on campus. Housing is guaranteed for all undergraduates. Campus can house 918 undergraduates. Single rooms are available for students with medical or special needs. A medical note is required.

EXPENSES

Tuition (2005-06): $14,544 per year.
Room & Board: $5,630.
There is no additional cost for LD program/services.

LD SERVICES

LD program size is not limited.

LD services available to:

■ Freshmen ■ Sophomores ■ Juniors ■ Seniors

Academic Accommodations

Curriculum		**In class**	
Foreign language waiver	☐	Early syllabus	☐
Lighter course load	☐	Note takers in class	■
Math waiver	☐	Priority seating	☐
Other special classes	☐	Tape recorders	■
Priority registrations	☐	Videotaped classes	☐
Substitution of courses	☐	Text on tape	■
Exams		**Services**	
Extended time	■	Diagnostic tests	☐
Oral exams	■	Learning centers	☐
Take home exams	☐	Proofreaders	☐
Exams on tape or computer	■	Readers	■
Untimed exams	☐	Reading Machines/Kurzweil	☐
Other accommodations	■	Special bookstore section	☐
		Typists	■

Credit toward degree is not given for remedial courses taken.

Counseling Services

- ■ Academic — Meets 2 times per academic year
- ☐ Psychological
- ☐ Student Support groups
- ☐ Vocational

Tutoring

Individual tutoring is available weekly.

Average size of tutoring groups: 3

	Individual	Group
Time management	■	☐
Organizational skills	■	☐
Learning strategies	■	☐
Study skills	■	☐
Content area	■	■
Writing lab	■	☐
Math lab	☐	☐

LD PROGRAM STAFF

There is an advisor/advocate from the LD program available to students. The advisor/advocate meets with students 1 time per month. 6 peer tutors are available to work with LD students.

Key staff person available to work with LD students: Becky Lambert, Director of Academic Assistance and Disability Services.

LD Program web site: www.jbu.edu/campus_life/stdev/disability/index.asp

Lyon College

Batesville, AR

Address: P.O. Box 2317, Batesville, AR, 72503-2317
Admissions telephone: 800 423-2542
Admissions FAX: 870 793-1791
Vice President for Enrollment Services: Denny G. Bardos
Admissions e-mail: admissions@lyon.edu
Web site: http://www.lyon.edu
SAT Code: 6009 ACT Code: 112

Vice President for Academic Services: Dr. John M. Peek
LD program telephone: 870 698-4202
LD program e-mail: jpeek@lyon.edu
LD program enrollment: 10, Total campus enrollment: 511

GENERAL

Lyon College is a private, coed, four-year institution. 136-acre campus in Batesville (population: 9,445), 90 miles from Little Rock. Major airports serve Little Rock and Memphis (120 miles). Semester system.

LD ADMISSIONS

A personal interview is not required. Essay is required and may be typed.

SECONDARY SCHOOL REQUIREMENTS

Graduation from secondary school required; GED accepted. The following course distribution required: 4 units of English, 3 units of math, 3 units of science, 2 units of foreign language, 1 unit of social studies, 2 units of history, 1 unit of academic electives.

TESTING

SAT Reasoning or ACT required. SAT Subject recommended.

All enrolled freshmen (fall 2004):

Average SAT I Scores:	Verbal: 570	Math: 560
Average ACT Scores:	Composite: 24	

Child Study Team report is not required. Tests required as part of this documentation:

- ☐ WAIS-IV
- ☐ WISC-IV
- ☐ SATA
- ☐ Woodcock-Johnson
- ☐ Nelson-Denny Reading Test
- ☐ Other

UNDERGRADUATE STUDENT BODY

Total undergraduate student enrollment: 227 Men, 299 Women.

Composition of student body (fall 2004):

	Undergraduate	Freshmen
International	1.4	4.1
Black	4.3	3.7
American Indian	1.4	1.6
Asian-American	2.1	1.0
Hispanic	0.7	1.6
White	86.6	85.5
Unreported	3.5	2.5
	100.0%	100.0%

17% are from out of state. 19% join a fraternity and 24% join a sorority. Average age of full-time undergraduates is 21. 70% of classes have fewer than 20 students, 29% have between 20 and 50 students, 1% have more than 50 students.

STUDENT HOUSING

89% of freshmen live in college housing. Freshmen are required to live on campus. Housing is guaranteed for all undergraduates. Campus can house 421 undergraduates. Single rooms are available for students with medical or special needs. A medical note is required.

EXPENSES

Tuition (2005-06): $13,475 per year.
Room: $2,500. Board: $3,585.
There is no additional cost for LD program/services.

LD SERVICES

LD program size is not limited.

LD services available to:

☑ Freshmen ☑ Sophomores ☑ Juniors ☑ Seniors

Academic Accommodations

Curriculum		In class	
Foreign language waiver	☐	Early syllabus	☐
Lighter course load	☐	Note takers in class	☐
Math waiver	☐	Priority seating	☐
Other special classes	☐	Tape recorders	☑
Priority registrations	☐	Videotaped classes	☐
Substitution of courses	☐	Text on tape	☐
Exams		**Services**	
Extended time	☑	Diagnostic tests	☐
Oral exams	☑	Learning centers	☐
Take home exams	☑	Proofreaders	☐
Exams on tape or computer	☐	Readers	☑
Untimed exams	☑	Reading Machines/Kurzweil	☐
Other accommodations	☑	Special bookstore section	☐
		Typists	☐

Credit toward degree is not given for remedial courses taken.

Counseling Services

- ☐ Academic
- ☐ Psychological
- ☐ Student Support groups
- ☐ Vocational

Tutoring

Individual tutoring is available twice per month.

	Individual	Group
Time management	☐	☐
Organizational skills	☐	☐
Learning strategies	☐	☐
Study skills	☐	☐
Content area	☐	☐
Writing lab	☑	☐
Math lab	☑	☐

Ouachita Baptist University

Arkadelphia, AR

Address: 410 Ouachita, Arkadelphia, AR, 71998
Admissions telephone: 800 342-5628
Admissions FAX: 870 245-5500
Director of Admissions Counseling: David Goodman
Admissions e-mail: admissions@obu.edu
Web site: http://www.obu.edu
SAT Code: 6549 ACT Code: 134

Director, Counseling Services: Neill Hunter
LD program telephone: 870 245-5591
LD program e-mail: huntern@obu.edu
LD program enrollment: 28, Total campus enrollment: 1,511

GENERAL

Ouachita Baptist University is a private, coed, four-year institution. 200-acre campus in Arkadelphia (population: 10,912), 65 miles from Little Rock. Served by bus; major airport and train serve Little Rock; smaller airport serves Hot Springs (40 miles). Semester system.

LD ADMISSIONS

A personal interview is recommended. Essay is not required.

For fall 2004, 6 completed self-identified LD applications were received. 6 applications were offered admission, and 6 enrolled.

SECONDARY SCHOOL REQUIREMENTS

Graduation from secondary school required; GED accepted. The following course distribution required: 4 units of English, 2 units of math, 2 units of science, 1 unit of social studies, 2 units of history.

TESTING

SAT Reasoning or ACT required. SAT Subject recommended.

All enrolled freshmen (fall 2004):

Average SAT I Scores: Verbal: 529 Math: 529
Average ACT Scores: Composite: 23

Child Study Team report is not required. Tests required as part of this documentation:

- [ ] WAIS-IV
- [ ] WISC-IV
- [ ] SATA
- [ ] Woodcock-Johnson
- [ ] Nelson-Denny Reading Test
- [ ] Other

UNDERGRADUATE STUDENT BODY

Total undergraduate student enrollment: 778 Men, 879 Women.

Composition of student body (fall 2004):

	Undergraduate	Freshmen
International	2.4	4.1
Black	5.0	6.1
American Indian	0.0	0.2
Asian-American	0.8	0.6
Hispanic	2.6	1.4
White	89.2	87.6
Unreported	0.0	0.0
	100.0%	100.0%

43% are from out of state. 20% join a fraternity and 30% join a sorority. Average age of full-time undergraduates is 20. 59% of classes have fewer than 20 students, 41% have between 20 and 50 students.

STUDENT HOUSING

99% of freshmen live in college housing. Freshmen are required to live on campus. Housing is guaranteed for all undergraduates. Campus can house 1,517 undergraduates.

EXPENSES

Tuition (2005-06): $15,580 per year.

Room & Board: $4,733-$5,000.
There is no additional cost for LD program/services.

LD SERVICES

LD program size is not limited.

LD services available to:

- [x] Freshmen
- [x] Sophomores
- [x] Juniors
- [x] Seniors

Academic Accommodations

Curriculum		In class	
Foreign language waiver	[ ]	Early syllabus	[ ]
Lighter course load	[ ]	Note takers in class	[x]
Math waiver	[ ]	Priority seating	[ ]
Other special classes	[x]	Tape recorders	[x]
Priority registrations	[ ]	Videotaped classes	[x]
Substitution of courses	[ ]	Text on tape	[ ]
Exams		**Services**	
Extended time	[x]	Diagnostic tests	[ ]
Oral exams	[x]	Learning centers	[ ]
Take home exams	[ ]	Proofreaders	[ ]
Exams on tape or computer	[ ]	Readers	[x]
Untimed exams	[ ]	Reading Machines/Kurzweil	[x]
Other accommodations	[ ]	Special bookstore section	[ ]
		Typists	[ ]

Credit toward degree is not given for remedial courses taken.

Counseling Services

- [ ] Academic
- [ ] Psychological
- [ ] Student Support groups
- [ ] Vocational

Tutoring

Individual tutoring is available twice per month.

Average size of tutoring groups: 1

	Individual	Group
Time management	[ ]	[ ]
Organizational skills	[ ]	[ ]
Learning strategies	[ ]	[ ]
Study skills	[ ]	[ ]
Content area	[ ]	[ ]
Writing lab	[ ]	[ ]
Math lab	[ ]	[ ]

LD PROGRAM STAFF

Total number of LD Program staff (including director):

Full Time: 1 Part Time: 1

33 peer tutors are available to work with LD students.

Key staff person available to work with LD students: Neill Hunter, Director, Counseling Services.

University of the Ozarks

Clarksville, AR

Address: 415 North College Avenue, Clarksville, AR, 72830
Admissions telephone: 800 264-8636
Admissions FAX: 479 979-1355
Director of Admissions: Jana Hart
Admissions e-mail: admiss@ozarks.edu
Web site: http://www.ozarks.edu
SAT Code: 6111 ACT Code: 120

LD program name: Jones Learning Center
Director: Julia Frost
LD program telephone: 479 979-1403
LD program e-mail: jlc@ozarks.edu
LD program enrollment: 78, Total campus enrollment: 628

GENERAL

University of the Ozarks is a private, coed, four-year institution. 40-acre campus in Clarksville (population: 7,719), 60 miles from Fort Smith and 100 miles from Little Rock. Served by bus; airports serve Little Rock and Fort Smith. Semester system.

LD ADMISSIONS

Students complete a separate application and are simultaneously accepted to the LD program. A member of the LD program does sit on the admissions committee. High school waivers are accepted for math. A personal interview is required. Essay is required and may not be typed.

For fall 2004, 50 completed self-identified LD applications were received. 30 applications were offered admission, and 27 enrolled.

SECONDARY SCHOOL REQUIREMENTS

Graduation from secondary school required; GED accepted. The following course distribution required: 4 units of English, 4 units of math, 3 units of science, 2 units of foreign language, 1 unit of social studies, 2 units of history.

TESTING

SAT Reasoning or ACT required. SAT Subject recommended.

All enrolled freshmen (fall 2004):

Average SAT I Scores: Verbal: 530 Math: 510
Average ACT Scores: Composite: 23

Child Study Team report is not required. A neuropsychological or comprehensive psycho-educational evaluation is required for admission. Must be dated within 12 months of application. Tests required as part of this documentation:

- [x] WAIS-IV
- [ ] WISC-IV
- [x] SATA
- [x] Woodcock-Johnson
- [ ] Nelson-Denny Reading Test
- [x] Other

UNDERGRADUATE STUDENT BODY

Total undergraduate student enrollment: 295 Men, 359 Women.

Composition of student body (fall 2004):

	Undergraduate	Freshmen
International	10.4	18.8
Black	1.5	2.4
American Indian	4.5	3.0
Asian-American	1.5	2.0
Hispanic	3.0	3.0
White	79.1	70.8
Unreported	0.0	0.0
	100.0%	100.0%

42% are from out of state. Average age of full-time undergraduates is 21. 76% of classes have fewer than 20 students, 24% have between 20 and 50 students.

STUDENT HOUSING

Freshmen are required to live on campus. Housing is guaranteed for all undergraduates. Campus can house 500 undergraduates. Single rooms are available for students with medical or special needs. A medical note is not required.

EXPENSES

Tuition (2005-06): $13,740 per year.
Room: $2,330. Board: $2,750.
Additional cost for LD program/services: $7,400 per semester.

LD SERVICES

LD program is limited to 1% students.

LD services available to:

- [x] Freshmen
- [x] Sophomores
- [x] Juniors
- [x] Seniors

Academic Accommodations

Curriculum

- [ ] Foreign language waiver
- [x] Lighter course load
- [ ] Math waiver
- [x] Other special classes
- [x] Priority registrations
- [ ] Substitution of courses

Exams

- [x] Extended time
- [x] Oral exams
- [ ] Take home exams
- [ ] Exams on tape or computer
- [ ] Untimed exams
- [ ] Other accommodations

In class

- [ ] Early syllabus
- [x] Note takers in class
- [ ] Priority seating
- [x] Tape recorders
- [ ] Videotaped classes
- [x] Text on tape

Services

- [x] Diagnostic tests
- [x] Learning centers
- [x] Proofreaders
- [x] Readers
- [x] Reading Machines/Kurzweil
- [ ] Special bookstore section
- [x] Typists

Credit toward degree is not given for remedial courses taken.

Counseling Services

- [x] Academic — Meets 168 times per academic year
- [ ] Psychological
- [ ] Student Support groups
- [ ] Vocational

Tutoring

Individual tutoring is available daily.

Average size of tutoring groups: 2

	Individual	Group
Time management	[x]	[x]
Organizational skills	[x]	[x]
Learning strategies	[x]	[x]
Study skills	[x]	[x]
Content area	[x]	[x]
Writing lab	[x]	[x]
Math lab	[x]	[x]

UNIQUE LD PROGRAM FEATURES

Admissions Requirements: average to above intellectual ability, LD or ADHD as primary disability; and strength in one or more academic areas.

LD PROGRAM STAFF

Total number of LD Program staff (including director):

Full Time: 18 Part Time: 18

There is an advisor/advocate from the LD program available to students. The advisor/advocate meets with faculty 2 times per month and student 20 times per month. 125 peer tutors are available to work with LD students.

Key staff person available to work with LD students: Debra Cline, Assistant Director/Program Coordinator.

LD Program web site: www.ozarks.edu/campusservices/jlc/index.html

Southern Arkansas University - Magnolia

Magnolia, AR

Address: Box 9392, Magnolia, AR, 71754-9392

Admissions telephone: 800 332-7286
Admissions FAX: 870 235-4931
Dean of Enrollment Services: Sarah Jennings
Admissions e-mail: muleriders@saumag.edu
Web site: http://www.saumag.edu
SAT Code: 6661 ACT Code: 142

Director of Counseling and Testing: Paula Washington-Woods
LD program telephone: 870 235-4145
LD program e-mail: pwwoods@saumag.edu
Total campus enrollment: 2,804

GENERAL

Southern Arkansas University-Magnolia is a public, coed, four-year institution. 750-acre campus in Magnolia (population: 10,585), 135 miles from Little Rock. Served by bus; major airport serves Little Rock; other airport and train serve Texarkana, Tex. (55 miles). Semester system.

LD ADMISSIONS

A personal interview is required. Essay is not required.

SECONDARY SCHOOL REQUIREMENTS

Graduation from secondary school required; GED accepted.

TESTING

SAT Reasoning recommended. ACT recommended. SAT Reasoning may be substituted. SAT Subject recommended.

All enrolled freshmen (fall 2004):

Average ACT Scores: Composite: 21

Child Study Team report is not required. Tests required as part of this documentation:

- ☐ WAIS-IV
- ☐ WISC-IV
- ☐ SATA
- ☐ Woodcock-Johnson
- ☐ Nelson-Denny Reading Test
- ☐ Other

UNDERGRADUATE STUDENT BODY

Total undergraduate student enrollment: 1,247 Men, 1,616 Women.

Composition of student body (fall 2004):

	Undergraduate	Freshmen
International	5.2	4.9
Black	28.0	26.2
American Indian	1.1	0.4
Asian-American	1.2	0.7
Hispanic	1.2	1.4
White	63.3	66.4
Unreported	0.0	0.0
	100.0%	100.0%

22% are from out of state. 10% join a fraternity and 10% join a sorority. Average age of full-time undergraduates is 24. 53% of classes have fewer than 20 students, 42% have between 20 and 50 students, 5% have more than 50 students.

STUDENT HOUSING

70% of freshmen live in college housing. Freshmen are required to live on campus. Housing is guaranteed for all undergraduates. Campus can house 1,399 undergraduates.

EXPENSES

Tuition (2005-06): $3,900 per year (in-state), $5,910 (out-of-state).
Room & Board: $3,790.
There is no additional cost for LD program/services.

LD SERVICES

LD program size is not limited.

LD services available to:

☐ Freshmen ☐ Sophomores ☐ Juniors ☐ Seniors

Academic Accommodations

Curriculum		**In class**	
Foreign language waiver	☐	Early syllabus	☐
Lighter course load	☐	Note takers in class	■
Math waiver	☐	Priority seating	☐
Other special classes	☐	Tape recorders	■
Priority registrations	☐	Videotaped classes	☐
Substitution of courses	☐	Text on tape	☐
Exams		**Services**	
Extended time	■	Diagnostic tests	☐
Oral exams	☐	Learning centers	■
Take home exams	☐	Proofreaders	☐
Exams on tape or computer	☐	Readers	■
Untimed exams	☐	Reading Machines/Kurzweil	☐
Other accommodations	☐	Special bookstore section	☐
		Typists	☐

Credit toward degree is not given for remedial courses taken.

Counseling Services

- ☐ Academic
- ☐ Psychological
- ☐ Student Support groups
- ☐ Vocational

Tutoring

	Individual	Group
Time management	☐	☐
Organizational skills	☐	☐
Learning strategies	☐	☐
Study skills	☐	☐
Content area	☐	☐
Writing lab	☐	☐
Math lab	☐	☐

LD PROGRAM STAFF

Key staff person available to work with LD students: Paula Washington-Woods, Director of Counseling and Testing.

Williams Baptist College

Walnut Ridge, AR

Address: P.O. Box 3665, Walnut Ridge, AR, 72476
Admissions telephone: 800 722-4434
Admissions FAX: 870 886-3924
Director of Admissions: Angela Flippo
Admissions e-mail: admissions@wbcoll.edu
Web site: http://www.wbcoll.edu
SAT Code: 6658 ACT Code: 140

LD program name: Learning Disability Coordinator
LD program address: P.O. Box 3457
Director of Counseling: Dr. Gary Gregory
LD program telephone: 870 759-4178
LD program e-mail: ggregory@wbcoll.edu
LD program enrollment: 10, Total campus enrollment: 632

GENERAL

Williams Baptist College is a private, coed, four-year institution. 180-acre campus in Walnut Ridge (population: 4,925), 30 miles from Jonesboro and 100 miles from Memphis, TN; branch campuses in Bradford, Ark., and Senath, MO. Served by bus; major airport serves Memphis, TN. Semester system.

LD ADMISSIONS

Students do not complete a separate application and are simultaneously accepted to the LD program. A member of the LD program does not sit on the admissions committee. A personal interview is recommended. Essay is not required.

For fall 2004, 6 completed self-identified LD applications were received. 6 applications were offered admission, and 6 enrolled.

SECONDARY SCHOOL REQUIREMENTS

Graduation from secondary school required; GED accepted.

TESTING

ACT required; SAT Reasoning may be substituted.

All enrolled freshmen (fall 2004):

Average ACT Scores: Composite: 22

Child Study Team report is not required. A neuropsychological or comprehensive psycho-educational evaluation is required for admission. Must be dated within 4 months of application. Tests required as part of this documentation:

☑ WAIS-IV	☑ Woodcock-Johnson
☑ WISC-IV	☐ Nelson-Denny Reading Test
☐ SATA	☑ Other

UNDERGRADUATE STUDENT BODY

Total undergraduate student enrollment: 632.

Composition of student body (fall 2004):

	Undergraduate	Freshmen
International	0.0	0.0
Black	1.4	2.0
American Indian	0.0	1.3
Asian-American	0.0	0.8
Hispanic	1.4	0.8
White	97.2	94.8
Unreported	0.0	0.3
	100.0%	100.0%

27% are from out of state. Average age of full-time undergraduates is 24. 62% of classes have fewer than 20 students, 37% have between 20 and 50 students, 1% have more than 50 students.

STUDENT HOUSING

85% of freshmen live in college housing. Freshmen are required to live on campus. Housing is guaranteed for all undergraduates. Single rooms are available for students with medical or special needs. A medical note is required.

EXPENSES

Tuition (2005-06): $8,600 per year.
Room: $2,000. Board: $2,200.
There is no additional cost for LD program/services.

LD SERVICES

LD program size is not limited.

LD services available to:

☑ Freshmen ☑ Sophomores ☑ Juniors ☑ Seniors

Academic Accommodations

Curriculum		**In class**	
Foreign language waiver	☐	Early syllabus	☐
Lighter course load	☑	Note takers in class	☑
Math waiver	☐	Priority seating	☑
Other special classes	☑	Tape recorders	☑
Priority registrations	☐	Videotaped classes	☐
Substitution of courses	☐	Text on tape	☑
Exams		**Services**	
Extended time	☑	Diagnostic tests	☐
Oral exams	☑	Learning centers	☑
Take home exams	☐	Proofreaders	☐
Exams on tape or computer	☑	Readers	☑
Untimed exams	☑	Reading Machines/Kurzweil	☑
Other accommodations	☐	Special bookstore section	☐
		Typists	☐

Credit toward degree is not given for remedial courses taken.

Counseling Services

☑ Academic
☑ Psychological
☐ Student Support groups
☐ Vocational

Tutoring

Individual tutoring is available weekly.

Average size of tutoring groups: 1

	Individual	Group
Time management	☑	☐
Organizational skills	☑	☐
Learning strategies	☑	☐
Study skills	☑	☐
Content area	☑	☐
Writing lab	☑	☐
Math lab	☑	☐

UNIQUE LD PROGRAM FEATURES

Faculty members are very cooperative in providing accommodations to help students with disabilities to be successful in the classroom.

LD PROGRAM STAFF

Total number of LD Program staff (including director):

Full Time: 1 Part Time: 1

There is an advisor/advocate from the LD program available to students. The advisor/advocate meets with faculty 1 time per month and student 2 times per month. 4 peer tutors are available to work with LD students.

Key staff person available to work with LD students: Dr. Gary Gregory, Director of Counseling.

Alliant International University

San Diego, CA

Address: 10455 Pomerado Road, San Diego, CA, 92131-1799
Admissions telephone: 858 635-4772
Admissions FAX: 858 635-4555
Vice President of Enrollment: Eric Gravenberg
Admissions e-mail: admissions@alliant.edu
Web site: http://www.alliant.edu
SAT Code: 4039 ACT Code: 443

LD program name: Office of Disability Services
Disabilities Coordinator: Baby Medina
LD program telephone: 858 635-4471
LD program e-mail: bmedina@alliant.edu
LD program enrollment: 10, Total campus enrollment: 326

GENERAL

Alliant International University is a private, coed, four-year institution. 160-acre, suburban campus in San Diego (population: 1,223,400); branch campuses in Fresno, Irvine, Los Angeles, Sacramento, and San Francisco Bay and abroad in Nairobi, Kenya and Mexico City, Mexico. Served by air and bus; train serves Del Mar (12 miles). School operates transportation to La Jolla and to off-campus activities. Public transportation serves campus. Semester system.

LD ADMISSIONS

Students do not complete a separate application and are not simultaneously accepted to the LD program. A member of the LD program does not sit on the admissions committee. A personal interview is not required. Essay is not required.

SECONDARY SCHOOL REQUIREMENTS

Graduation from secondary school required; GED accepted.

TESTING

Child Study Team report is not required. A neuropsychological or comprehensive psycho-education evaluation is not required for admission. Tests required as part of this documentation:

- ☐ WAIS-IV
- ☐ WISC-IV
- ☐ SATA
- ☐ Woodcock-Johnson
- ☐ Nelson-Denny Reading Test
- ☐ Other

UNDERGRADUATE STUDENT BODY

Total undergraduate student enrollment: 230 Men, 292 Women.

Composition of student body (fall 2004):

	Undergraduate	Freshmen
International	18.8	32.5
Black	12.5	6.1
American Indian	0.0	0.9
Asian-American	8.3	6.4
Hispanic	27.1	21.8
White	25.0	25.2
Unreported	8.3	7.1
	100.0%	100.0%

25% are from out of state. Average age of full-time undergraduates is 22. 70% of classes have fewer than 20 students, 30% have between 20 and 50 students.

STUDENT HOUSING

94% of freshmen live in college housing. Freshmen are required to live on campus. Housing is guaranteed for all undergraduates. Campus can house 320 undergraduates. Single rooms are available for students with medical or special needs.

EXPENSES

Tuition (2005-06): $18,990 per year.
Room & Board: $7,600.

There is no additional cost for LD program/services.

LD SERVICES

LD program size is not limited.

LD services available to:

☑ Freshmen ☑ Sophomores ☑ Juniors ☑ Seniors

Academic Accommodations

Curriculum		**In class**	
Foreign language waiver	☐	Early syllabus	☑
Lighter course load	☑	Note takers in class	☑
Math waiver	☐	Priority seating	☑
Other special classes	☐	Tape recorders	☑
Priority registrations	☑	Videotaped classes	☑
Substitution of courses	☐	Text on tape	☑
Exams		**Services**	
Extended time	☑	Diagnostic tests	☐
Oral exams	☑	Learning centers	☐
Take home exams	☑	Proofreaders	☑
Exams on tape or computer	☑	Readers	☑
Untimed exams	☑	Reading Machines/Kurzweil	☑
Other accommodations	☑	Special bookstore section	☐
		Typists	☑

Credit toward degree is not given for remedial courses taken.

Counseling Services

- ☐ Academic
- ☐ Psychological
- ☐ Student Support groups
- ☐ Vocational

Tutoring

Individual tutoring is available.

	Individual	Group
Time management	☑	☐
Organizational skills	☑	☐
Learning strategies	☑	☐
Study skills	☑	☐
Content area	☑	☐
Writing lab	☑	☐
Math lab	☑	☐

UNIQUE LD PROGRAM FEATURES

Students should request accommodations prior to the beginning of each term.

LD PROGRAM STAFF

Total number of LD Program staff (including director):

Full Time: 1 Part Time: 1

LD Program web site: http://www.alliant.edu/about/ADA.htm

Art Center College of Design

Pasadena, CA

Address: 1700 Lida Street, Pasadena, CA, 91103
Admissions telephone: 626 396-2373
Admissions FAX: 626 795-0578
Vice President of Student Services: Kit Baron
Admissions e-mail: admissions@artcenter.edu
Web site: http://www.artcenter.edu
SAT Code: 4009 ACT Code: 164

Vice President of Admissions: Kit Baron
LD program telephone: 626 396-2373
LD program e-mail: cbaron@artcenter.edu
Total campus enrollment: 1,394

GENERAL

Art Center College of Design is a private, coed, four-year institution. 175-acre, suburban campus in Pasadena (population: 133,936), nine miles from Los Angeles. Major airport, bus, and train serve Los Angeles; major airport serves Burbank (15 miles). Trimester system.

LD ADMISSIONS

A personal interview is not required. Essay is required and may be typed.

SECONDARY SCHOOL REQUIREMENTS

Graduation from secondary school required; GED accepted.

TESTING

SAT Reasoning or ACT required of some applicants.

All enrolled freshmen (fall 2004):

Average SAT I Scores: Verbal: 529 Math: 565

Child Study Team report is not required. Tests required as part of this documentation:

- ❑ WAIS-IV
- ❑ WISC-IV
- ❑ SATA
- ❑ Woodcock-Johnson
- ❑ Nelson-Denny Reading Test
- ❑ Other

UNDERGRADUATE STUDENT BODY

Total undergraduate student enrollment: 831 Men, 546 Women.

Composition of student body (fall 2004):

	Undergraduate	Freshmen
International	19.6	14.9
Black	4.3	1.8
American Indian	0.0	0.6
Asian-American	43.5	35.7
Hispanic	10.9	11.5
White	21.7	35.5
Unreported	0.0	0.0
	100.0%	100.0%

21% are from out of state. Average age of full-time undergraduates is 25. 90% of classes have fewer than 20 students, 10% have between 20 and 50 students.

EXPENSES

Tuition (2005-06): $24,844 per year.

There is no additional cost for LD program/services.

LD SERVICES

LD services available to:

❑ Freshmen ❑ Sophomores ❑ Juniors ❑ Seniors

Academic Accommodations

Curriculum		In class	
Foreign language waiver	❑	Early syllabus	❑
Lighter course load	❑	Note takers in class	❑
Math waiver	❑	Priority seating	❑
Other special classes	❑	Tape recorders	❑
Priority registrations	❑	Videotaped classes	❑
Substitution of courses	❑	Text on tape	❑
Exams		**Services**	
Extended time	■	Diagnostic tests	❑
Oral exams	❑	Learning centers	❑
Take home exams	❑	Proofreaders	❑
Exams on tape or computer	❑	Readers	❑
Untimed exams	❑	Reading Machines/Kurzweil	❑
Other accommodations	❑	Special bookstore section	❑
		Typists	❑

Credit toward degree is not given for remedial courses taken.

Counseling Services

- ❑ Academic
- ❑ Psychological
- ❑ Student Support groups
- ❑ Vocational

Tutoring

	Individual	Group
Time management	❑	❑
Organizational skills	❑	❑
Learning strategies	❑	❑
Study skills	❑	❑
Content area	❑	❑
Writing lab	❑	❑
Math lab	❑	❑

Azusa Pacific University

Azusa, CA

Address: 901 East Alosta Avenue, Azusa, CA, 91702
Admissions telephone: 800 TALK-APU
Admissions FAX: 626 812-3096
Dean of Enrollment: Dave Burke
Admissions e-mail: admissions@apu.edu
Web site: http://www.apu.edu
SAT Code: 4596   ACT Code: 166

Director Learning Center: Dr. Nina Ashur
LD program telephone: 626 969-3434
LD program e-mail: nashur@apu.edu
Total campus enrollment: 4, 441

GENERAL

Azusa Pacific University is a private, coed, four-year institution. 103-acre, suburban campus in Azusa (population: 44,712), 30 miles from Los Angeles and 12 miles from Pasadena; regional centers in Menifee, Orange, San Berandino, San Diego, Ventura, and Victorville. Major airport serves Ontario (20 miles); major airport and train serve Los Angeles; bus serves West Covina (eight miles). Public transportation serves campus. Semester system.

LD ADMISSIONS

A personal interview is not required. Essay is not required.

SECONDARY SCHOOL REQUIREMENTS

Graduation from secondary school required; GED accepted.

TESTING

SAT Reasoning or ACT required.

All enrolled freshmen (fall 2004):

Average SAT I Scores:	Verbal: 541	Math: 542
Average ACT Scores:	Composite: 23	

Child Study Team report is not required. Tests required as part of this documentation:

- [ ] WAIS-IV
- [ ] WISC-IV
- [ ] SATA
- [ ] Woodcock-Johnson
- [ ] Nelson-Denny Reading Test
- [ ] Other

UNDERGRADUATE STUDENT BODY

Total undergraduate student enrollment: 1,326 Men, 2,328 Women.

Composition of student body (fall 2004):

	Undergraduate	Freshmen
International	1.6	1.6
Black	2.3	3.2
American Indian	0.4	0.3
Asian-American	5.1	4.8
Hispanic	10.0	11.6
White	74.7	73.4
Unreported	5.9	5.1
	100.0%	100.0%

11% are from out of state. Average age of full-time undergraduates is 21. 54% of classes have fewer than 20 students, 44% have between 20 and 50 students, 2% have more than 50 students.

STUDENT HOUSING

96% of freshmen live in college housing. Campus can house 2,807 undergraduates.

EXPENSES

Tuition (2005-06): $21,550 per year.

Room: $3,510. Board: $3,130.

There is no additional cost for LD program/services.

LD SERVICES

LD program size is not limited.

LD services available to:

- [ ] Freshmen
- [ ] Sophomores
- [ ] Juniors
- [ ] Seniors

Academic Accommodations

Curriculum		**In class**	
Foreign language waiver	[ ]	Early syllabus	[ ]
Lighter course load	[ ]	Note takers in class	[x]
Math waiver	[ ]	Priority seating	[ ]
Other special classes	[ ]	Tape recorders	[ ]
Priority registrations	[ ]	Videotaped classes	[ ]
Substitution of courses	[ ]	Text on tape	[ ]
Exams		**Services**	
Extended time	[x]	Diagnostic tests	[ ]
Oral exams	[ ]	Learning centers	[x]
Take home exams	[ ]	Proofreaders	[ ]
Exams on tape or computer	[ ]	Readers	[ ]
Untimed exams	[ ]	Reading Machines/Kurzweil	[ ]
Other accommodations	[ ]	Special bookstore section	[ ]
		Typists	[ ]

Credit toward degree is not given for remedial courses taken.

Counseling Services

- [ ] Academic
- [ ] Psychological
- [ ] Student Support groups
- [ ] Vocational

Tutoring

	Individual	Group
Time management	[ ]	[ ]
Organizational skills	[ ]	[ ]
Learning strategies	[ ]	[ ]
Study skills	[ ]	[ ]
Content area	[ ]	[ ]
Writing lab	[ ]	[ ]
Math lab	[ ]	[ ]

LD PROGRAM STAFF

Total number of LD Program staff (including director):

Full Time: 2   Part Time: 2

Key staff person available to work with LD students: Dr. Nina Ashur, Director Learning Center.

Biola University

La Mirada, CA

Address: 13800 Biola Avenue, La Mirada, CA, 90639-0001
Admissions telephone: 800 OK-BIOLA
Admissions FAX: 562 903-4709
Director of Enrollment Management: Andre Stephens
Admissions e-mail: admissions@biola.edu
Web site: http://www.biola.edu
SAT Code: 4017 ACT Code: 172

Director of Disability Services: Tim Engle
LD program telephone: 562 944-0351
LD program e-mail: Tim.Engle@biola.edu
LD program enrollment: 50, Total campus enrollment: 3,595

GENERAL

Biola University is a private, coed, four-year institution. 95-acre campus in La Mirada (population: 46,782), 22 miles from Los Angeles. Major airports serve Los Angeles; smaller airport serves Santa Ana (30 miles); bus serves Whittier (five miles); train serves Fullerton (five miles). 4-1-4 system.

LD ADMISSIONS

Application Deadline: 03/01. A member of the LD program does sit on the admissions committee. High school waivers are accepted for math and foreign language. A personal interview is required. Essay is required and may be typed.

SECONDARY SCHOOL REQUIREMENTS

Graduation from secondary school required; GED accepted.

TESTING

SAT Reasoning required; ACT may be substituted. SAT Subject recommended.

All enrolled freshmen (fall 2004):

Average SAT I Scores:	Verbal: 568	Math: 557
Average ACT Scores:	Composite: 24	

Child Study Team report is not required. A neuropsychological or comprehensive psycho-educational evaluation is required for admission. Must be dated within 4 months of application. Tests required as part of this documentation:

- ☒ WAIS-IV
- ☒ WISC-IV
- ☐ SATA
- ☒ Woodcock-Johnson
- ☐ Nelson-Denny Reading Test
- ☐ Other

UNDERGRADUATE STUDENT BODY

Total undergraduate student enrollment: 1,152 Men, 1,797 Women.

Composition of student body (fall 2004):

	Undergraduate	Freshmen
International	2.6	2.4
Black	1.4	3.6
American Indian	0.7	0.4
Asian-American	9.2	8.1
Hispanic	8.0	10.7
White	72.5	72.0
Unreported	5.6	2.8
	100.0%	100.0%

STUDENT HOUSING

Freshmen are required to live on campus. Housing is guaranteed for all undergraduates. Campus can house 2,298 undergraduates. Single rooms are available for students with medical or special needs. A medical note is required.

EXPENSES

Tuition (2005-06): $22,602 per year.
Room: $3,900. Board: $3,200.

There is no additional cost for LD program/services.

LD SERVICES

LD program size is not limited.

LD services available to:

☒ Freshmen ☒ Sophomores ☒ Juniors ☒ Seniors

Academic Accommodations

Curriculum		In class	
Foreign language waiver	☒	Early syllabus	☒
Lighter course load	☐	Note takers in class	☒
Math waiver	☒	Priority seating	☒
Other special classes	☐	Tape recorders	☒
Priority registrations	☒	Videotaped classes	☐
Substitution of courses	☐	Text on tape	☒
Exams		**Services**	
Extended time	☒	Diagnostic tests	☒
Oral exams	☐	Learning centers	☐
Take home exams	☐	Proofreaders	☒
Exams on tape or computer	☒	Readers	☒
Untimed exams	☐	Reading Machines/Kurzweil	☒
Other accommodations	☒	Special bookstore section	☐
		Typists	☒

Credit toward degree is not given for remedial courses taken.

Counseling Services

- ☒ Academic
- ☐ Psychological
- ☒ Student Support groups
- ☒ Vocational

Tutoring

Individual tutoring is available daily.

Average size of tutoring groups: 6

	Individual	Group
Time management	☒	☒
Organizational skills	☒	☒
Learning strategies	☒	☒
Study skills	☒	☒
Content area	☒	☒
Writing lab	☒	☒
Math lab	☒	☒

LD PROGRAM STAFF

Total number of LD Program staff (including director):

Full Time: 2 Part Time: 2

There is an advisor/advocate from the LD program available to students.

Key staff person available to work with LD students: Tim Engle, Director of Disability Services.

California Baptist University

Riverside, CA

Address: 8432 Magnolia Avenue, Riverside, CA, 92504
Admissions telephone: 877 228-8866
Admissions FAX: 951 343-4525
Dean of Enrollment Services: Allen Johnson
Admissions e-mail: admissions@calbaptist.edu
Web site: http://www.calbaptist.edu
SAT Code: 4094 ACT Code: 175

LD program name: Disability Services
Director: Jim Paulus
LD program telephone: 951 343-4690
LD program e-mail: jpaulus@calbaptist.edu
LD program enrollment: 9, Total campus enrollment: 2,243

GENERAL

California Baptist University is a private, coed, four-year institution. 80-acre, urban campus in Riverside (population: 255,166), 60 miles from Los Angeles; branch campuses in San Bernardino and Victorville. Served by bus; major airports serve Ontario (19 miles) and Los Angeles; train serves San Bernardino (15 miles). Public transportation serves campus. Semester system.

LD ADMISSIONS

Students do not complete a separate application and are not simultaneously accepted to the LD program. A member of the LD program does not sit on the admissions committee. A personal interview is recommended. Essay is required and may be typed.

SECONDARY SCHOOL REQUIREMENTS

Graduation from secondary school required; GED accepted. The following course distribution required: 4 units of English, 3 units of math, 2 units of science, 2 units of foreign language, 2 units of social studies, 2 units of history.

TESTING

SAT Reasoning or ACT required. SAT Subject recommended.

All enrolled freshmen (fall 2004):

Average SAT I Scores:	Verbal: 494	Math: 493
Average ACT Scores:	Composite: 19	

Child Study Team report is not required. A neuropsychological or comprehensive psycho-education evaluation is not required for admission. Tests required as part of this documentation:

- ☐ WAIS-IV
- ☐ WISC-IV
- ☐ SATA
- ☐ Woodcock-Johnson
- ☐ Nelson-Denny Reading Test
- ☐ Other

UNDERGRADUATE STUDENT BODY

Total undergraduate student enrollment: 550 Men, 1,030 Women.

Composition of student body (fall 2004):

	Undergraduate	Freshmen
International	0.3	0.8
Black	7.1	7.5
American Indian	0.3	0.9
Asian-American	2.9	2.7
Hispanic	16.4	16.2
White	61.1	59.9
Unreported	11.9	12.0
	100.0%	100.0%

6% are from out of state. Average age of full-time undergraduates is 23. 51% of classes have fewer than 20 students, 45% have between 20 and 50 students, 4% have more than 50 students.

STUDENT HOUSING

83% of freshmen live in college housing. Freshmen are required to live on campus. Housing is guaranteed for all undergraduates. Campus can house 1,035 undergraduates. Single rooms are available for students with medical or special needs. A medical note is required.

EXPENSES

Tuition (2005-06): $16,250 per year.
Room: $3,960. Board: $3,670.
There is no additional cost for LD program/services.

LD SERVICES

LD program size is not limited.

LD services available to:

■ Freshmen ■ Sophomores ■ Juniors ■ Seniors

Academic Accommodations

Curriculum		In class	
Foreign language waiver	☐	Early syllabus	☐
Lighter course load	■	Note takers in class	■
Math waiver	☐	Priority seating	■
Other special classes	☐	Tape recorders	■
Priority registrations	■	Videotaped classes	☐
Substitution of courses	☐	Text on tape	■
Exams		**Services**	
Extended time	■	Diagnostic tests	☐
Oral exams	■	Learning centers	■
Take home exams	☐	Proofreaders	☐
Exams on tape or computer	☐	Readers	■
Untimed exams	☐	Reading Machines/Kurzweil	☐
Other accommodations	■	Special bookstore section	☐
		Typists	■

Credit toward degree is not given for remedial courses taken.

Counseling Services

- ☐ Academic
- ☐ Psychological
- ☐ Student Support groups
- ☐ Vocational

Tutoring

Individual tutoring is available weekly.

Average size of tutoring groups: 1

	Individual	Group
Time management	■	■
Organizational skills	■	■
Learning strategies	■	■
Study skills	■	■
Content area	■	■
Writing lab	☐	■
Math lab	☐	■

LD PROGRAM STAFF

There is an advisor/advocate from the LD program available to students.

Key staff person available to work with LD students: Cora Lee Staley, Coordinator, Academic Resources.

California College of Arts and Crafts

San Francisco, CA

Address: 1111 Eighth Street, San Francisco, CA, 94107
Admissions telephone: 800 447-1-ART
Admissions FAX: 415 703-9539
Associate Vice President of Enrollment: Kate Wees
Admissions e-mail: enroll@cca.edu
Web site: http://www.cca.edu
SAT Code: 4031 ACT Code: 176

LD program name: Academic Support Services
Associate Dean of Retention and Advising: Janice Grossman
LD program telephone: 510 594-5019
LD program e-mail: jgrossman@cca.edu
Total campus enrollment: 1284

GENERAL

California College of Arts and Crafts is a private, coed, four-year institution. Four-acre, urban campus in San Francisco (population: 776,733); fine arts campus in Oakland. Served by air, bus, and train. Semester system.

LD ADMISSIONS

A personal interview is recommended. Essay is required and may be typed.

SECONDARY SCHOOL REQUIREMENTS

Graduation from secondary school required; GED accepted.

TESTING

SAT Subject recommended.

All enrolled freshmen (fall 2004):

Average SAT I Scores:	Verbal: 535	Math: 535
Average ACT Scores:	Composite: 22	

Child Study Team report is not required. Tests required as part of this documentation:

☐ WAIS-IV ☐ Woodcock-Johnson
☐ WISC-IV ☐ Nelson-Denny Reading Test
☐ SATA ☐ Other

UNDERGRADUATE STUDENT BODY

Total undergraduate student enrollment: 466 Men, 698 Women.

Composition of student body (fall 2004):

	Undergraduate
International	2.9
Black	1.8
American Indian	1.2
Asian-American	13.5
Hispanic	7.6
White	63.1
Unreported	9.9
	100.0%

23% are from out of state. Average age of full-time undergraduates is 28. 88% of classes have fewer than 20 students, 12% have between 20 and 50 students.

STUDENT HOUSING

82% of freshmen live in college housing. Freshmen are not required to live on campus. Housing is guaranteed for all undergraduates. Campus can house 228 undergraduates.

EXPENSES

Tuition (2005-06): $25,810 per year.

Room & Board: $4,820-$6,000.

There is no additional cost for LD program/services.

LD SERVICES

LD program size is not limited.

LD services available to:

☐ Freshmen ☐ Sophomores ☐ Juniors ☐ Seniors

Academic Accommodations

Curriculum		In class	
Foreign language waiver	☐	Early syllabus	☐
Lighter course load	■	Note takers in class	■
Math waiver	☐	Priority seating	☐
Other special classes	☐	Tape recorders	■
Priority registrations	☐	Videotaped classes	☐
Substitution of courses	☐	Text on tape	☐
Exams		**Services**	
Extended time	■	Diagnostic tests	☐
Oral exams	☐	Learning centers	☐
Take home exams	☐	Proofreaders	☐
Exams on tape or computer	☐	Readers	☐
Untimed exams	■	Reading Machines/Kurzweil	☐
Other accommodations	☐	Special bookstore section	☐
		Typists	☐

Credit toward degree is given for remedial courses taken.

Counseling Services

☐ Academic
☐ Psychological
☐ Student Support groups
☐ Vocational

Tutoring

	Individual	Group
Time management	☐	☐
Organizational skills	☐	☐
Learning strategies	☐	☐
Study skills	☐	☐
Content area	☐	☐
Writing lab	☐	☐
Math lab	☐	☐

LD PROGRAM STAFF

Key staff person available to work with LD students: Virginia Jardim, Director of Tutorial Services.

California Institute of the Arts

Valencia, CA

Address: 24700 McBean Parkway, Valencia, CA, 91355
Admissions telephone: 661 255-1050
Admissions FAX: 661 253-7710
Director of Enrollment Services: Carol Kim
Admissions e-mail: admiss@calarts.edu
Web site: http://www.calarts.edu
SAT Code: 4049 ACT Code: 181

Dean of Student Affairs: Yvonne Guy
LD program telephone: 661 253-7891
LD program e-mail: yguy@calarts.edu
Total campus enrollment: 835

GENERAL

California Institute of the Arts is a private, coed, four-year institution. 60-acre, suburban campus in Valencia (population: 50,000), 30 miles from Los Angeles. Major airport and train serve Los Angeles; smaller airport serves Burbank (25 miles); bus serves San Fernando (15 miles). Semester system.

LD ADMISSIONS

Students do not complete a separate application and are not simultaneously accepted to the LD program. A member of the LD program does not sit on the admissions committee. High school waivers are accepted for foreign language. A personal interview is recommended. Essay is required and may be typed.

SECONDARY SCHOOL REQUIREMENTS

Graduation from secondary school required; GED accepted.

TESTING

Child Study Team report is not required. A neuropsychological or comprehensive psycho-educational evaluation is required for admission. Tests required as part of this documentation:

- ☐ WAIS-IV
- ☐ WISC-IV
- ☐ SATA
- ☐ Woodcock-Johnson
- ☐ Nelson-Denny Reading Test
- ☐ Other

UNDERGRADUATE STUDENT BODY

Total undergraduate student enrollment: 473 Men, 350 Women.

52% are from out of state.

STUDENT HOUSING

Freshmen are not required to live on campus. Housing is guaranteed for all undergraduates. Campus can house 449 undergraduates.

EXPENSES

Tuition (2005-06): $27,260 per year.
Room & Board: $7,697.
There is no additional cost for LD program/services.

LD SERVICES

LD program size is not limited.

LD services available to:

■ Freshmen ■ Sophomores ■ Juniors ■ Seniors

Academic Accommodations

Curriculum		**In class**	
Foreign language waiver	☐	Early syllabus	☐
Lighter course load	☐	Note takers in class	☐
Math waiver	☐	Priority seating	☐
Other special classes	☐	Tape recorders	☐
Priority registrations	☐	Videotaped classes	☐
Substitution of courses	☐	Text on tape	☐
Exams		**Services**	
Extended time	☐	Diagnostic tests	☐
Oral exams	☐	Learning centers	☐
Take home exams	☐	Proofreaders	☐
Exams on tape or computer	☐	Readers	☐
Untimed exams	☐	Reading Machines/Kurzweil	☐
Other accommodations	☐	Special bookstore section	☐
		Typists	☐

Credit toward degree is not given for remedial courses taken.

Counseling Services

- ☐ Academic
- ☐ Psychological
- ☐ Student Support groups
- ☐ Vocational

Tutoring

	Individual	Group
Time management	☐	☐
Organizational skills	☐	☐
Learning strategies	☐	☐
Study skills	☐	☐
Content area	☐	☐
Writing lab	☐	☐
Math lab	☐	☐

LD PROGRAM STAFF

Key staff person available to work with LD students: Yvonne Guy, Dean of Student Affairs.

California Institute of Technology

Pasadena, CA

Address: 1200 East California Boulevard, Pasadena, CA, 91125
Admissions telephone: 800 568-8324
Admissions FAX: 626 683-3026
Director of Admissions: Richard Bischoff
Admissions e-mail: ugadmissions@caltech.edu
Web site: http://www.caltech.edu
SAT Code: 4034 ACT Code: 182

Asst. Vice President for Student Affairs: Dr. Erica O'Neal
LD program telephone: 626 395-6322
LD program e-mail: eoneal@stuaff.caltech.edu
Total campus enrollment: 896

GENERAL

California Institute of Technology is a private, coed, four-year institution. 124-acre, suburban campus in Pasadena (population: 133,936), 10 miles from Los Angeles. Served by bus and train; major airport serves Los Angeles; smaller airport serves Burbank (15 miles). School operates transportation to Jet Propulsion Lab. Public transportation serves campus. Quarter system.

LD ADMISSIONS

A personal interview is not required. Essay is required and may be typed.

SECONDARY SCHOOL REQUIREMENTS

Graduation from secondary school not required. The following course distribution required: 3 units of English, 4 units of math, 2 units of science, 1 unit of social studies, 1 unit of history.

TESTING

SAT Subject recommended.

Child Study Team report is not required. Tests required as part of this documentation:

- ☐ WAIS-IV
- ☐ WISC-IV
- ☐ SATA
- ☐ Woodcock-Johnson
- ☐ Nelson-Denny Reading Test
- ☐ Other

UNDERGRADUATE STUDENT BODY

Total undergraduate student enrollment: 632 Men, 297 Women.

Composition of student body (fall 2004):

	Undergraduate	Freshmen
International	4.8	6.9
Black	0.5	1.1
American Indian	0.5	0.7
Asian-American	31.4	31.1
Hispanic	5.8	6.9
White	54.6	51.8
Unreported	2.4	1.5
	100.0%	100.0%

60% are from out of state. Average age of full-time undergraduates is 20. 63% of classes have fewer than 20 students, 28% have between 20 and 50 students, 9% have more than 50 students.

STUDENT HOUSING

100% of freshmen live in college housing. Freshmen are required to live on campus. Housing is guaranteed for all undergraduates. Campus can house 896 undergraduates. Single rooms are available for students with medical or special needs.

EXPENSES

Tuition (2005-06): $27,309 per year.
Room: $5,013. Board: $3,801.
There is no additional cost for LD program/services.

LD SERVICES

LD program size is not limited.

LD services available to:

■ Freshmen ■ Sophomores ■ Juniors ■ Seniors

Academic Accommodations

Curriculum		**In class**	
Foreign language waiver	☐	Early syllabus	☐
Lighter course load	■	Note takers in class	■
Math waiver	☐	Priority seating	☐
Other special classes	☐	Tape recorders	■
Priority registrations	☐	Videotaped classes	☐
Substitution of courses	☐	Text on tape	☐
Exams		**Services**	
Extended time	■	Diagnostic tests	■
Oral exams	■	Learning centers	☐
Take home exams	☐	Proofreaders	☐
Exams on tape or computer	☐	Readers	■
Untimed exams	■	Reading Machines/Kurzweil	☐
Other accommodations	☐	Special bookstore section	☐
		Typists	☐

Counseling Services

- ■ Academic
- ■ Psychological
- ☐ Student Support groups
- ☐ Vocational

Tutoring

	Individual	Group
Time management	☐	☐
Organizational skills	☐	☐
Learning strategies	☐	☐
Study skills	☐	☐
Content area	☐	☐
Writing lab	☐	☐
Math lab	☐	☐

LD PROGRAM STAFF

Key staff person available to work with LD students: Dr. Barbara Green, Associate Dean of Students.

California Lutheran University

Thousand Oaks, CA

Address: 60 West Olsen Road, Thousand Oaks, CA, 91360
Admissions telephone: 877 258-3678
Admissions FAX: 805 493-3114
Director of Admission: Darryl Calkins
Admissions e-mail: claudm@clunet.edu
Web site: http://www.clunet.edu
SAT Code: 4088 ACT Code: 183

LD program name: Center for Academic and Acessibility Resources
LD program address: 60 West Olsen Road, #5300
Director: Damien A. Pena, MSW
LD program telephone: 805 493-3878
LD program e-mail: dpena@clunet.edu
LD program enrollment: 98, total campus enrollment: 1,972

GENERAL

California Lutheran University is a private, coed, four-year institution. 290-acre, suburban campus in Thousand Oaks (population: 117,005), 40 miles from Los Angeles; branch campuses in Ventura and Woodland Hills. Served by bus; major airports serve Los Angeles and Burbank (30 miles); train serves Simi Valley (15 miles). Public transportation serves campus. Semester system.

LD ADMISSIONS

Students complete a separate application and are simultaneously accepted to the LD program. A member of the LD program does sit on the admissions committee. A personal interview is required. Essay is not required.

For fall 2004, 10 completed self-identified LD applications were received. 10 applications were offered admission, and 10 enrolled.

SECONDARY SCHOOL REQUIREMENTS

Graduation from secondary school required; GED accepted. The following course distribution required: 4 units of English, 3 units of math, 2 units of science, 2 units of foreign language, 2 units of social studies.

TESTING

SAT Reasoning or ACT required.

All enrolled freshmen (fall 2004):

Average SAT I Scores:	Verbal: 538	Math: 547
Average ACT Scores:	Composite: 23	

Child Study Team report is not required. A neuropsychological or comprehensive psycho-education evaluation is not required for admission. Tests required as part of this documentation:

- [ ] WAIS-IV
- [ ] WISC-IV
- [ ] SATA
- [ ] Woodcock-Johnson
- [ ] Nelson-Denny Reading Test
- [ ] Other

UNDERGRADUATE STUDENT BODY

Total undergraduate student enrollment: 796 Men, 1,020 Women.

Composition of student body (fall 2004):

	Undergraduate	Freshmen
International	3.0	1.7
Black	3.5	2.5
American Indian	1.7	1.4
Asian-American	5.5	5.0
Hispanic	14.7	15.4
White	60.9	64.0
Unreported	10.7	10.0
	100.0%	100.0%

17% are from out of state. Average age of full-time undergraduates is 20. 55% of classes have fewer than 20 students, 43% have between 20 and 50 students, 2% have more than 50 students.

STUDENT HOUSING

89% of freshmen live in college housing. Freshmen are required to live on campus. Housing is guaranteed for all undergraduates. Campus can house 1,100 undergraduates. Single rooms are not available for students with medical or special needs.

EXPENSES

Tuition (2005-06): $23,170 per year.

Room: $4,330. Board: $3,990.

There is no additional cost for LD program/services.

LD SERVICES

LD program size is not limited.

LD services available to:

- [x] Freshmen
- [x] Sophomores
- [x] Juniors
- [x] Seniors

Academic Accommodations

Curriculum		**In class**	
Foreign language waiver	[ ]	Early syllabus	[x]
Lighter course load	[ ]	Note takers in class	[x]
Math waiver	[ ]	Priority seating	[x]
Other special classes	[ ]	Tape recorders	[x]
Priority registrations	[x]	Videotaped classes	[ ]
Substitution of courses	[ ]	Text on tape	[ ]
Exams		**Services**	
Extended time	[x]	Diagnostic tests	[ ]
Oral exams	[x]	Learning centers	[x]
Take home exams	[ ]	Proofreaders	[ ]
Exams on tape or computer	[x]	Readers	[x]
Untimed exams	[x]	Reading Machines/Kurzweil	[ ]
Other accommodations	[x]	Special bookstore section	[ ]
		Typists	[ ]

Credit toward degree is not given for remedial courses taken.

Counseling Services

- [x] Academic — Meets 5 times per academic year
- [ ] Psychological
- [ ] Student Support groups
- [ ] Vocational

Tutoring

Individual tutoring is available weekly.

	Individual	Group
Time management	[x]	[x]
Organizational skills	[x]	[x]
Learning strategies	[x]	[x]
Study skills	[x]	[x]
Content area	[x]	[x]
Writing lab	[x]	[x]
Math lab	[x]	[x]

LD PROGRAM STAFF

Total number of LD Program staff (including director):

Full Time: 4 Part Time: 4

There is an advisor/advocate from the LD program available to students. The advisor/advocate meets with faculty 30 times per month and students 6 times per month. One graduate student and 15 peer tutors are available to work with LD students.

Key staff person available to work with LD students: Valerie Cirino-Perez, Coordinator for Students with Disabilities.

LD Program web site: http://ww2.clunet.edu/car/undergrad/disabilities/

California Polytechnic State University, San Luis Obispo

San Luis Obispo, CA

Address: 1 Grand Avenue, San Luis Obispo, CA, 93407
Admissions telephone: 805 756-2311
Admissions FAX: 805 756-5400
Director of Admissions: James Maraviglia
Admissions e-mail: admissions@calpoly.edu
Web site: http://www.calpoly.edu
SAT Code: 4038 ACT Code: 188

LD program name: Disability Resource Center
LD program address: Student Services Building
Assistant Director: Steven Kane
LD program telephone: 805 756-1437
LD program e-mail: skane@calpoly.edu
Total campus enrollment: 16,639

GENERAL

California Polytechnic State University, San Luis Obispo is a public, coed, four-year institution. 6,000-acre campus in San Luis Obispo (population: 44,174), 195 miles from Los Angeles. Served by air, bus, and train. Public transportation serves campus. Quarter system.

LD ADMISSIONS

Students do not complete a separate application and are not simultaneously accepted to the LD program. A member of the LD program does not sit on the admissions committee. A personal interview is not required. Essay is not required.

SECONDARY SCHOOL REQUIREMENTS

Graduation from secondary school required; GED accepted. The following course distribution required: 4 units of English, 3 units of math, 3 units of science, 2 units of foreign language.

TESTING

SAT Reasoning or ACT required. SAT Subject recommended.

All enrolled freshmen (fall 2004):

Average SAT I Scores: Verbal: 586 Math: 625

Child Study Team report is not required. A neuropsychological or comprehensive psycho-educational evaluation is required for admission. Must be dated within 36 months of application. Tests required as part of this documentation:

- [x] WAIS-IV
- [x] WISC-IV
- [x] SATA
- [x] Woodcock-Johnson
- [x] Nelson-Denny Reading Test
- [ ] Other

UNDERGRADUATE STUDENT BODY

Total undergraduate student enrollment: 9,446 Men, 7,620 Women.

Composition of student body (fall 2004):

	Undergraduate	Freshmen
International	0.4	0.5
Black	1.1	1.0
American Indian	0.6	0.7
Asian-American	11.7	11.6
Hispanic	10.7	9.8
White	65.1	64.3
Unreported	10.4	12.1
	100.0%	100.0%

4% are from out of state. 10% join a fraternity and 8% join a sorority. Average age of full-time undergraduates is 21. 31% of classes have fewer than 20 students, 62% have between 20 and 50 students, 7% have more than 50 students.

STUDENT HOUSING

Freshmen are not required to live on campus. Housing is not guaranteed for all undergraduates. Campus can house 3,577 undergraduates. Single rooms are available for students with medical or special needs. A medical note is required.

EXPENSES

Tuition 2004-05: No tuition for in-state, $6,480 (out-of-state).

Room: $4,408. Board: $3,393.

There is no additional cost for LD program/services.

LD SERVICES

LD program size is not limited.

LD services available to:

- [x] Freshmen
- [x] Sophomores
- [x] Juniors
- [x] Seniors

Academic Accommodations

Curriculum		In class	
Foreign language waiver	[ ]	Early syllabus	[ ]
Lighter course load	[ ]	Note takers in class	[x]
Math waiver	[ ]	Priority seating	[ ]
Other special classes	[ ]	Tape recorders	[x]
Priority registrations	[ ]	Videotaped classes	[ ]
Substitution of courses	[ ]	Text on tape	[x]
Exams		**Services**	
Extended time	[x]	Diagnostic tests	[ ]
Oral exams	[ ]	Learning centers	[ ]
Take home exams	[ ]	Proofreaders	[ ]
Exams on tape or computer	[x]	Readers	[ ]
Untimed exams	[ ]	Reading Machines/Kurzweil	[ ]
Other accommodations	[ ]	Special bookstore section	[x]
		Typists	[ ]

Credit toward degree is not given for remedial courses taken.

Counseling Services

- [ ] Academic
- [ ] Psychological
- [ ] Student Support groups
- [ ] Vocational

Tutoring

Individual tutoring is available weekly.

	Individual	Group
Time management	[ ]	[ ]
Organizational skills	[ ]	[ ]
Learning strategies	[ ]	[ ]
Study skills	[ ]	[ ]
Content area	[ ]	[ ]
Writing lab	[ ]	[ ]
Math lab	[ ]	[ ]

LD PROGRAM STAFF

Total number of LD Program staff (including director):

Full Time: 3 Part Time: 3

There is an advisor/advocate from the LD program available to students.

Key staff person available to work with LD students: Steven Kane, Assistant Director.

LD Program web site: drc.calpoly.edu

California State Polytechnic University, Pomona

Pomona, CA

Address: 3801 West Temple Avenue, Pomona, CA, 91768-2557
Admissions telephone: 909 869-3210
Admissions FAX: 909 869-4529
Associate Director of Admissions: Dr. George Bradshaw
Admissions e-mail: generalinfo@csupomona.edu
Web site: http://www.csupomona.edu
SAT Code: 4082 ACT Code: 4048

LD program name: Disability Resource Center
Senior Coordinator, DRC, LD Specialist: Dr. Micki Bryant
LD program telephone: 909 869-3333
LD program e-mail: mbryant@csupomona.edu
LD program enrollment: 445, Total campus enrollment: 16,955

GENERAL

California State Polytechnic University, Pomona is a public, coed, four-year institution. 1,437-acre campus in Pomona (population: 149,473), 30 miles from Los Angeles. Served by bus and train; major airport serves Los Angeles; smaller airport serves Ontario (13 miles). School operates transportation to off-campus housing and around Pomona. Public transportation serves campus. Quarter system.

LD ADMISSIONS

Students do not complete a separate application and are simultaneously accepted to the LD program. A member of the LD program does not sit on the admissions committee. High school waivers are accepted for math and foreign language. A personal interview is not required. Essay is not required. Some admission requirements may be waived upon approval by the major department and college in consultation with the Disability Resource Center.

SECONDARY SCHOOL REQUIREMENTS

Graduation from secondary school required; GED accepted. The following course distribution required: 4 units of English, 3 units of math, 2 units of science, 2 units of foreign language, 1 unit of social studies, 1 unit of history, 1 unit of academic electives.

TESTING

SAT Reasoning or ACT required. SAT Subject recommended.

All enrolled freshmen (fall 2004):

Average SAT I Scores:	Verbal: 484	Math: 525
Average ACT Scores:	Composite: 21	

Child Study Team report is not required. A neuropsychological or comprehensive psycho-education evaluation is not required for admission. Tests required as part of this documentation:

- ☑ WAIS-IV
- ☐ WISC-IV
- ☑ SATA
- ☑ Woodcock-Johnson
- ☑ Nelson-Denny Reading Test
- ☐ Other

UNDERGRADUATE STUDENT BODY

Total undergraduate student enrollment: 9,627 Men, 7,378 Women.

Composition of student body (fall 2004):

	Undergraduate	Freshmen
International	0.9	3.2
Black	3.9	3.5
American Indian	0.6	0.5
Asian-American	29.5	32.9
Hispanic	25.9	25.5
White	29.3	24.8
Unreported	9.9	9.6
	100.0%	100.0%

2% are from out of state. 3% join a fraternity and 3% join a sorority. Average age of full-time undergraduates is 22. 37% of classes have fewer than 20 students, 54% have between 20 and 50 students, 9% have more than 50 students.

STUDENT HOUSING

40% of freshmen live in college housing. Freshmen are not required to live on campus. Housing is guaranteed for all undergraduates. Campus can house 2,892 undergraduates. Single rooms are available for students with medical or special needs. A medical note is required.

EXPENSES

Tuition (2005-06): $2,520 per year (in-state), $10,656 (out-of-state).

Room: $4,431. Board: $3,075.

There is no additional cost for LD program/services.

LD SERVICES

LD program size is not limited.

LD services available to:

☑ Freshmen ☑ Sophomores ☑ Juniors ☑ Seniors

Academic Accommodations

Curriculum		**In class**	
Foreign language waiver	☐	Early syllabus	☐
Lighter course load	☐	Note takers in class	☑
Math waiver	☐	Priority seating	☐
Other special classes	☐	Tape recorders	☑
Priority registrations	☑	Videotaped classes	☐
Substitution of courses	☐	Text on tape	☐
Exams		**Services**	
Extended time	☑	Diagnostic tests	☐
Oral exams	☑	Learning centers	☑
Take home exams	☐	Proofreaders	☐
Exams on tape or computer	☐	Readers	☐
Untimed exams	☐	Reading Machines/Kurzweil	☑
Other accommodations	☐	Special bookstore section	☐
		Typists	☐

Credit toward degree is not given for remedial courses taken.

Counseling Services

- ☑ Academic
- ☑ Psychological
- ☐ Student Support groups
- ☑ Vocational

Tutoring

Individual tutoring is not available.

	Individual	Group
Time management	☐	☐
Organizational skills	☐	☐
Learning strategies	☐	☐
Study skills	☐	☐
Content area	☐	☐
Writing lab	☐	☐
Math lab	☐	☐

UNIQUE LD PROGRAM FEATURES

A separate grant funded program that offers a more intensive level of service is available for a maximum of 150 students who have any type of disability. Services include academic advising, peer tutoring and/or peer advising for organizational and learning strategies, and financial aid and scholarship assistance.

LD PROGRAM STAFF

Total number of LD Program staff (including director):

Full Time: 1 Part Time: 1

There is an advisor/advocate from the LD program available to students.

Key staff person available to work with LD students: Dr. Micki Bryant, Senior Coordinator, DRC, LD Specialist.

LD Program web site: http://www.dsa.csupomona.edu/drc/

California State University, Bakersfield

Bakersfield, CA

Address: 9001 Stockdale Highway, Bakersfield, CA, 93311
Admissions telephone: 661 664-3036
Admissions FAX: 661 664-3389
Associate Dean of Admissions and Records: Homer Montalvo
Admissions e-mail: admissions@csub.edu
Web site: http://www.csub.edu
SAT Code: 4110 ACT Code: 201

Director: Janice Clausen
LD program telephone: 661 664-3360
LD program e-mail: jclausen@csub.edu
Total campus enrollment: 5, 963

GENERAL

California State University, Bakersfield is a public, coed, four-year institution. 375-acre campus in Bakersfield (population: 247,057), 112 miles from Los Angeles. Served by air, bus, and train. Public transportation serves campus. Quarter system.

SECONDARY SCHOOL REQUIREMENTS

Graduation from secondary school required; GED accepted. The following course distribution required: 4 units of English, 3 units of math, 2 units of science, 2 units of foreign language, 1 unit of social studies, 1 unit of history, 1 unit of academic electives.

TESTING

SAT Reasoning or ACT required of some applicants. SAT Subject required.

All enrolled freshmen (fall 2004):

Average SAT I Scores:	Verbal: 464	Math: 479
Average ACT Scores:	Composite: 19	

Child Study Team report is not required. Tests required as part of this documentation:

- ☐ WAIS-IV
- ☐ WISC-IV
- ☐ SATA
- ☐ Woodcock-Johnson
- ☐ Nelson-Denny Reading Test
- ☐ Other

UNDERGRADUATE STUDENT BODY

Total undergraduate student enrollment: 5,963.

Composition of student body (fall 2004):

	Undergraduate	Freshmen
International	1.3	2.0
Black	9.5	7.1
American Indian	1.3	1.4
Asian-American	8.6	6.3
Hispanic	38.0	33.1
White	33.8	40.6
Unreported	7.5	9.5
	100.0%	100.0%

1% are from out of state. 49% of classes have fewer than 20 students, 46% have between 20 and 50 students, 5% have more than 50 students.

STUDENT HOUSING

Freshmen are not required to live on campus. Housing is guaranteed for all undergraduates.

EXPENSES

Tuition (2005-06): No tuition for in-state, $10,170 (out-of-state).
Room & Board: $5,946.

LD SERVICES

LD services available to:

☐ Freshmen ☐ Sophomores ☐ Juniors ☐ Seniors

Academic Accommodations

Curriculum		In class	
Foreign language waiver	☐	Early syllabus	☐
Lighter course load	☐	Note takers in class	■
Math waiver	☐	Priority seating	☐
Other special classes	☐	Tape recorders	■
Priority registrations	☐	Videotaped classes	■
Substitution of courses	☐	Text on tape	☐
Exams		**Services**	
Extended time	■	Diagnostic tests	■
Oral exams	■	Learning centers	☐
Take home exams	☐	Proofreaders	☐
Exams on tape or computer	☐	Readers	■
Untimed exams	■	Reading Machines/Kurzweil	■
Other accommodations	☐	Special bookstore section	☐
		Typists	☐

Counseling Services

- ☐ Academic
- ☐ Psychological
- ☐ Student Support groups
- ☐ Vocational

Tutoring

	Individual	Group
Time management	☐	☐
Organizational skills	☐	☐
Learning strategies	☐	☐
Study skills	☐	☐
Content area	☐	☐
Writing lab	☐	☐
Math lab	☐	☐

LD PROGRAM STAFF

Key staff person available to work with LD students: Jan Freshwater, Learning Disability Specialist.

California State University, Chico

Chico, CA

Address: 400 West First Street, Chico, CA, 95929-0722
Admissions telephone: 800 542-4426
Admissions FAX: 530 898-6456
Vice Provost for Enrollment Management: John Swiney
Admissions e-mail: info@csuchico.edu
Web site: http://www.csuchico.edu
SAT Code: 4048 ACT Code: 212

LD program name: Disability Support Services
Learning Disability Specialists: Van Alexander/Chris Prator
LD program telephone: 530 898-5959
LD program e-mail: valexander@csuchico.edu or cprator@csuchico.edu
LD program enrollment: 222, Total campus enrollment: 14,279

GENERAL

California State University, Chico is a public, coed, four-year institution. 119-acre campus plus 1,000-acre farm in Chico (population: 59,954), 100 miles from Sacramento. Served by air, bus, and train; major airport serves Sacramento. Public transportation serves campus. Semester system.

LD ADMISSIONS

A member of the LD program does not sit on the admissions committee. A personal interview is not required. Essay is not required.

SECONDARY SCHOOL REQUIREMENTS

Graduation from secondary school required; GED accepted. The following course distribution required: 4 units of English, 3 units of math, 2 units of science, 2 units of foreign language, 2 units of social studies, 1 unit of academic electives.

TESTING

SAT Reasoning or ACT required. SAT Subject recommended.

All enrolled freshmen (fall 2004):

Average SAT I Scores:	Verbal: 513	Math: 529
Average ACT Scores:	Composite: 21	

Child Study Team report is not required. A neuropsychological or comprehensive psycho-educational evaluation is required for admission. Must be dated within 60 months of application. Tests required as part of this documentation:

- [x] WAIS-IV
- [x] WISC-IV
- [ ] SATA
- [x] Woodcock-Johnson
- [x] Nelson-Denny Reading Test
- [x] Other

UNDERGRADUATE STUDENT BODY

Total undergraduate student enrollment: 6,860 Men, 7,774 Women.

Composition of student body (fall 2004):

	Undergraduate	Freshmen
International	0.9	1.9
Black	1.7	1.9
American Indian	1.1	1.3
Asian-American	6.6	5.3
Hispanic	12.0	10.8
White	67.8	65.6
Unreported	9.9	13.2
	100.0%	100.0%

1% are from out of state. 7% join a fraternity and 6% join a sorority. Average age of full-time undergraduates is 22. 39% of classes have fewer than 20 students, 55% have between 20 and 50 students, 6% have more than 50 students.

STUDENT HOUSING

67% of freshmen live in college housing. Freshmen are not required to live on campus. Housing is guaranteed for all undergraduates. Campus can house 1,765 undergraduates. Single rooms are available for students with medical or special needs. A medical note is required.

EXPENSES

Tuition (2005-06): $2,520 per year (in-state), $12,609 (out-of-state). Room: $5,550. Board: $2,443.
There is no additional cost for LD program/services.

LD SERVICES

LD program size is not limited.

LD services available to:

- [x] Freshmen
- [x] Sophomores
- [x] Juniors
- [x] Seniors

Academic Accommodations

Curriculum		In class	
Foreign language waiver	[ ]	Early syllabus	[ ]
Lighter course load	[x]	Note takers in class	[x]
Math waiver	[ ]	Priority seating	[x]
Other special classes	[ ]	Tape recorders	[x]
Priority registrations	[x]	Videotaped classes	[ ]
Substitution of courses	[ ]	Text on tape	[x]
Exams		**Services**	
Extended time	[x]	Diagnostic tests	[x]
Oral exams	[x]	Learning centers	[x]
Take home exams	[ ]	Proofreaders	[ ]
Exams on tape or computer	[x]	Readers	[x]
Untimed exams	[x]	Reading Machines/Kurzweil	[x]
Other accommodations	[x]	Special bookstore section	[ ]
		Typists	[x]

Credit toward degree is not given for remedial courses taken.

Counseling Services

- [ ] Academic
- [ ] Psychological
- [ ] Student Support groups
- [ ] Vocational

Tutoring

Individual tutoring is available weekly.

	Individual	Group
Time management	[x]	[x]
Organizational skills	[x]	[x]
Learning strategies	[x]	[x]
Study skills	[x]	[x]
Content area	[x]	[x]
Writing lab	[x]	[ ]
Math lab	[x]	[ ]

LD PROGRAM STAFF

Total number of LD Program staff (including director):

Full Time: 2 Part Time: 2

There is an advisor/advocate from the LD program available to students.

Key staff person available to work with LD students: Van Alexander/Chris Prator, Learning Disability Specialists.

LD Program web site: dssdept@csuchico.edu

California State University, East Bay

Hayward, CA

Address: 25800 Carlos Bee Boulevard, Hayward, CA, 94542
Admissions telephone: 510 885-2784
Admissions FAX: 510 885-4059
Admissions e-mail: askes@csuhayward.edu
Web site: http://www.csueastbay.edu
SAT Code: 4011 ACT Code: 154

Director, Student Disability Resource Center: Mary Cheng
LD program telephone: 510 885-3868
LD program e-mail: mcheng@csuhayward.edu
Total campus enrollment: 9,402

GENERAL

California State University, Hayward is a public, coed, four-year institution. 342-acre, suburban campus in Hayward (population: 140,030), 15 miles from Oakland and 20 miles from San Francisco; branch campus in Concord. Served by bus; major airports serve San Francisco; train serves Oakland. Public transportation serves campus. Quarter system.

LD ADMISSIONS

A personal interview is required. Essay is not required.

SECONDARY SCHOOL REQUIREMENTS

Graduation from secondary school required; GED accepted. The following course distribution required: 4 units of English, 3 units of math, 2 units of science, 2 units of foreign language, 2 units of history, 1 unit of academic electives.

TESTING

SAT Reasoning or ACT required of some applicants. SAT Subject recommended.

Child Study Team report is not required. Tests required as part of this documentation:

☐ WAIS-IV	☐ Woodcock-Johnson
☐ WISC-IV	☐ Nelson-Denny Reading Test
☐ SATA	☐ Other

UNDERGRADUATE STUDENT BODY

Total undergraduate student enrollment: 3,353 Men, 5,984 Women.

Composition of student body (fall 2004):

	Undergraduate	Freshmen
International	5.5	5.6
Black	13.2	10.9
American Indian	0.2	0.6
Asian-American	34.0	27.5
Hispanic	17.6	12.3
White	19.0	25.9
Unreported	10.5	17.2
	100.0%	100.0%

11% are from out of state. 22% of classes have fewer than 20 students, 63% have between 20 and 50 students, 15% have more than 50 students.

STUDENT HOUSING

Housing is guaranteed for all undergraduates. Campus can house 400 undergraduates.

EXPENSES

Tuition 2004-05: No tuition for in-state, $6,036 (out-of-state).

There is no additional cost for LD program/services.

LD SERVICES

LD program size is not limited.

LD services available to:

☐ Freshmen ☐ Sophomores ☐ Juniors ☐ Seniors

Academic Accommodations

Curriculum		**In class**	
Foreign language waiver	☐	Early syllabus	☐
Lighter course load	☐	Note takers in class	■
Math waiver	☐	Priority seating	☐
Other special classes	☐	Tape recorders	■
Priority registrations	☐	Videotaped classes	☐
Substitution of courses	☐	Text on tape	☐
Exams		**Services**	
Extended time	■	Diagnostic tests	☐
Oral exams	☐	Learning centers	■
Take home exams	☐	Proofreaders	☐
Exams on tape or computer	☐	Readers	■
Untimed exams	■	Reading Machines/Kurzweil	☐
Other accommodations	☐	Special bookstore section	☐
		Typists	☐

Credit toward degree is not given for remedial courses taken.

Counseling Services

☐ Academic
☐ Psychological
☐ Student Support groups
☐ Vocational

Tutoring

	Individual	Group
Time management	☐	☐
Organizational skills	☐	☐
Learning strategies	☐	☐
Study skills	☐	☐
Content area	☐	☐
Writing lab	☐	☐
Math lab	☐	☐

LD PROGRAM STAFF

Total number of LD Program staff (including director):

Full Time: 1 Part Time: 1

Key staff person available to work with LD students: Russell Wong, Learning Disability Resource Counselor.

California State University, Fullerton

Fullerton, CA

Address: 800 North State College Boulevard, Fullerton, CA, 92834
Admissions telephone: 714 278-2370
Admissions FAX: 714 278-2356
Admissions Officer: Nancy Dority
Admissions e-mail: admissions@fullerton.edu
Web site: http://www.fullerton.edu
SAT Code: 4589 ACT Code: 355

Director: Paul Miller
LD program telephone: 714 278-3779
LD program e-mail: pmiller@fullerton.edu
Total campus enrollment: 27, 335

GENERAL

California State University, Fullerton is a public, coed, four-year institution. 225-acre, suburban campus in Fullerton (population: 126,003), 35 miles from Los Angeles; branch campus in Mission Viejo. Served by bus and train; major airports serve Los Angeles; smaller airport serves Orange (20 miles). School operates transportation to satellite parking lots. Public transportation serves campus. Semester system.

LD ADMISSIONS

A personal interview is not required. Essay is not required.

SECONDARY SCHOOL REQUIREMENTS

Graduation from secondary school required; GED accepted. The following course distribution required: 4 units of English, 3 units of math, 2 units of science, 2 units of foreign language, 1 unit of social studies, 1 unit of history, 1 unit of academic electives.

TESTING

SAT Reasoning or ACT required. SAT Subject recommended.

All enrolled freshmen (fall 2004):

Average SAT I Scores: Verbal: 484 Math: 507
Average ACT Scores: Composite: 20

Child Study Team report is not required. Tests required as part of this documentation:

☐ WAIS-IV ☐ Woodcock-Johnson
☐ WISC-IV ☐ Nelson-Denny Reading Test
☐ SATA ☐ Other

UNDERGRADUATE STUDENT BODY

Total undergraduate student enrollment: 10,094 Men, 14,977 Women.

Composition of student body (fall 2004):

	Undergraduate	Freshmen
International	2.7	3.9
Black	4.9	3.1
American Indian	0.4	0.6
Asian-American	22.1	22.4
Hispanic	31.2	26.2
White	31.4	32.8
Unreported	7.3	11.0
	100.0%	100.0%

1% are from out of state. 3% join a fraternity and 3% join a sorority. Average age of full-time undergraduates is 22. 27% of classes have fewer than 20 students, 65% have between 20 and 50 students, 8% have more than 50 students.

STUDENT HOUSING

7% of freshmen live in college housing. Freshmen are not required to live on campus. Housing is guaranteed for all undergraduates. Campus can house 836 undergraduates.

EXPENSES

Tuition (2005-06): No tuition for in-state, $9,960 (out-of-state).
Room: $4,356.
There is no additional cost for LD program/services.

LD SERVICES

LD program size is not limited.

LD services available to:

☐ Freshmen ☐ Sophomores ☐ Juniors ☐ Seniors

Academic Accommodations

Curriculum		**In class**	
Foreign language waiver	☐	Early syllabus	☐
Lighter course load	☐	Note takers in class	■
Math waiver	☐	Priority seating	☐
Other special classes	☐	Tape recorders	■
Priority registrations	☐	Videotaped classes	☐
Substitution of courses	☐	Text on tape	☐
Exams		**Services**	
Extended time	■	Diagnostic tests	■
Oral exams	☐	Learning centers	■
Take home exams	☐	Proofreaders	☐
Exams on tape or computer	☐	Readers	■
Untimed exams	☐	Reading Machines/Kurzweil	☐
Other accommodations	■	Special bookstore section	☐
		Typists	☐

Credit toward degree is not given for remedial courses taken.

Counseling Services

☐ Academic
☐ Psychological
☐ Student Support groups
☐ Vocational

Tutoring

Individual tutoring is available.

	Individual	Group
Time management	☐	☐
Organizational skills	☐	☐
Learning strategies	☐	☐
Study skills	☐	☐
Content area	☐	☐
Writing lab	■	■
Math lab	■	■

LD PROGRAM STAFF

Total number of LD Program staff (including director):

Full Time: 8 Part Time: 8

There is an advisor/advocate from the LD program available to students.

Key staff person available to work with LD students: Debra Fletcher.

California State University, Long Beach

Long Beach, CA

Address: 1250 Bellflower Boulevard, Long Beach, CA, 90840
Admissions telephone: 562 985-5471
Admissions FAX: 562 985-4973
Assistant Vice President for Enrollment Services: Thomas Enders
Web site: http://www.csulb.edu
SAT Code: 4389 ACT Code: 302

Coordinator: Kathryn Holmes
LD program telephone: 562 985-1875
LD program e-mail: kholmes@csulb.edu
Total campus enrollment: 27,180

GENERAL

California State University, Long Beach is a public, coed, four-year institution. 322-acre, urban campus in Long Beach (population: 461,522), 20 miles from Los Angeles. Served by air, bus, and train; major airport serves Los Angeles. Public transportation serves campus. Semester system.

LD ADMISSIONS

Some admissions requirements may be waived for LD students.

SECONDARY SCHOOL REQUIREMENTS

Graduation from secondary school required; GED accepted. The following course distribution required: 4 units of English, 3 units of math, 2 units of science, 2 units of foreign language, 1 unit of social studies, 1 unit of history, 1 unit of academic electives.

TESTING

SAT Reasoning or ACT required. SAT Subject recommended.

All enrolled freshmen (fall 2004):

Average SAT I Scores:	Verbal: 503	Math: 529
Average ACT Scores:	Composite: 20	

Child Study Team report is not required. Tests required as part of this documentation:

- ☐ WAIS-IV
- ☐ WISC-IV
- ☐ SATA
- ☐ Woodcock-Johnson
- ☐ Nelson-Denny Reading Test
- ☐ Other

UNDERGRADUATE STUDENT BODY

Total undergraduate student enrollment: 11,254 Men, 16,051 Women.

Composition of student body (fall 2004):

	Undergraduate	Freshmen
International	2.3	4.9
Black	6.8	5.8
American Indian	0.9	0.7
Asian-American	23.2	21.7
Hispanic	29.0	24.5
White	30.1	32.5
Unreported	7.7	9.9
	100.0%	100.0%

3% are from out of state. 4% join a fraternity and 4% join a sorority. Average age of full-time undergraduates is 23. 28% of classes have fewer than 20 students, 62% have between 20 and 50 students, 10% have more than 50 students.

STUDENT HOUSING

30% of freshmen live in college housing. Housing is guaranteed for all undergraduates. Campus can house 1,962 undergraduates.

EXPENSES

Tuition (2005-06): No tuition for in-state, $10,170 (out-of-state).
Room & Board: $6,530.

There is no additional cost for LD program/services.

LD SERVICES

LD program size is not limited.

LD services available to:

☐ Freshmen ☐ Sophomores ☐ Juniors ☐ Seniors

Academic Accommodations

Curriculum		**In class**	
Foreign language waiver	☐	Early syllabus	☐
Lighter course load	☒	Note takers in class	☒
Math waiver	☐	Priority seating	☐
Other special classes	☐	Tape recorders	☒
Priority registrations	☐	Videotaped classes	☐
Substitution of courses	☐	Text on tape	☐
Exams		**Services**	
Extended time	☒	Diagnostic tests	☒
Oral exams	☒	Learning centers	☒
Take home exams	☐	Proofreaders	☐
Exams on tape or computer	☐	Readers	☒
Untimed exams	☒	Reading Machines/Kurzweil	☒
Other accommodations	☐	Special bookstore section	☐
		Typists	☐

Credit toward degree is not given for remedial courses taken.

Counseling Services

- ☐ Academic
- ☐ Psychological
- ☐ Student Support groups
- ☐ Vocational

Tutoring

	Individual	Group
Time management	☐	☐
Organizational skills	☐	☐
Learning strategies	☐	☐
Study skills	☐	☐
Content area	☐	☐
Writing lab	☐	☐
Math lab	☐	☐

UNIQUE LD PROGRAM FEATURES

Provide weekly counseling meeting with students in the program.

LD PROGRAM STAFF

Total number of LD Program staff (including director):

Full Time: 4 Part Time: 4

Key staff person available to work with LD students: Kathryn Holmes, Coordinator, Stephen Benson Program.

California State University, Los Angeles

Los Angeles, CA

Address: 5151 State University Drive, Los Angeles, CA, 90032
Admissions telephone: 323 343-3901
Admissions FAX: 323 343-3888
Admissions Officer: Joan Woosley
Admissions e-mail: admission@calstatela.edu
Web site: http://www.calstatela.edu
SAT Code: 4399 ACT Code: 320

LD program name: Office for Students with Disabilities
LD Specialist: Dr. R. Silverston
LD program telephone: 232 343-3140
LD program e-mail: rsilver@cslanet.calstatela.edu
Total campus enrollment: 15,108

GENERAL

California State University, Los Angeles is a public, coed, four-year institution. 200-acre campus in Los Angeles (population: 3,694,820). Served by air, bus, and train. Public transportation serves campus. Quarter system.

LD ADMISSIONS

Students do not complete a separate application and are not simultaneously accepted to the LD program. A member of the LD program does not sit on the admissions committee. A personal interview is required.

SECONDARY SCHOOL REQUIREMENTS

Graduation from secondary school required; GED accepted. The following course distribution required: 4 units of English, 3 units of math, 2 units of science, 2 units of foreign language, 1 unit of social studies, 1 unit of history, 1 unit of academic electives.

TESTING

SAT Reasoning or ACT required of some applicants. SAT Subject recommended.

All enrolled freshmen (fall 2004):

Average SAT I Scores:	Verbal: 439	Math: 459
Average ACT Scores:	Composite: 18	

Child Study Team report is not required. A neuropsychological or comprehensive psycho-education evaluation is not required for admission. Tests required as part of this documentation:

- [ ] WAIS-IV
- [ ] WISC-IV
- [ ] SATA
- [ ] Woodcock-Johnson
- [ ] Nelson-Denny Reading Test
- [ ] Other

UNDERGRADUATE STUDENT BODY

Total undergraduate student enrollment: 5,445 Men, 8,453 Women.

Composition of student body (fall 2004):

	Undergraduate	Freshmen
International	3.1	1.2
Black	9.4	7.9
American Indian	0.5	0.4
Asian-American	20.9	22.0
Hispanic	52.6	45.3
White	5.7	11.4
Unreported	7.8	11.8
	100.0%	100.0%

4% are from out of state. Average age of full-time undergraduates is 24. 60% of classes have fewer than 20 students, 38% have between 20 and 50 students, 2% have more than 50 students.

STUDENT HOUSING

17% of freshmen live in college housing. Freshmen are not required to live on campus. Housing is guaranteed for all undergraduates. Campus can house 850 undergraduates. Single rooms are available for students with medical or special needs. A medical note is required.

EXPENSES

Tuition (2005-06): $3,035 per year (in-state), $11,171 (out-of-state).

Room & Board: $7,353.

There is no additional cost for LD program/services.

LD SERVICES

LD program size is not limited.

LD services available to:

- [x] Freshmen
- [x] Sophomores
- [x] Juniors
- [x] Seniors

Academic Accommodations

Curriculum		In class	
Foreign language waiver	[ ]	Early syllabus	[ ]
Lighter course load	[x]	Note takers in class	[x]
Math waiver	[ ]	Priority seating	[ ]
Other special classes	[ ]	Tape recorders	[x]
Priority registrations	[x]	Videotaped classes	[ ]
Substitution of courses	[x]	Text on tape	[x]
Exams		**Services**	
Extended time	[x]	Diagnostic tests	[x]
Oral exams	[x]	Learning centers	[ ]
Take home exams	[ ]	Proofreaders	[ ]
Exams on tape or computer	[x]	Readers	[x]
Untimed exams	[ ]	Reading Machines/Kurzweil	[ ]
Other accommodations	[x]	Special bookstore section	[ ]
		Typists	[x]

Credit toward degree is not given for remedial courses taken.

Counseling Services

- [ ] Academic
- [ ] Psychological
- [ ] Student Support groups
- [ ] Vocational

Tutoring

Individual tutoring is not available.

	Individual	Group
Time management	[ ]	[x]
Organizational skills	[x]	[x]
Learning strategies	[x]	[ ]
Study skills	[x]	[x]
Content area	[ ]	[ ]
Writing lab	[ ]	[ ]
Math lab	[ ]	[ ]

LD PROGRAM STAFF

Total number of LD Program staff (including director):

Full Time: 2 Part Time: 2

There is an advisor/advocate from the LD program available to students. The advisor/advocate meets with faculty once per month and students once per month.

Key staff person available to work with LD students: Dr. R. Silverston, LD Specialist.

California State University, Monterey Bay

Seaside, CA

Address: 100 Campus Center, Seaside, CA, 93955-8001
Admissions telephone: 831 582-5100
Admissions FAX: 831 582-3783
Admissions Contact: Dennis Geyer
Admissions e-mail: admissions@csumb.edu
Web site: http://www.csumb.edu

LD program name: Student Disability Resources
Coordinator: Margaret Keith
LD program telephone: 831 582-3672
LD program e-mail: student_disability_resources@csumb.edu
LD program enrollment: 93, Total campus enrollment: 3,534

GENERAL

California State University, Monterey Bay is a public, four-year institution. Semester system.

LD ADMISSIONS

Students do not complete a separate application and are not simultaneously accepted to the LD program. A member of the LD program does not sit on the admissions committee. A personal interview is not required. Essay is not required. Course substitutions may be considered but requirements will not be waived. If an applicant is denied admission to California State University, Monterey Bay the applicant may appeal through Special Admissions. Students with learning disabilities are expected to attempt foreign language at the university/college level with accommodations and frequent use of tutors and the language lab.

SECONDARY SCHOOL REQUIREMENTS

The following course distribution required: 8 units of English, 6 units of math, 4 units of science, 4 units of foreign language, 2 units of social studies, 2 units of history, 2 units of academic electives.

TESTING

SAT Reasoning recommended. ACT recommended. SAT Reasoning or ACT required of some applicants. SAT Subject recommended.

All enrolled freshmen (fall 2004):

Average SAT I Scores:	Verbal: 489	Math: 487
Average ACT Scores:	Composite: 20	

Child Study Team report is not required. A neuropsychological or comprehensive psycho-educational evaluation is required for admission. Tests required as part of this documentation:

- [x] WAIS-IV
- [ ] WISC-IV
- [ ] SATA
- [x] Woodcock-Johnson
- [ ] Nelson-Denny Reading Test
- [x] Other

UNDERGRADUATE STUDENT BODY

Total undergraduate student enrollment: 3,534.

Composition of student body (fall 2004):

	Undergraduate	Freshmen
International	1.1	1.1
Black	2.8	4.3
American Indian	1.1	0.7
Asian-American	6.6	5.8
Hispanic	24.7	28.4
White	54.1	45.1
Unreported	9.6	14.6
	100.0%	100.0%

Average age of full-time undergraduates is 23. 33% of classes have fewer than 20 students, 61% have between 20 and 50 students, 6% have more than 50 students.

STUDENT HOUSING

85% of freshmen live in college housing. Freshmen are required to live on campus. Housing is guaranteed for all undergraduates. Campus can house 2,620 undergraduates. Single rooms are available for students with medical or special needs. A medical note is required.

EXPENSES

Tuition 2004-05: $2,250 per year (in-state), $6,768 (out-of-state).

Room & Board: $5,725-$6,958.

There is no additional cost for LD program/services.

LD SERVICES

LD program size is not limited.

LD services available to:

- [x] Freshmen
- [x] Sophomores
- [x] Juniors
- [x] Seniors

Academic Accommodations

Curriculum		In class	
Foreign language waiver	[ ]	Early syllabus	[ ]
Lighter course load	[x]	Note takers in class	[x]
Math waiver	[ ]	Priority seating	[ ]
Other special classes	[ ]	Tape recorders	[ ]
Priority registrations	[x]	Videotaped classes	[ ]
Substitution of courses	[ ]	Text on tape	[ ]
Exams		**Services**	
Extended time	[x]	Diagnostic tests	[ ]
Oral exams	[ ]	Learning centers	[x]
Take home exams	[ ]	Proofreaders	[ ]
Exams on tape or computer	[ ]	Readers	[ ]
Untimed exams	[ ]	Reading Machines/Kurzweil	[x]
Other accommodations	[x]	Special bookstore section	[ ]
		Typists	[ ]

Counseling Services

[x]	Academic	Meets 2 times per academic year
[x]	Psychological	Meets 8 times per academic year
[ ]	Student Support groups	
[x]	Vocational	Meets 20 times per academic year

Tutoring

Individual tutoring is available weekly.

Average size of tutoring groups: 5

	Individual	Group
Time management	[ ]	[x]
Organizational skills	[ ]	[x]
Learning strategies	[ ]	[ ]
Study skills	[ ]	[ ]
Content area	[ ]	[x]
Writing lab	[ ]	[x]
Math lab	[ ]	[x]

LD PROGRAM STAFF

There is an advisor/advocate from the LD program available to students. The advisor/advocate meets with faculty 3 times per month and students once per month.

Key staff person available to work with LD students: Michael Hancock, Disability Resources Advisor.

LD Program web site: http://sdr.csumb.edu

California State University, Sacramento

Sacramento, CA

Address: 6000 J Street, Sacramento, CA, 95819
Admissions telephone: 800 722-4748
Admissions FAX: 916 278-5603
Director of Admissions and Records: Emiliano Diaz
Admissions e-mail: admissions@csus.edu
Web site: http://www.csus.edu
SAT Code: 4671 ACT Code: 382

LD program name: Services to Students with Disabilities
LD program address: Lassen Hall Room 1008
Learning Disabled Specialist: Hannah Simonet
LD program telephone: 916 278-6955
LD program e-mail: simonetph@csus.edu
Total campus enrollment: 22,555

GENERAL

California State University, Sacramento is a public, coed, four-year institution. 282-acre, suburban campus in Sacramento (population: 407,018). Served by air, bus, and train. School operates transportation to local student apartment complexes. Public transportation serves campus. Semester system.

LD ADMISSIONS

Students do not complete a separate application and are not simultaneously accepted to the LD program. A personal interview is not required. Essay is not required.

SECONDARY SCHOOL REQUIREMENTS

Graduation from secondary school required; GED accepted. The following course distribution required: 4 units of English, 3 units of math, 2 units of science, 2 units of foreign language, 1 unit of social studies, 1 unit of history, 1 unit of academic electives.

TESTING

SAT Reasoning or ACT required of some applicants. SAT Subject recommended.

Child Study Team report is not required. Tests required as part of this documentation:

- [ ] WAIS-IV
- [ ] WISC-IV
- [ ] SATA
- [ ] Woodcock-Johnson
- [ ] Nelson-Denny Reading Test
- [ ] Other

UNDERGRADUATE STUDENT BODY

Total undergraduate student enrollment: 9,306 Men, 12,197 Women.

Composition of student body (fall 2004):

	Undergraduate	Freshmen
International	0.8	1.5
Black	8.6	5.9
American Indian	1.0	1.0
Asian-American	22.9	19.0
Hispanic	18.5	14.2
White	39.0	42.4
Unreported	9.2	16.0
	100.0%	100.0%

1% are from out of state. 7% join a fraternity and 5% join a sorority. Average age of full-time undergraduates is 23. 23% of classes have fewer than 20 students, 65% have between 20 and 50 students, 12% have more than 50 students.

STUDENT HOUSING

28% of freshmen live in college housing. Freshmen are not required to live on campus. Housing is guaranteed for all undergraduates. Campus can house 1,100 undergraduates.

EXPENSES

Tuition 2004-05: No tuition for in-state, $12,504 (out-of-state).

Room & Board: $6,574.

There is no additional cost for LD program/services.

LD SERVICES

LD program size is not limited.

LD services available to:

- [x] Freshmen
- [x] Sophomores
- [x] Juniors
- [x] Seniors

Academic Accommodations

Curriculum

- [ ] Foreign language waiver
- [ ] Lighter course load
- [ ] Math waiver
- [ ] Other special classes
- [ ] Priority registrations
- [x] Substitution of courses

Exams

- [ ] Extended time
- [ ] Oral exams
- [ ] Take home exams
- [ ] Exams on tape or computer
- [ ] Untimed exams
- [x] Other accommodations

In class

- [ ] Early syllabus
- [x] Note takers in class
- [ ] Priority seating
- [x] Tape recorders
- [ ] Videotaped classes
- [ ] Text on tape

Services

- [x] Diagnostic tests
- [x] Learning centers
- [ ] Proofreaders
- [x] Readers
- [ ] Reading Machines/Kurzweil
- [ ] Special bookstore section
- [ ] Typists

Credit toward degree is not given for remedial courses taken.

Counseling Services

- [ ] Academic
- [ ] Psychological
- [ ] Student Support groups
- [ ] Vocational

Tutoring

Individual tutoring is available daily.

	Individual	Group
Time management	[ ]	[x]
Organizational skills	[ ]	[ ]
Learning strategies	[ ]	[x]
Study skills	[ ]	[x]
Content area	[ ]	[ ]
Writing lab	[x]	[x]
Math lab	[x]	[x]

LD PROGRAM STAFF

Total number of LD Program staff (including director):

Full Time: 13 Part Time: 13

There is an advisor/advocate from the LD program available to students.

Key staff person available to work with LD students: Hannah Simonet, MSW, Learning Disabled Specialist.

LD Program web site: www.csus.edu/sswd

California State University, San Bernardino

San Bernardino, CA

Address: 5500 University Parkway, San Bernardino, CA, 92407
Admissions telephone: 909 880-5188
Admissions FAX: 909 880-7034
Director of Admissions and Records: Olivia Rosas
Admissions e-mail: moreinfo@csusb.edu
Web site: http://www.csusb.edu
SAT Code: 4099 ACT Code: 205

LD program name: Services to Students with Disabilities
LD program address: 5500 University Parkway, UH 183
Director: Laurie Flynn
LD program telephone: 909 880-5238
LD program e-mail: lflynn@csusb.edu
LD program enrollment: 73, Total campus enrollment: 12,109

GENERAL

California State University, San Bernardino is a public, coed, four-year institution. 430-acre, suburban campus in San Bernardino (population: 185,401), 55 miles from Los Angeles and 100 miles from San Diego; branch campus in Palm Desert. Served by bus and train; major airports serve Ontario (20 miles) and Los Angeles. Public transportation serves campus. Quarter system.

LD ADMISSIONS

Applicants with learning disabilities must follow the same application procedure as all applicants. Special admission may be requested through the Learning Disability Program if the applicant has a deficiency in course entrance requirements. The Director of the LD program provides recommendations on the admissibility of those students who do not meet regular admission requirements. If the applicant can demonstrate the presence and severity of current disability, as well as functional limitation, in the form of current documentation provided by a qualified heath or education provider, then the disability counselor could use this data to appeal to the admissions counselor.

For fall 2004, 36 completed self-identified LD applications were received.

SECONDARY SCHOOL REQUIREMENTS

Graduation from secondary school required; GED accepted. The following course distribution required: 4 units of English, 3 units of math, 2 units of science, 2 units of foreign language, 1 unit of social studies, 1 unit of history, 1 unit of academic electives.

TESTING

SAT Reasoning or ACT required.

All enrolled freshmen (fall 2004):

Average SAT I Scores:	Verbal: 445	Math: 461
Average ACT Scores:	Composite: 18	

Child Study Team report is not required. A neuropsychological or comprehensive psycho-educational evaluation is required for admission. Must be dated within 36 months of application. Tests required as part of this documentation:

☒ WAIS-IV ☒ Woodcock-Johnson
☒ WISC-IV ☒ Nelson-Denny Reading Test
☐ SATA ☒ Other

UNDERGRADUATE STUDENT BODY

Total undergraduate student enrollment: 4,125 Men, 6,894 Women.

Composition of student body (fall 2004):

	Undergraduate	Freshmen
International	3.4	3.1
Black	13.1	11.7
American Indian	0.6	0.8
Asian-American	8.9	7.6
Hispanic	44.1	32.8
White	22.0	32.9
Unreported	7.9	11.1
	100.0%	100.0%

4% join a fraternity and 2% join a sorority. Average age of full-time undergraduates is 22. 25% of classes have fewer than 20 students, 59% have between 20 and 50 students, 16% have more than 50 students.

STUDENT HOUSING

33% of freshmen live in college housing. Freshmen are not required to live on campus. Housing is not guaranteed for all undergraduates. Single rooms are available for students with medical or special needs.

EXPENSES

Tuition (2005-06): No tuition for in-state, $8,136 (out-of-state).

Room & Board: $7,517.

There is no additional cost for LD program/services.

LD SERVICES

LD program size is not limited.

LD services available to:

☒ Freshmen ☒ Sophomores ☒ Juniors ☒ Seniors

Academic Accommodations

Curriculum		In class	
Foreign language waiver	☐	Early syllabus	☐
Lighter course load	☐	Note takers in class	☒
Math waiver	☐	Priority seating	☒
Other special classes	☒	Tape recorders	☒
Priority registrations	☒	Videotaped classes	☐
Substitution of courses	☒	Text on tape	☒
Exams		**Services**	
Extended time	☒	Diagnostic tests	☒
Oral exams	☒	Learning centers	☒
Take home exams	☐	Proofreaders	☒
Exams on tape or computer	☒	Readers	☒
Untimed exams	☐	Reading Machines/Kurzweil	☒
Other accommodations	☒	Special bookstore section	☐
		Typists	☒

Credit toward degree is not given for remedial courses taken.

Counseling Services

☐ Academic
☐ Psychological
☐ Student Support groups
☐ Vocational

Tutoring

Individual tutoring is not available.

Average size of tutoring groups: 5

	Individual	Group
Time management	☐	☐
Organizational skills	☐	☐
Learning strategies	☐	☐
Study skills	☐	☐
Content area	☐	☐
Writing lab	☒	☒
Math lab	☐	☐

LD PROGRAM STAFF

Total number of LD Program staff (including director):

Full Time: 1 Part Time: 1

There is an advisor/advocate from the LD program available to students. The advisor/advocate meets with faculty once per month and students 2 times per month.

Key staff person available to work with LD students: Doron Dula, LD Specialist.

LD Program web site: ddula@csusb.edu

California State University, Stanislaus

Turlock, CA

Address: 801 West Monte Vista Avenue, Turlock, CA, 95382
Admissions telephone: 800 300-7420
Admissions FAX: 209 667-3788
Director of Admissions and Records: Lisa Bernardo
Admissions e-mail: Outreach_Help_Desk@csustan.edu
Web site: http://www.csustan.edu
SAT Code: 4713 ACT Code: 435

Administrative Support Assistant: Ona Baker
LD program telephone: 209 667-3159
LD program e-mail: obaker@csustan.edu
Total campus enrollment: 6,192

GENERAL

California State University, Stanislaus is a public, coed, four-year institution. 224-acre campus in Turlock (population: 55,810), 10 miles from Modesto and 115 miles from San Francisco; branch campuses in Sonora, Stockton, Tracy, and Castle Air Force Base/Merced. Served by bus; major airport serves San Francisco; smaller airport serves Modesto; train serves Denair (two miles). 4-1-4 system.

LD ADMISSIONS

A personal interview is not required. Essay is not required. Consideration of waiving entrance requirements is based on student's disability.

SECONDARY SCHOOL REQUIREMENTS

Graduation from secondary school required; GED accepted. The following course distribution required: 4 units of English, 3 units of math, 2 units of science, 2 units of foreign language, 2 units of history, 1 unit of academic electives.

TESTING

SAT Reasoning or ACT required. SAT Subject recommended.

All enrolled freshmen (fall 2004):

Average SAT I Scores: Verbal: 478 Math: 488
Average ACT Scores: Composite: 20

Child Study Team report is not required. Tests required as part of this documentation:

- [ ] WAIS-IV
- [ ] WISC-IV
- [ ] SATA
- [ ] Woodcock-Johnson
- [ ] Nelson-Denny Reading Test
- [ ] Other

UNDERGRADUATE STUDENT BODY

Total undergraduate student enrollment: 1,864 Men, 3,760 Women.

Composition of student body (fall 2004):

	Undergraduate	Freshmen
International	0.8	1.3
Black	5.8	3.2
American Indian	0.5	1.1
Asian-American	13.0	11.0
Hispanic	31.1	27.0
White	42.0	42.1
Unreported	6.8	14.3
	100.0%	100.0%

4% join a fraternity and 3% join a sorority. Average age of full-time undergraduates is 23. 33% of classes have fewer than 20 students, 58% have between 20 and 50 students, 9% have more than 50 students.

STUDENT HOUSING

31% of freshmen live in college housing. Freshmen are not required to live on campus. Housing is guaranteed for all undergraduates. Campus can house 648 undergraduates.

EXPENSES

Tuition 2004-05: No tuition for in-state, $10,170 (out-of-state).

Room & Board: $8,295.

There is no additional cost for LD program/services.

LD SERVICES

LD program size is not limited.

LD services available to:

- [ ] Freshmen
- [ ] Sophomores
- [ ] Juniors
- [ ] Seniors

Academic Accommodations

Curriculum		**In class**	
Foreign language waiver	[ ]	Early syllabus	[ ]
Lighter course load	[x]	Note takers in class	[x]
Math waiver	[ ]	Priority seating	[ ]
Other special classes	[ ]	Tape recorders	[x]
Priority registrations	[ ]	Videotaped classes	[ ]
Substitution of courses	[ ]	Text on tape	[ ]
Exams		**Services**	
Extended time	[x]	Diagnostic tests	[ ]
Oral exams	[ ]	Learning centers	[ ]
Take home exams	[ ]	Proofreaders	[ ]
Exams on tape or computer	[ ]	Readers	[x]
Untimed exams	[ ]	Reading Machines/Kurzweil	[x]
Other accommodations	[ ]	Special bookstore section	[ ]
		Typists	[ ]

Credit toward degree is not given for remedial courses taken.

Counseling Services

- [ ] Academic
- [ ] Psychological
- [ ] Student Support groups
- [ ] Vocational

Tutoring

	Individual	Group
Time management	[ ]	[ ]
Organizational skills	[ ]	[ ]
Learning strategies	[ ]	[ ]
Study skills	[ ]	[ ]
Content area	[ ]	[ ]
Writing lab	[ ]	[ ]
Math lab	[ ]	[ ]

LD PROGRAM STAFF

Total number of LD Program staff (including director):

Full Time: 3 Part Time: 3

Key staff person available to work with LD students: Lee Bettencourt, Interim Director.

University of California, Davis

Davis, CA

Address: 1 Shields Avenue, Davis, CA, 95616
Admissions telephone: 530 752-2971
Admissions FAX: 530 752-1280
Director of Undergraduate Admissions: Pamela L. Burnett
Admissions e-mail: undergraduateadmissions@ucdavis.edu
Web site: http://www.ucdavis.edu
SAT Code: 4834 ACT Code: 454

LD program telephone: 530 752-3184
LD program e-mail: sdc@ucdavis.edu
Total campus enrollment: 23,113

GENERAL

University of California, Davis is a public, coed, four-year institution. 5,200-acre campus in Davis (population: 60,308), 15 miles from Sacramento. Served by bus and train; small airport on campus; major airport serves Sacramento. School operates transportation to Sacramento Medical Center. Public transportation serves campus. Quarter system.

LD ADMISSIONS

SECONDARY SCHOOL REQUIREMENTS

Graduation from secondary school required; GED accepted. The following course distribution required: 4 units of English, 3 units of math, 2 units of science, 2 units of foreign language, 2 units of social studies, 1 unit of academic electives.

TESTING

SAT Reasoning or ACT required. SAT Subject required.

All enrolled freshmen (fall 2004):

Average SAT I Scores:	Verbal: 562	Math: 609
Average ACT Scores:	Composite: 24	

Child Study Team report is not required. Tests required as part of this documentation:

- ☐ WAIS-IV
- ☐ WISC-IV
- ☐ SATA
- ☐ Woodcock-Johnson
- ☐ Nelson-Denny Reading Test
- ☐ Other

UNDERGRADUATE STUDENT BODY

Total undergraduate student enrollment: 8,966 Men, 11,422 Women.

Composition of student body (fall 2004):

	Undergraduate	Freshmen
International	1.2	1.7
Black	2.6	2.6
American Indian	0.7	0.7
Asian-American	43.1	38.9
Hispanic	11.6	10.6
White	32.6	39.0
Unreported	8.2	6.5
	100.0%	100.0%

4% are from out of state. 33% of classes have fewer than 20 students, 38% have between 20 and 50 students, 29% have more than 50 students.

STUDENT HOUSING

Freshmen are not required to live on campus. Housing is not guaranteed for all undergraduates.

EXPENSES

Tuition (2005-06): $6,141 per year (in-state), $23,961 (out-of-state).
Room & Board: $10,791.
There is no additional cost for LD program/services.

LD SERVICES

LD services available to:

☐ Freshmen ☐ Sophomores ☐ Juniors ☐ Seniors

Academic Accommodations

Curriculum		In class	
Foreign language waiver	☐	Early syllabus	☐
Lighter course load	☐	Note takers in class	■
Math waiver	☐	Priority seating	☐
Other special classes	☐	Tape recorders	■
Priority registrations	☐	Videotaped classes	☐
Substitution of courses	☐	Text on tape	☐
Exams		**Services**	
Extended time	■	Diagnostic tests	☐
Oral exams	■	Learning centers	■
Take home exams	☐	Proofreaders	☐
Exams on tape or computer	☐	Readers	■
Untimed exams	☐	Reading Machines/Kurzweil	■
Other accommodations	☐	Special bookstore section	☐
		Typists	☐

Counseling Services

- ☐ Academic
- ☐ Psychological
- ☐ Student Support groups
- ☐ Vocational

Tutoring

	Individual	Group
Time management	☐	☐
Organizational skills	☐	☐
Learning strategies	☐	☐
Study skills	☐	☐
Content area	☐	☐
Writing lab	☐	☐
Math lab	☐	☐

LD PROGRAM STAFF

Total number of LD Program staff (including director):

Full Time: 2 Part Time: 2

University of California, Irvine

Irvine, CA

Address: Irvine, CA, 92697
Admissions telephone: 949 824-6703
Admissions FAX: 949 824-2711
Director of Admissions: Marguerite Bonous-Hammarth
Admissions e-mail: admissions@uci.edu
Web site: http://www.uci.edu
SAT Code: 4859 ACT Code: 446

LD program name: Disability Services Center
Assistant Director: Jennifer Gibson, Ph.D.
LD program telephone: 949 824-7494
LD program e-mail: jjgibson@uci.edu
LD program enrollment: 105, Total campus enrollment: 19,862

GENERAL

University of California, Irvine is a public, coed, four-year institution. 1,489-acre campus in Irvine (population: 143,072), 40 miles from Los Angeles. Served by bus and train; major airport serves Los Angeles; smaller airport serves Orange County (three miles). School operates transportation to UC Irvine Medical Ctr and to university owned apartments. Public transportation serves campus. Quarter system.

LD ADMISSIONS

Students do not complete a separate application and are not simultaneously accepted to the LD program. A member of the LD program does not sit on the admissions committee. A personal interview is not required. Essay is required and may be typed.

SECONDARY SCHOOL REQUIREMENTS

Graduation from secondary school required; GED accepted. The following course distribution required: 4 units of English, 3 units of math, 2 units of science, 2 units of foreign language, 2 units of history, 1 unit of academic electives.

TESTING

SAT Subject required.

All enrolled freshmen (fall 2004):

Average SAT I Scores: Verbal: 590 Math: 630

Child Study Team report is not required. A neuropsychological or comprehensive psycho-educational evaluation is required for admission. Must be dated within 36 months of application. Tests required as part of this documentation:

- [x] WAIS-IV
- [x] WISC-IV
- [x] SATA
- [x] Woodcock-Johnson
- [x] Nelson-Denny Reading Test
- [ ] Other

UNDERGRADUATE STUDENT BODY

Total undergraduate student enrollment: 8,553 Men, 9,170 Women.

Composition of student body (fall 2004):

	Undergraduate	Freshmen
International	0.7	2.6
Black	1.9	2.2
American Indian	0.3	0.4
Asian-American	49.4	49.2
Hispanic	12.4	11.7
White	27.1	25.1
Unreported	8.2	8.8
	100.0%	100.0%

2% are from out of state. 8% join a fraternity and 8% join a sorority. Average age of full-time undergraduates is 21. 39% of classes have fewer than 20 students, 38% have between 20 and 50 students, 23% have more than 50 students.

STUDENT HOUSING

82% of freshmen live in college housing. Freshmen are not required to live on campus. Housing is not guaranteed for all undergraduates. Housing guaranteed for first year only. Campus can house 6,420 undergraduates. Single rooms are available for students with medical or special needs. A medical note is required.

EXPENSES

Tuition (2005-06): $6,141 per year (in-state), $23,961 (out-of-state).
Room & Board: $9,176.
There is no additional cost for LD program/services.

LD SERVICES

LD program size is not limited.

LD services available to:

- [x] Freshmen
- [x] Sophomores
- [x] Juniors
- [x] Seniors

Academic Accommodations

Curriculum

- [ ] Foreign language waiver
- [x] Lighter course load
- [ ] Math waiver
- [ ] Other special classes
- [x] Priority registrations
- [ ] Substitution of courses

Exams

- [x] Extended time
- [ ] Oral exams
- [ ] Take home exams
- [ ] Exams on tape or computer
- [ ] Untimed exams
- [ ] Other accommodations

In class

- [ ] Early syllabus
- [x] Note takers in class
- [ ] Priority seating
- [x] Tape recorders
- [ ] Videotaped classes
- [x] Text on tape

Services

- [ ] Diagnostic tests
- [ ] Learning centers
- [ ] Proofreaders
- [x] Readers
- [x] Reading Machines/Kurzweil
- [ ] Special bookstore section
- [ ] Typists

Credit toward degree is not given for remedial courses taken.

Counseling Services

- [x] Academic — Meets 3 times per academic year
- [ ] Psychological
- [ ] Student Support groups
- [ ] Vocational

Tutoring

Individual tutoring is not available.

	Individual	Group
Time management	[ ]	[ ]
Organizational skills	[ ]	[ ]
Learning strategies	[ ]	[ ]
Study skills	[ ]	[ ]
Content area	[ ]	[ ]
Writing lab	[ ]	[x]
Math lab	[ ]	[ ]

LD PROGRAM STAFF

Total number of LD Program staff (including director):

Full Time: 1 Part Time: 1

There is an advisor/advocate from the LD program available to students. The advisor/advocate meets with students three times per month.

Key staff person available to work with LD students: Jennifer Gibson, Ph.D., Assistant Director.

LD Program web site: http://www.disability.uci.edu/

University of California, Los Angeles

Los Angeles, CA

Address: 405 Hilgard Avenue, Los Angeles, CA, 90095
Admissions telephone: 310 825-3101
Admissions FAX: 310 206-1206
Director of Undergraduate Admissions: Vu Tran
Admissions e-mail: ugadm@saonet.ucla.edu
Web site: http://www.ucla.edu/
SAT Code: 4837 ACT Code: 448

Learning Disabilities Program Coordinator: Julie Morris
LD program telephone: 310 794-5732
LD program e-mail: http://www.saonet.ucla.edu/osd/
Total campus enrollment: 24,946

GENERAL

University of California, Los Angeles is a public, coed, four-year institution. 419-acre, urban campus in Los Angeles (population: 3,694,820). Served by air and train; bus serves Santa Monica (three miles). School operates campus transportation system. Public transportation serves campus. Quarter system.

LD ADMISSIONS

Students do not complete a separate application and are not simultaneously accepted to the LD program. A member of the LD program does not sit on the admissions committee. A personal interview is not required.

SECONDARY SCHOOL REQUIREMENTS

Graduation from secondary school required; GED accepted. The following course distribution required: 4 units of English, 3 units of math, 2 units of science, 2 units of foreign language, 2 units of history, 1 unit of academic electives.

TESTING

SAT Reasoning or ACT required. SAT Subject required.

All enrolled freshmen (fall 2004):

Average SAT I Scores:	Verbal: 628	Math: 662
Average ACT Scores:	Composite: 27	

Child Study Team report is not required. A neuropsychological or comprehensive psycho-educational evaluation is required for admission. Tests required as part of this documentation:

- ☑ WAIS-IV
- ☐ WISC-IV
- ☑ SATA
- ☑ Woodcock-Johnson
- ☑ Nelson-Denny Reading Test
- ☐ Other

UNDERGRADUATE STUDENT BODY

Total undergraduate student enrollment: 11,381 Men, 13,947 Women.

Composition of student body (fall 2004):

	Undergraduate	Freshmen
International	3.0	3.9
Black	2.9	3.3
American Indian	0.3	0.5
Asian-American	40.1	37.4
Hispanic	13.9	15.3
White	35.4	33.2
Unreported	4.4	6.4
	100.0%	100.0%

3% are from out of state. 14% join a fraternity and 11% join a sorority. Average age of full-time undergraduates is 21. 50% of classes have fewer than 20 students, 28% have between 20 and 50 students, 22% have more than 50 students.

STUDENT HOUSING

92% of freshmen live in college housing. Freshmen are not required to live on campus. Housing is guaranteed for two years to first-year undergraduates and one year for transfer students. UCLA is working toward a four-year guarantee for housing for undergraduates including, two years for transfer students. Campus can house 9,753 undergraduates.

EXPENSES

Tuition (2005-06): $6,141 per year (in-state), $23,961 (out-of-state).
Room & Board: $11,928.
There is no additional cost for LD program/services.

LD SERVICES

LD program size is not limited.

LD services available to:

☑ Freshmen ☑ Sophomores ☑ Juniors ☑ Seniors

Academic Accommodations

Curriculum		**In class**	
Foreign language waiver	☐	Early syllabus	☐
Lighter course load	☑	Note takers in class	☑
Math waiver	☐	Priority seating	☐
Other special classes	☐	Tape recorders	☑
Priority registrations	☑	Videotaped classes	☐
Substitution of courses	☐	Text on tape	☑
Exams		**Services**	
Extended time	☑	Diagnostic tests	☑
Oral exams	☐	Learning centers	☐
Take home exams	☐	Proofreaders	☐
Exams on tape or computer	☐	Readers	☑
Untimed exams	☐	Reading Machines/Kurzweil	☑
Other accommodations	☑	Special bookstore section	☐
		Typists	☐

Credit toward degree is not given for remedial courses taken.

Counseling Services

- ☑ Academic
- ☑ Psychological
- ☑ Student Support groups
- ☑ Vocational

Tutoring

Individual tutoring is not available.

	Individual	Group
Time management	☑	☑
Organizational skills	☑	☑
Learning strategies	☑	☑
Study skills	☐	☐
Content area	☐	☐
Writing lab	☐	☐
Math lab	☐	☐

LD PROGRAM STAFF

Total number of LD Program staff (including director):

Full Time: 2 Part Time: 2

Key staff people available to work with LD students: Chana Bell, Sharon Teruya, and Julie Morris, Learning Disabilities Specialists.

University of California, Riverside

Riverside, CA

Address: 900 University Avenue, Riverside, CA, 92521
Admissions telephone: 951 827-3411
Admissions FAX: 951 827-4532
Director of Undergraduate Admissions: LaRae Lundgren
Admissions e-mail: discover@ucr.edu
Web site: http://www.ucr.edu
SAT Code: 4839 ACT Code: 456

LD program name: Services for Students with Disabilities
LD program address: 125 Costo Hall
Director: Marcia Schiffer
LD program telephone: 951 827-4538
LD program e-mail: marcia.schiffer@ucr.edu
LD program enrollment: 39, Total campus enrollment: 15,089

GENERAL

University of California, Riverside is a public, coed, four-year institution. 1,200-acre, suburban campus in Riverside (population: 255,166), 60 miles from Los Angeles. Served by bus and train; major airports serve Ontario (20 miles) and Los Angeles. School operates transportation around campus and to nearby housing and shopping areas. Public transportation serves campus. Quarter system.

SECONDARY SCHOOL REQUIREMENTS

Graduation from secondary school required; GED accepted. The following course distribution required: 4 units of English, 3 units of math, 2 units of science, 2 units of foreign language, 2 units of history, 1 unit of academic electives.

TESTING

SAT Reasoning or ACT required. SAT Subject required.

All enrolled freshmen (fall 2004):

Average SAT I Scores:	Verbal: 514	Math: 560
Average ACT Scores:	Composite: 21	

Child Study Team report is not required. A neuropsychological or comprehensive psycho-educational evaluation is required for admission. Must be dated within 36 months of application. Tests required as part of this documentation:

- ☑ WAIS-IV
- ☐ WISC-IV
- ☐ SATA
- ☑ Woodcock-Johnson
- ☐ Nelson-Denny Reading Test
- ☐ Other

UNDERGRADUATE STUDENT BODY

Total undergraduate student enrollment: 5,899 Men, 6,815 Women.

Composition of student body (fall 2004):

	Undergraduate	Freshmen
International	1.8	1.8
Black	5.8	6.6
American Indian	0.3	0.5
Asian-American	45.8	41.7
Hispanic	23.5	23.6
White	17.5	20.2
Unreported	5.3	5.6
	100.0%	100.0%

1% are from out of state. 7% join a fraternity and 7% join a sorority. Average age of full-time undergraduates is 20. 36% of classes have fewer than 20 students, 39% have between 20 and 50 students, 25% have more than 50 students.

STUDENT HOUSING

76% of freshmen live in college housing. Freshmen are not required to live on campus. Housing is guaranteed for first-time, first-year freshmen. Campus can house 4,354 undergraduates.

EXPENSES

Tuition (2005-06): $6,141 per year (in-state), $23,961 (out-of-state).
Room & Board: $10,200.
There is no additional cost for LD program/services.

LD SERVICES

LD program size is not limited.

LD services available to:

☑ Freshmen ☑ Sophomores ☑ Juniors ☑ Seniors

Academic Accommodations

Curriculum		**In class**	
Foreign language waiver	☐	Early syllabus	☐
Lighter course load	☐	Note takers in class	☐
Math waiver	☐	Priority seating	☐
Other special classes	☐	Tape recorders	☐
Priority registrations	☐	Videotaped classes	☐
Substitution of courses	☐	Text on tape	☐
Exams		**Services**	
Extended time	☐	Diagnostic tests	☐
Oral exams	☐	Learning centers	☐
Take home exams	☐	Proofreaders	☐
Exams on tape or computer	☐	Readers	☐
Untimed exams	☐	Reading Machines/Kurzweil	☐
Other accommodations	☐	Special bookstore section	☐
		Typists	☐

Counseling Services

- ☐ Academic
- ☐ Psychological
- ☐ Student Support groups
- ☐ Vocational

Tutoring

	Individual	Group
Time management	☐	☐
Organizational skills	☐	☐
Learning strategies	☐	☐
Study skills	☐	☐
Content area	☐	☐
Writing lab	☐	☐
Math lab	☐	☐

UNIQUE LD PROGRAM FEATURES

Accommodations are individually tailored to meet the student's disability-related needs and are based on the student's current functional limitations and the requirements of the specific class in which the student is enrolled.

LD PROGRAM STAFF

Key staff person available to work with LD students: Jean Dona, Learning Disabilities Specialist.

LD Program web site: www.specialservices.ucr.edu

University of California, San Diego

La Jolla, CA

Address: 9500 Gilman Drive, La Jolla, CA, 92093
Admissions telephone: 858 534-4831
Director of Admissions and Relations with Schools: Mae W. Brown
Admissions e-mail: admissionsinfo@ucsd.edu
Web site: http://www.ucsd.edu/
SAT Code: 4836 ACT Code: 459

Director of Disabled Student Services: Roberta Gimblett, M.Ed.
LD program telephone: 858 534-4382
LD program e-mail: rgimblett@ucsd.edu
Total campus enrollment: 20, 339

GENERAL

University of California, San Diego is a public, coed, four-year institution. 1,976-acre campus in LaJolla (population: 39,437), 12 miles from downtown San Diego. Major airport serves San Diego; train serves Del Mar (five miles). School operates transportation around campus and to medical center in San Diego. Public transportation serves campus. Quarter system.

LD ADMISSIONS

Students do not complete a separate application and are not simultaneously accepted to the LD program. A member of the LD program does not sit on the admissions committee. A personal interview is not required. Essay is required and may be typed.

SECONDARY SCHOOL REQUIREMENTS

Graduation from secondary school required; GED accepted. The following course distribution required: 4 units of English, 3 units of math, 2 units of science, 2 units of foreign language, 2 units of history, 1 unit of academic electives.

TESTING

SAT Reasoning or ACT required. SAT Subject required.

All enrolled freshmen (fall 2004):

Average SAT I Scores:	Verbal: 598	Math: 644
Average ACT Scores:	Composite: 26	

Child Study Team report is not required. A neuropsychological or comprehensive psycho-educational evaluation is required for admission. Tests required as part of this documentation:

- ☐ WAIS-IV
- ☐ WISC-IV
- ☐ SATA
- ■ Woodcock-Johnson
- ☐ Nelson-Denny Reading Test
- ■ Other

UNDERGRADUATE STUDENT BODY

Total undergraduate student enrollment: 7,891 Men, 8,605 Women.

Composition of student body (fall 2004):

	Undergraduate	Freshmen
International	2.2	3.0
Black	1.4	1.3
American Indian	0.4	0.4
Asian-American	43.2	38.1
Hispanic	11.3	10.4
White	29.9	33.6
Unreported	11.6	13.2
	100.0%	100.0%

3% are from out of state. 10% join a fraternity and 10% join a sorority. Average age of full-time undergraduates is 21. 47% of classes have fewer than 20 students, 25% have between 20 and 50 students, 28% have more than 50 students.

STUDENT HOUSING

95% of freshmen live in college housing. Freshmen are required to live on campus. Housing is guaranteed for all undergraduates. Campus can house 6,534 undergraduates. Single rooms are available for students with medical or special needs. A medical note is required.

EXPENSES

Tuition (2005-06): $6,141 per year (in-state), $23,961 (out-of-state).
Room & Board: $9,421.
There is no additional cost for LD program/services.

LD SERVICES

LD program size is not limited.

LD services available to:

■ Freshmen ■ Sophomores ■ Juniors ■ Seniors

Academic Accommodations

Curriculum		**In class**	
Foreign language waiver	☐	Early syllabus	☐
Lighter course load	☐	Note takers in class	■
Math waiver	☐	Priority seating	■
Other special classes	☐	Tape recorders	■
Priority registrations	■	Videotaped classes	☐
Substitution of courses	☐	Text on tape	■
Exams		**Services**	
Extended time	■	Diagnostic tests	■
Oral exams	■	Learning centers	■
Take home exams	☐	Proofreaders	■
Exams on tape or computer	■	Readers	■
Untimed exams	■	Reading Machines/Kurzweil	■
Other accommodations	■	Special bookstore section	■
		Typists	■

Credit toward degree is not given for remedial courses taken.

Counseling Services

- ■ Academic
- ■ Psychological
- ■ Student Support groups
- ■ Vocational

Tutoring

Individual tutoring is available daily.

	Individual	Group
Time management	■	■
Organizational skills	■	■
Learning strategies	■	■
Study skills	■	■
Content area	■	■
Writing lab	■	■
Math lab	■	■

LD PROGRAM STAFF

Total number of LD Program staff (including director):

Full Time: 3 Part Time: 3

There is an advisor/advocate from the LD program available to students.

Key staff person available to work with LD students: Judith Babbitt Gould, LD and ADHD Counselor.

LD Program web site: http://osd.ucsd.edu/index.html

University of California, Santa Cruz

Santa Cruz, CA

Address: 1156 High Street, Santa Cruz, CA, 95064
Admissions telephone: 831 459-4008
Admissions FAX: 831 459-4452
Associate Vice Chancellor of Outreach, Admissions, & Student Academics: Kevin Browne
Admissions e-mail: admissions@cats.ucsc.edu
Web site: http://www.ucsc.edu
SAT Code: 4860 ACT Code: 460

LD program name: Disability Resource Center
LD program address: 146 Hahn
Assistant Director: Barbara Duron
LD program telephone: 831 459-2089
LD program e-mail: drc@ucsc.edu
Total campus enrollment: 13, 694

GENERAL

University of California, Santa Cruz is a public, coed, four-year institution. 2,000-acre campus in Santa Cruz (population: 54,593), 75 miles from San Francisco and 30 miles from San Jose; branch campus in Silicon Valley and extension in downtown Santa Cruz. Served by bus; major airports serve San Francisco and San Jose; train serves San Jose. School operates transportation to the Bay Area. Public transportation serves campus. Quarter system.

LD ADMISSIONS

A personal interview is not required. Essay is required and may be typed.

SECONDARY SCHOOL REQUIREMENTS

Graduation from secondary school required; GED accepted. The following course distribution required: 4 units of English, 3 units of math, 2 units of science, 2 units of foreign language, 1 unit of social studies, 1 unit of history, 1 unit of academic electives.

TESTING

SAT Reasoning or ACT required. SAT Subject required.

All enrolled freshmen (fall 2004):

Average SAT I Scores:	Verbal: 573	Math: 584
Average ACT Scores:	Composite: 24	

Child Study Team report is not required. Tests required as part of this documentation:

- ☐ WAIS-IV
- ☐ WISC-IV
- ☐ SATA
- ☐ Woodcock-Johnson
- ☐ Nelson-Denny Reading Test
- ☐ Other

UNDERGRADUATE STUDENT BODY

Total undergraduate student enrollment: 4,731 Men, 6,344 Women.

Composition of student body (fall 2004):

	Undergraduate	Freshmen
International	0.9	1.5
Black	2.7	2.6
American Indian	0.8	0.9
Asian-American	20.9	18.0
Hispanic	14.0	14.4
White	50.9	51.5
Unreported	9.8	11.1
	100.0%	100.0%

6% are from out of state. 1% join a fraternity and 1% join a sorority. Average age of full-time undergraduates is 21. 43% of classes have fewer than 20 students, 37% have between 20 and 50 students, 20% have more than 50 students.

STUDENT HOUSING

94% of freshmen live in college housing. Freshmen are not required to live on campus. Housing is guaranteed for all undergraduates. Campus can house 6,637 undergraduates.

EXPENSES

Tuition (2005-06): $6,141 per year (in-state), $23,961 (out-of-state).
Room: $8,374. Board: $3,197.
There is no additional cost for LD program/services.

LD SERVICES

LD program size is not limited.

LD services available to:

☐ Freshmen ☐ Sophomores ☐ Juniors ☐ Seniors

Academic Accommodations

Curriculum		**In class**	
Foreign language waiver	☐	Early syllabus	☐
Lighter course load	■	Note takers in class	■
Math waiver	☐	Priority seating	☐
Other special classes	☐	Tape recorders	■
Priority registrations	☐	Videotaped classes	■
Substitution of courses	☐	Text on tape	☐
Exams		**Services**	
Extended time	■	Diagnostic tests	☐
Oral exams	■	Learning centers	■
Take home exams	☐	Proofreaders	☐
Exams on tape or computer	☐	Readers	■
Untimed exams	☐	Reading Machines/Kurzwell	■
Other accommodations	☐	Special bookstore section	☐
		Typists	☐

Credit toward degree is not given for remedial courses taken.

Counseling Services

- ☐ Academic
- ☐ Psychological
- ☐ Student Support groups
- ☐ Vocational

Tutoring

	Individual	Group
Time management	☐	☐
Organizational skills	☐	☐
Learning strategies	☐	☐
Study skills	☐	☐
Content area	☐	☐
Writing lab	☐	☐
Math lab	☐	☐

LD PROGRAM STAFF

Total number of LD Program staff (including director):

Full Time: 2 Part Time: 2

Key staff person available to work with LD students: Sharyn Martin, Director.

LD Program web site: http://www2.ucsc.edu/drc/

Chapman University

Orange, CA

Address: One University Drive, Orange, CA, 92866
Admissions telephone: 888 CUAPPLY
Admissions FAX: 714 997-6713
Chief Admissions Officer: Michael Drummy
Admissions e-mail: admit@chapman.edu
Web site: http://www.chapman.edu
SAT Code: 4047 ACT Code: 210

LD program name: Center for Academic Success
Director of the Center for Academic Success: Dr. Lynn Mayer
LD program telephone: 714 997-6857
LD program e-mail: lmayer@chapman.edu
LD program enrollment: 265, Total campus enrollment: 3,733

GENERAL

Chapman University is a private, coed, four-year institution. 75-acre, suburban campus in Orange (population: 128,821), 35 miles from Los Angeles. Served by bus and train; major airports serve Los Angeles; smaller airport serves Santa Ana (8 miles). Public transportation serves campus. 4-1-4 system.

LD ADMISSIONS

Students do not complete a separate application and are not simultaneously accepted to the LD program. A member of the LD program does not sit on the admissions committee. A personal interview is recommended. Essay is required and may be typed.

SECONDARY SCHOOL REQUIREMENTS

Graduation from secondary school required; GED accepted. The following course distribution required: 2 units of English, 2 units of math, 2 units of science, 2 units of foreign language, 3 units of social studies.

TESTING

SAT Reasoning or ACT required. SAT Subject required.

All enrolled freshmen (fall 2004):

Average SAT I Scores:	Verbal: 595	Math: 599
Average ACT Scores:	Composite: 25	

Child Study Team report is not required. A neuropsychological or comprehensive psycho-education evaluation is not required for admission. Tests required as part of this documentation:

- ☐ WAIS-IV
- ☐ WISC-IV
- ☐ SATA
- ☐ Woodcock-Johnson
- ☐ Nelson-Denny Reading Test
- ☐ Other

UNDERGRADUATE STUDENT BODY

Total undergraduate student enrollment: 1,385 Men, 1,742 Women.

Composition of student body (fall 2004):

	Undergraduate	Freshmen
International	2.4	2.6
Black	3.0	2.4
American Indian	1.1	0.6
Asian-American	8.9	8.4
Hispanic	10.1	10.4
White	64.1	64.8
Unreported	10.4	10.8
	100.0%	100.0%

33% are from out of state. 14% join a fraternity and 17% join a sorority. Average age of full-time undergraduates is 20. 33% of classes have fewer than 20 students, 66% have between 20 and 50 students, 1% have more than 50 students.

STUDENT HOUSING

83% of freshmen live in college housing. Freshmen are required to live on campus. Housing is guaranteed for all undergraduates. Campus can house 1,632 undergraduates. Single rooms are available for students with medical or special needs. A medical note is not required.

EXPENSES

Tuition (2005-06): $28,050 per year.

Room & Board: $10,471.

There is no additional cost for LD program/services.

LD SERVICES

LD program size is not limited.

LD services available to:

☒ Freshmen ☒ Sophomores ☒ Juniors ☒ Seniors

Academic Accommodations

Curriculum		In class	
Foreign language waiver	☐	Early syllabus	☐
Lighter course load	☒	Note takers in class	☒
Math waiver	☐	Priority seating	☐
Other special classes	☐	Tape recorders	☒
Priority registrations	☒	Videotaped classes	☐
Substitution of courses	☐	Text on tape	☐
Exams		**Services**	
Extended time	☒	Diagnostic tests	☐
Oral exams	☒	Learning centers	☒
Take home exams	☐	Proofreaders	☐
Exams on tape or computer	☐	Readers	☒
Untimed exams	☐	Reading Machines/Kurzweil	☐
Other accommodations	☐	Special bookstore section	☐
		Typists	☐

Credit toward degree is not given for remedial courses taken.

Counseling Services

- ☒ Academic
- ☒ Psychological
- ☒ Student Support groups
- ☐ Vocational

Tutoring

Individual tutoring is available weekly.

Average size of tutoring groups: 1

	Individual	Group
Time management	☒	☐
Organizational skills	☒	☐
Learning strategies	☒	☐
Study skills	☒	☐
Content area	☒	☐
Writing lab	☐	☐
Math lab	☐	☐

LD PROGRAM STAFF

Total number of LD Program staff (including director):

Full Time: 3 Part Time: 3

There is an advisor/advocate from the LD program available to students. Five peer tutors are available to work with LD students.

Key staff person available to work with LD students: Dr. Lynn Mayer, Director of the Center for Academic Success.

LD Program web site: http://www.chapman.edu/academics/cas/

Charles R. Drew University of Medicine and Science

Los Angeles, CA

Address: 1621 East 120th Street, Los Angeles, CA, 90059
Admissions FAX: 323 569-0597
Director of Admissions: Cesar Hernandez
Web site: http://www.cdrewu.edu
SAT Code: 4982

LD program name: Student Education & Service Center
LD program address: 1731 East 120th Street
Director of Student Affairs/SESC: Maranda Montgomery
LD program telephone: 323 563-3638
LD program e-mail: mmmontgo@cdrewu.edu

GENERAL

Charles R. Drew University of Medicine and Science is a private, coed, four-year institution. Urban campus in Los Angeles (population: 3,694,820). Served by air, bus, and train. Trimester system.

LD ADMISSIONS

Students do not complete a separate application and are not simultaneously accepted to the LD program. A member of the LD program does not sit on the admissions committee.

TESTING

Child Study Team report is not required. A neuropsychological or comprehensive psycho-education evaluation is not required for admission. Tests required as part of this documentation:

- [ ] WAIS-IV
- [ ] WISC-IV
- [ ] SATA
- [ ] Woodcock-Johnson
- [ ] Nelson-Denny Reading Test
- [ ] Other

UNDERGRADUATE STUDENT BODY

Total undergraduate student enrollment: 250.

Composition of student body (fall 2004):

	Undergraduate	Freshmen
International	0.0	0.0
Black	72.5	40.4
American Indian	0.1	0.6
Asian-American	8.7	17.4
Hispanic	10.1	26.4
White	4.3	12.4
Unreported	4.3	2.8
	100.0%	100.0%

Average age of full-time undergraduates is 35.

STUDENT HOUSING

Campus housing is not available.

EXPENSES

There is no additional cost for LD program/services.

LD SERVICES

LD program size is not limited.

LD services available to:

- [x] Freshmen
- [x] Sophomores
- [x] Juniors
- [x] Seniors

Academic Accommodations

Curriculum

- [ ] Foreign language waiver
- [ ] Lighter course load
- [ ] Math waiver
- [ ] Other special classes
- [x] Priority registrations
- [ ] Substitution of courses

Exams

- [x] Extended time
- [x] Oral exams
- [x] Take home exams
- [x] Exams on tape or computer
- [ ] Untimed exams
- [ ] Other accommodations

In class

- [x] Early syllabus
- [x] Note takers in class
- [x] Priority seating
- [x] Tape recorders
- [x] Videotaped classes
- [ ] Text on tape

Services

- [x] Diagnostic tests
- [x] Learning centers
- [x] Proofreaders
- [x] Readers
- [ ] Reading Machines/Kurzweil
- [ ] Special bookstore section
- [x] Typists

Credit toward degree is not given for remedial courses taken.

Counseling Services

- [x] Academic
- [x] Psychological
- [x] Student Support groups
- [x] Vocational

Tutoring

Individual tutoring is available weekly.

Average size of tutoring groups: 3

	Individual	Group
Time management	[x]	[x]
Organizational skills	[x]	[x]
Learning strategies	[x]	[x]
Study skills	[x]	[x]
Content area	[x]	[x]
Writing lab	[x]	[x]
Math lab	[x]	[x]

LD PROGRAM STAFF

Total number of LD Program staff (including director):

Full Time: 13 Part Time: 13

There is an advisor/advocate from the LD program available to students. The advisor/advocate meets with faculty once per month. Five peer tutors are available to work with LD students.

Key staff person available to work with LD students: Melanie Gordon, Academic Counselor.

LD Program web site: http://www.cdrewu.edu/kdhsl/sesc/index.htm

Claremont McKenna College

Claremont, CA

Address: 890 Columbia Avenue, Claremont, CA, 91711
Admissions telephone: 909 621-8088
Admissions FAX: 909 621-8516
Vice President/Dean of Admission and Financial Aid: Richard Vos
Admissions e-mail: admission@claremontmckenna.edu
Web site: http://www.claremontmckenna.edu
SAT Code: 4054 ACT Code: 224

LD program address: Heggblade Center
Psychologist: Dr. Nana Sadamura
LD program telephone: 909 621-8202
LD program enrollment: 28, Total campus enrollment: 1,124

GENERAL

Claremont McKenna College is a private, coed, four-year institution. 56-acre campus in Claremont (population: 33,998), 35 miles from Los Angeles. Served by bus and train; major airport serves Los Angeles; other airport serves Ontario (10 miles). School operates transportation to libraries and athletic, cultural, and entertainment events. Public transportation serves campus. Semester system.

LD ADMISSIONS

A personal interview is recommended. Essay is required and may be typed.

SECONDARY SCHOOL REQUIREMENTS

Graduation from secondary school not required. The following course distribution required: 4 units of English, 3 units of math, 2 units of science, 3 units of foreign language, 1 unit of social studies, 1 unit of history.

TESTING

SAT Reasoning or ACT required. SAT Subject required.

All enrolled freshmen (fall 2004):

Average SAT I Scores:	Verbal: 700	Math: 700
Average ACT Scores:	Composite: 31	

Child Study Team report is not required. Tests required as part of this documentation:

- [ ] WAIS-IV
- [ ] WISC-IV
- [ ] SATA
- [ ] Woodcock-Johnson
- [ ] Nelson-Denny Reading Test
- [ ] Other

UNDERGRADUATE STUDENT BODY

Total undergraduate student enrollment: 559 Men, 485 Women.

Composition of student body (fall 2004):

	Undergraduate	Freshmen
International	5.0	3.0
Black	6.1	4.2
American Indian	0.0	0.5
Asian-American	13.6	14.2
Hispanic	13.9	10.9
White	51.8	58.2
Unreported	9.6	9.0
	100.0%	100.0%

50% are from out of state. Average age of full-time undergraduates is 20. 86% of classes have fewer than 20 students, 14% have between 20 and 50 students.

STUDENT HOUSING

99% of freshmen live in college housing. Freshmen are required to live on campus. Housing is guaranteed for all undergraduates. Campus can house 984 undergraduates. Single rooms are available for students with medical or special needs. A medical note is required.

EXPENSES

Tuition (2005-06): $30,600 per year.
Room: $5,160. Board: $5,110.
There is no additional cost for LD program/services.

LD SERVICES

LD program size is not limited.

LD services available to:

- [x] Freshmen
- [x] Sophomores
- [x] Juniors
- [x] Seniors

Academic Accommodations

Curriculum		In class	
Foreign language waiver	[x]	Early syllabus	[ ]
Lighter course load	[ ]	Note takers in class	[x]
Math waiver	[ ]	Priority seating	[ ]
Other special classes	[ ]	Tape recorders	[x]
Priority registrations	[ ]	Videotaped classes	[ ]
Substitution of courses	[x]	Text on tape	[ ]
Exams		**Services**	
Extended time	[x]	Diagnostic tests	[ ]
Oral exams	[ ]	Learning centers	[ ]
Take home exams	[ ]	Proofreaders	[ ]
Exams on tape or computer	[ ]	Readers	[ ]
Untimed exams	[x]	Reading Machines/Kurzweil	[ ]
Other accommodations	[ ]	Special bookstore section	[ ]
		Typists	[ ]

Credit toward degree is not given for remedial courses taken.

Counseling Services

- [x] Academic — Meets 4 times per academic year
- [x] Psychological — Meets 6 times per academic year
- [ ] Student Support groups
- [ ] Vocational

Tutoring

Individual tutoring is available daily.

Average size of tutoring groups: 3

	Individual	Group
Time management	[x]	[ ]
Organizational skills	[x]	[ ]
Learning strategies	[x]	[ ]
Study skills	[x]	[ ]
Content area	[ ]	[ ]
Writing lab	[ ]	[ ]
Math lab	[ ]	[ ]

UNIQUE LD PROGRAM FEATURES

CMC works with students on a case-by-case basis to provide reasonable accommodations as required by law. Accommodations may include additional time to complete exams and a private testing facility. Any student may petition for these accommodations by submitting evidence of LD testing which is less than three years old.

LD PROGRAM STAFF

There is an advisor/advocate from the LD program available to students. The advisor/advocate meets with faculty 2 times per month and students once per month.

Key staff person available to work with LD students: Jefferson Huang, Dean of Students.

Concordia University

Irvine, CA

Address: 1530 Concordia W, Irvine, CA, 92612-3299
Admissions telephone: 800 229-1200
Admissions FAX: 949 854-6894
Vice President for Student Services: Lori McDonald
Admissions e-mail: admission@cui.edu
Web site: http://www.cui.edu
SAT Code: 4069 ACT Code: 227

Director of The Learning Center: Becky Peters
LD program telephone: 949 854-8002, extension 1836
LD program e-mail: becky.peters@cui.edu
Total campus enrollment: 1, 367

GENERAL

Concordia University is a private, coed, four-year institution. 70-acre campus in Irvine (population: 143,072), 40 miles from Los Angeles. Served by air, bus, and train; major airport serves Los Angeles. School operates transportation to shopping areas, church services, and off-campus events. Semester system.

LD ADMISSIONS

A personal interview is not required. Essay is not required.

SECONDARY SCHOOL REQUIREMENTS

Graduation from secondary school required; GED accepted. The following course distribution required: 4 units of English, 3 units of math, 3 units of science, 2 units of foreign language, 2 units of social studies.

TESTING

SAT Reasoning required; ACT may be substituted. SAT Subject recommended.

All enrolled freshmen (fall 2004):

Average SAT I Scores:	Verbal: 510	Math: 510
Average ACT Scores:	Composite: 22	

Child Study Team report is not required. Tests required as part of this documentation:

- [ ] WAIS-IV
- [ ] WISC-IV
- [ ] SATA
- [ ] Woodcock-Johnson
- [ ] Nelson-Denny Reading Test
- [ ] Other

UNDERGRADUATE STUDENT BODY

Total undergraduate student enrollment: 378 Men, 748 Women.

Composition of student body (fall 2004):

	Undergraduate	Freshmen
International	1.3	1.7
Black	5.7	3.5
American Indian	1.1	0.9
Asian-American	3.4	4.7
Hispanic	15.6	12.5
White	65.6	70.2
Unreported	7.3	6.5
	100.0%	100.0%

17% are from out of state. Average age of full-time undergraduates is 21. 50% of classes have fewer than 20 students, 48% have between 20 and 50 students, 2% have more than 50 students.

STUDENT HOUSING

99% of freshmen live in college housing. Freshmen are required to live on campus. Housing is guaranteed for all undergraduates. Campus can house 1,024 undergraduates.

EXPENSES

Tuition (2005-06): $19,930 per year.
Room: $4,250. Board: $2,800.
There is no additional cost for LD program/services.

LD SERVICES

LD program size is not limited.

LD services available to:

- [ ] Freshmen
- [ ] Sophomores
- [ ] Juniors
- [ ] Seniors

Academic Accommodations

Curriculum		In class	
Foreign language waiver	[ ]	Early syllabus	[ ]
Lighter course load	[ ]	Note takers in class	[ ]
Math waiver	[ ]	Priority seating	[ ]
Other special classes	[ ]	Tape recorders	[ ]
Priority registrations	[ ]	Videotaped classes	[ ]
Substitution of courses	[ ]	Text on tape	[ ]
Exams		**Services**	
Extended time	[x]	Diagnostic tests	[ ]
Oral exams	[x]	Learning centers	[x]
Take home exams	[ ]	Proofreaders	[ ]
Exams on tape or computer	[ ]	Readers	[ ]
Untimed exams	[x]	Reading Machines/Kurzweil	[ ]
Other accommodations	[ ]	Special bookstore section	[ ]
		Typists	[ ]

Credit toward degree is not given for remedial courses taken.

Counseling Services

- [ ] Academic
- [ ] Psychological
- [ ] Student Support groups
- [ ] Vocational

Tutoring

	Individual	Group
Time management	[ ]	[ ]
Organizational skills	[ ]	[ ]
Learning strategies	[ ]	[ ]
Study skills	[ ]	[ ]
Content area	[ ]	[ ]
Writing lab	[ ]	[ ]
Math lab	[ ]	[ ]

LD PROGRAM STAFF

Total number of LD Program staff (including director):

Full Time: 1 Part Time: 1

Key staff person available to work with LD students: Becky Peters, Director of the Learning Center.

Dominican University of California

San Rafael, CA

Address: 50 Acacia Avenue, San Rafael, CA, 94901-2298
Admissions telephone: 888 323-6763
Admissions FAX: 415 485-3214
Director of Admissions: Art Criss
Admissions e-mail: enroll@dominican.edu
Web site: http://www.dominican.edu
SAT Code: 4284 ACT Code: 256

LD program name: Tutoring and Disability Services
Director of Tutoring and Disability Services: Iris Crossley
LD program telephone: 415 257-0187
LD program e-mail: crossley@dominican.edu
LD program enrollment: 40, Total campus enrollment: 1,340

GENERAL

Dominican University of California is a private, coed, four-year institution. 80-acre, suburban campus in San Rafael (population: 56,063), 11 miles from San Francisco; branch campus in Ukiah. Served by bus; major airports serve San Francisco and Oakland (25 miles); train serves Richmond (15 miles). Public transportation serves campus. Semester system.

LD ADMISSIONS

Students do not complete a separate application and are not simultaneously accepted to the LD program. A member of the LD program does not sit on the admissions committee. A personal interview is recommended. Essay is required and may be typed.

SECONDARY SCHOOL REQUIREMENTS

Graduation from secondary school required; GED accepted.

TESTING

SAT Reasoning required; ACT may be substituted. SAT Subject required.

All enrolled freshmen (fall 2004):

Average SAT I Scores: Verbal: 514 Math: 501

Child Study Team report is not required. A neuropsychological or comprehensive psycho-educational evaluation is required for admission. Must be dated within 36 months of application. Tests required as part of this documentation:

- ■ WAIS-IV
- ■ WISC-IV
- ☐ SATA
- ■ Woodcock-Johnson
- ■ Nelson-Denny Reading Test
- ☐ Other

UNDERGRADUATE STUDENT BODY

Total undergraduate student enrollment: 213 Men, 733 Women.

Composition of student body (fall 2004):

	Undergraduate	Freshmen
International	1.1	3.3
Black	10.3	8.3
American Indian	0.4	1.0
Asian-American	17.0	16.4
Hispanic	22.3	15.5
White	39.3	44.6
Unreported	9.6	10.9
	100.0%	100.0%

5% are from out of state. Average age of full-time undergraduates is 23. 72% of classes have fewer than 20 students, 28% have between 20 and 50 students.

STUDENT HOUSING

88% of freshmen live in college housing. Freshmen are not required to live on campus. Housing is guaranteed for all undergraduates. Campus can house 560 undergraduates. Single rooms are available for students with medical or special needs. A medical note is required.

EXPENSES

Tuition (2005-06): $25,952 per year.

Room: $5,578. Board: $4,140.
There is no additional cost for LD program/services.

LD SERVICES

LD program size is not limited.

LD services available to:

■ Freshmen ■ Sophomores ■ Juniors ■ Seniors

Academic Accommodations

Curriculum		**In class**	
Foreign language waiver	☐	Early syllabus	☐
Lighter course load	■	Note takers in class	■
Math waiver	☐	Priority seating	■
Other special classes	☐	Tape recorders	■
Priority registrations	■	Videotaped classes	☐
Substitution of courses	☐	Text on tape	■
Exams		**Services**	
Extended time	■	Diagnostic tests	☐
Oral exams	☐	Learning centers	☐
Take home exams	☐	Proofreaders	☐
Exams on tape or computer	■	Readers	■
Untimed exams	☐	Reading Machines/Kurzweil	☐
Other accommodations	■	Special bookstore section	☐
		Typists	■

Credit toward degree is not given for remedial courses taken.

Counseling Services

- ☐ Academic
- ☐ Psychological
- ☐ Student Support groups
- ☐ Vocational

Tutoring

Individual tutoring is available daily.

Average size of tutoring groups: 4

	Individual	Group
Time management	☐	■
Organizational skills	☐	■
Learning strategies	■	■
Study skills	■	■
Content area	☐	☐
Writing lab	☐	☐
Math lab	☐	☐

LD PROGRAM STAFF

Total number of LD Program staff (including director):

Full Time: 1 Part Time: 1

There is an advisor/advocate from the LD program available to students. 20 peer tutors are available to work with LD students.

Key staff person available to work with LD students: Iris Crossley, Director of Tutoring and Disability Services.

Evergreen Valley College

San Jose, CA

Address: 3095 Yerba Buena Road, San Jose, CA 95135
Admissions telephone: 408 270-6441
Admissions FAX: 408 223-9351
Director of Admissions/Records: Kathleen Moberg
Web site: http://www.evc.edu
SAT Code: 4273

LD program name: Disabled Students Program
Coordinator, Disabled Students Program: Robin Salak
LD program telephone: 408 223-6756
LD program e-mail: robin.salak@evc.edu
LD program enrollment: 70, Total campus enrollment: 10,600

GENERAL

Evergreen Valley College is a public, coed, two-year institution. 175-acre, urban campus in San Jose (population: 976,000). Served by air, bus, and train. Public transportation serves campus. Semester system.

LD ADMISSIONS

No deadline for application. Students do not complete a separate application for admission and are not simultaneously accepted to the program. A member of the LD program does not sit on the admissions committee. A personal interview is not required. Essay is not required.

SECONDARY SCHOOL REQUIREMENTS

Graduation from secondary school required; GED accepted.

TESTING

Child Study Team report is not required. Documentation of a neuropsychological or comprehensive pscho-educational evaluation is required for admission. Tests required as part of this documentation:

- [x] WAIS-IV
- [x] WISC-IV
- [ ] SATA
- [x] Woodcock-Johnson
- [ ] Nelson-Denny Reading Test
- [ ] Other

STUDENT HOUSING

There is no campus housing available.

EXPENSES

There is no additional cost for LD program/services.

LD SERVICES

LD program size is not limited.

LD services available to:

- [x] Freshmen
- [x] Sophomores
- [x] Juniors
- [x] Seniors

Academic Accommodations

Curriculum
- [ ] Foreign language waiver
- [x] Lighter course load
- [ ] Math waiver
- [x] Other special classes
- [x] Priority registrations
- [ ] Substitution of courses

Exams
- [x] Extended time
- [x] Oral exams
- [ ] Take home exams
- [x] Exams on tape or computer
- [ ] Untimed exams
- [x] Other accommodations

In class
- [ ] Early syllabus
- [x] Note takers in class
- [ ] Priority seating
- [x] Tape recorders
- [ ] Videotaped classes
- [x] Text on tape

Services
- [x] Diagnostic tests
- [ ] Learning centers
- [ ] Proofreaders
- [ ] Readers
- [x] Reading Machines/Kurzweil
- [ ] Special bookstore section
- [ ] Typists

Credit toward degree is not given for remedial courses taken.

Counseling Services

- [x] Academic
- [ ] Psychological
- [ ] Student Support groups
- [ ] Vocational

Tutoring

Average size of tutoring groups is 1-6.

	Individual	Group
Time management	[ ]	[ ]
Organizational skills	[ ]	[ ]
Learning strategies	[ ]	[ ]
Study skills	[ ]	[ ]
Content area	[ ]	[ ]
Writing lab	[ ]	[x]
Math lab	[ ]	[x]

LD PROGRAM STAFF

Total number of LD Program staff (including director):

Part Time: 2

Key staff person available to work with LD students: Bonnie Clark, Learning Disability Specialist

Fresno Pacific University

Fresno, CA

Address: 1717 South Chestnut Avenue, Fresno, CA, 93702
Admissions telephone: 800 660-6089
Admissions FAX: 559 453-2007
Director of Admissions: Dina Gonzalez-Pina
Admissions e-mail: ugadmis@fresno.edu
Web site: http://www.fresno.edu
SAT Code: 4616 ACT Code: 357

Asst. Dean of Student Development Programs: Don Sparks
LD program telephone: 559 453-3696
LD program e-mail: drsparks@fresno.edu
LD program enrollment: 16, Total campus enrollment: 1,417

GENERAL

Fresno Pacific University is a private, coed, four-year institution. 42-acre campus in Fresno (population: 427,652), 150 miles from San Francisco. Served by air, bus, and train. Public transportation serves campus. Semester system.

LD ADMISSIONS

Application Deadline: 07/31. A personal interview is recommended. Essay is required and may be typed.

For fall 2004, 17 completed self-identified LD applications were received.

SECONDARY SCHOOL REQUIREMENTS

Graduation from secondary school required; GED accepted. The following course distribution required: 4 units of English, 3 units of math, 1 unit of science, 2 units of foreign language, 2 units of social studies.

TESTING

SAT Subject recommended.

All enrolled freshmen (fall 2004):

Average SAT I Scores:	Verbal: 506	Math: 506
Average ACT Scores:	Composite: 20	

Child Study Team report is not required. Tests required as part of this documentation:

- [ ] WAIS-IV
- [ ] WISC-IV
- [ ] SATA
- [ ] Woodcock-Johnson
- [ ] Nelson-Denny Reading Test
- [ ] Other

UNDERGRADUATE STUDENT BODY

Total undergraduate student enrollment: 290 Men, 619 Women.

Composition of student body (fall 2004):

	Undergraduate	Freshmen
International	1.1	2.4
Black	5.4	4.5
American Indian	0.5	0.9
Asian-American	7.5	2.4
Hispanic	25.8	24.1
White	58.1	57.2
Unreported	1.6	8.5
	100.0%	100.0%

3% are from out of state. Average age of full-time undergraduates is 23. 67% of classes have fewer than 20 students, 26% have between 20 and 50 students, 7% have more than 50 students.

STUDENT HOUSING

70% of freshmen live in college housing. Freshmen are required to live on campus. Housing is guaranteed for all undergraduates. Campus can house 572 undergraduates. Single rooms are available for students with medical or special needs. A medical note is required.

EXPENSES

Tuition (2005-06): $19,430 per year.
Room: $2,850. Board: $3,100.

There is no additional cost for LD program/services.

LD SERVICES

LD program size is not limited.

LD services available to:

- [x] Freshmen
- [x] Sophomores
- [x] Juniors
- [x] Seniors

Academic Accommodations

Curriculum		**In class**	
Foreign language waiver	[ ]	Early syllabus	[ ]
Lighter course load	[ ]	Note takers in class	[x]
Math waiver	[ ]	Priority seating	[ ]
Other special classes	[ ]	Tape recorders	[x]
Priority registrations	[ ]	Videotaped classes	[ ]
Substitution of courses	[ ]	Text on tape	[x]
Exams		**Services**	
Extended time	[x]	Diagnostic tests	[ ]
Oral exams	[x]	Learning centers	[x]
Take home exams	[x]	Proofreaders	[ ]
Exams on tape or computer	[ ]	Readers	[x]
Untimed exams	[ ]	Reading Machines/Kurzweil	[ ]
Other accommodations	[x]	Special bookstore section	[ ]
		Typists	[x]

Credit toward degree is given for remedial courses taken.

Counseling Services

- [x] Academic
- [x] Psychological
- [ ] Student Support groups
- [x] Vocational

Tutoring

Individual tutoring is available weekly.

	Individual	Group
Time management	[ ]	[ ]
Organizational skills	[ ]	[ ]
Learning strategies	[ ]	[ ]
Study skills	[ ]	[ ]
Content area	[ ]	[ ]
Writing lab	[ ]	[ ]
Math lab	[ ]	[ ]

UNIQUE LD PROGRAM FEATURES

Requirements for reduced course loads or "remedial" courses are based on past academic performance and do not consider disability.

LD PROGRAM STAFF

There is an advisor/advocate from the LD program available to students. 15 peer tutors are available to work with LD students.

Key staff person available to work with LD students: Don Sparks, Asst. Dean of Student Development Programs.

Harvey Mudd College

Claremont, CA

Address: 301 East 12th Street, Claremont, CA, 91711
Admissions telephone: 909 621-8011
Admissions FAX: 909 607-7046
Vice President and Dean of Admission and Financial Aid: Peter Osgood
Admissions e-mail: admission@hmc.edu
Web site: http://www.hmc.edu
SAT Code: 4341 ACT Code: 282

Dean of Students: Jeanne Noda
LD program telephone: 909 621-8125
LD program e-mail: jeanne_noda@hmc.edu
Total campus enrollment: 721

GENERAL

Harvey Mudd College is a private, coed, four-year institution. 33-acre campus in Claremont (population: 33,998), 35 miles from Los Angeles. Major airport serves Ontario (10 miles); smaller airport serves Rancho Cucamonga (nine miles); bus and train serve Pomona (six miles). Public transportation serves campus. Semester system.

SECONDARY SCHOOL REQUIREMENTS

Graduation from secondary school required; GED not accepted. The following course distribution required: 4 units of English, 4 units of math, 4 units of science, 2 units of social studies.

TESTING

ACT considered if submitted. SAT Subject required.

All enrolled freshmen (fall 2004):

Average SAT I Scores: Verbal: 700 Math: 750

Child Study Team report is not required. Tests required as part of this documentation:

☐ WAIS-IV	☐ Woodcock-Johnson
☐ WISC-IV	☐ Nelson-Denny Reading Test
☐ SATA	☐ Other

UNDERGRADUATE STUDENT BODY

Total undergraduate student enrollment: 483 Men, 223 Women.

Composition of student body (fall 2004):

	Undergraduate	Freshmen
International	6.7	3.9
Black	0.0	1.1
American Indian	0.0	0.4
Asian-American	32.1	18.2
Hispanic	3.0	5.7
White	41.0	48.8
Unreported	17.2	21.9
	100.0%	100.0%

57% are from out of state. Average age of full-time undergraduates is 20. 67% of classes have fewer than 20 students, 28% have between 20 and 50 students, 5% have more than 50 students.

STUDENT HOUSING

100% of freshmen live in college housing. Freshmen are required to live on campus. Housing is guaranteed for all undergraduates. Campus can house 712 undergraduates.

EXPENSES

Tuition (2005-06): $31,536 per year.

Room: $5,282. Board: $5,130.

There is no additional cost for LD program/services.

LD SERVICES

LD program size is not limited.

LD services available to:

☐ Freshmen ☐ Sophomores ☐ Juniors ☐ Seniors

Academic Accommodations

Curriculum		**In class**	
Foreign language waiver	☐	Early syllabus	☐
Lighter course load	■	Note takers in class	☐
Math waiver	☐	Priority seating	☐
Other special classes	☐	Tape recorders	■
Priority registrations	☐	Videotaped classes	☐
Substitution of courses	☐	Text on tape	☐
Exams		**Services**	
Extended time	■	Diagnostic tests	☐
Oral exams	☐	Learning centers	☐
Take home exams	☐	Proofreaders	☐
Exams on tape or computer	☐	Readers	☐
Untimed exams	■	Reading Machines/Kurzweil	☐
Other accommodations	☐	Special bookstore section	☐
		Typists	☐

Credit toward degree is not given for remedial courses taken.

Counseling Services

☐ Academic
☐ Psychological
☐ Student Support groups
☐ Vocational

Tutoring

	Individual	Group
Time management	☐	☐
Organizational skills	☐	☐
Learning strategies	☐	☐
Study skills	☐	☐
Content area	☐	☐
Writing lab	☐	☐
Math lab	☐	☐

LD PROGRAM STAFF

Key staff person available to work with LD students: Jeanne Noda, Dean of Students.

Holy Names University

Oakland, CA

Address: 3500 Mountain Boulevard, Oakland, CA, 94619
Admissions telephone: 800 430-1321
Admissions FAX: 510 436-1325
Vice President for Enrollment Management: Lonnie R. Morris, Jr.
Admissions e-mail: admissions@hnu.edu
Web site: http://www.hnu.edu
SAT Code: 4059 ACT Code: 230

LD program name: Disability Support Services
Director of Disability Support Services: Laura Lyndon
LD program telephone: 510 436-1356
LD program e-mail: DSS@hnu.edu
LD program enrollment: 40, total campus enrollment: 641

GENERAL

Holy Names University is a private, coed, four-year institution. 60-acre, urban campus in Oakland (population: 399,484), 20 miles from San Francisco. Served by air, bus, and train. Public transportation serves campus. Semester system.

LD ADMISSIONS

Students do not complete a separate application and are simultaneously accepted to the LD program. A member of the LD program does not sit on the admissions committee. A personal interview is recommended. Essay is required and may be typed. Admissions requirements that may be waived are considered on a case-by-case basis.

SECONDARY SCHOOL REQUIREMENTS

Graduation from secondary school required; GED accepted. The following course distribution required: 4 units of English, 3 units of math, 1 unit of science, 2 units of foreign language, 1 unit of history, 3 units of academic electives.

TESTING

SAT Reasoning required; ACT may be substituted. SAT Subject recommended.

All enrolled freshmen (fall 2004):

Average SAT I Scores:	Verbal: 465	Math: 469
Average ACT Scores:	Composite: 19	

Child Study Team report is not required. A neuropsychological or comprehensive psycho-education evaluation is not required for admission. Tests required as part of this documentation:

❑ WAIS-IV	❑ Woodcock-Johnson
❑ WISC-IV	❑ Nelson-Denny Reading Test
❑ SATA	❑ Other

UNDERGRADUATE STUDENT BODY

Total undergraduate student enrollment: 112 Men, 480 Women.

Composition of student body (fall 2004):

	Undergraduate	Freshmen
International	8.3	4.7
Black	17.4	30.0
American Indian	2.8	1.8
Asian-American	20.2	8.9
Hispanic	19.3	16.3
White	22.8	26.1
Unreported	9.2	12.2
	100.0%	100.0%

4% are from out of state. Average age of full-time undergraduates is 26. 73% of classes have fewer than 20 students, 27% have between 20 and 50 students.

STUDENT HOUSING

78% of freshmen live in college housing. Freshmen are not required to live on campus. Housing is guaranteed for all undergraduates. Campus can house 326 undergraduates. Single rooms are available for students with medical or special needs. A medical note is required.

EXPENSES

Tuition (2005-06): $21,400 per year.
Room: $4,000. Board: $3,800.
There is no additional cost for LD program/services.

LD SERVICES

LD program size is not limited.

LD services available to:

■ Freshmen ■ Sophomores ■ Juniors ■ Seniors

Academic Accommodations

Curriculum		**In class**	
Foreign language waiver	❑	Early syllabus	❑
Lighter course load	■	Note takers in class	■
Math waiver	❑	Priority seating	❑
Other special classes	❑	Tape recorders	■
Priority registrations	❑	Videotaped classes	■
Substitution of courses	■	Text on tape	■
Exams		**Services**	
Extended time	■	Diagnostic tests	❑
Oral exams	■	Learning centers	■
Take home exams	❑	Proofreaders	❑
Exams on tape or computer	❑	Readers	■
Untimed exams	❑	Reading Machines/Kurzweil	■
Other accommodations	■	Special bookstore section	❑
		Typists	❑

Credit toward degree is not given for remedial courses taken.

Counseling Services

■ Academic — Meets 6 times per academic year
❑ Psychological
❑ Student Support groups
❑ Vocational

Tutoring

Individual tutoring is available weekly.

	Individual	Group
Time management	■	■
Organizational skills	■	■
Learning strategies	❑	❑
Study skills	■	■
Content area	❑	❑
Writing lab	❑	❑
Math lab	❑	❑

LD PROGRAM STAFF

Total number of LD Program staff (including director):

Full Time: 1 Part Time: 1

There is an advisor/advocate from the LD program available to students. The advisor/advocate meets with faculty once per month and studentsonce per month.

Key staff person available to work with LD students: Laura Lyndon, Director of Disability Support Services.

Humboldt State University

Arcata, CA

Address: 1 Harpst Street, Arcata, CA, 95521-8299
Admissions telephone: 866 850-9556
Admissions FAX: 707 826-6194
Assistant Director of Admissions: Scott Hagg
Admissions e-mail: hsuinfo@humboldt.edu
Web site: http://www.humboldt.edu
SAT Code: 4345

Director, SDRC: Ralph McFarland
LD program telephone: 707 826-5394
LD program e-mail: rdm7001@humboldt.edu
Total campus enrollment: 6, 529

GENERAL

Humboldt State University is a public, coed, four-year institution. 161-acre campus in Arcata (population: 16,651), 275 miles from San Francisco. Served by air and bus. Public transportation serves campus.

LD ADMISSIONS

A member of the LD program does sit on the admissions committee. A personal interview is not required. Essay is not required. Course substitutions may be permitted but admissions requirements are not waived.

SECONDARY SCHOOL REQUIREMENTS

Graduation from secondary school required; GED accepted. The following course distribution required: 4 units of English, 3 units of math, 2 units of science, 2 units of foreign language, 1 unit of social studies, 1 unit of history, 1 unit of academic electives.

TESTING

SAT Reasoning or ACT required of some applicants. SAT Subject recommended.

All enrolled freshmen (fall 2004):

Average SAT I Scores:	Verbal:	Math:
Average ACT Scores:	Composite: 21	

Child Study Team report is not required. Tests required as part of this documentation:

- ❑ WAIS-IV
- ❑ WISC-IV
- ❑ SATA
- ❑ Woodcock-Johnson
- ❑ Nelson-Denny Reading Test
- ❑ Other

UNDERGRADUATE STUDENT BODY

Total undergraduate student enrollment: 2,888 Men, 3,530 Women.

Composition of student body (fall 2004):

	Undergraduate	Freshmen
International	0.6	0.6
Black	4.3	3.2
American Indian	2.0	2.4
Asian-American	4.9	3.6
Hispanic	8.9	8.5
White	55.7	59.8
Unreported	23.6	21.9
	100.0%	100.0%

4% are from out of state. Average age of full-time undergraduates is 23. 34% of classes have fewer than 20 students, 57% have between 20 and 50 students, 9% have more than 50 students.

STUDENT HOUSING

82% of freshmen live in college housing.

EXPENSES

Tuition 2004-05: $2,046 per year (in-state), $6,768 (out-of-state).

Room & Board: $6,861.

There is no additional cost for LD program/services.

LD SERVICES

LD program size is not limited.

LD services available to:

❑ Freshmen ❑ Sophomores ❑ Juniors ❑ Seniors

Academic Accommodations

Curriculum		**In class**	
Foreign language waiver	❑	Early syllabus	❑
Lighter course load	❑	Note takers in class	■
Math waiver	❑	Priority seating	❑
Other special classes	❑	Tape recorders	■
Priority registrations	❑	Videotaped classes	❑
Substitution of courses	❑	Text on tape	❑
Exams		**Services**	
Extended time	■	Diagnostic tests	❑
Oral exams	❑	Learning centers	■
Take home exams	❑	Proofreaders	❑
Exams on tape or computer	❑	Readers	■
Untimed exams	❑	Reading Machines/Kurzweil	■
Other accommodations	❑	Special bookstore section	❑
		Typists	❑

Credit toward degree is not given for remedial courses taken.

Counseling Services

- ❑ Academic
- ❑ Psychological
- ❑ Student Support groups
- ❑ Vocational

Tutoring

	Individual	Group
Time management	❑	❑
Organizational skills	❑	❑
Learning strategies	❑	❑
Study skills	❑	❑
Content area	❑	❑
Writing lab	❑	❑
Math lab	❑	❑

UNIQUE LD PROGRAM FEATURES

All students may access Tutorial Center. Students may choose a lighter course load, but may affect financial aid allocations. GED certification is accepted, however, additional achievement tests may be requested.

LD PROGRAM STAFF

Total number of LD Program staff (including director):

Full Time: 4 Part Time: 4

Key staff person available to work with LD students: Mary Smith, LD Resource Specialist.

Humphreys College

Stockton, CA

Address: 6650 Inglewood Avenue, Stockton, CA, 95207
Admissions telephone: 209 478-0800
Admissions FAX: 209 478-8721
Admissions Director: Santa Lopez
Admissions e-mail: ugadmission@humphreys.edu
Web site: http://www.humphreys.edu
SAT Code: 4346

Dean of Instruction: Jess Bonds
LD program telephone: 209 478-0800, extension 300
LD program e-mail: jbonds@humphreys.edu
Total campus enrollment: 909

GENERAL

Humphreys College is a private, coed, four-year institution. 10-acre, suburban campus in Stockton (population: 243,771); branch campuses in Sacramento and Modesto. Served by train and bus; major airport serves Sacramento (50 miles). Public transportation serves campus. Quarter system.

LD ADMISSIONS

High school waivers are accepted for math and foreign language.

SECONDARY SCHOOL REQUIREMENTS

Graduation from secondary school required; GED accepted.

TESTING

Child Study Team report is not required. A neuropsychological or comprehensive psycho-education evaluation is not required for admission. Tests required as part of this documentation:

- [ ] WAIS-IV
- [ ] WISC-IV
- [ ] SATA
- [ ] Woodcock-Johnson
- [ ] Nelson-Denny Reading Test
- [ ] Other

UNDERGRADUATE STUDENT BODY

Total undergraduate student enrollment: 89 Men, 469 Women.

Composition of student body (fall 2004):

	Undergraduate	Freshmen
International	0.0	0.0
Black	23.4	15.4
American Indian	2.2	1.4
Asian-American	12.4	10.7
Hispanic	29.1	34.5
White	26.3	35.5
Unreported	6.6	2.5
	100.0%	100.0%

5% are from out of state. Average age of full-time undergraduates is 31.

STUDENT HOUSING

1% of freshmen live in college housing. Housing is guaranteed for all undergraduates. Campus can house 64 undergraduates.

EXPENSES

Tuition (2005-06): $10,560 per year.
Room & Board: $6,534.
There is no additional cost for LD program/services.

LD SERVICES

LD program size is not limited.

LD services available to:

- [x] Freshmen
- [x] Sophomores
- [x] Juniors
- [x] Seniors

Academic Accommodations

Curriculum		In class	
Foreign language waiver	[ ]	Early syllabus	[ ]
Lighter course load	[ ]	Note takers in class	[ ]
Math waiver	[x]	Priority seating	[x]
Other special classes	[ ]	Tape recorders	[ ]
Priority registrations	[ ]	Videotaped classes	[ ]
Substitution of courses	[ ]	Text on tape	[ ]
Exams		**Services**	
Extended time	[x]	Diagnostic tests	[ ]
Oral exams	[ ]	Learning centers	[x]
Take home exams	[ ]	Proofreaders	[ ]
Exams on tape or computer	[ ]	Readers	[ ]
Untimed exams	[ ]	Reading Machines/Kurzweil	[ ]
Other accommodations	[ ]	Special bookstore section	[ ]
		Typists	[ ]

Credit toward degree is not given for remedial courses taken.

Counseling Services

- [x] Academic
- [ ] Psychological
- [ ] Student Support groups
- [x] Vocational

Tutoring

Individual tutoring is available daily.

Average size of tutoring groups: 1

	Individual	Group
Time management	[ ]	[ ]
Organizational skills	[ ]	[ ]
Learning strategies	[x]	[ ]
Study skills	[x]	[ ]
Content area	[ ]	[ ]
Writing lab	[x]	[ ]
Math lab	[x]	[ ]

LD PROGRAM STAFF

Total number of LD Program staff (including director):

Full Time: 1 Part Time: 1

There is no advisor/advocate from the LD program available to students. 2 peer tutors are available to work with LD students.

Key staff person available to work with LD students: Jess Bonds, Dean of Instruction.

University of Judaism

Bel Air, CA

Address: 15600 Mulholland Drive, Bel Air, CA, 90077
Admissions telephone: 888 UJ-FOR-ME
Admissions FAX: 310 471-3657
Dean of Admissions: Bryan Pisetsky
Admissions e-mail: admissions@uj.edu
Web site: http://www.uj.edu
SAT Code: 4876 ACT Code: 462

Total campus enrollment: 150

GENERAL

University of Judaism is a private, coed, four-year institution. 28-acre, suburban campus in Los Angeles (population: 3,694,820). Served by air, bus, and train. Semester system.

LD ADMISSIONS

A personal interview is required. Essay is required and may be typed.

SECONDARY SCHOOL REQUIREMENTS

Graduation from secondary school required; GED accepted.

TESTING

SAT Reasoning or ACT required.

Child Study Team report is not required. Tests required as part of this documentation:

- [ ] WAIS-IV
- [ ] WISC-IV
- [ ] SATA
- [ ] Woodcock-Johnson
- [ ] Nelson-Denny Reading Test
- [ ] Other

UNDERGRADUATE STUDENT BODY

Total undergraduate student enrollment: 46 Men, 60 Women.

STUDENT HOUSING

Housing is guaranteed for all undergraduates.

EXPENSES

Tuition (2005-06): $18,480 per year.
Room: $5,478. Board: $5,082.
There is no additional cost for LD program/services.

LD SERVICES

LD program size is not limited.

LD services available to:

[ ] Freshmen [ ] Sophomores [ ] Juniors [ ] Seniors

Academic Accommodations

Curriculum		In class	
Foreign language waiver	[ ]	Early syllabus	[ ]
Lighter course load	[x]	Note takers in class	[x]
Math waiver	[ ]	Priority seating	[ ]
Other special classes	[ ]	Tape recorders	[x]
Priority registrations	[ ]	Videotaped classes	[ ]
Substitution of courses	[ ]	Text on tape	[ ]
Exams		**Services**	
Extended time	[x]	Diagnostic tests	[ ]
Oral exams	[x]	Learning centers	[ ]
Take home exams	[ ]	Proofreaders	[ ]
Exams on tape or computer	[ ]	Readers	[x]
Untimed exams	[x]	Reading Machines/Kurzweil	[ ]
Other accommodations	[ ]	Special bookstore section	[ ]
		Typists	[ ]

Credit toward degree is not given for remedial courses taken.

Counseling Services

- [ ] Academic
- [ ] Psychological
- [ ] Student Support groups
- [ ] Vocational

Tutoring

	Individual	Group
Time management	[ ]	[ ]
Organizational skills	[ ]	[ ]
Learning strategies	[ ]	[ ]
Study skills	[ ]	[ ]
Content area	[ ]	[ ]
Writing lab	[ ]	[ ]
Math lab	[ ]	[ ]

University of La Verne

La Verne, CA

Address: 1950 Third Street, La Verne, CA, 91750
Admissions telephone: 800 876-4ULV
Admissions FAX: 909 392-2714
Dean of Undergraduate Admissions: Ana Liza V. Zell
Admissions e-mail: admissions@ulv.edu
Web site: http://www.ulv.edu
SAT Code: 4381   ACT Code: 295

Director: Cynthia Denne
LD program telephone: 909 593-3511, extension 4441
LD program e-mail: dennec@ulv.edu
LD program enrollment: 16, Total campus enrollment: 1,650

GENERAL

University of La Verne is a private, coed, four-year institution. 34-acre, suburban campus in LaVerne (population: 35,421), 26 miles from Los Angeles; continuing education branch campuses in Bakersfield, Riverside, Orange County, San Fernando Valley, and Ventura County, at military bases in Alaska, and abroad in Athens, Greece. Major airports serve Ontario (six miles) and Los Angeles; bus and train serve Pomona. 4-1-4 system.

LD ADMISSIONS

A personal interview is recommended. Essay is required and may be typed. Waivers or course substitutions in math and foreign language are subject to documentation of specific disability.

SECONDARY SCHOOL REQUIREMENTS

Graduation from secondary school required; GED not accepted. The following course distribution required: 4 units of English, 3 units of math, 2 units of science, 2 units of social studies, 3 units of history.

TESTING

SAT Reasoning or ACT required. SAT Subject recommended.

All enrolled freshmen (fall 2004):

Average SAT I Scores:	Verbal: 502	Math: 512
Average ACT Scores:	Composite: 21	

Child Study Team report is not required. A neuropsychological or comprehensive psycho-educational evaluation is required for admission. Tests required as part of this documentation:

- ☐ WAIS-IV
- ☒ WISC-IV
- ☐ SATA
- ☒ Woodcock-Johnson
- ☐ Nelson-Denny Reading Test
- ☐ Other

UNDERGRADUATE STUDENT BODY

Total undergraduate student enrollment: 571 Men, 851 Women.

Composition of student body (fall 2004):

	Undergraduate	Freshmen
International	0.0	0.8
Black	8.4	9.1
American Indian	0.8	0.7
Asian-American	3.2	4.6
Hispanic	40.1	37.5
White	34.8	35.6
Unreported	12.7	11.7
	100.0%	100.0%

5% are from out of state. 18% join a fraternity and 15% join a sorority. Average age of full-time undergraduates is 20. 66% of classes have fewer than 20 students, 34% have between 20 and 50 students.

STUDENT HOUSING

60% of freshmen live in college housing. Freshmen are not required to live on campus. Housing is not guaranteed for all undergraduates. Housing is limited. Campus can house 536 undergraduates. Single rooms are available for students with medical or special needs. A medical note is required.

EXPENSES

Tuition (2005-06): $22,800 per year.
Room: $4,490. Board: $4,620.

There is no additional cost for LD program/services.

LD SERVICES

LD program size is not limited.

LD services available to:

☒ Freshmen ☒ Sophomores ☒ Juniors ☒ Seniors

Academic Accommodations

Curriculum		In class	
Foreign language waiver	☒	Early syllabus	☒
Lighter course load	☐	Note takers in class	☒
Math waiver	☒	Priority seating	☒
Other special classes	☐	Tape recorders	☒
Priority registrations	☒	Videotaped classes	☐
Substitution of courses	☒	Text on tape	☒
Exams		**Services**	
Extended time	☒	Diagnostic tests	☐
Oral exams	☒	Learning centers	☒
Take home exams	☐	Proofreaders	☐
Exams on tape or computer	☒	Readers	☒
Untimed exams	☒	Reading Machines/Kurzweil	☒
Other accommodations	☒	Special bookstore section	☐
		Typists	☒

Credit toward degree is not given for remedial courses taken.

Counseling Services

- ☐ Academic
- ☐ Psychological
- ☐ Student Support groups
- ☐ Vocational

Tutoring

Individual tutoring is available daily.

Average size of tutoring groups: 1

	Individual	Group
Time management	☒	☐
Organizational skills	☒	☐
Learning strategies	☒	☐
Study skills	☒	☐
Content area	☒	☐
Writing lab	☐	☐
Math lab	☐	☐

LD PROGRAM STAFF

Total number of LD Program staff (including director):

Full Time: 1   Part Time: 1

There is an advisor/advocate from the LD program available to students. The advisor/advocate meets with faculty once per month and students once per month. Three graduate students and 24 peer tutors are available to work with LD students.

Key staff person available to work with LD students: Cynthia Denne, Director of Services for Students w/ Disabilities.

Life Pacific College

San Dimas, CA

Address: 1100 Covina Boulevard, San Dimas, CA, 91773-3298
Admissions telephone: 877 866-5433
Admissions FAX: 909 706-3070
Director of Admissions: Linda Hibdon
Web site: http://www.lifepacific.edu
SAT Code: 4264 ACT Code: 489

LD program name: LIFE Challenges & PCS
Dean of Students: Pat Crowder
LD program telephone: 909 599-5433, extension 330
LD program e-mail: pcrowder@lifepacific.edu
Total campus enrollment: 489

GENERAL

Life Pacific College is a private, coed, four-year institution. Nine-acre campus in San Dimas (population: 34,980), 40 miles from Los Angeles. Airport serves Ontario (15 miles); major airport serves Los Angeles; bus and train serve Pomona (10 miles). Public transportation serves campus. Semester system.

LD ADMISSIONS

Application Deadline: 07/01. Students do not complete a separate application and are simultaneously accepted to the LD program. A member of the LD program does sit on the admissions committee. A personal interview is recommended. Essay is not required.

SECONDARY SCHOOL REQUIREMENTS

Graduation from secondary school required; GED accepted.

TESTING

SAT Subject recommended.

All enrolled freshmen (fall 2004):

Average SAT I Scores:	Verbal: 513	Math:
Average ACT Scores:	Composite: 21	

Child Study Team report is not required. A neuropsychological or comprehensive psycho-education evaluation is not required for admission. Tests required as part of this documentation:

- [ ] WAIS-IV
- [ ] WISC-IV
- [ ] SATA
- [ ] Woodcock-Johnson
- [ ] Nelson-Denny Reading Test
- [ ] Other

UNDERGRADUATE STUDENT BODY

Total undergraduate student enrollment: 250 Men, 230 Women.

47% are from out of state. Average age of full-time undergraduates is 22. 63% of classes have fewer than 20 students, 29% have between 20 and 50 students, 8% have more than 50 students.

STUDENT HOUSING

93% of freshmen live in college housing. Housing is guaranteed for all undergraduates. Single rooms are available for students with medical or special needs. A medical note is not required.

EXPENSES

Tuition (2005-06): $9,750 per year.
Room & Board: $2,500.
There is no additional cost for LD program/services.

LD SERVICES

LD program size is not limited.

LD services available to:

- [x] Freshmen
- [x] Sophomores
- [x] Juniors
- [x] Seniors

Academic Accommodations

Curriculum		In class	
Foreign language waiver	[ ]	Early syllabus	[ ]
Lighter course load	[x]	Note takers in class	[x]
Math waiver	[ ]	Priority seating	[x]
Other special classes	[ ]	Tape recorders	[x]
Priority registrations	[ ]	Videotaped classes	[ ]
Substitution of courses	[ ]	Text on tape	[ ]
Exams		**Services**	
Extended time	[x]	Diagnostic tests	[ ]
Oral exams	[x]	Learning centers	[ ]
Take home exams	[x]	Proofreaders	[ ]
Exams on tape or computer	[ ]	Readers	[ ]
Untimed exams	[x]	Reading Machines/Kurzweil	[ ]
Other accommodations	[x]	Special bookstore section	[ ]
		Typists	[ ]

Credit toward degree is given for remedial courses taken.

Counseling Services

- [x] Academic
- [ ] Psychological
- [x] Student Support groups
- [ ] Vocational

Tutoring

Individual tutoring is not available.

	Individual	Group
Time management	[ ]	[x]
Organizational skills	[ ]	[x]
Learning strategies	[ ]	[x]
Study skills	[ ]	[x]
Content area	[ ]	[ ]
Writing lab	[ ]	[ ]
Math lab	[ ]	[ ]

LD PROGRAM STAFF

There is an advisor/advocate from the LD program available to students. The advisor/advocate meets with faculty once per month and students four times per month.

Key staff person available to work with LD students: Gayle Samples, Professor.

Loyola Marymount University

Los Angeles, CA

Address: 1 LMU Drive, Los Angeles, CA, 90045-2659
Admissions telephone: 310 338-2750
Admissions FAX: 310 338-2797
Director of Admissions: Matthew X. Fissinger
Admissions e-mail: admissions@lmu.edu
Web site: http://www.lmu.edu
SAT Code: 4403   ACT Code: 326

LD program name: Disability Support Services
Coordinator for Disability Support Services: Robert Scholz
LD program telephone: 310 338-4535
LD program e-mail: rscholz@lmu.edu
LD program enrollment: 134, Total campus enrollment: 5,721

GENERAL

Loyola Marymount University is a private, coed, four-year institution. 128-acre, suburban campus in Los Angeles (population: 3,694,820); branch campus (law school) downtown. Served by air, bus, and train. Public transportation serves campus. Semester system.

LD ADMISSIONS

Students do not complete a separate application and are not simultaneously accepted to the LD program. A member of the LD program does not sit on the admissions committee. A personal interview is not required. Essay is required and may be typed.

SECONDARY SCHOOL REQUIREMENTS

Graduation from secondary school required; GED accepted. The following course distribution required: 4 units of English, 3 units of math, 2 units of science, 3 units of foreign language, 3 units of social studies, 1 unit of academic electives.

TESTING

SAT Reasoning or ACT required. SAT Subject recommended.

All enrolled freshmen (fall 2004):

Average SAT I Scores: Verbal: 572   Math: 582

Child Study Team report is not required. A neuropsychological or comprehensive psycho-educational evaluation is required for admission. Must be dated within 36 months of application. Tests required as part of this documentation:

■ WAIS-IV	■ Woodcock-Johnson
■ WISC-IV	■ Nelson-Denny Reading Test
☐ SATA	☐ Other

UNDERGRADUATE STUDENT BODY

Total undergraduate student enrollment: 2,188 Men, 2,956 Women.

Composition of student body (fall 2004):

	Undergraduate	Freshmen
International	0.6	1.7
Black	8.1	7.0
American Indian	1.6	0.6
Asian-American	15.0	12.4
Hispanic	18.2	18.7
White	56.6	54.6
Unreported	0.0	4.9
	100.0%	100.0%

20% are from out of state. 10% join a fraternity and 17% join a sorority. Average age of full-time undergraduates is 20. 50% of classes have fewer than 20 students, 49% have between 20 and 50 students, 1% have more than 50 students.

STUDENT HOUSING

94% of freshmen live in college housing. Freshmen are not required to live on campus. Housing guaranteed for freshmen and sophomores; lottery for juniors and seniors. Campus can house 2,676 undergraduates. Single rooms are available for students with medical or special needs. A medical note is required.

EXPENSES

Tuition (2005-06): $27,162 per year.
Room: $7,890. Board: $2,450.
There is no additional cost for LD program/services.

LD SERVICES

LD program size is not limited.

LD services available to:

■ Freshmen ■ Sophomores ■ Juniors ■ Seniors

Academic Accommodations

Curriculum		In class	
Foreign language waiver	☐	Early syllabus	☐
Lighter course load	■	Note takers in class	■
Math waiver	☐	Priority seating	■
Other special classes	■	Tape recorders	■
Priority registrations	■	Videotaped classes	☐
Substitution of courses	☐	Text on tape	■
Exams		**Services**	
Extended time	■	Diagnostic tests	☐
Oral exams	■	Learning centers	■
Take home exams	☐	Proofreaders	☐
Exams on tape or computer	☐	Readers	■
Untimed exams	☐	Reading Machines/Kurzweil	■
Other accommodations	■	Special bookstore section	☐
		Typists	☐

Credit toward degree is not given for remedial courses taken.

Counseling Services

■ Academic	Meets 20 times per academic year
■ Psychological	Meets 15 times per academic year
■ Student Support groups	Meets 2 times per academic year
■ Vocational	Meets 10 times per academic year

Tutoring

Individual tutoring is available daily.

Average size of tutoring groups: 1

	Individual	Group
Time management	■	■
Organizational skills	■	■
Learning strategies	■	■
Study skills	■	■
Content area	■	■
Writing lab	■	■
Math lab	■	■

LD PROGRAM STAFF

Total number of LD Program staff (including director):

Full Time: 1   Part Time: 1

There is an advisor/advocate from the LD program available to students. The advisor/advocate meets with faculty seven times per month and students once per month. One graduate student and 20 peer tutors are available to work with LD students.

Key staff person available to work with LD students: Robert Scholz, M.A. LMFT, NLC, Coordinator for Disability Support Services.

The Master's College and Seminary

Santa Clarita, CA

Address: 21726 Placerita Canyon Road, Santa Clarita, CA, 91321-1200
Admissions telephone: 800 568-6248
Admissions FAX: 661 288-1037
Director of Enrollment: Yaphet Peterson
Admissions e-mail: enrollment@masters.edu
Web site: http://www.masters.edu
SAT Code: 4411 ACT Code: 303

Director of Human Resources: Kent Haney
LD program telephone: 661 259-3540, extension 3850
LD program e-mail: khaney@masters.edu
LD program enrollment: 2, Total campus enrollment: 1,134

GENERAL

The Master's College and Seminary is a private, coed, four-year institution. Two campuses totaling 103-acres in Newhall area of Santa Clarita (population: 151,088), 32 miles from Los Angeles; branch campus abroad in Jerusalem, Israel. Major airports serve Burbank (25 miles) and Los Angeles; bus serves San Fernando (15 miles); train serves Los Angeles. Public transportation serves campus. Semester system.

LD ADMISSIONS

A member of the LD program does not sit on the admissions committee. A personal interview is required. Essay is required and may be typed.

For fall 2004, one completed self-identified LD application was received. One application was offered admission, and one enrolled.

SECONDARY SCHOOL REQUIREMENTS

Graduation from secondary school required; GED accepted. The following course distribution required: 4 units of English, 3 units of math, 2 units of science, 2 units of history.

TESTING

SAT Reasoning or ACT required. SAT Subject required.

All enrolled freshmen (fall 2004):

Average SAT I Scores:	Verbal: 588	Math: 559
Average ACT Scores:	Composite: 24	

Child Study Team report is not required. A neuropsychological or comprehensive psycho-educational evaluation is required for admission. Must be dated within 36 months of application. Tests required as part of this documentation:

- ■ WAIS-IV
- ☐ WISC-IV
- ☐ SATA
- ☐ Woodcock-Johnson
- ☐ Nelson-Denny Reading Test
- ☐ Other

UNDERGRADUATE STUDENT BODY

Total undergraduate student enrollment: 573 Men, 602 Women.

Composition of student body (fall 2004):

	Undergraduate	Freshmen
International	4.6	3.1
Black	1.4	2.3
American Indian	0.9	0.8
Asian-American	3.7	4.4
Hispanic	5.0	7.7
White	84.4	81.3
Unreported	0.0	0.4
	100.0%	100.0%

35% are from out of state. Average age of full-time undergraduates is 20. 72% of classes have fewer than 20 students, 22% have between 20 and 50 students, 6% have more than 50 students.

STUDENT HOUSING

90% of freshmen live in college housing. Freshmen are required to live on campus. Housing is guaranteed for all undergraduates. Graduate housing is not available. Campus can house 775 undergraduates. Single rooms are not available for students with medical or special needs.

EXPENSES

Tuition (2005-06): $19,230 per year.
Room: $3,660. Board: $2,960.
There is no additional cost for LD program/services.

LD SERVICES

LD program size is not limited.

LD services available to:

■ Freshmen ■ Sophomores ■ Juniors ■ Seniors

Academic Accommodations

Curriculum		**In class**	
Foreign language waiver	☐	Early syllabus	☐
Lighter course load	☐	Note takers in class	☐
Math waiver	☐	Priority seating	☐
Other special classes	☐	Tape recorders	☐
Priority registrations	☐	Videotaped classes	☐
Substitution of courses	☐	Text on tape	☐
Exams		**Services**	
Extended time	■	Diagnostic tests	☐
Oral exams	☐	Learning centers	☐
Take home exams	☐	Proofreaders	☐
Exams on tape or computer	☐	Readers	☐
Untimed exams	☐	Reading Machines/Kurzweil	☐
Other accommodations	☐	Special bookstore section	☐
		Typists	☐

Credit toward degree is not given for remedial courses taken.

Counseling Services

- ■ Academic
- ☐ Psychological
- ☐ Student Support groups
- ☐ Vocational

Tutoring

Individual tutoring is available weekly.

Average size of tutoring groups: 3

	Individual	Group
Time management	■	☐
Organizational skills	■	☐
Learning strategies	■	☐
Study skills	■	☐
Content area	☐	☐
Writing lab	☐	☐
Math lab	■	☐

LD PROGRAM STAFF

There is an advisor/advocate from the LD program available to students.

Key staff person available to work with LD students: Marion McElwee, Academic Counselor.

Menlo College

Atherton, CA

Address: 1000 El Camino Real, Atherton, CA, 94027
Admissions telephone: 800 55-MENLO
Admissions FAX: 650 543-4496
Dean of Admissions: Greg Smith
Admissions e-mail: admissions@menlo.edu
Web site: http://www.menlo.edu
SAT Code: 4483 ACT Code: 330

Director of Academic Success Center: Janet Miller, M.A.
LD program telephone: 650 543-3854
LD program e-mail: jmiller@menlo.edu
Total campus enrollment: 749

GENERAL

Menlo College is a private, coed, four-year institution. 62-acre campus in Atherton (population: 7,194), 30 miles from San Francisco. Served by bus; major airport serves San Francisco. Public transportation serves campus. Semester system.

LD ADMISSIONS

A member of the LD program does not sit on the admissions committee. A personal interview is recommended. Essay is required and may be typed.

For fall 2004, 50 completed self-identified LD applications were received. 45 applications were offered admission, and 40 enrolled.

SECONDARY SCHOOL REQUIREMENTS

Graduation from secondary school required; GED accepted.

TESTING

SAT Reasoning or ACT required. SAT Subject recommended.

All enrolled freshmen (fall 2004):

Average SAT I Scores:	Verbal: 500	Math: 510
Average ACT Scores:	Composite: 17	

Child Study Team report is not required. A neuropsychological or comprehensive psycho-educational evaluation is required for admission. Tests required as part of this documentation:

- [ ] WAIS-IV
- [ ] WISC-IV
- [ ] SATA
- [ ] Woodcock-Johnson
- [ ] Nelson-Denny Reading Test
- [ ] Other

UNDERGRADUATE STUDENT BODY

Total undergraduate student enrollment: 385 Men, 287 Women.

Composition of student body (fall 2004):

	Undergraduate	Freshmen
International	6.3	11.7
Black	8.9	7.7
American Indian	0.5	0.6
Asian-American	15.6	12.2
Hispanic	15.1	13.1
White	37.5	38.2
Unreported	16.1	16.5
	100.0%	100.0%

16% are from out of state. Average age of full-time undergraduates is 20. 56% of classes have fewer than 20 students, 42% have between 20 and 50 students, 2% have more than 50 students.

STUDENT HOUSING

80% of freshmen live in college housing. Freshmen are required to live on campus. Housing is guaranteed for all undergraduates. Single rooms are available for students with medical or special needs. A medical note is required.

EXPENSES

Tuition (2005-06): $24,000 per year.
Room & Board: $9,600.

There is no additional cost for LD program/services.

LD SERVICES

LD program size is not limited.

LD services available to:

- [x] Freshmen
- [x] Sophomores
- [x] Juniors
- [x] Seniors

Academic Accommodations

Curriculum		In class	
Foreign language waiver	[x]	Early syllabus	[ ]
Lighter course load	[x]	Note takers in class	[x]
Math waiver	[x]	Priority seating	[ ]
Other special classes	[x]	Tape recorders	[x]
Priority registrations	[ ]	Videotaped classes	[ ]
Substitution of courses	[x]	Text on tape	[ ]
Exams		**Services**	
Extended time	[x]	Diagnostic tests	[ ]
Oral exams	[ ]	Learning centers	[x]
Take home exams	[ ]	Proofreaders	[ ]
Exams on tape or computer	[x]	Readers	[ ]
Untimed exams	[ ]	Reading Machines/Kurzweil	[ ]
Other accommodations	[x]	Special bookstore section	[ ]
		Typists	[x]

Credit toward degree is not given for remedial courses taken.

Counseling Services

[x]	Academic	Meets 9 times per academic year
[ ]	Psychological	
[x]	Student Support groups	Meets 112 times per academic year
[x]	Vocational	Meets 12 times per academic year

Tutoring

Individual tutoring is available weekly.

	Individual	Group
Time management	[ ]	[x]
Organizational skills	[ ]	[x]
Learning strategies	[ ]	[x]
Study skills	[ ]	[x]
Content area	[ ]	[ ]
Writing lab	[x]	[ ]
Math lab	[ ]	[ ]

LD PROGRAM STAFF

Total number of LD Program staff (including director):

Full Time: 2 Part Time: 2

There is an advisor/advocate from the LD program available to students. The advisor/advocate meets with students once per month. 10 peer tutors are available to work with LD students.

Key staff person available to work with LD students: Janet Miller, M.A., C.E.T., Director of Academic Success Center.

LD Program web site: www.menlo.edu/academics/asc

Mills College

Oakland, CA

Address: 5000 MacArthur Boulevard, Oakland, CA, 94613
Admissions telephone: 800 87-MILLS
Admissions FAX: 510 430-3298
Dean of Admission: Julie Richardson
Admissions e-mail: admission@mills.edu
Web site: http://www.mills.edu
SAT Code: 4485

Asst. to the Dean of Students: Kennedy Golden
LD program telephone: 510 430-2264
LD program e-mail: kennedyg@mills.edu
Total campus enrollment: 762

GENERAL

Mills College is a private, women's, four-year institution. 135-acre, suburban campus in Oakland (population: 399,480). Served by air, bus, and train. School operates transportation to UC Berkeley. Public transportation serves campus. Semester system.

LD ADMISSIONS

A personal interview is recommended. Essay is required and may be typed.

SECONDARY SCHOOL REQUIREMENTS

Graduation from secondary school required; GED accepted.

TESTING

SAT Reasoning required; ACT may be substituted. SAT Subject recommended.

All enrolled freshmen (fall 2004):

Average SAT I Scores:	Verbal: 602	Math: 549
Average ACT Scores:	Composite: 24	

Child Study Team report is not required. Tests required as part of this documentation:

- [ ] WAIS-IV
- [ ] WISC-IV
- [ ] SATA
- [ ] Woodcock-Johnson
- [ ] Nelson-Denny Reading Test
- [ ] Other

UNDERGRADUATE STUDENT BODY

Total undergraduate student enrollment: 684 Women.

Composition of student body (fall 2004):

	Undergraduate	Freshmen
International	2.9	4.8
Black	6.6	8.9
American Indian	0.8	1.0
Asian-American	8.1	8.7
Hispanic	10.3	9.0
White	36.0	44.7
Unreported	35.3	22.9
	100.0%	100.0%

23% are from out of state. Average age of full-time undergraduates is 23. 82% of classes have fewer than 20 students, 17% have between 20 and 50 students, 1% have more than 50 students.

STUDENT HOUSING

90% of freshmen live in college housing. Freshmen are not required to live on campus. Housing is guaranteed for all undergraduates. Campus can house 503 undergraduates. Single rooms are available for students with medical or special needs. A medical note is not required.

EXPENSES

Tuition (2005-06): $27,750 per year.

Room: $5,150. Board: $4,730.

There is no additional cost for LD program/services.

LD SERVICES

LD program size is not limited.

LD services available to:

- [x] Freshmen
- [x] Sophomores
- [x] Juniors
- [x] Seniors

Academic Accommodations

Curriculum

- [ ] Foreign language waiver
- [x] Lighter course load
- [ ] Math waiver
- [ ] Other special classes
- [ ] Priority registrations
- [ ] Substitution of courses

Exams

- [x] Extended time
- [ ] Oral exams
- [ ] Take home exams
- [ ] Exams on tape or computer
- [ ] Untimed exams
- [ ] Other accommodations

In class

- [ ] Early syllabus
- [x] Note takers in class
- [ ] Priority seating
- [x] Tape recorders
- [ ] Videotaped classes
- [ ] Text on tape

Services

- [ ] Diagnostic tests
- [ ] Learning centers
- [ ] Proofreaders
- [x] Readers
- [x] Reading Machines/Kurzweil
- [ ] Special bookstore section
- [ ] Typists

Credit toward degree is not given for remedial courses taken.

Counseling Services

- [x] Academic
- [x] Psychological
- [ ] Student Support groups
- [ ] Vocational

Tutoring

Individual tutoring is available.

	Individual	Group
Time management	[ ]	[x]
Organizational skills	[ ]	[x]
Learning strategies	[ ]	[x]
Study skills	[ ]	[x]
Content area	[ ]	[ ]
Writing lab	[x]	[x]
Math lab	[ ]	[ ]

LD PROGRAM STAFF

There is an advisor/advocate from the LD program available to students.

Key staff person available to work with LD students: Kennedy Golden, Assistant to the Dean of Students.

Mount St. Mary's College

Los Angeles, CA

Address: 12001 Chalon Road, Los Angeles, CA, 90049
Admissions telephone: 800 999-9893
Admissions FAX: 310 954-4259
Director of Admission: Dean Kilgour
Admissions e-mail: admissions@msmc.la.edu
Web site: http://www.msmc.la.edu
SAT Code: 4493 ACT Code: 338

LD program name: Learning Assistance Program
Director: Michele Lewis
Total campus enrollment: 1,804

GENERAL

Mount St. Mary's College is a private, coed, four-year institution. 53-acre campus in Los Angeles (population: 3,694,820) plus Doheny campus in Los Angeles. Served by air, bus, and train; airport serves Burbank (22 miles). School operates transportation between campuses. Public transportation serves Doheny campus. Semester system.

SECONDARY SCHOOL REQUIREMENTS

Graduation from secondary school required; GED accepted. The following course distribution required: 4 units of English, 3 units of math, 2 units of science, 2 units of foreign language, 2 units of social studies, 2 units of history.

TESTING

SAT Reasoning required; ACT may be substituted. SAT Subject recommended.

All enrolled freshmen (fall 2004):

Average SAT I Scores: Verbal: 519 Math: 507

Child Study Team report is not required. Tests required as part of this documentation:

- ☐ WAIS-IV
- ☐ WISC-IV
- ☐ SATA
- ☐ Woodcock-Johnson
- ☐ Nelson-Denny Reading Test
- ☐ Other

UNDERGRADUATE STUDENT BODY

Total undergraduate student enrollment: 1,804.

Composition of student body (fall 2004):

	Undergraduate	Freshmen
International	0.3	0.3
Black	5.8	10.6
American Indian	1.3	0.6
Asian-American	20.6	17.6
Hispanic	53.4	46.3
White	10.6	14.9
Unreported	8.0	9.7
	100.0%	100.0%

11% are from out of state. Average age of full-time undergraduates is 21. 68% of classes have fewer than 20 students, 32% have between 20 and 50 students.

STUDENT HOUSING

82% of freshmen live in college housing. Freshmen are not required to live on campus. Housing is guaranteed for all undergraduates. Campus can house 432 undergraduates.

EXPENSES

Tuition (2005-06): $22,054 per year.
Room & Board: $8,492.

LD SERVICES

LD program size is not limited.

LD services available to:

■ Freshmen ■ Sophomores ■ Juniors ■ Seniors

Academic Accommodations

Curriculum		**In class**	
Foreign language waiver	☐	Early syllabus	☐
Lighter course load	☐	Note takers in class	☐
Math waiver	☐	Priority seating	☐
Other special classes	☐	Tape recorders	☐
Priority registrations	☐	Videotaped classes	☐
Substitution of courses	☐	Text on tape	☐
Exams		**Services**	
Extended time	■	Diagnostic tests	☐
Oral exams	☐	Learning centers	■
Take home exams	☐	Proofreaders	☐
Exams on tape or computer	☐	Readers	☐
Untimed exams	☐	Reading Machines/Kurzweil	☐
Other accommodations	■	Special bookstore section	☐
		Typists	☐

Counseling Services

- ☐ Academic
- ☐ Psychological
- ☐ Student Support groups
- ☐ Vocational

Tutoring

	Individual	Group
Time management	☐	☐
Organizational skills	☐	☐
Learning strategies	☐	☐
Study skills	☐	☐
Content area	☐	☐
Writing lab	☐	☐
Math lab	☐	☐

LD PROGRAM STAFF

Key staff person available to work with LD students: Michele Lewis, Director, Learning Assistance Program.

National University

La Jolla, CA

Address: 11255 North Torrey Pines Road, La Jolla, CA, 92037
Admissions telephone: 800 NATUNIV
Admissions FAX: 858 642-8709
Associate Regional Dean: Walter Tobias
Admissions e-mail: advisor@nu.edu
Web site: http://www.nu.edu
SAT Code: 470

LD program name: Brain Jensen
Scholarships and Special Services: Brian Jensen
LD program telephone: 858 541-8185, extension 8185
LD program e-mail: bjensen@nu.edu
LD program enrollment: 30, Total campus enrollment: 5,820

GENERAL

National University is a private, coed, four-year institution. 15-acre, suburban campus in San Diego (population: 1,223,400); branch campuses in Bakersfield, Chula Vista, Costa Mesa, La Mesa, Redding, Sacramento, San Bernardino, San Jose, Sherman Oaks, Stockton, Twentynine Palms, and Vista. Served by air, bus, and train. Public transportation serves campus.

LD ADMISSIONS

Students do not complete a separate application and are not simultaneously accepted to the LD program. A member of the LD program does not sit on the admissions committee.

For fall 2004, 38 completed self-identified LD applications were received. 38 applications were offered admission, and 38 enrolled.

SECONDARY SCHOOL REQUIREMENTS

Graduation from secondary school required; GED accepted.

TESTING

Child Study Team report is not required. A neuropsychological or comprehensive psycho-education evaluation is not required for admission. Tests required as part of this documentation:

- [ ] WAIS-IV
- [ ] WISC-IV
- [ ] SATA
- [ ] Woodcock-Johnson
- [ ] Nelson-Denny Reading Test
- [ ] Other

UNDERGRADUATE STUDENT BODY

Total undergraduate student enrollment: 2,311 Men, 3,049 Women.

Composition of student body (fall 2004):

	Freshmen
International	1.4
Black	12.6
American Indian	1.0
Asian-American	8.7
Hispanic	19.0
White	51.2
Unreported	6.1
	100.0%

Average age of full-time undergraduates is 31. 82% of classes have fewer than 20 students, 18% have between 20 and 50 students.

EXPENSES

Tuition (2005-06): $9,950 per year.
There is no additional cost for LD program/services.

LD SERVICES

LD program size is not limited.

LD services available to:

- [x] Freshmen
- [x] Sophomores
- [x] Juniors
- [x] Seniors

Academic Accommodations

Curriculum

- [ ] Foreign language waiver
- [ ] Lighter course load
- [ ] Math waiver
- [ ] Other special classes
- [ ] Priority registrations
- [ ] Substitution of courses

Exams

- [x] Extended time
- [ ] Oral exams
- [ ] Take home exams
- [ ] Exams on tape or computer
- [x] Untimed exams
- [ ] Other accommodations

In class

- [ ] Early syllabus
- [x] Note takers in class
- [ ] Priority seating
- [x] Tape recorders
- [x] Videotaped classes
- [ ] Text on tape

Services

- [x] Diagnostic tests
- [ ] Learning centers
- [ ] Proofreaders
- [x] Readers
- [x] Reading Machines/Kurzweil
- [ ] Special bookstore section
- [ ] Typists

Credit toward degree is not given for remedial courses taken.

Counseling Services

- [x] Academic
- [ ] Psychological
- [ ] Student Support groups
- [ ] Vocational

Tutoring

Individual tutoring is available daily.

	Individual	Group
Time management	❑	❑
Organizational skills	❑	❑
Learning strategies	❑	❑
Study skills	❑	❑
Content area	❑	❑
Writing lab	■	❑
Math lab	❑	❑

LD PROGRAM STAFF

Key staff person available to work with LD students: Brian Jensen, Scholarships and Special Services.

Notre Dame de Namur University

Belmont, CA

Address: 1500 Ralston Avenue, Belmont, CA, 94002-1908
Admissions telephone: 800 263-0545
Admissions FAX: 650 508-3426
Director of Admission: Katy Murphy
Admissions e-mail: admissions@ndnu.edu
Web site: http://www.ndnu.edu
SAT Code: 4063 ACT Code: 236

LD program name: Program for Academic Services & Support (PASS)
Director: Dr. Joanne Rossi
LD program telephone: 650 508-3613
LD program e-mail: pass@ndnu.edu
LD program enrollment: 53, Total campus enrollment: 919

GENERAL

Notre Dame de Namur University is a private, coed, four-year institution. 50-acre, suburban campus in Belmont (population: 25,123), 25 miles from San Francisco. Served by train; major airports serve San Francisco and San Jose (25 miles). Public transportation serves campus. Semester system.

LD ADMISSIONS

Students do not complete a separate application and are not simultaneously accepted to the LD program. A member of the LD program does not sit on the admissions committee. A personal interview is not required. Essay is required and may be typed.

SECONDARY SCHOOL REQUIREMENTS

Graduation from secondary school required; GED accepted. The following course distribution required: 4 units of English, 2 units of math, 1 unit of science, 2 units of foreign language, 2 units of social studies, 1 unit of history, 3 units of academic electives.

TESTING

SAT Reasoning required; ACT may be substituted. SAT Subject required.

All enrolled freshmen (fall 2004):

Average SAT I Scores:	Verbal: 497	Math: 497
Average ACT Scores:	Composite: 20	

Child Study Team report is not required. A neuropsychological or comprehensive psycho-educational evaluation is required for admission. Must be dated within 36 months of application. Tests required as part of this documentation:

- [x] WAIS-IV
- [x] WISC-IV
- [ ] SATA
- [ ] Woodcock-Johnson
- [ ] Nelson-Denny Reading Test
- [ ] Other

UNDERGRADUATE STUDENT BODY

Total undergraduate student enrollment: 291 Men, 694 Women.

Composition of student body (fall 2004):

	Undergraduate	Freshmen
International	3.1	4.3
Black	5.6	6.6
American Indian	0.1	1.0
Asian-American	13.0	14.1
Hispanic	25.5	20.0
White	48.4	47.0
Unreported	4.3	7.0
	100.0%	100.0%

20% are from out of state. Average age of full-time undergraduates is 22. 68% of classes have fewer than 20 students, 32% have between 20 and 50 students.

STUDENT HOUSING

90% of freshmen live in college housing. Freshmen are required to live on campus. Housing is guaranteed for all undergraduates. Campus can house 520 undergraduates. Single rooms are available for students with medical or special needs. A medical note is required.

EXPENSES

Tuition (2005-06): $22,520 per year.
Room: $6,800. Board: $3,240.
There is no additional cost for LD program/services.

LD SERVICES

LD program size is not limited.

LD services available to:

- [x] Freshmen
- [x] Sophomores
- [x] Juniors
- [x] Seniors

Academic Accommodations

Curriculum		In class	
Foreign language waiver	[x]	Early syllabus	[x]
Lighter course load	[x]	Note takers in class	[x]
Math waiver	[ ]	Priority seating	[x]
Other special classes	[ ]	Tape recorders	[x]
Priority registrations	[ ]	Videotaped classes	[ ]
Substitution of courses	[x]	Text on tape	[x]
Exams		**Services**	
Extended time	[x]	Diagnostic tests	[x]
Oral exams	[x]	Learning centers	[x]
Take home exams	[x]	Proofreaders	[x]
Exams on tape or computer	[x]	Readers	[x]
Untimed exams	[x]	Reading Machines/Kurzweil	[ ]
Other accommodations	[x]	Special bookstore section	[ ]
		Typists	[x]

Credit toward degree is not given for remedial courses taken.

Counseling Services

- [x] Academic
- [ ] Psychological
- [ ] Student Support groups
- [ ] Vocational

Tutoring

Individual tutoring is available daily.

	Individual	Group
Time management	[x]	[ ]
Organizational skills	[x]	[ ]
Learning strategies	[x]	[ ]
Study skills	[x]	[ ]
Content area	[x]	[ ]
Writing lab	[x]	[ ]
Math lab	[x]	[ ]

LD PROGRAM STAFF

Total number of LD Program staff (including director):

Full Time: 1 Part Time: 1

There is an advisor/advocate from the LD program available to students.

Key staff person available to work with LD students: Dr. Joanne Rossi, Director, Program for Academic Services & Support.

LD Program web site: http://www.ndnu.edu/pass/

Occidental College

Los Angeles, CA

Address: 1600 Campus Road, Los Angeles, CA, 90041-3314
Admissions telephone: 800 852-5262
Admissions FAX: 323 341-4875
Director of Admissions: Vince Cuseo
Admissions e-mail: admission@oxy.edu
Web site: http://www.oxy.edu
SAT Code: 4581 ACT Code: 350

LD program name: Center for Academic Excellence
LD program address: F-10, 1600 Campus Road
Coordinator, Center for Academic Excellence: Linda Whitney
LD program telephone: 323 259-2849
LD program e-mail: lwhitney@oxy.edu
Total campus enrollment: 1, 866

GENERAL

Occidental College is a private, coed, four-year institution. 120-acre, suburban campus in northeast Los Angeles (population: 3,694,820). Served by air, bus, and train. School operates transportation to Pasadena, nearby shopping centers, and UCLA libraries. Semester system.

LD ADMISSIONS

Application Deadline: 01/10. Students do not complete a separate application and are simultaneously accepted to the LD program. A member of the LD program does not sit on the admissions committee. A personal interview is recommended. Essay is required and may be typed. Courses may be substituted in lieu of foreign language requirement depending on documentation.

SECONDARY SCHOOL REQUIREMENTS

Graduation from secondary school required; GED accepted.

TESTING

SAT Reasoning or ACT required. SAT Subject required.

All enrolled freshmen (fall 2004):

Average SAT I Scores:	Verbal: 640	Math: 630
Average ACT Scores:	Composite: 28	

Child Study Team report is not required. Tests required as part of this documentation:

- [ ] WAIS-IV
- [ ] WISC-IV
- [ ] SATA
- [ ] Woodcock-Johnson
- [ ] Nelson-Denny Reading Test
- [ ] Other

UNDERGRADUATE STUDENT BODY

Total undergraduate student enrollment: 1,866.

Composition of student body (fall 2004):

	Undergraduate	Freshmen
International	1.8	2.5
Black	8.7	7.3
American Indian	0.8	1.2
Asian-American	9.7	11.4
Hispanic	15.9	14.6
White	52.0	54.7
Unreported	11.1	8.3
	100.0%	100.0%

29% are from out of state. 6% join a fraternity and 13% join a sorority. Average age of full-time undergraduates is 20. 58% of classes have fewer than 20 students, 40% have between 20 and 50 students, 2% have more than 50 students.

STUDENT HOUSING

100% of freshmen live in college housing. Freshmen are required to live on campus. Housing is guaranteed for all undergraduates. Campus can house 1,310 undergraduates. Single rooms are available for students with medical or special needs. A medical note is required.

EXPENSES

Tuition (2005-06): $30,724 per year.

Room: $4,758. Board: $3,914.

There is no additional cost for LD program/services.

LD SERVICES

LD program size is not limited.

LD services available to:

- [x] Freshmen
- [x] Sophomores
- [x] Juniors
- [x] Seniors

Academic Accommodations

Curriculum		**In class**	
Foreign language waiver	[ ]	Early syllabus	[ ]
Lighter course load	[x]	Note takers in class	[ ]
Math waiver	[ ]	Priority seating	[ ]
Other special classes	[ ]	Tape recorders	[x]
Priority registrations	[ ]	Videotaped classes	[ ]
Substitution of courses	[ ]	Text on tape	[ ]
Exams		**Services**	
Extended time	[x]	Diagnostic tests	[ ]
Oral exams	[ ]	Learning centers	[x]
Take home exams	[ ]	Proofreaders	[ ]
Exams on tape or computer	[x]	Readers	[ ]
Untimed exams	[ ]	Reading Machines/Kurzweil	[ ]
Other accommodations	[ ]	Special bookstore section	[ ]
		Typists	[ ]

Credit toward degree is not given for remedial courses taken.

Counseling Services

- [ ] Academic
- [ ] Psychological
- [ ] Student Support groups
- [ ] Vocational

Tutoring

Individual tutoring is not available.

	Individual	Group
Time management	[x]	[x]
Organizational skills	[x]	[x]
Learning strategies	[x]	[x]
Study skills	[x]	[x]
Content area	[ ]	[ ]
Writing lab	[ ]	[ ]
Math lab	[ ]	[ ]

UNIQUE LD PROGRAM FEATURES

Services available to LD students are determined on an individual basis. A lighter course load is sometimes available, as appropriate. Documentation to establish ADA eligibility is required. Assistive technology is available to all students regardless of ADA eligibility. Occidental helps LD students find student notetakers, but all arrangements must be made by the LD student.

LD PROGRAM STAFF

Total number of LD Program staff (including director):

Full Time: 1 Part Time: 1

There is no advisor/advocate from the LD program available to students.

Key staff person available to work with LD students: Linda Whitney, Coordinator, Center for Academic Excellence.

Orange Coast College

Costa Mesa, CA

Address: 2701 Fairview Road, P.O. Box 5005, Costa Mesa, CA 92628
Admissions telephone: 714 432-5735
Administrative Dean of Admissions/Records: Nancy Kidder
Admissions e-mail: nkidder@occ.cccd.edu
Web site: http://www.occ.ccd.edu
SAT Code: 4584

LD program name: OCC Learning Center
Learning Specialist/Instructor: Kevin Smith
LD program telephone: 714 432-0202, extension 26247
LD program e-mail: ksmith@occ.cccd.edu
LD program enrollment: 306, Total campus enrollment: 25,628

GENERAL

Orange Coast College is a public, coed, two-year institution. 25-acre campus in Costa Mesa (population: 96,357). Served by bus. Major airport serves Los Angeles (50 miles), other airport serves Santa Ana (5 miles); train serves Irvine (10 miles). Public transportation serves campus. Semester system.

LD ADMISSIONS

Students do not complete a separate application and are not simultaneously accepted to the LD program. A member of the LD program does not sit on the admissions committee. A personal interview is required. Essay is not required.

SECONDARY SCHOOL REQUIREMENTS

Graduation from secondary school required; GED accepted.

TESTING

Child Study Team report is not required. A neuropsychological or comprehensive psycho-education evaluation is required for admission. Must be dated within 24 months of application. Tests required as part of this documentation:

■ WAIS-IV	■ Woodcock-Johnson
❑ WISC-IV	❑ Nelson-Denny Reading Test
❑ SATA	■ Other

UNDERGRADUATE STUDENT BODY

Composition of student body (fall 2004):

	Undergraduate	Freshmen
International	0.0	0.0
Black	0.0	0.0
American Indian	0.0	0.0
Asian-American	0.0	0.0
Hispanic	0.0	0.0
White	0.0	0.0
Unreported	0.0	0.0
	100.0%	100.0%

STUDENT HOUSING

No campus housing available.

EXPENSES

There is no additional cost for LD program/services.

LD SERVICES

LD program size is not limited.

LD services available to:

■ Freshmen ■ Sophomores ■ Juniors ■ Seniors

Academic Accommodations

Curriculum		In class	
Foreign language waiver	❑	Early syllabus	❑
Lighter course load	❑	Note takers in class	■
Math waiver	❑	Priority seating	❑
Other special classes	■	Tape recorders	■
Priority registrations	■	Videotaped classes	❑
Substitution of courses	❑	Text on tape	■
Exams		**Services**	
Extended time	■	Diagnostic tests	❑
Oral exams	■	Learning centers	■
Take home exams	❑	Proofreaders	❑
Exams on tape or computer	■	Readers	■
Untimed exams	❑	Reading Machines/Kurzweil	❑
Other accommodations	❑	Special bookstore section	❑
		Typists	❑

Credit toward degree is not given for remedial courses taken.

Counseling Services

■ Academic	Meets two to three times per academic year
❑ Psychological	
❑ Student Support groups	
■ Vocational	Meets one time per academic year

Tutoring

Individual tutoring is available daily.

Average size of tutoring groups: 3-5

	Individual	Group
Time management	❑	■
Organizational skills	❑	■
Learning strategies	❑	■
Study skills	❑	■
Content area	❑	■
Writing lab	❑	■
Math lab	❑	■

LD PROGRAM STAFF

Total number of LD Program staff (including director):

Full Time: 6 Part Time: 6

There is an advisor/advocate from the LD program available to students. The advisor/advocate meets with faculty and students daily.

There are 2 peer tutors available to work with students.

Key staff person available to work with LD students: Kevin Smith, Learning Specialist/Instructor

University of the Pacific

Stockton, CA

Address: 3601 Pacific Avenue, Stockton, CA, 95211
Admissions telephone: 800 959-2867
Admissions FAX: 209 946-2413
Associate Provost: Marc McGee
Admissions e-mail: admissions@pacific.edu
Web site: http://www.pacific.edu
SAT Code: 4065 ACT Code: 240

LD program name: Services for Students with Disabilities
Coordinator: Lisa Cooper
LD program telephone: 209 946-2879
LD program e-mail: SSD@pacific.edu
LD program enrollment: 180, Total campus enrollment: 3,459

GENERAL

University of the Pacific is a private, coed, four-year institution. 175-acre campus in Stockton (population: 243,771), 40 miles from Sacramento and 85 miles from San Francisco; branch campuses in Sacramento (McGeorge Sch of Law) and San Francisco (Sch of Dentistry). Served by bus and train; airport serves Sacramento. Public transportation serves campus. Semester system.

LD ADMISSIONS

Students complete a separate application and are not simultaneously accepted to the LD program. A member of the LD program does not sit on the admissions committee. A personal interview is not required. Essay is required and may be typed.

SECONDARY SCHOOL REQUIREMENTS

Graduation from secondary school required; GED accepted. The following course distribution required: 4 units of English, 3 units of math, 2 units of science, 2 units of foreign language, 1 unit of history, 3 units of academic electives.

TESTING

SAT Reasoning or ACT required. SAT Subject recommended.

All enrolled freshmen (fall 2004):

Average SAT I Scores:	Verbal: 574	Math: 600
Average ACT Scores:	Composite: 25	

Child Study Team report is not required. A neuropsychological or comprehensive psycho-educational evaluation is required for admission. Tests required as part of this documentation:

- ■ WAIS-IV
- ■ WISC-IV
- □ SATA
- ■ Woodcock-Johnson
- □ Nelson-Denny Reading Test
- ■ Other

UNDERGRADUATE STUDENT BODY

Total undergraduate student enrollment: 1,338 Men, 1,847 Women.

Composition of student body (fall 2004):

	Undergraduate	Freshmen
International	1.4	2.3
Black	2.3	3.0
American Indian	0.3	0.6
Asian-American	33.2	28.5
Hispanic	7.0	9.7
White	45.8	46.1
Unreported	10.0	9.8
	100.0%	100.0%

20% are from out of state. 20% join a fraternity and 21% join a sorority. Average age of full-time undergraduates is 20. 59% of classes have fewer than 20 students, 35% have between 20 and 50 students, 6% have more than 50 students.

STUDENT HOUSING

89% of freshmen live in college housing. Freshmen are required to live on campus. Housing is not guaranteed for all undergraduates. Our total enrollment surpasses our current living spaces. Freshmen and sophomores whose permanent address is outside of 50 miles from the school must reside on campus. Campus can house 2,232 undergraduates.

EXPENSES

Tuition (2005-06): $25,658 per year.
Room: $5,760. Board: $2,718.
There is no additional cost for LD program/services.

LD SERVICES

LD program size is not limited.

LD services available to:

■ Freshmen ■ Sophomores ■ Juniors ■ Seniors

Academic Accommodations

Curriculum		In class	
Foreign language waiver	□	Early syllabus	□
Lighter course load	■	Note takers in class	□
Math waiver	□	Priority seating	□
Other special classes	□	Tape recorders	□
Priority registrations	□	Videotaped classes	□
Substitution of courses	□	Text on tape	□
Exams		**Services**	
Extended time	■	Diagnostic tests	□
Oral exams	□	Learning centers	■
Take home exams	□	Proofreaders	□
Exams on tape or computer	□	Readers	□
Untimed exams	□	Reading Machines/Kurzweil	■
Other accommodations	□	Special bookstore section	□
		Typists	□

Credit toward degree is not given for remedial courses taken.

Counseling Services

- ■ Academic
- ■ Psychological
- ■ Student Support groups
- □ Vocational

Tutoring

Individual tutoring is available weekly.

	Individual	Group
Time management	□	□
Organizational skills	□	□
Learning strategies	□	□
Study skills	□	□
Content area	□	□
Writing lab	■	□
Math lab	□	■

LD PROGRAM STAFF

Total number of LD Program staff (including director):

Full Time: 2 Part Time: 2

There is an advisor/advocate from the LD program available to students.

Key staff person available to work with LD students: Lisa Cooper, Coordinator.

LD Program web site: www.pacific.edu

Pacific Oaks College

Pasadena, CA

Address: Five Westmoreland Place, Pasadena, CA, 91103
Admissions telephone: 800 684-0900
Admissions FAX: 626 577-3502
Director of Admissions: Teresa Cook
Admissions e-mail: admissions@pacificoaks.edu
Web site: http://www.pacificoaks.edu
SAT Code: 482

LD program name: Care Center
Director of care: Patricia Meda
LD program telephone: 626 397-1338
LD program e-mail: pmeda@pacificoaks.edu
LD program enrollment: 1, Total campus enrollment: 208

GENERAL

Pacific Oaks College is a private, coed, graduate institution. Four-acre, suburban campus in Pasadena (population: 133,936), 10 miles from Los Angeles; branch campuses in Oakland and Seattle. Served by bus; major airport and train serve Los Angeles; smaller airport serves Burbank (10 miles). Public transportation serves campus. Semester system.

LD ADMISSIONS

A personal interview is not required. Essay is required and may be typed.

TESTING

Child Study Team report is not required. Tests required as part of this documentation:

- [ ] WAIS-IV
- [ ] WISC-IV
- [ ] SATA
- [ ] Woodcock-Johnson
- [ ] Nelson-Denny Reading Test
- [ ] Other

UNDERGRADUATE STUDENT BODY

Total undergraduate student enrollment: 19 Men, 239 Women.

Composition of student body (fall 2004):

	Freshmen
International	0.5
Black	12.5
American Indian	1.9
Asian-American	5.8
Hispanic	35.1
White	26.9
Unreported	17.3
	100.0%

20% are from out of state.

STUDENT HOUSING

Housing is not guaranteed for all undergraduates.

EXPENSES

Tuition (2005-06): $16,320 per year.

There is no additional cost for LD program/services.

LD SERVICES

LD program size is not limited.

LD services available to:

- [ ] Freshmen
- [ ] Sophomores
- [x] Juniors
- [x] Seniors

Academic Accommodations

Curriculum

- [ ] Foreign language waiver
- [ ] Lighter course load
- [ ] Math waiver
- [ ] Other special classes
- [ ] Priority registrations
- [ ] Substitution of courses

Exams

- [ ] Extended time
- [ ] Oral exams
- [ ] Take home exams
- [ ] Exams on tape or computer
- [ ] Untimed exams
- [ ] Other accommodations

In class

- [ ] Early syllabus
- [x] Note takers in class
- [ ] Priority seating
- [ ] Tape recorders
- [ ] Videotaped classes
- [ ] Text on tape

Services

- [ ] Diagnostic tests
- [ ] Learning centers
- [ ] Proofreaders
- [ ] Readers
- [ ] Reading Machines/Kurzweil
- [ ] Special bookstore section
- [ ] Typists

Credit toward degree is not given for remedial courses taken.

Counseling Services

- [x] Academic
- [ ] Psychological
- [ ] Student Support groups
- [x] Vocational

Tutoring

Individual tutoring is available daily.

Average size of tutoring groups: 1

	Individual	Group
Time management	[x]	[ ]
Organizational skills	[x]	[ ]
Learning strategies	[x]	[ ]
Study skills	[ ]	[ ]
Content area	[ ]	[ ]
Writing lab	[ ]	[ ]
Math lab	[ ]	[ ]

LD PROGRAM STAFF

Total number of LD Program staff (including director):

Full Time: 4 Part Time: 4

There is an advisor/advocate from the LD program available to students.

Key staff person available to work with LD students: Patricia Meda, Director of care.

Pacific Union College

Angwin, CA

Address: One Angwin Avenue, Angwin, CA, 94508
Admissions telephone: 800 862-6336, 800 862-7080
Admissions FAX: 707 965-6432
Director of Admissions: Sean Kootsey
Admissions e-mail: enroll@puc.edu
Web site: http://www.puc.edu
SAT Code: 4600 ACT Code: 362

LD program name: Disabilities Support Services
Disabilities Support Services Coordinator: Nancy Jacobo
LD program telephone: 707 965-7685
LD program e-mail: njacobo@puc.edu
LD program enrollment: 125, Total campus enrollment: 1,545

GENERAL

Pacific Union College is a private, coed, four-year institution. 200-acre campus in Angwin (population: 3,148), 65 miles from San Francisco and 75 miles from Sacramento; branch campuses in Hanford and Los Angeles and in Orlando, Fla. Major airports serve San Francisco and Sacramento; bus serves Napa (30 miles). Quarter system.

LD ADMISSIONS

Students do not complete a separate application and are not simultaneously accepted to the LD program. A member of the LD program does not sit on the admissions committee. High school waivers are accepted for math and foreign language. A personal interview is not required. Essay is not required.

SECONDARY SCHOOL REQUIREMENTS

Graduation from secondary school required; GED accepted. The following course distribution required: 4 units of English, 2 units of math, 1 unit of science, 1 unit of history.

TESTING

All enrolled freshmen (fall 2004):

Average SAT I Scores: Verbal: 554 Math: 515
Average ACT Scores: Composite: 21

Child Study Team report is not required. A neuropsychological or comprehensive psycho-educational evaluation is required for admission. Must be dated within 36 months of application. Tests required as part of this documentation:

- [x] WAIS-IV
- [x] WISC-IV
- [x] SATA
- [x] Woodcock-Johnson
- [x] Nelson-Denny Reading Test
- [ ] Other

UNDERGRADUATE STUDENT BODY

Total undergraduate student enrollment: 695 Men, 818 Women.

Composition of student body (fall 2004):

	Undergraduate	Freshmen
International	5.5	7.5
Black	6.1	3.9
American Indian	0.9	0.6
Asian-American	21.5	20.2
Hispanic	12.4	10.9
White	44.5	43.0
Unreported	9.1	13.9
	100.0%	100.0%

21% are from out of state. Average age of full-time undergraduates is 19. 62% of classes have fewer than 20 students, 33% have between 20 and 50 students, 5% have more than 50 students.

STUDENT HOUSING

94% of freshmen live in college housing. Housing is not guaranteed for all undergraduates. Campus can house 1,288 undergraduates. Single rooms are available for students with medical or special needs. A medical note is required.

EXPENSES

Tuition (2005-06): $18,990 per year.

Room: $3,312. Board: $2,118.
There is no additional cost for LD program/services.

LD SERVICES

LD program size is not limited.

LD services available to:

- [x] Freshmen
- [x] Sophomores
- [x] Juniors
- [x] Seniors

Academic Accommodations

Curriculum		In class	
Foreign language waiver	[ ]	Early syllabus	[ ]
Lighter course load	[x]	Note takers in class	[x]
Math waiver	[ ]	Priority seating	[x]
Other special classes	[ ]	Tape recorders	[x]
Priority registrations	[ ]	Videotaped classes	[ ]
Substitution of courses	[x]	Text on tape	[x]
Exams		**Services**	
Extended time	[x]	Diagnostic tests	[x]
Oral exams	[x]	Learning centers	[x]
Take home exams	[ ]	Proofreaders	[x]
Exams on tape or computer	[x]	Readers	[x]
Untimed exams	[ ]	Reading Machines/Kurzweil	[x]
Other accommodations	[x]	Special bookstore section	[ ]
		Typists	[x]

Credit toward degree is not given for remedial courses taken.

Counseling Services

- [x] Academic
- [x] Psychological
- [x] Student Support groups
- [ ] Vocational

Tutoring

Individual tutoring is available weekly.

Average size of tutoring groups: 5

	Individual	Group
Time management	[x]	[ ]
Organizational skills	[x]	[ ]
Learning strategies	[x]	[ ]
Study skills	[x]	[ ]
Content area	[ ]	[ ]
Writing lab	[x]	[ ]
Math lab	[x]	[ ]

LD PROGRAM STAFF

Total number of LD Program staff (including director):

Full Time: 1 Part Time: 1

There is an advisor/advocate from the LD program available to students. The advisor/advocate meets with faculty once per month and students five times per month. 25 peer tutors are available to work with LD students.

Key staff person available to work with LD students: Nancy Jacobo, Disabilities Support Services Coordinator.

Patten University

Oakland, CA

Address: 2433 Coolidge Avenue, Oakland, CA, 94601
Admissions telephone: 877 472-8836
Admissions FAX: 510 534-4344
Director of Admissions: Inez Bailey
Admissions e-mail: Admissions@patten.edu
Web site: http://www.patten.edu/
SAT Code: 4620 ACT Code: 369

LD program name: Patten University Learning Center
Director: Clevum Smith
LD program telephone: 510 261-8500, extension 7765
LD program e-mail: inez.bailey@patten.edu
Total campus enrollment: 523

GENERAL

Patten University is a private, coed, four-year institution. Five-acre, urban campus in Oakland (population: 399,484). Served by air, bus, and train. Public transportation serves campus. Semester system.

LD ADMISSIONS

Application Deadline: 07/01. Students do not complete a separate application and are simultaneously accepted to the LD program. A member of the LD program does not sit on the admissions committee. A personal interview is recommended. Essay is required and may be typed. Admissions requirements that may be waived for LD students include timed assessment exams

SECONDARY SCHOOL REQUIREMENTS

Graduation from secondary school required; GED accepted. The following course distribution required: 4 units of English, 3 units of math, 3 units of science, 2 units of foreign language, 3 units of social studies, 3 units of history, 4 units of academic electives.

TESTING

SAT Reasoning or ACT required. SAT Subject required.

All enrolled freshmen (fall 2004):

Average SAT I Scores:	Verbal: 580	Math: 555
Average ACT Scores:	Composite: 25	

Child Study Team report is not required. A neuropsychological or comprehensive psycho-education evaluation is not required for admission. Tests required as part of this documentation:

- ☐ WAIS-IV
- ☐ WISC-IV
- ☐ SATA
- ☐ Woodcock-Johnson
- ☐ Nelson-Denny Reading Test
- ☐ Other

UNDERGRADUATE STUDENT BODY

Total undergraduate student enrollment: 345 Men, 264 Women.

Composition of student body (fall 2004):

	Undergraduate
International	0.0
Black	27.7
American Indian	1.3
Asian-American	38.9
Hispanic	32.1
White	0.0
Unreported	0.0
	100.0%

19% are from out of state. Average age of full-time undergraduates is 24. 91% of classes have fewer than 20 students, 9% have between 20 and 50 students.

STUDENT HOUSING

73% of freshmen live in college housing. Freshmen are not required to live on campus. Housing is guaranteed for all undergraduates. Single rooms are available for students with medical or special needs. A medical note is required.

EXPENSES

Tuition (2005-06): $11,520 per year.

Room & Board: $2,900.

There is no additional cost for LD program/services.

LD SERVICES

LD program size is not limited.

LD services available to:

■ Freshmen ■ Sophomores ■ Juniors ■ Seniors

Academic Accommodations

Curriculum		In class	
Foreign language waiver	☐	Early syllabus	☐
Lighter course load	■	Note takers in class	■
Math waiver	☐	Priority seating	☐
Other special classes	☐	Tape recorders	■
Priority registrations	☐	Videotaped classes	■
Substitution of courses	☐	Text on tape	☐
Exams		**Services**	
Extended time	■	Diagnostic tests	☐
Oral exams	■	Learning centers	■
Take home exams	■	Proofreaders	■
Exams on tape or computer	■	Readers	■
Untimed exams	■	Reading Machines/Kurzweil	☐
Other accommodations	☐	Special bookstore section	☐
		Typists	☐

Credit toward degree is not given for remedial courses taken.

Counseling Services

■	Academic	Meets 32 times per academic year
■	Psychological	Meets 32 times per academic year
☐	Student Support groups	
■	Vocational	Meets 32 times per academic year

Tutoring

Individual tutoring is available daily.

Average size of tutoring groups: 1

	Individual	Group
Time management	■	☐
Organizational skills	■	☐
Learning strategies	■	☐
Study skills	■	☐
Content area	■	☐
Writing lab	■	☐
Math lab	■	☐

LD PROGRAM STAFF

Total number of LD Program staff (including director):

Full Time: 3 Part Time: 3

There is an advisor/advocate from the LD program available to students. The advisor/advocate meets with faculty once per month and students four times per month.

Key staff person available to work with LD students: Clevon Smith, Learning Center Director.

LD Program web site: www.patten.edu

Pepperdine University

Malibu, CA

Address: 24255 Pacific Coast Highway, Malibu, CA, 90263
Admissions telephone: 310 506-4392
Admissions FAX: 310 506-4861
Dean of Admission: Paul Long
Admissions e-mail: admission-seaver@pepperdine.edu
Web site: http://www.pepperdine.edu
SAT Code: 4630   ACT Code: 373

LD program name: Disability Services
Director of Disability Services: Lauren B. Joyce
LD program telephone: 310 506-6500
LD program e-mail: lauren.joyce@pepperdine.edu
LD program enrollment: 131, Total campus enrollment: 3,201

GENERAL

Pepperdine University is a private, coed, four-year institution. 830-acre, suburban campus in Malibu (population: 12,575), 12 miles from Santa Monica and 35 miles from Los Angeles; branch campus (graduate level) in Culver City. Major airport, bus, and train serve Los Angeles. School operates transportation to local shopping areas and to special events. Public transportation serves campus. Semester system.

LD ADMISSIONS

A personal interview is recommended. Essay is not required.

SECONDARY SCHOOL REQUIREMENTS

Graduation from secondary school required; GED accepted.

TESTING

SAT Reasoning or ACT required. SAT Subject recommended.

All enrolled freshmen (fall 2004):

Average SAT I Scores:	Verbal: 594	Math: 609
Average ACT Scores:	Composite: 26	

Child Study Team report is not required. Tests required as part of this documentation:

- [ ] WAIS-IV
- [ ] WISC-IV
- [ ] SATA
- [ ] Woodcock-Johnson
- [ ] Nelson-Denny Reading Test
- [ ] Other

UNDERGRADUATE STUDENT BODY

Total undergraduate student enrollment: 1,158 Men, 1,691 Women.

Composition of student body (fall 2004):

	Undergraduate	Freshmen
International	5.9	6.1
Black	8.5	7.6
American Indian	1.2	1.8
Asian-American	13.8	11.1
Hispanic	9.1	12.6
White	59.3	52.6
Unreported	2.2	8.2
	100.0%	100.0%

50% are from out of state. 24% join a fraternity and 29% join a sorority. Average age of full-time undergraduates is 20. 62% of classes have fewer than 20 students, 34% have between 20 and 50 students, 4% have more than 50 students.

STUDENT HOUSING

100% of freshmen live in college housing. Freshmen are required to live on campus. Housing is guaranteed for all undergraduates. Campus can house 1,902 undergraduates. Single rooms are available for students with medical or special needs. A medical note is required.

EXPENSES

Tuition (2005-06): $30,770 per year.
Room: $7,000. Board: $2,100.

There is no additional cost for LD program/services.

LD SERVICES

LD program size is not limited.

LD services available to:

- [x] Freshmen
- [x] Sophomores
- [x] Juniors
- [x] Seniors

Academic Accommodations

Curriculum		**In class**	
Foreign language waiver	[ ]	Early syllabus	[ ]
Lighter course load	[ ]	Note takers in class	[x]
Math waiver	[ ]	Priority seating	[x]
Other special classes	[ ]	Tape recorders	[x]
Priority registrations	[x]	Videotaped classes	[ ]
Substitution of courses	[ ]	Text on tape	[ ]
Exams		**Services**	
Extended time	[x]	Diagnostic tests	[x]
Oral exams	[x]	Learning centers	[ ]
Take home exams	[ ]	Proofreaders	[ ]
Exams on tape or computer	[ ]	Readers	[x]
Untimed exams	[ ]	Reading Machines/Kurzweil	[x]
Other accommodations	[ ]	Special bookstore section	[ ]
		Typists	[ ]

Credit toward degree is not given for remedial courses taken.

Counseling Services

- [ ] Academic
- [ ] Psychological
- [ ] Student Support groups
- [ ] Vocational

Tutoring

Individual tutoring is not available.

	Individual	Group
Time management	[ ]	[ ]
Organizational skills	[ ]	[ ]
Learning strategies	[ ]	[ ]
Study skills	[ ]	[ ]
Content area	[ ]	[ ]
Writing lab	[ ]	[ ]
Math lab	[ ]	[ ]

LD PROGRAM STAFF

Total number of LD Program staff (including director):

Full Time: 2   Part Time: 2

There is an advisor/advocate from the LD program available to students.

Key staff person available to work with LD students: Lauren B. Joyce, Director of Disability Services.

LD Program web site: www.pepperdine.edu/disabilityservices/

Pitzer College

Claremont, CA

Address: 1050 North Mills Avenue, Claremont, CA, 91711-6101
Admissions telephone: 909 621-8129
Admissions FAX: 909 621-8770
Vice President for Admission and Financial Aid: Arnaldo Rodriguez
Admissions e-mail: admission@pitzer.edu
Web site: http://www.pitzer.edu
SAT Code: 4619 ACT Code: 363

LD program name: Academic Support Services
Director of Academic Support Services: Rochelle D. Brown
LD program telephone: 909 607-3553
LD program e-mail: rochelle_brown@pitzer.edu
LD program enrollment: 91, Total campus enrollment: 927

GENERAL

Pitzer College is a private, coed, four-year institution. 35-acre campus in Claremont (population: 33,998), 35 miles from Los Angeles. Major airport serves Ontario (10 miles); bus and train serve Pomona (five miles). Public transportation serves campus. Semester system.

LD ADMISSIONS

Application Deadline: 01/15. Students do not complete a separate application and are simultaneously accepted to the LD program. A member of the LD program does not sit on the admissions committee. A personal interview is recommended. Essay is required and may be typed.

25 applications were offered admission, and 25 enrolled.

SECONDARY SCHOOL REQUIREMENTS

Graduation from secondary school required; GED accepted.

TESTING

SAT Subject recommended.

All enrolled freshmen (fall 2004):

Average SAT I Scores: Verbal: 633 Math: 613

Child Study Team report is not required. A neuropsychological or comprehensive psycho-educational evaluation is required for admission. Must be dated within 36 months of application. Tests required as part of this documentation:

- [x] WAIS-IV
- [x] WISC-IV
- [x] SATA
- [x] Woodcock-Johnson
- [x] Nelson-Denny Reading Test
- [ ] Other

UNDERGRADUATE STUDENT BODY

Total undergraduate student enrollment: 346 Men, 575 Women.

Composition of student body (fall 2004):

	Undergraduate	Freshmen
International	1.8	2.5
Black	5.8	5.5
American Indian	0.5	0.8
Asian-American	11.2	10.2
Hispanic	7.6	12.8
White	50.7	44.4
Unreported	22.4	23.8
	100.0%	100.0%

46% are from out of state. Average age of full-time undergraduates is 21. 68% of classes have fewer than 20 students, 30% have between 20 and 50 students, 02% have more than 50 students.

STUDENT HOUSING

97% of freshmen live in college housing. Freshmen are required to live on campus. Housing is not guaranteed for all undergraduates. Senior year cannot be guaranteed. Campus can house 634 undergraduates. Single rooms are not available for students with medical or special needs.

EXPENSES

Tuition (2005-06): $29,520 per year.
Room: $5,402. Board: $3,230.
There is no additional cost for LD program/services.

LD SERVICES

LD program size is not limited.

LD services available to:

- [x] Freshmen
- [x] Sophomores
- [x] Juniors
- [x] Seniors

Academic Accommodations

Curriculum		In class	
Foreign language waiver	[ ]	Early syllabus	[ ]
Lighter course load	[x]	Note takers in class	[x]
Math waiver	[ ]	Priority seating	[ ]
Other special classes	[ ]	Tape recorders	[x]
Priority registrations	[ ]	Videotaped classes	[ ]
Substitution of courses	[ ]	Text on tape	[ ]
Exams		**Services**	
Extended time	[x]	Diagnostic tests	[ ]
Oral exams	[ ]	Learning centers	[ ]
Take home exams	[ ]	Proofreaders	[ ]
Exams on tape or computer	[ ]	Readers	[x]
Untimed exams	[ ]	Reading Machines/Kurzweil	[x]
Other accommodations	[ ]	Special bookstore section	[ ]
		Typists	[ ]

Credit toward degree is not given for remedial courses taken.

Counseling Services

- [x] Academic
- [x] Psychological
- [x] Student Support groups
- [x] Vocational

Tutoring

Individual tutoring is available daily.

Average size of tutoring groups: 4

	Individual	Group
Time management	[x]	[x]
Organizational skills	[x]	[x]
Learning strategies	[x]	[x]
Study skills	[x]	[x]
Content area	[x]	[x]
Writing lab	[x]	[x]
Math lab	[x]	[x]

UNIQUE LD PROGRAM FEATURES

All services are provided as often as needed by the students.

LD PROGRAM STAFF

Total number of LD Program staff (including director):

Full Time: 1 Part Time: 1

There is an advisor/advocate from the LD program available to students. 12 peer tutors are available to work with LD students.

Key staff person available to work with LD students: Rochelle D. Brown, Director of Academic Support Services.

Point Loma Nazarene University

San Diego, CA

Address: 3900 Lomaland Drive, San Diego, CA, 92106
Admissions telephone: 800 773-7770
Admissions FAX: 619 849-2601
Director of Admissions: Scott Shoemaker
Admissions e-mail: admissions@ptloma.edu
Web site: http://www.ptloma.edu
SAT Code: 4605 ACT Code: 370

LD program name: Academic Advising Office
Director of Special Academic Services: Jacqueline Escalante
LD program telephone: 619 849-2486
LD program e-mail: JacquelineEscalante@ptloma.edu
LD program enrollment: 79, Total campus enrollment: 2,361

GENERAL

Point Loma Nazarene University is a private, coed, four-year institution. 90-acre campus in San Diego (population: 1,223,400), five miles from downtown area; off-campus classes held in Arcadia and Bakersfield. Served by air, bus, and train. Public transportation serves campus. Semester system.

LD ADMISSIONS

Students do not complete a separate application and are not simultaneously accepted to the LD program. A personal interview is required. Essay is required and may be typed.

SECONDARY SCHOOL REQUIREMENTS

Graduation from secondary school required; GED accepted. The following course distribution required: 4 units of English, 2 units of math, 1 unit of science, 2 units of foreign language, 1 unit of history.

TESTING

SAT Reasoning required; ACT may be substituted. SAT Subject recommended.

All enrolled freshmen (fall 2004):

Average SAT I Scores:	Verbal: 572	Math: 575
Average ACT Scores:	Composite: 24	

Child Study Team report is not required. A neuropsychological or comprehensive psycho-educational evaluation is required for admission. Must be dated within 36 months of application. Tests required as part of this documentation:

- ■ WAIS-IV
- ■ WISC-IV
- ■ SATA
- ■ Woodcock-Johnson
- ■ Nelson-Denny Reading Test
- ☐ Other

UNDERGRADUATE STUDENT BODY

Total undergraduate student enrollment: 952 Men, 1,401 Women.

Composition of student body (fall 2004):

	Undergraduate	Freshmen
International	0.1	0.6
Black	2.6	2.3
American Indian	0.9	0.9
Asian-American	5.0	5.1
Hispanic	11.2	8.3
White	79.1	82.0
Unreported	1.1	0.8
	100.0%	100.0%

22% are from out of state. Average age of full-time undergraduates is 20. 41% of classes have fewer than 20 students, 54% have between 20 and 50 students, 5% have more than 50 students.

STUDENT HOUSING

Freshmen are required to live on campus. Housing is guaranteed for all undergraduates. Campus can house 1,637 undergraduates.

EXPENSES

Tuition (2005-06): $20,200 per year.

Room & Board: $7,150.

There is no additional cost for LD program/services.

LD SERVICES

LD program size is not limited.

LD services available to:

■ Freshmen ■ Sophomores ■ Juniors ■ Seniors

Academic Accommodations

Curriculum		**In class**	
Foreign language waiver	■	Early syllabus	■
Lighter course load	■	Note takers in class	■
Math waiver	☐	Priority seating	☐
Other special classes	☐	Tape recorders	■
Priority registrations	☐	Videotaped classes	☐
Substitution of courses	☐	Text on tape	■
Exams		**Services**	
Extended time	■	Diagnostic tests	☐
Oral exams	■	Learning centers	☐
Take home exams	☐	Proofreaders	■
Exams on tape or computer	☐	Readers	☐
Untimed exams	■	Reading Machines/Kurzweil	☐
Other accommodations	☐	Special bookstore section	☐
		Typists	☐

Credit toward degree is not given for remedial courses taken.

Counseling Services

- ■ Academic
- ■ Psychological
- ☐ Student Support groups
- ■ Vocational

Tutoring

Individual tutoring is available daily.

	Individual	Group
Time management	■	☐
Organizational skills	■	☐
Learning strategies	■	☐
Study skills	■	☐
Content area	☐	☐
Writing lab	☐	☐
Math lab	☐	☐

LD PROGRAM STAFF

Total number of LD Program staff (including director):

Full Time: 1 Part Time: 1

There is an advisor/advocate from the LD program available to students. 30 peer tutors are available to work with LD students.

Key staff person available to work with LD students: Jacqueline Escalante, Director of Special Academic Services.

Pomona College

Claremont, CA

Address: 550 North College Avenue, Claremont, CA, 91711
Admissions telephone: 909 621-8134
Admissions FAX: 909 621-8952
Dean of Admissions: Bruce Poch
Admissions e-mail: admissions@pomona.edu
Web site: http://www.pomona.edu
SAT Code: 4607 ACT Code: 372

Associate Dean of Students: Toni Clark
LD program telephone: 909 621-8017
LD program e-mail: Toni_Clark@pomona.edu
Total campus enrollment: 1,559

GENERAL

Pomona College is a private, coed, four-year institution. 140-acre campus in Claremont (population: 33,998), 35 miles from downtown Los Angeles. Served by bus and train; airport serves Ontario (10 miles); major airports serve Los Angeles. School operates transportation to downtown Los Angeles, Pasadena, Westwood, and UCLA. Public transportation serves campus. Semester system.

LD ADMISSIONS

Students do not complete a separate application and are not simultaneously accepted to the LD program. A member of the LD program does not sit on the admissions committee. A personal interview is recommended. Essay is required and may be typed.

SECONDARY SCHOOL REQUIREMENTS

Graduation from secondary school not required. The following course distribution required: 4 units of English, 3 units of math, 3 units of science, 3 units of foreign language, 2 units of social studies.

TESTING

SAT Subject recommended.

All enrolled freshmen (fall 2004):

Average SAT I Scores:	Verbal: 726	Math: 717
Average ACT Scores:	Composite: 32	

Child Study Team report is not required. A neuropsychological or comprehensive psycho-educational evaluation is required for admission. Must be dated within 36 months of application. Tests required as part of this documentation:

- ■ WAIS-IV
- ❑ WISC-IV
- ■ SATA
- ■ Woodcock-Johnson
- ❑ Nelson-Denny Reading Test
- ❑ Other

UNDERGRADUATE STUDENT BODY

Total undergraduate student enrollment: 800 Men, 765 Women.

Composition of student body (fall 2004):

	Undergraduate	Freshmen
International	3.8	2.5
Black	8.1	6.2
American Indian	0.0	0.5
Asian-American	13.7	12.7
Hispanic	9.6	8.7
White	51.4	55.7
Unreported	13.4	13.7
	100.0%	100.0%

63% are from out of state. 5% join a fraternity. Average age of full-time undergraduates is 20. 73% of classes have fewer than 20 students, 26% have between 20 and 50 students, 1% have more than 50 students.

STUDENT HOUSING

100% of freshmen live in college housing. Freshmen are required to live on campus. Housing is guaranteed for all undergraduates. Campus can house 1,361 undergraduates. Single rooms are available for students with medical or special needs. A medical note is required.

EXPENSES

Tuition (2005-06): $29,650 per year.
Room: $6,851. Board: $4,000.
There is no additional cost for LD program/services.

LD SERVICES

LD program size is not limited.

LD services available to:

■ Freshmen ■ Sophomores ■ Juniors ■ Seniors

Academic Accommodations

Curriculum		**In class**	
Foreign language waiver	❑	Early syllabus	❑
Lighter course load	■	Note takers in class	■
Math waiver	❑	Priority seating	❑
Other special classes	❑	Tape recorders	■
Priority registrations	❑	Videotaped classes	❑
Substitution of courses	❑	Text on tape	❑
Exams		**Services**	
Extended time	■	Diagnostic tests	❑
Oral exams	■	Learning centers	❑
Take home exams	❑	Proofreaders	❑
Exams on tape or computer	❑	Readers	■
Untimed exams	❑	Reading Machines/Kurzweil	❑
Other accommodations	❑	Special bookstore section	❑
		Typists	❑

Credit toward degree is not given for remedial courses taken.

Counseling Services

- ■ Academic
- ■ Psychological — Meets 14 times per academic year
- ■ Student Support groups
- ❑ Vocational

Tutoring

Individual tutoring is available weekly.

Average size of tutoring groups: 1

	Individual	Group
Time management	❑	❑
Organizational skills	❑	❑
Learning strategies	❑	❑
Study skills	❑	❑
Content area	❑	❑
Writing lab	❑	❑
Math lab	❑	❑

LD PROGRAM STAFF

Total number of LD Program staff (including director):

Full Time: 1 Part Time: 1

There is an advisor/advocate from the LD program available to students.

Key staff person available to work with LD students: Toni Clark, Associate Dean of Students.

University of Redlands

Redlands, CA

Address: P.O. Box 3080, Redlands, CA, 92373
Admissions telephone: 800 455-5064
Admissions FAX: 909 335-4089
Dean of Admissions: Paul M. Driscoll
Admissions e-mail: admissions@redlands.edu
Web site: http://www.redlands.edu
SAT Code: 4848   ACT Code: 464

LD program name: Disabled Student Services
Director: Judy Bowman
LD program telephone: 909 335-4079
LD program e-mail: judy_bowman@redlands.edu
LD program enrollment: 281, Total campus enrollment: 3,295

GENERAL

University of Redlands is a private, coed, four-year institution. 140-acre campus in Redlands (population: 63,591), 65 miles from Los Angeles and 45 miles from Palm Springs. Major airport serves Ontario (30 miles); bus and train serve San Bernardino (15 miles).

LD ADMISSIONS

Students do not complete a separate application and are not simultaneously accepted to the LD program. A member of the LD program does not sit on the admissions committee. High school waivers are accepted for math and foreign language. A personal interview is recommended. Essay is required and may be typed. Math and foreign language requirements may be waived depending on documentation.

SECONDARY SCHOOL REQUIREMENTS

Graduation from secondary school required; GED accepted. The following course distribution required: 4 units of English, 3 units of math, 2 units of science, 2 units of foreign language, 2 units of social studies.

TESTING

SAT Reasoning or ACT required. SAT Subject recommended.

All enrolled freshmen (fall 2004):

Average SAT I Scores:	Verbal: 584	Math: 580
Average ACT Scores:	Composite: 24	

Child Study Team report is not required. A neuropsychological or comprehensive psycho-educational evaluation is required for admission. Must be dated within 36 months of application. Tests required as part of this documentation:

- ■ WAIS-IV
- ☐ WISC-IV
- ☐ SATA
- ■ Woodcock-Johnson
- ☐ Nelson-Denny Reading Test
- ☐ Other

UNDERGRADUATE STUDENT BODY

Total undergraduate student enrollment: 816 Men, 1,130 Women.

Composition of student body (fall 2004):

	Undergraduate	Freshmen
International	0.5	0.9
Black	1.7	4.0
American Indian	0.5	0.7
Asian-American	6.0	6.1
Hispanic	13.6	15.1
White	57.8	57.2
Unreported	19.9	16.0
	100.0%	100.0%

27% are from out of state. 2% join a fraternity and 1% join a sorority. Average age of full-time undergraduates is 25. 75% of classes have fewer than 20 students, 24% have between 20 and 50 students, 1% have more than 50 students.

STUDENT HOUSING

93% of freshmen live in college housing. Freshmen are required to live on campus. Housing is guaranteed for all undergraduates. Campus can house 1,705 undergraduates. Single rooms are available for students with medical or special needs. A medical note is required.

EXPENSES

Tuition (2005-06): $26,864 per year.
Room: $5,020. Board: $3,980.
There is no additional cost for LD program/services.

LD SERVICES

LD program size is not limited.

LD services available to:

■ Freshmen ■ Sophomores ■ Juniors ■ Seniors

Academic Accommodations

Curriculum		**In class**	
Foreign language waiver	■	Early syllabus	☐
Lighter course load	■	Note takers in class	■
Math waiver	■	Priority seating	☐
Other special classes	☐	Tape recorders	■
Priority registrations	☐	Videotaped classes	☐
Substitution of courses	■	Text on tape	■
Exams		**Services**	
Extended time	■	Diagnostic tests	☐
Oral exams	■	Learning centers	☐
Take home exams	☐	Proofreaders	☐
Exams on tape or computer	☐	Readers	■
Untimed exams	■	Reading Machines/Kurzweil	☐
Other accommodations	■	Special bookstore section	☐
		Typists	■

Credit toward degree is not given for remedial courses taken.

Counseling Services

- ■ Academic
- ■ Psychological
- ☐ Student Support groups
- ■ Vocational

Tutoring

Individual tutoring is available weekly.

Average size of tutoring groups: 3

	Individual	Group
Time management	■	■
Organizational skills	■	■
Learning strategies	■	■
Study skills	■	■
Content area	■	☐
Writing lab	■	☐
Math lab	■	☐

LD PROGRAM STAFF

Total number of LD Program staff (including director):

Full Time: 1   Part Time: 1

There is an advisor/advocate from the LD program available to students. 35 peer tutors are available to work with LD students.

Key staff person available to work with LD students: Judy Bowman, Director, Academic Support and Disabled Student Services.

Saint Mary's College of California

Moraga, CA

Address: 1928 St. Mary's Road, Moraga, CA, 94556
Admissions telephone: 800 800-4762
Admissions FAX: 925 376-7193
Dean of Admissions: Dorothy Jones
Admissions e-mail: smcadmit@stmarys-ca.edu
Web site: http://www.stmarys-ca.edu
SAT Code: 4675 ACT Code: 386

LD program name: Academic Support Center
LD program address: P.O. Box 3326, Moraga, CA, 94575
Director Academic Support Center: Jeannine Chavez-Parfitt
LD program telephone: 925 631-4358
LD program e-mail: jparfitt@st.marys-ca.edu
LD program enrollment: 250, Total campus enrollment: 2,440

GENERAL

Saint Mary's College of California is a private, coed, four-year institution. 420-acre campus in Moraga (population: 16,290), 12 miles from Oakland and 20 miles from San Francisco. Major airport, bus, and train serve Oakland; other airport serves San Francisco. Public transportation serves campus. 4-1-4 system.

LD ADMISSIONS

A member of the LD program does not sit on the admissions committee. High school waivers are accepted for math and foreign language. A personal interview is recommended. Essay is required and may be typed. Course substitutions may be accepted but requirements may not be waived.

SECONDARY SCHOOL REQUIREMENTS

Graduation from secondary school required; GED accepted. The following course distribution required: 4 units of English, 3 units of math, 2 units of science, 2 units of foreign language, 1 unit of social studies, 1 unit of history, 2 units of academic electives.

TESTING

SAT Reasoning or ACT required. SAT Subject recommended.

All enrolled freshmen (fall 2004):

Average SAT I Scores: Verbal: 547 Math: 548

Child Study Team report is not required. A neuropsychological or comprehensive psycho-educational evaluation is required for admission. Must be dated within 3 months of application. Tests required as part of this documentation:

- ☒ WAIS-IV
- ☐ WISC-IV
- ☒ SATA
- ☒ Woodcock-Johnson
- ☒ Nelson-Denny Reading Test
- ☐ Other

UNDERGRADUATE STUDENT BODY

Total undergraduate student enrollment: 1,177 Men, 1,884 Women.

Composition of student body (fall 2004):

	Undergraduate	Freshmen
International	2.6	2.6
Black	7.2	6.2
American Indian	0.5	0.7
Asian-American	9.8	10.0
Hispanic	22.7	19.3
White	49.8	55.1
Unreported	7.4	6.1
	100.0%	100.0%

11% are from out of state. Average age of full-time undergraduates is 21. 53% of classes have fewer than 20 students, 47% have between 20 and 50 students.

STUDENT HOUSING

95% of freshmen live in college housing. Freshmen are not required to live on campus. Housing is guaranteed for all undergraduates. Campus can house 1,577 undergraduates. Single rooms are available for students with medical or special needs. A medical note is required.

EXPENSES

Tuition (2005-06): $27,130 per year.

Room: $5,590. Board: $4,420.

There is no additional cost for LD program/services.

LD SERVICES

LD program size is not limited.

LD services available to:

☒ Freshmen ☒ Sophomores ☒ Juniors ☒ Seniors

Academic Accommodations

Curriculum		In class	
Foreign language waiver	☒	Early syllabus	☒
Lighter course load	☒	Note takers in class	☒
Math waiver	☒	Priority seating	☐
Other special classes	☐	Tape recorders	☒
Priority registrations	☒	Videotaped classes	☐
Substitution of courses	☒	Text on tape	☐
Exams		**Services**	
Extended time	☒	Diagnostic tests	☐
Oral exams	☒	Learning centers	☐
Take home exams	☐	Proofreaders	☐
Exams on tape or computer	☒	Readers	☒
Untimed exams	☒	Reading Machines/Kurzweil	☒
Other accommodations	☒	Special bookstore section	☐
		Typists	☒

Credit toward degree is given for remedial courses taken.

Counseling Services

- ☒ Academic
- ☐ Psychological
- ☐ Student Support groups
- ☐ Vocational

Tutoring

Individual tutoring is available daily.

Average size of tutoring groups: 8

	Individual	Group
Time management	☒	☒
Organizational skills	☐	☐
Learning strategies	☒	☒
Study skills	☒	☒
Content area	☐	☐
Writing lab	☒	☒
Math lab	☒	☒

LD PROGRAM STAFF

Total number of LD Program staff (including director):

Full Time: 1 Part Time: 1

There is an advisor/advocate from the LD program available to students. 80 peer tutors are available to work with LD students.

Key staff person available to work with LD students: Jeannine Chavez-Parfitt, Director Academic Support Center.

University of San Diego

San Diego, CA

Address: 5998 Alcala Park, San Diego, CA, 92110-2492
Admissions telephone: 800 248-4873
Admissions FAX: 619 260-6836
Director of Admissions: Stephen F. Pultz
Admissions e-mail: admissions@SanDiego.edu
Web site: http://www.SanDiego.edu
SAT Code: 4849 ACT Code: 394

Director of Disability Services: Ken Chep, Ed.S
LD program telephone: 619 260-4655
LD program e-mail: kchep@SanDiego.edu
Total campus enrollment: 4,908

GENERAL

University of San Diego is a private, coed, four-year institution. 180-acre, suburban campus in San Diego (population: 1,223,400). Served by air, bus, and train. School operates transportation on campus. Public transportation serves campus. 4-1-4 system.

LD ADMISSIONS

A personal interview is not required. Essay is required and may be typed.

SECONDARY SCHOOL REQUIREMENTS

Graduation from secondary school required; GED accepted.

TESTING

SAT Reasoning required; ACT may be substituted. SAT Subject required.

All enrolled freshmen (fall 2004):

Average SAT I Scores: Verbal: 575 Math: 592
Average ACT Scores: Composite: 26

Child Study Team report is not required. Tests required as part of this documentation:

☐ WAIS-IV ☐ Woodcock-Johnson
☐ WISC-IV ☐ Nelson-Denny Reading Test
☐ SATA ☐ Other

UNDERGRADUATE STUDENT BODY

Total undergraduate student enrollment: 1,944 Men, 2,865 Women.

Composition of student body (fall 2004):

	Undergraduate	Freshmen
International	0.5	1.9
Black	1.4	2.0
American Indian	0.4	1.0
Asian-American	7.7	7.2
Hispanic	12.4	15.3
White	70.8	67.7
Unreported	6.8	4.9
	100.0%	100.0%

40% are from out of state. 10% join a fraternity and 19% join a sorority. Average age of full-time undergraduates is 20. 39% of classes have fewer than 20 students, 61% have between 20 and 50 students.

STUDENT HOUSING

94% of freshmen live in college housing. Freshmen are required to live on campus. Housing is guaranteed for all undergraduates.

EXPENSES

Tuition (2005-06): $28,760 per year.
Room & Board: $11,330.

There is no additional cost for LD program/services.

LD SERVICES

LD program size is not limited.

LD services available to:

☐ Freshmen ☐ Sophomores ☐ Juniors ☐ Seniors

Academic Accommodations

Curriculum		**In class**	
Foreign language waiver	☐	Early syllabus	☐
Lighter course load	☒	Note takers in class	☒
Math waiver	☐	Priority seating	☐
Other special classes	☐	Tape recorders	☒
Priority registrations	☐	Videotaped classes	☐
Substitution of courses	☐	Text on tape	☐
Exams		**Services**	
Extended time	☒	Diagnostic tests	☐
Oral exams	☐	Learning centers	☐
Take home exams	☐	Proofreaders	☐
Exams on tape or computer	☐	Readers	☐
Untimed exams	☐	Reading Machines/Kurzweil	☒
Other accommodations	☐	Special bookstore section	☐
		Typists	☐

Credit toward degree is not given for remedial courses taken.

Counseling Services

☐ Academic
☐ Psychological
☐ Student Support groups
☐ Vocational

Tutoring

	Individual	Group
Time management	☐	☐
Organizational skills	☐	☐
Learning strategies	☐	☐
Study skills	☐	☐
Content area	☐	☐
Writing lab	☐	☐
Math lab	☐	☐

LD PROGRAM STAFF

Total number of LD Program staff (including director):

Full Time: 1 Part Time: 1

Key staff person available to work with LD students: Ken Chep, Ed.S, Director of Disability Services.

San Diego State University

San Diego, CA

Address: 5500 Campanile Drive, San Diego, CA, 92182
Admissions telephone: 619 594-6336
Director of Admissions: Beverly Arata
Admissions e-mail: admissions@sdsu.edu
Web site: http://www.sdsu.edu
SAT Code: 4682 ACT Code: 398

Director, Disabled Student Services: Mary Shojai
LD program telephone: 619 594-6473
LD program enrollment: 217, Total campus enrollment: 26,853

GENERAL

San Diego State University is a public, coed, four-year institution. 300-acre, suburban campus in San Diego (population: 1,223,400); branch campus in Calexico. Served by air, bus, and train. Public transportation serves campus. Semester system.

LD ADMISSIONS

A personal interview is not required. Essay is not required. Requirements are not waived but limited substitutions may be accepted.

For fall 2004, 38 completed self-identified LD applications were received. 16 applications were offered admission, and 16 enrolled.

SECONDARY SCHOOL REQUIREMENTS

Graduation from secondary school required; GED accepted. The following course distribution required: 4 units of English, 3 units of math, 2 units of science, 2 units of foreign language, 1 unit of social studies, 1 unit of history, 1 unit of academic electives.

TESTING

SAT Reasoning or ACT required. SAT Subject recommended.

All enrolled freshmen (fall 2004):

Average SAT I Scores:	Verbal: 529	Math: 550
Average ACT Scores:	Composite: 22	

Child Study Team report is not required. Tests required as part of this documentation:

- ☐ WAIS-IV
- ☐ WISC-IV
- ☐ SATA
- ☐ Woodcock-Johnson
- ☐ Nelson-Denny Reading Test
- ☐ Other

UNDERGRADUATE STUDENT BODY

Total undergraduate student enrollment: 11,867 Men, 16,004 Women.

Composition of student body (fall 2004):

	Undergraduate	Freshmen
International	0.9	2.3
Black	3.5	3.9
American Indian	0.5	0.8
Asian-American	15.6	15.3
Hispanic	19.8	21.7
White	50.7	45.2
Unreported	9.0	10.8
	100.0%	100.0%

3% are from out of state. 9% join a fraternity and 7% join a sorority. 23% of classes have fewer than 20 students, 58% have between 20 and 50 students, 19% have more than 50 students.

STUDENT HOUSING

Freshmen are not required to live on campus. Housing is guaranteed for all undergraduates. Campus can house 3,059 undergraduates. Single rooms are available for students with medical or special needs.

EXPENSES

Tuition (2005-06): $2,520 per year (in-state), $12,690 (out-of-state).

Room & Board: $8,892.
There is no additional cost for LD program/services.

LD SERVICES

LD program size is not limited.

LD services available to:

■ Freshmen ■ Sophomores ■ Juniors ■ Seniors

Academic Accommodations

Curriculum		**In class**	
Foreign language waiver	☐	Early syllabus	☐
Lighter course load	☐	Note takers in class	☐
Math waiver	☐	Priority seating	☐
Other special classes	■	Tape recorders	☐
Priority registrations	☐	Videotaped classes	☐
Substitution of courses	☐	Text on tape	☐
Exams		**Services**	
Extended time	■	Diagnostic tests	☐
Oral exams	☐	Learning centers	■
Take home exams	☐	Proofreaders	☐
Exams on tape or computer	☐	Readers	☐
Untimed exams	☐	Reading Machines/Kurzweil	☐
Other accommodations	☐	Special bookstore section	☐
		Typists	☐

Credit toward degree is not given for remedial courses taken.

Counseling Services

- ☐ Academic
- ☐ Psychological
- ☐ Student Support groups
- ☐ Vocational

Tutoring

	Individual	Group
Time management	☐	☐
Organizational skills	☐	☐
Learning strategies	☐	☐
Study skills	☐	☐
Content area	☐	☐
Writing lab	☐	☐
Math lab	☐	☐

UNIQUE LD PROGRAM FEATURES

Lighter course load and additional time given to complete degree may be reviewed on an individual basis.

LD PROGRAM STAFF

Total number of LD Program staff (including director):

Full Time: 3 Part Time: 3

Key staff person available to work with LD students: Margo Behr, Learning Disabilities Coordinator.

University of San Francisco

San Francisco, CA

Address: Ignatian Heights, San Francisco, CA, 94117-1080
Admissions telephone: 800 CALL-USF
Admissions FAX: 415 422-2217
Director of Admissions: Mike Hughes
Admissions e-mail: admission@usfca.edu
Web site: http://www.usfca.edu
SAT Code: 4850 ACT Code: 466

LD program name: Student Disability Services
Disability Specialist: Teresa Ong
LD program telephone: 415 422-6876
LD program e-mail: ongt@usfca.edu
LD program enrollment: 190, Total campus enrollment: 4,967

GENERAL

University of San Francisco is a private, coed, four-year institution. 55-acre, urban campus in San Francisco (population: 776,733); branch campuses in Cupertino, Fresno, Oakland, Sacramento, San Ramon, and Santa Rosa. Served by air, bus, and train. School operates transportation on campus. Public transportation serves campus. 4-1-4 system.

LD ADMISSIONS

A personal interview is not required. Essay is required and may be typed. Foreign language requirement may be waived.

SECONDARY SCHOOL REQUIREMENTS

Graduation from secondary school required; GED accepted. The following course distribution required: 4 units of English, 3 units of math, 2 units of science, 2 units of foreign language, 3 units of social studies, 6 units of academic electives.

TESTING

SAT Reasoning required; ACT may be substituted. SAT Subject required.

All enrolled freshmen (fall 2004):

Average SAT I Scores:	Verbal: 559	Math: 561
Average ACT Scores:	Composite: 23	

Child Study Team report is not required. A neuropsychological or comprehensive psycho-educational evaluation is required for admission. Tests required as part of this documentation:

- [x] WAIS-IV
- [x] WISC-IV
- [x] SATA
- [x] Woodcock-Johnson
- [x] Nelson-Denny Reading Test
- [ ] Other

UNDERGRADUATE STUDENT BODY

Total undergraduate student enrollment: 1,772 Men, 2,915 Women.

Composition of student body (fall 2004):

	Undergraduate	Freshmen
International	4.4	7.1
Black	5.8	5.3
American Indian	0.5	0.4
Asian-American	26.8	26.0
Hispanic	13.6	13.4
White	38.7	37.4
Unreported	10.2	10.4
	100.0%	100.0%

22% are from out of state. 1% join a fraternity and 1% join a sorority. Average age of full-time undergraduates is 20. 51% of classes have fewer than 20 students, 46% have between 20 and 50 students, 3% have more than 50 students.

STUDENT HOUSING

90% of freshmen live in college housing. Freshmen are required to live on campus. Housing is limited and is not guaranteed for all undergraduates. Campus can house 2,200 undergraduates.

EXPENSES

Tuition (2005-06): $26,680 per year.
Room: $6,500. Board: $3,740.
There is no additional cost for LD program/services.

LD SERVICES

LD program size is not limited.

LD services available to:

- [x] Freshmen
- [x] Sophomores
- [x] Juniors
- [x] Seniors

Academic Accommodations

Curriculum

- [ ] Foreign language waiver
- [x] Lighter course load
- [ ] Math waiver
- [x] Other special classes
- [ ] Priority registrations
- [ ] Substitution of courses

Exams

- [x] Extended time
- [ ] Oral exams
- [ ] Take home exams
- [ ] Exams on tape or computer
- [x] Untimed exams
- [ ] Other accommodations

In class

- [ ] Early syllabus
- [x] Note takers in class
- [ ] Priority seating
- [x] Tape recorders
- [x] Videotaped classes
- [ ] Text on tape

Services

- [x] Diagnostic tests
- [x] Learning centers
- [ ] Proofreaders
- [x] Readers
- [x] Reading Machines/Kurzweil
- [ ] Special bookstore section
- [ ] Typists

Credit toward degree is not given for remedial courses taken.

Counseling Services

- [ ] Academic
- [ ] Psychological
- [ ] Student Support groups
- [ ] Vocational

Tutoring

Individual tutoring is available.

	Individual	Group
Time management	[x]	[ ]
Organizational skills	[x]	[ ]
Learning strategies	[x]	[ ]
Study skills	[x]	[ ]
Content area	[ ]	[ ]
Writing lab	[x]	[ ]
Math lab	[x]	[ ]

LD PROGRAM STAFF

Total number of LD Program staff (including director):

Full Time: 2 Part Time: 2

There is an advisor/advocate from the LD program available to students.

Key staff person available to work with LD students: Tom Merrell, LD Specialist.

San Francisco Art Institute

San Francisco, CA

Address: 800 Chestnut Street, San Francisco, CA, 94133
Admissions telephone: 800 345-SFAI
Admissions FAX: 415 749-4592
Admissions e-mail: admissions@sfai.edu
Web site: http://www.sfai.edu
SAT Code: 4036

Associate Director of Admissions: Renee Talmon
LD program telephone: 415 749-4500
LD program e-mail: rshearer@sfai.edu
Total campus enrollment: 407

GENERAL

San Francisco Art Institute is a private, coed, four-year institution. Four-acre, urban campus in San Francisco (population: 776,733). Served by air, bus, and train; other airport serves Oakland (20 miles). Public transportation serves campus. Semester system.

LD ADMISSIONS

A personal interview is required. Essay is required and may be typed.

SECONDARY SCHOOL REQUIREMENTS

Graduation from secondary school required; GED accepted.

TESTING

Child Study Team report is not required. Tests required as part of this documentation:

☐ WAIS-IV ☐ Woodcock-Johnson
☐ WISC-IV ☐ Nelson-Denny Reading Test
☐ SATA ☐ Other

UNDERGRADUATE STUDENT BODY

Total undergraduate student enrollment: 243 Men, 257 Women.

33% are from out of state.

STUDENT HOUSING

Housing is not guaranteed for all undergraduates. Campus can house 40 undergraduates.

EXPENSES

Tuition (2005-06): $25,640 per year.

Room & Board: $8,100.

There is no additional cost for LD program/services.

LD SERVICES

LD program size is not limited.

LD services available to:

☐ Freshmen ☐ Sophomores ☐ Juniors ☐ Seniors

Academic Accommodations

Curriculum		**In class**	
Foreign language waiver	☐	Early syllabus	☐
Lighter course load	☐	Note takers in class	☒
Math waiver	☐	Priority seating	☐
Other special classes	☐	Tape recorders	☒
Priority registrations	☐	Videotaped classes	☐
Substitution of courses	☐	Text on tape	☐
Exams		**Services**	
Extended time	☐	Diagnostic tests	☐
Oral exams	☐	Learning centers	☒
Take home exams	☐	Proofreaders	☐
Exams on tape or computer	☐	Readers	☐
Untimed exams	☐	Reading Machines/Kurzweil	☐
Other accommodations	☐	Special bookstore section	☐
		Typists	☐

Credit toward degree is not given for remedial courses taken.

Counseling Services

☐ Academic
☐ Psychological
☐ Student Support groups
☐ Vocational

Tutoring

	Individual	Group
Time management	☐	☐
Organizational skills	☐	☐
Learning strategies	☐	☐
Study skills	☐	☐
Content area	☐	☐
Writing lab	☐	☐
Math lab	☐	☐

LD PROGRAM STAFF

Total number of LD Program staff (including director):

Full Time: 1 Part Time: 1

Key staff person available to work with LD students: Susan Greene, Director Center for Individual Learning.

San Francisco State University

San Francisco, CA

Address: 1600 Holloway Avenue, San Francisco, CA, 94132
Admissions telephone: 415 338-1113
Director of Undergraduate Admissions: Patricia Wade
Admissions e-mail: ugadmit@sfsu.edu
Web site: http://www.sfsu.edu
SAT Code: 4684

Total campus enrollment: 22,018

GENERAL

San Francisco State University is a public, coed, four-year institution. 130-acre, urban campus in San Francisco (population: 776,733). Served by air and bus; train serves Oakland (30 miles). School operates transportation to Daly City and public transportation. Public transportation serves campus. Semester system.

LD ADMISSIONS

A personal interview is not required. Essay is required and may be typed. Foreign language requirement may be waived.

SECONDARY SCHOOL REQUIREMENTS

Graduation from secondary school required; GED accepted. The following course distribution required: 4 units of English, 3 units of math, 2 units of science, 2 units of foreign language, 1 unit of social studies, 1 unit of history.

TESTING

SAT Reasoning or ACT required of some applicants. SAT Subject recommended.

Child Study Team report is not required. Tests required as part of this documentation:

- ☐ WAIS-IV
- ☐ WISC-IV
- ☐ SATA
- ☐ Woodcock-Johnson
- ☐ Nelson-Denny Reading Test
- ☐ Other

UNDERGRADUATE STUDENT BODY

Total undergraduate student enrollment: 8,226 Men, 11,940 Women.

Composition of student body (fall 2004):

	Undergraduate	Freshmen
International	1.8	5.6
Black	7.0	6.0
American Indian	1.0	0.9
Asian-American	33.3	31.7
Hispanic	16.2	13.4
White	30.3	27.6
Unreported	10.4	14.8
	100.0%	100.0%

1% are from out of state. 1% join a fraternity and 1% join a sorority. Average age of full-time undergraduates is 23. 24% of classes have fewer than 20 students, 55% have between 20 and 50 students, 21% have more than 50 students.

STUDENT HOUSING

41% of freshmen live in college housing. Freshmen are not required to live on campus.

EXPENSES

Tuition (2005-06): No tuition for in-state, $8,136 (out-of-state).
Room & Board: $8,830-$10,458.

LD SERVICES

LD program size is not limited.

LD services available to:

☐ Freshmen ☐ Sophomores ☐ Juniors ☐ Seniors

Academic Accommodations

Curriculum		In class	
Foreign language waiver	☐	Early syllabus	☐
Lighter course load	☐	Note takers in class	■
Math waiver	☐	Priority seating	☐
Other special classes	■	Tape recorders	☐
Priority registrations	☐	Videotaped classes	☐
Substitution of courses	☐	Text on tape	☐
Exams		**Services**	
Extended time	☐	Diagnostic tests	☐
Oral exams	☐	Learning centers	☐
Take home exams	☐	Proofreaders	☐
Exams on tape or computer	☐	Readers	☐
Untimed exams	☐	Reading Machines/Kurzweil	☐
Other accommodations	☐	Special bookstore section	☐
		Typists	☐

Counseling Services

- ☐ Academic
- ☐ Psychological
- ☐ Student Support groups
- ☐ Vocational

Tutoring

	Individual	Group
Time management	☐	☐
Organizational skills	☐	☐
Learning strategies	☐	☐
Study skills	☐	☐
Content area	☐	☐
Writing lab	☐	☐
Math lab	☐	☐

San Jose State University

San Jose, CA

Address: One Washington Square, San Jose, CA, 95192
Admissions telephone: 408 924-2013
Admissions FAX: 408 924-2050
Director of Admissions: Susan Hoagland
Admissions e-mail: contact@sjsu.edu
Web site: http://www.sjsu.edu
SAT Code: 4687

LD program name: Disability Resource Center
Associate Director: Cindy Marota
LD program telephone: 408 924-6000
LD program e-mail: info@drc.sjsu.edu
LD program enrollment: 405, Total campus enrollment: 21,663

GENERAL

San Jose State University is a public, coed, four-year institution. 104-acre campus in San Jose (population: 894,943); branch campuses in Monterey and Salinas. Served by air, bus, and train; major airport serves San Francisco (40 miles). School operates transportation to off-campus parking lots. Public transportation serves campus. Semester system.

LD ADMISSIONS

Students do not complete a separate application and are not simultaneously accepted to the LD program. A member of the LD program does not sit on the admissions committee. High school waivers are accepted for foreign language. A personal interview is not required. Essay is not required.

For fall 2004, 125 completed self-identified LD applications were received.

SECONDARY SCHOOL REQUIREMENTS

Graduation from secondary school required; GED accepted. The following course distribution required: 4 units of English, 3 units of math, 2 units of science, 2 units of foreign language, 1 unit of social studies, 1 unit of history, 1 unit of academic electives.

TESTING

SAT Reasoning or ACT required. SAT Subject recommended.

All enrolled freshmen (fall 2004):

Average SAT I Scores:	Verbal: 485	Math: 517
Average ACT Scores:	Composite: 20	

Child Study Team report is not required. A neuropsychological or comprehensive psycho-educational evaluation is required for admission. Tests required as part of this documentation:

- ■ WAIS-IV
- ❑ WISC-IV
- ❑ SATA
- ■ Woodcock-Johnson
- ■ Nelson-Denny Reading Test
- ❑ Other

UNDERGRADUATE STUDENT BODY

Total undergraduate student enrollment: 10,902 Men, 11,339 Women.

Composition of student body (fall 2004):

	Undergraduate	Freshmen
International	1.0	3.6
Black	6.5	4.8
American Indian	0.5	0.5
Asian-American	37.2	38.0
Hispanic	21.0	15.2
White	26.4	23.5
Unreported	7.4	14.4
	100.0%	100.0%

1% are from out of state. 6% join a fraternity and 3% join a sorority. Average age of full-time undergraduates is 23. 25% of classes have fewer than 20 students, 61% have between 20 and 50 students, 14% have more than 50 students.

STUDENT HOUSING

23% of freshmen live in college housing. Freshmen are not required to live on campus. Housing is guaranteed for all undergraduates. Campus can house 1,650 undergraduates. Single rooms are available for students with medical or special needs. A medical note is required.

EXPENSES

Tuition 2004-05: $2,944 per year (in-state), $12,520 (out-of-state).

There is no additional cost for LD program/services.

LD SERVICES

LD program size is not limited.

LD services available to:

■ Freshmen ■ Sophomores ■ Juniors ■ Seniors

Academic Accommodations

Curriculum		In class	
Foreign language waiver	❑	Early syllabus	❑
Lighter course load	■	Note takers in class	■
Math waiver	❑	Priority seating	❑
Other special classes	❑	Tape recorders	■
Priority registrations	❑	Videotaped classes	❑
Substitution of courses	❑	Text on tape	❑
Exams		**Services**	
Extended time	■	Diagnostic tests	■
Oral exams	■	Learning centers	■
Take home exams	❑	Proofreaders	❑
Exams on tape or computer	❑	Readers	■
Untimed exams	❑	Reading Machines/Kurzweil	■
Other accommodations	❑	Special bookstore section	❑
		Typists	❑

Credit toward degree is not given for remedial courses taken.

Counseling Services

- ■ Academic
- ■ Psychological
- ❑ Student Support groups
- ■ Vocational

Tutoring

Individual tutoring is available weekly.

	Individual	Group
Time management	❑	❑
Organizational skills	❑	❑
Learning strategies	❑	❑
Study skills	❑	❑
Content area	■	■
Writing lab	■	■
Math lab	❑	❑

UNIQUE LD PROGRAM FEATURES

Accommodations are determined on an individual basis. An educational psychologist is available to meet with students individually and assess their needs.

The DRC works proactively with students in preparation for state licensing exams, state boards, and standardized entrance exams (i.e.: LSAT, GRE) to meet the requirements for LD documentation and test accommodations. Once registered with the DRC, students have the opportunity to meet with professional counselors for educational strategies, accommodation needs, academic advising, advocacy, and pre-employment information/direction.

LD PROGRAM STAFF

Total number of LD Program staff (including director):

Full Time: 4 Part Time: 4

There is an advisor/advocate from the LD program available to students.

Key staff person available to work with LD students: Gary Bonanno, Educational Psychologist.

LD Program web site: www.drc.sjsu.edu

Santa Barbara City College

Santa Barbara, CA

Address: 721 Cliff Drive, Santa Barbara CA, 93109
Admissions telephone: 805 965-0581, extension 2200
Director of Admissions/Records: Allison Curtis
Web site: http://www.sbcc.edu
SAT Code: 4690

LD program name: Disabled Students Program
DSPS Coordinator: Janet Shapiro
LD program telephone: 805 965-0581, extension 2365
LD program e-mail: shapiro@sbcc.edu
LD program enrollment: 1,863, Total campus enrollment: 15,456

GENERAL

Santa Barbara City College is a public, coed, two-year institution. 74-acre, campus in Santa Barbara (population: 92,325), 90 miles from Los Angeles. Served by air, bus, and train. Major airport serves Los Angeles. Public transportation serves campus. Semester system.

LD ADMISSIONS

No deadline for application. Students do not complete a separate application for admission and are simultaneously accepted to the program. A personal interview is required. Essay is not required.

SECONDARY SCHOOL REQUIREMENTS

Graduation from secondary school required; GED accepted.

TESTING

Child Study Team report is not required. Documentation of a neuropsychological or comprehensive pscho-educational evaluation is required for admission. Must be dated within 36 months of the application. Tests required as part of this documentation:

- ■ WAIS-IV
- ☐ WISC-IV
- ☐ SATA
- ■ Woodcock-Johnson
- ■ Nelson-Denny Reading Test
- ☐ Other

STUDENT HOUSING

There is no campus housing available.

EXPENSES

There is no additional cost for LD program/services.

LD SERVICES

LD program size is not limited.

LD services available to:

■ Freshmen ■ Sophomores ■ Juniors ■ Seniors

Academic Accommodations

Curriculum		**In class**	
Foreign language waiver	☐	Early syllabus	☐
Lighter course load	■	Note takers in class	☐
Math waiver	☐	Priority seating	☐
Other special classes	☐	Tape recorders	☐
Priority registrations	■	Videotaped classes	☐
Substitution of courses	☐	Text on tape	■
Exams		**Services**	
Extended time	■	Diagnostic tests	■
Oral exams	☐	Learning centers	■
Take home exams	☐	Proofreaders	☐
Exams on tape or computer	■	Readers	☐
Untimed exams	☐	Reading Machines/Kurzweil	■
Other accommodations	■	Special bookstore section	☐
		Typists	☐

Credit toward degree is not given for remedial courses taken.

Counseling Services

- ■ Academic
- ■ Psychological
- ■ Student Support groups
- ■ Vocational

Tutoring

Individual tutoring is available.

Average size of tutoring groups is 4.

	Individual	Group
Time management	■	■
Organizational skills	■	■
Learning strategies	■	■
Study skills	■	■
Content area	☐	☐
Writing lab	■	■
Math lab	■	■

LD PROGRAM STAFF

Total number of LD Program staff (including director):

Full Time: 9.6

There is an advisor/advocate from the LD program available to faculty and students. Six peer tutors are available to work with LD students.

Key staff person available to work with LD students: Janet Shapiro, DSPS Coordinator

LD program web site: http://www.sbcc.edu/dsps

Santa Clara University

Santa Clara, CA

Address: 500 El Camino Real, Santa Clara, CA, 95053
Admissions telephone: 408 554-4700
Admissions FAX: 408 554-5255
Dean of Admissions: Sandra Hayes
Admissions e-mail: ugadmissions@scu.edu
Web site: http://www.scu.edu
SAT Code: 4851 ACT Code: 468

LD program name: Disabilities Resources, Drahmann Academic Advising Center
Coordinator of Disabilities Resources: E. Ann Ravenscroft
LD program telephone: 408 554-4111
LD program e-mail: ERavenscroft@scu.edu
LD program enrollment: 105, Total campus enrollment: 4,434

GENERAL

Santa Clara University is a private, coed, four-year institution. 104-acre, suburban campus in Santa Clara (population: 102,361), three miles from San Jose and 46 miles from San Francisco. Served by bus and train; major airport serves San Jose; other major airport serves San Francisco. Public transportation serves campus. Quarter system.

LD ADMISSIONS

A member of the LD program does not sit on the admissions committee. High school waivers are accepted for foreign language. A personal interview is not required. Essay is required and may be typed.

19 applications were offered admission, and 19 enrolled.

SECONDARY SCHOOL REQUIREMENTS

Graduation from secondary school required; GED not accepted. The following course distribution required: 4 units of English, 4 units of math, 3 units of science, 3 units of foreign language, 1 unit of social studies, 1 unit of history, 2 units of academic electives.

TESTING

SAT Reasoning required; ACT may be substituted. SAT Subject recommended.

All enrolled freshmen (fall 2004):

Average SAT I Scores:	Verbal: 592	Math: 613
Average ACT Scores:	Composite: 26	

Child Study Team report is not required. A neuropsychological or comprehensive psycho-educational evaluation is required for admission. Must be dated within 36 months of application. Tests required as part of this documentation:

- [x] WAIS-IV
- [x] WISC-IV
- [ ] SATA
- [x] Woodcock-Johnson
- [x] Nelson-Denny Reading Test
- [ ] Other

UNDERGRADUATE STUDENT BODY

Total undergraduate student enrollment: 1,981 Men, 2,298 Women.

Composition of student body (fall 2004):

	Undergraduate	Freshmen
International	2.0	3.8
Black	3.3	2.8
American Indian	0.7	0.5
Asian-American	18.2	18.9
Hispanic	12.3	13.0
White	59.4	56.1
Unreported	4.1	4.9
	100.0%	100.0%

31% are from out of state. Average age of full-time undergraduates is 21. 31% of classes have fewer than 20 students, 66% have between 20 and 50 students, 3% have more than 50 students.

STUDENT HOUSING

88% of freshmen live in college housing. Freshmen are not required to live on campus. Housing is guaranteed for all undergraduates. Campus can house 2,450 undergraduates. Single rooms are available for students with medical or special needs. A medical note is required.

EXPENSES

Tuition (2005-06): $28,899 per year.

Room: $6,882. Board: $3,150.

There is no additional cost for LD program/services.

LD SERVICES

LD program size is not limited.

LD services available to:

- [x] Freshmen
- [x] Sophomores
- [x] Juniors
- [x] Seniors

Academic Accommodations

Curriculum		In class	
Foreign language waiver	[ ]	Early syllabus	[x]
Lighter course load	[x]	Note takers in class	[x]
Math waiver	[ ]	Priority seating	[x]
Other special classes	[ ]	Tape recorders	[x]
Priority registrations	[x]	Videotaped classes	[ ]
Substitution of courses	[x]	Text on tape	[x]
Exams		**Services**	
Extended time	[x]	Diagnostic tests	[ ]
Oral exams	[ ]	Learning centers	[ ]
Take home exams	[ ]	Proofreaders	[ ]
Exams on tape or computer	[ ]	Readers	[x]
Untimed exams	[ ]	Reading Machines/Kurzweil	[x]
Other accommodations	[x]	Special bookstore section	[ ]
		Typists	[ ]

Credit toward degree is not given for remedial courses taken.

Counseling Services

- [x] Academic
- [x] Psychological
- [x] Student Support groups
- [x] Vocational

Tutoring

Individual tutoring is available weekly.

	Individual	Group
Time management	[x]	[x]
Organizational skills	[x]	[x]
Learning strategies	[x]	[x]
Study skills	[x]	[x]
Content area	[x]	[x]
Writing lab	[x]	[x]
Math lab	[x]	[x]

UNIQUE LD PROGRAM FEATURES

Matriculated students must register with Disabilities Resources and provide complete documentation of their disability. Policy manual available online.

LD PROGRAM STAFF

Total number of LD Program staff (including director):

Full Time: 1 Part Time: 1

Key staff person available to work with LD students: E. Ann Ravenscroft, Coordinator of Disabilities Resources.

LD Program web site: www.scu.edu/advising/

Scripps College

Claremont, CA

Address: 1030 Columbia Avenue, Claremont, CA, 91711
Admissions telephone: 800 770-1333
Admissions FAX: 909 607-7508
Dean of Admission and Financial Aid: Patricia Goldsmith
Admissions e-mail: admission@scrippscollege.edu
Web site: http://www.scrippscol.edu
SAT Code: 4693 ACT Code: 426

Registrar: Carol Entler
LD program telephone: 909 621-8089
LD program e-mail: carol.entler@scrippscollege.edu
Total campus enrollment: 822

GENERAL

Scripps College is a private, women's, four-year institution. 30-acre campus in Claremont (population: 33,998), 35 miles from Los Angeles. Served by bus; major airports serve Los Angeles and Ontario (10 miles); train serves Pomona (five miles). Public transportation serves campus. Semester system.

LD ADMISSIONS

Students do not complete a separate application and are not simultaneously accepted to the LD program. A member of the LD program does not sit on the admissions committee. A personal interview is recommended. Essay is required and may be typed. Some courses may be substituted by petition.

SECONDARY SCHOOL REQUIREMENTS

Graduation from secondary school required; GED accepted. The following course distribution required: 4 units of English, 3 units of math, 3 units of science, 3 units of foreign language, 3 units of social studies.

TESTING

SAT Reasoning or ACT required. SAT Subject recommended.

All enrolled freshmen (fall 2004):

Average SAT I Scores:	Verbal: 681	Math: 653
Average ACT Scores:	Composite: 29	

Child Study Team report is not required. A neuropsychological or comprehensive psycho-educational evaluation is required for admission. Must be dated within 36 months of application. Tests required as part of this documentation:

- ☑ WAIS-IV
- ☑ WISC-IV
- ☑ SATA
- ☑ Woodcock-Johnson
- ☑ Nelson-Denny Reading Test
- ☐ Other

UNDERGRADUATE STUDENT BODY

Total undergraduate student enrollment: 798 Women.

Composition of student body (fall 2004):

	Undergraduate	Freshmen
International	1.0	1.2
Black	3.0	3.2
American Indian	0.0	0.0
Asian-American	14.4	13.3
Hispanic	7.5	6.0
White	49.7	59.6
Unreported	24.4	16.7
	100.0%	100.0%

52% are from out of state. Average age of full-time undergraduates is 20. 73% of classes have fewer than 20 students, 24% have between 20 and 50 students, 3% have more than 50 students.

STUDENT HOUSING

100% of freshmen live in college housing. Freshmen are required to live on campus. Housing is guaranteed for all undergraduates. Campus can house 715 undergraduates. Single rooms are available for students with medical or special needs. A medical note is required.

EXPENSES

Tuition (2005-06): $31,332 per year.
Room: $5,100. Board: $4,400.
There is no additional cost for LD program/services.

LD SERVICES

LD program size is not limited.

LD services available to:

☑ Freshmen ☑ Sophomores ☑ Juniors ☑ Seniors

Academic Accommodations

Curriculum		In class	
Foreign language waiver	☐	Early syllabus	☑
Lighter course load	☑	Note takers in class	☐
Math waiver	☑	Priority seating	☑
Other special classes	☐	Tape recorders	☑
Priority registrations	☑	Videotaped classes	☐
Substitution of courses	☑	Text on tape	☐
Exams		**Services**	
Extended time	☑	Diagnostic tests	☐
Oral exams	☐	Learning centers	☐
Take home exams	☑	Proofreaders	☐
Exams on tape or computer	☑	Readers	☑
Untimed exams	☑	Reading Machines/Kurzweil	☐
Other accommodations	☐	Special bookstore section	☐
		Typists	☑

Credit toward degree is not given for remedial courses taken.

Counseling Services

- ☐ Academic
- ☐ Psychological
- ☐ Student Support groups
- ☐ Vocational

Tutoring

Individual tutoring is available weekly.

Average size of tutoring groups: 3

	Individual	Group
Time management	☑	☑
Organizational skills	☑	☑
Learning strategies	☑	☑
Study skills	☑	☐
Content area	☐	☐
Writing lab	☑	☐
Math lab	☑	☐

LD PROGRAM STAFF

Total number of LD Program staff (including director):

Full Time: 2 Part Time: 2

There is an advisor/advocate from the LD program available to students.

Key staff person available to work with LD students: Debra Wood, Vice President and Dean of Students.

Simpson University

Redding, CA

Address: 2211 College View Drive, Redding, CA, 96003-8606
Admissions telephone: 800 598-2493
Admissions FAX: 530 226-4861
Director of Admissions and Enrollment Services: Richard Ruiz
Admissions e-mail: admissions@simpsonuniversity.edu
Web site: http://www.simpsonuniversity.edu
SAT Code: 4698 ACT Code: 430

LD program name: Growth and Development
Director of Growth and Development: Mike Schill
LD program telephone: 530 226-4179
LD program e-mail: mschill@simpsonuniversity.edu
LD program enrollment: 30, Total campus enrollment: 951

GENERAL

Simpson University is a private, coed, four-year institution. 60-acre campus in Redding (population: 80,865), 160 miles from Sacramento. Served by air, bus, and train. School operates transportation to airport and bus and train stations. Public transportation serves campus. Semester system.

LD ADMISSIONS

Students do not complete a separate application and are not simultaneously accepted to the LD program.

SECONDARY SCHOOL REQUIREMENTS

Graduation from secondary school required; GED accepted.

TESTING

SAT Reasoning or ACT required. SAT Subject required.

All enrolled freshmen (fall 2004):

Average SAT I Scores:	Verbal: 522	Math: 499
Average ACT Scores:	Composite: 20	

Child Study Team report is not required. A neuropsychological or comprehensive psycho-education evaluation is not required for admission. Tests required as part of this documentation:

- ☐ WAIS-IV
- ☐ WISC-IV
- ☐ SATA
- ☐ Woodcock-Johnson
- ☐ Nelson-Denny Reading Test
- ☐ Other

UNDERGRADUATE STUDENT BODY

Total undergraduate student enrollment: 338 Men, 648 Women.

Composition of student body (fall 2004):

	Undergraduate	Freshmen
International	1.1	0.8
Black	2.7	1.2
American Indian	0.5	0.6
Asian-American	4.8	5.6
Hispanic	9.7	3.7
White	65.1	75.7
Unreported	16.1	12.4
	100.0%	100.0%

25% are from out of state. Average age of full-time undergraduates is 20. 56% of classes have fewer than 20 students, 38% have between 20 and 50 students, 6% have more than 50 students.

STUDENT HOUSING

Freshmen are required to live on campus. Housing is guaranteed for all undergraduates. Campus can house 590 undergraduates. Single rooms are available for students with medical or special needs. A medical note is required.

EXPENSES

Tuition (2005-06): $17,000 per year.
Room & Board: $5,900.
There is no additional cost for LD program/services.

LD SERVICES

LD program size is not limited.

LD services available to:

☒ Freshmen ☒ Sophomores ☒ Juniors ☒ Seniors

Academic Accommodations

Curriculum		In class	
Foreign language waiver	☐	Early syllabus	☒
Lighter course load	☐	Note takers in class	☒
Math waiver	☐	Priority seating	☒
Other special classes	☐	Tape recorders	☐
Priority registrations	☒	Videotaped classes	☐
Substitution of courses	☐	Text on tape	☐
Exams		**Services**	
Extended time	☒	Diagnostic tests	☐
Oral exams	☒	Learning centers	☐
Take home exams	☐	Proofreaders	☐
Exams on tape or computer	☐	Readers	☒
Untimed exams	☒	Reading Machines/Kurzweil	☐
Other accommodations	☒	Special bookstore section	☐
		Typists	☒

Credit toward degree is not given for remedial courses taken.

Counseling Services

☒	Academic	Meets 4 times per academic year
☒	Psychological	Meets 8 times per academic year
☐	Student Support groups	
☒	Vocational	Meets 6 times per academic year

Tutoring

Individual tutoring is available weekly.

Average size of tutoring groups: 1

	Individual	Group
Time management	☒	☐
Organizational skills	☒	☐
Learning strategies	☒	☐
Study skills	☒	☐
Content area	☒	☐
Writing lab	☒	☐
Math lab	☒	☐

UNIQUE LD PROGRAM FEATURES

Academic accommodations and services are approved based on documented functional limitations resulting from a disability, however, a student may request help in the form of tutoring for an individual class without documentation.

LD PROGRAM STAFF

There is an advisor/advocate from the LD program available to students. The advisor/advocate meets with faculty once per month. 20 peer tutors are available to work with LD students.

Key staff person available to work with LD students: Sheri Polvogt, Learning Disabilities Specialist.

LD Program web site: www.simpsonuniversity.edu

Sonoma State University

Rohnert Park, CA

Address: 1801 East Cotati Avenue, Rohnert Park, CA, 94928
Admissions telephone: 707 664-2778
Admissions FAX: 707 664-2060
Vice Provost: Katharyn Crabbe
Admissions e-mail: student.outreach@sonoma.edu
Web site: http://www.sonoma.edu
SAT Code: 4723 ACT Code: 431

LD program name: Disabled Student Services
LD program address: 1049 Salazar Hall
Managing Director, Disabled Student Services: Linda Lipps
LD program telephone: 707 664-2677
LD program e-mail: linda.lipps@sonoma.edu
LD program enrollment: 200, Total campus enrollment: 6,798

GENERAL

Sonoma State University is a public, coed, four-year institution. 280-acre campus in Rohnert Park (population: 42,236), 45 miles from San Francisco; branch campus in Ukiah. Major airport serves San Francisco (70 miles); smaller airport and train serve Oakland (60 miles); bus serves Santa Rosa (10 miles). Public transportation serves campus. Semester system.

LD ADMISSIONS

Students do not complete a separate application and are not simultaneously accepted to the LD program. A member of the LD program does not sit on the admissions committee. A personal interview is not required. Essay is not required.

For fall 2004, 200 completed self-identified LD applications were received. 200 applications were offered admission, and 200 enrolled.

SECONDARY SCHOOL REQUIREMENTS

Graduation from secondary school required; GED accepted. The following course distribution required: 4 units of English, 3 units of math, 2 units of science, 2 units of foreign language, 1 unit of history, 3 units of academic electives.

TESTING

SAT Reasoning or ACT required. SAT Subject recommended.

All enrolled freshmen (fall 2004):

Average SAT I Scores:	Verbal: 519	Math: 524
Average ACT Scores:	Composite: 22	

Child Study Team report is not required. A neuropsychological or comprehensive psycho-educational evaluation is required for admission. Must be dated within 36 months of application. Tests required as part of this documentation:

☒ WAIS-IV	☒ Woodcock-Johnson
☐ WISC-IV	☐ Nelson-Denny Reading Test
☐ SATA	☒ Other

UNDERGRADUATE STUDENT BODY

Total undergraduate student enrollment: 2,279 Men, 3,999 Women.

Composition of student body (fall 2004):

	Undergraduate	Freshmen
International	0.5	1.2
Black	2.3	1.9
American Indian	0.5	0.8
Asian-American	5.3	4.8
Hispanic	11.8	10.8
White	70.7	67.2
Unreported	8.9	13.3
	100.0%	100.0%

4% are from out of state. 6% join a fraternity and 5% join a sorority. Average age of full-time undergraduates is 22. 37% of classes have fewer than 20 students, 54% have between 20 and 50 students, 9% have more than 50 students.

STUDENT HOUSING

91% of freshmen live in college housing. Housing is guaranteed for all undergraduates. Campus can house 2,480 undergraduates. Single rooms are available for students with medical or special needs. A medical note is required.

EXPENSES

Tuition (2005-06): No tuition for in-state, $8,136 (out-of-state).
Room: $6,052. Board: $2,838.
There is no additional cost for LD program/services.

LD SERVICES

LD program size is not limited.

LD services available to:

☒ Freshmen ☒ Sophomores ☒ Juniors ☒ Seniors

Academic Accommodations

Curriculum		In class	
Foreign language waiver	☐	Early syllabus	☐
Lighter course load	☐	Note takers in class	☒
Math waiver	☐	Priority seating	☐
Other special classes	☒	Tape recorders	☒
Priority registrations	☒	Videotaped classes	☐
Substitution of courses	☐	Text on tape	☒
Exams		**Services**	
Extended time	☒	Diagnostic tests	☐
Oral exams	☐	Learning centers	☒
Take home exams	☐	Proofreaders	☐
Exams on tape or computer	☒	Readers	☒
Untimed exams	☐	Reading Machines/Kurzweil	☒
Other accommodations	☒	Special bookstore section	☐
		Typists	☐

Credit toward degree is not given for remedial courses taken.

Counseling Services

☒ Academic
☐ Psychological
☐ Student Support groups
☐ Vocational

Tutoring

Individual tutoring is available monthly.

Average size of tutoring groups: 3

	Individual	Group
Time management	☒	☐
Organizational skills	☒	☐
Learning strategies	☒	☐
Study skills	☒	☐
Content area	☒	☐
Writing lab	☒	☐
Math lab	☒	☐

LD PROGRAM STAFF

Total number of LD Program staff (including director):

Full Time: 2 Part Time: 2

There is an advisor/advocate from the LD program available to students.

Key staff person available to work with LD students: Brent Boyer, Disability Management Advisor.

LD Program web site: www.sonoma.edu/sas/dss/

University of Southern California

Los Angeles, CA

Address: University Park, Los Angeles, CA, 90089
Admissions telephone: 213 740-1111
Admissions FAX: 213 740-1556
Director of Admission: Katherine Harrington
Admissions e-mail: admitusc@usc.edu
Web site: http://www.usc.edu/
SAT Code: 4852 ACT Code: 470

Coordinator of Disability Services and Programs: Tammy Tucker
LD program telephone: 213 740-0776
LD program e-mail: ability@usc.edu
Total campus enrollment: 16,474

GENERAL

University of Southern California is a private, coed, four-year institution. 155-acre campus in Los Angeles (population: 3,694,820); separate campus for health sciences, satellite centers in Sacramento and in Orange county, marine science center on Santa Catalina Island. Served by air, bus, and train. School operates transportion on campus, to health science campus, and to nearby housing. Public transportation serves campus. Semester system.

LD ADMISSIONS

Admissions requirements may be waived for LD students.

SECONDARY SCHOOL REQUIREMENTS

Graduation from secondary school required; GED not accepted. The following course distribution required: 4 units of English, 3 units of math, 2 units of science, 2 units of foreign language, 2 units of social studies, 3 units of academic electives.

TESTING

SAT Reasoning or ACT required. SAT Subject required.

All enrolled freshmen (fall 2004):

Average SAT I Scores:	Verbal: 665	Math: 685
Average ACT Scores:	Composite: 29	

Child Study Team report is not required. Tests required as part of this documentation:

- ☐ WAIS-IV
- ☐ WISC-IV
- ☐ SATA
- ☐ Woodcock-Johnson
- ☐ Nelson-Denny Reading Test
- ☐ Other

UNDERGRADUATE STUDENT BODY

Total undergraduate student enrollment: 8,049 Men, 7,971 Women.

Composition of student body (fall 2004):

	Undergraduate	Freshmen
International	7.0	8.5
Black	7.0	6.5
American Indian	0.5	0.8
Asian-American	19.2	21.1
Hispanic	15.7	13.1
White	47.7	47.8
Unreported	2.9	2.2
	100.0%	100.0%

31% are from out of state. 18% join a fraternity and 21% join a sorority. Average age of full-time undergraduates is 21. 61% of classes have fewer than 20 students, 28% have between 20 and 50 students, 11% have more than 50 students.

STUDENT HOUSING

96% of freshmen live in college housing. Freshmen are not required to live on campus. Housing is not guaranteed for all undergraduates. Campus can house 6,400 undergraduates. Single rooms are available for students with medical or special needs. A medical note is not required.

EXPENSES

Tuition (2005-06): $31,458 per year.
Room: $5,260. Board: $4,350.
There is no additional cost for LD program/services.

LD SERVICES

LD program size is not limited.

LD services available to:

■ Freshmen ■ Sophomores ■ Juniors ■ Seniors

Academic Accommodations

Curriculum		In class	
Foreign language waiver	☐	Early syllabus	☐
Lighter course load	■	Note takers in class	■
Math waiver	☐	Priority seating	☐
Other special classes	☐	Tape recorders	■
Priority registrations	☐	Videotaped classes	■
Substitution of courses	☐	Text on tape	☐
Exams		**Services**	
Extended time	■	Diagnostic tests	☐
Oral exams	☐	Learning centers	☐
Take home exams	☐	Proofreaders	☐
Exams on tape or computer	☐	Readers	■
Untimed exams	☐	Reading Machines/Kurzweil	■
Other accommodations	☐	Special bookstore section	☐
		Typists	☐

Credit toward degree is not given for remedial courses taken.

Counseling Services

- ■ Academic
- ■ Psychological
- ■ Student Support groups
- ☐ Vocational

Tutoring

Individual tutoring is available.

	Individual	Group
Time management	☐	☐
Organizational skills	☐	☐
Learning strategies	☐	☐
Study skills	☐	☐
Content area	☐	☐
Writing lab	☐	☐
Math lab	☐	☐

LD PROGRAM STAFF

Total number of LD Program staff (including director):

Full Time: 3 Part Time: 3

There is an advisor/advocate from the LD program available to students.

Key staff person available to work with LD students: Tammy Tucker, Coordinator of Disability Services and Programs.

Stanford University

Stanford, CA

Address: Stanford, CA, 94305
Admissions telephone: 650 723-2091
Admissions FAX: 650 723-6050
Dean of Undergraduate Admissions and Financial Aid: Anna Marie Porras
Admissions e-mail: admission@stanford.edu
Web site: http://www.stanford.edu
SAT Code: 4704 ACT Code: 434

LD program name: Schwab Learning Center
LD program address: 563 Salvatierra Walk
Director: Joan Bisagno, Ph.D.
LD program telephone: 650 723-1066
LD program e-mail: joan.bisagno@stanford.edu

GENERAL

Stanford University is a private, coed, four-year institution. 8,180-acre campus near Palo Alto (population: 58,598), 20 miles from San Jose and 30 miles from San Francisco; branch campuses in Washington, D.C., and abroad in Argentina, Chile, England, France, Germany, Italy, Japan, Mexico, and Russia. Served by bus; major airports serve San Francisco and San Jose; train serves San Jose. School operates transportation to local shopping center, downtown Palo Alto, and university medical center. Public transportation serves campus. Quarter system.

LD ADMISSIONS

Students do not complete a separate application and are not simultaneously accepted to the LD program. A member of the LD program does not sit on the admissions committee. A personal interview is not required.

SECONDARY SCHOOL REQUIREMENTS

Graduation from secondary school required; GED accepted.

TESTING

SAT Reasoning required; ACT may be substituted. SAT Subject required.

Child Study Team report is not required. A neuropsychological or comprehensive psycho-educational evaluation is required for admission. Tests required as part of this documentation:

- [x] WAIS-IV
- [x] WISC-IV
- [x] SATA
- [x] Woodcock-Johnson
- [x] Nelson-Denny Reading Test
- [x] Other

UNDERGRADUATE STUDENT BODY

Total undergraduate student enrollment: 3,597 Men, 3,682 Women.

Composition of student body (fall 2004):

	Undergraduate	Freshmen
International	5.8	5.9
Black	8.4	10.7
American Indian	2.1	2.1
Asian-American	23.9	24.3
Hispanic	10.8	11.7
White	44.0	40.9
Unreported	5.0	4.4
	100.0%	100.0%

53% are from out of state. 13% join a fraternity and 12% join a sorority. Average age of full-time undergraduates is 20. 69% of classes have fewer than 20 students, 19% have between 20 and 50 students, 12% have more than 50 students.

STUDENT HOUSING

100% of freshmen live in college housing. Freshmen are required to live on campus. Housing is guaranteed for all undergraduates. Campus can house 6,273 undergraduates. Single rooms are available for students with medical or special needs. A medical note is required.

EXPENSES

Tuition (2005-06): $31,200 per year.
Room: $5,276. Board: $4,656.
There is no additional cost for LD program/services.

LD SERVICES

LD program size is not limited.

LD services available to:

- [x] Freshmen
- [x] Sophomores
- [x] Juniors
- [x] Seniors

Academic Accommodations

Curriculum		In class	
Foreign language waiver	☐	Early syllabus	☐
Lighter course load	☑	Note takers in class	☑
Math waiver	☐	Priority seating	☐
Other special classes	☐	Tape recorders	☑
Priority registrations	☐	Videotaped classes	☐
Substitution of courses	☑	Text on tape	☑
Exams		**Services**	
Extended time	☑	Diagnostic tests	☑
Oral exams	☑	Learning centers	☑
Take home exams	☑	Proofreaders	☐
Exams on tape or computer	☑	Readers	☑
Untimed exams	☐	Reading Machines/Kurzweil	☑
Other accommodations	☑	Special bookstore section	☐
		Typists	☑

Credit toward degree is not given for remedial courses taken.

Counseling Services

- [x] Academic
- [x] Psychological
- [x] Student Support groups
- [x] Vocational

Tutoring

Individual tutoring is available weekly.

	Individual	Group
Time management	☑	☑
Organizational skills	☑	☑
Learning strategies	☑	☑
Study skills	☑	☑
Content area	☑	☑
Writing lab	☑	☑
Math lab	☑	☑

UNIQUE LD PROGRAM FEATURES

The Schwab Learning Center was established to offer a service program for academically gifted students with learning differences and Attention Deficit Hyperactivity Disorder (ADHD). The center provides services based on a "best practices" model in the field of higher education.

LD PROGRAM STAFF

Total number of LD Program staff (including director):

Full Time: 2 Part Time: 2

There is an advisor/advocate from the LD program available to students. 14 graduate students are available to work with LD students.

Key staff people available to work with LD students: Barbara Leeson and Laurel Weeks, Learning Strategies Coordinators.

Vanguard University of Southern California

Costa Mesa, CA

Address: 55 Fair Drive, Costa Mesa, CA, 92626
Admissions telephone: 800 722-6279
Admissions FAX: 714 966-5471
Director of Admissions: Jennifer Purga
Admissions e-mail: admissions@vanguard.edu
Web site: http://www.vanguard.edu
SAT Code: 4701 ACT Code: 432

LD program name: Learning Enrichment
Admissions Office: Barbi Rouse
LD program telephone: 714 556-3610
LD program e-mail: brouse@vanguard.edu
LD program enrollment: 31, Total campus enrollment: 1,800

GENERAL

Vanguard University of Southern California is a private, coed, four-year institution. 38-acre, suburban campus in Costa Mesa (population: 108,724), 45 miles from Los Angeles. Served by air; major airport serves Los Angeles; bus and train serve Santa Ana (10 miles). Public transportation serves campus. Semester system.

LD ADMISSIONS

Students do not complete a separate application and are not simultaneously accepted to the LD program. A member of the LD program does sit on the admissions committee. A personal interview is recommended. Essay is not required.

SECONDARY SCHOOL REQUIREMENTS

Graduation from secondary school required; GED accepted.

TESTING

SAT Reasoning or ACT recommended. SAT Subject recommended.

All enrolled freshmen (fall 2004):

Average SAT I Scores: Verbal: 502 Math: 497
Average ACT Scores: Composite: 22

Child Study Team report is not required. A neuropsychological or comprehensive psycho-educational evaluation is required for admission. Must be dated within 36 months of application. Tests required as part of this documentation:

- [x] WAIS-IV
- [x] WISC-IV
- [x] SATA
- [x] Woodcock-Johnson
- [x] Nelson-Denny Reading Test
- [x] Other

UNDERGRADUATE STUDENT BODY

Total undergraduate student enrollment: 638 Men, 940 Women.

Composition of student body (fall 2004):

	Undergraduate	Freshmen
International	0.3	0.9
Black	4.2	4.0
American Indian	1.1	0.7
Asian-American	3.1	4.8
Hispanic	18.9	18.4
White	69.0	65.8
Unreported	3.4	5.4
	100.0%	100.0%

9% are from out of state. Average age of full-time undergraduates is 20. 56% of classes have fewer than 20 students, 38% have between 20 and 50 students, 6% have more than 50 students.

STUDENT HOUSING

96% of freshmen live in college housing. Housing is not guaranteed for all undergraduates, however, undergraduates receive housing priority. Campus can house 1,054 undergraduates.

EXPENSES

Tuition (2005-06): $19,900 per year.
Room: $3,366. Board: $3,390.
There is no additional cost for LD program/services.

LD SERVICES

LD program size is not limited.

LD services available to:

- [x] Freshmen
- [x] Sophomores
- [x] Juniors
- [x] Seniors

Academic Accommodations

Curriculum		In class	
Foreign language waiver	[ ]	Early syllabus	[ ]
Lighter course load	[ ]	Note takers in class	[x]
Math waiver	[ ]	Priority seating	[ ]
Other special classes	[ ]	Tape recorders	[ ]
Priority registrations	[ ]	Videotaped classes	[ ]
Substitution of courses	[ ]	Text on tape	[ ]
Exams		**Services**	
Extended time	[x]	Diagnostic tests	[ ]
Oral exams	[x]	Learning centers	[ ]
Take home exams	[ ]	Proofreaders	[ ]
Exams on tape or computer	[ ]	Readers	[ ]
Untimed exams	[x]	Reading Machines/Kurzweil	[ ]
Other accommodations	[ ]	Special bookstore section	[ ]
		Typists	[ ]

Credit toward degree is not given for remedial courses taken.

Counseling Services

- [x] Academic
- [x] Psychological
- [ ] Student Support groups
- [x] Vocational

Tutoring

Individual tutoring is available monthly.

	Individual	Group
Time management	[x]	[ ]
Organizational skills	[x]	[ ]
Learning strategies	[x]	[ ]
Study skills	[x]	[ ]
Content area	[ ]	[ ]
Writing lab	[x]	[ ]
Math lab	[ ]	[ ]

LD PROGRAM STAFF

There is an advisor/advocate from the LD program available to students.

Key staff person available to work with LD students: Barbi Rouse, Director of Learning Skills.

Westmont College

Santa Barbara, CA

Address: 955 La Paz Road, Santa Barbara, CA, 93108
Admissions telephone: 800 777-9011
Admissions FAX: 805 565-6234
Director of Admissions: Joyce Luy
Admissions e-mail: admissions@westmont.edu
Web site: http://www.westmont.edu
SAT Code: 4950 ACT Code: 478

LD program name: Academic Resource Office
Director: Michelle Hardley
LD program telephone: 805 565-6159
LD program e-mail: mhardley@westmont.edu
LD program enrollment: 71, total campus enrollment: 1,369

GENERAL

Westmont College is a private, coed, four-year institution. 133-acre, suburban campus in Santa Barbara (population: 92,325), 90 miles from Los Angeles. Served by air, bus, and train; major airport serves Los Angeles. School operates transportation within Santa Barbara. Semester system.

LD ADMISSIONS

Students do not complete a separate application and are simultaneously accepted to the LD program. A member of the LD program does sit on the admissions committee. A personal interview is recommended. Essay is required and may be typed.

For fall 2004, 29 completed self-identified LD applications were received. 19 applications were offered admission, and 14 enrolled.

SECONDARY SCHOOL REQUIREMENTS

Graduation from secondary school required; GED accepted. The following course distribution required: 4 units of English, 3 units of math, 3 units of science, 2 units of foreign language, 1 unit of social studies, 2 units of history, 1 unit of academic electives.

TESTING

SAT Reasoning or ACT required. SAT Subject recommended.

All enrolled freshmen (fall 2004):

Average SAT I Scores:	Verbal: 610	Math: 610
Average ACT Scores:	Composite: 26	

Child Study Team report is not required. A neuropsychological or comprehensive psycho-educational evaluation is required for admission. Must be dated within 48 months of application. Tests required as part of this documentation:

- [x] WAIS-IV
- [ ] WISC-IV
- [ ] SATA
- [x] Woodcock-Johnson
- [x] Nelson-Denny Reading Test
- [ ] Other

UNDERGRADUATE STUDENT BODY

Total undergraduate student enrollment: 515 Men, 859 Women.

Composition of student body (fall 2004):

	Undergraduate	Freshmen
International	1.4	1.0
Black	3.6	1.6
American Indian	2.2	1.8
Asian-American	6.7	6.2
Hispanic	10.3	7.7
White	71.4	78.1
Unreported	4.4	3.6
	100.0%	100.0%

34% are from out of state. Average age of full-time undergraduates is 20. 62% of classes have fewer than 20 students, 34% have between 20 and 50 students, 4% have more than 50 students.

STUDENT HOUSING

100% of freshmen live in college housing. Freshmen are not required to live on campus. Housing is guaranteed for all undergraduates. Campus can house 1,125 undergraduates. Single rooms are available for students with medical or special needs. A medical note is not required.

EXPENSES

Tuition (2005-06): $27,076 per year.
Room: $5,376. Board: $3,490.
There is no additional cost for LD program/services.

LD SERVICES

LD program size is not limited.

LD services available to:

- [x] Freshmen
- [x] Sophomores
- [x] Juniors
- [x] Seniors

Academic Accommodations

Curriculum		In class	
Foreign language waiver	[ ]	Early syllabus	[ ]
Lighter course load	[x]	Note takers in class	[x]
Math waiver	[ ]	Priority seating	[ ]
Other special classes	[ ]	Tape recorders	[x]
Priority registrations	[x]	Videotaped classes	[ ]
Substitution of courses	[ ]	Text on tape	[x]
Exams		**Services**	
Extended time	[x]	Diagnostic tests	[ ]
Oral exams	[x]	Learning centers	[ ]
Take home exams	[ ]	Proofreaders	[ ]
Exams on tape or computer	[x]	Readers	[x]
Untimed exams	[x]	Reading Machines/Kurzweil	[ ]
Other accommodations	[x]	Special bookstore section	[ ]
		Typists	[x]

Credit toward degree is not given for remedial courses taken.

Counseling Services

- [x] Academic — Meets 5 times per academic year
- [x] Psychological
- [ ] Student Support groups
- [ ] Vocational

Tutoring

Individual tutoring is available weekly.

Average size of tutoring groups: 1

	Individual	Group
Time management	[x]	[x]
Organizational skills	[x]	[x]
Learning strategies	[x]	[x]
Study skills	[x]	[x]
Content area	[x]	[ ]
Writing lab	[x]	[ ]
Math lab	[ ]	[x]

LD PROGRAM STAFF

Total number of LD Program staff (including director):

Full Time: 1 Part Time: 1

There is an advisor/advocate from the LD program available to students. The advisor/advocate meets with faculty four times per month and students 4 times per month.

Key staff person available to work with LD students: Michelle Hardley, Director of Academic Advising and Disability Services.

Whittier College

Whittier, CA

Address: 13406 Philadelphia Street, P.O. Box 634, Whittier, CA, 90608
Admissions telephone: 562 907-4238
Admissions FAX: 562 907-4870
Dean of Enrollment: Lisa Meyer
Admissions e-mail: admission@whittier.edu
Web site: http://www.whittier.edu
SAT Code: 4952

LD program name: Disability Services
Director of Disability Services: Joan Smith
LD program telephone: 562 907-4840
LD program e-mail: jsmith@whittier.edu
LD program enrollment: 127, Total campus enrollment: 1,343

GENERAL

Whittier College is a private, coed, four-year institution. 95-acre campus in Whittier (population: 83,680), 20 miles from Los Angeles. Airport serves Los Angeles; train serves Fullerton (15 miles). Public transportation serves campus. 4-1-4 system.

LD ADMISSIONS

A personal interview is recommended. Essay is required and may be typed.

SECONDARY SCHOOL REQUIREMENTS

Graduation from secondary school required; GED not accepted. The following course distribution required: 4 units of English, 3 units of math, 1 unit of science, 2 units of foreign language, 1 unit of social studies.

TESTING

SAT Reasoning or ACT required. SAT Subject required.

All enrolled freshmen (fall 2004):

Average SAT I Scores:	Verbal: 544	Math: 545
Average ACT Scores:	Composite: 22	

Child Study Team report is not required. A neuropsychological or comprehensive psycho-educational evaluation is required for admission. Must be dated within 36 months of application. Tests required as part of this documentation:

■ WAIS-IV
■ WISC-IV
■ SATA
■ Woodcock-Johnson
■ Nelson-Denny Reading Test
☐ Other

UNDERGRADUATE STUDENT BODY

Total undergraduate student enrollment: 567 Men, 712 Women.

Composition of student body (fall 2004):

	Undergraduate	Freshmen
International	3.0	4.4
Black	3.3	3.4
American Indian	1.4	1.2
Asian-American	8.6	9.0
Hispanic	20.3	24.6
White	48.7	45.0
Unreported	14.7	12.4
	100.0%	100.0%

27% are from out of state. 5% join a fraternity and 11% join a sorority. Average age of full-time undergraduates is 20. 56% of classes have fewer than 20 students, 41% have between 20 and 50 students, 3% have more than 50 students.

STUDENT HOUSING

88% of freshmen live in college housing. Freshmen are required to live on campus. Housing is guaranteed for all undergraduates. Campus can house 800 undergraduates. Single rooms are available for students with medical or special needs. A medical note is required.

EXPENSES

Tuition (2005-06): $25,838 per year.
Room & Board: $8,252.
There is no additional cost for LD program/services.

LD SERVICES

LD program size is not limited.

LD services available to:

■ Freshmen ■ Sophomores ■ Juniors ■ Seniors

Academic Accommodations

Curriculum		In class	
Foreign language waiver	☐	Early syllabus	☐
Lighter course load	■	Note takers in class	■
Math waiver	☐	Priority seating	☐
Other special classes	☐	Tape recorders	■
Priority registrations	☐	Videotaped classes	☐
Substitution of courses	■	Text on tape	■
Exams		**Services**	
Extended time	■	Diagnostic tests	☐
Oral exams	■	Learning centers	■
Take home exams	☐	Proofreaders	☐
Exams on tape or computer	☐	Readers	■
Untimed exams	☐	Reading Machines/Kurzweil	■
Other accommodations	☐	Special bookstore section	☐
		Typists	■

Counseling Services

☐ Academic
■ Psychological
☐ Student Support groups
☐ Vocational

Tutoring

Individual tutoring is available weekly.

Average size of tutoring groups: 2

	Individual	Group
Time management	■	☐
Organizational skills	■	☐
Learning strategies	■	☐
Study skills	■	☐
Content area	☐	■
Writing lab	■	☐
Math lab	■	☐

LD PROGRAM STAFF

Key staff person available to work with LD students: Joan Smith, Director of Disability Services.

LD Program web site: www.whittier.edu/student/life/disabilityservices.htm

Woodbury University

Burbank, CA

Address: 7500 Glenoaks Boulevard, Burbank, CA, 91510
Admissions telephone: 818 767-0888
Admissions FAX: 818 767-7520
Associate Dean of Academic Affairs: Mauro Diaz
Admissions e-mail: info@woodbury.edu
Web site: http://www.woodbury.edu
SAT Code: 4955 ACT Code: 481

Director, Academic Advising: Julie Oinonen
LD program telephone: 818 767-0888, extension 322
LD program e-mail: julie.oinonen@woodbury.edu
LD program enrollment: 3, Total campus enrollment: 1,270

GENERAL

Woodbury University is a private, coed, four-year institution. 22-acre, suburban campus in Burbank (population: 100,316), 17 miles from Los Angeles; branch campus in San Diego. Served by air, bus, and train; major airport serves Los Angeles. Public transportation serves campus. Semester system.

LD ADMISSIONS

For fall 2004, 20 completed self-identified LD applications were received.

SECONDARY SCHOOL REQUIREMENTS

Graduation from secondary school required; GED accepted.

TESTING

SAT Reasoning required; ACT may be substituted. SAT Subject recommended.

All enrolled freshmen (fall 2004):

Average SAT I Scores: Verbal: 550 Math: 550

Child Study Team report is not required. Tests required as part of this documentation:

- ☐ WAIS-IV
- ☐ WISC-IV
- ☐ SATA
- ☐ Woodcock-Johnson
- ☐ Nelson-Denny Reading Test
- ☐ Other

UNDERGRADUATE STUDENT BODY

Total undergraduate student enrollment: 1,270.

Composition of student body (fall 2004):

	Undergraduate	Freshmen
International	0.8	7.1
Black	10.6	6.5
American Indian	0.0	0.2
Asian-American	5.7	11.8
Hispanic	37.4	35.6
White	45.5	38.8
Unreported	0.0	0.0
	100.0%	100.0%

6% join a fraternity and 6% join a sorority. Average age of full-time undergraduates is 20. 76% of classes have fewer than 20 students, 24% have between 20 and 50 students.

STUDENT HOUSING

Freshmen are not required to live on campus. Housing is guaranteed for all undergraduates. Campus can house 226 undergraduates.

EXPENSES

Tuition (2005-06): $22,128 per year.
Room: $4,762. Board: $3,046.

LD SERVICES

LD program size is not limited.

LD services available to:

■ Freshmen ■ Sophomores ■ Juniors ■ Seniors

Academic Accommodations

Curriculum		In class	
Foreign language waiver	☐	Early syllabus	☐
Lighter course load	☐	Note takers in class	■
Math waiver	☐	Priority seating	☐
Other special classes	☐	Tape recorders	■
Priority registrations	■	Videotaped classes	☐
Substitution of courses	☐	Text on tape	■
Exams		**Services**	
Extended time	■	Diagnostic tests	☐
Oral exams	☐	Learning centers	■
Take home exams	☐	Proofreaders	☐
Exams on tape or computer	☐	Readers	☐
Untimed exams	■	Reading Machines/Kurzweil	☐
Other accommodations	■	Special bookstore section	☐
		Typists	☐

Credit toward degree is not given for remedial courses taken.

Counseling Services

- ■ Academic
- ☐ Psychological
- ☐ Student Support groups
- ☐ Vocational

Tutoring

Individual tutoring is available daily.

Average size of tutoring groups: 3

	Individual	Group
Time management	☐	☐
Organizational skills	☐	☐
Learning strategies	☐	☐
Study skills	☐	☐
Content area	☐	☐
Writing lab	☐	☐
Math lab	☐	☐

LD PROGRAM STAFF

Total number of LD Program staff (including director):

Full Time: 3 Part Time: 3

There is an advisor/advocate from the LD program available to students. The advisor/advocate meets with faculty and students three times per month. 28 peer tutors are available to work with LD students.

Key staff person available to work with LD students: Dr. Phyllis Cremer, Associate Dean.

University of Alberta

Edmonton, CN

Address: Edmonton
Admissions telephone: 780 492-3111
Admissions FAX: 780 492-7172
Associate Registrar and Director of Admissions: Deborah Gougeon
Web site: http://www.registrar.ualberta.ca
SAT Code: 963

LD program contact: Specialized Support & Disability Services
LD program telephone: 780 492-3381
Total campus enrollment: 28, 467

GENERAL

University of Alberta is a public, coed, four-year institution. 216-acre main campus in Edmonton (population: 616,306); bilingual campus (Faculte Saint-Jean) five miles from main campus. Served by air, bus, and train. School operates transportation between campuses. Public transportation serves campus. Semester system.

SECONDARY SCHOOL REQUIREMENTS

Graduation from secondary school not required.

TESTING

SAT Subject recommended.

Child Study Team report is not required. Tests required as part of this documentation:

- [ ] WAIS-IV
- [ ] WISC-IV
- [ ] SATA
- [ ] Woodcock-Johnson
- [ ] Nelson-Denny Reading Test
- [ ] Other

UNDERGRADUATE STUDENT BODY

Total undergraduate student enrollment: 11,916 Men, 15,325 Women.

STUDENT HOUSING

Freshmen are not required to live on campus. Housing is guaranteed for all undergraduates. Campus can house 4,000 undergraduates.

EXPENSES

Tuition (2005-06): $3,891 per year (Canadian residents), $10,000 (nonresidents).

There is no additional cost for LD program/services.

LD SERVICES

LD services available to:

- [x] Freshmen
- [x] Sophomores
- [x] Juniors
- [x] Seniors

Academic Accommodations

Curriculum

- [ ] Foreign language waiver
- [ ] Lighter course load
- [ ] Math waiver
- [ ] Other special classes
- [ ] Priority registrations
- [ ] Substitution of courses

Exams

- [x] Extended time
- [x] Oral exams
- [ ] Take home exams
- [x] Exams on tape or computer
- [ ] Untimed exams
- [x] Other accommodations

In class

- [ ] Early syllabus
- [x] Note takers in class
- [x] Priority seating
- [ ] Tape recorders
- [ ] Videotaped classes
- [x] Text on tape

Services

- [x] Diagnostic tests
- [ ] Learning centers
- [ ] Proofreaders
- [x] Readers
- [x] Reading Machines/Kurzweil
- [ ] Special bookstore section
- [x] Typists

Counseling Services

- [ ] Academic
- [ ] Psychological
- [ ] Student Support groups
- [ ] Vocational

Tutoring

Individual tutoring is available.

	Individual	Group
Time management	[ ]	[ ]
Organizational skills	[ ]	[ ]
Learning strategies	[ ]	[ ]
Study skills	[ ]	[ ]
Content area	[ ]	[ ]
Writing lab	[ ]	[ ]
Math lab	[ ]	[ ]

LD PROGRAM STAFF

There is an advisor/advocate from the LD program available to students.

University of Calgary

Calgary, CN

Address: 2500 University Drive NW, Calgary, AB,
Admissions telephone: 403 220-6645
Admissions FAX: 403 220-0762
Admissions e-mail: applinfo@ucalgary.ca
Web site: http://www.ucalgary.ca/admissions
SAT Code: 813

LD program name: Disability Resource Centre
LD program contact: Patricia Pardo
LD program telephone: 403 220-8237
Total campus enrollment: 22, 794

GENERAL

University of Calgary is a public, coed, four-year institution. Campus of over 300 acres in Calgary (population: 768,082). Served by air and bus. Public transportation serves campus. Semester system.

SECONDARY SCHOOL REQUIREMENTS

Graduation from secondary school required; GED not accepted.

TESTING

Child Study Team report is not required. Tests required as part of this documentation:

- ❑ WAIS-IV
- ❑ WISC-IV
- ❑ SATA
- ❑ Woodcock-Johnson
- ❑ Nelson-Denny Reading Test
- ❑ Other

UNDERGRADUATE STUDENT BODY

Total undergraduate student enrollment: 10,222 Men, 12,657 Women.

STUDENT HOUSING

Freshmen are not required to live on campus. Housing is not guaranteed for all undergraduates.

EXPENSES

Tuition (2005-06): $4,860 per year. $4,120 (Canadian residents), $8,240 (nonresidents).

Room: $2,245. Board: $3,500.

LD SERVICES

LD services available to:

❑ Freshmen ❑ Sophomores ❑ Juniors ❑ Seniors

Academic Accommodations

Curriculum		**In class**	
Foreign language waiver	❑	Early syllabus	❑
Lighter course load	❑	Note takers in class	❑
Math waiver	❑	Priority seating	❑
Other special classes	❑	Tape recorders	❑
Priority registrations	❑	Videotaped classes	❑
Substitution of courses	❑	Text on tape	❑
Exams		**Services**	
Extended time	❑	Diagnostic tests	❑
Oral exams	❑	Learning centers	❑
Take home exams	❑	Proofreaders	❑
Exams on tape or computer	❑	Readers	❑
Untimed exams	❑	Reading Machines/Kurzweil	❑
Other accommodations	❑	Special bookstore section	❑
		Typists	❑

Counseling Services

- ❑ Academic
- ❑ Psychological
- ❑ Student Support groups
- ❑ Vocational

Tutoring

	Individual	Group
Time management	❑	❑
Organizational skills	❑	❑
Learning strategies	❑	❑
Study skills	❑	❑
Content area	❑	❑
Writing lab	❑	❑
Math lab	❑	❑

LD PROGRAM STAFF

Key staff person available to work with LD students: Patricia Pardo, Director, Disability Resource Centre.

Dalhousie University

Halifax, CN

Address: 1236 Henry Street, Halifax, NS,
Admissions FAX: 902 494-1630
Associate Registrar, Admissions, and Awards: Susan Tanner
Web site: www.dal.ca
SAT Code: 915

LD program name: Accessibility Services
Accessibility Services : Lynn Shokry
LD program telephone: 902 494-2836
LD program e-mail: lynn.shokry@dal.ca
Total campus enrollment: 11, 050

GENERAL

Dalhousie University is a public, coed, four-year institution. 80-acre, urban campus in Halifax, Nova Scotia (population: 350,000). Served by air, bus, and train. Public transportation serves campus. Semester system.

LD ADMISSIONS

Application Deadline: 06/01. Students do not complete a separate application and are not simultaneously accepted to the LD program. A member of the LD program does not sit on the admissions committee. A personal interview is not required. Essay is not required.

SECONDARY SCHOOL REQUIREMENTS

Graduation from secondary school required; GED not accepted.

TESTING

SAT Subject recommended.

Child Study Team report is not required. Tests required as part of this documentation:

- [ ] WAIS-IV
- [ ] WISC-IV
- [ ] SATA
- [ ] Woodcock-Johnson
- [ ] Nelson-Denny Reading Test
- [ ] Other

UNDERGRADUATE STUDENT BODY

Total undergraduate student enrollment: 4,071 Men, 5,242 Women.

STUDENT HOUSING

Freshmen are not required to live on campus. Housing is guaranteed for all undergraduates. Single rooms are available for students with medical or special needs. A medical note is required.

EXPENSES

Tuition (2005-06): $3,285 per year (Canadian residents), $7,423 (nonresidents). Tuition varies by program.

There is no additional cost for LD program/services.

LD SERVICES

LD program size is not limited.

LD services available to:

- [x] Freshmen
- [x] Sophomores
- [x] Juniors
- [x] Seniors

Academic Accommodations

Curriculum

- [ ] Foreign language waiver
- [ ] Lighter course load
- [ ] Math waiver
- [ ] Other special classes
- [ ] Priority registrations
- [ ] Substitution of courses

Exams

- [x] Extended time
- [x] Oral exams
- [ ] Take home exams
- [ ] Exams on tape or computer
- [ ] Untimed exams
- [x] Other accommodations

In class

- [ ] Early syllabus
- [x] Note takers in class
- [x] Priority seating
- [x] Tape recorders
- [ ] Videotaped classes
- [x] Text on tape

Services

- [ ] Diagnostic tests
- [x] Learning centers
- [ ] Proofreaders
- [x] Readers
- [x] Reading Machines/Kurzweil
- [ ] Special bookstore section
- [x] Typists

Counseling Services

- [ ] Academic
- [ ] Psychological
- [ ] Student Support groups
- [ ] Vocational

Tutoring

	Individual	Group
Time management	[ ]	[x]
Organizational skills	[ ]	[x]
Learning strategies	[ ]	[x]
Study skills	[ ]	[x]
Content area	[ ]	[ ]
Writing lab	[ ]	[x]
Math lab	[ ]	[x]

LD PROGRAM STAFF

There is an advisor/advocate from the LD program available to students.

Key staff person available to work with LD students: Lynn Shokry, Accessibility Services.

McGill University

Montreal, CN

Address: 845 Sherbrooke Street West, Montreal, QC,
Admissions FAX: 514 398-4183
Director of Admissions: Kim Bartlett
Web site: http://www.mcgill.ca
SAT Code: 935 ACT Code: 5231

LD program name: Office for Students with Disabilities
LD program address: Brown Student Services Building, 3600 McTavish Street, Montreal, QC, H3A 1Y2
Director Office for Students with Disabilities: Dr. Joan Wolforth
LD program telephone: 514 398-6009
LD program e-mail: joan.wolforth@mcgill.ca
LD program enrollment: 131, Total campus enrollment: 20,629

GENERAL

McGill University is a public, coed, four-year institution. 80-acre main campus in downtown Montreal (population: 1,016,376; 1,600-acre Macdonald campus in Ste. Anne-de-Bellevue). Bus and train serve Montreal; airport serves Dorval (15 miles). School operates transportation to Macdonald campus and for disabled students around campus. Public transportation serves campus. Semester system.

LD ADMISSIONS

Students do not complete a separate application and are not simultaneously accepted to the LD program. A member of the LD program does not sit on the admissions committee. A personal interview is not required. Essay is not required. McGill University has no differential admissions policy for LD students. They are admitted on the same basis as all other students.

SECONDARY SCHOOL REQUIREMENTS

Graduation from secondary school required; GED not accepted.

TESTING

SAT Subject recommended.

All enrolled freshmen (fall 2004):

Average SAT I Scores: Verbal: 657 Math: 668
Average ACT Scores: Composite:

Child Study Team report is not required. A neuropsychological or comprehensive psycho-educational evaluation is required for admission. Must be dated within 24 months of application. Tests required as part of this documentation:

- [x] WAIS-IV
- [x] WISC-IV
- [ ] SATA
- [x] Woodcock-Johnson
- [x] Nelson-Denny Reading Test
- [x] Other

UNDERGRADUATE STUDENT BODY

Total undergraduate student enrollment: 6,953 Men, 10,616 Women.

Average age of full-time undergraduates is 21.

STUDENT HOUSING

38% of freshmen live in college housing. Freshmen are not required to live on campus. Housing is guaranteed for all undergraduates. Priority is given to incoming first year students (approximately 92% of spaces). Any leftover spaces after first year students are placed are made available to other undergraduate students. Campus can house 2,202 undergraduates. Single rooms are available for students with medical or special needs. A medical note is required.

EXPENSES

Tuition (2005-06): $1,366 per year (in-state), $3,604 (out-of-state). $1,668 per year (in-province Canadian residents), $4,013 (out-of-province Canadian residents), $8,763-$15,000 (nonresidents). Tuition varies by program for international students.

Room: $3,784. Board: $2,426.

There is no additional cost for LD program/services.

LD SERVICES

LD program size is not limited.

LD services available to:

- [x] Freshmen
- [x] Sophomores
- [x] Juniors
- [x] Seniors

Academic Accommodations

Curriculum		In class	
Foreign language waiver	[ ]	Early syllabus	[ ]
Lighter course load	[x]	Note takers in class	[x]
Math waiver	[ ]	Priority seating	[ ]
Other special classes	[ ]	Tape recorders	[x]
Priority registrations	[ ]	Videotaped classes	[ ]
Substitution of courses	[ ]	Text on tape	[x]
Exams		**Services**	
Extended time	[x]	Diagnostic tests	[ ]
Oral exams	[x]	Learning centers	[ ]
Take home exams	[ ]	Proofreaders	[x]
Exams on tape or computer	[x]	Readers	[x]
Untimed exams	[ ]	Reading Machines/Kurzweil	[x]
Other accommodations	[ ]	Special bookstore section	[ ]
		Typists	[x]

Credit toward degree is not given for remedial courses taken.

Counseling Services

- [x] Academic
- [x] Psychological
- [x] Student Support groups
- [x] Vocational

Tutoring

Individual tutoring is available weekly.

Average size of tutoring groups: 1

	Individual	Group
Time management	[x]	[ ]
Organizational skills	[x]	[ ]
Learning strategies	[x]	[ ]
Study skills	[x]	[ ]
Content area	[ ]	[ ]
Writing lab	[x]	[ ]
Math lab	[ ]	[ ]

UNIQUE LD PROGRAM FEATURES

No special admissions requirements for LD students. Inclusive program in a large, urban, competitive University.

LD PROGRAM STAFF

Total number of LD Program staff (including director):

Full Time: 1 Part Time: 1

There is an advisor/advocate from the LD program available to students. 2 graduate students are available to work with LD students.

Key staff person available to work with LD students: Elaine Ransom-Hodges, M.Ed., Learning Skills Specialist.

LD Program web site: www.mcgill.ca/osd

NSCAD University

Halifax, CN

Address: 5163 Duke Street, Halifax, NS,
Admissions telephone: 902 494-8129
Admissions FAX: 902 425-2987
Coordinator of Admissions: Terrence Bailey
Admissions e-mail: admiss@nscad.ns.ca
Web site: http://www.nscad.ca

LD program name: Bill Travis
LD program address: Rm D210, 5163 Duke St,
Disability Resource Facilitator: Bill Travis
LD program telephone: 902 494-8313
LD program e-mail: btravis@nscad.ns.ca
LD program enrollment: 27, Total campus enrollment: 935

GENERAL

NSCAD University is a public, coed, four-year institution. 150,000-square-foot campus in Halifax (population: 350,000). Served by air, bus, and train. Public transportation serves campus. Semester system.

LD ADMISSIONS

Students do not complete a separate application and are simultaneously accepted to the LD program. A member of the LD program does not sit on the admissions committee. A personal interview is not required. Essay is not required.

SECONDARY SCHOOL REQUIREMENTS

Graduation from secondary school required; GED accepted.

TESTING

Child Study Team report is not required. A neuropsychological or comprehensive psycho-education evaluation is not required for admission. Tests required as part of this documentation:

- [ ] WAIS-IV
- [ ] WISC-IV
- [ ] SATA
- [ ] Woodcock-Johnson
- [ ] Nelson-Denny Reading Test
- [ ] Other

UNDERGRADUATE STUDENT BODY

Total undergraduate student enrollment: 271 Men, 571 Women.

79% of classes have fewer than 20 students, 18% have between 20 and 50 students, 3% have more than 50 students.

STUDENT HOUSING

Housing is not guaranteed for all undergraduates.

EXPENSES

Tuition 2004-05: $4,436 per year (Canadian residents), $8,884 (non-residents).

There is no additional cost for LD program/services.

LD SERVICES

LD program size is not limited.

LD services available to:

- [x] Freshmen
- [x] Sophomores
- [x] Juniors
- [x] Seniors

Academic Accommodations

Curriculum		In class	
Foreign language waiver	[ ]	Early syllabus	[ ]
Lighter course load	[ ]	Note takers in class	[x]
Math waiver	[ ]	Priority seating	[ ]
Other special classes	[ ]	Tape recorders	[x]
Priority registrations	[ ]	Videotaped classes	[ ]
Substitution of courses	[ ]	Text on tape	[ ]
Exams		**Services**	
Extended time	[x]	Diagnostic tests	[x]
Oral exams	[x]	Learning centers	[ ]
Take home exams	[ ]	Proofreaders	[x]
Exams on tape or computer	[x]	Readers	[x]
Untimed exams	[x]	Reading Machines/Kurzweil	[ ]
Other accommodations	[ ]	Special bookstore section	[ ]
		Typists	[x]

Credit toward degree is not given for remedial courses taken.

Counseling Services

- [ ] Academic
- [ ] Psychological
- [ ] Student Support groups
- [ ] Vocational

Tutoring

Individual tutoring is available weekly.

Average size of tutoring groups: 1

	Individual	Group
Time management	[x]	[x]
Organizational skills	[ ]	[x]
Learning strategies	[ ]	[x]
Study skills	[x]	[x]
Content area	[x]	[ ]
Writing lab	[ ]	[x]
Math lab	[ ]	[ ]

LD PROGRAM STAFF

Total number of LD Program staff (including director):

Full Time: 1 Part Time: 1

There is an advisor/advocate from the LD program available to students. The advisor/advocate meets with students1 time per month. 2 graduate students and 16 peer tutors are available to work with LD students.

Key staff person available to work with LD students: Bill Travis, Disability Resource Facilitator.

University of Prince Edward Island

Charlottetown, CN

Address: 550 University Avenue, Charlottetown, PE, C1A 4P3
Admissions telephone: 902 628-4353
Admissions FAX: 902 566-0795
Admissions Contact: Paul Cantelo
Admissions e-mail: newstudent@upei.ca
Web site: http://www.upei.ca/registrar/
SAT Code: 941

Coordinator of Students with Learning Disabilities: Joanne McCabe
Total campus enrollment: 3, 211

GENERAL

University of Prince Edward Island is a public, coed, four-year institution. 130-acre campus in Charlottetown (population: 15,776). Served by air and bus. Semester system.

LD ADMISSIONS

Students do not complete a separate application and are not simultaneously accepted to the LD program. A member of the LD program does not sit on the admissions committee. If documentation is received by the Coordinator of Students with Disabilities, accommodations can be set in place.

SECONDARY SCHOOL REQUIREMENTS

The following course distribution required: 4 units of English.

TESTING

SAT Subject recommended.

Child Study Team report is not required. A neuropsychological or comprehensive psycho-educational evaluation is required for admission. Must be dated within 12 months of application. Tests required as part of this documentation:

- ☐ WAIS-IV
- ☐ WISC-IV
- ■ SATA
- ■ Woodcock-Johnson
- ☐ Nelson-Denny Reading Test
- ☐ Other

UNDERGRADUATE STUDENT BODY

Total undergraduate student enrollment: 3,211.

STUDENT HOUSING

Freshmen are not required to live on campus. Housing is guaranteed for all undergraduates. Single rooms are available for students with medical or special needs. A medical note is required.

EXPENSES

Tuition (2005-06): $4,620 per year. $3,690 per year (Canadian residents), $7,090 (nonresidents).

Room & Board: $6,754.

There is no additional cost for LD program/services.

LD SERVICES

LD program size is not limited.

LD services available to:

■ Freshmen ■ Sophomores ■ Juniors ■ Seniors

Academic Accommodations

Curriculum		**In class**	
Foreign language waiver	☐	Early syllabus	☐
Lighter course load	☐	Note takers in class	☐
Math waiver	☐	Priority seating	☐
Other special classes	☐	Tape recorders	☐
Priority registrations	☐	Videotaped classes	☐
Substitution of courses	☐	Text on tape	☐
Exams		**Services**	
Extended time	☐	Diagnostic tests	☐
Oral exams	☐	Learning centers	☐
Take home exams	☐	Proofreaders	☐
Exams on tape or computer	☐	Readers	☐
Untimed exams	☐	Reading Machines/Kurzweil	☐
Other accommodations	☐	Special bookstore section	☐
		Typists	☐

Credit toward degree is not given for remedial courses taken.

Counseling Services

- ☐ Academic
- ☐ Psychological
- ☐ Student Support groups
- ☐ Vocational

Tutoring

Individual tutoring is available.

	Individual	Group
Time management	☐	☐
Organizational skills	☐	☐
Learning strategies	☐	☐
Study skills	☐	☐
Content area	☐	☐
Writing lab	☐	☐
Math lab	☐	☐

LD PROGRAM STAFF

Total number of LD Program staff (including director):

Full Time: 1 Part Time: 1

There is an advisor/advocate from the LD program available to students.

Key staff person available to work with LD students: Joanne McCabe, Coordinator of Students with Learning Disabilities.

Simon Fraser University

Burnaby, CN

Address: 8888 University Drive, Burnaby, BC,
Admissions telephone: 604 291-3224
Admissions FAX: 604 291-4969
Director of Admissions and Assistant Registrar: Nick Heath
Admissions e-mail: undergraduate-admissions@sfu.ca
Web site: http://www.sfu.ca
SAT Code: 651

Learning Specialist: Ron Snitz
LD program telephone: 604 291-5381
LD program e-mail: rsnitz@sfu.ca
LD program enrollment: 44, Total campus enrollment: 17,185

GENERAL

Simon Fraser University is a public, coed, four-year institution. 400-acre, urban campus in Burnaby (population: 180,000), 9 miles from downtown Vancouver; branch campus in Vancouver. Airport, bus, and train serve Vancouver. Public transportation serves campus. Trimester system.

LD ADMISSIONS

Students do not complete a separate application and are not simultaneously accepted to the LD program. A member of the LD program does not sit on the admissions committee. A personal interview is not required. Essay is not required.

SECONDARY SCHOOL REQUIREMENTS

Graduation from secondary school required; GED not accepted. The following course distribution required: 4 units of English, 3 units of math, 2 units of science, 2 units of foreign language, 1 unit of social studies, 1 unit of history.

TESTING

SAT Reasoning required. ACT required. SAT Reasoning or ACT required.

Child Study Team report is not required. A neuropsychological or comprehensive psycho-education evaluation is not required for admission. Tests required as part of this documentation:

- [ ] WAIS-IV
- [ ] WISC-IV
- [ ] SATA
- [ ] Woodcock-Johnson
- [ ] Nelson-Denny Reading Test
- [ ] Other

UNDERGRADUATE STUDENT BODY

Total undergraduate student enrollment: 7,418 Men, 9,767 Women.

STUDENT HOUSING

Freshmen are not required to live on campus. Housing is guaranteed for all undergraduates.

EXPENSES

Tuition 2004-05: $2,760 per year (in-state), $10,202 (out-of-state).

There is no additional cost for LD program/services.

LD SERVICES

LD program size is not limited.

LD services available to:

- [x] Freshmen
- [x] Sophomores
- [x] Juniors
- [x] Seniors

Academic Accommodations

Curriculum

- [ ] Foreign language waiver
- [x] Lighter course load
- [ ] Math waiver
- [ ] Other special classes
- [ ] Priority registrations
- [ ] Substitution of courses

Exams

- [x] Extended time
- [x] Oral exams
- [ ] Take home exams
- [ ] Exams on tape or computer
- [ ] Untimed exams
- [ ] Other accommodations

In class

- [ ] Early syllabus
- [x] Note takers in class
- [ ] Priority seating
- [x] Tape recorders
- [ ] Videotaped classes
- [ ] Text on tape

Services

- [ ] Diagnostic tests
- [x] Learning centers
- [ ] Proofreaders
- [x] Readers
- [x] Reading Machines/Kurzweil
- [ ] Special bookstore section
- [ ] Typists

Credit toward degree is not given for remedial courses taken.

Counseling Services

- [ ] Academic
- [ ] Psychological
- [ ] Student Support groups
- [ ] Vocational

Tutoring

	Individual	Group
Time management	[ ]	[ ]
Organizational skills	[ ]	[ ]
Learning strategies	[ ]	[ ]
Study skills	[ ]	[ ]
Content area	[ ]	[ ]
Writing lab	[ ]	[ ]
Math lab	[ ]	[ ]

LD PROGRAM STAFF

Total number of LD Program staff (including director):

Full Time: 3 Part Time: 3

Key staff person available to work with LD students: Ron Snitz, Learning Specialist.

University of Victoria

Victoria, CN

Address: 3800 Finnerty Road, Victoria, BC, V8W 3P2
Admissions FAX: 250 721-6225
Acting Director of Admission Services: David Glen
Web site: http://www.uvic.ca

LD program address: P.O. Box 1700 STN CSC
LD program enrollment: 161, Total campus enrollment: 15,816

GENERAL

University of Victoria is a public, four-year institution. 385-acre campus in Victoria (population: 300,000). Served by air and bus. Public transportation serves campus.

LD ADMISSIONS

Application Deadline: 02/28. Students do not complete a separate application and are not simultaneously accepted to the LD program. A member of the LD program does not sit on the admissions committee. High school waivers are accepted for foreign language. A personal interview is recommended. Essay is not required. Subject requirements may be waived on a case by case basis.

SECONDARY SCHOOL REQUIREMENTS

Graduation from secondary school required; GED accepted. The following course distribution required: 4 units of English, 3 units of math, 2 units of science, 2 units of foreign language, 3 units of social studies.

TESTING

Child Study Team report is not required. A neuropsychological or comprehensive psycho-educational evaluation is required for admission. Must be dated within 24 months of application. Tests required as part of this documentation:

- [x] WAIS-IV
- [x] WISC-IV
- [x] SATA
- [x] Woodcock-Johnson
- [x] Nelson-Denny Reading Test
- [ ] Other

UNDERGRADUATE STUDENT BODY

Total undergraduate student enrollment: 6,309 Men, 9,224 Women.

39% of classes have fewer than 20 students, 41% have between 20 and 50 students, 20% have more than 50 students.

STUDENT HOUSING

Freshmen are not required to live on campus. Housing is guaranteed for all undergraduates. Campus can house 2,386 undergraduates. Single rooms are available for students with medical or special needs. A medical note is required.

EXPENSES

Tuition (2005-06): $4,324 per year. $2,796 per year (Canadian residents), $8,834 (nonresidents). Tuition varies by program.

Room: $3,670. Board: $2,090.

There is no additional cost for LD program/services.

LD SERVICES

LD program size is not limited.

LD services available to:

- [x] Freshmen
- [x] Sophomores
- [x] Juniors
- [x] Seniors

Academic Accommodations

Curriculum		In class	
Foreign language waiver	[x]	Early syllabus	[x]
Lighter course load	[x]	Note takers in class	[x]
Math waiver	[x]	Priority seating	[x]
Other special classes	[ ]	Tape recorders	[x]
Priority registrations	[ ]	Videotaped classes	[x]
Substitution of courses	[ ]	Text on tape	[x]
Exams		**Services**	
Extended time	[x]	Diagnostic tests	[ ]
Oral exams	[x]	Learning centers	[x]
Take home exams	[x]	Proofreaders	[ ]
Exams on tape or computer	[x]	Readers	[x]
Untimed exams	[ ]	Reading Machines/Kurzweil	[x]
Other accommodations	[ ]	Special bookstore section	[ ]
		Typists	[x]

Credit toward degree is not given for remedial courses taken.

Counseling Services

- [x] Academic
- [x] Psychological
- [x] Student Support groups
- [x] Vocational

Tutoring

Individual tutoring is available weekly.

Average size of tutoring groups: 1

	Individual	Group
Time management	[x]	[x]
Organizational skills	[x]	[x]
Learning strategies	[x]	[x]
Study skills	[x]	[x]
Content area	[x]	[x]
Writing lab	[ ]	[ ]
Math lab	[ ]	[ ]

LD PROGRAM STAFF

Total number of LD Program staff (including director):

Full Time: 3 Part Time: 3

There is an advisor/advocate from the LD program available to students.

Key staff person available to work with LD students: Anna Stein, Student Advisor.

LD Program web site: http://rcsd.uvic.ca/

York University

Toronto, CN

Address: 4700 Keele Street, Toronto
Admissions FAX: 416 736-5741
Director of Admissions: Krista Larson
Web site: http://www.yorku.ca/web/index.htm
SAT Code: 894

Total campus enrollment: 34,248

GENERAL

York University is a public, coed, four-year institution. 650-acre, urban campus in Toronto (metropolitan population: 4,263,757); separate 85-acre Glendon College campus. Served by air, bus, and train. School operates transportation to Glendon campus. Public transportation serves campus. Semester system.

LD ADMISSIONS

A personal interview is not required. Essay is not required.

SECONDARY SCHOOL REQUIREMENTS

Graduation from secondary school required; GED not accepted.

TESTING

SAT Reasoning or ACT required.

Child Study Team report is not required. A neuropsychological or comprehensive psycho-education evaluation is not required for admission. Tests required as part of this documentation:

- ■ WAIS-IV
- ☐ WISC-IV
- ☐ SATA
- ■ Woodcock-Johnson
- ☐ Nelson-Denny Reading Test
- ■ Other

UNDERGRADUATE STUDENT BODY

Total undergraduate student enrollment: 12,950 Men, 21,298 Women.

STUDENT HOUSING

Freshmen are not required to live on campus. Housing is not guaranteed for all undergraduates. Campus housing is available for any unmarried student interested in living on-campus, regardless of year. Single rooms are available for students with medical or special needs. A medical note is required.

EXPENSES

Tuition (2005-06): $4,184 per year. Tuition: $4,636 per year (Canadian residents), $11,195 (nonresidents). Tuition is higher for some programs.

Room: $3,719. Board: $2,400.

LD SERVICES

LD services available to:

■ Freshmen ■ Sophomores ■ Juniors ■ Seniors

Academic Accommodations

Curriculum		In class	
Foreign language waiver	☐	Early syllabus	■
Lighter course load	■	Note takers in class	■
Math waiver	☐	Priority seating	☐
Other special classes	■	Tape recorders	☐
Priority registrations	☐	Videotaped classes	☐
Substitution of courses	☐	Text on tape	■
Exams		**Services**	
Extended time	■	Diagnostic tests	■
Oral exams	■	Learning centers	■
Take home exams	☐	Proofreaders	■
Exams on tape or computer	■	Readers	☐
Untimed exams	☐	Reading Machines/Kurzweil	☐
Other accommodations	■	Special bookstore section	☐
		Typists	■

Counseling Services

- ☐ Academic
- ☐ Psychological
- ☐ Student Support groups
- ☐ Vocational

Tutoring

Individual tutoring is available.

	Individual	Group
Time management	☐	☐
Organizational skills	☐	☐
Learning strategies	☐	☐
Study skills	☐	☐
Content area	☐	☐
Writing lab	■	☐
Math lab	☐	☐

LD PROGRAM STAFF

There is an advisor/advocate from the LD program available to students.

University of Colorado at Boulder

Boulder, CO

Address: Regent Administration Center, Room 125, 552 UCB, Boulder, CO, 80309-0552
Admissions telephone: 303 492-6301
Admissions FAX: 303 492-7115
Executive Director of Admissions: Barbara L. Schneider
Admissions e-mail: apply@colorado.edu
Web site: http://www.colorado.edu
SAT Code: 4841 ACT Code: 532

LD program name: Academic Access and Resources Program
LD program address: 107 UCB, Boulder, CO, 80309-0107
Coordinator: Jayne MacArthur
LD program telephone: 303 492-8671
LD program e-mail: dsinfo@colorado.edu
LD program enrollment: 220, Total campus enrollment: 26,182

GENERAL

University of Colorado at Boulder is a public, coed, four-year institution. 600-acre, suburban campus in Boulder (population: 94,673), 30 miles from Denver. Served by bus; major airport and train serve Denver. School operates transportation to off-campus apartment complex. Public transportation serves campus. Semester system.

LD ADMISSIONS

Students do not complete a separate application and are not simultaneously accepted to the LD program. A member of the LD program does not sit on the admissions committee. A personal interview is not required. Essay is required and may be typed.

SECONDARY SCHOOL REQUIREMENTS

Graduation from secondary school required; GED accepted. The following course distribution required: 4 units of English, 3 units of math, 3 units of science, 3 units of foreign language, 1 unit of social studies, 1 unit of history.

TESTING

SAT Reasoning or ACT required. SAT Subject recommended.

All enrolled freshmen (fall 2004):

Average SAT I Scores:	Verbal: 579	Math: 596
Average ACT Scores:	Composite: 25	

Child Study Team report is not required. A neuropsychological or comprehensive psycho-educational evaluation is required for admission. Must be dated within 36 months of application. Tests required as part of this documentation:

- [x] WAIS-IV
- [x] WISC-IV
- [x] SATA
- [x] Woodcock-Johnson
- [x] Nelson-Denny Reading Test
- [x] Other

UNDERGRADUATE STUDENT BODY

Total undergraduate student enrollment: 12,596 Men, 11,402 Women.

Composition of student body (fall 2004):

	Undergraduate	Freshmen
International	0.8	1.3
Black	1.3	1.6
American Indian	0.8	0.8
Asian-American	6.5	6.0
Hispanic	6.6	5.9
White	78.6	78.5
Unreported	5.4	5.9
	100.0%	100.0%

33% are from out of state. 8% join a fraternity and 11% join a sorority. Average age of full-time undergraduates is 21. 45% of classes have fewer than 20 students, 39% have between 20 and 50 students, 16% have more than 50 students.

STUDENT HOUSING

96% of freshmen live in college housing. Freshmen are required to live on campus. Housing is guaranteed for all undergraduates, on a space available basis. The Williams Village housing addition (Bear Creek Apartments) adds another 1,900 beds to the housing available to students. Campus can house 7,100 undergraduates. Single rooms are not available for students with medical or special needs.

EXPENSES

Tuition (2005-06): $4,446 per year (in-state), $21,900 (out-of-state).
Room: $4,450.

Additional cost for LD program/services: $300 per optional diagnostic .

LD SERVICES

LD program size is not limited.

LD services available to:

- [x] Freshmen
- [x] Sophomores
- [x] Juniors
- [x] Seniors

Academic Accommodations

Curriculum		In class	
Foreign language waiver	[ ]	Early syllabus	[ ]
Lighter course load	[ ]	Note takers in class	[x]
Math waiver	[ ]	Priority seating	[ ]
Other special classes	[ ]	Tape recorders	[ ]
Priority registrations	[ ]	Videotaped classes	[ ]
Substitution of courses	[ ]	Text on tape	[x]
Exams		**Services**	
Extended time	[x]	Diagnostic tests	[x]
Oral exams	[ ]	Learning centers	[x]
Take home exams	[ ]	Proofreaders	[x]
Exams on tape or computer	[x]	Readers	[x]
Untimed exams	[ ]	Reading Machines/Kurzweil	[x]
Other accommodations	[ ]	Special bookstore section	[ ]
		Typists	[ ]

Credit toward degree is not given for remedial courses taken.

Counseling Services

[x] Academic	Meets 48 times per academic year
[x] Psychological	Meets 8 times per academic year
[x] Student Support groups	Meets 30 times per academic year
[x] Vocational	

Tutoring

Individual tutoring is available.

	Individual	Group
Time management	[x]	[ ]
Organizational skills	[x]	[ ]
Learning strategies	[x]	[ ]
Study skills	[x]	[ ]
Content area	[x]	[ ]
Writing lab	[x]	[ ]
Math lab	[ ]	[x]

UNIQUE LD PROGRAM FEATURES

When students with learning disabilities contact Disability Services, they are assigned to a Disability Specialist who will work with them on an individual basis at their request. The Specialist can be supportive in a variety of areas.

LD PROGRAM STAFF

Total number of LD Program staff (including director):

Full Time: 4 Part Time: 4

There is an advisor/advocate from the LD program available to students.

Key staff person available to work with LD students: Jayne MacArthur, Coordinator of Academic Access and Resources Program.

LD Program web site: www.colorado.edu/disabilityservices

University of Colorado at Colorado Springs

Colorado Springs, CO

Address: 1420 Austin Bluffs Parkway, Colorado Springs, CO, 80918
Admissions telephone: 719 262-3383
Admissions FAX: 719 262-3116
Director of Admissions: Steven Ellis
Admissions e-mail: admrecor@uccs.edu
Web site: http://www.uccs.edu
SAT Code: 4874 ACT Code: 535

LD program name: Disability Services
LD program address: Main Hall 105, Colorado Springs
Coordinator, Disability Services: Katherine Simonton
LD program telephone: 719 262-3259
LD program e-mail: ksimonto@uccs.edu
Total campus enrollment: 6,233

GENERAL

University of Colorado at Colorado Springs is a public, coed, four-year institution. 501-acre campus in Colorado Springs (population: 360,890), 60 miles from Denver. Served by air and bus; major airport and train serve Denver. School operates transportation to statellite parking lots. Public transportation serves campus. Semester system.

SECONDARY SCHOOL REQUIREMENTS

Graduation from secondary school required; GED accepted. The following course distribution required: 4 units of English, 3 units of math, 3 units of science, 2 units of foreign language, 2 units of social studies, 1 unit of academic electives.

TESTING

SAT Reasoning or ACT required. SAT Subject recommended.

All enrolled freshmen (fall 2004):

Average SAT I Scores: Verbal: 534 Math: 529
Average ACT Scores: Composite: 23

Child Study Team report is not required. Tests required as part of this documentation:

- ☐ WAIS-IV
- ☐ WISC-IV
- ☐ SATA
- ☐ Woodcock-Johnson
- ☐ Nelson-Denny Reading Test
- ☐ Other

UNDERGRADUATE STUDENT BODY

Total undergraduate student enrollment: 2,065 Men, 3,179 Women.

Composition of student body (fall 2004):

	Undergraduate	Freshmen
International	0.4	0.6
Black	4.0	4.0
American Indian	0.9	1.0
Asian-American	5.0	4.7
Hispanic	9.4	8.7
White	77.1	76.6
Unreported	3.2	4.4
	100.0%	100.0%

14% are from out of state. Average age of full-time undergraduates is 22. 38% of classes have fewer than 20 students, 50% have between 20 and 50 students, 12% have more than 50 students.

STUDENT HOUSING

20% of freshmen live in college housing. Freshmen are not required to live on campus. Housing is guaranteed for all undergraduates. Campus can house 900 undergraduates. Single rooms are available for students with medical or special needs.

EXPENSES

Tuition (2005-06): $3,730 per year (in-state), $15,540 (out-of-state). Tuition varies by program.

Room: $4,050. Board: $3,098.

LD SERVICES

LD program size is not limited.

LD services available to:

☑ Freshmen ☑ Sophomores ☑ Juniors ☑ Seniors

Academic Accommodations

Curriculum		In class	
Foreign language waiver	☐	Early syllabus	☐
Lighter course load	☑	Note takers in class	☑
Math waiver	☐	Priority seating	☑
Other special classes	☑	Tape recorders	☑
Priority registrations	☐	Videotaped classes	☑
Substitution of courses	☐	Text on tape	☐
Exams		**Services**	
Extended time	☑	Diagnostic tests	☑
Oral exams	☑	Learning centers	☑
Take home exams	☐	Proofreaders	☐
Exams on tape or computer	☐	Readers	☑
Untimed exams	☐	Reading Machines/Kurzweil	☑
Other accommodations	☑	Special bookstore section	☐
		Typists	☑

Credit toward degree is not given for remedial courses taken.

Counseling Services

- ☐ Academic
- ☐ Psychological
- ☐ Student Support groups
- ☐ Vocational

Tutoring

Individual tutoring is available daily.

	Individual	Group
Time management	☑	☑
Organizational skills	☑	☑
Learning strategies	☑	☐
Study skills	☑	☑
Content area	☑	☑
Writing lab	☑	☑
Math lab	☑	☑

LD PROGRAM STAFF

Total number of LD Program staff (including director):

Full Time: 1 Part Time: 1

There is an advisor/advocate from the LD program available to students.

Key staff person available to work with LD students: Katherine Simonton, Coordinator, Disability Services.

LD Program web site: http://web.uccs.edu/dss/Default.htm

University of Colorado at Denver Health Sciences Center

Denver, CO

Address: Campus Box 167 PO Box 173364, Denver, CO, 80217-3364
Admissions telephone: 303 556-2704
Admissions FAX: 303 556-4838
Director of Admissions: Barbara Edwards
Admissions e-mail: admissions@carbon.cudenver.edu
Web site: http://www.cudenver.edu
SAT Code: 4875 ACT Code: 533

Director of Disability Resources and Services: Lisa McGill
LD program telephone: 303 556-3450
LD program e-mail: lisa.mcgill@cudenver.edu
Total campus enrollment: 9, 921

GENERAL

University of Colorado at Denver Health Sciences Center is a public, coed, four-year institution. 127-acre, urban campus in Denver (population: 554,636); branch campuses in Boulder and Colorado Springs. Served by air, bus, and train. Public transportation serves campus. Semester system.

LD ADMISSIONS

A personal interview is not required. Essay is not required.

SECONDARY SCHOOL REQUIREMENTS

Graduation from secondary school required; GED accepted. The following course distribution required: 4 units of English, 3 units of math, 3 units of science, 2 units of foreign language, 2 units of social studies, 1 unit of history.

TESTING

SAT Reasoning or ACT required. SAT Subject recommended.

All enrolled freshmen (fall 2004):

Average SAT I Scores: Verbal: 530 Math: 528
Average ACT Scores: Composite: 22

Child Study Team report is not required. Tests required as part of this documentation:

- [ ] WAIS-IV
- [ ] WISC-IV
- [ ] SATA
- [ ] Woodcock-Johnson
- [ ] Nelson-Denny Reading Test
- [ ] Other

UNDERGRADUATE STUDENT BODY

Total undergraduate student enrollment: 3,736 Men, 5,054 Women.

Composition of student body (fall 2004):

	Undergraduate	Freshmen
International	0.9	3.3
Black	4.5	4.3
American Indian	1.2	1.2
Asian-American	13.4	10.3
Hispanic	14.5	10.7
White	61.1	62.4
Unreported	4.4	7.8
	100.0%	100.0%

3% are from out of state. Average age of full-time undergraduates is 23. 34% of classes have fewer than 20 students, 57% have between 20 and 50 students, 9% have more than 50 students.

EXPENSES

Tuition (2005-06): $3,300 per year (in-state), $15,242 (out-of-state).
Room: $8,874. Board: $5,598.
There is no additional cost for LD program/services.

LD SERVICES

LD program size is not limited.

LD services available to:

- [ ] Freshmen
- [ ] Sophomores
- [ ] Juniors
- [ ] Seniors

Academic Accommodations

Curriculum

- [ ] Foreign language waiver
- [ ] Lighter course load
- [ ] Math waiver
- [ ] Other special classes
- [ ] Priority registrations
- [ ] Substitution of courses

Exams

- [x] Extended time
- [x] Oral exams
- [ ] Take home exams
- [ ] Exams on tape or computer
- [ ] Untimed exams
- [ ] Other accommodations

In class

- [ ] Early syllabus
- [x] Note takers in class
- [ ] Priority seating
- [ ] Tape recorders
- [ ] Videotaped classes
- [ ] Text on tape

Services

- [x] Diagnostic tests
- [ ] Learning centers
- [ ] Proofreaders
- [x] Readers
- [x] Reading Machines/Kurzweil
- [ ] Special bookstore section
- [ ] Typists

Credit toward degree is not given for remedial courses taken.

Counseling Services

- [ ] Academic
- [ ] Psychological
- [ ] Student Support groups
- [ ] Vocational

Tutoring

	Individual	Group
Time management	[ ]	[ ]
Organizational skills	[ ]	[ ]
Learning strategies	[ ]	[ ]
Study skills	[ ]	[x]
Content area	[ ]	[x]
Writing lab	[x]	[ ]
Math lab	[x]	[ ]

UNIQUE LD PROGRAM FEATURES

Support Staff: A variety of support staff are available to implement accommodations including approximately 8 interpreters, 6-8 carptionists (CART), 4 readers/scribes for examinations, 24 readers to assist with providing textbooks onto tape, and accommodation aides on an as needed basis for internships, student teaching, etc.

LD PROGRAM STAFF

Total number of LD Program staff (including director):

Full Time: 1 Part Time: 1

Key staff person available to work with LD students: Lisa McGill, Director of Disability Resources and Services.

Colorado Christian University

Lakewood, CO

Address: 180 S. Garrison Street, Lakewood, CO, 80226
Admissions telephone: 800 44-FAITH
Admissions FAX: 303 963-3201
Vice President for Enrollment Management: Rodney Stanford
Admissions e-mail: admission@ccu.edu
Web site: http://www.ccu.edu
SAT Code: 4659 ACT Code: 523

Director of Prior Learning & Evaluation: Cynthia Swift
LD program telephone: 303 963-3267
LD program e-mail: cswift@ccu.edu
Total campus enrollment: 1,763

GENERAL

Colorado Christian University is a private, coed, four-year institution. 26-acre, suburban campus in Lakewood (population: 144,126), 10 miles from Denver; branch campuses in Colorado Springs, Denver, Fort Collins, and Grand Junction. Major airport, bus, and train serve Denver. Public transportation serves campus. Semester system.

LD ADMISSIONS

A personal interview is not required. Essay is required and may be typed.

SECONDARY SCHOOL REQUIREMENTS

Graduation from secondary school required; GED accepted.

TESTING

Child Study Team report is not required. Tests required as part of this documentation:

- ❑ WAIS-IV
- ❑ WISC-IV
- ❑ SATA
- ❑ Woodcock-Johnson
- ❑ Nelson-Denny Reading Test
- ❑ Other

UNDERGRADUATE STUDENT BODY

Total undergraduate student enrollment: 795 Men, 968 Women.

32% are from out of state.

STUDENT HOUSING

Housing is guaranteed for all undergraduates. Campus can house 722 undergraduates.

EXPENSES

Tuition (2005-06): $16,590 per year.

There is no additional cost for LD program/services.

LD SERVICES

LD program size is not limited.

LD services available to:

❑ Freshmen ❑ Sophomores ❑ Juniors ❑ Seniors

Academic Accommodations

Curriculum		In class	
Foreign language waiver	❑	Early syllabus	❑
Lighter course load	❑	Note takers in class	❑
Math waiver	❑	Priority seating	❑
Other special classes	■	Tape recorders	■
Priority registrations	❑	Videotaped classes	❑
Substitution of courses	❑	Text on tape	❑
Exams		**Services**	
Extended time	❑	Diagnostic tests	❑
Oral exams	❑	Learning centers	■
Take home exams	❑	Proofreaders	❑
Exams on tape or computer	❑	Readers	❑
Untimed exams	❑	Reading Machines/Kurzweil	❑
Other accommodations	❑	Special bookstore section	❑
		Typists	❑

Credit toward degree is not given for remedial courses taken.

Counseling Services

- ❑ Academic
- ❑ Psychological
- ❑ Student Support groups
- ❑ Vocational

Tutoring

	Individual	Group
Time management	❑	❑
Organizational skills	❑	❑
Learning strategies	❑	❑
Study skills	❑	❑
Content area	❑	❑
Writing lab	❑	❑
Math lab	❑	❑

LD PROGRAM STAFF

Total number of LD Program staff (including director):

Full Time: 1 Part Time: 1

Key staff person available to work with LD students: Cynthia Swift, Director of Prior Learning & Evaluation.

Colorado College

Colorado Springs, CO

Address: 14 East Cache La Poudre Street, Colorado Springs, CO, 80903
Admissions telephone: 800 542-7214
Admissions FAX: 719 389-6816
Dean of Admissions and Financial Aid: Mark Hatch
Admissions e-mail: admission@ColoradoCollege.edu
Web site: http://www.ColoradoCollege.edu
SAT Code: 4072 ACT Code: 498

LD program name: Disability Services
Coordinator, Disability Services: Jan Edwards
LD program telephone: 719 227-8285
LD program e-mail: jedwards@coloradocollege.edu
LD program enrollment: 90, Total campus enrollment: 2,011

GENERAL

Colorado College is a private, coed, four-year institution. 90-acre, urban campus in Colorado Springs (population: 360,890), 70 miles from Denver; branch campus in Crestone. Served by air and bus; larger airport and train serve Denver. School operates transportation to Colorado Springs airport for breaks. Public transportation serves campus. Semester system.

LD ADMISSIONS

Students complete a separate application and are not simultaneously accepted to the LD program. A member of the LD program does not sit on the admissions committee. A personal interview is recommended. Essay is required and may be typed.

SECONDARY SCHOOL REQUIREMENTS

Graduation from secondary school not required.

TESTING

SAT Reasoning or ACT required. SAT Subject recommended.

All enrolled freshmen (fall 2004):

Average SAT I Scores: Verbal: 632 Math: 630
Average ACT Scores: Composite: 27

Child Study Team report is not required. A neuropsychological or comprehensive psycho-educational evaluation is required for admission. Must be dated within 36 months of application. Tests required as part of this documentation:

- [ ] WAIS-IV
- [ ] WISC-IV
- [ ] SATA
- [ ] Woodcock-Johnson
- [ ] Nelson-Denny Reading Test
- [ ] Other

UNDERGRADUATE STUDENT BODY

Total undergraduate student enrollment: 879 Men, 1,055 Women.

Composition of student body (fall 2004):

	Undergraduate	Freshmen
International	0.9	1.8
Black	1.5	1.6
American Indian	1.4	1.3
Asian-American	4.5	4.4
Hispanic	8.8	6.9
White	78.8	79.5
Unreported	4.1	4.5
	100.0%	100.0%

69% are from out of state. 11% join a fraternity and 16% join a sorority. Average age of full-time undergraduates is 20. 73% of classes have fewer than 20 students, 27% have between 20 and 50 students.

STUDENT HOUSING

98% of freshmen live in college housing. Freshmen are required to live on campus. Housing is guaranteed for all undergraduates. Campus can house 1,423 undergraduates. Single rooms are available for students with medical or special needs. A medical note is required.

EXPENSES

Tuition (2005-06): $30,048 per year.

Room: $4,116. Board: $3,504.

There is no additional cost for LD program/services.

LD SERVICES

LD program size is not limited.

LD services available to:

- [x] Freshmen
- [x] Sophomores
- [x] Juniors
- [x] Seniors

Academic Accommodations

Curriculum		In class	
Foreign language waiver	[ ]	Early syllabus	[x]
Lighter course load	[ ]	Note takers in class	[x]
Math waiver	[ ]	Priority seating	[x]
Other special classes	[ ]	Tape recorders	[x]
Priority registrations	[ ]	Videotaped classes	[ ]
Substitution of courses	[x]	Text on tape	[x]
Exams		**Services**	
Extended time	[x]	Diagnostic tests	[ ]
Oral exams	[ ]	Learning centers	[x]
Take home exams	[ ]	Proofreaders	[ ]
Exams on tape or computer	[x]	Readers	[x]
Untimed exams	[ ]	Reading Machines/Kurzweil	[ ]
Other accommodations	[x]	Special bookstore section	[ ]
		Typists	[ ]

Credit toward degree is not given for remedial courses taken.

Counseling Services

- [x] Academic
- [x] Psychological
- [ ] Student Support groups
- [ ] Vocational

Tutoring

Individual tutoring is available.

	Individual	Group
Time management	[x]	[ ]
Organizational skills	[x]	[ ]
Learning strategies	[x]	[ ]
Study skills	[x]	[ ]
Content area	[x]	[ ]
Writing lab	[x]	[ ]
Math lab	[x]	[ ]

UNIQUE LD PROGRAM FEATURES

Colorado College is committed to being an exciting place of learning and discovery for all of its students and strives to provide equal educational opportunities to students with disabilities. The College offers a variety of services and resources to help students succeed and, in accordance with the Americans with Disabilities Act (ADA) and Section 504 of the Rehabilitation Act of 1973, Colorado College staff members work closely with students who have documented disabilities requiring accommodation to ensure equal access to the College's programs, activities, services, and facilities.

Accommodations are provided to students who request support through the disability services program and submit appropriate documentation of disability. Accommodations, which are determined on an individual basis, will be made depending on the nature of the particular disability and based upon the documentation provided.

LD PROGRAM STAFF

Total number of LD Program staff (including director):

Full Time: 1 Part Time: 1

There is an advisor/advocate from the LD program available to students.

Key staff person available to work with LD students: Jan Edwards, Coordinator, Disability Services.

LD Program web site: www.coloradocollege.edu/disabilityservices

Colorado School of Mines

Golden, CO

Address: 1600 Maple Street, Golden, CO, 80401
Admissions telephone: 800 446-9488, extension 3220
Admissions FAX: 303 273-3509
Director of Enrollment Management: Bill Young
Admissions e-mail: admit@mines.edu
Web site: http://www.mines.edu
SAT Code: 4073 ACT Code: 500

LD program name: Office of Services for Students with Disabilities
LD program address: 1600 Maple Street #8
Director: Ron Brummett
LD program telephone: 303 273-3377
LD program e-mail: rbrummet@is.mines.edu
LD program enrollment: 27, Total campus enrollment: 2,873

GENERAL

Colorado School of Mines is a public, coed, four-year institution. 373-acre, suburban campus in Golden (population: 17,159), 15 miles from Denver. Major airport, bus, and train serve Denver. Public transportation serves campus. Semester system.

LD ADMISSIONS

Application Deadline: 05/01. Students do not complete a separate application and are not simultaneously accepted to the LD program. A member of the LD program does not sit on the admissions committee. A personal interview is not required. Essay is not required.

For fall 2004, 10 completed self-identified LD applications were received. 10 applications were offered admission, and 10 enrolled.

SECONDARY SCHOOL REQUIREMENTS

Graduation from secondary school required; GED accepted. The following course distribution required: 4 units of English, 4 units of math, 3 units of science, 2 units of social studies, 3 units of academic electives.

TESTING

SAT Subject recommended.

All enrolled freshmen (fall 2004):

Average SAT I Scores:	Verbal: 600	Math: 645
Average ACT Scores:	Composite: 27	

Child Study Team report is not required. A neuropsychological or comprehensive psycho-education evaluation is not required for admission. Tests required as part of this documentation:

- ☐ WAIS-IV
- ☐ WISC-IV
- ☐ SATA
- ☐ Woodcock-Johnson
- ☐ Nelson-Denny Reading Test
- ☐ Other

UNDERGRADUATE STUDENT BODY

Total undergraduate student enrollment: 1,925 Men, 631 Women.

Composition of student body (fall 2004):

	Undergraduate	Freshmen
International	2.9	3.3
Black	1.2	1.4
American Indian	0.4	0.8
Asian-American	5.2	5.2
Hispanic	5.5	6.1
White	78.8	76.8
Unreported	6.0	6.4
	100.0%	100.0%

21% are from out of state. 20% join a fraternity and 20% join a sorority. Average age of full-time undergraduates is 20. 43% of classes have fewer than 20 students, 49% have between 20 and 50 students, 8% have more than 50 students.

STUDENT HOUSING

80% of freshmen live in college housing. Freshmen are not required to live on campus. Housing is guaranteed for all undergraduates. Campus can house 1,397 undergraduates. Single rooms are available for students with medical or special needs. A medical note is required.

EXPENSES

Tuition (2005-06): $6,464 per year (in-state), $19,624 (out-of-state).
Room: $3,500. Board: $3,100.
There is no additional cost for LD program/services.

LD SERVICES

LD program size is not limited.

LD services available to:

■ Freshmen ■ Sophomores ■ Juniors ■ Seniors

Academic Accommodations

Curriculum		In class	
Foreign language waiver	☐	Early syllabus	☐
Lighter course load	☐	Note takers in class	■
Math waiver	☐	Priority seating	■
Other special classes	☐	Tape recorders	☐
Priority registrations	☐	Videotaped classes	☐
Substitution of courses	☐	Text on tape	☐
Exams		**Services**	
Extended time	■	Diagnostic tests	☐
Oral exams	☐	Learning centers	☐
Take home exams	☐	Proofreaders	☐
Exams on tape or computer	☐	Readers	☐
Untimed exams	☐	Reading Machines/Kurzweil	☐
Other accommodations	☐	Special bookstore section	☐
		Typists	☐

Credit toward degree is not given for remedial courses taken.

Counseling Services

- ■ Academic
- ■ Psychological
- ☐ Student Support groups
- ☐ Vocational

Tutoring

Individual tutoring is not available.

Average size of tutoring groups: 12

	Individual	Group
Time management	■	■
Organizational skills	■	■
Learning strategies	☐	☐
Study skills	■	■
Content area	☐	☐
Writing lab	☐	☐
Math lab	☐	☐

LD PROGRAM STAFF

There is no advisor/advocate from the LD program available to students. 26 peer tutors are available to work with LD students.

Key staff person available to work with LD students: Ron Brummett, Director, Student Development & Academic Services.

LD Program web site: www.mines.edu/stu_life/dss

Colorado State University

Fort Collins, CO

Address: 8020 Campus Delivery, Fort Collins, CO, 80523
Admissions telephone: 970 491-6909
Admissions FAX: 970 491-7799
Director of Admissions: Mary Ontiveros
Admissions e-mail: admissions@colostate.edu
Web site: http://www.colostate.edu
SAT Code: 4075 ACT Code: 504

LD program name: Resources for Disabled Students
LD program address: 100 General Services
Director, Resources for Disabled Students: Rose Kreston
LD program telephone: 970 491-6385
LD program e-mail: rkreston@lamar.colostate.edu
LD program enrollment: 363, Total campus enrollment: 21,729

GENERAL

Colorado State University is a public, coed, four-year institution. 562-acre main campus and 1,703-acre research campus in Fort Collins (population: 118,652), 65 miles from Denver. Served by air and bus; major airport and train serve Denver. Public transportation serves campus. Semester system.

LD ADMISSIONS

Students do not complete a separate application and are simultaneously accepted to the LD program. A member of the LD program does not sit on the admissions committee. A personal interview is recommended. Essay is not required.

SECONDARY SCHOOL REQUIREMENTS

Graduation from secondary school required; GED accepted. The following course distribution required: 4 units of English, 3 units of math, 2 units of science, 2 units of foreign language, 3 units of social studies.

TESTING

SAT Reasoning or ACT required. SAT Subject recommended.

All enrolled freshmen (fall 2004):

Average SAT I Scores:	Verbal: 557	Math: 563
Average ACT Scores:	Composite: 24	

Child Study Team report is not required. A neuropsychological or comprehensive psycho-educational evaluation is required for admission. Tests required as part of this documentation:

- [x] WAIS-IV
- [x] WISC-IV
- [x] SATA
- [x] Woodcock-Johnson
- [x] Nelson-Denny Reading Test
- [x] Other

UNDERGRADUATE STUDENT BODY

Total undergraduate student enrollment: 10,395 Men, 11,128 Women.

Composition of student body (fall 2004):

	Undergraduate	Freshmen
International	0.5	1.1
Black	1.9	2.0
American Indian	1.0	1.2
Asian-American	3.4	2.8
Hispanic	6.3	5.9
White	84.4	83.4
Unreported	2.5	3.6
	100.0%	100.0%

20% are from out of state. 8% join a fraternity and 8% join a sorority. Average age of full-time undergraduates is 21. 37% of classes have fewer than 20 students, 45% have between 20 and 50 students, 18% have more than 50 students.

STUDENT HOUSING

92% of freshmen live in college housing. Freshmen are required to live on campus. Housing is guaranteed for all undergraduates, if space permits. Campus can house 5,031 undergraduates. Single rooms are available for students with medical or special needs. A medical note is required.

EXPENSES

Tuition (2005-06): $3,381 per year (in-state), $14,343 (out-of-state).

Room & Board: $6,768.

There is no additional cost for LD program/services.

LD SERVICES

LD program size is not limited.

LD services available to:

- [x] Freshmen
- [x] Sophomores
- [x] Juniors
- [x] Seniors

Academic Accommodations

Curriculum		**In class**	
Foreign language waiver	[ ]	Early syllabus	[ ]
Lighter course load	[x]	Note takers in class	[x]
Math waiver	[ ]	Priority seating	[ ]
Other special classes	[ ]	Tape recorders	[x]
Priority registrations	[x]	Videotaped classes	[ ]
Substitution of courses	[x]	Text on tape	[x]
Exams		**Services**	
Extended time	[x]	Diagnostic tests	[x]
Oral exams	[ ]	Learning centers	[ ]
Take home exams	[ ]	Proofreaders	[ ]
Exams on tape or computer	[x]	Readers	[x]
Untimed exams	[ ]	Reading Machines/Kurzweil	[x]
Other accommodations	[x]	Special bookstore section	[ ]
		Typists	[ ]

Credit toward degree is not given for remedial courses taken.

Counseling Services

- [x] Academic — Meets 2 times per academic year
- [ ] Psychological
- [ ] Student Support groups
- [ ] Vocational

Tutoring

Individual tutoring is available weekly.

	Individual	Group
Time management	[x]	[ ]
Organizational skills	[x]	[ ]
Learning strategies	[x]	[ ]
Study skills	[x]	[ ]
Content area	[ ]	[ ]
Writing lab	[x]	[ ]
Math lab	[ ]	[ ]

LD PROGRAM STAFF

Total number of LD Program staff (including director):

Full Time: 4 Part Time: 4

There is an advisor/advocate from the LD program available to students. The advisor/advocate meets with faculty 2 times per month and students 2 times per month.

Key staff person available to work with LD students: Rose Kreston, Director, Resources for Disabled Students.

LD Program web site: www.colostate.edu/depts/rds

Colorado State University - Pueblo

Pueblo, CO

Address: 2200 Bonforte Boulevard, Pueblo, CO, 81001
Admissions telephone: 877 USC-WOLF
Admissions FAX: 719 549-2419
Director of Admissions and Records: Joseph C. Marshall
Admissions e-mail: info@colostate-pueblo.edu
Web site: http://www.colostate-pueblo.edu
SAT Code: 4611 ACT Code: 524

Disability Resource Coordinator: Pam Chambers
LD program telephone: 719 549-2663
LD program e-mail: pam.chambers@colostate-pueblo.edu
LD program enrollment: 30, Total campus enrollment: 5,189

GENERAL

Colorado State University - Pueblo is a public, coed, four-year institution. 275-acre, suburban campus in Pueblo (population: 102,121), 35 miles from Colorado Springs. Served by bus and train; airport serves Colorado Springs; major airport serves Denver (119 miles). Public transportation serves campus. Semester system.

LD ADMISSIONS

A personal interview is not required. Essay is not required.

SECONDARY SCHOOL REQUIREMENTS

Graduation from secondary school required; GED accepted.

TESTING

SAT Reasoning or ACT required.

All enrolled freshmen (fall 2004):

Average SAT I Scores:	Verbal: 471	Math: 478
Average ACT Scores:	Composite: 20	

Child Study Team report is not required. Tests required as part of this documentation:

☐ WAIS-IV	☐ Woodcock-Johnson
☐ WISC-IV	☐ Nelson-Denny Reading Test
☐ SATA	☐ Other

UNDERGRADUATE STUDENT BODY

Total undergraduate student enrollment: 2,274 Men, 3,050 Women.

Composition of student body (fall 2004):

	Undergraduate	Freshmen
International	0.6	1.7
Black	6.4	4.5
American Indian	1.3	2.0
Asian-American	3.4	2.3
Hispanic	24.1	27.2
White	59.6	57.8
Unreported	4.6	4.5
	100.0%	100.0%

3% join a fraternity and 2% join a sorority. Average age of full-time undergraduates is 23. 41% of classes have fewer than 20 students, 50% have between 20 and 50 students, 9% have more than 50 students.

STUDENT HOUSING

48% of freshmen live in college housing. Freshmen are required to live on campus. Housing is guaranteed for all undergraduates. Campus can house 500 undergraduates. Single rooms are available for students with medical or special needs. A medical note is required.

EXPENSES

Tuition (2005-06): $2,650 per year (in-state), $13,542 (out-of-state).
Room: $2,876. Board: $3,036.

There is no additional cost for LD program/services.

LD SERVICES

LD program size is not limited.

LD services available to:

☐ Freshmen ☐ Sophomores ☐ Juniors ☐ Seniors

Academic Accommodations

Curriculum		**In class**	
Foreign language waiver	☐	Early syllabus	☐
Lighter course load	☐	Note takers in class	■
Math waiver	☐	Priority seating	☐
Other special classes	☐	Tape recorders	■
Priority registrations	☐	Videotaped classes	☐
Substitution of courses	☐	Text on tape	☐
Exams		**Services**	
Extended time	■	Diagnostic tests	☐
Oral exams	☐	Learning centers	☐
Take home exams	☐	Proofreaders	☐
Exams on tape or computer	☐	Readers	■
Untimed exams	☐	Reading Machines/Kurzweil	☐
Other accommodations	☐	Special bookstore section	☐
		Typists	☐

Credit toward degree is not given for remedial courses taken.

Counseling Services

☐ Academic
☐ Psychological
☐ Student Support groups
☐ Vocational

Tutoring

	Individual	Group
Time management	☐	☐
Organizational skills	☐	☐
Learning strategies	☐	☐
Study skills	☐	☐
Content area	☐	☐
Writing lab	■	☐
Math lab	■	☐

UNIQUE LD PROGRAM FEATURES

We have no separate LD Program available at this time.

LD PROGRAM STAFF

Total number of LD Program staff (including director):

Full Time: 1 Part Time: 1

Key staff person available to work with LD students: Pam Chambers, Disability Resource Coordinator.

University of Denver

Denver, CO

Address: 2199 S. University Boulevard, Denver, CO, 80208
Admissions telephone: 800 525-9495
Admissions FAX: 303 871-3301
Dean of Admission: Tom Willoughby
Admissions e-mail: admission@du.edu
Web site: http://www.du.edu
SAT Code: 4842 ACT Code: 534

LD program name: Learning Effectiveness Program
LD program address: 2050 East Evans Avenue
Director, University Disability Services: Ted May
LD program telephone: 303 871-4155
LD program e-mail: dluker@du.edu
LD program enrollment: 210, Total campus enrollment: 4,360

GENERAL

University of Denver is a private, coed, four-year institution. 125-acre, urban campus in Denver (population: 554,636). Served by air, bus, and train. Public transportation serves campus. Quarter system.

LD ADMISSIONS

Students do not complete a separate application and are not simultaneously accepted to the LD program. A member of the LD program does not sit on the admissions committee. A personal interview is required. Essay is required and may be typed.

For fall 2004, 251 completed self-identified LD applications were received. 130 applications were offered admission, and 78 enrolled.

SECONDARY SCHOOL REQUIREMENTS

Graduation from secondary school required; GED accepted.

TESTING

SAT Reasoning or ACT required. SAT Subject recommended.

All enrolled freshmen (fall 2004):

Average SAT I Scores: Verbal: 570 Math: 576
Average ACT Scores: Composite: 25

Child Study Team report is not required. A neuropsychological or comprehensive psycho-educational evaluation is required for admission. Must be dated within 36 months of application. Tests required as part of this documentation:

- ■ WAIS-IV
- ☐ WISC-IV
- ☐ SATA
- ■ Woodcock-Johnson
- ■ Nelson-Denny Reading Test
- ■ Other

UNDERGRADUATE STUDENT BODY

Total undergraduate student enrollment: 1,768 Men, 2,342 Women.

Composition of student body (fall 2004):

	Undergraduate	Freshmen
International	2.6	3.9
Black	1.8	5.9
American Indian	1.1	1.0
Asian-American	6.1	4.7
Hispanic	5.8	5.7
White	82.2	78.6
Unreported	0.4	0.2
	100.0%	100.0%

50% are from out of state. 20% join a fraternity and 19% join a sorority. Average age of full-time undergraduates is 20. 59% of classes have fewer than 20 students, 38% have between 20 and 50 students, 3% have more than 50 students.

STUDENT HOUSING

92% of freshmen live in college housing. Freshmen are required to live on campus. Housing is not guaranteed for all undergraduates. The University lacks the capacity to provide for all requests. Campus can house 2,300 undergraduates. Single rooms are available for students with medical or special needs. A medical note is required.

EXPENSES

Tuition (2005-06): $27,756 per year.

Room: $5,355. Board: $3,394.

Additional cost for LD program/services: $2,860 per academic year.

LD SERVICES

LD program is limited to 1% students.

LD services available to:

■ Freshmen ■ Sophomores ■ Juniors ■ Seniors

Academic Accommodations

Curriculum		In class	
Foreign language waiver	☐	Early syllabus	■
Lighter course load	■	Note takers in class	■
Math waiver	☐	Priority seating	☐
Other special classes	☐	Tape recorders	■
Priority registrations	■	Videotaped classes	■
Substitution of courses	■	Text on tape	■
Exams		**Services**	
Extended time	■	Diagnostic tests	■
Oral exams	■	Learning centers	■
Take home exams	■	Proofreaders	☐
Exams on tape or computer	■	Readers	■
Untimed exams	☐	Reading Machines/Kurzweil	■
Other accommodations	☐	Special bookstore section	☐
		Typists	■

Credit toward degree is not given for remedial courses taken.

Counseling Services

- ■ Academic
- ■ Psychological
- ■ Student Support groups
- ■ Vocational

Tutoring

Individual tutoring is available daily.

Average size of tutoring groups: 2

	Individual	Group
Time management	■	■
Organizational skills	■	■
Learning strategies	■	■
Study skills	■	■
Content area	■	■
Writing lab	■	■
Math lab	■	■

UNIQUE LD PROGRAM FEATURES

The Learning Effectiveness Program is a comprehensive program for students with LD and ADHD. Students with other disabilities are welcome to apply.

LD PROGRAM STAFF

Total number of LD Program staff (including director):

Full Time: 12 Part Time: 12

There is an advisor/advocate from the LD program available to students. The advisor/advocate meets with students 5 times per month. 20 graduate students and 4 peer tutors are available to work with LD students.

Key staff person available to work with LD students: Dave Luker, Assoc. Dir., Learning Effectiveness Program.

Fort Lewis College

Durango, CO

Address: 1000 Rim Drive, Durango, CO, 81301
Admissions telephone: 970 247-7184
Admissions FAX: 970 247-7179
Dean of Admission and Development: Gretchen Foster
Admissions e-mail: admission@fortlewis.edu
Web site: http://www.fortlewis.edu
SAT Code: 4310 ACT Code: 510

LD program name: Academic Success Program
Coordinator of Disability Services: Dian Jenkins
LD program telephone: 970 247-7459
LD program e-mail: jenkins_d@fortlewis.edu
LD program enrollment: 160, Total campus enrollment: 4,190

GENERAL

Fort Lewis College is a public, coed, four-year institution. 362-acre campus in Durango (population: 13,922), 174 miles from Grand Junction. Served by air and bus; train serves Grand Junction. Public transportation serves campus. Semester system.

LD ADMISSIONS

Students do not complete a separate application and are not simultaneously accepted to the LD program. A member of the LD program does not sit on the admissions committee. A personal interview is required. Essay is not required.

SECONDARY SCHOOL REQUIREMENTS

Graduation from secondary school required; GED accepted.

TESTING

SAT Reasoning or ACT required. SAT Subject recommended.

All enrolled freshmen (fall 2004):

Average SAT I Scores:	Verbal: 505	Math: 505
Average ACT Scores:	Composite: 21	

Child Study Team report is not required. A neuropsychological or comprehensive psycho-educational evaluation is required for admission. Must be dated within 36 months of application. Tests required as part of this documentation:

- ■ WAIS-IV
- ☐ WISC-IV
- ☐ SATA
- ■ Woodcock-Johnson
- ■ Nelson-Denny Reading Test
- ☐ Other

UNDERGRADUATE STUDENT BODY

Total undergraduate student enrollment: 2,342 Men, 2,099 Women.

Composition of student body (fall 2004):

	Undergraduate	Freshmen
International	0.1	1.1
Black	0.8	1.0
American Indian	15.6	17.9
Asian-American	1.5	0.9
Hispanic	6.3	5.7
White	69.5	68.1
Unreported	6.2	5.3
	100.0%	100.0%

34% are from out of state. Average age of full-time undergraduates is 22. 42% of classes have fewer than 20 students, 55% have between 20 and 50 students, 3% have more than 50 students.

STUDENT HOUSING

86% of freshmen live in college housing. Freshmen are required to live on campus. Housing is guaranteed for all undergraduates. Campus can house 1,486 undergraduates. Single rooms are not available for students with medical or special needs.

EXPENSES

Tuition (2005-06): $2,464 per year (in-state), $12,870 (out-of-state).

Room & Board: $6,524.

There is no additional cost for LD program/services.

LD SERVICES

LD program size is not limited.

LD services available to:

■ Freshmen ■ Sophomores ■ Juniors ■ Seniors

Academic Accommodations

Curriculum		In class	
Foreign language waiver	☐	Early syllabus	☐
Lighter course load	☐	Note takers in class	■
Math waiver	☐	Priority seating	☐
Other special classes	☐	Tape recorders	■
Priority registrations	☐	Videotaped classes	☐
Substitution of courses	☐	Text on tape	☐
Exams		**Services**	
Extended time	■	Diagnostic tests	☐
Oral exams	■	Learning centers	☐
Take home exams	☐	Proofreaders	☐
Exams on tape or computer	☐	Readers	■
Untimed exams	☐	Reading Machines/Kurzweil	☐
Other accommodations	☐	Special bookstore section	☐
		Typists	☐

Credit toward degree is not given for remedial courses taken.

Counseling Services

- ☐ Academic
- ☐ Psychological
- ☐ Student Support groups
- ☐ Vocational

Tutoring

Individual tutoring is available weekly.

Average size of tutoring groups: 4

	Individual	Group
Time management	☐	■
Organizational skills	☐	■
Learning strategies	☐	■
Study skills	☐	■
Content area	■	■
Writing lab	■	☐
Math lab	■	■

LD PROGRAM STAFF

There is an advisor/advocate from the LD program available to students. 80 peer tutors are available to work with LD students.

Key staff person available to work with LD students: Dian Jenkins, Coordinator of Disability Services.

Mesa State College

Grand Junction, CO

Address: 1100 North Avenue, Grand Junction, CO, 81501-3122
Admissions telephone: 800 982-6372 (in-state)
Admissions FAX: 970 248-1464
Dean of Enrollment Management: Tyre Bush
Admissions e-mail: admissions@mesastate.edu
Web site: http://www.mesastate.edu
SAT Code: 4484 ACT Code: 518

Coordinator of Educational Access Services: Sandra Wymore
LD program telephone: 970 248-1801
LD program e-mail: swymore@mesastate.edu
Total campus enrollment: 6,192

GENERAL

Mesa State College is a public, coed, four-year institution. 42-acre campus in Grand Junction (area population: 41,986), 250 miles from Denver; branch campus in Montrose. Served by air, bus, and train; major airport serves Denver. Public transportation serves campus. Semester system.

LD ADMISSIONS

A personal interview is not required. Essay is not required.

SECONDARY SCHOOL REQUIREMENTS

Graduation from secondary school required; GED accepted.

TESTING

SAT Reasoning or ACT required. SAT Subject recommended.

All enrolled freshmen (fall 2004):

Average SAT I Scores:	Verbal: 500	Math: 492
Average ACT Scores:	Composite: 20	

Child Study Team report is not required. Tests required as part of this documentation:

☐ WAIS-IV	☐ Woodcock-Johnson
☐ WISC-IV	☐ Nelson-Denny Reading Test
☐ SATA	☐ Other

UNDERGRADUATE STUDENT BODY

Total undergraduate student enrollment: 2,237 Men, 3,060 Women.

Composition of student body (fall 2004):

	Undergraduate	Freshmen
International	0.5	0.8
Black	2.4	1.4
American Indian	1.0	1.4
Asian-American	2.3	1.8
Hispanic	9.4	7.7
White	78.1	82.4
Unreported	6.3	4.5
	100.0%	100.0%

8% are from out of state. Average age of full-time undergraduates is 23. 49% of classes have fewer than 20 students, 45% have between 20 and 50 students, 6% have more than 50 students.

STUDENT HOUSING

46% of freshmen live in college housing. Freshmen are required to live on campus. Housing is guaranteed for all undergraduates. Campus can house 959 undergraduates.

EXPENSES

Tuition (2005-06): $2,359 per year (in-state), $9,546 (out-of-state).

Room: $3,364. Board: $3,339.
There is no additional cost for LD program/services.

LD SERVICES

LD program size is not limited.

LD services available to:

☐ Freshmen ☐ Sophomores ☐ Juniors ☐ Seniors

Academic Accommodations

Curriculum		**In class**	
Foreign language waiver	☐	Early syllabus	☐
Lighter course load	■	Note takers in class	■
Math waiver	☐	Priority seating	☐
Other special classes	☐	Tape recorders	■
Priority registrations	☐	Videotaped classes	☐
Substitution of courses	☐	Text on tape	☐
Exams		**Services**	
Extended time	■	Diagnostic tests	☐
Oral exams	■	Learning centers	■
Take home exams	☐	Proofreaders	☐
Exams on tape or computer	☐	Readers	☐
Untimed exams	☐	Reading Machines/Kurzweil	■
Other accommodations	☐	Special bookstore section	☐
		Typists	☐

Credit toward degree is not given for remedial courses taken.

Counseling Services

☐ Academic
☐ Psychological
☐ Student Support groups
☐ Vocational

Tutoring

	Individual	Group
Time management	☐	☐
Organizational skills	☐	☐
Learning strategies	☐	☐
Study skills	☐	☐
Content area	☐	☐
Writing lab	☐	☐
Math lab	☐	☐

LD PROGRAM STAFF

Total number of LD Program staff (including director):

Full Time: 2 Part Time: 2

Key staff person available to work with LD students: Sandra Wymore, Coordinator of Educational Access Services.

Metropolitan State College of Denver

Denver, CO

Address: 1201 Fifth Street, Denver, CO, 80217-3362
Admissions telephone: 303 556-3058
Admissions FAX: 303 556-6345
Director of Admissions: William Hathaway-Clark
Admissions e-mail: askmetro@mscd.edu
Web site: http://www.mscd.edu
SAT Code: 4505 ACT Code: 519

Total campus enrollment: 20,761

GENERAL

Metropolitan State College of Denver is a public, coed, four-year institution. 175-acre campus in Denver (population: 554,636); branch campuses in Englewood and Northglenn. Served by air, bus, and train. School operates transportation to parking lots. Public transportation serves campus. Semester system.

LD ADMISSIONS

Application Deadline: 08/01. Students do not complete a separate application and are not simultaneously accepted to the LD program. A member of the LD program does not sit on the admissions committee. A personal interview is not required. Essay is not required.

SECONDARY SCHOOL REQUIREMENTS

Graduation from secondary school required; GED accepted. The following course distribution required: 4 units of English, 3 units of math, 3 units of science, 2 units of foreign language, 2 units of social studies, 1 unit of history.

TESTING

SAT Reasoning or ACT required.

All enrolled freshmen (fall 2004):

Average SAT I Scores:	Verbal: 507	Math: 496
Average ACT Scores:	Composite: 20	

Child Study Team report is not required. A neuropsychological or comprehensive psycho-education evaluation is not required for admission. Tests required as part of this documentation:

- ☐ WAIS-IV
- ☐ WISC-IV
- ☐ SATA
- ☐ Woodcock-Johnson
- ☐ Nelson-Denny Reading Test
- ☐ Other

UNDERGRADUATE STUDENT BODY

Total undergraduate student enrollment: 7,863 Men, 10,582 Women.

Composition of student body (fall 2004):

	Undergraduate	Freshmen
International	0.4	0.9
Black	6.1	6.0
American Indian	1.0	1.1
Asian-American	4.3	4.0
Hispanic	16.5	13.8
White	66.7	69.0
Unreported	5.0	5.2
	100.0%	100.0%

1% are from out of state. Average age of full-time undergraduates is 24. 32% of classes have fewer than 20 students, 60% have between 20 and 50 students, 8% have more than 50 students.

STUDENT HOUSING

Housing is not guaranteed for all undergraduates. Single rooms are not available for students with medical or special needs.

EXPENSES

Tuition (2005-06): $2,192 per year (in-state), $9,420 (out-of-state).

LD SERVICES

LD program size is not limited.

LD services available to:

■ Freshmen ■ Sophomores ■ Juniors ■ Seniors

Academic Accommodations

Curriculum		**In class**	
Foreign language waiver	☐	Early syllabus	☐
Lighter course load	☐	Note takers in class	☐
Math waiver	☐	Priority seating	☐
Other special classes	☐	Tape recorders	☐
Priority registrations	☐	Videotaped classes	☐
Substitution of courses	☐	Text on tape	☐
Exams		**Services**	
Extended time	■	Diagnostic tests	☐
Oral exams	■	Learning centers	■
Take home exams	☐	Proofreaders	■
Exams on tape or computer	☐	Readers	■
Untimed exams	☐	Reading Machines/Kurzweil	☐
Other accommodations	☐	Special bookstore section	☐
		Typists	☐

Credit toward degree is not given for remedial courses taken.

Counseling Services

- ☐ Academic
- ☐ Psychological
- ☐ Student Support groups
- ☐ Vocational

Tutoring

Individual tutoring is available weekly.

Average size of tutoring groups: 20

	Individual	Group
Time management	☐	☐
Organizational skills	☐	☐
Learning strategies	■	☐
Study skills	■	☐
Content area	☐	☐
Writing lab	■	☐
Math lab	■	☐

University of Northern Colorado

Greeley, CO

Address: Greeley, CO, 80639
Admissions telephone: 800 700-4UNC
Admissions FAX: 970 351-2984
Director of Admissions: Mr. Gary Gullickson
Admissions e-mail: admissions.help@unco.edu
Web site: http://www.unco.edu
SAT Code: 4074 ACT Code: 502

LD program name: Disability Support Services
LD program address: Harrison 159A, Campus Box 139
Director, Disability Support Services: Nancy Kauffman
LD program telephone: 970 351-2289
LD program e-mail: nancy.kauffman@unco.edu
Total campus enrollment: 10,811

GENERAL

University of Northern Colorado is a public, coed, four-year institution. 236-acre campus in Greeley (population: 76,930), 50 miles from Denver. Served by bus; major airport and train serve Denver. Public transportation serves campus. Semester system.

LD ADMISSIONS

Students do not complete a separate application and are not simultaneously accepted to the LD program. A member of the LD program does not sit on the admissions committee.

SECONDARY SCHOOL REQUIREMENTS

Graduation from secondary school required; GED accepted. The following course distribution required: 3 units of math.

TESTING

SAT Reasoning or ACT required. SAT Subject recommended.

All enrolled freshmen (fall 2004):

Average SAT I Scores: Verbal: 519 Math: 516
Average ACT Scores: Composite: 22

Child Study Team report is not required. Tests required as part of this documentation:

- ❑ WAIS-IV
- ❑ WISC-IV
- ❑ SATA
- ❑ Woodcock-Johnson
- ❑ Nelson-Denny Reading Test
- ❑ Other

UNDERGRADUATE STUDENT BODY

Total undergraduate student enrollment: 3,995 Men, 6,166 Women.

Composition of student body (fall 2004):

	Undergraduate	Freshmen
International	0.2	0.4
Black	2.9	2.5
American Indian	1.4	1.2
Asian-American	4.5	3.4
Hispanic	8.9	8.1
White	78.9	79.7
Unreported	3.2	4.7
	100.0%	100.0%

11% are from out of state. 2% join a fraternity and 2% join a sorority. Average age of full-time undergraduates is 21. 24% of classes have fewer than 20 students, 60% have between 20 and 50 students, 16% have more than 50 students.

STUDENT HOUSING

91% of freshmen live in college housing. Freshmen are required to live on campus. Housing is not guaranteed for all undergraduates. Residence hall capacity limitations. Campus can house 3,101 undergraduates. Single rooms are available for students with medical or special needs.

EXPENSES

Tuition (2005-06): $3,192 per year (in-state), $11,736 (out-of-state). Room & Board: $6,133.

LD SERVICES

LD program size is not limited.

LD services available to:

■ Freshmen ■ Sophomores ■ Juniors ■ Seniors

Academic Accommodations

Curriculum		In class	
Foreign language waiver	❑	Early syllabus	❑
Lighter course load	❑	Note takers in class	■
Math waiver	❑	Priority seating	❑
Other special classes	❑	Tape recorders	■
Priority registrations	❑	Videotaped classes	❑
Substitution of courses	❑	Text on tape	❑
Exams		**Services**	
Extended time	■	Diagnostic tests	❑
Oral exams	❑	Learning centers	❑
Take home exams	❑	Proofreaders	❑
Exams on tape or computer	❑	Readers	■
Untimed exams	❑	Reading Machines/Kurzweil	❑
Other accommodations	■	Special bookstore section	❑
		Typists	❑

Credit toward degree is not given for remedial courses taken.

Counseling Services

- ❑ Academic
- ❑ Psychological
- ❑ Student Support groups
- ❑ Vocational

Tutoring

	Individual	Group
Time management	❑	❑
Organizational skills	❑	❑
Learning strategies	❑	❑
Study skills	❑	❑
Content area	❑	❑
Writing lab	❑	❑
Math lab	❑	❑

LD PROGRAM STAFF

Total number of LD Program staff (including director):

Full Time: 1 Part Time: 1

There is an advisor/advocate from the LD program available to students.

Key staff person available to work with LD students: Nancy Kauffman, Director, Disability Support Services.

Regis University

Denver, CO

Address: 3333 Regis Boulevard, B-20, Denver, CO, 80221
Admissions telephone: 800 388-2366, extension 4900
Admissions FAX: 303 964-5534
Acting Director of Admissions: Victor Davolt
Admissions e-mail: regisadm@regis.edu
Web site: http://www.regis.edu
SAT Code: 4656 ACT Code: 526

LD program name: Disability Services
LD program address: CO, 80221
Director of Disability Services: Joie Williams
LD program telephone: 303 458-4941
LD program e-mail: jwilliams@regis.edu
LD program enrollment: 237, Total campus enrollment: 6,123

GENERAL

Regis University is a private, coed, four-year institution. 90-acre, suburban campus in Denver (population: 554,636). Served by air, bus, and train. Public transportation serves campus. Semester system.

LD ADMISSIONS

Students do not complete a separate application and are not simultaneously accepted to the LD program. A member of the LD program does not sit on the admissions committee. A personal interview is recommended. Essay is required and may be typed.

For fall 2004, 84 completed self-identified LD applications were received. 84 applications were offered admission, and 84 enrolled.

SECONDARY SCHOOL REQUIREMENTS

Graduation from secondary school required; GED accepted.

TESTING

SAT Reasoning or ACT required. SAT Subject recommended.

All enrolled freshmen (fall 2004):

Average SAT I Scores:	Verbal: 534	Math: 530
Average ACT Scores:	Composite: 23	

Child Study Team report is not required. A neuropsychological or comprehensive psycho-educational evaluation is required for admission. Must be dated within 12 months of application. Tests required as part of this documentation:

- ■ WAIS-IV
- ☐ WISC-IV
- ☐ SATA
- ■ Woodcock-Johnson
- ☐ Nelson-Denny Reading Test
- ☐ Other

UNDERGRADUATE STUDENT BODY

Total undergraduate student enrollment: 466 Men, 556 Women.

Composition of student body (fall 2004):

	Undergraduate	Freshmen
International	0.2	0.9
Black	2.8	4.6
American Indian	0.0	0.6
Asian-American	3.9	3.1
Hispanic	12.9	8.3
White	69.0	64.5
Unreported	11.2	18.0
	100.0%	100.0%

53% are from out of state. Average age of full-time undergraduates is 20. 90% of classes have fewer than 20 students, 10% have between 20 and 50 students.

STUDENT HOUSING

86% of freshmen live in college housing. Freshmen are required to live on campus. Housing is guaranteed for all undergraduates. Campus can house 780 undergraduates. Single rooms are available for students with medical or special needs. A medical note is required.

EXPENSES

Tuition (2005-06): $23,500 per year.
Room: $4,700. Board: $3,490.

There is no additional cost for LD program/services.

LD SERVICES

LD program size is not limited.

LD services available to:

■ Freshmen ■ Sophomores ■ Juniors ■ Seniors

Academic Accommodations

Curriculum		In class	
Foreign language waiver	☐	Early syllabus	☐
Lighter course load	■	Note takers in class	■
Math waiver	☐	Priority seating	☐
Other special classes	☐	Tape recorders	■
Priority registrations	☐	Videotaped classes	☐
Substitution of courses	☐	Text on tape	■
Exams		**Services**	
Extended time	■	Diagnostic tests	☐
Oral exams	■	Learning centers	■
Take home exams	☐	Proofreaders	☐
Exams on tape or computer	■	Readers	■
Untimed exams	☐	Reading Machines/Kurzweil	■
Other accommodations	☐	Special bookstore section	☐
		Typists	☐

Credit toward degree is not given for remedial courses taken.

Counseling Services

- ■ Academic
- ☐ Psychological
- ☐ Student Support groups
- ☐ Vocational

Tutoring

Individual tutoring is not available.

	Individual	Group
Time management	☐	☐
Organizational skills	☐	☐
Learning strategies	☐	☐
Study skills	☐	☐
Content area	☐	☐
Writing lab	■	☐
Math lab	☐	☐

UNIQUE LD PROGRAM FEATURES

Regis University provides services to disabled students; Regis does not offer an LD program.

LD PROGRAM STAFF

Total number of LD Program staff (including director):

Full Time: 2 Part Time: 2

There is an advisor/advocate from the LD program available to students. The advisor/advocate meets with faculty 3 times per month and students 2 times per month.

Key staff person available to work with LD students: Joie Williams, Director of Disability Services.

Western State College of Colorado

Gunnison, CO

Address: 600 North Adams Street, Gunnison, CO, 81231
Admissions telephone: 800 876-5309
Admissions FAX: 970 943-2212
Director of Admissions: Tim Albers
Admissions e-mail: discover@western.edu
Web site: http://www.western.edu
SAT Code: 4946 ACT Code: 536

Director of Learning Services: Jan Edwards
LD program telephone: 970 943-7056
LD program e-mail: jedwards@western.edu
Total campus enrollment: 2, 270

GENERAL

Western State College of Colorado is a public, coed, four-year institution. 228-acre campus in Gunnison (population: 5,409), 166 miles from Colorado Springs. Served by air and bus; major airport serves Denver (200 miles); train serves Grand Junction (125 miles). Semester system.

LD ADMISSIONS

Students do not complete a separate application and are not simultaneously accepted to the LD program. A member of the LD program does not sit on the admissions committee. A personal interview is recommended. Essay is not required.

SECONDARY SCHOOL REQUIREMENTS

Graduation from secondary school required; GED accepted. The following course distribution required: 4 units of English, 3 units of math, 2 units of science, 2 units of social studies, 2 units of history, 3 units of academic electives.

TESTING

SAT Reasoning or ACT required. SAT Subject recommended.

All enrolled freshmen (fall 2004):

Average SAT I Scores:	Verbal: 497	Math: 499
Average ACT Scores:	Composite: 21	

Child Study Team report is not required. Tests required as part of this documentation:

- ☐ WAIS-IV
- ☐ WISC-IV
- ☐ SATA
- ☐ Woodcock-Johnson
- ☐ Nelson-Denny Reading Test
- ☐ Other

UNDERGRADUATE STUDENT BODY

Total undergraduate student enrollment: 1,342 Men, 960 Women.

Composition of student body (fall 2004):

	Undergraduate	Freshmen
International	0.0	0.0
Black	1.8	1.3
American Indian	0.3	0.9
Asian-American	1.0	0.9
Hispanic	6.5	5.4
White	85.1	85.0
Unreported	5.3	6.5
	100.0%	100.0%

30% are from out of state. 46% of classes have fewer than 20 students, 53% have between 20 and 50 students, 1% have more than 50 students.

STUDENT HOUSING

Housing is guaranteed for all undergraduates. Campus can house 1,200 undergraduates.

EXPENSES

Tuition (2005-06): $2,352 per year (in-state), $10,968 (out-of-state).
Room: $3,701. Board: $3,105.
There is no additional cost for LD program/services.

LD SERVICES

LD program size is not limited.

LD services available to:

☐ Freshmen ☐ Sophomores ☐ Juniors ☐ Seniors

Academic Accommodations

Curriculum		**In class**	
Foreign language waiver	☐	Early syllabus	☐
Lighter course load	☑	Note takers in class	☐
Math waiver	☐	Priority seating	☐
Other special classes	☐	Tape recorders	☐
Priority registrations	☐	Videotaped classes	☐
Substitution of courses	☐	Text on tape	☐
Exams		**Services**	
Extended time	☑	Diagnostic tests	☑
Oral exams	☐	Learning centers	☐
Take home exams	☐	Proofreaders	☐
Exams on tape or computer	☐	Readers	☐
Untimed exams	☐	Reading Machines/Kurzweil	☐
Other accommodations	☐	Special bookstore section	☐
		Typists	☐

Credit toward degree is not given for remedial courses taken.

Counseling Services

- ☐ Academic
- ☐ Psychological
- ☐ Student Support groups
- ☐ Vocational

Tutoring

	Individual	Group
Time management	☐	☐
Organizational skills	☐	☐
Learning strategies	☐	☐
Study skills	☐	☐
Content area	☐	☐
Writing lab	☐	☐
Math lab	☐	☐

LD PROGRAM STAFF

Total number of LD Program staff (including director):

Full Time: 1 Part Time: 1

Key staff person available to work with LD students: Jan Edwards, Director of Learning Services.

Albertus Magnus College

New Haven, CT

Address: 700 Prospect Street, New Haven, CT, 06511
Admissions telephone: 800 578-9160
Admissions FAX: 203 773-5248
Dean of Admission and Financial Aid: Richard Lolatte
Admissions e-mail: admissions@albertus.edu
Web site: http://www.albertus.edu
SAT Code: 3001 ACT Code: 549

Director of Academic Development Center: Deborah Frattini
LD program telephone: 203 772-8590
LD program e-mail: frattini@albertus.edu
Total campus enrollment: 1,906

GENERAL

Albertus Magnus College is a private, coed, four-year institution. 50-acre, suburban campus in New Haven (population: 123,626), 73 miles from New York City; branch campuses in Danbury, Hartford, New London, Stamford, Stratford, and Waterbury. Served by air, bus, and train; major airport serves Hartford (42 miles). School operates transportation to New Haven. Public transportation serves campus. Semester system.

LD ADMISSIONS

Application Deadline: 08/15. High school waivers are accepted for math and foreign language. A personal interview is recommended. Essay is required and may be typed.

SECONDARY SCHOOL REQUIREMENTS

Graduation from secondary school required; GED accepted. The following course distribution required: 4 units of English, 3 units of math, 1 unit of science, 3 units of foreign language, 1 unit of history, 3 units of academic electives.

TESTING

SAT Reasoning recommended. ACT considered if submitted. SAT Subject recommended.

All enrolled freshmen (fall 2004):

Average SAT I Scores: Verbal: 451 Math: 437

Child Study Team report is not required. Tests required as part of this documentation:

- ❑ WAIS-IV
- ❑ WISC-IV
- ❑ SATA
- ❑ Woodcock-Johnson
- ❑ Nelson-Denny Reading Test
- ❑ Other

UNDERGRADUATE STUDENT BODY

Total undergraduate student enrollment: 637 Men, 1,235 Women.

Composition of student body (fall 2004):

	Undergraduate	Freshmen
International	1.0	0.3
Black	16.1	23.3
American Indian	1.6	0.3
Asian-American	0.5	0.9
Hispanic	13.0	8.9
White	63.0	60.2
Unreported	4.7	5.9
	100.0%	100.0%

5% are from out of state, 78% of classes have fewer than 20 students, 22% have between 20 and 50 students.

STUDENT HOUSING

12% of freshmen live in college housing. Freshmen are not required to live on campus. Housing is guaranteed for all undergraduates.

EXPENSES

Tuition (2005-06): $17,268 per year.

Room & Board: $7,928.

There is no additional cost for LD program/services.

LD SERVICES

LD program size is not limited.

LD services available to:

❑ Freshmen ❑ Sophomores ❑ Juniors ❑ Seniors

Academic Accommodations

Curriculum		In class	
Foreign language waiver	❑	Early syllabus	❑
Lighter course load	■	Note takers in class	❑
Math waiver	❑	Priority seating	❑
Other special classes	❑	Tape recorders	■
Priority registrations	❑	Videotaped classes	❑
Substitution of courses	❑	Text on tape	❑
Exams		**Services**	
Extended time	■	Diagnostic tests	❑
Oral exams	❑	Learning centers	■
Take home exams	❑	Proofreaders	❑
Exams on tape or computer	❑	Readers	❑
Untimed exams	■	Reading Machines/Kurzweil	❑
Other accommodations	❑	Special bookstore section	❑
		Typists	❑

Credit toward degree is not given for remedial courses taken.

Counseling Services

- ❑ Academic
- ❑ Psychological
- ❑ Student Support groups
- ❑ Vocational

Tutoring

	Individual	Group
Time management	❑	❑
Organizational skills	❑	❑
Learning strategies	❑	❑
Study skills	❑	❑
Content area	❑	❑
Writing lab	❑	❑
Math lab	❑	❑

LD PROGRAM STAFF

Total number of LD Program staff (including director):

Full Time: 2 Part Time: 2

There is an advisor/advocate from the LD program available to students.

Key staff person available to work with LD students: Deborah Frattini, Director of Academic Development Center.

University of Bridgeport

Bridgeport, CT

Address: 126 Park Avenue, Bridgeport, CT, 06604
Admissions telephone: 800 EXCEL-UB
Admissions FAX: 203 576-4941
Dean of Admissions: Barbara L. Maryak
Admissions e-mail: admit@bridgeport.edu
Web site: http://www.bridgeport.edu
SAT Code: 3914 ACT Code: 602

Director of Counseling Services: Carole Weiner
LD program telephone: 203 576-4454
LD program e-mail: weiner@bridgeport.edu
Total campus enrollment: 1,374

GENERAL

University of Bridgeport is a private, coed, four-year institution. 86-acre, urban campus in Bridgeport (population: 139,529), 60 miles from New York City; branch campuses in Riverbend, Trumbull, and Waterbury; graduate center in Stamford. Served by air, bus, and train; major airport serves New York City. School operates transportation on campus. Public transportation serves campus. Semester system.

LD ADMISSIONS

A personal interview is recommended. Essay is required and may be typed.

SECONDARY SCHOOL REQUIREMENTS

Graduation from secondary school required; GED accepted. The following course distribution required: 4 units of English, 3 units of math, 2 units of science, 2 units of social studies, 5 units of academic electives.

TESTING

SAT Reasoning or ACT required. SAT Subject recommended.

All enrolled freshmen (fall 2004):

Average SAT I Scores: Verbal: 445 Math: 453
Average ACT Scores: Composite: 20

Child Study Team report is not required. Tests required as part of this documentation:

- ☐ WAIS-IV
- ☐ WISC-IV
- ☐ SATA
- ☐ Woodcock-Johnson
- ☐ Nelson-Denny Reading Test
- ☐ Other

UNDERGRADUATE STUDENT BODY

Total undergraduate student enrollment: 524 Men, 657 Women.

Composition of student body (fall 2004):

	Undergraduate	Freshmen
International	11.8	16.1
Black	35.7	32.8
Asian-American	5.1	4.5
Hispanic	17.6	13.4
White	25.1	29.5
Unreported	4.7	3.6
	100.0%	100.0%

39% are from out of state. 2% join a fraternity and 2% join a sorority. Average age of full-time undergraduates is 23, 66% of classes have fewer than 20 students, 33% have between 20 and 50 students.

STUDENT HOUSING

75% of freshmen live in college housing. Freshmen are required to live on campus. Housing is guaranteed for all undergraduates. Campus can house 976 undergraduates.

EXPENSES

Tuition (2005-06): $19,200 per year. Tuition is higher for some programs. Room: $4,600. Board: $4,400.
There is no additional cost for LD program/services.

LD SERVICES

LD program size is not limited.

LD services available to:

☑ Freshmen ☑ Sophomores ☑ Juniors ☑ Seniors

Academic Accommodations

Curriculum		**In class**	
Foreign language waiver	☐	Early syllabus	☐
Lighter course load	☑	Note takers in class	☐
Math waiver	☐	Priority seating	☐
Other special classes	☐	Tape recorders	☐
Priority registrations	☐	Videotaped classes	☐
Substitution of courses	☐	Text on tape	☐
Exams		**Services**	
Extended time	☐	Diagnostic tests	☐
Oral exams	☐	Learning centers	☑
Take home exams	☐	Proofreaders	☐
Exams on tape or computer	☐	Readers	☐
Untimed exams	☑	Reading Machines/Kurzweil	☐
Other accommodations	☐	Special bookstore section	☐
		Typists	☐

Credit toward degree is not given for remedial courses taken.

Counseling Services

- ☑ Academic
- ☑ Psychological
- ☐ Student Support groups
- ☐ Vocational

Tutoring

Individual tutoring is available daily.

	Individual	Group
Time management	☑	☑
Organizational skills	☑	☑
Learning strategies	☑	☑
Study skills	☑	☑
Content area	☑	☑
Writing lab	☑	☑
Math lab	☑	☑

LD PROGRAM STAFF

Key staff person available to work with LD students: Carole Weiner, Director of Counseling Services.

Central Connecticut State University

New Britain, CT

Address: 1615 Stanley Street, New Britain, CT, 06050
Admissions telephone: 888 733-2278
Admissions FAX: 860 832-2295
Director of Admissions: vacant
Admissions e-mail: admissions@ccsu.edu
Web site: http://www.ccsu.edu
SAT Code: 3898 ACT Code: 596

LD program name: Special Student Services
Director: Dr. George Tenney
Total campus enrollment: 9,604

GENERAL

Central Connecticut State University is a public, coed, four-year institution. 294-acre campus in New Britain (population: 71,538), nine miles from Hartford. Airport serves Windsor Locks (23 miles); train serves Berlin (three miles). Public transportation serves campus. Semester system.

LD ADMISSIONS

Students do not complete a separate application and are not simultaneously accepted to the LD program. A member of the LD program does not sit on the admissions committee. A personal interview is not required. Essay is required and may be typed.

SECONDARY SCHOOL REQUIREMENTS

Graduation from secondary school required; GED accepted. The following course distribution required: 4 units of English, 3 units of math, 2 units of science, 2 units of social studies, 1 unit of history.

TESTING

SAT Reasoning required; ACT may be substituted. SAT Subject recommended.

All enrolled freshmen (fall 2004):

Average SAT I Scores: Verbal: 514 Math: 518

Child Study Team report is not required. Tests required as part of this documentation:

- ☐ WAIS-IV
- ☐ WISC-IV
- ☐ SATA
- ☐ Woodcock-Johnson
- ☐ Nelson-Denny Reading Test
- ☐ Other

UNDERGRADUATE STUDENT BODY

Total undergraduate student enrollment: 4,615 Men, 4,936 Women.

Composition of student body (fall 2004):

	Undergraduate	Freshmen
International	1.2	1.6
Black	6.5	8.1
American Indian	1.4	0.5
Asian-American	2.9	2.7
Hispanic	5.7	5.8
White	76.5	74.1
Unreported	5.7	7.2
	100.0%	100.0%

6% are from out of state. 1% join a fraternity and 1% join a sorority. Average age of full-time undergraduates is 21, 43% of classes have fewer than 20 students, 56% have between 20 and 50 students.

STUDENT HOUSING

48% of freshmen live in college housing. Freshmen are not required to live on campus. Housing is guaranteed for all undergraduates. Campus can house 2,427 undergraduates.

EXPENSES

Tuition (2005-06): $3,034 per year (in-state), $9,820 (out-of-state).
Room & Board: $7,456.
There is no additional cost for LD program/services.

LD SERVICES

LD services available to:

■ Freshmen ■ Sophomores ■ Juniors ■ Seniors

Academic Accommodations

Curriculum		**In class**	
Foreign language waiver	☐	Early syllabus	☐
Lighter course load	☐	Note takers in class	■
Math waiver	☐	Priority seating	☐
Other special classes	☐	Tape recorders	■
Priority registrations	☐	Videotaped classes	☐
Substitution of courses	☐	Text on tape	☐
Exams		**Services**	
Extended time	■	Diagnostic tests	☐
Oral exams	■	Learning centers	■
Take home exams	☐	Proofreaders	☐
Exams on tape or computer	☐	Readers	■
Untimed exams	☐	Reading Machines/Kurzweil	■
Other accommodations	☐	Special bookstore section	☐
		Typists	☐

Credit toward degree is not given for remedial courses taken.

Counseling Services

- ☐ Academic
- ☐ Psychological
- ☐ Student Support groups
- ☐ Vocational

Tutoring

	Individual	Group
Time management	☐	☐
Organizational skills	☐	☐
Learning strategies	☐	☐
Study skills	☐	☐
Content area	☐	☐
Writing lab	☐	☐
Math lab	☐	☐

LD PROGRAM STAFF

There is an advisor/advocate from the LD program available to students.

Key staff person available to work with LD students: Dr. George Tenney, Director of Special Student Services.

Connecticut College

New London, CT

Address: 270 Mohegan Avenue, New London, CT, 06320-4196
Admissions telephone: 860 439-2200
Admissions FAX: 860 439-4301
Dean of Admissions and Financial Aid: Martha Merrill
Admissions e-mail: admission@conncoll.edu
Web site: http://www.conncoll.edu
SAT Code: 3284 ACT Code: 556

Director of Disability Services: Susan L. Duques, Ph.D.
LD program telephone: 860 439-5428
LD program e-mail: slduq@conncoll.edu
Total campus enrollment: 1,894

GENERAL

Connecticut College is a private, coed, four-year institution. 700-acre campus in New London (population: 25,671). Served by bus and train; major airport serves Hartford (50 miles); smaller airport serves Groton (10 miles). Semester system.

LD ADMISSIONS

A personal interview is recommended. Essay is required and may be typed.

SECONDARY SCHOOL REQUIREMENTS

Graduation from secondary school required; GED accepted.

TESTING

SAT Reasoning considered if submitted. ACT considered if submitted. SAT Subject recommended.

All enrolled freshmen (fall 2004):

Average SAT I Scores:	Verbal: 663	Math: 665
Average ACT Scores:	Composite: 28	

Child Study Team report is not required. Tests required as part of this documentation:

☐ WAIS-IV ☐ Woodcock-Johnson
☐ WISC-IV ☐ Nelson-Denny Reading Test
☐ SATA ☐ Other

UNDERGRADUATE STUDENT BODY

Total undergraduate student enrollment: 748 Men, 1,087 Women.

Composition of student body (fall 2004):

	Undergraduate	Freshmen
International	6.0	7.2
Black	4.0	3.8
American Indian	0.0	0.2
Asian-American	2.4	3.6
Hispanic	5.2	4.3
White	74.1	71.2
Unreported	8.2	9.7
	100.0%	100.0%

77% are from out of state. Average age of full-time undergraduates is 20, 61% of classes have fewer than 20 students, 36% have between 20 and 50 students.

STUDENT HOUSING

100% of freshmen live in college housing. Freshmen are required to live on campus. Housing is not guaranteed for all undergraduates. Available only to traditional full-time students. Campus can house 1,732 undergraduates.

EXPENSES

Tuition (2005-06): $41,975 per year (comprehensive).

There is no additional cost for LD program/services.

LD SERVICES

LD services available to:

☐ Freshmen ☐ Sophomores ☐ Juniors ☐ Seniors

Academic Accommodations

Curriculum		**In class**	
Foreign language waiver	☐	Early syllabus	☐
Lighter course load	■	Note takers in class	■
Math waiver	☐	Priority seating	☐
Other special classes	☐	Tape recorders	☐
Priority registrations	☐	Videotaped classes	☐
Substitution of courses	☐	Text on tape	☐
Exams		**Services**	
Extended time	■	Diagnostic tests	☐
Oral exams	☐	Learning centers	☐
Take home exams	☐	Proofreaders	☐
Exams on tape or computer	■	Readers	☐
Untimed exams	☐	Reading Machines/Kurzweil	☐
Other accommodations	■	Special bookstore section	☐
		Typists	☐

Credit toward degree is not given for remedial courses taken.

Counseling Services

☐ Academic
☐ Psychological
☐ Student Support groups
☐ Vocational

Tutoring

	Individual	Group
Time management	☐	☐
Organizational skills	☐	☐
Learning strategies	☐	☐
Study skills	☐	☐
Content area	☐	☐
Writing lab	☐	☐
Math lab	☐	☐

UNIQUE LD PROGRAM FEATURES

Connecticut College's Office of Student Disability Services determines eligibility for reasonable accommodations for documented disabilities to ensure equal access. We have no "LD" program, only services available to all qualified students with disabilities.

LD PROGRAM STAFF

Key staff person available to work with LD students: Susan L. Duques, Ph.D., Director of Student Disability Services.

University of Connecticut

Storrs, CT

Address: 2131 Hillside Road, Unit 3088, Storrs, CT, 06269-3088
Admissions telephone: 860 486-3137
Admissions FAX: 860 486-1476
Director of Admissions: Lee H. Melvin
Admissions e-mail: beahusky@uconn.edu
Web site: http://www.uconn.edu
SAT Code: 3915 ACT Code: 604

LD program name: University Program for Students with Learning Disabilities
LD program address: 249 Glenbrook Road Unit 2064, Storrs
Director, UPLD: David Parker, Ph.D.
LD program telephone: 860 486-0178
LD program e-mail: david.parker@uconn.edu
Total campus enrollment: 15,751

GENERAL

University of Connecticut is a public, coed, four-year institution. 4,104-acre campus in Storrs (population: 10,996), 25 miles from Hartford; branch campuses in Avery Point, Hartford, Stamford, Torrington, and Waterbury. Airports serve Windsor Locks (40 miles) and Boston (75 miles); bus serves Willimantic (15 miles); train serves Hartford. School operates shuttle on campus and to off-campus apartment complexes. Public transportation serves campus. Semester system.

LD ADMISSIONS

Students do not complete a separate application and are not simultaneously accepted to the LD program. A member of the LD program does not sit on the admissions committee. A personal interview is not required. Essay is required and may be typed. Foreign language requirement may be waived.

SECONDARY SCHOOL REQUIREMENTS

Graduation from secondary school required; GED accepted. The following course distribution required: 4 units of English, 3 units of math, 2 units of science, 2 units of foreign language, 2 units of social studies, 3 units of academic electives.

TESTING

SAT Reasoning or ACT required. SAT Subject recommended.

All enrolled freshmen (fall 2004):

Average SAT I Scores:	Verbal: 580	Math: 597
Average ACT Scores:	Composite: 24	

Child Study Team report is not required. A neuropsychological or comprehensive psycho-educational evaluation is required for admission. Tests required as part of this documentation:

- [x] WAIS-IV
- [x] WISC-IV
- [x] SATA
- [x] Woodcock-Johnson
- [x] Nelson-Denny Reading Test
- [x] Other

UNDERGRADUATE STUDENT BODY

Total undergraduate student enrollment: 6,776 Men, 7,274 Women.

Composition of student body (fall 2004):

	Undergraduate	Freshmen
International	0.6	0.9
Black	5.4	4.8
American Indian	0.4	0.3
Asian-American	6.6	6.6
Hispanic	4.4	4.4
White	74.3	74.7
Unreported	8.4	8.4
	100.0%	100.0%

23% are from out of state. 10% join a fraternity and 7% join a sorority. Average age of full-time undergraduates is 20, 39% of classes have fewer than 20 students, 45% have between 20 and 50 students, 16% have more than 50 students.

STUDENT HOUSING

97% of freshmen live in college housing. Freshmen are not required to live on campus. Housing is not guaranteed for all undergraduates. If demand for on-campus housing exceeds the supply, returning students who have lived on campus six or more semesters are subject to a lottery. Students are limited to 8 semesters of on-campus housing. Campus can house 10,652 undergraduates. Single rooms are not available for students with medical or special needs.

EXPENSES

Tuition (2005-06): $6,096 per year (in-state), $18,600 (out-of-state).

Room: $4,104. Board: $3,744.

There is no additional cost for LD program/services.

LD SERVICES

LD program size is not limited.

LD services available to:

- [x] Freshmen
- [x] Sophomores
- [x] Juniors
- [x] Seniors

Academic Accommodations

Curriculum		In class	
Foreign language waiver	[ ]	Early syllabus	[ ]
Lighter course load	[x]	Note takers in class	[x]
Math waiver	[ ]	Priority seating	[ ]
Other special classes	[ ]	Tape recorders	[x]
Priority registrations	[x]	Videotaped classes	[ ]
Substitution of courses	[x]	Text on tape	[x]
Exams		**Services**	
Extended time	[x]	Diagnostic tests	[ ]
Oral exams	[x]	Learning centers	[ ]
Take home exams	[ ]	Proofreaders	[ ]
Exams on tape or computer	[x]	Readers	[x]
Untimed exams	[x]	Reading Machines/Kurzweil	[x]
Other accommodations	[ ]	Special bookstore section	[ ]
		Typists	[ ]

Credit toward degree is not given for remedial courses taken.

Counseling Services

- [x] Academic
- [ ] Psychological
- [ ] Student Support groups
- [ ] Vocational

Tutoring

Individual tutoring is available weekly.

Average size of tutoring groups: 1

	Individual	Group
Time management	[x]	[ ]
Organizational skills	[x]	[ ]
Learning strategies	[x]	[ ]
Study skills	[x]	[ ]
Content area	[ ]	[ ]
Writing lab	[ ]	[ ]
Math lab	[ ]	[ ]

UNIQUE LD PROGRAM FEATURES

Eligibility for accommodations/services through the University Program for Students with Learning Disabilities (UPLD) are provided to students who present documentation that meets institutional guidelines at any point after being admitted.

LD PROGRAM STAFF

Total number of LD Program staff (including director):

Full Time: 1 Part Time: 1

There is an advisor/advocate from the LD program available to students. 5 graduate students are available to work with LD students.

Key staff person available to work with LD students: David Parker, Ph.D., Director, UPLD.

LD Program web site: www.cped.uconn.edu

Eastern Connecticut State University

Willimantic, CT

Address: 83 Windham Street, Willimantic, CT, 06226
Admissions telephone: 877 353-3278
Admissions FAX: 860 465-5544
Director of Admissions and Enrollment Management: Kimberly M. Crone
Admissions e-mail: admissions@easternct.edu
Web site: http://www.easternct.edu
SAT Code: 3966

LD program name: Access Ability Services
LD program address: 83 Windham St, Wood 240
Secretary: Hazel Gage
LD program telephone: 860 465-0189
LD program e-mail: GAGE@easternct.edu
LD program enrollment: 80, Total campus enrollment: 4,720

GENERAL

Eastern Connecticut State University is a public, coed, four-year institution. 200-acre campus in Willimantic (population: 15,823), 25 miles from both Hartford and New London. Served by bus; airports serve Windsor Locks (35 miles) and Boston (100 miles); train serves Hartford. School operates shuttle service on campus. Public transportation serves campus. Semester system.

LD ADMISSIONS

Students do not complete a separate application and are not simultaneously accepted to the LD program. A member of the LD program does not sit on the admissions committee. A personal interview is recommended. Essay is required and may be typed.

SECONDARY SCHOOL REQUIREMENTS

Graduation from secondary school required; GED accepted. The following course distribution required: 4 units of English, 3 units of math, 2 units of science, 2 units of foreign language, 2 units of social studies, 3 units of history.

TESTING

SAT Reasoning or ACT required. SAT Subject recommended.

All enrolled freshmen (fall 2004):

Average SAT I Scores:	Verbal: 512	Math: 509
Average ACT Scores:	Composite:	

Child Study Team report is required if student is classified. A neuropsychological or comprehensive psycho-educational evaluation is required for admission. Must be dated within 36 months of application. Tests required as part of this documentation:

■ WAIS-IV	■ Woodcock-Johnson
■ WISC-IV	☐ Nelson-Denny Reading Test
☐ SATA	☐ Other

UNDERGRADUATE STUDENT BODY

Total undergraduate student enrollment: 2,116 Men, 2,878 Women.

Composition of student body (fall 2004):

	Undergraduate	Freshmen
International	0.0	0.8
Black	8.2	7.0
American Indian	0.7	0.8
Asian-American	1.7	1.3
Hispanic	5.4	4.1
White	82.1	82.9
Unreported	1.9	3.1
	100.0%	100.0%

8% are from out of state. Average age of full-time undergraduates is 21, 30% of classes have fewer than 20 students, 70% have between 20 and 50 students.

STUDENT HOUSING

87% of freshmen live in college housing. Freshmen are not required to live on campus. Housing is guaranteed for all undergraduates. Campus can house 2,500 undergraduates. Single rooms are available for students with medical or special needs. A medical note is required.

EXPENSES

Tuition (2005-06): $3,034 per year (in-state), $9,820 (out-of-state).
Room: $5,250. Board: $3,350.
There is no additional cost for LD program/services.

LD SERVICES

LD program size is not limited.

LD services available to:

■ Freshmen ■ Sophomores ■ Juniors ■ Seniors

Academic Accommodations

Curriculum		**In class**	
Foreign language waiver	☐	Early syllabus	■
Lighter course load	■	Note takers in class	■
Math waiver	☐	Priority seating	■
Other special classes	☐	Tape recorders	■
Priority registrations	■	Videotaped classes	☐
Substitution of courses	■	Text on tape	■
Exams		**Services**	
Extended time	■	Diagnostic tests	☐
Oral exams	■	Learning centers	■
Take home exams	☐	Proofreaders	■
Exams on tape or computer	■	Readers	■
Untimed exams	☐	Reading Machines/Kurzweil	■
Other accommodations	■	Special bookstore section	☐
		Typists	■

Credit toward degree is not given for remedial courses taken.

Counseling Services

■ Academic
■ Psychological
☐ Student Support groups
■ Vocational

Tutoring

Individual tutoring is available.

	Individual	Group
Time management	■	☐
Organizational skills	■	☐
Learning strategies	■	☐
Study skills	■	☐
Content area	■	☐
Writing lab	☐	☐
Math lab	☐	☐

UNIQUE LD PROGRAM FEATURES

The Office of Access Ability Services works with students who have any sort of self-identified disability, including LD. All services are determined on a case-by-case basis. Services are provided as needed by students.

LD PROGRAM STAFF

Total number of LD Program staff (including director):

Full Time: 1 Part Time: 1

There is an advisor/advocate from the LD program available to students. 5 peer tutors are available to work with LD students.

Key staff person available to work with LD students: Dr. Pamela Starr, Coordinator/Counselor.

LD Program web site: http://www.easternct.edu/depts/stuaff/ods/

Fairfield University

Fairfield, CT

Address: 1073 North Benson Road, Fairfield, CT, 06824-5195
Admissions telephone: 203 254-4100
Admissions FAX: 203 254-4199
Director of Admission: Karen A. Pellegrino
Admissions e-mail: admis@mail.fairfield.edu
Web site: http://www.fairfield.edu
SAT Code: 3390 ACT Code: 560

Director of Student Support Services: W. Laurence O'Neil, S.J.
LD program e-mail: wloneil@mail.fairfield.edu
LD program enrollment: 119, Total campus enrollment: 3,942

GENERAL

Fairfield University is a private, coed, four-year institution. 200-acre, suburban campus in Fairfield (population: 57,340), five miles from Bridgeport and 60 miles from New York City. Major airport serves New York City; smaller airport serves New Haven (20 miles); bus and train serve Bridgeport. School operates transportation around Fairfield. Semester system.

LD ADMISSIONS

A personal interview is not required. Essay is required and may be typed. Math and foreign language requirements may be waived.

SECONDARY SCHOOL REQUIREMENTS

Graduation from secondary school required; GED not accepted. The following course distribution required: 4 units of English, 3 units of math, 3 units of science, 2 units of foreign language, 3 units of social studies.

TESTING

SAT Reasoning or ACT required. SAT Subject recommended.

All enrolled freshmen (fall 2004):

Average SAT I Scores:	Verbal: 592	Math: 608
Average ACT Scores:	Composite: 25	

Child Study Team report is not required. Tests required as part of this documentation:

- [ ] WAIS-IV
- [ ] WISC-IV
- [ ] SATA
- [ ] Woodcock-Johnson
- [ ] Nelson-Denny Reading Test
- [ ] Other

UNDERGRADUATE STUDENT BODY

Total undergraduate student enrollment: 1,884 Men, 2,280 Women.

Composition of student body (fall 2004):

	Undergraduate	Freshmen
International	0.7	1.0
Black	1.1	1.8
American Indian	0.0	0.2
Asian-American	2.0	3.4
Hispanic	4.6	5.1
White	91.1	88.3
Unreported	0.6	0.3
	100.0%	100.0%

76% are from out of state. Average age of full-time undergraduates is 20, 36% of classes have fewer than 20 students, 64% have between 20 and 50 students.

STUDENT HOUSING

97% of freshmen live in college housing. Freshmen are required to live on campus. Housing is guaranteed for all undergraduates. Campus can house 2,590 undergraduates. Single rooms are available for students with medical or special needs. A medical note is required.

EXPENSES

Tuition (2005-06): $29,730 per year.
Room & Board: $9,600.
There is no additional cost for LD program/services.

LD SERVICES

LD program size is not limited.

LD services available to:

- [x] Freshmen
- [x] Sophomores
- [x] Juniors
- [x] Seniors

Academic Accommodations

Curriculum		In class	
Foreign language waiver	[ ]	Early syllabus	[ ]
Lighter course load	[x]	Note takers in class	[x]
Math waiver	[ ]	Priority seating	[ ]
Other special classes	[ ]	Tape recorders	[x]
Priority registrations	[ ]	Videotaped classes	[ ]
Substitution of courses	[ ]	Text on tape	[ ]
Exams		**Services**	
Extended time	[x]	Diagnostic tests	[ ]
Oral exams	[x]	Learning centers	[ ]
Take home exams	[ ]	Proofreaders	[ ]
Exams on tape or computer	[ ]	Readers	[x]
Untimed exams	[ ]	Reading Machines/Kurzweil	[x]
Other accommodations	[ ]	Special bookstore section	[ ]
		Typists	[ ]

Credit toward degree is not given for remedial courses taken.

Counseling Services

- [ ] Academic
- [ ] Psychological
- [ ] Student Support groups
- [ ] Vocational

Tutoring

Individual tutoring is available weekly.

Average size of tutoring groups: 1

	Individual	Group
Time management	[x]	[ ]
Organizational skills	[x]	[ ]
Learning strategies	[x]	[ ]
Study skills	[x]	[ ]
Content area	[x]	[ ]
Writing lab	[x]	[ ]
Math lab	[x]	[ ]

UNIQUE LD PROGRAM FEATURES

We provide accommodations for students with disabilities and a variety of support services are available to all undergraduates.

LD PROGRAM STAFF

Total number of LD Program staff (including director):

Full Time: 1 Part Time: 1

There is no advisor/advocate from the LD program available to students. 2 graduate students and 100 peer tutors are available to work with LD students.

Key staff person available to work with LD students: David Ryan-Soderlund, Assistant Director of Student Support Services.

University of Hartford

West Hartford, CT

Address: 200 Bloomfield Avenue, West Hartford, CT, 06117-1599
Admissions telephone: 800 947-4303
Admissions FAX: 860 768-4961
Dean of Admissions: Richard Zeiser
Admissions e-mail: admission@hartford.edu
Web site: http://www.hartford.edu
SAT Code: 3436 ACT Code: 606

Director of Learning Plus: E. Lynne Golden
LD program e-mail: LDsupport@hartford.eduLD program
LD program telephone: 860 768-4522
Total campus enrollment: 5,566

GENERAL

University of Hartford is a private, coed, four-year institution. 320-acre, suburban campus in West Hartford (population: 63,589), two miles from downtown Hartford. Served by bus and train; major airport serves Windsor Locks (13 miles). School operates transportation to consortium schools. Public transportation serves campus. Semester system.

LD ADMISSIONS

SECONDARY SCHOOL REQUIREMENTS

Graduation from secondary school required; GED accepted. The following course distribution required: 4 units of English, 2 units of math, 2 units of science, 2 units of social studies, 2 units of history, 4 units of academic electives.

TESTING

ACT considered if submitted. SAT Reasoning required; ACT may be substituted.

All enrolled freshmen (fall 2004):

Average SAT I Scores: Verbal: 533 Math: 539
Average ACT Scores: Composite: 23

Child Study Team report is not required. Tests required as part of this documentation:

- [ ] WAIS-IV
- [ ] WISC-IV
- [ ] SATA
- [ ] Woodcock-Johnson
- [ ] Nelson-Denny Reading Test
- [ ] Other

UNDERGRADUATE STUDENT BODY

Total undergraduate student enrollment: 2,582 Men, 2,843 Women.

Composition of student body (fall 2004):

	Undergraduate	Freshmen
International	2.6	2.8
Black	9.6	10.2
American Indian	0.2	0.2
Asian-American	2.9	2.4
Hispanic	4.3	4.2
White	64.9	67.6
Unreported	15.6	12.4
	100.0%	100.0%

61% are from out of state. 9% join a fraternity and 13% join a sorority. Average age of full-time undergraduates is 20, 61% of classes have fewer than 20 students, 38% have between 20 and 50 students, 1% have more than 50 students.

STUDENT HOUSING

92% of freshmen live in college housing. Freshmen are not required to live on campus. Housing is not guaranteed for all undergraduates. No graduate housing Campus can house 3,472 undergraduates.

EXPENSES

Tuition (2005-06): $23,406 per year.
Room: $5,826. Board: $3,622.
There is no additional cost for LD program/services.

LD SERVICES

LD program size is not limited.

LD services available to:

[ ] Freshmen [ ] Sophomores [ ] Juniors [ ] Seniors

Academic Accommodations

Curriculum		**In class**	
Foreign language waiver	[ ]	Early syllabus	[ ]
Lighter course load	[ ]	Note takers in class	[x]
Math waiver	[ ]	Priority seating	[ ]
Other special classes	[ ]	Tape recorders	[x]
Priority registrations	[ ]	Videotaped classes	[ ]
Substitution of courses	[ ]	Text on tape	[ ]
Exams		**Services**	
Extended time	[x]	Diagnostic tests	[ ]
Oral exams	[ ]	Learning centers	[x]
Take home exams	[ ]	Proofreaders	[ ]
Exams on tape or computer	[ ]	Readers	[x]
Untimed exams	[ ]	Reading Machines/Kurzweil	[ ]
Other accommodations	[ ]	Special bookstore section	[ ]
		Typists	[ ]

Credit toward degree is not given for remedial courses taken.

Counseling Services

- [ ] Academic
- [ ] Psychological
- [ ] Student Support groups
- [ ] Vocational

Tutoring

	Individual	Group
Time management	[ ]	[ ]
Organizational skills	[ ]	[ ]
Learning strategies	[ ]	[ ]
Study skills	[ ]	[ ]
Content area	[ ]	[ ]
Writing lab	[ ]	[ ]
Math lab	[ ]	[ ]

LD PROGRAM STAFF

Key staff person available to work with LD students: E. Lynne Golden, Director of Learning Plus.

The LD Support Website is: uhaweb.hartford.edu\LDsupport

Mitchell College

New London, CT

Address: New London, CT
Admissions telephone: 800 443-2811
Admissions FAX: 860 444-1209
Director of Admissions: Kimberly S. Hodges
Web site: http://www.mitchell.edu
SAT Code: 3528 ACT Code: 572

LD program name: Academic Sucess Center
LD program address: 437 Pequot Ave, New London
LRC Admissions Liasion: Joanne Carnevale
LD program telephone: 860 701-5071
LD program e-mail: carnevale_j@mitchell.edu
Total campus enrollment: 561

GENERAL

Mitchell College is a private, coed, four-year institution. 65-acre campus in New London (population: 25,674). Served by bus and train; airport serves Windsor Locks (40 miles). School operates transportation to local transportation depot and shopping center. Public transportation serves campus. Semester system.

LD ADMISSIONS

Students do not complete a separate application and are not simultaneously accepted to the LD program. A member of the LD program does sit on the admissions committee. High school waivers are accepted for math and foreign language. A personal interview is recommended. Essay is required and may be typed.

SECONDARY SCHOOL REQUIREMENTS

Graduation from secondary school required; GED accepted. The following course distribution required: 4 units of English, 3 units of math, 3 units of science, 1 unit of foreign language, 2 units of social studies, 1 unit of history, 2 units of academic electives.

TESTING

SAT Reasoning or ACT required. SAT Subject recommended.

All enrolled freshmen (fall 2004):

Average SAT I Scores: Verbal: 420 Math: 400

Child Study Team report is not required. A neuropsychological or comprehensive psycho-educational evaluation is required for admission. Tests required as part of this documentation:

- ■ WAIS-IV
- ■ WISC-IV
- ☐ SATA
- ■ Woodcock-Johnson
- ■ Nelson-Denny Reading Test
- ■ Other

UNDERGRADUATE STUDENT BODY

Total undergraduate student enrollment: 348 Men, 360 Women.

Composition of student body (fall 2004):

	Undergraduate	Freshmen
International	0.4	3.3
Black	15.8	6.2
American Indian	2.4	7.1
Asian-American	0.4	0.5
Hispanic	7.3	1.4
White	69.2	66.4
Unreported	4.5	15.2
	100.0%	100.0%

47% are from out of state, 69% of classes have fewer than 20 students, 31% have between 20 and 50 students.

STUDENT HOUSING

90% of freshmen live in college housing. Freshmen are required to live on campus. Housing is guaranteed for all undergraduates. Campus can house 450 undergraduates. Single rooms are available for students with medical or special needs. A medical note is not required.

EXPENSES

Tuition 2002-03: $16,380 per year.

Room: $4,095. Board: $3,780.

Additional cost for LD program/services: $6,500 per year.

LD SERVICES

LD program size is limited.

LD services available to:

■ Freshmen ■ Sophomores ■ Juniors ■ Seniors

Academic Accommodations

Curriculum		In class	
Foreign language waiver	☐	Early syllabus	■
Lighter course load	■	Note takers in class	■
Math waiver	☐	Priority seating	☐
Other special classes	☐	Tape recorders	■
Priority registrations	■	Videotaped classes	☐
Substitution of courses	■	Text on tape	■
Exams		**Services**	
Extended time	■	Diagnostic tests	☐
Oral exams	■	Learning centers	■
Take home exams	☐	Proofreaders	☐
Exams on tape or computer	■	Readers	☐
Untimed exams	■	Reading Machines/Kurzweil	■
Other accommodations	■	Special bookstore section	☐
		Typists	■

Credit toward degree is not given for remedial courses taken.

Counseling Services

- ■ Academic
- ■ Psychological
- ■ Student Support groups
- ■ Vocational

Tutoring

Individual tutoring is available daily.

Average size of tutoring groups: 1

	Individual	Group
Time management	■	■
Organizational skills	■	■
Learning strategies	■	■
Study skills	■	■
Content area	■	■
Writing lab	■	■
Math lab	■	■

LD PROGRAM STAFF

There is an advisor/advocate from the LD program available to students.

Key staff person available to work with LD students: Joanne Carnevale, LRC Admissions Liasion.

University of New Haven

West Haven, CT

Address: 300 Boston Post Road, West Haven, CT, 06516
Admissions telephone: 800 DIAL-UNH
Admissions FAX: 203 931-6093
Director of Undergraduate Admissions: Jane C. Sangeloty
Admissions e-mail: adminfo@newhaven.edu
Web site: http://www.newhaven.edu
SAT Code: 3663 ACT Code: 576

LD program name: Office of Disability Services and Resources
Director of Disability Services/Resources: Linda O'Keke
LD program telephone: 203 932-7331
LD program e-mail: lokeke@newhaven.edu
Total campus enrollment: 2,570

GENERAL

University of New Haven is a private, coed, four-year institution. 78-acre campus in West Haven (population: 52,360), two miles from New Haven; branch campus in Groton. Airport, bus, and train serve New Haven; major airports serve Hartford (50 miles) and New York City (73 miles). Public transportation serves campus. 4-1-4 system.

LD ADMISSIONS

A personal interview is not required. Essay is required and may be typed.

SECONDARY SCHOOL REQUIREMENTS

Graduation from secondary school required; GED accepted. The following course distribution required: 4 units of English, 3 units of math, 2 units of science, 2 units of foreign language, 2 units of social studies.

TESTING

SAT Reasoning required; ACT may be substituted. SAT Subject recommended.

All enrolled freshmen (fall 2004):

Average SAT I Scores:	Verbal: 512	Math: 518
Average ACT Scores:	Composite: 23	

Child Study Team report is not required. Tests required as part of this documentation:

- ☐ WAIS-IV
- ☐ WISC-IV
- ☐ SATA
- ☐ Woodcock-Johnson
- ☐ Nelson-Denny Reading Test
- ☐ Other

UNDERGRADUATE STUDENT BODY

Total undergraduate student enrollment: 1,474 Men, 1,058 Women.

Composition of student body (fall 2004):

	Undergraduate	Freshmen
International	1.5	3.1
Black	6.8	9.0
American Indian	0.3	0.7
Asian-American	2.4	1.6
Hispanic	6.6	6.1
White	75.8	66.7
Unreported	6.6	12.8
	100.0%	100.0%

30% are from out of state. 3% join a fraternity and 4% join a sorority. Average age of full-time undergraduates is 21, 48% of classes have fewer than 20 students, 51% have between 20 and 50 students.

STUDENT HOUSING

78% of freshmen live in college housing. Freshmen are not required to live on campus. Housing is not guaranteed for all undergraduates. Campus housing is not guaranteed for all students, but every attempt is made to accommodate those interested in living on campus. Campus can house 1,335 undergraduates. Single rooms are available for students with medical or special needs. A medical note is required.

EXPENSES

Tuition (2005-06): $22,380 per year.

Room: $5,796. Board: $3,754.
There is no additional cost for LD program/services.

LD SERVICES

LD program size is not limited.

LD services available to:

■ Freshmen ■ Sophomores ■ Juniors ■ Seniors

Academic Accommodations

Curriculum		**In class**	
Foreign language waiver	☐	Early syllabus	☐
Lighter course load	■	Note takers in class	■
Math waiver	☐	Priority seating	■
Other special classes	☐	Tape recorders	■
Priority registrations	☐	Videotaped classes	☐
Substitution of courses	☐	Text on tape	■
Exams		**Services**	
Extended time	■	Diagnostic tests	■
Oral exams	☐	Learning centers	■
Take home exams	☐	Proofreaders	■
Exams on tape or computer	■	Readers	■
Untimed exams	☐	Reading Machines/Kurzweil	■
Other accommodations	■	Special bookstore section	☐
		Typists	■

Credit toward degree is not given for remedial courses taken.

Counseling Services

- ■ Academic
- ■ Psychological
- ☐ Student Support groups
- ■ Vocational

Tutoring

Individual tutoring is available daily.

Average size of tutoring groups: 5

	Individual	Group
Time management	■	☐
Organizational skills	■	☐
Learning strategies	■	☐
Study skills	■	☐
Content area	■	☐
Writing lab	■	☐
Math lab	■	☐

LD PROGRAM STAFF

Total number of LD Program staff (including director):

Full Time: 1 Part Time: 1

There is an advisor/advocate from the LD program available to students. 3 graduate students and 6 peer tutors are available to work with LD students.

Key staff person available to work with LD students: Linda O'Keke, Director.

LD Program web site: www.newhaven.edu/campuslife/disabilities.html

Quinnipiac University

Hamden, CT

Address: 275 Mount Carmel Avenue, Hamden, CT, 06518
Admissions telephone: 800 462-1944
Admissions FAX: 203 582-8906
Vice President and Dean of Admissions: Carla M. Knowlton
Admissions e-mail: admissions@quinnipiac.edu
Web site: http://www.quinnipiac.edu
SAT Code: 3712 ACT Code: 582

Coordinator of Learning Services: John Jarvis
Total campus enrollment: 5, 464

GENERAL

Quinnipiac University is a private, coed, four-year institution. 300-acre, suburban campus in Hamden (population: 56,913), eight miles from New Haven. Major airport serves Windsor Locks (35 miles); smaller airport, bus, and train serve New Haven. School operates transportation to area conveniences and train station. Public transportation serves campus. Semester system.

LD ADMISSIONS

A personal interview is recommended. Essay is required and may be typed. LD students may self-disclose to the coordinator of LD services in the Learning Center at any time following their acceptance to the University. Prior to that, we do not ask students to self-disclose their information.

SECONDARY SCHOOL REQUIREMENTS

Graduation from secondary school required; GED accepted. The following course distribution required: 4 units of English, 3 units of math, 2 units of science, 2 units of foreign language, 3 units of social studies, 2 units of academic electives.

TESTING

SAT Reasoning required; ACT may be substituted. SAT Subject required.

All enrolled freshmen (fall 2004):

Average SAT I Scores:	Verbal: 565	Math: 584
Average ACT Scores:	Composite: 26	

Child Study Team report is not required. Tests required as part of this documentation:

- ☐ WAIS-IV
- ☐ WISC-IV
- ☐ SATA
- ☐ Woodcock-Johnson
- ☐ Nelson-Denny Reading Test
- ☐ Other

UNDERGRADUATE STUDENT BODY

Total undergraduate student enrollment: 1,864 Men, 3,192 Women.

Composition of student body (fall 2004):

	Undergraduate	Freshmen
International	1.1	1.2
Black	1.2	2.3
American Indian	0.1	0.2
Asian-American	2.2	2.3
Hispanic	4.6	3.9
White	78.8	80.8
Unreported	12.0	9.3
	100.0%	100.0%

70% are from out of state. 4% join a fraternity and 4% join a sorority. Average age of full-time undergraduates is 21, 54% of classes have fewer than 20 students, 46% have between 20 and 50 students.

STUDENT HOUSING

95% of freshmen live in college housing. Freshmen are not required to live on campus. Housing is not guaranteed for all undergraduates. Housing is guaranteed for three years to entering freshmen, and for two years to entering transfer students in on-campus residence halls and nearby houses owned by the University. Senior year students are not housed on campus, but find apartments in nearby areas of Hamden, Cheshire, North Haven, Wallingford and Meriden. Campus can house 3,200 undergraduates. Single rooms are not available for students with medical or special needs.

EXPENSES

Tuition (2005-06): $23,360 per year.
Room & Board: $10,300.
There is no additional cost for LD program/services.

LD SERVICES

LD program size is not limited.

LD services available to:

☐ Freshmen ☐ Sophomores ☐ Juniors ☐ Seniors

Academic Accommodations

Curriculum		In class	
Foreign language waiver	☐	Early syllabus	☐
Lighter course load	☐	Note takers in class	☐
Math waiver	☐	Priority seating	☐
Other special classes	☐	Tape recorders	☐
Priority registrations	☐	Videotaped classes	☐
Substitution of courses	☐	Text on tape	☐
Exams		**Services**	
Extended time	☐	Diagnostic tests	☐
Oral exams	☐	Learning centers	■
Take home exams	☐	Proofreaders	☐
Exams on tape or computer	☐	Readers	☐
Untimed exams	☐	Reading Machines/Kurzweil	☐
Other accommodations	☐	Special bookstore section	☐
		Typists	☐

Credit toward degree is not given for remedial courses taken.

Counseling Services

- ☐ Academic
- ☐ Psychological
- ☐ Student Support groups
- ☐ Vocational

Tutoring

Individual tutoring is available daily.

	Individual	Group
Time management	☐	☐
Organizational skills	☐	☐
Learning strategies	☐	☐
Study skills	☐	☐
Content area	☐	☐
Writing lab	☐	☐
Math lab	☐	☐

UNIQUE LD PROGRAM FEATURES

Students are encouraged to self-advocate for services needed. Students can self-disclose at any point following their admissions decision.

LD PROGRAM STAFF

Total number of LD Program staff (including director):

Full Time: 1 Part Time: 1

Key staff person available to work with LD students: John Jarvis, Coordinator of Learning Services.

Sacred Heart University

Fairfield, CT

Address: 5151 Park Avenue, Fairfield, CT, 06825
Admissions telephone: 203 371-7880
Admissions FAX: 203 365-7607
Dean of Undergraduate Admissions: Karen N. Guastelle
Admissions e-mail: enroll@sacredheart.edu
Web site: http://www.sacredheart.edu
SAT Code: 3780 ACT Code: 589

LD program name: Office of Special Services
Director of Special Services: Jill Angotta
LD program telephone: 203 365-4730
LD program e-mail: angottaj@sacredheart.edu
LD program enrollment: 232, Total campus enrollment: 4,081

GENERAL

Sacred Heart University is a private, coed, four-year institution. 56-acre campus in Fairfield (population: 57,340), 55 miles from New York City; branch campuses in Derby, Lisbon, and Stamford and abroad in Luxembourg. Served by train; bus serves Bridgeport (10 miles); major airports serve New Haven (25 miles) and New York City. School operates transportation to local malls, businesses, banks, and transportation centers. Public transportation serves campus. Semester system.

LD ADMISSIONS

Students do not complete a separate application and are simultaneously accepted to the LD program. A member of the LD program does not sit on the admissions committee. High school waivers are accepted for foreign language. A personal interview is recommended. Essay is required and may be typed.

SECONDARY SCHOOL REQUIREMENTS

Graduation from secondary school required; GED accepted. The following course distribution required: 4 units of English, 3 units of math, 3 units of science, 2 units of foreign language, 3 units of social studies, 3 units of history, 3 units of academic electives.

TESTING

SAT Reasoning or ACT required. SAT Subject recommended.

All enrolled freshmen (fall 2004):

Average SAT I Scores: Verbal: 533 Math: 539
Average ACT Scores: Composite:

Child Study Team report is required if student is classified. A neuropsychological or comprehensive psycho-educational evaluation is required for admission. Must be dated within 12 months of application. Tests required as part of this documentation:

- [x] WAIS-IV
- [x] WISC-IV
- [ ] SATA
- [x] Woodcock-Johnson
- [ ] Nelson-Denny Reading Test
- [ ] Other

UNDERGRADUATE STUDENT BODY

Total undergraduate student enrollment: 1,528 Men, 2,603 Women.

Composition of student body (fall 2004):

	Undergraduate	Freshmen
International	0.6	1.2
Black	3.2	6.0
American Indian	0.5	0.2
Asian-American	1.4	1.3
Hispanic	2.9	5.8
White	91.6	85.7
Unreported	0.0	0.0
	100.0%	100.0%

42% are from out of state. 4% join a fraternity and 5% join a sorority. Average age of full-time undergraduates is 20, 54% of classes have fewer than 20 students, 46% have between 20 and 50 students.

STUDENT HOUSING

93% of freshmen live in college housing. Freshmen are not required to live on campus. Housing is guaranteed for all undergraduates. Campus can house 2,115 undergraduates. Single rooms are available for students with medical or special needs. A medical note is required.

EXPENSES

Tuition (2005-06): $23,750 per year. $17,000 per year (full-time first-time freshmen and transfers), $16,328 (all others).

Room: $7,111. Board: $2,583.

Additional cost for LD program/services: $1,054 per semester.

LD SERVICES

LD program size is not limited.

LD services available to:

- [x] Freshmen
- [x] Sophomores
- [x] Juniors
- [x] Seniors

Academic Accommodations

Curriculum		In class	
Foreign language waiver	[ ]	Early syllabus	[ ]
Lighter course load	[x]	Note takers in class	[x]
Math waiver	[ ]	Priority seating	[ ]
Other special classes	[ ]	Tape recorders	[x]
Priority registrations	[ ]	Videotaped classes	[ ]
Substitution of courses	[x]	Text on tape	[ ]
Exams		**Services**	
Extended time	[x]	Diagnostic tests	[ ]
Oral exams	[x]	Learning centers	[x]
Take home exams	[ ]	Proofreaders	[ ]
Exams on tape or computer	[ ]	Readers	[x]
Untimed exams	[x]	Reading Machines/Kurzweil	[x]
Other accommodations	[x]	Special bookstore section	[ ]
		Typists	[x]

Credit toward degree is not given for remedial courses taken.

Counseling Services

- [x] Academic
- [x] Psychological
- [ ] Student Support groups
- [ ] Vocational

Tutoring

Individual tutoring is available weekly.

Average size of tutoring groups: 4

	Individual	Group
Time management	[x]	[ ]
Organizational skills	[x]	[ ]
Learning strategies	[x]	[ ]
Study skills	[x]	[x]
Content area	[x]	[x]
Writing lab	[ ]	[ ]
Math lab	[ ]	[ ]

UNIQUE LD PROGRAM FEATURES

Mandatory LD services are free. The $1,054 per semester charge for first-year students covers additional, non-mandated services. After the first year the cost is $817 per semester. Academic and psychological counseling services are available as often as students require. Referrals for diagnostic testing available.

LD PROGRAM STAFF

Total number of LD Program staff (including director):

Full Time: 6 Part Time: 6

There is an advisor/advocate from the LD program available to students.

Key staff person available to work with LD students: Jill Angotta, Director of Special Services.

LD Program web site: www.sacredheart.edu/academics/academicsupport

Saint Joseph College

West Hartford, CT

Address: 1678 Asylum Avenue, West Hartford, CT, 06117
Admissions telephone: 860 231-5216
Admissions FAX: 860 231-5744
Director of Admissions: Kim Manning
Admissions e-mail: admissions@sjc.edu
Web site: http://www.sjc.edu
SAT Code: 3754 ACT Code: 588

ADA Coordinator: Barbara Maddaloni
LD program telephone: 860 231-5428
LD program enrollment: 30, Total campus enrollment: 1,172

GENERAL

Saint Joseph College is a private, women's, four-year institution. 84-acre campus in West Hartford (population: 63,589), three miles from Hartford. Served by bus and train; major airport serves Windsor Locks (10 miles). School operates transportation to shopping malls, Hartford Civic Center, and consortium schools. Public transportation serves campus. Semester system.

LD ADMISSIONS

SECONDARY SCHOOL REQUIREMENTS

Graduation from secondary school required; GED accepted. The following course distribution required: 4 units of English, 3 units of math, 3 units of science, 3 units of foreign language, 3 units of social studies.

TESTING

SAT Reasoning or ACT required.

All enrolled freshmen (fall 2004):

Average SAT I Scores: Verbal: 488 Math: 475

Child Study Team report is not required. Tests required as part of this documentation:

☐ WAIS-IV	☐ Woodcock-Johnson
☐ WISC-IV	☐ Nelson-Denny Reading Test
☐ SATA	☐ Other

UNDERGRADUATE STUDENT BODY

Total undergraduate student enrollment: 51 Men, 1,236 Women.

Composition of student body (fall 2004):

	Undergraduate	Freshmen
International	0.5	0.1
Black	13.8	14.3
American Indian	0.0	0.2
Asian-American	3.2	1.7
Hispanic	9.5	7.9
White	61.4	65.4
Unreported	11.6	10.2
	100.0%	100.0%

10% are from out of state. Average age of full-time undergraduates is 21, 71% of classes have fewer than 20 students, 28% have between 20 and 50 students.

STUDENT HOUSING

72% of freshmen live in college housing. Freshmen are not required to live on campus. Housing is guaranteed for all undergraduates. Campus can house 430 undergraduates. Single rooms are available for students with medical or special needs. A medical note is required.

EXPENSES

Tuition (2005-06): $21,370 per year.

Room & Board: $9,725.

LD SERVICES

LD program size is not limited.

LD services available to:

■ Freshmen ■ Sophomores ■ Juniors ■ Seniors

Academic Accommodations

Curriculum		**In class**	
Foreign language waiver	☐	Early syllabus	■
Lighter course load	■	Note takers in class	■
Math waiver	☐	Priority seating	■
Other special classes	☐	Tape recorders	■
Priority registrations	■	Videotaped classes	☐
Substitution of courses	■	Text on tape	■
Exams		**Services**	
Extended time	■	Diagnostic tests	☐
Oral exams	■	Learning centers	■
Take home exams	■	Proofreaders	■
Exams on tape or computer	■	Readers	■
Untimed exams	■	Reading Machines/Kurzweil	☐
Other accommodations	■	Special bookstore section	☐
		Typists	☐

Counseling Services

■ Academic
■ Psychological
☐ Student Support groups
☐ Vocational

Tutoring

Individual tutoring is available daily.

Average size of tutoring groups: 1

	Individual	Group
Time management	■	☐
Organizational skills	■	☐
Learning strategies	■	■
Study skills	■	☐
Content area	■	■
Writing lab	■	☐
Math lab	■	☐

LD PROGRAM STAFF

There is an advisor/advocate from the LD program available to students. The advisor/advocate meets with faculty once per month and students once per month.

Key staff person available to work with LD students: Barbara Maddaloni, ADA Coordinator.

Southern Connecticut State University

New Haven, CT

Address: 501 Crescent Street, New Haven, CT, 06515-1355
Admissions telephone: 203 392-5656
Admissions FAX: 203 392-5727
Director of Admissions: Sharon A. Brennan
Admissions e-mail: adminfo@southernct.edu
Web site: http://www.southernct.edu
SAT Code: 3662

Coordinator: Suzanne Tucker
LD program telephone: 203 392-6825
LD program e-mail: tuckers1@southernct.edu
Total campus enrollment: 8,314

GENERAL

Southern Connecticut State University is a public, coed, four-year institution. 168-acre campus in New Haven (population: 123,626), 35 miles from Hartford. Served by bus and train; major airports serve Windsor Locks, CT., and New York City (65 miles). School operates transportation to commuter parking lot. Public transportation serves campus. Semester system.

LD ADMISSIONS

A personal interview is not required. Essay is required and may be typed. Admissions requirements that may be waived for LD students include foreign language requirement.

SECONDARY SCHOOL REQUIREMENTS

Graduation from secondary school required; GED accepted. The following course distribution required: 4 units of English, 3 units of math, 2 units of science, 2 units of foreign language, 2 units of social studies, 2 units of history, 1 unit of academic electives.

TESTING

SAT Reasoning required. SAT Subject recommended.

All enrolled freshmen (fall 2004):

Average SAT I Scores: Verbal: 481 Math: 475

Child Study Team report is not required. Tests required as part of this documentation:

❑ WAIS-IV	❑ Woodcock-Johnson
❑ WISC-IV	❑ Nelson-Denny Reading Test
❑ SATA	❑ Other

UNDERGRADUATE STUDENT BODY

Total undergraduate student enrollment: 8,314.

Composition of student body (fall 2004):

	Undergraduate	Freshmen
International	1.1	1.5
Black	11.4	12.4
American Indian	0.1	0.3
Asian-American	1.5	2.3
Hispanic	6.2	6.4
White	73.5	69.8
Unreported	6.2	7.3
	100.0%	100.0%

7% are from out of state, 31% of classes have fewer than 20 students, 67% have between 20 and 50 students.

STUDENT HOUSING

Housing is guaranteed for all undergraduates. Campus can house 2,613 undergraduates.

EXPENSES

Tuition (2005-06): $3,034 per year (in-state), $9,820 (out-of-state).
Room: $4,234. Board: $3,414.

There is no additional cost for LD program/services.

LD SERVICES

LD program size is not limited.

LD services available to:

❑ Freshmen ❑ Sophomores ❑ Juniors ❑ Seniors

Academic Accommodations

Curriculum		**In class**	
Foreign language waiver	❑	Early syllabus	❑
Lighter course load	■	Note takers in class	■
Math waiver	❑	Priority seating	❑
Other special classes	■	Tape recorders	■
Priority registrations	❑	Videotaped classes	❑
Substitution of courses	❑	Text on tape	❑
Exams		**Services**	
Extended time	■	Diagnostic tests	❑
Oral exams	❑	Learning centers	❑
Take home exams	❑	Proofreaders	❑
Exams on tape or computer	❑	Readers	■
Untimed exams	❑	Reading Machines/Kurzweil	■
Other accommodations	❑	Special bookstore section	❑
		Typists	❑

Credit toward degree is not given for remedial courses taken.

Counseling Services

❑ Academic
❑ Psychological
❑ Student Support groups
❑ Vocational

Tutoring

	Individual	Group
Time management	❑	❑
Organizational skills	❑	❑
Learning strategies	❑	❑
Study skills	❑	❑
Content area	❑	❑
Writing lab	❑	❑
Math lab	❑	❑

UNIQUE LD PROGRAM FEATURES

University's Center for Adaptive Technology evaluates and trains students with disabilites.

LD PROGRAM STAFF

Total number of LD Program staff (including director):

Full Time: 2 Part Time: 2

Key staff person available to work with LD students: DRC Specialists.

Teikyo Post University

Waterbury, CT

Address: 800 Country Club Road, P.O. Box 2540, Waterbury, CT, 06723
Admissions telephone: 800 345-2562
Admissions FAX: 203 756-5810
Dean of Admissions: William Johnson
Admissions e-mail: admissions@post.edu
Web site: http://www.post.edu
SAT Code: 3698 ACT Code: 580

Assistant Coordinator for LD Program: Edith Cass
LD program telephone: 203 596-4511
LD program e-mail: ECass@post.edu
LD program enrollment: 18, Total campus enrollment: 1,198

GENERAL

Teikyo Post University is a private, coed, four-year institution. 60-acre, suburban campus in Waterbury (population: 107,271), 40 miles from Hartford; branch campuses in Danbury, Meriden, Trumbull, and West Hartford. Served by bus and train; major airport serves Hartford. School operates transportation to malls and surrounding communities and between campus and off-campus housing. Semester system.

LD ADMISSIONS

Students do not complete a separate application and are not simultaneously accepted to the LD program. A member of the LD program does not sit on the admissions committee. A personal interview is recommended. Essay is required and may be typed.

For fall 2004, 4 completed self-identified LD applications were received. 3 applications were offered admission, and 3 enrolled.

SECONDARY SCHOOL REQUIREMENTS

Graduation from secondary school required; GED accepted. The following course distribution required: 4 units of English, 2 units of math, 2 units of science, 2 units of foreign language, 1 unit of social studies, 2 units of history, 2 units of academic electives.

TESTING

SAT Reasoning or ACT recommended. SAT Subject recommended.

All enrolled freshmen (fall 2004):

Average SAT I Scores:	Verbal: 549	Math: 478
Average ACT Scores:	Composite: 18	

Child Study Team report is required if student is classified. A neuropsychological or comprehensive psycho-education evaluation is not required for admission. Tests required as part of this documentation:

☐ WAIS-IV ☐ Woodcock-Johnson
☐ WISC-IV ☐ Nelson-Denny Reading Test
☐ SATA ☐ Other

UNDERGRADUATE STUDENT BODY

Total undergraduate student enrollment: 473 Men, 877 Women.

Composition of student body (fall 2004):

	Undergraduate	Freshmen
International	0.9	5.0
Black	26.2	18.4
American Indian	0.9	0.4
Asian-American	1.8	1.8
Hispanic	13.6	10.8
White	52.5	61.8
Unreported	4.1	1.8
	100.0%	100.0%

14% are from out of state. Average age of full-time undergraduates is 22, 77% of classes have fewer than 20 students, 23% have between 20 and 50 students.

STUDENT HOUSING

50% of freshmen live in college housing. Freshmen are not required to live on campus. Housing is guaranteed for all undergraduates. Campus can house 410 undergraduates. Single rooms are available for students with medical or special needs. A medical note is required.

EXPENSES

Tuition (2005-06): $19,500 per year.
Room & Board: $8,300.
There is no additional cost for LD program/services.

LD SERVICES

LD program size is not limited.

LD services available to:

☑ Freshmen ☑ Sophomores ☑ Juniors ☑ Seniors

Academic Accommodations

Curriculum		In class	
Foreign language waiver	☑	Early syllabus	☐
Lighter course load	☑	Note takers in class	☐
Math waiver	☐	Priority seating	☐
Other special classes	☐	Tape recorders	☐
Priority registrations	☐	Videotaped classes	☐
Substitution of courses	☑	Text on tape	☐
Exams		**Services**	
Extended time	☑	Diagnostic tests	☐
Oral exams	☐	Learning centers	☑
Take home exams	☐	Proofreaders	☐
Exams on tape or computer	☐	Readers	☐
Untimed exams	☑	Reading Machines/Kurzweil	☐
Other accommodations	☑	Special bookstore section	☐
		Typists	☐

Credit toward degree is given for remedial courses taken.

Counseling Services

☑ Academic
☐ Psychological
☑ Student Support groups
☐ Vocational

Tutoring

Individual tutoring is available daily.

	Individual	Group
Time management	☑	☐
Organizational skills	☐	☐
Learning strategies	☑	☐
Study skills	☑	☑
Content area	☐	☐
Writing lab	☑	☑
Math lab	☑	☑

LD PROGRAM STAFF

Total number of LD Program staff (including director):

Full Time: 2 Part Time: 2

There is an advisor/advocate from the LD program available to students.

Key staff person available to work with LD students: Edith Cass, Assistant Coordinator.

Trinity College

Hartford, CT

Address: 300 Summit Street, Hartford, CT, 06106
Admissions telephone: 860 297-2180
Admissions FAX: 860 297-2287
Dean of Admissions and Financial Aid: Larry Dow
Admissions e-mail: admissions.office@trincoll.edu
Web site: http://www.trincoll.edu
SAT Code: 3899 ACT Code: 598

Dean of Students: Fred Alford
LD program telephone: 860 297-2157
LD program e-mail: dean-students@trincoll.edu
LD program enrollment: 180, Total campus enrollment: 2,317

GENERAL

Trinity College is a private, coed, four-year institution. 100-acre campus in Hartford (population: 121,578). Served by bus and train; major airport serves Windsor Locks (15 miles). Public transportation serves campus. School operates transportation around campus and Hartford. Semester system.

LD ADMISSIONS

A member of the LD program does not sit on the admissions committee. A personal interview is recommended.

SECONDARY SCHOOL REQUIREMENTS

Graduation from secondary school required; GED accepted. The following course distribution required: 4 units of English, 3 units of math, 2 units of science, 3 units of foreign language, 2 units of history.

TESTING

SAT Reasoning or ACT required. SAT Subject recommended.

All enrolled freshmen (fall 2004):

Average SAT I Scores:	Verbal: 647	Math: 653
Average ACT Scores:	Composite: 27	

Child Study Team report is not required. A neuropsychological or comprehensive psycho-educational evaluation is required for admission. Must be dated within 36 months of application. Tests required as part of this documentation:

☐ WAIS-IV ☐ Woodcock-Johnson
☐ WISC-IV ☐ Nelson-Denny Reading Test
☐ SATA ☐ Other

UNDERGRADUATE STUDENT BODY

Total undergraduate student enrollment: 1,011 Men, 1,063 Women.

Composition of student body (fall 2004):

	Undergraduate	Freshmen
International	3.3	1.8
Black	6.5	4.6
American Indian	0.2	0.0
Asian-American	5.8	5.7
Hispanic	5.1	4.7
White	52.9	61.1
Unreported	26.2	22.0
	100.0%	100.0%

80% are from out of state. 20% join a fraternity and 16% join a sorority. Average age of full-time undergraduates is 20, 65% of classes have fewer than 20 students, 31% have between 20 and 50 students.

STUDENT HOUSING

99% of freshmen live in college housing. Freshmen are not required to live on campus. Housing is guaranteed for all undergraduates. Campus can house 1,861 undergraduates. Single rooms are available for students with medical or special needs. A medical note is required.

EXPENSES

Tuition (2005-06): $32,000 per year.
Room: $5,550. Board: $3,040.
There is no additional cost for LD program/services.

LD SERVICES

LD program size is not limited.

LD services available to:

■ Freshmen ■ Sophomores ■ Juniors ■ Seniors

Academic Accommodations

Curriculum		**In class**	
Foreign language waiver	☐	Early syllabus	☐
Lighter course load	☐	Note takers in class	■
Math waiver	☐	Priority seating	■
Other special classes	☐	Tape recorders	■
Priority registrations	☐	Videotaped classes	☐
Substitution of courses	☐	Text on tape	■
Exams		**Services**	
Extended time	■	Diagnostic tests	☐
Oral exams	■	Learning centers	☐
Take home exams	☐	Proofreaders	☐
Exams on tape or computer	■	Readers	■
Untimed exams	☐	Reading Machines/Kurzweil	☐
Other accommodations	■	Special bookstore section	☐
		Typists	■

Credit toward degree is not given for remedial courses taken.

Counseling Services

■ Academic
■ Psychological
☐ Student Support groups
☐ Vocational

Tutoring

Individual tutoring is available.

	Individual	Group
Time management	■	■
Organizational skills	■	■
Learning strategies	■	■
Study skills	■	■
Content area	☐	☐
Writing lab	■	■
Math lab	■	■

LD PROGRAM STAFF

There is an advisor/advocate from the LD program available to students.

Key staff person available to work with LD students: Mark Brown, Consultant for Students with LD and other special needs.

Wesleyan University

Middletown, CT

Address: 237 High Street, Middletown, CT, 06459
Admissions telephone: 860 685-3000
Admissions FAX: 860 685-3001
Dean of Admission and Financial Aid: Nancy Hargrave Meislahn
Admissions e-mail: admissions@wesleyan.edu
Web site: http://www.wesleyan.edu
SAT Code: 3959 ACT Code: 614

LD program name: Disabilities Services
Interim Associate Dean/Student Academic Resources: Shelley Stephenson
LD program telephone: 860 685-2332
LD program e-mail: sstephenson@wesleyan.edu
LD program enrollment: 114, Total campus enrollment: 2,777

GENERAL

Wesleyan University is a private, coed, four-year institution. 240-acre campus in Middletown (population: 43,167), 15 miles from Hartford and 20 miles from New Haven. Served by bus; major airport serves Windsor Locks (35 miles); train serves Meriden (seven miles). School operates transportation to airport. Semester system.

LD ADMISSIONS

A member of the LD program does not sit on the admissions committee. High school waivers are accepted for math and foreign language. A personal interview is recommended. Essay is required and may be typed.

SECONDARY SCHOOL REQUIREMENTS

Graduation from secondary school required; GED not accepted. The following course distribution required: 4 units of English, 3 units of math, 3 units of science, 3 units of foreign language, 3 units of social studies.

TESTING

SAT Subject recommended.

All enrolled freshmen (fall 2004):

Average SAT I Scores: Verbal: 700 Math: 700
Average ACT Scores: Composite: 31

Child Study Team report is not required. A neuropsychological or comprehensive psycho-educational evaluation is required for admission. Tests required as part of this documentation:

- ☑ WAIS-IV
- ☑ WISC-IV
- ☑ SATA
- ☑ Woodcock-Johnson
- ☑ Nelson-Denny Reading Test
- ☑ Other

UNDERGRADUATE STUDENT BODY

Total undergraduate student enrollment: 1,322 Men, 1,470 Women.

Composition of student body (fall 2004):

	Undergraduate	Freshmen
International	7.3	6.1
Black	5.4	6.9
American Indian	0.7	0.5
Asian-American	11.1	9.0
Hispanic	7.3	7.3
White	58.8	61.8
Unreported	9.5	8.4
	100.0%	100.0%

84% are from out of state. 3% join a fraternity and 1% join a sorority. Average age of full-time undergraduates is 20, 62% of classes have fewer than 20 students, 32% have between 20 and 50 students, 5% have more than 50 students.

STUDENT HOUSING

100% of freshmen live in college housing. Housing is guaranteed for all undergraduates. Campus can house 2,568 undergraduates. Single rooms are available for students with medical or special needs. A medical note is required.

EXPENSES

Tuition (2005-06): $32,976 per year.
Room: $5,378. Board: $3,554.

There is no additional cost for LD program/services.

LD SERVICES

LD program size is not limited.

LD services available to:

☑ Freshmen ☑ Sophomores ☑ Juniors ☑ Seniors

Academic Accommodations

Curriculum		In class	
Foreign language waiver	☐	Early syllabus	☑
Lighter course load	☐	Note takers in class	☑
Math waiver	☐	Priority seating	☐
Other special classes	☐	Tape recorders	☐
Priority registrations	☑	Videotaped classes	☐
Substitution of courses	☐	Text on tape	☑
Exams		**Services**	
Extended time	☑	Diagnostic tests	☐
Oral exams	☐	Learning centers	☐
Take home exams	☐	Proofreaders	☐
Exams on tape or computer	☑	Readers	☐
Untimed exams	☐	Reading Machines/Kurzweil	☐
Other accommodations	☐	Special bookstore section	☐
		Typists	☐

Credit toward degree is not given for remedial courses taken.

Counseling Services

- ☑ Academic
- ☑ Psychological
- ☐ Student Support groups
- ☐ Vocational

Tutoring

Individual tutoring is available weekly.

	Individual	Group
Time management	☐	☐
Organizational skills	☐	☐
Learning strategies	☐	☐
Study skills	☐	☐
Content area	☑	☐
Writing lab	☑	☐
Math lab	☑	☐

UNIQUE LD PROGRAM FEATURES

We do not maintain separate admission for students with learning disabilities.

Services are available to all students with learning disabilities whose documentation warrants that service.

LD PROGRAM STAFF

There is an advisor/advocate from the LD program available to students. 3 graduate students and 12 peer tutors are available to work with LD students.

Key staff person available to work with LD students: Shelley Stephenson, Interim Associate Dean/ Student Academic Resources.

LD Program web site: htttp://www.wesleyan.edu/deans/disabilities.html

Yale University

New Haven, CT

Address: P.O. Box 208234, New Haven, CT, 06520
Admissions telephone: 203 432-9316
Admissions FAX: 203 432-9392
Dean of Undergraduate Admissions: Richard H. Shaw
Admissions e-mail: undergraduate.admissions@yale.edu
Web site: http://www.yale.edu
SAT Code: 3987 ACT Code: 618

LD program name: Resource Office on Disabilities
LD program address: P.O. Box 208305
Senior Administrative Assistant: Carolyn Barrett
LD program telephone: 203 432-2324
LD program e-mail: carolyn.barrett@yale.edu
LD program enrollment: 67, Total campus enrollment: 5,319

GENERAL

Yale University is a private, coed, four-year institution. 295-acre, urban campus in New Haven (population: 123,626), 42 miles from Hartford. Served by air, bus, and train; larger airport serves Hartford. School operates campus shuttle service. Public transportation serves campus. Semester system.

LD ADMISSIONS

A personal interview is not required. Essay is not required.

SECONDARY SCHOOL REQUIREMENTS

Graduation from secondary school not required.

TESTING

SAT Subject recommended.

All enrolled freshmen (fall 2004):

Average SAT I Scores: Verbal: 750 Math: 740
Average ACT Scores: Composite: 33

Child Study Team report is not required. Tests required as part of this documentation:

- ❑ WAIS-IV
- ❑ WISC-IV
- ❑ SATA
- ❑ Woodcock-Johnson
- ❑ Nelson-Denny Reading Test
- ❑ Other

UNDERGRADUATE STUDENT BODY

Total undergraduate student enrollment: 2,678 Men, 2,608 Women.

Composition of student body (fall 2004):

	Undergraduate	Freshmen
International	8.0	8.6
Black	9.0	7.8
American Indian	1.2	0.8
Asian-American	13.8	13.6
Hispanic	8.1	7.0
White	49.8	51.3
Unreported	10.1	11.0
	100.0%	100.0%

90% are from out of state. Average age of full-time undergraduates is 20, 74% of classes have fewer than 20 students, 18% have between 20 and 50 students.

STUDENT HOUSING

100% of freshmen live in college housing. Freshmen are required to live on campus. Housing is guaranteed for all undergraduates.

EXPENSES

Tuition (2005-06): $31,460 per year.

Room: $5,200. Board: $4,340.
There is no additional cost for LD program/services.

LD SERVICES

LD program size is not limited.

LD services available to:

❑ Freshmen ❑ Sophomores ❑ Juniors ❑ Seniors

Academic Accommodations

Curriculum		In class	
Foreign language waiver	❑	Early syllabus	❑
Lighter course load	❑	Note takers in class	❑
Math waiver	❑	Priority seating	❑
Other special classes	❑	Tape recorders	❑
Priority registrations	❑	Videotaped classes	❑
Substitution of courses	❑	Text on tape	❑
Exams		**Services**	
Extended time	❑	Diagnostic tests	❑
Oral exams	❑	Learning centers	❑
Take home exams	❑	Proofreaders	❑
Exams on tape or computer	❑	Readers	❑
Untimed exams	❑	Reading Machines/Kurzweil	❑
Other accommodations	❑	Special bookstore section	❑
		Typists	❑

Counseling Services

- ❑ Academic
- ❑ Psychological
- ❑ Student Support groups
- ❑ Vocational

Tutoring

	Individual	Group
Time management	❑	❑
Organizational skills	❑	❑
Learning strategies	❑	❑
Study skills	❑	❑
Content area	❑	❑
Writing lab	❑	❑
Math lab	❑	❑

LD PROGRAM STAFF

Total number of LD Program staff (including director):

Full Time: 1 Part Time: 1

Key staff person available to work with LD students: Judy York, Director.

LD Program web site: http://www.yale.edu/rod

University of Delaware

Newark, DE

Address: Newark, DE, 19716
Admissions telephone: 302 831-8123
Admissions FAX: 302 831-6905
Director of Admissions: Lou Hirsh
Admissions e-mail: admissions@udel.edu
Web site: http://www.udel.edu/
SAT Code: 5811 ACT Code: 634

LD program name: Academic Enrichment Center
LD program address: 148-150 South College Ave.,
Associate Director: Lysbet Murray
LD program telephone: 302 831-3025
LD program e-mail: lysbet@udel.edu
LD program enrollment: 183, Total campus enrollment: 17,318

GENERAL

University of Delaware is a public, coed, four-year institution. 1,000-acre campus in Newark (population: 28,547), 12 miles from Wilmington, 30 miles from Philadelphia, and 50 miles from Baltimore; branch campuses in Dover, Georgetown, and Wilmington. Served by bus; major airports serve Baltimore and Philadelphia; train serves Newark and Wilmington. School operates transportation to southern Delaware. Public transportation serves campus. 4-1-4 system.

LD ADMISSIONS

Students do not complete a separate application and are not simultaneously accepted to the LD program. A member of the LD program does not sit on the admissions committee. All decisions are made by Admissions Office.

SECONDARY SCHOOL REQUIREMENTS

Graduation from secondary school required; GED accepted. The following course distribution required: 4 units of English, 3 units of math, 3 units of science, 2 units of foreign language, 2 units of social studies, 2 units of history, 2 units of academic electives.

TESTING

SAT Reasoning or ACT required. SAT Subject required.

All enrolled freshmen (fall 2004):

Average SAT I Scores:	Verbal: 587	Math: 602
Average ACT Scores:	Composite: 27	

Child Study Team report is not required. A neuropsychological or comprehensive psycho-educational evaluation is required for admission. Must be dated within 36 months of application. Tests required as part of this documentation:

- [x] WAIS-IV
- [ ] WISC-IV
- [ ] SATA
- [x] Woodcock-Johnson
- [x] Nelson-Denny Reading Test
- [x] Other

UNDERGRADUATE STUDENT BODY

Total undergraduate student enrollment: 7,259 Men, 10,172 Women.

Composition of student body (fall 2004):

	Undergraduate	Freshmen
International	0.4	1.0
Black	5.8	5.6
American Indian	0.2	0.3
Asian-American	3.6	3.4
Hispanic	4.8	3.6
White	84.3	84.9
Unreported	1.0	1.3
	100.0%	100.0%

59% are from out of state. 13% join a fraternity and 13% join a sorority. Average age of full-time undergraduates is 20, 35% of classes have fewer than 20 students, 46% have between 20 and 50 students, 18% have more than 50 students.

STUDENT HOUSING

92% of freshmen live in college housing. Freshmen are required to live on campus. Housing is guaranteed for all undergraduates. Campus can house 7,244 undergraduates. Single rooms are available for students with medical or special needs. A medical note is required.

EXPENSES

Tuition (2005-06): $6,614 per year (in-state), $16,770 (out-of-state).
Room: $3,924. Board: $2,900.
There is no additional cost for LD program/services.

LD SERVICES

LD program size is not limited.

LD services available to:

- [x] Freshmen
- [x] Sophomores
- [x] Juniors
- [x] Seniors

Academic Accommodations

Curriculum		**In class**	
Foreign language waiver	[ ]	Early syllabus	[ ]
Lighter course load	[ ]	Note takers in class	[ ]
Math waiver	[ ]	Priority seating	[ ]
Other special classes	[ ]	Tape recorders	[ ]
Priority registrations	[ ]	Videotaped classes	[ ]
Substitution of courses	[ ]	Text on tape	[ ]
Exams		**Services**	
Extended time	[ ]	Diagnostic tests	[ ]
Oral exams	[ ]	Learning centers	[ ]
Take home exams	[ ]	Proofreaders	[ ]
Exams on tape or computer	[ ]	Readers	[ ]
Untimed exams	[ ]	Reading Machines/Kurzweil	[ ]
Other accommodations	[ ]	Special bookstore section	[ ]
		Typists	[ ]

Credit toward degree is not given for remedial courses taken.

Counseling Services

- [ ] Academic
- [ ] Psychological
- [ ] Student Support groups
- [ ] Vocational

Tutoring

Individual tutoring is available weekly.

Average size of tutoring groups: 10

	Individual	Group
Time management	[x]	[x]
Organizational skills	[ ]	[ ]
Learning strategies	[x]	[x]
Study skills	[x]	[x]
Content area	[ ]	[ ]
Writing lab	[x]	[x]
Math lab	[x]	[x]

UNIQUE LD PROGRAM FEATURES

The University of Delaware's LD/ADHD services office is available to matriculated students with documentation meeting the guidelines. Accommodations are determined on an individual basis to students whose disabilities substantially limit their ability to learn. The Academic Enrichment Center provides support to the entire University community in the form of reasonably priced individual tutoring, free group tutoring, study skills workshops and one-credit classes and academic counseling. Accommodations for nonmatriculated students are provided through the Professional and Continuing Education Division.

LD PROGRAM STAFF

Total number of LD Program staff (including director):

Full Time: 3 Part Time: 3

There is an advisor/advocate from the LD program available to students. 1 graduate student and 80 peer tutors are available to work with LD students.

Key staff person available to work with LD students: Barbara Lewis-Kvszyk, LD/ADHD Coordinator.

LD Program web site: www.aec.udel.edu

Delaware State University

Dover, DE

Address: 1200 North Dupont Highway, Dover, DE, 19901
Admissions telephone: 302 857-6353
Admissions FAX: 302 857-6352
Director of Admissions: Germaine Scott-Cheatham
Admissions e-mail: admissions@desu.edu
Web site: http://www.desu.edu
SAT Code: 5153 ACT Code: 630

Disabilities Service Coordinator: Laura Kurtz
LD program telephone: 302 857-6388
LD program e-mail: lkurtz@dsc.edu
Total campus enrollment: 3,074

GENERAL

Delaware State University is a public, coed, four-year institution. 400-acre campus in Dover (population: 32,135), 45 miles from Wilmington; branch campuses in Georgetown and Wilmington. Served by bus; major airport serves Philadelphia (75 miles); train serves Wilmington. School operates transportation to shopping areas and internship locations. Public transportation serves campus. Semester system.

SECONDARY SCHOOL REQUIREMENTS

Graduation from secondary school required; GED accepted. The following course distribution required: 4 units of English, 3 units of math, 3 units of science, 2 units of social studies, 4 units of academic electives.

TESTING

SAT Reasoning or ACT required.

All enrolled freshmen (fall 2004):

Average SAT I Scores:	Verbal: 410	Math: 409
Average ACT Scores:	Composite: 15	

Child Study Team report is not required. Tests required as part of this documentation:

☐ WAIS-IV ☐ Woodcock-Johnson
☐ WISC-IV ☐ Nelson-Denny Reading Test
☐ SATA ☐ Other

UNDERGRADUATE STUDENT BODY

Total undergraduate student enrollment: 3,074.

Composition of student body (fall 2004):

	Undergraduate	Freshmen
International	0.0	0.1
Black	85.4	81.5
American Indian	0.1	0.4
Asian-American	0.5	0.7
Hispanic	1.7	1.8
White	9.1	12.9
Unreported	3.1	2.6
	100.0%	100.0%

34% are from out of state.

STUDENT HOUSING

Campus can house 416 undergraduates.

EXPENSES

Tuition (2005-06): $5,089 per year (in-state), $11,333 (out-of-state).
Room & Board: $8,298.
There is no additional cost for LD program/services.

LD SERVICES

LD program size is not limited.

LD services available to:

☐ Freshmen ☐ Sophomores ☐ Juniors ☐ Seniors

Academic Accommodations

Curriculum		**In class**	
Foreign language waiver	☐	Early syllabus	☐
Lighter course load	■	Note takers in class	■
Math waiver	☐	Priority seating	☐
Other special classes	☐	Tape recorders	■
Priority registrations	☐	Videotaped classes	☐
Substitution of courses	☐	Text on tape	☐
Exams		**Services**	
Extended time	■	Diagnostic tests	☐
Oral exams	■	Learning centers	■
Take home exams	☐	Proofreaders	☐
Exams on tape or computer	☐	Readers	■
Untimed exams	■	Reading Machines/Kurzweil	☐
Other accommodations	☐	Special bookstore section	☐
		Typists	☐

Credit toward degree is not given for remedial courses taken.

Counseling Services

☐ Academic
☐ Psychological
☐ Student Support groups
☐ Vocational

Tutoring

	Individual	Group
Time management	☐	☐
Organizational skills	☐	☐
Learning strategies	☐	☐
Study skills	☐	☐
Content area	☐	☐
Writing lab	☐	☐
Math lab	☐	☐

LD PROGRAM STAFF

Total number of LD Program staff (including director):

Full Time: 1 Part Time: 1

Key staff person available to work with LD students: Laura Kurtz, Disabilities Service Coordinator.

Wesley College

Dover, DE

Address: 120 North State Street, Dover, DE, 19901-3875
Admissions telephone: 800 937-5398
Admissions FAX: 302 736-2301
Director of Admissions: Arthur Jacobs
Admissions e-mail: admissions@wesley.edu
Web site: http://www.wesley.edu
SAT Code: 5894 ACT Code: 636

Director of Academic Support Services: Jean Zipke
LD program telephone: 302 736-2505
LD program e-mail: zipkeje@wesley.edu
LD program enrollment: 50, Total campus enrollment: 1,901

GENERAL

Wesley College is a private, coed, four-year institution. 60-acre campus in Dover (population: 32,135), 50 miles from Wilmington and 70 miles from Philadelphia, PA. Served by bus; major airport serves Philadelphia, PA; train serves Wilmington. Public transportation serves campus. Semester system.

LD ADMISSIONS

Students do not complete a separate application and are not simultaneously accepted to the LD program. A member of the LD program does not sit on the admissions committee. A personal interview is required. Essay is not required.

For fall 2004, 40 completed self-identified LD applications were received. 30 applications were offered admission, and 20 enrolled.

SECONDARY SCHOOL REQUIREMENTS

Graduation from secondary school required; GED accepted.

TESTING

SAT Reasoning recommended; ACT may be substituted.

All enrolled freshmen (fall 2004):

Average SAT I Scores: Verbal: 490 Math: 495

Child Study Team report is not required. A neuropsychological or comprehensive psycho-educational evaluation is required for admission. Tests required as part of this documentation:

- [ ] WAIS-IV
- [ ] WISC-IV
- [ ] SATA
- [ ] Woodcock-Johnson
- [ ] Nelson-Denny Reading Test
- [ ] Other

UNDERGRADUATE STUDENT BODY

Total undergraduate student enrollment: 635 Men, 761 Women.

Composition of student body (fall 2004):

	Undergraduate	Freshmen
International	0.6	0.9
Black	22.0	22.6
American Indian	0.0	0.3
Asian-American	3.3	1.8
Hispanic	2.1	2.3
White	72.1	71.4
Unreported	0.0	0.8
	100.0%	100.0%

59% are from out of state. 3% join a fraternity and 3% join a sorority. Average age of full-time undergraduates is 20, 48% of classes have fewer than 20 students, 52% have between 20 and 50 students.

STUDENT HOUSING

86% of freshmen live in college housing. Freshmen are required to live on campus. Housing is guaranteed for all undergraduates. Campus can house 829 undergraduates.

EXPENSES

Tuition (2005-06): $14,600 per year.

Board: $3,480.

There is no additional cost for LD program/services.

LD SERVICES

LD program size is not limited.

LD services available to:

- [x] Freshmen
- [x] Sophomores
- [x] Juniors
- [x] Seniors

Academic Accommodations

Curriculum

- [ ] Foreign language waiver
- [x] Lighter course load
- [ ] Math waiver
- [ ] Other special classes
- [ ] Priority registrations
- [ ] Substitution of courses

Exams

- [x] Extended time
- [ ] Oral exams
- [ ] Take home exams
- [ ] Exams on tape or computer
- [x] Untimed exams
- [ ] Other accommodations

In class

- [ ] Early syllabus
- [x] Note takers in class
- [ ] Priority seating
- [x] Tape recorders
- [ ] Videotaped classes
- [ ] Text on tape

Services

- [ ] Diagnostic tests
- [ ] Learning centers
- [ ] Proofreaders
- [ ] Readers
- [ ] Reading Machines/Kurzweil
- [ ] Special bookstore section
- [ ] Typists

Credit toward degree is given for remedial courses taken.

Counseling Services

- [x] Academic
- [x] Psychological
- [x] Student Support groups
- [x] Vocational

Tutoring

Average size of tutoring groups: 5

	Individual	Group
Time management	[ ]	[x]
Organizational skills	[ ]	[x]
Learning strategies	[x]	[ ]
Study skills	[ ]	[x]
Content area	[ ]	[x]
Writing lab	[ ]	[x]
Math lab	[ ]	[x]

LD PROGRAM STAFF

Total number of LD Program staff (including director):

Full Time: 2 Part Time: 2

There is an advisor/advocate from the LD program available to students.

Key staff person available to work with LD students: Jean Zipke, Director of Academic Support Services.

American University

Washington, DC

Address: 4400 Massachusetts Avenue NW, Washington, DC, 20016
Admissions telephone: 202 885-6000
Admissions FAX: 202 885-1025
Director of Admissions: Dr. Sharon M. Alston
Admissions e-mail: admissions@american.edu
Web site: http://www.american.edu
SAT Code: 5007 ACT Code: 648

LD program name: Learning Service Program
LD program address: MGC 243
Director, Academic Support Center: Kathy Schwartz
LD program telephone: 202 885-3360
LD program e-mail: acs@american.edu
Total campus enrollment: 5,811

GENERAL

American University is a private, coed, four-year institution. 84-acre, suburban campus in northwest Washington, DC (population: 607,000); branch campuses in Spring Valley (law school) and Tenleytown (Washington Semester program). Served by airport, bus, and train. School operates transportation to branch campuses, off-campus housing, and subway. Public transportation serves campus. Semester system.

LD ADMISSIONS

Application Deadline: 01/15. Students complete a separate application and are simultaneously accepted to the LD program. A member of the LD program does not sit on the admissions committee. High school waivers are accepted for foreign language. A personal interview is not required. Essay is required and may be typed. Foreign language requirement may be waived based upon review of appropriate documentation.

For fall 2004, 95 completed self-identified LD applications were received. 34 applications were offered admission, and 18 enrolled.

SECONDARY SCHOOL REQUIREMENTS

Graduation from secondary school required; GED accepted. The following course distribution required: 4 units of English, 3 units of math, 2 units of science, 2 units of foreign language, 2 units of social studies, 3 units of academic electives.

TESTING

SAT Reasoning or ACT required. SAT Subject required.

All enrolled freshmen (fall 2004):

Average SAT I Scores: Verbal: 635 Math: 614
Average ACT Scores: Composite: 27

Child Study Team report is not required. A neuropsychological or comprehensive psycho-educational evaluation is required for admission. Tests required as part of this documentation:

- [x] WAIS-IV
- [x] WISC-IV
- [ ] SATA
- [x] Woodcock-Johnson
- [ ] Nelson-Denny Reading Test
- [x] Other

UNDERGRADUATE STUDENT BODY

Total undergraduate student enrollment: 2,240 Men, 3,611 Women.

Composition of student body (fall 2004):

	Undergraduate	Freshmen
International	3.7	6.5
Black	4.8	5.7
American Indian	0.7	0.4
Asian-American	4.1	4.8
Hispanic	4.5	4.6
White	67.2	62.7
Unreported	15.0	15.3
	100.0%	100.0%

93% are from out of state. 16% join a fraternity and 17% join a sorority. Average age of full-time undergraduates is 20, 41% of classes have fewer than 20 students, 55% have between 20 and 50 students.

STUDENT HOUSING

99% of freshmen live in college housing. Freshmen are not required to live on campus. Housing is guaranteed for all undergraduates. Campus can house 4,050 undergraduates. Single rooms are not available for students with medical or special needs.

EXPENSES

Tuition (2005-06): $27,552 per year.
Room: $6,970. Board: $3,730.

Additional cost for LD program/services: $1,000 one-time fee.

LD SERVICES

LD program size is not limited.

LD services available to:

- [x] Freshmen
- [x] Sophomores
- [x] Juniors
- [x] Seniors

Academic Accommodations

Curriculum

- [ ] Foreign language waiver
- [x] Lighter course load
- [ ] Math waiver
- [ ] Other special classes
- [x] Priority registrations
- [ ] Substitution of courses

Exams

- [x] Extended time
- [ ] Oral exams
- [ ] Take home exams
- [ ] Exams on tape or computer
- [ ] Untimed exams
- [x] Other accommodations

In class

- [ ] Early syllabus
- [x] Note takers in class
- [ ] Priority seating
- [ ] Tape recorders
- [ ] Videotaped classes
- [ ] Text on tape

Services

- [ ] Diagnostic tests
- [x] Learning centers
- [ ] Proofreaders
- [x] Readers
- [ ] Reading Machines/Kurzweil
- [ ] Special bookstore section
- [ ] Typists

Counseling Services

- [ ] Academic
- [ ] Psychological
- [ ] Student Support groups
- [ ] Vocational

Tutoring

Individual tutoring is available weekly.

	Individual	Group
Time management	[x]	[x]
Organizational skills	[x]	[ ]
Learning strategies	[x]	[x]
Study skills	[x]	[x]
Content area	[ ]	[ ]
Writing lab	[x]	[ ]
Math lab	[ ]	[ ]

UNIQUE LD PROGRAM FEATURES

The focus of the Program is to assist students with learning disabilities with their transition from high school to college during their freshmen year. It is a small, mainstream program offering weekly individual meetings wth the program coordinator throughout the student's first year, additional writing support in the college writing class, and free course-content tutoring as needed. There is a one time fee for the program. Students with learning disabilities who are not in the program may receive services through the Academic Support Center (ASC). Numbers provided earlier for LD applicants are for the Program, not for the ASC.

LD PROGRAM STAFF

Total number of LD Program staff (including director):

Full Time: 9 Part Time: 9

There is an advisor/advocate from the LD program available to students.

Key staff person available to work with LD students: Melissa Scarfone, Coordinator of Learning Services Program.

LD Program web site: www.american.edu/asc

The Catholic University of America

Washington, DC

Address: 620 Michigan Avenue NE, Washington, DC, 20064
Admissions telephone: 800 673-2772
Admissions FAX: 202 319-6533
Admissions Contact: Christine Mica
Admissions e-mail: cua-admissions@cua.edu
Web site: http://www.cua.edu
SAT Code: 5104 ACT Code: 654

LD program name: Disability Support Services
Director, Disability Support Services: Bonnie McClellan
LD program telephone: 202 319-5211
LD program e-mail: cua-disabilityservices@cua.edu
LD program enrollment: 200, Total campus enrollment: 2,910

GENERAL

The Catholic University of America is a private, coed, four-year institution. 144-acre, suburban campus in Washington, DC (population: 572,059). Served by airport, bus, and train. School operates transportation to adjacent apartment complexes and residential community. Public transportation serves campus. Semester system.

LD ADMISSIONS

Application Deadline: 02/01. Students do not complete a separate application and are not simultaneously accepted to the LD program. A member of the LD program does not sit on the admissions committee. High school waivers are accepted for foreign language. A personal interview is not required. Essay is required and may be typed.

For fall 2004, 28 completed self-identified LD applications were received. 23 applications were offered admission, and 15 enrolled.

SECONDARY SCHOOL REQUIREMENTS

Graduation from secondary school required; GED accepted.

TESTING

SAT Reasoning or ACT required. SAT Subject recommended.

All enrolled freshmen (fall 2004):

Average SAT I Scores: Verbal: 583 Math: 569
Average ACT Scores: Composite: 24

Child Study Team report is not required. A neuropsychological or comprehensive psycho-educational evaluation is required for admission. Tests required as part of this documentation:

- ☑ WAIS-IV
- ☑ WISC-IV
- ☐ SATA
- ☑ Woodcock-Johnson
- ☑ Nelson-Denny Reading Test
- ☐ Other

UNDERGRADUATE STUDENT BODY

Total undergraduate student enrollment: 1,204 Men, 1,405 Women.

Composition of student body (fall 2004):

	Undergraduate	Freshmen
International	1.4	1.6
Black	4.2	7.0
American Indian	0.0	0.1
Asian-American	3.9	3.1
Hispanic	6.4	4.6
White	75.8	71.3
Unreported	8.3	12.2
	100.0%	100.0%

92% are from out of state. 1% join a fraternity and 1% join a sorority. Average age of full-time undergraduates is 20, 56% of classes have fewer than 20 students, 41% have between 20 and 50 students.

STUDENT HOUSING

94% of freshmen live in college housing. Freshmen are required to live on campus. Housing is not guaranteed for all undergraduates. Single rooms are available for students with medical or special needs. A medical note is required.

EXPENSES

Tuition (2005-06): $24,800 per year.
Room: $5,646. Board: $4,192.

There is no additional cost for LD program/services.

LD SERVICES

LD program size is not limited.

LD services available to:

☑ Freshmen ☑ Sophomores ☑ Juniors ☑ Seniors

Academic Accommodations

Curriculum		In class	
Foreign language waiver	☑	Early syllabus	☑
Lighter course load	☑	Note takers in class	☑
Math waiver	☐	Priority seating	☑
Other special classes	☐	Tape recorders	☑
Priority registrations	☑	Videotaped classes	☑
Substitution of courses	☑	Text on tape	☑
Exams		**Services**	
Extended time	☑	Diagnostic tests	☐
Oral exams	☑	Learning centers	☑
Take home exams	☑	Proofreaders	☐
Exams on tape or computer	☑	Readers	☑
Untimed exams	☑	Reading Machines/Kurzweil	☑
Other accommodations	☑	Special bookstore section	☐
		Typists	☑

Credit toward degree is not given for remedial courses taken.

Counseling Services

- ☑ Academic
- ☑ Psychological
- ☐ Student Support groups
- ☐ Vocational

Tutoring

Individual tutoring is available weekly.

	Individual	Group
Time management	☑	☑
Organizational skills	☑	☑
Learning strategies	☑	☑
Study skills	☑	☑
Content area	☑	☑
Writing lab	☑	☑
Math lab	☑	☑

UNIQUE LD PROGRAM FEATURES

Comprehensive Support Services. Self-disclosure initiates services. Documentation required.

LD PROGRAM STAFF

Total number of LD Program staff (including director):

Full Time: 2 Part Time: 2

There is an advisor/advocate from the LD program available to students.

Key staff person available to work with LD students: Bonnie McClellan, Director, Disability Support Services.

LD Program web site: http://disabilityservices.cua.edu

Corcoran College of Art and Design

Washington, DC

Address: 500 17th Street NW, Washington, DC, 20006-4804
Admissions telephone: 202 639-1814
Admissions FAX: 202 639-1830
Director of Admissions: Elizabeth C. Smith
Admissions e-mail: admissions@corcoran.org
Web site: http://www.corcoran.edu
SAT Code: 5705 ACT Code: 671

LD program contact: Office of Admissions
LD program telephone: 202 639-1814
LD program e-mail: admissions@corcoran.org
Total campus enrollment: 481

GENERAL

Corcoran College of Art and Design is a private, coed, four-year institution. Seven-acre, urban campus in Washington, DC (population: 572,059); branch campuses on H Street and in Georgetown. Served by airport, bus, and train. Public transportation serves campus. Semester system.

LD ADMISSIONS

A personal interview is required. Essay is not required.

For fall 2004, 11 completed self-identified LD applications were received. 7 applications were offered admission, and 2 enrolled.

SECONDARY SCHOOL REQUIREMENTS

Graduation from secondary school required; GED accepted. The following course distribution required: 4 units of English, 4 units of history.

TESTING

SAT Reasoning required; ACT may be substituted. SAT Subject recommended.

All enrolled freshmen (fall 2004):

Average SAT I Scores:	Verbal: 555	Math: 504
Average ACT Scores:	Composite: 22	

Child Study Team report is not required. Tests required as part of this documentation:

- [ ] WAIS-IV
- [ ] WISC-IV
- [ ] SATA
- [ ] Woodcock-Johnson
- [ ] Nelson-Denny Reading Test
- [ ] Other

UNDERGRADUATE STUDENT BODY

Total undergraduate student enrollment: 100 Men, 193 Women.

Composition of student body (fall 2004):

	Undergraduate	Freshmen
International	0.0	7.3
Black	7.7	6.9
American Indian	0.0	0.2
Asian-American	9.6	7.5
Hispanic	7.7	6.0
White	69.2	60.1
Unreported	5.8	12.1
	100.0%	100.0%

86% are from out of state. Average age of full-time undergraduates is 22, 94% of classes have fewer than 20 students.

STUDENT HOUSING

88% of freshmen live in college housing. Freshmen are not required to live on campus. Housing is guaranteed for all undergraduates. Campus can house 105 undergraduates.

EXPENSES

Tuition (2005-06): $22,700 per year.

Room: $8,150. Board: $1,900.

There is no additional cost for LD program/services.

LD SERVICES

LD program size is not limited.

LD services available to:

- [ ] Freshmen
- [ ] Sophomores
- [ ] Juniors
- [ ] Seniors

Academic Accommodations

Curriculum		In class	
Foreign language waiver	[ ]	Early syllabus	[ ]
Lighter course load	[ ]	Note takers in class	[ ]
Math waiver	[ ]	Priority seating	[ ]
Other special classes	[ ]	Tape recorders	[ ]
Priority registrations	[ ]	Videotaped classes	[ ]
Substitution of courses	[ ]	Text on tape	[ ]
Exams		**Services**	
Extended time	[x]	Diagnostic tests	[ ]
Oral exams	[ ]	Learning centers	[x]
Take home exams	[ ]	Proofreaders	[ ]
Exams on tape or computer	[ ]	Readers	[ ]
Untimed exams	[ ]	Reading Machines/Kurzweil	[ ]
Other accommodations	[ ]	Special bookstore section	[ ]
		Typists	[ ]

Credit toward degree is not given for remedial courses taken.

Counseling Services

- [ ] Academic
- [ ] Psychological
- [ ] Student Support groups
- [ ] Vocational

Tutoring

Individual tutoring is available.

	Individual	Group
Time management	[ ]	[ ]
Organizational skills	[ ]	[ ]
Learning strategies	[ ]	[ ]
Study skills	[ ]	[ ]
Content area	[ ]	[ ]
Writing lab	[ ]	[ ]
Math lab	[ ]	[ ]

University of the District of Columbia

Washington, DC

Address: 4200 Connecticut Avenue NW, Washington, DC, 20008
Admissions telephone: 202 274-5010
Admissions FAX: 202 274-5552
Director of Admission: LaVerne Hill-Flannigan
Web site: http://www.udc.edu/
SAT Code: 5929 ACT Code: 695

LD program name: Services to Students w/Disabilities
Director: Sandra Majid Carter
LD program telephone: 202 274-5531
LD program e-mail: SCarter@udc.edu
Total campus enrollment: 4,966

GENERAL

University of the District of Columbia is a public, coed, four-year institution. 21-acre, urban campus in Washington, DC (population: 572,059). Served by airport, bus, and train. Public transportation serves campus. Semester system.

LD ADMISSIONS

A personal interview is recommended. Essay is not required.

SECONDARY SCHOOL REQUIREMENTS

Graduation from secondary school required; GED accepted. The following course distribution required: 4 units of English, 2 units of math, 2 units of science, 2 units of foreign language.

TESTING

Child Study Team report is not required. Tests required as part of this documentation:

- [ ] WAIS-IV
- [ ] WISC-IV
- [ ] SATA
- [ ] Woodcock-Johnson
- [ ] Nelson-Denny Reading Test
- [ ] Other

UNDERGRADUATE STUDENT BODY

Total undergraduate student enrollment: 1,946 Men, 3,194 Women.

Composition of student body (fall 2004):

	Undergraduate	Freshmen
International	0.0	0.0
Black	81.9	81.7
American Indian	0.0	0.1
Asian-American	2.3	2.4
Hispanic	5.7	5.7
White	4.6	5.2
Unreported	5.6	4.8
	100.0%	100.0%

5% are from out of state. 3% join a fraternity and 4% join a sorority. Average age of full-time undergraduates is 34, 53% of classes have fewer than 20 students, 26% have between 20 and 50 students, 21% have more than 50 students.

STUDENT HOUSING

Housing is not guaranteed for all undergraduates. The University of the Disrict of Columbia is a commuter school.

EXPENSES

Tuition 2004-05: $1,800 per year (in-state), $4,440 (out-of-state).

There is no additional cost for LD program/services.

LD SERVICES

LD program size is not limited.

LD services available to:

- [ ] Freshmen
- [ ] Sophomores
- [ ] Juniors
- [ ] Seniors

Academic Accommodations

Curriculum

- [ ] Foreign language waiver
- [ ] Lighter course load
- [ ] Math waiver
- [x] Other special classes
- [ ] Priority registrations
- [ ] Substitution of courses

Exams

- [x] Extended time
- [x] Oral exams
- [ ] Take home exams
- [ ] Exams on tape or computer
- [x] Untimed exams
- [ ] Other accommodations

In class

- [ ] Early syllabus
- [x] Note takers in class
- [ ] Priority seating
- [x] Tape recorders
- [ ] Videotaped classes
- [ ] Text on tape

Services

- [x] Diagnostic tests
- [x] Learning centers
- [ ] Proofreaders
- [x] Readers
- [x] Reading Machines/Kurzweil
- [ ] Special bookstore section
- [ ] Typists

Credit toward degree is not given for remedial courses taken.

Counseling Services

- [ ] Academic
- [ ] Psychological
- [ ] Student Support groups
- [ ] Vocational

Tutoring

	Individual	Group
Time management	[ ]	[ ]
Organizational skills	[ ]	[ ]
Learning strategies	[ ]	[ ]
Study skills	[ ]	[ ]
Content area	[ ]	[ ]
Writing lab	[ ]	[ ]
Math lab	[ ]	[ ]

LD PROGRAM STAFF

Total number of LD Program staff (including director):

Full Time: 2 Part Time: 2

Key staff person available to work with LD students: A. Jamal Reed, Educational Specialist.

Gallaudet University

Washington, DC

Address: 800 Florida Avenue NE, Washington, DC, 20002
Admissions telephone: 800 995-0550
Admissions FAX: 202 651-5744
Director of Admissions: Charity Reedy-Hines
Admissions e-mail: admissions.studentvisits@gallaudet.edu
Web site: http://www.gallaudet.edu
SAT Code: 5240 ACT Code: 662

LD program name: Office for Students with Disabilities
Director, Office of Students with Disabilities: Edgar Palmer
LD program telephone: 202 651-5256
LD program e-mail: oswd@gallaudet.edu
Total campus enrollment: 1,207

GENERAL

Gallaudet University is a private, coed, four-year institution. 93-acre, urban campus in Washington, DC (population: 572,059). Served by airport, bus, and train. School operates transportation to subway and Union Station. Public transportation serves campus. Semester system.

LD ADMISSIONS

Students do not complete a separate application and are not simultaneously accepted to the LD program. A member of the LD program does not sit on the admissions committee.

SECONDARY SCHOOL REQUIREMENTS

Graduation from secondary school required; GED accepted. The following course distribution required: 4 units of English, 4 units of math, 4 units of science, 4 units of social studies, 4 units of history.

TESTING

ACT required; SAT Reasoning may be substituted. SAT Subject recommended.

Child Study Team report is not required. A neuropsychological or comprehensive psycho-educational evaluation is required for admission. Tests required as part of this documentation:

- ☒ WAIS-IV
- ☐ WISC-IV
- ☐ SATA
- ☐ Woodcock-Johnson
- ☒ Nelson-Denny Reading Test
- ☐ Other

UNDERGRADUATE STUDENT BODY

Total undergraduate student enrollment: 572 Men, 628 Women.

Composition of student body (fall 2004):

	Undergraduate	Freshmen
International	9.3	11.6
Black	14.5	11.6
American Indian	7.5	3.0
Asian-American	5.3	4.7
Hispanic	6.6	7.3
White	56.4	59.4
Unreported	0.4	2.4
	100.0%	100.0%

98% are from out of state. 10% join a fraternity and 9% join a sorority, 92% of classes have fewer than 20 students.

STUDENT HOUSING

96% of freshmen live in college housing. Freshmen are not required to live on campus. Housing is guaranteed for all undergraduates. Campus can house 1,220 undergraduates. Single rooms are available for students with medical or special needs. A medical note is required.

EXPENSES

Tuition (2005-06): $9,920 per year (in-state), $19,840 (out-of-state). International student tuition is $16,840.

Room: $4,850. Board: $3,650.

There is no additional cost for LD program/services.

LD SERVICES

LD program size is not limited.

LD services available to:

☒ Freshmen ☒ Sophomores ☒ Juniors ☒ Seniors

Academic Accommodations

Curriculum		**In class**	
Foreign language waiver	☐	Early syllabus	☐
Lighter course load	☒	Note takers in class	☒
Math waiver	☐	Priority seating	☒
Other special classes	☒	Tape recorders	☒
Priority registrations	☐	Videotaped classes	☐
Substitution of courses	☐	Text on tape	☒
Exams		**Services**	
Extended time	☒	Diagnostic tests	☒
Oral exams	☐	Learning centers	☒
Take home exams	☒	Proofreaders	☐
Exams on tape or computer	☒	Readers	☒
Untimed exams	☒	Reading Machines/Kurzweil	☒
Other accommodations	☐	Special bookstore section	☐
		Typists	☐

Credit toward degree is not given for remedial courses taken.

Counseling Services

- ☐ Academic
- ☐ Psychological
- ☐ Student Support groups
- ☐ Vocational

Tutoring

Individual tutoring is available weekly.

Average size of tutoring groups: 5

	Individual	Group
Time management	☒	☐
Organizational skills	☒	☐
Learning strategies	☒	☐
Study skills	☒	☐
Content area	☒	☐
Writing lab	☒	☐
Math lab	☒	☐

LD PROGRAM STAFF

Total number of LD Program staff (including director):

Full Time: 6 Part Time: 6

There is an advisor/advocate from the LD program available to students. 10 graduate students and 50 peer tutors are available to work with LD students.

Key staff person available to work with LD students: Patricia Tesar, Coordinator, Office for Students with Disabilities.

LD Program web site: http://depts.gallaudet.edu/OSWD/index.htm

Georgetown University

Washington, DC

Address: 37th and O Streets NW, Washington, DC, 20057
Admissions telephone: 202 687-3600
Admissions FAX: 202 687-5084
Dean of Undergraduate Admissions: Charles A. Deacon
Admissions e-mail: guadmiss@georgetown.edu
Web site: http://www.georgetown.edu
SAT Code: 5244 ACT Code: 668

Director of Disability & Academic Support Service: Jane Holahan
LD program telephone: 202 687-8354
LD program e-mail: arc@georgetown.edu
Total campus enrollment: 6,522

GENERAL

Georgetown University is a private, coed, four-year institution. 110-acre, urban campus in Washington, DC (population: 572,059). Served by airport, bus, and train; other airport serves Dulles, VA (25 miles). School operates transportation to local subway stations. Public transportation serves campus. Semester system.

LD ADMISSIONS

A personal interview is required. Essay is required and may be typed.

SECONDARY SCHOOL REQUIREMENTS

Graduation from secondary school required; GED accepted. The following course distribution required: 4 units of English, 2 units of math, 2 units of science, 2 units of foreign language, 2 units of social studies.

TESTING

SAT Reasoning or ACT required. SAT Subject recommended.

All enrolled freshmen (fall 2004):

Average SAT I Scores:	Verbal: 684	Math: 683
Average ACT Scores:	Composite: 29	

Child Study Team report is not required. Tests required as part of this documentation:

- [ ] WAIS-IV
- [ ] WISC-IV
- [ ] SATA
- [ ] Woodcock-Johnson
- [ ] Nelson-Denny Reading Test
- [ ] Other

UNDERGRADUATE STUDENT BODY

Total undergraduate student enrollment: 3,047 Men, 3,375 Women.

Composition of student body (fall 2004):

	Undergraduate	Freshmen
International	3.4	3.9
Black	6.6	6.7
American Indian	0.3	0.1
Asian-American	9.7	9.6
Hispanic	6.5	5.6
White	68.6	69.3
Unreported	4.9	4.7
	100.0%	100.0%

99% are from out of state. Average age of full-time undergraduates is 20, 57% of classes have fewer than 20 students, 33% have between 20 and 50 students, 10% have more than 50 students.

STUDENT HOUSING

100% of freshmen live in college housing. Freshmen are required to live on campus. Housing is not guaranteed for all undergraduates. Freshmen and sophomores are required to live on campus. Juniors and seniors may request housing and are assigned as space is available. Campus can house 5,053 undergraduates.

EXPENSES

Tuition (2005-06): $31,656 per year.

Room: $7,410. Board: $3,329.

There is no additional cost for LD program/services.

LD SERVICES

LD program size is not limited.

LD services available to:

- [x] Freshmen
- [x] Sophomores
- [x] Juniors
- [x] Seniors

Academic Accommodations

Curriculum		In class	
Foreign language waiver	[ ]	Early syllabus	[ ]
Lighter course load	[x]	Note takers in class	[x]
Math waiver	[ ]	Priority seating	[ ]
Other special classes	[ ]	Tape recorders	[x]
Priority registrations	[x]	Videotaped classes	[ ]
Substitution of courses	[ ]	Text on tape	[ ]
Exams		**Services**	
Extended time	[x]	Diagnostic tests	[ ]
Oral exams	[ ]	Learning centers	[ ]
Take home exams	[ ]	Proofreaders	[ ]
Exams on tape or computer	[ ]	Readers	[x]
Untimed exams	[ ]	Reading Machines/Kurzweil	[ ]
Other accommodations	[ ]	Special bookstore section	[ ]
		Typists	[ ]

Counseling Services

- [x] Academic
- [x] Psychological
- [ ] Student Support groups
- [ ] Vocational

Tutoring

Individual tutoring is available weekly.

Average size of tutoring groups: 4

	Individual	Group
Time management	[ ]	[x]
Organizational skills	[ ]	[x]
Learning strategies	[ ]	[x]
Study skills	[ ]	[x]
Content area	[ ]	[x]
Writing lab	[ ]	[x]
Math lab	[ ]	[x]

LD PROGRAM STAFF

Total number of LD Program staff (including director):

Full Time: 2 Part Time: 2

There is an advisor/advocate from the LD program available to students.

Key staff person available to work with LD students: Jane Holahan, Director of Disability & Academic Support Service.

The George Washington University

Washington, DC

Address: 2121 I Street NW, Washington, DC, 20052
Admissions telephone: 800 447-3765
Admissions FAX: 202 994-0325
Director of Admission: Kathryn M. Napper
Admissions e-mail: gwadm@gwu.edu
Web site: http://www.gwu.edu
SAT Code: 5246 ACT Code: 664

LD program name: Disability Support Services
LD program address: 800 21st Street, NW
Director of Disability Support Services: Christy Lynne Willis
LD program telephone: 202 994-8250
LD program e-mail: cwillis@gwu.edu
LD program enrollment: 365, Total campus enrollment: 10,967

GENERAL

The George Washington University is a private, coed, four-year institution. 36-acre campus in Washington, DC (population: 572,059); branch campuses at various sites in Washington, DC, MD, and VA. Served by airport, bus, and train. School operates transportation around campus and to the Mt. Vernon campus. Public transportation serves campus. Semester system.

LD ADMISSIONS

Students do not complete a separate application and are not simultaneously accepted to the LD program. A member of the LD program does not sit on the admissions committee. High school waivers are accepted for foreign language. A personal interview is recommended. Essay is required and may be typed.

SECONDARY SCHOOL REQUIREMENTS

Graduation from secondary school required; GED not accepted. The following course distribution required: 4 units of English, 2 units of math, 2 units of science, 2 units of foreign language, 2 units of social studies.

TESTING

SAT Reasoning required; ACT may be substituted. SAT Subject recommended.

All enrolled freshmen (fall 2004):

Average SAT I Scores:	Verbal: 640	Math: 640
Average ACT Scores:	Composite: 28	

Child Study Team report is not required. A neuropsychological or comprehensive psycho-educational evaluation is required for admission. Must be dated within 36 months of application. Tests required as part of this documentation:

- ■ WAIS-IV
- ■ WISC-IV
- ☐ SATA
- ■ Woodcock-Johnson
- ■ Nelson-Denny Reading Test
- ☐ Other

UNDERGRADUATE STUDENT BODY

Total undergraduate student enrollment: 4,412 Men, 5,651 Women.

Composition of student body (fall 2004):

	Undergraduate	Freshmen
International	3.7	4.1
Black	5.7	6.1
American Indian	0.3	0.3
Asian-American	8.9	9.4
Hispanic	4.6	4.6
White	66.5	63.9
Unreported	10.3	11.5
	100.0%	100.0%

96% are from out of state. 15% join a fraternity and 13% join a sorority. Average age of full-time undergraduates is 20, 50% of classes have fewer than 20 students, 39% have between 20 and 50 students, 11% have more than 50 students.

STUDENT HOUSING

91% of freshmen live in college housing. Freshmen are required to live on campus. Housing is guaranteed for all undergraduates. Campus can house 7,015 undergraduates.

EXPENSES

Tuition (2005-06): $36,370 per year. Higher tuition for media and public affairs programs.
Room: $7,470. Board: $3,000.
There is no additional cost for LD program/services.

LD SERVICES

LD program size is not limited.

LD services available to:

■ Freshmen ■ Sophomores ■ Juniors ■ Seniors

Academic Accommodations

Curriculum		In class	
Foreign language waiver	☐	Early syllabus	☐
Lighter course load	■	Note takers in class	■
Math waiver	☐	Priority seating	■
Other special classes	☐	Tape recorders	■
Priority registrations	■	Videotaped classes	☐
Substitution of courses	■	Text on tape	■
Exams		**Services**	
Extended time	■	Diagnostic tests	☐
Oral exams	☐	Learning centers	☐
Take home exams	☐	Proofreaders	■
Exams on tape or computer	■	Readers	■
Untimed exams	■	Reading Machines/Kurzweil	■
Other accommodations	■	Special bookstore section	☐
		Typists	☐

Credit toward degree is not given for remedial courses taken.

Counseling Services

- ■ Academic
- ■ Psychological
- ■ Student Support groups
- ☐ Vocational

Tutoring

Individual tutoring is available.

	Individual	Group
Time management	■	☐
Organizational skills	■	☐
Learning strategies	■	☐
Study skills	■	☐
Content area	☐	☐
Writing lab	■	☐
Math lab	☐	☐

LD PROGRAM STAFF

Total number of LD Program staff (including director):

Full Time: 3 Part Time: 3

There is an advisor/advocate from the LD program available to students.

Key staff person available to work with LD students: Susan McMenamin, Associate Director.

LD Program web site: http://gwired.gwu.edu/dss/

Howard University

Washington, DC

Address: 2400 Sixth Street NW, Washington, DC, 20059
Admissions telephone: 800 469-2738
Admissions FAX: 202 806-4467
Admissions e-mail: admission@howard.edu
Web site: http://www.howard.edu
SAT Code: 5297 ACT Code: 4102

LD program name: Office of the Dean for Special Students Services
LD program address: 2225 Georgia Avenue, NW, Suite 725
Dean, Special Student Services: Dr. Barbara Williams
LD program telephone: 202 238-2420
LD program e-mail: bwilliams@howard.edu
LD program enrollment: 400, Total campus enrollment: 7,112

GENERAL

Howard University is a private, coed, four-year institution. 89-acre main campus in Washington, DC (population: 572,059) plus 108-acre Beltsville campus, 22-acre West campus, Divinity School campus, and Silver Spring campus. Served by airport, bus, and train. School operates transportation to some off-campus university housing. Public transportation serves campus. Semester system.

LD ADMISSIONS

Students do not complete a separate application and are not simultaneously accepted to the LD program. A member of the LD program does not sit on the admissions committee. A personal interview is not required. Essay is not required.

For fall 2004, 425 completed self-identified LD applications were received.

SECONDARY SCHOOL REQUIREMENTS

Graduation from secondary school required; GED accepted. The following course distribution required: 4 units of English, 2 units of math, 2 units of science, 2 units of foreign language, 2 units of social studies, 2 units of history.

TESTING

SAT Reasoning or ACT required. SAT Subject required.

All enrolled freshmen (fall 2004):

Average SAT I Scores:	Verbal: 544	Math: 538
Average ACT Scores:	Composite: 22	

Child Study Team report is not required. Tests required as part of this documentation:

☐ WAIS-IV	☐ Woodcock-Johnson
☐ WISC-IV	☐ Nelson-Denny Reading Test
☐ SATA	☐ Other

UNDERGRADUATE STUDENT BODY

Total undergraduate student enrollment: 2,245 Men, 3,854 Women.

Composition of student body (fall 2004):

	Undergraduate	Freshmen
International	0.6	7.0
Black	85.0	84.1
American Indian	0.0	0.1
Asian-American	0.1	0.5
Hispanic	0.0	0.3
White	0.0	0.3
Unreported	14.3	7.7
	100.0%	100.0%

67% are from out of state. 2% join a fraternity and 1% join a sorority. Average age of full-time undergraduates is 20, 64% of classes have fewer than 20 students, 32% have between 20 and 50 students.

STUDENT HOUSING

92% of freshmen live in college housing. Freshmen are required to live on campus. Housing is not guaranteed for all undergraduates. There is not enough housing available. Any undergraduate may apply. Assignments are made to the extent of availability. A block of rooms are reserved for incoming freshmen. Campus can house 6,500 undergraduates. Single rooms are available for students with medical or special needs. A medical note is required.

EXPENSES

Tuition (2005-06): $11,490 per year.

Room: $3,736. Board: $2,450.

LD SERVICES

LD program size is not limited.

LD services available to:

■ Freshmen ■ Sophomores ■ Juniors ■ Seniors

Academic Accommodations

Curriculum		**In class**	
Foreign language waiver	☐	Early syllabus	☐
Lighter course load	☐	Note takers in class	■
Math waiver	☐	Priority seating	■
Other special classes	☐	Tape recorders	■
Priority registrations	☐	Videotaped classes	☐
Substitution of courses	☐	Text on tape	■
Exams		**Services**	
Extended time	■	Diagnostic tests	☐
Oral exams	☐	Learning centers	☐
Take home exams	☐	Proofreaders	☐
Exams on tape or computer	■	Readers	■
Untimed exams	☐	Reading Machines/Kurzweil	■
Other accommodations	■	Special bookstore section	☐
		Typists	■

Credit toward degree is not given for remedial courses taken.

Counseling Services

■ Academic
■ Psychological
■ Student Support groups
■ Vocational

Tutoring

Individual tutoring is available weekly.

Average size of tutoring groups: 1

	Individual	Group
Time management	■	■
Organizational skills	☐	☐
Learning strategies	☐	☐
Study skills	■	■
Content area	☐	☐
Writing lab	☐	☐
Math lab	■	■

UNIQUE LD PROGRAM FEATURES

Admission requirements for LD student are the same as those for regular students. The same staff members in the office of Special Student Services that work with regular students also work with LD students. We try to support LD students but try to be as unintrusive as possible.

LD PROGRAM STAFF

Total number of LD Program staff (including director):

Full Time: 4 Part Time: 4

There is an advisor/advocate from the LD program available to students. The advisor/advocate meets with faculty once per month. 1 graduate student is available to work with LD students.

Key staff person available to work with LD students: Dr. Barbara W. Williams, Dean, Special Student Services.

Trinity University

Washington, DC

Address: 125 Michigan Avenue NE, Washington, DC, 20017
Admissions telephone: 800 492-6882
Admissions FAX: 202 884-9403
Director of Undergraduate Admission: Mariea Noblitt
Admissions e-mail: admissions@trinitydc.edu
Web site: http://www.trinitydc.edu
SAT Code: 5796   ACT Code: 696

Coordinator, Disability Support Services: Melissa Earnest
LD program telephone: 202 884-9681
LD program e-mail: earnestm@trinitydc.edu
LD program enrollment: 15, Total campus enrollment: 968

GENERAL

Trinity University is a private, women's, four-year institution. 26-acre, urban campus in Washington, DC (population: 572,059). Served by air, bus, and train. School operates transportation to metro rail station. Public transportation serves campus. Semester system.

LD ADMISSIONS

A personal interview is recommended.

SECONDARY SCHOOL REQUIREMENTS

Graduation from secondary school required; GED accepted. The following course distribution required: 4 units of English, 3 units of math, 2 units of science, 2 units of foreign language, 3 units of social studies, 2 units of history.

TESTING

SAT Reasoning or ACT recommended. SAT Subject recommended.

All enrolled freshmen (fall 2004):

Average SAT I Scores:	Verbal: 420	Math: 400
Average ACT Scores:	Composite: 16	

Child Study Team report is not required. Tests required as part of this documentation:

☐ WAIS-IV   ☐ Woodcock-Johnson
☐ WISC-IV   ☐ Nelson-Denny Reading Test
☐ SATA   ☐ Other

UNDERGRADUATE STUDENT BODY

Total undergraduate student enrollment: 1,035 Women.

Composition of student body (fall 2004):

	Undergraduate	Freshmen
International	0.0	1.4
Black	58.3	67.7
American Indian	2.1	0.6
Asian-American	2.1	2.5
Hispanic	22.2	10.8
White	6.9	7.1
Unreported	8.3	10.0
	100.0%	100.0%

14% are from out of state. Average age of full-time undergraduates is 22, 65% of classes have fewer than 20 students, 35% have between 20 and 50 students.

STUDENT HOUSING

42% of freshmen live in college housing. Freshmen are not required to live on campus. Housing is guaranteed for all undergraduates. Campus can house 230 undergraduates. Single rooms are available for students with medical or special needs. A medical note is not required.

EXPENSES

Tuition (2005-06): $17,200 per year.
Room: $3,350. Board: $4,224.
There is no additional cost for LD program/services.

LD SERVICES

LD program size is not limited.

LD services available to:

■ Freshmen   ■ Sophomores   ■ Juniors   ■ Seniors

Academic Accommodations

Curriculum		In class	
Foreign language waiver	☐	Early syllabus	☐
Lighter course load	☐	Note takers in class	■
Math waiver	☐	Priority seating	☐
Other special classes	☐	Tape recorders	■
Priority registrations	☐	Videotaped classes	☐
Substitution of courses	☐	Text on tape	■
Exams		**Services**	
Extended time	■	Diagnostic tests	☐
Oral exams	☐	Learning centers	☐
Take home exams	☐	Proofreaders	☐
Exams on tape or computer	☐	Readers	■
Untimed exams	☐	Reading Machines/Kurzweil	☐
Other accommodations	☐	Special bookstore section	☐
		Typists	☐

Counseling Services

☐ Academic
☐ Psychological
☐ Student Support groups
☐ Vocational

Tutoring

Individual tutoring is available weekly.

	Individual	Group
Time management	☐	■
Organizational skills	☐	☐
Learning strategies	☐	■
Study skills	☐	■
Content area	☐	☐
Writing lab	☐	☐
Math lab	☐	☐

LD PROGRAM STAFF

There is an advisor/advocate from the LD program available to students. The advisor/advocate meets with students twice per month.

Key staff person available to work with LD students: Melissa Earnest, Coordinator, Disability Support Services.

Baptist College of Florida

Graceville, FL

Address: 5400 College Drive, Graceville, FL, 32440
Admissions telephone: 800 328-2660
Admissions FAX: 850 263-9026
Director of Admissions: Chris Bishop
Admissions e-mail: admissions@baptistcollege.edu
Web site: http://www.baptistcollege.edu
SAT Code: 7322 ACT Code: 6870

ADA Coordinator: Stephanie W. Orr
LD program e-mail: sworr@baptistcollege.edu
Total campus enrollment: 575

GENERAL

Baptist College of Florida is a private, coed, four-year institution. 217-acre campus in Graceville (population: 2,402), 20 miles from Dothan, AL; branch campuses in Jacksonville, Miami, and Orlando. Major airport serves Panama City (60 miles); smaller airport serves Dothan; bus serves Chipley (15 miles). Semester system.

LD ADMISSIONS

A personal interview is recommended.

SECONDARY SCHOOL REQUIREMENTS

Graduation from secondary school required; GED accepted.

TESTING

Child Study Team report is not required. Tests required as part of this documentation:

- ☐ WAIS-IV
- ☐ WISC-IV
- ☐ SATA
- ☐ Woodcock-Johnson
- ☐ Nelson-Denny Reading Test
- ☐ Other

UNDERGRADUATE STUDENT BODY

Total undergraduate student enrollment: 382 Men, 193 Women.

30% are from out of state.

STUDENT HOUSING

Housing is not guaranteed for all undergraduates. Available units are in proportion to demand. Campus can house 209 undergraduates.

EXPENSES

There is no additional cost for LD program/services.

LD SERVICES

LD program size is not limited.

LD services available to:

☐ Freshmen ☐ Sophomores ☐ Juniors ☐ Seniors

Academic Accommodations

Curriculum		In class	
Foreign language waiver	☐	Early syllabus	☐
Lighter course load	■	Note takers in class	■
Math waiver	☐	Priority seating	☐
Other special classes	☐	Tape recorders	■
Priority registrations	☐	Videotaped classes	☐
Substitution of courses	☐	Text on tape	☐
Exams		**Services**	
Extended time	■	Diagnostic tests	☐
Oral exams	■	Learning centers	☐
Take home exams	☐	Proofreaders	☐
Exams on tape or computer	☐	Readers	■
Untimed exams	■	Reading Machines/Kurzweil	☐
Other accommodations	☐	Special bookstore section	☐
		Typists	☐

Credit toward degree is given for remedial courses taken.

Counseling Services

- ☐ Academic
- ☐ Psychological
- ☐ Student Support groups
- ☐ Vocational

Tutoring

	Individual	Group
Time management	☐	☐
Organizational skills	☐	☐
Learning strategies	☐	☐
Study skills	☐	☐
Content area	☐	☐
Writing lab	☐	☐
Math lab	☐	☐

LD PROGRAM STAFF

Total number of LD Program staff (including director):

Full Time: 3 Part Time: 3

Key staff person available to work with LD students: Stephanie W. Orr, ADA Coordinator.

Barry University

Miami Shores, FL

Address: 11300 N.E. Second Avenue, Miami Shores, FL, 33161-6695
Admissions telephone: 305 899-3100
Admissions FAX: 305 899-2971
Director of Admissions: Helen Corpuz
Admissions e-mail: admissions@mail.barry.edu
Web site: http://www.barry.edu
SAT Code: 5053 ACT Code: 718

Director, CAL Program: Vivian Castro
LD program telephone: 305 899-3461
LD program e-mail: vcastro@mail.barry.edu
Total campus enrollment: 5,942

GENERAL

Barry University is a private, coed, four-year institution. 122-acre campus in Miami Shores (population: 10,380), seven miles from Miami and 14 miles from Fort Lauderdale. Major airport, bus, and train serve Miami. Public transportation serves campus. Semester system.

LD ADMISSIONS

Students do not complete a separate application and are simultaneously accepted to the LD program. A personal interview is required. Students are admitted to the CAL program on a case-by-case basis upon the recommendation of the Program Director and the Division of Enrollment Services.

SECONDARY SCHOOL REQUIREMENTS

Graduation from secondary school required; GED accepted.

TESTING

SAT Reasoning or ACT required.

All enrolled freshmen (fall 2004):

Average SAT I Scores:	Verbal: 483	Math: 477
Average ACT Scores:	Composite: 20	

Child Study Team report is required if student is classified. Tests required as part of this documentation:

- ☐ WAIS-IV
- ☐ WISC-IV
- ☐ SATA
- ☐ Woodcock-Johnson
- ☐ Nelson-Denny Reading Test
- ☐ Other

UNDERGRADUATE STUDENT BODY

Total undergraduate student enrollment: 2,045 Men, 3,732 Women.

Composition of student body (fall 2004):

	Undergraduate
International	5.8
Black	26.0
American Indian	0.2
Asian-American	2.0
Hispanic	27.5
White	28.9
Unreported	9.6
	100.0%

10% are from out of state. Average age of full-time undergraduates is 28, 68% of classes have fewer than 20 students, 32% have between 20 and 50 students.

STUDENT HOUSING

67% of freshmen live in college housing. Freshmen are not required to live on campus. Housing is guaranteed for all undergraduates. Campus can house 1,000 undergraduates.

EXPENSES

Tuition (2005-06): $22,430 per year.
Room & Board: $7,620.
Additional cost for LD program/services: $2,150 per semester.

LD SERVICES

LD program size is limited.

LD services available to:

☐ Freshmen ☐ Sophomores ☐ Juniors ☐ Seniors

Academic Accommodations

Curriculum		**In class**	
Foreign language waiver	☐	Early syllabus	☐
Lighter course load	■	Note takers in class	■
Math waiver	☐	Priority seating	☐
Other special classes	■	Tape recorders	■
Priority registrations	☐	Videotaped classes	☐
Substitution of courses	☐	Text on tape	☐
Exams		**Services**	
Extended time	■	Diagnostic tests	☐
Oral exams	■	Learning centers	■
Take home exams	☐	Proofreaders	☐
Exams on tape or computer	☐	Readers	■
Untimed exams	☐	Reading Machines/Kurzweil	■
Other accommodations	☐	Special bookstore section	☐
		Typists	☐

Credit toward degree is not given for remedial courses taken.

Counseling Services

- ☐ Academic
- ☐ Psychological
- ☐ Student Support groups
- ☐ Vocational

Tutoring

	Individual	Group
Time management	☐	☐
Organizational skills	☐	☐
Learning strategies	☐	☐
Study skills	☐	☐
Content area	☐	☐
Writing lab	☐	☐
Math lab	☐	☐

LD PROGRAM STAFF

Total number of LD Program staff (including director):

Full Time: 1 Part Time: 1

Key staff person available to work with LD students: Vivian Castro, Director, CAL Program.

University of Central Florida

Orlando, FL

Address: 4000 Central Florida Boulevard, Orlando, FL, 32816
Admissions telephone: 407 823-3000
Admissions FAX: 407 823-5625
Executive Director of Admissions: Dr. Gordon Chavis Jr.
Admissions e-mail: admission@mail.ucf.edu
Web site: http://www.ucf.edu
SAT Code: 5233   ACT Code: 735

Director of Student Disability Services: Dr. Philip Kalfin
LD program telephone: 407 823-2371
Total campus enrollment: 35,159

GENERAL

University of Central Florida is a public, coed, four-year institution. 1,415-acre campus in Orlando (population: 185,951); branch campuses in Cocoa and Daytona Beach. Served by airport, bus, and train. Public transportation serves campus. Semester system.

LD ADMISSIONS

A personal interview is recommended. Essay is required and may be typed.

SECONDARY SCHOOL REQUIREMENTS

Graduation from secondary school required; GED accepted. The following course distribution required: 4 units of English, 3 units of math, 3 units of science, 2 units of foreign language, 3 units of social studies, 4 units of academic electives.

TESTING

SAT Reasoning or ACT required. SAT Subject required.

All enrolled freshmen (fall 2004):

Average SAT I Scores:	Verbal: 570	Math: 581
Average ACT Scores:	Composite: 25	

Child Study Team report is not required. Tests required as part of this documentation:

- ☐ WAIS-IV
- ☐ WISC-IV
- ☐ SATA
- ☐ Woodcock-Johnson
- ☐ Nelson-Denny Reading Test
- ☐ Other

UNDERGRADUATE STUDENT BODY

Total undergraduate student enrollment: 13,585 Men, 16,451 Women.

Composition of student body (fall 2004):

	Undergraduate	Freshmen
International	0.5	1.3
Black	8.5	8.4
American Indian	0.4	0.5
Asian-American	5.3	5.0
Hispanic	13.9	12.5
White	69.4	69.1
Unreported	2.0	3.3
	100.0%	100.0%

8% are from out of state. 13% join a fraternity and 12% join a sorority. Average age of full-time undergraduates is 21, 28% of classes have fewer than 20 students, 53% have between 20 and 50 students, 19% have more than 50 students.

STUDENT HOUSING

66% of freshmen live in college housing. Freshmen are not required to live on campus. Housing is not guaranteed for all undergraduates. Campus can house 8,090 undergraduates.

EXPENSES

Tuition (2005-06): $3,141 per year (in-state), $16,273 (out-of-state).
Room: $4,300. Board: $3,100.
There is no additional cost for LD program/services.

LD SERVICES

LD program size is not limited.

LD services available to:

☐ Freshmen ☐ Sophomores ☐ Juniors ☐ Seniors

Academic Accommodations

Curriculum		**In class**	
Foreign language waiver	☐	Early syllabus	☐
Lighter course load	☐	Note takers in class	■
Math waiver	☐	Priority seating	☐
Other special classes	☐	Tape recorders	■
Priority registrations	☐	Videotaped classes	■
Substitution of courses	☐	Text on tape	☐
Exams		**Services**	
Extended time	■	Diagnostic tests	■
Oral exams	☐	Learning centers	☐
Take home exams	☐	Proofreaders	☐
Exams on tape or computer	☐	Readers	■
Untimed exams	☐	Reading Machines/Kurzweil	■
Other accommodations	☐	Special bookstore section	☐
		Typists	☐

Credit toward degree is not given for remedial courses taken.

Counseling Services

- ☐ Academic
- ☐ Psychological
- ☐ Student Support groups
- ☐ Vocational

Tutoring

	Individual	Group
Time management	■	☐
Organizational skills	■	☐
Learning strategies	■	☐
Study skills	■	☐
Content area	☐	☐
Writing lab	■	☐
Math lab	■	☐

LD PROGRAM STAFF

Total number of LD Program staff (including director):

Full Time: 5   Part Time: 5

Clearwater Christian College

Clearwater, FL

Address: 3400 Gulf-to-Bay Boulevard, Clearwater, FL, 33759-4595
Admissions telephone: 800 348-4463
Admissions FAX: 727 726-8597
Dean of Enrollment Services: Mr. Benjamin J. Puckett
Admissions e-mail: admissions@clearwater.edu
Web site: http://www.clearwater.edu
SAT Code: 5142

Director of Guidance: Linda Wiggins
LD program telephone: 727 726-1153
LD program e-mail: lindawiggins@clearwater.edu
Total campus enrollment: 628

GENERAL

Clearwater Christian College is a private, coed, four-year institution. 148-acre campus in Clearwater (population: 108,787), 20 miles from Tampa. Served by air and bus. Semester system.

LD ADMISSIONS

Students do not complete a separate application and are simultaneously accepted to the LD program. A member of the LD program does not sit on the admissions committee. A personal interview is required. Essay is not required.

SECONDARY SCHOOL REQUIREMENTS

Graduation from secondary school not required.

TESTING

SAT Reasoning or ACT required. SAT Subject recommended.

All enrolled freshmen (fall 2004):

Average SAT I Scores: Verbal: 538 Math: 513

Child Study Team report is required if student is classified. A neuropsychological or comprehensive psycho-educational evaluation is required for admission. Must be dated within 48 months of application. Tests required as part of this documentation:

- ☐ WAIS-IV
- ☐ WISC-IV
- ☐ SATA
- ☐ Woodcock-Johnson
- ☐ Nelson-Denny Reading Test
- ■ Other

UNDERGRADUATE STUDENT BODY

Total undergraduate student enrollment: 628.

Composition of student body (fall 2004):

	Undergraduate	Freshmen
International	0.0	0.0
Black	2.2	2.6
American Indian	0.0	0.3
Asian-American	1.1	1.0
Hispanic	7.1	5.2
White	88.5	90.0
Unreported	1.1	0.9
	100.0%	100.0%

Average age of full-time undergraduates is 19, 67% of classes have fewer than 20 students, 27% have between 20 and 50 students.

STUDENT HOUSING

90% of freshmen live in college housing. Freshmen are not required to live on campus. Housing is guaranteed for all undergraduates. Campus can house 600 undergraduates. Single rooms are not available for students with medical or special needs.

EXPENSES

Tuition (2005-06): $11,220 per year.
Room: $3,090. Board: $1,980.
There is no additional cost for LD program/services.

LD SERVICES

LD program size is not limited.

LD services available to:

■ Freshmen ■ Sophomores ■ Juniors ■ Seniors

Academic Accommodations

Curriculum		In class	
Foreign language waiver	☐	Early syllabus	☐
Lighter course load	■	Note takers in class	☐
Math waiver	☐	Priority seating	☐
Other special classes	☐	Tape recorders	■
Priority registrations	☐	Videotaped classes	■
Substitution of courses	☐	Text on tape	☐
Exams		**Services**	
Extended time	■	Diagnostic tests	☐
Oral exams	■	Learning centers	☐
Take home exams	☐	Proofreaders	☐
Exams on tape or computer	☐	Readers	■
Untimed exams	■	Reading Machines/Kurzweil	☐
Other accommodations	☐	Special bookstore section	☐
		Typists	☐

Credit toward degree is not given for remedial courses taken.

Counseling Services

- ☐ Academic
- ☐ Psychological
- ☐ Student Support groups
- ☐ Vocational

Tutoring

Individual tutoring is available daily.

Average size of tutoring groups: 1

	Individual	Group
Time management	■	☐
Organizational skills	■	☐
Learning strategies	■	☐
Study skills	■	☐
Content area	☐	☐
Writing lab	☐	☐
Math lab	☐	☐

LD PROGRAM STAFF

Total number of LD Program staff (including director):

Full Time: 1 Part Time: 1

There is an advisor/advocate from the LD program available to students. The advisor/advocate meets with students 4 times per month. 10 peer tutors are available to work with LD students.

Key staff person available to work with LD students: Linda Wiggins, Director of Guidance.

Eckerd College

St. Petersburg, FL

Address: 4200 54th Avenue South, St. Petersburg, FL, 33711
Admissions telephone: 800 456-9009
Admissions FAX: 727 866-2304
Dean of Admissions: Laura E. Schlack
Admissions e-mail: admissions@eckerd.edu
Web site: http://www.eckerd.edu
SAT Code: 5223 ACT Code: 731

LD program name: Disability Support Services
Dean of Admissions: Laura E. Schlack
LD program telephone: 727 864-8331
LD program e-mail: admissions@eckerd.edu
Total campus enrollment: 1,684

GENERAL

Eckerd College is a private, coed, four-year institution. 267-acre, suburban campus in St. Petersburg (population: 248,232), 25 miles from Tampa. Served by airport, bus, and train; major airport serves Tampa. School operates transportation to inter-collegiate sporting events. Public transportation serves campus. 4-1-4 system.

LD ADMISSIONS

SECONDARY SCHOOL REQUIREMENTS

Graduation from secondary school required; GED accepted. The following course distribution required: 4 units of English, 3 units of math, 3 units of science, 2 units of foreign language, 2 units of social studies, 1 unit of history, 3 units of academic electives.

TESTING

SAT Reasoning or ACT required. SAT Subject recommended.

All enrolled freshmen (fall 2004):

Average SAT I Scores:	Verbal: 576	Math: 562
Average ACT Scores:	Composite: 24	

Child Study Team report is not required. Tests required as part of this documentation:

- ❑ WAIS-IV
- ❑ WISC-IV
- ❑ SATA
- ❑ Woodcock-Johnson
- ❑ Nelson-Denny Reading Test
- ❑ Other

UNDERGRADUATE STUDENT BODY

Total undergraduate student enrollment: 703 Men, 879 Women.

Composition of student body (fall 2004):

	Undergraduate	Freshmen
International	3.2	6.4
Black	3.0	3.3
American Indian	0.9	0.2
Asian-American	2.4	1.8
Hispanic	3.2	3.7
White	78.0	77.3
Unreported	9.4	7.2
	100.0%	100.0%

73% are from out of state. Average age of full-time undergraduates is 20, 50% of classes have fewer than 20 students, 49% have between 20 and 50 students.

STUDENT HOUSING

93% of freshmen live in college housing. Freshmen are not required to live on campus. Housing is guaranteed for all undergraduates. Campus can house 1,325 undergraduates.

EXPENSES

Tuition (2005-06): $25,804 per year.
Room: $3,572. Board: $3,580.

LD SERVICES

LD services available to:

❑ Freshmen ❑ Sophomores ❑ Juniors ❑ Seniors

Academic Accommodations

Curriculum		In class	
Foreign language waiver	❑	Early syllabus	❑
Lighter course load	❑	Note takers in class	❑
Math waiver	❑	Priority seating	❑
Other special classes	❑	Tape recorders	❑
Priority registrations	❑	Videotaped classes	❑
Substitution of courses	❑	Text on tape	❑
Exams		**Services**	
Extended time	❑	Diagnostic tests	❑
Oral exams	❑	Learning centers	❑
Take home exams	❑	Proofreaders	❑
Exams on tape or computer	❑	Readers	❑
Untimed exams	❑	Reading Machines/Kurzweil	❑
Other accommodations	❑	Special bookstore section	❑
		Typists	❑

Counseling Services

- ❑ Academic
- ❑ Psychological
- ❑ Student Support groups
- ❑ Vocational

Tutoring

	Individual	Group
Time management	❑	❑
Organizational skills	❑	❑
Learning strategies	❑	❑
Study skills	❑	❑
Content area	❑	❑
Writing lab	❑	❑
Math lab	❑	❑

LD PROGRAM STAFF

Key staff person available to work with LD students: Sherri Rings, Ph.D, Staff Psychologist and Coordinator of DSS.

Edward Waters Coll

Jacksonville, FL

Address: 1658 Kings Road, Jacksonville, FL, 32209
Admissions telephone: 904 470-8200
Admissions FAX: 904 470-8048
Director of Admissions: Tony A. Baldwin
Admissions e-mail: admissions@ewc.edu
Web site: http://www.ewc.edu
SAT Code: 5182

Dean, Division of General Studies: Dr. Emmanuel Okakor
LD program telephone: 904 470-8052
Total campus enrollment: 1,206

GENERAL

Edward Waters Coll is a private, coed, four-year institution. 21-acre campus in Jacksonville (population: 735,617). Served by airport, bus, and train. Semester system.

LD ADMISSIONS

Students do not complete a separate application and are simultaneously accepted to the LD program. A member of the LD program does not sit on the admissions committee. A personal interview is required. Essay is not required.

SECONDARY SCHOOL REQUIREMENTS

Graduation from secondary school required; GED accepted. The following course distribution required: 4 units of English, 3 units of math, 3 units of science, 3 units of social studies, 5 units of academic electives.

TESTING

Child Study Team report is not required. A neuropsychological or comprehensive psycho-education evaluation is not required for admission. Tests required as part of this documentation:

- ☐ WAIS-IV
- ☐ WISC-IV
- ☐ SATA
- ☐ Woodcock-Johnson
- ☐ Nelson-Denny Reading Test
- ☐ Other

UNDERGRADUATE STUDENT BODY

Total undergraduate student enrollment: 1,206.

Composition of student body (fall 2004):

	Undergraduate	Freshmen
International	0.3	0.0
Black	92.8	95.7
American Indian	0.0	0.0
Asian-American	0.0	0.1
Hispanic	1.2	0.7
White	4.0	1.6
Unreported	1.7	1.9
	100.0%	100.0%

17% are from out of state.

STUDENT HOUSING

Freshmen are not required to live on campus. Housing is guaranteed for all undergraduates.

EXPENSES

Tuition 2004-05: $9,176 per year.

Room: $3,124. Board: $3,350.

There is no additional cost for LD program/services.

LD SERVICES

LD program size is not limited.

LD services available to:

☐ Freshmen ☐ Sophomores ☐ Juniors ☐ Seniors

Academic Accommodations

Curriculum		**In class**	
Foreign language waiver	☐	Early syllabus	☐
Lighter course load	■	Note takers in class	■
Math waiver	☐	Priority seating	☐
Other special classes	☐	Tape recorders	■
Priority registrations	☐	Videotaped classes	☐
Substitution of courses	☐	Text on tape	☐
Exams		**Services**	
Extended time	■	Diagnostic tests	☐
Oral exams	■	Learning centers	☐
Take home exams	☐	Proofreaders	☐
Exams on tape or computer	☐	Readers	■
Untimed exams	■	Reading Machines/Kurzweil	☐
Other accommodations	☐	Special bookstore section	☐
		Typists	☐

Credit toward degree is not given for remedial courses taken.

Counseling Services

- ☐ Academic
- ☐ Psychological
- ☐ Student Support groups
- ☐ Vocational

Tutoring

	Individual	Group
Time management	☐	☐
Organizational skills	☐	☐
Learning strategies	☐	☐
Study skills	☐	☐
Content area	☐	☐
Writing lab	☐	☐
Math lab	☐	☐

LD PROGRAM STAFF

Key staff person available to work with LD students: Dr. Emmanuel Okakor, Dean, Division of General Studies.

Embry-Riddle Aeronautical University

Daytona Beach, FL

Address: 600 South Clyde Morris Boulevard, Daytona Beach, FL, 32114
Admissions telephone: 800 862-2416
Admissions FAX: 386 226-7070
Director of Admissions: Michael Novak
Admissions e-mail: dbadmit@erau.edu
Web site: http://www.embryriddle.edu
SAT Code: 5190 ACT Code: 725

Coordinator, Disability Support Services: Maureen Bridger
LD program telephone: 386 226-7919
LD program e-mail: bridgerm@erau.edu
Total campus enrollment: 4,407

GENERAL

Embry-Riddle Aeronautical University is a private, coed, four-year institution. 178-acre campus in Daytona Beach (population: 64,112), 50 miles from Orlando; affiliated campus in Prescott, AZ. Served by airport and bus; major airport serves Orlando; train serves Deland (20 miles). Public transportation serves campus. Semester system.

LD ADMISSIONS

Students do not complete a separate application and are not simultaneously accepted to the LD program. A member of the LD program does not sit on the admissions committee. A personal interview is not required. Essay is not required.

SECONDARY SCHOOL REQUIREMENTS

Graduation from secondary school required; GED accepted. The following course distribution required: 4 units of English, 3 units of math, 3 units of science, 3 units of social studies, 1 unit of history, 3 units of academic electives.

TESTING

SAT Reasoning required. ACT required. SAT Subject recommended.

All enrolled freshmen (fall 2004):

Average SAT I Scores:	Verbal: 538	Math: 568
Average ACT Scores:	Composite: 23	

Child Study Team report is not required. A neuropsychological or comprehensive psycho-education evaluation is not required for admission. Tests required as part of this documentation:

- [ ] WAIS-IV
- [ ] WISC-IV
- [ ] SATA
- [ ] Woodcock-Johnson
- [ ] Nelson-Denny Reading Test
- [ ] Other

UNDERGRADUATE STUDENT BODY

Total undergraduate student enrollment: 3,882 Men, 759 Women.

Composition of student body (fall 2004):

	Undergraduate	Freshmen
International	3.9	7.9
Black	4.6	4.5
American Indian	0.0	0.4
Asian-American	4.3	3.8
Hispanic	8.7	6.6
White	69.2	66.9
Unreported	9.3	10.0
	100.0%	100.0%

70% are from out of state. 12% join a fraternity and 14% join a sorority. Average age of full-time undergraduates is 20, 24% of classes have fewer than 20 students, 73% have between 20 and 50 students.

STUDENT HOUSING

96% of freshmen live in college housing. Freshmen are required to live on campus. Housing is not guaranteed for all undergraduates. Assignments made on a space available basis. Campus can house 1,889 undergraduates. Single rooms are not available for students with medical or special needs.

EXPENSES

Tuition (2005-06): $22,820 per year. $17,850 per year (freshmen), $16,600 (upperclass students).

Room: $3,800. Board: $3,136.

There is no additional cost for LD program/services.

LD SERVICES

LD program size is not limited.

LD services available to:

- [x] Freshmen
- [x] Sophomores
- [x] Juniors
- [x] Seniors

Academic Accommodations

Curriculum		In class	
Foreign language waiver	[ ]	Early syllabus	[ ]
Lighter course load	[x]	Note takers in class	[x]
Math waiver	[ ]	Priority seating	[ ]
Other special classes	[ ]	Tape recorders	[x]
Priority registrations	[ ]	Videotaped classes	[ ]
Substitution of courses	[ ]	Text on tape	[ ]
Exams		**Services**	
Extended time	[ ]	Diagnostic tests	[ ]
Oral exams	[ ]	Learning centers	[ ]
Take home exams	[ ]	Proofreaders	[ ]
Exams on tape or computer	[ ]	Readers	[ ]
Untimed exams	[x]	Reading Machines/Kurzweil	[x]
Other accommodations	[ ]	Special bookstore section	[ ]
		Typists	[ ]

Credit toward degree is not given for remedial courses taken.

Counseling Services

- [ ] Academic
- [ ] Psychological
- [ ] Student Support groups
- [ ] Vocational

Tutoring

Individual tutoring is available.

	Individual	Group
Time management	[ ]	[ ]
Organizational skills	[ ]	[ ]
Learning strategies	[ ]	[ ]
Study skills	[ ]	[ ]
Content area	[ ]	[ ]
Writing lab	[ ]	[ ]
Math lab	[ ]	[ ]

UNIQUE LD PROGRAM FEATURES

Work with each student on an individual basis.

LD PROGRAM STAFF

Total number of LD Program staff (including director):

Full Time: 1 Part Time: 1

Key staff person available to work with LD students: Vanessa Lloyd, Disability Services Advocate.

Flagler College

St. Augustine, FL

Address: 74 King Street, St. Augustine, FL, 32084
Admissions telephone: 800 304-4208, extension 220
Admissions FAX: 904 819-6466
Director of Admissions: Marc G. Williar
Admissions e-mail: admiss@flagler.edu
Web site: http://www.flagler.edu
SAT Code: 5235   ACT Code: 772

LD program name: Office of Services for Students with Disabilities
Coordinator: Deborah Larew
LD program telephone: 904 819-6460
LD program e-mail: OSSD@flagler.edu
LD program enrollment: 47, Total campus enrollment: 2,106

GENERAL

Flagler College is a private, coed, four-year institution. 38-acre campus in Saint Augustine (population: 11,592), 35 miles south of Jacksonville. Served by bus; airports serve Jacksonville and Daytona Beach (55 miles); train serves Jacksonville. Semester system.

LD ADMISSIONS

Students do not complete a separate application and are not simultaneously accepted to the LD program. A member of the LD program does not sit on the admissions committee. A personal interview is recommended. Essay is required and may be typed.

For fall 2004, 12 completed self-identified LD applications were received. 8 applications were offered admission, and 8 enrolled.

SECONDARY SCHOOL REQUIREMENTS

Graduation from secondary school required; GED accepted. The following course distribution required: 4 units of English, 3 units of math, 2 units of science, 3 units of social studies, 1 unit of history, 3 units of academic electives.

TESTING

SAT Reasoning or ACT required. SAT Subject recommended.

All enrolled freshmen (fall 2004):

Average SAT I Scores: Verbal: 568 Math: 560
Average ACT Scores: Composite: 24

Child Study Team report is not required. A neuropsychological or comprehensive psycho-educational evaluation is required for admission. Must be dated within 36 months of application. Tests required as part of this documentation:

- ■ WAIS-IV
- ☐ WISC-IV
- ■ SATA
- ■ Woodcock-Johnson
- ■ Nelson-Denny Reading Test
- ☐ Other

UNDERGRADUATE STUDENT BODY

Total undergraduate student enrollment: 680 Men, 1,150 Women.

Composition of student body (fall 2004):

	Undergraduate	Freshmen
International	0.2	1.3
Black	1.4	1.6
American Indian	0.7	0.3
Asian-American	0.8	0.6
Hispanic	3.9	3.9
White	90.5	90.2
Unreported	2.5	2.1
	100.0%	100.0%

31% are from out of state. Average age of full-time undergraduates is 21, 30% of classes have fewer than 20 students, 69% have between 20 and 50 students.

STUDENT HOUSING

81% of freshmen live in college housing. Freshmen are required to live on campus. Housing is guaranteed for all undergraduates. Campus can house 710 undergraduates.

EXPENSES

Tuition (2005-06): $8,600 per year.
Room: $2,130. Board: $3,060.

There is no additional cost for LD program/services.

LD SERVICES

LD program size is not limited.

LD services available to:

■ Freshmen ■ Sophomores ■ Juniors ■ Seniors

Academic Accommodations

Curriculum		In class	
Foreign language waiver	☐	Early syllabus	☐
Lighter course load	■	Note takers in class	■
Math waiver	☐	Priority seating	☐
Other special classes	☐	Tape recorders	☐
Priority registrations	■	Videotaped classes	☐
Substitution of courses	☐	Text on tape	☐
Exams		**Services**	
Extended time	■	Diagnostic tests	☐
Oral exams	■	Learning centers	☐
Take home exams	☐	Proofreaders	☐
Exams on tape or computer	☐	Readers	☐
Untimed exams	☐	Reading Machines/Kurzweil	■
Other accommodations	■	Special bookstore section	☐
		Typists	☐

Credit toward degree is not given for remedial courses taken.

Counseling Services

- ■ Academic
- ■ Psychological
- ☐ Student Support groups
- ☐ Vocational

Tutoring

Individual tutoring is available.

	Individual	Group
Time management	☐	☐
Organizational skills	☐	☐
Learning strategies	■	☐
Study skills	■	☐
Content area	☐	☐
Writing lab	■	■
Math lab	■	■

UNIQUE LD PROGRAM FEATURES

Services for students with disabilities are determined on an individual basis according to the documented significant limitation of the disability. The admission process, while allowing for reasonable accommodations, still looks for students who are otherwise qualified.

LD PROGRAM STAFF

Total number of LD Program staff (including director):

Full Time: 1   Part Time: 1

There is an advisor/advocate from the LD program available to students.

Key staff person available to work with LD students: Deborah Larew, Coordinator of Services for Students with Disabilities.

University of Florida

Gainesville, FL

Address: 201 Criser Hall, Gainesville, FL, 32611
Admissions telephone: 352 392-1365
Director of Admissions: Pat Herring
Admissions e-mail: freshman@ufl.edu
Web site: http://www.ufl.edu
SAT Code: 5812 ACT Code: 758

LD program name: Disability Resources
LD program address: P.O. Box 114075
Director: John Denny
LD program e-mail: jdenny@ufl.edu
LD program enrollment: 768, Total campus enrollment: 33,694

GENERAL

University of Florida is a public, coed, four-year institution. 2,000-acre suburban campus in Gainesville (population: 95,447), 70 miles from Jacksonville. Served by airport and bus; major airport serves Orlando (90 miles); train serves Waldo (10 miles). School operates transportation to downtown area. Public transportation serves campus. Semester system.

LD ADMISSIONS

Students do not complete a separate application and are simultaneously accepted to the LD program. A member of the LD program does not sit on the admissions committee. High school waivers are accepted for math and foreign language. A personal interview is not required. Essay is required and may be typed. Foreign language and math requirements may be waived or substituted.

SECONDARY SCHOOL REQUIREMENTS

Graduation from secondary school required; GED accepted. The following course distribution required: 4 units of English, 3 units of math, 3 units of science, 2 units of foreign language, 3 units of social studies.

TESTING

SAT Reasoning or ACT required. SAT Subject required.

All enrolled freshmen (fall 2004):

Average SAT I Scores:	Verbal: 618	Math: 635
Average ACT Scores:	Composite: 27	

Child Study Team report is not required. A neuropsychological or comprehensive psycho-educational evaluation is required for admission. Must be dated within 36 months of application. Tests required as part of this documentation:

- ■ WAIS-IV
- ■ WISC-IV
- ☐ SATA
- ■ Woodcock-Johnson
- ■ Nelson-Denny Reading Test
- ☐ Other

UNDERGRADUATE STUDENT BODY

Total undergraduate student enrollment: 15,943 Men, 17,696 Women.

Composition of student body (fall 2004):

	Undergraduate	Freshmen
International	0.7	0.9
Black	10.7	8.7
American Indian	0.3	0.4
Asian-American	7.7	6.9
Hispanic	11.8	12.2
White	67.6	69.8
Unreported	1.2	1.0
	100.0%	100.0%

5% are from out of state. 15% join a fraternity and 15% join a sorority. Average age of full-time undergraduates is 21, 37% of classes have fewer than 20 students, 42% have between 20 and 50 students, 21% have more than 50 students.

STUDENT HOUSING

81% of freshmen live in college housing. Freshmen are not required to live on campus. Housing is guaranteed for all undergraduates. Campus housing available on a first-come, first-served basis. Campus can house 7,552 undergraduates. Single rooms are not available for students with medical or special needs.

EXPENSES

There is no additional cost for LD program/services.

LD SERVICES

LD program size is not limited.

LD services available to:

■ Freshmen ■ Sophomores ■ Juniors ■ Seniors

Academic Accommodations

Curriculum		**In class**	
Foreign language waiver	☐	Early syllabus	☐
Lighter course load	■	Note takers in class	■
Math waiver	☐	Priority seating	☐
Other special classes	☐	Tape recorders	■
Priority registrations	☐	Videotaped classes	☐
Substitution of courses	☐	Text on tape	☐
Exams		**Services**	
Extended time	■	Diagnostic tests	■
Oral exams	☐	Learning centers	☐
Take home exams	☐	Proofreaders	☐
Exams on tape or computer	☐	Readers	■
Untimed exams	☐	Reading Machines/Kurzweil	■
Other accommodations	☐	Special bookstore section	☐
		Typists	☐

Credit toward degree is not given for remedial courses taken.

Counseling Services

- ■ Academic
- ☐ Psychological
- ☐ Student Support groups
- ☐ Vocational

Tutoring

Individual tutoring is available weekly.

	Individual	Group
Time management	■	☐
Organizational skills	■	☐
Learning strategies	■	☐
Study skills	■	☐
Content area	☐	☐
Writing lab	■	■
Math lab	■	■

UNIQUE LD PROGRAM FEATURES

Students are encouraged to submit a personal statement explaining how their learning disabilities affected standardized test scores, GPA, or course selection.

LD PROGRAM STAFF

Total number of LD Program staff (including director):

Full Time: 6 Part Time: 6

There is an advisor/advocate from the LD program available to students.

Key staff person available to work with LD students: John Denny, LCSW, Director, Disability Resources.

LD Program web site: www.dso.ufl.edu/drp

Florida Agricultural and Mechanical University

Tallahassee, FL

Address: Tallahassee, FL, 32307
Admissions telephone: 866 642-1198
Admissions FAX: 850 561-2428
Director of Admissions: Kimberly A. Davis
Admissions e-mail: admissions@famu.edu
Web site: http://www.famu.edu
SAT Code: 5215 ACT Code: 726

LD program name: Learning Development & Evaluation Center
LD program address: 667 Arcadelia Court
Associate Director: Donna Shell
LD program telephone: 850 599-3180
LD program e-mail: donna.shell@famu.edu
LD program enrollment: 160, Total campus enrollment: 10,584

GENERAL

Florida Agricultural and Mechanical University is a public, coed, four-year institution. 419-acre campus in Tallahassee (population: 150,624). Served by airport, bus and train. School operates transportation to Florida St U. Public transportation serves campus. Semester system.

LD ADMISSIONS

Application Deadline: 04/30. Students complete a separate application and are not simultaneously accepted to the LD program. A member of the LD program does not sit on the admissions committee. A personal interview is recommended. Essay is required and may be typed.

For fall 2004, 44 completed self-identified LD applications were received. 44 applications were offered admission, and 44 enrolled.

SECONDARY SCHOOL REQUIREMENTS

Graduation from secondary school required; GED accepted. The following course distribution required: 4 units of English, 3 units of math, 3 units of science, 2 units of foreign language, 3 units of social studies, 3 units of history, 3 units of academic electives.

TESTING

SAT Reasoning or ACT required. SAT Subject recommended.

All enrolled freshmen (fall 2004):

Average ACT Scores: Composite: 19

Child Study Team report is not required. A neuropsychological or comprehensive psycho-educational evaluation is required for admission. Must be dated within 36 months of application. Tests required as part of this documentation:

- ☒ WAIS-IV
- ☐ WISC-IV
- ☐ SATA
- ☒ Woodcock-Johnson
- ☐ Nelson-Denny Reading Test
- ☒ Other

UNDERGRADUATE STUDENT BODY

Total undergraduate student enrollment: 10,584.

Composition of student body (fall 2004):

	Undergraduate	Freshmen
International	0.3	0.7
Black	97.1	96.4
American Indian	0.0	0.0
Asian-American	0.5	0.2
Hispanic	1.0	0.8
White	1.1	1.8
Unreported	0.0	0.0
	100.0%	100.0%

25% are from out of state. 1% join a fraternity and 1% join a sorority. Average age of full-time undergraduates is 25, 37% of classes have fewer than 20 students, 52% have between 20 and 50 students, 11% have more than 50 students.

STUDENT HOUSING

95% of freshmen live in college housing. Freshmen are required to live on campus. Housing is guaranteed for all undergraduates. Campus can house 3,146 undergraduates. Single rooms are available for students with medical or special needs. A medical note is required.

EXPENSES

Tuition (2005-06): $2,960 per year (in-state), $14,950 (out-of-state).
Room: $3,616. Board: $2,224.
There is no additional cost for LD program/services.

LD SERVICES

LD program size is not limited.

LD services available to:

☒ Freshmen ☒ Sophomores ☒ Juniors ☒ Seniors

Academic Accommodations

Curriculum		In class	
Foreign language waiver	☒	Early syllabus	☐
Lighter course load	☒	Note takers in class	☐
Math waiver	☒	Priority seating	☐
Other special classes	☒	Tape recorders	☒
Priority registrations	☐	Videotaped classes	☐
Substitution of courses	☒	Text on tape	☐
Exams		**Services**	
Extended time	☒	Diagnostic tests	☐
Oral exams	☐	Learning centers	☒
Take home exams	☐	Proofreaders	☒
Exams on tape or computer	☒	Readers	☒
Untimed exams	☐	Reading Machines/Kurzweil	☒
Other accommodations	☐	Special bookstore section	☐
		Typists	☐

Credit toward degree is not given for remedial courses taken.

Counseling Services

- ☒ Academic — Meets 2 times per academic year
- ☐ Psychological
- ☐ Student Support groups
- ☒ Vocational — Meets once per academic year

Tutoring

Individual tutoring is available daily.

Average size of tutoring groups: 4

	Individual	Group
Time management	☒	☐
Organizational skills	☒	☐
Learning strategies	☒	☐
Study skills	☒	☐
Content area	☒	☐
Writing lab	☒	☐
Math lab	☒	☐

LD PROGRAM STAFF

Total number of LD Program staff (including director):

Full Time: 6 Part Time: 6

There is an advisor/advocate from the LD program available to students. The advisor/advocate meets with students once per month. 7 peer tutors are available to work with LD students.

Key staff person available to work with LD students: Dr. Sharon Wooten, Director.

Florida Atlantic University

Boca Raton, FL

Address: 777 Glades Road, P.O. Box 3091, Boca Raton, FL, 33431
Admissions telephone: 800 299-4FAU
Admissions FAX: 561 297-2758
Director of Admissions: Albert Colom
Admissions e-mail: admisweb@fau.edu
Web site: http://www.fau.edu
SAT Code: 5229 ACT Code: 729

LD program name: Office for Students with Disabilities
Director, Office of Students with Disabiltiies: Nicole Rokos
LD program telephone: 561 297-3880
LD program e-mail: nrokos@fau.edu
LD program enrollment: 364, Total campus enrollment: 21,551

GENERAL

Florida Atlantic University is a public, coed, four-year institution. 860-acre, suburban campus in Boca Raton (population: 74,764), 15 miles from Fort Lauderdale; branch campuses in Dania, Davie, Fort Lauderdale, North Palm Beach, and Port St. Lucie. Served by bus and train; major airports serve Fort Lauderdale and West Palm Beach (20 miles). Public transportation serves campus. Semester system.

LD ADMISSIONS

Students do not complete a separate application and are not simultaneously accepted to the LD program. A member of the LD program does not sit on the admissions committee. High school waivers are accepted for foreign language. A personal interview is not required. Essay is not required.

For fall 2004, 92 completed self-identified LD applications were received. 87 applications were offered admission, and 81 enrolled.

SECONDARY SCHOOL REQUIREMENTS

Graduation from secondary school required; GED accepted. The following course distribution required: 4 units of English, 3 units of math, 3 units of science, 2 units of foreign language, 1 unit of social studies, 2 units of history, 3 units of academic electives.

TESTING

SAT Reasoning or ACT required. SAT Subject required.

All enrolled freshmen (fall 2004):

Average SAT I Scores:	Verbal: 517	Math: 520
Average ACT Scores:	Composite: 21	

Child Study Team report is not required. A neuropsychological or comprehensive psycho-educational evaluation is required for admission. Must be dated within 1 months of application. Tests required as part of this documentation:

- ☑ WAIS-IV
- ☐ WISC-IV
- ☑ SATA
- ☑ Woodcock-Johnson
- ☑ Nelson-Denny Reading Test
- ☐ Other

UNDERGRADUATE STUDENT BODY

Total undergraduate student enrollment: 7,301 Men, 11,456 Women.

Composition of student body (fall 2004):

	Undergraduate	Freshmen
International	1.9	4.2
Black	16.2	18.2
American Indian	0.3	0.4
Asian-American	4.6	4.5
Hispanic	17.0	15.8
White	59.8	56.8
Unreported	0.1	0.0
	100.0%	100.0%

9% are from out of state. 2% join a fraternity and 2% join a sorority. Average age of full-time undergraduates is 22, 38% of classes have fewer than 20 students, 52% have between 20 and 50 students, 11% have more than 50 students.

STUDENT HOUSING

50% of freshmen live in college housing. Freshmen are required to live on campus. Housing is guaranteed for all undergraduates. Campus can house 2,200 undergraduates. Single rooms are available for students with medical or special needs. A medical note is required.

EXPENSES

Tuition (2005-06): $2,254 per year (in-state), $15,386 (out-of-state).

Room: $5,290. Board: $2,522.
There is no additional cost for LD program/services.

LD SERVICES

LD program size is not limited.

LD services available to:

☑ Freshmen ☑ Sophomores ☑ Juniors ☑ Seniors

Academic Accommodations

Curriculum		In class	
Foreign language waiver	☐	Early syllabus	☐
Lighter course load	☑	Note takers in class	☐
Math waiver	☐	Priority seating	☐
Other special classes	☐	Tape recorders	☑
Priority registrations	☐	Videotaped classes	☐
Substitution of courses	☐	Text on tape	☐
Exams		**Services**	
Extended time	☐	Diagnostic tests	☐
Oral exams	☐	Learning centers	☐
Take home exams	☐	Proofreaders	☐
Exams on tape or computer	☐	Readers	☐
Untimed exams	☐	Reading Machines/Kurzweil	☑
Other accommodations	☐	Special bookstore section	☐
		Typists	☐

Credit toward degree is not given for remedial courses taken.

Counseling Services

- ☑ Academic — Meets 3 times per academic year
- ☐ Psychological
- ☐ Student Support groups
- ☑ Vocational

Tutoring

Individual tutoring is not available.

	Individual	Group
Time management	☑	☑
Organizational skills	☑	☑
Learning strategies	☑	☑
Study skills	☑	☑
Content area	☐	☐
Writing lab	☐	☐
Math lab	☐	☐

UNIQUE LD PROGRAM FEATURES

Services are offered on an individual basis.

LD PROGRAM STAFF

Total number of LD Program staff (including director):

Full Time: 3 Part Time: 3

There is an advisor/advocate from the LD program available to students. 2 graduate students and 30 peer tutors are available to work with LD students.

Key staff person available to work with LD students: Nicole Rokos, Director, Office of Students with Disabilities.

LD Program web site: http://www.osd.fau.edu/

Florida Gulf Coast University

Fort Myers, FL

Address: 10501 FGCU Boulevard South, Fort Myers, FL, 33965-6565
Admissions telephone: 239 590-7878
Admissions FAX: 239 590-7894
Director of Admissions: F. Larry Stiles
Admissions e-mail: admissions@fgcu.edu
Web site: http://www.fgcu.edu
SAT Code: 5221 ACT Code: 733

Coordinator: Cori Bright
LD program telephone: 239 590-7956
LD program enrollment: 240, Total campus enrollment: 4,959

GENERAL

Florida Gulf Coast University is a public, coed, four-year institution. 760-acre campus in Fort Myers (population: 48,208). Served by airport and bus; train serves Tampa (123 miles). Public transportation serves campus. Semester system.

LD ADMISSIONS

Students do not complete a separate application and are simultaneously accepted to the LD program. A member of the LD program does sit on the admissions committee. High school waivers are accepted for math and foreign language. A personal interview is not required. Essay is not required. Test scores may be waived.

For fall 2004, 129 completed self-identified LD applications were received. 77 applications were offered admission, and 44 enrolled.

SECONDARY SCHOOL REQUIREMENTS

Graduation from secondary school required; GED accepted. The following course distribution required: 4 units of English, 3 units of math, 3 units of science, 2 units of foreign language, 3 units of social studies, 3 units of academic electives.

TESTING

SAT Reasoning or ACT required. SAT Subject required.

All enrolled freshmen (fall 2004):

Average SAT I Scores:	Verbal: 521	Math: 527
Average ACT Scores:	Composite: 22	

Child Study Team report is not required. A neuropsychological or comprehensive psycho-educational evaluation is required for admission. Must be dated within 36 months of application. Tests required as part of this documentation:

- [x] WAIS-IV
- [x] WISC-IV
- [ ] SATA
- [x] Woodcock-Johnson
- [x] Nelson-Denny Reading Test
- [ ] Other

UNDERGRADUATE STUDENT BODY

Total undergraduate student enrollment: 1,181 Men, 2,222 Women.

Composition of student body (fall 2004):

	Undergraduate	Freshmen
International	0.3	0.9
Black	3.4	5.4
American Indian	0.2	0.3
Asian-American	2.5	1.7
Hispanic	9.7	8.9
White	82.5	81.2
Unreported	1.4	1.7
	100.0%	100.0%

5% are from out of state. 6% join a fraternity and 3% join a sorority. Average age of full-time undergraduates is 21, 27% of classes have fewer than 20 students, 68% have between 20 and 50 students.

STUDENT HOUSING

61% of freshmen live in college housing. Freshmen are not required to live on campus. Housing is not guaranteed for all undergraduates. Housing is limited to 1, 662 of the student body on a first come basis. Single rooms are available for students with medical or special needs. A medical note is required.

EXPENSES

Tuition (2005-06): $3,260 per year (in-state), $15,249 (out-of-state).
Room: $4,420. Board: $1,972.
There is no additional cost for LD program/services.

LD SERVICES

LD program size is not limited.

LD services available to:

- [x] Freshmen
- [x] Sophomores
- [x] Juniors
- [x] Seniors

Academic Accommodations

Curriculum		In class	
Foreign language waiver	[ ]	Early syllabus	[x]
Lighter course load	[x]	Note takers in class	[x]
Math waiver	[ ]	Priority seating	[x]
Other special classes	[ ]	Tape recorders	[x]
Priority registrations	[x]	Videotaped classes	[ ]
Substitution of courses	[x]	Text on tape	[x]
Exams		**Services**	
Extended time	[x]	Diagnostic tests	[x]
Oral exams	[ ]	Learning centers	[x]
Take home exams	[ ]	Proofreaders	[ ]
Exams on tape or computer	[x]	Readers	[x]
Untimed exams	[x]	Reading Machines/Kurzweil	[x]
Other accommodations	[x]	Special bookstore section	[ ]
		Typists	[x]

Credit toward degree is not given for remedial courses taken.

Counseling Services

- [x] Academic
- [x] Psychological
- [ ] Student Support groups
- [x] Vocational

Tutoring

Individual tutoring is available daily.

	Individual	Group
Time management	[x]	[ ]
Organizational skills	[x]	[ ]
Learning strategies	[x]	[ ]
Study skills	[x]	[ ]
Content area	[x]	[ ]
Writing lab	[x]	[ ]
Math lab	[x]	[ ]

LD PROGRAM STAFF

Total number of LD Program staff (including director):

Full Time: 1 Part Time: 1

There is an advisor/advocate from the LD program available to students. 6 peer tutors are available to work with LD students.

Key staff person available to work with LD students: Cori Bright, Coordinator.

Florida Institute of Technology

Melbourne, FL

Address: 150 West University Boulevard, Melbourne, FL, 32901-6975
Admissions telephone: 800 888-4348
Admissions FAX: 321 723-9468
Director of Admissions: Judith Marino
Admissions e-mail: admissions@fit.edu
Web site: http://www.fit.edu
SAT Code: 5080 ACT Code: 716

LD program name: Academic Support Services
Director Academic Support Center: Rodney Bowers
LD program telephone: 321 674-7110
LD program e-mail: rbowers@fit.edu
LD program enrollment: 26, Total campus enrollment: 2,319

GENERAL

Florida Institute of Technology is a private, coed, four-year institution. 130-acre campus in Melbourne (population: 71,382), 75 miles from Orlando. Served by airport, bus, and train; major airport serves Orlando. School operates transportation to shopping centers and Melbourne airport. Semester system.

LD ADMISSIONS

Students do not complete a separate application and are simultaneously accepted to the LD program. A member of the LD program does not sit on the admissions committee. A personal interview is recommended. Essay is not required.

SECONDARY SCHOOL REQUIREMENTS

Graduation from secondary school required; GED accepted. The following course distribution required: 4 units of English, 4 units of math, 3 units of science.

TESTING

SAT Reasoning required; ACT may be substituted. SAT Subject recommended.

All enrolled freshmen (fall 2004):

Average SAT I Scores:	Verbal: 564	Math: 603
Average ACT Scores:	Composite: 25	

Child Study Team report is not required. A neuropsychological or comprehensive psycho-educational evaluation is required for admission. Must be dated within 36 months of application. Tests required as part of this documentation:

- ■ WAIS-IV
- ■ WISC-IV
- ☐ SATA
- ■ Woodcock-Johnson
- ☐ Nelson-Denny Reading Test
- ☐ Other

UNDERGRADUATE STUDENT BODY

Total undergraduate student enrollment: 1,533 Men, 658 Women.

Composition of student body (fall 2004):

	Undergraduate	Freshmen
International	9.4	17.2
Black	5.6	3.7
American Indian	0.4	0.3
Asian-American	4.0	2.9
Hispanic	7.1	6.6
White	61.2	56.1
Unreported	12.3	13.1
	100.0%	100.0%

43% are from out of state. 16% join a fraternity and 10% join a sorority. Average age of full-time undergraduates is 20, 56% of classes have fewer than 20 students, 41% have between 20 and 50 students.

STUDENT HOUSING

94% of freshmen live in college housing. Freshmen are required to live on campus. Housing is guaranteed for all undergraduates. Campus can house 1,333 undergraduates. Single rooms are available for students with medical or special needs. A medical note is required.

EXPENSES

Tuition (2005-06): $25,150 per year. $19,600 per year, $20,900 for engineering and science programs.

Room: $4,000. Board: $2,800.

There is no additional cost for LD program/services.

LD SERVICES

LD program size is not limited.

LD services available to:

■ Freshmen ■ Sophomores ■ Juniors ■ Seniors

Academic Accommodations

Curriculum		**In class**	
Foreign language waiver	☐	Early syllabus	☐
Lighter course load	☐	Note takers in class	■
Math waiver	☐	Priority seating	☐
Other special classes	☐	Tape recorders	■
Priority registrations	☐	Videotaped classes	☐
Substitution of courses	☐	Text on tape	☐
Exams		**Services**	
Extended time	■	Diagnostic tests	■
Oral exams	☐	Learning centers	■
Take home exams	☐	Proofreaders	☐
Exams on tape or computer	☐	Readers	☐
Untimed exams	■	Reading Machines/Kurzweil	☐
Other accommodations	☐	Special bookstore section	☐
		Typists	☐

Credit toward degree is not given for remedial courses taken.

Counseling Services

- ■ Academic
- ■ Psychological
- ☐ Student Support groups
- ■ Vocational

Tutoring

Individual tutoring is available daily.

Average size of tutoring groups: 10

	Individual	Group
Time management	■	■
Organizational skills	■	☐
Learning strategies	■	■
Study skills	■	☐
Content area	■	☐
Writing lab	■	☐
Math lab	■	■

LD PROGRAM STAFF

There is an advisor/advocate from the LD program available to students. 15 peer tutors are available to work with LD students.

Key staff person available to work with LD students: Rodney Bowers, Director.

Florida International University

Miami, FL

Address: University Park, Miami, FL, 33199
Admissions telephone: 305 348-2363
Admissions FAX: 305 348-3648
Director of Admissions: Ms. Carmen Brown
Admissions e-mail: admiss@fiu.edu
Web site: http://www.fiu.edu
SAT Code: 5206 ACT Code: 776

Director: Dr. Julio Garcia
LD program telephone: 305 348-3532
LD program e-mail: garciaj@fiu.edu
Total campus enrollment: 28,865

GENERAL

Florida International University is a public, coed, four-year institution. 573-acre, urban campus in Miami (population: 362,470); branch campuses in Davie, Ft. Lauderdale, and North Miami. Served by airport, bus, and train. Public transportation serves campus. Semester system.

LD ADMISSIONS

A personal interview is recommended. Essay is not required. Minimum SAT score may be waived.

SECONDARY SCHOOL REQUIREMENTS

Graduation from secondary school required; GED accepted. The following course distribution required: 4 units of English, 3 units of math, 3 units of science, 2 units of foreign language, 3 units of social studies, 4 units of academic electives.

TESTING

SAT Reasoning or ACT required. SAT Subject recommended.

All enrolled freshmen (fall 2004):

Average SAT I Scores: Verbal: 563 Math: 565
Average ACT Scores: Composite: 24

Child Study Team report is not required. Tests required as part of this documentation:

☐ WAIS-IV ☐ Woodcock-Johnson
☐ WISC-IV ☐ Nelson-Denny Reading Test
☐ SATA ☐ Other

UNDERGRADUATE STUDENT BODY

Total undergraduate student enrollment: 11,302 Men, 14,669 Women.

Composition of student body (fall 2004):

	Undergraduate	Freshmen
International	3.0	6.3
Black	11.6	12.9
American Indian	0.1	0.2
Asian-American	3.6	3.7
Hispanic	63.4	58.3
White	16.7	17.9
Unreported	1.6	0.7
	100.0%	100.0%

11% are from out of state. Average age of full-time undergraduates is 21, 29% of classes have fewer than 20 students, 52% have between 20 and 50 students, 19% have more than 50 students.

STUDENT HOUSING

Housing is guaranteed for all undergraduates. Campus can house 2,050 undergraduates.

EXPENSES

Tuition (2005-06): $3,062 per year (in-state), $15,461 (out-of-state).

Room: $5,253. Board: $3,000.

There is no additional cost for LD program/services.

LD SERVICES

LD program size is not limited.

LD services available to:

☐ Freshmen ☐ Sophomores ☐ Juniors ☐ Seniors

Academic Accommodations

Curriculum		**In class**	
Foreign language waiver	☐	Early syllabus	☐
Lighter course load	■	Note takers in class	■
Math waiver	☐	Priority seating	☐
Other special classes	■	Tape recorders	■
Priority registrations	☐	Videotaped classes	■
Substitution of courses	☐	Text on tape	☐
Exams		**Services**	
Extended time	■	Diagnostic tests	■
Oral exams	■	Learning centers	■
Take home exams	☐	Proofreaders	☐
Exams on tape or computer	☐	Readers	■
Untimed exams	■	Reading Machines/Kurzweil	■
Other accommodations	☐	Special bookstore section	☐
		Typists	☐

Credit toward degree is not given for remedial courses taken.

Counseling Services

☐ Academic
☐ Psychological
☐ Student Support groups
☐ Vocational

Tutoring

	Individual	Group
Time management	☐	☐
Organizational skills	☐	☐
Learning strategies	☐	☐
Study skills	☐	☐
Content area	☐	☐
Writing lab	☐	☐
Math lab	☐	☐

LD PROGRAM STAFF

Total number of LD Program staff (including director):

Full Time: 6 Part Time: 6

Key staff person available to work with LD students: Dr. Beverly Paden, Assistant Director.

Florida Memorial College

Miami, FL

Address: 15800 N.W. 42nd Avenue, Miami, FL, 33054
Admissions telephone: 305 626-3750
Admissions FAX: 305 623-1462
Director of Admissions: Lenora V. Edwards
Admissions e-mail: ledwards@fmc.edu
Web site: http://www.fmc.edu/
SAT Code: 5217 ACT Code: 730

Vice President: Dr. Harold R. Clarke, Jr
LD program telephone: 305 626-3711
LD program e-mail: pclarke@fmc.edu

GENERAL

Florida Memorial College is a private, coed, four-year institution. 50-acre campus in metropolitan Miami (population: 362,470). Served by airport, bus, and train. Semester system.

LD ADMISSIONS

A personal interview is not required. Essay is not required. GPA and high school course distribution requirements may be waived.

SECONDARY SCHOOL REQUIREMENTS

Graduation from secondary school required; GED accepted. The following course distribution required: 4 units of English, 3 units of math, 3 units of science, 2 units of foreign language, 3 units of social studies, 4 units of academic electives.

TESTING

Child Study Team report is not required. Tests required as part of this documentation:

- ☐ WAIS-IV
- ☐ WISC-IV
- ☐ SATA
- ☐ Woodcock-Johnson
- ☐ Nelson-Denny Reading Test
- ☐ Other

COMPOSITION OF STUDENT BODY (FALL 2004):

20% are from out of state.

STUDENT HOUSING

Housing is guaranteed for all undergraduates. Campus can house 776 undergraduates.

EXPENSES

Tuition (2005-06): $10,104 per year.

Room: $2,738. Board: $2,396.

There is no additional cost for LD program/services.

LD SERVICES

LD program size is not limited.

LD services available to:

☐ Freshmen ☐ Sophomores ☐ Juniors ☐ Seniors

Academic Accommodations

Curriculum		**In class**	
Foreign language waiver	☐	Early syllabus	☐
Lighter course load	■	Note takers in class	☐
Math waiver	☐	Priority seating	☐
Other special classes	☐	Tape recorders	☐
Priority registrations	☐	Videotaped classes	☐
Substitution of courses	☐	Text on tape	☐
Exams		**Services**	
Extended time	■	Diagnostic tests	■
Oral exams	☐	Learning centers	■
Take home exams	☐	Proofreaders	☐
Exams on tape or computer	☐	Readers	☐
Untimed exams	☐	Reading Machines/Kurzweil	☐
Other accommodations	☐	Special bookstore section	☐
		Typists	☐

Credit toward degree is not given for remedial courses taken.

Counseling Services

- ☐ Academic
- ☐ Psychological
- ☐ Student Support groups
- ☐ Vocational

Tutoring

	Individual	Group
Time management	☐	☐
Organizational skills	☐	☐
Learning strategies	☐	☐
Study skills	☐	☐
Content area	☐	☐
Writing lab	☐	☐
Math lab	☐	☐

UNIQUE LD PROGRAM FEATURES

FMC did not have any self-identified LD students in 2003-2004. However, two students were diagnosed and were supported during the academic year.

LD PROGRAM STAFF

Key staff person available to work with LD students: Argerine Williams, Director.

Florida State University

Tallahassee, FL

Address: Tallahassee, FL, 32306
Admissions telephone: 850 644-6200
Admissions FAX: 850 644-0197
Director of Admissions: Janice Finney
Admissions e-mail: admissions@admin.fsu.edu
Web site: http://www.fsu.edu
SAT Code: 5219 ACT Code: 734

LD program name: Student Disability Resource Center
LD program address: 97 Woodward Ave South, 108 Student Service Bldg
Academic Access Coordinator: Alison Guest
LD program telephone: 850 644-9566
LD program e-mail: SDRC@admin.fsu.edu
LD program enrollment: 215, Total campus enrollment: 30,373

GENERAL

Florida State University is a public, coed, four-year institution. 463-acre, suburban campus in Tallahassee (population: 150,624); branch campuses in Panama City and abroad in Panama. Served by airport, bus, and train; major airport serves Jacksonville (170 miles). Public transportation serves campus. Semester system.

LD ADMISSIONS

Students do not complete a separate application and are not simultaneously accepted to the LD program. A member of the LD program does sit on the admissions committee. High school waivers are accepted for math and foreign language. A personal interview is not required. Essay is required and may be typed. May request special consideration based on disability.

For fall 2004, 1,233 completed self-identified LD applications were received. 371 applications were offered admission, and 242 enrolled.

SECONDARY SCHOOL REQUIREMENTS

Graduation from secondary school required; GED accepted. The following course distribution required: 4 units of English, 3 units of math, 3 units of science, 2 units of foreign language, 2 units of social studies, 1 unit of history, 4 units of academic electives.

TESTING

SAT Reasoning or ACT required. SAT Subject recommended.

All enrolled freshmen (fall 2004):

Average SAT I Scores:	Verbal: 580	Math: 584
Average ACT Scores:	Composite: 25	

Child Study Team report is not required. A neuropsychological or comprehensive psycho-educational evaluation is required for admission. Tests required as part of this documentation:

- ■ WAIS-IV
- ☐ WISC-IV
- ☐ SATA
- ■ Woodcock-Johnson
- ■ Nelson-Denny Reading Test
- ■ Other

UNDERGRADUATE STUDENT BODY

Total undergraduate student enrollment: 12,242 Men, 15,989 Women.

Composition of student body (fall 2004):

	Undergraduate	Freshmen
International	0.3	0.5
Black	10.4	11.7
American Indian	0.4	0.4
Asian-American	2.7	3.0
Hispanic	11.2	10.5
White	73.0	72.6
Unreported	2.1	1.4
	100.0%	100.0%

19% are from out of state. 15% join a fraternity and 13% join a sorority. Average age of full-time undergraduates is 21, 34% of classes have fewer than 20 students, 51% have between 20 and 50 students, 15% have more than 50 students.

STUDENT HOUSING

58% of freshmen live in college housing. Freshmen are not required to live on campus. Housing is guaranteed for all undergraduates. Campus can house 4,436 undergraduates. Single rooms are available for students with medical or special needs. A medical note is required.

EXPENSES

Tuition (2005-06): $2,397 per year (in-state), $15,528 (out-of-state).
Room & Board: $7,774.
There is no additional cost for LD program/services.

LD SERVICES

LD program size is not limited.

LD services available to:

■ Freshmen ■ Sophomores ■ Juniors ■ Seniors

Academic Accommodations

Curriculum		In class	
Foreign language waiver	■	Early syllabus	■
Lighter course load	■	Note takers in class	■
Math waiver	■	Priority seating	☐
Other special classes	☐	Tape recorders	■
Priority registrations	☐	Videotaped classes	☐
Substitution of courses	■	Text on tape	■
Exams		**Services**	
Extended time	■	Diagnostic tests	■
Oral exams	■	Learning centers	☐
Take home exams	☐	Proofreaders	☐
Exams on tape or computer	☐	Readers	■
Untimed exams	■	Reading Machines/Kurzweil	■
Other accommodations	☐	Special bookstore section	■
		Typists	☐

Credit toward degree is not given for remedial courses taken.

Counseling Services

- ■ Academic
- ■ Psychological
- ■ Student Support groups
- ■ Vocational

Tutoring

Individual tutoring is available weekly.

	Individual	Group
Time management	■	☐
Organizational skills	■	☐
Learning strategies	■	☐
Study skills	■	☐
Content area	■	☐
Writing lab	■	☐
Math lab	■	☐

LD PROGRAM STAFF

Total number of LD Program staff (including director):

Full Time: 8 Part Time: 8

There is an advisor/advocate from the LD program available to students.

Key staff person available to work with LD students: Robin Leach, Interim Dir. of Student Disability Resource Center.

LD Program web site: www.disabilitycenter.fsu.edu

Jacksonville University

Jacksonville, FL

Address: 2800 University Boulevard North, Jacksonville, FL, 32211
Admissions telephone: 800 225-2027
Admissions FAX: 904 256-7012
Director of Admissions: Miriam King
Admissions e-mail: admissions@ju.edu
Web site: http://www.jacksonville.edu
SAT Code: 5331 ACT Code: 740

Vice President for Student Life: Dr. John A. Balog
LD program telephone: 904 256-7070
LD program e-mail: jbalog@ju.edu
Total campus enrollment: 2, 561

GENERAL

Jacksonville University is a private, coed, four-year institution. 260-acre, suburban campus in Jacksonville (population: 735,617). Served by air, bus, and train. Public transportation serves campus. Semester system.

LD ADMISSIONS

Students do not complete a separate application and are simultaneously accepted to the LD program. A member of the LD program does not sit on the admissions committee. A personal interview is recommended. Essay is not required.

SECONDARY SCHOOL REQUIREMENTS

Graduation from secondary school required; GED accepted. The following course distribution required: 4 units of English, 3 units of math, 2 units of science, 3 units of social studies.

TESTING

SAT Reasoning or ACT required. SAT Subject recommended.

All enrolled freshmen (fall 2004):

Average SAT I Scores:	Verbal: 509	Math: 517
Average ACT Scores:	Composite: 22	

Child Study Team report is not required. A neuropsychological or comprehensive psycho-educational evaluation is required for admission. Must be dated within 36 months of application. Tests required as part of this documentation:

- ■ WAIS-IV
- ■ WISC-IV
- ■ SATA
- ■ Woodcock-Johnson
- ■ Nelson-Denny Reading Test
- ☐ Other

UNDERGRADUATE STUDENT BODY

Total undergraduate student enrollment: 885 Men, 932 Women.

Composition of student body (fall 2004):

	Undergraduate	Freshmen
International	2.8	2.5
Black	18.0	14.9
American Indian	0.0	0.7
Asian-American	1.3	2.7
Hispanic	5.4	4.8
White	61.6	65.9
Unreported	10.9	8.4
	100.0%	100.0%

13% join a fraternity and 17% join a sorority. Average age of full-time undergraduates is 21, 54% of classes have fewer than 20 students, 45% have between 20 and 50 students.

STUDENT HOUSING

84% of freshmen live in college housing. Freshmen are required to live on campus. Housing is guaranteed for all undergraduates. Campus can house 1,085 undergraduates. Single rooms are available for students with medical or special needs. A medical note is required.

EXPENSES

Tuition (2005-06): $19,970 per year.
Room: $3,030. Board: $3,430.
There is no additional cost for LD program/services.

LD SERVICES

LD program size is not limited.

LD services available to:

■ Freshmen ■ Sophomores ■ Juniors ■ Seniors

Academic Accommodations

Curriculum		**In class**	
Foreign language waiver	☐	Early syllabus	☐
Lighter course load	■	Note takers in class	■
Math waiver	☐	Priority seating	■
Other special classes	■	Tape recorders	■
Priority registrations	☐	Videotaped classes	■
Substitution of courses	■	Text on tape	■
Exams		**Services**	
Extended time	■	Diagnostic tests	☐
Oral exams	■	Learning centers	■
Take home exams	☐	Proofreaders	☐
Exams on tape or computer	☐	Readers	■
Untimed exams	■	Reading Machines/Kurzweil	■
Other accommodations	■	Special bookstore section	■
		Typists	☐

Credit toward degree is not given for remedial courses taken.

Counseling Services

- ■ Academic — Meets 2 times per academic year
- ☐ Psychological
- ■ Student Support groups — Meets 2 times per academic year
- ☐ Vocational

Tutoring

Individual tutoring is available daily.

	Individual	Group
Time management	■	■
Organizational skills	■	■
Learning strategies	☐	☐
Study skills	■	■
Content area	☐	☐
Writing lab	■	☐
Math lab	■	☐

LD PROGRAM STAFF

Total number of LD Program staff (including director):

Full Time: 2 Part Time: 2

There is an advisor/advocate from the LD program available to students.

Key staff person available to work with LD students: Dr. John A. Balog, Vice President for Student Life.

Lynn University

Boca Raton, FL

Address: 3601 North Military Trail, Boca Raton, FL, 33431
Admissions telephone: 800 544-8035, extension 1
Admissions FAX: 561 237-7100
Vice President for Enrollment: Brett Ormandy
Admissions e-mail: admission@lynn.edu
Web site: http://www.lynn.edu
SAT Code: 5437 ACT Code: 706

LD program name: Comprehensive Support Program
LD program contact: Admissions Office
LD program telephone: 561 237-7900
LD program e-mail: admission@lynn.edu
Total campus enrollment: 2,091

GENERAL

Lynn University is a private, coed, four-year institution. 123-acre campus in Boca Raton (population: 74,764), 23 miles from Fort Lauderdale and Palm Beach and 50 miles from Miami; branch campuses abroad in Argentina and Ireland. Served by air, bus, and train; larger airports serve West Palm Beach and Fort Lauderdale; major airport serves Miami. School operates transportation to cinema, malls, and beach. Public transportation serves campus. Semester system.

LD ADMISSIONS

A personal interview is recommended. Essay is required and may be typed.

SECONDARY SCHOOL REQUIREMENTS

Graduation from secondary school required; GED accepted. The following course distribution required: 4 units of English, 4 units of math, 4 units of science, 2 units of social studies, 2 units of history.

TESTING

SAT Reasoning or ACT required. SAT Subject recommended.

All enrolled freshmen (fall 2004):

Average SAT I Scores:	Verbal: 454	Math: 458
Average ACT Scores:	Composite: 19	

Child Study Team report is not required. Tests required as part of this documentation:

☐ WAIS-IV ☐ Woodcock-Johnson
☐ WISC-IV ☐ Nelson-Denny Reading Test
☐ SATA ☐ Other

UNDERGRADUATE STUDENT BODY

Total undergraduate student enrollment: 873 Men, 948 Women.

Composition of student body (fall 2004):

	Undergraduate	Freshmen
International	10.4	13.1
Black	3.2	6.3
American Indian	0.2	0.7
Asian-American	1.0	0.6
Hispanic	4.5	6.9
White	57.3	54.7
Unreported	23.5	17.7
	100.0%	100.0%

45% are from out of state. Average age of full-time undergraduates is 21, 53% of classes have fewer than 20 students, 47% have between 20 and 50 students.

STUDENT HOUSING

Freshmen are required to live on campus. Housing is guaranteed for all undergraduates. Campus can house 1,138 undergraduates.

EXPENSES

Tuition (2005-06): $24,700 per year.
Board: $1,820.
Additional cost for LD program/services: $5,100 per semester.

LD SERVICES

LD program size is not limited.

LD services available to:

☐ Freshmen ☐ Sophomores ☐ Juniors ☐ Seniors

Academic Accommodations

Curriculum		**In class**	
Foreign language waiver	☐	Early syllabus	☐
Lighter course load	☐	Note takers in class	☐
Math waiver	☐	Priority seating	☐
Other special classes	■	Tape recorders	■
Priority registrations	☐	Videotaped classes	☐
Substitution of courses	☐	Text on tape	☐
Exams		**Services**	
Extended time	■	Diagnostic tests	☐
Oral exams	■	Learning centers	■
Take home exams	☐	Proofreaders	☐
Exams on tape or computer	☐	Readers	■
Untimed exams	■	Reading Machines/Kurzweil	■
Other accommodations	☐	Special bookstore section	☐
		Typists	☐

Credit toward degree is not given for remedial courses taken.

Counseling Services

☐ Academic
☐ Psychological
☐ Student Support groups
☐ Vocational

Tutoring

	Individual	Group
Time management	☐	☐
Organizational skills	☐	☐
Learning strategies	☐	☐
Study skills	☐	☐
Content area	☐	☐
Writing lab	☐	☐
Math lab	☐	☐

LD PROGRAM STAFF

Total number of LD Program staff (including director):

Full Time: 12 Part Time: 12

Key staff person available to work with LD students: Dr. Marsha Glines, Executive Director, The Institute for Achievement.

University of Miami

Coral Gables, FL

Address: P.O. Box 248025, Coral Gables, FL, 33124
Admissions telephone: 305 284-4323
Admissions FAX: 305 284-2507
Director of Admission and Associate Dean of Enrollments: Edward M. Gillis
Admissions e-mail: admission@miami.edu
Web site: http://www.miami.edu
SAT Code: 5815 ACT Code: 760

Director, Accessibility Resources: Judith Antinarella
LD program telephone: 305 284-2374
LD program e-mail: jantinarella@miami.edu
Total campus enrollment: 10,104

GENERAL

University of Miami is a private, coed, four-year institution. 260-acre campus in Coral Gables (population: 42,249), four miles from Miami; branch campuses in Miami and Virginia Key. Served by bus; major airport and train serve Miami. School operates transportation to local shopping area and around campus. Public transportation serves campus. Semester system.

LD ADMISSIONS

Students do not complete a separate application and are not simultaneously accepted to the LD program. A member of the LD program does not sit on the admissions committee. A personal interview is not required. Essay is required and may be typed.

SECONDARY SCHOOL REQUIREMENTS

Graduation from secondary school required; GED accepted.

TESTING

SAT Reasoning or ACT required. SAT Subject recommended.

Child Study Team report is not required. A neuropsychological or comprehensive psycho-education evaluation is not required for admission. Tests required as part of this documentation:

- [ ] WAIS-IV
- [ ] WISC-IV
- [ ] SATA
- [ ] Woodcock-Johnson
- [ ] Nelson-Denny Reading Test
- [ ] Other

UNDERGRADUATE STUDENT BODY

Total undergraduate student enrollment: 4,069 Men, 5,290 Women.

Composition of student body (fall 2004):

	Undergraduate	Freshmen
International	3.5	6.0
Black	9.4	9.4
American Indian	0.4	0.3
Asian-American	6.7	5.6
Hispanic	19.2	23.9
White	57.2	52.1
Unreported	3.7	2.9
	100.0%	100.0%

44% are from out of state, 47% of classes have fewer than 20 students, 47% have between 20 and 50 students.

STUDENT HOUSING

Freshmen are required to live on campus. Housing is not guaranteed for all undergraduates. We only house undergraduate students in on-campus housing. Campus can house 4,213 undergraduates.

EXPENSES

Tuition (2005-06): $29,020 per year.
Room: $5,224. Board: $3,682.

There is no additional cost for LD program/services.

LD SERVICES

LD program size is not limited.

LD services available to:

- [x] Freshmen
- [x] Sophomores
- [x] Juniors
- [x] Seniors

Academic Accommodations

Curriculum

- [ ] Foreign language waiver
- [ ] Lighter course load
- [ ] Math waiver
- [ ] Other special classes
- [ ] Priority registrations
- [ ] Substitution of courses

Exams

- [x] Extended time
- [ ] Oral exams
- [ ] Take home exams
- [ ] Exams on tape or computer
- [ ] Untimed exams
- [ ] Other accommodations

In class

- [ ] Early syllabus
- [ ] Note takers in class
- [ ] Priority seating
- [x] Tape recorders
- [ ] Videotaped classes
- [ ] Text on tape

Services

- [ ] Diagnostic tests
- [x] Learning centers
- [ ] Proofreaders
- [x] Readers
- [ ] Reading Machines/Kurzweil
- [ ] Special bookstore section
- [ ] Typists

Counseling Services

- [ ] Academic
- [ ] Psychological
- [ ] Student Support groups
- [ ] Vocational

Tutoring

Individual tutoring is available weekly.

Average size of tutoring groups: 1

	Individual	Group
Time management	[x]	[ ]
Organizational skills	[x]	[ ]
Learning strategies	[x]	[ ]
Study skills	[x]	[ ]
Content area	[ ]	[ ]
Writing lab	[ ]	[ ]
Math lab	[ ]	[ ]

LD PROGRAM STAFF

Total number of LD Program staff (including director):

Full Time: 2 Part Time: 2

Key staff person available to work with LD students: Judith Antinarella, Director, Accessibility Resources.

Miami International University of Art & Design

Miami, FL

Address: 1501 Biscayne Boulevard, Suite 100, Miami, FL, 33132
Admissions telephone: 305 428-5700
Admissions FAX: 305 374-5933
Admissions Contact: Elsia Suarez
Web site: www.aimiu.artinstitutes.edu
SAT Code: 5327

LD program name: Student Affairs, Counseling Department
Dean of Student Affairs: Shari Saperstein
LD program telephone: 305 428-5900
LD program e-mail: ssaperstein@aii.edu
LD program enrollment: 26, Total campus enrollment: 1,328

GENERAL

Miami International University of Art & Design is a private, coed, four-year institution. Campus in Miami (population: 362,470). Served by air, bus, and train. Quarter system.

LD ADMISSIONS

Students do not complete a separate application and are not simultaneously accepted to the LD program. A member of the LD program does not sit on the admissions committee. A personal interview is required. Essay is required and may be typed.

For fall 2004, 22 completed self-identified LD applications were received. 22 applications were offered admission, and 22 enrolled.

SECONDARY SCHOOL REQUIREMENTS

Graduation from secondary school required; GED accepted.

TESTING

Child Study Team report is not required. A neuropsychological or comprehensive psycho-educational evaluation is required for admission. Must be dated within 60 months of application. Tests required as part of this documentation:

- ■ WAIS-IV
- ■ WISC-IV
- ■ SATA
- ■ Woodcock-Johnson
- ■ Nelson-Denny Reading Test
- ☐ Other

UNDERGRADUATE STUDENT BODY

Total undergraduate student enrollment: 844 Men.

Composition of student body (fall 2004):

	Undergraduate	Freshmen
International	0.0	0.0
Black	11.5	8.9
American Indian	0.5	0.2
Asian-American	2.0	1.8
Hispanic	43.0	47.3
White	13.0	16.2
Unreported	30.0	25.5
	100.0%	100.0%

89% of classes have fewer than 20 students, 11% have between 20 and 50 students.

STUDENT HOUSING

Freshmen are not required to live on campus. Housing is guaranteed for all undergraduates. Campus can house 2 undergraduates.

EXPENSES

Tuition (2005-06): Tuition: $12,800-$15,900.
Room: $4,880.
There is no additional cost for LD program/services.

LD SERVICES

LD program size is not limited.

LD services available to:

■ Freshmen ■ Sophomores ■ Juniors ■ Seniors

Academic Accommodations

Curriculum		**In class**	
Foreign language waiver	☐	Early syllabus	■
Lighter course load	■	Note takers in class	■
Math waiver	☐	Priority seating	■
Other special classes	☐	Tape recorders	☐
Priority registrations	☐	Videotaped classes	☐
Substitution of courses	☐	Text on tape	☐
Exams		**Services**	
Extended time	■	Diagnostic tests	■
Oral exams	■	Learning centers	■
Take home exams	■	Proofreaders	☐
Exams on tape or computer	■	Readers	☐
Untimed exams	■	Reading Machines/Kurzweil	☐
Other accommodations	☐	Special bookstore section	■
		Typists	☐

Credit toward degree is not given for remedial courses taken.

Counseling Services

- ■ Academic — Meets 4 times per academic year
- ■ Psychological — Meets 8 times per academic year
- ☐ Student Support groups
- ☐ Vocational

Tutoring

Individual tutoring is available daily.

Average size of tutoring groups: 4

	Individual	Group
Time management	☐	■
Organizational skills	☐	■
Learning strategies	■	■
Study skills	■	■
Content area	■	☐
Writing lab	☐	☐
Math lab	■	■

LD PROGRAM STAFF

Total number of LD Program staff (including director):

Full Time: 2 Part Time: 2

There is an advisor/advocate from the LD program available to students. The advisor/advocate meets with faculty 2 times per month and students 2 times per month.

Key staff person available to work with LD students: Jose Rodriguez, Counselor.

New College of Florida

Sarasota, FL

Address: 5700 North Tamiami Trail, Sarasota, FL, 34243-2197
Admissions telephone: 941 359-4269
Admissions FAX: 941 359-4435
Dean of Admissions and Financial Aid: Kathy Killion
Admissions e-mail: admissions@ncf.edu
Web site: http://www.ncf.edu
SAT Code: 5506 ACT Code: 750

LD program name: Student Disability Services
Coordinator: Christopher J. Pantzis
LD program telephone: 941 359-4254
LD program e-mail: pantzis@ncf.edu
LD program enrollment: 11, Total campus enrollment: 692

GENERAL

New College of Florida is a public, coed, four-year institution. 140-acre campus in Sarasota (population: 52,715), 50 miles south of Tampa. Served by air, bus, and train; major airport serves Tampa. Public transportation serves campus. 4-1-4 system.

LD ADMISSIONS

Students do not complete a separate application and are not simultaneously accepted to the LD program. A member of the LD program does not sit on the admissions committee. High school waivers are accepted for math and foreign language. A personal interview is not required. Essay is required and may be typed.

SECONDARY SCHOOL REQUIREMENTS

Graduation from secondary school required; GED accepted. The following course distribution required: 4 units of English, 3 units of math, 3 units of science, 2 units of foreign language, 3 units of social studies, 3 units of academic electives.

TESTING

SAT Reasoning or ACT required. SAT Subject recommended.

All enrolled freshmen (fall 2004):

Average SAT I Scores:	Verbal: 677	Math: 634
Average ACT Scores:	Composite: 29	

Child Study Team report is not required. A neuropsychological or comprehensive psycho-educational evaluation is required for admission. Must be dated within 60 months of application. Tests required as part of this documentation:

■ WAIS-IV	■ Woodcock-Johnson
■ WISC-IV	☐ Nelson-Denny Reading Test
☐ SATA	☐ Other

UNDERGRADUATE STUDENT BODY

Total undergraduate student enrollment: 223 Men, 411 Women.

Composition of student body (fall 2004):

	Undergraduate	Freshmen
International	1.1	2.2
Black	1.6	1.6
American Indian	0.0	0.1
Asian-American	3.2	3.0
Hispanic	11.1	9.1
White	81.0	82.4
Unreported	2.1	1.6
	100.0%	100.0%

25% are from out of state. Average age of full-time undergraduates is 20, 64% of classes have fewer than 20 students, 34% have between 20 and 50 students.

STUDENT HOUSING

91% of freshmen live in college housing. Freshmen are required to live on campus. Housing is guaranteed for all undergraduates. Campus can house 471 undergraduates. Single rooms are available for students with medical or special needs. A medical note is required.

EXPENSES

Tuition (2005-06): $3,679 per year (in-state), $19,475 (out-of-state).
Room: $3,910. Board: $2,420.
There is no additional cost for LD program/services.

LD SERVICES

LD program size is not limited.

LD services available to:

■ Freshmen ■ Sophomores ■ Juniors ■ Seniors

Academic Accommodations

Curriculum		**In class**	
Foreign language waiver	☐	Early syllabus	■
Lighter course load	☐	Note takers in class	■
Math waiver	☐	Priority seating	■
Other special classes	☐	Tape recorders	■
Priority registrations	☐	Videotaped classes	☐
Substitution of courses	☐	Text on tape	☐
Exams		**Services**	
Extended time	■	Diagnostic tests	☐
Oral exams	■	Learning centers	☐
Take home exams	☐	Proofreaders	☐
Exams on tape or computer	☐	Readers	■
Untimed exams	☐	Reading Machines/Kurzweil	☐
Other accommodations	☐	Special bookstore section	☐
		Typists	■

Credit toward degree is not given for remedial courses taken.

Counseling Services

☐ Academic
■ Psychological — Meets 12 times per academic year
☐ Student Support groups
☐ Vocational

Tutoring

Individual tutoring is available weekly.

	Individual	Group
Time management	■	☐
Organizational skills	■	☐
Learning strategies	☐	☐
Study skills	■	☐
Content area	☐	☐
Writing lab	■	☐
Math lab	■	☐

LD PROGRAM STAFF

There is an advisor/advocate from the LD program available to students.

Key staff person available to work with LD students: Christopher J. Pantzis, Coordinator.

University of North Florida

Jacksonville, FL

Address: 4567 St. Johns Bluff Road South, Jacksonville, FL, 32224-2645
Admissions telephone: 904 620-2624
Admissions FAX: 904 620-2414
Director of Admissions: John Yancey
Admissions e-mail: admissions@unf.edu
Web site: http://www.unf.edu
SAT Code: 5490 ACT Code: 3970

LD program name: Disability Resource Center
Director, Disability Resource Center: Dr. Robert E. Lee
LD program telephone: 904 620-2769
LD program e-mail: rlee@unf.edu
LD program enrollment: 150, Total campus enrollment: 12,668

GENERAL

University of North Florida is a public, coed, four-year institution. 1,300-acre campus in Jacksonville (population: 735,617). Served by air, bus, and train. Public transportation serves campus. Semester system.

LD ADMISSIONS

Students do not complete a separate application and are not simultaneously accepted to the LD program. A member of the LD program does not sit on the admissions committee. A personal interview is not required. Essay is not required. SAT, ACT, and GPA requirements may be waived.

SECONDARY SCHOOL REQUIREMENTS

Graduation from secondary school required; GED accepted. The following course distribution required: 4 units of English, 3 units of math, 3 units of science, 2 units of foreign language, 3 units of social studies, 4 units of academic electives.

TESTING

SAT Reasoning or ACT required. SAT Subject recommended.

All enrolled freshmen (fall 2004):

Average SAT I Scores:	Verbal: 553	Math: 550
Average ACT Scores:	Composite: 22	

Child Study Team report is not required. A neuropsychological or comprehensive psycho-educational evaluation is required for admission. Must be dated within 36 months of application. Tests required as part of this documentation:

- [x] WAIS-IV
- [x] WISC-IV
- [ ] SATA
- [x] Woodcock-Johnson
- [ ] Nelson-Denny Reading Test
- [ ] Other

UNDERGRADUATE STUDENT BODY

Total undergraduate student enrollment: 4,617 Men, 6,517 Women.

Composition of student body (fall 2004):

	Undergraduate	Freshmen
International	0.3	0.8
Black	9.2	9.6
American Indian	0.7	0.5
Asian-American	4.4	5.2
Hispanic	7.3	5.8
White	77.5	76.7
Unreported	0.6	1.3
	100.0%	100.0%

5% are from out of state. 7% join a fraternity and 6% join a sorority. Average age of full-time undergraduates is 22, 23% of classes have fewer than 20 students, 65% have between 20 and 50 students, 11% have more than 50 students.

STUDENT HOUSING

85% of freshmen live in college housing. Freshmen are not required to live on campus. Housing is guaranteed for all undergraduates. Campus can house 2,000 undergraduates. Single rooms are available for students with medical or special needs. A medical note is required.

EXPENSES

Tuition (2005-06): $2,254 per year (in-state), $13,896 (out-of-state). Room: $3,780. Board: $2,831.

There is no additional cost for LD program/services.

LD SERVICES

LD program size is not limited.

LD services available to:

- [x] Freshmen
- [x] Sophomores
- [x] Juniors
- [x] Seniors

Academic Accommodations

Curriculum

- [ ] Foreign language waiver
- [ ] Lighter course load
- [ ] Math waiver
- [ ] Other special classes
- [ ] Priority registrations
- [ ] Substitution of courses

Exams

- [x] Extended time
- [x] Oral exams
- [ ] Take home exams
- [ ] Exams on tape or computer
- [x] Untimed exams
- [ ] Other accommodations

In class

- [ ] Early syllabus
- [x] Note takers in class
- [ ] Priority seating
- [x] Tape recorders
- [ ] Videotaped classes
- [ ] Text on tape

Services

- [ ] Diagnostic tests
- [x] Learning centers
- [ ] Proofreaders
- [x] Readers
- [x] Reading Machines/Kurzweil
- [ ] Special bookstore section
- [ ] Typists

Credit toward degree is not given for remedial courses taken.

Counseling Services

- [x] Academic
- [x] Psychological
- [ ] Student Support groups
- [x] Vocational

Tutoring

Individual tutoring is available.

	Individual	Group
Time management	[ ]	[x]
Organizational skills	[ ]	[x]
Learning strategies	[ ]	[x]
Study skills	[ ]	[x]
Content area	[ ]	[x]
Writing lab	[ ]	[x]
Math lab	[ ]	[x]

UNIQUE LD PROGRAM FEATURES

There is no LD specialist on staff.

LD PROGRAM STAFF

Total number of LD Program staff (including director):

Full Time: 3 Part Time: 3

There is no advisor/advocate from the LD program available to students. 33 peer tutors are available to work with LD students.

Key staff person available to work with LD students: Dr. Robert E. Lee, Director, Disability Resource Center.

Northwood University - Florida Campus

West Palm Beach, FL

Address: 2600 North Military Trail, West Palm Beach, FL, 33409
Admissions telephone: 800 458-8325
Admissions FAX: 561 640-3328
Director of Admissions: Jack Letvinchuk
Admissions e-mail: fladmit@northwood.edu
Web site: http://www.northwood.edu
SAT Code: 5162 ACT Code: 6736

LD program name: Academics
Academic Dean: Cheryl Pridgeon
LD program telephone: 561 478-5526
LD program e-mail: pridgeon@northwood.edu
Total campus enrollment: 956

GENERAL

Northwood University - Florida Campus is a private, coed, four-year institution. 83-acre campus in West Palm Beach (population: 82,103). Major airport, bus, and train serve Palm Beach (10 miles). Public transportation serves campus. Quarter system.

SECONDARY SCHOOL REQUIREMENTS

Graduation from secondary school required; GED accepted.

TESTING

SAT Reasoning or ACT required. SAT Subject recommended.

All enrolled freshmen (fall 2004):

Average SAT I Scores: Verbal: 467 Math: 480
Average ACT Scores: Composite: 20

Child Study Team report is not required. A neuropsychological or comprehensive psycho-educational evaluation is required for admission. Must be dated within 24 months of application. Tests required as part of this documentation:

- [x] WAIS-IV
- [x] WISC-IV
- [x] SATA
- [x] Woodcock-Johnson
- [ ] Nelson-Denny Reading Test
- [ ] Other

UNDERGRADUATE STUDENT BODY

Total undergraduate student enrollment: 497 Men, 466 Women.

Composition of student body (fall 2004):

	Undergraduate	Freshmen
International	11.9	21.1
Black	14.0	10.3
American Indian	0.0	0.1
Asian-American	2.1	1.5
Hispanic	12.4	9.7
White	57.0	55.1
Unreported	2.6	2.2
	100.0%	100.0%

70% are from out of state. Average age of full-time undergraduates is 20, 41% of classes have fewer than 20 students, 59% have between 20 and 50 students.

STUDENT HOUSING

76% of freshmen live in college housing. Freshmen are required to live on campus. Housing is guaranteed for all undergraduates. Campus can house 400 undergraduates.

EXPENSES

Tuition (2005-06): $14,625 per year.
Room: $3,696. Board: $3,561.

There is no additional cost for LD program/services.

LD SERVICES

LD services available to:

- [ ] Freshmen
- [ ] Sophomores
- [ ] Juniors
- [ ] Seniors

Academic Accommodations

Curriculum		**In class**	
Foreign language waiver	[ ]	Early syllabus	[ ]
Lighter course load	[ ]	Note takers in class	[ ]
Math waiver	[ ]	Priority seating	[ ]
Other special classes	[ ]	Tape recorders	[ ]
Priority registrations	[ ]	Videotaped classes	[ ]
Substitution of courses	[ ]	Text on tape	[ ]
Exams		**Services**	
Extended time	[ ]	Diagnostic tests	[ ]
Oral exams	[ ]	Learning centers	[ ]
Take home exams	[ ]	Proofreaders	[ ]
Exams on tape or computer	[ ]	Readers	[ ]
Untimed exams	[ ]	Reading Machines/Kurzweil	[ ]
Other accommodations	[ ]	Special bookstore section	[ ]
		Typists	[ ]

Credit toward degree is not given for remedial courses taken.

Counseling Services

- [ ] Academic
- [ ] Psychological
- [ ] Student Support groups
- [ ] Vocational

Tutoring

Individual tutoring is available weekly.

Average size of tutoring groups: 3

	Individual	Group
Time management	[ ]	[ ]
Organizational skills	[ ]	[ ]
Learning strategies	[ ]	[ ]
Study skills	[ ]	[ ]
Content area	[ ]	[ ]
Writing lab	[x]	[x]
Math lab	[x]	[x]

LD PROGRAM STAFF

Key staff person available to work with LD students: Cheryl Pridgeon, Academic Dean.

Nova Southeastern University

Ft. Lauderdale, FL

Address: 3301 College Avenue, Ft. Lauderdale, FL, 33314
Admissions telephone: 800 338-4723, extension 8001
Admissions FAX: 954 262-3811
Associate Director of Admissions: Maria Dillard
Admissions e-mail: ncsinfo@nova.edu
Web site: http://www.nova.edu
SAT Code: 5514 ACT Code: 6706

LD program name: Academic Services
Assistant Director of Academic Services: Sue Mills
LD program telephone: 954 262-8405
LD program e-mail: smills@nsu.nova.edu
Total campus enrollment: 5,355

GENERAL

Nova Southeastern University is a private, coed, four-year institution. 232-acre, suburban campus in Fort Lauderdale (population: 152,397). Served by air, bus, and train; major airport serves Miami (26 miles). School operates transportation on main campus. Public transportation serves campus. Trimester system.

LD ADMISSIONS

Students do not complete a separate application and are not simultaneously accepted to the LD program. A personal interview is recommended.

SECONDARY SCHOOL REQUIREMENTS

Graduation from secondary school required; GED accepted. The following course distribution required: 4 units of English, 3 units of math, 3 units of science, 1 unit of social studies, 2 units of history.

TESTING

SAT Reasoning or ACT required.

All enrolled freshmen (fall 2004):

Average SAT I Scores: Verbal: 495 Math: 503
Average ACT Scores: Composite: 21

Child Study Team report is not required. Tests required as part of this documentation:

- ☐ WAIS-IV
- ☐ WISC-IV
- ☐ SATA
- ☐ Woodcock-Johnson
- ☐ Nelson-Denny Reading Test
- ☐ Other

UNDERGRADUATE STUDENT BODY

Total undergraduate student enrollment: 1,056 Men, 2,958 Women.

Composition of student body (fall 2004):

	Undergraduate	Freshmen
International	3.8	7.1
Black	20.7	27.4
American Indian	0.2	0.4
Asian-American	9.0	3.7
Hispanic	22.4	24.9
White	37.6	29.9
Unreported	6.2	6.7
	100.0%	100.0%

Average age of full-time undergraduates is 27, 69% of classes have fewer than 20 students, 30% have between 20 and 50 students.

STUDENT HOUSING

48% of freshmen live in college housing. Housing is guaranteed for all undergraduates. Campus can house 464 undergraduates. Single rooms are available for students with medical or special needs.

EXPENSES

Tuition (2005-06): $17,250 per year.
Room: $4,848. Board: $2,400.
There is no additional cost for LD program/services.

LD SERVICES

LD program size is not limited.

LD services available to:

■ Freshmen ■ Sophomores ■ Juniors ■ Seniors

Academic Accommodations

Curriculum		In class	
Foreign language waiver	☐	Early syllabus	☐
Lighter course load	■	Note takers in class	■
Math waiver	☐	Priority seating	☐
Other special classes	☐	Tape recorders	■
Priority registrations	☐	Videotaped classes	☐
Substitution of courses	☐	Text on tape	☐
Exams		**Services**	
Extended time	■	Diagnostic tests	■
Oral exams	■	Learning centers	■
Take home exams	☐	Proofreaders	☐
Exams on tape or computer	☐	Readers	■
Untimed exams	☐	Reading Machines/Kurzweil	■
Other accommodations	☐	Special bookstore section	☐
		Typists	☐

Credit toward degree is not given for remedial courses taken.

Counseling Services

- ☐ Academic
- ☐ Psychological
- ☐ Student Support groups
- ☐ Vocational

Tutoring

Individual tutoring is available.

	Individual	Group
Time management	■	■
Organizational skills	☐	☐
Learning strategies	☐	■
Study skills	■	■
Content area	☐	☐
Writing lab	■	■
Math lab	■	■

UNIQUE LD PROGRAM FEATURES

Services are determined on an individual basis.

LD PROGRAM STAFF

Total number of LD Program staff (including director):

Full Time: 2 Part Time: 2

There is an advisor/advocate from the LD program available to students.

Key staff person available to work with LD students: Sue Mills, Assistant Director of Academic Services.

LD Program web site: http://www.undergrad.nova.edu/academic services

Ringling School of Art and Design

Sarasota, FL

Address: 2700 North Tamiami Trail, Sarasota, FL, 34234-5895
Admissions telephone: 800 255-7695
Admissions FAX: 941 359-7517
Dean of Admissions: James H. Dean
Admissions e-mail: admissions@ringling.edu
Web site: http://www.ringling.edu
SAT Code: 5573 ACT Code: 6724

LD program name: Academic Resource Center
Director of Academic Resource Center: Virginia Demers
LD program e-mail: vdemers@ringling.edu
Total campus enrollment: 1, 008

GENERAL

Ringling School of Art and Design is a private, coed, four-year institution. 30-acre campus in Sarasota (population: 52,715), 50 miles from Tampa. Served by air and bus; major airport and train serve Tampa. Public transportation serves campus. Semester system.

LD ADMISSIONS

A member of the LD program does not sit on the admissions committee. A personal interview is recommended. Essay is required and may be typed.

For fall 2004, 9 completed self-identified LD applications were received.

SECONDARY SCHOOL REQUIREMENTS

Graduation from secondary school required; GED accepted.

TESTING

Child Study Team report is not required. A neuropsychological or comprehensive psycho-educational evaluation is required for admission. Must be dated within 36 months of application. Tests required as part of this documentation:

☑ WAIS-IV	☑ Woodcock-Johnson
☐ WISC-IV	☐ Nelson-Denny Reading Test
☐ SATA	☐ Other

UNDERGRADUATE STUDENT BODY

Total undergraduate student enrollment: 517 Men, 452 Women.

Composition of student body (fall 2004):

	Undergraduate	Freshmen
International	3.4	4.9
Black	1.5	2.0
American Indian	1.0	1.0
Asian-American	3.4	4.0
Hispanic	10.8	9.2
White	79.4	78.8
Unreported	0.5	0.2
	100.0%	100.0%

43% are from out of state. 3% join a fraternity and 1% join a sorority. Average age of full-time undergraduates is 21, 66% of classes have fewer than 20 students, 33% have between 20 and 50 students.

STUDENT HOUSING

79% of freshmen live in college housing. Freshmen are not required to live on campus. Housing is guaranteed for all undergraduates. Campus can house 474 undergraduates. Single rooms are available for students with medical or special needs. A medical note is required.

EXPENSES

Tuition (2005-06): $22,450 per year.

Room: $7,358. Board: $4,544.

There is no additional cost for LD program/services.

LD SERVICES

LD program size is not limited.

LD services available to:

☑ Freshmen ☑ Sophomores ☑ Juniors ☑ Seniors

Academic Accommodations

Curriculum		**In class**	
Foreign language waiver	☐	Early syllabus	☐
Lighter course load	☐	Note takers in class	☑
Math waiver	☐	Priority seating	☐
Other special classes	☐	Tape recorders	☑
Priority registrations	☐	Videotaped classes	☐
Substitution of courses	☐	Text on tape	☑
Exams		**Services**	
Extended time	☑	Diagnostic tests	☐
Oral exams	☐	Learning centers	☑
Take home exams	☐	Proofreaders	☐
Exams on tape or computer	☐	Readers	☐
Untimed exams	☐	Reading Machines/Kurzweil	☑
Other accommodations	☐	Special bookstore section	☐
		Typists	☐

Credit toward degree is not given for remedial courses taken.

Counseling Services

☐ Academic
☐ Psychological
☐ Student Support groups
☐ Vocational

Tutoring

Individual tutoring is available weekly.
Average size of tutoring groups: 2

	Individual	Group
Time management	☑	☐
Organizational skills	☑	☐
Learning strategies	☑	☐
Study skills	☑	☐
Content area	☐	☐
Writing lab	☑	☐
Math lab	☐	☐

UNIQUE LD PROGRAM FEATURES

Students may request books on tape and text to speech software is available on some of our campus computers. Writing support is generally individualized and most students with language learning disabilities work with professional tutors. To receive special accommodations, students must document their specific learning disabilities and provide professional verification of their need for particular accommodations. When the school receives notice of a student's disability (whether through a health form or a personal request), we provide a set of guidelines specific to that disability to clarify what documentation is required. When we receive the documentation, the student may come to request reasonable accommodations, and provided they are warranted by the documentary information, such requests will be granted. Students with disabilities do not generally identify themselves during the admissions process, and the school cannot consider disability as a factor in the admitting process.

LD PROGRAM STAFF

Total number of LD Program staff (including director):

Full Time: 1 Part Time: 1

There is no advisor/advocate from the LD program available to students. 5 peer tutors are available to work with LD students.

Key staff person available to work with LD students: Virginia Demers, Director of Academic Resource Center.

Rollins College

Winter Park, FL

Address: 1000 Holt Avenue, Winter Park, FL, 32789-4499
Admissions telephone: 407 646-2161
Admissions FAX: 407 646-1502
Dean of Admissions: Mike Lynch
Admissions e-mail: admission@rollins.edu
Web site: http://www.rollins.edu
SAT Code: 5572 ACT Code: 748

Director, Student Resource Center: Thomas P. Johnson
Dr. Karen Hater
LD program telephone: 407 646-2354
LD program e-mail: klhater@rollins.edu
Total campus enrollment: 1,759

GENERAL

Rollins College is a private, coed, four-year institution. 67-acre, suburban campus in Winter Park (population: 24,090), five miles from Orlando; branch campus in West Melbourne. Served by train; major airport and bus serve Orlando. Public transportation serves campus. Semester system.

LD ADMISSIONS

A personal interview is recommended. Essay is required and may be typed.

SECONDARY SCHOOL REQUIREMENTS

Graduation from secondary school required; GED accepted. The following course distribution required: 4 units of English, 3 units of math, 2 units of science, 2 units of foreign language, 2 units of social studies, 2 units of history, 2 units of academic electives.

TESTING

SAT Reasoning or ACT required. SAT Subject recommended.

All enrolled freshmen (fall 2004):

Average SAT I Scores: Verbal: 592 Math: 592
Average ACT Scores: Composite: 25

Child Study Team report is not required. Tests required as part of this documentation:

☐ WAIS-IV ☐ Woodcock-Johnson
☐ WISC-IV ☐ Nelson-Denny Reading Test
☐ SATA ☐ Other

UNDERGRADUATE STUDENT BODY

Total undergraduate student enrollment: 660 Men, 1,017 Women.

Composition of student body (fall 2004):

	Undergraduate	Freshmen
International	2.5	2.6
Black	4.9	4.8
American Indian	0.2	0.5
Asian-American	3.9	3.5
Hispanic	10.3	7.6
White	70.2	74.2
Unreported	8.0	6.7
	100.0%	100.0%

47% are from out of state. 38% join a fraternity and 40% join a sorority. Average age of full-time undergraduates is 20, 61% of classes have fewer than 20 students, 39% have between 20 and 50 students.

STUDENT HOUSING

90% of freshmen live in college housing. Freshmen are required to live on campus. Housing is guaranteed for all undergraduates. Campus can house 1,231 undergraduates.

EXPENSES

Tuition (2005-06): $28,390 per year.
Room: $5,376. Board: $3,766.
There is no additional cost for LD program/services.

LD SERVICES

LD program size is not limited.

LD services available to:

☐ Freshmen ☐ Sophomores ☐ Juniors ☐ Seniors

Academic Accommodations

Curriculum		**In class**	
Foreign language waiver	☐	Early syllabus	☐
Lighter course load	■	Note takers in class	■
Math waiver	☐	Priority seating	☐
Other special classes	☐	Tape recorders	■
Priority registrations	☐	Videotaped classes	☐
Substitution of courses	☐	Text on tape	☐
Exams		**Services**	
Extended time	■	Diagnostic tests	☐
Oral exams	☐	Learning centers	■
Take home exams	☐	Proofreaders	☐
Exams on tape or computer	☐	Readers	■
Untimed exams	■	Reading Machines/Kurzweil	■
Other accommodations	☐	Special bookstore section	☐
		Typists	☐

Credit toward degree is not given for remedial courses taken.

Counseling Services

☐ Academic
☐ Psychological
☐ Student Support groups
☐ Vocational

Tutoring

	Individual	Group
Time management	☐	☐
Organizational skills	☐	☐
Learning strategies	☐	☐
Study skills	☐	☐
Content area	☐	☐
Writing lab	☐	☐
Math lab	☐	☐

LD PROGRAM STAFF

Total number of LD Program staff (including director):

Full Time: 1 Part Time: 1

Key staff person available to work with LD students: Dr. Karen Hater, Director, Thomas P. Johnson Student Resource Center.

St. Thomas University

Miami Gardens, FL

Address: 16401 N.W. 37th Avenue, Miami Gardens, FL, 33054
Admissions telephone: 800 367-9010, 800 367-9006 (in-state)
Admissions FAX: 305 628-6591
Director of Admissions: Lydia Amy
Admissions e-mail: signup@stu.edu
Web site: http://www.stu.edu
SAT Code: 5076 ACT Code: 719

Academic Enhancement Center Coordinator: Maritza Rivera
LD program telephone: 305 628-6564
LD program e-mail: mrivera@stu.edu
Total campus enrollment: 1,169

GENERAL

St. Thomas University is a private, coed, four-year institution. 140-acre, urban campus in Miami (population: 362,470); branch campus at St. Brendan's High School. Served by air, bus, and train; smaller airport serves Fort Lauderdale (20 miles). Public transportation serves campus. Semester system.

LD ADMISSIONS

A personal interview is recommended. Essay is required and may be typed.

SECONDARY SCHOOL REQUIREMENTS

Graduation from secondary school required; GED accepted. The following course distribution required: 4 units of English, 3 units of math, 2 units of science, 3 units of social studies, 6 units of academic electives.

TESTING

ACT considered if submitted. SAT Reasoning or ACT required. SAT Subject recommended.

All enrolled freshmen (fall 2004):

Average SAT I Scores:	Verbal: 456	Math: 440
Average ACT Scores:	Composite: 22	

Child Study Team report is not required. Tests required as part of this documentation:

- ☐ WAIS-IV
- ☐ WISC-IV
- ☐ SATA
- ☐ Woodcock-Johnson
- ☐ Nelson-Denny Reading Test
- ☐ Other

UNDERGRADUATE STUDENT BODY

Total undergraduate student enrollment: 517 Men, 704 Women.

Composition of student body (fall 2004):

	Undergraduate	Freshmen
International	12.5	11.5
Black	25.5	28.1
American Indian	0.5	0.3
Asian-American	0.5	0.5
Hispanic	44.8	44.7
White	14.1	13.4
Unreported	2.1	1.5
	100.0%	100.0%

3% are from out of state. Average age of full-time undergraduates is 25, 66% of classes have fewer than 20 students, 34% have between 20 and 50 students.

STUDENT HOUSING

23% of freshmen live in college housing. Freshmen are not required to live on campus. Housing is guaranteed for all undergraduates. Campus can house 135 undergraduates. Single rooms are not available for students with medical or special needs.

EXPENSES

Tuition (2005-06): $17,860 per year.

Room & Board: $5,630.

There is no additional cost for LD program/services.

LD SERVICES

LD program size is not limited.

LD services available to:

☐ Freshmen ☐ Sophomores ☐ Juniors ☐ Seniors

Academic Accommodations

Curriculum		**In class**	
Foreign language waiver	☐	Early syllabus	☐
Lighter course load	☐	Note takers in class	■
Math waiver	☐	Priority seating	☐
Other special classes	☐	Tape recorders	■
Priority registrations	☐	Videotaped classes	☐
Substitution of courses	☐	Text on tape	☐
Exams		**Services**	
Extended time	■	Diagnostic tests	☐
Oral exams	☐	Learning centers	■
Take home exams	☐	Proofreaders	■
Exams on tape or computer	☐	Readers	☐
Untimed exams	■	Reading Machines/Kurzweil	☐
Other accommodations	☐	Special bookstore section	☐
		Typists	☐

Credit toward degree is not given for remedial courses taken.

Counseling Services

- ☐ Academic
- ☐ Psychological
- ☐ Student Support groups
- ☐ Vocational

Tutoring

Individual tutoring is available weekly.

	Individual	Group
Time management	☐	☐
Organizational skills	☐	☐
Learning strategies	☐	☐
Study skills	☐	☐
Content area	☐	☐
Writing lab	☐	☐
Math lab	☐	☐

LD PROGRAM STAFF

Total number of LD Program staff (including director):

Full Time: 1 Part Time: 1

Key staff person available to work with LD students: Maritza Rivera, Academic Enhancement Center Coordinator.

Saint Leo University

Saint Leo, FL

Address: P.O. Box 6665, Saint Leo, FL, 33574-6665
Admissions telephone: 800 334-5532
Admissions FAX: 352 588-8257
Dean of Admission and Financial Aid: Gary Bracken
Admissions e-mail: admission@saintleo.edu
Web site: http://www.saintleo.edu
SAT Code: 5638 ACT Code: 755

Director, Learning Resource Center: Dr. Joanne MacEachran
LD program telephone: 352 588-8462
LD program e-mail: joanne.maceachran@saintleo.edu
Total campus enrollment: 1,241

GENERAL

Saint Leo University is a private, coed, four-year institution. 153-acre, rural campus in Saint Leo (population: 595), 25 miles northeast of Tampa. Major airport serves Tampa; bus and train serve Dade City (eight miles). School operates transportation to Tampa airport by arrangement and to local shopping areas weekly. Semester system.

LD ADMISSIONS

A personal interview is recommended. Essay is required and may be typed.

SECONDARY SCHOOL REQUIREMENTS

Graduation from secondary school required; GED accepted.

TESTING

SAT Reasoning or ACT required. SAT Subject recommended.

All enrolled freshmen (fall 2004):

Average SAT I Scores:	Verbal: 510	Math: 508
Average ACT Scores:	Composite: 21	

Child Study Team report is not required. Tests required as part of this documentation:

- [ ] WAIS-IV
- [ ] WISC-IV
- [ ] SATA
- [ ] Woodcock-Johnson
- [ ] Nelson-Denny Reading Test
- [ ] Other

UNDERGRADUATE STUDENT BODY

Total undergraduate student enrollment: 407 Men, 505 Women.

Composition of student body (fall 2004):

	Undergraduate	Freshmen
International	7.8	6.1
Black	7.8	7.3
American Indian	1.0	0.6
Asian-American	1.3	1.1
Hispanic	7.3	7.2
White	66.2	67.4
Unreported	8.6	10.3
	100.0%	100.0%

24% are from out of state. 20% join a fraternity and 14% join a sorority. Average age of full-time undergraduates is 21, 61% of classes have fewer than 20 students, 39% have between 20 and 50 students.

STUDENT HOUSING

84% of freshmen live in college housing. Freshmen are required to live on campus. Housing is guaranteed for all undergraduates. Campus can house 887 undergraduates.

EXPENSES

Tuition (2005-06): $14,250 per year.

Room: $3,920. Board: $3,540.

There is no additional cost for LD program/services.

LD SERVICES

LD program size is not limited.

LD services available to:

- [ ] Freshmen
- [ ] Sophomores
- [ ] Juniors
- [ ] Seniors

Academic Accommodations

Curriculum		In class	
Foreign language waiver	[ ]	Early syllabus	[ ]
Lighter course load	[x]	Note takers in class	[x]
Math waiver	[ ]	Priority seating	[ ]
Other special classes	[ ]	Tape recorders	[x]
Priority registrations	[ ]	Videotaped classes	[ ]
Substitution of courses	[ ]	Text on tape	[ ]
Exams		**Services**	
Extended time	[x]	Diagnostic tests	[ ]
Oral exams	[x]	Learning centers	[x]
Take home exams	[ ]	Proofreaders	[ ]
Exams on tape or computer	[ ]	Readers	[x]
Untimed exams	[ ]	Reading Machines/Kurzweil	[x]
Other accommodations	[ ]	Special bookstore section	[ ]
		Typists	[ ]

Credit toward degree is not given for remedial courses taken.

Counseling Services

- [ ] Academic
- [ ] Psychological
- [ ] Student Support groups
- [ ] Vocational

Tutoring

	Individual	Group
Time management	[ ]	[ ]
Organizational skills	[ ]	[ ]
Learning strategies	[ ]	[ ]
Study skills	[ ]	[ ]
Content area	[ ]	[ ]
Writing lab	[ ]	[ ]
Math lab	[ ]	[ ]

LD PROGRAM STAFF

Total number of LD Program staff (including director):

Full Time: 1 Part Time: 1

Key staff person available to work with LD students: Dr. Karen Hahn, Director of ADA Student Services.

University of South Florida

Tampa, FL

Address: 4202 East Fowler Avenue, Tampa, FL, 33620-9951
Admissions telephone: 813 974-3350
Admissions FAX: 813 974-9689
Director of Admissions: Julie Hite, Interim
Admissions e-mail: admissions@grad.usf.edu
Web site: http://www.usf.edu
SAT Code: 5828 ACT Code: 761

LD program name: Office of Academic Support and Accommodations for Students with Disabilities
LD program address: 4202 East Fowler Avenue, SVC 1133
Director: Mary Sarver
LD program telephone: 813 974-8135
LD program e-mail: msarver@admin.usf.edu
Total campus enrollment: 33,266

GENERAL

University of South Florida is a public, coed, four-year institution. 1,931-acre campus in Tampa (population: 303,447); branch campuses in Lakeland, Pasco/Hernando County, St. Petersburg, and Sarasota. Served by air, bus, and train. School operates transportation on campus and locally. Public transportation serves campus. Semester system.

LD ADMISSIONS

Students do not complete a separate application and are not simultaneously accepted to the LD program. A member of the LD program does not sit on the admissions committee. A personal interview is required. Essay is required and may be typed. Student must be admitted to USF (some academic minimums may be waived for acceptance); then, provide documentation of the disability to be admitted into the Disability Services benefits.

SECONDARY SCHOOL REQUIREMENTS

Graduation from secondary school required; GED accepted. The following course distribution required: 4 units of English, 3 units of math, 3 units of science, 2 units of foreign language, 3 units of social studies, 3 units of academic electives.

TESTING

SAT Subject recommended.

All enrolled freshmen (fall 2004):

Average SAT I Scores: Verbal: 540 Math: 545
Average ACT Scores: Composite: 23

Child Study Team report is not required. Tests required as part of this documentation:

- ☐ WAIS-IV
- ☐ WISC-IV
- ☐ SATA
- ☐ Woodcock-Johnson
- ☐ Nelson-Denny Reading Test
- ☐ Other

UNDERGRADUATE STUDENT BODY

Total undergraduate student enrollment: 11,846 Men, 16,923 Women.

Composition of student body (fall 2004):

	Undergraduate	Freshmen
International	1.3	2.8
Black	12.2	12.5
American Indian	0.2	0.4
Asian-American	5.9	5.6
Hispanic	11.8	10.6
White	66.3	65.9
Unreported	2.2	2.1
	100.0%	100.0%

5% are from out of state. 6% join a fraternity and 4% join a sorority. Average age of full-time undergraduates is 22, 27% of classes have fewer than 20 students, 57% have between 20 and 50 students, 17% have more than 50 students.

STUDENT HOUSING

54% of freshmen live in college housing. Freshmen are not required to live on campus. Housing is not guaranteed for all undergraduates. Not enough capacity. Campus can house 4,176 undergraduates. Single rooms are available for students with medical or special needs. A medical note is not required.

EXPENSES

Tuition 2004-05: $3,092 per year (in-state), $15,966 (out-of-state).

Room & Board: $6,730.

There is no additional cost for LD program/services.

LD SERVICES

LD program size is not limited.

LD services available to:

☒ Freshmen ☒ Sophomores ☒ Juniors ☒ Seniors

Academic Accommodations

Curriculum		**In class**	
Foreign language waiver	☐	Early syllabus	☐
Lighter course load	☒	Note takers in class	☒
Math waiver	☐	Priority seating	☐
Other special classes	☐	Tape recorders	☒
Priority registrations	☐	Videotaped classes	☐
Substitution of courses	☐	Text on tape	☐
Exams		**Services**	
Extended time	☒	Diagnostic tests	☐
Oral exams	☒	Learning centers	☐
Take home exams	☐	Proofreaders	☐
Exams on tape or computer	☐	Readers	☒
Untimed exams	☐	Reading Machines/Kurzweil	☒
Other accommodations	☐	Special bookstore section	☐
		Typists	☐

Credit toward degree is not given for remedial courses taken.

Counseling Services

- ☐ Academic
- ☐ Psychological
- ☐ Student Support groups
- ☐ Vocational

Tutoring

Individual tutoring is available.

	Individual	Group
Time management	☐	☐
Organizational skills	☐	☐
Learning strategies	☐	☐
Study skills	☐	☐
Content area	☐	☐
Writing lab	☐	☐
Math lab	☐	☐

LD PROGRAM STAFF

There is an advisor/advocate from the LD program available to students.

Key staff person available to work with LD students: Mary Sarver, Director, ASASD.

LD Program web site: http://www.asasd.usf.edu

Southeastern College of the Assemblies of God

Lakeland, FL

Address: 1000 Longfellow Boulevard, Lakeland, FL, 33801
Admissions telephone: 800 500-8760
Admissions FAX: 863 667-5200
Director of Admission: Omar Rashed
Admissions e-mail: admission@seuniversity.edu
Web site: http://www.seuniversity.edu
SAT Code: 5621 ACT Code: 754

Academic Services Coordinator: Misty Mancini
LD program telephone: 863 667-5157
LD program e-mail: mmancini@seuniversity.edu
LD program enrollment: 31, Total campus enrollment: 1,964

GENERAL

Southeastern College of the Assemblies of God is a private, coed, four-year institution. 61-acre campus in Lakeland (population: 78,452), 40 miles from Tampa. Served by bus and train; major airports serve Tampa and Orlando (50 miles). Public transportation serves campus. Semester system.

LD ADMISSIONS

A member of the LD program does not sit on the admissions committee.

SECONDARY SCHOOL REQUIREMENTS

Graduation from secondary school required; GED accepted. The following course distribution required: 3 units of English, 3 units of math, 3 units of science, 3 units of social studies.

TESTING

SAT Reasoning or ACT required. SAT Subject recommended.

All enrolled freshmen (fall 2004):

Average ACT Scores: Composite: 22

Child Study Team report is not required. Tests required as part of this documentation:

- [ ] WAIS-IV
- [ ] WISC-IV
- [ ] SATA
- [ ] Woodcock-Johnson
- [ ] Nelson-Denny Reading Test
- [ ] Other

UNDERGRADUATE STUDENT BODY

Total undergraduate student enrollment: 645 Men, 718 Women.

Composition of student body (fall 2004):

	Undergraduate	Freshmen
International	0.5	0.4
Black	5.7	5.9
American Indian	0.2	0.4
Asian-American	0.7	1.8
Hispanic	14.9	10.5
White	74.5	74.9
Unreported	3.4	6.1
	100.0%	100.0%

42% are from out of state. Average age of full-time undergraduates is 22, 38% of classes have fewer than 20 students, 48% have between 20 and 50 students, 14% have more than 50 students.

STUDENT HOUSING

86% of freshmen live in college housing. Freshmen are required to live on campus. Housing is guaranteed for all undergraduates. Campus can house 1,463 undergraduates. Single rooms are available for students with medical or special needs. A medical note is required.

EXPENSES

Tuition (2005-06): $11,040 per year.

Room & Board: $5,678.

There is no additional cost for LD program/services.

LD SERVICES

LD program size is not limited.

LD services available to:

- [x] Freshmen
- [x] Sophomores
- [x] Juniors
- [x] Seniors

Academic Accommodations

Curriculum		**In class**	
Foreign language waiver	[ ]	Early syllabus	[ ]
Lighter course load	[x]	Note takers in class	[x]
Math waiver	[ ]	Priority seating	[ ]
Other special classes	[ ]	Tape recorders	[x]
Priority registrations	[ ]	Videotaped classes	[ ]
Substitution of courses	[ ]	Text on tape	[x]
Exams		**Services**	
Extended time	[x]	Diagnostic tests	[x]
Oral exams	[x]	Learning centers	[x]
Take home exams	[ ]	Proofreaders	[x]
Exams on tape or computer	[ ]	Readers	[x]
Untimed exams	[x]	Reading Machines/Kurzweil	[x]
Other accommodations	[x]	Special bookstore section	[ ]
		Typists	[ ]

Credit toward degree is not given for remedial courses taken.

Counseling Services

[x]	Academic	Meets 30 times per academic year
[x]	Psychological	Meets 30 times per academic year
[x]	Student Support groups	Meets 30 times per academic year
[x]	Vocational	Meets 30 times per academic year

Tutoring

Individual tutoring is available daily.

Average size of tutoring groups: 5

	Individual	Group
Time management	[x]	[x]
Organizational skills	[x]	[x]
Learning strategies	[x]	[x]
Study skills	[x]	[x]
Content area	[ ]	[ ]
Writing lab	[x]	[x]
Math lab	[x]	[ ]

LD PROGRAM STAFF

Total number of LD Program staff (including director):

Full Time: 1 Part Time: 1

There is an advisor/advocate from the LD program available to students. The advisor/advocate meets with students 3 times per month. 14 peer tutors are available to work with LD students.

Key staff person available to work with LD students: Misty Mancini, Academic Services Coordinator.

Stetson University

Deland, FL

Address: 421 North Woodland Boulevard, Deland, FL, 32723
Admissions telephone: 800 688-0101
Admissions FAX: 386 822-7112
Vice President for Enrollment Management: Deborah Thompson
Admissions e-mail: admissions@stetson.edu
Web site: http://www.stetson.edu
SAT Code: 5630 ACT Code: 756

LD program name: Academic Resource Center
LD program address: 421 North Woodland Blvd, Unit 8366
Director, Academic Support Office: Karen Cole, Ph.D.
LD program telephone: 386 822-7127
LD program e-mail: kcole@stetson.edu
LD program enrollment: 34, Total campus enrollment: 2,230

GENERAL

Stetson University is a private, coed, four-year institution. 170-acre campus in DeLand (population: 20,904), 50 miles from Orlando and 25 miles from Daytona Beach. Served by bus and train; airports serve Orlando and Daytona Beach. Public transportation serves campus. Semester system.

LD ADMISSIONS

Students do not complete a separate application and are not simultaneously accepted to the LD program. A member of the LD program does not sit on the admissions committee. A personal interview is recommended. Essay is required and may be typed.

SECONDARY SCHOOL REQUIREMENTS

Graduation from secondary school required; GED accepted. The following course distribution required: 4 units of English, 3 units of math, 3 units of science, 2 units of foreign language, 2 units of social studies.

TESTING

SAT Reasoning or ACT required. SAT Subject recommended.

All enrolled freshmen (fall 2004):

Average SAT I Scores:	Verbal: 571	Math: 561
Average ACT Scores:	Composite: 24	

Child Study Team report is not required. A neuropsychological or comprehensive psycho-educational evaluation is required for admission. Must be dated within 36 months of application. Tests required as part of this documentation:

- [x] WAIS-IV
- [ ] WISC-IV
- [ ] SATA
- [x] Woodcock-Johnson
- [ ] Nelson-Denny Reading Test
- [ ] Other

UNDERGRADUATE STUDENT BODY

Total undergraduate student enrollment: 931 Men, 1,243 Women.

Composition of student body (fall 2004):

	Undergraduate	Freshmen
International	2.8	3.1
Black	2.8	3.6
American Indian	0.2	0.3
Asian-American	1.5	1.8
Hispanic	7.2	5.6
White	79.2	81.2
Unreported	6.3	4.5
	100.0%	100.0%

20% are from out of state. 26% join a fraternity and 24% join a sorority. Average age of full-time undergraduates is 20, 54% of classes have fewer than 20 students, 46% have between 20 and 50 students.

STUDENT HOUSING

91% of freshmen live in college housing. Freshmen are required to live on campus. Housing is guaranteed for all undergraduates. Campus can house 1,547 undergraduates. Single rooms are available for students with medical or special needs. A medical note is required.

EXPENSES

Tuition (2005-06): $23,975 per year.
Room: $4,075. Board: $3,200.
There is no additional cost for LD program/services.

LD SERVICES

LD program size is not limited.

LD services available to:

- [x] Freshmen
- [x] Sophomores
- [x] Juniors
- [x] Seniors

Academic Accommodations

Curriculum		In class	
Foreign language waiver	[ ]	Early syllabus	[ ]
Lighter course load	[x]	Note takers in class	[x]
Math waiver	[ ]	Priority seating	[ ]
Other special classes	[ ]	Tape recorders	[x]
Priority registrations	[ ]	Videotaped classes	[ ]
Substitution of courses	[ ]	Text on tape	[ ]
Exams		**Services**	
Extended time	[x]	Diagnostic tests	[ ]
Oral exams	[x]	Learning centers	[x]
Take home exams	[ ]	Proofreaders	[ ]
Exams on tape or computer	[ ]	Readers	[x]
Untimed exams	[ ]	Reading Machines/Kurzweil	[ ]
Other accommodations	[ ]	Special bookstore section	[ ]
		Typists	[ ]

Credit toward degree is not given for remedial courses taken.

Counseling Services

- [x] Academic
- [x] Psychological
- [x] Student Support groups
- [ ] Vocational

Tutoring

Individual tutoring is available daily.

Average size of tutoring groups: 2

	Individual	Group
Time management	[x]	[x]
Organizational skills	[x]	[x]
Learning strategies	[x]	[x]
Study skills	[x]	[ ]
Content area	[ ]	[ ]
Writing lab	[x]	[x]
Math lab	[x]	[x]

LD PROGRAM STAFF

Total number of LD Program staff (including director):

Full Time: 1 Part Time: 1

There is an advisor/advocate from the LD program available to students. The advisor/advocate meets with students 2 times per month. 1 graduate student is available to work with LD students.

Key staff person available to work with LD students: Karen Cole, Ph.D., Director, Academic Resource Center.

Tallahassee Community College

Tallahassee, FL

Address: 444 Appleyard Drive
Admissions telephone: 850 201-8555
Admissions FAX: 850 201-8474
Distributed Information Specialist: Jay Gelin
Admissions e-mail: enrollment@tcc.fl.edu
Web site: http://www.tcc.cc.fl.us
SAT Code: 5794

LD program name: Disability Support Services
Counselor: Judy Barnes
LD program telephone: 850 201-8430
LD program enrollment: 923, Total campus enrollment: 12,784

GENERAL

Tallahassee Community College is a public, coed, two-year institution. 192-acre campus in Tallahassee (population: 125,000). Served by air, bus, and train. Public transportation serves campus.

LD ADMISSIONS

Students do not complete a separate application and are not simultaneously accepted to the LD program. A member of the LD program does not sit on the admissions committee. A personal interview is recommended. Essay is not required. Documentation is required for admission.

SECONDARY SCHOOL REQUIREMENTS

Graduation from secondary school required; GED accepted.

TESTING

Child Study Team report is not required. Tests required as part of this documentation:

- ■ WAIS-IV
- ■ WISC-IV
- ☐ SATA
- ■ Woodcock-Johnson
- ■ Nelson-Denny Reading Test
- ☐ Other

STUDENT HOUSING

There is no campus housing.

EXPENSES

Tuition 2004-05: $56 per credit hour (state residents), $211 (out-of-state).

There is no additional cost for LD program/services.

LD SERVICES

LD program size is not limited.

LD services available to:

■ Freshmen ■ Sophomores ■ Juniors ■ Seniors

Academic Accommodations

Curriculum		In class	
Foreign language waiver	☐	Early syllabus	☐
Lighter course load	■	Note takers in class	■
Math waiver	■	Priority seating	■
Other special classes	■	Tape recorders	■
Priority registrations	■	Videotaped classes	☐
Substitution of courses	■	Text on tape	■
Exams		**Services**	
Extended time	■	Diagnostic tests	☐
Oral exams	■	Learning centers	■
Take home exams	☐	Proofreaders	☐
Exams on tape or computer	■	Readers	■
Untimed exams	■	Reading Machines/Kurzweil	■
Other accommodations	☐	Special bookstore section	☐
		Typists	■

Counseling Services

- ■ Academic
- ☐ Psychological
- ☐ Student Support groups
- ■ Vocational

Tutoring

Individual tutoring is available weekly.

Average size of tutoring groups: 1

	Individual	Group
Time management	☐	☐
Organizational skills	☐	☐
Learning strategies	☐	☐
Study skills	☐	☐
Content area	☐	☐
Writing lab	■	☐
Math lab	■	☐

LD PROGRAM STAFF

There is an advisor/advocate from the LD program available to students.

Key staff person available to work with LD students: Mark Lineham, Counselor; Judy Barnes, Counselor

LD program website: http://www.tcc.fl.edu/generalinfo/dss.htm

University of Tampa

Tampa, FL

Address: 401 West Kennedy Boulevard, Tampa, FL, 33606-1490
Admissions telephone: 888 MINARET
Admissions FAX: 813 258-7398
Vice President for Enrollment: Barbara P. Strickler
Admissions e-mail: admissions@ut.edu
Web site: http://www.ut.edu
SAT Code: 5819 ACT Code: 762

Academic Coordinator: Cheri Kittrell
LD program telephone: 813 258-7251
LD program e-mail: ckittrell@ut.edu
LD program enrollment: 93, Total campus enrollment: 4,348

GENERAL

University of Tampa is a private, coed, four-year institution. 85-acre, urban campus in Tampa (population: 303,447). Served by air, bus, and train. Public transportation serves campus. Semester system.

LD ADMISSIONS

Students complete a separate application and are simultaneously accepted to the LD program. A member of the LD program does not sit on the admissions committee. A personal interview is recommended. Essay is required and may be typed.

SECONDARY SCHOOL REQUIREMENTS

Graduation from secondary school required; GED accepted. The following course distribution required: 4 units of English, 3 units of math, 3 units of science, 2 units of foreign language, 3 units of social studies, 4 units of academic electives.

TESTING

SAT Reasoning or ACT required. SAT Subject recommended.

All enrolled freshmen (fall 2004):

Average SAT I Scores:	Verbal: 540	Math: 542
Average ACT Scores:	Composite: 23	

Child Study Team report is not required. A neuropsychological or comprehensive psycho-educational evaluation is required for admission. Must be dated within 36 months of application. Tests required as part of this documentation:

- [x] WAIS-IV
- [ ] WISC-IV
- [ ] SATA
- [ ] Woodcock-Johnson
- [ ] Nelson-Denny Reading Test
- [x] Other

UNDERGRADUATE STUDENT BODY

Total undergraduate student enrollment: 1,283 Men, 2,044 Women.

Composition of student body (fall 2004):

	Undergraduate	Freshmen
International	3.7	5.0
Black	5.1	6.4
American Indian	0.3	0.6
Asian-American	2.2	1.9
Hispanic	7.6	8.7
White	65.5	63.5
Unreported	15.6	13.9
	100.0%	100.0%

49% are from out of state. Average age of full-time undergraduates is 20, 43% of classes have fewer than 20 students, 57% have between 20 and 50 students.

STUDENT HOUSING

88% of freshmen live in college housing. Freshmen are not required to live on campus. Housing is guaranteed for all undergraduates. Campus can house 2,504 undergraduates. Single rooms are available for students with medical or special needs. A medical note is required.

EXPENSES

Tuition (2005-06): $17,906 per year.
Room: $3,710. Board: $3,226.
There is no additional cost for LD program/services.

LD SERVICES

LD program size is not limited.

LD services available to:

- [x] Freshmen
- [x] Sophomores
- [x] Juniors
- [x] Seniors

Academic Accommodations

Curriculum		In class	
Foreign language waiver	[ ]	Early syllabus	[ ]
Lighter course load	[x]	Note takers in class	[x]
Math waiver	[ ]	Priority seating	[ ]
Other special classes	[ ]	Tape recorders	[ ]
Priority registrations	[ ]	Videotaped classes	[ ]
Substitution of courses	[ ]	Text on tape	[ ]
Exams		**Services**	
Extended time	[x]	Diagnostic tests	[ ]
Oral exams	[ ]	Learning centers	[x]
Take home exams	[ ]	Proofreaders	[ ]
Exams on tape or computer	[ ]	Readers	[ ]
Untimed exams	[ ]	Reading Machines/Kurzweil	[ ]
Other accommodations	[ ]	Special bookstore section	[ ]
		Typists	[ ]

Credit toward degree is not given for remedial courses taken.

Counseling Services

- [ ] Academic
- [ ] Psychological
- [ ] Student Support groups
- [ ] Vocational

Tutoring

Individual tutoring is available daily.

	Individual	Group
Time management	[x]	[x]
Organizational skills	[x]	[x]
Learning strategies	[ ]	[x]
Study skills	[ ]	[x]
Content area	[ ]	[ ]
Writing lab	[x]	[ ]
Math lab	[x]	[ ]

LD PROGRAM STAFF

Total number of LD Program staff (including director):

Full Time: 1 Part Time: 1

There is an advisor/advocate from the LD program available to students.

Key staff person available to work with LD students: Ms. Cheri Kittrell, Academic Coordinator.

Trinity Baptist College

Jacksonville, FL

Address: 800 Hammond Boulevard, Jacksonville, FL, 32221
Admissions telephone: 800 786-2206
Admissions FAX: 904 596-2531
Director of Admissions: Larry Appleby
Admissions e-mail: admissions@tbc.edu
Web site: http://www.tbc.edu
SAT Code: 5780 ACT Code: 4745

Total campus enrollment: 392

GENERAL

Trinity Baptist College is a private, coed, four-year institution. 148-acre campus in Jacksonville (population: 735,617). Served by air, bus, and train. Semester system.

LD ADMISSIONS

A personal interview is recommended. Essay is required and may be typed.

SECONDARY SCHOOL REQUIREMENTS

Graduation from secondary school required; GED accepted. The following course distribution required: 3 units of English, 2 units of math, 1 unit of science, 2 units of foreign language, 2 units of social studies, 6 units of academic electives.

TESTING

Child Study Team report is not required. Tests required as part of this documentation:

- [ ] WAIS-IV
- [ ] WISC-IV
- [ ] SATA
- [ ] Woodcock-Johnson
- [ ] Nelson-Denny Reading Test
- [ ] Other

UNDERGRADUATE STUDENT BODY

Total undergraduate student enrollment: 205 Men, 195 Women.

Composition of student body (fall 2004):

	Undergraduate	Freshmen
International	0.9	1.1
Black	3.6	5.0
American Indian	0.0	0.0
Asian-American	0.0	1.1
Hispanic	0.9	2.8
White	94.6	90.0
Unreported	0.0	0.0
	100.0%	100.0%

40% are from out of state.

STUDENT HOUSING

freshmen are required to live on campus. Housing is guaranteed for all undergraduates. Campus can house 230 undergraduates.

EXPENSES

There is no additional cost for LD program/services.

LD SERVICES

LD services available to:

- [ ] Freshmen
- [ ] Sophomores
- [ ] Juniors
- [ ] Seniors

Academic Accommodations

Curriculum		**In class**	
Foreign language waiver	[ ]	Early syllabus	[ ]
Lighter course load	[x]	Note takers in class	[ ]
Math waiver	[ ]	Priority seating	[ ]
Other special classes	[ ]	Tape recorders	[ ]
Priority registrations	[ ]	Videotaped classes	[ ]
Substitution of courses	[ ]	Text on tape	[ ]
Exams		**Services**	
Extended time	[x]	Diagnostic tests	[x]
Oral exams	[x]	Learning centers	[ ]
Take home exams	[ ]	Proofreaders	[ ]
Exams on tape or computer	[ ]	Readers	[ ]
Untimed exams	[x]	Reading Machines/Kurzweil	[ ]
Other accommodations	[ ]	Special bookstore section	[ ]
		Typists	[ ]

Credit toward degree is not given for remedial courses taken.

Counseling Services

- [ ] Academic
- [ ] Psychological
- [ ] Student Support groups
- [ ] Vocational

Tutoring

	Individual	Group
Time management	[ ]	[ ]
Organizational skills	[ ]	[ ]
Learning strategies	[ ]	[ ]
Study skills	[ ]	[ ]
Content area	[ ]	[ ]
Writing lab	[ ]	[ ]
Math lab	[ ]	[ ]

LD PROGRAM STAFF

Total number of LD Program staff (including director):

Full Time: 2 Part Time: 2

Warner Southern College

Lake Wales, FL

Address: 13895 US 27, Lake Wales, FL, 33859
Admissions telephone: 800 949-7248
Admissions FAX: 863 638-7290
Director of Admissions: Jason Roe
Admissions e-mail: admissions@warner.edu
Web site: http://www.warner.edu
SAT Code: 5883 ACT Code: 777

Admissions Director: Jason Roe
LD program telephone: 863 638-7212
LD program e-mail: roej@warner.edu
Total campus enrollment: 973

GENERAL

Warner Southern College is a private, coed, four-year institution. 300-acre campus near Lake Wales (population: 10,194), 60 miles from Orlando; classroom sites in Brandon, Deland, Ft. Pierce, Lakeland, Leesburg, Melbourne, Orlando, Plant City, and Titusville. Served by bus; airports serve Orlando and Tampa (65 miles); train serves Winter Haven (20 miles). Semester system.

LD ADMISSIONS

Students do not complete a separate application and are simultaneously accepted to the LD program. A member of the LD program does sit on the admissions committee. High school waivers are accepted for foreign language. A personal interview is recommended. Essay is not required. Any admission requirements may be waived when reviewed. We are a small school and have few LD student applicants. When students apply, we meet with them personally and one-on-one. What's important is that they notify us of any LD as early as possible.

SECONDARY SCHOOL REQUIREMENTS

Graduation from secondary school required; GED accepted.

TESTING

SAT Reasoning or ACT required. SAT Subject recommended.

Child Study Team report is not required. A neuropsychological or comprehensive psycho-education evaluation is not required for admission. Tests required as part of this documentation:

- [ ] WAIS-IV
- [ ] WISC-IV
- [ ] SATA
- [ ] Woodcock-Johnson
- [ ] Nelson-Denny Reading Test
- [ ] Other

UNDERGRADUATE STUDENT BODY

Total undergraduate student enrollment: 436 Men, 646 Women.

Composition of student body (fall 2004):

	Undergraduate	Freshmen
International	0.8	2.3
Black	18.8	18.1
American Indian	0.0	0.7
Asian-American	1.6	0.8
Hispanic	16.4	10.9
White	60.9	65.0
Unreported	1.6	2.2
	100.0%	100.0%

12% are from out of state. Average age of full-time undergraduates is 27, 71% of classes have fewer than 20 students, 28% have between 20 and 50 students.

STUDENT HOUSING

96% of freshmen live in college housing. Freshmen are required to live on campus. Housing is guaranteed for all undergraduates. Available for all who request it. Single rooms are available for students with medical or special needs. A medical note is required.

EXPENSES

Tuition (2005-06): $11,740 per year.
Room & Board: $5,523.
There is no additional cost for LD program/services.

LD SERVICES

LD program size is not limited.

LD services available to:

- [x] Freshmen
- [x] Sophomores
- [x] Juniors
- [ ] Seniors

Academic Accommodations

Curriculum

- [ ] Foreign language waiver
- [ ] Lighter course load
- [ ] Math waiver
- [ ] Other special classes
- [ ] Priority registrations
- [ ] Substitution of courses

Exams

- [x] Extended time
- [x] Oral exams
- [ ] Take home exams
- [ ] Exams on tape or computer
- [ ] Untimed exams
- [ ] Other accommodations

In class

- [ ] Early syllabus
- [ ] Note takers in class
- [ ] Priority seating
- [ ] Tape recorders
- [ ] Videotaped classes
- [ ] Text on tape

Services

- [ ] Diagnostic tests
- [x] Learning centers
- [x] Proofreaders
- [x] Readers
- [x] Reading Machines/Kurzweil
- [ ] Special bookstore section
- [ ] Typists

Credit toward degree is not given for remedial courses taken.

Counseling Services

- [ ] Academic
- [ ] Psychological
- [ ] Student Support groups
- [ ] Vocational

Tutoring

Individual tutoring is available daily.

	Individual	Group
Time management	[ ]	[x]
Organizational skills	[ ]	[x]
Learning strategies	[x]	[x]
Study skills	[ ]	[x]
Content area	[x]	[x]
Writing lab	[x]	[ ]
Math lab	[x]	[ ]

LD PROGRAM STAFF

Total number of LD Program staff (including director):

Full Time: 1 Part Time: 1

There is no advisor/advocate from the LD program available to students.

University of West Florida

Pensacola, FL

Address: 11000 University Parkway, Pensacola, FL, 32514-5750
Admissions telephone: 850 474-2230
Admissions FAX: 850 474-3360
Director of Admissions: Mr. Matt Hulett
Admissions e-mail: admissions@uwf.edu
Web site: http://uwf.edu
SAT Code: 5833 ACT Code: 771

LD program name: Student Disability Resource Center
Director: Barbara Fitzpatrick
LD program telephone: 850 474-2387
LD program e-mail: bfitzpat@uwf.edu
LD program enrollment: 130, Total campus enrollment: 7,974

GENERAL

University of West Florida is a public, coed, four-year institution. 1,600-acre campus in Pensacola (population: 56,255); branch campus at Ft. Walton Beach. Served by air, bus, and train. Public transportation serves campus. Semester system.

LD ADMISSIONS

A personal interview is not required. Essay is not required. All waivers vary and are considered on an individual basis.

SECONDARY SCHOOL REQUIREMENTS

Graduation from secondary school required; GED accepted. The following course distribution required: 4 units of English, 3 units of math, 3 units of science, 2 units of foreign language, 3 units of social studies, 4 units of academic electives.

TESTING

SAT Reasoning or ACT required. SAT Subject recommended.

All enrolled freshmen (fall 2004):

Average SAT I Scores:	Verbal: 561	Math: 550
Average ACT Scores:	Composite: 24	

Child Study Team report is not required. A neuropsychological or comprehensive psycho-educational evaluation is required for admission. Tests required as part of this documentation:

- ■ WAIS-IV
- ■ WISC-IV
- ■ SATA
- ■ Woodcock-Johnson
- ■ Nelson-Denny Reading Test
- ☐ Other

UNDERGRADUATE STUDENT BODY

Total undergraduate student enrollment: 3,156 Men, 4,266 Women.

Composition of student body (fall 2004):

	Undergraduate	Freshmen
International	0.4	0.8
Black	8.1	9.9
American Indian	0.6	1.1
Asian-American	5.0	4.3
Hispanic	5.3	5.0
White	78.2	76.1
Unreported	2.3	2.9
	100.0%	100.0%

13% are from out of state. 5% join a fraternity and 5% join a sorority. Average age of full-time undergraduates is 23, 35% of classes have fewer than 20 students, 58% have between 20 and 50 students.

STUDENT HOUSING

Freshmen are not required to live on campus. Housing is guaranteed for all undergraduates.

EXPENSES

Tuition (2005-06): $2,147 per year (in-state), $14,058 (out-of-state).
Room: $3,560. Board: $2,968.
There is no additional cost for LD program/services.

LD SERVICES

LD program size is not limited.

LD services available to:

■ Freshmen ■ Sophomores ■ Juniors ■ Seniors

Academic Accommodations

Curriculum		In class	
Foreign language waiver	☐	Early syllabus	☐
Lighter course load	■	Note takers in class	■
Math waiver	☐	Priority seating	☐
Other special classes	☐	Tape recorders	☐
Priority registrations	☐	Videotaped classes	☐
Substitution of courses	☐	Text on tape	☐
Exams		**Services**	
Extended time	■	Diagnostic tests	☐
Oral exams	☐	Learning centers	■
Take home exams	☐	Proofreaders	☐
Exams on tape or computer	☐	Readers	■
Untimed exams	☐	Reading Machines/Kurzweil	■
Other accommodations	☐	Special bookstore section	☐
		Typists	☐

Credit toward degree is not given for remedial courses taken.

Counseling Services

- ☐ Academic
- ☐ Psychological
- ☐ Student Support groups
- ☐ Vocational

Tutoring

	Individual	Group
Time management	☐	☐
Organizational skills	☐	☐
Learning strategies	☐	☐
Study skills	☐	☐
Content area	☐	☐
Writing lab	☐	☐
Math lab	☐	☐

LD PROGRAM STAFF

Key staff person available to work with LD students: Barbara Fitzpatrick, Director, Student Disability Resource Center.

Agnes Scott College

Decatur, GA

Address: 141 East College Avenue, Decatur, GA, 30030
Admissions telephone: 800 868-8602
Admissions FAX: 404 471-6414
Associate Vice President for Enrollment/Director of Admissions: Stephanie Balmer
Admissions e-mail: admission@agnesscott.edu
Web site: http://www.agnesscott.edu
SAT Code: 5002 ACT Code: 780

LD program name: Office of Academic Advising
Director: Sibby Anderson-Thompkins
LD program telephone: 404 471-5186
LD program e-mail: asanderson-thompkins@agnesscott.edu
LD program enrollment: 28, Total campus enrollment: 973

GENERAL

Agnes Scott College is a private, women's, four-year institution. 100-acre, urban campus in Decatur (population: 18,147), six miles from downtown Atlanta. Major airport, bus, and train serve Atlanta. School operates transportation to local colleges and off-campus events. Public transportation serves campus. Semester system.

LD ADMISSIONS

Students do not complete a separate application and are simultaneously accepted to the LD program. A member of the LD program does not sit on the admissions committee. A personal interview is recommended. Essay is required and may be typed.

SECONDARY SCHOOL REQUIREMENTS

Graduation from secondary school required; GED accepted.

TESTING

SAT Reasoning or ACT required. SAT Subject recommended.

All enrolled freshmen (fall 2004):

Average SAT I Scores:	Verbal: 611	Math: 563
Average ACT Scores:	Composite: 25	

Child Study Team report is not required. A neuropsychological or comprehensive psycho-educational evaluation is required for admission. Must be dated within 36 months of application. Tests required as part of this documentation:

- [x] WAIS-IV
- [ ] WISC-IV
- [x] SATA
- [x] Woodcock-Johnson
- [x] Nelson-Denny Reading Test
- [x] Other

UNDERGRADUATE STUDENT BODY

Total undergraduate student enrollment: 1 Men, 868 Women.

Composition of student body (fall 2004):

	Undergraduate	Freshmen
International	2.3	6.5
Black	25.8	21.8
American Indian	0.5	0.3
Asian-American	6.6	6.1
Hispanic	5.1	4.3
White	52.7	53.2
Unreported	7.0	7.8
	100.0%	100.0%

48% are from out of state. Average age of full-time undergraduates is 20. 67% of classes have fewer than 20 students, 33% have between 20 and 50 students.

STUDENT HOUSING

97% of freshmen live in college housing. Housing is guaranteed for all undergraduates. Woodruff scholars and fifth-year students are not required to live on campus, but may petition to do so. Other students wishing to live off-campus must petition for permission to do so. Campus can house 940 undergraduates. Single rooms are available for students with medical or special needs. A medical note is required.

EXPENSES

Tuition (2005-06): $23,260 per year.
Room & Board: $4,250.
There is no additional cost for LD program/services.

LD SERVICES

LD program size is not limited.

LD services available to:

- [x] Freshmen
- [x] Sophomores
- [x] Juniors
- [x] Seniors

Academic Accommodations

Curriculum		In class	
Foreign language waiver	[ ]	Early syllabus	[ ]
Lighter course load	[x]	Note takers in class	[x]
Math waiver	[ ]	Priority seating	[ ]
Other special classes	[ ]	Tape recorders	[x]
Priority registrations	[ ]	Videotaped classes	[ ]
Substitution of courses	[ ]	Text on tape	[ ]
Exams		**Services**	
Extended time	[x]	Diagnostic tests	[ ]
Oral exams	[x]	Learning centers	[ ]
Take home exams	[ ]	Proofreaders	[ ]
Exams on tape or computer	[ ]	Readers	[x]
Untimed exams	[x]	Reading Machines/Kurzweil	[x]
Other accommodations	[ ]	Special bookstore section	[ ]
		Typists	[ ]

Credit toward degree is not given for remedial courses taken.

Counseling Services

- [ ] Academic
- [ ] Psychological
- [ ] Student Support groups
- [ ] Vocational

Tutoring

Individual tutoring is available daily.

	Individual	Group
Time management	[ ]	[x]
Organizational skills	[ ]	[ ]
Learning strategies	[ ]	[ ]
Study skills	[ ]	[x]
Content area	[ ]	[ ]
Writing lab	[ ]	[x]
Math lab	[ ]	[x]

UNIQUE LD PROGRAM FEATURES

Tutoring and counseling services are available for all students.

LD PROGRAM STAFF

Total number of LD Program staff (including director):

Full Time: 1 Part Time: 1

There is an advisor/advocate from the LD program available to students.

Key staff person available to work with LD students: Sibby Anderson-Thompkins, Director of Academic Advising

Armstrong Atlantic State University

Savannah, GA

Address: 11935 Abercorn Street, Savannah, GA, 31419
Admissions telephone: 912 927-5277
Admissions FAX: 912 921-5462
Director of Admissions/Registrar: Kim West
Admissions e-mail: adm-info@mail.armstrong.edu
Web site: http://www.armstrong.edu
SAT Code: 5012 ACT Code: 162

Director of Disability Services: Amelia Bunch
LD program telephone: 912 927-5271
LD program e-mail: bunchame@mail.armstrong.edu
Total campus enrollment: 6,147

GENERAL

Armstrong Atlantic State University is a public, coed, four-year institution. 250-acre campus in Savannah (population: 138,000), 10 miles from downtown; branch campuses in Brunswick and in Liberty County. Served by airport, bus, and train. Public transportation serves campus. Semester system.

LD ADMISSIONS

Students do not complete a separate application and are simultaneously accepted to the LD program. A member of the LD program does not sit on the admissions committee. High school waivers are accepted for math and foreign language. A personal interview is required. Essay is not required.

SECONDARY SCHOOL REQUIREMENTS

Graduation from secondary school required; GED accepted. The following course distribution required: 4 units of English, 3 units of math, 3 units of science, 2 units of foreign language, 3 units of social studies.

TESTING

SAT Reasoning recommended. ACT recommended.

All enrolled freshmen (fall 2004):

Average SAT I Scores: Verbal: 519 Math: 507
Average ACT Scores: Composite: 21

Child Study Team report is not required. Tests required as part of this documentation:

- [ ] WAIS-IV
- [ ] WISC-IV
- [ ] SATA
- [ ] Woodcock-Johnson
- [ ] Nelson-Denny Reading Test
- [ ] Other

UNDERGRADUATE STUDENT BODY

Total undergraduate student enrollment: 1,641 Men, 3,420 Women.

Composition of student body (fall 2004):

	Undergraduate	Freshmen
International	1.4	1.6
Black	18.5	23.1
American Indian	0.4	0.4
Asian-American	2.8	3.0
Hispanic	3.9	2.9
White	73.0	69.0
Unreported	0.0	0.0
	100.0%	100.0%

2% are from out of state. Average age of full-time undergraduates is 23.

STUDENT HOUSING

Housing is guaranteed for all undergraduates. Campus can house 600 undergraduates.

EXPENSES

Tuition (2005-06): $2,438 per year (in-state), $9,754 (out-of-state).

Room & Board: $6,192.
There is no additional cost for LD program/services.

LD SERVICES

LD program size is not limited.

LD services available to:

- [ ] Freshmen
- [ ] Sophomores
- [ ] Juniors
- [ ] Seniors

Academic Accommodations

Curriculum
- [ ] Foreign language waiver
- [ ] Lighter course load
- [ ] Math waiver
- [x] Other special classes
- [ ] Priority registrations
- [ ] Substitution of courses

Exams
- [x] Extended time
- [ ] Oral exams
- [ ] Take home exams
- [ ] Exams on tape or computer
- [ ] Untimed exams
- [ ] Other accommodations

In class
- [ ] Early syllabus
- [x] Note takers in class
- [ ] Priority seating
- [x] Tape recorders
- [ ] Videotaped classes
- [ ] Text on tape

Services
- [x] Diagnostic tests
- [x] Learning centers
- [ ] Proofreaders
- [x] Readers
- [x] Reading Machines/Kurzweil
- [ ] Special bookstore section
- [ ] Typists

Credit toward degree is not given for remedial courses taken.

Counseling Services

- [ ] Academic
- [ ] Psychological
- [ ] Student Support groups
- [ ] Vocational

Tutoring

	Individual	Group
Time management	☐	☐
Organizational skills	☐	☐
Learning strategies	☐	☐
Study skills	☐	☐
Content area	☐	☐
Writing lab	☐	☐
Math lab	☐	☐

LD PROGRAM STAFF

Total number of LD Program staff (including director):

Full Time: 2 Part Time: 2

Key staff person available to work with LD students: Amelia Bunch, Director of Disability Services

The Art Institute of Atlanta

Atlanta, GA

Address: 6600 Peachtree Dunwoody Road, 100 Embassy Row, Atlanta, GA, 30328
Admissions telephone: 770 394-8300
Admissions FAX: 770 394-0008
Director of Admissions: Donna Scott
Admissions e-mail: aiaadm@aii.edu
Web site: www.aia.artinstitutes.edu
SAT Code: 5429 ACT Code: 859

Counselor: April Shavkin
LD program telephone: 770 689-4908
LD program e-mail: ashavkin@aii.edu
Total campus enrollment: 2,651

GENERAL

The Art Institute of Atlanta is a private, coed, four-year institution. Two-acre, suburban campus in Dunwoody, five miles north of Atlanta (population: 416,474); 24 Art Institute International campuses nationwide. Airport, bus, and train serve Atlanta. School operates transportation to local commuter rail stations and dormitories. Public transportation serves campus. Quarter system.

LD ADMISSIONS

A personal interview is required. Essay is required and may be typed.

SECONDARY SCHOOL REQUIREMENTS

Graduation from secondary school required; GED accepted.

TESTING

SAT Reasoning or ACT considered if submitted. SAT Subject recommended.

Child Study Team report is not required. Tests required as part of this documentation:

- ☐ WAIS-IV
- ☐ WISC-IV
- ☐ SATA
- ☐ Woodcock-Johnson
- ☐ Nelson-Denny Reading Test
- ☐ Other

UNDERGRADUATE STUDENT BODY

Total undergraduate student enrollment: 1,279 Men, 1,158 Women.

Composition of student body (fall 2004):

	Undergraduate	Freshmen
International	1.4	3.5
Black	39.8	32.2
American Indian	0.6	0.4
Asian-American	2.8	2.9
Hispanic	4.2	3.9
White	42.3	48.8
Unreported	8.9	8.3
	100.0%	100.0%

22% are from out of state. Average age of full-time undergraduates is 23. 45% of classes have fewer than 20 students, 55% have between 20 and 50 students.

STUDENT HOUSING

23% of freshmen live in college housing. Freshmen are not required to live on campus. Housing is guaranteed for all undergraduates.

EXPENSES

Room: $6,645.

There is no additional cost for LD program/services.

LD SERVICES

LD program size is not limited.

LD services available to:

■ Freshmen ■ Sophomores ■ Juniors ■ Seniors

Academic Accommodations

Curriculum		In class	
Foreign language waiver	☐	Early syllabus	☐
Lighter course load	☐	Note takers in class	■
Math waiver	☐	Priority seating	☐
Other special classes	☐	Tape recorders	☐
Priority registrations	☐	Videotaped classes	☐
Substitution of courses	☐	Text on tape	☐
Exams		**Services**	
Extended time	■	Diagnostic tests	☐
Oral exams	■	Learning centers	☐
Take home exams	☐	Proofreaders	☐
Exams on tape or computer	☐	Readers	☐
Untimed exams	☐	Reading Machines/Kurzweil	☐
Other accommodations	☐	Special bookstore section	☐
		Typists	☐

Credit toward degree is not given for remedial courses taken.

Counseling Services

- ■ Academic
- ■ Psychological
- ☐ Student Support groups
- ☐ Vocational

Tutoring

Individual tutoring is available.

	Individual	Group
Time management	☐	☐
Organizational skills	☐	☐
Learning strategies	☐	☐
Study skills	☐	☐
Content area	☐	☐
Writing lab	☐	☐
Math lab	☐	☐

LD PROGRAM STAFF

Total number of LD Program staff (including director):

Full Time: 1 Part Time: 1

There is an advisor/advocate from the LD program available to students.

Key staff person available to work with LD students: April Shavkin, Counselor

Atlanta College of Art

Atlanta, GA

Address: 1280 Peachtree Street NE, Atlanta, GA, 30309
Admissions telephone: 800 832-2104
Admissions FAX: 404 733-5107
Vice President of Enrollment Management: Lucy Leusch
Admissions e-mail: acainfo@woodruffcenter.org
Web site: http://www.aca.edu
SAT Code: 5014 ACT Code: 829

Assistant Dean: Remi Stewart
LD program telephone: 404 733-5090
LD program e-mail: remi.stewart@woodruffcenter.org
Total campus enrollment: 330

GENERAL

Atlanta College of Art is a private, coed, four-year institution. Six-acre, urban campus in Atlanta (population: 416,474). Served by airport, bus, and train. Public transportation serves campus. Semester system.

LD ADMISSIONS

Students do not complete a separate application and are simultaneously accepted to the LD program. A member of the LD program does sit on the admissions committee. A personal interview is not required. Essay is required and may be typed.

SECONDARY SCHOOL REQUIREMENTS

Graduation from secondary school required; GED accepted.

TESTING

SAT Reasoning or ACT required. SAT Subject required.

All enrolled freshmen (fall 2004):

Average SAT I Scores:	Verbal: 515	Math: 486
Average ACT Scores:	Composite: 20	

Child Study Team report is not required. A neuropsychological or comprehensive psycho-education evaluation is not required for admission. Tests required as part of this documentation:

- ☐ WAIS-IV
- ☐ WISC-IV
- ☐ SATA
- ☐ Woodcock-Johnson
- ☐ Nelson-Denny Reading Test
- ☐ Other

UNDERGRADUATE STUDENT BODY

Total undergraduate student enrollment: 330.

Composition of student body (fall 2004):

	Undergraduate	Freshmen
International	0.1	4.9
Black	34.7	24.7
American Indian	0.0	0.0
Asian-American	2.8	4.0
Hispanic	9.7	5.6
White	44.4	54.3
Unreported	8.3	6.5
	100.0%	100.0%

52% are from out of state. Average age of full-time undergraduates is 22. 76% of classes have fewer than 20 students, 24% have between 20 and 50 students.

STUDENT HOUSING

82% of freshmen live in college housing. Freshmen are not required to live on campus. Housing is guaranteed for all undergraduates. Campus can house 150 undergraduates. Single rooms are not available for students with medical or special needs.

EXPENSES

Tuition (2005-06): $17,900 per year.
Room: $5,400.
There is no additional cost for LD program/services.

LD SERVICES

LD program size is not limited.

LD services available to:

☒ Freshmen ☒ Sophomores ☒ Juniors ☒ Seniors

Academic Accommodations

Curriculum		In class	
Foreign language waiver	☐	Early syllabus	☐
Lighter course load	☐	Note takers in class	☒
Math waiver	☐	Priority seating	☐
Other special classes	☐	Tape recorders	☐
Priority registrations	☐	Videotaped classes	☐
Substitution of courses	☐	Text on tape	☐
Exams		**Services**	
Extended time	☒	Diagnostic tests	☐
Oral exams	☒	Learning centers	☐
Take home exams	☐	Proofreaders	☐
Exams on tape or computer	☐	Readers	☐
Untimed exams	☒	Reading Machines/Kurzweil	☐
Other accommodations	☐	Special bookstore section	☐
		Typists	☐

Credit toward degree is given for remedial courses taken.

Counseling Services

- ☐ Academic
- ☐ Psychological
- ☐ Student Support groups
- ☐ Vocational

Tutoring

Individual tutoring is not available.

	Individual	Group
Time management	☐	☐
Organizational skills	☐	☐
Learning strategies	☐	☐
Study skills	☐	☐
Content area	☐	☐
Writing lab	☐	☐
Math lab	☐	☐

LD PROGRAM STAFF

Total number of LD Program staff (including director):

Full Time: 1 Part Time: 1

There is no advisor/advocate from the LD program available to students.

Key staff person available to work with LD students: Remi Stewart, Assistant Dean

Augusta State University

Augusta, GA

Address: 2500 Walton Way, Augusta, GA, 30904-2200
Admissions telephone: 800 341-4373
Admissions FAX: 706 667-4355
Acting Director of Admissions and Registrar: Katherine Sweeney
Admissions e-mail: admissions@aug.edu
Web site: http://www.aug.edu
SAT Code: 5336 ACT Code: 796

LD program name: Testing & Disability Services
Coordinator of Disability Services: Angie Kitchens
LD program telephone: 706 737-1469
LD program e-mail: akitchens@aug.edu
LD program enrollment: 23, Total campus enrollment: 5,502

GENERAL

Augusta State University is a public, coed, four-year institution. 77-acre campus in Augusta (population: 195,182), 150 miles from Atlanta. Served by airport and bus; major airport serves Atlanta; train serves Denmark, SC. (70 miles). Public transportation serves campus. Semester system.

LD ADMISSIONS

Students do not complete a separate application and are not simultaneously accepted to the LD program. A member of the LD program does not sit on the admissions committee. A personal interview is not required. Essay is not required.

For fall 2004, 12 completed self-identified LD applications were received. 12 applications were offered admission, and 12 enrolled.

SECONDARY SCHOOL REQUIREMENTS

Graduation from secondary school required; GED accepted. The following course distribution required: 4 units of English, 4 units of math, 3 units of science, 2 units of foreign language, 3 units of social studies, 2 units of academic electives.

TESTING

SAT Reasoning or ACT required. SAT Subject recommended.

All enrolled freshmen (fall 2004):

Average SAT I Scores:	Verbal:491	Math:483
Average ACT Scores:	Composite:18	

Child Study Team report is not required. A neuropsychological or comprehensive psycho-education evaluation is not required for admission. Tests required as part of this documentation:

- ☐ WAIS-IV
- ☐ WISC-IV
- ☐ SATA
- ☐ Woodcock-Johnson
- ☐ Nelson-Denny Reading Test
- ☑ Other

UNDERGRADUATE STUDENT BODY

Total undergraduate student enrollment: 1,704 Men, 2,976 Women.

Composition of student body (fall 2004):

	Undergraduate	Freshmen
International	0.7	0.9
Black	27.0	27.8
American Indian	0.3	0.3
Asian-American	3.6	2.7
Hispanic	2.8	2.9
White	65.6	65.4
Unreported	0.0	0.0
	100.0%	100.0%

1% join a fraternity and 1% join a sorority. 31% of classes have fewer than 20 students, 66% have between 20 and 50 students, 3% have more than 50 students.

STUDENT HOUSING

Housing is not guaranteed for all undergraduates.

EXPENSES

Tuition (2005-06): $2,438 per year (in-state), $9,754 (out-of-state). There is no additional cost for LD program/services.

LD SERVICES

LD program size is not limited.

LD services available to:

☑ Freshmen ☑ Sophomores ☑ Juniors ☑ Seniors

Academic Accommodations

Curriculum		**In class**	
Foreign language waiver	☐	Early syllabus	☐
Lighter course load	☑	Note takers in class	☑
Math waiver	☐	Priority seating	☑
Other special classes	☐	Tape recorders	☑
Priority registrations	☑	Videotaped classes	☐
Substitution of courses	☑	Text on tape	☑
Exams		**Services**	
Extended time	☑	Diagnostic tests	☑
Oral exams	☑	Learning centers	☑
Take home exams	☐	Proofreaders	☑
Exams on tape or computer	☑	Readers	☑
Untimed exams	☐	Reading Machines/Kurzweil	☑
Other accommodations	☑	Special bookstore section	☐
		Typists	☑

Credit toward degree is not given for remedial courses taken.

Counseling Services

- ☑ Academic
- ☑ Psychological
- ☑ Student Support groups
- ☑ Vocational

Tutoring

Individual tutoring is available.

	Individual	Group
Time management	☑	☑
Organizational skills	☑	☑
Learning strategies	☑	☐
Study skills	☑	☑
Content area	☐	☐
Writing lab	☐	☑
Math lab	☐	☑

LD PROGRAM STAFF

Total number of LD Program staff (including director):

Full Time: 1 Part Time: 1

There is an advisor/advocate from the LD program available to students.

Key staff person available to work with LD students: Angie Kitchens, Coordinator of Disability Services.

Berry College

Mount Berry, GA

Address: P.O. Box 490279, Mount Berry, GA, 30149
Admissions telephone: 800 237-7942
Admissions FAX: 706 290-2178
Dean of Admissions: Garreth M. Johnson
Admissions e-mail: admissions@berry.edu
Web site: http://www.berry.edu
SAT Code: 5059 ACT Code: 798

LD program name: Academic Support Center
LD program address: 2277 Martha Berry Hwy, NW
Director of Academic Support Center: Martha Van Cise
LD program telephone: 706 233-4080
LD program e-mail: mvancise@berry.edu
LD program enrollment: 54, Total campus enrollment: 1,878

GENERAL

Berry College is a private, coed, four-year institution. 28,000-acre campus in Mount Berry, bordering Rome (population: 34,980) and 65 miles from both Atlanta and Chattanooga, TN. Served by bus; major airport and train serve Atlanta; smaller airport serves Chattanooga, TN. School operates transportation on campus. Public transportation serves campus. Semester system.

LD ADMISSIONS

Application Deadline: 07/22. Students do not complete a separate application and are simultaneously accepted to the LD program. A member of the LD program does sit on the admissions committee. A personal interview is recommended. Essay is not required.

SECONDARY SCHOOL REQUIREMENTS

Graduation from secondary school required; GED accepted. The following course distribution required: 4 units of English, 4 units of math, 3 units of science, 2 units of foreign language, 3 units of social studies.

TESTING

SAT Reasoning or ACT required. SAT Subject required.

Child Study Team report is not required. A neuropsychological or comprehensive psycho-educational evaluation is required for admission. Must be dated within 36 months of application. Tests required as part of this documentation:

- [x] WAIS-IV
- [ ] WISC-IV
- [ ] SATA
- [x] Woodcock-Johnson
- [x] Nelson-Denny Reading Test
- [ ] Other

UNDERGRADUATE STUDENT BODY

Total undergraduate student enrollment: 681 Men, 1,165 Women.

Composition of student body (fall 2004):

	Undergraduate	Freshmen
International	1.2	1.5
Black	3.1	3.2
American Indian	0.2	0.1
Asian-American	1.6	1.4
Hispanic	2.5	1.2
White	89.8	90.9
Unreported	1.6	1.7
	100.0%	100.0%

15% are from out of state. Average age of full-time undergraduates is 20. 59% of classes have fewer than 20 students, 41% have between 20 and 50 students.

STUDENT HOUSING

97% of freshmen live in college housing. Freshmen are required to live on campus. Housing is guaranteed for all undergraduates. Campus can house 1,414 undergraduates. Single rooms are available for students with medical or special needs. A medical note is required.

EXPENSES

Tuition (2005-06): $17,570 per year.
Room: $3,832. Board: $2,990.
There is no additional cost for LD program/services.

LD SERVICES

LD program size is not limited.

LD services available to:

- [x] Freshmen
- [x] Sophomores
- [x] Juniors
- [x] Seniors

Academic Accommodations

Curriculum

- [ ] Foreign language waiver
- [ ] Lighter course load
- [ ] Math waiver
- [ ] Other special classes
- [x] Priority registrations
- [ ] Substitution of courses

Exams

- [x] Extended time
- [x] Oral exams
- [ ] Take home exams
- [x] Exams on tape or computer
- [ ] Untimed exams
- [ ] Other accommodations

In class

- [ ] Early syllabus
- [x] Note takers in class
- [x] Priority seating
- [x] Tape recorders
- [ ] Videotaped classes
- [ ] Text on tape

Services

- [ ] Diagnostic tests
- [ ] Learning centers
- [ ] Proofreaders
- [x] Readers
- [ ] Reading Machines/Kurzweil
- [ ] Special bookstore section
- [x] Typists

Credit toward degree is not given for remedial courses taken.

Counseling Services

- [x] Academic
- [ ] Psychological
- [ ] Student Support groups
- [ ] Vocational

Meets 2 times per academic year

Tutoring

Individual tutoring is available weekly.

Average size of tutoring groups: 1

	Individual	Group
Time management	[ ]	[ ]
Organizational skills	[ ]	[ ]
Learning strategies	[ ]	[ ]
Study skills	[ ]	[ ]
Content area	[ ]	[ ]
Writing lab	[x]	[ ]
Math lab	[x]	[ ]

LD PROGRAM STAFF

Key staff person available to work with LD students: Martha Van Cise, Director of Academic Support Center

Brenau University Women's College

Gainesville, GA

Address: 500 Washington Street, SE, Gainesville, GA, 30501
Admissions telephone: 770 534-6100
Admissions FAX: 770 538-4306
Coordinator of Women's College Admissions: Ms. Christina White
Admissions e-mail: wcadmissions@lib.brenau.edu
Web site: http://www.brenau.edu
SAT Code: 5066 ACT Code: 800

LD program name: Learning Center
Professor of Education/Director of Learning Center: Vincent Yamilkoski
LD program telephone: 770 534-6134
LD program e-mail: vyamilkoski@lib.brenau.edu
LD program enrollment: 50, Total campus enrollment: 680

GENERAL

Brenau University Women's College is a private, women's, four-year institution. 57-acre, suburban campus in Gainesville (population: 25,578), 50 miles northeast of Atlanta. Served by bus and train; major airport serves Atlanta. Public transportation serves campus. Semester system.

LD ADMISSIONS

Students do not complete a separate application and are not simultaneously accepted to the LD program. A member of the LD program does sit on the admissions committee. A personal interview is required. Essay is not required. Students with SAT/ACT scores and/or high school grades below regular admissions standards will receive a faculty interview.

For fall 2004, 19 completed self-identified LD applications were received. 18 applications were offered admission, and 18 enrolled.

SECONDARY SCHOOL REQUIREMENTS

Graduation from secondary school required; GED accepted. The following course distribution required: 4 units of English, 3 units of math, 2 units of science, 3 units of foreign language.

TESTING

SAT Reasoning or ACT required. SAT Subject required.

All enrolled freshmen (fall 2004):

Average SAT I Scores: Verbal: 516 Math: 494

Child Study Team report is required if student is classified. A neuropsychological or comprehensive psycho-educational evaluation is required for admission. Tests required as part of this documentation:

- ■ WAIS-IV
- ■ WISC-IV
- ☐ SATA
- ■ Woodcock-Johnson
- ■ Nelson-Denny Reading Test
- ■ Other

UNDERGRADUATE STUDENT BODY

Total undergraduate student enrollment: 572 Women.

Composition of student body (fall 2004):

	Undergraduate	Freshmen
International	1.0	2.7
Black	23.5	16.4
American Indian	0.6	0.5
Asian-American	2.0	2.0
Hispanic	1.5	2.7
White	66.3	68.6
Unreported	5.1	7.1
	100.0%	100.0%

18% are from out of state. 32% join a sorority. Average age of full-time undergraduates is 22. 82% of classes have fewer than 20 students, 18% have between 20 and 50 students.

STUDENT HOUSING

78% of freshmen live in college housing. Housing is guaranteed for all undergraduates. Campus can house 458 undergraduates. Single rooms are available for students with medical or special needs. A medical note is required.

EXPENSES

Tuition (2005-06): $15,450 per year.
Room & Board: $8,350.
Additional cost for LD program/services: $900

LD SERVICES

LD program size is not limited.

LD services available to:

■ Freshmen ■ Sophomores ■ Juniors ■ Seniors

Academic Accommodations

Curriculum		In class	
Foreign language waiver	☐	Early syllabus	☐
Lighter course load	■	Note takers in class	■
Math waiver	☐	Priority seating	■
Other special classes	■	Tape recorders	■
Priority registrations	■	Videotaped classes	☐
Substitution of courses	☐	Text on tape	■
Exams		**Services**	
Extended time	■	Diagnostic tests	■
Oral exams	■	Learning centers	■
Take home exams	☐	Proofreaders	■
Exams on tape or computer	☐	Readers	■
Untimed exams	■	Reading Machines/Kurzweil	■
Other accommodations	☐	Special bookstore section	☐
		Typists	☐

Credit toward degree is given for remedial courses taken.

Counseling Services

- ■ Academic
- ■ Psychological
- ■ Student Support groups
- ☐ Vocational

Tutoring

Individual tutoring is available weekly.

Average size of tutoring groups: 1

	Individual	Group
Time management	☐	■
Organizational skills	☐	■
Learning strategies	☐	■
Study skills	☐	■
Content area	■	☐
Writing lab	■	☐
Math lab	■	☐

UNIQUE LD PROGRAM FEATURES

Full-time students enroll in three or four courses per semester and receive tutoring in one to four courses, depending on individual need. For each course, students receive tutoring two hours per week from a content-area specialist. They also receive additional tutoring sessions in reading, math, or any area of special need. Each Brenau tutor holds at least one college degree. All students enrolled in the Learning Center may take tests in an extended-time format where oral assistance is available. Learning Center students are given the opportunity to register early for their courses. For students with a reading deficit who qualify, taped textbooks are available.

LD PROGRAM STAFF

Total number of LD Program staff (including director):

Full Time: 2 Part Time : 2

There is an advisor/advocate from the LD program available to students.

Key staff person available to work with LD students: Vincent Yamilkoski, Ed.D., Professor of Education/Director of Learning Center

Brewton-Parker College

Mount Vernon, GA

Address: Highway 280, Mount Vernon, GA, 30445
Admissions telephone: 912 583-3265
Admissions FAX: 912 583-3598
Director of Admissions: Brad Kissell
Admissions e-mail: admissions@bpc.edu
Web site: http://www.bpc.edu
SAT Code: 5068

Director of Counseling Services: Juanita Kissell
LD program telephone: 912 583-3222
LD program e-mail: jkissell@bpc.edu
Total campus enrollment: 1,111

GENERAL

Brewton-Parker College is a private, coed, four-year institution. 285-acre campus in Mt. Vernon (population: 2,082), 85 miles from Macon; branch campuses in Baxley, Cordele, Hazlehurst, Hinesville, Norman Park, Reidsville, Richmond Hill, Savannah, and Swainsboro. Major airport serves Atlanta (180 miles); smaller airport and train serve Savannah (120 miles); bus serves Vidalia (12 miles). Semester system.

LD ADMISSIONS

A personal interview is not required. Essay is not required.

SECONDARY SCHOOL REQUIREMENTS

Graduation from secondary school not required. The following course distribution required: 4 units of English, 3 units of math, 3 units of science, 3 units of social studies.

TESTING

SAT Reasoning required of some applicants. ACT required of some applicants. SAT Subject recommended.

Child Study Team report is not required. Tests required as part of this documentation:

- ☐ WAIS-IV
- ☐ WISC-IV
- ☐ SATA
- ☐ Woodcock-Johnson
- ☐ Nelson-Denny Reading Test
- ☐ Other

UNDERGRADUATE STUDENT BODY

Total undergraduate student enrollment: 1,111.

Composition of student body (fall 2004):

	Undergraduate	Freshmen
International	1.3	1.5
Black	23.4	19.5
American Indian	0.1	0.1
Asian-American	0.4	0.4
Hispanic	3.0	2.0
White	59.7	64.1
Unreported	12.1	12.4
	100.0%	100.0%

6% are from out of state. 88% of classes have fewer than 20 students, 12% have between 20 and 50 students.

STUDENT HOUSING

Housing is guaranteed for all undergraduates. Campus can house 455 undergraduates.

EXPENSES

Tuition (2005-06): $11,584 per year.
Room & Board: $4,550.

There is no additional cost for LD program/services.

LD SERVICES

LD program size is not limited.

LD services available to:

☐ Freshmen ☐ Sophomores ☐ Juniors ☐ Seniors

Academic Accommodations

Curriculum		In class	
Foreign language waiver	☐	Early syllabus	☐
Lighter course load	☐	Note takers in class	■
Math waiver	☐	Priority seating	☐
Other special classes	☐	Tape recorders	☐
Priority registrations	☐	Videotaped classes	☐
Substitution of courses	☐	Text on tape	☐
Exams		**Services**	
Extended time	■	Diagnostic tests	☐
Oral exams	☐	Learning centers	■
Take home exams	☐	Proofreaders	☐
Exams on tape or computer	☐	Readers	■
Untimed exams	☐	Reading Machines/Kurzweil	☐
Other accommodations	☐	Special bookstore section	☐
		Typists	☐

Credit toward degree is not given for remedial courses taken.

Counseling Services

- ☐ Academic
- ☐ Psychological
- ☐ Student Support groups
- ☐ Vocational

Tutoring

	Individual	Group
Time management	☐	☐
Organizational skills	☐	☐
Learning strategies	☐	☐
Study skills	☐	☐
Content area	☐	☐
Writing lab	☐	☐
Math lab	☐	☐

LD PROGRAM STAFF

Total number of LD Program staff (including director):

Full Time: 1 Part Time: 1

Key staff person available to work with LD students: Juanita Kissell, Director of Counseling Services

Clark Atlanta University

Atlanta, GA

Address: 223 James P. Brawley Drive, SW, Atlanta, GA, 30314
Admissions telephone: 800 688-3228
Admissions FAX: 404 880-6174
Director of Admissions: Julius Dodds
Admissions e-mail: jdodds@cau.edu
Web site: http://www.cau.edu
SAT Code: 5110 ACT Code: 804

Interim Director: Gay Linn E. Gatewood-Jasho
LD program telephone: 404 880-8709
LD program e-mail: gjasho@cau.edu
Total campus enrollment: 3,701

GENERAL

Clark Atlanta University is a private, coed, four-year institution. 126-acre campus in Atlanta (population: 416,471), one mile west of downtown area. Served by airport, bus, and train. Public transportation serves campus. Semester system.

LD ADMISSIONS

A personal interview is required. Essay is not required. Admissions requirements that may be waived for LD students include not applicable

SECONDARY SCHOOL REQUIREMENTS

Graduation from secondary school required; GED accepted. The following course distribution required: 4 units of English, 3 units of math, 2 units of science, 2 units of foreign language, 3 units of social studies, 3 units of academic electives.

TESTING

All enrolled freshmen (fall 2004):

Average SAT I Scores:	Verbal: 451	Math: 459
Average ACT Scores:	Composite: 18	

Child Study Team report is not required. Tests required as part of this documentation:

- ❑ WAIS-IV
- ❑ WISC-IV
- ❑ SATA
- ❑ Woodcock-Johnson
- ❑ Nelson-Denny Reading Test
- ❑ Other

UNDERGRADUATE STUDENT BODY

Total undergraduate student enrollment: 1,135 Men, 2,788 Women.

Composition of student body (fall 2004):

	Undergraduate	Freshmen
International	0.0	0.0
Black	85.1	94.9
American Indian	0.1	0.0
Asian-American	0.2	0.1
Hispanic	0.1	0.1
White	0.2	0.0
Unreported	14.3	4.9
	100.0%	100.0%

60% are from out of state. 46% of classes have fewer than 20 students, 50% have between 20 and 50 students, 4% have more than 50 students.

STUDENT HOUSING

Freshmen are not required to live on campus. Housing is not guaranteed for all undergraduates. Campus can house 1,422 undergraduates.

EXPENSES

Tuition (2005-06): $13,972 per year.
Room: $3,970-$4,042. Board: $2,846.
There is no additional cost for LD program/services.

LD SERVICES

LD program size is not limited.

LD services available to:

❑ Freshmen ❑ Sophomores ❑ Juniors ❑ Seniors

Academic Accommodations

Curriculum		In class	
Foreign language waiver	❑	Early syllabus	❑
Lighter course load	■	Note takers in class	❑
Math waiver	❑	Priority seating	❑
Other special classes	❑	Tape recorders	■
Priority registrations	❑	Videotaped classes	❑
Substitution of courses	❑	Text on tape	❑
Exams		**Services**	
Extended time	■	Diagnostic tests	❑
Oral exams	❑	Learning centers	❑
Take home exams	❑	Proofreaders	❑
Exams on tape or computer	❑	Readers	■
Untimed exams	■	Reading Machines/Kurzweil	❑
Other accommodations	❑	Special bookstore section	❑
		Typists	❑

Credit toward degree is not given for remedial courses taken.

Counseling Services

- ❑ Academic
- ❑ Psychological
- ❑ Student Support groups
- ❑ Vocational

Tutoring

	Individual	Group
Time management	❑	❑
Organizational skills	❑	❑
Learning strategies	❑	❑
Study skills	❑	❑
Content area	❑	❑
Writing lab	❑	❑
Math lab	❑	❑

LD PROGRAM STAFF

Total number of LD Program staff (including director):

Full Time: 1 Part Time: 1

Key staff person available to work with LD students: Gay Linn E. Gatewood-Jasho, Director

Clayton College and State University

Morrow, GA

Address: 5900 North Lee Street, Morrow, GA, 30260
Admissions telephone: 770 961-3500
Admissions FAX: 770 961-3752
Director of Admissions: Jeff Hammer
Admissions e-mail: ccsu-info@mail.clayton.edu
Web site: http://www.clayton.edu
SAT Code: 5145 ACT Code: 806

LD program name: Disability Services
Director, Disability Services: Dr. Elaine Manglitz
LD program telephone: 770 961-3719
LD program enrollment: 12, Total campus enrollment: 5,954

GENERAL

Clayton College and State University is a public, coed, four-year institution. 163-acre, suburban campus in Morrow (population: 4,882), 10 miles from Atlanta. Major airport, bus, and train serve Atlanta. Semester system.

LD ADMISSIONS

Students do not complete a separate application and are not simultaneously accepted to the LD program. A member of the LD program does not sit on the admissions committee. A personal interview is not required. Essay is not required.

SECONDARY SCHOOL REQUIREMENTS

Graduation from secondary school required; GED not accepted. The following course distribution required: 4 units of English, 4 units of math, 3 units of science, 2 units of foreign language, 3 units of social studies.

TESTING

SAT Reasoning or ACT required. SAT Subject recommended.

All enrolled freshmen (fall 2004):

Average SAT I Scores:	Verbal: 499	Math: 495
Average ACT Scores:	Composite: 19	

Child Study Team report is not required. A neuropsychological or comprehensive psycho-educational evaluation is required for admission. Must be dated within 36 months of application. Tests required as part of this documentation:

- [x] WAIS-IV
- [x] WISC-IV
- [x] SATA
- [x] Woodcock-Johnson
- [x] Nelson-Denny Reading Test
- [ ] Other

UNDERGRADUATE STUDENT BODY

Total undergraduate student enrollment: 1,623 Men, 3,052 Women.

Composition of student body (fall 2004):

	Undergraduate	Freshmen
International	5.3	2.0
Black	43.5	47.8
American Indian	0.1	0.4
Asian-American	3.0	4.2
Hispanic	2.5	2.2
White	38.3	37.8
Unreported	7.3	5.6
	100.0%	100.0%

2% are from out of state. 1% join a fraternity and 1% join a sorority. Average age of full-time undergraduates is 24. 42% of classes have fewer than 20 students, 54% have between 20 and 50 students, 4% have more than 50 students.

STUDENT HOUSING

30% of freshmen live in college housing. Freshmen are not required to live on campus. Housing is guaranteed for all undergraduates. Campus can house 854 undergraduates.

EXPENSES

Tuition (2005-06): $2,438 per year (in-state), $9,754 (out-of-state). There is no additional cost for LD program/services.

LD SERVICES

LD program size is not limited.

LD services available to:

- [x] Freshmen
- [x] Sophomores
- [x] Juniors
- [x] Seniors

Academic Accommodations

Curriculum		**In class**	
Foreign language waiver	[ ]	Early syllabus	[ ]
Lighter course load	[x]	Note takers in class	[x]
Math waiver	[ ]	Priority seating	[x]
Other special classes	[ ]	Tape recorders	[x]
Priority registrations	[x]	Videotaped classes	[ ]
Substitution of courses	[ ]	Text on tape	[x]
Exams		**Services**	
Extended time	[x]	Diagnostic tests	[ ]
Oral exams	[ ]	Learning centers	[ ]
Take home exams	[ ]	Proofreaders	[ ]
Exams on tape or computer	[x]	Readers	[x]
Untimed exams	[ ]	Reading Machines/Kurzweil	[x]
Other accommodations	[x]	Special bookstore section	[ ]
		Typists	[ ]

Credit toward degree is not given for remedial courses taken.

Counseling Services

- [ ] Academic
- [ ] Psychological
- [ ] Student Support groups
- [ ] Vocational

Tutoring

Individual tutoring is available.

	Individual	Group
Time management	[ ]	[ ]
Organizational skills	[ ]	[ ]
Learning strategies	[ ]	[ ]
Study skills	[ ]	[ ]
Content area	[ ]	[ ]
Writing lab	[ ]	[ ]
Math lab	[ ]	[ ]

LD PROGRAM STAFF

Total number of LD Program staff (including director):

Full Time: 2 Part Time: 2

There is an advisor/advocate from the LD program available to students.

Key staff person available to work with LD students: Dr. Elaine Manglitz, Director, Disability Services

LD Program web site: http://adminservices.clayton.edu/disability/

Columbus State University

Columbus, GA

Address: 4225 University Avenue, Columbus, GA, 31907
Admissions telephone: 706 568-2035
Admissions FAX: 706 568-2462
Director of Admissions: Susan Lovell
Admissions e-mail: admissions@colstate.edu
Web site: http://www.colstate.edu
SAT Code: 5123 ACT Code: 807

LD program name: Office of Disability Services
Coordinator of Disability Services: Joy Norman
LD program telephone: (706) 568-2330
LD program e-mail: norman_joy@colstate.edu
Total campus enrollment: 6,300

GENERAL

Columbus State University is a public, coed, four-year institution. 132-acre campus in Columbus (population: 185,781), 94 miles from Atlanta; classes offered at Ft. Benning and in Americus, Griffin, LaGrange, and Thomaston. Served by airport and bus; major airport serves Atlanta. Public transportation serves campus. Semester system.

LD ADMISSIONS

A personal interview is not required. Essay is not required.

SECONDARY SCHOOL REQUIREMENTS

Graduation from secondary school required; GED accepted. The following course distribution required: 4 units of English, 4 units of math, 3 units of science, 2 units of foreign language, 3 units of social studies.

TESTING

SAT Reasoning or ACT required. SAT Subject recommended.

All enrolled freshmen (fall 2004):

Average SAT I Scores: Verbal: 495 Math: 485
Average ACT Scores: Composite: 19

Child Study Team report is not required. Tests required as part of this documentation:

- ☐ WAIS-IV
- ☐ WISC-IV
- ☐ SATA
- ☐ Woodcock-Johnson
- ☐ Nelson-Denny Reading Test
- ☐ Other

UNDERGRADUATE STUDENT BODY

Total undergraduate student enrollment: 1,748 Men, 2,876 Women.

Composition of student body (fall 2004):

	Undergraduate	Freshmen
International	1.4	1.3
Black	32.2	30.4
American Indian	0.3	0.5
Asian-American	1.9	1.9
Hispanic	4.1	3.5
White	56.0	59.0
Unreported	4.1	3.4
	100.0%	100.0%

14% are from out of state. 1% join a fraternity and 1% join a sorority. Average age of full-time undergraduates is 22. 29% of classes have fewer than 20 students, 66% have between 20 and 50 students, 5% have more than 50 students.

STUDENT HOUSING

35% of freshmen live in college housing. Freshmen are not required to live on campus. Housing is guaranteed for all undergraduates. Campus can house 965 undergraduates.

EXPENSES

Tuition (2005-06): $2,438 per year (in-state), $9,754 (out-of-state).

Room: $3,600. Board: $2,280.
There is no additional cost for LD program/services.

LD SERVICES

LD program size is not limited.

LD services available to:

■ Freshmen ■ Sophomores ■ Juniors ■ Seniors

Academic Accommodations

Curriculum		In class	
Foreign language waiver	☐	Early syllabus	☐
Lighter course load	☐	Note takers in class	■
Math waiver	☐	Priority seating	☐
Other special classes	☐	Tape recorders	■
Priority registrations	☐	Videotaped classes	■
Substitution of courses	☐	Text on tape	☐
Exams		**Services**	
Extended time	■	Diagnostic tests	■
Oral exams	■	Learning centers	■
Take home exams	☐	Proofreaders	☐
Exams on tape or computer	☐	Readers	■
Untimed exams	■	Reading Machines/Kurzweil	■
Other accommodations	☐	Special bookstore section	☐
		Typists	☐

Credit toward degree is not given for remedial courses taken.

Counseling Services

- ■ Academic
- ■ Psychological
- ■ Student Support groups
- ■ Vocational

Tutoring

Individual tutoring is available daily.

	Individual	Group
Time management	■	☐
Organizational skills	■	☐
Learning strategies	■	☐
Study skills	■	☐
Content area	■	☐
Writing lab	■	☐
Math lab	■	☐

LD PROGRAM STAFF

Total number of LD Program staff (including director):

Full Time: 1 Part Time: 1

There is an advisor/advocate from the LD program available to students.

Key staff person available to work with LD students: Joy Norman, Coordinator of Disability Services

Covenant College

Lookout Mountain, GA

Address: 14049 Scenic Highway, Lookout Mountain, GA, 30750
Admissions telephone: 888 451-2683
Admissions FAX: 706 820-0893
Vice President for Development and Admissions: Beth Nedelisky
Admissions e-mail: admissions@covenant.edu
Web site: http://www.covenant.edu
SAT Code: 6124 ACT Code: 3951

LD program name: Office of Records
Dean of Records: Rodney Miller
LD program telephone: 706 419-1135
LD program e-mail: miller@covenant.edu
LD program enrollment: 5, Total campus enrollment: 1,258

GENERAL

Covenant College is a private, coed, four-year institution. 300-acre, suburban campus in Lookout Mountain (population: 1,617), 10 miles from Chattanooga, TN and 120 miles from Atlanta. Major airport and train serve Atlanta; smaller airport and bus serve Chattanooga, TN. Semester system.

LD ADMISSIONS

Students do not complete a separate application and are simultaneously accepted to the LD program. A member of the LD program does sit on the admissions committee. A personal interview is required. Essay is required and may be typed.

For fall 2004, 2 completed self-identified LD applications were received. 2 applications were offered admission, and 2 enrolled.

SECONDARY SCHOOL REQUIREMENTS

Graduation from secondary school required; GED accepted. The following course distribution required: 4 units of English, 3 units of math, 2 units of science, 2 units of foreign language, 2 units of social studies, 3 units of academic electives.

TESTING

SAT Reasoning required; ACT may be substituted. SAT Subject required.

All enrolled freshmen (fall 2004):

Average SAT I Scores:	Verbal: 600	Math: 560
Average ACT Scores:	Composite: 25	

Child Study Team report is not required. A neuropsychological or comprehensive psycho-educational evaluation is required for admission. Must be dated within 36 months of application. Tests required as part of this documentation:

- ■ WAIS-IV
- ■ WISC-IV
- ■ SATA
- ■ Woodcock-Johnson
- ■ Nelson-Denny Reading Test
- ☐ Other

UNDERGRADUATE STUDENT BODY

Total undergraduate student enrollment: 459 Men, 720 Women.

Composition of student body (fall 2004):

	Undergraduate	Freshmen
International	0.4	0.6
Black	1.6	6.0
American Indian	0.6	0.4
Asian-American	0.6	0.9
Hispanic	1.0	1.5
White	94.2	89.6
Unreported	1.6	1.0
	100.0%	100.0%

77% are from out of state. Average age of full-time undergraduates is 20. 56% of classes have fewer than 20 students, 43% have between 20 and 50 students, 1% have more than 50 students.

STUDENT HOUSING

99% of freshmen live in college housing. Freshmen are required to live on campus. Housing is guaranteed for all undergraduates. Campus can house 772 undergraduates. Single rooms are available for students with medical or special needs. A medical note is required.

EXPENSES

Tuition (2005-06): $20,100 per year.

Room & Board: $5,880.

There is no additional cost for LD program/services.

LD SERVICES

LD program size is not limited.

LD services available to:

■ Freshmen ■ Sophomores ■ Juniors ■ Seniors

Academic Accommodations

Curriculum		**In class**	
Foreign language waiver	☐	Early syllabus	☐
Lighter course load	■	Note takers in class	☐
Math waiver	☐	Priority seating	☐
Other special classes	☐	Tape recorders	☐
Priority registrations	☐	Videotaped classes	☐
Substitution of courses	☐	Text on tape	☐
Exams		**Services**	
Extended time	■	Diagnostic tests	■
Oral exams	☐	Learning centers	☐
Take home exams	☐	Proofreaders	☐
Exams on tape or computer	☐	Readers	☐
Untimed exams	☐	Reading Machines/Kurzweil	☐
Other accommodations	☐	Special bookstore section	☐
		Typists	☐

Credit toward degree is not given for remedial courses taken.

Counseling Services

■	Academic	Meets 120 times/academic year
■	Psychological	Meets 30 times per academic year
☐	Student Support groups	
☐	Vocational	

Tutoring

Individual tutoring is available daily.

Average size of tutoring groups: 3

	Individual	Group
Time management	☐	■
Organizational skills	☐	■
Learning strategies	☐	■
Study skills	☐	■
Content area	☐	☐
Writing lab	■	☐
Math lab	■	☐

LD PROGRAM STAFF

Total number of LD Program staff (including director):

Full Time: 1 Part Time: 1

There is an advisor/advocate from the LD program available to students. The advisor/advocate meets with faculty 4 times per month and students once per month. 15 peer tutors are available to work with LD students.

Key staff person available to work with LD students: Rodney Miller, Dean of Records

Emmanuel College

Franklin Springs, GA

Address: P.O. Box 129, Franklin Springs, GA, 30639
Admissions telephone: 800 860-8800
Admissions FAX: 706 245-4424
Director of Admissions: Kirk McConnell
Admissions e-mail: admissions@eclions.net
Web site: http://www.emmanuelcollege.edu
SAT Code: 5184 ACT Code: 808

LD program name: Academic Assistance
Director: Vicki White
LD program telephone: 706 245-7226, extension 2632
LD program e-mail: vwhite@emmanuelcollege.edu
Total campus enrollment: 754

GENERAL

Emmanuel College is a private, coed, four-year institution. 80-acre, rural campus in Franklin Springs (population: 762), 30 miles from both Athens and Toccoa. Airports serve Atlanta (80 miles) and Greenville, SC. (70 miles); bus serves Athens; train serves Toccoa. Semester system.

LD ADMISSIONS

Application Deadline: 08/01. Students do not complete a separate application and are not simultaneously accepted to the LD program. A member of the LD program does sit on the admissions committee. A personal interview is recommended. Essay is not required.

SECONDARY SCHOOL REQUIREMENTS

Graduation from secondary school required; GED accepted.

TESTING

SAT Reasoning required; ACT may be substituted. SAT Subject recommended.

All enrolled freshmen (fall 2004):

Average SAT I Scores: Verbal: 505 Math: 500

Child Study Team report is not required. A neuropsychological or comprehensive psycho-education evaluation is not required for admission. Tests required as part of this documentation:

- ☐ WAIS-IV
- ☐ WISC-IV
- ☐ SATA
- ☐ Woodcock-Johnson
- ☐ Nelson-Denny Reading Test
- ☐ Other

UNDERGRADUATE STUDENT BODY

Total undergraduate student enrollment: 344 Men, 418 Women.

Composition of student body (fall 2004):

	Undergraduate	Freshmen
International	0.5	0.5
Black	14.9	16.2
American Indian	0.0	0.3
Asian-American	0.0	1.3
Hispanic	1.5	0.9
White	83.1	80.8
Unreported	0.0	0.0
	100.0%	100.0%

26% are from out of state. Average age of full-time undergraduates is 20. 70% of classes have fewer than 20 students, 28% have between 20 and 50 students, 2% have more than 50 students.

STUDENT HOUSING

41% of freshmen live in college housing. Freshmen are not required to live on campus. Housing is guaranteed for all undergraduates. Campus can house 370 undergraduates. Single rooms are available for students with medical or special needs. A medical note is not required.

EXPENSES

Tuition (2005-06): $9,800 per year.

Room: $2,150. Board: $2,550.

There is no additional cost for LD program/services.

LD SERVICES

LD program size is not limited.

LD services available to:

■ Freshmen ■ Sophomores ■ Juniors ■ Seniors

Academic Accommodations

Curriculum		**In class**	
Foreign language waiver	☐	Early syllabus	☐
Lighter course load	☐	Note takers in class	☐
Math waiver	☐	Priority seating	☐
Other special classes	☐	Tape recorders	☐
Priority registrations	☐	Videotaped classes	☐
Substitution of courses	☐	Text on tape	☐
Exams		**Services**	
Extended time	☐	Diagnostic tests	☐
Oral exams	☐	Learning centers	☐
Take home exams	☐	Proofreaders	☐
Exams on tape or computer	☐	Readers	☐
Untimed exams	☐	Reading Machines/Kurzweil	☐
Other accommodations	☐	Special bookstore section	☐
		Typists	☐

Credit toward degree is not given for remedial courses taken.

Counseling Services

- ■ Academic
- ☐ Psychological
- ☐ Student Support groups
- ☐ Vocational

Tutoring

Individual tutoring is available daily.

Average size of tutoring groups: 3

	Individual	Group
Time management	☐	☐
Organizational skills	☐	☐
Learning strategies	☐	☐
Study skills	☐	☐
Content area	☐	☐
Writing lab	☐	☐
Math lab	☐	☐

LD PROGRAM STAFF

Total number of LD Program staff (including director):

Full Time: 1 Part Time: 1

There is an advisor/advocate from the LD program available to students.

Key staff person available to work with LD students: Vicki White, Director

Emory University

Atlanta, GA

Address: 201 Dowman Drive, Atlanta, GA, 30322
Admissions telephone: 800 727-6036
Admissions FAX: 404 727-4303
Dean of Admissions: Daniel C. Walls
Admissions e-mail: admiss@emory.edu
Web site: http://www.emory.edu
SAT Code: 5187 ACT Code: 810

LD program name: Disability Services
Coordinator: Jessalyn Smiley
Total campus enrollment: 6,346

GENERAL

Emory University is a private, coed, four-year institution. 631-acre campus in Atlanta (population: 416,474), five miles from city center; branch campus in Oxford. Served by airport, bus, and train. Public transportation serves campus. Semester system.

SECONDARY SCHOOL REQUIREMENTS

Graduation from secondary school required; GED not accepted. The following course distribution required: 4 units of English, 3 units of math, 2 units of science, 2 units of foreign language, 2 units of social studies, 2 units of history, 3 units of academic electives.

TESTING

SAT Reasoning or ACT required. SAT Subject recommended.

Child Study Team report is not required. Tests required as part of this documentation:

- [ ] WAIS IV
- [ ] WISC-IV
- [ ] SATA
- [ ] Woodcock-Johnson
- [ ] Nelson-Denny Reading Test
- [ ] Other

UNDERGRADUATE STUDENT BODY

Total undergraduate student enrollment: 2,863 Men, 3,511 Women.

Composition of student body (fall 2004):

	Undergraduate	Freshmen
International	5.2	3.6
Black	8.1	9.1
American Indian	0.3	0.2
Asian-American	15.5	15.7
Hispanic	2.8	2.8
White	57.8	61.2
Unreported	10.3	7.4
	100.0%	100.0%

81% are from out of state. 31% join a fraternity and 33% join a sorority. Average age of full-time undergraduates is 20. 67% of classes have fewer than 20 students, 26% have between 20 and 50 students, 7% have more than 50 students.

STUDENT HOUSING

97% of freshmen live in college housing. Freshmen are required to live on campus. Housing is guaranteed for all undergraduates. Campus can house 3,913 undergraduates.

EXPENSES

Tuition (2005-06): $30,400 per year.
Room: $6,112. Board: $3,640.

There is no additional cost for LD program/services.

LD SERVICES

LD program size is not limited.

LD services available to:

- [ ] Freshmen
- [ ] Sophomores
- [ ] Juniors
- [ ] Seniors

Academic Accommodations

Curriculum

- [ ] Foreign language waiver
- [x] Lighter course load
- [ ] Math waiver
- [x] Other special classes
- [ ] Priority registrations
- [ ] Substitution of courses

Exams

- [x] Extended time
- [x] Oral exams
- [ ] Take home exams
- [ ] Exams on tape or computer
- [ ] Untimed exams
- [ ] Other accommodations

In class

- [ ] Early syllabus
- [x] Note takers in class
- [ ] Priority seating
- [ ] Tape recorders
- [ ] Videotaped classes
- [ ] Text on tape

Services

- [ ] Diagnostic tests
- [ ] Learning centers
- [ ] Proofreaders
- [x] Readers
- [ ] Reading Machines/Kurzweil
- [ ] Special bookstore section
- [ ] Typists

Credit toward degree is not given for remedial courses taken.

Counseling Services

- [ ] Academic
- [ ] Psychological
- [ ] Student Support groups
- [ ] Vocational

Tutoring

	Individual	Group
Time management	[ ]	[ ]
Organizational skills	[ ]	[ ]
Learning strategies	[ ]	[ ]
Study skills	[ ]	[ ]
Content area	[ ]	[ ]
Writing lab	[ ]	[ ]
Math lab	[ ]	[ ]

LD PROGRAM STAFF

Key staff person available to work with LD students: Jessalyn Smiley, Coordinator, Disability Services.

Fort Valley State University

Fort Valley, GA

Address: 1005 State University Drive, Fort Valley, GA, 31030-4313
Admissions telephone: 478 825-6307
Admissions FAX: 478 825-6057
Dean of Admissions and Enrollment Management: Debra McGhee
Admissions e-mail: admissap@mail.fvsu.edu
Web site: http://www.fvsu.edu
SAT Code: 5220 ACT Code: 814

LD program name: Differently Abled Services
Director: Alfred Conteh
LD program telephone: 478 825-6744
LD program e-mail: conteha@fvsu.edu
Total campus enrollment: 2313

GENERAL

Fort Valley State University is a public, coed, four-year institution. 630-acre campus in Fort Valley (population: 8,005), 20 miles southeast of Macon; branch campuses in Dublin, Macon, and Warner Robins. Served by bus; airport serves Macon; major airport serves Atlanta (100 miles). Semester system.

LD ADMISSIONS

A personal interview is not required. Essay is not required.

SECONDARY SCHOOL REQUIREMENTS

Graduation from secondary school required; GED accepted. The following course distribution required: 4 units of English, 3 units of math, 3 units of science, 2 units of foreign language, 3 units of social studies, 1 unit of history.

TESTING

SAT Reasoning or ACT required.

All enrolled freshmen (fall 2004):

Average SAT I Scores:	Verbal: 450	Math: 490
Average ACT Scores:	Composite: 20	

Child Study Team report is not required. Tests required as part of this documentation:

- [ ] WAIS-IV
- [ ] WISC-IV
- [ ] SATA
- [ ] Woodcock-Johnson
- [ ] Nelson-Denny Reading Test
- [ ] Other

UNDERGRADUATE STUDENT BODY

Total undergraduate student enrollment: 1,039 Men, 1,293 Women.

Composition of student body (fall 2004):

	Undergraduate	Freshmen
International	0.9	1.7
Black	97.2	94.9
American Indian	0.0	0.0
Asian-American	0.0	0.0
Hispanic	0.2	0.0
White	1.7	3.4
Unreported	0.0	0.0
	100.0%	100.0%

6% are from out of state. 36% of classes have fewer than 20 students, 63% have between 20 and 50 students, 1% have more than 50 students.

STUDENT HOUSING

Freshmen are not required to live on campus. Housing is guaranteed for all undergraduates. Campus can house 1,032 undergraduates.

EXPENSES

Tuition (2005-06): $2,438 per year (in-state), $9,754 (out-of-state).
Room: $2,200. Board: $2,296.
There is no additional cost for LD program/services.

LD SERVICES

LD program size is limited.

LD services available to:

- [x] Freshmen
- [x] Sophomores
- [x] Juniors
- [x] Seniors

Academic Accommodations

Curriculum		In class	
Foreign language waiver	[ ]	Early syllabus	[ ]
Lighter course load	[x]	Note takers in class	[x]
Math waiver	[ ]	Priority seating	[ ]
Other special classes	[ ]	Tape recorders	[x]
Priority registrations	[ ]	Videotaped classes	[ ]
Substitution of courses	[ ]	Text on tape	[ ]
Exams		**Services**	
Extended time	[ ]	Diagnostic tests	[ ]
Oral exams	[x]	Learning centers	[x]
Take home exams	[ ]	Proofreaders	[ ]
Exams on tape or computer	[ ]	Readers	[x]
Untimed exams	[x]	Reading Machines/Kurzweil	[x]
Other accommodations	[ ]	Special bookstore section	[ ]
		Typists	[ ]

Credit toward degree is not given for remedial courses taken.

Counseling Services

- [ ] Academic
- [ ] Psychological
- [ ] Student Support groups
- [ ] Vocational

Tutoring

Individual tutoring is available daily.

Average size of tutoring groups: 3

	Individual	Group
Time management	[x]	[ ]
Organizational skills	[x]	[ ]
Learning strategies	[x]	[ ]
Study skills	[x]	[ ]
Content area	[x]	[ ]
Writing lab	[x]	[x]
Math lab	[x]	[x]

LD PROGRAM STAFF

Total number of LD Program staff (including director):

Full Time: 2 Part Time: 2

There is an advisor/advocate from the LD program available to students. The advisor/advocate meets with faculty once per month and students two times per month.

Key staff person available to work with LD students: Alfred Conteh, Director

Georgia College and State University

Milledgeville, GA

Address: 231 West Hancock Street, Milledgeville, GA, 31061
Admissions telephone: 800 342-0471 (in-state)
Admissions FAX: 478 445-1914
Associate Vice President for Enrollment Services: Mike Augustine
Admissions e-mail: info@gcsu.edu
Web site: http://www.gcsu.edu
SAT Code: 5252 ACT Code: 828

Chair, Dept of Special Education & Administration: Dr. Craig Smith
LD program telephone: 478 445-4577
LD program e-mail: craig.smith@gcsu.edu
LD program enrollment: 108, Total campus enrollment: 4,566

GENERAL

Georgia College and State University is a public, coed, four-year institution. 666-acre campus in Milledgeville (population: 18,757), 30 miles from Macon; branch campuses in Macon and Warner Robins. Major airport serves Atlanta (90 miles); bus serves Macon. School operates transportation on campus. Semester system.

LD ADMISSIONS

Students do not complete a separate application and are not simultaneously accepted to the LD program. A member of the LD program does not sit on the admissions committee. A personal interview is not required. Essay is not required.

SECONDARY SCHOOL REQUIREMENTS

Graduation from secondary school required; GED accepted. The following course distribution required: 4 units of English, 4 units of math, 3 units of science, 2 units of foreign language, 3 units of social studies.

TESTING

SAT Reasoning or ACT required. SAT Subject required.

All enrolled freshmen (fall 2004):

Average SAT I Scores:	Verbal: 559	Math: 558
Average ACT Scores:	Composite: 23	

Child Study Team report is not required. A neuropsychological or comprehensive psycho-educational evaluation is required for admission. Must be dated within 36 months of application. Tests required as part of this documentation:

- ■ WAIS-IV
- ■ WISC-IV
- ■ SATA
- ■ Woodcock-Johnson
- ☐ Nelson-Denny Reading Test
- ■ Other

UNDERGRADUATE STUDENT BODY

Total undergraduate student enrollment: 1,566 Men, 2,517 Women.

Composition of student body (fall 2004):

	Undergraduate	Freshmen
International	1.2	1.9
Black	4.2	8.8
American Indian	0.3	0.4
Asian-American	1.1	1.1
Hispanic	1.8	1.0
White	91.4	86.8
Unreported	0.0	0.0
	100.0%	100.0%

1% are from out of state. 12% join a fraternity and 8% join a sorority. Average age of full-time undergraduates is 21. 44% of classes have fewer than 20 students, 55% have between 20 and 50 students, 1% have more than 50 students.

STUDENT HOUSING

97% of freshmen live in college housing. Freshmen are required to live on campus. Housing is guaranteed for all undergraduates. Campus can house 1,777 undergraduates. Single rooms are available for students with medical or special needs. A medical note is required.

EXPENSES

Tuition (2005-06): $3,404 per year (in-state), $13,616 (out-of-state).
Room: $3,690. Board: $3,188.
There is no additional cost for LD program/services.

LD SERVICES

LD program size is not limited.

LD services available to:

■ Freshmen ■ Sophomores ■ Juniors ■ Seniors

Academic Accommodations

Curriculum		**In class**	
Foreign language waiver	☐	Early syllabus	☐
Lighter course load	■	Note takers in class	☐
Math waiver	☐	Priority seating	☐
Other special classes	☐	Tape recorders	■
Priority registrations	■	Videotaped classes	☐
Substitution of courses	☐	Text on tape	☐
Exams		**Services**	
Extended time	■	Diagnostic tests	■
Oral exams	■	Learning centers	☐
Take home exams	☐	Proofreaders	☐
Exams on tape or computer	☐	Readers	■
Untimed exams	■	Reading Machines/Kurzweil	☐
Other accommodations	☐	Special bookstore section	☐
		Typists	☐

Credit toward degree is not given for remedial courses taken.

Counseling Services

- ■ Academic
- ■ Psychological
- ■ Student Support groups
- ■ Vocational

Tutoring

Individual tutoring is available weekly.

Average size of tutoring groups: 4

	Individual	Group
Time management	☐	■
Organizational skills	☐	■
Learning strategies	☐	■
Study skills	☐	■
Content area	☐	■
Writing lab	■	☐
Math lab	■	☐

LD PROGRAM STAFF

Total number of LD Program staff (including director):

Full Time: 3 Part Time: 3

There is an advisor/advocate from the LD program available to students.

Key staff person available to work with LD students: Dr. Craig Smith, Chair, Dept. of Special Education & Administration

Georgia Institute of Technology

Atlanta, GA

Address: 225 North Avenue, NW, Atlanta, GA, 30332
Admissions telephone: 404 894-4154
Admissions FAX: 404 894-9511
Director of Admissions: Ingrid Hayes
Admissions e-mail: admission@gatech.edu
Web site: http://www.gatech.edu
SAT Code: 5248 ACT Code: 818

LD program name: Access Disabled Assistance Programs for Tech Students (ADAPTS)
LD program address: 353 Ferst Drive, Suite 210
Disability Services Specialist: Tameeka Hunter
LD program telephone: 404 894-2564
LD program e-mail: tameeka.hunter@vpss.gatech.edu
LD program enrollment: 215, Total campus enrollment: 11,546

GENERAL

Georgia Institute of Technology is a public, coed, four-year institution. 400-acre, urban campus in Atlanta (population: 416,474); branch campus abroad in Lorraine, France. Served by airport, bus, and train. School operates transportation to local transit stations. Public transportation serves campus. Semester system.

LD ADMISSIONS

Students do not complete a separate application and are not simultaneously accepted to the LD program. A member of the LD program does not sit on the admissions committee. High school waivers are accepted for foreign language. A personal interview is not required. Essay is not required. Some course requirements may be substituted.

SECONDARY SCHOOL REQUIREMENTS

Graduation from secondary school required; GED accepted. The following course distribution required: 4 units of English, 4 units of math, 3 units of science, 2 units of foreign language, 3 units of social studies.

TESTING

SAT Reasoning required; ACT may be substituted. SAT Subject required.

All enrolled freshmen (fall 2004):

Average SAT I Scores: Verbal: 644 Math: 690
Average ACT Scores: Composite: 28

Child Study Team report is required if student is classified. A neuropsychological or comprehensive psycho-educational evaluation is required for admission. Must be dated within 36 months of application. Tests required as part of this documentation:

■ WAIS-IV
■ WISC-IV
□ SATA
■ Woodcock-Johnson
■ Nelson-Denny Reading Test
□ Other

UNDERGRADUATE STUDENT BODY

Total undergraduate student enrollment: 7,872 Men, 3,171 Women.

Composition of student body (fall 2004):

	Undergraduate	Freshmen
International	4.0	4.7
Black	5.7	7.4
American Indian	0.4	0.3
Asian-American	15.1	15.1
Hispanic	3.8	3.4
White	70.5	68.4
Unreported	0.5	0.7
	100.0%	100.0%

32% are from out of state. 21% join a fraternity and 24% join a sorority. Average age of full-time undergraduates is 20. 38% of classes have fewer than 20 students, 42% have between 20 and 50 students, 20% have more than 50 students.

STUDENT HOUSING

94% of freshmen live in college housing. Freshmen are not required to live on campus. Housing is guaranteed for all undergraduates. Campus can house 5,633 undergraduates. Single rooms are available for students with medical or special needs. A medical note is required.

EXPENSES

Tuition (2005-06): $3,638 per year (in-state), $17,980 (out-of-state).
Room: $3,858-$4,200. Board: $2,600.
There is no additional cost for LD program/services.

LD SERVICES

LD program size is not limited.

LD services available to:

■ Freshmen ■ Sophomores ■ Juniors ■ Seniors

Academic Accommodations

Curriculum		In class	
Foreign language waiver	■	Early syllabus	□
Lighter course load	■	Note takers in class	■
Math waiver	□	Priority seating	■
Other special classes	□	Tape recorders	■
Priority registrations	■	Videotaped classes	■
Substitution of courses	□	Text on tape	■
Exams		**Services**	
Extended time	■	Diagnostic tests	■
Oral exams	■	Learning centers	■
Take home exams	□	Proofreaders	□
Exams on tape or computer	■	Readers	■
Untimed exams	□	Reading Machines/Kurzweil	□
Other accommodations	■	Special bookstore section	□
		Typists	■

Credit toward degree is not given for remedial courses taken.

Counseling Services

■ Academic
■ Psychological
■ Student Support groups
■ Vocational

Tutoring

Individual tutoring is available weekly.

	Individual	Group
Time management	■	■
Organizational skills	■	■
Learning strategies	■	■
Study skills	■	■
Content area	□	■
Writing lab	□	□
Math lab	■	■

LD PROGRAM STAFF

Total number of LD Program staff (including director):

Full Time: 2 Part Time: 2

There is an advisor/advocate from the LD program available to students. 2 graduate students are available to work with LD students.

Key staff person available to work with LD students: Tameeka Hunter, Disability Services Specialist

LD Program web site: http://www.adapts.gatech.edu

Georgia Southern University

Statesboro, GA

Address: P.O. Box 8033, Statesboro, GA, 30460
Admissions telephone: 912 681-5391
Admissions FAX: 912 486-7240
Director of Admissions: Susan Davies
Admissions e-mail: admissions@georgiasouthern.edu
Web site: http://www.georgiasouthern.edu
SAT Code: 5253 ACT Code: 830

LD program name: Student Disability Resource Center
LD program address: P.O. Box 8037
Director, Student Disability Resource Center: Wayne Akins
LD program telephone: 912 871-1566
LD program e-mail: cwakins@georgiasouthern.edu
LD program enrollment: 134, Total campus enrollment: 14,092

GENERAL

Georgia Southern University is a public, coed, four-year institution. 630-acre campus in Statesboro (population: 22,698), 50 miles from Savannah; satellite campuses in Augusta, Dublin, Hinesville, and Savannah. Served by bus; major airport and train serve Savannah. Semester system.

LD ADMISSIONS

Application Deadline: 05/01. Students do not complete a separate application and are not simultaneously accepted to the LD program. A member of the LD program does not sit on the admissions committee. High school waivers are accepted for foreign language. A personal interview is not required. Essay is not required.

For fall 2004, 41 completed self-identified LD applications were received. 41 applications were offered admission, and 40 enrolled.

SECONDARY SCHOOL REQUIREMENTS

Graduation from secondary school required; GED not accepted. The following course distribution required: 4 units of English, 4 units of math, 3 units of science, 2 units of foreign language, 3 units of social studies.

TESTING

SAT Reasoning or ACT required. SAT Subject required.

All enrolled freshmen (fall 2004):

Average SAT I Scores:	Verbal: 539	Math: 541
Average ACT Scores:	Composite: 21	

Child Study Team report is not required. A neuropsychological or comprehensive psycho-educational evaluation is required for admission. Must be dated within 36 months of application. Tests required as part of this documentation:

- ■ WAIS-IV
- ☐ WISC-IV
- ☐ SATA
- ■ Woodcock-Johnson
- ■ Nelson-Denny Reading Test
- ■ Other

UNDERGRADUATE STUDENT BODY

Total undergraduate student enrollment: 6,193 Men, 6,605 Women.

Composition of student body (fall 2004):

	Undergraduate	Freshmen
International	0.4	0.9
Black	20.4	23.4
American Indian	0.2	0.2
Asian-American	1.4	1.2
Hispanic	2.2	1.4
White	75.4	72.9
Unreported	0.0	0.0
	100.0%	100.0%

5% are from out of state. 13% join a fraternity and 14% join a sorority. Average age of full-time undergraduates is 21. 29% of classes have fewer than 20 students, 60% have between 20 and 50 students, 11% have more than 50 students.

STUDENT HOUSING

68% of freshmen live in college housing. Freshmen are not required to live on campus. Housing is guaranteed for all undergraduates. Campus can house 3,925 undergraduates. Single rooms are available for students with medical or special needs. A medical note is required.

EXPENSES

Tuition (2005-06): $2,438 per year (in-state), $9,754 (out-of-state).
Room: $4,034. Board: $2,266.
There is no additional cost for LD program/services.

LD SERVICES

LD program size is not limited.

LD services available to:

■ Freshmen ■ Sophomores ■ Juniors ■ Seniors

Academic Accommodations

Curriculum		**In class**	
Foreign language waiver	■	Early syllabus	☐
Lighter course load	■	Note takers in class	■
Math waiver	☐	Priority seating	■
Other special classes	■	Tape recorders	■
Priority registrations	■	Videotaped classes	☐
Substitution of courses	■	Text on tape	■
Exams		**Services**	
Extended time	■	Diagnostic tests	■
Oral exams	■	Learning centers	■
Take home exams	☐	Proofreaders	■
Exams on tape or computer	■	Readers	■
Untimed exams	☐	Reading Machines/Kurzweil	■
Other accommodations	■	Special bookstore section	☐
		Typists	■

Credit toward degree is not given for remedial courses taken.

Counseling Services

- ☐ Academic
- ☐ Psychological
- ☐ Student Support groups
- ☐ Vocational

Tutoring

Individual tutoring is available daily.

Average size of tutoring groups: 5

	Individual	Group
Time management	■	■
Organizational skills	■	■
Learning strategies	■	■
Study skills	☐	☐
Content area	☐	☐
Writing lab	■	■
Math lab	☐	■

LD PROGRAM STAFF

Total number of LD Program staff (including director):

Full Time: 4 Part Time: 4

There is an advisor/advocate from the LD program available to students. 2 graduate students are available to work with LD students.

Key staff person available to work with LD students: Wayne Akins, Director

Georgia State University

Atlanta, GA

Address: University Plaza, Atlanta, GA, 30303-3083
Admissions telephone: 404 651-2365
Admissions FAX: 404 651-4811
Director of Admissions: Diane Weber
Admissions e-mail: admissions@gsu.edu
Web site: http://www.gsu.edu
SAT Code: 5251 ACT Code: 826

LD program name: Disability Services
LD program address: P.O. Box 3973
Director of Disability Services: Rodney Pennamon
LD program telephone: 404 651-3523
LD program e-mail: disrep@langate.gsu.edu
LD program enrollment: 150, Total campus enrollment: 19,894

GENERAL

Georgia State University is a public, coed, four-year institution. 57-acre, urban campus in Atlanta (population: 416,474); branch campus in Alpharetta. Served by airport, bus, and train. School operates transportation to dorms and off-campus parking. Public transportation serves campus. Semester system.

LD ADMISSIONS

Students do not complete a separate application and are simultaneously accepted to the LD program. A member of the LD program does not sit on the admissions committee. A personal interview is not required. Essay is not required.

SECONDARY SCHOOL REQUIREMENTS

Graduation from secondary school required; GED not accepted. The following course distribution required: 4 units of English, 4 units of math, 3 units of science, 2 units of foreign language, 2 units of social studies, 1 unit of history.

TESTING

SAT Reasoning or ACT required. SAT Subject required.

All enrolled freshmen (fall 2004):

Average SAT I Scores:	Verbal: 542	Math: 546
Average ACT Scores:	Composite: 22	

Child Study Team report is not required. A neuropsychological or comprehensive psycho-educational evaluation is required for admission. Tests required as part of this documentation:

- [x] WAIS-IV
- [x] WISC-IV
- [ ] SATA
- [x] Woodcock-Johnson
- [x] Nelson-Denny Reading Test
- [x] Other

UNDERGRADUATE STUDENT BODY

Total undergraduate student enrollment: 6,330 Men, 10,114 Women.

Composition of student body (fall 2004):

	Undergraduate	Freshmen
International	2.7	2.9
Black	29.2	31.8
American Indian	0.2	0.3
Asian-American	13.1	9.7
Hispanic	4.1	3.1
White	42.2	38.5
Unreported	8.5	13.7
	100.0%	100.0%

1% are from out of state. 3% join a fraternity and 4% join a sorority. Average age of full-time undergraduates is 22. 14% of classes have fewer than 20 students, 73% have between 20 and 50 students, 13% have more than 50 students.

STUDENT HOUSING

Freshmen are not required to live on campus. Housing is guaranteed for all undergraduates. Campus can house 2,435 undergraduates. Single rooms are available for students with medical or special needs. A medical note is not required.

EXPENSES

Tuition (2005-06): $3,638 per year (in-state), $14,552 (out-of-state).
Room & Board: $6,980.
There is no additional cost for LD program/services.

LD SERVICES

LD program size is not limited.

LD services available to:

- [x] Freshmen
- [x] Sophomores
- [x] Juniors
- [x] Seniors

Academic Accommodations

Curriculum		In class	
Foreign language waiver	[ ]	Early syllabus	[ ]
Lighter course load	[x]	Note takers in class	[x]
Math waiver	[ ]	Priority seating	[x]
Other special classes	[ ]	Tape recorders	[ ]
Priority registrations	[x]	Videotaped classes	[ ]
Substitution of courses	[x]	Text on tape	[x]
Exams		**Services**	
Extended time	[x]	Diagnostic tests	[x]
Oral exams	[x]	Learning centers	[ ]
Take home exams	[ ]	Proofreaders	[ ]
Exams on tape or computer	[x]	Readers	[ ]
Untimed exams	[ ]	Reading Machines/Kurzweil	[x]
Other accommodations	[x]	Special bookstore section	[ ]
		Typists	[ ]

Credit toward degree is not given for remedial courses taken.

Counseling Services

- [x] Academic
- [x] Psychological
- [x] Student Support groups
- [x] Vocational

Tutoring

Individual tutoring is available weekly.

	Individual	Group
Time management	[x]	[ ]
Organizational skills	[x]	[ ]
Learning strategies	[x]	[ ]
Study skills	[x]	[ ]
Content area	[ ]	[ ]
Writing lab	[x]	[ ]
Math lab	[x]	[ ]

LD PROGRAM STAFF

Total number of LD Program staff (including director):

Full Time: 4 Part Time: 4

There is an advisor/advocate from the LD program available to students.

Key staff person available to work with LD students: Louise Bedrossian, Cognitive Disabliity Specialist.

University of Georgia

Athens, GA

Address: Terrell Hall, Athens, GA, 30602
Admissions telephone: 706 542-8776
Admissions FAX: 706 542-1466
Director of Admissions: Nancy G. McDuff
Admissions e-mail: undergrad@admissions.uga.edu
Web site: http://www.uga.edu
SAT Code: 5813 ACT Code: 872

LD program name: Learning Disabilities Center
LD program address: 331 Milledge Hall,
Senior Disability Specialist: Patricia Marshall
LD program telephone: 706 542-7034
LD program enrollment: 200, Total campus enrollment: 25,019

GENERAL

University of Georgia is a public, coed, four-year institution. 614-acre main campus in Athens (population: 100,266), 80 miles from Atlanta. Served by airport and bus; major airport and train serve Atlanta. School operates transportation on campus. Public transportation serves campus. Semester system.

LD ADMISSIONS

Students do not complete a separate application and are not simultaneously accepted to the LD program. A member of the LD program does not sit on the admissions committee. A personal interview is not required. Essay is required and may be typed.

For fall 2004, 50 completed self-identified LD applications were received. 48 applications were offered admission, and 47 enrolled.

SECONDARY SCHOOL REQUIREMENTS

Graduation from secondary school required; GED accepted. The following course distribution required: 4 units of English, 4 units of math, 3 units of science, 2 units of foreign language, 1 unit of social studies, 2 units of history.

TESTING

SAT Reasoning or ACT required. SAT Subject required.

All enrolled freshmen (fall 2004):

Average SAT I Scores:	Verbal: 616	Math: 618
Average ACT Scores:	Composite: 27	

Child Study Team report is not required. A neuropsychological or comprehensive psycho-educational evaluation is required for admission. Must be dated within 36 months of application. Tests required as part of this documentation:

- [x] WAIS-IV
- [ ] WISC-IV
- [x] SATA
- [x] Woodcock-Johnson
- [x] Nelson-Denny Reading Test
- [x] Other

UNDERGRADUATE STUDENT BODY

Total undergraduate student enrollment: 10,949 Men, 13,091 Women.

Composition of student body (fall 2004):

	Undergraduate	Freshmen
International	0.8	0.7
Black	4.9	4.7
American Indian	0.2	0.2
Asian-American	5.6	4.6
Hispanic	1.7	1.8
White	86.8	88.0
Unreported	0.0	0.0
	100.0%	100.0%

10% are from out of state. 15% join a fraternity and 18% join a sorority. Average age of full-time undergraduates is 21. 35% of classes have fewer than 20 students, 54% have between 20 and 50 students, 11% have more than 50 students.

STUDENT HOUSING

97% of freshmen live in college housing. Freshmen are required to live on campus. Housing is guaranteed for all undergraduates. First priority is given to freshmen. Campus can house 7,529 undergraduates. Single rooms are available for students with medical or special needs. A medical note is required.

EXPENSES

Tuition (2005-06): $3,638 per year (in-state), $15,858 (out-of-state). Tuition is different for forestry and pharmacy programs.
Room & Board: $6,376.
There is no additional cost for LD program/services.

LD SERVICES

LD program size is not limited.

LD services available to:

- [x] Freshmen
- [x] Sophomores
- [x] Juniors
- [x] Seniors

Academic Accommodations

Curriculum

- [ ] Foreign language waiver
- [x] Lighter course load
- [ ] Math waiver
- [ ] Other special classes
- [x] Priority registrations
- [ ] Substitution of courses

Exams

- [x] Extended time
- [x] Oral exams
- [ ] Take home exams
- [ ] Exams on tape or computer
- [ ] Untimed exams
- [ ] Other accommodations

In class

- [ ] Early syllabus
- [x] Note takers in class
- [ ] Priority seating
- [x] Tape recorders
- [ ] Videotaped classes
- [x] Text on tape

Services

- [x] Diagnostic tests
- [x] Learning centers
- [ ] Proofreaders
- [x] Readers
- [x] Reading Machines/Kurzweil
- [ ] Special bookstore section
- [x] Typists

Credit toward degree is not given for remedial courses taken.

Counseling Services

- [x] Academic
- [x] Psychological
- [x] Student Support groups — Meets 24 times per academic year
- [x] Vocational

Tutoring

Individual tutoring is available daily.

Average size of tutoring groups: 3

	Individual	Group
Time management	[x]	[ ]
Organizational skills	[x]	[ ]
Learning strategies	[x]	[ ]
Study skills	[x]	[ ]
Content area	[x]	[x]
Writing lab	[x]	[x]
Math lab	[x]	[x]

LD PROGRAM STAFF

Total number of LD Program staff (including director):

Full Time: 8 Part Time: 8

There is an advisor/advocate from the LD program available to students.

Key staff person available to work with LD students: Patricia Marshall, Senior Disability Specialist

LD Program web site: www.coe.uga.edu/ldcenter/index.html

Kennesaw State University

Kennesaw, GA

Address: 1000 Chastain Road, Kennesaw, GA, 30144-5591
Admissions telephone: 770 423-6300
Admissions FAX: 770 423-6541
Director of Admissions: Joe F. Head
Admissions e-mail: ksuadmit@kennesaw.edu
Web site: http://www.kennesaw.edu
SAT Code: 5359 ACT Code: 833

LD program name: Disabled Student Support Services
LD program address: 1000 Chastain Road, #0502
Assistant Director: Carol Pope
LD program telephone: 770 423-6443
LD program e-mail: cpope@kennesaw.edu
LD program enrollment: 53, Total campus enrollment: 16,073

GENERAL

Kennesaw State University is a public, coed, four-year institution. 196-acre campus in Kennesaw (population: 21,675), 25 miles from Atlanta. Major airport and train serve Atlanta; bus serves Marietta (10 miles). Public transportation serves campus. Semester system.

LD ADMISSIONS

Students do not complete a separate application and are not simultaneously accepted to the LD program. A member of the LD program does not sit on the admissions committee. High school waivers are accepted for foreign language. A personal interview is not required. Essay is not required.

SECONDARY SCHOOL REQUIREMENTS

Graduation from secondary school required; GED accepted. The following course distribution required: 4 units of English, 4 units of math, 3 units of science, 2 units of foreign language, 3 units of social studies.

TESTING

SAT Reasoning or ACT required. SAT Subject recommended.

All enrolled freshmen (fall 2004):

Average SAT I Scores: Verbal: 533 Math: 536
Average ACT Scores: Composite: 22

Child Study Team report is not required. A neuropsychological or comprehensive psycho-educational evaluation is required for admission. Must be dated within 36 months of application. Tests required as part of this documentation:

- ■ WAIS-IV
- ■ WISC-IV
- ■ SATA
- ■ Woodcock-Johnson
- ■ Nelson-Denny Reading Test
- ■ Other

UNDERGRADUATE STUDENT BODY

Total undergraduate student enrollment: 4,398 Men, 7,266 Women.

Composition of student body (fall 2004):

	Undergraduate	Freshmen
International	3.2	3.1
Black	5.2	9.5
American Indian	0.3	0.3
Asian-American	4.0	2.9
Hispanic	3.7	2.7
White	83.6	81.5
Unreported	0.0	0.0
	100.0%	100.0%

1% are from out of state. 1% join a fraternity and 1% join a sorority. Average age of full-time undergraduates is 23. 23% of classes have fewer than 20 students, 64% have between 20 and 50 students, 13% have more than 50 students.

STUDENT HOUSING

33% of freshmen live in college housing. Freshmen are not required to live on campus. Housing is not guaranteed for all undergraduates. Limited number of beds. Campus can house 2,059 undergraduates. Single rooms are not available for students with medical or special needs.

EXPENSES

Tuition (2005-06): $2,438 per year (in-state), $9,754 (out-of-state).
Room: $4,900.

There is no additional cost for LD program/services.

LD SERVICES

LD program size is not limited.

LD services available to:

■ Freshmen ■ Sophomores ■ Juniors ■ Seniors

Academic Accommodations

Curriculum		In class	
Foreign language waiver	☐	Early syllabus	☐
Lighter course load	☐	Note takers in class	☐
Math waiver	☐	Priority seating	■
Other special classes	☐	Tape recorders	■
Priority registrations	■	Videotaped classes	☐
Substitution of courses	☐	Text on tape	■
Exams		**Services**	
Extended time	■	Diagnostic tests	■
Oral exams	■	Learning centers	☐
Take home exams	☐	Proofreaders	☐
Exams on tape or computer	■	Readers	☐
Untimed exams	☐	Reading Machines/Kurzweil	■
Other accommodations	☐	Special bookstore section	☐
		Typists	☐

Credit toward degree is not given for remedial courses taken.

Counseling Services

- ■ Academic
- ■ Psychological
- ■ Student Support groups — Meets 12 times per academic year
- ■ Vocational

Tutoring

Individual tutoring is available weekly.

Average size of tutoring groups: 5

	Individual	Group
Time management	■	■
Organizational skills	■	☐
Learning strategies	■	■
Study skills	■	■
Content area	☐	☐
Writing lab	■	■
Math lab	■	☐

LD PROGRAM STAFF

Total number of LD Program staff (including director):

Full Time: 1 Part Time: 1

There is an advisor/advocate from the LD program available to students. Three peer tutors are available to work with LD students.

Key staff person available to work with LD students: Carol Pope, Assistant Director

LD Program web site: www.kennesaw.edu/stu_dev/dsss

LaGrange College

LaGrange, GA

Address: 601 Broad Street, LaGrange, GA, 30240
Admissions telephone: 800 593-2885
Admissions FAX: 706 880-8010
Director of Admissions: Wells Shepard
Admissions e-mail: admission@lagrange.edu
Web site: http://www.lagrange.edu
SAT Code: 5362 ACT Code: 834

Director of Counseling Services: Pamela Tremblay
LD program telephone: 706 880-8313
LD program e-mail: pscotto@lagrange.edu
LD program enrollment: 15, Total campus enrollment: 993

GENERAL

LaGrange College is a private, coed, four-year institution. 120-acre campus in LaGrange (population: 25,998), 70 miles southwest of Atlanta; branch campus in Albany. Served by bus; major airport and train serve Atlanta. 4-1-4 system.

LD ADMISSIONS

A personal interview is recommended. Essay is required and may be typed.

SECONDARY SCHOOL REQUIREMENTS

Graduation from secondary school required; GED accepted. The following course distribution required: 4 units of English, 4 units of math, 3 units of science, 3 units of social studies.

TESTING

SAT Reasoning or ACT required. SAT Subject required.

All enrolled freshmen (fall 2004):

Average SAT I Scores:	Verbal: 516	Math: 517
Average ACT Scores:	Composite: 20	

Child Study Team report is not required. A neuropsychological or comprehensive psycho-educational evaluation is required for admission. Must be dated within 36 months of application. Tests required as part of this documentation:

- ■ WAIS-IV
- ■ WISC-IV
- ■ SATA
- ■ Woodcock-Johnson
- ☐ Nelson-Denny Reading Test
- ☐ Other

UNDERGRADUATE STUDENT BODY

Total undergraduate student enrollment: 336 Men, 566 Women.

Composition of student body (fall 2004):

	Undergraduate	Freshmen
International	0.0	0.0
Black	16.8	19.2
American Indian	1.4	0.6
Asian-American	0.9	1.3
Hispanic	1.8	1.1
White	76.8	75.4
Unreported	2.3	2.4
	100.0%	100.0%

10% are from out of state. 37% join a fraternity and 28% join a sorority. Average age of full-time undergraduates is 21. 87% of classes have fewer than 20 students, 13% have between 20 and 50 students.

STUDENT HOUSING

84% of freshmen live in college housing. Freshmen are required to live on campus. Housing is guaranteed for all undergraduates. Campus can house 647 undergraduates. Single rooms are available for students with medical or special needs. A medical note is required.

EXPENSES

Tuition (2005-06): $16,200 per year.

Room & Board: $6,674.

There is no additional cost for LD program/services.

LD SERVICES

LD program size is not limited.

LD services available to:

■ Freshmen ■ Sophomores ■ Juniors ■ Seniors

Academic Accommodations

Curriculum		**In class**	
Foreign language waiver	☐	Early syllabus	☐
Lighter course load	■	Note takers in class	■
Math waiver	☐	Priority seating	☐
Other special classes	☐	Tape recorders	■
Priority registrations	☐	Videotaped classes	☐
Substitution of courses	☐	Text on tape	☐
Exams		**Services**	
Extended time	■	Diagnostic tests	☐
Oral exams	■	Learning centers	☐
Take home exams	☐	Proofreaders	☐
Exams on tape or computer	☐	Readers	■
Untimed exams	■	Reading Machines/Kurzweil	☐
Other accommodations	☐	Special bookstore section	☐
		Typists	☐

Credit toward degree is not given for remedial courses taken.

Counseling Services

■	Academic	Meets 32 times per academic year
■	Psychological	Meets 32 times per academic year
☐	Student Support groups	
☐	Vocational	

Tutoring

Individual tutoring is available daily.

	Individual	Group
Time management	☐	■
Organizational skills	☐	■
Learning strategies	☐	■
Study skills	☐	■
Content area	■	■
Writing lab	■	■
Math lab	☐	☐

LD PROGRAM STAFF

There is an advisor/advocate from the LD program available to students. The advisor/advocate meets with students four times per month. 12 peer tutors are available to work with LD students.

Key staff person available to work with LD students: Pamela Tremblay, Dirctor of Counseling Services

Life University

Marietta, GA

Address: 1269 Barclay Circle, Marietta, GA, 30060
Admissions telephone: 800 543-3202
Admissions FAX: 770 426-2895
Director of Admissions: Dr. Deborah Heairlston
Web site: http://www.life.edu
SAT Code: 7006 ACT Code: 845

LD program name: Student Success Center
Director: Dr. Lisa Rubin
LD program telephone: 770 426-2725
LD program e-mail: lrubin@life.edu
Total campus enrollment: 467

GENERAL

Life University is a private, coed, four-year institution. 100-acre campus in Marietta (population: 58,748), 20 miles from Atlanta. Served by bus; major airport and train serve Atlanta. Public transportation serves campus. Quarter system.

LD ADMISSIONS

A personal interview is not required. Essay is not required.

SECONDARY SCHOOL REQUIREMENTS

Graduation from secondary school required; GED accepted.

TESTING

SAT Reasoning required; ACT may be substituted. SAT Subject recommended.

All enrolled freshmen (fall 2004):

Average SAT I Scores:	Verbal: 473	Math: 468
Average ACT Scores:	Composite: 19	

Child Study Team report is not required. Tests required as part of this documentation:

- [ ] WAIS-IV
- [ ] WISC-IV
- [ ] SATA
- [ ] Woodcock-Johnson
- [ ] Nelson-Denny Reading Test
- [ ] Other

UNDERGRADUATE STUDENT BODY

Total undergraduate student enrollment: 405 Men, 188 Women.

Composition of student body (fall 2004):

	Undergraduate	Freshmen
International	10.7	16.5
Black	0.0	10.9
American Indian	0.0	0.1
Asian-American	0.0	1.5
Hispanic	0.0	1.7
White	10.7	12.2
Unreported	78.6	57.1
	100.0%	100.0%

70% are from out of state. Average age of full-time undergraduates is 27. 92% of classes have fewer than 20 students, 8% have between 20 and 50 students.

STUDENT HOUSING

Freshmen are not required to live on campus. Housing is guaranteed for all undergraduates. Campus can house 280 undergraduates. Single rooms are available for students with medical or special needs. A medical note is not required.

EXPENSES

Tuition (2005-06): $6,660 per year.
There is no additional cost for LD program/services.

LD SERVICES

LD program size is not limited.

LD services available to:

- [x] Freshmen
- [x] Sophomores
- [x] Juniors
- [x] Seniors

Academic Accommodations

Curriculum		In class	
Foreign language waiver	[ ]	Early syllabus	[ ]
Lighter course load	[ ]	Note takers in class	[x]
Math waiver	[ ]	Priority seating	[ ]
Other special classes	[ ]	Tape recorders	[x]
Priority registrations	[x]	Videotaped classes	[x]
Substitution of courses	[ ]	Text on tape	[ ]
Exams		**Services**	
Extended time	[x]	Diagnostic tests	[ ]
Oral exams	[x]	Learning centers	[ ]
Take home exams	[ ]	Proofreaders	[ ]
Exams on tape or computer	[ ]	Readers	[ ]
Untimed exams	[ ]	Reading Machines/Kurzweil	[ ]
Other accommodations	[x]	Special bookstore section	[ ]
		Typists	[ ]

Credit toward degree is not given for remedial courses taken.

Counseling Services

- [x] Academic
- [x] Psychological
- [ ] Student Support groups
- [ ] Vocational

Tutoring

Individual tutoring is available daily.

Average size of tutoring groups: 3

	Individual	Group
Time management	[ ]	[x]
Organizational skills	[ ]	[ ]
Learning strategies	[ ]	[ ]
Study skills	[ ]	[x]
Content area	[ ]	[ ]
Writing lab	[x]	[ ]
Math lab	[x]	[ ]

LD PROGRAM STAFF

Total number of LD Program staff (including director):

Full Time: 1 Part Time: 1

There is an advisor/advocate from the LD program available to students. 20 graduate students are available to work with LD students.

Key staff person available to work with LD students: Dr. Lisa Rubin, Director

LD Program web site: http://www.life.edu/newlife/academics/aacenter.html

Mercer University

Macon, GA

Address: 1400 Coleman Avenue, Macon, GA, 31207-0003
Admissions telephone: 800 840-8577
Admissions FAX: 478 301-2828
Associate Vice President/Director of Freshmen Admissions: John P. Cole
Admissions e-mail: admissions@mercer.edu
Web site: http://www.mercer.edu
SAT Code: 5409 ACT Code: 838

Interim Coordinator of TRIO Programs: Michele Currie
LD program telephone: 478 301-2686
LD program e-mail: Currie_m@mercer.edu
Total campus enrollment: 4, 628

GENERAL

Mercer University is a private, coed, four-year institution. 150-acre campus in Macon (population: 97,255), 85 miles south of Atlanta; branch campus in Atlanta. Served by air and bus; major airport and train serve Atlanta. Public transportation serves campus. Semester system.

LD ADMISSIONS

A personal interview is not required. Essay is not required. Course substitution for foreign language is possible.

SECONDARY SCHOOL REQUIREMENTS

Graduation from secondary school required; GED accepted. The following course distribution required: 4 units of English, 4 units of math, 3 units of science, 2 units of foreign language, 1 unit of social studies, 2 units of history.

TESTING

SAT Reasoning or ACT required. SAT Subject required.

All enrolled freshmen (fall 2004):

Average SAT I Scores:	Verbal: 588	Math: 587
Average ACT Scores:	Composite: 25	

Child Study Team report is not required. Tests required as part of this documentation:

❑ WAIS-IV	❑ Woodcock-Johnson
❑ WISC-IV	❑ Nelson-Denny Reading Test
❑ SATA	❑ Other

UNDERGRADUATE STUDENT BODY

Total undergraduate student enrollment: 1,549 Men, 3,191 Women.

Composition of student body (fall 2004):

	Undergraduate	Freshmen
International	1.8	2.5
Black	20.1	28.7
American Indian	0.2	0.2
Asian-American	4.7	3.2
Hispanic	2.0	1.7
White	69.5	60.8
Unreported	1.7	2.9
	100.0%	100.0%

16% are from out of state. 26% join a fraternity and 27% join a sorority. Average age of full-time undergraduates is 20. 51% of classes have fewer than 20 students, 46% have between 20 and 50 students, 3% have more than 50 students.

STUDENT HOUSING

89% of freshmen live in college housing. Freshmen are required to live on campus. Housing is guaranteed for all undergraduates. Campus can house 1,781 undergraduates. Single rooms are not available for students with medical or special needs.

EXPENSES

Tuition (2005-06): $23,460 per year.
Room: $3,570. Board: $3,843.
There is no additional cost for LD program/services.

LD SERVICES

LD program size is not limited.

LD services available to:

■ Freshmen ■ Sophomores ■ Juniors ■ Seniors

Academic Accommodations

Curriculum		In class	
Foreign language waiver	■	Early syllabus	❑
Lighter course load	■	Note takers in class	❑
Math waiver	❑	Priority seating	■
Other special classes	❑	Tape recorders	■
Priority registrations	■	Videotaped classes	❑
Substitution of courses	■	Text on tape	■
Exams		**Services**	
Extended time	■	Diagnostic tests	❑
Oral exams	❑	Learning centers	■
Take home exams	❑	Proofreaders	❑
Exams on tape or computer	❑	Readers	❑
Untimed exams	❑	Reading Machines/Kurzweil	❑
Other accommodations	❑	Special bookstore section	❑
		Typists	❑

Credit toward degree is not given for remedial courses taken.

Counseling Services

■ Academic
■ Psychological
■ Student Support groups
❑ Vocational

Tutoring

Individual tutoring is available weekly.

	Individual	Group
Time management	■	❑
Organizational skills	■	❑
Learning strategies	■	❑
Study skills	■	❑
Content area	■	❑
Writing lab	❑	❑
Math lab	❑	❑

LD PROGRAM STAFF

There is an advisor/advocate from the LD program available to students. The advisor/advocate meets with faculty and students four times per month.

Key staff person available to work with LD students: Tamara Martin, Counselor

Morehouse College

Atlanta, GA

Address: 830 Westview Drive, SW, Atlanta, GA, 30314
Admissions telephone: 800 851-1254
Admissions FAX: 404 524-5635
Associate Dean of Admissions and Recruitment: Terrance Dixon
Admissions e-mail: admissions@morehouse.edu
Web site: http://www.morehouse.edu
SAT Code: 5415 ACT Code: 792

LD program name: Disability Service Office
Disability Services Coordinator: Carolyn S. Walker
LD program telephone: 404 215-2636
LD program e-mail: cwalker@morehouse.edu
LD program enrollment: 20, Total campus enrollment: 2,891

GENERAL

Morehouse College is a private, men's, four-year institution. 61-acre campus in Atlanta (population: 416,474). Served by air, bus, and train. School operates transportation to library and subway stations. Public transportation serves campus. Semester system.

LD ADMISSIONS

Students do not complete a separate application and are not simultaneously accepted to the LD program. A member of the LD program does not sit on the admissions committee. High school waivers are accepted for math and foreign language. A personal interview is recommended. Essay is required and may be typed.

SECONDARY SCHOOL REQUIREMENTS

Graduation from secondary school required; GED accepted. The following course distribution required: 4 units of English, 3 units of math, 2 units of science, 2 units of foreign language, 2 units of social studies.

TESTING

SAT Reasoning required; ACT may be substituted. SAT Subject required.

All enrolled freshmen (fall 2004):

Average SAT I Scores:	Verbal: 525	Math: 530
Average ACT Scores:	Composite: 21	

Child Study Team report is not required. A neuropsychological or comprehensive psycho-educational evaluation is required for admission. Tests required as part of this documentation:

- ■ WAIS-IV
- ☐ WISC-IV
- ☐ SATA
- ■ Woodcock-Johnson
- ☐ Nelson-Denny Reading Test
- ■ Other

UNDERGRADUATE STUDENT BODY

Total undergraduate student enrollment: 2,729 Men.

Composition of student body (fall 2004):

	Undergraduate	Freshmen
International	3.7	3.1
Black	94.6	94.5
American Indian	0.1	0.1
Asian-American	0.0	0.0
Hispanic	0.1	0.2
White	0.1	0.2
Unreported	1.4	1.9
	100.0%	100.0%

66% are from out of state. 3% join a fraternity. Average age of full-time undergraduates is 20. 53% of classes have fewer than 20 students, 45% have between 20 and 50 students, 2% have more than 50 students.

STUDENT HOUSING

93% of freshmen live in college housing. Freshmen are required to live on campus. Housing is guaranteed for all undergraduates. Campus can house 1,676 undergraduates. Single rooms are available for students with medical or special needs. A medical note is required.

EXPENSES

Tuition (2005-06): $15,178 per year.
Room & Board: $9,066.
There is no additional cost for LD program/services.

LD SERVICES

LD program size is not limited.

LD services available to:

■ Freshmen ■ Sophomores ■ Juniors ■ Seniors

Academic Accommodations

Curriculum		In class	
Foreign language waiver	■	Early syllabus	☐
Lighter course load	■	Note takers in class	■
Math waiver	■	Priority seating	■
Other special classes	☐	Tape recorders	■
Priority registrations	☐	Videotaped classes	☐
Substitution of courses	■	Text on tape	☐
Exams		**Services**	
Extended time	■	Diagnostic tests	■
Oral exams	■	Learning centers	■
Take home exams	☐	Proofreaders	☐
Exams on tape or computer	☐	Readers	■
Untimed exams	■	Reading Machines/Kurzweil	☐
Other accommodations	■	Special bookstore section	■
		Typists	■

Credit toward degree is not given for remedial courses taken.

Counseling Services

■	Academic	Meets 3 times per academic year
■	Psychological	Meets 3 times per academic year
☐	Student Support groups	
☐	Vocational	

Tutoring

Individual tutoring is available daily.

	Individual	Group
Time management	■	■
Organizational skills	■	■
Learning strategies	■	■
Study skills	■	■
Content area	☐	☐
Writing lab	■	☐
Math lab	■	☐

LD PROGRAM STAFF

Total number of LD Program staff (including director):

Full Time: 1 Part Time: 1

Key staff person available to work with LD students: Carolyn S. Walker, Disability Services Coordinator

North Georgia College & State University

Dahlonega, GA

Address: College Circle, Dahlonega, GA, 30597
Admissions telephone: 800 498-9581
Admissions FAX: 706 864-1478
Director of Admissions: Robert LaVerriere
Admissions e-mail: admissions@ngcsu.edu
Web site: http://www.ngcsu.edu
SAT Code: 5497 ACT Code: 848

LD program name: Student Disability Resources
LD program address: 82 College Circle, Barnes Hall
Coordinator: Elizabeth McIntosh
LD program telephone: 706 867-2782
LD program e-mail: emcintosh@ngcsu.edu
LD program enrollment: 100, Total campus enrollment: 4,014

GENERAL

North Georgia College & State University is a public, coed, four-year institution. 150-acre campus in Dahlonega (population: 3,638), 70 miles from Atlanta; branch campuses in Cumming and Gainesville. Major airport serves Atlanta; bus and train serve Gainesville (20 miles). Semester system.

LD ADMISSIONS

Students do not complete a separate application and are not simultaneously accepted to the LD program. A member of the LD program does not sit on the admissions committee. High school waivers are accepted for math and foreign language. A personal interview is recommended. Essay is not required.

For fall 2004, 50 completed self-identified LD applications were received. 50 applications were offered admission, and 50 enrolled.

SECONDARY SCHOOL REQUIREMENTS

Graduation from secondary school required; GED accepted. The following course distribution required: 4 units of English, 4 units of math, 3 units of science, 2 units of foreign language, 3 units of social studies.

TESTING

SAT Subject recommended.

All enrolled freshmen (fall 2004):

Average SAT I Scores:	Verbal: 541	Math: 539
Average ACT Scores:	Composite: 22	

Child Study Team report is not required. A neuropsychological or comprehensive psycho-educational evaluation is required for admission. Must be dated within 36 months of application. Tests required as part of this documentation:

■ WAIS-IV
☐ WISC-IV
☐ SATA
■ Woodcock-Johnson
☐ Nelson-Denny Reading Test
☐ Other

UNDERGRADUATE STUDENT BODY

Total undergraduate student enrollment: 1,202 Men, 2,230 Women.

Composition of student body (fall 2004):

	Undergraduate	Freshmen
International	0.8	1.3
Black	1.6	1.8
American Indian	0.6	0.4
Asian-American	1.7	1.5
Hispanic	1.3	1.9
White	94.0	93.1
Unreported	0.0	0.0
	100.0%	100.0%

10% join a fraternity and 6% join a sorority. Average age of full-time undergraduates is 22. 38% of classes have fewer than 20 students, 61% have between 20 and 50 students, 1% have more than 50 students.

STUDENT HOUSING

63% of freshmen live in college housing. Freshmen are not required to live on campus. Housing is guaranteed for all undergraduates. Campus can house 1,478 undergraduates. Single rooms are available for students with medical or special needs. A medical note is required.

EXPENSES

Tuition (2005-06): $2,438 per year (in-state), $9,754 (out-of-state).
Room: $2,292. Board: $2,304.
There is no additional cost for LD program/services.

LD SERVICES

LD program size is not limited.

LD services available to:

■ Freshmen ■ Sophomores ■ Juniors ■ Seniors

Academic Accommodations

Curriculum
Foreign language waiver ☐
Lighter course load ☐
Math waiver ☐
Other special classes ☐
Priority registrations ■
Substitution of courses ■

Exams
Extended time ■
Oral exams ☐
Take home exams ☐
Exams on tape or computer ■
Untimed exams ■
Other accommodations ☐

In class
Early syllabus ☐
Note takers in class ■
Priority seating ■
Tape recorders ■
Videotaped classes ☐
Text on tape ☐

Services
Diagnostic tests ■
Learning centers ☐
Proofreaders ☐
Readers ■
Reading Machines/Kurzweil ■
Special bookstore section ☐
Typists ■

Credit toward degree is not given for remedial courses taken.

Counseling Services

☐ Academic
☐ Psychological
☐ Student Support groups
☐ Vocational

Tutoring

Individual tutoring is not available.

	Individual	Group
Time management	■	☐
Organizational skills	■	☐
Learning strategies	■	☐
Study skills	■	☐
Content area	■	☐
Writing lab	■	■
Math lab	■	■

LD PROGRAM STAFF

Total number of LD Program staff (including director):

Full Time: 1 Part Time: 1

There is an advisor/advocate from the LD program available to students.

Key staff person available to work with LD students: Elizabeth McIntosh, Coordinator, Student Disability Resources

Paine College

Augusta, GA

Address: 1235 15th Street, Augusta, GA, 30901-3182
Admissions telephone: 800 476-7703
Admissions FAX: 706 821-8648
Director of Admission: Joseph Tinsley
Admissions e-mail: tinsleyj@mail.paine.edu
Web site: http://www.paine.edu
SAT Code: 5530 ACT Code: 852

Dean of Student Affairs: Dr. Elias Etinge
LD program telephone: 706 821-8302
LD program e-mail: etingee@mail.paine.edu
Total campus enrollment: 882

GENERAL

Paine College is a private, coed, four-year institution. 54-acre campus in Augusta (population: 195,182), 75 miles from Columbia, S.C., and 145 miles from Atlanta; branch campus at Ft. Gordon Army Base. Served by air and bus; major airport serves Atlanta; airport and train serve Columbia. Public transportation serves campus. Semester system.

LD ADMISSIONS

A personal interview is not required. Essay is required and may be typed.

SECONDARY SCHOOL REQUIREMENTS

Graduation from secondary school required; GED accepted. The following course distribution required: 4 units of English, 3 units of math, 3 units of science, 3 units of social studies, 1 unit of history, 3 units of academic electives.

TESTING

SAT Reasoning required; ACT may be substituted. SAT Subject recommended.

All enrolled freshmen (fall 2004):

Average SAT I Scores: Verbal: 399 Math: 398
Average ACT Scores: Composite: 17

Child Study Team report is not required. Tests required as part of this documentation:

- ❑ WAIS-IV
- ❑ WISC-IV
- ❑ SATA
- ❑ Woodcock-Johnson
- ❑ Nelson-Denny Reading Test
- ❑ Other

UNDERGRADUATE STUDENT BODY

Total undergraduate student enrollment: 257 Men, 601 Women.

Composition of student body (fall 2004):

	Undergraduate	Freshmen
International	0.0	0.6
Black	97.9	98.3
American Indian	0.0	0.0
Asian-American	0.0	0.0
Hispanic	0.1	0.2
White	1.0	0.6
Unreported	1.0	0.3
	100.0%	100.0%

21% are from out of state. 10% join a fraternity and 10% join a sorority. Average age of full-time undergraduates is 22. 75% of classes have fewer than 20 students, 25% have between 20 and 50 students.

STUDENT HOUSING

82% of freshmen live in college housing. Freshmen are not required to live on campus. Housing is guaranteed for all undergraduates. Campus can house 506 undergraduates.

EXPENSES

Tuition (2005-06): $8,952 per year.
Room: $2,122. Board: $2,606.
There is no additional cost for LD program/services.

LD SERVICES

LD program size is not limited.

LD services available to:

❑ Freshmen ❑ Sophomores ❑ Juniors ❑ Seniors

Academic Accommodations

Curriculum		In class	
Foreign language waiver	❑	Early syllabus	❑
Lighter course load	❑	Note takers in class	❑
Math waiver	❑	Priority seating	❑
Other special classes	❑	Tape recorders	❑
Priority registrations	❑	Videotaped classes	❑
Substitution of courses	❑	Text on tape	❑
Exams		**Services**	
Extended time	❑	Diagnostic tests	❑
Oral exams	❑	Learning centers	❑
Take home exams	❑	Proofreaders	❑
Exams on tape or computer	❑	Readers	❑
Untimed exams	❑	Reading Machines/Kurzweil	❑
Other accommodations	❑	Special bookstore section	❑
		Typists	❑

Credit toward degree is not given for remedial courses taken.

Counseling Services

- ❑ Academic
- ❑ Psychological
- ❑ Student Support groups
- ❑ Vocational

Tutoring

Individual tutoring is available.

	Individual	Group
Time management	❑	❑
Organizational skills	❑	❑
Learning strategies	❑	❑
Study skills	❑	❑
Content area	❑	❑
Writing lab	❑	❑
Math lab	■	■

LD PROGRAM STAFF

There is no advisor/advocate from the LD program available to students.

Piedmont College

Demorest, GA

Address: P.O. Box 10, Demorest, GA, 30535
Admissions telephone: 800 277-7020
Admissions FAX: 706 776-6635
Director of Undergraduate Admissions: Cynthia Peterson
Admissions e-mail: ugrad@piedmont.edu
Web site: http://www.piedmont.edu
SAT Code: 5537 ACT Code: 853

Director of Academic Support: Debra Taylor
LD program telephone: 706 778-3000
LD program e-mail: dtaylor@piedmont.edu
Total campus enrollment: 1, 096

GENERAL

Piedmont College is a private, coed, four-year institution. 115-acre campus in Demorest (population: 1,465), 75 miles from Atlanta and 70 miles from Greenville, S.C.; branch campus in Athens. Major airport serves Atlanta; smaller airport serves Greenville; bus serves Gainsville (25 miles); train serves Toccoa (15 miles). Semester system.

LD ADMISSIONS

A personal interview is recommended. Essay is not required.

SECONDARY SCHOOL REQUIREMENTS

Graduation from secondary school required; GED accepted.

TESTING

All enrolled freshmen (fall 2004):

Average SAT I Scores:	Verbal: 507	Math: 512
Average ACT Scores:	Composite: 21	

Child Study Team report is not required. Tests required as part of this documentation:

☐ WAIS-IV ☐ Woodcock-Johnson
☐ WISC-IV ☐ Nelson-Denny Reading Test
☐ SATA ☐ Other

UNDERGRADUATE STUDENT BODY

Total undergraduate student enrollment: 365 Men, 625 Women.

Composition of student body (fall 2004):

	Undergraduate	Freshmen
International	0.0	0.4
Black	3.9	5.0
American Indian	0.0	0.1
Asian-American	1.1	0.9
Hispanic	2.2	2.0
White	87.2	89.5
Unreported	5.6	2.1
	100.0%	100.0%

22% are from out of state. 75% of classes have fewer than 20 students, 25% have between 20 and 50 students.

STUDENT HOUSING

83% of freshmen live in college housing. Housing is guaranteed for all undergraduates. Campus can house 410 undergraduates.

EXPENSES

Tuition (2005-06): $15,500 per year.
Room: $2,600. Board: $2,400.

There is no additional cost for LD program/services.

LD SERVICES

LD program size is not limited.

LD services available to:

☐ Freshmen ☐ Sophomores ☐ Juniors ☐ Seniors

Academic Accommodations

Curriculum		**In class**	
Foreign language waiver	☐	Early syllabus	☐
Lighter course load	■	Note takers in class	☐
Math waiver	☐	Priority seating	☐
Other special classes	☐	Tape recorders	■
Priority registrations	☐	Videotaped classes	☐
Substitution of courses	☐	Text on tape	☐
Exams		**Services**	
Extended time	☐	Diagnostic tests	☐
Oral exams	■	Learning centers	■
Take home exams	☐	Proofreaders	☐
Exams on tape or computer	☐	Readers	☐
Untimed exams	■	Reading Machines/Kurzweil	☐
Other accommodations	☐	Special bookstore section	☐
		Typists	☐

Counseling Services

☐ Academic
☐ Psychological
☐ Student Support groups
☐ Vocational

Tutoring

Individual tutoring is available daily.

	Individual	Group
Time management	☐	☐
Organizational skills	☐	☐
Learning strategies	☐	☐
Study skills	☐	☐
Content area	☐	☐
Writing lab	☐	☐
Math lab	☐	☐

LD PROGRAM STAFF

Total number of LD Program staff (including director):

Full Time: 1 Part Time: 1

Key staff person available to work with LD students: Debra Taylor, Director of Academic Support

Reinhardt College

Waleska, GA

Address: 7300 Reinhardt College Circle, Waleska, GA, 30183-0128
Admissions telephone: 770 720-5526
Admissions FAX: 770 720-5899
Director of Admissions: Julie Fleming
Admissions e-mail: admissions@reinhardt.edu
Web site: http://www.reinhardt.edu/
SAT Code: 5568 ACT Code: 856

LD program name: Academic Support Office
Dir Academic Support: Sylvia Robertson
LD program telephone: 770 720-5567
LD program e-mail: srr@reinhardt.edu
LD program enrollment: 120, Total campus enrollment: 1,079

GENERAL

Reinhardt College is a private, coed, four-year institution. 600-acre campus in Waleska (population: 616), 38 miles from Atlanta; branch campusin Alpharetta. Major airport, bus, and train serve Atlanta. Semester system.

LD ADMISSIONS

Students do not complete a separate application and are simultaneously accepted to the LD program. A member of the LD program does sit on the admissions committee. A personal interview is required. Essay is required and may not be typed.

For fall 2004, 33 completed self-identified LD applications were received. 31 applications were offered admission, and 28 enrolled.

SECONDARY SCHOOL REQUIREMENTS

Graduation from secondary school required; GED accepted. The following course distribution required: 4 units of English, 4 units of math, 3 units of science, 4 units of social studies.

TESTING

SAT Reasoning required; ACT may be substituted. SAT Subject recommended.

All enrolled freshmen (fall 2004):

Average SAT I Scores:	Verbal: 488	Math: 479
Average ACT Scores:	Composite: 19	

Child Study Team report is required if student is classified. A neuropsychological or comprehensive psycho-educational evaluation is required for admission. Must be dated within 36 months of application. Tests required as part of this documentation:

- ☒ WAIS-IV
- ☒ WISC-IV
- ☒ SATA
- ☒ Woodcock-Johnson
- ☒ Nelson-Denny Reading Test
- ☒ Other

UNDERGRADUATE STUDENT BODY

Total undergraduate student enrollment: 386 Men, 692 Women.

Composition of student body (fall 2004):

	Undergraduate	Freshmen
International	1.8	0.9
Black	3.9	7.3
American Indian	0.4	0.6
Asian-American	0.4	1.0
Hispanic	2.1	2.4
White	86.1	83.0
Unreported	5.3	4.8
	100.0%	100.0%

1% are from out of state. Average age of full-time undergraduates is 24. 69% of classes have fewer than 20 students, 31% have between 20 and 50 students.

STUDENT HOUSING

17% of freshmen live in college housing. Freshmen are not required to live on campus. Housing is guaranteed for all undergraduates. Campus can house 608 undergraduates. Single rooms are available for students with medical or special needs. A medical note is required.

EXPENSES

Tuition (2005-06): $13,020 per year.
Room & Board: $6,500.
Additional cost for LD program/services: $990 per course.

LD SERVICES

LD program size is not limited.

LD services available to:

☒ Freshmen ☒ Sophomores ☒ Juniors ☒ Seniors

Academic Accommodations

Curriculum		In class	
Foreign language waiver	☐	Early syllabus	☐
Lighter course load	☒	Note takers in class	☒
Math waiver	☐	Priority seating	☒
Other special classes	☐	Tape recorders	☒
Priority registrations	☒	Videotaped classes	☐
Substitution of courses	☐	Text on tape	☒
Exams		**Services**	
Extended time	☒	Diagnostic tests	☐
Oral exams	☒	Learning centers	☒
Take home exams	☐	Proofreaders	☒
Exams on tape or computer	☐	Readers	☒
Untimed exams	☐	Reading Machines/Kurzweil	☐
Other accommodations	☒	Special bookstore section	☐
		Typists	☐

Credit toward degree is not given for remedial courses taken.

Counseling Services

- ☒ Academic — Meets 2 times per academic year
- ☐ Psychological
- ☐ Student Support groups
- ☐ Vocational

Tutoring

Individual tutoring is available weekly.

Average size of tutoring groups: 4

	Individual	Group
Time management	☐	☐
Organizational skills	☐	☐
Learning strategies	☐	☐
Study skills	☐	☐
Content area	☐	☒
Writing lab	☒	☐
Math lab	☒	☐

LD PROGRAM STAFF

Total number of LD Program staff (including director):

Full Time: 4 Part Time: 4

There is an advisor/advocate from the LD program available to students.

Key staff person available to work with LD students: Sylvia Robertson, Director, Academic Support

The Savannah College of Art and Design

Savannah, GA

Address: 342 Bull Street, P.O. Box 3146, Savannah, GA, 31402-3146
Admissions telephone: 800 869-SCAD
Admissions FAX: 912 525-5986
Vice President for Admissions: Pamela Rhame
Admissions e-mail: admission@scad.edu
Web site: http://www.scad.edu
SAT Code: 5631 ACT Code: 855

LD program name: Disabilities Services
Director of Disabilities Services: Lita Clary
LD program telephone: 912 525-4665
LD program enrollment: 227, Total campus enrollment: 5,741

GENERAL

The Savannah College of Art and Design is a private, coed, four-year institution. Urban campus in Savannah (population: 131,510). Served by air, bus, and train. School operates transportation to all academic, administrative, and student resident buildings. Public transportation serves campus. Quarter system.

LD ADMISSIONS

Students do not complete a separate application and are not simultaneously accepted to the LD program. A member of the LD program does not sit on the admissions committee. A personal interview is recommended. Essay is not required.

SECONDARY SCHOOL REQUIREMENTS

Graduation from secondary school required; GED accepted.

TESTING

SAT Reasoning or ACT required. SAT Subject recommended.

All enrolled freshmen (fall 2004):

Average SAT I Scores:	Verbal: 554	Math: 540
Average ACT Scores:	Composite: 23	

Child Study Team report is not required. A neuropsychological or comprehensive psycho-education evaluation is not required for admission. Tests required as part of this documentation:

- ☐ WAIS-IV
- ☐ WISC-IV
- ☐ SATA
- ☐ Woodcock-Johnson
- ☐ Nelson-Denny Reading Test
- ☐ Other

UNDERGRADUATE STUDENT BODY

Total undergraduate student enrollment: 2,560 Men, 2,147 Women.

Composition of student body (fall 2004):

	Undergraduate	Freshmen
International	1.9	4.3
Black	5.8	5.0
American Indian	0.2	0.2
Asian-American	2.0	2.1
Hispanic	3.0	3.0
White	46.0	44.7
Unreported	41.1	40.7
	100.0%	100.0%

79% are from out of state. Average age of full-time undergraduates is 21. 71% of classes have fewer than 20 students, 29% have between 20 and 50 students.

STUDENT HOUSING

90% of freshmen live in college housing. Freshmen are not required to live on campus. Housing is guaranteed for all undergraduates. Campus can house 2,300 undergraduates. Single rooms are not available for students with medical or special needs.

EXPENSES

Tuition (2005-06): $21,600 per year.

Room: $5,550. Board: $3,150.

There is no additional cost for LD program/services.

LD SERVICES

LD program size is not limited.

LD services available to:

■ Freshmen ■ Sophomores ■ Juniors ■ Seniors

Academic Accommodations

Curriculum		In class	
Foreign language waiver	☐	Early syllabus	☐
Lighter course load	☐	Note takers in class	■
Math waiver	☐	Priority seating	☐
Other special classes	☐	Tape recorders	■
Priority registrations	☐	Videotaped classes	☐
Substitution of courses	☐	Text on tape	☐
Exams		**Services**	
Extended time	☐	Diagnostic tests	☐
Oral exams	☐	Learning centers	☐
Take home exams	☐	Proofreaders	☐
Exams on tape or computer	☐	Readers	■
Untimed exams	☐	Reading Machines/Kurzweil	☐
Other accommodations	☐	Special bookstore section	☐
		Typists	☐

Credit toward degree is not given for remedial courses taken.

Counseling Services

- ☐ Academic
- ☐ Psychological
- ☐ Student Support groups
- ☐ Vocational

Tutoring

Individual tutoring is available.

	Individual	Group
Time management	☐	■
Organizational skills	☐	■
Learning strategies	☐	■
Study skills	☐	■
Content area	☐	☐
Writing lab	☐	☐
Math lab	☐	☐

LD PROGRAM STAFF

Total number of LD Program staff (including director):

Full Time: 2 Part Time: 2

There is an advisor/advocate from the LD program available to students.

Key staff person available to work with LD students: Lita Clary, Director of Disabilities Services

Shorter College

Rome, GA

Address: 315 Shorter Avenue, Rome, GA, 30165-4298
Admissions telephone: 800 868-6980
Admissions FAX: 706 233-7224
Director of Admissions: John Head
Admissions e-mail: admissions@shorter.edu
Web site: http://www.shorter.edu
SAT Code: 5616 ACT Code: 860

Director of Academic Support: Terri Cordle
LD program telephone: 706 233-7323
LD program e-mail: tcordle@shorter.edu
Total campus enrollment: 896

GENERAL

Shorter College is a private, coed, four-year institution. 150-acre campus in Rome (population: 34,980), 60 miles from both Atlanta and Chattanooga. Served by bus; major airport serves Atlanta. Semester system.

SECONDARY SCHOOL REQUIREMENTS

Graduation from secondary school required; GED accepted. The following course distribution required: 4 units of English, 4 units of math, 3 units of science, 2 units of foreign language, 3 units of history.

TESTING

SAT Reasoning or ACT required. SAT Subject required.

All enrolled freshmen (fall 2004):

Average SAT I Scores:	Verbal: 551	Math: 534
Average ACT Scores:	Composite: 22	

Child Study Team report is not required. Tests required as part of this documentation:

- ❑ WAIS-IV
- ❑ WISC-IV
- ❑ SATA
- ❑ Woodcock-Johnson
- ❑ Nelson-Denny Reading Test
- ❑ Other

UNDERGRADUATE STUDENT BODY

Total undergraduate student enrollment: 318 Men, 652 Women.

Composition of student body (fall 2004):

	Undergraduate	Freshmen
International	6.2	5.8
Black	4.4	5.9
American Indian	0.0	0.0
Asian-American	0.5	1.1
Hispanic	1.3	1.4
White	85.8	83.6
Unreported	1.8	2.2
	100.0%	100.0%

8% are from out of state. 10% join a fraternity and 24% join a sorority. Average age of full-time undergraduates is 21. 60% of classes have fewer than 20 students, 39% have between 20 and 50 students, 1% have more than 50 students.

STUDENT HOUSING

77% of freshmen live in college housing. Freshmen are required to live on campus. Housing is guaranteed for all undergraduates. Campus can house 587 undergraduates.

EXPENSES

Tuition (2005-06): $13,200 per year.
Room: $3,400. Board: $2,800.

LD SERVICES

LD program size is not limited.

LD services available to:

❑ Freshmen ❑ Sophomores ❑ Juniors ❑ Seniors

Academic Accommodations

Curriculum		**In class**	
Foreign language waiver	❑	Early syllabus	❑
Lighter course load	❑	Note takers in class	❑
Math waiver	❑	Priority seating	❑
Other special classes	❑	Tape recorders	❑
Priority registrations	❑	Videotaped classes	❑
Substitution of courses	❑	Text on tape	❑
Exams		**Services**	
Extended time	❑	Diagnostic tests	❑
Oral exams	❑	Learning centers	❑
Take home exams	❑	Proofreaders	❑
Exams on tape or computer	❑	Readers	❑
Untimed exams	❑	Reading Machines/Kurzweil	❑
Other accommodations	❑	Special bookstore section	❑
		Typists	❑

Counseling Services

- ❑ Academic
- ❑ Psychological
- ❑ Student Support groups
- ❑ Vocational

Tutoring

	Individual	Group
Time management	❑	❑
Organizational skills	❑	❑
Learning strategies	❑	❑
Study skills	❑	❑
Content area	❑	❑
Writing lab	❑	❑
Math lab	❑	❑

LD PROGRAM STAFF

Key staff person available to work with LD students: Terri Cordle, Director of Academic Support

South University-Georgia

Savannah, GA

Address: 709 Mall Boulevard, Savannah, GA, 33411
Admissions FAX: 912 201-8070
Director of Admissions: Michael Thompson
SAT Code: 5157 ACT Code: 866
Web site: http://www.southuniversity.edu

LD program name: Student Services
Dean of Student Services: Gabriella Fischer
LD program telephone: 912 201-8000, extension 6041
LD program e-mail: gfischer@southuniversity.edu
Total campus enrollment: 562

GENERAL

South University (Georgia) is a private, coed, four-year institution. 6 1/2-acre campus in Savannah (population: 131,510); branch campuses in Montgomery, AL and West Palm Beach, FL. Served by air, bus, and train. Public transportation serves campus. Quarter system.

LD ADMISSIONS

Students complete a separate application and are not simultaneously accepted to the LD program. A member of the LD program does not sit on the admissions committee. A personal interview is required. Essay is not required.

SECONDARY SCHOOL REQUIREMENTS

Graduation from secondary school required; GED accepted.

TESTING

SAT Reasoning or ACT considered if submitted. SAT Subject recommended.

Child Study Team report is not required. A neuropsychological or comprehensive psycho-education evaluation is not required for admission. Tests required as part of this documentation:

- [ ] WAIS-IV
- [ ] WISC-IV
- [ ] SATA
- [ ] Woodcock-Johnson
- [ ] Nelson-Denny Reading Test
- [ ] Other

UNDERGRADUATE STUDENT BODY

Total undergraduate student enrollment: 562.

Composition of student body (fall 2004):

	Undergraduate	Freshmen
International	2.5	1.4
Black	31.7	36.5
American Indian	1.5	0.8
Asian-American	2.0	1.4
Hispanic	2.5	1.4
White	49.2	51.6
Unreported	10.6	6.9
	100.0%	100.0%

2% are from out of state. Average age of full-time undergraduates is 24. 79% of classes have fewer than 20 students, 14% have between 20 and 50 students, 7% have more than 50 students.

STUDENT HOUSING

No campus housing available.

EXPENSES

Tuition (2005-06): $14,780 per year (comprehensive). Tuition is higher for physician assistant program.
There is no additional cost for LD program/services.

LD SERVICES

LD services available to:

[x] Freshmen [x] Sophomores [x] Juniors [x] Seniors

Academic Accommodations

Curriculum		In class	
Foreign language waiver	[ ]	Early syllabus	[ ]
Lighter course load	[x]	Note takers in class	[ ]
Math waiver	[ ]	Priority seating	[x]
Other special classes	[ ]	Tape recorders	[x]
Priority registrations	[ ]	Videotaped classes	[ ]
Substitution of courses	[ ]	Text on tape	[ ]
Exams		**Services**	
Extended time	[x]	Diagnostic tests	[ ]
Oral exams	[x]	Learning centers	[x]
Take home exams	[ ]	Proofreaders	[ ]
Exams on tape or computer	[x]	Readers	[ ]
Untimed exams	[x]	Reading Machines/Kurzweil	[ ]
Other accommodations	[x]	Special bookstore section	[ ]
		Typists	[ ]

Credit toward degree is not given for remedial courses taken.

Counseling Services

- [ ] Academic
- [ ] Psychological
- [ ] Student Support groups
- [ ] Vocational

Tutoring

Individual tutoring is available daily.

Average size of tutoring groups: 3

	Individual	Group
Time management	[x]	[ ]
Organizational skills	[x]	[ ]
Learning strategies	[ ]	[x]
Study skills	[ ]	[x]
Content area	[ ]	[ ]
Writing lab	[ ]	[ ]
Math lab	[ ]	[ ]

LD PROGRAM STAFF

Total number of LD Program staff (including director):

Full Time: 1 Part Time: 1

There is an advisor/advocate from the LD program available to students. The advisor/advocate meets with faculty and students once per month.

Key staff person available to work with LD students: Gabriella Fischer, Dean of Student Services

Spelman College

Atlanta, GA

Address: 350 Spelman Lane, SW, Atlanta, GA, 30314-4399
Admissions telephone: 800 982-2411
Admissions FAX: 404 270-5201
Director of Admissions and Orientation Services: Arlene Cash
Admissions e-mail: admiss@spelman.edu
Web site: http://www.spelman.edu
SAT Code: 5628 ACT Code: 794

Director, Learning Disabilities Program: Merrine McDonald
LD program telephone: 404 270-5289, extension 5289
LD program e-mail: mmcdonald@spelman.edu
LD program enrollment: 15, Total campus enrollment: 2,186

GENERAL

Spelman College is a private, women's, four-year institution. 32-acre campus in Atlanta (population: 416,474). Served by air, bus, and train. Public transportation serves campus. Semester system.

LD ADMISSIONS

Application Deadline: 02/01. Students do not complete a separate application and are not simultaneously accepted to the LD program. A member of the LD program does not sit on the admissions committee. A personal interview is not required. Essay is required and may be typed.

SECONDARY SCHOOL REQUIREMENTS

Graduation from secondary school required; GED accepted. The following course distribution required: 4 units of English, 2 units of math, 2 units of science, 2 units of foreign language, 2 units of social studies, 3 units of history, 2 units of academic electives.

TESTING

SAT Reasoning or ACT required. SAT Subject recommended.

All enrolled freshmen (fall 2004):

Average SAT I Scores:	Verbal: 541	Math: 524
Average ACT Scores:	Composite: 22	

Child Study Team report is not required. A neuropsychological or comprehensive psycho-educational evaluation is required for admission. Must be dated within 36 months of application. Tests required as part of this documentation:

- [x] WAIS-IV
- [x] WISC-IV
- [ ] SATA
- [x] Woodcock-Johnson
- [x] Nelson-Denny Reading Test
- [x] Other

UNDERGRADUATE STUDENT BODY

Total undergraduate student enrollment: 2,139 Women.

Composition of student body (fall 2004):

	Undergraduate	Freshmen
International	1.2	1.6
Black	93.2	94.1
American Indian	0.0	0.1
Asian-American	0.0	0.0
Hispanic	0.2	0.2
White	0.0	0.0
Unreported	5.4	4.0
	100.0%	100.0%

70% are from out of state. 2% join a sorority. Average age of full-time undergraduates is 20. 58% of classes have fewer than 20 students, 40% have between 20 and 50 students, 2% have more than 50 students.

STUDENT HOUSING

92% of freshmen live in college housing. Freshmen are required to live on campus. Housing is guaranteed for all undergraduates. Campus can house 1,174 undergraduates. Single rooms are available for students with medical or special needs. A medical note is required.

EXPENSES

Tuition (2005-06): $13,525 per year.
Room: $5,130. Board: $3,325.
There is no additional cost for LD program/services.

LD SERVICES

LD program size is not limited.

LD services available to:

- [x] Freshmen
- [x] Sophomores
- [x] Juniors
- [x] Seniors

Academic Accommodations

Curriculum

- [ ] Foreign language waiver
- [ ] Lighter course load
- [ ] Math waiver
- [ ] Other special classes
- [x] Priority registrations
- [x] Substitution of courses

Exams

- [x] Extended time
- [x] Oral exams
- [ ] Take home exams
- [ ] Exams on tape or computer
- [ ] Untimed exams
- [x] Other accommodations

In class

- [ ] Early syllabus
- [x] Note takers in class
- [x] Priority seating
- [x] Tape recorders
- [ ] Videotaped classes
- [x] Text on tape

Services

- [ ] Diagnostic tests
- [x] Learning centers
- [ ] Proofreaders
- [x] Readers
- [ ] Reading Machines/Kurzweil
- [ ] Special bookstore section
- [ ] Typists

Credit toward degree is not given for remedial courses taken.

Counseling Services

- [x] Academic
- [x] Psychological
- [x] Student Support groups
- [ ] Vocational

Tutoring

Individual tutoring is available daily.

	Individual	Group
Time management	[x]	[ ]
Organizational skills	[x]	[ ]
Learning strategies	[ ]	[ ]
Study skills	[ ]	[ ]
Content area	[ ]	[ ]
Writing lab	[x]	[ ]
Math lab	[x]	[ ]

LD PROGRAM STAFF

Total number of LD Program staff (including director):

Full Time: 1 Part Time: 1

There is an advisor/advocate from the LD program available to students.

Key staff person available to work with LD students: Merrine McDonald, Director

Toccoa Falls College

Toccoa Falls, GA

Address: 325 Chapel Drive, Toccoa Falls, GA, 30598
Admissions telephone: 800 868-3257
Admissions FAX: 706 282-6012
Director of Admissions: Christy Meadows
Admissions e-mail: admissions@tfc.edu
Web site: http://www.tfc.edu
SAT Code: 5799 ACT Code: 868

VP for Academic Affairs: Dr. David Reese
LD program telephone: 706 886-6831, extension 5250
LD program e-mail: dreese@tfc.edu
Total campus enrollment: 829

GENERAL

Toccoa Falls College is a private, coed, four-year institution. 1,100-acre campus two miles outside Toccoa (population: 9,323), 45 miles from Gainesville. Served by train; major airport serves Atlanta (110 miles); smaller airport serves Greenville-Spartanburg, SC (75 miles); bus serves Gainesville. Semester system.

LD ADMISSIONS

Students do not complete a separate application and are simultaneously accepted to the LD program. A member of the LD program does not sit on the admissions committee. A personal interview is recommended. Essay is required and may be typed.

SECONDARY SCHOOL REQUIREMENTS

Graduation from secondary school required; GED accepted. The following course distribution required: 4 units of English, 3 units of math, 3 units of science, 3 units of social studies, 6 units of academic electives.

TESTING

SAT Reasoning or ACT required. SAT Subject recommended.

All enrolled freshmen (fall 2004):

Average SAT I Scores:	Verbal: 532	Math: 517
Average ACT Scores:	Composite: 21	

Child Study Team report is not required. A neuropsychological or comprehensive psycho-education evaluation is not required for admission. Tests required as part of this documentation:

- ☐ WAIS-IV
- ☐ WISC-IV
- ☐ SATA
- ☐ Woodcock-Johnson
- ☐ Nelson-Denny Reading Test
- ☐ Other

UNDERGRADUATE STUDENT BODY

Total undergraduate student enrollment: 393 Men, 523 Women.

Composition of student body (fall 2004):

	Undergraduate	Freshmen
International	0.0	2.0
Black	3.6	2.8
American Indian	0.0	0.1
Asian-American	5.6	5.0
Hispanic	2.0	2.0
White	88.8	88.0
Unreported	0.0	0.1
	100.0%	100.0%

61% are from out of state. Average age of full-time undergraduates is 21. 58% of classes have fewer than 20 students, 40% have between 20 and 50 students, 2% have more than 50 students.

STUDENT HOUSING

94% of freshmen live in college housing. Freshmen are required to live on campus. Housing is guaranteed for all undergraduates. Campus can house 622 undergraduates. Single rooms are available for students with medical or special needs. A medical note is required.

EXPENSES

Tuition (2005-06): $12,050 per year.
Room & Board: $4,600.
There is no additional cost for LD program/services.

LD SERVICES

LD program size is not limited.

LD services available to:

■ Freshmen ■ Sophomores ■ Juniors ■ Seniors

Academic Accommodations

Curriculum		**In class**	
Foreign language waiver	☐	Early syllabus	☐
Lighter course load	☐	Note takers in class	■
Math waiver	☐	Priority seating	■
Other special classes	☐	Tape recorders	☐
Priority registrations	☐	Videotaped classes	☐
Substitution of courses	☐	Text on tape	☐
Exams		**Services**	
Extended time	■	Diagnostic tests	☐
Oral exams	■	Learning centers	■
Take home exams	☐	Proofreaders	☐
Exams on tape or computer	☐	Readers	■
Untimed exams	■	Reading Machines/Kurzweil	☐
Other accommodations	■	Special bookstore section	☐
		Typists	■

Credit toward degree is not given for remedial courses taken.

Counseling Services

- ■ Academic
- ☐ Psychological
- ☐ Student Support groups
- ☐ Vocational

Tutoring

Individual tutoring is available daily.

	Individual	Group
Time management	■	☐
Organizational skills	■	☐
Learning strategies	☐	☐
Study skills	■	☐
Content area	☐	■
Writing lab	☐	■
Math lab	☐	☐

LD PROGRAM STAFF

Total number of LD Program staff (including director):

Full Time: 1 Part Time: 1

There is an advisor/advocate from the LD program available to students. The advisor/advocate meets with faculty four times per month and students six times per month. Four peer tutors are available to work with LD students.

Truett-McConnell College

Cleveland, GA

Address: Cleveland, GA, 30528
Admissions FAX: 706 865-7615
Admissions Contact: Penny Loggins
Web site: http://www.truett.edu
SAT Code: 5798 ACT Code: 870

LD program name: Special Support Services
LD program address: 100 Alumni Drive,
Director of Special Support Services: Nell Hoyle
LD program telephone: 706 865-2134, extension 172
LD program e-mail: nhoyle@truett.edu
LD program enrollment: 15, Total campus enrollment: 359

GENERAL

Truett-McConnell College is a private, coed, four-year institution. Semester system.

LD ADMISSIONS

Application Deadline: 08/01. Students do not complete a separate application and are simultaneously accepted to the LD program. A member of the LD program does sit on the admissions committee. A personal interview is not required. Essay is not required.

For fall 2004, 15 completed self-identified LD applications were received. 15 applications were offered admission, and 15 enrolled.

TESTING

SAT Reasoning or ACT required. SAT Subject recommended.

All enrolled freshmen (fall 2004):

Average SAT I Scores:	Verbal: 463	Math: 470
Average ACT Scores:	Composite: 19	

Child Study Team report is not required. A neuropsychological or comprehensive psycho-educational evaluation is required for admission. Must be dated within 12 months of application. Tests required as part of this documentation:

- ☐ WAIS-IV
- ☐ WISC-IV
- ☐ SATA
- ☐ Woodcock-Johnson
- ☐ Nelson-Denny Reading Test
- ☑ Other

UNDERGRADUATE STUDENT BODY

Total undergraduate student enrollment: 359.

Composition of student body (fall 2004):

	Undergraduate	Freshmen
International	0.0	0.0
Black	10.5	12.5
American Indian	0.6	0.3
Asian-American	1.2	1.2
Hispanic	1.9	1.8
White	82.1	81.8
Unreported	3.7	2.4
	100.0%	100.0%

STUDENT HOUSING

66% of freshmen live in college housing. Freshmen are required to live on campus. Housing is guaranteed for all undergraduates. Campus can house 358 undergraduates. Single rooms are available for students with medical or special needs. A medical note is required.

EXPENSES

Tuition (2005-06): $11,550 per year.
Room: $2,200. Board: $2,400.
There is no additional cost for LD program/services.

LD SERVICES

LD program size is not limited.

LD services available to:

☑ Freshmen ☑ Sophomores ☑ Juniors ☑ Seniors

Academic Accommodations

Curriculum		In class	
Foreign language waiver	☐	Early syllabus	☐
Lighter course load	☐	Note takers in class	☑
Math waiver	☐	Priority seating	☑
Other special classes	☐	Tape recorders	☑
Priority registrations	☐	Videotaped classes	☐
Substitution of courses	☐	Text on tape	☑
Exams		**Services**	
Extended time	☑	Diagnostic tests	☐
Oral exams	☑	Learning centers	☑
Take home exams	☐	Proofreaders	☐
Exams on tape or computer	☑	Readers	☑
Untimed exams	☑	Reading Machines/Kurzweil	☑
Other accommodations	☑	Special bookstore section	☑
		Typists	☐

Credit toward degree is not given for remedial courses taken.

Counseling Services

☑	Academic	Meets 4 times per academic year
☑	Psychological	Meets 10 times per academic year
☑	Student Support groups	
☑	Vocational	Meets 2 times per academic year

Tutoring

Individual tutoring is available weekly.

Average size of tutoring groups: 1

	Individual	Group
Time management	☐	☐
Organizational skills	☐	☐
Learning strategies	☐	☐
Study skills	☐	☑
Content area	☐	☐
Writing lab	☐	☐
Math lab	☐	☑

LD PROGRAM STAFF

There is an advisor/advocate from the LD program available to students. The advisor/advocate meets with faculty students once per month.

Key staff person available to work with LD students: Nell Hoyle, Director of Special Support Services

Valdosta State University

Valdosta, GA

Address: 1500 North Patterson Street, Valdosta, GA, 31698
Admissions telephone: 800 618-1878
Admissions FAX: 229 333-5482
Director of Admissions: Walter Peacock
Admissions e-mail: admissions@valdosta.edu
Web site: http://www.valdosta.edu
SAT Code: 5855 ACT Code: 874

LD program name: Access Office for Students with Disabilities
Acting Director, Access Office: Kimberly Godden
LD program telephone: 229 245-2498
LD program e-mail: kgodden@valdosta.edu
LD program enrollment: 50, Total campus enrollment: 9,013

GENERAL

Valdosta State University is a public, coed, four-year institution. Two campuses totaling 200 acres in Valdosta (population: 43,724), 115 miles from Jacksonville, FL; branch campuses in Bainbridge, Douglas, Tifton, and Waycross. Served by air and bus; major airport and train serve Jacksonville, FL; other major airport serves Tallahassee, FL. (100 miles). School operates transportation to parking lots, north campus, and shopping center. Semester system.

LD ADMISSIONS

Students do not complete a separate application and are not simultaneously accepted to the LD program. A member of the LD program does not sit on the admissions committee. High school waivers are accepted for foreign language. A personal interview is recommended. Essay is not required. Students may be eligible for foreign language substitution if approved by Board of Regents.

SECONDARY SCHOOL REQUIREMENTS

Graduation from secondary school required; GED accepted. The following course distribution required: 4 units of English, 4 units of math, 3 units of science, 2 units of foreign language, 3 units of social studies.

TESTING

SAT Reasoning or ACT required. SAT Subject recommended.

All enrolled freshmen (fall 2004):

Average SAT I Scores:	Verbal: 515	Math: 510
Average ACT Scores:	Composite: 21	

Child Study Team report is not required. A neuropsychological or comprehensive psycho-educational evaluation is required for admission. Tests required as part of this documentation:

☐ WAIS-IV	☐ Woodcock-Johnson
☐ WISC-IV	☐ Nelson-Denny Reading Test
☐ SATA	☑ Other

UNDERGRADUATE STUDENT BODY

Total undergraduate student enrollment: 3,013 Men, 4,498 Women.

Composition of student body (fall 2004):

	Undergraduate	Freshmen
International	0.4	1.3
Black	21.0	21.3
American Indian	0.2	0.3
Asian-American	1.1	1.1
Hispanic	1.6	1.6
White	75.7	74.4
Unreported	0.0	0.0
	100.0%	100.0%

8% are from out of state. 1% join a fraternity and 2% join a sorority. Average age of full-time undergraduates is 22. 29% of classes have fewer than 20 students, 68% have between 20 and 50 students, 3% have more than 50 students.

STUDENT HOUSING

56% of freshmen live in college housing. Freshmen are not required to live on campus. Housing is guaranteed for all undergraduates. Campus can house 1,928 undergraduates. Single rooms are available for students with medical or special needs. A medical note is required.

EXPENSES

Tuition (2005-06): $2,322 per year (in-state), $9,290 (out-of-state). Room: $2,664. Board: $2,544.
There is no additional cost for LD program/services.

LD SERVICES

LD program size is not limited.

LD services available to:

☑ Freshmen ☑ Sophomores ☑ Juniors ☑ Seniors

Academic Accommodations

Curriculum		In class	
Foreign language waiver	☐	Early syllabus	☐
Lighter course load	☑	Note takers in class	☑
Math waiver	☐	Priority seating	☑
Other special classes	☐	Tape recorders	☑
Priority registrations	☑	Videotaped classes	☐
Substitution of courses	☑	Text on tape	☑
Exams		**Services**	
Extended time	☑	Diagnostic tests	☐
Oral exams	☐	Learning centers	☐
Take home exams	☐	Proofreaders	☐
Exams on tape or computer	☑	Readers	☑
Untimed exams	☐	Reading Machines/Kurzweil	☑
Other accommodations	☑	Special bookstore section	☐
		Typists	☑

Credit toward degree is not given for remedial courses taken.

Counseling Services

☑ Academic
☑ Psychological
☐ Student Support groups
☐ Vocational

Tutoring

Individual tutoring is available daily.

Average size of tutoring groups: 1

	Individual	Group
Time management	☑	☐
Organizational skills	☑	☐
Learning strategies	☑	☐
Study skills	☑	☐
Content area	☐	☐
Writing lab	☐	☐
Math lab	☐	☐

LD PROGRAM STAFF

Total number of LD Program staff (including director):

Full Time: 2 Part Time: 2

There is an advisor/advocate from the LD program available to students. Two graduate students are available to work with LD students.

Key staff person available to work with LD students: Kimberly Godden, Acting Director, Access Office

LD Program web site: www.valdosta.edu/access

Wesleyan College

Macon, GA

Address: 4760 Forsyth Road, Macon, GA, 31210-4462
Admissions telephone: 800 447-6610
Admissions FAX: 478 757-4030
Vice President for Enrollment and Marketing: Patricia M. Gibbs
Admissions e-mail: admissions@wesleyancollege.edu
Web site: http://www.wesleyancollege.edu
SAT Code: 5895 ACT Code: 876

LD program name: Academic Center
LD program enrollment: 7, Total campus enrollment: 565

GENERAL

Wesleyan College is a private, women's, four-year institution. 200-acre, suburban campus in Macon (population: 97,255), 90 miles from Atlanta. Served by air and bus; major airport and train serve Atlanta. School operates transportation to downtown Macon and shopping areas. Semester system.

LD ADMISSIONS

Application Deadline: 08/01. Students do not complete a separate application and are not simultaneously accepted to the LD program. A member of the LD program does not sit on the admissions committee. A personal interview is recommended. Essay is required and may be typed.

SECONDARY SCHOOL REQUIREMENTS

Graduation from secondary school required; GED accepted. The following course distribution required: 4 units of English, 3 units of math, 3 units of science, 2 units of foreign language, 3 units of social studies.

TESTING

SAT Reasoning or ACT required. SAT Subject recommended.

All enrolled freshmen (fall 2004):

Average SAT I Scores:	Verbal: 574	Math: 562
Average ACT Scores:	Composite: 24	

Child Study Team report is not required. A neuropsychological or comprehensive psycho-education evaluation is not required for admission. Tests required as part of this documentation:

- ☐ WAIS-IV
- ☐ WISC-IV
- ☐ SATA
- ☐ Woodcock-Johnson
- ☐ Nelson-Denny Reading Test
- ☐ Other

UNDERGRADUATE STUDENT BODY

Total undergraduate student enrollment: 674 Women.

Composition of student body (fall 2004):

	Undergraduate	Freshmen
International	14.3	17.6
Black	36.3	31.1
American Indian	0.0	0.0
Asian-American	2.2	2.4
Hispanic	4.4	2.4
White	41.7	43.8
Unreported	1.1	2.7
	100.0%	100.0%

19% are from out of state. Average age of full-time undergraduates is 22. 89% of classes have fewer than 20 students, 11% have between 20 and 50 students.

STUDENT HOUSING

95% of freshmen live in college housing. Freshmen are required to live on campus. Housing is guaranteed for all undergraduates. Campus can house 622 undergraduates. Single rooms are available for students with medical or special needs. A medical note is required.

University of West Georgia

Carrollton, GA

Address: 1601 Maple Street, Carrollton, GA, 30118
Admissions telephone: 678 839-4000
Admissions FAX: 678 839-4747
Director of Admissions: Dr. Bobby Johnson
Admissions e-mail: admiss@westga.edu
Web site: http://www.westga.edu
SAT Code: 5900 ACT Code: 878

LD program name: Disability Services
Coordinator of Disabled Student Services: Ann Phillips, Ph.D.
LD program telephone: 678 839-6428
LD program e-mail: aphillip@westga.edu
LD program enrollment: 100, Total campus enrollment: 8,279

GENERAL

State University of West Georgia is a public, coed, four-year institution. 394-acre campus in Carrollton (population: 19,843), 45 miles from Atlanta; branch campuses in Dalton and Newnan. Major airport, bus, and train serve Atlanta. School operates transportation on campus. Semester system.

LD ADMISSIONS

Students complete a separate application and are not simultaneously accepted to the LD program. A member of the LD program does not sit on the admissions committee. High school waivers are accepted for foreign language. A personal interview is required. Essay is not required.

For fall 2004, 15 completed self-identified LD applications were received. 15 applications were offered admission, and 15 enrolled.

SECONDARY SCHOOL REQUIREMENTS

Graduation from secondary school required; GED not accepted. The following course distribution required: 4 units of English, 4 units of math, 3 units of science, 2 units of foreign language, 3 units of social studies.

TESTING

SAT Reasoning or ACT required. SAT Subject recommended.

All enrolled freshmen (fall 2004):

Average SAT I Scores:	Verbal: 507	Math: 498
Average ACT Scores:	Composite: 20	

Child Study Team report is not required. A neuropsychological or comprehensive psycho-educational evaluation is required for admission. Must be dated within 36 months of application. Tests required as part of this documentation:

- ■ WAIS-IV
- ☐ WISC-IV
- ■ SATA
- ■ Woodcock-Johnson
- ■ Nelson-Denny Reading Test
- ■ Other

UNDERGRADUATE STUDENT BODY

Total undergraduate student enrollment: 2,860 Men, 4,394 Women.

Composition of student body (fall 2004):

	Undergraduate	Freshmen
International	0.6	1.1
Black	24.6	22.9
American Indian	0.3	0.3
Asian-American	1.6	1.3
Hispanic	1.5	1.4
White	69.8	71.4
Unreported	1.6	1.6
	100.0%	100.0%

5% are from out of state. Average age of full-time undergraduates is 21. 39% of classes have fewer than 20 students, 49% have between 20 and 50 students, 12% have more than 50 students.

STUDENT HOUSING

65% of freshmen live in college housing. Freshmen are required to live on campus. Housing is guaranteed for all undergraduates. Campus can house 2,500 undergraduates. Single rooms are not available for students with medical or special needs.

EXPENSES

Tuition (2005-06): $2,438 per year (in-state), $9,754 (out-of-state).

Room: $2,360. Board: $2,028.
There is no additional cost for LD program/services.

LD SERVICES

LD program size is not limited.

LD services available to:

■ Freshmen ■ Sophomores ■ Juniors ■ Seniors

Academic Accommodations

Curriculum		In class	
Foreign language waiver	■	Early syllabus	☐
Lighter course load	☐	Note takers in class	■
Math waiver	☐	Priority seating	☐
Other special classes	☐	Tape recorders	■
Priority registrations	■	Videotaped classes	☐
Substitution of courses	☐	Text on tape	☐
Exams		**Services**	
Extended time	■	Diagnostic tests	☐
Oral exams	■	Learning centers	☐
Take home exams	☐	Proofreaders	☐
Exams on tape or computer	☐	Readers	■
Untimed exams	■	Reading Machines/Kurzweil	■
Other accommodations	☐	Special bookstore section	☐
		Typists	☐

Credit toward degree is not given for remedial courses taken.

Counseling Services

- ■ Academic
- ■ Psychological
- ☐ Student Support groups
- ■ Vocational

Tutoring

Individual tutoring is available weekly.

	Individual	Group
Time management	☐	■
Organizational skills	☐	■
Learning strategies	■	☐
Study skills	☐	■
Content area	☐	☐
Writing lab	■	☐
Math lab	■	☐

LD PROGRAM STAFF

Total number of LD Program staff (including director):

Full Time: 1 Part Time: 1

There is an advisor/advocate from the LD program available to students. The advisor/advocate meets with students once per month. Two graduate students and 10 peer tutors are available to work with LD students.

Key staff person available to work with LD students: Ann Phillips, Ph.D, Coordinator of Disabled Student Services

Room & Board: $7,450.
There is no additional cost for LD program/services.

Brigham Young University - Hawaii Campus

Laie Oahu, HI

Address: 55-220 Kulanui Street, Laie Oahu, HI, 96762-1294
Admissions telephone: 808 293-3738
Admissions FAX: 808 293-3741
Dean of Admissions and Records: Jeffery Bunker
Admissions e-mail: admissions@byuh.edu
Web site: http://www.byuh.edu
SAT Code: 4106 ACT Code: 899

LD program name: Services for Students with Special Needs
Coordinator: Leilani Auna
LD program telephone: 808 293-3518
LD program e-mail: aunal@byuh.edu
LD program enrollment: 58, Total campus enrollment: 2,486

GENERAL

Brigham Young University - Hawaii Campus is a private, coed, four-year institution. 60-acre campus in Laie (population: 4,585), 38 miles from Honolulu. Major airport serves Honolulu. School operates transportation to airport. Public transportation serves campus. Semester system.

LD ADMISSIONS

Application Deadline: 02/15. Students do not complete a separate application and are not simultaneously accepted to the LD program. A member of the LD program does not sit on the admissions committee. A personal interview is recommended. Essay is not required.

SECONDARY SCHOOL REQUIREMENTS

Graduation from secondary school required; GED not accepted.

TESTING

ACT recommended.

All enrolled freshmen (fall 2004):

Average SAT I Scores: Verbal: 465 Math: 515
Average ACT Scores: Composite: 24

Child Study Team report is required if student is classified. A neuropsychological or comprehensive psycho-educational evaluation is required for admission. Must be dated within 24 months of application. Tests required as part of this documentation:

- [x] WAIS-IV
- [x] WISC-IV
- [x] SATA
- [x] Woodcock-Johnson
- [x] Nelson-Denny Reading Test
- [ ] Other

UNDERGRADUATE STUDENT BODY

Total undergraduate student enrollment: 989 Men, 1,289 Women.

Composition of student body (fall 2004):

	Undergraduate	Freshmen
International	44.2	45.3
Black	1.0	0.4
American Indian	0.0	0.6
Asian-American	39.8	22.2
Hispanic	0.5	1.5
White	14.1	28.7
Unreported	0.5	1.3
	100.0%	100.0%

41% are from out of state. Average age of full-time undergraduates is 24. 57% of classes have fewer than 20 students, 39% have between 20 and 50 students.

STUDENT HOUSING

100% of freshmen live in college housing. Freshmen are required to live on campus. Housing is guaranteed for all undergraduates. Campus can house 1,372 undergraduates. Single rooms are available for students with medical or special needs. A medical note is not required.

EXPENSES

Tuition (2005-06): $2,760 per year. $2,490 per year (Latter-Day Saints members), $3,740 (non-members).

Room & Board: $4,980.

There is no additional cost for LD program/services.

LD SERVICES

LD program size is not limited.

LD services available to:

- [x] Freshmen
- [x] Sophomores
- [x] Juniors
- [x] Seniors

Academic Accommodations

Curriculum		In class	
Foreign language waiver	☐	Early syllabus	☐
Lighter course load	☐	Note takers in class	☒
Math waiver	☐	Priority seating	☐
Other special classes	☐	Tape recorders	☒
Priority registrations	☒	Videotaped classes	☒
Substitution of courses	☐	Text on tape	☐
Exams		**Services**	
Extended time	☒	Diagnostic tests	☒
Oral exams	☒	Learning centers	☒
Take home exams	☐	Proofreaders	☐
Exams on tape or computer	☐	Readers	☒
Untimed exams	☒	Reading Machines/Kurzweil	☒
Other accommodations	☐	Special bookstore section	☐
		Typists	☐

Credit toward degree is not given for remedial courses taken.

Counseling Services

- [ ] Academic
- [ ] Psychological
- [ ] Student Support groups
- [ ] Vocational

Tutoring

Individual tutoring is available.

Average size of tutoring groups: 1

	Individual	Group
Time management	☒	☐
Organizational skills	☒	☐
Learning strategies	☒	☐
Study skills	☒	☐
Content area	☒	☐
Writing lab	☒	☐
Math lab	☒	☐

UNIQUE LD PROGRAM FEATURES

The number of students with special needs is increasing due to the publicity of our office, the flat terrain, the warm climate, and the small class size of BYUH. These factors make this university ideal for students with a physical disability as well as a learning disability. In addition, we are constantly seeking ways to help international students with hidden disabilities.

LD PROGRAM STAFF

Total number of LD Program staff (including director):

Full Time: 1 Part Time: 1

There is an advisor/advocate from the LD program available to students. 1 graduate student is available to work with LD students.

Key staff person available to work with LD students: Leilani Auna, Coordinator, Services for Students w/ Special Needs.

Chaminade University of Honolulu

Honolulu, HI

Address: 3140 Waialae Avenue, Honolulu, HI, 96816-1578
Admissions telephone: 808 735-4735
Admissions FAX: 808 739-4647
Dean of Enrollment Management: Joy Bouey, Dean of EM
Admissions e-mail: admissions@chaminade.edu
Web site: http://www.chaminade.edu
SAT Code: 4105 ACT Code: 898

Personal Counselor: June Yasuhara
LD program telephone: 808 739-4603
LD program e-mail: jyasuhar@chaminade.edu
Total campus enrollment: 1,079

GENERAL

Chaminade University of Honolulu is a private, coed, four-year institution. 67-acre, urban campus four miles from downtown Honolulu (population: 371,657); eight branch campuses in metropolitan area. Served by air. Public transportation serves campus. Semester system.

LD ADMISSIONS

Students do not complete a separate application and are not simultaneously accepted to the LD program. A member of the LD program does not sit on the admissions committee.

SECONDARY SCHOOL REQUIREMENTS

Graduation from secondary school required; GED accepted. The following course distribution required: 4 units of English, 3 units of math, 2 units of science, 3 units of social studies.

TESTING

SAT Reasoning or ACT required. SAT Subject recommended.

All enrolled freshmen (fall 2004):

Average SAT I Scores:	Verbal: 468	Math: 478
Average ACT Scores:	Composite: 21	

Child Study Team report is not required. A neuropsychological or comprehensive psycho-education evaluation is not required for admission. Tests required as part of this documentation:

- ☐ WAIS-IV
- ☐ WISC-IV
- ☐ SATA
- ☐ Woodcock-Johnson
- ☐ Nelson-Denny Reading Test
- ☐ Other

UNDERGRADUATE STUDENT BODY

Total undergraduate student enrollment: 803 Men, 1,171 Women.

Composition of student body (fall 2004):

	Undergraduate	Freshmen
International	1.2	2.3
Black	1.2	3.7
American Indian	0.4	0.7
Asian-American	63.7	64.4
Hispanic	8.1	6.4
White	25.4	22.6
Unreported	0.0	0.0
	100.0%	100.0%

43% are from out of state. Average age of full-time undergraduates is 22. 64% of classes have fewer than 20 students, 36% have between 20 and 50 students.

STUDENT HOUSING

65% of freshmen live in college housing. Housing is not guaranteed for all undergraduates. Housing space is limited. Campus can house 380 undergraduates. Single rooms are available for students with medical or special needs. A medical note is required.

EXPENSES

Tuition (2005-06): $14,330 per year.

Room: $4,680. Board: $4,190.
There is no additional cost for LD program/services.

LD SERVICES

LD program size is not limited.

LD services available to:

■ Freshmen ■ Sophomores ■ Juniors ■ Seniors

Academic Accommodations

Curriculum		In class	
Foreign language waiver	☐	Early syllabus	☐
Lighter course load	■	Note takers in class	☐
Math waiver	☐	Priority seating	☐
Other special classes	☐	Tape recorders	☐
Priority registrations	☐	Videotaped classes	☐
Substitution of courses	☐	Text on tape	☐
Exams		**Services**	
Extended time	☐	Diagnostic tests	☐
Oral exams	☐	Learning centers	☐
Take home exams	☐	Proofreaders	☐
Exams on tape or computer	☐	Readers	☐
Untimed exams	☐	Reading Machines/Kurzweil	☐
Other accommodations	☐	Special bookstore section	☐
		Typists	☐

Credit toward degree is not given for remedial courses taken.

Counseling Services

- ☐ Academic
- ☐ Psychological
- ☐ Student Support groups
- ☐ Vocational

Tutoring

	Individual	Group
Time management	☐	☐
Organizational skills	☐	☐
Learning strategies	☐	☐
Study skills	☐	☐
Content area	☐	☐
Writing lab	☐	☐
Math lab	☐	☐

UNIQUE LD PROGRAM FEATURES

We do not collect information about students with learning disabilities during the application process. We have the same admissions criterion for everyone. When a student matriculates and lets us know about their disability then we make the neccessary accommodations to meet the student's needs.

LD PROGRAM STAFF

Key staff person available to work with LD students: Donald Kopf, Director of Personal Counseling.

University of Hawaii at Hilo

Hilo, HI

Address: 200 West Kawili Street, Hilo, HI, 96720-4091
Admissions telephone: 800 897-4456
Admissions FAX: 808 933-0861
Admissions Coordinator: James Cromwell
Admissions e-mail: uhhadm@hawaii.edu
Web site: http://www.uhh.hawaii.edu
SAT Code: 4869 ACT Code: 904

Director, University Disability Services: Susan Shirachi-Gonsalves
LD program telephone: 808 933-0816
LD program e-mail: shirachi@hawaii.edu
Total campus enrollment: 3,182

GENERAL

University of Hawaii at Hilo is a public, coed, four-year institution. 115-acre campus in Hilo (population: 40,759), 200 air miles from Honolulu. Served by air and bus; airport serves Honolulu. Semester system.

LD ADMISSIONS

A personal interview is required. Essay is not required.

SECONDARY SCHOOL REQUIREMENTS

Graduation from secondary school required; GED accepted. The following course distribution required: 4 units of English, 3 units of math, 3 units of science, 2 units of social studies, 2 units of history, 3 units of academic electives.

TESTING

ACT considered if submitted. SAT Reasoning required; ACT may be substituted. SAT Subject recommended.

All enrolled freshmen (fall 2004):

Average SAT I Scores: Verbal: 500 Math: 510

Child Study Team report is required if student is classified. Tests required as part of this documentation:

- [ ] WAIS-IV
- [ ] WISC-IV
- [ ] SATA
- [ ] Woodcock-Johnson
- [ ] Nelson-Denny Reading Test
- [ ] Other

UNDERGRADUATE STUDENT BODY

Total undergraduate student enrollment: 1,082 Men, 1,642 Women.

Composition of student body (fall 2004):

	Freshmen
International	11.0
Black	1.4
American Indian	0.7
Asian-American	37.2
Hispanic	3.1
White	36.6
Unreported	9.9
	100.0%

31% are from out of state. Average age of full-time undergraduates is 25. 40% of classes have fewer than 20 students, 56% have between 20 and 50 students.

STUDENT HOUSING

41% of freshmen live in college housing. Freshmen are not required to live on campus. Housing is not guaranteed for all undergraduates. Plans for two more housing complexes with 1,000 more bed spaces are currently underway, approximately 450 bed spaces in off-campus affiliated housing are available in the interim. Campus can house 800 undergraduates.

EXPENSES

Tuition (2005-06): $2,472 per year (in-state), $8,040 (out-of-state). $1,608 per year (state residents, lower division), $2,328 (state residents, upper division), $7,344 (out-of-state, lower division), $7,896 (out-of-state, upper division).

Room: $2,680. Board: $2,792.

There is no additional cost for LD program/services.

LD SERVICES

LD program size is not limited.

LD services available to:

- [ ] Freshmen
- [ ] Sophomores
- [ ] Juniors
- [ ] Seniors

Academic Accommodations

Curriculum

- [ ] Foreign language waiver
- [ ] Lighter course load
- [ ] Math waiver
- [x] Other special classes
- [ ] Priority registrations
- [ ] Substitution of courses

Exams

- [x] Extended time
- [x] Oral exams
- [ ] Take home exams
- [ ] Exams on tape or computer
- [ ] Untimed exams
- [ ] Other accommodations

In class

- [ ] Early syllabus
- [x] Note takers in class
- [ ] Priority seating
- [x] Tape recorders
- [x] Videotaped classes
- [ ] Text on tape

Services

- [ ] Diagnostic tests
- [x] Learning centers
- [ ] Proofreaders
- [x] Readers
- [x] Reading Machines/Kurzweil
- [ ] Special bookstore section
- [ ] Typists

Credit toward degree is not given for remedial courses taken.

Counseling Services

- [ ] Academic
- [ ] Psychological
- [ ] Student Support groups
- [ ] Vocational

Tutoring

	Individual	Group
Time management	[ ]	[ ]
Organizational skills	[ ]	[ ]
Learning strategies	[ ]	[ ]
Study skills	[ ]	[ ]
Content area	[ ]	[ ]
Writing lab	[ ]	[ ]
Math lab	[ ]	[ ]

UNIQUE LD PROGRAM FEATURES

Forty percent of students enrolled with the Disability Services Office are learning disabled.

LD PROGRAM STAFF

Total number of LD Program staff (including director):

Full Time: 1 Part Time: 1

Key staff person available to work with LD students: Susan Shirachi-Gonsalves, Director, University Disability Services.

University of Hawaii at Manoa

Honolulu, HI

Address: 2444 Dole Street, Honolulu, HI, 96822
Admissions telephone: 800 823-9771
Admissions FAX: 808 956-4148
Interim Director of Admissions and Records: Janice Heu
Admissions e-mail: ar-info@hawaii.edu
Web site: http://www.hawaii.edu
SAT Code: 4867 ACT Code: 902

LD program name: KOKUA Program
LD program address: 2660 Campus Road, QLCSS Room #013
Director: Ann Ito
LD program telephone: 808 956-7511
LD program e-mail: lanning@hawaii.edu
LD program enrollment: 300, Total campus enrollment: 14,251

GENERAL

University of Hawaii at Manoa is a public, coed, four-year institution. 320-acre, urban campus in Honolulu (population: 371,657); seven community college branch campuses. Served by air. School operates transportation to student and faculty housing. Public transportation serves campus. Semester system.

LD ADMISSIONS

Students do not complete a separate application and are not simultaneously accepted to the LD program. A member of the LD program does not sit on the admissions committee. A personal interview is not required. Essay is required and may be typed.

SECONDARY SCHOOL REQUIREMENTS

Graduation from secondary school required; GED accepted. The following course distribution required: 4 units of English, 3 units of math, 3 units of science, 3 units of social studies, 5 units of academic electives.

TESTING

SAT Reasoning or ACT required. SAT Subject required.

All enrolled freshmen (fall 2004):

Average SAT I Scores: Verbal: 537 Math: 568
Average ACT Scores: Composite: 23

Child Study Team report is not required. A neuropsychological or comprehensive psycho-educational evaluation is required for admission. Must be dated within 36 months of application. Tests required as part of this documentation:

■ WAIS-IV
☐ WISC-IV
■ SATA
■ Woodcock-Johnson
■ Nelson-Denny Reading Test
☐ Other

UNDERGRADUATE STUDENT BODY

Total undergraduate student enrollment: 5,333 Men, 6,721 Women.

Composition of student body (fall 2004):

	Undergraduate	Freshmen
International	1.7	4.7
Black	0.9	1.0
American Indian	0.5	0.3
Asian-American	63.0	63.1
Hispanic	2.6	2.1
White	30.5	25.3
Unreported	0.8	3.6
	100.0%	100.0%

17% are from out of state. Average age of full-time undergraduates is 21. 45% of classes have fewer than 20 students, 45% have between 20 and 50 students, 10% have more than 50 students.

STUDENT HOUSING

49% of freshmen live in college housing. Freshmen are not required to live on campus. Housing is guaranteed for all undergraduates. Campus can house 3,128 undergraduates. Single rooms are available for students with medical or special needs. A medical note is required.

EXPENSES

Tuition (2005-06): $3,504 per year (in-state), $9,984 (out-of-state).
Room: $4,232. Board: $2,485.
There is no additional cost for LD program/services.

LD SERVICES

LD program size is not limited.

LD services available to:

■ Freshmen ■ Sophomores ■ Juniors ■ Seniors

Academic Accommodations

Curriculum		In class	
Foreign language waiver	☐	Early syllabus	■
Lighter course load	■	Note takers in class	■
Math waiver	☐	Priority seating	☐
Other special classes	☐	Tape recorders	■
Priority registrations	■	Videotaped classes	☐
Substitution of courses	■	Text on tape	■
Exams		**Services**	
Extended time	■	Diagnostic tests	■
Oral exams	☐	Learning centers	☐
Take home exams	☐	Proofreaders	■
Exams on tape or computer	■	Readers	■
Untimed exams	☐	Reading Machines/Kurzweil	■
Other accommodations	☐	Special bookstore section	☐
		Typists	■

Credit toward degree is not given for remedial courses taken.

Counseling Services

■ Academic — Meets 3 times per academic year
☐ Psychological
☐ Student Support groups
☐ Vocational

Tutoring

Individual tutoring is available weekly.

Average size of tutoring groups: 1

	Individual	Group
Time management	☐	☐
Organizational skills	☐	☐
Learning strategies	☐	☐
Study skills	☐	☐
Content area	■	☐
Writing lab	☐	☐
Math lab	☐	☐

UNIQUE LD PROGRAM FEATURES

Campus does not have a specific learning disabilities program, but a general disabilities program called KOKUA. Striving to create equity of educational opportunity, KOKUA serves undergraduate and graduate students with learning, mental, and physical disabilities.

LD PROGRAM STAFF

Total number of LD Program staff (including director):

Full Time: 6 Part Time: 6

There is an advisor/advocate from the LD program available to students. 4 peer tutors are available to work with LD students.

Key staff person available to work with LD students: Dr. Lanning Lee, Learning Resource Specialist.

Hawaii Pacific University

Honolulu, HI

Address: 1164 Bishop Street, Honolulu, HI, 96813
Admissions telephone: 866 CALL-HPU
Admissions FAX: 808 544-1136
Associate Vice President, Enrollment Management: Scott Stensrud
Admissions e-mail: admissions@hpu.edu
Web site: http://www.hpu.edu
SAT Code: 4352 ACT Code: 900

Director of Admission: Cherie Andrade
LD program telephone: 808 544-0238
LD program e-mail: candrade@hpu.edu
LD program enrollment: 57, Total campus enrollment: 6,615

GENERAL

Hawaii Pacific University is a private, coed, four-year institution. Five-acre, urban campus plus 135-acre, suburban campus in Honolulu (population: 371,657); branch campuses at several military installations on Oahu. Served by air. School operates transportation between campuses. Public transportation serves campus. 4-1-4 system.

LD ADMISSIONS

Application Deadline: 08/01. Students do not complete a separate application and are not simultaneously accepted to the LD program. A member of the LD program does not sit on the admissions committee. A personal interview is recommended. Essay is not required.

SECONDARY SCHOOL REQUIREMENTS

Graduation from secondary school required; GED accepted.

TESTING

SAT Reasoning or ACT required. SAT Subject recommended.

All enrolled freshmen (fall 2004):

Average SAT I Scores:	Verbal: 498	Math: 508
Average ACT Scores:	Composite: 22	

Child Study Team report is not required. A neuropsychological or comprehensive psycho-educational evaluation is required for admission. Tests required as part of this documentation:

- [x] WAIS-IV
- [ ] WISC-IV
- [x] SATA
- [x] Woodcock-Johnson
- [x] Nelson-Denny Reading Test
- [ ] Other

UNDERGRADUATE STUDENT BODY

Total undergraduate student enrollment: 3,074 Men, 3,685 Women.

Composition of student body (fall 2004):

	Undergraduate	Freshmen
International	11.3	12.7
Black	5.1	7.8
American Indian	0.7	1.1
Asian-American	31.6	32.5
Hispanic	6.0	7.1
White	44.6	38.2
Unreported	0.7	0.5
	100.0%	100.0%

48% are from out of state. Average age of full-time undergraduates is 22. 47% of classes have fewer than 20 students, 53% have between 20 and 50 students.

STUDENT HOUSING

10% of freshmen live in college housing. Freshmen are not required to live on campus. Housing is guaranteed for all undergraduates. Campus can house 800 undergraduates. Single rooms are not available for students with medical or special needs.

EXPENSES

Tuition (2005-06): $11,550 per year.
Room & Board: $8,950.

There is no additional cost for LD program/services.

LD SERVICES

LD program size is not limited.

LD services available to:

- [x] Freshmen
- [x] Sophomores
- [x] Juniors
- [x] Seniors

Academic Accommodations

Curriculum		**In class**	
Foreign language waiver	[x]	Early syllabus	[ ]
Lighter course load	[ ]	Note takers in class	[ ]
Math waiver	[ ]	Priority seating	[x]
Other special classes	[ ]	Tape recorders	[x]
Priority registrations	[x]	Videotaped classes	[ ]
Substitution of courses	[x]	Text on tape	[x]
Exams		**Services**	
Extended time	[x]	Diagnostic tests	[ ]
Oral exams	[x]	Learning centers	[x]
Take home exams	[x]	Proofreaders	[x]
Exams on tape or computer	[x]	Readers	[x]
Untimed exams	[x]	Reading Machines/Kurzweil	[ ]
Other accommodations	[x]	Special bookstore section	[ ]
		Typists	[x]

Credit toward degree is not given for remedial courses taken.

Counseling Services

- [x] Academic
- [ ] Psychological
- [ ] Student Support groups
- [ ] Vocational

Tutoring

Individual tutoring is available daily.

Average size of tutoring groups: 2

	Individual	Group
Time management	[ ]	[ ]
Organizational skills	[ ]	[ ]
Learning strategies	[ ]	[ ]
Study skills	[ ]	[ ]
Content area	[ ]	[ ]
Writing lab	[ ]	[ ]
Math lab	[ ]	[ ]

LD PROGRAM STAFF

Total number of LD Program staff (including director):

Full Time: 2 Part Time: 2

There is an advisor/advocate from the LD program available to students. The advisor/advocate meets with faculty 12 times per month and students 8 times per month. 10 peer tutors are available to work with LD students.

Key staff person available to work with LD students: Tiffany Shiraishi, ADA Coordinator/Academic Advisor.

Albertson College of Idaho

Caldwell, ID

Address: 2112 Cleveland Boulevard, Caldwell, ID, 83605
Admissions telephone: 800 224-3246
Admissions FAX: 208 459-5757
Dean of Enrollment Management: Warren Muller
Admissions e-mail: admission@albertson.edu
Web site: http://www.albertson.edu
SAT Code: 4060 ACT Code: 916

LD program name: Disability Services
Study Skills Coordinator: Dorothy Gerber
LD program telephone: 208 459-5683
LD program e-mail: dgerber@albertson.edu
LD program enrollment: 20, Total campus enrollment: 789

GENERAL

Albertson College of Idaho is a private, coed, four-year institution. 43-acre campus in Caldwell (population: 25,967), 30 miles from Boise. Served by bus; major airport serves Boise. School operates transportation to Bogus Basin Ski Area in winter and to events in Boise. Public transportation serves campus.

LD ADMISSIONS

Application Deadline: 05/01. Students do not complete a separate application and are not simultaneously accepted to the LD program. A member of the LD program does sit on the admissions committee. A personal interview is recommended. Essay is required and may be typed.

12 applications were offered admission, and 5 enrolled.

SECONDARY SCHOOL REQUIREMENTS

Graduation from secondary school required; GED accepted. The following course distribution required: 4 units of English, 3 units of math, 2 units of science, 3 units of history, 3 units of academic electives.

TESTING

SAT Reasoning or ACT required. SAT Subject required.

All enrolled freshmen (fall 2004):

Average SAT I Scores:	Verbal: 584	Math: 567
Average ACT Scores:	Composite: 24	

Child Study Team report is not required. A neuropsychological or comprehensive psycho-educational evaluation is required for admission. Must be dated within 36 months of application. Tests required as part of this documentation:

- [x] WAIS-IV
- [x] WISC-IV
- [ ] SATA
- [x] Woodcock-Johnson
- [x] Nelson-Denny Reading Test
- [x] Other

UNDERGRADUATE STUDENT BODY

Total undergraduate student enrollment: 358 Men, 420 Women.

Composition of student body (fall 2004):

	Undergraduate	Freshmen
International	2.6	2.3
Black	1.1	0.8
American Indian	0.0	0.5
Asian-American	4.2	3.0
Hispanic	5.3	3.9
White	69.5	74.4
Unreported	17.4	15.2
	100.0%	100.0%

21% are from out of state. 7% join a fraternity and 7% join a sorority. Average age of full-time undergraduates is 20. 73% of classes have fewer than 20 students, 26% have between 20 and 50 students, 1% have more than 50 students.

STUDENT HOUSING

83% of freshmen live in college housing. Freshmen are required to live on campus. Housing is guaranteed for all undergraduates. Campus can house 555 undergraduates. Single rooms are available for students with medical or special needs. A medical note is required.

EXPENSES

Tuition (2005-06): $15,200 per year. $19,800 per year (freshmen), $17,100 (returning students).

Room & Board: $5,624.

There is no additional cost for LD program/services.

LD SERVICES

LD program size is not limited.

LD services available to:

- [x] Freshmen
- [x] Sophomores
- [x] Juniors
- [x] Seniors

Academic Accommodations

Curriculum		In class	
Foreign language waiver	[ ]	Early syllabus	[ ]
Lighter course load	[x]	Note takers in class	[x]
Math waiver	[ ]	Priority seating	[ ]
Other special classes	[ ]	Tape recorders	[x]
Priority registrations	[ ]	Videotaped classes	[ ]
Substitution of courses	[ ]	Text on tape	[ ]
Exams		**Services**	
Extended time	[x]	Diagnostic tests	[ ]
Oral exams	[x]	Learning centers	[x]
Take home exams	[x]	Proofreaders	[ ]
Exams on tape or computer	[ ]	Readers	[x]
Untimed exams	[x]	Reading Machines/Kurzweil	[ ]
Other accommodations	[x]	Special bookstore section	[ ]
		Typists	[ ]

Credit toward degree is not given for remedial courses taken.

Counseling Services

- [x] Academic
- [x] Psychological
- [x] Student Support groups
- [ ] Vocational

Tutoring

Individual tutoring is available daily.

Average size of tutoring groups: 1

	Individual	Group
Time management	[x]	[x]
Organizational skills	[x]	[x]
Learning strategies	[x]	[x]
Study skills	[x]	[x]
Content area	[x]	[x]
Writing lab	[ ]	[ ]
Math lab	[ ]	[ ]

LD PROGRAM STAFF

Total number of LD Program staff (including director):

Full Time: 1 Part Time: 1

There is no advisor/advocate from the LD program available to students.

Key staff person available to work with LD students: Dorothy Gerber, Study Skills Coordinator.

Boise State University

Boise, ID

Address: 1910 University Drive, Boise, ID, 83725
Admissions telephone: 800 824-7017
Admissions FAX: 208 426-3765
Dean of Enrollment Services: Barbara Fortin
Admissions e-mail: bsuinfo@boisestate.edu
Web site: http://www.BoiseState.edu
SAT Code: 4018 ACT Code: 914

Total campus enrollment: 16,719

GENERAL

Boise State University is a public, coed, four-year institution. 113-acre, urban campus in Boise (population: 185,787); branch campuses in Canyon County, Gowen Field, MacCall, and Mountain Home. Served by air, bus, and train. Public transportation serves campus. Semester system.

LD ADMISSIONS

SECONDARY SCHOOL REQUIREMENTS

Graduation from secondary school required; GED accepted. The following course distribution required: 8 units of English, 6 units of math, 6 units of science, 5 units of social studies, 2 units of history, 3 units of academic electives.

TESTING

SAT Reasoning or ACT required. SAT Subject recommended.

All enrolled freshmen (fall 2004):

Average SAT I Scores: Verbal: 508 Math: 514

Child Study Team report is not required. Tests required as part of this documentation:

- ☐ WAIS-IV
- ☐ WISC-IV
- ☐ SATA
- ☐ Woodcock-Johnson
- ☐ Nelson-Denny Reading Test
- ☐ Other

UNDERGRADUATE STUDENT BODY

Total undergraduate student enrollment: 6,639 Men, 8,111 Women.

Composition of student body (fall 2004):

	Undergraduate	Freshmen
International	2.1	2.3
Black	1.6	1.1
American Indian	0.9	1.0
Asian-American	2.6	2.1
Hispanic	6.3	4.9
White	81.2	82.0
Unreported	5.4	6.5
	100.0%	100.0%

8% are from out of state. 1% join a fraternity and 1% join a sorority. Average age of full-time undergraduates is 25. 45% of classes have fewer than 20 students, 49% have between 20 and 50 students, 6% have more than 50 students.

STUDENT HOUSING

20% of freshmen live in college housing. Freshmen are not required to live on campus. Housing is guaranteed for all undergraduates.

EXPENSES

Tuition (2005-06): $2,568 per year (in-state), $9,784 (out-of-state).
Room & Board: $5,545.

LD SERVICES

LD program size is not limited.

LD services available to:

☐ Freshmen ☐ Sophomores ☐ Juniors ☐ Seniors

Academic Accommodations

Curriculum		In class	
Foreign language waiver	☐	Early syllabus	☐
Lighter course load	☐	Note takers in class	☐
Math waiver	☐	Priority seating	☐
Other special classes	☐	Tape recorders	■
Priority registrations	☐	Videotaped classes	☐
Substitution of courses	☐	Text on tape	☐
Exams		**Services**	
Extended time	☐	Diagnostic tests	■
Oral exams	■	Learning centers	■
Take home exams	☐	Proofreaders	☐
Exams on tape or computer	☐	Readers	☐
Untimed exams	☐	Reading Machines/Kurzweil	☐
Other accommodations	☐	Special bookstore section	☐
		Typists	☐

Credit toward degree is not given for remedial courses taken.

Counseling Services

- ☐ Academic
- ☐ Psychological
- ☐ Student Support groups
- ☐ Vocational

Tutoring

	Individual	Group
Time management	☐	☐
Organizational skills	☐	☐
Learning strategies	☐	☐
Study skills	☐	☐
Content area	☐	☐
Writing lab	☐	☐
Math lab	☐	☐

Idaho State University

Pocatello, ID

Address: 741 South Seventh Avenue, Pocatello, ID, 83209
Admissions telephone: 208 282-2475
Admissions FAX: 208 282-4511
Director of Admissions: Nathan Peterson
Admissions e-mail: info@isu.edu
Web site: http://www.isu.edu
SAT Code: 4355 ACT Code: 918

LD program name: ADA Disabilities and Resource Center
LD program address: Gravely Hall 123, Campus Box 8121
Director: Dennis Toney
LD program telephone: 208 282-3599
LD program e-mail: Tonedenn@isu.edu
LD program enrollment: 140, Total campus enrollment: 11,663

GENERAL

Idaho State University is a public, coed, four-year institution. 236-acre campus in Pocatello (population: 51,466), 100 miles from Ogden, Utah; branch campuses in Boise, Idaho Falls, and Twin Falls. Served by air and bus; major aiport serves Salt Lake City (150 miles). School operates transportation to Blackfoot, Idaho Falls, Rexburg, Rigby, Soda Springs, and Twin Falls. Public transportation serves campus. Semester system.

LD ADMISSIONS

Students do not complete a separate application and are not simultaneously accepted to the LD program. A member of the LD program does not sit on the admissions committee. A personal interview is recommended. Essay is not required.

SECONDARY SCHOOL REQUIREMENTS

Graduation from secondary school required; GED accepted. The following course distribution required: 4 units of English, 3 units of math, 3 units of science, 1 unit of foreign language, 3 units of social studies.

TESTING

SAT Reasoning or ACT considered if submitted; ACT preferred. SAT Subject recommended.

All enrolled freshmen (fall 2004):

Average SAT I Scores: Verbal: 527 Math: 537
Average ACT Scores: Composite: 21

Child Study Team report is not required. A neuropsychological or comprehensive psycho-educational evaluation is required for admission. Must be dated within 36 months of application. Tests required as part of this documentation:

- [x] WAIS-IV
- [x] WISC-IV
- [x] SATA
- [x] Woodcock-Johnson
- [x] Nelson-Denny Reading Test
- [ ] Other

UNDERGRADUATE STUDENT BODY

Total undergraduate student enrollment: 4,993 Men, 6,174 Women.

Composition of student body (fall 2004):

	Undergraduate	Freshmen
International	1.1	1.9
Black	1.2	0.8
American Indian	1.9	1.9
Asian-American	1.9	1.2
Hispanic	6.2	4.2
White	84.2	87.1
Unreported	3.5	2.9
	100.0%	100.0%

4% are from out of state. 1% join a fraternity and 1% join a sorority. Average age of full-time undergraduates is 25. 62% of classes have fewer than 20 students, 33% have between 20 and 50 students, 5% have more than 50 students.

STUDENT HOUSING

3% of freshmen live in college housing. Freshmen are not required to live on campus. Housing is guaranteed for all undergraduates. Campus can house 654 undergraduates. Single rooms are available for students with medical or special needs. A medical note is required.

EXPENSES

Tuition (2005-06): No tuition for in-state, $7,080 (out-of-state).
Room: $2,060. Board: $2,790.
There is no additional cost for LD program/services.

LD SERVICES

LD program size is not limited.

LD services available to:

- [x] Freshmen
- [x] Sophomores
- [x] Juniors
- [x] Seniors

Academic Accommodations

Curriculum		**In class**	
Foreign language waiver	[x]	Early syllabus	[ ]
Lighter course load	[ ]	Note takers in class	[x]
Math waiver	[x]	Priority seating	[ ]
Other special classes	[ ]	Tape recorders	[x]
Priority registrations	[x]	Videotaped classes	[ ]
Substitution of courses	[ ]	Text on tape	[ ]
Exams		**Services**	
Extended time	[x]	Diagnostic tests	[x]
Oral exams	[x]	Learning centers	[x]
Take home exams	[ ]	Proofreaders	[ ]
Exams on tape or computer	[x]	Readers	[x]
Untimed exams	[x]	Reading Machines/Kurzweil	[x]
Other accommodations	[x]	Special bookstore section	[ ]
		Typists	[x]

Credit toward degree is not given for remedial courses taken.

Counseling Services

- [x] Academic
- [x] Psychological
- [x] Student Support groups
- [x] Vocational

Tutoring

Individual tutoring is available daily.

	Individual	Group
Time management	[ ]	[ ]
Organizational skills	[ ]	[ ]
Learning strategies	[x]	[x]
Study skills	[x]	[x]
Content area	[x]	[x]
Writing lab	[x]	[x]
Math lab	[x]	[x]

LD PROGRAM STAFF

Total number of LD Program staff (including director):

Full Time: 5 Part Time: 5

There is an advisor/advocate from the LD program available to students.

Key staff person available to work with LD students: Todd Devries, Assistant Tech. Coordinator.

University of Idaho

Moscow, ID

Address: 875 Perimeter Drive, P.O. Box 442282, Moscow, ID, 83844-2282
Admissions telephone: 888 884-3246
Admissions FAX: 208 885-9119
Director of Admissions and Financial Aid: Dr. Dan Davenport
Admissions e-mail: admappl@uidaho.edu
Web site: http://www.its.uidaho.edu/uihome/
SAT Code: 4843 ACT Code: 928

Interim Coordinator: Gloria Jensen
LD program telephone: 208 885-7200
LD program e-mail: dds@uidaho.edu
Total campus enrollment: 9,550

GENERAL

University of Idaho is a public, coed, four-year institution. 800-acre campus and university farm in Moscow (population: 21,291), 85 miles from Spokane; branch campuses in Boise, Coeur d'Alene, and Idaho Falls. Served by bus; major airport and train serve Spokane; smaller airport serves Pullman, Wash. (eight miles). School operates transportation to Pullman. Public transportation serves campus. Semester system.

LD ADMISSIONS

A personal interview is not required. Essay is not required.

SECONDARY SCHOOL REQUIREMENTS

Graduation from secondary school required; GED accepted. The following course distribution required: 4 units of English, 3 units of math, 3 units of science, 1 unit of foreign language, 3 units of social studies, 2 units of academic electives.

TESTING

SAT Reasoning or ACT required. SAT Subject recommended.

All enrolled freshmen (fall 2004):

Average SAT I Scores:	Verbal: 548	Math: 553
Average ACT Scores:	Composite: 23	

Child Study Team report is not required. Tests required as part of this documentation:

☐ WAIS-IV
☐ WISC-IV
☐ SATA
☐ Woodcock-Johnson
☐ Nelson-Denny Reading Test
☐ Other

UNDERGRADUATE STUDENT BODY

Total undergraduate student enrollment: 4,946 Men, 4,188 Women.

Composition of student body (fall 2004):

	Undergraduate	Freshmen
International	1.0	2.3
Black	1.2	0.8
American Indian	1.6	1.2
Asian-American	2.8	2.3
Hispanic	4.7	3.7
White	84.4	84.6
Unreported	4.5	4.9
	100.0%	100.0%

19% are from out of state. Average age of full-time undergraduates is 22. 49% of classes have fewer than 20 students, 44% have between 20 and 50 students, 8% have more than 50 students.

STUDENT HOUSING

48% of freshmen live in college housing. Freshmen are not required to live on campus. Housing is guaranteed for all undergraduates. Campus can house 2,226 undergraduates.

EXPENSES

Tuition (2005-06): No tuition for in-state, $8,770 (out-of-state).

Room & Board: $5,342.
There is no additional cost for LD program/services.

LD SERVICES

LD program size is not limited.

LD services available to:

☐ Freshmen ☐ Sophomores ☐ Juniors ☐ Seniors

Academic Accommodations

Curriculum		**In class**	
Foreign language waiver	☐	Early syllabus	☐
Lighter course load	☑	Note takers in class	☑
Math waiver	☐	Priority seating	☐
Other special classes	☐	Tape recorders	☑
Priority registrations	☐	Videotaped classes	☑
Substitution of courses	☐	Text on tape	☐
Exams		**Services**	
Extended time	☑	Diagnostic tests	☐
Oral exams	☑	Learning centers	☑
Take home exams	☐	Proofreaders	☐
Exams on tape or computer	☐	Readers	☑
Untimed exams	☐	Reading Machines/Kurzweil	☑
Other accommodations	☐	Special bookstore section	☐
		Typists	☐

Credit toward degree is not given for remedial courses taken.

Counseling Services

☐ Academic
☐ Psychological
☐ Student Support groups
☐ Vocational

Tutoring

	Individual	Group
Time management	☐	☐
Organizational skills	☐	☐
Learning strategies	☐	☐
Study skills	☐	☐
Content area	☐	☐
Writing lab	☐	☐
Math lab	☐	☐

UNIQUE LD PROGRAM FEATURES

Diagnostic Testing Service through Counseling and Testing Center.

LD PROGRAM STAFF

Total number of LD Program staff (including director):

Full Time: 1 Part Time: 1

Key staff person available to work with LD students: Rosie Pavlov, Learning Disabilities Specialist.

Lewis-Clark State College

Lewiston, ID

Address: 500 Eighth Avenue, Lewiston, ID, 83501
Admissions telephone: 800 933-5272
Admissions FAX: 208 792-2876
Director of Enrollment Management: Steven Bussolini
Admissions e-mail: admissions@lcsc.edu
Web site: http://www.lcsc.edu
SAT Code: 4385 ACT Code: 920

Coordinator of Advising & Disability Services: Debi Mundell
LD program telephone: 208 792-2378
LD program e-mail: dmundell@lcsc.edu
Total campus enrollment: 3,325

GENERAL

Lewis-Clark State College is a public, coed, four-year institution. 44-acre campus in Lewiston (population: 30,904), 105 miles from Spokane; branch campus in Coeur d'Alene. Served by bus; major airport serves Spokane. Semester system.

LD ADMISSIONS

Students do not complete a separate application and are not simultaneously accepted to the LD program. A member of the LD program does not sit on the admissions committee. A personal interview is not required. Essay is not required.

SECONDARY SCHOOL REQUIREMENTS

Graduation from secondary school required; GED accepted. The following course distribution required: 4 units of English, 3 units of math, 3 units of science, 3 units of social studies, 2 units of academic electives.

TESTING

ACT required of some applicants; SAT Reasoning may be substituted. SAT Subject recommended.

All enrolled freshmen (fall 2004):

Average SAT I Scores:	Verbal: 463	Math: 473
Average ACT Scores:	Composite: 20	

Child Study Team report is not required. A neuropsychological or comprehensive psycho-education evaluation is not required for admission. Tests required as part of this documentation:

- ☐ WAIS-IV
- ☐ WISC-IV
- ☐ SATA
- ☐ Woodcock-Johnson
- ☐ Nelson-Denny Reading Test
- ☐ Other

UNDERGRADUATE STUDENT BODY

Total undergraduate student enrollment: 1,125 Men, 1,828 Women.

15% are from out of state. Average age of full-time undergraduates is 25. 67% of classes have fewer than 20 students, 32% have between 20 and 50 students.

STUDENT HOUSING

21% of freshmen live in college housing. Freshmen are not required to live on campus. Housing is guaranteed for all undergraduates. Campus can house 200 undergraduates.

EXPENSES

Tuition (2005-06): $3,714 per year (in-state), $10,484 (out-of-state).
Room: $1,785. Board: $2,415.
There is no additional cost for LD program/services.

LD SERVICES

LD program size is not limited.

LD services available to:

☑ Freshmen ☑ Sophomores ☑ Juniors ☑ Seniors

Academic Accommodations

Curriculum		**In class**	
Foreign language waiver	☐	Early syllabus	☐
Lighter course load	☑	Note takers in class	☐
Math waiver	☐	Priority seating	☐
Other special classes	☐	Tape recorders	☑
Priority registrations	☐	Videotaped classes	☐
Substitution of courses	☐	Text on tape	☑
Exams		**Services**	
Extended time	☑	Diagnostic tests	☐
Oral exams	☐	Learning centers	☑
Take home exams	☐	Proofreaders	☑
Exams on tape or computer	☐	Readers	☑
Untimed exams	☐	Reading Machines/Kurzweil	☑
Other accommodations	☑	Special bookstore section	☐
		Typists	☐

Credit toward degree is not given for remedial courses taken.

Counseling Services

- ☑ Academic
- ☑ Psychological
- ☐ Student Support groups
- ☑ Vocational

Tutoring

Individual tutoring is available.

	Individual	Group
Time management	☐	☐
Organizational skills	☐	☐
Learning strategies	☐	☐
Study skills	☐	☐
Content area	☐	☐
Writing lab	☐	☐
Math lab	☐	☐

LD PROGRAM STAFF

Total number of LD Program staff (including director):

Full Time: 1 Part Time: 1

There is an advisor/advocate from the LD program available to students.

Key staff person available to work with LD students: Debi Mundell, Coordinator of Advising & Disability Services.

Northwest Nazarene University

Nampa, ID

Address: 623 Holly Street, Nampa, ID, 83686
Admissions telephone: 877 668-4968
Admissions FAX: 208 467-8645
Director of Admissions: Dianna Gibney
Admissions e-mail: Admissions@nnu.edu
Web site: http://www.nnu.edu
SAT Code: 4544 ACT Code: 924

LD program name: Advising for Students with Learning Disabilities
Advisor to Students with LD: Barbara Howard
LD program telephone: 208 467-8669
LD program e-mail: bshoward@nnu.edu
LD program enrollment: 6, Total campus enrollment: 1,163

GENERAL

Northwest Nazarene University is a private, coed, four-year institution. 119-acre campus in Nampa (population: 51,867), 20 miles from Boise. Served by bus and train; airport serves Boise. Public transportation serves campus. Semester system.

LD ADMISSIONS

Students do not complete a separate application and are not simultaneously accepted to the LD program. A member of the LD program does sit on the admissions committee. A personal interview is not required. Essay is not required. All students not meeting full admissions requirements may be considered for provisional admission.

SECONDARY SCHOOL REQUIREMENTS

Graduation from secondary school required; GED accepted. The following course distribution required: 4 units of English, 3 units of math, 3 units of science, 2 units of foreign language, 3 units of social studies.

TESTING

SAT Reasoning or ACT considered if submitted; ACT preferred.

All enrolled freshmen (fall 2004):

Average SAT I Scores: Verbal: Math:
Average ACT Scores: Composite:

Child Study Team report is not required. A neuropsychological or comprehensive psycho-educational evaluation is required for admission. Must be dated within 48 months of application. Tests required as part of this documentation:

- [x] WAIS-IV
- [x] WISC-IV
- [x] SATA
- [x] Woodcock-Johnson
- [x] Nelson-Denny Reading Test
- [x] Other

UNDERGRADUATE STUDENT BODY

Total undergraduate student enrollment: 467 Men, 629 Women.

Composition of student body (fall 2004):

	Undergraduate	Freshmen
International	0.4	0.6
Black	0.0	0.8
American Indian	0.7	0.4
Asian-American	1.4	1.3
Hispanic	1.4	1.3
White	62.7	67.6
Unreported	33.3	27.9
	100.0%	100.0%

65% are from out of state. Average age of full-time undergraduates is 21. 67% of classes have fewer than 20 students, 29% have between 20 and 50 students, 3% have more than 50 students.

STUDENT HOUSING

90% of freshmen live in college housing. Freshmen are required to live on campus. Housing is guaranteed for all undergraduates. Campus can house 862 undergraduates. Single rooms are available for students with medical or special needs. A medical note is not required.

EXPENSES

Tuition (2005-06): $17,280 per year.
Room & Board: $4,860.
There is no additional cost for LD program/services.

LD SERVICES

LD program size is not limited.

LD services available to:

- [x] Freshmen
- [x] Sophomores
- [x] Juniors
- [x] Seniors

Academic Accommodations

Curriculum

- [ ] Foreign language waiver
- [x] Lighter course load
- [ ] Math waiver
- [x] Other special classes
- [x] Priority registrations
- [ ] Substitution of courses

Exams

- [x] Extended time
- [x] Oral exams
- [ ] Take home exams
- [x] Exams on tape or computer
- [x] Untimed exams
- [x] Other accommodations

In class

- [x] Early syllabus
- [x] Note takers in class
- [x] Priority seating
- [x] Tape recorders
- [ ] Videotaped classes
- [x] Text on tape

Services

- [ ] Diagnostic tests
- [x] Learning centers
- [x] Proofreaders
- [x] Readers
- [ ] Reading Machines/Kurzweil
- [ ] Special bookstore section
- [x] Typists

Credit toward degree is given for remedial courses taken.

Counseling Services

- [ ] Academic
- [ ] Psychological
- [ ] Student Support groups
- [ ] Vocational

Tutoring

Individual tutoring is available daily.

Average size of tutoring groups: 1

	Individual	Group
Time management	[x]	[x]
Organizational skills	[x]	[x]
Learning strategies	[x]	[x]
Study skills	[x]	[x]
Content area	[x]	[x]
Writing lab	[x]	[x]
Math lab	[x]	[x]

LD PROGRAM STAFF

Total number of LD Program staff (including director):

Full Time: 1 Part Time: 1

There is an advisor/advocate from the LD program available to students. The advisor/advocate meets with faculty 2 times per month and students 8 times per month. 2 graduate students and 7 peer tutors are available to work with LD students.

Key staff person available to work with LD students: Barbara Howard, Advisor to Students with Learning Disabilities.

Augustana College

Rock Island, IL

Address: 639 38th Street, Rock Island, IL, 61201-2296
Admissions telephone: 800 798-8100
Admissions FAX: 309 794-7174
Director of Admissions/Associate Dean for Enrollment: Martin Sauer
Admissions e-mail: admissions@augustana.edu
Web site: http://www.augustana.edu
SAT Code: 6015 ACT Code: 946

Dean of Students: Evelyn Campbell, Ph.D.
LD program telephone: 309 794-7533
LD program e-mail: adsec@augustana.edu
Total campus enrollment: 2,292

GENERAL

Augustana College is a private, coed, four-year institution. 115-acre campus in Rock Island (population: 39,684), 165 miles from Chicago. Major airport serves Chicago; smaller airport and bus serve Moline (five miles); train serves Galesburg (45 miles). School operates van service as needed. Public transportation serves campus. Quarter system.

LD ADMISSIONS

A personal interview is not required. Essay is not required.

SECONDARY SCHOOL REQUIREMENTS

Graduation from secondary school required; GED accepted. The following course distribution required: 4 units of English, 3 units of math, 2 units of science, 1 unit of foreign language, 1 unit of social studies, 1 unit of history, 4 units of academic electives.

TESTING

SAT Reasoning or ACT required.

All enrolled freshmen (fall 2004):

Average ACT Scores: Composite: 26

Child Study Team report is not required. Tests required as part of this documentation:

- ❑ WAIS-IV
- ❑ WISC-IV
- ❑ SATA
- ❑ Woodcock-Johnson
- ❑ Nelson-Denny Reading Test
- ❑ Other

UNDERGRADUATE STUDENT BODY

Total undergraduate student enrollment: 956 Men, 1,276 Women.

Composition of student body (fall 2004):

	Undergraduate	Freshmen
International	0.8	0.4
Black	2.2	2.2
American Indian	0.5	0.3
Asian-American	2.5	2.2
Hispanic	2.8	2.6
White	91.2	92.2
Unreported	0.0	0.0
	100.0%	100.0%

12% are from out of state. 21% join a fraternity and 27% join a sorority. Average age of full-time undergraduates is 20, 55% of classes have fewer than 20 students, 43% have between 20 and 50 students.

STUDENT HOUSING

95% of freshmen live in college housing. Freshmen are required to live on campus. Housing is not guaranteed for all undergraduates. Senior students generally live in apartments in the surrounding community. Campus can house 1,600 undergraduates.

EXPENSES

Tuition (2005-06): $22,971 per year.
Room & Board: $6,405.
There is no additional cost for LD program/services.

LD SERVICES

LD program size is not limited.

LD services available to:

❑ Freshmen ❑ Sophomores ❑ Juniors ❑ Seniors

Academic Accommodations

Curriculum		**In class**	
Foreign language waiver	❑	Early syllabus	❑
Lighter course load	❑	Note takers in class	❑
Math waiver	❑	Priority seating	❑
Other special classes	❑	Tape recorders	❑
Priority registrations	❑	Videotaped classes	❑
Substitution of courses	❑	Text on tape	❑
Exams		**Services**	
Extended time	❑	Diagnostic tests	❑
Oral exams	❑	Learning centers	❑
Take home exams	❑	Proofreaders	❑
Exams on tape or computer	❑	Readers	❑
Untimed exams	❑	Reading Machines/Kurzweil	❑
Other accommodations	❑	Special bookstore section	❑
		Typists	❑

Credit toward degree is not given for remedial courses taken.

Counseling Services

- ❑ Academic
- ❑ Psychological
- ❑ Student Support groups
- ❑ Vocational

Tutoring

	Individual	Group
Time management	❑	❑
Organizational skills	❑	❑
Learning strategies	❑	❑
Study skills	❑	❑
Content area	❑	❑
Writing lab	❑	❑
Math lab	❑	❑

LD PROGRAM STAFF

Key staff person available to work with LD students: Evelyn Campbell, Ph.D., Dean of Students.

Aurora University

Aurora, IL

Address: 347 South Gladstone Avenue, Aurora, IL, 60506-4892
Admissions telephone: 800 742-5281
Admissions FAX: 630 844-5535
Vice President for Enrollment: Dr. Carol Dunn
Admissions e-mail: admission@aurora.edu
Web site: http://www.aurora.edu
SAT Code: 1027 ACT Code: 950

LD program name: Learning Center
LD program address: 347 S Gladstone Avenue
Disabilities Services Coordinator: Susan Lausier
LD program telephone: 630 844-5267
LD program e-mail: slausier@aurora.edu
LD program enrollment: 42, Total campus enrollment: 1,719

GENERAL

Aurora University is a private, coed, four-year institution. 27-acre, suburban campus in Aurora (population: 142,990), 40 miles from Chicago; branch campus in Lake Geneva, Wis. Served by bus and train; major airport serves Chicago. Public transportation serves campus. Semester system.

LD ADMISSIONS

Students do not complete a separate application and are not simultaneously accepted to the LD program. A member of the LD program does not sit on the admissions committee. A personal interview is required. Essay is not required.

SECONDARY SCHOOL REQUIREMENTS

Graduation from secondary school required; GED accepted.

TESTING

ACT recommended; SAT Reasoning may be substituted. SAT Subject recommended.

All enrolled freshmen (fall 2004):

Average SAT I Scores:	Verbal: 534	Math: 525
Average ACT Scores:	Composite: 21	

Child Study Team report is not required. A neuropsychological or comprehensive psycho-educational evaluation is required for admission. Must be dated within 36 months of application. Tests required as part of this documentation:

- ☒ WAIS-IV
- ☐ WISC-IV
- ☐ SATA
- ☒ Woodcock-Johnson
- ☐ Nelson-Denny Reading Test
- ☒ Other

UNDERGRADUATE STUDENT BODY

Total undergraduate student enrollment: 532 Men, 791 Women.

Composition of student body (fall 2004):

	Undergraduate	Freshmen
International	0.0	0.1
Black	12.6	13.8
American Indian	0.0	0.2
Asian-American	1.0	2.4
Hispanic	15.6	12.5
White	69.7	70.6
Unreported	1.0	0.5
	100.0%	100.0%

4% are from out of state. 1% join a fraternity and 1% join a sorority. Average age of full-time undergraduates is 22, 37% of classes have fewer than 20 students, 63% have between 20 and 50 students.

STUDENT HOUSING

69% of freshmen live in college housing. Freshmen are not required to live on campus. Campus can house 501 undergraduates. Single rooms are available for students with medical or special needs. A medical note is required.

EXPENSES

Tuition (2005-06): $15,500 per year.

Room: $3,020. Board: $3,820.
There is no additional cost for LD program/services.

LD SERVICES

LD program size is not limited.

LD services available to:

☒ Freshmen ☒ Sophomores ☒ Juniors ☒ Seniors

Academic Accommodations

Curriculum		**In class**	
Foreign language waiver	☐	Early syllabus	☒
Lighter course load	☒	Note takers in class	☒
Math waiver	☐	Priority seating	☒
Other special classes	☐	Tape recorders	☒
Priority registrations	☐	Videotaped classes	☐
Substitution of courses	☒	Text on tape	☒
Exams		**Services**	
Extended time	☒	Diagnostic tests	☐
Oral exams	☒	Learning centers	☒
Take home exams	☐	Proofreaders	☒
Exams on tape or computer	☒	Readers	☒
Untimed exams	☐	Reading Machines/Kurzweil	☒
Other accommodations	☒	Special bookstore section	☐
		Typists	☐

Credit toward degree is not given for remedial courses taken.

Counseling Services

- ☒ Academic
- ☐ Psychological
- ☐ Student Support groups
- ☐ Vocational

Tutoring

Individual tutoring is available daily.

Average size of tutoring groups: 2

	Individual	Group
Time management	☒	☐
Organizational skills	☒	☐
Learning strategies	☒	☐
Study skills	☒	☐
Content area	☒	☒
Writing lab	☒	☒
Math lab	☒	☐

LD PROGRAM STAFF

Total number of LD Program staff (including director):

Full Time: 2 Part Time: 2

There is an advisor/advocate from the LD program available to students.

Key staff person available to work with LD students: Susan Lausier, Disabilities Services Coordinator.

LD Program web site: http://www.aurora.edu/ada/index.htm

Benedictine University

Lisle, IL

Address: 5700 College Road, Lisle, IL, 60532
Admissions telephone: 888 829-6363
Admissions FAX: 630 829-6301
Dean of Undergraduate Admissions: Kari Gibbons
Admissions e-mail: admissions@ben.edu
Web site: http://www.ben.edu
SAT Code: 1707 ACT Code: 1132

LD program name: Academic Resource Center
LD program address: 5700 College Road, Lisle, IL, 60532
Coordinator of Special Programs: Tina Sonderby
LD program telephone: 630 829-6512
LD program e-mail: tsonderby@ben.edu
Total campus enrollment: 2,148

GENERAL

Benedictine University is a private, coed, four-year institution. 108-acre, suburban campus in Lisle (population: 21,182), 25 miles from Chicago. Major airports and train serve Chicago; bus serves Joliet (17 miles). Semester system.

LD ADMISSIONS

Students do not complete a separate application and are simultaneously accepted to the LD program. A member of the LD program does sit on the admissions committee. A personal interview is required. Essay is not required.

SECONDARY SCHOOL REQUIREMENTS

Graduation from secondary school required; GED accepted. The following course distribution required: 4 units of English, 3 units of math, 2 units of science, 2 units of foreign language, 1 unit of history.

TESTING

SAT Subject recommended.

All enrolled freshmen (fall 2004):

Average ACT Scores: Composite: 23

Child Study Team report is not required. A neuropsychological or comprehensive psycho-educational evaluation is required for admission. Tests required as part of this documentation:

- [x] WAIS-IV
- [x] WISC-IV
- [x] SATA
- [x] Woodcock-Johnson
- [x] Nelson-Denny Reading Test
- [ ] Other

UNDERGRADUATE STUDENT BODY

Total undergraduate student enrollment: 686 Men, 1,230 Women.

Composition of student body (fall 2004):

	Undergraduate	Freshmen
International	1.0	1.0
Black	4.3	9.5
American Indian	0.7	0.2
Asian-American	21.5	13.3
Hispanic	8.9	7.5
White	41.7	47.7
Unreported	21.9	20.9
	100.0%	100.0%

3% are from out of state. Average age of full-time undergraduates is 21, 63% of classes have fewer than 20 students, 38% have between 20 and 50 students.

STUDENT HOUSING

41% of freshmen live in college housing. Freshmen are not required to live on campus. Housing is guaranteed for all undergraduates. Campus can house 670 undergraduates. Single rooms are available for students with medical or special needs. A medical note is not required.

EXPENSES

Tuition (2005-06): $18,700 per year.

There is no additional cost for LD program/services.

LD SERVICES

LD program size is not limited.

LD services available to:

- [x] Freshmen
- [x] Sophomores
- [x] Juniors
- [x] Seniors

Academic Accommodations

Curriculum

- [ ] Foreign language waiver
- [x] Lighter course load
- [ ] Math waiver
- [ ] Other special classes
- [ ] Priority registrations
- [x] Substitution of courses

Exams

- [x] Extended time
- [x] Oral exams
- [x] Take home exams
- [x] Exams on tape or computer
- [x] Untimed exams
- [x] Other accommodations

In class

- [x] Early syllabus
- [x] Note takers in class
- [x] Priority seating
- [x] Tape recorders
- [x] Videotaped classes
- [x] Text on tape

Services

- [ ] Diagnostic tests
- [x] Learning centers
- [x] Proofreaders
- [x] Readers
- [x] Reading Machines/Kurzweil
- [ ] Special bookstore section
- [x] Typists

Credit toward degree is not given for remedial courses taken.

Counseling Services

- [x] Academic
- [x] Psychological
- [x] Student Support groups
- [x] Vocational

Tutoring

Individual tutoring is available daily.

Average size of tutoring groups: 2

	Individual	Group
Time management	[x]	[x]
Organizational skills	[x]	[x]
Learning strategies	[x]	[x]
Study skills	[x]	[x]
Content area	[x]	[x]
Writing lab	[x]	[x]
Math lab	[x]	[x]

LD PROGRAM STAFF

Total number of LD Program staff (including director):

Full Time: 2 Part Time: 2

There is an advisor/advocate from the LD program available to students. 15 peer tutors are available to work with LD students.

Key staff person available to work with LD students: Tina Sonderby, Coordinator of Special Programs.

Blackburn College

Carlinville, IL

Address: 700 College Avenue, Carlinville, IL, 62626
Admissions telephone: 800 233-3550
Admissions FAX: 217 854-3713
Director of Admissions: Ron Bryan
Admissions e-mail: admit@mail.blackburn.edu
Web site: http://www.blackburn.edu
SAT Code: 1065 ACT Code: 958

LD program name: Counseling Office / Learning Center
Director of Counseling Services: Rob Weis
LD program e-mail: rweis@blackburn.edu
Total campus enrollment: 594

GENERAL

Blackburn College is a private, coed, four-year institution. 80-acre campus in Carlinville (population: 5,686), 60 miles from St. Louis. Served by train; major airport serves St. Louis; smaller airport and bus serve Springfield (50 miles). School operates transportation to airport, bus, and train. Semester system.

LD ADMISSIONS

A personal interview is recommended. Essay is not required.

SECONDARY SCHOOL REQUIREMENTS

Graduation from secondary school required; GED accepted. The following course distribution required: 4 units of English, 3 units of math, 2 units of science, 2 units of foreign language, 2 units of social studies, 2 units of history, 3 units of academic electives.

TESTING

SAT Subject recommended.

All enrolled freshmen (fall 2004):

Average ACT Scores: Composite: 21

Child Study Team report is not required. Tests required as part of this documentation:

- [ ] WAIS-IV
- [ ] WISC-IV
- [ ] SATA
- [ ] Woodcock-Johnson
- [ ] Nelson-Denny Reading Test
- [ ] Other

UNDERGRADUATE STUDENT BODY

Total undergraduate student enrollment: 254 Men, 317 Women.

Composition of student body (fall 2004):

	Undergraduate	Freshmen
International	1.1	2.7
Black	7.9	8.4
American Indian	0.6	0.5
Asian-American	0.6	0.5
Hispanic	2.3	1.2
White	83.1	82.8
Unreported	4.5	3.9
	100.0%	100.0%

10% are from out of state. Average age of full-time undergraduates is 20, 70% of classes have fewer than 20 students, 28% have between 20 and 50 students.

STUDENT HOUSING

91% of freshmen live in college housing. Freshmen are required to live on campus. Housing is guaranteed for all undergraduates. Single rooms are available for students with medical or special needs. A medical note is required.

EXPENSES

Tuition (2005-06): $15,040 per year.
Room: $1,795. Board: $1,900.
There is no additional cost for LD program/services.

LD SERVICES

LD services available to:

- [x] Freshmen
- [x] Sophomores
- [x] Juniors
- [x] Seniors

Academic Accommodations

Curriculum

- [ ] Foreign language waiver
- [ ] Lighter course load
- [ ] Math waiver
- [ ] Other special classes
- [ ] Priority registrations
- [x] Substitution of courses

Exams

- [x] Extended time
- [x] Oral exams
- [ ] Take home exams
- [ ] Exams on tape or computer
- [x] Untimed exams
- [ ] Other accommodations

In class

- [x] Early syllabus
- [x] Note takers in class
- [x] Priority seating
- [x] Tape recorders
- [x] Videotaped classes
- [x] Text on tape

Services

- [ ] Diagnostic tests
- [x] Learning centers
- [x] Proofreaders
- [x] Readers
- [x] Reading Machines/Kurzweil
- [ ] Special bookstore section
- [x] Typists

Credit toward degree is given for remedial courses taken.

Counseling Services

- [x] Academic
- [x] Psychological
- [x] Student Support groups
- [x] Vocational

Tutoring

Individual tutoring is available weekly.

	Individual	Group
Time management	[x]	[ ]
Organizational skills	[x]	[ ]
Learning strategies	[x]	[ ]
Study skills	[x]	[ ]
Content area	[x]	[ ]
Writing lab	[x]	[x]
Math lab	[x]	[x]

LD PROGRAM STAFF

Total number of LD Program staff (including director):

Full Time: 2 Part Time: 2

There is an advisor/advocate from the LD program available to students.

Key staff person available to work with LD students: Pat Kowal, Director of Learning Center.

Bradley University

Peoria, IL

Address: 1501 West Bradley Avenue, Peoria, IL, 61625
Admissions telephone: 800 447-6460
Admissions FAX: 309 677-2797
Associate Provost for Enrollment Management: Ms. Nicki Roberson
Admissions e-mail: admissions@bradley.edu
Web site: http://www.bradley.edu
SAT Code: 1070 ACT Code: 960

Director, Center for Learning Assistance: Carolyn Griffith
LD program telephone: 309 677-3654
LD program e-mail: griffith@bradley.edu
LD program enrollment: 100, Total campus enrollment: 5,315

GENERAL

Bradley University is a private, coed, four-year institution. 75-acre, suburban campus in Peoria (population: 112,936), 75 miles from Springfield and 157 miles from Chicago. Served by air and bus; major airport serves Chicago; train serves Bloomington (40 miles). Public transportation serves campus. Semester system.

LD ADMISSIONS

Students do not complete a separate application and are simultaneously accepted to the LD program. A member of the LD program does not sit on the admissions committee.

For fall 2004, 18 completed self-identified LD applications were received.

SECONDARY SCHOOL REQUIREMENTS

Graduation from secondary school required; GED accepted. The following course distribution required: 4 units of English, 3 units of math, 2 units of science, 2 units of social studies.

TESTING

SAT Reasoning or ACT required. SAT Subject recommended.

All enrolled freshmen (fall 2004):

Average SAT I Scores:	Verbal: 552	Math: 564
Average ACT Scores:	Composite: 25	

Child Study Team report is not required. A neuropsychological or comprehensive psycho-educational evaluation is required for admission. Must be dated within 36 months of application. Tests required as part of this documentation:

☒ WAIS-IV	☒ Woodcock-Johnson
☐ WISC-IV	☐ Nelson-Denny Reading Test
☐ SATA	☐ Other

UNDERGRADUATE STUDENT BODY

Total undergraduate student enrollment: 2,363 Men, 2,804 Women.

Composition of student body (fall 2004):

	Undergraduate	Freshmen
International	0.8	1.3
Black	5.7	5.5
American Indian	0.2	0.2
Asian-American	3.2	2.8
Hispanic	2.0	2.0
White	86.2	83.9
Unreported	2.0	4.2
	100.0%	100.0%

14% are from out of state. 31% join a fraternity and 26% join a sorority. Average age of full-time undergraduates is 21, 49% of classes have fewer than 20 students, 48% have between 20 and 50 students.

STUDENT HOUSING

94% of freshmen live in college housing. Freshmen are required to live on campus. Housing is guaranteed for all undergraduates. Campus can house 2,850 undergraduates.

EXPENSES

Tuition (2005-06): $18,700 per year.
Room & Board: $6,450.
There is no additional cost for LD program/services.

LD SERVICES

LD program size is not limited.

LD services available to:

☐ Freshmen ☐ Sophomores ☐ Juniors ☐ Seniors

Academic Accommodations

Curriculum		**In class**	
Foreign language waiver	☐	Early syllabus	☐
Lighter course load	☒	Note takers in class	☐
Math waiver	☐	Priority seating	☐
Other special classes	☐	Tape recorders	☒
Priority registrations	☐	Videotaped classes	☒
Substitution of courses	☐	Text on tape	☐
Exams		**Services**	
Extended time	☒	Diagnostic tests	☐
Oral exams	☐	Learning centers	☒
Take home exams	☐	Proofreaders	☐
Exams on tape or computer	☐	Readers	☐
Untimed exams	☒	Reading Machines/Kurzweil	☐
Other accommodations	☐	Special bookstore section	☐
		Typists	☐

Counseling Services

☐ Academic
☐ Psychological
☐ Student Support groups
☐ Vocational

Tutoring

Individual tutoring is available.

	Individual	Group
Time management	☒	☒
Organizational skills	☐	☐
Learning strategies	☐	☒
Study skills	☒	☒
Content area	☐	☐
Writing lab	☒	☐
Math lab	☐	☐

UNIQUE LD PROGRAM FEATURES

While not offering a learning disabilities program, The Center for Learning Assistance can assist those students with certain learning disabilities by providing "select coordinated accommodations" as defined by standardized national service-delivery models. This includes the provision of a contact person, generic support services, peer tutors, and student referral service for off-campus testing resources. These services are available only during the academic year. To be eligible for accommodations the student must provide current documentation of the learning disability (testing data from within the last three years) and possess strong self-advocacy skills.

LD PROGRAM STAFF

Total number of LD Program staff (including director):

Full Time: 3 Part Time: 3

There is an advisor/advocate from the LD program available to students. The advisor/advocate meets with students 4 times per month. 60 peer tutors are available to work with LD students.

Key staff person available to work with LD students: Carolyn Griffith, Director, Center for Learning Assistance.

Chicago State University

Chicago, IL

Address: 9501 South King Drive, Chicago, IL, 60628
Admissions telephone: 773 995-2513
Admissions FAX: 773 995-3820
Director of Admissions: Ms. Addie Epps
Admissions e-mail: ug-admissions@csu.edu
Web site: http://www.csu.edu
SAT Code: 1118 ACT Code: 992

LD program name: Abilities Office
LD program address: Chicago State University, Sub 190
LD program enrollment: 17, Total campus enrollment: 4,867

GENERAL

Chicago State University is a public, coed, four-year institution. 152-acre campus in Chicago (population: 2,896,016). Served by air, bus, and train. Public transportation serves campus. Semester system.

LD ADMISSIONS

Students do not complete a separate application and are not simultaneously accepted to the LD program. A member of the LD program does not sit on the admissions committee. High school waivers are accepted for math and foreign language. A personal interview is not required. Essay is not required.

SECONDARY SCHOOL REQUIREMENTS

Graduation from secondary school required; GED accepted. The following course distribution required: 4 units of English, 3 units of math, 3 units of science, 2 units of academic electives.

TESTING

SAT Reasoning or ACT required. SAT Subject recommended.

All enrolled freshmen (fall 2004):

Average ACT Scores: Composite: 18

Child Study Team report is not required. A neuropsychological or comprehensive psycho-educational evaluation is required for admission. Must be dated within 12 months of application. Tests required as part of this documentation:

- [x] WAIS-IV
- [x] WISC-IV
- [ ] SATA
- [x] Woodcock-Johnson
- [x] Nelson-Denny Reading Test
- [ ] Other

UNDERGRADUATE STUDENT BODY

Total undergraduate student enrollment: 1,356 Men, 3,704 Women.

Composition of student body (fall 2004):

	Undergraduate	Freshmen
International	1.0	0.6
Black	85.4	86.7
American Indian	0.0	0.1
Asian-American	0.5	0.4
Hispanic	7.4	6.4
White	2.4	3.1
Unreported	3.4	2.6
	100.0%	100.0%

1% are from out of state. 1% join a fraternity and 1% join a sorority. Average age of full-time undergraduates is 26, 43% of classes have fewer than 20 students, 55% have between 20 and 50 students.

STUDENT HOUSING

20% of freshmen live in college housing. Freshmen are not required to live on campus. Housing is guaranteed for all undergraduates. Campus can house 384 undergraduates. Single rooms are available for students with medical or special needs. A medical note is required.

EXPENSES

Tuition (2005-06): $2,610 per year (in-state), $5,205 (out-of-state).
Room: $3,182. Board: $3,030.

There is no additional cost for LD program/services.

LD SERVICES

LD program size is not limited.

LD services available to:

- [x] Freshmen
- [x] Sophomores
- [x] Juniors
- [x] Seniors

Academic Accommodations

Curriculum

- Foreign language waiver [ ]
- Lighter course load [x]
- Math waiver [ ]
- Other special classes [ ]
- Priority registrations [x]
- Substitution of courses [x]

Exams

- Extended time [x]
- Oral exams [x]
- Take home exams [ ]
- Exams on tape or computer [x]
- Untimed exams [ ]
- Other accommodations [x]

In class

- Early syllabus [x]
- Note takers in class [x]
- Priority seating [x]
- Tape recorders [x]
- Videotaped classes [ ]
- Text on tape [x]

Services

- Diagnostic tests [x]
- Learning centers [x]
- Proofreaders [ ]
- Readers [x]
- Reading Machines/Kurzweil [x]
- Special bookstore section [ ]
- Typists [x]

Credit toward degree is not given for remedial courses taken.

Counseling Services

- [x] Academic — Meets 20 times per academic year
- [x] Psychological — Meets 20 times per academic year
- [ ] Student Support groups
- [ ] Vocational

Tutoring

Individual tutoring is available daily.

Average size of tutoring groups: 2

	Individual	Group
Time management	[ ]	[x]
Organizational skills	[ ]	[x]
Learning strategies	[ ]	[x]
Study skills	[ ]	[ ]
Content area	[ ]	[ ]
Writing lab	[ ]	[x]
Math lab	[x]	[ ]

LD PROGRAM STAFF

Total number of LD Program staff (including director):

Full Time: 2 Part Time: 2

There is an advisor/advocate from the LD program available to students. The advisor/advocate meets with faculty 2 times per month and students 2 times per month. 4 peer tutors are available to work with LD students.

Key staff person available to work with LD students: Elois McMillian, Coordinator for Disability Services.

Columbia College Chicago

Chicago, IL

Address: 600 South Michigan Avenue, Chicago, IL, 60605-1996
Admissions telephone: 312 344-7130
Admissions FAX: 312 344-8024
Director of Admissions: Murphy Monroe
Admissions e-mail: admissions@colum.edu
Web site: http://www.colum.edu
SAT Code: 1135 ACT Code: 1002

Coordinator: Susan Snook
LD program telephone: 312 344-8134
LD program e-mail: ssnook@colum.edu
Total campus enrollment: 9,708

GENERAL

Columbia College Chicago is a private, coed, four-year institution. Urban campus of nine high-rise buildings in Chicago (population: 2,896,016). Served by air, bus, and train. School operates transportation to residence hall. Public transportation serves campus. Semester system.

LD ADMISSIONS

A personal interview is not required. Essay is required and may be typed.

SECONDARY SCHOOL REQUIREMENTS

Graduation from secondary school required; GED accepted.

TESTING

SAT Reasoning or ACT considered if submitted.

All enrolled freshmen (fall 2004):

Average ACT Scores: Composite: 21

Child Study Team report is not required. Tests required as part of this documentation:

- ❑ WAIS-IV
- ❑ WISC-IV
- ❑ SATA
- ❑ Woodcock-Johnson
- ❑ Nelson-Denny Reading Test
- ❑ Other

UNDERGRADUATE STUDENT BODY

Total undergraduate student enrollment: 4,382 Men, 4,529 Women.

Composition of student body (fall 2004):

	Undergraduate	Freshmen
International	0.6	1.8
Black	20.8	15.6
American Indian	1.3	0.9
Asian-American	2.7	3.4
Hispanic	10.7	10.0
White	58.4	62.8
Unreported	5.5	5.4
	100.0%	100.0%

19% are from out of state, 77% of classes have fewer than 20 students, 23% have between 20 and 50 students.

STUDENT HOUSING

Housing is not guaranteed for all undergraduates. Campus can house 1,136 undergraduates.

EXPENSES

Tuition (2005-06): $15,888 per year.

Room & Board: $7,600.

LD SERVICES

LD program size is not limited.

LD services available to:

❑ Freshmen ❑ Sophomores ❑ Juniors ❑ Seniors

Academic Accommodations

Curriculum		In class	
Foreign language waiver	❑	Early syllabus	❑
Lighter course load	❑	Note takers in class	■
Math waiver	❑	Priority seating	❑
Other special classes	❑	Tape recorders	❑
Priority registrations	❑	Videotaped classes	❑
Substitution of courses	❑	Text on tape	❑
Exams		**Services**	
Extended time	■	Diagnostic tests	❑
Oral exams	❑	Learning centers	❑
Take home exams	❑	Proofreaders	❑
Exams on tape or computer	❑	Readers	❑
Untimed exams	❑	Reading Machines/Kurzweil	❑
Other accommodations	❑	Special bookstore section	❑
		Typists	❑

Credit toward degree is given for remedial courses taken.

Counseling Services

- ❑ Academic
- ❑ Psychological
- ❑ Student Support groups
- ❑ Vocational

Tutoring

	Individual	Group
Time management	❑	❑
Organizational skills	❑	❑
Learning strategies	❑	❑
Study skills	❑	❑
Content area	❑	❑
Writing lab	❑	❑
Math lab	❑	❑

LD PROGRAM STAFF

Key staff person available to work with LD students: Susan Snook, Coord., Services for Students w/ Disabilities.

Concordia University, River Forest

River Forest, IL

Address: 7400 Augusta Street, River Forest, IL, 60305-1499
Admissions telephone: 800 285-2668
Admissions FAX: 708 209-3473
Acting Director of Undergraduate Admissions: Michelle Mega
Admissions e-mail: crfadmis@curf.edu
Web site: http://www.curf.edu
SAT Code: 1140 ACT Code: 1004

Director of Learning Assistance: Carol Gilbert
LD program telephone: 708 209-3042
LD program e-mail: Carol.Gilbert@curf.edu
Total campus enrollment: 1,134

GENERAL

Concordia University, River Forest is a private, coed, four-year institution. 40-acre campus in River Forest (population: 11,635), 10 miles from Chicago. Major airport, bus, and train serve Chicago. School operates transportation to airports and to train and bus stations before and after breaks. Semester system.

SECONDARY SCHOOL REQUIREMENTS

Graduation from secondary school required; GED accepted. The following course distribution required: 4 units of English, 3 units of math, 2 units of science, 2 units of social studies.

TESTING

ACT required; SAT Reasoning may be substituted. SAT Subject recommended.

All enrolled freshmen (fall 2004):

Average SAT I Scores: Verbal: Math:
Average ACT Scores: Composite: 22

Child Study Team report is not required. Tests required as part of this documentation:

- ☐ WAIS-IV
- ☐ WISC-IV
- ☐ SATA
- ☐ Woodcock-Johnson
- ☐ Nelson-Denny Reading Test
- ☐ Other

UNDERGRADUATE STUDENT BODY

Total undergraduate student enrollment: 428 Men, 852 Women.

Composition of student body (fall 2004):

	Undergraduate	Freshmen
International	0.0	0.4
Black	10.5	6.7
American Indian	0.8	0.3
Asian-American	2.0	1.5
Hispanic	9.4	6.2
White	71.1	72.3
Unreported	6.3	12.7
	100.0%	100.0%

32% are from out of state, 71% of classes have fewer than 20 students, 29% have between 20 and 50 students.

STUDENT HOUSING

Freshmen are not required to live on campus. Housing is guaranteed for all undergraduates. Campus can house 753 undergraduates.

EXPENSES

Tuition (2005-06): $19,500 per year.
Room & Board: $6,300.

LD SERVICES

LD services available to:

☐ Freshmen ☐ Sophomores ☐ Juniors ☐ Seniors

Academic Accommodations

Curriculum		In class	
Foreign language waiver	☐	Early syllabus	☐
Lighter course load	☐	Note takers in class	☐
Math waiver	☐	Priority seating	☐
Other special classes	☐	Tape recorders	☐
Priority registrations	☐	Videotaped classes	☐
Substitution of courses	☐	Text on tape	☐
Exams		**Services**	
Extended time	☐	Diagnostic tests	☐
Oral exams	☐	Learning centers	☐
Take home exams	☐	Proofreaders	☐
Exams on tape or computer	☐	Readers	☐
Untimed exams	☐	Reading Machines/Kurzweil	☐
Other accommodations	☐	Special bookstore section	☐
		Typists	☐

Counseling Services

- ☐ Academic
- ☐ Psychological
- ☐ Student Support groups
- ☐ Vocational

Tutoring

	Individual	Group
Time management	☐	☐
Organizational skills	☐	☐
Learning strategies	☐	☐
Study skills	☐	☐
Content area	☐	☐
Writing lab	☐	☐
Math lab	☐	☐

UNIQUE LD PROGRAM FEATURES

Students with disabilities should contact the Learning Assistance Center for information concerning accommodations in the classroom. A diagnosis and documentation of testing by a licensed professional must be submitted before services may be received.

DePaul University

Chicago, IL

Address: 1 East Jackson Boulevard, Chicago, IL, 60604-2287
Admissions telephone: 800 433-7285
Admissions FAX: 312 362-5749
Director of Undergraduate Admissions: Carlene Klaas
Admissions e-mail: admitdpu@depaul.edu
Web site: http://www.depaul.edu
SAT Code: 1165 ACT Code: 1012

LD program name: PLuS (Productive Learning Strategies)
LD program address: 2320 North Kenmore Ave, SAC 220
Director of PLuS: Stamatios Miras
LD program telephone: 773 325-4239
LD program e-mail: smiras@depaul.edu
LD program enrollment: 205, Total campus enrollment: 14,717

GENERAL

DePaul University is a private, coed, four-year institution. 36-acre, urban campus in Chicago (population: 2,896,016); branch campuses in Chicago, Des Plaines, Lake County, Naperville, Oak Brook, Oak Forest, and Rolling Meadows. Served by air, bus, and train. School operates transportation to basketball games. Public transportation serves campus. Quarter system.

LD ADMISSIONS

A member of the LD program does not sit on the admissions committee. High school waivers are accepted for foreign language. A personal interview is required. Essay is required and may be typed. LD and/or AD/HD students do not have separate admissions procedures through PLuS however, PLuS might send a memo to the admission counselor addressing an area which might not be representing the student's potential accurately due to the LD and/or AD/HD. Placement tests in math and English (essay) are taken by all entering students. The tests are online, and students may take them at home. Timed portions of those tests, are adjusted to double time for LD and/or AD/HD students. Foreign language requirement may be substituted unless it is a major component of the program, like in International Studies, Anthropology, and Archaeology majors.

SECONDARY SCHOOL REQUIREMENTS

Graduation from secondary school required; GED accepted. The following course distribution required: 4 units of English, 2 units of math, 2 units of science, 2 units of social studies, 4 units of academic electives.

TESTING

SAT Reasoning or ACT required. SAT Subject recommended.

All enrolled freshmen (fall 2004):

Average SAT I Scores:	Verbal: 569	Math: 560
Average ACT Scores:	Composite: 24	

Child Study Team report is not required. A neuropsychological or comprehensive psycho-educational evaluation is required for admission. Must be dated within 36 months of application. Tests required as part of this documentation:

- [x] WAIS-IV
- [x] WISC-IV
- [ ] SATA
- [x] Woodcock-Johnson
- [x] Nelson-Denny Reading Test
- [x] Other

UNDERGRADUATE STUDENT BODY

Total undergraduate student enrollment: 5,350 Men, 7,670 Women.

Composition of student body (fall 2004):

	Undergraduate	Freshmen
International	1.0	1.7
Black	7.3	10.4
American Indian	0.3	0.4
Asian-American	8.2	9.1
Hispanic	15.1	12.9
White	61.8	59.7
Unreported	6.2	5.7
	100.0%	100.0%

10% are from out of state. Average age of full-time undergraduates is 21, 42% of classes have fewer than 20 students, 56% have between 20 and 50 students, 2% have more than 50 students.

STUDENT HOUSING

43% of freshmen live in college housing. Housing is not guaranteed for all undergraduates. Housing is available to all unmarried undergraduate students but we do not have sufficient housing for all the students who want to live on campus. On the Lincoln Park campus, only single undergraduates are housed. DePaul on Michigan will house both undergraduate and graduate students. Campus can house 3,030 undergraduates.

EXPENSES

Tuition (2005-06): $20,500 per year, $16,380 (School of Music), $20,000 (School of Theatre).

Additional cost for LD program/services: $600 per quarter.

LD SERVICES

LD program size is not limited.

LD services available to:

- [x] Freshmen
- [x] Sophomores
- [x] Juniors
- [x] Seniors

Academic Accommodations

Curriculum		In class	
Foreign language waiver	[x]	Early syllabus	[ ]
Lighter course load	[x]	Note takers in class	[ ]
Math waiver	[ ]	Priority seating	[ ]
Other special classes	[ ]	Tape recorders	[x]
Priority registrations	[x]	Videotaped classes	[ ]
Substitution of courses	[ ]	Text on tape	[x]
Exams		**Services**	
Extended time	[x]	Diagnostic tests	[x]
Oral exams	[ ]	Learning centers	[ ]
Take home exams	[ ]	Proofreaders	[ ]
Exams on tape or computer	[x]	Readers	[x]
Untimed exams	[x]	Reading Machines/Kurzweil	[ ]
Other accommodations	[ ]	Special bookstore section	[ ]
		Typists	[ ]

Credit toward degree is given for remedial courses taken.

Counseling Services

- [x] Academic
- [ ] Psychological
- [ ] Student Support groups
- [ ] Vocational

Meets 4 times per academic year

Tutoring

Individual tutoring is available.

	Individual	Group
Time management	[x]	[ ]
Organizational skills	[x]	[ ]
Learning strategies	[x]	[ ]
Study skills	[x]	[ ]
Content area	[ ]	[ ]
Writing lab	[x]	[ ]
Math lab	[ ]	[ ]

UNIQUE LD PROGRAM FEATURES

Weekly meetings with LD specialists who will monitor progress and work on time management, organization, reading comprehension and written language skills and strategies, are available for a fee.

LD PROGRAM STAFF

Total number of LD Program staff (including director):

Full Time: 2 Part Time: 2

Key staff person available to work with LD students: Stamatios Miras, Director of PLuS.

LD Program web site: http://condor.depaul.edu/~plus/

Eastern Illinois University

Charleston, IL

Address: 600 Lincoln Avenue, Charleston, IL, 61920-3099
Admissions telephone: 800 252-5711
Admissions FAX: 217 581-7060
Director of Admissions: Brenda Ross
Admissions e-mail: admissns@www.eiu.edu
Web site: http://www.eiu.edu
SAT Code: 1199 ACT Code: 1016

LD program name: Office of Disability Services
Assistant Director, Disability Services: Kathryn Waggoner
LD program telephone: 217 581-6583
LD program e-mail: cfkw@eiu.edu
LD program enrollment: 97, Total campus enrollment: 9,928

GENERAL

Eastern Illinois University is a public, coed, four-year institution. 320-acre campus in Charleston (population: 21,039), 55 miles from Urbana-Champaign. Served by air and bus; major airports serve Chicago (190 miles) and St. Louis (130 miles); train serves Mattoon (10 miles). School operates transportation to Chicago area on weekends. Semester system.

LD ADMISSIONS

Students do not complete a separate application and are not simultaneously accepted to the LD program. A member of the LD program does not sit on the admissions committee. High school waivers are accepted for math and foreign language. A personal interview is recommended. Essay is not required.

For fall 2004, 97 completed self-identified LD applications were received. 97 applications were offered admission, and 97 enrolled.

SECONDARY SCHOOL REQUIREMENTS

Graduation from secondary school required; GED accepted. The following course distribution required: 4 units of English, 3 units of math, 3 units of science, 3 units of social studies, 2 units of academic electives.

TESTING

SAT Reasoning or ACT required. SAT Subject recommended.

All enrolled freshmen (fall 2004):

Average ACT Scores: Composite: 22

Child Study Team report is not required. A neuropsychological or comprehensive psycho-educational evaluation is required for admission. Must be dated within 60 months of application. Tests required as part of this documentation:

- ■ WAIS-IV
- ☐ WISC-IV
- ☐ SATA
- ■ Woodcock-Johnson
- ☐ Nelson-Denny Reading Test
- ■ Other

UNDERGRADUATE STUDENT BODY

Total undergraduate student enrollment: 3,888 Men, 5,227 Women.

Composition of student body (fall 2004):

	Undergraduate	Freshmen
International	0.3	0.6
Black	6.1	6.3
American Indian	0.2	0.2
Asian-American	1.1	1.0
Hispanic	2.1	2.3
White	88.3	87.5
Unreported	2.0	2.0
	100.0%	100.0%

2% are from out of state. 14% join a fraternity and 14% join a sorority. Average age of full-time undergraduates is 20, 35% of classes have fewer than 20 students, 61% have between 20 and 50 students.

STUDENT HOUSING

84% of freshmen live in college housing. Freshmen are required to live on campus. Housing is guaranteed for all undergraduates. Campus can house 5,551 undergraduates. Single rooms are available for students with medical or special needs. A medical note is required.

EXPENSES

Tuition (2005-06): $4,629 per year (in-state), $13,887 (out-of-state).
Room & Board: $6,196.

There is no additional cost for LD program/services.

LD SERVICES

LD program size is not limited.

LD services available to:

■ Freshmen ■ Sophomores ■ Juniors ■ Seniors

Academic Accommodations

Curriculum		In class	
Foreign language waiver	☐	Early syllabus	☐
Lighter course load	■	Note takers in class	■
Math waiver	☐	Priority seating	■
Other special classes	■	Tape recorders	■
Priority registrations	■	Videotaped classes	☐
Substitution of courses	■	Text on tape	■
Exams		**Services**	
Extended time	■	Diagnostic tests	☐
Oral exams	■	Learning centers	■
Take home exams	☐	Proofreaders	☐
Exams on tape or computer	■	Readers	■
Untimed exams	☐	Reading Machines/Kurzweil	■
Other accommodations	■	Special bookstore section	☐
		Typists	☐

Credit toward degree is given for remedial courses taken.

Counseling Services

- ■ Academic
- ■ Psychological
- ☐ Student Support groups
- ■ Vocational

Tutoring

Individual tutoring is available.

	Individual	Group
Time management	■	☐
Organizational skills	■	☐
Learning strategies	■	☐
Study skills	☐	■
Content area	☐	■
Writing lab	■	☐
Math lab	☐	☐

UNIQUE LD PROGRAM FEATURES

Tutors are not only offered for LD students but are available through some departments for all students. Also provided as support for students, is the writing center, reading center and Academic Success Center.

LD PROGRAM STAFF

Total number of LD Program staff (including director):

Full Time: 3 Part Time: 3

There is not an advisor/advocate from the LD program available to students. 1 graduate student is available to work with LD students.

Key staff person available to work with LD students: Kathryn Waggoner, Assistant Director, Disability Services.

LD Program web site: www.eiu.edu/~disablty/

Elmhurst College

Elmhurst, IL

Address: 190 Prospect Avenue, Elmhurst, IL, 60126
Admissions telephone: 800 697-1871
Admissions FAX: 630 617-5501
Dean of Admission: Andrew Sison, M.A.
Admissions e-mail: admit@elmhurst.edu
Web site: http://www.elmhurst.edu
SAT Code: 1204 ACT Code: 1020

Disability Services Provider: Maureen Connolly
LD program telephone: 630 617-3753
LD program e-mail: maureenc@elmhurst.edu
Total campus enrollment: 2,484

GENERAL

Elmhurst College is a private, coed, four-year institution. 38-acre, suburban campus in Elmhurst (population: 42,762), 15 miles from Chicago. Served by train; major airport serves Chicago; bus serves Norridge (10 miles). 4-1-4 system.

LD ADMISSIONS

SECONDARY SCHOOL REQUIREMENTS

Graduation from secondary school required; GED accepted. The following course distribution required: 4 units of English, 2 units of math, 2 units of science, 1 unit of foreign language, 2 units of social studies, 1 unit of history, 4 units of academic electives.

TESTING

SAT Reasoning or ACT required. SAT Subject recommended.

All enrolled freshmen (fall 2004):

Average SAT I Scores: Verbal: 558 Math: 569
Average ACT Scores: Composite: 23

Child Study Team report is not required. Tests required as part of this documentation:

- ❑ WAIS-IV
- ❑ WISC-IV
- ❑ SATA
- ❑ Woodcock-Johnson
- ❑ Nelson-Denny Reading Test
- ❑ Other

UNDERGRADUATE STUDENT BODY

Total undergraduate student enrollment: 866 Men, 1,544 Women.

Composition of student body (fall 2004):

	Undergraduate	Freshmen
International	0.3	0.9
Black	5.7	5.3
American Indian	0.3	0.4
Asian-American	2.6	2.9
Hispanic	6.2	5.2
White	77.7	78.7
Unreported	7.3	6.6
	100.0%	100.0%

9% are from out of state. 11% join a fraternity and 10% join a sorority. Average age of full-time undergraduates is 21, 66% of classes have fewer than 20 students, 34% have between 20 and 50 students.

STUDENT HOUSING

67% of freshmen live in college housing. Freshmen are not required to live on campus. Housing is guaranteed for all undergraduates. Campus can house 810 undergraduates.

EXPENSES

Tuition (2005-06): $21,600 per year.
Room: $3,816. Board: $2,740.

LD SERVICES

LD services available to:

❑ Freshmen ❑ Sophomores ❑ Juniors ❑ Seniors

Academic Accommodations

Curriculum		In class	
Foreign language waiver	❑	Early syllabus	❑
Lighter course load	❑	Note takers in class	❑
Math waiver	❑	Priority seating	❑
Other special classes	❑	Tape recorders	❑
Priority registrations	❑	Videotaped classes	❑
Substitution of courses	❑	Text on tape	❑
Exams		**Services**	
Extended time	❑	Diagnostic tests	❑
Oral exams	❑	Learning centers	❑
Take home exams	❑	Proofreaders	❑
Exams on tape or computer	❑	Readers	❑
Untimed exams	❑	Reading Machines/Kurzweil	❑
Other accommodations	❑	Special bookstore section	❑
		Typists	❑

Counseling Services

- ❑ Academic
- ❑ Psychological
- ❑ Student Support groups
- ❑ Vocational

Tutoring

	Individual	Group
Time management	❑	❑
Organizational skills	❑	❑
Learning strategies	❑	❑
Study skills	❑	❑
Content area	❑	❑
Writing lab	❑	❑
Math lab	❑	❑

UNIQUE LD PROGRAM FEATURES

Elmhurst College accepts students with disabilities in accordance with the Americans with Disabilities Act. Accommodations are made available on an individual basis according to documented need.

Eureka College

Eureka, IL

Address: 300 East College Avenue, Eureka, IL, 61530-1500
Admissions telephone: 888 4EUREKA
Admissions FAX: 309 467-6576
Dean of Admissions and Financial Aid: Brian Sajko
Admissions e-mail: admissions@eureka.edu
Web site: http://www.eureka.edu
SAT Code: 1206 ACT Code: 1022

LD program enrollment: 5, Total campus enrollment: 520

GENERAL

Eureka College is a private, coed, four-year institution. 112-acre, rural campus in Eureka (population: 4,871), 25 miles from Peoria. Major airport serves Chicago (140 miles); airport and bus serve Peoria; train serves Normal (25 miles). School operates transportation to airport in Peoria and to train station. Semester system.

LD ADMISSIONS

Students do not complete a separate application and are not simultaneously accepted to the LD program. A member of the LD program does not sit on the admissions committee.

For fall 2004, 5 completed self-identified LD applications were received. 2 applications were offered admission, and 2 enrolled.

SECONDARY SCHOOL REQUIREMENTS

Graduation from secondary school required; GED accepted. The following course distribution required: 4 units of English, 3 units of math, 3 units of science, 2 units of foreign language, 3 units of social studies, 2 units of history.

TESTING

ACT required; SAT Reasoning may be substituted. SAT Subject recommended.

Child Study Team report is not required. A neuropsychological or comprehensive psycho-education evaluation is not required for admission. Tests required as part of this documentation:

- ☐ WAIS-IV
- ☐ WISC-IV
- ☐ SATA
- ☐ Woodcock-Johnson
- ☐ Nelson-Denny Reading Test
- ☐ Other

UNDERGRADUATE STUDENT BODY

Total undergraduate student enrollment: 219 Men, 295 Women.

Composition of student body (fall 2004):

	Undergraduate	Freshmen
International	0.0	1.0
Black	12.7	8.6
American Indian	0.0	0.4
Asian-American	0.8	1.2
Hispanic	1.7	1.2
White	84.7	87.7
Unreported	0.0	0.0
	100.0%	100.0%

7% are from out of state. 30% join a fraternity and 31% join a sorority. Average age of full-time undergraduates is 21, 70% of classes have fewer than 20 students, 30% have between 20 and 50 students.

STUDENT HOUSING

78% of freshmen live in college housing. Freshmen are required to live on campus. Housing is guaranteed for all undergraduates. Campus can house 525 undergraduates.

EXPENSES

Tuition (2005-06): $13,000 per year.
Room: $2,820. Board: $3,060.
There is no additional cost for LD program/services.

LD SERVICES

LD program size is not limited.

LD services available to:

☐ Freshmen ☐ Sophomores ☐ Juniors ☐ Seniors

Academic Accommodations

Curriculum		In class	
Foreign language waiver	☐	Early syllabus	☐
Lighter course load	■	Note takers in class	☐
Math waiver	☐	Priority seating	☐
Other special classes	☐	Tape recorders	☐
Priority registrations	☐	Videotaped classes	☐
Substitution of courses	☐	Text on tape	☐
Exams		**Services**	
Extended time	☐	Diagnostic tests	☐
Oral exams	☐	Learning centers	■
Take home exams	☐	Proofreaders	☐
Exams on tape or computer	☐	Readers	☐
Untimed exams	☐	Reading Machines/Kurzweil	☐
Other accommodations	☐	Special bookstore section	☐
		Typists	☐

Credit toward degree is not given for remedial courses taken.

Counseling Services

- ☐ Academic
- ☐ Psychological
- ☐ Student Support groups
- ☐ Vocational

Tutoring

	Individual	Group
Time management	☐	☐
Organizational skills	☐	☐
Learning strategies	☐	☐
Study skills	☐	☐
Content area	☐	☐
Writing lab	☐	☐
Math lab	☐	☐

LD PROGRAM STAFF

Key staff person available to work with LD students: Martha Lister, Director, Learning Center.

Governors State University

University Park, IL

Address: 1 University Parkway, University Park, IL, 60466
Admissions telephone: 708 534-4490
Admissions FAX: 708 534-1640
Director, Admissions/Student Recruitment: Larry Polselli
Web site: www.govst.edu
SAT Code: 807 ACT Code: 1028

Total campus enrollment: 2, 752

GENERAL

Governors State University is a public, coed, graduate institution. 767-acre campus in University Park (population: 6,662), 35 miles from Chicago. Served by bus; major airport serves Chicago. School operates evening transportation to Metra station. Public transportation serves campus. Semester system.

LD ADMISSIONS

Students do not complete a separate application and are simultaneously accepted to the LD program. A personal interview is not required. Essay is not required. All students must be junior transfers.

TESTING

Child Study Team report is not required. A neuropsychological or comprehensive psycho-education evaluation is not required for admission. Tests required as part of this documentation:

- ☐ WAIS-IV
- ☐ WISC-IV
- ☐ SATA
- ☐ Woodcock-Johnson
- ☐ Nelson-Denny Reading Test
- ☐ Other

UNDERGRADUATE STUDENT BODY

Total undergraduate student enrollment: 921 Men, 2,059 Women.

Composition of student body (fall 2004):

	Freshmen
International	1.4
Black	36.4
American Indian	0.2
Asian-American	1.3
Hispanic	6.2
White	54.0
Unreported	0.5
	100.0%

3% are from out of state. Average age of full-time undergraduates is 34, 42% of classes have fewer than 20 students, 58% have between 20 and 50 students.

EXPENSES

Tuition (2005-06): $3,552 per year (in-state), $10,656 (out-of-state).

There is no additional cost for LD program/services.

LD SERVICES

LD services available to:

☐ Freshmen ☐ Sophomores ■ Juniors ■ Seniors

Academic Accommodations

Curriculum		**In class**	
Foreign language waiver	☐	Early syllabus	■
Lighter course load	■	Note takers in class	■
Math waiver	☐	Priority seating	☐
Other special classes	☐	Tape recorders	■
Priority registrations	☐	Videotaped classes	☐
Substitution of courses	☐	Text on tape	■
Exams		**Services**	
Extended time	■	Diagnostic tests	☐
Oral exams	■	Learning centers	■
Take home exams	☐	Proofreaders	☐
Exams on tape or computer	☐	Readers	☐
Untimed exams	■	Reading Machines/Kurzweil	☐
Other accommodations	■	Special bookstore section	☐
		Typists	☐

Credit toward degree is not given for remedial courses taken.

Counseling Services

- ■ Academic
- ☐ Psychological
- ☐ Student Support groups
- ☐ Vocational

Tutoring

Individual tutoring is available.

	Individual	Group
Time management	■	☐
Organizational skills	■	☐
Learning strategies	■	☐
Study skills	■	☐
Content area	■	■
Writing lab	■	■
Math lab	■	■

LD PROGRAM STAFF

Total number of LD Program staff (including director):

Full Time: 2 Part Time: 2

There is an advisor/advocate from the LD program available to students.

Greenville College

Greenville, IL

Address: 315 East College Avenue, Greenville, IL, 62246-0159
Admissions telephone: 800 248-2288 (in-state), 800 345-4440 (out-of-state)
Admissions FAX: 618 664-9841
Dean of Admissions: Michael Ritter
Admissions e-mail: admissions@greenville.edu
Web site: http://www.greenville.edu
SAT Code: 1256 ACT Code: 1032

Assistant Director Academic Enrichment Center: Tonya Holman
LD program telephone: 618 664-6613
LD program e-mail: tonya.holman@greenville.edu
Total campus enrollment: 1,170

GENERAL

Greenville College is a private, coed, four-year institution. 40-acre campus in Greenville (population: 6,955), 50 miles from Alton, Effingham, and St. Louis and 60 miles from Springfield. Airport serves St. Louis; bus serves Effingham; train serves Alton. School operates transportation to airport and to bus and train stations. 4-1-4 system.

LD ADMISSIONS

A personal interview is recommended. Essay is required and may be typed.

SECONDARY SCHOOL REQUIREMENTS

Graduation from secondary school required; GED accepted.

TESTING

ACT required; SAT Reasoning may be substituted. SAT Subject recommended.

All enrolled freshmen (fall 2004):

Average SAT I Scores:	Verbal: 510	Math: 530
Average ACT Scores:	Composite: 23	

Child Study Team report is not required. Tests required as part of this documentation:

- ☐ WAIS-IV
- ☐ WISC-IV
- ☐ SATA
- ☐ Woodcock-Johnson
- ☐ Nelson-Denny Reading Test
- ☐ Other

UNDERGRADUATE STUDENT BODY

Total undergraduate student enrollment: 483 Men, 566 Women.

Composition of student body (fall 2004):

	Undergraduate	Freshmen
International	0.8	1.8
Black	7.9	6.7
American Indian	0.4	0.5
Asian-American	0.8	0.9
Hispanic	3.3	2.3
White	82.4	83.9
Unreported	4.2	4.0
	100.0%	100.0%

31% are from out of state. Average age of full-time undergraduates is 24, 63% of classes have fewer than 20 students, 33% have between 20 and 50 students.

STUDENT HOUSING

95% of freshmen live in college housing. Freshmen are required to live on campus. Housing is guaranteed for all undergraduates. Campus can house 757 undergraduates. Single rooms are available for students with medical or special needs. A medical note is required.

EXPENSES

Tuition (2005-06): $17,142 per year.
Room: $2,794-$2,952. Board: $3,110.
There is no additional cost for LD program/services.

LD SERVICES

LD program size is not limited.

LD services available to:

☒ Freshmen ☒ Sophomores ☒ Juniors ☒ Seniors

Academic Accommodations

Curriculum		**In class**	
Foreign language waiver	☐	Early syllabus	☐
Lighter course load	☒	Note takers in class	☐
Math waiver	☐	Priority seating	☐
Other special classes	☐	Tape recorders	☐
Priority registrations	☐	Videotaped classes	☐
Substitution of courses	☐	Text on tape	☐
Exams		**Services**	
Extended time	☒	Diagnostic tests	☐
Oral exams	☐	Learning centers	☐
Take home exams	☐	Proofreaders	☐
Exams on tape or computer	☐	Readers	☐
Untimed exams	☐	Reading Machines/Kurzweil	☐
Other accommodations	☐	Special bookstore section	☐
		Typists	☐

Credit toward degree is not given for remedial courses taken.

Counseling Services

- ☐ Academic
- ☐ Psychological
- ☐ Student Support groups
- ☐ Vocational

Tutoring

Individual tutoring is available daily.

	Individual	Group
Time management	☐	☐
Organizational skills	☐	☐
Learning strategies	☐	☐
Study skills	☐	☒
Content area	☐	☐
Writing lab	☐	☐
Math lab	☐	☐

LD PROGRAM STAFF

Key staff person available to work with LD students: Tonya Holman, Assistant Director Academic Enrichment Center.

Illinois College

Jacksonville, IL

Address: 1101 West College Avenue, Jacksonville, IL, 62650-2299
Admissions telephone: 866 464-5265
Admissions FAX: 217 245-3034
Director of Admissions: Scott Belobrajdic
Admissions e-mail: admissions@ic.edu
Web site: http://www.ic.edu
SAT Code: 1315 ACT Code: 1034

LD program name: Templeton Counseling Center
Director, Counseling Center: Judy Norris
LD program telephone: 217 245-3073
LD program e-mail: jnorris@ic.edu
LD program enrollment: 13, Total campus enrollment: 1,037

GENERAL

Illinois College is a private, coed, four-year institution. 62-acre campus in Jacksonville (population: 18,940), 35 miles from Springfield. Airport, bus, and train serve Springfield; major airport serves St. Louis (90 miles). Semester system.

LD ADMISSIONS

Application Deadline: 08/01. Students do not complete a separate application and are simultaneously accepted to the LD program. A member of the LD program does not sit on the admissions committee. A personal interview is recommended. Essay is required and may be typed.

SECONDARY SCHOOL REQUIREMENTS

Graduation from secondary school required; GED accepted. The following course distribution required: 3 units of English.

TESTING

SAT Reasoning or ACT required. SAT Subject recommended.

All enrolled freshmen (fall 2004):

Average SAT I Scores:	Verbal: 552	Math: 559
Average ACT Scores:	Composite: 24	

Child Study Team report is not required. A neuropsychological or comprehensive psycho-education evaluation is not required for admission. Tests required as part of this documentation:

- □ WAIS-IV
- □ WISC-IV
- □ SATA
- □ Woodcock-Johnson
- □ Nelson-Denny Reading Test
- □ Other

UNDERGRADUATE STUDENT BODY

Total undergraduate student enrollment: 395 Men, 479 Women.

Composition of student body (fall 2004):

	Undergraduate	Freshmen
International	1.2	1.1
Black	3.1	2.6
American Indian	0.4	0.4
Asian-American	0.4	0.6
Hispanic	1.2	1.7
White	93.0	92.0
Unreported	0.8	1.7
	100.0%	100.0%

2% are from out of state. Average age of full-time undergraduates is 20, 62% of classes have fewer than 20 students, 36% have between 20 and 50 students.

STUDENT HOUSING

91% of freshmen live in college housing. Freshmen are required to live on campus. Housing is guaranteed for all undergraduates. Campus can house 772 undergraduates. Single rooms are available for students with medical or special needs. A medical note is not required.

EXPENSES

Tuition (2005-06): $15,500 per year.
Room: $2,600. Board: $3,800.
There is no additional cost for LD program/services.

LD SERVICES

LD program size is not limited.

LD services available to:

■ Freshmen ■ Sophomores ■ Juniors ■ Seniors

Academic Accommodations

Curriculum		**In class**	
Foreign language waiver	■	Early syllabus	■
Lighter course load	■	Note takers in class	■
Math waiver	■	Priority seating	■
Other special classes	□	Tape recorders	■
Priority registrations	■	Videotaped classes	□
Substitution of courses	■	Text on tape	□
Exams		**Services**	
Extended time	■	Diagnostic tests	■
Oral exams	■	Learning centers	□
Take home exams	□	Proofreaders	□
Exams on tape or computer	□	Readers	■
Untimed exams	■	Reading Machines/Kurzweil	□
Other accommodations	■	Special bookstore section	□
		Typists	□

Credit toward degree is not given for remedial courses taken.

Counseling Services

- ■ Academic
- ■ Psychological
- □ Student Support groups
- □ Vocational

Tutoring

Individual tutoring is available daily.

	Individual	Group
Time management	□	□
Organizational skills	□	□
Learning strategies	□	□
Study skills	□	□
Content area	■	□
Writing lab	■	□
Math lab	■	□

LD PROGRAM STAFF

There is an advisor/advocate from the LD program available to students.

Key staff person available to work with LD students: Judy Norris, Director, Counseling Center.

Illinois Institute of Technology

Chicago, IL

Address: 3300 South Federal Street, Chicago, IL, 60616-3793
Admissions telephone: 800 448-2329
Admissions e-mail: admission@iit.edu
Web site: http://www.iit.edu
SAT Code: 1318 ACT Code: 1040

Director, Center for Disability Resources: GleeAnn L. Kehr
LD program telephone: 312 567-5744
Total campus enrollment: 2,089

GENERAL

Illinois Institute of Technology is a private, coed, four-year institution. 128-acre, urban campus in Chicago (population: 2,896,016); branch campuses in downtown Chicago and in Wheaton. Served by air, bus, and train. School operates transportation to downtown Chicago. Public transportation serves campus. Semester system.

LD ADMISSIONS

A personal interview is not required. Essay is required and may be typed.

SECONDARY SCHOOL REQUIREMENTS

Graduation from secondary school required; GED not accepted. The following course distribution required: 4 units of English, 4 units of math, 3 units of science, 2 units of social studies, 2 units of history.

TESTING

SAT Subject recommended.

All enrolled freshmen (fall 2004):

Average SAT I Scores:	Verbal: 619	Math: 675
Average ACT Scores:	Composite: 28	

Child Study Team report is not required. Tests required as part of this documentation:

- ☐ WAIS-IV
- ☐ WISC-IV
- ☐ SATA
- ☐ Woodcock-Johnson
- ☐ Nelson-Denny Reading Test
- ☐ Other

UNDERGRADUATE STUDENT BODY

Total undergraduate student enrollment: 1,380 Men, 462 Women.

Composition of student body (fall 2004):

	Undergraduate	Freshmen
International	8.2	16.2
Black	4.7	5.4
American Indian	0.0	0.3
Asian-American	14.2	13.8
Hispanic	7.3	7.3
White	56.9	47.9
Unreported	8.6	9.1
	100.0%	100.0%

46% are from out of state. 15% join a fraternity and 17% join a sorority. Average age of full-time undergraduates is 20.

STUDENT HOUSING

86% of freshmen live in college housing. Freshmen are not required to live on campus. Housing is not guaranteed for all undergraduates. Only full time students can live in campus housing. Campus can house 1,225 undergraduates.

EXPENSES

Tuition (2005-06): $22,218 per year.
Room: $3,900. Board: $3,618.
There is no additional cost for LD program/services.

LD SERVICES

LD program size is not limited.

LD services available to:

■ Freshmen ■ Sophomores ■ Juniors ■ Seniors

Academic Accommodations

Curriculum		In class	
Foreign language waiver	☐	Early syllabus	☐
Lighter course load	■	Note takers in class	■
Math waiver	☐	Priority seating	☐
Other special classes	☐	Tape recorders	■
Priority registrations	☐	Videotaped classes	■
Substitution of courses	☐	Text on tape	☐
Exams		**Services**	
Extended time	■	Diagnostic tests	☐
Oral exams	■	Learning centers	■
Take home exams	☐	Proofreaders	☐
Exams on tape or computer	☐	Readers	■
Untimed exams	■	Reading Machines/Kurzweil	☐
Other accommodations	☐	Special bookstore section	☐
		Typists	☐

Credit toward degree is not given for remedial courses taken.

Counseling Services

- ☐ Academic
- ☐ Psychological
- ☐ Student Support groups
- ☐ Vocational

Tutoring

Individual tutoring is available.

	Individual	Group
Time management	☐	☐
Organizational skills	☐	☐
Learning strategies	☐	☐
Study skills	☐	☐
Content area	☐	☐
Writing lab	☐	☐
Math lab	☐	☐

LD PROGRAM STAFF

There is an advisor/advocate from the LD program available to students.

Key staff person available to work with LD students: GleeAnn L. Kehr, MSCRC, Director, Center for Disability Resources.

Illinois State University

Normal, IL

Address: School and North Streets, Normal, IL, 61790
Admissions telephone: 800 366-2478
Admissions FAX: 309 438-3932
Director of Admissions: Molly Arnold
Admissions e-mail: admissions@ilstu.edu
Web site: http://www.ilstu.edu
SAT Code: 1319 ACT Code: 1042

LD program name: Disability Concerns
LD program address: Campus Box 1290
Director, Disability Concerns: Ann M. Caldwell
LD program telephone: 309 438-5853
LD program e-mail: ableisu@ilstu.edu
LD program enrollment: 105, Total campus enrollment: 17,878

GENERAL

Illinois State University is a public, coed, four-year institution. 850-acre campus in Normal (population: 45,386), 40 miles from Peoria. Served by train; airport and bus serve Bloomington (three miles); major airport serves Chicago (130 miles). School operates evening transportation to local residences and stores. Public transportation serves campus. Semester system.

LD ADMISSIONS

Students do not complete a separate application and are not simultaneously accepted to the LD program. A member of the LD program does sit on the admissions committee. A personal interview is not required. Essay is not required. An Admissions Review Committee is available for all students who may not meet admission requirements, but have special circumstances that need consideration. Students with learning disabilities who are borderline admits or who are denied admission may self-disclose and submit a letter of appeal to this committee.

SECONDARY SCHOOL REQUIREMENTS

Graduation from secondary school required; GED accepted. The following course distribution required: 4 units of English, 3 units of math, 2 units of science, 2 units of foreign language, 2 units of social studies, 2 units of academic electives.

TESTING

ACT required; SAT Reasoning may be substituted. SAT Subject recommended.

All enrolled freshmen (fall 2004):

Average ACT Scores: Composite: 24

Child Study Team report is required if student is classified. A neuropsychological or comprehensive psycho-educational evaluation is required for admission. Must be dated within 24 months of application. Tests required as part of this documentation:

- [x] WAIS-IV
- [ ] WISC-IV
- [ ] SATA
- [x] Woodcock-Johnson
- [ ] Nelson-Denny Reading Test
- [x] Other

UNDERGRADUATE STUDENT BODY

Total undergraduate student enrollment: 7,692 Men, 10,780 Women.

Composition of student body (fall 2004):

	Undergraduate	Freshmen
International	0.7	0.8
Black	7.7	6.2
American Indian	0.5	0.3
Asian-American	1.9	1.6
Hispanic	3.4	3.0
White	81.1	86.3
Unreported	4.7	1.8
	100.0%	100.0%

4% are from out of state. 9% join a fraternity and 9% join a sorority. Average age of full-time undergraduates is 21, 29% of classes have fewer than 20 students, 61% have between 20 and 50 students, 10% have more than 50 students.

STUDENT HOUSING

97% of freshmen live in college housing. Freshmen are required to live on campus. Housing is guaranteed for all undergraduates. Campus can house 6,901 undergraduates. Single rooms are available for students with medical or special needs. A medical note is required.

EXPENSES

Tuition (2005-06): $5,400 per year (in-state), $11,280 (out-of-state).
Room: $3,010. Board: $2,738.
There is no additional cost for LD program/services.

LD SERVICES

LD program size is not limited.

LD services available to:

- [x] Freshmen
- [x] Sophomores
- [x] Juniors
- [x] Seniors

Academic Accommodations

Curriculum		In class	
Foreign language waiver	[ ]	Early syllabus	[ ]
Lighter course load	[ ]	Note takers in class	[x]
Math waiver	[ ]	Priority seating	[ ]
Other special classes	[ ]	Tape recorders	[ ]
Priority registrations	[ ]	Videotaped classes	[ ]
Substitution of courses	[ ]	Text on tape	[ ]
Exams		**Services**	
Extended time	[x]	Diagnostic tests	[x]
Oral exams	[ ]	Learning centers	[x]
Take home exams	[ ]	Proofreaders	[ ]
Exams on tape or computer	[x]	Readers	[x]
Untimed exams	[ ]	Reading Machines/Kurzweil	[x]
Other accommodations	[x]	Special bookstore section	[ ]
		Typists	[x]

Credit toward degree is not given for remedial courses taken.

Counseling Services

- [x] Academic
- [x] Psychological
- [x] Student Support groups
- [x] Vocational

Tutoring

Individual tutoring is not available.

Average size of tutoring groups: 4

	Individual	Group
Time management	[x]	[x]
Organizational skills	[x]	[x]
Learning strategies	[x]	[x]
Study skills	[x]	[x]
Content area	[ ]	[x]
Writing lab	[x]	[ ]
Math lab	[ ]	[x]

LD PROGRAM STAFF

Total number of LD Program staff (including director):

Full Time: 1 Part Time: 1

There is an advisor/advocate from the LD program available to students. 2 graduate students and 20 peer tutors are available to work with LD students.

Key staff person available to work with LD students: Sheryl Hogan, Coordinator for Learning Disability Services.

LD Program web site: www.disabilityconcerns.ilstu.edu

University of Illinois at Chicago

Chicago, IL

Address: 601 South Morgan M/C 102, Chicago, IL, 60607
Admissions telephone: 312 996-4350
Admissions FAX: 312 413-7628
Executive Director of Admissions and Records: Thomas E. Glenn
Admissions e-mail: uicadmit@uic.edu
Web site: http://www.uic.edu
SAT Code: 1851 ACT Code: 1155

Interim Coordinator: William Rodriguez
LD program telephone: 312 413-9467
LD program e-mail: willie@uic.edu
Total campus enrollment: 15,457

GENERAL

University of Illinois at Chicago is a public, coed, four-year institution. 216-acre, urban campus in Chicago (population: 2,896,016). Served by air, bus, and train. School operates shuttle on campus and to rail stations during rush hour. Public transportation serves campus. Semester system.

LD ADMISSIONS

A personal interview is not required. Essay is not required.

SECONDARY SCHOOL REQUIREMENTS

Graduation from secondary school required; GED accepted. The following course distribution required: 4 units of English, 3 units of math, 3 units of science, 2 units of foreign language, 3 units of social studies, 1 unit of academic electives.

TESTING

ACT required; SAT Reasoning may be substituted.

All enrolled freshmen (fall 2004):

Average ACT Scores: Composite: 23

Child Study Team report is not required. Tests required as part of this documentation:

- [ ] WAIS-IV
- [ ] WISC-IV
- [ ] SATA
- [ ] Woodcock-Johnson
- [ ] Nelson-Denny Reading Test
- [ ] Other

UNDERGRADUATE STUDENT BODY

Total undergraduate student enrollment: 7,154 Men, 8,733 Women.

Composition of student body (fall 2004):

	Undergraduate	Freshmen
International	0.7	1.5
Black	10.2	8.3
American Indian	0.2	0.2
Asian-American	25.1	25.0
Hispanic	18.5	16.3
White	36.5	43.2
Unreported	8.8	5.5
	100.0%	100.0%

3% are from out of state. 1% join a fraternity and 1% join a sorority. Average age of full-time undergraduates is 21, 39% of classes have fewer than 20 students, 44% have between 20 and 50 students, 18% have more than 50 students.

STUDENT HOUSING

25% of freshmen live in college housing. Housing is not guaranteed for all undergraduates. The campus can only accommodate 10% of the student body in campus housing. Campus can house 2,600 undergraduates.

EXPENSES

Tuition (2005-06): $6,194 per year (in-state), $18,584 (out-of-state). Additional $400 per year for engineering program.
Room & Board: $7,160.

LD SERVICES

LD program size is not limited.

LD services available to:

- [ ] Freshmen
- [ ] Sophomores
- [ ] Juniors
- [ ] Seniors

Academic Accommodations

Curriculum		In class	
Foreign language waiver	[ ]	Early syllabus	[ ]
Lighter course load	[ ]	Note takers in class	[x]
Math waiver	[ ]	Priority seating	[ ]
Other special classes	[ ]	Tape recorders	[x]
Priority registrations	[ ]	Videotaped classes	[ ]
Substitution of courses	[ ]	Text on tape	[ ]
Exams		**Services**	
Extended time	[x]	Diagnostic tests	[ ]
Oral exams	[x]	Learning centers	[x]
Take home exams	[ ]	Proofreaders	[ ]
Exams on tape or computer	[ ]	Readers	[x]
Untimed exams	[ ]	Reading Machines/Kurzweil	[x]
Other accommodations	[ ]	Special bookstore section	[ ]
		Typists	[ ]

Credit toward degree is not given for remedial courses taken.

Counseling Services

- [ ] Academic
- [ ] Psychological
- [ ] Student Support groups
- [ ] Vocational

Tutoring

	Individual	Group
Time management	[ ]	[ ]
Organizational skills	[ ]	[ ]
Learning strategies	[ ]	[ ]
Study skills	[ ]	[ ]
Content area	[ ]	[ ]
Writing lab	[ ]	[ ]
Math lab	[ ]	[ ]

LD PROGRAM STAFF

Total number of LD Program staff (including director):

Full Time: 4 Part Time: 4

Key staff person available to work with LD students: William Rodriguez, Interim Coordinator/Disability Specialist.

University of Illinois at Springfield

Springfield, IL

Address: 1 University Plaza, Springfield, IL, 62703-5407
Admissions telephone: 217 206-4847
Admissions FAX: 217 206-6620
Director of Admissions and Records: Darren L. Bush
Admissions e-mail: admissions@uis.edu
Web site: http://www.uis.edu
SAT Code: 834 ACT Code: 1137

LD program name: Disability Services
Director: Karla Carwile
LD program telephone: 217 206-6666
LD program e-mail: kcarwl@uis.edu
LD program enrollment: 48, Total campus enrollment: 2,507

GENERAL

University of Illinois at Springfield is a public, coed, graduate institution. Five-acre campus in Springfield (population: 111,454), 90 miles from St. Louis; branch campus in Peoria. Served by air, bus, and train. School operates transportation to downtown Springfield. Public transportation serves campus. Semester system.

LD ADMISSIONS

A personal interview is not required. Essay is required and may be typed.

For fall 2004, 45 completed self-identified LD applications were received. 45 applications were offered admission, and 15 enrolled.

SECONDARY SCHOOL REQUIREMENTS

The following course distribution required: 4 units of English, 3 units of math, 3 units of science, 2 units of foreign language, 3 units of social studies.

TESTING

SAT Reasoning or ACT required. SAT Subject recommended.

All enrolled freshmen (fall 2004):

Average ACT Scores: Composite: 25

Child Study Team report is not required. Tests required as part of this documentation:

☐	WAIS-IV	☐	Woodcock-Johnson
☐	WISC-IV	☐	Nelson-Denny Reading Test
☐	SATA	☐	Other

UNDERGRADUATE STUDENT BODY

Total undergraduate student enrollment: 834 Men, 1,466 Women.

Composition of student body (fall 2004):

	Undergraduate	Freshmen
International	2.2	0.7
Black	7.8	8.3
American Indian	1.1	0.3
Asian-American	4.4	2.4
Hispanic	1.1	1.9
White	80.0	81.4
Unreported	3.3	5.0
	100.0%	100.0%

Average age of full-time undergraduates is 25, 60% of classes have fewer than 20 students, 39% have between 20 and 50 students.

STUDENT HOUSING

100% of freshmen live in college housing. Freshmen are required to live on campus. Campus can house 846 undergraduates. Single rooms are available for students with medical or special needs. A medical note is required.

EXPENSES

Tuition (2005-06): $4,575 per year (in-state), $13,725 (out-of-state).
Room: $2,860-$4,760. Board: $2,350.
There is no additional cost for LD program/services.

LD SERVICES

LD program size is not limited.

LD services available to:

■ Freshmen ■ Sophomores ■ Juniors ■ Seniors

Academic Accommodations

Curriculum		**In class**	
Foreign language waiver	☐	Early syllabus	■
Lighter course load	☐	Note takers in class	■
Math waiver	☐	Priority seating	■
Other special classes	☐	Tape recorders	■
Priority registrations	■	Videotaped classes	☐
Substitution of courses	■	Text on tape	■
Exams		**Services**	
Extended time	■	Diagnostic tests	☐
Oral exams	■	Learning centers	■
Take home exams	☐	Proofreaders	■
Exams on tape or computer	■	Readers	■
Untimed exams	☐	Reading Machines/Kurzweil	☐
Other accommodations	■	Special bookstore section	☐
		Typists	■

Credit toward degree is not given for remedial courses taken.

Counseling Services

■ Academic
☐ Psychological
■ Student Support groups — Meets 36 times per academic year
☐ Vocational

Tutoring

Individual tutoring is available daily.

Average size of tutoring groups: 1

	Individual	Group
Time management	■	☐
Organizational skills	■	☐
Learning strategies	■	☐
Study skills	■	☐
Content area	■	☐
Writing lab	■	☐
Math lab	■	☐

LD PROGRAM STAFF

Total number of LD Program staff (including director):

Full Time: 3 Part Time: 3

There is an advisor/advocate from the LD program available to students. 1 graduate student is available to work with LD students.

Key staff person available to work with LD students: Kimberly Rutherford, Disability Services/Learning Specialist.

LD Program web site: http://www.uis.edu/disabilityservices

University of Illinois at Urbana-Champaign

Champaign, IL

Address: 601 East John Street, Champaign, IL, 61820-5711
Admissions telephone: 217 333-0302
Admissions FAX: 217 244-0903
Director of Admissions and Records: Stacey Kostell
Admissions e-mail: undergraduate@admissions.uiuc.edu
Web site: http://www.uiuc.edu
SAT Code: 1836 ACT Code: 1154

LD program name: Division of Rehab-Educ Services
LD program address: 1207 South Oak
LD Specialist: Karen Wold
LD program telephone: 217 333-8705
LD program e-mail: kwold2@uiuc.edu
LD program enrollment: 182, Total campus enrollment: 29,632

GENERAL

University of Illinois at Urbana-Champaign is a public, coed, four-year institution. 1,470-acre campus in Urbana-Champaign (population: 103,863), 130 miles from Chicago. Served by bus and train; major airport serves Chicago; airport also serves Savoy (four miles). Public transportation serves campus. Semester system.

LD ADMISSIONS

Application Deadline: 12/15. Students do not complete a separate application and are simultaneously accepted to the LD program. A member of the LD program does sit on the admissions committee. A personal interview is recommended. Essay is required and may be typed. Requirements may be substituted when there is evidence that the student's ability to meet the requirements is significantly compromised by a disability. LD applicants are required to provide neuro-psychological documentation which can be used to determine their specific disability-related needs and to optimize their accommodation service planning.

SECONDARY SCHOOL REQUIREMENTS

Graduation from secondary school required; GED accepted. The following course distribution required: 4 units of English, 3 units of math, 2 units of science, 2 units of foreign language, 2 units of social studies, 2 units of academic electives.

TESTING

SAT Reasoning or ACT required. SAT Subject recommended.

All enrolled freshmen (fall 2004):

Average SAT I Scores: Verbal: 614 Math: 674
Average ACT Scores: Composite: 28

Child Study Team report is not required. A neuropsychological or comprehensive psycho-education evaluation is not required for admission. Tests required as part of this documentation:

- [x] WAIS-IV
- [ ] WISC-IV
- [ ] SATA
- [x] Woodcock-Johnson
- [ ] Nelson-Denny Reading Test
- [ ] Other

UNDERGRADUATE STUDENT BODY

Total undergraduate student enrollment: 15,080 Men, 13,666 Women.

Composition of student body (fall 2004):

	Undergraduate	Freshmen
International	3.9	3.8
Black	5.7	6.8
American Indian	0.2	0.3
Asian-American	13.3	12.9
Hispanic	6.6	6.4
White	67.8	68.2
Unreported	2.4	1.6
	100.0%	100.0%

7% are from out of state. 20% join a fraternity and 22% join a sorority. Average age of full-time undergraduates is 21, 33% of classes have fewer than 20 students, 47% have between 20 and 50 students, 20% have more than 50 students.

STUDENT HOUSING

97% of freshmen live in college housing. Freshmen are required to live on campus. Housing is guaranteed for all undergraduates. Campus can house 11,034 undergraduates. Single rooms are available for students with medical or special needs. A medical note is required.

EXPENSES

Tuition (2005-06): $7,042 per year (in-state), $21,128 (out-of-state). Tuition is higher for some programs and varies by year of study.

Room: $2,970. Board: $4,206.

There is no additional cost for LD program/services.

LD SERVICES

LD program size is not limited.

LD services available to:

- [x] Freshmen
- [x] Sophomores
- [x] Juniors
- [x] Seniors

Academic Accommodations

Curriculum		In class	
Foreign language waiver	[ ]	Early syllabus	[x]
Lighter course load	[x]	Note takers in class	[x]
Math waiver	[ ]	Priority seating	[x]
Other special classes	[x]	Tape recorders	[x]
Priority registrations	[x]	Videotaped classes	[ ]
Substitution of courses	[ ]	Text on tape	[x]
Exams		**Services**	
Extended time	[x]	Diagnostic tests	[x]
Oral exams	[x]	Learning centers	[x]
Take home exams	[x]	Proofreaders	[x]
Exams on tape or computer	[x]	Readers	[x]
Untimed exams	[x]	Reading Machines/Kurzweil	[x]
Other accommodations	[x]	Special bookstore section	[x]
		Typists	[x]

Credit toward degree is not given for remedial courses taken.

Counseling Services

[x]	Academic	Meets 72 times per academic year
[x]	Psychological	Meets 36 times per academic year
[x]	Student Support groups	Meets 6 times per academic year
[x]	Vocational	Meets 3 times per academic year

Tutoring

Individual tutoring is available weekly.

Average size of tutoring groups: 5

	Individual	Group
Time management	[x]	[x]
Organizational skills	[x]	[ ]
Learning strategies	[x]	[x]
Study skills	[x]	[x]
Content area	[ ]	[x]
Writing lab	[x]	[x]
Math lab	[x]	[x]

LD PROGRAM STAFF

Total number of LD Program staff (including director):

Full Time: 7 Part Time: 7

There is an advisor/advocate from the LD program available to students. The advisor/advocate meets with faculty 10 times per month and students 8 times per month. 2 graduate students are available to work with LD students.

Key staff person available to work with LD students: Karen Wold, LD Specialist.

LD Program web site: http://www.disability.uiuc.edu/

Illinois Wesleyan University

Bloomington, IL

Address: Box 2900, Bloomington, IL, 61702-2900
Admissions telephone: 800 332-2498
Admissions FAX: 309 556-3820
Dean of Admissions: Jerry Pope
Admissions e-mail: iwuadmit@iwu.edu
Web site: http://www.iwu.edu
SAT Code: 1320 ACT Code: 1044

Associate Provost: Roger Schnaitter
LD program telephone: 309 556-3255
LD program e-mail: rschnait@iwu.edu
LD program enrollment: 20, Total campus enrollment: 2,118

GENERAL

Illinois Wesleyan University is a private, coed, four-year institution. 76-acre campus in Bloomington (population: 64,808), 130 miles from Chicago. Served by air, bus, and train; major airport serves Chicago. Public transportation serves campus.

LD ADMISSIONS

Students do not complete a separate application and are not simultaneously accepted to the LD program. A member of the LD program does sit on the admissions committee. A personal interview is recommended. Essay is required and may be typed.

SECONDARY SCHOOL REQUIREMENTS

Graduation from secondary school required; GED accepted.

TESTING

SAT Reasoning or ACT required. SAT Subject recommended.

All enrolled freshmen (fall 2004):

Average SAT I Scores: Verbal: 638 Math: 640
Average ACT Scores: Composite: 29

Child Study Team report is not required. Tests required as part of this documentation:

- [ ] WAIS-IV
- [ ] WISC-IV
- [ ] SATA
- [ ] Woodcock-Johnson
- [ ] Nelson-Denny Reading Test
- [ ] Other

UNDERGRADUATE STUDENT BODY

Total undergraduate student enrollment: 899 Men, 1,165 Women.

Composition of student body (fall 2004):

	Undergraduate	Freshmen
International	0.7	1.6
Black	4.0	3.2
American Indian	0.4	0.2
Asian-American	2.2	2.2
Hispanic	3.1	2.7
White	84.3	85.5
Unreported	5.3	4.7
	100.0%	100.0%

11% are from out of state. 34% join a fraternity and 26% join a sorority. Average age of full-time undergraduates is 20, 59% of classes have fewer than 20 students, 40% have between 20 and 50 students.

STUDENT HOUSING

100% of freshmen live in college housing. Freshmen are required to live on campus. Housing is guaranteed for all undergraduates. Campus can house 1,745 undergraduates. Single rooms are available for students with medical or special needs. A medical note is required.

EXPENSES

Tuition (2005-06): $27,474 per year.
Room: $3,892. Board: $2,534.
There is no additional cost for LD program/services.

LD SERVICES

LD program size is not limited.

LD services available to:

[x] Freshmen [x] Sophomores [x] Juniors [x] Seniors

Academic Accommodations

Curriculum		**In class**	
Foreign language waiver	[ ]	Early syllabus	[ ]
Lighter course load	[x]	Note takers in class	[ ]
Math waiver	[ ]	Priority seating	[ ]
Other special classes	[ ]	Tape recorders	[x]
Priority registrations	[ ]	Videotaped classes	[ ]
Substitution of courses	[x]	Text on tape	[ ]
Exams		**Services**	
Extended time	[x]	Diagnostic tests	[ ]
Oral exams	[x]	Learning centers	[ ]
Take home exams	[ ]	Proofreaders	[ ]
Exams on tape or computer	[ ]	Readers	[ ]
Untimed exams	[ ]	Reading Machines/Kurzweil	[ ]
Other accommodations	[ ]	Special bookstore section	[ ]
		Typists	[ ]

Credit toward degree is not given for remedial courses taken.

Counseling Services

- [ ] Academic
- [ ] Psychological
- [ ] Student Support groups
- [ ] Vocational

Tutoring

Individual tutoring is available.

	Individual	Group
Time management	[x]	[ ]
Organizational skills	[x]	[ ]
Learning strategies	[ ]	[ ]
Study skills	[x]	[ ]
Content area	[x]	[ ]
Writing lab	[x]	[ ]
Math lab	[x]	[ ]

UNIQUE LD PROGRAM FEATURES

Illinois Wesleyan does not have a formal Learning Disabilities "program" in the sense that it appears to be meant here. We have a number of "services" for students with learning disabilities, and all are tailored to each student indivdiually. For example, the number of times tutoring is available to an LD student depends on his/her specific needs and often varies within the academic year even for an individual student.

LD PROGRAM STAFF

There is no advisor/advocate from the LD program available to students.

Key staff person available to work with LD students: Roger Schnaitter, Associate Provost.

Knox College

Galesburg, IL

Address: 2 East South Street, Galesburg, IL, 61401
Admissions telephone: 800 678-5669
Admissions FAX: 309 341-7070
Director of Admissions: Paul Steenis
Admissions e-mail: admission@knox.edu
Web site: http://www.knox.edu
SAT Code: 1372 ACT Code: 1052

LD program name: Center for Teaching and Learning
Director, Center for Teaching and Learning: John Haslem
LD program telephone: 309 341-7151
LD program e-mail: jhaslem@knox.edu
LD program enrollment: 41, Total campus enrollment: 1,205

GENERAL

Knox College is a private, coed, four-year institution. 82-acre campus in Galesburg (population: 33,706), 45 miles from both Moline and Peoria. Served by bus and train; airports serve Moline and Peoria. Public transportation serves campus. Trimester system.

LD ADMISSIONS

Students do not complete a separate application and are simultaneously accepted to the LD program. A member of the LD program does not sit on the admissions committee. A personal interview is recommended. Essay is required and may be typed.

SECONDARY SCHOOL REQUIREMENTS

Graduation from secondary school required; GED accepted.

TESTING

SAT Reasoning or ACT required. SAT Subject recommended.

All enrolled freshmen (fall 2004):

Average SAT I Scores:	Verbal: 635	Math: 615
Average ACT Scores:	Composite: 27	

Child Study Team report is not required. A neuropsychological or comprehensive psycho-educational evaluation is required for admission. Must be dated within 36 months of application. Tests required as part of this documentation:

- ■ WAIS-IV
- ■ WISC-IV
- ☐ SATA
- ■ Woodcock-Johnson
- ■ Nelson-Denny Reading Test
- ☐ Other

UNDERGRADUATE STUDENT BODY

Total undergraduate student enrollment: 508 Men, 635 Women.

Composition of student body (fall 2004):

	Undergraduate	Freshmen
International	7.4	7.6
Black	5.2	4.5
American Indian	0.3	0.3
Asian-American	5.8	4.9
Hispanic	6.1	4.5
White	71.1	72.5
Unreported	4.1	5.7
	100.0%	100.0%

51% are from out of state. 28% join a fraternity and 17% join a sorority. Average age of full-time undergraduates is 20, 65% of classes have fewer than 20 students, 35% have between 20 and 50 students.

STUDENT HOUSING

98% of freshmen live in college housing. Freshmen are required to live on campus. Housing is guaranteed for all undergraduates. Campus can house 1,110 undergraduates. Single rooms are available for students with medical or special needs. A medical note is required.

EXPENSES

Tuition (2005-06): $25,815 per year.
Room: $2,784. Board: $3,501.
There is no additional cost for LD program/services.

LD SERVICES

LD program size is not limited.

LD services available to:

■ Freshmen ■ Sophomores ■ Juniors ■ Seniors

Academic Accommodations

Curriculum		**In class**	
Foreign language waiver	☐	Early syllabus	☐
Lighter course load	■	Note takers in class	■
Math waiver	☐	Priority seating	☐
Other special classes	☐	Tape recorders	■
Priority registrations	☐	Videotaped classes	☐
Substitution of courses	☐	Text on tape	☐
Exams		**Services**	
Extended time	■	Diagnostic tests	☐
Oral exams	■	Learning centers	■
Take home exams	☐	Proofreaders	☐
Exams on tape or computer	☐	Readers	■
Untimed exams	■	Reading Machines/Kurzweil	☐
Other accommodations	☐	Special bookstore section	☐
		Typists	☐

Credit toward degree is given for remedial courses taken.

Counseling Services

- ■ Academic
- ■ Psychological
- ☐ Student Support groups
- ☐ Vocational

Tutoring

Individual tutoring is available daily.

Average size of tutoring groups: 2

	Individual	Group
Time management	■	■
Organizational skills	■	■
Learning strategies	■	■
Study skills	■	■
Content area	■	■
Writing lab	■	■
Math lab	☐	☐

LD PROGRAM STAFF

Total number of LD Program staff (including director):

Full Time: 7 Part Time: 7

There is an advisor/advocate from the LD program available to students. 60 peer tutors are available to work with LD students.

Key staff person available to work with LD students: John Haslem, Director, Center for Teaching and Learning.

Lake Forest College

Lake Forest, IL

Address: 555 North Sheridan Road, Lake Forest, IL, 60045
Admissions telephone: 800 828-4751
Admissions FAX: 847 735-6271
Director of Admissions: William G. Motzer, Jr.
Admissions e-mail: admissions@lakeforest.edu
Web site: http://www.lakeforest.edu
SAT Code: 1392 ACT Code: 1054

Interim Director of Counseling Center: Patrice L. Pohl
LD program telephone: 847 735-5240
LD program e-mail: pohl@lakeforest.edu
Total campus enrollment: 1,391

GENERAL

Lake Forest College is a private, coed, four-year institution. 107-acre, suburban campus in Lake Forest (population: 20,059), 25 miles from Chicago. Served by train; major airports serve Chicago and Milwaukee (47 miles). Public transportation serves campus. Semester system.

LD ADMISSIONS

A personal interview is recommended. Essay is required and may be typed.

SECONDARY SCHOOL REQUIREMENTS

Graduation from secondary school required, GED accepted. The following course distribution required: 4 units of English, 3 units of math, 2 units of science, 2 units of foreign language, 1 unit of social studies, 1 unit of history, 3 units of academic electives.

TESTING

SAT Reasoning or ACT required. SAT Subject recommended.

All enrolled freshmen (fall 2004):

Average SAT I Scores:	Verbal: 593	Math: 584
Average ACT Scores:	Composite: 26	

Child Study Team report is not required. Tests required as part of this documentation:

- [ ] WAIS-IV
- [ ] WISC-IV
- [ ] SATA
- [ ] Woodcock-Johnson
- [ ] Nelson-Denny Reading Test
- [ ] Other

UNDERGRADUATE STUDENT BODY

Total undergraduate student enrollment: 524 Men, 736 Women.

Composition of student body (fall 2004):

	Undergraduate	Freshmen
International	5.7	9.0
Black	3.5	4.1
American Indian	0.5	0.3
Asian-American	4.0	3.6
Hispanic	6.9	5.4
White	79.5	77.5
Unreported	0.0	0.0
	100.0%	100.0%

50% are from out of state. 10% join a fraternity and 17% join a sorority. Average age of full-time undergraduates is 20, 60% of classes have fewer than 20 students, 40% have between 20 and 50 students.

STUDENT HOUSING

88% of freshmen live in college housing. Housing is not guaranteed for all undergraduates. Campus can house 1,105 undergraduates. Single rooms are available for students with medical or special needs. A medical note is required.

EXPENSES

Tuition (2005-06): $27,000 per year.
Room: $3,456. Board: $3,070.
There is no additional cost for LD program/services.

LD SERVICES

LD program size is not limited.

LD services available to:

- [ ] Freshmen
- [ ] Sophomores
- [ ] Juniors
- [ ] Seniors

Academic Accommodations

Curriculum		In class	
Foreign language waiver	[ ]	Early syllabus	[ ]
Lighter course load	[ ]	Note takers in class	[x]
Math waiver	[ ]	Priority seating	[ ]
Other special classes	[ ]	Tape recorders	[x]
Priority registrations	[ ]	Videotaped classes	[ ]
Substitution of courses	[ ]	Text on tape	[x]
Exams		**Services**	
Extended time	[x]	Diagnostic tests	[ ]
Oral exams	[x]	Learning centers	[x]
Take home exams	[x]	Proofreaders	[ ]
Exams on tape or computer	[ ]	Readers	[x]
Untimed exams	[x]	Reading Machines/Kurzweil	[x]
Other accommodations	[ ]	Special bookstore section	[ ]
		Typists	[x]

Counseling Services

- [ ] Academic
- [ ] Psychological
- [ ] Student Support groups
- [ ] Vocational

Tutoring

Individual tutoring is available weekly.

	Individual	Group
Time management	[x]	[ ]
Organizational skills	[ ]	[ ]
Learning strategies	[x]	[ ]
Study skills	[x]	[ ]
Content area	[x]	[ ]
Writing lab	[x]	[ ]
Math lab	[ ]	[ ]

LD PROGRAM STAFF

There is no advisor/advocate from the LD program available to students.

Key staff person available to work with LD students: Patrice L. Pohl, Interim Director of Counseling Center.

Lewis University

Romeoville, IL

Address: 1 University Parkway, Romeoville, IL, 60446-2200
Admissions telephone: 800 897 9000
Admissions FAX: 815 836-5002
Admissions Contact: Patrick Hughes
Admissions e-mail: admissions@lewisu.edu
Web site: http://www.lewisu.edu
SAT Code: 1404 ACT Code: 1058

LD program name: Leckrone Academic Resource Center
Academic Skills Coordinator: Denise Rich
LD program telephone: 815 836-5284
LD program e-mail: richde@lewisu.edu
Total campus enrollment: 3,457

GENERAL

Lewis University is a private, coed, four-year institution. 350-acre campus in Romeoville (population: 21,153), three miles from Joliet and 30 miles from Chicago; branch campuses in Hickory Hills, Oak Brook, and Schaumburg. Major airport serves Chicago; train and bus serve Joliet. Public transportation serves campus. Semester system.

LD ADMISSIONS

A personal interview is recommended. Essay is not required.

SECONDARY SCHOOL REQUIREMENTS

Graduation from secondary school required; GED accepted. The following course distribution required: 3 units of English, 2 units of math, 2 units of science, 2 units of social studies, 1 unit of history, 8 units of academic electives.

TESTING

ACT required; SAT Reasoning may be substituted. SAT Subject recommended.

All enrolled freshmen (fall 2004):

Average SAT I Scores:	Verbal: 515	Math: 527
Average ACT Scores:	Composite: 22	

Child Study Team report is required if student is classified. Tests required as part of this documentation:

- ☐ WAIS-IV
- ☐ WISC-IV
- ☐ SATA
- ☐ Woodcock-Johnson
- ☐ Nelson-Denny Reading Test
- ☐ Other

UNDERGRADUATE STUDENT BODY

Total undergraduate student enrollment: 1,434 Men, 1,949 Women.

Composition of student body (fall 2004):

	Undergraduate	freshmen
International	2.0	3.5
Black	13.3	14.0
American Indian	0.0	0.1
Asian-American	2.4	2.8
Hispanic	10.0	7.4
White	72.2	68.7
Unreported	0.2	3.6
	100.0%	100.0%

3% are from out of state. 3% join a fraternity and 5% join a sorority. Average age of full-time undergraduates is 22, 68% of classes have fewer than 20 students, 32% have between 20 and 50 students.

STUDENT HOUSING

60% of freshmen live in college housing. Freshmen are not required to live on campus. Housing is guaranteed for all undergraduates. Campus can house 1,005 undergraduates. Single rooms are available for students with medical or special needs. A medical note is required.

EXPENSES

Tuition (2005-06): $17,990 per year.
Room: $5,050. Board: $2,450.

There is no additional cost for LD program/services.

LD SERVICES

LD program size is not limited.

LD services available to:

☑ Freshmen ☑ Sophomores ☑ Juniors ☑ Seniors

Academic Accommodations

Curriculum		In class	
Foreign language waiver	☐	Early syllabus	☐
Lighter course load	☐	Note takers in class	☑
Math waiver	☐	Priority seating	☐
Other special classes	☐	Tape recorders	☐
Priority registrations	☐	Videotaped classes	☐
Substitution of courses	☐	Text on tape	☐
Exams		**Services**	
Extended time	☑	Diagnostic tests	☐
Oral exams	☑	Learning centers	☐
Take home exams	☐	Proofreaders	☐
Exams on tape or computer	☐	Readers	☐
Untimed exams	☑	Reading Machines/Kurzweil	☐
Other accommodations	☐	Special bookstore section	☐
		Typists	☐

Credit toward degree is not given for remedial courses taken.

Counseling Services

- ☐ Academic
- ☐ Psychological
- ☐ Student Support groups
- ☐ Vocational

Tutoring

Individual tutoring is available weekly.

Average size of tutoring groups: 2

	Individual	Group
Time management	☐	☐
Organizational skills	☐	☐
Learning strategies	☐	☐
Study skills	☑	☐
Content area	☑	☐
Writing lab	☑	☐
Math lab	☑	☐

UNIQUE LD PROGRAM FEATURES

Documentation of accommodations is required prior to delivery of services.

LD PROGRAM STAFF

There is an advisor/advocate from the LD program available to students. The advisor/advocate meets with faculty 2 times per month and students 3 times per month.

Key staff person available to work with LD students: Denise Rich, Academic Skills Coordinator.

Loyola University, Chicago

Chicago, IL

Address: 820 North Michigan Avenue, Chicago, IL, 60611-9810
Admissions telephone: 800 262-2373
Admissions FAX: 312 915-7216
Director of Admissions: April Hansen
Admissions e-mail: admission@luc.edu
Web site: http://www.luc.edu
SAT Code: 1412 ACT Code: 1064

LD program name: Services for Students with Disabilities
LD program address: Damen Hall 105, 6525 Sheridan
Coordinator: Maggie Rogers
LD program telephone: 773 508-3197
LD program e-mail: aroger1@luc.edu
LD program enrollment: 28, Total campus enrollment: 8,319

GENERAL

Loyola University, Chicago is a private, coed, four-year institution. Four campuses totaling 105 acres in Chicago (population: 2,896,016). Served by air, bus, and train. School operates transportation between campuses. Public transportation serves campus. Semester system.

LD ADMISSIONS

Students do not complete a separate application and are not simultaneously accepted to the LD program. A member of the LD program does not sit on the admissions committee. A personal interview is not required. Essay is not required.

SECONDARY SCHOOL REQUIREMENTS

Graduation from secondary school required; GED accepted. The following course distribution required: 4 units of English, 2 units of math, 2 units of science, 2 units of social studies, 1 unit of history.

TESTING

SAT Reasoning or ACT required. SAT Subject recommended.

All enrolled freshmen (fall 2004):

Average SAT I Scores: Verbal: 587 Math: 580
Average ACT Scores: Composite: 25

Child Study Team report is not required. A neuropsychological or comprehensive psycho-educational evaluation is required for admission. Tests required as part of this documentation:

- [x] WAIS-IV
- [x] WISC-IV
- [x] SATA
- [x] Woodcock-Johnson
- [x] Nelson-Denny Reading Test
- [ ] Other

UNDERGRADUATE STUDENT BODY

Total undergraduate student enrollment: 2,587 Men, 4,910 Women.

Composition of student body (fall 2004):

	Undergraduate	Freshmen
International	1.1	1.6
Black	5.3	6.9
American Indian	0.3	0.2
Asian-American	12.7	10.6
Hispanic	9.3	10.2
White	61.3	59.2
Unreported	10.0	11.3
	100.0%	100.0%

20% are from out of state. 7% join a fraternity and 5% join a sorority. Average age of full-time undergraduates is 20, 37% of classes have fewer than 20 students, 55% have between 20 and 50 students.

STUDENT HOUSING

68% of freshmen live in college housing. Freshmen are required to live on campus. Housing is not guaranteed for all undergraduates. Housing is offered, but not guaranteed, to third-year and fourth-year students. Campus can house 3,215 undergraduates. Single rooms are available for students with medical or special needs. A medical note is required.

EXPENSES

Tuition (2005-06): $23,900 per year.
Room & Board: $9,060.
There is no additional cost for LD program/services.

LD SERVICES

LD program size is not limited.

LD services available to:

- [x] Freshmen
- [x] Sophomores
- [x] Juniors
- [x] Seniors

Academic Accommodations

Curriculum		In class	
Foreign language waiver	[x]	Early syllabus	[x]
Lighter course load	[ ]	Note takers in class	[x]
Math waiver	[x]	Priority seating	[ ]
Other special classes	[ ]	Tape recorders	[x]
Priority registrations	[ ]	Videotaped classes	[ ]
Substitution of courses	[x]	Text on tape	[x]
Exams		**Services**	
Extended time	[x]	Diagnostic tests	[ ]
Oral exams	[x]	Learning centers	[x]
Take home exams	[ ]	Proofreaders	[ ]
Exams on tape or computer	[x]	Readers	[x]
Untimed exams	[ ]	Reading Machines/Kurzweil	[x]
Other accommodations	[ ]	Special bookstore section	[ ]
		Typists	[x]

Credit toward degree is not given for remedial courses taken.

Counseling Services

- [ ] Academic
- [ ] Psychological
- [ ] Student Support groups
- [ ] Vocational

Tutoring

Individual tutoring is not available.

	Individual	Group
Time management	[x]	[ ]
Organizational skills	[x]	[ ]
Learning strategies	[x]	[ ]
Study skills	[x]	[ ]
Content area	[x]	[ ]
Writing lab	[x]	[ ]
Math lab	[ ]	[x]

UNIQUE LD PROGRAM FEATURES

Students are eligible for accommodations and services through the SSWD office, if they self-identify with appropriate documentation. Services available to all students regardless of disability status include individual and group tutoring, individual academic skills assistance, and academic advising.

LD PROGRAM STAFF

Total number of LD Program staff (including director):

Full Time: 1 Part Time: 1

There is no advisor/advocate from the LD program available to students. 14 peer tutors are available to work with LD students.

Key staff person available to work with LD students: Maggie Rogers, Coordinator of Services for Students with Disabilities.

LD Program web site: www.luc.edu/depts/luc/disabilities

MacMurray College

Jacksonville, IL

Address: 447 East College, Jacksonville, IL, 62650
Admissions telephone: 800 252-7485
Admissions FAX: 217 291-0702
Dean of Enrollment: Rhonda Cors
Admissions e-mail: admissions@mac.edu
Web site: http://www.mac.edu
SAT Code: 1435 ACT Code: 1068

Director of Special Services: Laura Covell
LD program telephone: 217 479-7222
LD program e-mail: laura.covell@mac.edu
Total campus enrollment: 655

GENERAL

MacMurray College is a private, coed, four-year institution. 60-acre campus in Jacksonville (population: 18,940), 30 miles from Springfield. Airport, bus, and train serve Springfield; major airport serves St. Louis (90 miles). Semester system.

LD ADMISSIONS

A personal interview is recommended. Essay is not required.

SECONDARY SCHOOL REQUIREMENTS

Graduation from secondary school required; GED accepted.

TESTING

SAT Reasoning or ACT required.

Child Study Team report is not required. Tests required as part of this documentation:

- ☐ WAIS-IV
- ☐ WISC-IV
- ☐ SATA
- ☐ Woodcock-Johnson
- ☐ Nelson-Denny Reading Test
- ☐ Other

UNDERGRADUATE STUDENT BODY

Total undergraduate student enrollment: 309 Men, 346 Women.

18% are from out of state.

STUDENT HOUSING

Housing is guaranteed for all undergraduates. Campus can house 900 undergraduates.

EXPENSES

Tuition (2005-06): $15,000 per year.
Room: $2,652. Board: $3,162.
There is no additional cost for LD program/services.

LD SERVICES

LD program size is not limited.

LD services available to:

☐ Freshmen ☐ Sophomores ☐ Juniors ☐ Seniors

Academic Accommodations

Curriculum		**In class**	
Foreign language waiver	☐	Early syllabus	☐
Lighter course load	■	Note takers in class	■
Math waiver	☐	Priority seating	☐
Other special classes	☐	Tape recorders	☐
Priority registrations	☐	Videotaped classes	☐
Substitution of courses	☐	Text on tape	☐
Exams		**Services**	
Extended time	☐	Diagnostic tests	☐
Oral exams	■	Learning centers	■
Take home exams	☐	Proofreaders	☐
Exams on tape or computer	☐	Readers	■
Untimed exams	■	Reading Machines/Kurzweil	☐
Other accommodations	☐	Special bookstore section	☐
		Typists	☐

Credit toward degree is not given for remedial courses taken.

Counseling Services

- ☐ Academic
- ☐ Psychological
- ☐ Student Support groups
- ☐ Vocational

Tutoring

	Individual	Group
Time management	☐	☐
Organizational skills	☐	☐
Learning strategies	☐	☐
Study skills	☐	☐
Content area	☐	☐
Writing lab	☐	☐
Math lab	☐	☐

LD PROGRAM STAFF

Total number of LD Program staff (including director):

Full Time: 2 Part Time: 2

Key staff person available to work with LD students: Laura Covell, Director of Special Services.

McKendree College

Lebanon, IL

Address: 701 College Road, Lebanon, IL, 62254-1299
Admissions telephone: 800 BEAR CAT, extension 6831
Admissions FAX: 618 537-6259
Vice President of Admissions and Financial Aid: Mark Campbell
Admissions e-mail: inquiry@mckendree.edu
Web site: http://www.mckendree.edu
SAT Code: 1456   ACT Code: 1076

Coordinator, Learning Resource Center: Lynn Cross Schwartzhoff
LD program telephone: 618 537-6850
LD program enrollment: 2, Total campus enrollment: 2,156

GENERAL

McKendree College is a private, coed, four-year institution. 110-acre campus in Lebanon (population: 3,523), 23 miles from St. Louis, MO; branch campuses in Louisville and Radcliff, KY; satellite campuses in Belleville, Carterville, Centralia, Godfrey, Harrisburg, IN, and Ullin and at Scott Air Force Base. Major airport and bus serve St. Louis, MO; train serves Belleville (15 miles). School operates transportation to various locations on campus. Public transportation serves campus. Semester system.

LD ADMISSIONS

Students do not complete a separate application and are not simultaneously accepted to the LD program. A member of the LD program does not sit on the admissions committee. High school waivers are accepted for foreign language. A personal interview is recommended. Essay is not required.

For fall 2004, 2 completed self-identified LD applications were received. 2 applications were offered admission, and 2 enrolled.

SECONDARY SCHOOL REQUIREMENTS

Graduation from secondary school required; GED accepted.

TESTING

ACT required; SAT Reasoning may be substituted. SAT Subject recommended.

All enrolled freshmen (fall 2004):

Average ACT Scores: Composite: 25

Child Study Team report is not required. A neuropsychological or comprehensive psycho-education evaluation is not required for admission. Tests required as part of this documentation:

☐ WAIS-IV   ☐ Woodcock-Johnson
☐ WISC-IV   ☐ Nelson-Denny Reading Test
☐ SATA   ☐ Other

UNDERGRADUATE STUDENT BODY

Total undergraduate student enrollment: 811 Men, 1,296 Women.

Composition of student body (fall 2004):

	Undergraduate	Freshmen
International	3.5	1.4
Black	10.9	12.1
American Indian	0.0	0.1
Asian-American	0.3	1.0
Hispanic	2.1	1.5
White	79.4	81.9
Unreported	3.8	1.9
	100.0%	100.0%

31% are from out of state. 5% join a fraternity and 3% join a sorority. Average age of full-time undergraduates is 21, 66% of classes have fewer than 20 students, 34% have between 20 and 50 students.

STUDENT HOUSING

79% of freshmen live in college housing. Freshmen are required to live on campus. Housing is not guaranteed for all undergraduates. Campus can house 690 undergraduates. Single rooms are not available for students with medical or special needs.

EXPENSES

Tuition (2005-06): $17,500 per year.
Room: $3,700. Board: $3,300.
There is no additional cost for LD program/services.

LD SERVICES

LD program size is not limited.

LD services available to:

■ Freshmen   ■ Sophomores   ■ Juniors   ■ Seniors

Academic Accommodations

Curriculum		**In class**	
Foreign language waiver	☐	Early syllabus	☐
Lighter course load	■	Note takers in class	☐
Math waiver	■	Priority seating	■
Other special classes	☐	Tape recorders	■
Priority registrations	☐	Videotaped classes	☐
Substitution of courses	☐	Text on tape	■
Exams		**Services**	
Extended time	■	Diagnostic tests	☐
Oral exams	■	Learning centers	■
Take home exams	■	Proofreaders	☐
Exams on tape or computer	■	Readers	☐
Untimed exams	■	Reading Machines/Kurzweil	■
Other accommodations	☐	Special bookstore section	☐
		Typists	☐

Credit toward degree is not given for remedial courses taken.

Counseling Services

■ Academic
☐ Psychological
☐ Student Support groups
☐ Vocational

Tutoring

Individual tutoring is available weekly.

Average size of tutoring groups: 2

	Individual	Group
Time management	■	☐
Organizational skills	■	☐
Learning strategies	■	☐
Study skills	■	☐
Content area	■	☐
Writing lab	■	☐
Math lab	■	☐

LD PROGRAM STAFF

There is no advisor/advocate from the LD program available to students. 10 peer tutors are available to work with LD students.

Key staff person available to work with LD students: Lynn Cross Schwartzhoff, Coordinator, Learning Resource Center.

Millikin University

Decatur, IL

Address: 1184 West Main Street, Decatur, IL, 62522-2084
Admissions telephone: 800 373-7733
Admissions FAX: 217 425-4669
Dean of Admissions: Lin Stoner
Admissions e-mail: admis@millikin.edu
Web site: http://www.millikin.edu
SAT Code: 1470 ACT Code: 1080

Director, Academic Development: Linda M. Slagell
LD program telephone: 217 420-6622
LD program e-mail: lslagell@mail.millikin.edu
LD program enrollment: 48, Total campus enrollment: 2,645

GENERAL

Millikin University is a private, coed, four-year institution. 70-acre, suburban campus in Decatur (population: 81860), 38 miles from Springfield and 130 miles from St. Louis. Served by air and bus; major airport serves St. Louis; train serves Springfield. Public transportation serves campus. Semester system.

LD ADMISSIONS

Students do not complete a separate application and are simultaneously accepted to the LD program. A member of the LD program does not sit on the admissions committee. A personal interview is recommended. Essay is not required.

SECONDARY SCHOOL REQUIREMENTS

Graduation from secondary school required; GED accepted. The following course distribution required:.

TESTING

SAT Reasoning or ACT required. SAT Subject recommended.

All enrolled freshmen (fall 2004):

Average SAT I Scores: Verbal: 539 Math: 525
Average ACT Scores: Composite: 23

Child Study Team report is not required. A neuropsychological or comprehensive psycho-educational evaluation is required for admission. Must be dated within 48 months of application. Tests required as part of this documentation:

- ■ WAIS-IV
- ■ WISC-IV
- ■ SATA
- ■ Woodcock-Johnson
- ■ Nelson-Denny Reading Test
- ☐ Other

UNDERGRADUATE STUDENT BODY

Total undergraduate student enrollment: 1,005 Men, 1,384 Women.

Composition of student body (fall 2004):

	Undergraduate	Freshmen
International	0.8	0.6
Black	10.7	8.9
American Indian	0.0	0.1
Asian-American	1.1	1.0
Hispanic	3.0	2.4
White	79.7	82.7
Unreported	4.7	4.3
	100.0%	100.0%

15% are from out of state. 16% join a fraternity and 13% join a sorority. Average age of full-time undergraduates is 22, 52% of classes have fewer than 20 students, 46% have between 20 and 50 students.

STUDENT HOUSING

88% of freshmen live in college housing. Freshmen are required to live on campus. Housing is guaranteed for all undergraduates. Campus can house 1,612 undergraduates. Single rooms are available for students with medical or special needs. A medical note is required.

EXPENSES

Tuition (2005-06): $20,696 per year.
Room: $3,763. Board: $2,950.
There is no additional cost for LD program/services.

LD SERVICES

LD program size is not limited.

LD services available to:

■ Freshmen ■ Sophomores ■ Juniors ■ Seniors

Academic Accommodations

Curriculum		In class	
Foreign language waiver	☐	Early syllabus	☐
Lighter course load	■	Note takers in class	■
Math waiver	☐	Priority seating	☐
Other special classes	■	Tape recorders	■
Priority registrations	☐	Videotaped classes	☐
Substitution of courses	☐	Text on tape	☐
Exams		**Services**	
Extended time	■	Diagnostic tests	☐
Oral exams	■	Learning centers	■
Take home exams	☐	Proofreaders	☐
Exams on tape or computer	☐	Readers	■
Untimed exams	■	Reading Machines/Kurzweil	☐
Other accommodations	☐	Special bookstore section	☐
		Typists	☐

Credit toward degree is given for remedial courses taken.

Counseling Services

- ☐ Academic
- ☐ Psychological
- ☐ Student Support groups
- ☐ Vocational

Tutoring

Individual tutoring is available weekly.

Average size of tutoring groups: 3

	Individual	Group
Time management	☐	☐
Organizational skills	☐	☐
Learning strategies	☐	☐
Study skills	☐	☐
Content area	☐	☐
Writing lab	☐	☐
Math lab	☐	☐

LD PROGRAM STAFF

Total number of LD Program staff (including director):

Full Time: 1 Part Time: 1

Key staff person available to work with LD students: Linda M. Slagell, Director, Academic Development.

Monmouth College

Monmouth, IL

Address: 700 East Broadway, Monmouth, IL, 61462
Admissions telephone: 800 74-SCOTS
Admissions FAX: 309 457-2141
Vice President for Admission: John Klockentager
Admissions e-mail: admit@monm.edu
Web site: http://www.monm.edu
SAT Code: 1484 ACT Code: 1084

LD program name: Student Affairs
LD program address: 700 E. Broadway
Vice President for Student Life: Jacquelyn Condon
LD program telephone: 309 457-2113
LD program e-mail: jackiec@monm.edu
Total campus enrollment: 1,252

GENERAL

Monmouth College is a private, coed, four-year institution. 40-acre campus in Monmouth (population: 9,841), 60 miles from Peoria. Airport serves Moline (40 miles); smaller airport, bus, and train serve Galesburg (15 miles). School operates transportation to Galesburg and Moline. Semester system.

LD ADMISSIONS

Students do not complete a separate application and are not simultaneously accepted to the LD program. A member of the LD program does not sit on the admissions committee. A personal interview is not required. Essay is not required. Admissions requirements that may be waived for LD students include recommendations and an on campus interview.

SECONDARY SCHOOL REQUIREMENTS

Graduation from secondary school required; GED accepted. The following course distribution required: 4 units of English, 3 units of math, 2 units of science, 2 units of foreign language, 2 units of social studies, 1 unit of history.

TESTING

ACT required; SAT Reasoning may be substituted. SAT Subject recommended.

All enrolled freshmen (fall 2004):

Average SAT I Scores:	Verbal: 550	Math: 560
Average ACT Scores:	Composite: 23	

Child Study Team report is not required. A neuropsychological or comprehensive psycho-education evaluation is not required for admission. Tests required as part of this documentation:

- ☐ WAIS-IV
- ☐ WISC-IV
- ☐ SATA
- ☐ Woodcock-Johnson
- ☐ Nelson-Denny Reading Test
- ☐ Other

UNDERGRADUATE STUDENT BODY

Total undergraduate student enrollment: 488 Men, 576 Women.

Composition of student body (fall 2004):

	Undergraduate	Freshmen
International	1.0	1.1
Black	4.6	3.4
American Indian	0.0	0.1
Asian-American	0.3	0.8
Hispanic	3.3	3.1
White	90.7	91.3
Unreported	0.0	0.2
	100.0%	100.0%

6% are from out of state. 23% join a fraternity and 26% join a sorority. Average age of full-time undergraduates is 20, 51% of classes have fewer than 20 students, 49% have between 20 and 50 students.

STUDENT HOUSING

91% of freshmen live in college housing. Freshmen are required to live on campus. Housing is guaranteed for all undergraduates. Campus can house 1,062 undergraduates. Single rooms are not available for students with medical or special needs.

EXPENSES

Tuition (2005-06): $20,200 per year.
Room: $3,240. Board: $2,510.
There is no additional cost for LD program/services.

LD SERVICES

LD program size is not limited.

LD services available to:

■ Freshmen ■ Sophomores ■ Juniors ■ Seniors

Academic Accommodations

Curriculum		**In class**	
Foreign language waiver	☐	Early syllabus	☐
Lighter course load	☐	Note takers in class	■
Math waiver	☐	Priority seating	■
Other special classes	☐	Tape recorders	■
Priority registrations	☐	Videotaped classes	☐
Substitution of courses	☐	Text on tape	☐
Exams		**Services**	
Extended time	■	Diagnostic tests	☐
Oral exams	■	Learning centers	■
Take home exams	☐	Proofreaders	☐
Exams on tape or computer	☐	Readers	■
Untimed exams	■	Reading Machines/Kurzweil	☐
Other accommodations	■	Special bookstore section	☐
		Typists	■

Credit toward degree is not given for remedial courses taken.

Counseling Services

- ☐ Academic
- ☐ Psychological
- ☐ Student Support groups
- ☐ Vocational

Tutoring

Individual tutoring is available weekly.

	Individual	Group
Time management	■	■
Organizational skills	■	■
Learning strategies	■	■
Study skills	■	■
Content area	☐	☐
Writing lab	■	■
Math lab	☐	☐

LD PROGRAM STAFF

There is no advisor/advocate from the LD program available to students.

Key staff person available to work with LD students: Jacquelyn Condon, Vice President for Student Life.

Moraine Valley Community College

Palos Hills, IL

Address: 10900 South 88th Avenue, Palos Hills IL, 60465
Admissions telephone: 708 974-2110
Admissions FAX: 708 974-0681
Dean, Enrollment Services: Wendy Manser
Admissions e-mail: manser@morainevalley.edu
Web site: http://www.morainevalley.edu
SAT Code: 1524 ACT Code: 1087

LD program name: Center for Disability Services
Director: Debbie Sievers
LD program telephone: 708 974-5711
LD program enrollment: 92, Total campus enrollment: 16,077

GENERAL

Moraine Valley Community College is a public, coed, two-year institution. 294-acre campus in Palos Hills (population: 17,803), 20 miles from Chicago. Major airport and bus serve Chicago; train serves Worth (2 miles). Public transportation serves campus. Semester system.

LD ADMISSIONS

No application deadline. Students do not complete a separate application and are not simultaneously accepted to the LD program. A member of the LD program does not sit on the admissions committee. A personal interview is required. Essay is not required.

SECONDARY SCHOOL REQUIREMENTS

Graduation from secondary school required; GED accepted.

TESTING

Child Study Team report is not required. Documentation of a neuropsychological or comprehensive psycho-educational evaluation is required for admission to the program. Must be dated within 36 months of application. Tests required as part of this documentation:

- ■ WAIS-IV
- ☐ WISC-IV
- ☐ SATA
- ■ Woodcock-Johnson
- ☐ Nelson-Denny Reading Test
- ■ Other

STUDENT HOUSING

There is no campus housing.

EXPENSES

Tuition (2005-06): $64 per credit hour (in-state), $242 (out-of-state).

There is no additional cost for LD program/services.

LD SERVICES

LD program size is not limited.

LD services available to:

■ Freshmen ■ Sophomores ■ Juniors ■ Seniors

Academic Accommodations

Curriculum		In class	
Foreign language waiver	☐	Early syllabus	■
Lighter course load	☐	Note takers in class	■
Math waiver	☐	Priority seating	■
Other special classes	■	Tape recorders	■
Priority registrations	■	Videotaped classes	☐
Substitution of courses	☐	Text on tape	■
Exams		**Services**	
Extended time	■	Diagnostic tests	■
Oral exams	■	Learning centers	■
Take home exams	☐	Proofreaders	☐
Exams on tape or computer	■	Readers	■
Untimed exams	☐	Reading Machines/Kurzweil	☐
Other accommodations	■	Special bookstore section	☐
		Typists	☐

Counseling Services

- ■ Academic
- ■ Psychological
- ■ Student Support groups
- ■ Vocational

Tutoring

Individual tutoring is available on a weekly basis.

Average size of tutoring groups: 1

	Individual	Group
Time management	☐	■
Organizational skills	☐	■
Learning strategies	☐	☐
Study skills	☐	■
Content area	☐	☐
Writing lab	☐	☐
Math lab	☐	☐

LD PROGRAM STAFF

Total number of LD Program staff (including director):

Part Time: 1

There is an advisor/advocate from the LD program available to students. One peer tutor is available to work with LD students.

Key staff person available to work with LD students: Katie Landers, Educational Case Manager

National-Louis University

Chicago, IL

Address: 122 S. Michigan Avenue, Chicago, IL, 60603
Admissions telephone: 888 NLU-TODAY
Admissions FAX: 847 465-0594
Vice President for University Services: Pat Petillo
Admissions e-mail: nluinfo@nl.edu
Web site: http://www.nl.edu
SAT Code: 1551 ACT Code: 1094

Director, PACE Program: Carol Burns
LD program e-mail: CBurns@nl.edu
Total campus enrollment: 2,113

GENERAL

National-Louis University is a private, coed, four-year institution. Urban campus in downtown Chicago (population: 2,896,016); branch campuses in Elgin, Evanston, Wheaton, and Wheeling, in Atlanta, GA; McLean, VA; Milwaukee, WI; Orlando and Tampa, FL; St. Louis, MO; and abroad in Heidelberg, Germany. Served by air, bus, and train. Public transportation serves campus. Quarter system.

LD ADMISSIONS

A personal interview is required. Essay is not required.

SECONDARY SCHOOL REQUIREMENTS

Graduation from secondary school required; GED accepted.

TESTING

SAT Reasoning or ACT required.

Child Study Team report is required if student is classified. Tests required as part of this documentation:

- ☐ WAIS-IV
- ☐ WISC-IV
- ☐ SATA
- ☐ Woodcock-Johnson
- ☐ Nelson-Denny Reading Test
- ☐ Other

UNDERGRADUATE STUDENT BODY

Total undergraduate student enrollment: 892 Men, 2,449 Women.

Composition of student body (fall 2004):

	Undergraduate	Freshmen
International	0.0	0.0
Black	12.0	21.9
American Indian	0.0	0.3
Asian-American	2.0	1.5
Hispanic	4.0	6.5
White	14.0	17.1
Unreported	68.0	52.5
	100.0%	100.0%

1% are from out of state, 88% of classes have fewer than 20 students, 12% have between 20 and 50 students.

STUDENT HOUSING

Housing is guaranteed for all undergraduates. Campus can house 126 undergraduates.

EXPENSES

Tuition (2005-06): $16,875 per year. $13,995-$15,705 per year. Tuition varies by program.

LD SERVICES

LD program size is limited.

LD services available to:

☐ Freshmen ☐ Sophomores ☐ Juniors ☐ Seniors

Academic Accommodations

Curriculum		**In class**	
Foreign language waiver	☐	Early syllabus	☐
Lighter course load	☐	Note takers in class	☐
Math waiver	☐	Priority seating	☐
Other special classes	■	Tape recorders	■
Priority registrations	☐	Videotaped classes	■
Substitution of courses	☐	Text on tape	☐
Exams		**Services**	
Extended time	☐	Diagnostic tests	■
Oral exams	■	Learning centers	■
Take home exams	☐	Proofreaders	☐
Exams on tape or computer	☐	Readers	■
Untimed exams	☐	Reading Machines/Kurzweil	■
Other accommodations	☐	Special bookstore section	☐
		Typists	☐

Credit toward degree is given for remedial courses taken.

Counseling Services

- ☐ Academic
- ☐ Psychological
- ☐ Student Support groups
- ☐ Vocational

Tutoring

	Individual	Group
Time management	☐	☐
Organizational skills	☐	☐
Learning strategies	☐	☐
Study skills	☐	☐
Content area	☐	☐
Writing lab	☐	☐
Math lab	☐	☐

UNIQUE LD PROGRAM FEATURES

Founded in 1986, PACE (the Professional Assistant Center for Education), is a two-year, non-credit post-seconary certificate program located on the campus of National-Louis University in Evanston, Illinois. The PACE program is designed especially to meet the transitional needs of students with multiple learning disabilities in a university setting. The Program commits to educating the whole person, preparing young adults for independent living by integrating instruction in four areas: academics, career preparation, life skills, socialization.

An apartment living program is available to qualified graduates of the Program, allowing students to remain in a familiar environment among friends while transitioning to the next step of independent living.

LD PROGRAM STAFF

Total number of LD Program staff (including director):

Full Time: 11 Part Time: 11

Key staff person available to work with LD students: Carol Burns, Director, PACE Program.

North Central College

Naperville, IL

Address: 30 North Brainard Street, P.O. Box 3063, Naperville, IL, 60540
Admissions telephone: 800 411-1861
Admissions FAX: 630 637-5819
Dean of Admission: Marguerite Waters
Admissions e-mail: ncadm@noctrl.edu
Web site: http://www.noctrl.edu
SAT Code: 1555 ACT Code: 1096

LD program name: Academic Support Center
Coordinator of Disability Services: Dee Wiedeman
LD program telephone: 630 637-5264
LD program e-mail: dmwiedeman@noctrl.edu
LD program enrollment: 62, Total campus enrollment: 2,036

GENERAL

North Central College is a private, coed, four-year institution. 56-acre, suburban campus in Naperville (population: 28,358), 29 miles from downtown Chicago. Served by bus and train; major airport serves Chicago. Public transportation serves campus. Trimester system.

LD ADMISSIONS

Students do not complete a separate application and are simultaneously accepted to the LD program. A member of the LD program does not sit on the admissions committee. A personal interview is recommended. Essay is not required.

SECONDARY SCHOOL REQUIREMENTS

Graduation from secondary school required; GED accepted. The following course distribution required: 4 units of English, 3 units of math, 3 units of science, 2 units of social studies, 2 units of history, 3 units of academic electives.

TESTING

ACT required; SAT Reasoning may be substituted. SAT Subject recommended.

All enrolled freshmen (fall 2004):

Average SAT I Scores:	Verbal: 570	Math: 603
Average ACT Scores:	Composite: 24	

Child Study Team report is not required. A neuropsychological or comprehensive psycho-educational evaluation is required for admission. Tests required as part of this documentation:

- [x] WAIS-IV
- [x] WISC-IV
- [ ] SATA
- [x] Woodcock-Johnson
- [ ] Nelson-Denny Reading Test
- [ ] Other

UNDERGRADUATE STUDENT BODY

Total undergraduate student enrollment: 924 Men, 1,238 Women.

Composition of student body (fall 2004):

	Undergraduate	Freshmen
International	2.1	1.9
Black	4.2	3.4
American Indian	0.0	0.1
Asian-American	4.2	2.5
Hispanic	4.5	4.7
White	78.2	82.7
Unreported	6.8	4.7
	100.0%	100.0%

11% are from out of state. Average age of full-time undergraduates is 21, 54% of classes have fewer than 20 students, 46% have between 20 and 50 students.

STUDENT HOUSING

86% of freshmen live in college housing. Freshmen are not required to live on campus. Housing is guaranteed for all undergraduates. Campus can house 1,030 undergraduates. Single rooms are available for students with medical or special needs. A medical note is required.

EXPENSES

Tuition (2005-06): $21,528 per year.
Room: $4,719. Board: $2,274.
There is no additional cost for LD program/services.

LD SERVICES

LD program size is not limited.

LD services available to:

- [x] Freshmen
- [x] Sophomores
- [x] Juniors
- [x] Seniors

Academic Accommodations

Curriculum

- [ ] Foreign language waiver
- [x] Lighter course load
- [ ] Math waiver
- [ ] Other special classes
- [ ] Priority registrations
- [ ] Substitution of courses

Exams

- [x] Extended time
- [x] Oral exams
- [ ] Take home exams
- [x] Exams on tape or computer
- [x] Untimed exams
- [x] Other accommodations

In class

- [ ] Early syllabus
- [x] Note takers in class
- [x] Priority seating
- [x] Tape recorders
- [ ] Videotaped classes
- [x] Text on tape

Services

- [x] Diagnostic tests
- [x] Learning centers
- [ ] Proofreaders
- [x] Readers
- [x] Reading Machines/Kurzweil
- [ ] Special bookstore section
- [x] Typists

Credit toward degree is not given for remedial courses taken.

Counseling Services

- [x] Academic
- [x] Psychological
- [ ] Student Support groups
- [ ] Vocational

Tutoring

Individual tutoring is available daily.

	Individual	Group
Time management	[x]	[x]
Organizational skills	[x]	[x]
Learning strategies	[x]	[x]
Study skills	[x]	[x]
Content area	[x]	[ ]
Writing lab	[x]	[ ]
Math lab	[ ]	[ ]

UNIQUE LD PROGRAM FEATURES

The program is part of a larger Academic Support Program available to all students on a no-charge basis. LD students are integrated into the life of the campus.

LD PROGRAM STAFF

Total number of LD Program staff (including director):

Full Time: 1 Part Time: 1

There is an advisor/advocate from the LD program available to students.

Key staff person available to work with LD students: Dee Wiedeman, Coordinator of Disability Services.

North Park University

Chicago, IL

Address: 3225 West Foster Avenue, Chicago, IL, 60625-4895
Admissions telephone: 800 888-6728
Admissions FAX: 773 244-4953
Director of Admissions: Mark Olson
Admissions e-mail: admissions@northpark.edu
Web site: http://www.northpark.edu
SAT Code: 1556 ACT Code: 1098

LD program name: Center for Academic Services
LD program telephone: 773 244-5737
LD program e-mail: esnezek@northpark.edu
LD program enrollment: 35, Total campus enrollment: 1,716

GENERAL

North Park University is a private, coed, four-year institution. 30-acre, urban campus in Chicago (population: 2,896,016). Served by air, bus, and train. Public transportation serves campus. Semester system.

LD ADMISSIONS

Students do not complete a separate application and are not simultaneously accepted to the LD program. A member of the LD program does sit on the admissions committee. A personal interview is not required. Essay is required and may be typed.

SECONDARY SCHOOL REQUIREMENTS

Graduation from secondary school required; GED accepted. The following course distribution required: 3 units of English, 3 units of math, 1 unit of foreign language, 1 unit of social studies.

TESTING

SAT Reasoning or ACT required.

All enrolled freshmen (fall 2004):

Average SAT I Scores:	Verbal: 560	Math: 536
Average ACT Scores:	Composite: 22	

Child Study Team report is not required. A neuropsychological or comprehensive psycho-educational evaluation is required for admission. Must be dated within 36 months of application. Tests required as part of this documentation:

- [x] WAIS-IV
- [ ] WISC-IV
- [ ] SATA
- [x] Woodcock-Johnson
- [x] Nelson-Denny Reading Test
- [x] Other

UNDERGRADUATE STUDENT BODY

Total undergraduate student enrollment: 632 Men, 1,023 Women.

Composition of student body (fall 2004):

	Undergraduate	Freshmen
International	0.3	2.8
Black	12.7	11.7
American Indian	0.7	0.4
Asian-American	7.0	8.3
Hispanic	6.3	9.4
White	67.7	59.1
Unreported	5.3	8.4
	100.0%	100.0%

38% are from out of state, 57% of classes have fewer than 20 students, 40% have between 20 and 50 students.

STUDENT HOUSING

Single rooms are available for students with medical or special needs. A medical note is required.

EXPENSES

Tuition (2005-06): $13,900 per year.
Room: $3,800. Board: $2,980.

There is no additional cost for LD program/services.

LD SERVICES

LD program size is not limited.

LD services available to:

- [x] Freshmen
- [x] Sophomores
- [x] Juniors
- [x] Seniors

Academic Accommodations

Curriculum		In class	
Foreign language waiver	[ ]	Early syllabus	[ ]
Lighter course load	[x]	Note takers in class	[x]
Math waiver	[ ]	Priority seating	[ ]
Other special classes	[ ]	Tape recorders	[x]
Priority registrations	[ ]	Videotaped classes	[ ]
Substitution of courses	[x]	Text on tape	[x]
Exams		**Services**	
Extended time	[x]	Diagnostic tests	[ ]
Oral exams	[x]	Learning centers	[x]
Take home exams	[x]	Proofreaders	[ ]
Exams on tape or computer	[x]	Readers	[ ]
Untimed exams	[x]	Reading Machines/Kurzweil	[ ]
Other accommodations	[x]	Special bookstore section	[ ]
		Typists	[ ]

Credit toward degree is given for remedial courses taken.

Counseling Services

- [x] Academic
- [x] Psychological
- [ ] Student Support groups
- [ ] Vocational

Tutoring

Individual tutoring is available daily.

Average size of tutoring groups: 1

	Individual	Group
Time management	[x]	[x]
Organizational skills	[x]	[x]
Learning strategies	[x]	[ ]
Study skills	[x]	[x]
Content area	[x]	[ ]
Writing lab	[x]	[ ]
Math lab	[x]	[ ]

LD PROGRAM STAFF

Total number of LD Program staff (including director):

Full Time: 3 Part Time: 3

There is an advisor/advocate from the LD program available to students. 37 peer tutors are available to work with LD students.

Key staff person available to work with LD students: Elizabeth Snezek, Director of Academic Services.

Northeastern Illinois University

Chicago, IL

Address: 5500 North St. Louis Avenue, Chicago, IL, 60625
Admissions telephone: 773 442-4000
Admissions FAX: 773 442-4020
Director of Admissions and Records: Dr. Janice Harring-Hendon
Admissions e-mail: admrec@neiu.edu
Web site: http://www.neiu.edu
SAT Code: 1090 ACT Code: 993

Director: Victoria Amey-Flippin
LD program telephone: 773 442-5495
Total campus enrollment: 9,305

GENERAL

Northeastern Illinois University is a public, coed, four-year institution. 63-acre campus in Chicago (population: 2,896,016). Served by air, bus, and train. Public transportation serves campus. Semester system.

LD ADMISSIONS

Students do not complete a separate application and are not simultaneously accepted to the LD program. A member of the LD program does not sit on the admissions committee. A personal interview is required. Essay is not required. Once a student with a disability is admitted to the university, he/she self identifies his/her disability to the Accessability Center.

SECONDARY SCHOOL REQUIREMENTS

Graduation from secondary school required; GED accepted. The following course distribution required: 4 units of English, 3 units of math, 3 units of science, 3 units of social studies.

TESTING

SAT Reasoning or ACT considered if submitted; ACT preferred.

All enrolled freshmen (fall 2004):

Average SAT I Scores: Verbal: Math:

Average ACT Scores: Composite: 19

Child Study Team report is not required. A neuropsychological or comprehensive psycho-education evaluation is not required for admission. Tests required as part of this documentation:

- [ ] WAIS-IV
- [ ] WISC-IV
- [ ] SATA
- [ ] Woodcock-Johnson
- [ ] Nelson-Denny Reading Test
- [ ] Other

UNDERGRADUATE STUDENT BODY

Total undergraduate student enrollment: 3,171 Men, 5,034 Women.

Composition of student body (fall 2004):

	Undergraduate	Freshmen
International	3.2	3.6
Black	10.9	12.1
American Indian	0.5	0.3
Asian-American	14.6	10.8
Hispanic	35.7	29.3
White	35.1	43.8
Unreported	0.0	0.0
	100.0%	100.0%

4% are from out of state. Average age of full-time undergraduates is 23, 43% of classes have fewer than 20 students, 54% have between 20 and 50 students.

EXPENSES

Tuition (2005-06): $3,840 per year (in-state), $7,680 (out-of-state).

There is no additional cost for LD program/services.

LD SERVICES

LD program size is not limited.

LD services available to:

- [ ] Freshmen
- [ ] Sophomores
- [ ] Juniors
- [ ] Seniors

Academic Accommodations

Curriculum		**In class**	
Foreign language waiver	[ ]	Early syllabus	[ ]
Lighter course load	[ ]	Note takers in class	[x]
Math waiver	[ ]	Priority seating	[ ]
Other special classes	[ ]	Tape recorders	[x]
Priority registrations	[ ]	Videotaped classes	[ ]
Substitution of courses	[ ]	Text on tape	[ ]
Exams		**Services**	
Extended time	[x]	Diagnostic tests	[ ]
Oral exams	[x]	Learning centers	[ ]
Take home exams	[ ]	Proofreaders	[ ]
Exams on tape or computer	[ ]	Readers	[x]
Untimed exams	[x]	Reading Machines/Kurzweil	[x]
Other accommodations	[ ]	Special bookstore section	[ ]
		Typists	[ ]

Credit toward degree is not given for remedial courses taken.

Tutoring

Individual tutoring is not available.

	Individual	Group
Time management	[ ]	[ ]
Organizational skills	[ ]	[ ]
Learning strategies	[ ]	[ ]
Study skills	[ ]	[ ]
Content area	[ ]	[ ]
Writing lab	[ ]	[ ]
Math lab	[ ]	[ ]

UNIQUE LD PROGRAM FEATURES

Tutor support available from Accessability Center if student is a client of Department of Rehabilitation Services.

LD PROGRAM STAFF

Total number of LD Program staff (including director):

Full Time: 2 Part Time: 2

There is not an advisor/advocate from the LD program available to students.

Key staff person available to work with LD students: Victoria Amey-Flippin, Director.

Northern Illinois University

DeKalb, IL

Address: P.O. Box 3001, DeKalb, IL, 60115
Admissions telephone: 815 753-0446
Admissions FAX: 815 753-1783
Admissions e-mail: admission-info@niu.edu
Web site: http://www.niu.edu/
SAT Code: 1559 ACT Code: 1102

LD program name: Center for Access-Ability Resources
Coordinator: Garth Rubin
LD program telephone: 815 753-1303
LD program e-mail: grubin@niu.edu
LD program enrollment: 163, Total campus enrollment: 18,031

GENERAL

Northern Illinois University is a public, coed, four-year institution. 755-acre campus in DeKalb (population: 94,487), 65 miles from Chicago; branch campuses in Hoffman Estates and Rockford. Served by bus; major airport serves Chicago; smaller airport serves Rockford (40 miles); train serves Geneva (35 miles). School operates transportation to Chicago on weekends. Semester system.

LD ADMISSIONS

Students do not complete a separate application and are not simultaneously accepted to the LD program. A member of the LD program does not sit on the admissions committee. High school waivers are accepted for foreign language. A personal interview is not required. Essay is not required. Admissions requirements may be waived and special admission granted.

For fall 2004, 106 completed self-identified LD applications were received. 57 applications were offered admission, and 40 enrolled.

SECONDARY SCHOOL REQUIREMENTS

Graduation from secondary school required; GED accepted. The following course distribution required: 4 units of English, 2 units of math, 2 units of science, 1 unit of foreign language, 2 units of social studies, 1 unit of history.

TESTING

SAT Reasoning or ACT required. SAT Subject recommended.

All enrolled freshmen (fall 2004):

Average ACT Scores: Composite: 22

Child Study Team report is not required. A neuropsychological or comprehensive psycho-educational evaluation is required for admission. Must be dated within 36 months of application. Tests required as part of this documentation:

■ WAIS-IV
■ WISC-IV
☐ SATA
■ Woodcock-Johnson
☐ Nelson-Denny Reading Test
☐ Other

UNDERGRADUATE STUDENT BODY

Total undergraduate student enrollment: 8,174 Men, 9,294 Women.

Composition of student body (fall 2004):

	Undergraduate	Freshmen
International	0.3	0.9
Black	16.1	12.4
American Indian	0.2	0.2
Asian-American	4.7	5.7
Hispanic	7.4	6.5
White	68.7	71.2
Unreported	2.6	3.1
	100.0%	100.0%

3% are from out of state. 2% join a fraternity and 2% join a sorority, 39% of classes have fewer than 20 students, 49% have between 20 and 50 students, 12% have more than 50 students.

STUDENT HOUSING

Housing is not guaranteed for all undergraduates. Campus can house 5,998 undergraduates. Single rooms are available for students with medical or special needs. A medical note is required.

EXPENSES

Tuition (2005-06): $5,061 per year (in-state), $10,123 (out-of-state).
Room: $3,724. Board: $3,200.
There is no additional cost for LD program/services.

LD SERVICES

LD program size is not limited.

LD services available to:

■ Freshmen ■ Sophomores ■ Juniors ■ Seniors

Academic Accommodations

Curriculum		**In class**	
Foreign language waiver	☐	Early syllabus	☐
Lighter course load	■	Note takers in class	■
Math waiver	☐	Priority seating	■
Other special classes	☐	Tape recorders	■
Priority registrations	■	Videotaped classes	☐
Substitution of courses	☐	Text on tape	■
Exams		**Services**	
Extended time	■	Diagnostic tests	☐
Oral exams	■	Learning centers	■
Take home exams	☐	Proofreaders	☐
Exams on tape or computer	■	Readers	■
Untimed exams	☐	Reading Machines/Kurzweil	■
Other accommodations	☐	Special bookstore section	☐
		Typists	☐

Credit toward degree is not given for remedial courses taken.

Counseling Services

☐ Academic
☐ Psychological
☐ Student Support groups
☐ Vocational

Tutoring

	Individual	Group
Time management	■	■
Organizational skills	■	■
Learning strategies	■	■
Study skills	■	■
Content area	☐	☐
Writing lab	☐	☐
Math lab	☐	☐

LD PROGRAM STAFF

Total number of LD Program staff (including director):

Full Time: 5 Part Time: 5

There is an advisor/advocate from the LD program available to students.

Key staff person available to work with LD students: Garth Rubin, Coordinator, Center for Access-Ability Resources.

LD Program web site: www.niu.edu/caar

Northwestern University

Evanston, IL

Address: 633 Clark Street, Evanston, IL, 60208
Admissions telephone: 847 491-7271
Director of Undergraduate Admissions: Keith Todd
Admissions e-mail: ug-admission@northwestern.edu
Web site: http://www.northwestern.edu
SAT Code: 1565 ACT Code: 1106

LD program telephone: 847 467-5530
LD program e-mail: ssd@northwestern.edu
Total campus enrollment: 8,031

GENERAL

Northwestern University is a private, coed, four-year institution. 250-acre, suburban campus in Evanston (population: 74,239), 12 miles from Chicago; branch campus (law and medical schools) in Chicago. Major airport, bus, and train serve Chicago. Public transportation serves campus. Quarter system.

LD ADMISSIONS

A personal interview is not required. Essay is required and may be typed.

SECONDARY SCHOOL REQUIREMENTS

Graduation from secondary school not required.

TESTING

SAT Reasoning or ACT required. SAT Subject required.

All enrolled freshmen (fall 2004):

Average SAT I Scores:	Verbal: 689	Math: 709
Average ACT Scores:	Composite: 30	

Child Study Team report is not required. Tests required as part of this documentation:

☐ WAIS-IV	☐ Woodcock-Johnson
☐ WISC-IV	☐ Nelson-Denny Reading Test
☐ SATA	☐ Other

UNDERGRADUATE STUDENT BODY

Total undergraduate student enrollment: 3,697 Men, 4,119 Women.

Composition of student body (fall 2004):

	Undergraduate	Freshmen
International	4.9	5.2
Black	5.5	5.3
American Indian	0.3	0.3
Asian-American	16.4	16.8
Hispanic	6.4	5.5
White	61.5	60.5
Unreported	5.1	6.4
	100.0%	100.0%

78% are from out of state. 30% join a fraternity and 39% join a sorority. Average age of full-time undergraduates is 20, 73% of classes have fewer than 20 students, 19% have between 20 and 50 students.

STUDENT HOUSING

99% of freshmen live in college housing. Freshmen are not required to live on campus. Housing is not guaranteed for all undergraduates. We guarantee housing for freshmen year only. Campus can house 5,050 undergraduates. Single rooms are available for students with medical or special needs. A medical note is required.

EXPENSES

Tuition (2005-06): $31,644 per year.

Room: $5,613. Board: $4,260.
There is no additional cost for LD program/services.

LD SERVICES

LD program size is not limited.

LD services available to:

■ Freshmen ■ Sophomores ■ Juniors ■ Seniors

Academic Accommodations

Curriculum		**In class**	
Foreign language waiver	☐	Early syllabus	☐
Lighter course load	■	Note takers in class	■
Math waiver	☐	Priority seating	■
Other special classes	☐	Tape recorders	■
Priority registrations	■	Videotaped classes	☐
Substitution of courses	■	Text on tape	■
Exams		**Services**	
Extended time	■	Diagnostic tests	■
Oral exams	■	Learning centers	☐
Take home exams	☐	Proofreaders	■
Exams on tape or computer	■	Readers	■
Untimed exams	☐	Reading Machines/Kurzweil	■
Other accommodations	■	Special bookstore section	☐
		Typists	■

Credit toward degree is not given for remedial courses taken.

Counseling Services

☐ Academic
☐ Psychological
☐ Student Support groups
☐ Vocational

Tutoring

	Individual	Group
Time management	■	☐
Organizational skills	■	☐
Learning strategies	■	☐
Study skills	■	☐
Content area	☐	☐
Writing lab	☐	☐
Math lab	☐	☐

LD PROGRAM STAFF

Total number of LD Program staff (including director):

Full Time: 3 Part Time: 3

Key staff person available to work with LD students: Kiriko Takahashi, Disability Specialist.

Olivet Nazarene University

Bourbonnais, IL

Address: 1 University Avenue, Bourbonnais, IL, 60914
Admissions telephone: 800 648-1463
Admissions FAX: 815 935-4998
Director of Admissions: Brian Parker
Admissions e-mail: admissions@olivet.edu
Web site: http://www.olivet.edu
SAT Code: 1596 ACT Code: 1112

Director of Academic Support: Sue Rattin
LD program telephone: 815 939-5150
LD program e-mail: srattin@olivet.edu
LD program enrollment: 74, Total campus enrollment: 2,633

GENERAL

Olivet Nazarene University is a private, coed, four-year institution. 168-acre campus in Bourbonnais (population: 15,256), 50 miles from Chicago. Major airports serve Chicago; bus and train serve Kankakee (seven miles). Public transportation serves campus. Semester system.

LD ADMISSIONS

Application Deadline: 05/15. Students do not complete a separate application and are simultaneously accepted to the LD program. A member of the LD program does sit on the admissions committee. A personal interview is required. Essay is not required.

For fall 2004, 10 completed self-identified LD applications were received. 10 applications were offered admission, and 10 enrolled.

SECONDARY SCHOOL REQUIREMENTS

Graduation from secondary school required; GED accepted. The following course distribution required: 4 units of English, 3 units of math, 3 units of science, 3 units of social studies, 2 units of history.

TESTING

SAT Reasoning considered if submitted. ACT required.

All enrolled freshmen (fall 2004):

Average SAT I Scores:	Verbal: 550	Math: 540
Average ACT Scores:	Composite: 23	

Child Study Team report is not required. A neuropsychological or comprehensive psycho-educational evaluation is required for admission. Tests required as part of this documentation:

- [x] WAIS-IV
- [x] WISC-IV
- [ ] SATA
- [x] Woodcock-Johnson
- [ ] Nelson-Denny Reading Test
- [ ] Other

UNDERGRADUATE STUDENT BODY

Total undergraduate student enrollment: 762 Men, 1,104 Women.

Composition of student body (fall 2004):

	Undergraduate	Freshmen
International	0.1	1.1
Black	7.0	8.5
American Indian	0.1	0.2
Asian-American	1.7	1.4
Hispanic	3.4	2.8
White	87.6	86.0
Unreported	0.0	0.0
	100.0%	100.0%

40% are from out of state. Average age of full-time undergraduates is 21, 35% of classes have fewer than 20 students, 53% have between 20 and 50 students, 12% have more than 50 students.

STUDENT HOUSING

90% of freshmen live in college housing. Freshmen are not required to live on campus. Housing is not guaranteed for all undergraduates. Housing is not provided for students 23 and older. Campus can house 2,019 undergraduates. Single rooms are not available for students with medical or special needs.

EXPENSES

Tuition (2005-06): $15,650 per year.
Room & Board: $3,050.
There is no additional cost for LD program/services.

LD SERVICES

LD program size is not limited.

LD services available to:

- [x] Freshmen
- [x] Sophomores
- [x] Juniors
- [x] Seniors

Academic Accommodations

Curriculum		In class	
Foreign language waiver	[ ]	Early syllabus	[ ]
Lighter course load	[x]	Note takers in class	[x]
Math waiver	[ ]	Priority seating	[x]
Other special classes	[ ]	Tape recorders	[x]
Priority registrations	[ ]	Videotaped classes	[ ]
Substitution of courses	[ ]	Text on tape	[ ]
Exams		**Services**	
Extended time	[x]	Diagnostic tests	[x]
Oral exams	[x]	Learning centers	[x]
Take home exams	[ ]	Proofreaders	[ ]
Exams on tape or computer	[x]	Readers	[x]
Untimed exams	[x]	Reading Machines/Kurzweil	[x]
Other accommodations	[x]	Special bookstore section	[ ]
		Typists	[ ]

Credit toward degree is not given for remedial courses taken.

Counseling Services

- [x] Academic
- [x] Psychological
- [x] Student Support groups
- [x] Vocational

Tutoring

Individual tutoring is available weekly.

Average size of tutoring groups: 5

	Individual	Group
Time management	[x]	[ ]
Organizational skills	[x]	[ ]
Learning strategies	[x]	[x]
Study skills	[x]	[x]
Content area	[x]	[ ]
Writing lab	[ ]	[x]
Math lab	[ ]	[x]

LD PROGRAM STAFF

Total number of LD Program staff (including director):

Full Time: 1 Part Time: 1

There is an advisor/advocate from the LD program available to students. 65 peer tutors are available to work with LD students.

Key staff person available to work with LD students: Sue Rattin, Director of Academic Support.

Quincy University

Quincy, IL

Address: 1800 College Avenue, Quincy, IL, 62301
Admissions telephone: 217 228-5210
Admissions FAX: 217 228-5479
Director of Admissions: Mark P. Clynes
Admissions e-mail: admissions@quincy.edu
Web site: http://www.quincy.edu
SAT Code: 1645 ACT Code: 1120

Dean of Academic Support Services: Linda Godley
LD program telephone: 217 228-5288
LD program e-mail: godley@quincy.edu
Total campus enrollment: 1,086

GENERAL

Quincy University is a private, coed, four-year institution. 82-acre campus in Quincy (population: 40,366), 100 miles from Springfield. Served by air, bus, and train; major airport serves Springfield. School operates transportation to north campus. Public transportation serves campus. Semester system.

LD ADMISSIONS

Students do not complete a separate application and are simultaneously accepted to the LD program. A member of the LD program does sit on the admissions committee. A personal interview is recommended. Essay is required and may be typed.

SECONDARY SCHOOL REQUIREMENTS

Graduation from secondary school required; GED accepted. The following course distribution required: 4 units of English.

TESTING

SAT Reasoning or ACT required. SAT Subject recommended.

All enrolled freshmen (fall 2004):

Average SAT I Scores: Verbal: 510 Math: 520
Average ACT Scores: Composite: 21

Child Study Team report is not required. Tests required as part of this documentation:

- ☐ WAIS-IV
- ☐ WISC-IV
- ☐ SATA
- ☐ Woodcock-Johnson
- ☐ Nelson-Denny Reading Test
- ☐ Other

UNDERGRADUATE STUDENT BODY

Total undergraduate student enrollment: 500 Men, 647 Women.

Composition of student body (fall 2004):

	Undergraduate	Freshmen
International	0.4	0.7
Black	10.1	6.3
American Indian	0.0	0.1
Asian-American	0.9	0.8
Hispanic	3.5	2.8
White	72.8	77.4
Unreported	12.3	11.9
	100.0%	100.0%

25% are from out of state. 5% join a fraternity and 15% join a sorority. Average age of full-time undergraduates is 22, 70% of classes have fewer than 20 students, 30% have between 20 and 50 students.

STUDENT HOUSING

77% of freshmen live in college housing. Housing is guaranteed for all undergraduates. Campus can house 831 undergraduates.

EXPENSES

Tuition (2005-06): $24,920 per year (in-state), $17,800 (out-of-state).
Room: $3,540. Board: $3,050.
There is no additional cost for LD program/services.

LD SERVICES

LD program size is not limited.

LD services available to:

☑ Freshmen ☑ Sophomores ☑ Juniors ☑ Seniors

Academic Accommodations

Curriculum

- Foreign language waiver ☐
- Lighter course load ☑
- Math waiver ☐
- Other special classes ☐
- Priority registrations ☐
- Substitution of courses ☐

Exams

- Extended time ☑
- Oral exams ☑
- Take home exams ☐
- Exams on tape or computer ☐
- Untimed exams ☑
- Other accommodations ☐

In class

- Early syllabus ☐
- Note takers in class ☑
- Priority seating ☐
- Tape recorders ☑
- Videotaped classes ☐
- Text on tape ☐

Services

- Diagnostic tests ☐
- Learning centers ☑
- Proofreaders ☐
- Readers ☑
- Reading Machines/Kurzweil ☑
- Special bookstore section ☐
- Typists ☐

Credit toward degree is not given for remedial courses taken.

Counseling Services

- ☐ Academic
- ☐ Psychological
- ☐ Student Support groups
- ☐ Vocational

Tutoring

Individual tutoring is available weekly.

	Individual	Group
Time management	☐	☐
Organizational skills	☐	☐
Learning strategies	☐	☐
Study skills	☐	☐
Content area	☐	☐
Writing lab	☐	☐
Math lab	☐	☐

LD PROGRAM STAFF

Key staff person available to work with LD students: Linda Godley, Dean of Academic Support Services.

Robert Morris College

Chicago, IL

Address: 401 South State Street, Chicago, IL, 60605
Admissions telephone: 800 225-1520
Admissions FAX: 312 935-6819
Senior Vice President for Academics: Candace Goodwin
Admissions e-mail: enroll@robertmorris.edu
Web site: http://www.robertmorris.edu/
SAT Code: 1670   ACT Code: 1121

Director of Student Services/Special Services: Monique Jones
LD program telephone: 312 935-6213
LD program e-mail: mqjones@robertmorris.edu
LD program enrollment: 21, Total campus enrollment: 5,520

GENERAL

Robert Morris College is a private, coed, four-year institution. Urban campus in Chicago (population: 2,896,016); branch campuses in Dupage, Orland Park, and Springfield. Served by air, bus, and train. Public transportation serves campus.

LD ADMISSIONS

Students do not complete a separate application and are simultaneously accepted to the LD program. A member of the LD program does not sit on the admissions committee. A personal interview is recommended. Essay is not required.

For fall 2004, 21 completed self-identified LD applications were received. 21 applications were offered admission, and 21 enrolled.

SECONDARY SCHOOL REQUIREMENTS

Graduation from secondary school required; GED accepted.

TESTING

Child Study Team report is not required. A neuropsychological or comprehensive psycho-educational evaluation is required for admission. Must be dated within 36 months of application. Tests required as part of this documentation:

- ☐ WAIS-IV
- ☐ WISC-IV
- ☐ SATA
- ☐ Woodcock-Johnson
- ☐ Nelson-Denny Reading Test
- ■ Other

UNDERGRADUATE STUDENT BODY

Total undergraduate student enrollment: 1,720 Men, 3,599 Women.

Composition of student body (fall 2004):

	Undergraduate	Freshmen
International	0.2	0.5
Black	42.0	41.3
American Indian	0.6	0.4
Asian-American	1.2	2.2
Hispanic	24.3	23.6
White	29.9	30.0
Unreported	1.9	2.1
	100.0%	100.0%

1% are from out of state. Average age of full-time undergraduates is 25, 38% of classes have fewer than 20 students, 61% have between 20 and 50 students.

STUDENT HOUSING

5% of freshmen live in college housing. Freshmen are not required to live on campus. Housing is guaranteed for all undergraduates. Campus can house 119 undergraduates. Single rooms are not available for students with medical or special needs.

EXPENSES

Tuition (2005-06): $15,375 per year.
Room: $6,060. Board: $2,250.
There is no additional cost for LD program/services.

LD SERVICES

LD program size is not limited.

LD services available to:

■ Freshmen ■ Sophomores ■ Juniors ■ Seniors

Academic Accommodations

Curriculum		In class	
Foreign language waiver	☐	Early syllabus	☐
Lighter course load	■	Note takers in class	■
Math waiver	☐	Priority seating	☐
Other special classes	☐	Tape recorders	■
Priority registrations	☐	Videotaped classes	☐
Substitution of courses	☐	Text on tape	■
Exams		**Services**	
Extended time	■	Diagnostic tests	☐
Oral exams	■	Learning centers	■
Take home exams	☐	Proofreaders	☐
Exams on tape or computer	☐	Readers	■
Untimed exams	☐	Reading Machines/Kurzweil	☐
Other accommodations	■	Special bookstore section	☐
		Typists	☐

Credit toward degree is not given for remedial courses taken.

Counseling Services

- ■ Academic
- ■ Psychological
- ■ Student Support groups
- ■ Vocational

Tutoring

Individual tutoring is available daily.

Average size of tutoring groups: 3

	Individual	Group
Time management	☐	■
Organizational skills	☐	■
Learning strategies	☐	■
Study skills	☐	■
Content area	☐	■
Writing lab	☐	■
Math lab	☐	☐

LD PROGRAM STAFF

Total number of LD Program staff (including director):

Full Time: 2   Part Time: 2

There is an advisor/advocate from the LD program available to students. The advisor/advocate meets with faculty 2 times per month and students 4 times per month.

Key staff person available to work with LD students: Monique Jones, Director of Student Services/Special Services.

Rockford College

Rockford, IL

Address: 5050 East State Street, Rockford, IL, 61108-2393
Admissions telephone: 800 892-2984
Admissions FAX: 815 226-2822
Vice President for Enrollment Management: Mike Plocinski
Admissions e-mail: rcadmissions@rockford.edu
Web site: http://www.rockford.edu
SAT Code: 1665   ACT Code: 1122

LD program name: Disability Support Services
Disability Support Services: Lorraine Hoover
LD program telephone: 815 226-4022
LD program e-mail: lhoover@rockford.edu
LD program enrollment: 29, Total campus enrollment: 887

GENERAL

Rockford College is a private, coed, four-year institution. 130-acre campus in Rockford (population: 150,115), 90 miles from Chicago. Served by air and bus; train serves Elgin (45 miles). School operates transportation to malls, bus station, and Catholic church. Public transportation serves campus. Semester system.

LD ADMISSIONS

Students do not complete a separate application and are not simultaneously accepted to the LD program. A member of the LD program does not sit on the admissions committee. A personal interview is recommended. Essay is not required. If students do not meet minimum requirements they can write a personal essay and provide two letters of recommendation. The entire application and IEP will be reviewed by the Admission Retention Committee.

For fall 2004, 12 completed self-identified LD applications were received.

SECONDARY SCHOOL REQUIREMENTS

Graduation from secondary school required; GED accepted. The following course distribution required: 4 units of English, 3 units of math, 3 units of science, 2 units of foreign language, 3 units of social studies, 3 units of history, 2 units of academic electives.

TESTING

ACT required; SAT Reasoning may be substituted. SAT Subject recommended.

All enrolled freshmen (fall 2004):

Average SAT I Scores:	Verbal: 520	Math: 510
Average ACT Scores:	Composite: 22	

Child Study Team report is not required. A neuropsychological or comprehensive psycho-educational evaluation is required for admission. Tests required as part of this documentation:

- [x] WAIS-IV
- [x] WISC-IV
- [x] SATA
- [x] Woodcock-Johnson
- [x] Nelson-Denny Reading Test
- [x] Other

UNDERGRADUATE STUDENT BODY

Total undergraduate student enrollment: 392 Men, 664 Women.

Composition of student body (fall 2004):

	Undergraduate	Freshmen
International	0.0	0.9
Black	10.5	8.1
American Indian	0.0	0.3
Asian-American	1.1	1.9
Hispanic	5.3	5.0
White	62.6	77.0
Unreported	20.5	6.8
	100.0%	100.0%

21% are from out of state.

STUDENT HOUSING

Freshmen are not required to live on campus. Housing is guaranteed for all undergraduates. Campus can house 572 undergraduates. Single rooms are available for students with medical or special needs. A medical note is not required.

EXPENSES

Tuition (2005-06): $22,460 per year.
Room: $4,410. Board: $2,780.
There is no additional cost for LD program/services.

LD SERVICES

LD program size is not limited.

LD services available to:

- [x] Freshmen
- [x] Sophomores
- [x] Juniors
- [x] Seniors

Academic Accommodations

Curriculum

- [ ] Foreign language waiver
- [x] Lighter course load
- [ ] Math waiver
- [ ] Other special classes
- [x] Priority registrations
- [ ] Substitution of courses

Exams

- [x] Extended time
- [x] Oral exams
- [ ] Take home exams
- [x] Exams on tape or computer
- [x] Untimed exams
- [x] Other accommodations

In class

- [x] Early syllabus
- [x] Note takers in class
- [x] Priority seating
- [x] Tape recorders
- [ ] Videotaped classes
- [x] Text on tape

Services

- [x] Diagnostic tests
- [x] Learning centers
- [x] Proofreaders
- [x] Readers
- [x] Reading Machines/Kurzweil
- [x] Special bookstore section
- [x] Typists

Credit toward degree is not given for remedial courses taken.

Counseling Services

- [x] Academic
- [x] Psychological
- [ ] Student Support groups
- [ ] Vocational

Tutoring

Individual tutoring is available daily.

Average size of tutoring groups: 2

	Individual	Group
Time management	[x]	[ ]
Organizational skills	[x]	[ ]
Learning strategies	[x]	[ ]
Study skills	[x]	[ ]
Content area	[ ]	[ ]
Writing lab	[x]	[ ]
Math lab	[x]	[ ]

UNIQUE LD PROGRAM FEATURES

There may be some additional costs attributed to the LD program.

LD PROGRAM STAFF

Total number of LD Program staff (including director):

Full Time: 1   Part Time: 1

There is an advisor/advocate from the LD program available to students. The advisor/advocate meets with students 2 times per month.

Key staff person available to work with LD students: Lorraine Hoover, Disability Support Services.

Roosevelt University

Chicago, IL

Address: 430 South Michigan Avenue, Chicago, IL, 60605
Admissions telephone: 877 APPLY RU
Admissions FAX: 312 341-3523
Director of Admissions: Gwen Kanelos
Admissions e-mail: applyRU@roosevelt.edu
Web site: http://www.roosevelt.edu
SAT Code: 1666 ACT Code: 1124

Director of Learning Support Services: Nancy Litke
LD program telephone: 312 341-3810
LD program e-mail: nlitke@roosevelt.edu
Total campus enrollment: 4,103

GENERAL

Roosevelt University is a private, coed, four-year institution. Main campuses in Chicago (population: 2,896,016) and Schaumburg (population: 68,586); branch campuses in Logan Square and La Villita areas of Chicago. Served by air, bus, and train. School operates transportation between campuses. Public transportation serves campus. Semester system.

SECONDARY SCHOOL REQUIREMENTS

Graduation from secondary school required; GED accepted. The following course distribution required: 4 units of English, 3 units of math, 3 units of science, 2 units of social studies, 1 unit of history, 2 units of academic electives.

TESTING

SAT Reasoning or ACT required. SAT Subject recommended.

All enrolled freshmen (fall 2004):

Average SAT I Scores:	Verbal: 573	Math: 533
Average ACT Scores:	Composite: 21	

Child Study Team report is not required. Tests required as part of this documentation:

- ☐ WAIS-IV
- ☐ WISC-IV
- ☐ SATA
- ☐ Woodcock-Johnson
- ☐ Nelson-Denny Reading Test
- ☐ Other

UNDERGRADUATE STUDENT BODY

Total undergraduate student enrollment: 4,103.

Composition of student body (fall 2004):

	Undergraduate	Freshmen
International	1.7	2.4
Black	20.2	25.5
American Indian	0.8	0.4
Asian-American	5.9	4.6
Hispanic	13.4	10.6
White	52.9	47.7
Unreported	5.0	8.7
	100.0%	100.0%

10% are from out of state. 1% join a fraternity and 2% join a sorority. Average age of full-time undergraduates is 24, 65% of classes have fewer than 20 students, 34% have between 20 and 50 students.

STUDENT HOUSING

51% of freshmen live in college housing. Freshmen are required to live on campus. Housing is guaranteed for all undergraduates. Campus can house 600 undergraduates.

EXPENSES

Tuition (2005-06): $14,180 per year.
Room: $5,800. Board: $2,190.
Additional cost for LD program/services: $1,000 per full-time semester.

LD SERVICES

LD program size is not limited.

LD services available to:

☐ Freshmen ☐ Sophomores ☐ Juniors ☐ Seniors

Academic Accommodations

Curriculum		In class	
Foreign language waiver	☐	Early syllabus	☐
Lighter course load	■	Note takers in class	■
Math waiver	☐	Priority seating	☐
Other special classes	☐	Tape recorders	☐
Priority registrations	☐	Videotaped classes	☐
Substitution of courses	☐	Text on tape	☐
Exams		**Services**	
Extended time	■	Diagnostic tests	■
Oral exams	☐	Learning centers	■
Take home exams	☐	Proofreaders	☐
Exams on tape or computer	☐	Readers	☐
Untimed exams	■	Reading Machines/Kurzweil	☐
Other accommodations	☐	Special bookstore section	☐
		Typists	☐

Credit toward degree is given for remedial courses taken.

Counseling Services

- ☐ Academic
- ☐ Psychological
- ☐ Student Support groups
- ☐ Vocational

Tutoring

	Individual	Group
Time management	☐	☐
Organizational skills	☐	☐
Learning strategies	☐	☐
Study skills	☐	☐
Content area	☐	☐
Writing lab	☐	☐
Math lab	☐	☐

LD PROGRAM STAFF

Total number of LD Program staff (including director):

Full Time: 1 Part Time: 1

Key staff person available to work with LD students: Nancy Litke, Director of Learning Support Services.

Saint Anthony College of Nursing

Rockford, IL

Address: 5658 East State Street, Rockford, IL, 61108-2468
Director of Student Services: Nancy Sanders
Admissions e-mail: cheryldelgado@sacn.edu
Web site: http://www.sacn.edu

Assistant Dean for Admissions & Student Affairs: Nancy Sanders
LD program telephone: 815 395-5100
LD program e-mail: nancysanders@sacn.edu
Total campus enrollment: 112

GENERAL

Saint Anthony College of Nursing is a private, coed, four-year institution. 17-acre campus in Rockford (population: 150,115), 75 miles from Chicago. Served by air and bus; major airport and train serve Chicago. Public transportation serves campus. Semester system.

LD ADMISSIONS

A personal interview is required. Essay is required and may be typed.

TESTING

Child Study Team report is not required. A neuropsychological or comprehensive psycho-education evaluation is not required for admission. Tests required as part of this documentation:

☐ WAIS-IV	☐ Woodcock-Johnson
☐ WISC-IV	☐ Nelson-Denny Reading Test
☐ SATA	☐ Other

UNDERGRADUATE STUDENT BODY

Total undergraduate student enrollment: 6 Men, 65 Women.

10% are from out of state. Average age of full-time undergraduates is 29.

STUDENT HOUSING

Housing is not guaranteed for all undergraduates. There are no residence halls--all students must provide their own housing. Single rooms are not available for students with medical or special needs.

EXPENSES

Tuition 2004-05: $14,700 per year.

There is no additional cost for LD program/services.

LD SERVICES

LD program size is not limited.

LD services available to:

☐ Freshmen ☐ Sophomores ☐ Juniors ☐ Seniors

Academic Accommodations

Curriculum		**In class**	
Foreign language waiver	☐	Early syllabus	☐
Lighter course load	☑	Note takers in class	☐
Math waiver	☐	Priority seating	☐
Other special classes	☐	Tape recorders	☑
Priority registrations	☐	Videotaped classes	☐
Substitution of courses	☐	Text on tape	☐
Exams		**Services**	
Extended time	☑	Diagnostic tests	☐
Oral exams	☐	Learning centers	☐
Take home exams	☐	Proofreaders	☐
Exams on tape or computer	☐	Readers	☑
Untimed exams	☐	Reading Machines/Kurzweil	☐
Other accommodations	☐	Special bookstore section	☐
		Typists	☐

Credit toward degree is not given for remedial courses taken.

Counseling Services

☐ Academic
☐ Psychological
☐ Student Support groups
☐ Vocational

Tutoring

Individual tutoring is available.

Average size of tutoring groups: 2

	Individual	Group
Time management	☐	☐
Organizational skills	☐	☐
Learning strategies	☐	☐
Study skills	☐	☐
Content area	☐	☐
Writing lab	☐	☐
Math lab	☐	☐

LD PROGRAM STAFF

2 peer tutors are available to work with LD students.

Saint Francis Medical Center College of Nursing

Peoria, IL

Address: 511 N.E. Greenleaf Street, Peoria, IL, 61603
Admissions FAX: 309 624-8973
Director of Admissions and Registrar: Janice Farquharson
Web site: http://www.sfmccon.edu
SAT Code: 1756 ACT Code: 1138

Health Nurse, Lab Assistant: Maureen Hermann
Total campus enrollment: 220

GENERAL

St. Francis Medical Center College of Nursing is a private, coed, upper-division institution. Campus in Peoria (population: 112,936), 157 miles from Chicago. Served by air and bus; major airport serves Chicago; train serves Bloomington (40 miles). Public transportation serves campus. Semester system.

LD ADMISSIONS

Students do not complete a separate application and are not simultaneously accepted to the LD program. A member of the LD program does not sit on the admissions committee. A personal interview is not required. Essay is required and may be typed.

TESTING

Child Study Team report is not required. A neuropsychological or comprehensive psycho-education evaluation is not required for admission. Tests required as part of this documentation:

- ☐ WAIS-IV
- ☐ WISC-IV
- ☐ SATA
- ☐ Woodcock-Johnson
- ☐ Nelson-Denny Reading Test
- ☐ Other

UNDERGRADUATE STUDENT BODY

Total undergraduate student enrollment: 10 Men, 134 Women.

25% of classes have fewer than 20 students, 55% have between 20 and 50 students, 20% have more than 50 students.

STUDENT HOUSING

Housing is not guaranteed for all undergraduates. Campus can house 92 undergraduates. Single rooms are available for students with medical or special needs. A medical note is not required.

EXPENSES

Tuition (2005-06): $10,200 per year.

LD SERVICES

LD services available to:

☐ Freshmen ☐ Sophomores ☐ Juniors ☐ Seniors

Academic Accommodations

Curriculum		**In class**	
Foreign language waiver	☐	Early syllabus	☐
Lighter course load	☐	Note takers in class	☐
Math waiver	☐	Priority seating	☐
Other special classes	☐	Tape recorders	☐
Priority registrations	☐	Videotaped classes	☐
Substitution of courses	☐	Text on tape	☐
Exams		**Services**	
Extended time	■	Diagnostic tests	☐
Oral exams	☐	Learning centers	☐
Take home exams	☐	Proofreaders	☐
Exams on tape or computer	☐	Readers	☐
Untimed exams	☐	Reading Machines/Kurzweil	☐
Other accommodations	■	Special bookstore section	☐
		Typists	☐

Credit toward degree is not given for remedial courses taken.

Counseling Services

- ☐ Academic
- ☐ Psychological
- ☐ Student Support groups
- ☐ Vocational

Tutoring

	Individual	Group
Time management	☐	☐
Organizational skills	☐	☐
Learning strategies	☐	☐
Study skills	☐	☐
Content area	☐	☐
Writing lab	☐	☐
Math lab	☐	☐

LD PROGRAM STAFF

Key staff person available to work with LD students: Maureen Hermann, Health Nurse, Lab Assistant.

Saint Xavier University

Chicago, IL

Address: 3700 West 103rd Street, Chicago, IL, 60655
Admissions telephone: 800 462-9288
Admissions FAX: 773 298-3076
Managing Director of Admissions: Beth Gierach
Admissions e-mail: admission@sxu.edu
Web site: http://www.sxu.edu
SAT Code: 1708 ACT Code: 1134

Director: Sue Zientara
LD program telephone: 773 298-3308
LD program e-mail: zientara@sxu.edu
LD program enrollment: 85, Total campus enrollment: 3,075

GENERAL

Saint Xavier University is a private, coed, four-year institution. 70-acre, suburban campus in Chicago (population: 2,896,016); branch campus in Tinley Park. Served by air, bus, and train. Public transportation serves campus. Semester system.

LD ADMISSIONS

A member of the LD program does not sit on the admissions committee. A personal interview is recommended. Essay is not required.

For fall 2004, 12 completed self-identified LD applications were received.

SECONDARY SCHOOL REQUIREMENTS

Graduation from secondary school required; GED accepted. The following course distribution required: 4 units of English, 3 units of math, 2 units of science, 2 units of foreign language, 2 units of social studies, 2 units of history, 3 units of academic electives.

TESTING

ACT required; SAT Reasoning may be substituted. SAT Subject recommended.

All enrolled freshmen (fall 2004):

Average ACT Scores: Composite: 22

Child Study Team report is not required. Tests required as part of this documentation:

- [ ] WAIS-IV
- [ ] WISC-IV
- [ ] SATA
- [ ] Woodcock-Johnson
- [ ] Nelson-Denny Reading Test
- [ ] Other

UNDERGRADUATE STUDENT BODY

Total undergraduate student enrollment: 806 Men, 2,009 Women.

Composition of student body (fall 2004):

	Undergraduate	Freshmen
International	0.0	0.3
Black	15.7	18.3
American Indian	0.2	0.3
Asian-American	1.2	1.8
Hispanic	15.2	11.9
White	60.4	62.2
Unreported	7.2	5.2
	100.0%	100.0%

3% are from out of state. Average age of full-time undergraduates is 22, 45% of classes have fewer than 20 students, 54% have between 20 and 50 students.

STUDENT HOUSING

55% of freshmen live in college housing. Freshmen are not required to live on campus. Housing is guaranteed for all undergraduates. Campus can house 592 undergraduates. Single rooms are available for students with medical or special needs. A medical note is required.

EXPENSES

Tuition (2005-06): $18,350 per year.

Room: $4,428. Board: $2,650.

There is no additional cost for LD program/services.

LD SERVICES

LD program size is not limited.

LD services available to:

- [x] Freshmen
- [x] Sophomores
- [x] Juniors
- [x] Seniors

Academic Accommodations

Curriculum		In class	
Foreign language waiver	[ ]	Early syllabus	[ ]
Lighter course load	[ ]	Note takers in class	[x]
Math waiver	[ ]	Priority seating	[ ]
Other special classes	[ ]	Tape recorders	[x]
Priority registrations	[ ]	Videotaped classes	[ ]
Substitution of courses	[ ]	Text on tape	[x]
Exams		**Services**	
Extended time	[x]	Diagnostic tests	[ ]
Oral exams	[x]	Learning centers	[x]
Take home exams	[ ]	Proofreaders	[ ]
Exams on tape or computer	[x]	Readers	[ ]
Untimed exams	[ ]	Reading Machines/Kurzweil	[ ]
Other accommodations	[ ]	Special bookstore section	[ ]
		Typists	[x]

Credit toward degree is not given for remedial courses taken.

Counseling Services

- [x] Academic
- [x] Psychological
- [x] Student Support groups
- [ ] Vocational

Tutoring

Individual tutoring is available daily.

	Individual	Group
Time management	[ ]	[x]
Organizational skills	[ ]	[x]
Learning strategies	[ ]	[x]
Study skills	[ ]	[x]
Content area	[ ]	[x]
Writing lab	[ ]	[x]
Math lab	[ ]	[x]

LD PROGRAM STAFF

Total number of LD Program staff (including director):

Full Time: 2 Part Time: 2

There is an advisor/advocate from the LD program available to students. 25 peer tutors are available to work with LD students.

Key staff person available to work with LD students: Sue Zientara, Director of Learning Assistance & Disability Services

The School of the Art Institute of Chicago

Chicago, IL

Address: 37 South Wabash, Chicago, IL, 60603
Admissions telephone: 800 232-7242
Admissions FAX: 312 899-1840
Executive Director of Admissions and Marketing: Scott Ramon
Admissions e-mail: admiss@artic.edu
Web site: http://www.artic.edu/saic
SAT Code: 1713 ACT Code: 1136

LD program name: The Learning Center
LD program address: 112 South Michigan
Director of the Learning Center: Heather Walsh
LD program telephone: 312 345-9478
LD program e-mail: hwalsh@artic.edu
LD program enrollment: 92, Total campus enrollment: 2,093

GENERAL

The School of the Art Institute of Chicago is a private, coed, four-year institution. Urban campus in Chicago (population: 2,896,016). Served by air, bus, and train. School operates transportation to all campus facilities. Public transportation serves campus. Semester system.

LD ADMISSIONS

Students do not complete a separate application and are simultaneously accepted to the LD program. A member of the LD program does not sit on the admissions committee. A personal interview is recommended. Essay is required and may be typed.

SECONDARY SCHOOL REQUIREMENTS

Graduation from secondary school required; GED accepted.

TESTING

SAT Reasoning or ACT required. SAT Subject recommended.

Child Study Team report is not required. A neuropsychological or comprehensive psycho-educational evaluation is required for admission. Must be dated within 36 months of application. Tests required as part of this documentation:

- [x] WAIS-IV
- [x] WISC-IV
- [ ] SATA
- [x] Woodcock-Johnson
- [x] Nelson-Denny Reading Test
- [ ] Other

UNDERGRADUATE STUDENT BODY

Total undergraduate student enrollment: 767 Men, 1,381 Women.

Composition of student body (fall 2004):

	Undergraduate	Freshmen
International	17.0	15.1
Black	2.7	3.0
American Indian	0.0	0.8
Asian-American	11.5	9.9
Hispanic	6.1	7.2
White	60.9	61.2
Unreported	1.8	2.8
	100.0%	100.0%

77% are from out of state. Average age of full-time undergraduates is 21, 82% of classes have fewer than 20 students, 16% have between 20 and 50 students.

STUDENT HOUSING

85% of freshmen live in college housing. Freshmen are not required to live on campus. Housing is not guaranteed for all undergraduates. Housing available on a first-come, first-served basis. Campus can house 704 undergraduates. Single rooms are available for students with medical or special needs. A medical note is required.

EXPENSES

Tuition (2005-06): $27,150 per year.

Room: $8,200.

There is no additional cost for LD program/services.

LD SERVICES

LD program size is not limited.

LD services available to:

- [x] Freshmen
- [x] Sophomores
- [x] Juniors
- [x] Seniors

Academic Accommodations

Curriculum

- [ ] Foreign language waiver
- [x] Lighter course load
- [ ] Math waiver
- [ ] Other special classes
- [x] Priority registrations
- [ ] Substitution of courses

Exams

- [x] Extended time
- [x] Oral exams
- [ ] Take home exams
- [ ] Exams on tape or computer
- [x] Untimed exams
- [x] Other accommodations

In class

- [ ] Early syllabus
- [x] Note takers in class
- [ ] Priority seating
- [x] Tape recorders
- [ ] Videotaped classes
- [x] Text on tape

Services

- [ ] Diagnostic tests
- [x] Learning centers
- [ ] Proofreaders
- [x] Readers
- [ ] Reading Machines/Kurzweil
- [ ] Special bookstore section
- [ ] Typists

Credit toward degree is given for remedial courses taken.

Counseling Services

- [x] Academic
- [x] Psychological
- [ ] Student Support groups
- [x] Vocational

Tutoring

Individual tutoring is not available.

	Individual	Group
Time management	[ ]	[ ]
Organizational skills	[ ]	[ ]
Learning strategies	[ ]	[ ]
Study skills	[ ]	[ ]
Content area	[ ]	[ ]
Writing lab	[ ]	[ ]
Math lab	[ ]	[ ]

UNIQUE LD PROGRAM FEATURES

To identify as a student with a learning disability, students must submit a recent psycho-educational evaluation. Through the Learning Center, LD students are eligible for a weekly appointment to work on academic assignments, time management, organization, and study strategies. Accommodations are provided on an individual basis as needed.

LD PROGRAM STAFF

Total number of LD Program staff (including director):

Full Time: 2 Part Time: 2

There is an advisor/advocate from the LD program available to students. 1 graduate student is available to work with LD students.

Key staff person available to work with LD students: Heather Walsh, Director of the Learning Center.

LD Program web site: www.artic.edu/saic/life/sdd.html

Southern Illinois University Carbondale

Carbondale, IL

Address: Carbondale, IL, 62901-6899
Admissions telephone: 618 536-4405
Admissions FAX: 618 453-4609
Director of Admissions and Records: Dr. Anne De Luca
Admissions e-mail: joinsiuc@siu.edu
Web site: http://www.siuc.edu
SAT Code: 1726 ACT Code: 1144

LD program name: Disability Support Services/Achieve
LD program address: SIUC Woody Hall B150
LD program contact: Roger Pugh/Michael Whitney
LD program telephone: 618 453-2369
LD program e-mail: rpugh@siu.edu
LD program enrollment: 121, Total campus enrollment: 16,872

GENERAL

Southern Illinois University Carbondale is a public, coed, four-year institution. 1,133-acre campus in Carbondale (population: 20,681), 100 miles from St. Louis; medical school branch campus in Springfield; branch campus abroad in Nakajo, Japan. Served by bus and train; major airport serves St. Louis; smaller airport serves Marion (20 miles). Semester system.

LD ADMISSIONS

Students do not complete a separate application and are simultaneously accepted to the LD program. A member of the LD program does not sit on the admissions committee. A personal interview is not required. Essay is not required. Disability Support Service students meet admissions requirements or are admitted through Center for Basic Skills. Achieve Program students must submit through standard process; Achieve will make recommendation for admission if students do not meet standards.

SECONDARY SCHOOL REQUIREMENTS

Graduation from secondary school required; GED accepted. The following course distribution required: 4 units of English, 3 units of math, 3 units of science, 3 units of social studies, 2 units of academic electives.

TESTING

ACT required; SAT Reasoning may be substituted. SAT Subject recommended.

All enrolled freshmen (fall 2004):

Average SAT I Scores:	Verbal: 521	Math: 528
Average ACT Scores:	Composite: 22	

Child Study Team report is not required. A neuropsychological or comprehensive psycho-education evaluation is not required for admission. Tests required as part of this documentation:

- [x] WAIS-IV
- [x] WISC-IV
- [x] SATA
- [x] Woodcock-Johnson
- [x] Nelson-Denny Reading Test
- [ ] Other

UNDERGRADUATE STUDENT BODY

Total undergraduate student enrollment: 9,490 Men, 7,312 Women.

Composition of student body (fall 2004):

	Undergraduate	Freshmen
International	0.8	2.5
Black	21.9	15.2
American Indian	0.3	0.4
Asian-American	2.3	1.9
Hispanic	3.9	3.3
White	68.5	69.8
Unreported	2.2	6.9
	100.0%	100.0%

20% are from out of state. 4% join a fraternity and 5% join a sorority. Average age of full-time undergraduates is 23, 42% of classes have fewer than 20 students, 50% have between 20 and 50 students.

STUDENT HOUSING

Freshmen are required to live on campus. Housing is not guaranteed for all undergraduates. We have traditionally been able to house all students requesting housing. However, we could not house all admitted students. Campus can house 4,892 undergraduates. Single rooms are not available for students with medical or special needs.

EXPENSES

Tuition (2005-06): $5,310 per year (in-state), $13,275 (out-of-state).

Room: $3,058. Board: $2,502.
Additional cost for LD program/services: $2,200 per full-time enrollment.

LD SERVICES

LD program size is not limited.

LD services available to:

- [x] Freshmen
- [x] Sophomores
- [x] Juniors
- [x] Seniors

Academic Accommodations

Curriculum		In class	
Foreign language waiver	[ ]	Early syllabus	[ ]
Lighter course load	[x]	Note takers in class	[x]
Math waiver	[ ]	Priority seating	[ ]
Other special classes	[x]	Tape recorders	[x]
Priority registrations	[ ]	Videotaped classes	[x]
Substitution of courses	[x]	Text on tape	[x]
Exams		**Services**	
Extended time	[x]	Diagnostic tests	[x]
Oral exams	[x]	Learning centers	[x]
Take home exams	[ ]	Proofreaders	[ ]
Exams on tape or computer	[ ]	Readers	[x]
Untimed exams	[ ]	Reading Machines/Kurzweil	[x]
Other accommodations	[ ]	Special bookstore section	[ ]
		Typists	[ ]

Credit toward degree is not given for remedial courses taken.

Counseling Services

- [x] Academic
- [x] Psychological
- [x] Student Support groups
- [x] Vocational

Tutoring

Individual tutoring is available daily.

	Individual	Group
Time management	[ ]	[ ]
Organizational skills	[ ]	[ ]
Learning strategies	[ ]	[ ]
Study skills	[ ]	[ ]
Content area	[ ]	[ ]
Writing lab	[ ]	[ ]
Math lab	[ ]	[ ]

UNIQUE LD PROGRAM FEATURES

SIUC offers two seperate programs, the Achieve Program and Disability Support Services. Both programs make extraordinary efforts to ensure that students make informed choices.

LD PROGRAM STAFF

Total number of LD Program staff (including director):

Full Time: 4 Part Time: 4

There is an advisor/advocate from the LD program available to students. 2 graduate students and 100 peer tutors are available to work with LD students.

Key staff person available to work with LD students: Michael Whitney/Roger Pugh, Disability Support Services/Achieve.

Southern Illinois University Edwardsville

Edwardsville, IL

Address: Box 1600, Edwardsville, IL, 62026
Admissions telephone: 800 447-SIUE
Admissions FAX: 618 650-2031
Director of Admission: Todd Burrell
Admissions e-mail: admissions@siue.edu
Web site: http://www.siue.edu
SAT Code: 1759 ACT Code: 1147

LD program name: SIUE Disability Support Services
LD program address: Campus Box 1617
Learning Disabilities Specialist: Jim Boyle
LD program telephone: 618 650-2568
LD program e-mail: jboyle@siue.edu
LD program enrollment: 133, Total campus enrollment: 10,811

GENERAL

Southern Illinois University Edwardsville is a public, coed, four-year institution. 2,660-acre, suburban campus in Edwardsville (population: 21,491), 18 miles from St. Louis, MO; branch campuses in Alton and East St. Louis, MO. Major airport and bus serve St. Louis, MO; smaller airport serves Bethalto (12 miles); train serves Alton (15 miles). Public transportation serves campus. Semester system.

LD ADMISSIONS

A member of the LD program does not sit on the admissions committee. A personal interview is recommended. Essay is not required. May take into consideration low ACT/SAT scores if student does well in school, but does not test well. Lower class rank may be considered if student comes form competitive college prep school.

SECONDARY SCHOOL REQUIREMENTS

Graduation from secondary school required; GED accepted. The following course distribution required: 4 units of English, 3 units of math, 3 units of science, 3 units of social studies, 2 units of academic electives.

TESTING

ACT required. SAT Subject recommended.

All enrolled freshmen (fall 2004):

Average SAT I Scores:	Verbal:	Math:
Average ACT Scores:	Composite: 22	

Child Study Team report is not required. A neuropsychological or comprehensive psycho-educational evaluation is required for admission. Must be dated within 36 months of application. Tests required as part of this documentation:

- [x] WAIS-IV
- [x] WISC-IV
- [x] SATA
- [x] Woodcock-Johnson
- [x] Nelson-Denny Reading Test
- [x] Other

UNDERGRADUATE STUDENT BODY

Total undergraduate student enrollment: 4,186 Men, 5,613 Women.

Composition of student body (fall 2004):

	Undergraduate	Freshmen
International	0.2	1.0
Black	9.2	10.8
American Indian	0.1	0.3
Asian-American	2.5	2.0
Hispanic	1.3	1.6
White	86.7	84.4
Unreported	0.0	0.0
	100.0%	100.0%

10% are from out of state. Average age of full-time undergraduates is 21, 37% of classes have fewer than 20 students, 49% have between 20 and 50 students, 14% have more than 50 students.

STUDENT HOUSING

57% of freshmen live in college housing. Housing is guaranteed for all undergraduates. Campus can house 2,950 undergraduates. Single rooms are available for students with medical or special needs. A medical note is required.

EXPENSES

Tuition (2005-06): $4,320 per year (in-state), $10,800 (out-of-state).
Room: $3,389. Board: $2,430.
There is no additional cost for LD program/services.

LD SERVICES

LD program size is not limited.

LD services available to:

- [ ] Freshmen
- [ ] Sophomores
- [ ] Juniors
- [ ] Seniors

Academic Accommodations

Curriculum		In class	
Foreign language waiver	[ ]	Early syllabus	[x]
Lighter course load	[x]	Note takers in class	[x]
Math waiver	[ ]	Priority seating	[x]
Other special classes	[x]	Tape recorders	[x]
Priority registrations	[x]	Videotaped classes	[ ]
Substitution of courses	[x]	Text on tape	[ ]
Exams		**Services**	
Extended time	[x]	Diagnostic tests	[x]
Oral exams	[x]	Learning centers	[x]
Take home exams	[ ]	Proofreaders	[x]
Exams on tape or computer	[x]	Readers	[x]
Untimed exams	[x]	Reading Machines/Kurzweil	[x]
Other accommodations	[ ]	Special bookstore section	[ ]
		Typists	[x]

Credit toward degree is not given for remedial courses taken.

Counseling Services

- [ ] Academic
- [ ] Psychological
- [ ] Student Support groups
- [ ] Vocational

Tutoring

Individual tutoring is available daily.

	Individual	Group
Time management	[x]	[ ]
Organizational skills	[x]	[ ]
Learning strategies	[x]	[ ]
Study skills	[ ]	[x]
Content area	[x]	[ ]
Writing lab	[x]	[ ]
Math lab	[ ]	[ ]

LD PROGRAM STAFF

Total number of LD Program staff (including director):

Full Time: 3 Part Time: 3

There is an advisor/advocate from the LD program available to students.

Key staff person available to work with LD students: Jim Boyle, Learning Disabilities Specialist.

LD Program web site: www.siue.edu/DSS

Trinity Christian College

Palos Heights, IL

Address: 6601 West College Drive, Palos Heights, IL, 60463
Admissions telephone: 800 748-0085
Admissions FAX: 708 239-4826
Dean of Admissions and Financial Aid: Josh Lenarz
Admissions e-mail: admissions@trnty.edu
Web site: http://www.trnty.edu
SAT Code: 1820 ACT Code: 1165

LD program name: Services for Student Success
LD program telephone: 708 239-4765
LD program e-mail: nancy.kwasteniet@trnty.edu
Total campus enrollment: 1,234

GENERAL

Trinity Christian College is a private, coed, four-year institution. 47-acre, suburban campus in Palos Heights (population: 11,260, 25 miles from Chicago Loop. Major airport, bus, and train serve Chicago. School operates shuttle to airport. Public transportation serves campus. Semester system.

LD ADMISSIONS

Students do not complete a separate application and are simultaneously accepted to the LD program. A member of the LD program does sit on the admissions committee. A personal interview is not required. Essay is required and may be typed.

SECONDARY SCHOOL REQUIREMENTS

Graduation from secondary school required; GED accepted. The following course distribution required: 3 units of English, 3 units of math, 2 units of science, 2 units of social studies.

TESTING

ACT recommended; SAT Reasoning may be substituted. SAT Subject recommended.

All enrolled freshmen (fall 2004):

Average SAT I Scores:	Verbal: 538	Math: 518
Average ACT Scores:	Composite: 23	

Child Study Team report is not required. A neuropsychological or comprehensive psycho-educational evaluation is required for admission. Tests required as part of this documentation:

☑ WAIS-IV	☑ Woodcock-Johnson
☑ WISC-IV	☐ Nelson-Denny Reading Test
☐ SATA	☐ Other

UNDERGRADUATE STUDENT BODY

Total undergraduate student enrollment: 359 Men, 614 Women.

Composition of student body (fall 2004):

	Undergraduate	Freshmen
International	1.4	1.9
Black	7.3	6.7
American Indian	0.0	0.3
Asian-American	0.9	2.2
Hispanic	6.0	4.3
White	81.7	80.5
Unreported	2.8	4.1
	100.0%	100.0%

45% are from out of state. Average age of full-time undergraduates is 23, 66% of classes have fewer than 20 students, 34% have between 20 and 50 students.

STUDENT HOUSING

88% of freshmen live in college housing. Freshmen are required to live on campus. Housing is guaranteed for all undergraduates. Campus can house 810 undergraduates. Single rooms are available for students with medical or special needs. A medical note is required.

EXPENSES

Tuition (2005-06): $16,986 per year.

Room: $3,400. Board: $3,000.

There is no additional cost for LD program/services.

LD SERVICES

LD program size is not limited.

LD services available to:

☑ Freshmen ☑ Sophomores ☑ Juniors ☑ Seniors

Academic Accommodations

Curriculum		**In class**	
Foreign language waiver	☐	Early syllabus	☐
Lighter course load	☐	Note takers in class	☑
Math waiver	☐	Priority seating	☐
Other special classes	☐	Tape recorders	☑
Priority registrations	☐	Videotaped classes	☐
Substitution of courses	☐	Text on tape	☑
Exams		**Services**	
Extended time	☑	Diagnostic tests	☐
Oral exams	☑	Learning centers	☑
Take home exams	☐	Proofreaders	☐
Exams on tape or computer	☐	Readers	☑
Untimed exams	☑	Reading Machines/Kurzweil	☐
Other accommodations	☐	Special bookstore section	☐
		Typists	☑

Credit toward degree is not given for remedial courses taken.

Counseling Services

☑ Academic
☐ Psychological
☐ Student Support groups
☐ Vocational

Tutoring

Individual tutoring is available weekly.

Average size of tutoring groups: 2

	Individual	Group
Time management	☑	☑
Organizational skills	☑	☐
Learning strategies	☑	☐
Study skills	☑	☑
Content area	☑	☑
Writing lab	☑	☑
Math lab	☑	☑

LD PROGRAM STAFF

Total number of LD Program staff (including director):

Full Time: 1 Part Time: 1

There is an advisor/advocate from the LD program available to students. The advisor/advocate meets with faculty 20 times per month and student 1 times per month. 20 peer tutors are available to work with LD students.

Key staff person available to work with LD students: Nancy Kwasteniet, Director of Services for Student Success.

Trinity International University

Deerfield, IL

Address: 2065 Half Day Road, Deerfield, IL, 60015
Admissions telephone: 800 822-3225
Admissions FAX: 847 317-8097
Director of Undergraduate Admissions: Matthew Yoder
Admissions e-mail: tcdadm@tiu.edu
Web site: http://www.tiu.edu
SAT Code: 1810 ACT Code: 1150

Associate Dean of Students: Matthew Perrault
LD program telephone: 847 317-8192
LD program e-mail: mperraul@tiu.edu
Total campus enrollment: 1, 309

GENERAL

Trinity International University is a private, coed, four-year institution. 111-acre, suburban campus in Deerfield (population: 18,420), 20 miles from Chicago; branch campus in Miami, FL. Served by bus and train; major airport serves Chicago. Semester system.

LD ADMISSIONS

A personal interview is not required. Essay is not required.

SECONDARY SCHOOL REQUIREMENTS

Graduation from secondary school required; GED accepted. The following course distribution required: 3 units of English, 2 units of math, 2 units of science, 2 units of foreign language, 2 units of social studies, 3 units of academic electives.

TESTING

SAT Reasoning or ACT required. SAT Subject recommended.

All enrolled freshmen (fall 2004):

Average SAT I Scores:	Verbal: 512	Math: 521
Average ACT Scores:	Composite: 23	

Child Study Team report is not required. Tests required as part of this documentation:

- ❑ WAIS-IV
- ❑ WISC-IV
- ❑ SATA
- ❑ Woodcock-Johnson
- ❑ Nelson-Denny Reading Test
- ❑ Other

UNDERGRADUATE STUDENT BODY

Total undergraduate student enrollment: 501 Men, 699 Women.

Composition of student body (fall 2004):

	Undergraduate	Freshmen
International	0.0	0.5
Black	6.8	10.7
American Indian	0.7	0.2
Asian-American	5.2	2.5
Hispanic	2.6	1.7
White	79.5	60.3
Unreported	5.2	24.2
	100.0%	100.0%

54% are from out of state. Average age of full-time undergraduates is 24, 66% of classes have fewer than 20 students, 31% have between 20 and 50 students.

STUDENT HOUSING

85% of freshmen live in college housing. Freshmen are required to live on campus. Housing is guaranteed for all undergraduates. Campus can house 850 undergraduates.

EXPENSES

Tuition (2005-06): $19,080 per year.
Room: $3,430. Board: $2,890.

LD SERVICES

LD program size is not limited.

LD services available to:

❑ Freshmen ❑ Sophomores ❑ Juniors ❑ Seniors

Academic Accommodations

Curriculum		**In class**	
Foreign language waiver	❑	Early syllabus	❑
Lighter course load	❑	Note takers in class	❑
Math waiver	❑	Priority seating	❑
Other special classes	❑	Tape recorders	❑
Priority registrations	❑	Videotaped classes	❑
Substitution of courses	❑	Text on tape	❑
Exams		**Services**	
Extended time	❑	Diagnostic tests	❑
Oral exams	❑	Learning centers	❑
Take home exams	❑	Proofreaders	❑
Exams on tape or computer	❑	Readers	❑
Untimed exams	❑	Reading Machines/Kurzweil	❑
Other accommodations	❑	Special bookstore section	❑
		Typists	❑

Credit toward degree is not given for remedial courses taken.

Counseling Services

- ❑ Academic
- ❑ Psychological
- ❑ Student Support groups
- ❑ Vocational

Tutoring

	Individual	Group
Time management	❑	❑
Organizational skills	❑	❑
Learning strategies	❑	❑
Study skills	❑	❑
Content area	❑	❑
Writing lab	❑	❑
Math lab	❑	❑

LD PROGRAM STAFF

Total number of LD Program staff (including director):

Full Time: 2 Part Time: 2

Key staff person available to work with LD students: Matthew Perrault, Associate Dean of Students.

University of St. Francis

Joliet, IL

Address: 500 Wilcox Street, Joliet, IL, 60435
Admissions telephone: 800 735-7500
Admissions FAX: 815 740-5032
Director, Freshmen Recruitment and Marketing: Ron Clement
Admissions e-mail: information@stfrancis.edu
Web site: http://www.stfrancis.edu
SAT Code: 1130 ACT Code: 1000

LD program name: Office of Disability Services
Administrator for Students with Disabilities: Pat Vivio
LD program telephone: 815 740-3204
LD program e-mail: pvivio@stfrancis.edu
LD program enrollment: 15, Total campus enrollment: 1,249

GENERAL

University of St. Francis is a private, coed, four-year institution. 14-acre, suburban campus in Joliet (population: 106,221), 35 miles from Chicago; off-campus sites in 19 states. Served by bus and train; major airport serves Chicago. Public transportation serves campus. Semester system.

LD ADMISSIONS

Students do not complete a separate application and are not simultaneously accepted to the LD program. A member of the LD program does sit on the admissions committee. A personal interview is recommended. Essay is not required.

SECONDARY SCHOOL REQUIREMENTS

Graduation from secondary school required; GED accepted. The following course distribution required: 4 units of English, 2 units of math, 2 units of science, 2 units of social studies, 3 units of academic electives.

TESTING

ACT required; SAT Reasoning may be substituted. SAT Subject recommended.

All enrolled freshmen (fall 2004):

Average ACT Scores: Composite: 23

Child Study Team report is not required. A neuropsychological or comprehensive psycho-educational evaluation is required for admission. Must be dated within 12 months of application. Tests required as part of this documentation:

- ☑ WAIS-IV
- ☑ WISC-IV
- ☐ SATA
- ☑ Woodcock-Johnson
- ☐ Nelson-Denny Reading Test
- ☑ Other

UNDERGRADUATE STUDENT BODY

Total undergraduate student enrollment: 458 Men, 1,014 Women.

Composition of student body (fall 2004):

	Undergraduate	Freshmen
International	2.5	1.3
Black	7.0	8.2
American Indian	0.6	0.3
Asian-American	2.5	2.6
Hispanic	8.3	6.8
White	77.7	78.1
Unreported	1.3	2.8
	100.0%	100.0%

1% are from out of state. Average age of full-time undergraduates is 22, 70% of classes have fewer than 20 students, 30% have between 20 and 50 students.

STUDENT HOUSING

42% of freshmen live in college housing. Freshmen are not required to live on campus. Housing is guaranteed for all undergraduates. Campus can house 332 undergraduates. Single rooms are available for students with medical or special needs. A medical note is not required.

EXPENSES

Tuition (2005-06): $18,170 per year.

Room & Board: $6,900.

There is no additional cost for LD program/services.

LD SERVICES

LD program size is not limited.

LD services available to:

☑ Freshmen ☑ Sophomores ☑ Juniors ☑ Seniors

Academic Accommodations

Curriculum		In class	
Foreign language waiver	☐	Early syllabus	☐
Lighter course load	☐	Note takers in class	☑
Math waiver	☐	Priority seating	☑
Other special classes	☐	Tape recorders	☑
Priority registrations	☐	Videotaped classes	☐
Substitution of courses	☐	Text on tape	☑
Exams		**Services**	
Extended time	☑	Diagnostic tests	☐
Oral exams	☑	Learning centers	☑
Take home exams	☐	Proofreaders	☐
Exams on tape or computer	☐	Readers	☑
Untimed exams	☑	Reading Machines/Kurzweil	☐
Other accommodations	☑	Special bookstore section	☐
		Typists	☐

Credit toward degree is not given for remedial courses taken.

Counseling Services

- ☑ Academic
- ☑ Psychological
- ☐ Student Support groups
- ☐ Vocational

Tutoring

Individual tutoring is available daily.

Average size of tutoring groups: 1

	Individual	Group
Time management	☑	☑
Organizational skills	☑	☑
Learning strategies	☑	☑
Study skills	☑	☑
Content area	☑	☐
Writing lab	☑	☐
Math lab	☑	☑

LD PROGRAM STAFF

Total number of LD Program staff (including director):

Full Time: 2 Part Time: 2

There is an advisor/advocate from the LD program available to students. The advisor/advocate meets with student once per month.

Key staff person available to work with LD students: Pat Vivio, Administrator for Students with Disabilities.

Waubonsee Community College

Sugar Grove, IL

Address: Route 47 at Waubonsee Drive, Sugar Grove, IL
Admissions telephone: 630 466-5756
Admissions FAX: 630 466-4964
Recruitment/Retention Manager: Faith Marston
Admissions e-mail: recruitment@waubonsee.edu
Web site: http://www.waubonsee.edu
SAT Code: 1938   ACT Code: 11590

LD program name: Access Center for Students with Disabilities
Access Center Manager: Iris Hansen
LD program telephone: 630 466-7900, extension 5702
LD program e-mail: ihansen@waubonsee.edu
Total campus enrollment: 14,450

GENERAL

Waubonsee Community College is a public, coed, two-year institution. 243-acre campus in Sugar Grove (population: 3,909), six miles from Aurora.

LD ADMISSIONS

Students do not complete a separate application and are simultaneously accepted to the LD program. A member of the LD program does not sit on the admissions committee. A personal interview is not required. Essay is required.

SECONDARY SCHOOL REQUIREMENTS

Graduation from secondary school required; GED accepted.

TESTING

Child Study Team report is not required. Tests required as part of this documentation:

- ■ WAIS-IV
- ■ WISC-IV
- ■ SATA
- ■ Woodcock-Johnson
- ■ Nelson-Denny Reading Test
- ■ Other

UNDERGRADUATE STUDENT BODY

Total undergraduate student enrollment: 5,973 Men, 8,477 Women.

STUDENT HOUSING

There is no campus housing.

EXPENSES

Tuition 2004-05: $1,860 per year (state residents), $6,358 (state residents out-of-district), $7,290 (out-of-state).

There is no additional cost for LD program/services.

LD SERVICES

LD program size is not limited.

LD services available to:

■ Freshmen ■ Sophomores ■ Juniors ■ Seniors

Academic Accommodations

Curriculum		**In class**	
Foreign language waiver	☐	Early syllabus	■
Lighter course load	☐	Note takers in class	■
Math waiver	☐	Priority seating	☐
Other special classes	☐	Tape recorders	■
Priority registrations	☐	Videotaped classes	☐
Substitution of courses	■	Text on tape	■
Exams		**Services**	
Extended time	■	Diagnostic tests	☐
Oral exams	■	Learning centers	■
Take home exams	■	Proofreaders	■
Exams on tape or computer	■	Readers	■
Untimed exams	■	Reading Machines/Kurzweil	■
Other accommodations	☐	Special bookstore section	☐
		Typists	■

Credit toward some degree programs is given for remedial courses taken.

Counseling Services

- ■ Academic
- ■ Psychological
- ☐ Student Support groups
- ■ Vocational

Tutoring

Individual tutoring is available.

Average size of tutoring groups: 3

	Individual	Group
Time management	☐	☐
Organizational skills	☐	☐
Learning strategies	☐	☐
Study skills	☐	☐
Content area	☐	☐
Writing lab	☐	☐
Math lab	☐	☐

LD PROGRAM STAFF

There is an advisor/advocate from the LD program available to students.

Key staff person available to work with LD students: Iris Hansen, Access Center Manager.

Western Illinois University

Macomb, IL

Address: 1 University Circle, Macomb, IL, 61455
Admissions telephone: 877 PICK-WIU
Admissions FAX: 309 298-3111
Director of Admissions: David Garcia
Admissions e-mail: admissions@wiu.edu
Web site: http://www.wiu.edu
SAT Code: 1900 ACT Code: 1158

Learning Specialist: Gretchen Steil Weiss
LD program telephone: 309 298-2512
LD program e-mail: GE-Steilweiss@wiu.edu
Total campus enrollment: 11,310

GENERAL

Western Illinois University is a public, coed, four-year institution. 1,050-acre campus in Macomb (population: 18,558), 70 miles from Peoria; branch campus in Moline. Served by bus and train; major airport serves St. Louis; smaller airport serves Peoria. School operates transportation to downtown area and shopping locations. Public transportation serves campus. Semester system.

LD ADMISSIONS

A personal interview is not required. Essay is not required.

SECONDARY SCHOOL REQUIREMENTS

Graduation from secondary school required; GED accepted.

TESTING

SAT Reasoning or ACT required. SAT Subject recommended.

All enrolled freshmen (fall 2004):

Average ACT Scores: Composite: 21

Child Study Team report is not required. Tests required as part of this documentation:

- ☐ WAIS-IV
- ☐ WISC-IV
- ☐ SATA
- ☐ Woodcock-Johnson
- ☐ Nelson-Denny Reading Test
- ☐ Other

UNDERGRADUATE STUDENT BODY

Total undergraduate student enrollment: 5,310 Men, 5,445 Women.

Composition of student body (fall 2004):

	Undergraduate	Freshmen
International	0.7	1.3
Black	7.4	6.8
American Indian	0.3	0.2
Asian-American	1.6	1.3
Hispanic	4.3	3.7
White	80.9	82.4
Unreported	4.7	4.3
	100.0%	100.0%

3% are from out of state. 9% join a fraternity and 8% join a sorority. Average age of full-time undergraduates is 21, 30% of classes have fewer than 20 students, 61% have between 20 and 50 students.

STUDENT HOUSING

93% of freshmen live in college housing. Freshmen are required to live on campus. Housing is guaranteed for all undergraduates. Campus can house 5,200 undergraduates. Single rooms are available for students with medical or special needs. A medical note is required.

EXPENSES

Tuition (2005-06): $4,968 per year (in-state), $7,452 (out-of-state).
Room: $3,428-$3,693. Board: $2,340-$2,450.
There is no additional cost for LD program/services.

LD SERVICES

LD program size is not limited.

LD services available to:

☐ Freshmen ☐ Sophomores ☐ Juniors ☐ Seniors

Academic Accommodations

Curriculum		**In class**	
Foreign language waiver	☐	Early syllabus	☐
Lighter course load	☐	Note takers in class	☐
Math waiver	☐	Priority seating	☐
Other special classes	☐	Tape recorders	■
Priority registrations	☐	Videotaped classes	☐
Substitution of courses	☐	Text on tape	☐
Exams		**Services**	
Extended time	■	Diagnostic tests	☐
Oral exams	■	Learning centers	☐
Take home exams	☐	Proofreaders	☐
Exams on tape or computer	☐	Readers	■
Untimed exams	☐	Reading Machines/Kurzweil	☐
Other accommodations	☐	Special bookstore section	☐
		Typists	☐

Credit toward degree is given for remedial courses taken.

Counseling Services

- ☐ Academic
- ☐ Psychological
- ☐ Student Support groups
- ☐ Vocational

Tutoring

Individual tutoring is not available.

	Individual	Group
Time management	☐	☐
Organizational skills	☐	☐
Learning strategies	☐	☐
Study skills	☐	☐
Content area	☐	☐
Writing lab	☐	☐
Math lab	☐	☐

UNIQUE LD PROGRAM FEATURES

Individual tutoring in math, science, & writing on first-come, first-served basis.

LD PROGRAM STAFF

Total number of LD Program staff (including director):

Full Time: 1 Part Time: 1

There is no advisor/advocate from the LD program available to students.

Key staff person available to work with LD students: Gretchen Steil Weiss, Learning Specialist.

Wheaton College

Wheaton, IL

Address: 501 College Avenue, Wheaton, IL, 60187
Admissions telephone: 800 222-2419
Admissions FAX: 603 752-5285
Director of Admissions: Shawn Leftwich
Admissions e-mail: admissions@wheaton.edu
Web site: http://www.wheaton.edu
SAT Code: 1905 ACT Code: 1160

Registrar: Paul E. Johnson
LD program telephone: 630 752-5044
LD program e-mail: Paul.E.Johnson@wheaton.edu
Total campus enrollment: 2,439

GENERAL

Wheaton College is a private, coed, four-year institution. 80-acre campus in Wheaton (population: 55,416), 25 miles from Chicago. Major airport, bus, and train serve Chicago. Semester system.

LD ADMISSIONS

A personal interview is required. Essay is required and may be typed.

SECONDARY SCHOOL REQUIREMENTS

Graduation from secondary school required; GED accepted.

TESTING

SAT Reasoning or ACT required. SAT Subject required.

All enrolled freshmen (fall 2004):

Average SAT I Scores:	Verbal: 664	Math: 655
Average ACT Scores:	Composite: 29	

Child Study Team report is not required. Tests required as part of this documentation:

- ❑ WAIS-IV
- ❑ WISC-IV
- ❑ SATA
- ❑ Woodcock-Johnson
- ❑ Nelson-Denny Reading Test
- ❑ Other

UNDERGRADUATE STUDENT BODY

Total undergraduate student enrollment: 1,165 Men, 1,221 Women.

Composition of student body (fall 2004):

	Undergraduate	Freshmen
International	1.8	1.4
Black	1.3	2.2
American Indian	0.2	0.4
Asian-American	7.9	7.4
Hispanic	3.9	2.8
White	84.2	85.1
Unreported	0.7	0.7
	100.0%	100.0%

77% are from out of state. Average age of full-time undergraduates is 20, 50% of classes have fewer than 20 students, 48% have between 20 and 50 students.

STUDENT HOUSING

100% of freshmen live in college housing. Freshmen are required to live on campus. Housing is guaranteed for all undergraduates. Campus can house 2,146 undergraduates.

EXPENSES

Tuition (2005-06): $21,100 per year.
Room: $3,900. Board: $2,760.
There is no additional cost for LD program/services.

LD SERVICES

LD services available to:

■ Freshmen ■ Sophomores ■ Juniors ■ Seniors

Academic Accommodations

Curriculum		**In class**	
Foreign language waiver	❑	Early syllabus	❑
Lighter course load	❑	Note takers in class	❑
Math waiver	❑	Priority seating	❑
Other special classes	❑	Tape recorders	❑
Priority registrations	❑	Videotaped classes	❑
Substitution of courses	❑	Text on tape	❑
Exams		**Services**	
Extended time	❑	Diagnostic tests	❑
Oral exams	❑	Learning centers	❑
Take home exams	❑	Proofreaders	❑
Exams on tape or computer	❑	Readers	❑
Untimed exams	❑	Reading Machines/Kurzweil	❑
Other accommodations	❑	Special bookstore section	❑
		Typists	❑

Credit toward degree is not given for remedial courses taken.

Counseling Services

- ❑ Academic
- ❑ Psychological
- ❑ Student Support groups
- ❑ Vocational

Tutoring

	Individual	Group
Time management	❑	❑
Organizational skills	❑	❑
Learning strategies	❑	❑
Study skills	❑	❑
Content area	❑	❑
Writing lab	❑	❑
Math lab	❑	❑

UNIQUE LD PROGRAM FEATURES

Students who are learning disabled are admitted on the same basis as all others. They must contact the Registrar to request services and must present a medical diagnosis and prescription. Services are provided as needed on a case-by-case basis. The same is true for those who are physically disabled.

LD PROGRAM STAFF

Key staff person available to work with LD students: Paul E. Johnson, Registrar.

Indiana University-Purdue University Indianapolis

Indianapolis, IN

Address: 425 North University Boulevard, Indianapolis, IN, 46202-5143
Admissions telephone: 317 274-4591
Admissions FAX: 317 278-1862
Director of Admissions Assessment and Recruitment Services: Mike Donahue
Admissions e-mail: apply@iupui.edu
Web site: http://www.iupui.edu
SAT Code: 1325 ACT Code: 1214

Total campus enrollment: 21,172

GENERAL

Indiana University-Purdue University Indianapolis is a public, coed, four-year institution. 511-acre, urban campus in Indianapolis (population: 781,870); branch campus in Columbus. Served by air, bus, and train. Public transportation serves campus. Semester system.

LD ADMISSIONS

A personal interview is recommended. Essay is not required. Admissions requirements that may be waived for LD students include language and some math requirements.

SECONDARY SCHOOL REQUIREMENTS

Graduation from secondary school required; GED accepted. The following course distribution required: 4 units of English, 3 units of math, 3 units of science, 1 unit of social studies, 2 units of history, 4 units of academic electives.

TESTING

SAT Reasoning required; ACT may be substituted. SAT Subject recommended.

All enrolled freshmen (fall 2004):

Average SAT I Scores:	Verbal: 494	Math: 499
Average ACT Scores:	Composite: 21	

Child Study Team report is not required. Tests required as part of this documentation:

- [ ] WAIS-IV
- [ ] WISC-IV
- [ ] SATA
- [ ] Woodcock-Johnson
- [ ] Nelson-Denny Reading Test
- [ ] Other

UNDERGRADUATE STUDENT BODY

Total undergraduate student enrollment: 8,479 Men, 12,216 Women.

Composition of student body (fall 2004):

	Undergraduate	Freshmen
International	1.5	1.8
Black	9.5	10.8
American Indian	0.3	0.3
Asian-American	2.5	2.5
Hispanic	2.8	2.0
White	80.4	80.0
Unreported	2.9	2.7
	100.0%	100.0%

3% are from out of state. 1% join a fraternity and 1% join a sorority. Average age of full-time undergraduates is 23. 38% of classes have fewer than 20 students, 54% have between 20 and 50 students, 8% have more than 50 students.

STUDENT HOUSING

12% of freshmen live in college housing. Freshmen are not required to live on campus. Housing is not guaranteed for all undergraduates.

EXPENSES

Tuition (2005-06): $5,625 per year (in-state), $15,953 (out-of-state). Room: $2,358. Board: $2,400.

LD SERVICES

LD program size is not limited.

LD services available to:

- [ ] Freshmen
- [ ] Sophomores
- [ ] Juniors
- [ ] Seniors

Academic Accommodations

Curriculum		In class	
Foreign language waiver	[ ]	Early syllabus	[ ]
Lighter course load	[x]	Note takers in class	[x]
Math waiver	[ ]	Priority seating	[ ]
Other special classes	[ ]	Tape recorders	[x]
Priority registrations	[ ]	Videotaped classes	[x]
Substitution of courses	[ ]	Text on tape	[ ]
Exams		**Services**	
Extended time	[ ]	Diagnostic tests	[x]
Oral exams	[x]	Learning centers	[x]
Take home exams	[ ]	Proofreaders	[ ]
Exams on tape or computer	[ ]	Readers	[x]
Untimed exams	[x]	Reading Machines/Kurzweil	[x]
Other accommodations	[ ]	Special bookstore section	[ ]
		Typists	[ ]

Credit toward degree is not given for remedial courses taken.

Counseling Services

- [ ] Academic
- [ ] Psychological
- [ ] Student Support groups
- [ ] Vocational

Tutoring

	Individual	Group
Time management	[ ]	[ ]
Organizational skills	[ ]	[ ]
Learning strategies	[ ]	[ ]
Study skills	[ ]	[ ]
Content area	[ ]	[ ]
Writing lab	[ ]	[ ]
Math lab	[ ]	[ ]

LD PROGRAM STAFF

Total number of LD Program staff (including director):

Full Time: 3 Part Time: 3

Key staff person available to work with LD students: Pamela King, Director.

Indiana University Bloomington

Bloomington, IN

Address: 107 S. Indiana Ave., Bloomington, IN, 47405-7000
Admissions telephone: 812 855-0661
Admissions FAX: 812 855-5102
Director of Admissions: Mary Ellen Anderson
Admissions e-mail: iuadmit@indiana.edu
Web site: http://www.iub.edu
SAT Code: 1324 ACT Code: 1210

LD program name: Learning Disability Services/Disability Services for Students
LD program address: 601 East Kirkwood Avenue, #327
Learning Disabilities Coordinator: Jody K. Ferguson
LD program telephone: 812 855-3508
LD program e-mail: iubdss@indiana.edu
LD program enrollment: 500, Total campus enrollment: 29,549

GENERAL

Indiana University Bloomington is a public, coed, four-year institution. 1,878-acre campus in Bloomington (population: 69,291); branch campuses in Fort Wayne, Gary, Indianapolis, Kokomo, New Albany, Richmond, and South Bend. Served by bus; major airport and train serve Indianapolis (50 miles). Public transportation serves campus. Semester system.

LD ADMISSIONS

Students do not complete a separate application and are not simultaneously accepted to the LD program. A member of the LD program does not sit on the admissions committee. A personal interview is not required. Essay is not required. There is no separate admission process for students with disabilities - all students applying to the university meet the same entry criteria.

SECONDARY SCHOOL REQUIREMENTS

Graduation from secondary school required; GED accepted. The following course distribution required: 4 units of English, 3 units of math, 1 unit of science, 2 units of social studies, 4 units of academic electives.

TESTING

SAT Reasoning or ACT required. SAT Subject required.

All enrolled freshmen (fall 2004):

Average SAT I Scores: Verbal: 544 Math: 560
Average ACT Scores: Composite: 24

Child Study Team report is required if student is classified. A neuropsychological or comprehensive psycho-educational evaluation is required for admission. Must be dated within 24 months of application. Tests required as part of this documentation:

- ■ WAIS-IV
- ☐ WISC-IV
- ■ SATA
- ■ Woodcock-Johnson
- ■ Nelson-Denny Reading Test
- ■ Other

UNDERGRADUATE STUDENT BODY

Total undergraduate student enrollment: 14,168 Men, 15,989 Women.

Composition of student body (fall 2004):

	Undergraduate	Freshmen
International	2.8	4.2
Black	5.6	4.2
American Indian	0.2	0.2
Asian-American	2.9	3.2
Hispanic	2.5	2.2
White	84.7	84.8
Unreported	1.4	1.3
	100.0%	100.0%

28% are from out of state. 16% join a fraternity and 18% join a sorority. Average age of full-time undergraduates is 20. 42% of classes have fewer than 20 students, 39% have between 20 and 50 students, 18% have more than 50 students.

STUDENT HOUSING

96% of freshmen live in college housing. Housing is guaranteed for all undergraduates. Single rooms are available for students with medical or special needs. A medical note is required.

EXPENSES

Tuition (2005-06): $6,291 per year (in state), $18,687 (out-of-state).

Room: $3,760. Board: $2,480.

There is no additional cost for LD program/services.

LD SERVICES

LD program size is not limited.

LD services available to:

■ Freshmen ■ Sophomores ■ Juniors ■ Seniors

Academic Accommodations

Curriculum

- Foreign language waiver ☐
- Lighter course load ■
- Math waiver ☐
- Other special classes ☐
- Priority registrations ■
- Substitution of courses ■

Exams

- Extended time ■
- Oral exams ■
- Take home exams ☐
- Exams on tape or computer ■
- Untimed exams ☐
- Other accommodations ■

In class

- Early syllabus ☐
- Note takers in class ■
- Priority seating ■
- Tape recorders ■
- Videotaped classes ☐
- Text on tape ■

Services

- Diagnostic tests ☐
- Learning centers ☐
- Proofreaders ☐
- Readers ■
- Reading Machines/Kurzweil ■
- Special bookstore section ☐
- Typists ■

Credit toward degree is not given for remedial courses taken.

Counseling Services

- ☐ Academic
- ☐ Psychological
- ☐ Student Support groups
- ☐ Vocational

Tutoring

Individual tutoring is not available.

	Individual	Group
Time management	☐	☐
Organizational skills	☐	☐
Learning strategies	☐	☐
Study skills	☐	☐
Content area	☐	☐
Writing lab	☐	☐
Math lab	☐	☐

LD PROGRAM STAFF

Total number of LD Program staff (including director):

Full Time: 2 Part Time: 2

There is an advisor/advocate from the LD program available to students.

Key staff person available to work with LD students: Jody K. Ferguson, Learning Disabilities Coordinator.

LD Program web site: http://www.indiana.edu/~iubdss/

University of Saint Francis

Fort Wayne, IN

Address: 2701 Spring Street, Fort Wayne, IN, 46808
Admissions telephone: 800 729-4732
Admissions FAX: 260 434-7590
Interim Director of Admissions: Ronald Schumacher
Admissions e-mail: admis@sf.edu
Web site: http://www.sf.edu
SAT Code: 1693 ACT Code: 1238

LD program name: Student Learning Center
LD program address: 2701 Spring St,
Director: Michelle Kruyer
LD program telephone: 260 434-7677
LD program e-mail: mkruyer@sf.edu
LD program enrollment: 36, Total campus enrollment: 1,650

GENERAL

University of Saint Francis is a private, coed, four-year institution. 73-acre, suburban campus in Fort Wayne (population: 205,727). Served by air and bus; train serves Garrett (20 miles). Public transportation serves campus. Semester system.

LD ADMISSIONS

Students do not complete a separate application and are simultaneously accepted to the LD program. A member of the LD program does not sit on the admissions committee. A personal interview is recommended. Essay is required and may be typed.

SECONDARY SCHOOL REQUIREMENTS

Graduation from secondary school not required. The following course distribution required: 4 units of English, 2 units of math, 2 units of science, 2 units of social studies, 1 unit of history, 1 unit of academic electives.

TESTING

SAT Reasoning or ACT required of some applicants. SAT Subject recommended.

All enrolled freshmen (fall 2004):

Average SAT I Scores:	Verbal: 493	Math: 492
Average ACT Scores:	Composite: 21	

Child Study Team report is not required. Tests required as part of this documentation:

- ☐ WAIS-IV
- ☐ WISC-IV
- ☐ SATA
- ☐ Woodcock-Johnson
- ☐ Nelson-Denny Reading Test
- ☐ Other

UNDERGRADUATE STUDENT BODY

Total undergraduate student enrollment: 1,650.

Composition of student body (fall 2004):

	Undergraduate	Freshmen
International	0.0	0.2
Black	2.0	4.3
American Indian	0.3	0.3
Asian-American	1.7	1.0
Hispanic	1.0	1.7
White	69.3	69.8
Unreported	25.6	22.6
	100.0%	100.0%

16% are from out of state. Average age of full-time undergraduates is 23. 58% of classes have fewer than 20 students, 40% have between 20 and 50 students, 2% have more than 50 students.

STUDENT HOUSING

47% of freshmen live in college housing. Freshmen are not required to live on campus. Housing is guaranteed for all undergraduates. Campus can house 337 undergraduates. Single rooms are available for students with medical or special needs. A medical note is required.

EXPENSES

Tuition (2005-06): $16,750 per year.
Room & Board: $5,610.
There is no additional cost for LD program/services.

LD SERVICES

LD program size is not limited.

LD services available to:

■ Freshmen ■ Sophomores ■ Juniors ■ Seniors

Academic Accommodations

Curriculum		In class	
Foreign language waiver	■	Early syllabus	☐
Lighter course load	■	Note takers in class	☐
Math waiver	☐	Priority seating	■
Other special classes	☐	Tape recorders	■
Priority registrations	☐	Videotaped classes	☐
Substitution of courses	■	Text on tape	☐
Exams		**Services**	
Extended time	■	Diagnostic tests	☐
Oral exams	■	Learning centers	■
Take home exams	☐	Proofreaders	■
Exams on tape or computer	■	Readers	■
Untimed exams	■	Reading Machines/Kurzweil	■
Other accommodations	■	Special bookstore section	☐
		Typists	■

Credit toward degree is not given for remedial courses taken.

Counseling Services

- ■ Academic
- ☐ Psychological
- ☐ Student Support groups
- ☐ Vocational

Meets 4 times per academic year

Tutoring

Individual tutoring is available daily.

	Individual	Group
Time management	■	☐
Organizational skills	■	☐
Learning strategies	■	☐
Study skills	■	■
Content area	☐	☐
Writing lab	■	■
Math lab	■	■

LD PROGRAM STAFF

Total number of LD Program staff (including director):

Full Time: 1 Part Time: 1

There is an advisor/advocate from the LD program available to students. 3 peer tutors are available to work with LD students.

Key staff person available to work with LD students: Michelle L. Kruyer, Director, Student Learning Center.

Saint Mary-of-the-Woods College

St.Mary-of-the-Woods, IN

Address: , St.Mary-of-the-Woods, IN, 47876
Admissions telephone: 800 926-SMWC
Admissions FAX: 812 535-5010
Director of Enrollment Management and Marketing: Jim Malley
Admissions e-mail: smwcadms@smwc.edu
Web site: http://www.smwc.edu
SAT Code: 1704 ACT Code: 1242

LD program name: SMWC Learning Resource Center
LD program address: Le Fer Hall # 148
LD Program Contact: John Lotz
LD program telephone: 812 535-5271
LD program e-mail: jlotz@smwc.edu
LD program enrollment: 15, Total campus enrollment: 1,577

GENERAL

Saint Mary-of-the-Woods College is a private, women's, four-year institution. 212-acre campus in St. Mary-of-the-Woods, three miles from Terre Haute (population: 59,617) and 70 miles from Indianapolis. Major airport serves Indianapolis; smaller airport and bus serve Terre Haute; train serves Mattoon, Ill. (40 miles). Public transportation serves campus. Semester system.

LD ADMISSIONS

Students do not complete a separate application and are simultaneously accepted to the LD program. A member of the LD program does not sit on the admissions committee. A personal interview is required. Essay is required and may be typed.

For fall 2004, 3 completed self-identified LD applications were received. 3 applications were offered admission, and 3 enrolled.

SECONDARY SCHOOL REQUIREMENTS

Graduation from secondary school required; GED accepted. The following course distribution required: 4 units of English, 3 units of math, 3 units of science, 2 units of foreign language, 3 units of social studies.

TESTING

SAT Reasoning or ACT required.

All enrolled freshmen (fall 2004):

Average SAT I Scores: Verbal: Math:
Average ACT Scores: Composite:

Child Study Team report is not required. A neuropsychological or comprehensive psycho-educational evaluation is required for admission. Tests required as part of this documentation:

- ■ WAIS-IV
- ■ WISC-IV
- ■ SATA
- ■ Woodcock-Johnson
- ■ Nelson-Denny Reading Test
- ■ Other

UNDERGRADUATE STUDENT BODY

Total undergraduate student enrollment: 1,377 Women.

25% are from out of state.

STUDENT HOUSING

Housing is guaranteed for all undergraduates. Single rooms are available for students with medical or special needs. A medical note is required.

EXPENSES

Tuition (2005-06): $18,060 per year.
Room & Board: $6,820.
There is no additional cost for LD program/services.

LD SERVICES

LD program size is not limited.

LD services available to:

■ Freshmen ■ Sophomores ■ Juniors ■ Seniors

Academic Accommodations

Curriculum		**In class**	
Foreign language waiver	■	Early syllabus	☐
Lighter course load	☐	Note takers in class	■
Math waiver	☐	Priority seating	☐
Other special classes	■	Tape recorders	■
Priority registrations	☐	Videotaped classes	☐
Substitution of courses	■	Text on tape	☐
Exams		**Services**	
Extended time	■	Diagnostic tests	☐
Oral exams	■	Learning centers	■
Take home exams	☐	Proofreaders	☐
Exams on tape or computer	■	Readers	■
Untimed exams	■	Reading Machines/Kurzweil	☐
Other accommodations	■	Special bookstore section	☐
		Typists	☐

Credit toward degree is not given for remedial courses taken.

Counseling Services

■ Academic
■ Psychological
■ Student Support groups
■ Vocational

Meets 2 times per academic year

Tutoring

Individual tutoring is available daily.

Average size of tutoring groups: 1

	Individual	Group
Time management	■	■
Organizational skills	■	■
Learning strategies	■	■
Study skills	■	■
Content area	■	■
Writing lab	■	■
Math lab	■	■

UNIQUE LD PROGRAM FEATURES

Intensive one-on-one tutoring is available in or via the Learning Resource Center.Strict confidentiality is observed when students self-declare.

LD PROGRAM STAFF

Total number of LD Program staff (including director):

Full Time: 1 Part Time: 1

There is an advisor/advocate from the LD program available to students. 15 peer tutors are available to work with LD students.

Key staff person available to work with LD students: John Lotz, Learning Resource Center Director.

Indiana University Southeast

New Albany, IN

Address: 4201 Grant Line Road, New Albany, IN, 47150-6405
Admissions telephone: 800 852-8835 (in-state and Kentucky only)
Admissions FAX: 812 941-2595
Admissions e-mail: admissions@ius.edu
Web site: http://www.ius.edu
SAT Code: 1314 ACT Code: 1229

LD program telephone: 812 941-2579
Total campus enrollment: 5,419

GENERAL

Indiana University Southeast is a public, coed, four-year institution. 177-acre campus in New Albany (population: 37,603), just outside Louisville, Ky. Major airport, bus, and train serve Louisville. Semester system.

LD ADMISSIONS

A personal interview is recommended. Essay is not required.

SECONDARY SCHOOL REQUIREMENTS

Graduation from secondary school required; GED accepted. The following course distribution required: 4 units of English, 3 units of math, 1 unit of science, 2 units of social studies, 4 units of academic electives.

TESTING

SAT Reasoning or ACT required. SAT Subject required.

All enrolled freshmen (fall 2004):

Average SAT I Scores:	Verbal: 474	Math: 472
Average ACT Scores:	Composite: 20	

Child Study Team report is not required. Tests required as part of this documentation:

☐ WAIS-IV ☐ Woodcock-Johnson
☐ WISC-IV ☐ Nelson-Denny Reading Test
☐ SATA ☐ Other

UNDERGRADUATE STUDENT BODY

Total undergraduate student enrollment: 2,117 Men, 3,551 Women.

Composition of student body (fall 2004):

	Undergraduate	Freshmen
International	0.5	0.3
Black	2.1	3.4
American Indian	0.2	0.3
Asian-American	0.7	0.9
Hispanic	1.6	0.9
White	92.9	90.9
Unreported	2.0	3.3
	100.0%	100.0%

15% are from out of state. Average age of full-time undergraduates is 23. 45% of classes have fewer than 20 students, 54% have between 20 and 50 students, 2% have more than 50 students.

EXPENSES

Tuition (2005-06): $4,475 per year (in-state), $11,153 (out-of-state).
There is no additional cost for LD program/services.

LD SERVICES

LD program size is not limited.

LD services available to:

☐ Freshmen ☐ Sophomores ☐ Juniors ☐ Seniors

Academic Accommodations

Curriculum		**In class**	
Foreign language waiver	☐	Early syllabus	☐
Lighter course load	☑	Note takers in class	☑
Math waiver	☐	Priority seating	☐
Other special classes	☑	Tape recorders	☐
Priority registrations	☐	Videotaped classes	☐
Substitution of courses	☐	Text on tape	☐
Exams		**Services**	
Extended time	☐	Diagnostic tests	☐
Oral exams	☑	Learning centers	☐
Take home exams	☐	Proofreaders	☐
Exams on tape or computer	☐	Readers	☐
Untimed exams	☑	Reading Machines/Kurzweil	☑
Other accommodations	☐	Special bookstore section	☑
		Typists	☐

Credit toward degree is not given for remedial courses taken.

Counseling Services

☐ Academic
☐ Psychological
☐ Student Support groups
☐ Vocational

Tutoring

	Individual	Group
Time management	☐	☐
Organizational skills	☐	☐
Learning strategies	☐	☐
Study skills	☐	☐
Content area	☐	☐
Writing lab	☐	☐
Math lab	☐	☐

LD PROGRAM STAFF

Total number of LD Program staff (including director):

Full Time: 2 Part Time: 2

Indiana University South Bend

South Bend, IN

Address: 1700 Mishawaka Avenue, PO Box 7111, South Bend, IN, 46634
Admissions telephone: 574 520-4839
Admissions FAX: 574 520-4834
Director of Admissions: Jeff Johnston
Admissions e-mail: admissions@iusb.edu
Web site: http://www.iusb.edu
SAT Code: 1339

Coordinator, Disabled Student Services: Mark Dosch
LD program telephone: 574 520-4479
Total campus enrollment: 6322

GENERAL

Indiana University South Bend is a public, coed, four-year institution. 80-acre, suburban campus in South Bend (population: 107,789), 60 miles from Chicago. Served by air, bus, and train; major airport serves Chicago. Public transportation serves campus. Semester system.

LD ADMISSIONS

A personal interview is recommended. Essay is not required.

SECONDARY SCHOOL REQUIREMENTS

Graduation from secondary school required; GED accepted. The following course distribution required: 4 units of English, 3 units of math, 1 unit of science, 2 units of social studies.

TESTING

SAT Reasoning or ACT required.

All enrolled freshmen (fall 2004):

Average SAT I Scores: Verbal: 486 Math: 479
Average ACT Scores: Composite: 20

Child Study Team report is not required. Tests required as part of this documentation:

- ☐ WAIS-IV
- ☐ WISC-IV
- ☐ SATA
- ☐ Woodcock-Johnson
- ☐ Nelson-Denny Reading Test
- ☐ Other

UNDERGRADUATE STUDENT BODY

Total undergraduate student enrollment: 2,212 Men, 3,858 Women.

Composition of student body (fall 2004):

	Undergraduate	Freshmen
International	1.1	2.1
Black	6.6	6.8
American Indian	1.0	0.5
Asian-American	1.2	1.2
Hispanic	3.6	2.9
White	83.0	83.4
Unreported	3.5	3.1
	100.0%	100.0%

3% are from out of state. Average age of full-time undergraduates is 23. 48% of classes have fewer than 20 students, 47% have between 20 and 50 students, 5% have more than 50 students.

STUDENT HOUSING

Housing is not guaranteed for all undergraduates. Campus has limited housing. Housing that is available is for international students, visiting scholars, and some atheletes.

EXPENSES

Tuition (2005-06): $4,583 per year (in-state), $12,002 (out-of-state). There is no additional cost for LD program/services.

LD SERVICES

LD program size is not limited.

LD services available to:

☐ Freshmen ☐ Sophomores ☐ Juniors ☐ Seniors

Academic Accommodations

Curriculum		In class	
Foreign language waiver	☐	Early syllabus	☐
Lighter course load	■	Note takers in class	☐
Math waiver	☐	Priority seating	☐
Other special classes	☐	Tape recorders	☐
Priority registrations	☐	Videotaped classes	☐
Substitution of courses	☐	Text on tape	☐
Exams		**Services**	
Extended time	☐	Diagnostic tests	■
Oral exams	☐	Learning centers	■
Take home exams	☐	Proofreaders	☐
Exams on tape or computer	☐	Readers	☐
Untimed exams	☐	Reading Machines/Kurzweil	☐
Other accommodations	☐	Special bookstore section	☐
		Typists	☐

Credit toward degree is not given for remedial courses taken.

Counseling Services

- ☐ Academic
- ☐ Psychological
- ☐ Student Support groups
- ☐ Vocational

Tutoring

	Individual	Group
Time management	☐	☐
Organizational skills	☐	☐
Learning strategies	☐	☐
Study skills	☐	☐
Content area	☐	☐
Writing lab	☐	☐
Math lab	☐	☐

LD PROGRAM STAFF

Key staff person available to work with LD students: Donna Lamborn, Learning Disabilities Specialist.

Indiana University Northwest

Gary, IN

Address: 3400 Broadway, Gary, IN, 46408
Admissions telephone: (888) YOUR-IUN
Admissions FAX: 219 981-4219
Director of Admissions: Linda Templeton
Admissions e-mail: admit@iun.edu
Web site: http://www.iun.edu
SAT Code: 1338

Coordinator for Students with Special Needs: Ron Thornton
LD program telephone: 219 980-6943
LD program e-mail: rthornto@iun.edu
Total campus enrollment: 4,536

GENERAL

Indiana University Northwest is a public, coed, four-year institution. 38-acre, urban campus in Gary (population: 102,746). Served by air, bus, and train; major airport serves Chicago. Semester system.

LD ADMISSIONS

A personal interview is recommended. Essay is not required.

SECONDARY SCHOOL REQUIREMENTS

Graduation from secondary school required; GED accepted. The following course distribution required: 4 units of English, 3 units of math, 1 unit of science, 2 units of social studies, 4 units of academic electives.

TESTING

SAT Reasoning or ACT required.

All enrolled freshmen (fall 2004):

Average SAT I Scores:	Verbal: 451	Math: 446
Average ACT Scores:	Composite: 18	

Child Study Team report is not required. Tests required as part of this documentation:

- ☐ WAIS-IV
- ☐ WISC-IV
- ☐ SATA
- ☐ Woodcock-Johnson
- ☐ Nelson-Denny Reading Test
- ☐ Other

UNDERGRADUATE STUDENT BODY

Total undergraduate student enrollment: 1,208 Men, 2,819 Women.

Composition of student body (fall 2004):

	Undergraduate	Freshmen
International	0.0	0.2
Black	19.6	21.4
American Indian	0.1	0.4
Asian-American	0.9	1.3
Hispanic	12.2	11.8
White	64.6	62.2
Unreported	2.6	2.7
	100.0%	100.0%

1% are from out of state. Average age of full-time undergraduates is 24. 48% of classes have fewer than 20 students, 47% have between 20 and 50 students, 5% have more than 50 students.

STUDENT HOUSING

Housing is not guaranteed for all undergraduates.

EXPENSES

Tuition (2005-06): $4,475 per year (in-state), $11,153 (out-of-state). There is no additional cost for LD program/services.

LD SERVICES

LD program size is not limited.

LD services available to:

☐ Freshmen ☐ Sophomores ☐ Juniors ☐ Seniors

Academic Accommodations

Curriculum		In class	
Foreign language waiver	☐	Early syllabus	☐
Lighter course load	■	Note takers in class	☐
Math waiver	☐	Priority seating	☐
Other special classes	☐	Tape recorders	☐
Priority registrations	☐	Videotaped classes	☐
Substitution of courses	☐	Text on tape	☐
Exams		**Services**	
Extended time	☐	Diagnostic tests	■
Oral exams	☐	Learning centers	■
Take home exams	☐	Proofreaders	☐
Exams on tape or computer	☐	Readers	☐
Untimed exams	☐	Reading Machines/Kurzweil	☐
Other accommodations	☐	Special bookstore section	☐
		Typists	☐

Credit toward degree is not given for remedial courses taken.

Counseling Services

- ☐ Academic
- ☐ Psychological
- ☐ Student Support groups
- ☐ Vocational

Tutoring

	Individual	Group
Time management	☐	☐
Organizational skills	☐	☐
Learning strategies	☐	☐
Study skills	☐	☐
Content area	☐	☐
Writing lab	☐	☐
Math lab	☐	☐

Bethel College

Mishawaka, IN

Address: 1001 W. McKinley Avenue, Mishawaka, IN, 46545
Admissions telephone: 800 422-4101
Admissions FAX: 574 257-3335
Director of Admissions: Randy Beachy
Admissions e-mail: admissions@bethelcollege.edu
Web site: http://www.bethelcollege.edu
SAT Code: 1079 ACT Code: 1178

LD program name: Academic Support Center
Director of Academic Support Services: Carolyn Arthur
LD program telephone: 574 257-3356
LD program e-mail: arthurc@bethelcollege.edu
LD program enrollment: 36, Total campus enrollment: 1,868

GENERAL

Bethel College is a private, coed, four-year institution. 70-acre, suburban campus in Mishawaka (population: 46,577), less than one mile from South Bend and 90 miles from Chicago. Major airport serves Chicago; smaller airport, bus, and train serve South Bend. Public transportation serves campus. Semester system.

LD ADMISSIONS

A personal interview is recommended. Essay is required and may be typed.

SECONDARY SCHOOL REQUIREMENTS

Graduation from secondary school required; GED accepted. The following course distribution required: 4 units of English, 3 units of math, 3 units of science, 2 units of foreign language, 2 units of social studies, 2 units of history, 2 units of academic electives.

TESTING

SAT Reasoning or ACT required. SAT Subject recommended.

All enrolled freshmen (fall 2004):

Average SAT I Scores: Verbal: 520 Math: 520
Average ACT Scores: Composite: 22

Child Study Team report is not required. A neuropsychological or comprehensive psycho-educational evaluation is required for admission. Tests required as part of this documentation:

- [ ] WAIS-IV
- [ ] WISC-IV
- [ ] SATA
- [ ] Woodcock-Johnson
- [x] Nelson-Denny Reading Test
- [x] Other

UNDERGRADUATE STUDENT BODY

Total undergraduate student enrollment: 552 Men, 989 Women.

Composition of student body (fall 2004):

	Undergraduate	Freshmen
International	2.8	1.9
Black	2.8	10.4
American Indian	0.3	0.5
Asian-American	1.9	1.4
Hispanic	2.2	2.7
White	89.9	83.0
Unreported	0.0	0.0
	100.0%	100.0%

27% are from out of state. Average age of full-time undergraduates is 21. 70% of classes have fewer than 20 students, 28% have between 20 and 50 students, 2% have more than 50 students.

STUDENT HOUSING

83% of freshmen live in college housing. Freshmen are required to live on campus. Housing is guaranteed for all undergraduates. Campus can house 860 undergraduates. Single rooms are available for students with medical or special needs. A medical note is required.

EXPENSES

Tuition (2005-06): $15,950 per year.
Room: $2,930. Board: $2,800.
There is no additional cost for LD program/services.

LD SERVICES

LD program size is not limited.

LD services available to:

- [x] Freshmen
- [x] Sophomores
- [x] Juniors
- [x] Seniors

Academic Accommodations

Curriculum

- [ ] Foreign language waiver
- [ ] Lighter course load
- [ ] Math waiver
- [ ] Other special classes
- [ ] Priority registrations
- [ ] Substitution of courses

Exams

- [x] Extended time
- [x] Oral exams
- [ ] Take home exams
- [ ] Exams on tape or computer
- [x] Untimed exams
- [ ] Other accommodations

In class

- [ ] Early syllabus
- [ ] Note takers in class
- [ ] Priority seating
- [ ] Tape recorders
- [ ] Videotaped classes
- [ ] Text on tape

Services

- [ ] Diagnostic tests
- [x] Learning centers
- [ ] Proofreaders
- [ ] Readers
- [ ] Reading Machines/Kurzweil
- [ ] Special bookstore section
- [ ] Typists

Credit toward degree is not given for remedial courses taken.

Counseling Services

- [x] Academic
- [x] Psychological
- [ ] Student Support groups
- [ ] Vocational

Tutoring

Individual tutoring is available weekly.

Average size of tutoring groups: 2

	Individual	Group
Time management	[ ]	[ ]
Organizational skills	[ ]	[ ]
Learning strategies	[ ]	[ ]
Study skills	[ ]	[ ]
Content area	[ ]	[ ]
Writing lab	[ ]	[ ]
Math lab	[ ]	[ ]

LD PROGRAM STAFF

Total number of LD Program staff (including director):

Full Time: 3 Part Time: 3

There is an advisor/advocate from the LD program available to students.

Key staff person available to work with LD students: Carolyn Arthur, Director of Academic Support Services.

Taylor University

Upland, IN

Address: 236 W. Reade Avenue, Upland, IN, 46989-1002
Admissions telephone: 800 882-3456
Admissions FAX: 765 998-4925
Director of Admissions: Steve Mortland
Admissions e-mail: admissions_u@taylor.edu
Web site: http://www.taylor.edu
SAT Code: 1802 ACT Code: 1248

LD program name: Academic Support Services
Coordinator: Dr. R. Edwin Welch
LD program telephone: 765 998-5523
LD program e-mail: edwelch@tayloru.edu
LD program enrollment: 23, Total campus enrollment: 1,868

GENERAL

Taylor University is a private, coed, four-year institution. 250-acre campus in Upland (population: 3,000), 13 miles from Marion; branch campus in Fort Wayne. Served by bus; major airport and train serve Indianapolis (65 miles); smaller airport serves Fort Wayne (50 miles). School operates transportation to airport at school breaks. 4-1-4 system.

LD ADMISSIONS

Students do not complete a separate application and are not simultaneously accepted to the LD program. A personal interview is required. Essay is required and may be typed.

SECONDARY SCHOOL REQUIREMENTS

Graduation from secondary school required; GED accepted. The following course distribution required: 4 units of English, 3 units of math, 3 units of science, 2 units of social studies.

TESTING

SAT Reasoning or ACT required. SAT Subject recommended.

All enrolled freshmen (fall 2004):

Average SAT I Scores:	Verbal: 595	Math: 587
Average ACT Scores:	Composite: 26	

Child Study Team report is not required. A neuropsychological or comprehensive psycho-educational evaluation is required for admission. Must be dated within 36 months of application. Tests required as part of this documentation:

- ☒ WAIS-IV
- ☒ WISC-IV
- ☐ SATA
- ☒ Woodcock-Johnson
- ☐ Nelson-Denny Reading Test
- ☐ Other

UNDERGRADUATE STUDENT BODY

Total undergraduate student enrollment: 890 Men, 971 Women.

Composition of student body (fall 2004):

	Undergraduate	Freshmen
International	1.3	1.1
Black	1.3	1.4
American Indian	0.0	0.3
Asian-American	1.5	1.4
Hispanic	0.8	0.9
White	93.7	93.9
Unreported	1.5	1.1
	100.0%	100.0%

70% are from out of state. Average age of full-time undergraduates is 20. 55% of classes have fewer than 20 students, 42% have between 20 and 50 students, 3% have more than 50 students.

STUDENT HOUSING

99% of freshmen live in college housing. Freshmen are required to live on campus. Housing is guaranteed for all undergraduates. Campus can house 1,478 undergraduates. Single rooms are available for students with medical or special needs.

EXPENSES

Tuition (2005-06): $20,520 per year.

Room: $2,732. Board: $2,898.
There is no additional cost for LD program/services.

LD SERVICES

LD program size is not limited.

LD services available to:

☒ Freshmen ☒ Sophomores ☒ Juniors ☒ Seniors

Academic Accommodations

Curriculum		In class	
Foreign language waiver	☐	Early syllabus	☐
Lighter course load	☐	Note takers in class	☒
Math waiver	☐	Priority seating	☐
Other special classes	☐	Tape recorders	☒
Priority registrations	☒	Videotaped classes	☐
Substitution of courses	☒	Text on tape	☒
Exams		**Services**	
Extended time	☒	Diagnostic tests	☐
Oral exams	☒	Learning centers	☒
Take home exams	☐	Proofreaders	☐
Exams on tape or computer	☒	Readers	☒
Untimed exams	☐	Reading Machines/Kurzweil	☒
Other accommodations	☒	Special bookstore section	☐
		Typists	☐

Credit toward degree is given for remedial courses taken.

Counseling Services

- ☒ Academic
- ☒ Psychological
- ☐ Student Support groups
- ☐ Vocational

Tutoring

Individual tutoring is available weekly.

Average size of tutoring groups: 7

	Individual	Group
Time management	☒	☐
Organizational skills	☒	☐
Learning strategies	☒	☐
Study skills	☒	☐
Content area	☒	☐
Writing lab	☒	☐
Math lab	☐	☒

LD PROGRAM STAFF

Total number of LD Program staff (including director):

Full Time: 1 Part Time: 1

There is an advisor/advocate from the LD program available to students. 47 peer tutors are available to work with LD students.

Key staff person available to work with LD students: Dr. R. Edwin Welch, Coordinator of Academic Support Services.

LD Program web site: www.taylor.edu

Purdue University - North Central

Westville, IN

Address: 1401 S. U.S. Highway 421, Westville, IN, 46391
Admissions telephone: 219 785-5455
Admissions FAX: 219 785-5538
Director of Admissions: Cathy Buckman
Admissions e-mail: admissions@pnc.edu
Web site: http://www.pnc.edu
SAT Code: 1640 ACT Code: 1231

LD program name: Disability Services
LD program address: 1401 S US 421, Westville, IN, 46391
Director, Student Services: Gail Barker
LD program telephone: 219 785-5549
LD program e-mail: Gbarker@pnc.edu
LD program enrollment: 30, Total campus enrollment: 3,414

GENERAL

Purdue University - North Central is a public, coed, four-year institution. 264-acre campus in Westville (population: 2,116), 75 miles from Chicago; branch campus in West Lafayette. Major airport, bus, and train serve Chicago; smaller airport serves South Bend (40 miles). Semester system.

LD ADMISSIONS

Students do not complete a separate application and are not simultaneously accepted to the LD program. A member of the LD program does not sit on the admissions committee. A personal interview is recommended. Essay is not required.

For fall 2004, 5 completed self-identified LD applications were received. 5 applications were offered admission, and 5 enrolled.

SECONDARY SCHOOL REQUIREMENTS

Graduation from secondary school required; GED accepted. The following course distribution required: 4 units of English, 3 units of math, 2 units of science, 1 unit of social studies, 5 units of academic electives.

TESTING

SAT Reasoning or ACT considered if submitted. SAT Subject recommended.

All enrolled freshmen (fall 2004):

Average SAT I Scores: Verbal: 475 Math: 469
Average ACT Scores: Composite: 20

Child Study Team report is not required. A neuropsychological or comprehensive psycho-educational evaluation is required for admission. Must be dated within 36 months of application. Tests required as part of this documentation:

- [x] WAIS-IV
- [x] WISC-IV
- [x] SATA
- [x] Woodcock-Johnson
- [x] Nelson-Denny Reading Test
- [ ] Other

UNDERGRADUATE STUDENT BODY

Total undergraduate student enrollment: 1,379 Men, 2,093 Women.

Composition of student body (fall 2004):

	Undergraduate	Freshmen
International	0.2	0.3
Black	3.3	3.7
American Indian	0.9	0.9
Asian-American	0.9	0.9
Hispanic	5.4	4.1
White	89.3	90.1
Unreported	0.0	0.0
	100.0%	100.0%

1% are from out of state. Average age of full-time undergraduates is 23. 59% of classes have fewer than 20 students, 40% have between 20 and 50 students, 1% have more than 50 students.

STUDENT HOUSING

Single rooms are not available for students with medical or special needs.

EXPENSES

Tuition (2005-06): $4,699 per year (in-state), $10,890 (out-of-state).

There is no additional cost for LD program/services.

LD SERVICES

LD program size is not limited.

LD services available to:

- [x] Freshmen
- [x] Sophomores
- [x] Juniors
- [x] Seniors

Academic Accommodations

Curriculum

- [ ] Foreign language waiver
- [x] Lighter course load
- [ ] Math waiver
- [ ] Other special classes
- [ ] Priority registrations
- [x] Substitution of courses

Exams

- [x] Extended time
- [x] Oral exams
- [ ] Take home exams
- [x] Exams on tape or computer
- [ ] Untimed exams
- [x] Other accommodations

In class

- [ ] Early syllabus
- [x] Note takers in class
- [ ] Priority seating
- [x] Tape recorders
- [ ] Videotaped classes
- [x] Text on tape

Services

- [ ] Diagnostic tests
- [x] Learning centers
- [ ] Proofreaders
- [x] Readers
- [ ] Reading Machines/Kurzweil
- [ ] Special bookstore section
- [x] Typists

Credit toward degree is not given for remedial courses taken.

Counseling Services

- [ ] Academic
- [ ] Psychological
- [ ] Student Support groups
- [ ] Vocational

Tutoring

Individual tutoring is available weekly.

Average size of tutoring groups: 2

	Individual	Group
Time management	[x]	[ ]
Organizational skills	[x]	[ ]
Learning strategies	[x]	[ ]
Study skills	[x]	[ ]
Content area	[x]	[ ]
Writing lab	[x]	[ ]
Math lab	[x]	[ ]

LD PROGRAM STAFF

Total number of LD Program staff (including director):

Full Time: 1 Part Time: 1

There is an advisor/advocate from the LD program available to students. The advisor/advocate meets with students 2 times per month. 10 peer tutors are available to work with LD students.

Key staff person available to work with LD students: Jodi James, Disability Services Coordinator.

LD Program web site: www.pnc.edu/s3/dss.htm

Calumet College of St. Joseph

Whiting, IN

Address: 2400 New York Avenue, Whiting, IN, 46394
Admissions telephone: 219 473-4215
Admissions FAX: 219 473-4259
Vice President for Enrollment Management: Chuck Walz
Admissions e-mail: admissions@ccsj.edu
Web site: http://www.ccsj.edu
SAT Code: 1776 ACT Code: 1245

LD program name: Student Support Services
Director of Student Support Services: Valerie Rister
LD program telephone: 219 473-4388
LD program e-mail: vrister@ccsj.edu
Total campus enrollment: 1, 260

GENERAL

Calumet College of St. Joseph is a private, coed, four-year institution. 20-acre campus in Whiting (population: 5,137), 35 miles from Chicago; branch campus in Merrillville. Major airport serves Chicago; bus and train serve Hammond (four miles). Public transportation serves campus. Trimester system.

LD ADMISSIONS

Students do not complete a separate application and are not simultaneously accepted to the LD program. A member of the LD program does not sit on the admissions committee.

For fall 2004, 3 completed self-identified LD applications were received.

SECONDARY SCHOOL REQUIREMENTS

Graduation from secondary school required; GED accepted.

TESTING

SAT Reasoning considered if submitted. ACT considered if submitted. SAT Reasoning or ACT considered if submitted. SAT Subject recommended.

All enrolled freshmen (fall 2004):

Average SAT I Scores: Verbal: 437 Math: 436
Average ACT Scores: Composite:

Child Study Team report is not required. A neuropsychological or comprehensive psycho-educational evaluation is required for admission. Must be dated within 36 months of application. Tests required as part of this documentation:

- [x] WAIS-IV
- [x] WISC-IV
- [ ] SATA
- [x] Woodcock-Johnson
- [ ] Nelson-Denny Reading Test
- [ ] Other

UNDERGRADUATE STUDENT BODY

Total undergraduate student enrollment: 1,260.

Composition of student body (fall 2004):

	Undergraduate	Freshmen
International	0.0	0.1
Black	12.5	30.2
American Indian	0.0	0.3
Asian-American	1.0	0.5
Hispanic	26.0	19.7
White	60.6	49.2
Unreported	0.0	0.1
	100.0%	100.0%

25% are from out of state. 2% join a sorority. 78% of classes have fewer than 20 students, 21% have between 20 and 50 students, 1% have more than 50 students.

EXPENSES

Tuition (2005-06): $9,900 per year.
There is no additional cost for LD program/services.

LD SERVICES

LD program size is not limited.

LD services available to:

- [x] Freshmen
- [x] Sophomores
- [x] Juniors
- [x] Seniors

Academic Accommodations

Curriculum

- [ ] Foreign language waiver
- [ ] Lighter course load
- [ ] Math waiver
- [ ] Other special classes
- [ ] Priority registrations
- [ ] Substitution of courses

Exams

- [x] Extended time
- [x] Oral exams
- [ ] Take home exams
- [ ] Exams on tape or computer
- [x] Untimed exams
- [ ] Other accommodations

In class

- [ ] Early syllabus
- [x] Note takers in class
- [ ] Priority seating
- [x] Tape recorders
- [ ] Videotaped classes
- [x] Text on tape

Services

- [ ] Diagnostic tests
- [x] Learning centers
- [x] Proofreaders
- [x] Readers
- [ ] Reading Machines/Kurzweil
- [ ] Special bookstore section
- [ ] Typists

Credit toward degree is not given for remedial courses taken.

Counseling Services

- [x] Academic — Meets 4 times per academic year
- [ ] Psychological
- [x] Student Support groups — Meets 30 times per academic year
- [x] Vocational — Meets 10 times per academic year

Tutoring

Individual tutoring is available daily.

Average size of tutoring groups: 2

	Individual	Group
Time management	[x]	[x]
Organizational skills	[x]	[x]
Learning strategies	[x]	[x]
Study skills	[x]	[x]
Content area	[x]	[x]
Writing lab	[x]	[x]
Math lab	[x]	[x]

LD PROGRAM STAFF

Total number of LD Program staff (including director):

Full Time: 1 Part Time: 1

There is an advisor/advocate from the LD program available to students. The advisor/advocate meets with faculty 1 time per month and students 2 times per month. 10 peer tutors are available to work with LD students.

Key staff person available to work with LD students: Valerie Rister, Director of Student Support Services.

Indiana University East

Richmond, IN

Address: 2325 Chester Boulevard, Richmond, IN, 47374-1289
Admissions telephone: 800 959-EAST
Admissions FAX: 765 973-8288
Director of Admissions:
Admissions e-mail: eaadmit@indiana.edu
Web site: http://www.iue.edu
SAT Code: 1194 ACT Code: 1216

Director, Student Support Services: Cheryl Stafford
Total campus enrollment: 2449

GENERAL

Indiana University East is a public, coed, four-year institution. 194-acre campus in Richmond (population: 39,124), 45 miles from Dayton. Served by bus; major airports serve Dayton and Indianapolis (70 miles). Public transportation serves campus. Semester system.

LD ADMISSIONS

A personal interview is recommended. Essay is not required.

SECONDARY SCHOOL REQUIREMENTS

Graduation from secondary school required; GED accepted. The following course distribution required: 4 units of English, 3 units of math, 1 unit of science, 2 units of social studies.

TESTING

SAT Reasoning or ACT recommended.

All enrolled freshmen (fall 2004):

Average SAT I Scores: Verbal: 456 Math: 441
Average ACT Scores: Composite: 19

Child Study Team report is not required. Tests required as part of this documentation:

- [ ] WAIS-IV
- [ ] WISC-IV
- [ ] SATA
- [ ] Woodcock-Johnson
- [ ] Nelson-Denny Reading Test
- [ ] Other

UNDERGRADUATE STUDENT BODY

Total undergraduate student enrollment: 709 Men, 1,696 Women.

Composition of student body (fall 2004):

	Undergraduate	Freshmen
International	0.2	0.2
Black	4.4	4.6
American Indian	0.0	0.4
Asian-American	0.7	0.5
Hispanic	1.0	0.7
White	91.9	90.8
Unreported	1.7	2.8
	100.0%	100.0%

5% are from out of state. Average age of full-time undergraduates is 25. 59% of classes have fewer than 20 students, 40% have between 20 and 50 students, 1% have more than 50 students.

EXPENSES

Tuition (2005-06): $4,475 per year (in-state), $11,153 (out-of-state).
There is no additional cost for LD program/services.

LD SERVICES

LD program size is not limited.

LD services available to:

- [ ] Freshmen
- [ ] Sophomores
- [ ] Juniors
- [ ] Seniors

Academic Accommodations

Curriculum

- [ ] Foreign language waiver
- [x] Lighter course load
- [ ] Math waiver
- [ ] Other special classes
- [ ] Priority registrations
- [ ] Substitution of courses

Exams

- [ ] Extended time
- [x] Oral exams
- [ ] Take home exams
- [ ] Exams on tape or computer
- [x] Untimed exams
- [ ] Other accommodations

In class

- [ ] Early syllabus
- [x] Note takers in class
- [ ] Priority seating
- [x] Tape recorders
- [ ] Videotaped classes
- [ ] Text on tape

Services

- [x] Diagnostic tests
- [x] Learning centers
- [ ] Proofreaders
- [x] Readers
- [x] Reading Machines/Kurzweil
- [ ] Special bookstore section
- [ ] Typists

Credit toward degree is not given for remedial courses taken.

Counseling Services

- [ ] Academic
- [ ] Psychological
- [ ] Student Support groups
- [ ] Vocational

Tutoring

	Individual	Group
Time management	[ ]	[ ]
Organizational skills	[ ]	[ ]
Learning strategies	[ ]	[ ]
Study skills	[ ]	[ ]
Content area	[ ]	[ ]
Writing lab	[ ]	[ ]
Math lab	[ ]	[ ]

LD PROGRAM STAFF

Total number of LD Program staff (including director):

Full Time: 1 Part Time: 1

Key staff person available to work with LD students: Cheryl Stafford, Director, Student Support Services.

Earlham College

Richmond, IN

Address: 801 National Road W, Richmond, IN, 47374
Admissions telephone: 800 327-5426
Admissions FAX: 765 983-1560
Dean of Admissions and Financial Aid: Jeff Rickey
Admissions e-mail: admission@earlham.edu
Web site: http://www.earlham.edu
SAT Code: 1195 ACT Code: 1186

LD program name: Center for Academic Enrichment
Director: Donna Keesling
LD program telephone: 765 983-1341
LD program e-mail: keesldo@earlham.edu
LD program enrollment: 98, Total campus enrollment: 1,190

GENERAL

Earlham College is a private, coed, four-year institution. 800-acre campus in Richmond (population: 39,124), 70 miles from Indianapolis and 45 miles from Dayton. Served by bus; airport serves Dayton; larger airport and train serve Indianapolis. School operates shuttle to Dayton airport for holiday breaks. Public transportation serves campus. Semester system.

LD ADMISSIONS

Students do not complete a separate application and are not simultaneously accepted to the LD program. A member of the LD program does not sit on the admissions committee. A personal interview is recommended. Essay is required and may be typed.

SECONDARY SCHOOL REQUIREMENTS

Graduation from secondary school required; GED accepted. The following course distribution required: 4 units of English, 3 units of math, 2 units of science, 2 units of foreign language, 1 unit of social studies, 1 unit of history, 2 units of academic electives.

TESTING

SAT Reasoning required; ACT may be substituted. SAT Subject recommended.

All enrolled freshmen (fall 2004):

Average SAT I Scores: Verbal: 640 Math: 600
Average ACT Scores: Composite: 27

Child Study Team report is not required. A neuropsychological or comprehensive psycho-educational evaluation is required for admission. Tests required as part of this documentation:

- ■ WAIS-IV
- ■ WISC-IV
- ☐ SATA
- ■ Woodcock-Johnson
- ■ Nelson-Denny Reading Test
- ☐ Other

UNDERGRADUATE STUDENT BODY

Total undergraduate student enrollment: 481 Men, 597 Women.

Composition of student body (fall 2004):

	Undergraduate	Freshmen
International	9.2	5.9
Black	6.3	7.0
American Indian	0.9	0.3
Asian-American	1.2	1.9
Hispanic	2.1	2.8
White	68.2	76.4
Unreported	12.2	5.7
	100.0%	100.0%

72% are from out of state. Average age of full-time undergraduates is 20. 61% of classes have fewer than 20 students,37% have between 20 and 50 students, 3% have more than 50 students.

STUDENT HOUSING

99% of freshmen live in college housing. Freshmen are required to live on campus. Housing is guaranteed for all undergraduates. Campus can house 1,002 undergraduates. Single rooms are available for students with medical or special needs. A medical note is required.

EXPENSES

Tuition (2005-06): $26,984 per year.
Room: $2,900. Board: $3,020.
There is no additional cost for LD program/services.

LD SERVICES

LD program size is not limited.

LD services available to:

■ Freshmen ■ Sophomores ■ Juniors ■ Seniors

Academic Accommodations

Curriculum
- Foreign language waiver ☐
- Lighter course load ☐
- Math waiver ☐
- Other special classes ☐
- Priority registrations ☐
- Substitution of courses ☐

Exams
- Extended time ☐
- Oral exams ☐
- Take home exams ☐
- Exams on tape or computer ☐
- Untimed exams ☐
- Other accommodations ☐

In class
- Early syllabus ☐
- Note takers in class ☐
- Priority seating ☐
- Tape recorders ☐
- Videotaped classes ☐
- Text on tape ☐

Services
- Diagnostic tests ☐
- Learning centers ☐
- Proofreaders ☐
- Readers ☐
- Reading Machines/Kurzweil ☐
- Special bookstore section ☐
- Typists ☐

Counseling Services

- ■ Academic
- ☐ Psychological
- ☐ Student Support groups
- ☐ Vocational

Meets 8 times per academic year

Tutoring

Individual tutoring is available weekly.

	Individual	Group
Time management	■	☐
Organizational skills	■	☐
Learning strategies	■	☐
Study skills	☐	☐
Content area	☐	☐
Writing lab	■	☐
Math lab	☐	☐

UNIQUE LD PROGRAM FEATURES

Many of these services are available, but not all services are available to all LD students.

An advisor from the LD program is available to students on an as-needed basis to meet with faculty and/or students.

Total number of peer tutors available to work with LD students varies.

LD PROGRAM STAFF

Total number of LD Program staff (including director):

Full Time: 1 Part Time: 1

There is an advisor/advocate from the LD program available to students.

Key staff person available to work with LD students: Donna Keesling, Director of the Center for Academic Enrichment.

LD Program web site: www.earlham.edu/~sas/support

Rose-Hulman Institute of Technology

Terre Haute, IN

Address: 5500 Wabash Avenue, Terre Haute, IN, 47803
Admissions telephone: 800 248-7448 (out-of-state), 800 552-0725 (in-state)
Admissions FAX: 812 877-8941
Vice President and Dean of Admissions: James A. Goecker
Admissions e-mail: admis.ofc@rose-hulman.edu
Web site: http://www.rose-hulman.edu
SAT Code: 1668   ACT Code: 1232

Director of Special Programs: Karen DeGrange
LD program telephone: 812 877-8285
LD program e-mail: Karen.DeGrange@rose-hulman.edu
LD program enrollment: 20, Total campus enrollment: 1,765

GENERAL

Rose-Hulman Institute of Technology is a private, coed, four-year institution. 400-acre campus in Terre Haute (population: 59,614), 75 miles from Indianapolis. Served by bus; major airport and train serve Indianapolis. Public transportation serves campus. Quarter system.

LD ADMISSIONS

Students do not complete a separate application and are not simultaneously accepted to the LD program. A member of the LD program does not sit on the admissions committee. A personal interview is not required. Essay is not required.

SECONDARY SCHOOL REQUIREMENTS

Graduation from secondary school required; GED not accepted. The following course distribution required: 4 units of English, 4 units of math, 2 units of science, 2 units of social studies, 4 units of academic electives.

TESTING

SAT Reasoning or ACT required. SAT Subject recommended.

All enrolled freshmen (fall 2004):

Average SAT I Scores:	Verbal: 627	Math: 677
Average ACT Scores:	Composite: 29	

Child Study Team report is not required. A neuropsychological or comprehensive psycho-education evaluation is not required for admission. Tests required as part of this documentation:

- ☐ WAIS-IV
- ☐ WISC-IV
- ☐ SATA
- ☐ Woodcock-Johnson
- ☐ Nelson-Denny Reading Test
- ☐ Other

UNDERGRADUATE STUDENT BODY

Total undergraduate student enrollment: 1,283 Men, 290 Women.

Composition of student body (fall 2004):

	Undergraduate	Freshmen
International	1.3	1.0
Black	3.2	2.6
American Indian	0.0	0.1
Asian-American	3.6	3.5
Hispanic	1.5	1.6
White	90.3	91.3
Unreported	0.2	0.1
	100.0%	100.0%

51% are from out of state. 37% join a fraternity and 43% join a sorority. Average age of full-time undergraduates is 20. 37% of classes have fewer than 20 students, 63% have between 20 and 50 students.

STUDENT HOUSING

98% of freshmen live in college housing. Freshmen are required to live on campus. Housing is guaranteed for all undergraduates. Campus can house 1,164 undergraduates. Single rooms are not available for students with medical or special needs.

EXPENSES

Tuition (2005-06): $26,688 per year.

Room: $4,236. Board: $3,183.
There is no additional cost for LD program/services.

LD SERVICES

LD program size is not limited.

LD services available to:

☒ Freshmen ☒ Sophomores ☒ Juniors ☒ Seniors

Academic Accommodations

Curriculum		**In class**	
Foreign language waiver	☐	Early syllabus	☐
Lighter course load	☐	Note takers in class	☒
Math waiver	☐	Priority seating	☐
Other special classes	☐	Tape recorders	☒
Priority registrations	☐	Videotaped classes	☐
Substitution of courses	☐	Text on tape	☐
Exams		**Services**	
Extended time	☒	Diagnostic tests	☐
Oral exams	☐	Learning centers	☒
Take home exams	☐	Proofreaders	☐
Exams on tape or computer	☐	Readers	☐
Untimed exams	☒	Reading Machines/Kurzweil	☐
Other accommodations	☐	Special bookstore section	☐
		Typists	☐

Credit toward degree is not given for remedial courses taken.

Counseling Services

- ☒ Academic
- ☐ Psychological
- ☐ Student Support groups
- ☐ Vocational

Tutoring

Individual tutoring is available daily.

	Individual	Group
Time management	☐	☐
Organizational skills	☐	☐
Learning strategies	☐	☐
Study skills	☒	☐
Content area	☒	☐
Writing lab	☒	☐
Math lab	☒	☐

LD PROGRAM STAFF

Total number of LD Program staff (including director):

Full Time: 2   Part Time: 2

There is an advisor/advocate from the LD program available to students. 56 peer tutors are available to work with LD students.

Key staff person available to work with LD students: Susan Smith, Director of the Learning Center.

Indiana University-Purdue University Fort Wayne

Fort Wayne, IN

Address: 2101 E. Coliseum Boulevard, Fort Wayne, IN, 46805-1499
Admissions telephone: 800 324-4739 (in-state only)
Admissions FAX: 260 481-6880
Director of Admissions: Carol B. Isaacs
Admissions e-mail: ipfwadms@ipfw.edu
Web site: http://www.ipfw.edu
SAT Code: 1336 ACT Code: 1217

LD program name: Services for Students with Disabilities
Director: Susan Borror
LD program telephone: 260 481-6657
LD program e-mail: borrors@ipfw.edu
Total campus enrollment: 11, 089

GENERAL

Indiana University-Purdue University Fort Wayne is a public, coed, four-year institution. 565-acre campus in Fort Wayne (population: 205,727), 110 miles from Indianapolis. Served by air, bus, and train; major airport serves Indianapolis. Public transportation serves campus. Semester system.

LD ADMISSIONS

Students do not complete a separate application and are not simultaneously accepted to the LD program. A member of the LD program does not sit on the admissions committee. A personal interview is recommended. Essay is not required.

SECONDARY SCHOOL REQUIREMENTS

Graduation from secondary school required; GED accepted. The following course distribution required: 4 units of English, 3 units of math, 1 unit of science, 1 unit of foreign language, 1 unit of social studies.

TESTING

SAT Reasoning or ACT required. SAT Subject recommended.

All enrolled freshmen (fall 2004):

Average SAT I Scores:	Verbal: 484	Math: 493
Average ACT Scores:	Composite: 20	

Child Study Team report is not required. A neuropsychological or comprehensive psycho-education evaluation is not required for admission. Tests required as part of this documentation:

- ☐ WAIS-IV
- ☐ WISC-IV
- ☐ SATA
- ☐ Woodcock-Johnson
- ☐ Nelson-Denny Reading Test
- ☐ Other

UNDERGRADUATE STUDENT BODY

Total undergraduate student enrollment: 4,436 Men, 5,846 Women.

Composition of student body (fall 2004):

	Undergraduate	Freshmen
International	0.6	1.2
Black	6.0	5.1
American Indian	0.6	0.4
Asian-American	2.1	2.1
Hispanic	2.5	2.5
White	85.8	86.5
Unreported	2.4	2.2
	100.0%	100.0%

7% are from out of state. 2% join a fraternity and 3% join a sorority. Average age of full-time undergraduates is 22. 42% of classes have fewer than 20 students, 53% have between 20 and 50 students, 4% have more than 50 students.

STUDENT HOUSING

15% of freshmen live in college housing. Freshmen are not required to live on campus. Housing is guaranteed for all undergraduates. Campus can house 568 undergraduates. Single rooms are not available for students with medical or special needs.

EXPENSES

Tuition (2005-06): $5,630 per year (in-state), $12,984 (out-of-state).
Room: $4,628. Board: $1,766.
There is no additional cost for LD program/services.

LD SERVICES

LD program size is not limited.

LD services available to:

■ Freshmen ■ Sophomores ■ Juniors ■ Seniors

Academic Accommodations

Curriculum		In class	
Foreign language waiver	☐	Early syllabus	☐
Lighter course load	☐	Note takers in class	☐
Math waiver	☐	Priority seating	☐
Other special classes	☐	Tape recorders	■
Priority registrations	☐	Videotaped classes	☐
Substitution of courses	☐	Text on tape	☐
Exams		**Services**	
Extended time	☐	Diagnostic tests	☐
Oral exams	☐	Learning centers	☐
Take home exams	☐	Proofreaders	☐
Exams on tape or computer	☐	Readers	■
Untimed exams	☐	Reading Machines/Kurzweil	■
Other accommodations	■	Special bookstore section	☐
		Typists	☐

Credit toward degree is not given for remedial courses taken.

Counseling Services

- ■ Academic
- ☐ Psychological
- ☐ Student Support groups
- ☐ Vocational

Tutoring

Individual tutoring is available weekly.

	Individual	Group
Time management	■	☐
Organizational skills	■	☐
Learning strategies	■	☐
Study skills	■	☐
Content area	☐	☐
Writing lab	■	☐
Math lab	☐	☐

UNIQUE LD PROGRAM FEATURES

Services are also available through the Center for Academic Support and Advancement.

LD PROGRAM STAFF

Total number of LD Program staff (including director):

Full Time: 2 Part Time: 2

There is an advisor/advocate from the LD program available to students.

Grace College and Seminary

Winona Lake, IN

Address: 200 Seminary Drive, Winona Lake, IN, 46590
Admissions telephone: 800 54-GRACE
Admissions FAX: 574 372-5114
Director of Admissions: Anecia Miller
Admissions e-mail: enroll@grace.edu
Web site: http://www.grace.edu
SAT Code: 1252 ACT Code: 1198

LD program name: Student Academic Achievement Center (SAAC)
Director: Peggy Underwood
LD program telephone: 574 372-5100
LD program e-mail: underwps@grace.edu
LD program enrollment: 23, Total campus enrollment: 1,113

GENERAL

Grace College and Seminary is a private, coed, four-year institution. 160-acre campus in Winona Lake (population: 3,987), 45 miles from Ft. Wayne. Major airport serves Indianapolis (120 miles); smaller airport serves Ft. Wayne; bus serves Warsaw (two miles); train serves Syracuse (23 miles). Semester system.

LD ADMISSIONS

Students do not complete a separate application and are simultaneously accepted to the LD program. A member of the LD program does sit on the admissions committee. A personal interview is recommended. Essay is not required. Admissions may be waived. Test scores.

SECONDARY SCHOOL REQUIREMENTS

Graduation from secondary school required; GED accepted.

TESTING

SAT Reasoning or ACT required. SAT Subject recommended.

All enrolled freshmen (fall 2004):

Average SAT I Scores: Verbal: Math:
Average ACT Scores: Composite:

Child Study Team report is not required. A neuropsychological or comprehensive psycho-educational evaluation is required for admission. Must be dated within 60 months of application. Tests required as part of this documentation:

- ■ WAIS-IV
- ■ WISC-IV
- ■ SATA
- ■ Woodcock-Johnson
- ■ Nelson-Denny Reading Test
- ☐ Other

UNDERGRADUATE STUDENT BODY

Total undergraduate student enrollment: 553 Men, 592 Women.

Composition of student body (fall 2004):

	Undergraduate	Freshmen
International	0.0	0.7
Black	1.7	9.1
American Indian	0.6	0.6
Asian-American	1.1	0.4
Hispanic	3.3	1.9
White	93.3	87.4
Unreported	0.0	0.0
	100.0%	100.0%

53% are from out of state. Average age of full-time undergraduates is 23. 60% of classes have fewer than 20 students, 39% have between 20 and 50 students, 1% have more than 50 students.

STUDENT HOUSING

72% of freshmen live in college housing. Freshmen are required to live on campus. Housing is guaranteed for all undergraduates. Campus can house 724 undergraduates. Single rooms are available for students with medical or special needs. A medical note is not required.

EXPENSES

Tuition (2005-06): $15,620 per year.
Room: $3,070. Board: $3,080.
There is no additional cost for LD program/services.

LD SERVICES

LD program size is limited.

LD services available to:

■ Freshmen ■ Sophomores ■ Juniors ■ Seniors

Academic Accommodations

Curriculum		**In class**	
Foreign language waiver	☐	Early syllabus	☐
Lighter course load	■	Note takers in class	■
Math waiver	☐	Priority seating	☐
Other special classes	☐	Tape recorders	■
Priority registrations	☐	Videotaped classes	☐
Substitution of courses	☐	Text on tape	☐
Exams		**Services**	
Extended time	■	Diagnostic tests	☐
Oral exams	■	Learning centers	■
Take home exams	☐	Proofreaders	■
Exams on tape or computer	■	Readers	■
Untimed exams	■	Reading Machines/Kurzweil	■
Other accommodations	■	Special bookstore section	☐
		Typists	☐

Credit toward degree is not given for remedial courses taken.

Counseling Services

- ■ Academic
- ■ Psychological
- ■ Student Support groups
- ■ Vocational

Tutoring

Individual tutoring is available daily.

Average size of tutoring groups: 3

	Individual	Group
Time management	■	■
Organizational skills	■	■
Learning strategies	■	☐
Study skills	■	■
Content area	■	■
Writing lab	■	☐
Math lab	■	■

LD PROGRAM STAFF

Total number of LD Program staff (including director):

Full Time: 1 Part Time: 1

There is an advisor/advocate from the LD program available to students. 3 peer tutors are available to work with LD students.

Key staff person available to work with LD students: Peggy Underwood, Director, Student Academic Achievement Center.

Goshen College

Goshen, IN

Address: 1700 S. Main Street, Goshen, IN, 46526
Admissions telephone: 800 348-7422
Admissions FAX: 574 535-7609
Interim Director of Admissions: Karen Raftus
Admissions e-mail: admissions@goshen.edu
Web site: http://www.goshen.edu
SAT Code: 1251 ACT Code: 1196

V.P. for Student Life: Bill Born
LD program telephone: 574 535-7543
LD program e-mail: billjb@goshen.edu
LD program enrollment: 19, Total campus enrollment: 908

GENERAL

Goshen College is a private, coed, four-year institution. 135-acre campus in Goshen (population: 29,383), 120 miles from Chicago. Served by bus; airports serve Chicago and South Bend (35 miles); train serves Elkhart (10 miles). Semester system.

LD ADMISSIONS

A personal interview is recommended. Essay is required and may be typed. We look at GPA, SAT/ACT plus strategies used for success & make determination on admission requirements.

SECONDARY SCHOOL REQUIREMENTS

Graduation from secondary school required; GED accepted. The following course distribution required: 4 units of English, 3 units of math, 2 units of science, 2 units of foreign language, 2 units of social studies, 2 units of history.

TESTING

SAT Reasoning or ACT required. SAT Subject recommended.

All enrolled freshmen (fall 2004):

Average SAT I Scores:	Verbal: 576	Math: 561
Average ACT Scores:	Composite: 24	

Child Study Team report is not required. Tests required as part of this documentation:

- ☐ WAIS-IV
- ☐ WISC-IV
- ☐ SATA
- ☐ Woodcock-Johnson
- ☐ Nelson-Denny Reading Test
- ☐ Other

UNDERGRADUATE STUDENT BODY

Total undergraduate student enrollment: 388 Men, 598 Women.

Composition of student body (fall 2004):

	Undergraduate	Freshmen
International	6.0	7.5
Black	1.8	3.3
American Indian	0.6	0.2
Asian-American	1.8	1.0
Hispanic	4.2	4.2
White	85.1	83.7
Unreported	0.6	0.1
	100.0%	100.0%

51% are from out of state. 65% of classes have fewer than 20 students, 31% have between 20 and 50 students, 4% have more than 50 students.

STUDENT HOUSING

85% of freshmen live in college housing. Freshmen are required to live on campus. Housing is guaranteed for all undergraduates. Campus can house 681 undergraduates. Single rooms are available for students with medical or special needs. A medical note is required.

EXPENSES

Tuition (2005-06): $19,300 per year.
Room: $3,450. Board: $3,000.
There is no additional cost for LD program/services.

LD SERVICES

LD program size is not limited.

LD services available to:

☑ Freshmen ☑ Sophomores ☑ Juniors ☑ Seniors

Academic Accommodations

Curriculum		In class	
Foreign language waiver	☐	Early syllabus	☑
Lighter course load	☐	Note takers in class	☑
Math waiver	☐	Priority seating	☐
Other special classes	☐	Tape recorders	☑
Priority registrations	☐	Videotaped classes	☐
Substitution of courses	☐	Text on tape	☐
Exams		**Services**	
Extended time	☑	Diagnostic tests	☐
Oral exams	☐	Learning centers	☑
Take home exams	☐	Proofreaders	☐
Exams on tape or computer	☑	Readers	☑
Untimed exams	☑	Reading Machines/Kurzweil	☑
Other accommodations	☐	Special bookstore section	☑
		Typists	☐

Credit toward degree is not given for remedial courses taken.

Counseling Services

- ☑ Academic — Meets 2 times per academic year
- ☑ Psychological — Meets 12 times per academic year
- ☐ Student Support groups
- ☐ Vocational

Tutoring

Individual tutoring is available weekly.

Average size of tutoring groups: 2

	Individual	Group
Time management	☑	☐
Organizational skills	☑	☐
Learning strategies	☑	☐
Study skills	☑	☐
Content area	☐	☐
Writing lab	☑	☐
Math lab	☐	☐

LD PROGRAM STAFF

39 peer tutors are available to work with LD students.

Key staff person available to work with LD students: Margot Zahner, Director of Academic Support Center.

University of Indianapolis

Indianapolis, IN

Address: 1400 E. Hanna Avenue, Indianapolis, IN, 46227-3697
Admissions telephone: 800 232-8634
Admissions FAX: 317 788-3300
Director of Admissions: Ron Wilks
Admissions e-mail: admissions@uindy.edu
Web site: http://www.uindy.edu
SAT Code: 1321 ACT Code: 1204

LD program name: B.U.I.L.D Program
Director: Deborah L. Spinney
LD program telephone: 317 788-3536
LD program e-mail: http://build.uindy.edu
LD program enrollment: 60, Total campus enrollment: 2,926

GENERAL

University of Indianapolis is a private, coed, four-year institution. 64-acre, suburban campus in Indianapolis (population: 781,870), five miles from downtown; branch campuses abroad in China, Cyprus, Greece, and Taiwan. Served by air, bus, and train. Public transportation serves campus.

LD ADMISSIONS

Application Deadline: 08/01. Students complete a separate application and are simultaneously accepted to the LD program. A member of the LD program does not sit on the admissions committee. High school waivers are accepted for math and foreign language. A personal interview is recommended. Essay is not required. Some course requirements may be substituted or modified.

For fall 2004, 38 completed self-identified LD applications were received. 37 applications were offered admission, and 23 enrolled.

SECONDARY SCHOOL REQUIREMENTS

Graduation from secondary school required; GED accepted. The following course distribution required: 4 units of English, 3 units of math, 3 units of science, 2 units of foreign language, 3 units of social studies.

TESTING

SAT Reasoning or ACT required. SAT Subject recommended.

All enrolled freshmen (fall 2004):

Average SAT I Scores: Verbal: 502 Math: 512
Average ACT Scores: Composite: 21

Child Study Team report is not required. A neuropsychological or comprehensive psycho-educational evaluation is required for admission. Must be dated within 36 months of application. Tests required as part of this documentation:

■	WAIS-IV	■	Woodcock-Johnson
☐	WISC-IV	☐	Nelson-Denny Reading Test
☐	SATA	☐	Other

UNDERGRADUATE STUDENT BODY

Total undergraduate student enrollment: 981 Men, 1,873 Women.

Composition of student body (fall 2004):

	Undergraduate	Freshmen
International	1.8	3.4
Black	11.1	9.8
American Indian	0.6	0.3
Asian-American	1.9	1.2
Hispanic	2.4	1.5
White	79.6	79.7
Unreported	2.6	4.0
	100.0%	100.0%

8% are from out of state. Average age of full-time undergraduates is 22. 68% of classes have fewer than 20 students, 31% have between 20 and 50 students, 1% have more than 50 students.

STUDENT HOUSING

81% of freshmen live in college housing. Freshmen are not required to live on campus. Housing is guaranteed for all undergraduates. Campus can house 1,342 undergraduates. Single rooms are not available for students with medical or special needs.

EXPENSES

Tuition (2005-06): $17,980 per year.

Room: $3,270. Board: $3,740.

Additional cost for LD program/services: $4,100 per year.

LD SERVICES

LD program size is not limited.

LD services available to:

■ Freshmen ■ Sophomores ■ Juniors ■ Seniors

Academic Accommodations

Curriculum		**In class**	
Foreign language waiver	☐	Early syllabus	☐
Lighter course load	■	Note takers in class	☐
Math waiver	☐	Priority seating	■
Other special classes	■	Tape recorders	■
Priority registrations	☐	Videotaped classes	☐
Substitution of courses	■	Text on tape	■
Exams		**Services**	
Extended time	■	Diagnostic tests	■
Oral exams	■	Learning centers	■
Take home exams	☐	Proofreaders	■
Exams on tape or computer	☐	Readers	■
Untimed exams	■	Reading Machines/Kurzweil	■
Other accommodations	■	Special bookstore section	☐
		Typists	☐

Credit toward degree is given for remedial courses taken.

Counseling Services

■	Academic	Meets 96 times per academic year
■	Psychological	Meets 96 times per academic year
■	Student Support groups	Meets 96 times per academic year
☐	Vocational	

Tutoring

Individual tutoring is available daily.

Average size of tutoring groups: 1

	Individual	Group
Time management	■	☐
Organizational skills	■	☐
Learning strategies	■	☐
Study skills	■	☐
Content area	■	☐
Writing lab	■	☐
Math lab	■	☐

UNIQUE LD PROGRAM FEATURES

There are two programs offered at the University of Indianapolis which provide for students with learning disabilities---compliance through the Disabilities Office and a comprehensive program through B.U.I.L.D.

LD PROGRAM STAFF

Total number of LD Program staff (including director):

Full Time: 2 Part Time: 2

There is an advisor/advocate from the LD program available to students. The advisor/advocate meets with faculty 2 times per month and students1 time per month. 1 graduate student and 3 peer tutors are available to work with LD students.

Key staff person available to work with LD students: Deborah L. Spinney, Director.

LD Program web site: www.uindy.edu

Wabash College

Crawfordsville, IN

Address: PO Box 352, Crawfordsville, IN, 47933
Admissions telephone: 800 345-5385
Admissions FAX: 765 361-6437
Director of Admissions: Steven J. Klein
Admissions e-mail: admissions@wabash.edu
Web site: http://www.wabash.edu
SAT Code: 1895 ACT Code: 1260

LD program name: Academic Support Services
Director, Academic Support Services: Julia Rosenberg
LD program telephone: 765 361-6024
LD program e-mail: rosenbj@wabash.edu
Total campus enrollment: 853

GENERAL

Wabash College is a private, men's, four-year institution. 55-acre campus in Crawfordsville (population: 15,243), 45 miles from Indianapolis. Served by bus and train; major airport serves Indianapolis. Semester system.

LD ADMISSIONS

Application Deadline: 03/01. Students do not complete a separate application and are not simultaneously accepted to the LD program. A member of the LD program does not sit on the admissions committee. A personal interview is recommended. Essay is required and may be typed.

SECONDARY SCHOOL REQUIREMENTS

Graduation from secondary school not required.

TESTING

SAT Reasoning required; ACT may be substituted. SAT Subject recommended.

All enrolled freshmen (fall 2004):

Average SAT I Scores:	Verbal: 592	Math: 604
Average ACT Scores:	Composite: 26	

Child Study Team report is not required. A neuropsychological or comprehensive psycho-education evaluation is not required for admission. Tests required as part of this documentation:

- [ ] WAIS-IV
- [ ] WISC-IV
- [ ] SATA
- [ ] Woodcock-Johnson
- [ ] Nelson-Denny Reading Test
- [ ] Other

UNDERGRADUATE STUDENT BODY

Total undergraduate student enrollment: 849 Men.

Composition of student body (fall 2004):

	Undergraduate	Freshmen
International	4.0	3.7
Black	5.2	7.0
American Indian	0.0	0.1
Asian-American	2.8	3.2
Hispanic	4.0	4.1
White	82.4	79.9
Unreported	1.6	2.0
	100.0%	100.0%

24% are from out of state. 60% join a fraternity. Average age of full-time undergraduates is 20. 77% of classes have fewer than 20 students, 21% have between 20 and 50 students, 3% have more than 50 students.

STUDENT HOUSING

100% of freshmen live in college housing. Freshmen are not required to live on campus. Housing is guaranteed for all undergraduates. Campus can house 900 undergraduates. Single rooms are available for students with medical or special needs. A medical note is required.

EXPENSES

Tuition (2005-06): $22,964 per year.

Room: $2,740. Board: $3,988.

There is no additional cost for LD program/services.

LD SERVICES

LD program size is not limited.

LD services available to:

[x] Freshmen [x] Sophomores [x] Juniors [x] Seniors

Academic Accommodations

Curriculum		In class	
Foreign language waiver	[ ]	Early syllabus	[ ]
Lighter course load	[ ]	Note takers in class	[ ]
Math waiver	[ ]	Priority seating	[ ]
Other special classes	[ ]	Tape recorders	[x]
Priority registrations	[ ]	Videotaped classes	[ ]
Substitution of courses	[ ]	Text on tape	[ ]
Exams		**Services**	
Extended time	[x]	Diagnostic tests	[ ]
Oral exams	[ ]	Learning centers	[x]
Take home exams	[ ]	Proofreaders	[ ]
Exams on tape or computer	[ ]	Readers	[ ]
Untimed exams	[x]	Reading Machines/Kurzweil	[ ]
Other accommodations	[ ]	Special bookstore section	[ ]
		Typists	[ ]

Credit toward degree is not given for remedial courses taken.

Counseling Services

- [x] Academic
- [x] Psychological
- [ ] Student Support groups
- [x] Vocational

Tutoring

Individual tutoring is available daily.

Average size of tutoring groups: 1

	Individual	Group
Time management	[ ]	[ ]
Organizational skills	[ ]	[ ]
Learning strategies	[ ]	[ ]
Study skills	[x]	[ ]
Content area	[ ]	[ ]
Writing lab	[x]	[x]
Math lab	[x]	[ ]

UNIQUE LD PROGRAM FEATURES

Wabash works individually, one on one, with students who have learning disabilities. Each student has a program tailored to meet his needs, utilizing the Director and peer tutors.

LD PROGRAM STAFF

Total number of LD Program staff (including director):

Full Time: 1 Part Time: 1

There is an advisor/advocate from the LD program available to students. The advisor/advocate meets with faculty 2 times per month. 12 peer tutors are available to work with LD students.

Key staff person available to work with LD students: Julia Rosenberg, Director, Academic Support Services.

University of Notre Dame

Notre Dame, IN

Address: , Notre Dame, IN, 46556
Admissions telephone: 574 631-7505
Admissions FAX: 574 631-8865
Assistant Provost for Enrollment: Daniel Saracino
Admissions e-mail: admissio.1@nd.edu
Web site: http://www.nd.edu
SAT Code: 1841 ACT Code: 1252

LD program name: Office for Students with Disabilities
Program Coordinator: Scott Howland
LD program telephone: 574 631-7157
LD program e-mail: nd.osd.1@nd.edu
Total campus enrollment: 8,332

GENERAL

University of Notre Dame is a private, coed, four-year institution. 1,250-acre campus in Notre Dame, near South Bend (population: 107,789); environmental studies center in Wisconsin. Airport, bus, and train serve South Bend; major airport serves Chicago (90 miles). Public transportation serves campus. Semester system.

LD ADMISSIONS

Application Deadline: 12/31. Students do not complete a separate application and are not simultaneously accepted to the LD program. A personal interview is not required.

SECONDARY SCHOOL REQUIREMENTS

Graduation from secondary school required; GED not accepted. The following course distribution required: 4 units of English, 3 units of math, 2 units of science, 2 units of foreign language, 2 units of history, 3 units of academic electives.

TESTING

SAT Reasoning or ACT required. SAT Subject recommended.

All enrolled freshmen (fall 2004):

Average SAT I Scores: Verbal: 676 Math: 693
Average ACT Scores: Composite: 31

Child Study Team report is not required. Tests required as part of this documentation:

- ☐ WAIS-IV
- ☐ WISC-IV
- ☐ SATA
- ☐ Woodcock-Johnson
- ☐ Nelson-Denny Reading Test
- ☐ Other

UNDERGRADUATE STUDENT BODY

Total undergraduate student enrollment: 4,406 Men, 3,802 Women.

Composition of student body (fall 2004):

	Undergraduate	Freshmen
International	3.4	3.8
Black	4.6	3.7
American Indian	0.9	0.7
Asian-American	6.6	5.4
Hispanic	9.5	8.2
White	75.0	78.3
Unreported	0.0	0.0
	100.0%	100.0%

88% are from out of state. Average age of full-time undergraduates is 20. 56% of classes have fewer than 20 students, 34% have between 20 and 50 students, 10% have more than 50 students.

STUDENT HOUSING

100% of freshmen live in college housing. Freshmen are required to live on campus. Housing is not guaranteed for all undergraduates. Housing is usually available, but not guaranteed for upperclass students. Campus can house 6,284 undergraduates.

EXPENSES

Tuition (2005-06): $31,100 per year.
Room & Board: $8,010.
There is no additional cost for LD program/services.

LD SERVICES

LD program size is not limited.

LD services available to:

☒ Freshmen ☒ Sophomores ☒ Juniors ☒ Seniors

Academic Accommodations

Curriculum

- Foreign language waiver ☐
- Lighter course load ☐
- Math waiver ☐
- Other special classes ☐
- Priority registrations ☐
- Substitution of courses ☐

Exams

- Extended time ☒
- Oral exams ☒
- Take home exams ☐
- Exams on tape or computer ☐
- Untimed exams ☒
- Other accommodations ☐

In class

- Early syllabus ☐
- Note takers in class ☒
- Priority seating ☐
- Tape recorders ☒
- Videotaped classes ☒
- Text on tape ☒

Services

- Diagnostic tests ☒
- Learning centers ☒
- Proofreaders ☐
- Readers ☒
- Reading Machines/Kurzweil ☒
- Special bookstore section ☐
- Typists ☐

Credit toward degree is not given for remedial courses taken.

Counseling Services

- ☐ Academic
- ☐ Psychological
- ☐ Student Support groups
- ☐ Vocational

Tutoring

	Individual	Group
Time management	☐	☐
Organizational skills	☐	☐
Learning strategies	☐	☐
Study skills	☐	☐
Content area	☐	☐
Writing lab	☐	☐
Math lab	☐	☐

LD PROGRAM STAFF

Key staff person available to work with LD students: Scott Howland, Program Coordinator.

LD Program web site: http://www.nd.edu/~osd/

Franklin College

Franklin, IN

Address: 101 Branigin Boulevard, Franklin, IN, 46131-2623
Admissions telephone: 800 852-0232
Admissions FAX: 317 738-8274
Vice President for Enrollment and Student Affairs: Alan Hill
Admissions e-mail: admissions@franklincollege.edu
Web site: http://www.franklincollege.edu
SAT Code: 1228 ACT Code: 1194

LD program name: Disabilities Services
LD program address: Academic Resource Center, 101 Branigin Boulevard
Director of Academic Resources: Claudia Bramon
LD program telephone: 317 738-8288
LD program e-mail: abraman@franklincollege.edu
Total campus enrollment: 994

GENERAL

Franklin College is a private, coed, four-year institution. 110-acre, semirural campus in Franklin (population: 19,463), 20 miles from Indianapolis. Served by bus; major airport and train serve Indianapolis. 4-1-4 system.

LD ADMISSIONS

Students do not complete a separate application and are not simultaneously accepted to the LD program. A member of the LD program does not sit on the admissions committee. A personal interview is recommended. Essay is not required.

SECONDARY SCHOOL REQUIREMENTS

Graduation from secondary school required; GED accepted. The following course distribution required: 4 units of English, 3 units of math, 1 unit of science, 2 units of social studies, 2 units of history.

TESTING

SAT Reasoning required; ACT may be substituted. SAT Subject required.

All enrolled freshmen (fall 2004):

Average SAT I Scores:	Verbal: 516	Math: 522
Average ACT Scores:	Composite: 22	

Child Study Team report is not required. A neuropsychological or comprehensive psycho-education evaluation is not required for admission. Tests required as part of this documentation:

☐ WAIS-IV	☐ Woodcock-Johnson
☐ WISC-IV	☐ Nelson-Denny Reading Test
☐ SATA	☐ Other

UNDERGRADUATE STUDENT BODY

Total undergraduate student enrollment: 465 Men, 563 Women.

Composition of student body (fall 2004):

	Undergraduate	Freshmen
International	1.1	0.7
Black	7.2	4.4
American Indian	0.4	0.3
Asian-American	1.4	0.6
Hispanic	1.8	1.5
White	79.7	86.2
Unreported	8.3	6.2
	100.0%	100.0%

7% are from out of state. 32% join a fraternity and 39% join a sorority. Average age of full-time undergraduates is 20. 64% of classes have fewer than 20 students, 35% have between 20 and 50 students.

STUDENT HOUSING

90% of freshmen live in college housing. Freshmen are required to live on campus. Housing is guaranteed for all undergraduates. Campus can house 814 undergraduates.

EXPENSES

Tuition (2005-06): $19,190 per year.
Room: $3,340. Board: $2,390.

There is no additional cost for LD program/services.

LD SERVICES

LD program size is not limited.

LD services available to:

■ Freshmen ■ Sophomores ■ Juniors ■ Seniors

Academic Accommodations

Curriculum		**In class**	
Foreign language waiver	☐	Early syllabus	☐
Lighter course load	■	Note takers in class	■
Math waiver	☐	Priority seating	☐
Other special classes	■	Tape recorders	■
Priority registrations	■	Videotaped classes	■
Substitution of courses	☐	Text on tape	■
Exams		**Services**	
Extended time	■	Diagnostic tests	☐
Oral exams	■	Learning centers	■
Take home exams	☐	Proofreaders	☐
Exams on tape or computer	■	Readers	■
Untimed exams	■	Reading Machines/Kurzweil	☐
Other accommodations	☐	Special bookstore section	☐
		Typists	☐

Credit toward degree is not given for remedial courses taken.

Counseling Services

■ Academic
■ Psychological
☐ Student Support groups
☐ Vocational

Tutoring

Individual tutoring is available daily.

Average size of tutoring groups: 3

	Individual	Group
Time management	■	■
Organizational skills	■	■
Learning strategies	■	■
Study skills	■	■
Content area	■	■
Writing lab	■	■
Math lab	■	■

LD PROGRAM STAFF

Total number of LD Program staff (including director):

Full Time: 1 Part Time: 1

There is an advisor/advocate from the LD program available to students. 15 peer tutors are available to work with LD students.

Key staff person available to work with LD students: Claudia Bramon, Director of Academic Resources.

LD Program web site: www.franklincollege.edu/ARCweb\ADA,htm

Valparaiso University

Valparaiso, IN

Address: Kretzmann Hall, 1700 Chapel Drive, Valparaiso, IN, 46383
Admissions telephone: 888 GO-VALPO
Admissions FAX: 219 464-6898
Director of Admissions: Joyce Lantz
Admissions e-mail: undergrad.admissions@valpo.edu
Web site: http://www.valpo.edu
SAT Code: 1874 ACT Code: 1256

LD program name: Disability Support Services
LD program address: 132 Huegli Hall, 1409 Chapel Drive
Director, Disability Support Services: Sheryl DeMik
LD program telephone: 219 464-5318
LD program e-mail: sheryl.demik@valpo.edu
LD program enrollment: 55, Total campus enrollment: 3,067

GENERAL

Valparaiso University is a private, coed, four-year institution. 310-acre campus in Valparaiso (population: 27,428), 50 miles from South Bend and 60 miles from Chicago; served by bus. Major airport serves Chicago; inter-urban train serves Chesterton (13 miles). Semester system.

LD ADMISSIONS

Students complete a separate application and are not simultaneously accepted to the LD program. A member of the LD program does not sit on the admissions committee. A personal interview is recommended. Essay is required and may be typed.

For fall 2004, 34 completed self-identified LD applications were received. 28 applications were offered admission, and 5 enrolled.

SECONDARY SCHOOL REQUIREMENTS

Graduation from secondary school required; GED accepted. The following course distribution required: 4 units of English, 3 units of math, 2 units of science, 3 units of social studies, 3 units of academic electives.

TESTING

SAT Reasoning or ACT required. SAT Subject required.

All enrolled freshmen (fall 2004):

Average SAT I Scores:	Verbal: 578	Math: 587
Average ACT Scores:	Composite: 26	

Child Study Team report is required if student is classified. A neuropsychological or comprehensive psycho-educational evaluation is required for admission. Must be dated within 36 months of application. Tests required as part of this documentation:

- [ ] WAIS-IV
- [ ] WISC-IV
- [ ] SATA
- [ ] Woodcock-Johnson
- [ ] Nelson-Denny Reading Test
- [x] Other

UNDERGRADUATE STUDENT BODY

Total undergraduate student enrollment: 1,347 Men, 1,526 Women.

Composition of student body (fall 2004):

	Undergraduate	Freshmen
International	1.1	1.5
Black	4.2	3.7
American Indian	0.3	0.2
Asian-American	1.1	1.6
Hispanic	2.6	3.0
White	83.9	86.0
Unreported	6.9	4.0
	100.0%	100.0%

65% are from out of state. 25% join a fraternity and 18% join a sorority. Average age of full-time undergraduates is 20. 51% of classes have fewer than 20 students, 45% have between 20 and 50 students, 4% have more than 50 students.

STUDENT HOUSING

92% of freshmen live in college housing. Freshmen are required to live on campus. Housing is guaranteed for all undergraduates. Campus can house 1,988 undergraduates. Single rooms are available for students with medical or special needs. A medical note is required.

EXPENSES

Tuition (2005-06): $22,000 per year.

Room: $3,910. Board: $2,310.
There is no additional cost for LD program/services.

LD SERVICES

LD program size is not limited.

LD services available to:

- [x] Freshmen
- [x] Sophomores
- [x] Juniors
- [x] Seniors

Academic Accommodations

Curriculum		In class	
Foreign language waiver	[ ]	Early syllabus	[ ]
Lighter course load	[ ]	Note takers in class	[x]
Math waiver	[ ]	Priority seating	[x]
Other special classes	[x]	Tape recorders	[x]
Priority registrations	[x]	Videotaped classes	[x]
Substitution of courses	[ ]	Text on tape	[ ]
Exams		**Services**	
Extended time	[x]	Diagnostic tests	[ ]
Oral exams	[x]	Learning centers	[ ]
Take home exams	[x]	Proofreaders	[ ]
Exams on tape or computer	[x]	Readers	[x]
Untimed exams	[x]	Reading Machines/Kurzweil	[x]
Other accommodations	[x]	Special bookstore section	[ ]
		Typists	[ ]

Credit toward degree is not given for remedial courses taken.

Counseling Services

- [x] Academic
- [x] Psychological
- [x] Student Support groups
- [x] Vocational

Tutoring

Individual tutoring is available.

	Individual	Group
Time management	[x]	[x]
Organizational skills	[x]	[x]
Learning strategies	[x]	[x]
Study skills	[x]	[x]
Content area	[x]	[x]
Writing lab	[x]	[x]
Math lab	[x]	[x]

UNIQUE LD PROGRAM FEATURES

Students should submit documentation to the DSS office following admission into the University.

LD PROGRAM STAFF

Total number of LD Program staff (including director):

Full Time: 1 Part Time: 1

There is an advisor/advocate from the LD program available to students.

Key staff person available to work with LD students: Sheryl DeMik, Director, Disability Support Services.

LD Program web site: http://www.valpo.edu/cas/dss/

Indiana University Kokomo

Kokomo, IN

Address: 2300 S. Washington Street, PO Box 9003, Kokomo, IN, 46904-9003
Admissions telephone: 888 875-4485
Admissions FAX: 765 455-9537
Director of Admissions: Patty Young
Admissions e-mail: luadmiss@iuk.edu
Web site: http://www.iuk.edu
SAT Code: 1337 ACT Code: 1219

Director, University Division: Gerry Stroman
LD program telephone: 765 455-9309
LD program e-mail: gstroman@iuk.edu
Total campus enrollment: 2, 732

GENERAL

Indiana University Kokomo is a public, coed, four-year institution. 51-acre campus in Kokomo (population: 47,800), 50 miles from Indianapolis. Major airport, bus, and train serve Indianapolis. Semester system.

LD ADMISSIONS

A personal interview is recommended. Essay is not required.

SECONDARY SCHOOL REQUIREMENTS

Graduation from secondary school required; GED accepted. The following course distribution required: 4 units of English, 3 units of math, 1 unit of science, 2 units of social studies.

TESTING

SAT Reasoning or ACT required. SAT Subject required.

All enrolled freshmen (fall 2004):

Average SAT I Scores:	Verbal: 487	Math: 480
Average ACT Scores:	Composite: 19	

Child Study Team report is not required. Tests required as part of this documentation:

- ☐ WAIS-IV
- ☐ WISC-IV
- ☐ SATA
- ☐ Woodcock-Johnson
- ☐ Nelson-Denny Reading Test
- ☐ Other

UNDERGRADUATE STUDENT BODY

Total undergraduate student enrollment: 767 Men, 1,752 Women.

Composition of student body (fall 2004):

	Undergraduate	Freshmen
International	0.2	0.3
Black	2.4	3.4
American Indian	0.4	0.5
Asian-American	0.6	0.8
Hispanic	0.9	1.1
White	92.7	91.0
Unreported	2.8	3.0
	100.0%	100.0%

1% are from out of state. 2% join a sorority. Average age of full-time undergraduates is 23. 46% of classes have fewer than 20 students, 50% have between 20 and 50 students, 4% have more than 50 students.

EXPENSES

Tuition (2005-06): $4,475 per year (in-state), $11,153 (out-of-state).

There is no additional cost for LD program/services.

LD SERVICES

LD program size is not limited.

LD services available to:

☐ Freshmen ☐ Sophomores ☐ Juniors ☐ Seniors

Academic Accommodations

Curriculum		**In class**	
Foreign language waiver	☐	Early syllabus	☐
Lighter course load	■	Note takers in class	■
Math waiver	☐	Priority seating	☐
Other special classes	☐	Tape recorders	☐
Priority registrations	☐	Videotaped classes	☐
Substitution of courses	☐	Text on tape	☐
Exams		**Services**	
Extended time	☐	Diagnostic tests	■
Oral exams	■	Learning centers	■
Take home exams	☐	Proofreaders	☐
Exams on tape or computer	☐	Readers	■
Untimed exams	■	Reading Machines/Kurzweil	☐
Other accommodations	☐	Special bookstore section	☐
		Typists	☐

Credit toward degree is not given for remedial courses taken.

Counseling Services

- ☐ Academic
- ☐ Psychological
- ☐ Student Support groups
- ☐ Vocational

Tutoring

	Individual	Group
Time management	☐	☐
Organizational skills	☐	☐
Learning strategies	☐	☐
Study skills	☐	☐
Content area	☐	☐
Writing lab	☐	☐
Math lab	☐	☐

LD PROGRAM STAFF

Key staff person available to work with LD students: Gerry Stroman, Director, University Division.

Hanover College

Hanover, IN

Address: Box 108, Hanover, IN, 47243
Admissions telephone: 800 213-2178
Admissions FAX: 812 866-7098
Dean of Admission: Ken Moyer
Admissions e-mail: admission@hanover.edu
Web site: http://www.hanover.edu
SAT Code: 1290 ACT Code: 1200

Assoicate Registrar: Dr. Kenneth Prince
LD program telephone: 812 866-7051
LD program e-mail: princek@hanover.edu
Total campus enrollment: 1, 062

GENERAL

Hanover College is a private, coed, four-year institution. 650-acre campus in Hanover (population: 2,834), four miles from Madison and 40 miles from Louisville, Ky. Major airport serves Louisville; airport and train serve Cincinnati (65 miles); bus serves Scottsburg (18 miles). School operates transportation to Louisville. OTHER.

LD ADMISSIONS

A personal interview is recommended. Essay is required and may be typed.

SECONDARY SCHOOL REQUIREMENTS

Graduation from secondary school required; GED not accepted. The following course distribution required: 3 units of English, 3 units of math, 3 units of science, 2 units of foreign language, 2 units of social studies, 2 units of history, 2 units of academic electives.

TESTING

SAT Reasoning or ACT required. SAT Subject required.

All enrolled freshmen (fall 2004):

Average SAT I Scores: Verbal: 584 Math: 586
Average ACT Scores: Composite: 25

Child Study Team report is not required. Tests required as part of this documentation:

- ❑ WAIS-IV
- ❑ WISC-IV
- ❑ SATA
- ❑ Woodcock-Johnson
- ❑ Nelson-Denny Reading Test
- ❑ Other

UNDERGRADUATE STUDENT BODY

Total undergraduate student enrollment: 513 Men, 598 Women.

Composition of student body (fall 2004):

	Undergraduate	Freshmen
International	3.2	4.1
Black	1.8	2.0
American Indian	0.5	0.2
Asian-American	3.7	3.0
Hispanic	1.3	1.2
White	83.2	84.7
Unreported	6.3	4.8
	100.0%	100.0%

34% are from out of state. 29% join a fraternity and 33% join a sorority. Average age of full-time undergraduates is 19. 75% of classes have fewer than 20 students, 25% have between 20 and 50 students.

STUDENT HOUSING

98% of freshmen live in college housing. Freshmen are required to live on campus. Housing is guaranteed for all undergraduates. Campus can house 1,070 undergraduates.

EXPENSES

Tuition (2005-06): $21,150 per year.
Room: $3,100. Board: $3,400.
There is no additional cost for LD program/services.

LD SERVICES

LD services available to:

❑ Freshmen ❑ Sophomores ❑ Juniors ❑ Seniors

Academic Accommodations

Curriculum		**In class**	
Foreign language waiver	❑	Early syllabus	❑
Lighter course load	❑	Note takers in class	■
Math waiver	❑	Priority seating	❑
Other special classes	❑	Tape recorders	■
Priority registrations	❑	Videotaped classes	❑
Substitution of courses	❑	Text on tape	❑
Exams		**Services**	
Extended time	■	Diagnostic tests	❑
Oral exams	❑	Learning centers	❑
Take home exams	❑	Proofreaders	❑
Exams on tape or computer	❑	Readers	❑
Untimed exams	■	Reading Machines/Kurzweil	❑
Other accommodations	❑	Special bookstore section	❑
		Typists	❑

Credit toward degree is not given for remedial courses taken.

Counseling Services

- ❑ Academic
- ❑ Psychological
- ❑ Student Support groups
- ❑ Vocational

Tutoring

Individual tutoring is available weekly.

	Individual	Group
Time management	❑	❑
Organizational skills	❑	❑
Learning strategies	❑	❑
Study skills	❑	❑
Content area	❑	❑
Writing lab	■	❑
Math lab	❑	❑

LD PROGRAM STAFF

Key staff person available to work with LD students: Dr. Kenneth Prince, Associate Registrar.

Purdue University - Calumet

Hammond, IN

Address: 2200 169th Street, Hammond, IN, 46323-2094
Admissions telephone: 800 288-0799
Admissions FAX: 219 989-2775
Director of Admissions and Recruitment: Paul McGuinness
Admissions e-mail: adms@calumet.purdue.edu
Web site: http://www.calumet.purdue.edu/
SAT Code: 1638 ACT Code: 1233

LD program name: Student Support Services
Coordinator of Services for Students with Disabilities:
Mrs. Michaeline Florek
LD program telephone: 219 989-2920
LD program e-mail: florekms@calumet.purdue.edu
LD program enrollment: 510, Total campus enrollment: 8,283

GENERAL

Purdue University - Calumet is a public, coed, four-year institution. 180-acre campus in Hammond (population: 83,048), 26 miles from Chicago; branch campuses in Crown Point, East Chicago, Merrillville, and St. John. Served by bus and train; major airports serve Chicago. Public transportation serves campus. Semester system.

LD ADMISSIONS

Students do not complete a separate application and are not simultaneously accepted to the LD program. A member of the LD program does not sit on the admissions committee. A personal interview is not required. Essay is not required.

SECONDARY SCHOOL REQUIREMENTS

Graduation from secondary school required; GED accepted. The following course distribution required: 4 units of English, 2 units of math, 2 units of science, 2 units of foreign language, 1 unit of social studies, 1 unit of history.

TESTING

SAT Reasoning required of some applicants; ACT may be substituted. SAT Subject required.

All enrolled freshmen (fall 2004):

Average SAT I Scores: Verbal: 456 Math: 453
Average ACT Scores: Composite:

Child Study Team report is not required. A neuropsychological or comprehensive psycho-educational evaluation is required for admission. Tests required as part of this documentation:

- [x] WAIS-IV
- [x] WISC-IV
- [x] SATA
- [x] Woodcock-Johnson
- [x] Nelson-Denny Reading Test
- [ ] Other

UNDERGRADUATE STUDENT BODY

Total undergraduate student enrollment: 8,283.

Composition of student body (fall 2004):

	Undergraduate	Freshmen
International	0.5	0.8
Black	16.3	14.8
American Indian	0.2	0.3
Asian-American	1.3	1.5
Hispanic	16.8	15.0
White	64.9	67.6
Unreported	0.0	0.0
	100.0%	100.0%

7% are from out of state. Average age of full-time undergraduates is 22. 40% of classes have fewer than 20 students, 56% have between 20 and 50 students, 4% have more than 50 students.

STUDENT HOUSING

Freshmen are not required to live on campus. Housing is guaranteed for all undergraduates. Campus can house undergraduates. Single rooms are not available for students with medical or special needs.

EXPENSES

Tuition (2005-06): $4,680 per year (in-state), $10,994 (out-of-state).

Room: $3,990.
There is no additional cost for LD program/services.

LD SERVICES

LD program size is not limited.

LD services available to:

- [x] Freshmen
- [x] Sophomores
- [x] Juniors
- [x] Seniors

Academic Accommodations

Curriculum
- [ ] Foreign language waiver
- [ ] Lighter course load
- [ ] Math waiver
- [ ] Other special classes
- [ ] Priority registrations
- [x] Substitution of courses

Exams
- [x] Extended time
- [x] Oral exams
- [ ] Take home exams
- [x] Exams on tape or computer
- [ ] Untimed exams
- [ ] Other accommodations

In class
- [ ] Early syllabus
- [x] Note takers in class
- [x] Priority seating
- [x] Tape recorders
- [ ] Videotaped classes
- [x] Text on tape

Services
- [ ] Diagnostic tests
- [ ] Learning centers
- [ ] Proofreaders
- [x] Readers
- [x] Reading Machines/Kurzweil
- [ ] Special bookstore section
- [x] Typists

Credit toward degree is not given for remedial courses taken.

Counseling Services

- [x] Academic
- [x] Psychological
- [x] Student Support groups
- [ ] Vocational

Meets 2 times per academic year

Tutoring

Individual tutoring is available weekly.

Average size of tutoring groups: 1

	Individual	Group
Time management	[x]	[x]
Organizational skills	[x]	[x]
Learning strategies	[x]	[x]
Study skills	[x]	[x]
Content area	[x]	[x]
Writing lab	[x]	[x]
Math lab	[x]	[x]

LD PROGRAM STAFF

Total number of LD Program staff (including director):

Full Time: 7 Part Time: 7

There is an advisor/advocate from the LD program available to students.

Key staff person available to work with LD students: Mrs. Michaeline Florek, Coord. of Services for Students w/ Disabilities.

LD Program web site: http://www.calumet.purdue.edu/stusuprt

Purdue University

West Lafayette, IN

Address: Schleman Hall, 475 Stadium Mall Drive, West Lafayette, IN, 47907
Admissions telephone: 765 494-1776
Admissions FAX: 765 494-0544
Director of Admissions: Dr. Douglas L.Christiansen
Admissions e-mail: admissions@purdue.edu
Web site: http://www.purdue.edu
SAT Code: 1631 ACT Code: 1230

LD program name: Adaptive Programs
LD program address: Young Hall, 302 Wood Street, West Lafayette, IN, 47907-2108
Psychologist: Carole Dunning
LD program telephone: 765 494-6673
LD program e-mail: csdunning@purdue.edu
Total campus enrollment: 30747

GENERAL

Purdue University is a public, coed, four-year institution. 1,579-acre campus in West Lafayette (population: 28,778), 65 miles from Indianapolis; branch campuses in Fort Wayne, Hammond, and Westville. Served by air, bus, and train; major airport serves Indianapolis. Public transportation serves campus. Semester system.

LD ADMISSIONS

Students do not complete a separate application and are not simultaneously accepted to the LD program. A member of the LD program does not sit on the admissions committee. A personal interview is not required. Essay is not required. Each case is reviewed individually and holistically, and admission decisions are made based on information provided.

SECONDARY SCHOOL REQUIREMENTS

Graduation from secondary school required; GED accepted. The following course distribution required: 4 units of English, 3 units of math, 2 units of science, 2 units of foreign language.

TESTING

SAT Reasoning or ACT required. SAT Subject required.

All enrolled freshmen (fall 2004):

Average SAT I Scores:	Verbal: 558	Math: 591
Average ACT Scores:	Composite: 25	

Child Study Team report is not required. A neuropsychological or comprehensive psycho-educational evaluation is required for admission. Tests required as part of this documentation:

- [x] WAIS-IV
- [x] WISC-IV
- [x] SATA
- [x] Woodcock-Johnson
- [x] Nelson-Denny Reading Test
- [x] Other

UNDERGRADUATE STUDENT BODY

Total undergraduate student enrollment: 18,036 Men, 12,951 Women.

Composition of student body (fall 2004):

	Undergraduate	Freshmen
International	3.7	6.7
Black	3.7	3.4
American Indian	0.6	0.4
Asian-American	5.6	4.8
Hispanic	2.9	2.3
White	83.4	82.4
Unreported	0.0	0.0
	100.0%	100.0%

21% are from out of state. 18% join a fraternity and 17% join a sorority. Average age of full-time undergraduates is 20. 36% of classes have fewer than 20 students, 45% have between 20 and 50 students, 19% have more than 50 students.

STUDENT HOUSING

90% of freshmen live in college housing. Freshmen are not required to live on campus. Housing is guaranteed for all undergraduates. Campus can house 10,600 undergraduates. Single rooms are available for students with medical or special needs. A medical note is required.

EXPENSES

Tuition (2005-06): $6,320 per year (in-state), $19,686 (out-of-state).
Room: $2,904. Board: $3,926.
There is no additional cost for LD program/services.

LD SERVICES

LD program size is not limited.

LD services available to:

- [x] Freshmen
- [x] Sophomores
- [x] Juniors
- [x] Seniors

Academic Accommodations

Curriculum		**In class**	
Foreign language waiver	[ ]	Early syllabus	[ ]
Lighter course load	[ ]	Note takers in class	[x]
Math waiver	[ ]	Priority seating	[x]
Other special classes	[ ]	Tape recorders	[x]
Priority registrations	[x]	Videotaped classes	[ ]
Substitution of courses	[x]	Text on tape	[x]
Exams		**Services**	
Extended time	[x]	Diagnostic tests	[x]
Oral exams	[x]	Learning centers	[x]
Take home exams	[ ]	Proofreaders	[ ]
Exams on tape or computer	[x]	Readers	[x]
Untimed exams	[ ]	Reading Machines/Kurzweil	[x]
Other accommodations	[x]	Special bookstore section	[ ]
		Typists	[x]

Credit toward degree is not given for remedial courses taken.

Counseling Services

- [ ] Academic
- [ ] Psychological
- [ ] Student Support groups
- [ ] Vocational

Tutoring

Individual tutoring is not available.

	Individual	Group
Time management	[ ]	[ ]
Organizational skills	[ ]	[ ]
Learning strategies	[ ]	[ ]
Study skills	[ ]	[ ]
Content area	[ ]	[ ]
Writing lab	[ ]	[ ]
Math lab	[ ]	[ ]

LD PROGRAM STAFF

Total number of LD Program staff (including director):

Full Time: 3 Part Time: 3

There is no advisor/advocate from the LD program available to students.

Key staff person available to work with LD students: Carole Dunning, Psychologist.

LD Program web site: http://www.purdue.edu/odos/adpro/Welcome.html

Saint Joseph's College

Rensselaer, IN

Address: PO Box 890, Rensselaer, IN, 47978
Admissions telephone: 800 447-8781
Admissions FAX: 219 866-6122
Director of Admissions, Assistant Vice President of Enrollment Management: Jeremy Spencer
Admissions e-mail: admissions@saintjoe.edu
Web site: http://www.saintjoe.edu
SAT Code: 1697 ACT Code: 1240

Director of Academic Services: Stacey Russo
LD program telephone: 219 866-6116
LD program e-mail: srusso@saintjoe.edu
LD program enrollment: 5, Total campus enrollment: 1,010

GENERAL

Saint Joseph's College is a private, coed, four-year institution. 340-acre campus in Rensselaer (population: 5,294), 80 miles from Chicago and 45 miles from Lafayette. Served by bus and train; major airports serve Chicago and Indianapolis (80 miles); smaller airport serves Lafayette. Semester system.

LD ADMISSIONS

Students do not complete a separate application and are not simultaneously accepted to the LD program. A member of the LD program does not sit on the admissions committee. A personal interview is required. Essay is required and may be typed. Requirement for high school GPA may be waived on an individual basis. LD and/or ADHD documentation should be submitted only after the student has been accepted, they will not be considered in the application process.

SECONDARY SCHOOL REQUIREMENTS

Graduation from secondary school required; GED accepted. The following course distribution required:.

TESTING

SAT Reasoning or ACT required. SAT Subject recommended.

All enrolled freshmen (fall 2004):

Average SAT I Scores:	Verbal: 494	Math: 491
Average ACT Scores:	Composite: 22	

Child Study Team report is not required. A neuropsychological or comprehensive psycho-educational evaluation is required for admission. Must be dated within 36 months of application. Tests required as part of this documentation:

- [ ] WAIS-IV
- [ ] WISC-IV
- [ ] SATA
- [ ] Woodcock-Johnson
- [ ] Nelson-Denny Reading Test
- [ ] Other

UNDERGRADUATE STUDENT BODY

Total undergraduate student enrollment: 408 Men, 527 Women.

Composition of student body (fall 2004):

	Undergraduate	Freshmen
International	1.7	1.0
Black	5.5	4.6
American Indian	0.0	0.2
Asian-American	0.3	0.4
Hispanic	3.4	4.1
White	87.3	88.4
Unreported	1.7	1.4
	100.0%	100.0%

28% are from out of state. Average age of full-time undergraduates is 20. 81% of classes have fewer than 20 students, 18% have between 20 and 50 students, 1% have more than 50 students.

STUDENT HOUSING

90% of freshmen live in college housing. Freshmen are required to live on campus. Housing is guaranteed for all undergraduates. Campus can house 806 undergraduates.

EXPENSES

Tuition (2005-06): $19,600 per year.
Room: $2,960. Board: $3,520.

There is no additional cost for LD program/services.

LD SERVICES

LD program size is not limited.

LD services available to:

- [x] Freshmen
- [x] Sophomores
- [x] Juniors
- [x] Seniors

Academic Accommodations

Curriculum		**In class**	
Foreign language waiver	[ ]	Early syllabus	[ ]
Lighter course load	[x]	Note takers in class	[ ]
Math waiver	[ ]	Priority seating	[ ]
Other special classes	[x]	Tape recorders	[x]
Priority registrations	[ ]	Videotaped classes	[ ]
Substitution of courses	[ ]	Text on tape	[ ]
Exams		**Services**	
Extended time	[x]	Diagnostic tests	[ ]
Oral exams	[x]	Learning centers	[ ]
Take home exams	[ ]	Proofreaders	[ ]
Exams on tape or computer	[ ]	Readers	[ ]
Untimed exams	[x]	Reading Machines/Kurzweil	[ ]
Other accommodations	[ ]	Special bookstore section	[ ]
		Typists	[ ]

Credit toward degree is given for remedial courses taken.

Counseling Services

- [ ] Academic
- [ ] Psychological
- [ ] Student Support groups
- [ ] Vocational

Tutoring

	Individual	Group
Time management	[ ]	[ ]
Organizational skills	[ ]	[ ]
Learning strategies	[ ]	[ ]
Study skills	[ ]	[ ]
Content area	[ ]	[ ]
Writing lab	[ ]	[ ]
Math lab	[ ]	[ ]

UNIQUE LD PROGRAM FEATURES

If an LD student fails to meet normal admissions requirements, he/she may be accepted through the College's Freshmen Academic Support Program (FASP). FASP is not limited to LD students, but provided to students who would not typically be admitted to SJC based on high school achievement and/or standardized testing but who are motivated to succeed and willing to actively take advantage of the services provided by the program.

LD PROGRAM STAFF

Total number of LD Program staff (including director):

Full Time: 2 Part Time: 2

Key staff person available to work with LD students: Stacey Russo, Director of Academic Services.

Butler University

Indianapolis, IN

Address: 4600 Sunset Avenue, Indianapolis, IN, 46208
Admissions telephone: 888 940-8100
Admissions FAX: 317 940-8150
Director of Admission: William Preble
Admissions e-mail: admission@butler.edu
Web site: http://www.butler.edu
SAT Code: 1073 ACT Code: 1180

LD program name: Michele Atterson, M.A,
LD program telephone: 317 940-9308
LD program e-mail: matterso@butler.edu
LD program enrollment: 52, Total campus enrollment: 3,722

GENERAL

Butler University is a private, coed, four-year institution. 290-acre, suburban campus five miles from the center of Indianapolis (population: 781,870). Served by air, bus, and train. School operates transportation to local shopping centers. Public transportation serves campus. Semester system.

LD ADMISSIONS

Students do not complete a separate application and are not simultaneously accepted to the LD program. A member of the LD program does not sit on the admissions committee. High school waivers are accepted for foreign language. A personal interview is not required. Essay is required and may be typed. All accommodation requests are individually considered on a case by case basis.

SECONDARY SCHOOL REQUIREMENTS

Graduation from secondary school required; GED accepted. The following course distribution required: 4 units of English, 3 units of math, 3 units of science, 2 units of foreign language, 2 units of history, 2 units of academic electives.

TESTING

SAT Reasoning or ACT required. SAT Subject required.

All enrolled freshmen (fall 2004):

Average SAT I Scores:	Verbal: 581	Math: 593
Average ACT Scores:	Composite: 27	

Child Study Team report is not required. A neuropsychological or comprehensive psycho-educational evaluation is required for admission. Tests required as part of this documentation:

- ■ WAIS-IV
- ■ WISC-IV
- ■ SATA
- ■ Woodcock-Johnson
- ■ Nelson-Denny Reading Test
- ■ Other

UNDERGRADUATE STUDENT BODY

Total undergraduate student enrollment: 1,267 Men, 2,157 Women.

Composition of student body (fall 2004):

	Undergraduate	Freshmen
International	3.0	2.0
Black	3.1	3.8
American Indian	0.1	0.2
Asian-American	1.2	1.8
Hispanic	1.7	1.6
White	86.3	85.7
Unreported	4.5	5.0
	100.0%	100.0%

40% are from out of state. 22% join a fraternity and 25% join a sorority. Average age of full-time undergraduates is 20. 53% of classes have fewer than 20 students, 44% have between 20 and 50 students, 4% have more than 50 students.

STUDENT HOUSING

95% of freshmen live in college housing. Freshmen are required to live on campus. Housing is guaranteed for all undergraduates. Campus can house 1,587 undergraduates. Single rooms are available for students with medical or special needs. A medical note is required.

EXPENSES

Tuition (2005-06): $23,530 per year. $19,990 per year, $21,360 (pharmacy and physician assistant programs).

Room: $3,980. Board: $4,190.

There is no additional cost for LD program/services.

LD SERVICES

LD program size is not limited.

LD services available to:

■ Freshmen ■ Sophomores ■ Juniors ■ Seniors

Academic Accommodations

Curriculum		**In class**	
Foreign language waiver	☐	Early syllabus	☐
Lighter course load	■	Note takers in class	■
Math waiver	☐	Priority seating	■
Other special classes	☐	Tape recorders	■
Priority registrations	■	Videotaped classes	☐
Substitution of courses	■	Text on tape	■
Exams		**Services**	
Extended time	■	Diagnostic tests	☐
Oral exams	☐	Learning centers	■
Take home exams	☐	Proofreaders	☐
Exams on tape or computer	■	Readers	■
Untimed exams	☐	Reading Machines/Kurzweil	■
Other accommodations	■	Special bookstore section	☐
		Typists	■

Credit toward degree is not given for remedial courses taken.

Counseling Services

- ■ Academic
- ■ Psychological
- ☐ Student Support groups
- ☐ Vocational

Tutoring

Individual tutoring is available weekly.

Average size of tutoring groups: 1

	Individual	Group
Time management	■	☐
Organizational skills	■	☐
Learning strategies	■	☐
Study skills	■	☐
Content area	■	☐
Writing lab	■	☐
Math lab	■	☐

LD PROGRAM STAFF

Total number of LD Program staff (including director):

Full Time: 2 Part Time: 2

There is an advisor/advocate from the LD program available to students.

Key staff person available to work with LD students: Linda Brooks Williams, M.S.ED., Learning Disabilities Specialist.

Manchester College

North Manchester, IN

Address: 604 E. College Avenue, North Manchester, IN, 46962
Admissions telephone: 800 852-3648
Admissions FAX: 260 982-5239
Director of Admissions: Jolane Rohr
Admissions e-mail: admitinfo@manchester.edu
Web site: http://www.manchester.edu
SAT Code: 1440 ACT Code: 1222

Total campus enrollment: 1,056

GENERAL

Manchester College is a private, coed, four-year institution. 124-acre campus in North Manchester (population: 6,260), 35 miles from Fort Wayne. Major airport serves Fort Wayne; bus and train serve Warsaw (30 miles). 4-1-4 system.

LD ADMISSIONS

Students do not complete a separate application and are simultaneously accepted to the LD program. A member of the LD program does sit on the admissions committee. A personal interview is recommended. Essay is not required.

SECONDARY SCHOOL REQUIREMENTS

Graduation from secondary school required; GED accepted. The following course distribution required: 4 units of English, 2 units of math, 2 units of science, 2 units of foreign language, 2 units of social studies, 1 unit of history, 1 unit of academic electives.

TESTING

SAT Reasoning or ACT required. SAT Subject recommended.

All enrolled freshmen (fall 2004):

Average SAT I Scores: Verbal: 510 Math: 516
Average ACT Scores: Composite: 22

Child Study Team report is not required. A neuropsychological or comprehensive psycho-educational evaluation is required for admission. Tests required as part of this documentation:

- ☐ WAIS-IV
- ☐ WISC-IV
- ☐ SATA
- ☐ Woodcock-Johnson
- ☐ Nelson-Denny Reading Test
- ☐ Other

UNDERGRADUATE STUDENT BODY

Total undergraduate student enrollment: 508 Men, 627 Women.

Composition of student body (fall 2004):

	Undergraduate	Freshmen
International	4.7	6.9
Black	3.2	3.0
American Indian	1.1	0.7
Asian-American	1.4	0.8
Hispanic	1.1	2.0
White	87.7	86.2
Unreported	0.7	0.4
	100.0%	100.0%

11% are from out of state. Average age of full-time undergraduates is 20. 56% of classes have fewer than 20 students, 44% have between 20 and 50 students.

STUDENT HOUSING

95% of freshmen live in college housing. Housing is guaranteed for all undergraduates. Single rooms are available for students with medical or special needs. A medical note is required.

EXPENSES

Tuition (2005-06): $18,750 per year.
Room: $4,250. Board: $2,600.
There is no additional cost for LD program/services.

LD SERVICES

LD program size is not limited.

LD services available to:

☐ Freshmen ☐ Sophomores ☐ Juniors ☐ Seniors

Academic Accommodations

Curriculum		**In class**	
Foreign language waiver	☐	Early syllabus	☐
Lighter course load	☒	Note takers in class	☒
Math waiver	☐	Priority seating	☐
Other special classes	☐	Tape recorders	☒
Priority registrations	☐	Videotaped classes	☐
Substitution of courses	☐	Text on tape	☐
Exams		**Services**	
Extended time	☒	Diagnostic tests	☐
Oral exams	☒	Learning centers	☒
Take home exams	☐	Proofreaders	☐
Exams on tape or computer	☐	Readers	☒
Untimed exams	☒	Reading Machines/Kurzweil	☐
Other accommodations	☐	Special bookstore section	☐
		Typists	☐

Credit toward degree is not given for remedial courses taken.

Counseling Services

- ☐ Academic
- ☐ Psychological
- ☐ Student Support groups
- ☐ Vocational

Tutoring

Individual tutoring is available.

	Individual	Group
Time management	☐	☒
Organizational skills	☐	☒
Learning strategies	☐	☒
Study skills	☒	☒
Content area	☒	☒
Writing lab	☒	☒
Math lab	☒	☒

LD PROGRAM STAFF

Total number of LD Program staff (including director):

Full Time: 1 Part Time: 1

Key staff person available to work with LD students: Denise Howe, Learning Center Director.

Indiana Wesleyan University

Marion, IN

Address: 4201 S. Washington Street, Marion, IN, 46953-4999
Admissions telephone: 800 332-6901
Admissions FAX: 765 677-2333
Vice President for Enrollment Management: Dr. John S. Gredy
Admissions e-mail: admissions@indwes.edu
Web site: http://www.indwes.edu
SAT Code: 1446 ACT Code: 1226

Director of Student Support Services: Jerry Harrell
LD program telephone: 765 677-2257
LD program e-mail: csss@indwes.edu
Total campus enrollment: 7,609

GENERAL

Indiana Wesleyan University is a private, coed, four-year institution. 132-acre campus in Marion (population: 31,320), 60 miles from Indianapolis; branch campuses in Fort Wayne and Indianapolis. Served by bus and train; major airport serves Indianapolis. Public transportation serves campus. Semester system.

LD ADMISSIONS

A personal interview is recommended. Essay is not required. Admissions requirements that may be waived for LD students are determined upon request.

SECONDARY SCHOOL REQUIREMENTS

Graduation from secondary school required; GED accepted.

TESTING

SAT Reasoning or ACT required.

All enrolled freshmen (fall 2004):

Average SAT I Scores: Verbal: 549 Math: 540
Average ACT Scores: Composite: 24

Child Study Team report is not required. Tests required as part of this documentation:

☐ WAIS-IV ☐ Woodcock-Johnson
☐ WISC-IV ☐ Nelson-Denny Reading Test
☐ SATA ☐ Other

UNDERGRADUATE STUDENT BODY

Total undergraduate student enrollment: 1,918 Men, 3,302 Women.

Composition of student body (fall 2004):

	Undergraduate	Freshmen
International	0.1	0.3
Black	10.7	13.1
American Indian	0.6	0.4
Asian-American	0.3	0.8
Hispanic	2.3	1.7
White	83.2	80.1
Unreported	2.8	3.6
	100.0%	100.0%

STUDENT HOUSING

Housing is guaranteed for all undergraduates. This applies to the main campus in Marion (approximately 2700 students). Campus can house 2,000 undergraduates.

EXPENSES

Tuition (2005-06): $16,184 per year.
Room: $2,800. Board: $3,090.

There is no additional cost for LD program/services.

LD SERVICES

LD program size is not limited.

LD services available to:

☐ Freshmen ☐ Sophomores ☐ Juniors ☐ Seniors

Academic Accommodations

Curriculum		**In class**	
Foreign language waiver	☐	Early syllabus	☐
Lighter course load	☐	Note takers in class	■
Math waiver	☐	Priority seating	☐
Other special classes	☐	Tape recorders	■
Priority registrations	☐	Videotaped classes	■
Substitution of courses	☐	Text on tape	☐
Exams		**Services**	
Extended time	■	Diagnostic tests	☐
Oral exams	■	Learning centers	■
Take home exams	☐	Proofreaders	☐
Exams on tape or computer	☐	Readers	■
Untimed exams	■	Reading Machines/Kurzweil	■
Other accommodations	☐	Special bookstore section	☐
		Typists	☐

Credit toward degree is not given for remedial courses taken.

Counseling Services

☐ Academic
☐ Psychological
☐ Student Support groups
☐ Vocational

Tutoring

	Individual	Group
Time management	☐	☐
Organizational skills	☐	☐
Learning strategies	☐	☐
Study skills	☐	☐
Content area	☐	☐
Writing lab	☐	☐
Math lab	☐	☐

LD PROGRAM STAFF

Total number of LD Program staff (including director):

Full Time: 4 Part Time: 4

Key staff person available to work with LD students: Jerry Harrell, Director of Student Support Services.

Marian College

Indianapolis, IN

Address: 3200 Cold Spring Road, Indianapolis, IN, 46222
Admissions telephone: 800 772-7264
Admissions FAX: 317 955-6401
Vice President for Enrollment Management: Mrs. Luann Brames
Admissions e-mail: admissions@marian.edu
Web site: http://www.marian.edu
SAT Code: 1442

Director, Academic Support Services: Marjorie Batic
LD program telephone: 317 955-6150
LD program e-mail: mbatic@marian.edu
Total campus enrollment: 1,271

GENERAL

Marian College is a private, coed, four-year institution. 114-acre, suburban campus in Indianapolis (population: 781,870). Served by air, bus, and train. Public transportation serves campus. Semester system.

SECONDARY SCHOOL REQUIREMENTS

Graduation from secondary school required; GED accepted. The following course distribution required: 4 units of English, 2 units of math, 2 units of science, 2 units of foreign language, 1 unit of social studies, 1 unit of history, 9 units of academic electives.

TESTING

SAT Reasoning or ACT required.

Child Study Team report is not required. Tests required as part of this documentation:

- [ ] WAIS-IV
- [ ] WISC-IV
- [ ] SATA
- [ ] Woodcock-Johnson
- [ ] Nelson-Denny Reading Test
- [ ] Other

UNDERGRADUATE STUDENT BODY

Total undergraduate student enrollment: 318 Men, 953 Women.

6% are from out of state.

STUDENT HOUSING

Housing is guaranteed for all undergraduates. Campus can house 554 undergraduates.

EXPENSES

Tuition (2005-06): $18,400 per year.

Room & Board: $6,300.

There is no additional cost for LD program/services.

LD SERVICES

LD program size is not limited.

LD services available to:

- [ ] Freshmen
- [ ] Sophomores
- [ ] Juniors
- [ ] Seniors

Academic Accommodations

Curriculum		In class	
Foreign language waiver	[ ]	Early syllabus	[ ]
Lighter course load	[x]	Note takers in class	[x]
Math waiver	[ ]	Priority seating	[ ]
Other special classes	[x]	Tape recorders	[ ]
Priority registrations	[ ]	Videotaped classes	[ ]
Substitution of courses	[ ]	Text on tape	[ ]
Exams		**Services**	
Extended time	[x]	Diagnostic tests	[x]
Oral exams	[ ]	Learning centers	[x]
Take home exams	[ ]	Proofreaders	[ ]
Exams on tape or computer	[ ]	Readers	[x]
Untimed exams	[x]	Reading Machines/Kurzweil	[ ]
Other accommodations	[ ]	Special bookstore section	[ ]
		Typists	[ ]

Credit toward degree is not given for remedial courses taken.

Counseling Services

- [ ] Academic
- [ ] Psychological
- [ ] Student Support groups
- [ ] Vocational

Tutoring

	Individual	Group
Time management	[ ]	[ ]
Organizational skills	[ ]	[ ]
Learning strategies	[ ]	[ ]
Study skills	[ ]	[ ]
Content area	[ ]	[ ]
Writing lab	[ ]	[ ]
Math lab	[ ]	[ ]

LD PROGRAM STAFF

Total number of LD Program staff (including director):

Full Time: 2 Part Time: 2

Key staff person available to work with LD students: Marjorie Batic, Director, Academic Support Services.

DePauw University

Greencastle, IN

Address: 313 S. Locust Street, Greencastle, IN, 46135
Admissions telephone: 800 447-2495
Admissions FAX: 765 658-4007
Vice President for Admission and Financial Aid: Ms. Madeleine Eagon
Admissions e-mail: admission@depauw.edu
Web site: http://www.depauw.edu
SAT Code: 1166 ACT Code: 1184

LD program name: Student Academic Support Services
LD program address: 302 Harrison Hall, DePauw University
ADA Coordinator: Diane D. Hightower
LD program telephone: 765 658-4027
LD program e-mail: dhightower@depauw.edu
LD program enrollment: 50, Total campus enrollment: 2,391

GENERAL

DePauw University is a private, coed, four-year institution. 175-acre, suburban campus in Greencastle (population: 9,880), 40 miles west of Indianapolis. Major airport and bus serve Indianapolis; train serves Crawfordsville (30 miles). School operates transportation to airport and bus station. 4-1-4 system.

LD ADMISSIONS

SECONDARY SCHOOL REQUIREMENTS

Graduation from secondary school required; GED accepted.

TESTING

SAT Reasoning or ACT required. SAT Subject required.

All enrolled freshmen (fall 2004):

Average SAT I Scores:	Verbal: 605	Math: 610
Average ACT Scores:	Composite: 26	

Child Study Team report is not required. Tests required as part of this documentation:

- ☐ WAIS-IV
- ☐ WISC-IV
- ☐ SATA
- ☐ Woodcock-Johnson
- ☐ Nelson-Denny Reading Test
- ☐ Other

UNDERGRADUATE STUDENT BODY

Total undergraduate student enrollment: 969 Men, 1,250 Women.

Composition of student body (fall 2004):

	Undergraduate	Freshmen
International	0.8	1.8
Black	5.9	5.4
American Indian	0.8	0.4
Asian-American	2.4	2.2
Hispanic	2.6	3.1
White	86.5	85.9
Unreported	1.1	1.1
	100.0%	100.0%

45% are from out of state. 75% join a fraternity and 74% join a sorority. Average age of full-time undergraduates is 20. 64% of classes have fewer than 20 students, 36% have between 20 and 50 students.

STUDENT HOUSING

100% of freshmen live in college housing. Freshmen are required to live on campus. Housing is guaranteed for all undergraduates. Campus can house 1,380 undergraduates. Single rooms are available for students with medical or special needs. A medical note is required.

EXPENSES

Tuition (2005-06): $26,100 per year. $21,100 per year (freshmen, sophomores, and juniors), $20,150 (seniors).

Room: $3,900. Board: $3,600.

There is no additional cost for LD program/services.

LD SERVICES

LD program size is not limited.

LD services available to:

■ Freshmen ■ Sophomores ■ Juniors ■ Seniors

Academic Accommodations

Curriculum		In class	
Foreign language waiver	☐	Early syllabus	■
Lighter course load	■	Note takers in class	■
Math waiver	☐	Priority seating	■
Other special classes	☐	Tape recorders	■
Priority registrations	■	Videotaped classes	☐
Substitution of courses	☐	Text on tape	■
Exams		**Services**	
Extended time	■	Diagnostic tests	■
Oral exams	■	Learning centers	■
Take home exams	☐	Proofreaders	☐
Exams on tape or computer	■	Readers	■
Untimed exams	■	Reading Machines/Kurzweil	■
Other accommodations	■	Special bookstore section	☐
		Typists	■

Credit toward degree is not given for remedial courses taken.

Counseling Services

- ■ Academic
- ■ Psychological
- ■ Student Support groups
- ☐ Vocational

Tutoring

Individual tutoring is available daily.

Average size of tutoring groups: 8

	Individual	Group
Time management	■	■
Organizational skills	■	■
Learning strategies	■	■
Study skills	■	■
Content area	■	■
Writing lab	■	■
Math lab	■	■

UNIQUE LD PROGRAM FEATURES

Academic, psychological, and student support group counseling services are offered as needed and can vary from daily to weekly or monthly, depending on the identified need. All other LD services are available on an as needed basis based upon student needs.

LD PROGRAM STAFF

Total number of LD Program staff (including director):

Full Time: 1 Part Time: 1

There is an advisor/advocate from the LD program available to students. The advisor/advocate meets with faculty 1 time per month and students 20 times per month. 15 peer tutors are available to work with LD students.

Key staff person available to work with LD students: Diane D. Hightower, ADA Coordinator.

Ball State University

Muncie, IN

Address: 2000 University Avenue, Muncie, IN, 47306
Admissions telephone: 800 482-4BSU
Admissions FAX: 765 285-1632
Dean of Admissions and Enrollment Services: Dr. Larry Waters
Admissions e-mail: askus@bsu.edu
Web site: http://www.bsu.edu
SAT Code: 1051 ACT Code: 1176

Director, Disability Services: Richard Harris
LD program telephone: 765 285-5293
LD program e-mail: rharris@bsu.edu
LD program enrollment: 225, Total campus enrollment: 17,535

GENERAL

Ball State University is a public, coed, four-year institution. 955-acre campus in Muncie (population: 67,430), 56 miles from Indianapolis; satellite campuses in Brown County, Carmel, Fishers, Ft. Wayne, Indianapolis, Lafayette, Marion, New Castle, Noblesville, and Westfield. Served by bus and train; major airport serves Indianapolis; smaller airport serves Dayton (70 miles). School operates transportation to locations on campus. Public transportation serves campus. Semester system.

LD ADMISSIONS

A member of the LD program does not sit on the admissions committee. A personal interview is not required. Essay is not required.

SECONDARY SCHOOL REQUIREMENTS

Graduation from secondary school required; GED accepted. The following course distribution required: 4 units of English, 3 units of math, 3 units of science, 3 units of social studies.

TESTING

SAT Subject required.

All enrolled freshmen (fall 2004):

Average SAT I Scores:	Verbal: 523	Math: 527
Average ACT Scores:	Composite: 22	

Child Study Team report is not required. A neuropsychological or comprehensive psycho-education evaluation is not required for admission. Tests required as part of this documentation:

- ☐ WAIS-IV
- ☐ WISC-IV
- ☐ SATA
- ☐ Woodcock-Johnson
- ☐ Nelson-Denny Reading Test
- ☐ Other

UNDERGRADUATE STUDENT BODY

Total undergraduate student enrollment: 7,780 Men, 8,755 Women.

Composition of student body (fall 2004):

	Undergraduate	Freshmen
International	0.0	0.0
Black	8.1	7.0
American Indian	0.3	0.3
Asian-American	0.6	0.7
Hispanic	1.5	1.4
White	88.1	88.4
Unreported	1.3	2.3
	100.0%	100.0%

8% are from out of state. 8% join a fraternity and 10% join a sorority. Average age of full-time undergraduates is 21. 35% of classes have fewer than 20 students, 56% have between 20 and 50 students, 9% have more than 50 students.

STUDENT HOUSING

89% of freshmen live in college housing. Freshmen are required to live on campus. Housing is guaranteed for all undergraduates. Campus can house 6,173 undergraduates.

EXPENSES

Tuition (2005-06): $5,752 per year (in-state), $14,928 (out-of-state).

Room & Board: $6,328.

There is no additional cost for LD program/services.

LD SERVICES

LD program size is not limited.

LD services available to:

■ Freshmen ■ Sophomores ■ Juniors ■ Seniors

Academic Accommodations

Curriculum		In class	
Foreign language waiver	☐	Early syllabus	☐
Lighter course load	■	Note takers in class	■
Math waiver	☐	Priority seating	☐
Other special classes	☐	Tape recorders	■
Priority registrations	☐	Videotaped classes	☐
Substitution of courses	☐	Text on tape	☐
Exams		**Services**	
Extended time	■	Diagnostic tests	☐
Oral exams	■	Learning centers	■
Take home exams	☐	Proofreaders	☐
Exams on tape or computer	☐	Readers	■
Untimed exams	☐	Reading Machines/Kurzweil	■
Other accommodations	☐	Special bookstore section	☐
		Typists	☐

Credit toward degree is given for remedial courses taken.

Counseling Services

- ☐ Academic
- ☐ Psychological
- ☐ Student Support groups
- ☐ Vocational

Tutoring

Individual tutoring is available weekly.

Average size of tutoring groups: 1

	Individual	Group
Time management	☐	☐
Organizational skills	☐	☐
Learning strategies	☐	☐
Study skills	☐	☐
Content area	☐	☐
Writing lab	☐	☐
Math lab	☐	☐

LD PROGRAM STAFF

Total number of LD Program staff (including director):

Full Time: 3 Part Time: 3

There is an advisor/advocate from the LD program available to students.

Key staff person available to work with LD students: Dr. Jackie Harris, Coordinator of Academic Svcs for Students w/Dis.

University of Evansville

Evansville, IN

Address: 1800 Lincoln Avenue, Evansville, IN, 47722
Admissions telephone: 812 479-2468
Admissions FAX: 812 474-4076
Dean of Admissions: Dr. Tom Bear
Admissions e-mail: admission@evansville.edu
Web site: http://www.evansville.edu
SAT Code: 1208 ACT Code: 1188

LD program name: Counseling and Health Education
Director: Ms. Sylvia Buck, LCSW
LD program telephone: 812 488-2720
LD program e-mail: sb79@evansville.edu
LD program enrollment: 38, Total campus enrollment: 2, 632

GENERAL

University of Evansville is a private, coed, four-year institution. 75-acre, suburban campus in Evansville (population: 121,582); branch campus abroad in Grantham, England. Served by air and bus. Public transportation serves campus. Semester system.

LD ADMISSIONS

Application Deadline: 05/01. A member of the LD program does not sit on the admissions committee. A personal interview is not required. Essay is required and may be typed.

SECONDARY SCHOOL REQUIREMENTS

Graduation from secondary school required; GED accepted. The following course distribution required: 3 units of English, 2 units of math, 2 units of science, 2 units of foreign language.

TESTING

SAT Reasoning or ACT required. SAT Subject required.

All enrolled freshmen (fall 2004):

Average SAT I Scores:	Verbal: 575	Math: 568
Average ACT Scores:	Composite: 25	

Child Study Team report is not required. A neuropsychological or comprehensive psycho-educational evaluation is required for admission. Must be dated within 36 months of application. Tests required as part of this documentation:

- [x] WAIS-IV
- [x] WISC-IV
- [x] SATA
- [x] Woodcock-Johnson
- [x] Nelson-Denny Reading Test
- [ ] Other

UNDERGRADUATE STUDENT BODY

Total undergraduate student enrollment: 1,055 Men, 1,618 Women.

Composition of student body (fall 2004):

	Undergraduate	Freshmen
International	4.2	5.2
Black	2.4	2.2
American Indian	0.5	0.2
Asian-American	1.3	1.1
Hispanic	2.2	1.0
White	80.0	67.8
Unreported	9.4	22.4
	100.0%	100.0%

43% are from out of state. 28% join a fraternity and 23% join a sorority. Average age of full-time undergraduates is 20. 60% of classes have fewer than 20 students, 39% have between 20 and 50 students, 2% have more than 50 students.

STUDENT HOUSING

87% of freshmen live in college housing. Freshmen are required to live on campus. Housing is guaranteed for all undergraduates. Campus can house 1,789 undergraduates. Single rooms are available for students with medical or special needs. A medical note is required.

EXPENSES

Tuition (2005-06): $21,120 per year.
Room: $3,460. Board: $3,380.
There is no additional cost for LD program/services.

LD SERVICES

LD program size is not limited.

LD services available to:

- [x] Freshmen
- [x] Sophomores
- [x] Juniors
- [x] Seniors

Academic Accommodations

Curriculum

- [ ] Foreign language waiver
- [ ] Lighter course load
- [ ] Math waiver
- [ ] Other special classes
- [ ] Priority registrations
- [ ] Substitution of courses

Exams

- [x] Extended time
- [ ] Oral exams
- [ ] Take home exams
- [ ] Exams on tape or computer
- [ ] Untimed exams
- [x] Other accommodations

In class

- [ ] Early syllabus
- [x] Note takers in class
- [x] Priority seating
- [x] Tape recorders
- [ ] Videotaped classes
- [x] Text on tape

Services

- [ ] Diagnostic tests
- [ ] Learning centers
- [x] Proofreaders
- [ ] Readers
- [ ] Reading Machines/Kurzweil
- [ ] Special bookstore section
- [ ] Typists

Credit toward degree is not given for remedial courses taken.

Counseling Services

- [x] Academic
- [x] Psychological
- [ ] Student Support groups
- [ ] Vocational

Tutoring

Individual tutoring is available weekly.

	Individual	Group
Time management	[ ]	[ ]
Organizational skills	[ ]	[ ]
Learning strategies	[ ]	[ ]
Study skills	[ ]	[ ]
Content area	[ ]	[x]
Writing lab	[ ]	[x]
Math lab	[ ]	[ ]

LD PROGRAM STAFF

There is an advisor/advocate from the LD program available to students.

Key staff person available to work with LD students: Ms. Sylvia Buck, LCSW, Director of Counseling and Health Education.

Anderson University

Anderson, IN

Address: 1100 E. Fifth Street, Anderson, IN, 46012
Admissions telephone: 800 428-6414
Admissions FAX: 765 641-4091
Director of Admissions: Jim King
Admissions e-mail: info@anderson.edu
Web site: http://www.anderson.edu
SAT Code: 1016 ACT Code: 1174

LD program name: Office of Disabled Student Services/LD Program
Coordinator, LD Program: Teresa Coplin
LD program telephone: 765 641-4223
LD program e-mail: rsvogelgesang@anderson.edu
LD program enrollment: 47, Total campus enrollment: 2,270

GENERAL

Anderson University is a private, coed, four-year institution. 100-acre campus in Anderson (population: 59,734), 48 miles from Indianapolis. Served by bus; major airport and train serve Indianapolis. Public transportation serves campus. Semester system.

LD ADMISSIONS

Application Deadline: 08/01. Students do not complete a separate application and are simultaneously accepted to the LD program. A member of the LD program does sit on the admissions committee. High school waivers are accepted for foreign language. A personal interview is required. Essay is not required. May consider those students who do not meet standard AU scores (SAT/ACT scores; class rank).

For fall 2004, 24 completed self-identified LD applications were received. 16 applications were offered admission, and 12 enrolled.

SECONDARY SCHOOL REQUIREMENTS

Graduation from secondary school required; GED accepted. The following course distribution required: 4 units of English, 3 units of math, 3 units of science, 2 units of foreign language, 1 unit of social studies, 1 unit of history.

TESTING

SAT Reasoning or ACT required.

All enrolled freshmen (fall 2004):

Average SAT I Scores:	Verbal: 531	Math: 531
Average ACT Scores:	Composite: 23	

Child Study Team report is not required. Tests required as part of this documentation:

- ☑ WAIS-IV
- ☑ WISC-IV
- ☐ SATA
- ☐ Woodcock-Johnson
- ☐ Nelson-Denny Reading Test
- ☐ Other

UNDERGRADUATE STUDENT BODY

Total undergraduate student enrollment: 894 Men, 1,196 Women.

Composition of student body (fall 2004):

	Undergraduate	Freshmen
International	0.0	0.1
Black	5.9	7.0
American Indian	0.0	0.2
Asian-American	2.4	1.9
Hispanic	0.7	1.1
White	89.2	88.1
Unreported	1.9	1.5
	100.0%	100.0%

36% are from out of state. Average age of full-time undergraduates is 20. 51% of classes have fewer than 20 students, 45% have between 20 and 50 students, 4% have more than 50 students.

STUDENT HOUSING

90% of freshmen live in college housing. Freshmen are required to live on campus. Housing is guaranteed for all undergraduates. Campus can house 1,368 undergraduates. Single rooms are available for students with medical or special needs. A medical note is not required.

EXPENSES

Tuition (2005-06): $18,900 per year.

Room: $3,730. Board: $2,420.

There is no additional cost for LD program/services.

LD SERVICES

LD program size is not limited.

LD services available to:

☑ Freshmen ☑ Sophomores ☑ Juniors ☑ Seniors

Academic Accommodations

Curriculum		In class	
Foreign language waiver	☑	Early syllabus	☐
Lighter course load	☑	Note takers in class	☑
Math waiver	☐	Priority seating	☐
Other special classes	☑	Tape recorders	☑
Priority registrations	☐	Videotaped classes	☐
Substitution of courses	☐	Text on tape	☐
Exams		**Services**	
Extended time	☑	Diagnostic tests	☐
Oral exams	☑	Learning centers	☑
Take home exams	☐	Proofreaders	☑
Exams on tape or computer	☑	Readers	☑
Untimed exams	☑	Reading Machines/Kurzweil	☐
Other accommodations	☐	Special bookstore section	☐
		Typists	☑

Credit toward degree is not given for remedial courses taken.

Counseling Services

- ☑ Academic
- ☑ Psychological
- ☑ Student Support groups
- ☑ Vocational

Tutoring

Individual tutoring is available.

	Individual	Group
Time management	☑	☑
Organizational skills	☑	☑
Learning strategies	☑	☑
Study skills	☑	☑
Content area	☑	☑
Writing lab	☑	☐
Math lab	☐	☐

LD PROGRAM STAFF

Total number of LD Program staff (including director):

Full Time: 1 Part Time: 1

There is an advisor/advocate from the LD program available to students.

Key staff person available to work with LD students: Rinda Vogelgesang, Director, Disabled Student Services.

LD Program web site: http://www.anderson.edu/kissinger/dss.html

University of Southern Indiana

Evansville, IN

Address: 8600 University Boulevard, Evansville, IN, 47712
Admissions telephone: 800 467-1965
Admissions FAX: 812 465-7154
Director of Admission: Mr. Eric Otto
Admissions e-mail: enroll@usi.edu
Web site: http://www.usi.edu
SAT Code: 1335 ACT Code: 1207

LD program name: Counseling Center
Assistant Director of Counseling: Leslie M. Smith
LD program telephone: 812 464-1867
LD program e-mail: lmsmith@usi.edu
LD program enrollment: 275, Total campus enrollment: 9,217

GENERAL

University of Southern Indiana is a public, coed, four-year institution. 300-acre campus in Evansville (population: 121,582), 112 miles from Louisville, Ky. Served by air, bus, and train. School operates transportation to local public transportation system. Semester system.

LD ADMISSIONS

Students complete a separate application and are not simultaneously accepted to the LD program. A member of the LD program does not sit on the admissions committee. A personal interview is recommended. Essay is not required.

For fall 2004, 275 completed self-identified LD applications were received.

SECONDARY SCHOOL REQUIREMENTS

Graduation from secondary school required; GED accepted.

TESTING

SAT Reasoning or ACT required. SAT Subject recommended.

All enrolled freshmen (fall 2004):

Average SAT I Scores: Verbal: 473 Math: 476
Average ACT Scores: Composite: 19

Child Study Team report is not required. A neuropsychological or comprehensive psycho-educational evaluation is required for admission. Must be dated within 60 months of application. Tests required as part of this documentation:

- ☑ WAIS-IV
- ☑ WISC-IV
- ☑ SATA
- ☑ Woodcock-Johnson
- ☑ Nelson-Denny Reading Test
- ☐ Other

UNDERGRADUATE STUDENT BODY

Total undergraduate student enrollment: 3,533 Men, 5,250 Women.

Composition of student body (fall 2004):

	Undergraduate	Freshmen
International	0.3	0.5
Black	5.8	4.6
American Indian	0.4	0.2
Asian-American	0.7	0.6
Hispanic	1.1	0.7
White	91.7	93.4
Unreported	0.0	0.0
	100.0%	100.0%

10% are from out of state. 4% join a fraternity and 3% join a sorority. Average age of full-time undergraduates is 21. 37% of classes have fewer than 20 students, 58% have between 20 and 50 students, 6% have more than 50 students.

STUDENT HOUSING

63% of freshmen live in college housing. Freshmen are not required to live on campus. Housing is guaranteed for all undergraduates. Campus can house 3,227 undergraduates. Single rooms are available for students with medical or special needs. A medical note is required.

EXPENSES

Tuition (2005-06): $4,244 per year (in-state), $10,118 (out-of-state).
Room: $3,170. Board: $2,580.
There is no additional cost for LD program/services.

LD SERVICES

LD program size is not limited.

LD services available to:

☑ Freshmen ☑ Sophomores ☑ Juniors ☑ Seniors

Academic Accommodations

Curriculum		**In class**	
Foreign language waiver	☐	Early syllabus	☐
Lighter course load	☐	Note takers in class	☑
Math waiver	☐	Priority seating	☑
Other special classes	☐	Tape recorders	☐
Priority registrations	☑	Videotaped classes	☐
Substitution of courses	☑	Text on tape	☑
Exams		**Services**	
Extended time	☑	Diagnostic tests	☐
Oral exams	☑	Learning centers	☑
Take home exams	☐	Proofreaders	☐
Exams on tape or computer	☑	Readers	☑
Untimed exams	☐	Reading Machines/Kurzweil	☐
Other accommodations	☑	Special bookstore section	☐
		Typists	☑

Credit toward degree is not given for remedial courses taken.

Counseling Services

- ☐ Academic
- ☑ Psychological
- ☐ Student Support groups
- ☐ Vocational

Tutoring

Individual tutoring is not available.

	Individual	Group
Time management	☐	☑
Organizational skills	☐	☑
Learning strategies	☐	☑
Study skills	☐	☑
Content area	☐	☑
Writing lab	☐	☑
Math lab	☐	☑

LD PROGRAM STAFF

There is an advisor/advocate from the LD program available to students.

Key staff person available to work with LD students: Leslie M. Smith, Assistant Director of Counseling.

LD Program web site: www.usi.edu

Indiana State University

Terre Haute, IN

Address: 210 N. Seventh Street, Terre Haute, IN, 47809
Admissions telephone: 800 742-0891
Admissions FAX: 812 237-8023
Director of Admissions: Richard Toomey
Admissions e-mail: admissions@indstate.edu
Web site: http://web.indstate.edu/
SAT Code: 1322 ACT Code: 1206

LD program name: Student Support Services
LD program address: 204A Gillum Hall
Director, Student Support Services: Rita Worrall
LD program telephone: 812 237-2300
LD program e-mail: sacworra@isugw.indstate.edu
LD program enrollment: 135, Total campus enrollment: 9,321

GENERAL

Indiana State University is a public, coed, four-year institution. 92-acre campus in Terre Haute (population: 59,614). Served by air and bus; major airport and train serve Indianapolis (75 miles). Public transportation serves campus. Semester system.

LD ADMISSIONS

Students complete a separate application and are not simultaneously accepted to the LD program. A member of the LD program does not sit on the admissions committee. A personal interview is recommended. Essay is not required.

SECONDARY SCHOOL REQUIREMENTS

Graduation from secondary school required; GED accepted. The following course distribution required: 8 units of English, 8 units of math, 6 units of science, 2 units of foreign language, 4 units of social studies, 2 units of history, 4 units of academic electives.

TESTING

SAT Reasoning or ACT required. SAT Subject required.

All enrolled freshmen (fall 2004):

Average SAT I Scores: Verbal: 474 Math: 477
Average ACT Scores: Composite: 20

Child Study Team report is not required. A neuropsychological or comprehensive psycho-educational evaluation is required for admission. Tests required as part of this documentation:

- ■ WAIS-IV
- ■ WISC-IV
- ☐ SATA
- ■ Woodcock-Johnson
- ☐ Nelson-Denny Reading Test
- ☐ Other

UNDERGRADUATE STUDENT BODY

Total undergraduate student enrollment: 4,587 Men, 5,147 Women.

Composition of student body (fall 2004):

	Undergraduate	Freshmen
International	1.3	1.6
Black	13.1	12.0
American Indian	0.5	0.4
Asian-American	1.1	0.7
Hispanic	1.1	1.2
White	79.4	81.6
Unreported	3.5	2.6
	100.0%	100.0%

7% are from out of state. 13% join a fraternity and 9% join a sorority. Average age of full-time undergraduates is 22. 49% of classes have fewer than 20 students, 46% have between 20 and 50 students, 6% have more than 50 students.

STUDENT HOUSING

67% of freshmen live in college housing. Freshmen are required to live on campus. Housing is guaranteed for all undergraduates. Campus can house 4,150 undergraduates. Single rooms are available for students with medical or special needs. A medical note is required.

EXPENSES

Tuition (2005-06): $5,756 per year (in-state), $11,672 (out-of-state).
Room: $2,972-$3,150. Board: $2,643-$2,788.
There is no additional cost for LD program/services.

LD SERVICES

LD program size is not limited.

LD services available to:

■ Freshmen ■ Sophomores ■ Juniors ■ Seniors

Academic Accommodations

Curriculum		In class	
Foreign language waiver	☐	Early syllabus	☐
Lighter course load	■	Note takers in class	■
Math waiver	☐	Priority seating	☐
Other special classes	☐	Tape recorders	☐
Priority registrations	☐	Videotaped classes	☐
Substitution of courses	☐	Text on tape	☐
Exams		**Services**	
Extended time	■	Diagnostic tests	☐
Oral exams	■	Learning centers	■
Take home exams	☐	Proofreaders	☐
Exams on tape or computer	☐	Readers	■
Untimed exams	☐	Reading Machines/Kurzweil	☐
Other accommodations	☐	Special bookstore section	☐
		Typists	☐

Credit toward degree is not given for remedial courses taken.

Counseling Services

- ☐ Academic
- ☐ Psychological
- ☐ Student Support groups
- ☐ Vocational

Tutoring

Individual tutoring is available daily.

	Individual	Group
Time management	■	☐
Organizational skills	■	☐
Learning strategies	■	☐
Study skills	■	☐
Content area	■	☐
Writing lab	■	☐
Math lab	■	☐

LD PROGRAM STAFF

Total number of LD Program staff (including director):

Full Time: 3 Part Time: 3

There is an advisor/advocate from the LD program available to students. 1 graduate student and 30 peer tutors are available to work with LD students.

Key staff person available to work with LD students: Rita Worrall, Director, Student Support Services.

Huntington College

Huntington, IN

Address: 2303 College Avenue, Huntington, IN, 46750
Admissions telephone: 800 642-6493
Admissions FAX: 260 358-3699
Vice President of Enrollment Management: Jeff Berggren
Admissions e-mail: admissions@huntington.edu
Web site: http://www.huntington.edu
SAT Code: 1304 ACT Code: 1202

LD program name: Learning Center
Director of Learning Assistance: Kris Chafin
LD program telephone: 260 359-4290
LD program e-mail: kchafin@huntington.edu
LD program enrollment: 8, Total campus enrollment: 915

GENERAL

Huntington College is a private, coed, four-year institution. 170-acre campus in Huntington (population: 17,450), 20 miles from Ft. Wayne. Served by air and bus; major airport and train serve Ft. Wayne. School operates transportation to airports. 4-1-4 system.

LD ADMISSIONS

A member of the LD program does not sit on the admissions committee.

SECONDARY SCHOOL REQUIREMENTS

Graduation from secondary school required; GED accepted. The following course distribution required: 4 units of English, 2 units of math, 2 units of science, 2 units of foreign language, 3 units of social studies, 2 units of history.

TESTING

SAT Reasoning or ACT required. SAT Subject recommended.

All enrolled freshmen (fall 2004):

Average SAT I Scores: Verbal: 500 Math: 540
Average ACT Scores: Composite: 24

Child Study Team report is not required. A neuropsychological or comprehensive psycho-educational evaluation is required for admission. Tests required as part of this documentation:

- ☐ WAIS-IV
- ☐ WISC-IV
- ☐ SATA
- ☐ Woodcock-Johnson
- ☐ Nelson-Denny Reading Test
- ☐ Other

UNDERGRADUATE STUDENT BODY

Total undergraduate student enrollment: 401 Men, 567 Women.

Composition of student body (fall 2004):

	Undergraduate	Freshmen
International	0.9	2.4
Black	0.9	0.9
American Indian	0.0	0.1
Asian-American	2.3	1.0
Hispanic	0.5	0.6
White	95.4	95.0
Unreported	0.0	0.0
	100.0%	100.0%

40% are from out of state. Average age of full-time undergraduates is 19. 72% of classes have fewer than 20 students, 28% have between 20 and 50 students.

STUDENT HOUSING

91% of freshmen live in college housing. Freshmen are required to live on campus. Housing is guaranteed for all undergraduates. Single rooms are available for students with medical or special needs. A medical note is required.

EXPENSES

Tuition (2005-06): $18,060 per year.
Room & Board: $6,340.

There is no additional cost for LD program/services.

LD SERVICES

LD program size is not limited.

LD services available to:

☒ Freshmen ☒ Sophomores ☒ Juniors ☒ Seniors

Academic Accommodations

Curriculum		**In class**	
Foreign language waiver	☐	Early syllabus	☐
Lighter course load	☐	Note takers in class	☒
Math waiver	☐	Priority seating	☒
Other special classes	☐	Tape recorders	☐
Priority registrations	☒	Videotaped classes	☐
Substitution of courses	☐	Text on tape	☒
Exams		**Services**	
Extended time	☒	Diagnostic tests	☐
Oral exams	☒	Learning centers	☒
Take home exams	☐	Proofreaders	☒
Exams on tape or computer	☒	Readers	☒
Untimed exams	☐	Reading Machines/Kurzweil	☐
Other accommodations	☐	Special bookstore section	☐
		Typists	☒

Credit toward degree is not given for remedial courses taken.

Counseling Services

- ☒ Academic
- ☒ Psychological
- ☐ Student Support groups
- ☒ Vocational

Tutoring

Individual tutoring is available weekly.

Average size of tutoring groups: 2

	Individual	Group
Time management	☒	☐
Organizational skills	☒	☐
Learning strategies	☐	☐
Study skills	☒	☐
Content area	☒	☐
Writing lab	☐	☐
Math lab	☐	☐

UNIQUE LD PROGRAM FEATURES

Any student with a disability not just students with LD may rquest accommadations. Accommodations are provided based on the student's individual needs, as supported in the student's documentation.

LD PROGRAM STAFF

There is an advisor/advocate from the LD program available to students.

Key staff person available to work with LD students: Kris Chafin, Director of Learning Assistance.

Ivy Tech State College-Southwest

Evansville, IN

Address: 3501 First Avenue, Evansville, IN 47710
Admissions telephone: 812 429-1435
Admissions FAX: 812 429-9878
Director of Admissions: Denise Johnson Kincaid
Web site: http://www.ivytech.edu/evansville
SAT Code: 1277

LD program name: Disability Support Services
DSS/Professor of Skills Advancement: Peg Ehlen
LD program telephone: 812 429-1386
LD program e-mail: pehlen@ivytech.edu
LD program enrollment: 49, Total campus enrollment: 5,500

GENERAL

Ivy Tech College-Southwest is a public, two-year institution. Campus is in Evansville (population: 126,000). Served by air and bus. Public transportation serves campus. Semester system.

LD ADMISSIONS

Students do not complete a separate application and are not simultaneously accepted to the LD program. A member of the LD program does not sit on the admissions committee. Personal interview and Essay are not required.

SECONDARY SCHOOL REQUIREMENTS

Graduation from secondary school required; GED accepted.

TESTING

Child Study Team report is not required. A neuropsychological or comprehensive psycho-educational evaluation is required for admission. Tests required as part of this documentation:

- ☒ WAIS-IV
- ☐ WISC-IV
- ☐ SATA
- ☒ Woodcock-Johnson
- ☐ Nelson-Denny Reading Test
- ☐ Other

UNDERGRADUATE STUDENT BODY

Composition of student body (fall 2004):

	Undergraduate	Freshmen
International	0.0	0.0
Black	0.0	0.0
American Indian	0.0	0.0
Asian-American	0.0	0.0
Hispanic	0.0	0.0
White	0.0	0.0
Unreported	0.0	0.0
	100.0%	100.0%

STUDENT HOUSING

There is no student housing available.

EXPENSES

Tuition (2005-06): $83.95 per credit hour.

There is no additional cost for LD program/services.

LD SERVICES

LD program size is not limited.

LD services available to:

☒ Freshmen ☒ Sophomores ☒ Juniors ☒ Seniors

Academic Accommodations

Curriculum		In class	
Foreign language waiver	☐	Early syllabus	☒
Lighter course load	☐	Note takers in class	☒
Math waiver	☐	Priority seating	☐
Other special classes	☐	Tape recorders	☐
Priority registrations	☐	Videotaped classes	☐
Substitution of courses	☐	Text on tape	☒
Exams		**Services**	
Extended time	☒	Diagnostic tests	☐
Oral exams	☒	Learning centers	☒
Take home exams	☐	Proofreaders	☐
Exams on tape or computer	☒	Readers	☐
Untimed exams	☐	Reading Machines/Kurzweil	☒
Other accommodations	☒	Special bookstore section	☐
		Typists	☐

Credit toward degree is not given for remedial courses taken.

Counseling Services

- ☒ Academic
- ☐ Psychological
- ☐ Student Support groups
- ☐ Vocational

Meets 3 times per academic year

Tutoring

	Individual	Group
Time management	☐	☐
Organizational skills	☐	☐
Learning strategies	☐	☐
Study skills	☐	☐
Content area	☐	☐
Writing lab	☒	☒
Math lab	☒	☒

LD PROGRAM STAFF

There is an advisor/advocate from the LD program available to students.

Key staff person available to work with LD students: Peg Ehlen, Disability Support Services/Professor of Skills Advancement

Briar Cliff University

Sioux City, IA

Address: 3303 Rebecca Street, Box 2100, Sioux City, IA, 51104
Admissions telephone: 800 662-3303
Admissions FAX: 712 279-1632
Vice President for Enrollment Management: Sharisue Wilcoxon
Admissions e-mail: admissions@briarcliff.edu
Web site: http://www.briarcliff.edu
SAT Code: 6046 ACT Code: 1276

Director of Student Support Services: Sister Jean Beringer
LD program telephone: 712 279-5232
LD program e-mail: jean.beringer@briarcliff.edu
LD program enrollment: 7, Total campus enrollment: 1,084

GENERAL

Briar Cliff University is a private, coed, four-year institution. 70-acre campus in Sioux City (population: 85,013), 90 miles from Omaha, NE; branch campuses in Algona, Denison, and Storm Lake. Served by air and bus; major airport and train serve Omaha. Public transportation serves campus. Trimester system.

LD ADMISSIONS

A personal interview is required. Essay is not required.

For fall 2004, 2 completed self-identified LD applications were received. 2 applications were offered admission, and 2 enrolled.

SECONDARY SCHOOL REQUIREMENTS

Graduation from secondary school required; GED accepted.

TESTING

ACT required; SAT Reasoning may be substituted. SAT Subject recommended.

All enrolled freshmen (fall 2004):

Average SAT I Scores:	Verbal: 514	Math: 456
Average ACT Scores:	Composite: 22	

Child Study Team report is not required. Tests required as part of this documentation:

- ☐ WAIS-IV
- ☐ WISC-IV
- ☐ SATA
- ☐ Woodcock-Johnson
- ☐ Nelson-Denny Reading Test
- ☐ Other

UNDERGRADUATE STUDENT BODY

Total undergraduate student enrollment: 1,084.

Composition of student body (fall 2004):

	Undergraduate	Freshmen
International	0.4	0.3
Black	3.9	2.2
American Indian	0.1	1.1
Asian-American	0.8	1.2
Hispanic	3.9	3.4
White	90.9	91.8
Unreported	0.0	0.0
	100.0%	100.0%

29% are from out of state. Average age of full-time undergraduates is 23. 63% of classes have fewer than 20 students, 35% have between 20 and 50 students, 2% have more than 50 students.

STUDENT HOUSING

85% of freshmen live in college housing. Freshmen are required to live on campus. Housing is guaranteed for all undergraduates. Campus can house 565 undergraduates.

EXPENSES

Tuition (2005-06): $17,490 per year.

Room: $2,760. Board: $2,805.
There is no additional cost for LD program/services.

LD SERVICES

LD program size is not limited.

LD services available to:

☐ Freshmen ☐ Sophomores ☐ Juniors ☐ Seniors

Academic Accommodations

Curriculum		**In class**	
Foreign language waiver	☐	Early syllabus	☐
Lighter course load	☒	Note takers in class	☒
Math waiver	☐	Priority seating	☐
Other special classes	☐	Tape recorders	☒
Priority registrations	☒	Videotaped classes	☐
Substitution of courses	☐	Text on tape	☐
Exams		**Services**	
Extended time	☒	Diagnostic tests	☐
Oral exams	☒	Learning centers	☐
Take home exams	☐	Proofreaders	☐
Exams on tape or computer	☐	Readers	☐
Untimed exams	☐	Reading Machines/Kurzweil	☒
Other accommodations	☒	Special bookstore section	☐
		Typists	☐

Credit toward degree is given for remedial courses taken.

Counseling Services

- ☐ Academic
- ☐ Psychological
- ☐ Student Support groups
- ☐ Vocational

Tutoring

Individual tutoring is available weekly.

Average size of tutoring groups: 4

	Individual	Group
Time management	☐	☐
Organizational skills	☐	☐
Learning strategies	☐	☐
Study skills	☐	☒
Content area	☐	☐
Writing lab	☐	☒
Math lab	☐	☐

LD PROGRAM STAFF

Total number of LD Program staff (including director):

Full Time: 1 Part Time: 1

There is an advisor/advocate from the LD program available to students.

Key staff person available to work with LD students: Sister Jean Beringer, Director of Student Support Services

Buena Vista University

Storm Lake, IA

Address: 610 West Fourth Street, Storm Lake, IA, 50588
Admissions telephone: 800 383-9600
Admissions FAX: 712 749-2035
Director of Admissions: Julie Keehner
Admissions e-mail: admissions@bvu.edu
Web site: http://www.bvu.edu
SAT Code: 6047 ACT Code: 1278

Associate Dean of Faculty: Mary Gill
LD program telephone: 712 749-2205
LD program e-mail: gill@bvu.edu
LD program enrollment: 15, Total campus enrollment: 1,276

GENERAL

Buena Vista University is a private, coed, four-year institution. 60-acre campus in Storm Lake (population: 10,076), 60 miles from Sioux City; branch campuses in Cherokee, Council Bluffs, Creston, Denison, Emmesburg, Estherville, Fort Dodge, Iowa Falls, LeMars, Marshalltown, Mason City, Ottumwa, Spencer, and Spirit Lake. Served by bus; major airport serves Omaha (120 miles); smaller airport serves Sioux City; train serves Council Bluffs (120 miles). 4-1-4 system.

LD ADMISSIONS

Students do not complete a separate application and are not simultaneously accepted to the LD program. A member of the LD program does not sit on the admissions committee. A personal interview is not required. Essay is not required.

For fall 2004, 8 completed self-identified LD applications were received. 8 applications were offered admission, and 8 enrolled.

SECONDARY SCHOOL REQUIREMENTS

Graduation from secondary school required; GED accepted. The following course distribution required: 4 units of English, 2 units of science, 2 units of social studies.

TESTING

ACT required; SAT Reasoning may be substituted. SAT Subject recommended.

All enrolled freshmen (fall 2004):

Average SAT I Scores: Verbal: 569 Math: 570
Average ACT Scores: Composite: 22

Child Study Team report is not required. A neuropsychological or comprehensive psycho-educational evaluation is required for admission. Tests required as part of this documentation:

- [x] WAIS-IV
- [x] WISC-IV
- [ ] SATA
- [x] Woodcock-Johnson
- [x] Nelson-Denny Reading Test
- [ ] Other

UNDERGRADUATE STUDENT BODY

Total undergraduate student enrollment: 633 Men, 659 Women.

Composition of student body (fall 2004):

	Undergraduate	Freshmen
International	0.0	0.1
Black	4.8	2.1
American Indian	0.1	0.2
Asian-American	2.4	1.9
Hispanic	2.7	1.7
White	84.6	89.5
Unreported	5.4	4.5
	100.0%	100.0%

15% are from out of state. Average age of full-time undergraduates is 21. 63% of classes have fewer than 20 students, 36% have between 20 and 50 students, 1% have more than 50 students.

STUDENT HOUSING

97% of freshmen live in college housing. Freshmen are required to live on campus. Housing is guaranteed for all undergraduates. Campus can house 1,137 undergraduates.

EXPENSES

Tuition (2005-06): $21,688 per year.
Room: $3,042. Board: $3,012.
There is no additional cost for LD program/services.

LD SERVICES

LD program size is not limited.

LD services available to:

- [x] Freshmen
- [x] Sophomores
- [x] Juniors
- [x] Seniors

Academic Accommodations

Curriculum

- [ ] Foreign language waiver
- [ ] Lighter course load
- [ ] Math waiver
- [ ] Other special classes
- [ ] Priority registrations
- [ ] Substitution of courses

Exams

- [ ] Extended time
- [ ] Oral exams
- [ ] Take home exams
- [ ] Exams on tape or computer
- [ ] Untimed exams
- [ ] Other accommodations

In class

- [ ] Early syllabus
- [ ] Note takers in class
- [ ] Priority seating
- [x] Tape recorders
- [ ] Videotaped classes
- [ ] Text on tape

Services

- [ ] Diagnostic tests
- [x] Learning centers
- [ ] Proofreaders
- [ ] Readers
- [ ] Reading Machines/Kurzweil
- [ ] Special bookstore section
- [ ] Typists

Credit toward degree is not given for remedial courses taken.

Counseling Services

- [x] Academic
- [x] Psychological
- [x] Student Support groups
- [ ] Vocational

Tutoring

Individual tutoring is available daily.

Average size of tutoring groups: 1

	Individual	Group
Time management	[x]	[ ]
Organizational skills	[x]	[ ]
Learning strategies	[x]	[ ]
Study skills	[x]	[ ]
Content area	[x]	[ ]
Writing lab	[x]	[ ]
Math lab	[x]	[ ]

LD PROGRAM STAFF

Total number of LD Program staff (including director):

Full Time: 1 Part Time: 1

There is an advisor/advocate from the LD program available to students. 20 peer tutors are available to work with LD students.

Key staff person available to work with LD students: Donna Musel, Director of Center for Academic Excellence

Central College

Pella, IA

Address: 812 University Street, Pella, IA, 50219
Admissions telephone: 800 458-5503
Admissions FAX: 641 628-5316
Director of Admissions: Carol Williamson
Admissions e-mail: admissions@central.edu
Web site: http://www.central.edu
SAT Code: 6087 ACT Code: 1284

Total campus enrollment: 1750

GENERAL

Central College is a private, coed, four-year institution. 133-acre campus in Pella (population: 9,832), 45 miles southeast of Des Moines. Served by bus; major airport serves Des Moines; train serves Ottumwa (45 miles). Semester system.

LD ADMISSIONS

A personal interview is recommended. Essay is not required.

SECONDARY SCHOOL REQUIREMENTS

Graduation from secondary school required; GED accepted.

TESTING

ACT required; SAT Reasoning may be substituted. SAT Subject recommended.

All enrolled freshmen (fall 2004):

Average SAT I Scores:	Verbal: 546	Math: 579
Average ACT Scores:	Composite: 24	

Child Study Team report is not required. Tests required as part of this documentation:

☐ WAIS-IV ☐ Woodcock-Johnson
☐ WISC-IV ☐ Nelson-Denny Reading Test
☐ SATA ☐ Other

UNDERGRADUATE STUDENT BODY

Total undergraduate student enrollment: 568 Men, 768 Women.

Composition of student body (fall 2004):

	Undergraduate	Freshmen
International	0.5	0.8
Black	0.5	0.8
American Indian	0.0	0.2
Asian-American	1.8	1.3
Hispanic	1.4	1.3
White	95.1	95.2
Unreported	0.7	0.4
	100.0%	100.0%

20% are from out of state. Average age of full-time undergraduates is 20. 69% of classes have fewer than 20 students, 31% have between 20 and 50 students.

STUDENT HOUSING

98% of freshmen live in college housing. Housing is guaranteed for all undergraduates. Campus can house 1,357 undergraduates. Single rooms are available for students with medical or special needs.

EXPENSES

Tuition (2005-06): $19,684 per year.
Room: $3,356. Board: $3,490.
There is no additional cost for LD program/services.

LD SERVICES

LD program size is not limited.

LD services available to:

■ Freshmen ■ Sophomores ■ Juniors ■ Seniors

Academic Accommodations

Curriculum		**In class**	
Foreign language waiver	☐	Early syllabus	☐
Lighter course load	■	Note takers in class	■
Math waiver	☐	Priority seating	☐
Other special classes	☐	Tape recorders	■
Priority registrations	☐	Videotaped classes	■
Substitution of courses	■	Text on tape	■
Exams		**Services**	
Extended time	■	Diagnostic tests	■
Oral exams	■	Learning centers	■
Take home exams	☐	Proofreaders	☐
Exams on tape or computer	■	Readers	■
Untimed exams	■	Reading Machines/Kurzweil	■
Other accommodations	☐	Special bookstore section	☐
		Typists	☐

Credit toward degree is not given for remedial courses taken.

Counseling Services

■ Academic
■ Psychological
■ Student Support groups
■ Vocational

Tutoring

Individual tutoring is available daily.

Average size of tutoring groups: 1

	Individual	Group
Time management	■	☐
Organizational skills	■	☐
Learning strategies	■	☐
Study skills	■	☐
Content area	■	☐
Writing lab	■	☐
Math lab	☐	☐

LD PROGRAM STAFF

Total number of LD Program staff (including director):

Full Time: 3 Part Time: 3

There is an advisor/advocate from the LD program available to students.

Key staff person available to work with LD students: Nancy Kroese, Director, Student Support Services

Clarke College

Dubuque, IA

Address: 1550 Clarke Drive, Dubuque, IA, 52001
Admissions telephone: 800 383-2345
Admissions FAX: 563 588-6789
Director of Admissions: Omar G. Correa
Admissions e-mail: admissions@clarke.edu
Web site: http://www.clarke.edu
SAT Code: 6099 ACT Code: 1290

Learning Center Director: Myra Benzer
LD program telephone: 563 588-8107
LD program e-mail: myra.benzer@clarke.edu
Total campus enrollment: 1,053

GENERAL

Clarke College is a private, coed, four-year institution. 55-acre campus in Dubuque (population: 57,686). Served by air and bus; major airport and train serve Chicago (150 miles). Public transportation serves campus. Semester system.

LD ADMISSIONS

A personal interview is recommended. Essay is not required. Secondary school class rank requirement may be waived.

SECONDARY SCHOOL REQUIREMENTS

Graduation from secondary school required; GED accepted. The following course distribution required: 4 units of English, 3 units of math, 3 units of science, 2 units of foreign language, 3 units of social studies, 4 units of academic electives.

TESTING

SAT Reasoning or ACT required. SAT Subject recommended.

All enrolled freshmen (fall 2004):

Average SAT I Scores:	Verbal: 498	Math: 498
Average ACT Scores:	Composite: 22	

Child Study Team report is not required. Tests required as part of this documentation:

- [ ] WAIS-IV
- [ ] WISC-IV
- [ ] SATA
- [ ] Woodcock-Johnson
- [ ] Nelson-Denny Reading Test
- [ ] Other

UNDERGRADUATE STUDENT BODY

Total undergraduate student enrollment: 344 Men, 708 Women.

Composition of student body (fall 2004):

	Undergraduate	Freshmen
International	0.0	1.0
Black	2.5	2.5
American Indian	0.5	0.3
Asian-American	0.5	0.4
Hispanic	3.4	2.4
White	92.1	93.1
Unreported	1.0	0.3
	100.0%	100.0%

40% are from out of state. Average age of full-time undergraduates is 22. 82% of classes have fewer than 20 students, 18% have between 20 and 50 students.

STUDENT HOUSING

86% of freshmen live in college housing. Campus can house 571 undergraduates.

EXPENSES

Tuition (2005-06): $18,360 per year.
Room: $3,135. Board: $3,310.
There is no additional cost for LD program/services.

LD SERVICES

LD program size is not limited.

LD services available to:

- [ ] Freshmen
- [ ] Sophomores
- [ ] Juniors
- [ ] Seniors

Academic Accommodations

Curriculum		In class	
Foreign language waiver	[ ]	Early syllabus	[ ]
Lighter course load	[x]	Note takers in class	[ ]
Math waiver	[ ]	Priority seating	[ ]
Other special classes	[ ]	Tape recorders	[ ]
Priority registrations	[ ]	Videotaped classes	[ ]
Substitution of courses	[ ]	Text on tape	[ ]
Exams		**Services**	
Extended time	[x]	Diagnostic tests	[ ]
Oral exams	[x]	Learning centers	[x]
Take home exams	[ ]	Proofreaders	[ ]
Exams on tape or computer	[ ]	Readers	[x]
Untimed exams	[x]	Reading Machines/Kurzweil	[ ]
Other accommodations	[ ]	Special bookstore section	[ ]
		Typists	[ ]

Credit toward degree is not given for remedial courses taken.

Counseling Services

- [ ] Academic
- [ ] Psychological
- [ ] Student Support groups
- [ ] Vocational

Tutoring

	Individual	Group
Time management	[ ]	[ ]
Organizational skills	[ ]	[ ]
Learning strategies	[ ]	[ ]
Study skills	[ ]	[ ]
Content area	[ ]	[ ]
Writing lab	[ ]	[ ]
Math lab	[ ]	[ ]

LD PROGRAM STAFF

Total number of LD Program staff (including director):

Full Time: 3 Part Time: 3

Key staff person available to work with LD students: Heather Kues, Learning Specialist

Coe College

Cedar Rapids, IA

Address: 1220 First Avenue, NE, Cedar Rapids, IA, 52402
Admissions telephone: 877 CALL COE
Admissions FAX: 319 399-8816
Vice President of Admission and Financial Aid: John Grundig
Admissions e-mail: admission@coe.edu
Web site: http://www.coe.edu
SAT Code: 6101 ACT Code: 1294

Director of Academic Achievement Program: Lois Kabela-Coates
LD program telephone: 319 399-8547
LD program e-mail: lkabela@coe.edu
Total campus enrollment: 1,321

GENERAL

Coe College is a private, coed, four-year institution. 55-acre, urban campus in Cedar Rapids (population: 120,758). Served by air and bus; train serves Mt. Pleasant (60 miles). Public transportation serves campus. Semester system.

LD ADMISSIONS

Students do not complete a separate application and are not simultaneously accepted to the LD program. A member of the LD program does sit on the admissions committee. A personal interview is recommended. Essay is required and may be typed.

SECONDARY SCHOOL REQUIREMENTS

Graduation from secondary school required; GED accepted. The following course distribution required: 4 units of English, 3 units of math, 3 units of science, 2 units of foreign language, 3 units of social studies, 2 units of academic electives.

TESTING

SAT Reasoning or ACT required. SAT Subject recommended.

All enrolled freshmen (fall 2004):

Average SAT I Scores:	Verbal: 587	Math: 583
Average ACT Scores:	Composite: 24	

Child Study Team report is not required. A neuropsychological or comprehensive psycho-educational evaluation is required for admission. Must be dated within 36 months of application. Tests required as part of this documentation:

- [x] WAIS-IV
- [x] WISC-IV
- [x] SATA
- [x] Woodcock-Johnson
- [x] Nelson-Denny Reading Test
- [ ] Other

UNDERGRADUATE STUDENT BODY

Total undergraduate student enrollment: 566 Men, 714 Women.

Composition of student body (fall 2004):

	Undergraduate	Freshmen
International	2.5	3.6
Black	3.2	1.8
American Indian	0.6	0.4
Asian-American	1.6	0.8
Hispanic	2.5	1.5
White	88.3	90.6
Unreported	1.3	1.3
	100.0%	100.0%

38% are from out of state. 25% join a fraternity and 19% join a sorority. Average age of full-time undergraduates is 20. 70% of classes have fewer than 20 students, 29% have between 20 and 50 students, 1% have more than 50 students.

STUDENT HOUSING

95% of freshmen live in college housing. Freshmen are required to live on campus. Housing is guaranteed for all undergraduates. Campus can house 1,030 undergraduates. Single rooms are available for students with medical or special needs. A medical note is required.

EXPENSES

Tuition (2005-06): $23,570 per year.
Room: $2,880. Board: $3,380.
There is no additional cost for LD program/services.

LD SERVICES

LD program size is not limited.

LD services available to:

- [x] Freshmen
- [x] Sophomores
- [x] Juniors
- [x] Seniors

Academic Accommodations

Curriculum

- [ ] Foreign language waiver
- [x] Lighter course load
- [ ] Math waiver
- [ ] Other special classes
- [ ] Priority registrations
- [ ] Substitution of courses

Exams

- [x] Extended time
- [x] Oral exams
- [ ] Take home exams
- [ ] Exams on tape or computer
- [x] Untimed exams
- [x] Other accommodations

In class

- [ ] Early syllabus
- [x] Note takers in class
- [ ] Priority seating
- [x] Tape recorders
- [ ] Videotaped classes
- [x] Text on tape

Services

- [ ] Diagnostic tests
- [x] Learning centers
- [x] Proofreaders
- [ ] Readers
- [ ] Reading Machines/Kurzweil
- [ ] Special bookstore section
- [x] Typists

Credit toward degree is not given for remedial courses taken.

Counseling Services

- [x] Academic
- [x] Psychological
- [ ] Student Support groups
- [ ] Vocational

Tutoring

Individual tutoring is available weekly.

	Individual	Group
Time management	[x]	[ ]
Organizational skills	[x]	[ ]
Learning strategies	[x]	[ ]
Study skills	[x]	[ ]
Content area	[ ]	[ ]
Writing lab	[ ]	[x]
Math lab	[x]	[ ]

LD PROGRAM STAFF

Total number of LD Program staff (including director):

Full Time: 3 Part Time: 3

Key staff person available to work with LD students: Carol Smith, Reading Specialist

Cornell College

Mount Vernon, IA

Address: 600 First Street, Mount Vernon, IA, 52314
Admissions telephone: 800 747-1112
Admissions FAX: 319 895-4451
Vice President for Admissions and Financial Assistance: Jonathan Stroud
Admissions e-mail: admissions@cornellcollege.edu
Web site: http://www.cornellcollege.edu
SAT Code: 6119 ACT Code: 1296

Registrar: Jackie Wallace
LD program telephone: 319 895-4371
LD program e-mail: jwallace@cornellcollege.edu
LD program enrollment: 22, Total campus enrollment: 1,155

GENERAL

Cornell College is a private, coed, four-year institution. 129-acre campus in Mount Vernon (population: 3,390), 15 miles from Cedar Rapids. Airport and bus serve Cedar Rapids; train serves Mt. Pleasant (70 miles).

LD ADMISSIONS

Students do not complete a separate application and are not simultaneously accepted to the LD program. A member of the LD program does not sit on the admissions committee. A personal interview is recommended. Essay is required and may be typed.

SECONDARY SCHOOL REQUIREMENTS

Graduation from secondary school required; GED accepted.

TESTING

SAT Reasoning or ACT required. SAT Subject recommended.

All enrolled freshmen (fall 2004):

Average SAT I Scores:	Verbal: 616	Math: 623
Average ACT Scores:	Composite: 26	

Child Study Team report is not required. A neuropsychological or comprehensive psycho-education evaluation is not required for admission. Tests required as part of this documentation:

- ☐ WAIS-IV
- ☐ WISC-IV
- ☐ SATA
- ☐ Woodcock-Johnson
- ☐ Nelson-Denny Reading Test
- ☐ Other

UNDERGRADUATE STUDENT BODY

Total undergraduate student enrollment: 417 Men, 569 Women.

Composition of student body (fall 2004):

	Undergraduate	Freshmen
International	3.4	2.2
Black	3.1	2.6
American Indian	0.0	0.3
Asian-American	2.1	1.1
Hispanic	4.5	3.3
White	82.1	86.1
Unreported	4.8	4.4
	100.0%	100.0%

70% are from out of state. 30% join a fraternity and 32% join a sorority. Average age of full-time undergraduates is 20. 59% of classes have fewer than 20 students, 41% have between 20 and 50 students.

STUDENT HOUSING

99% of freshmen live in college housing. Freshmen are required to live on campus. Housing is guaranteed for all undergraduates. Campus can house 1,037 undergraduates. Single rooms are not available for students with medical or special needs.

EXPENSES

Tuition (2005-06): $23,500 per year.
Room: $3,010. Board: $3,420.
There is no additional cost for LD program/services.

LD SERVICES

LD program size is not limited.

LD services available to:

☒ Freshmen ☒ Sophomores ☒ Juniors ☒ Seniors

Academic Accommodations

Curriculum		**In class**	
Foreign language waiver	☐	Early syllabus	☒
Lighter course load	☐	Note takers in class	☐
Math waiver	☐	Priority seating	☒
Other special classes	☐	Tape recorders	☒
Priority registrations	☐	Videotaped classes	☐
Substitution of courses	☐	Text on tape	☒
Exams		**Services**	
Extended time	☒	Diagnostic tests	☐
Oral exams	☒	Learning centers	☒
Take home exams	☐	Proofreaders	☐
Exams on tape or computer	☐	Readers	☐
Untimed exams	☒	Reading Machines/Kurzweil	☐
Other accommodations	☒	Special bookstore section	☐
		Typists	☐

Credit toward degree is not given for remedial courses taken.

Counseling Services

- ☐ Academic
- ☐ Psychological
- ☐ Student Support groups
- ☐ Vocational

Tutoring

Individual tutoring is available.

	Individual	Group
Time management	☐	☐
Organizational skills	☐	☐
Learning strategies	☐	☐
Study skills	☐	☐
Content area	☐	☐
Writing lab	☐	☐
Math lab	☐	☐

LD PROGRAM STAFF

There is an advisor/advocate from the LD program available to students.

Key staff person available to work with LD students: Jackie Wallace, Registrar

Dordt College

Sioux Center, IA

Address: 498 Fourth Avenue, NE, Sioux Center, IA, 51250
Admissions telephone: 800 343-6738
Admissions FAX: 712 722-1967
Executive Director of Admissions: Quentin Van Essen
Admissions e-mail: admissions@dordt.edu
Web site: http://www.dordt.edu
SAT Code: 6171 ACT Code: 1301

LD program name: Services for Students with Disabilities
LD program address: Academic Skills Center
Coordinator: Marliss Van Der Zwaag
LD program telephone: 712 722-6490
LD program enrollment: 23, Total campus enrollment: 1,290

GENERAL

Dordt College is a private, coed, four-year institution. 65-acre campus in Sioux Center (population: 6,002), 45 miles from Sioux City and 55 miles from Sioux Falls, SD. Served by air; major airport and bus serve Sioux City. School operates transportation to Sioux City, Sioux Falls, SD, and local airport. Semester system.

LD ADMISSIONS

A member of the LD program does not sit on the admissions committee. High school waivers are accepted for foreign language. A personal interview is recommended. Essay is not required. ACT or SAT test requirements may be waived.

SECONDARY SCHOOL REQUIREMENTS

Graduation from secondary school required; GED accepted. The following course distribution required: 3 units of English, 2 units of math, 2 units of science, 2 units of foreign language, 2 units of history, 6 units of academic electives.

TESTING

SAT Reasoning or ACT required.

All enrolled freshmen (fall 2004):

Average SAT I Scores:	Verbal: 560	Math: 585
Average ACT Scores:	Composite: 24	

Child Study Team report is not required. A neuropsychological or comprehensive psycho-educational evaluation is required for admission. Must be dated within 36 months of application. Tests required as part of this documentation:

- ■ WAIS-IV
- ■ WISC-IV
- ☐ SATA
- ■ Woodcock-Johnson
- ☐ Nelson-Denny Reading Test
- ☐ Other

UNDERGRADUATE STUDENT BODY

Total undergraduate student enrollment: 621 Men, 775 Women.

Composition of student body (fall 2004):

	Undergraduate	Freshmen
International	9.6	8.8
Black	0.0	0.2
American Indian	0.0	0.0
Asian-American	0.6	1.0
Hispanic	0.6	0.1
White	88.6	89.9
Unreported	0.6	0.0
	100.0%	100.0%

53% are from out of state. 57% of classes have fewer than 20 students, 39% have between 20 and 50 students, 4% have more than 50 students.

STUDENT HOUSING

98% of freshmen live in college housing. Freshmen are required to live on campus. Housing is guaranteed for all undergraduates. Campus can house 1,335 undergraduates. Single rooms are available for students with medical or special needs. A medical note is required.

EXPENSES

Tuition (2005-06): $17,400 per year.
Room: $2,580. Board: $2,320.

There is no additional cost for LD program/services.

LD SERVICES

LD program size is not limited.

LD services available to:

■ Freshmen ■ Sophomores ■ Juniors ■ Seniors

Academic Accommodations

Curriculum		In class	
Foreign language waiver	■	Early syllabus	■
Lighter course load	■	Note takers in class	■
Math waiver	☐	Priority seating	■
Other special classes	☐	Tape recorders	■
Priority registrations	☐	Videotaped classes	☐
Substitution of courses	■	Text on tape	■
Exams		**Services**	
Extended time	■	Diagnostic tests	☐
Oral exams	■	Learning centers	■
Take home exams	☐	Proofreaders	■
Exams on tape or computer	■	Readers	■
Untimed exams	■	Reading Machines/Kurzweil	☐
Other accommodations	■	Special bookstore section	☐
		Typists	☐

Credit toward degree is not given for remedial courses taken.

Counseling Services

- ■ Academic — Meets 32 times per academic year
- ☐ Psychological
- ☐ Student Support groups
- ☐ Vocational

Tutoring

Individual tutoring is available weekly.

Average size of tutoring groups: 2

	Individual	Group
Time management	■	☐
Organizational skills	■	☐
Learning strategies	■	☐
Study skills	■	☐
Content area	■	☐
Writing lab	■	☐
Math lab	■	☐

UNIQUE LD PROGRAM FEATURES

Although we do not offer diagnostic testing, we do provide preliminary screening for disabilities.

LD PROGRAM STAFF

There is an advisor/advocate from the LD program available to students. The advisor/advocate meets with faculty once per month and students four times per month. 20 peer tutors are available to work with LD students.

Key staff person available to work with LD students: Marliss Van Der Zwaag, Coordinator of Services for Students with Disabilities

Drake University

Des Moines, IA

Address: 2507 University Avenue, Des Moines, IA, 50311
Admissions telephone: 800 44-DRAKE
Admissions FAX: 515 271-2831
Dean of Admission and Financial Aid: Thomas F. Delahunt
Admissions e-mail: admission@drake.edu
Web site: http://www.drake.edu
SAT Code: 6168 ACT Code: 1302

LD program name: Student Disability Services
Student Disability Services Coordinator: Michelle Laughlin
LD program telephone: 515 271-1835
LD program e-mail: michelle.laughlin@drake.edu
LD program enrollment: 54, Total campus enrollment: 2,835

GENERAL

Drake University is a private, coed, four-year institution. 120-acre, suburban campus in Des Moines (population: 198,682). Served by air and bus; train serves Osceola (40 miles). Public transportation serves campus. Semester system.

LD ADMISSIONS

Students do not complete a separate application and are not simultaneously accepted to the LD program. A member of the LD program does not sit on the admissions committee. A personal interview is recommended. Essay is not required.

For fall 2004, 27 completed self-identified LD applications were received. 27 applications were offered admission, and 27 enrolled.

SECONDARY SCHOOL REQUIREMENTS

Graduation from secondary school required; GED accepted.

TESTING

SAT Reasoning or ACT required. SAT Subject recommended.

All enrolled freshmen (fall 2004):

Average SAT I Scores:	Verbal: 591	Math: 609
Average ACT Scores:	Composite: 26	

Child Study Team report is not required. A neuropsychological or comprehensive psycho-educational evaluation is required for admission. Must be dated within 60 months of application. Tests required as part of this documentation:

■ WAIS-IV
■ WISC-IV
☐ SATA
■ Woodcock-Johnson
■ Nelson-Denny Reading Test
☐ Other

UNDERGRADUATE STUDENT BODY

Total undergraduate student enrollment: 1,381 Men, 2,145 Women.

Composition of student body (fall 2004):

	Undergraduate	Freshmen
International	4.0	5.0
Black	3.3	3.6
American Indian	0.2	0.3
Asian-American	3.0	2.8
Hispanic	1.4	1.5
White	81.4	79.3
Unreported	6.7	7.5
	100.0%	100.0%

59% are from out of state. 29% join a fraternity and 31% join a sorority. Average age of full-time undergraduates is 21. 48% of classes have fewer than 20 students, 41% have between 20 and 50 students, 11% have more than 50 students.

STUDENT HOUSING

96% of freshmen live in college housing. Freshmen are required to live on campus. Housing is guaranteed for all undergraduates. Campus can house 2,282 undergraduates. Single rooms are available for students with medical or special needs. A medical note is required.

EXPENSES

Tuition (2005-06): $21,100 per year.
Room: $3,000. Board: $3,170.
There is no additional cost for LD program/services.

LD SERVICES

LD program size is not limited.

LD services available to:

■ Freshmen ■ Sophomores ■ Juniors ■ Seniors

Academic Accommodations

Curriculum		In class	
Foreign language waiver	☐	Early syllabus	☐
Lighter course load	■	Note takers in class	■
Math waiver	☐	Priority seating	■
Other special classes	☐	Tape recorders	■
Priority registrations	☐	Videotaped classes	☐
Substitution of courses	☐	Text on tape	■
Exams		**Services**	
Extended time	■	Diagnostic tests	☐
Oral exams	☐	Learning centers	☐
Take home exams	☐	Proofreaders	☐
Exams on tape or computer	■	Readers	■
Untimed exams	☐	Reading Machines/Kurzweil	■
Other accommodations	■	Special bookstore section	☐
		Typists	■

Credit toward degree is not given for remedial courses taken.

Counseling Services

■ Academic
■ Psychological
☐ Student Support groups
☐ Vocational

Tutoring

Individual tutoring is not available.

	Individual	Group
Time management	■	■
Organizational skills	■	☐
Learning strategies	■	☐
Study skills	■	■
Content area	☐	☐
Writing lab	■	■
Math lab	■	■

LD PROGRAM STAFF

Total number of LD Program staff (including director):

Full Time: 1 Part Time: 1

There is an advisor/advocate from the LD program available to students.

Key staff person available to work with LD students: Michelle Laughlin, Student Disability Services Coordinator

LD Program web site: http://www.drake.edu/sds/

University of Dubuque

Dubuque, IA

Address: 2000 University Avenue, Dubuque, IA, 52001
Admissions telephone: 800 722-5583
Admissions FAX: 563 589-3690
Director of Admission: Jesse James
Admissions e-mail: admssns@univ.dbq.edu
Web site: http://www.dbq.edu
SAT Code: 6869 ACT Code: 1358

Director of Academic Resource Center: Susanna Robey
LD program telephone: 563 589-3218
LD program e-mail: srobey@dbq.edu
LD program enrollment: 28, Total campus enrollment: 1,101

GENERAL

University of Dubuque is a private, coed, four-year institution. 56-acre campus in Dubuque (population: 57,686), 180 miles from Chicago, IL. Served by air and bus; major airport serves Chicago, IL; train serves Galesburg, IL. (100 miles). School operates transportation to Clarke Coll and Loras Coll. Public transportation serves campus. Semester system.

LD ADMISSIONS

Students do not complete a separate application and are not simultaneously accepted to the LD program. A member of the LD program does not sit on the admissions committee. High school waivers are accepted for foreign language. A personal interview is recommended. Essay is required and may be typed. After acceptance, LD students that self-iendify may ask for accommodations and the college will grant those accommodations if possible.

For fall 2004, 3 completed self-identified LD applications were received.

SECONDARY SCHOOL REQUIREMENTS

Graduation from secondary school required; GED accepted. The following course distribution required: 4 units of English, 3 units of math, 3 units of science, 3 units of social studies, 3 units of academic electives.

TESTING

SAT Reasoning or ACT required. SAT Subject recommended.

All enrolled freshmen (fall 2004):

Average SAT I Scores:	Verbal: 450	Math: 470
Average ACT Scores:	Composite: 21	

Child Study Team report is not required. A neuropsychological or comprehensive psycho-education evaluation is not required for admission. Tests required as part of this documentation:

- [ ] WAIS-IV
- [ ] WISC-IV
- [ ] SATA
- [ ] Woodcock-Johnson
- [ ] Nelson-Denny Reading Test
- [ ] Other

UNDERGRADUATE STUDENT BODY

Total undergraduate student enrollment: 474 Men, 282 Women.

Composition of student body (fall 2004):

	Undergraduate	Freshmen
International	1.0	0.5
Black	14.2	1.3
American Indian	3.3	2.6
Asian-American	2.0	1.3
Hispanic	6.3	3.9
White	67.2	78.4
Unreported	6.0	12.0
	100.0%	100.0%

60% are from out of state. 13% join a fraternity and 25% join a sorority. Average age of full-time undergraduates is 18. 69% of classes have fewer than 20 students, 31% have between 20 and 50 students.

STUDENT HOUSING

55% of freshmen live in college housing. Freshmen are required to live on campus. Housing is guaranteed for all undergraduates. Campus can house 700 undergraduates. Single rooms are not available for students with medical or special needs.

EXPENSES

Tuition (2005-06): $17,250 per year.
Room: $2,920. Board: $3,030.
There is no additional cost for LD program/services.

LD SERVICES

LD program size is not limited.

LD services available to:

- [x] Freshmen
- [x] Sophomores
- [x] Juniors
- [x] Seniors

Academic Accommodations

Curriculum

- [ ] Foreign language waiver
- [x] Lighter course load
- [ ] Math waiver
- [x] Other special classes
- [ ] Priority registrations
- [ ] Substitution of courses

Exams

- [x] Extended time
- [x] Oral exams
- [ ] Take home exams
- [ ] Exams on tape or computer
- [x] Untimed exams
- [ ] Other accommodations

In class

- [ ] Early syllabus
- [x] Note takers in class
- [ ] Priority seating
- [x] Tape recorders
- [ ] Videotaped classes
- [ ] Text on tape

Services

- [ ] Diagnostic tests
- [x] Learning centers
- [ ] Proofreaders
- [ ] Readers
- [ ] Reading Machines/Kurzweil
- [x] Special bookstore section
- [ ] Typists

Credit toward degree is given for remedial courses taken.

Counseling Services

- [x] Academic
- [x] Psychological
- [ ] Student Support groups
- [x] Vocational

Tutoring

Individual tutoring is available daily.

Average size of tutoring groups: 1

	Individual	Group
Time management	[x]	[ ]
Organizational skills	[x]	[ ]
Learning strategies	[x]	[ ]
Study skills	[x]	[ ]
Content area	[x]	[ ]
Writing lab	[x]	[ ]
Math lab	[x]	[ ]

LD PROGRAM STAFF

Total number of LD Program staff (including director):

Full Time: 4 Part Time: 4

There is an advisor/advocate from the LD program available to students.

Key staff person available to work with LD students: Susanna Robey, Director of Academic Resource Center

Faith Baptist Bible College and Theological Seminary

Ankeny, IA

Address: 1900 N.W. Fourth Street, Ankeny, IA, 50021
Admissions telephone: 888 FAITH4U
Admissions FAX: 515 964-1638
Vice President of Enrollment and Constituency Services: Tim Nilius
Admissions e-mail: admissions@faith.edu
Web site: www.faith.edu
SAT Code: 6214 ACT Code: 1315

LD program contact: Mrs. Cole
LD program e-mail: colea@faith.edu
LD program enrollment: 5, Total campus enrollment: 358

GENERAL

Faith Baptist Bible College and Theological Seminary is a private, coed, four-year institution. 52-acre, suburban campus in Ankeny (population: 27,117), six miles from Des Moines. Airport and bus serve Des Moines; train serves Osceola (55 miles). Semester system.

LD ADMISSIONS

Application Deadline: 08/01. A member of the LD program does sit on the admissions committee. A personal interview is recommended. Essay is required and may be typed. English requirements may be waived on an individual basis.

For fall 2004, 2 completed self-identified LD applications were received.

SECONDARY SCHOOL REQUIREMENTS

Graduation from secondary school required; GED accepted.

TESTING

ACT required; SAT Reasoning may be substituted. SAT Subject recommended.

All enrolled freshmen (fall 2004):

Average SAT I Scores:	Verbal: 510	Math: 514
Average ACT Scores:	Composite: 22	

Child Study Team report is not required. A neuropsychological or comprehensive psycho-education evaluation is not required for admission. Tests required as part of this documentation:

- [ ] WAIS-IV
- [ ] WISC-IV
- [ ] SATA
- [ ] Woodcock-Johnson
- [ ] Nelson-Denny Reading Test
- [ ] Other

UNDERGRADUATE STUDENT BODY

Total undergraduate student enrollment: 159 Men, 213 Women.

Composition of student body (fall 2004):

	Undergraduate	Freshmen
International	0.0	0.0
Black	1.0	0.3
American Indian	1.0	0.3
Asian-American	1.0	0.9
Hispanic	1.0	1.7
White	96.0	96.8
Unreported	0.0	0.0
	100.0%	100.0%

54% are from out of state. Average age of full-time undergraduates is 20. 58% of classes have fewer than 20 students, 25% have between 20 and 50 students, 17% have more than 50 students.

STUDENT HOUSING

99% of freshmen live in college housing. Freshmen are required to live on campus. Housing is guaranteed for all undergraduates. Single rooms are available for students with medical or special needs. A medical note is required.

EXPENSES

Tuition (2005-06): $10,804 per year.
Room: $2,010. Board: $2,306.
There is no additional cost for LD program/services.

LD SERVICES

LD program size is not limited.

LD services available to:

- [x] Freshmen
- [x] Sophomores
- [x] Juniors
- [x] Seniors

Academic Accommodations

Curriculum		**In class**	
Foreign language waiver	[ ]	Early syllabus	[ ]
Lighter course load	[x]	Note takers in class	[ ]
Math waiver	[ ]	Priority seating	[ ]
Other special classes	[ ]	Tape recorders	[ ]
Priority registrations	[ ]	Videotaped classes	[ ]
Substitution of courses	[ ]	Text on tape	[ ]
Exams		**Services**	
Extended time	[x]	Diagnostic tests	[ ]
Oral exams	[ ]	Learning centers	[ ]
Take home exams	[ ]	Proofreaders	[ ]
Exams on tape or computer	[ ]	Readers	[ ]
Untimed exams	[ ]	Reading Machines/Kurzweil	[ ]
Other accommodations	[ ]	Special bookstore section	[ ]
		Typists	[ ]

Credit toward degree is not given for remedial courses taken.

Counseling Services

- [ ] Academic
- [ ] Psychological
- [ ] Student Support groups
- [ ] Vocational

Tutoring

Individual tutoring is available monthly.

Average size of tutoring groups: 2

	Individual	Group
Time management	[ ]	[x]
Organizational skills	[ ]	[x]
Learning strategies	[ ]	[x]
Study skills	[ ]	[x]
Content area	[x]	[ ]
Writing lab	[x]	[ ]
Math lab	[x]	[ ]

LD PROGRAM STAFF

There is an advisor/advocate from the LD program available to students.

Key staff person available to work with LD students: Sharon Gutwein, Dean of Women

Graceland University

Lamoni, IA

Address: 1 University Place, Lamoni, IA, 50140-1698
Admissions telephone: 866 GRACELAND
Admissions FAX: 641 784-5480
Vice Provost for Enrollment Management/Dean of Admissions: Brian Shantz
Admissions e-mail: admissions@graceland.edu
Web site: http://www.graceland.edu
SAT Code: 6249 ACT Code: 1314

LD program name: Chance Program
Director: Susan Knotts
LD program telephone: 641 784-5421
LD program e-mail: knotts@graceland.edu
Total campus enrollment: 2, 283

GENERAL

Graceland University is a private, coed, four-year institution. 169-acre campus in Lamoni (population: 2,444), 75 miles south of Des Moines; branch campuses in Centerville, Creston, and Des Moines and in Independence and Trenton, Mo. Served by bus; airport serves Des Moines; train serves Osceola (30 miles). School operates transportation to airport for major holidays and at start and end of school year. 4-1-4 system.

LD ADMISSIONS

A personal interview is recommended. Essay is not required. Applicants that do not meet the normal admission criteria may be considered individually and they will be required to take developmental courses. Some applicants may be requested to test for the Chance Program prior to being considered for acceptance.

SECONDARY SCHOOL REQUIREMENTS

Graduation from secondary school required; GED accepted.

TESTING

ACT required; SAT Reasoning may be substituted.

Child Study Team report is not required. Tests required as part of this documentation:

- ☐ WAIS-IV
- ☐ WISC-IV
- ☐ SATA
- ☐ Woodcock-Johnson
- ☐ Nelson-Denny Reading Test
- ☐ Other

UNDERGRADUATE STUDENT BODY

Total undergraduate student enrollment: 701 Men, 1,582 Women.

61% are from out of state.

STUDENT HOUSING

Housing is guaranteed for all undergraduates.

EXPENSES

Tuition (2005-06): $16,000 per year.

Room: $2,100. Board: $3,300.

Additional cost for LD program/services: $1,350 per semester.

LD SERVICES

LD program size is not limited.

LD services available to:

☐ Freshmen ☐ Sophomores ☐ Juniors ☐ Seniors

Academic Accommodations

Curriculum		In class	
Foreign language waiver	☐	Early syllabus	☐
Lighter course load	☑	Note takers in class	☑
Math waiver	☐	Priority seating	☐
Other special classes	☐	Tape recorders	☑
Priority registrations	☐	Videotaped classes	☐
Substitution of courses	☐	Text on tape	☐
Exams		**Services**	
Extended time	☑	Diagnostic tests	☑
Oral exams	☑	Learning centers	☑
Take home exams	☐	Proofreaders	☐
Exams on tape or computer	☐	Readers	☑
Untimed exams	☑	Reading Machines/Kurzweil	☐
Other accommodations	☐	Special bookstore section	☐
		Typists	☐

Credit toward degree is given for remedial courses taken.

Counseling Services

- ☐ Academic
- ☐ Psychological
- ☐ Student Support groups
- ☐ Vocational

Tutoring

	Individual	Group
Time management	☐	☐
Organizational skills	☐	☐
Learning strategies	☐	☐
Study skills	☐	☐
Content area	☐	☐
Writing lab	☐	☐
Math lab	☐	☐

UNIQUE LD PROGRAM FEATURES

LD students who are not in the Chance Program do not have additional costs. Specialized clinical and counseling services are provided to students who have the potential to do college work, but whose past academic performance has been inhibited by certain learning dysfunctions. Services provided by this program supplement a carefully structured academic program designed in cooperation with the student and the program clinicians. The central objective of the Chance Program is to remediate poor reading, writing, and oral language skills so the student may come to participate fully in the university's educational program. The program offers diagnostic tests to determine the nature and severity of a student's learning dysfunction(s). Students may begin the Chance Program during a three-week summer or winter term session.

LD PROGRAM STAFF

Total number of LD Program staff (including director):

Full Time: 8 Part Time: 8

Key staff person available to work with LD students: Susan Knotts, Director, Student Disability Services & Chance Program

Grand View College

Des Moines, IA

Address: 1200 Grandview Avenue, Des Moines, IA, 50316
Admissions telephone: 800 444-6083
Admissions FAX: 515 263-2974
Vice President for Enrollment Management: Diane Schaefer Johnson
Admissions e-mail: admissions@gvc.edu
Web site: http://www.gvc.edu
SAT Code: 6251 ACT Code: 1316

Director of Academic Sucess: Carolyn Wassenaar
LD program telephone: (515) 263-2971
LD program e-mail: cwassenaar@gvc.edu
Total campus enrollment: 1,759

GENERAL

Grand View College is a private, coed, four-year institution. 35-acre campus in Des Moines (population: 198,682); branch campus in Johnston. Served by air and bus; train serves Osceola (35 miles). Public transportation serves campus. Semester system.

LD ADMISSIONS

A personal interview is not required. Essay is not required.

SECONDARY SCHOOL REQUIREMENTS

Graduation from secondary school required; GED not accepted.

TESTING

ACT required.

All enrolled freshmen (fall 2004):

Average SAT I Scores:	Verbal: 502	Math: 474
Average ACT Scores:	Composite: 21	

Child Study Team report is not required. Tests required as part of this documentation:

- ☐ WAIS-IV
- ☐ WISC-IV
- ☐ SATA
- ☐ Woodcock-Johnson
- ☐ Nelson-Denny Reading Test
- ☐ Other

UNDERGRADUATE STUDENT BODY

Total undergraduate student enrollment: 467 Men, 935 Women.

Composition of student body (fall 2004):

	Undergraduate	Freshmen
International	0.7	0.7
Black	2.3	2.8
American Indian	0.0	0.5
Asian-American	1.4	1.8
Hispanic	3.2	1.2
White	90.1	64.6
Unreported	2.3	28.2
	100.0%	100.0%

7% are from out of state. Average age of full-time undergraduates is 23. 70% of classes have fewer than 20 students, 30% have between 20 and 50 students.

STUDENT HOUSING

68% of freshmen live in college housing. Freshmen are required to live on campus. Housing is guaranteed for all undergraduates. Campus can house 446 undergraduates.

EXPENSES

Tuition (2005-06): $15,750 per year.

Room & Board: $5,422.
There is no additional cost for LD program/services.

LD SERVICES

LD program size is not limited.

LD services available to:

☐ Freshmen ☐ Sophomores ☐ Juniors ☐ Seniors

Academic Accommodations

Curriculum		**In class**	
Foreign language waiver	☐	Early syllabus	☐
Lighter course load	■	Note takers in class	■
Math waiver	☐	Priority seating	☐
Other special classes	☐	Tape recorders	■
Priority registrations	☐	Videotaped classes	■
Substitution of courses	☐	Text on tape	☐
Exams		**Services**	
Extended time	■	Diagnostic tests	☐
Oral exams	■	Learning centers	■
Take home exams	☐	Proofreaders	☐
Exams on tape or computer	☐	Readers	■
Untimed exams	■	Reading Machines/Kurzweil	■
Other accommodations	☐	Special bookstore section	☐
		Typists	☐

Credit toward degree is given for remedial courses taken.

Counseling Services

- ☐ Academic
- ☐ Psychological
- ☐ Student Support groups
- ☐ Vocational

Tutoring

	Individual	Group
Time management	☐	☐
Organizational skills	☐	☐
Learning strategies	☐	☐
Study skills	☐	☐
Content area	☐	☐
Writing lab	☐	☐
Math lab	☐	☐

LD PROGRAM STAFF

Total number of LD Program staff (including director):

Full Time: 1 Part Time: 1

Key staff person available to work with LD students: Carolyn Wassenaar, Director of Academic Sucess

Grinnell College

Grinnell, IA

Address: 1103 Park Street, Grinnell, IA, 50112-1690
Admissions telephone: 800 247-0113
Admissions FAX: 641 269-4800
Dean of Admissions and Financial Aid: James M. Sumner
Admissions e-mail: askgrin@grinnell.edu
Web site: http://www.grinnell.edu
SAT Code: 6252   ACT Code: 1318

Director of Academic Advising: Joyce Stern
LD program telephone: 641 269-3702
LD program e-mail: sternjm@grinnell.edu
LD program enrollment: 28, Total campus enrollment: 1,556

GENERAL

Grinnell College is a private, coed, four-year institution. 109-acre campus in Grinnell (population: 9,105), 55 miles from Des Moines; branch campuses in Washington, DC and abroad in London, England. Served by bus; airports serve Des Moines and Cedar Rapids (63 miles); train serves Ottumwa (56 miles). School operates transportation to Des Moines at beginning and end of each semester. Semester system.

LD ADMISSIONS

A personal interview is recommended. Essay is required and may be typed.

SECONDARY SCHOOL REQUIREMENTS

Graduation from secondary school required; GED accepted.

TESTING

SAT Reasoning or ACT required. SAT Subject required.

All enrolled freshmen (fall 2004):

Average SAT I Scores: Verbal: Math:
Average ACT Scores: Composite:

Child Study Team report is not required. Tests required as part of this documentation:

- [ ] WAIS-IV
- [ ] WISC-IV
- [ ] SATA
- [ ] Woodcock-Johnson
- [ ] Nelson-Denny Reading Test
- [ ] Other

UNDERGRADUATE STUDENT BODY

Total undergraduate student enrollment: 622 Men, 716 Women.

Composition of student body (fall 2004):

	Undergraduate	Freshmen
International	10.8	10.9
Black	3.9	4.0
American Indian	0.2	0.7
Asian-American	5.8	5.0
Hispanic	3.9	3.6
White	69.4	68.8
Unreported	6.0	7.0
	100.0%	100.0%

86% are from out of state. Average age of full-time undergraduates is 20. 63% of classes have fewer than 20 students, 37% have between 20 and 50 students.

STUDENT HOUSING

100% of freshmen live in college housing. Freshmen are required to live on campus. Housing is guaranteed for all undergraduates. Campus can house 1,252 undergraduates.

EXPENSES

Tuition (2005-06): $27,060 per year.
Room: $3,424. Board: $3,886.

There is no additional cost for LD program/services.

LD SERVICES

LD program size is not limited.

LD services available to:

- [x] Freshmen
- [x] Sophomores
- [x] Juniors
- [x] Seniors

Academic Accommodations

Curriculum		**In class**	
Foreign language waiver	[ ]	Early syllabus	[ ]
Lighter course load	[x]	Note takers in class	[x]
Math waiver	[ ]	Priority seating	[ ]
Other special classes	[ ]	Tape recorders	[x]
Priority registrations	[ ]	Videotaped classes	[ ]
Substitution of courses	[ ]	Text on tape	[ ]
Exams		**Services**	
Extended time	[x]	Diagnostic tests	[ ]
Oral exams	[x]	Learning centers	[ ]
Take home exams	[ ]	Proofreaders	[ ]
Exams on tape or computer	[ ]	Readers	[x]
Untimed exams	[x]	Reading Machines/Kurzweil	[ ]
Other accommodations	[ ]	Special bookstore section	[ ]
		Typists	[ ]

Credit toward degree is not given for remedial courses taken.

Counseling Services

- [ ] Academic
- [ ] Psychological
- [ ] Student Support groups
- [ ] Vocational

Tutoring

Individual tutoring is available.

	Individual	Group
Time management	[x]	[ ]
Organizational skills	[x]	[ ]
Learning strategies	[x]	[ ]
Study skills	[x]	[ ]
Content area	[x]	[ ]
Writing lab	[x]	[ ]
Math lab	[x]	[ ]

UNIQUE LD PROGRAM FEATURES

Tutoring and all other academic support services are available to all students who request them.

LD PROGRAM STAFF

There is an advisor/advocate from the LD program available to students.

Key staff person available to work with LD students: Joyce Stern, Director of Academic Advising

Hawkeye Community College

Waterloo, IA

Address: 1501 East Orange Road, Waterloo, IA 50704
Admissions telephone: 800 670-4769
Admissions FAX: 319 296-2505
Director of Enrollment Management/Registrar: Patricia East
Admissions e-mail: admission@hawkeyecollege.edu
Web site: http://www.hawkeyecollege.edu
SAT Code: 6288 ACT Code: 1309

Assistant Coordinator: Nancy Dallenbach
LD program telephone: 319 296-4238
LD program e-mail: ndallenbach@hawkeyecollege.edu
LD program enrollment: 58, Total campus enrollment: 5,374

GENERAL

Hawkeye Community College is a public, coed, two-year institution. 320-acre campus in Waterloo (population: 75,000). Served by air and bus; other airport serves Cedar Rapids (75 miles); train serves Ottumwa (100 miles). Public transportation serves campus. Semester system.

LD ADMISSIONS

Students do not complete a separate application process and are not simultaneously accepted. A member of the LD program does not sit on the admissions committee. A personal interview is required. Essay is not required.

SECONDARY SCHOOL REQUIREMENTS

Graduation from secondary school required; GED accepted.

TESTING

Child Study Team report is not required. A neuropsychological or comprehensive psycho-educational evaluation is required for admission. Must be dated within 36 months of application. Tests required as part of this documentation:

- ■ WAIS-IV
- □ WISC-IV
- □ SATA
- ■ Woodcock-Johnson
- □ Nelson-Denny Reading Test
- □ Other

STUDENT HOUSING

There is no student housing available.

LD SERVICES

There is no additional cost for LD program/services.

LD services available to:

■ Freshmen ■ Sophomores ■ Juniors ■ Seniors

Academic Accommodations

Curriculum		**In class**	
Foreign language waiver	□	Early syllabus	□
Lighter course load	■	Note takers in class	■
Math waiver	□	Priority seating	■
Other special classes	□	Tape recorders	■
Priority registrations	■	Videotaped classes	□
Substitution of courses	■	Text on tape	■
Exams		**Services**	
Extended time	■	Diagnostic tests	□
Oral exams	■	Learning centers	■
Take home exams	□	Proofreaders	■
Exams on tape or computer	□	Readers	■
Untimed exams	□	Reading Machines/Kurzweil	■
Other accommodations	■	Special bookstore section	□
		Typists	■

Credit toward degree is not given for remedial courses taken.

Counseling Services

- ■ Academic
- ■ Psychological
- ■ Student Support groups
- ■ Vocational

Tutoring

Individual tutoring is available.

Average size of tutoring groups is 2.

	Individual	Group
Time management	■	■
Organizational skills	□	□
Learning strategies	■	■
Study skills	■	■
Content area	■	■
Writing lab	■	■
Math lab	■	■

LD PROGRAM STAFF

Total number of LD Program staff (including director):

Full Time: 5 Part Time: 35

There is an advisor/advocate from the LD program available to work with students. There are three to six peer tutors available to work with students.

Key staff person available to work with LD students: Barb Hill, Counselor

University of Iowa

Iowa City, IA

Address: 107 Calvin Hall, Iowa City, IA, 52242-1396
Admissions telephone: 800 553-4692
Admissions FAX: 319 335-1535
Director of Admissions: Michael Barron
Admissions e-mail: admissions@uiowa.edu
Web site: http://www.uiowa.edu
SAT Code: 6681 ACT Code: 1356

LD program name: Office of Student Disability Services
LD program address: 3100 Burge Hall
Director of Student Disability Services: Dau-shen Ju
LD program telephone: 319 335-1462
LD program e-mail: sds-information@uiowa.edu
LD program enrollment: 273, Total campus enrollment: 20,135

GENERAL

University of Iowa is a public, coed, four-year institution. 1,900-acre campus in Iowa City (population: 62,220), 24 miles from Cedar Rapids. Served by bus; airport serves Cedar Rapids; train serves Mt. Pleasant (60 miles). Public transportation serves campus. Semester system.

LD ADMISSIONS

Students complete a separate application and are not simultaneously accepted to the LD program. A member of the LD program does not sit on the admissions committee. A personal interview is not required. Essay is not required.

For fall 2004, 80 completed self-identified LD applications were received.

SECONDARY SCHOOL REQUIREMENTS

Graduation from secondary school required; GED accepted. The following course distribution required: 4 units of English, 3 units of math, 3 units of science, 2 units of foreign language, 3 units of social studies.

TESTING

SAT Reasoning or ACT required. SAT Subject recommended.

Child Study Team report is not required. A neuropsychological or comprehensive psycho-educational evaluation is required for admission. Must be dated within 36 months of application. Tests required as part of this documentation:

- [x] WAIS-IV
- [x] WISC-IV
- [x] SATA
- [x] Woodcock-Johnson
- [x] Nelson-Denny Reading Test
- [ ] Other

UNDERGRADUATE STUDENT BODY

Total undergraduate student enrollment: 8,898 Men, 10,705 Women.

Composition of student body (fall 2004):

	Undergraduate	Freshmen
International	0.7	1.2
Black	2.2	2.2
American Indian	0.6	0.5
Asian-American	3.8	3.6
Hispanic	2.1	2.3
White	88.9	87.3
Unreported	1.7	2.9
	100.0%	100.0%

31% are from out of state. 8% join a fraternity and 12% join a sorority. Average age of full-time undergraduates is 21. 49% of classes have fewer than 20 students, 40% have between 20 and 50 students, 11% have more than 50 students.

STUDENT HOUSING

90% of freshmen live in college housing. Housing is guaranteed for all undergraduates. Campus can house 5,600 undergraduates. Single rooms are available for students with medical or special needs. A medical note is required.

EXPENSES

Tuition (2005-06): $5,612 per year (in-state), $16,988 (out-of-state). Room: $4,210. Board: $2,350.
There is no additional cost for LD program/services.

LD SERVICES

LD program size is not limited.

LD services available to:

- [x] Freshmen
- [x] Sophomores
- [x] Juniors
- [x] Seniors

Academic Accommodations

Curriculum		**In class**	
Foreign language waiver	[ ]	Early syllabus	[ ]
Lighter course load	[ ]	Note takers in class	[x]
Math waiver	[ ]	Priority seating	[x]
Other special classes	[ ]	Tape recorders	[x]
Priority registrations	[x]	Videotaped classes	[ ]
Substitution of courses	[ ]	Text on tape	[x]
Exams		**Services**	
Extended time	[x]	Diagnostic tests	[ ]
Oral exams	[ ]	Learning centers	[ ]
Take home exams	[ ]	Proofreaders	[ ]
Exams on tape or computer	[x]	Readers	[x]
Untimed exams	[ ]	Reading Machines/Kurzweil	[x]
Other accommodations	[x]	Special bookstore section	[ ]
		Typists	[x]

Credit toward degree is not given for remedial courses taken.

Counseling Services

- [ ] Academic
- [ ] Psychological
- [ ] Student Support groups
- [ ] Vocational

Tutoring

Individual tutoring is available.

	Individual	Group
Time management	[ ]	[ ]
Organizational skills	[ ]	[ ]
Learning strategies	[ ]	[ ]
Study skills	[ ]	[ ]
Content area	[ ]	[ ]
Writing lab	[ ]	[ ]
Math lab	[ ]	[ ]

LD PROGRAM STAFF

Total number of LD Program staff (including director):

Full Time: 6 Part Time: 6

There is an advisor/advocate from the LD program available to students. Three graduate students are available to work with LD students.

Key staff person available to work with LD students: Dau-shen Ju, Director of Student Disability Services

LD Program web site: www.uiowa.edu/~sds

Iowa State University

Ames, IA

Address: 100 Alumni Hall, Ames, IA, 50011
Admissions telephone: 800 262-3810
Admissions FAX: 515 294-2592
Director of Admissions: Marc Harding
Admissions e-mail: admissions@iastate.edu
Web site: http://www.iastate.edu
SAT Code: 6306   ACT Code: 1320

LD program name: Disability Resources
LD program address: 1076 Student Services, ISU
Coordinator, Disability Resources: Bea O. Awoniyi
LD program telephone: 515 294-6624
LD program e-mail: Awoniyib@iastate.edu
LD program enrollment: 212, Total campus enrollment: 21,354

GENERAL

Iowa State University is a public, coed, four-year institution. 1,788-acre campus in Ames (population: 50,731), 30 miles from Des Moines. Served by bus; major airport serves Des Moines; train serves Osceola (90 miles). Public transportation serves campus. Semester system.

LD ADMISSIONS

Application Deadline: 07/01. Students do not complete a separate application and are not simultaneously accepted to the LD program. A member of the LD program does not sit on the admissions committee. A personal interview is not required. Essay is not required. Exceptions may be made for the class rank and ACT/SAT requirements, but not for the high school course requirements.

SECONDARY SCHOOL REQUIREMENTS

Graduation from secondary school required; GED accepted. The following course distribution required: 4 units of English, 3 units of math, 3 units of science, 2 units of foreign language, 3 units of social studies.

TESTING

SAT Reasoning or ACT required. SAT Subject recommended.

All enrolled freshmen (fall 2004):

Average ACT Scores: Composite: 25

Child Study Team report is not required. A neuropsychological or comprehensive psycho-educational evaluation is required for admission. Tests required as part of this documentation:

- [x] WAIS-IV
- [ ] WISC-IV
- [ ] SATA
- [x] Woodcock-Johnson
- [ ] Nelson-Denny Reading Test
- [ ] Other

UNDERGRADUATE STUDENT BODY

Total undergraduate student enrollment: 12,827 Men, 10,233 Women.

Composition of student body (fall 2004):

	Undergraduate	Freshmen
International	1.3	3.1
Black	3.0	2.8
American Indian	0.5	0.4
Asian-American	3.5	3.1
Hispanic	2.3	2.1
White	85.3	83.5
Unreported	4.1	5.0
	100.0%	100.0%

19% are from out of state. 12% join a fraternity and 12% join a sorority. 33% of classes have fewer than 20 students, 47% have between 20 and 50 students, 20% have more than 50 students.

STUDENT HOUSING

87% of freshmen live in college housing. Freshmen are not required to live on campus. Housing is guaranteed for all undergraduates. Campus can house 10,047 undergraduates.

EXPENSES

Tuition (2005-06): $4,890 per year (in-state), $14,980 (out-of-state). Room: $3,295. Board: $2,902.

There is no additional cost for LD program/services.

LD SERVICES

LD program size is not limited.

LD services available to:

- [x] Freshmen
- [x] Sophomores
- [x] Juniors
- [x] Seniors

Academic Accommodations

Curriculum		In class	
Foreign language waiver	[x]	Early syllabus	[x]
Lighter course load	[x]	Note takers in class	[x]
Math waiver	[ ]	Priority seating	[x]
Other special classes	[ ]	Tape recorders	[x]
Priority registrations	[x]	Videotaped classes	[x]
Substitution of courses	[x]	Text on tape	[x]
Exams		**Services**	
Extended time	[x]	Diagnostic tests	[ ]
Oral exams	[ ]	Learning centers	[x]
Take home exams	[ ]	Proofreaders	[ ]
Exams on tape or computer	[x]	Readers	[x]
Untimed exams	[ ]	Reading Machines/Kurzweil	[x]
Other accommodations	[x]	Special bookstore section	[ ]
		Typists	[ ]

Credit toward degree is not given for remedial courses taken.

Counseling Services

- [ ] Academic
- [ ] Psychological
- [ ] Student Support groups
- [ ] Vocational

Tutoring

Individual tutoring is available weekly.

Average size of tutoring groups: 3

	Individual	Group
Time management	[x]	[x]
Organizational skills	[x]	[x]
Learning strategies	[x]	[x]
Study skills	[x]	[x]
Content area	[x]	[x]
Writing lab	[x]	[x]
Math lab	[x]	[x]

LD PROGRAM STAFF

Total number of LD Program staff (including director):

Full Time: 3   Part Time: 3

There is an advisor/advocate from the LD program available to students. The advisor/advocate meets with faculty five times per month and students 20 times per month. Two graduate students and 20 peer tutors are available to work with LD students.

Key staff person available to work with LD students: Bea O. Awoniyi, Coordinator, Disability Resources

Iowa Wesleyan College

Mount Pleasant, IA

Address: 601 North Main Street, Mount Pleasant, IA, 52641
Admissions telephone: 800 582-2383
Admissions FAX: 319 385-6240
Director of Admissions: Cary A. Owens
Admissions e-mail: admit@iwc.edu
Web site: http://www.iwc.edu
SAT Code: 6308 ACT Code: 1324

LD program name: Learning Center
Director of Learning Center: Kay Brouwer
LD program telephone: 319 385-6334
LD program e-mail: kbrouwer@iwc.edu
LD program enrollment: 26, Total campus enrollment: 776

GENERAL

Iowa Wesleyan College is a private, coed, four-year institution. 60-acre campus in Mount Pleasant (population: 8,751), 70 miles from Cedar Rapids. Served by bus and train; airports serve Burlington (30 miles) and Cedar Rapids. Semester system.

LD ADMISSIONS

Students do not complete a separate application and are not simultaneously accepted to the LD program. A member of the LD program does not sit on the admissions committee. A personal interview is recommended. Essay is not required.

SECONDARY SCHOOL REQUIREMENTS

Graduation from secondary school required; GED accepted. The following course distribution required: 4 units of English, 3 units of math, 2 units of science, 3 units of social studies.

TESTING

ACT required; SAT Reasoning may be substituted. SAT Subject recommended.

All enrolled freshmen (fall 2004):

Average ACT Scores: Composite: 20

Child Study Team report is not required. A neuropsychological or comprehensive psycho-education evaluation is not required for admission. Tests required as part of this documentation:

- ☐ WAIS-IV
- ☐ WISC-IV
- ☐ SATA
- ☐ Woodcock-Johnson
- ☐ Nelson-Denny Reading Test
- ☐ Other

UNDERGRADUATE STUDENT BODY

Total undergraduate student enrollment: 322 Men, 490 Women.

Composition of student body (fall 2004):

	Undergraduate	Freshmen
International	12.9	5.7
Black	5.4	10.5
American Indian	0.0	0.3
Asian-American	0.0	0.9
Hispanic	3.2	7.9
White	78.5	72.8
Unreported	0.0	1.9
	100.0%	100.0%

27% are from out of state. Average age of full-time undergraduates is 25. 80% of classes have fewer than 20 students, 20% have between 20 and 50 students.

STUDENT HOUSING

Housing is guaranteed for all undergraduates. Campus can house 465 undergraduates. Single rooms are available for students with medical or special needs. A medical note is not required.

EXPENSES

Tuition (2005-06): $16,950 per year.
Room: $2,160. Board: $3,030.

There is no additional cost for LD program/services.

LD SERVICES

LD program size is not limited.

LD services available to:

■ Freshmen ■ Sophomores ■ Juniors ■ Seniors

Academic Accommodations

Curriculum		**In class**	
Foreign language waiver	☐	Early syllabus	☐
Lighter course load	☐	Note takers in class	■
Math waiver	☐	Priority seating	☐
Other special classes	■	Tape recorders	■
Priority registrations	☐	Videotaped classes	☐
Substitution of courses	☐	Text on tape	☐
Exams		**Services**	
Extended time	■	Diagnostic tests	■
Oral exams	■	Learning centers	■
Take home exams	☐	Proofreaders	■
Exams on tape or computer	☐	Readers	■
Untimed exams	■	Reading Machines/Kurzweil	■
Other accommodations	■	Special bookstore section	☐
		Typists	■

Credit toward degree is not given for remedial courses taken.

Counseling Services

- ■ Academic — Meets 30 times per academic year
- ☐ Psychological
- ☐ Student Support groups
- ☐ Vocational

Tutoring

Individual tutoring is available weekly.

Average size of tutoring groups: 1

	Individual	Group
Time management	■	☐
Organizational skills	■	☐
Learning strategies	■	☐
Study skills	■	☐
Content area	■	☐
Writing lab	■	☐
Math lab	■	☐

LD PROGRAM STAFF

Total number of LD Program staff (including director):

Full Time: 2 Part Time: 2

There is an advisor/advocate from the LD program available to students. The advisor/advocate meets with faculty once per month and students 8 times per month. 10 peer tutors are available to work with LD students.

Key staff person available to work with LD students: Kay Brouwer, Director of Learning Center

Loras College

Dubuque, IA

Address: 1450 Alta Vista, Dubuque, IA, 52004-0178
Admissions telephone: 800 245-6727
Admissions FAX: 563 588-7119
Director of Admissions: Tim Hauber
Admissions e-mail: adms@loras.edu
Web site: http://www.loras.edu
SAT Code: 6370 ACT Code: 1328

Secretary: Rochelle Fury
LD program telephone: 563 588-7134
LD program e-mail: rfury@loras.edu
LD program enrollment: 125, Total campus enrollment: 1,618

GENERAL

Loras College is a private, coed, four-year institution. 60-acre campus in Dubuque (population: 57,686), 80 miles from Cedar Rapids. Served by air and bus; major airport serves Chicago, IL (150 miles); train serves Cedar Rapids. School operates transportation to local colleges. Public transportation serves campus. Semester system.

LD ADMISSIONS

A member of the LD program does not sit on the admissions committee. A personal interview is required. Essay is required and may be typed. Students applying for the Enhanced Program should take a rigorous college preparatory curriculum. GPA is not weighed as heavily as coursework.

For fall 2004, 42 completed self-identified LD applications were received. 40 applications were offered admission, and 25 enrolled.

SECONDARY SCHOOL REQUIREMENTS

Graduation from secondary school required; GED accepted.

TESTING

SAT Reasoning considered if submitted. ACT recommended.

All enrolled freshmen (fall 2004):

Average ACT Scores: Composite: 22

Child Study Team report is not required. A neuropsychological or comprehensive psycho-educational evaluation is required for admission. Tests required as part of this documentation:

- [x] WAIS-IV
- [x] WISC-IV
- [ ] SATA
- [x] Woodcock-Johnson
- [ ] Nelson-Denny Reading Test
- [ ] Other

UNDERGRADUATE STUDENT BODY

Total undergraduate student enrollment: 801 Men, 835 Women.

Composition of student body (fall 2004):

	Undergraduate	Freshmen
International	2.7	1.7
Black	1.0	1.1
American Indian	0.3	0.1
Asian-American	1.2	0.7
Hispanic	0.7	1.1
White	90.4	92.1
Unreported	3.7	3.2
	100.0%	100.0%

42% are from out of state. 3% join a sorority. Average age of full-time undergraduates is 20. 58% of classes have fewer than 20 students, 42% have between 20 and 50 students.

STUDENT HOUSING

94% of freshmen live in college housing. Freshmen are required to live on campus. Housing is guaranteed for all undergraduates. Campus can house 1,119 undergraduates.

EXPENSES

Tuition (2005-06): $19,990 per year.
Room: $3,100. Board: $2,995.

LD SERVICES

LD program is limited to %1 students.

LD services available to:

- [x] Freshmen
- [x] Sophomores
- [x] Juniors
- [x] Seniors

Academic Accommodations

Curriculum		In class	
Foreign language waiver	[ ]	Early syllabus	[ ]
Lighter course load	[x]	Note takers in class	[x]
Math waiver	[ ]	Priority seating	[ ]
Other special classes	[x]	Tape recorders	[x]
Priority registrations	[ ]	Videotaped classes	[ ]
Substitution of courses	[ ]	Text on tape	[ ]
Exams		**Services**	
Extended time	[x]	Diagnostic tests	[ ]
Oral exams	[ ]	Learning centers	[x]
Take home exams	[ ]	Proofreaders	[ ]
Exams on tape or computer	[ ]	Readers	[ ]
Untimed exams	[x]	Reading Machines/Kurzweil	[x]
Other accommodations	[ ]	Special bookstore section	[ ]
		Typists	[ ]

Credit toward degree is not given for remedial courses taken.

Counseling Services

- [ ] Academic
- [ ] Psychological
- [ ] Student Support groups
- [ ] Vocational

Tutoring

Individual tutoring is available.

	Individual	Group
Time management	[x]	[ ]
Organizational skills	[x]	[ ]
Learning strategies	[x]	[ ]
Study skills	[ ]	[ ]
Content area	[x]	[ ]
Writing lab	[x]	[ ]
Math lab	[x]	[ ]

LD PROGRAM STAFF

Total number of LD Program staff (including director):

Full Time: 4 Part Time: 4

Key staff person available to work with LD students: Dianne Gibson, Director of LD Program

Luther College

Decorah, IA

Address: 700 College Drive, Decorah, IA, 52101-1045
Admissions telephone: 800 458-8437
Admissions FAX: 563 387-2159
Vice President for Enrollment and Marketing: Jon Lund
Admissions e-mail: admissions@luther.edu
Web site: http://www.luther.edu
SAT Code: 6375 ACT Code: 1330

LD program name: Student Academic Support Center
LD program address: Preus Library 108
Director, Student Academic Support Services: G. R. Rosales
LD program telephone: 563 387-1270
LD program e-mail: SASC@luther.edu
LD program enrollment: 18, Total campus enrollment: 2,573

GENERAL

Luther College is a private, coed, four-year institution. 800-acre campus in Decorah (population: 8,172), 120 miles from Minneapolis-St. Paul, MN and 350 miles from Chicago, IL. Major airport serves Minneapolis-St. Paul, MN; smaller airport and train serve LaCrosse, WI (50 miles); bus serves Rochester, MN (50 miles). School operates transportation to Chicago, IL at end of fall semester. 4-1-4 system.

LD ADMISSIONS

Students do not complete a separate application and are simultaneously accepted to the LD program. A member of the LD program does not sit on the admissions committee. High school waivers are accepted for math and foreign language. A personal interview is not required. Essay is not required.

For fall 2004, 6 completed self-identified LD applications were received. 4 applications were offered admission, and 4 enrolled.

SECONDARY SCHOOL REQUIREMENTS

Graduation from secondary school required; GED accepted. The following course distribution required: 4 units of English, 3 units of math, 2 units of science, 2 units of foreign language, 3 units of social studies.

TESTING

SAT Reasoning or ACT required. SAT Subject recommended.

All enrolled freshmen (fall 2004):

Average SAT I Scores:	Verbal: 598	Math: 612
Average ACT Scores:	Composite: 25	

Child Study Team report is not required. A neuropsychological or comprehensive psycho-educational evaluation is required for admission. Must be dated within 36 months of application. Tests required as part of this documentation:

- ■ WAIS-IV
- ■ WISC-IV
- ■ SATA
- ■ Woodcock-Johnson
- ■ Nelson-Denny Reading Test
- ☐ Other

UNDERGRADUATE STUDENT BODY

Total undergraduate student enrollment: 1,019 Men, 1,556 Women.

Composition of student body (fall 2004):

	Undergraduate	Freshmen
International	0.8	3.1
Black	1.1	0.7
American Indian	0.5	0.3
Asian-American	1.5	1.4
Hispanic	1.5	1.2
White	91.0	90.0
Unreported	3.6	3.3
	100.0%	100.0%

63% are from out of state. 7% join a fraternity and 9% join a sorority. Average age of full-time undergraduates is 20. 42% of classes have fewer than 20 students, 55% have between 20 and 50 students, 3% have more than 50 students.

STUDENT HOUSING

100% of freshmen live in college housing. Freshmen are required to live on campus. Housing is guaranteed for all undergraduates. Campus can house 2,133 undergraduates. Single rooms are available for students with medical or special needs. A medical note is required.

EXPENSES

Tuition (2005-06): $24,570 per year.

Room: $2,070. Board: $2,160.
There is no additional cost for LD program/services.

LD SERVICES

LD program size is not limited.

LD services available to:

■ Freshmen ■ Sophomores ■ Juniors ■ Seniors

Academic Accommodations

Curriculum		In class	
Foreign language waiver	■	Early syllabus	☐
Lighter course load	☐	Note takers in class	■
Math waiver	■	Priority seating	☐
Other special classes	☐	Tape recorders	■
Priority registrations	■	Videotaped classes	☐
Substitution of courses	■	Text on tape	■
Exams		**Services**	
Extended time	■	Diagnostic tests	☐
Oral exams	■	Learning centers	■
Take home exams	☐	Proofreaders	☐
Exams on tape or computer	☐	Readers	☐
Untimed exams	☐	Reading Machines/Kurzweil	☐
Other accommodations	■	Special bookstore section	☐
		Typists	■

Credit toward degree is given for remedial courses taken.

Counseling Services

- ■ Academic
- ■ Psychological
- ☐ Student Support groups
- ☐ Vocational

Tutoring

Individual tutoring is available weekly.

Average size of tutoring groups: 1

	Individual	Group
Time management	■	☐
Organizational skills	■	☐
Learning strategies	■	☐
Study skills	■	☐
Content area	■	☐
Writing lab	■	☐
Math lab	■	☐

LD PROGRAM STAFF

Total number of LD Program staff (including director):

Full Time: 2 Part Time: 2

There is an advisor/advocate from the LD program available to students. The advisor/advocate meets with faculty and students once per month. 25 peer tutors are available to work with LD students.

Key staff person available to work with LD students: Mary Klimesh, Coordinator Disability Services

LD Program web site: www.sasc.luther.edu

Morningside College

Sioux City, IA

Address: 1501 Morningside Avenue, Sioux City, IA, 51106
Admissions telephone: 800 831-0806, extension 5111
Admissions FAX: 712 274-5101
Director of Admissions: Joel Weyand
Admissions e-mail: mscadm@morningside.edu
Web site: http://www.morningside.edu
SAT Code: 6415 ACT Code: 1338

LD program name: FOCUS
Dean of Students: Robbie Rohlena
LD program telephone: 712 274-5426
LD program e-mail: rohlena@morningside.edu
LD program enrollment: 28, Total campus enrollment: 1,037

GENERAL

Morningside College is a private, coed, four-year institution. 41-acre, suburban campus in Sioux City (population: 85,013). Served by air and bus. Public transportation serves campus. Semester system.

LD ADMISSIONS

Application Deadline: 08/25. Students do not complete a separate application and are not simultaneously accepted to the LD program. A member of the LD program does not sit on the admissions committee. High school waivers are accepted for math and foreign language. A personal interview is recommended. Essay is not required.

For fall 2004, 30 completed self-identified LD applications were received. 21 applications were offered admission, and 16 enrolled.

SECONDARY SCHOOL REQUIREMENTS

Graduation from secondary school required; GED accepted. The following course distribution required: 3 units of English, 2 units of math, 2 units of science, 3 units of social studies.

TESTING

ACT required; SAT Reasoning may be substituted. SAT Subject recommended.

All enrolled freshmen (fall 2004):

Average ACT Scores: Composite: 21

Child Study Team report is not required. A neuropsychological or comprehensive psycho-education evaluation is not required for admission. Tests required as part of this documentation:

- [ ] WAIS-IV
- [ ] WISC-IV
- [ ] SATA
- [ ] Woodcock-Johnson
- [ ] Nelson-Denny Reading Test
- [ ] Other

UNDERGRADUATE STUDENT BODY

Total undergraduate student enrollment: 317 Men, 533 Women.

Composition of student body (fall 2004):

	Undergraduate	Freshmen
International	1.3	2.1
Black	2.5	2.6
American Indian	0.0	0.3
Asian-American	1.9	1.3
Hispanic	5.7	3.9
White	80.4	81.4
Unreported	8.2	8.4
	100.0%	100.0%

22% are from out of state. 9% join a fraternity and 4% join a sorority. Average age of full-time undergraduates is 21. 52% of classes have fewer than 20 students, 46% have between 20 and 50 students, 2% have more than 50 students.

STUDENT HOUSING

85% of freshmen live in college housing. Freshmen are required to live on campus. Housing is guaranteed for all undergraduates. Campus can house 700 undergraduates. Single rooms are available for students with medical or special needs. A medical note is required.

EXPENSES

Tuition (2005-06): $17,170 per year.
Room: $2,940. Board: $2,684.
Additional cost for LD program/services: $1,550 per semester - freshmen.

LD SERVICES

LD program is limited.

LD services available to:

- [x] Freshmen
- [x] Sophomores
- [x] Juniors
- [x] Seniors

Academic Accommodations

Curriculum		**In class**	
Foreign language waiver	[x]	Early syllabus	[ ]
Lighter course load	[ ]	Note takers in class	[x]
Math waiver	[ ]	Priority seating	[x]
Other special classes	[ ]	Tape recorders	[x]
Priority registrations	[ ]	Videotaped classes	[ ]
Substitution of courses	[x]	Text on tape	[x]
Exams		**Services**	
Extended time	[x]	Diagnostic tests	[x]
Oral exams	[x]	Learning centers	[x]
Take home exams	[ ]	Proofreaders	[x]
Exams on tape or computer	[x]	Readers	[x]
Untimed exams	[x]	Reading Machines/Kurzweil	[x]
Other accommodations	[ ]	Special bookstore section	[ ]
		Typists	[ ]

Credit toward degree is given for remedial courses taken.

Counseling Services

- [x] Academic — Meets 2 times per academic year
- [ ] Psychological
- [x] Student Support groups — Meets 30 times per academic year
- [ ] Vocational

Tutoring

Individual tutoring is available daily.

Average size of tutoring groups: 1

	Individual	Group
Time management	[x]	[ ]
Organizational skills	[x]	[ ]
Learning strategies	[x]	[ ]
Study skills	[x]	[ ]
Content area	[x]	[ ]
Writing lab	[x]	[ ]
Math lab	[x]	[ ]

LD PROGRAM STAFF

Total number of LD Program staff (including director):

Full Time: 2 Part Time: 2

There is an advisor/advocate from the LD program available to students. The advisor/advocate meets with faculty once per month and students four times per month. 12 peer tutors are available to work with LD students.

Key staff person available to work with LD students: Karmen Ten Napel, LD Specialist/Tutor

Mount Mercy College

Cedar Rapids, IA

Address: 1330 Elmhurst Drive, NE, Cedar Rapids, IA, 52402
Admissions telephone: 800 248-4504, extension 6460
Admissions FAX: 319 363-5270
Dean of Admission: Jim Krystofiak
Admissions e-mail: admission@mtmercy.edu
Web site: http://www.mtmercy.edu
SAT Code: 6417 ACT Code: 1340

Director of Academic Achievement: Mary Jean Stanton
LD program telephone: 319 363-8213
LD program e-mail: mstanton@mtmercy.edu
LD program enrollment: 61, Total campus enrollment: 1,486

GENERAL

Mount Mercy College is a private, coed, four-year institution. 40-acre, suburban campus in Cedar Rapids (population: 120,758). Served by air and bus. School operates transportation to downtown and malls. Public transportation serves campus. 4-1-4 system.

LD ADMISSIONS

A member of the LD program does not sit on the admissions committee. A personal interview is recommended. Essay is not required.

SECONDARY SCHOOL REQUIREMENTS

Graduation from secondary school required; GED accepted.

TESTING

SAT Reasoning or ACT required. SAT Subject recommended.

All enrolled freshmen (fall 2004):

Average ACT Scores: Composite: 22

Child Study Team report is not required. A neuropsychological or comprehensive psycho-educational evaluation is required for admission. Must be dated within 36 months of application. Tests required as part of this documentation:

- ■ WAIS-IV
- ☐ WISC-IV
- ☐ SATA
- ■ Woodcock-Johnson
- ■ Nelson-Denny Reading Test
- ☐ Other

UNDERGRADUATE STUDENT BODY

Total undergraduate student enrollment: 437 Men, 950 Women.

10% are from out of state. 78% of classes have fewer than 20 students. 20% have between 20 and 50 students, 2% have more than 50 students.

STUDENT HOUSING

88% of freshmen live in college housing. Freshmen are required to live on campus. Housing is guaranteed for all undergraduates. Campus can house 518 undergraduates. Single rooms are available for students with medical or special needs. A medical note is required.

EXPENSES

Tuition (2005-06): $18,030 per year.
Room & Board: $5,680.
There is no additional cost for LD program/services.

LD SERVICES

LD program size is not limited.

LD services available to:

■ Freshmen ■ Sophomores ■ Juniors ■ Seniors

Academic Accommodations

Curriculum		In class	
Foreign language waiver	☐	Early syllabus	☐
Lighter course load	■	Note takers in class	■
Math waiver	☐	Priority seating	■
Other special classes	☐	Tape recorders	■
Priority registrations	■	Videotaped classes	■
Substitution of courses	☐	Text on tape	☐
Exams		**Services**	
Extended time	■	Diagnostic tests	☐
Oral exams	■	Learning centers	■
Take home exams	☐	Proofreaders	■
Exams on tape or computer	■	Readers	■
Untimed exams	☐	Reading Machines/Kurzweil	■
Other accommodations	■	Special bookstore section	☐
		Typists	■

Credit toward degree is given for remedial courses taken.

Counseling Services

- ■ Academic
- ■ Psychological
- ■ Student Support groups
- ■ Vocational

Tutoring

Individual tutoring is available daily.

	Individual	Group
Time management	■	☐
Organizational skills	■	☐
Learning strategies	■	■
Study skills	■	■
Content area	■	☐
Writing lab	■	☐
Math lab	■	☐

LD PROGRAM STAFF

Total number of LD Program staff (including director):

Full Time: 2 Part Time: 2

There is an advisor/advocate from the LD program available to students. The advisor/advocate meets with faculty three times per month and students eight times per month. 12 peer tutors are available to work with LD students.

Key staff person available to work with LD students: Mary Jean Stanton, Director of Academic Achievement

LD Program web site: www.mtmercy.edu/ace/index.htm

University of Northern Iowa

Cedar Falls, IA

Address: 1227 West 27th Street, Cedar Falls, IA, 50614
Admissions telephone: 800 772-2037
Admissions FAX: 319 273-2885
Director of Enrollment Management and Admissions: Roland Carrillo
Admissions e-mail: admissions@uni.edu
Web site: http://www.uni.edu/
SAT Code: 6307 ACT Code: 1322

LD program name: Office of Disability Services
LD program address: 103 Student Health Center
Coordinator, Disability Services: Jane Slykhuis
LD program telephone: 319 273-2676
LD program e-mail: DisabilityServices@uni.edu
LD program enrollment: 81, Total campus enrollment: 11,266

GENERAL

University of Northern Iowa is a public, coed, four-year institution. 788-acre campus in Cedar Falls (population: 36,145), seven miles from Waterloo. Served by air and bus. Public transportation serves campus. Semester system.

LD ADMISSIONS

Students do not complete a separate application and are not simultaneously accepted to the LD program. A member of the LD program does not sit on the admissions committee. A personal interview is not required. Essay is not required.

SECONDARY SCHOOL REQUIREMENTS

Graduation from secondary school required; GED accepted. The following course distribution required: 4 units of English, 3 units of math, 3 units of science, 3 units of social studies, 2 units of academic electives.

TESTING

ACT required; SAT Reasoning may be substituted. SAT Subject recommended.

All enrolled freshmen (fall 2004):

Average SAT I Scores:	Verbal: 518	Math: 540
Average ACT Scores:	Composite: 23	

Child Study Team report is not required. A neuropsychological or comprehensive psycho-educational evaluation is required for admission. Must be dated within 24 months of application. Tests required as part of this documentation:

■ WAIS-IV
☐ WISC-IV
☐ SATA
■ Woodcock-Johnson
☐ Nelson-Denny Reading Test
■ Other

UNDERGRADUATE STUDENT BODY

Total undergraduate student enrollment: 5,286 Men, 7,394 Women.

Composition of student body (fall 2004):

	Undergraduate	Freshmen
International	1.3	1.8
Black	3.1	2.9
American Indian	0.4	0.3
Asian-American	0.8	1.0
Hispanic	1.4	1.7
White	93.0	92.3
Unreported	0.0	0.0
	100.0%	100.0%

5% are from out of state. 3% join a fraternity and 3% join a sorority. Average age of full-time undergraduates is 21. 33% of classes have fewer than 20 students, 58% have between 20 and 50 students, 9% have more than 50 students.

STUDENT HOUSING

87% of freshmen live in college housing. Freshmen are not required to live on campus. Housing is guaranteed for all undergraduates. Campus can house 5,285 undergraduates. Single rooms are available for students with medical or special needs. A medical note is required.

EXPENSES

Tuition (2005-06): $4,890 per year (in-state), $12,502 (out-of-state). Room: $2,565. Board: $2,972.
There is no additional cost for LD program/services.

LD SERVICES

LD program size is not limited.

LD services available to:

■ Freshmen ■ Sophomores ■ Juniors ■ Seniors

Academic Accommodations

Curriculum		In class	
Foreign language waiver	☐	Early syllabus	☐
Lighter course load	☐	Note takers in class	■
Math waiver	☐	Priority seating	■
Other special classes	☐	Tape recorders	■
Priority registrations	■	Videotaped classes	☐
Substitution of courses	■	Text on tape	■
Exams		**Services**	
Extended time	■	Diagnostic tests	☐
Oral exams	☐	Learning centers	☐
Take home exams	☐	Proofreaders	☐
Exams on tape or computer	■	Readers	■
Untimed exams	☐	Reading Machines/Kurzweil	■
Other accommodations	■	Special bookstore section	☐
		Typists	■

Credit toward degree is not given for remedial courses taken.

Counseling Services

■ Academic
■ Psychological
■ Student Support groups
■ Vocational

Tutoring

Individual tutoring is available daily.

	Individual	Group
Time management	■	■
Organizational skills	■	■
Learning strategies	■	■
Study skills	■	■
Content area	■	☐
Writing lab	■	☐
Math lab	■	☐

LD PROGRAM STAFF

Total number of LD Program staff (including director):

Full Time: 1 Part Time: 1

There is an advisor/advocate from the LD program available to students. The advisor/advocate meets with faculty ten times per month and students two times per month. Two graduate students and five peer tutors are available to work with LD students.

Key staff person available to work with LD students: Jane Slykhuis, Coordinator, Disability Services

LD Program web site: www.uni.edu/disability

Northwestern College

Orange City, IA

Address: 101 Seventh Street, SW, Orange City, IA, 51041
Admissions telephone: 800 747-4757
Admissions FAX: 712 707-7164
Dean of Admissions: Mark Bloemendaal
Admissions e-mail: admissions@nwciowa.edu
Web site: http://www.nwciowa.edu
SAT Code: 6490 ACT Code: 1346

LD program name: Academic Support Services
Director Academic Support Services: Patti Thayer
LD program telephone: 712 707-7045
LD program e-mail: pthayer@nwciowa.edu
LD program enrollment: 20, Total campus enrollment: 1,284

GENERAL

Northwestern College is a private, coed, four-year institution. 50-acre campus in Orange City (population: 5,582), 50 miles from Sioux City and 70 miles from Sioux Falls, SD. Airports serve Sioux City and Sioux Falls, SD; bus serves Sioux City; train serves Omaha, NE (130 miles). Semester system.

LD ADMISSIONS

Students do not complete a separate application and are not simultaneously accepted to the LD program. A member of the LD program does sit on the admissions committee. A personal interview is required. Essay is not required.

SECONDARY SCHOOL REQUIREMENTS

Graduation from secondary school required; GED accepted.

TESTING

All enrolled freshmen (fall 2004):

Average ACT Scores: Composite: 24

Child Study Team report is not required. A neuropsychological or comprehensive psycho-educational evaluation is required for admission. Must be dated within 36 months of application. Tests required as part of this documentation:

- [x] WAIS-IV
- [ ] WISC-IV
- [ ] SATA
- [x] Woodcock-Johnson
- [ ] Nelson-Denny Reading Test
- [ ] Other

UNDERGRADUATE STUDENT BODY

Total undergraduate student enrollment: 486 Men, 808 Women.

Composition of student body (fall 2004):

	Undergraduate	Freshmen
International	1.7	2.8
Black	0.6	0.4
American Indian	0.3	0.1
Asian-American	0.6	0.9
Hispanic	0.3	1.1
White	96.5	94.7
Unreported	0.0	0.0
	100.0%	100.0%

41% are from out of state. Average age of full-time undergraduates is 21. 59% of classes have fewer than 20 students, 40% have between 20 and 50 students, 1% have more than 50 students.

STUDENT HOUSING

100% of freshmen live in college housing. Freshmen are required to live on campus. Housing is not guaranteed for all undergraduates. Campus can house 1,295 undergraduates. Single rooms are available for students with medical or special needs. A medical note is required.

EXPENSES

Tuition (2005-06): $17,260 per year.
Room: $2,090. Board: $2,824.

There is no additional cost for LD program/services.

LD SERVICES

LD program size is not limited.

LD services available to:

- [x] Freshmen
- [x] Sophomores
- [x] Juniors
- [x] Seniors

Academic Accommodations

Curriculum		In class	
Foreign language waiver	[ ]	Early syllabus	[ ]
Lighter course load	[ ]	Note takers in class	[x]
Math waiver	[ ]	Priority seating	[ ]
Other special classes	[ ]	Tape recorders	[x]
Priority registrations	[ ]	Videotaped classes	[ ]
Substitution of courses	[ ]	Text on tape	[ ]
Exams		**Services**	
Extended time	[x]	Diagnostic tests	[ ]
Oral exams	[x]	Learning centers	[x]
Take home exams	[x]	Proofreaders	[x]
Exams on tape or computer	[x]	Readers	[ ]
Untimed exams	[x]	Reading Machines/Kurzweil	[ ]
Other accommodations	[ ]	Special bookstore section	[ ]
		Typists	[x]

Credit toward degree is not given for remedial courses taken.

Counseling Services

- [x] Academic
- [x] Psychological
- [x] Student Support groups
- [ ] Vocational

Tutoring

Individual tutoring is available daily.

Average size of tutoring groups: 10

	Individual	Group
Time management	[x]	[x]
Organizational skills	[x]	[x]
Learning strategies	[x]	[x]
Study skills	[x]	[x]
Content area	[x]	[x]
Writing lab	[x]	[x]
Math lab	[x]	[x]

LD PROGRAM STAFF

Total number of LD Program staff (including director):

Full Time: 1 Part Time: 1

There is an advisor/advocate from the LD program available to students. The advisor/advocate meets with faculty and student once per month. 100 peer tutors are available to work with LD students.

Key staff person available to work with LD students: Patti Thayer, Director, Academic Support Services

Simpson College

Indianola, IA

Address: 701 North C Street, Indianola, IA, 50125
Admissions telephone: 800 362-2454
Admissions FAX: 515 961-1870
Vice President for Enrollment: Deb Tierney
Admissions e-mail: admiss@simpson.edu
Web site: http://www.simpson.edu
SAT Code: 6650 ACT Code: 1354

LD program name: Hawley Academic Resource Center
Director, Hawley Academic Resource Center: Todd Little
LD program telephone: 515 961-1524
LD program e-mail: little@simpson.edu
Total campus enrollment: 1,955

GENERAL

Simpson College is a private, coed, four-year institution. 68-acre campus in Indianola (population: 12,998); branch campus in West Des Moines. Airport and bus serve Des Moines (12 miles); train serves Osceola (30 miles). Semester system.

LD ADMISSIONS

A personal interview is recommended. Essay is not required.

SECONDARY SCHOOL REQUIREMENTS

Graduation from secondary school required; GED accepted.

TESTING

SAT Reasoning or ACT required. SAT Subject recommended.

All enrolled freshmen (fall 2004):

Average ACT Scores: Composite: 24

Child Study Team report is not required. Tests required as part of this documentation:

- [ ] WAIS-IV
- [ ] WISC-IV
- [ ] SATA
- [ ] Woodcock-Johnson
- [ ] Nelson-Denny Reading Test
- [ ] Other

UNDERGRADUATE STUDENT BODY

Total undergraduate student enrollment: 787 Men, 1,029 Women.

Composition of student body (fall 2004):

	Undergraduate	Freshmen
International	0.5	1.7
Black	1.5	1.8
American Indian	0.3	0.1
Asian-American	0.8	1.2
Hispanic	1.5	1.3
White	94.9	92.3
Unreported	0.5	1.6
	100.0%	100.0%

7% are from out of state. 21% join a fraternity and 21% join a sorority. Average age of full-time undergraduates is 20. 69% of classes have fewer than 20 students, 30% have between 20 and 50 students, 1% have more than 50 students.

STUDENT HOUSING

96% of freshmen live in college housing. Freshmen are required to live on campus. Housing is guaranteed for all undergraduates. Campus can house 1,124 undergraduates. Single rooms are available for students with medical or special needs. A medical note is required.

EXPENSES

Tuition (2005-06): $20,693 per year.
Room: $2,842. Board: $3,080.
There is no additional cost for LD program/services.

LD SERVICES

LD program size is not limited.

LD services available to:

- [ ] Freshmen
- [ ] Sophomores
- [ ] Juniors
- [ ] Seniors

Academic Accommodations

Curriculum
- [ ] Foreign language waiver
- [x] Lighter course load
- [ ] Math waiver
- [ ] Other special classes
- [ ] Priority registrations
- [ ] Substitution of courses

Exams
- [x] Extended time
- [x] Oral exams
- [ ] Take home exams
- [ ] Exams on tape or computer
- [x] Untimed exams
- [ ] Other accommodations

In class
- [ ] Early syllabus
- [x] Note takers in class
- [ ] Priority seating
- [x] Tape recorders
- [ ] Videotaped classes
- [ ] Text on tape

Services
- [ ] Diagnostic tests
- [x] Learning centers
- [ ] Proofreaders
- [x] Readers
- [ ] Reading Machines/Kurzweil
- [ ] Special bookstore section
- [ ] Typists

Credit toward degree is not given for remedial courses taken.

Counseling Services

- [ ] Academic
- [ ] Psychological
- [ ] Student Support groups
- [ ] Vocational

Tutoring

Individual tutoring is available daily.

Average size of tutoring groups: 1

	Individual	Group
Time management	[x]	[ ]
Organizational skills	[x]	[ ]
Learning strategies	[x]	[ ]
Study skills	[x]	[ ]
Content area	[x]	[x]
Writing lab	[x]	[ ]
Math lab	[x]	[x]

LD PROGRAM STAFF

Total number of LD Program staff (including director):

Full Time: 2 Part Time: 2

There is an advisor/advocate from the LD program available to students. The advisor/advocate meets with faculty once per month. 12 peer tutors are available to work with LD students.

Key staff person available to work with LD students: Todd Little, Director, Hawley Academic Resource Center

LD Program web site: http://www.simpson.edu/hawley

St. Ambrose University

Davenport, IA

Address: 518 West Locust Street, Davenport, IA, 52803-2898
Admissions telephone: 800 383-2627
Admissions FAX: 319 333-6321
Director of Admissions: Meg Halligan
Admissions e-mail: admit@sau.edu
Web site: http://www.sau.edu
SAT Code: 6617 ACT Code: 1352

LD program name: Office of Students with Disabilities
Director, Office of Students with Disabilities: Ryan Saddler
LD program telephone: 563 333-6627
LD program e-mail: SaddlerRyanC@sau.edu
LD program enrollment: 143, Total campus enrollment: 2,639

GENERAL

St. Ambrose University is a private, coed, four-year institution. 20-acre campus in Davenport (population: 98,359), 180 miles from Chicago, IL. Served by air and bus; major airport serves Moline, IL (nine miles); train serves Galesburg, IL (90 miles). Public transportation serves campus. 4-1-4 system.

LD ADMISSIONS

Students do not complete a separate application and are not simultaneously accepted to the LD program. A member of the LD program does sit on the admissions committee. A personal interview is required. Essay is not required.

SECONDARY SCHOOL REQUIREMENTS

Graduation from secondary school required; GED accepted. The following course distribution required: 4 units of English, 3 units of math, 2 units of science, 1 unit of foreign language, 1 unit of social studies, 1 unit of history, 4 units of academic electives.

TESTING

SAT Subject recommended.

All enrolled freshmen (fall 2004):

Average ACT Scores: Composite: 22

Child Study Team report is not required. A neuropsychological or comprehensive psycho-education evaluation is not required for admission. Tests required as part of this documentation:

- [ ] WAIS-IV
- [ ] WISC-IV
- [ ] SATA
- [ ] Woodcock-Johnson
- [ ] Nelson-Denny Reading Test
- [ ] Other

UNDERGRADUATE STUDENT BODY

Total undergraduate student enrollment: 853 Men, 1,263 Women.

Composition of student body (fall 2004):

	Undergraduate	Freshmen
International	0.6	0.4
Black	1.2	2.6
American Indian	0.0	0.4
Asian-American	0.8	1.4
Hispanic	3.1	3.5
White	94.3	91.7
Unreported	0.0	0.0
	100.0%	100.0%

36% are from out of state. Average age of full-time undergraduates is 21. 57% of classes have fewer than 20 students, 43% have between 20 and 50 students.

STUDENT HOUSING

91% of freshmen live in college housing. Freshmen are required to live on campus. Housing is guaranteed for all undergraduates. Campus can house 1,284 undergraduates.

EXPENSES

Tuition (2005-06): $18,530 per year.

Room: $3,550. Board: $3,415.
There is no additional cost for LD program/services.

LD SERVICES

LD program size is not limited.

LD services available to:

- [x] Freshmen
- [x] Sophomores
- [x] Juniors
- [x] Seniors

Academic Accommodations

Curriculum
- [ ] Foreign language waiver
- [ ] Lighter course load
- [ ] Math waiver
- [ ] Other special classes
- [ ] Priority registrations
- [ ] Substitution of courses

Exams
- [x] Extended time
- [x] Oral exams
- [ ] Take home exams
- [ ] Exams on tape or computer
- [x] Untimed exams
- [x] Other accommodations

In class
- [ ] Early syllabus
- [ ] Note takers in class
- [ ] Priority seating
- [x] Tape recorders
- [ ] Videotaped classes
- [ ] Text on tape

Services
- [x] Diagnostic tests
- [x] Learning centers
- [ ] Proofreaders
- [ ] Readers
- [ ] Reading Machines/Kurzweil
- [ ] Special bookstore section
- [ ] Typists

Credit toward degree is not given for remedial courses taken.

Counseling Services

- [x] Academic
- [x] Psychological
- [ ] Student Support groups
- [ ] Vocational

Tutoring

Individual tutoring is available daily.

Average size of tutoring groups: 1

	Individual	Group
Time management	[x]	[ ]
Organizational skills	[x]	[ ]
Learning strategies	[x]	[ ]
Study skills	[x]	[ ]
Content area	[x]	[ ]
Writing lab	[x]	[ ]
Math lab	[x]	[ ]

LD PROGRAM STAFF

Total number of LD Program staff (including director):

Full Time: 2 Part Time: 2

There is an advisor/advocate from the LD program available to students. 25 peer tutors are available to work with LD students.

Key staff person available to work with LD students: Ryan Saddler, Director, Office of Students with Disabilities

LD Program web site: www.sau.edu

Waldorf College

Forest City, IA

Address: 106 South Sixth Street, Forest City, IA, 50436
Admissions telephone: 800 292-1903
Admissions FAX: 641 585-8194
Dean of Admissions/Financial Aid: Steve Lovik
Admissions e-mail: admissions@waldorf.edu
Web site: http://www.waldorf.edu
SAT Code: 6925 ACT Code: 1362

LD program name: Waldorf College LD Program
Director: Michelle Sprout Murray
LD program telephone: 641 585-8207
LD program e-mail: murraym@waldorf.edu
LD program enrollment: 20, Total campus enrollment: 629

GENERAL

Waldorf College is a private, coed, four-year institution. 40-acre campus in Forest City (population: 4,362), 40 miles from Mason City and 120 miles from both Des Moines and Minneapolis, MN. Major airports serve Des Moines and Minneapolis, MN; smaller airport, bus, and train serve Mason City. Semester system.

LD ADMISSIONS

Application Deadline: 08/01. Students do not complete a separate application and are simultaneously accepted to the LD program. A member of the LD program does sit on the admissions committee. High school waivers are accepted for foreign language. A personal interview is recommended. Essay is not required.

For fall 2004, 15 completed self-identified LD applications were received. 8 applications were offered admission, and 6 enrolled.

SECONDARY SCHOOL REQUIREMENTS

Graduation from secondary school required; GED accepted.

TESTING

SAT Reasoning or ACT required. SAT Subject recommended.

All enrolled freshmen (fall 2004):

Average ACT Scores: Composite: 21

Child Study Team report is required if student is classified. A neuropsychological or comprehensive psycho-educational evaluation is required for admission. Must be dated within 36 months of application. Tests required as part of this documentation:

- [x] WAIS-IV
- [x] WISC-IV
- [x] SATA
- [ ] Woodcock-Johnson
- [x] Nelson-Denny Reading Test
- [x] Other

UNDERGRADUATE STUDENT BODY

Total undergraduate student enrollment: 344 Men, 297 Women.

Composition of student body (fall 2004):

	Undergraduate	Freshmen
International	4.6	5.7
Black	8.2	3.9
American Indian	0.0	0.0
Asian-American	0.6	0.5
Hispanic	1.0	0.5
White	85.6	89.4
Unreported	0.0	0.0
	100.0%	100.0%

39% are from out of state. Average age of full-time undergraduates is 20. 62% of classes have fewer than 20 students, 38% have between 20 and 50 students.

STUDENT HOUSING

99% of freshmen live in college housing. Freshmen are required to live on campus. Housing is guaranteed for all undergraduates. Campus can house 521 undergraduates. Single rooms are available for students with medical or special needs.

EXPENSES

Tuition (2005-06): $14,985 per year.
Room: $2,150. Board: $2,470.
Additional cost for LD program/services: $450 per semester.

LD SERVICES

LD program size is not limited.

LD services available to:

- [x] Freshmen
- [x] Sophomores
- [x] Juniors
- [x] Seniors

Academic Accommodations

Curriculum

- Foreign language waiver [ ]
- Lighter course load [x]
- Math waiver [ ]
- Other special classes [x]
- Priority registrations [ ]
- Substitution of courses [ ]

Exams

- Extended time [x]
- Oral exams [x]
- Take home exams [ ]
- Exams on tape or computer [ ]
- Untimed exams [x]
- Other accommodations [x]

In class

- Early syllabus [ ]
- Note takers in class [x]
- Priority seating [ ]
- Tape recorders [x]
- Videotaped classes [ ]
- Text on tape [x]

Services

- Diagnostic tests [ ]
- Learning centers [x]
- Proofreaders [ ]
- Readers [x]
- Reading Machines/Kurzweil [ ]
- Special bookstore section [ ]
- Typists [ ]

Credit toward degree is given for remedial courses taken.

Counseling Services

- [x] Academic — Meets 4 times per academic year
- [ ] Psychological
- [x] Student Support groups — Meets 2 times per academic year
- [ ] Vocational

Tutoring

Average size of tutoring groups: 4

	Individual	Group
Time management	[x]	[x]
Organizational skills	[x]	[x]
Learning strategies	[x]	[x]
Study skills	[x]	[x]
Content area	[x]	[x]
Writing lab	[x]	[x]
Math lab	[ ]	[ ]

LD PROGRAM STAFF

Total number of LD Program staff (including director):

Full Time: 2 Part Time: 2

There is an advisor/advocate from the LD program available to students. The advisor/advocate meets with faculty and students four times per month.

Key staff person available to work with LD students: Michelle Sprout Murray, Director of Academic Achievement Center

Wartburg College

Waverly, IA

Address: P.O. Box 1003, Waverly, IA, 50677-0903
Admissions telephone: 800 772-2085
Admissions FAX: 319 352-8579
Dean of Admissions and Financial Aid: Doug Bowman
Admissions e-mail: admissions@wartburg.edu
Web site: http://www.wartburg.edu
SAT Code: 6926 ACT Code: 1364

Vice President for Student Life: Alexander Smith
LD program telephone: 319 352-8260
LD program e-mail: alexander.smith
Total campus enrollment: 1,804

GENERAL

Wartburg College is a private, coed, four-year institution. 118-acre campus in Waverly (population: 8,968), 15 miles from Waterloo-Cedar Falls and 100 miles from Des Moines. Served by bus; airport serves Waterloo. School operates transportation to airport.

SECONDARY SCHOOL REQUIREMENTS

Graduation from secondary school required; GED accepted.

TESTING

ACT required; SAT Reasoning may be substituted. SAT Subject recommended.

All enrolled freshmen (fall 2004):

Average SAT I Scores:	Verbal: 553	Math: 565
Average ACT Scores:	Composite: 24	

Child Study Team report is not required. Tests required as part of this documentation:

- ☐ WAIS-IV
- ☐ WISC-IV
- ☐ SATA
- ☐ Woodcock-Johnson
- ☐ Nelson-Denny Reading Test
- ☐ Other

UNDERGRADUATE STUDENT BODY

Total undergraduate student enrollment: 691 Men, 958 Women.

Composition of student body (fall 2004):

	Undergraduate	Freshmen
International	6.2	5.3
Black	3.0	3.4
American Indian	0.0	0.2
Asian-American	2.4	1.5
Hispanic	1.8	1.1
White	84.2	83.5
Unreported	2.4	5.0
	100.0%	100.0%

21% are from out of state. Average age of full-time undergraduates is 20. 42% of classes have fewer than 20 students, 56% have between 20 and 50 students, 2% have more than 50 students.

STUDENT HOUSING

98% of freshmen live in college housing. Freshmen are required to live on campus. Housing is guaranteed for all undergraduates. Campus can house 1,435 undergraduates.

EXPENSES

Tuition (2005-06): $20,500 per year.
Room: $2,815. Board: $2,950.

There is no additional cost for LD program/services.

LD SERVICES

LD program size is not limited.

LD services available to:

☐ Freshmen ☐ Sophomores ☐ Juniors ☐ Seniors

Academic Accommodations

Curriculum		In class	
Foreign language waiver	☐	Early syllabus	☐
Lighter course load	☐	Note takers in class	☐
Math waiver	☐	Priority seating	☐
Other special classes	☐	Tape recorders	■
Priority registrations	☐	Videotaped classes	☐
Substitution of courses	☐	Text on tape	☐
Exams		**Services**	
Extended time	■	Diagnostic tests	☐
Oral exams	■	Learning centers	☐
Take home exams	☐	Proofreaders	☐
Exams on tape or computer	☐	Readers	■
Untimed exams	☐	Reading Machines/Kurzweil	☐
Other accommodations	☐	Special bookstore section	☐
		Typists	☐

Credit toward degree is not given for remedial courses taken.

Counseling Services

- ☐ Academic
- ☐ Psychological
- ☐ Student Support groups
- ☐ Vocational

Tutoring

	Individual	Group
Time management	☐	☐
Organizational skills	☐	☐
Learning strategies	☐	☐
Study skills	☐	☐
Content area	☐	☐
Writing lab	☐	☐
Math lab	☐	☐

LD PROGRAM STAFF

Total number of LD Program staff (including director):

Full Time: 2 Part Time: 2

Key staff person available to work with LD students: Kayah-Bah Malecek, Pathways Center Testing Services Coordinator

William Penn University

Oskaloosa, IA

Address: 201 Trueblood Avenue, Oskaloosa, IA, 52577
Admissions telephone: 800 779-7366
Admissions FAX: 641 673-2113
Director of Admissions: John Ottosson
Admissions e-mail: admissions@wmpenn.edu
Web site: http://www.wmpenn.edu
SAT Code: 6943 ACT Code: 1372

LD program name: Academic Resource Center
Academic Dean: Dr. Fred Allen
LD program telephone: 641 673-1102
LD program e-mail: allenf@wmpenn.edu
LD program enrollment: 12, Total campus enrollment: 1,685

GENERAL

William Penn University is a private, coed, four-year institution. 40-acre campus in Oskaloosa (population: 10,938), 60 miles from Des Moines. Served by bus; airport serves Des Moines; train serves Ottumwa (26 miles). Semester system.

LD ADMISSIONS

Students do not complete a separate application and are simultaneously accepted to the LD program. A member of the LD program does sit on the admissions committee. A personal interview is recommended. Essay is not required.

SECONDARY SCHOOL REQUIREMENTS

Graduation from secondary school required; GED accepted.

TESTING

SAT Reasoning or ACT considered if submitted. SAT Subject recommended.

All enrolled freshmen (fall 2004):

Average SAT I Scores:	Verbal: 460	Math: 440
Average ACT Scores:	Composite: 20	

Child Study Team report is not required. A neuropsychological or comprehensive psycho-educational evaluation is required for admission. Must be dated within 24 months of application. Tests required as part of this documentation:

- [x] WAIS-IV
- [x] WISC-IV
- [x] SATA
- [x] Woodcock-Johnson
- [x] Nelson-Denny Reading Test
- [ ] Other

UNDERGRADUATE STUDENT BODY

Total undergraduate student enrollment: 812 Men, 735 Women.

Composition of student body (fall 2004):

	Undergraduate	Freshmen
International	0.9	0.5
Black	16.0	11.7
American Indian	1.8	0.8
Asian-American	3.0	1.6
Hispanic	3.3	2.9
White	71.4	71.9
Unreported	3.6	10.6
	100.0%	100.0%

27% are from out of state. 7% join a fraternity and 4% join a sorority. Average age of full-time undergraduates is 21. 67% of classes have fewer than 20 students, 30% have between 20 and 50 students, 3% have more than 50 students.

STUDENT HOUSING

95% of freshmen live in college housing. Freshmen are required to live on campus. Housing is guaranteed for all undergraduates. Campus can house 534 undergraduates. Single rooms are available for students with medical or special needs. A medical note is required.

EXPENSES

Tuition (2005-06): $14,964 per year.
Room & Board: $4,896.
There is no additional cost for LD program/services.

LD SERVICES

LD program size is not limited.

LD services available to:

- [x] Freshmen
- [x] Sophomores
- [x] Juniors
- [x] Seniors

Academic Accommodations

Curriculum		In class	
Foreign language waiver	☐	Early syllabus	☐
Lighter course load	☑	Note takers in class	☑
Math waiver	☐	Priority seating	☐
Other special classes	☐	Tape recorders	☑
Priority registrations	☐	Videotaped classes	☐
Substitution of courses	☐	Text on tape	☐
Exams		**Services**	
Extended time	☑	Diagnostic tests	☐
Oral exams	☐	Learning centers	☐
Take home exams	☐	Proofreaders	☐
Exams on tape or computer	☐	Readers	☐
Untimed exams	☑	Reading Machines/Kurzweil	☐
Other accommodations	☐	Special bookstore section	☐
		Typists	☐

Credit toward degree is not given for remedial courses taken.

Counseling Services

- [x] Academic
- [x] Psychological
- [x] Student Support groups
- [ ] Vocational

Meets 6 times per academic year

Tutoring

Individual tutoring is available daily.

Average size of tutoring groups: 5

	Individual	Group
Time management	☐	☑
Organizational skills	☐	☐
Learning strategies	☐	☑
Study skills	☑	☑
Content area	☑	☐
Writing lab	☑	☑
Math lab	☑	☑

LD PROGRAM STAFF

Total number of LD Program staff (including director):

Full Time: 2 Part Time: 2

There is an advisor/advocate from the LD program available to students. The advisor/advocate meets with faculty and students once per month. 12 peer tutors are available to work with LD students.

Key staff person available to work with LD students: Dan Coffey, Director of Academic Resource Center

Baker University

Baldwin City, KS

Address: P.O. Box 65, Baldwin City, KS, 66006
Admissions telephone: 800 873-4282
Admissions FAX: 785 594-4282
Director of Admissions: Daniel McKinney
Admissions e-mail: admission@bakeru.edu
Web site: http://www.bakeru.edu
SAT Code: 6031 ACT Code: 1386

LD program name: Learning Resource Center: Disability Services Office
Special Services Coordinator: Cindy Novelo
LD program telephone: 785 594-8349
LD program e-mail: cindy.novelo@bakeru.edu
LD program enrollment: 11, Total campus enrollment: 1,802

GENERAL

Baker University is a private, coed, four-year institution. 36-acre campus in Baldwin City (population: 3,400), 15 miles from Lawrence; branch campuses in Kansas City, Topeka, and Wichita and in Lee's Summit, MO. Major airport and train serve Kansas City (50 miles); bus serves Lawrence. 4-1-4 system.

LD ADMISSIONS

Students do not complete a separate application and are not simultaneously accepted to the LD program. A member of the LD program does not sit on the admissions committee. A personal interview is recommended. Essay is not required.

SECONDARY SCHOOL REQUIREMENTS

Graduation from secondary school required; GED accepted.

TESTING

SAT Reasoning or ACT required. SAT Subject recommended.

All enrolled freshmen (fall 2004):

Average SAT I Scores: Verbal: 513 Math: 524
Average ACT Scores: Composite: 24

Child Study Team report is not required. A neuropsychological or comprehensive psycho-educational evaluation is required for admission. Must be dated within 36 months of application. Tests required as part of this documentation:

- ■ WAIS-IV
- ☐ WISC-IV
- ■ SATA
- ■ Woodcock-Johnson
- ■ Nelson-Denny Reading Test
- ☐ Other

UNDERGRADUATE STUDENT BODY

Total undergraduate student enrollment: 415 Men, 587 Women.

Composition of student body (fall 2004):

	Undergraduate	Freshmen
International	0.0	0.3
Black	7.3	7.2
American Indian	0.0	0.8
Asian-American	1.4	1.3
Hispanic	5.5	3.8
White	80.0	77.4
Unreported	5.8	9.2
	100.0%	100.0%

25% are from out of state. 41% join a fraternity and 47% join a sorority. Average age of full-time undergraduates is 20. 78% of classes have fewer than 20 students, 21% have between 20 and 50 students, 1% have more than 50 students.

STUDENT HOUSING

94% of freshmen live in college housing. Freshmen are required to live on campus. Housing is guaranteed for all undergraduates. Campus can house 868 undergraduates.

EXPENSES

Tuition (2005-06): $16,100 per year.

Room: $2,580. Board: $3,050.
There is no additional cost for LD program/services.

LD SERVICES

LD program size is not limited.

LD services available to:

■ Freshmen ■ Sophomores ■ Juniors ■ Seniors

Academic Accommodations

Curriculum		**In class**	
Foreign language waiver	☐	Early syllabus	☐
Lighter course load	■	Note takers in class	■
Math waiver	☐	Priority seating	■
Other special classes	☐	Tape recorders	■
Priority registrations	☐	Videotaped classes	☐
Substitution of courses	☐	Text on tape	☐
Exams		**Services**	
Extended time	■	Diagnostic tests	☐
Oral exams	■	Learning centers	■
Take home exams	☐	Proofreaders	☐
Exams on tape or computer	■	Readers	■
Untimed exams	☐	Reading Machines/Kurzweil	☐
Other accommodations	☐	Special bookstore section	☐
		Typists	■

Credit toward degree is not given for remedial courses taken.

Counseling Services

- ■ Academic
- ■ Psychological
- ☐ Student Support groups
- ☐ Vocational

Tutoring

Individual tutoring is available.

Average size of tutoring groups: 3

	Individual	Group
Time management	■	☐
Organizational skills	■	☐
Learning strategies	■	☐
Study skills	■	☐
Content area	■	☐
Writing lab	☐	☐
Math lab	☐	☐

LD PROGRAM STAFF

Total number of LD Program staff (including director):

Full Time: 3 Part Time: 3

There is an advisor/advocate from the LD program available to students. 12 peer tutors are available to work with LD students.

Key staff person available to work with LD students: Cindy Novelo, Special Services Coordinator

Benedictine College

Atchison, KS

Address: 1020 North Second Street, Atchison, KS, 66002
Admissions telephone: 800 467-5340
Admissions FAX: 913 367-5462
Dean of Enrollment Management: Kelly Vowels
Admissions e-mail: bcadmiss@benedictine.edu
Web site: http://www.benedictine.edu
SAT Code: 6056 ACT Code: 1444

LD program name: General Studies Program
Director of General Studies Center: Camille Osborn
LD program telephone: 913 360-7517
LD program e-mail: cosborn@benedictine.edu
LD program enrollment: 65, Total campus enrollment: 1,394

GENERAL

Benedictine College is a private, coed, four-year institution. 100-acre campus in Atchison (population: 10,232), 25 miles from Kansas City. Major airport and train serve Kansas City; bus serves St. Joseph, MO (20 miles). School operates transportation to airport and bus and train stations. Public transportation serves campus. Semester system.

LD ADMISSIONS

Students do not complete a separate application and are not simultaneously accepted to the LD program. A member of the LD program does sit on the admissions committee. A personal interview is recommended. Essay is not required.

For fall 2004, 19 completed self-identified LD applications were received. 18 applications were offered admission, and 11 enrolled.

SECONDARY SCHOOL REQUIREMENTS

Graduation from secondary school required; GED accepted. The following course distribution required: 4 units of English, 3 units of math, 2 units of science, 2 units of foreign language, 2 units of social studies, 1 unit of history.

TESTING

SAT Subject recommended.

All enrolled freshmen (fall 2004):

Average SAT I Scores:	Verbal: 508	Math: 528
Average ACT Scores:	Composite: 23	

Child Study Team report is required if student is classified. A neuropsychological or comprehensive psycho-education evaluation is not required for admission. Tests required as part of this documentation:

- ☐ WAIS-IV
- ☐ WISC-IV
- ☐ SATA
- ☐ Woodcock-Johnson
- ☐ Nelson-Denny Reading Test
- ☐ Other

UNDERGRADUATE STUDENT BODY

Total undergraduate student enrollment: 629 Men, 668 Women.

Composition of student body (fall 2004):

	Undergraduate	Freshmen
International	1.6	3.0
Black	3.2	3.7
American Indian	0.0	0.2
Asian-American	1.0	1.7
Hispanic	5.8	7.5
White	85.2	81.7
Unreported	3.2	2.2
	100.0%	100.0%

54% are from out of state. Average age of full-time undergraduates is 20. 50% of classes have fewer than 20 students, 50% have between 20 and 50 students.

STUDENT HOUSING

98% of freshmen live in college housing. Freshmen are required to live on campus. Housing is guaranteed for all undergraduates. Campus can house 766 undergraduates. Single rooms are available for students with medical or special needs. A medical note is required.

EXPENSES

Tuition (2005-06): $15,110 per year.
Room: $2,730-$2,800. Board: $3,478.
There is no additional cost for LD program/services.

LD SERVICES

LD program size is not limited.

LD services available to:

■ Freshmen ■ Sophomores ■ Juniors ■ Seniors

Academic Accommodations

Curriculum		In class	
Foreign language waiver	■	Early syllabus	☐
Lighter course load	☐	Note takers in class	■
Math waiver	■	Priority seating	☐
Other special classes	☐	Tape recorders	■
Priority registrations	☐	Videotaped classes	☐
Substitution of courses	☐	Text on tape	☐
Exams		**Services**	
Extended time	■	Diagnostic tests	☐
Oral exams	■	Learning centers	■
Take home exams	☐	Proofreaders	☐
Exams on tape or computer	☐	Readers	■
Untimed exams	■	Reading Machines/Kurzweil	☐
Other accommodations	☐	Special bookstore section	☐
		Typists	■

Credit toward degree is not given for remedial courses taken.

Counseling Services

- ■ Academic
- ■ Psychological
- ☐ Student Support groups
- ☐ Vocational

Tutoring

Individual tutoring is available daily.

Average size of tutoring groups: 1

	Individual	Group
Time management	■	■
Organizational skills	■	■
Learning strategies	■	■
Study skills	■	■
Content area	■	☐
Writing lab	☐	☐
Math lab	☐	☐

LD PROGRAM STAFF

There is an advisor/advocate from the LD program available to students. 20 peer tutors are available to work with LD students.

Key staff person available to work with LD students: Camille Osborn, Director of General Studies Center

LD Program web site: www.benedictine.edu

Bethany College

Lindsborg, KS

Address: 421 North First Street, Lindsborg, KS, 67456-1897
Admissions telephone: 800 826-2281
Admissions FAX: 785 227-8993
Dean of Admissions and Financial Aid: Thandabantu Maceo
Admissions e-mail: admissions@bethanylb.edu
Web site: http://www.bethanylb.edu
SAT Code: 6034 ACT Code: 1388

Director of Academic Support Services: Tamara Korenman, Ph.D.
LD program telephone: 785 227-3311
LD program e-mail: tamarak@bethanylb.edu
Total campus enrollment: 585

GENERAL

Bethany College is a private, coed, four-year institution. 56-acre campus in Lindsborg (population: 3,321), 20 miles from Salina and 70 miles from Wichita. Major airport serves Wichita; smaller airport and bus serve Salina; train serves Newton (40 miles). 4-1-4 system.

LD ADMISSIONS

A personal interview is required. Essay is not required.

SECONDARY SCHOOL REQUIREMENTS

Graduation from secondary school required; GED accepted.

TESTING

ACT required; SAT Reasoning may be substituted.

All enrolled freshmen (fall 2004):

Average SAT I Scores: Verbal: 475 Math: 478
Average ACT Scores: Composite: 21

Child Study Team report is not required. Tests required as part of this documentation:

☐ WAIS-IV ☐ Woodcock-Johnson
☐ WISC-IV ☐ Nelson-Denny Reading Test
☐ SATA ☐ Other

UNDERGRADUATE STUDENT BODY

Total undergraduate student enrollment: 329 Men, 293 Women.

Composition of student body (fall 2004):

	Undergraduate	Freshmen
International	1.9	2.6
Black	9.7	8.3
American Indian	1.4	1.2
Asian-American	1.9	0.9
Hispanic	3.9	4.0
White	76.0	78.4
Unreported	5.2	4.6
	100.0%	100.0%

37% are from out of state. 15% join a fraternity and 18% join a sorority. Average age of full-time undergraduates is 20. 81% of classes have fewer than 20 students, 19% have between 20 and 50 students.

STUDENT HOUSING

91% of freshmen live in college housing. Housing is guaranteed for all undergraduates. Campus can house 609 undergraduates.

EXPENSES

Tuition (2005-06): $15,250 per year.
Room: $2,850. Board: $2,350.

There is no additional cost for LD program/services.

LD SERVICES

LD program size is not limited.

LD services available to:

☐ Freshmen ☐ Sophomores ☐ Juniors ☐ Seniors

Academic Accommodations

Curriculum		**In class**	
Foreign language waiver	☐	Early syllabus	☐
Lighter course load	☐	Note takers in class	■
Math waiver	☐	Priority seating	☐
Other special classes	■	Tape recorders	■
Priority registrations	☐	Videotaped classes	☐
Substitution of courses	☐	Text on tape	☐
Exams		**Services**	
Extended time	■	Diagnostic tests	■
Oral exams	■	Learning centers	■
Take home exams	☐	Proofreaders	☐
Exams on tape or computer	☐	Readers	■
Untimed exams	■	Reading Machines/Kurzweil	☐
Other accommodations	☐	Special bookstore section	☐
		Typists	☐

Credit toward degree is not given for remedial courses taken.

Counseling Services

☐ Academic
☐ Psychological
☐ Student Support groups
☐ Vocational

Tutoring

	Individual	Group
Time management	☐	☐
Organizational skills	☐	☐
Learning strategies	☐	☐
Study skills	☐	☐
Content area	☐	☐
Writing lab	☐	☐
Math lab	☐	☐

LD PROGRAM STAFF

Total number of LD Program staff (including director):

Full Time: 1 Part Time: 1

Key staff person available to work with LD students: Tamara Korenman, Ph.D., Director of Academic Support Services

Bethel College

North Newton, KS

Address: 300 East 27th Street, North Newton, KS, 67117-0531
Admissions telephone: 800 522-1887, extension 230
Admissions FAX: 316 284-5870
Dean of Enrollment Services: Allan Bartel
Admissions e-mail: admissions@bethelks.edu
Web site: http://www.bethelks.edu
SAT Code: 6037 ACT Code: 1390

Director of Center for Academic Development: Dan Quinlin
LD program telephone: 316 284-5333
LD program e-mail: dquinlin@bethelks.edu
Total campus enrollment: 509

GENERAL

Bethel College is a private, coed, four-year institution. 60-acre campus in North Newton (population: 1,533), 25 miles from Wichita. Major airport and bus serve Wichita; train serves Newton (four miles). 4-1-4 system.

LD ADMISSIONS

A personal interview is recommended. Essay is not required. Consideration is given to all students not meeting automatic admission requirements.

SECONDARY SCHOOL REQUIREMENTS

Graduation from secondary school required; GED accepted. The following course distribution required: 4 units of English, 4 units of math, 3 units of science, 2 units of foreign language, 3 units of social studies, 1 unit of history.

TESTING

SAT Reasoning or ACT required. SAT Subject recommended.

All enrolled freshmen (fall 2004):

Average SAT I Scores:	Verbal: 591	Math: 603
Average ACT Scores:	Composite: 24	

Child Study Team report is not required. A neuropsychological or comprehensive psycho-educational evaluation is required for admission. Must be dated within 24 months of application. Tests required as part of this documentation:

- ■ WAIS-IV
- ■ WISC-IV
- ■ SATA
- ■ Woodcock-Johnson
- ☐ Nelson-Denny Reading Test
- ☐ Other

UNDERGRADUATE STUDENT BODY

Total undergraduate student enrollment: 263 Men, 262 Women.

Composition of student body (fall 2004):

	Undergraduate	Freshmen
International	2.5	3.7
Black	2.5	5.5
American Indian	0.9	0.6
Asian-American	0.8	2.4
Hispanic	4.2	4.7
White	89.1	83.1
Unreported	0.0	0.0
	100.0%	100.0%

31% are from out of state. Average age of full-time undergraduates is 21. 72% of classes have fewer than 20 students, 27% have between 20 and 50 students, 1% have more than 50 students.

STUDENT HOUSING

94% of freshmen live in college housing. Freshmen are required to live on campus. Housing is guaranteed for all undergraduates. Campus can house 458 undergraduates. Single rooms are available for students with medical or special needs. A medical note is required.

EXPENSES

Tuition (2005-06): $15,550 per year.
Room: $3,200. Board: $2,900.
There is no additional cost for LD program/services.

LD SERVICES

LD program size is not limited.

LD services available to:

■ Freshmen ■ Sophomores ■ Juniors ■ Seniors

Academic Accommodations

Curriculum		In class	
Foreign language waiver	☐	Early syllabus	☐
Lighter course load	■	Note takers in class	■
Math waiver	☐	Priority seating	☐
Other special classes	☐	Tape recorders	■
Priority registrations	☐	Videotaped classes	■
Substitution of courses	☐	Text on tape	☐
Exams		**Services**	
Extended time	■	Diagnostic tests	☐
Oral exams	■	Learning centers	■
Take home exams	☐	Proofreaders	☐
Exams on tape or computer	☐	Readers	■
Untimed exams	■	Reading Machines/Kurzweil	☐
Other accommodations	☐	Special bookstore section	☐
		Typists	☐

Credit toward degree is not given for remedial courses taken.

Counseling Services

- ☐ Academic
- ☐ Psychological
- ☐ Student Support groups
- ☐ Vocational

Tutoring

Individual tutoring is available daily.

	Individual	Group
Time management	■	☐
Organizational skills	■	☐
Learning strategies	■	☐
Study skills	■	☐
Content area	■	☐
Writing lab	■	☐
Math lab	■	☐

LD PROGRAM STAFF

There is an advisor/advocate from the LD program available to students.

Key staff person available to work with LD students: Dan Quinlin, Director of Center for Academic Development

Central Christian College of Kansas

McPherson, KS

Address: 1200 South Main, P.O. Box 1403, McPherson, KS, 67460-5799
Admissions telephone: 800 835-0078
Admissions FAX: 620 241-6032
Dean of Admissions: Dr. David Ferrell
Admissions e-mail: david.ferrell@centralchristian.edu
Web site: http://www.centralchristian.edu/index.html
SAT Code: 6088 ACT Code: 1394

LD program name: Guidance Center
Director of Guidance Center: Karen Mayse
LD program telephone: 620 241-0723
LD program e-mail: karen.mayse@centralchristian.edu
LD program enrollment: 9, Total campus enrollment: 324

GENERAL

Central Christian College of Kansas is a private, coed, four-year institution. 15-acre campus in McPherson (population: 13,770), 50 miles from Wichita. Served by bus; major airport serves Wichita; train serves Newton (30 miles). 4-1-4 system.

LD ADMISSIONS

Students do not complete a separate application and are simultaneously accepted to the LD program. A member of the LD program does sit on the admissions committee. High school waivers are accepted for math and foreign language. A personal interview is recommended. Essay is not required.

For fall 2004, 6 completed self-identified LD applications were received. 4 applications were offered admission, and 3 enrolled.

SECONDARY SCHOOL REQUIREMENTS

Graduation from secondary school required; GED accepted.

TESTING

SAT Subject recommended.

All enrolled freshmen (fall 2004):

Average SAT I Scores: Verbal: 422 Math: 429
Average ACT Scores: Composite: 20

Child Study Team report is not required. A neuropsychological or comprehensive psycho-education evaluation is not required for admission. Tests required as part of this documentation:

- [ ] WAIS-IV
- [ ] WISC-IV
- [ ] SATA
- [ ] Woodcock-Johnson
- [ ] Nelson-Denny Reading Test
- [ ] Other

UNDERGRADUATE STUDENT BODY

Total undergraduate student enrollment: 150 Men, 164 Women.

Composition of student body (fall 2004):

	Undergraduate	Freshmen
International	2.2	2.6
Black	16.1	9.6
American Indian	4.3	2.3
Asian-American	0.0	0.4
Hispanic	11.8	7.3
White	65.6	77.8
Unreported	0.0	0.0
	100.0%	100.0%

60% are from out of state. Average age of full-time undergraduates is 22. 79% of classes have fewer than 20 students, 18% have between 20 and 50 students, 3% have more than 50 students.

STUDENT HOUSING

90% of freshmen live in college housing. Freshmen are required to live on campus. Housing is guaranteed for all undergraduates. Campus can house 300 undergraduates. Single rooms are available for students with medical or special needs. A medical note is required.

EXPENSES

Tuition (2005-06): $13,100 per year.
Room: $2,100. Board: $2,400.
There is no additional cost for LD program/services.

LD SERVICES

LD program size is not limited.

LD services available to:

- [x] Freshmen
- [x] Sophomores
- [x] Juniors
- [x] Seniors

Academic Accommodations

Curriculum		In class	
Foreign language waiver	[ ]	Early syllabus	[ ]
Lighter course load	[x]	Note takers in class	[x]
Math waiver	[ ]	Priority seating	[ ]
Other special classes	[x]	Tape recorders	[ ]
Priority registrations	[ ]	Videotaped classes	[ ]
Substitution of courses	[ ]	Text on tape	[ ]
Exams		**Services**	
Extended time	[x]	Diagnostic tests	[ ]
Oral exams	[x]	Learning centers	[ ]
Take home exams	[ ]	Proofreaders	[ ]
Exams on tape or computer	[ ]	Readers	[x]
Untimed exams	[x]	Reading Machines/Kurzweil	[ ]
Other accommodations	[ ]	Special bookstore section	[ ]
		Typists	[ ]

Credit toward degree is given for remedial courses taken.

Counseling Services

- [x] Academic — Meets 6 times per academic year
- [ ] Psychological
- [ ] Student Support groups
- [x] Vocational — Meets 2 times per academic year

Tutoring

Individual tutoring is available weekly.

Average size of tutoring groups: 4

	Individual	Group
Time management	[x]	[x]
Organizational skills	[x]	[x]
Learning strategies	[x]	[x]
Study skills	[x]	[x]
Content area	[ ]	[ ]
Writing lab	[ ]	[ ]
Math lab	[ ]	[ ]

LD PROGRAM STAFF

There is an advisor/advocate from the LD program available to students. The advisor/advocate meets with faculty once per month and students three times per month. Three peer tutors are available to work with LD students.

Key staff person available to work with LD students: Karen Mayse, Director of Guidance Center

Emporia State University

Emporia, KS

Address: 1200 Commercial, Emporia, KS, 66801-5087
Admissions telephone: 877 GO-TO-ESU
Admissions FAX: 620 341-5599
Director of Admissions: Laura Eddy
Admissions e-mail: go2esu@emporia.edu
Web site: http://www.emporia.edu
SAT Code: 6335 ACT Code: 1430

LD program name: Office of Disability Services
LD program address: ESU, Campus Box 4023
Director, Office of Disability Services: Shanti Ramcharan
LD program telephone: 620 341-6637
LD program e-mail: disabser@emporia.edu
LD program enrollment: 78, Total campus enrollment: 4,370

GENERAL

Emporia State University is a public, coed, four-year institution. 207-acre campus in Emporia (population: 26,760), 50 miles from Topeka. Served by bus; major airport serves Kansas City (110 miles); smaller airport and train serve Topeka. Semester system.

LD ADMISSIONS

Students do not complete a separate application and are not simultaneously accepted to the LD program. A member of the LD program does not sit on the admissions committee. A personal interview is not required. Essay is not required.

SECONDARY SCHOOL REQUIREMENTS

Graduation from secondary school required; GED accepted. The following course distribution required: 4 units of English, 3 units of math, 3 units of science, 3 units of social studies.

TESTING

ACT required; SAT Reasoning may be substituted. SAT Subject recommended.

All enrolled freshmen (fall 2004):

Average ACT Scores: Composite: 22

Child Study Team report is not required. A neuropsychological or comprehensive psycho-educational evaluation is required for admission. Must be dated within 36 months of application. Tests required as part of this documentation:

■ WAIS-IV ■ Woodcock-Johnson
■ WISC-IV ☐ Nelson-Denny Reading Test
☐ SATA ■ Other

UNDERGRADUATE STUDENT BODY

Total undergraduate student enrollment: 1,665 Men, 2,622 Women.

Composition of student body (fall 2004):

	Undergraduate	Freshmen
International	1.2	1.8
Black	4.3	4.0
American Indian	1.5	0.7
Asian-American	1.0	0.8
Hispanic	5.5	4.4
White	84.7	86.0
Unreported	1.8	2.3
	100.0%	100.0%

8% are from out of state. 10% join a fraternity and 7% join a sorority. Average age of full-time undergraduates is 22. 39% of classes have fewer than 20 students, 54% have between 20 and 50 students, 7% have more than 50 students.

STUDENT HOUSING

85% of freshmen live in college housing. Freshmen are required to live on campus. Housing is guaranteed for all undergraduates. Campus can house 1,226 undergraduates. Single rooms are available for students with medical or special needs. A medical note is required.

EXPENSES

Tuition (2005-06): $2,638 per year (in-state), $9,990 (out-of-state). Room: $2,363. Board: $2,424.
There is no additional cost for LD program/services.

LD SERVICES

LD program size is not limited.

LD services available to:

■ Freshmen ■ Sophomores ■ Juniors ■ Seniors

Academic Accommodations

Curriculum		In class	
Foreign language waiver	■	Early syllabus	■
Lighter course load	■	Note takers in class	■
Math waiver	■	Priority seating	■
Other special classes	☐	Tape recorders	■
Priority registrations	■	Videotaped classes	☐
Substitution of courses	■	Text on tape	■
Exams		**Services**	
Extended time	■	Diagnostic tests	■
Oral exams	■	Learning centers	☐
Take home exams	☐	Proofreaders	☐
Exams on tape or computer	■	Readers	■
Untimed exams	☐	Reading Machines/Kurzweil	■
Other accommodations	■	Special bookstore section	☐
		Typists	■

Credit toward degree is not given for remedial courses taken.

Counseling Services

☐ Academic
☐ Psychological
☐ Student Support groups
☐ Vocational

Tutoring

Individual tutoring is not available.

	Individual	Group
Time management	■	☐
Organizational skills	■	☐
Learning strategies	■	☐
Study skills	■	☐
Content area	■	☐
Writing lab	■	■
Math lab	■	■

LD PROGRAM STAFF

Total number of LD Program staff (including director):

Full Time: 1 Part Time: 1

There is an advisor/advocate from the LD program available to students. One graduate student is available to work with LD students.

Key staff person available to work with LD students: Shanti Ramcharan, Director, Office of Disability Services

LD Program web site: www.emporia.edu/disability

Friends University

Wichita, KS

Address: 2100 West University Street, Wichita, KS, 67213
Admissions telephone: 316 295-5100
Admissions FAX: 316 295-5101
Vice President of Enrollment Management: Tony Myers
Admissions e-mail: learn@friends.edu
Web site: http://www.friends.edu
SAT Code: 6224 ACT Code: 1412

LD program name: Disability Services
Associate Vice President of Student Affairs: Cynthia Jacobson
LD program telephone: 316 295-5779
LD program e-mail: ada@friends.edu
LD program enrollment: 15, Total campus enrollment: 2,271

GENERAL

Friends University is a private, coed, four-year institution. 46-acre, urban campus in Wichita (population: 344,284); branch campuses in Kansas City, Liberal, and Topeka. Served by air and bus; train serves Newton (25 miles). Public transportation serves campus. Semester system.

LD ADMISSIONS

Students do not complete a separate application and are not simultaneously accepted to the LD program. A member of the LD program does not sit on the admissions committee. A personal interview is not required. Essay is not required.

For fall 2004, 21 completed self-identified LD applications were received. 21 applications were offered admission, and 16 enrolled.

SECONDARY SCHOOL REQUIREMENTS

Graduation from secondary school required; GED accepted.

TESTING

ACT recommended; SAT Reasoning may be substituted. SAT Subject recommended.

All enrolled freshmen (fall 2004):

Average SAT I Scores:	Verbal: 511	Math: 495
Average ACT Scores:	Composite: 21	

Child Study Team report is not required. A neuropsychological or comprehensive psycho-educational evaluation is required for admission. Tests required as part of this documentation:

■ WAIS-IV	■ Woodcock-Johnson
■ WISC-IV	■ Nelson-Denny Reading Test
■ SATA	☐ Other

UNDERGRADUATE STUDENT BODY

Total undergraduate student enrollment: 452 Men, 571 Women.

Composition of student body (fall 2004):

	Undergraduate	Freshmen
International	4.7	1.3
Black	18.0	11.4
American Indian	2.4	1.8
Asian-American	1.4	1.5
Hispanic	10.0	5.3
White	63.5	78.7
Unreported	0.0	0.0
	100.0%	100.0%

12% are from out of state. 1% join a fraternity. Average age of full-time undergraduates is 22. 60% of classes have fewer than 20 students, 40% have between 20 and 50 students.

STUDENT HOUSING

56% of freshmen live in college housing. Freshmen are not required to live on campus. Housing is guaranteed for all undergraduates. Campus can house 329 undergraduates. Single rooms are available for students with medical or special needs. A medical note is required.

EXPENSES

Tuition (2005-06): $15,150 per year.

Room: $2,420. Board: $2,500.

There is no additional cost for LD program/services.

LD SERVICES

LD program size is not limited.

LD services available to:

■ Freshmen ■ Sophomores ■ Juniors ■ Seniors

Academic Accommodations

Curriculum		**In class**	
Foreign language waiver	☐	Early syllabus	☐
Lighter course load	☐	Note takers in class	■
Math waiver	☐	Priority seating	☐
Other special classes	■	Tape recorders	■
Priority registrations	☐	Videotaped classes	■
Substitution of courses	☐	Text on tape	■
Exams		**Services**	
Extended time	■	Diagnostic tests	☐
Oral exams	■	Learning centers	■
Take home exams	☐	Proofreaders	☐
Exams on tape or computer	■	Readers	■
Untimed exams	■	Reading Machines/Kurzweil	■
Other accommodations	☐	Special bookstore section	☐
		Typists	■

Credit toward degree is not given for remedial courses taken.

Counseling Services

■ Academic — Meets 2 times per academic year
☐ Psychological
☐ Student Support groups
☐ Vocational

Tutoring

Individual tutoring is available daily.

Average size of tutoring groups: 1

	Individual	Group
Time management	■	☐
Organizational skills	■	☐
Learning strategies	■	☐
Study skills	■	☐
Content area	■	☐
Writing lab	■	■
Math lab	■	■

LD PROGRAM STAFF

Total number of LD Program staff (including director):

Full Time: 2 Part Time: 2

There is an advisor/advocate from the LD program available to students. The advisor/advocate meets with faculty four times per month and students 15 times per month. 10 peer tutors are available to work with LD students.

Key staff person available to work with LD students: Cynthia Jacobson, Associate Vice President of Student Affairs

Kansas State University

Manhattan, KS

Address: Anderson Hall, Manhattan, KS, 66506
Admissions telephone: 800 432-8270 (in-state)
Admissions FAX: 785 532-6393
Director of Admissions: Larry Moeder
Admissions e-mail: kstate@ksu.edu
Web site: http://www.ksu.edu
SAT Code: 6334 ACT Code: 1428

LD program name: Disability Support Services
LD program address: 202 Holton Hall
Director: Gretchen Holden
LD program telephone: 785 532-6441
LD program e-mail: gretch@ksu.edu
LD program enrollment: 170, Total campus enrollment: 19,098

GENERAL

Kansas State University is a public, coed, four-year institution. 668-acre campus in Manhattan (population: 44,831), 55 miles from Topeka; branch campus in Salina. Served by air and bus; major airport serves Kansas City (116 miles); train serves Topeka. School operates transportation to two off-campus buildings and for students with disabilities. Semester system.

LD ADMISSIONS

Students complete a separate application and are not simultaneously accepted to the LD program. A member of the LD program does not sit on the admissions committee. A personal interview is not required. Essay is not required.

SECONDARY SCHOOL REQUIREMENTS

Graduation from secondary school required; GED accepted.

TESTING

ACT required; SAT Reasoning may be substituted. SAT Subject recommended.

All enrolled freshmen (fall 2004):

Average ACT Scores: Composite: 24

Child Study Team report is not required. A neuropsychological or comprehensive psycho-educational evaluation is required for admission. Must be dated within 36 months of application. Tests required as part of this documentation:

- ■ WAIS-IV
- ■ WISC-IV
- ■ SATA
- ■ Woodcock-Johnson
- ■ Nelson-Denny Reading Test
- ■ Other

UNDERGRADUATE STUDENT BODY

Total undergraduate student enrollment: 9,856 Men, 8,914 Women.

Composition of student body (fall 2004):

	Undergraduate	Freshmen
International	1.2	1.0
Black	3.4	2.9
American Indian	0.8	0.6
Asian-American	1.5	1.3
Hispanic	2.8	2.4
White	86.6	88.4
Unreported	3.7	3.4
	100.0%	100.0%

9% are from out of state. 20% join a fraternity and 20% join a sorority. 49% of classes have fewer than 20 students, 41% have between 20 and 50 students, 10% have more than 50 students.

STUDENT HOUSING

Freshmen are not required to live on campus. Housing is guaranteed for all undergraduates. Campus can house 5,987 undergraduates. Single rooms are available for students with medical or special needs. A medical note is required.

EXPENSES

Tuition (2005-06): $4,560 per year (in-state), $13,890 (out-of-state).

Room & Board: $6,024.
There is no additional cost for LD program/services.

LD SERVICES

LD program size is not limited.

LD services available to:

■ Freshmen ■ Sophomores ■ Juniors ■ Seniors

Academic Accommodations

Curriculum		In class	
Foreign language waiver	☐	Early syllabus	☐
Lighter course load	■	Note takers in class	■
Math waiver	☐	Priority seating	☐
Other special classes	☐	Tape recorders	☐
Priority registrations	■	Videotaped classes	☐
Substitution of courses	■	Text on tape	■
Exams		**Services**	
Extended time	■	Diagnostic tests	☐
Oral exams	■	Learning centers	☐
Take home exams	☐	Proofreaders	■
Exams on tape or computer	■	Readers	■
Untimed exams	☐	Reading Machines/Kurzweil	■
Other accommodations	■	Special bookstore section	☐
		Typists	☐

Credit toward degree is not given for remedial courses taken.

Counseling Services

- ■ Academic
- ■ Psychological
- ■ Student Support groups
- ■ Vocational

Tutoring

Individual tutoring is available weekly.

	Individual	Group
Time management	☐	☐
Organizational skills	☐	☐
Learning strategies	☐	☐
Study skills	☐	☐
Content area	☐	☐
Writing lab	☐	☐
Math lab	☐	☐

LD PROGRAM STAFF

Total number of LD Program staff (including director):

Full Time: 1 Part Time: 1

There is an advisor/advocate from the LD program available to students. One graduate student is available to work with LD students.

Key staff person available to work with LD students: Andrea Blair, Learning Disabilities Specialist

LD Program web site: www.ksu.edu/dss

University of Kansas

Lawrence, KS

Address: 1502 Iowa Street, Lawrence, KS, 66045-7576
Admissions telephone: 785 864-3911
Admissions FAX: 785 864-5006
Director of Admissions and Scholarships: Lisa Pinamonti Kress
Admissions e-mail: adm@ku.edu
Web site: http://www.ku.edu
SAT Code: 6871 ACT Code: 1470

LD program name: Academic Achievement & Access Center/Disability Resources
LD program address: 1450 Jayhwak Blvd, Rm 22
Learning Disability Specialist: Andrew Shoemaker
LD program telephone: 785 864-2620
LD program e-mail: shoe@ku.edu
LD program enrollment: 253, Total campus enrollment: 21,343

GENERAL

University of Kansas is a public, coed, four-year institution. 1,000-acre campus in Lawrence (population: 80,089), 40 miles from Kansas City; branch campus and medical center in Kansas City. Served by bus and train; major airport serves Kansas City. Public transportation serves campus. Semester system.

LD ADMISSIONS

Students do not complete a separate application and are simultaneously accepted to the LD program. A member of the LD program does sit on the admissions committee. A personal interview is not required. Essay is not required.

SECONDARY SCHOOL REQUIREMENTS

Graduation from secondary school required; GED accepted. The following course distribution required: 4 units of English, 3 units of math, 3 units of science, 3 units of social studies.

TESTING

SAT Reasoning or ACT required. SAT Subject recommended.

All enrolled freshmen (fall 2004):

Average ACT Scores: Composite: 24

Child Study Team report is not required. A neuropsychological or comprehensive psycho-educational evaluation is required for admission. Must be dated within 24 months of application. Tests required as part of this documentation:

- [x] WAIS-IV
- [x] WISC-IV
- [ ] SATA
- [x] Woodcock-Johnson
- [ ] Nelson-Denny Reading Test
- [ ] Other

UNDERGRADUATE STUDENT BODY

Total undergraduate student enrollment: 9,462 Men, 10,600 Women.

Composition of student body (fall 2004):

	Undergraduate	Freshmen
International	1.8	3.0
Black	4.4	3.5
American Indian	1.0	1.3
Asian-American	4.0	4.0
Hispanic	3.8	3.2
White	81.7	82.6
Unreported	3.3	2.4
	100.0%	100.0%

24% are from out of state. 14% join a fraternity and 17% join a sorority. Average age of full-time undergraduates is 21. 31% of classes have fewer than 20 students, 56% have between 20 and 50 students, 13% have more than 50 students.

STUDENT HOUSING

55% of freshmen live in college housing. Freshmen are not required to live on campus. Housing is not guaranteed for all undergraduates. Campus can house 5,299 undergraduates. Single rooms are available for students with medical or special needs. A medical note is required.

EXPENSES

Tuition (2005-06): $4,824 per year (in-state), $13,277 (out-of-state).
Room: $2,752. Board: $2,750.
There is no additional cost for LD program/services.

LD SERVICES

LD program size is not limited.

LD services available to:

- [x] Freshmen
- [x] Sophomores
- [x] Juniors
- [x] Seniors

Academic Accommodations

Curriculum		In class	
Foreign language waiver	[ ]	Early syllabus	[ ]
Lighter course load	[ ]	Note takers in class	[x]
Math waiver	[ ]	Priority seating	[x]
Other special classes	[ ]	Tape recorders	[x]
Priority registrations	[x]	Videotaped classes	[ ]
Substitution of courses	[ ]	Text on tape	[x]
Exams		**Services**	
Extended time	[x]	Diagnostic tests	[x]
Oral exams	[x]	Learning centers	[x]
Take home exams	[ ]	Proofreaders	[ ]
Exams on tape or computer	[x]	Readers	[x]
Untimed exams	[ ]	Reading Machines/Kurzweil	[ ]
Other accommodations	[x]	Special bookstore section	[ ]
		Typists	[x]

Credit toward degree is not given for remedial courses taken.

Counseling Services

- [x] Academic
- [x] Psychological
- [x] Student Support groups — Meets 28 times per academic year
- [x] Vocational

Tutoring

Individual tutoring is available weekly.

Average size of tutoring groups: 3

	Individual	Group
Time management	[x]	[ ]
Organizational skills	[x]	[ ]
Learning strategies	[x]	[ ]
Study skills	[x]	[x]
Content area	[ ]	[x]
Writing lab	[x]	[ ]
Math lab	[x]	[ ]

LD PROGRAM STAFF

Total number of LD Program staff (including director):

Full Time: 1 Part Time: 1

There is an advisor/advocate from the LD program available to students. Two peer tutors are available to work with LD students.

Key staff person available to work with LD students: Andrew Shoemaker, Learning Disability Specialist

LD Program web site: www.disability.ku.edu

Manhattan Christian College

Manhattan, KS

Address: 1415 Anderson Avenue, Manhattan, KS, 66502
Admissions telephone: 877 2GO-4MCC
Admissions FAX: 785 776-9251
Director of Admissions and Recruitment: Pam Schmidt
Web site: http://www.mccks.edu
SAT Code: 6392 ACT Code: 1436

LD program name: Student Development
LD program contact: Rachael Lenz
LD program telephone: 785 539-3571
LD program e-mail: rlenz@mccks.edu
Total campus enrollment: 331

GENERAL

Manhattan Christian College is a private, coed, four-year institution. 16-acre campus in Manhattan (population: 44,831), 48 miles from Topeka and 115 miles from Kansas City. Served by bus; major airport serves Kansas City; smaller airport and train serve Topeka. Semester system.

LD ADMISSIONS

Application Deadline: 08/15. Students do not complete a separate application and are not simultaneously accepted to the LD program. A member of the LD program does not sit on the admissions committee. A personal interview is not required. Essay is required and may be typed.

SECONDARY SCHOOL REQUIREMENTS

Graduation from secondary school required; GED accepted.

TESTING

ACT required; SAT Reasoning may be substituted. SAT Subject recommended.

All enrolled freshmen (fall 2004):

Average ACT Scores: Composite: 22

Child Study Team report is not required. Tests required as part of this documentation:

- [ ] WAIS-IV
- [ ] WISC-IV
- [ ] SATA
- [ ] Woodcock-Johnson
- [ ] Nelson-Denny Reading Test
- [ ] Other

UNDERGRADUATE STUDENT BODY

Total undergraduate student enrollment: 184 Men, 228 Women.

Composition of student body (fall 2004):

	Undergraduate	Freshmen
International	0.0	0.4
Black	2.3	4.1
American Indian	0.0	0.0
Asian-American	0.0	0.5
Hispanic	0.0	2.0
White	95.4	91.4
Unreported	2.3	1.6
	100.0%	100.0%

30% are from out of state. 69% of classes have fewer than 20 students, 29% have between 20 and 50 students, 2% have more than 50 students.

STUDENT HOUSING

Freshmen are required to live on campus. Housing is not guaranteed for all undergraduates. Housing for upperclassmen is available if space allows. Campus can house 275 undergraduates. Single rooms are not available for students with medical or special needs.

EXPENSES

Tuition (2005-06): $9,444 per year.

Room & Board: $4,796.

There is no additional cost for LD program/services.

LD SERVICES

LD program size is not limited.

LD services available to:

[x] Freshmen [x] Sophomores [x] Juniors [x] Seniors

Academic Accommodations

Curriculum		**In class**	
Foreign language waiver	[ ]	Early syllabus	[ ]
Lighter course load	[x]	Note takers in class	[x]
Math waiver	[ ]	Priority seating	[x]
Other special classes	[ ]	Tape recorders	[ ]
Priority registrations	[ ]	Videotaped classes	[ ]
Substitution of courses	[ ]	Text on tape	[ ]
Exams		**Services**	
Extended time	[x]	Diagnostic tests	[ ]
Oral exams	[x]	Learning centers	[ ]
Take home exams	[ ]	Proofreaders	[ ]
Exams on tape or computer	[ ]	Readers	[x]
Untimed exams	[x]	Reading Machines/Kurzweil	[ ]
Other accommodations	[ ]	Special bookstore section	[ ]
		Typists	[ ]

Credit toward degree is not given for remedial courses taken.

Counseling Services

- [ ] Academic
- [ ] Psychological
- [ ] Student Support groups
- [ ] Vocational

Tutoring

Individual tutoring is available weekly.

	Individual	Group
Time management	[x]	[ ]
Organizational skills	[x]	[ ]
Learning strategies	[x]	[ ]
Study skills	[x]	[ ]
Content area	[x]	[ ]
Writing lab	[x]	[ ]
Math lab	[x]	[ ]

LD PROGRAM STAFF

Total number of LD Program staff (including director):

Full Time: 1 Part Time: 1

There is no advisor/advocate from the LD program available to students. Five peer tutors are available to work with LD students.

Key staff person available to work with LD students: Rachael Lenz

McPherson College

McPherson, KS

Address: P.O. Box 1402, McPherson, KS, 67460
Admissions telephone: 800 365-7402, extension 1270
Admissions FAX: 620 241-8443
Dean of Enrollment/Director of Admissions: Carol Williams
Admissions e-mail: admiss@mcpherson.edu
Web site: http://www.mcpherson.edu
SAT Code: 6404 ACT Code: 1440

Director of Academic Development: Kevin Hadduck
LD program telephone: 620 241-0731
LD program e-mail: hadduckk@mcpherson.edu
Total campus enrollment: 464

GENERAL

McPherson College is a private, coed, four-year institution. 23-acre campus in McPherson (population: 13,770), 60 miles from Wichita. Served by bus; major airport serves Wichita; train serves Hutchinson (25 miles). 4-1-4 system.

SECONDARY SCHOOL REQUIREMENTS

Graduation from secondary school required; GED accepted.

TESTING

SAT Subject recommended.

Child Study Team report is not required. Tests required as part of this documentation:

- ☐ WAIS-IV
- ☐ WISC-IV
- ☐ SATA
- ☐ Woodcock-Johnson
- ☐ Nelson-Denny Reading Test
- ☐ Other

UNDERGRADUATE STUDENT BODY

Total undergraduate student enrollment: 208 Men, 189 Women.

56% are from out of state. 72% of classes have fewer than 20 students, 25% have between 20 and 50 students, 3% have more than 50 students.

STUDENT HOUSING

Freshmen are required to live on campus. Housing is guaranteed for all undergraduates. Campus can house 416 undergraduates.

EXPENSES

Tuition (2005-06): $14,900 per year.

Room: $2,400. Board: $3,450.

There is no additional cost for LD program/services.

LD SERVICES

LD services available to:

☐ Freshmen ☐ Sophomores ☐ Juniors ☐ Seniors

Academic Accommodations

Curriculum		**In class**	
Foreign language waiver	☐	Early syllabus	☐
Lighter course load	☐	Note takers in class	■
Math waiver	☐	Priority seating	☐
Other special classes	☐	Tape recorders	☐
Priority registrations	☐	Videotaped classes	☐
Substitution of courses	☐	Text on tape	☐
Exams		**Services**	
Extended time	■	Diagnostic tests	☐
Oral exams	■	Learning centers	■
Take home exams	☐	Proofreaders	☐
Exams on tape or computer	☐	Readers	☐
Untimed exams	☐	Reading Machines/Kurzweil	■
Other accommodations	☐	Special bookstore section	☐
		Typists	☐

Credit toward degree is given for remedial courses taken.

Counseling Services

- ☐ Academic
- ☐ Psychological
- ☐ Student Support groups
- ☐ Vocational

Tutoring

	Individual	Group
Time management	☐	☐
Organizational skills	☐	☐
Learning strategies	☐	☐
Study skills	☐	☐
Content area	☐	☐
Writing lab	☐	☐
Math lab	☐	☐

LD PROGRAM STAFF

Key staff person available to work with LD students: Kevin Hadduck, Director of Academic Development

MidAmerica Nazarene University

Olathe, KS

Address: 2030 East College Way, Olathe, KS, 66062
Admissions telephone: 800 800-8887
Admissions FAX: 913 791-3481
Vice President of Enrollment Development: Mike Redwine
Admissions e-mail: admissions@mnu.edu
Web site: http://www.mnu.edu
SAT Code: 6437 ACT Code: 1445

LD program name: Kresge Academic Support Services
Director of Support Services: Cynthia K. Chamberlin
LD program telephone: 913 791-3387
LD program e-mail: ckchamberlin@mnu.edu
LD program enrollment: 20, Total campus enrollment: 1,466

GENERAL

MidAmerica Nazarene University is a private, coed, four-year institution. 105-acre campus in Olathe (population: 92,962), 20 miles from Kansas City. Major airport serves Kansas City, MO (38 miles); bus and train serve Kansas City. Public transportation serves campus. Semester system.

LD ADMISSIONS

A member of the LD program does not sit on the admissions committee. A personal interview is required. Essay is not required.

For fall 2004, 27 completed self-identified LD applications were received. 27 applications were offered admission, and 27 enrolled.

SECONDARY SCHOOL REQUIREMENTS

Graduation from secondary school required; GED accepted. The following course distribution required: 4 units of English, 3 units of math, 3 units of science, 1 unit of foreign language, 3 units of social studies.

TESTING

ACT required; SAT Reasoning may be substituted. SAT Subject recommended.

All enrolled freshmen (fall 2004):

Average ACT Scores: Composite: 22

Child Study Team report is not required. A neuropsychological or comprehensive psycho-educational evaluation is required for admission. Must be dated within 12 months of application. Tests required as part of this documentation:

- ☑ WAIS-IV
- ☑ WISC-IV
- ☐ SATA
- ☑ Woodcock-Johnson
- ☑ Nelson-Denny Reading Test
- ☐ Other

UNDERGRADUATE STUDENT BODY

Total undergraduate student enrollment: 603 Men, 687 Women.

Composition of student body (fall 2004):

	Undergraduate	Freshmen
International	0.4	1.6
Black	6.8	7.2
American Indian	0.8	1.1
Asian-American	0.8	0.9
Hispanic	5.6	3.0
White	85.1	85.0
Unreported	0.5	1.2
	100.0%	100.0%

38% are from out of state. Average age of full-time undergraduates is 24. 66% of classes have fewer than 20 students, 31% have between 20 and 50 students, 3% have more than 50 students.

STUDENT HOUSING

90% of freshmen live in college housing. Freshmen are required to live on campus. Housing is guaranteed for all undergraduates. Campus can house 715 undergraduates. Single rooms are not available for students with medical or special needs.

EXPENSES

Tuition (2005-06): $13,754 per year.

Room & Board: $2,915.

There is no additional cost for LD program/services.

LD SERVICES

LD program size is not limited.

LD services available to:

☑ Freshmen ☑ Sophomores ☑ Juniors ☑ Seniors

Academic Accommodations

Curriculum		**In class**	
Foreign language waiver	☐	Early syllabus	☑
Lighter course load	☐	Note takers in class	☑
Math waiver	☐	Priority seating	☑
Other special classes	☐	Tape recorders	☑
Priority registrations	☐	Videotaped classes	☑
Substitution of courses	☐	Text on tape	☑
Exams		**Services**	
Extended time	☑	Diagnostic tests	☑
Oral exams	☑	Learning centers	☑
Take home exams	☐	Proofreaders	☐
Exams on tape or computer	☑	Readers	☑
Untimed exams	☑	Reading Machines/Kurzweil	☐
Other accommodations	☐	Special bookstore section	☐
		Typists	☐

Credit toward degree is given for remedial courses taken.

Counseling Services

- ☑ Academic
- ☐ Psychological
- ☑ Student Support groups
- ☐ Vocational

Tutoring

Individual tutoring is available daily.

	Individual	Group
Time management	☑	☐
Organizational skills	☑	☐
Learning strategies	☑	☐
Study skills	☑	☐
Content area	☑	☐
Writing lab	☐	☐
Math lab	☐	☐

LD PROGRAM STAFF

Total number of LD Program staff (including director):

Full Time: 1 Part Time: 1

There is an advisor/advocate from the LD program available to students. Three graduate students and 25 peer tutors are available to work with LD students.

Key staff person available to work with LD students: Cynthia K. Chamberlin, Director of Support Services

LD Program web site: www.mnu.edu

Newman University

Wichita, KS

Address: 3100 McCormick Avenue, Wichita, KS, 67213
Admissions telephone: 877 NEWMANU
Admissions FAX: 316 942-4483
Admissions e-mail: admissions@newmanu.edu
Web site: http://www.newmanu.edu
SAT Code: 6615 ACT Code: 1452

Coordinator, Student Support Services: Susan Miller
LD program telephone: (316) 942-4291
LD program e-mail: millers@newman.edu
Total campus enrollment: 1,843

GENERAL

Newman University is a private, coed, four-year institution. 53-acre, suburban campus in Wichita (population: 344,284); branch campuses at McConnell Air Force Base and in Andover, Dodge City, Garden City, Great Bend, and Hutchison. Served by air and bus; train serves Newton (35 miles). Semester system.

SECONDARY SCHOOL REQUIREMENTS

Graduation from secondary school required; GED accepted.

TESTING

ACT required.

Child Study Team report is not required. Tests required as part of this documentation:

- ☐ WAIS-IV
- ☐ WISC-IV
- ☐ SATA
- ☐ Woodcock-Johnson
- ☐ Nelson-Denny Reading Test
- ☐ Other

UNDERGRADUATE STUDENT BODY

Total undergraduate student enrollment: 524 Men, 1,000 Women.

12% are from out of state.

STUDENT HOUSING

Freshmen are required to live on campus. Housing is guaranteed for all undergraduates. Campus can house 264 undergraduates.

EXPENSES

Tuition (2005-06): $15,822 per year.

Room & Board: $5,296.

There is no additional cost for LD program/services.

LD SERVICES

LD services available to:

☐ Freshmen ☐ Sophomores ☐ Juniors ☐ Seniors

Academic Accommodations

Curriculum		**In class**	
Foreign language waiver	☐	Early syllabus	☐
Lighter course load	☐	Note takers in class	■
Math waiver	☐	Priority seating	☐
Other special classes	☐	Tape recorders	■
Priority registrations	☐	Videotaped classes	☐
Substitution of courses	☐	Text on tape	☐
Exams		**Services**	
Extended time	■	Diagnostic tests	☐
Oral exams	■	Learning centers	■
Take home exams	☐	Proofreaders	☐
Exams on tape or computer	☐	Readers	■
Untimed exams	■	Reading Machines/Kurzweil	■
Other accommodations	☐	Special bookstore section	☐
		Typists	☐

Credit toward degree is not given for remedial courses taken.

Counseling Services

- ☐ Academic
- ☐ Psychological
- ☐ Student Support groups
- ☐ Vocational

Tutoring

	Individual	Group
Time management	☐	☐
Organizational skills	☐	☐
Learning strategies	☐	☐
Study skills	☐	☐
Content area	☐	☐
Writing lab	☐	☐
Math lab	☐	☐

LD PROGRAM STAFF

Total number of LD Program staff (including director):

Full Time: 2 Part Time: 2

Key staff person available to work with LD students: Julie Wright Connolly - ADA Accommodations Coordinator, Learning Specialist

Pittsburg State University

Pittsburg, KS

Address: 1701 South Broadway, Pittsburg, KS, 66762
Admissions telephone: 800 854-PITT
Admissions FAX: 620 235-6003
Director of Admissions and Enrollment Services: Angie Peterson
Admissions e-mail: psuadmit@pittstate.edu
Web site: http://www.pittstate.edu
SAT Code: 6336 ACT Code: 1449

LD program name: Learning Center
Director of Learning Center: Dr. Jamie Wood
LD program telephone: 620 235-4193
LD program e-mail: jwood@pittstate.edu
LD program enrollment: 133, Total campus enrollment: 5,493

GENERAL

Pittsburg State University is a public, coed, four-year institution. 233-acre campus in Pittsburg (population: 19,243), 120 miles from both Kansas City and Tulsa, OK; branch campus in Kansas City. Served by bus; major airport and train serve Kansas City; smaller airport serves Joplin, MO (30 miles). Semester system.

LD ADMISSIONS

Students do not complete a separate application and are not simultaneously accepted to the LD program. A member of the LD program does not sit on the admissions committee. A personal interview is not required. Essay is not required.

For fall 2004, 30 completed self-identified LD applications were received. 28 applications were offered admission, and 28 enrolled.

SECONDARY SCHOOL REQUIREMENTS

Graduation from secondary school required; GED accepted. The following course distribution required: 4 units of English, 3 units of math, 3 units of science, 2 units of social studies, 1 unit of history.

TESTING

ACT required.

All enrolled freshmen (fall 2004):

Average ACT Scores: Composite: 22

Child Study Team report is not required. A neuropsychological or comprehensive psycho-education evaluation is not required for admission. Tests required as part of this documentation:

- [ ] WAIS-IV
- [ ] WISC-IV
- [ ] SATA
- [ ] Woodcock-Johnson
- [ ] Nelson-Denny Reading Test
- [ ] Other

UNDERGRADUATE STUDENT BODY

Total undergraduate student enrollment: 2,823 Men, 2,647 Women.

Composition of student body (fall 2004):

	Undergraduate	Freshmen
International	1.2	4.8
Black	2.8	2.3
American Indian	1.8	2.0
Asian-American	1.0	0.5
Hispanic	1.6	1.6
White	88.4	86.0
Unreported	3.2	2.8
	100.0%	100.0%

7% join a fraternity and 7% join a sorority. Average age of full-time undergraduates is 23. 45% of classes have fewer than 20 students, 45% have between 20 and 50 students, 10% have more than 50 students.

STUDENT HOUSING

Freshmen are required to live on campus. Housing is guaranteed for all undergraduates. Campus can house 979 undergraduates.

EXPENSES

Tuition (2005-06): $3,562 per year (in-state), $10,444 (out-of-state). Tuition varies for technology courses.
Room: $2,270. Board: $2,280.
There is no additional cost for LD program/services.

LD SERVICES

LD program size is not limited.

LD services available to:

- [x] Freshmen
- [x] Sophomores
- [x] Juniors
- [x] Seniors

Academic Accommodations

Curriculum		In class	
Foreign language waiver	[ ]	Early syllabus	[ ]
Lighter course load	[ ]	Note takers in class	[x]
Math waiver	[ ]	Priority seating	[ ]
Other special classes	[ ]	Tape recorders	[x]
Priority registrations	[ ]	Videotaped classes	[ ]
Substitution of courses	[ ]	Text on tape	[ ]
Exams		**Services**	
Extended time	[x]	Diagnostic tests	[x]
Oral exams	[x]	Learning centers	[x]
Take home exams	[ ]	Proofreaders	[ ]
Exams on tape or computer	[ ]	Readers	[x]
Untimed exams	[x]	Reading Machines/Kurzweil	[ ]
Other accommodations	[x]	Special bookstore section	[ ]
		Typists	[ ]

Credit toward degree is not given for remedial courses taken.

Counseling Services

- [ ] Academic
- [ ] Psychological
- [ ] Student Support groups
- [ ] Vocational

Tutoring

Individual tutoring is available.

	Individual	Group
Time management	[ ]	[ ]
Organizational skills	[ ]	[ ]
Learning strategies	[ ]	[ ]
Study skills	[ ]	[ ]
Content area	[ ]	[ ]
Writing lab	[x]	[ ]
Math lab	[x]	[ ]

LD PROGRAM STAFF

There is an advisor/advocate from the LD program available to students. One graduate student and three peer tutors are available to work with LD students.

Key staff person available to work with LD students: Dr. Jamie Wood, Director of Learning Center

University of Saint Mary

Leavenworth, KS

Address: 4100 South Fourth Street Trafficway, Leavenworth, KS, 66048
Admissions telephone: 800 752-7043
Admissions FAX: 913 758-6140
Director of Enrollment Services: Judy Wiedower
Admissions e-mail: admiss@stmary.edu
Web site: http://www.stmary.edu
SAT Code: 6630 ACT Code: 1455

Vice President Student Life: Keith Hansen
LD program telephone: 913 682-5151
LD program e-mail: hansenk@stmary.edu
Total campus enrollment: 537

GENERAL

University of Saint Mary is a private, coed, four-year institution. 240-acre campus in Leavenworth (population: 35,421), 25 miles from Kansas City; two branch campuses in Kansas City. Major airport, bus, and train serve Kansas City. Semester system.

LD ADMISSIONS

A personal interview is recommended. Essay is not required.

SECONDARY SCHOOL REQUIREMENTS

Graduation from secondary school required; GED accepted. The following course distribution required: 4 units of English, 2 units of math, 2 units of science, 2 units of history, 2 units of academic electives.

TESTING

ACT required; SAT Reasoning may be substituted. SAT Subject recommended.

Child Study Team report is not required. Tests required as part of this documentation:

☐	WAIS-IV	☐	Woodcock-Johnson
☐	WISC-IV	☐	Nelson-Denny Reading Test
☐	SATA	☐	Other

UNDERGRADUATE STUDENT BODY

Total undergraduate student enrollment: 177 Men, 329 Women.

Composition of student body (fall 2004):

	Undergraduate	Freshmen
International	2.0	2.0
Black	14.3	12.6
American Indian	0.1	0.2
Asian-American	1.0	2.5
Hispanic	6.1	7.2
White	66.3	63.3
Unreported	10.2	12.2
	100.0%	100.0%

24% are from out of state. Average age of full-time undergraduates is 22. 79% of classes have fewer than 20 students, 20% have between 20 and 50 students, 1% have more than 50 students.

STUDENT HOUSING

73% of freshmen live in college housing. Freshmen are required to live on campus. Housing is not guaranteed for all undergraduates. Campus can house 351 undergraduates.

EXPENSES

Tuition (2005-06): $15,300 per year.
Room: $2,500. Board: $3,350.
There is no additional cost for LD program/services.

LD SERVICES

LD program size is not limited.

LD services available to:

☐ Freshmen ☐ Sophomores ☐ Juniors ☐ Seniors

Academic Accommodations

Curriculum		In class	
Foreign language waiver	☐	Early syllabus	☐
Lighter course load	■	Note takers in class	☐
Math waiver	☐	Priority seating	☐
Other special classes	☐	Tape recorders	■
Priority registrations	☐	Videotaped classes	☐
Substitution of courses	☐	Text on tape	☐
Exams		**Services**	
Extended time	■	Diagnostic tests	☐
Oral exams	☐	Learning centers	■
Take home exams	☐	Proofreaders	☐
Exams on tape or computer	☐	Readers	☐
Untimed exams	■	Reading Machines/Kurzweil	☐
Other accommodations	☐	Special bookstore section	☐
		Typists	☐

Credit toward degree is not given for remedial courses taken.

Counseling Services

☐ Academic
☐ Psychological
☐ Student Support groups
☐ Vocational

Tutoring

	Individual	Group
Time management	☐	☐
Organizational skills	☐	☐
Learning strategies	☐	☐
Study skills	☐	☐
Content area	☐	☐
Writing lab	☐	☐
Math lab	☐	☐

UNIQUE LD PROGRAM FEATURES

Accomodations are dealt with on an individual basis.

LD PROGRAM STAFF

Total number of LD Program staff (including director):

Full Time: 2 Part Time: 2

Key staff person available to work with LD students: Laura Ng, Director of Learning Center

Sterling College

Sterling, KS

Address: P.O. Box 98, Sterling, KS, 67579
Admissions telephone: 800 346-1017
Admissions FAX: 620 278-4416
Vice President for Enrollment Services: Dennis Dutton
Admissions e-mail: admissions@sterling.edu
Web site: http://www.sterling.edu
SAT Code: 6684 ACT Code: 1466

Director of Academic Support: Jan Schierling
LD program telephone: 620 278-4202
LD program e-mail: jschierling@sterling.edu
LD program enrollment: 10, Total campus enrollment: 487

GENERAL

Sterling College is a private, coed, four-year institution. 42-acre, rural campus in Sterling (population: 2,642), 65 miles from Wichita. Major airport serves Wichita; bus and train serve Hutchinson (20 miles). 4-1-4 system.

LD ADMISSIONS

Students do not complete a separate application and are simultaneously accepted to the LD program. A member of the LD program does sit on the admissions committee. A personal interview is recommended. Essay is required and may be typed. Composite ACT score may be waived.

For fall 2004, 3 completed self-identified LD applications were received. 3 applications were offered admission, and 3 enrolled.

SECONDARY SCHOOL REQUIREMENTS

Graduation from secondary school required; GED accepted. The following course distribution required: 4 units of English, 3 units of math, 3 units of science, 2 units of foreign language, 1 unit of social studies, 2 units of history, 1 unit of academic electives.

TESTING

SAT Reasoning or ACT required. SAT Subject recommended.

All enrolled freshmen (fall 2004):

Average SAT I Scores:	Verbal: 473	Math: 501
Average ACT Scores:	Composite: 22	

Child Study Team report is required if student is classified. A neuropsychological or comprehensive psycho-educational evaluation is required for admission. Must be dated within 12 months of application. Tests required as part of this documentation:

- [x] WAIS-IV
- [x] WISC-IV
- [x] SATA
- [x] Woodcock-Johnson
- [x] Nelson-Denny Reading Test
- [ ] Other

UNDERGRADUATE STUDENT BODY

Total undergraduate student enrollment: 220 Men, 241 Women.

Composition of student body (fall 2004):

	Undergraduate	Freshmen
International	0.7	2.1
Black	10.3	6.6
American Indian	3.7	2.3
Asian-American	0.0	0.5
Hispanic	3.7	5.3
White	80.9	82.7
Unreported	0.7	0.5
	100.0%	100.0%

35% are from out of state. Average age of full-time undergraduates is 20. 75% of classes have fewer than 20 students, 24% have between 20 and 50 students, 1% have more than 50 students.

STUDENT HOUSING

98% of freshmen live in college housing. Freshmen are required to live on campus. Housing is guaranteed for all undergraduates. Campus can house 490 undergraduates. Single rooms are available for students with medical or special needs. A medical note is required.

EXPENSES

Tuition (2005-06): $13,806 per year.
Room: $2,400. Board: $3,686.
There is no additional cost for LD program/services.

LD SERVICES

LD program size is not limited.

LD services available to:

- [x] Freshmen
- [x] Sophomores
- [x] Juniors
- [x] Seniors

Academic Accommodations

Curriculum		In class	
Foreign language waiver	[ ]	Early syllabus	[ ]
Lighter course load	[x]	Note takers in class	[x]
Math waiver	[ ]	Priority seating	[ ]
Other special classes	[ ]	Tape recorders	[x]
Priority registrations	[ ]	Videotaped classes	[ ]
Substitution of courses	[ ]	Text on tape	[ ]
Exams		**Services**	
Extended time	[x]	Diagnostic tests	[x]
Oral exams	[x]	Learning centers	[x]
Take home exams	[ ]	Proofreaders	[x]
Exams on tape or computer	[ ]	Readers	[x]
Untimed exams	[x]	Reading Machines/Kurzweil	[ ]
Other accommodations	[ ]	Special bookstore section	[ ]
		Typists	[ ]

Credit toward degree is not given for remedial courses taken.

Counseling Services

- [ ] Academic
- [ ] Psychological
- [ ] Student Support groups
- [ ] Vocational

Tutoring

Individual tutoring is available weekly.

Average size of tutoring groups: 1

	Individual	Group
Time management	[x]	[ ]
Organizational skills	[x]	[ ]
Learning strategies	[x]	[ ]
Study skills	[x]	[x]
Content area	[ ]	[ ]
Writing lab	[x]	[x]
Math lab	[x]	[x]

LD PROGRAM STAFF

Total number of LD Program staff (including director):

Full Time: 1 Part Time: 1

20 peer tutors are available to work with LD students.

Key staff person available to work with LD students: Jan Schierling, Director of Academic Support

Tabor College

Hillsboro, KS

Address: 400 South Jefferson, Hillsboro, KS, 67063
Admissions telephone: 800 TABOR-99
Admissions FAX: 620 947-6276
Vice President for Enrollment Management: Rusty Allen
Admissions e-mail: admissions@tabor.edu
Web site: http://www.tabor.edu
SAT Code: 6815 ACT Code: 1468

Dean of Student Development: James Fischer
LD program telephone: 620 947-3121, extension 1033
LD program e-mail: jamesf@tabor.edu
LD program enrollment: 5, Total campus enrollment: 586

GENERAL

Tabor College is a private, coed, four-year institution. 30-acre campus in Hillsboro (population: 2,854), 50 miles from Wichita. Major airport and bus serve Wichita; train serves Newton (30 miles). School operates transportation from airport and bus station at start of each semester. 4-1-4 system.

LD ADMISSIONS

Students do not complete a separate application and are not simultaneously accepted to the LD program. A member of the LD program does sit on the admissions committee. A personal interview is not required. Essay is required and may be typed.

For fall 2004, 4 completed self-identified LD applications were received. 3 applications were offered admission, and 2 enrolled.

SECONDARY SCHOOL REQUIREMENTS

Graduation from secondary school required; GED accepted.

TESTING

ACT required; SAT Reasoning may be substituted. SAT Subject recommended.

All enrolled freshmen (fall 2004):

Average ACT Scores: Composite: 23

Child Study Team report is not required. A neuropsychological or comprehensive psycho-educational evaluation is required for admission. Must be dated within 36 months of application. Tests required as part of this documentation:

- [x] WAIS-IV
- [x] WISC-IV
- [ ] SATA
- [x] Woodcock-Johnson
- [ ] Nelson-Denny Reading Test
- [x] Other

UNDERGRADUATE STUDENT BODY

Total undergraduate student enrollment: 278 Men, 294 Women.

Composition of student body (fall 2004):

	Undergraduate	Freshmen
International	0.8	0.7
Black	5.0	5.0
American Indian	1.4	1.2
Asian-American	0.0	0.9
Hispanic	2.2	2.8
White	89.9	88.4
Unreported	0.7	1.0
	100.0%	100.0%

33% are from out of state. Average age of full-time undergraduates is 20. 72% of classes have fewer than 20 students, 28% have between 20 and 50 students.

STUDENT HOUSING

99% of freshmen live in college housing. Freshmen are required to live on campus. Housing is guaranteed for all undergraduates. Campus can house 441 undergraduates. Single rooms are available for students with medical or special needs. A medical note is not required.

EXPENSES

Tuition (2005-06): $15,574 per year.
Room: $2,200. Board: $3,470.
There is no additional cost for LD program/services.

LD SERVICES

LD program size is not limited.

LD services available to:

- [x] Freshmen
- [x] Sophomores
- [x] Juniors
- [x] Seniors

Academic Accommodations

Curriculum		**In class**	
Foreign language waiver	[ ]	Early syllabus	[ ]
Lighter course load	[x]	Note takers in class	[x]
Math waiver	[ ]	Priority seating	[ ]
Other special classes	[x]	Tape recorders	[x]
Priority registrations	[ ]	Videotaped classes	[ ]
Substitution of courses	[ ]	Text on tape	[ ]
Exams		**Services**	
Extended time	[x]	Diagnostic tests	[ ]
Oral exams	[x]	Learning centers	[x]
Take home exams	[ ]	Proofreaders	[x]
Exams on tape or computer	[ ]	Readers	[x]
Untimed exams	[x]	Reading Machines/Kurzweil	[ ]
Other accommodations	[ ]	Special bookstore section	[ ]
		Typists	[ ]

Credit toward degree is given for remedial courses taken.

Counseling Services

- [x] Academic — Meets 30 times per academic year
- [ ] Psychological
- [ ] Student Support groups
- [ ] Vocational

Tutoring

Individual tutoring is available weekly.

	Individual	Group
Time management	[ ]	[x]
Organizational skills	[ ]	[x]
Learning strategies	[ ]	[x]
Study skills	[ ]	[x]
Content area	[x]	[ ]
Writing lab	[x]	[ ]
Math lab	[ ]	[ ]

LD PROGRAM STAFF

Total number of LD Program staff (including director):

Full Time: 2 Part Time: 2

There is an advisor/advocate from the LD program available to students. The advisor/advocate meets with faculty once per month and students four times per month.

Key staff person available to work with LD students: James Fischer, Dean of Student Development

Washburn University

Topeka, KS

Address: 1700 S.W. College, Topeka, KS, 66621
Admissions telephone: 800 332-0291
Admissions FAX: 785 231-1113
Director of Admissions: Kirk Haskins
Admissions e-mail: admissions@washburn.edu
Web site: http://www.washburn.edu
SAT Code: 6928 ACT Code: 1474

LD program name: Student Services
Director of Student Services: Jeannene D. Kessler
LD program telephone: 785 231-1010
LD program enrollment: 35, Total campus enrollment: 6,398

GENERAL

Washburn University is a public, coed, four-year institution. 160-acre campus in Topeka (population: 122,377), 60 miles from Kansas City. Served by air, bus, and train; major airport serves Kansas City. Public transportation serves campus. Semester system.

LD ADMISSIONS

Application Deadline: 08/01. Students do not complete a separate application and are not simultaneously accepted to the LD program. A member of the LD program does not sit on the admissions committee. A personal interview is not required. Essay is not required.

SECONDARY SCHOOL REQUIREMENTS

Graduation from secondary school required; GED accepted.

TESTING

SAT Reasoning or ACT considered if submitted.

All enrolled freshmen (fall 2004):

Average ACT Scores: Composite: 22

Child Study Team report is not required. A neuropsychological or comprehensive psycho-educational evaluation is required for admission. Tests required as part of this documentation:

- [x] WAIS-IV
- [x] WISC-IV
- [x] SATA
- [x] Woodcock-Johnson
- [x] Nelson-Denny Reading Test
- [x] Other

UNDERGRADUATE STUDENT BODY

Total undergraduate student enrollment: 2,028 Men, 3,257 Women.

Composition of student body (fall 2004):

	Undergraduate	Freshmen
International	0.2	0.9
Black	1.3	4.7
American Indian	1.0	1.4
Asian-American	0.6	0.8
Hispanic	2.0	2.9
White	44.9	55.4
Unreported	50.0	33.9
	100.0%	100.0%

2% are from out of state. 3% join a fraternity and 5% join a sorority. Average age of full-time undergraduates is 23. 46% of classes have fewer than 20 students, 52% have between 20 and 50 students, 2% have more than 50 students.

STUDENT HOUSING

42% of freshmen live in college housing. Freshmen are not required to live on campus. Housing is guaranteed for all undergraduates. Campus can house 941 undergraduates. Single rooms are available for students with medical or special needs. A medical note is required.

EXPENSES

Tuition (2005-06): $4,920 per year (in-state), $11,130 (out-of-state).
Room: $2,358. Board: $3,570.
There is no additional cost for LD program/services.

LD SERVICES

LD program size is not limited.

LD services available to:

- [x] Freshmen
- [x] Sophomores
- [x] Juniors
- [x] Seniors

Academic Accommodations

Curriculum		In class	
Foreign language waiver	[ ]	Early syllabus	[ ]
Lighter course load	[x]	Note takers in class	[x]
Math waiver	[ ]	Priority seating	[ ]
Other special classes	[ ]	Tape recorders	[x]
Priority registrations	[ ]	Videotaped classes	[ ]
Substitution of courses	[ ]	Text on tape	[ ]
Exams		**Services**	
Extended time	[x]	Diagnostic tests	[ ]
Oral exams	[x]	Learning centers	[x]
Take home exams	[ ]	Proofreaders	[ ]
Exams on tape or computer	[ ]	Readers	[x]
Untimed exams	[ ]	Reading Machines/Kurzweil	[x]
Other accommodations	[x]	Special bookstore section	[ ]
		Typists	[ ]

Credit toward degree is not given for remedial courses taken.

Counseling Services

- [x] Academic
- [x] Psychological
- [x] Student Support groups
- [x] Vocational

Tutoring

Individual tutoring is available weekly.

	Individual	Group
Time management	[x]	[x]
Organizational skills	[x]	[x]
Learning strategies	[x]	[x]
Study skills	[x]	[x]
Content area	[ ]	[ ]
Writing lab	[x]	[ ]
Math lab	[x]	[ ]

LD PROGRAM STAFF

Total number of LD Program staff (including director):

Full Time: 2 Part Time: 2

There is an advisor/advocate from the LD program available to students.

Key staff person available to work with LD students: Jeannene D. Kessler, Director of Student Services

Wichita State University

Wichita, KS

Address: 1845 Fairmount, Wichita, KS, 67260
Admissions telephone: 800 362-2594
Admissions FAX: 316 978-3174
Director of Admissions: Gina Crabtree
Admissions e-mail: admissions@wichita.edu
Web site: http://www.wichita.edu
SAT Code: 6884   ACT Code: 1472

Director: Corinne Nilsen
LD program telephone: 316 978-5949
LD program e-mail: corinne.nilsen@wichita.edu
Total campus enrollment: 11,199

GENERAL

Wichita State University is a public, coed, four-year institution. 330-acre, urban campus in Wichita (population: 344,284); centers in downtown, west, and south Wichita. Served by air and bus; train serves Newton (30 miles). School operates transportation to local public transportation. Public transportation serves campus. Semester system.

LD ADMISSIONS

A personal interview is not required. Essay is not required.

SECONDARY SCHOOL REQUIREMENTS

Graduation from secondary school required; GED accepted. The following course distribution required: 4 units of English, 3 units of math, 3 units of science, 3 units of social studies.

TESTING

SAT Subject recommended.

All enrolled freshmen (fall 2004):

Average SAT I Scores:	Verbal: 525	Math: 560
Average ACT Scores:	Composite: 23	

Child Study Team report is not required. Tests required as part of this documentation:

- ☐ WAIS-IV
- ☐ WISC-IV
- ☐ SATA
- ☐ Woodcock-Johnson
- ☐ Nelson-Denny Reading Test
- ☐ Other

UNDERGRADUATE STUDENT BODY

Total undergraduate student enrollment: 4,934 Men, 6,369 Women.

Composition of student body (fall 2004):

	Undergraduate	Freshmen
International	3.9	4.8
Black	7.1	6.8
American Indian	1.3	1.4
Asian-American	7.7	7.1
Hispanic	5.6	5.1
White	72.4	70.0
Unreported	2.0	4.8
	100.0%	100.0%

3% are from out of state. 8% join a fraternity and 5% join a sorority. Average age of full-time undergraduates is 23. 51% of classes have fewer than 20 students, 42% have between 20 and 50 students, 7% have more than 50 students.

STUDENT HOUSING

27% of freshmen live in college housing. Housing is guaranteed for all undergraduates. Campus can house 1,453 undergraduates.

EXPENSES

Tuition (2005 06): $3,434 per year (in-state), $10,887 (out-of-state).
Room: $2,800. Board: $2,188.

There is no additional cost for LD program/services.

LD SERVICES

LD program size is not limited.

LD services available to:

☐ Freshmen ☐ Sophomores ☐ Juniors ☐ Seniors

Academic Accommodations

Curriculum		**In class**	
Foreign language waiver	☐	Early syllabus	☐
Lighter course load	☐	Note takers in class	☑
Math waiver	☐	Priority seating	☐
Other special classes	☐	Tape recorders	☑
Priority registrations	☐	Videotaped classes	☑
Substitution of courses	☐	Text on tape	☐
Exams		**Services**	
Extended time	☑	Diagnostic tests	☑
Oral exams	☑	Learning centers	☐
Take home exams	☐	Proofreaders	☐
Exams on tape or computer	☐	Readers	☑
Untimed exams	☑	Reading Machines/Kurzweil	☑
Other accommodations	☐	Special bookstore section	☐
		Typists	☐

Credit toward degree is not given for remedial courses taken.

Counseling Services

- ☐ Academic
- ☐ Psychological
- ☐ Student Support groups
- ☐ Vocational

Tutoring

	Individual	Group
Time management	☐	☐
Organizational skills	☐	☐
Learning strategies	☐	☐
Study skills	☐	☐
Content area	☐	☐
Writing lab	☐	☐
Math lab	☐	☐

UNIQUE LD PROGRAM FEATURES

Individual plans are developed to determine the services the program will provide. Services include tutors, study skills workshops offered twice per semester, and academic advisors. In addition, Disability Support Services has scholarships available.

LD PROGRAM STAFF

Total number of LD Program staff (including director):

Full Time: 7   Part Time: 7

Key staff person available to work with LD students: Corinne Nilsen, Director

Bellarmine University

Louisville, KY

Address: 2001 Newburg Road, Louisville, KY, 40205
Admissions telephone: 502 452-8131
Admissions FAX: 502 452-8002
Dean of Admissions: Timothy A. Sturgeon
Admissions e-mail: admissions@bellarmine.edu
Web site: http://www.bellarmine.edu
SAT Code: 1056 ACT Code: 1490

Disability Services Coordinator: Dr. Fred Ehrman
LD program telephone: 502 452-8150
LD program e-mail: fehrman@bellarmine.edu
LD program enrollment: 120, Total campus enrollment: 2,327

GENERAL

Bellarmine University is a private, coed, four-year institution. 120-acre, suburban campus in Louisville (population: 256,231), 100 miles from both Cincinnati and Indianapolis. Served by airport and bus; major airports serve Cincinnati, OH and Indianapolis, IN; train serves Indianapolis, IN. Public transportation serves campus. Semester system.

LD ADMISSIONS

A member of the LD program does not sit on the admissions committee. A personal interview is required. Essay is not required.

SECONDARY SCHOOL REQUIREMENTS

Graduation from secondary school required; GED accepted. The following course distribution required: 4 units of English, 3 units of math, 2 units of science, 2 units of social studies, 1 unit of history.

TESTING

SAT Reasoning or ACT required. SAT Subject recommended.

All enrolled freshmen (fall 2004):

Average SAT I Scores:	Verbal: 561	Math: 555
Average ACT Scores:	Composite: 24	

Child Study Team report is not required. Tests required as part of this documentation:

- [ ] WAIS-IV
- [ ] WISC-IV
- [ ] SATA
- [ ] Woodcock-Johnson
- [ ] Nelson-Denny Reading Test
- [ ] Other

UNDERGRADUATE STUDENT BODY

Total undergraduate student enrollment: 852 Men, 1,521 Women.

Composition of student body (fall 2004):

	Undergraduate	Freshmen
International	2.3	0.8
Black	2.5	4.6
American Indian	0.2	0.2
Asian-American	2.1	1.5
Hispanic	1.6	1.3
White	91.1	90.8
Unreported	0.2	0.8
	100.0%	100.0%

31% are from out of state. 53% of classes have fewer than 20 students, 46% have between 20 and 50 students.

STUDENT HOUSING

63% of freshmen live in college housing. Freshmen are required to live on campus. The university owns 5 residential halls, 1 apartment complex, and 4 houses. Campus can house 667 undergraduates. Single rooms are available for students with medical or special needs. A medical note is required.

EXPENSES

Tuition (2005-06): $20,800 per year.
Room: $3,480. Board: $2,670.
There is no additional cost for LD program/services.

LD SERVICES

LD program size is not limited.

LD services available to:

- [x] Freshmen
- [x] Sophomores
- [x] Juniors
- [x] Seniors

Academic Accommodations

Curriculum

- [ ] Foreign language waiver
- [ ] Lighter course load
- [ ] Math waiver
- [ ] Other special classes
- [ ] Priority registrations
- [ ] Substitution of courses

Exams

- [x] Extended time
- [x] Oral exams
- [ ] Take home exams
- [ ] Exams on tape or computer
- [x] Untimed exams
- [x] Other accommodations

In class

- [ ] Early syllabus
- [x] Note takers in class
- [ ] Priority seating
- [x] Tape recorders
- [x] Videotaped classes
- [ ] Text on tape

Services

- [x] Diagnostic tests
- [x] Learning centers
- [ ] Proofreaders
- [x] Readers
- [ ] Reading Machines/Kurzweil
- [ ] Special bookstore section
- [x] Typists

Credit toward degree is not given for remedial courses taken.

Counseling Services

- [ ] Academic
- [x] Psychological
- [ ] Student Support groups
- [ ] Vocational

Tutoring

Individual tutoring is available daily.

Average size of tutoring groups: 5

	Individual	Group
Time management	[x]	[x]
Organizational skills	[x]	[x]
Learning strategies	[x]	[x]
Study skills	[x]	[x]
Content area	[x]	[x]
Writing lab	[x]	[x]
Math lab	[x]	[x]

UNIQUE LD PROGRAM FEATURES

LD Advisor/Advocate can meet with faculty on an as needed basis.

LD PROGRAM STAFF

Total number of LD Program staff (including director):

Full Time: 2 Part Time: 2

There is an advisor/advocate from the LD program available to students.

Key staff person available to work with LD students: Dr. Fred Ehrman, Disability Services Coordinator.

Berea College

Berea, KY

Address: CPO Box 2142, Berea, KY, 40404
Admissions telephone: 800 326-5948
Admissions FAX: 859 985-3512
Director of Admissions: Jamie Ealy
Admissions e-mail: admissions@berea.edu
Web site: http://www.berea.edu
SAT Code: 1060 ACT Code: 1492

Executive Assistant/Special Needs Services Coordinator:
Bev Penkalski
LD program telephone: 859 985-3150
LD program e-mail: bev_penkalski@berea.edu
LD program enrollment: 35, Total campus enrollment: 1,556

GENERAL

Berea College is a private, coed, four-year institution. 140-acre campus in Berea (population: 9,851), 40 miles south of Lexington. Served by bus; major airports serve Cincinnati (100 miles), Lexington, and Louisville (100 miles); train serves Lexington. School operates transportation to area shopping and to Lexington. 4-1-4 system.

LD ADMISSIONS

A member of the LD program does not sit on the admissions committee. A personal interview is not required. Essay is required and may be typed.

SECONDARY SCHOOL REQUIREMENTS

Graduation from secondary school required; GED accepted.

TESTING

SAT Reasoning or ACT required. SAT Subject recommended.

All enrolled freshmen (fall 2004):

Average SAT I Scores:	Verbal: 551	Math: 554
Average ACT Scores:	Composite: 24	

Child Study Team report is not required. A neuropsychological or comprehensive psycho-educational evaluation is required for admission. Must be dated within 24 months of application. Tests required as part of this documentation:

- [x] WAIS-IV
- [x] WISC-IV
- [x] SATA
- [x] Woodcock-Johnson
- [x] Nelson-Denny Reading Test
- [x] Other

UNDERGRADUATE STUDENT BODY

Total undergraduate student enrollment: 729 Men, 944 Women.

Composition of student body (fall 2004):

	Undergraduate	Freshmen
International	6.8	7.3
Black	21.3	18.7
American Indian	0.0	0.5
Asian-American	1.8	1.5
Hispanic	1.8	1.7
White	66.3	68.6
Unreported	2.3	1.8
	100.0%	100.0%

57% are from out of state. Average age of full-time undergraduates is 20. 62% of classes have fewer than 20 students, 37% have between 20 and 50 students.

STUDENT HOUSING

97% of freshmen live in college housing. Freshmen are required to live on campus. Housing is guaranteed for all undergraduates. Campus can house 1,245 undergraduates. Single rooms are available for students with medical or special needs. A medical note is required.

EXPENSES

Tuition (2005-06): No tuition. School pays for students through grants and scholarships.

Room: $2,660. Board: $2,320.
There is no additional cost for LD program/services.

LD SERVICES

LD program size is not limited.

LD services available to:

- [ ] Freshmen
- [ ] Sophomores
- [ ] Juniors
- [ ] Seniors

Academic Accommodations

Curriculum

- [ ] Foreign language waiver
- [x] Lighter course load
- [ ] Math waiver
- [ ] Other special classes
- [ ] Priority registrations
- [ ] Substitution of courses

Exams

- [x] Extended time
- [ ] Oral exams
- [ ] Take home exams
- [ ] Exams on tape or computer
- [ ] Untimed exams
- [x] Other accommodations

In class

- [ ] Early syllabus
- [x] Note takers in class
- [x] Priority seating
- [x] Tape recorders
- [ ] Videotaped classes
- [ ] Text on tape

Services

- [x] Diagnostic tests
- [x] Learning centers
- [ ] Proofreaders
- [ ] Readers
- [ ] Reading Machines/Kurzweil
- [ ] Special bookstore section
- [ ] Typists

Credit toward degree is not given for remedial courses taken.

Counseling Services

- [x] Academic
- [x] Psychological
- [ ] Student Support groups
- [x] Vocational

Tutoring

	Individual	Group
Time management	[x]	[ ]
Organizational skills	[x]	[ ]
Learning strategies	[x]	[x]
Study skills	[x]	[x]
Content area	[ ]	[ ]
Writing lab	[ ]	[x]
Math lab	[ ]	[ ]

LD PROGRAM STAFF

Total number of LD Program staff (including director):

Full Time: 1 Part Time: 1

There is an advisor/advocate from the LD program available to students.

Key staff person available to work with LD students: Bev Penkalski, Executive Assistant/Special Needs Services Coordinator.

Centre College

Danville, KY

Address: 600 West Walnut Street, Danville, KY, 40422
Admissions telephone: 800 423-6236
Admissions FAX: 859 238-5373
Dean of Admissions and Student Financial Planning: J. Carey Thompson
Admissions e-mail: admission@centre.edu
Web site: http://www.centre.edu
SAT Code: 1109 ACT Code: 1506

LD program name: Disability Services
Assistant Dean for Advising: Mary R. Gulley
LD program telephone: 859 238-5223
LD program e-mail: gulley@centre.edu
LD program enrollment: 22, Total campus enrollment: 1,069

GENERAL

Centre College is a private, coed, four-year institution. 100-acre campus in Danville (population: 15,477), 35 miles from Lexington and 70 miles from Louisville; branch campuses abroad in London, England, Strasbourg, France, Japan, and Merida, Mexico. Airports serve Lexington and Louisville; bus serves Lexington; train serves Cincinnati (120 miles). 4-1-4 system.

LD ADMISSIONS

A personal interview is recommended. Essay is required and may be typed.

For fall 2004, 22 completed self-identified LD applications were received.

SECONDARY SCHOOL REQUIREMENTS

Graduation from secondary school not required. The following course distribution required: 4 units of English, 4 units of math, 2 units of science, 2 units of foreign language, 2 units of social studies, 2 units of academic electives.

TESTING

SAT Reasoning or ACT required. SAT Subject recommended.

All enrolled freshmen (fall 2004):

Average SAT I Scores:	Verbal: 642	Math: 624
Average ACT Scores:	Composite: 28	

Child Study Team report is not required. A neuropsychological or comprehensive psycho-educational evaluation is required for admission. Must be dated within 36 months of application. Tests required as part of this documentation:

- ☑ WAIS-IV
- ☑ WISC-IV
- ☑ SATA
- ☑ Woodcock-Johnson
- ☑ Nelson-Denny Reading Test
- ☑ Other

UNDERGRADUATE STUDENT BODY

Total undergraduate student enrollment: 482 Men, 588 Women.

Composition of student body (fall 2004):

	Undergraduate	Freshmen
International	1.3	1.5
Black	3.4	2.4
American Indian	0.3	0.2
Asian-American	2.4	2.6
Hispanic	1.3	0.6
White	90.6	92.5
Unreported	0.7	0.2
	100.0%	100.0%

28% are from out of state. 51% join a fraternity and 52% join a sorority. Average age of full-time undergraduates is 20. 56% of classes have fewer than 20 students, 44% have between 20 and 50 students.

STUDENT HOUSING

99% of freshmen live in college housing. Freshmen are required to live on campus. Housing is guaranteed for all undergraduates. Campus can house 1,002 undergraduates. Single rooms are available for students with medical or special needs. A medical note is required.

EXPENSES

Tuition (2005-06): $23,110 per year.
Room: $3,900. Board: $3,800.
There is no additional cost for LD program/services.

LD SERVICES

LD program size is not limited.

LD services available to:

☑ Freshmen ☑ Sophomores ☑ Juniors ☑ Seniors

Academic Accommodations

Curriculum		In class	
Foreign language waiver	☐	Early syllabus	☐
Lighter course load	☑	Note takers in class	☑
Math waiver	☐	Priority seating	☑
Other special classes	☑	Tape recorders	☑
Priority registrations	☑	Videotaped classes	☑
Substitution of courses	☐	Text on tape	☑
Exams		**Services**	
Extended time	☑	Diagnostic tests	☐
Oral exams	☑	Learning centers	☑
Take home exams	☐	Proofreaders	☑
Exams on tape or computer	☑	Readers	☑
Untimed exams	☑	Reading Machines/Kurzweil	☐
Other accommodations	☑	Special bookstore section	☐
		Typists	☑

Credit toward degree is not given for remedial courses taken.

Counseling Services

- ☑ Academic — Meets 2 times per academic year
- ☑ Psychological
- ☐ Student Support groups
- ☑ Vocational

Tutoring

Individual tutoring is available daily.

Average size of tutoring groups: 1

	Individual	Group
Time management	☐	☐
Organizational skills	☐	☐
Learning strategies	☐	☐
Study skills	☐	☐
Content area	☐	☐
Writing lab	☑	☑
Math lab	☑	☑

UNIQUE LD PROGRAM FEATURES

Our LD program accommodates students on an individual needs basis.

LD PROGRAM STAFF

There is an advisor/advocate from the LD program available to students. The advisor/advocate meets with faculty 4 times per month and students 15 times per month. 30 peer tutors are available to work with LD students.

Key staff person available to work with LD students: Mary R. Gulley, Assistant Dean for Advising.

Cumberland College

Williamsburg, KY

Address: 6178 College Station Drive, Williamsburg, KY, 40769
Admissions telephone: 800 343-1609
Admissions FAX: 606 539-4303
Director of Admissions: Erica Harris
Admissions e-mail: admiss@cumberlandcollege.edu
Web site: http://www.cumberlandcollege.edu
SAT Code: 1145 ACT Code: 1510

Vice President of Academic Affairs: Don Good
LD program telephone: 606 539-4214
LD program e-mail: dgood@cumberlandcollege.edu
Total campus enrollment: 1,603

GENERAL

Cumberland College is a private, coed, four-year institution. 50-acre campus in Williamsburg (population: 5,143), 60 miles from Knoxville, TN, and 100 miles from Lexington. Major airport serves Knoxville; bus serves Corbin (15 miles). School operates transportation to Knoxville and Lexington airports by arrangement. Semester system.

LD ADMISSIONS

Application Deadline: 08/15. A personal interview is not required. Essay is required and may be typed.

SECONDARY SCHOOL REQUIREMENTS

Graduation from secondary school required; GED accepted. The following course distribution required: 4 units of English, 3 units of math, 2 units of science, 1 unit of social studies.

TESTING

SAT Reasoning or ACT required. SAT Subject recommended.

All enrolled freshmen (fall 2004):

Average SAT I Scores: Verbal: 483 Math: 495
Average ACT Scores: Composite: 22

Child Study Team report is not required. Tests required as part of this documentation:

- ❑ WAIS-IV
- ❑ WISC-IV
- ❑ SATA
- ❑ Woodcock-Johnson
- ❑ Nelson-Denny Reading Test
- ❑ Other

UNDERGRADUATE STUDENT BODY

Total undergraduate student enrollment: 742 Men, 827 Women.

Composition of student body (fall 2004):

	Undergraduate	Freshmen
International	2.1	2.5
Black	6.6	6.7
American Indian	0.0	0.4
Asian-American	0.9	0.4
Hispanic	2.1	1.6
White	88.2	88.3
Unreported	0.0	0.2
	100.0%	100.0%

42% are from out of state. Average age of full-time undergraduates is 19. 55% of classes have fewer than 20 students, 44% have between 20 and 50 students.

STUDENT HOUSING

84% of freshmen live in college housing. Freshmen are required to live on campus. Housing is guaranteed for all undergraduates. Campus can house 1,100 undergraduates. Single rooms are not available for students with medical or special needs.

EXPENSES

Tuition 2004-05: $11,498 per year.

Room & Board: $5,126.

There is no additional cost for LD program/services.

LD SERVICES

LD program size is not limited.

LD services available to:

❑ Freshmen ❑ Sophomores ❑ Juniors ❑ Seniors

Academic Accommodations

Curriculum		In class	
Foreign language waiver	❑	Early syllabus	❑
Lighter course load	❑	Note takers in class	❑
Math waiver	❑	Priority seating	❑
Other special classes	❑	Tape recorders	❑
Priority registrations	❑	Videotaped classes	❑
Substitution of courses	❑	Text on tape	❑
Exams		**Services**	
Extended time	❑	Diagnostic tests	❑
Oral exams	❑	Learning centers	❑
Take home exams	❑	Proofreaders	❑
Exams on tape or computer	❑	Readers	❑
Untimed exams	❑	Reading Machines/Kurzweil	❑
Other accommodations	❑	Special bookstore section	❑
		Typists	❑

Counseling Services

- ❑ Academic
- ❑ Psychological
- ❑ Student Support groups
- ❑ Vocational

Tutoring

Individual tutoring is available daily.

	Individual	Group
Time management	❑	❑
Organizational skills	❑	❑
Learning strategies	❑	❑
Study skills	❑	❑
Content area	❑	❑
Writing lab	❑	❑
Math lab	❑	❑

LD PROGRAM STAFF

Total number of LD Program staff (including director):

Full Time: 2 Part Time: 2

Key staff person available to work with LD students: Don Good, Vice President of Academic Affairs.

Eastern Kentucky University

Richmond, KY

Address: 521 Lancaster Avenue, Richmond, KY, 40475
Admissions telephone: 800 465-9191
Admissions FAX: 859 622-8024
Director of Admissions: Stephen Byrn
Admissions e-mail: admissions@eku.edu
Web site: http://www.eku.edu
SAT Code: 1200 ACT Code: 1512

LD program name: Project SUCCESS
Assistant Director, Disabilities: Teresa Belluscio
LD program telephone: 859 622-2933
LD program e-mail: teresa.belluscio@eku.edu
LD program enrollment: 260, Total campus enrollment: 13,837

GENERAL

Eastern Kentucky University is a public, coed, four-year institution. 628-acre campus in Richmond (population: 27,152), 30 miles from Lexington; branch campuses in Corbin, Danville, Manchester, and Somerset. Served by bus; major airport serves Lexington. Semester system.

LD ADMISSIONS

Students do not complete a separate application and are not simultaneously accepted to the LD program. A member of the LD program does not sit on the admissions committee. A personal interview is recommended. Essay is not required. Admission for students with Specified Learning Disabilities are considered on an individual basis. Individual decisions are based on a number of factors, including disability, high school status, prior college work, and other related factors.

For fall 2004, 60 completed self-identified LD applications were received. 58 applications were offered admission, and 58 enrolled.

SECONDARY SCHOOL REQUIREMENTS

Graduation from secondary school required; GED accepted. The following course distribution required: 4 units of English, 3 units of math, 3 units of science, 3 units of social studies, 1 unit of history, 7 units of academic electives.

TESTING

SAT Reasoning considered if submitted. ACT required. SAT Subject recommended.

All enrolled freshmen (fall 2004):

Average SAT I Scores:	Verbal: 500	Math: 494
Average ACT Scores:	Composite: 21	

Child Study Team report is not required. A neuropsychological or comprehensive psycho-education evaluation is not required for admission. Tests required as part of this documentation:

- □ WAIS-IV
- □ WISC-IV
- □ SATA
- □ Woodcock-Johnson
- □ Nelson-Denny Reading Test
- □ Other

UNDERGRADUATE STUDENT BODY

Total undergraduate student enrollment: 5,240 Men, 7,564 Women.

Composition of student body (fall 2004):

	Undergraduate	Freshmen
International	0.0	0.6
Black	4.0	4.4
American Indian	0.4	0.4
Asian-American	0.7	1.0
Hispanic	0.4	0.7
White	93.1	91.6
Unreported	1.2	1.2
	100.0%	100.0%

7% are from out of state. 8% join a fraternity and 6% join a sorority. Average age of full-time undergraduates is 22. 48% of classes have fewer than 20 students, 48% have between 20 and 50 students.

STUDENT HOUSING

65% of freshmen live in college housing. Freshmen are required to live on campus. Housing is guaranteed for all undergraduates. Campus can house 5,885 undergraduates. Single rooms are available for students with medical or special needs.

EXPENSES

Tuition (2005-06): $4,200 per year (in-state), $12,610 (out-of-state).
Room: $2,208. Board: $2,500.
There is no additional cost for LD program/services.

LD SERVICES

LD program is limited to 1% students.

LD services available to:

■ Freshmen ■ Sophomores ■ Juniors ■ Seniors

Academic Accommodations

Curriculum		**In class**	
Foreign language waiver	□	Early syllabus	□
Lighter course load	□	Note takers in class	■
Math waiver	□	Priority seating	□
Other special classes	■	Tape recorders	■
Priority registrations	□	Videotaped classes	□
Substitution of courses	□	Text on tape	□
Exams		**Services**	
Extended time	■	Diagnostic tests	■
Oral exams	■	Learning centers	■
Take home exams	□	Proofreaders	□
Exams on tape or computer	□	Readers	■
Untimed exams	□	Reading Machines/Kurzweil	■
Other accommodations	□	Special bookstore section	□
		Typists	□

Credit toward degree is not given for remedial courses taken.

Counseling Services

- ■ Academic
- ■ Psychological
- ■ Student Support groups
- □ Vocational

Tutoring

Individual tutoring is available.

	Individual	Group
Time management	■	□
Organizational skills	■	□
Learning strategies	■	□
Study skills	■	□
Content area	■	□
Writing lab	■	□
Math lab	■	□

LD PROGRAM STAFF

Total number of LD Program staff (including director):

Full Time: 1 Part Time: 1

There is an advisor/advocate from the LD program available to students.

Key staff person available to work with LD students: Teresa Belluscio, Assistant Director, Disabilities-Project SUCCESS.

Georgetown College

Georgetown, KY

Address: 400 East College Street, Georgetown, KY, 40324
Admissions telephone: 800 788-9985
Admissions FAX: 502 868-7733
Director of Admissions: Johnnie Johnson
Admissions e-mail: admissions@georgetowncollege.edu
Web site: http://www.georgetowncollege.edu
SAT Code: 1249 ACT Code: 1514

Director of Counseling: Edward Marshall
LD program telephone: 502 863-7074
LD program e-mail:
Edward_Marshall@georgetowncollege.edu
Total campus enrollment: 1334

GENERAL

Georgetown College is a private, coed, four-year institution. 104-acre campus in Georgetown (population: 18,080), 15 miles from Lexington. Airport and bus serve Lexington; major airport and train serve Cincinnati (60 miles). Semester system.

LD ADMISSIONS

A personal interview is recommended. Essay is required and may be typed.

SECONDARY SCHOOL REQUIREMENTS

Graduation from secondary school required; GED accepted.

TESTING

ACT required; SAT Reasoning may be substituted. SAT Subject recommended.

All enrolled freshmen (fall 2004):

Average ACT Scores: Composite: 23

Child Study Team report is not required. Tests required as part of this documentation:

- ☐ WAIS-IV
- ☐ WISC-IV
- ☐ SATA
- ☐ Woodcock-Johnson
- ☐ Nelson-Denny Reading Test
- ☐ Other

UNDERGRADUATE STUDENT BODY

Total undergraduate student enrollment: 590 Men, 771 Women.

Composition of student body (fall 2004):

	Undergraduate	Freshmen
International	0.6	1.1
Black	3.1	3.8
American Indian	0.6	0.2
Asian-American	1.1	0.8
Hispanic	0.6	0.7
White	94.1	93.3
Unreported	0.0	0.0
	100.0%	100.0%

16% are from out of state. 28% join a fraternity and 40% join a sorority. Average age of full-time undergraduates is 20. 63% of classes have fewer than 20 students, 37% have between 20 and 50 students.

STUDENT HOUSING

95% of freshmen live in college housing. Freshmen are required to live on campus. Housing is guaranteed for all undergraduates. Campus can house 1,238 undergraduates.

EXPENSES

Tuition (2005-06): $19,170 per year.

Room: $2,790. Board: $2,990.

There is no additional cost for LD program/services.

LD SERVICES

LD program size is not limited.

LD services available to:

☐ Freshmen ☐ Sophomores ☐ Juniors ☐ Seniors

Academic Accommodations

Curriculum		In class	
Foreign language waiver	☐	Early syllabus	☐
Lighter course load	☐	Note takers in class	■
Math waiver	☐	Priority seating	☐
Other special classes	☐	Tape recorders	☐
Priority registrations	☐	Videotaped classes	☐
Substitution of courses	☐	Text on tape	☐
Exams		**Services**	
Extended time	■	Diagnostic tests	☐
Oral exams	☐	Learning centers	☐
Take home exams	☐	Proofreaders	☐
Exams on tape or computer	☐	Readers	■
Untimed exams	■	Reading Machines/Kurzweil	☐
Other accommodations	☐	Special bookstore section	☐
		Typists	☐

Counseling Services

- ☐ Academic
- ☐ Psychological
- ☐ Student Support groups
- ☐ Vocational

Tutoring

	Individual	Group
Time management	☐	☐
Organizational skills	☐	☐
Learning strategies	☐	☐
Study skills	☐	☐
Content area	☐	☐
Writing lab	☐	☐
Math lab	☐	☐

LD PROGRAM STAFF

Total number of LD Program staff (including director):

Full Time: 1 Part Time: 1

Key staff person available to work with LD students: Edward Marshall, Director of Counseling.

Kentucky Christian University

Grayson, KY

Address: 100 Academic Parkway, Grayson, KY, 41143
Admissions telephone: 800 522-3181
Admissions FAX: 606 474-3251
Vice President of Enrollment Management: Mrs. Sandra Deakins
Admissions e-mail: knights@kcu.edu
Web site: http://www.kcu.edu
SAT Code: 1377 ACT Code: 1523

Coordinator of Special Student Services: Chad Leach
LD program telephone: 606 474-3257
LD program e-mail: cleach@kcu.edu
Total campus enrollment: 584

GENERAL

Kentucky Christian University is a private, coed, four-year institution. 121-acre, rural campus in Grayson (population: 3,877), 30 miles from both Huntington, WV, and Ashland. Major airport serves Lexington (95 miles); airport also serves Huntington; bus and train serve Ashland. Semester system.

LD ADMISSIONS

A personal interview is recommended. Essay is required and may be typed.

SECONDARY SCHOOL REQUIREMENTS

Graduation from secondary school required; GED accepted.

TESTING

ACT required; SAT Reasoning may be substituted.

All enrolled freshmen (fall 2004):

Average SAT I Scores: Verbal: 501 Math: 507
Average ACT Scores: Composite: 21

Child Study Team report is not required. Tests required as part of this documentation:

- ☐ WAIS-IV
- ☐ WISC-IV
- ☐ SATA
- ☐ Woodcock-Johnson
- ☐ Nelson-Denny Reading Test
- ☐ Other

UNDERGRADUATE STUDENT BODY

Total undergraduate student enrollment: 276 Men, 302 Women.

Composition of student body (fall 2004):

	Undergraduate	Freshmen
International	1.4	1.6
Black	0.7	0.2
American Indian	0.0	0.3
Asian-American	0.0	0.0
Hispanic	0.0	0.2
White	97.9	95.7
Unreported	0.0	2.1
	100.0%	100.0%

66% are from out of state. Average age of full-time undergraduates is 22. 67% of classes have fewer than 20 students, 31% have between 20 and 50 students, 2% have more than 50 students.

STUDENT HOUSING

90% of freshmen live in college housing. Freshmen are not required to live on campus. Housing is guaranteed for all undergraduates. Campus can house 589 undergraduates. Single rooms are available for students with medical or special needs. A medical note is required.

EXPENSES

Tuition (2005-06): $11,520 per year.

Room & Board: $4,514.

There is no additional cost for LD program/services.

LD SERVICES

LD program size is not limited.

LD services available to:

☐ Freshmen ☐ Sophomores ☐ Juniors ☐ Seniors

Academic Accommodations

Curriculum		In class	
Foreign language waiver	☐	Early syllabus	☐
Lighter course load	☐	Note takers in class	☑
Math waiver	☐	Priority seating	☐
Other special classes	☐	Tape recorders	☐
Priority registrations	☐	Videotaped classes	☐
Substitution of courses	☐	Text on tape	☐
Exams		**Services**	
Extended time	☑	Diagnostic tests	☐
Oral exams	☑	Learning centers	☑
Take home exams	☐	Proofreaders	☐
Exams on tape or computer	☐	Readers	☑
Untimed exams	☑	Reading Machines/Kurzweil	☐
Other accommodations	☐	Special bookstore section	☐
		Typists	☐

Credit toward degree is not given for remedial courses taken.

Counseling Services

- ☐ Academic
- ☐ Psychological
- ☐ Student Support groups
- ☐ Vocational

Tutoring

Individual tutoring is available daily.

	Individual	Group
Time management	☐	☐
Organizational skills	☐	☐
Learning strategies	☐	☐
Study skills	☐	☐
Content area	☐	☐
Writing lab	☐	☐
Math lab	☐	☐

LD PROGRAM STAFF

Total number of LD Program staff (including director):

Full Time: 1 Part Time: 1

There is an advisor/advocate from the LD program available to students. 6 peer tutors are available to work with LD students.

Kentucky Wesleyan College

Owensboro, KY

Address: 3000 Frederica Street, P.O. Box 1039, Owensboro, KY, 42302
Admissions telephone: 800 999-0592
Admissions FAX: 270 926-3196
Dean of Admissions and Financial Aid: Mr. Ken R. Rasp
Admissions e-mail: admitme@kwc.edu
Web site: http://www.kwc.edu
SAT Code: 1369 ACT Code: 1518

LD program name: PLUS Center
LD program contact: Marisue Coy
LD program e-mail: marisuec@kwc.edu
Total campus enrollment: 679

GENERAL

Kentucky Wesleyan College is a private, coed, four-year institution. 63-acre campus in Owensboro (population: 54,067), 100 miles from Nashville and 141 miles from Louisville. Served by bus; major airport serves Louisville; smaller airport and bus serve Evansville, Ind. (40 miles); train serves Carbondale, Ill. (150 miles). Semester system.

LD ADMISSIONS

SECONDARY SCHOOL REQUIREMENTS

Graduation from secondary school required; GED accepted. The following course distribution required: 4 units of English, 3 units of math, 3 units of science, 3 units of social studies.

TESTING

ACT required; SAT Reasoning may be substituted. SAT Subject recommended.

All enrolled freshmen (fall 2004):

Average SAT I Scores: Verbal: 538 Math: 528
Average ACT Scores: Composite: 22

Child Study Team report is not required. Tests required as part of this documentation:

- ☐ WAIS-IV
- ☐ WISC-IV
- ☐ SATA
- ☐ Woodcock-Johnson
- ☐ Nelson-Denny Reading Test
- ☐ Other

UNDERGRADUATE STUDENT BODY

Total undergraduate student enrollment: 361 Men, 310 Women.

Composition of student body (fall 2004):

	Undergraduate	Freshmen
International	1.4	1.7
Black	11.0	7.9
American Indian	0.5	0.2
Asian-American	1.0	0.6
Hispanic	3.3	2.0
White	78.1	82.0
Unreported	4.8	5.6
	100.0%	100.0%

23% are from out of state. 15% join a fraternity and 20% join a sorority. Average age of full-time undergraduates is 21. 77% of classes have fewer than 20 students, 23% have between 20 and 50 students.

STUDENT HOUSING

66% of freshmen live in college housing. Freshmen are required to live on campus. Housing is guaranteed for all undergraduates. Campus can house 470 undergraduates.

EXPENSES

Tuition (2005-06): $12,590 per year.
Room: $2,550. Board: $3,050.

LD SERVICES

LD program size is not limited.

LD services available to:

☐ Freshmen ☐ Sophomores ☐ Juniors ☐ Seniors

Academic Accommodations

Curriculum

- Foreign language waiver ☐
- Lighter course load ☐
- Math waiver ☐
- Other special classes ☐
- Priority registrations ☐
- Substitution of courses ☐

Exams

- Extended time ☐
- Oral exams ☐
- Take home exams ☐
- Exams on tape or computer ☐
- Untimed exams ☐
- Other accommodations ☐

In class

- Early syllabus ☐
- Note takers in class ■
- Priority seating ☐
- Tape recorders ☐
- Videotaped classes ☐
- Text on tape ☐

Services

- Diagnostic tests ☐
- Learning centers ■
- Proofreaders ☐
- Readers ☐
- Reading Machines/Kurzweil ☐
- Special bookstore section ☐
- Typists ☐

Counseling Services

- ☐ Academic
- ☐ Psychological
- ☐ Student Support groups
- ☐ Vocational

Tutoring

	Individual	Group
Time management	☐	☐
Organizational skills	☐	☐
Learning strategies	☐	☐
Study skills	☐	☐
Content area	☐	☐
Writing lab	☐	☐
Math lab	☐	☐

LD PROGRAM STAFF

Key staff person available to work with LD students: Marisue Coy, PLUS Center Director.

University of Kentucky

Lexington, KY

Address: 101 Main Building, Lexington, KY, 40506
Admissions telephone: 859 257-2000
Admissions FAX: 859 257-3823
Director of Admissions: Don Witt
Web site: http://www.uky.edu
SAT Code: 1837 ACT Code: 1554

LD program name: Disability Resource Center
LD program address: Alumni Gym, Room 2
Cognitive Disabilities Specialist: Leisa Pickering
LD program telephone: 859 257-2754
LD program e-mail: lmpick@uky.edu
LD program enrollment: 515, Total campus enrollment: 18,434

GENERAL

University of Kentucky is a public, coed, four-year institution. 779-acre campus in Lexington (population: 260,512), 75 miles from both Cincinnati, OH and Louisville. Served by air and bus; train serves Naysville (40 miles). School operates campus shuttle. Public transportation serves campus. Semester system.

LD ADMISSIONS

Students do not complete a separate application and are not simultaneously accepted to the LD program. A member of the LD program does not sit on the admissions committee. A personal interview is required. Essay is not required.

For fall 2004, 184 completed self-identified LD applications were received. 184 applications were offered admission, and 184 enrolled.

SECONDARY SCHOOL REQUIREMENTS

Graduation from secondary school required; GED accepted. The following course distribution required: 4 units of English, 3 units of math, 3 units of science, 2 units of foreign language, 3 units of social studies, 5 units of academic electives.

TESTING

SAT Subject recommended.

All enrolled freshmen (fall 2004):

Average SAT I Scores: Verbal: 563 Math: 574
Average ACT Scores: Composite: 24

Child Study Team report is not required. A neuropsychological or comprehensive psycho-educational evaluation is required for admission. Must be dated within 36 months of application. Tests required as part of this documentation:

- ■ WAIS-IV
- ☐ WISC-IV
- ■ SATA
- ■ Woodcock-Johnson
- ■ Nelson-Denny Reading Test
- ■ Other

UNDERGRADUATE STUDENT BODY

Total undergraduate student enrollment: 8,295 Men, 8,842 Women.

Composition of student body (fall 2004):

	Undergraduate	Freshmen
International	0.3	1.0
Black	6.7	5.7
American Indian	0.2	0.1
Asian-American	1.8	1.7
Hispanic	0.8	1.0
White	88.0	88.6
Unreported	2.2	2.0
	100.0%	100.0%

12% are from out of state. 15% join a fraternity and 19% join a sorority. Average age of full-time undergraduates is 21. 27% of classes have fewer than 20 students, 57% have between 20 and 50 students, 16% have more than 50 students.

STUDENT HOUSING

Freshmen are not required to live on campus. Housing is not guaranteed for all undergraduates. Housing is available on a first-come, first-served basis with freshmen and underclassmen having first priority. Campus can house 6,123 undergraduates. Single rooms are available for students with medical or special needs. A medical note is required.

EXPENSES

Tuition (2005-06): $5,162 per year (in-state), $12,148 (out-of-state).
Room: $3,363. Board: $1,766.
There is no additional cost for LD program/services.

LD SERVICES

LD program size is not limited.

LD services available to:

■ Freshmen ■ Sophomores ■ Juniors ■ Seniors

Academic Accommodations

Curriculum		In class	
Foreign language waiver	☐	Early syllabus	☐
Lighter course load	☐	Note takers in class	☐
Math waiver	☐	Priority seating	☐
Other special classes	☐	Tape recorders	■
Priority registrations	■	Videotaped classes	☐
Substitution of courses	■	Text on tape	■
Exams		**Services**	
Extended time	■	Diagnostic tests	■
Oral exams	■	Learning centers	☐
Take home exams	☐	Proofreaders	☐
Exams on tape or computer	■	Readers	■
Untimed exams	☐	Reading Machines/Kurzweil	■
Other accommodations	■	Special bookstore section	☐
		Typists	■

Credit toward degree is not given for remedial courses taken.

Counseling Services

- ☐ Academic
- ☐ Psychological
- ■ Student Support groups
- ☐ Vocational

Tutoring

Individual tutoring is not available.

	Individual	Group
Time management	■	■
Organizational skills	■	■
Learning strategies	■	■
Study skills	■	■
Content area	■	■
Writing lab	■	☐
Math lab	☐	■

LD PROGRAM STAFF

Total number of LD Program staff (including director):

Full Time: 1 Part Time: 1

There is an advisor/advocate from the LD program available to students.

Key staff person available to work with LD students: Leisa Pickering, Cognitive Disabilities Specialist.

Lindsey Wilson College

Columbia, KY

Address: 210 Lindsey Wilson Street, Columbia, KY, 42728
Admissions telephone: 800 264-0138
Admissions FAX: 270 384-8591
Director of Admissions: Traci Pooler
Admissions e-mail: admissions@lindsey.edu
Web site: http://www.lindsey.edu
SAT Code: 1409 ACT Code: 1522

Learning Disabilities Coordinator: David Ludden
LD program telephone: 270 384-8080
LD program e-mail: luddend@lindsey.edu
LD program enrollment: 15, Total campus enrollment: 1,565

GENERAL

Lindsey Wilson College is a private, coed, four-year institution. 43-acre campus in Columbia (population: 4,014), 100 miles from Lexington and Louisville and from Nashville, TN; branch campus in Scottsville. Major airports serve Louisville and Nashville, TN; bus serves Elizabethtown (50 miles); train serves Cincinnati, OH (180 miles). Semester system.

LD ADMISSIONS

Students do not complete a separate application and are not simultaneously accepted to the LD program. A member of the LD program does not sit on the admissions committee. A personal interview is required. Essay is not required.

SECONDARY SCHOOL REQUIREMENTS

Graduation from secondary school not required.

TESTING

ACT required of some applicants. SAT Reasoning or ACT considered if submitted. SAT Subject recommended.

All enrolled freshmen (fall 2004):

Average ACT Scores: Composite: 19

Child Study Team report is not required. A neuropsychological or comprehensive psycho-education evaluation is not required for admission. Tests required as part of this documentation:

- ☐ WAIS-IV
- ☐ WISC-IV
- ☐ SATA
- ☐ Woodcock-Johnson
- ☐ Nelson-Denny Reading Test
- ☐ Other

UNDERGRADUATE STUDENT BODY

Total undergraduate student enrollment: 556 Men, 821 Women.

Composition of student body (fall 2004):

	Undergraduate	Freshmen
International	0.3	5.1
Black	13.1	5.5
American Indian	0.5	0.3
Asian-American	0.5	0.6
Hispanic	2.0	1.3
White	79.1	85.0
Unreported	4.5	2.2
	100.0%	100.0%

8% are from out of state. Average age of full-time undergraduates is 24. 64% of classes have fewer than 20 students, 35% have between 20 and 50 students.

STUDENT HOUSING

74% of freshmen live in college housing. Freshmen are required to live on campus. Housing is guaranteed for all undergraduates. Campus can house 805 undergraduates. Single rooms are available for students with medical or special needs. A medical note is required.

EXPENSES

Tuition (2005-06): $13,584 per year.

Room: $2,184. Board: $3,742.
There is no additional cost for LD program/services.

LD SERVICES

LD program size is not limited.

LD services available to:

■ Freshmen ■ Sophomores ■ Juniors ■ Seniors

Academic Accommodations

Curriculum		**In class**	
Foreign language waiver	☐	Early syllabus	☐
Lighter course load	■	Note takers in class	■
Math waiver	☐	Priority seating	■
Other special classes	☐	Tape recorders	■
Priority registrations	☐	Videotaped classes	☐
Substitution of courses	☐	Text on tape	☐
Exams		**Services**	
Extended time	■	Diagnostic tests	☐
Oral exams	■	Learning centers	■
Take home exams	☐	Proofreaders	☐
Exams on tape or computer	☐	Readers	■
Untimed exams	■	Reading Machines/Kurzweil	■
Other accommodations	☐	Special bookstore section	☐
		Typists	☐

Credit toward degree is given for remedial courses taken.

Counseling Services

- ■ Academic
- ■ Psychological
- ☐ Student Support groups
- ☐ Vocational

Tutoring

Individual tutoring is available daily.

Average size of tutoring groups: 1

	Individual	Group
Time management	☐	☐
Organizational skills	☐	☐
Learning strategies	☐	☐
Study skills	☐	■
Content area	☐	☐
Writing lab	☐	☐
Math lab	☐	■

LD PROGRAM STAFF

Total number of LD Program staff (including director):

Full Time: 1 Part Time: 1

There is no advisor/advocate from the LD program available to students. 49 peer tutors are available to work with LD students.

Key staff person available to work with LD students: Jan Green, Tutor Coordinator.

University of Louisville

Louisville, KY

Address: 2301 South Third Street, Louisville, KY, 40292
Admissions telephone: 800 334-8635
Admissions FAX: 502 852-4776
Director of Admissions: Jenny L. Sawyer
Admissions e-mail: admitme@gwise.louisville.edu
Web site: http://www.louisville.edu
SAT Code: 1838 ACT Code: 1556

Assistant Director: Kathy Pendleton
LD program telephone: 502 852-6938
LD program e-mail: kjpend01@louisville.edu
Total campus enrollment: 14,872

GENERAL

University of Louisville is a public, coed, four-year institution. 170-acre, urban campus in Louisville (population: 256,231); branch campuses in downtown and eastern Louisville and at Fort Knox. Served by air and bus. Public transportation serves campus. Semester system.

LD ADMISSIONS

Application Deadline: 08/22. Students do not complete a separate application and are not simultaneously accepted to the LD program. A member of the LD program does not sit on the admissions committee. A personal interview is not required. Essay is not required.

SECONDARY SCHOOL REQUIREMENTS

Graduation from secondary school required; GED accepted. The following course distribution required: 4 units of English, 3 units of math, 3 units of science, 2 units of foreign language, 3 units of social studies, 5 units of academic electives.

TESTING

ACT required; SAT Reasoning may be substituted. SAT Subject recommended.

All enrolled freshmen (fall 2004):

Average ACT Scores: Composite: 23

Child Study Team report is not required. Tests required as part of this documentation:

- ☐ WAIS-IV
- ☐ WISC-IV
- ☐ SATA
- ☐ Woodcock-Johnson
- ☐ Nelson-Denny Reading Test
- ☐ Other

UNDERGRADUATE STUDENT BODY

Total undergraduate student enrollment: 6,515 Men, 7,594 Women.

Composition of student body (fall 2004):

	Undergraduate	Freshmen
International	0.9	1.2
Black	13.1	13.7
American Indian	0.3	0.2
Asian-American	2.5	2.8
Hispanic	1.7	1.2
White	81.0	80.1
Unreported	0.5	0.8
	100.0%	100.0%

11% are from out of state. 9% join a fraternity and 6% join a sorority. Average age of full-time undergraduates is 23. 26% of classes have fewer than 20 students, 63% have between 20 and 50 students, 11% have more than 50 students.

STUDENT HOUSING

51% of freshmen live in college housing. Housing is guaranteed for all undergraduates. Campus can house 2,656 undergraduates.

EXPENSES

Tuition (2005-06): $5,532 per year (in-state), $15,092 (out-of-state).
Room: $4,490. Board: $1,546.
There is no additional cost for LD program/services.

LD SERVICES

LD program size is not limited.

LD services available to:

☐ Freshmen ☐ Sophomores ☐ Juniors ☐ Seniors

Academic Accommodations

Curriculum		In class	
Foreign language waiver	☐	Early syllabus	☐
Lighter course load	☐	Note takers in class	■
Math waiver	☐	Priority seating	☐
Other special classes	☐	Tape recorders	■
Priority registrations	☐	Videotaped classes	☐
Substitution of courses	☐	Text on tape	☐
Exams		**Services**	
Extended time	■	Diagnostic tests	☐
Oral exams	■	Learning centers	☐
Take home exams	☐	Proofreaders	☐
Exams on tape or computer	☐	Readers	■
Untimed exams	☐	Reading Machines/Kurzweil	■
Other accommodations	☐	Special bookstore section	☐
		Typists	☐

Credit toward degree is not given for remedial courses taken.

Counseling Services

- ☐ Academic
- ☐ Psychological
- ☐ Student Support groups
- ☐ Vocational

Tutoring

	Individual	Group
Time management	☐	☐
Organizational skills	☐	☐
Learning strategies	☐	☐
Study skills	☐	☐
Content area	☐	☐
Writing lab	☐	☐
Math lab	☐	☐

LD PROGRAM STAFF

Key staff person available to work with LD students: Kathy Pendleton, Assistant Director.

Mid-Continent College

Mayfield, KY

Address: 99 Powell Road East, Mayfield, KY, 42066
Admissions telephone: 270 247-8521
Admissions FAX: 270 247-3115
Director, Enrollment and Retention: Dr. Butch Booth
Admissions e-mail: admissions@midcontinent.edu
Web site: http://www.midcontinent.edu
SAT Code: 254 ACT Code: 1524

Learning Disabled Coordinator/Instructor: Debra McCuiston
LD program telephone: 270 247-8521, extension 354
LD program e-mail: dmccuiston@midcontinent.edu
Total campus enrollment: 814

GENERAL

Mid-Continent College is a private, coed, four-year institution. Campus in Mayfield (population: 10,349), 15 miles from Paducah; classes offered in Fulton, Hopkinsville, Owensboro, and Paducah and in Benton, IL. Served by bus; major airport serves Nashville, TN (125 miles); smaller airport serves Paducah. Semester system.

LD ADMISSIONS

A personal interview is recommended. Essay is required and may be typed.

SECONDARY SCHOOL REQUIREMENTS

Graduation from secondary school required; GED accepted. The following course distribution required: 4 units of English, 2 units of math, 2 units of science, 1 unit of foreign language, 2 units of social studies, 1 unit of history.

TESTING

SAT Reasoning or ACT required.

All enrolled freshmen (fall 2004):

Average SAT I Scores:	Verbal: 465	Math: 560
Average ACT Scores:	Composite: 19	

Child Study Team report is not required. Tests required as part of this documentation:

❑ WAIS-IV	❑ Woodcock-Johnson
❑ WISC-IV	❑ Nelson-Denny Reading Test
❑ SATA	❑ Other

UNDERGRADUATE STUDENT BODY

Total undergraduate student enrollment: 341 Men, 311 Women.

Composition of student body (fall 2004):

	Undergraduate	Freshmen
International	10.5	3.9
Black	3.5	12.5
American Indian	0.0	0.0
Asian-American	1.2	0.4
Hispanic	1.2	0.7
White	81.4	81.9
Unreported	2.3	0.5
	100.0%	100.0%

87% of classes have fewer than 20 students, 13% have between 20 and 50 students.

STUDENT HOUSING

52% of freshmen live in college housing. Freshmen are required to live on campus. Housing is not guaranteed for all undergraduates. Campus housing is recommended for the full-time traditional college aged student. Campus can house 88 undergraduates.

EXPENSES

Tuition (2005-06): $8,850 per year.

Room: $2,500. Board: $3,200.

There is no additional cost for LD program/services.

LD SERVICES

LD program size is not limited.

LD services available to:

❑ Freshmen ❑ Sophomores ❑ Juniors ❑ Seniors

Academic Accommodations

Curriculum		**In class**	
Foreign language waiver	❑	Early syllabus	❑
Lighter course load	■	Note takers in class	■
Math waiver	❑	Priority seating	❑
Other special classes	❑	Tape recorders	■
Priority registrations	❑	Videotaped classes	■
Substitution of courses	❑	Text on tape	❑
Exams		**Services**	
Extended time	■	Diagnostic tests	❑
Oral exams	■	Learning centers	❑
Take home exams	❑	Proofreaders	❑
Exams on tape or computer	❑	Readers	■
Untimed exams	■	Reading Machines/Kurzweil	❑
Other accommodations	❑	Special bookstore section	❑
		Typists	❑

Credit toward degree is not given for remedial courses taken.

Counseling Services

❑ Academic
❑ Psychological
❑ Student Support groups
❑ Vocational

Tutoring

	Individual	Group
Time management	❑	❑
Organizational skills	❑	❑
Learning strategies	❑	❑
Study skills	❑	❑
Content area	❑	❑
Writing lab	❑	❑
Math lab	❑	❑

LD PROGRAM STAFF

Total number of LD Program staff (including director):

Full Time: 1 Part Time: 1

Key staff person available to work with LD students: Debra McCuiston, Learning Disabled Coordinator/Instructor.

Midway College

Midway, KY

Address: 512 East Stephens Street, Midway, KY, 40347
Admissions telephone: 800 755-0031
Admissions FAX: 859 846-5823
Director of Admissions: Dr. Jim Wombles
Admissions e-mail: admissions@midway.edu
Web site: http://www.Midway.edu
SAT Code: 1467 ACT Code: 1528

LD program enrollment: 6, Total campus enrollment: 1,271

GENERAL

Midway College is a private, women's, four-year institution. 105-acre campus in Midway (population: 1,620), 12 miles from Lexington; branch campus in Danville. Airport and bus serve Lexington; airport and train serve Louisville (67 miles); major airport serves Cincinnati, OH (85 miles). School operates transportation to local shopping malls and athletic and musical events. Semester system.

LD ADMISSIONS

For fall 2004, 6 completed self-identified LD applications were received. 6 applications were offered admission, and 6 enrolled.

SECONDARY SCHOOL REQUIREMENTS

Graduation from secondary school required; GED accepted. The following course distribution required: 4 units of English.

TESTING

SAT Subject recommended.

All enrolled freshmen (fall 2004):

Average SAT I Scores: Verbal: 530 Math: 476
Average ACT Scores: Composite: 21

Child Study Team report is not required. Tests required as part of this documentation:

- □ WAIS-IV
- □ WISC-IV
- □ SATA
- □ Woodcock-Johnson
- □ Nelson-Denny Reading Test
- □ Other

UNDERGRADUATE STUDENT BODY

Total undergraduate student enrollment: 118 Men, 756 Women.

Composition of student body (fall 2004):

	Undergraduate	Freshmen
International	0.5	0.6
Black	3.3	5.1
American Indian	0.0	0.5
Asian-American	0.0	0.2
Hispanic	0.0	0.2
White	91.3	91.2
Unreported	4.9	2.4
	100.0%	100.0%

12% are from out of state. Average age of full-time undergraduates is 29. 79% of classes have fewer than 20 students, 20% have between 20 and 50 students, 1% have more than 50 students.

STUDENT HOUSING

47% of freshmen live in college housing. Freshmen are required to live on campus. Housing is guaranteed for all undergraduates.

EXPENSES

Tuition (2005-06): $13,800 per year.
Room: $3,000. Board: $3,200.

LD SERVICES

LD program size is not limited.

LD services available to:

■ Freshmen ■ Sophomores ■ Juniors ■ Seniors

Academic Accommodations

Curriculum		In class	
Foreign language waiver	□	Early syllabus	□
Lighter course load	□	Note takers in class	□
Math waiver	□	Priority seating	■
Other special classes	□	Tape recorders	■
Priority registrations	□	Videotaped classes	□
Substitution of courses	□	Text on tape	■
Exams		**Services**	
Extended time	■	Diagnostic tests	□
Oral exams	■	Learning centers	□
Take home exams	■	Proofreaders	□
Exams on tape or computer	□	Readers	□
Untimed exams	■	Reading Machines/Kurzweil	□
Other accommodations	■	Special bookstore section	□
		Typists	□

Counseling Services

- ■ Academic
- □ Psychological
- □ Student Support groups
- □ Vocational

Tutoring

Individual tutoring is available.

	Individual	Group
Time management	□	□
Organizational skills	□	□
Learning strategies	□	□
Study skills	□	□
Content area	□	□
Writing lab	□	□
Math lab	□	□

Morehead State University

Morehead, KY

Address: 150 University Boulevard, Morehead, KY, 40351
Admissions telephone: 800 585-6781
Admissions FAX: 601 783-5038
Assistant Vice President for Admissions, Financial Aid, and Housing: Joel Pace
Admissions e-mail: admissions@moreheadstate.edu
Web site: http://www.moreheadstate.edu
SAT Code: 1487 ACT Code: 1530

LD program name: Center for Academic Services
LD program address: 322 Allie Young Hall
Counselor: Debra Reed
LD program telephone: 606 783-5188
LD program e-mail: d.reed@moreheadstate.edu
LD program enrollment: 27, Total campus enrollment: 7,757

GENERAL

Morehead State University is a public, coed, four-year institution. 1,039-acre campus in Morehead (population: 5,914), 65 miles from Lexington. Served by bus; major airport serves Lexington. School operates transportation to university farm, off-campus parking areas, and golf course. Public transportation serves campus. Semester system.

LD ADMISSIONS

A member of the LD program does not sit on the admissions committee. A personal interview is not required. Essay is not required.

SECONDARY SCHOOL REQUIREMENTS

Graduation from secondary school required; GED accepted. The following course distribution required: 4 units of English, 3 units of math, 3 units of science, 3 units of social studies, 7 units of academic electives.

TESTING

ACT required; SAT Reasoning may be substituted. SAT Subject recommended.

All enrolled freshmen (fall 2004):

Average ACT Scores: Composite: 20

Child Study Team report is not required. Tests required as part of this documentation:

☐ WAIS-IV ☐ Woodcock-Johnson
☐ WISC-IV ☐ Nelson-Denny Reading Test
☐ SATA ☐ Other

UNDERGRADUATE STUDENT BODY

Total undergraduate student enrollment: 2,833 Men, 4,366 Women.

Composition of student body (fall 2004):

	Undergraduate	Freshmen
International	0.3	0.6
Black	4.8	3.4
American Indian	0.3	0.2
Asian-American	0.2	0.3
Hispanic	0.5	0.6
White	93.8	94.9
Unreported	0.0	0.0
	100.0%	100.0%

15% are from out of state. Average age of full-time undergraduates is 22. 51% of classes have fewer than 20 students, 45% have between 20 and 50 students, 4% have more than 50 students.

STUDENT HOUSING

65% of freshmen live in college housing. Freshmen are required to live on campus. Housing is guaranteed for all undergraduates. Campus can house 3,553 undergraduates. Single rooms are available for students with medical or special needs. A medical note is required.

EXPENSES

Tuition (2005-06): $4,320 per year (in-state), $11,480 (out-of-state).

Room & Board: $4,830.
There is no additional cost for LD program/services.

LD SERVICES

LD program size is not limited.

LD services available to:

■ Freshmen ■ Sophomores ■ Juniors ■ Seniors

Academic Accommodations

Curriculum		**In class**	
Foreign language waiver	☐	Early syllabus	☐
Lighter course load	■	Note takers in class	■
Math waiver	☐	Priority seating	☐
Other special classes	☐	Tape recorders	■
Priority registrations	☐	Videotaped classes	☐
Substitution of courses	☐	Text on tape	☐
Exams		**Services**	
Extended time	■	Diagnostic tests	☐
Oral exams	☐	Learning centers	☐
Take home exams	☐	Proofreaders	☐
Exams on tape or computer	☐	Readers	☐
Untimed exams	☐	Reading Machines/Kurzweil	■
Other accommodations	■	Special bookstore section	☐
		Typists	☐

Credit toward degree is not given for remedial courses taken.

Counseling Services

■ Academic
☐ Psychological
☐ Student Support groups
☐ Vocational

Tutoring

Individual tutoring is available weekly.

Average size of tutoring groups: 5

	Individual	Group
Time management	■	☐
Organizational skills	■	☐
Learning strategies	■	☐
Study skills	■	☐
Content area	■	☐
Writing lab	☐	☐
Math lab	■	☐

LD PROGRAM STAFF

Total number of LD Program staff (including director):

Full Time: 1 Part Time: 1

There is an advisor/advocate from the LD program available to students.

Key staff person available to work with LD students: Debra Reed, Counselor.

LD Program web site: www.moreheadstate.edu/units/acadsupport/retention

Murray State University

Murray, KY

Address: P.O. Box 9, Murray, KY, 42071
Admissions telephone: 800 272-4678
Admissions FAX: 270 762-3780
Acting Dean of Admissions and Registrar: Jim Vaughan
Admissions e-mail: admissions@murraystate.edu
Web site: http://www.murraystate.edu
SAT Code: 1494 ACT Code: 1532

LD program name: Services for Students with Learning Disabilities
LD program address: 423 Wells Hall
Coordinator, SSLD Office: Cindy Clemson
LD program telephone: 270 762-2018
LD program e-mail: Cindy.Clemson@murraystate.edu
LD program enrollment: 297, Total campus enrollment: 8,363

GENERAL

Murray State University is a public, coed, four-year institution. 232-acre campus in Murray (population: 14,950), 50 miles from Paducah. Major airport serves Nashville, TN (130 miles); smaller airport and bus serve Paducah; train serves Fulton (40 miles). Semester system.

LD ADMISSIONS

Students do not complete a separate application and are simultaneously accepted to the LD program. A member of the LD program does not sit on the admissions committee. High school waivers are accepted for math and foreign language. A personal interview is recommended. Essay is not required. Any student not meeting minimum university standards for admissions may go through the admissions appeal process.

SECONDARY SCHOOL REQUIREMENTS

Graduation from secondary school required; GED accepted. The following course distribution required: 4 units of English, 3 units of math, 3 units of science, 2 units of foreign language, 3 units of social studies, 5 units of academic electives.

TESTING

SAT Reasoning considered if submitted. ACT required.

All enrolled freshmen (fall 2004):

Average ACT Scores: Composite: 23

Child Study Team report is not required. A neuropsychological or comprehensive psycho-educational evaluation is required for admission. Must be dated within 36 months of application. Tests required as part of this documentation:

☒ WAIS-IV	☒ Woodcock-Johnson
☒ WISC-IV	☐ Nelson-Denny Reading Test
☐ SATA	☐ Other

UNDERGRADUATE STUDENT BODY

Total undergraduate student enrollment: 3,258 Men, 4,505 Women.

Composition of student body (fall 2004):

	Undergraduate	Freshmen
International	0.8	2.1
Black	5.4	5.7
American Indian	0.6	0.5
Asian-American	0.9	0.8
Hispanic	0.7	0.8
White	90.6	89.4
Unreported	1.1	0.8
	100.0%	100.0%

27% are from out of state. 17% join a fraternity and 10% join a sorority. Average age of full-time undergraduates is 20. 53% of classes have fewer than 20 students, 42% have between 20 and 50 students, 5% have more than 50 students.

STUDENT HOUSING

60% of freshmen live in college housing. Freshmen are required to live on campus. Housing is guaranteed for all undergraduates. Campus can house 3,000 undergraduates. Single rooms are available for students with medical or special needs. A medical note is required.

EXPENSES

Tuition (2005-06): $3,864 per year (in-state), $5,536 (out-of-state). Tuition is lower for new students from Illinois, Indiana, Missouri, and Tennessee. Room: $2,366. Board: $2,106.

Additional cost for LD program/services: $15 per hour for tutoring.

LD SERVICES

LD program size is not limited.

LD services available to:

☒ Freshmen ☒ Sophomores ☒ Juniors ☒ Seniors

Academic Accommodations

Curriculum		In class	
Foreign language waiver	☐	Early syllabus	☐
Lighter course load	☒	Note takers in class	☒
Math waiver	☐	Priority seating	☐
Other special classes	☒	Tape recorders	☒
Priority registrations	☐	Videotaped classes	☐
Substitution of courses	☐	Text on tape	☒
Exams		**Services**	
Extended time	☒	Diagnostic tests	☒
Oral exams	☒	Learning centers	☒
Take home exams	☐	Proofreaders	☐
Exams on tape or computer	☐	Readers	☒
Untimed exams	☒	Reading Machines/Kurzweil	☒
Other accommodations	☐	Special bookstore section	☒
		Typists	☐

Credit toward degree is not given for remedial courses taken.

Counseling Services

☒ Academic — Meets 2 times per academic year
☐ Psychological
☐ Student Support groups
☐ Vocational

Tutoring

Individual tutoring is available daily.

Average size of tutoring groups: 1

	Individual	Group
Time management	☒	☒
Organizational skills	☒	☒
Learning strategies	☒	☒
Study skills	☒	☒
Content area	☒	☒
Writing lab	☒	☒
Math lab	☐	☒

LD PROGRAM STAFF

Total number of LD Program staff (including director):

Full Time: 3 Part Time: 3

There is an advisor/advocate from the LD program available to students. 5 graduate students and 47 peer tutors are available to work with LD students.

Key staff person available to work with LD students: Cindy Clemson, Coordinator, SSLD Office.

LD Program web site: www.murraystate.edu/secsv/ssld

Northern Kentucky University

Highland Heights, KY

Address: Nunn Drive, Highland Heights, KY, 41099
Admissions telephone: 800 637-9948
Admissions FAX: 859 572-6665
Associate Director of Admissions for Recruitment: Melissa Gorbandt
Admissions e-mail: admitnku@nku.edu
Web site: http://www.nku.edu
SAT Code: 1574 ACT Code: 1566

LD program name: Testing & Disability Services
LD program address: UC 320, 41099
Director, Testing/Disability Services: A. Dale Adams
LD program telephone: 859 572-5180
LD program e-mail: adamsad@nku.edu
LD program enrollment: 89, Total campus enrollment: 12,052

GENERAL

Northern Kentucky University is a public, coed, four-year institution. Campus of more than 300 acres in Highland Heights (population: 6,554), seven miles from Cincinnati, OH; branch campus in Covington. Airport, bus, and train serve Cincinnati, OH; smaller airport serves Florence (10 miles). Public transportation serves campus. Semester system.

LD ADMISSIONS

Students do not complete a separate application and are not simultaneously accepted to the LD program. A member of the LD program does not sit on the admissions committee. High school waivers are accepted for foreign language. A personal interview is required. Essay is not required. Minimum class rank accepted is top 30%.

For fall 2004, 8 completed self-identified LD applications were received. 8 applications were offered admission, and 8 enrolled.

SECONDARY SCHOOL REQUIREMENTS

Graduation from secondary school required; GED accepted. The following course distribution required: 4 units of English, 3 units of math, 3 units of science, 2 units of foreign language, 3 units of social studies, 6 units of academic electives.

TESTING

ACT required.

All enrolled freshmen (fall 2004):

Average SAT I Scores:	Verbal: 489	Math: 481
Average ACT Scores:	Composite: 20	

Child Study Team report is not required. A neuropsychological or comprehensive psycho-educational evaluation is required for admission. Must be dated within 36 months of application. Tests required as part of this documentation:

- [x] WAIS-IV
- [x] WISC-IV
- [x] SATA
- [x] Woodcock-Johnson
- [x] Nelson-Denny Reading Test
- [ ] Other

UNDERGRADUATE STUDENT BODY

Total undergraduate student enrollment: 4,587 Men, 6,682 Women.

Composition of student body (fall 2004):

	Undergraduate	Freshmen
International	0.6	1.7
Black	6.2	4.9
American Indian	0.3	0.2
Asian-American	0.9	0.9
Hispanic	1.2	1.0
White	90.8	91.3
Unreported	0.0	0.0
	100.0%	100.0%

24% are from out of state. 4% join a fraternity and 4% join a sorority. Average age of full-time undergraduates is 22. 32% of classes have fewer than 20 students, 64% have between 20 and 50 students, 4% have more than 50 students.

STUDENT HOUSING

28% of freshmen live in college housing. Freshmen are required to live on campus. Housing is guaranteed for all undergraduates. Campus can house 1,400 undergraduates.

EXPENSES

Tuition (2005-06): $4,968 per year (in-state), $9,696 (out-of-state). $2,754 per year (in-state), $3,234 (seven Indiana counties close to northern Kentucky border), $7,002 (other out-of-state).
Room & Board: $2,679.
There is no additional cost for LD program/services.

LD SERVICES

LD program size is not limited.

LD services available to:

- [x] Freshmen
- [x] Sophomores
- [x] Juniors
- [x] Seniors

Academic Accommodations

Curriculum		In class	
Foreign language waiver	[ ]	Early syllabus	[ ]
Lighter course load	[ ]	Note takers in class	[ ]
Math waiver	[ ]	Priority seating	[x]
Other special classes	[x]	Tape recorders	[x]
Priority registrations	[x]	Videotaped classes	[ ]
Substitution of courses	[ ]	Text on tape	[ ]
Exams		**Services**	
Extended time	[x]	Diagnostic tests	[ ]
Oral exams	[ ]	Learning centers	[x]
Take home exams	[ ]	Proofreaders	[ ]
Exams on tape or computer	[x]	Readers	[x]
Untimed exams	[ ]	Reading Machines/Kurzweil	[x]
Other accommodations	[ ]	Special bookstore section	[ ]
		Typists	[ ]

Credit toward degree is not given for remedial courses taken.

Counseling Services

- [x] Academic
- [x] Psychological
- [ ] Student Support groups
- [x] Vocational

Tutoring

Individual tutoring is available weekly.

Average size of tutoring groups: 1

	Individual	Group
Time management	[x]	[ ]
Organizational skills	[x]	[ ]
Learning strategies	[x]	[ ]
Study skills	[x]	[ ]
Content area	[ ]	[ ]
Writing lab	[x]	[ ]
Math lab	[x]	[ ]

LD PROGRAM STAFF

Total number of LD Program staff (including director):

Full Time: 1 Part Time: 1

There is an advisor/advocate from the LD program available to students. 20 peer tutors are available to work with LD students.

Key staff person available to work with LD students: A. Dale Adams, Director, Testing/Disability Services.

LD Program web site: www.nku.edu/~disability

Pikeville College

Pikeville, KY

Address: 147 Sycamore Street, Pikeville, KY, 41501-1194
Admissions telephone: 866 232-7700
Admissions FAX: 606 432-9328
Director of Admissions: Melinda Lynch
Admissions e-mail: wewantyou@pc.edu
Web site: http://www.pc.edu/
SAT Code: 1625 ACT Code: 1540

LD program enrollment: 5, Total campus enrollment: 801

GENERAL

Pikeville College is a private, coed, four-year institution. 20-acre campus in Pikeville (population: 6,295), 100 miles from Huntington, WV. Major airport serves Lexington (150 miles); smaller airport serves Huntington, WV; bus and train serve Ashland (85 miles). Semester system.

LD ADMISSIONS

Students do not complete a separate application and are not simultaneously accepted to the LD program. A member of the LD program does not sit on the admissions committee. A personal interview is not required. Essay is not required.

SECONDARY SCHOOL REQUIREMENTS

Graduation from secondary school required; GED accepted.

TESTING

All enrolled freshmen (fall 2004):

Average ACT Scores: Composite: 20

Child Study Team report is not required. A neuropsychological or comprehensive psycho-educational evaluation is required for admission. Tests required as part of this documentation:

- ■ WAIS-IV
- ■ WISC-IV
- ■ SATA
- ■ Woodcock-Johnson
- ■ Nelson-Denny Reading Test
- ☐ Other

UNDERGRADUATE STUDENT BODY

Total undergraduate student enrollment: 391 Men, 557 Women.

Composition of student body (fall 2004):

	Undergraduate	Freshmen
International	0.0	0.3
Black	4.0	6.4
American Indian	0.6	0.4
Asian-American	0.0	0.3
Hispanic	0.0	0.8
White	95.5	92.0
Unreported	0.0	0.0
	100.0%	100.0%

18% are from out of state. Average age of full-time undergraduates is 22. 57% of classes have fewer than 20 students, 43% have between 20 and 50 students.

STUDENT HOUSING

50% of freshmen live in college housing. Freshmen are not required to live on campus. Housing is guaranteed for all undergraduates. Campus can house 525 undergraduates. Single rooms are not available for students with medical or special needs.

EXPENSES

Tuition (2005-06): $11,500 per year.
Room & Board: $5,000.

There is no additional cost for LD program/services.

LD SERVICES

LD program size is not limited.

LD services available to:

■ Freshmen ■ Sophomores ■ Juniors ■ Seniors

Academic Accommodations

Curriculum		In class	
Foreign language waiver	☐	Early syllabus	☐
Lighter course load	☐	Note takers in class	☐
Math waiver	☐	Priority seating	☐
Other special classes	☐	Tape recorders	☐
Priority registrations	☐	Videotaped classes	☐
Substitution of courses	☐	Text on tape	☐
Exams		**Services**	
Extended time	■	Diagnostic tests	☐
Oral exams	■	Learning centers	☐
Take home exams	☐	Proofreaders	☐
Exams on tape or computer	☐	Readers	■
Untimed exams	■	Reading Machines/Kurzweil	☐
Other accommodations	☐	Special bookstore section	☐
		Typists	☐

Credit toward degree is not given for remedial courses taken.

Counseling Services

- ■ Academic
- ☐ Psychological
- ☐ Student Support groups
- ☐ Vocational

Tutoring

Individual tutoring is available daily.

	Individual	Group
Time management	☐	☐
Organizational skills	☐	☐
Learning strategies	☐	☐
Study skills	☐	☐
Content area	■	☐
Writing lab	■	☐
Math lab	■	☐

LD PROGRAM STAFF

Total number of LD Program staff (including director):

Full Time: 1 Part Time: 1

There is an advisor/advocate from the LD program available to students.

Key staff person available to work with LD students: Kathy Petot, Student Services: Testing Coordinator.

Spalding University

Louisville, KY

Address: 851 South Fourth Street, Louisville, KY, 40203-2188
Admissions telephone: 502 585-7111
Admissions FAX: 502 585-7158
Director of Admissions: Vicki Prince
Admissions e-mail: admissions@spalding.edu
Web site: http://www.spalding.edu
SAT Code: 1552 ACT Code: 1534

Dean of Students: Dan Fox
LD program telephone: 502 585-9911
LD program e-mail: dfox@spalding.edu
Total campus enrollment: 989

GENERAL

Spalding University is a private, coed, four-year institution. Six-acre, urban campus in Louisville (population: 256,231). Served by air and bus; train serves Cincinnati, OH and Indianapolis, IN (both 100 miles). Public transportation serves campus.

LD ADMISSIONS

A personal interview is required. Essay is not required.

SECONDARY SCHOOL REQUIREMENTS

Graduation from secondary school required; GED accepted. The following course distribution required: 4 units of English, 3 units of math, 2 units of science, 2 units of foreign language, 2 units of social studies.

TESTING

SAT Reasoning or ACT required. SAT Subject recommended.

All enrolled freshmen (fall 2004):

Average SAT I Scores:	Verbal: 508	Math: 477
Average ACT Scores:	Composite: 19	

Child Study Team report is not required. Tests required as part of this documentation:

- ☐ WAIS-IV
- ☐ WISC-IV
- ☐ SATA
- ☐ Woodcock-Johnson
- ☐ Nelson-Denny Reading Test
- ☐ Other

UNDERGRADUATE STUDENT BODY

Total undergraduate student enrollment: 245 Men, 843 Women.

Composition of student body (fall 2004):

	Undergraduate	Freshmen
International	3.9	4.5
Black	17.4	17.1
American Indian	0.6	0.4
Asian-American	2.6	1.4
Hispanic	0.0	0.8
White	50.3	47.0
Unreported	25.2	28.8
	100.0%	100.0%

3% are from out of state.

STUDENT HOUSING

Freshmen are not required to live on campus. Housing is guaranteed for all undergraduates. Campus can house 326 undergraduates.

EXPENSES

Tuition (2005-06): $14,400 per year.
Room: $2,286. Board: $1,572.

There is no additional cost for LD program/services.

LD SERVICES

LD program size is not limited.

LD services available to:

☐ Freshmen ☐ Sophomores ☐ Juniors ☐ Seniors

Academic Accommodations

Curriculum		**In class**	
Foreign language waiver	☐	Early syllabus	☐
Lighter course load	■	Note takers in class	■
Math waiver	☐	Priority seating	☐
Other special classes	■	Tape recorders	■
Priority registrations	☐	Videotaped classes	☐
Substitution of courses	☐	Text on tape	☐
Exams		**Services**	
Extended time	■	Diagnostic tests	■
Oral exams	■	Learning centers	■
Take home exams	☐	Proofreaders	☐
Exams on tape or computer	☐	Readers	☐
Untimed exams	■	Reading Machines/Kurzweil	☐
Other accommodations	☐	Special bookstore section	☐
		Typists	☐

Credit toward degree is not given for remedial courses taken.

Counseling Services

- ☐ Academic
- ☐ Psychological
- ☐ Student Support groups
- ☐ Vocational

Tutoring

	Individual	Group
Time management	☐	☐
Organizational skills	☐	☐
Learning strategies	☐	☐
Study skills	☐	☐
Content area	☐	☐
Writing lab	☐	☐
Math lab	☐	☐

LD PROGRAM STAFF

Total number of LD Program staff (including director):

Full Time: 1 Part Time: 1

Key staff person available to work with LD students: Dan Fox, Dean of Students.

Thomas More College

Crestview Hills, KY

Address: 333 Thomas More Parkway, Crestview Hills, KY, 41017-3495
Admissions telephone: 800 825-4557
Admissions FAX: 859 344-3444
Director of Admissions: Angela Griffin Jones
Admissions e-mail: admissions@thomasmore.edu
Web site: http://www.thomasmore.edu
SAT Code: 1876 ACT Code: 1560

LD program name: Student Services and Advising
Director of Student Services and Advising: Barb Davis
LD program telephone: 859 344-3521
LD program e-mail: barb.davis@thomasmore.edu
LD program enrollment: 18, Total campus enrollment: 1,339

GENERAL

Thomas More College is a private, coed, four-year institution. 100-acre campus in Crestview Hills (population: 2,889), 10 miles from Cincinnati, OH. Major airport and train serve Cincinnati, OH; bus serves Covington (seven miles). Public transportation serves campus. Semester system.

LD ADMISSIONS

Application Deadline: 08/15. Students do not complete a separate application and are simultaneously accepted to the LD program. A member of the LD program does sit on the admissions committee. A personal interview is not required. Essay is not required. All students are under the same admission requirements. To receive accommodations for disability, documentation of specific needs is required and must be submitted after acceptance to the college.

For fall 2004, 4 completed self-identified LD applications were received. 4 applications were offered admission, and 4 enrolled.

SECONDARY SCHOOL REQUIREMENTS

Graduation from secondary school required; GED accepted. The following course distribution required: 4 units of English, 3 units of math, 3 units of science, 2 units of foreign language, 3 units of social studies.

TESTING

SAT Reasoning or ACT required. SAT Subject recommended.

All enrolled freshmen (fall 2004):

Average SAT I Scores:	Verbal: 504	Math: 515
Average ACT Scores:	Composite: 21	

Child Study Team report is not required. A neuropsychological or comprehensive psycho-educational evaluation is required for admission. Must be dated within 36 months of application. Tests required as part of this documentation:

■ WAIS-IV	■ Woodcock-Johnson
■ WISC-IV	☐ Nelson-Denny Reading Test
☐ SATA	☐ Other

UNDERGRADUATE STUDENT BODY

Total undergraduate student enrollment: 675 Men, 747 Women.

Composition of student body (fall 2004):

	Undergraduate	Freshmen
International	0.0	0.7
Black	5.7	4.9
American Indian	0.0	0.2
Asian-American	0.6	0.5
Hispanic	0.6	0.6
White	85.2	74.0
Unreported	8.0	19.1
	100.0%	100.0%

34% are from out of state. Average age of full-time undergraduates is 20. 76% of classes have fewer than 20 students, 24% have between 20 and 50 students.

STUDENT HOUSING

49% of freshmen live in college housing. Freshmen are not required to live on campus. Housing is not guaranteed for all undergraduates. Housing is not available for graduate students. Campus can house 432 undergraduates. Single rooms are available for students with medical or special needs. A medical note is required.

EXPENSES

Tuition (2005-06): $17,600 per year.
Room: $2,900. Board: $3,250.
There is no additional cost for LD program/services.

LD SERVICES

LD program size is not limited.

LD services available to:

■ Freshmen ■ Sophomores ■ Juniors ■ Seniors

Academic Accommodations

Curriculum		In class	
Foreign language waiver	☐	Early syllabus	☐
Lighter course load	■	Note takers in class	■
Math waiver	☐	Priority seating	■
Other special classes	■	Tape recorders	■
Priority registrations	☐	Videotaped classes	☐
Substitution of courses	☐	Text on tape	■
Exams		**Services**	
Extended time	■	Diagnostic tests	☐
Oral exams	■	Learning centers	■
Take home exams	■	Proofreaders	■
Exams on tape or computer	■	Readers	■
Untimed exams	■	Reading Machines/Kurzweil	☐
Other accommodations	☐	Special bookstore section	☐
		Typists	☐

Credit toward degree is not given for remedial courses taken.

Counseling Services

■ Academic	Meets 20 times per academic year
■ Psychological	Meets 50 times per academic year
☐ Student Support groups	
☐ Vocational	

Tutoring

Individual tutoring is available daily.

Average size of tutoring groups: 2

	Individual	Group
Time management	■	☐
Organizational skills	■	☐
Learning strategies	■	☐
Study skills	■	☐
Content area	■	☐
Writing lab	■	☐
Math lab	■	☐

LD PROGRAM STAFF

There is an advisor/advocate from the LD program available to students. The advisor/advocate meets with faculty 2 times per month and students 5 times per month. 15 peer tutors are available to work with LD students.

Key staff person available to work with LD students: Barb Davis, Director of Student Services and Advising.

Transylvania University

Lexington, KY

Admissions telephone: 800 872-6798
Admissions FAX: 859 233-8797
Director of Admissions: Sarah Coen
Admissions e-mail: admissions@transy.edu
Web site: http://www.transy.edu
SAT Code: 1808 ACT Code: 1550

Coordinator of Learning Disability Students: Marian Baker
LD program telephone: 859 233-8215
LD program e-mail: mhbaker@transy.edu
Total campus enrollment: 1,114

GENERAL

Transylvania University is a private, coed, four-year institution. 48-acre, urban campus in Lexington (population: 260,512), 80 miles from both Cincinnati, OH and Louisville. Served by air and bus; major airports serve Cincinnati, OH and Louisville; train serves Maysville (55 miles). School operates transportation to U of Kentucky library. Public transportation serves campus.

LD ADMISSIONS

A personal interview is not required. Essay is not required.

SECONDARY SCHOOL REQUIREMENTS

Graduation from secondary school required; GED accepted. The following course distribution required: 4 units of English, 3 units of math, 3 units of science, 2 units of social studies, 1 unit of history.

TESTING

SAT Reasoning or ACT required. SAT Subject recommended.

All enrolled freshmen (fall 2004):

Average SAT I Scores:	Verbal: 590	Math: 563
Average ACT Scores:	Composite: 26	

Child Study Team report is required if student is classified. Tests required as part of this documentation:

- [ ] WAIS-IV
- [ ] WISC-IV
- [ ] SATA
- [ ] Woodcock-Johnson
- [ ] Nelson-Denny Reading Test
- [ ] Other

UNDERGRADUATE STUDENT BODY

Total undergraduate student enrollment: 457 Men, 595 Women.

Composition of student body (fall 2004):

	Undergraduate	Freshmen
International	0.0	0.1
Black	2.2	2.0
American Indian	0.3	0.5
Asian-American	0.9	1.4
Hispanic	1.9	1.4
White	88.2	87.6
Unreported	6.5	7.1
	100.0%	100.0%

18% are from out of state. 50% join a fraternity and 50% join a sorority. Average age of full-time undergraduates is 20. 60% of classes have fewer than 20 students, 40% have between 20 and 50 students.

STUDENT HOUSING

96% of freshmen live in college housing. Freshmen are required to live on campus. Housing is guaranteed for all undergraduates. Campus can house 900 undergraduates. Single rooms are not available for students with medical or special needs.

EXPENSES

Tuition (2005-06): $18,880 per year.
Room: $3,690. Board: $2,900.

There is no additional cost for LD program/services.

LD SERVICES

LD program size is not limited.

LD services available to:

[x] Freshmen [x] Sophomores [x] Juniors [x] Seniors

Academic Accommodations

Curriculum		In class	
Foreign language waiver	[ ]	Early syllabus	[x]
Lighter course load	[ ]	Note takers in class	[x]
Math waiver	[ ]	Priority seating	[x]
Other special classes	[ ]	Tape recorders	[ ]
Priority registrations	[ ]	Videotaped classes	[ ]
Substitution of courses	[ ]	Text on tape	[ ]
Exams		**Services**	
Extended time	[x]	Diagnostic tests	[ ]
Oral exams	[ ]	Learning centers	[ ]
Take home exams	[ ]	Proofreaders	[ ]
Exams on tape or computer	[ ]	Readers	[ ]
Untimed exams	[x]	Reading Machines/Kurzweil	[ ]
Other accommodations	[ ]	Special bookstore section	[ ]
		Typists	[x]

Credit toward degree is not given for remedial courses taken.

Counseling Services

- [x] Academic
- [x] Psychological
- [ ] Student Support groups
- [ ] Vocational

Tutoring

Individual tutoring is available daily.

Average size of tutoring groups: 1

	Individual	Group
Time management	[ ]	[ ]
Organizational skills	[ ]	[ ]
Learning strategies	[ ]	[ ]
Study skills	[ ]	[ ]
Content area	[ ]	[ ]
Writing lab	[x]	[ ]
Math lab	[x]	[ ]

UNIQUE LD PROGRAM FEATURES

Services to disabled students are arranged and provided on an as-needed basis.

LD PROGRAM STAFF

There is an advisor/advocate from the LD program available to students.

Key staff person available to work with LD students: Marian Baker, Coordinator of Learning Disability Students.

Western Kentucky University

Bowling Green, KY

Address: 1 Big Red Way, Bowling Green, KY, 42101-3576
Admissions telephone: 800 495-8463
Admissions FAX: 270 745-6133
Director of Admissions and Academic Services: Dr. Dean R. Kahler
Admissions e-mail: admission@wku.edu
Web site: http://www.wku.edu
SAT Code: 1901 ACT Code: 1562

LD program name: Student Disability Services
LD program address: 101 Garrett Conference Center, WKU
Coordinator, Student Disability Services: Matt Davis
LD program telephone: 270 745-5004
LD program e-mail: matt.davis@wku.edu
LD program enrollment: 214, Total campus enrollment: 15,815

GENERAL

Western Kentucky University is a public, coed, four-year institution. 200-acre campus in Bowling Green (population: 50,000), 65 miles north of Nashville, TN; branch campus in Glasgow. Served by bus; major airport serves Nashville, TN. School operates transportation on campus and to Bowling Green. Public transportation serves campus. Semester system.

LD ADMISSIONS

Students do not complete a separate application and are simultaneously accepted to the LD program. A member of the LD program does not sit on the admissions committee. High school waivers are accepted for foreign language. A personal interview is recommended. Essay is not required.

SECONDARY SCHOOL REQUIREMENTS

Graduation from secondary school required; GED accepted. The following course distribution required: 4 units of English, 3 units of math, 3 units of science, 2 units of foreign language, 3 units of social studies.

TESTING

SAT Subject recommended.

Child Study Team report is not required. A neuropsychological or comprehensive psycho-educational evaluation is required for admission. Must be dated within 36 months of application. Tests required as part of this documentation:

- [x] WAIS-IV
- [x] WISC-IV
- [ ] SATA
- [x] Woodcock-Johnson
- [ ] Nelson-Denny Reading Test
- [ ] Other

UNDERGRADUATE STUDENT BODY

Total undergraduate student enrollment: 5,599 Men, 7,636 Women.

Composition of student body (fall 2004):

	Undergraduate	Freshmen
International	0.8	1.3
Black	12.1	9.0
American Indian	0.3	0.3
Asian-American	0.9	1.0
Hispanic	0.9	0.9
White	83.9	86.4
Unreported	1.1	1.1
	100.0%	100.0%

16% are from out of state. 9% join a fraternity and 8% join a sorority. Average age of full-time undergraduates is 22. 37% of classes have fewer than 20 students, 57% have between 20 and 50 students, 6% have more than 50 students.

STUDENT HOUSING

69% of freshmen live in college housing. Freshmen are required to live on campus. Housing is guaranteed for all undergraduates. Campus can house 4,953 undergraduates. Single rooms are available for students with medical or special needs. A medical note is required.

EXPENSES

Tuition (2005-06): $5,391 per year (in-state), $13,167 (out-of-state).
Room: $2,990. Board: $2,244.
There is no additional cost for LD program/services.

LD SERVICES

LD program size is not limited.

LD services available to:

- [x] Freshmen
- [x] Sophomores
- [x] Juniors
- [x] Seniors

Academic Accommodations

Curriculum		In class	
Foreign language waiver	[ ]	Early syllabus	[ ]
Lighter course load	[ ]	Note takers in class	[x]
Math waiver	[ ]	Priority seating	[x]
Other special classes	[ ]	Tape recorders	[x]
Priority registrations	[x]	Videotaped classes	[x]
Substitution of courses	[ ]	Text on tape	[x]
Exams		**Services**	
Extended time	[x]	Diagnostic tests	[x]
Oral exams	[x]	Learning centers	[x]
Take home exams	[ ]	Proofreaders	[x]
Exams on tape or computer	[ ]	Readers	[x]
Untimed exams	[ ]	Reading Machines/Kurzweil	[x]
Other accommodations	[ ]	Special bookstore section	[ ]
		Typists	[ ]

Credit toward degree is not given for remedial courses taken.

Counseling Services

- [x] Academic
- [x] Psychological
- [x] Student Support groups
- [x] Vocational

Tutoring

Individual tutoring is available weekly.

Average size of tutoring groups: 2

	Individual	Group
Time management	[x]	[ ]
Organizational skills	[x]	[ ]
Learning strategies	[x]	[ ]
Study skills	[x]	[ ]
Content area	[ ]	[ ]
Writing lab	[ ]	[x]
Math lab	[ ]	[x]

LD PROGRAM STAFF

Total number of LD Program staff (including director):

Full Time: 1 Part Time: 1

There is an advisor/advocate from the LD program available to students.

Key staff person available to work with LD students: Matt Davis, Coordinator, Student Disability Services.

LD Program web site: www.wku.edu/dept/support/legal/eoo/sds.htm

Centenary College of Louisiana

Shreveport, LA

Address: P.O. Box 41188, Shreveport, LA, 71134-1188
Admissions telephone: 800 234-4448
Admissions FAX: 318 869-5005
Director of Admissions: Tim Crowley
Admissions e-mail: admissions@centenary.edu
Web site: http://www.centenary.edu
SAT Code: 6082 ACT Code: 1576

Director of Admissions: Tim Crowley
LD program telephone: 318 869-5131
LD program e-mail: tcrowley@centenary.edu
LD program enrollment: 15, Total campus enrollment: 905

GENERAL

Centenary College of Louisiana is a private, coed, four-year institution. 68-acre, suburban campus in Shreveport (population: 200,145). Served by airport and bus; train serves Marshall, TX. (30 miles). Public transportation serves campus.

LD ADMISSIONS

A personal interview is recommended. Essay is required and may be typed.

SECONDARY SCHOOL REQUIREMENTS

Graduation from secondary school required; GED accepted.

TESTING

SAT Reasoning or ACT required. SAT Subject recommended.

All enrolled freshmen (fall 2004):

Average SAT I Scores:	Verbal: 575	Math: 574
Average ACT Scores:	Composite: 26	

Child Study Team report is not required. Tests required as part of this documentation:

☐ WAIS-IV	☐ Woodcock-Johnson
☐ WISC-IV	☐ Nelson-Denny Reading Test
☐ SATA	☐ Other

UNDERGRADUATE STUDENT BODY

Total undergraduate student enrollment: 335 Men, 523 Women.

Composition of student body (fall 2004):

	Undergraduate	Freshmen
International	0.4	2.0
Black	6.7	7.5
American Indian	0.0	0.6
Asian-American	2.8	2.7
Hispanic	2.8	2.4
White	86.9	84.5
Unreported	0.4	0.3
	100.0%	100.0%

38% are from out of state. 26% join a fraternity and 28% join a sorority. Average age of full-time undergraduates is 19. 71% of classes have fewer than 20 students, 29% have between 20 and 50 students.

STUDENT HOUSING

90% of freshmen live in college housing. Freshmen are required to live on campus. Housing is guaranteed for all undergraduates. Campus can house 648 undergraduates. Single rooms are available for students with medical or special needs. A medical note is required.

EXPENSES

Tuition (2005-06): $17,750 per year.
Room: $3,270. Board: $3,220.

There is no additional cost for LD program/services.

LD SERVICES

LD program size is not limited.

LD services available to:

■ Freshmen ■ Sophomores ■ Juniors ■ Seniors

Academic Accommodations

Curriculum		In class	
Foreign language waiver	☐	Early syllabus	☐
Lighter course load	☐	Note takers in class	■
Math waiver	☐	Priority seating	■
Other special classes	☐	Tape recorders	■
Priority registrations	☐	Videotaped classes	☐
Substitution of courses	☐	Text on tape	■
Exams		**Services**	
Extended time	■	Diagnostic tests	☐
Oral exams	■	Learning centers	■
Take home exams	☐	Proofreaders	☐
Exams on tape or computer	☐	Readers	■
Untimed exams	■	Reading Machines/Kurzweil	■
Other accommodations	☐	Special bookstore section	☐
		Typists	☐

Credit toward degree is not given for remedial courses taken.

Counseling Services

- ☐ Academic
- ■ Psychological
- ☐ Student Support groups
- ☐ Vocational

Tutoring

Individual tutoring is available daily.

	Individual	Group
Time management	☐	☐
Organizational skills	☐	☐
Learning strategies	☐	☐
Study skills	☐	☐
Content area	☐	☐
Writing lab	☐	☐
Math lab	☐	☐

LD PROGRAM STAFF

Total number of LD Program staff (including director):

Full Time: 2 Part Time: 2

1 graduate student is available to work with LD students.

Key staff person available to work with LD students: Tina Feldt, Director of Counseling/Disability Services.

Dillard University

New Orleans, LA

Address: 2601 Gentilly Boulevard, New Orleans, LA, 70122
Admissions telephone: 800 216-6637
Admissions FAX: 504 816-4895
Vice President of Enrollment Management and Admissions: Linda Nash
Admissions e-mail: admissions@dillard.edu
Web site: http://www.dillard.edu
SAT Code: 6164 ACT Code: 1578

Director of Support Services: Dr. Kevin Bastian
LD program telephone: 504 816-4714
LD program e-mail: kbastian@dillard.edu
LD program enrollment: 12, Total campus enrollment: 2,155

GENERAL

Dillard University is a private, coed, four-year institution. 48-acre campus in New Orleans (population: 484,674). Served by airport, bus, and train. Public transportation serves campus. Semester system.

LD ADMISSIONS

Application Deadline: 06/01. Students do not complete a separate application and are simultaneously accepted to the LD program. A member of the LD program does sit on the admissions committee. A personal interview is recommended. Essay is not required.

For fall 2004, 15 completed self-identified LD applications were received. 5 applications were offered admission, and 5 enrolled.

SECONDARY SCHOOL REQUIREMENTS

Graduation from secondary school required; GED accepted. The following course distribution required: 4 units of English, 3 units of math, 3 units of science, 3 units of social studies, 6 units of academic electives.

TESTING

SAT Reasoning or ACT required. SAT Subject required.

All enrolled freshmen (fall 2004):

Average SAT I Scores:	Verbal:	Math:
Average ACT Scores:	Composite: 22	

Child Study Team report is not required. A neuropsychological or comprehensive psycho-educational evaluation is required for admission. Must be dated within 36 months of application. Tests required as part of this documentation:

☑ WAIS-IV	☑ Woodcock-Johnson
☑ WISC-IV	☑ Nelson-Denny Reading Test
☑ SATA	☐ Other

UNDERGRADUATE STUDENT BODY

Total undergraduate student enrollment: 497 Men, 1,640 Women.

Composition of student body (fall 2004):

	Undergraduate	Freshmen
International	0.2	0.3
Black	99.4	99.3
American Indian	0.0	0.0
Asian-American	0.0	0.0
Hispanic	0.0	0.1
White	0.2	0.3
Unreported	0.2	0.0
	100.0%	100.0%

49% are from out of state. 5% join a fraternity and 2% join a sorority. Average age of full-time undergraduates is 19. 60% of classes have fewer than 20 students, 38% have between 20 and 50 students.

STUDENT HOUSING

72% of freshmen live in college housing. Freshmen are not required to live on campus. Housing is guaranteed for all undergraduates. Campus can house 1,168 undergraduates. Single rooms are not available for students with medical or special needs.

EXPENSES

Tuition (2005-06): $11,760 per year.
There is no additional cost for LD program/services.

LD SERVICES

LD program size is not limited.

LD services available to:

☑ Freshmen ☑ Sophomores ☑ Juniors ☑ Seniors

Academic Accommodations

Curriculum		**In class**	
Foreign language waiver	☐	Early syllabus	☐
Lighter course load	☐	Note takers in class	☑
Math waiver	☐	Priority seating	☑
Other special classes	☐	Tape recorders	☑
Priority registrations	☑	Videotaped classes	☐
Substitution of courses	☐	Text on tape	☐
Exams		**Services**	
Extended time	☑	Diagnostic tests	☐
Oral exams	☑	Learning centers	☑
Take home exams	☑	Proofreaders	☑
Exams on tape or computer	☐	Readers	☑
Untimed exams	☑	Reading Machines/Kurzweil	☐
Other accommodations	☑	Special bookstore section	☐
		Typists	☐

Credit toward degree is not given for remedial courses taken.

Counseling Services

☑ Academic	Meets 6 times per academic year
☑ Psychological	Meets 3 times per academic year
☑ Student Support groups	Meets 3 times per academic year
☑ Vocational	Meets 3 times per academic year

Tutoring

Individual tutoring is available weekly.

Average size of tutoring groups: 3

	Individual	Group
Time management	☑	☑
Organizational skills	☑	☑
Learning strategies	☑	☑
Study skills	☑	☑
Content area	☑	☑
Writing lab	☑	☑
Math lab	☑	☑

LD PROGRAM STAFF

Total number of LD Program staff (including director):

Full Time: 1 Part Time: 1

There is an advisor/advocate from the LD program available to students. The advisor/advocate meets with faculty once per month and students 2 times per month. 5 peer tutors are available to work with LD students.

Key staff person available to work with LD students: Dr. Kevin Bastian, Director of Support Services.

Grambling State University

Grambling, LA

Address: Box 607, Grambling, LA, 71245
Admissions telephone: 318 274-6183
Admissions FAX: 318 274-3292
Acting Director of Admissions/Recruitment: Nora Taylor
Admissions e-mail: admissions@gram.edu
Web site: http://www.gram.edu/
SAT Code: 6250 ACT Code: 1582

LD program name: ADA Student Services
Director of SIRC: Ruth Osborne
LD program telephone: 318 274-3163
LD program e-mail: osborner@gram.edu
Total campus enrollment: 4260

GENERAL

Grambling State University is a public, coed, four-year institution. 340-acre campus in Grambling (population: 4,692), five miles from Ruston and 75 miles from Shreveport. Served by bus; major airport serves Monroe (40 miles); train serves Jackson, MS (140 miles). School operates transportation to Jackson Parish, Monroe, and Ruston. Semester system.

LD ADMISSIONS

A personal interview is not required. Essay is not required.

SECONDARY SCHOOL REQUIREMENTS

Graduation from secondary school required; GED accepted. The following course distribution required: 4 units of English, 4 units of math, 4 units of science, 1 unit of foreign language, 2 units of social studies, 2 units of history.

TESTING

Child Study Team report is not required. Tests required as part of this documentation:

- ☐ WAIS-IV
- ☐ WISC-IV
- ☐ SATA
- ☐ Woodcock-Johnson
- ☐ Nelson-Denny Reading Test
- ☐ Other

UNDERGRADUATE STUDENT BODY

Total undergraduate student enrollment: 1,862 Men, 2,398 Women.

36% are from out of state.

STUDENT HOUSING

Housing is guaranteed for all undergraduates. Campus can house 2,479 undergraduates.

EXPENSES

Tuition 2004-05: $1,068 per year (in-state), $3,743 (out-of-state).

Room: $969. Board: $815.

There is no additional cost for LD program/services.

LD SERVICES

LD program size is not limited.

LD services available to:

☐ Freshmen ☐ Sophomores ☐ Juniors ☐ Seniors

Academic Accommodations

Curriculum		**In class**	
Foreign language waiver	☐	Early syllabus	☐
Lighter course load	■	Note takers in class	☐
Math waiver	☐	Priority seating	☐
Other special classes	☐	Tape recorders	☐
Priority registrations	☐	Videotaped classes	☐
Substitution of courses	☐	Text on tape	☐
Exams		**Services**	
Extended time	☐	Diagnostic tests	■
Oral exams	☐	Learning centers	☐
Take home exams	☐	Proofreaders	☐
Exams on tape or computer	☐	Readers	☐
Untimed exams	☐	Reading Machines/Kurzweil	☐
Other accommodations	☐	Special bookstore section	☐
		Typists	☐

Credit toward degree is not given for remedial courses taken.

Counseling Services

- ☐ Academic
- ☐ Psychological
- ☐ Student Support groups
- ☐ Vocational

Tutoring

	Individual	Group
Time management	☐	☐
Organizational skills	☐	☐
Learning strategies	☐	☐
Study skills	☐	☐
Content area	☐	☐
Writing lab	☐	☐
Math lab	☐	☐

LD PROGRAM STAFF

Total number of LD Program staff (including director):

Full Time: 5 Part Time: 5

Key staff person available to work with LD students: Ruth Osborne, Director of SIRC.

Louisiana College

Pineville, LA

Address: 1140 College Drive, Pineville, LA, 71360
Admissions telephone: 800 487-1906
Admissions FAX: 318 487-7550
Director of Admissions: Mr. Byron McGee
Admissions e-mail: admissions@lacollege.edu
Web site: http://www.lacollege.edu
SAT Code: 6371 ACT Code: 1586

LD program name: Program to Assist Student Sucess (PASS)
LD program address: P.O. Box 545
Director: Betty Matthews
LD program telephone: 318 487-7629
LD program e-mail: matthews@lacollege.edu
LD program enrollment: 10, Total campus enrollment: 1,085

GENERAL

Louisiana College is a private, coed, four-year institution. 81-acre campus in Pineville (population: 13,829), two miles from Alexandria. Airport and bus serve Alexandria. Semester system.

LD ADMISSIONS

Students do not complete a separate application and are not simultaneously accepted to the LD program. A member of the LD program does not sit on the admissions committee. A personal interview is required. Essay is required and may be typed.

For fall 2004, 6 completed self-identified LD applications were received. 4 applications were offered admission, and 4 enrolled.

SECONDARY SCHOOL REQUIREMENTS

Graduation from secondary school required; GED accepted. The following course distribution required: 4 units of English, 3 units of math, 3 units of science, 2 units of social studies, 1 unit of history, 4 units of academic electives.

TESTING

ACT required; SAT Reasoning may be substituted. SAT Subject recommended.

All enrolled freshmen (fall 2004):

Average SAT I Scores:	Verbal: 534	Math: 519
Average ACT Scores:	Composite: 22	

Child Study Team report is not required. A neuropsychological or comprehensive psycho-educational evaluation is required for admission. Must be dated within 24 months of application. Tests required as part of this documentation:

■ WAIS-IV	■ Woodcock-Johnson
■ WISC-IV	□ Nelson-Denny Reading Test
□ SATA	■ Other

UNDERGRADUATE STUDENT BODY

Total undergraduate student enrollment: 506 Men, 698 Women.

Composition of student body (fall 2004):

	Undergraduate	Freshmen
International	0.0	0.9
Black	8.9	8.8
American Indian	0.4	0.3
Asian-American	2.1	1.4
Hispanic	2.5	1.6
White	85.7	86.7
Unreported	0.4	0.2
	100.0%	100.0%

7% are from out of state. Average age of full-time undergraduates is 21. 71% of classes have fewer than 20 students, 29% have between 20 and 50 students.

STUDENT HOUSING

80% of freshmen live in college housing. Freshmen are required to live on campus. Housing is guaranteed for all undergraduates. Campus can house 674 undergraduates. Single rooms are available for students with medical or special needs. A medical note is not required.

EXPENSES

Tuition (2005-06): $10,080 per year.
Room: $1,660. Board: $2,400.

Additional cost for LD program/services: $850 per semester.

LD SERVICES

LD program size is not limited.

LD services available to:

■ Freshmen ■ Sophomores ■ Juniors ■ Seniors

Academic Accommodations

Curriculum		**In class**	
Foreign language waiver	□	Early syllabus	□
Lighter course load	□	Note takers in class	■
Math waiver	□	Priority seating	□
Other special classes	□	Tape recorders	■
Priority registrations	□	Videotaped classes	□
Substitution of courses	□	Text on tape	■
Exams		**Services**	
Extended time	■	Diagnostic tests	□
Oral exams	■	Learning centers	■
Take home exams	□	Proofreaders	□
Exams on tape or computer	■	Readers	■
Untimed exams	■	Reading Machines/Kurzweil	□
Other accommodations	■	Special bookstore section	□
		Typists	■

Credit toward degree is not given for remedial courses taken.

Counseling Services

■ Academic — Meets 19 times per academic year
□ Psychological
□ Student Support groups
□ Vocational

Tutoring

Individual tutoring is available daily.

Average size of tutoring groups: 1

	Individual	Group
Time management	■	□
Organizational skills	■	□
Learning strategies	■	□
Study skills	■	□
Content area	■	□
Writing lab	□	□
Math lab	□	□

UNIQUE LD PROGRAM FEATURES

Each student is scheduled to meet with the PASS director weekly to monitor tutoring schedule, assignments and grades. Students are encouraged to meet with PASS counselors prior to semester registration for planning course schedule to meet specific needs.

LD PROGRAM STAFF

Total number of LD Program staff (including director):

Full Time: 1 Part Time: 1

There is an advisor/advocate from the LD program available to students. The advisor/advocate meets with faculty once per month and students 4 times per month. 50 peer tutors are available to work with LD students.

University of Louisiana at Lafayette

Lafayette, LA

Address: P.O. Drawer 41008, Lafayette, LA, 70504-1008
Admissions telephone: 337 482-6467
Admissions FAX: 337 482-6195
Director of Admissions: Leroy Broussard, Jr.
Admissions e-mail: enroll@louisiana.edu
Web site: http://www.louisiana.edu
SAT Code: 6672 ACT Code: 1612

LD program name: Services for Students with Disabilities
Coordinator: Carol Landry, Ph.D.
LD program telephone: 337 482-5252
LD program e-mail: carollandry@louisiana.edu
LD program enrollment: 135, Total campus enrollment: 15,043

GENERAL

University of Louisiana at Lafayette is a public, coed, four-year institution. 1,375-acre, suburban campus in Lafayette (population: 110,257), 50 miles from Baton Rouge and 125 miles from New Orleans; branch campuses in Cade and New Iberia. Served by air, bus, and train; major airports serve New Orleans and Baton Rouge. Public transportation serves campus. Semester system.

LD ADMISSIONS

Students do not complete a separate application and are simultaneously accepted to the LD program. A member of the LD program does not sit on the admissions committee. A personal interview is required. Essay is not required. Students may apply to be allowed in the University as an admissions exception.

For fall 2004, 142 completed self-identified LD applications were received. 142 applications were offered admission, and 142 enrolled.

SECONDARY SCHOOL REQUIREMENTS

Graduation from secondary school required; GED accepted. The following course distribution required: 4 units of English, 3 units of math, 3 units of science, 2 units of social studies, 1 unit of history, 5 units of academic electives.

TESTING

ACT required; SAT Reasoning may be substituted. SAT Subject recommended.

All enrolled freshmen (fall 2004):

Average ACT Scores: Composite: 21

Child Study Team report is not required. A neuropsychological or comprehensive psycho-education evaluation is not required for admission. Tests required as part of this documentation:

- ☐ WAIS-IV
- ☐ WISC-IV
- ☐ SATA
- ☐ Woodcock-Johnson
- ☐ Nelson-Denny Reading Test
- ☐ Other

UNDERGRADUATE STUDENT BODY

Total undergraduate student enrollment: 5,916 Men, 7,997 Women.

Composition of student body (fall 2004):

	Undergraduate	Freshmen
International	0.8	1.7
Black	19.1	19.0
American Indian	0.5	0.5
Asian-American	1.4	1.4
Hispanic	2.1	1.7
White	74.5	74.4
Unreported	1.6	1.3
	100.0%	100.0%

6% are from out of state. 3% join a fraternity and 4% join a sorority. Average age of full-time undergraduates is 21. 28% of classes have fewer than 20 students, 62% have between 20 and 50 students, 10% have more than 50 students.

STUDENT HOUSING

23% of freshmen live in college housing. Freshmen are required to live on campus. Housing is guaranteed for all undergraduates. Campus can house 2,399 undergraduates.

EXPENSES

Tuition (2005-06): $3,364 per year (in-state), $9,544 (out-of-state).

Room & Board: $3,566.

There is no additional cost for LD program/services.

LD SERVICES

LD program size is not limited.

LD services available to:

☑ Freshmen ☑ Sophomores ☑ Juniors ☑ Seniors

Academic Accommodations

Curriculum		In class	
Foreign language waiver	☐	Early syllabus	☐
Lighter course load	☐	Note takers in class	☑
Math waiver	☐	Priority seating	☐
Other special classes	☑	Tape recorders	☑
Priority registrations	☐	Videotaped classes	☐
Substitution of courses	☐	Text on tape	☐
Exams		**Services**	
Extended time	☑	Diagnostic tests	☑
Oral exams	☑	Learning centers	☑
Take home exams	☐	Proofreaders	☐
Exams on tape or computer	☐	Readers	☑
Untimed exams	☑	Reading Machines/Kurzweil	☑
Other accommodations	☐	Special bookstore section	☐
		Typists	☐

Credit toward degree is not given for remedial courses taken.

Counseling Services

- ☐ Academic
- ☐ Psychological
- ☐ Student Support groups
- ☐ Vocational

Tutoring

Individual tutoring is available.

	Individual	Group
Time management	☐	☐
Organizational skills	☐	☐
Learning strategies	☐	☐
Study skills	☐	☐
Content area	☐	☐
Writing lab	☐	☐
Math lab	☐	☐

UNIQUE LD PROGRAM FEATURES

Math study groups, special five day math classes, videos available in remedial math and college algebra classes, online tutoring. SMART THINKING is available through the university and a writing lab is available in the English department. Workshops in study skills, time management and individual counseling.

LD PROGRAM STAFF

Total number of LD Program staff (including director):

Full Time: 3 Part Time: 3

There is no advisor/advocate from the LD program available to students.

Key staff person available to work with LD students: Carol Landry, Ph.D., Coordinator of Services for Students with Disabilities.

University of Louisiana at Monroe

Monroe, LA

Address: 700 University Avenue, Monroe, LA, 71209
Admissions telephone: 318 342-5430
Admissions FAX: 318 342-1915
Associate Director of Admissions: Lisa Miller
Admissions e-mail: admissions@ulm.edu
Web site: http://www.ulm.edu
SAT Code: 6482 ACT Code: 1598

Total campus enrollment: 7475

GENERAL

University of Louisiana at Monroe is a public, coed, four-year institution. 238-acre campus in Monroe (population: 53,107), 100 miles from Shreveport. Served by air and bus; major airport serves Jackson, MS. (125 miles). Public transportation serves campus. Semester system.

SECONDARY SCHOOL REQUIREMENTS

Graduation from secondary school required; GED accepted. The following course distribution required: 4 units of English, 3 units of math, 3 units of science, 2 units of foreign language, 1 unit of social studies, 2 units of history.

TESTING

SAT Reasoning considered if submitted. ACT required.

All enrolled freshmen (fall 2004):

Average ACT Scores: Composite: 21

Child Study Team report is not required. Tests required as part of this documentation:

- ☐ WAIS-IV
- ☐ WISC-IV
- ☐ SATA
- ☐ Woodcock-Johnson
- ☐ Nelson-Denny Reading Test
- ☐ Other

UNDERGRADUATE STUDENT BODY

Total undergraduate student enrollment: 3,342 Men, 5,327 Women.

Composition of student body (fall 2004):

	Undergraduate	Freshmen
International	0.7	1.0
Black	29.7	28.1
American Indian	0.3	0.4
Asian-American	2.2	2.2
Hispanic	0.6	0.6
White	66.4	67.7
Unreported	0.1	0.0
	100.0%	100.0%

7% are from out of state. 6% join a fraternity and 5% join a sorority. Average age of full-time undergraduates is 22. 36% of classes have fewer than 20 students, 54% have between 20 and 50 students, 10% have more than 50 students.

STUDENT HOUSING

45% of freshmen live in college housing. Freshmen are not required to live on campus. Housing is guaranteed for all undergraduates. Campus can house 3,000 undergraduates.

EXPENSES

Tuition 2004-05: $3,075 per year (in-state), $9,028 (out-of-state).

Room: $3,290. Board: $1,790.

LD SERVICES

LD services available to:

☑ Freshmen ☑ Sophomores ☑ Juniors ☑ Seniors

Academic Accommodations

Curriculum		In class	
Foreign language waiver	☐	Early syllabus	☐
Lighter course load	☐	Note takers in class	☐
Math waiver	☐	Priority seating	☐
Other special classes	☐	Tape recorders	☐
Priority registrations	☐	Videotaped classes	☐
Substitution of courses	☐	Text on tape	☐
Exams		**Services**	
Extended time	☐	Diagnostic tests	☐
Oral exams	☐	Learning centers	☐
Take home exams	☐	Proofreaders	☐
Exams on tape or computer	☐	Readers	☐
Untimed exams	☐	Reading Machines/Kurzweil	☐
Other accommodations	☐	Special bookstore section	☐
		Typists	☐

Counseling Services

- ☑ Academic
- ☐ Psychological
- ☐ Student Support groups
- ☐ Vocational

Tutoring

	Individual	Group
Time management	☐	☐
Organizational skills	☐	☐
Learning strategies	☐	☐
Study skills	☐	☐
Content area	☐	☐
Writing lab	☐	☐
Math lab	☐	☐

Louisiana State University and Agricultural and Mechanical College

Baton Rouge, LA

Address: 156 Thomas Boyd Hall, Baton Rouge, LA, 70803
Admissions telephone: 225 578-1175
Admissions FAX: 225 578-4433
Director of Admissions: Cleve Brooks
Admissions e-mail: admissions@lsu.edu
Web site: http://www.lsu.edu
SAT Code: 6373 ACT Code: 1590

LD program name: Office of Disability Services
LD program address: 112 Johnston Hall
LD program telephone: 225 578-5919
LD program e-mail: disability@lsu.edu
LD program enrollment: 175, Total campus enrollment: 26,387

GENERAL

Louisiana State University and Agricultural and Mechanical College is a public, coed, four-year institution. 2,000-acre, urban campus in Baton Rouge (population: 227,818). Served by bus; airport serves New Orleans (80 miles); train serves Hammond (40 miles). Public transportation serves campus. Semester system.

LD ADMISSIONS

Students do not complete a separate application and are not simultaneously accepted to the LD program. A member of the LD program does not sit on the admissions committee. A personal interview is not required. Essay is not required.

SECONDARY SCHOOL REQUIREMENTS

Graduation from secondary school required; GED accepted. The following course distribution required: 4 units of English, 3 units of math, 3 units of science, 2 units of foreign language, 3 units of social studies, 2 units of academic electives.

TESTING

SAT Reasoning or ACT required. SAT Subject recommended.

All enrolled freshmen (fall 2004):

Average SAT I Scores:	Verbal: 574	Math: 586
Average ACT Scores:	Composite: 25	

Child Study Team report is not required. A neuropsychological or comprehensive psycho-educational evaluation is required for admission. Must be dated within 60 months of application. Tests required as part of this documentation:

- [x] WAIS-IV
- [ ] WISC-IV
- [ ] SATA
- [x] Woodcock-Johnson
- [ ] Nelson-Denny Reading Test
- [ ] Other

UNDERGRADUATE STUDENT BODY

Total undergraduate student enrollment: 12,553 Men, 13,965 Women.

Composition of student body (fall 2004):

	Undergraduate	Freshmen
International	1.1	2.0
Black	8.8	8.9
American Indian	0.5	0.4
Asian-American	2.5	2.9
Hispanic	2.8	2.5
White	80.9	80.7
Unreported	3.3	2.7
	100.0%	100.0%

8% are from out of state. 10% join a fraternity and 17% join a sorority. Average age of full-time undergraduates is 21. 31% of classes have fewer than 20 students, 52% have between 20 and 50 students, 17% have more than 50 students.

STUDENT HOUSING

43% of freshmen live in college housing. Freshmen are not required to live on campus. Housing is guaranteed for all undergraduates. Campus can house 6,021 undergraduates. Single rooms are available for students with medical or special needs. A medical note is required.

EXPENSES

Tuition (2005-06): $2,981 per year (in-state), $11,281 (out-of-state). Room: $3,670. Board: $2,258.
There is no additional cost for LD program/services.

LD SERVICES

LD program size is not limited.

LD services available to:

- [x] Freshmen
- [x] Sophomores
- [x] Juniors
- [x] Seniors

Academic Accommodations

Curriculum		**In class**	
Foreign language waiver	[ ]	Early syllabus	[ ]
Lighter course load	[ ]	Note takers in class	[x]
Math waiver	[ ]	Priority seating	[ ]
Other special classes	[x]	Tape recorders	[x]
Priority registrations	[x]	Videotaped classes	[ ]
Substitution of courses	[ ]	Text on tape	[x]
Exams		**Services**	
Extended time	[x]	Diagnostic tests	[ ]
Oral exams	[x]	Learning centers	[ ]
Take home exams	[ ]	Proofreaders	[ ]
Exams on tape or computer	[x]	Readers	[x]
Untimed exams	[ ]	Reading Machines/Kurzweil	[ ]
Other accommodations	[ ]	Special bookstore section	[ ]
		Typists	[ ]

Credit toward degree is not given for remedial courses taken.

Counseling Services

- [ ] Academic
- [ ] Psychological
- [ ] Student Support groups
- [ ] Vocational

Tutoring

Individual tutoring is not available.

	Individual	Group
Time management	[ ]	[ ]
Organizational skills	[ ]	[ ]
Learning strategies	[ ]	[ ]
Study skills	[x]	[ ]
Content area	[ ]	[ ]
Writing lab	[ ]	[x]
Math lab	[ ]	[x]

LD PROGRAM STAFF

Total number of LD Program staff (including director):

Full Time: 1 Part Time: 1

There is an advisor/advocate from the LD program available to students.

LD Program web site: www.lsu.edu/disability

Loyola University New Orleans

New Orleans, LA

Address: 6363 St. Charles Avenue, New Orleans, LA, 70118-6195
Admissions telephone: 800 4-LOYOLA
Admissions FAX: 504 865-3383
Dean of Admissions and Enrollment Management: Deborah C. Stieffel
Admissions e-mail: admit@loyno.edu
Web site: http://www.loyno.edu
SAT Code: 6374 ACT Code: 1592

LD program address: Box 41
Director or Special Needs Counselor: Sarah Mead Smith or Kacey McNalley
LD program telephone: 504 865-2990
LD program e-mail: ssmith@loyno.edu

GENERAL

Loyola University New Orleans is a private, coed, four-year institution. 19-acre, urban campus in New Orleans (population: 484,674); four-acre branch campus on Broadway Street. Served by air, bus, and train. School operates transportation to Broadway campus. Public transportation serves campus. Semester system.

LD ADMISSIONS

Students do not complete a separate application and are simultaneously accepted to the LD program. A member of the LD program does not sit on the admissions committee. A personal interview is recommended. Essay is required and may be typed.

SECONDARY SCHOOL REQUIREMENTS

Graduation from secondary school required; GED accepted. The following course distribution required: 4 units of English, 2 units of math, 2 units of science, 2 units of social studies.

TESTING

SAT Reasoning or ACT required. SAT Subject required.

All enrolled freshmen (fall 2004):

Average SAT I Scores:	Verbal: 625	Math: 603
Average ACT Scores:	Composite: 27	

Child Study Team report is not required. A neuropsychological or comprehensive psycho-education evaluation is not required for admission. Tests required as part of this documentation:

- [x] WAIS-IV
- [ ] WISC-IV
- [x] SATA
- [x] Woodcock-Johnson
- [x] Nelson-Denny Reading Test
- [x] Other

UNDERGRADUATE STUDENT BODY

Total undergraduate student enrollment: 1,349 Men, 2,443 Women.

Composition of student body (fall 2004):

	Undergraduate	Freshmen
International	2.7	3.3
Black	8.5	10.0
American Indian	1.1	0.5
Asian-American	4.7	4.2
Hispanic	14.4	10.9
White	61.6	64.7
Unreported	7.1	6.4
	100.0%	100.0%

47% are from out of state. 19% join a fraternity and 20% join a sorority. Average age of full-time undergraduates is 20. 52% of classes have fewer than 20 students, 46% have between 20 and 50 students.

STUDENT HOUSING

81% of freshmen live in college housing. Freshmen are required to live on campus. Housing is guaranteed for all undergraduates. Campus can house 1,381 undergraduates.

EXPENSES

Tuition (2005-06): $2,981 per year (in-state), $11,281 (out-of-state). Room: $3,670. Board: $2,258.

There is no additional cost for LD program/services.

LD SERVICES

LD program size is not limited.

LD services available to:

- [x] Freshmen
- [x] Sophomores
- [x] Juniors
- [x] Seniors

Academic Accommodations

Curriculum		In class	
Foreign language waiver	[x]	Early syllabus	[ ]
Lighter course load	[x]	Note takers in class	[x]
Math waiver	[x]	Priority seating	[x]
Other special classes	[ ]	Tape recorders	[x]
Priority registrations	[ ]	Videotaped classes	[ ]
Substitution of courses	[x]	Text on tape	[x]
Exams		**Services**	
Extended time	[x]	Diagnostic tests	[ ]
Oral exams	[ ]	Learning centers	[x]
Take home exams	[ ]	Proofreaders	[x]
Exams on tape or computer	[x]	Readers	[x]
Untimed exams	[ ]	Reading Machines/Kurzweil	[x]
Other accommodations	[ ]	Special bookstore section	[ ]
		Typists	[x]

Credit toward degree is not given for remedial courses taken.

Counseling Services

- [x] Academic
- [x] Psychological
- [x] Student Support groups
- [ ] Vocational

Tutoring

Individual tutoring is available daily.

	Individual	Group
Time management	[x]	[x]
Organizational skills	[x]	[ ]
Learning strategies	[x]	[ ]
Study skills	[x]	[ ]
Content area	[x]	[ ]
Writing lab	[x]	[ ]
Math lab	[x]	[ ]

LD PROGRAM STAFF

Total number of LD Program staff (including director):

Full Time: 4 Part Time: 4

There is an advisor/advocate from the LD program available to students. 25 peer tutors are available to work with LD students.

Key staff person available to work with LD students: Sarah Mead Smith, Director of Disability Services.

LD Program web site: http://www.loyno.edu/arc/disabilityservices.html

McNeese State University

Lake Charles, LA

Address: 4100 Ryan Street, Lake Charles, LA, 70609
Admissions telephone: 337 475-5356
Admissions FAX: 337 475-5151
Director of Admissions: Ms. Tammie Pettis
Admissions e-mail: info@mcneese.edu
Web site: http://www.mcneese.edu
SAT Code: 6403 ACT Code: 1594

LD program name: Services for Sudents with Disabilities
Director: Timothy Delany
LD program telephone: 337 475-5916
LD program e-mail: tdelany@mcneese.edu
Total campus enrollment: 7,726

GENERAL

McNeese State University is a public, coed, four-year institution. 171-acre campus in Lake Charles (population: 71,757), 80 miles west of New Orleans and 60 miles east of Beaumont, TX. Served by air, bus, and train; major airport serves Houston, TX (135 miles). Public transportation serves campus. Semester system.

LD ADMISSIONS

A personal interview is required. Essay is not required.

SECONDARY SCHOOL REQUIREMENTS

Graduation from secondary school required; GED accepted.

TESTING

ACT required; SAT Reasoning may be substituted.

All enrolled freshmen (fall 2004):

Average ACT Scores: Composite: 20

Child Study Team report is not required. Tests required as part of this documentation:

- [ ] WAIS-IV
- [ ] WISC-IV
- [ ] SATA
- [ ] Woodcock-Johnson
- [ ] Nelson-Denny Reading Test
- [ ] Other

UNDERGRADUATE STUDENT BODY

Total undergraduate student enrollment: 2,924 Men, 3,941 Women.

Composition of student body (fall 2004):

	Undergraduate	Freshmen
International	1.1	1.6
Black	21.5	20.1
American Indian	0.7	0.7
Asian-American	0.6	0.8
Hispanic	1.4	1.4
White	73.8	74.8
Unreported	0.9	0.5
	100.0%	100.0%

9% are from out of state.

STUDENT HOUSING

10% of freshmen live in college housing. Housing is guaranteed for all undergraduates.

EXPENSES

Tuition (2005-06): $2,226 per year (in-state), $8,292 (out-of-state).
Room & Board: $4,637.

There is no additional cost for LD program/services.

LD SERVICES

LD program size is not limited.

LD services available to:

- [ ] Freshmen
- [ ] Sophomores
- [ ] Juniors
- [ ] Seniors

Academic Accommodations

Curriculum		In class	
Foreign language waiver	[ ]	Early syllabus	[ ]
Lighter course load	[ ]	Note takers in class	[x]
Math waiver	[ ]	Priority seating	[ ]
Other special classes	[x]	Tape recorders	[ ]
Priority registrations	[ ]	Videotaped classes	[ ]
Substitution of courses	[ ]	Text on tape	[ ]
Exams		**Services**	
Extended time	[x]	Diagnostic tests	[ ]
Oral exams	[x]	Learning centers	[x]
Take home exams	[ ]	Proofreaders	[ ]
Exams on tape or computer	[ ]	Readers	[x]
Untimed exams	[ ]	Reading Machines/Kurzweil	[x]
Other accommodations	[ ]	Special bookstore section	[ ]
		Typists	[ ]

Credit toward degree is not given for remedial courses taken.

Counseling Services

- [ ] Academic
- [ ] Psychological
- [ ] Student Support groups
- [ ] Vocational

Tutoring

	Individual	Group
Time management	[ ]	[ ]
Organizational skills	[ ]	[ ]
Learning strategies	[ ]	[ ]
Study skills	[ ]	[ ]
Content area	[ ]	[ ]
Writing lab	[ ]	[ ]
Math lab	[ ]	[ ]

LD PROGRAM STAFF

Total number of LD Program staff (including director):

Full Time: 2 Part Time: 2

Key staff person available to work with LD students: Timothy Delany, Director, Services for Students with Disabilities.

University of New Orleans

New Orleans, LA

Address: 2000 Lakeshore Drive, New Orleans, LA, 70148
Admissions telephone: 504 280-6595
Admissions FAX: 504 280-5522
Director of Admissions: Roslyn Sheley
Admissions e-mail: admissions@uno.edu
Web site: http://www.uno.edu
SAT Code: 6379 ACT Code: 1591

LD program name: Disabled Student Services
Associate Dean, Director: Janice Lyn
LD program telephone: 504 280-6222
LD program e-mail: jlyn@uno.edu
Total campus enrollment: 13, 225

GENERAL

University of New Orleans is a public, coed, four-year institution. 195-acre, urban campus in New Orleans (population: 484,674); branch campuses in Metairie and the central business district. Served by air, bus, and train. School operates shuttle service. Public transportation serves campus. Semester system.

LD ADMISSIONS

A personal interview is not required. Essay is not required.

SECONDARY SCHOOL REQUIREMENTS

Graduation from secondary school required; GED accepted. The following course distribution required: 4 units of English, 3 units of math, 3 units of science, 2 units of foreign language, 3 units of history, 1 unit of academic electives.

TESTING

SAT Reasoning or ACT required. SAT Subject recommended.

All enrolled freshmen (fall 2004):

Average SAT I Scores: Verbal: 529 Math: 523
Average ACT Scores: Composite: 21

Child Study Team report is not required. Tests required as part of this documentation:

- ❑ WAIS-IV
- ❑ WISC-IV
- ❑ SATA
- ❑ Woodcock-Johnson
- ❑ Nelson-Denny Reading Test
- ❑ Other

UNDERGRADUATE STUDENT BODY

Total undergraduate student enrollment: 5,613 Men, 7,354 Women.

Composition of student body (fall 2004):

	Undergraduate	Freshmen
International	1.4	2.5
Black	30.0	24.8
American Indian	0.4	0.4
Asian-American	6.0	5.6
Hispanic	6.6	6.6
White	51.5	54.7
Unreported	4.0	5.4
	100.0%	100.0%

5% are from out of state. 2% join a fraternity and 2% join a sorority. Average age of full-time undergraduates is 22. 40% of classes have fewer than 20 students, 51% have between 20 and 50 students.

STUDENT HOUSING

9% of freshmen live in college housing. Freshmen are not required to live on campus. Housing is guaranteed for all undergraduates. Campus can house 1,426 undergraduates.

EXPENSES

Tuition (2005-06): $3,292 per year (in-state), $10,336 (out-of-state).
Room: $4,590.
There is no additional cost for LD program/services.

LD SERVICES

LD program size is not limited.

LD services available to:

❑ Freshmen ❑ Sophomores ❑ Juniors ❑ Seniors

Academic Accommodations

Curriculum		**In class**	
Foreign language waiver	❑	Early syllabus	❑
Lighter course load	❑	Note takers in class	❑
Math waiver	❑	Priority seating	❑
Other special classes	❑	Tape recorders	❑
Priority registrations	❑	Videotaped classes	❑
Substitution of courses	❑	Text on tape	❑
Exams		**Services**	
Extended time	❑	Diagnostic tests	❑
Oral exams	❑	Learning centers	❑
Take home exams	❑	Proofreaders	❑
Exams on tape or computer	❑	Readers	❑
Untimed exams	❑	Reading Machines/Kurzweil	❑
Other accommodations	❑	Special bookstore section	❑
		Typists	❑

Credit toward degree is not given for remedial courses taken.

Counseling Services

- ❑ Academic
- ❑ Psychological
- ❑ Student Support groups
- ❑ Vocational

Tutoring

	Individual	Group
Time management	❑	❑
Organizational skills	❑	❑
Learning strategies	❑	❑
Study skills	❑	❑
Content area	❑	❑
Writing lab	❑	❑
Math lab	❑	❑

LD PROGRAM STAFF

Total number of LD Program staff (including director):

Full Time: 3 Part Time: 3

Key staff person available to work with LD students: Janice Lyn, Assoc. Dean, Director of Disabled Student Services.

Nicholls State University

Thibodaux, LA

Address: P.O. Box 2004, University Station, Thibodaux, LA, 70310
Admissions telephone: 877 642-4655
Admissions FAX: 985 448-4929
Director of Admissions: Becky Leblanc-Durocher
Admissions e-mail: nicholls@nicholls.edu
Web site: http://www.nicholls.edu
SAT Code: 6221 ACT Code: 1580

LD program name: The Office of Disability Services
LD program address: P.O. Box 2186
Director: Jerry Saunders
LD program telephone: 985 448-4430
LD program e-mail: Jerry.Saunders@nicholls.edu
Total campus enrollment: 6,784

GENERAL

Nicholls State University is a public, coed, four-year institution. 210-acre campus in Thibodaux (population: 14,431), 60 miles from New Orleans; seven satellite campuses. Served by bus; major airport and train serve New Orleans; smaller airport serves Baton Rouge (75 miles). Public transportation serves campus. Semester system.

LD ADMISSIONS

Application Deadline: 09/06. Students complete a separate application and are not simultaneously accepted to the LD program. A personal interview is not required. Essay is not required.

SECONDARY SCHOOL REQUIREMENTS

Graduation from secondary school required; GED accepted.

TESTING

All enrolled freshmen (fall 2004):

Average ACT Scores: Composite: 20

Child Study Team report is not required. Tests required as part of this documentation:

- [ ] WAIS-IV
- [ ] WISC-IV
- [ ] SATA
- [ ] Woodcock-Johnson
- [ ] Nelson-Denny Reading Test
- [ ] Other

UNDERGRADUATE STUDENT BODY

Total undergraduate student enrollment: 2,461 Men, 4,095 Women.

Composition of student body (fall 2004):

	Undergraduate	Freshmen
International	0.8	0.7
Black	24.7	18.5
American Indian	1.9	2.0
Asian-American	1.4	0.9
Hispanic	1.6	1.5
White	68.8	74.4
Unreported	0.9	2.0
	100.0%	100.0%

2% are from out of state. 2% join a fraternity and 3% join a sorority. Average age of full-time undergraduates is 22. 37% of classes have fewer than 20 students, 54% have between 20 and 50 students.

STUDENT HOUSING

33% of freshmen live in college housing. Freshmen are required to live on campus. Housing is guaranteed for all undergraduates. Campus can house 1,563 undergraduates.

EXPENSES

Tuition (2005-06): $2,231 per year (in-state), $7,679 (out-of-state).
Room: $1,800. Board: $1,820.
There is no additional cost for LD program/services.

LD SERVICES

LD program size is not limited.

LD services available to:

- [x] Freshmen
- [x] Sophomores
- [x] Juniors
- [x] Seniors

Academic Accommodations

Curriculum		In class	
Foreign language waiver	[ ]	Early syllabus	[ ]
Lighter course load	[x]	Note takers in class	[x]
Math waiver	[ ]	Priority seating	[ ]
Other special classes	[ ]	Tape recorders	[x]
Priority registrations	[ ]	Videotaped classes	[ ]
Substitution of courses	[ ]	Text on tape	[ ]
Exams		**Services**	
Extended time	[x]	Diagnostic tests	[ ]
Oral exams	[x]	Learning centers	[x]
Take home exams	[ ]	Proofreaders	[ ]
Exams on tape or computer	[ ]	Readers	[ ]
Untimed exams	[x]	Reading Machines/Kurzweil	[ ]
Other accommodations	[ ]	Special bookstore section	[ ]
		Typists	[ ]

Credit toward degree is not given for remedial courses taken.

Counseling Services

- [x] Academic
- [x] Psychological
- [x] Student Support groups
- [x] Vocational

Tutoring

	Individual	Group
Time management	[ ]	[ ]
Organizational skills	[ ]	[ ]
Learning strategies	[ ]	[ ]
Study skills	[ ]	[ ]
Content area	[ ]	[ ]
Writing lab	[ ]	[ ]
Math lab	[ ]	[ ]

LD PROGRAM STAFF

Total number of LD Program staff (including director):

Full Time: 3 Part Time: 3

There is an advisor/advocate from the LD program available to students.

Key staff person available to work with LD students: Jerry Saunders, Director.

LD Program web site: http://www.nicholls.edu/disability/

Northwestern State University of Louisiana

Natchitoches, LA

Address: College Avenue, Natchitoches, LA, 71497
Admissions telephone: 800 426-3754 (in-state), 800 327-1903 (out-of-state)
Admissions FAX: 318 357-5567
Director of Enrollment Services: Jana Lucky
Admissions e-mail: admissions@nsula.edu
Web site: http://www.nsula.edu
SAT Code: 6492

LD program name: Disability Services
LD program address: Kyser Hall 237
Disabilities Service Coordinator: Steve Hicks
LD program telephone: 318 357-6950
LD program e-mail: hickss@nsula.edu
LD program enrollment: 170, Total campus enrollment: 9,414

GENERAL

Northwestern State University of Louisiana is a public, coed, four-year institution. 940-acre campus in Natchitoches (population: 17,865), 60 miles southeast of Shreveport; branch campuses in Alexandria, Leesville, and Shreveport. Served by bus; major airports serve Shreveport and Alexandria (50 miles). Public transportation serves campus. Semester system.

LD ADMISSIONS

Students do not complete a separate application and are not simultaneously accepted to the LD program. A member of the LD program does not sit on the admissions committee. A personal interview is not required. Essay is not required.

For fall 2004, 35 completed self-identified LD applications were received. 35 applications were offered admission, and 35 enrolled.

SECONDARY SCHOOL REQUIREMENTS

Graduation from secondary school required; GED accepted. The following course distribution required: 4 units of English, 3 units of math, 3 units of science, 2 units of foreign language, 1 unit of social studies, 2 units of history.

TESTING

ACT required; SAT Reasoning may be substituted. SAT Subject recommended.

All enrolled freshmen (fall 2004):

Average SAT I Scores:	Verbal: 504	Math: 504
Average ACT Scores:	Composite: 19	

Child Study Team report is not required. A neuropsychological or comprehensive psycho-education evaluation is not required for admission. Tests required as part of this documentation:

- ☐ WAIS-IV
- ☐ WISC-IV
- ☐ SATA
- ☐ Woodcock-Johnson
- ☐ Nelson-Denny Reading Test
- ☐ Other

UNDERGRADUATE STUDENT BODY

Total undergraduate student enrollment: 2,943 Men, 5,430 Women.

Composition of student body (fall 2004):

	Undergraduate	Freshmen
International	0.3	0.4
Black	37.7	31.8
American Indian	2.1	1.9
Asian-American	0.5	0.9
Hispanic	2.0	1.8
White	51.4	58.3
Unreported	6.0	4.9
	100.0%	100.0%

6% are from out of state. 5% join a fraternity and 6% join a sorority. Average age of full-time undergraduates is 22. 35% of classes have fewer than 20 students, 50% have between 20 and 50 students, 15% have more than 50 students.

STUDENT HOUSING

52% of freshmen live in college housing. Freshmen are required to live on campus. Housing is guaranteed for all undergraduates. Campus can house 2,122 undergraduates.

EXPENSES

Tuition (2005-06): $2,240 per year (in-state), $8,318 (out-of-state).
Room & Board: $3,554.
There is no additional cost for LD program/services.

LD SERVICES

LD program size is not limited.

LD services available to:

☑ Freshmen ☑ Sophomores ☑ Juniors ☑ Seniors

Academic Accommodations

Curriculum		In class	
Foreign language waiver	☐	Early syllabus	☐
Lighter course load	☐	Note takers in class	☑
Math waiver	☐	Priority seating	☐
Other special classes	☑	Tape recorders	☑
Priority registrations	☐	Videotaped classes	☐
Substitution of courses	☐	Text on tape	☐
Exams		**Services**	
Extended time	☑	Diagnostic tests	☐
Oral exams	☑	Learning centers	☑
Take home exams	☐	Proofreaders	☐
Exams on tape or computer	☐	Readers	☑
Untimed exams	☑	Reading Machines/Kurzweil	☑
Other accommodations	☐	Special bookstore section	☐
		Typists	☐

Credit toward degree is not given for remedial courses taken.

Counseling Services

- ☐ Academic
- ☐ Psychological
- ☐ Student Support groups
- ☐ Vocational

Tutoring

Individual tutoring is available weekly.

Average size of tutoring groups: 2

	Individual	Group
Time management	☐	☑
Organizational skills	☐	☑
Learning strategies	☐	☑
Study skills	☐	☑
Content area	☐	☑
Writing lab	☐	☑
Math lab	☐	☑

LD PROGRAM STAFF

Total number of LD Program staff (including director):

Full Time: 1 Part Time: 1

Key staff person available to work with LD students: Steve Hicks, Disabilities Service Coordinator.

LD Program web site:
www.nsula.edu/universitycollege/disabilityservices.asp

Our Lady of Holy Cross College

New Orleans, LA

Address: 4123 Woodland Drive, New Orleans, LA, 70131
Admissions telephone: 800 259-7744
Admissions FAX: 504 391-2421
Vice President for Student Affairs: Kristine Kopecky
Admissions e-mail: admissions@olhcc.edu
Web site: http://www.olhcc.edu
SAT Code: 6002 ACT Code: 1574

Vice President for Enrollment Services: Kristine Kopecky
LD program telephone: 504 398-2185
LD program e-mail: kkopecky@olhcc.edu
Total campus enrollment: 1,316

GENERAL

Our Lady of Holy Cross College is a private, coed, four-year institution. 40-acre, suburban campus in New Orleans (population: 484,674). Served by air and bus. Semester system.

LD ADMISSIONS

A personal interview is not required. Essay is not required.

SECONDARY SCHOOL REQUIREMENTS

Graduation from secondary school required; GED accepted.

TESTING

SAT Reasoning or ACT required. SAT Subject recommended.

All enrolled freshmen (fall 2004):

Average ACT Scores: Composite: 20

Child Study Team report is not required. Tests required as part of this documentation:

- ☐ WAIS-IV
- ☐ WISC-IV
- ☐ SATA
- ☐ Woodcock-Johnson
- ☐ Nelson-Denny Reading Test
- ☐ Other

UNDERGRADUATE STUDENT BODY

Total undergraduate student enrollment: 306 Men, 944 Women.

Composition of student body (fall 2004):

	Undergraduate	Freshmen
International	0.0	0.0
Black	15.3	17.4
American Indian	2.4	0.5
Asian-American	4.0	1.4
Hispanic	4.0	4.0
White	68.5	72.1
Unreported	5.6	4.5
	100.0%	100.0%

1% are from out of state. Average age of full-time undergraduates is 24. 56% of classes have fewer than 20 students, 44% have between 20 and 50 students.

STUDENT HOUSING

We do not offer campus housing. We are a commuter college.

EXPENSES

Tuition (2005-06): $5,928 per year (in-state), $10,848 (out-of-state). $4,920 per year, $5,280 for nursing program. Tuition is based on $205 per credit ($240 per credit for nursing program).

There is no additional cost for LD program/services.

LD SERVICES

LD program size is not limited.

LD services available to:

☐ Freshmen ☐ Sophomores ☐ Juniors ☐ Seniors

Academic Accommodations

Curriculum		**In class**	
Foreign language waiver	☐	Early syllabus	☐
Lighter course load	☐	Note takers in class	■
Math waiver	☐	Priority seating	☐
Other special classes	☐	Tape recorders	■
Priority registrations	☐	Videotaped classes	☐
Substitution of courses	☐	Text on tape	☐
Exams		**Services**	
Extended time	■	Diagnostic tests	☐
Oral exams	■	Learning centers	☐
Take home exams	☐	Proofreaders	☐
Exams on tape or computer	☐	Readers	■
Untimed exams	■	Reading Machines/Kurzweil	☐
Other accommodations	☐	Special bookstore section	☐
		Typists	☐

Credit toward degree is not given for remedial courses taken.

Counseling Services

- ☐ Academic
- ☐ Psychological
- ☐ Student Support groups
- ☐ Vocational

Tutoring

	Individual	Group
Time management	☐	☐
Organizational skills	☐	☐
Learning strategies	☐	☐
Study skills	☐	☐
Content area	☐	☐
Writing lab	☐	☐
Math lab	☐	☐

LD PROGRAM STAFF

Total number of LD Program staff (including director):

Full Time: 1 Part Time: 1

Key staff person available to work with LD students: Kristine Kopecky, Vice President for Enrollment Services.

Southeastern Louisiana University

Hammond, LA

Address: SLU 10752, Hammond, LA, 70402
Admissions telephone: 800 222-7358
Admissions FAX: 985 549-5632
Associate Director of Admissions: Richard Beaugh
Admissions e-mail: admissions@selu.edu
Web site: http://www.selu.edu
SAT Code: 6656 ACT Code: 1608

LD program name: Office of Disabilty Services
LD program address: SLU 10496, Hammond, LA, 70402
Director, Disability Services: Sharon Eaton
LD program telephone: 985 549-2247
LD program e-mail: seaton@selu.edu
LD program enrollment: 190, Total campus enrollment: 13,664

GENERAL

Southeastern Louisiana University is a public, coed, four-year institution. 375-acre campus in Hammond (population: 17,639), 55 miles from New Orleans and 40 miles from Baton Rouge; branch campuses in Baton Rouge and Mandeville. Served by bus and train; major airport serves New Orleans; smaller airport serves Baton Rouge. Semester system.

LD ADMISSIONS

Application Deadline: 07/15. Students do not complete a separate application and are not simultaneously accepted to the LD program. A member of the LD program does not sit on the admissions committee. A personal interview is not required. Essay is not required.

SECONDARY SCHOOL REQUIREMENTS

Graduation from secondary school required; GED accepted. The following course distribution required: 4 units of English, 3 units of math, 3 units of science, 2 units of foreign language, 3 units of social studies, 2 units of academic electives.

TESTING

SAT Subject recommended.

All enrolled freshmen (fall 2004):

Average ACT Scores: Composite: 21

Child Study Team report is not required. A neuropsychological or comprehensive psycho-educational evaluation is required for admission. Must be dated within 36 months of application. Tests required as part of this documentation:

- [x] WAIS-IV
- [ ] WISC-IV
- [ ] SATA
- [x] Woodcock-Johnson
- [ ] Nelson-Denny Reading Test
- [ ] Other

UNDERGRADUATE STUDENT BODY

Total undergraduate student enrollment: 4,734 Men, 8,087 Women.

Composition of student body (fall 2004):

	Undergraduate	Freshmen
International	0.9	0.7
Black	18.9	16.1
American Indian	0.5	0.4
Asian-American	0.8	0.6
Hispanic	1.3	1.4
White	75.1	78.9
Unreported	2.6	2.0
	100.0%	100.0%

1% are from out of state. 2% join a fraternity and 2% join a sorority. Average age of full-time undergraduates is 22. 30% of classes have fewer than 20 students, 61% have between 20 and 50 students.

STUDENT HOUSING

27% of freshmen live in college housing. Freshmen are required to live on campus. Housing is not guaranteed for all undergraduates. First-come, first-served basis. Campus can house 2,000 undergraduates. Single rooms are available for students with medical or special needs. A medical note is required.

EXPENSES

Tuition (2005-06): $3,191 per year (in-state), $8,519 (out-of-state).
Room: $2,300. Board: $1,990.
There is no additional cost for LD program/services.

LD SERVICES

LD program size is not limited.

LD services available to:

- [x] Freshmen
- [x] Sophomores
- [x] Juniors
- [x] Seniors

Academic Accommodations

Curriculum		In class	
Foreign language waiver	[ ]	Early syllabus	[x]
Lighter course load	[ ]	Note takers in class	[x]
Math waiver	[ ]	Priority seating	[ ]
Other special classes	[ ]	Tape recorders	[x]
Priority registrations	[x]	Videotaped classes	[ ]
Substitution of courses	[x]	Text on tape	[ ]
Exams		**Services**	
Extended time	[x]	Diagnostic tests	[ ]
Oral exams	[x]	Learning centers	[ ]
Take home exams	[ ]	Proofreaders	[x]
Exams on tape or computer	[x]	Readers	[ ]
Untimed exams	[ ]	Reading Machines/Kurzweil	[x]
Other accommodations	[x]	Special bookstore section	[ ]
		Typists	[x]

Credit toward degree is not given for remedial courses taken.

Counseling Services

- [x] Academic
- [x] Psychological
- [x] Student Support groups
- [x] Vocational

Tutoring

Individual tutoring is available weekly.

	Individual	Group
Time management	[ ]	[x]
Organizational skills	[ ]	[x]
Learning strategies	[ ]	[x]
Study skills	[ ]	[x]
Content area	[ ]	[ ]
Writing lab	[x]	[ ]
Math lab	[x]	[ ]

LD PROGRAM STAFF

Total number of LD Program staff (including director):

Full Time: 2 Part Time: 2

There is an advisor/advocate from the LD program available to students. 1 graduate student is available to work with LD students.

Key staff person available to work with LD students: Sharon Eaton, Director, Disability Services.

LD Program web site: http://www.selu.edu/StudentAffairs/DisabilityServices

Southern University and Agricultural and Mechanical College

Baton Rouge, LA

Address: P.O. Box 9374, Baton Rouge, LA, 70813
Admissions telephone: 800 256-1531
Admissions FAX: 225 771-2500
Director of Admissions: Nathaniel Harrison
Admissions e-mail: admit@subr.edu
Web site: http://www.subr.edu/
SAT Code: 6663 ACT Code: 1610

LD program name: Office of Disability Services
LD program address: P.O. Box 11275
Assistant Professor/Special Education Coordinator: Patricia R. Hebert
LD program telephone: 225 771-3950
LD program e-mail: patricia_hebert@cxs.subr.edu
LD program enrollment: 224, Total campus enrollment: 8,053

GENERAL

Southern University and Agricultural and Mechanical College is a public, coed, four-year institution. 884-acre campus in Baton Rouge (population: 227,818). Served by air and bus; train serves Hammond (40 miles). Public transportation serves campus. Semester system.

LD ADMISSIONS

Students do not complete a separate application and are not simultaneously accepted to the LD program. A member of the LD program does not sit on the admissions committee. A personal interview is required. Essay is not required.

SECONDARY SCHOOL REQUIREMENTS

Graduation from secondary school not required. The following course distribution required: 4 units of English, 3 units of math, 3 units of science, 2 units of foreign language, 2 units of social studies, 1 unit of history.

TESTING

SAT Reasoning or ACT required. SAT Subject recommended.

All enrolled freshmen (fall 2004):

Average SAT I Scores:	Verbal: 425	Math: 428
Average ACT Scores:	Composite: 17	

Child Study Team report is not required. A neuropsychological or comprehensive psycho-educational evaluation is required for admission. Must be dated within 36 months of application. Tests required as part of this documentation:

- ■ WAIS-IV
- ■ WISC-IV
- ■ SATA
- ■ Woodcock-Johnson
- ☐ Nelson-Denny Reading Test
- ☐ Other

UNDERGRADUATE STUDENT BODY

Total undergraduate student enrollment: 3,091 Men, 4,381 Women.

Composition of student body (fall 2004):

	Undergraduate	Freshmen
International	2.7	1.2
Black	96.5	96.7
American Indian	0.0	0.1
Asian-American	0.3	0.4
Hispanic	0.2	0.1
White	0.3	1.6
Unreported	0.0	0.0
	100.0%	100.0%

14% are from out of state. 1% join a fraternity and 2% join a sorority. Average age of full-time undergraduates is 22. 30% of classes have fewer than 20 students, 62% have between 20 and 50 students.

STUDENT HOUSING

74% of freshmen live in college housing. Freshmen are required to live on campus. Housing is guaranteed for all undergraduates. Campus can house 3,015 undergraduates. Single rooms are available for students with medical or special needs. A medical note is required.

EXPENSES

Tuition (2005-06): $3,488 per year (in-state), $9,280 (out-of-state). Room: $2,756. Board: $1,780.

There is no additional cost for LD program/services.

LD SERVICES

LD program size is not limited.

LD services available to:

■ Freshmen ■ Sophomores ■ Juniors ■ Seniors

Academic Accommodations

Curriculum		In class	
Foreign language waiver	☐	Early syllabus	☐
Lighter course load	☐	Note takers in class	■
Math waiver	☐	Priority seating	■
Other special classes	☐	Tape recorders	■
Priority registrations	■	Videotaped classes	☐
Substitution of courses	☐	Text on tape	■
Exams		**Services**	
Extended time	■	Diagnostic tests	☐
Oral exams	■	Learning centers	■
Take home exams	☐	Proofreaders	☐
Exams on tape or computer	■	Readers	■
Untimed exams	☐	Reading Machines/Kurzweil	☐
Other accommodations	■	Special bookstore section	☐
		Typists	☐

Credit toward degree is not given for remedial courses taken.

Counseling Services

■	Academic	Meets 4 times per academic year
☐	Psychological	
☐	Student Support groups	
■	Vocational	Meets 1 times per academic year

Tutoring

Individual tutoring is available weekly.

Average size of tutoring groups: 3

	Individual	Group
Time management	■	■
Organizational skills	☐	☐
Learning strategies	☐	☐
Study skills	☐	☐
Content area	☐	☐
Writing lab	■	■
Math lab	■	■

LD PROGRAM STAFF

Total number of LD Program staff (including director):

Full Time: 1 Part Time: 1

There is an advisor/advocate from the LD program available to students.

Key staff person available to work with LD students: Patricia R. Hebert, Assist. Prof. Spec. Educ., Coord Disability Services.

Tulane University

New Orleans, LA

Address: 6823 St. Charles Avenue, 218 Gibson Hall, New Orleans, LA, 70118
Admissions telephone: 800 873-9283
Admissions FAX: 504 862-8715
Vice President of Enrollment Management and Institutional Research: Richard Whiteside
Admissions e-mail: undergrad.admission@tulane.edu
Web site: http://www.tulane.edu
SAT Code: 6832 ACT Code: 1616

LD program name: Office of Disability Services
Manager of Disability Services: David Tylicki
LD program telephone: 504 862-8433
LD program e-mail: dtylicki@tulane.edu
LD program enrollment: 208, Total campus enrollment: 7,978

GENERAL

Tulane University is a private, coed, four-year institution. 110-acre, urban campus four miles from downtown New Orleans (population: 484,674). Served by air, bus, and train. School operates transportation to Tulane Medical Ctr and within a one-mile radius of campus. Public transportation serves campus. Semester system.

LD ADMISSIONS

Students do not complete a separate application and are not simultaneously accepted to the LD program. A member of the LD program does sit on the admissions committee. High school waivers are accepted for math and foreign language. A personal interview is not required. Essay is required and may be typed. Admissions requirements that may be waived for LD students are determined on a case by case basis.

SECONDARY SCHOOL REQUIREMENTS

Graduation from secondary school required; GED accepted. The following course distribution required: 4 units of English, 3 units of math, 3 units of science, 2 units of foreign language, 3 units of social studies, 3 units of history, 2 units of academic electives.

TESTING

SAT Reasoning or ACT required. SAT Subject recommended.

All enrolled freshmen (fall 2004):

Average SAT I Scores:	Verbal: 667	Math: 653
Average ACT Scores:	Composite: 30	

Child Study Team report is not required. A neuropsychological or comprehensive psycho-educational evaluation is required for admission. Must be dated within 36 months of application. Tests required as part of this documentation:

- [x] WAIS-IV
- [x] WISC-IV
- [ ] SATA
- [x] Woodcock-Johnson
- [x] Nelson-Denny Reading Test
- [x] Other

UNDERGRADUATE STUDENT BODY

Total undergraduate student enrollment: 3,522 Men, 4,000 Women.

Composition of student body (fall 2004):

	Undergraduate	Freshmen
International	1.8	2.5
Black	4.4	10.5
American Indian	0.4	0.5
Asian-American	5.7	3.9
Hispanic	2.1	3.8
White	81.1	70.0
Unreported	4.6	8.8
	100.0%	100.0%

64% are from out of state. 33% join a fraternity and 35% join a sorority. Average age of full-time undergraduates is 20. 57% of classes have fewer than 20 students, 35% have between 20 and 50 students.

STUDENT HOUSING

99% of freshmen live in college housing. Freshmen are required to live on campus. Housing is guaranteed for all undergraduates. Campus can house 3,346 undergraduates. Single rooms are available for students with medical or special needs. A medical note is required.

EXPENSES

Tuition (2005-06): $30,350 per year.

Room: $4,841-$5,104. Board: $3,311.
There is no additional cost for LD program/services.

LD SERVICES

LD program size is not limited.

LD services available to:

- [x] Freshmen
- [x] Sophomores
- [x] Juniors
- [x] Seniors

Academic Accommodations

Curriculum		In class	
Foreign language waiver	[ ]	Early syllabus	[ ]
Lighter course load	[ ]	Note takers in class	[x]
Math waiver	[ ]	Priority seating	[x]
Other special classes	[ ]	Tape recorders	[x]
Priority registrations	[ ]	Videotaped classes	[ ]
Substitution of courses	[x]	Text on tape	[x]
Exams		**Services**	
Extended time	[x]	Diagnostic tests	[x]
Oral exams	[x]	Learning centers	[x]
Take home exams	[ ]	Proofreaders	[x]
Exams on tape or computer	[x]	Readers	[x]
Untimed exams	[x]	Reading Machines/Kurzweil	[x]
Other accommodations	[x]	Special bookstore section	[ ]
		Typists	[x]

Credit toward degree is not given for remedial courses taken.

Counseling Services

- [x] Academic
- [x] Psychological
- [x] Student Support groups — Meets 12 times per academic year
- [x] Vocational

Tutoring

Individual tutoring is available daily.

Average size of tutoring groups: 2

	Individual	Group
Time management	[x]	[x]
Organizational skills	[x]	[x]
Learning strategies	[x]	[x]
Study skills	[x]	[x]
Content area	[x]	[x]
Writing lab	[x]	[x]
Math lab	[x]	[x]

LD PROGRAM STAFF

Total number of LD Program staff (including director):

Full Time: 3 Part Time: 3

There is an advisor/advocate from the LD program available to students. 40 peer tutors are available to work with LD students.

Key staff person available to work with LD students: David Tylicki, Manager of Disability Services.

Bates College

Lewiston, ME

Address: Two Andrews Road, Lewiston, ME, 04240
Admissions telephone: 207 786-6000
Admissions FAX: 207 786-6025
Dean of Admissions: Wylie L. Mitchell
Admissions e-mail: admissions@bates.edu
Web site: http://www.bates.edu
SAT Code: 3076   ACT Code: 1634

Total campus enrollment: 1,743

GENERAL

Bates College is a private, coed, four-year institution. 109-acre campus in Lewiston (Lewiston population: 35,690), 35 miles from Portland and 145 miles from Boston. Served by air and bus; major airport serves Portland. School operates transportation in the local area. Public transportation serves campus.

LD ADMISSIONS

Application Deadline: 01/01. A personal interview is recommended. Essay is required and may be typed.

SECONDARY SCHOOL REQUIREMENTS

Graduation from secondary school not required. The following course distribution required: 4 units of English, 3 units of math, 2 units of science, 2 units of foreign language.

TESTING

SAT Reasoning or ACT considered if submitted. SAT Subject recommended.

All enrolled freshmen (fall 2004):

Average SAT I Scores: Verbal: 668 Math: 667

Child Study Team report is not required. Tests required as part of this documentation:

- [ ] WAIS-IV
- [ ] WISC-IV
- [ ] SATA
- [ ] Woodcock-Johnson
- [ ] Nelson-Denny Reading Test
- [ ] Other

UNDERGRADUATE STUDENT BODY

Total undergraduate student enrollment: 871 Men, 896 Women.

Composition of student body (fall 2004):

	Undergraduate	Freshmen
International	3.4	5.6
Black	2.4	2.2
American Indian	0.4	0.2
Asian-American	2.8	3.6
Hispanic	3.2	2.8
White	85.9	82.6
Unreported	1.9	2.9
	100.0%	100.0%

89% are from out of state. Average age of full-time undergraduates is 20. 64% of classes have fewer than 20 students, 31% have between 20 and 50 students, 4% have more than 50 students.

STUDENT HOUSING

100% of freshmen live in college housing. Housing is guaranteed for all undergraduates. Campus can house 1,592 undergraduates.

EXPENSES

Tuition (2005-06): $42,100 per year (comprehensive).
There is no additional cost for LD program/services.

LD SERVICES

LD program size is not limited.

LD services available to:

- [x] Freshmen
- [x] Sophomores
- [x] Juniors
- [x] Seniors

Academic Accommodations

Curriculum

- [ ] Foreign language waiver
- [ ] Lighter course load
- [ ] Math waiver
- [ ] Other special classes
- [ ] Priority registrations
- [ ] Substitution of courses

Exams

- [x] Extended time
- [x] Oral exams
- [ ] Take home exams
- [ ] Exams on tape or computer
- [x] Untimed exams
- [ ] Other accommodations

In class

- [ ] Early syllabus
- [x] Note takers in class
- [ ] Priority seating
- [x] Tape recorders
- [ ] Videotaped classes
- [ ] Text on tape

Services

- [ ] Diagnostic tests
- [ ] Learning centers
- [ ] Proofreaders
- [x] Readers
- [ ] Reading Machines/Kurzweil
- [ ] Special bookstore section
- [ ] Typists

Counseling Services

- [ ] Academic
- [ ] Psychological
- [ ] Student Support groups
- [ ] Vocational

Tutoring

	Individual	Group
Time management	[ ]	[ ]
Organizational skills	[ ]	[ ]
Learning strategies	[ ]	[ ]
Study skills	[ ]	[ ]
Content area	[ ]	[ ]
Writing lab	[ ]	[ ]
Math lab	[ ]	[ ]

LD PROGRAM STAFF

Key staff person available to work with LD students: Holly Gurney, Associate Dean of Students.

Bowdoin College

Brunswick, ME

Address: 5700 College Station, Brunswick, ME, 04011-8448
Admissions telephone: 207 725-3100
Admissions FAX: 207 725-3101
Dean of Admissions and Student Aid: James S. Miller
Admissions e-mail: admissions@bowdoin.edu
Web site: http://www.bowdoin.edu
SAT Code: 3089 ACT Code: 1636

Director: Joann E. Canning
LD program telephone: 207 725-3866
LD program e-mail: jcanning@bowdoin.edu
LD program enrollment: 76, Total campus enrollment: 1,677

GENERAL

Bowdoin College is a private, coed, four-year institution. 200-acre campus in Brunswick (population: 21,172), 26 miles from Portland; 118-acre coastal studies center on Orr's Island, 13 miles from campus; scientific station on Kent Island (New Brunswick, Canada). Airport and train serve Portland; larger airport serves Boston (120 miles). School operates transportation around Brunswick and to Portland and Boston. Semester system.

LD ADMISSIONS

A personal interview is recommended. Essay is required and may be typed.

SECONDARY SCHOOL REQUIREMENTS

Graduation from secondary school not required.

TESTING

SAT Reasoning or ACT considered if submitted. SAT Subject recommended.

All enrolled freshmen (fall 2004):

Average SAT I Scores: Verbal: 690 Math: 690

Child Study Team report is not required. Tests required as part of this documentation:

☐ WAIS-IV	☐ Woodcock-Johnson
☐ WISC-IV	☐ Nelson-Denny Reading Test
☐ SATA	☐ Other

UNDERGRADUATE STUDENT BODY

Total undergraduate student enrollment: 827 Men, 808 Women.

Composition of student body (fall 2004):

	Undergraduate	Freshmen
International	3.2	3.1
Black	5.5	5.4
American Indian	1.7	0.8
Asian-American	13.4	11.1
Hispanic	6.6	5.7
White	66.4	71.8
Unreported	3.2	2.2
	100.0%	100.0%

85% are from out of state. Average age of full-time undergraduates is 20. 63% of classes have fewer than 20 students, 33% have between 20 and 50 students, 4% have more than 50 students.

STUDENT HOUSING

100% of freshmen live in college housing. Freshmen are required to live on campus. Housing is guaranteed for all undergraduates. Campus can house 1,611 undergraduates.

EXPENSES

Tuition (2005-06): $32,650 per year.
Room: $3,900. Board: $4,770.
There is no additional cost for LD program/services.

LD SERVICES

LD program size is not limited.

LD services available to:

☑ Freshmen ☑ Sophomores ☑ Juniors ☑ Seniors

Academic Accommodations

Curriculum		**In class**	
Foreign language waiver	☐	Early syllabus	☐
Lighter course load	☐	Note takers in class	☑
Math waiver	☐	Priority seating	☐
Other special classes	☐	Tape recorders	☑
Priority registrations	☐	Videotaped classes	☐
Substitution of courses	☐	Text on tape	☐
Exams		**Services**	
Extended time	☑	Diagnostic tests	☐
Oral exams	☑	Learning centers	☑
Take home exams	☐	Proofreaders	☐
Exams on tape or computer	☐	Readers	☑
Untimed exams	☐	Reading Machines/Kurzweil	☑
Other accommodations	☐	Special bookstore section	☐
		Typists	☐

Credit toward degree is not given for remedial courses taken.

Counseling Services

☐ Academic
☐ Psychological
☐ Student Support groups
☐ Vocational

Tutoring

	Individual	Group
Time management	☐	☐
Organizational skills	☐	☐
Learning strategies	☐	☐
Study skills	☐	☐
Content area	☐	☐
Writing lab	☐	☐
Math lab	☐	☐

UNIQUE LD PROGRAM FEATURES

Students with disabilities are not asked to self-identify on their Bowdoin admissions application. Bowdoin does not offer a formal LD Program; services are provided on a case-by-case basis.

LD PROGRAM STAFF

Total number of LD Program staff (including director):

Full Time: 2 Part Time: 2

Key staff person available to work with LD students: Joann E. Canning, Dir, Accommodations for Students with Disabilities.

Colby College

Waterville, ME

Address: 4000 Mayflower Hill, Waterville, ME, 04901-8840
Admissions telephone: 800 723-3032
Admissions FAX: 207 859-4828
Dean of Admissions and Financial Aid: Parker J. Beverage
Admissions e-mail: admissions@colby.edu
Web site: http://www.colby.edu
SAT Code: 3280 ACT Code: 1638

Total campus enrollment: 1,821

GENERAL

Colby College is a private, coed, four-year institution. 714-acre campus in Waterville (population: 15,605), 75 miles from Portland. Served by bus; major airport serves Portland; smaller airport serves Augusta (15 miles). School operates transportation into Waterville. Public transportation serves campus. 4-1-4 system.

LD ADMISSIONS

A personal interview is recommended. Essay is required and may be typed.

SECONDARY SCHOOL REQUIREMENTS

Graduation from secondary school not required. The following course distribution required: 4 units of English, 3 units of math, 2 units of science, 3 units of foreign language, 2 units of social studies, 2 units of academic electives.

TESTING

SAT Reasoning or ACT required. SAT Subject recommended.

All enrolled freshmen (fall 2004):

Average SAT I Scores: Verbal: 680 Math: 680
Average ACT Scores: Composite: 29

Child Study Team report is not required. Tests required as part of this documentation:

- ☐ WAIS-IV
- ☐ WISC-IV
- ☐ SATA
- ☐ Woodcock-Johnson
- ☐ Nelson-Denny Reading Test
- ☐ Other

UNDERGRADUATE STUDENT BODY

Total undergraduate student enrollment: 867 Men, 942 Women.

Composition of student body (fall 2004):

	Undergraduate	Freshmen
International	6.1	7.5
Black	1.8	1.4
American Indian	0.8	0.6
Asian-American	5.3	5.3
Hispanic	2.6	2.6
White	83.4	82.5
Unreported	0.0	0.0
	100.0%	100.0%

89% are from out of state. Average age of full-time undergraduates is 20. 62% of classes have fewer than 20 students, 34% have between 20 and 50 students, 4% have more than 50 students.

STUDENT HOUSING

100% of freshmen live in college housing. Freshmen are required to live on campus. Housing is guaranteed for all undergraduates. Campus can house 1,722 undergraduates.

EXPENSES

Tuition (2005-06): $41,770 per year (comprehensive).
There is no additional cost for LD program/services.

LD SERVICES

LD program size is not limited.

LD services available to:

☑ Freshmen ☑ Sophomores ☑ Juniors ☑ Seniors

Academic Accommodations

Curriculum		In class	
Foreign language waiver	☐	Early syllabus	☐
Lighter course load	☑	Note takers in class	☑
Math waiver	☐	Priority seating	☐
Other special classes	☐	Tape recorders	☑
Priority registrations	☐	Videotaped classes	☐
Substitution of courses	☐	Text on tape	☐
Exams		**Services**	
Extended time	☑	Diagnostic tests	☐
Oral exams	☐	Learning centers	☐
Take home exams	☐	Proofreaders	☐
Exams on tape or computer	☐	Readers	☑
Untimed exams	☐	Reading Machines/Kurzweil	☑
Other accommodations	☐	Special bookstore section	☐
		Typists	☐

Credit toward degree is not given for remedial courses taken.

Counseling Services

- ☐ Academic
- ☐ Psychological
- ☐ Student Support groups
- ☐ Vocational

Tutoring

	Individual	Group
Time management	☐	☐
Organizational skills	☐	☐
Learning strategies	☐	☐
Study skills	☐	☐
Content area	☐	☐
Writing lab	☐	☐
Math lab	☐	☐

LD PROGRAM STAFF

Total number of LD Program staff (including director):

Full Time: 1 Part Time: 1

Key staff person available to work with LD students: Mark R. Serdjenian, Associate Dean of Students.

College of the Atlantic

Bar Harbor, ME

Address: 105 Eden Street, Bar Harbor, ME, 04609
Admissions telephone: 800 528-0025
Admissions FAX: 207 288-4126
Director of Admissions: Sarah Baker
Admissions e-mail: inquiry@ecology.coa.edu
Web site: http://www.coa.edu/
SAT Code: 3305 ACT Code: 1637

Associate Dean of Academic Services: Ken Hill
LD program e-mail: khill@coa.edu
Total campus enrollment: 272

GENERAL

College of the Atlantic is a private, coed, four-year institution. 25-acre campus in Bar Harbor (population: 4,820), 20 miles from Ellsworth and 45 miles from Bangor. Airport serves Bangor; smaller airport serves Trenton (15 miles); bus serves Ellsworth. Trimester system.

LD ADMISSIONS

Students do not complete a separate application and are not simultaneously accepted to the LD program. A member of the LD program does not sit on the admissions committee. High school waivers are accepted for foreign language. A personal interview is recommended. Essay is required and may be typed.

SECONDARY SCHOOL REQUIREMENTS

Graduation from secondary school required; GED accepted. The following course distribution required: 4 units of English, 3 units of math, 2 units of science, 2 units of social studies.

TESTING

SAT Reasoning or ACT considered if submitted. SAT Subject required.

All enrolled freshmen (fall 2004):

Average SAT I Scores:	Verbal: 624	Math: 586
Average ACT Scores:	Composite: 28	

Child Study Team report is not required. Tests required as part of this documentation:

- [ ] WAIS-IV
- [ ] WISC-IV
- [ ] SATA
- [ ] Woodcock-Johnson
- [ ] Nelson-Denny Reading Test
- [ ] Other

UNDERGRADUATE STUDENT BODY

Total undergraduate student enrollment: 111 Men, 158 Women.

Composition of student body (fall 2004):

	Undergraduate	Freshmen
International	22.1	18.7
Black	0.0	0.0
American Indian	0.0	0.0
Asian-American	0.0	0.0
Hispanic	0.0	0.0
White	0.0	0.0
Unreported	77.9	81.3
	100.0%	100.0%

63% are from out of state. Average age of full-time undergraduates is 21. 88% of classes have fewer than 20 students, 12% have between 20 and 50 students.

STUDENT HOUSING

99% of freshmen live in college housing. Housing is not guaranteed for all undergraduates. Campus can house 104 undergraduates. Single rooms are available for students with medical or special needs. A medical note is required.

EXPENSES

Tuition (2005-06): $26,238 per year.
Room: $4,368. Board: $2,721.

There is no additional cost for LD program/services.

LD SERVICES

LD program size is not limited.

LD services available to:

- [x] Freshmen
- [x] Sophomores
- [x] Juniors
- [x] Seniors

Academic Accommodations

Curriculum

- [ ] Foreign language waiver
- [x] Lighter course load
- [ ] Math waiver
- [x] Other special classes
- [ ] Priority registrations
- [ ] Substitution of courses

Exams

- [x] Extended time
- [ ] Oral exams
- [x] Take home exams
- [ ] Exams on tape or computer
- [x] Untimed exams
- [x] Other accommodations

In class

- [ ] Early syllabus
- [x] Note takers in class
- [ ] Priority seating
- [x] Tape recorders
- [ ] Videotaped classes
- [ ] Text on tape

Services

- [ ] Diagnostic tests
- [ ] Learning centers
- [x] Proofreaders
- [ ] Readers
- [ ] Reading Machines/Kurzweil
- [ ] Special bookstore section
- [ ] Typists

Credit toward degree is given for remedial courses taken.

Counseling Services

- [x] Academic — Meets 27 times per academic year
- [x] Psychological
- [x] Student Support groups — Meets 25 times per academic year
- [ ] Vocational

Tutoring

Individual tutoring is available daily.

Average size of tutoring groups: 1

	Individual	Group
Time management	[x]	[x]
Organizational skills	[x]	[x]
Learning strategies	[x]	[x]
Study skills	[x]	[x]
Content area	[x]	[ ]
Writing lab	[x]	[ ]
Math lab	[x]	[ ]

UNIQUE LD PROGRAM FEATURES

Rooms for disabled students located within campus dorms.

LD PROGRAM STAFF

Total number of LD Program staff (including director):

Full Time: 2 Part Time: 2

There is an advisor/advocate from the LD program available to students. The advisor/advocate meets with faculty 2 times per month and students 4 times per month. 8 peer tutors are available to work with LD students.

Key staff person available to work with LD students: Ken Hill, Associate Dean of Academic Services.

Husson College

Bangor, ME

Address: 1 College Circle, Bangor, ME, 04401
Admissions telephone: 800 448-7766
Admissions FAX: 207 941-7935
Director of Admissions: Jane Goodwin
Admissions e-mail: admit@husson.edu
Web site: http://www.husson.edu
SAT Code: 3440 ACT Code: 1646

Dean of the College: John Rubino
LD program telephone: 207 941-7109
LD program e-mail: rubinoj@husson.edu
Total campus enrollment: 1,778

GENERAL

Husson College is a private, coed, four-year institution. 170-acre campus in Bangor (population: 31,473), 125 miles from Portland. Served by air and bus; other airport and train serve Portland. Semester system.

LD ADMISSIONS

A personal interview is recommended. Essay is required and may be typed.

SECONDARY SCHOOL REQUIREMENTS

Graduation from secondary school required; GED accepted.

TESTING

SAT Reasoning required; ACT may be substituted. SAT Subject required.

All enrolled freshmen (fall 2004):

Average SAT I Scores:	Verbal: 459	Math: 469
Average ACT Scores:	Composite: 21	

Child Study Team report is not required. Tests required as part of this documentation:

- ☐ WAIS-IV
- ☐ WISC-IV
- ☐ SATA
- ☐ Woodcock-Johnson
- ☐ Nelson-Denny Reading Test
- ☐ Other

UNDERGRADUATE STUDENT BODY

Total undergraduate student enrollment: 521 Men, 1,015 Women.

Composition of student body (fall 2004):

	Undergraduate	Freshmen
International	0.4	1.9
Black	0.4	1.7
American Indian	0.0	0.2
Asian-American	0.8	1.3
Hispanic	0.4	0.3
White	98.1	94.5
Unreported	0.0	0.0
	100.0%	100.0%

15% are from out of state. 3% join a fraternity and 3% join a sorority. Average age of full-time undergraduates is 21. 53% of classes have fewer than 20 students, 45% have between 20 and 50 students, 2% have more than 50 students.

STUDENT HOUSING

60% of freshmen live in college housing. Freshmen are required to live on campus. Housing is guaranteed for all undergraduates. Campus can house 800 undergraduates.

EXPENSES

Tuition (2005-06): $11,130 per year.
Room: $3,015. Board: $3,015.
There is no additional cost for LD program/services.

LD SERVICES

LD program size is not limited.

LD services available to:

☐ Freshmen ☐ Sophomores ☐ Juniors ☐ Seniors

Academic Accommodations

Curriculum		In class	
Foreign language waiver	☐	Early syllabus	☐
Lighter course load	■	Note takers in class	■
Math waiver	☐	Priority seating	☐
Other special classes	☐	Tape recorders	■
Priority registrations	☐	Videotaped classes	☐
Substitution of courses	☐	Text on tape	☐
Exams		**Services**	
Extended time	■	Diagnostic tests	☐
Oral exams	☐	Learning centers	☐
Take home exams	☐	Proofreaders	☐
Exams on tape or computer	☐	Readers	☐
Untimed exams	■	Reading Machines/Kurzweil	■
Other accommodations	☐	Special bookstore section	☐
		Typists	☐

Credit toward degree is not given for remedial courses taken.

Counseling Services

- ☐ Academic
- ☐ Psychological
- ☐ Student Support groups
- ☐ Vocational

Tutoring

	Individual	Group
Time management	☐	☐
Organizational skills	☐	☐
Learning strategies	☐	☐
Study skills	☐	☐
Content area	☐	☐
Writing lab	☐	☐
Math lab	☐	☐

Maine College of Art

Portland, ME

Address: 97 Spring Street, Portland, ME, 04101
Admissions telephone: 800 639-4808
Admissions FAX: 207 772-5069
Director of Admissions: Joshua D. Bergey
Admissions e-mail: admissions@meca.edu
Web site: http://www.meca.edu
SAT Code: 3701 ACT Code: 6908

Dean of Students/Director, Student Affairs: Carmita McCoy
LD program telephone: 207 879-5742, extension 224
LD program e-mail: cmccoy@meca.edu
Total campus enrollment: 410

GENERAL

Maine College of Art is a private, coed, four-year institution. Urban campus in Portland (population: 64,249), 100 miles from Boston. Served by air, bus, and train; major airport serves Boston. Public transportation serves campus. Semester system.

LD ADMISSIONS

A personal interview is recommended. Essay is required and may be typed.

SECONDARY SCHOOL REQUIREMENTS

Graduation from secondary school required; GED accepted.

TESTING

SAT Reasoning or ACT required.

Child Study Team report is not required. Tests required as part of this documentation:

- [ ] WAIS-IV
- [ ] WISC-IV
- [ ] SATA
- [ ] Woodcock-Johnson
- [ ] Nelson-Denny Reading Test
- [ ] Other

UNDERGRADUATE STUDENT BODY

Total undergraduate student enrollment: 175 Men, 235 Women.

52% are from out of state.

STUDENT HOUSING

Housing is guaranteed for all undergraduates. Campus can house 110 undergraduates.

EXPENSES

Tuition (2005-06): $23,380 per year.

Room & Board: $8,826.

There is no additional cost for LD program/services.

LD SERVICES

LD program size is not limited.

LD services available to:

- [ ] Freshmen
- [ ] Sophomores
- [ ] Juniors
- [ ] Seniors

Academic Accommodations

Curriculum

- [ ] Foreign language waiver
- [ ] Lighter course load
- [ ] Math waiver
- [ ] Other special classes
- [ ] Priority registrations
- [ ] Substitution of courses

Exams

- [x] Extended time
- [x] Oral exams
- [ ] Take home exams
- [ ] Exams on tape or computer
- [x] Untimed exams
- [ ] Other accommodations

In class

- [ ] Early syllabus
- [x] Note takers in class
- [ ] Priority seating
- [x] Tape recorders
- [ ] Videotaped classes
- [ ] Text on tape

Services

- [ ] Diagnostic tests
- [x] Learning centers
- [ ] Proofreaders
- [x] Readers
- [ ] Reading Machines/Kurzweil
- [ ] Special bookstore section
- [ ] Typists

Counseling Services

- [ ] Academic
- [ ] Psychological
- [ ] Student Support groups
- [ ] Vocational

Tutoring

	Individual	Group
Time management	[ ]	[ ]
Organizational skills	[ ]	[ ]
Learning strategies	[ ]	[ ]
Study skills	[ ]	[ ]
Content area	[ ]	[ ]
Writing lab	[ ]	[ ]
Math lab	[ ]	[ ]

UNIQUE LD PROGRAM FEATURES

In addition to staff persons who work with LD students, Maine College of Art offers peer tutoring by a student who is specially trained to work with LD students.

LD PROGRAM STAFF

Total number of LD Program staff (including director):

Full Time: 1 Part Time: 1

Key staff person available to work with LD students: Carmita McCoy, Director of Student Affairs.

Maine Maritime Academy

Castine, ME

Address: Pleasant Street, Castine, ME, 04420-001
Admissions telephone: 207 326-2206
Admissions FAX: 207 326-2515
Director of Admissions: Jeff Wright
Admissions e-mail: admissions@mma.edu
Web site: http://www.mainemaritime.edu/index.php
SAT Code: 3505   ACT Code: 1648

Associate Dean: Donald Dobbin
LD program telephone: 207 326-2370
LD program e-mail: ddobb@mma.edu
LD program enrollment: 31, Total campus enrollment: 828

GENERAL

Maine Maritime Academy is a public, coed, four-year institution. 35-acre campus in Castine (population: 1,343), 40 miles from Bangor and 130 miles from Portland. Airport and bus serve Bangor; larger airport and train serve Portland. School operates transportation to Bangor. Semester system.

LD ADMISSIONS

Students do not complete a separate application and are simultaneously accepted to the LD program. A member of the LD program does not sit on the admissions committee. A personal interview is recommended. Essay is not required.

SECONDARY SCHOOL REQUIREMENTS

Graduation from secondary school required; GED accepted. The following course distribution required: 4 units of English, 4 units of math, 3 units of science, 2 units of social studies, 2 units of history.

TESTING

All enrolled freshmen (fall 2004):

Average SAT I Scores:	Verbal: 510	Math: 526
Average ACT Scores:	Composite: 22	

Child Study Team report is not required. A neuropsychological or comprehensive psycho-educational evaluation is required for admission. Must be dated within 36 months of application. Tests required as part of this documentation:

- [x] WAIS-IV
- [x] WISC-IV
- [x] SATA
- [x] Woodcock-Johnson
- [x] Nelson-Denny Reading Test
- [x] Other

UNDERGRADUATE STUDENT BODY

Total undergraduate student enrollment: 607 Men, 106 Women.

Composition of student body (fall 2004):

	Undergraduate	Freshmen
International	0.9	0.7
Black	0.0	0.5
American Indian	0.5	0.2
Asian-American	0.5	0.7
Hispanic	0.5	1.2
White	97.3	95.5
Unreported	0.5	1.2
	100.0%	100.0%

40% are from out of state. 41% of classes have fewer than 20 students, 57% have between 20 and 50 students, 2% have more than 50 students.

STUDENT HOUSING

98% of freshmen live in college housing. Freshmen are required to live on campus. Housing is guaranteed for all undergraduates. We have the space for those who are required to live on campus. Campus can house 640 undergraduates. Single rooms are available for students with medical or special needs. A medical note is required.

EXPENSES

Tuition (2005-06): $6,380 per year (in-state), $12,310 (out-of-state). Room: $2,420. Board: $4,300.

There is no additional cost for LD program/services.

LD SERVICES

LD program size is not limited.

LD services available to:

- [x] Freshmen
- [x] Sophomores
- [x] Juniors
- [x] Seniors

Academic Accommodations

Curriculum		In class	
Foreign language waiver	[ ]	Early syllabus	[ ]
Lighter course load	[ ]	Note takers in class	[x]
Math waiver	[ ]	Priority seating	[x]
Other special classes	[ ]	Tape recorders	[x]
Priority registrations	[ ]	Videotaped classes	[x]
Substitution of courses	[ ]	Text on tape	[x]
Exams		**Services**	
Extended time	[x]	Diagnostic tests	[ ]
Oral exams	[x]	Learning centers	[ ]
Take home exams	[ ]	Proofreaders	[ ]
Exams on tape or computer	[x]	Readers	[x]
Untimed exams	[x]	Reading Machines/Kurzweil	[ ]
Other accommodations	[x]	Special bookstore section	[ ]
		Typists	[ ]

Credit toward degree is not given for remedial courses taken.

Counseling Services

- [x] Academic
- [x] Psychological
- [x] Student Support groups
- [ ] Vocational

Tutoring

Individual tutoring is available daily.

Average size of tutoring groups: 1

	Individual	Group
Time management	[ ]	[x]
Organizational skills	[ ]	[x]
Learning strategies	[ ]	[x]
Study skills	[ ]	[x]
Content area	[x]	[ ]
Writing lab	[x]	[x]
Math lab	[x]	[x]

UNIQUE LD PROGRAM FEATURES

Our program is very flexible and informal. LD students are given a letter of accommodations that they may or may not show to their professors, using their own judgement.

LD PROGRAM STAFF

There is an advisor/advocate from the LD program available to students. 10 peer tutors are available to work with LD students.

Key staff person available to work with LD students: Donald Dobbin, Associate Dean.

University of Maine at Augusta

Augusta, ME

Address: 46 University Drive, Augusta, ME, 04330
Admissions telephone: 207 621-3185
Admissions FAX: 207 621-3333
Director of Admissions and Records: Sheri Cranston-Fraser
Admissions e-mail: umaar@maine.edu
Web site: http://www.uma.edu
SAT Code: 3929

Director of Learning Support Services: Donald Osier
LD program telephone: 207 621-3066
LD program e-mail: donald.osier@maine.edu
LD program enrollment: 38, Total campus enrollment: 5,538

GENERAL

University of Maine at Augusta is a public, coed, four-year institution. 165-acre campus in Augusta (population: 18,560), 60 miles from Portland; branch campuses in Brunswick, East Millinocket, Ellsworth, Lewiston, Rumford, Saco, Sanford, and Thomaston. Served by air and bus; major airports serve Bangor (65 miles) and Portland. Public transportation serves campus. Semester system.

LD ADMISSIONS

A member of the LD program does not sit on the admissions committee. A personal interview is not required. Essay is not required.

SECONDARY SCHOOL REQUIREMENTS

Graduation from secondary school required; GED accepted.

TESTING

All enrolled freshmen (fall 2004):

Average SAT I Scores: Verbal: 467 Math: 447

Child Study Team report is not required. Tests required as part of this documentation:

- [ ] WAIS-IV
- [ ] WISC-IV
- [ ] SATA
- [ ] Woodcock-Johnson
- [ ] Nelson-Denny Reading Test
- [ ] Other

UNDERGRADUATE STUDENT BODY

Total undergraduate student enrollment: 5,538.

Composition of student body (fall 2004):

	Undergraduate	Freshmen
International	0.0	0.0
Black	0.8	0.8
American Indian	2.8	2.8
Asian-American	0.3	0.4
Hispanic	0.6	0.6
White	95.5	95.4
Unreported	0.0	0.0
	100.0%	100.0%

70% of classes have fewer than 20 students, 29% have between 20 and 50 students, 1% have more than 50 students.

STUDENT HOUSING

Housing is not guaranteed for all undergraduates. Institution does not provide student housing.

EXPENSES

Tuition (2005-06): $4,290 per year (in-state), $10,380 (out-of-state).
There is no additional cost for LD program/services.

LD SERVICES

LD program size is not limited.

LD services available to:

- [x] Freshmen
- [x] Sophomores
- [x] Juniors
- [x] Seniors

Academic Accommodations

Curriculum

- [ ] Foreign language waiver
- [x] Lighter course load
- [ ] Math waiver
- [ ] Other special classes
- [ ] Priority registrations
- [ ] Substitution of courses

Exams

- [x] Extended time
- [ ] Oral exams
- [ ] Take home exams
- [ ] Exams on tape or computer
- [ ] Untimed exams
- [ ] Other accommodations

In class

- [ ] Early syllabus
- [x] Note takers in class
- [ ] Priority seating
- [ ] Tape recorders
- [ ] Videotaped classes
- [ ] Text on tape

Services

- [ ] Diagnostic tests
- [ ] Learning centers
- [ ] Proofreaders
- [ ] Readers
- [ ] Reading Machines/Kurzweil
- [ ] Special bookstore section
- [ ] Typists

Credit toward degree is not given for remedial courses taken.

Counseling Services

- [x] Academic
- [x] Psychological
- [ ] Student Support groups
- [x] Vocational

Tutoring

Individual tutoring is available weekly.

Average size of tutoring groups: 1

	Individual	Group
Time management	[x]	[x]
Organizational skills	[ ]	[ ]
Learning strategies	[x]	[x]
Study skills	[ ]	[ ]
Content area	[ ]	[ ]
Writing lab	[x]	[ ]
Math lab	[x]	[ ]

UNIQUE LD PROGRAM FEATURES

Students with learning disabilities may be eligible for amplified services through a federally funded student support services program.

LD PROGRAM STAFF

Total number of LD Program staff (including director):

Full Time: 2 Part Time: 2

There is no advisor/advocate from the LD program available to students. 8 peer tutors are available to work with LD students.

Key staff person available to work with LD students: Donald Osier, Director of Learning Support Services.

University of Maine at Farmington

Farmington, ME

Address: 111 South Street, Farmington, ME, 04938
Admissions telephone: 207 778-7050
Admissions FAX: 207 778-8182
Director of Admissions: William W. Geller
Admissions e-mail: umfadmit@maine.edu
Web site: http://www.umf.maine.edu
SAT Code: 3506 ACT Code: 1640

Coordinator: Claire Nelson
LD program telephone: 207 778-7295
LD program e-mail: claire@maine.edu
LD program enrollment: 35, Total campus enrollment: 2,349

GENERAL

University of Maine at Farmington is a public, coed, four-year institution. 50-acre campus in Farmington (population: 7,410), 38 miles from Augusta. Airport and train serve Portland (80 miles); smaller airport serves Bangor (78 miles); bus serves Lewiston (46 miles). School operates transportation to Portland airport before and after holidays. Semester system.

LD ADMISSIONS

A member of the LD program does not sit on the admissions committee. A personal interview is recommended. Essay is required and may be typed. Documentation is required in order to receive accommodations.

SECONDARY SCHOOL REQUIREMENTS

Graduation from secondary school required; GED accepted. The following course distribution required: 4 units of English, 3 units of math, 2 units of science, 2 units of foreign language, 2 units of social studies.

TESTING

SAT Subject recommended.

All enrolled freshmen (fall 2004):

Average SAT I Scores: Verbal: 524 Math: 507

Child Study Team report is not required. Tests required as part of this documentation:

- ☐ WAIS-IV
- ☐ WISC-IV
- ☐ SATA
- ☐ Woodcock-Johnson
- ☐ Nelson-Denny Reading Test
- ☐ Other

UNDERGRADUATE STUDENT BODY

Total undergraduate student enrollment: 793 Men, 1,642 Women.

Composition of student body (fall 2004):

	Undergraduate	Freshmen
International	0.2	0.3
Black	0.2	0.2
American Indian	1.2	0.8
Asian-American	1.2	0.8
Hispanic	0.4	0.7
White	96.9	97.2
Unreported	0.0	0.0
	100.0%	100.0%

21% are from out of state. Average age of full-time undergraduates is 23. 64% of classes have fewer than 20 students, 35% have between 20 and 50 students, 1% have more than 50 students.

STUDENT HOUSING

97% of freshmen live in college housing. Freshmen are not required to live on campus. Housing is guaranteed for all undergraduates. Campus can house 1,031 undergraduates. Single rooms are available for students with medical or special needs. A medical note is required.

EXPENSES

Tuition (2005-06): $5,010 per year (in-state), $12,240 (out-of-state).
Room: $3,200. Board: $2,646.
There is no additional cost for LD program/services.

LD SERVICES

LD program size is not limited.

LD services available to:

■ Freshmen ■ Sophomores ■ Juniors ■ Seniors

Academic Accommodations

Curriculum		**In class**	
Foreign language waiver	☐	Early syllabus	☐
Lighter course load	■	Note takers in class	■
Math waiver	☐	Priority seating	■
Other special classes	☐	Tape recorders	■
Priority registrations	☐	Videotaped classes	☐
Substitution of courses	☐	Text on tape	■
Exams		**Services**	
Extended time	■	Diagnostic tests	☐
Oral exams	☐	Learning centers	■
Take home exams	☐	Proofreaders	☐
Exams on tape or computer	☐	Readers	☐
Untimed exams	☐	Reading Machines/Kurzweil	☐
Other accommodations	■	Special bookstore section	☐
		Typists	■

Credit toward degree is not given for remedial courses taken.

Counseling Services

- ☐ Academic
- ☐ Psychological
- ☐ Student Support groups
- ☐ Vocational

Tutoring

Individual tutoring is available weekly.

	Individual	Group
Time management	☐	☐
Organizational skills	☐	☐
Learning strategies	☐	☐
Study skills	☐	☐
Content area	■	☐
Writing lab	■	☐
Math lab	■	☐

LD PROGRAM STAFF

There is no advisor/advocate from the LD program available to students.

University of Maine at Fort Kent

Fort Kent, ME

Address: 23 University Drive, Fort Kent, ME, 04743
Admissions telephone: 888 TRY-UMFK
Admissions FAX: 207 834-7609
Associate Director of Admissions: Melik P. Khoury
Admissions e-mail: umfkadm@maine.edu
Web site: http://www.umfk.maine.edu
SAT Code: 3393 ACT Code: 1642

LD program contact: Angela Theriault
LD program telephone: 207 834-7530
LD program e-mail: asaucier@maine.edu
Total campus enrollment: 1,076

GENERAL

University of Maine at Fort Kent is a public, coed, four-year institution. 52-acre campus in Fort Kent (population: 4,233), 200 miles from Bangor. Airport serves Presque Isle (60 miles); larger airport serves Bangor; bus serves Caribou (45 miles). School operates transportation to Caribou and Presque Isle. Semester system.

LD ADMISSIONS

A personal interview is recommended. Essay is required and may be typed.

SECONDARY SCHOOL REQUIREMENTS

Graduation from secondary school required; GED accepted. The following course distribution required: 4 units of English, 2 units of math, 2 units of science, 2 units of social studies.

TESTING

SAT Reasoning recommended; ACT may be substituted. SAT Subject recommended.

Child Study Team report is not required. Tests required as part of this documentation:

- ☐ WAIS-IV
- ☐ WISC-IV
- ☐ SATA
- ☐ Woodcock-Johnson
- ☐ Nelson-Denny Reading Test
- ☐ Other

UNDERGRADUATE STUDENT BODY

Total undergraduate student enrollment: 325 Men, 561 Women.

38% are from out of state. 1% join a fraternity and 1% join a sorority. Average age of full-time undergraduates is 20.

STUDENT HOUSING

Freshmen are not required to live on campus. Housing is guaranteed for all undergraduates.

EXPENSES

Tuition (2005-06): $4,290 per year (in-state), $10,380 (out-of-state).
Room: $3,324. Board: $2,664.
There is no additional cost for LD program/serv

LD SERVICES

LD program size is not limited.

LD services available to:

☐ Freshmen ☐ Sophomores ☐ Juniors ☐ Seniors

Academic Accommodations

Curriculum		In class	
Foreign language waiver	☐	Early syllabus	☐
Lighter course load	■	Note takers in class	☐
Math waiver	☐	Priority seating	☐
Other special classes	☐	Tape recorders	■
Priority registrations	☐	Videotaped classes	■
Substitution of courses	☐	Text on tape	☐
Exams		**Services**	
Extended time	■	Diagnostic tests	☐
Oral exams	■	Learning centers	☐
Take home exams	☐	Proofreaders	☐
Exams on tape or computer	☐	Readers	■
Untimed exams	■	Reading Machines/Kurzweil	☐
Other accommodations	☐	Special bookstore section	☐
		Typists	☐

Counseling Services

- ☐ Academic
- ☐ Psychological
- ☐ Student Support groups
- ☐ Vocational

Tutoring

	Individual	Group
Time management	☐	☐
Organizational skills	☐	☐
Learning strategies	☐	☐
Study skills	☐	☐
Content area	☐	☐
Writing lab	☐	☐
Math lab	☐	☐

University of Maine at Machias

Machias, ME

Address: 9 O'Brien Avenue, Machias, ME, 04654
Admissions telephone: 888 468-6866
Admissions FAX: 207 255-1363
Director of Admissions: Stewart Bennett
Admissions e-mail: ummadmissions@maine.edu
Web site: http://www.umm.maine.edu
SAT Code: 3956 ACT Code: 1666

LD program name: Disability Services - EEO
Disability Services - EEO: Jean Schild
LD program telephone: 207 255-1228
LD program e-mail: schild@maine.edu
LD program enrollment: 63, Total campus enrollment: 1,191

GENERAL

University of Maine at Machias is a public, coed, four-year institution. 42-acre campus in Machias (population: 2,353), 85 miles from Bangor. Airports serve Bangor and Bar Harbor (65 miles); bus serves Ellsworth (60 miles); special bus service from Machias to airport and bus stations in Bangor. Semester system.

LD ADMISSIONS

Students do not complete a separate application and are not simultaneously accepted to the LD program. A member of the LD program does not sit on the admissions committee. A personal interview is recommended. Essay is required and may be typed.

For fall 2004, 17 completed self-identified LD applications were received. 10 applications were offered admission, and 8 enrolled.

SECONDARY SCHOOL REQUIREMENTS

Graduation from secondary school required; GED accepted. The following course distribution required: 4 units of English, 3 units of math, 2 units of science, 2 units of social studies.

TESTING

SAT Reasoning required; ACT may be substituted. SAT Subject recommended.

All enrolled freshmen (fall 2004):

Average SAT I Scores:	Verbal: 470	Math: 463
Average ACT Scores:	Composite: 20	

Child Study Team report is not required. A neuropsychological or comprehensive psycho-educational evaluation is required for admission. Must be dated within 36 months of application. Tests required as part of this documentation:

- [x] WAIS-IV
- [ ] WISC-IV
- [ ] SATA
- [x] Woodcock-Johnson
- [ ] Nelson-Denny Reading Test
- [ ] Other

UNDERGRADUATE STUDENT BODY

Total undergraduate student enrollment: 318 Men, 699 Women.

Composition of student body (fall 2004):

	Undergraduate	Freshmen
International	4.6	7.5
Black	0.0	1.1
American Indian	3.4	4.3
Asian-American	0.0	0.2
Hispanic	3.4	1.8
White	88.5	85.1
Unreported	0.0	0.0
	100.0%	100.0%

22% are from out of state. 9% join a fraternity and 4% join a sorority. Average age of full-time undergraduates is 23. 70% of classes have fewer than 20 students, 30% have between 20 and 50 students.

STUDENT HOUSING

71% of freshmen live in college housing. Freshmen are not required to live on campus. Housing is guaranteed for all undergraduates. Campus can house 297 undergraduates. Single rooms are available for students with medical or special needs. A medical note is required.

EXPENSES

Tuition (2005-06): $4,290 per year (in-state), $11,340 (out-of-state). Room: $2,958. Board: $2,920.
There is no additional cost for LD program/services.

LD SERVICES

LD program size is not limited.

LD services available to:

- [x] Freshmen
- [x] Sophomores
- [x] Juniors
- [x] Seniors

Academic Accommodations

Curriculum		In class	
Foreign language waiver	[ ]	Early syllabus	[ ]
Lighter course load	[x]	Note takers in class	[x]
Math waiver	[ ]	Priority seating	[x]
Other special classes	[ ]	Tape recorders	[x]
Priority registrations	[ ]	Videotaped classes	[ ]
Substitution of courses	[ ]	Text on tape	[x]
Exams		**Services**	
Extended time	[x]	Diagnostic tests	[ ]
Oral exams	[ ]	Learning centers	[x]
Take home exams	[ ]	Proofreaders	[ ]
Exams on tape or computer	[ ]	Readers	[x]
Untimed exams	[x]	Reading Machines/Kurzweil	[x]
Other accommodations	[x]	Special bookstore section	[ ]
		Typists	[x]

Credit toward degree is not given for remedial courses taken.

Counseling Services

- [x] Academic
- [ ] Psychological
- [ ] Student Support groups
- [x] Vocational

Tutoring

Individual tutoring is available weekly.

Average size of tutoring groups: 2

	Individual	Group
Time management	[x]	[ ]
Organizational skills	[x]	[ ]
Learning strategies	[x]	[ ]
Study skills	[x]	[ ]
Content area	[x]	[ ]
Writing lab	[x]	[ ]
Math lab	[x]	[ ]

LD PROGRAM STAFF

Total number of LD Program staff (including director):

Full Time: 1 Part Time: 1

There is an advisor/advocate from the LD program available to students. 10 peer tutors are available to work with LD students.

Key staff person available to work with LD students: Jean Schild, Disability Services - EEO.

LD Program web site:
http://www.umm.maine.edu/life/EEODISABILITIES/disability.shtml

University of Maine at Orono

Orono, ME

Address: 168 College Avenue, Orono, ME, 04469
Admissions telephone: 877 486-2364
Admissions FAX: 207 581-1213
Admissions Director: Sharon M. Oliver
Admissions e-mail: um-admit@maine.edu
Web site: http://www.umaine.edu
SAT Code: 3916 ACT Code: 1664

LD program name: College Success Programs
LD program address: 125 East Annex
Director of Disability Support Services: Ann Smith
LD program telephone: 207 581-2319
LD program e-mail: ann.smith@umit.maine.edu
Total campus enrollment: 9,085

GENERAL

University of Maine is a public, coed, four-year institution. 3,300-acre campus in Orono (population: 9,112), 12 miles from Bangor. Airport and bus serve Bangor; larger airport and train serve Portland (125 miles). Public transportation serves campus. Semester system.

LD ADMISSIONS

Students do not complete a separate application and are not simultaneously accepted to the LD program. A member of the LD program does not sit on the admissions committee. A personal interview is not required. Essay is required and may be typed.

SECONDARY SCHOOL REQUIREMENTS

Graduation from secondary school required; GED accepted. The following course distribution required: 4 units of English, 3 units of math, 2 units of science, 2 units of foreign language, 2 units of social studies, 2 units of academic electives.

TESTING

SAT Reasoning required; ACT may be substituted. SAT Subject recommended.

All enrolled freshmen (fall 2004):

Average SAT I Scores:	Verbal: 539	Math: 543
Average ACT Scores:	Composite: 24	

Child Study Team report is not required. A neuropsychological or comprehensive psycho-education evaluation is not required for admission. Tests required as part of this documentation:

- [ ] WAIS-IV
- [ ] WISC-IV
- [ ] SATA
- [ ] Woodcock-Johnson
- [ ] Nelson-Denny Reading Test
- [ ] Other

UNDERGRADUATE STUDENT BODY

Total undergraduate student enrollment: 4,037 Men, 4,474 Women.

Composition of student body (fall 2004):

	Undergraduate	Freshmen
International	1.7	1.7
Black	1.0	1.0
American Indian	1.4	1.8
Asian-American	1.6	1.3
Hispanic	0.8	0.8
White	92.5	92.8
Unreported	1.0	0.6
	100.0%	100.0%

14% are from out of state. Average age of full-time undergraduates is 22. 46% of classes have fewer than 20 students, 42% have between 20 and 50 students, 12% have more than 50 students.

STUDENT HOUSING

86% of freshmen live in college housing. Freshmen are required to live on campus. Housing is guaranteed for all undergraduates. Campus can house 3,875 undergraduates. Single rooms are available for students with medical or special needs. A medical note is required.

EXPENSES

Tuition (2005-06): $5,520 per year (in-state), $15,660 (out-of-state).

Room: $3,390. Board: $3,342.

There is no additional cost for LD program/services.

LD SERVICES

LD program size is not limited.

LD services available to:

- [x] Freshmen
- [x] Sophomores
- [x] Juniors
- [x] Seniors

Academic Accommodations

Curriculum

- [ ] Foreign language waiver
- [x] Lighter course load
- [ ] Math waiver
- [ ] Other special classes
- [ ] Priority registrations
- [ ] Substitution of courses

Exams

- [x] Extended time
- [x] Oral exams
- [ ] Take home exams
- [ ] Exams on tape or computer
- [ ] Untimed exams
- [x] Other accommodations

In class

- [ ] Early syllabus
- [x] Note takers in class
- [ ] Priority seating
- [ ] Tape recorders
- [ ] Videotaped classes
- [ ] Text on tape

Services

- [ ] Diagnostic tests
- [ ] Learning centers
- [ ] Proofreaders
- [x] Readers
- [ ] Reading Machines/Kurzweil
- [ ] Special bookstore section
- [ ] Typists

Credit toward degree is not given for remedial courses taken.

Counseling Services

- [x] Academic
- [x] Psychological
- [ ] Student Support groups
- [x] Vocational

Tutoring

Individual tutoring is not available.

Average size of tutoring groups: 4

	Individual	Group
Time management	[ ]	[ ]
Organizational skills	[ ]	[ ]
Learning strategies	[ ]	[x]
Study skills	[ ]	[x]
Content area	[ ]	[ ]
Writing lab	[ ]	[ ]
Math lab	[ ]	[ ]

LD PROGRAM STAFF

Total number of LD Program staff (including director):

Full Time: 1 Part Time: 1

There is an advisor/advocate from the LD program available to students.

Key staff person available to work with LD students: Ann Smith, Director of Disability Support Services.

LD Program web site: http://www.umaine.edu/onward/

University of Maine at Presque Isle

Presque Isle, ME

Address: 181 Main Street, Presque Isle, ME, 04769
Admissions telephone: 207 768-9532
Admissions FAX: 207 768-9777
Director of Admissions: Brian Manter
Admissions e-mail: adventure@umpi.maine.edu
Web site: http://www.umpi.maine.edu
SAT Code: 3008 ACT Code: 1630

Director of Student Support Services: Myrna McGaffin
LD program telephone: 207 768-9613
LD program e-mail: mcgaffin@umpi.maine.edu
Total campus enrollment: 1,652

GENERAL

University of Maine at Presque Isle is a public, coed, four-year institution. 150-acre campus in Presque Isle (population: 9,511), 130 miles from Bangor; branch campuses in Houlton. Served by air and bus; larger airport serves Bangor. Semester system.

LD ADMISSIONS

A personal interview is required. Essay is required and may be typed.

SECONDARY SCHOOL REQUIREMENTS

Graduation from secondary school required; GED accepted. The following course distribution required: 4 units of English, 3 units of math, 2 units of science, 2 units of foreign language, 3 units of social studies, 2 units of academic electives.

TESTING

Child Study Team report is not required. Tests required as part of this documentation:

☐ WAIS-IV ☐ Woodcock-Johnson
☐ WISC-IV ☐ Nelson-Denny Reading Test
☐ SATA ☐ Other

UNDERGRADUATE STUDENT BODY

Total undergraduate student enrollment: 494 Men, 873 Women.

Composition of student body (fall 2004):

	Undergraduate	Freshmen
International	1.2	7.6
Black	0.4	0.5
American Indian	5.3	3.9
Asian-American	2.0	0.8
Hispanic	0.4	0.7
White	90.6	86.6
Unreported	0.0	0.0
	100.0%	100.0%

5% are from out of state. 1% join a fraternity and 1% join a sorority. Average age of full-time undergraduates is 23. 67% of classes have fewer than 20 students, 33% have between 20 and 50 students, 1% have more than 50 students.

STUDENT HOUSING

49% of freshmen live in college housing. Housing is guaranteed for all undergraduates. Campus can house 360 undergraduates.

EXPENSES

Tuition (2005-06): $4,290 per year (in-state), $10,680 (out-of-state). Room: $3,000. Board: $2,246.

There is no additional cost for LD program/services.

LD SERVICES

LD program size is not limited.

LD services available to:

☐ Freshmen ☐ Sophomores ☐ Juniors ☐ Seniors

Academic Accommodations

Curriculum		**In class**	
Foreign language waiver	☐	Early syllabus	☐
Lighter course load	■	Note takers in class	■
Math waiver	☐	Priority seating	☐
Other special classes	☐	Tape recorders	■
Priority registrations	☐	Videotaped classes	■
Substitution of courses	☐	Text on tape	☐
Exams		**Services**	
Extended time	■	Diagnostic tests	☐
Oral exams	■	Learning centers	☐
Take home exams	☐	Proofreaders	☐
Exams on tape or computer	☐	Readers	■
Untimed exams	☐	Reading Machines/Kurzweil	☐
Other accommodations	☐	Special bookstore section	☐
		Typists	☐

Credit toward degree is not given for remedial courses taken.

Counseling Services

☐ Academic
☐ Psychological
☐ Student Support groups
☐ Vocational

Tutoring

	Individual	Group
Time management	☐	☐
Organizational skills	☐	☐
Learning strategies	☐	☐
Study skills	☐	☐
Content area	☐	☐
Writing lab	☐	☐
Math lab	☐	☐

LD PROGRAM STAFF

Total number of LD Program staff (including director):

Full Time: 5 Part Time: 5

Key staff person available to work with LD students: Myrna McGaffin, Director of Student Support Services.

University of New England

Biddeford, ME

Address: 11 Hills Beach Road, Biddeford, ME, 04005
Admissions telephone: 800 477-4863
Admissions FAX: 207 294-5900
Dean of Admissions and Enrollment Management: Alan Liebrecht
Admissions e-mail: admissions@une.edu
Web site: http://www.une.edu
SAT Code: 3751 ACT Code: 1660

Coordinator Disability Services: Susan Church
LD program telephone: 207 283-0170, extension 2815
LD program e-mail: schurch@une.edu
Total campus enrollment: 1,695

GENERAL

University of New England is a private, coed, four-year institution. 550-acre campus in Biddeford (population: 20,942), 18 miles from Portland and 90 miles from Boston; branch campus in Portland. Served by bus; airport and train serve Portland; larger airport serves Boston. Semester system.

LD ADMISSIONS

A personal interview is not required. Essay is not required.

SECONDARY SCHOOL REQUIREMENTS

Graduation from secondary school required; GED accepted. The following course distribution required: 4 units of English, 3 units of math, 2 units of science.

TESTING

SAT Reasoning recommended; ACT may be substituted. SAT Subject recommended.

All enrolled freshmen (fall 2004):

Average SAT I Scores: Verbal: 512 Math: 511

Child Study Team report is not required. Tests required as part of this documentation:

- ☐ WAIS-IV
- ☐ WISC-IV
- ☐ SATA
- ☐ Woodcock-Johnson
- ☐ Nelson-Denny Reading Test
- ☐ Other

UNDERGRADUATE STUDENT BODY

Total undergraduate student enrollment: 336 Men, 1,053 Women.

Composition of student body (fall 2004):

	Undergraduate	Freshmen
International	0.2	0.2
Black	0.0	0.7
American Indian	0.2	0.2
Asian-American	0.4	0.8
Hispanic	0.4	0.8
White	97.1	95.9
Unreported	1.6	1.3
	100.0%	100.0%

53% are from out of state. Average age of full-time undergraduates is 21. 51% of classes have fewer than 20 students, 45% have between 20 and 50 students, 4% have more than 50 students.

STUDENT HOUSING

92% of freshmen live in college housing. Freshmen are required to live on campus. Housing is not guaranteed for all undergraduates. Campus housing is not guaranteed to seniors or those who have fulfilled the 3-year residency requirement. Campus can house 699 undergraduates. Single rooms are not available for students with medical or special needs.

EXPENSES

Tuition (2005-06): $21,540 per year.
Room: $4,365. Board: $4,365.
There is no additional cost for LD program/services.

LD SERVICES

LD program size is not limited.

LD services available to:

☐ Freshmen ☐ Sophomores ☐ Juniors ☐ Seniors

Academic Accommodations

Curriculum		In class	
Foreign language waiver	☐	Early syllabus	☐
Lighter course load	■	Note takers in class	■
Math waiver	☐	Priority seating	■
Other special classes	☐	Tape recorders	☐
Priority registrations	■	Videotaped classes	☐
Substitution of courses	☐	Text on tape	■
Exams		**Services**	
Extended time	■	Diagnostic tests	☐
Oral exams	☐	Learning centers	■
Take home exams	☐	Proofreaders	☐
Exams on tape or computer	■	Readers	■
Untimed exams	☐	Reading Machines/Kurzweil	■
Other accommodations	☐	Special bookstore section	☐
		Typists	☐

Credit toward degree is not given for remedial courses taken.

Counseling Services

- ☐ Academic
- ☐ Psychological
- ☐ Student Support groups
- ☐ Vocational

Tutoring

Individual tutoring is available weekly.

	Individual	Group
Time management	■	☐
Organizational skills	■	☐
Learning strategies	■	☐
Study skills	■	■
Content area	☐	■
Writing lab	■	■
Math lab	■	■

LD PROGRAM STAFF

Total number of LD Program staff (including director):

Full Time: 2 Part Time: 2

There is an advisor/advocate from the LD program available to students.

Key staff person available to work with LD students: Susan Church, Coordinator Disability Services.

Saint Joseph's College

Standish, ME

Address: 278 Whites Bridge Road, Standish, ME, 04084
Admissions telephone: 800 338-7057
Admissions FAX: 207 893-7862
Vice President for Enrollment Management: Vincent Kloskowski
Admissions e-mail: admission@sjcme.edu
Web site: http://www.sjcme.edu
SAT Code: 3755 ACT Code: 1659

LD program telephone: 207 893-6642
LD program enrollment: 57, Total campus enrollment: 986

GENERAL

Saint Joseph's College is a private, coed, four-year institution. 331-acre campus in Standish (population: 9,285), 16 miles from Portland and 120 miles from Boston, MA. Airport and bus serve Portland; major airport and train serve Boston, MA. School operates transportation to Windham, Portland, and South Portland. Semester system.

LD ADMISSIONS

A personal interview is recommended. Essay is required and may be typed.

SECONDARY SCHOOL REQUIREMENTS

Graduation from secondary school required; GED accepted.

TESTING

SAT Reasoning required; ACT may be substituted. SAT Subject recommended.

All enrolled freshmen (fall 2004):

Average SAT I Scores: Verbal: 512 Math: 505

Child Study Team report is not required. Tests required as part of this documentation:

- [ ] WAIS-IV
- [ ] WISC-IV
- [ ] SATA
- [ ] Woodcock-Johnson
- [ ] Nelson-Denny Reading Test
- [ ] Other

UNDERGRADUATE STUDENT BODY

Total undergraduate student enrollment: 313 Men, 579 Women.

Composition of student body (fall 2004):

	Undergraduate	Freshmen
International	0.0	0.1
Black	1.0	1.1
American Indian	0.0	0.0
Asian-American	1.0	0.5
Hispanic	0.3	0.5
White	83.5	84.8
Unreported	14.1	12.9
	100.0%	100.0%

37% are from out of state. Average age of full-time undergraduates is 20. 56% of classes have fewer than 20 students, 44% have between 20 and 50 students, 1% have more than 50 students.

STUDENT HOUSING

90% of freshmen live in college housing. Freshmen are required to live on campus. Housing is guaranteed for all undergraduates. Campus can house 829 undergraduates. Single rooms are available for students with medical or special needs.

EXPENSES

Tuition (2005-06): $19,890 per year.
Room & Board: $8,580.
There is no additional cost for LD program/services.

LD SERVICES

LD program size is not limited.

LD services available to:

- [x] Freshmen
- [x] Sophomores
- [x] Juniors
- [x] Seniors

Academic Accommodations

Curriculum

- [ ] Foreign language waiver
- [ ] Lighter course load
- [ ] Math waiver
- [ ] Other special classes
- [ ] Priority registrations
- [ ] Substitution of courses

Exams

- [x] Extended time
- [x] Oral exams
- [ ] Take home exams
- [ ] Exams on tape or computer
- [ ] Untimed exams
- [ ] Other accommodations

In class

- [ ] Early syllabus
- [x] Note takers in class
- [ ] Priority seating
- [x] Tape recorders
- [ ] Videotaped classes
- [ ] Text on tape

Services

- [ ] Diagnostic tests
- [ ] Learning centers
- [ ] Proofreaders
- [x] Readers
- [x] Reading Machines/Kurzweil
- [ ] Special bookstore section
- [ ] Typists

Credit toward degree is not given for remedial courses taken.

Counseling Services

- [ ] Academic
- [ ] Psychological
- [ ] Student Support groups
- [ ] Vocational

Tutoring

	Individual	Group
Time management	[ ]	[ ]
Organizational skills	[ ]	[ ]
Learning strategies	[ ]	[ ]
Study skills	[ ]	[ ]
Content area	[ ]	[ ]
Writing lab	[ ]	[ ]
Math lab	[ ]	[ ]

LD PROGRAM STAFF

Key staff person available to work with LD students: Joyce Coburn, Associate Dean of the College.

University of Southern Maine

Gorham, ME

Address: 37 College Avenue, Gorham, ME, 04038
Admissions telephone: 800 800-4USM
Admissions FAX: 207 780-5640
Director of Admissions: Dee Gardner
Admissions e-mail: usmadm@usm.maine.edu
Web site: http://www.usm.maine.edu
SAT Code: 3691 ACT Code: 1644

LD program address: 242 Luther Bonney Hall, Portland, ME, 04104
Support for Students with Disabilities: Joyce Branaman
LD program telephone: 207 780-4706
LD program e-mail: branaman@usm.maine.du
LD program enrollment: 53, Total campus enrollment: 8,736

GENERAL

University of Southern Maine is a public, coed, four-year institution. Three campuses totaling 126 acres in Portland (population: 64,249), Gorham, and Lewiston; branch campus in Sanford. Served by air and bus; major airport and train serve Boston (150 miles). School operates transportation between Portland and Gorham campuses and to other locations in Portland. Public transportation serves campus. Semester system.

LD ADMISSIONS

A personal interview is recommended. Essay is required and may be typed.

SECONDARY SCHOOL REQUIREMENTS

Graduation from secondary school required; GED accepted. The following course distribution required: 4 units of English, 3 units of math, 2 units of science, 2 units of foreign language, 2 units of social studies, 2 units of history.

TESTING

SAT Reasoning required; ACT may be substituted. SAT Subject recommended.

All enrolled freshmen (fall 2004):

Average SAT I Scores: Verbal: 509 Math: 504
Average ACT Scores: Composite: 21

Child Study Team report is not required. A neuropsychological or comprehensive psycho-educational evaluation is required for admission. Must be dated within 48 months of application. Tests required as part of this documentation:

- [x] WAIS-IV
- [ ] WISC-IV
- [ ] SATA
- [x] Woodcock-Johnson
- [x] Nelson-Denny Reading Test
- [ ] Other

UNDERGRADUATE STUDENT BODY

Total undergraduate student enrollment: 3,448 Men, 5,383 Women.

Composition of student body (fall 2004):

	Undergraduate	Freshmen
International	0.0	0.0
Black	0.9	1.1
American Indian	1.3	1.2
Asian-American	1.3	1.4
Hispanic	0.6	0.9
White	95.9	95.4
Unreported	0.0	0.0
	100.0%	100.0%

9% are from out of state. 1% join a fraternity and 1% join a sorority. Average age of full-time undergraduates is 22. 53% of classes have fewer than 20 students, 44% have between 20 and 50 students, 3% have more than 50 students.

STUDENT HOUSING

64% of freshmen live in college housing. Housing is guaranteed for all undergraduates. Campus can house 1,587 undergraduates. Single rooms are available for students with medical or special needs. A medical note is required.

EXPENSES

Tuition (2005-06): $4,212 per year (in-state), $11,622 (out-of-state).
Room: $3,780. Board: $3,045.
There is no additional cost for LD program/services.

LD SERVICES

LD program size is not limited.

LD services available to:

- [x] Freshmen
- [x] Sophomores
- [x] Juniors
- [x] Seniors

Academic Accommodations

Curriculum		In class	
Foreign language waiver	[ ]	Early syllabus	[x]
Lighter course load	[ ]	Note takers in class	[x]
Math waiver	[x]	Priority seating	[ ]
Other special classes	[x]	Tape recorders	[x]
Priority registrations	[ ]	Videotaped classes	[ ]
Substitution of courses	[x]	Text on tape	[x]
Exams		**Services**	
Extended time	[x]	Diagnostic tests	[ ]
Oral exams	[ ]	Learning centers	[x]
Take home exams	[ ]	Proofreaders	[x]
Exams on tape or computer	[x]	Readers	[x]
Untimed exams	[x]	Reading Machines/Kurzweil	[x]
Other accommodations	[x]	Special bookstore section	[ ]
		Typists	[x]

Credit toward degree is not given for remedial courses taken.

Counseling Services

- [ ] Academic
- [ ] Psychological
- [ ] Student Support groups
- [ ] Vocational

Tutoring

Individual tutoring is available weekly.

	Individual	Group
Time management	[ ]	[ ]
Organizational skills	[ ]	[ ]
Learning strategies	[ ]	[ ]
Study skills	[x]	[ ]
Content area	[ ]	[ ]
Writing lab	[ ]	[ ]
Math lab	[ ]	[ ]

LD PROGRAM STAFF

Total number of LD Program staff (including director):

Full Time: 1 Part Time: 1

There is an advisor/advocate from the LD program available to students.

Key staff person available to work with LD students: Bill Ferreira, Learning Disability Specialist.

LD Program web site: www.usm.maine.edu/oassd/

Thomas College

Waterville, ME

Address: 180 West River Road, Waterville, ME, 04901
Admissions telephone: 800 339-7001
Admissions FAX: 207 859-1114
Vice President for Enrollment Management: Robert Callahan
Admissions e-mail: admiss@thomas.edu
Web site: http://www.thomas.edu
SAT Code: 3903 ACT Code: 1663

LD program name: Center for Academic Support
Director, Center for Academic Support: Ellen McQuiston
LD program telephone: 207 859-1214
LD program e-mail: mcquiston@thomas.edu
LD program enrollment: 16, Total campus enrollment: 737

GENERAL

Thomas College is a private, coed, four-year institution. 70-acre campus in Waterville (population: 15,605), 70 miles from Portland and 55 miles from Bangor; branch campus in Portland (graduate programs only). Served by bus; airports serve Portland and Bangor. Semester system.

LD ADMISSIONS

Students do not complete a separate application and are not simultaneously accepted to the LD program. A member of the LD program does not sit on the admissions committee. A personal interview is recommended. Essay is required and may be typed.

SECONDARY SCHOOL REQUIREMENTS

Graduation from secondary school required; GED accepted.

TESTING

SAT Reasoning required of some applicants; ACT may be substituted. SAT Subject recommended.

All enrolled freshmen (fall 2004):

Average SAT I Scores: Verbal: 454 Math: 446

Child Study Team report is not required. A neuropsychological or comprehensive psycho-educational evaluation is required for admission. Must be dated within 36 months of application. Tests required as part of this documentation:

- ☑ WAIS-IV
- ☑ WISC-IV
- ☐ SATA
- ☑ Woodcock-Johnson
- ☐ Nelson-Denny Reading Test
- ☑ Other

UNDERGRADUATE STUDENT BODY

Total undergraduate student enrollment: 265 Men, 333 Women.

Composition of student body (fall 2004):

	Undergraduate	Freshmen
International	0.0	0.0
Black	2.2	0.4
American Indian	0.5	0.6
Asian-American	0.0	0.4
Hispanic	1.1	1.0
White	88.2	89.5
Unreported	8.1	8.1
	100.0%	100.0%

8% are from out of state. 2% join a fraternity and 3% join a sorority. Average age of full-time undergraduates is 19. 57% of classes have fewer than 20 students, 43% have between 20 and 50 students.

STUDENT HOUSING

80% of freshmen live in college housing. Freshmen are not required to live on campus. Housing is guaranteed for all undergraduates. Campus can house 383 undergraduates.

EXPENSES

Tuition (2005-06): $16,300 per year.
Room & Board: $7,410.
There is no additional cost for LD program/services.

LD SERVICES

LD program size is not limited.

LD services available to:

☑ Freshmen ☑ Sophomores ☑ Juniors ☑ Seniors

Academic Accommodations

Curriculum

- Foreign language waiver ☐
- Lighter course load ☑
- Math waiver ☐
- Other special classes ☐
- Priority registrations ☑
- Substitution of courses ☐

Exams

- Extended time ☑
- Oral exams ☑
- Take home exams ☐
- Exams on tape or computer ☑
- Untimed exams ☐
- Other accommodations ☐

In class

- Early syllabus ☐
- Note takers in class ☑
- Priority seating ☑
- Tape recorders ☑
- Videotaped classes ☐
- Text on tape ☑

Services

- Diagnostic tests ☐
- Learning centers ☑
- Proofreaders ☐
- Readers ☐
- Reading Machines/Kurzweil ☐
- Special bookstore section ☐
- Typists ☑

Credit toward degree is not given for remedial courses taken.

Counseling Services

- ☑ Academic
- ☐ Psychological
- ☐ Student Support groups
- ☐ Vocational

Tutoring

Individual tutoring is available weekly.

Average size of tutoring groups: 1

	Individual	Group
Time management	☑	☑
Organizational skills	☑	☑
Learning strategies	☑	☑
Study skills	☑	☑
Content area	☐	☐
Writing lab	☑	☑
Math lab	☑	☑

UNIQUE LD PROGRAM FEATURES

Essay is required for all students applying to the college. Decisions about services for LD students are made individually. Application for LD services is made separately from application to the college. Students with learning disabilities have access to tutoring and academic-support services consistent with the access available to all other students.

LD PROGRAM STAFF

There is an advisor/advocate from the LD program available to students. 6 peer tutors are available to work with LD students.

Key staff person available to work with LD students: Ellen McQuiston, Director, Center for Academic Support.

Unity College

Unity, ME

Address: 90 Quaker Hill Road, Unity, ME, 04988
Admissions telephone: 800 624-1024
Admissions FAX: 207 948-2928
Director of Admissions: Kay Fiedler
Admissions e-mail: admissions@unity.edu
Web site: http://www.unity.edu
SAT Code: 3925 ACT Code: 1665

Resource Center Director: James Horan
LD program telephone: 207 948-3131, extension 263
LD program e-mail: jhoran@unity.edu
Total campus enrollment: 521

GENERAL

Unity College is a private, coed, four-year institution. 235-acre campus in Unity (population: 1,889), 18 miles from Waterville and 100 miles from Portland. Airports serve Bangor (35 miles) and Portland; bus serves Waterville. Semester system.

LD ADMISSIONS

A personal interview is not required. Essay is required and may be typed.

SECONDARY SCHOOL REQUIREMENTS

Graduation from secondary school required; GED accepted. The following course distribution required: 4 units of English, 2 units of math, 2 units of science, 2 units of social studies, 2 units of history.

TESTING

SAT Reasoning or ACT considered if submitted; SAT Reasoning preferred.

All enrolled freshmen (fall 2004):

Average SAT I Scores: Verbal: 520 Math: 490

Child Study Team report is not required. Tests required as part of this documentation:

❑ WAIS-IV ❑ Woodcock-Johnson
❑ WISC-IV ❑ Nelson-Denny Reading Test
❑ SATA ❑ Other

UNDERGRADUATE STUDENT BODY

Total undergraduate student enrollment: 340 Men, 166 Women.

Composition of student body (fall 2004):

	Undergraduate	Freshmen
International	0.0	0.6
Black	0.7	0.4
American Indian	0.0	0.0
Asian-American	0.0	0.0
Hispanic	0.7	0.4
White	98.7	98.7
Unreported	0.0	0.0
	100.0%	100.0%

60% are from out of state.

STUDENT HOUSING

Housing is guaranteed for all undergraduates. Campus can house 310 undergraduates.

EXPENSES

Tuition (2005-06): $16,740 per year.

Room: $3,880. Board: $2,750.

There is no additional cost for LD program/services.

LD SERVICES

LD program size is not limited.

LD services available to:

❑ Freshmen ❑ Sophomores ❑ Juniors ❑ Seniors

Academic Accommodations

Curriculum		In class	
Foreign language waiver	❑	Early syllabus	❑
Lighter course load	❑	Note takers in class	■
Math waiver	❑	Priority seating	❑
Other special classes	❑	Tape recorders	❑
Priority registrations	❑	Videotaped classes	❑
Substitution of courses	❑	Text on tape	❑
Exams		**Services**	
Extended time	■	Diagnostic tests	❑
Oral exams	❑	Learning centers	■
Take home exams	❑	Proofreaders	❑
Exams on tape or computer	❑	Readers	■
Untimed exams	❑	Reading Machines/Kurzweil	❑
Other accommodations	❑	Special bookstore section	❑
		Typists	❑

Credit toward degree is given for remedial courses taken.

Counseling Services

❑ Academic
❑ Psychological
❑ Student Support groups
❑ Vocational

Tutoring

	Individual	Group
Time management	❑	❑
Organizational skills	❑	❑
Learning strategies	❑	❑
Study skills	❑	❑
Content area	❑	❑
Writing lab	❑	❑
Math lab	❑	❑

LD PROGRAM STAFF

Key staff person available to work with LD students: Ann Dailey, Learning Disability Specialist.

University of Baltimore

Baltimore, MD

Address: 1420 North Charles Street, Baltimore, MD, 21201
Admissions telephone: 877 ApplyUB
Admissions FAX: 410 837-4793
Web site: http://www.ubalt.edu
SAT Code: 5810 ACT Code: 1744

Director: Jacquelyn Trvelove-DeSimone
LD program telephone: 410 837-4141
LD program e-mail: jtrvelove@ubalt.edu
LD program enrollment: 59, Total campus enrollment: 2,117

GENERAL

University of Baltimore is a public, coed, graduate institution. 14-acre, urban campus in Baltimore (population: 651,154). Served by airport, bus, and train. School operates transportation to Coppin St Coll and to parking lots and garages. Public transportation serves campus. Semester system.

TESTING

Child Study Team report is not required. A neuropsychological or comprehensive psycho-educational evaluation is required for admission. Must be dated within 36 months of application. Tests required as part of this documentation:

■ WAIS-IV
❑ WISC-IV
❑ SATA
■ Woodcock-Johnson
❑ Nelson-Denny Reading Test
❑ Other

UNDERGRADUATE STUDENT BODY

Total undergraduate student enrollment: 890 Men, 1,103 Women.

Composition of student body (fall 2004):

	Freshmen
International	6.0
Black	32.7
American Indian	0.8
Asian-American	2.9
Hispanic	1.6
White	47.1
Unreported	8.9
	100.0%

8% are from out of state. Average age of full-time undergraduates is 27. 36% of classes have fewer than 20 students, 60% have between 20 and 50 students, 4% have more than 50 students.

EXPENSES

Tuition (2005-06): $5,324 per year (in-state), $16,904 (out-of-state).

There is no additional cost for LD program/services.

LD SERVICES

LD program size is not limited.

LD services available to:

❑ Freshmen ❑ Sophomores ■ Juniors ■ Seniors

Academic Accommodations

Curriculum		In class	
Foreign language waiver	❑	Early syllabus	■
Lighter course load	❑	Note takers in class	■
Math waiver	❑	Priority seating	❑
Other special classes	❑	Tape recorders	■
Priority registrations	❑	Videotaped classes	■
Substitution of courses	❑	Text on tape	■
Exams		**Services**	
Extended time	■	Diagnostic tests	❑
Oral exams	■	Learning centers	■
Take home exams	❑	Proofreaders	❑
Exams on tape or computer	■	Readers	■
Untimed exams	❑	Reading Machines/Kurzweil	■
Other accommodations	❑	Special bookstore section	❑
		Typists	■

Credit toward degree is not given for remedial courses taken.

Counseling Services

■ Academic — Meets 4 times per academic year
■ Psychological — Meets 6 times per academic year
❑ Student Support groups
❑ Vocational

Tutoring

Individual tutoring is available weekly.

Average size of tutoring groups: 6

	Individual	Group
Time management	■	■
Organizational skills	■	■
Learning strategies	■	■
Study skills	❑	❑
Content area	■	■
Writing lab	■	■
Math lab	■	■

LD PROGRAM STAFF

Total number of LD Program staff (including director):

Full Time: 2 Part Time: 2

There is an advisor/advocate from the LD program available to students. The advisor/advocate meets with faculty two times per month and students four times per month. Four peer tutors are available to work with LD students.

Key staff person available to work with LD students: Jacquelyn Trvelove-Desimone, Director

LD Program web site: www.ubalt.edu/disability

Capitol College

Laurel, MD

Address: 11301 Springfield Road, Laurel, MD, 20708
Admissions telephone: 800 950-1992
Admissions FAX: 301 953-1442
Director of Admissions: Darnell Edwards
Admissions e-mail: admissions@capitol-college.edu
Web site: http://www.capitol-college.edu
SAT Code: 5101 ACT Code: 1683

LD program name: Dean of Student's Office
Dean of Students: Melinda Bunnell-Rhyne
LD program telephone: 301 369-2800, extension 3046
LD program e-mail: deanofstudents@capitol-college.edu
LD program enrollment: 11, Total campus enrollment: 324

GENERAL

Capitol College is a private, coed, four-year institution. 52-acre, suburban campus in Laurel (population: 19,960), 25 miles from Baltimore and Washington, DC. Served by bus; major airports and train serve Baltimore and Washington, DC. School operates transportation to bank, metropolitan area, and shopping center. Semester system.

SECONDARY SCHOOL REQUIREMENTS

Graduation from secondary school required; GED accepted. The following course distribution required: 4 units of English, 3 units of math, 2 units of science, 2 units of social studies, 1 unit of history.

TESTING

SAT Reasoning or ACT considered if submitted; SAT Reasoning preferred. SAT Subject required.

All enrolled freshmen (fall 2004):

Average SAT I Scores: Verbal:420 Math:440

Child Study Team report is not required. Tests required as part of this documentation:

- ❑ WAIS-IV
- ❑ WISC-IV
- ❑ SATA
- ❑ Woodcock-Johnson
- ❑ Nelson-Denny Reading Test
- ❑ Other

UNDERGRADUATE STUDENT BODY

Total undergraduate student enrollment: 502 Men, 182 Women.

Composition of student body (fall 2004):

	Undergraduate	Freshmen
International	2.3	3.4
Black	54.5	42.6
American Indian	0.0	0.0
Asian-American	4.5	7.1
Hispanic	0.0	3.7
White	36.4	42.3
Unreported	2.3	0.9
	100.0%	100.0%

14% are from out of state. 92% of classes have fewer than 20 students, 8% have between 20 and 50 students.

STUDENT HOUSING

Freshmen are not required to live on campus. Housing is guaranteed for all undergraduates. Campus can house 90 undergraduates. Single rooms are available for students with medical or special needs. A medical note is required.

EXPENSES

Tuition (2005-06): $17,688 per year.

Room: $4,084.

There is no additional cost for LD program/services.

LD SERVICES

LD program size is not limited.

LD services available to:

■ Freshmen ■ Sophomores ■ Juniors ■ Seniors

Academic Accommodations

Curriculum		**In class**	
Foreign language waiver	❑	Early syllabus	■
Lighter course load	■	Note takers in class	■
Math waiver	❑	Priority seating	■
Other special classes	❑	Tape recorders	■
Priority registrations	❑	Videotaped classes	■
Substitution of courses	❑	Text on tape	■
Exams		**Services**	
Extended time	■	Diagnostic tests	❑
Oral exams	■	Learning centers	❑
Take home exams	❑	Proofreaders	■
Exams on tape or computer	■	Readers	❑
Untimed exams	❑	Reading Machines/Kurzweil	❑
Other accommodations	■	Special bookstore section	❑
		Typists	■

Credit toward degree is not given for remedial courses taken.

Counseling Services

- ■ Academic — Meets 2 times per academic year
- ❑ Psychological
- ❑ Student Support groups
- ❑ Vocational

Tutoring

Individual tutoring is available daily.

Average size of tutoring groups: 3

	Individual	Group
Time management	■	❑
Organizational skills	■	❑
Learning strategies	■	❑
Study skills	■	❑
Content area	■	❑
Writing lab	■	❑
Math lab	❑	❑

LD PROGRAM STAFF

Total number of LD Program staff (including director):

Full Time: 1 Part Time: 1

There is an advisor/advocate from the LD program available to students. The advisor/advocate meets with faculty and students once per month.

Key staff person available to work with LD students: Melinda Bunnell-Rhyne, Dean of Students.

Columbia Union College

Takoma Park, MD

Address: 7600 Flower Avenue, Takoma Park, MD, 20912
Admissions telephone: 301 891-4080
Admissions FAX: 301 891-4230
Director of Admissions: Emile John
Admissions e-mail: enroll@cuc.edu
Web site: http://www.cuc.edu
SAT Code: 5890 ACT Code: 1687

LD program name: The Center for Learning Resources
Assistant Director, Academic Support: Dr. Selma Chaij
LD program telephone: 301 891-4184
LD program e-mail: schaij@cuc.edu
Total campus enrollment: 1,086

GENERAL

Columbia Union College is a private, coed, four-year institution. 19-acre, suburban campus in Takoma Park (population: 17,299), seven miles from Washington, DC. Major airport, bus, and train serve Washington, DC. Public transportation serves campus. Semester system.

LD ADMISSIONS

A personal interview is recommended. Essay is not required.

SECONDARY SCHOOL REQUIREMENTS

Graduation from secondary school required; GED accepted. The following course distribution required: 4 units of English, 2 units of math, 2 units of science, 2 units of foreign language, 2 units of social studies, 4 units of history.

TESTING

SAT Reasoning or ACT required. SAT Subject required.

All enrolled freshmen (fall 2004):

Average SAT I Scores: Verbal: 463 Math: 432
Average ACT Scores: Composite: 20

Child Study Team report is not required. A neuropsychological or comprehensive psycho-educational evaluation is required for admission. Must be dated within 36 months of application. Tests required as part of this documentation:

- ■ WAIS-IV
- ■ WISC-IV
- ☐ SATA
- ■ Woodcock-Johnson
- ☐ Nelson-Denny Reading Test
- ☐ Other

UNDERGRADUATE STUDENT BODY

Total undergraduate student enrollment: 420 Men, 649 Women.

Composition of student body (fall 2004):

	Undergraduate	Freshmen
International	0.0	3.3
Black	58.6	55.1
American Indian	0.0	0.2
Asian-American	11.1	5.4
Hispanic	10.6	8.5
White	17.8	16.8
Unreported	1.9	10.7
	100.0%	100.0%

38% are from out of state. Average age of full-time undergraduates is 23. 75% of classes have fewer than 20 students, 24% have between 20 and 50 students, 1% have more than 50 students.

STUDENT HOUSING

79% of freshmen live in college housing. Housing is guaranteed for all undergraduates.

EXPENSES

Tuition (2005-06): $16,514 per year.

Room: $3,232. Board: $2,717.
There is no additional cost for LD program/services.

LD SERVICES

LD program size is not limited.

LD services available to:

■ Freshmen ■ Sophomores ■ Juniors ■ Seniors

Academic Accommodations

Curriculum		In class	
Foreign language waiver	☐	Early syllabus	☐
Lighter course load	■	Note takers in class	☐
Math waiver	☐	Priority seating	☐
Other special classes	☐	Tape recorders	☐
Priority registrations	☐	Videotaped classes	☐
Substitution of courses	☐	Text on tape	☐
Exams		**Services**	
Extended time	■	Diagnostic tests	☐
Oral exams	☐	Learning centers	■
Take home exams	☐	Proofreaders	☐
Exams on tape or computer	☐	Readers	☐
Untimed exams	■	Reading Machines/Kurzweil	☐
Other accommodations	☐	Special bookstore section	☐
		Typists	☐

Credit toward degree is not given for remedial courses taken.

Counseling Services

- ☐ Academic
- ☐ Psychological
- ☐ Student Support groups
- ☐ Vocational

Tutoring

Individual tutoring is available.

	Individual	Group
Time management	☐	☐
Organizational skills	☐	☐
Learning strategies	☐	☐
Study skills	☐	☐
Content area	☐	☐
Writing lab	☐	☐
Math lab	☐	☐

LD PROGRAM STAFF

Total number of LD Program staff (including director):

Full Time: 2 Part Time: 2

There is an advisor/advocate from the LD program available to students.

Key staff person available to work with LD students: Dr. Selma Chaij, Assistant Director, Academic Support

Coppin State University

Baltimore, MD

Address: 2500 West North Avenue, Baltimore, MD, 21216-3698
Admissions telephone: 410 951-3600
Admissions FAX: 410 523-7351
Director of Admissions: Michelle Gross
Admissions e-mail: admissions@coppin.edu
Web site: http://www.coppin.edu
SAT Code: 5122 ACT Code: 1688

LD program name: Counseling Center
Director of Counseling Center: Gillian Hallmen
LD program telephone: 410 951-3939
LD program e-mail: ghallmen@coppin.edu
Total campus enrollment: 3,290

GENERAL

Coppin State University is a public, coed, four-year institution. 33-acre, urban campus in Baltimore (population: 651,154). Served by airport, bus, and train. Public transportation serves campus. Semester system.

SECONDARY SCHOOL REQUIREMENTS

Graduation from secondary school required; GED accepted. The following course distribution required: 4 units of English, 3 units of math, 2 units of science, 2 units of foreign language, 3 units of social studies.

TESTING

SAT Reasoning required; ACT may be substituted. SAT Subject recommended.

Child Study Team report is not required. Tests required as part of this documentation:

- ☐ WAIS-IV
- ☐ WISC-IV
- ☐ SATA
- ☐ Woodcock-Johnson
- ☐ Nelson-Denny Reading Test
- ☐ Other

UNDERGRADUATE STUDENT BODY

Total undergraduate student enrollment: 3,290.

Composition of student body (fall 2004):

	Undergraduate	Freshmen
International	2.7	3.0
Black	96.6	94.6
American Indian	0.0	0.1
Asian-American	0.2	0.3
Hispanic	0.0	0.2
White	0.3	1.5
Unreported	0.2	0.3
	100.0%	100.0%

10% are from out of state. Average age of full-time undergraduates is 25.

STUDENT HOUSING

43% of freshmen live in college housing. Housing is guaranteed for all undergraduates. Campus can house 650 undergraduates. Single rooms are available for students with medical or special needs. A medical note is required.

EXPENSES

Tuition (2005-06): $3,527 per year (in-state), $10,048 (out-of-state).
Room: $3,881. Board: $2,358.

LD SERVICES

LD program size is not limited.

LD services available to:

☐ Freshmen ☐ Sophomores ☐ Juniors ☐ Seniors

Academic Accommodations

Curriculum		**In class**	
Foreign language waiver	☐	Early syllabus	☐
Lighter course load	☐	Note takers in class	☐
Math waiver	☐	Priority seating	☐
Other special classes	☐	Tape recorders	☐
Priority registrations	☐	Videotaped classes	☐
Substitution of courses	☐	Text on tape	☐
Exams		**Services**	
Extended time	■	Diagnostic tests	☐
Oral exams	☐	Learning centers	☐
Take home exams	☐	Proofreaders	☐
Exams on tape or computer	☐	Readers	☐
Untimed exams	■	Reading Machines/Kurzweil	☐
Other accommodations	☐	Special bookstore section	☐
		Typists	☐

Credit toward degree is not given for remedial courses taken.

Counseling Services

- ☐ Academic
- ☐ Psychological
- ☐ Student Support groups
- ☐ Vocational

Tutoring

	Individual	Group
Time management	☐	☐
Organizational skills	☐	☐
Learning strategies	☐	☐
Study skills	☐	☐
Content area	☐	☐
Writing lab	☐	☐
Math lab	☐	☐

LD PROGRAM STAFF

Key staff person available to work with LD students: Gillian Hallmen, Director of Counseling Center

LD Program web site: www.coppin.edu/counseling_center/dss.asp

Frostburg State University

Frostburg, MD

Address: 101 Braddock Road, Frostburg, MD, 21532
Admissions telephone: 301 687-4201
Admissions FAX: 301 687-7074
Vice President for Enrollment Management: James Antonio
Admissions e-mail: fsuadmissions@frostburg.edu
Web site: http://www.frostburg.edu
SAT Code: 5402

LD program name: Disability Support Services
Director, Disability Support Services: Lee Pullen
LD program telephone: 301 687-4441
LD program e-mail: lpullen@frostburg.edu
LD program enrollment: 260, Total campus enrollment: 4,522

GENERAL

Frostburg State University is a public, coed, four-year institution. 260-acre campus in Frostburg (population: 7,873), 11 miles from Cumberland; branch campuses in Frederick and Hagerstown. Served by bus; major airports serve Pittsburgh (100 miles) and Baltimore (150 miles); smaller airport and train serve Cumberland. Public transportation serves campus. Semester system.

LD ADMISSIONS

A personal interview is not required. Essay is not required.

SECONDARY SCHOOL REQUIREMENTS

Graduation from secondary school required; GED accepted. The following course distribution required: 4 units of English, 3 units of math, 3 units of science, 2 units of foreign language, 3 units of history.

TESTING

SAT Reasoning required; ACT may be substituted. SAT Subject recommended.

Child Study Team report is not required. Tests required as part of this documentation:

- [ ] WAIS-IV
- [ ] WISC-IV
- [ ] SATA
- [ ] Woodcock-Johnson
- [ ] Nelson-Denny Reading Test
- [ ] Other

UNDERGRADUATE STUDENT BODY

Total undergraduate student enrollment: 2,074 Men, 2,280 Women.

Composition of student body (fall 2004):

	Undergraduate	Freshmen
International	0.6	0.7
Black	15.8	12.8
American Indian	0.3	0.5
Asian-American	2.2	1.5
Hispanic	2.0	1.9
White	77.4	80.3
Unreported	1.7	2.3
	100.0%	100.0%

12% are from out of state. 10% join a fraternity and 10% join a sorority. Average age of full-time undergraduates is 21. 48% of classes have fewer than 20 students, 49% have between 20 and 50 students, 3% have more than 50 students.

STUDENT HOUSING

73% of freshmen live in college housing. Freshmen are not required to live on campus. Housing is guaranteed for all undergraduates. Campus can house 1,700 undergraduates.

EXPENSES

Tuition (2005-06): $5,000 per year (in-state), $13,250 (out-of-state). Out-of-state tuition is lower for residents of some counties bordering Maryland.

Room: $3,132. Board: $3,310.

There is no additional cost for LD program/services.

LD SERVICES

LD program size is not limited.

LD services available to:

- [x] Freshmen
- [x] Sophomores
- [x] Juniors
- [x] Seniors

Academic Accommodations

Curriculum

- [ ] Foreign language waiver
- [ ] Lighter course load
- [ ] Math waiver
- [ ] Other special classes
- [ ] Priority registrations
- [ ] Substitution of courses

Exams

- [x] Extended time
- [ ] Oral exams
- [ ] Take home exams
- [ ] Exams on tape or computer
- [x] Untimed exams
- [ ] Other accommodations

In class

- [ ] Early syllabus
- [x] Note takers in class
- [ ] Priority seating
- [x] Tape recorders
- [ ] Videotaped classes
- [ ] Text on tape

Services

- [ ] Diagnostic tests
- [ ] Learning centers
- [ ] Proofreaders
- [x] Readers
- [ ] Reading Machines/Kurzweil
- [ ] Special bookstore section
- [ ] Typists

Credit toward degree is not given for remedial courses taken.

Counseling Services

- [ ] Academic
- [ ] Psychological
- [ ] Student Support groups
- [ ] Vocational

Tutoring

Individual tutoring is available.

	Individual	Group
Time management	[ ]	[ ]
Organizational skills	[ ]	[ ]
Learning strategies	[ ]	[ ]
Study skills	[ ]	[ ]
Content area	[ ]	[ ]
Writing lab	[ ]	[ ]
Math lab	[ ]	[ ]

LD PROGRAM STAFF

Key staff person available to work with LD students: Lee Pullen, Director, Disability Support Services

Goucher College

Baltimore, MD

Address: 1021 Dulaney Valley Road, Baltimore, MD, 21204
Admissions telephone: 410 337-6100
Admissions FAX: 410 337-6354
Director of Admissions: Carlton E. Surbeck III
Admissions e-mail: admissions@goucher.edu
Web site: http://www.goucher.edu
SAT Code: 5257 ACT Code: 1696

Disability Specialist: Frona Brown
LD program telephone: 410 337-6178
Total campus enrollment: 1,366

GENERAL

Goucher College is a private, coed, four-year institution. 287-acre campus in Towson (population: 51,793), eight miles north of Baltimore. Served by airport, bus, and train; major airport serves Washington, DC (30 miles). School operates transportation to Johns Hopkins U and Towson U. Public transportation serves campus. Semester system.

LD ADMISSIONS

A personal interview is recommended. Essay is required and may be typed.

SECONDARY SCHOOL REQUIREMENTS

Graduation from secondary school required; GED accepted. The following course distribution required: 4 units of English, 3 units of math, 2 units of science, 2 units of foreign language, 3 units of social studies, 2 units of academic electives.

TESTING

SAT Reasoning or ACT required. SAT Subject required.

All enrolled freshmen (fall 2004):

Average SAT I Scores:	Verbal: 607	Math: 581
Average ACT Scores:	Composite: 26	

Child Study Team report is not required. Tests required as part of this documentation:

- [ ] WAIS-IV
- [ ] WISC-IV
- [ ] SATA
- [ ] Woodcock-Johnson
- [ ] Nelson-Denny Reading Test
- [ ] Other

UNDERGRADUATE STUDENT BODY

Total undergraduate student enrollment: 333 Men, 862 Women.

Composition of student body (fall 2004):

	Undergraduate	Freshmen
International	0.1	0.6
Black	3.2	4.6
American Indian	0.2	0.4
Asian-American	3.5	3.3
Hispanic	3.5	3.1
White	70.1	64.7
Unreported	19.4	23.3
	100.0%	100.0%

60% are from out of state. Average age of full-time undergraduates is 20. 76% of classes have fewer than 20 students, 23% have between 20 and 50 students, 1% have more than 50 students.

STUDENT HOUSING

94% of freshmen live in college housing. Freshmen are required to live on campus. Housing is guaranteed for all undergraduates. Campus can house 930 undergraduates.

EXPENSES

Tuition (2005-06): $27,100 per year.
Room: $5,625. Board: $3,075.
There is no additional cost for LD program/services.

LD SERVICES

LD program size is not limited.

LD services available to:

- [ ] Freshmen
- [ ] Sophomores
- [ ] Juniors
- [ ] Seniors

Academic Accommodations

Curriculum

- [ ] Foreign language waiver
- [x] Lighter course load
- [ ] Math waiver
- [ ] Other special classes
- [ ] Priority registrations
- [ ] Substitution of courses

Exams

- [x] Extended time
- [ ] Oral exams
- [ ] Take home exams
- [ ] Exams on tape or computer
- [ ] Untimed exams
- [ ] Other accommodations

In class

- [ ] Early syllabus
- [x] Note takers in class
- [ ] Priority seating
- [x] Tape recorders
- [ ] Videotaped classes
- [ ] Text on tape

Services

- [ ] Diagnostic tests
- [x] Learning centers
- [ ] Proofreaders
- [ ] Readers
- [x] Reading Machines/Kurzweil
- [ ] Special bookstore section
- [ ] Typists

Credit toward degree is not given for remedial courses taken.

Counseling Services

- [ ] Academic
- [ ] Psychological
- [ ] Student Support groups
- [ ] Vocational

Tutoring

	Individual	Group
Time management	[ ]	[ ]
Organizational skills	[ ]	[ ]
Learning strategies	[ ]	[ ]
Study skills	[ ]	[ ]
Content area	[ ]	[ ]
Writing lab	[ ]	[ ]
Math lab	[ ]	[ ]

LD PROGRAM STAFF

Key staff person available to work with LD students: Gretchen Marcus, Director of the Academic Center for Excellence

Hood College

Frederick, MD

Address: 401 Rosemont Avenue, Frederick, MD, 21701
Admissions telephone: 800 922-1599
Admissions FAX: 301 696-3819
Dean of Admissions: Susan Hallenbeck
Admissions e-mail: admissions@hood.edu
Web site: http://www.hood.edu
SAT Code: 5296 ACT Code: 1702

LD program name: Disability Services
Disability Services Coordinator: Tom Kranz
LD program telephone: 301 696-3421
LD program e-mail: kranz@hood.edu
LD program enrollment: 21, Total campus enrollment: 1,027

GENERAL

Hood College is a private, women's, four-year institution. 50-acre campus in Frederick (population: 52,767), 40 miles northwest of Washington, DC, and 45 miles west of Baltimore. Served by bus; major airports and train serve Baltimore and Washington, DC. School operates transportation to Washington, DC metro shuttle and subway stops, and to airports for semester breaks. Semester system.

LD ADMISSIONS

Students do not complete a separate application and are not simultaneously accepted to the LD program. A member of the LD program does not sit on the admissions committee. A personal interview is recommended. Essay is required and may be typed.

For fall 2004, 7 completed self-identified LD applications were received.

SECONDARY SCHOOL REQUIREMENTS

Graduation from secondary school required; GED accepted. The following course distribution required: 4 units of English, 3 units of math, 3 units of science, 2 units of foreign language, 3 units of social studies, 1 unit of academic electives.

TESTING

SAT Reasoning required; ACT may be substituted. SAT Subject recommended.

All enrolled freshmen (fall 2004):

Average SAT I Scores:	Verbal: 555	Math: 541
Average ACT Scores:	Composite: 23	

Child Study Team report is not required. A neuropsychological or comprehensive psycho-educational evaluation is required for admission. Must be dated within 36 months of application. Tests required as part of this documentation:

■ WAIS-IV	■ Woodcock-Johnson
■ WISC-IV	☐ Nelson-Denny Reading Test
☐ SATA	☐ Other

UNDERGRADUATE STUDENT BODY

Total undergraduate student enrollment: 97 Men, 687 Women.

Composition of student body (fall 2004):

	Undergraduate	Freshmen
International	2.1	3.7
Black	11.9	11.6
American Indian	0.4	0.3
Asian-American	2.5	1.9
Hispanic	4.9	2.4
White	71.2	70.1
Unreported	7.0	10.0
	100.0%	100.0%

23% are from out of state. Average age of full-time undergraduates is 21. 67% of classes have fewer than 20 students, 33% have between 20 and 50 students.

STUDENT HOUSING

83% of freshmen live in college housing. Freshmen are required to live on campus. Housing is guaranteed for all undergraduates. Campus can house 646 undergraduates. Single rooms are available for students with medical or special needs. A medical note is required.

EXPENSES

Tuition (2005-06): $22,000 per year.
Room: $4,050. Board: $3,700.
There is no additional cost for LD program/services.

LD SERVICES

LD program size is not limited.

LD services available to:

■ Freshmen ■ Sophomores ■ Juniors ■ Seniors

Academic Accommodations

Curriculum		**In class**	
Foreign language waiver	☐	Early syllabus	☐
Lighter course load	■	Note takers in class	■
Math waiver	☐	Priority seating	■
Other special classes	■	Tape recorders	■
Priority registrations	☐	Videotaped classes	☐
Substitution of courses	■	Text on tape	☐
Exams		**Services**	
Extended time	■	Diagnostic tests	☐
Oral exams	■	Learning centers	☐
Take home exams	■	Proofreaders	☐
Exams on tape or computer	■	Readers	☐
Untimed exams	■	Reading Machines/Kurzweil	■
Other accommodations	■	Special bookstore section	☐
		Typists	■

Credit toward degree is not given for remedial courses taken.

Counseling Services

☐ Academic
☐ Psychological
☐ Student Support groups
☐ Vocational

Tutoring

Individual tutoring is available daily.

	Individual	Group
Time management	☐	☐
Organizational skills	☐	☐
Learning strategies	☐	☐
Study skills	☐	☐
Content area	■	☐
Writing lab	■	☐
Math lab	■	☐

We work with students on a case-by-case basis.

LD PROGRAM STAFF

There is an advisor/advocate from the LD program available to students. Five peer tutors are available to work with LD students.

Key staff person available to work with LD students: Tom Kranz, Disability Services Coordinator

LD Program web site: http://www.hood.edu/academic/services/ds/

The Johns Hopkins University

Baltimore, MD

Address: 3400 North Charles Street, Baltimore, MD, 21218
Admissions telephone: 410 516-8171
Admissions FAX: 410 516-6025
Interim Director of Undergraduate Admissions: John Latting
Admissions e-mail: gotojhu@jhu.edu
Web site: http://www.jhu.edu
SAT Code: 5332   ACT Code: 1704

LD program name: Disability Services
Associate Director Disability Services: Peggy Hayeslip
LD program telephone: 410 516-8075
LD program e-mail: phayeslip@jhu.edu
LD program enrollment: 85, Total campus enrollment: 5,454

GENERAL

The Johns Hopkins University is a private, coed, four-year institution. 140-acre campus in Baltimore (population: 651,154); branch campuses in East Baltimore and Washington, DC. Served by air, bus, and train; airport also serves Washington, DC (40 miles). School operates transportation to area schools, John Hopkins Medical Sch, Peabody Conservatory, and train station. Public transportation serves campus. Semester system.

LD ADMISSIONS

A personal interview is not required. Essay is required and may be typed.

SECONDARY SCHOOL REQUIREMENTS

Graduation from secondary school not required. The following course distribution required: 4 units of English, 3 units of math, 3 units of science, 3 units of social studies.

TESTING

SAT Reasoning required; ACT may be substituted. SAT Subject recommended.

All enrolled freshmen (fall 2004):

Average SAT I Scores:	Verbal: 680	Math: 706
Average ACT Scores:	Composite: 29	

Child Study Team report is not required. Tests required as part of this documentation:

- ☐ WAIS-IV
- ☐ WISC-IV
- ☐ SATA
- ☐ Woodcock-Johnson
- ☐ Nelson-Denny Reading Test
- ☐ Other

UNDERGRADUATE STUDENT BODY

Total undergraduate student enrollment: 2,342 Men, 1,619 Women.

Composition of student body (fall 2004):

	Undergraduate	Freshmen
International	5.9	5.1
Black	6.0	6.2
American Indian	0.7	0.4
Asian-American	22.3	19.2
Hispanic	6.5	4.8
White	58.6	64.3
Unreported	0.0	0.0
	100.0%	100.0%

78% are from out of state. 22% join a fraternity and 20% join a sorority. Average age of full-time undergraduates is 20. 55% of classes have fewer than 20 students, 28% have between 20 and 50 students, 17% have more than 50 students.

STUDENT HOUSING

100% of freshmen live in college housing. Freshmen are required to live on campus. Housing is not guaranteed for all undergraduates. Campus can house 2,115 undergraduates. Single rooms are available for students with medical or special needs. A medical note is required.

EXPENSES

Tuition (2005-06): $31,620 per year.
Room: $5,698. Board: $4,226.
There is no additional cost for LD program/services.

LD SERVICES

LD program size is not limited.

LD services available to:

■ Freshmen ■ Sophomores ■ Juniors ■ Seniors

Academic Accommodations

Curriculum		**In class**	
Foreign language waiver	☐	Early syllabus	☐
Lighter course load	■	Note takers in class	■
Math waiver	☐	Priority seating	■
Other special classes	☐	Tape recorders	■
Priority registrations	■	Videotaped classes	☐
Substitution of courses	■	Text on tape	■
Exams		**Services**	
Extended time	■	Diagnostic tests	☐
Oral exams	■	Learning centers	☐
Take home exams	☐	Proofreaders	☐
Exams on tape or computer	■	Readers	■
Untimed exams	■	Reading Machines/Kurzweil	■
Other accommodations	■	Special bookstore section	☐
		Typists	■

Credit toward degree is not given for remedial courses taken.

Counseling Services

- ■ Academic
- ■ Psychological
- ☐ Student Support groups
- ☐ Vocational

Tutoring

Individual tutoring is available weekly.

Average size of tutoring groups: 1

	Individual	Group
Time management	■	☐
Organizational skills	■	☐
Learning strategies	■	☐
Study skills	■	☐
Content area	■	■
Writing lab	■	☐
Math lab	■	☐

LD PROGRAM STAFF

Total number of LD Program staff (including director):

Full Time: 1   Part Time: 1

There is an advisor/advocate from the LD program available to students.

Key staff person available to work with LD students: Richard J. Sanders, Undergraduate Disability Services Coordinator

Loyola College

Baltimore, MD

Address: 4501 North Charles Street, Baltimore, MD, 21210
Admissions telephone: 800 221-9107
Admissions FAX: 410 617-2176
Dean of Admissions: David duKor-Jackson
Web site: http://www.loyola.edu
SAT Code: 5370 ACT Code: 1708

LD program name: Academic Services
Assistant Director: Stacey Grady
LD program telephone: 410 617-2663
LD program e-mail: sgrady@loyola.edu
LD program enrollment: 124, Total campus enrollment: 3,441

GENERAL

Loyola College is a private, coed, four-year institution. 89-acre, suburban campus in Baltimore (population: 651,154); branch campuses in Columbia and Timonium. Served by air, bus, and train. School operates shuttle bus to off-campus parking facilities. Public transportation serves campus. Semester system.

LD ADMISSIONS

Application Deadline: 01/15. Students do not complete a separate application and are not simultaneously accepted to the LD program. A member of the LD program does not sit on the admissions committee. A personal interview is recommended. Essay is required and may be typed.

For fall 2004, 30 completed self-identified LD applications were received.

SECONDARY SCHOOL REQUIREMENTS

Graduation from secondary school required; GED accepted. The following course distribution required: 4 units of English, 3 units of math, 3 units of science, 3 units of foreign language, 2 units of history.

TESTING

SAT Reasoning required; ACT may be substituted. SAT Subject recommended.

All enrolled freshmen (fall 2004):

Average SAT I Scores:	Verbal: 606	Math: 610
Average ACT Scores:	Composite: 27	

Child Study Team report is not required. A neuropsychological or comprehensive psycho-educational evaluation is required for admission. Tests required as part of this documentation:

- ■ WAIS-IV
- ■ WISC-IV
- ☐ SATA
- ■ Woodcock-Johnson
- ☐ Nelson-Denny Reading Test
- ☐ Other

UNDERGRADUATE STUDENT BODY

Total undergraduate student enrollment: 1,483 Men, 1,994 Women.

Composition of student body (fall 2004):

	Undergraduate	Freshmen
International	0.3	0.6
Black	5.2	4.9
American Indian	0.0	0.0
Asian-American	2.1	1.8
Hispanic	2.6	2.1
White	86.7	87.3
Unreported	3.1	3.3
	100.0%	100.0%

77% are from out of state. Average age of full-time undergraduates is 20. 43% of classes have fewer than 20 students, 56% have between 20 and 50 students, 1% have more than 50 students.

STUDENT HOUSING

98% of freshmen live in college housing. Freshmen are not required to live on campus. Housing is not guaranteed for all undergraduates. Campus can house 2,798 undergraduates. Single rooms are not available for students with medical or special needs.

EXPENSES

Tuition (2005-06): $29,500 per year. $20,973 per year, $22,930 for freshmen.
Room & Board: $8,435-$9,200.
There is no additional cost for LD program/services.

LD SERVICES

LD program size is not limited.

LD services available to:

■ Freshmen ■ Sophomores ■ Juniors ■ Seniors

Academic Accommodations

Curriculum		**In class**	
Foreign language waiver	☐	Early syllabus	☐
Lighter course load	■	Note takers in class	■
Math waiver	☐	Priority seating	☐
Other special classes	☐	Tape recorders	■
Priority registrations	☐	Videotaped classes	☐
Substitution of courses	☐	Text on tape	☐
Exams		**Services**	
Extended time	■	Diagnostic tests	☐
Oral exams	■	Learning centers	☐
Take home exams	☐	Proofreaders	☐
Exams on tape or computer	☐	Readers	■
Untimed exams	☐	Reading Machines/Kurzweil	■
Other accommodations	☐	Special bookstore section	☐
		Typists	☐

Credit toward degree is not given for remedial courses taken.

Counseling Services

- ■ Academic
- ☐ Psychological
- ■ Student Support groups
- ☐ Vocational

Tutoring

Individual tutoring is available weekly.

Average size of tutoring groups: 4

	Individual	Group
Time management	■	☐
Organizational skills	■	☐
Learning strategies	■	☐
Study skills	■	☐
Content area	☐	☐
Writing lab	☐	☐
Math lab	☐	☐

LD PROGRAM STAFF

Total number of LD Program staff (including director):

Full Time: 1 Part Time: 1

There is an advisor/advocate from the LD program available to students. Three graduate students are available to work with LD students.

Key staff person available to work with LD students: Stacey Grady, Assistant Director

University of Maryland Baltimore County

Baltimore, MD

Address: 1000 Hilltop Circle, Baltimore, MD, 21250
Admissions telephone: 800 UMBC-4U2
Admissions FAX: 410 455-1094
Director of Admissions: Yvette Mozie-Ross
Admissions e-mail: admissions@umbc.edu
Web site: http://www.umbc.edu
SAT Code: 5835 ACT Code: 1751

LD program name: Student Support Services
Director, Student Support Services: Cynthia M. Hill
LD program telephone: 410 455-2459
LD program e-mail: chill@umbc.edu
LD program enrollment: 100, Total campus enrollment: 9,668

GENERAL

University of Maryland Baltimore County is a public, coed, four-year institution. 500-acre, suburban campus in Catonsville (population: 39,820), five miles from downtown Baltimore and 40 miles from Washington, DC; branch campus in Shady Grove. Major airport, bus, and train serve Baltimore; other major airport serves Washington, DC. Public transportation serves campus. School operates transportation to surrounding communities and to the schools and campuses of U of Maryland--Baltimore. 4-1-4 system.

LD ADMISSIONS

A personal interview is not required. Essay is required and may be typed. Upon request by student, admissions committee can review/consider student under an Individual Admission (IA) process with appropriate LD documentation. Upon admission, there are provisions made for LD students who can provide documentation with reference to trouble with the foreign language requirement.

SECONDARY SCHOOL REQUIREMENTS

Graduation from secondary school required; GED not accepted. The following course distribution required: 4 units of English, 3 units of math, 3 units of science, 2 units of foreign language, 2 units of social studies, 2 units of history, 4 units of academic electives.

TESTING

SAT Reasoning or ACT required. SAT Subject recommended.

All enrolled freshmen (fall 2004):

Average SAT I Scores:	Verbal: 597	Math: 624
Average ACT Scores:	Composite: 25	

Child Study Team report is not required. Tests required as part of this documentation:

- ☐ WAIS-IV
- ☐ WISC-IV
- ☐ SATA
- ☐ Woodcock-Johnson
- ☐ Nelson-Denny Reading Test
- ☐ Other

UNDERGRADUATE STUDENT BODY

Total undergraduate student enrollment: 4,694 Men, 4,634 Women.

Composition of student body (fall 2004):

	Undergraduate	Freshmen
International	3.1	4.3
Black	9.4	14.5
American Indian	0.4	0.4
Asian-American	21.3	19.8
Hispanic	2.7	3.3
White	61.6	56.2
Unreported	1.5	1.5
	100.0%	100.0%

8% are from out of state. 4% join a fraternity and 4% join a sorority. Average age of full-time undergraduates is 21. 41% of classes have fewer than 20 students, 47% have between 20 and 50 students, 12% have more than 50 students.

STUDENT HOUSING

74% of freshmen live in college housing. Freshmen are not required to live on campus. Housing is guaranteed for all undergraduates. Campus can house 3,850 undergraduates. Single rooms are available for students with medical or special needs. A medical note is required.

EXPENSES

Tuition (2005-06): $6,484 per year (in-state), $14,560 (out-of-state).
Room: $5,204. Board: $3,160.
There is no additional cost for LD program/services.

LD SERVICES

LD program size is not limited.

LD services available to:

■ Freshmen ■ Sophomores ■ Juniors ■ Seniors

Academic Accommodations

Curriculum		In class	
Foreign language waiver	☐	Early syllabus	☐
Lighter course load	☐	Note takers in class	■
Math waiver	☐	Priority seating	■
Other special classes	☐	Tape recorders	■
Priority registrations	■	Videotaped classes	■
Substitution of courses	■	Text on tape	☐
Exams		**Services**	
Extended time	■	Diagnostic tests	☐
Oral exams	■	Learning centers	■
Take home exams	☐	Proofreaders	☐
Exams on tape or computer	■	Readers	■
Untimed exams	■	Reading Machines/Kurzweil	☐
Other accommodations	■	Special bookstore section	☐
		Typists	■

Credit toward degree is not given for remedial courses taken.

Counseling Services

- ■ Academic
- ☐ Psychological
- ☐ Student Support groups
- ☐ Vocational

Tutoring

Individual tutoring is available weekly.

Average size of tutoring groups: 1

	Individual	Group
Time management	■	☐
Organizational skills	■	☐
Learning strategies	■	☐
Study skills	■	☐
Content area	■	☐
Writing lab	■	☐
Math lab	■	☐

LD PROGRAM STAFF

Total number of LD Program staff (including director):

Full Time: 5 Part Time: 5

There is an advisor/advocate from the LD program available to students. One graduate student and 30 peer tutors are available to work with LD students.

Key staff person available to work with LD students: Cynthia M. Hill, Director, Student Support Services

University of Maryland, College Park

College Park, MD

Address: College Park, MD, 20742-5025
Admissions telephone: 800 422-5867
Admissions FAX: 301 314-9693
Director of Undergraduate Admissions: Barbara Gill
Admissions e-mail: um-admit@uga.umd.edu
Web site: http://www.maryland.edu
SAT Code: 5814 ACT Code: 1746

LD program name: Disability Support Services
LD program address: 0126 Shoemaker Building
Coordinator, DSS-LD Services: Diane Hallila
LD program telephone: 301 314-9969
LD program e-mail: dhallila@umd.edu
Total campus enrollment: 25,065

GENERAL

University of Maryland, College Park is a public, coed, four-year institution. 1,212-acre campus in College Park (population: 24,657), nine miles from downtown Washington, DC, plus 2,438-acre agricultural extension; branch campus in Shady Grove. Served by train; major airport and bus serve Washington, DC; other airport serves Baltimore (20 miles). School operates transportation around College Park and to Greenbelt and Landover. Public transportation serves campus. Semester system.

LD ADMISSIONS

Students do not complete a separate application and are not simultaneously accepted to the LD program. A member of the LD program does sit on the admissions committee. A personal interview is recommended. Essay is required and may be typed.

SECONDARY SCHOOL REQUIREMENTS

Graduation from secondary school required; GED accepted. The following course distribution required: 4 units of English, 3 units of math, 3 units of science, 2 units of foreign language, 3 units of social studies.

TESTING

SAT Reasoning required; ACT may be substituted. SAT Subject required.

Child Study Team report is not required. A neuropsychological or comprehensive psycho-educational evaluation is required for admission. Must be dated within 36 months of application. Tests required as part of this documentation:

- ■ WAIS-IV
- ■ WISC-IV
- ☐ SATA
- ■ Woodcock-Johnson
- ■ Nelson-Denny Reading Test
- ■ Other

UNDERGRADUATE STUDENT BODY

Total undergraduate student enrollment: 12,899 Men, 12,200 Women.

Composition of student body (fall 2004):

	Undergraduate	Freshmen
International	1.6	2.3
Black	12.3	12.1
American Indian	0.4	0.3
Asian-American	13.4	13.8
Hispanic	5.3	5.6
White	58.2	58.4
Unreported	8.8	7.5
	100.0%	100.0%

26% are from out of state. 11% join a fraternity and 11% join a sorority. Average age of full-time undergraduates is 20. 36% of classes have fewer than 20 students, 48% have between 20 and 50 students, 16% have more than 50 students.

STUDENT HOUSING

89% of freshmen live in college housing. Freshmen are not required to live on campus. Housing is not guaranteed for all undergraduates. Housing is not available beyond the third year. Campus can house 12,157 undergraduates. Single rooms are available for students with medical or special needs. A medical note is required.

EXPENSES

Tuition (2005-06): $6,566 per year (in-state), $18,890 (out-of-state).

Room: $4,784. Board: $3,291.

There is no additional cost for LD program/services.

LD SERVICES

LD program size is not limited.

LD services available to:

■ Freshmen ■ Sophomores ■ Juniors ■ Seniors

Academic Accommodations

Curriculum		In class	
Foreign language waiver	☐	Early syllabus	■
Lighter course load	■	Note takers in class	■
Math waiver	☐	Priority seating	■
Other special classes	☐	Tape recorders	■
Priority registrations	■	Videotaped classes	☐
Substitution of courses	■	Text on tape	☐
Exams		**Services**	
Extended time	■	Diagnostic tests	☐
Oral exams	■	Learning centers	■
Take home exams	■	Proofreaders	■
Exams on tape or computer	■	Readers	■
Untimed exams	☐	Reading Machines/Kurzweil	■
Other accommodations	☐	Special bookstore section	☐
		Typists	■

Credit toward degree is not given for remedial courses taken.

Counseling Services

- ■ Academic
- ■ Psychological — Meets 12 times per academic year
- ■ Student Support groups
- ■ Vocational

Tutoring

Individual tutoring is not available.

	Individual	Group
Time management	■	■
Organizational skills	■	■
Learning strategies	■	■
Study skills	■	■
Content area	☐	☐
Writing lab	■	■
Math lab	■	■

LD PROGRAM STAFF

Total number of LD Program staff (including director):

Full Time: 2 Part Time: 2

There is an advisor/advocate from the LD program available to students. The advisor/advocate meets with students three times per month. Four graduate students are available to work with LD students.

Key staff person available to work with LD students: Diane Hallila, Coordinator, DSS-LD Services

University of Maryland Eastern Shore

Princess Anne, MD

Address: J.T. Williams Hall, Room 2106, Princess Anne, MD, 21853
Admissions telephone: 410 651-6410
Admissions FAX: 410 651-7922
Acting Director of Admissions: Cheryll Collier-Mills
Admissions e-mail: umesadmissions@umes.edu
Web site: http://www.umes.edu
SAT Code: 5400 ACT Code: 1752

Coordinator: Dorling Joseph
LD program telephone: 410 651-6461
LD program e-mail: djoseph@mail.umes.edu
Total campus enrollment: 2,969

GENERAL

University of Maryland Eastern Shore is a public, coed, four-year institution. 620-acre campus in Princess Anne (population: 2,313), 12 miles from Salisbury (metropolitan population: 42,000). Served by bus; airport serves Salisbury; major airport and train serve Baltimore (125 miles). School operates transportation to Salisbury. Semester system.

LD ADMISSIONS

A personal interview is recommended. Essay is not required.

SECONDARY SCHOOL REQUIREMENTS

Graduation from secondary school required; GED accepted. The following course distribution required: 4 units of English, 3 units of math, 2 units of science, 2 units of foreign language, 3 units of social studies.

TESTING

Child Study Team report is not required. Tests required as part of this documentation:

- [ ] WAIS-IV
- [ ] WISC-IV
- [ ] SATA
- [ ] Woodcock-Johnson
- [ ] Nelson-Denny Reading Test
- [ ] Other

UNDERGRADUATE STUDENT BODY

Total undergraduate student enrollment: 1,255 Men, 1,714 Women.

26% are from out of state.

STUDENT HOUSING

Housing is guaranteed for all undergraduates. Campus can house 2,092 undergraduates.

EXPENSES

Tuition (2005-06): $4,112 per year (in-state), $10,268 (out-of-state).
Room: $3,430. Board: $2,700.
There is no additional cost for LD program/services.

LD SERVICES

LD program size is not limited.

LD services available to:

- [ ] Freshmen
- [ ] Sophomores
- [ ] Juniors
- [ ] Seniors

Academic Accommodations

Curriculum		**In class**	
Foreign language waiver	[ ]	Early syllabus	[ ]
Lighter course load	[ ]	Note takers in class	[x]
Math waiver	[ ]	Priority seating	[ ]
Other special classes	[ ]	Tape recorders	[x]
Priority registrations	[ ]	Videotaped classes	[ ]
Substitution of courses	[ ]	Text on tape	[ ]
Exams		**Services**	
Extended time	[x]	Diagnostic tests	[ ]
Oral exams	[ ]	Learning centers	[ ]
Take home exams	[ ]	Proofreaders	[ ]
Exams on tape or computer	[ ]	Readers	[ ]
Untimed exams	[x]	Reading Machines/Kurzweil	[ ]
Other accommodations	[ ]	Special bookstore section	[ ]
		Typists	[ ]

Credit toward degree is not given for remedial courses taken.

Counseling Services

- [ ] Academic
- [ ] Psychological
- [ ] Student Support groups
- [ ] Vocational

Tutoring

	Individual	Group
Time management	[ ]	[ ]
Organizational skills	[ ]	[ ]
Learning strategies	[ ]	[ ]
Study skills	[ ]	[ ]
Content area	[ ]	[ ]
Writing lab	[ ]	[ ]
Math lab	[ ]	[ ]

LD PROGRAM STAFF

Total number of LD Program staff (including director):

Full Time: 1 Part Time: 1

Key staff person available to work with LD students: Dorling Joseph, Coordinator, Services for Students with Disabilities

University of Maryland University College

Adelphi, MD

Address: 3501 University Boulevard East, Adelphi, MD, 20783
Admissions telephone: 800 888-UMUC
Admissions FAX: 301 985-7364
Technical Director, Admissions: Anne Rahill
Admissions e-mail: umucinfo@umuc.edu
Web site: http://umuc.edu/
SAT Code: 551

Technical Director: Noelle Atwell
LD program telephone: 301 985-7260
LD program e-mail: natwell@umuc.edu
Total campus enrollment: 19,857

GENERAL

University of Maryland University College is a public, coed, four-year institution. Suburban campus in College Park (population: 24,657), 10 miles from Washington, DC; branch campuses in Annapolis, Shady Grove, and Waldorf. Served by bus; airports and train serve Washington, DC. Public transportation serves campus. Semester system.

LD ADMISSIONS

A personal interview is not required. Essay is not required.

SECONDARY SCHOOL REQUIREMENTS

Graduation from secondary school required; GED accepted.

TESTING

Child Study Team report is not required. Tests required as part of this documentation:

- [ ] WAIS-IV
- [ ] WISC-IV
- [ ] SATA
- [ ] Woodcock-Johnson
- [ ] Nelson-Denny Reading Test
- [ ] Other

UNDERGRADUATE STUDENT BODY

Total undergraduate student enrollment: 6,721 Men, 9,341 Women.

Composition of student body (fall 2004):

	Undergraduate	Freshmen
International	0.9	1.6
Black	39.2	33.6
American Indian	0.8	0.8
Asian-American	3.4	5.1
Hispanic	6.8	5.0
White	40.3	45.8
Unreported	8.6	8.1
	100.0%	100.0%

29% are from out of state. Average age of full-time undergraduates is 29. 47% of classes have fewer than 20 students, 53% have between 20 and 50 students.

EXPENSES

Tuition (2005-06): $5,520 per year (in-state), $10,152 (out-of-state).
There is no additional cost for LD program/services.

LD SERVICES

LD program size is not limited.

LD services available to:

- [x] Freshmen
- [x] Sophomores
- [x] Juniors
- [x] Seniors

Academic Accommodations

Curriculum		**In class**	
Foreign language waiver	[ ]	Early syllabus	[ ]
Lighter course load	[x]	Note takers in class	[x]
Math waiver	[ ]	Priority seating	[ ]
Other special classes	[ ]	Tape recorders	[x]
Priority registrations	[ ]	Videotaped classes	[ ]
Substitution of courses	[ ]	Text on tape	[ ]
Exams		**Services**	
Extended time	[ ]	Diagnostic tests	[ ]
Oral exams	[x]	Learning centers	[ ]
Take home exams	[ ]	Proofreaders	[ ]
Exams on tape or computer	[ ]	Readers	[x]
Untimed exams	[x]	Reading Machines/Kurzweil	[ ]
Other accommodations	[ ]	Special bookstore section	[ ]
		Typists	[ ]

Credit toward degree is not given for remedial courses taken.

Counseling Services

- [ ] Academic
- [ ] Psychological
- [ ] Student Support groups
- [ ] Vocational

Tutoring

	Individual	Group
Time management	[ ]	[ ]
Organizational skills	[ ]	[ ]
Learning strategies	[ ]	[ ]
Study skills	[ ]	[ ]
Content area	[ ]	[ ]
Writing lab	[ ]	[ ]
Math lab	[ ]	[ ]

LD PROGRAM STAFF

Total number of LD Program staff (including director):

Full Time: 1 Part Time: 1

There is an advisor/advocate from the LD program available to students.

Key staff person available to work with LD students: Noelle Atwell, Technical Director, Veteran & Disabled Student Services

McDaniel College

Westminster, MD

Address: 2 College Hill, Westminster, MD, 21157
Admissions telephone: 800 638-5005
Admissions FAX: 410 857-2757
Dean of Admissions: Martha O'Connell
Admissions e-mail: admissions@mcdaniel.edu
Web site: http://www.mcdaniel.edu
SAT Code: 5898 ACT Code: 1756

LD program name: Academic Skills Program
Director: Kevin Selby
LD program telephone: 410 857-2479
LD program e-mail: kselby@mcdaniel.edu
LD program enrollment: 141, Total campus enrollment: 1,619

GENERAL

McDaniel College is a private, coed, four-year institution. 160-acre campus in Westminster (population: 16,731), 35 miles from Baltimore and 55 miles from Washington, DC; branch campus abroad in Budapest, Hungary. Served by bus; major airport and train serve Baltimore; other airport also serves Washington, DC. School operates transportation to Baltimore. 4-1-4 system.

LD ADMISSIONS

Students do not complete a separate application and are simultaneously accepted to the LD program. A member of the LD program does not sit on the admissions committee. High school waivers are accepted for foreign language. A personal interview is not required. Essay is required and may be typed.

SECONDARY SCHOOL REQUIREMENTS

Graduation from secondary school required; GED accepted. The following course distribution required: 4 units of English, 3 units of math, 3 units of science, 3 units of foreign language, 2 units of social studies, 2 units of history.

TESTING

SAT Reasoning or ACT required of some applicants. SAT Subject recommended.

All enrolled freshmen (fall 2004):

Average SAT I Scores: Verbal: 555 Math: 555

Child Study Team report is not required. A neuropsychological or comprehensive psycho-educational evaluation is required for admission. Must be dated within 36 months of application. Tests required as part of this documentation:

- [x] WAIS-IV
- [x] WISC-IV
- [ ] SATA
- [x] Woodcock-Johnson
- [ ] Nelson-Denny Reading Test
- [ ] Other

UNDERGRADUATE STUDENT BODY

Total undergraduate student enrollment: 721 Men, 920 Women.

Composition of student body (fall 2004):

	Undergraduate	Freshmen
International	0.3	1.3
Black	5.9	8.3
American Indian	1.4	0.9
Asian-American	2.5	1.6
Hispanic	1.7	1.5
White	82.9	80.4
Unreported	5.3	6.0
	100.0%	100.0%

30% are from out of state. 18% join a fraternity and 22% join a sorority. Average age of full-time undergraduates is 20. 64% of classes have fewer than 20 students, 36% have between 20 and 50 students.

STUDENT HOUSING

91% of freshmen live in college housing. Freshmen are required to live on campus. Housing is guaranteed for all undergraduates. Campus can house 1,315 undergraduates. Single rooms are available for students with medical or special needs. A medical note is required.

EXPENSES

Tuition (2005-06): $24,500 per year.
Room: $3,000. Board: $2,600.
Additional cost for LD program/services: $1,500 per year.

LD SERVICES

LD program size is not limited.

LD services available to:

- [x] Freshmen
- [x] Sophomores
- [x] Juniors
- [x] Seniors

Academic Accommodations

Curriculum		In class	
Foreign language waiver	[ ]	Early syllabus	[ ]
Lighter course load	[ ]	Note takers in class	[x]
Math waiver	[ ]	Priority seating	[ ]
Other special classes	[ ]	Tape recorders	[x]
Priority registrations	[ ]	Videotaped classes	[ ]
Substitution of courses	[x]	Text on tape	[x]
Exams		**Services**	
Extended time	[x]	Diagnostic tests	[ ]
Oral exams	[ ]	Learning centers	[x]
Take home exams	[ ]	Proofreaders	[ ]
Exams on tape or computer	[ ]	Readers	[x]
Untimed exams	[ ]	Reading Machines/Kurzweil	[x]
Other accommodations	[ ]	Special bookstore section	[ ]
		Typists	[ ]

Credit toward degree is not given for remedial courses taken.

Counseling Services

- [x] Academic — Meets 29 times per academic year
- [ ] Psychological
- [ ] Student Support groups
- [ ] Vocational

Tutoring

Individual tutoring is available weekly.

	Individual	Group
Time management	[x]	[ ]
Organizational skills	[x]	[ ]
Learning strategies	[x]	[ ]
Study skills	[x]	[ ]
Content area	[ ]	[ ]
Writing lab	[x]	[ ]
Math lab	[ ]	[ ]

LD PROGRAM STAFF

Total number of LD Program staff (including director):

Full Time: 2 Part Time: 2

There is an advisor/advocate from the LD program available to students. The advisor/advocate meets with students three times per month. Three graduate students are available to work with LD students.

Key staff person available to work with LD students: Kevin Selby, Director, Student Academic Support Services

Montgomery College-Rockville Campus

Baltimore, MD

Address: 51 Mannakee Street, Rockville, MD 20850
Admissions telephone: 301 279-5034
Director of Communications: Steve Simon
Web site: http://www.montgomerycollege.edu
SAT Code: 5440

LD program name: College Access Program
Director, Disability Support Services: Brenda Williams
LD program telephone: 301 279-5050
LD program enrollment: 490

GENERAL

Montgomery College-Rockville is a public, coed, two-year institution. Campus in Rockville (population: 47,388), fifteen miles from Washington, DC. Major airport serves Washington DC (25 miles); train serves Gaithersburg (10 miles).

LD ADMISSIONS

Separate application is required for admission but students are not simultaneously accepted to the institution and LD program. A member of the LD program does sit on the admissions committee. A personal interview is required. Essay is required and may be typed.

SECONDARY SCHOOL REQUIREMENTS

Graduation from secondary school required; GED is accepted.

TESTING

Child Study Team report is not required. IEP and 504 Plan are required. Tests required as part of this documentation:

- ■ WAIS-IV
- ☐ WISC-IV
- ☐ SATA
- ■ Woodcock-Johnson
- ☐ Nelson-Denny Reading Test
- ☐ Other

STUDENT HOUSING

There is no campus housing.

EXPENSES

Tuition 2004-05: $3,564 (state residents, in-district), $6,948 (state residents, out-of-district), $9,180 (out-of-state).

There are no additional costs for LD program/services.

LD SERVICES

LD program size is limited to approximately 30 students per semester.

LD services available to:

■ Freshmen ■ Sophomores ■ Juniors ■ Seniors

Academic Accommodations

Curriculum		**In class**	
Foreign language waiver	☐	Early syllabus	■
Lighter course load	■	Note takers in class	■
Math waiver	■	Priority seating	■
Other special classes	■	Tape recorders	■
Priority registrations	☐	Videotaped classes	■
Substitution of courses	■	Text on tape	■
Exams		**Services**	
Extended time	■	Diagnostic tests	☐
Oral exams	☐	Learning centers	■
Take home exams	☐	Proofreaders	■
Exams on tape or computer	■	Readers	■
Untimed exams	■	Reading Machines/Kurzweil	☐
Other accommodations	■	Special bookstore section	☐
		Typists	■

Credit toward degree is not given for remedial courses taken.

Counseling Services

- ■ Academic
- ■ Psychological
- ■ Student Support groups
- ☐ Vocational

Tutoring

Individual tutoring is available daily.

Average size of tutoring groups: 5-12

	Individual	Group
Time management	■	■
Organizational skills	■	■
Learning strategies	■	■
Study skills	☐	■
Content area	☐	■
Writing lab	☐	■
Math lab	☐	■

LD PROGRAM STAFF

Total number of LD Program staff (including director):

Full Time: 4

There is an advisor/advocate from the LD program available to students.

Key staff person available to work with LD students: Brenda C. Williams, Director, Disability Support Services

Morgan State University

Baltimore, MD

Address: 1700 East Cold Spring Lane, Baltimore, MD, 21251
Admissions telephone: 800 332-6674
Admissions FAX: 443 885-3684
Director of Admissions and Recruitment: Edwin Johnson
Web site: http://www.morgan.edu
SAT Code: 5416 ACT Code: 1722

Director: Nina Hopkins
LD program telephone: 443 885-3103
LD program e-mail: nhopkins@moac.morgan.edu
LD program enrollment: 45, Total campus enrollment: 6,244

GENERAL

Morgan State University is a public, coed, four-year institution. 125-acre, suburban campus in Baltimore (population: 651,154), 45 miles from Washington, DC. Served by air, bus, and train. School operates transportation on campus. Public transportation serves campus.

LD ADMISSIONS

A member of the LD program does not sit on the admissions committee. A personal interview is not required. Essay is not required.

For fall 2004, 20 completed self-identified LD applications were received.

SECONDARY SCHOOL REQUIREMENTS

Graduation from secondary school required; GED accepted. The following course distribution required: 4 units of English, 3 units of math, 3 units of science, 2 units of foreign language, 3 units of social studies, 3 units of history, 3 units of academic electives.

TESTING

SAT Reasoning or ACT required. SAT Subject recommended.

All enrolled freshmen (fall 2004):

Average SAT I Scores: Verbal: 453 Math: 451

Child Study Team report is not required. A neuropsychological or comprehensive psycho-educational evaluation is required for admission. Tests required as part of this documentation:

- [x] WAIS-IV
- [ ] WISC-IV
- [ ] SATA
- [x] Woodcock-Johnson
- [ ] Nelson-Denny Reading Test
- [x] Other

UNDERGRADUATE STUDENT BODY

Total undergraduate student enrollment: 6,244.

Composition of student body (fall 2004):

	Undergraduate	Freshmen
International	0.1	2.2
Black	94.4	92.6
American Indian	0.2	0.2
Asian-American	0.7	0.6
Hispanic	0.5	0.5
White	0.7	1.0
Unreported	3.4	2.9
	100.0%	100.0%

33% are from out of state. Average age of full-time undergraduates is 21. 44% of classes have fewer than 20 students, 54% have between 20 and 50 students, 2% have more than 50 students.

STUDENT HOUSING

Freshmen are not required to live on campus. Housing is not guaranteed for all undergraduates. Preference is given to freshmen and students attending on a scholarship. The remainder of housing is assigned by order of receipt of application. Campus can house 2,647 undergraduates.

EXPENSES

Tuition (2005-06): $2,140 per year (in-state), $5,845 (out-of-state).
Room: $2,215. Board: $1,280.
There is no additional cost for LD program/services.

LD SERVICES

LD program size is not limited.

LD services available to:

- [x] Freshmen
- [x] Sophomores
- [x] Juniors
- [x] Seniors

Academic Accommodations

Curriculum		In class	
Foreign language waiver	[ ]	Early syllabus	[ ]
Lighter course load	[x]	Note takers in class	[x]
Math waiver	[ ]	Priority seating	[x]
Other special classes	[x]	Tape recorders	[x]
Priority registrations	[x]	Videotaped classes	[ ]
Substitution of courses	[ ]	Text on tape	[ ]
Exams		**Services**	
Extended time	[x]	Diagnostic tests	[ ]
Oral exams	[x]	Learning centers	[x]
Take home exams	[ ]	Proofreaders	[ ]
Exams on tape or computer	[ ]	Readers	[x]
Untimed exams	[ ]	Reading Machines/Kurzweil	[ ]
Other accommodations	[x]	Special bookstore section	[ ]
		Typists	[ ]

Credit toward degree is not given for remedial courses taken.

Counseling Services

[x]	Academic	Meets 8 times per academic year
[x]	Psychological	Meets 8 times per academic year
[x]	Student Support groups	Meets 4 times per academic year
[x]	Vocational	Meets 4 times per academic year

Tutoring

	Individual	Group
Time management	[ ]	[ ]
Organizational skills	[ ]	[ ]
Learning strategies	[ ]	[ ]
Study skills	[ ]	[ ]
Content area	[ ]	[ ]
Writing lab	[ ]	[ ]
Math lab	[ ]	[ ]

LD PROGRAM STAFF

There is an advisor/advocate from the LD program available to students.
Key staff person available to work with LD students: Nina Hopkins, Director

Mount Saint Mary's University

Emmitsburg, MD

Address: 16300 Old Emmitsburg Road, Emmitsburg, MD, 21727
Admissions telephone: 800 448-4347
Admissions FAX: 301 447-5860
Executive Director of Admissions and Financial Aid: Stephen Neitz
Admissions e-mail: admissions@msmary.edu
Web site: http://www.msmary.edu
SAT Code: 5421 ACT Code: 1726

Director Learning Services: Denise Marjarum
LD program telephone: 301 447-5006
LD program e-mail: marjarum@msmary.edu
Total campus enrollment: 1,612

GENERAL

Mount Saint Mary's University is a private, coed, four-year institution. 1,400-acre campus in Emmitsburg (population: 2,290), 12 miles from Gettysburg, PA and 25 miles from Frederick; branch campus in Frederick. Major airports serve Baltimore (55 miles) and Washington, DC (60 miles); bus serves Gettysburg, PA; train serves Baltimore. Semester system.

LD ADMISSIONS

A personal interview is recommended. Essay is not required.

SECONDARY SCHOOL REQUIREMENTS

Graduation from secondary school required; GED accepted. The following course distribution required: 4 units of English, 3 units of math, 3 units of science, 2 units of foreign language, 3 units of social studies, 1 unit of academic electives.

TESTING

SAT Reasoning required; ACT may be substituted. SAT Subject recommended.

All enrolled freshmen (fall 2004):

Average SAT I Scores: Verbal: 538 Math: 529

Child Study Team report is not required. Tests required as part of this documentation:

- [ ] WAIS-IV
- [ ] WISC-IV
- [ ] SATA
- [ ] Woodcock-Johnson
- [ ] Nelson-Denny Reading Test
- [ ] Other

UNDERGRADUATE STUDENT BODY

Total undergraduate student enrollment: 637 Men, 905 Women.

Composition of student body (fall 2004):

	Undergraduate	Freshmen
International	1.0	0.9
Black	6.9	5.6
American Indian	0.3	0.3
Asian-American	3.6	2.4
Hispanic	4.3	3.2
White	82.6	86.5
Unreported	1.3	1.1
	100.0%	100.0%

41% are from out of state. Average age of full-time undergraduates is 20. 47% of classes have fewer than 20 students, 52% have between 20 and 50 students, 1% have more than 50 students.

STUDENT HOUSING

96% of freshmen live in college housing. Freshmen are required to live on campus. Housing is guaranteed for all undergraduates. Campus can house 1,185 undergraduates. Single rooms are available for students with medical or special needs. A medical note is required.

EXPENSES

Tuition (2005-06): $22,500 per year.

Room: $3,930. Board: $4,100.
There is no additional cost for LD program/services.

LD SERVICES

LD program size is not limited.

LD services available to:

- [x] Freshmen
- [x] Sophomores
- [x] Juniors
- [x] Seniors

Academic Accommodations

Curriculum		In class	
Foreign language waiver	[ ]	Early syllabus	[ ]
Lighter course load	[x]	Note takers in class	[x]
Math waiver	[ ]	Priority seating	[ ]
Other special classes	[ ]	Tape recorders	[x]
Priority registrations	[ ]	Videotaped classes	[ ]
Substitution of courses	[x]	Text on tape	[x]
Exams		**Services**	
Extended time	[x]	Diagnostic tests	[ ]
Oral exams	[x]	Learning centers	[x]
Take home exams	[ ]	Proofreaders	[x]
Exams on tape or computer	[x]	Readers	[x]
Untimed exams	[ ]	Reading Machines/Kurzweil	[x]
Other accommodations	[ ]	Special bookstore section	[ ]
		Typists	[x]

Credit toward degree is not given for remedial courses taken.

Counseling Services

- [x] Academic
- [ ] Psychological
- [ ] Student Support groups
- [ ] Vocational

Tutoring

Individual tutoring is available daily.

	Individual	Group
Time management	[x]	[x]
Organizational skills	[x]	[x]
Learning strategies	[ ]	[x]
Study skills	[x]	[x]
Content area	[x]	[x]
Writing lab	[x]	[x]
Math lab	[ ]	[x]

LD PROGRAM STAFF

Total number of LD Program staff (including director):

Full Time: 2 Part Time: 2

There is an advisor/advocate from the LD program available to students. Two graduate students and 100 peer tutors are available to work with LD students.

Key staff person available to work with LD students: Denise Marjarum, Director Learning Services

College of Notre Dame of Maryland

Baltimore, MD

Address: 4701 North Charles Street, Baltimore, MD, 21210
Admissions telephone: 800 435-0300
Admissions FAX: 410 532-6287
Admissions e-mail: admiss@ndm.edu
Web site: http://www.ndm.edu
SAT Code: 5114 ACT Code: 1727

LD program name: Disability Support Services
LD program address: Theresa Hall
Director: Winifred Daisley, Ph.D.
LD program telephone: 410 532-5379
LD program e-mail: wdaisley@ndm.edu
LD program enrollment: 86, Total campus enrollment: 1,686

GENERAL

College of Notre Dame of Maryland is a private, women's, four-year institution. 58-acre, suburban campus in Baltimore (population: 651,154); satellite campuses at Anne Arundel Comm College, Harford Comm College, Heat Ctr (Harford County), Frederick Comm College, and in southern Maryland. Served by air, bus, and train. School operates transportation to consortium colleges and Towson area. Public transportation serves campus. Semester system.

LD ADMISSIONS

Students do not complete a separate application and are not simultaneously accepted to the LD program. A member of the LD program does not sit on the admissions committee. A personal interview is recommended. Essay is required and may be typed. Documentation on special needs is reviewed and evaluated by the Director of Counseling and necessary accommodations will be made with each individual student based on the testing documentation provided and the interview process. Based on documented LD, some students are evaluated, given a language requirement waiver, and additional courses are assigned to the core requirement. It is recommended that all students with learning disabilities meet with the Director of Counseling to discuss any accommodations needed. This should occur the first semester so as to help students throughout their full program of study at Notre Dame.

SECONDARY SCHOOL REQUIREMENTS

Graduation from secondary school required; GED accepted. The following course distribution required: 4 units of English, 3 units of math, 2 units of science, 3 units of foreign language, 2 units of social studies, 4 units of academic electives.

TESTING

SAT Reasoning required; ACT may be substituted. SAT Subject required.

All enrolled freshmen (fall 2004):

Average SAT I Scores:	Verbal: 535	Math: 504
Average ACT Scores:	Composite: 21	

Child Study Team report is not required. Tests required as part of this documentation:

- [ ] WAIS-IV
- [ ] WISC-IV
- [ ] SATA
- [ ] Woodcock-Johnson
- [ ] Nelson-Denny Reading Test
- [ ] Other

UNDERGRADUATE STUDENT BODY

Total undergraduate student enrollment: 106 Men, 1,824 Women.

Composition of student body (fall 2004):

	Undergraduate	Freshmen
International	0.7	1.6
Black	22.8	26.4
American Indian	0.0	0.5
Asian-American	6.7	2.8
Hispanic	9.4	2.6
White	59.7	65.4
Unreported	0.7	0.7
	100.0%	100.0%

14% are from out of state. Average age of full-time undergraduates is 19. 78% of classes have fewer than 20 students, 22% have between 20 and 50 students.

STUDENT HOUSING

71% of freshmen live in college housing. Freshmen are not required to live on campus. Housing is guaranteed for all undergraduates. Campus can house 406 undergraduates. Single rooms are available for students with medical or special needs. A medical note is required.

EXPENSES

Tuition (2005-06): $21,100 per year.
Room & Board: $8,000.
There is no additional cost for LD program/services.

LD SERVICES

LD program size is not limited.

LD services available to:

- [x] Freshmen
- [x] Sophomores
- [x] Juniors
- [x] Seniors

Academic Accommodations

Curriculum		In class	
Foreign language waiver	[x]	Early syllabus	[x]
Lighter course load	[x]	Note takers in class	[ ]
Math waiver	[ ]	Priority seating	[x]
Other special classes	[ ]	Tape recorders	[x]
Priority registrations	[ ]	Videotaped classes	[ ]
Substitution of courses	[x]	Text on tape	[x]
Exams		**Services**	
Extended time	[x]	Diagnostic tests	[ ]
Oral exams	[x]	Learning centers	[ ]
Take home exams	[ ]	Proofreaders	[x]
Exams on tape or computer	[x]	Readers	[ ]
Untimed exams	[x]	Reading Machines/Kurzweil	[ ]
Other accommodations	[x]	Special bookstore section	[ ]
		Typists	[ ]

Credit toward degree is not given for remedial courses taken.

Counseling Services

[x]	Academic	Meets 6 times per academic year
[x]	Psychological	Meets 25 times per academic year
[x]	Student Support groups	Meets 6 times per academic year
[ ]	Vocational	

Tutoring

Individual tutoring is available weekly.

	Individual	Group
Time management	[x]	[x]
Organizational skills	[x]	[x]
Learning strategies	[x]	[x]
Study skills	[x]	[x]
Content area	[ ]	[ ]
Writing lab	[x]	[ ]
Math lab	[ ]	[ ]

LD PROGRAM STAFF

Total number of LD Program staff (including director):

Full Time: 1 Part Time: 1

There is an advisor/advocate from the LD program available to students. The advisor/advocate meets with faculty and students once per month. Three graduate students are available to work with LD students.

Key staff person available to work with LD students: Winifred Daisley, Ph.D.

Salisbury University

Salisbury, MD

Address: 1101 Camden Avenue, Salisbury, MD, 21801
Admissions telephone: 410 543-6161
Admissions FAX: 410 546-6016
Dean of Enrollment Management: Laura Thorpe
Admissions e-mail: admissions@salisbury.edu
Web site: http://www.salisbury.edu/
SAT Code: 5403 ACT Code: 1716

Executive Administrative Assistant: Lea Wimbrow
LD program telephone: 410 543-6080
LD program e-mail: lmwimbrow@salisbury.edu
LD program enrollment: 157, Total campus enrollment: 6,366

GENERAL

Salisbury University is a public, coed, four-year institution. 144-acre campus in Salisbury (population: 24,000), 100 miles from both Baltimore and Washington, DC. Served by air and bus; major airports serve Baltimore and Washington, DC. School operates transportation to U of Maryland--Eastern Shore, off-campus housing, bus station, and shopping malls. 4-1-4 system.

LD ADMISSIONS

A personal interview is not required. Essay is not required.

SECONDARY SCHOOL REQUIREMENTS

Graduation from secondary school required; GED accepted. The following course distribution required: 4 units of English, 3 units of math, 3 units of science, 2 units of foreign language, 3 units of social studies.

TESTING

SAT Reasoning required; ACT may be substituted. SAT Subject required.

All enrolled freshmen (fall 2004):

Average SAT I Scores: Verbal: 553 Math: 568

Child Study Team report is not required. Tests required as part of this documentation:

- ☐ WAIS-IV
- ☐ WISC-IV
- ☐ SATA
- ☐ Woodcock-Johnson
- ☐ Nelson-Denny Reading Test
- ☐ Other

UNDERGRADUATE STUDENT BODY

Total undergraduate student enrollment: 2,628 Men, 3,432 Women.

Composition of student body (fall 2004):

	Undergraduate	Freshmen
International	0.5	0.5
Black	7.6	8.4
American Indian	0.3	0.4
Asian-American	2.5	2.6
Hispanic	2.3	2.3
White	81.3	80.3
Unreported	5.5	5.5
	100.0%	100.0%

18% are from out of state. 6% join a fraternity and 5% join a sorority. Average age of full-time undergraduates is 21. 30% of classes have fewer than 20 students, 66% have between 20 and 50 students, 4% have more than 50 students.

STUDENT HOUSING

91% of freshmen live in college housing. Freshmen are not required to live on campus. Housing is guaranteed for all undergraduates. Campus can house 1,721 undergraduates.

EXPENSES

Tuition (2005-06): $4,814 per year (in-state), $12,492 (out-of-state).
Room & Board: $6,752.

There is no additional cost for LD program/services.

LD SERVICES

LD program size is not limited.

LD services available to:

☒ Freshmen ☒ Sophomores ☒ Juniors ☒ Seniors

Academic Accommodations

Curriculum		In class	
Foreign language waiver	☐	Early syllabus	☐
Lighter course load	☒	Note takers in class	☒
Math waiver	☐	Priority seating	☐
Other special classes	☐	Tape recorders	☐
Priority registrations	☐	Videotaped classes	☐
Substitution of courses	☐	Text on tape	☐
Exams		**Services**	
Extended time	☒	Diagnostic tests	☐
Oral exams	☒	Learning centers	☐
Take home exams	☐	Proofreaders	☐
Exams on tape or computer	☐	Readers	☒
Untimed exams	☐	Reading Machines/Kurzweil	☐
Other accommodations	☐	Special bookstore section	☐
		Typists	☐

Credit toward degree is not given for remedial courses taken.

Counseling Services

- ☐ Academic
- ☐ Psychological
- ☐ Student Support groups
- ☐ Vocational

Tutoring

Individual tutoring is available.

	Individual	Group
Time management	☐	☐
Organizational skills	☐	☐
Learning strategies	☐	☐
Study skills	☐	☐
Content area	☐	☐
Writing lab	☐	☐
Math lab	☐	☐

UNIQUE LD PROGRAM FEATURES

90% of the campus is accessible to physically disabled persons.

LD PROGRAM STAFF

Total number of LD Program staff (including director):

Full Time: 1 Part Time: 1

Key staff person available to work with LD students: Lea Wimbrow, Executive Administrative Assistant, Student Affairs Office

St. Mary's College of Maryland

St. Mary's City, MD

Address: 18952 East Fisher Road, St. Mary's City, MD, 20686-3001
Admissions telephone: 800 492-7181
Admissions FAX: 240 895-5001
Director of Admissions: Richard Edgar
Admissions e-mail: admissions@smcm.edu
Web site: http://www.smcm.edu
SAT Code: 5601 ACT Code: 1736

LD program name: Academic Services
Coordinator of Advising Programs: Nancy Danganan
LD program telephone: 240 895-4388
LD program e-mail: nadanganan@smcm.edu
LD program enrollment: 29, Total campus enrollment: 1,935

GENERAL

St. Mary's College of Maryland is a public, coed, four-year institution. 275-acre campus in St. Mary's City (population: 3,000), 70 miles from Washington, DC. Airport, bus, and train serve Washington, DC. Semester system.

LD ADMISSIONS

A member of the LD program does not sit on the admissions committee. A personal interview is recommended. Essay is required and may be typed.

SECONDARY SCHOOL REQUIREMENTS

Graduation from secondary school required; GED accepted. The following course distribution required: 4 units of English, 3 units of math, 3 units of science, 1 unit of social studies, 2 units of history, 7 units of academic electives.

TESTING

SAT Reasoning required; ACT may be substituted. SAT Subject recommended.

All enrolled freshmen (fall 2004):

Average SAT I Scores: Verbal: 631 Math: 616

Child Study Team report is not required. A neuropsychological or comprehensive psycho-education evaluation is not required for admission. Tests required as part of this documentation:

- [ ] WAIS-IV
- [ ] WISC-IV
- [ ] SATA
- [ ] Woodcock-Johnson
- [ ] Nelson-Denny Reading Test
- [ ] Other

UNDERGRADUATE STUDENT BODY

Total undergraduate student enrollment: 656 Men, 1,032 Women.

Composition of student body (fall 2004):

	Undergraduate	Freshmen
International	1.2	0.6
Black	7.2	6.5
American Indian	0.0	0.2
Asian-American	3.9	3.9
Hispanic	2.8	2.6
White	78.4	79.5
Unreported	6.5	6.7
	100.0%	100.0%

14% are from out of state. Average age of full-time undergraduates is 20. 58% of classes have fewer than 20 students, 41% have between 20 and 50 students, 1% have more than 50 students.

STUDENT HOUSING

98% of freshmen live in college housing. Freshmen are not required to live on campus. Housing is guaranteed for all undergraduates. Campus can house 1,486 undergraduates. Single rooms are available for students with medical or special needs. A medical note is required.

EXPENSES

Tuition (2005-06): $9,063 per year (in-state), $17,940 (out-of-state).

Room: $4,455. Board: $3,525.
There is no additional cost for LD program/services.

LD SERVICES

LD program size is not limited.

LD services available to:

- [x] Freshmen
- [x] Sophomores
- [x] Juniors
- [x] Seniors

Academic Accommodations

Curriculum		**In class**	
Foreign language waiver	[ ]	Early syllabus	[ ]
Lighter course load	[x]	Note takers in class	[x]
Math waiver	[ ]	Priority seating	[x]
Other special classes	[ ]	Tape recorders	[x]
Priority registrations	[x]	Videotaped classes	[ ]
Substitution of courses	[x]	Text on tape	[x]
Exams		**Services**	
Extended time	[x]	Diagnostic tests	[ ]
Oral exams	[x]	Learning centers	[ ]
Take home exams	[ ]	Proofreaders	[x]
Exams on tape or computer	[ ]	Readers	[ ]
Untimed exams	[x]	Reading Machines/Kurzweil	[ ]
Other accommodations	[x]	Special bookstore section	[ ]
		Typists	[ ]

Credit toward degree is not given for remedial courses taken.

Counseling Services

- [x] Academic
- [x] Psychological
- [ ] Student Support groups
- [ ] Vocational

Tutoring

Individual tutoring is available weekly.

Average size of tutoring groups: 15

	Individual	Group
Time management	[x]	[ ]
Organizational skills	[x]	[ ]
Learning strategies	[x]	[ ]
Study skills	[x]	[ ]
Content area	[x]	[x]
Writing lab	[x]	[x]
Math lab	[ ]	[ ]

LD PROGRAM STAFF

Total number of LD Program staff (including director):

Full Time: 1 Part Time: 1

There is no advisor/advocate from the LD program available to students.

Key staff person available to work with LD students: Nancy Danganan, Coordinator of Advising Programs

Villa Julie College

Stevenson, MD

Address: 1525 Greenspring Valley Road, Stevenson, MD, 21153
Admissions telephone: 410 486-7001
Admissions FAX: 443 334-2600
Dean of Admissions: Mark Hergan
Admissions e-mail: admissions@mail.vjc.edu
Web site: http://www.vjc.edu
SAT Code: 5856 ACT Code: 1753

LD program name: Academic Support Services
Associate Dean: Christine Noya
LD program telephone: 443 334-2224
LD program e-mail: dea-chri@mail.vjc.edu
Total campus enrollment: 2,659

GENERAL

Villa Julie College is a private, coed, four-year institution. 62-acre, semirural campus in Stevenson, 10 miles from Baltimore (population: 651,154). Major airport, bus, and train serve Baltimore. School operates transportation to off-campus housing. Public transportation serves campus. Semester system.

LD ADMISSIONS

Students do not complete a separate application and are not simultaneously accepted to the LD program. A member of the LD program does not sit on the admissions committee. High school waivers are accepted for math and foreign language. A personal interview is recommended. Essay is not required.

SECONDARY SCHOOL REQUIREMENTS

Graduation from secondary school required; GED accepted. The following course distribution required: 4 units of English, 3 units of math, 3 units of science, 2 units of social studies, 1 unit of history, 4 units of academic electives.

TESTING

SAT Reasoning required; ACT may be substituted. SAT Subject recommended.

All enrolled freshmen (fall 2004):

Average SAT I Scores: Verbal: 549 Math: 552

Child Study Team report is not required. A neuropsychological or comprehensive psycho-education evaluation is not required for admission. Tests required as part of this documentation:

- ☐ WAIS-IV
- ☐ WISC-IV
- ☐ SATA
- ☐ Woodcock-Johnson
- ☐ Nelson-Denny Reading Test
- ☐ Other

UNDERGRADUATE STUDENT BODY

Total undergraduate student enrollment: 677 Men, 1,699 Women.

Composition of student body (fall 2004):

	Undergraduate	Freshmen
International	0.7	0.4
Black	12.8	13.1
American Indian	0.5	0.3
Asian-American	4.0	2.6
Hispanic	1.1	1.3
White	76.1	78.3
Unreported	4.8	4.0
	100.0%	100.0%

3% are from out of state. 2% join a sorority. Average age of full-time undergraduates is 24. 67% of classes have fewer than 20 students, 33% have between 20 and 50 students.

STUDENT HOUSING

52% of freshmen live in college housing. Freshmen are not required to live on campus. Housing is guaranteed for all undergraduates. Campus can house 548 undergraduates. Single rooms are available for students with medical or special needs. A medical note is required.

EXPENSES

Tuition (2005-06): $14,674 per year.

Room: $5,967. Board: $3,000.

There is no additional cost for LD program/services.

LD SERVICES

LD program size is not limited.

LD services available to:

■ Freshmen ■ Sophomores ■ Juniors ■ Seniors

Academic Accommodations

Curriculum		**In class**	
Foreign language waiver	■	Early syllabus	■
Lighter course load	☐	Note takers in class	■
Math waiver	☐	Priority seating	■
Other special classes	☐	Tape recorders	■
Priority registrations	■	Videotaped classes	☐
Substitution of courses	■	Text on tape	☐
Exams		**Services**	
Extended time	■	Diagnostic tests	☐
Oral exams	■	Learning centers	■
Take home exams	■	Proofreaders	■
Exams on tape or computer	☐	Readers	■
Untimed exams	■	Reading Machines/Kurzweil	■
Other accommodations	■	Special bookstore section	☐
		Typists	■

Credit toward degree is not given for remedial courses taken.

Counseling Services

- ■ Academic — Meets 2 times per academic year
- ☐ Psychological
- ☐ Student Support groups
- ☐ Vocational

Tutoring

Individual tutoring is available daily.

Average size of tutoring groups: 2

	Individual	Group
Time management	■	■
Organizational skills	■	■
Learning strategies	■	■
Study skills	■	■
Content area	■	■
Writing lab	■	■
Math lab	■	■

LD PROGRAM STAFF

Total number of LD Program staff (including director):

Full Time: 1 Part Time: 1

There is an advisor/advocate from the LD program available to students. The advisor/advocate meets with students two times per month. 50 peer tutors are available to work with LD students.

Key staff person available to work with LD students: Deborah Blake, Office Manager of Academic Support Services

Washington College

Chestertown, MD

Address: 300 Washington Avenue, Chestertown, MD, 21620
Admissions telephone: 800 422-1782
Admissions FAX: 410 778-7287
Vice President for Admissions: Kevin Coveney
Admissions e-mail: ivictorius2@washcoll.edu
Web site: http://www.washcoll.edu
SAT Code: 5888 ACT Code: 1754

Associate Dean: Mark Hoesly
LD program telephone: 410 778-7206
LD program e-mail: mhoesly2@washcoll.edu
Total campus enrollment: 1,349

GENERAL

Washington College is a private, coed, four-year institution. 120-acre campus in Chestertown (population: 4,746), 75 miles from Baltimore, Philadelphia, PA and Washington, DC. Major airports serve Baltimore and Washington, DC; bus and train serve Wilmington, DE (50 miles). Semester system.

LD ADMISSIONS

A personal interview is recommended. Essay is not required.

SECONDARY SCHOOL REQUIREMENTS

Graduation from secondary school required; GED accepted. The following course distribution required: 4 units of English, 3 units of math, 3 units of science, 2 units of foreign language, 3 units of social studies.

TESTING

SAT Reasoning or ACT required. SAT Subject recommended.

All enrolled freshmen (fall 2004):

Average SAT I Scores: Verbal: 578 Math: 565
Average ACT Scores: Composite: 25

Child Study Team report is not required. Tests required as part of this documentation:

- ☐ WAIS-IV
- ☐ WISC-IV
- ☐ SATA
- ☐ Woodcock-Johnson
- ☐ Nelson-Denny Reading Test
- ☐ Other

UNDERGRADUATE STUDENT BODY

Total undergraduate student enrollment: 464 Men, 744 Women.

Composition of student body (fall 2004):

	Undergraduate	Freshmen
International	2.0	3.3
Black	5.6	3.9
American Indian	0.1	0.2
Asian-American	2.3	1.7
Hispanic	1.3	1.0
White	86.1	82.7
Unreported	2.6	7.2
	100.0%	100.0%

50% are from out of state. 69% of classes have fewer than 20 students, 30% have between 20 and 50 students, 1% have more than 50 students.

STUDENT HOUSING

Freshmen are required to live on campus. Housing is not guaranteed for all undergraduates.

EXPENSES

Tuition (2005-06): $28,230 per year.
Room: $3,000. Board: $3,200.
There is no additional cost for LD program/services.

LD SERVICES

LD program size is not limited.

LD services available to:

☐ Freshmen ☐ Sophomores ☐ Juniors ☐ Seniors

Academic Accommodations

Curriculum		**In class**	
Foreign language waiver	☐	Early syllabus	☐
Lighter course load	☐	Note takers in class	☐
Math waiver	☐	Priority seating	☐
Other special classes	☐	Tape recorders	■
Priority registrations	☐	Videotaped classes	☐
Substitution of courses	☐	Text on tape	☐
Exams		**Services**	
Extended time	■	Diagnostic tests	☐
Oral exams	☐	Learning centers	☐
Take home exams	☐	Proofreaders	☐
Exams on tape or computer	☐	Readers	☐
Untimed exams	☐	Reading Machines/Kurzweil	☐
Other accommodations	☐	Special bookstore section	☐
		Typists	☐

Credit toward degree is not given for remedial courses taken.

Counseling Services

- ☐ Academic
- ☐ Psychological
- ☐ Student Support groups
- ☐ Vocational

Tutoring

	Individual	Group
Time management	☐	☐
Organizational skills	☐	☐
Learning strategies	☐	☐
Study skills	☐	☐
Content area	☐	☐
Writing lab	☐	☐
Math lab	☐	☐

LD PROGRAM STAFF

Key staff person available to work with LD students: Mark Hoesly, Associate Dean

American International College

Springfield, MA

Address: 1000 State Street, Springfield, MA, 01109
Admissions telephone: 800 242-3142
Admissions FAX: 413 205-3051
Dean of Admissions: Peter J. Miller
Admissions e-mail: inquiry@acad.aic.edu
Web site: http://www.aic.edu
SAT Code: 3002 ACT Code: 1772

LD program name: Supportive Learning Services
Administrative Assistant: Anne Midura
LD program telephone: 413 205-3426
LD program enrollment: 31, Total campus enrollment: 1,227

GENERAL

American International College is a private, coed, four-year institution. 58-acre, urban campus in Springfield (population: 152,082), 20 miles from Hartford and 90 miles from Boston. Served by air, bus, and train; major airport serves Hartford, CT. School provides on-campus shuttle service. Public transportation serves campus. Semester system.

LD ADMISSIONS

Students do not complete a separate application and are not simultaneously accepted to the LD program. A member of the LD program does not sit on the admissions committee. High school waivers are accepted for foreign language. A personal interview is required. Essay is not required.

For fall 2004, 103 completed self-identified LD applications were received. 89 applications were offered admission, and 31 enrolled.

SECONDARY SCHOOL REQUIREMENTS

Graduation from secondary school required; GED accepted. The following course distribution required: 4 units of English, 2 units of math, 2 units of science, 2 units of social studies, 2 units of history, 3 units of academic electives.

TESTING

SAT Reasoning required; ACT may be substituted. SAT Subject recommended.

All enrolled freshmen (fall 2004):

Average SAT I Scores: Verbal: 490 Math: 500

Child Study Team report is not required. A neuropsychological or comprehensive psycho-educational evaluation is required for admission. Tests required as part of this documentation:

- [x] WAIS-IV
- [x] WISC-IV
- [ ] SATA
- [x] Woodcock-Johnson
- [ ] Nelson-Denny Reading Test
- [ ] Other

UNDERGRADUATE STUDENT BODY

Total undergraduate student enrollment: 500 Men, 574 Women.

41% are from out of state. Average age of full-time undergraduates is 21. 69% of classes have fewer than 20 students, 31% have between 20 and 50 students.

STUDENT HOUSING

64% of freshmen live in college housing. Freshmen are not required to live on campus. Housing is guaranteed for all undergraduates. Campus can house 700 undergraduates. Single rooms are available for students with medical or special needs. A medical note is required.

EXPENSES

Tuition (2005-06): $19,800 per year.
Room: $4,600. Board: $4,310.
Additional cost for LD program/services: $2,040 per semester.

LD SERVICES

LD program size is not limited.

LD services available to:

- [x] Freshmen
- [x] Sophomores
- [x] Juniors
- [x] Seniors

Academic Accommodations

Curriculum

- [ ] Foreign language waiver
- [x] Lighter course load
- [ ] Math waiver
- [ ] Other special classes
- [ ] Priority registrations
- [ ] Substitution of courses

Exams

- [x] Extended time
- [x] Oral exams
- [ ] Take home exams
- [ ] Exams on tape or computer
- [x] Untimed exams
- [ ] Other accommodations

In class

- [ ] Early syllabus
- [x] Note takers in class
- [ ] Priority seating
- [x] Tape recorders
- [ ] Videotaped classes
- [ ] Text on tape

Services

- [x] Diagnostic tests
- [x] Learning centers
- [ ] Proofreaders
- [x] Readers
- [x] Reading Machines/Kurzweil
- [ ] Special bookstore section
- [ ] Typists

Credit toward degree is not given for remedial courses taken.

Counseling Services

- [x] Academic
- [ ] Psychological
- [ ] Student Support groups
- [ ] Vocational

Tutoring

Individual tutoring is available daily.

Average size of tutoring groups: 1

	Individual	Group
Time management	[x]	[ ]
Organizational skills	[x]	[ ]
Learning strategies	[x]	[ ]
Study skills	[x]	[ ]
Content area	[x]	[ ]
Writing lab	[x]	[ ]
Math lab	[x]	[ ]

LD PROGRAM STAFF

Total number of LD Program staff (including director):

Full Time: 11 Part Time: 11

There is an advisor/advocate from the LD program available to students. The advisor/advocate meets with faculty two times per month and students 16 times per month.

Key staff person available to work with LD students: Mary Saltus, Coordinator, Supportive Learning Services

Amherst College

Amherst, MA

Address: P.O. Box 5000, Amherst, MA, 01002
Admissions telephone: 413 542-2328
Admissions FAX: 413 542-2040
Dean of Admissions and Financial Aid: Katharine Fretwell
Admissions e-mail: admission@amherst.edu
Web site: http://www.amherst.edu
SAT Code: 3003 ACT Code: 1774

Associate Dean of Students: Frances Tuleja
LD program telephone: 413 542-2529
LD program e-mail: fetuleja@amherst.edu
Total campus enrollment: 1, 638

GENERAL

Amherst College is a private, coed, four-year institution. 978-acre campus in Amherst (population: 34,874), 50 miles from Hartford, CT and 90 miles from Boston. Served by bus and train; major airport serves Boston; smaller airport serves Windsor Locks, CT (50 miles). School operates shuttle buses to five college campuses. Public transportation serves campus. Semester system.

LD ADMISSIONS

A personal interview is not required. Essay is required and may be typed.

TESTING

SAT Subject recommended.

All enrolled freshmen (fall 2004):

Average SAT I Scores:	Verbal: 722	Math: 721
Average ACT Scores:	Composite: 31	

Child Study Team report is not required. Tests required as part of this documentation:

☐ WAIS-IV	☐ Woodcock-Johnson
☐ WISC-IV	☐ Nelson-Denny Reading Test
☐ SATA	☐ Other

UNDERGRADUATE STUDENT BODY

Total undergraduate student enrollment: 835 Men, 796 Women.

Composition of student body (fall 2004):

	Undergraduate	Freshmen
International	6.1	6.2
Black	5.2	9.0
American Indian	0.5	0.2
Asian-American	15.9	12.9
Hispanic	7.3	7.1
White	47.4	46.3
Unreported	17.6	18.3
	100.0%	100.0%

84% are from out of state. Average age of full-time undergraduates is 20. 71% of classes have fewer than 20 students, 25% have between 20 and 50 students, 4% have more than 50 students.

STUDENT HOUSING

100% of freshmen live in college housing. Freshmen are required to live on campus. Housing is guaranteed for all undergraduates. Campus can house 1,620 undergraduates.

EXPENSES

Tuition (2005-06): $32,395 per year.

Room: $4,600. Board: $3,985.
There is no additional cost for LD program/services.

LD SERVICES

LD program size is not limited.

LD services available to:

☐ Freshmen ☐ Sophomores ☐ Juniors ☐ Seniors

Academic Accommodations

Curriculum		**In class**	
Foreign language waiver	☐	Early syllabus	☐
Lighter course load	☐	Note takers in class	■
Math waiver	☐	Priority seating	☐
Other special classes	☐	Tape recorders	■
Priority registrations	☐	Videotaped classes	☐
Substitution of courses	☐	Text on tape	☐
Exams		**Services**	
Extended time	■	Diagnostic tests	☐
Oral exams	☐	Learning centers	☐
Take home exams	☐	Proofreaders	☐
Exams on tape or computer	☐	Readers	■
Untimed exams	☐	Reading Machines/Kurzweil	☐
Other accommodations	☐	Special bookstore section	☐
		Typists	☐

Credit toward degree is not given for remedial courses taken.

Counseling Services

☐ Academic
☐ Psychological
☐ Student Support groups
☐ Vocational

Tutoring

	Individual	Group
Time management	☐	☐
Organizational skills	☐	☐
Learning strategies	☐	☐
Study skills	☐	☐
Content area	☐	☐
Writing lab	☐	☐
Math lab	☐	☐

LD PROGRAM STAFF

Key staff person available to work with LD students: Frances Tuleja, Associate Dean of Students

The Art Institute of Boston at Lesley University

Boston, MA

Address: 700 Beacon Street, Boston, MA, 02215-2598
Admissions telephone: 800 773-0494
Admissions FAX: 617 585-6720
Director of Admissions: Bonnie Roth
Admissions e-mail: admissions@aiboston.edu
Web site: http://www.aiboston.edu
SAT Code: 3777

LD program name: LD/ADD Academic Support Program
Director: Maureen Riley, Professor of Special Education
LD program telephone: 617 349-8464
LD program e-mail: mriley@mail.lesley.edu
Total campus enrollment: 1,042

GENERAL

The Art Institute of Boston at Lesley University is a private, coed, four-year institution. Urban campus in Boston (population: 589,141). Served by air, bus, and train. School operates transportation to Lesley U. Public transportation serves campus. Semester system.

LD ADMISSIONS

A personal interview is recommended. Essay is required and may be typed.

SECONDARY SCHOOL REQUIREMENTS

Graduation from secondary school required; GED accepted. The following course distribution required: 4 units of English.

TESTING

SAT Reasoning required; ACT may be substituted.

Child Study Team report is not required. Tests required as part of this documentation:

- [ ] WAIS-IV
- [ ] WISC-IV
- [ ] SATA
- [ ] Woodcock-Johnson
- [ ] Nelson-Denny Reading Test
- [ ] Other

UNDERGRADUATE STUDENT BODY

Total undergraduate student enrollment: 330 Men, 461 Women.

Composition of student body (fall 2004):

	Undergraduate	Freshmen
International	4.4	4.6
Black	9.6	6.6
American Indian	0.1	0.5
Asian-American	4.8	4.7
Hispanic	7.9	4.3
White	58.3	63.1
Unreported	14.9	16.2
	100.0%	100.0%

58% are from out of state. Average age of full-time undergraduates is 21. 76% of classes have fewer than 20 students, 24% have between 20 and 50 students.

STUDENT HOUSING

85% of freshmen live in college housing. Housing is not guaranteed for all undergraduates. Campus can house 137 undergraduates.

EXPENSES

Tuition 2004-05: $18,000 per year.

Room: $5,645. Board: $3,725.

There is no additional cost for LD program/services.

LD SERVICES

LD program size is not limited.

LD services available to:

- [ ] Freshmen
- [ ] Sophomores
- [ ] Juniors
- [ ] Seniors

Academic Accommodations

Curriculum		**In class**	
Foreign language waiver	☐	Early syllabus	☐
Lighter course load	■	Note takers in class	■
Math waiver	☐	Priority seating	☐
Other special classes	■	Tape recorders	■
Priority registrations	☐	Videotaped classes	☐
Substitution of courses	☐	Text on tape	☐
Exams		**Services**	
Extended time	■	Diagnostic tests	☐
Oral exams	■	Learning centers	■
Take home exams	☐	Proofreaders	☐
Exams on tape or computer	☐	Readers	■
Untimed exams	☐	Reading Machines/Kurzweil	■
Other accommodations	☐	Special bookstore section	☐
		Typists	☐

Credit toward degree is not given for remedial courses taken.

Counseling Services

- [ ] Academic
- [ ] Psychological
- [ ] Student Support groups
- [ ] Vocational

Tutoring

	Individual	Group
Time management	☐	☐
Organizational skills	☐	☐
Learning strategies	☐	☐
Study skills	☐	☐
Content area	☐	☐
Writing lab	☐	☐
Math lab	☐	☐

UNIQUE LD PROGRAM FEATURES

The tutorial program is accredited by the College Reading and Language Association (CRLA). Tutors are trained weekly by senior faculty. The course selection and academic needs of students with learning disabilities and attention disorders are assessed by the program director. Students are then matched to tutors and tutors are supervised individually. The Center provided over 6,000 hours of free tutoring last year. Students with special learning needs may have as many tutorial hours per week as they need.

LD PROGRAM STAFF

Total number of LD Program staff (including director):

Full Time: 2 Part Time: 2

Key staff person available to work with LD students: Maureen Riley, Professor of Special Education and Director, LD/ADD Academic Support Program

Assumption College

Worcester, MA

Address: 500 Salisbury Street, Worcester, MA, 01609
Admissions telephone: 888 882-7786
Admissions FAX: 508 799-4412
Dean of Admissions: Kathleen Murphy
Admissions e-mail: admiss@assumption.edu
Web site: http://www.assumption.edu
SAT Code: 3009 ACT Code: 1782

LD program name: Office of the Dean of Studies
Dean of Studies: Sr. Ellen Guerin, RSM
LD program telephone: 508 767-7487
LD program e-mail: eguerin@assumption.edu
LD program enrollment: 103, Total campus enrollment: 2,184

GENERAL

Assumption College is a private, coed, four-year institution. 175-acre campus in Worcester (population: 170,000), 50 miles from Boston. Served by air, bus, and train; major airport serves Boston. School operates transportation to consortium schools. Public transportation serves campus. Semester system.

LD ADMISSIONS

Application Deadline: 02/15. Students do not complete a separate application and are simultaneously accepted to the LD program. A member of the LD program does not sit on the admissions committee. A personal interview is recommended. Essay is not required.

SECONDARY SCHOOL REQUIREMENTS

Graduation from secondary school required; GED accepted. The following course distribution required: 4 units of English, 3 units of math, 2 units of science, 2 units of foreign language, 2 units of history, 5 units of academic electives.

TESTING

SAT Reasoning or ACT required. SAT Subject recommended.

All enrolled freshmen (fall 2004):

Average SAT I Scores:	Verbal: 545	Math: 543
Average ACT Scores:	Composite: 22	

Child Study Team report is not required. A neuropsychological or comprehensive psycho-educational evaluation is required for admission. Must be dated within 36 months of application. Tests required as part of this documentation:

- ■ WAIS-IV
- ☐ WISC-IV
- ☐ SATA
- ■ Woodcock-Johnson
- ☐ Nelson-Denny Reading Test
- ☐ Other

UNDERGRADUATE STUDENT BODY

Total undergraduate student enrollment: 812 Men, 1,282 Women.

Composition of student body (fall 2004):

	Undergraduate	Freshmen
International	0.0	0.0
Black	1.3	1.1
American Indian	0.0	0.0
Asian-American	0.8	1.3
Hispanic	1.4	1.8
White	85.4	85.0
Unreported	11.1	10.8
	100.0%	100.0%

32% are from out of state. Average age of full-time undergraduates is 20. 41% of classes have fewer than 20 students, 59% have between 20 and 50 students.

STUDENT HOUSING

94% of freshmen live in college housing. Freshmen are not required to live on campus. Housing is guaranteed for all undergraduates. Campus can house 1,942 undergraduates. Single rooms are available for students with medical or special needs. A medical note is required.

EXPENSES

Tuition (2005-06): $23,930 per year.
Room: $5,500. Board: $3,280.
There is no additional cost for LD program/services.

LD SERVICES

LD program size is not limited.

LD services available to:

■ Freshmen ■ Sophomores ■ Juniors ■ Seniors

Academic Accommodations

Curriculum		In class	
Foreign language waiver	☐	Early syllabus	☐
Lighter course load	☐	Note takers in class	■
Math waiver	☐	Priority seating	■
Other special classes	☐	Tape recorders	■
Priority registrations	■	Videotaped classes	☐
Substitution of courses	☐	Text on tape	☐
Exams		**Services**	
Extended time	■	Diagnostic tests	☐
Oral exams	■	Learning centers	■
Take home exams	☐	Proofreaders	☐
Exams on tape or computer	☐	Readers	☐
Untimed exams	■	Reading Machines/Kurzweil	■
Other accommodations	☐	Special bookstore section	☐
		Typists	☐

Credit toward degree is not given for remedial courses taken.

Counseling Services

- ☐ Academic
- ☐ Psychological
- ☐ Student Support groups
- ☐ Vocational

Tutoring

Individual tutoring is available weekly.

	Individual	Group
Time management	■	■
Organizational skills	■	■
Learning strategies	■	■
Study skills	■	■
Content area	■	■
Writing lab	■	■
Math lab	■	■

LD PROGRAM STAFF

Total number of LD Program staff (including director):

Full Time: 2 Part Time: 2

There is an advisor/advocate from the LD program available to students. The advisor/advocate meets with faculty once per month and students four times per month. One graduate student and 42 peer tutors are available to work with LD students.

Key staff person available to work with LD students: Allen Bruehl, Director, Academic Support Center

Babson College

Babson Park, MA

Address: 231 Forest Street, Babson Park, MA, 02457-0310
Admissions telephone: 800 488-3696
Admissions FAX: 781 239-4135
Dean, Undergraduate Admissions and Student Financial Svcs: Alan Kines
Admissions e-mail: ugradadmission@babson.edu
Web site: http://www.babson.edu
SAT Code: 3075 ACT Code: 1780

LD program name: Disability Services
Manager of Disability Services: Erin Evans
LD program telephone: 781 239-4508
LD program e-mail: eevans@babson.edu
Total campus enrollment: 1, 697

GENERAL

Babson College is a private, coed, four-year institution. 370-acre, suburban campus in Wellesley (population: 26,613), 14 miles from Boston. Major airport, bus, and train serve Boston. Semester system.

LD ADMISSIONS

A member of the LD program does not sit on the admissions committee. A personal interview is recommended. Essay is required and may be typed.

SECONDARY SCHOOL REQUIREMENTS

Graduation from secondary school required; GED accepted. The following course distribution required: 4 units of English, 4 units of math, 3 units of science, 2 units of foreign language, 2 units of social studies, 1 unit of history.

TESTING

SAT Reasoning or ACT required. SAT Subject required.

All enrolled freshmen (fall 2004):

Average SAT I Scores: Verbal: 597 Math: 655

Child Study Team report is not required. Tests required as part of this documentation:

- [ ] WAIS-IV
- [ ] WISC-IV
- [ ] SATA
- [ ] Woodcock-Johnson
- [ ] Nelson-Denny Reading Test
- [ ] Other

UNDERGRADUATE STUDENT BODY

Total undergraduate student enrollment: 1,080 Men, 639 Women.

Composition of student body (fall 2004):

	Undergraduate	Freshmen
International	16.0	17.2
Black	4.7	3.3
American Indian	0.0	0.4
Asian-American	5.9	7.6
Hispanic	5.4	5.1
White	47.6	44.1
Unreported	20.4	22.3
	100.0%	100.0%

53% are from out of state. 10% join a fraternity and 10% join a sorority. Average age of full-time undergraduates is 20. 23% of classes have fewer than 20 students, 74% have between 20 and 50 students, 3% have more than 50 students.

STUDENT HOUSING

100% of freshmen live in college housing. Freshmen are required to live on campus. Housing is guaranteed for all undergraduates. Campus can house 1,435 undergraduates. Single rooms are available for students with medical or special needs. A medical note is required.

EXPENSES

Tuition (2005-06): $30,496 per year.
Room: $6,964. Board: $3,828.

There is no additional cost for LD program/services.

LD SERVICES

LD program size is not limited.

LD services available to:

- [x] Freshmen
- [x] Sophomores
- [x] Juniors
- [x] Seniors

Academic Accommodations

Curriculum		In class	
Foreign language waiver	[ ]	Early syllabus	[ ]
Lighter course load	[x]	Note takers in class	[x]
Math waiver	[ ]	Priority seating	[ ]
Other special classes	[ ]	Tape recorders	[x]
Priority registrations	[ ]	Videotaped classes	[ ]
Substitution of courses	[ ]	Text on tape	[ ]
Exams		**Services**	
Extended time	[x]	Diagnostic tests	[ ]
Oral exams	[ ]	Learning centers	[ ]
Take home exams	[ ]	Proofreaders	[ ]
Exams on tape or computer	[ ]	Readers	[ ]
Untimed exams	[ ]	Reading Machines/Kurzweil	[x]
Other accommodations	[ ]	Special bookstore section	[ ]
		Typists	[ ]

Credit toward degree is not given for remedial courses taken.

Counseling Services

- [ ] Academic
- [ ] Psychological
- [ ] Student Support groups
- [ ] Vocational

Tutoring

Individual tutoring is not available.

	Individual	Group
Time management	[ ]	[ ]
Organizational skills	[ ]	[ ]
Learning strategies	[ ]	[ ]
Study skills	[ ]	[ ]
Content area	[ ]	[ ]
Writing lab	[ ]	[ ]
Math lab	[ ]	[ ]

LD PROGRAM STAFF

Total number of LD Program staff (including director):

Full Time: 1 Part Time: 1

There is no advisor/advocate from the LD program available to students.

Key staff person available to work with LD students: Erin Evans, Manager of Disability Services

LD Program web site: www.babson.edu/classdeans

Bay Path College

Longmeadow, MA

Address: 588 Longmeadow Street, Longmeadow, MA, 01106
Admissions telephone: 800 782-7284
Admissions FAX: 413 565-1105
Director of Enrollment Services: Brenda Wishart
Admissions e-mail: admiss@baypath.edu
Web site: http://www.baypath.edu
SAT Code: 3078 ACT Code: 1785

LD program name: Office of Disability Services
Director: Brenda Hardin
LD program telephone: 413 565-1353
LD program e-mail: bhardin@baypath.edu
Total campus enrollment: 1,347

GENERAL

Bay Path College is a private, women's, four-year institution. 44-acre, suburban campus in Longmeadow (population: 15,633), three miles from Springfield. Airport serves Windsor Locks, CT (15 miles); bus and train serve Springfield. School operates transportation to local shopping malls and to cultural activities in Boston, New York City, NY, and Springfield. Semester system.

LD ADMISSIONS

A personal interview is recommended. Essay is required and may be typed.

SECONDARY SCHOOL REQUIREMENTS

Graduation from secondary school required; GED accepted. The following course distribution required: 4 units of English, 3 units of math, 2 units of science, 2 units of history.

TESTING

SAT Reasoning or ACT required. SAT Subject required.

All enrolled freshmen (fall 2004):

Average SAT I Scores: Verbal: 512 Math: 499
Average ACT Scores: Composite: 22

Child Study Team report is not required. Tests required as part of this documentation:

- ☐ WAIS-IV
- ☐ WISC-IV
- ☐ SATA
- ☐ Woodcock-Johnson
- ☐ Nelson-Denny Reading Test
- ☐ Other

UNDERGRADUATE STUDENT BODY

Total undergraduate student enrollment: 918 Women.

Composition of student body (fall 2004):

	Freshmen
International	1.1
Black	11.0
American Indian	0.5
Asian-American	1.0
Hispanic	7.1
White	79.3
Unreported	0.0
	100.0%

40% are from out of state. Average age of full-time undergraduates is 20. 65% of classes have fewer than 20 students, 35% have between 20 and 50 students.

STUDENT HOUSING

85% of freshmen live in college housing. Freshmen are required to live on campus. Housing is guaranteed for all undergraduates. Campus can house 400 undergraduates. Single rooms are available for students with medical or special needs. A medical note is required.

EXPENSES

Tuition (2005-06): $20,606 per year.

Room & Board: $8,756.

There is no additional cost for LD program/services.

LD SERVICES

LD program size is not limited.

LD services available to:

■ Freshmen ■ Sophomores ■ Juniors ■ Seniors

Academic Accommodations

Curriculum		**In class**	
Foreign language waiver	☐	Early syllabus	☐
Lighter course load	■	Note takers in class	■
Math waiver	☐	Priority seating	■
Other special classes	☐	Tape recorders	■
Priority registrations	☐	Videotaped classes	☐
Substitution of courses	☐	Text on tape	■
Exams		**Services**	
Extended time	■	Diagnostic tests	☐
Oral exams	☐	Learning centers	■
Take home exams	☐	Proofreaders	☐
Exams on tape or computer	☐	Readers	☐
Untimed exams	■	Reading Machines/Kurzweil	☐
Other accommodations	■	Special bookstore section	☐
		Typists	■

Credit toward degree is not given for remedial courses taken.

Counseling Services

- ■ Academic
- ■ Psychological
- ☐ Student Support groups
- ☐ Vocational

Tutoring

Individual tutoring is available daily.

	Individual	Group
Time management	■	■
Organizational skills	■	■
Learning strategies	■	■
Study skills	■	■
Content area	■	■
Writing lab	■	■
Math lab	☐	☐

LD PROGRAM STAFF

Total number of LD Program staff (including director):

Full Time: 1 Part Time: 1

There is an advisor/advocate from the LD program available to students. 10 peer tutors are available to work with LD students.

Key staff person available to work with LD students: Brenda Hardin, Director of Bashevkin Academic Development Center

Becker College

Worcester, MA

Address: 61 Sever Street, Worcester, MA, 01609
Admissions telephone: 877 5-BECKER
Admissions FAX: 508 890-1500
Vice President of Enrollment Management: Pamela Hawkins
Admissions e-mail: admissions@beckercollege.edu
Web site: http://www.beckercollege.edu
SAT Code: 3079 ACT Code: 1787

LD program name: Center for Academic Success
Administrator: Madeleine Entel
LD program telephone: 508 791-9241
Total campus enrollment: 1,660

GENERAL

Becker College is a private, coed, four-year institution. 100-acre, urban campus in Worcester (population: 172,648), 40 miles from both Boston and Providence, RI; branch campus in Leicester. Served by bus; major airport and train serve Boston; smaller airport serves Providence, RI. School operates transportation to Leicester campus. Public transportation serves campus. Semester system.

LD ADMISSIONS

A personal interview is recommended. Essay is not required.

SECONDARY SCHOOL REQUIREMENTS

Graduation from secondary school required; GED accepted.

TESTING

SAT Reasoning required; ACT may be substituted.

Child Study Team report is not required. Tests required as part of this documentation:

- ☐ WAIS-IV
- ☐ WISC-IV
- ☐ SATA
- ☐ Woodcock-Johnson
- ☐ Nelson-Denny Reading Test
- ☐ Other

UNDERGRADUATE STUDENT BODY

Total undergraduate student enrollment: 277 Men, 1,021 Women.

Composition of student body (fall 2004):

	Undergraduate	Freshmen
International	0.2	0.3
Black	6.0	5.2
American Indian	0.5	0.4
Asian-American	1.6	1.6
Hispanic	3.8	2.8
White	59.3	55.0
Unreported	28.6	34.7
	100.0%	100.0%

31% are from out of state. 61% of classes have fewer than 20 students, 35% have between 20 and 50 students, 4% have more than 50 students.

STUDENT HOUSING

Housing is guaranteed for all undergraduates. Campus can house 596 undergraduates.

EXPENSES

Tuition (2005-06): $18,000 per year.
Room & Board: $8,000.

There is no additional cost for LD program/services.

LD SERVICES

LD program size is not limited.

LD services available to:

☐ Freshmen ☐ Sophomores ☐ Juniors ☐ Seniors

Academic Accommodations

Curriculum		**In class**	
Foreign language waiver	☐	Early syllabus	☐
Lighter course load	☐	Note takers in class	■
Math waiver	☐	Priority seating	☐
Other special classes	☐	Tape recorders	■
Priority registrations	☐	Videotaped classes	☐
Substitution of courses	☐	Text on tape	☐
Exams		**Services**	
Extended time	■	Diagnostic tests	☐
Oral exams	■	Learning centers	■
Take home exams	☐	Proofreaders	☐
Exams on tape or computer	☐	Readers	☐
Untimed exams	☐	Reading Machines/Kurzweil	☐
Other accommodations	☐	Special bookstore section	☐
		Typists	☐

Counseling Services

- ☐ Academic
- ☐ Psychological
- ☐ Student Support groups
- ☐ Vocational

Tutoring

	Individual	Group
Time management	☐	☐
Organizational skills	☐	☐
Learning strategies	☐	☐
Study skills	☐	☐
Content area	☐	☐
Writing lab	☐	☐
Math lab	☐	☐

LD PROGRAM STAFF

Total number of LD Program staff (including director):

Full Time: 2 Part Time: 2

Key staff person available to work with LD students: Madeleine Entel, Administrator for the Center for Academic Success

Bentley College

Waltham, MA

Address: 175 Forest Street, Waltham, MA, 02452-4705
Admissions telephone: 800 523-2354
Admissions FAX: 781 891-3414
Dean of Undergraduate Admissions and Financial Assistance: Kenton W Rinehart
Admissions e-mail: ugadmission@bentley.edu
Web site: http://www.bentley.edu
SAT Code: 3096 ACT Code: 1783

LD program name: Counseling and Student Development
Coordinator of Disability Services: Christopher Kennedy
LD program telephone: 781 891-2274
LD program e-mail: ckennedy@bentley.edu
LD program enrollment: 165, Total campus enrollment: 4,257

GENERAL

Bentley College is a private, coed, four-year institution. 163-acre, suburban campus in Waltham (population: 59,226), 10 miles from Boston. Airport, bus, and train serve Boston. School operates transportation around Waltham and to Boston and Cambridge. Semester system.

LD ADMISSIONS

Application Deadline: 02/01. Students do not complete a separate application and are simultaneously accepted to the LD program. A member of the LD program does not sit on the admissions committee. High school waivers are accepted for foreign language. A personal interview is not required. Essay is required and may be typed.

SECONDARY SCHOOL REQUIREMENTS

Graduation from secondary school required; GED accepted.

TESTING

SAT Reasoning or ACT required. SAT Subject required.

All enrolled freshmen (fall 2004):

Average SAT I Scores: Verbal: 576 Math: 623
Average ACT Scores: Composite: 25

Child Study Team report is not required. A neuropsychological or comprehensive psycho-educational evaluation is required for admission. Must be dated within 36 months of application. Tests required as part of this documentation:

- [x] WAIS-IV
- [x] WISC-IV
- [x] SATA
- [x] Woodcock-Johnson
- [x] Nelson-Denny Reading Test
- [ ] Other

UNDERGRADUATE STUDENT BODY

Total undergraduate student enrollment: 2,417 Men, 1,839 Women.

Composition of student body (fall 2004):

	Undergraduate	Freshmen
International	5.5	8.2
Black	3.0	3.6
American Indian	0.0	0.1
Asian-American	6.4	7.2
Hispanic	3.7	4.0
White	71.2	69.6
Unreported	10.2	7.3
	100.0%	100.0%

38% are from out of state. Average age of full-time undergraduates is 20. 25% of classes have fewer than 20 students, 75% have between 20 and 50 students.

STUDENT HOUSING

97% of freshmen live in college housing. Freshmen are not required to live on campus. Housing is guaranteed for all undergraduates. Campus can house 3,170 undergraduates. Single rooms are available for students with medical or special needs. A medical note is required.

EXPENSES

Tuition (2005-06): $28,390 per year.
Room: $6,060. Board: $4,110.
There is no additional cost for LD program/services.

LD SERVICES

LD program size is not limited.

LD services available to:

- [x] Freshmen
- [x] Sophomores
- [x] Juniors
- [x] Seniors

Academic Accommodations

Curriculum
- [x] Foreign language waiver
- [x] Lighter course load
- [ ] Math waiver
- [ ] Other special classes
- [x] Priority registrations
- [x] Substitution of courses

Exams
- [x] Extended time
- [x] Oral exams
- [ ] Take home exams
- [x] Exams on tape or computer
- [ ] Untimed exams
- [x] Other accommodations

In class
- [x] Early syllabus
- [x] Note takers in class
- [x] Priority seating
- [x] Tape recorders
- [ ] Videotaped classes
- [ ] Text on tape

Services
- [ ] Diagnostic tests
- [x] Learning centers
- [x] Proofreaders
- [x] Readers
- [x] Reading Machines/Kurzweil
- [ ] Special bookstore section
- [x] Typists

Credit toward degree is not given for remedial courses taken.

Counseling Services

- [x] Academic
- [x] Psychological
- [x] Student Support groups
- [ ] Vocational

Tutoring

Individual tutoring is available weekly.

	Individual	Group
Time management	[x]	[ ]
Organizational skills	[x]	[ ]
Learning strategies	[x]	[ ]
Study skills	[x]	[x]
Content area	[x]	[ ]
Writing lab	[x]	[ ]
Math lab	[x]	[ ]

LD PROGRAM STAFF

Total number of LD Program staff (including director):

Full Time: 1 Part Time: 1

There is an advisor/advocate from the LD program available to students. 25 peer tutors are available to work with LD students.

Key staff person available to work with LD students: Christopher Kennedy, Coordinator of Disability Services

LD Program web site: http://ecampus.bentley.edu/dept/counsel

Berkleee College of Music

Boston, MA

Address: 1140 Boylston Street, Boston, MA, 02215
Admissions telephone: 800 BERKLEE
Admissions FAX: 617 747-2047
Director of Admissions: Damien Bracken
Admissions e-mail: admissions@berklee.edu
Web site: http://www.berklee.edu
SAT Code: 3107 ACT Code: 1789

Associate Director for Special Services: Bob Mulvey
LD program telephone: 617 747-2351
LD program e-mail: bmulvey@berklee.edu
Total campus enrollment: 3,882

GENERAL

Berklee College of Music is a private, coed, four-year institution. Urban campus in Boston (population: 589,141). Served by air, bus, and train. Public transportation serves campus. Semester system.

LD ADMISSIONS

A personal interview is recommended. Essay is required and may be typed.

SECONDARY SCHOOL REQUIREMENTS

Graduation from secondary school required; GED accepted. The following course distribution required: 4 units of English, 1 unit of math, 1 unit of science, 2 units of social studies, 6 units of history, 2 units of academic electives.

TESTING

SAT Reasoning or ACT required of some applicants.

Child Study Team report is not required. Tests required as part of this documentation:

- ☐ WAIS-IV
- ☐ WISC-IV
- ☐ SATA
- ☐ Woodcock-Johnson
- ☐ Nelson-Denny Reading Test
- ☐ Other

UNDERGRADUATE STUDENT BODY

Total undergraduate student enrollment: 2,581 Men, 834 Women.

79% are from out of state.

STUDENT HOUSING

Housing is guaranteed for all undergraduates. Campus can house 846 undergraduates.

EXPENSES

Tuition (2005-06): $21,790 per year.
Room & Board: $11,690.
There is no additional cost for LD program/services.

LD SERVICES

LD program size is not limited.

LD services available to:

☐ Freshmen ☐ Sophomores ☐ Juniors ☐ Seniors

Academic Accommodations

Curriculum		**In class**	
Foreign language waiver	☐	Early syllabus	☐
Lighter course load	☐	Note takers in class	☐
Math waiver	☐	Priority seating	☐
Other special classes	☐	Tape recorders	☐
Priority registrations	☐	Videotaped classes	☐
Substitution of courses	☐	Text on tape	☐
Exams		**Services**	
Extended time	■	Diagnostic tests	☐
Oral exams	☐	Learning centers	■
Take home exams	☐	Proofreaders	☐
Exams on tape or computer	☐	Readers	■
Untimed exams	■	Reading Machines/Kurzweil	☐
Other accommodations	☐	Special bookstore section	☐
		Typists	☐

Counseling Services

- ☐ Academic
- ☐ Psychological
- ☐ Student Support groups
- ☐ Vocational

Tutoring

	Individual	Group
Time management	☐	☐
Organizational skills	☐	☐
Learning strategies	☐	☐
Study skills	☐	☐
Content area	☐	☐
Writing lab	☐	☐
Math lab	☐	☐

LD PROGRAM STAFF

Key staff person available to work with LD students: Bob Mulvey, Associate Director for Special Services

Boston Architectural Center

Boston, MA

Address: 320 Newbury Street, Boston, MA, 02115
Admissions telephone: 617 585-0123
Admissions FAX: 617 585-0121
Director of Admission and Enrollment Management: Jeff Cutting
Admissions e-mail: admissions@the-bac.edu
Web site: http://www.the-bac.edu
SAT Code: 1168

LD program name: Advising Department
Director of Advising: Jenifer Marshall
LD program telephone: 617 585-0259
LD program e-mail: jenifer.marshall@the-bac.edu
Total campus enrollment: 507

GENERAL

Boston Architectural Center is a private, coed, four-year institution. Urban campus in Boston (population: 589,141). Served by air, bus, and train. Public transportation serves campus. Semester system.

LD ADMISSIONS

Students do not complete a separate application and are simultaneously accepted to the LD program. A member of the LD program does not sit on the admissions committee. A personal interview is not required. Essay is not required.

SECONDARY SCHOOL REQUIREMENTS

Graduation from secondary school required; GED accepted.

TESTING

Child Study Team report is not required. A neuropsychological or comprehensive psycho-education evaluation is not required for admission. Tests required as part of this documentation:

- ☐ WAIS-IV
- ☐ WISC-IV
- ☐ SATA
- ☐ Woodcock-Johnson
- ☐ Nelson-Denny Reading Test
- ☐ Other

UNDERGRADUATE STUDENT BODY

Total undergraduate student enrollment: 484 Men, 311 Women.

Composition of student body (fall 2004):

	Undergraduate	Freshmen
International	0.0	0.0
Black	2.8	2.0
American Indian	0.0	0.2
Asian-American	2.8	3.4
Hispanic	5.6	4.1
White	40.3	40.6
Unreported	48.5	49.7
	100.0%	100.0%

40% are from out of state. Average age of full-time undergraduates is 25. 81% of classes have fewer than 20 students, 14% have between 20 and 50 students, 5% have more than 50 students.

STUDENT HOUSING

Freshmen are not required to live on campus. Housing is not guaranteed for all undergraduates.

EXPENSES

Tuition (2005-06): $8,610 per year.
There is no additional cost for LD program/services.

LD SERVICES

LD program size is not limited.

LD services available to:

■ Freshmen ■ Sophomores ■ Juniors ■ Seniors

Academic Accommodations

Curriculum		**In class**	
Foreign language waiver	☐	Early syllabus	☐
Lighter course load	■	Note takers in class	■
Math waiver	☐	Priority seating	■
Other special classes	☐	Tape recorders	■
Priority registrations	☐	Videotaped classes	■
Substitution of courses	☐	Text on tape	☐
Exams		**Services**	
Extended time	■	Diagnostic tests	☐
Oral exams	■	Learning centers	■
Take home exams	☐	Proofreaders	■
Exams on tape or computer	■	Readers	■
Untimed exams	■	Reading Machines/Kurzweil	☐
Other accommodations	■	Special bookstore section	☐
		Typists	☐

Credit toward degree is not given for remedial courses taken.

Counseling Services

- ■ Academic
- ☐ Psychological
- ☐ Student Support groups
- ☐ Vocational

Tutoring

Individual tutoring is available weekly.

Average size of tutoring groups: 1

	Individual	Group
Time management	■	☐
Organizational skills	■	☐
Learning strategies	■	☐
Study skills	■	☐
Content area	■	☐
Writing lab	■	☐
Math lab	■	☐

LD PROGRAM STAFF

Total number of LD Program staff (including director):

Full Time: 4 Part Time: 4

There is an advisor/advocate from the LD program available to students.

Key staff person available to work with LD students: Jenifer Marshall, Director of Advising/ADA Coordinator

Boston College

Chestnut Hill, MA

Address: 140 Commonwealth Avenue, Chestnut Hill, MA, 02467
Admissions telephone: 617 552-3100
Admissions FAX: 617 552-0498
Director of Admissions: John L. Mahoney, Jr.
Admissions e-mail: ugadmis@bc.edu
Web site: http://www.bc.edu
SAT Code: 3083 ACT Code: 1788

LD program name: Connors Family Learning Center
Assistant Director: Kathy Duggan
LD program telephone: 617 552-8093
LD program e-mail: dugganka@bc.edu
LD program enrollment: 385, Total campus enrollment: 9,059

GENERAL

Boston College is a private, coed, four-year institution. 200-acre, suburban campus in Chestnut Hill and 40-acre, suburban campus in Newton (population: 84,000), both six miles from Boston. Major airport, bus, and train serve Boston. School operates transportation between campuses and in surrounding neighborhood. Public transportation serves campus. Semester system.

LD ADMISSIONS

Students do not complete a separate application and are not simultaneously accepted to the LD program. A member of the LD program does not sit on the admissions committee. A personal interview is not required. Essay is required and may be typed. SAT Subject exams may be waived if appropriate documentation is provided.

For fall 2004, 75 completed self-identified LD applications were received. 18 applications were offered admission, and 11 enrolled.

SECONDARY SCHOOL REQUIREMENTS

Graduation from secondary school required; GED accepted.

TESTING

SAT Subject required.

All enrolled freshmen (fall 2004):

Average SAT I Scores: Verbal: 650 Math: 667

Child Study Team report is not required. A neuropsychological or comprehensive psycho-education evaluation is not required for admission. Tests required as part of this documentation:

- ❑ WAIS-IV
- ❑ WISC-IV
- ❑ SATA
- ❑ Woodcock-Johnson
- ❑ Nelson-Denny Reading Test
- ❑ Other

UNDERGRADUATE STUDENT BODY

Total undergraduate student enrollment: 4,260 Men, 4,740 Women.

Composition of student body (fall 2004):

	Undergraduate	Freshmen
International	2.3	1.9
Black	5.7	5.8
American Indian	0.4	0.3
Asian-American	9.1	8.9
Hispanic	9.1	7.3
White	69.2	74.5
Unreported	4.2	1.3
	100.0%	100.0%

72% are from out of state. Average age of full-time undergraduates is 20. 39% of classes have fewer than 20 students, 53% have between 20 and 50 students, 8% have more than 50 students.

STUDENT HOUSING

100% of freshmen live in college housing. Freshmen are not required to live on campus. Housing is not guaranteed for all undergraduates. Campus can house 7,235 undergraduates. Single rooms are available for students with medical or special needs.

EXPENSES

Tuition (2005-06): $30,950 per year.
Room: $6,270-$6,945. Board: $3,900.
There is no additional cost for LD program/services.

LD SERVICES

LD program size is not limited.

LD services available to:

■ Freshmen ■ Sophomores ■ Juniors ■ Seniors

Academic Accommodations

Curriculum		In class	
Foreign language waiver	❑	Early syllabus	❑
Lighter course load	■	Note takers in class	■
Math waiver	❑	Priority seating	❑
Other special classes	❑	Tape recorders	■
Priority registrations	■	Videotaped classes	❑
Substitution of courses	■	Text on tape	■
Exams		**Services**	
Extended time	■	Diagnostic tests	❑
Oral exams	❑	Learning centers	■
Take home exams	❑	Proofreaders	❑
Exams on tape or computer	■	Readers	■
Untimed exams	❑	Reading Machines/Kurzweil	■
Other accommodations	■	Special bookstore section	❑
		Typists	❑

Credit toward degree is not given for remedial courses taken.

Counseling Services

- ■ Academic
- ■ Psychological
- ❑ Student Support groups
- ❑ Vocational

Tutoring

Individual tutoring is available daily.

Average size of tutoring groups: 1

	Individual	Group
Time management	■	❑
Organizational skills	■	❑
Learning strategies	■	❑
Study skills	■	❑
Content area	■	❑
Writing lab	■	❑
Math lab	❑	❑

LD PROGRAM STAFF

Total number of LD Program staff (including director):

Full Time: 1 Part Time: 1

There is an advisor/advocate from the LD program available to students. 65 peer tutors are available to work with LD students.

Key staff person available to work with LD students: Dr. Kathy Duggan, Assistant Director

LD Program web site: http://www.bc.edu/libraries/centers/connors/

Boston University

Boston, MA

Address: 1 Sherborn Street, Boston, MA, 02215
Admissions telephone: 617 353-2300
Admissions FAX: 617 353-9695
Director of Admissions: Kelly Walter
Admissions e-mail: admissions@bu.edu
Web site: http://www.bu.edu
SAT Code: 3087 ACT Code: 1794

LD program name: Office of Disability Services
LD program address: 19 Deerfield Street
Clinical Director: Lorraine Wolf
LD program telephone: 617 353-3658
LD program e-mail: access@bu.edu
LD program enrollment: 450, Total campus enrollment: 17,740

GENERAL

Boston University is a private, coed, four-year institution. Urban campus in Boston (population: 589,141) plus 133 acres along the Charles River; medical center campus in downtown Boston. Served by air, bus, and train. Public transportation serves campus. Semester system.

LD ADMISSIONS

A personal interview is not required. Essay is required and may be typed.

SECONDARY SCHOOL REQUIREMENTS

Graduation from secondary school required; GED accepted. The following course distribution required: 4 units of English, 3 units of math, 3 units of science, 2 units of foreign language, 3 units of social studies, 3 units of history.

TESTING

SAT Reasoning or ACT required. SAT Subject required.

All enrolled freshmen (fall 2004):

Average SAT I Scores:	Verbal: 645	Math: 654
Average ACT Scores:	Composite: 28	

Child Study Team report is not required. Tests required as part of this documentation:

- [ ] WAIS-IV
- [ ] WISC-IV
- [ ] SATA
- [ ] Woodcock-Johnson
- [ ] Nelson-Denny Reading Test
- [ ] Other

UNDERGRADUATE STUDENT BODY

Total undergraduate student enrollment: 7,100 Men, 10,502 Women.

Composition of student body (fall 2004):

	Undergraduate	Freshmen
International	5.3	6.6
Black	2.6	2.5
American Indian	0.4	0.4
Asian-American	13.1	13.2
Hispanic	6.3	5.3
White	56.4	57.7
Unreported	15.9	14.3
	100.0%	100.0%

76% are from out of state. 3% join a fraternity and 5% join a sorority. Average age of full-time undergraduates is 20. 56% of classes have fewer than 20 students, 34% have between 20 and 50 students, 10% have more than 50 students.

STUDENT HOUSING

98% of freshmen live in college housing. Freshmen are required to live on campus. Housing is guaranteed for all undergraduates. Campus can house 10,816 undergraduates. Single rooms are available for students with medical or special needs. A medical note is required.

EXPENSES

Tuition (2005-06): $31,530 per year.

Room: $6,450. Board: $3,630.

Additional cost for LD program/services: $1,600 per semester for services beyond state mandate. Tutoring may be an additional cost.

LD SERVICES

LD program size is not limited.

LD services available to:

- [x] Freshmen
- [x] Sophomores
- [x] Juniors
- [x] Seniors

Academic Accommodations

Curriculum		In class	
Foreign language waiver	[ ]	Early syllabus	[ ]
Lighter course load	[x]	Note takers in class	[x]
Math waiver	[ ]	Priority seating	[ ]
Other special classes	[ ]	Tape recorders	[x]
Priority registrations	[ ]	Videotaped classes	[ ]
Substitution of courses	[ ]	Text on tape	[ ]
Exams		**Services**	
Extended time	[x]	Diagnostic tests	[ ]
Oral exams	[x]	Learning centers	[x]
Take home exams	[ ]	Proofreaders	[ ]
Exams on tape or computer	[ ]	Readers	[x]
Untimed exams	[ ]	Reading Machines/Kurzweil	[x]
Other accommodations	[x]	Special bookstore section	[ ]
		Typists	[ ]

Credit toward degree is not given for remedial courses taken.

Counseling Services

- [ ] Academic
- [ ] Psychological
- [ ] Student Support groups
- [ ] Vocational

Tutoring

Individual tutoring is available.

	Individual	Group
Time management	[ ]	[ ]
Organizational skills	[ ]	[ ]
Learning strategies	[ ]	[ ]
Study skills	[ ]	[ ]
Content area	[ ]	[ ]
Writing lab	[ ]	[ ]
Math lab	[ ]	[ ]

UNIQUE LD PROGRAM FEATURES

LD advocate and counseling are available as needed.

LD PROGRAM STAFF

Total number of LD Program staff (including director):

Full Time: 2 Part Time: 2

There is an advisor/advocate from the LD program available to students.

Key staff person available to work with LD students: Lorraine Wolf, Clinical Director, Office of Disability Services

LD Program web site: bu.edu/disability

Brandeis University

Waltham, MA

Address: 415 South Street, Waltham, MA, 02454-9110
Admissions telephone: 800 622-0622 (out-of-state)
Admissions FAX: 781 736-3536
Director of Enrollment: Deena Whitfield
Admissions e-mail: sendinfo@brandeis.edu
Web site: http://www.brandeis.edu
SAT Code: 3092 ACT Code: 1802

LD program name: Disabilities Services and Support
Coordinator: Beth Rodgers-Kay
LD program address: MS001 Kutz 108
LD program enrollment: 93, Total campus enrollment: 3,200

GENERAL

Brandeis University is a private, coed, four-year institution. 235-acre, suburban campus in Waltham (population: 59,226), 10 miles from Boston. Major airport, bus, and train serve Boston. School operates weekend transportation to Cambridge and Boston. Public transportation serves campus. Semester system.

LD ADMISSIONS

Students do not complete a separate application and are not simultaneously accepted to the LD program. A member of the LD program does not sit on the admissions committee. A personal interview is recommended. Essay is required and may be typed.

SECONDARY SCHOOL REQUIREMENTS

Graduation from secondary school required; GED accepted.

TESTING

SAT Subject required.

All enrolled freshmen (fall 2004):

Average SAT I Scores: Verbal: 671 Math: 680

Child Study Team report is not required. A neuropsychological or comprehensive psycho-educational evaluation is required for admission. Must be dated within 36 months of application. Tests required as part of this documentation:

- [x] WAIS-IV
- [ ] WISC-IV
- [ ] SATA
- [x] Woodcock-Johnson
- [x] Nelson-Denny Reading Test
- [x] Other

UNDERGRADUATE STUDENT BODY

Total undergraduate student enrollment: 1,344 Men, 1,737 Women.

Composition of student body (fall 2004):

	Undergraduate	Freshmen
International	5.8	6.9
Black	2.4	2.6
American Indian	0.1	0.2
Asian-American	7.5	7.6
Hispanic	3.9	2.8
White	65.2	67.3
Unreported	15.1	12.6
	100.0%	100.0%

75% are from out of state. Average age of full-time undergraduates is 20. 58% of classes have fewer than 20 students, 33% have between 20 and 50 students, 9% have more than 50 students.

STUDENT HOUSING

99% of freshmen live in college housing. Freshmen are not required to live on campus. Housing is guaranteed for freshmen and sophomores only. Campus can house 2,600 undergraduates. Single rooms are available for students with medical or special needs. A medical note is required.

EXPENSES

Tuition (2005-06): $31,532 per year.

Room: $5,083. Board: $3,967.
There is no additional cost for LD program/services.

LD SERVICES

LD program size is not limited.

LD services available to:

- [x] Freshmen
- [x] Sophomores
- [x] Juniors
- [x] Seniors

Academic Accommodations

Curriculum
- [ ] Foreign language waiver
- [ ] Lighter course load
- [ ] Math waiver
- [ ] Other special classes
- [ ] Priority registrations
- [x] Substitution of courses

Exams
- [x] Extended time
- [ ] Oral exams
- [ ] Take home exams
- [x] Exams on tape or computer
- [ ] Untimed exams
- [x] Other accommodations

In class
- [ ] Early syllabus
- [x] Note takers in class
- [ ] Priority seating
- [x] Tape recorders
- [ ] Videotaped classes
- [x] Text on tape

Services
- [ ] Diagnostic tests
- [ ] Learning centers
- [ ] Proofreaders
- [ ] Readers
- [x] Reading Machines/Kurzweil
- [ ] Special bookstore section
- [ ] Typists

Credit toward degree is not given for remedial courses taken.

Counseling Services

- [x] Academic
- [x] Psychological
- [ ] Student Support groups
- [ ] Vocational

Tutoring

Individual tutoring is not available.

	Individual	Group
Time management	[ ]	[ ]
Organizational skills	[ ]	[ ]
Learning strategies	[ ]	[ ]
Study skills	[ ]	[ ]
Content area	[ ]	[ ]
Writing lab	[ ]	[ ]
Math lab	[ ]	[ ]

LD PROGRAM STAFF

Total number of LD Program staff (including director):

Full Time: 1 Part Time: 1

There is an advisor/advocate from the LD program available to students.

Key staff person available to work with LD students: Beth Rodgers-Kay, Coordinator of Disabilities Services and Support

Bridgewater State College

Bridgewater, MA

Address: Boyden Hall, Bridgewater, MA, 02325
Admissions telephone: 508 531-1237
Admissions FAX: 508 531-1746
Director of Admissions: Gregg Meyer
Admissions e-mail: admission@bridgew.edu
Web site: http://www.bridgew.edu
SAT Code: 3517 ACT Code: 1900

LD program name: Disability Resources
LD program address: Maxwell Library 001
Learning Disabilities Specialist: Pamela Spillane
LD program telephone: 508 531-1214
LD program e-mail: pspillane@bridgew.edu
Total campus enrollment: 7,753

GENERAL

Bridgewater State College is a public, coed, four-year institution. 235-acre campus in Bridgewater (population: 25,185), 30 miles from Boston and 35 miles from Providence, RI. Served by bus and train; major airport serves Boston; smaller airport serves Providence, RI. School operates transportation in Bridgewater and to Brockton. Public transportation serves campus. Semester system.

LD ADMISSIONS

Students do not complete a separate application and are simultaneously accepted to the LD program. A member of the LD program does not sit on the admissions committee. A personal interview is not required. Essay is required and may be typed.

SECONDARY SCHOOL REQUIREMENTS

Graduation from secondary school required; GED accepted. The following course distribution required: 4 units of English, 3 units of math, 3 units of science, 2 units of foreign language, 1 unit of social studies, 1 unit of history, 2 units of academic electives.

TESTING

SAT Reasoning or ACT required. SAT Subject recommended.

All enrolled freshmen (fall 2004):

Average SAT I Scores:	Verbal: 507	Math: 511
Average ACT Scores:	Composite: 21	

Child Study Team report is not required. A neuropsychological or comprehensive psycho-educational evaluation is required for admission. Must be dated within 36 months of application. Tests required as part of this documentation:

- [x] WAIS-IV
- [ ] WISC-IV
- [ ] SATA
- [x] Woodcock-Johnson
- [ ] Nelson-Denny Reading Test
- [ ] Other

UNDERGRADUATE STUDENT BODY

Total undergraduate student enrollment: 2,783 Men, 4,416 Women.

Composition of student body (fall 2004):

	Undergraduate	Freshmen
International	0.8	2.0
Black	5.4	3.6
American Indian	0.3	0.4
Asian-American	1.8	1.1
Hispanic	2.2	1.5
White	82.1	68.6
Unreported	7.4	22.8
	100.0%	100.0%

3% are from out of state. Average age of full-time undergraduates is 21. 35% of classes have fewer than 20 students, 63% have between 20 and 50 students, 2% have more than 50 students.

STUDENT HOUSING

49% of freshmen live in college housing. Freshmen are not required to live on campus. Housing is guaranteed for all undergraduates. Campus can house 2,045 undergraduates. Single rooms are available for students with medical or special needs. A medical note is required.

EXPENSES

Tuition (2005-06): $910 per year (in-state), $7,050 (out-of-state).
Room: $4,114. Board: $2,500.
There is no additional cost for LD program/services.

LD SERVICES

LD program size is not limited.

LD services available to:

- [x] Freshmen
- [x] Sophomores
- [x] Juniors
- [x] Seniors

Academic Accommodations

Curriculum

- [ ] Foreign language waiver
- [x] Lighter course load
- [ ] Math waiver
- [ ] Other special classes
- [ ] Priority registrations
- [ ] Substitution of courses

Exams

- [x] Extended time
- [x] Oral exams
- [ ] Take home exams
- [ ] Exams on tape or computer
- [x] Untimed exams
- [ ] Other accommodations

In class

- [ ] Early syllabus
- [x] Note takers in class
- [ ] Priority seating
- [x] Tape recorders
- [ ] Videotaped classes
- [ ] Text on tape

Services

- [ ] Diagnostic tests
- [x] Learning centers
- [ ] Proofreaders
- [x] Readers
- [ ] Reading Machines/Kurzweil
- [ ] Special bookstore section
- [ ] Typists

Credit toward degree is not given for remedial courses taken.

Counseling Services

- [ ] Academic
- [ ] Psychological
- [ ] Student Support groups
- [ ] Vocational

Tutoring

Individual tutoring is available weekly.

Average size of tutoring groups: 1

	Individual	Group
Time management	[x]	[x]
Organizational skills	[x]	[x]
Learning strategies	[x]	[x]
Study skills	[x]	[x]
Content area	[x]	[x]
Writing lab	[x]	[x]
Math lab	[x]	[x]

LD PROGRAM STAFF

Total number of LD Program staff (including director):

Full Time: 2 Part Time: 2

There is an advisor/advocate from the LD program available to students.

Key staff person available to work with LD students: Pamela Spillane, Learning Disabilities Specialist

LD Program web site: www.bridgew.edu/AAC/Disability_Resources.cfm

Clark University

Worcester, MA

Address: 950 Main Street, Worcester, MA, 01610-1477
Admissions telephone: 800 GO-CLARK
Dean of Admissions: Harold Wingood
Admissions e-mail: admissions@clarku.edu
Web site: http://www.clarku.edu
SAT Code: 3279 ACT Code: 1808

LD program name: Academic Advising Center - Disability Services
Coordinator of Disability Services: Sharon de Klerk
LD program telephone: 508 793-7468
LD program e-mail: sdeklerk@clarku.edu
LD program enrollment: 135, Total campus enrollment: 2,204

GENERAL

Clark University is a private, coed, four-year institution. 50-acre, urban campus in Worcester (population: 172,648), 50 miles from Boston; branch campus in Framingham. Served by air, bus, and train; major airport serves Boston. School operates transportation to consortium schools and to Boston and Worcester locations on weekends. Public transportation serves campus. Semester system.

LD ADMISSIONS

A member of the LD program does not sit on the admissions committee. A personal interview is recommended. Essay is required and may be typed.

SECONDARY SCHOOL REQUIREMENTS

Graduation from secondary school required; GED accepted.

TESTING

SAT Reasoning or ACT required. SAT Subject recommended.

All enrolled freshmen (fall 2004):

Average SAT I Scores: Verbal: 593 Math: 588
Average ACT Scores: Composite: 25

Child Study Team report is not required. A neuropsychological or comprehensive psycho-educational evaluation is required for admission. Must be dated within 36 months of application. Tests required as part of this documentation:

- [x] WAIS-IV
- [ ] WISC-IV
- [x] SATA
- [x] Woodcock-Johnson
- [x] Nelson-Denny Reading Test
- [x] Other

UNDERGRADUATE STUDENT BODY

Total undergraduate student enrollment: 846 Men, 1,292 Women.

Composition of student body (fall 2004):

	Undergraduate	Freshmen
International	8.3	7.2
Black	3.0	2.7
American Indian	0.6	0.3
Asian-American	5.9	3.8
Hispanic	2.5	3.1
White	61.9	63.8
Unreported	17.8	19.1
	100.0%	100.0%

60% are from out of state. Average age of full-time undergraduates is 20. 57% of classes have fewer than 20 students, 38% have between 20 and 50 students, 5% have more than 50 students.

STUDENT HOUSING

97% of freshmen live in college housing. Freshmen are required to live on campus. Housing is guaranteed for all undergraduates. Campus can house 1,570 undergraduates. Single rooms are available for students with medical or special needs. A medical note is required.

EXPENSES

Tuition (2005-06): $29,300 per year.
Room: $3,400. Board: $2,200.

There is no additional cost for LD program/services.

LD SERVICES

LD program size is not limited.

LD services available to:

- [x] Freshmen
- [x] Sophomores
- [x] Juniors
- [x] Seniors

Academic Accommodations

Curriculum		In class	
Foreign language waiver	[ ]	Early syllabus	[ ]
Lighter course load	[x]	Note takers in class	[ ]
Math waiver	[ ]	Priority seating	[ ]
Other special classes	[ ]	Tape recorders	[ ]
Priority registrations	[ ]	Videotaped classes	[ ]
Substitution of courses	[ ]	Text on tape	[x]
Exams		**Services**	
Extended time	[x]	Diagnostic tests	[ ]
Oral exams	[x]	Learning centers	[ ]
Take home exams	[ ]	Proofreaders	[ ]
Exams on tape or computer	[ ]	Readers	[x]
Untimed exams	[ ]	Reading Machines/Kurzweil	[ ]
Other accommodations	[ ]	Special bookstore section	[ ]
		Typists	[ ]

Credit toward degree is not given for remedial courses taken.

Counseling Services

- [ ] Academic
- [x] Psychological — Meets 16 times per academic year
- [ ] Student Support groups
- [ ] Vocational

Tutoring

Individual tutoring is not available.

	Individual	Group
Time management	[x]	[ ]
Organizational skills	[x]	[ ]
Learning strategies	[ ]	[ ]
Study skills	[x]	[ ]
Content area	[ ]	[ ]
Writing lab	[x]	[ ]
Math lab	[x]	[ ]

LD PROGRAM STAFF

Total number of LD Program staff (including director):

Full Time: 1 Part Time: 1

There is an advisor/advocate from the LD program available to students. The advisor/advocate meets with students four times per month. One graduate student is available to work with LD students.

Key staff person available to work with LD students: Sharon de Klerk, Coordinator of Disability Services

LD Program web site: www.clarku.edu/offices/aac/ada/

College of the Holy Cross

Worcester, MA

Address: 1 College Street, Worcester, MA, 01610
Admissions telephone: 800 442-2421
Admissions FAX: 508 793-3888
Director of Admissions: Ann Bowe McDermott
Admissions e-mail: admissions@holycross.edu
Web site: http://www.holycross.edu
SAT Code: 3282 ACT Code: 1810

Assistant Dean for Student Development: Dr. Matthew Toth
LD program telephone: 508 793-3693
Total campus enrollment: 2,745

GENERAL

College of the Holy Cross is a private, coed, four-year institution. 174-acre, suburban campus in Worcester (population: 172,648), 45 miles from Boston. Served by air, bus, and train; major airport serves Boston. School operates transportation to consortium schools and Worcester Art Museum. Public transportation serves campus. Semester system.

LD ADMISSIONS

A personal interview is recommended. Essay is required and may be typed. Language requirement may be waived or substituted

SECONDARY SCHOOL REQUIREMENTS

Graduation from secondary school required; GED accepted.

TESTING

SAT Subject recommended.

All enrolled freshmen (fall 2004):

Average SAT I Scores: Verbal: 631 Math: 629

Child Study Team report is not required. Tests required as part of this documentation:

- ☐ WAIS-IV
- ☐ WISC-IV
- ☐ SATA
- ☐ Woodcock-Johnson
- ☐ Nelson-Denny Reading Test
- ☐ Other

UNDERGRADUATE STUDENT BODY

Total undergraduate student enrollment: 1,339 Men, 1,472 Women.

Composition of student body (fall 2004):

	Undergraduate	Freshmen
International	0.9	1.0
Black	4.0	3.3
American Indian	0.6	0.3
Asian-American	5.4	4.5
Hispanic	4.1	4.8
White	74.6	76.6
Unreported	10.4	9.5
	100.0%	100.0%

66% are from out of state. Average age of full-time undergraduates is 20. 52% of classes have fewer than 20 students, 47% have between 20 and 50 students, 1% have more than 50 students.

STUDENT HOUSING

100% of freshmen live in college housing. Freshmen are required to live on campus. Housing is guaranteed for all undergraduates. Campus can house 2,350 undergraduates. Single rooms are available for students with medical or special needs. A medical note is required.

EXPENSES

Tuition (2005-06): $30,960 per year.
Room & Board: $4,610.

There is no additional cost for LD program/services.

LD SERVICES

LD program size is not limited.

LD services available to:

☐ Freshmen ☐ Sophomores ☐ Juniors ☐ Seniors

Academic Accommodations

Curriculum		**In class**	
Foreign language waiver	☐	Early syllabus	☐
Lighter course load	☐	Note takers in class	☐
Math waiver	☐	Priority seating	☐
Other special classes	☐	Tape recorders	☐
Priority registrations	☐	Videotaped classes	☐
Substitution of courses	☐	Text on tape	☐
Exams		**Services**	
Extended time	☒	Diagnostic tests	☐
Oral exams	☐	Learning centers	☒
Take home exams	☐	Proofreaders	☐
Exams on tape or computer	☐	Readers	☐
Untimed exams	☐	Reading Machines/Kurzweil	☐
Other accommodations	☐	Special bookstore section	☐
		Typists	☐

Credit toward degree is not given for remedial courses taken.

Counseling Services

- ☐ Academic
- ☐ Psychological
- ☐ Student Support groups
- ☐ Vocational

Tutoring

	Individual	Group
Time management	☐	☐
Organizational skills	☐	☐
Learning strategies	☐	☐
Study skills	☒	☐
Content area	☐	☐
Writing lab	☒	☐
Math lab	☒	☐

UNIQUE LD PROGRAM FEATURES

All services are granted based on documentation.

LD PROGRAM STAFF

Total number of LD Program staff (including director):

Full Time: 1 Part Time: 1

Key staff person available to work with LD students: Dr. Matthew Toth, Assistant Dean for Student Development

Curry College

Milton, MA

Address: 1071 Blue Hill Avenue, Milton, MA, 02186
Admissions telephone: 800 669-0686
Admissions FAX: 617 333-2114
Dean of Admissions: Jane P. Fidler
Admissions e-mail: curryadm@curry.edu
Web site: http://www.curry.edu
SAT Code: 3285 ACT Code: 1814

LD program name: Program for Advancement of Learning (PAL)
PAL Admissions Counselor: Anna Langenfeld
LD program telephone: 617 333-2250, extension 2079
LD program e-mail: alangenf@curry.edu
LD program enrollment: 375, Total campus enrollment: 2,695

GENERAL

Curry College is a private, coed, four-year institution. 131-acre, suburban campus in Milton (population: 26,062), seven miles from Boston; continuing education campus in Plymouth. Major airport, bus, and train serve Boston. School operates transportation to public transportation and downtown Boston. Semester system.

LD ADMISSIONS

Application Deadline: 03/01. Students complete a separate application and are simultaneously accepted to the LD program. A member of the LD program does sit on the admissions committee. High school waivers are accepted for foreign language. A personal interview is recommended. Essay is required and may be typed.

For fall 2004, 703 completed self-identified LD applications were received. 402 applications were offered admission, and 174 enrolled.

SECONDARY SCHOOL REQUIREMENTS

Graduation from secondary school required; GED accepted. The following course distribution required: 4 units of English, 3 units of math, 2 units of science, 2 units of foreign language, 2 units of social studies, 2 units of history.

TESTING

SAT Reasoning or ACT required of some applicants. SAT Subject recommended.

All enrolled freshmen (fall 2004):

Average SAT I Scores: Verbal: 470 Math: 450

Child Study Team report is not required. A neuropsychological or comprehensive psycho-educational evaluation is required for admission. Must be dated within 36 months of application. Tests required as part of this documentation:

■ WAIS-IV	■ Woodcock-Johnson
■ WISC-IV	■ Nelson-Denny Reading Test
❑ SATA	■ Other

UNDERGRADUATE STUDENT BODY

Total undergraduate student enrollment: 2,695.

Composition of student body (fall 2004):

	Undergraduate	Freshmen
International	0.7	1.1
Black	6.9	7.0
American Indian	0.4	0.2
Asian-American	1.7	1.5
Hispanic	2.1	2.6
White	73.6	59.5
Unreported	14.6	28.1
	100.0%	100.0%

35% are from out of state. Average age of full-time undergraduates is 22. 60% of classes have fewer than 20 students, 39% have between 20 and 50 students, 1% have more than 50 students.

STUDENT HOUSING

85% of freshmen live in college housing. Freshmen are not required to live on campus. Housing is guaranteed for all undergraduates. Campus can house 1,327 undergraduates. Single rooms are available for students with medical or special needs. A medical note is required.

EXPENSES

Tuition (2005-06): $21,900 per year.

Room: $5,000. Board: $4,140.

Additional cost for LD program/services: $4,800.

LD SERVICES

LD program size is not limited.

LD services available to:

■ Freshmen ■ Sophomores ■ Juniors ■ Seniors

Academic Accommodations

Curriculum		In class	
Foreign language waiver	❑	Early syllabus	❑
Lighter course load	■	Note takers in class	■
Math waiver	❑	Priority seating	❑
Other special classes	■	Tape recorders	■
Priority registrations	❑	Videotaped classes	❑
Substitution of courses	❑	Text on tape	■
Exams		**Services**	
Extended time	■	Diagnostic tests	■
Oral exams	■	Learning centers	■
Take home exams	❑	Proofreaders	❑
Exams on tape or computer	■	Readers	■
Untimed exams	■	Reading Machines/Kurzweil	■
Other accommodations	■	Special bookstore section	❑
		Typists	❑

Credit toward degree is given for remedial courses taken.

Counseling Services

■ Academic — Meets 60 times per academic year
❑ Psychological
❑ Student Support groups
❑ Vocational

Tutoring

Individual tutoring is available weekly.

Average size of tutoring groups: 2

	Individual	Group
Time management	■	■
Organizational skills	■	■
Learning strategies	■	■
Study skills	■	■
Content area	■	■
Writing lab	■	■
Math lab	■	■

UNIQUE LD PROGRAM FEATURES

Summer PAL prepares students for the transition to college life.

LD PROGRAM STAFF

Total number of LD Program staff (including director):

Full Time: 16 Part Time: 16

There is an advisor/advocate from the LD program available to students. The advisor/advocate meets with faculty once per month and students eight times per month.

Key staff person available to work with LD students: Dr. Susan Pratt, Coordinator, PAL

Dean College

Franklin, MA

Address: 99 Main Street, Franklin, MA, 02038
Admissions telephone: 508 541-1508
Admissions FAX: 508 541-8726
Admissions Contact: Paul J. Vaccaro
Admissions e-mail: admission@dean.edu
Web site: http://www.dean.edu

LD program name: Dean Arch Program
VP Student Development & Retention: Cindy Kozil
LD program telephone: 508 541-1551
LD program e-mail: ckozil@dean.edu
LD program enrollment: 81, Total campus enrollment: 1,298

GENERAL

Dean College is a private, four-year institution. Campus in suburban Franklin (population 30,189); 35 miles from Boston and 20 miles from Providence, RI. Public transportation serves campus. Semester system.

LD ADMISSIONS

Students do not complete a separate application and are simultaneously accepted to the LD program. A member of the LD program does sit on the admissions committee. High school waivers are accepted for foreign language. A personal interview is required. Essay is required and may be typed.

For fall 2004, 144 completed self-identified LD applications were received. 95 applications were offered admission, and 41 enrolled.

SECONDARY SCHOOL REQUIREMENTS

The following course distribution required: 4 units of English, 2 units of math, 2 units of science, 3 units of social studies, 1 unit of history, 2 units of academic electives.

TESTING

SAT Reasoning or ACT required. SAT Subject recommended.

All enrolled freshmen (fall 2004):

Average SAT I Scores:	Verbal: 440	Math: 443
Average ACT Scores:	Composite: 17	

Child Study Team report is not required. A neuropsychological or comprehensive psycho-educational evaluation is required for admission. Must be dated within 36 months of application. Tests required as part of this documentation:

- ■ WAIS-IV
- ■ WISC-IV
- □ SATA
- ■ Woodcock-Johnson
- ■ Nelson-Denny Reading Test
- □ Other

UNDERGRADUATE STUDENT BODY

Total undergraduate student enrollment: 1,298.

Composition of student body (fall 2004):

	Undergraduate	Freshmen
International	1.9	4.4
Black	4.5	6.2
American Indian	0.4	0.3
Asian-American	0.7	1.0
Hispanic	3.0	2.4
White	32.6	39.4
Unreported	56.9	46.3
	100.0%	100.0%

Average age of full-time undergraduates is 20. 64% of classes have fewer than 20 students, 35% have between 20 and 50 students, 1% have more than 50 students.

STUDENT HOUSING

92% of freshmen live in college housing. Freshmen are required to live on campus. Housing is guaranteed for all undergraduates. Campus can house 808 undergraduates. Single rooms are not available for students with medical or special needs.

EXPENSES

Tuition (2005-06): $22,650 per year.
Room: $6,174. Board: $3,590.
Additional cost for LD program/services: $2,500 per semester.

LD SERVICES

LD program size is not limited.

LD services available to:

■ Freshmen ■ Sophomores ■ Juniors ■ Seniors

Academic Accommodations

Curriculum		In class	
Foreign language waiver	□	Early syllabus	□
Lighter course load	■	Note takers in class	■
Math waiver	□	Priority seating	□
Other special classes	■	Tape recorders	■
Priority registrations	□	Videotaped classes	□
Substitution of courses	□	Text on tape	□
Exams		**Services**	
Extended time	■	Diagnostic tests	□
Oral exams	■	Learning centers	■
Take home exams	□	Proofreaders	□
Exams on tape or computer	□	Readers	■
Untimed exams	■	Reading Machines/Kurzweil	■
Other accommodations	□	Special bookstore section	□
		Typists	□

Credit toward degree is not given for remedial courses taken.

Counseling Services

- ■ Academic
- ■ Psychological
- □ Student Support groups
- □ Vocational

Tutoring

Individual tutoring is available weekly.

Average size of tutoring groups: 4

	Individual	Group
Time management	□	■
Organizational skills	□	■
Learning strategies	□	■
Study skills	□	■
Content area	■	□
Writing lab	□	■
Math lab	□	■

LD PROGRAM STAFF

Total number of LD Program staff (including director):

Full Time: 1 Part Time: 1

There is an advisor/advocate from the LD program available to students. The advisor/advocate meets with faculty once per month and students four times per month. 10 peer tutors are available to work with LD students.

Key staff person available to work with LD students: Erin Lowery-Corkran, Director of Learning Services

Eastern Nazarene College

Quincy, MA

Address: 23 East Elm Avenue, Quincy, MA, 02170
Admissions telephone: 800 88-ENC-88
Admissions FAX: 617 745-3992
Director of Admissions: Doris Webb
Admissions e-mail: admissio@enc.edu
Web site: http://www.enc.edu
SAT Code: 3365 ACT Code: 1818

Director of Academic Services: Joyce Klittich
LD program telephone: 617 745-3837
LD program e-mail: klitticj@enc.edu
LD program enrollment: 36, Total campus enrollment: 1,065

GENERAL

Eastern Nazarene College is a private, coed, four-year institution. 20-acre, suburban campus in Quincy (population: 88,025), six miles from Boston. Major airport, bus, and train serve Boston. Public transportation serves campus. 4-1-4 system.

LD ADMISSIONS

Students do not complete a separate application and are simultaneously accepted to the LD program. A member of the LD program does sit on the admissions committee. A personal interview is recommended. Essay is not required. Foreign language and math requirements may be waived.

20 applications were offered admission, and 15 enrolled.

SECONDARY SCHOOL REQUIREMENTS

Graduation from secondary school required; GED accepted.

TESTING

SAT Reasoning required. ACT considered if submitted. SAT Subject required.

All enrolled freshmen (fall 2004):

Average SAT I Scores:	Verbal: 520	Math: 520
Average ACT Scores:	Composite: 21	

Child Study Team report is not required. A neuropsychological or comprehensive psycho-education evaluation is not required for admission. Tests required as part of this documentation:

- [x] WAIS-IV
- [x] WISC-IV
- [ ] SATA
- [x] Woodcock-Johnson
- [ ] Nelson-Denny Reading Test
- [ ] Other

UNDERGRADUATE STUDENT BODY

Total undergraduate student enrollment: 435 Men, 640 Women.

Composition of student body (fall 2004):

	Undergraduate	Freshmen
International	1.7	1.3
Black	5.8	12.5
American Indian	0.0	0.7
Asian-American	2.9	2.4
Hispanic	5.8	4.8
White	79.2	72.5
Unreported	4.6	5.8
	100.0%	100.0%

53% are from out of state. Average age of full-time undergraduates is 19. 70% of classes have fewer than 20 students, 29% have between 20 and 50 students, 1% have more than 50 students.

STUDENT HOUSING

93% of freshmen live in college housing. Freshmen are required to live on campus. Housing is guaranteed for all undergraduates. Campus can house 630 undergraduates. Single rooms are available for students with medical or special needs. A medical note is required.

EXPENSES

Tuition 2004-05: $16,855 per year.

Room & Board: $5,920.

There is no additional cost for LD program/services.

LD SERVICES

LD program size is not limited.

LD services available to:

- [x] Freshmen
- [x] Sophomores
- [x] Juniors
- [x] Seniors

Academic Accommodations

Curriculum		In class	
Foreign language waiver	[ ]	Early syllabus	[ ]
Lighter course load	[x]	Note takers in class	[x]
Math waiver	[ ]	Priority seating	[ ]
Other special classes	[ ]	Tape recorders	[x]
Priority registrations	[ ]	Videotaped classes	[ ]
Substitution of courses	[ ]	Text on tape	[ ]
Exams		**Services**	
Extended time	[x]	Diagnostic tests	[x]
Oral exams	[x]	Learning centers	[x]
Take home exams	[ ]	Proofreaders	[ ]
Exams on tape or computer	[ ]	Readers	[ ]
Untimed exams	[x]	Reading Machines/Kurzweil	[x]
Other accommodations	[ ]	Special bookstore section	[ ]
		Typists	[ ]

Credit toward degree is not given for remedial courses taken.

Counseling Services

- [x] Academic
- [x] Psychological
- [ ] Student Support groups
- [x] Vocational

Meets 2 times per academic year

Tutoring

Individual tutoring is available daily.

Average size of tutoring groups: 6

	Individual	Group
Time management	[x]	[ ]
Organizational skills	[x]	[ ]
Learning strategies	[x]	[ ]
Study skills	[x]	[ ]
Content area	[x]	[ ]
Writing lab	[ ]	[ ]
Math lab	[ ]	[ ]

LD PROGRAM STAFF

Total number of LD Program staff (including director):

Full Time: 1 Part Time: 1

There is an advisor/advocate from the LD program available to students. 40 peer tutors are available to work with LD students.

Key staff person available to work with LD students: Joyce Klittich, Director of Academic Services

Elms College (College of Our Lady of the Elms)

Chicopee, MA

Address: 291 Springfield Street, Chicopee, MA, 01013
Admissions telephone: 800 255-ELMS
Admissions FAX: 413 594-2781
Director of Admissions: Joseph P. Wagner
Admissions e-mail: admissions@elms.edu
Web site: http://www.elms.edu
SAT Code: 3283 ACT Code: 1812

LD program name: Office of Student Disability Services
Student Disability Coordinator: Anne Marie Smith
LD program telephone: 413 265-2333
LD program e-mail: smitha@elms.edu
Total campus enrollment: 823

GENERAL

Elms College (College of Our Lady of the Elms) is a private, coed, four-year institution. 32-acre, suburban campus in Chicopee (population: 54,653), two miles from Springfield and 90 miles from Boston. Major airports serve Windsor Locks, CT (25 miles) and Boston; bus and train serve Springfield. Public transportation serves campus. Semester system.

LD ADMISSIONS

Students do not complete a separate application and are simultaneously accepted to the LD program. A member of the LD program does not sit on the admissions committee. High school waivers are accepted for foreign language. Essay is required and may be typed.

SECONDARY SCHOOL REQUIREMENTS

Graduation from secondary school required; GED accepted. The following course distribution required: 4 units of English, 3 units of math, 2 units of science, 2 units of foreign language, 1 unit of social studies, 1 unit of history.

TESTING

SAT Reasoning or ACT required. SAT Subject recommended.

All enrolled freshmen (fall 2004):

Average SAT I Scores: Verbal: 490 Math: 450

Child Study Team report is not required. A neuropsychological or comprehensive psycho-educational evaluation is required for admission. Must be dated within 12 months of application. Tests required as part of this documentation:

- ☐ WAIS-IV
- ☐ WISC-IV
- ☐ SATA
- ■ Woodcock-Johnson
- ■ Nelson-Denny Reading Test
- ☐ Other

UNDERGRADUATE STUDENT BODY

Total undergraduate student enrollment: 90 Men, 564 Women.

Composition of student body (fall 2004):

	Undergraduate	Freshmen
International	0.0	0.3
Black	4.9	4.9
American Indian	0.1	0.2
Asian-American	0.8	1.4
Hispanic	1.6	3.3
White	78.7	69.5
Unreported	13.9	20.4
	100.0%	100.0%

12% are from out of state. Average age of full-time undergraduates is 23. 76% of classes have fewer than 20 students, 24% have between 20 and 50 students.

STUDENT HOUSING

65% of freshmen live in college housing. Freshmen are not required to live on campus. Housing is guaranteed for all undergraduates. Single rooms are available for students with medical or special needs. A medical note is not required.

EXPENSES

Tuition 2004-05: $19,250 per year.

Room & Board: $7,750.

LD SERVICES

LD program size is not limited.

LD services available to:

■ Freshmen ■ Sophomores ■ Juniors ■ Seniors

Academic Accommodations

Curriculum		In class	
Foreign language waiver	☐	Early syllabus	☐
Lighter course load	☐	Note takers in class	☐
Math waiver	☐	Priority seating	☐
Other special classes	☐	Tape recorders	☐
Priority registrations	☐	Videotaped classes	☐
Substitution of courses	☐	Text on tape	☐
Exams		**Services**	
Extended time	☐	Diagnostic tests	☐
Oral exams	☐	Learning centers	☐
Take home exams	☐	Proofreaders	☐
Exams on tape or computer	☐	Readers	☐
Untimed exams	☐	Reading Machines/Kurzweil	☐
Other accommodations	☐	Special bookstore section	☐
		Typists	☐

Counseling Services

- ☐ Academic
- ☐ Psychological
- ☐ Student Support groups
- ☐ Vocational

Tutoring

Individual tutoring is available.

	Individual	Group
Time management	☐	☐
Organizational skills	☐	☐
Learning strategies	☐	☐
Study skills	☐	☐
Content area	☐	☐
Writing lab	☐	☐
Math lab	☐	☐

LD PROGRAM STAFF

There is an advisor/advocate from the LD program available to students. The advisor/advocate meets with students twice per month.

Key staff person available to work with LD students: Anne Marie Smith, Student Disability Coordinator

Emerson College

Boston, MA

Address: 120 Boylston Street, Boston, MA, 02116-4624
Admissions telephone: 617 824-8600
Admissions FAX: 617 824-8609
Director of Undergraduate Admissions: Sara S. Ramirez
Admissions e-mail: admission@emerson.edu
Web site: http://www.emerson.edu
SAT Code: 3367 ACT Code: 1820

LD program name: Learning Assistance Center
Coordinator of Academic Disability Services: Anthony Bashir
LD program telephone: 617 824-8415
LD program e-mail: dso@emerson.edu
LD program enrollment: 60, Total campus enrollment: 3,418

GENERAL

Emerson College is a private, coed, four-year institution. Urban campus in Boston (population: 589,141); branch sites in Los Angeles, CA and abroad in the Netherlands. Served by air, bus, and train. Public transportation serves campus. Semester system.

LD ADMISSIONS

Students do not complete a separate application and are not simultaneously accepted to the LD program. A member of the LD program does not sit on the admissions committee. A personal interview is not required. Essay is required and may be typed.

SECONDARY SCHOOL REQUIREMENTS

Graduation from secondary school required; GED accepted. The following course distribution required: 4 units of English, 3 units of math, 3 units of science, 3 units of foreign language, 3 units of social studies.

TESTING

SAT Reasoning or ACT required. SAT Subject required.

All enrolled freshmen (fall 2004):

Average SAT I Scores:	Verbal: 628	Math: 591
Average ACT Scores:	Composite: 26	

Child Study Team report is not required. A neuropsychological or comprehensive psycho-education evaluation is not required for admission. Tests required as part of this documentation:

- ☐ WAIS-IV
- ☐ WISC-IV
- ☐ SATA
- ☐ Woodcock-Johnson
- ☐ Nelson-Denny Reading Test
- ☐ Other

UNDERGRADUATE STUDENT BODY

Total undergraduate student enrollment: 1,362 Men, 2,050 Women.

Composition of student body (fall 2004):

	Undergraduate	Freshmen
International	2.9	3.0
Black	3.0	2.5
American Indian	0.1	0.4
Asian-American	5.4	4.1
Hispanic	6.0	5.0
White	73.6	76.3
Unreported	9.0	8.7
	100.0%	100.0%

65% are from out of state. 3% join a fraternity and 3% join a sorority. Average age of full-time undergraduates is 21. 62% of classes have fewer than 20 students, 29% have between 20 and 50 students, 9% have more than 50 students.

STUDENT HOUSING

97% of freshmen live in college housing. Freshmen are not required to live on campus. Housing is not guaranteed for all undergraduates. Campus can house 1,207 undergraduates. Single rooms are available for students with medical or special needs. A medical note is required.

EXPENSES

Tuition (2005-06): $24,064 per year.
Room: $6,200. Board: $4,220.
There is no additional cost for LD program/services.

LD SERVICES

LD program size is not limited.

LD services available to:

■ Freshmen ■ Sophomores ■ Juniors ■ Seniors

Academic Accommodations

Curriculum		**In class**	
Foreign language waiver	☐	Early syllabus	☐
Lighter course load	■	Note takers in class	■
Math waiver	☐	Priority seating	☐
Other special classes	☐	Tape recorders	■
Priority registrations	☐	Videotaped classes	☐
Substitution of courses	☐	Text on tape	■
Exams		**Services**	
Extended time	■	Diagnostic tests	☐
Oral exams	■	Learning centers	■
Take home exams	☐	Proofreaders	■
Exams on tape or computer	■	Readers	☐
Untimed exams	☐	Reading Machines/Kurzweil	■
Other accommodations	☐	Special bookstore section	☐
		Typists	■

Credit toward degree is not given for remedial courses taken.

Counseling Services

- ■ Academic
- ■ Psychological
- ☐ Student Support groups
- ■ Vocational

Tutoring

Individual tutoring is available weekly.

	Individual	Group
Time management	■	☐
Organizational skills	■	☐
Learning strategies	■	☐
Study skills	■	☐
Content area	■	☐
Writing lab	■	☐
Math lab	■	☐

LD PROGRAM STAFF

Total number of LD Program staff (including director):

Full Time: 2 Part Time: 2

There is no advisor/advocate from the LD program available to students.

Key staff person available to work with LD students: Anthony Bashir, Coordinator of Academic Disability Services

LD Program web site: http://www.emerson.edu/learning_assistance

Emmanuel College

Boston, MA

Address: 400 The Fenway, Boston, MA, 02115
Admissions telephone: 617 735-9715
Admissions FAX: 617 735-9801
Dean of Admissions: Sandra Robbins
Admissions e-mail: enroll@emmanuel.edu
Web site: http://www.emmanuel.edu
SAT Code: 3368 ACT Code: 1822

Disabilities Coordinator: Susan Mayo
LD program telephone: 617 735-9923
LD program e-mail: mayos@emmanuel.edu
LD program enrollment: 24, Total campus enrollment: 1,947

GENERAL

Emmanuel College is a private, coed, four-year institution. 16-acre, urban campus in Boston (population: 589,141); branch campuses in Charlestown, Framingham, Leominster, Quincy, and Woburn. Served by air, bus, and train. School operates transportation to local transit stops, Boston Public Library, and Northeastern U. Public transportation serves campus. Semester system.

LD ADMISSIONS

A personal interview is recommended. Essay is required and may be typed.

SECONDARY SCHOOL REQUIREMENTS

Graduation from secondary school required; GED accepted. The following course distribution required: 4 units of English, 3 units of math, 2 units of science, 2 units of foreign language, 2 units of social studies.

TESTING

SAT Reasoning or ACT required.

All enrolled freshmen (fall 2004):

Average SAT I Scores:	Verbal: 530	Math: 510
Average ACT Scores:	Composite: 21	

Child Study Team report is not required. Tests required as part of this documentation:

❑ WAIS-IV	❑ Woodcock-Johnson
❑ WISC-IV	❑ Nelson-Denny Reading Test
❑ SATA	❑ Other

UNDERGRADUATE STUDENT BODY

Total undergraduate student enrollment: 156 Men, 1,204 Women.

Composition of student body (fall 2004):

	Undergraduate	Freshmen
International	4.2	3.0
Black	4.2	8.0
American Indian	0.0	0.2
Asian-American	4.0	3.6
Hispanic	4.6	4.4
White	63.2	63.0
Unreported	19.8	17.8
	100.0%	100.0%

12% are from out of state. Average age of full-time undergraduates is 20. 63% of classes have fewer than 20 students, 37% have between 20 and 50 students.

STUDENT HOUSING

92% of freshmen live in college housing. Freshmen are not required to live on campus. Housing is guaranteed for all undergraduates. Campus can house 1,023 undergraduates. Single rooms are available for students with medical or special needs. A medical note is required.

EXPENSES

Tuition (2005-06): $21,900 per year.
Room & Board: $9,700.

There is no additional cost for LD program/services.

LD SERVICES

LD program size is not limited.

LD services available to:

■ Freshmen ■ Sophomores ■ Juniors ■ Seniors

Academic Accommodations

Curriculum		**In class**	
Foreign language waiver	❑	Early syllabus	❑
Lighter course load	■	Note takers in class	■
Math waiver	❑	Priority seating	❑
Other special classes	■	Tape recorders	■
Priority registrations	❑	Videotaped classes	❑
Substitution of courses	❑	Text on tape	❑
Exams		**Services**	
Extended time	■	Diagnostic tests	❑
Oral exams	■	Learning centers	■
Take home exams	❑	Proofreaders	❑
Exams on tape or computer	❑	Readers	■
Untimed exams	❑	Reading Machines/Kurzweil	❑
Other accommodations	❑	Special bookstore section	❑
		Typists	❑

Credit toward degree is not given for remedial courses taken.

Counseling Services

■ Academic — Meets 2 times per academic year
❑ Psychological
❑ Student Support groups
❑ Vocational

Tutoring

Individual tutoring is available weekly.

Average size of tutoring groups: 2

	Individual	Group
Time management	■	❑
Organizational skills	■	❑
Learning strategies	■	❑
Study skills	■	❑
Content area	■	❑
Writing lab	■	❑
Math lab	■	❑

LD PROGRAM STAFF

Total number of LD Program staff (including director):

Full Time: 3 Part Time: 3

There is an advisor/advocate from the LD program available to students. 40 peer tutors are available to work with LD students.

Key staff person available to work with LD students: Susan Mayo, Disabilities Coordinator

Endicott College

Beverly, MA

Address: 376 Hale Street, Beverly, MA, 01915
Admissions telephone: 978 921-1000
Admissions FAX: 978 232-2520
Vice President for Admissions and Financial Aid: Thomas Redman
Admissions e-mail: admissio@endicott.edu
Web site: http://www.endicott.edu
SAT Code: 3369 ACT Code: 1824

Vice President/Dean: Laura Rossile
LD program telephone: 978 232-2057
LD program e-mail: lrossile@endicott.edu
Total campus enrollment: 1,973

GENERAL

Endicott College is a private, coed, four-year institution. 200-acre, suburban campus in Beverly (population: 39,862), 20 miles from Boston; branch campuses abroad in Mexico City, Mexico and Madrid, Spain. Served by train; major airport and bus serve Boston. School operates transportation to train station and local malls. 4-1-4 system.

LD ADMISSIONS

Essay is required and may be typed.

SECONDARY SCHOOL REQUIREMENTS

Graduation from secondary school required; GED accepted.

TESTING

SAT Reasoning required; ACT may be substituted. SAT Subject recommended.

All enrolled freshmen (fall 2004):

Average SAT I Scores: Verbal: 530 Math: 536

Child Study Team report is not required. Tests required as part of this documentation:

- ☐ WAIS-IV
- ☐ WISC-IV
- ☐ SATA
- ☐ Woodcock-Johnson
- ☐ Nelson-Denny Reading Test
- ☐ Other

UNDERGRADUATE STUDENT BODY

Total undergraduate student enrollment: 536 Men, 1,048 Women.

Composition of student body (fall 2004):

	Undergraduate	Freshmen
International	1.7	4.7
Black	2.1	1.0
American Indian	0.0	0.3
Asian-American	0.0	0.8
Hispanic	1.7	1.7
White	90.2	72.2
Unreported	4.3	19.3
	100.0%	100.0%

46% are from out of state. Average age of full-time undergraduates is 20. 54% of classes have fewer than 20 students, 46% have between 20 and 50 students.

STUDENT HOUSING

97% of freshmen live in college housing. Freshmen are required to live on campus. Housing is guaranteed for all undergraduates. Campus can house 1,368 undergraduates. Single rooms are available for students with medical or special needs. A medical note is required.

EXPENSES

Tuition (2005-06): $19,690 per year.

Room: $6,846. Board: $2,920.
Additional cost for LD program/services: $1,000 per semester for tutoring.

LD SERVICES

LD services available to:

☐ Freshmen ☐ Sophomores ☐ Juniors ☐ Seniors

Academic Accommodations

Curriculum		**In class**	
Foreign language waiver	☐	Early syllabus	☐
Lighter course load	■	Note takers in class	■
Math waiver	☐	Priority seating	■
Other special classes	☐	Tape recorders	■
Priority registrations	☐	Videotaped classes	☐
Substitution of courses	☐	Text on tape	■
Exams		**Services**	
Extended time	■	Diagnostic tests	☐
Oral exams	■	Learning centers	■
Take home exams	■	Proofreaders	■
Exams on tape or computer	☐	Readers	■
Untimed exams	■	Reading Machines/Kurzweil	☐
Other accommodations	☐	Special bookstore section	☐
		Typists	☐

Counseling Services

- ☐ Academic
- ☐ Psychological
- ☐ Student Support groups
- ☐ Vocational

Tutoring

Individual tutoring is available weekly.

	Individual	Group
Time management	■	☐
Organizational skills	■	☐
Learning strategies	■	☐
Study skills	■	☐
Content area	■	☐
Writing lab	■	☐
Math lab	■	☐

LD PROGRAM STAFF

Total number of LD Program staff (including director):

Full Time: 2 Part Time: 2

There is an advisor/advocate from the LD program available to students. 45 peer tutors are available to work with LD students.

Key staff person available to work with LD students: Kathy Bloomfield, Coordinator of Student Support

Fitchburg State College

Fitchburg, MA

Address: 160 Pearl Street, Fitchburg, MA, 01420-2697
Admissions telephone: 800 705-9692
Admissions FAX: 978 665-4540
Dean of Enrollment Management: Karen Schedin
Admissions e-mail: admissions@fsc.edu
Web site: http://www.fsc.edu
SAT Code: 3518 ACT Code: 1902

LD program name: Disabilities Services
Director, Disabilities Services: Willa Peterson
LD program telephone: 978 665-3427
LD program e-mail: wpeterson@fsc.edu
Total campus enrollment: 3,522

GENERAL

Fitchburg State College is a public, coed, four-year institution. 45-acre campus in Fitchburg (population: 39,102), 25 miles from Worcester and 50 miles from Boston. Served by bus and train; major airport serves Boston; smaller airport serves Worcester. School operates transportation to bus and train stations. Public transportation serves campus. Semester system.

LD ADMISSIONS

Students do not complete a separate application and are not simultaneously accepted to the LD program. A member of the LD program does not sit on the admissions committee. High school waivers are accepted for foreign language. A personal interview is not required. Essay is required and may be typed.

SECONDARY SCHOOL REQUIREMENTS

Graduation from secondary school required; GED accepted. The following course distribution required: 4 units of English, 3 units of math, 3 units of science, 2 units of foreign language, 1 unit of social studies, 1 unit of history, 2 units of academic electives.

TESTING

SAT Reasoning required; ACT may be substituted. SAT Subject recommended.

All enrolled freshmen (fall 2004):

Average SAT I Scores:	Verbal: 507	Math: 510
Average ACT Scores:	Composite: 21	

Child Study Team report is not required. A neuropsychological or comprehensive psycho-education evaluation is not required for admission. Tests required as part of this documentation:

- [ ] WAIS-IV
- [ ] WISC-IV
- [ ] SATA
- [ ] Woodcock-Johnson
- [ ] Nelson-Denny Reading Test
- [ ] Other

UNDERGRADUATE STUDENT BODY

Total undergraduate student enrollment: 1,393 Men, 1,826 Women.

Composition of student body (fall 2004):

	Undergraduate	Freshmen
International	1.0	1.0
Black	3.3	3.0
American Indian	0.3	0.2
Asian-American	1.9	1.9
Hispanic	2.5	3.3
White	83.2	83.9
Unreported	7.8	6.7
	100.0%	100.0%

8% are from out of state. Average age of full-time undergraduates is 20. 55% of classes have fewer than 20 students, 45% have between 20 and 50 students.

STUDENT HOUSING

80% of freshmen live in college housing. Freshmen are not required to live on campus. Housing is guaranteed for all undergraduates. Campus can house 1,445 undergraduates. Single rooms are available for students with medical or special needs.

EXPENSES

Tuition (2005-06): $970 per year (in-state), $7,050 (out-of-state).
Room: $3,840. Board: $2,100.
There is no additional cost for LD program/services.

LD SERVICES

LD program size is not limited.

LD services available to:

- [x] Freshmen
- [x] Sophomores
- [x] Juniors
- [x] Seniors

Academic Accommodations

Curriculum

- [ ] Foreign language waiver
- [x] Lighter course load
- [ ] Math waiver
- [ ] Other special classes
- [ ] Priority registrations
- [ ] Substitution of courses

Exams

- [x] Extended time
- [x] Oral exams
- [ ] Take home exams
- [ ] Exams on tape or computer
- [ ] Untimed exams
- [ ] Other accommodations

In class

- [ ] Early syllabus
- [x] Note takers in class
- [ ] Priority seating
- [x] Tape recorders
- [ ] Videotaped classes
- [ ] Text on tape

Services

- [ ] Diagnostic tests
- [ ] Learning centers
- [ ] Proofreaders
- [ ] Readers
- [ ] Reading Machines/Kurzweil
- [ ] Special bookstore section
- [ ] Typists

Credit toward degree is not given for remedial courses taken.

Counseling Services

- [x] Academic
- [x] Psychological
- [x] Student Support groups
- [x] Vocational

Tutoring

Individual tutoring is available weekly.

	Individual	Group
Time management	[x]	[x]
Organizational skills	[x]	[x]
Learning strategies	[x]	[x]
Study skills	[x]	[x]
Content area	[x]	[x]
Writing lab	[x]	[x]
Math lab	[x]	[x]

LD PROGRAM STAFF

Total number of LD Program staff (including director):

Full Time: 3 Part Time: 3

There is an advisor/advocate from the LD program available to students.

Key staff person available to work with LD students: Willa Peterson, Director, Disabilities Services

LD Program web site: http://www.fsc.edu/disability

Framingham State College

Framingham, MA

Address: 100 State Street, P.O. Box 9101, Framingham, MA, 01701-9101
Admissions telephone: 508 626-4500
Admissions FAX: 508 626-4017
Dean of Admissions and Enrollment Services: Philip M. Dooher
Admissions e-mail: admiss@frc.mass.edu
Web site: http://www.framingham.edu
SAT Code: 3519 ACT Code: 1904

LD program name: Center for Academic Support & Advising
LD program telephone: 508 626-4905
Total campus enrollment: 3,873

GENERAL

Framingham State College is a public, coed, four-year institution. 72-acre, suburban campus in Framingham (population: 66,910), 20 miles from Boston. Served by bus and train; major airport serves Boston. School operates transportation to campus parking lots. Public transportation serves campus. Semester system.

LD ADMISSIONS

A personal interview is not required. Essay is not required. Students with diagnosed language disfunction may substitute two college preparatory electives for the foreign language requirement.

SECONDARY SCHOOL REQUIREMENTS

Graduation from secondary school required; GED accepted. The following course distribution required: 4 units of English, 3 units of math, 3 units of science, 2 units of foreign language, 2 units of history, 2 units of academic electives.

TESTING

SAT Reasoning required; ACT may be substituted. SAT Subject required.

All enrolled freshmen (fall 2004):

Average SAT I Scores: Verbal: 534 Math: 522

Child Study Team report is required if student is classified. Tests required as part of this documentation:

- ☐ WAIS-IV
- ☐ WISC-IV
- ☐ SATA
- ☐ Woodcock-Johnson
- ☐ Nelson-Denny Reading Test
- ☐ Other

UNDERGRADUATE STUDENT BODY

Total undergraduate student enrollment: 1,469 Men, 2,716 Women.

Composition of student body (fall 2004):

	Undergraduate	Freshmen
International	0.3	1.7
Black	3.1	3.3
American Indian	0.2	0.5
Asian-American	2.3	2.5
Hispanic	3.5	3.4
White	85.2	82.3
Unreported	5.4	6.3
	100.0%	100.0%

8% are from out of state. Average age of full-time undergraduates is 22. 38% of classes have fewer than 20 students, 61% have between 20 and 50 students, 1% have more than 50 students.

STUDENT HOUSING

75% of freshmen live in college housing. Freshmen are not required to live on campus. Housing is not guaranteed for all undergraduates. Priority in housing is for returning upperclass students who submit their deposit by March 15 th for the upcoming year and for accepted students who make their admissions deposit by May 1st. All other students who apply for housing will be placed on a waiting list. Campus can house 1,484 undergraduates.

EXPENSES

Tuition (2005-06): $970 per year (in-state), $7,050 (out-of-state).
Room: $3,997. Board: $2,160.
There is no additional cost for LD program/services.

LD SERVICES

LD program size is not limited.

LD services available to:

☑ Freshmen ☑ Sophomores ☑ Juniors ☑ Seniors

Academic Accommodations

Curriculum		In class	
Foreign language waiver	☐	Early syllabus	☐
Lighter course load	☑	Note takers in class	☐
Math waiver	☐	Priority seating	☐
Other special classes	☐	Tape recorders	☐
Priority registrations	☐	Videotaped classes	☐
Substitution of courses	☐	Text on tape	☐
Exams		**Services**	
Extended time	☐	Diagnostic tests	☐
Oral exams	☐	Learning centers	☑
Take home exams	☐	Proofreaders	☐
Exams on tape or computer	☐	Readers	☐
Untimed exams	☐	Reading Machines/Kurzweil	☐
Other accommodations	☐	Special bookstore section	☐
		Typists	☐

Credit toward degree is not given for remedial courses taken.

Counseling Services

- ☑ Academic
- ☐ Psychological
- ☐ Student Support groups
- ☐ Vocational

Tutoring

	Individual	Group
Time management	☐	☐
Organizational skills	☐	☐
Learning strategies	☐	☐
Study skills	☐	☐
Content area	☐	☐
Writing lab	☐	☐
Math lab	☐	☐

LD PROGRAM STAFF

Total number of LD Program staff (including director):

Full Time: 1 Part Time: 1

Gordon College

Wenham, MA

Address: 255 Grapevine Road, Wenham, MA, 01984
Admissions telephone: 866 464-6736
Admissions FAX: 978 867-4682
Dean of Admissions: Nancy Mering
Admissions e-mail: admissions@hope.gordon.edu
Web site: http://www.gordon.edu
SAT Code: 3417 ACT Code: 1838

LD program e-mail: seavey@hope.gordon.edu
LD program enrollment: 98, Total campus enrollment: 1,617

GENERAL

Gordon College is a private, coed, four-year institution. 550-acre campus in Wenham (population: 4,440), 25 miles from Boston. Major airport and bus serve Boston; train serves Beverly Farms (three miles). School provides transportation to local churches for Sunday services and to special college events in Boston and surrounding communities. Semester system.

LD ADMISSIONS

A personal interview is required. Essay is required and may be typed. Some requirements may be substituted.

SECONDARY SCHOOL REQUIREMENTS

Graduation from secondary school required; GED accepted. The following course distribution required: 4 units of English, 2 units of math, 2 units of science, 2 units of foreign language, 2 units of social studies, 5 units of academic electives.

TESTING

SAT Reasoning required; ACT may be substituted. SAT Subject required.

Child Study Team report is not required. Tests required as part of this documentation:

- [ ] WAIS-IV
- [ ] WISC-IV
- [ ] SATA
- [ ] Woodcock-Johnson
- [ ] Nelson-Denny Reading Test
- [ ] Other

UNDERGRADUATE STUDENT BODY

Total undergraduate student enrollment: 545 Men, 1,079 Women.

Composition of student body (fall 2004):

	Undergraduate	Freshmen
International	2.5	2.4
Black	1.7	1.4
American Indian	0.8	0.3
Asian-American	1.5	2.2
Hispanic	3.5	2.2
White	85.3	87.7
Unreported	4.7	3.8
	100.0%	100.0%

72% are from out of state. 63% of classes have fewer than 20 students, 31% have between 20 and 50 students, 6% have more than 50 students.

STUDENT HOUSING

Housing is guaranteed for all undergraduates. Campus can house 1,420 undergraduates. Single rooms are available for students with medical or special needs. A medical note is required.

EXPENSES

Tuition (2005-06): $21,930 per year.
Room: $4,200. Board: $2,070.
There is no additional cost for LD program/services.

LD SERVICES

LD program size is not limited.

LD services available to:

- [x] Freshmen
- [x] Sophomores
- [x] Juniors
- [x] Seniors

Academic Accommodations

Curriculum

- [ ] Foreign language waiver
- [x] Lighter course load
- [ ] Math waiver
- [ ] Other special classes
- [ ] Priority registrations
- [ ] Substitution of courses

Exams

- [ ] Extended time
- [ ] Oral exams
- [ ] Take home exams
- [ ] Exams on tape or computer
- [ ] Untimed exams
- [ ] Other accommodations

In class

- [ ] Early syllabus
- [ ] Note takers in class
- [ ] Priority seating
- [ ] Tape recorders
- [ ] Videotaped classes
- [ ] Text on tape

Services

- [ ] Diagnostic tests
- [x] Learning centers
- [ ] Proofreaders
- [ ] Readers
- [ ] Reading Machines/Kurzweil
- [ ] Special bookstore section
- [ ] Typists

Credit toward degree is not given for remedial courses taken.

Counseling Services

- [ ] Academic
- [ ] Psychological
- [ ] Student Support groups
- [ ] Vocational

Tutoring

Individual tutoring is available.

	Individual	Group
Time management	[x]	[ ]
Organizational skills	[x]	[ ]
Learning strategies	[x]	[ ]
Study skills	[x]	[x]
Content area	[x]	[x]
Writing lab	[x]	[ ]
Math lab	[ ]	[x]

UNIQUE LD PROGRAM FEATURES

Accommodations such as extended time, books on tape, copies of notes, etc. are available on an individual basis after careful consideration of a student's documentation. Students who wish to request accommodations must submit recent (completed within 3 years) comprehensive documentation that identifies the disability and verifies accommodation needs.

LD PROGRAM STAFF

Total number of LD Program staff (including director):

Full Time: 2 Part Time: 2

Key staff person available to work with LD students: Ann Seavey, Director of Academic Support Center

Hampshire College

Amherst, MA

Address: 893 West Street, Amherst, MA, 01002
Admissions telephone: 877 YES-HAMP
Admissions FAX: 413 559-5631
Director of Admissions: Karen S. Parker
Admissions e-mail: admissions@hampshire.edu
Web site: http://www.hampshire.edu
SAT Code: 3447 ACT Code: 1842

Disabilities Service Coordinator: Joel Dansky
LD program telephone: 413 559-5423
LD program e-mail: jdansky@hampshire.edu

GENERAL

Hampshire College is a private, coed, four-year institution. 800-acre campus in Amherst (population: 34,874), 90 miles from Boston and 20 miles from Springfield. Served by bus; major airport serves Windsor Locks, CT (30 miles); train serves Springfield. School operates transportation to consortium schools. Public transportation serves campus. 4-1-4 system.

LD ADMISSIONS

A member of the LD program does not sit on the admissions committee. High school waivers are accepted for math and foreign language. A personal interview is recommended. Essay is required and may be typed.

SECONDARY SCHOOL REQUIREMENTS

Graduation from secondary school is not required.

TESTING

SAT Reasoning or ACT considered if submitted. SAT Subject recommended.

All enrolled freshmen (fall 2004):

Average SAT I Scores: Verbal: 651 Math: 601
Average ACT Scores: Composite: 27

Child Study Team report is not required. Tests required as part of this documentation:

- ☐ WAIS-IV
- ☐ WISC-IV
- ☐ SATA
- ☐ Woodcock-Johnson
- ☐ Nelson-Denny Reading Test
- ☐ Other

UNDERGRADUATE STUDENT BODY

Total undergraduate student enrollment: 513 Men, 706 Women.

Composition of student body (fall 2004):

	Undergraduate	Freshmen
International	3.0	3.0
Black	4.6	3.1
American Indian	0.3	0.5
Asian-American	3.2	3.6
Hispanic	5.1	5.0
White	62.2	72.2
Unreported	21.6	12.6
	100.0%	100.0%

81% are from out of state. Average age of full-time undergraduates is 20. 68% of classes have fewer than 20 students, 32% have between 20 and 50 students.

STUDENT HOUSING

100% of freshmen live in college housing. Freshmen are required to live on campus. Housing is guaranteed for all undergraduates. Campus can house 1,179 undergraduates. Single rooms are available for students with medical or special needs.

EXPENSES

Tuition (2005-06): $31,939 per year.
Room: $5,433. Board: $3,086.
There is no additional cost for LD program/services.

LD SERVICES

LD program size is not limited.

LD services available to:

☒ Freshmen ☒ Sophomores ☒ Juniors ☒ Seniors

Academic Accommodations

Curriculum		In class	
Foreign language waiver	☐	Early syllabus	☐
Lighter course load	☒	Note takers in class	☒
Math waiver	☐	Priority seating	☐
Other special classes	☐	Tape recorders	☒
Priority registrations	☐	Videotaped classes	☐
Substitution of courses	☐	Text on tape	☐
Exams		**Services**	
Extended time	☒	Diagnostic tests	☐
Oral exams	☐	Learning centers	☐
Take home exams	☐	Proofreaders	☐
Exams on tape or computer	☐	Readers	☒
Untimed exams	☐	Reading Machines/Kurzweil	☒
Other accommodations	☐	Special bookstore section	☐
		Typists	☐

Credit toward degree is not given for remedial courses taken.

Counseling Services

- ☒ Academic
- ☒ Psychological
- ☐ Student Support groups
- ☐ Vocational

Tutoring

	Individual	Group
Time management	☐	☐
Organizational skills	☐	☐
Learning strategies	☐	☐
Study skills	☐	☐
Content area	☐	☐
Writing lab	☐	☐
Math lab	☐	☐

LD PROGRAM STAFF

Total number of LD Program staff (including director):

Full Time: 2 Part Time: 2

There is an advisor/advocate from the LD program available to students.

Key staff person available to work with LD students: Joel Dansky, Disabilities Service Coordinator

Harvard University

Cambridge, MA

Address: Undergraduate Admissions Office, Byerly Hall, 8 Garden Street, Cambridge, MA, 02138
Admissions telephone: 617 495-1551
Admissions FAX: 617 495-8821
Director of Admissions: Dr. Marlyn McGrath Lewis
Admissions e-mail: college@fas.harvard.edu
Web site: http://www.college.harvard.edu
SAT Code: 3434   ACT Code: 1840

LD program name: Student Disability Resource Center
Director: Louise H. Russell
LD program telephone: 617 496-8707
LD program e-mail: lrussell@fas.harvard.edu
Total campus enrollment: 6,562

GENERAL

Harvard University is a private, coed, four-year institution. 380-acre, urban campus in Cambridge (population: 101,355), three miles from Boston; medical school campus in Boston. Major airport, bus, and train serve Boston. School operates transportation to medical school area, to Boston, and within Cambridge. Public transportation serves campus. Semester system.

SECONDARY SCHOOL REQUIREMENTS

Graduation from secondary school is not required.

TESTING

SAT Reasoning or ACT required. SAT Subject recommended.

Child Study Team report is not required. Tests required as part of this documentation:

☐ WAIS-IV   ☐ Woodcock-Johnson
☐ WISC-IV   ☐ Nelson-Denny Reading Test
☐ SATA   ☐ Other

UNDERGRADUATE STUDENT BODY

Total undergraduate student enrollment: 3,592 Men, 3,092 Women.

Composition of student body (fall 2004):

	Undergraduate	Freshmen
International	9.1	8.9
Black	8.8	7.6
American Indian	1.1	0.9
Asian-American	20.0	17.4
Hispanic	8.7	7.8
White	46.9	48.1
Unreported	5.4	9.3
	100.0%	100.0%

86% are from out of state. Average age of full-time undergraduates is 20. 69% of classes have fewer than 20 students, 18% have between 20 and 50 students, 13% have more than 50 students.

STUDENT HOUSING

Housing is guaranteed for all undergraduates.

EXPENSES

Tuition (2005-06): $28,752 per year.
Room: $5,148. Board: $4,430.
There is no additional cost for LD program/services.

LD SERVICES

LD program size is not limited.

LD services available to:

☐ Freshmen   ☐ Sophomores   ☐ Juniors   ☐ Seniors

Academic Accommodations

Curriculum		**In class**	
Foreign language waiver	☐	Early syllabus	☐
Lighter course load	☐	Note takers in class	☐
Math waiver	☐	Priority seating	☐
Other special classes	☐	Tape recorders	■
Priority registrations	☐	Videotaped classes	■
Substitution of courses	☐	Text on tape	☐
Exams		**Services**	
Extended time	■	Diagnostic tests	☐
Oral exams	☐	Learning centers	☐
Take home exams	☐	Proofreaders	☐
Exams on tape or computer	☐	Readers	■
Untimed exams	■	Reading Machines/Kurzweil	☐
Other accommodations	☐	Special bookstore section	☐
		Typists	☐

Counseling Services

☐ Academic
☐ Psychological
☐ Student Support groups
☐ Vocational

Tutoring

	Individual	Group
Time management	☐	☐
Organizational skills	☐	☐
Learning strategies	☐	☐
Study skills	☐	☐
Content area	☐	☐
Writing lab	☐	☐
Math lab	☐	☐

LD PROGRAM STAFF

Key staff person available to work with LD students: Louise H. Russell, Director, Student Disability Resource Center

Lasell College

Newton, MA

Address: 1844 Commonwealth Avenue, Newton, MA, 02466
Admissions telephone: 888 527-3554
Admissions FAX: 617 243-2380
Director of Admissions: James Tweed
Admissions e-mail: info@lasell.edu
Web site: http://www.lasell.edu
SAT Code: 3481 ACT Code: 1848

LD program contact: Rosalie Frolick
LD program telephone: 617 243-2306
LD program e-mail: rfrolick@lasell.edu
LD program enrollment: 22, Total campus enrollment: 1,170

GENERAL

Lasell College is a private, coed, four-year institution. 50-acre, suburban campus in Newton (population: 83,829), eight miles from Boston. Served by bus and train; major airport and train serve Boston. School operates transportation to local shopping area and public transportation. Semester system.

LD ADMISSIONS

Students do not complete a separate application and are not simultaneously accepted to the LD program. A member of the LD program does not sit on the admissions committee. A personal interview is recommended. Essay is not required.

SECONDARY SCHOOL REQUIREMENTS

Graduation from secondary school required; GED accepted. The following course distribution required: 4 units of English, 3 units of math, 2 units of science, 2 units of social studies, 2 units of history, 2 units of academic electives.

TESTING

SAT Reasoning required; ACT may be substituted. SAT Subject recommended.

All enrolled freshmen (fall 2004):

Average SAT I Scores:	Verbal: 470	Math: 490
Average ACT Scores:	Composite: 20	

Child Study Team report is not required. Tests required as part of this documentation:

- ☐ WAIS-IV
- ☐ WISC-IV
- ☐ SATA
- ☐ Woodcock-Johnson
- ☐ Nelson-Denny Reading Test
- ☐ Other

UNDERGRADUATE STUDENT BODY

Total undergraduate student enrollment: 229 Men, 665 Women.

Composition of student body (fall 2004):

	Undergraduate	Freshmen
International	2.1	4.2
Black	4.9	6.5
American Indian	0.5	0.4
Asian-American	2.3	3.9
Hispanic	4.1	5.8
White	81.7	75.3
Unreported	4.4	3.9
	100.0%	100.0%

50% are from out of state. Average age of full-time undergraduates is 20. 32% of classes have fewer than 20 students, 68% have between 20 and 50 students.

STUDENT HOUSING

92% of freshmen live in college housing. Freshmen are not required to live on campus. Housing is guaranteed for all undergraduates. Campus can house 912 undergraduates. Single rooms are available for students with medical or special needs. A medical note is required.

EXPENSES

Tuition (2005-06): $18,700 per year.
Room & Board: $8,800.
There is no additional cost for LD program/services.

LD SERVICES

LD program size is not limited.

LD services available to:

■ Freshmen ■ Sophomores ■ Juniors ■ Seniors

Academic Accommodations

Curriculum		**In class**	
Foreign language waiver	☐	Early syllabus	☐
Lighter course load	■	Note takers in class	■
Math waiver	☐	Priority seating	☐
Other special classes	☐	Tape recorders	■
Priority registrations	☐	Videotaped classes	☐
Substitution of courses	☐	Text on tape	☐
Exams		**Services**	
Extended time	■	Diagnostic tests	☐
Oral exams	■	Learning centers	■
Take home exams	☐	Proofreaders	☐
Exams on tape or computer	☐	Readers	■
Untimed exams	■	Reading Machines/Kurzweil	■
Other accommodations	☐	Special bookstore section	☐
		Typists	☐

Credit toward degree is not given for remedial courses taken.

Counseling Services

- ■ Academic
- ■ Psychological
- ☐ Student Support groups
- ☐ Vocational

Tutoring

	Individual	Group
Time management	☐	☐
Organizational skills	☐	☐
Learning strategies	☐	☐
Study skills	☐	☐
Content area	☐	☐
Writing lab	☐	☐
Math lab	☐	☐

LD PROGRAM STAFF

Total number of LD Program staff (including director):

Full Time: 1 Part Time: 1

There is an advisor/advocate from the LD program available to students.

Key staff person available to work with LD students: Rosalie Frolick, Director of Learning Center

Lesley University

Cambridge, MA

Address: 29 Everett Street, Cambridge, MA, 02138
Admissions telephone: 800 999-1959, extension 8800
Admissions FAX: 617 349-8810
Director of Undergraduate Admissions: Deb Kocar
Admissions e-mail: ugadm@mail.lesley.edu
Web site: http://www.lesley.edu
SAT Code: 3483 ACT Code: 1850

Director LD/ADD Academic Support Program: Maureen Riley
LD program telephone: 617 349-8464
LD program e-mail: mriley@mail.lesley.edu
Total campus enrollment: 1,042

GENERAL

Lesley University is a private, women's, four-year institution. Five-acre campus in Cambridge (population: 101,355), four miles from downtown Boston; sites in 14 other states and throughout Massachusetts for graduate and alternative programs. Major airport, bus, and train serve Boston. School operates transportation to Porter Exchange building. Public transportation serves campus. Semester system.

LD ADMISSIONS

A personal interview is recommended. Essay is required and may be typed.

SECONDARY SCHOOL REQUIREMENTS

Graduation from secondary school required; GED accepted. The following course distribution required: 4 units of English, 3 units of math, 3 units of science, 1 unit of social studies, 1 unit of history, 7 units of academic electives.

TESTING

SAT Reasoning or ACT required. SAT Subject recommended.

All enrolled freshmen (fall 2004):

Average SAT I Scores: Verbal: 540 Math: 519

Child Study Team report is not required. Tests required as part of this documentation:

☐ WAIS-IV ☐ Woodcock-Johnson
☐ WISC-IV ☐ Nelson-Denny Reading Test
☐ SATA ☐ Other

UNDERGRADUATE STUDENT BODY

Total undergraduate student enrollment: 553 Women.

Composition of student body (fall 2004):

	Undergraduate	Freshmen
International	4.4	4.6
Black	9.6	6.6
American Indian	0.1	0.5
Asian-American	4.8	4.7
Hispanic	7.9	4.3
White	58.3	63.1
Unreported	14.9	16.2
	100.0%	100.0%

Average age of full-time undergraduates is 21. 76% of classes have fewer than 20 students, 24% have between 20 and 50 students.

STUDENT HOUSING

85% of freshmen live in college housing. Housing is not guaranteed for all undergraduates. Campus can house 487 undergraduates.

EXPENSES

Tuition (2005-06): $21,000 per year.
Room: $6,100. Board: $3,850.
There is no additional cost for LD program/services.

LD SERVICES

LD program size is not limited.

LD services available to:

☐ Freshmen ☐ Sophomores ☐ Juniors ☐ Seniors

Academic Accommodations

Curriculum		**In class**	
Foreign language waiver	☐	Early syllabus	☐
Lighter course load	■	Note takers in class	■
Math waiver	☐	Priority seating	☐
Other special classes	■	Tape recorders	■
Priority registrations	☐	Videotaped classes	☐
Substitution of courses	☐	Text on tape	☐
Exams		**Services**	
Extended time	■	Diagnostic tests	☐
Oral exams	■	Learning centers	■
Take home exams	☐	Proofreaders	☐
Exams on tape or computer	☐	Readers	■
Untimed exams	■	Reading Machines/Kurzweil	■
Other accommodations	☐	Special bookstore section	☐
		Typists	☐

Credit toward degree is not given for remedial courses taken.

Counseling Services

☐ Academic
☐ Psychological
☐ Student Support groups
☐ Vocational

Tutoring

	Individual	Group
Time management	☐	☐
Organizational skills	☐	☐
Learning strategies	☐	☐
Study skills	☐	☐
Content area	☐	☐
Writing lab	☐	☐
Math lab	☐	☐

UNIQUE LD PROGRAM FEATURES

The tutorial program is accredited by the College Reading and Language Association (CRLA). Tutors are trained weekly by senior faculty. The course selection and academic needs of students with learning disabilities and attention disorders are assessed by the program director. Students are then matched to tutors and tutors are supervised individually. The Center provided over 6,000 hours of free tutoring last year. Students with special learning needs may have as many tutorial hours per week as they need.

LD PROGRAM STAFF

Total number of LD Program staff (including director):

Full Time: 2 Part Time: 2

Key staff person available to work with LD students: Maureen Riley, Director, LD/ADD Academic Support Program/ Professor

Massachusetts College of Liberal Arts

North Adams, MA

Address: 375 Church Street, North Adams, MA, 01247
Admissions telephone: 800 292-6632
Admissions FAX: 413 662-5179
Dean of Enrollment Management: Mr. Steven King
Admissions e-mail: admissions@mcla.edu
Web site: http://www.mcla.edu
SAT Code: 3521 ACT Code: 1908

Coordinator of Academic Support Svcs: Claire Smith
LD program telephone: (413) 662-5318
LD program e-mail: msmith1@mcla.edu
Total campus enrollment: 1,430

GENERAL

Massachusetts College of Liberal Arts is a public, coed, four-year institution. 75-acre campus in North Adams (population: 14,681), 50 miles from Albany, NY, and 20 miles from Pittsfield. Served by bus; major airport serves Albany, NY; smaller airport serves Hartford, CT (80 miles); train serves Rensselaer, NY (45 miles). Public transportation serves campus. Semester system.

LD ADMISSIONS

Students do not complete a separate application and are simultaneously accepted to the LD program. A personal interview is not required. Essay is not required. Summer seminar requires an additional application.

For fall 2004, 31 completed self-identified LD applications were received. 28 applications were offered admission, and 11 enrolled.

SECONDARY SCHOOL REQUIREMENTS

Graduation from secondary school required; GED accepted. The following course distribution required: 4 units of English, 3 units of math, 3 units of science, 2 units of foreign language, 2 units of history, 2 units of academic electives.

TESTING

ACT considered if submitted. SAT Subject recommended.

All enrolled freshmen (fall 2004):

Average SAT I Scores:	Verbal: 532	Math: 504
Average ACT Scores:	Composite: 20	

Child Study Team report is not required. Tests required as part of this documentation:

❑ WAIS-IV ❑ Woodcock-Johnson
❑ WISC-IV ❑ Nelson-Denny Reading Test
❑ SATA ❑ Other

UNDERGRADUATE STUDENT BODY

Total undergraduate student enrollment: 544 Men, 848 Women.

Composition of student body (fall 2004):

	Undergraduate	Freshmen
International	0.0	0.3
Black	4.2	4.0
American Indian	0.0	0.3
Asian-American	1.9	1.4
Hispanic	3.8	2.4
White	87.8	90.0
Unreported	2.3	1.6
	100.0%	100.0%

16% are from out of state. Average age of full-time undergraduates is 21. 63% of classes have fewer than 20 students, 37% have between 20 and 50 students.

STUDENT HOUSING

87% of freshmen live in college housing. Freshmen are required to live on campus. Housing is guaranteed for all undergraduates. Campus can house 867 undergraduates.

EXPENSES

Tuition (2005-06): $1,030 per year (in-state), $9,975 (out-of-state).
Room: $3,316. Board: $2,966.
There is no additional cost for LD program/services.

LD SERVICES

LD program size is not limited.

LD services available to:

❑ Freshmen ❑ Sophomores ❑ Juniors ❑ Seniors

Academic Accommodations

Curriculum		**In class**	
Foreign language waiver	❑	Early syllabus	❑
Lighter course load	■	Note takers in class	■
Math waiver	❑	Priority seating	❑
Other special classes	❑	Tape recorders	■
Priority registrations	❑	Videotaped classes	❑
Substitution of courses	❑	Text on tape	❑
Exams		**Services**	
Extended time	■	Diagnostic tests	■
Oral exams	■	Learning centers	■
Take home exams	❑	Proofreaders	❑
Exams on tape or computer	❑	Readers	■
Untimed exams	■	Reading Machines/Kurzweil	❑
Other accommodations	❑	Special bookstore section	❑
		Typists	❑

Credit toward degree is not given for remedial courses taken.

Counseling Services

❑ Academic
❑ Psychological
❑ Student Support groups
❑ Vocational

Tutoring

	Individual	Group
Time management	❑	❑
Organizational skills	❑	❑
Learning strategies	❑	❑
Study skills	❑	❑
Content area	❑	❑
Writing lab	❑	❑
Math lab	❑	❑

LD PROGRAM STAFF

Key staff person available to work with LD students: Claire Smith, Coordinator of Academic Support Services

Massachusetts College of Pharmacy and Health Sciences

Boston, MA

Address: 179 Longwood Avenue, Boston, MA, 02115-5896
Admissions telephone: 800 225-5506
Admissions FAX: 617 732-2118
Executive Director of Admissions: William Dunfey
Admissions e-mail: admissions@bos.mcphs.edu
Web site: http://www.mcphs.edu
SAT Code: 3512 ACT Code: 1860

LD program name: Academic Support Services
LD program address: Room WB 12
Director: Carol Sitterly, Ed.D.
LD program telephone: 617 732-2860
LD program e-mail: csitterly@bos.mcphs.edu
Total campus enrollment: 1,632

GENERAL

Massachusetts College of Pharmacy and Health Sciences is a private, coed, four-year institution. One-acre campus in Boston (population: 589,141); branch campus in Worcester. Served by air, bus, and train. Public transportation serves campus. Semester system.

SECONDARY SCHOOL REQUIREMENTS

Graduation from secondary school required; GED accepted. The following course distribution required: 4 units of English, 3 units of math, 2 units of science, 1 unit of social studies, 1 unit of history, 5 units of academic electives.

TESTING

SAT Reasoning required; ACT may be substituted. SAT Subject required.

All enrolled freshmen (fall 2004):

Average SAT I Scores:	Verbal: 527	Math: 570
Average ACT Scores:	Composite: 22	

Child Study Team report is not required. A neuropsychological or comprehensive psycho-educational evaluation is required for admission. Tests required as part of this documentation:

- [ ] WAIS-IV
- [ ] WISC-IV
- [ ] SATA
- [ ] Woodcock-Johnson
- [ ] Nelson-Denny Reading Test
- [ ] Other

UNDERGRADUATE STUDENT BODY

Total undergraduate student enrollment: 380 Men, 785 Women.

53% are from out of state. 25% join a fraternity and 11% join a sorority. Average age of full-time undergraduates is 23. 34% of classes have fewer than 20 students, 49% have between 20 and 50 students, 17% have more than 50 students.

STUDENT HOUSING

72% of freshmen live in college housing. Freshmen are not required to live on campus. Housing is not guaranteed for all undergraduates. Campus can house 495 undergraduates.

EXPENSES

Tuition (2005-06): $19,600 per year. $17,721-$27,300 for Worcester campus.
Room: $7,400. Board: $3,170.
There is no additional cost for LD program/services.

LD SERVICES

LD services available to:

- [x] Freshmen
- [x] Sophomores
- [x] Juniors
- [x] Seniors

Academic Accommodations

Curriculum		In class	
Foreign language waiver	[ ]	Early syllabus	[ ]
Lighter course load	[ ]	Note takers in class	[x]
Math waiver	[ ]	Priority seating	[ ]
Other special classes	[ ]	Tape recorders	[ ]
Priority registrations	[ ]	Videotaped classes	[ ]
Substitution of courses	[ ]	Text on tape	[ ]
Exams		**Services**	
Extended time	[ ]	Diagnostic tests	[ ]
Oral exams	[ ]	Learning centers	[x]
Take home exams	[ ]	Proofreaders	[ ]
Exams on tape or computer	[ ]	Readers	[ ]
Untimed exams	[ ]	Reading Machines/Kurzweil	[ ]
Other accommodations	[x]	Special bookstore section	[ ]
		Typists	[ ]

Credit toward degree is not given for remedial courses taken.

Counseling Services

- [ ] Academic
- [ ] Psychological
- [ ] Student Support groups
- [ ] Vocational

Tutoring

Individual tutoring is available.

	Individual	Group
Time management	[x]	[ ]
Organizational skills	[x]	[ ]
Learning strategies	[x]	[ ]
Study skills	[x]	[ ]
Content area	[x]	[ ]
Writing lab	[x]	[ ]
Math lab	[x]	[ ]

LD PROGRAM STAFF

Total number of LD Program staff (including director):

Full Time: 3 Part Time: 3

Key staff person available to work with LD students: Carol Sitterly, Ed.D., Director, Academic Support Services

Massachusetts Institute of Technology

Cambridge, MA

Address: 77 Massachusetts Avenue, Cambridge, MA, 02139
Admissions telephone: 617 253-4791
Admissions FAX: 617 258-8304
Dean of Admissions: Marilee Jones
Admissions e-mail: admissions@mit.edu
Web site: http://www.mit.edu/
SAT Code: 3514 ACT Code: 1858

Program Specialist, Administrative Assistant: Kathleen Monagle, Carol Clark
LD program telephone: 617 253-1674
LD program e-mail: monaglek@mit.edu, cclark@mit.edu
Total campus enrollment: 4,136

GENERAL

Massachusetts Institute of Technology is a private, coed, four-year institution. 155-acre, urban campus in Cambridge (population: 101,355), across the Charles River from Boston. Major airport, bus, and train serve Boston. School operates transportation around campus, to independent living groups in Boston, and to Logan Airport. Public transportation serves campus. 4-1-4 system.

LD ADMISSIONS

Application Deadline: 01/01. A personal interview is recommended. Essay is required and may be typed.

For fall 2004, 13 completed self-identified LD applications were received. 4 applications were offered admission, and 2 enrolled.

TESTING

SAT Reasoning or ACT required. SAT Subject recommended.

All enrolled freshmen (fall 2004):

Average SAT I Scores:	Verbal: 712	Math: 755
Average ACT Scores:	Composite: 32	

Child Study Team report is not required. A neuropsychological or comprehensive psycho-education evaluation is not required for admission. Tests required as part of this documentation:

☐ WAIS-IV ☐ Woodcock-Johnson
☐ WISC-IV ☐ Nelson-Denny Reading Test
☐ SATA ☐ Other

UNDERGRADUATE STUDENT BODY

Total undergraduate student enrollment: 2,455 Men, 1,765 Women.

Composition of student body (fall 2004):

	Undergraduate	Freshmen
International	6.3	7.4
Black	5.8	6.0
American Indian	1.9	1.6
Asian-American	26.1	27.8
Hispanic	11.6	11.5
White	35.5	35.3
Unreported	12.8	10.4
	100.0%	100.0%

90% are from out of state. 48% join a fraternity and 26% join a sorority. Average age of full-time undergraduates is 20. 61% of classes have fewer than 20 students, 23% have between 20 and 50 students, 16% have more than 50 students.

STUDENT HOUSING

100% of freshmen live in college housing. Freshmen are required to live on campus. Housing is guaranteed for all undergraduates. Campus can house 4,500 undergraduates.

EXPENSES

Tuition (2005-06): $32,100 per year.
Room: $5,250. Board: $4,250.

There is no additional cost for LD program/services.

LD SERVICES

LD program size is not limited.

LD services available to:

☐ Freshmen ☐ Sophomores ☐ Juniors ☐ Seniors

Academic Accommodations

Curriculum		In class	
Foreign language waiver	☐	Early syllabus	☐
Lighter course load	☐	Note takers in class	☒
Math waiver	☐	Priority seating	☐
Other special classes	☐	Tape recorders	☒
Priority registrations	☐	Videotaped classes	☐
Substitution of courses	☐	Text on tape	☐
Exams		**Services**	
Extended time	☒	Diagnostic tests	☐
Oral exams	☐	Learning centers	☐
Take home exams	☐	Proofreaders	☐
Exams on tape or computer	☐	Readers	☒
Untimed exams	☐	Reading Machines/Kurzweil	☒
Other accommodations	☐	Special bookstore section	☐
		Typists	☐

Credit toward degree is not given for remedial courses taken.

Counseling Services

☐ Academic
☐ Psychological
☐ Student Support groups
☐ Vocational

Tutoring

	Individual	Group
Time management	☐	☐
Organizational skills	☐	☐
Learning strategies	☐	☐
Study skills	☐	☐
Content area	☐	☐
Writing lab	☐	☐
Math lab	☐	☐

UNIQUE LD PROGRAM FEATURES

MIT is an elite, highly selective institution. Students with disablilities are expected to meet the same standards as other students.

LD PROGRAM STAFF

Total number of LD Program staff (including director):

Full Time: 1 Part Time: 1

Key staff person available to work with LD students: Kathleen Monagle, Program Specialist

Massachusetts Maritime Academy

Buzzards Bay, MA

Address: 101 Academy Drive, Buzzards Bay, MA, 02532-1803
Admissions telephone: 800 544-3411
Admissions FAX: 508 830-5077
Dean of Enrollment Management: Francis McDonald
Admissions e-mail: admissions@maritime.edu
Web site: http://www.maritime.edu
SAT Code: 3515

Disability Resource Coordinator: Betty Anne Bevis
LD program telephone: 508 830-5000, extension 1409
LD program e-mail: bbevis@maritime.edu
Total campus enrollment: 831

GENERAL

Massachusetts Maritime Academy is a public, coed, four-year institution. 55-acre campus in Buzzards Bay (population: 3,545), 50 miles from Boston. Major airport and train serve Boston; smaller airport serves Providence, RI (50 miles); bus serves Bourne (three miles). Semester system.

LD ADMISSIONS

A personal interview is recommended. Essay is required and may be typed.

SECONDARY SCHOOL REQUIREMENTS

Graduation from secondary school required; GED accepted. The following course distribution required: 4 units of English, 3 units of math, 3 units of science, 2 units of foreign language, 1 unit of social studies, 1 unit of history, 2 units of academic electives.

TESTING

Child Study Team report is not required. Tests required as part of this documentation:

- ☐ WAIS-IV
- ☐ WISC-IV
- ☐ SATA
- ☐ Woodcock-Johnson
- ☐ Nelson-Denny Reading Test
- ☐ Other

UNDERGRADUATE STUDENT BODY

Total undergraduate student enrollment: 721 Men, 110 Women.

23% are from out of state.

STUDENT HOUSING

Housing is guaranteed for all undergraduates.

EXPENSES

Tuition (2005-06): $1,030 per year (state residents and Connecticut, Delaware, Florida, Maryland, New Jersey, Pennsylvania, Rhode Island, Virginia, and Washington, DC residents), $9,170 (other out-of-state).
There is no additional cost for LD program/services.

LD SERVICES

LD program size is not limited.

LD services available to:

☐ Freshmen ☐ Sophomores ☐ Juniors ☐ Seniors

Academic Accommodations

Curriculum		In class	
Foreign language waiver	☐	Early syllabus	☐
Lighter course load	☐	Note takers in class	☐
Math waiver	☐	Priority seating	☐
Other special classes	☐	Tape recorders	■
Priority registrations	☐	Videotaped classes	☐
Substitution of courses	☐	Text on tape	☐
Exams		**Services**	
Extended time	■	Diagnostic tests	☐
Oral exams	☐	Learning centers	■
Take home exams	☐	Proofreaders	☐
Exams on tape or computer	☐	Readers	☐
Untimed exams	☐	Reading Machines/Kurzweil	☐
Other accommodations	☐	Special bookstore section	☐
		Typists	☐

Credit toward degree is not given for remedial courses taken.

Counseling Services

- ☐ Academic
- ☐ Psychological
- ☐ Student Support groups
- ☐ Vocational

Tutoring

	Individual	Group
Time management	☐	☐
Organizational skills	☐	☐
Learning strategies	☐	☐
Study skills	☐	☐
Content area	☐	☐
Writing lab	☐	☐
Math lab	☐	☐

LD PROGRAM STAFF

Key staff person available to work with LD students: Betty Anne Bevis, Disability Resource Coordinator

University of Massachusetts Amherst

Amherst, MA

Address: 181 President's Drive, Amherst, MA, 01003-9313
Admissions telephone: 413 545-0222
Admissions FAX: 413 545-4312
Assistant Vice Chancellor of Enrollment Services: Michael Gargano
Web site: http://www.umass.edu
SAT Code: 3917 ACT Code: 1924

LD program name: Disability Services
LD program address: 231 Whitmore Administration Building
LD program contact: Margarita Hydal
LD program telephone: 413 545-0892
Total campus enrollment: 18,966

GENERAL

University of Massachusetts Amherst is a public, coed, four-year institution. 1,463-acre campus in Amherst (population: 34,874), 30 miles from Springfield and 90 miles from Boston. Served by bus and train; major airport serves Hartford, CT (40 miles). School operates transportation to consortium schools, local apartments, and surrounding towns. Semester system.

LD ADMISSIONS

A personal interview is recommended. Essay is not required. Massachusetts residents can get SAT waived; diagnostic tests are required if SAT is waived.

SECONDARY SCHOOL REQUIREMENTS

Graduation from secondary school required; GED accepted. The following course distribution required: 4 units of English, 3 units of math, 3 units of science, 2 units of foreign language, 2 units of social studies, 2 units of academic electives.

TESTING

SAT Reasoning or ACT required. SAT Subject recommended.

All enrolled freshmen (fall 2004):

Average SAT I Scores: Verbal: 561 Math: 576

Child Study Team report is not required. Tests required as part of this documentation:

- ☐ WAIS-IV
- ☐ WISC-IV
- ☐ SATA
- ☐ Woodcock-Johnson
- ☐ Nelson-Denny Reading Test
- ☐ Other

UNDERGRADUATE STUDENT BODY

Total undergraduate student enrollment: 9,405 Men, 9,963 Women.

Composition of student body (fall 2004):

	Undergraduate	Freshmen
International	1.0	1.3
Black	3.6	4.3
American Indian	0.4	0.3
Asian-American	7.3	7.3
Hispanic	3.6	3.3
White	76.9	76.6
Unreported	7.2	6.9
	100.0%	100.0%

23% are from out of state. 3% join a fraternity and 7% join a sorority. Average age of full-time undergraduates is 20. 41% of classes have fewer than 20 students, 44% have between 20 and 50 students, 15% have more than 50 students.

STUDENT HOUSING

95% of freshmen live in college housing. Freshmen are required to live on campus. Housing is guaranteed for all undergraduates. Campus can house 11,000 undergraduates. Single rooms are available for students with medical or special needs. A medical note is required.

EXPENSES

Tuition (2005-06): $1,714 per year (in-state), $9,937 (out-of-state).

Room: $3,605. Board: $2,912.

There is no additional cost for LD program/services.

LD SERVICES

LD program size is not limited.

LD services available to:

☑ Freshmen ☑ Sophomores ☑ Juniors ☑ Seniors

Academic Accommodations

Curriculum		**In class**	
Foreign language waiver	☐	Early syllabus	☑
Lighter course load	☑	Note takers in class	☑
Math waiver	☐	Priority seating	☑
Other special classes	☑	Tape recorders	☑
Priority registrations	☐	Videotaped classes	☐
Substitution of courses	☐	Text on tape	☑
Exams		**Services**	
Extended time	☑	Diagnostic tests	☐
Oral exams	☑	Learning centers	☐
Take home exams	☐	Proofreaders	☑
Exams on tape or computer	☑	Readers	☑
Untimed exams	☑	Reading Machines/Kurzweil	☑
Other accommodations	☑	Special bookstore section	☐
		Typists	☑

Counseling Services

- ☐ Academic
- ☐ Psychological
- ☐ Student Support groups
- ☐ Vocational

Tutoring

Individual tutoring is not available.

	Individual	Group
Time management	☐	☑
Organizational skills	☐	☑
Learning strategies	☐	☑
Study skills	☐	☐
Content area	☐	☑
Writing lab	☐	☐
Math lab	☐	☐

LD PROGRAM STAFF

Total number of LD Program staff (including director):

Full Time: 14 Part Time: 14

There is an advisor/advocate from the LD program available to students. Nine graduate students are available to work with LD students.

Key staff person available to work with LD students: Madeline L. Peters, Director, Disability Services

LD Program web site: http://www.umass.edu/disability/

University of Massachusetts at Boston

Boston, MA

Address: 100 Morrissey Boulevard, Boston, MA, 02125-3393
Admissions telephone: 617 287-6100
Admissions FAX: 617 287-5999
Director of Undergraduate Admissions: Liliana Mickle
Admissions e-mail: undergrad@umb.edu
Web site: http://www.umb.edu
SAT Code: 3924 ACT Code: 3924

Assistant Director: Renee Goldberg, Ed.D
LD program telephone: 617 287-7439
LD program e-mail: renee.goldberg@umb.edu
Total campus enrollment: 8,832

GENERAL

University of Massachusetts at Boston is a public, coed, four-year institution. 177-acre, urban campus in Boston (population: 589,141). Served by air, bus, and train. School operates transportation to train station. Public transportation serves campus. Semester system.

LD ADMISSIONS

A personal interview is not required. Essay is required and may be typed. Foreign language requirement may be waived with proper documentation.

SECONDARY SCHOOL REQUIREMENTS

Graduation from secondary school required; GED accepted. The following course distribution required: 4 units of English, 3 units of math, 3 units of science, 2 units of foreign language, 2 units of history, 2 units of academic electives.

TESTING

SAT Reasoning or ACT required. SAT Subject recommended.

All enrolled freshmen (fall 2004):

Average SAT I Scores: Verbal:475 Math:496

Child Study Team report is not required. Tests required as part of this documentation:

❑ WAIS-IV
❑ WISC-IV
❑ SATA
❑ Woodcock-Johnson
❑ Nelson-Denny Reading Test
❑ Other

UNDERGRADUATE STUDENT BODY

Total undergraduate student enrollment: 4,632 Men, 5,933 Women.

Composition of student body (fall 2004):

	Undergraduate	Freshmen
International	3.9	3.6
Black	15.8	15.2
American Indian	0.9	0.5
Asian-American	19.6	12.2
Hispanic	8.1	6.5
White	42.1	48.1
Unreported	9.6	13.9
	100.0%	100.0%

4% are from out of state. Average age of full-time undergraduates is 25. 53% of classes have fewer than 20 students, 44% have between 20 and 50 students, 3% have more than 50 students.

STUDENT HOUSING

Housing is not guaranteed for all undergraduates.

EXPENSES

Tuition (2005-06): $1,714 per year (in-state), $9,758 (out-of-state).

There is no additional cost for LD program/services.

LD SERVICES

LD program size is not limited.

LD services available to:

❑ Freshmen ❑ Sophomores ❑ Juniors ❑ Seniors

Academic Accommodations

Curriculum		**In class**	
Foreign language waiver	❑	Early syllabus	❑
Lighter course load	■	Note takers in class	■
Math waiver	❑	Priority seating	❑
Other special classes	❑	Tape recorders	■
Priority registrations	❑	Videotaped classes	❑
Substitution of courses	❑	Text on tape	❑
Exams		**Services**	
Extended time	■	Diagnostic tests	❑
Oral exams	■	Learning centers	❑
Take home exams	❑	Proofreaders	❑
Exams on tape or computer	❑	Readers	■
Untimed exams	❑	Reading Machines/Kurzweil	■
Other accommodations	❑	Special bookstore section	❑
		Typists	❑

Credit toward degree is not given for remedial courses taken.

Counseling Services

❑ Academic
❑ Psychological
❑ Student Support groups
❑ Vocational

Tutoring

	Individual	Group
Time management	❑	❑
Organizational skills	❑	❑
Learning strategies	❑	❑
Study skills	❑	❑
Content area	❑	❑
Writing lab	❑	❑
Math lab	❑	❑

LD PROGRAM STAFF

Total number of LD Program staff (including director):

Full Time: 4 Part Time: 4

Key staff person available to work with LD students: Renee L. Goldberg, Ed.D, Assistant Director, Ross Center for Disability Services

University of Massachusetts at Dartmouth

North Dartmouth, MA

Address: 285 Old Westport Road, North Dartmouth, MA, 02747-2300
Admissions telephone: 508 999-8605
Admissions FAX: 508 999-8755
Director of Admissions: Steven T. Briggs
Admissions e-mail: admissions@umassd.edu
Web site: http://www.umassd.edu
SAT Code: 3786 ACT Code: 1906

LD program name: Disabled Student Services
Director, Disabled Student Services: Carole J. Johnson
LD program telephone: 508 999-8711
LD program e-mail: cjohnson@umassd.edu
Total campus enrollment: 7,290

GENERAL

University of Massachusetts at Dartmouth is a public, coed, four-year institution. 710-acre campus in Dartmouth (population: 30,666), five miles from New Bedford and 60 miles from Boston; branch campus (for art studio classes) in New Bedford. Major airport serves Boston; smaller airport and train serve Providence, RI (35 miles); bus serves New Bedford. School operates transportation to New Bedford for studio art courses. Public transportation serves campus. Semester system.

LD ADMISSIONS

A personal interview is recommended. Essay is required and may be typed. State residents may submit diagnostic test in lieu of SAT.

SECONDARY SCHOOL REQUIREMENTS

Graduation from secondary school required; GED accepted. The following course distribution required: 4 units of English, 3 units of math, 3 units of science, 2 units of foreign language, 1 unit of social studies, 1 unit of history, 2 units of academic electives.

TESTING

SAT Reasoning required; ACT may be substituted. SAT Subject recommended.

All enrolled freshmen (fall 2004):

Average SAT I Scores:	Verbal: 530	Math: 544
Average ACT Scores:	Composite: 21	

Child Study Team report is not required. Tests required as part of this documentation:

- [ ] WAIS-IV
- [ ] WISC-IV
- [ ] SATA
- [ ] Woodcock-Johnson
- [ ] Nelson-Denny Reading Test
- [ ] Other

UNDERGRADUATE STUDENT BODY

Total undergraduate student enrollment: 3,117 Men, 3,521 Women.

Composition of student body (fall 2004):

	Undergraduate	Freshmen
International	0.5	0.7
Black	6.5	6.4
American Indian	0.5	0.5
Asian-American	2.9	2.5
Hispanic	2.6	2.3
White	80.6	78.2
Unreported	6.4	9.4
	100.0%	100.0%

6% are from out of state. Average age of full-time undergraduates is 21. 38% of classes have fewer than 20 students, 54% have between 20 and 50 students, 8% have more than 50 students.

STUDENT HOUSING

74% of freshmen live in college housing. Freshmen are not required to live on campus. Housing is guaranteed for all undergraduates. Campus can house 3,580 undergraduates. Single rooms are available for students with medical or special needs. A medical note is required.

EXPENSES

Tuition (2005-06): $1,417 per year (in-state), $8,099 (out-of-state).
Room: $4,612. Board: $3,174.
There is no additional cost for LD program/services.

LD SERVICES

LD program size is not limited.

LD services available to:

- [x] Freshmen
- [x] Sophomores
- [x] Juniors
- [x] Seniors

Academic Accommodations

Curriculum		**In class**	
Foreign language waiver	[ ]	Early syllabus	[ ]
Lighter course load	[x]	Note takers in class	[x]
Math waiver	[ ]	Priority seating	[ ]
Other special classes	[ ]	Tape recorders	[x]
Priority registrations	[ ]	Videotaped classes	[ ]
Substitution of courses	[ ]	Text on tape	[x]
Exams		**Services**	
Extended time	[x]	Diagnostic tests	[ ]
Oral exams	[x]	Learning centers	[x]
Take home exams	[ ]	Proofreaders	[ ]
Exams on tape or computer	[ ]	Readers	[x]
Untimed exams	[x]	Reading Machines/Kurzweil	[x]
Other accommodations	[x]	Special bookstore section	[ ]
		Typists	[ ]

Credit toward degree is not given for remedial courses taken.

Counseling Services

- [x] Academic
- [x] Psychological
- [x] Student Support groups
- [ ] Vocational

Tutoring

Individual tutoring is available daily.

	Individual	Group
Time management	[x]	[ ]
Organizational skills	[x]	[ ]
Learning strategies	[x]	[ ]
Study skills	[x]	[ ]
Content area	[x]	[ ]
Writing lab	[x]	[ ]
Math lab	[x]	[ ]

LD PROGRAM STAFF

Total number of LD Program staff (including director):

Full Time: 1 Part Time: 1

There is an advisor/advocate from the LD program available to students. Three graduate students and 100 peer tutors are available to work with LD students.

Key staff person available to work with LD students: Carole J. Johnson, Director, Disabled Student Services

University of Massachusetts at Lowell

Lowell, MA

Address: One University Avenue, Lowell, MA, 01854
Admissions telephone: 800 410-4607
Admissions FAX: 978 934-3086
Assistant Vice Chancellor for Admissions: Kerri Mead/Michael Belcher
Admissions e-mail: admissions@uml.edu
Web site: http://www.uml.edu
SAT Code: 3911 ACT Code: 1854

LD program name: Office of Disability Services
LD program address: 240 O'Leary Library - 61 Wilder Street
LD program contact: Chandrika Sharma
LD program telephone: 978 934-4574
LD program e-mail: Chandrika_Sharma@uml.edu
LD program enrollment: 202, Total campus enrollment: 8,662

GENERAL

University of Massachusetts at Lowell is a public, coed, four-year institution. Two major campuses of 105 acres in Lowell (population: 105,167), 25 miles north of Boston. Served by bus; major airport, bus, and train serve Boston. School operates free shuttle bus on campus. Public transportation serves campus. Semester system.

LD ADMISSIONS

Students do not complete a separate application and are simultaneously accepted to the LD program. A member of the LD program does not sit on the admissions committee. A personal interview is required.

SECONDARY SCHOOL REQUIREMENTS

Graduation from secondary school required; GED accepted. The following course distribution required: 4 units of English, 3 units of math, 3 units of science, 2 units of foreign language, 2 units of social studies, 2 units of academic electives.

TESTING

SAT Reasoning required; ACT may be substituted. SAT Subject recommended.

All enrolled freshmen (fall 2004):

Average SAT I Scores: Verbal: 534 Math: 557

Child Study Team report is not required. A neuropsychological or comprehensive psycho-educational evaluation is required for admission. Must be dated within 48 months of application. Tests required as part of this documentation:

- [x] WAIS-IV
- [x] WISC-IV
- [ ] SATA
- [x] Woodcock-Johnson
- [ ] Nelson-Denny Reading Test
- [x] Other

UNDERGRADUATE STUDENT BODY

Total undergraduate student enrollment: 5,668 Men, 3,982 Women.

Composition of student body (fall 2004):

	Undergraduate	Freshmen
International	0.8	1.3
Black	2.4	3.0
American Indian	0.2	0.3
Asian-American	6.9	5.9
Hispanic	5.5	3.8
White	79.1	50.7
Unreported	5.1	35.0
	100.0%	100.0%

13% are from out of state. 57% of classes have fewer than 20 students, 37% have between 20 and 50 students, 6% have more than 50 students.

STUDENT HOUSING

Freshmen are not required to live on campus. Housing is guaranteed for all undergraduates. Campus can house 2,239 undergraduates. Single rooms are available for students with medical or special needs. A medical note is required.

EXPENSES

Tuition 2004-05: $1,454 per year (in-state), $8,567 (out-of-state).

Room: $3,567. Board: $2,444.

There is no additional cost for LD program/services.

LD SERVICES

LD program size is not limited.

LD services available to:

- [x] Freshmen
- [x] Sophomores
- [x] Juniors
- [x] Seniors

Academic Accommodations

Curriculum		In class	
Foreign language waiver	[x]	Early syllabus	[ ]
Lighter course load	[x]	Note takers in class	[x]
Math waiver	[ ]	Priority seating	[x]
Other special classes	[ ]	Tape recorders	[x]
Priority registrations	[x]	Videotaped classes	[ ]
Substitution of courses	[ ]	Text on tape	[ ]
Exams		**Services**	
Extended time	[x]	Diagnostic tests	[ ]
Oral exams	[x]	Learning centers	[x]
Take home exams	[x]	Proofreaders	[x]
Exams on tape or computer	[x]	Readers	[x]
Untimed exams	[x]	Reading Machines/Kurzweil	[ ]
Other accommodations	[x]	Special bookstore section	[ ]
		Typists	[x]

Credit toward degree is not given for remedial courses taken.

Counseling Services

- [x] Academic
- [x] Psychological
- [ ] Student Support groups
- [x] Vocational

Tutoring

Individual tutoring is available weekly.

Average size of tutoring groups: 5

	Individual	Group
Time management	[x]	[ ]
Organizational skills	[x]	[ ]
Learning strategies	[x]	[ ]
Study skills	[x]	[ ]
Content area	[x]	[ ]
Writing lab	[x]	[x]
Math lab	[ ]	[x]

LD PROGRAM STAFF

Total number of LD Program staff (including director):

Full Time: 2 Part Time: 2

There is an advisor/advocate from the LD program available to students. The advisor/advocate meets with faculty and students once per month. 50 graduate students are available to work with LD students.

Key staff person available to work with LD students: Chandrika Sharma Ed.D, Assistant Director of Disability Services

LD Program web site: www.uml.edu/dis

Merrimack College

North Andover, MA

Address: 315 Turnpike Street, North Andover, MA, 01845
Admissions telephone: 978 837-5100
Admissions FAX: 978 837-5133
Assistant Dean/Coordinator of Transfer Affairs: Joyce Caruso
Admissions e-mail: Admission@Merrimack.edu
Web site: http://www.merrimack.edu
SAT Code: 3525 ACT Code: 1864

ADA Academic Advisor: Timothy Montgomery
LD program telephone: 978 837-5140
LD program e-mail: Timothy.Montgomery@merrimack.edu
LD program enrollment: 109, Total campus enrollment: 2,304

GENERAL

Merrimack College is a private, coed, four-year institution. 220-acre, suburban campus in North Andover (population: 27,202), 25 miles north of Boston. Served by bus and train; major airport serves Boston; smaller airport serves Manchester, NH (25 miles). School operates transportation to Boston. Public transportation serves campus. Semester system.

LD ADMISSIONS

Application Deadline: 02/01. A personal interview is recommended. Essay is required and may be typed.

SECONDARY SCHOOL REQUIREMENTS

Graduation from secondary school required; GED not accepted. The following course distribution required: 4 units of English, 3 units of math, 3 units of science, 2 units of foreign language, 2 units of social studies, 2 units of history, 1 unit of academic electives.

TESTING

SAT Reasoning required; ACT may be substituted. SAT Subject required.

All enrolled freshmen (fall 2004):

Average SAT I Scores:	Verbal: 530	Math: 560
Average ACT Scores:	Composite: 24	

Child Study Team report is not required. Tests required as part of this documentation:

- ☐ WAIS-IV
- ☐ WISC-IV
- ☐ SATA
- ☐ Woodcock-Johnson
- ☐ Nelson-Denny Reading Test
- ☐ Other

UNDERGRADUATE STUDENT BODY

Total undergraduate student enrollment: 1,209 Men, 1,359 Women.

Composition of student body (fall 2004):

	Undergraduate	Freshmen
International	1.2	1.4
Black	0.6	0.6
American Indian	0.4	0.2
Asian-American	2.8	1.6
Hispanic	4.1	2.2
White	74.4	65.5
Unreported	16.5	28.5
	100.0%	100.0%

26% are from out of state. 3% join a fraternity and 5% join a sorority. Average age of full-time undergraduates is 20. 67% of classes have fewer than 20 students, 32% have between 20 and 50 students, 1% have more than 50 students.

STUDENT HOUSING

92% of freshmen live in college housing. Freshmen are not required to live on campus. Housing is guaranteed for all undergraduates. Campus can house 1,585 undergraduates. Single rooms are available for students with medical or special needs. A medical note is required.

EXPENSES

Tuition (2005-06): $24,200 per year.

Room: $5,500. Board: $4,230.

There is no additional cost for LD program/services.

LD SERVICES

LD program size is not limited.

LD services available to:

■ Freshmen ■ Sophomores ■ Juniors ■ Seniors

Academic Accommodations

Curriculum		**In class**	
Foreign language waiver	☐	Early syllabus	☐
Lighter course load	■	Note takers in class	■
Math waiver	☐	Priority seating	☐
Other special classes	☐	Tape recorders	■
Priority registrations	☐	Videotaped classes	☐
Substitution of courses	☐	Text on tape	☐
Exams		**Services**	
Extended time	■	Diagnostic tests	☐
Oral exams	■	Learning centers	■
Take home exams	☐	Proofreaders	☐
Exams on tape or computer	☐	Readers	■
Untimed exams	☐	Reading Machines/Kurzweil	☐
Other accommodations	☐	Special bookstore section	☐
		Typists	☐

Credit toward degree is not given for remedial courses taken.

Counseling Services

- ■ Academic
- ■ Psychological
- ☐ Student Support groups
- ☐ Vocational

Tutoring

Individual tutoring is available weekly.

Average size of tutoring groups: 2

	Individual	Group
Time management	■	☐
Organizational skills	■	☐
Learning strategies	■	☐
Study skills	■	☐
Content area	■	☐
Writing lab	■	☐
Math lab	■	☐

LD PROGRAM STAFF

Total number of LD Program staff (including director):

Full Time: 1 Part Time: 1

There is an advisor/advocate from the LD program available to students. 25 peer tutors are available to work with LD students.

Key staff person available to work with LD students: Timothy Montgomery, ADA Academic Advisor

Montserrat College of Art

Beverly, MA

Address: P.O. Box 26, 23 Essex Street, Beverly, MA, 01915
Admissions telephone: 800 836-0487
Admissions FAX: 978 921-4241
Dean of Admissions and Enrollment Management: Jessica Sarin-Perry
Admissions e-mail: admiss@montserrrat.edu
Web site: http://www.montserrat.edu
SAT Code: 9101 ACT Code: 1847

Director of Academic Services: Brian Pellinen
LD program telephone: 978 922-2356
LD program e-mail: bpellinen@montserrat.edu
LD program enrollment: 23, Total campus enrollment: 353

GENERAL

Montserrat College of Art is a private, coed, four-year institution. 12-acre campus in Beverly (population: 39,862), 23 miles from Boston. Served by train; major airport and bus serve Boston. Semester system.

LD ADMISSIONS

Students do not complete a separate application and are simultaneously accepted to the LD program. A member of the LD program does not sit on the admissions committee. High school waivers are accepted for math and foreign language. A personal interview is required. Essay is required and may be typed. SAT/ACT score requirement may be waived for applicants to a diploma program.

For fall 2004, 29 completed self-identified LD applications were received. 29 applications were offered admission, and 8 enrolled.

SECONDARY SCHOOL REQUIREMENTS

Graduation from secondary school required; GED accepted. The following course distribution required: 4 units of English, 2 units of social studies, 2 units of history.

TESTING

SAT Reasoning or ACT required of some applicants. SAT Subject recommended.

All enrolled freshmen (fall 2004):

Average SAT I Scores:	Verbal: 533	Math: 475
Average ACT Scores:	Composite: 21	

Child Study Team report is not required. Tests required as part of this documentation:

- ☐ WAIS-IV
- ☐ WISC-IV
- ☐ SATA
- ☐ Woodcock-Johnson
- ☐ Nelson-Denny Reading Test
- ☐ Other

UNDERGRADUATE STUDENT BODY

Total undergraduate student enrollment: 165 Men, 227 Women.

Composition of student body (fall 2004):

	Undergraduate	Freshmen
International	0.0	0.8
Black	0.0	0.8
American Indian	1.4	0.0
Asian-American	0.0	3.3
Hispanic	2.9	0.8
White	82.8	74.5
Unreported	12.9	19.8
	100.0%	100.0%

50% are from out of state. Average age of full-time undergraduates is 22.

STUDENT HOUSING

77% of freshmen live in college housing. Freshmen are not required to live on campus. Housing is guaranteed for all undergraduates. Campus can house 153 undergraduates. Single rooms are available for students with medical or special needs. A medical note is not required.

EXPENSES

Tuition (2005-06): $19,934 per year.

Room: $5,300.

There is no additional cost for LD program/services.

LD SERVICES

LD program size is not limited.

LD services available to:

■ Freshmen ■ Sophomores ■ Juniors ■ Seniors

Academic Accommodations

Curriculum		In class	
Foreign language waiver	☐	Early syllabus	☐
Lighter course load	■	Note takers in class	☐
Math waiver	☐	Priority seating	☐
Other special classes	☐	Tape recorders	■
Priority registrations	☐	Videotaped classes	☐
Substitution of courses	☐	Text on tape	■
Exams		**Services**	
Extended time	■	Diagnostic tests	☐
Oral exams	■	Learning centers	■
Take home exams	☐	Proofreaders	☐
Exams on tape or computer	☐	Readers	☐
Untimed exams	☐	Reading Machines/Kurzweil	■
Other accommodations	☐	Special bookstore section	☐
		Typists	☐

Credit toward degree is not given for remedial courses taken.

Counseling Services

- ■ Academic
- ■ Psychological
- ☐ Student Support groups
- ☐ Vocational

Tutoring

Individual tutoring is available.

	Individual	Group
Time management	☐	☐
Organizational skills	☐	☐
Learning strategies	☐	☐
Study skills	☐	☐
Content area	☐	☐
Writing lab	☐	☐
Math lab	☐	☐

UNIQUE LD PROGRAM FEATURES

We are institutional members of recording for the blind and dyslexic.

LD PROGRAM STAFF

Total number of LD Program staff (including director):

Full Time: 1 Part Time: 1

There is an advisor/advocate from the LD program available to students.

Key staff person available to work with LD students: Brian Pellinen, Director of Academic Services

Mount Holyoke College

South Hadley, MA

Address: 50 College Street, South Hadley, MA, 01075
Admissions telephone: 413 538-2023
Admissions FAX: 413 538-2409
Dean of Admissions: Diane Anci
Admissions e-mail: admission@mtholyoke.edu
Web site: http://www.mtholyoke.edu
SAT Code: 3529 ACT Code: 1866

Associate Dean of Learning Skills: John Body III
LD program telephone: 413 538-2504
LD program e-mail: jbody@mtholyoke.edu
LD program enrollment: 117, Total campus enrollment: 2,143

GENERAL

Mount Holyoke College is a private, women's, four-year institution. 800-acre campus in South Hadley (population: 17,196), 15 miles from Springfield and 25 miles north of Hartford, CT. Served by bus; airport serves Boston (90 miles); smaller airport serves Hartford, CT; train serves Springfield. Free bus service connects Five College Consortium schools. School operates shuttle service to airports at breaks. Public transportation serves campus. Semester system.

LD ADMISSIONS

A member of the LD program does not sit on the admissions committee. A personal interview is recommended. Essay is required and may be typed.

SECONDARY SCHOOL REQUIREMENTS

Graduation from secondary school required; GED accepted.

TESTING

SAT Reasoning or ACT considered if submitted. SAT Subject recommended.

All enrolled freshmen (fall 2004):

Average SAT I Scores:	Verbal: 648	Math: 625
Average ACT Scores:	Composite: 28	

Child Study Team report is not required. A neuropsychological or comprehensive psycho-educational evaluation is required for admission. Must be dated within 36 months of application. Tests required as part of this documentation:

- [x] WAIS-IV
- [ ] WISC-IV
- [ ] SATA
- [x] Woodcock-Johnson
- [ ] Nelson-Denny Reading Test
- [ ] Other

UNDERGRADUATE STUDENT BODY

Total undergraduate student enrollment: 6 Men, 2,059 Women.

Composition of student body (fall 2004):

	Undergraduate	Freshmen
International	12.9	14.5
Black	4.7	4.2
American Indian	0.9	0.7
Asian-American	12.4	10.7
Hispanic	5.0	5.1
White	52.8	52.2
Unreported	11.3	12.6
	100.0%	100.0%

74% are from out of state. Average age of full-time undergraduates is 20. 76% of classes have fewer than 20 students, 21% have between 20 and 50 students, 3% have more than 50 students.

STUDENT HOUSING

99% of freshmen live in college housing. Freshmen are required to live on campus. Housing is guaranteed for all undergraduates. Campus can house 1,940 undergraduates. Single rooms are available for students with medical or special needs.

EXPENSES

Tuition (2005-06): $32,430 per year.
Room: $4,670. Board: $4,880.
There is no additional cost for LD program/services.

LD SERVICES

LD program size is not limited.

LD services available to:

- [x] Freshmen
- [x] Sophomores
- [x] Juniors
- [x] Seniors

Academic Accommodations

Curriculum		**In class**	
Foreign language waiver	[ ]	Early syllabus	[x]
Lighter course load	[x]	Note takers in class	[x]
Math waiver	[ ]	Priority seating	[x]
Other special classes	[ ]	Tape recorders	[x]
Priority registrations	[ ]	Videotaped classes	[ ]
Substitution of courses	[x]	Text on tape	[x]
Exams		**Services**	
Extended time	[x]	Diagnostic tests	[x]
Oral exams	[x]	Learning centers	[ ]
Take home exams	[ ]	Proofreaders	[x]
Exams on tape or computer	[x]	Readers	[x]
Untimed exams	[ ]	Reading Machines/Kurzweil	[ ]
Other accommodations	[x]	Special bookstore section	[ ]
		Typists	[x]

Credit toward degree is not given for remedial courses taken.

Counseling Services

- [x] Academic
- [x] Psychological
- [ ] Student Support groups
- [ ] Vocational

Tutoring

Individual tutoring is available weekly.

	Individual	Group
Time management	[x]	[x]
Organizational skills	[x]	[ ]
Learning strategies	[x]	[x]
Study skills	[x]	[x]
Content area	[x]	[x]
Writing lab	[x]	[x]
Math lab	[x]	[x]

LD PROGRAM STAFF

There is an advisor/advocate from the LD program available to students.

Key staff person available to work with LD students: John Body III, Associate Dean of Learning Skills

LD Program web site: http://www.mtholyoke.edu/offices/dcoll/learning.shtml

Mount Ida College

Newton, MA

Address: 777 Dedham Street, Newton, MA, 02159
Admissions telephone: 617 928-4535
Admissions FAX: 617 928-4507
Dean of Admissions: Elizabeth Storinge
Admissions e-mail: admissions@mountida.edu
Web site: http://www.mountida.edu
SAT Code: 3530 ACT Code: 1868

LD program name: Learning Opportunities Program
LD program address: Halden Hall, 777 Dedham Street
Dean of Academic Services: Alyce Curtis
LD program telephone: 617 928-4500
LD program e-mail: acurtis@mountida.edu
Total campus enrollment: 1,297

GENERAL

Mount Ida College is a private, coed, four-year institution. 85-acre, suburban campus in Newton (population: 83,829), eight miles from Boston. Major airport, bus, and train serve Boston. School operates transportation to public transit line. Public transportation serves campus. Semester system.

LD ADMISSIONS

Students do not complete a separate application and are simultaneously accepted to the LD program. A member of the LD program does sit on the admissions committee. High school waivers are accepted for foreign language. A personal interview is recommended. Essay is required and may not be typed.

SECONDARY SCHOOL REQUIREMENTS

Graduation from secondary school required; GED accepted. The following course distribution required: 4 units of English, 3 units of math, 2 units of science, 2 units of social studies.

TESTING

SAT Reasoning or ACT required. SAT Subject recommended.

All enrolled freshmen (fall 2004):

Average SAT I Scores: Verbal: 450 Math: 441

Child Study Team report is not required. A neuropsychological or comprehensive psycho-educational evaluation is required for admission. Must be dated within 36 months of application. Tests required as part of this documentation:

- ■ WAIS-IV
- ☐ WISC-IV
- ☐ SATA
- ■ Woodcock-Johnson
- ☐ Nelson-Denny Reading Test
- ☐ Other

UNDERGRADUATE STUDENT BODY

Total undergraduate student enrollment: 1,297.

Composition of student body (fall 2004):

	Undergraduate	Freshmen
International	4.5	8.2
Black	11.4	12.2
American Indian	0.0	0.1
Asian-American	2.9	2.9
Hispanic	6.9	5.9
White	61.1	58.7
Unreported	13.2	12.0
	100.0%	100.0%

43% are from out of state. Average age of full-time undergraduates is 21. 65% of classes have fewer than 20 students, 35% have between 20 and 50 students.

STUDENT HOUSING

80% of freshmen live in college housing. Freshmen are not required to live on campus. Housing is guaranteed for all undergraduates. Single rooms are available for students with medical or special needs. A medical note is required.

EXPENSES

Tuition (2005-06): $18,500 per year.
Room & Board: $9,830.
Additional cost for LD program/services: $2,900 per year.

LD SERVICES

LD program size is not limited.

LD services available to:

■ Freshmen ■ Sophomores ■ Juniors ■ Seniors

Academic Accommodations

Curriculum		In class	
Foreign language waiver	☐	Early syllabus	☐
Lighter course load	■	Note takers in class	■
Math waiver	☐	Priority seating	☐
Other special classes	☐	Tape recorders	☐
Priority registrations	☐	Videotaped classes	☐
Substitution of courses	☐	Text on tape	☐
Exams		**Services**	
Extended time	■	Diagnostic tests	☐
Oral exams	☐	Learning centers	■
Take home exams	☐	Proofreaders	☐
Exams on tape or computer	☐	Readers	☐
Untimed exams	■	Reading Machines/Kurzweil	☐
Other accommodations	☐	Special bookstore section	☐
		Typists	☐

Credit toward degree is not given for remedial courses taken.

Counseling Services

- ■ Academic — Meets 60 times per academic year
- ■ Psychological
- ☐ Student Support groups
- ■ Vocational

Tutoring

Individual tutoring is available daily.

Average size of tutoring groups: 6

	Individual	Group
Time management	■	■
Organizational skills	■	■
Learning strategies	■	☐
Study skills	☐	■
Content area	■	■
Writing lab	☐	■
Math lab	☐	■

LD PROGRAM STAFF

Total number of LD Program staff (including director):

Full Time: 3 Part Time: 3

There is an advisor/advocate from the LD program available to students. The advisor/advocate meets with faculty four times per month and students eight times per month.

Key staff person available to work with LD students: Alyce Curtis, Dean of Academic Services

LD Program web site: http://www.mountida.edu

Mount Wachusett Community College

Gardner, MA

Address: 444 Green Street, Gardner, MA 01440-1000
Admissions telephone: 978 630-9110
Senior Institutional Research & Assessment Analyst: Rebecca Forest
Admissions e-mail: admissions@mwcc.mass.edu
Web site: http://www.mwcc.mass.edu
SAT Code: 3545

Counselor: Saul Torres
LD program telephone: 978 630-9120
LD program e-mail: storres@mwcc.mass.edu
LD program enrollment: 141

GENERAL

Mount Wachusett Community College is a public, coed, two-year institution. 153-acre, campus in Gardner (population: 20,770). Served by bus; major airport serves Boston (55 miles). Smaller airport serves Worcester (30 miles); train serves Fitchburg (12 miles). Public transportation serves campus. Semester system.

LD ADMISSIONS

Students do not complete a separate application and are simultaneously accepted to the LD program. A member of the LD program does not sit on the admissions committee. A personal interview is required.

SECONDARY SCHOOL REQUIREMENTS

Graduation from secondary school required; GED accepted.

TESTING

IEP is recommended. Tests required as part of this documentation:

- ☐ WAIS-IV
- ☐ WISC-IV
- ☐ SATA
- ☐ Woodcock-Johnson
- ☐ Nelson-Denny Reading Test
- ☐ Other

STUDENT HOUSING

Single rooms are available to students with specific disabilities; documentation is required.

EXPENSES

Tuition (2005-06): $131 per credit hour (in-state), $336 (out-of-state). Tuition includes fees.

There is no additional cost for LD program/services.

LD SERVICES

LD program size is not limited.

LD services available to:

☒ Freshmen ☒ Sophomores ☒ Juniors ☒ Seniors

Academic Accommodations

Curriculum		**In class**	
Foreign language waiver	☐	Early syllabus	☒
Lighter course load	☒	Note takers in class	☒
Math waiver	☐	Priority seating	☐
Other special classes	☐	Tape recorders	☒
Priority registrations	☐	Videotaped classes	☐
Substitution of courses	☒	Text on tape	☒
Exams		**Services**	
Extended time	☒	Diagnostic tests	☐
Oral exams	☒	Learning centers	☒
Take home exams	☐	Proofreaders	☐
Exams on tape or computer	☒	Readers	☒
Untimed exams	☐	Reading Machines/Kurzweil	☒
Other accommodations	☒	Special bookstore section	☐
		Typists	☒

Credit toward degree is not given for remedial courses taken.

Counseling Services

- ☒ Academic
- ☒ Psychological
- ☒ Student Support groups
- ☒ Vocational

Tutoring

Individual tutoring is available for all students on a weekly basis.

Average size of tutoring groups is 1.

	Individual	Group
Time management	☒	☐
Organizational skills	☒	☐
Learning strategies	☒	☐
Study skills	☒	☐
Content area	☒	☐
Writing lab	☒	☐
Math lab	☒	☐

LD PROGRAM STAFF

Total number of LD Program staff (including director):

Full Time: 2

Key staff person available to work with LD students: Saul Torres, Counselor for Students with Disabilities; Joyce Kulig, Visions LD Specialist

Nichols College

Dudley, MA

Address: Box 5000, Dudley, MA, 01571
Admissions telephone: 800 470-3379
Admissions FAX: 508 943-9885
Dean of Admissions and Financial Aid: R. Joseph Bellavance
Admissions e-mail: admissions@nichols.edu
Web site: http://www.nichols.edu/
SAT Code: 3666 ACT Code: 1878

LD program name: Advising Services
Assistant Dean of Advising & Academic Services: Edward J. Kolek, Jr., Ph.D.
LD program telephone: 508 213-2293
LD program e-mail: edward.kolek@nichols.edu
LD program enrollment: 70, Total campus enrollment: 1,434

GENERAL

Nichols College is a private, coed, four-year institution. 200-acre campus in Dudley (population: 10,036), 20 miles from Worcester; branch campuses in Auburn and Marlboro. Airport, bus, and train serve Worcester; major airports serve Providence, RI (45 miles), Hartford, CT (50 miles), and Boston (55 miles). Semester system.

LD ADMISSIONS

Students do not complete a separate application and are not simultaneously accepted to the LD program. A member of the LD program does not sit on the admissions committee. A personal interview is recommended. Essay is required and may be typed.

SECONDARY SCHOOL REQUIREMENTS

Graduation from secondary school required; GED accepted. The following course distribution required: 4 units of English, 2 units of math, 2 units of science, 2 units of social studies, 2 units of history.

TESTING

SAT Reasoning or ACT considered if submitted; SAT Reasoning preferred.

All enrolled freshmen (fall 2004):

Average SAT I Scores: Verbal: 451 Math: 462

Child Study Team report is not required. A neuropsychological or comprehensive psycho-educational evaluation is required for admission. Must be dated within 36 months of application. Tests required as part of this documentation:

- [x] WAIS-IV
- [ ] WISC-IV
- [ ] SATA
- [x] Woodcock-Johnson
- [x] Nelson-Denny Reading Test
- [x] Other

UNDERGRADUATE STUDENT BODY

Total undergraduate student enrollment: 724 Men, 573 Women.

Composition of student body (fall 2004):

	Undergraduate	Freshmen
International	0.0	0.0
Black	4.5	7.9
American Indian	0.3	0.4
Asian-American	1.3	1.8
Hispanic	4.8	3.3
White	89.1	86.6
Unreported	0.0	0.0
	100.0%	100.0%

40% are from out of state. Average age of full-time undergraduates is 20. 51% of classes have fewer than 20 students, 49% have between 20 and 50 students.

STUDENT HOUSING

88% of freshmen live in college housing. Freshmen are not required to live on campus. Housing is guaranteed for all undergraduates. Campus can house 741 undergraduates. Single rooms are available for students with medical or special needs. A medical note is required.

EXPENSES

Tuition (2005-06): $22,000 per year.
Room: $4,490. Board: $3,800.
There is no additional cost for LD program/services.

LD SERVICES

LD program size is not limited.

LD services available to:

- [x] Freshmen
- [x] Sophomores
- [x] Juniors
- [x] Seniors

Academic Accommodations

Curriculum		In class	
Foreign language waiver	[ ]	Early syllabus	[ ]
Lighter course load	[x]	Note takers in class	[ ]
Math waiver	[ ]	Priority seating	[ ]
Other special classes	[ ]	Tape recorders	[ ]
Priority registrations	[ ]	Videotaped classes	[ ]
Substitution of courses	[ ]	Text on tape	[ ]
Exams		**Services**	
Extended time	[x]	Diagnostic tests	[ ]
Oral exams	[ ]	Learning centers	[x]
Take home exams	[ ]	Proofreaders	[ ]
Exams on tape or computer	[ ]	Readers	[ ]
Untimed exams	[x]	Reading Machines/Kurzweil	[x]
Other accommodations	[ ]	Special bookstore section	[ ]
		Typists	[ ]

Credit toward degree is not given for remedial courses taken.

Counseling Services

- [ ] Academic
- [ ] Psychological
- [ ] Student Support groups
- [ ] Vocational

Tutoring

Individual tutoring is available weekly.

	Individual	Group
Time management	[x]	[ ]
Organizational skills	[x]	[ ]
Learning strategies	[x]	[ ]
Study skills	[x]	[ ]
Content area	[x]	[ ]
Writing lab	[x]	[ ]
Math lab	[x]	[ ]

LD PROGRAM STAFF

Total number of LD Program staff (including director):

Full Time: 1 Part Time: 1

There is an advisor/advocate from the LD program available to students.

Key staff person available to work with LD students: Edward J. Kolek, Jr., Ph.D., Assistant Dean of Advising & Academic Services

Northeastern University

Boston, MA

Address: 360 Huntington Avenue, Boston, MA, 02115
Admissions telephone: 617 373-2200
Admissions FAX: 617 373-8780
Director of Undergraduate Admissions: Ronne Turner, Dean
Admissions e-mail: admissions@neu.edu
Web site: http://www.northeastern.edu/
SAT Code: 3667 ACT Code: 1880

Service Coordinator: Debbie Auerbach
LD program telephone: 617 373-2675
LD program e-mail: d.auerbach@neu.edu
LD program enrollment: 300, Total campus enrollment: 14,618

GENERAL

Northeastern University is a private, coed, four-year institution. 60-acre, urban campus in Boston (population: 589,141); branch campuses in Burlington, Dedham, and Nahant. Served by air, bus, and train. Public transportation serves campus. Semester system.

LD ADMISSIONS

Essay is not required. Some courses may be substituted.

SECONDARY SCHOOL REQUIREMENTS

Graduation from secondary school required; GED accepted. The following course distribution required: 4 units of English, 3 units of math, 3 units of science, 2 units of foreign language, 3 units of social studies, 2 units of history.

TESTING

SAT Reasoning required; ACT may be substituted. SAT Subject required.

All enrolled freshmen (fall 2004):

Average SAT I Scores:	Verbal: 596	Math: 615
Average ACT Scores:	Composite: 26	

Child Study Team report is not required. A neuropsychological or comprehensive psycho-educational evaluation is required for admission. Must be dated within 12 months of application. Tests required as part of this documentation:

- [x] WAIS-IV
- [x] WISC-IV
- [x] SATA
- [x] Woodcock-Johnson
- [x] Nelson-Denny Reading Test
- [x] Other

UNDERGRADUATE STUDENT BODY

Total undergraduate student enrollment: 7,063 Men, 6,900 Women.

Composition of student body (fall 2004):

	Undergraduate	Freshmen
International	3.6	4.7
Black	4.9	5.8
American Indian	0.5	0.4
Asian-American	7.0	7.4
Hispanic	4.8	4.9
White	67.5	66.6
Unreported	11.7	10.2
	100.0%	100.0%

60% are from out of state. 4% join a fraternity and 4% join a sorority. Average age of full-time undergraduates is 21. 41% of classes have fewer than 20 students, 50% have between 20 and 50 students, 9% have more than 50 students.

STUDENT HOUSING

93% of freshmen live in college housing. Freshmen are not required to live on campus. Housing is guaranteed for all undergraduates. Campus can house 7,244 undergraduates.

EXPENSES

Tuition (2005-06): $28,400 per year.
Room: $5,780. Board: $4,550.
There are additional costs for LD program/services.

LD SERVICES

LD program size is limited.

LD services available to:

- [x] Freshmen
- [x] Sophomores
- [x] Juniors
- [x] Seniors

Academic Accommodations

Curriculum		**In class**	
Foreign language waiver	[ ]	Early syllabus	[ ]
Lighter course load	[x]	Note takers in class	[x]
Math waiver	[ ]	Priority seating	[ ]
Other special classes	[ ]	Tape recorders	[x]
Priority registrations	[ ]	Videotaped classes	[x]
Substitution of courses	[x]	Text on tape	[x]
Exams		**Services**	
Extended time	[x]	Diagnostic tests	[x]
Oral exams	[x]	Learning centers	[x]
Take home exams	[ ]	Proofreaders	[ ]
Exams on tape or computer	[ ]	Readers	[x]
Untimed exams	[ ]	Reading Machines/Kurzweil	[x]
Other accommodations	[x]	Special bookstore section	[ ]
		Typists	[ ]

Credit toward degree is not given for remedial courses taken.

Counseling Services

- [ ] Academic
- [ ] Psychological
- [ ] Student Support groups
- [ ] Vocational

Tutoring

	Individual	Group
Time management	[ ]	[ ]
Organizational skills	[ ]	[ ]
Learning strategies	[ ]	[ ]
Study skills	[ ]	[ ]
Content area	[ ]	[ ]
Writing lab	[x]	[ ]
Math lab	[ ]	[x]

UNIQUE LD PROGRAM FEATURES

Northeastern University has both a self-directed program (currently serving approximately 350 students) and a structured program (currently serving about 45 students at a cost of $2,200 per semester, per student).

Students in the self-directed program can meet regularly with their specialist as they choose. Students in the structured program meet with their specialist two to three times per week.

LD PROGRAM STAFF

Total number of LD Program staff (including director):

Full Time: 2 Part Time: 2

There is an advisor/advocate from the LD program available to students.

Key staff person available to work with LD students: Barbara Sherbondy, LD Specialist

LD Program web site: www.access-disability-deaf.neu.edu

Pine Manor College

Chestnut Hill, MA

Address: 400 Heath Street, Chestnut Hill, MA, 02467
Admissions telephone: 800 762-1357
Admissions FAX: 617 731-7102
Dean of Admissions: Bill Nichols
Admissions e-mail: admission@pmc.edu
Web site: http://www.pmc.edu
SAT Code: 3689 ACT Code: 1882

LD program name: Learning Resource Center
Director of Learning Resource Center: Mary Walsh
LD program telephone: 617 731-7167
LD program e-mail: admissions@pmc.edu
Total campus enrollment: 478

GENERAL

Pine Manor College is a private, women's, four-year institution. 60-acre, suburban campus in Chestnut Hill, five miles from downtown Boston (population: 589,141). Major airport, bus, and train serve Boston. Semester system.

LD ADMISSIONS

A member of the LD program does sit on the admissions committee. A personal interview is recommended. Essay is required and may be typed.

SECONDARY SCHOOL REQUIREMENTS

Graduation from secondary school required; GED accepted.

TESTING

SAT Reasoning or ACT required. SAT Subject recommended.

All enrolled freshmen (fall 2004):

Average SAT I Scores: Verbal: 420 Math: 400
Average ACT Scores: Composite: 17

Child Study Team report is not required. Tests required as part of this documentation:

- ☐ WAIS-IV
- ☐ WISC-IV
- ☐ SATA
- ☐ Woodcock-Johnson
- ☐ Nelson-Denny Reading Test
- ☐ Other

UNDERGRADUATE STUDENT BODY

Total undergraduate student enrollment: 406 Women.

Composition of student body (fall 2004):

	Undergraduate	Freshmen
International	6.5	8.9
Black	46.1	40.8
American Indian	0.1	0.6
Asian-American	4.5	3.5
Hispanic	11.0	11.4
White	21.4	26.3
Unreported	10.4	8.5
	100.0%	100.0%

28% are from out of state. Average age of full-time undergraduates is 20. 79% of classes have fewer than 20 students, 21% have between 20 and 50 students.

STUDENT HOUSING

93% of freshmen live in college housing. Freshmen are not required to live on campus. Housing is guaranteed for all undergraduates. Campus can house 481 undergraduates. Single rooms are available for students with medical or special needs. A medical note is required.

EXPENSES

Tuition (2005-06): $15,538 per year.
Room & Board: $9,500.

There is no additional cost for LD program/services.

LD SERVICES

LD program size is not limited.

LD services available to:

☑ Freshmen ☑ Sophomores ☑ Juniors ☑ Seniors

Academic Accommodations

Curriculum		**In class**	
Foreign language waiver	☐	Early syllabus	☐
Lighter course load	☑	Note takers in class	☑
Math waiver	☐	Priority seating	☐
Other special classes	☐	Tape recorders	☐
Priority registrations	☐	Videotaped classes	☐
Substitution of courses	☐	Text on tape	☐
Exams		**Services**	
Extended time	☑	Diagnostic tests	☐
Oral exams	☑	Learning centers	☑
Take home exams	☐	Proofreaders	☐
Exams on tape or computer	☐	Readers	☑
Untimed exams	☑	Reading Machines/Kurzweil	☐
Other accommodations	☑	Special bookstore section	☐
		Typists	☐

Credit toward degree is given for remedial courses taken.

Counseling Services

- ☐ Academic
- ☐ Psychological
- ☐ Student Support groups
- ☐ Vocational

Tutoring

Individual tutoring is available.

	Individual	Group
Time management	☑	☑
Organizational skills	☑	☑
Learning strategies	☑	☑
Study skills	☑	☑
Content area	☐	☐
Writing lab	☑	☑
Math lab	☑	☑

LD PROGRAM STAFF

Total number of LD Program staff (including director):

Full Time: 5 Part Time: 5

There is an advisor/advocate from the LD program available to students.

Key staff person available to work with LD students: Mary Walsh, Director of the Learning Resource Center

LD Program web site: http://www.pmc.edu/academic/LRC/lrc.html

Regis College

Weston, MA

Address: 235 Wellesley Street, Weston, MA, 02493-1571
Admissions telephone: 800 456-1820
Admissions FAX: 781 768-7071
Director of Admissions: Emily Keily
Admissions e-mail: admission@regiscollege.edu
Web site: http://www.regiscollege.edu
SAT Code: 3723 ACT Code: 1886

Associate Director of Admissions: Wanda Suriel
LD program telephone: 781 768-7100
LD program e-mail: wanda.suriel@regiscollege.edu
LD program enrollment: 60, Total campus enrollment: 897

GENERAL

Regis College is a private, women's, four-year institution. 168-acre, suburban campus in Weston (population: 11,469), 12 miles from Boston. Major airport, bus, and train serve Boston. School operates transportation to Boston and Cambridge and to Babson College, Bentley College, and Boston College. Semester system.

LD ADMISSIONS

A member of the LD program does not sit on the admissions committee. A personal interview is recommended. Essay is required and may be typed.

SECONDARY SCHOOL REQUIREMENTS

Graduation from secondary school required; GED accepted. The following course distribution required: 4 units of English, 3 units of math, 2 units of science, 2 units of foreign language, 2 units of social studies, 3 units of academic electives.

TESTING

SAT Reasoning required. ACT required. ACT may be substituted. SAT Subject recommended.

All enrolled freshmen (fall 2004):

Average SAT I Scores: Verbal: 470 Math: 466

Child Study Team report is not required. A neuropsychological or comprehensive psycho-educational evaluation is required for admission. Must be dated within 36 months of application. Tests required as part of this documentation:

- ■ WAIS-IV
- ■ WISC-IV
- ■ SATA
- ■ Woodcock-Johnson
- ■ Nelson-Denny Reading Test
- ■ Other

UNDERGRADUATE STUDENT BODY

Total undergraduate student enrollment: 11 Men, 840 Women.

Composition of student body (fall 2004):

	Undergraduate	Freshmen
International	1.3	1.1
Black	21.5	11.3
American Indian	0.0	0.2
Asian-American	8.2	5.4
Hispanic	10.8	8.6
White	43.0	40.3
Unreported	15.2	33.1
	100.0%	100.0%

17% are from out of state. Average age of full-time undergraduates is 21.67% of classes have fewer than 20 students, 33% have between 20 and 50 students.

STUDENT HOUSING

85% of freshmen live in college housing. Freshmen are not required to live on campus. Housing is guaranteed for all undergraduates. Campus can house 600 undergraduates. Single rooms are available for students with medical or special needs. A medical note is required.

EXPENSES

Tuition (2005-06): $21,525 per year.

Room: $4,995. Board: $4,830.
There is no additional cost for LD program/services.

LD SERVICES

LD program size is not limited.

LD services available to:

■ Freshmen ■ Sophomores ■ Juniors ■ Seniors

Academic Accommodations

Curriculum		In class	
Foreign language waiver	☐	Early syllabus	☐
Lighter course load	■	Note takers in class	■
Math waiver	■	Priority seating	☐
Other special classes	☐	Tape recorders	■
Priority registrations	☐	Videotaped classes	☐
Substitution of courses	☐	Text on tape	☐
Exams		**Services**	
Extended time	■	Diagnostic tests	☐
Oral exams	■	Learning centers	■
Take home exams	☐	Proofreaders	☐
Exams on tape or computer	☐	Readers	■
Untimed exams	■	Reading Machines/Kurzweil	☐
Other accommodations	■	Special bookstore section	☐
		Typists	☐

Credit toward degree is given for remedial courses taken.

Counseling Services

- ☐ Academic
- ☐ Psychological
- ☐ Student Support groups
- ☐ Vocational

Tutoring

Individual tutoring is available.

	Individual	Group
Time management	■	☐
Organizational skills	■	☐
Learning strategies	■	☐
Study skills	■	☐
Content area	■	☐
Writing lab	■	☐
Math lab	■	☐

UNIQUE LD PROGRAM FEATURES

LD services works closely with academic advising and the Student Success Center.

LD PROGRAM STAFF

There is an advisor/advocate from the LD program available to students.

Key staff person available to work with LD students: Elaine LeClair, Coordinator Learning Disability Services

Simmons College

Boston, MA

Address: 300 The Fenway, Boston, MA, 02115
Admissions telephone: 800 345-8468
Admissions FAX: 617 521-3190
Interim Director of Undergraduate Admissions: Jennifer O'Loughlin Hiebe
Admissions e-mail: ugadm@simmons.edu
Web site: http://www.simmons.edu
SAT Code: 3761 ACT Code: 1892

LD program name: Disability Services
ADA Compliance Officer/Coordinator: Todd Herriott
LD program telephone: 617 521-2473
LD program e-mail: todd.herriott@simmons.edu
Total campus enrollment: 1,812

GENERAL

Simmons College is a private, women's, four-year institution. 12-acre, urban campus in Boston (population: 589,141). Served by air, bus, and train. Public transportation serves campus. Semester system.

LD ADMISSIONS

A personal interview is recommended. Essay is not required.

SECONDARY SCHOOL REQUIREMENTS

Graduation from secondary school required; GED accepted. The following course distribution required: 4 units of English, 3 units of math, 3 units of science, 3 units of foreign language, 3 units of social studies, 3 units of history.

TESTING

SAT Reasoning or ACT required. SAT Subject recommended.

All enrolled freshmen (fall 2004):

Average SAT I Scores:	Verbal: 564	Math: 546
Average ACT Scores:	Composite: 23	

Child Study Team report is not required. Tests required as part of this documentation:

- ☐ WAIS-IV
- ☐ WISC-IV
- ☐ SATA
- ☐ Woodcock-Johnson
- ☐ Nelson-Denny Reading Test
- ☐ Other

UNDERGRADUATE STUDENT BODY

Total undergraduate student enrollment: 1,275 Women.

Composition of student body (fall 2004):

	Undergraduate	Freshmen
International	2.0	1.8
Black	4.0	6.7
American Indian	0.8	0.4
Asian-American	9.6	7.4
Hispanic	3.8	3.3
White	79.5	79.6
Unreported	0.3	0.8
	100.0%	100.0%

40% are from out of state. Average age of full-time undergraduates is 22. 65% of classes have fewer than 20 students, 30% have between 20 and 50 students, 5% have more than 50 students.

STUDENT HOUSING

100% of freshmen live in college housing. Freshmen are not required to live on campus. Housing is guaranteed for all undergraduates. Campus can house 825 undergraduates.

EXPENSES

Tuition (2005-06): $24,680 per year.

Room & Board: $10,200.
There is no additional cost for LD program/services.

LD SERVICES

LD program size is not limited.

LD services available to:

☒ Freshmen ☒ Sophomores ☒ Juniors ☒ Seniors

Academic Accommodations

Curriculum		**In class**	
Foreign language waiver	☒	Early syllabus	☐
Lighter course load	☐	Note takers in class	☒
Math waiver	☐	Priority seating	☐
Other special classes	☐	Tape recorders	☒
Priority registrations	☐	Videotaped classes	☐
Substitution of courses	☒	Text on tape	☐
Exams		**Services**	
Extended time	☒	Diagnostic tests	☐
Oral exams	☒	Learning centers	☒
Take home exams	☐	Proofreaders	☐
Exams on tape or computer	☐	Readers	☒
Untimed exams	☒	Reading Machines/Kurzweil	☒
Other accommodations	☒	Special bookstore section	☐
		Typists	☐

Credit toward degree is not given for remedial courses taken.

Counseling Services

- ☒ Academic
- ☐ Psychological
- ☐ Student Support groups
- ☐ Vocational

Tutoring

Individual tutoring is available weekly.

	Individual	Group
Time management	☒	☐
Organizational skills	☒	☐
Learning strategies	☒	☐
Study skills	☒	☐
Content area	☒	☐
Writing lab	☒	☐
Math lab	☒	☐

LD PROGRAM STAFF

There is an advisor/advocate from the LD program available to students.

Key staff person available to work with LD students: Todd Herriott, ADA Compliance Officer/Coordinator, Disability Services

Smith College

Northampton, MA

Address: 7 College Lane, Northampton, MA, 01063
Admissions telephone: 413 585-2500
Admissions FAX: 413 585-2527
Director of Admissions: Debra Shaver
Admissions e-mail: admission@smith.edu
Web site: http://www.smith.edu
SAT Code: 3762 ACT Code: 1894

LD program name: Disability Services
Disability Services Director: Laura Rauscher
LD program telephone: 413 585-2071
LD program e-mail: lrausch@email.smith.edu
LD program enrollment: 82, Total campus enrollment: 2,692

GENERAL

Smith College is a private, women's, four-year institution. 125-acre campus in Northampton (population: 28,978), 20 miles from Springfield. Served by bus; major airport serves Hartford, CT. (35 miles); train serves Springfield. School operates transportation to consortium schools, local shopping malls, and local businesses. Public transportation serves campus. Semester system.

LD ADMISSIONS

A personal interview is recommended. Essay is required and may be typed.

TESTING

SAT Reasoning or ACT required. SAT Subject recommended.

All enrolled freshmen (fall 2004):

Average SAT I Scores:	Verbal:650	Math:620
Average ACT Scores:	Composite:27	

Child Study Team report is not required. Tests required as part of this documentation:

- ☐ WAIS-IV
- ☐ WISC-IV
- ☐ SATA
- ☐ Woodcock-Johnson
- ☐ Nelson-Denny Reading Test
- ☐ Other

UNDERGRADUATE STUDENT BODY

Total undergraduate student enrollment: 2,665 Women.

Composition of student body (fall 2004):

	Undergraduate	Freshmen
International	6.8	6.7
Black	6.8	5.7
American Indian	1.0	1.1
Asian-American	11.8	9.8
Hispanic	6.2	5.9
White	53.2	54.1
Unreported	14.2	16.7
	100.0%	100.0%

76% are from out of state. Average age of full-time undergraduates is 21. 68% of classes have fewer than 20 students, 27% have between 20 and 50 students, 5% have more than 50 students.

STUDENT HOUSING

100% of freshmen live in college housing. Freshmen are required to live on campus. Housing is guaranteed for all undergraduates. Campus can house 2,449 undergraduates. Single rooms are available for students with medical or special needs. A medical note is required.

EXPENSES

Tuition (2005-06): $30,520 per year.
Room & Board: $10,270.

There is no additional cost for LD program/services.

LD SERVICES

LD program size is not limited.

LD services available to:

■ Freshmen ■ Sophomores ■ Juniors ■ Seniors

Academic Accommodations

Curriculum		In class	
Foreign language waiver	☐	Early syllabus	☐
Lighter course load	☐	Note takers in class	■
Math waiver	☐	Priority seating	☐
Other special classes	☐	Tape recorders	■
Priority registrations	☐	Videotaped classes	☐
Substitution of courses	☐	Text on tape	■
Exams		**Services**	
Extended time	■	Diagnostic tests	☐
Oral exams	☐	Learning centers	☐
Take home exams	☐	Proofreaders	☐
Exams on tape or computer	■	Readers	■
Untimed exams	■	Reading Machines/Kurzweil	■
Other accommodations	■	Special bookstore section	☐
		Typists	■

Credit toward degree is not given for remedial courses taken.

Counseling Services

- ☐ Academic
- ☐ Psychological
- ☐ Student Support groups
- ☐ Vocational

Tutoring

	Individual	Group
Time management	☐	☐
Organizational skills	☐	☐
Learning strategies	☐	☐
Study skills	☐	☐
Content area	☐	☐
Writing lab	☐	☐
Math lab	☐	☐

LD PROGRAM STAFF

Total number of LD Program staff (including director):

Full Time: 1 Part Time: 1

Key staff person available to work with LD students: Laura Rauscher, Disability Services Director

Springfield College

Springfield, MA

Address: 263 Alden Street, Springfield, MA, 01109
Admissions telephone: 800 343-1257
Admissions FAX: 413 748-3694
Director of Admissions: Mary N. DeAngelo
Admissions e-mail: admissions@spfldcol.edu
Web site: http://www.springfieldcollege.edu
SAT Code: 3763 ACT Code: 1896

LD program name: Student Support Services
Director: Deborah Dickens
LD program telephone: 413 748-3768
LD program e-mail: ddickens@spfldcol.edu
LD program enrollment: 138, Total campus enrollment: 3,621

GENERAL

Springfield College is a private, coed, four-year institution. 167-acre, suburban campus in Springfield (population: 152,082), 23 miles from Hartford, CT. Served by bus and train; major airport serves Windsor Locks, CT. Public transportation serves campus. Semester system.

LD ADMISSIONS

Students do not complete a separate application and are simultaneously accepted to the LD program. A member of the LD program does not sit on the admissions committee. High school waivers are accepted for foreign language. A personal interview is recommended. Essay is required and may be typed.

For fall 2004, 28 completed self-identified LD applications were received.

SECONDARY SCHOOL REQUIREMENTS

Graduation from secondary school required; GED accepted. The following course distribution required: 4 units of English, 3 units of math, 3 units of science, 2 units of foreign language, 3 units of history.

TESTING

SAT Reasoning required; ACT may be substituted. SAT Subject recommended.

All enrolled freshmen (fall 2004):

Average SAT I Scores: Verbal:509 Math:527

Child Study Team report is not required. A neuropsychological or comprehensive psycho-educational evaluation is required for admission. Must be dated within 36 months of application. Tests required as part of this documentation:

- [x] WAIS-IV
- [ ] WISC-IV
- [ ] SATA
- [x] Woodcock-Johnson
- [ ] Nelson-Denny Reading Test
- [ ] Other

UNDERGRADUATE STUDENT BODY

Total undergraduate student enrollment: 1,086 Men, 973 Women.

Composition of student body (fall 2004):

	Undergraduate	Freshmen
International	0.1	0.2
Black	4.1	22.4
American Indian	0.5	0.3
Asian-American	1.4	1.0
Hispanic	2.0	7.1
White	77.3	51.4
Unreported	14.6	17.6
	100.0%	100.0%

76% are from out of state. Average age of full-time undergraduates is 21. 46% of classes have fewer than 20 students, 52% have between 20 and 50 students, 2% have more than 50 students.

STUDENT HOUSING

97% of freshmen live in college housing. Freshmen are required to live on campus. Housing is guaranteed for all undergraduates. Campus can house 1,900 undergraduates. Single rooms are available for students with medical or special needs. A medical note is required.

EXPENSES

Tuition (2005-06): $21,320 per year.
Room: $4,230. Board: $3,540.
There is no additional cost for LD program/services.

LD SERVICES

LD program size is not limited.

LD services available to:

- [x] Freshmen
- [x] Sophomores
- [x] Juniors
- [x] Seniors

Academic Accommodations

Curriculum
- [ ] Foreign language waiver
- [x] Lighter course load
- [ ] Math waiver
- [ ] Other special classes
- [ ] Priority registrations
- [ ] Substitution of courses

Exams
- [x] Extended time
- [ ] Oral exams
- [ ] Take home exams
- [ ] Exams on tape or computer
- [x] Untimed exams
- [ ] Other accommodations

In class
- [ ] Early syllabus
- [x] Note takers in class
- [ ] Priority seating
- [x] Tape recorders
- [ ] Videotaped classes
- [ ] Text on tape

Services
- [ ] Diagnostic tests
- [ ] Learning centers
- [ ] Proofreaders
- [x] Readers
- [x] Reading Machines/Kurzweil
- [ ] Special bookstore section
- [ ] Typists

Credit toward degree is not given for remedial courses taken.

Counseling Services

- [ ] Academic
- [ ] Psychological
- [ ] Student Support groups
- [ ] Vocational

Tutoring

Individual tutoring is available weekly.

	Individual	Group
Time management	[x]	[ ]
Organizational skills	[x]	[ ]
Learning strategies	[x]	[ ]
Study skills	[x]	[ ]
Content area	[ ]	[ ]
Writing lab	[ ]	[ ]
Math lab	[ ]	[ ]

LD PROGRAM STAFF

Total number of LD Program staff (including director):

Full Time: 2 Part Time: 2

Key staff person available to work with LD students: Deborah Dickens, Director, Student Support Services

Stonehill College

Easton, MA

Address: 320 Washington Street, Easton, MA, 02357
Admissions telephone: 508 565-1373
Admissions FAX: 508 565-1545
Dean of Admissions and Enrollment: Brian P. Murphy
Admissions e-mail: admissions@stonehill.edu
Web site: http://www.stonehill.edu
SAT Code: 3770 ACT Code: 1918

LD program name: Center for Academic Achievement
Director: Autumn Grant-Kimball
LD program telephone: 508 565-1033
LD program e-mail: akimball@stonehill.edu
LD program enrollment: 12, Total campus enrollment: 2,466

GENERAL

Stonehill College is a private, coed, four-year institution. 375-acre campus in Easton (population: 22,299), less than one mile from Brockton and 20 miles from Boston. Major airport serves Boston; bus and train serve Brockton. School operates transportation to Boston subway system, Amtrak, and area malls and cinemas. Public transportation serves campus. Semester system.

LD ADMISSIONS

Students do not complete a separate application and are simultaneously accepted to the LD program. A member of the LD program does not sit on the admissions committee. High school waivers are accepted for foreign language. A personal interview is not required. Essay is required and may be typed. Foreign language requirements may be substituted or waived.

For fall 2004, 2 completed self-identified LD applications were received.

SECONDARY SCHOOL REQUIREMENTS

Graduation from secondary school required; GED accepted. The following course distribution required: 4 units of English, 3 units of math, 1 unit of science, 2 units of foreign language, 3 units of history, 3 units of academic electives.

TESTING

SAT Reasoning or ACT required. SAT Subject required.

All enrolled freshmen (fall 2004):

Average SAT I Scores:	Verbal: 590	Math: 590
Average ACT Scores:	Composite: 25	

Child Study Team report is not required. A neuropsychological or comprehensive psycho-educational evaluation is required for admission. Tests required as part of this documentation:

- [x] WAIS-IV
- [ ] WISC-IV
- [ ] SATA
- [x] Woodcock-Johnson
- [x] Nelson-Denny Reading Test
- [ ] Other

UNDERGRADUATE STUDENT BODY

Total undergraduate student enrollment: 1,057 Men, 1,556 Women.

Composition of student body (fall 2004):

	Undergraduate	Freshmen
International	0.4	0.6
Black	2.1	2.8
American Indian	0.3	0.4
Asian-American	2.4	2.9
Hispanic	4.6	3.0
White	90.2	90.3
Unreported	0.0	0.0
	100.0%	100.0%

40% are from out of state. Average age of full-time undergraduates is 20. 43% of classes have fewer than 20 students, 56% have between 20 and 50 students, 1% have more than 50 students.

STUDENT HOUSING

95% of freshmen live in college housing. Freshmen are not required to live on campus. Housing is guaranteed for all undergraduates. Students must first be accepted as resident students. Campus can house 1,825 undergraduates. Single rooms are available for students with medical or special needs. A medical note is required.

EXPENSES

Tuition (2005-06): $25,540 per year.
Room: $8,584. Board: $1,980.
There is no additional cost for LD program/services.

LD SERVICES

LD program size is not limited.

LD services available to:

- [x] Freshmen
- [x] Sophomores
- [x] Juniors
- [x] Seniors

Academic Accommodations

Curriculum		In class	
Foreign language waiver	[ ]	Early syllabus	[ ]
Lighter course load	[x]	Note takers in class	[x]
Math waiver	[ ]	Priority seating	[ ]
Other special classes	[ ]	Tape recorders	[x]
Priority registrations	[ ]	Videotaped classes	[ ]
Substitution of courses	[ ]	Text on tape	[x]
Exams		**Services**	
Extended time	[x]	Diagnostic tests	[x]
Oral exams	[ ]	Learning centers	[x]
Take home exams	[ ]	Proofreaders	[ ]
Exams on tape or computer	[ ]	Readers	[x]
Untimed exams	[ ]	Reading Machines/Kurzweil	[x]
Other accommodations	[ ]	Special bookstore section	[x]
		Typists	[ ]

Credit toward degree is not given for remedial courses taken.

Counseling Services

- [x] Academic
- [x] Psychological
- [ ] Student Support groups
- [ ] Vocational

Tutoring

Individual tutoring is available daily.

Average size of tutoring groups: 8

	Individual	Group
Time management	[ ]	[ ]
Organizational skills	[ ]	[ ]
Learning strategies	[ ]	[ ]
Study skills	[ ]	[ ]
Content area	[x]	[x]
Writing lab	[x]	[ ]
Math lab	[ ]	[ ]

LD PROGRAM STAFF

Total number of LD Program staff (including director):

Full Time: 1 Part Time: 1

There is an advisor/advocate from the LD program available to students. 80 peer tutors are available to work with LD students.

Key staff person available to work with LD students: Autumn Grant-Kimball, Director, Center for Academic Achievement

Suffolk University

Boston, MA

Address: 8 Ashburton Place, Boston, MA, 02108
Admissions telephone: 800-6-SUFFOL
Admissions FAX: 617 742-4291
Dean of Enrollment Management: John Hamel
Admissions e-mail: admission@suffolk.edu
Web site: http://www.suffolk.edu
SAT Code: 3771 ACT Code: 1920

LD program name: Ballotti Learning Center
Director of Specialized Services: Joyce Atkinson
LD program telephone: 617 573-8235
LD program e-mail: jatkiso@suffolk.edu
LD program enrollment: 150, Total campus enrollment: 4,477

GENERAL

Suffolk University is a private, coed, four-year institution. Urban campus in Boston (population: 589,141); branch campuses in Cape Cod, Franklin, and Merrimack and abroad in Madrid, Spain and Senegal. Served by air, bus, and train. Public transportation serves campus. Semester system.

LD ADMISSIONS

Students do not complete a separate application and are simultaneously accepted to the LD program. A member of the LD program does not sit on the admissions committee. A personal interview is recommended. Essay is required and may be typed.

SECONDARY SCHOOL REQUIREMENTS

Graduation from secondary school required; GED accepted. The following course distribution required: 4 units of English, 3 units of math, 2 units of science, 2 units of foreign language, 1 unit of history, 4 units of academic electives.

TESTING

SAT Reasoning or ACT required.

All enrolled freshmen (fall 2004):

Average SAT I Scores: Verbal: 506 Math: 497

Child Study Team report is not required. A neuropsychological or comprehensive psycho-educational evaluation is required for admission. Tests required as part of this documentation:

- [x] WAIS-IV
- [x] WISC-IV
- [ ] SATA
- [x] Woodcock-Johnson
- [ ] Nelson-Denny Reading Test
- [ ] Other

UNDERGRADUATE STUDENT BODY

Total undergraduate student enrollment: 1,462 Men, 1,975 Women.

Composition of student body (fall 2004):

	Undergraduate	Freshmen
International	4.1	9.7
Black	3.8	3.4
American Indian	0.5	0.4
Asian-American	7.8	6.6
Hispanic	5.6	4.6
White	63.1	60.6
Unreported	15.1	14.7
	100.0%	100.0%

15% are from out of state. Average age of full-time undergraduates is 20. 41% of classes have fewer than 20 students, 58% have between 20 and 50 students, 1% have more than 50 students.

STUDENT HOUSING

47% of freshmen live in college housing. Freshmen are not required to live on campus. Housing is not guaranteed for all undergraduates. We do offer assistance in locating housing. Campus can house 850 undergraduates. Single rooms are available for students with medical or special needs. A medical note is required.

EXPENSES

Tuition (2005-06): $21,140 per year.

Room: $10,020. Board: $1,920.
There is no additional cost for LD program/services.

LD SERVICES

LD program size is not limited.

LD services available to:

- [x] Freshmen
- [x] Sophomores
- [x] Juniors
- [x] Seniors

Academic Accommodations

Curriculum

- [ ] Foreign language waiver
- [x] Lighter course load
- [ ] Math waiver
- [ ] Other special classes
- [x] Priority registrations
- [x] Substitution of courses

Exams

- [x] Extended time
- [x] Oral exams
- [ ] Take home exams
- [ ] Exams on tape or computer
- [x] Untimed exams
- [x] Other accommodations

In class

- [ ] Early syllabus
- [x] Note takers in class
- [x] Priority seating
- [x] Tape recorders
- [ ] Videotaped classes
- [x] Text on tape

Services

- [ ] Diagnostic tests
- [x] Learning centers
- [ ] Proofreaders
- [x] Readers
- [x] Reading Machines/Kurzweil
- [ ] Special bookstore section
- [x] Typists

Credit toward degree is not given for remedial courses taken.

Counseling Services

- [ ] Academic
- [ ] Psychological
- [ ] Student Support groups
- [ ] Vocational

Tutoring

Individual tutoring is available weekly.

Average size of tutoring groups: 1

	Individual	Group
Time management	[x]	[ ]
Organizational skills	[x]	[ ]
Learning strategies	[x]	[ ]
Study skills	[x]	[ ]
Content area	[x]	[x]
Writing lab	[x]	[ ]
Math lab	[x]	[ ]

LD PROGRAM STAFF

Total number of LD Program staff (including director):

Full Time: 2 Part Time: 2

There is an advisor/advocate from the LD program available to students. 15 graduate students and 60 peer tutors are available to work with LD students.

Key staff person available to work with LD students: Joyce Atkinson, Assistant Director

Tufts University

Medford, MA

Address: Medford, MA, 02155
Admissions telephone: 617 627-3170
Admissions FAX: 617 627-3860
Dean of Admissions: Lee C. Coffin
Admissions e-mail: admissions.inquiry@ase.tufts.edu
Web site: http://www.tufts.edu
SAT Code: 3901 ACT Code: 1922

LD program name: Disability Services
Disability Services Coordinator: Sandra Baer
LD program telephone: 617 627-2000
Total campus enrollment: 4,913

GENERAL

Tufts University is a private, coed, four-year institution. 150-acre, suburban campus in Medford (population: 55,765), five miles from Boston; medical center campus in downtown Boston. Served by air, bus, and train. School operates transportation between campuses. Public transportation serves campus. Semester system.

LD ADMISSIONS

A personal interview is recommended. Essay is required and may be typed.

SECONDARY SCHOOL REQUIREMENTS

Graduation from secondary school required; GED accepted.

TESTING

SAT Subject required.

Child Study Team report is not required. Tests required as part of this documentation:

- ☐ WAIS-IV
- ☐ WISC-IV
- ☐ SATA
- ☐ Woodcock-Johnson
- ☐ Nelson-Denny Reading Test
- ☐ Other

UNDERGRADUATE STUDENT BODY

Total undergraduate student enrollment: 2,187 Men, 2,568 Women.

Composition of student body (fall 2004):

	Undergraduate	Freshmen
International	5.6	6.4
Black	7.1	7.3
American Indian	0.6	0.4
Asian-American	9.6	12.5
Hispanic	7.0	7.7
White	60.6	55.8
Unreported	9.5	9.9
	100.0%	100.0%

77% are from out of state. 15% join a fraternity and 4% join a sorority. 76% of classes have fewer than 20 students, 20% have between 20 and 50 students, 4% have more than 50 students.

STUDENT HOUSING

98% of freshmen live in college housing. Freshmen are required to live on campus.

EXPENSES

Tuition (2005-06): $31,828 per year.
Room: $4,827. Board: $4,570.

There is no additional cost for LD program/services.

LD SERVICES

LD services available to:

☐ Freshmen ☐ Sophomores ☐ Juniors ☐ Seniors

Academic Accommodations

Curriculum		In class	
Foreign language waiver	☐	Early syllabus	☐
Lighter course load	☐	Note takers in class	☒
Math waiver	☐	Priority seating	☐
Other special classes	☐	Tape recorders	☒
Priority registrations	☐	Videotaped classes	☐
Substitution of courses	☐	Text on tape	☐
Exams		**Services**	
Extended time	☒	Diagnostic tests	☐
Oral exams	☒	Learning centers	☒
Take home exams	☐	Proofreaders	☐
Exams on tape or computer	☐	Readers	☒
Untimed exams	☐	Reading Machines/Kurzweil	☐
Other accommodations	☐	Special bookstore section	☐
		Typists	☐

Credit toward degree is not given for remedial courses taken.

Counseling Services

- ☐ Academic
- ☐ Psychological
- ☐ Student Support groups
- ☐ Vocational

Tutoring

Individual tutoring is available.

	Individual	Group
Time management	☐	☐
Organizational skills	☐	☐
Learning strategies	☐	☐
Study skills	☐	☐
Content area	☐	☐
Writing lab	☐	☐
Math lab	☐	☐

LD PROGRAM STAFF

Key staff person available to work with LD students: Sandra Baer, Disability Services Coordinator

Wellesley College

Wellesley, MA

Address: 106 Central Street, Wellesley, MA, 02481-8203
Admissions telephone: 781 283-2270
Admissions FAX: 781 283-3678
Dean of Admissions: Jennifer Desjarlais
Admissions e-mail: admission@wellesley.edu
Web site: http://www.wellesley.edu
SAT Code: 3957   ACT Code: 1926

Director, Pforzheimer Learning & Teaching Center: Barbara Boger
LD program telephone: 781 283-2092
LD program e-mail: bboger@wellesley.edu
Total campus enrollment: 2,289

GENERAL

Wellesley College is a private, women's, four-year institution. 500-acre, suburban campus in Wellesley (population: 26,613), 12 miles from Boston. Major airport, bus, and train serve Boston. School operates transportation to Cambridge. Public transportation serves campus. Semester system.

LD ADMISSIONS

A personal interview is recommended. Essay is required and may be typed.

TESTING

SAT Subject required.

All enrolled freshmen (fall 2004):

Average SAT I Scores:	Verbal: 689	Math: 678
Average ACT Scores:	Composite: 29	

Child Study Team report is not required. Tests required as part of this documentation:

- ☐ WAIS-IV
- ☐ WISC-IV
- ☐ SATA
- ☐ Woodcock-Johnson
- ☐ Nelson-Denny Reading Test
- ☐ Other

UNDERGRADUATE STUDENT BODY

Total undergraduate student enrollment: 12 Men, 2,261 Women.

Composition of student body (fall 2004):

	Undergraduate	Freshmen
International	8.1	8.0
Black	6.5	6.1
American Indian	0.6	0.4
Asian-American	28.2	28.1
Hispanic	8.3	6.6
White	41.5	43.6
Unreported	6.8	7.2
	100.0%	100.0%

80% are from out of state. Average age of full-time undergraduates is 20. 65% of classes have fewer than 20 students, 34% have between 20 and 50 students, 1% have more than 50 students.

STUDENT HOUSING

100% of freshmen live in college housing. Freshmen are not required to live on campus. Housing is guaranteed for all undergraduates. Campus can house 2,187 undergraduates.

EXPENSES

Tuition (2005-06): $30,696 per year.

Room: $4,906. Board: $4,776.

There is no additional cost for LD program/services.

LD SERVICES

LD services available to:

■ Freshmen ■ Sophomores ■ Juniors ■ Seniors

Academic Accommodations

Curriculum		In class	
Foreign language waiver	☐	Early syllabus	☐
Lighter course load	☐	Note takers in class	■
Math waiver	☐	Priority seating	☐
Other special classes	■	Tape recorders	■
Priority registrations	☐	Videotaped classes	☐
Substitution of courses	☐	Text on tape	■
Exams		**Services**	
Extended time	■	Diagnostic tests	☐
Oral exams	■	Learning centers	■
Take home exams	☐	Proofreaders	☐
Exams on tape or computer	■	Readers	☐
Untimed exams	☐	Reading Machines/Kurzweil	☐
Other accommodations	■	Special bookstore section	☐
		Typists	☐

Credit toward degree is not given for remedial courses taken.

Counseling Services

- ☐ Academic
- ☐ Psychological
- ☐ Student Support groups
- ☐ Vocational

Tutoring

Individual tutoring is available daily.

	Individual	Group
Time management	■	☐
Organizational skills	■	☐
Learning strategies	■	☐
Study skills	■	☐
Content area	■	☐
Writing lab	■	☐
Math lab	■	☐

UNIQUE LD PROGRAM FEATURES

Reasonable accommodations for a student with learning and/or attention disabilities are highly individualized and can only be determined in consultation with the student, the Director of the PLTC and the faculty member.

LD PROGRAM STAFF

Key staff person available to work with LD students: Barbara Boger, Director, Pforzheimer Learning & Teaching Center

Wentworth Institute of Technology

Boston, MA

Address: 550 Huntington Avenue, Boston, MA, 02115-5998
Admissions telephone: 800 556-0610
Admissions FAX: 617 989-4010
Director of Admissions: Kathleen A. Lynch
Admissions e-mail: admissions@wit.edu
Web site: http://www.wit.edu
SAT Code: 3958

Disability Specialist: Judith Moss
LD program telephone: 617 989-4393
LD program e-mail: mossj@wit.edu
Total campus enrollment: 3,597

GENERAL

Wentworth Institute of Technology is a private, coed, four-year institution. 35-acre, urban campus in Boston (population: 589,141). Served by air, bus, and train. School operates transportation to consortium schools. Public transportation serves campus. Semester system.

LD ADMISSIONS

A personal interview is recommended.

SECONDARY SCHOOL REQUIREMENTS

Graduation from secondary school required; GED accepted. The following course distribution required: 4 units of English, 3 units of math, 1 unit of science.

TESTING

SAT Reasoning or ACT required.

All enrolled freshmen (fall 2004):

Average SAT I Scores: Verbal: 510 Math: 553

Child Study Team report is required if student is classified. Tests required as part of this documentation:

- ❑ WAIS-IV
- ❑ WISC-IV
- ❑ SATA
- ❑ Woodcock-Johnson
- ❑ Nelson-Denny Reading Test
- ❑ Other

UNDERGRADUATE STUDENT BODY

Total undergraduate student enrollment: 2,594 Men, 609 Women.

Composition of student body (fall 2004):

	Freshmen
International	3.0
Black	4.3
American Indian	0.2
Asian-American	5.4
Hispanic	3.8
White	76.2
Unreported	7.1
	100.0%

40% are from out of state.

STUDENT HOUSING

Housing is guaranteed for all undergraduates.

EXPENSES

Tuition (2005-06): $18,500 per year.

Room: $7,000. Board: $2,000.

There is no additional cost for LD program/services.

LD SERVICES

LD program size is not limited.

LD services available to:

❑ Freshmen ❑ Sophomores ❑ Juniors ❑ Seniors

Academic Accommodations

Curriculum		**In class**	
Foreign language waiver	❑	Early syllabus	❑
Lighter course load	❑	Note takers in class	■
Math waiver	❑	Priority seating	❑
Other special classes	❑	Tape recorders	■
Priority registrations	❑	Videotaped classes	❑
Substitution of courses	❑	Text on tape	❑
Exams		**Services**	
Extended time	■	Diagnostic tests	❑
Oral exams	■	Learning centers	■
Take home exams	❑	Proofreaders	❑
Exams on tape or computer	❑	Readers	■
Untimed exams	■	Reading Machines/Kurzweil	❑
Other accommodations	❑	Special bookstore section	❑
		Typists	❑

Counseling Services

- ❑ Academic
- ❑ Psychological
- ❑ Student Support groups
- ❑ Vocational

Tutoring

	Individual	Group
Time management	❑	❑
Organizational skills	❑	❑
Learning strategies	❑	❑
Study skills	❑	❑
Content area	❑	❑
Writing lab	❑	❑
Math lab	❑	❑

LD PROGRAM STAFF

Key staff person available to work with LD students: Judith Moss, Disability Specialist

Western New England College

Springfield, MA

Address: 1215 Wilbraham Road, Springfield, MA, 01119-2684
Admissions telephone: 800 325-1122, extension 1321
Admissions FAX: 413 782-1777
Vice President of Enrollment Management: Dr. Charles Pollock
Admissions e-mail: ugradmis@wnec.edu
Web site: http://www.wnec.edu
SAT Code: 3962 ACT Code: 1930

LD program telephone: 413 782-1257
LD program e-mail: balpert@wnec.edu
Total campus enrollment: 3,038

GENERAL

Western New England College is a private, coed, four-year institution. 215-acre, suburban campus in Springfield (population: 152,082), 90 miles from Boston; branch campuses in numerous locations, including military bases and community colleges. Served by bus and train; major airport serves Hartford, CT. (25 miles). Public transportation serves campus. Semester system.

LD ADMISSIONS

A personal interview is recommended. Essay is not required.

SECONDARY SCHOOL REQUIREMENTS

Graduation from secondary school required; GED accepted. The following course distribution required: 4 units of English, 2 units of math, 1 unit of science, 1 unit of social studies, 1 unit of history.

TESTING

SAT Reasoning required; ACT may be substituted. SAT Subject recommended.

All enrolled freshmen (fall 2004):

Average SAT I Scores: Verbal: 520 Math: 541

Child Study Team report is required if student is classified. Tests required as part of this documentation:

- [ ] WAIS-IV
- [ ] WISC-IV
- [ ] SATA
- [ ] Woodcock-Johnson
- [ ] Nelson-Denny Reading Test
- [ ] Other

UNDERGRADUATE STUDENT BODY

Total undergraduate student enrollment: 1,975 Men, 1,116 Women.

Composition of student body (fall 2004):

	Undergraduate	Freshmen
International	0.2	0.2
Black	2.0	3.0
American Indian	0.2	0.3
Asian-American	4.0	2.2
Hispanic	3.2	3.2
White	87.7	84.6
Unreported	2.7	6.5
	100.0%	100.0%

56% are from out of state. Average age of full-time undergraduates is 20. 43% of classes have fewer than 20 students, 57% have between 20 and 50 students.

STUDENT HOUSING

86% of freshmen live in college housing. Housing is guaranteed for all undergraduates. Campus can house 1,950 undergraduates.

EXPENSES

Tuition (2005-06): $21,600 per year. Tuition varies by program.
Room: $4,660. Board: $4,230.
There is no additional cost for LD program/services.

LD SERVICES

LD program size is not limited.

LD services available to:

- [ ] Freshmen
- [ ] Sophomores
- [ ] Juniors
- [ ] Seniors

Academic Accommodations

Curriculum		**In class**	
Foreign language waiver	[ ]	Early syllabus	[ ]
Lighter course load	[x]	Note takers in class	[x]
Math waiver	[ ]	Priority seating	[ ]
Other special classes	[ ]	Tape recorders	[x]
Priority registrations	[ ]	Videotaped classes	[ ]
Substitution of courses	[ ]	Text on tape	[ ]
Exams		**Services**	
Extended time	[x]	Diagnostic tests	[ ]
Oral exams	[ ]	Learning centers	[x]
Take home exams	[ ]	Proofreaders	[ ]
Exams on tape or computer	[ ]	Readers	[x]
Untimed exams	[ ]	Reading Machines/Kurzweil	[x]
Other accommodations	[ ]	Special bookstore section	[ ]
		Typists	[ ]

Credit toward degree is given for remedial courses taken.

Counseling Services

- [ ] Academic
- [ ] Psychological
- [ ] Student Support groups
- [ ] Vocational

Tutoring

	Individual	Group
Time management	[ ]	[ ]
Organizational skills	[ ]	[ ]
Learning strategies	[ ]	[ ]
Study skills	[ ]	[ ]
Content area	[ ]	[ ]
Writing lab	[ ]	[ ]
Math lab	[ ]	[ ]

LD PROGRAM STAFF

Total number of LD Program staff (including director):

Full Time: 2 Part Time: 2

Key staff person available to work with LD students: Bonni Alpert, Director

Wheaton College

Norton, MA

Address: East Main Street, Norton, MA, 02766
Admissions telephone: 800 394-6003
Admissions FAX: 508 286-8271
Vice President for Enrollment/Dean of Admissions and Student Aid: Gail Berson
Admissions e-mail: admission@wheatoncollege.edu
Web site: http://www.wheatoncollege.edu
SAT Code: 3963 ACT Code: 1932

LD program name: College Skills
LD program address: 26 East Main Street
Assistant Dean for College Skills: Marty Bledsoe
LD program telephone: 508 286-8215
LD program e-mail: mbledsoe@wheatoncollege.edu
LD program enrollment: 86, Total campus enrollment: 1,538

GENERAL

Wheaton College is a private, coed, four-year institution. 385-acre campus in Norton (population: 18,036), 15 miles from Providence, RI and 35 miles from Boston. Major airport serves Boston; smaller airport serves Providence, RI; train serves Mansfield (five miles); bus serves Taunton-Attleboro (six miles). School operates transportation to Boston and Mansfield. Public transportation serves campus. Semester system.

LD ADMISSIONS

Students do not complete a separate application and are not simultaneously accepted to the LD program. A member of the LD program does not sit on the admissions committee. A personal interview is recommended. Essay is required and may be typed. Foreign language requirement may be substituted.

For fall 2004, 138 completed self-identified LD applications were received. 71 applications were offered admission, and 15 enrolled.

SECONDARY SCHOOL REQUIREMENTS

Graduation from secondary school required; GED accepted.

TESTING

SAT Reasoning or ACT considered if submitted. SAT Subject recommended.

All enrolled freshmen (fall 2004):

Average SAT I Scores:	Verbal: 620	Math: 610
Average ACT Scores:	Composite: 27	

Child Study Team report is not required. A neuropsychological or comprehensive psycho-educational evaluation is required for admission. Must be dated within 36 months of application. Tests required as part of this documentation:

- ■ WAIS-IV
- ■ WISC-IV
- ☐ SATA
- ■ Woodcock-Johnson
- ■ Nelson-Denny Reading Test
- ■ Other

UNDERGRADUATE STUDENT BODY

Total undergraduate student enrollment: 537 Men, 1,014 Women.

Composition of student body (fall 2004):

	Undergraduate	Freshmen
International	3.4	2.7
Black	3.6	3.1
American Indian	0.2	0.3
Asian-American	3.2	3.0
Hispanic	3.4	3.8
White	77.2	78.5
Unreported	9.0	8.6
	100.0%	100.0%

65% are from out of state. Average age of full-time undergraduates is 20. 66% of classes have fewer than 20 students, 29% have between 20 and 50 students, 5% have more than 50 students.

STUDENT HOUSING

100% of freshmen live in college housing. Freshmen are not required to live on campus. Housing is guaranteed for all undergraduates. Campus can house 1,525 undergraduates. Single rooms are available for students with medical or special needs. A medical note is required.

EXPENSES

Tuition (2005-06): $32,115 per year.

Room: $4,130. Board: $3,700.

There is no additional cost for LD program/services.

LD SERVICES

LD program size is not limited.

LD services available to:

■ Freshmen ■ Sophomores ■ Juniors ■ Seniors

Academic Accommodations

Curriculum		**In class**	
Foreign language waiver	☐	Early syllabus	☐
Lighter course load	■	Note takers in class	■
Math waiver	☐	Priority seating	☐
Other special classes	☐	Tape recorders	■
Priority registrations	☐	Videotaped classes	☐
Substitution of courses	☐	Text on tape	☐
Exams		**Services**	
Extended time	■	Diagnostic tests	☐
Oral exams	■	Learning centers	■
Take home exams	☐	Proofreaders	☐
Exams on tape or computer	☐	Readers	■
Untimed exams	☐	Reading Machines/Kurzweil	■
Other accommodations	☐	Special bookstore section	☐
		Typists	☐

Credit toward degree is not given for remedial courses taken.

Counseling Services

- ■ Academic
- ■ Psychological
- ☐ Student Support groups
- ☐ Vocational

Tutoring

Individual tutoring is available weekly.

Average size of tutoring groups: 3

	Individual	Group
Time management	■	■
Organizational skills	■	■
Learning strategies	■	■
Study skills	■	■
Content area	■	■
Writing lab	■	☐
Math lab	☐	■

LD PROGRAM STAFF

Total number of LD Program staff (including director):

Full Time: 1 Part Time: 1

There is an advisor/advocate from the LD program available to students. 52 peer tutors are available to work with LD students.

Key staff person available to work with LD students: Marty Bledsoe, Assistant Dean for College Skills

LD Program web site: www.wheatoncollege.edu/Advising/Help/ADA.html

Wheelock College

Boston, MA

Address: 200 The Riverway, Boston, MA, 02215
Admissions telephone: 800 734-5212
Admissions FAX: 617 566-4453
Dean of Admissions: Lynne Harding
Admissions e-mail: undergrad@wheelock.edu
Web site: http://www.wheelock.edu
SAT Code: 3964 ACT Code: 1934

LD program name: Disability and Support Services
Coordinator: Paul Hastings
LD program telephone: 617 879-2304
LD program e-mail: phastings@wheelock.edu
Total campus enrollment: 616

GENERAL

Wheelock College is a private, coed, four-year institution. 5-1/2-acre, urban campus in Boston (population: 589,141). Served by air, bus, and train. Public transportation serves campus. Semester system.

LD ADMISSIONS

A personal interview is recommended. Essay is required and may be typed.

SECONDARY SCHOOL REQUIREMENTS

Graduation from secondary school required; GED accepted. The following course distribution required: 4 units of English, 3 units of math, 2 units of science, 2 units of social studies.

TESTING

SAT Reasoning or ACT required.

Child Study Team report is not required. Tests required as part of this documentation:

- ☐ WAIS-IV
- ☐ WISC-IV
- ☐ SATA
- ☐ Woodcock-Johnson
- ☐ Nelson-Denny Reading Test
- ☐ Other

UNDERGRADUATE STUDENT BODY

Total undergraduate student enrollment: 36 Men, 580 Women.

48% are from out of state.

STUDENT HOUSING

Housing is guaranteed for all undergraduates. Campus can house 475 undergraduates.

EXPENSES

Tuition (2005-06): $23,100 per year.
Room & Board: $9,450.
There is no additional cost for LD program/services.

LD SERVICES

LD program size is not limited.

LD services available to:

☐ Freshmen ☐ Sophomores ☐ Juniors ☐ Seniors

Academic Accommodations

Curriculum		In class	
Foreign language waiver	☐	Early syllabus	☐
Lighter course load	■	Note takers in class	■
Math waiver	☐	Priority seating	☐
Other special classes	☐	Tape recorders	☐
Priority registrations	☐	Videotaped classes	☐
Substitution of courses	☐	Text on tape	☐
Exams		**Services**	
Extended time	■	Diagnostic tests	☐
Oral exams	■	Learning centers	■
Take home exams	☐	Proofreaders	☐
Exams on tape or computer	☐	Readers	■
Untimed exams	☐	Reading Machines/Kurzweil	■
Other accommodations	☐	Special bookstore section	☐
		Typists	☐

Credit toward degree is not given for remedial courses taken.

Counseling Services

- ☐ Academic
- ☐ Psychological
- ☐ Student Support groups
- ☐ Vocational

Tutoring

	Individual	Group
Time management	☐	☐
Organizational skills	☐	☐
Learning strategies	☐	☐
Study skills	☐	☐
Content area	☐	☐
Writing lab	☐	☐
Math lab	☐	☐

LD PROGRAM STAFF

Total number of LD Program staff (including director):

Full Time: 3 Part Time: 3

Key staff person available to work with LD students: Paul Hastings, Coordinator of Disability and Support Services

Williams College

Williamstown, MA

Address: 988 Main Street, Williamstown, MA, 01267
Admissions telephone: 413 597-2211
Admissions FAX: 413 597-4052
Director of Admissions: Richard L. Nesbitt
Admissions e-mail: admission@williams.edu
Web site: http://www.williams.edu
SAT Code: 3965

Associate Dean for Student Services: Charles Toomajian
LD program telephone: 413 597-4010
LD program e-mail: Charles.Toomajian@williams.edu
Total campus enrollment: 1,991

GENERAL

Williams College is a private, coed, four-year institution. 450-acre campus in Williamstown (population: 8,424), 38 miles from Albany, NY and 140 miles from Boston. Served by bus; major airport serves Boston; smaller airport and train serve Albany, NY. School operates transportation to airport and train station at vacations. Public transportation serves campus. 4-1-4 system.

LD ADMISSIONS

A personal interview is not required. Essay is required and may be typed.

SECONDARY SCHOOL REQUIREMENTS

Graduation from secondary school not required.

TESTING

SAT Subject recommended.

All enrolled freshmen (fall 2004):

Average SAT I Scores: Verbal: 705 Math: 708

Child Study Team report is not required. Tests required as part of this documentation:

- ☐ WAIS-IV
- ☐ WISC-IV
- ☐ SATA
- ☐ Woodcock-Johnson
- ☐ Nelson-Denny Reading Test
- ☐ Other

UNDERGRADUATE STUDENT BODY

Total undergraduate student enrollment: 1,035 Men, 962 Women.

Composition of student body (fall 2004):

	Undergraduate	Freshmen
International	5.8	5.6
Black	10.5	9.9
American Indian	0.4	0.2
Asian-American	9.2	9.2
Hispanic	8.5	7.7
White	65.6	67.4
Unreported	0.0	0.0
	100.0%	100.0%

78% are from out of state. Average age of full-time undergraduates is 20. 71% of classes have fewer than 20 students, 25% have between 20 and 50 students, 4% have more than 50 students.

STUDENT HOUSING

100% of freshmen live in college housing. Freshmen are required to live on campus. Housing is guaranteed for all undergraduates. Campus can house 1,972 undergraduates. Single rooms are available for students with medical or special needs.

EXPENSES

Tuition (2005-06): $31,548 per year.

Room: $4,330. Board: $4,220.
There is no additional cost for LD program/services.

LD SERVICES

LD program size is not limited.

LD services available to:

☑ Freshmen ☑ Sophomores ☑ Juniors ☑ Seniors

Academic Accommodations

Curriculum		In class	
Foreign language waiver	☐	Early syllabus	☐
Lighter course load	☐	Note takers in class	☑
Math waiver	☐	Priority seating	☐
Other special classes	☐	Tape recorders	☑
Priority registrations	☐	Videotaped classes	☐
Substitution of courses	☐	Text on tape	☐
Exams		**Services**	
Extended time	☑	Diagnostic tests	☐
Oral exams	☐	Learning centers	☐
Take home exams	☐	Proofreaders	☐
Exams on tape or computer	☐	Readers	☐
Untimed exams	☐	Reading Machines/Kurzweil	☐
Other accommodations	☐	Special bookstore section	☐
		Typists	☐

Counseling Services

- ☐ Academic
- ☐ Psychological
- ☐ Student Support groups
- ☐ Vocational

Tutoring

Individual tutoring is available.

Average size of tutoring groups: 1

	Individual	Group
Time management	☐	☐
Organizational skills	☐	☐
Learning strategies	☐	☐
Study skills	☐	☐
Content area	☐	☐
Writing lab	☑	☑
Math lab	☑	☑

LD PROGRAM STAFF

LD Program web site: http://www.williams.edu/dean/disable.html

Worcester Polytechnic Institute

Worcester, MA

Address: 100 Institute Road, Worcester, MA, 01609
Admissions telephone: 508 831-5286
Admissions FAX: 508 831-5875
Director of Admissions: Kristin R. Tichenor
Admissions e-mail: admissions@wpi.edu
Web site: http://www.wpi.edu
SAT Code: 3969 ACT Code: 1942

Total campus enrollment: 2,868

GENERAL

Worcester Polytechnic Institute is a private, coed, four-year institution. 80-acre, suburban campus in Worcester (population: 172,648), 45 miles from Boston. Served by air, bus, and train; major airport serves Boston. School operates transportation to consortium schools and downtown Worcester. Public transportation serves campus. Quarter system.

SECONDARY SCHOOL REQUIREMENTS

Graduation from secondary school required; GED not accepted. The following course distribution required: 4 units of math, 2 units of science.

TESTING

SAT Reasoning or ACT required. SAT Subject recommended.

All enrolled freshmen (fall 2004):

Average SAT I Scores:	Verbal: 620	Math: 674
Average ACT Scores:	Composite: 29	

Child Study Team report is not required. Tests required as part of this documentation:

- ☐ WAIS-IV
- ☐ WISC-IV
- ☐ SATA
- ☐ Woodcock-Johnson
- ☐ Nelson-Denny Reading Test
- ☐ Other

UNDERGRADUATE STUDENT BODY

Total undergraduate student enrollment: 2,186 Men, 637 Women.

Composition of student body (fall 2004):

	Undergraduate	Freshmen
International	7.2	4.6
Black	3.3	1.7
American Indian	0.5	0.6
Asian-American	6.6	6.3
Hispanic	3.3	3.4
White	77.4	81.0
Unreported	1.7	2.4
	100.0%	100.0%

29% join a fraternity and 28% join a sorority. Average age of full-time undergraduates is 20. 76% of classes have fewer than 20 students, 20% have between 20 and 50 students, 4% have more than 50 students.

STUDENT HOUSING

94% of freshmen live in college housing. Freshmen are not required to live on campus. Housing is guaranteed for all freshmen. Campus can house 1,754 undergraduates. Single rooms are available for students with medical or special needs. A medical note is required.

EXPENSES

Tuition (2005-06): $30,990 per year.
Room: $5,500. Board: $3,960.
There is no additional cost for LD program/services.

LD SERVICES

LD program size is not limited.

LD services available to:

☑ Freshmen ☑ Sophomores ☑ Juniors ☑ Seniors

Academic Accommodations

Curriculum		In class	
Foreign language waiver	☐	Early syllabus	☐
Lighter course load	☑	Note takers in class	☑
Math waiver	☐	Priority seating	☐
Other special classes	☐	Tape recorders	☑
Priority registrations	☐	Videotaped classes	☐
Substitution of courses	☐	Text on tape	☐
Exams		**Services**	
Extended time	☑	Diagnostic tests	☐
Oral exams	☑	Learning centers	☑
Take home exams	☐	Proofreaders	☐
Exams on tape or computer	☐	Readers	☑
Untimed exams	☐	Reading Machines/Kurzweil	☑
Other accommodations	☐	Special bookstore section	☐
		Typists	☐

Credit toward degree is not given for remedial courses taken.

Counseling Services

- ☐ Academic
- ☐ Psychological
- ☐ Student Support groups
- ☐ Vocational

Tutoring

Individual tutoring is not available.

	Individual	Group
Time management	☐	☐
Organizational skills	☐	☐
Learning strategies	☐	☐
Study skills	☐	☐
Content area	☐	☐
Writing lab	☐	☐
Math lab	☐	☐

UNIQUE LD PROGRAM FEATURES

If a student's documentation necessitates a reduced course load this can be arranged but it will result in additional time to complete the degree requirements.

LD PROGRAM STAFF

Total number of LD Program staff (including director):

Full Time: 1 Part Time: 1

Key staff person available to work with LD students: JoAnn VanDyke, Director, Academic Resources/Disabilities Service Coordinator

Worcester State College

Worcester, MA

Address: 486 Chandler Street, Worcester, MA, 01602-2597
Admissions telephone: 508 929-8758
Admissions FAX: 508 929-8183
Dean of Enrollment Management: E. Alan Kines
Admissions e-mail: admissions@worcester.edu
Web site: http://www.worcester.edu
SAT Code: 3524 ACT Code: 1914

Coordinator, Disability Services Office: Dennis Lindblom
LD program telephone: 508 929-8733
LD program e-mail: dlindblom@worcester.edu
LD program enrollment: 82, Total campus enrollment: 4,554

GENERAL

Worcester State College is a public, coed, four-year institution. 58-acre campus in Worcester (population: 172,648), 45 miles from Boston. Served by air, bus, and train; major airport serves Boston. Colleges of Worcester Consortium operates transportation between campuses. Public transportation serves campus. Semester system.

LD ADMISSIONS

Application Deadline: 06/01. Students do not complete a separate application and are not simultaneously accepted to the LD program. A member of the LD program does not sit on the admissions committee. High school waivers are accepted for foreign language. A personal interview is not required. Essay is not required. GPA, SAT/ACT, and foreign language requirements may be waived.

SECONDARY SCHOOL REQUIREMENTS

Graduation from secondary school required; GED not accepted. The following course distribution required: 4 units of English, 3 units of math, 3 units of science, 2 units of foreign language, 1 unit of social studies, 1 unit of history, 2 units of academic electives.

TESTING

SAT Reasoning required of some applicants; ACT may be substituted. SAT Subject recommended.

All enrolled freshmen (fall 2004):

Average SAT I Scores:	Verbal: 498	Math: 507
Average ACT Scores:	Composite: 20	

Child Study Team report is not required. A neuropsychological or comprehensive psycho-educational evaluation is required for admission. Must be dated within 12 months of application. Tests required as part of this documentation:

- [x] WAIS-IV
- [x] WISC-IV
- [x] SATA
- [x] Woodcock-Johnson
- [ ] Nelson-Denny Reading Test
- [ ] Other

UNDERGRADUATE STUDENT BODY

Total undergraduate student enrollment: 1,886 Men, 3,029 Women.

Composition of student body (fall 2004):

	Undergraduate	Freshmen
International	6.8	5.5
Black	1.7	3.5
American Indian	0.3	0.3
Asian-American	2.8	2.8
Hispanic	3.3	3.4
White	78.5	77.8
Unreported	6.6	6.7
	100.0%	100.0%

3% are from out of state. Average age of full-time undergraduates is 22. 49% of classes have fewer than 20 students, 51% have between 20 and 50 students.

STUDENT HOUSING

53% of freshmen live in college housing. Freshmen are not required to live on campus. Housing is not guaranteed for all undergraduates. Housing is not available to gradaute students. Campus can house 1,000 undergraduates. Single rooms are available for students with medical or special needs. A medical note is required.

EXPENSES

Tuition (2005-06): $970 per year (in-state), $7,050 (out-of-state).
Room & Board: $6,182.
There is no additional cost for LD program/services.

LD SERVICES

LD program size is not limited.

LD services available to:

- [x] Freshmen
- [x] Sophomores
- [x] Juniors
- [x] Seniors

Academic Accommodations

Curriculum		In class	
Foreign language waiver	[x]	Early syllabus	[ ]
Lighter course load	[x]	Note takers in class	[x]
Math waiver	[ ]	Priority seating	[x]
Other special classes	[ ]	Tape recorders	[x]
Priority registrations	[x]	Videotaped classes	[ ]
Substitution of courses	[ ]	Text on tape	[ ]
Exams		**Services**	
Extended time	[x]	Diagnostic tests	[ ]
Oral exams	[x]	Learning centers	[x]
Take home exams	[ ]	Proofreaders	[x]
Exams on tape or computer	[x]	Readers	[x]
Untimed exams	[x]	Reading Machines/Kurzweil	[x]
Other accommodations	[ ]	Special bookstore section	[ ]
		Typists	[ ]

Credit toward degree is not given for remedial courses taken.

Counseling Services

- [x] Academic
- [ ] Psychological
- [ ] Student Support groups
- [ ] Vocational

Tutoring

Individual tutoring is available weekly.

	Individual	Group
Time management	[x]	[ ]
Organizational skills	[x]	[ ]
Learning strategies	[x]	[ ]
Study skills	[x]	[ ]
Content area	[ ]	[ ]
Writing lab	[ ]	[ ]
Math lab	[ ]	[ ]

LD PROGRAM STAFF

Total number of LD Program staff (including director):

Full Time: 1 Part Time: 1

There is an advisor/advocate from the LD program available to students.

Key staff person available to work with LD students: Dennis Lindblom, Coordinator, Disability Services Office

Monterrey Institute of Technology and Higher Education - Central Campus of Veracruz

Cordoba, MX

Address: Avenida Eugenio Garza Sada No. 1, Apartado Postal 314, Cordoba, VZ, 94500
Admissions FAX: 271 717-0581
Director of Academic Services: Angela Salgado
Admissions e-mail: ip_mty@itesm.mx
LD program telephone: 271 713-2300, extension 6580
LD program e-mail: asalgado@itesm.mx
Total campus enrollment: 394

GENERAL

Monterrey Institute of Technology and Higher Education - Central Campus of Veracruz is a private, coed, four-year institution. 63-acre, semi-rural campus in Cordoba (population: 600,000). Served by bus and train; major airport serves Veracruz City (75 miles). Public transportation serves campus. Semester system.

LD ADMISSIONS

Application Deadline: 01/15. Students do not complete a separate application and are simultaneously accepted to the LD program. A member of the LD program does not sit on the admissions committee. A personal interview is recommended. Essay is not required.

SECONDARY SCHOOL REQUIREMENTS

Graduation from secondary school required; GED not accepted.

TESTING

SAT Reasoning required. SAT Subject recommended.

All enrolled freshmen (fall 2004):

Average SAT I Scores: Verbal: 562 Math: 530

Child Study Team report is not required. A neuropsychological or comprehensive psycho-education evaluation is not required for admission. Tests required as part of this documentation:

- [ ] WAIS-IV
- [ ] WISC-IV
- [ ] SATA
- [ ] Woodcock-Johnson
- [ ] Nelson-Denny Reading Test
- [ ] Other

UNDERGRADUATE STUDENT BODY

Total undergraduate student enrollment: 248 Men, 160 Women.

Average age of full-time undergraduates is 22. 79% of classes have fewer than 20 students, 21% have between 20 and 50 students.

STUDENT HOUSING

Housing is not guaranteed for all undergraduates. Single rooms are not available for students with medical or special needs.

EXPENSES

Tuition 2004-05: $8,876 per year.

LD SERVICES

LD program size is not limited.

LD services available to:

- [x] Freshmen
- [x] Sophomores
- [x] Juniors
- [x] Seniors

Academic Accommodations

Curriculum		In class	
Foreign language waiver	[ ]	Early syllabus	[ ]
Lighter course load	[ ]	Note takers in class	[ ]
Math waiver	[ ]	Priority seating	[ ]
Other special classes	[ ]	Tape recorders	[ ]
Priority registrations	[ ]	Videotaped classes	[ ]
Substitution of courses	[ ]	Texts on tape	[ ]
Exams		**Services**	
Extended time	[x]	Diagnostic tests	[ ]
Oral exams	[ ]	Learning centers	[ ]
Take home exams	[ ]	Proofreaders	[ ]
Exams on tape or computer	[ ]	Readers	[ ]
Untimed exams	[ ]	Reading Machines/Kurzweil	[ ]
Other accommodations	[ ]	Special bookstore section	[ ]
		Typists	[ ]

Credit toward degree is not given for remedial courses taken.

Counseling Services

- [x] Academic
- [ ] Psychological
- [ ] Student Support groups
- [x] Vocational

Tutoring

Individual tutoring is not available.

	Individual	Group
Time management	[ ]	[ ]
Organizational skills	[ ]	[ ]
Learning strategies	[ ]	[ ]
Study skills	[ ]	[ ]
Content area	[ ]	[ ]
Writing lab	[ ]	[ ]
Math lab	[ ]	[ ]

LD PROGRAM STAFF

There is no advisor/advocate from the LD program available to students.

Monterrey Institute of Technology and Higher Education - Juarez City

Juarez, MX

Address: Av. Tomas Fernadez Campus No. 8945, Juarez, CI,
Admissions FAX: 656 629-9100
Director of Admissions: Jorge Arturo Montes Figueroa
Web site: http://www.cdj.itesm.mx

Directora: Irma Durón Madrid
Total campus enrollment: 827

GENERAL

Monterrey Institute of Technology and Higher Education - Juarez City is a private, coed, four-year institution. 35-acre, urban campus in Juarez City (population: 1,500,000). Served by air, bus, and train. Public transportation serves campus. Semester system.

LD ADMISSIONS

A personal interview is recommended.

SECONDARY SCHOOL REQUIREMENTS

Graduation from secondary school required; GED not accepted.

TESTING

All enrolled freshmen (fall 2004):

Average SAT I Scores: Verbal: 542 Math: 526

Child Study Team report is not required. Tests required as part of this documentation:

- ❑ WAIS-IV
- ❑ WISC-IV
- ❑ SATA
- ❑ Woodcock-Johnson
- ❑ Nelson-Denny Reading Test
- ❑ Other

UNDERGRADUATE STUDENT BODY

Total undergraduate student enrollment: 372 Men, 297 Women.

Average age of full-time undergraduates is 22. 58% of classes have fewer than 20 students, 42% have between 20 and 50 students.

EXPENSES

There is no additional cost for LD program/services.

LD SERVICES

LD services available to:

❑ Freshmen ❑ Sophomores ❑ Juniors ❑ Seniors

Academic Accommodations

Curriculum		**In class**	
Foreign language waiver	❑	Early syllabus	❑
Lighter course load	❑	Note takers in class	❑
Math waiver	❑	Priority seating	❑
Other special classes	❑	Tape recorders	❑
Priority registrations	❑	Videotaped classes	■
Substitution of courses	❑	Texts on tape	❑
Exams		**Services**	
Extended time	❑	Diagnostic tests	❑
Oral exams	■	Learning centers	❑
Take home exams	❑	Proofreaders	❑
Exams on tape or computer	❑	Readers	❑
Untimed exams	❑	Reading Machines/Kurzweil	❑
Other accommodations	❑	Special bookstore section	❑
		Typists	❑

Counseling Services

- ❑ Academic
- ❑ Psychological
- ❑ Student Support groups
- ❑ Vocational

Tutoring

	Individual	Group
Time management	❑	❑
Organizational skills	❑	❑
Learning strategies	❑	❑
Study skills	❑	❑
Content area	❑	❑
Writing lab	❑	❑
Math lab	❑	❑

LD PROGRAM STAFF

Key staff person available to work with LD students: Irma Durón Madrid, Directora.

Monterrey Institute of Technology and Higher Education - Leon

Leon, MX

Address: E. Garza Sada S/N, Col. Cerro Gordo, Leon, GJ, 37190
Admissions telephone: 477 710-9032
Admissions FAX: 477 710-9014
Director of Academic Services: Sergio Arturo Sánchez Dávila
Web site: http://www.leo.itesm.mx

Director: Sergio Arturo Sánchez
LD program telephone: 477 710-9000
LD program e-mail: sergio.sanchez@itesm.mx
Total campus enrollment: 1,072

GENERAL

Monterrey Institute of Technology and Higher Education - Leon is a private, coed, four-year institution. 38-acre, suburban campus in Leon (population: 1,500,000). Served by air, bus, and train. Public transportation serves campus. Semester system.

LD ADMISSIONS

Application Deadline: 01/15. Students do not complete a separate application and are simultaneously accepted to the LD program. A member of the LD program does not sit on the admissions committee. A personal interview is recommended. Essay is not required.

SECONDARY SCHOOL REQUIREMENTS

Graduation from secondary school required; GED not accepted.

TESTING

SAT Reasoning required. SAT Subject recommended.

All enrolled freshmen (fall 2004):

Average SAT I Scores: Verbal: 570 Math: 552

Child Study Team report is not required. A neuropsychological or comprehensive psycho-education evaluation is not required for admission. Tests required as part of this documentation:

- ☐ WAIS-IV
- ☐ WISC-IV
- ☐ SATA
- ☐ Woodcock-Johnson
- ☐ Nelson-Denny Reading Test
- ☐ Other

UNDERGRADUATE STUDENT BODY

Total undergraduate student enrollment: 618 Men, 459 Women.

Average age of full-time undergraduates is 22. 51% of classes have fewer than 20 students, 49% have between 20 and 50 students.

STUDENT HOUSING

Freshmen are not required to live on campus. Housing is not guaranteed for all undergraduates. Housing is limited. Single rooms are not available for students with medical or special needs.

EXPENSES

Tuition 2004-05: $8,875 per year.

There is no additional cost for LD program/services.

LD SERVICES

LD program size is not limited.

LD services available to:

☑ Freshmen ☑ Sophomores ☑ Juniors ☑ Seniors

Academic Accommodations

Curriculum		In class	
Foreign language waiver	☐	Early syllabus	☐
Lighter course load	☐	Note takers in class	☐
Math waiver	☐	Priority seating	☐
Other special classes	☐	Tape recorders	☐
Priority registrations	☐	Videotaped classes	☑
Substitution of courses	☐	Texts on tape	☐
Exams		**Services**	
Extended time	☑	Diagnostic tests	☐
Oral exams	☐	Learning centers	☐
Take home exams	☐	Proofreaders	☐
Exams on tape or computer	☐	Readers	☐
Untimed exams	☐	Reading Machines/Kurzweil	☐
Other accommodations	☐	Special bookstore section	☐
		Typists	☐

Credit toward degree is not given for remedial courses taken.

Counseling Services

- ☑ Academic
- ☑ Psychological
- ☐ Student Support groups
- ☑ Vocational

Tutoring

Individual tutoring is not available.

	Individual	Group
Time management	☐	☐
Organizational skills	☐	☐
Learning strategies	☐	☐
Study skills	☐	☐
Content area	☐	☐
Writing lab	☐	☐
Math lab	☐	☐

LD PROGRAM STAFF

There is no advisor/advocate from the LD program available to students.

Monterrey Institute of Technology and Higher Education - Mazatlan

Mazatlan, MX

Address: Apartado Postal 799, Carretera a Mazatlan-Higueras Km 3, Mazatlan, SI, 82000
Admissions FAX: 989 205-2051
Director of Academic Services: Isela Calderon

Psycologist: Nancy Ortega
LD program e-mail: nancy.ortega@itesm.mx
Total campus enrollment: 376

GENERAL

Monterrey Institute of Technology and Higher Education - Mazatlan is a private, coed, four-year institution. 50-acre campus in Mazatlan (population: 400,830). Served by air, bus, and train. Public transportation serves campus. Semester system.

LD ADMISSIONS

A personal interview is recommended.

SECONDARY SCHOOL REQUIREMENTS

Graduation from secondary school required; GED not accepted.

TESTING

SAT Reasoning required.

All enrolled freshmen (fall 2004):

Average SAT I Scores: Verbal: 549 Math: 555

Child Study Team report is not required. Tests required as part of this documentation:

- ❑ WAIS-IV
- ❑ WISC-IV
- ❑ SATA
- ❑ Woodcock-Johnson
- ❑ Nelson-Denny Reading Test
- ❑ Other

UNDERGRADUATE STUDENT BODY

Total undergraduate student enrollment: 254 Men, 191 Women.

Average age of full-time undergraduates is 21. 68% of classes have fewer than 20 students, 32% have between 20 and 50 students.

EXPENSES

There is no additional cost for LD program/services.

LD SERVICES

LD program size is not limited.

LD services available to:

❑ Freshmen ❑ Sophomores ❑ Juniors ❑ Seniors

Academic Accommodations

Curriculum		In class	
Foreign language waiver	❑	Early syllabus	❑
Lighter course load	❑	Note takers in class	❑
Math waiver	❑	Priority seating	❑
Other special classes	❑	Tape recorders	❑
Priority registrations	❑	Videotaped classes	❑
Substitution of courses	❑	Texts on tape	❑
Exams		**Services**	
Extended time	❑	Diagnostic tests	❑
Oral exams	❑	Learning centers	❑
Take home exams	❑	Proofreaders	❑
Exams on tape or computer	❑	Readers	❑
Untimed exams	❑	Reading Machines/Kurzweil	❑
Other accommodations	❑	Special bookstore section	❑
		Typists	❑

Counseling Services

- ❑ Academic
- ❑ Psychological
- ❑ Student Support groups
- ❑ Vocational

Tutoring

	Individual	Group
Time management	❑	❑
Organizational skills	❑	❑
Learning strategies	❑	❑
Study skills	❑	❑
Content area	❑	❑
Writing lab	❑	❑
Math lab	❑	❑

LD PROGRAM STAFF

Key staff person available to work with LD students: Nancy Ortega.

Monterrey Institute of Technology and Higher Education - Monterrey

Monterrey, MX

Address: Avenida Eugenio Garza Sada 2501, Sucursal de Correos J, Monterrey, NL, 64849
Admissions telephone: 835 466-6601
Admissions FAX: 835 819-1954
Director of Academic Services: Alejandra García
Admissions e-mail: admisiones.mty@itesm.mx
Web site: http://www.mty.itesm.mx/profesional/admision/home.html
SAT Code: 843

LD program contact: Thelma Páez
LD program telephone: 818 328-4458
LD program e-mail: thelma.paez@itesm.mx
Total campus enrollment: 17,049

GENERAL

Monterrey Institute of Technology and Higher Education - Monterrey is a private, coed, four-year institution. 125-acre, urban campus in Monterrey (population: 1,000,000). Served by air, bus, and train. Public transportation serves campus. Semester system.

LD ADMISSIONS

A personal interview is recommended.

SECONDARY SCHOOL REQUIREMENTS

Graduation from secondary school required; GED not accepted.

TESTING

SAT Reasoning required.

Child Study Team report is not required. Tests required as part of this documentation:

- ☐ WAIS-IV
- ☐ WISC-IV
- ☐ SATA
- ☐ Woodcock-Johnson
- ☐ Nelson-Denny Reading Test
- ☐ Other

UNDERGRADUATE STUDENT BODY

Total undergraduate student enrollment: 10,041 Men, 6,365 Women.

Average age of full-time undergraduates is 22. 31% of classes have fewer than 20 students, 68% have between 20 and 50 students, 1% have more than 50 students.

STUDENT HOUSING

Housing is not guaranteed for all undergraduates. Housing is limited. Campus can house 1,508 undergraduates.

EXPENSES

There is no additional cost for LD program/services.

LD SERVICES

LD program size is not limited.

LD services available to:

☐ Freshmen ☐ Sophomores ☐ Juniors ☐ Seniors

Academic Accommodations

Curriculum		**In class**	
Foreign language waiver	☐	Early syllabus	☐
Lighter course load	☐	Note takers in class	■
Math waiver	☐	Priority seating	☐
Other special classes	☐	Tape recorders	☐
Priority registrations	☐	Videotaped classes	■
Substitution of courses	☐	Texts on tape	☐
Exams		**Services**	
Extended time	■	Diagnostic tests	☐
Oral exams	■	Learning centers	☐
Take home exams	☐	Proofreaders	☐
Exams on tape or computer	☐	Readers	☐
Untimed exams	☐	Reading Machines/Kurzweil	☐
Other accommodations	☐	Special bookstore section	☐
		Typists	☐

Counseling Services

- ☐ Academic
- ☐ Psychological
- ☐ Student Support groups
- ☐ Vocational

Tutoring

	Individual	Group
Time management	☐	☐
Organizational skills	☐	☐
Learning strategies	☐	☐
Study skills	☐	☐
Content area	☐	☐
Writing lab	☐	☐
Math lab	☐	☐

LD PROGRAM STAFF

Key staff person available to work with LD students: Francisco Javier Menoza.

Monterrey Institute of Technology and Higher Education - Obregon City

Obregon, MX

Address: Apartado Postal 662, Zacatecas 158 Nte, 85000
Ciudad Obregon, SO, Mexico
Admissions FAX: 644 415-0364
Director of Admissions: Dora Alicia Valenzuela Leyva
Web site: http://www.cob.itesm.mx

Director: Dora Alicia Valenzuela
LD program telephone: 644 415-0624
LD program e-mail: dora.valenzuela@itesm.mx
Total campus enrollment: 164

GENERAL

Monterrey Institute of Technology and Higher Education - Obregon City is a private, coed, four-year institution. 150-acre campus in Obregon City (population: 350,000). Served by air, bus, and train. Public transportation serves campus. Semester system.

LD ADMISSIONS

Application Deadline: 01/15. Students do not complete a separate application and are simultaneously accepted to the LD program. A member of the LD program does not sit on the admissions committee. A personal interview is recommended. Essay is not required.

SECONDARY SCHOOL REQUIREMENTS

Graduation from secondary school required; GED not accepted.

TESTING

SAT Reasoning required. SAT Subject recommended.

All enrolled freshmen (fall 2004):

Average SAT I Scores: Verbal: 541 Math: 568

Child Study Team report is not required. A neuropsychological or comprehensive psycho-education evaluation is not required for admission. Tests required as part of this documentation:

- ☐ WAIS-IV
- ☐ WISC-IV
- ☐ SATA
- ☐ Woodcock-Johnson
- ☐ Nelson-Denny Reading Test
- ☐ Other

UNDERGRADUATE STUDENT BODY

Total undergraduate student enrollment: 83 Men, 63 Women.

Average age of full-time undergraduates is 21. 73% of classes have fewer than 20 students, 27% have between 20 and 50 students.

STUDENT HOUSING

Housing is not guaranteed for all undergraduates. Single rooms are not available for students with medical or special needs.

EXPENSES

Tuition 2004-05: $8,876 per year.

There is no additional cost for LD program/services.

LD SERVICES

LD program size is not limited.

LD services available to:

■ Freshmen ■ Sophomores ■ Juniors ■ Seniors

Academic Accommodations

Curriculum		In class	
Foreign language waiver	☐	Early syllabus	☐
Lighter course load	☐	Note takers in class	☐
Math waiver	☐	Priority seating	☐
Other special classes	☐	Tape recorders	☐
Priority registrations	☐	Videotaped classes	☐
Substitution of courses	☐	Texts on tape	☐
Exams		**Services**	
Extended time	■	Diagnostic tests	☐
Oral exams	☐	Learning centers	☐
Take home exams	☐	Proofreaders	☐
Exams on tape or computer	☐	Readers	☐
Untimed exams	☐	Reading Machines/Kurzweil	☐
Other accommodations	☐	Special bookstore section	☐
		Typists	☐

Credit toward degree is not given for remedial courses taken.

Counseling Services

- ■ Academic
- ■ Psychological
- ☐ Student Support groups
- ■ Vocational

Tutoring

Individual tutoring is not available.

	Individual	Group
Time management	☐	☐
Organizational skills	☐	☐
Learning strategies	☐	☐
Study skills	☐	☐
Content area	☐	☐
Writing lab	☐	☐
Math lab	☐	☐

LD PROGRAM STAFF

There is no advisor/advocate from the LD program available to students.

Monterrey Institute of Technology and Higher Education - University System

64849 Monterrey, MX

Address: Ave Eugenio Garza, Sada #2501 Col. Tecnologico, 64849
Monterrey, NL, 64849

Director: Carlos Mijares
LD program telephone: 818 514-2004, extension 270
LD program e-mail: cmijares@itesm.mx
Total campus enrollment: 57,022

GENERAL

Monterrey Institute of Technology and Higher Education - University System is a private, coed, four-year institution. Semester system.

LD ADMISSIONS

Application Deadline: 01/15. Students do not complete a separate application and are simultaneously accepted to the LD program. A member of the LD program does not sit on the admissions committee. A personal interview is recommended. Essay is not required.

SECONDARY SCHOOL REQUIREMENTS

Graduation from secondary school required; GED not accepted.

TESTING

SAT Reasoning required. SAT Subject recommended.

All enrolled freshmen (fall 2004):

Average SAT I Scores: Verbal: 578 Math: 567

Child Study Team report is not required. A neuropsychological or comprehensive psycho-education evaluation is not required for admission. Tests required as part of this documentation:

- [ ] WAIS-IV
- [ ] WISC-IV
- [ ] SATA
- [ ] Woodcock-Johnson
- [ ] Nelson-Denny Reading Test
- [ ] Other

UNDERGRADUATE STUDENT BODY

Total undergraduate student enrollment: 30,787 Men, 21,363 Women.

Average age of full-time undergraduates is 22. 39% of classes have fewer than 20 students, 59% have between 20 and 50 students, 2% have more than 50 students.

STUDENT HOUSING

Housing is not guaranteed for all undergraduates. Housing is limited. Single rooms are not available for students with medical or special needs.

EXPENSES

Tuition 2004-05: $8,876 per year.

There is no additional cost for LD program/services.

LD SERVICES

LD program size is not limited.

LD services available to:

- [x] Freshmen
- [x] Sophomores
- [x] Juniors
- [x] Seniors

Academic Accommodations

Curriculum		In class	
Foreign language waiver	[ ]	Early syllabus	[ ]
Lighter course load	[ ]	Note takers in class	[ ]
Math waiver	[ ]	Priority seating	[ ]
Other special classes	[ ]	Tape recorders	[ ]
Priority registrations	[ ]	Videotaped classes	[x]
Substitution of courses	[ ]	Texts on tape	[ ]
Exams		**Services**	
Extended time	[x]	Diagnostic tests	[ ]
Oral exams	[ ]	Learning centers	[ ]
Take home exams	[ ]	Proofreaders	[ ]
Exams on tape or computer	[ ]	Readers	[ ]
Untimed exams	[ ]	Reading Machines/Kurzweil	[ ]
Other accommodations	[ ]	Special bookstore section	[ ]
		Typists	[ ]

Credit toward degree is not given for remedial courses taken.

Counseling Services

- [x] Academic
- [x] Psychological
- [ ] Student Support groups
- [x] Vocational

Tutoring

Individual tutoring is not available.

	Individual	Group
Time management	[ ]	[ ]
Organizational skills	[ ]	[ ]
Learning strategies	[ ]	[ ]
Study skills	[ ]	[ ]
Content area	[ ]	[ ]
Writing lab	[ ]	[ ]
Math lab	[ ]	[ ]

LD PROGRAM STAFF

There is not an advisor/advocate from the LD program available to students.

Adrian College

Adrian, MI

Address: 110 S. Madison Street, Adrian, MI, 49221
Admissions telephone: 800 877-2246
Admissions FAX: 517 264-3331
Admissions e-mail: admissions@adrian.edu
Web site: http://www.adrian.edu
SAT Code: 1001 ACT Code: 1954

Director of Academic Services: Jane McCloskey
LD program telephone: 517 265-5161
LD program e-mail: jmccloskey@adrian.edu
Total campus enrollment: 1,013

GENERAL

Adrian College is a private, coed, four-year institution. 100-acre campus in Adrian (population: 21,574), 35 miles northwest of Toledo. Major airport serves Detroit (30 miles); bus and train serve Toledo; train also serves Jackson (35 miles). Public transportation serves campus. School operates transportation to airports and bus stations for semester breaks. Semester system.

LD ADMISSIONS

Students do not complete a separate application and are simultaneously accepted to the LD program. A member of the LD program does not sit on the admissions committee. A personal interview is recommended. Essay is not required.

SECONDARY SCHOOL REQUIREMENTS

Graduation from secondary school required; GED accepted.

TESTING

ACT recommended. SAT Reasoning may be substituted. SAT Subject recommended.

All enrolled freshmen (fall 2004):

Average ACT Scores: Composite: 22

Child Study Team report is not required. Tests required as part of this documentation:

- ☐ WAIS-IV
- ☐ WISC-IV
- ☐ SATA
- ☐ Woodcock-Johnson
- ☐ Nelson-Denny Reading Test
- ☐ Other

UNDERGRADUATE STUDENT BODY

Total undergraduate student enrollment: 458 Men, 597 Women.

Composition of student body (fall 2004):

	Undergraduate	Freshmen
International	0.0	1.3
Black	8.5	6.1
American Indian	0.3	0.4
Asian-American	1.0	0.7
Hispanic	2.7	1.4
White	76.9	75.1
Unreported	10.6	15.0
	100.0%	100.0%

76% are from out of state. 30% join a fraternity and 30% join a sorority. Average age of full-time undergraduates is 19. 78% of classes have fewer than 20 students, 22% have between 20 and 50 students.

STUDENT HOUSING

77% of freshmen live in college housing. Freshmen are required to live on campus. Housing is guaranteed for all undergraduates. Campus can house 1,150 undergraduates. Single rooms are available for students with medical or special needs. A medical note is required.

EXPENSES

Tuition (2005-06): $18,530 per year.
Room: $2,800. Board: $3,810.

There is no additional cost for LD program/services.

LD SERVICES

LD program size is not limited.

LD services available to:

☒ Freshmen ☒ Sophomores ☒ Juniors ☐ Seniors

Academic Accommodations

Curriculum		**In class**	
Foreign language waiver	☐	Early syllabus	☐
Lighter course load	☐	Note takers in class	☒
Math waiver	☐	Priority seating	☐
Other special classes	☒	Tape recorders	☒
Priority registrations	☐	Videotaped classes	☐
Substitution of courses	☐	Text on tape	☐
Exams		**Services**	
Extended time	☒	Diagnostic tests	☒
Oral exams	☒	Learning centers	☒
Take home exams	☐	Proofreaders	☐
Exams on tape or computer	☐	Readers	☒
Untimed exams	☒	Reading Machines/Kurzweil	☒
Other accommodations	☒	Special bookstore section	☐
		Typists	☐

Credit toward degree is not given for remedial courses taken.

Counseling Services

- ☒ Academic
- ☒ Psychological
- ☒ Student Support groups
- ☐ Vocational

Tutoring

Individual tutoring is available weekly.

Average size of tutoring groups: 5

	Individual	Group
Time management	☒	☒
Organizational skills	☒	☒
Learning strategies	☒	☒
Study skills	☒	☒
Content area	☒	☒
Writing lab	☒	☒
Math lab	☒	☒

UNIQUE LD PROGRAM FEATURES

We do not track the number of LD applicants who apply or are admitted.

LD PROGRAM STAFF

Total number of LD Program staff (including director):

Full Time: 4 Part Time: 4

There is an advisor/advocate from the LD program available to students.

Key staff person available to work with LD students: Jane McCloskey, Director of Academic Services.

Albion College

Albion, MI

Address: 611 E. Porter, Albion, MI, 49224
Admissions telephone: 800 858-6770
Admissions FAX: 517 629-0569
Associate Vice President for Enrollment: Doug Kellar
Admissions e-mail: admissions@albion.edu
Web site: http://www.albion.edu
SAT Code: 1007 ACT Code: 1956

LD program telephone: 517 629-0825
LD program e-mail: pschwartz@albion.edu
LD program enrollment: 118, Total campus enrollment: 1,867

GENERAL

Albion College is a private, coed, four-year institution. 225-acre campus in Albion (population: 9,144), about 20 miles west of Jackson and 30 miles east of Battle Creek. Served by bus and train; major airport serves Detroit (90 miles); smaller airport serves Jackson. School operates transportation to U of Michigan-Ann Arbor libraries. Semester system.

LD ADMISSIONS

Students do not complete a separate application and are simultaneously accepted to the LD program. A member of the LD program does not sit on the admissions committee. A personal interview is recommended. Admissions requirements that may be waived for LD students include Standardized Tests such as SAT or ACT.

SECONDARY SCHOOL REQUIREMENTS

Graduation from secondary school required; GED accepted. The following course distribution required: 4 units of English, 3 units of math, 3 units of science, 2 units of foreign language, 3 units of social studies.

TESTING

SAT Reasoning or ACT required. SAT Subject recommended.

All enrolled freshmen (fall 2004):

Average SAT I Scores:	Verbal: 562	Math: 582
Average ACT Scores:	Composite: 25	

Child Study Team report is not required. A neuropsychological or comprehensive psycho-educational evaluation is required for admission. Must be dated within 60 months of application. Tests required as part of this documentation:

- ☑ WAIS-IV
- ☑ WISC-IV
- ☑ SATA
- ☑ Woodcock-Johnson
- ☑ Nelson-Denny Reading Test
- ☑ Other

UNDERGRADUATE STUDENT BODY

Total undergraduate student enrollment: 687 Men, 861 Women.

Composition of student body (fall 2004):

	Undergraduate	Freshmen
International	0.4	1.0
Black	6.6	3.6
American Indian	0.5	0.4
Asian-American	1.8	2.0
Hispanic	1.1	1.0
White	86.6	88.2
Unreported	3.0	3.8
	100.0%	100.0%

11% are from out of state. 42% join a fraternity and 46% join a sorority. Average age of full-time undergraduates is 19. 62% of classes have fewer than 20 students, 38% have between 20 and 50 students.

STUDENT HOUSING

99% of freshmen live in college housing. Freshmen are required to live on campus. Housing is guaranteed for all undergraduates. Campus can house 1,751 undergraduates. Single rooms are available for students with medical or special needs. A medical note is not required.

EXPENSES

Tuition (2005-06): $24,012 per year.
Room: $3,388. Board: $3,540.
There is no additional cost for LD program/services.

LD SERVICES

LD program size is not limited.

LD services available to:

☑ Freshmen ☑ Sophomores ☑ Juniors ☑ Seniors

Academic Accommodations

Curriculum		In class	
Foreign language waiver	☐	Early syllabus	☐
Lighter course load	☑	Note takers in class	☑
Math waiver	☐	Priority seating	☑
Other special classes	☐	Tape recorders	☑
Priority registrations	☐	Videotaped classes	☑
Substitution of courses	☐	Text on tape	☑
Exams		**Services**	
Extended time	☑	Diagnostic tests	☐
Oral exams	☑	Learning centers	☑
Take home exams	☐	Proofreaders	☑
Exams on tape or computer	☑	Readers	☑
Untimed exams	☑	Reading Machines/Kurzweil	☑
Other accommodations	☑	Special bookstore section	☐
		Typists	☑

Credit toward degree is not given for remedial courses taken.

Counseling Services

- ☑ Academic
- ☑ Psychological
- ☑ Student Support groups
- ☑ Vocational

Tutoring

Individual tutoring is available weekly.

	Individual	Group
Time management	☑	☐
Organizational skills	☑	☐
Learning strategies	☑	☐
Study skills	☑	☐
Content area	☑	☐
Writing lab	☑	☐
Math lab	☑	☐

LD PROGRAM STAFF

Total number of LD Program staff (including director):

Full Time: 2 Part Time: 2

There is an advisor/advocate from the LD program available to students. 5 peer tutors are available to work with LD students.

Key staff person available to work with LD students: Pam Schwartz, Ph.D., Director, Learning Center.

Alma College

Alma, MI

Address: 614 W. Superior Street, Alma, MI, 48801-1599
Admissions telephone: 800 321-ALMA
Admissions FAX: 989 463-7057
Director of Admissions: Anne Monroe
Admissions e-mail: admissions@alma.edu
Web site: http://www.alma.edu
SAT Code: 1010 ACT Code: 1958

LD program name: The Center for Student Development
Director of Student Development: Dr. Patricia Chase
LD program telephone: 989 463-7225
LD program e-mail: chase@alma.edu
LD program enrollment: 75, Total campus enrollment: 1,268

GENERAL

Alma College is a private, coed, four-year institution. 100-acre, suburban campus in Alma (population: 9,275), 50 miles from Lansing. Served by bus; airport and train serve Lansing; smaller airport serves Saginaw (35 miles).

LD ADMISSIONS

A member of the LD program does sit on the admissions committee. A personal interview is recommended. Essay is not required. Students are encouraged to self-identify learning disabilities during their first week on campus and provide documentation for review to determine appropriate waivers or substitutions.

SECONDARY SCHOOL REQUIREMENTS

Graduation from secondary school required; GED accepted. The following course distribution required: 4 units of English, 3 units of math, 3 units of science, 3 units of social studies, 1 unit of academic electives.

TESTING

ACT required; SAT Reasoning may be substituted. SAT Subject recommended.

All enrolled freshmen (fall 2004):

Average SAT I Scores:	Verbal: 565	Math: 561
Average ACT Scores:	Composite: 24	

Child Study Team report is not required. Tests required as part of this documentation:

☐ WAIS-IV	☐ Woodcock-Johnson
☐ WISC-IV	☐ Nelson-Denny Reading Test
☐ SATA	☐ Other

UNDERGRADUATE STUDENT BODY

Total undergraduate student enrollment: 563 Men, 808 Women.

Composition of student body (fall 2004):

	Undergraduate	Freshmen
International	0.0	0.8
Black	1.5	2.1
American Indian	0.0	0.5
Asian-American	1.2	1.3
Hispanic	1.5	1.5
White	95.8	93.7
Unreported	0.0	0.1
	100.0%	100.0%

5% are from out of state. 19% join a fraternity and 28% join a sorority. Average age of full-time undergraduates is 20. 59% of classes have fewer than 20 students, 39% have between 20 and 50 students, 2% have more than 50 students.

STUDENT HOUSING

97% of freshmen live in college housing. Freshmen are required to live on campus. Housing is guaranteed for all undergraduates. Campus can house 1,211 undergraduates.

EXPENSES

Tuition (2005-06): $20,934 per year.
Room: $3,650. Board: $3,760.
There is no additional cost for LD program/services.

LD SERVICES

LD program size is not limited.

LD services available to:

■ Freshmen ■ Sophomores ■ Juniors ■ Seniors

Academic Accommodations

Curriculum		**In class**	
Foreign language waiver	☐	Early syllabus	☐
Lighter course load	☐	Note takers in class	■
Math waiver	☐	Priority seating	■
Other special classes	☐	Tape recorders	■
Priority registrations	☐	Videotaped classes	☐
Substitution of courses	■	Text on tape	■
Exams		**Services**	
Extended time	■	Diagnostic tests	■
Oral exams	■	Learning centers	☐
Take home exams	☐	Proofreaders	☐
Exams on tape or computer	☐	Readers	■
Untimed exams	■	Reading Machines/Kurzweil	■
Other accommodations	☐	Special bookstore section	☐
		Typists	☐

Credit toward degree is not given for remedial courses taken.

Counseling Services

■ Academic
■ Psychological
☐ Student Support groups
☐ Vocational

Tutoring

Individual tutoring is available weekly.

	Individual	Group
Time management	☐	☐
Organizational skills	☐	☐
Learning strategies	☐	☐
Study skills	■	☐
Content area	☐	☐
Writing lab	■	☐
Math lab	■	☐

LD PROGRAM STAFF

There is no advisor/advocate from the LD program available to students. 87 peer tutors are available to work with LD students.

Key staff person available to work with LD students: Janet Tissue, Assistant Director of Student Development.

Andrews University

Berrien Springs, MI

Address: Berrien Springs, MI, 49104
Admissions telephone: 800 253-2874
Admissions FAX: 269 471-2670
Vice President for Enrollment Management: Stephan Payne
Admissions e-mail: enroll@andrews.edu
Web site: http://www.andrews.edu
SAT Code: 1030 ACT Code: 1992

Student Success Consultant: Karen Tilstra
LD program telephone: 269 471-6205
Total campus enrollment: 1,730

GENERAL

Andrews University is a private, coed, four-year institution. 1,600-acre campus in Berrien Springs (population: 1,862), 25 miles from South Bend, Ind., and 50 miles from Kalamazoo; branch campus in Kettering, Ohio. Airport serves South Bend; smaller airport and bus serve Benton Harbor (12 miles); train serves Niles (10 miles). Semester system.

LD ADMISSIONS

A personal interview is required. Essay is required and may be typed. Admissions requirements that may be waived for LD students are considered on a case-by-case basis.

SECONDARY SCHOOL REQUIREMENTS

Graduation from secondary school required; GED accepted. The following course distribution required: 3 units of English, 2 units of math, 2 units of science, 1 unit of social studies, 2 units of history.

TESTING

ACT required; SAT Reasoning may be substituted. SAT Subject recommended.

All enrolled freshmen (fall 2004):

Average SAT I Scores:	Verbal: 530	Math: 520
Average ACT Scores:	Composite: 23	

Child Study Team report is required if student is classified. Tests required as part of this documentation:

- ☐ WAIS-IV
- ☐ WISC-IV
- ☐ SATA
- ☐ Woodcock-Johnson
- ☐ Nelson-Denny Reading Test
- ☐ Other

UNDERGRADUATE STUDENT BODY

Total undergraduate student enrollment: 731 Men, 912 Women.

Composition of student body (fall 2004):

	Undergraduate	Freshmen
International	7.5	11.9
Black	19.9	19.7
American Indian	0.7	0.4
Asian-American	10.4	9.0
Hispanic	10.4	10.8
White	51.1	48.2
Unreported	0.0	0.0
	100.0%	100.0%

71% are from out of state. Average age of full-time undergraduates is 21. 64% of classes have fewer than 20 students, 29% have between 20 and 50 students, 7% have more than 50 students.

STUDENT HOUSING

81% of freshmen live in college housing. Housing is guaranteed for all undergraduates. Campus can house 1,148 undergraduates.

EXPENSES

Tuition (2005-06): $16,030 per year.
Room: $2,850. Board: $2,430.

LD SERVICES

LD program size is not limited.

LD services available to:

☐ Freshmen ☐ Sophomores ☐ Juniors ☐ Seniors

Academic Accommodations

Curriculum		In class	
Foreign language waiver	☐	Early syllabus	☐
Lighter course load	■	Note takers in class	■
Math waiver	☐	Priority seating	☐
Other special classes	■	Tape recorders	■
Priority registrations	☐	Videotaped classes	■
Substitution of courses	☐	Text on tape	☐
Exams		**Services**	
Extended time	■	Diagnostic tests	■
Oral exams	■	Learning centers	■
Take home exams	☐	Proofreaders	☐
Exams on tape or computer	☐	Readers	■
Untimed exams	■	Reading Machines/Kurzweil	■
Other accommodations	☐	Special bookstore section	☐
		Typists	☐

Credit toward degree is not given for remedial courses taken.

Counseling Services

- ☐ Academic
- ☐ Psychological
- ☐ Student Support groups
- ☐ Vocational

Tutoring

	Individual	Group
Time management	☐	☐
Organizational skills	☐	☐
Learning strategies	☐	☐
Study skills	☐	☐
Content area	☐	☐
Writing lab	☐	☐
Math lab	☐	☐

LD PROGRAM STAFF

Total number of LD Program staff (including director):

Full Time: 5 Part Time: 5

Key staff person available to work with LD students: Carletta Witzel, Education Specialist.

Aquinas College

Grand Rapids, MI

Address: 1607 Robinson Road SE, Grand Rapids, MI, 49506-1799
Admissions telephone: 800 678-9593
Admissions FAX: 616 732-4469
Director of Admissions: Tom Mikowski
Admissions e-mail: admissions@aquinas.edu
Web site: http://www.aquinas.edu
SAT Code: 1018 ACT Code: 1962

LD program name: Academic Achievement Center
Director, Disability Coordinator: Jacquelyn Sweeney
LD program telephone: 616 632-2166
LD program e-mail: sweenjac@aquinas.edu
LD program enrollment: 91, Total campus enrollment: 1,813

GENERAL

Aquinas College is a private, coed, four-year institution. 107-acre, suburban campus in Grand Rapids (population: 197,800); branch campuses in Holland and Lansing. Served by air, bus, and train. Public transportation serves campus. Semester system.

LD ADMISSIONS

Students complete a separate application and are simultaneously accepted to the LD program. A member of the LD program does not sit on the admissions committee. A personal interview is not required. Essay is not required. Admissions requirements that may be waived for LD students include In the case of an exceptional student, the requirement of graduation from a secondary school may be waived at the discretion of the Committee on Admissions.

For fall 2004, 19 completed self-identified LD applications were received. 19 applications were offered admission, and 19 enrolled.

SECONDARY SCHOOL REQUIREMENTS

Graduation from secondary school required; GED not accepted. The following course distribution required: 4 units of English, 4 units of math, 3 units of science, 4 units of social studies.

TESTING

SAT Reasoning considered if submitted. ACT recommended. SAT Subject recommended.

All enrolled freshmen (fall 2004):

Average ACT Scores: Composite: 23

Child Study Team report is not required. A neuropsychological or comprehensive psycho-educational evaluation is required for admission. Must be dated within 36 months of application. Tests required as part of this documentation:

- ☑ WAIS-IV
- ☐ WISC-IV
- ☐ SATA
- ☑ Woodcock-Johnson
- ☑ Nelson-Denny Reading Test
- ☐ Other

UNDERGRADUATE STUDENT BODY

Total undergraduate student enrollment: 643 Men, 1,373 Women.

Composition of student body (fall 2004):

	Undergraduate	Freshmen
International	0.0	0.5
Black	4.4	4.2
American Indian	0.3	0.2
Asian-American	1.6	1.4
Hispanic	3.8	3.8
White	89.6	89.5
Unreported	0.3	0.4
	100.0%	100.0%

7% are from out of state. Average age of full-time undergraduates is 22. 66% of classes have fewer than 20 students, 34% have between 20 and 50 students.

STUDENT HOUSING

82% of freshmen live in college housing. Freshmen are required to live on campus. Housing is guaranteed for all undergraduates. Campus can house 704 undergraduates. Single rooms are available for students with medical or special needs. A medical note is required.

EXPENSES

Tuition (2005-06): $17,926 per year. Tuition is different for continuing education programs.
Room: $2,690. Board: $3,134.
There is no additional cost for LD program/services.

LD SERVICES

LD program size is not limited.

LD services available to:

☑ Freshmen ☑ Sophomores ☑ Juniors ☑ Seniors

Academic Accommodations

Curriculum		In class	
Foreign language waiver	☑	Early syllabus	☐
Lighter course load	☑	Note takers in class	☑
Math waiver	☑	Priority seating	☐
Other special classes	☑	Tape recorders	☑
Priority registrations	☑	Videotaped classes	☐
Substitution of courses	☑	Text on tape	☑
Exams		**Services**	
Extended time	☑	Diagnostic tests	☐
Oral exams	☑	Learning centers	☑
Take home exams	☐	Proofreaders	☐
Exams on tape or computer	☑	Readers	☑
Untimed exams	☐	Reading Machines/Kurzweil	☐
Other accommodations	☐	Special bookstore section	☐
		Typists	☑

Credit toward degree is given for remedial courses taken.

Counseling Services

☑	Academic	Meets 32 times per academic year
☐	Psychological	
☑	Student Support groups	Meets 32 times per academic year
☐	Vocational	

Tutoring

Individual tutoring is available weekly.

Average size of tutoring groups: 12

	Individual	Group
Time management	☑	☐
Organizational skills	☑	☐
Learning strategies	☑	☐
Study skills	☑	☐
Content area	☑	☐
Writing lab	☑	☐
Math lab	☑	☐

LD PROGRAM STAFF

Total number of LD Program staff (including director):

Full Time: 2 Part Time: 2

There is an advisor/advocate from the LD program available to students. The advisor/advocate meets with faculty 5 times per month and students 4 times per month.

Key staff person available to work with LD students: Jacquelyn Sweeney

LD Program web site: www.aquinas.edu

Calvin College

Grand Rapids, MI

Address: 3201 Burton Street SE, Grand Rapids, MI, 49546
Admissions telephone: 800 688-0122
Admissions FAX: 616 526-6777
Director of Admissions: Dale Kuiper
Admissions e-mail: admissions@calvin.edu
Web site: http://www.calvin.edu
SAT Code: 1095 ACT Code: 1968

LD program name: Services to Students with Disabilities
LD program address: Heimenga Hall 1846 Knollcrest Circle SE
Coordinator: June DeBoer
LD program telephone: 616 526-6937
LD program e-mail: jed4@calvin.edu
LD program enrollment: 110, Total campus enrollment: 4,127

GENERAL

Calvin College is a private, coed, four-year institution. 370-acre, suburban campus in Grand Rapids (population: 197,800), 150 miles from Detroit. Served by air, bus, and train. Public transportation serves campus. 4-1-4 system.

LD ADMISSIONS

A member of the LD program does not sit on the admissions committee. A personal interview is recommended. Essay is not required.

For fall 2004, 35 completed self-identified LD applications were received. 35 applications were offered admission, and 30 enrolled.

SECONDARY SCHOOL REQUIREMENTS

Graduation from secondary school required; GED accepted. The following course distribution required: 3 units of English, 3 units of math, 2 units of science, 2 units of social studies, 3 units of academic electives.

TESTING

ACT required; SAT Reasoning may be substituted. SAT Subject recommended.

All enrolled freshmen (fall 2004):

Average SAT I Scores:	Verbal: 599	Math: 605
Average ACT Scores:	Composite: 26	

Child Study Team report is not required. A neuropsychological or comprehensive psycho-educational evaluation is required for admission. Must be dated within 36 months of application. Tests required as part of this documentation:

- ☑ WAIS-IV
- ☑ WISC-IV
- ☐ SATA
- ☑ Woodcock-Johnson
- ☑ Nelson-Denny Reading Test
- ☑ Other

UNDERGRADUATE STUDENT BODY

Total undergraduate student enrollment: 1,858 Men, 2,363 Women.

Composition of student body (fall 2004):

	Undergraduate	Freshmen
International	5.9	7.7
Black	2.3	1.1
American Indian	0.1	0.3
Asian-American	2.8	2.7
Hispanic	1.7	1.1
White	85.1	84.7
Unreported	2.1	2.4
	100.0%	100.0%

39% are from out of state. Average age of full-time undergraduates is 20. 37% of classes have fewer than 20 students, 62% have between 20 and 50 students, 1% have more than 50 students.

STUDENT HOUSING

97% of freshmen live in college housing. Freshmen are required to live on campus. Housing is guaranteed for all undergraduates. Campus can house 2,559 undergraduates. Single rooms are available for students with medical or special needs. A medical note is required.

EXPENSES

Tuition (2005-06): $18,925 per year.
Room: $3,580. Board: $3,005.
There is no additional cost for LD program/services.

LD SERVICES

LD program size is not limited.

LD services available to:

☑ Freshmen ☑ Sophomores ☑ Juniors ☑ Seniors

Academic Accommodations

Curriculum		**In class**	
Foreign language waiver	☐	Early syllabus	☐
Lighter course load	☑	Note takers in class	☑
Math waiver	☐	Priority seating	☐
Other special classes	☐	Tape recorders	☑
Priority registrations	☑	Videotaped classes	☐
Substitution of courses	☐	Text on tape	☑
Exams		**Services**	
Extended time	☑	Diagnostic tests	☐
Oral exams	☐	Learning centers	☐
Take home exams	☐	Proofreaders	☐
Exams on tape or computer	☑	Readers	☑
Untimed exams	☐	Reading Machines/Kurzweil	☐
Other accommodations	☑	Special bookstore section	☐
		Typists	☐

Credit toward degree is not given for remedial courses taken.

Counseling Services

- ☑ Academic
- ☐ Psychological
- ☐ Student Support groups
- ☐ Vocational

Tutoring

Individual tutoring is available weekly.

Average size of tutoring groups: 2

	Individual	Group
Time management	☑	☑
Organizational skills	☑	☑
Learning strategies	☑	☑
Study skills	☑	☐
Content area	☑	☑
Writing lab	☐	☐
Math lab	☐	☐

LD PROGRAM STAFF

Total number of LD Program staff (including director):

Full Time: 2 Part Time: 2

There is an advisor/advocate from the LD program available to students. 60 peer tutors are available to work with LD students.

Key staff person available to work with LD students: Karen Broekstra, Coordinator for Services to Students.

Central Michigan University

Mount Pleasant, MI

Address: 105 Warriner Hall, Mount Pleasant, MI, 48859
Admissions telephone: 989 774-3076
Admissions FAX: 989 774-7267
Director of Admissions: Betty J. Wagner
Admissions e-mail: cmuadmit@cmich.edu
Web site: http://www.cmich.edu
SAT Code: 1106 ACT Code: 1972

LD program name: Student Disability Services
LD program address: 120 Library Central Michigan University
Assistant Director/Learning Disabilities: Dennis McCue
LD program telephone: 989 774-3018
LD program e-mail: mccue1d@cmich.edu
LD program enrollment: 132, Total campus enrollment: 19,916

GENERAL

Central Michigan University is a public, coed, four-year institution. 854-acre campus in Mount Pleasant (population: 25,946), 60 miles from Saginaw; over 50 off-campus sites across the country. Served by bus; airport serves Saginaw; train serves Lansing (60 miles). Public transportation serves campus. Semester system.

LD ADMISSIONS

Students do not complete a separate application and are not simultaneously accepted to the LD program. A member of the LD program does not sit on the admissions committee. A personal interview is recommended. Essay is not required.

SECONDARY SCHOOL REQUIREMENTS

Graduation from secondary school required; GED accepted.

TESTING

SAT Reasoning considered if submitted. ACT required. SAT Subject recommended.

All enrolled freshmen (fall 2004):

Average SAT I Scores:	Verbal: 523	Math: 526
Average ACT Scores:	Composite: 22	

Child Study Team report is required if student is classified. A neuropsychological or comprehensive psycho-educational evaluation is required for admission. Must be dated within 36 months of application. Tests required as part of this documentation:

- [x] WAIS-IV
- [x] WISC-IV
- [x] SATA
- [x] Woodcock-Johnson
- [x] Nelson-Denny Reading Test
- [ ] Other

UNDERGRADUATE STUDENT BODY

Total undergraduate student enrollment: 7,880 Men, 11,650 Women.

Composition of student body (fall 2004):

	Undergraduate	Freshmen
International	0.4	0.6
Black	6.8	6.2
American Indian	0.7	0.8
Asian-American	1.5	1.1
Hispanic	1.6	1.8
White	83.6	83.9
Unreported	5.4	5.6
	100.0%	100.0%

3% are from out of state. 6% join a fraternity and 7% join a sorority. Average age of full-time undergraduates is 21. 26% of classes have fewer than 20 students, 57% have between 20 and 50 students, 17% have more than 50 students.

STUDENT HOUSING

94% of freshmen live in college housing. Freshmen are required to live on campus. Housing is guaranteed for all undergraduates. Campus can house 5,939 undergraduates. Single rooms are available for students with medical or special needs. A medical note is required.

EXPENSES

Tuition (2005-06): $6,390 per year (in-state), $14,850 (out-of-state).

There is no additional cost for LD program/services.

LD SERVICES

LD program size is not limited.

LD services available to:

- [x] Freshmen
- [x] Sophomores
- [x] Juniors
- [x] Seniors

Academic Accommodations

Curriculum		**In class**	
Foreign language waiver	[ ]	Early syllabus	[ ]
Lighter course load	[ ]	Note takers in class	[x]
Math waiver	[x]	Priority seating	[x]
Other special classes	[ ]	Tape recorders	[x]
Priority registrations	[ ]	Videotaped classes	[ ]
Substitution of courses	[ ]	Text on tape	[ ]
Exams		**Services**	
Extended time	[x]	Diagnostic tests	[ ]
Oral exams	[x]	Learning centers	[ ]
Take home exams	[ ]	Proofreaders	[ ]
Exams on tape or computer	[ ]	Readers	[x]
Untimed exams	[x]	Reading Machines/Kurzweil	[x]
Other accommodations	[ ]	Special bookstore section	[ ]
		Typists	[x]

Credit toward degree is not given for remedial courses taken.

Counseling Services

- [x] Academic
- [x] Psychological
- [ ] Student Support groups
- [ ] Vocational

Tutoring

Individual tutoring is available weekly.

Average size of tutoring groups: 1

	Individual	Group
Time management	[x]	[x]
Organizational skills	[x]	[x]
Learning strategies	[x]	[x]
Study skills	[x]	[x]
Content area	[x]	[x]
Writing lab	[x]	[x]
Math lab	[x]	[x]

UNIQUE LD PROGRAM FEATURES

Kurzweil 3000 reading and writing software, Text help and Inspiration available in library and dorms.

LD PROGRAM STAFF

Total number of LD Program staff (including director):

Full Time: 2 Part Time: 2

There is an advisor/advocate from the LD program available to students.

Key staff person available to work with LD students: Dennis McCue, Assistant Director/Learning Disabilities.

LD Program web site: http://www.cmich.edu/student-disability/default.htm

College for Creative Studies

Detroit, MI

Address: 201 E. Kirby, Detroit, MI, 48202
Admissions telephone: 800 952-ARTS
Admissions FAX: 313 872-2739
Admissions e-mail: admissions@ccscad.edu
Web site: http://www.ccscad.edu
SAT Code: 1035 ACT Code: 1989

Director of the Student Success Center: Sylvia Austermiller
LD program telephone: 313 664-7680
Total campus enrollment: 1,265

GENERAL

College for Creative Studies is a private, coed, four-year institution. 11-acre, urban campus in Detroit (population: 951,270). Served by air, bus, and train. Public transportation serves campus. Semester system.

LD ADMISSIONS

A personal interview is recommended. Essay is not required.

SECONDARY SCHOOL REQUIREMENTS

Graduation from secondary school required; GED accepted.

TESTING

SAT Reasoning or ACT required. SAT Subject recommended.

Child Study Team report is not required. Tests required as part of this documentation:

- ☐ WAIS-IV
- ☐ WISC-IV
- ☐ SATA
- ☐ Woodcock-Johnson
- ☐ Nelson-Denny Reading Test
- ☐ Other

UNDERGRADUATE STUDENT BODY

Total undergraduate student enrollment: 681 Men, 471 Women.

Composition of student body (fall 2004):

	Undergraduate	Freshmen
International	4.4	5.4
Black	10.0	6.2
American Indian	1.7	0.4
Asian-American	4.4	5.6
Hispanic	3.9	4.2
White	65.6	67.0
Unreported	10.0	11.2
	100.0%	100.0%

17% are from out of state. Average age of full-time undergraduates is 22.

STUDENT HOUSING

37% of freshmen live in college housing. Freshmen are not required to live on campus. Housing is guaranteed for all undergraduates. Campus can house 263 undergraduates. Single rooms are not available for students with medical or special needs.

EXPENSES

Tuition (2005-06): $21,990 per year.

Room: $3,900.

There is no additional cost for LD program/services.

LD SERVICES

LD services available to:

☑ Freshmen ☑ Sophomores ☑ Juniors ☑ Seniors

Academic Accommodations

Curriculum

- Foreign language waiver ☐
- Lighter course load ☑
- Math waiver ☐
- Other special classes ☐
- Priority registrations ☐
- Substitution of courses ☐

Exams

- Extended time ☐
- Oral exams ☑
- Take home exams ☐
- Exams on tape or computer ☐
- Untimed exams ☑
- Other accommodations ☐

In class

- Early syllabus ☐
- Note takers in class ☑
- Priority seating ☐
- Tape recorders ☑
- Videotaped classes ☐
- Text on tape ☐

Services

- Diagnostic tests ☑
- Learning centers ☑
- Proofreaders ☐
- Readers ☑
- Reading Machines/Kurzweil ☐
- Special bookstore section ☐
- Typists ☐

Credit toward degree is not given for remedial courses taken.

Counseling Services

- ☐ Academic
- ☐ Psychological
- ☐ Student Support groups
- ☐ Vocational

Tutoring

Individual tutoring is available daily.

	Individual	Group
Time management	☑	☑
Organizational skills	☑	☑
Learning strategies	☐	☐
Study skills	☑	☑
Content area	☐	☐
Writing lab	☑	☑
Math lab	☐	☐

LD PROGRAM STAFF

There is an advisor/advocate from the LD program available to students.

Key staff person available to work with LD students: Sylvia Austermiller, Director of the Student Success Center.

Concordia University

Ann Arbor, MI

Address: 4090 Geddes Road, Ann Arbor, MI, 48105
Admissions telephone: 800 253-0680
Admissions FAX: 734 995-4610
Director of Admissions: Gary Neumann
Admissions e-mail: admissions@cuaa.edu
Web site: http://www.cuaa.edu
SAT Code: 1094 ACT Code: 1977

LD program name: Academic Resource Center
Director: Kathryn Klintworth
LD program telephone: 734 995-7479
LD program e-mail: klintk@cuaa.edu
Total campus enrollment: 530

GENERAL

Concordia University is a private, coed, four-year institution. 234-acre, suburban campus in Ann Arbor (population: 114,024), 45 miles from Detroit. Served by air, bus, and train; major airport serves Detroit. School operates transportation to local churches. Public transportation serves campus. Semester system.

LD ADMISSIONS

A personal interview is not required. Essay is not required.

SECONDARY SCHOOL REQUIREMENTS

Graduation from secondary school required; GED accepted.

TESTING

ACT required; SAT Reasoning may be substituted. SAT Subject recommended.

All enrolled freshmen (fall 2004):

Average SAT I Scores: Verbal: 529 Math: 525
Average ACT Scores: Composite: 22

Child Study Team report is not required. Tests required as part of this documentation:

- ☐ WAIS-IV
- ☐ WISC-IV
- ☐ SATA
- ☐ Woodcock-Johnson
- ☐ Nelson-Denny Reading Test
- ☐ Other

UNDERGRADUATE STUDENT BODY

Total undergraduate student enrollment: 235 Men, 298 Women.

Composition of student body (fall 2004):

	Undergraduate	Freshmen
International	0.0	0.6
Black	8.1	10.5
American Indian	0.8	1.4
Asian-American	1.6	1.0
Hispanic	3.3	2.8
White	86.2	83.7
Unreported	0.0	0.0
	100.0%	100.0%

22% are from out of state. Average age of full-time undergraduates is 24. 71% of classes have fewer than 20 students, 26% have between 20 and 50 students, 3% have more than 50 students.

STUDENT HOUSING

95% of freshmen live in college housing. Freshmen are required to live on campus. Housing is guaranteed for all undergraduates. Campus can house 512 undergraduates. Single rooms are available for students with medical or special needs.

EXPENSES

Tuition (2005-06): $18,035 per year.

Room: $5,042. Board: $1,906.

There is no additional cost for LD program/services.

LD SERVICES

LD program size is not limited.

LD services available to:

■ Freshmen ■ Sophomores ■ Juniors ■ Seniors

Academic Accommodations

Curriculum		In class	
Foreign language waiver	■	Early syllabus	☐
Lighter course load	■	Note takers in class	☐
Math waiver	☐	Priority seating	☐
Other special classes	☐	Tape recorders	☐
Priority registrations	☐	Videotaped classes	☐
Substitution of courses	■	Text on tape	☐
Exams		**Services**	
Extended time	■	Diagnostic tests	☐
Oral exams	■	Learning centers	■
Take home exams	☐	Proofreaders	☐
Exams on tape or computer	☐	Readers	☐
Untimed exams	■	Reading Machines/Kurzweil	☐
Other accommodations	■	Special bookstore section	☐
		Typists	☐

Credit toward degree is not given for remedial courses taken.

Counseling Services

- ☐ Academic
- ☐ Psychological
- ☐ Student Support groups
- ☐ Vocational

Tutoring

Individual tutoring is available daily.

	Individual	Group
Time management	■	☐
Organizational skills	■	☐
Learning strategies	■	☐
Study skills	■	☐
Content area	■	☐
Writing lab	■	☐
Math lab	■	☐

LD PROGRAM STAFF

Key staff person available to work with LD students: Kathryn Klintworth, Director of the Academic Resource Center.

LD Program web site: http://www.cuaa.edu/~arc/

Cornerstone University

Grand Rapids, MI

Address: 1001 East Beltline NE, Grand Rapids, MI, 49525
Admissions telephone: 800 787-9778
Admissions FAX: 616 222-1400
Director of Admissions: Brent Rudin
Admissions e-mail: admissions@cornerstone.edu
Web site: http://www.cornerstone.edu
SAT Code: 1253 ACT Code: 2002

Director of Cornerstone Learning Center:Stephen Neynaber
LD program telephone: 616 949-5300
LD program e-mail: stephen_neynaber@cornerstone.edu
Total campus enrollment: 2,085

GENERAL

Cornerstone University is a private, coed, four-year institution. 132-acre campus in Grand Rapids (population: 197,800), 150 miles from both Detroit and Chicago; branch campuses in Kalamazoo and Troy. Served by air, bus, and train. Semester system.

SECONDARY SCHOOL REQUIREMENTS

Graduation from secondary school required; GED accepted.

TESTING

ACT required; SAT Reasoning may be substituted. SAT Subject recommended.

All enrolled freshmen (fall 2004):

Average SAT I Scores: Verbal: 540 Math: 530
Average ACT Scores: Composite: 23

Child Study Team report is not required. Tests required as part of this documentation:

- ❑ WAIS-IV
- ❑ WISC-IV
- ❑ SATA
- ❑ Woodcock-Johnson
- ❑ Nelson-Denny Reading Test
- ❑ Other

UNDERGRADUATE STUDENT BODY

Total undergraduate student enrollment: 665 Men, 1,051 Women.

Composition of student body (fall 2004):

	Undergraduate	Freshmen
International	0.3	0.9
Black	19.0	19.0
American Indian	0.3	0.3
Asian-American	1.1	1.1
Hispanic	2.2	2.0
White	77.1	76.7
Unreported	0.0	0.0
	100.0%	100.0%

20% are from out of state. 53% of classes have fewer than 20 students, 45% have between 20 and 50 students, 2% have more than 50 students.

STUDENT HOUSING

Housing is guaranteed for all undergraduates.

EXPENSES

Tuition (2005-06): $15,550 per year.
Room & Board: $5,800.
There is no additional cost for LD program/services.

LD SERVICES

LD program size is not limited.

LD services available to:

❑ Freshmen ❑ Sophomores ❑ Juniors ❑ Seniors

Academic Accommodations

Curriculum		In class	
Foreign language waiver	❑	Early syllabus	❑
Lighter course load	❑	Note takers in class	■
Math waiver	❑	Priority seating	❑
Other special classes	■	Tape recorders	■
Priority registrations	❑	Videotaped classes	■
Substitution of courses	❑	Text on tape	❑
Exams		**Services**	
Extended time	■	Diagnostic tests	■
Oral exams	■	Learning centers	■
Take home exams	❑	Proofreaders	❑
Exams on tape or computer	❑	Readers	■
Untimed exams	■	Reading Machines/Kurzweil	❑
Other accommodations	❑	Special bookstore section	❑
		Typists	❑

Counseling Services

- ❑ Academic
- ❑ Psychological
- ❑ Student Support groups
- ❑ Vocational

Tutoring

	Individual	Group
Time management	❑	❑
Organizational skills	❑	❑
Learning strategies	❑	❑
Study skills	❑	❑
Content area	❑	❑
Writing lab	❑	❑
Math lab	❑	❑

LD PROGRAM STAFF

Total number of LD Program staff (including director):

Full Time: 2 Part Time: 2

Key staff person available to work with LD students: Stephen Neynaber, Director of Cornerstone Learning Center.

Davenport U

Grand Rapids, MI

Address: 415 E. Fulton Street, Grand Rapids, MI, 49503
Admissions telephone: 800 455-2669
Admissions Contact: Susan Backofen
Admissions e-mail: Davenport.Admissions@davenport.edu
Web site: http://www.davenport.edu
SAT Code: 1183

Total campus enrollment: 12,323

GENERAL

Davenport U is a private, coed, four-year institution. Campus in Grand Rapids (population: 197,800). Served by air. Semester system.

LD ADMISSIONS

A personal interview is not required. Essay is not required.

SECONDARY SCHOOL REQUIREMENTS

Graduation from secondary school not required.

TESTING

All enrolled freshmen (fall 2004):

Average SAT I Scores: Verbal: Math:
Average ACT Scores: Composite:

Child Study Team report is not required. Tests required as part of this documentation:

- ☐ WAIS-IV
- ☐ WISC-IV
- ☐ SATA
- ☐ Woodcock-Johnson
- ☐ Nelson-Denny Reading Test
- ☐ Other

UNDERGRADUATE STUDENT BODY

Total undergraduate student enrollment: 12,323.

Composition of student body (fall 2004):

	Undergraduate	Freshmen
International	0.4	0.3
Black	20.6	25.0
American Indian	0.2	0.4
Asian-American	2.7	1.6
Hispanic	3.9	3.7
White	52.9	56.8
Unreported	19.3	12.2
	100.0%	100.0%

Average age of full-time undergraduates is 27. 87% of classes have fewer than 20 students, 13% have between 20 and 50 students.

STUDENT HOUSING

Housing is not guaranteed for all undergraduates. Limited by space available.

EXPENSES

Tuition (2005-06): $8,760 per year.

Room: $3,400.

There is no additional cost for LD program/services.

LD SERVICES

LD program size is not limited.

LD services available to:

☐ Freshmen ☐ Sophomores ☐ Juniors ☐ Seniors

Academic Accommodations

Curriculum

- Foreign language waiver ☐
- Lighter course load ☐
- Math waiver ☐
- Other special classes ☐
- Priority registrations ☐
- Substitution of courses ☐

Exams

- Extended time ☐
- Oral exams ☐
- Take home exams ☐
- Exams on tape or computer ☐
- Untimed exams ☐
- Other accommodations ☐

In class

- Early syllabus ☐
- Note takers in class ☒
- Priority seating ☐
- Tape recorders ☒
- Videotaped classes ☐
- Text on tape ☐

Services

- Diagnostic tests ☐
- Learning centers ☒
- Proofreaders ☐
- Readers ☐
- Reading Machines/Kurzweil ☒
- Special bookstore section ☐
- Typists ☐

Credit toward degree is not given for remedial courses taken.

Counseling Services

- ☐ Academic
- ☐ Psychological
- ☐ Student Support groups
- ☐ Vocational

Tutoring

	Individual	Group
Time management	☐	☐
Organizational skills	☐	☐
Learning strategies	☐	☐
Study skills	☐	☐
Content area	☐	☐
Writing lab	☐	☐
Math lab	☐	☐

Eastern Michigan University

Ypsilanti, MI

Address: Ypsilanti, MI, 48197
Admissions telephone: 800 GOTOEMU
Admissions FAX: 734 487-6559
Director of Admissions: Judy Tatum
Admissions e-mail: undergraduate.admissions@emich.edu
Web site: http://www.emich.edu/
SAT Code: 1201   ACT Code: 1990

LD program name: Access Services Office
LD program address: 203 King Hall
Director, Access Services: Donald J. Anderson
LD program telephone: 734 487-2470
LD program e-mail: donald.anderson@emich.edu
Total campus enrollment: 18,868

GENERAL

Eastern Michigan University is a public, coed, four-year institution. 460-acre campus in Ypsilanti (population: 49,182), seven miles from Ann Arbor and 30 miles from Detroit. Served by bus; major airport serves Detroit; other airport serves Romulus (15 miles); train serves Ann Arbor. School operates transportation around campus in conjunction with Ann Arbor Transit Authority. Public transportation serves campus. Semester system.

LD ADMISSIONS

Students do not complete a separate application and are not simultaneously accepted to the LD program. A member of the LD program does not sit on the admissions committee. A personal interview is not required. Essay is not required.

SECONDARY SCHOOL REQUIREMENTS

Graduation from secondary school required; GED accepted. The following course distribution required: 4 units of English, 3 units of math, 2 units of science, 2 units of foreign language, 2 units of social studies, 1 unit of history.

TESTING

SAT Reasoning considered if submitted. ACT recommended.

All enrolled freshmen (fall 2004):

Average SAT I Scores:	Verbal: 503	Math: 508
Average ACT Scores:	Composite: 21	

Child Study Team report is not required. A neuropsychological or comprehensive psycho-educational evaluation is required for admission. Must be dated within 60 months of application. Tests required as part of this documentation:

■ WAIS-IV   ■ Woodcock-Johnson
■ WISC-IV   ■ Nelson-Denny Reading Test
☐ SATA   ■ Other

UNDERGRADUATE STUDENT BODY

Total undergraduate student enrollment: 7,271 Men, 11,231 Women.

Composition of student body (fall 2004):

	Undergraduate	Freshmen
International	0.9	1.5
Black	23.0	17.4
American Indian	0.5	0.5
Asian-American	1.8	2.1
Hispanic	2.4	2.1
White	66.0	70.7
Unreported	5.4	5.7
	100.0%	100.0%

10% are from out of state. 4% join a fraternity and 4% join a sorority. Average age of full-time undergraduates is 22. 38% of classes have fewer than 20 students, 54% have between 20 and 50 students, 8% have more than 50 students.

STUDENT HOUSING

67% of freshmen live in college housing. Freshmen are required to live on campus. Housing is guaranteed for all undergraduates. Campus can house 4,200 undergraduates. Single rooms are available for students with medical or special needs. A medical note is required.

EXPENSES

Tuition (2005-06): $4,905 per year (in-state), $15,405 (out-of-state).
Room: $2,970. Board: $3,355.
There is no additional cost for LD program/services.

LD SERVICES

LD program size is not limited.

LD services available to:

■ Freshmen ■ Sophomores ■ Juniors ■ Seniors

Academic Accommodations

Curriculum		In class	
Foreign language waiver	☐	Early syllabus	■
Lighter course load	■	Note takers in class	■
Math waiver	☐	Priority seating	■
Other special classes	☐	Tape recorders	■
Priority registrations	■	Videotaped classes	☐
Substitution of courses	■	Text on tape	■
Exams		**Services**	
Extended time	■	Diagnostic tests	■
Oral exams	☐	Learning centers	■
Take home exams	☐	Proofreaders	☐
Exams on tape or computer	■	Readers	■
Untimed exams	☐	Reading Machines/Kurzweil	■
Other accommodations	■	Special bookstore section	☐
		Typists	☐

Credit toward degree is not given for remedial courses taken.

Counseling Services

■ Academic
■ Psychological
☐ Student Support groups
☐ Vocational

Tutoring

Individual tutoring is available weekly.

	Individual	Group
Time management	■	■
Organizational skills	■	■
Learning strategies	■	■
Study skills	■	■
Content area	■	■
Writing lab	☐	☐
Math lab	☐	☐

LD PROGRAM STAFF

Total number of LD Program staff (including director):

Full Time: 1   Part Time: 1

There is an advisor/advocate from the LD program available to students. 1 graduate student and 80 peer tutors are available to work with LD students.

Key staff person available to work with LD students: Donald J. Anderson, Director, Access Services.

Ferris State University

Big Rapids, MI

Address: 1201 South State Street CSS201, Big Rapids, MI, 49307
Admissions telephone: 800 4-FERRIS
Admissions FAX: 231 591-3944
Director of Admissions/Records/Associate Dean/Enrollment Services: Dr. Craig Westman
Admissions e-mail: admissions@ferris.edu
Web site: http://www.ferris.edu
SAT Code: 1222 ACT Code: 1994

Educational Counselor for Students w/Disabilities: Eunice Merwin, LPC
LD program telephone: 231 591-3772, extension 3772
LD program e-mail: merwine@ferris.edu
Total campus enrollment: 10, 711

GENERAL

Ferris State University is a public, coed, four-year institution. 800-acre campus in Big Rapids (population: 10,849), 50 miles from Grand Rapids; branch campus in Grand Rapids. Served by bus; airport and train serve Grand Rapids. Public transportation serves campus. Semester system.

LD ADMISSIONS

Application Deadline: 08/05. Students do not complete a separate application and are not simultaneously accepted to the LD program. A member of the LD program does not sit on the admissions committee. High school waivers are accepted for foreign language. A personal interview is not required. Essay is not required.

SECONDARY SCHOOL REQUIREMENTS

Graduation from secondary school required; GED accepted.

TESTING

ACT required; SAT Reasoning may be substituted. SAT Subject recommended.

All enrolled freshmen (fall 2004):

Average SAT I Scores: Verbal: Math:
Average ACT Scores: Composite: 21

Child Study Team report is not required. Tests required as part of this documentation:

- ☐ WAIS-IV
- ☐ WISC-IV
- ☐ SATA
- ☐ Woodcock-Johnson
- ☐ Nelson-Denny Reading Test
- ☐ Other

UNDERGRADUATE STUDENT BODY

Total undergraduate student enrollment: 5,454 Men, 4,638 Women.

Composition of student body (fall 2004):

	Undergraduate	Freshmen
International	1.5	1.7
Black	6.3	7.0
American Indian	1.2	0.9
Asian-American	1.3	1.8
Hispanic	1.2	1.4
White	80.8	80.4
Unreported	7.7	6.8
	100.0%	100.0%

6% are from out of state. 4% join a fraternity and 4% join a sorority. Average age of full-time undergraduates is 25. 45% of classes have fewer than 20 students, 51% have between 20 and 50 students, 4% have more than 50 students.

STUDENT HOUSING

Freshmen are required to live on campus. Housing is guaranteed for all undergraduates. Campus can house 4,200 undergraduates. Single rooms are available for students with medical or special needs. A medical note is required.

EXPENSES

Tuition 2004-05: $6,090 (in-state), $12,178 (out-of-state).
There is no additional cost for LD program/services.

LD SERVICES

LD program size is not limited.

LD services available to:

☑ Freshmen ☑ Sophomores ☑ Juniors ☑ Seniors

Academic Accommodations

Curriculum		In class	
Foreign language waiver	☐	Early syllabus	☐
Lighter course load	☑	Note takers in class	☑
Math waiver	☐	Priority seating	☐
Other special classes	☑	Tape recorders	☑
Priority registrations	☐	Videotaped classes	☐
Substitution of courses	☐	Text on tape	☑
Exams		**Services**	
Extended time	☑	Diagnostic tests	☐
Oral exams	☐	Learning centers	☑
Take home exams	☐	Proofreaders	☐
Exams on tape or computer	☐	Readers	☑
Untimed exams	☐	Reading Machines/Kurzweil	☑
Other accommodations	☐	Special bookstore section	☐
		Typists	☑

Credit toward degree is given for remedial courses taken.

Counseling Services

- ☑ Academic
- ☑ Psychological
- ☐ Student Support groups
- ☐ Vocational

Tutoring

Individual tutoring is available daily.

Average size of tutoring groups: 1

	Individual	Group
Time management	☑	☐
Organizational skills	☑	☐
Learning strategies	☑	☐
Study skills	☑	☐
Content area	☑	☐
Writing lab	☑	☐
Math lab	☑	☐

LD PROGRAM STAFF

Total number of LD Program staff (including director):

Full Time: 1 Part Time: 1

There is an advisor/advocate from the LD program available to students.

Key staff person available to work with LD students: Eunice Merwin, LPC, Educational Counselor for Students w/Disabilities.

Grand Valley State University

Allendale, MI

Address: 1 Campus Drive, Allendale, MI, 49401
Admissions telephone: 800 748-0246
Admissions FAX: 616 331-2000
Director of Admissions: Jodi Chycinski
Admissions e-mail: go2gvsu@gvsu.edu
Web site: http://www.gvsu.edu
SAT Code: 1258 ACT Code: 2005

Vice Provost & Dean: Lynn M Blue
LD program telephone: 616 331-3327
LD program e-mail: bluel@gvsu.edu
Total campus enrollment: 18,393

GENERAL

Grand Valley State University is a public, coed, four-year institution. 897-acre campus in Allendale (population: 6,950), 12 miles from Grand Rapids; branch campuses in Grand Rapids, Holland, and Muskegon. Airport, bus, and train serve Grand Rapids. School operates transportation to Grand Rapids. Public transportation serves campus. Semester system.

LD ADMISSIONS

A personal interview is not required. Essay is not required.

SECONDARY SCHOOL REQUIREMENTS

Graduation from secondary school required; GED accepted.

TESTING

ACT required; SAT Reasoning may be substituted. SAT Subject recommended.

All enrolled freshmen (fall 2004):

Average ACT Scores: Composite: 24

Child Study Team report is required if student is classified. Tests required as part of this documentation:

- ☐ WAIS-IV
- ☐ WISC-IV
- ☐ SATA
- ☐ Woodcock-Johnson
- ☐ Nelson-Denny Reading Test
- ☐ Other

UNDERGRADUATE STUDENT BODY

Total undergraduate student enrollment: 6,625 Men, 9,760 Women.

Composition of student body (fall 2004):

	Undergraduate	Freshmen
International	0.1	0.5
Black	4.7	4.7
American Indian	0.5	0.6
Asian-American	3.5	2.3
Hispanic	3.6	2.8
White	86.7	87.9
Unreported	0.9	1.2
	100.0%	100.0%

4% are from out of state. 4% join a fraternity and 3% join a sorority. Average age of full-time undergraduates is 21. 30% of classes have fewer than 20 students, 64% have between 20 and 50 students, 6% have more than 50 students.

STUDENT HOUSING

78% of freshmen live in college housing. Freshmen are not required to live on campus. Housing is not guaranteed for all undergraduates. Priority is given to single first year students, then returning undergraduates. Campus can house 5,292 undergraduates.

EXPENSES

Tuition (2005-06): $6,220 per year (in-state), $12,510 (out-of-state). $4,660 per year (state residents, lower division), $10,080 (out-of-state, lower division), $4,830 (state residents, upper division), $10,420 (out-of-state, upper division).

Room & Board: $0-$6,360.

There is no additional cost for LD program/services.

LD SERVICES

LD program size is not limited.

LD services available to:

☐ Freshmen ☐ Sophomores ☐ Juniors ☐ Seniors

Academic Accommodations

Curriculum		**In class**	
Foreign language waiver	☐	Early syllabus	☐
Lighter course load	■	Note takers in class	■
Math waiver	☐	Priority seating	☐
Other special classes	☐	Tape recorders	■
Priority registrations	☐	Videotaped classes	■
Substitution of courses	☐	Text on tape	☐
Exams		**Services**	
Extended time	■	Diagnostic tests	☐
Oral exams	☐	Learning centers	☐
Take home exams	☐	Proofreaders	☐
Exams on tape or computer	☐	Readers	■
Untimed exams	■	Reading Machines/Kurzweil	■
Other accommodations	☐	Special bookstore section	☐
		Typists	☐

Credit toward degree is not given for remedial courses taken.

Counseling Services

- ☐ Academic
- ☐ Psychological
- ☐ Student Support groups
- ☐ Vocational

Tutoring

	Individual	Group
Time management	☐	☐
Organizational skills	☐	☐
Learning strategies	☐	☐
Study skills	☐	☐
Content area	☐	☐
Writing lab	☐	☐
Math lab	☐	☐

LD PROGRAM STAFF

Total number of LD Program staff (including director):

Full Time: 2 Part Time: 2

There is an advisor/advocate from the LD program available to students.

Hillsdale College

Hillsdale, MI

Address: 33 E. College Street, Hillsdale, MI, 49242
Admissions telephone: 517 607-2327
Admissions FAX: 517 607-2223
Director of Admissions: Jeffrey S. Lantis
Admissions e-mail: admissions@hillsdale.edu
Web site: http://www.hillsdale.edu
SAT Code: 1295 ACT Code: 2010

LD program name: Student Affairs
Vice President for Student Affairs: CarolAnn Barker
LD program telephone: 517 437-7341
Total campus enrollment: 1,273

GENERAL

Hillsdale College is a private, coed, four-year institution. 200-acre campus in Hillsdale (population: 8,233), 70 miles from Ann Arbor, 75 miles from Lansing, and 110 miles from Detroit. Served by air; major airports serve Detroit and Toledo (75 miles); bus and train serve Jackson (40 miles). School operates transportation to airports and bus and train stations. Semester system.

LD ADMISSIONS

Students do not complete a separate application and are not simultaneously accepted to the LD program. A member of the LD program does not sit on the admissions committee. A personal interview is recommended. Essay is required and may be typed.

SECONDARY SCHOOL REQUIREMENTS

Graduation from secondary school required; GED accepted. The following course distribution required: 4 units of English, 4 units of math, 3 units of science, 2 units of foreign language, 1 unit of social studies, 2 units of history.

TESTING

SAT Reasoning or ACT required. SAT Subject recommended.

All enrolled freshmen (fall 2004):

Average SAT I Scores:	Verbal: 660	Math: 610
Average ACT Scores:	Composite: 27	

Child Study Team report is not required. Tests required as part of this documentation:

☐ WAIS-IV	☐ Woodcock-Johnson
☐ WISC-IV	☐ Nelson-Denny Reading Test
☐ SATA	☐ Other

UNDERGRADUATE STUDENT BODY

Total undergraduate student enrollment: 583 Men, 625 Women.

49% are from out of state. 35% join a fraternity and 45% join a sorority. Average age of full-time undergraduates is 20. 74% of classes have fewer than 20 students, 25% have between 20 and 50 students, 1% have more than 50 students.

STUDENT HOUSING

99% of freshmen live in college housing. Freshmen are required to live on campus. Housing is guaranteed for all undergraduates. Campus can house 1,100 undergraduates.

EXPENSES

Tuition (2005-06): $17,000 per year.
Room: $3,350. Board: $3,400.
There is no additional cost for LD program/services.

LD SERVICES

LD program size is not limited.

LD services available to:

☐ Freshmen ☐ Sophomores ☐ Juniors ☐ Seniors

Academic Accommodations

Curriculum		**In class**	
Foreign language waiver	☐	Early syllabus	☐
Lighter course load	■	Note takers in class	☐
Math waiver	☐	Priority seating	☐
Other special classes	☐	Tape recorders	☐
Priority registrations	☐	Videotaped classes	☐
Substitution of courses	☐	Text on tape	☐
Exams		**Services**	
Extended time	■	Diagnostic tests	☐
Oral exams	☐	Learning centers	■
Take home exams	☐	Proofreaders	☐
Exams on tape or computer	☐	Readers	☐
Untimed exams	☐	Reading Machines/Kurzweil	☐
Other accommodations	☐	Special bookstore section	☐
		Typists	☐

Credit toward degree is not given for remedial courses taken.

Counseling Services

■ Academic
■ Psychological
☐ Student Support groups
☐ Vocational

Tutoring

Individual tutoring is available.

	Individual	Group
Time management	■	☐
Organizational skills	■	☐
Learning strategies	■	☐
Study skills	■	■
Content area	☐	☐
Writing lab	☐	■
Math lab	■	■

LD PROGRAM STAFF

There is an advisor/advocate from the LD program available to students.

Key staff person available to work with LD students: CarolAnn Barker, Vice President for Student Affairs.

Hope College

Holland, MI

Address: PO Box 9000, Holland, MI, 49422-9000
Admissions telephone: 800 968-7850
Admissions FAX: 616 395-7130
Vice President for Admissions: Gary Camp
Admissions e-mail: admissions@hope.edu
Web site: http://www.hope.edu
SAT Code: 1301 ACT Code: 2012

LD program name: Academic Support Center
LD program telephone: 616 395-7830
LD program e-mail: jheisler@hope.edu
Total campus enrollment: 3,112

GENERAL

Hope College is a private, coed, four-year institution. 45-acre campus in Holland (population: 26,300), 30 miles from both Grand Rapids and Muskegon. Served by bus and train; airports serve Grand Rapids and Muskegon. School operates transportation to off-campus employment locations. Semester system.

LD ADMISSIONS

A member of the LD program does not sit on the admissions committee. High school waivers are accepted for foreign language. A personal interview is recommended. Essay is required and may be typed.

SECONDARY SCHOOL REQUIREMENTS

Graduation from secondary school required; GED accepted. The following course distribution required: 4 units of English, 2 units of math, 1 unit of science, 1 unit of foreign language, 2 units of social studies, 1 unit of history, 5 units of academic electives.

TESTING

All enrolled freshmen (fall 2004):

Average SAT I Scores:	Verbal: 595	Math: 601
Average ACT Scores:	Composite: 26	

Child Study Team report is required if student is classified. A neuropsychological or comprehensive psycho-educational evaluation is required for admission. Tests required as part of this documentation:

■ WAIS-IV	■ Woodcock-Johnson
☐ WISC-IV	■ Nelson-Denny Reading Test
☐ SATA	☐ Other

UNDERGRADUATE STUDENT BODY

Total undergraduate student enrollment: 1,190 Men, 1,809 Women.

Composition of student body (fall 2004):

	Undergraduate	Freshmen
International	1.0	1.2
Black	2.4	1.5
American Indian	0.5	0.2
Asian-American	2.9	2.0
Hispanic	2.0	1.8
White	89.9	92.6
Unreported	1.3	0.7
	100.0%	100.0%

26% are from out of state. 17% join a fraternity and 19% join a sorority. Average age of full-time undergraduates is 20. 52% of classes have fewer than 20 students, 46% have between 20 and 50 students, 2% have more than 50 students.

STUDENT HOUSING

99% of freshmen live in college housing. Housing is guaranteed for all undergraduates. Campus can house 2,362 undergraduates. Single rooms are available for students with medical or special needs. A medical note is required.

EXPENSES

Tuition (2005-06): $21,420 per year.
Room: $3,040. Board: $3,628.

There is no additional cost for LD program/services.

LD SERVICES

LD program size is not limited.

LD services available to:

■ Freshmen ■ Sophomores ■ Juniors ■ Seniors

Academic Accommodations

Curriculum		**In class**	
Foreign language waiver	☐	Early syllabus	☐
Lighter course load	■	Note takers in class	■
Math waiver	☐	Priority seating	☐
Other special classes	☐	Tape recorders	■
Priority registrations	■	Videotaped classes	☐
Substitution of courses	■	Text on tape	■
Exams		**Services**	
Extended time	■	Diagnostic tests	☐
Oral exams	■	Learning centers	■
Take home exams	☐	Proofreaders	☐
Exams on tape or computer	■	Readers	■
Untimed exams	■	Reading Machines/Kurzweil	■
Other accommodations	☐	Special bookstore section	☐
		Typists	■

Credit toward degree is not given for remedial courses taken.

Counseling Services

■ Academic — Meets 10 times per academic year

☐ Psychological
■ Student Support groups
■ Vocational

Tutoring

Individual tutoring is available weekly.

Average size of tutoring groups: 1

	Individual	Group
Time management	■	☐
Organizational skills	■	☐
Learning strategies	■	☐
Study skills	■	☐
Content area	■	■
Writing lab	■	☐
Math lab	■	■

LD PROGRAM STAFF

Total number of LD Program staff (including director):

Full Time: 1 Part Time: 1

There is an advisor/advocate from the LD program available to students. The advisor/advocate meets with faculty 2 times per month and students 2 times per month. 10 peer tutors are available to work with LD students.

Key staff person available to work with LD students: Jacqueline Heisler, Director of Academic Support Center.

LD Program web site: www.hope.edu/admin/acadsupport

Kalamazoo College

Kalamazoo, MI

Address: 1200 Academy Street, Kalamazoo, MI, 49006
Admissions telephone: 800 253-3602
Admissions FAX: 269 337-7390
Director of Admissions: John M. Carroll
Admissions e-mail: admission@kzoo.edu
Web site: http://www.kzoo.edu
SAT Code: 1365 ACT Code: 2018

Associate Dean of Students: Karen Joshua-Wathel
LD program telephone: 269 337-7209
LD program e-mail: kjoshua@kzoo.edu
Total campus enrollment: 1,234

GENERAL

Kalamazoo College is a private, coed, four-year institution. 60-acre, suburban campus in Kalamazoo (population: 77,145), 140 miles from Chicago. Served by air, bus, and train. Public transportation serves campus. Quarter system.

LD ADMISSIONS

Application Deadline: 02/15. A personal interview is recommended. Essay is required and may be typed.

SECONDARY SCHOOL REQUIREMENTS

Graduation from secondary school required; GED accepted.

TESTING

SAT Reasoning or ACT required. SAT Subject required.

All enrolled freshmen (fall 2004):

Average SAT I Scores:	Verbal: 631	Math: 630
Average ACT Scores:	Composite: 28	

Child Study Team report is not required. Tests required as part of this documentation:

- [ ] WAIS-IV
- [ ] WISC-IV
- [ ] SATA
- [ ] Woodcock-Johnson
- [ ] Nelson-Denny Reading Test
- [ ] Other

UNDERGRADUATE STUDENT BODY

Total undergraduate student enrollment: 603 Men, 781 Women.

Composition of student body (fall 2004):

	Undergraduate	Freshmen
International	0.0	0.0
Black	0.3	2.5
American Indian	0.0	0.1
Asian-American	4.3	4.6
Hispanic	3.3	2.1
White	79.8	79.7
Unreported	12.3	11.0
	100.0%	100.0%

24% are from out of state. Average age of full-time undergraduates is 20. 68% of classes have fewer than 20 students 32% have between 20 and 50 students.

STUDENT HOUSING

100% of freshmen live in college housing. Freshmen are required to live on campus. Housing is guaranteed for all undergraduates. Campus can house 855 undergraduates. Single rooms are available for students with medical or special needs. A medical note is required.

EXPENSES

Tuition (2005-06): $25,644 per year.

Room: $3,273. Board: $3,435.

There is no additional cost for LD program/services.

LD SERVICES

LD program size is not limited.

LD services available to:

- [x] Freshmen
- [x] Sophomores
- [x] Juniors
- [x] Seniors

Academic Accommodations

Curriculum

- [ ] Foreign language waiver
- [ ] Lighter course load
- [ ] Math waiver
- [ ] Other special classes
- [ ] Priority registrations
- [ ] Substitution of courses

Exams

- [x] Extended time
- [ ] Oral exams
- [ ] Take home exams
- [ ] Exams on tape or computer
- [ ] Untimed exams
- [ ] Other accommodations

In class

- [ ] Early syllabus
- [ ] Note takers in class
- [ ] Priority seating
- [x] Tape recorders
- [ ] Videotaped classes
- [ ] Text on tape

Services

- [x] Diagnostic tests
- [x] Learning centers
- [ ] Proofreaders
- [ ] Readers
- [ ] Reading Machines/Kurzweil
- [ ] Special bookstore section
- [ ] Typists

Credit toward degree is not given for remedial courses taken.

Counseling Services

- [ ] Academic
- [ ] Psychological
- [ ] Student Support groups
- [ ] Vocational

Tutoring

	Individual	Group
Time management	[ ]	[ ]
Organizational skills	[ ]	[ ]
Learning strategies	[ ]	[ ]
Study skills	[ ]	[ ]
Content area	[ ]	[ ]
Writing lab	[ ]	[ ]
Math lab	[ ]	[ ]

LD PROGRAM STAFF

Total number of LD Program staff (including director):

Full Time: 1 Part Time: 1

Key staff person available to work with LD students: Karen Joshua-Wathel, Associate Dean of Students.

Kettering University

Flint, MI

Address: 1700 W. Third Avenue, Flint, MI, 48504
Admissions telephone: 800 955-4464
Admissions FAX: 810 762-9837
Director of Admissions: Barbara Sosin
Admissions e-mail: admissions@kettering.edu
Web site: http://www.kettering.edu
SAT Code: 1246 ACT Code: 1998

Director of Wellness Center: Deborah Williams-Roberts
LD program telephone: 810 762-9650, extension 9650
LD program e-mail: droberts@kettering.edu
Total campus enrollment: 2,512

GENERAL

Kettering University is a private, coed, four-year institution. 54-acre, suburban campus in Flint (population: 124,943), 75 miles north of Detroit. Served by air, bus, and train; major airport serves Detroit. Public transportation serves campus. Semester system.

LD ADMISSIONS

A personal interview is recommended.

SECONDARY SCHOOL REQUIREMENTS

Graduation from secondary school required; GED not accepted. The following course distribution required: 3 units of English, 4 units of math, 2 units of science, 5 units of academic electives.

TESTING

SAT Reasoning or ACT required. SAT Subject recommended.

All enrolled freshmen (fall 2004):

Average SAT I Scores:	Verbal: 600	Math: 650
Average ACT Scores:	Composite: 26	

Child Study Team report is required if student is classified. Tests required as part of this documentation:

- ☐ WAIS-IV
- ☐ WISC-IV
- ☐ SATA
- ☐ Woodcock-Johnson
- ☐ Nelson-Denny Reading Test
- ☐ Other

UNDERGRADUATE STUDENT BODY

Total undergraduate student enrollment: 2,152 Men, 501 Women.

Composition of student body (fall 2004):

	Undergraduate	Freshmen
International	0.9	3.6
Black	3.8	6.0
American Indian	0.4	0.3
Asian-American	4.3	5.3
Hispanic	2.7	2.2
White	77.7	73.6
Unreported	10.2	9.0
	100.0%	100.0%

40% are from out of state. 40% join a fraternity and 33% join a sorority. Average age of full-time undergraduates is 20. 40% of classes have fewer than 20 students, 54% have between 20 and 50 students, 6% have more than 50 students.

STUDENT HOUSING

99% of freshmen live in college housing. Freshmen are required to live on campus. Housing is not guaranteed for all undergraduates. Campus can house 620 undergraduates.

EXPENSES

Tuition (2005-06): $23,360 per year.

Room: $3,432. Board: $1,930.
There is no additional cost for LD program/services.

LD SERVICES

LD program size is not limited.

LD services available to:

☐ Freshmen ☐ Sophomores ☐ Juniors ☐ Seniors

Academic Accommodations

Curriculum		In class	
Foreign language waiver	☐	Early syllabus	☐
Lighter course load	☐	Note takers in class	■
Math waiver	☐	Priority seating	☐
Other special classes	☐	Tape recorders	■
Priority registrations	☐	Videotaped classes	☐
Substitution of courses	☐	Text on tape	☐
Exams		**Services**	
Extended time	■	Diagnostic tests	■
Oral exams	☐	Learning centers	☐
Take home exams	☐	Proofreaders	☐
Exams on tape or computer	☐	Readers	■
Untimed exams	☐	Reading Machines/Kurzweil	■
Other accommodations	☐	Special bookstore section	☐
		Typists	☐

Credit toward degree is not given for remedial courses taken.

Counseling Services

- ☐ Academic
- ☐ Psychological
- ☐ Student Support groups
- ☐ Vocational

Tutoring

	Individual	Group
Time management	☐	☐
Organizational skills	☐	☐
Learning strategies	☐	☐
Study skills	☐	☐
Content area	☐	☐
Writing lab	☐	☐
Math lab	☐	☐

UNIQUE LD PROGRAM FEATURES

Applicants with learning disabilities are encouraged to advise the Admissions Office of the nature of their needs so that the student and the university can assess readiness for studies and if needs can be met.

LD PROGRAM STAFF

Key staff person available to work with LD students: Deborah Williams-Roberts, Director of Wellness Center.

Lawrence Technological University

Southfield, MI

Address: 21000 W. Ten Mile Road, Southfield, MI, 48075
Admissions telephone: 800 CALL-LTU
Admissions FAX: 248 204-3188
Director of Admissions: Jane Rohrback
Admissions e-mail: admissions@ltu.edu
Web site: http://www.ltu.edu
SAT Code: 1399   ACT Code: 2020

Coordinator, Academic Achievement Center: Diana Richard
LD program telephone: 248 204-4120
LD program e-mail: richard@ltu.edu
LD program enrollment: 18, Total campus enrollment: 2,906

GENERAL

Lawrence Technological University is a private, coed, four-year institution. 110-acre campus in Southfield (population: 78,296), 30 miles from Detroit; branch campus in Vancouver, British Columbia, Canada. Served by bus; major airport and bus serve Detroit; train serves Dearborn (15 miles). Public transportation serves campus. Semester system.

LD ADMISSIONS

A personal interview is not required. Essay is not required. Acommodations provided for placement assessments if appropriate.

SECONDARY SCHOOL REQUIREMENTS

Graduation from secondary school required; GED accepted.

TESTING

SAT Reasoning considered if submitted. ACT recommended. SAT Subject recommended.

All enrolled freshmen (fall 2004):

Average SAT I Scores:	Verbal: 525	Math: 587
Average ACT Scores:	Composite: 23	

Child Study Team report is required if student is classified. A neuropsychological or comprehensive psycho-educational evaluation is required for admission. Must be dated within 48 months of application. Tests required as part of this documentation:

- ☑ WAIS-IV
- ☑ WISC-IV
- ☑ SATA
- ☑ Woodcock-Johnson
- ☐ Nelson-Denny Reading Test
- ☐ Other

UNDERGRADUATE STUDENT BODY

Total undergraduate student enrollment: 2,202 Men, 773 Women.

Composition of student body (fall 2004):

	Undergraduate	Freshmen
International	0.3	1.7
Black	14.5	12.5
American Indian	0.0	0.4
Asian-American	2.5	2.8
Hispanic	2.5	1.8
White	70.7	69.5
Unreported	9.5	11.3
	100.0%	100.0%

5% are from out of state. 5% join a fraternity and 8% join a sorority. Average age of full-time undergraduates is 21. 73% of classes have fewer than 20 students, 26% have between 20 and 50 students, 1% have more than 50 students.

STUDENT HOUSING

38% of freshmen live in college housing. Freshmen are not required to live on campus. Housing is guaranteed for all undergraduates. Campus can house 563 undergraduates. Single rooms are available for students with medical or special needs. A medical note is required.

EXPENSES

Tuition (2005-06): $17,978 per year. Tuition varies by level and program. Room: $5,286. Board: $1,941.

There is no additional cost for LD program/services.

LD SERVICES

LD program size is not limited.

LD services available to:

☑ Freshmen ☑ Sophomores ☑ Juniors ☑ Seniors

Academic Accommodations

Curriculum		In class	
Foreign language waiver	☐	Early syllabus	☐
Lighter course load	☑	Note takers in class	☑
Math waiver	☐	Priority seating	☑
Other special classes	☐	Tape recorders	☑
Priority registrations	☐	Videotaped classes	☐
Substitution of courses	☐	Text on tape	☑
Exams		**Services**	
Extended time	☑	Diagnostic tests	☐
Oral exams	☑	Learning centers	☑
Take home exams	☐	Proofreaders	☐
Exams on tape or computer	☐	Readers	☑
Untimed exams	☑	Reading Machines/Kurzweil	☑
Other accommodations	☑	Special bookstore section	☐
		Typists	☑

Credit toward degree is not given for remedial courses taken.

Counseling Services

- ☑ Academic — Meets 2 times per academic year
- ☑ Psychological — Meets 10 times per academic year
- ☐ Student Support groups
- ☐ Vocational

Tutoring

Individual tutoring is available daily.

	Individual	Group
Time management	☑	☐
Organizational skills	☑	☐
Learning strategies	☐	☐
Study skills	☐	☑
Content area	☐	☐
Writing lab	☐	☐
Math lab	☐	☐

UNIQUE LD PROGRAM FEATURES

Acommodations for LD students are provided based on documented need by a qualified professional.

LD PROGRAM STAFF

Total number of LD Program staff (including director):

Full Time: 1   Part Time: 1

20 peer tutors are available to work with LD students.

Key staff person available to work with LD students: Diana Richard, Coordinator, Academic Achievement Center.

Madonna University

Livonia, MI

Address: 36600 Schoolcraft Road, Livonia, MI, 48150
Admissions telephone: 800 852-4951
Director of Admissions: Frank Hribar
Web site: http://www.madonna.edu
SAT Code: 1437 ACT Code: 2022

LD program name: Office of Disability Resources
Director: Michael Meldrum
LD program telephone: 734 432-5641
LD program e-mail: mmeldrum@madonna.edu
LD program enrollment: 42, Total campus enrollment: 3,259

GENERAL

Madonna University is a private, coed, four-year institution. 49-acre, suburban campus in Livonia (population: 100,545), just outside Detroit. Major airport serves Detroit; train serves Ann Arbor (20 miles). Semester system.

LD ADMISSIONS

Students do not complete a separate application and are not simultaneously accepted to the LD program. A member of the LD program does sit on the admissions committee. A personal interview is recommended. Essay is required and may be typed. Provisional acceptance is available after testing/evaluation by Admissions.

For fall 2004, 42 completed self-identified LD applications were received. 42 applications were offered admission, and 42 enrolled.

SECONDARY SCHOOL REQUIREMENTS

Graduation from secondary school not required. The following course distribution required: 3 units of English, 2 units of math, 3 units of science, 3 units of social studies.

TESTING

SAT Reasoning or ACT required. SAT Subject recommended.

All enrolled freshmen (fall 2004):

Average SAT I Scores: Verbal: Math:
Average ACT Scores: Composite: 22

Child Study Team report is not required. A neuropsychological or comprehensive psycho-educational evaluation is required for admission. Must be dated within 36 months of application. Tests required as part of this documentation:

- ■ WAIS-IV
- ■ WISC-IV
- ■ SATA
- ■ Woodcock-Johnson
- ■ Nelson-Denny Reading Test
- ☐ Other

UNDERGRADUATE STUDENT BODY

Total undergraduate student enrollment: 789 Men, 2,821 Women.

Composition of student body (fall 2004):

	Undergraduate	Freshmen
International	2.2	3.7
Black	10.5	13.1
American Indian	0.0	0.3
Asian-American	0.6	1.5
Hispanic	3.3	2.9
White	81.7	77.9
Unreported	1.7	0.6
	100.0%	100.0%

2% are from out of state. Average age of full-time undergraduates is 26. 66% of classes have fewer than 20 students, 33% have between 20 and 50 students, 1% have more than 50 students.

STUDENT HOUSING

2% of freshmen live in college housing. Freshmen are not required to live on campus. Housing is guaranteed for all undergraduates. Campus can house 250 undergraduates. Single rooms are available for students with medical or special needs. A medical note is required.

EXPENSES

Tuition (2005-06): $10,200 per year.
Room & Board: $5,768-$5,768.
There is no additional cost for LD program/services.

LD SERVICES

LD program size is not limited.

LD services available to:

■ Freshmen ■ Sophomores ■ Juniors ■ Seniors

Academic Accommodations

Curriculum		**In class**	
Foreign language waiver	☐	Early syllabus	■
Lighter course load	■	Note takers in class	■
Math waiver	☐	Priority seating	■
Other special classes	☐	Tape recorders	■
Priority registrations	☐	Videotaped classes	☐
Substitution of courses	■	Text on tape	■
Exams		**Services**	
Extended time	■	Diagnostic tests	■
Oral exams	■	Learning centers	■
Take home exams	■	Proofreaders	■
Exams on tape or computer	■	Readers	■
Untimed exams	☐	Reading Machines/Kurzweil	■
Other accommodations	■	Special bookstore section	☐
		Typists	■

Credit toward degree is given for remedial courses taken.

Counseling Services

- ■ Academic
- ☐ Psychological
- ☐ Student Support groups
- ☐ Vocational

Tutoring

Individual tutoring is available weekly.

Average size of tutoring groups: 5

	Individual	Group
Time management	■	■
Organizational skills	■	■
Learning strategies	■	■
Study skills	■	■
Content area	■	■
Writing lab	■	■
Math lab	■	■

LD PROGRAM STAFF

Total number of LD Program staff (including director):

Full Time: 10 Part Time: 10

There is an advisor/advocate from the LD program available to students. 35 peer tutors are available to work with LD students.

Key staff person available to work with LD students: Michael Meldrum, Director.

LD Program web site: www.madonna.edu/pages/odr.cfm

University of Michigan - Ann Arbor

Ann Arbor, MI

Address: Ann Arbor, MI, 48109
Admissions telephone: 734 764-7433
Admissions FAX: 734 936-0740
Director of Admissions: Theodore Spencer
Admissions e-mail: ugadmiss@umich.edu
Web site: http://www.umich.edu
SAT Code: 1839 ACT Code: 2062

Coordinator: Stuart Segal
LD program telephone: 734 763-3000
Total campus enrollment: 24,828

GENERAL

University of Michigan - Ann Arbor is a public, coed, four-year institution. 3,177-acre, suburban campus in Ann Arbor (population: 114,024), 50 miles west of Detroit. Served by bus and train; major airport serves Detroit. School operates campus transportation system. Public transportation serves campus. Trimester system.

LD ADMISSIONS

A personal interview is not required. Essay is required and may be typed.

SECONDARY SCHOOL REQUIREMENTS

Graduation from secondary school required; GED accepted. The following course distribution required: 4 units of English, 3 units of math, 2 units of science, 2 units of foreign language, 3 units of social studies.

TESTING

SAT Reasoning or ACT required. SAT Subject required.

All enrolled freshmen (fall 2004):

Average SAT I Scores:	Verbal: 630	Math: 672
Average ACT Scores:	Composite: 28	

Child Study Team report is not required. Tests required as part of this documentation:

☐ WAIS-IV	☐ Woodcock-Johnson
☐ WISC-IV	☐ Nelson-Denny Reading Test
☐ SATA	☐ Other

UNDERGRADUATE STUDENT BODY

Total undergraduate student enrollment: 12,159 Men, 12,388 Women.

Composition of student body (fall 2004):

	Undergraduate	Freshmen
International	5.1	4.8
Black	5.8	7.6
American Indian	1.0	0.9
Asian-American	11.6	12.2
Hispanic	4.4	4.6
White	63.7	63.0
Unreported	8.4	6.9
	100.0%	100.0%

32% are from out of state. 16% join a fraternity and 15% join a sorority. Average age of full-time undergraduates is 20. 46% of classes have fewer than 20 students, 38% have between 20 and 50 students, 16% have more than 50 students.

STUDENT HOUSING

98% of freshmen live in college housing. Freshmen are required to live on campus. Housing is not guaranteed for all undergraduates. Campus can house 10,639 undergraduates.

EXPENSES

Tuition (2005-06): $8,202 per year (in-state), $26,028 (out-of-state). Tuition varies by program and year of study.
Room & Board: $7,374.
There is no additional cost for LD program/services.

LD SERVICES

LD program size is not limited.

LD services available to:

☐ Freshmen ☐ Sophomores ☐ Juniors ☐ Seniors

Academic Accommodations

Curriculum		**In class**	
Foreign language waiver	☐	Early syllabus	☐
Lighter course load	■	Note takers in class	■
Math waiver	☐	Priority seating	☐
Other special classes	☐	Tape recorders	■
Priority registrations	☐	Videotaped classes	■
Substitution of courses	☐	Text on tape	☐
Exams		**Services**	
Extended time	■	Diagnostic tests	■
Oral exams	■	Learning centers	☐
Take home exams	☐	Proofreaders	☐
Exams on tape or computer	☐	Readers	☐
Untimed exams	■	Reading Machines/Kurzweil	■
Other accommodations	☐	Special bookstore section	☐
		Typists	☐

Counseling Services

☐ Academic
☐ Psychological
☐ Student Support groups
☐ Vocational

Tutoring

	Individual	Group
Time management	☐	☐
Organizational skills	☐	☐
Learning strategies	☐	☐
Study skills	☐	☐
Content area	☐	☐
Writing lab	☐	☐
Math lab	☐	☐

LD PROGRAM STAFF

Total number of LD Program staff (including director):

Full Time: 2 Part Time: 2

University of Michigan - Dearborn

Dearborn, MI

Address: 4901 Evergreen, Dearborn, MI, 48128-1491
Admissions telephone: 313 593-5100
Admissions FAX: 313 436-9167
Director of Admissions: Ray Metz
Admissions e-mail: admissions@umd.umich.edu
Web site: http://www.umd.umich.edu
SAT Code: 1861 ACT Code: 2074

LD program name: Counseling & Support Services
Coordinator: Dennis Underwood
LD program telephone: 313 593-5430
LD program e-mail: dennisu@umd.umich.edu
LD program enrollment: 18, Total campus enrollment: 6,449

GENERAL

University of Michigan - Dearborn is a public, coed, four-year institution. 210-acre, suburban campus in Dearborn (population: 97,775), 10 miles from Detroit. Served by train; major airport and bus serve Detroit; bus serves Lincoln Park (six miles). Public transportation serves campus. Semester system.

LD ADMISSIONS

Students do not complete a separate application and are not simultaneously accepted to the LD program. A member of the LD program does not sit on the admissions committee. High school waivers are accepted for math and foreign language. A personal interview is not required. Essay is required and may be typed.

SECONDARY SCHOOL REQUIREMENTS

Graduation from secondary school required; GED accepted. The following course distribution required:.

TESTING

SAT Reasoning considered if submitted. ACT considered if submitted. SAT Subject recommended.

All enrolled freshmen (fall 2004):

Average SAT I Scores:	Verbal: 547	Math: 585
Average ACT Scores:	Composite: 23	

Child Study Team report is not required. A neuropsychological or comprehensive psycho-educational evaluation is required for admission. Must be dated within 60 months of application. Tests required as part of this documentation:

- ■ WAIS-IV
- ☐ WISC-IV
- ■ SATA
- ■ Woodcock-Johnson
- ☐ Nelson-Denny Reading Test
- ☐ Other

UNDERGRADUATE STUDENT BODY

Total undergraduate student enrollment: 3,087 Men, 3,528 Women.

Composition of student body (fall 2004):

	Undergraduate	Freshmen
International	1.6	1.7
Black	5.5	7.6
American Indian	0.3	0.4
Asian-American	10.6	6.6
Hispanic	2.7	3.0
White	70.0	71.4
Unreported	9.3	9.3
	100.0%	100.0%

2% join a fraternity and 2% join a sorority. Average age of full-time undergraduates is 22. 38% of classes have fewer than 20 students, 55% have between 20 and 50 students, 7% have more than 50 students.

EXPENSES

Tuition (2005-06): $6,577 per year (in-state), $14,167 (out-of-state).

There is no additional cost for LD program/services.

LD SERVICES

LD program size is not limited.

LD services available to:

■ Freshmen ■ Sophomores ■ Juniors ■ Seniors

Academic Accommodations

Curriculum		In class	
Foreign language waiver	■	Early syllabus	☐
Lighter course load	■	Note takers in class	■
Math waiver	■	Priority seating	■
Other special classes	☐	Tape recorders	■
Priority registrations	■	Videotaped classes	☐
Substitution of courses	☐	Text on tape	■
Exams		**Services**	
Extended time	■	Diagnostic tests	☐
Oral exams	■	Learning centers	☐
Take home exams	☐	Proofreaders	☐
Exams on tape or computer	■	Readers	■
Untimed exams	☐	Reading Machines/Kurzweil	■
Other accommodations	☐	Special bookstore section	☐
		Typists	■

Credit toward degree is not given for remedial courses taken.

Counseling Services

- ■ Academic
- ■ Psychological
- ☐ Student Support groups
- ☐ Vocational

Tutoring

Individual tutoring is available weekly.

	Individual	Group
Time management	☐	☐
Organizational skills	☐	☐
Learning strategies	☐	☐
Study skills	☐	☐
Content area	☐	☐
Writing lab	■	☐
Math lab	■	☐

LD PROGRAM STAFF

Total number of LD Program staff (including director):

Full Time: 1 Part Time: 1

There is an advisor/advocate from the LD program available to students.

Key staff person available to work with LD students: Dennis Underwood, Coordinator of Disability Resource Services.

University of Michigan - Flint

Flint, MI

Address: 303 E. Kearsley, Flint, MI, 48502-1950
Admissions telephone: 810 762-3300
Admissions FAX: 810 762-3272
Interim Director of Admissions: Kimberley Buster-Williams
Admissions e-mail: admissions@umflint.edu
Web site: http://www.umflint.edu
SAT Code: 1853 ACT Code: 2063

Accessibility Coordinator: Becky Armour
LD program telephone: 810 762-3431
Total campus enrollment: 5,620

GENERAL

University of Michigan - Flint is a public, coed, four-year institution. 70-acre, urban campus in Flint (population: 124,943). Served by air, bus, and train. Public transportation serves campus. Semester system.

LD ADMISSIONS

A personal interview is not required. Essay is not required.

SECONDARY SCHOOL REQUIREMENTS

Graduation from secondary school required; GED accepted. The following course distribution required: 4 units of English, 3 units of math, 2 units of science, 3 units of social studies.

TESTING

ACT required; SAT Reasoning may be substituted. SAT Subject recommended.

All enrolled freshmen (fall 2004):

Average SAT I Scores:	Verbal: 508	Math: 525
Average ACT Scores:	Composite: 21	

Child Study Team report is not required. Tests required as part of this documentation:

❑ WAIS-IV ❑ Woodcock-Johnson
❑ WISC-IV ❑ Nelson-Denny Reading Test
❑ SATA ❑ Other

UNDERGRADUATE STUDENT BODY

Total undergraduate student enrollment: 2,062 Men, 3,817 Women.

Composition of student body (fall 2004):

	Undergraduate	Freshmen
International	0.5	0.9
Black	8.5	10.4
American Indian	0.5	0.7
Asian-American	1.6	1.5
Hispanic	2.5	2.1
White	82.2	77.4
Unreported	4.2	7.0
	100.0%	100.0%

1% are from out of state. 1% join a fraternity and 1% join a sorority. Average age of full-time undergraduates is 24. 41% of classes have fewer than 20 students, 54% have between 20 and 50 students, 5% have more than 50 students.

EXPENSES

Tuition (2005-06): Tuition is different for physical therapy and nursing programs.

There is no additional cost for LD program/services.

LD SERVICES

LD program size is not limited.

LD services available to:

❑ Freshmen ❑ Sophomores ❑ Juniors ❑ Seniors

Academic Accommodations

Curriculum		**In class**	
Foreign language waiver	❑	Early syllabus	❑
Lighter course load	❑	Note takers in class	■
Math waiver	❑	Priority seating	❑
Other special classes	❑	Tape recorders	❑
Priority registrations	❑	Videotaped classes	❑
Substitution of courses	❑	Text on tape	❑
Exams		**Services**	
Extended time	■	Diagnostic tests	❑
Oral exams	❑	Learning centers	❑
Take home exams	❑	Proofreaders	❑
Exams on tape or computer	❑	Readers	❑
Untimed exams	❑	Reading Machines/Kurzweil	❑
Other accommodations	❑	Special bookstore section	❑
		Typists	❑

Credit toward degree is given for remedial courses taken.

Counseling Services

❑ Academic
❑ Psychological
❑ Student Support groups
❑ Vocational

Tutoring

	Individual	Group
Time management	❑	❑
Organizational skills	❑	❑
Learning strategies	❑	❑
Study skills	❑	❑
Content area	❑	❑
Writing lab	❑	❑
Math lab	❑	❑

LD PROGRAM STAFF

Total number of LD Program staff (including director):

Full Time: 2 Part Time: 2

Key staff person available to work with LD students: Becky Armour, Accessibility Coordinator.

Michigan State University

East Lansing, MI

Address: East Lansing, MI, 48824
Admissions telephone: 517 355-8332
Admissions FAX: 517 353-1647
Director of Admissions: Pamela Horne
Admissions e-mail: admis@msu.edu
Web site: http://www.msu.edu/
SAT Code: 1465 ACT Code: 2032

LD program name: Disability Resource Center
LD program address: 120 Bessey Hall
LD Senior Specialist: Valerie Nilson
LD program telephone: 517 353-9642, extension 226
LD program e-mail: nilson@msu.edu
LD program enrollment: 412, Total campus enrollment: 35,408

GENERAL

Michigan State University is a public, coed, four-year institution. 5,315-acre, suburban campus in East Lansing (population: 46,525), 80 miles from Detroit. Served by bus and train; major airport serves Detroit; smaller airport serves Lansing (10 miles). School operates transportation around campus. Public transportation serves campus. Semester system.

LD ADMISSIONS

Students do not complete a separate application and are not simultaneously accepted to the LD program. A member of the LD program does not sit on the admissions committee. A personal interview is recommended. Essay is required and may not be typed. LD students, as all other applicants, must meet general admissions criteria and are reviewed from holistic perspectives.

For fall 2004, 129 completed self-identified LD applications were received.

SECONDARY SCHOOL REQUIREMENTS

Graduation from secondary school required; GED accepted. The following course distribution required: 4 units of English, 3 units of math, 2 units of science, 2 units of foreign language, 3 units of social studies.

TESTING

SAT Reasoning or ACT required. SAT Subject required.

All enrolled freshmen (fall 2004):

Average SAT I Scores: Verbal: 556 Math: 579
Average ACT Scores: Composite: 24

Child Study Team report is required if student is classified. A neuropsychological or comprehensive psycho-educational evaluation is required for admission. Must be dated within 36 months of application. Tests required as part of this documentation:

- [x] WAIS-IV
- [x] WISC-IV
- [x] SATA
- [x] Woodcock-Johnson
- [x] Nelson-Denny Reading Test
- [ ] Other

UNDERGRADUATE STUDENT BODY

Total undergraduate student enrollment: 16,084 Men, 18,258 Women.

Composition of student body (fall 2004):

	Undergraduate	Freshmen
International	2.5	2.8
Black	8.6	8.4
American Indian	0.7	0.7
Asian-American	5.1	5.5
Hispanic	2.7	2.8
White	79.3	79.0
Unreported	1.1	0.8
	100.0%	100.0%

9% are from out of state. Average age of full-time undergraduates is 20. 21% of classes have fewer than 20 students, 56% have between 20 and 50 students, 23% have more than 50 students.

STUDENT HOUSING

96% of freshmen live in college housing. Freshmen are required to live on campus. Housing is guaranteed for all undergraduates. Campus can house 22,200 undergraduates. Single rooms are available for students with medical or special needs. A medical note is required.

EXPENSES

Tuition (2005-06): $4,973 per year (state residents, lower division), $13,320 (out-of-state, lower division), $5,543 (state residents, upper division), $13,800 (out-of-state, upper division).

There is no additional cost for LD program/services.

LD SERVICES

LD program size is not limited.

LD services available to:

- [x] Freshmen
- [x] Sophomores
- [x] Juniors
- [x] Seniors

Academic Accommodations

Curriculum		In class	
Foreign language waiver	[ ]	Early syllabus	[ ]
Lighter course load	[x]	Note takers in class	[ ]
Math waiver	[ ]	Priority seating	[ ]
Other special classes	[ ]	Tape recorders	[ ]
Priority registrations	[x]	Videotaped classes	[ ]
Substitution of courses	[ ]	Text on tape	[ ]
Exams		**Services**	
Extended time	[ ]	Diagnostic tests	[x]
Oral exams	[ ]	Learning centers	[ ]
Take home exams	[ ]	Proofreaders	[ ]
Exams on tape or computer	[ ]	Readers	[ ]
Untimed exams	[ ]	Reading Machines/Kurzweil	[ ]
Other accommodations	[ ]	Special bookstore section	[ ]
		Typists	[ ]

Credit toward degree is not given for remedial courses taken.

Counseling Services

- [x] Academic
- [x] Psychological
- [x] Student Support groups
- [x] Vocational

Tutoring

Individual tutoring is available weekly.

Average size of tutoring groups: 3

	Individual	Group
Time management	[x]	[x]
Organizational skills	[x]	[x]
Learning strategies	[x]	[x]
Study skills	[x]	[x]
Content area	[x]	[x]
Writing lab	[x]	[ ]
Math lab	[x]	[x]

LD PROGRAM STAFF

Total number of LD Program staff (including director):

Full Time: 2 Part Time: 2

There is an advisor/advocate from the LD program available to students. 32 peer tutors are available to work with LD students.

Key staff person available to work with LD students: Valerie Nilson

LD Program web site: www.rcpd.msu.edu

Michigan Technological University

Houghton, MI

Address: 1400 Townsend Drive, Houghton, MI, 49931
Admissions telephone: 888 688-1885
Admissions FAX: 906 487-2125
Director of Undergraduate Admissions: Robert Forget
Admissions e-mail: mtu4u@mtu.edu
Web site: http://www.mtu.edu
SAT Code: 1464 ACT Code: 2030

LD program name: Services for Students with Disabilities
Associate Dean of Student Affairs: Gloria B. Melton
LD program telephone: 906 487-2212
LD program e-mail: gbmelton@mtu.edu
LD program enrollment: 30, Total campus enrollment: 5,709

GENERAL

Michigan Technological University is a public, coed, four-year institution. 240-acre campus in Houghton (population: 7,010) on Michigan's Upper Peninsula. Served by bus; airport serves Hancock (seven miles). Public transportation serves campus. Semester system.

LD ADMISSIONS

A personal interview is not required. Essay is not required.

SECONDARY SCHOOL REQUIREMENTS

Graduation from secondary school required; GED accepted. The following course distribution required: 3 units of English, 3 units of math, 2 units of science.

TESTING

SAT Reasoning or ACT required. SAT Subject recommended.

All enrolled freshmen (fall 2004):

Average SAT I Scores:	Verbal: 588	Math: 619
Average ACT Scores:	Composite: 25	

Child Study Team report is not required. Tests required as part of this documentation:

- [ ] WAIS-IV
- [ ] WISC-IV
- [ ] SATA
- [ ] Woodcock-Johnson
- [ ] Nelson-Denny Reading Test
- [ ] Other

UNDERGRADUATE STUDENT BODY

Total undergraduate student enrollment: 4,214 Men, 1,452 Women.

Composition of student body (fall 2004):

	Undergraduate	Freshmen
International	1.5	4.5
Black	1.6	2.1
American Indian	1.3	0.9
Asian-American	1.2	1.1
Hispanic	1.1	1.1
White	90.5	86.4
Unreported	2.8	3.9
	100.0%	100.0%

18% are from out of state. 8% join a fraternity and 13% join a sorority. Average age of full-time undergraduates is 21. 46% of classes have fewer than 20 students, 43% have between 20 and 50 students, 11% have more than 50 students.

STUDENT HOUSING

89% of freshmen live in college housing. Freshmen are required to live on campus. Housing is guaranteed for all undergraduates. Campus can house 2,639 undergraduates. Single rooms are available for students with medical or special needs. A medical note is required.

EXPENSES

Tuition (2005-06): $6,978 per year (in-state), $18,150 (out-of-state). $5,028 per year (state residents, lower division), $5,456 (state residents, upper division), $12,306 (out-of-state, lower division), $13,552 (out-of-state, upper division).
Room: $2,965-$3,100. Board: $3,131-$3,255.
There is no additional cost for LD program/services.

LD SERVICES

LD program size is not limited.

LD services available to:

- [x] Freshmen
- [x] Sophomores
- [x] Juniors
- [x] Seniors

Academic Accommodations

Curriculum		**In class**	
Foreign language waiver	[ ]	Early syllabus	[ ]
Lighter course load	[x]	Note takers in class	[x]
Math waiver	[ ]	Priority seating	[ ]
Other special classes	[x]	Tape recorders	[x]
Priority registrations	[ ]	Videotaped classes	[ ]
Substitution of courses	[ ]	Text on tape	[ ]
Exams		**Services**	
Extended time	[x]	Diagnostic tests	[ ]
Oral exams	[x]	Learning centers	[x]
Take home exams	[ ]	Proofreaders	[ ]
Exams on tape or computer	[ ]	Readers	[x]
Untimed exams	[x]	Reading Machines/Kurzweil	[x]
Other accommodations	[ ]	Special bookstore section	[ ]
		Typists	[ ]

Credit toward degree is not given for remedial courses taken.

Counseling Services

- [x] Academic
- [x] Psychological
- [ ] Student Support groups
- [ ] Vocational

Tutoring

Individual tutoring is not available.

	Individual	Group
Time management	[x]	[x]
Organizational skills	[x]	[x]
Learning strategies	[x]	[x]
Study skills	[x]	[x]
Content area	[x]	[x]
Writing lab	[x]	[x]
Math lab	[x]	[x]

LD PROGRAM STAFF

Total number of LD Program staff (including director):

Full Time: 1 Part Time: 1

There is an advisor/advocate from the LD program available to students.

Key staff person available to work with LD students: Gloria B. Melton, Associate Dean of Student Affairs.

Northern Michigan University

Marquette, MI

Address: 1401 Presque Isle Avenue, Marquette, MI, 49855
Admissions telephone: 800 682-9797
Admissions FAX: 906 227-1747
Director of Admissions: Gerri Daniels
Admissions e-mail: admiss@nmu.edu
Web site: http://www.nmu.edu
SAT Code: 1560 ACT Code: 2038

Coordinator-Disability Services: Lynn Walden
LD program telephone: 906 227-1737
LD program e-mail: lwalden@nmu.edu
Total campus enrollment: 9159

GENERAL

Northern Michigan University is a public, coed, four-year institution. 320-acre campus in Marquette (population: 19,661), 300 miles from Milwaukee. Served by air and bus; train serves Milwaukee. Public transportation serves campus. Semester system.

LD ADMISSIONS

A personal interview is not required. Essay is not required.

SECONDARY SCHOOL REQUIREMENTS

Graduation from secondary school required; GED accepted.

TESTING

SAT Reasoning or ACT required.

All enrolled freshmen (fall 2004):

Average SAT I Scores: Verbal: Math:
Average ACT Scores: Composite: 22

Child Study Team report is not required. Tests required as part of this documentation:

- ☐ WAIS-IV
- ☐ WISC-IV
- ☐ SATA
- ☐ Woodcock-Johnson
- ☐ Nelson-Denny Reading Test
- ☐ Other

UNDERGRADUATE STUDENT BODY

Total undergraduate student enrollment: 3,598 Men, 4,126 Women.

Composition of student body (fall 2004):

	Undergraduate	Freshmen
International	0.2	0.1
Black	1.5	1.9
American Indian	0.9	1.9
Asian-American	0.9	0.7
Hispanic	1.1	0.9
White	91.1	90.7
Unreported	4.3	3.8
	100.0%	100.0%

15% are from out of state.

STUDENT HOUSING

Housing is guaranteed for all undergraduates. Campus can house 2,360 undergraduates.

EXPENSES

Tuition 2004-05: $5,334 per year (in-state), $8,742 (out-of-state).

Room & Board: $6,182.

There is no additional cost for LD program/services.

LD SERVICES

LD program size is not limited.

LD services available to:

☐ Freshmen ☐ Sophomores ☐ Juniors ☐ Seniors

Academic Accommodations

Curriculum		**In class**	
Foreign language waiver	☐	Early syllabus	☐
Lighter course load	☐	Note takers in class	☑
Math waiver	☐	Priority seating	☐
Other special classes	☐	Tape recorders	☐
Priority registrations	☐	Videotaped classes	☐
Substitution of courses	☐	Text on tape	☐
Exams		**Services**	
Extended time	☑	Diagnostic tests	☐
Oral exams	☐	Learning centers	☑
Take home exams	☐	Proofreaders	☐
Exams on tape or computer	☐	Readers	☑
Untimed exams	☐	Reading Machines/Kurzweil	☐
Other accommodations	☐	Special bookstore section	☐
		Typists	☐

Credit toward degree is not given for remedial courses taken.

Counseling Services

- ☐ Academic
- ☐ Psychological
- ☐ Student Support groups
- ☐ Vocational

Tutoring

	Individual	Group
Time management	☐	☐
Organizational skills	☐	☐
Learning strategies	☐	☐
Study skills	☐	☐
Content area	☐	☐
Writing lab	☐	☐
Math lab	☐	☐

Northwood University - Midland

Midland, MI

Address: 4000 Whiting Drive, Midland, MI, 48640
Admissions telephone: 800 457-7878
Admissions FAX: 989 837-4490
Vice President of Enrollment Management: Daniel F. Toland
Admissions e-mail: admissions@northwood.edu
Web site: http://www.northwood.edu
SAT Code: 1568 ACT Code: 2041

LD program name: Special Needs Services
Special Needs Counselor: Rachelle Puffpaff
LD program telephone: 989 837-4216
LD program e-mail: puffpaff@northwood.edu
LD program enrollment: 77, Total campus enrollment: 3,432

GENERAL

Northwood University - Midland is a private, coed, four-year institution. 434-acre, suburban campus in Midland (population: 41,685), 135 miles from Detroit; branch campuses in Cedar Hill, Tex., and West Palm Beach, Fla. Served by air and bus; major airport serves Detroit. Public transportation serves campus. Quarter system.

LD ADMISSIONS

Students do not complete a separate application and are not simultaneously accepted to the LD program. A member of the LD program does sit on the admissions committee. A personal interview is recommended. Essay is required and may be typed. May make exceptions to minimum GPA and ACT/SAT score requirements.

SECONDARY SCHOOL REQUIREMENTS

Graduation from secondary school required; GED accepted.

TESTING

SAT Reasoning or ACT required. SAT Subject recommended.

All enrolled freshmen (fall 2004):

Average SAT I Scores:	Verbal: 462	Math: 490
Average ACT Scores:	Composite: 21	

Child Study Team report is not required. A neuropsychological or comprehensive psycho-educational evaluation is required for admission. Tests required as part of this documentation:

- [x] WAIS-IV
- [x] WISC-IV
- [ ] SATA
- [x] Woodcock-Johnson
- [ ] Nelson-Denny Reading Test
- [ ] Other

UNDERGRADUATE STUDENT BODY

Total undergraduate student enrollment: 1,834 Men, 1,580 Women.

18% are from out of state. Average age of full-time undergraduates is 20. 37% of classes have fewer than 20 students, 58% have between 20 and 50 students, 5% have more than 50 students.

STUDENT HOUSING

86% of freshmen live in college housing. Freshmen are required to live on campus. Housing is guaranteed for all undergraduates. Campus can house 812 undergraduates. Single rooms are available for students with medical or special needs. A medical note is not required.

EXPENSES

Tuition (2005-06): $14,625 per year.
Room: $3,405. Board: $3,291.
There is no additional cost for LD program/services.

LD SERVICES

LD program size is not limited.

LD services available to:

- [x] Freshmen
- [x] Sophomores
- [x] Juniors
- [x] Seniors

Academic Accommodations

Curriculum		In class	
Foreign language waiver	[ ]	Early syllabus	[ ]
Lighter course load	[x]	Note takers in class	[ ]
Math waiver	[ ]	Priority seating	[ ]
Other special classes	[ ]	Tape recorders	[ ]
Priority registrations	[x]	Videotaped classes	[ ]
Substitution of courses	[ ]	Text on tape	[ ]
Exams		**Services**	
Extended time	[x]	Diagnostic tests	[ ]
Oral exams	[x]	Learning centers	[x]
Take home exams	[ ]	Proofreaders	[x]
Exams on tape or computer	[ ]	Readers	[ ]
Untimed exams	[x]	Reading Machines/Kurzweil	[x]
Other accommodations	[ ]	Special bookstore section	[ ]
		Typists	[ ]

Credit toward degree is not given for remedial courses taken.

Counseling Services

- [x] Academic
- [x] Psychological
- [ ] Student Support groups
- [ ] Vocational

Tutoring

Individual tutoring is available daily.

Average size of tutoring groups: 2

	Individual	Group
Time management	[x]	[ ]
Organizational skills	[x]	[ ]
Learning strategies	[x]	[ ]
Study skills	[x]	[ ]
Content area	[ ]	[ ]
Writing lab	[ ]	[ ]
Math lab	[ ]	[ ]

LD PROGRAM STAFF

Total number of LD Program staff (including director):

Full Time: 1 Part Time: 1

There is an advisor/advocate from the LD program available to students. 10 peer tutors are available to work with LD students.

Key staff person available to work with LD students: Rachelle Puffpaff, Special Needs Counselor.

Oakland University

Rochester, MI

Address: 2200 N. Squirrel Road, Rochester, MI, 48309-4401
Admissions telephone: 800 OAK-UNIV
Admissions FAX: 248 370-4462
Associate Vice President for Enrollment Management: Eleanor Reynolds
Admissions e-mail: ouinfo@oakland.edu
Web site: http://www.oakland.edu
SAT Code: 1497 ACT Code: 2033

Office of Disability Support Services: Linda Sisson
LD program telephone: 248 370-3266
LD program e-mail: lgsisson@oakland.edu
LD program enrollment: 200, Total campus enrollment: 13,114

GENERAL

Oakland University is a public, coed, four-year institution. 1,444-acre campus in Rochester (population: 10,467), 25 miles from Detroit. Major airports serve Detroit and Flint (35 miles); bus and train serve Pontiac (five miles). Semester system.

LD ADMISSIONS

A member of the LD program does not sit on the admissions committee. A personal interview is required. Essay is not required.

SECONDARY SCHOOL REQUIREMENTS

Graduation from secondary school required; GED accepted. The following course distribution required: 4 units of English, 3 units of math, 3 units of science, 3 units of social studies.

TESTING

All enrolled freshmen (fall 2004):

Average SAT I Scores: Verbal: Math:
Average ACT Scores: Composite: 21

Child Study Team report is not required. A neuropsychological or comprehensive psycho-educational evaluation is required for admission. Must be dated within 36 months of application. Tests required as part of this documentation:

- [x] WAIS-IV
- [ ] WISC-IV
- [ ] SATA
- [x] Woodcock-Johnson
- [x] Nelson-Denny Reading Test
- [ ] Other

UNDERGRADUATE STUDENT BODY

Total undergraduate student enrollment: 4,581 Men, 7,948 Women.

Composition of student body (fall 2004):

	Undergraduate	Freshmen
International	0.4	0.8
Black	15.7	9.3
American Indian	0.4	0.5
Asian-American	3.1	3.2
Hispanic	1.6	1.6
White	74.6	77.5
Unreported	4.2	7.1
	100.0%	100.0%

2% are from out of state. 1% join a fraternity and 1% join a sorority. Average age of full-time undergraduates is 21. 33% of classes have fewer than 20 students, 49% have between 20 and 50 students, 18% have more than 50 students.

STUDENT HOUSING

31% of freshmen live in college housing. Freshmen are not required to live on campus. Housing is guaranteed for all undergraduates. Campus can house 2,324 undergraduates.

EXPENSES

Tuition 2004-05: $4,868 per year (in-state), $11,468 (out-of-state).

Room & Board: $5,790.

There is no additional cost for LD program/services.

LD SERVICES

LD program size is not limited.

LD services available to:

- [x] Freshmen
- [x] Sophomores
- [x] Juniors
- [x] Seniors

Academic Accommodations

Curriculum		In class	
Foreign language waiver	[ ]	Early syllabus	[ ]
Lighter course load	[x]	Note takers in class	[x]
Math waiver	[ ]	Priority seating	[x]
Other special classes	[ ]	Tape recorders	[x]
Priority registrations	[x]	Videotaped classes	[x]
Substitution of courses	[ ]	Text on tape	[x]
Exams		**Services**	
Extended time	[x]	Diagnostic tests	[x]
Oral exams	[ ]	Learning centers	[x]
Take home exams	[ ]	Proofreaders	[ ]
Exams on tape or computer	[x]	Readers	[x]
Untimed exams	[ ]	Reading Machines/Kurzweil	[x]
Other accommodations	[ ]	Special bookstore section	[ ]
		Typists	[x]

Credit toward degree is not given for remedial courses taken.

Counseling Services

- [x] Academic
- [x] Psychological
- [x] Student Support groups
- [ ] Vocational

Meets 2 times per academic year

Tutoring

Individual tutoring is available daily.

	Individual	Group
Time management	[x]	[ ]
Organizational skills	[x]	[ ]
Learning strategies	[x]	[ ]
Study skills	[x]	[ ]
Content area	[x]	[ ]
Writing lab	[x]	[ ]
Math lab	[x]	[ ]

LD PROGRAM STAFF

Total number of LD Program staff (including director):

Full Time: 2 Part Time: 2

There is an advisor/advocate from the LD program available to students.

Key staff person available to work with LD students: Linda Sisson, Director of Disability Support Services.

Olivet College

Olivet, MI

Address: 320 South Main Street, Olivet, MI, 49076
Admissions telephone: 800 456-7189
Admissions FAX: 269 749-6617
Director of Admissions: Tom Shaw
Admissions e-mail: admissions@olivetcollege.edu
Web site: http://www.olivetcollege.edu
SAT Code: 1595 ACT Code: 2042

LD program name: Academic Resource Center
Academic Resource Center Advisor: Jason Meadows
LD program telephone: 269 749-6637
LD program e-mail: jmeadows@olivetcollege.edu
LD program enrollment: 19, Total campus enrollment: 1,023

GENERAL

Olivet College is a private, coed, four-year institution. 92-acre campus in Olivet (population: 1,758), 30 miles from Lansing and 23 miles from Battle Creek. Major airport serves Detroit (120 miles); smaller airport and bus serve Lansing; train serves Battle Creek. Semester system.

LD ADMISSIONS

Application Deadline: 08/19. Students do not complete a separate application and are not simultaneously accepted to the LD program. A member of the LD program does not sit on the admissions committee. A personal interview is recommended. Essay is not required.

For fall 2004, 19 completed self-identified LD applications were received. 4 applications were offered admission, and 4 enrolled.

SECONDARY SCHOOL REQUIREMENTS

Graduation from secondary school required; GED accepted.

TESTING

SAT Reasoning or ACT considered if submitted; ACT preferred.

All enrolled freshmen (fall 2004):

Average SAT I Scores:	Verbal: 542	Math: 555
Average ACT Scores:	Composite: 20	

Child Study Team report is required if student is classified. A neuropsychological or comprehensive psycho-educational evaluation is required for admission. Tests required as part of this documentation:

- ☐ WAIS-IV
- ☐ WISC-IV
- ☐ SATA
- ☐ Woodcock-Johnson
- ☐ Nelson-Denny Reading Test
- ■ Other

UNDERGRADUATE STUDENT BODY

Total undergraduate student enrollment: 1,023.

Composition of student body (fall 2004):

	Undergraduate	Freshmen
International	1.0	3.8
Black	19.2	15.9
American Indian	1.5	1.1
Asian-American	0.0	0.3
Hispanic	3.5	2.1
White	69.7	75.2
Unreported	5.1	1.6
	100.0%	100.0%

18% are from out of state. 4% join a fraternity and 1% join a sorority. Average age of full-time undergraduates is 22. 52% of classes have fewer than 20 students, 46% have between 20 and 50 students, 2% have more than 50 students.

STUDENT HOUSING

64% of freshmen live in college housing. Freshmen are required to live on campus. Housing is guaranteed for all undergraduates. Campus can house 728 undergraduates. Single rooms are available for students with medical or special needs. A medical note is required.

EXPENSES

Tuition (2005-06): $15,970 per year.

Room: $2,980. Board: $2,500.
There is no additional cost for LD program/services

LD SERVICES

LD program size is not limited.

LD services available to:

■ Freshmen ■ Sophomores ■ Juniors ■ Seniors

Academic Accommodations

Curriculum		In class	
Foreign language waiver	☐	Early syllabus	■
Lighter course load	■	Note takers in class	■
Math waiver	☐	Priority seating	■
Other special classes	☐	Tape recorders	■
Priority registrations	☐	Videotaped classes	☐
Substitution of courses	☐	Text on tape	☐
Exams		**Services**	
Extended time	■	Diagnostic tests	☐
Oral exams	■	Learning centers	☐
Take home exams	☐	Proofreaders	■
Exams on tape or computer	☐	Readers	■
Untimed exams	■	Reading Machines/Kurzweil	☐
Other accommodations	☐	Special bookstore section	☐
		Typists	☐

Credit toward degree is not given for remedial courses taken.

Counseling Services

- ■ Academic
- ☐ Psychological
- ☐ Student Support groups
- ☐ Vocational

Tutoring

Individual tutoring is available weekly.

Average size of tutoring groups: 2

	Individual	Group
Time management	■	☐
Organizational skills	■	☐
Learning strategies	☐	☐
Study skills	■	☐
Content area	■	☐
Writing lab	☐	☐
Math lab	☐	☐

LD PROGRAM STAFF

Total number of LD Program staff (including director):

Full Time: 2 Part Time: 2

There is an advisor/advocate from the LD program available to students. The advisor/advocate meets with faculty 1 time per month and students 2 times per month. 15 peer tutors are available to work with LD students.

Key staff person available to work with LD students: Jason Meadows

Reformed Bible College

Grand Rapids, MI

Address: 3333 East Beltline Avenue NE, Grand Rapids, MI, 49525
Admissions telephone: 800 511-3749
Admissions FAX: 616 222-3045
Director of Enrollment Management: Larissa Lighthiser
Admissions e-mail: admissions@reformed.edu
Web site: http://www.reformed.edu
SAT Code: 1672 ACT Code: 2049

Vice President for Academic Affairs: Dr. Melvin Flikkema
LD program telephone: 616 222-3000
LD program e-mail: mjf@reformed.edu
LD program enrollment: 32, Total campus enrollment: 286

GENERAL

Reformed Bible College is a private, coed, four-year institution. 34-acre campus in Grand Rapids (population: 197,800). Served by air, bus, and train. Semester system.

LD ADMISSIONS

Application Deadline: 08/19. Students do not complete a separate application and are simultaneously accepted to the LD program. A member of the LD program does sit on the admissions committee. A personal interview is recommended. Essay is required and may be typed.

For fall 2004, 10 completed self-identified LD applications were received. 10 applications were offered admission, and 6 enrolled.

SECONDARY SCHOOL REQUIREMENTS

Graduation from secondary school required; GED accepted. The following course distribution required: 3 units of English, 2 units of math, 2 units of science, 3 units of social studies, 2 units of history, 4 units of academic electives.

TESTING

SAT Subject recommended.

All enrolled freshmen (fall 2004):

Average SAT I Scores:	Verbal: 530	Math: 510
Average ACT Scores:	Composite: 22	

Child Study Team report is not required. A neuropsychological or comprehensive psycho-educational evaluation is required for admission. Must be dated within 36 months of application. Tests required as part of this documentation:

- ■ WAIS-IV
- ■ WISC-IV
- ■ SATA
- ■ Woodcock-Johnson
- ■ Nelson-Denny Reading Test
- ☐ Other

UNDERGRADUATE STUDENT BODY

Total undergraduate student enrollment: 154 Men, 140 Women.

Composition of student body (fall 2004):

	Undergraduate	Freshmen
International	6.3	7.1
Black	2.1	2.5
American Indian	0.0	0.0
Asian-American	2.1	3.2
Hispanic	2.1	2.1
White	87.4	85.1
Unreported	0.0	0.0
	100.0%	100.0%

20% are from out of state. Average age of full-time undergraduates is 23. 67% of classes have fewer than 20 students, 33% have between 20 and 50 students.

STUDENT HOUSING

40% of freshmen live in college housing. Freshmen are required to live on campus. Housing is guaranteed for all undergraduates. Single rooms are available for students with medical or special needs. A medical note is not required.

EXPENSES

Tuition (2005-06): $10,900 per year.
Room: $2,300. Board: $3,000.

There is no additional cost for LD program/services.

LD SERVICES

LD program size is not limited.

LD services available to:

■ Freshmen ■ Sophomores ■ Juniors ■ Seniors

Academic Accommodations

Curriculum		**In class**	
Foreign language waiver	☐	Early syllabus	☐
Lighter course load	■	Note takers in class	■
Math waiver	☐	Priority seating	☐
Other special classes	☐	Tape recorders	■
Priority registrations	☐	Videotaped classes	☐
Substitution of courses	☐	Text on tape	■
Exams		**Services**	
Extended time	■	Diagnostic tests	■
Oral exams	■	Learning centers	■
Take home exams	☐	Proofreaders	☐
Exams on tape or computer	☐	Readers	■
Untimed exams	☐	Reading Machines/Kurzweil	☐
Other accommodations	■	Special bookstore section	☐
		Typists	■

Credit toward degree is not given for remedial courses taken.

Counseling Services

■	Academic	Meets 30 times per academic year
■	Psychological	Meets 36 times per academic year
■	Student Support groups	Meets 30 times per academic year
☐	Vocational	

Tutoring

Individual tutoring is available weekly.

Average size of tutoring groups: 1

	Individual	Group
Time management	■	■
Organizational skills	■	■
Learning strategies	☐	■
Study skills	☐	■
Content area	☐	☐
Writing lab	■	☐
Math lab	☐	☐

LD PROGRAM STAFF

Total number of LD Program staff (including director):

Full Time: 1 Part Time: 1

There is an advisor/advocate from the LD program available to students. The advisor/advocate meets with faculty 5 times per month and students 5 times per month. 8 peer tutors are available to work with LD students.

Key staff person available to work with LD students: Sarah Behm, Academic Support Services Coordinator.

Rochester College

Rochester Hills, MI

Address: 800 West Avon Road, Rochester Hills, MI, 48307
Admissions telephone: 800 521-6010
Admissions FAX: 248 218-2035
Vice President of Enrollment Services: Kelvin Brown
Admissions e-mail: admissions@rc.edu
Web site: http://www.rc.edu
SAT Code: 1516 ACT Code: 2072

Accommodations Officer: Janice Kern
LD program telephone: 248 218-2014
LD program e-mail: jkern@rc.edu
LD program enrollment: 21, Total campus enrollment: 1,011

GENERAL

Rochester College is a private, coed, four-year institution. 83-acre, suburban campus in Rochester Hills (population: 68,825), 25 miles from Detroit. Major airport and train serve Detroit; bus serves Pontiac (10 miles). Semester system.

LD ADMISSIONS

Students do not complete a separate application and are not simultaneously accepted to the LD program. A member of the LD program does not sit on the admissions committee. A personal interview is recommended. Essay is not required.

For fall 2004, 10 completed self-identified LD applications were received. 10 applications were offered admission, and 9 enrolled.

SECONDARY SCHOOL REQUIREMENTS

Graduation from secondary school required; GED accepted.

TESTING

ACT required; SAT Reasoning may be substituted. SAT Subject recommended.

All enrolled freshmen (fall 2004):

Average SAT I Scores:	Verbal: 528	Math: 488
Average ACT Scores:	Composite: 21	

Child Study Team report is not required. A neuropsychological or comprehensive psycho-educational evaluation is required for admission. Must be dated within 36 months of application. Tests required as part of this documentation:

- [x] WAIS-IV
- [x] WISC-IV
- [x] SATA
- [x] Woodcock-Johnson
- [x] Nelson-Denny Reading Test
- [x] Other

UNDERGRADUATE STUDENT BODY

Total undergraduate student enrollment: 402 Men, 525 Women.

Composition of student body (fall 2004):

	Undergraduate	Freshmen
International	3.7	1.6
Black	4.6	14.6
American Indian	0.9	0.2
Asian-American	0.9	1.3
Hispanic	0.9	1.3
White	88.1	79.0
Unreported	0.9	2.0
	100.0%	100.0%

14% are from out of state. 1% join a fraternity. 82% of classes have fewer than 20 students, 18% have between 20 and 50 students.

STUDENT HOUSING

Freshmen are required to live on campus. Housing is guaranteed for all undergraduates. Campus can house 338 undergraduates. Single rooms are available for students with medical or special needs. A medical note is required.

EXPENSES

Tuition (2005-06): $11,120 per year.

Room: $3,620. Board: $2,940.
There is no additional cost for LD program/services.

LD SERVICES

LD program size is not limited.

LD services available to:

- [x] Freshmen
- [x] Sophomores
- [x] Juniors
- [x] Seniors

Academic Accommodations

Curriculum

- [ ] Foreign language waiver
- [x] Lighter course load
- [ ] Math waiver
- [ ] Other special classes
- [ ] Priority registrations
- [ ] Substitution of courses

Exams

- [x] Extended time
- [x] Oral exams
- [ ] Take home exams
- [ ] Exams on tape or computer
- [x] Untimed exams
- [ ] Other accommodations

In class

- [ ] Early syllabus
- [x] Note takers in class
- [x] Priority seating
- [x] Tape recorders
- [ ] Videotaped classes
- [x] Text on tape

Services

- [ ] Diagnostic tests
- [ ] Learning centers
- [x] Proofreaders
- [ ] Readers
- [x] Reading Machines/Kurzweil
- [ ] Special bookstore section
- [ ] Typists

Credit toward degree is not given for remedial courses taken.

Counseling Services

- [x] Academic — Meets 2 times per academic year
- [ ] Psychological
- [x] Student Support groups — Meets 30 times per academic year
- [x] Vocational

Tutoring

Individual tutoring is available daily.

Average size of tutoring groups: 4

	Individual	Group
Time management	[x]	[x]
Organizational skills	[x]	[x]
Learning strategies	[x]	[x]
Study skills	[x]	[x]
Content area	[x]	[x]
Writing lab	[x]	[ ]
Math lab	[x]	[ ]

LD PROGRAM STAFF

Total number of LD Program staff (including director):

Full Time: 1 Part Time: 1

There is an advisor/advocate from the LD program available to students. 13 peer tutors are available to work with LD students.

Key staff person available to work with LD students: Janice Kern, Accommodations Officer.

Saginaw Valley State University

University Center, MI

Address: 7400 Bay Road, University Center, MI, 48710
Admissions telephone: 800 968-9500
Admissions FAX: 989 790-0180
Director of Admissions: James Dwyer
Admissions e-mail: admissions@svsu.edu
Web site: http://www.svsu.edu
SAT Code: 1766 ACT Code: 2057

LD program name: Disability Services
Director of Disability Services: Cynthia Woiderski
LD program telephone: 989 964-7000
LD program e-mail: clbw@svsu.edu
Total campus enrollment: 7,789

GENERAL

Saginaw Valley State University is a public, coed, four-year institution. 782-acre campus in University Center, 10 miles from Saginaw (population: 77,500). Airport serves Freeland (five miles); bus serves Saginaw; train serves Flint (45 miles). Public transportation serves campus. Semester system.

LD ADMISSIONS

Students do not complete a separate application and are not simultaneously accepted to the LD program. A personal interview is not required. Essay is not required.

SECONDARY SCHOOL REQUIREMENTS

Graduation from secondary school required; GED accepted. The following course distribution required: 4 units of English, 3 units of math, 2 units of science, 3 units of social studies.

TESTING

ACT required.

All enrolled freshmen (fall 2004):

Average ACT Scores: Composite: 21

Child Study Team report is not required. A neuropsychological or comprehensive psycho-educational evaluation is required for admission. Must be dated within 36 months of application. Tests required as part of this documentation:

- [x] WAIS-IV
- [ ] WISC-IV
- [ ] SATA
- [x] Woodcock-Johnson
- [ ] Nelson-Denny Reading Test
- [ ] Other

UNDERGRADUATE STUDENT BODY

Total undergraduate student enrollment: 2,931 Men, 4,389 Women.

Composition of student body (fall 2004):

	Undergraduate	Freshmen
International	1.6	3.0
Black	6.0	6.0
American Indian	0.4	0.3
Asian-American	0.8	0.7
Hispanic	1.7	2.2
White	85.8	83.3
Unreported	3.7	4.5
	100.0%	100.0%

Average age of full-time undergraduates is 22. 27% of classes have fewer than 20 students, 66% have between 20 and 50 students, 7% have more than 50 students.

STUDENT HOUSING

60% of freshmen live in college housing. Freshmen are not required to live on campus. Housing is guaranteed for all undergraduates. Campus can house 1,700 undergraduates. Single rooms are available for students with medical or special needs. A medical note is required.

EXPENSES

Tuition (2005-06): $4,877 per year (in-state), $11,486 (out-of-state). Room: $3,500. Board: $2,100.
There is no additional cost for LD program/services.

LD SERVICES

LD program size is not limited.

LD services available to:

- [x] Freshmen
- [x] Sophomores
- [x] Juniors
- [x] Seniors

Academic Accommodations

Curriculum		In class	
Foreign language waiver	[ ]	Early syllabus	[ ]
Lighter course load	[x]	Note takers in class	[ ]
Math waiver	[ ]	Priority seating	[ ]
Other special classes	[ ]	Tape recorders	[x]
Priority registrations	[ ]	Videotaped classes	[ ]
Substitution of courses	[ ]	Text on tape	[ ]
Exams		**Services**	
Extended time	[x]	Diagnostic tests	[ ]
Oral exams	[x]	Learning centers	[ ]
Take home exams	[ ]	Proofreaders	[ ]
Exams on tape or computer	[x]	Readers	[x]
Untimed exams	[ ]	Reading Machines/Kurzweil	[x]
Other accommodations	[ ]	Special bookstore section	[ ]
		Typists	[ ]

Counseling Services

- [ ] Academic
- [ ] Psychological
- [ ] Student Support groups
- [ ] Vocational

Tutoring

Individual tutoring is available weekly.

	Individual	Group
Time management	[ ]	[ ]
Organizational skills	[ ]	[ ]
Learning strategies	[ ]	[ ]
Study skills	[ ]	[ ]
Content area	[ ]	[ ]
Writing lab	[ ]	[ ]
Math lab	[ ]	[ ]

LD PROGRAM STAFF

Total number of LD Program staff (including director):

Full Time: 1 Part Time: 1

There is not an advisor/advocate from the LD program available to students.

Key staff person available to work with LD students: Cynthia Woiderski, Director of Disability Services.

LD Program web site: www.svsu.edu/disabilityservices

Spring Arbor University

Spring Arbor, MI

Address: 106 E. Main Street, Spring Arbor, MI, 49283-9799
Admissions telephone: 800 968-0011
Admissions FAX: 517 750-6620
Director of Enrollment Services: Randy Comfort
Admissions e-mail: admissions@arbor.edu
Web site: http://www.arbor.edu
SAT Code: 1732 ACT Code: 2056

Director of Learning Center: Carolee Hamilton
LD program telephone: 517 750-6479
LD program e-mail: caroleeh@arbor.edu
LD program enrollment: 7, Total campus enrollment: 2,510

GENERAL

Spring Arbor University is a private, coed, four-year institution. 120-acre campus in Spring Arbor (population: 2,188), eight miles from Jackson and 45 miles from Lansing. Major airport serves Detroit (70 miles); bus and train serve Jackson. Semester system.

LD ADMISSIONS

Students do not complete a separate application and are simultaneously accepted to the LD program. A member of the LD program does sit on the admissions committee. High school waivers are accepted for foreign language. A personal interview is recommended. Essay is not required.

For fall 2004, 10 completed self-identified LD applications were received. 10 applications were offered admission, and 6 enrolled.

SECONDARY SCHOOL REQUIREMENTS

Graduation from secondary school required; GED accepted. The following course distribution required: 4 units of English, 2 units of math, 2 units of science, 2 units of foreign language, 2 units of social studies.

TESTING

SAT Subject recommended.

All enrolled freshmen (fall 2004):

Average SAT I Scores:	Verbal: 534	Math: 529
Average ACT Scores:	Composite: 23	

Child Study Team report is not required. A neuropsychological or comprehensive psycho-educational evaluation is required for admission. Must be dated within 36 months of application. Tests required as part of this documentation:

- [x] WAIS-IV
- [x] WISC-IV
- [ ] SATA
- [x] Woodcock-Johnson
- [x] Nelson-Denny Reading Test
- [ ] Other

UNDERGRADUATE STUDENT BODY

Total undergraduate student enrollment: 713 Men, 1,430 Women.

Composition of student body (fall 2004):

	Undergraduate	Freshmen
International	2.3	0.9
Black	5.6	7.5
American Indian	0.0	0.4
Asian-American	1.3	0.9
Hispanic	3.0	1.8
White	87.5	83.4
Unreported	0.3	5.1
	100.0%	100.0%

12% are from out of state. 56% of classes have fewer than 20 students, 42% have between 20 and 50 students, 2% have more than 50 students.

STUDENT HOUSING

93% of freshmen live in college housing. Freshmen are required to live on campus. Housing is guaranteed for all undergraduates. Campus can house 919 undergraduates. Single rooms are not available for students with medical or special needs.

EXPENSES

Tuition (2005-06): $16,270 per year.
Room: $2,730. Board: $3,080.
There is no additional cost for LD program/services.

LD SERVICES

LD program size is not limited.

LD services available to:

- [x] Freshmen
- [x] Sophomores
- [x] Juniors
- [x] Seniors

Academic Accommodations

Curriculum		In class	
Foreign language waiver	[ ]	Early syllabus	[ ]
Lighter course load	[x]	Note takers in class	[x]
Math waiver	[ ]	Priority seating	[ ]
Other special classes	[ ]	Tape recorders	[x]
Priority registrations	[ ]	Videotaped classes	[ ]
Substitution of courses	[ ]	Text on tape	[ ]
Exams		**Services**	
Extended time	[x]	Diagnostic tests	[ ]
Oral exams	[x]	Learning centers	[x]
Take home exams	[ ]	Proofreaders	[ ]
Exams on tape or computer	[ ]	Readers	[x]
Untimed exams	[x]	Reading Machines/Kurzweil	[ ]
Other accommodations	[ ]	Special bookstore section	[ ]
		Typists	[ ]

Credit toward degree is given for remedial courses taken.

Counseling Services

- [x] Academic — Meets 2 times per academic year
- [ ] Psychological
- [x] Student Support groups — Meets 4 times per academic year
- [ ] Vocational

Tutoring

Individual tutoring is available.

Average size of tutoring groups: 3

	Individual	Group
Time management	[x]	[x]
Organizational skills	[x]	[x]
Learning strategies	[x]	[x]
Study skills	[x]	[x]
Content area	[x]	[ ]
Writing lab	[x]	[ ]
Math lab	[x]	[ ]

LD PROGRAM STAFF

Total number of LD Program staff (including director):

Full Time: 1 Part Time: 1

There is an advisor/advocate from the LD program available to students. The advisor/advocate meets with faculty 1 time per month and students 1 time per month. 6 peer tutors are available to work with LD students.

Key staff person available to work with LD students: Carolee Hamilton, Director of Learning Center.

Walsh College of Accountancy and Business Administration

Troy, MI

Address: PO Box 7006, Troy, MI, 48007-7006
Admissions telephone: 248 823-1610
Admissions FAX: 248 689-0938
Director of Admissions: Karen Mahaffey
Admissions e-mail: admissions@walshcollege.edu
Web site: http://www.walshcollege.edu
SAT Code: 372 ACT Code: 3349

Admissions/Academic Advisor: Kathy Bentley
LD program telephone: 248 823-1386
LD program e-mail: kbentley@walshcollege.edu
Total campus enrollment: 906

GENERAL

Walsh College of Accountancy and Business Administration is a private, coed, graduate institution. 20-acre, suburban campus in Troy (population: 80,959), 17 miles from Detroit; branch campuses in Clinton Township, Novi, and Port Huron. Major airports and bus serve Detroit; train serves Dearborn (25 miles). Public transportation serves campus. Semester system.

LD ADMISSIONS

A personal interview is recommended. Essay is not required.

TESTING

All enrolled freshmen (fall 2004):

Average SAT I Scores: Verbal: Math:
Average ACT Scores: Composite:

Child Study Team report is not required. Tests required as part of this documentation:

- ❑ WAIS-IV
- ❑ WISC-IV
- ❑ SATA
- ❑ Woodcock-Johnson
- ❑ Nelson-Denny Reading Test
- ❑ Other

UNDERGRADUATE STUDENT BODY

Total undergraduate student enrollment: 440 Men, 730 Women.

EXPENSES

Tuition (2005-06): $11,208 per year.

There is no additional cost for LD program/services.

LD SERVICES

LD program size is not limited.

LD services available to:

❑ Freshmen ❑ Sophomores ❑ Juniors ❑ Seniors

Academic Accommodations

Curriculum		In class	
Foreign language waiver	❑	Early syllabus	❑
Lighter course load	❑	Note takers in class	■
Math waiver	❑	Priority seating	❑
Other special classes	❑	Tape recorders	■
Priority registrations	❑	Videotaped classes	❑
Substitution of courses	❑	Text on tape	❑
Exams		**Services**	
Extended time	■	Diagnostic tests	❑
Oral exams	❑	Learning centers	❑
Take home exams	❑	Proofreaders	❑
Exams on tape or computer	❑	Readers	❑
Untimed exams	❑	Reading Machines/Kurzweil	❑
Other accommodations	❑	Special bookstore section	❑
		Typists	❑

Credit toward degree is not given for remedial courses taken.

Counseling Services

- ❑ Academic
- ❑ Psychological
- ❑ Student Support groups
- ❑ Vocational

Tutoring

	Individual	Group
Time management	❑	❑
Organizational skills	❑	❑
Learning strategies	❑	❑
Study skills	❑	❑
Content area	❑	❑
Writing lab	❑	❑
Math lab	❑	❑

LD PROGRAM STAFF

Key staff person available to work with LD students: Kathy Bentley, Admissions/Academic Advisor.

Wayne State University

Detroit, MI

Address: 656 W. Kirby, Detroit, MI, 48202
Admissions telephone: 313 577-3577
Admissions FAX: 313 577-7536
Director of Admissions: Susan Zwieg
Admissions e-mail: admissions@wayne.edu
Web site: http://www.wayne.edu/
SAT Code: 1898 ACT Code: 2064

LD program name: Educational Accessibility Services
LD program address: 1600 Undergraduate Library
Learning Specialist: Jane DePriester-Morandini
LD program telephone: 313 577-1851
LD program e-mail: AA7740@wayne.edu
Total campus enrollment: 20, 712

GENERAL

Wayne State University is a public, coed, four-year institution. 203-acre, urban campus in Detroit (population: 951,270); branch campuses in Macomb County and in Harper Woods and Oakland Center. Served by air, bus, and train. Public transportation serves campus. Semester system.

LD ADMISSIONS

Students do not complete a separate application and are not simultaneously accepted to the LD program. A member of the LD program does not sit on the admissions committee. A personal interview is not required. Essay is not required.

SECONDARY SCHOOL REQUIREMENTS

Graduation from secondary school required; GED accepted.

TESTING

All enrolled freshmen (fall 2004):

Average SAT I Scores: Verbal: Math:
Average ACT Scores: Composite: 20

Child Study Team report is not required. A neuropsychological or comprehensive psycho-educational evaluation is required for admission. Must be dated within 60 months of application. Tests required as part of this documentation:

- ■ WAIS-IV
- ■ WISC-IV
- ☐ SATA
- ☐ Woodcock-Johnson
- ☐ Nelson-Denny Reading Test
- ☐ Other

UNDERGRADUATE STUDENT BODY

Total undergraduate student enrollment: 7,381 Men, 11,108 Women.

Composition of student body (fall 2004):

	Undergraduate	Freshmen
International	3.2	4.4
Black	40.9	32.3
American Indian	0.4	0.5
Asian-American	6.0	5.3
Hispanic	3.3	2.6
White	39.8	47.5
Unreported	6.4	7.4
	100.0%	100.0%

1% are from out of state. 1% join a fraternity and 1% join a sorority. Average age of full-time undergraduates is 22. 47% of classes have fewer than 20 students, 48% have between 20 and 50 students, 5% have more than 50 students.

STUDENT HOUSING

29% of freshmen live in college housing. Freshmen are not required to live on campus. Housing is guaranteed for all undergraduates. Campus can house 1,229 undergraduates. Single rooms are available for students with medical or special needs. A medical note is required.

EXPENSES

Tuition (2005-06): $3,888 per year (state residents, lower division), $4,209 (state residents, upper division), $8,175 per year (out-of-state, lower division), $9,675 (out-of-state, upper division). (Tuition based on $118.90 per credit [in-state, lower division], $140.30 per credit [in-state, lower division], $272.50 per credit [out-of-state, upper division], and $322.50 per credit [out-of-state, upper division] for an estimated 30 credits per year.)

There is no additional cost for LD program/services.

LD SERVICES

LD program size is not limited.

LD services available to:

■ Freshmen ■ Sophomores ■ Juniors ■ Seniors

Academic Accommodations

Curriculum		**In class**	
Foreign language waiver	☐	Early syllabus	☐
Lighter course load	■	Note takers in class	■
Math waiver	☐	Priority seating	☐
Other special classes	☐	Tape recorders	■
Priority registrations	☐	Videotaped classes	☐
Substitution of courses	☐	Text on tape	■
Exams		**Services**	
Extended time	■	Diagnostic tests	■
Oral exams	☐	Learning centers	■
Take home exams	☐	Proofreaders	☐
Exams on tape or computer	■	Readers	☐
Untimed exams	■	Reading Machines/Kurzweil	■
Other accommodations	☐	Special bookstore section	☐
		Typists	☐

Credit toward degree is not given for remedial courses taken.

Counseling Services

- ☐ Academic
- ☐ Psychological
- ☐ Student Support groups
- ☐ Vocational

Tutoring

Individual tutoring is available weekly.

Average size of tutoring groups: 1

	Individual	Group
Time management	☐	■
Organizational skills	■	☐
Learning strategies	■	☐
Study skills	■	☐
Content area	■	☐
Writing lab	■	☐
Math lab	■	☐

LD PROGRAM STAFF

Total number of LD Program staff (including director):

Full Time: 6 Part Time: 6

There is an advisor/advocate from the LD program available to students. The advisor/advocate meets with students 3 times per month.

Key staff person available to work with LD students: Jane DePriester-Morandini, Learning Specialist.

LD Program web site: www.eas.wayne.edu

Western Michigan University

Kalamazoo, MI

Address: 1903 West Michigan Avenue, Kalamazoo, MI, 49008
Admissions telephone: 800 400-4968
Admissions FAX: 269 387-2096
Dean of Admissions and Orientation: Pam Liberacki
Admissions e-mail: ask-wmu@wmich.edu
Web site: http://www.wmich.edu
SAT Code: 1902 ACT Code: 2066

Assistant Director: Dorothy Fancher
LD program telephone: 269 387-4128
LD program e-mail: dorothy.fancher@wmich.edu
LD program enrollment: 111, Total campus enrollment: 22,502

GENERAL

Western Michigan University is a public, coed, four-year institution. 541-acre campus in Kalamazoo (population: 77,145), 145 miles from both Chicago and Detroit; branch campuses in Battle Creek, Benton Harbor, Grand Rapids, Lansing, Muskegon, and Traverse City. Served by air, bus, and train. Public transportation serves campus. Semester system.

LD ADMISSIONS

Students do not complete a separate application and are not simultaneously accepted to the LD program. A member of the LD program does not sit on the admissions committee. A personal interview is not required. Essay is not required.

SECONDARY SCHOOL REQUIREMENTS

Graduation from secondary school required; GED accepted. The following course distribution required: 4 units of English, 3 units of math, 2 units of science, 1 unit of foreign language, 2 units of social studies, 1 unit of history, 2 units of academic electives.

TESTING

All enrolled freshmen (fall 2004):

Average ACT Scores: Composite: 22

Child Study Team report is not required. A neuropsychological or comprehensive psycho-educational evaluation is required for admission. Tests required as part of this documentation:

☑ WAIS-IV	☑ Woodcock-Johnson
☑ WISC-IV	☐ Nelson-Denny Reading Test
☑ SATA	☑ Other

UNDERGRADUATE STUDENT BODY

Total undergraduate student enrollment: 11,145 Men, 12,011 Women.

Composition of student body (fall 2004):

	Undergraduate	Freshmen
International	1.6	2.8
Black	6.8	5.5
American Indian	0.4	0.4
Asian-American	1.8	1.4
Hispanic	2.3	2.0
White	87.1	87.7
Unreported	0.0	0.2
	100.0%	100.0%

6% are from out of state. 8% join a fraternity and 8% join a sorority. Average age of full-time undergraduates is 21. 40% of classes have fewer than 20 students, 48% have between 20 and 50 students, 12% have more than 50 students.

STUDENT HOUSING

89% of freshmen live in college housing. Freshmen are not required to live on campus. Housing is guaranteed for all undergraduates. Campus can house 6,200 undergraduates. Single rooms are available for students with medical or special needs. A medical note is not required.

EXPENSES

Tuition 2004-05: $5,668 per year (in-state), $13,823 (out-of-state).

Room & Board: $6,496.

There is no additional cost for LD program/services.

LD SERVICES

LD program size is not limited.

LD services available to:

☑ Freshmen ☑ Sophomores ☑ Juniors ☑ Seniors

Academic Accommodations

Curriculum		In class	
Foreign language waiver	☐	Early syllabus	☐
Lighter course load	☑	Note takers in class	☐
Math waiver	☐	Priority seating	☑
Other special classes	☐	Tape recorders	☑
Priority registrations	☑	Videotaped classes	☐
Substitution of courses	☑	Text on tape	☑
Exams		**Services**	
Extended time	☑	Diagnostic tests	☐
Oral exams	☐	Learning centers	☑
Take home exams	☐	Proofreaders	☐
Exams on tape or computer	☑	Readers	☑
Untimed exams	☐	Reading Machines/Kurzweil	☑
Other accommodations	☑	Special bookstore section	☐
		Typists	☐

Credit toward degree is not given for remedial courses taken.

Counseling Services

☑ Academic
☑ Psychological
☐ Student Support groups
☐ Vocational

Tutoring

Individual tutoring is not available.

	Individual	Group
Time management	☑	☑
Organizational skills	☑	☐
Learning strategies	☑	☑
Study skills	☑	☑
Content area	☑	☑
Writing lab	☑	☐
Math lab	☑	☐

LD PROGRAM STAFF

Total number of LD Program staff (including director):

Full Time: 3 Part Time: 3

There is an advisor/advocate from the LD program available to students.

Key staff person available to work with LD students: Beth DenHartigh, Director.

LD Program web site: www.dsrs.wmich.edu

Augsburg College

Minneapolis, MN

Address: 2211 Riverside Avenue South, Minneapolis, MN, 55454
Admissions telephone: 800 788-5678
Admissions FAX: 612 330-1590
Director of Admissions: Sally Daniels
Admissions e-mail: admissions@augsburg.edu
Web site: http://www.augsburg.edu
SAT Code: 6014 ACT Code: 2080

LD program name: Center for Learning and Adaptive Student Services
LD program address: Campus Box 57
CLASS Program Assistant: Emily Nugent
LD program telephone: 612 330-1053
LD program e-mail: class@augsburg.edu
LD program enrollment: 77, Total campus enrollment: 2,916

GENERAL

Augsburg College is a private, coed, four-year institution. 23-acre campus in Minneapolis (Twin Cities population: 669,769), one mile from downtown area. Served by air, bus, and train. School operates transportation to consortium schools. Public transportation serves campus. Semester system.

LD ADMISSIONS

Students complete a separate application and are not simultaneously accepted to the LD program. A member of the LD program does not sit on the admissions committee. A personal interview is recommended. Essay is required and may be typed.

For fall 2004, 38 completed self-identified LD applications were received. 32 applications were offered admission, and 29 enrolled.

SECONDARY SCHOOL REQUIREMENTS

Graduation from secondary school required; GED accepted. The following course distribution required: 4 units of English, 3 units of math, 3 units of science, 2 units of foreign language, 3 units of social studies.

TESTING

All enrolled freshmen (fall 2004):

Average SAT I Scores: Verbal: 559 Math: 548
Average ACT Scores: Composite: 23

Child Study Team report is not required. A neuropsychological or comprehensive psycho-educational evaluation is required for admission. Must be dated within 36 months of application. Tests required as part of this documentation:

- [x] WAIS-IV
- [ ] WISC-IV
- [ ] SATA
- [x] Woodcock-Johnson
- [ ] Nelson-Denny Reading Test
- [ ] Other

UNDERGRADUATE STUDENT BODY

Total undergraduate student enrollment: 1,163 Men, 1,617 Women.

Composition of student body (fall 2004):

	Undergraduate	Freshmen
International	2.2	1.3
Black	4.4	5.2
American Indian	0.3	1.2
Asian-American	4.4	3.1
Hispanic	1.7	1.5
White	85.9	68.1
Unreported	1.1	19.6
	100.0%	100.0%

10% are from out of state. Average age of full-time undergraduates is 24. 63% of classes have fewer than 20 students, 37% have between 20 and 50 students.

STUDENT HOUSING

84% of freshmen live in college housing. Housing is guaranteed for all undergraduates. Campus can house 950 undergraduates. Single rooms are available for students with medical or special needs. A medical note is required.

EXPENSES

Tuition (2005-06): $21,460 per year. Tuition varies for weekend college program.

Room: $3,250. Board: $3,090.

There is no additional cost for LD program/services.

LD SERVICES

LD program size is not limited.

LD services available to:

- [x] Freshmen
- [x] Sophomores
- [x] Juniors
- [x] Seniors

Academic Accommodations

Curriculum

- [ ] Foreign language waiver
- [ ] Lighter course load
- [ ] Math waiver
- [ ] Other special classes
- [ ] Priority registrations
- [ ] Substitution of courses

Exams

- [x] Extended time
- [x] Oral exams
- [ ] Take home exams
- [ ] Exams on tape or computer
- [ ] Untimed exams
- [x] Other accommodations

In class

- [ ] Early syllabus
- [x] Note takers in class
- [ ] Priority seating
- [x] Tape recorders
- [ ] Videotaped classes
- [x] Text on tape

Services

- [ ] Diagnostic tests
- [x] Learning centers
- [ ] Proofreaders
- [x] Readers
- [x] Reading Machines/Kurzweil
- [ ] Special bookstore section
- [x] Typists

Credit toward degree is not given for remedial courses taken.

Counseling Services

- [x] Academic — Meets 30 times per academic year
- [ ] Psychological
- [ ] Student Support groups
- [ ] Vocational

Tutoring

Individual tutoring is available weekly.

Average size of tutoring groups: 4

	Individual	Group
Time management	[x]	[ ]
Organizational skills	[x]	[ ]
Learning strategies	[x]	[ ]
Study skills	[x]	[ ]
Content area	[ ]	[ ]
Writing lab	[x]	[ ]
Math lab	[x]	[ ]

UNIQUE LD PROGRAM FEATURES

CLASS provides accommodations and academic support to students with a broad range of specific cognitive and psychological disabilities, including dyslexia, ADHD, and Asperger syndrome, psychiatric disabilities, anxiety disorder, depression and PTSD, and those with acquired or developmental neurological conditions. Students whose disabilities are primarily physical or sensory in nature are served by a separate program, the Access Center. Full-time disability specialists are available to design an appropriate accommodation plan which might include a classroom note-taker, taped text, extended testing time, reduced distraction testing environment, use of a computer for testing, or a test reader. Students have access to the Groves Computer Lab. Our assistive technology programs include the Kurzweil 3000 text-to-speech system, Dragon Naturally Speaking dictation software, and recorded text from Recordings for the Blind and Dyslexic. Students are responsible for providing their own playback devices for RFB&D tapes and CDs.

LD PROGRAM STAFF

Total number of LD Program staff (including director):

Full Time: 6 Part Time: 6

Bemidji State University

Bemidji, MN

Address: 1500 Birchmont Drive NE, Bemidji, MN, 56601
Admissions telephone: 888 345-1721
Admissions FAX: 218 755-2074
Director of Admissions: Russ Kreager
Admissions e-mail: admissions@bemidjistate.edu
Web site: http://www.bemidjistate.edu
SAT Code: 6676 ACT Code: 2084

LD program name: Disability Services
Coordinator, Disabilities Services Office: Kathi Hagen
LD program telephone: 218 755-3883
LD program e-mail: khagen@bemidjistate.edu
Total campus enrollment: 4,554

GENERAL

Bemidji State University is a public, coed, four-year institution. 90-acre campus in Bemidji (population: 11,917), 100 miles from Grand Forks, N.Dak.; branch campuses in Hibbing and abroad in Akita, Japan. Served by air and bus. Public transportation serves campus. Semester system.

LD ADMISSIONS

Students do not complete a separate application and are not simultaneously accepted to the LD program. A member of the LD program does not sit on the admissions committee. High school waivers are accepted for foreign language. A personal interview is recommended. Essay is not required.

SECONDARY SCHOOL REQUIREMENTS

Graduation from secondary school required; GED accepted. The following course distribution required: 4 units of English, 3 units of math, 3 units of science, 2 units of foreign language, 3 units of social studies, 1 unit of history.

TESTING

ACT required.

Child Study Team report is not required. A neuropsychological or comprehensive psycho-educational evaluation is required for admission. Must be dated within 36 months of application. Tests required as part of this documentation:

- ☑ WAIS-IV
- ☑ WISC-IV
- ☐ SATA
- ☑ Woodcock-Johnson
- ☐ Nelson-Denny Reading Test
- ☐ Other

UNDERGRADUATE STUDENT BODY

Total undergraduate student enrollment: 1,889 Men, 2,585 Women.

7% are from out of state. Average age of full-time undergraduates is 24. 58% of classes have fewer than 20 students, 39% have between 20 and 50 students, 3% have more than 50 students.

STUDENT HOUSING

50% of freshmen live in college housing. Freshmen are not required to live on campus. Housing is guaranteed for all undergraduates. Campus can house 1,500 undergraduates. Single rooms are available for students with medical or special needs. A medical note is required.

EXPENSES

Tuition (2005-06): $5,294 per year.
Room: $3,368. Board: $1,798.
There is no additional cost for LD program/services.

LD SERVICES

LD program size is not limited.

LD services available to:

☑ Freshmen ☑ Sophomores ☑ Juniors ☑ Seniors

Academic Accommodations

Curriculum		In class	
Foreign language waiver	☐	Early syllabus	☑
Lighter course load	☑	Note takers in class	☑
Math waiver	☐	Priority seating	☑
Other special classes	☐	Tape recorders	☑
Priority registrations	☑	Videotaped classes	☐
Substitution of courses	☑	Text on tape	☑
Exams		**Services**	
Extended time	☑	Diagnostic tests	☐
Oral exams	☑	Learning centers	☐
Take home exams	☐	Proofreaders	☑
Exams on tape or computer	☑	Readers	☑
Untimed exams	☐	Reading Machines/Kurzweil	☑
Other accommodations	☑	Special bookstore section	☐
		Typists	☑

Credit toward degree is not given for remedial courses taken.

Counseling Services

- ☑ Academic
- ☑ Psychological
- ☐ Student Support groups
- ☐ Vocational

Tutoring

Individual tutoring is available daily.

Average size of tutoring groups: 1

	Individual	Group
Time management	☑	☑
Organizational skills	☑	☑
Learning strategies	☑	☑
Study skills	☑	☑
Content area	☐	☐
Writing lab	☑	☐
Math lab	☐	☐

LD PROGRAM STAFF

Total number of LD Program staff (including director):

Full Time: 2 Part Time: 2

There is an advisor/advocate from the LD program available to students. 10 peer tutors are available to work with LD students.

Key staff person available to work with LD students: Kathi Hagen, Coordinator, Disability Services Office.

Bethel University

St. Paul, MN

Address: 3900 Bethel Drive, St. Paul, MN, 55112
Admissions telephone: 800 255-8706
Admissions FAX: 651 635-1490
Director of Admissions: Jay Fedje
Admissions e-mail: BUadmissions-cas@bethel.edu
Web site: http://www.bethel.edu
SAT Code: 6038 ACT Code: 2088

LD program name: Office of Diversity Services
Director of Disability Services: Kathy McGillivray
LD program telephone: 651 635-8759
LD program e-mail: k-mcgillivray@bethel.edu
LD program enrollment: 75, Total campus enrollment: 3,051

GENERAL

Bethel University is a private, coed, four-year institution. 231-acre, suburban campus in Arden Hills (population: 9,652), 10 miles from Minneapolis-St. Paul. Airport, bus, and train serve Minneapolis-St. Paul. School operates transportation to college-owned apartments, local shopping centers, and mass transit connections. 4-1-4 system.

LD ADMISSIONS

Students do not complete a separate application and are not simultaneously accepted to the LD program. A member of the LD program does not sit on the admissions committee. A personal interview is recommended. Essay is required and may be typed.

SECONDARY SCHOOL REQUIREMENTS

Graduation from secondary school required; GED accepted.

TESTING

SAT Reasoning or ACT required.

All enrolled freshmen (fall 2004):

Average SAT I Scores:	Verbal: 592	Math: 592
Average ACT Scores:	Composite: 25	

Child Study Team report is not required. A neuropsychological or comprehensive psycho-educational evaluation is required for admission. Tests required as part of this documentation:

- ■ WAIS-IV
- ■ WISC-IV
- ■ SATA
- ■ Woodcock-Johnson
- ■ Nelson-Denny Reading Test
- ■ Other

UNDERGRADUATE STUDENT BODY

Total undergraduate student enrollment: 1,053 Men, 1,647 Women.

Composition of student body (fall 2004):

	Undergraduate	Freshmen
International	0.4	0.5
Black	1.8	1.9
American Indian	0.6	0.3
Asian-American	3.1	2.7
Hispanic	1.9	1.3
White	92.2	93.3
Unreported	0.0	0.0
	100.0%	100.0%

29% are from out of state. Average age of full-time undergraduates is 20. 42% of classes have fewer than 20 students, 54% have between 20 and 50 students, 5% have more than 50 students.

STUDENT HOUSING

97% of freshmen live in college housing. Freshmen are required to live on campus. Housing is guaranteed for all undergraduates. Campus can house 2,169 undergraduates. Single rooms are available for students with medical or special needs. A medical note is required.

EXPENSES

Tuition (2005-06): $21,190 per year.
Room: $4,020. Board: $2,780.
There is no additional cost for LD program/services.

LD SERVICES

LD program size is not limited.

LD services available to:

■ Freshmen ■ Sophomores ■ Juniors ■ Seniors

Academic Accommodations

Curriculum		**In class**	
Foreign language waiver	☐	Early syllabus	■
Lighter course load	■	Note takers in class	■
Math waiver	☐	Priority seating	■
Other special classes	☐	Tape recorders	■
Priority registrations	■	Videotaped classes	☐
Substitution of courses	■	Text on tape	■
Exams		**Services**	
Extended time	■	Diagnostic tests	☐
Oral exams	■	Learning centers	■
Take home exams	☐	Proofreaders	☐
Exams on tape or computer	■	Readers	■
Untimed exams	☐	Reading Machines/Kurzweil	■
Other accommodations	■	Special bookstore section	☐
		Typists	■

Credit toward degree is not given for remedial courses taken.

Counseling Services

- ■ Academic
- ☐ Psychological
- ☐ Student Support groups
- ☐ Vocational

Tutoring

Individual tutoring is available.

	Individual	Group
Time management	■	☐
Organizational skills	■	☐
Learning strategies	■	■
Study skills	☐	☐
Content area	■	☐
Writing lab	■	☐
Math lab	■	☐

UNIQUE LD PROGRAM FEATURES

The Disability Services Office serves physical, psychiatric, and learning disabilities.

LD PROGRAM STAFF

Total number of LD Program staff (including director):

Full Time: 1 Part Time: 1

There is an advisor/advocate from the LD program available to students.

Key staff person available to work with LD students: Kathy McGillivray, Director of Disability Services.

LD Program web site: www.bethel.edu/disability

Carleton College

Northfield, MN

Address: 1 N. College Street, Northfield, MN, 55057
Admissions telephone: 800 995-2275
Admissions FAX: 507 646-4526
Dean of Admissions: Paul Thiboutot
Admissions e-mail: admissions@acs.carleton.edu
Web site: http://www.carleton.edu
SAT Code: 6081 ACT Code: 2092

Coordinator of Disability Services for Students: Sue Keesey
LD program e-mail: skeesey@acs.carleton.edu
Total campus enrollment: 1,951

GENERAL

Carleton College is a private, coed, four-year institution. 955-acre campus in Northfield (population: 17,147), 35 miles south of Minneapolis-St. Paul. Airport serves Minneapolis-St. Paul; bus serves Faribault (15 miles); train serves Red Wing (25 miles). School operates transportation in Northfield and to Minneapolis-St. Paul. Public transportation serves campus. Trimester system.

LD ADMISSIONS

Students do not complete a separate application and are not simultaneously accepted to the LD program. A member of the LD program does not sit on the admissions committee.

SECONDARY SCHOOL REQUIREMENTS

Graduation from secondary school required; GED accepted.

TESTING

SAT Reasoning or ACT required. SAT Subject required.

Child Study Team report is not required. A neuropsychological or comprehensive psycho-educational evaluation is required for admission. Tests required as part of this documentation:

- [x] WAIS-IV
- [x] WISC-IV
- [ ] SATA
- [x] Woodcock-Johnson
- [x] Nelson-Denny Reading Test
- [x] Other

UNDERGRADUATE STUDENT BODY

Total undergraduate student enrollment: 927 Men, 1,021 Women.

Composition of student body (fall 2004):

	Undergraduate	Freshmen
International	5.1	4.9
Black	5.5	5.6
American Indian	0.6	0.6
Asian-American	10.1	9.3
Hispanic	5.7	4.4
White	73.0	75.2
Unreported	0.0	0.0
	100.0%	100.0%

77% are from out of state. Average age of full-time undergraduates is 20. 66% of classes have fewer than 20 students, 33% have between 20 and 50 students, 1% have more than 50 students.

STUDENT HOUSING

100% of freshmen live in college housing. Freshmen are required to live on campus. Housing is guaranteed for all undergraduates. Campus can house 1,627 undergraduates. Single rooms are available for students with medical or special needs. A medical note is required.

EXPENSES

Tuition (2005-06): $32,460 per year.
Room: $3,738. Board: $4,080.

There is no additional cost for LD program/services.

LD SERVICES

LD program size is not limited.

LD services available to:

[x] Freshmen [x] Sophomores [x] Juniors [x] Seniors

Academic Accommodations

Curriculum		**In class**	
Foreign language waiver	[x]	Early syllabus	[x]
Lighter course load	[ ]	Note takers in class	[x]
Math waiver	[ ]	Priority seating	[ ]
Other special classes	[ ]	Tape recorders	[x]
Priority registrations	[ ]	Videotaped classes	[ ]
Substitution of courses	[x]	Text on tape	[x]
Exams		**Services**	
Extended time	[x]	Diagnostic tests	[x]
Oral exams	[ ]	Learning centers	[x]
Take home exams	[ ]	Proofreaders	[ ]
Exams on tape or computer	[x]	Readers	[ ]
Untimed exams	[ ]	Reading Machines/Kurzweil	[x]
Other accommodations	[x]	Special bookstore section	[ ]
		Typists	[ ]

Credit toward degree is not given for remedial courses taken.

Counseling Services

- [x] Academic
- [x] Psychological
- [ ] Student Support groups
- [ ] Vocational

Tutoring

Individual tutoring is available daily.

Average size of tutoring groups: 1

	Individual	Group
Time management	[x]	[ ]
Organizational skills	[x]	[ ]
Learning strategies	[x]	[ ]
Study skills	[x]	[ ]
Content area	[x]	[x]
Writing lab	[x]	[x]
Math lab	[x]	[x]

LD PROGRAM STAFF

Total number of LD Program staff (including director):

Full Time: 1 Part Time: 1

There is an advisor/advocate from the LD program available to students.

Key staff person available to work with LD students: Sue Keesey, Coordinator of Disability Services for Students.

College of Saint Benedict

St. Joseph, MN

Address: 37 S. College Avenue, St. Joseph, MN, 56374
Admissions telephone: 800 544-1489
Admissions FAX: 320 363-2750
Dean of Admissions: Mary Milbert
Admissions e-mail: admissions@csbsju.edu
Web site: http://www.csbsju.edu
SAT Code: 6104 ACT Code: 2140

Associate Director of Academic Advising: Michelle Sauer
LD program telephone: 320 363-5687
LD program e-mail: msauer@csbsju.edu
Total campus enrollment: 2,033

GENERAL

College of Saint Benedict is a private, women's, four-year institution. 315-acre campus in St. Joseph (population: 5,000), 75 miles from Minneapolis-St. Paul. Served by bus; major airport serves Minneapolis-St. Paul; smaller airport and train serve St. Cloud (20 miles). School operates transportation to St. John's U and to St. Cloud and St. Joseph. Semester system.

LD ADMISSIONS

A personal interview is recommended. Essay is required and may be typed.

SECONDARY SCHOOL REQUIREMENTS

Graduation from secondary school required; GED accepted.

TESTING

SAT Reasoning or ACT required. SAT Subject recommended.

All enrolled freshmen (fall 2004):

Average SAT I Scores:	Verbal: 590	Math: 593
Average ACT Scores:	Composite: 25	

Child Study Team report is not required. Tests required as part of this documentation:

- [ ] WAIS-IV
- [ ] WISC-IV
- [ ] SATA
- [ ] Woodcock-Johnson
- [ ] Nelson-Denny Reading Test
- [ ] Other

UNDERGRADUATE STUDENT BODY

Total undergraduate student enrollment: 2,100 Women.

Composition of student body (fall 2004):

	Undergraduate	Freshmen
International	1.7	3.3
Black	0.6	0.5
American Indian	0.0	0.0
Asian-American	2.7	2.2
Hispanic	1.2	1.0
White	93.8	93.0
Unreported	0.0	0.0
	100.0%	100.0%

14% are from out of state. Average age of full-time undergraduates is 20. 52% of classes have fewer than 20 students, 48% have between 20 and 50 students.

STUDENT HOUSING

99% of freshmen live in college housing. Freshmen are required to live on campus. Housing is guaranteed for all undergraduates. Campus can house 1,532 undergraduates. Single rooms are available for students with medical or special needs.

EXPENSES

Tuition (2005-06): $23,064 per year.
Room: $3,419. Board: $3,218.

There is no additional cost for LD program/services.

LD SERVICES

LD program size is not limited.

LD services available to:

- [x] Freshmen
- [x] Sophomores
- [x] Juniors
- [x] Seniors

Academic Accommodations

Curriculum		In class	
Foreign language waiver	[ ]	Early syllabus	[ ]
Lighter course load	[ ]	Note takers in class	[ ]
Math waiver	[ ]	Priority seating	[ ]
Other special classes	[ ]	Tape recorders	[ ]
Priority registrations	[ ]	Videotaped classes	[ ]
Substitution of courses	[ ]	Text on tape	[ ]
Exams		**Services**	
Extended time	[x]	Diagnostic tests	[ ]
Oral exams	[ ]	Learning centers	[ ]
Take home exams	[ ]	Proofreaders	[ ]
Exams on tape or computer	[ ]	Readers	[ ]
Untimed exams	[x]	Reading Machines/Kurzweil	[x]
Other accommodations	[ ]	Special bookstore section	[ ]
		Typists	[ ]

Credit toward degree is not given for remedial courses taken.

Counseling Services

- [ ] Academic
- [ ] Psychological
- [ ] Student Support groups
- [ ] Vocational

Tutoring

Individual tutoring is available.

	Individual	Group
Time management	[ ]	[ ]
Organizational skills	[ ]	[ ]
Learning strategies	[ ]	[ ]
Study skills	[x]	[ ]
Content area	[ ]	[ ]
Writing lab	[x]	[ ]
Math lab	[x]	[ ]

UNIQUE LD PROGRAM FEATURES

LD services are coordinated through the Academic Advising Department. While our disability services are limited, we are committed to providing academic accommodations on a case-by-case basis for enrolled students who provide adequate documentation of a disability.

LD PROGRAM STAFF

Key staff person available to work with LD students: Michelle Sauer, Associate Director of Academic Advising.

Concordia College (Minnesota)

Moorhead, MN

Address: 901 Eighth Street S, Moorhead, MN, 56562
Admissions telephone: 800 699-9897
Admissions FAX: 218 299-4720
Director of Admissions: Scott Ellingson
Admissions e-mail: admissions@cord.edu
Web site: http://www.cord.edu
SAT Code: 6113 ACT Code: 2104

Director of the Counseling Center: Monica Kersting
LD program telephone: 218 299-3514
LD program e-mail: kersting@cord.edu
LD program enrollment: 18, Total campus enrollment: 2,812

GENERAL

Concordia College (Minnesota) is a private, coed, four-year institution. 120-acre campus in Moorhead (population 32,177), one mile from Fargo, ND Served by bus; airport and train serve Fargo. School operates transportation to Fargo and consortium colleges. Public transportation serves campus. Semester system.

LD ADMISSIONS

Students do not complete a separate application and are simultaneously accepted to the LD program. A member of the LD program does not sit on the admissions committee. A personal interview is recommended. Essay is not required.

SECONDARY SCHOOL REQUIREMENTS

Graduation from secondary school required; GED accepted.

TESTING

SAT Reasoning or ACT required. SAT Subject recommended.

All enrolled freshmen (fall 2004):

Average SAT I Scores:	Verbal: 582	Math: 582
Average ACT Scores:	Composite: 24	

Child Study Team report is required if student is classified. A neuropsychological or comprehensive psycho-educational evaluation is required for admission. Must be dated within 36 months of application. Tests required as part of this documentation:

- ☒ WAIS-IV
- ☐ WISC-IV
- ☒ SATA
- ☒ Woodcock-Johnson
- ☒ Nelson-Denny Reading Test
- ☐ Other

UNDERGRADUATE STUDENT BODY

Total undergraduate student enrollment: 1,048 Men, 1,718 Women.

Composition of student body (fall 2004):

	Undergraduate	Freshmen
International	2.3	4.9
Black	0.9	0.7
American Indian	0.8	0.4
Asian-American	2.0	1.6
Hispanic	1.3	0.9
White	91.5	90.6
Unreported	1.2	0.9
	100.0%	100.0%

40% are from out of state. 44% of classes have fewer than 20 students, 54% have between 20 and 50 students, 2% have more than 50 students.

STUDENT HOUSING

Freshmen are required to live on campus. Housing is guaranteed for all undergraduates. Campus can house 1,853 undergraduates. Single rooms are available for students with medical or special needs. A medical note is required.

EXPENSES

Tuition (2005-06): $19,366 per year.

Room: $2,300. Board: $2,690.
There is no additional cost for LD program/services.

LD SERVICES

LD program size is not limited.

LD services available to:

☒ Freshmen ☒ Sophomores ☒ Juniors ☒ Seniors

Academic Accommodations

Curriculum		**In class**	
Foreign language waiver	☐	Early syllabus	☐
Lighter course load	☒	Note takers in class	☒
Math waiver	☐	Priority seating	☒
Other special classes	☐	Tape recorders	☒
Priority registrations	☒	Videotaped classes	☐
Substitution of courses	☐	Text on tape	☒
Exams		**Services**	
Extended time	☒	Diagnostic tests	☐
Oral exams	☐	Learning centers	☒
Take home exams	☐	Proofreaders	☒
Exams on tape or computer	☒	Readers	☒
Untimed exams	☐	Reading Machines/Kurzweil	☒
Other accommodations	☐	Special bookstore section	☐
		Typists	☒

Credit toward degree is not given for remedial courses taken.

Counseling Services

- ☒ Academic
- ☒ Psychological
- ☐ Student Support groups
- ☒ Vocational

Tutoring

Individual tutoring is available daily.

Average size of tutoring groups: 3

	Individual	Group
Time management	☒	☐
Organizational skills	☒	☐
Learning strategies	☒	☐
Study skills	☒	☐
Content area	☒	☐
Writing lab	☒	☐
Math lab	☐	☐

LD PROGRAM STAFF

Total number of LD Program staff (including director):

Full Time: 1 Part Time: 1

There is an advisor/advocate from the LD program available to students.

Key staff person available to work with LD students: Monica Kersting, Director of the Counseling Center.

Concordia University, St. Paul

St. Paul, MN

Address: 275 Syndicate Street N, St. Paul, MN, 55104-5494
Admissions telephone: 800 333-4705
Admissions FAX: 651 603-6320
Director of Freshmen Admissions: Thomas Larson
Admissions e-mail: admiss@csp.edu
Web site: http://www.csp.edu
SAT Code: 6114 ACT Code: 2106

Disabilities Specialist: Melissa Fletcher
LD program telephone: 651 641-8272
LD program e-mail: fletcher@csp.edu
Total campus enrollment: 1,835

GENERAL

Concordia University, St. Paul is a private, coed, four-year institution. 37-acre, urban campus in St. Paul (Twin Cities population: 669,769). Served by air, bus, and train. Public transportation serves campus. Semester system.

LD ADMISSIONS

A personal interview is recommended. Essay is not required.

SECONDARY SCHOOL REQUIREMENTS

Graduation from secondary school required; GED accepted. The following course distribution required: 4 units of English, 2 units of math, 2 units of science, 1 unit of social studies, 1 unit of history.

TESTING

SAT Reasoning considered if submitted. ACT required.

All enrolled freshmen (fall 2004):

Average SAT I Scores: Verbal: 530 Math: 550
Average ACT Scores: Composite: 22

Child Study Team report is not required. Tests required as part of this documentation:

☐ WAIS-IV ☐ Woodcock-Johnson
☐ WISC-IV ☐ Nelson-Denny Reading Test
☐ SATA ☐ Other

UNDERGRADUATE STUDENT BODY

Total undergraduate student enrollment: 605 Men, 906 Women.

Composition of student body (fall 2004):

	Undergraduate	Freshmen
International	1.1	0.6
Black	8.0	6.5
American Indian	1.1	0.5
Asian-American	9.7	4.6
Hispanic	1.1	1.4
White	71.6	68.7
Unreported	7.4	17.7
	100.0%	100.0%

25% are from out of state. Average age of full-time undergraduates is 26. 81% of classes have fewer than 20 students, 19% have between 20 and 50 students.

STUDENT HOUSING

78% of freshmen live in college housing. Housing is guaranteed for all undergraduates. Campus can house 480 undergraduates.

EXPENSES

Tuition (2005-06): $21,312 per year. For students in non-traditional adult degree completion programs, tuition is $220, $242, or $299 per credit hour.

Room & Board: $6,464-$6,464.
There is no additional cost for LD program/services.

LD SERVICES

LD program size is not limited.

LD services available to:

☐ Freshmen ☐ Sophomores ☐ Juniors ☐ Seniors

Academic Accommodations

Curriculum		**In class**	
Foreign language waiver	☐	Early syllabus	☐
Lighter course load	☐	Note takers in class	■
Math waiver	☐	Priority seating	☐
Other special classes	☐	Tape recorders	■
Priority registrations	☐	Videotaped classes	■
Substitution of courses	☐	Text on tape	☐
Exams		**Services**	
Extended time	■	Diagnostic tests	☐
Oral exams	■	Learning centers	■
Take home exams	☐	Proofreaders	☐
Exams on tape or computer	☐	Readers	■
Untimed exams	■	Reading Machines/Kurzweil	■
Other accommodations	☐	Special bookstore section	☐
		Typists	☐

Credit toward degree is not given for remedial courses taken.

Counseling Services

☐ Academic
☐ Psychological
☐ Student Support groups
☐ Vocational

Tutoring

	Individual	Group
Time management	☐	☐
Organizational skills	☐	☐
Learning strategies	☐	☐
Study skills	☐	☐
Content area	☐	☐
Writing lab	☐	☐
Math lab	☐	☐

LD PROGRAM STAFF

Total number of LD Program staff (including director):

Full Time: 1 Part Time: 1

Key staff person available to work with LD students: Melissa Fletcher, Disabilities Specialist.

Crown College

St. Bonifacius, MN

Address: 8700 College View Drive, St. Bonifacius, MN, 55375
Admissions telephone: 800 68-CROWN
Admissions FAX: 952 446-4149
Vice President of Enrollment Services: Mitch Fisk
Admissions e-mail: info@crown.edu
Web site: http://www.crown.edu
SAT Code: 6639 ACT Code: 2152

LD program name: Crown Study Lab
Director of Academic Success: Don Bouchard
LD program telephone: 952 446-4216
LD program e-mail: bouchardd@crown.edu
LD program enrollment: 6, Total campus enrollment: 1,047

GENERAL

Crown College is a private, coed, four-year institution. 193-acre campus in St. Bonifacius (population: 1,873), 20 miles from Minneapolis-St. Paul. Major airport and bus serve Minneapolis; train serves St. Paul. Semester system.

LD ADMISSIONS

Students do not complete a separate application and are not simultaneously accepted to the LD program. A member of the LD program does not sit on the admissions committee. A personal interview is recommended. Essay is required and may be typed.

For fall 2004, 10 completed self-identified LD applications were received.

SECONDARY SCHOOL REQUIREMENTS

Graduation from secondary school required; GED accepted.

TESTING

SAT Subject recommended.

All enrolled freshmen (fall 2004):

Average SAT I Scores:	Verbal: 512	Math: 497
Average ACT Scores:	Composite: 22	

Child Study Team report is required if student is classified. A neuropsychological or comprehensive psycho-educational evaluation is required for admission. Tests required as part of this documentation:

- [x] WAIS-IV
- [ ] WISC-IV
- [x] SATA
- [x] Woodcock-Johnson
- [ ] Nelson-Denny Reading Test
- [ ] Other

UNDERGRADUATE STUDENT BODY

Total undergraduate student enrollment: 388 Men, 474 Women.

Composition of student body (fall 2004):

	Undergraduate	Freshmen
International	0.0	0.2
Black	2.1	2.1
American Indian	0.7	0.4
Asian-American	8.6	6.5
Hispanic	2.1	2.3
White	86.5	86.4
Unreported	0.0	2.1
	100.0%	100.0%

25% are from out of state. Average age of full-time undergraduates is 24. 75% of classes have fewer than 20 students, 25% have between 20 and 50 students.

STUDENT HOUSING

94% of freshmen live in college housing. Freshmen are not required to live on campus. Housing is guaranteed for all undergraduates. Campus can house 529 undergraduates. Single rooms are available for students with medical or special needs. A medical note is required.

EXPENSES

Tuition (2005-06): $15,646 per year.
Room & Board: $6,232-$6,232.

There is no additional cost for LD program/services.

LD SERVICES

LD program size is not limited.

LD services available to:

- [x] Freshmen
- [x] Sophomores
- [x] Juniors
- [x] Seniors

Academic Accommodations

Curriculum		In class	
Foreign language waiver	[ ]	Early syllabus	[ ]
Lighter course load	[x]	Note takers in class	[x]
Math waiver	[ ]	Priority seating	[x]
Other special classes	[ ]	Tape recorders	[x]
Priority registrations	[x]	Videotaped classes	[ ]
Substitution of courses	[ ]	Text on tape	[ ]
Exams		**Services**	
Extended time	[x]	Diagnostic tests	[ ]
Oral exams	[x]	Learning centers	[x]
Take home exams	[ ]	Proofreaders	[x]
Exams on tape or computer	[ ]	Readers	[x]
Untimed exams	[x]	Reading Machines/Kurzweil	[ ]
Other accommodations	[x]	Special bookstore section	[ ]
		Typists	[ ]

Credit toward degree is not given for remedial courses taken.

Counseling Services

- [x] Academic — Meets 30 times per academic year
- [ ] Psychological
- [ ] Student Support groups
- [ ] Vocational

Tutoring

Individual tutoring is available weekly.

Average size of tutoring groups: 5

	Individual	Group
Time management	[x]	[ ]
Organizational skills	[x]	[ ]
Learning strategies	[x]	[ ]
Study skills	[x]	[ ]
Content area	[x]	[ ]
Writing lab	[x]	[ ]
Math lab	[x]	[ ]

LD PROGRAM STAFF

Total number of LD Program staff (including director):

Full Time: 1 Part Time: 1

There is an advisor/advocate from the LD program available to students. 1 graduate student and 7 peer tutors are available to work with LD students.

Key staff person available to work with LD students: Don Bouchard, Director of Academic Success.

LD Program web site: www.crown.edu/Crown_Study_Lab.263.0html

Gustavus Adolphus College

St. Peter, MN

Address: 800 West College Avenue, St. Peter, MN, 56082
Admissions telephone: 800 487-8288
Admissions FAX: 507 933-7474
Dean of Admissions: Mark Anderson
Admissions e-mail: admission@gac.edu
Web site: http://www.gac.edu
SAT Code: 6253 ACT Code: 2112

Disability Services Coordinator: Jane Lalim
LD program telephone: 507 933-6124
LD program e-mail: jpatchin@gustavus.edu
Total campus enrollment: 2,577

GENERAL

Gustavus Adolphus College is a private, coed, four-year institution. 340-acre campus in St. Peter (population: 9,747), 60 miles from Minneapolis-St. Paul. Served by bus; major airport and train serve Minneapolis-St. Paul; smaller airport serves Mankato (10 miles). Public transportation serves campus. 4-1-4 system.

LD ADMISSIONS

A personal interview is recommended. Essay is required and may be typed.

SECONDARY SCHOOL REQUIREMENTS

Graduation from secondary school required; GED accepted. The following course distribution required: 4 units of English, 3 units of math, 2 units of science, 2 units of foreign language, 2 units of social studies, 2 units of history.

TESTING

SAT Reasoning considered if submitted. ACT recommended. SAT Subject recommended.

All enrolled freshmen (fall 2004):

Average SAT I Scores: Verbal: 600 Math: 620
Average ACT Scores: Composite: 26

Child Study Team report is not required. Tests required as part of this documentation:

- ☐ WAIS-IV
- ☐ WISC-IV
- ☐ SATA
- ☐ Woodcock-Johnson
- ☐ Nelson-Denny Reading Test
- ☐ Other

UNDERGRADUATE STUDENT BODY

Total undergraduate student enrollment: 1,093 Men, 1,499 Women.

Composition of student body (fall 2004):

	Undergraduate	Freshmen
International	1.2	1.1
Black	1.7	0.8
American Indian	0.2	0.3
Asian-American	4.4	3.9
Hispanic	2.0	1.1
White	89.7	92.7
Unreported	0.8	0.1
	100.0%	100.0%

22% are from out of state. 27% join a fraternity and 22% join a sorority. Average age of full-time undergraduates is 20. 52% of classes have fewer than 20 students, 46% have between 20 and 50 students, 2% have more than 50 students.

STUDENT HOUSING

100% of freshmen live in college housing. Freshmen are required to live on campus. Housing is guaranteed for all undergraduates. Campus can house 2,156 undergraduates.

EXPENSES

Tuition (2005-06): $24,500 per year.
Room: $3,655. Board: $2,400.
There is no additional cost for LD program/services.

LD SERVICES

LD program size is not limited.

LD services available to:

☐ Freshmen ☐ Sophomores ☐ Juniors ☐ Seniors

Academic Accommodations

Curriculum		In class	
Foreign language waiver	☐	Early syllabus	☐
Lighter course load	☐	Note takers in class	■
Math waiver	☐	Priority seating	☐
Other special classes	☐	Tape recorders	■
Priority registrations	☐	Videotaped classes	☐
Substitution of courses	☐	Text on tape	☐
Exams		**Services**	
Extended time	■	Diagnostic tests	☐
Oral exams	■	Learning centers	■
Take home exams	☐	Proofreaders	☐
Exams on tape or computer	☐	Readers	■
Untimed exams	☐	Reading Machines/Kurzweil	■
Other accommodations	☐	Special bookstore section	☐
		Typists	☐

Credit toward degree is not given for remedial courses taken.

Counseling Services

- ☐ Academic
- ☐ Psychological
- ☐ Student Support groups
- ☐ Vocational

Tutoring

	Individual	Group
Time management	☐	☐
Organizational skills	☐	☐
Learning strategies	☐	☐
Study skills	☐	☐
Content area	☐	☐
Writing lab	☐	☐
Math lab	☐	☐

LD PROGRAM STAFF

Total number of LD Program staff (including director):

Full Time: 4 Part Time: 4

Key staff person available to work with LD students: Jane Lalim, Disability Services Coordinator.

Hamline University

St. Paul, MN

Address: 1536 Hewitt Avenue, St. Paul, MN, 55104-1284
Admissions telephone: 800 753-9753
Admissions FAX: 651 523-2458
Director of Undergraduate Admissions: Steve Bjork
Admissions e-mail: cla-admis@hamline.edu
Web site: http://www.hamline.edu
SAT Code: 6265 ACT Code: 2114

LD program name: Disability Services
Disability Specialist: Deb Holtz
LD program telephone: 651 523-2204
LD program e-mail: dholtz02@gw.hamline.edu
LD program enrollment: 42, Total campus enrollment: 1,992

GENERAL

Hamline University is a private, coed, four-year institution. 50-acre campus in St. Paul (Twin Cities population: 669,769). Served by air, bus, and train. School operates transportation to member institutions of Associated Colleges of Twin Cities. Public transportation serves campus. 4-1-4 system.

LD ADMISSIONS

A personal interview is recommended. Essay is required and may be typed.

SECONDARY SCHOOL REQUIREMENTS

Graduation from secondary school required; GED accepted.

TESTING

SAT Reasoning or ACT required. SAT Subject recommended.

All enrolled freshmen (fall 2004):

Average SAT I Scores: Verbal: 585 Math: 567
Average ACT Scores: Composite: 24

Child Study Team report is not required. Tests required as part of this documentation:

☐ WAIS-IV	☐ Woodcock-Johnson
☐ WISC-IV	☐ Nelson-Denny Reading Test
☐ SATA	☐ Other

UNDERGRADUATE STUDENT BODY

Total undergraduate student enrollment: 624 Men, 1,209 Women.

Composition of student body (fall 2004):

	Undergraduate	Freshmen
International	1.1	2.9
Black	5.2	4.3
American Indian	0.7	0.6
Asian-American	7.6	6.3
Hispanic	1.3	2.0
White	80.5	80.6
Unreported	3.6	3.3
	100.0%	100.0%

28% are from out of state. 2% join a fraternity and 3% join a sorority. Average age of full-time undergraduates is 20. 50% of classes have fewer than 20 students, 45% have between 20 and 50 students, 5% have more than 50 students.

STUDENT HOUSING

89% of freshmen live in college housing. Freshmen are not required to live on campus. Housing is guaranteed for all undergraduates. Campus can house 922 undergraduates. Single rooms are available for students with medical or special needs. A medical note is required.

EXPENSES

Tuition (2005-06): $23,130 per year. $17,670 per year (returning third-and fourth-year undergraduates), $18,290 per year (returning second-year undergraduates), $18,970 (new undergraduates).
Room: $3,484. Board: $3,426.

There is no additional cost for LD program/services.

LD SERVICES

LD program size is not limited.

LD services available to:

■ Freshmen ■ Sophomores ■ Juniors ■ Seniors

Academic Accommodations

Curriculum		In class	
Foreign language waiver	☐	Early syllabus	■
Lighter course load	☐	Note takers in class	■
Math waiver	☐	Priority seating	■
Other special classes	☐	Tape recorders	■
Priority registrations	■	Videotaped classes	☐
Substitution of courses	☐	Text on tape	■
Exams		**Services**	
Extended time	■	Diagnostic tests	☐
Oral exams	■	Learning centers	■
Take home exams	☐	Proofreaders	☐
Exams on tape or computer	■	Readers	■
Untimed exams	■	Reading Machines/Kurzweil	■
Other accommodations	■	Special bookstore section	☐
		Typists	■

Credit toward degree is not given for remedial courses taken.

Counseling Services

■ Academic
■ Psychological
■ Student Support groups
■ Vocational

Tutoring

Individual tutoring is available daily.

Average size of tutoring groups: 3

	Individual	Group
Time management	■	■
Organizational skills	■	■
Learning strategies	■	■
Study skills	■	■
Content area	■	■
Writing lab	■	■
Math lab	☐	☐

LD PROGRAM STAFF

Total number of LD Program staff (including director):

Full Time: 1 Part Time: 1

There is an advisor/advocate from the LD program available to students. 5 peer tutors are available to work with LD students.

Key staff person available to work with LD students: Deb Holtz, Disability Specialist.

Macalester College

St. Paul, MN

Address: 1600 Grand Avenue, St. Paul, MN, 55105
Admissions telephone: 800 231-7974
Admissions FAX: 651 696-6724
Dean of Admissions and Financial Aid: Lorne T. Robinson
Admissions e-mail: admissions@macalester.edu
Web site: http://www.macalester.edu
SAT Code: 6390 ACT Code: 2122

Dean of Students: Laurie Hamre
LD program telephone: 651 696-6220
LD program e-mail: hamre@macalester.edu
LD program enrollment: 36, Total campus enrollment: 1,900

GENERAL

Macalester College is a private, coed, four-year institution. 53-acre, suburban campus in St. Paul (population: 287,151). Served by bus and train; major airport serves Minneapolis (eight miles). School operates transportation to consortium schools. Public transportation serves campus. Semester system.

LD ADMISSIONS

A member of the LD program does not sit on the admissions committee.

SECONDARY SCHOOL REQUIREMENTS

Graduation from secondary school not required.

TESTING

SAT Reasoning or ACT required. SAT Subject recommended.

All enrolled freshmen (fall 2004):

Average SAT I Scores:	Verbal: 684	Math: 660
Average ACT Scores:	Composite: 30	

Child Study Team report is not required. Tests required as part of this documentation:

- [x] WAIS-IV
- [ ] WISC-IV
- [ ] SATA
- [x] Woodcock-Johnson
- [ ] Nelson-Denny Reading Test
- [ ] Other

UNDERGRADUATE STUDENT BODY

Total undergraduate student enrollment: 759 Men, 1,063 Women.

Composition of student body (fall 2004):

	Undergraduate	Freshmen
International	14.6	13.8
Black	6.4	3.4
American Indian	0.6	0.9
Asian-American	9.7	6.4
Hispanic	2.7	2.8
White	66.0	72.7
Unreported	0.0	0.0
	100.0%	100.0%

73% are from out of state. Average age of full-time undergraduates is 20. 68% of classes have fewer than 20 students, 30% have between 20 and 50 students, 2% have more than 50 students.

STUDENT HOUSING

100% of freshmen live in college housing. Freshmen are required to live on campus. Housing is guaranteed for all undergraduates. Campus can house 1,323 undergraduates. Single rooms are available for students with medical or special needs. A medical note is required.

EXPENSES

Tuition (2005-06): $28,474 per year.
Room: $4,084. Board: $3,774.
There is no additional cost for LD program/services.

LD SERVICES

LD program size is not limited.

LD services available to:

- [x] Freshmen
- [x] Sophomores
- [x] Juniors
- [x] Seniors

Academic Accommodations

Curriculum		**In class**	
Foreign language waiver	[ ]	Early syllabus	[ ]
Lighter course load	[x]	Note takers in class	[x]
Math waiver	[ ]	Priority seating	[ ]
Other special classes	[ ]	Tape recorders	[x]
Priority registrations	[ ]	Videotaped classes	[ ]
Substitution of courses	[ ]	Text on tape	[ ]
Exams		**Services**	
Extended time	[x]	Diagnostic tests	[ ]
Oral exams	[x]	Learning centers	[x]
Take home exams	[ ]	Proofreaders	[x]
Exams on tape or computer	[ ]	Readers	[x]
Untimed exams	[x]	Reading Machines/Kurzweil	[x]
Other accommodations	[ ]	Special bookstore section	[ ]
		Typists	[ ]

Credit toward degree is not given for remedial courses taken.

Counseling Services

- [x] Academic
- [x] Psychological — Meets 10 times per academic year
- [x] Student Support groups
- [ ] Vocational

Tutoring

Individual tutoring is available weekly.

	Individual	Group
Time management	[x]	[x]
Organizational skills	[x]	[x]
Learning strategies	[x]	[x]
Study skills	[x]	[x]
Content area	[x]	[x]
Writing lab	[x]	[x]
Math lab	[x]	[x]

LD PROGRAM STAFF

Total number of LD Program staff (including director):

Full Time: 3 Part Time: 3

There is an advisor/advocate from the LD program available to students. 3 graduate students are available to work with LD students.

Key staff person available to work with LD students: Becky Graham, Director of Health Services.

Minneapolis College of Art and Design

Minneapolis, MN

Address: 2501 Stevens Avenue S, Minneapolis, MN, 55404
Admissions telephone: 800 874-6223
Admissions FAX: 612 874-3701
Director of Admissions: William Mullen
Admissions e-mail: admissions@mcad.edu
Web site: http://www.mcad.edu
SAT Code: 6411 ACT Code: 2130

Director, Learning Center: Margaret McGee
LD program telephone: 612 874-3633
LD program e-mail: margaret_mcgee@mcad.edu
LD program enrollment: 13, Total campus enrollment: 643

GENERAL

Minneapolis College of Art and Design is a private, coed, four-year institution. Seven-acre, urban campus in Minneapolis (Twin Cities population: 669,469). Served by air, bus, and train. Public transportation serves campus. Semester system.

LD ADMISSIONS

A personal interview is recommended. Essay is required and may be typed. Minimum GPA and test scores are mitigated by LD disclosure.

SECONDARY SCHOOL REQUIREMENTS

Graduation from secondary school required; GED accepted.

TESTING

SAT Reasoning or ACT required. SAT Subject recommended.

All enrolled freshmen (fall 2004):

Average SAT I Scores: Verbal: 602 Math: 492
Average ACT Scores: Composite: 23

Child Study Team report is not required. Tests required as part of this documentation:

- [ ] WAIS-IV
- [ ] WISC-IV
- [ ] SATA
- [ ] Woodcock-Johnson
- [ ] Nelson-Denny Reading Test
- [ ] Other

UNDERGRADUATE STUDENT BODY

Total undergraduate student enrollment: 337 Men, 253 Women.

Composition of student body (fall 2004):

	Undergraduate	Freshmen
International	0.0	0.0
Black	0.9	2.4
American Indian	0.9	1.1
Asian-American	2.8	3.2
Hispanic	0.9	2.8
White	71.1	70.7
Unreported	23.4	19.8
	100.0%	100.0%

44% are from out of state. Average age of full-time undergraduates is 21. 76% of classes have fewer than 20 students, 23% have between 20 and 50 students, 1% have more than 50 students.

STUDENT HOUSING

60% of freshmen live in college housing. Freshmen are not required to live on campus. Housing is not guaranteed for all undergraduates. Junior and senior-level students obtain right to live on campus via random lottery process. Campus can house 275 undergraduates.

EXPENSES

Tuition (2005-06): $24,800 per year.
Room: $3,770.

There is no additional cost for LD program/services.

LD SERVICES

LD program size is not limited.

LD services available to:

- [x] Freshmen
- [x] Sophomores
- [x] Juniors
- [x] Seniors

Academic Accommodations

Curriculum		**In class**	
Foreign language waiver	[ ]	Early syllabus	[ ]
Lighter course load	[ ]	Note takers in class	[x]
Math waiver	[ ]	Priority seating	[ ]
Other special classes	[ ]	Tape recorders	[x]
Priority registrations	[ ]	Videotaped classes	[ ]
Substitution of courses	[ ]	Text on tape	[ ]
Exams		**Services**	
Extended time	[x]	Diagnostic tests	[ ]
Oral exams	[ ]	Learning centers	[x]
Take home exams	[ ]	Proofreaders	[ ]
Exams on tape or computer	[ ]	Readers	[x]
Untimed exams	[ ]	Reading Machines/Kurzweil	[ ]
Other accommodations	[ ]	Special bookstore section	[ ]
		Typists	[ ]

Credit toward degree is not given for remedial courses taken.

Counseling Services

- [ ] Academic
- [ ] Psychological
- [ ] Student Support groups
- [ ] Vocational

Tutoring

Individual tutoring is available weekly.

Average size of tutoring groups: 1

	Individual	Group
Time management	[x]	[ ]
Organizational skills	[ ]	[ ]
Learning strategies	[x]	[ ]
Study skills	[x]	[ ]
Content area	[x]	[ ]
Writing lab	[x]	[ ]
Math lab	[ ]	[ ]

LD PROGRAM STAFF

Total number of LD Program staff (including director):

Full Time: 1 Part Time: 1

There is an advisor/advocate from the LD program available to students.

Key staff person available to work with LD students: Margaret McGee, Director, Learning Center.

University of Minnesota - Crookston

Crookston, MN

Address: 2900 University Avenue, Crookston, MN, 56716
Admissions telephone: 800 862-6466
Admissions FAX: 218 281-8575
Director of Enrollment Management: Mary Feller
Admissions e-mail: info@mail.crk.umn.edu
Web site: http://www.umcrookston.edu
SAT Code: 6893 ACT Code: 2129

Coordinator, UMC Disability Services: Laurie Wilson
LD program telephone: 218 281-8587
LD program e-mail: lwilson@UMCrookston.edu
LD program enrollment: 25, Total campus enrollment: 2,088

GENERAL

University of Minnesota - Crookston is a public, coed, four-year institution. 95-acre, suburban campus in Crookston (population: 8,192). Served by bus; airport and train serve Grand Forks, N.Dak. (35 miles). Semester system.

LD ADMISSIONS

Students do not complete a separate application and are not simultaneously accepted to the LD program. High school waivers are accepted for math and foreign language. A personal interview is not required. Essay is not required.

10 applications were offered admission, and 8 enrolled.

SECONDARY SCHOOL REQUIREMENTS

Graduation from secondary school required; GED accepted.

TESTING

SAT Reasoning considered if submitted. ACT required. SAT Subject recommended.

All enrolled freshmen (fall 2004):

Average SAT I Scores:	Verbal: 512	Math: 520
Average ACT Scores:	Composite: 21	

Child Study Team report is not required. A neuropsychological or comprehensive psycho-education evaluation is not required for admission. Tests required as part of this documentation:

- [ ] WAIS-IV
- [ ] WISC-IV
- [ ] SATA
- [ ] Woodcock-Johnson
- [ ] Nelson-Denny Reading Test
- [ ] Other

UNDERGRADUATE STUDENT BODY

Total undergraduate student enrollment: 1,116 Men, 1,344 Women.

Composition of student body (fall 2004):

	Undergraduate	Freshmen
International	1.4	3.1
Black	4.7	2.3
American Indian	0.5	0.9
Asian-American	0.9	1.4
Hispanic	1.4	1.6
White	82.7	83.1
Unreported	8.4	7.6
	100.0%	100.0%

38% are from out of state. 1% join a fraternity. Average age of full-time undergraduates is 23. 50% of classes have fewer than 20 students, 46% have between 20 and 50 students, 4% have more than 50 students.

STUDENT HOUSING

67% of freshmen live in college housing. Freshmen are not required to live on campus. Housing is guaranteed for all undergraduates. Campus can house 480 undergraduates. Single rooms are available for students with medical or special needs. A medical note is required.

EXPENSES

Tuition (2005-06): $5,792 per year.
Room: $2,459. Board: $2,580.

There is no additional cost for LD program/services.

LD SERVICES

LD program size is not limited.

LD services available to:

- [x] Freshmen
- [x] Sophomores
- [x] Juniors
- [x] Seniors

Academic Accommodations

Curriculum		In class	
Foreign language waiver	[ ]	Early syllabus	[ ]
Lighter course load	[x]	Note takers in class	[x]
Math waiver	[ ]	Priority seating	[x]
Other special classes	[ ]	Tape recorders	[x]
Priority registrations	[x]	Videotaped classes	[ ]
Substitution of courses	[ ]	Text on tape	[ ]
Exams		**Services**	
Extended time	[x]	Diagnostic tests	[ ]
Oral exams	[x]	Learning centers	[x]
Take home exams	[ ]	Proofreaders	[ ]
Exams on tape or computer	[x]	Readers	[x]
Untimed exams	[x]	Reading Machines/Kurzweil	[x]
Other accommodations	[x]	Special bookstore section	[ ]
		Typists	[ ]

Credit toward degree is not given for remedial courses taken.

Counseling Services

- [x] Academic
- [x] Psychological
- [x] Student Support groups
- [x] Vocational

Tutoring

Individual tutoring is available weekly.

	Individual	Group
Time management	[x]	[ ]
Organizational skills	[x]	[ ]
Learning strategies	[x]	[ ]
Study skills	[x]	[ ]
Content area	[x]	[ ]
Writing lab	[ ]	[ ]
Math lab	[ ]	[ ]

UNIQUE LD PROGRAM FEATURES

UMC does not have a separate program for students with LD. We have services available to students with disabilities who are individually accommodated.

LD PROGRAM STAFF

There is an advisor/advocate from the LD program available to students.

Key staff person available to work with LD students: Laurie Wilson, Coordinator, UMC Disability Services.

University of Minnesota - Duluth

Duluth, MN

Address: 1049 University Drive, Duluth, MN, 55812-2496
Admissions telephone: 800 232-1339
Admissions FAX: 218 726-7040
Director of Admissions: Beth Esselstrom
Admissions e-mail: umdadmis@d.umn.edu
Web site: http://www.d.umn.edu
SAT Code: 6873 ACT Code: 2157

LD Program Name: Access Center/Disability Services
Coordinator, Cognitive Disabilities Program: Judy Bromen
Access Center/Disability Services: Penny Cragun
LD program telephone: 218 726-8727
LD program e-mail: pcragun@d.umn.edu
Total campus enrollment: 9,441

GENERAL

University of Minnesota - Duluth is a public, coed, four-year institution. 247-acre, suburban campus in Duluth (population: 86,918). Served by air and bus; major airport and train serve Minneapolis-St. Paul (130 miles). Public transportation serves campus. Semester system.

LD ADMISSIONS

A personal interview is recommended. Essay is not required. Applications of students who voluntarily disclose that they have a disability will be reviewed on an individual basis.

SECONDARY SCHOOL REQUIREMENTS

Graduation from secondary school required; GED accepted. The following course distribution required: 4 units of English, 3 units of math, 3 units of science, 2 units of foreign language, 2 units of social studies.

TESTING

ACT required; SAT Reasoning may be substituted. SAT Subject required.

All enrolled freshmen (fall 2004):

Average ACT Scores: Composite: 23

Child Study Team report is not required. Tests required as part of this documentation:

- ☐ WAIS-IV
- ☐ WISC-IV
- ☐ SATA
- ☐ Woodcock-Johnson
- ☐ Nelson-Denny Reading Test
- ☐ Other

UNDERGRADUATE STUDENT BODY

Total undergraduate student enrollment: 4,301 Men, 4,479 Women.

Composition of student body (fall 2004):

	Undergraduate	Freshmen
International	0.6	1.7
Black	1.3	1.3
American Indian	0.7	0.6
Asian-American	3.2	2.5
Hispanic	0.9	0.8
White	91.4	91.3
Unreported	1.9	1.8
	100.0%	100.0%

13% are from out of state. 41% of classes have fewer than 20 students, 50% have between 20 and 50 students, 9% have more than 50 students.

STUDENT HOUSING

61% of freshmen live in college housing. Freshmen are not required to live on campus. Housing is not guaranteed for all undergraduates. Not enough units to house all students. Campus can house 3,018 undergraduates.

EXPENSES

Tuition (2005-06): $7,157 per year (in-state), $18,264 (out-of-state).

Room: $2,624. Board: $2,922.

There is no additional cost for LD program/services.

LD SERVICES

LD program size is not limited.

LD services available to:

☐ Freshmen ☐ Sophomores ☐ Juniors ☐ Seniors

Academic Accommodations

Curriculum		**In class**	
Foreign language waiver	☐	Early syllabus	☐
Lighter course load	■	Note takers in class	■
Math waiver	☐	Priority seating	☐
Other special classes	☐	Tape recorders	■
Priority registrations	☐	Videotaped classes	☐
Substitution of courses	☐	Text on tape	☐
Exams		**Services**	
Extended time	■	Diagnostic tests	■
Oral exams	☐	Learning centers	■
Take home exams	☐	Proofreaders	☐
Exams on tape or computer	☐	Readers	■
Untimed exams	☐	Reading Machines/Kurzweil	■
Other accommodations	☐	Special bookstore section	☐
		Typists	☐

Credit toward degree is given for remedial courses taken.

Counseling Services

- ☐ Academic
- ☐ Psychological
- ☐ Student Support groups
- ☐ Vocational

Tutoring

	Individual	Group
Time management	☐	☐
Organizational skills	☐	☐
Learning strategies	☐	☐
Study skills	☐	☐
Content area	☐	☐
Writing lab	☐	☐
Math lab	☐	☐

LD PROGRAM STAFF

Total number of LD Program staff (including director):

Full Time: 2 Part Time: 2

Key staff person available to work with LD students: Judy Bromen, Cognitive Disabilities Program Coordinator.

University of Minnesota - Morris

Morris, MN

Address: 600 E. Fourth Street, Morris, MN, 56267
Admissions telephone: 800 992-8863
Admissions FAX: 320 589-1673
Director of Admissions: James Morales
Admissions e-mail: admissions@morris.umn.edu
Web site: http://www.morris.umn.edu
SAT Code: 6890 ACT Code: 2155

LD program name: Academic Assistance Center
Director: Ferolyn Angell
LD program telephone: 320 589-6178
LD program e-mail: angfa@morris.umn.edu
Total campus enrollment: 1,839

GENERAL

University of Minnesota - Morris is a public, coed, four-year institution. 130-acre campus in Morris (population: 5,068), 150 miles from Minneapolis-St. Paul. Served by air; major airport serves Minneapolis-St. Paul; bus serves Benson (25 miles); train serves Fargo, N.Dak. (100 miles). School operates transportation to Twin Cities campus. Public transportation serves campus. Semester system.

LD ADMISSIONS

A member of the LD program does not sit on the admissions committee. A personal interview is recommended. Essay is required and may be typed.

SECONDARY SCHOOL REQUIREMENTS

Graduation from secondary school required; GED accepted.

TESTING

ACT required; SAT Reasoning may be substituted. SAT Subject required.

All enrolled freshmen (fall 2004):

Average SAT I Scores:	Verbal: 600	Math: 620
Average ACT Scores:	Composite: 25	

Child Study Team report is not required. A neuropsychological or comprehensive psycho-education evaluation is not required for admission. Tests required as part of this documentation:

- [ ] WAIS-IV
- [ ] WISC-IV
- [ ] SATA
- [ ] Woodcock-Johnson
- [ ] Nelson-Denny Reading Test
- [ ] Other

UNDERGRADUATE STUDENT BODY

Total undergraduate student enrollment: 784 Men, 1,143 Women.

Composition of student body (fall 2004):

	Undergraduate	Freshmen
International	4.8	3.2
Black	1.5	2.4
American Indian	9.3	8.2
Asian-American	4.3	3.2
Hispanic	1.8	1.4
White	76.3	79.9
Unreported	2.0	1.7
	100.0%	100.0%

18% are from out of state. Average age of full-time undergraduates is 21. 69% of classes have fewer than 20 students, 25% have between 20 and 50 students, 6% have more than 50 students.

STUDENT HOUSING

99% of freshmen live in college housing. Freshmen are not required to live on campus. Housing is guaranteed for all undergraduates. Campus can house 1,022 undergraduates. Single rooms are available for students with medical or special needs. A medical note is not required.

EXPENSES

Tuition (2005-06): $8,204 per year.
Room: $2,730. Board: $3,020.

There is no additional cost for LD program/services.

LD SERVICES

LD program size is not limited.

LD services available to:

- [x] Freshmen
- [x] Sophomores
- [x] Juniors
- [x] Seniors

Academic Accommodations

Curriculum		In class	
Foreign language waiver	[ ]	Early syllabus	[x]
Lighter course load	[x]	Note takers in class	[x]
Math waiver	[ ]	Priority seating	[x]
Other special classes	[x]	Tape recorders	[x]
Priority registrations	[x]	Videotaped classes	[x]
Substitution of courses	[ ]	Text on tape	[x]
Exams		**Services**	
Extended time	[x]	Diagnostic tests	[ ]
Oral exams	[x]	Learning centers	[x]
Take home exams	[ ]	Proofreaders	[x]
Exams on tape or computer	[x]	Readers	[x]
Untimed exams	[x]	Reading Machines/Kurzweil	[x]
Other accommodations	[x]	Special bookstore section	[ ]
		Typists	[x]

Credit toward degree is not given for remedial courses taken.

Counseling Services

- [x] Academic
- [x] Psychological
- [x] Student Support groups
- [x] Vocational

Tutoring

Individual tutoring is available weekly.

Average size of tutoring groups: 3

	Individual	Group
Time management	[x]	[x]
Organizational skills	[x]	[x]
Learning strategies	[x]	[x]
Study skills	[x]	[x]
Content area	[x]	[ ]
Writing lab	[x]	[x]
Math lab	[x]	[x]

LD PROGRAM STAFF

Total number of LD Program staff (including director):

Full Time: 3 Part Time: 3

There is an advisor/advocate from the LD program available to students. 56 peer tutors are available to work with LD students.

Key staff person available to work with LD students: Ferolyn Angell, Director of Disability Services/Academic Assistance.

LD Program web site: http://www.morris.umn.edu/services/dsoaac/dso/

Minnesota State University, Mankato

Mankato, MN

Address: 309 Wigley Administration Center, Mankato, MN, 56001
Admissions telephone: 800 722-0544
Admissions FAX: 507 389-5114
Director of Admissions: Walt Wolff
Admissions e-mail: admissions@mnsu.edu
Web site: http://www.mnsu.edu
SAT Code: 6677 ACT Code: 2126

LD program name: Office of Disability Services
LD program address: 132 Memorial Library
Director, Office of Disability Services: Julie Snow
LD program telephone: 507 389-2825
LD program e-mail: julie.snow@mnsu.edu
LD program enrollment: 121, Total campus enrollment: 12,464

GENERAL

Minnesota State University, Mankato is a public, coed, four-year institution. 400-acre campus in Mankato (population: 32,427), 85 miles from Minneapolis-St. Paul; branch campuses in Bloomington, Burnsville, Fairmont, Farbault, Owatonna, New Ulm, and St. Louis Park. Served by bus; major airport and train serve Minneapolis-St. Paul. Public transportation serves campus. School operates transportation to remote campus parking lots. Semester system.

LD ADMISSIONS

Students do not complete a separate application and are not simultaneously accepted to the LD program. A member of the LD program does not sit on the admissions committee. A personal interview is not required. Essay is not required.

SECONDARY SCHOOL REQUIREMENTS

Graduation from secondary school required; GED accepted. The following course distribution required: 4 units of English, 3 units of math, 3 units of science, 2 units of foreign language, 2 units of social studies, 1 unit of history.

TESTING

ACT required of some applicants. SAT Reasoning or ACT considered if submitted; ACT preferred. SAT Subject recommended.

All enrolled freshmen (fall 2004):

Average ACT Scores: Composite: 21

Child Study Team report is required if student is classified. A neuropsychological or comprehensive psycho-educational evaluation is required for admission. Must be dated within 36 months of application. Tests required as part of this documentation:

- [x] WAIS-IV
- [x] WISC-IV
- [ ] SATA
- [ ] Woodcock-Johnson
- [ ] Nelson-Denny Reading Test
- [ ] Other

UNDERGRADUATE STUDENT BODY

Total undergraduate student enrollment: 5,614 Men, 6,026 Women.

Composition of student body (fall 2004):

	Undergraduate	Freshmen
International	0.9	3.0
Black	2.5	1.7
American Indian	0.7	0.3
Asian-American	2.1	1.6
Hispanic	0.5	0.6
White	80.8	66.2
Unreported	12.5	26.6
	100.0%	100.0%

17% are from out of state. Average age of full-time undergraduates is 21. 34% of classes have fewer than 20 students, 56% have between 20 and 50 students, 10% have more than 50 students.

STUDENT HOUSING

80% of freshmen live in college housing. Freshmen are not required to live on campus. Housing is guaranteed for all undergraduates. Campus can house 2,932 undergraduates. Single rooms are available for students with medical or special needs. A medical note is required.

EXPENSES

Tuition (2005-06): $4,682 per year (in-state), $10,030 (out-of-state).

Room: $3,300. Board: $1,470.

There is no additional cost for LD program/services.

LD SERVICES

LD program size is not limited.

LD services available to:

- [x] Freshmen
- [x] Sophomores
- [x] Juniors
- [x] Seniors

Academic Accommodations

Curriculum		In class	
Foreign language waiver	[x]	Early syllabus	[ ]
Lighter course load	[x]	Note takers in class	[x]
Math waiver	[x]	Priority seating	[ ]
Other special classes	[ ]	Tape recorders	[x]
Priority registrations	[ ]	Videotaped classes	[ ]
Substitution of courses	[ ]	Text on tape	[ ]
Exams		**Services**	
Extended time	[x]	Diagnostic tests	[ ]
Oral exams	[x]	Learning centers	[x]
Take home exams	[ ]	Proofreaders	[ ]
Exams on tape or computer	[x]	Readers	[x]
Untimed exams	[ ]	Reading Machines/Kurzweil	[x]
Other accommodations	[ ]	Special bookstore section	[ ]
		Typists	[ ]

Credit toward degree is not given for remedial courses taken.

Counseling Services

- [ ] Academic
- [ ] Psychological
- [ ] Student Support groups
- [ ] Vocational

Tutoring

Individual tutoring is available daily.

Average size of tutoring groups: 3

	Individual	Group
Time management	[ ]	[x]
Organizational skills	[ ]	[x]
Learning strategies	[ ]	[x]
Study skills	[ ]	[x]
Content area	[ ]	[x]
Writing lab	[ ]	[x]
Math lab	[ ]	[x]

LD PROGRAM STAFF

Total number of LD Program staff (including director):

Full Time: 1 Part Time: 1

There is an advisor/advocate from the LD program available to students. 2 graduate students are available to work with LD students.

Key staff person available to work with LD students: Julie Snow, Director, Disability Services.

University of Minnesota - Twin Cities

Minneapolis, MN

Address: 100 Church Street SE, Minneapolis, MN, 55455-0213
Admissions telephone: 800 752-1000
Admissions FAX: 612 626-1693
Director of Admissions: Wayne Sigler, Ph.D.
Admissions e-mail: admissions@tc.umn.edu
Web site: http://www1.umn.edu/twincities/
SAT Code: 6874 ACT Code: 2156

LD program name: Disability Services
LD program address: 230 McNamara Center
Director, Disability Services: Roberta J. Cordano
LD program telephone: 612 624-4120
LD program e-mail: corda001@umn.edu
Total campus enrollment: 32,716

GENERAL

University of Minnesota - Twin Cities is a public, coed, four-year institution. 2,000-acre, urban campus in Minneapolis with additional 730 acres in St. Paul (Twin Cities population: 669,769). Served by air; bus serves Minneapolis; train serves St. Paul. School operates transportation between campuses. Public transportation serves campus. Semester system.

LD ADMISSIONS

SECONDARY SCHOOL REQUIREMENTS

Graduation from secondary school required; GED accepted. The following course distribution required: 4 units of English, 3 units of math, 3 units of science, 2 units of foreign language, 3 units of social studies.

TESTING

SAT Reasoning or ACT required. SAT Subject recommended.

All enrolled freshmen (fall 2004):

Average SAT I Scores:	Verbal: 595	Math: 616
Average ACT Scores:	Composite: 25	

Child Study Team report is not required. A neuropsychological or comprehensive psycho-educational evaluation is required for admission. Must be dated within 60 months of application. Tests required as part of this documentation:

- [x] WAIS-IV
- [x] WISC-IV
- [x] SATA
- [x] Woodcock-Johnson
- [x] Nelson-Denny Reading Test
- [x] Other

UNDERGRADUATE STUDENT BODY

Total undergraduate student enrollment: 15,237 Men, 16,899 Women.

Composition of student body (fall 2004):

	Undergraduate	Freshmen
International	0.7	1.8
Black	4.8	4.5
American Indian	0.9	0.7
Asian-American	10.8	9.2
Hispanic	1.9	2.0
White	79.6	79.3
Unreported	1.3	2.5
	100.0%	100.0%

25% are from out of state. Average age of full-time undergraduates is 21. 44% of classes have fewer than 20 students, 40% have between 20 and 50 students, 16% have more than 50 students.

STUDENT HOUSING

77% of freshmen live in college housing. Freshmen are not required to live on campus. Housing is guaranteed for all undergraduates. Campus can house 6,500 undergraduates.

EXPENSES

Tuition (2005-06): $7,140 per year (in-state), $18,770 (out-of-state). Room: $3,886. Board: $2,836.

There is no additional cost for LD program/services.

LD SERVICES

LD program size is not limited.

LD services available to:

- [x] Freshmen
- [x] Sophomores
- [x] Juniors
- [x] Seniors

Academic Accommodations

Curriculum

- [ ] Foreign language waiver
- [ ] Lighter course load
- [ ] Math waiver
- [x] Other special classes
- [x] Priority registrations
- [x] Substitution of courses

Exams

- [ ] Extended time
- [x] Oral exams
- [ ] Take home exams
- [x] Exams on tape or computer
- [ ] Untimed exams
- [ ] Other accommodations

In class

- [x] Early syllabus
- [x] Note takers in class
- [ ] Priority seating
- [x] Tape recorders
- [x] Videotaped classes
- [x] Text on tape

Services

- [ ] Diagnostic tests
- [ ] Learning centers
- [ ] Proofreaders
- [x] Readers
- [x] Reading Machines/Kurzweil
- [ ] Special bookstore section
- [ ] Typists

Counseling Services

- [ ] Academic
- [ ] Psychological
- [ ] Student Support groups
- [ ] Vocational

Tutoring

Individual tutoring is available.

	Individual	Group
Time management	[ ]	[ ]
Organizational skills	[ ]	[ ]
Learning strategies	[ ]	[ ]
Study skills	[ ]	[ ]
Content area	[ ]	[ ]
Writing lab	[ ]	[ ]
Math lab	[ ]	[ ]

LD PROGRAM STAFF

LD Program web site: ds.umn.edu

North Central University

Minneapolis, MN

Address: 910 Elliot Avenue S, Minneapolis, MN, 55404
Admissions telephone: 800 289-6222
Admissions FAX: 612 343-4146
Director of Admissions: Jim Hubert
Admissions e-mail: admissions@northcentral.edu
Web site: http://www.northcentral.edu
SAT Code: 51 ACT Code: 2136

LD program contact: Dr. Farella Shaka
LD program telephone: 612 343-4190
LD program e-mail: farella.shaka@northcentral.edu
Total campus enrollment: 1,235

GENERAL

North Central University is a private, coed, four-year institution. Nine-acre, urban campus in Minneapolis (population: 382,618). Served by air and bus; train serves St. Paul (10 miles). Public transportation serves campus. Semester system.

LD ADMISSIONS

A personal interview is recommended. Essay is required and may be typed.

SECONDARY SCHOOL REQUIREMENTS

Graduation from secondary school required; GED accepted.

TESTING

ACT required; SAT Reasoning may be substituted. SAT Subject recommended.

All enrolled freshmen (fall 2004):

Average SAT I Scores: Verbal: 555 Math: 509
Average ACT Scores: Composite: 21

Child Study Team report is not required. Tests required as part of this documentation:

- ❑ WAIS-IV
- ❑ WISC-IV
- ❑ SATA
- ❑ Woodcock-Johnson
- ❑ Nelson-Denny Reading Test
- ❑ Other

UNDERGRADUATE STUDENT BODY

Total undergraduate student enrollment: 502 Men, 670 Women.

Composition of student body (fall 2004):

	Undergraduate	Freshmen
International	1.1	1.1
Black	3.0	2.9
American Indian	0.4	0.3
Asian-American	1.9	1.7
Hispanic	2.6	2.5
White	89.1	89.9
Unreported	1.9	1.6
	100.0%	100.0%

50% are from out of state. 48% of classes have fewer than 20 students, 46% have between 20 and 50 students, 6% have more than 50 students.

STUDENT HOUSING

90% of freshmen live in college housing. Freshmen are required to live on campus. Housing is guaranteed for all undergraduates. Campus can house 1,000 undergraduates.

EXPENSES

Tuition (2005-06): $11,280 per year.

Room: $2,270. Board: $2,520.

LD SERVICES

LD services available to:

❑ Freshmen ❑ Sophomores ❑ Juniors ❑ Seniors

Academic Accommodations

Curriculum		In class	
Foreign language waiver	❑	Early syllabus	❑
Lighter course load	❑	Note takers in class	❑
Math waiver	❑	Priority seating	❑
Other special classes	■	Tape recorders	■
Priority registrations	❑	Videotaped classes	❑
Substitution of courses	❑	Text on tape	❑
Exams		**Services**	
Extended time	■	Diagnostic tests	❑
Oral exams	❑	Learning centers	■
Take home exams	❑	Proofreaders	❑
Exams on tape or computer	❑	Readers	❑
Untimed exams	❑	Reading Machines/Kurzweil	❑
Other accommodations	❑	Special bookstore section	❑
		Typists	❑

Credit toward degree is not given for remedial courses taken.

Counseling Services

- ❑ Academic
- ❑ Psychological
- ❑ Student Support groups
- ❑ Vocational

Tutoring

Individual tutoring is available weekly.

	Individual	Group
Time management	❑	❑
Organizational skills	❑	❑
Learning strategies	❑	❑
Study skills	❑	❑
Content area	❑	❑
Writing lab	❑	❑
Math lab	❑	❑

LD PROGRAM STAFF

Total number of LD Program staff (including director):

Full Time: 1 Part Time: 1

Key staff person available to work with LD students: Dr. Farella Shaka.

Northwestern College

St. Paul, MN

Address: 3003 Snelling Avenue North, St. Paul, MN, 55113-1598
Admissions telephone: 800 827-6827
Admissions FAX: 651 631-5680
Dean of Admissions and Records: Kenneth K. Faffler
Admissions e-mail: admissions@nwc.edu
Web site: http://www.nwc.edu
SAT Code: 6489 ACT Code: 2138

Associate Professor: Dr. Yvonne Banks
LD program telephone: 651 631-5221
LD program e-mail: yrb@nwc.edu
LD program enrollment: 43, Total campus enrollment: 2,734

GENERAL

Northwestern College is a private, coed, four-year institution. 103-acre, suburban campus in St. Paul (Twin Cities population: 669,769). Served by air, bus, and train. Public transportation serves campus. Semester system.

LD ADMISSIONS

Application Deadline: 08/01. Students do not complete a separate application and are not simultaneously accepted to the LD program. A member of the LD program does not sit on the admissions committee. A personal interview is recommended. Essay is required and may be typed.

SECONDARY SCHOOL REQUIREMENTS

Graduation from secondary school required; GED accepted.

TESTING

ACT required; SAT Reasoning may be substituted. SAT Subject recommended.

All enrolled freshmen (fall 2004):

Average SAT I Scores:	Verbal: 596	Math: 593
Average ACT Scores:	Composite: 23	

Child Study Team report is not required. A neuropsychological or comprehensive psycho-educational evaluation is required for admission. Must be dated within 36 months of application. Tests required as part of this documentation:

- [x] WAIS-IV
- [x] WISC-IV
- [ ] SATA
- [x] Woodcock-Johnson
- [ ] Nelson-Denny Reading Test
- [ ] Other

UNDERGRADUATE STUDENT BODY

Total undergraduate student enrollment: 791 Men, 1,293 Women.

Composition of student body (fall 2004):

	Undergraduate	Freshmen
International	0.2	0.4
Black	1.2	3.4
American Indian	0.5	0.4
Asian-American	3.5	2.8
Hispanic	1.6	1.6
White	92.1	90.7
Unreported	0.9	0.7
	100.0%	100.0%

41% are from out of state. Average age of full-time undergraduates is 23. 49% of classes have fewer than 20 students, 45% have between 20 and 50 students, 6% have more than 50 students.

STUDENT HOUSING

94% of freshmen live in college housing. Freshmen are required to live on campus. Housing is not guaranteed for all undergraduates. All full-time, single students under age 20 by the start of the semester(except those who are part-time, are married, have more than 60 credit hours, or are living with one or both parents) are required to live in campus housing. Campus can house 1,056 undergraduates. Single rooms are available for students with medical or special needs. A medical note is not required.

EXPENSES

Tuition (2005-06): $19,100 per year.

Room: $3,400. Board: $2,720.

There is no additional cost for LD program/services.

LD SERVICES

LD program size is not limited.

LD services available to:

- [x] Freshmen
- [x] Sophomores
- [x] Juniors
- [x] Seniors

Academic Accommodations

Curriculum

- [ ] Foreign language waiver
- [x] Lighter course load
- [ ] Math waiver
- [x] Other special classes
- [x] Priority registrations
- [ ] Substitution of courses

Exams

- [x] Extended time
- [x] Oral exams
- [ ] Take home exams
- [x] Exams on tape or computer
- [x] Untimed exams
- [x] Other accommodations

In class

- [x] Early syllabus
- [x] Note takers in class
- [ ] Priority seating
- [x] Tape recorders
- [ ] Videotaped classes
- [x] Text on tape

Services

- [ ] Diagnostic tests
- [x] Learning centers
- [ ] Proofreaders
- [x] Readers
- [x] Reading Machines/Kurzweil
- [ ] Special bookstore section
- [x] Typists

Credit toward degree is not given for remedial courses taken.

Counseling Services

- [x] Academic
- [x] Psychological
- [x] Student Support groups — Meets 8 times per academic year
- [ ] Vocational

Tutoring

Individual tutoring is available daily.

Average size of tutoring groups: 1

	Individual	Group
Time management	[x]	[ ]
Organizational skills	[x]	[ ]
Learning strategies	[x]	[ ]
Study skills	[x]	[ ]
Content area	[ ]	[ ]
Writing lab	[ ]	[ ]
Math lab	[ ]	[ ]

UNIQUE LD PROGRAM FEATURES

Documentation of high school LD services is recommended.

LD PROGRAM STAFF

There is an advisor/advocate from the LD program available to students. 10 peer tutors are available to work with LD students.

Key staff person available to work with LD students: Dr. Yvonne Banks, Assoc Prof of Educ/Dir of Disability Services.

Saint John's University

Collegeville, MN

Address: PO Box 7155, Collegeville, MN, 56321
Admissions telephone: 800 245-6467
Admissions FAX: 320 363-2750
Dean of Admissions: Mary Milbert, Dean
Admissions e-mail: admissions@csbsju.edu
Web site: http://www.csbsju.edu
SAT Code: 6624 ACT Code: 2140

Director of Academic Advising: Susan Douma
LD program telephone: 320 363-2246
LD program e-mail: sdouma@csbsju.edu
Total campus enrollment: 1,895

GENERAL

Saint John's University is a private, men's, four-year institution. 2,400-acre campus in Collegeville (population: 3,516), 75 miles from Minneapolis-St. Paul. Served by bus; major airport serves Minneapolis-St. Paul; smaller airport and train serve St. Cloud (15 miles). School operates transportation to Coll. of St. Benedict and to St. Cloud and St. Joseph. Semester system.

LD ADMISSIONS

A personal interview is recommended. Essay is required and may be typed. Students may take untimed ACT.

SECONDARY SCHOOL REQUIREMENTS

Graduation from secondary school required; GED accepted.

TESTING

SAT Reasoning or ACT required. SAT Subject recommended.

All enrolled freshmen (fall 2004):

Average SAT I Scores:	Verbal: 579	Math: 619
Average ACT Scores:	Composite: 25	

Child Study Team report is not required. Tests required as part of this documentation:

- ☐ WAIS-IV
- ☐ WISC-IV
- ☐ SATA
- ☐ Woodcock-Johnson
- ☐ Nelson-Denny Reading Test
- ☐ Other

UNDERGRADUATE STUDENT BODY

Total undergraduate student enrollment: 1,888 Men.

Composition of student body (fall 2004):

	Undergraduate	Freshmen
International	2.1	2.9
Black	0.6	0.8
American Indian	0.2	0.3
Asian-American	2.1	2.2
Hispanic	1.2	1.1
White	93.8	92.7
Unreported	0.0	0.0
	100.0%	100.0%

14% are from out of state. Average age of full-time undergraduates is 20. 52% of classes have fewer than 20 students, 48% have between 20 and 50 students.

STUDENT HOUSING

99% of freshmen live in college housing. Freshmen are required to live on campus. Housing is not guaranteed for all undergraduates. Campus can house 1,488 undergraduates. Single rooms are available for students with medical or special needs.

EXPENSES

Tuition (2005-06): $23,064 per year.
Room: $3,151. Board: $3,124.

There is no additional cost for LD program/services.

LD SERVICES

LD program size is not limited.

LD services available to:

■ Freshmen ■ Sophomores ■ Juniors ■ Seniors

Academic Accommodations

Curriculum		In class	
Foreign language waiver	☐	Early syllabus	☐
Lighter course load	☐	Note takers in class	☐
Math waiver	☐	Priority seating	☐
Other special classes	☐	Tape recorders	☐
Priority registrations	☐	Videotaped classes	☐
Substitution of courses	☐	Text on tape	☐
Exams		**Services**	
Extended time	■	Diagnostic tests	☐
Oral exams	☐	Learning centers	☐
Take home exams	☐	Proofreaders	☐
Exams on tape or computer	☐	Readers	☐
Untimed exams	■	Reading Machines/Kurzweil	■
Other accommodations	☐	Special bookstore section	☐
		Typists	☐

Credit toward degree is not given for remedial courses taken.

Counseling Services

- ☐ Academic
- ☐ Psychological
- ☐ Student Support groups
- ☐ Vocational

Tutoring

Individual tutoring is available.

	Individual	Group
Time management	☐	☐
Organizational skills	☐	☐
Learning strategies	☐	☐
Study skills	■	☐
Content area	☐	☐
Writing lab	■	☐
Math lab	■	☐

UNIQUE LD PROGRAM FEATURES

LD services are coordinated through the Academic Advising Office. While our disability services are limited, we are committed to providing academic accommodations on a case-by-case basis for enrolled students who provide adequate documentation of a disability.

LD PROGRAM STAFF

Key staff person available to work with LD students: Susan Douma, Director of Academic Advising.

Saint Mary's University of Minnesota

Winona, MN

Address: 700 Terrace Heights, Winona, MN, 55987-1399
Admissions telephone: 800 635-5987
Admissions FAX: 507 457-1722
Vice President for Admissions: Anthony Piscitiello
Admissions e-mail: admissions@smumn.edu
Web site: http://www.smumn.edu
SAT Code: 6632 ACT Code: 2148

LD program name: Academic Skills Center
Disability Services Coordinator: Bonnie Smith
LD program telephone: 507 457-1465
LD program e-mail: bsmith@smumn.edu
LD program enrollment: 20, Total campus enrollment: 1,644

GENERAL

Saint Mary's University of Minnesota is a private, coed, four-year institution. 400-acre campus in Winona (population: 27,069), 110 miles from Minneapolis-St. Paul; graduate-level branch campuses in Minneapolis and Rochester. Served by bus and train; airports serve LaCrosse, Wis. (30 miles) and Rochester (45 miles). Public transportation serves campus. Semester system.

LD ADMISSIONS

A personal interview is not required. Essay is required and may be typed.

SECONDARY SCHOOL REQUIREMENTS

Graduation from secondary school required; GED accepted. The following course distribution required: 4 units of English, 3 units of math, 3 units of science, 2 units of social studies, 6 units of academic electives.

TESTING

ACT required; SAT Reasoning may be substituted. SAT Subject recommended.

All enrolled freshmen (fall 2004):

Average SAT I Scores:	Verbal: 506	Math: 498
Average ACT Scores:	Composite: 22	

Child Study Team report is not required. A neuropsychological or comprehensive psycho-educational evaluation is required for admission. Must be dated within 36 months of application. Tests required as part of this documentation:

- ■ WAIS-IV
- ☐ WISC-IV
- ■ SATA
- ■ Woodcock-Johnson
- ■ Nelson-Denny Reading Test
- ■ Other

UNDERGRADUATE STUDENT BODY

Total undergraduate student enrollment: 751 Men, 870 Women.

Composition of student body (fall 2004):

	Undergraduate	Freshmen
International	0.3	0.8
Black	3.0	3.6
American Indian	0.6	0.5
Asian-American	2.2	1.9
Hispanic	4.1	2.6
White	85.4	78.5
Unreported	4.4	12.1
	100.0%	100.0%

38% are from out of state. 2% join a fraternity and 1% join a sorority. Average age of full-time undergraduates is 20. 59% of classes have fewer than 20 students, 41% have between 20 and 50 students.

STUDENT HOUSING

97% of freshmen live in college housing. Freshmen are required to live on campus. Housing is guaranteed for all undergraduates. Campus can house 1,103 undergraduates. Single rooms are available for students with medical or special needs. A medical note is required.

EXPENSES

Tuition (2005-06): $18,704 per year.

Room: $3,200. Board: $2,520.

There is no additional cost for LD program/services

LD SERVICES

LD program size is not limited.

LD services available to:

■ Freshmen ■ Sophomores ■ Juniors ■ Seniors

Academic Accommodations

Curriculum		**In class**	
Foreign language waiver	☐	Early syllabus	☐
Lighter course load	☐	Note takers in class	■
Math waiver	☐	Priority seating	☐
Other special classes	☐	Tape recorders	■
Priority registrations	☐	Videotaped classes	☐
Substitution of courses	■	Text on tape	■
Exams		**Services**	
Extended time	■	Diagnostic tests	☐
Oral exams	■	Learning centers	■
Take home exams	☐	Proofreaders	☐
Exams on tape or computer	■	Readers	■
Untimed exams	☐	Reading Machines/Kurzweil	■
Other accommodations	■	Special bookstore section	☐
		Typists	■

Credit toward degree is not given for remedial courses taken.

Counseling Services

- ■ Academic
- ■ Psychological
- ■ Student Support groups
- ☐ Vocational

Tutoring

Individual tutoring is available weekly.

Average size of tutoring groups: 3

	Individual	Group
Time management	☐	☐
Organizational skills	☐	☐
Learning strategies	☐	☐
Study skills	☐	☐
Content area	☐	☐
Writing lab	■	☐
Math lab	☐	■

LD PROGRAM STAFF

Total number of LD Program staff (including director):

Full Time: 2 Part Time: 2

There is no advisor/advocate from the LD program available to students.

Key staff person available to work with LD students: Bonnie Smith

LD Program web site:
http://www2.smumn.edu/deptpages/~asc/disabilityservices.html

Saint Olaf College

Northfield, MN

Address: 1520 St. Olaf Avenue, Northfield, MN, 55057
Admissions telephone: 800 800-3025
Admissions FAX: 507 646-3832
Vice President and Dean of Enrollment: Jennifer Krengel Olsen
Admissions e-mail: admissions@stolaf.edu
Web site: http://www.stolaf.edu
SAT Code: 6638 ACT Code: 2150

LD Specialist: Ruth Boldstad
LD program telephone: 507 646-3288
LD program e-mail: bolstadr@stolaf.edu
Total campus enrollment: 3,046

GENERAL

Saint Olaf College is a private, coed, four-year institution. 300-acre campus in Northfield (population: 17,147), 35 miles from Minneapolis-St. Paul. Major airport and bus serve Minneapolis-St. Paul; smaller airport serves Stanton (10 miles); train serves Red Wing (25 miles). School operates transportation to Carleton Coll and to Minneapolis-St. Paul. 4-1-4 system.

LD ADMISSIONS

A personal interview is recommended. Essay is required and may be typed.

SECONDARY SCHOOL REQUIREMENTS

Graduation from secondary school required; GED accepted. The following course distribution required: 4 units of English, 2 units of math, 2 units of science, 2 units of foreign language, 1 unit of social studies, 1 unit of history, 2 units of academic electives.

TESTING

SAT Reasoning or ACT required. SAT Subject recommended.

All enrolled freshmen (fall 2004):

Average SAT I Scores:	Verbal: 650	Math: 640
Average ACT Scores:	Composite: 27	

Child Study Team report is not required. Tests required as part of this documentation:

- [ ] WAIS-IV
- [ ] WISC-IV
- [ ] SATA
- [ ] Woodcock-Johnson
- [ ] Nelson-Denny Reading Test
- [ ] Other

UNDERGRADUATE STUDENT BODY

Total undergraduate student enrollment: 1,258 Men, 1,753 Women.

Composition of student body (fall 2004):

	Undergraduate	Freshmen
International	0.5	0.6
Black	0.6	1.1
American Indian	0.3	0.2
Asian-American	4.9	4.2
Hispanic	1.8	1.6
White	81.3	84.7
Unreported	10.6	7.6
	100.0%	100.0%

46% are from out of state. Average age of full-time undergraduates is 20. 44% of classes have fewer than 20 students, 52% have between 20 and 50 students, 4% have more than 50 students.

STUDENT HOUSING

100% of freshmen live in college housing. Freshmen are required to live on campus. Housing is not guaranteed for all undergraduates. For all full time students housing is guaranteed. Campus can house 2,725 undergraduates. Single rooms are available for students with medical or special needs. A medical note is required.

EXPENSES

Tuition (2005-06): $26,500 per year.

Room: $3,100. Board: $3,200.
There is no additional cost for LD program/services.

LD SERVICES

LD program size is not limited.

LD services available to:

- [x] Freshmen
- [x] Sophomores
- [x] Juniors
- [x] Seniors

Academic Accommodations

Curriculum		In class	
Foreign language waiver	[ ]	Early syllabus	[ ]
Lighter course load	[x]	Note takers in class	[x]
Math waiver	[ ]	Priority seating	[ ]
Other special classes	[ ]	Tape recorders	[x]
Priority registrations	[ ]	Videotaped classes	[ ]
Substitution of courses	[ ]	Text on tape	[x]
Exams		**Services**	
Extended time	[x]	Diagnostic tests	[ ]
Oral exams	[x]	Learning centers	[ ]
Take home exams	[ ]	Proofreaders	[ ]
Exams on tape or computer	[x]	Readers	[x]
Untimed exams	[ ]	Reading Machines/Kurzweil	[ ]
Other accommodations	[ ]	Special bookstore section	[ ]
		Typists	[x]

Credit toward degree is not given for remedial courses taken.

Counseling Services

- [x] Academic
- [x] Psychological
- [x] Student Support groups
- [x] Vocational

Tutoring

Individual tutoring is available daily.

Average size of tutoring groups: 1

	Individual	Group
Time management	[x]	[x]
Organizational skills	[x]	[x]
Learning strategies	[x]	[x]
Study skills	[x]	[x]
Content area	[x]	[x]
Writing lab	[x]	[ ]
Math lab	[x]	[x]

LD PROGRAM STAFF

Total number of LD Program staff (including director):

Full Time: 1 Part Time: 1

There is an advisor/advocate from the LD program available to students.

Key staff person available to work with LD students: Ruth Boldstad, Student Disability Services & Tutoring Specialist.

Southwest Minnesota State University

Marshall, MN

Address: 1501 State Street, Marshall, MN, 56258
Admissions telephone: 800 642-0684
Admissions FAX: 507 537-7154
Director of Enrollment Services: Richard Shearer
Admissions e-mail: shearerr@southwestmsu.edu
Web site: http://www.southwestmsu.edu
SAT Code: 6703 ACT Code: 2151

LD program name: Learning Resources Center
Director of Learning Resources: Marilyn Leach
LD program telephone: 507 537-6169
LD program e-mail: leach@southwestmsu.edu
Total campus enrollment: 5,370

GENERAL

Southwest Minnesota State University is a public, coed, four-year institution. 216-acre campus in Marshall (population: 12,735), 90 miles from Sioux Falls, S.Dak. Served by bus; major airport serves Minneapolis-St. Paul (150 miles); smaller airport serves Sioux Falls; train serves Willmar (70 miles). Public transportation serves campus. Semester system.

LD ADMISSIONS

A personal interview is required. Essay is not required. Admission of LD students is based on the recommendation of the Learning Resources Staff.

SECONDARY SCHOOL REQUIREMENTS

Graduation from secondary school required; GED accepted. The following course distribution required: 4 units of English, 3 units of math, 3 units of science, 2 units of foreign language, 3 units of social studies.

TESTING

ACT required. SAT Subject recommended.

All enrolled freshmen (fall 2004):

Average ACT Scores: Composite: 22

Child Study Team report is not required. Tests required as part of this documentation:

- [ ] WAIS-IV
- [ ] WISC-IV
- [ ] SATA
- [ ] Woodcock-Johnson
- [ ] Nelson-Denny Reading Test
- [ ] Other

UNDERGRADUATE STUDENT BODY

Total undergraduate student enrollment: 1,689 Men, 2,310 Women.

Composition of student body (fall 2004):

	Undergraduate	Freshmen
International	4.0	6.1
Black	3.0	3.6
American Indian	0.2	0.6
Asian-American	2.8	1.7
Hispanic	2.3	1.3
White	84.7	74.6
Unreported	3.0	12.1
	100.0%	100.0%

21% are from out of state. 48% of classes have fewer than 20 students, 45% have between 20 and 50 students, 7% have more than 50 students.

STUDENT HOUSING

Freshmen are required to live on campus. Housing is guaranteed for all undergraduates. Campus can house 731 undergraduates. Single rooms are available for students with medical or special needs. A medical note is not required.

EXPENSES

Tuition (2005-06): $4,720 per year.
Room: $3,660. Board: $1,460.

There is no additional cost for LD program/services

LD SERVICES

LD program size is not limited.

LD services available to:

- [ ] Freshmen
- [ ] Sophomores
- [ ] Juniors
- [ ] Seniors

Academic Accommodations

Curriculum

- [ ] Foreign language waiver
- [x] Lighter course load
- [ ] Math waiver
- [x] Other special classes
- [ ] Priority registrations
- [ ] Substitution of courses

Exams

- [x] Extended time
- [x] Oral exams
- [ ] Take home exams
- [ ] Exams on tape or computer
- [x] Untimed exams
- [ ] Other accommodations

In class

- [ ] Early syllabus
- [x] Note takers in class
- [ ] Priority seating
- [x] Tape recorders
- [ ] Videotaped classes
- [ ] Text on tape

Services

- [x] Diagnostic tests
- [x] Learning centers
- [ ] Proofreaders
- [x] Readers
- [ ] Reading Machines/Kurzweil
- [ ] Special bookstore section
- [ ] Typists

Credit toward degree is not given for remedial courses taken.

Counseling Services

- [ ] Academic
- [ ] Psychological
- [ ] Student Support groups
- [ ] Vocational

Tutoring

Individual tutoring is available monthly.

	Individual	Group
Time management	[x]	[x]
Organizational skills	[x]	[ ]
Learning strategies	[x]	[ ]
Study skills	[x]	[x]
Content area	[x]	[ ]
Writing lab	[x]	[ ]
Math lab	[x]	[ ]

LD PROGRAM STAFF

Total number of LD Program staff (including director):

Full Time: 4 Part Time: 4

There is an advisor/advocate from the LD program available to students. The advisor/advocate meets with students once per month.

Key staff person available to work with LD students: Marilyn Leach, Director of Learning Resources.

St. Cloud State University

St. Cloud, MN

Address: 720 S. Fourth Avenue, St. Cloud, MN, 56301
Admissions telephone: 800 369-4260
Admissions FAX: 320 308-2243
Director of Enrollment Management: Pat Krueger
Admissions e-mail: scsu4u@stcloudstate.edu
Web site: http://www.stcloudstate.edu
SAT Code: 6679 ACT Code: 2144

LD program contact: Owen Zimpel
LD program telephone: 320 308-3117
LD program e-mail: ojzimpel@stcloudstate.edu
Total campus enrollment: 14,209

GENERAL

St. Cloud State University is a public, coed, four-year institution. 108-acre campus in St. Cloud (population: 59,107), 70 miles from Minneapolis-St. Paul. Served by bus and train; major airport serves Minneapolis. Public transportation serves campus. Semester system.

LD ADMISSIONS

A personal interview is not required. Essay is not required.

SECONDARY SCHOOL REQUIREMENTS

Graduation from secondary school required; GED accepted. The following course distribution required: 4 units of English, 3 units of math, 3 units of science, 2 units of foreign language, 3 units of social studies, 1 unit of history.

TESTING

ACT required; SAT Reasoning may be substituted. SAT Subject recommended.

All enrolled freshmen (fall 2004):

Average ACT Scores: Composite: 21

Child Study Team report is not required. Tests required as part of this documentation:

- [ ] WAIS-IV
- [ ] WISC-IV
- [ ] SATA
- [ ] Woodcock-Johnson
- [ ] Nelson-Denny Reading Test
- [ ] Other

UNDERGRADUATE STUDENT BODY

Total undergraduate student enrollment: 6,702 Men, 8,012 Women.

Composition of student body (fall 2004):

	Undergraduate	Freshmen
International	2.2	4.7
Black	2.2	1.8
American Indian	0.7	0.7
Asian-American	2.8	1.9
Hispanic	0.8	0.6
White	85.4	77.4
Unreported	5.9	12.9
	100.0%	100.0%

12% are from out of state. Average age of full-time undergraduates is 21. 30% of classes have fewer than 20 students, 62% have between 20 and 50 students, 8% have more than 50 students.

STUDENT HOUSING

72% of freshmen live in college housing. Housing is not guaranteed for all undergraduates. Campus can house 3,000 undergraduates.

EXPENSES

Tuition 2004: $4,577 per year (in-state), $9,935 (out-of-state).

There is no additional cost for LD program/services.

LD SERVICES

LD program size is not limited.

LD services available to:

- [ ] Freshmen
- [ ] Sophomores
- [ ] Juniors
- [ ] Seniors

Academic Accommodations

Curriculum

- [ ] Foreign language waiver
- [x] Lighter course load
- [ ] Math waiver
- [ ] Other special classes
- [ ] Priority registrations
- [ ] Substitution of courses

Exams

- [x] Extended time
- [x] Oral exams
- [ ] Take home exams
- [ ] Exams on tape or computer
- [ ] Untimed exams
- [ ] Other accommodations

In class

- [ ] Early syllabus
- [x] Note takers in class
- [ ] Priority seating
- [ ] Tape recorders
- [ ] Videotaped classes
- [ ] Text on tape

Services

- [ ] Diagnostic tests
- [x] Learning centers
- [ ] Proofreaders
- [x] Readers
- [ ] Reading Machines/Kurzweil
- [ ] Special bookstore section
- [ ] Typists

Counseling Services

- [ ] Academic
- [ ] Psychological
- [ ] Student Support groups
- [ ] Vocational

Tutoring

	Individual	Group
Time management	☐	☐
Organizational skills	☐	☐
Learning strategies	☐	☐
Study skills	☐	☐
Content area	☐	☐
Writing lab	☐	☐
Math lab	☐	☐

LD PROGRAM STAFF

Total number of LD Program staff (including director):

Full Time: 2 Part Time: 2

Key staff person available to work with LD students: Owen Zimpel, Director of Student Disablity Services.

University of St. Thomas

St. Paul, MN

Address: 2115 Summit Avenue, St. Paul, MN, 55105-1096
Admissions telephone: 800 328-6819, extension 2-6150
Admissions FAX: 651 962-6160
Associate Vice President for Enrollment Management: Marla Friederichs
Admissions e-mail: admissions@stthomas.edu
Web site: http://www.stthomas.edu
SAT Code: 6110 ACT Code: 2102

LD program name: Enhancement Program
LD program address: Mail No. 4016
Director: Kimberly Schumann
LD program telephone: 651 962-6315
LD program e-mail: kjschumann@stthomas.edu
LD program enrollment: 175, Total campus enrollment: 5,302

GENERAL

University of St. Thomas is a private, coed, four-year institution. 87-acre, urban campus in St. Paul (population: 287,151); branch campuses in Minneapolis and Owatonna; off-campus class sites in Anoka, Bloomington, Chaska, East St. Paul, and Rochester and abroad in Canada, Italy, and Taiwan. Served by air, bus, and train. School operates transportation to nearby schools and downtown Minneapolis. Public transportation serves campus. 4-1-4 system.

LD ADMISSIONS

Students do not complete a separate application and are not simultaneously accepted to the LD program. A member of the LD program does not sit on the admissions committee. A personal interview is recommended. Essay is required and may be typed.

SECONDARY SCHOOL REQUIREMENTS

Graduation from secondary school required; GED accepted. The following course distribution required: 3 units of math.

TESTING

ACT required; SAT Reasoning may be substituted.

All enrolled freshmen (fall 2004):

Average SAT I Scores:	Verbal: 575	Math: 587
Average ACT Scores:	Composite: 25	

Child Study Team report is not required. A neuropsychological or comprehensive psycho-educational evaluation is required for admission. Must be dated within 36 months of application. Tests required as part of this documentation:

- ■ WAIS-IV
- □ WISC-IV
- □ SATA
- ■ Woodcock-Johnson
- □ Nelson-Denny Reading Test
- □ Other

UNDERGRADUATE STUDENT BODY

Total undergraduate student enrollment: 2,560 Men, 2,856 Women.

Composition of student body (fall 2004):

	Undergraduate	Freshmen
International	1.0	1.1
Black	4.6	2.8
American Indian	0.3	0.5
Asian-American	5.0	5.1
Hispanic	2.0	1.9
White	83.6	87.3
Unreported	3.5	1.3
	100.0%	100.0%

21% are from out of state. Average age of full-time undergraduates is 20. 51% of classes have fewer than 20 students, 47% have between 20 and 50 students, 2% have more than 50 students.

STUDENT HOUSING

91% of freshmen live in college housing. Freshmen are not required to live on campus. Housing is guaranteed for all undergraduates. Campus can house 2,000 undergraduates. Single rooms are available for students with medical or special needs. A medical note is required.

EXPENSES

Tuition (2005-06): $22,880 per year.

Room: $4,100. Board: $2,606.

There is no additional cost for LD program/services.

LD SERVICES

LD program size is not limited.

LD services available to:

■ Freshmen ■ Sophomores ■ Juniors ■ Seniors

Academic Accommodations

Curriculum		In class	
Foreign language waiver	■	Early syllabus	■
Lighter course load	□	Note takers in class	■
Math waiver	■	Priority seating	□
Other special classes	□	Tape recorders	■
Priority registrations	□	Videotaped classes	□
Substitution of courses	■	Text on tape	■
Exams		**Services**	
Extended time	■	Diagnostic tests	□
Oral exams	■	Learning centers	■
Take home exams	□	Proofreaders	■
Exams on tape or computer	■	Readers	■
Untimed exams	□	Reading Machines/Kurzweil	■
Other accommodations	■	Special bookstore section	□
		Typists	■

Counseling Services

- ■ Academic
- ■ Psychological
- □ Student Support groups
- □ Vocational

Tutoring

Individual tutoring is available weekly.

	Individual	Group
Time management	■	□
Organizational skills	■	□
Learning strategies	■	□
Study skills	■	□
Content area	■	□
Writing lab	■	□
Math lab	■	□

UNIQUE LD PROGRAM FEATURES

Students can make weekly appointments for time management study skills assistance.

LD PROGRAM STAFF

Total number of LD Program staff (including director):

Full Time: 1 Part Time: 1

There is an advisor/advocate from the LD program available to students.

Key staff person available to work with LD students: Kimberly Schumann, Director.

LD Program web site: www.stthomas.edu/enhancementprog/

The College of St. Catherine

St. Paul, MN

Address: 2004 Randolph Avenue, St. Paul, MN, 55105
Admissions telephone: 800 945-4599
Assistant to the President for Admissions: Cal Mosely
Admissions e-mail: admissions@stkate.edu
Web site: http://www.stkate.edu
SAT Code: 6105 ACT Code: 2096

Disabilities Coordinator: Barbara Mandel
LD program telephone: 651 690-6563
LD program e-mail: bjmandel@stkate.edu
Total campus enrollment: 3,582

GENERAL

The College of St. Catherine is a private, women's, four-year institution. 110-acre, suburban campus in St. Paul (population: 287,151); branch campus in Minneapolis. Served by air, bus, and train. School operates transportation to consortium schools. Public transportation serves campus. 4-1-4 system.

LD ADMISSIONS

A personal interview is recommended. Essay is required and may be typed.

SECONDARY SCHOOL REQUIREMENTS

Graduation from secondary school required; GED accepted.

TESTING

SAT Reasoning or ACT required. SAT Subject recommended.

All enrolled freshmen (fall 2004):

Average SAT I Scores: Verbal: 620 Math: 557
Average ACT Scores: Composite: 24

Child Study Team report is not required. Tests required as part of this documentation:

☐ WAIS-IV ☐ Woodcock-Johnson
☐ WISC-IV ☐ Nelson-Denny Reading Test
☐ SATA ☐ Other

UNDERGRADUATE STUDENT BODY

Total undergraduate student enrollment: 89 Men, 3,511 Women.

Composition of student body (fall 2004):

	Undergraduate	Freshmen
International	1.9	2.0
Black	6.1	6.8
American Indian	0.5	0.6
Asian-American	10.9	5.7
Hispanic	3.4	2.3
White	70.6	75.0
Unreported	6.6	7.6
	100.0%	100.0%

10% are from out of state. Average age of full-time undergraduates is 21. 74% of classes have fewer than 20 students, 24% have between 20 and 50 students, 2% have more than 50 students.

STUDENT HOUSING

76% of freshmen live in college housing. Housing is guaranteed for all undergraduates.

EXPENSES

Tuition (2005-06): $21,060 per year.
Room: $3,420. Board: $2,700.
There is no additional cost for LD program/services.

LD SERVICES

LD program size is not limited.

LD services available to:

☐ Freshmen ☐ Sophomores ☐ Juniors ☐ Seniors

Academic Accommodations

Curriculum		**In class**	
Foreign language waiver	☐	Early syllabus	☐
Lighter course load	☑	Note takers in class	☑
Math waiver	☐	Priority seating	☐
Other special classes	☐	Tape recorders	☑
Priority registrations	☐	Videotaped classes	☐
Substitution of courses	☐	Text on tape	☐
Exams		**Services**	
Extended time	☑	Diagnostic tests	☑
Oral exams	☑	Learning centers	☑
Take home exams	☐	Proofreaders	☐
Exams on tape or computer	☐	Readers	☑
Untimed exams	☑	Reading Machines/Kurzweil	☑
Other accommodations	☐	Special bookstore section	☐
		Typists	☐

Credit toward degree is not given for remedial courses taken.

Counseling Services

☐ Academic
☐ Psychological
☐ Student Support groups
☐ Vocational

Tutoring

	Individual	Group
Time management	☐	☐
Organizational skills	☐	☐
Learning strategies	☐	☐
Study skills	☐	☐
Content area	☐	☐
Writing lab	☐	☐
Math lab	☐	☐

LD PROGRAM STAFF

Key staff person available to work with LD students: Barbara Mandel, Disabilities Coordinator.

The College of St. Scholastica

Duluth, MN

Address: 1200 Kenwood Avenue, Duluth, MN, 55811
Admissions telephone: 800 249-6412
Admissions FAX: 218 723-5991
Vice President for Enrollment Management: Brian Dalton
Admissions e-mail: admissions@css.edu
Web site: http://www.css.edu
SAT Code: 6107 ACT Code: 2098

Director of Academic Support Services: Jay Newcomb
LD program telephone: 218 723-6552
LD program e-mail: jnewcomb@css.edu
Total campus enrollment: 2,441

GENERAL

The College of St. Scholastica is a private, coed, four-year institution. 160-acre, suburban campus in Duluth (population: 86,918). Served by air and bus; major airport and train serve Minneapolis (150 miles). Public transportation serves campus. Semester system.

LD ADMISSIONS

A personal interview is not required. Essay is not required.

SECONDARY SCHOOL REQUIREMENTS

Graduation from secondary school required; GED accepted.

TESTING

SAT Reasoning considered if submitted. ACT considered if submitted. SAT Subject recommended.

All enrolled freshmen (fall 2004):

Average SAT I Scores:	Verbal: 538	Math: 532
Average ACT Scores:	Composite: 23	

Child Study Team report is not required. Tests required as part of this documentation:

☐ WAIS-IV	☐ Woodcock-Johnson
☐ WISC-IV	☐ Nelson-Denny Reading Test
☐ SATA	☐ Other

UNDERGRADUATE STUDENT BODY

Total undergraduate student enrollment: 505 Men, 1,195 Women.

Composition of student body (fall 2004):

	Undergraduate	Freshmen
International	3.6	2.0
Black	0.9	1.2
American Indian	0.9	1.9
Asian-American	2.0	1.5
Hispanic	0.2	0.7
White	87.2	87.5
Unreported	5.2	5.2
	100.0%	100.0%

11% are from out of state. Average age of full-time undergraduates is 23. 65% of classes have fewer than 20 students, 30% have between 20 and 50 students, 5% have more than 50 students.

STUDENT HOUSING

73% of freshmen live in college housing. Freshmen are required to live on campus. Housing is guaranteed for all undergraduates. Campus can house 742 undergraduates. Single rooms are available for students with medical or special needs. A medical note is required.

EXPENSES

Tuition (2005-06): $22,110 per year.

Room: $3,556. Board: $2,660.

There is no additional cost for LD program/services.

LD SERVICES

LD program size is not limited.

LD services available to:

☑ Freshmen ☑ Sophomores ☑ Juniors ☑ Seniors

Academic Accommodations

Curriculum		**In class**	
Foreign language waiver	☐	Early syllabus	☐
Lighter course load	☐	Note takers in class	☑
Math waiver	☐	Priority seating	☐
Other special classes	☐	Tape recorders	☑
Priority registrations	☑	Videotaped classes	☐
Substitution of courses	☑	Text on tape	☑
Exams		**Services**	
Extended time	☑	Diagnostic tests	☐
Oral exams	☐	Learning centers	☐
Take home exams	☐	Proofreaders	☑
Exams on tape or computer	☑	Readers	☑
Untimed exams	☐	Reading Machines/Kurzweil	☑
Other accommodations	☐	Special bookstore section	☐
		Typists	☑

Credit toward degree is not given for remedial courses taken.

Counseling Services

☑ Academic — Meets 6 times per academic year
☑ Psychological
☐ Student Support groups
☐ Vocational

Tutoring

Individual tutoring is available daily.

Average size of tutoring groups: 10

	Individual	Group
Time management	☑	☐
Organizational skills	☑	☐
Learning strategies	☑	☐
Study skills	☑	☑
Content area	☑	☐
Writing lab	☑	☐
Math lab	☑	☐

UNIQUE LD PROGRAM FEATURES

Our services focus on Disabled Student Services providing required accommodations. Policies and accommodations are approved by an access committee made up of faculty and staff. Individual counseling and support are provided through the Student Support Services Program.

LD PROGRAM STAFF

There is an advisor/advocate from the LD program available to students.

Key staff person available to work with LD students: Jay Newcomb, Director of Academic Support Services.

Winona State University

Winona, MN

Address: PO Box 5838, Winona, MN, 55987-5838
Admissions telephone: 800 DIAL-WSU
Admissions FAX: 507 457-5620
Director of Admissions: Carl Stange
Admissions e-mail: admissions@winona.edu
Web site: http://www.winona.edu
SAT Code: 6680 ACT Code: 2162

LD program name: Advising and Retention
Office Manager, Disability Resource Center: Deb Huegel
LD program telephone: 507 457-2391, extension 507
LD program e-mail: dhuegel@winona.edu
Total campus enrollment: 7,582

GENERAL

Winona State University is a public, coed, four-year institution. 40-acre campus in Winona (population: 27,069), 90 miles from Minneapolis-St. Paul; branch campus in Rochester (45 miles). Served by bus and train; major airport serves Minneapolis-St. Paul; smaller airport serves LaCrosse, Wis. (24 miles). Public transportation serves campus. Semester system.

LD ADMISSIONS

Students do not complete a separate application and are not simultaneously accepted to the LD program. A member of the LD program does not sit on the admissions committee. High school waivers are accepted for foreign language. A personal interview is recommended. Essay is not required.

SECONDARY SCHOOL REQUIREMENTS

Graduation from secondary school required; GED accepted. The following course distribution required: 4 units of English, 3 units of math, 3 units of science, 2 units of foreign language, 3 units of social studies, 1 unit of history, 1 unit of academic electives.

TESTING

SAT Reasoning considered if submitted. ACT required. SAT Subject recommended.

All enrolled freshmen (fall 2004):

Average ACT Scores: Composite: 22

Child Study Team report is not required. A neuropsychological or comprehensive psycho-educational evaluation is required for admission. Must be dated within 36 months of application. Tests required as part of this documentation:

☒	WAIS-IV	☒	Woodcock-Johnson
☒	WISC-IV	☐	Nelson-Denny Reading Test
☐	SATA	☐	Other

UNDERGRADUATE STUDENT BODY

Total undergraduate student enrollment: 2,621 Men, 4,493 Women.

Composition of student body (fall 2004):

	Undergraduate	Freshmen
International	1.3	4.2
Black	0.6	1.1
American Indian	0.3	0.3
Asian-American	1.5	1.7
Hispanic	1.1	1.1
White	92.1	67.8
Unreported	3.1	23.8
	100.0%	100.0%

40% are from out of state. Average age of full-time undergraduates is 22. 36% of classes have fewer than 20 students, 58% have between 20 and 50 students, 6% have more than 50 students.

STUDENT HOUSING

81% of freshmen live in college housing. Freshmen are not required to live on campus. Housing is guaranteed for all undergraduates. Campus can house 2,700 undergraduates. Single rooms are available for students with medical or special needs. A medical note is required.

EXPENSES

Tuition (2005-06): $4,940 per year (in-state), $9,160 (out-of-state).
Room & Board: $6,060.
There is no additional cost for LD program/services.

LD SERVICES

LD program size is not limited.

LD services available to:

☒ Freshmen ☒ Sophomores ☒ Juniors ☒ Seniors

Academic Accommodations

Curriculum		In class	
Foreign language waiver	☐	Early syllabus	☐
Lighter course load	☒	Note takers in class	☒
Math waiver	☐	Priority seating	☒
Other special classes	☐	Tape recorders	☐
Priority registrations	☒	Videotaped classes	☐
Substitution of courses	☐	Text on tape	☒
Exams		**Services**	
Extended time	☒	Diagnostic tests	☐
Oral exams	☒	Learning centers	☒
Take home exams	☐	Proofreaders	☐
Exams on tape or computer	☒	Readers	☐
Untimed exams	☐	Reading Machines/Kurzweil	☒
Other accommodations	☒	Special bookstore section	☐
		Typists	☐

Credit toward degree is not given for remedial courses taken.

Counseling Services

☒ Academic
☒ Psychological
☒ Student Support groups
☐ Vocational

Tutoring

Individual tutoring is available weekly.

Average size of tutoring groups: 1

	Individual	Group
Time management	☒	☐
Organizational skills	☒	☐
Learning strategies	☒	☐
Study skills	☒	☐
Content area	☒	☐
Writing lab	☒	☐
Math lab	☒	☐

LD PROGRAM STAFF

Total number of LD Program staff (including director):

Full Time: 1 Part Time: 1

There is an advisor/advocate from the LD program available to students. 2 graduate students and 16 peer tutors are available to work with LD students.

Key staff person available to work with LD students: Nancy Dumke, Coordinator, Disability Resource Center.

Belhaven College

Jackson, MS

Address: 1500 Peachtree Street, Jackson, MS, 39202
Admissions telephone: 800 960-5940
Admissions FAX: 601 968-8946
Director of Admissions: Suzanne T. Sullivan
Admissions e-mail: admissions@belhaven.edu
Web site: http://www.belhaven.edu
SAT Code: 1055 ACT Code: 2180

Director of Academic Support/Career Center: Erin Price
LD program telephone: 601 968-5961
LD program e-mail: eprice@belhaven.edu
Total campus enrollment: 2,145

GENERAL

Belhaven College is a private, coed, four-year institution. 42-acre, suburban campus in Jackson (population: 184,256); branch campuses in Memphis and Orlando. Served by airport, bus, and train. Public transportation serves campus. Semester system.

LD ADMISSIONS

A personal interview is recommended. Essay is not required.

SECONDARY SCHOOL REQUIREMENTS

Graduation from secondary school required; GED accepted. The following course distribution required: 4 units of English, 2 units of math, 1 unit of science, 1 unit of history, 8 units of academic electives.

TESTING

ACT required; SAT Reasoning may be substituted. SAT Subject recommended.

All enrolled freshmen (fall 2004):

Average SAT I Scores: Verbal: 597 Math: 560
Average ACT Scores: Composite: 24

Child Study Team report is not required. Tests required as part of this documentation:

- ❑ WAIS-IV
- ❑ WISC-IV
- ❑ SATA
- ❑ Woodcock-Johnson
- ❑ Nelson-Denny Reading Test
- ❑ Other

UNDERGRADUATE STUDENT BODY

Total undergraduate student enrollment: 621 Men, 1,045 Women.

Composition of student body (fall 2004):

	Undergraduate	Freshmen
International	1.7	1.4
Black	20.6	38.7
American Indian	0.0	0.6
Asian-American	0.4	0.4
Hispanic	2.9	1.6
White	69.3	50.0
Unreported	5.0	7.2
	100.0%	100.0%

34% are from out of state.

STUDENT HOUSING

Freshmen are required to live on campus. Housing is guaranteed for all undergraduates. Campus can house 532 undergraduates.

EXPENSES

Tuition (2005-06): $13,450 per year.

Room & Board: $5,430.

There is no additional cost for LD program/services.

LD SERVICES

LD program size is not limited.

LD services available to:

❑ Freshmen ❑ Sophomores ❑ Juniors ❑ Seniors

Academic Accommodations

Curriculum		In class	
Foreign language waiver	❑	Early syllabus	❑
Lighter course load	■	Note takers in class	❑
Math waiver	❑	Priority seating	❑
Other special classes	❑	Tape recorders	❑
Priority registrations	❑	Videotaped classes	❑
Substitution of courses	❑	Text on tape	❑
Exams		**Services**	
Extended time	❑	Diagnostic tests	❑
Oral exams	❑	Learning centers	❑
Take home exams	❑	Proofreaders	❑
Exams on tape or computer	❑	Readers	❑
Untimed exams	■	Reading Machines/Kurzweil	❑
Other accommodations	❑	Special bookstore section	❑
		Typists	❑

Credit toward degree is not given for remedial courses taken.

Counseling Services

- ❑ Academic
- ❑ Psychological
- ❑ Student Support groups
- ❑ Vocational

Tutoring

	Individual	Group
Time management	❑	❑
Organizational skills	❑	❑
Learning strategies	❑	❑
Study skills	❑	❑
Content area	❑	❑
Writing lab	❑	❑
Math lab	❑	❑

LD PROGRAM STAFF

Key staff person available to work with LD students: Erin Price, Director of Academic Support/Career Center.

Blue Mountain College

Blue Mountain, MS

Address: PO Box 160, Blue Mountain, MS, 38610-0160
Admissions telephone: 800 235-0136
Admissions FAX: 662 685-4776
Director of Admissions: Tina Barkley
Admissions e-mail: admissions@bmc.edu
Web site: http://www.bmc.edu
SAT Code: 1066 ACT Code: 2182

Vice President for Academic Affairs: Sharon B. Enzor
LD program telephone: 662 685-477, extension 1136
LD program e-mail: senzor@bmc.edu
Total campus enrollment: 388

GENERAL

Blue Mountain College is a private, women's, four-year institution. 44-acre campus in Blue Mountain (population: 670), 69 miles from Memphis, TN. Major airport and train serve Memphis, TN; smaller airport serves Ripley (five miles); bus serves New Albany (15 miles). Semester system.

LD ADMISSIONS

Students do not complete a separate application and are not simultaneously accepted to the LD program. A member of the LD program does not sit on the admissions committee. A personal interview is required. Essay is not required.

SECONDARY SCHOOL REQUIREMENTS

Graduation from secondary school required; GED accepted. The following course distribution required: 4 units of English, 3 units of math, 3 units of science, 2 units of foreign language, 1 unit of social studies, 2 units of history.

TESTING

ACT required; SAT Reasoning may be substituted. SAT Subject recommended.

All enrolled freshmen (fall 2004):

Average SAT I Scores: Verbal: Math:
Average ACT Scores: Composite: 20

Child Study Team report is not required. Tests required as part of this documentation:

☐ WAIS-IV	☐ Woodcock-Johnson
☐ WISC-IV	☐ Nelson-Denny Reading Test
☐ SATA	☐ Other

UNDERGRADUATE STUDENT BODY

Total undergraduate student enrollment: 68 Men, 327 Women.

Composition of student body (fall 2004):

	Undergraduate	Freshmen
International	0.0	0.5
Black	11.3	13.0
American Indian	0.0	0.3
Asian-American	0.0	0.0
Hispanic	0.0	0.0
White	88.7	86.2
Unreported	0.0	0.0
	100.0%	100.0%

11% are from out of state. Average age of full-time undergraduates is 24. 73% of classes have fewer than 20 students, 25% have between 20 and 50 students, 2% have more than 50 students.

STUDENT HOUSING

60% of freshmen live in college housing. Housing is guaranteed for all undergraduates. Campus can house 250 undergraduates. Single rooms are available for students with medical or special needs. A medical note is required.

EXPENSES

Tuition (2005-06): $6,780 per year.
Room: $1,400.
There is no additional cost for LD program/services.

LD SERVICES

LD program size is not limited.

LD services available to:

☐ Freshmen ☐ Sophomores ☐ Juniors ☐ Seniors

Academic Accommodations

Curriculum		In class	
Foreign language waiver	☐	Early syllabus	☐
Lighter course load	■	Note takers in class	■
Math waiver	☐	Priority seating	☐
Other special classes	☐	Tape recorders	■
Priority registrations	☐	Videotaped classes	☐
Substitution of courses	☐	Text on tape	☐
Exams		**Services**	
Extended time	■	Diagnostic tests	☐
Oral exams	■	Learning centers	■
Take home exams	☐	Proofreaders	☐
Exams on tape or computer	☐	Readers	■
Untimed exams	■	Reading Machines/Kurzweil	☐
Other accommodations	☐	Special bookstore section	☐
		Typists	☐

Credit toward degree is not given for remedial courses taken.

Counseling Services

☐ Academic
☐ Psychological
☐ Student Support groups
☐ Vocational

Tutoring

Individual tutoring is available.

	Individual	Group
Time management	☐	☐
Organizational skills	☐	☐
Learning strategies	☐	☐
Study skills	☐	☐
Content area	☐	☐
Writing lab	☐	☐
Math lab	☐	☐

LD PROGRAM STAFF

There is an advisor/advocate from the LD program available to students. 1 peer tutor is available to work with LD students.

Key staff person available to work with LD students: Audrey Hector, Dir. of the Ctr. for the Advancement of Learning.

Jackson State University

Jackson, MS

Address: 1400 J.R. Lynch Street, Jackson, MS, 39217
Admissions telephone: 601 979-2100
Admissions FAX: 601 979-3445
Director of Admissions: Stephanie Chatman
Admissions e-mail: admappl@ccaix.jsums.edu
Web site: http://www.jsums.edu
SAT Code: 1341 ACT Code: 2204

ADA Coordinator: Vinson Ballard
LD program telephone: 601 979-3704
LD program e-mail: vinson.ballard@jsums.edu
Total campus enrollment: 5,471

GENERAL

Jackson State University is a public, coed, four-year institution. 150-acre, urban campus in Jackson (population: 184,256). Served by air, bus, and train. Public transportation serves campus. Semester system.

LD ADMISSIONS

A personal interview is not required. Essay is not required.

SECONDARY SCHOOL REQUIREMENTS

Graduation from secondary school not required. The following course distribution required: 4 units of English, 3 units of math, 3 units of science, 1 unit of foreign language, 1 unit of social studies, 2 units of history, 1 unit of academic electives.

TESTING

Child Study Team report is not required. Tests required as part of this documentation:

- ☐ WAIS-IV
- ☐ WISC-IV
- ☐ SATA
- ☐ Woodcock-Johnson
- ☐ Nelson-Denny Reading Test
- ☐ Other

UNDERGRADUATE STUDENT BODY

Total undergraduate student enrollment: 2,158 Men, 3,313 Women.

22% are from out of state.

STUDENT HOUSING

Housing is guaranteed for all undergraduates. Campus can house 2,458 undergraduates.

EXPENSES

Tuition (2005-06): $3,964 per year (in-state), $8,872 (out-of-state).
Room: $2,998. Board: $1,997.
There is no additional cost for LD program/services.

LD SERVICES

LD program size is not limited.

LD services available to:

☐ Freshmen ☐ Sophomores ☐ Juniors ☐ Seniors

Academic Accommodations

Curriculum		**In class**	
Foreign language waiver	☐	Early syllabus	☐
Lighter course load	☑	Note takers in class	☑
Math waiver	☐	Priority seating	☐
Other special classes	☑	Tape recorders	☑
Priority registrations	☐	Videotaped classes	☐
Substitution of courses	☐	Text on tape	☐
Exams		**Services**	
Extended time	☑	Diagnostic tests	☑
Oral exams	☑	Learning centers	☑
Take home exams	☐	Proofreaders	☐
Exams on tape or computer	☐	Readers	☑
Untimed exams	☐	Reading Machines/Kurzweil	☑
Other accommodations	☐	Special bookstore section	☑
		Typists	☐

Credit toward degree is not given for remedial courses taken.

Counseling Services

- ☐ Academic
- ☐ Psychological
- ☐ Student Support groups
- ☐ Vocational

Tutoring

	Individual	Group
Time management	☐	☐
Organizational skills	☐	☐
Learning strategies	☐	☐
Study skills	☐	☐
Content area	☐	☐
Writing lab	☐	☐
Math lab	☐	☐

LD PROGRAM STAFF

Total number of LD Program staff (including director):

Full Time: 2 Part Time: 2

Key staff person available to work with LD students: Vinson Ballard, ADA Coordinator.

Millsaps College

Jackson, MS

Address: 1701 N. State Street, Jackson, MS, 39210-0001
Admissions telephone: 800 352-1050
Admissions FAX: 601 974-1059
Director of Admissions: Ann Hendrick
Admissions e-mail: admissions@millsaps.edu
Web site: http://www.millsaps.edu
SAT Code: 1471 ACT Code: 2212

LD program name: ADA Services for Students
Director, ADA Services for Students: Sherryl E. Wilburn
LD program telephone: 601 974-1208
LD program e-mail: wilbuse@millsaps.edu
LD program enrollment: 76, Total campus enrollment: 1,086

GENERAL

Millsaps College is a private, coed, four-year institution. 100-acre campus in Jackson (population: 184,256), 180 miles from New Orleans and 190 miles from Memphis. Served by air, bus, and train. Public transportation serves campus. Semester system.

LD ADMISSIONS

Students do not complete a separate application and are simultaneously accepted to the LD program. A member of the LD program does not sit on the admissions committee. A personal interview is required. Essay is required and may be typed.

For fall 2004, 21 completed self-identified LD applications were received.

SECONDARY SCHOOL REQUIREMENTS

Graduation from secondary school required; GED accepted. The following course distribution required: 4 units of English, 3 units of math, 3 units of science, 2 units of social studies, 2 units of history.

TESTING

SAT Reasoning or ACT required. SAT Subject recommended.

All enrolled freshmen (fall 2004):

Average SAT I Scores:	Verbal: 593	Math: 590
Average ACT Scores:	Composite: 26	

Child Study Team report is not required. A neuropsychological or comprehensive psycho-educational evaluation is required for admission. Tests required as part of this documentation:

- ■ WAIS-IV
- ■ WISC-IV
- ■ SATA
- ■ Woodcock-Johnson
- ■ Nelson-Denny Reading Test
- ■ Other

UNDERGRADUATE STUDENT BODY

Total undergraduate student enrollment: 555 Men, 666 Women.

Composition of student body (fall 2004):

	Undergraduate	Freshmen
International	0.0	0.4
Black	15.8	11.2
American Indian	0.0	0.4
Asian-American	4.0	3.5
Hispanic	1.4	1.4
White	78.8	81.6
Unreported	0.0	1.6
	100.0%	100.0%

42% are from out of state. 54% join a fraternity and 56% join a sorority. Average age of full-time undergraduates is 20. 73% of classes have fewer than 20 students, 27% have between 20 and 50 students.

STUDENT HOUSING

96% of freshmen live in college housing. Freshmen are required to live on campus. Housing is guaranteed for all undergraduates. Campus can house 991 undergraduates. Single rooms are available for students with medical or special needs. A medical note is required.

EXPENSES

Tuition (2005-06): $19,490 per year.

Room: $4,248. Board: $3,318.

There is no additional cost for LD program/services.

LD SERVICES

LD program size is not limited.

LD services available to:

■ Freshmen ■ Sophomores ■ Juniors ■ Seniors

Academic Accommodations

Curriculum		In class	
Foreign language waiver	☐	Early syllabus	☐
Lighter course load	■	Note takers in class	■
Math waiver	☐	Priority seating	■
Other special classes	■	Tape recorders	■
Priority registrations	☐	Videotaped classes	☐
Substitution of courses	☐	Text on tape	☐
Exams		**Services**	
Extended time	■	Diagnostic tests	☐
Oral exams	■	Learning centers	■
Take home exams	☐	Proofreaders	☐
Exams on tape or computer	☐	Readers	■
Untimed exams	■	Reading Machines/Kurzweil	☐
Other accommodations	☐	Special bookstore section	☐
		Typists	☐

Credit toward degree is not given for remedial courses taken.

Counseling Services

- ■ Academic — Meets 4 times per academic year
- ☐ Psychological
- ☐ Student Support groups
- ☐ Vocational

Tutoring

Individual tutoring is available.

Average size of tutoring groups: 2

	Individual	Group
Time management	■	☐
Organizational skills	■	☐
Learning strategies	☐	☐
Study skills	■	☐
Content area	☐	☐
Writing lab	■	☐
Math lab	■	☐

LD PROGRAM STAFF

Total number of LD Program staff (including director):

Full Time: 2 Part Time: 2

There is an advisor/advocate from the LD program available to students. The advisor/advocate meets with students 2 times per month.

Key staff person available to work with LD students: Sherryl E. Wilburn, Director, ADA Services for Students.

LD Program web site:
http://www.millsaps.edu/stuafr/disabilityservices.html

Mississippi College

Clinton, MS

Address: MC Box 4001, Clinton, MS, 39058
Admissions telephone: 800 738-1236
Admissions FAX: 601 925-3950
Director of Admissions: Chad Phillips
Admissions e-mail: enrollment-services@mc.edu
Web site: http://www.mc.edu
SAT Code: 1477 ACT Code: 2214

LD program name: Counseling & Testing Center
LD program address: Box 4016
Director of Counseling & Testing Center: Dr. Buddy Wagner
LD program telephone: 601 925-3354
LD program e-mail: bwagner@mc.edu
LD program enrollment: 35, Total campus enrollment: 2,422

GENERAL

Mississippi College is a private, coed, four-year institution. 320-acre campus in Clinton (population: 23,341), 10 miles from Jackson. Airport and bus serve Jackson. Semester system.

LD ADMISSIONS

Students do not complete a separate application and are not simultaneously accepted to the LD program. A member of the LD program does not sit on the admissions committee. A personal interview is not required. Essay is not required. LD students must meet the same requirements as other students.

SECONDARY SCHOOL REQUIREMENTS

Graduation from secondary school required; GED accepted.

TESTING

SAT Reasoning considered if submitted. ACT required. SAT Subject recommended.

All enrolled freshmen (fall 2004):

Average SAT I Scores:	Verbal: 597	Math: 569
Average ACT Scores:	Composite: 24	

Child Study Team report is not required. A neuropsychological or comprehensive psycho-education evaluation is not required for admission. Tests required as part of this documentation:

- ☐ WAIS-IV
- ☐ WISC-IV
- ☐ SATA
- ☐ Woodcock-Johnson
- ☐ Nelson-Denny Reading Test
- ☐ Other

UNDERGRADUATE STUDENT BODY

Total undergraduate student enrollment: 948 Men, 1,341 Women.

Composition of student body (fall 2004):

	Undergraduate	Freshmen
International	0.3	0.2
Black	12.7	17.8
American Indian	0.0	0.2
Asian-American	1.0	0.8
Hispanic	1.3	0.4
White	84.5	80.0
Unreported	0.3	0.5
	100.0%	100.0%

18% are from out of state. Average age of full-time undergraduates is 22. 52% of classes have fewer than 20 students, 47% have between 20 and 50 students, 1% have more than 50 students.

STUDENT HOUSING

86% of freshmen live in college housing. Freshmen are required to live on campus. Housing is guaranteed for all undergraduates. Campus can house 1,667 undergraduates. Single rooms are available for students with medical or special needs. A medical note is required.

EXPENSES

Tuition (2005-06): $11,400 per year.
Room: $2,492. Board: $2,750.
There is no additional cost for LD program/services.

LD SERVICES

LD program size is not limited.

LD services available to:

☑ Freshmen ☑ Sophomores ☑ Juniors ☑ Seniors

Academic Accommodations

Curriculum		**In class**	
Foreign language waiver	☐	Early syllabus	☐
Lighter course load	☐	Note takers in class	☑
Math waiver	☐	Priority seating	☐
Other special classes	☐	Tape recorders	☑
Priority registrations	☐	Videotaped classes	☐
Substitution of courses	☐	Text on tape	☐
Exams		**Services**	
Extended time	☑	Diagnostic tests	☐
Oral exams	☑	Learning centers	☐
Take home exams	☐	Proofreaders	☐
Exams on tape or computer	☐	Readers	☑
Untimed exams	☐	Reading Machines/Kurzweil	☐
Other accommodations	☐	Special bookstore section	☐
		Typists	☐

Credit toward degree is not given for remedial courses taken.

Counseling Services

- ☑ Academic
- ☑ Psychological
- ☐ Student Support groups
- ☐ Vocational

Tutoring

Individual tutoring is available weekly.

Average size of tutoring groups: 1

	Individual	Group
Time management	☑	☐
Organizational skills	☑	☐
Learning strategies	☑	☐
Study skills	☑	☑
Content area	☐	☐
Writing lab	☐	☑
Math lab	☐	☑

LD PROGRAM STAFF

Total number of LD Program staff (including director):

Full Time: 1 Part Time: 1

There is an advisor/advocate from the LD program available to students.

Key staff person available to work with LD students: Dr. Buddy Wagner, Director of Counseling & Testing Center.

Mississippi State University

Mississippi State, MS

Address: PO Box 6334, Mississippi State, MS, 39762
Admissions telephone: 662 325-2224
Admissions FAX: 662 325-1678
Director of Admissions: Lisa Harris, Interim
Admissions e-mail: admit@admissions.msstate.edu
Web site: http://www.msstate.edu
SAT Code: 1480 ACT Code: 2220

LD program address: P.O. Box 806
LD Specialist: Susan Felker
LD program telephone: 662 325-3335
LD program e-mail: sfelker@saffairs.msstate.edu
LD program enrollment: 86, Total campus enrollment: 12,495

GENERAL

Mississippi State University is a public, coed, four-year institution. 4,200-acre campus in Starkville (population: 21,869), 120 miles from Jackson; branch campuses in Meridian and Vicksburg and at Stennis Space Center. Served by bus; major airport serves Jackson; smaller airport serves Columbus (16 miles); train serves Greenwood (84 miles). School operates transportation to Jackson, Meridian, Stennis Space Center, and Vicksburg. Semester system.

LD ADMISSIONS

Students do not complete a separate application and are not simultaneously accepted to the LD program. A member of the LD program does not sit on the admissions committee. A personal interview is required. Essay is not required.

For fall 2004, 98 completed self-identified LD applications were received.

SECONDARY SCHOOL REQUIREMENTS

Graduation from secondary school required; GED accepted. The following course distribution required: 4 units of English, 3 units of math, 3 units of science, 1 unit of foreign language, 1 unit of social studies, 2 units of history, 1 unit of academic electives.

TESTING

SAT Reasoning or ACT required. SAT Subject recommended.

All enrolled freshmen (fall 2004):

Average ACT Scores: Composite: 23

Child Study Team report is not required. A neuropsychological or comprehensive psycho-educational evaluation is required for admission. Must be dated within 36 months of application. Tests required as part of this documentation:

- [x] WAIS-IV
- [x] WISC-IV
- [ ] SATA
- [x] Woodcock-Johnson
- [ ] Nelson-Denny Reading Test
- [x] Other

UNDERGRADUATE STUDENT BODY

Total undergraduate student enrollment: 7,221 Men, 6,383 Women.

Composition of student body (fall 2004):

	Undergraduate	Freshmen
International	0.4	0.9
Black	22.1	19.8
American Indian	0.5	0.6
Asian-American	1.9	1.3
Hispanic	1.0	0.8
White	74.2	76.6
Unreported	0.0	0.0
	100.0%	100.0%

21% are from out of state. 17% join a fraternity and 18% join a sorority. Average age of full-time undergraduates is 22. 40% of classes have fewer than 20 students, 48% have between 20 and 50 students, 11% have more than 50 students.

STUDENT HOUSING

85% of freshmen live in college housing. Freshmen are not required to live on campus. Housing is guaranteed for all undergraduates. Campus can house 4,000 undergraduates. Single rooms are available for students with medical or special needs. A medical note is required.

EXPENSES

Tuition (2005-06): $4,312 per year (in-state), $9,772 (out-of-state). Room: $2,824. Board: $3,035.

There is no additional cost for LD program/services.

LD SERVICES

LD program size is not limited.

LD services available to:

- [x] Freshmen
- [x] Sophomores
- [x] Juniors
- [x] Seniors

Academic Accommodations

Curriculum

- [ ] Foreign language waiver
- [x] Lighter course load
- [ ] Math waiver
- [ ] Other special classes
- [x] Priority registrations
- [x] Substitution of courses

Exams

- [x] Extended time
- [x] Oral exams
- [ ] Take home exams
- [x] Exams on tape or computer
- [ ] Untimed exams
- [ ] Other accommodations

In class

- [ ] Early syllabus
- [x] Note takers in class
- [x] Priority seating
- [x] Tape recorders
- [ ] Videotaped classes
- [x] Text on tape

Services

- [ ] Diagnostic tests
- [x] Learning centers
- [ ] Proofreaders
- [x] Readers
- [x] Reading Machines/Kurzweil
- [ ] Special bookstore section
- [ ] Typists

Credit toward degree is not given for remedial courses taken.

Counseling Services

- [ ] Academic
- [ ] Psychological
- [ ] Student Support groups
- [ ] Vocational

Tutoring

Individual tutoring is not available.

	Individual	Group
Time management	[ ]	[ ]
Organizational skills	[ ]	[ ]
Learning strategies	[ ]	[ ]
Study skills	[ ]	[ ]
Content area	[ ]	[ ]
Writing lab	[ ]	[ ]
Math lab	[ ]	[ ]

UNIQUE LD PROGRAM FEATURES

Mississippi State University does not have a formal program for students with disabilities. Accommodations are made based on documentation and student requests.

LD PROGRAM STAFF

There is an advisor/advocate from the LD program available to students. The advisor/advocate meets with faculty once per month.

Key staff person available to work with LD students: Susan Felker

LD Program web site: http://www.msstate.edu/dept/sss/

Mississippi University for Women

Columbus, MS

Address: 1100 College Street, Columbus, MS, 39701
Admissions telephone: 662 329-7106
Admissions FAX: 662 241-7481
Director of Admissions: Dr. Bucky Wesley
Admissions e-mail: admissions@muw.edu
Web site: http://www.muw.edu
SAT Code: 1481 ACT Code: 2222

LD program name: Academic Support Services
LD program address: W-1633
Coord. of Academic Support Services: Carol Frazier
LD program telephone: 662 241-7471
LD program e-mail: cfrazier@muw.edu
LD program enrollment: 6, Total campus enrollment: 2,063

GENERAL

Mississippi University for Women is a public, coed, four-year institution. 110-acre campus in Columbus (population: 25,944), 120 miles from Birmingham, Ala.; branch campuses at Columbus Air Force Base and in Tupelo. Served by air and bus; major airport serves Birmingham; train serves Tuscaloosa, Ala. (60 miles). Semester system.

LD ADMISSIONS

Students do not complete a separate application and are not simultaneously accepted to the LD program. A member of the LD program does not sit on the admissions committee. A personal interview is not required. Essay is not required.

SECONDARY SCHOOL REQUIREMENTS

Graduation from secondary school not required. The following course distribution required: 4 units of English, 3 units of math, 3 units of science, 3 units of social studies, 1 unit of academic electives.

TESTING

ACT required; SAT Reasoning may be substituted. SAT Subject recommended.

All enrolled freshmen (fall 2004):

Average SAT I Scores:	Verbal:	Math:
Average ACT Scores:	Composite: 21	

Child Study Team report is not required. A neuropsychological or comprehensive psycho-educational evaluation is required for admission. Must be dated within 36 months of application. Tests required as part of this documentation:

- ■ WAIS-IV
- ■ WISC-IV
- ☐ SATA
- ☐ Woodcock-Johnson
- ☐ Nelson-Denny Reading Test
- ☐ Other

UNDERGRADUATE STUDENT BODY

Total undergraduate student enrollment: 2,063.

Composition of student body (fall 2004):

	Undergraduate	Freshmen
International	2.4	1.5
Black	29.0	31.8
American Indian	0.4	0.5
Asian-American	1.6	1.4
Hispanic	0.4	0.7
White	66.1	64.1
Unreported	0.0	0.0
	100.0%	100.0%

11% are from out of state. 7% join a fraternity and 13% join a sorority. Average age of full-time undergraduates is 24. 59% of classes have fewer than 20 students, 39% have between 20 and 50 students, 2% have more than 50 students.

STUDENT HOUSING

61% of freshmen live in college housing. Freshmen are not required to live on campus. Housing is guaranteed for all undergraduates. Campus can house 848 undergraduates. Single rooms are available for students with medical or special needs. A medical note is required.

EXPENSES

Tuition (2005-06): $3,495 per year (in-state), $8,442 (out-of-state).
Room & Board: $3,778.
There is no additional cost for LD program/services.

LD SERVICES

LD program size is not limited.

LD services available to:

■ Freshmen ■ Sophomores ■ Juniors ■ Seniors

Academic Accommodations

Curriculum		**In class**	
Foreign language waiver	☐	Early syllabus	☐
Lighter course load	☐	Note takers in class	■
Math waiver	☐	Priority seating	■
Other special classes	☐	Tape recorders	■
Priority registrations	☐	Videotaped classes	☐
Substitution of courses	☐	Text on tape	☐
Exams		**Services**	
Extended time	■	Diagnostic tests	☐
Oral exams	■	Learning centers	■
Take home exams	☐	Proofreaders	☐
Exams on tape or computer	☐	Readers	■
Untimed exams	☐	Reading Machines/Kurzweil	☐
Other accommodations	☐	Special bookstore section	☐
		Typists	☐

Credit toward degree is not given for remedial courses taken.

Counseling Services

- ■ Academic
- ■ Psychological
- ☐ Student Support groups
- ■ Vocational

Tutoring

Individual tutoring is not available.

Average size of tutoring groups: 3

	Individual	Group
Time management	■	☐
Organizational skills	■	☐
Learning strategies	■	☐
Study skills	■	☐
Content area	☐	☐
Writing lab	☐	☐
Math lab	☐	☐

LD PROGRAM STAFF

Total number of LD Program staff (including director):

Full Time: 2 Part Time: 2

There is no advisor/advocate from the LD program available to students.

Key staff person available to work with LD students: Carol Frazier, Coordinator of Academic Support Services.

University of Mississippi

University, MS

Address: PO Box 1848, University, MS, 38677-1848
Admissions telephone: 800 OLEMISS (in-state)
Admissions FAX: 662 915-5869
Director of Admissions: Dr. Charlotte Fant
Admissions e-mail: admissions@olemiss.edu
Web site: http://www.olemiss.edu
SAT Code: 1840 ACT Code: 2250

LD program name: Office of Student Disability Services
LD program address: 234 Martindale
Assistant Director: Stacey Reycraft
LD program telephone: 662 915-7128
LD program e-mail: sds@olemiss.edu
Total campus enrollment: 11,820

GENERAL

University of Mississippi is a public, coed, four-year institution. 2,500-acre campus in Oxford (population: 11,756), 70 miles from Memphis; branch campuses in Iuka, Southaven, and Tupelo. Served by bus; major airport serves Memphis; smaller airport serves Tupelo (50 miles); train serves Greenwood (70 miles). Semester system.

LD ADMISSIONS

Students do not complete a separate application and are not simultaneously accepted to the LD program.

SECONDARY SCHOOL REQUIREMENTS

Graduation from secondary school required; GED accepted. The following course distribution required: 4 units of English, 3 units of math, 3 units of science, 1 unit of foreign language, 1 unit of social studies, 2 units of history, 2 units of academic electives.

TESTING

SAT Reasoning or ACT required of some applicants.

All enrolled freshmen (fall 2004):

Average SAT I Scores: Verbal: Math:
Average ACT Scores: Composite: 23

Child Study Team report is not required. A neuropsychological or comprehensive psycho-educational evaluation is required for admission. Must be dated within 36 months of application. Tests required as part of this documentation:

- [x] WAIS-IV
- [x] WISC-IV
- [ ] SATA
- [x] Woodcock-Johnson
- [ ] Nelson-Denny Reading Test
- [x] Other

UNDERGRADUATE STUDENT BODY

Total undergraduate student enrollment: 4,637 Men, 4,971 Women.

Composition of student body (fall 2004):

	Undergraduate	Freshmen
International	0.3	0.6
Black	13.3	13.3
American Indian	0.2	0.3
Asian-American	0.8	0.9
Hispanic	1.1	0.7
White	83.8	83.8
Unreported	0.5	0.4
	100.0%	100.0%

35% are from out of state. 40% of classes have fewer than 20 students, 42% have between 20 and 50 students, 18% have more than 50 students.

STUDENT HOUSING

Freshmen are required to live on campus. Housing is guaranteed for all undergraduates. Campus can house 4,410 undergraduates.

EXPENSES

Tuition (2005-06): $4,320 per year (in-state), $9,744 (out-of-state). (Tuition is higher for upper-division pharmacy students.)

Room & Board: $5,762.

LD SERVICES

LD services available to:

- [ ] Freshmen
- [ ] Sophomores
- [ ] Juniors
- [ ] Seniors

Academic Accommodations

Curriculum		In class	
Foreign language waiver	☐	Early syllabus	☐
Lighter course load	☐	Note takers in class	☐
Math waiver	☐	Priority seating	☐
Other special classes	☐	Tape recorders	☐
Priority registrations	☐	Videotaped classes	☐
Substitution of courses	☐	Text on tape	☐
Exams		**Services**	
Extended time	☐	Diagnostic tests	☐
Oral exams	☐	Learning centers	☐
Take home exams	☐	Proofreaders	☐
Exams on tape or computer	☐	Readers	☐
Untimed exams	☐	Reading Machines/Kurzweil	☐
Other accommodations	☐	Special bookstore section	☐
		Typists	☐

Counseling Services

- [ ] Academic
- [ ] Psychological
- [ ] Student Support groups
- [ ] Vocational

Tutoring

	Individual	Group
Time management	☐	☐
Organizational skills	☐	☐
Learning strategies	☐	☐
Study skills	☐	☐
Content area	☐	☐
Writing lab	☐	☐
Math lab	☐	☐

LD PROGRAM STAFF

Key staff person available to work with LD students: Stacey Reycraft, Assistant Director.

LD Program web site: www.olemiss.edu/depts/sds

Rust College

Holly Springs, MS

Address: 150 Rust Avenue, Holly Springs, MS, 38635
Admissions telephone: 888 886-8492, extension 4065
Admissions FAX: 662 252-8895
Director of Enrollment Services: Johnny B. McDonald
Admissions e-mail: admissions@rustcollege.edu
Web site: http://www.rustcollege.edu
SAT Code: 1669 ACT Code: 2240

Director, Student Support Services: Chiquita Walls
LD program telephone: 662 252-8000, extension 4909
LD program e-mail: cwalls@rustcollege.edu
Total campus enrollment: 1,001

GENERAL

Rust College is a private, coed, four-year institution. 126-acre campus in Holly Springs (population: 7,957), 45 miles from Memphis. Served by bus; major airport and train serve Memphis. Semester system.

LD ADMISSIONS

A personal interview is not required. Essay is not required.

SECONDARY SCHOOL REQUIREMENTS

Graduation from secondary school required; GED accepted. The following course distribution required: 4 units of English, 3 units of math, 3 units of science, 3 units of social studies, 6 units of academic electives.

TESTING

All enrolled freshmen (fall 2004):

Average SAT I Scores: Verbal: Math:
Average ACT Scores: Composite: 16

Child Study Team report is not required. Tests required as part of this documentation:

- ❑ WAIS-IV
- ❑ WISC-IV
- ❑ SATA
- ❑ Woodcock-Johnson
- ❑ Nelson-Denny Reading Test
- ❑ Other

UNDERGRADUATE STUDENT BODY

Total undergraduate student enrollment: 303 Men, 498 Women.

2% join a fraternity and 6% join a sorority. Average age of full-time undergraduates is 19. 48% of classes have fewer than 20 students, 45% have between 20 and 50 students, 7% have more than 50 students.

STUDENT HOUSING

Housing is guaranteed for all undergraduates. Campus can house 856 undergraduates.

EXPENSES

Tuition (2005-06): $6,000 per year.
Room & Board: $2,600.
There is no additional cost for LD program/services.

LD SERVICES

LD services available to:

❑ Freshmen ❑ Sophomores ❑ Juniors ❑ Seniors

Academic Accommodations

Curriculum		**In class**	
Foreign language waiver	❑	Early syllabus	❑
Lighter course load	■	Note takers in class	❑
Math waiver	❑	Priority seating	❑
Other special classes	❑	Tape recorders	❑
Priority registrations	❑	Videotaped classes	❑
Substitution of courses	❑	Text on tape	❑
Exams		**Services**	
Extended time	❑	Diagnostic tests	■
Oral exams	❑	Learning centers	❑
Take home exams	❑	Proofreaders	❑
Exams on tape or computer	❑	Readers	❑
Untimed exams	❑	Reading Machines/Kurzweil	❑
Other accommodations	❑	Special bookstore section	❑
		Typists	❑

Credit toward degree is not given for remedial courses taken.

Counseling Services

- ❑ Academic
- ❑ Psychological
- ❑ Student Support groups
- ❑ Vocational

Tutoring

	Individual	Group
Time management	❑	❑
Organizational skills	❑	❑
Learning strategies	❑	❑
Study skills	❑	❑
Content area	❑	❑
Writing lab	❑	❑
Math lab	❑	❑

LD PROGRAM STAFF

Total number of LD Program staff (including director):

Full Time: 4 Part Time: 4

Key staff person available to work with LD students: Pamela McKinney, Academic Educational Specialist.

University of Southern Mississippi

Hattiesburg, MS

Address: 118 College Drive, Hattiesburg, MS, 39406-0001
Admissions telephone: 601 266-5000
Admissions FAX: 601 266-5148
Director of Admissions: Dr. Matthew Cox
Admissions e-mail: admissions@USM.EDU
Web site: http://www.usm.edu
SAT Code: 1479   ACT Code: 2218

LD program name: Office of Disability Accommodations
Coordinator: Suzy Hebert
LD program telephone: 601 266-5024
LD program e-mail: Suzy.Hebert@usm.edu
LD program enrollment: 42, Total campus enrollment: 12,520

GENERAL

University of Southern Mississippi is a public, coed, four-year institution. 1,090-acre, suburban campus in Hattiesburg (population: 44,779), 90 miles from both Jackson and New Orleans; branch campuses in Jackson County and Long Beach and at Keesler Air Force Base. Served by air, bus, and train; major airports serve Jackson and New Orleans. Public transportation serves campus. Semester system.

LD ADMISSIONS

Students do not complete a separate application and are not simultaneously accepted to the LD program. A member of the LD program does not sit on the admissions committee. A personal interview is not required. Essay is not required.

For fall 2004, 52 completed self-identified LD applications were received. 52 applications were offered admission, and 52 enrolled.

SECONDARY SCHOOL REQUIREMENTS

Graduation from secondary school required; GED accepted. The following course distribution required: 4 units of English, 3 units of math, 3 units of science, 1 unit of social studies, 2 units of history, 2 units of academic electives.

TESTING

ACT required; SAT Reasoning may be substituted. SAT Subject recommended.

All enrolled freshmen (fall 2004):

Average SAT I Scores:	Verbal: 527	Math: 517
Average ACT Scores:	Composite: 21	

Child Study Team report is not required. A neuropsychological or comprehensive psycho-educational evaluation is required for admission. Must be dated within 36 months of application. Tests required as part of this documentation:

- [x] WAIS-IV
- [x] WISC-IV
- [x] SATA
- [x] Woodcock-Johnson
- [x] Nelson-Denny Reading Test
- [ ] Other

UNDERGRADUATE STUDENT BODY

Total undergraduate student enrollment: 5,048 Men, 7,796 Women.

Composition of student body (fall 2004):

	Undergraduate	Freshmen
International	0.6	1.1
Black	37.7	27.8
American Indian	0.2	0.4
Asian-American	1.4	1.2
Hispanic	1.2	1.0
White	57.5	67.2
Unreported	1.3	1.2
	100.0%	100.0%

9% are from out of state. 5% join a fraternity and 5% join a sorority. Average age of full-time undergraduates is 23. 48% of classes have fewer than 20 students, 43% have between 20 and 50 students, 9% have more than 50 students.

STUDENT HOUSING

65% of freshmen live in college housing. Freshmen are not required to live on campus. Housing is not guaranteed for all undergraduates. Limited facilities which make it impossible to house all enrolled students. Campus can house 2,283 undergraduates. Single rooms are not available for students with medical or special needs.

EXPENSES

Tuition (2005-06): $4,106 per year (in-state), $9,276 (out-of-state).
Room: $2,620. Board: $1,800.
There is no additional cost for LD program/services.

LD SERVICES

LD program size is not limited.

LD services available to:

- [x] Freshmen
- [x] Sophomores
- [x] Juniors
- [x] Seniors

Academic Accommodations

Curriculum
- [ ] Foreign language waiver
- [x] Lighter course load
- [ ] Math waiver
- [x] Other special classes
- [ ] Priority registrations
- [x] Substitution of courses

Exams
- [x] Extended time
- [x] Oral exams
- [ ] Take home exams
- [x] Exams on tape or computer
- [x] Untimed exams
- [x] Other accommodations

In class
- [x] Early syllabus
- [x] Note takers in class
- [x] Priority seating
- [x] Tape recorders
- [x] Videotaped classes
- [x] Text on tape

Services
- [x] Diagnostic tests
- [x] Learning centers
- [x] Proofreaders
- [x] Readers
- [x] Reading Machines/Kurzweil
- [x] Special bookstore section
- [x] Typists

Credit toward degree is not given for remedial courses taken.

Counseling Services

- [x] Academic
- [ ] Psychological
- [x] Student Support groups — Meets 9 times per academic year
- [ ] Vocational

Tutoring

Individual tutoring is not available.

	Individual	Group
Time management	[ ]	[ ]
Organizational skills	[ ]	[ ]
Learning strategies	[ ]	[ ]
Study skills	[ ]	[ ]
Content area	[ ]	[ ]
Writing lab	[ ]	[ ]
Math lab	[ ]	[ ]

LD PROGRAM STAFF

Total number of LD Program staff (including director):

Full Time: 3   Part Time: 3

There is an advisor/advocate from the LD program available to students. 2 graduate students are available to work with LD students.

Key staff person available to work with LD students: Suzy Hebert, Coordinator.

William Carey College

Hattiesburg, MS

Address: 498 Tuscan Avenue, Hattiesburg, MS, 39401-5499
Admissions telephone: 800 962-5991
Admissions FAX: 601 318-6765
Director of Admissions: William N. Curry
Admissions e-mail: admissions@wmcarey.edu
Web site: http://www.wmcarey.edu
SAT Code: 1907 ACT Code: 2254

Director of Student Support Services: Sonny Woodard
LD program telephone: 601 318-6212
LD program e-mail: sonny.woodard@wmcarey.edu
LD program enrollment: 12, Total campus enrollment: 1,853

GENERAL

William Carey College is a private, coed, four-year institution. 64-acre campus in Hattiesburg (population: 44,779), 85 miles from Jackson; branch campuses in Gulfport and New Orleans. Served by air and train. Trimester system.

LD ADMISSIONS

Students do not complete a separate application and are simultaneously accepted to the LD program. A member of the LD program does sit on the admissions committee. A personal interview is not required. Essay is not required.

For fall 2004, 3 completed self-identified LD applications were received. 3 applications were offered admission, and 3 enrolled.

SECONDARY SCHOOL REQUIREMENTS

Graduation from secondary school required; GED accepted.

TESTING

ACT required; SAT Reasoning may be substituted. SAT Subject recommended.

All enrolled freshmen (fall 2004):

Average SAT I Scores:	Verbal: 480	Math: 508
Average ACT Scores:	Composite: 21	

Child Study Team report is not required. Tests required as part of this documentation:

- ☑ WAIS-IV
- ☐ WISC-IV
- ☐ SATA
- ☑ Woodcock-Johnson
- ☐ Nelson-Denny Reading Test
- ☑ Other

UNDERGRADUATE STUDENT BODY

Total undergraduate student enrollment: 527 Men, 1,102 Women.

Composition of student body (fall 2004):

	Undergraduate	Freshmen
International	7.3	1.8
Black	12.9	34.2
American Indian	0.8	0.5
Asian-American	3.2	0.9
Hispanic	0.8	2.1
White	75.0	59.9
Unreported	0.0	0.6
	100.0%	100.0%

18% are from out of state. Average age of full-time undergraduates is 26. 61% of classes have fewer than 20 students, 39% have between 20 and 50 students.

STUDENT HOUSING

65% of freshmen live in college housing. Housing is guaranteed for all undergraduates. Campus can house 540 undergraduates. Single rooms are available for students with medical or special needs.

EXPENSES

Tuition (2005-06): $8,100 per year.
Room: $1,305. Board: $1,920.
There is no additional cost for LD program/services.

LD SERVICES

LD program size is not limited.

LD services available to:

☑ Freshmen ☑ Sophomores ☑ Juniors ☑ Seniors

Academic Accommodations

Curriculum		In class	
Foreign language waiver	☐	Early syllabus	☐
Lighter course load	☐	Note takers in class	☑
Math waiver	☐	Priority seating	☐
Other special classes	☐	Tape recorders	☑
Priority registrations	☐	Videotaped classes	☐
Substitution of courses	☐	Text on tape	☐
Exams		**Services**	
Extended time	☑	Diagnostic tests	☑
Oral exams	☑	Learning centers	☐
Take home exams	☐	Proofreaders	☐
Exams on tape or computer	☐	Readers	☐
Untimed exams	☑	Reading Machines/Kurzweil	☑
Other accommodations	☐	Special bookstore section	☐
		Typists	☐

Credit toward degree is given for remedial courses taken.

Counseling Services

- ☐ Academic
- ☐ Psychological
- ☐ Student Support groups
- ☐ Vocational

Tutoring

Individual tutoring is available weekly.

Average size of tutoring groups: 1

	Individual	Group
Time management	☐	☑
Organizational skills	☑	☐
Learning strategies	☑	☐
Study skills	☐	☑
Content area	☑	☐
Writing lab	☐	☑
Math lab	☐	☑

LD PROGRAM STAFF

Total number of LD Program staff (including director):

Full Time: 5 Part Time: 5

3 peer tutors are available to work with LD students.

Key staff person available to work with LD students: Sonny Woodard, Director of Student Support Services.

Avila University

Kansas City, MO

Address: 11901 Wornall Road, Kansas City, MO, 64145
Admissions telephone: 800 GO-AVILA
Admissions FAX: 816 501-2453
Assistant Vice President for Undergraduate Admissions: Paige Illum
Admissions e-mail: admissions@mail.avila.edu
Web site: http://www.Avila.edu
SAT Code: 6109 ACT Code: 2278

Coordinator: Suzanne R. Franklin
LD program telephone: 816 501-3666
LD program e-mail: FranklinSR@mail.Avila.edu
Total campus enrollment: 1,579

GENERAL

Avila University is a private, coed, four-year institution. 48-acre, suburban campus in Kansas City (population: 441,545), 10 miles from downtown. Served by air, bus, and train. Public transportation serves campus. Semester system.

LD ADMISSIONS

A personal interview is recommended. Essay is not required.

SECONDARY SCHOOL REQUIREMENTS

Graduation from secondary school required; GED accepted. The following course distribution required: 4 units of English, 3 units of math, 2 units of science, 3 units of foreign language, 3 units of social studies.

TESTING

ACT required; SAT Reasoning may be substituted. SAT Subject recommended.

All enrolled freshmen (fall 2004):

Average SAT I Scores: Verbal: 490 Math: 495
Average ACT Scores: Composite: 22

Child Study Team report is not required. Tests required as part of this documentation:

☐ WAIS-IV
☐ WISC-IV
☐ SATA
☐ Woodcock-Johnson
☐ Nelson-Denny Reading Test
☐ Other

UNDERGRADUATE STUDENT BODY

Total undergraduate student enrollment: 424 Men, 811 Women.

Composition of student body (fall 2004):

	Undergraduate	Freshmen
International	1.5	2.2
Black	6.1	17.0
American Indian	3.0	1.0
Asian-American	0.0	1.8
Hispanic	4.5	3.2
White	81.1	72.2
Unreported	3.8	2.6
	100.0%	100.0%

30% are from out of state. Average age of full-time undergraduates is 24. 73% of classes have fewer than 20 students, 27% have between 20 and 50 students.

STUDENT HOUSING

61% of freshmen live in college housing. Housing is guaranteed for all undergraduates. Campus can house 220 undergraduates.

EXPENSES

Tuition (2005-06): $16,300 per year.
Room & Board: $6,720.
There is no additional cost for LD program/services.

LD SERVICES

LD program size is not limited.

LD services available to:

☐ Freshmen ☐ Sophomores ☐ Juniors ☐ Seniors

Academic Accommodations

Curriculum		**In class**	
Foreign language waiver	☐	Early syllabus	☐
Lighter course load	☒	Note takers in class	☒
Math waiver	☐	Priority seating	☐
Other special classes	☒	Tape recorders	☒
Priority registrations	☐	Videotaped classes	☐
Substitution of courses	☐	Text on tape	☐
Exams		**Services**	
Extended time	☒	Diagnostic tests	☐
Oral exams	☒	Learning centers	☒
Take home exams	☐	Proofreaders	☐
Exams on tape or computer	☐	Readers	☒
Untimed exams	☐	Reading Machines/Kurzweil	☐
Other accommodations	☐	Special bookstore section	☐
		Typists	☐

Credit toward degree is not given for remedial courses taken.

Counseling Services

☐ Academic
☐ Psychological
☐ Student Support groups
☐ Vocational

Tutoring

	Individual	Group
Time management	☐	☐
Organizational skills	☐	☐
Learning strategies	☐	☐
Study skills	☐	☐
Content area	☐	☐
Writing lab	☐	☐
Math lab	☐	☐

LD PROGRAM STAFF

Total number of LD Program staff (including director):

Full Time: 2 Part Time: 2

Key staff person available to work with LD students: Suzanne R. Franklin, Coordinator - College Skills & Disability Services.

Central Methodist University

Fayette, MO

Address: 411 Central Methodist Square, Fayette, MO, 65248
Admissions telephone: 660 248-6251
Admissions FAX: 660 248-1872
Dean of Admissions and Financial Assistance: Edward Lamm
Admissions e-mail: admissions@centralmethodist.edu
Web site: http://www.centralmethodist.edu
SAT Code: 6089 ACT Code: 2270

Total campus enrollment: 781

GENERAL

Central Methodist College is a private, coed, four-year institution. 100-acre campus in Fayette (population: 2,793), 25 miles from Columbia; branch campuses in Parks Hills and Union. Airport serves Columbia; major airports serve St. Louis and Kansas City (both 125 miles); bus serves Booneville (15 miles); train serves Jefferson City (50 miles). Semester system.

LD ADMISSIONS

A personal interview is not required. Essay is not required.

SECONDARY SCHOOL REQUIREMENTS

Graduation from secondary school required; GED accepted.

TESTING

ACT required; SAT Reasoning may be substituted. SAT Subject recommended.

All enrolled freshmen (fall 2004):

Average ACT Scores: Composite: 21

Child Study Team report is not required. Tests required as part of this documentation:

☐ WAIS-IV	☐ Woodcock-Johnson
☐ WISC-IV	☐ Nelson-Denny Reading Test
☐ SATA	☐ Other

UNDERGRADUATE STUDENT BODY

Total undergraduate student enrollment: 474 Men, 752 Women.

Composition of student body (fall 2004):

	Undergraduate	Freshmen
International	1.0	2.3
Black	6.7	9.1
American Indian	1.0	0.5
Asian-American	0.5	0.5
Hispanic	1.0	1.7
White	87.2	84.2
Unreported	2.6	1.7
	100.0%	100.0%

6% are from out of state. 17% join a fraternity and 20% join a sorority. Average age of full-time undergraduates is 21. 67% of classes have fewer than 20 students, 31% have between 20 and 50 students, 2% have more than 50 students.

STUDENT HOUSING

95% of freshmen live in college housing. Housing is not guaranteed for all undergraduates. Housing is available up to capacity of housing units. Campus can house 650 undergraduates.

EXPENSES

Tuition (2005-06): $14,490 per year.

Room: $2,640. Board: $2,720.
There is no additional cost for LD program/services.

LD SERVICES

LD program size is not limited.

LD services available to:

☐ Freshmen ☐ Sophomores ☐ Juniors ☐ Seniors

Academic Accommodations

Curriculum		**In class**	
Foreign language waiver	☐	Early syllabus	☐
Lighter course load	■	Note takers in class	☐
Math waiver	☐	Priority seating	☐
Other special classes	☐	Tape recorders	☐
Priority registrations	☐	Videotaped classes	☐
Substitution of courses	☐	Text on tape	☐
Exams		**Services**	
Extended time	■	Diagnostic tests	☐
Oral exams	☐	Learning centers	■
Take home exams	☐	Proofreaders	☐
Exams on tape or computer	☐	Readers	■
Untimed exams	☐	Reading Machines/Kurzweil	☐
Other accommodations	☐	Special bookstore section	☐
		Typists	☐

Credit toward degree is not given for remedial courses taken.

Counseling Services

☐ Academic
☐ Psychological
☐ Student Support groups
☐ Vocational

Tutoring

	Individual	Group
Time management	☐	☐
Organizational skills	☐	☐
Learning strategies	☐	☐
Study skills	☐	☐
Content area	☐	☐
Writing lab	☐	☐
Math lab	☐	☐

LD PROGRAM STAFF

Total number of LD Program staff (including director):

Full Time: 1 Part Time: 1

Key staff person available to work with LD students: Maryann Rustemeyer, Director of Learning Center.

Central Missouri State University

Warrensburg, MO

Address: Administration Building, Suite 304, Warrensburg, MO, 64093
Admissions telephone: 660 543-4290
Admissions FAX: 660 543-8517
Executive Director of Enrollment Management: Dr. Matt Melvin
Admissions e-mail: admit@cmsu1.cmsu.edu
Web site: http://www.cmsu.edu
SAT Code: 6090 ACT Code: 2272

LD program name: Accessibility Services
LD program address: Elliott Union 222
Director/ADA Coordinator: Barbara Mayfield
LD program telephone: 660 543-4421
LD program e-mail: mayfield@cmsu1.cmsu.edu
LD program enrollment: 125, Total campus enrollment: 8,303

GENERAL

Central Missouri State University is a public, coed, four-year institution. 1,300-acre campus in Warrensburg (population: 16,340), 50 miles from Kansas City; branch campus in Lee's Summit. Served by bus and train; major airport serves Kansas City. Semester system.

LD ADMISSIONS

Application Deadline: 08/05. Students do not complete a separate application and are not simultaneously accepted to the LD program. A member of the LD program does not sit on the admissions committee. A personal interview is not required. Essay is not required. Admissions requirements that may be waived for LD students include the ACT score, and class rank.

SECONDARY SCHOOL REQUIREMENTS

Graduation from secondary school required; GED accepted. The following course distribution required: 4 units of English, 3 units of math, 2 units of science, 3 units of social studies, 3 units of academic electives.

TESTING

ACT required; SAT Reasoning may be substituted. SAT Subject recommended.

All enrolled freshmen (fall 2004):

Average ACT Scores: Composite: 22

Child Study Team report is not required. A neuropsychological or comprehensive psycho-educational evaluation is required for admission. Must be dated within 60 months of application. Tests required as part of this documentation:

- [x] WAIS-IV
- [x] WISC-IV
- [ ] SATA
- [x] Woodcock-Johnson
- [ ] Nelson-Denny Reading Test
- [x] Other

UNDERGRADUATE STUDENT BODY

Total undergraduate student enrollment: 4,271 Men, 4,797 Women.

Composition of student body (fall 2004):

	Undergraduate	Freshmen
International	3.1	2.6
Black	6.3	5.7
American Indian	0.5	0.6
Asian-American	1.1	1.0
Hispanic	1.9	1.8
White	85.5	84.2
Unreported	1.6	4.1
	100.0%	100.0%

6% are from out of state. 18% join a fraternity and 12% join a sorority. Average age of full-time undergraduates is 22. 44% of classes have fewer than 20 students, 53% have between 20 and 50 students, 3% have more than 50 students.

STUDENT HOUSING

81% of freshmen live in college housing. Freshmen are required to live on campus. Housing is guaranteed for all undergraduates. Campus can house 3,527 undergraduates. Single rooms are available for students with medical or special needs. A medical note is required.

EXPENSES

Tuition (2005-06): $5,550 per year (in-state), $10,680 (out-of-state).
Room: $3,244. Board: $1,936.
There is no additional cost for LD program/services.

LD SERVICES

LD program size is not limited.

LD services available to:

- [x] Freshmen
- [x] Sophomores
- [x] Juniors
- [x] Seniors

Academic Accommodations

Curriculum		In class	
Foreign language waiver	[x]	Early syllabus	[ ]
Lighter course load	[x]	Note takers in class	[x]
Math waiver	[x]	Priority seating	[x]
Other special classes	[x]	Tape recorders	[x]
Priority registrations	[x]	Videotaped classes	[x]
Substitution of courses	[x]	Text on tape	[x]
Exams		**Services**	
Extended time	[x]	Diagnostic tests	[ ]
Oral exams	[x]	Learning centers	[x]
Take home exams	[ ]	Proofreaders	[x]
Exams on tape or computer	[x]	Readers	[x]
Untimed exams	[ ]	Reading Machines/Kurzweil	[x]
Other accommodations	[x]	Special bookstore section	[x]
		Typists	[x]

Credit toward degree is given for remedial courses taken.

Counseling Services

- [x] Academic
- [x] Psychological
- [ ] Student Support groups
- [ ] Vocational

Tutoring

Individual tutoring is available weekly.

Average size of tutoring groups: 4

	Individual	Group
Time management	[x]	[x]
Organizational skills	[x]	[x]
Learning strategies	[x]	[x]
Study skills	[x]	[x]
Content area	[x]	[x]
Writing lab	[x]	[x]
Math lab	[x]	[ ]

LD PROGRAM STAFF

Total number of LD Program staff (including director):

Full Time: 3 Part Time: 3

There is an advisor/advocate from the LD program available to students. The advisor/advocate meets with faculty 1 time per month and students 2 times per month. 2 graduate students are available to work with LD students.

Key staff person available to work with LD students: Barbara Mayfield, Director/Accessibility Services, ADA 504 Coordinator.

LD Program web site: cmsu.edu/access

Columbia College

Columbia, MO

Address: 1001 Rogers Street, Columbia, MO, 65216
Admissions telephone: 800 231-2391, extension 7352
Admissions FAX: 573 875-7506
Director of Admissions: Regina Morin
Admissions e-mail: admissions@ccis.edu
Web site: http://www.ccis.edu
SAT Code: 6095 ACT Code: 2276

ADA Coordinator: Shirley Wilbur
LD program telephone: 573 875-7626
LD program e-mail: sawilbur@ccis.edu
LD program enrollment: 13, Total campus enrollment: 953

GENERAL

Columbia College is a private, coed, four-year institution. 29-acre campus in Columbia (population: 84,531), 125 miles from both Kansas City and St. Louis; branch campuses in Independence, Jefferson City, Lake Ozark, Moberly, and St. Louis and at Ft. Leonard Wood and numerous other locations. Served by air and bus; major airports serve Kansas City and St. Louis; train serves Jefferson City (30 miles). School operates transportation to local attractions. Public transportation serves campus. Semester system.

LD ADMISSIONS

Application Deadline: 08/01. Students do not complete a separate application and are not simultaneously accepted to the LD program. A member of the LD program does not sit on the admissions committee. A personal interview is required. Essay is not required.

SECONDARY SCHOOL REQUIREMENTS

Graduation from secondary school required; GED accepted. The following course distribution required: 4 units of English, 3 units of math, 2 units of science, 2 units of social studies.

TESTING

ACT required; SAT Reasoning may be substituted. SAT Subject recommended.

All enrolled freshmen (fall 2004):

Average SAT I Scores:	Verbal: 554	Math: 528
Average ACT Scores:	Composite: 22	

Child Study Team report is not required. A neuropsychological or comprehensive psycho-education evaluation is not required for admission. Tests required as part of this documentation:

- [ ] WAIS-IV
- [ ] WISC-IV
- [ ] SATA
- [ ] Woodcock-Johnson
- [ ] Nelson-Denny Reading Test
- [ ] Other

UNDERGRADUATE STUDENT BODY

Total undergraduate student enrollment: 364 Men, 491 Women.

Composition of student body (fall 2004):

	Undergraduate	Freshmen
International	4.2	5.8
Black	2.4	5.1
American Indian	0.6	0.4
Asian-American	0.6	1.3
Hispanic	0.6	1.9
White	88.6	80.3
Unreported	3.0	5.2
	100.0%	100.0%

6% are from out of state. Average age of full-time undergraduates is 22. 72% of classes have fewer than 20 students, 28% have between 20 and 50 students.

STUDENT HOUSING

70% of freshmen live in college housing. Freshmen are required to live on campus. Housing is guaranteed for all undergraduates. Campus can house 320 undergraduates. Single rooms are not available for students with medical or special needs.

EXPENSES

Tuition (2005-06): $11,599 per year.
Room: $3,152. Board: $1,859.
There is no additional cost for LD program/services.

LD SERVICES

LD program size is not limited.

LD services available to:

- [x] Freshmen
- [x] Sophomores
- [x] Juniors
- [x] Seniors

Academic Accommodations

Curriculum		**In class**	
Foreign language waiver	[ ]	Early syllabus	[ ]
Lighter course load	[x]	Note takers in class	[ ]
Math waiver	[ ]	Priority seating	[ ]
Other special classes	[ ]	Tape recorders	[ ]
Priority registrations	[ ]	Videotaped classes	[ ]
Substitution of courses	[ ]	Text on tape	[ ]
Exams		**Services**	
Extended time	[x]	Diagnostic tests	[ ]
Oral exams	[ ]	Learning centers	[ ]
Take home exams	[ ]	Proofreaders	[ ]
Exams on tape or computer	[ ]	Readers	[ ]
Untimed exams	[ ]	Reading Machines/Kurzweil	[ ]
Other accommodations	[ ]	Special bookstore section	[ ]
		Typists	[ ]

Credit toward degree is not given for remedial courses taken.

Counseling Services

- [ ] Academic
- [ ] Psychological
- [ ] Student Support groups
- [ ] Vocational

Tutoring

Individual tutoring is available.

	Individual	Group
Time management	[ ]	[ ]
Organizational skills	[ ]	[ ]
Learning strategies	[ ]	[ ]
Study skills	[ ]	[ ]
Content area	[ ]	[ ]
Writing lab	[ ]	[ ]
Math lab	[ ]	[ ]

UNIQUE LD PROGRAM FEATURES

Columbia College has a part-time ADA coordinator to facilitate application to LD services and to process documentation, but we do not have an LD program as such, and the ADA coordinator is also responsible for accommodating physical disabilities. Tutoring available to LD students is also available to all students, and is delivered outside the LD/ADA office -- hence those staff persons are not listed or counted above.

LD PROGRAM STAFF

There is not an advisor/advocate from the LD program available to students.

Culver-Stockton College

Canton, MO

Address: 1 College Hill, Canton, MO, 63435
Admissions telephone: 800 537-1883
Admissions FAX: 573 288-6618
Director of Enrollment Services: Betty Smith
Admissions e-mail: enrollment@culver.edu
Web site: http://www.culver.edu
SAT Code: 6123 ACT Code: 2290

Director of Support Services: Christie Mennenga
LD program telephone: 573 288-6451
LD program e-mail: cmennenga@culver.edu
LD program enrollment: 9, Total campus enrollment: 855

GENERAL

Culver-Stockton College is a private, coed, four-year institution. 139-acre campus in Canton (population: 2,557), 20 miles from Quincy, Ill., and 120 miles from St. Louis. Served by bus; major airport serves St. Louis; smaller airport and train serve Quincy. Semester system.

LD ADMISSIONS

Students do not complete a separate application and are not simultaneously accepted to the LD program. A member of the LD program does not sit on the admissions committee. A personal interview is recommended. Essay is not required.

SECONDARY SCHOOL REQUIREMENTS

Graduation from secondary school required; GED accepted.

TESTING

SAT Reasoning or ACT considered if submitted; ACT preferred. SAT Subject recommended.

All enrolled freshmen (fall 2004):

Average ACT Scores: Composite: 22

Child Study Team report is not required. A neuropsychological or comprehensive psycho-education evaluation is not required for admission. Tests required as part of this documentation:

- [ ] WAIS-IV
- [ ] WISC-IV
- [ ] SATA
- [ ] Woodcock-Johnson
- [ ] Nelson-Denny Reading Test
- [ ] Other

UNDERGRADUATE STUDENT BODY

Total undergraduate student enrollment: 369 Men, 452 Women.

Composition of student body (fall 2004):

	Undergraduate	Freshmen
International	0.5	0.9
Black	8.8	6.8
American Indian	0.0	0.2
Asian-American	0.0	0.5
Hispanic	0.5	2.7
White	90.2	88.9
Unreported	0.0	0.0
	100.0%	100.0%

45% are from out of state. 33% join a fraternity and 31% join a sorority. Average age of full-time undergraduates is 19. 59% of classes have fewer than 20 students, 39% have between 20 and 50 students, 2% have more than 50 students.

STUDENT HOUSING

81% of freshmen live in college housing. Freshmen are required to live on campus. Housing is guaranteed for all undergraduates. Campus can house 596 undergraduates. Single rooms are available for students with medical or special needs. A medical note is required.

EXPENSES

Tuition (2005-06): $14,250 per year.
Room: $2,860. Board: $3,315.

There is no additional cost for LD program/services.

LD SERVICES

LD program size is not limited.

LD services available to:

- [x] Freshmen
- [x] Sophomores
- [x] Juniors
- [x] Seniors

Academic Accommodations

Curriculum		In class	
Foreign language waiver	[ ]	Early syllabus	[ ]
Lighter course load	[x]	Note takers in class	[x]
Math waiver	[ ]	Priority seating	[ ]
Other special classes	[ ]	Tape recorders	[x]
Priority registrations	[ ]	Videotaped classes	[x]
Substitution of courses	[ ]	Text on tape	[ ]
Exams		**Services**	
Extended time	[x]	Diagnostic tests	[ ]
Oral exams	[x]	Learning centers	[x]
Take home exams	[ ]	Proofreaders	[ ]
Exams on tape or computer	[ ]	Readers	[x]
Untimed exams	[x]	Reading Machines/Kurzweil	[ ]
Other accommodations	[ ]	Special bookstore section	[ ]
		Typists	[ ]

Credit toward degree is not given for remedial courses taken.

Counseling Services

- [x] Academic
- [x] Psychological
- [x] Student Support groups
- [ ] Vocational

Tutoring

Individual tutoring is available daily.

Average size of tutoring groups: 5

	Individual	Group
Time management	[x]	[ ]
Organizational skills	[x]	[ ]
Learning strategies	[x]	[ ]
Study skills	[x]	[ ]
Content area	[x]	[ ]
Writing lab	[ ]	[x]
Math lab	[ ]	[x]

LD PROGRAM STAFF

Total number of LD Program staff (including director):

Full Time: 1 Part Time: 1

There is an advisor/advocate from the LD program available to students. The advisor/advocate meets with faculty 1 time per month and students 4 times per month. 10 peer tutors are available to work with LD students.

Key staff person available to work with LD students: Christie Mennenga, Director of Support Services.

Drury University

Springfield, MO

Address: 900 N. Benton Avenue, Springfield, MO, 65802
Admissions telephone: 800 922-2274
Admissions FAX: 417 866-3873
Director of Admissions: Chip Parker
Admissions e-mail: druryad@drury.edu
Web site: http://www.drury.edu
SAT Code: 6169 ACT Code: 2292

Coordinator of Disability Services: Lawrence Anderson
LD program telephone: 417 873-7457
LD program e-mail: landerso@drury.edu
Total campus enrollment: 1,562

GENERAL

Drury University is a private, coed, four-year institution. 60-acre, urban campus in Springfield (population: 151,580), 200 miles from St. Louis; branch campus abroad in Greece. Served by air and bus; major airports serve St. Louis and Kansas City (169 miles); train serves Jefferson City (80 miles). Public transportation serves campus. Semester system.

LD ADMISSIONS

Students do not complete a separate application and are not simultaneously accepted to the LD program. A member of the LD program does not sit on the admissions committee. A personal interview is recommended. Essay is required and may be typed.

SECONDARY SCHOOL REQUIREMENTS

Graduation from secondary school required; GED accepted. The following course distribution required: 4 units of English, 3 units of math, 3 units of science, 2 units of foreign language, 3 units of social studies.

TESTING

SAT Reasoning or ACT required. SAT Subject recommended.

All enrolled freshmen (fall 2004):

Average SAT I Scores:	Verbal: 558	Math: 565
Average ACT Scores:	Composite: 26	

Child Study Team report is not required. Tests required as part of this documentation:

- [ ] WAIS-IV
- [ ] WISC-IV
- [ ] SATA
- [ ] Woodcock-Johnson
- [ ] Nelson-Denny Reading Test
- [ ] Other

UNDERGRADUATE STUDENT BODY

Total undergraduate student enrollment: 632 Men, 818 Women.

Composition of student body (fall 2004):

	Undergraduate	Freshmen
International	1.6	3.5
Black	0.5	1.1
American Indian	0.8	0.3
Asian-American	2.2	2.2
Hispanic	2.5	1.6
White	92.4	91.3
Unreported	0.0	0.0
	100.0%	100.0%

20% are from out of state. 14% join a fraternity and 14% join a sorority. Average age of full-time undergraduates is 21. 63% of classes have fewer than 20 students, 36% have between 20 and 50 students, 1% have more than 50 students.

STUDENT HOUSING

76% of freshmen live in college housing. Freshmen are required to live on campus. Housing is guaranteed for all undergraduates. Campus can house 952 undergraduates.

EXPENSES

Tuition (2005-06): $14,348 per year.
Room & Board: $5,430
There is no additional cost for LD program/services.

LD SERVICES

LD program size is not limited.

LD services available to:

- [x] Freshmen
- [x] Sophomores
- [x] Juniors
- [x] Seniors

Academic Accommodations

Curriculum		In class	
Foreign language waiver	[ ]	Early syllabus	[ ]
Lighter course load	[x]	Note takers in class	[x]
Math waiver	[ ]	Priority seating	[x]
Other special classes	[x]	Tape recorders	[x]
Priority registrations	[x]	Videotaped classes	[ ]
Substitution of courses	[ ]	Text on tape	[x]
Exams		**Services**	
Extended time	[x]	Diagnostic tests	[ ]
Oral exams	[x]	Learning centers	[ ]
Take home exams	[ ]	Proofreaders	[ ]
Exams on tape or computer	[ ]	Readers	[x]
Untimed exams	[x]	Reading Machines/Kurzweil	[ ]
Other accommodations	[ ]	Special bookstore section	[ ]
		Typists	[ ]

Credit toward degree is not given for remedial courses taken.

Counseling Services

- [ ] Academic
- [ ] Psychological
- [ ] Student Support groups
- [ ] Vocational

Tutoring

	Individual	Group
Time management	[ ]	[ ]
Organizational skills	[ ]	[ ]
Learning strategies	[ ]	[ ]
Study skills	[ ]	[ ]
Content area	[ ]	[ ]
Writing lab	[ ]	[ ]
Math lab	[ ]	[ ]

LD PROGRAM STAFF

Total number of LD Program staff (including director):

Full Time: 1 Part Time: 1

There is an advisor/advocate from the LD program available to students.

Key staff person available to work with LD students: Lawrence Anderson, Coordinator of Disability Services.

Evangel University

Springfield, MO

Address: 1111 North Glenstone, Springfield, MO, 65802
Admissions telephone: 800 EVANGEL
Admissions FAX: 417 865-9599
Director of Admissions: Charity Waltner
Admissions e-mail: admissions@evangel.edu
Web site: http://www.evangel.edu
SAT Code: 6198 ACT Code: 2296

LD program name: Career Development
LD program telephone: 417 865-2811, extension 7321
LD program e-mail: phillipss@evangel.edu
LD program enrollment: 17, Total campus enrollment: 1,721

GENERAL

Evangel University is a private, coed, four-year institution. 80-acre campus in Springfield (population: 151,580), 169 miles from Kansas City. Served by air, bus, and train; major airport serves Kansas City. Semester system.

LD ADMISSIONS

Application Deadline: 08/01. Students do not complete a separate application and are simultaneously accepted to the LD program. A member of the LD program does not sit on the admissions committee. A personal interview is recommended. Essay is not required.

SECONDARY SCHOOL REQUIREMENTS

Graduation from secondary school required; GED accepted. The following course distribution required: 3 units of English, 2 units of math, 3 units of science, 2 units of social studies.

TESTING

ACT required; SAT Reasoning may be substituted. SAT Subject required.

All enrolled freshmen (fall 2004):

Average ACT Scores: Composite: 22

Child Study Team report is not required. A neuropsychological or comprehensive psycho-education evaluation is not required for admission. Tests required as part of this documentation:

- [ ] WAIS-IV
- [ ] WISC-IV
- [ ] SATA
- [ ] Woodcock-Johnson
- [ ] Nelson-Denny Reading Test
- [ ] Other

UNDERGRADUATE STUDENT BODY

Total undergraduate student enrollment: 662 Men, 867 Women.

Composition of student body (fall 2004):

	Undergraduate	Freshmen
International	0.9	0.2
Black	2.8	2.9
American Indian	0.9	1.3
Asian-American	1.9	1.5
Hispanic	4.7	2.5
White	88.8	91.4
Unreported	0.0	0.2
	100.0%	100.0%

61% are from out of state. Average age of full-time undergraduates is 20. 60% of classes have fewer than 20 students, 37% have between 20 and 50 students, 3% have more than 50 students.

STUDENT HOUSING

68% of freshmen live in college housing. Housing is guaranteed for all undergraduates. Campus can house 1,254 undergraduates. Single rooms are available for students with medical or special needs. A medical note is required.

EXPENSES

Tuition (2005-06): $12,040 per year.

Room: $2,270. Board: $2,350.

There is no additional cost for LD program/services.

LD SERVICES

LD program size is not limited.

LD services available to:

- [x] Freshmen
- [x] Sophomores
- [x] Juniors
- [x] Seniors

Academic Accommodations

Curriculum		In class	
Foreign language waiver	[ ]	Early syllabus	[ ]
Lighter course load	[ ]	Note takers in class	[ ]
Math waiver	[ ]	Priority seating	[ ]
Other special classes	[ ]	Tape recorders	[x]
Priority registrations	[ ]	Videotaped classes	[ ]
Substitution of courses	[ ]	Text on tape	[ ]
Exams		**Services**	
Extended time	[x]	Diagnostic tests	[x]
Oral exams	[x]	Learning centers	[x]
Take home exams	[ ]	Proofreaders	[ ]
Exams on tape or computer	[x]	Readers	[x]
Untimed exams	[x]	Reading Machines/Kurzweil	[ ]
Other accommodations	[x]	Special bookstore section	[ ]
		Typists	[ ]

Credit toward degree is given for remedial courses taken.

Counseling Services

- [x] Academic
- [x] Psychological
- [x] Student Support groups
- [ ] Vocational

Tutoring

Individual tutoring is available weekly.

	Individual	Group
Time management	[x]	[x]
Organizational skills	[x]	[x]
Learning strategies	[x]	[x]
Study skills	[x]	[x]
Content area	[x]	[x]
Writing lab	[x]	[x]
Math lab	[x]	[x]

UNIQUE LD PROGRAM FEATURES

This service is offered on an as-needed basis. Individual plans are developed by the staff to meet the needs of the student.

LD PROGRAM STAFF

Total number of LD Program staff (including director):

Full Time: 3 Part Time: 3

There is an advisor/advocate from the LD program available to students. 35 peer tutors are available to work with LD students.

Key staff person available to work with LD students: Sheri Phillips, Director.

Fontbonne University

St. Louis, MO

Address: 6800 Wydown Boulevard, St. Louis, MO, 63105
Admissions telephone: 314 889-1400
Admissions FAX: 314 719-8021
Associate Dean of Enrollment Management: Peggy Musen
Admissions e-mail: admissions@fontbonne.edu
Web site: http://www.fontbonne.edu
SAT Code: 6216 ACT Code: 2298

Director of Academic Resources: Jane Snyder
LD program telephone: 314 719-3627
LD program e-mail: jsnyder@fontbonne.edu
Total campus enrollment: 2,016

GENERAL

Fontbonne University is a private, coed, four-year institution. 13-acre, suburban campus in St. Louis (population: 348,189). Served by air, bus, and train. Semester system.

LD ADMISSIONS

A personal interview is required. Essay is not required. Admissions requirements that may be waived for LD students include ACT Score, and GPA.

SECONDARY SCHOOL REQUIREMENTS

Graduation from secondary school required; GED accepted. The following course distribution required: 4 units of English, 3 units of math, 3 units of science, 3 units of social studies, 3 units of academic electives.

TESTING

All enrolled freshmen (fall 2004):

Average ACT Scores: Composite: 22

Child Study Team report is not required. Tests required as part of this documentation:

- [ ] WAIS-IV
- [ ] WISC-IV
- [ ] SATA
- [ ] Woodcock-Johnson
- [ ] Nelson-Denny Reading Test
- [ ] Other

UNDERGRADUATE STUDENT BODY

Total undergraduate student enrollment: 407 Men, 970 Women.

Composition of student body (fall 2004):

	Undergraduate	Freshmen
International	0.5	0.4
Black	24.5	32.3
American Indian	0.0	0.4
Asian-American	0.5	0.8
Hispanic	0.0	1.3
White	71.0	63.4
Unreported	3.5	1.4
	100.0%	100.0%

Average age of full-time undergraduates is 26. 80% of classes have fewer than 20 students, 20% have between 20 and 50 students.

STUDENT HOUSING

47% of freshmen live in college housing. Freshmen are not required to live on campus. Housing is guaranteed for all undergraduates.

EXPENSES

Tuition (2005-06): $16,000 per year.

Room & Board: $6,988.

There is no additional cost for LD program/services.

LD SERVICES

LD program size is not limited.

LD services available to:

- [ ] Freshmen
- [ ] Sophomores
- [ ] Juniors
- [ ] Seniors

Academic Accommodations

Curriculum		In class	
Foreign language waiver	[ ]	Early syllabus	[ ]
Lighter course load	[ ]	Note takers in class	[x]
Math waiver	[ ]	Priority seating	[ ]
Other special classes	[x]	Tape recorders	[x]
Priority registrations	[ ]	Videotaped classes	[ ]
Substitution of courses	[ ]	Text on tape	[ ]
Exams		**Services**	
Extended time	[x]	Diagnostic tests	[ ]
Oral exams	[x]	Learning centers	[x]
Take home exams	[ ]	Proofreaders	[ ]
Exams on tape or computer	[ ]	Readers	[x]
Untimed exams	[x]	Reading Machines/Kurzweil	[x]
Other accommodations	[ ]	Special bookstore section	[x]
		Typists	[ ]

Credit toward degree is not given for remedial courses taken.

Counseling Services

- [ ] Academic
- [ ] Psychological
- [ ] Student Support groups
- [ ] Vocational

Tutoring

	Individual	Group
Time management	[ ]	[ ]
Organizational skills	[ ]	[ ]
Learning strategies	[ ]	[ ]
Study skills	[ ]	[ ]
Content area	[ ]	[ ]
Writing lab	[ ]	[ ]
Math lab	[ ]	[ ]

LD PROGRAM STAFF

Total number of LD Program staff (including director):

Full Time: 2 Part Time: 2

Key staff person available to work with LD students: Jane Snyder, Director of Academic Resources.

Hannibal-LaGrange College

Hannibal, MO

Address: 2800 Palmyra Road, Hannibal, MO, 63401
Admissions telephone: 800 454-1119
Admissions FAX: 573 221-6594
Dean of Enrollment Management: Ray Carty
Admissions e-mail: admissio@hlg.edu
Web site: http://www.hlg.edu
SAT Code: 6266 ACT Code: 2320

LD program name: Dr. David Pelletier
Vice President for Academic Affairs: Dr. Gary Breland
LD program telephone: 573 221-3675
LD program e-mail: gbreland@hlg.edu
Total campus enrollment: 1,067

GENERAL

Hannibal-LaGrange College is a private, coed, four-year institution. 110-acre campus in Hannibal (population: 17,757), 100 miles from St. Louis. Airport, bus, and train serve Quincy, Ill. (25 miles). Semester system.

LD ADMISSIONS

Students do not complete a separate application and are not simultaneously accepted to the LD program. A personal interview is recommended. Essay is not required.

SECONDARY SCHOOL REQUIREMENTS

Graduation from secondary school required; GED accepted.

TESTING

SAT Subject recommended.

All enrolled freshmen (fall 2004):

Average ACT Scores: Composite: 23

Child Study Team report is not required. Tests required as part of this documentation:

☐ WAIS-IV	☐ Woodcock-Johnson
☐ WISC-IV	☐ Nelson-Denny Reading Test
☐ SATA	☐ Other

UNDERGRADUATE STUDENT BODY

Total undergraduate student enrollment: 409 Men, 690 Women.

Composition of student body (fall 2004):

	Freshmen
International	0.9
Black	1.9
American Indian	0.4
Asian-American	0.2
Hispanic	0.9
White	95.4
Unreported	0.3
	100.0%

30% are from out of state. Average age of full-time undergraduates is 24.

STUDENT HOUSING

86% of freshmen live in college housing. Housing is guaranteed for all undergraduates. Campus can house 457 undergraduates. Single rooms are available for students with medical or special needs. A medical note is required.

EXPENSES

Tuition (2005-06): $11,420 per year.

Room & Board: $4,610

There is no additional cost for LD program/services.

LD SERVICES

LD program size is not limited.

LD services available to:

☐ Freshmen ☐ Sophomores ☐ Juniors ☐ Seniors

Academic Accommodations

Curriculum		**In class**	
Foreign language waiver	☐	Early syllabus	☐
Lighter course load	☐	Note takers in class	■
Math waiver	☐	Priority seating	■
Other special classes	☐	Tape recorders	☐
Priority registrations	☐	Videotaped classes	☐
Substitution of courses	☐	Text on tape	☐
Exams		**Services**	
Extended time	■	Diagnostic tests	☐
Oral exams	■	Learning centers	☐
Take home exams	☐	Proofreaders	☐
Exams on tape or computer	☐	Readers	☐
Untimed exams	■	Reading Machines/Kurzweil	☐
Other accommodations	☐	Special bookstore section	☐
		Typists	☐

Credit toward degree is not given for remedial courses taken.

Counseling Services

■ Academic
☐ Psychological
☐ Student Support groups
☐ Vocational

Tutoring

Individual tutoring is available weekly.

Average size of tutoring groups: 1

	Individual	Group
Time management	■	☐
Organizational skills	■	☐
Learning strategies	■	☐
Study skills	■	☐
Content area	☐	☐
Writing lab	☐	☐
Math lab	☐	☐

LD PROGRAM STAFF

Total number of LD Program staff (including director):

Full Time: 1 Part Time: 1

There is an advisor/advocate from the LD program available to students. The advisor/advocate meets with faculty 1 time per month and students 1 time per month.

Key staff person available to work with LD students: Carol Bunch, Instructor.

Harris-Stowe State College

St. Louis, MO

Address: 3026 Laclede Avenue, St. Louis, MO, 63103
Admissions telephone: 314 340-3300
Admissions FAX: 314 340-3555
Director of Admissions and Academic Advisement: Lashanda Boone
Admissions e-mail: admissions@hssc.edu
Web site: http://www.hssc.edu
SAT Code: 6269 ACT Code: 2302

Academic Support Coordinator: Robert Bandon
LD program telephone: 314 340-3648
LD program e-mail: brandonr@hssc.edu
LD program enrollment: 23, Total campus enrollment: 1,605

GENERAL

Harris-Stowe State College is a public, coed, four-year institution. 22-acre, urban campus in St. Louis (population: 348,189). Served by air, bus, and train. School operates transportation to nearby Metrolink stations. Public transportation serves campus. Semester system.

LD ADMISSIONS

A personal interview is recommended. Essay is not required.

For fall 2004, 17 completed self-identified LD applications were received. 17 applications were offered admission, and 17 enrolled.

SECONDARY SCHOOL REQUIREMENTS

Graduation from secondary school required; GED accepted. The following course distribution required: 4 units of English, 3 units of math, 2 units of science, 2 units of social studies, 1 unit of history, 3 units of academic electives.

TESTING

ACT required.

All enrolled freshmen (fall 2004):

Average ACT Scores: Composite: 17

Child Study Team report is not required. A neuropsychological or comprehensive psycho-education evaluation is not required for admission. Tests required as part of this documentation:

- [ ] WAIS-IV
- [ ] WISC-IV
- [ ] SATA
- [ ] Woodcock-Johnson
- [ ] Nelson-Denny Reading Test
- [ ] Other

UNDERGRADUATE STUDENT BODY

Total undergraduate student enrollment: 513 Men, 1,408 Women.

Composition of student body (fall 2004):

	Undergraduate	Freshmen
International	0.0	0.0
Black	93.7	82.2
American Indian	0.0	0.2
Asian-American	0.0	0.0
Hispanic	0.0	0.2
White	6.3	16.6
Unreported	0.0	0.8
	100.0%	100.0%

5% are from out of state. Average age of full-time undergraduates is 25. 73% of classes have fewer than 20 students, 26% have between 20 and 50 students, 1% have more than 50 students.

STUDENT HOUSING

Housing is not guaranteed for all undergraduates. Campus housing is not offered at this time. Single rooms are not available for students with medical or special needs.

EXPENSES

Tuition 2004: $4,095 per year (in-state), $8,070 (out-of-state).
There is no additional cost for LD program/services.

LD SERVICES

LD program size is not limited.

LD services available to:

- [x] Freshmen
- [x] Sophomores
- [x] Juniors
- [x] Seniors

Academic Accommodations

Curriculum

- [ ] Foreign language waiver
- [ ] Lighter course load
- [ ] Math waiver
- [ ] Other special classes
- [ ] Priority registrations
- [ ] Substitution of courses

Exams

- [x] Extended time
- [ ] Oral exams
- [ ] Take home exams
- [ ] Exams on tape or computer
- [ ] Untimed exams
- [ ] Other accommodations

In class

- [ ] Early syllabus
- [x] Note takers in class
- [ ] Priority seating
- [x] Tape recorders
- [ ] Videotaped classes
- [ ] Text on tape

Services

- [ ] Diagnostic tests
- [x] Learning centers
- [ ] Proofreaders
- [x] Readers
- [ ] Reading Machines/Kurzweil
- [ ] Special bookstore section
- [ ] Typists

Credit toward degree is not given for remedial courses taken.

Counseling Services

- [ ] Academic
- [ ] Psychological
- [ ] Student Support groups
- [ ] Vocational

Tutoring

Individual tutoring is not available.

	Individual	Group
Time management	☐	☐
Organizational skills	☐	☐
Learning strategies	☐	☐
Study skills	☐	☐
Content area	☐	☐
Writing lab	☐	☐
Math lab	☐	☐

LD PROGRAM STAFF

There are no advisors/advocates from the LD program available to students.

Key staff person available to work with LD students: Robert Bandon, Academic Support Coordinator.

Jewish Hospital College of Nursing and Allied Health

St. Louis, MO

Address: 306 South Kingshighway Boulevard, St. Louis, MO, 33132
Admissions telephone: 800 832-9009
Admissions FAX: 314 454-5239
Chief Admissions Officer: Christie Schneider
ACT Code: 2305

Total campus enrollment: 804

GENERAL

Jewish Hospital College of Nursing and Allied Health is a private, coed, four-year institution. Two-acre, urban campus in St. Louis (population: 348,189). Served by air and bus; train serves Kirkwood (five miles). School operates transportation to medical center and Washington U-St. Louis. Public transportation serves campus. Semester system.

LD ADMISSIONS

Application Deadline: 05/01.

SECONDARY SCHOOL REQUIREMENTS

Graduation from secondary school required; GED accepted.

TESTING

SAT Reasoning or ACT required. SAT Subject recommended.

Child Study Team report is not required. Tests required as part of this documentation:

☐	WAIS-IV	☐	Woodcock-Johnson
☐	WISC-IV	☐	Nelson-Denny Reading Test
☐	SATA	☐	Other

UNDERGRADUATE STUDENT BODY

Total undergraduate student enrollment: 50 Men, 299 Women.

Composition of student body (fall 2004):

	Undergraduate	Freshmen
International	0.0	0.0
Black	37.0	19.9
American Indian	0.0	0.5
Asian-American	2.2	3.1
Hispanic	0.0	1.6
White	43.4	60.1
Unreported	17.4	14.8
	100.0%	100.0%

20% are from out of state. Average age of full-time undergraduates is 26. 33% of classes have fewer than 20 students, 64% have between 20 and 50 students, 3% have more than 50 students.

STUDENT HOUSING

1% of freshmen live in college housing. Freshmen are not required to live on campus. Housing is guaranteed for all undergraduates. Campus can house 40 undergraduates. Single rooms are available for students with medical or special needs. A medical note is required.

EXPENSES

Tuition (2005-06): $8,808 per year.
There is no additional cost for LD program/services.

LD SERVICES

LD program size is not limited.

LD services available to:

☑ Freshmen ☑ Sophomores ☑ Juniors ☑ Seniors

Academic Accommodations

Curriculum		**In class**	
Foreign language waiver	☐	Early syllabus	☐
Lighter course load	☑	Note takers in class	☐
Math waiver	☐	Priority seating	☐
Other special classes	☐	Tape recorders	☑
Priority registrations	☐	Videotaped classes	☐
Substitution of courses	☐	Text on tape	☐
Exams		**Services**	
Extended time	☑	Diagnostic tests	☑
Oral exams	☑	Learning centers	☐
Take home exams	☐	Proofreaders	☐
Exams on tape or computer	☐	Readers	☐
Untimed exams	☑	Reading Machines/Kurzweil	☐
Other accommodations	☐	Special bookstore section	☐
		Typists	☐

Credit toward degree is not given for remedial courses taken.

Counseling Services

☑ Academic
☑ Psychological
☑ Student Support groups
☐ Vocational

Tutoring

Individual tutoring is available weekly.

Average size of tutoring groups: 1

	Individual	Group
Time management	☑	☐
Organizational skills	☑	☐
Learning strategies	☑	☐
Study skills	☑	☐
Content area	☑	☐
Writing lab	☑	☐
Math lab	☑	☐

LD PROGRAM STAFF

Total number of LD Program staff (including director):

Full Time: 1 Part Time: 1

There is no advisor/advocate from the LD program available to students. 5 peer tutors are available to work with LD students.

Kansas City Art Institute

Kansas City, MO

Address: 4415 Warwick Boulevard, Kansas City, MO, 64111
Admissions telephone: 800 522-5224
Admissions FAX: 816 802-3309
Vice President of Enrollment Management: Larry Stone
Admissions e-mail: admiss@kcai.edu
Web site: http://www.kcai.edu
SAT Code: 6330 ACT Code: 2277

LD program name: Academic Resource Center
Dean of Academic Resources: Bambi Burgard, Ph.D.
LD program telephone: 816 802-3376
LD program e-mail: bburgard@kcai.edu
LD program enrollment: 35, Total campus enrollment: 612

GENERAL

Kansas City Art Institute is a private, coed, four-year institution. 15-acre campus in Kansas City (population: 441,545). Served by air, bus, and train. Public transportation serves campus. Semester system.

LD ADMISSIONS

Students do not complete a separate application and are simultaneously accepted to the LD program. A member of the LD program does sit on the admissions committee. A personal interview is recommended. Essay is required and may be typed. Minimum SAT/ACT or GPA may be lowered.

15 applications were offered admission, and 15 enrolled.

SECONDARY SCHOOL REQUIREMENTS

Graduation from secondary school required; GED accepted.

TESTING

SAT Reasoning or ACT required.

All enrolled freshmen (fall 2004):

Average SAT I Scores:	Verbal: 542	Math: 494
Average ACT Scores:	Composite: 23	

Child Study Team report is not required. A neuropsychological or comprehensive psycho-education evaluation is not required for admission. Tests required as part of this documentation:

- [x] WAIS-IV
- [x] WISC-IV
- [ ] SATA
- [x] Woodcock-Johnson
- [x] Nelson-Denny Reading Test
- [ ] Other

UNDERGRADUATE STUDENT BODY

Total undergraduate student enrollment: 254 Men, 283 Women.

Composition of student body (fall 2004):

	Undergraduate	Freshmen
International	0.7	1.0
Black	2.2	3.1
American Indian	1.5	1.6
Asian-American	3.7	3.8
Hispanic	6.0	6.7
White	83.7	82.8
Unreported	2.2	1.0
	100.0%	100.0%

62% are from out of state. Average age of full-time undergraduates is 21. 72% of classes have fewer than 20 students, 28% have between 20 and 50 students.

STUDENT HOUSING

75% of freshmen live in college housing. Housing is not guaranteed for all undergraduates. On-campus housing is available only for freshmen. Campus can house 230 undergraduates. Single rooms are available for students with medical or special needs. A medical note is not required.

EXPENSES

Tuition (2005-06): $21,446 per year.
Room & Board: $7,150.

There is no additional cost for LD program/services.

LD SERVICES

LD program size is not limited.

LD services available to:

- [x] Freshmen
- [x] Sophomores
- [x] Juniors
- [x] Seniors

Academic Accommodations

Curriculum		In class	
Foreign language waiver	[ ]	Early syllabus	[ ]
Lighter course load	[x]	Note takers in class	[x]
Math waiver	[ ]	Priority seating	[ ]
Other special classes	[ ]	Tape recorders	[x]
Priority registrations	[ ]	Videotaped classes	[ ]
Substitution of courses	[ ]	Text on tape	[x]
Exams		**Services**	
Extended time	[x]	Diagnostic tests	[ ]
Oral exams	[x]	Learning centers	[x]
Take home exams	[ ]	Proofreaders	[ ]
Exams on tape or computer	[ ]	Readers	[x]
Untimed exams	[x]	Reading Machines/Kurzweil	[ ]
Other accommodations	[x]	Special bookstore section	[ ]
		Typists	[ ]

Credit toward degree is not given for remedial courses taken.

Counseling Services

- [x] Academic — Meets 30 times per academic year
- [x] Psychological — Meets 30 times per academic year
- [ ] Student Support groups
- [ ] Vocational

Tutoring

Individual tutoring is available daily.

	Individual	Group
Time management	[x]	[ ]
Organizational skills	[x]	[ ]
Learning strategies	[x]	[ ]
Study skills	[x]	[ ]
Content area	[x]	[ ]
Writing lab	[ ]	[ ]
Math lab	[ ]	[ ]

LD PROGRAM STAFF

Total number of LD Program staff (including director):

Full Time: 3 Part Time: 3

There is an advisor/advocate from the LD program available to students. The advisor/advocate meets with students 4 times per month. 1 peer tutor is available to work with LD students.

Key staff person available to work with LD students: Bambi Burgard, Ph.D., Dean of Academic Resources.

Lincoln University

Jefferson City, MO

Address: PO Box 29, Jefferson City, MO, 65102-0029
Admissions telephone: 800 521-5052
Admissions FAX: 573 681-5889
Associate Director of Admissions: Debra Cooper
Admissions e-mail: enroll@lincolnu.edu
Web site: http://www.lincolnu.edu
ACT Code: 6366

Director, Counseling and Career Center: Ron Nelson
LD program telephone: 573 681-5162
Total campus enrollment: 2,539

GENERAL

Lincoln University is a public, coed, four-year institution. 155-acre campus in Jefferson City (population: 39,630), 20 miles from Columbia; branch campus in Fort Leonardwood and Caruthersville, MO. Served by bus and train; airport serves Columbia; larger airports serve St. Louis (125 miles) and Kansas City (145 miles). Public transportation serves campus. Semester system.

LD ADMISSIONS

A personal interview is not required. Essay is not required.

SECONDARY SCHOOL REQUIREMENTS

Graduation from secondary school required; GED accepted.

TESTING

All enrolled freshmen (fall 2004):

Average ACT Scores: Composite: 17

Child Study Team report is not required. Tests required as part of this documentation:

- ☐ WAIS-IV
- ☐ WISC-IV
- ☐ SATA
- ☐ Woodcock-Johnson
- ☐ Nelson-Denny Reading Test
- ☐ Other

UNDERGRADUATE STUDENT BODY

Total undergraduate student enrollment: 1,267 Men, 1,857 Women.

15% are from out of state. Average age of full-time undergraduates is 22. 49% of classes have fewer than 20 students, 50% have between 20 and 50 students, 1% have more than 50 students.

STUDENT HOUSING

57% of freshmen live in college housing. freshmen are not required to live on campus. Housing is not guaranteed for all undergraduates. Insufficient capacity to house all unmarried students. Campus can house 845 undergraduates.

EXPENSES

Tuition (2005-06): $4,412 per year (in-state), $8,059 (out-of-state).
Room: $1,850. Board: $1,940.
There is no additional cost for LD program/services.

LD SERVICES

LD program size is not limited.

LD services available to:

☐ Freshmen ☐ Sophomores ☐ Juniors ☐ Seniors

Academic Accommodations

Curriculum		In class	
Foreign language waiver	☐	Early syllabus	☐
Lighter course load	☐	Note takers in class	☐
Math waiver	☐	Priority seating	☐
Other special classes	☐	Tape recorders	■
Priority registrations	☐	Videotaped classes	☐
Substitution of courses	☐	Text on tape	☐
Exams		**Services**	
Extended time	■	Diagnostic tests	☐
Oral exams	☐	Learning centers	☐
Take home exams	☐	Proofreaders	☐
Exams on tape or computer	☐	Readers	■
Untimed exams	☐	Reading Machines/Kurzweil	☐
Other accommodations	☐	Special bookstore section	☐
		Typists	☐

Credit toward degree is not given for remedial courses taken.

Counseling Services

- ☐ Academic
- ☐ Psychological
- ☐ Student Support groups
- ☐ Vocational

Tutoring

	Individual	Group
Time management	☐	☐
Organizational skills	☐	☐
Learning strategies	☐	☐
Study skills	☐	☐
Content area	☐	☐
Writing lab	☐	☐
Math lab	☐	☐

LD PROGRAM STAFF

Total number of LD Program staff (including director):

Full Time: 3 Part Time: 3

Key staff person available to work with LD students: Ron Nelson, Director, Counseling and Career Center.

Lindenwood University

St. Charles, MO

Address: 209 S. Kingshighway, St. Charles, MO, 63301-1695
Admissions telephone: 636 949-4949
Admissions FAX: 636 949-4989
Dean of Admissions: John Guffey
Admissions e-mail: admissions@lindenwood.edu
Web site: http://www.lindenwood.edu
SAT Code: 6367 ACT Code: 2324

Coordinator: Tonie Isenhour
LD program telephone: 636 949-8784
LD program e-mail: tisenhour@lindenwood.edu
Total campus enrollment: 5,512

GENERAL

Lindenwood University is a private, coed, four-year institution. 1,250-acre campus in St. Charles (population: 60,321), 20 miles from St. Louis; branch campuses in O'Fallon, Washington, Wentzville, and Westport. Major airport, bus, and train serve St. Louis. 4-1-4 system.

LD ADMISSIONS

A personal interview is recommended. Essay is not required.

SECONDARY SCHOOL REQUIREMENTS

Graduation from secondary school required; GED accepted.

TESTING

SAT Reasoning or ACT required. SAT Subject recommended.

All enrolled freshmen (fall 2004):

Average ACT Scores: Composite: 23

Child Study Team report is not required. Tests required as part of this documentation:

- [ ] WAIS-IV
- [ ] WISC-IV
- [ ] SATA
- [ ] Woodcock-Johnson
- [ ] Nelson-Denny Reading Test
- [ ] Other

UNDERGRADUATE STUDENT BODY

Total undergraduate student enrollment: 1,808 Men, 2,391 Women.

Composition of student body (fall 2004):

	Undergraduate	Freshmen
International	5.7	6.9
Black	6.2	11.3
American Indian	0.7	0.4
Asian-American	0.5	0.6
Hispanic	2.7	1.7
White	68.7	72.4
Unreported	15.5	6.7
	100.0%	100.0%

8% are from out of state. 5% join a fraternity and 10% join a sorority. Average age of full-time undergraduates is 25. 61% of classes have fewer than 20 students, 39% have between 20 and 50 students.

STUDENT HOUSING

89% of freshmen live in college housing. Housing is guaranteed for all undergraduates. Campus can house 3,200 undergraduates.

EXPENSES

Tuition (2005-06): $12,000 per year.
Room: $3,000. Board: $3,000.

There is no additional cost for LD program/services.

LD SERVICES

LD program size is not limited.

LD services available to:

- [ ] Freshmen
- [ ] Sophomores
- [ ] Juniors
- [ ] Seniors

Academic Accommodations

Curriculum

- [ ] Foreign language waiver
- [x] Lighter course load
- [ ] Math waiver
- [ ] Other special classes
- [ ] Priority registrations
- [ ] Substitution of courses

Exams

- [x] Extended time
- [x] Oral exams
- [ ] Take home exams
- [ ] Exams on tape or computer
- [x] Untimed exams
- [ ] Other accommodations

In class

- [ ] Early syllabus
- [x] Note takers in class
- [ ] Priority seating
- [ ] Tape recorders
- [ ] Videotaped classes
- [ ] Text on tape

Services

- [ ] Diagnostic tests
- [ ] Learning centers
- [ ] Proofreaders
- [x] Readers
- [x] Reading Machines/Kurzweil
- [ ] Special bookstore section
- [ ] Typists

Credit toward degree is not given for remedial courses taken.

Counseling Services

- [ ] Academic
- [ ] Psychological
- [ ] Student Support groups
- [ ] Vocational

Tutoring

	Individual	Group
Time management	[ ]	[ ]
Organizational skills	[ ]	[ ]
Learning strategies	[ ]	[ ]
Study skills	[ ]	[ ]
Content area	[ ]	[ ]
Writing lab	[ ]	[ ]
Math lab	[ ]	[ ]

LD PROGRAM STAFF

Total number of LD Program staff (including director):

Full Time: 1 Part Time: 1

Key staff person available to work with LD students: Tonie Isenhour, Coordinator for Campus Accessibility Services.

Maryville University of St. Louis

St Louis, MO

Address: 13550 Conway Road, St Louis, MO, 63141-7299
Admissions telephone: 800 627-9855
Admissions FAX: 314 529-9927
Vice President, Enrollment: Lynn Jackson
Admissions e-mail: admissions@maryville.edu
Web site: http://www.maryville.edu
SAT Code: 6399 ACT Code: 2326

Director, Academic Success Center: Julie Kindred, M.Ed
LD program telephone: 314 529-9374
LD program e-mail: jkindred@maryville.edu
LD program enrollment: 42, Total campus enrollment: 2,584

GENERAL

Maryville University of St. Louis is a private, coed, four-year institution. 130-acre, suburban campus in St. Louis (population: 348,189), 20 miles from downtown; branch campuses in St. Charles County and southwest St. Louis County. Served by air, bus, and train. Public transportation serves campus. Semester system.

LD ADMISSIONS

Students do not complete a separate application and are simultaneously accepted to the LD program. A member of the LD program does sit on the admissions committee. A personal interview is not required. Essay is not required.

SECONDARY SCHOOL REQUIREMENTS

Graduation from secondary school required; GED accepted. The following course distribution required: 4 units of English, 3 units of math, 2 units of science, 2 units of social studies, 8 units of academic electives.

TESTING

SAT Reasoning or ACT required. SAT Subject recommended.

All enrolled freshmen (fall 2004):

Average ACT Scores: Composite: 24

Child Study Team report is not required. A neuropsychological or comprehensive psycho-educational evaluation is required for admission. Must be dated within 36 months of application. Tests required as part of this documentation:

- [x] WAIS-IV
- [ ] WISC-IV
- [ ] SATA
- [x] Woodcock-Johnson
- [ ] Nelson-Denny Reading Test
- [ ] Other

UNDERGRADUATE STUDENT BODY

Total undergraduate student enrollment: 683 Men, 1,949 Women.

Composition of student body (fall 2004):

	Undergraduate	Freshmen
International	0.9	1.3
Black	5.3	6.4
American Indian	0.3	0.3
Asian-American	1.9	1.1
Hispanic	2.2	1.5
White	85.0	75.9
Unreported	4.4	13.5
	100.0%	100.0%

8% are from out of state. Average age of full-time undergraduates is 22. 69% of classes have fewer than 20 students, 31% have between 20 and 50 students.

STUDENT HOUSING

60% of freshmen live in college housing. Freshmen are not required to live on campus. Housing is guaranteed for all undergraduates. Campus can house 550 undergraduates. Single rooms are available for students with medical or special needs. A medical note is required.

EXPENSES

Tuition (2005-06): $17,000 per year.

Room & Board: $7,350

There is no additional cost for LD program/services.

LD SERVICES

LD program size is not limited.

LD services available to:

- [x] Freshmen
- [x] Sophomores
- [x] Juniors
- [x] Seniors

Academic Accommodations

Curriculum

- [ ] Foreign language waiver
- [x] Lighter course load
- [ ] Math waiver
- [ ] Other special classes
- [ ] Priority registrations
- [ ] Substitution of courses

Exams

- [x] Extended time
- [x] Oral exams
- [ ] Take home exams
- [ ] Exams on tape or computer
- [x] Untimed exams
- [ ] Other accommodations

In class

- [ ] Early syllabus
- [x] Note takers in class
- [ ] Priority seating
- [x] Tape recorders
- [ ] Videotaped classes
- [ ] Text on tape

Services

- [ ] Diagnostic tests
- [x] Learning centers
- [ ] Proofreaders
- [x] Readers
- [ ] Reading Machines/Kurzweil
- [ ] Special bookstore section
- [ ] Typists

Credit toward degree is not given for remedial courses taken.

Counseling Services

- [x] Academic
- [x] Psychological
- [x] Student Support groups
- [x] Vocational

Tutoring

Individual tutoring is available daily.

Average size of tutoring groups: 1

	Individual	Group
Time management	[x]	[ ]
Organizational skills	[x]	[ ]
Learning strategies	[x]	[ ]
Study skills	[x]	[ ]
Content area	[x]	[ ]
Writing lab	[x]	[ ]
Math lab	[x]	[ ]

LD PROGRAM STAFF

Total number of LD Program staff (including director):

Full Time: 1 Part Time: 1

There is an advisor/advocate from the LD program available to students. 50 peer tutors are available to work with LD students.

Key staff person available to work with LD students: Julie Kindred, M.Ed, Director, Academic Success Center.

University of Missouri - Columbia

Columbia, MO

Address: 305 Jesse Hall, Columbia, MO, 65211
Admissions telephone: 800 225-6075 (in-state)
Admissions FAX: 573 882-7887
Director of Admissions: Barbara Rupp
Admissions e-mail: mu4u@missouri.edu
Web site: http://www.missouri.edu
SAT Code: 6875 ACT Code: 2382

LD program name: Disability Services Office
LD program address: A038 Brady Commons
Director, Disability Services: Sarah C. Weaver
LD program telephone: 573 882-4696
LD program e-mail: weavers@missouri.edu
Total campus enrollment: 20,883

GENERAL

University of Missouri - Columbia is a public, coed, four-year institution. 1,377-acre campus in Columbia (population: 84,531), 125 miles from both Kansas City and St. Louis. Served by air and bus; major airports serve Kansas City and St. Louis; train serves Jefferson City. Public transportation serves campus. Semester system.

LD ADMISSIONS

A personal interview is not required. Essay is not required.

SECONDARY SCHOOL REQUIREMENTS

Graduation from secondary school required; GED accepted. The following course distribution required: 4 units of English, 4 units of math, 3 units of science, 2 units of foreign language, 3 units of social studies.

TESTING

ACT required; SAT Reasoning may be substituted. SAT Subject recommended.

All enrolled freshmen (fall 2004):

Average ACT Scores: Composite: 25

Child Study Team report is not required. Tests required as part of this documentation:

☐ WAIS-IV	☐ Woodcock-Johnson
☐ WISC-IV	☐ Nelson-Denny Reading Test
☐ SATA	☐ Other

UNDERGRADUATE STUDENT BODY

Total undergraduate student enrollment: 8,803 Men, 9,628 Women.

Composition of student body (fall 2004):

	Undergraduate	Freshmen
International	0.6	1.3
Black	6.4	5.6
American Indian	0.6	0.6
Asian-American	2.6	2.8
Hispanic	1.7	1.6
White	85.3	84.9
Unreported	2.8	3.2
	100.0%	100.0%

12% are from out of state. 20% join a fraternity and 20% join a sorority. Average age of full-time undergraduates is 20. 44% of classes have fewer than 20 students, 43% have between 20 and 50 students, 13% have more than 50 students.

STUDENT HOUSING

68% of freshmen live in college housing. Freshmen are required to live on campus. Housing is guaranteed for all undergraduates. Campus can house 9,207 undergraduates. Single rooms are available for students with medical or special needs. A medical note is required.

EXPENSES

Tuition (2005-06): $6,495 per year (in-state), $16,272 (out-of-state).
Room & Board: $6,540

There is no additional cost for LD program/services.

LD SERVICES

LD program size is not limited.

LD services available to:

☑ Freshmen ☑ Sophomores ☑ Juniors ☑ Seniors

Academic Accommodations

Curriculum		**In class**	
Foreign language waiver	☐	Early syllabus	☐
Lighter course load	☑	Note takers in class	☑
Math waiver	☐	Priority seating	☐
Other special classes	☐	Tape recorders	☑
Priority registrations	☐	Videotaped classes	☐
Substitution of courses	☐	Text on tape	☐
Exams		**Services**	
Extended time	☑	Diagnostic tests	☑
Oral exams	☑	Learning centers	☑
Take home exams	☐	Proofreaders	☐
Exams on tape or computer	☐	Readers	☑
Untimed exams	☑	Reading Machines/Kurzweil	☑
Other accommodations	☑	Special bookstore section	☐
		Typists	☑

Credit toward degree is not given for remedial courses taken.

Counseling Services

☑ Academic
☑ Psychological
☑ Student Support groups
☑ Vocational

Tutoring

	Individual	Group
Time management	☐	☐
Organizational skills	☐	☐
Learning strategies	☐	☐
Study skills	☐	☐
Content area	☐	☐
Writing lab	☐	☐
Math lab	☐	☐

UNIQUE LD PROGRAM FEATURES

MU Office of Disability Services trains volunteer students to be notetakers, readers, tutors, proctors, etc., to work with LD students when necessary.

LD PROGRAM STAFF

Total number of LD Program staff (including director):

Full Time: 4 Part Time: 4

There is an advisor/advocate from the LD program available to students.

Key staff person available to work with LD students: Sarah C. Weaver, Director, Disability Services.

LD Program web site: http://www.missouri.edu/~accesscm/

University of Missouri - Kansas City

Kansas City, MO

Address: 5100 Rockhill Road, Kansas City, MO, 64110
Admissions telephone: 800 775-8652
Admissions FAX: 816 235-5544
Director of Admissions: Jennifer DeHaemers
Admissions e-mail: admit@umkc.edu
Web site: http://www.umkc.edu
SAT Code: 6872 ACT Code: 2380

LD program name: Office of Svs for Students with Disabilities
LD program address: UC LL23
Coordinator: Scott Laurent
LD program telephone: 816 235-5696
LD program e-mail: disability@umkc.edu
LD program enrollment: 120, Total campus enrollment: 9,393

GENERAL

University of Missouri - Kansas City is a public, coed, four-year institution. 191-acre, urban campus in Kansas City (population: 441,545); branch campuses in downtown Kansas City and in Independence. Served by air, bus, and train. School operates transportation to branch campuses. Public transportation serves campus. Semester system.

LD ADMISSIONS

Students do not complete a separate application and are simultaneously accepted to the LD program. A personal interview is not required. Essay is not required.

SECONDARY SCHOOL REQUIREMENTS

Graduation from secondary school required; GED accepted. The following course distribution required: 4 units of English, 4 units of math, 3 units of science, 2 units of foreign language, 3 units of social studies.

TESTING

ACT required; SAT Reasoning may be substituted. SAT Subject recommended.

All enrolled freshmen (fall 2004):

Average ACT Scores: Composite: 24

Child Study Team report is not required. A neuropsychological or comprehensive psycho-education evaluation is not required for admission. Tests required as part of this documentation:

☐	WAIS-IV	☐	Woodcock-Johnson
☐	WISC-IV	☐	Nelson-Denny Reading Test
☐	SATA	☐	Other

UNDERGRADUATE STUDENT BODY

Total undergraduate student enrollment: 3,446 Men, 4,853 Women.

Composition of student body (fall 2004):

	Undergraduate	Freshmen
International	2.3	2.9
Black	16.7	13.9
American Indian	0.5	0.8
Asian-American	8.9	5.3
Hispanic	4.8	4.1
White	59.4	63.2
Unreported	7.4	9.8
	100.0%	100.0%

14% are from out of state. 4% join a fraternity and 5% join a sorority. Average age of full-time undergraduates is 23. 53% of classes have fewer than 20 students, 40% have between 20 and 50 students, 7% have more than 50 students.

STUDENT HOUSING

40% of freshmen live in college housing. Freshmen are not required to live on campus. Housing is not guaranteed for all undergraduates. Housing is available on a first-come, first-serve basis. Campus can house 972 undergraduates.

EXPENSES

Tuition (2005-06): $6,495 per year (in-state), $16,272 (out-of-state).

Room: $4,265. Board: $2,405.
There is no additional cost for LD program/services.

LD SERVICES

LD program size is not limited.

LD services available to:

■ Freshmen ■ Sophomores ■ Juniors ■ Seniors

Academic Accommodations

Curriculum		**In class**	
Foreign language waiver	☐	Early syllabus	☐
Lighter course load	■	Note takers in class	■
Math waiver	☐	Priority seating	■
Other special classes	☐	Tape recorders	■
Priority registrations	☐	Videotaped classes	☐
Substitution of courses	☐	Text on tape	■
Exams		**Services**	
Extended time	■	Diagnostic tests	■
Oral exams	☐	Learning centers	■
Take home exams	☐	Proofreaders	☐
Exams on tape or computer	☐	Readers	■
Untimed exams	☐	Reading Machines/Kurzweil	■
Other accommodations	☐	Special bookstore section	☐
		Typists	■

Credit toward degree is not given for remedial courses taken.

Counseling Services

■ Academic
■ Psychological
■ Student Support groups
☐ Vocational

Tutoring

Individual tutoring is available daily.

	Individual	Group
Time management	☐	☐
Organizational skills	☐	■
Learning strategies	☐	■
Study skills	☐	☐
Content area	☐	☐
Writing lab	■	■
Math lab	■	■

LD PROGRAM STAFF

Total number of LD Program staff (including director):

Full Time: 2 Part Time: 2

There is an advisor/advocate from the LD program available to students.

Key staff person available to work with LD students: Scott Laurent, Coordinator.

LD Program web site: http://www.umkc.edu/disability/

University of Missouri - Rolla

Rolla, MO

Address: 207 Parker Hall - 1870 Miner Circle, Rolla, MO, 65409-0910
Admissions telephone: 800 522-0938
Admissions FAX: 573 341-4082
Acting Director of Admissions: Lynn Stichnote
Admissions e-mail: admissions@umr.edu
Web site: http://www.umr.edu
SAT Code: 6876 ACT Code: 2398

Disability Support Services Advisor: Connie Arthur
LD program telephone: 573 341-4211
LD program e-mail: conniea@umr.edu
Total campus enrollment: 4,121

GENERAL

University of Missouri - Rolla is a public, coed, four-year institution. 284-acre campus in Rolla (population: 15,000), 100 miles from St. Louis. Served by bus; major airport serves St. Louis; smaller airport serves Springfield (100 miles); train serves Jefferson City (60 miles). Semester system.

LD ADMISSIONS

A personal interview is not required. Essay is not required.

SECONDARY SCHOOL REQUIREMENTS

Graduation from secondary school required; GED accepted. The following course distribution required: 4 units of English, 4 units of math, 3 units of science, 2 units of foreign language, 3 units of social studies.

TESTING

SAT Reasoning or ACT required. SAT Subject recommended.

All enrolled freshmen (fall 2004):

Average ACT Scores: Composite: 27

Child Study Team report is required if student is classified. Tests required as part of this documentation:

- ☐ WAIS-IV
- ☐ WISC-IV
- ☐ SATA
- ☐ Woodcock-Johnson
- ☐ Nelson-Denny Reading Test
- ☐ Other

UNDERGRADUATE STUDENT BODY

Total undergraduate student enrollment: 2,889 Men, 867 Women.

Composition of student body (fall 2004):

	Undergraduate	Freshmen
International	0.6	2.4
Black	3.0	4.3
American Indian	0.4	0.5
Asian-American	2.5	2.6
Hispanic	1.9	2.0
White	86.0	83.5
Unreported	5.6	4.7
	100.0%	100.0%

22% are from out of state. 25% join a fraternity and 25% join a sorority. Average age of full-time undergraduates is 21. 42% of classes have fewer than 20 students, 50% have between 20 and 50 students, 8% have more than 50 students.

STUDENT HOUSING

95% of freshmen live in college housing. Freshmen are required to live on campus. Housing is guaranteed for all undergraduates. Campus can house 2,500 undergraduates.

EXPENSES

Tuition (2005-06): $6,495 per year (in-state), $16,272 (out-of-state). Additional fee of $42.60 per credit for engineering programs.

Room: $3,570. Board: $2,270.
There is no additional cost for LD program/services.

LD SERVICES

LD program size is not limited.

LD services available to:

☐ Freshmen ☐ Sophomores ☐ Juniors ☐ Seniors

Academic Accommodations

Curriculum		**In class**	
Foreign language waiver	☐	Early syllabus	☐
Lighter course load	☑	Note takers in class	☑
Math waiver	☐	Priority seating	☐
Other special classes	☐	Tape recorders	☑
Priority registrations	☐	Videotaped classes	☐
Substitution of courses	☐	Text on tape	☐
Exams		**Services**	
Extended time	☑	Diagnostic tests	☐
Oral exams	☑	Learning centers	☑
Take home exams	☐	Proofreaders	☐
Exams on tape or computer	☐	Readers	☑
Untimed exams	☐	Reading Machines/Kurzweil	☑
Other accommodations	☐	Special bookstore section	☐
		Typists	☐

Credit toward degree is not given for remedial courses taken.

Counseling Services

- ☐ Academic
- ☐ Psychological
- ☐ Student Support groups
- ☐ Vocational

Tutoring

Individual tutoring is available.

	Individual	Group
Time management	☐	☐
Organizational skills	☐	☐
Learning strategies	☐	☐
Study skills	☐	☐
Content area	☐	☐
Writing lab	☐	☐
Math lab	☐	☐

LD PROGRAM STAFF

Total number of LD Program staff (including director):

Full Time: 1 Part Time: 1

Key staff person available to work with LD students: Connie Arthur, Disability Support Services; Student Services Advisor.

University of Missouri - St. Louis

St. Louis, MO

Address: 1 University Boulevard, St. Louis, MO, 63121-4400
Admissions telephone: 314 516-5451
Admissions FAX: 314 516-5310
Director of Admissions: Melissa Hattman
Admissions e-mail: admissions@umsl.edu
Web site: http://www.umsl.edu
SAT Code: 6889 ACT Code: 2383

Director, Disability Access Services: Marilyn Ditto-Pernell
LD program telephone: 314 516-6554
LD program e-mail: mditto@umsl.edu
LD program enrollment: 62, Total campus enrollment: 12,586

GENERAL

University of Missouri - St. Louis is a public, coed, four-year institution. 275-acre campus in St. Louis (population: 348,189); branch campuses in Hillsboro and St. Charles. Served by air, bus, and train. School operates shuttle service. Public transportation serves campus. Semester system.

LD ADMISSIONS

A personal interview is not required. Essay is not required.

SECONDARY SCHOOL REQUIREMENTS

Graduation from secondary school required; GED accepted. The following course distribution required: 4 units of English, 4 units of math, 3 units of science, 2 units of foreign language, 3 units of social studies.

TESTING

ACT required; SAT Reasoning may be substituted. SAT Subject recommended.

All enrolled freshmen (fall 2004):

Average SAT I Scores:	Verbal: 556	Math: 557
Average ACT Scores:	Composite: 23	

Child Study Team report is not required. A neuropsychological or comprehensive psycho-educational evaluation is required for admission. Must be dated within 36 months of application. Tests required as part of this documentation:

- ☑ WAIS-IV
- ☐ WISC-IV
- ☑ SATA
- ☑ Woodcock-Johnson
- ☐ Nelson-Denny Reading Test
- ☐ Other

UNDERGRADUATE STUDENT BODY

Total undergraduate student enrollment: 4,036 Men, 5,576 Women.

Composition of student body (fall 2004):

	Undergraduate	Freshmen
International	3.6	2.3
Black	18.3	15.9
American Indian	0.4	0.3
Asian-American	3.1	3.1
Hispanic	1.6	1.7
White	67.9	69.6
Unreported	5.1	7.1
	100.0%	100.0%

3% are from out of state. 1% join a fraternity and 1% join a sorority. Average age of full-time undergraduates is 23. 44% of classes have fewer than 20 students, 48% have between 20 and 50 students, 8% have more than 50 students.

STUDENT HOUSING

Freshmen are not required to live on campus. Housing is guaranteed for all undergraduates. Campus can house 1,000 undergraduates. Single rooms are available for students with medical or special needs. A medical note is required.

EXPENSES

Tuition (2005-06): $6,495 per year (in-state), $16,272 (out-of-state).

Room: $4,561. Board: $1,867.
There is no additional cost for LD program/services.

LD SERVICES

LD program size is not limited.

LD services available to:

☑ Freshmen ☑ Sophomores ☑ Juniors ☑ Seniors

Academic Accommodations

Curriculum		**In class**	
Foreign language waiver	☐	Early syllabus	☐
Lighter course load	☑	Note takers in class	☑
Math waiver	☐	Priority seating	☑
Other special classes	☐	Tape recorders	☑
Priority registrations	☐	Videotaped classes	☐
Substitution of courses	☐	Text on tape	☑
Exams		**Services**	
Extended time	☑	Diagnostic tests	☐
Oral exams	☑	Learning centers	☐
Take home exams	☐	Proofreaders	☐
Exams on tape or computer	☑	Readers	☑
Untimed exams	☐	Reading Machines/Kurzweil	☑
Other accommodations	☐	Special bookstore section	☐
		Typists	☐

Credit toward degree is not given for remedial courses taken.

Counseling Services

- ☐ Academic
- ☐ Psychological
- ☐ Student Support groups
- ☐ Vocational

Tutoring

Individual tutoring is not available.

	Individual	Group
Time management	☐	☐
Organizational skills	☐	☐
Learning strategies	☐	☐
Study skills	☐	☑
Content area	☐	☐
Writing lab	☑	☐
Math lab	☑	☐

UNIQUE LD PROGRAM FEATURES

No specific LD program.

LD PROGRAM STAFF

Total number of LD Program staff (including director):

Full Time: 1 Part Time: 1

There is an advisor/advocate from the LD program available to students.

Key staff person available to work with LD students: Marilyn Ditto-Pernell, Director.

Missouri Southern State University

Joplin, MO

Address: 3950 E. Newman Road, Joplin, MO, 64801-1595
Admissions telephone: 800 606-6772
Admissions FAX: 417 659-4429
Director of Enrollment Services: Derek Skaggs
Admissions e-mail: admissions@mssu.edu
Web site: http://www.mssu.edu
SAT Code: 6322 ACT Code: 2304

Coordinator of Disability Services: Melissa Locher
LD program telephone: 417 625-9373
LD program e-mail: locher-m@mssu.edu
LD program enrollment: 7, Total campus enrollment: 5,256

GENERAL

Missouri Southern State University is a public, coed, four-year institution. 340-acre campus in Joplin (population: 45,504), 60 miles from Springfield; instruction sites in Carthage, Cassville, Lamar, and Monett and in Neosho, Nev. Served by air and bus; major airport and train serve Kansas City (150 miles); smaller airports serve Springfield and Tulsa (120 miles). Semester system.

LD ADMISSIONS

Students do not complete a separate application and are simultaneously accepted to the LD program. A member of the LD program does sit on the admissions committee. High school waivers are accepted for math and foreign language. A personal interview is not required. Essay is not required.

For fall 2004, 7 completed self-identified LD applications were received. 7 applications were offered admission, and 7 enrolled.

SECONDARY SCHOOL REQUIREMENTS

Graduation from secondary school required; GED accepted. The following course distribution required: 4 units of English, 3 units of math, 2 units of science, 2 units of foreign language, 3 units of social studies, 3 units of academic electives.

TESTING

SAT Reasoning considered if submitted. ACT required; SAT Reasoning may be substituted. SAT Subject recommended.

All enrolled freshmen (fall 2004):

Average ACT Scores: Composite: 22

Child Study Team report is not required. A neuropsychological or comprehensive psycho-educational evaluation is required for admission. Must be dated within 48 months of application. Tests required as part of this documentation:

- ■ WAIS-IV
- ☐ WISC-IV
- ☐ SATA
- ■ Woodcock-Johnson
- ☐ Nelson-Denny Reading Test
- ■ Other

UNDERGRADUATE STUDENT BODY

Total undergraduate student enrollment: 2,534 Men, 3,365 Women.

Composition of student body (fall 2004):

	Undergraduate	Freshmen
International	0.3	2.4
Black	3.5	2.6
American Indian	2.4	2.5
Asian-American	0.9	1.1
Hispanic	2.8	2.1
White	90.1	89.3
Unreported	0.0	0.0
	100.0%	100.0%

13% are from out of state. 1% join a fraternity and 1% join a sorority. Average age of full-time undergraduates is 24. 50% of classes have fewer than 20 students, 49% have between 20 and 50 students, 1% have more than 50 students.

STUDENT HOUSING

30% of freshmen live in college housing. Freshmen are required to live on campus. Housing is guaranteed for all undergraduates. Campus can house 700 undergraduates. Single rooms are available for students with medical or special needs. A medical note is required.

EXPENSES

Tuition (2005-06): $3,750 per year (in-state), $7,500 (out-of-state).
Room & Board: $4,480
There is no additional cost for LD program/services.

LD SERVICES

LD program size is not limited.

LD services available to:

■ Freshmen ■ Sophomores ■ Juniors ■ Seniors

Academic Accommodations

Curriculum
- Foreign language waiver ☐
- Lighter course load ☐
- Math waiver ☐
- Other special classes ☐
- Priority registrations ■
- Substitution of courses ■

Exams
- Extended time ■
- Oral exams ■
- Take home exams ☐
- Exams on tape or computer ■
- Untimed exams ☐
- Other accommodations ■

In class
- Early syllabus ☐
- Note takers in class ■
- Priority seating ■
- Tape recorders ■
- Videotaped classes ☐
- Text on tape ■

Services
- Diagnostic tests ☐
- Learning centers ■
- Proofreaders ☐
- Readers ■
- Reading Machines/Kurzweil ☐
- Special bookstore section ☐
- Typists ■

Credit toward degree is not given for remedial courses taken.

Counseling Services

- ■ Academic
- ■ Psychological
- ☐ Student Support groups
- ☐ Vocational

Tutoring

Individual tutoring is available.

	Individual	Group
Time management	☐	■
Organizational skills	☐	■
Learning strategies	☐	■
Study skills	☐	■
Content area	■	☐
Writing lab	■	☐
Math lab	☐	☐

LD PROGRAM STAFF

Total number of LD Program staff (including director):

Full Time: 1 Part Time: 1

There is an advisor/advocate from the LD program available to students. 20 peer tutors are available to work with LD students.

Key staff person available to work with LD students: Ms. Melissa Locher, Coordinator of Disability Services.

Northwest Missouri State University

Maryville, MO

Address: 800 University Drive, Maryville, MO, 64468
Admissions telephone: 800 633-1175
Admissions FAX: 660 562-1821
Dean of Enrollment Management: Bev Schenkel
Admissions e-mail: admissions@mail.nwmissouri.edu
Web site: http://www.nwmissouri.edu
SAT Code: 6488 ACT Code: 2338

504 Coordinator: Angel Harris-Lewis
LD program telephone: 660 562-1110
LD program e-mail: ahlewis@mail.nwmissouri.edu
Total campus enrollment: 5,600

GENERAL

Northwest Missouri State University is a public, coed, four-year institution. 240-acre campus in Maryville (population: 10,581), 72 miles from Kansas City. Served by bus; major airport serves Kansas City. School operates transportation to Kansas City airport at vacation and special times. Trimester system.

LD ADMISSIONS

A personal interview is not required. Essay is not required.

SECONDARY SCHOOL REQUIREMENTS

Graduation from secondary school required; GED accepted. The following course distribution required: 4 units of English, 3 units of math, 2 units of science, 3 units of social studies, 4 units of academic electives.

TESTING

Child Study Team report is not required. Tests required as part of this documentation:

- [ ] WAIS-IV
- [ ] WISC-IV
- [ ] SATA
- [ ] Woodcock-Johnson
- [ ] Nelson-Denny Reading Test
- [ ] Other

UNDERGRADUATE STUDENT BODY

Total undergraduate student enrollment: 2,474 Men, 3,126 Women.

35% are from out of state.

STUDENT HOUSING

Housing is guaranteed for all undergraduates. Campus can house 2,393 undergraduates.

EXPENSES

Tuition (2005-06): $4,005 per year (in-state), $8,010 (out-of-state).
Room: $3,466. Board: $2,320.
There is no additional cost for LD program/services.

LD SERVICES

LD program size is not limited.

LD services available to:

- [ ] Freshmen
- [ ] Sophomores
- [ ] Juniors
- [ ] Seniors

Academic Accommodations

Curriculum		**In class**	
Foreign language waiver	[ ]	Early syllabus	[ ]
Lighter course load	[x]	Note takers in class	[ ]
Math waiver	[ ]	Priority seating	[ ]
Other special classes	[ ]	Tape recorders	[x]
Priority registrations	[ ]	Videotaped classes	[ ]
Substitution of courses	[ ]	Text on tape	[ ]
Exams		**Services**	
Extended time	[x]	Diagnostic tests	[ ]
Oral exams	[ ]	Learning centers	[x]
Take home exams	[ ]	Proofreaders	[ ]
Exams on tape or computer	[ ]	Readers	[x]
Untimed exams	[ ]	Reading Machines/Kurzweil	[x]
Other accommodations	[ ]	Special bookstore section	[ ]
		Typists	[ ]

Credit toward degree is given for remedial courses taken.

Counseling Services

- [ ] Academic
- [ ] Psychological
- [ ] Student Support groups
- [ ] Vocational

Tutoring

	Individual	Group
Time management	[ ]	[ ]
Organizational skills	[ ]	[ ]
Learning strategies	[ ]	[ ]
Study skills	[ ]	[ ]
Content area	[ ]	[ ]
Writing lab	[ ]	[ ]
Math lab	[ ]	[ ]

LD PROGRAM STAFF

Total number of LD Program staff (including director):

Full Time: 17 Part Time: 17

Key staff person available to work with LD students: Angel Harris-Lewis, 504 Coordinator.

College of the Ozarks

Point Lookout, MO

Address: PO Box 17, Point Lookout, MO, 65726
Admissions telephone: 800 222-0525
Admissions FAX: 417 335-2618
Dean of Admissions: Marci Linson
Admissions e-mail: admiss4@cofo.edu
Web site: http://www.cofo.edu
SAT Code: 6713 ACT Code: 120

Registrar: Fran Forman
LD program telephone: 417 334-6411, extension 4223
LD program e-mail: fforman@cofo.edu
LD program enrollment: 20, Total campus enrollment: 1,348

GENERAL

College of the Ozarks is a private, coed, four-year institution. 1,000-acre campus at Point Lookout (population: 6,050), three miles from Branson and 40 miles from Springfield. Major airport serves Kansas City (210 miles); smaller airport serves Springfield; bus serves Hollister (three miles). School operates transportation to Branson. Public transportation serves campus. Semester system.

LD ADMISSIONS

Application Deadline: 02/15. Students do not complete a separate application and are not simultaneously accepted to the LD program. A member of the LD program does not sit on the admissions committee. A personal interview is required. Essay is not required.

SECONDARY SCHOOL REQUIREMENTS

Graduation from secondary school is not required.

TESTING

ACT required.

All enrolled freshmen (fall 2004):

Average ACT Scores: Composite: 22

Child Study Team report is not required. A neuropsychological or comprehensive psycho-education evaluation is not required for admission. Tests required as part of this documentation:

- [ ] WAIS-IV
- [ ] WISC-IV
- [ ] SATA
- [ ] Woodcock-Johnson
- [ ] Nelson-Denny Reading Test
- [ ] Other

UNDERGRADUATE STUDENT BODY

Total undergraduate student enrollment: 622 Men, 777 Women.

Composition of student body (fall 2004):

	Undergraduate	Freshmen
International	0.4	2.3
Black	0.7	0.7
American Indian	1.9	0.7
Asian-American	0.0	0.5
Hispanic	0.7	1.0
White	95.2	94.1
Unreported	1.1	0.7
	100.0%	100.0%

31% are from out of state. Average age of full-time undergraduates is 21. 53% of classes have fewer than 20 students, 45% have between 20 and 50 students, 2% have more than 50 students.

STUDENT HOUSING

99% of freshmen live in college housing. Freshmen are required to live on campus. Housing is guaranteed for all undergraduates. Campus can house 1,031 undergraduates. Single rooms are not available for students with medical or special needs.

EXPENSES

Tuition (2005-06): $14,900 per year.
Room: $1,850. Board: $1,950.
There is no additional cost for LD program/services.

LD SERVICES

LD program size is not limited.

LD services available to:

- [x] Freshmen
- [x] Sophomores
- [x] Juniors
- [x] Seniors

Academic Accommodations

Curriculum		In class	
Foreign language waiver	[ ]	Early syllabus	[ ]
Lighter course load	[x]	Note takers in class	[x]
Math waiver	[ ]	Priority seating	[ ]
Other special classes	[ ]	Tape recorders	[x]
Priority registrations	[ ]	Videotaped classes	[ ]
Substitution of courses	[x]	Text on tape	[x]
Exams		**Services**	
Extended time	[x]	Diagnostic tests	[ ]
Oral exams	[ ]	Learning centers	[ ]
Take home exams	[ ]	Proofreaders	[ ]
Exams on tape or computer	[x]	Readers	[ ]
Untimed exams	[ ]	Reading Machines/Kurzweil	[ ]
Other accommodations	[x]	Special bookstore section	[ ]
		Typists	[ ]

Credit toward degree is not given for remedial courses taken.

Counseling Services

- [x] Academic
- [x] Psychological
- [ ] Student Support groups
- [x] Vocational

Tutoring

Individual tutoring is available daily.

Average size of tutoring groups: 1

	Individual	Group
Time management	[ ]	[x]
Organizational skills	[ ]	[x]
Learning strategies	[ ]	[x]
Study skills	[ ]	[x]
Content area	[x]	[ ]
Writing lab	[x]	[ ]
Math lab	[x]	[x]

LD PROGRAM STAFF

There is no advisor/advocate from the LD program available to students.

Park University

Parkville, MO

Address: 8700 N.W. River Park Drive, Parkville, MO, 64152
Admissions telephone: 800 745-7275
Admissions FAX: 816 741-4462
Director of Student Recruiting and Marketing: Cathy Colapietro
Admissions e-mail: admissions@mail.park.edu
Web site: http://www.park.edu
SAT Code: 6574 ACT Code: 2340

LD program address: Box 46
Director of Academic Support Services: Debra McArthur
LD program telephone: 816 584-6332
LD program e-mail: debra.mcarthur@park.edu
LD program enrollment: 22, Total campus enrollment: 12,077

GENERAL

Park University is a private, coed, four-year institution. 800-acre campus in Parkville (population: 4,059), 12 miles from Kansas City. Major airport, bus, and train serve Kansas City. Semester system.

SECONDARY SCHOOL REQUIREMENTS

Graduation from secondary school required; GED accepted.

TESTING

ACT required.

Child Study Team report is not required. Tests required as part of this documentation:

- ☐ WAIS-IV
- ☐ WISC-IV
- ☐ SATA
- ☐ Woodcock-Johnson
- ☐ Nelson-Denny Reading Test
- ☐ Other

UNDERGRADUATE STUDENT BODY

Total undergraduate student enrollment: 4,771 Men, 4,491 Women.

Composition of student body (fall 2004):

	Undergraduate	Freshmen
International	1.6	1.6
Black	25.2	21.4
American Indian	0.0	0.6
Asian-American	3.1	2.6
Hispanic	7.9	15.5
White	62.2	58.3
Unreported	0.0	0.0
	100.0%	100.0%

72% are from out of state.

STUDENT HOUSING

35% of freshmen live in college housing.

EXPENSES

Tuition (2005-06): $6,870 per year.

Room & Board: $5,180

LD SERVICES

LD program size is not limited.

LD services available to:

■ Freshmen ■ Sophomores ■ Juniors ■ Seniors

Academic Accommodations

Curriculum		**In class**	
Foreign language waiver	☐	Early syllabus	☐
Lighter course load	☐	Note takers in class	■
Math waiver	☐	Priority seating	☐
Other special classes	■	Tape recorders	■
Priority registrations	☐	Videotaped classes	■
Substitution of courses	■	Text on tape	■
Exams		**Services**	
Extended time	■	Diagnostic tests	☐
Oral exams	■	Learning centers	■
Take home exams	■	Proofreaders	■
Exams on tape or computer	■	Readers	■
Untimed exams	■	Reading Machines/Kurzweil	■
Other accommodations	■	Special bookstore section	☐
		Typists	■

Credit toward degree is not given for remedial courses taken.

Counseling Services

- ☐ Academic
- ☐ Psychological
- ☐ Student Support groups
- ☐ Vocational

Tutoring

Individual tutoring is available daily.

Average size of tutoring groups: 1

	Individual	Group
Time management	■	☐
Organizational skills	■	☐
Learning strategies	■	☐
Study skills	■	☐
Content area	■	☐
Writing lab	■	☐
Math lab	■	☐

LD PROGRAM STAFF

Total number of LD Program staff (including director):

Full Time: 1 Part Time: 1

There is an advisor/advocate from the LD program available to students. 3 graduate students and 10 peer tutors are available to work with LD students.

Key staff person available to work with LD students: Debra McArthur, Director of Academic Support Services.

LD Program web site: www.park.edu/support/policy.asp

Saint Louis University

St. Louis, MO

Address: 221 N. Grand Boulevard, St. Louis, MO, 63103
Admissions telephone: 800 SLU-FORU
Admissions FAX: 314 977-7136
Associate Provost: Shani Lenore
Admissions e-mail: admitme@slu.edu
Web site: http://www.slu.edu
SAT Code: 6629 ACT Code: 2352

LD program name: Disabilities Services
LD program address: Room 36
Counselor for Student Disabilities: Adam Meyer
LD program telephone: 314 977-8885
LD program e-mail: meyerah@slu.edu
LD program enrollment: 70, Total campus enrollment: 7,086

GENERAL

Saint Louis University is a private, coed, four-year institution. 300-acre campus in St. Louis (population: 348,189); remote sites in mid-town St. Louis and abroad in Madrid, Spain. Served by air, bus, and train. School operates transportation to mid-town campus, Parks Coll, and nearby off-campus housing. Public transportation serves campus. Semester system.

LD ADMISSIONS

Students do not complete a separate application and are not simultaneously accepted to the LD program. A member of the LD program does not sit on the admissions committee. A personal interview is not required. Essay is required and may be typed.

SECONDARY SCHOOL REQUIREMENTS

Graduation from secondary school required; GED accepted. The following course distribution required: 4 units of English, 4 units of math, 3 units of science, 2 units of foreign language, 3 units of social studies, 3 units of academic electives.

TESTING

SAT Reasoning or ACT required. SAT Subject recommended.

All enrolled freshmen (fall 2004):

Average ACT Scores: Composite: 26

Child Study Team report is not required. A neuropsychological or comprehensive psycho-educational evaluation is required for admission. Must be dated within 36 months of application. Tests required as part of this documentation:

- ■ WAIS-IV
- ■ WISC-IV
- ☐ SATA
- ■ Woodcock-Johnson
- ■ Nelson-Denny Reading Test
- ☐ Other

UNDERGRADUATE STUDENT BODY

Total undergraduate student enrollment: 3,280 Men, 3,948 Women.

Composition of student body (fall 2004):

	Undergraduate	Freshmen
International	0.3	2.1
Black	6.1	7.6
American Indian	0.5	0.4
Asian-American	6.0	4.7
Hispanic	2.7	2.3
White	71.1	71.3
Unreported	13.3	11.6
	100.0%	100.0%

48% are from out of state. 23% join a fraternity and 16% join a sorority. Average age of full-time undergraduates is 21. 49% of classes have fewer than 20 students, 45% have between 20 and 50 students, 6% have more than 50 students.

STUDENT HOUSING

85% of freshmen live in college housing. Freshmen are not required to live on campus. Housing is guaranteed for all undergraduates. Campus can house 3,442 undergraduates. Single rooms are available for students with medical or special needs. A medical note is required.

EXPENSES

Tuition (2005-06): $24,760 per year.
Room: $4,490. Board: $3,710.
There is no additional cost for LD program/services.

LD SERVICES

LD program size is not limited.

LD services available to:

■ Freshmen ■ Sophomores ■ Juniors ■ Seniors

Academic Accommodations

Curriculum		**In class**	
Foreign language waiver	☐	Early syllabus	☐
Lighter course load	☐	Note takers in class	■
Math waiver	☐	Priority seating	■
Other special classes	■	Tape recorders	■
Priority registrations	■	Videotaped classes	☐
Substitution of courses	■	Text on tape	■
Exams		**Services**	
Extended time	■	Diagnostic tests	■
Oral exams	☐	Learning centers	☐
Take home exams	☐	Proofreaders	■
Exams on tape or computer	■	Readers	■
Untimed exams	☐	Reading Machines/Kurzweil	■
Other accommodations	■	Special bookstore section	☐
		Typists	☐

Credit toward degree is not given for remedial courses taken.

Counseling Services

- ■ Academic
- ■ Psychological
- ■ Student Support groups
- ■ Vocational

Tutoring

Individual tutoring is available daily.

Average size of tutoring groups: 1

	Individual	Group
Time management	☐	■
Organizational skills	☐	■
Learning strategies	☐	■
Study skills	☐	■
Content area	☐	☐
Writing lab	■	☐
Math lab	■	■

LD PROGRAM STAFF

Total number of LD Program staff (including director):

Full Time: 3 Part Time: 3

There is an advisor/advocate from the LD program available to students. 10 graduate students and 30 peer tutors are available to work with LD students.

Key staff person available to work with LD students: Adam Meyer, Counselor for Student Disabilities.

Southeast Missouri State University

Cape Girardeau, MO

Address: 1 University Plaza, Cape Girardeau, MO, 63701
Admissions telephone: 573 651-2590
Admissions FAX: 573 651-5936
Director of Admissions: Deborah Below
Admissions e-mail: admissions@semo.edu
Web site: http://www.semo.edu
SAT Code: 6655 ACT Code: 2366

LD program name: Learning Enrichment Center
LD program address: MS 1300
Assistant Director: Melanie Thompson
LD program telephone: 573 651-2273
LD program e-mail: mvthompson@semo.edu
LD program enrollment: 104, Total campus enrollment: 8,460

GENERAL

Southeast Missouri State University is a public, coed, four-year institution. 200-plus-acre campus in Cape Girardeau (population: 35,349), 120 miles from St. Louis. Served by air and bus; major airport serves St. Louis. Semester system.

LD ADMISSIONS

A member of the LD program does not sit on the admissions committee. A personal interview is not required. Essay is not required.

SECONDARY SCHOOL REQUIREMENTS

Graduation from secondary school required; GED accepted. The following course distribution required: 4 units of English, 3 units of math, 3 units of science, 2 units of social studies, 1 unit of history, 3 units of academic electives.

TESTING

SAT Reasoning or ACT considered if submitted; ACT preferred. SAT Subject recommended.

All enrolled freshmen (fall 2004):

Average ACT Scores: Composite: 22

Child Study Team report is not required. A neuropsychological or comprehensive psycho-educational evaluation is required for admission. Must be dated within 36 months of application. Tests required as part of this documentation:

- [x] WAIS-IV
- [ ] WISC-IV
- [x] SATA
- [x] Woodcock-Johnson
- [x] Nelson-Denny Reading Test
- [ ] Other

UNDERGRADUATE STUDENT BODY

Total undergraduate student enrollment: 3,234 Men, 4,864 Women.

Composition of student body (fall 2004):

	Undergraduate	Freshmen
International	1.1	1.9
Black	9.5	7.9
American Indian	0.5	0.5
Asian-American	0.7	0.6
Hispanic	1.1	1.0
White	87.1	88.1
Unreported	0.0	0.0
	100.0%	100.0%

10% are from out of state. 15% join a fraternity and 10% join a sorority. Average age of full-time undergraduates is 22. 39% of classes have fewer than 20 students, 60% have between 20 and 50 students, 1% have more than 50 students.

STUDENT HOUSING

64% of freshmen live in college housing. Freshmen are required to live on campus. Housing is guaranteed for all undergraduates. Campus can house 2,748 undergraduates. Single rooms are available for students with medical or special needs. A medical note is required.

EXPENSES

Tuition (2005-06): $4,554 per year (in-state), $8,139 (out-of-state).
Room: $3,205. Board: $1,982.
There is no additional cost for LD program/services.

LD SERVICES

LD program size is not limited.

LD services available to:

- [x] Freshmen
- [x] Sophomores
- [x] Juniors
- [x] Seniors

Academic Accommodations

Curriculum		In class	
Foreign language waiver	[ ]	Early syllabus	[ ]
Lighter course load	[ ]	Note takers in class	[x]
Math waiver	[ ]	Priority seating	[ ]
Other special classes	[ ]	Tape recorders	[x]
Priority registrations	[ ]	Videotaped classes	[ ]
Substitution of courses	[ ]	Text on tape	[x]
Exams		**Services**	
Extended time	[x]	Diagnostic tests	[ ]
Oral exams	[x]	Learning centers	[x]
Take home exams	[ ]	Proofreaders	[ ]
Exams on tape or computer	[ ]	Readers	[x]
Untimed exams	[x]	Reading Machines/Kurzweil	[x]
Other accommodations	[x]	Special bookstore section	[ ]
		Typists	[ ]

Credit toward degree is not given for remedial courses taken.

Counseling Services

- [x] Academic
- [x] Psychological
- [x] Student Support groups
- [x] Vocational

Tutoring

Individual tutoring is available daily.

	Individual	Group
Time management	[ ]	[ ]
Organizational skills	[ ]	[ ]
Learning strategies	[x]	[ ]
Study skills	[x]	[ ]
Content area	[x]	[ ]
Writing lab	[x]	[ ]
Math lab	[x]	[ ]

LD PROGRAM STAFF

Total number of LD Program staff (including director):

Full Time: 2 Part Time: 2

There is an advisor/advocate from the LD program available to students. 1 graduate student is available to work with LD students.

Key staff person available to work with LD students: Melanie Thompson, Assistant Director.

Southwest Baptist University

Bolivar, MO

Address: 1600 University Avenue, Bolivar, MO, 65613
Admissions telephone: 800 526-5859
Admissions FAX: 417 328-1514
Director of Admissions: Darren Crowder
Admissions e-mail: admitme@sbuniv.edu
Web site: http://www.sbuniv.edu
SAT Code: 6664 ACT Code: 2368

LD program name: Enrollment Management
Vice President Enrollment Mgmt: Dr. Stephanie Miller
LD program telephone: 417 328-1797
LD program e-mail: smiller@sbuniv.edu
LD program enrollment: 49, Total campus enrollment: 2,746

GENERAL

Southwest Baptist University is a private, coed, four-year institution. 152-acre campus in Bolivar (population: 9,143), 28 miles from Springfield; branch campuses in Mountain View and Springfield. Major airport and bus serve Springfield; other major airport serves Kansas City (120 miles); train serves Warrensburg (75 miles). 4-1-4 system.

LD ADMISSIONS

Students do not complete a separate application and are not simultaneously accepted to the LD program. A member of the LD program does sit on the admissions committee. A personal interview is not required. Essay is required and may be typed.

For fall 2004, 12 completed self-identified LD applications were received. 12 applications were offered admission, and 8 enrolled.

SECONDARY SCHOOL REQUIREMENTS

Graduation from secondary school required; GED accepted.

TESTING

ACT required; SAT Reasoning may be substituted. SAT Subject recommended.

All enrolled freshmen (fall 2004):

Average SAT I Scores: Verbal: 492 Math: 486
Average ACT Scores: Composite: 23

Child Study Team report is not required. A neuropsychological or comprehensive psycho-educational evaluation is required for admission. Must be dated within 36 months of application. Tests required as part of this documentation:

- ■ WAIS-IV
- ■ WISC-IV
- ■ SATA
- ■ Woodcock-Johnson
- ■ Nelson-Denny Reading Test
- ☐ Other

UNDERGRADUATE STUDENT BODY

Total undergraduate student enrollment: 915 Men, 1,799 Women.

Composition of student body (fall 2004):

	Undergraduate	Freshmen
International	0.5	0.7
Black	4.0	2.4
American Indian	0.7	0.5
Asian-American	1.2	0.7
Hispanic	1.2	0.9
White	90.7	92.3
Unreported	1.7	2.5
	100.0%	100.0%

24% are from out of state. Average age of full-time undergraduates is 21. 60% of classes have fewer than 20 students, 39% have between 20 and 50 students, 1% have more than 50 students.

STUDENT HOUSING

96% of freshmen live in college housing. Freshmen are required to live on campus. Housing is guaranteed for all undergraduates. Campus can house 1,123 undergraduates. Single rooms are available for students with medical or special needs. A medical note is required.

EXPENSES

Tuition (2005-06): $12,450 per year.
Room: $2,050. Board: $1,900.
There is no additional cost for LD program/services.

LD SERVICES

LD program size is not limited.

LD services available to:

■ Freshmen ■ Sophomores ■ Juniors ■ Seniors

Academic Accommodations

Curriculum		**In class**	
Foreign language waiver	☐	Early syllabus	■
Lighter course load	■	Note takers in class	☐
Math waiver	☐	Priority seating	■
Other special classes	☐	Tape recorders	■
Priority registrations	☐	Videotaped classes	■
Substitution of courses	☐	Text on tape	■
Exams		**Services**	
Extended time	■	Diagnostic tests	☐
Oral exams	■	Learning centers	■
Take home exams	☐	Proofreaders	■
Exams on tape or computer	■	Readers	■
Untimed exams	■	Reading Machines/Kurzweil	☐
Other accommodations	■	Special bookstore section	☐
		Typists	☐

Credit toward degree is not given for remedial courses taken.

Counseling Services

- ■ Academic
- ■ Psychological
- ■ Student Support groups
- ☐ Vocational

Tutoring

Individual tutoring is available weekly.

Average size of tutoring groups: 1

	Individual	Group
Time management	☐	■
Organizational skills	☐	■
Learning strategies	☐	■
Study skills	■	■
Content area	■	■
Writing lab	■	■
Math lab	■	■

LD PROGRAM STAFF

Total number of LD Program staff (including director):

Full Time: 1 Part Time: 1

There is an advisor/advocate from the LD program available to students. The advisor/advocate meets with students 1 time per month. 1 graduate student and 20 peer tutors are available to work with LD students.

Key staff person available to work with LD students: Dr. Stephanie Miller, Vice President Enrollment Management.

Southwest Missouri State University

Springfield, MO

Address: 901 S. National, Springfield, MO, 65804-0094
Admissions telephone: 800 492-7900
Admissions FAX: 417 836-6334
Director of Admissions: Donald E. Simpson
Admissions e-mail: smsuinfo@smsu.edu
Web site: http://www.smsu.edu
SAT Code: 6665 ACT Code: 2370

LD program name: Learning Diagnostic Clinic
Director of the Learning Diagnostic Clinic: Dr. Steven Kapps
LD program telephone: 417 836-4787
LD program e-mail: LearningDiagnosticClinic@smsu.edu
Total campus enrollment: 16,269

GENERAL

Southwest Missouri State University is a public, coed, four-year institution. 225-acre, suburban campus in Springfield (population: 146,866); branch campus in West Plains. Served by air and bus; smaller airport and train serve Kansas City (180 miles). School operates transportation to classrooms and residence halls. Public transportation serves campus. Semester system.

LD ADMISSIONS

A personal interview is recommended. Essay is not required.

SECONDARY SCHOOL REQUIREMENTS

Graduation from secondary school required; GED accepted. The following course distribution required: 4 units of English, 3 units of math, 2 units of science, 3 units of social studies, 3 units of academic electives.

TESTING

ACT required; SAT Reasoning may be substituted.

Child Study Team report is not required. Tests required as part of this documentation:

☐ WAIS-IV
☐ WISC-IV
☐ SATA
☐ Woodcock-Johnson
☐ Nelson-Denny Reading Test
☐ Other

UNDERGRADUATE STUDENT BODY

Total undergraduate student enrollment: 6,618 Men, 8,081 Women.

Composition of student body (fall 2004):

	Undergraduate	Freshmen
International	0.7	1.8
Black	3.3	2.6
American Indian	0.7	0.9
Asian-American	1.6	1.3
Hispanic	1.5	1.4
White	88.6	87.2
Unreported	3.6	4.8
	100.0%	100.0%

8% are from out of state. 10% join a fraternity and 10% join a sorority. Average age of full-time undergraduates is 21. 44% of classes have fewer than 20 students, 50% have between 20 and 50 students, 6% have more than 50 students.

STUDENT HOUSING

80% of freshmen live in college housing. Housing is guaranteed for all undergraduates. Campus can house 4,034 undergraduates.

EXPENSES

Tuition (2005-06): $4,920 per year (in-state), $9,840 (out-of-state).

Room & Board: $5,294.
There is no additional cost for LD program/services.

LD SERVICES

LD program size is not limited.

LD services available to:

☐ Freshmen ☐ Sophomores ☐ Juniors ☐ Seniors

Academic Accommodations

Curriculum		In class	
Foreign language waiver	☐	Early syllabus	☐
Lighter course load	■	Note takers in class	■
Math waiver	☐	Priority seating	☐
Other special classes	☐	Tape recorders	☐
Priority registrations	☐	Videotaped classes	☐
Substitution of courses	☐	Text on tape	☐
Exams		**Services**	
Extended time	■	Diagnostic tests	■
Oral exams	■	Learning centers	■
Take home exams	☐	Proofreaders	☐
Exams on tape or computer	☐	Readers	■
Untimed exams	■	Reading Machines/Kurzweil	☐
Other accommodations	☐	Special bookstore section	☐
		Typists	☐

Counseling Services

☐ Academic
☐ Psychological
☐ Student Support groups
☐ Vocational

Tutoring

	Individual	Group
Time management	☐	☐
Organizational skills	☐	☐
Learning strategies	☐	☐
Study skills	☐	☐
Content area	☐	☐
Writing lab	☐	☐
Math lab	☐	☐

LD PROGRAM STAFF

Total number of LD Program staff (including director):

Full Time: 4 Part Time: 4

Key staff person available to work with LD students: Dr. Steven Kapps, Director of the Learning Diagnostic Clinic.

Stephens College

Columbia, MO

Address: 1200 E. Broadway Box 2121, Columbia, MO, 65215
Admissions telephone: 800 876-7207
Admissions FAX: 573 876-7237
Dean of Enrollment Services: Samantha White
Admissions e-mail: apply@stephens.edu
Web site: http://www.stephens.edu
SAT Code: 6683 ACT Code: 2374

Total campus enrollment: 633

GENERAL

Stephens College is a private, women's, four-year institution. 86-acre campus in Columbia (population: 84,531), 126 miles from both St. Louis and Kansas City. Served by air and bus; major airports serve St. Louis and Kansas City; train serves Jefferson City (30 miles). Public transportation serves campus. Semester system.

LD ADMISSIONS

A personal interview is recommended. Essay is required and may be typed.

SECONDARY SCHOOL REQUIREMENTS

Graduation from secondary school required; GED accepted. The following course distribution required: 4 units of English, 2 units of math, 2 units of science, 2 units of foreign language, 2 units of social studies.

TESTING

SAT Reasoning or ACT considered if submitted.

All enrolled freshmen (fall 2004):

Average SAT I Scores: Verbal: 531 Math: 470
Average ACT Scores: Composite: 23

Child Study Team report is not required. Tests required as part of this documentation:

- ❑ WAIS-IV
- ❑ WISC-IV
- ❑ SATA
- ❑ Woodcock-Johnson
- ❑ Nelson-Denny Reading Test
- ❑ Other

UNDERGRADUATE STUDENT BODY

Total undergraduate student enrollment: 32 Men, 586 Women.

Composition of student body (fall 2004):

	Undergraduate	Freshmen
International	0.0	0.3
Black	15.3	7.9
American Indian	0.6	0.6
Asian-American	3.2	1.6
Hispanic	1.9	2.5
White	77.7	85.8
Unreported	1.3	1.3
	100.0%	100.0%

52% are from out of state. 8% join a sorority. Average age of full-time undergraduates is 21. 76% of classes have fewer than 20 students, 24% have between 20 and 50 students.

STUDENT HOUSING

95% of freshmen live in college housing. Housing is guaranteed for all undergraduates. Campus can house 778 undergraduates.

EXPENSES

Tuition (2005-06): $19,300 per year.

Room & Board: $7,630.

LD SERVICES

LD program size is not limited.

LD services available to:

❑ Freshmen ❑ Sophomores ❑ Juniors ❑ Seniors

Academic Accommodations

Curriculum		In class	
Foreign language waiver	❑	Early syllabus	❑
Lighter course load	❑	Note takers in class	❑
Math waiver	❑	Priority seating	❑
Other special classes	❑	Tape recorders	❑
Priority registrations	❑	Videotaped classes	❑
Substitution of courses	❑	Text on tape	❑
Exams		**Services**	
Extended time	❑	Diagnostic tests	❑
Oral exams	❑	Learning centers	■
Take home exams	❑	Proofreaders	❑
Exams on tape or computer	❑	Readers	❑
Untimed exams	❑	Reading Machines/Kurzweil	❑
Other accommodations	❑	Special bookstore section	❑
		Typists	❑

Credit toward degree is not given for remedial courses taken.

Counseling Services

- ❑ Academic
- ❑ Psychological
- ❑ Student Support groups
- ❑ Vocational

Tutoring

	Individual	Group
Time management	❑	❑
Organizational skills	❑	❑
Learning strategies	❑	❑
Study skills	❑	❑
Content area	❑	❑
Writing lab	❑	❑
Math lab	❑	❑

LD PROGRAM STAFF

Total number of LD Program staff (including director):

Full Time: 1 Part Time: 1

Key staff person available to work with LD students: Deb Duren, Vice President for Student Services.

Truman State University

Kirksville, MO

Address: 100 East Normal Street, Kirksville, MO, 63501
Admissions telephone: 800 892-7792 (in-state)
Admissions FAX: 660 785-7456
Dean of Admission and Records: Garry Gordon
Admissions e-mail: admissions@truman.edu
Web site: http://www.truman.edu
SAT Code: 6483 ACT Code: 2336

LD program name: Services for Individuals with Disabilities
Director: Vicky Wehner
LD program telephone: 660 785-4478
LD program e-mail: sids@truman.edu
LD program enrollment: 55, Total campus enrollment: 5,616

GENERAL

Truman State University is a public, coed, four-year institution. 140-acre campus in Kirksville (population: 16,988), 200 miles from both Kansas City and St. Louis. Major airports serve Kansas City and St. Louis; smaller airport serves Columbia (90 miles); bus and train serve LaPlata (10 miles). School operates transportation to train station at holiday breaks. Semester system.

LD ADMISSIONS

Application Deadline: 03/01. Students do not complete a separate application and are not simultaneously accepted to the LD program. A member of the LD program does not sit on the admissions committee. A personal interview is recommended. Essay is required and may be typed. We do not distinguish between LD students and other students during the admissions process.

SECONDARY SCHOOL REQUIREMENTS

Graduation from secondary school required; GED accepted. The following course distribution required: 4 units of English, 3 units of math, 3 units of science, 2 units of foreign language, 3 units of social studies.

TESTING

ACT required; SAT Reasoning may be substituted. SAT Subject recommended.

All enrolled freshmen (fall 2004):

Average SAT I Scores:	Verbal: 622	Math: 620
Average ACT Scores:	Composite: 27	

Child Study Team report is required if student is classified. A neuropsychological or comprehensive psycho-educational evaluation is required for admission. Tests required as part of this documentation:

- [x] WAIS-IV
- [x] WISC-IV
- [x] SATA
- [x] Woodcock-Johnson
- [x] Nelson-Denny Reading Test
- [x] Other

UNDERGRADUATE STUDENT BODY

Total undergraduate student enrollment: 2,395 Men, 3,290 Women.

Composition of student body (fall 2004):

	Undergraduate	Freshmen
International	2.2	3.7
Black	3.2	3.6
American Indian	0.5	0.5
Asian-American	1.8	2.1
Hispanic	1.9	1.8
White	88.8	86.0
Unreported	1.6	2.3
	100.0%	100.0%

25% are from out of state. 31% join a fraternity and 22% join a sorority. Average age of full-time undergraduates is 20. 33% of classes have fewer than 20 students, 64% have between 20 and 50 students, 3% have more than 50 students.

STUDENT HOUSING

99% of freshmen live in college housing. Freshmen are required to live on campus. Housing is guaranteed for all undergraduates. Campus can house 2,979 undergraduates. Single rooms are available for students with medical or special needs. A medical note is required.

EXPENSES

Tuition (2005-06): $5,740 per year (in-state), $9,920 (out-of-state).
Room & Board: $5,380.
There is no additional cost for LD program/services.

LD SERVICES

LD program size is not limited.

LD services available to:

- [x] Freshmen
- [x] Sophomores
- [x] Juniors
- [x] Seniors

Academic Accommodations

Curriculum		In class	
Foreign language waiver	[ ]	Early syllabus	[x]
Lighter course load	[x]	Note takers in class	[x]
Math waiver	[ ]	Priority seating	[x]
Other special classes	[ ]	Tape recorders	[ ]
Priority registrations	[x]	Videotaped classes	[ ]
Substitution of courses	[ ]	Text on tape	[ ]
Exams		**Services**	
Extended time	[x]	Diagnostic tests	[ ]
Oral exams	[x]	Learning centers	[ ]
Take home exams	[ ]	Proofreaders	[ ]
Exams on tape or computer	[x]	Readers	[x]
Untimed exams	[ ]	Reading Machines/Kurzweil	[x]
Other accommodations	[x]	Special bookstore section	[ ]
		Typists	[x]

Credit toward degree is not given for remedial courses taken.

Counseling Services

- [x] Academic
- [x] Psychological
- [x] Student Support groups
- [ ] Vocational

Tutoring

Individual tutoring is available weekly.

Average size of tutoring groups: 1

	Individual	Group
Time management	[x]	[ ]
Organizational skills	[x]	[ ]
Learning strategies	[x]	[ ]
Study skills	[x]	[ ]
Content area	[x]	[ ]
Writing lab	[x]	[ ]
Math lab	[ ]	[ ]

LD PROGRAM STAFF

Total number of LD Program staff (including director):

Full Time: 1 Part Time: 1

There is an advisor/advocate from the LD program available to students.

Key staff person available to work with LD students: Vicky Wehner.

LD Program web site: http://disabilityservices.truman.edu/

Washington University in St. Louis

St. Louis, MO

Address: 1 Brookings Drive, St. Louis, MO, 63130-4899
Admissions telephone: 800 638-0700
Admissions FAX: 314 935-4290
Director of Admissions: Nanette Tarbouni
Admissions e-mail: admissions@wustl.edu
Web site: http://www.wustl.edu
SAT Code: 6929 ACT Code: 2386

Disability Resource Coordinator: Zac McBee
LD program telephone: 314 935-4062
Total campus enrollment: 7,350

GENERAL

Washington University in St. Louis is a private, coed, four-year institution. 169-acre, suburban campus in St. Louis (population: 348,189); medical school branch campus in St. Louis. Served by air, bus, and train. School operates transportation to medical school, nearby Metrolink station, and surrounding suburbs. Public transportation serves campus. Semester system.

LD ADMISSIONS

Students do not complete a separate application and are not simultaneously accepted to the LD program. A member of the LD program does not sit on the admissions committee. A personal interview is recommended. Essay is required and may be typed.

SECONDARY SCHOOL REQUIREMENTS

Graduation from secondary school not required.

TESTING

SAT Reasoning or ACT required. SAT Subject recommended.

Child Study Team report is not required. A neuropsychological or comprehensive psycho-educational evaluation is required for admission. Tests required as part of this documentation:

- ☑ WAIS-IV
- ☐ WISC-IV
- ☐ SATA
- ☑ Woodcock-Johnson
- ☑ Nelson-Denny Reading Test
- ☐ Other

UNDERGRADUATE STUDENT BODY

Total undergraduate student enrollment: 3,289 Men, 3,483 Women.

Composition of student body (fall 2004):

	Undergraduate	Freshmen
International	4.0	4.6
Black	9.0	9.0
American Indian	0.1	0.2
Asian-American	12.3	9.4
Hispanic	2.9	3.3
White	60.4	64.3
Unreported	11.3	9.2
	100.0%	100.0%

89% are from out of state. 25% join a fraternity and 25% join a sorority. Average age of full-time undergraduates is 20. 74% of classes have fewer than 20 students, 18% have between 20 and 50 students, 8% have more than 50 students.

STUDENT HOUSING

99% of freshmen live in college housing. Freshmen are required to live on campus. Housing is guaranteed for all undergraduates. Campus can house 4,583 undergraduates.

EXPENSES

Tuition (2005-06): $31,100 per year.

Room: $6,096. Board: $3,968.
There is no additional cost for LD program/services.

LD SERVICES

LD program size is not limited.

LD services available to:

☑ Freshmen ☑ Sophomores ☑ Juniors ☑ Seniors

Academic Accommodations

Curriculum		In class	
Foreign language waiver	☐	Early syllabus	☐
Lighter course load	☑	Note takers in class	☑
Math waiver	☐	Priority seating	☐
Other special classes	☐	Tape recorders	☑
Priority registrations	☐	Videotaped classes	☐
Substitution of courses	☐	Text on tape	☑
Exams		**Services**	
Extended time	☑	Diagnostic tests	☐
Oral exams	☐	Learning centers	☑
Take home exams	☐	Proofreaders	☐
Exams on tape or computer	☐	Readers	☑
Untimed exams	☐	Reading Machines/Kurzweil	☐
Other accommodations	☑	Special bookstore section	☐
		Typists	☑

Credit toward degree is not given for remedial courses taken.

Counseling Services

- ☐ Academic
- ☐ Psychological
- ☐ Student Support groups
- ☐ Vocational

Tutoring

Individual tutoring is available.

Average size of tutoring groups: 5

	Individual	Group
Time management	☑	☐
Organizational skills	☐	☐
Learning strategies	☐	☐
Study skills	☑	☐
Content area	☐	☐
Writing lab	☑	☐
Math lab	☐	☐

LD PROGRAM STAFF

Total number of LD Program staff (including director):

Full Time: 2 Part Time: 2

Key staff person available to work with LD students: Robert Koff, Ph.D., Director of Center for Advanced Learning.

Webster University

St. Louis, MO

Address: 470 E. Lockwood Avenue, St. Louis, MO, 63119
Admissions telephone: 800 753-6765
Admissions FAX: 314 968-7115
Director of Undergraduate Admissions: Niel DeVasto
Admissions e-mail: admit@webster.edu
Web site: http://www.webster.edu
SAT Code: 6933 ACT Code: 2388

LD program name: Academic Resource Center
LD program telephone: 314 968-7495
LD program e-mail: mcleespa@webster.edu
Total campus enrollment: 4,709

GENERAL

Webster University is a private, coed, four-year institution. 47-acre, suburban campus in Webster Groves (population: 23,230), 12 miles from St. Louis; branch campuses in St. Anne and St. Louis, the District of Columbia, and in 17 states and abroad in Austria, Bermuda, China, England, the Netherlands, Switzerland, and Thailand. Major airport, bus, and train serve St. Louis. Public transportation serves campus. Semester system.

LD ADMISSIONS

Students do not complete a separate application and are not simultaneously accepted to the LD program. A member of the LD program does sit on the admissions committee. A personal interview is recommended. Essay is required and may be typed.

SECONDARY SCHOOL REQUIREMENTS

Graduation from secondary school required; GED accepted.

TESTING

SAT Reasoning or ACT required. SAT Subject recommended.

All enrolled freshmen (fall 2004):

Average SAT I Scores:	Verbal: 585	Math: 570
Average ACT Scores:	Composite: 24	

Child Study Team report is not required. A neuropsychological or comprehensive psycho-educational evaluation is required for admission. Must be dated within 50 months of application. Tests required as part of this documentation:

- [x] WAIS-IV
- [x] WISC-IV
- [ ] SATA
- [x] Woodcock-Johnson
- [ ] Nelson-Denny Reading Test
- [ ] Other

UNDERGRADUATE STUDENT BODY

Total undergraduate student enrollment: 1,856 Men, 2,855 Women.

Composition of student body (fall 2004):

	Undergraduate	Freshmen
International	4.0	16.6
Black	5.9	10.9
American Indian	0.2	0.2
Asian-American	1.3	1.2
Hispanic	2.0	2.3
White	79.6	60.9
Unreported	7.0	7.9
	100.0%	100.0%

27% are from out of state. Average age of full-time undergraduates is 22. 85% of classes have fewer than 20 students, 15% have between 20 and 50 students.

STUDENT HOUSING

45% of freshmen live in college housing. Freshmen are not required to live on campus. Housing is not guaranteed for all undergraduates. Campus can house 500 undergraduates. Single rooms are available for students with medical or special needs. A medical note is required.

EXPENSES

Tuition (2005-06): $17,210 per year. $14,600 per year (most programs), $17,600 (theatre conservatory programs).

Room: $4,516. Board: $3,484.
There is no additional cost for LD program/services.

LD SERVICES

LD program size is not limited.

LD services available to:

- [x] Freshmen
- [x] Sophomores
- [x] Juniors
- [x] Seniors

Academic Accommodations

Curriculum		**In class**	
Foreign language waiver	[ ]	Early syllabus	[ ]
Lighter course load	[x]	Note takers in class	[x]
Math waiver	[ ]	Priority seating	[x]
Other special classes	[ ]	Tape recorders	[x]
Priority registrations	[ ]	Videotaped classes	[ ]
Substitution of courses	[ ]	Text on tape	[x]
Exams		**Services**	
Extended time	[x]	Diagnostic tests	[ ]
Oral exams	[x]	Learning centers	[x]
Take home exams	[ ]	Proofreaders	[x]
Exams on tape or computer	[x]	Readers	[x]
Untimed exams	[x]	Reading Machines/Kurzweil	[x]
Other accommodations	[ ]	Special bookstore section	[ ]
		Typists	[x]

Credit toward degree is not given for remedial courses taken.

Counseling Services

- [x] Academic — Meets 32 times per academic year
- [x] Psychological — Meets 32 times per academic year
- [ ] Student Support groups
- [ ] Vocational

Tutoring

Individual tutoring is available.

Average size of tutoring groups: 3

	Individual	Group
Time management	[x]	[x]
Organizational skills	[x]	[x]
Learning strategies	[x]	[x]
Study skills	[x]	[ ]
Content area	[x]	[ ]
Writing lab	[x]	[ ]
Math lab	[x]	[ ]

LD PROGRAM STAFF

Total number of LD Program staff (including director):

Full Time: 2 Part Time: 2

There is an advisor/advocate from the LD program available to students. The advisor/advocate meets with students 4 times per month. 20 peer tutors are available to work with LD students.

Key staff person available to work with LD students: Patricia A. McLeese, Ph.D., Director, Academic Resource Center.

Westminster College

Fulton, MO

Address: 501 Westminster Avenue, Fulton, MO, 65251
Admissions telephone: 800 475-3361
Admissions FAX: 573 592-5255
Vice President/Dean of Enrollment Services: Patrick Kirby
Admissions e-mail: admissions@westminster-mo.edu
Web site: http://www.westminster-mo.edu
SAT Code: 6937 ACT Code: 2392

LD program name: Learning Disabilities Program
Director/Assoc. Professor: Hank Ottinger
LD program telephone: 573 592-5304
LD program e-mail: ottingh@westminster-mo.edu
LD program enrollment: 46, Total campus enrollment: 861

GENERAL

Westminster College is a private, coed, four-year institution. 65-acre campus in Fulton (population: 12,128), 80 miles from St. Louis and 25 miles from Columbia and Jefferson City. Major airport serves St. Louis; smaller airport serves Columbia; bus serves Kingdom City (seven miles); train serves Jefferson City. Semester system.

LD ADMISSIONS

Students complete a separate application and are simultaneously accepted to the LD program. A member of the LD program does sit on the admissions committee. High school waivers are accepted for foreign language. A personal interview is required. Essay is required and may be typed.

For fall 2004, 52 completed self-identified LD applications were received. 29 applications were offered admission, and 20 enrolled.

SECONDARY SCHOOL REQUIREMENTS

Graduation from secondary school required; GED accepted. The following course distribution required: 4 units of English, 3 units of math, 2 units of science.

TESTING

ACT required; SAT Reasoning may be substituted.

All enrolled freshmen (fall 2004):

Average SAT I Scores: Verbal: 565 Math: 541
Average ACT Scores: Composite: 25

Child Study Team report is required if student is classified. A neuropsychological or comprehensive psycho-educational evaluation is required for admission. Must be dated within 24 months of application. Tests required as part of this documentation:

- [x] WAIS-IV
- [x] WISC-IV
- [ ] SATA
- [x] Woodcock-Johnson
- [ ] Nelson-Denny Reading Test
- [x] Other

UNDERGRADUATE STUDENT BODY

Total undergraduate student enrollment: 391 Men, 295 Women.

Composition of student body (fall 2004):

	Undergraduate	Freshmen
International	8.2	5.5
Black	5.6	4.3
American Indian	0.4	2.0
Asian-American	1.3	1.3
Hispanic	3.0	1.4
White	79.8	84.4
Unreported	1.7	1.1
	100.0%	100.0%

28% are from out of state. 51% join a fraternity and 40% join a sorority. Average age of full-time undergraduates is 20. 66% of classes have fewer than 20 students, 34% have between 20 and 50 students.

STUDENT HOUSING

95% of freshmen live in college housing. Freshmen are required to live on campus. Housing is guaranteed for all undergraduates. Campus can house 621 undergraduates. Single rooms are not available for students with medical or special needs.

EXPENSES

Tuition 2004-05: $12,990 per year.

Room: $2,880. Board: $2,770.

Additional cost for LD program/services: $2,000 per semester in first yr.

LD SERVICES

LD program is limited to %1 students.

LD services available to:

- [x] Freshmen
- [x] Sophomores
- [x] Juniors
- [x] Seniors

Academic Accommodations

Curriculum		In class	
Foreign language waiver	[ ]	Early syllabus	[ ]
Lighter course load	[x]	Note takers in class	[x]
Math waiver	[ ]	Priority seating	[ ]
Other special classes	[x]	Tape recorders	[x]
Priority registrations	[ ]	Videotaped classes	[ ]
Substitution of courses	[ ]	Text on tape	[x]
Exams		**Services**	
Extended time	[x]	Diagnostic tests	[ ]
Oral exams	[x]	Learning centers	[x]
Take home exams	[ ]	Proofreaders	[x]
Exams on tape or computer	[x]	Readers	[x]
Untimed exams	[x]	Reading Machines/Kurzweil	[x]
Other accommodations	[x]	Special bookstore section	[ ]
		Typists	[x]

Credit toward degree is given for remedial courses taken.

Counseling Services

- [ ] Academic
- [ ] Psychological
- [ ] Student Support groups
- [ ] Vocational

Tutoring

Individual tutoring is available daily.

Average size of tutoring groups: 1

	Individual	Group
Time management	[x]	[ ]
Organizational skills	[x]	[ ]
Learning strategies	[x]	[ ]
Study skills	[x]	[ ]
Content area	[x]	[ ]
Writing lab	[x]	[ ]
Math lab	[x]	[ ]

LD PROGRAM STAFF

Total number of LD Program staff (including director):

Full Time: 2 Part Time: 2

There is an advisor/advocate from the LD program available to students. The advisor/advocate meets with faculty 1 time per month and students 8 times per month. 3 peer tutors are available to work with LD students.

Key staff person available to work with LD students: Tirza Kroeker

William Jewell College

Liberty, MO

Address: 500 College Hill, Liberty, MO, 64068
Admissions telephone: 800 753-7009
Admissions FAX: 816 415-5040
Dean of Enrollment Development: Edwin Harris
Admissions e-mail: admission@william.jewell.edu
Web site: http://www.jewell.edu
SAT Code: 6941 ACT Code: 2394

Director of Counseling Services: Dr. Shawn Anderson
LD program telephone: 816 781-7700
LD program e-mail: anderson@william.jewell.edu
Total campus enrollment: 1,310

GENERAL

William Jewell College is a private, coed, four-year institution. 149-acre, suburban campus in Liberty (population: 26,232), 15 miles from Kansas City. Major airport, bus, and train serve Kansas City. Public transportation serves campus. Semester system.

LD ADMISSIONS

A personal interview is recommended.

SECONDARY SCHOOL REQUIREMENTS

Graduation from secondary school required; GED accepted.

TESTING

SAT Reasoning required of some applicants. ACT required of some applicants. SAT Subject recommended.

All enrolled freshmen (fall 2004):

Average SAT I Scores: Verbal: 626 Math: 595
Average ACT Scores: Composite: 25

Child Study Team report is not required. Tests required as part of this documentation:

- ❑ WAIS-IV
- ❑ WISC-IV
- ❑ SATA
- ❑ Woodcock-Johnson
- ❑ Nelson-Denny Reading Test
- ❑ Other

UNDERGRADUATE STUDENT BODY

Total undergraduate student enrollment: 451 Men, 638 Women.

Composition of student body (fall 2004):

	Undergraduate	Freshmen
International	1.2	0.8
Black	4.0	3.7
American Indian	1.5	0.7
Asian-American	0.9	0.8
Hispanic	3.6	2.3
White	87.3	89.9
Unreported	1.5	1.8
	100.0%	100.0%

20% are from out of state. 33% join a fraternity and 35% join a sorority. Average age of full-time undergraduates is 20. 69% of classes have fewer than 20 students, 30% have between 20 and 50 students, 1% have more than 50 students.

STUDENT HOUSING

94% of freshmen live in college housing. Freshmen are required to live on campus. Housing is guaranteed for all undergraduates. Campus can house 874 undergraduates.

EXPENSES

Tuition (2005-06): $18,200 per year.
Room: $2,250. Board: $3,100.
There is no additional cost for LD program/services.

LD SERVICES

LD program size is not limited.

LD services available to:

❑ Freshmen ❑ Sophomores ❑ Juniors ❑ Seniors

Academic Accommodations

Curriculum		In class	
Foreign language waiver	❑	Early syllabus	❑
Lighter course load	❑	Note takers in class	■
Math waiver	❑	Priority seating	❑
Other special classes	❑	Tape recorders	■
Priority registrations	❑	Videotaped classes	❑
Substitution of courses	❑	Text on tape	❑
Exams		**Services**	
Extended time	■	Diagnostic tests	❑
Oral exams	❑	Learning centers	❑
Take home exams	❑	Proofreaders	❑
Exams on tape or computer	❑	Readers	❑
Untimed exams	■	Reading Machines/Kurzweil	❑
Other accommodations	❑	Special bookstore section	❑
		Typists	❑

Counseling Services

- ❑ Academic
- ❑ Psychological
- ❑ Student Support groups
- ❑ Vocational

Tutoring

	Individual	Group
Time management	❑	❑
Organizational skills	❑	❑
Learning strategies	❑	❑
Study skills	❑	❑
Content area	❑	❑
Writing lab	❑	❑
Math lab	❑	❑

William Woods University

Fulton, MO

Address: 1 University Avenue, Fulton, MO, 65251
Admissions telephone: 800 995-3159
Admissions FAX: 573 592-1146
Executive Director of Enrollment Services: Jimmy Clay
Admissions e-mail: admissions@williamwoods.edu
Web site: http://www.williamwoods.edu
SAT Code: 6944 ACT Code: 2396

Disabiliy Service Coordinator: Carrie McCray
LD program telephone: 573 592-1194
LD program e-mail: cmccray@williamwoods.edu
LD program enrollment: 37, Total campus enrollment: 1,038

GENERAL

William Woods University is a private, coed, four-year institution. 170-acre campus in Fulton (population: 12,128), 25 miles from both Columbia and Jefferson City and 100 miles from St. Louis; branch campuses in Columbia and Jefferson City. Major airport serves St. Louis; smaller airport and bus serve Columbia; train serves Jefferson City. Semester system.

LD ADMISSIONS

Students do not complete a separate application and are not simultaneously accepted to the LD program. A member of the LD program does not sit on the admissions committee. A personal interview is recommended. Essay is not required.

SECONDARY SCHOOL REQUIREMENTS

Graduation from secondary school required; GED accepted. The following course distribution required: 4 units of English, 3 units of math, 3 units of science, 2 units of foreign language, 2 units of social studies, 3 units of history.

TESTING

SAT Reasoning considered if submitted. ACT considered if submitted. SAT Subject recommended.

All enrolled freshmen (fall 2004):

Average SAT I Scores:	Verbal: 500	Math: 490
Average ACT Scores:	Composite: 22	

Child Study Team report is not required. A neuropsychological or comprehensive psycho-education evaluation is not required for admission. Tests required as part of this documentation:

- [ ] WAIS-IV
- [ ] WISC-IV
- [ ] SATA
- [ ] Woodcock-Johnson
- [ ] Nelson-Denny Reading Test
- [ ] Other

UNDERGRADUATE STUDENT BODY

Total undergraduate student enrollment: 287 Men, 702 Women.

Composition of student body (fall 2004):

	Undergraduate	Freshmen
International	0.0	0.5
Black	1.6	3.6
American Indian	0.5	0.5
Asian-American	1.0	2.4
Hispanic	2.6	1.4
White	91.2	89.4
Unreported	3.1	2.2
	100.0%	100.0%

25% are from out of state. 47% join a fraternity and 48% join a sorority. Average age of full-time undergraduates is 22. 74% of classes have fewer than 20 students, 26% have between 20 and 50 students.

STUDENT HOUSING

87% of freshmen live in college housing. Freshmen are required to live on campus. Housing is guaranteed for all undergraduates. Campus can house 670 undergraduates. Single rooms are available for students with medical or special needs. A medical note is required.

EXPENSES

Tuition (2005-06): $14,700 per year.

Room: $2,900. Board: $3,000.
There is no additional cost for LD program/services.

LD SERVICES

LD program size is not limited.

LD services available to:

- [x] Freshmen
- [x] Sophomores
- [x] Juniors
- [x] Seniors

Academic Accommodations

Curriculum

- [ ] Foreign language waiver
- [ ] Lighter course load
- [ ] Math waiver
- [ ] Other special classes
- [ ] Priority registrations
- [ ] Substitution of courses

Exams

- [x] Extended time
- [x] Oral exams
- [ ] Take home exams
- [x] Exams on tape or computer
- [x] Untimed exams
- [x] Other accommodations

In class

- [ ] Early syllabus
- [x] Note takers in class
- [ ] Priority seating
- [x] Tape recorders
- [ ] Videotaped classes
- [x] Text on tape

Services

- [ ] Diagnostic tests
- [ ] Learning centers
- [ ] Proofreaders
- [x] Readers
- [ ] Reading Machines/Kurzweil
- [ ] Special bookstore section
- [ ] Typists

Credit toward degree is not given for remedial courses taken.

Counseling Services

- [x] Academic — Meets 2 times per academic year
- [ ] Psychological
- [ ] Student Support groups
- [ ] Vocational

Tutoring

Individual tutoring is available daily.

Average size of tutoring groups: 2

	Individual	Group
Time management	[ ]	[x]
Organizational skills	[ ]	[x]
Learning strategies	[ ]	[x]
Study skills	[ ]	[x]
Content area	[ ]	[x]
Writing lab	[x]	[ ]
Math lab	[x]	[ ]

LD PROGRAM STAFF

Total number of LD Program staff (including director):

Full Time: 1 Part Time: 1

There is an advisor/advocate from the LD program available to students. The advisor/advocate meets with faculty 2 times per month and students 3 times per month. 9 peer tutors are available to work with LD students.

Key staff person available to work with LD students: Carrie McCray, Disability Service Coordinator.

Carroll College

Helena, MT

Address: 1601 North Benton Avenue, Helena, MT, 59625-0002
Admissions telephone: 800 992-3648
Admissions FAX: 406 447-4533
Director of Admissions: Cynthia Thornquist
Admissions e-mail: enroll@carroll.edu
Web site: http://www.carroll.edu
SAT Code: 4041 ACT Code: 2408

LD program contact: Joan Stottlemyer
LD program telephone: 406 447-4504
LD program e-mail: jstottle@carroll.edu
Total campus enrollment: 1,441

GENERAL

Carroll College is a private, coed, four-year institution. 64-acre campus in Helena (population: 25,780), 91 miles from Great Falls. Served by air and bus; larger airport serves Great Falls. Public transportation serves campus. Semester system.

LD ADMISSIONS

Application Deadline: 06/01. Students do not complete a separate application and are simultaneously accepted to the LD program. A member of the LD program does not sit on the admissions committee. A personal interview is recommended. Essay is not required.

SECONDARY SCHOOL REQUIREMENTS

Graduation from secondary school required; GED accepted.

TESTING

SAT Reasoning or ACT required. SAT Subject recommended.

All enrolled freshmen (fall 2004):

Average SAT I Scores:	Verbal: 555	Math: 548
Average ACT Scores:	Composite: 24	

Child Study Team report is not required. A neuropsychological or comprehensive psycho-education evaluation is not required for admission. Tests required as part of this documentation:

- [ ] WAIS-IV
- [ ] WISC-IV
- [ ] SATA
- [ ] Woodcock-Johnson
- [ ] Nelson-Denny Reading Test
- [ ] Other

UNDERGRADUATE STUDENT BODY

Total undergraduate student enrollment: 527 Men, 820 Women.

Composition of student body (fall 2004):

	Undergraduate	Freshmen
International	0.3	0.7
Black	0.6	0.4
American Indian	0.8	0.8
Asian-American	1.1	0.8
Hispanic	1.4	1.5
White	72.8	73.0
Unreported	23.0	22.8
	100.0%	100.0%

32% are from out of state. Average age of full-time undergraduates is 21. 59% of classes have fewer than 20 students, 39% have between 20 and 50 students, 2% have more than 50 students.

STUDENT HOUSING

94% of freshmen live in college housing. Freshmen are required to live on campus. Housing is guaranteed for all undergraduates. Campus can house 830 undergraduates. Single rooms are available for students with medical or special needs. A medical note is not required.

EXPENSES

Tuition (2005-06): $16,778 per year.
Room: $3,046. Board: $3,200.
There is no additional cost for LD program/services.

LD SERVICES

LD program size is not limited.

LD services available to:

- [x] Freshmen
- [x] Sophomores
- [x] Juniors
- [x] Seniors

Academic Accommodations

Curriculum		In class	
Foreign language waiver	[ ]	Early syllabus	[ ]
Lighter course load	[x]	Note takers in class	[x]
Math waiver	[ ]	Priority seating	[ ]
Other special classes	[ ]	Tape recorders	[ ]
Priority registrations	[ ]	Videotaped classes	[ ]
Substitution of courses	[ ]	Text on tape	[ ]
Exams		**Services**	
Extended time	[x]	Diagnostic tests	[ ]
Oral exams	[x]	Learning centers	[x]
Take home exams	[ ]	Proofreaders	[ ]
Exams on tape or computer	[ ]	Readers	[x]
Untimed exams	[ ]	Reading Machines/Kurzweil	[ ]
Other accommodations	[ ]	Special bookstore section	[ ]
		Typists	[ ]

Credit toward degree is not given for remedial courses taken.

Counseling Services

- [ ] Academic
- [ ] Psychological
- [ ] Student Support groups
- [ ] Vocational

Tutoring

Individual tutoring is available daily.

	Individual	Group
Time management	[ ]	[ ]
Organizational skills	[ ]	[ ]
Learning strategies	[ ]	[ ]
Study skills	[ ]	[ ]
Content area	[ ]	[ ]
Writing lab	[ ]	[ ]
Math lab	[ ]	[ ]

LD PROGRAM STAFF

There is an advisor/advocate from the LD program available to students.

Key staff person available to work with LD students: Joan Stottlemyer, Director of Academic Resource Center

University of Great Falls

Great Falls, MT

Address: 1301 20th Street South, Great Falls, MT, 59405
Admissions telephone: 800 856-9544
Admissions FAX: 406 791-5209
Director of Admissions: Brian Best
Admissions e-mail: enroll@ugf.edu
Web site: http://www.ugf.edu
SAT Code: 4058 ACT Code: 2410

Disabilities Advocate: Kathryn Meier
LD program telephone: 406 791-5224
LD program e-mail: kmeier01@ugf.edu
LD program enrollment: 122, Total campus enrollment: 671

GENERAL

University of Great Falls is a private, coed, four-year institution. 44-acre campus in Great Falls (population: 56,690). Served by air and bus; train serves Shelby (90 miles). Public transportation serves campus. Semester system.

LD ADMISSIONS

Students do not complete a separate application and are not simultaneously accepted to the LD program. A member of the LD program does not sit on the admissions committee. High school waivers are accepted for foreign language. A personal interview is required. Essay is required and may be typed.

SECONDARY SCHOOL REQUIREMENTS

Graduation from secondary school required; GED accepted. The following course distribution required: 4 units of English, 3 units of math, 3 units of science, 1 unit of social studies, 3 units of history, 5 units of academic electives.

TESTING

SAT Reasoning or ACT recommended. SAT Subject recommended.

All enrolled freshmen (fall 2004):

Average SAT I Scores:	Verbal: 467	Math: 449
Average ACT Scores:	Composite: 22	

Child Study Team report is not required. A neuropsychological or comprehensive psycho-educational evaluation is required for admission. Tests required as part of this documentation:

- [ ] WAIS-IV
- [ ] WISC-IV
- [ ] SATA
- [ ] Woodcock-Johnson
- [ ] Nelson-Denny Reading Test
- [ ] Other

UNDERGRADUATE STUDENT BODY

Total undergraduate student enrollment: 236 Men, 520 Women.

Composition of student body (fall 2004):

	Undergraduate	Freshmen
International	0.0	1.9
Black	4.3	2.9
American Indian	9.6	5.9
Asian-American	1.7	1.8
Hispanic	2.6	2.9
White	69.6	78.3
Unreported	12.2	6.3
	100.0%	100.0%

7% are from out of state. Average age of full-time undergraduates is 27. 87% of classes have fewer than 20 students, 13% have between 20 and 50 students.

STUDENT HOUSING

32% of freshmen live in college housing. Freshmen are required to live on campus. Housing is guaranteed for all undergraduates. Campus can house 200 undergraduates. Single rooms are available for students with medical or special needs. A medical note is required.

EXPENSES

Tuition (2005-06): $13,500 per year.

Room: $2,330. Board: $3,340.
There is no additional cost for LD program/services.

LD SERVICES

LD program size is not limited.

LD services available to:

- [x] Freshmen
- [x] Sophomores
- [x] Juniors
- [x] Seniors

Academic Accommodations

Curriculum		**In class**	
Foreign language waiver	[ ]	Early syllabus	[ ]
Lighter course load	[ ]	Note takers in class	[x]
Math waiver	[ ]	Priority seating	[ ]
Other special classes	[ ]	Tape recorders	[x]
Priority registrations	[ ]	Videotaped classes	[x]
Substitution of courses	[ ]	Text on tape	[x]
Exams		**Services**	
Extended time	[x]	Diagnostic tests	[x]
Oral exams	[x]	Learning centers	[x]
Take home exams	[ ]	Proofreaders	[ ]
Exams on tape or computer	[x]	Readers	[x]
Untimed exams	[x]	Reading Machines/Kurzweil	[x]
Other accommodations	[x]	Special bookstore section	[ ]
		Typists	[ ]

Credit toward degree is not given for remedial courses taken.

Counseling Services

- [x] Academic
- [ ] Psychological
- [ ] Student Support groups
- [ ] Vocational

Tutoring

Individual tutoring is available daily.

Average size of tutoring groups: 2

	Individual	Group
Time management	[x]	[x]
Organizational skills	[x]	[x]
Learning strategies	[x]	[x]
Study skills	[x]	[x]
Content area	[x]	[x]
Writing lab	[x]	[x]
Math lab	[x]	[x]

LD PROGRAM STAFF

Total number of LD Program staff (including director):

Full Time: 1 Part Time: 1

There is an advisor/advocate from the LD program available to students. Five peer tutors are available to work with LD students.

Key staff person available to work with LD students: Kathryn Meier, Disabilities Advocate

Montana State University - Billings

Billings, MT

Address: 1500 University Drive, Billings, MT, 59101
Admissions telephone: 800 565-MSUB
Admissions FAX: 406 657-2302
Director of Admissions and Records: Cheri Johannes
Admissions e-mail: admissions@msubillings.edu
Web site: http://www.msubillings.edu
SAT Code: 4298 ACT Code: 2416

LD program name: Disability Support Services
Coordinator, Disability Support Services: Trudy Carey
LD program telephone: 406 657-2283
LD program e-mail: tcarey@msubillings.edu
LD program enrollment: 58, Total campus enrollment: 4,230

GENERAL

Montana State University - Billings is a public, coed, four-year institution. 92-acre campus in Billings (population: 89,847). Served by air and bus. Public transportation serves campus. Semester system.

LD ADMISSIONS

Students do not complete a separate application and are not simultaneously accepted to the LD program. A member of the LD program does not sit on the admissions committee. A personal interview is required. Essay is not required.

SECONDARY SCHOOL REQUIREMENTS

Graduation from secondary school required; GED accepted. The following course distribution required: 4 units of English, 3 units of math, 2 units of science, 3 units of social studies.

TESTING

ACT required; SAT Reasoning may be substituted. SAT Subject recommended.

All enrolled freshmen (fall 2004):

Average SAT I Scores: Verbal: 507 Math: 497
Average ACT Scores: Composite: 21

Child Study Team report is not required. A neuropsychological or comprehensive psycho-educational evaluation is required for admission. Must be dated within 36 months of application. Tests required as part of this documentation:

☑ WAIS-IV ☑ Woodcock-Johnson
☑ WISC-IV ☑ Nelson-Denny Reading Test
☑ SATA ☑ Other

UNDERGRADUATE STUDENT BODY

Total undergraduate student enrollment: 1,385 Men, 2,485 Women.

Composition of student body (fall 2004):

	Undergraduate	Freshmen
International	0.9	0.7
Black	0.7	0.6
American Indian	5.4	5.6
Asian-American	1.0	1.2
Hispanic	3.8	2.9
White	83.8	84.5
Unreported	4.4	4.5
	100.0%	100.0%

9% are from out of state. Average age of full-time undergraduates is 24. 45% of classes have fewer than 20 students, 52% have between 20 and 50 students, 3% have more than 50 students.

STUDENT HOUSING

27% of freshmen live in college housing. Freshmen are required to live on campus. Housing is guaranteed for all undergraduates. Campus can house 558 undergraduates. Single rooms are available for students with medical or special needs. A medical note is required.

EXPENSES

Tuition 2004-05: $4,550 per year (in-state), $12,831 (out-of-state).

There is no additional cost for LD program/services.

LD SERVICES

LD program size is not limited.

LD services available to:

☑ Freshmen ☑ Sophomores ☑ Juniors ☑ Seniors

Academic Accommodations

Curriculum		In class	
Foreign language waiver	☐	Early syllabus	☐
Lighter course load	☐	Note takers in class	☑
Math waiver	☐	Priority seating	☑
Other special classes	☐	Tape recorders	☑
Priority registrations	☑	Videotaped classes	☐
Substitution of courses	☐	Text on tape	☑
Exams		**Services**	
Extended time	☑	Diagnostic tests	☐
Oral exams	☑	Learning centers	☑
Take home exams	☐	Proofreaders	☐
Exams on tape or computer	☑	Readers	☑
Untimed exams	☐	Reading Machines/Kurzweil	☑
Other accommodations	☑	Special bookstore section	☐
		Typists	☑

Credit toward degree is not given for remedial courses taken.

Counseling Services

☐ Academic
☐ Psychological
☐ Student Support groups
☐ Vocational

Tutoring

Individual tutoring is not available.

	Individual	Group
Time management	☐	☐
Organizational skills	☐	☐
Learning strategies	☐	☐
Study skills	☐	☑
Content area	☐	☐
Writing lab	☑	☐
Math lab	☑	☐

UNIQUE LD PROGRAM FEATURES

Disability Support Services (DSS) is the contact agency for all students with documented disabilities. The school admissions process does not ask if a student has a disability. Students must self-identify and provide documentation of a disability to the DSS office. The coordinator does not do academic advising but does serve as an advocate and liaison between students and faculty. DSS does not provide tutoring, but a tutoring center is available free of charge to all students. All student accommodations are implemented through the DSS office.

LD PROGRAM STAFF

Total number of LD Program staff (including director):

Full Time: 2 Part Time: 2

There is no advisor/advocate from the LD program available to students.

Key staff person available to work with LD students: Trudy Carey, Coordinator, Disability Support Services

Montana State University - Bozeman

Bozeman, MT

Address: Bozeman, MT, 59717
Admissions telephone: 888 MSU-CATS
Admissions FAX: 406 994-1923
Director of Admissions: Ronda Russell
Admissions e-mail: admissions@montana.edu
Web site: http://www.montana.edu
SAT Code: 4488 ACT Code: 2420

LD program name: Disability, Re-entry & Veteran Services
Interim Director: Brenda York
LD program telephone: 406 994-2824
LD program e-mail: byork@montana.edu
LD program enrollment: 189, Total campus enrollment: 10,668

GENERAL

Montana State University-Bozeman is a public, coed, four-year institution. 1,170-acre campus in Bozeman (population: 27,509), 139 miles from Billings. Served by bus; airport serves Belgrade (eight miles); train serves Havre (290 miles). School operates transportation within Bozeman. Semester system.

LD ADMISSIONS

Students complete a separate application and are not simultaneously accepted to the LD program. A member of the LD program does not sit on the admissions committee. High school waivers are accepted for math and foreign language. A personal interview is not required. Essay is not required. Some courses may be substituted.

For fall 2004, 125 completed self-identified LD applications were received.

SECONDARY SCHOOL REQUIREMENTS

Graduation from secondary school required; GED accepted. The following course distribution required: 4 units of English, 3 units of math, 2 units of science, 3 units of social studies.

TESTING

SAT Reasoning or ACT required. SAT Subject recommended.

All enrolled freshmen (fall 2004):

Average SAT I Scores:	Verbal: 550	Math: 561
Average ACT Scores:	Composite: 23	

Child Study Team report is not required. A neuropsychological or comprehensive psycho-educational evaluation is required for admission. Must be dated within 60 months of application. Tests required as part of this documentation:

- [x] WAIS-IV
- [x] WISC-IV
- [x] SATA
- [x] Woodcock-Johnson
- [x] Nelson-Denny Reading Test
- [x] Other

UNDERGRADUATE STUDENT BODY

Total undergraduate student enrollment: 5,699 Men, 4,763 Women.

Composition of student body (fall 2004):

	Undergraduate	Freshmen
International	0.6	1.1
Black	0.5	0.6
American Indian	2.5	2.1
Asian-American	1.3	1.2
Hispanic	1.5	1.2
White	91.1	89.6
Unreported	2.5	4.2
	100.0%	100.0%

27% are from out of state. 2% join a fraternity and 1% join a sorority. Average age of full-time undergraduates is 22. 40% of classes have fewer than 20 students, 45% have between 20 and 50 students, 15% have more than 50 students.

STUDENT HOUSING

83% of freshmen live in college housing. Freshmen are required to live on campus. Housing is guaranteed for all undergraduates. Campus can house 3,200 undergraduates. Single rooms are available for students with medical or special needs. A medical note is required.

EXPENSES

Tuition (2005-06): $4,106 per year (in-state), $13,745 (out-of-state).
Room & Board: $5,956.
There is no additional cost for LD program/services.

LD SERVICES

LD program size is not limited.

LD services available to:

- [x] Freshmen
- [x] Sophomores
- [x] Juniors
- [x] Seniors

Academic Accommodations

Curriculum		In class	
Foreign language waiver	[ ]	Early syllabus	[ ]
Lighter course load	[x]	Note takers in class	[x]
Math waiver	[ ]	Priority seating	[x]
Other special classes	[ ]	Tape recorders	[x]
Priority registrations	[x]	Videotaped classes	[ ]
Substitution of courses	[ ]	Text on tape	[x]
Exams		**Services**	
Extended time	[x]	Diagnostic tests	[ ]
Oral exams	[x]	Learning centers	[x]
Take home exams	[ ]	Proofreaders	[ ]
Exams on tape or computer	[x]	Readers	[x]
Untimed exams	[ ]	Reading Machines/Kurzweil	[x]
Other accommodations	[x]	Special bookstore section	[ ]
		Typists	[ ]

Credit toward degree is not given for remedial courses taken.

Counseling Services

- [x] Academic
- [ ] Psychological
- [ ] Student Support groups
- [ ] Vocational

Tutoring

Individual tutoring is available weekly.

Average size of tutoring groups: 1

	Individual	Group
Time management	[x]	[x]
Organizational skills	[x]	[x]
Learning strategies	[x]	[x]
Study skills	[x]	[x]
Content area	[ ]	[ ]
Writing lab	[x]	[ ]
Math lab	[x]	[ ]

LD PROGRAM STAFF

Total number of LD Program staff (including director):

Full Time: 2 Part Time: 2

There is an advisor/advocate from the LD program available to students.

Key staff person available to work with LD students: Brenda York, Director

LD Program web site: http://www.montana.edu/wwwres/

Montana Tech of The U of Montana

Butte, MT

Address: 1300 West Park Street, Butte, MT, 59701
Admissions telephone: 800 445-TECH
Admissions FAX: 406 496-4710
Director of College Relations and Marketing: Tony Campeau
Admissions e-mail: admissions@mtech.edu
Web site: http://www.mtech.edu
SAT Code: 4487 ACT Code: 2418

Counselor: Lee Barnett
LD program telephone: 406 496-3730
LD program e-mail: lbarnett@mtech.edu
Total campus enrollment: 2,089

GENERAL

Montana Tech of The U of Montana is a public, coed, four-year institution. 56-acre campus in Butte (Buute-Silver Bow population: 33,892), 65 miles from Helena. Served by air and bus. Public transportation serves campus. Semester system.

LD ADMISSIONS

A personal interview is recommended. Essay is not required.

SECONDARY SCHOOL REQUIREMENTS

Graduation from secondary school required; GED accepted. The following course distribution required: 4 units of English, 3 units of math, 3 units of science, 3 units of social studies, 3 units of history, 2 units of academic electives.

TESTING

SAT Subject recommended.

All enrolled freshmen (fall 2004):

Average SAT I Scores:	Verbal: 522	Math: 559
Average ACT Scores:	Composite: 24	

Child Study Team report is not required. Tests required as part of this documentation:

- ☐ WAIS-IV
- ☐ WISC-IV
- ☐ SATA
- ☐ Woodcock-Johnson
- ☐ Nelson-Denny Reading Test
- ☐ Other

UNDERGRADUATE STUDENT BODY

Total undergraduate student enrollment: 1,097 Men, 908 Women.

Composition of student body (fall 2004):

	Undergraduate	Freshmen
International	2.3	2.9
Black	0.8	0.3
American Indian	1.5	1.4
Asian-American	0.3	0.7
Hispanic	1.0	1.4
White	84.2	86.2
Unreported	9.9	7.1
	100.0%	100.0%

13% are from out of state. 61% of classes have fewer than 20 students, 36% have between 20 and 50 students, 3% have more than 50 students.

STUDENT HOUSING

Freshmen are required to live on campus. Housing is guaranteed for all undergraduates. Campus can house 400 undergraduates.

EXPENSES

Tuition (2005-06): $4,044 per year (in-state), $9,241 (out-of-state).

Room: $2,294. Board: $3,062.
There is no additional cost for LD program/services.

LD SERVICES

LD program size is not limited.

LD services available to:

☐ Freshmen ☐ Sophomores ☐ Juniors ☐ Seniors

Academic Accommodations

Curriculum		In class	
Foreign language waiver	☐	Early syllabus	☐
Lighter course load	■	Note takers in class	☐
Math waiver	☐	Priority seating	☐
Other special classes	☐	Tape recorders	■
Priority registrations	☐	Videotaped classes	☐
Substitution of courses	☐	Text on tape	☐
Exams		**Services**	
Extended time	■	Diagnostic tests	☐
Oral exams	■	Learning centers	■
Take home exams	☐	Proofreaders	☐
Exams on tape or computer	☐	Readers	☐
Untimed exams	☐	Reading Machines/Kurzweil	☐
Other accommodations	☐	Special bookstore section	☐
		Typists	☐

Credit toward degree is not given for remedial courses taken.

Counseling Services

- ☐ Academic
- ☐ Psychological
- ☐ Student Support groups
- ☐ Vocational

Tutoring

	Individual	Group
Time management	☐	☐
Organizational skills	☐	☐
Learning strategies	☐	☐
Study skills	☐	☐
Content area	☐	☐
Writing lab	☐	☐
Math lab	☐	☐

LD PROGRAM STAFF

Total number of LD Program staff (including director):

Full Time: 2 Part Time: 2

Key staff person available to work with LD students: Paul Beatty, Dean of Students

The University of Montana

Missoula, MT

Address: 32 Campus Drive, Missoula, MT, 59812
Admissions telephone: 800 462-8636
Admissions FAX: 406 243-5711
Director of Admissions and New Student Services: Jed Liston
Admissions e-mail: admiss@umontana.edu
Web site: http://www.umt.edu
SAT Code: 4489 ACT Code: 2422

LD program name: Disability Services for Students
LD program address: LC 154
Director, Disability Services for Students: Jim Marks
LD program telephone: 406 243-2373
LD program e-mail: Jim.Marks@umontana.edu
LD program enrollment: 150, Total campus enrollment: 10,362

GENERAL

The University of Montana is a public, coed, four-year institution. 220-acre campus in Missoula (population: 57,053), 112 miles from Helena; branch campuses in Butte, Dillon, and Helena. Served by air and bus; train serves Whitefish (120 miles). Public transportation serves campus. Semester system.

LD ADMISSIONS

Students do not complete a separate application and are not simultaneously accepted to the LD program. A member of the LD program does sit on the admissions committee. A personal interview is not required. Essay is not required.

For fall 2004, 190 completed self-identified LD applications were received.

SECONDARY SCHOOL REQUIREMENTS

Graduation from secondary school required; GED accepted. The following course distribution required: 4 units of English, 3 units of math, 2 units of science, 2 units of social studies, 1 unit of history.

TESTING

SAT Reasoning or ACT required. SAT Subject recommended.

All enrolled freshmen (fall 2004):

Average SAT I Scores:	Verbal: 547	Math: 540
Average ACT Scores:	Composite: 23	

Child Study Team report is not required. A neuropsychological or comprehensive psycho-educational evaluation is required for admission. Must be dated within 5 months of application. Tests required as part of this documentation:

■ WAIS-IV	■ Woodcock-Johnson
■ WISC-IV	■ Nelson-Denny Reading Test
■ SATA	☐ Other

UNDERGRADUATE STUDENT BODY

Total undergraduate student enrollment: 5,037 Men, 5,629 Women.

Composition of student body (fall 2004):

	Undergraduate	Freshmen
International	0.9	1.5
Black	0.6	0.6
American Indian	2.5	3.7
Asian-American	1.3	1.2
Hispanic	1.9	1.4
White	84.5	84.4
Unreported	8.3	7.2
	100.0%	100.0%

30% are from out of state. 44% of classes have fewer than 20 students, 43% have between 20 and 50 students, 13% have more than 50 students.

STUDENT HOUSING

Freshmen are required to live on campus. Housing is guaranteed for all undergraduates. Campus can house 3,037 undergraduates. Single rooms are available for students with medical or special needs. A medical note is required.

EXPENSES

Tuition (2005-06): $3,470 per year (in-state), $12,186 (out-of-state).

Room: $2,546. Board: $3,100.
There are no additional cost for LD program/services.

LD SERVICES

LD program size is not limited.

LD services available to:

■ Freshmen ■ Sophomores ■ Juniors ■ Seniors

Academic Accommodations

Curriculum		**In class**	
Foreign language waiver	☐	Early syllabus	☐
Lighter course load	■	Note takers in class	■
Math waiver	☐	Priority seating	■
Other special classes	☐	Tape recorders	■
Priority registrations	■	Videotaped classes	☐
Substitution of courses	■	Text on tape	■
Exams		**Services**	
Extended time	■	Diagnostic tests	☐
Oral exams	■	Learning centers	☐
Take home exams	☐	Proofreaders	■
Exams on tape or computer	■	Readers	■
Untimed exams	☐	Reading Machines/Kurzweil	■
Other accommodations	■	Special bookstore section	☐
		Typists	■

Credit toward degree is not given for remedial courses taken.

Counseling Services

■ Academic
■ Psychological
■ Student Support groups
■ Vocational

Tutoring

Individual tutoring is available daily.

	Individual	Group
Time management	☐	☐
Organizational skills	☐	☐
Learning strategies	☐	■
Study skills	☐	■
Content area	☐	☐
Writing lab	■	■
Math lab	■	■

UNIQUE LD PROGRAM FEATURES

Programs are 100 percent accessible. Heavy focus on self-determination and focus on accessible learning environment, not on disability.

LD PROGRAM STAFF

Total number of LD Program staff (including director):

Full Time: 9 Part Time: 9

There is an advisor/advocate from the LD program available to students.

Key staff person available to work with LD students: Jim Marks, Director, Disability Services for Students

LD Program web site: www.umt.edu/dss

The University of Montana - Western

Dillon, MT

Address: 710 South Atlantic, Dillon, MT, 59725
Admissions telephone: 406 683-7331
Admissions FAX: 406 683-7493
Director of Student Services: Arlene Williams
Admissions e-mail: admissions@umwestern.edu
Web site: http://www.umwestern.edu
SAT Code: 4945 ACT Code: 2428

LD program name: Disability Services
LD program address: 750 East Cornell Street
Dean of Students: Eric Murray
LD program telephone: 406 683-7565
LD program e-mail: e_murray@umwestern.edu
LD program enrollment: 32, Total campus enrollment: 1,146

GENERAL

The University of Montana - Western is a public, coed, four-year institution. 35-acre campus in Dillon (population: 3,752), 65 miles from Butte. Served by bus; airport serves Butte; train serves Missoula (175 miles). Semester system.

LD ADMISSIONS

Students do not complete a separate application and are not simultaneously accepted to the LD program. A member of the LD program does not sit on the admissions committee. A personal interview is required. Essay is not required.

For fall 2004, 15 completed self-identified LD applications were received. 15 applications were offered admission, and 15 enrolled.

SECONDARY SCHOOL REQUIREMENTS

Graduation from secondary school required; GED accepted. The following course distribution required: 4 units of English, 3 units of math, 2 units of science, 3 units of social studies, 4 units of academic electives.

TESTING

SAT Reasoning or ACT required. SAT Subject recommended.

All enrolled freshmen (fall 2004):

Average SAT I Scores:	Verbal: 426	Math: 466
Average ACT Scores:	Composite: 20	

Child Study Team report is not required. A neuropsychological or comprehensive psycho-educational evaluation is required for admission. Must be dated within 36 months of application. Tests required as part of this documentation:

■ WAIS-IV	■ Woodcock-Johnson
☐ WISC-IV	☐ Nelson-Denny Reading Test
☐ SATA	☐ Other

UNDERGRADUATE STUDENT BODY

Total undergraduate student enrollment: 1,146.

Composition of student body (fall 2004):

	Undergraduate	Freshmen
International	0.0	0.0
Black	0.0	0.6
American Indian	3.1	4.0
Asian-American	2.7	2.1
Hispanic	1.3	1.9
White	81.3	84.5
Unreported	11.6	6.9
	100.0%	100.0%

11% are from out of state. Average age of full-time undergraduates is 25. 67% of classes have fewer than 20 students, 33% have between 20 and 50 students.

STUDENT HOUSING

88% of freshmen live in college housing. Freshmen are required to live on campus. Housing is guaranteed for all undergraduates. Campus can house 481 undergraduates. Single rooms are available for students with medical or special needs. A medical note is required.

EXPENSES

Tuition (2005-06): $2,705 per year (in-state), $11,270 (out-of-state).
Room: $1,890. Board: $2,850.
There is no additional cost for LD program/services.

LD SERVICES

LD program size is not limited.

LD services available to:

■ Freshmen ■ Sophomores ■ Juniors ■ Seniors

Academic Accommodations

Curriculum		**In class**	
Foreign language waiver	☐	Early syllabus	☐
Lighter course load	☐	Note takers in class	■
Math waiver	☐	Priority seating	☐
Other special classes	☐	Tape recorders	■
Priority registrations	■	Videotaped classes	■
Substitution of courses	☐	Text on tape	■
Exams		**Services**	
Extended time	■	Diagnostic tests	☐
Oral exams	■	Learning centers	■
Take home exams	☐	Proofreaders	☐
Exams on tape or computer	■	Readers	■
Untimed exams	■	Reading Machines/Kurzweil	■
Other accommodations	☐	Special bookstore section	☐
		Typists	■

Credit toward degree is not given for remedial courses taken.

Counseling Services

■ Academic
■ Psychological
☐ Student Support groups
☐ Vocational

Tutoring

Individual tutoring is available daily.

Average size of tutoring groups: 4

	Individual	Group
Time management	☐	☐
Organizational skills	☐	☐
Learning strategies	☐	■
Study skills	☐	■
Content area	☐	☐
Writing lab	☐	■
Math lab	☐	☐

LD PROGRAM STAFF

There is an advisor/advocate from the LD program available to students. Four peer tutors are available to work with LD students.

Key staff person available to work with LD students: Eric Murray, Dean of Students

LD Program web site: http:\\www.umwestern.edu/studentlife/disabilities

Rocky Mountain College

Billings, MT

Address: 1511 Poly Drive, Billings, MT, 59102
Admissions telephone: 800 877-6259
Admissions FAX: 406 657-1189
Director of Admissions: Bonnie Knapp
Admissions e-mail: admissions@rocky.edu
Web site: http://www.rocky.edu
SAT Code: 4660 ACT Code: 2426

LD program name: Services for Academic Success (SAS)
Director, Services for Academic Success: Jane Van Dyk
LD program telephone: 406 657-1070
LD program e-mail: vandykj@rocky.edu
LD program enrollment: 31, Total campus enrollment: 946

GENERAL

Rocky Mountain College is a private, coed, four-year institution. 60-acre, suburban campus in Billings (population: 89,847). Served by air and bus; train serves Havre (200 miles). Public transportation serves campus. Semester system.

LD ADMISSIONS

Students do not complete a separate application and are not simultaneously accepted to the LD program. A member of the LD program does not sit on the admissions committee. A personal interview is recommended. Essay is not required. Conditional admission may be offered to students who do not meet admissions requirements.

For fall 2004, 10 completed self-identified LD applications were received. 10 applications were offered admission, and 10 enrolled.

SECONDARY SCHOOL REQUIREMENTS

Graduation from secondary school required; GED accepted. The following course distribution required: 4 units of English, 2 units of math, 2 units of science, 1 unit of foreign language, 2 units of social studies, 2 units of history.

TESTING

ACT required; SAT Reasoning may be substituted. SAT Subject recommended.

All enrolled freshmen (fall 2004):

Average SAT I Scores:	Verbal: 510	Math: 531
Average ACT Scores:	Composite: 22	

Child Study Team report is not required. A neuropsychological or comprehensive psycho-educational evaluation is required for admission. Must be dated within 36 months of application. Tests required as part of this documentation:

■ WAIS-IV	■ Woodcock-Johnson
■ WISC-IV	☐ Nelson-Denny Reading Test
☐ SATA	☐ Other

UNDERGRADUATE STUDENT BODY

Total undergraduate student enrollment: 363 Men, 414 Women.

Composition of student body (fall 2004):

	Undergraduate	Freshmen
International	7.4	6.7
Black	0.5	1.0
American Indian	6.1	8.6
Asian-American	2.6	1.3
Hispanic	1.7	2.7
White	81.7	79.7
Unreported	0.0	0.0
	100.0%	100.0%

26% are from out of state. Average age of full-time undergraduates is 22. 67% of classes have fewer than 20 students, 32% have between 20 and 50 students, 1% have more than 50 students.

STUDENT HOUSING

84% of freshmen live in college housing. Freshmen are required to live on campus. Housing is guaranteed for all undergraduates. Campus can house 477 undergraduates. Single rooms are available for students with medical or special needs. A medical note is required.

EXPENSES

Tuition (2005-06): $15,080 per year. Tuition differs for degree completion, information technology/computer applications, and physician assistant programs.

Room: $2,600. Board: $2,872.

There is no additional cost for LD program/services.

LD SERVICES

LD program size is not limited.

LD services available to:

■ Freshmen ■ Sophomores ■ Juniors ■ Seniors

Academic Accommodations

Curriculum		**In class**	
Foreign language waiver	☐	Early syllabus	☐
Lighter course load	■	Note takers in class	■
Math waiver	☐	Priority seating	☐
Other special classes	■	Tape recorders	■
Priority registrations	☐	Videotaped classes	☐
Substitution of courses	☐	Text on tape	☐
Exams		**Services**	
Extended time	■	Diagnostic tests	☐
Oral exams	☐	Learning centers	☐
Take home exams	☐	Proofreaders	☐
Exams on tape or computer	☐	Readers	■
Untimed exams	■	Reading Machines/Kurzweil	☐
Other accommodations	☐	Special bookstore section	☐
		Typists	☐

Credit toward degree is not given for remedial courses taken.

Counseling Services

■ Academic — Meets 5 times per academic year
■ Psychological
■ Student Support groups
■ Vocational

Tutoring

Individual tutoring is available weekly.

Average size of tutoring groups: 3

	Individual	Group
Time management	■	■
Organizational skills	■	■
Learning strategies	■	■
Study skills	■	■
Content area	☐	☐
Writing lab	■	☐
Math lab	■	■

UNIQUE LD PROGRAM FEATURES

Services for Academic Success is a comprehensive support program which provides the skills, support, and encouragement needed for students with learning disabilities to successfully complete college. Students with disabilities are responsible for identifying themselves, providing appropriate documentation, and requesting reasonable accommodations. SAS is a TRIO program funded through a grant from the U.S. Department of Education.

LD PROGRAM STAFF

Total number of LD Program staff (including director):

Full Time: 3 Part Time: 3

There is an advisor/advocate from the LD program available to students. The advisor/advocate meets with students four times per month. 25 peer tutors are available to work with LD students.

Key staff person available to work with LD students: Jane Van Dyk, Director, Services for Academic Success

Bellevue University

Bellevue, NE

Address: 1000 Galvin Road South, Bellevue, NE, 68005
Admissions telephone: 800 756-7920
Admissions FAX: 402 293-3730
Director of Marketing and Enrollment: Roberta Mersch
Admissions e-mail: info@bellevue.edu
Web site: http://www.bellevue.edu
SAT Code: 6053 ACT Code: 2437

LD program name: Academic Support Services
Student Support Specialist: Terra Beethe
LD program telephone: 402 682-4012
LD program e-mail: specialneeds@bellevue.edu
LD program enrollment: 24, Total campus enrollment: 4,293

GENERAL

Bellevue University is a private, coed, four-year institution. 12-acre suburban campus in Bellevue (population: 44,382), 15 miles from Omaha; branch campuses in Grand Island and Omaha. Major airport, bus, and train serve Omaha. Public transportation serves campus. Quarter system.

LD ADMISSIONS

Students do not complete a separate application and are simultaneously accepted to the LD program. A member of the LD program does not sit on the admissions committee. A personal interview is recommended. Essay is not required.

For fall 2004, 9 completed self-identified LD applications were received.

SECONDARY SCHOOL REQUIREMENTS

Graduation from secondary school required; GED accepted.

TESTING

Child Study Team report is not required. A neuropsychological or comprehensive psycho-educational evaluation is required for admission. Must be dated within 36 months of application. Tests required as part of this documentation:

- ☑ WAIS-IV
- ☑ WISC-IV
- ☐ SATA
- ☑ Woodcock-Johnson
- ☐ Nelson-Denny Reading Test
- ☐ Other

UNDERGRADUATE STUDENT BODY

Total undergraduate student enrollment: 1,599 Men, 1,606 Women.

Composition of student body (fall 2004):

	Undergraduate	Freshmen
International	20.0	7.4
Black	4.0	10.1
American Indian	0.6	0.6
Asian-American	1.7	2.2
Hispanic	20.0	6.6
White	52.0	71.0
Unreported	1.7	2.1
	100.0%	100.0%

59% of classes have fewer than 20 students, 41% have between 20 and 50 students.

STUDENT HOUSING

1% of freshmen live in college housing. Freshmen are not required to live on campus. Housing is not guaranteed for all undergraduates. Campus can house 28 undergraduates.

EXPENSES

Tuition (2005-06): $4,575 per year.

There is no additional cost for LD program/services.

LD SERVICES

LD program size is not limited.

LD services available to:

☑ Freshmen ☑ Sophomores ☑ Juniors ☑ Seniors

Academic Accommodations

Curriculum		In class	
Foreign language waiver	☐	Early syllabus	☑
Lighter course load	☐	Note takers in class	☑
Math waiver	☐	Priority seating	☑
Other special classes	☐	Tape recorders	☑
Priority registrations	☐	Videotaped classes	☑
Substitution of courses	☑	Text on tape	☑
Exams		**Services**	
Extended time	☑	Diagnostic tests	☑
Oral exams	☑	Learning centers	☐
Take home exams	☑	Proofreaders	☑
Exams on tape or computer	☑	Readers	☑
Untimed exams	☐	Reading Machines/Kurzweil	☑
Other accommodations	☑	Special bookstore section	☐
		Typists	☑

Credit toward degree is not given for remedial courses taken.

Counseling Services

- ☐ Academic
- ☐ Psychological
- ☐ Student Support groups
- ☐ Vocational

Tutoring

Individual tutoring is available daily.

Average size of tutoring groups: 2

	Individual	Group
Time management	☑	☑
Organizational skills	☑	☑
Learning strategies	☑	☑
Study skills	☑	☑
Content area	☑	☑
Writing lab	☑	☑
Math lab	☑	☑

LD PROGRAM STAFF

Total number of LD Program staff (including director):

Full Time: 2 Part Time: 2

There is an advisor/advocate from the LD program available to students. 4 graduate students and 12 peer tutors are available to work with LD students.

Key staff person available to work with LD students: Inge Jacobs, Director, Academic Support Services.

LD Program web site: http://www.bellevue.edu/resources/special.asp

Concordia University

Seward, NE

Address: 800 North Columbia, Seward, NE, 68434
Admissions telephone: 800 535-5494
Admissions FAX: 402 643-4073
Director of Admission: Chad Thies
Admissions e-mail: admiss@seward.cune.edu
Web site: http://www.cune.edu
SAT Code: 6116 ACT Code: 2442

Director, Academic Support Services: Margene Schmidt
LD program telephone: 402 643-7365
LD program e-mail: mschmidt@seward.cune.edu
Total campus enrollment: 1,179

GENERAL

Concordia University is a private, coed, four-year institution. 120-acre campus in Seward (population: 6,319), 25 miles from Lincoln. Airport, bus, and train serve Lincoln; major airport serves Omaha (85 miles). Semester system.

LD ADMISSIONS

Students do not complete a separate application and are not simultaneously accepted to the LD program. A member of the LD program does not sit on the admissions committee. A personal interview is not required. Essay is not required.

SECONDARY SCHOOL REQUIREMENTS

Graduation from secondary school required; GED accepted.

TESTING

ACT required; SAT Reasoning may be substituted. SAT Subject recommended.

All enrolled freshmen (fall 2004):

Average SAT I Scores:	Verbal: 533	Math: 533
Average ACT Scores:	Composite: 23	

Child Study Team report is not required. A neuropsychological or comprehensive psycho-educational evaluation is required for admission. Must be dated within 24 months of application. Tests required as part of this documentation:

- ■ WAIS-IV
- ■ WISC-IV
- ☐ SATA
- ■ Woodcock-Johnson
- ☐ Nelson-Denny Reading Test
- ■ Other

UNDERGRADUATE STUDENT BODY

Total undergraduate student enrollment: 515 Men, 651 Women.

Composition of student body (fall 2004):

	Undergraduate	Freshmen
International	0.0	0.2
Black	1.2	1.1
American Indian	0.8	0.1
Asian-American	0.0	0.9
Hispanic	0.8	1.0
White	86.8	90.4
Unreported	10.4	6.3
	100.0%	100.0%

60% are from out of state. 54% of classes have fewer than 20 students, 46% have between 20 and 50 students.

STUDENT HOUSING

90% of freshmen live in college housing. Freshmen are required to live on campus. Housing is guaranteed for all undergraduates. Campus can house 867 undergraduates.

EXPENSES

Tuition (2005-06): $17,724 per year.

Room: $2,070. Board: $2,640.

There is no additional cost for LD program/services.

LD SERVICES

LD program size is not limited.

LD services available to:

■ Freshmen ■ Sophomores ■ Juniors ■ Seniors

Academic Accommodations

Curriculum		In class	
Foreign language waiver	☐	Early syllabus	☐
Lighter course load	■	Note takers in class	■
Math waiver	☐	Priority seating	☐
Other special classes	☐	Tape recorders	■
Priority registrations	☐	Videotaped classes	■
Substitution of courses	☐	Text on tape	☐
Exams		**Services**	
Extended time	■	Diagnostic tests	☐
Oral exams	☐	Learning centers	■
Take home exams	☐	Proofreaders	■
Exams on tape or computer	☐	Readers	■
Untimed exams	☐	Reading Machines/Kurzweil	■
Other accommodations	■	Special bookstore section	☐
		Typists	☐

Counseling Services

- ■ Academic
- ☐ Psychological
- ■ Student Support groups
- ☐ Vocational

Tutoring

Individual tutoring is available weekly.

Average size of tutoring groups: 3

	Individual	Group
Time management	■	■
Organizational skills	■	■
Learning strategies	■	■
Study skills	■	■
Content area	☐	☐
Writing lab	■	☐
Math lab	☐	☐

LD PROGRAM STAFF

There is an advisor/advocate from the LD program available to students. The advisor/advocate meets with students 4 times per month. 50 peer tutors are available to work with LD students.

Key staff person available to work with LD students: Margene Schmidt, Director of Academic Support Services.

Creighton University

Omaha, NE

Address: 2500 California Plaza, Omaha, NE, 68178
Admissions telephone: 800 282-5835
Admissions FAX: 402 280-2685
Director of Admissions: Mary Chase
Admissions e-mail: admissions@creighton.edu
Web site: http://www.creighton.edu
SAT Code: 6121 ACT Code: 2444

Coordinator: Wade Pearson
LD program telephone: 402 280-2749
LD program e-mail: chess@creighton.edu
LD program enrollment: 125, Total campus enrollment: 3,888

GENERAL

Creighton University is a private, coed, four-year institution. 9-acre, urban campus in Omaha (metropolitan population: 390,007); branch campus in Hastings. Served by air, bus, and train. School operates shuttle system. Public transportation serves campus. Semester system.

LD ADMISSIONS

Application Deadline: 08/01. Students do not complete a separate application and are simultaneously accepted to the LD program. A member of the LD program does not sit on the admissions committee. A personal interview is not required. Essay is required and may be typed.

For fall 2004, 9 completed self-identified LD applications were received. 8 applications were offered admission, and 6 enrolled.

SECONDARY SCHOOL REQUIREMENTS

Graduation from secondary school required; GED accepted. The following course distribution required: 4 units of English, 3 units of math, 2 units of science, 2 units of foreign language, 1 unit of social studies, 1 unit of history, 3 units of academic electives.

TESTING

SAT Reasoning or ACT required. SAT Subject recommended.

All enrolled freshmen (fall 2004):

Average SAT I Scores:	Verbal: 600	Math: 605
Average ACT Scores:	Composite: 26	

Child Study Team report is not required. A neuropsychological or comprehensive psycho-education evaluation is not required for admission. Tests required as part of this documentation:

- ☐ WAIS-IV
- ☐ WISC-IV
- ☐ SATA
- ☐ Woodcock-Johnson
- ☐ Nelson-Denny Reading Test
- ☐ Other

UNDERGRADUATE STUDENT BODY

Total undergraduate student enrollment: 1,540 Men, 2,139 Women.

Composition of student body (fall 2004):

	Undergraduate	Freshmen
International	0.7	1.4
Black	2.7	3.4
American Indian	2.1	1.4
Asian-American	8.5	6.8
Hispanic	3.7	3.3
White	82.2	83.6
Unreported	0.1	0.1
	100.0%	100.0%

50% are from out of state. 21% join a fraternity and 28% join a sorority. Average age of full-time undergraduates is 20. 46% of classes have fewer than 20 students, 49% have between 20 and 50 students, 5% have more than 50 students.

STUDENT HOUSING

90% of freshmen live in college housing. Freshmen are required to live on campus. Housing is guaranteed for all undergraduates. Campus can house 2,115 undergraduates. Single rooms are available for students with medical or special needs. A medical note is required.

EXPENSES

Tuition (2005-06): $21,576 per year.
Room: $4,250. Board: $3,290.
There is no additional cost for LD program/services.

LD SERVICES

LD program size is not limited.

LD services available to:

■ Freshmen ■ Sophomores ■ Juniors ■ Seniors

Academic Accommodations

Curriculum		In class	
Foreign language waiver	☐	Early syllabus	☐
Lighter course load	■	Note takers in class	■
Math waiver	☐	Priority seating	☐
Other special classes	☐	Tape recorders	■
Priority registrations	☐	Videotaped classes	☐
Substitution of courses	☐	Text on tape	☐
Exams		**Services**	
Extended time	■	Diagnostic tests	■
Oral exams	■	Learning centers	☐
Take home exams	☐	Proofreaders	☐
Exams on tape or computer	☐	Readers	■
Untimed exams	☐	Reading Machines/Kurzweil	■
Other accommodations	☐	Special bookstore section	☐
		Typists	☐

Credit toward degree is not given for remedial courses taken.

Counseling Services

- ■ Academic
- ■ Psychological
- ☐ Student Support groups
- ☐ Vocational

Tutoring

Individual tutoring is available daily.

	Individual	Group
Time management	☐	■
Organizational skills	☐	■
Learning strategies	☐	■
Study skills	☐	■
Content area	☐	☐
Writing lab	■	☐
Math lab	■	☐

LD PROGRAM STAFF

There is an advisor/advocate from the LD program available to students.

Key staff person available to work with LD students: Wade Pearson, Coordinator, Office of Disability Accommodations.

Dana College

Blair, NE

Address: 2848 College Drive, Blair, NE, 68008-1099
Admissions telephone: 800 444-3262
Admissions FAX: 402 426-7386
Director of Admissions: Jim Lynes
Admissions e-mail: admissions@dana.edu
Web site: http://www.dana.edu
SAT Code: 6157 ACT Code: 2446

LD program contact: Dr. Diane Mann
LD program telephone: 402 426-7361
LD program e-mail: dmann@dana.edu
Total campus enrollment: 639

GENERAL

Dana College is a private, coed, four-year institution. 150-acre, rural campus in Blair (population: 7,000), 20 miles from Omaha. Major airport, bus, and train serve Omaha. School operates transportation to Omaha. 4-1-4 system.

LD ADMISSIONS

Students do not complete a separate application and are not simultaneously accepted to the LD program. A member of the LD program does not sit on the admissions committee. High school waivers are accepted for foreign language. A personal interview is recommended. Essay is not required.

SECONDARY SCHOOL REQUIREMENTS

Graduation from secondary school required; GED accepted.

TESTING

SAT Reasoning considered if submitted. ACT considered if submitted.

All enrolled freshmen (fall 2004):

Average ACT Scores: Composite:22

Child Study Team report is not required. A neuropsychological or comprehensive psycho-education evaluation is not required for admission. Tests required as part of this documentation:

- [ ] WAIS-IV
- [ ] WISC-IV
- [ ] SATA
- [ ] Woodcock-Johnson
- [ ] Nelson-Denny Reading Test
- [ ] Other

UNDERGRADUATE STUDENT BODY

Total undergraduate student enrollment: 307 Men, 258 Women.

Composition of student body (fall 2004):

	Undergraduate	Freshmen
International	0.5	0.3
Black	2.4	4.9
American Indian	0.0	0.3
Asian-American	0.5	0.6
Hispanic	2.9	3.9
White	93.7	90.0
Unreported	0.0	0.0
	100.0%	100.0%

47% are from out of state. Average age of full-time undergraduates is 20. 64% of classes have fewer than 20 students, 34% have between 20 and 50 students, 2% have more than 50 students.

STUDENT HOUSING

94% of freshmen live in college housing. Freshmen are required to live on campus. Housing is guaranteed for all undergraduates. Campus can house 600 undergraduates. Single rooms are available for students with medical or special needs. A medical note is required.

EXPENSES

Tuition (2005-06): $16,850 per year.
Room: $2,060. Board: $3,260.
There is no additional cost for LD program/services.

LD SERVICES

LD program size is not limited.

LD services available to:

- [x] Freshmen
- [x] Sophomores
- [x] Juniors
- [x] Seniors

Academic Accommodations

Curriculum		In class	
Foreign language waiver	[ ]	Early syllabus	[ ]
Lighter course load	[ ]	Note takers in class	[ ]
Math waiver	[ ]	Priority seating	[ ]
Other special classes	[ ]	Tape recorders	[x]
Priority registrations	[ ]	Videotaped classes	[ ]
Substitution of courses	[ ]	Text on tape	[ ]
Exams		**Services**	
Extended time	[x]	Diagnostic tests	[x]
Oral exams	[ ]	Learning centers	[x]
Take home exams	[ ]	Proofreaders	[x]
Exams on tape or computer	[ ]	Readers	[ ]
Untimed exams	[x]	Reading Machines/Kurzweil	[ ]
Other accommodations	[ ]	Special bookstore section	[ ]
		Typists	[ ]

Credit toward degree is not given for remedial courses taken.

Counseling Services

- [x] Academic — Meets 30 times per academic year
- [x] Psychological — Meets 30 times per academic year
- [ ] Student Support groups
- [ ] Vocational

Tutoring

Individual tutoring is available weekly.

Average size of tutoring groups: 3

	Individual	Group
Time management	[ ]	[x]
Organizational skills	[ ]	[x]
Learning strategies	[ ]	[x]
Study skills	[ ]	[x]
Content area	[ ]	[x]
Writing lab	[ ]	[ ]
Math lab	[ ]	[ ]

LD PROGRAM STAFF

Total number of LD Program staff (including director):

Full Time: 1 Part Time: 1

There is an advisor/advocate from the LD program available to students. The advisor/advocate meets with faculty 1 time per month and students 2 times per month.

Key staff person available to work with LD students: Lori Neilson, Director of Learning Center.

Doane College

Crete, NE

Address: 1014 Boswell Avenue, Crete, NE, 68333
Admissions telephone: 800 333-6263
Admissions FAX: 402 826-8600
Dean of Admissions: Dan Kunzman
Admissions e-mail: admissions@doane.edu
Web site: http://www.doane.edu
SAT Code: 6165 ACT Code: 2448

Director Student Support Services: Sherri Hanigan
LD program telephone: 402 826-8586
LD program e-mail: sheri.hanigan@doane.edu
Total campus enrollment: 1,655

GENERAL

Doane College is a private, coed, four-year institution. 300-acre campus in Crete (population: 6,028), 75 miles from Omaha; non-traditional student campus in Lincoln. Major airport serves Omaha; airport, bus, and train serve Lincoln (25 miles). 4-1-4 system.

LD ADMISSIONS

SECONDARY SCHOOL REQUIREMENTS

Graduation from secondary school required; GED accepted.

TESTING

SAT Reasoning considered if submitted. ACT recommended.

All enrolled freshmen (fall 2004):

Average ACT Scores: Composite:23

Child Study Team report is not required. Tests required as part of this documentation:

- [ ] WAIS-IV
- [ ] WISC-IV
- [ ] SATA
- [ ] Woodcock-Johnson
- [ ] Nelson-Denny Reading Test
- [ ] Other

UNDERGRADUATE STUDENT BODY

Total undergraduate student enrollment: 490 Men, 486 Women.

17% are from out of state. 31% join a fraternity and 28% join a sorority. Average age of full-time undergraduates is 20. 77% of classes have fewer than 20 students, 23% have between 20 and 50 students.

STUDENT HOUSING

100% of freshmen live in college housing. Freshmen are required to live on campus. Housing is guaranteed for all undergraduates. Campus can house 881 undergraduates.

EXPENSES

Tuition (2005-06): $17,186 per year.

Room: $1,880. Board: $3,042.

There is no additional cost for LD program/services.

LD SERVICES

LD program size is not limited.

LD services available to:

- [ ] Freshmen
- [ ] Sophomores
- [ ] Juniors
- [ ] Seniors

Academic Accommodations

Curriculum

- [ ] Foreign language waiver
- [x] Lighter course load
- [ ] Math waiver
- [ ] Other special classes
- [ ] Priority registrations
- [ ] Substitution of courses

Exams

- [x] Extended time
- [ ] Oral exams
- [ ] Take home exams
- [ ] Exams on tape or computer
- [ ] Untimed exams
- [ ] Other accommodations

In class

- [ ] Early syllabus
- [x] Note takers in class
- [ ] Priority seating
- [x] Tape recorders
- [ ] Videotaped classes
- [ ] Text on tape

Services

- [ ] Diagnostic tests
- [x] Learning centers
- [ ] Proofreaders
- [ ] Readers
- [ ] Reading Machines/Kurzweil
- [ ] Special bookstore section
- [ ] Typists

Credit toward degree is not given for remedial courses taken.

Counseling Services

- [ ] Academic
- [ ] Psychological
- [ ] Student Support groups
- [ ] Vocational

Tutoring

	Individual	Group
Time management	[ ]	[ ]
Organizational skills	[ ]	[ ]
Learning strategies	[ ]	[ ]
Study skills	[ ]	[ ]
Content area	[ ]	[ ]
Writing lab	[ ]	[ ]
Math lab	[ ]	[ ]

LD PROGRAM STAFF

Total number of LD Program staff (including director):

Full Time: 2 Part Time: 2

Key staff person available to work with LD students: Sherri Hanigan, Director, Student Support Services.

Grace University

Omaha, NE

Address: 1311 South Ninth Street, Omaha, NE, 68108-3629
Admissions telephone: 800 383-1422
Admissions FAX: 402 341-9587
Director of Admissions: Diane Lee
Admissions e-mail: admissions@graceuniversity.edu
Web site: http://www.graceuniversity.edu
SAT Code: 6248 ACT Code: 2454

Director of Learning Assistance Lab: Doris Fyfe
LD program telephone: 402 449-2923
Total campus enrollment: 440

GENERAL

Grace University is a private, coed, four-year institution. 22-acre campus in Omaha (population: 390,007). Served by air, bus, and train. Semester system.

SECONDARY SCHOOL REQUIREMENTS

Graduation from secondary school required; GED accepted. The following course distribution required: 4 units of English, 3 units of math, 3 units of science, 2 units of foreign language, 3 units of social studies.

TESTING

ACT required; SAT Reasoning may be substituted.

All enrolled freshmen (fall 2004):

Average SAT I Scores:	Verbal: 563	Math: 504
Average ACT Scores:	Composite: 23	

Child Study Team report is not required. Tests required as part of this documentation:

- ☐ WAIS-IV
- ☐ WISC-IV
- ☐ SATA
- ☐ Woodcock-Johnson
- ☐ Nelson-Denny Reading Test
- ☐ Other

UNDERGRADUATE STUDENT BODY

Total undergraduate student enrollment: 233 Men, 286 Women.

Composition of student body (fall 2004):

	Undergraduate	Freshmen
International	0.0	1.1
Black	5.3	6.7
American Indian	3.5	1.1
Asian-American	0.0	0.0
Hispanic	1.7	1.4
White	89.5	89.7
Unreported	0.0	0.0
	100.0%	100.0%

61% are from out of state.

STUDENT HOUSING

Freshmen are required to live on campus. Housing is guaranteed for all undergraduates. Campus can house 317 undergraduates.

EXPENSES

Tuition (2005-06): $11,700 per year.
Room: $2,400. Board: $3,000.
There is no additional cost for LD program/services.

LD SERVICES

LD services available to:

☐ Freshmen ☐ Sophomores ☐ Juniors ☐ Seniors

Academic Accommodations

Curriculum		**In class**	
Foreign language waiver	☐	Early syllabus	☐
Lighter course load	☑	Note takers in class	☑
Math waiver	☐	Priority seating	☐
Other special classes	☐	Tape recorders	☐
Priority registrations	☐	Videotaped classes	☐
Substitution of courses	☐	Text on tape	☐
Exams		**Services**	
Extended time	☐	Diagnostic tests	☐
Oral exams	☐	Learning centers	☐
Take home exams	☐	Proofreaders	☐
Exams on tape or computer	☐	Readers	☑
Untimed exams	☑	Reading Machines/Kurzweil	☐
Other accommodations	☐	Special bookstore section	☐
		Typists	☐

Credit toward degree is not given for remedial courses taken.

Counseling Services

- ☐ Academic
- ☐ Psychological
- ☐ Student Support groups
- ☐ Vocational

Tutoring

	Individual	Group
Time management	☐	☐
Organizational skills	☐	☐
Learning strategies	☐	☐
Study skills	☐	☐
Content area	☐	☐
Writing lab	☐	☐
Math lab	☐	☐

LD PROGRAM STAFF

Total number of LD Program staff (including director):

Full Time: 5 Part Time: 5

Key staff person available to work with LD students: Christi Jensen, Dean of Women.

Hastings College

Hastings, NE

Address: 710 N. Turner Avenue, Hastings, NE, 68901-7621
Admissions telephone: 800 532-7642
Admissions FAX: 402 461-7490
Director of Admissions: Mary Molliconi
Admissions e-mail: mmolliconi@hastings.edu
Web site: http://www.hastings.edu
SAT Code: 6270 ACT Code: 2456

LD program name: Learning Center
Director of the Learning Center: Kathleen Haverly
LD program telephone: 402 461-7386
LD program e-mail: khaverly@hastings.edu
LD program enrollment: 41, Total campus enrollment: 1,105

GENERAL

Hastings College is a private, coed, four-year institution. 104-acre campus in Hastings (population: 24,064), 100 miles from Lincoln. Served by air and train; major airport serves Lincoln; bus serves Grand Island (30 miles). 4-1-4 system.

LD ADMISSIONS

Students do not complete a separate application and are simultaneously accepted to the LD program. A member of the LD program does sit on the admissions committee. High school waivers are accepted for foreign language. A personal interview is recommended. Essay is not required.

SECONDARY SCHOOL REQUIREMENTS

Graduation from secondary school required; GED accepted. The following course distribution required: 3 units of English, 3 units of math, 3 units of science, 4 units of social studies, 3 units of history.

TESTING

SAT Reasoning considered if submitted. ACT considered if submitted. SAT Subject recommended.

All enrolled freshmen (fall 2004):

Average SAT I Scores:	Verbal: 500	Math: 515
Average ACT Scores:	Composite: 23	

Child Study Team report is not required. A neuropsychological or comprehensive psycho-educational evaluation is required for admission. Must be dated within 12 months of application. Tests required as part of this documentation:

- ☐ WAIS-IV
- ☐ WISC-IV
- ☐ SATA
- ☐ Woodcock-Johnson
- ☐ Nelson-Denny Reading Test
- ☐ Other

UNDERGRADUATE STUDENT BODY

Total undergraduate student enrollment: 525 Men, 542 Women.

Composition of student body (fall 2004):

	Undergraduate	Freshmen
International	0.3	0.7
Black	3.5	2.7
American Indian	0.3	0.2
Asian-American	0.7	0.8
Hispanic	3.2	1.6
White	91.7	93.4
Unreported	0.3	0.6
	100.0%	100.0%

16% join a fraternity and 32% join a sorority. Average age of full-time undergraduates is 21. 67% of classes have fewer than 20 students, 32% have between 20 and 50 students, 1% have more than 50 students.

STUDENT HOUSING

95% of freshmen live in college housing. Freshmen are required to live on campus. Housing is guaranteed for all undergraduates. Campus can house 900 undergraduates. Single rooms are available for students with medical or special needs. A medical note is not required.

EXPENSES

Tuition (2005-06): $16,578 per year.
Room: $2,116. Board: $2,834.
There is no additional cost for LD program/services.

LD SERVICES

LD program size is not limited.

LD services available to:

■ Freshmen ■ Sophomores ■ Juniors ■ Seniors

Academic Accommodations

Curriculum		In class	
Foreign language waiver	■	Early syllabus	☐
Lighter course load	■	Note takers in class	■
Math waiver	☐	Priority seating	☐
Other special classes	☐	Tape recorders	☐
Priority registrations	☐	Videotaped classes	☐
Substitution of courses	☐	Text on tape	☐
Exams		**Services**	
Extended time	■	Diagnostic tests	☐
Oral exams	■	Learning centers	■
Take home exams	☐	Proofreaders	■
Exams on tape or computer	■	Readers	■
Untimed exams	■	Reading Machines/Kurzweil	☐
Other accommodations	■	Special bookstore section	☐
		Typists	☐

Credit toward degree is not given for remedial courses taken.

Counseling Services

- ■ Academic
- ■ Psychological
- ☐ Student Support groups
- ☐ Vocational

Tutoring

Individual tutoring is available daily.

Average size of tutoring groups: 5

	Individual	Group
Time management	■	☐
Organizational skills	■	☐
Learning strategies	☐	■
Study skills	☐	■
Content area	■	■
Writing lab	■	☐
Math lab	☐	☐

LD PROGRAM STAFF

Total number of LD Program staff (including director):

Full Time: 1 Part Time: 1

There is an advisor/advocate from the LD program available to students. 3 graduate students are available to work with LD students.

Key staff person available to work with LD students: Kathleen Haverly, Director of the Learning Center.

Midland Lutheran College

Fremont, NE

Address: 900 North Clarkson Street, Fremont, NE, 68025
Admissions telephone: 402 941-6501
Admissions FAX: 402 941-6513
Vice President for Enrollment Management:
Admissions e-mail: admissions@mlc.edu
Web site: http://www.mlc.edu
SAT Code: 6406 ACT Code: 2462

Director, Academic Support Services: Dr. Lori Moseman
LD program telephone: 402 941-6257
LD program e-mail: moseman@mlc.edu
Total campus enrollment: 955

GENERAL

Midland Lutheran College is a private, coed, four-year institution. 33-acre campus in Fremont (population: 25,174), 35 miles from Omaha. Airport, bus, and train serve Omaha. 4-1-4 system.

LD ADMISSIONS

A personal interview is recommended. Essay is not required.

SECONDARY SCHOOL REQUIREMENTS

Graduation from secondary school required; GED accepted.

TESTING

ACT recommended. SAT Subject recommended.

All enrolled freshmen (fall 2004):

Average SAT I Scores:	Verbal: 454	Math: 471
Average ACT Scores:	Composite: 22	

Child Study Team report is not required. Tests required as part of this documentation:

- [ ] WAIS-IV
- [ ] WISC-IV
- [ ] SATA
- [ ] Woodcock-Johnson
- [ ] Nelson-Denny Reading Test
- [ ] Other

UNDERGRADUATE STUDENT BODY

Total undergraduate student enrollment: 424 Men, 567 Women.

Composition of student body (fall 2004):

	Undergraduate	Freshmen
International	0.0	0.1
Black	1.6	2.7
American Indian	0.4	0.1
Asian-American	1.2	0.7
Hispanic	0.7	0.6
White	79.3	86.9
Unreported	16.8	8.9
	100.0%	100.0%

23% are from out of state. 49% of classes have fewer than 20 students, 49% have between 20 and 50 students, 2% have more than 50 students.

STUDENT HOUSING

94% of freshmen live in college housing. Freshmen are required to live on campus. Housing is guaranteed for all undergraduates. Campus can house 640 undergraduates.

EXPENSES

Tuition (2005-06): $18,140 per year.
Room: $2,070. Board: $2,630.
There is no additional cost for LD program/services.

LD SERVICES

LD program size is not limited.

LD services available to:

- [ ] Freshmen
- [ ] Sophomores
- [ ] Juniors
- [ ] Seniors

Academic Accommodations

Curriculum		In class	
Foreign language waiver	[ ]	Early syllabus	[ ]
Lighter course load	[ ]	Note takers in class	[x]
Math waiver	[ ]	Priority seating	[ ]
Other special classes	[ ]	Tape recorders	[x]
Priority registrations	[ ]	Videotaped classes	[x]
Substitution of courses	[ ]	Text on tape	[ ]
Exams		**Services**	
Extended time	[x]	Diagnostic tests	[x]
Oral exams	[x]	Learning centers	[x]
Take home exams	[ ]	Proofreaders	[ ]
Exams on tape or computer	[ ]	Readers	[x]
Untimed exams	[ ]	Reading Machines/Kurzweil	[ ]
Other accommodations	[ ]	Special bookstore section	[ ]
		Typists	[ ]

Credit toward degree is not given for remedial courses taken.

Counseling Services

- [ ] Academic
- [ ] Psychological
- [ ] Student Support groups
- [ ] Vocational

Tutoring

	Individual	Group
Time management	[ ]	[ ]
Organizational skills	[ ]	[ ]
Learning strategies	[ ]	[ ]
Study skills	[ ]	[ ]
Content area	[ ]	[ ]
Writing lab	[ ]	[ ]
Math lab	[ ]	[ ]

LD PROGRAM STAFF

Total number of LD Program staff (including director):

Full Time: 2 Part Time: 2

12 peer tutors are available to work with LD students.

Key staff person available to work with LD students: Dr. Lori Moseman, Director of Academic Support Services.

University of Nebraska, Kearney

Kearney, NE

Address: 905 West 25th Street, Kearney, NE, 68849
Admissions telephone: 800 KEARNEY
Admissions FAX: 308 865-8987
Interim Director of Admissions: Dusty Newton
Admissions e-mail: admissionsug@unk.edu
Web site: http://www.unk.edu
SAT Code: 6467 ACT Code: 2468

LD program telephone: 308 865-8248
Total campus enrollment: 5,380

GENERAL

University of Nebraska at Kearney is a public, coed, four-year institution. 235-acre campus in Kearney (population: 27,431), 180 miles from Omaha. Served by air, bus, and train. Public transportation serves campus. Semester system.

SECONDARY SCHOOL REQUIREMENTS

Graduation from secondary school required; GED accepted. The following course distribution required: 4 units of English, 3 units of math, 3 units of science, 2 units of foreign language, 3 units of social studies, 1 unit of academic electives.

TESTING

SAT Reasoning or ACT required. SAT Subject recommended.

All enrolled freshmen (fall 2004):

Average SAT I Scores:	Verbal: 444	Math: 534
Average ACT Scores:	Composite: 22	

Child Study Team report is not required. Tests required as part of this documentation:

- ❑ WAIS-IV
- ❑ WISC-IV
- ❑ SATA
- ❑ Woodcock-Johnson
- ❑ Nelson-Denny Reading Test
- ❑ Other

UNDERGRADUATE STUDENT BODY

Total undergraduate student enrollment: 2,532 Men, 3,273 Women.

Composition of student body (fall 2004):

	Undergraduate	Freshmen
International	8.5	6.8
Black	0.7	0.8
American Indian	0.2	0.2
Asian-American	0.8	0.7
Hispanic	3.3	2.8
White	80.9	83.4
Unreported	5.6	5.3
	100.0%	100.0%

9% are from out of state. 9% join a fraternity and 8% join a sorority. Average age of full-time undergraduates is 21. 34% of classes have fewer than 20 students, 60% have between 20 and 50 students, 6% have more than 50 students.

STUDENT HOUSING

83% of freshmen live in college housing. Freshmen are required to live on campus. Housing is guaranteed for all undergraduates. Campus can house 2,057 undergraduates. Single rooms are available for students with medical or special needs.

EXPENSES

Tuition (2005-06): $3,668 per year (in-state), $7,508 (out-of-state). Room: $2,752. Board: $2,574.

LD SERVICES

LD program size is not limited.

LD services available to:

■ Freshmen ■ Sophomores ■ Juniors ■ Seniors

Academic Accommodations

Curriculum		In class	
Foreign language waiver	❑	Early syllabus	❑
Lighter course load	❑	Note takers in class	❑
Math waiver	❑	Priority seating	❑
Other special classes	❑	Tape recorders	❑
Priority registrations	❑	Videotaped classes	❑
Substitution of courses	❑	Text on tape	❑
Exams		**Services**	
Extended time	❑	Diagnostic tests	❑
Oral exams	❑	Learning centers	❑
Take home exams	❑	Proofreaders	❑
Exams on tape or computer	❑	Readers	❑
Untimed exams	❑	Reading Machines/Kurzweil	❑
Other accommodations	❑	Special bookstore section	❑
		Typists	❑

Credit toward degree is not given for remedial courses taken.

Counseling Services

- ❑ Academic
- ❑ Psychological
- ❑ Student Support groups
- ❑ Vocational

Tutoring

	Individual	Group
Time management	❑	❑
Organizational skills	❑	❑
Learning strategies	❑	❑
Study skills	❑	❑
Content area	❑	❑
Writing lab	❑	❑
Math lab	❑	❑

University of Nebraska, Lincoln

Lincoln, NE

Address: 14th and R Streets, Lincoln, NE, 68588
Admissions telephone: 800 742-8800
Admissions FAX: 402 472-0670
Interim Director of Admissions: Alan Cerveny
Admissions e-mail: Admissions@unl.edu
Web site: http://www.unl.edu
SAT Code: 6877 ACT Code: 2482

LD program name: Services for Students with Disabilities
LD program address: 132 Canfield Administration Bldg.
Director: Veva Cheney
LD program telephone: 402 472-3787
LD program e-mail: vcheney2@unl.edu
LD program enrollment: 182, Total campus enrollment: 17,137

GENERAL

University of Nebraska, Lincoln is a public, coed, four-year institution. 628-acre campus in Lincoln (population: 225,581), 60 miles from Omaha. Served by air, bus, and train; major airport serves Omaha. School operates transportation between East Campus and City Campus and to remote parking lots. Public transportation serves campus. Semester system.

LD ADMISSIONS

Application Deadline: 05/01. Students do not complete a separate application and are not simultaneously accepted to the LD program. A member of the LD program does not sit on the admissions committee. A personal interview is not required. Essay is not required. There is an appeals process for students with disabilities who have been deferred admission. Those appeals are reviewed by the ADA Compliance Officer on an individual basis.

SECONDARY SCHOOL REQUIREMENTS

Graduation from secondary school required; GED accepted. The following course distribution required: 4 units of English, 4 units of math, 3 units of science, 2 units of foreign language, 3 units of social studies.

TESTING

ACT required of some applicants; SAT Reasoning may be substituted. SAT Subject recommended.

All enrolled freshmen (fall 2004):

Average SAT I Scores:	Verbal: 576	Math: 596
Average ACT Scores:	Composite: 25	

Child Study Team report is not required. A neuropsychological or comprehensive psycho-educational evaluation is required for admission. Tests required as part of this documentation:

- ■ WAIS-IV
- ■ WISC-IV
- ☐ SATA
- ■ Woodcock-Johnson
- ☐ Nelson-Denny Reading Test
- ■ Other

UNDERGRADUATE STUDENT BODY

Total undergraduate student enrollment: 9,518 Men, 8,467 Women.

Composition of student body (fall 2004):

	Undergraduate	Freshmen
International	1.6	2.8
Black	2.6	2.1
American Indian	0.6	0.5
Asian-American	2.3	2.5
Hispanic	2.9	2.3
White	86.8	85.9
Unreported	3.2	3.9
	100.0%	100.0%

14% are from out of state. 13% join a fraternity and 18% join a sorority. Average age of full-time undergraduates is 21. 34% of classes have fewer than 20 students, 52% have between 20 and 50 students, 14% have more than 50 students.

STUDENT HOUSING

77% of freshmen live in college housing. Freshmen are required to live on campus. Housing is guaranteed for all undergraduates. Limited number available Campus can house 5,592 undergraduates. Single rooms are available for students with medical or special needs. A medical note is required.

EXPENSES

Tuition (2005-06): $4,530 per year (in-state), $13,440 (out-of-state).
Room: $3,239. Board: $2,769.
There is no additional cost for LD program/services.

LD SERVICES

LD program size is not limited.

LD services available to:

■ Freshmen ■ Sophomores ■ Juniors ■ Seniors

Academic Accommodations

Curriculum		**In class**	
Foreign language waiver	☐	Early syllabus	☐
Lighter course load	■	Note takers in class	■
Math waiver	☐	Priority seating	■
Other special classes	☐	Tape recorders	■
Priority registrations	■	Videotaped classes	☐
Substitution of courses	■	Text on tape	■
Exams		**Services**	
Extended time	■	Diagnostic tests	☐
Oral exams	■	Learning centers	☐
Take home exams	☐	Proofreaders	☐
Exams on tape or computer	■	Readers	■
Untimed exams	☐	Reading Machines/Kurzweil	■
Other accommodations	■	Special bookstore section	☐
		Typists	■

Credit toward degree is not given for remedial courses taken.

Counseling Services

- ■ Academic
- ■ Psychological
- ☐ Student Support groups
- ■ Vocational

Tutoring

Individual tutoring is not available.

	Individual	Group
Time management	■	■
Organizational skills	■	■
Learning strategies	■	■
Study skills	■	■
Content area	■	☐
Writing lab	☐	■
Math lab	☐	■

LD PROGRAM STAFF

Total number of LD Program staff (including director):

Full Time: 4 Part Time: 4

There is an advisor/advocate from the LD program available to students.

Key staff person available to work with LD students: Veva Cheney, Director.

LD Program web site: http://www.unl.edu/ssd/

University of Nebraska, Medical Center

Omaha, NE

Address: 984265 Nebraska Medical Center, Omaha, NE, 68198-4265
Admissions telephone: 800 626-8431
Admissions FAX: 402 559-6796
Director of Admissions and Records: Tymaree Q Tonjes
SAT Code: 6896 ACT Code: 2487

LD program name: Student Disability Services
Coordinator, Student Disability Services: Ronda Stevens
LD program telephone: 402 559-5553
LD program e-mail: rstevens@unmc.edu
Total campus enrollment: 779

GENERAL

University of Nebraska Medical Center is a public, coed, Upper-division institution. Urban campus in Omaha (population: 390,007). Served by air, bus, and train. Semester system.

LD ADMISSIONS

Students do not complete a separate application and are not simultaneously accepted to the LD program. A personal interview is recommended. Essay is not required.

TESTING

Child Study Team report is not required. A neuropsychological or comprehensive psycho-educational evaluation is required for admission. Tests required as part of this documentation:

- [x] WAIS-IV
- [x] WISC-IV
- [x] SATA
- [x] Woodcock-Johnson
- [x] Nelson-Denny Reading Test
- [ ] Other

UNDERGRADUATE STUDENT BODY

Total undergraduate student enrollment: 779.

Composition of student body (fall 2004):

	Freshmen
International	1.3
Black	1.8
American Indian	0.3
Asian-American	0.8
Hispanic	2.3
White	93.1
Unreported	0.4
	100.0%

Average age of full-time undergraduates is 23.

STUDENT HOUSING

Freshmen are not required to live on campus. Housing is guaranteed for all undergraduates. Campus can house 212 undergraduates. Single rooms are not available for students with medical or special needs.

EXPENSES

There is no additional cost for LD program/services.

LD SERVICES

LD program size is limited.

LD services available to:

- [x] Freshmen
- [x] Sophomores
- [x] Juniors
- [x] Seniors

Academic Accommodations

Curriculum

- [ ] Foreign language waiver
- [x] Lighter course load
- [ ] Math waiver
- [ ] Other special classes
- [ ] Priority registrations
- [ ] Substitution of courses

Exams

- [x] Extended time
- [ ] Oral exams
- [ ] Take home exams
- [ ] Exams on tape or computer
- [ ] Untimed exams
- [ ] Other accommodations

In class

- [ ] Early syllabus
- [ ] Note takers in class
- [x] Priority seating
- [x] Tape recorders
- [ ] Videotaped classes
- [x] Text on tape

Services

- [ ] Diagnostic tests
- [ ] Learning centers
- [ ] Proofreaders
- [ ] Readers
- [ ] Reading Machines/Kurzweil
- [ ] Special bookstore section
- [ ] Typists

Credit toward degree is given for remedial courses taken.

Counseling Services

- [x] Academic
- [x] Psychological
- [ ] Student Support groups
- [ ] Vocational

Tutoring

Individual tutoring is available weekly.

	Individual	Group
Time management	[x]	[ ]
Organizational skills	[x]	[ ]
Learning strategies	[x]	[ ]
Study skills	[x]	[ ]
Content area	[x]	[ ]
Writing lab	[ ]	[ ]
Math lab	[ ]	[ ]

LD PROGRAM STAFF

There is an advisor/advocate from the LD program available to students.

Key staff person available to work with LD students: Ronda Stevens, Coordinator, Student Disability Services.

University of Nebraska, Omaha

Omaha, NE

Address: 6001 Dodge Street, Omaha, NE, 68182
Admissions telephone: 800 858-8648 (Nebraska and Iowa)
Admissions FAX: 402 554-3472
Director of Admissions: Wade Robinson
Admissions e-mail: unoadm@unomaha.edu
Web site: http://www.unomaha.edu
SAT Code: 6420 ACT Code: 2464

Disability Services Coordinator: Kate Clark
LD program telephone: 402 554-2872
LD program e-mail: mkclark@mail.unomaha.edu
LD program enrollment: 150, Total campus enrollment: 11,041

GENERAL

University of Nebraska, Omaha is a public, coed, four-year institution. 158-acre main campus and 70-acre College of Information Systems and Technology campus in Omaha (population: 390,007). Served by air, bus, and train. School operates transportation to campus parking lots, dormitories, and information systems/technology building. Public transportation serves campus. Semester system.

LD ADMISSIONS

Students do not complete a separate application and are not simultaneously accepted to the LD program. A member of the LD program does not sit on the admissions committee. A personal interview is not required. Essay is not required. Requirements are not waived but course substitutions may be available.

SECONDARY SCHOOL REQUIREMENTS

Graduation from secondary school required; GED accepted. The following course distribution required: 4 units of English, 3 units of math, 3 units of science, 2 units of foreign language, 1 unit of social studies, 2 units of history, 1 unit of academic electives.

TESTING

ACT required; SAT Reasoning may be substituted. SAT Subject recommended.

All enrolled freshmen (fall 2004):

Average SAT I Scores:	Verbal: 542	Math: 538
Average ACT Scores:	Composite: 22	

Child Study Team report is not required. A neuropsychological or comprehensive psycho-educational evaluation is required for admission. Must be dated within 12 months of application. Tests required as part of this documentation:

☐ WAIS-IV ☐ Woodcock-Johnson
☐ WISC-IV ☐ Nelson-Denny Reading Test
☐ SATA ■ Other

UNDERGRADUATE STUDENT BODY

Total undergraduate student enrollment: 5,160 Men, 5,978 Women.

Composition of student body (fall 2004):

	Undergraduate	Freshmen
International	0.5	2.4
Black	4.1	5.4
American Indian	0.7	0.5
Asian-American	2.4	2.7
Hispanic	3.9	3.2
White	86.3	82.5
Unreported	2.1	3.3
	100.0%	100.0%

8% are from out of state. 5% join a fraternity and 4% join a sorority. Average age of full-time undergraduates is 21. 35% of classes have fewer than 20 students, 51% have between 20 and 50 students, 14% have more than 50 students.

STUDENT HOUSING

27% of freshmen live in college housing. Freshmen are not required to live on campus. Housing is guaranteed for all undergraduates. Campus can house 1,212 undergraduates. Single rooms are not available for students with medical or special needs.

EXPENSES

Tuition (2005-06): $4,133 per year (in-state), $12,180 (out-of-state).
Room: $3,570. Board: $2,390.
There is no additional cost for LD program/services.

LD SERVICES

LD program size is not limited.

LD services available to:

■ Freshmen ■ Sophomores ■ Juniors ■ Seniors

Academic Accommodations

Curriculum		**In class**	
Foreign language waiver	☐	Early syllabus	☐
Lighter course load	☐	Note takers in class	■
Math waiver	☐	Priority seating	■
Other special classes	■	Tape recorders	■
Priority registrations	■	Videotaped classes	■
Substitution of courses	■	Text on tape	■
Exams		**Services**	
Extended time	■	Diagnostic tests	☐
Oral exams	■	Learning centers	☐
Take home exams	☐	Proofreaders	☐
Exams on tape or computer	☐	Readers	■
Untimed exams	☐	Reading Machines/Kurzweil	■
Other accommodations	☐	Special bookstore section	☐
		Typists	■

Credit toward degree is not given for remedial courses taken.

Counseling Services

■ Academic — Meets 2 times per academic year
☐ Psychological
☐ Student Support groups
☐ Vocational

Tutoring

Individual tutoring is available weekly.

	Individual	Group
Time management	☐	☐
Organizational skills	☐	☐
Learning strategies	☐	☐
Study skills	☐	☐
Content area	☐	☐
Writing lab	■	■
Math lab	☐	☐

LD PROGRAM STAFF

Total number of LD Program staff (including director):

Full Time: 1 Part Time: 1

There is an advisor/advocate from the LD program available to students.

Key staff person available to work with LD students: Kate Clark, Disability Services Coordinator.

Nebraska Methodist College

Omaha, NE

Address: 8501 West Dodge Road, Omaha, NE, 68114
Admissions telephone: 800 335-5510
Admissions FAX: 402 354-8875
Director of Admissions: Deann Sterner
SAT Code: 6510 ACT Code: 2465

LD program name: Student Developmental Services
Dean of Students: Gina Toman
LD program telephone: 402 354-4977
LD program e-mail: Gina.Toman@methodistcollege.edu
LD program enrollment: 1, Total campus enrollment: 477

GENERAL

Nebraska Methodist College is a private, coed, four-year institution. Five-acre, urban campus in Omaha (population: 390,007); branch campuses in central Omaha and in Council Bluffs, Iowa. Served by air, bus, and train. Public transportation serves campus. Semester system.

LD ADMISSIONS

Students do not complete a separate application and are not simultaneously accepted to the LD program. A member of the LD program does not sit on the admissions committee. A personal interview is required. Essay is required and may be typed.

SECONDARY SCHOOL REQUIREMENTS

Graduation from secondary school required; GED accepted. The following course distribution required: 4 units of English, 2 units of math, 2 units of science, 2 units of social studies.

TESTING

Child Study Team report is not required. A neuropsychological or comprehensive psycho-education evaluation is not required for admission. Tests required as part of this documentation:

- [ ] WAIS-IV
- [ ] WISC-IV
- [ ] SATA
- [ ] Woodcock-Johnson
- [ ] Nelson-Denny Reading Test
- [ ] Other

UNDERGRADUATE STUDENT BODY

Total undergraduate student enrollment: 36 Men, 311 Women.

Composition of student body (fall 2004):

	Undergraduate
International	0.0
Black	66.7
American Indian	0.0
Asian-American	0.0
Hispanic	33.3
White	0.0
Unreported	0.0
	100.0%

20% are from out of state. 5% join a sorority. Average age of full-time undergraduates is 25. 1% of classes have fewer than 20 students.

STUDENT HOUSING

Freshmen are not required to live on campus. Housing is not guaranteed for all undergraduates. Limited capacity. Campus can house 80 undergraduates. Single rooms are available for students with medical or special needs. A medical note is required.

EXPENSES

There is no additional cost for LD program/services.

LD SERVICES

LD program size is not limited.

LD services available to:

- [x] Freshmen
- [x] Sophomores
- [x] Juniors
- [x] Seniors

Academic Accommodations

Curriculum		In class	
Foreign language waiver	[ ]	Early syllabus	[ ]
Lighter course load	[ ]	Note takers in class	[ ]
Math waiver	[ ]	Priority seating	[x]
Other special classes	[ ]	Tape recorders	[x]
Priority registrations	[ ]	Videotaped classes	[x]
Substitution of courses	[ ]	Text on tape	[x]
Exams		**Services**	
Extended time	[x]	Diagnostic tests	[ ]
Oral exams	[x]	Learning centers	[x]
Take home exams	[x]	Proofreaders	[x]
Exams on tape or computer	[x]	Readers	[x]
Untimed exams	[x]	Reading Machines/Kurzweil	[ ]
Other accommodations	[x]	Special bookstore section	[ ]
		Typists	[ ]

Credit toward degree is not given for remedial courses taken.

Counseling Services

- [ ] Academic
- [ ] Psychological
- [ ] Student Support groups
- [ ] Vocational

Tutoring

Individual tutoring is available weekly.

Average size of tutoring groups: 1

	Individual	Group
Time management	[x]	[x]
Organizational skills	[x]	[x]
Learning strategies	[x]	[x]
Study skills	[x]	[x]
Content area	[x]	[x]
Writing lab	[x]	[x]
Math lab	[x]	[x]

LD PROGRAM STAFF

Total number of LD Program staff (including director):

Full Time: 3 Part Time: 3

There is an advisor/advocate from the LD program available to students. The advisor/advocate meets with faculty 4 times per month and students 5 times per month. 5 peer tutors are available to work with LD students.

Key staff person available to work with LD students: Carol Moore, Academic Skills Specialist.

Nebraska Wesleyan University

Lincoln, NE

Address: 5000 St. Paul Avenue, Lincoln, NE, 68504-2794
Admissions telephone: 800 541-3818
Admissions FAX: 402 465-2179
VP Enrollment & Marketing: Patricia F. Karthauser
Admissions e-mail: admissions@nebrwesleyan.edu
Web site: http://www.nebrwesleyan.edu
SAT Code: 6470 ACT Code: 2474

VP Enrollment & Marketing: Patricia F. Karthauser
LD program telephone: 402 465-2218
LD program e-mail: pkart@nebrwesleyan.edu
Total campus enrollment: 1,797

GENERAL

Nebraska Wesleyan University is a private, coed, four-year institution. 50-acre, suburban campus in Lincoln (population: 225,581). Served by air, bus, and train; major airport serves Omaha (50 miles). Public transportation serves campus. Semester system.

LD ADMISSIONS

A personal interview is not required. Essay is not required.

SECONDARY SCHOOL REQUIREMENTS

Graduation from secondary school required; GED accepted.

TESTING

SAT Reasoning or ACT required. SAT Subject recommended.

All enrolled freshmen (fall 2004):

Average ACT Scores: Composite: 24

Child Study Team report is not required. Tests required as part of this documentation:

- ☐ WAIS-IV
- ☐ WISC-IV
- ☐ SATA
- ☐ Woodcock-Johnson
- ☐ Nelson-Denny Reading Test
- ☐ Other

UNDERGRADUATE STUDENT BODY

Total undergraduate student enrollment: 698 Men, 923 Women.

Composition of student body (fall 2004):

	Undergraduate	Freshmen
International	0.0	0.6
Black	0.5	1.2
American Indian	0.7	0.3
Asian-American	1.6	1.4
Hispanic	1.9	1.6
White	94.8	94.1
Unreported	0.5	0.8
	100.0%	100.0%

6% are from out of state. 11% join a fraternity and 12% join a sorority. Average age of full-time undergraduates is 20. 55% of classes have fewer than 20 students, 42% have between 20 and 50 students, 3% have more than 50 students.

STUDENT HOUSING

87% of freshmen live in college housing. Freshmen are required to live on campus. Housing is not guaranteed for all undergraduates. Campus can house 988 undergraduates.

EXPENSES

Tuition (2005-06): $18,100 per year.
Room & Board: $5,015
There is no additional cost for LD program/services.

LD SERVICES

LD program size is not limited.

LD services available to:

☐ Freshmen ☐ Sophomores ☐ Juniors ☐ Seniors

Academic Accommodations

Curriculum		**In class**	
Foreign language waiver	☐	Early syllabus	☐
Lighter course load	☐	Note takers in class	■
Math waiver	☐	Priority seating	☐
Other special classes	☐	Tape recorders	■
Priority registrations	☐	Videotaped classes	■
Substitution of courses	☐	Text on tape	☐
Exams		**Services**	
Extended time	■	Diagnostic tests	☐
Oral exams	■	Learning centers	☐
Take home exams	☐	Proofreaders	☐
Exams on tape or computer	☐	Readers	■
Untimed exams	■	Reading Machines/Kurzweil	☐
Other accommodations	☐	Special bookstore section	☐
		Typists	☐

Counseling Services

- ☐ Academic
- ☐ Psychological
- ☐ Student Support groups
- ☐ Vocational

Tutoring

	Individual	Group
Time management	☐	☐
Organizational skills	☐	☐
Learning strategies	☐	☐
Study skills	☐	☐
Content area	☐	☐
Writing lab	☐	☐
Math lab	☐	☐

LD PROGRAM STAFF

Key staff person available to work with LD students: Gretchen Naugle, Coordinator for Students with Disabilities.

Peru State College

Peru, NE

Address: P.O. Box 10, Peru, NE, 68421-0010
Admissions telephone: 800 742-4412
Admissions FAX: 402 872-2296
Director of Enrollment Management: Janelle Moran
Admissions e-mail: Admissions@oakmail.peru.edu
Web site: http://www.peru.edu
SAT Code: 6468 ACT Code: 2470

Interim Director Student Support Services: Marie Meland
LD program telephone: 402 872-2440
LD program e-mail: mmeland@oakmail.peru.edu
LD program enrollment: 20, Total campus enrollment: 1,493

GENERAL

Peru State College is a public, coed, four-year institution. 103-acre campus in Peru (population: 1,569), 60 miles from Omaha; branch campuses in Beatrice, Falls City, Lincoln, Milford, Nebraska City, Omaha, and Ralston and at Offutt Air Force Base. Major airport and train serve Omaha; bus serves Auburn (13 miles). Semester system.

LD ADMISSIONS

Students do not complete a separate application and are not simultaneously accepted to the LD program. A personal interview is recommended. Essay is not required. We are an open enrollment institution.

SECONDARY SCHOOL REQUIREMENTS

Graduation from secondary school required; GED accepted.

TESTING

ACT recommended; SAT Reasoning may be substituted.

All enrolled freshmen (fall 2004):

Average ACT Scores: Composite:19

Child Study Team report is not required. A neuropsychological or comprehensive psycho-education evaluation is not required for admission. Tests required as part of this documentation:

- ☐ WAIS-IV
- ☐ WISC-IV
- ☐ SATA
- ☐ Woodcock-Johnson
- ☐ Nelson-Denny Reading Test
- ☐ Other

UNDERGRADUATE STUDENT BODY

Total undergraduate student enrollment: 658 Men, 796 Women.

Composition of student body (fall 2004):

	Undergraduate	Freshmen
International	2.3	0.9
Black	5.0	4.1
American Indian	0.5	0.5
Asian-American	0.0	0.0
Hispanic	1.4	1.9
White	87.2	86.5
Unreported	3.6	6.1
	100.0%	100.0%

11% are from out of state. Average age of full-time undergraduates is 25. 55% of classes have fewer than 20 students, 42% have between 20 and 50 students, 3% have more than 50 students.

STUDENT HOUSING

75% of freshmen live in college housing. Freshmen are required to live on campus. Housing is guaranteed for all undergraduates. Campus can house 546 undergraduates. Single rooms are available for students with medical or special needs.

EXPENSES

Tuition (2005-06): $2,933 per year (in-state), $5,865 (out-of-state).
Room & Board: $4,676.
There is no additional cost for LD program/services.

LD SERVICES

LD program size is not limited.

LD services available to:

☑ Freshmen ☑ Sophomores ☑ Juniors ☐ Seniors

Academic Accommodations

Curriculum		**In class**	
Foreign language waiver	☐	Early syllabus	☐
Lighter course load	☐	Note takers in class	☑
Math waiver	☐	Priority seating	☑
Other special classes	☐	Tape recorders	☑
Priority registrations	☐	Videotaped classes	☑
Substitution of courses	☐	Text on tape	☑
Exams		**Services**	
Extended time	☑	Diagnostic tests	☐
Oral exams	☑	Learning centers	☑
Take home exams	☐	Proofreaders	☐
Exams on tape or computer	☐	Readers	☑
Untimed exams	☐	Reading Machines/Kurzweil	☐
Other accommodations	☑	Special bookstore section	☐
		Typists	☑

Credit toward degree is not given for remedial courses taken.

Counseling Services

- ☑ Academic
- ☐ Psychological
- ☑ Student Support groups
- ☐ Vocational

Tutoring

Individual tutoring is available daily.

	Individual	Group
Time management	☑	☐
Organizational skills	☑	☐
Learning strategies	☐	☐
Study skills	☑	☐
Content area	☑	☐
Writing lab	☑	☐
Math lab	☑	☐

UNIQUE LD PROGRAM FEATURES

Many of our services are available on an as-needed basis so limits are not applicable.

LD PROGRAM STAFF

Total number of LD Program staff (including director):

Full Time: 3 Part Time: 3

There is an advisor/advocate from the LD program available to students.

Key staff person available to work with LD students: Marie Meland, Interim Director Student Support Services.

College of Saint Mary

Omaha, NE

Address: 1901 S. 72nd Street, Omaha, NE, 68124-2377
Admissions telephone: 800 926-5534
Admissions FAX: 402 399-2412
Vice President for Enrollment and Student Services: Lori Werth
Admissions e-mail: enroll@csm.edu
Web site: http://www.csm.edu
SAT Code: 6106 ACT Code: 2440

LD program name: Achievement Center
Learning Support Specialist: Mary Schlueter
LD program telephone: 402 399-2634
LD program e-mail: mschlueter@csm.edu
Total campus enrollment: 969

GENERAL

College of Saint Mary is a private, women's, four-year institution. 25-acre, urban campus in Omaha (population: 390,007); branch campus located in Lincoln. Served by air, bus, and train. Public transportation serves campus. Semester system.

LD ADMISSIONS

Students do not complete a separate application and are not simultaneously accepted to the LD program. A member of the LD program does not sit on the admissions committee. A personal interview is recommended. Essay is not required. All admission requirements are subject to waiver or revision as appropriate in a case-by-case review.

SECONDARY SCHOOL REQUIREMENTS

Graduation from secondary school required; GED accepted.

TESTING

All enrolled freshmen (fall 2004):

Average ACT Scores: Composite: 21

Child Study Team report is not required. A neuropsychological or comprehensive psycho-education evaluation is not required for admission. Tests required as part of this documentation:

- ☐ WAIS-IV
- ☐ WISC-IV
- ☐ SATA
- ☐ Woodcock-Johnson
- ☐ Nelson-Denny Reading Test
- ☐ Other

UNDERGRADUATE STUDENT BODY

Total undergraduate student enrollment: 19 Men, 911 Women.

Composition of student body (fall 2004):

	Undergraduate	Freshmen
International	0.0	1.1
Black	6.9	6.2
American Indian	0.0	0.7
Asian-American	0.0	1.1
Hispanic	12.9	5.3
White	80.2	85.6
Unreported	0.0	0.0
	100.0%	100.0%

12% are from out of state. Average age of full-time undergraduates is 26. 76% of classes have fewer than 20 students, 23% have between 20 and 50 students, 1% have more than 50 students.

STUDENT HOUSING

51% of freshmen live in college housing. Freshmen are required to live on campus. Housing is guaranteed for all undergraduates. Campus can house 274 undergraduates. Single rooms are available for students with medical or special needs. A medical note is required.

EXPENSES

Tuition (2005-06): $17,750 per year.
Room: $2,950. Board: $2,950.

There is no additional cost for LD program/services.

LD SERVICES

LD program size is not limited.

LD services available to:

■ Freshmen ■ Sophomores ■ Juniors ■ Seniors

Academic Accommodations

Curriculum		In class	
Foreign language waiver	☐	Early syllabus	☐
Lighter course load	■	Note takers in class	■
Math waiver	☐	Priority seating	☐
Other special classes	☐	Tape recorders	■
Priority registrations	☐	Videotaped classes	☐
Substitution of courses	☐	Text on tape	☐
Exams		**Services**	
Extended time	■	Diagnostic tests	■
Oral exams	■	Learning centers	■
Take home exams	☐	Proofreaders	■
Exams on tape or computer	☐	Readers	■
Untimed exams	☐	Reading Machines/Kurzweil	☐
Other accommodations	■	Special bookstore section	☐
		Typists	☐

Credit toward degree is not given for remedial courses taken.

Counseling Services

- ☐ Academic
- ☐ Psychological
- ☐ Student Support groups
- ☐ Vocational

Tutoring

Individual tutoring is available weekly.

Average size of tutoring groups: 3

	Individual	Group
Time management	■	■
Organizational skills	■	■
Learning strategies	■	■
Study skills	■	■
Content area	■	■
Writing lab	☐	☐
Math lab	☐	☐

LD PROGRAM STAFF

There is an advisor/advocate from the LD program available to students. 8 peer tutors are available to work with LD students.

Key staff person available to work with LD students: Mary Schlueter, Learning Support Specialist.

LD Program web site: http://www.csm.edu

Union College

Lincoln, NE

Address: 3800 S. 48th Street, Lincoln, NE, 68506
Admissions telephone: 800 228-4600
Admissions FAX: 402 486-2566
Vice President of Enrollment Services: Rob Weaver
Admissions e-mail: ucenroll@ucollege.edu
Web site: http://www.ucollege.edu
SAT Code: 6865   ACT Code: 2480

LD program name: Teaching Learning Center
Director of TLC: Debbie Forshee-Sweeney
LD program telephone: 402 486-2600, extension 2080
LD program e-mail: deforshe@ucollege.edu
LD program enrollment: 43, Total campus enrollment: 912

GENERAL

Union College is a private, coed, four-year institution. 26-acre campus in Lincoln (population: 225,581). Served by air, bus, and train; airport also serves Omaha (55 miles). Public transportation serves campus. Semester system.

LD ADMISSIONS

Students complete a separate application and are not simultaneously accepted to the LD program. A member of the LD program does not sit on the admissions committee. A personal interview is required. Essay is not required.

For fall 2004, 43 completed self-identified LD applications were received.

SECONDARY SCHOOL REQUIREMENTS

Graduation from secondary school required; GED accepted. The following course distribution required: 3 units of English, 2 units of math, 2 units of science, 1 unit of social studies, 1 unit of history, 3 units of academic electives.

TESTING

ACT required.

All enrolled freshmen (fall 2004):

Average ACT Scores: Composite: 22

Child Study Team report is not required. A neuropsychological or comprehensive psycho-educational evaluation is required for admission. Must be dated within 36 months of application. Tests required as part of this documentation:

- ■ WAIS-IV
- ☐ WISC-IV
- ☐ SATA
- ■ Woodcock-Johnson
- ☐ Nelson-Denny Reading Test
- ☐ Other

UNDERGRADUATE STUDENT BODY

Total undergraduate student enrollment: 430 Men, 492 Women.

Composition of student body (fall 2004):

	Undergraduate	Freshmen
International	2.4	15.1
Black	0.0	3.2
American Indian	1.2	1.3
Asian-American	3.7	1.6
Hispanic	9.8	6.7
White	78.0	59.0
Unreported	4.9	13.1
	100.0%	100.0%

77% are from out of state. Average age of full-time undergraduates is 22. 70% of classes have fewer than 20 students, 26% have between 20 and 50 students, 4% have more than 50 students.

STUDENT HOUSING

89% of freshmen live in college housing. Freshmen are required to live on campus. Housing is not guaranteed for all undergraduates. Campus can house 22 undergraduates. Single rooms are available for students with medical or special needs. A medical note is required.

EXPENSES

Tuition (2005-06): $13,990 per year.
Room: $2,680. Board: $1,270.
Additional cost for LD program/services: $575 per semester.

LD SERVICES

LD program size is not limited.

LD services available to:

■ Freshmen   ■ Sophomores   ■ Juniors   ■ Seniors

Academic Accommodations

Curriculum		**In class**	
Foreign language waiver	☐	Early syllabus	☐
Lighter course load	■	Note takers in class	■
Math waiver	☐	Priority seating	☐
Other special classes	☐	Tape recorders	■
Priority registrations	☐	Videotaped classes	■
Substitution of courses	☐	Text on tape	■
Exams		**Services**	
Extended time	■	Diagnostic tests	■
Oral exams	■	Learning centers	■
Take home exams	☐	Proofreaders	☐
Exams on tape or computer	■	Readers	■
Untimed exams	■	Reading Machines/Kurzweil	■
Other accommodations	■	Special bookstore section	☐
		Typists	■

Credit toward degree is not given for remedial courses taken.

Counseling Services

- ■ Academic — Meets 72 times per academic year
- ☐ Psychological
- ☐ Student Support groups
- ☐ Vocational

Tutoring

Individual tutoring is available weekly.

Average size of tutoring groups: 1

	Individual	Group
Time management	■	☐
Organizational skills	■	☐
Learning strategies	■	☐
Study skills	■	☐
Content area	■	☐
Writing lab	■	☐
Math lab	■	☐

LD PROGRAM STAFF

Total number of LD Program staff (including director):

Full Time: 3   Part Time: 3

There is an advisor/advocate from the LD program available to students. The advisor/advocate meets with students 8 times per month.

Key staff person available to work with LD students: Debbie Forshee-Sweeney, Director of TLC.

Wayne State College

Wayne, NE

Address: 1111 Main Street, Wayne, NE, 68787
Admissions telephone: 800 228-9972
Admissions FAX: 402 375-7204
Director of Admissions: R. Lincoln Morris
Admissions e-mail: admit1@wsc.edu
Web site: http://www.wsc.edu
SAT Code: 6469 ACT Code: 2472

Assistant Dean for Student Life: Dr. Jeff B. Carstens
LD program telephone: 402 375-7213
LD program e-mail: jecarst1@wsc.edu
Total campus enrollment: 2,750

GENERAL

Wayne State College is a public, coed, four-year institution. 128-acre campus in Wayne (population: 5,583), 45 miles from Sioux City and 100 miles from Omaha. Served by bus; major airport and train serve Omaha; smaller airport serves Sioux City. Semester system.

LD ADMISSIONS

A personal interview is not required. Essay is not required.

SECONDARY SCHOOL REQUIREMENTS

Graduation from secondary school required; GED accepted.

TESTING

All enrolled freshmen (fall 2004):

Average ACT Scores: Composite: 21

Child Study Team report is not required. Tests required as part of this documentation:

☐ WAIS-IV	☐ Woodcock-Johnson
☐ WISC-IV	☐ Nelson-Denny Reading Test
☐ SATA	☐ Other

UNDERGRADUATE STUDENT BODY

Total undergraduate student enrollment: 1,183 Men, 1,652 Women.

Composition of student body (fall 2004):

	Undergraduate	Freshmen
International	0.0	0.5
Black	4.6	3.2
American Indian	1.8	1.1
Asian-American	0.2	0.5
Hispanic	1.4	2.6
White	89.2	88.6
Unreported	2.8	3.5
	100.0%	100.0%

14% are from out of state. Average age of full-time undergraduates is 21. 43% of classes have fewer than 20 students, 55% have between 20 and 50 students, 2% have more than 50 students.

STUDENT HOUSING

90% of freshmen live in college housing. Freshmen are required to live on campus. Housing is guaranteed for all undergraduates. Campus can house 1,587 undergraduates.

EXPENSES

Tuition 2004-05: $2,850 per year (in-state), $5,700 (out-of-state).

Room: $2,000. Board: $2,120.

There is no additional cost for LD program/services.

LD SERVICES

LD services available to:

■ Freshmen ■ Sophomores ■ Juniors ■ Seniors

Academic Accommodations

Curriculum		In class	
Foreign language waiver	☐	Early syllabus	☐
Lighter course load	☐	Note takers in class	■
Math waiver	☐	Priority seating	☐
Other special classes	☐	Tape recorders	■
Priority registrations	☐	Videotaped classes	☐
Substitution of courses	☐	Text on tape	☐
Exams		**Services**	
Extended time	■	Diagnostic tests	■
Oral exams	☐	Learning centers	■
Take home exams	☐	Proofreaders	☐
Exams on tape or computer	☐	Readers	■
Untimed exams	☐	Reading Machines/Kurzweil	■
Other accommodations	☐	Special bookstore section	☐
		Typists	☐

Credit toward degree is not given for remedial courses taken.

Counseling Services

■ Academic
■ Psychological
☐ Student Support groups
☐ Vocational

Tutoring

Individual tutoring is available daily.

	Individual	Group
Time management	■	■
Organizational skills	■	■
Learning strategies	■	■
Study skills	■	■
Content area	■	☐
Writing lab	■	☐
Math lab	■	☐

UNIQUE LD PROGRAM FEATURES

Wayne State College faculty and staff provide a high level of individual assistance and support to all students. Students with LD thrive in the smaller, nurturing environment of the college.

LD PROGRAM STAFF

Total number of LD Program staff (including director):

Full Time: 1 Part Time: 1

Key staff person available to work with LD students: Dr. Jeff B. Carstens, Assistant Dean for Student Life.

York College

York, NE

Address: 1125 East Eighth Street, York, NE, 68467
Admissions telephone: 800 950-9675
Admissions FAX: 402 363-5623
Vice President of Enrollment Management: Tod Martin
Admissions e-mail: enroll@york.edu
Web site: http://www.york.edu
SAT Code: 6984 ACT Code: 2484

Director of Tutoring Center: Glenda McEuen
LD program telephone: 402 363-5702
LD program e-mail: gdmceuen@york.edu
LD program enrollment: 7, Total campus enrollment: 443

GENERAL

York College is a private, coed, four-year institution. 45-acre campus in York (population: 8,081), 45 miles from Lincoln. Airport, bus, and train serve Lincoln. Semester system.

LD ADMISSIONS

Students do not complete a separate application and are not simultaneously accepted to the LD program. A member of the LD program does not sit on the admissions committee. A personal interview is recommended. Essay is not required.

SECONDARY SCHOOL REQUIREMENTS

Graduation from secondary school required; GED accepted. The following course distribution required: 3 units of English, 2 units of math, 2 units of science, 1 unit of social studies, 1 unit of history.

TESTING

SAT Reasoning considered if submitted. ACT recommended. SAT Subject recommended.

All enrolled freshmen (fall 2004):

Average SAT I Scores:	Verbal: 499	Math: 509
Average ACT Scores:	Composite: 22	

Child Study Team report is not required. A neuropsychological or comprehensive psycho-educational evaluation is required for admission. Must be dated within 36 months of application. Tests required as part of this documentation:

- ☑ WAIS-IV
- ☐ WISC-IV
- ☑ SATA
- ☑ Woodcock-Johnson
- ☑ Nelson-Denny Reading Test
- ☑ Other

UNDERGRADUATE STUDENT BODY

Total undergraduate student enrollment: 194 Men, 261 Women.

Composition of student body (fall 2004):

	Undergraduate	Freshmen
International	2.8	0.0
Black	1.9	3.8
American Indian	0.0	0.6
Asian-American	1.9	2.7
Hispanic	0.8	3.6
White	88.0	86.6
Unreported	4.6	2.7
	100.0%	100.0%

65% are from out of state. 60% join a fraternity and 66% join a sorority. Average age of full-time undergraduates is 20. 81% of classes have fewer than 20 students, 18% have between 20 and 50 students, 1% have more than 50 students.

STUDENT HOUSING

94% of freshmen live in college housing. Freshmen are required to live on campus. Housing is guaranteed for all undergraduates. Campus can house 420 undergraduates.

EXPENSES

Tuition (2005-06): $11,400 per year.
Room & Board: $3,900.
There is no additional cost for LD program/services.

LD SERVICES

LD program size is not limited.

LD services available to:

☑ Freshmen ☑ Sophomores ☑ Juniors ☑ Seniors

Academic Accommodations

Curriculum		**In class**	
Foreign language waiver	☑	Early syllabus	☑
Lighter course load	☑	Note takers in class	☑
Math waiver	☐	Priority seating	☑
Other special classes	☐	Tape recorders	☑
Priority registrations	☐	Videotaped classes	☐
Substitution of courses	☐	Text on tape	☑
Exams		**Services**	
Extended time	☑	Diagnostic tests	☑
Oral exams	☑	Learning centers	☑
Take home exams	☐	Proofreaders	☑
Exams on tape or computer	☑	Readers	☑
Untimed exams	☑	Reading Machines/Kurzweil	☐
Other accommodations	☑	Special bookstore section	☐
		Typists	☐

Credit toward degree is not given for remedial courses taken.

Counseling Services

- ☑ Academic
- ☑ Psychological
- ☐ Student Support groups
- ☐ Vocational

Tutoring

Individual tutoring is available.

Average size of tutoring groups: 1

	Individual	Group
Time management	☑	☐
Organizational skills	☑	☐
Learning strategies	☑	☐
Study skills	☑	☐
Content area	☐	☐
Writing lab	☐	☐
Math lab	☐	☐

LD PROGRAM STAFF

There is an advisor/advocate from the LD program available to students. 8 peer tutors are available to work with LD students.

Key staff person available to work with LD students: Glenda McEuen, Counselor for Special Populations.

University of Nevada - Las Vegas

Las Vegas, NV

Address: 4505 Maryland Parkway, Las Vegas, NV, 89154
Admissions telephone: 702 895-3443
Admissions FAX: 702 895-1118
Associate Director of Admissions: Pam Hicks
Admissions e-mail: gounlv@ccmail.nevada.edu
Web site: http://www.unlv.edu
SAT Code: 4861 ACT Code: 2496

Director: Antita H. Stockbauer
LD program telephone: 702 895-0866
LD program e-mail: anitas@ccmail.nevada.edu
Total campus enrollment: 21,783

GENERAL

University of Nevada, Las Vegas is a public, coed, four-year institution. 335-acre, urban campus in Las Vegas (population: 478,434); branch campus at Nellis Air Force Base. Served by air, bus, and train. Public transportation serves campus. Semester system.

LD ADMISSIONS

Application Deadline: 04/02. Students do not complete a separate application and are not simultaneously accepted to the LD program. A member of the LD program does not sit on the admissions committee. A personal interview is not required. Essay is not required.

SECONDARY SCHOOL REQUIREMENTS

Graduation from secondary school required; GED accepted. The following course distribution required: 4 units of English, 3 units of math, 3 units of science, 3 units of social studies.

TESTING

SAT Reasoning or ACT required of some applicants. SAT Subject recommended.

All enrolled freshmen (fall 2004):

Average SAT I Scores:	Verbal: 503	Math: 513
Average ACT Scores:	Composite: 21	

Child Study Team report is not required. A neuropsychological or comprehensive psycho-educational evaluation is required for admission. Must be dated within 36 months of application. Tests required as part of this documentation:

- [x] WAIS-IV
- [x] WISC-IV
- [ ] SATA
- [x] Woodcock-Johnson
- [x] Nelson-Denny Reading Test
- [x] Other

UNDERGRADUATE STUDENT BODY

Total undergraduate student enrollment: 8,327 Men, 10,279 Women.

Composition of student body (fall 2004):

	Undergraduate	Freshmen
International	1.3	3.6
Black	8.9	8.1
American Indian	0.8	1.0
Asian-American	16.4	13.8
Hispanic	12.4	10.7
White	51.6	53.4
Unreported	8.6	9.4
	100.0%	100.0%

20% are from out of state. 5% join a fraternity and 3% join a sorority. Average age of full-time undergraduates is 21. 31% of classes have fewer than 20 students, 54% have between 20 and 50 students, 15% have more than 50 students.

STUDENT HOUSING

26% of freshmen live in college housing. Freshmen are required to live on campus. Housing is guaranteed for all undergraduates. Campus can house 2,000 undergraduates.

EXPENSES

Tuition (2005-06): $3,270 per year (in-state), $12,740 (out-of-state). Room: $5,860. Board: $3,750.

There is no additional cost for LD program/services.

LD SERVICES

LD program size is not limited.

LD services available to:

- [x] Freshmen
- [x] Sophomores
- [x] Juniors
- [x] Seniors

Academic Accommodations

Curriculum		**In class**	
Foreign language waiver	[ ]	Early syllabus	[ ]
Lighter course load	[ ]	Note takers in class	[x]
Math waiver	[ ]	Priority seating	[x]
Other special classes	[x]	Tape recorders	[x]
Priority registrations	[x]	Videotaped classes	[ ]
Substitution of courses	[x]	Text on tape	[x]
Exams		**Services**	
Extended time	[x]	Diagnostic tests	[ ]
Oral exams	[x]	Learning centers	[x]
Take home exams	[ ]	Proofreaders	[ ]
Exams on tape or computer	[ ]	Readers	[x]
Untimed exams	[ ]	Reading Machines/Kurzweil	[x]
Other accommodations	[x]	Special bookstore section	[ ]
		Typists	[x]

Credit toward degree is not given for remedial courses taken.

Counseling Services

- [x] Academic
- [x] Psychological
- [ ] Student Support groups
- [ ] Vocational

Tutoring

	Individual	Group
Time management	[ ]	[ ]
Organizational skills	[ ]	[ ]
Learning strategies	[ ]	[ ]
Study skills	[ ]	[ ]
Content area	[ ]	[ ]
Writing lab	[ ]	[ ]
Math lab	[ ]	[ ]

LD PROGRAM STAFF

Total number of LD Program staff (including director):

Full Time: 2 Part Time: 2

There is an advisor/advocate from the LD program available to students.

University of Nevada - Reno

Reno, NV

Address: Reno, NV, 89557
Admissions telephone: 775 784-4700
Admissions FAX: 775 784-4283
Assistant Vice President of Enrollment Services: Melisa N. Choroszy
Admissions e-mail: asknevada@unr.edu
Web site: http://www.unr.edu
SAT Code: 4844 ACT Code: 2497

LD program name: Disability Resource Center
LD program address: Reno DRC/079
Director, Disability Resource Center: Mary Zabel
LD program telephone: 775 784-6000
LD program e-mail: mzabel@unr.edu
LD program enrollment: 357, Total campus enrollment: 12,524

GENERAL

University of Nevada - Reno is a public, coed, four-year institution. 200-acre campus in Reno (population: 180,480). Served by air, bus, and train. Public transportation serves campus. School operates on-campus shuttle service. Semester system.

LD ADMISSIONS

Application Deadline: 11/30. Students do not complete a separate application and are not simultaneously accepted to the LD program. A member of the LD program does sit on the admissions committee. A personal interview is required. Essay is not required. Special Admissions can be considered on a case-by-case basis.

SECONDARY SCHOOL REQUIREMENTS

Graduation from secondary school required; GED not accepted. The following course distribution required: 4 units of English, 3 units of math, 3 units of science, 3 units of social studies.

TESTING

All enrolled freshmen (fall 2004):

Average SAT I Scores:	Verbal: 521	Math: 531
Average ACT Scores:	Composite: 22	

Child Study Team report is not required. Tests required as part of this documentation:

- [x] WAIS-IV
- [x] WISC-IV
- [x] SATA
- [x] Woodcock-Johnson
- [x] Nelson-Denny Reading Test
- [ ] Other

UNDERGRADUATE STUDENT BODY

Total undergraduate student enrollment: 4,955 Men, 6,120 Women.

Composition of student body (fall 2004):

	Undergraduate	Freshmen
International	2.0	2.6
Black	2.5	2.4
American Indian	1.1	1.3
Asian-American	6.6	6.6
Hispanic	7.1	7.0
White	68.2	71.5
Unreported	12.5	8.6
	100.0%	100.0%

18% are from out of state. 6% join a fraternity and 6% join a sorority. Average age of full-time undergraduates is 21. 31% of classes have fewer than 20 students, 55% have between 20 and 50 students, 14% have more than 50 students.

STUDENT HOUSING

52% of freshmen live in college housing. Freshmen are not required to live on campus. Housing is guaranteed for all undergraduates. Campus can house 1,721 undergraduates. Single rooms are available for students with medical or special needs. A medical note is required.

EXPENSES

Tuition (2005-06): $2,490 per year (state residents), $9,940 (out-of-state), $10,090 (international).

There is no additional cost for LD program/services.

LD SERVICES

LD program size is not limited.

LD services available to:

- [x] Freshmen
- [x] Sophomores
- [x] Juniors
- [x] Seniors

Academic Accommodations

Curriculum		In class	
Foreign language waiver	[ ]	Early syllabus	[ ]
Lighter course load	[x]	Note takers in class	[x]
Math waiver	[ ]	Priority seating	[x]
Other special classes	[x]	Tape recorders	[x]
Priority registrations	[ ]	Videotaped classes	[ ]
Substitution of courses	[x]	Text on tape	[x]
Exams		**Services**	
Extended time	[x]	Diagnostic tests	[x]
Oral exams	[x]	Learning centers	[x]
Take home exams	[ ]	Proofreaders	[ ]
Exams on tape or computer	[x]	Readers	[x]
Untimed exams	[ ]	Reading Machines/Kurzweil	[x]
Other accommodations	[ ]	Special bookstore section	[ ]
		Typists	[x]

Credit toward degree is not given for remedial courses taken.

Counseling Services

[x] Academic	Meets 2 times per academic year
[x] Psychological	Meets 10 times per academic year
[x] Student Support groups	Meets 30 times per academic year
[ ] Vocational	

Tutoring

Individual tutoring is available weekly.

Average size of tutoring groups: 4

	Individual	Group
Time management	[ ]	[x]
Organizational skills	[ ]	[x]
Learning strategies	[ ]	[ ]
Study skills	[ ]	[ ]
Content area	[ ]	[ ]
Writing lab	[x]	[ ]
Math lab	[x]	[ ]

UNIQUE LD PROGRAM FEATURES

Services and accommodations are provided on an individual case by case basis assessing functional limitations, the impact that the student's disability has on accessing campus programs and services and the specific class schedule.

LD PROGRAM STAFF

Total number of LD Program staff (including director):

Full Time: 7 Part Time: 7

There is not an advisor/advocate from the LD program available to students. 2 graduate students and 40 peer tutors are available to work with LD students.

Key staff person available to work with LD students: Mary Zabel, Director, Disability Resource Center.

LD Program web site: www.unr.edu/stsv/slservices/drc/indes.html

Sierra Nevada College

Incline Village, NV

Address: 999 Tahoe Boulevard, Incline Village, NV, 89451
Admissions telephone: 800 332-8666
Admissions FAX: 775 831-1347
Dean of Admissions: Charles Timinsky
Admissions e-mail: admissions@sierranevada.edu
Web site: http://www.sierranevada.edu
SAT Code: 4757 ACT Code: 2497

Total campus enrollment: 329

GENERAL

Sierra Nevada College is a private, coed, four-year institution. 25-acre campus in Incline Village (Incline Village-Crystal Bay population: 9,952), 35 miles from Reno; branch campuses in Fallon and Las Vegas. Major airport serves Reno; smaller airport serves South Lake Tahoe (25 miles); bus and train serve Truckee, Calif. (20 miles). School operates transportation between campuses. Public transportation serves campus. Semester system.

LD ADMISSIONS

A personal interview is recommended. Essay is required and may be typed.

SECONDARY SCHOOL REQUIREMENTS

Graduation from secondary school required; GED accepted.

TESTING

SAT Subject recommended.

All enrolled freshmen (fall 2004):

Average SAT I Scores: Verbal: 540 Math: 520
Average ACT Scores: Composite:

Child Study Team report is not required. Tests required as part of this documentation:

- ☐ WAIS-IV
- ☐ WISC-IV
- ☐ SATA
- ☐ Woodcock-Johnson
- ☐ Nelson-Denny Reading Test
- ☐ Other

UNDERGRADUATE STUDENT BODY

Total undergraduate student enrollment: 185 Men, 155 Women.

Composition of student body (fall 2004):

	Undergraduate	Freshmen
International	0.0	3.0
Black	1.5	1.5
American Indian	3.1	1.1
Asian-American	1.5	0.8
Hispanic	1.5	1.5
White	46.2	42.9
Unreported	46.2	49.2
	100.0%	100.0%

85% are from out of state.

STUDENT HOUSING

Housing is guaranteed for all undergraduates. Campus can house 250 undergraduates.

EXPENSES

Tuition (2005-06): $19,500 per year. Tuition is different for teacher education program.
Room: $3,990. Board: $3,460.

There is no additional cost for LD program/services.

LD SERVICES

LD program size is not limited.

LD services available to:

☐ Freshmen ☐ Sophomores ☐ Juniors ☐ Seniors

Academic Accommodations

Curriculum		**In class**	
Foreign language waiver	☐	Early syllabus	☐
Lighter course load	☒	Note takers in class	☒
Math waiver	☐	Priority seating	☐
Other special classes	☐	Tape recorders	☐
Priority registrations	☐	Videotaped classes	☐
Substitution of courses	☐	Text on tape	☐
Exams		**Services**	
Extended time	☐	Diagnostic tests	☐
Oral exams	☒	Learning centers	☐
Take home exams	☐	Proofreaders	☐
Exams on tape or computer	☐	Readers	☐
Untimed exams	☒	Reading Machines/Kurzweil	☐
Other accommodations	☐	Special bookstore section	☐
		Typists	☐

Credit toward degree is not given for remedial courses taken.

Counseling Services

- ☐ Academic
- ☐ Psychological
- ☐ Student Support groups
- ☐ Vocational

Tutoring

	Individual	Group
Time management	☐	☐
Organizational skills	☐	☐
Learning strategies	☐	☐
Study skills	☐	☐
Content area	☐	☐
Writing lab	☐	☐
Math lab	☐	☐

LD PROGRAM STAFF

Total number of LD Program staff (including director):

Full Time: 2 Part Time: 2

Key staff person available to work with LD students: LeeAnn Malone, Director of Student Services.

Truckee Meadows Community College

Reno, NV

Address: 7000 Dandini Boulevard, Reno, NV, 89512
Admissions telephone: 775 673-7042
Admissions FAX: 775 673-7028
Admissions/Records Supervisor
Admissions e-mail: admissions@tmcc.edu
Web site: http://www.tmcc.edu
SAT Code: 1096

LD program name: Disability Resource Center
LD program address: RDMT 120
Disability Resource Center Manager: Lee Geldmacher
LD program telephone: 775 673-7277
LD program e-mail: lgeldmacher@tmcc.edu
LD program enrollment: 151, Total campus enrollment: 11,412

GENERAL

Truckee Meadows Community College is a public, coed, two-year institution. Campus in Reno (population: 180,480). Served by air, bus, and train. Public transportation serves campus. Semester system.

LD ADMISSIONS

Students do not complete a separate application and are simultaneously accepted to the LD program. There is no admissions committee. A personal interview is required. Essay is not required.

SECONDARY SCHOOL REQUIREMENTS

Graduation from secondary school required; GED not accepted.

TESTING

Tests required as part of this documentation:

- ■ WAIS-IV
- ■ WISC-IV
- ☐ SATA
- ■ Woodcock-Johnson
- ■ Nelson-Denny Reading Test
- ☐ Other

UNDERGRADUATE STUDENT BODY

Total undergraduate student enrollment: 0 Men, 0 Women.

Composition of student body (fall 2004):

	Undergraduate	Freshmen
International	0.0	0.0
Black	0.0	0.0
American Indian	0.0	0.0
Asian-American	0.0	0.0
Hispanic	0.0	0.0
White	0.0	0.0
Unreported	0.0	0.0
	100.0%	100.0%

STUDENT HOUSING

No housing is available.

EXPENSES

Tuition 2004-05:

There is no additional cost for LD program/services.

LD SERVICES

LD program size is not limited.

LD services available to:

■ Freshmen ■ Sophomores ■ Juniors ■ Seniors

Academic Accommodations

Curriculum		**In class**	
Foreign language waiver	☐	Early syllabus	☐
Lighter course load	■	Note takers in class	■
Math waiver	☐	Priority seating	■
Other special classes	■	Tape recorders	☐
Priority registrations	■	Videotaped classes	☐
Substitution of courses	■	Text on tape	■
Exams		**Services**	
Extended time	■	Diagnostic tests	☐
Oral exams	■	Learning centers	☐
Take home exams	☐	Proofreaders	☐
Exams on tape or computer	■	Readers	■
Untimed exams	☐	Reading Machines/Kurzweil	☐
Other accommodations	■	Special bookstore section	☐
		Typists	☐

Credit toward degree is not given for remedial courses taken.

Counseling Services

■ Academic	Meets 2 times per academic year
☐ Psychological	Meets 10 times per academic year
☐ Student Support groups	Meets 30 times per academic year
☐ Vocational	

Tutoring

Individual tutoring is available weekly.

Average size of tutoring groups: 1

	Individual	Group
Time management	■	☐
Organizational skills	■	☐
Learning strategies	■	☐
Study skills	☐	☐
Content area	■	☐
Writing lab	☐	☐
Math lab	☐	☐

LD PROGRAM STAFF

Total number of LD Program staff (including director):

Part Time: 2

There is an advisor/advocate from the LD program available to students.

Key staff person available to work with LD students: Lee Geldmacher, Disability Resource Center Manager

LD Program web site: http://www.tmcc.edu/outreachservices/drc

Colby-Sawyer College

New London, NH

Address: 541 Main Street, New London, NH, 03257-7835
Admissions telephone: 800 272-1015
Admissions FAX: 603 526-3452
Vice President for Enrollment Management: Joseph Chillo
Admissions e-mail: csadmiss@colby-sawyer.edu
Web site: http://www.colby-sawyer.edu
SAT Code: 3281 ACT Code: 2506

Director of Learning Services: Ann Chalker
LD program telephone: 603 526-3711
LD program e-mail: jameshouse@colby-sawyer.edu
LD program enrollment: 92, Total campus enrollment: 964

GENERAL

Colby-Sawyer College is a private, coed, four-year institution. 200-acre campus in New London (population: 4,116), 50 miles from Manchester and 100 miles from Boston. Served by bus; major airport serves Boston; smaller airport serves Manchester; train serves White River Junction, Vt. (35 miles). Semester system.

LD ADMISSIONS

A personal interview is recommended. Essay is required and may be typed.

SECONDARY SCHOOL REQUIREMENTS

Graduation from secondary school required; GED accepted. The following course distribution required: 4 units of English, 3 units of math, 2 units of science, 2 units of foreign language, 3 units of social studies.

TESTING

SAT Reasoning or ACT required. SAT Subject recommended.

All enrolled freshmen (fall 2004):

Average SAT I Scores: Verbal: 505 Math: 504
Average ACT Scores: Composite: 20

Child Study Team report is not required. Tests required as part of this documentation:

- [ ] WAIS-IV
- [ ] WISC-IV
- [ ] SATA
- [ ] Woodcock-Johnson
- [ ] Nelson-Denny Reading Test
- [ ] Other

UNDERGRADUATE STUDENT BODY

Total undergraduate student enrollment: 327 Men, 574 Women.

Composition of student body (fall 2004):

	Undergraduate	Freshmen
International	0.8	1.0
Black	0.4	0.5
American Indian	0.0	0.1
Asian-American	2.3	1.5
Hispanic	0.0	0.2
White	94.7	93.2
Unreported	1.8	3.5
	100.0%	100.0%

69% are from out of state. Average age of full-time undergraduates is 20. 59% of classes have fewer than 20 students, 41% have between 20 and 50 students.

STUDENT HOUSING

99% of freshmen live in college housing. Freshmen are required to live on campus. Housing is guaranteed for all undergraduates. Campus can house 867 undergraduates.

EXPENSES

Tuition (2005-06): $24,700 per year.

Room: $5,280. Board: $4,210.
There is no additional cost for LD program/services.

LD SERVICES

LD program size is not limited.

LD services available to:

- [x] Freshmen
- [x] Sophomores
- [x] Juniors
- [x] Seniors

Academic Accommodations

Curriculum		In class	
Foreign language waiver	[ ]	Early syllabus	[ ]
Lighter course load	[x]	Note takers in class	[ ]
Math waiver	[ ]	Priority seating	[ ]
Other special classes	[ ]	Tape recorders	[x]
Priority registrations	[ ]	Videotaped classes	[ ]
Substitution of courses	[ ]	Text on tape	[ ]
Exams		**Services**	
Extended time	[x]	Diagnostic tests	[ ]
Oral exams	[ ]	Learning centers	[x]
Take home exams	[ ]	Proofreaders	[ ]
Exams on tape or computer	[ ]	Readers	[ ]
Untimed exams	[ ]	Reading Machines/Kurzweil	[ ]
Other accommodations	[ ]	Special bookstore section	[ ]
		Typists	[ ]

Counseling Services

- [x] Academic
- [ ] Psychological
- [ ] Student Support groups
- [ ] Vocational

Tutoring

Individual tutoring is available.

	Individual	Group
Time management	[x]	[x]
Organizational skills	[x]	[x]
Learning strategies	[x]	[x]
Study skills	[x]	[x]
Content area	[x]	[x]
Writing lab	[x]	[x]
Math lab	[x]	[x]

LD PROGRAM STAFF

Total number of LD Program staff (including director):

Full Time: 2 Part Time: 2

18 peer tutors are available to work with LD students.

Key staff person available to work with LD students: Ann Chalker, Director of Learning Services.

Dartmouth College

Hanover, NH

Address: 6016 McNutt Hall, Hanover, NH, 03755
Admissions telephone: 603 646-2875
Admissions FAX: 603 646-1216
Dean of Admissions and Financial Aid: Karl M. Furstenberg
Admissions e-mail: admissions.office@dartmouth.edu
Web site: http://www.dartmouth.edu
SAT Code: 3351 ACT Code: 2508

LD program name: Student Disability Services
LD program address: 301 Collis Center
Director of Student Disabilities Services: Nancy Pompian
LD program telephone: 603 646-2014
LD program e-mail: Nancy.Pompian@Dartmouth.edu
Total campus enrollment: 4,079

GENERAL

Dartmouth College is a private, coed, four-year institution. 265-acre campus in Hanover (population: 10,850), 53 miles from Concord and 130 miles from Boston. Served by bus; major airport serves Boston; smaller airport serves Lebanon (six miles); train serves White River Junction, VT (seven miles). School operates transportation to towns in the upper valley. Public transportation serves campus. Quarter system.

LD ADMISSIONS

Students do not complete a separate application and are not simultaneously accepted to the LD program. A member of the LD program does not sit on the admissions committee.

SECONDARY SCHOOL REQUIREMENTS

Graduation from secondary school not required.

TESTING

SAT Subject recommended.

All enrolled freshmen (fall 2004):

Average SAT I Scores:	Verbal: 713	Math: 719
Average ACT Scores:	Composite: 30	

Child Study Team report is not required. A neuropsychological or comprehensive psycho-education evaluation is not required for admission. Tests required as part of this documentation:

☐ WAIS-IV ☐ Woodcock-Johnson
☐ WISC-IV ☐ Nelson-Denny Reading Test
☐ SATA ☐ Other

UNDERGRADUATE STUDENT BODY

Total undergraduate student enrollment: 2,115 Men, 2,003 Women.

Composition of student body (fall 2004):

	Undergraduate	Freshmen
International	5.0	5.2
Black	7.3	6.8
American Indian	3.5	3.5
Asian-American	13.6	13.5
Hispanic	6.7	6.5
White	58.3	57.6
Unreported	5.6	6.9
	100.0%	100.0%

97% are from out of state. 39% join a fraternity and 34% join a sorority. Average age of full-time undergraduates is 20. 61% of classes have fewer than 20 students, 29% have between 20 and 50 students, 10% have more than 50 students.

STUDENT HOUSING

100% of freshmen live in college housing. Freshmen are required to live on campus. Housing is not guaranteed for all undergraduates. Housing is not guaranteed beyond the first-year, though most students who want to live on campus are able to. Campus can house 3,352 undergraduates. Single rooms are available for students with medical or special needs. A medical note is required.

EXPENSES

Tuition (2005-06): $31,770 per year.
Room: $5,640. Board: $3,750.
There is no additional cost for LD program/services.

LD SERVICES

LD program size is not limited.

LD services available to:

■ Freshmen ■ Sophomores ■ Juniors ■ Seniors

Academic Accommodations

Curriculum		In class	
Foreign language waiver	■	Early syllabus	☐
Lighter course load	■	Note takers in class	■
Math waiver	☐	Priority seating	■
Other special classes	☐	Tape recorders	■
Priority registrations	☐	Videotaped classes	☐
Substitution of courses	☐	Text on tape	■
Exams		**Services**	
Extended time	■	Diagnostic tests	☐
Oral exams	☐	Learning centers	■
Take home exams	■	Proofreaders	☐
Exams on tape or computer	■	Readers	■
Untimed exams	☐	Reading Machines/Kurzweil	☐
Other accommodations	☐	Special bookstore section	☐
		Typists	☐

Counseling Services

■ Academic
■ Psychological
■ Student Support groups
■ Vocational

Tutoring

Individual tutoring is available weekly.

Average size of tutoring groups: 8

	Individual	Group
Time management	■	■
Organizational skills	■	■
Learning strategies	■	■
Study skills	■	■
Content area	☐	☐
Writing lab	☐	☐
Math lab	☐	☐

UNIQUE LD PROGRAM FEATURES

There are no special courses or teachers, so our services are not a program.

LD PROGRAM STAFF

Total number of LD Program staff (including director):

Full Time: 1 Part Time: 1

There is an advisor/advocate from the LD program available to students.

Key staff person available to work with LD students: Nancy Pompian, Director of Student Disabilities Services.

Franklin Pierce College

Rindge, NH

Address: 20 College Road, Rindge, NH, 03461
Admissions telephone: 800 437-0048
Admissions FAX: 603 899-4394
Director of Admissions: Lucy Shonk
Admissions e-mail: admissions@fpc.edu
Web site: http://www.fpc.edu
SAT Code: 3395 ACT Code: 2509

LD program name: Academic Services
Coordinator of Academic Accommodations: Patrica Moore
LD program telephone: 603 899-4283, extension 4044
LD program e-mail: moorep@fpc.edu
LD program enrollment: 55, Total campus enrollment: 1,608

GENERAL

Franklin Pierce College is a private, coed, four-year institution. 1,200-acre campus in Rindge (population: 5,451), 50 miles from Manchester and 65 miles from Boston; branch campuses in Concord, Keene, Lebanon, Nashua, Portsmouth, and Salem. Served by bus; major airport serves Boston; smaller airport serves Manchester; train serves Brattleboro, VT (40 miles). School operates transportation in town and to Keene. Semester system.

LD ADMISSIONS

Students do not complete a separate application and are not simultaneously accepted to the LD program. A member of the LD program does not sit on the admissions committee. A personal interview is recommended. Essay is required and may be typed.

SECONDARY SCHOOL REQUIREMENTS

Graduation from secondary school required; GED accepted. The following course distribution required: 4 units of English, 3 units of math, 2 units of science, 3 units of social studies, 4 units of academic electives.

TESTING

SAT Reasoning or ACT required. SAT Subject recommended.

All enrolled freshmen (fall 2004):

Average SAT I Scores: Verbal: 503 Math: 491

Child Study Team report is not required. A neuropsychological or comprehensive psycho-educational evaluation is required for admission. Must be dated within 36 months of application. Tests required as part of this documentation:

- [x] WAIS-IV
- [x] WISC-IV
- [x] SATA
- [x] Woodcock-Johnson
- [x] Nelson-Denny Reading Test
- [x] Other

UNDERGRADUATE STUDENT BODY

Total undergraduate student enrollment: 752 Men, 737 Women.

Composition of student body (fall 2004):

	Undergraduate	Freshmen
International	1.8	2.8
Black	3.3	3.7
American Indian	0.0	0.1
Asian-American	1.1	0.9
Hispanic	1.9	1.8
White	79.6	78.6
Unreported	12.3	12.1
	100.0%	100.0%

86% are from out of state. Average age of full-time undergraduates is 20. 69% of classes have fewer than 20 students, 29% have between 20 and 50 students, 2% have more than 50 students.

STUDENT HOUSING

96% of freshmen live in college housing. Freshmen are required to live on campus. Housing is guaranteed for all undergraduates. Campus can house 1,400 undergraduates. Single rooms are available for students with medical or special needs. A medical note is required.

EXPENSES

Tuition (2005-06): $23,100 per year.
Room: $4,480. Board: $3,510.
There is no additional cost for LD program/services.

LD SERVICES

LD program size is not limited.

LD services available to:

- [ ] Freshmen
- [ ] Sophomores
- [ ] Juniors
- [ ] Seniors

Academic Accommodations

Curriculum

- [ ] Foreign language waiver
- [x] Lighter course load
- [ ] Math waiver
- [ ] Other special classes
- [ ] Priority registrations
- [ ] Substitution of courses

Exams

- [x] Extended time
- [ ] Oral exams
- [ ] Take home exams
- [ ] Exams on tape or computer
- [x] Untimed exams
- [ ] Other accommodations

In class

- [ ] Early syllabus
- [x] Note takers in class
- [x] Priority seating
- [ ] Tape recorders
- [ ] Videotaped classes
- [ ] Text on tape

Services

- [ ] Diagnostic tests
- [ ] Learning centers
- [x] Proofreaders
- [x] Readers
- [ ] Reading Machines/Kurzweil
- [ ] Special bookstore section
- [ ] Typists

Credit toward degree is not given for remedial courses taken.

Counseling Services

- [ ] Academic
- [ ] Psychological
- [ ] Student Support groups
- [ ] Vocational

Tutoring

Individual tutoring is available weekly.

Average size of tutoring groups: 5

	Individual	Group
Time management	[x]	[x]
Organizational skills	[x]	[x]
Learning strategies	[x]	[x]
Study skills	[x]	[x]
Content area	[x]	[x]
Writing lab	[x]	[x]
Math lab	[x]	[x]

LD PROGRAM STAFF

Total number of LD Program staff (including director):

Full Time: 1 Part Time: 1

There is an advisor/advocate from the LD program available to students. 15 peer tutors are available to work with LD students.

Key staff person available to work with LD students: Patrica Moore, Coordinator of Academic Accommodations.

Keene State College

Keene, NH

Address: 229 Main Street, Keene, NH, 03435
Admissions telephone: 800 KSC-1909
Admissions FAX: 603 358-2767
Director of Admissions: Margaret Richmond
Admissions e-mail: admissions@keene.edu
Web site: http://www.keene.edu
SAT Code: 3472 ACT Code: 2510

LD program name: Office of Disability Services
Program Support Assistant: Mary Leonard
LD program telephone: 603 358-2353
LD program e-mail: mleonard@keene.edu
Total campus enrollment: 4,797

GENERAL

Keene State College is a public, coed, four-year institution. 160-acre campus in Keene (population: 22,563), 50 miles from Manchester and 90 miles from Boston; training center in Manchester. Served by air and bus; major airport serves Windsor Locks, Conn. (75 miles); train serves Brattleboro, Vt. (15 miles). School operates transportation to parking lot. Semester system.

LD ADMISSIONS

A personal interview is recommended. Essay is required and may be typed.

SECONDARY SCHOOL REQUIREMENTS

Graduation from secondary school required; GED accepted. The following course distribution required: 4 units of English, 3 units of math, 3 units of science, 2 units of social studies, 2 units of academic electives.

TESTING

SAT Reasoning required; ACT may be substituted. SAT Subject required.

All enrolled freshmen (fall 2004):

Average SAT I Scores:	Verbal: 501	Math: 496
Average ACT Scores:	Composite: 20	

Child Study Team report is not required. Tests required as part of this documentation:

☐ WAIS-IV ☐ Woodcock-Johnson
☐ WISC-IV ☐ Nelson-Denny Reading Test
☐ SATA ☐ Other

UNDERGRADUATE STUDENT BODY

Total undergraduate student enrollment: 1,861 Men, 2,539 Women.

Composition of student body (fall 2004):

	Undergraduate	Freshmen
International	0.1	0.5
Black	0.6	0.3
American Indian	0.0	0.2
Asian-American	0.5	0.8
Hispanic	1.2	1.0
White	94.0	94.1
Unreported	3.6	3.1
	100.0%	100.0%

53% are from out of state. 2% join a fraternity and 4% join a sorority. Average age of full-time undergraduates is 20. 57% of classes have fewer than 20 students, 39% have between 20 and 50 students, 4% have more than 50 students.

STUDENT HOUSING

93% of freshmen live in college housing. Freshmen are not required to live on campus. Housing is guaranteed for all undergraduates. Campus can house 2,356 undergraduates. Single rooms are available for students with medical or special needs. A medical note is required.

EXPENSES

Tuition (2005-06): $5,410 per year (in-state), $12,250 (out-of-state).

Room: $4,268. Board: $2,216.

There is no additional cost for LD program/services.

LD SERVICES

LD program size is not limited.

LD services available to:

■ Freshmen ■ Sophomores ■ Juniors ■ Seniors

Academic Accommodations

Curriculum		In class	
Foreign language waiver	☐	Early syllabus	☐
Lighter course load	■	Note takers in class	■
Math waiver	☐	Priority seating	☐
Other special classes	☐	Tape recorders	■
Priority registrations	☐	Videotaped classes	☐
Substitution of courses	☐	Text on tape	☐
Exams		**Services**	
Extended time	■	Diagnostic tests	☐
Oral exams	■	Learning centers	☐
Take home exams	☐	Proofreaders	☐
Exams on tape or computer	☐	Readers	■
Untimed exams	■	Reading Machines/Kurzweil	■
Other accommodations	☐	Special bookstore section	☐
		Typists	☐

Credit toward degree is not given for remedial courses taken.

Counseling Services

■ Academic
☐ Psychological
☐ Student Support groups
☐ Vocational

Tutoring

Individual tutoring is available weekly.

	Individual	Group
Time management	☐	■
Organizational skills	☐	■
Learning strategies	☐	■
Study skills	☐	■
Content area	■	☐
Writing lab	■	☐
Math lab	■	☐

LD PROGRAM STAFF

Total number of LD Program staff (including director):

Full Time: 1 Part Time: 1

Key staff person available to work with LD students: Lisa David, Counselor, Office of Disability Services.

LD Program web site: http://www.keene.edu/aspire

New England College

Henniker, NH

Address: 7 Main Street, Henniker, NH, 03242
Admissions telephone: 800 521-7642
Admissions FAX: 603 428-3155
Dean of Admission: Paul Miller
Admissions e-mail: admission@nec.edu
Web site: http://www.nec.edu
SAT Code: 3657 ACT Code: 2513

LD program name: Pathways
LD program address: 24 Bridge Street
Director: Anna Carlson
LD program telephone: 603 428-2218
LD program e-mail: acarlson@nec.edu
LD program enrollment: 79, Total campus enrollment: 936

GENERAL

New England College is a private, coed, four-year institution. 225-acre campus in Henniker (population: 4,433), 17 miles from Concord and 85 miles from Boston; branch campus abroad in Israel. Airport serves Manchester (30 miles); bus serves Concord; train serves Boston. Semester system.

LD ADMISSIONS

Students do not complete a separate application and are simultaneously accepted to the LD program. A member of the LD program does not sit on the admissions committee. A personal interview is recommended. Essay is required and may be typed. Services are provided upon documentation of need. Admission requirements are identical for all students.

For fall 2004, 120 completed self-identified LD applications were received. 109 applications were offered admission, and 31 enrolled.

SECONDARY SCHOOL REQUIREMENTS

Graduation from secondary school required; GED accepted.

TESTING

SAT Reasoning or ACT considered if submitted.

All enrolled freshmen (fall 2004):

Average SAT I Scores:	Verbal: 470	Math: 455
Average ACT Scores:	Composite: 19	

Child Study Team report is not required. A neuropsychological or comprehensive psycho-education evaluation is not required for admission. Tests required as part of this documentation:

- ☐ WAIS-IV
- ☐ WISC-IV
- ☐ SATA
- ☐ Woodcock-Johnson
- ☐ Nelson-Denny Reading Test
- ☐ Other

UNDERGRADUATE STUDENT BODY

Total undergraduate student enrollment: 354 Men, 370 Women.

Composition of student body (fall 2004):

	Undergraduate	Freshmen
International	5.6	6.4
Black	2.0	1.8
American Indian	0.0	0.2
Asian-American	0.7	0.7
Hispanic	2.7	2.3
White	89.0	88.6
Unreported	0.0	0.0
	100.0%	100.0%

76% are from out of state. 10% join a fraternity and 7% join a sorority. Average age of full-time undergraduates is 21. 63% of classes have fewer than 20 students, 36% have between 20 and 50 students, 1% have more than 50 students.

STUDENT HOUSING

92% of freshmen live in college housing. Freshmen are required to live on campus. Housing is guaranteed for all undergraduates. Campus can house 671 undergraduates. Single rooms are available for students with medical or special needs. A medical note is required.

EXPENSES

Tuition (2005-06): $22,366 per year.
Room: $4,398. Board: $4,058.
There is no additional cost for LD program/services.

LD SERVICES

LD program size is not limited.

LD services available to:

■ Freshmen ■ Sophomores ■ Juniors ■ Seniors

Academic Accommodations

Curriculum		**In class**	
Foreign language waiver	☐	Early syllabus	☐
Lighter course load	■	Note takers in class	■
Math waiver	■	Priority seating	☐
Other special classes	☐	Tape recorders	■
Priority registrations	☐	Videotaped classes	☐
Substitution of courses	■	Text on tape	☐
Exams		**Services**	
Extended time	■	Diagnostic tests	☐
Oral exams	■	Learning centers	■
Take home exams	☐	Proofreaders	■
Exams on tape or computer	■	Readers	☐
Untimed exams	■	Reading Machines/Kurzweil	☐
Other accommodations	■	Special bookstore section	☐
		Typists	☐

Credit toward degree is given for remedial courses taken.

Counseling Services

- ■ Academic
- ■ Psychological
- ■ Student Support groups
- ■ Vocational

Tutoring

Individual tutoring is available daily.

Average size of tutoring groups: 5

	Individual	Group
Time management	■	☐
Organizational skills	■	☐
Learning strategies	■	☐
Study skills	■	■
Content area	■	☐
Writing lab	■	☐
Math lab	■	☐

UNIQUE LD PROGRAM FEATURES

Services are provided on an as needed basis.

LD PROGRAM STAFF

Total number of LD Program staff (including director):

Full Time: 7 Part Time: 7

There is an advisor/advocate from the LD program available to students. The advisor/advocate meets with faculty 4 times per month and students 4 times per month. 7 peer tutors are available to work with LD students.

Key staff person available to work with LD students: Anna Carlson, Director of Academic Advising and Support Services.

LD Program web site: http://www.nec.edu/academics/pathways.html

University of New Hampshire

Durham, NH

Address: Thompson Hall, Durham, NH, 03824
Admissions telephone: 603 862-1360
Admissions FAX: 603 862-0077
Executive Director of Admissions: Robert McGann
Admissions e-mail: admissions@unh.edu
Web site: http://www.unh.edu
SAT Code: 3918 ACT Code: 2524

LD program name: Access Office
LD program address: 118 Memorial Union Building
Assistant Director/LD Specialist: Brandee Franciosi
LD program telephone: 603 862-2607
LD program e-mail: b.franciosi@unh.edu
LD program enrollment: 224, Total campus enrollment: 11,394

GENERAL

University of New Hampshire is a public, coed, four-year institution. 2,600-acre campus in Durham (population: 12,664), 65 miles from Boston; branch campus in Manchester. Served by train (on weekends); major airport serves Boston; smaller airport serves Manchester (50 miles); bus serves Portsmouth (10 miles); train serves Dover (10 miles). School operates transportation to local communities. Semester system.

LD ADMISSIONS

Students do not complete a separate application and are not simultaneously accepted to the LD program. A member of the LD program does not sit on the admissions committee. A personal interview is recommended. Essay is required and may be typed. If clear documentation of a language-based learning disability is provided, the admissions requirement for foreign language study may be waived. Students with language-based LD may petition to substitute foreign culture courses for language study at UNH.

For fall 2004, 231 completed self-identified LD applications were received. 102 applications were offered admission, and 22 enrolled.

SECONDARY SCHOOL REQUIREMENTS

Graduation from secondary school required; GED accepted. The following course distribution required: 4 units of English, 4 units of math, 4 units of science, 3 units of foreign language, 3 units of social studies.

TESTING

SAT Reasoning or ACT required. SAT Subject required.

All enrolled freshmen (fall 2004):

Average SAT I Scores: Verbal: 550 Math: 561

Child Study Team report is not required. A neuropsychological or comprehensive psycho-educational evaluation is required for admission. Must be dated within 36 months of application. Tests required as part of this documentation:

- [x] WAIS-IV
- [x] WISC-IV
- [x] SATA
- [x] Woodcock-Johnson
- [x] Nelson-Denny Reading Test
- [ ] Other

UNDERGRADUATE STUDENT BODY

Total undergraduate student enrollment: 4,704 Men, 6,336 Women.

Composition of student body (fall 2004):

	Undergraduate	Freshmen
International	1.0	0.8
Black	1.4	1.3
American Indian	0.3	0.3
Asian-American	2.3	2.1
Hispanic	1.9	1.5
White	82.9	86.9
Unreported	10.2	7.1
	100.0%	100.0%

40% are from out of state. 4% join a fraternity and 5% join a sorority. Average age of full-time undergraduates is 21. 49% of classes have fewer than 20 students, 38% have between 20 and 50 students, 13% have more than 50 students.

STUDENT HOUSING

96% of freshmen live in college housing. Freshmen are not required to live on campus. Housing is guaranteed for all undergraduates. Campus can house 6,180 undergraduates. Single rooms are available for students with medical or special needs. A medical note is required.

EXPENSES

Tuition (2005-06): $7,710 per year (in-state), $19,430 (out-of-state). Tuition differs for business, computer science, economics, engineering, and hospitality management majors.

Room: $4,196. Board: $2,836.

There is no additional cost for LD program/services.

LD SERVICES

LD program size is not limited.

LD services available to:

- [x] Freshmen
- [x] Sophomores
- [x] Juniors
- [x] Seniors

Academic Accommodations

Curriculum		In class	
Foreign language waiver	[ ]	Early syllabus	[ ]
Lighter course load	[x]	Note takers in class	[x]
Math waiver	[ ]	Priority seating	[x]
Other special classes	[ ]	Tape recorders	[x]
Priority registrations	[x]	Videotaped classes	[ ]
Substitution of courses	[ ]	Text on tape	[x]
Exams		**Services**	
Extended time	[x]	Diagnostic tests	[ ]
Oral exams	[x]	Learning centers	[ ]
Take home exams	[ ]	Proofreaders	[ ]
Exams on tape or computer	[x]	Readers	[x]
Untimed exams	[ ]	Reading Machines/Kurzweil	[x]
Other accommodations	[x]	Special bookstore section	[ ]
		Typists	[x]

Credit toward degree is not given for remedial courses taken.

Counseling Services

- [x] Academic
- [x] Psychological
- [ ] Student Support groups
- [x] Vocational

Meets 2 times per academic year

Tutoring

	Individual	Group
Time management	[ ]	[ ]
Organizational skills	[ ]	[ ]
Learning strategies	[ ]	[ ]
Study skills	[ ]	[ ]
Content area	[ ]	[ ]
Writing lab	[ ]	[ ]
Math lab	[ ]	[ ]

LD PROGRAM STAFF

Total number of LD Program staff (including director):

Full Time: 1 Part Time: 1

There is an advisor/advocate from the LD program available to students.

Key staff person available to work with LD students: Brandee Franciosi, Access Assistant Director/LD Specialist

LD Program web site: http://www.unh.edu/access/

New Hampshire Community Technical College

Nashua, NH

Address: 505 Amherst Street, Nashua NH 03061
Admissions telephone: 603 882-6923, extension 1520
Vice President for Student Affairs/Provost: John Fischer
Admissions e-mail: nashua@nhctc.edu
Web site: http://www.nashua.nhctc.edu

Disability Coordinator: Mary Oswald
LD program telephone: 603 882-6423, extension 1451
LD program e-mail: moswald@nhctc.edu
LD program enrollment: 45

GENERAL

New Hampshire Community Technical College is a public, coed, two-year institution. Campus in Nashua (population: 86,605), 40 miles north of Boston, MA. Served by bus; major airport and train serve Boston, MA; other airport serves Manchester (13 miles). Public transportation serves campus. Semester system.

LD ADMISSIONS

Students complete a separate application and are simultaneously accepted to the LD program. A member of the LD program does not sit on the admissions committee. A personal interview is required. Essay is required. Documentation is required for admission to the program.

SECONDARY SCHOOL REQUIREMENTS

Graduation from secondary school required; GED accepted.

TESTING

Child Study Team report is not required. Tests required as part of this documentation:

- [x] WAIS-IV
- [ ] WISC-IV
- [ ] SATA
- [x] Woodcock-Johnson
- [ ] Nelson-Denny Reading Test
- [x] Other

STUDENT HOUSING

No housing available.

EXPENSES

Tuition (2005-06): $2, 625 (in-state); $6, 016 (out-of-state).

There is no additional cost for LD program/services.

LD SERVICES

LD program size is not limited.

LD services available to:

- [x] Freshmen
- [x] Sophomores
- [x] Juniors
- [x] Seniors

Academic Accommodations

Curriculum		**In class**	
Foreign language waiver	☐	Early syllabus	☐
Lighter course load	☐	Note takers in class	☐
Math waiver	☐	Priority seating	☐
Other special classes	☐	Tape recorders	☐
Priority registrations	☐	Videotaped classes	☐
Substitution of courses	☐	Text on tape	☐
Exams		**Services**	
Extended time	☐	Diagnostic tests	☐
Oral exams	☐	Learning centers	☐
Take home exams	☐	Proofreaders	☐
Exams on tape or computer	☐	Readers	☐
Untimed exams	☐	Reading Machines/Kurzweil	☐
Other accommodations	☐	Special bookstore section	☐
		Typists	☐

Credit toward degree is not given for remedial courses taken.

Counseling Services

- [ ] Academic
- [ ] Psychological
- [ ] Student Support groups
- [ ] Vocational

Tutoring

Individual tutoring is available twice per month.

Average size of tutoring groups: 2

	Individual	Group
Time management	☐	☐
Organizational skills	☐	☐
Learning strategies	☐	☐
Study skills	☐	☐
Content area	☐	☐
Writing lab	☐	☐
Math lab	☐	☐

LD PROGRAM STAFF

There is an advisor/advocate from the LD program available to students.

Key staff person available to work with LD students: Mary Oswald, Disability Coordinator.

Plymouth State University

Plymouth, NH

Address: 17 High Street, Plymouth, NH, 03264-1595
Admissions telephone: 800 842-6900
Admissions FAX: 603 535-2714
Senior Associate Director of Admission: Eugene D. Fahey
Admissions e-mail: plymouthadmit@plymouth.edu
Web site: http://www.plymouth.edu
SAT Code: 3690 ACT Code: 2518

Counselor: Susan Keefe
LD program telephone: 603 535-2270
LD program e-mail: susank@plymouth.edu
Total campus enrollment: 4,108

GENERAL

Plymouth State University is a public, coed, four-year institution. 170-acre campus in Plymouth (population: 5,892), 45 miles from Concord. Served by bus; major airport and train serve Boston (115 miles); smaller airport serves Manchester (60 miles). School operates shuttle service on campus. Semester system.

LD ADMISSIONS

A personal interview is not required. Essay is required and may be typed.

SECONDARY SCHOOL REQUIREMENTS

Graduation from secondary school required; GED accepted. The following course distribution required: 4 units of English, 3 units of math, 2 units of science, 2 units of social studies, 1 unit of history.

TESTING

SAT Reasoning required; ACT may be substituted. SAT Subject required.

All enrolled freshmen (fall 2004):

Average SAT I Scores: Verbal: 484 Math: 485
Average ACT Scores: Composite: 21

Child Study Team report is not required. Tests required as part of this documentation:

- [ ] WAIS-IV
- [ ] WISC-IV
- [ ] SATA
- [ ] Woodcock-Johnson
- [ ] Nelson-Denny Reading Test
- [ ] Other

UNDERGRADUATE STUDENT BODY

Total undergraduate student enrollment: 1,726 Men, 1,839 Women.

Composition of student body (fall 2004):

	Undergraduate	Freshmen
International	0.4	0.3
Black	1.2	0.6
American Indian	0.4	0.2
Asian-American	0.6	0.9
Hispanic	1.1	1.1
White	91.2	89.8
Unreported	5.1	7.1
	100.0%	100.0%

44% are from out of state. 4% join a fraternity and 7% join a sorority. Average age of full-time undergraduates is 20. 48% of classes have fewer than 20 students, 49% have between 20 and 50 students, 3% have more than 50 students.

STUDENT HOUSING

93% of freshmen live in college housing. Freshmen are required to live on campus. Housing is guaranteed for all undergraduates. If space is available, and recently we have housed all who wanted housing and followed the appropriate sign-up procedure. Campus can house 2,106 undergraduates. Single rooms are not available for students with medical or special needs.

EXPENSES

There is no additional cost for LD program/services.

LD SERVICES

LD program size is not limited.

LD services available to:

- [x] Freshmen
- [x] Sophomores
- [x] Juniors
- [x] Seniors

Academic Accommodations

Curriculum		In class	
Foreign language waiver	[ ]	Early syllabus	[ ]
Lighter course load	[ ]	Note takers in class	[x]
Math waiver	[ ]	Priority seating	[ ]
Other special classes	[ ]	Tape recorders	[ ]
Priority registrations	[ ]	Videotaped classes	[ ]
Substitution of courses	[ ]	Text on tape	[x]
Exams		**Services**	
Extended time	[x]	Diagnostic tests	[ ]
Oral exams	[x]	Learning centers	[ ]
Take home exams	[ ]	Proofreaders	[ ]
Exams on tape or computer	[ ]	Readers	[x]
Untimed exams	[x]	Reading Machines/Kurzweil	[ ]
Other accommodations	[ ]	Special bookstore section	[ ]
		Typists	[ ]

Credit toward degree is not given for remedial courses taken.

Counseling Services

- [x] Academic — Meets 7 times per academic year
- [ ] Psychological
- [ ] Student Support groups
- [ ] Vocational

Tutoring

Individual tutoring is available weekly.

Average size of tutoring groups: 3

	Individual	Group
Time management	[x]	[ ]
Organizational skills	[x]	[ ]
Learning strategies	[x]	[ ]
Study skills	[x]	[ ]
Content area	[x]	[ ]
Writing lab	[x]	[ ]
Math lab	[x]	[ ]

UNIQUE LD PROGRAM FEATURES

Our admission process does not track LD students separately.

LD PROGRAM STAFF

Total number of LD Program staff (including director):

Full Time: 2 Part Time: 2

There is no advisor/advocate from the LD program available to students.

Key staff person available to work with LD students: Susan Keefe, Counselor.

Rivier College

Nashua, NH

Address: 420 Main Street, Nashua, NH, 03060
Admissions telephone: 800 44-RIVIER
Admissions FAX: 603 891-1799
Director of Undergraduate Admissions: David Boisvert
Admissions e-mail: rivadmit@rivier.edu
Web site: http://www.rivier.edu
SAT Code: 3728 ACT Code: 2520

Special Services Coordinator: Kate Ricci
LD program telephone: 603 897-8497
Total campus enrollment: 1,447

GENERAL

Rivier College is a private, coed, four-year institution. 68-acre, suburban campus in Nashua (population: 86,605), 20 miles from Manchester and 45 miles from Boston. Served by bus; major airport serves Boston; smaller airport serves Manchester; train serves Lowell, MA (15 miles). Public transportation serves campus. Semester system.

LD ADMISSIONS

A personal interview is recommended. Essay is required and may be typed.

SECONDARY SCHOOL REQUIREMENTS

Graduation from secondary school required; GED accepted. The following course distribution required: 4 units of English, 3 units of math, 1 unit of science, 2 units of foreign language, 4 units of academic electives.

TESTING

SAT Reasoning considered if submitted. ACT considered if submitted.

All enrolled freshmen (fall 2004):

Average SAT I Scores: Verbal: 494 Math: 492

Child Study Team report is not required. Tests required as part of this documentation:

- [ ] WAIS-IV
- [ ] WISC-IV
- [ ] SATA
- [ ] Woodcock-Johnson
- [ ] Nelson-Denny Reading Test
- [ ] Other

UNDERGRADUATE STUDENT BODY

Total undergraduate student enrollment: 286 Men, 1,182 Women.

Composition of student body (fall 2004):

	Undergraduate	Freshmen
International	0.1	0.1
Black	0.4	2.0
American Indian	0.0	0.3
Asian-American	0.4	2.0
Hispanic	4.6	2.7
White	82.8	90.0
Unreported	11.7	2.9
	100.0%	100.0%

40% are from out of state. 60% of classes have fewer than 20 students, 40% have between 20 and 50 students.

STUDENT HOUSING

Housing is not guaranteed for all undergraduates. Campus housing is available to only full-time students. Campus can house 416 undergraduates.

EXPENSES

Tuition (2005-06): $19,980 per year.
Room: $4,188. Board: $3,376.
There is no additional cost for LD program/services.

LD SERVICES

LD program size is not limited.

LD services available to:

- [ ] Freshmen
- [ ] Sophomores
- [ ] Juniors
- [ ] Seniors

Academic Accommodations

Curriculum		**In class**	
Foreign language waiver	[ ]	Early syllabus	[ ]
Lighter course load	[ ]	Note takers in class	[ ]
Math waiver	[ ]	Priority seating	[ ]
Other special classes	[ ]	Tape recorders	[x]
Priority registrations	[ ]	Videotaped classes	[ ]
Substitution of courses	[ ]	Text on tape	[ ]
Exams		**Services**	
Extended time	[x]	Diagnostic tests	[ ]
Oral exams	[x]	Learning centers	[ ]
Take home exams	[ ]	Proofreaders	[ ]
Exams on tape or computer	[ ]	Readers	[ ]
Untimed exams	[x]	Reading Machines/Kurzweil	[ ]
Other accommodations	[ ]	Special bookstore section	[ ]
		Typists	[ ]

Counseling Services

- [ ] Academic
- [ ] Psychological
- [ ] Student Support groups
- [ ] Vocational

Tutoring

	Individual	Group
Time management	[ ]	[ ]
Organizational skills	[ ]	[ ]
Learning strategies	[ ]	[ ]
Study skills	[ ]	[ ]
Content area	[ ]	[ ]
Writing lab	[ ]	[ ]
Math lab	[ ]	[ ]

LD PROGRAM STAFF

Key staff person available to work with LD students: Kate Ricci, Special Services Coordinator.

Saint Anselm College

Manchester, NH

Address: 100 St. Anselm Drive, Manchester, NH, 03102-1310
Admissions telephone: 888 426-7356
Admissions FAX: 603 641-7550
Director of Admissions/Freshmen Contact: Nancy Davis Griffin
Admissions e-mail: admission@anselm.edu
Web site: http://www.anselm.edu
SAT Code: 3748 ACT Code: 2522

LD program name: Office of Academic Advisement
Director of Academic Advisement: Anne Harrington
LD program telephone: 603 641-7464
LD program e-mail: aharrington@anselm.edu
LD program enrollment: 45, Total campus enrollment: 1,987

GENERAL

Saint Anselm College is a private, coed, four-year institution. 404-acre campus in Manchester (population: 107,006), 50 miles north of Boston and 18 miles south of Concord. Served by air and bus; major airport and train serve Boston. Public transportation serves campus. Semester system.

LD ADMISSIONS

A personal interview is recommended.

SECONDARY SCHOOL REQUIREMENTS

Graduation from secondary school required; GED accepted. The following course distribution required: 4 units of English, 3 units of math, 3 units of science, 2 units of foreign language, 2 units of social studies, 1 unit of history, 3 units of academic electives.

TESTING

SAT Reasoning or ACT required. SAT Subject recommended.

All enrolled freshmen (fall 2004):

Average SAT I Scores:	Verbal: 560	Math: 559
Average ACT Scores:	Composite: 27	

Child Study Team report is not required. Tests required as part of this documentation:

- ☐ WAIS-IV
- ☐ WISC-IV
- ☐ SATA
- ☐ Woodcock-Johnson
- ☐ Nelson-Denny Reading Test
- ☐ Other

UNDERGRADUATE STUDENT BODY

Total undergraduate student enrollment: 886 Men, 1,078 Women.

Composition of student body (fall 2004):

	Undergraduate	Freshmen
International	0.4	1.1
Black	0.6	0.5
American Indian	0.0	0.1
Asian-American	1.6	0.7
Hispanic	0.4	1.1
White	45.8	78.2
Unreported	51.2	18.3
	100.0%	100.0%

74% are from out of state. Average age of full-time undergraduates is 20. 49% of classes have fewer than 20 students, 47% between 20 and 50 students, 4% have more than 50 students.

STUDENT HOUSING

95% of freshmen live in college housing. Freshmen are not required to live on campus. Housing is guaranteed for all undergraduates. Campus can house 1,644 undergraduates. Single rooms are available for students with medical or special needs. A medical note is required.

EXPENSES

Tuition (2005-06): $23,990 per year.
Room & Board: $9,070.

There is no additional cost for LD program/services.

LD SERVICES

LD program size is not limited.

LD services available to:

■ Freshmen ■ Sophomores ■ Juniors ■ Seniors

Academic Accommodations

Curriculum		In class	
Foreign language waiver	☐	Early syllabus	☐
Lighter course load	■	Note takers in class	☐
Math waiver	☐	Priority seating	■
Other special classes	☐	Tape recorders	■
Priority registrations	☐	Videotaped classes	☐
Substitution of courses	☐	Text on tape	■
Exams		**Services**	
Extended time	■	Diagnostic tests	☐
Oral exams	☐	Learning centers	■
Take home exams	☐	Proofreaders	☐
Exams on tape or computer	■	Readers	☐
Untimed exams	■	Reading Machines/Kurzweil	☐
Other accommodations	■	Special bookstore section	☐
		Typists	☐

Credit toward degree is not given for remedial courses taken.

Counseling Services

- ■ Academic
- ■ Psychological
- ■ Student Support groups
- ☐ Vocational

Tutoring

Individual tutoring is available twice per month.

Average size of tutoring groups: 2

	Individual	Group
Time management	■	■
Organizational skills	■	■
Learning strategies	■	■
Study skills	■	■
Content area	■	■
Writing lab	■	☐
Math lab	☐	■

LD PROGRAM STAFF

Total number of LD Program staff (including director):

Full Time: 1 Part Time: 1

There is an advisor/advocate from the LD program available to students. 90 peer tutors are available to work with LD students.

Key staff person available to work with LD students: Anne Harrington, Director of Academic Advisement.

Southern New Hampshire University

Manchester, NH

Address: 2500 N. River Road, Manchester, NH, 03106
Admissions telephone: 800 642-4968
Admissions FAX: 603 645-9693
Director of Admission and Enrollment Planning: Steven Soba
Admissions e-mail: admission@snhu.edu
Web site: http://www.snhu.edu
SAT Code: 3649 ACT Code: 2514

Director of Disability Services: Hyla Jaffe
LD program telephone: 603 668-2211, extension 2386
LD program e-mail: h.jaffe@snhu.edu
LD program enrollment: 85, Total campus enrollment: 1,844

GENERAL

Southern New Hampshire University is a private, coed, four-year institution. 280-acre campus in Manchester (population: 107,006), 40 miles from Boston; branch campuses in Laconia; Manchester; Nashua; Portsmouth, Brunswick, ME.; in Puerto Rico, and Klang, Malaysia. Served by air and bus; major airport and train serve Boston. Public transportation serves campus. Semester system.

LD ADMISSIONS

A personal interview is recommended. Essay is required and may be typed.

SECONDARY SCHOOL REQUIREMENTS

Graduation from secondary school required; GED accepted. The following course distribution required: 4 units of English, 2 units of math, 2 units of science, 2 units of social studies, 1 unit of history, 2 units of academic electives.

TESTING

SAT Reasoning required; ACT may be substituted. SAT Subject required.

All enrolled freshmen (fall 2004):

Average SAT I Scores: Verbal: 488 Math: 490

Child Study Team report is not required. Tests required as part of this documentation:

- ☐ WAIS-IV
- ☐ WISC-IV
- ☐ SATA
- ☐ Woodcock-Johnson
- ☐ Nelson-Denny Reading Test
- ☐ Other

UNDERGRADUATE STUDENT BODY

Total undergraduate student enrollment: 1,777 Men, 2,130 Women.

54% are from out of state. 10% join a fraternity and 10% join a sorority. Average age of full-time undergraduates is 19. 49% of classes have fewer than 20 students, 51% have between 20 and 50 students.

STUDENT HOUSING

78% of freshmen live in college housing. Freshmen are required to live on campus. Housing is guaranteed for all undergraduates. Campus can house 1,387 undergraduates. Single rooms are available for students with medical or special needs. A medical note is required.

EXPENSES

Tuition (2005-06): $20,184 per year.
Room: $5,850. Board: $2,400.
There is no additional cost for LD program/services.

LD SERVICES

LD program size is not limited.

LD services available to:

■ Freshmen ■ Sophomores ■ Juniors ■ Seniors

Academic Accommodations

Curriculum		In class	
Foreign language waiver	☐	Early syllabus	■
Lighter course load	■	Note takers in class	■
Math waiver	☐	Priority seating	■
Other special classes	☐	Tape recorders	■
Priority registrations	■	Videotaped classes	☐
Substitution of courses	☐	Text on tape	■
Exams		**Services**	
Extended time	■	Diagnostic tests	☐
Oral exams	■	Learning centers	■
Take home exams	☐	Proofreaders	☐
Exams on tape or computer	■	Readers	■
Untimed exams	■	Reading Machines/Kurzweil	■
Other accommodations	☐	Special bookstore section	☐
		Typists	■

Credit toward degree is not given for remedial courses taken.

Counseling Services

- ■ Academic
- ■ Psychological
- ☐ Student Support groups
- ☐ Vocational

Tutoring

Individual tutoring is available daily.

Average size of tutoring groups: 3

	Individual	Group
Time management	■	■
Organizational skills	■	■
Learning strategies	■	■
Study skills	■	■
Content area	■	■
Writing lab	■	■
Math lab	■	■

LD PROGRAM STAFF

Total number of LD Program staff (including director):

Full Time: 1 Part Time: 1

There is an advisor/advocate from the LD program available to students. The advisor/advocate meets with faculty 2 times per month and students 2 times per month.

Key staff person available to work with LD students: Hyla Jaffe, MMHS, Director of Disability Services.

Bloomfield College

Bloomfield, NJ

Address: 467 Franklin Street, Bloomfield, NJ, 07003
Admissions telephone: 800 848-4555
Admissions FAX: 973 748-0916
Vice President of Admission: Lourdes Delgado
Admissions e-mail: admission@bloomfield.edu
Web site: http://www.bloomfield.edu
SAT Code: 2044 ACT Code: 2540

Learning Needs Specialist: Janette Lawrence
LD program telephone: 973 748-9000, extension 654
LD program e-mail: janette_lawrence@bloomfield.edu
LD program enrollment: 29, Total campus enrollment: 2,164

GENERAL

Bloomfield College is a private, coed, four-year institution. 12-acre campus in Bloomfield (population: 47,683), 20 miles from New York City and seven miles from Newark. Major airport, bus, and train serve Newark. Public transportation serves campus. Semester system.

LD ADMISSIONS

Students do not complete a separate application and are not simultaneously accepted to the LD program. A member of the LD program does not sit on the admissions committee. A personal interview is required. Essay is not required.

SECONDARY SCHOOL REQUIREMENTS

Graduation from secondary school required; GED accepted.

TESTING

SAT Reasoning required; ACT may be substituted. SAT Subject recommended.

All enrolled freshmen (fall 2004):

Average SAT I Scores: Verbal: 413 Math: 415

Child Study Team report is required if student is classified. A neuropsychological or comprehensive psycho-educational evaluation is required for admission. Tests required as part of this documentation:

- ☒ WAIS-IV
- ☒ WISC-IV
- ☐ SATA
- ☒ Woodcock-Johnson
- ☒ Nelson-Denny Reading Test
- ☐ Other

UNDERGRADUATE STUDENT BODY

Total undergraduate student enrollment: 545 Men, 1,226 Women.

Composition of student body (fall 2004):

	Undergraduate	Freshmen
International	0.4	1.3
Black	55.4	54.0
American Indian	0.2	0.3
Asian-American	3.5	3.2
Hispanic	21.9	19.4
White	14.4	14.3
Unreported	4.2	7.5
	100.0%	100.0%

3% are from out of state. 1% join a fraternity and 1% join a sorority. Average age of full-time undergraduates is 23. 74% of classes have fewer than 20 students, 26% have between 20 and 50 students.

STUDENT HOUSING

27% of freshmen live in college housing. Freshmen are not required to live on campus. Housing is not guaranteed for all undergraduates. Limited space is available. Campus can house 264 undergraduates. Single rooms are available for students with medical or special needs. A medical note is required.

EXPENSES

Tuition (2005-06): $14,850 per year.
Room: $3,700. Board: $3,700.
There is no additional cost for LD program/services.

LD SERVICES

LD program size is not limited.

LD services available to:

☒ Freshmen ☒ Sophomores ☒ Juniors ☒ Seniors

Academic Accommodations

Curriculum		In class	
Foreign language waiver	☐	Early syllabus	☐
Lighter course load	☒	Note takers in class	☐
Math waiver	☐	Priority seating	☐
Other special classes	☐	Tape recorders	☒
Priority registrations	☐	Videotaped classes	☐
Substitution of courses	☐	Text on tape	☒
Exams		**Services**	
Extended time	☒	Diagnostic tests	☒
Oral exams	☐	Learning centers	☒
Take home exams	☐	Proofreaders	☐
Exams on tape or computer	☒	Readers	☒
Untimed exams	☐	Reading Machines/Kurzweil	☒
Other accommodations	☐	Special bookstore section	☐
		Typists	☒

Credit toward degree is not given for remedial courses taken.

Counseling Services

- ☐ Academic
- ☐ Psychological
- ☒ Student Support groups — Meets 6 times per academic year
- ☐ Vocational

Tutoring

Individual tutoring is available weekly.

Average size of tutoring groups: 1

	Individual	Group
Time management	☒	☐
Organizational skills	☒	☐
Learning strategies	☒	☐
Study skills	☒	☐
Content area	☒	☒
Writing lab	☒	☒
Math lab	☒	☒

LD PROGRAM STAFF

Total number of LD Program staff (including director):

Full Time: 1 Part Time: 1

There is an advisor/advocate from the LD program available to students. The advisor/advocate meets with students 2 times per month.

Key staff person available to work with LD students: Janette Lawrence, Learning Needs Specialist.

Caldwell College

Caldwell, NJ

Address: 9 Ryerson Avenue, Caldwell, NJ, 07006
Admissions telephone: 888 864-9516
Admissions FAX: 973 618-3600
Vice President for Enrollment: Kathryn Reilly
Admissions e-mail: admissions@caldwell.edu
Web site: http://www.caldwell.edu
SAT Code: 2072 ACT Code: 2542

Disabilities Coordinator: Judith Kuperstein
LD program telephone: 973 618-3645
LD program e-mail: jkuperstein@caldwell.edu
Total campus enrollment: 1,712

GENERAL

Caldwell College is a private, coed, four-year institution. 70-acre, suburban campus in Caldwell (population: 7,584), 20 miles from New York City and 10 miles from Newark. Major airport and train serve Newark; bus serves Caldwell. Public transportation serves campus. Semester system.

LD ADMISSIONS

Students do not complete a separate application and are not simultaneously accepted to the LD program. A member of the LD program does not sit on the admissions committee. High school waivers are accepted for math and foreign language. A personal interview is recommended. Essay is required and may be typed.

SECONDARY SCHOOL REQUIREMENTS

Graduation from secondary school required; GED accepted. The following course distribution required: 4 units of English, 2 units of math, 2 units of science, 2 units of foreign language, 1 unit of history, 5 units of academic electives.

TESTING

SAT Reasoning or ACT required. SAT Subject recommended.

All enrolled freshmen (fall 2004):

Average SAT I Scores: Verbal: 476 Math: 465

Child Study Team report is required if student is classified. A neuropsychological or comprehensive psycho-education evaluation is not required for admission. Tests required as part of this documentation:

- ☐ WAIS-IV
- ☐ WISC-IV
- ☐ SATA
- ☐ Woodcock-Johnson
- ☐ Nelson-Denny Reading Test
- ☐ Other

UNDERGRADUATE STUDENT BODY

Total undergraduate student enrollment: 610 Men, 1,313 Women.

Composition of student body (fall 2004):

	Undergraduate	Freshmen
International	6.3	6.3
Black	14.9	13.3
American Indian	0.1	0.2
Asian-American	2.2	0.8
Hispanic	12.0	11.7
White	60.4	64.3
Unreported	4.1	3.4
	100.0%	100.0%

3% are from out of state. Average age of full-time undergraduates is 21. 79% of classes have fewer than 20 students, 21% have between 20 and 50 students.

STUDENT HOUSING

50% of freshmen live in college housing. Freshmen are not required to live on campus. Housing is guaranteed for all undergraduates. Campus can house 371 undergraduates. Single rooms are available for students with medical or special needs. A medical note is required.

EXPENSES

Tuition (2005-06): $18,700 per year.
Room: $3,950. Board: $3,780.
There is no additional cost for LD program/services.

LD SERVICES

LD program size is not limited.

LD services available to:

☑ Freshmen ☑ Sophomores ☑ Juniors ☑ Seniors

Academic Accommodations

Curriculum		**In class**	
Foreign language waiver	☐	Early syllabus	☐
Lighter course load	☑	Note takers in class	☑
Math waiver	☐	Priority seating	☐
Other special classes	☑	Tape recorders	☑
Priority registrations	☐	Videotaped classes	☐
Substitution of courses	☐	Text on tape	☐
Exams		**Services**	
Extended time	☑	Diagnostic tests	☐
Oral exams	☑	Learning centers	☑
Take home exams	☐	Proofreaders	☐
Exams on tape or computer	☐	Readers	☑
Untimed exams	☑	Reading Machines/Kurzweil	☑
Other accommodations	☐	Special bookstore section	☐
		Typists	☐

Credit toward degree is not given for remedial courses taken.

Counseling Services

- ☑ Academic
- ☑ Psychological
- ☑ Student Support groups
- ☐ Vocational

Tutoring

Individual tutoring is available.

	Individual	Group
Time management	☑	☑
Organizational skills	☑	☑
Learning strategies	☑	☑
Study skills	☐	☐
Content area	☐	☐
Writing lab	☑	☑
Math lab	☑	☑

LD PROGRAM STAFF

Total number of LD Program staff (including director):

Full Time: 4 Part Time: 4

Key staff person available to work with LD students: Judith Kuperstein, Disabilities Coordinator.

Centenary College

Hackettstown, NJ

Address: 400 Jefferson Street, Hackettstown, NJ, 07840
Admissions telephone: 800 236-8679
Admissions FAX: 908 852-3454
Vice President for Enrollment Management: Diane Finnan
Admissions e-mail: admissions@centenarycollege.edu
Web site: http://www.centenarycollege.edu
SAT Code: 2080 ACT Code: 2544

LD program name: Project ABLE
Admissions Counselor for Special Needs: Jane Ozga
LD program telephone: 908 852-1400, extension 2274
LD program e-mail: ozgaj@centenarycollege.edu
Total campus enrollment: 1,827

GENERAL

Centenary College is a private, coed, four-year institution. 42-acre campus in Hackettstown (population: 10,403), 55 miles from New York City. Served by bus and train; major airports serve Newark (50 miles) and New York City. School operates transportation to equestrian center. Semester system.

LD ADMISSIONS

A personal interview is required. Essay is required and may be typed.

SECONDARY SCHOOL REQUIREMENTS

Graduation from secondary school required; GED accepted. The following course distribution required: 4 units of English, 3 units of math, 2 units of science.

TESTING

SAT Reasoning or ACT required.

All enrolled freshmen (fall 2004):

Average SAT I Scores:	Verbal: 462	Math: 459
Average ACT Scores:	Composite: 17	

Child Study Team report is required if student is classified. Tests required as part of this documentation:

- ☐ WAIS-IV
- ☐ WISC-IV
- ☐ SATA
- ☐ Woodcock-Johnson
- ☐ Nelson-Denny Reading Test
- ☐ Other

UNDERGRADUATE STUDENT BODY

Total undergraduate student enrollment: 230 Men, 710 Women.

Composition of student body (fall 2004):

	Undergraduate	Freshmen
International	2.2	1.3
Black	7.7	3.5
American Indian	1.0	0.4
Asian-American	3.5	2.3
Hispanic	6.4	3.4
White	67.0	46.3
Unreported	12.2	42.8
	100.0%	100.0%

15% are from out of state. 1% join a fraternity and 1% join a sorority. Average age of full-time undergraduates is 23. 71% of classes have fewer than 20 students, 29% have between 20 and 50 students.

STUDENT HOUSING

87% of freshmen live in college housing. Freshmen are not required to live on campus. Housing is guaranteed for all undergraduates. Campus can house 620 undergraduates.

EXPENSES

Tuition (2005-06): $19,440 per year.

Room & Board: $8,600.

Additional cost for LD program/services: $925 per semester.

LD SERVICES

LD program size is not limited.

LD services available to:

☐ Freshmen ☐ Sophomores ☐ Juniors ☐ Seniors

Academic Accommodations

Curriculum		**In class**	
Foreign language waiver	☐	Early syllabus	☐
Lighter course load	■	Note takers in class	■
Math waiver	☐	Priority seating	☐
Other special classes	☐	Tape recorders	■
Priority registrations	☐	Videotaped classes	☐
Substitution of courses	☐	Text on tape	☐
Exams		**Services**	
Extended time	■	Diagnostic tests	☐
Oral exams	■	Learning centers	■
Take home exams	☐	Proofreaders	☐
Exams on tape or computer	☐	Readers	■
Untimed exams	■	Reading Machines/Kurzweil	■
Other accommodations	☐	Special bookstore section	☐
		Typists	☐

Credit toward degree is not given for remedial courses taken.

Counseling Services

- ☐ Academic
- ☐ Psychological
- ☐ Student Support groups
- ☐ Vocational

Tutoring

	Individual	Group
Time management	☐	☐
Organizational skills	☐	☐
Learning strategies	☐	☐
Study skills	☐	☐
Content area	☐	☐
Writing lab	☐	☐
Math lab	☐	☐

LD PROGRAM STAFF

Total number of LD Program staff (including director):

Full Time: 3 Part Time: 3

Key staff person available to work with LD students: Sandra Moore, Academic Support.

Drew University

Madison, NJ

Address: 36 Madison Avenue, Madison, NJ, 07940-1493
Admissions telephone: 973 408-3739
Admissions FAX: 973 408-3068
Dean of Admissions: Mary Beth Carey
Admissions e-mail: cadm@drew.edu
Web site: http://www.drew.edu
SAT Code: 2193 ACT Code: 2550

LD program name: Educational and Student Affairs
Dean of Educational and Student Affairs: Dr. Edye Lawler
LD program telephone: 973 408-3327
LD program e-mail: elawler@drew.edu
LD program enrollment: 40, Total campus enrollment: 1,629

GENERAL

Drew University is a private, coed, four-year institution. 186-acre campus in Madison (population: 16,530), 24 miles from New York City. Served by bus and train; major airport serves Newark (15 miles). Public transportation serves campus. Semester system.

LD ADMISSIONS

Essay is required and may be typed.

SECONDARY SCHOOL REQUIREMENTS

Graduation from secondary school is not required.

TESTING

SAT Reasoning required; ACT may be substituted. SAT Subject required.

All enrolled freshmen (fall 2004):

Average SAT I Scores:	Verbal: 618	Math: 600
Average ACT Scores:	Composite: 26	

Child Study Team report is not required. Tests required as part of this documentation:

- [ ] WAIS-IV
- [ ] WISC-IV
- [ ] SATA
- [ ] Woodcock-Johnson
- [ ] Nelson-Denny Reading Test
- [ ] Other

UNDERGRADUATE STUDENT BODY

Total undergraduate student enrollment: 592 Men, 944 Women.

Composition of student body (fall 2004):

	Undergraduate	Freshmen
International	1.7	0.9
Black	3.3	3.9
American Indian	0.3	0.5
Asian-American	6.2	5.5
Hispanic	5.5	5.8
White	69.4	64.1
Unreported	13.6	19.3
	100.0%	100.0%

42% are from out of state. Average age of full-time undergraduates is 20. 71% of classes have fewer than 20 students, 25% have between 20 and 50 students, 4% have more than 50 students.

STUDENT HOUSING

94% of freshmen live in college housing. Freshmen are not required to live on campus. Housing is guaranteed for all undergraduates. Campus can house 1,337 undergraduates. Single rooms are available for students with medical or special needs. A medical note is required.

EXPENSES

Tuition (2005-06): $30,740 per year.
Room: $5,438. Board: $2,974.
There is no additional cost for LD program/services.

LD SERVICES

LD program size is not limited.

LD services available to:

- [x] Freshmen
- [x] Sophomores
- [x] Juniors
- [x] Seniors

Academic Accommodations

Curriculum		In class	
Foreign language waiver	[ ]	Early syllabus	[ ]
Lighter course load	[x]	Note takers in class	[x]
Math waiver	[ ]	Priority seating	[ ]
Other special classes	[ ]	Tape recorders	[x]
Priority registrations	[ ]	Videotaped classes	[ ]
Substitution of courses	[ ]	Text on tape	[x]
Exams		**Services**	
Extended time	[x]	Diagnostic tests	[ ]
Oral exams	[ ]	Learning centers	[ ]
Take home exams	[ ]	Proofreaders	[ ]
Exams on tape or computer	[ ]	Readers	[ ]
Untimed exams	[ ]	Reading Machines/Kurzweil	[ ]
Other accommodations	[ ]	Special bookstore section	[ ]
		Typists	[ ]

Credit toward degree is not given for remedial courses taken.

Counseling Services

- [x] Academic
- [x] Psychological
- [x] Student Support groups
- [ ] Vocational

Tutoring

Individual tutoring is available weekly.

Average size of tutoring groups: 1

	Individual	Group
Time management	[ ]	[x]
Organizational skills	[ ]	[x]
Learning strategies	[ ]	[x]
Study skills	[ ]	[x]
Content area	[ ]	[ ]
Writing lab	[ ]	[ ]
Math lab	[ ]	[ ]

LD PROGRAM STAFF

Key staff person available to work with LD students: Dr. Elizabeth O'Brien, Assistant Director, Educational Services.

Fairleigh Dickinson University

Teaneck, NJ

Address: 1000 River Road, Teaneck, NJ, 07666
Admissions telephone: 800 338-8803
Admissions FAX: 201 692-2560
Vice President for Enrollment and Career Management: Gary Hamme
Admissions e-mail: globaleducation@fdu.edu
Web site: http://www.fdu.edu
SAT Code: 2263 ACT Code: 2552

Director: Dr. Mary L. Farrell
LD program telephone: 201 692-2716
LD program enrollment: 39, Total campus enrollment: 4,113

GENERAL

Fairleigh Dickinson University is a private, coed, four-year institution. 88-acre campus in Teaneck (population: 39,260), 17 miles from Newark and 25 miles from New York City; branch campuses in Madison and abroad in England and Israel. Major airports, bus, and train serve Newark and New York City; train also serves Hackensack (one mile). School operates transportation to New York City. Public transportation serves campus. Semester system.

LD ADMISSIONS

Students do not complete a separate application and are not simultaneously accepted to the LD program. A member of the LD program does not sit on the admissions committee. A personal interview is not required. Essay is not required. Minimum SAT I score requirement may be waived.

For fall 2004, 62 completed self-identified LD applications were received. 25 applications were offered admission, and 13 enrolled.

SECONDARY SCHOOL REQUIREMENTS

Graduation from secondary school required; GED accepted. The following course distribution required: 4 units of English, 3 units of math, 2 units of science, 2 units of foreign language, 2 units of history, 4 units of academic electives.

TESTING

SAT Reasoning or ACT required. SAT Subject recommended.

Child Study Team report is required if student is classified. A neuropsychological or comprehensive psycho-education evaluation is not required for admission. Tests required as part of this documentation:

- ❑ WAIS-IV
- ❑ WISC-IV
- ❑ SATA
- ❑ Woodcock-Johnson
- ❑ Nelson-Denny Reading Test
- ❑ Other

UNDERGRADUATE STUDENT BODY

Total undergraduate student enrollment: 1,728 Men, 2,385 Women.

Composition of student body (fall 2004):

	Undergraduate	Freshmen
International	10.1	11.1
Black	25.7	21.0
American Indian	0.2	0.5
Asian-American	3.8	5.6
Hispanic	19.5	13.8
White	27.2	35.8
Unreported	13.5	12.2
	100.0%	100.0%

12% are from out of state. 4% join a fraternity and 2% join a sorority. Average age of full-time undergraduates is 21.

STUDENT HOUSING

52% of freshmen live in college housing. Housing is guaranteed for all undergraduates. Single rooms are not available for students with medical or special needs.

EXPENSES

Tuition (2005-06): $22,604 per year.
Room: $5,878. Board: $3,604.
There is no additional cost for LD program/services.

LD SERVICES

LD program is limited to %1 students.

LD services available to:

❑ Freshmen ❑ Sophomores ❑ Juniors ❑ Seniors

Academic Accommodations

Curriculum		In class	
Foreign language waiver	❑	Early syllabus	❑
Lighter course load	❑	Note takers in class	❑
Math waiver	❑	Priority seating	❑
Other special classes	❑	Tape recorders	❑
Priority registrations	❑	Videotaped classes	❑
Substitution of courses	❑	Text on tape	❑
Exams		**Services**	
Extended time	❑	Diagnostic tests	❑
Oral exams	❑	Learning centers	❑
Take home exams	❑	Proofreaders	❑
Exams on tape or computer	❑	Readers	❑
Untimed exams	❑	Reading Machines/Kurzweil	❑
Other accommodations	❑	Special bookstore section	❑
		Typists	❑

Credit toward degree is not given for remedial courses taken.

Counseling Services

- ❑ Academic
- ❑ Psychological
- ❑ Student Support groups
- ❑ Vocational

Tutoring

Individual tutoring is not available.

	Individual	Group
Time management	❑	❑
Organizational skills	❑	❑
Learning strategies	❑	❑
Study skills	❑	❑
Content area	❑	❑
Writing lab	❑	❑
Math lab	❑	❑

LD PROGRAM STAFF

Total number of LD Program staff (including director):

Full Time: 1 Part Time: 1

There is no advisor/advocate from the LD program available to students.

Key staff person available to work with LD students: Vincent J. Varrassi, Campus Dir., Regional Center, College Students with Learning Disabilities.

Georgian Court University

Lakewood, NJ

Address: 900 Lakewood Avenue, Lakewood, NJ, 08701-2697
Admissions telephone: 800 458-8422, extension 760
Admissions FAX: 732 987-2000
Vice President for Enrollment: Kathie DeBona
Admissions e-mail: admissions@georgian.edu
Web site: http://www.georgian.edu
SAT Code: 2274 ACT Code: 2562

Director of Learning Center: Patricia A. Cohen
LD program telephone: 732 364-2200
LD program e-mail: cohenp@georgian.edu
Total campus enrollment: 2,046

GENERAL

Georgian Court University is a private, women's, four-year institution. 150-acre campus in Lakewood (population: 60,352), 60 miles from Philadelphia. Served by bus; major airports serve Philadelphia and Newark (48 miles); train serves Trenton (30 miles). Semester system.

LD ADMISSIONS

Students do not complete a separate application and are not simultaneously accepted to the LD program. A member of the LD program does not sit on the admissions committee. A personal interview is required. Essay is not required.

SECONDARY SCHOOL REQUIREMENTS

Graduation from secondary school required; GED accepted. The following course distribution required: 4 units of English, 2 units of math, 1 unit of science, 2 units of foreign language, 1 unit of history, 6 units of academic electives.

TESTING

SAT Reasoning required; ACT may be substituted. SAT Subject recommended.

All enrolled freshmen (fall 2004):

Average SAT I Scores: Verbal: 465 Math: 455

Child Study Team report is required if student is classified. Tests required as part of this documentation:

- ☐ WAIS-IV
- ☐ WISC-IV
- ☐ SATA
- ☐ Woodcock-Johnson
- ☐ Nelson-Denny Reading Test
- ☐ Other

UNDERGRADUATE STUDENT BODY

Total undergraduate student enrollment: 186 Men, 1,581 Women.

Composition of student body (fall 2004):

	Undergraduate	Freshmen
International	1.1	0.7
Black	11.2	5.3
American Indian	0.5	0.2
Asian-American	2.7	2.0
Hispanic	11.8	6.4
White	70.0	78.4
Unreported	2.7	7.0
	100.0%	100.0%

6% are from out of state. Average age of full-time undergraduates is 24. 74% of classes have fewer than 20 students, 26% have between 20 and 50 students.

STUDENT HOUSING

56% of freshmen live in college housing. Freshmen are not required to live on campus. Housing is guaranteed for all undergraduates. Campus can house 356 undergraduates.

EXPENSES

Tuition (2005-06): $18,380 per year.

Room: $4,560. Board: $3,040.

Additional cost for LD program/services: $2,400 per academic year.

LD SERVICES

LD program size is limited.

LD services available to:

■ Freshmen ■ Sophomores ■ Juniors ■ Seniors

Academic Accommodations

Curriculum		In class	
Foreign language waiver	☐	Early syllabus	☐
Lighter course load	■	Note takers in class	■
Math waiver	☐	Priority seating	☐
Other special classes	☐	Tape recorders	■
Priority registrations	☐	Videotaped classes	☐
Substitution of courses	☐	Text on tape	☐
Exams		**Services**	
Extended time	☐	Diagnostic tests	■
Oral exams	■	Learning centers	■
Take home exams	☐	Proofreaders	☐
Exams on tape or computer	☐	Readers	■
Untimed exams	■	Reading Machines/Kurzweil	☐
Other accommodations	■	Special bookstore section	☐
		Typists	☐

Credit toward degree is not given for remedial courses taken.

Counseling Services

- ■ Academic
- ■ Psychological
- ☐ Student Support groups
- ☐ Vocational

Tutoring

Individual tutoring is available.

	Individual	Group
Time management	■	☐
Organizational skills	■	☐
Learning strategies	■	☐
Study skills	■	■
Content area	☐	☐
Writing lab	☐	☐
Math lab	☐	☐

LD PROGRAM STAFF

Total number of LD Program staff (including director):

Full Time: 2 Part Time: 2

There is an advisor/advocate from the LD program available to students.

Key staff person available to work with LD students: Luann Fahr, Instruction Consultant.

LD Program web site: http://www.georgian.edu/learningcenter

Kean University

Union, NJ

Address: P.O. Box 411, Union, NJ, 07083
Admissions telephone: 908 737-7100
Admissions FAX: 908 737-7105
Director of Admissions: Audley Bridges
Admissions e-mail: admitme@kean.edu
Web site: http://www.kean.edu
SAT Code: 2517 ACT Code: 2582

Professor: Dr. Marie Segal
LD program telephone: 908 737-5400
LD program e-mail: msegal@kean.edu
Total campus enrollment: 9,947

GENERAL

Kean University is a public, coed, four-year institution. 150-acre, suburban campus in Union (population 54,405), 12 miles from New York City; branch campus in Hillside. Major airport and bus serve Newark (eight miles); train serves Elizabeth (three miles). School operates transportation between campuses. Public transportation serves campus. 4-1-4 system.

LD ADMISSIONS

A personal interview is required. Essay is not required.

SECONDARY SCHOOL REQUIREMENTS

Graduation from secondary school required; GED accepted. The following course distribution required: 4 units of English, 3 units of math, 2 units of science, 2 units of social studies, 5 units of academic electives.

TESTING

SAT Reasoning recommended; ACT may be substituted. SAT Subject recommended.

All enrolled freshmen (fall 2004):

Average SAT I Scores: Verbal: 460 Math: 475

Child Study Team report is required if student is classified. Tests required as part of this documentation:

- ☐ WAIS-IV
- ☐ WISC-IV
- ☐ SATA
- ☐ Woodcock-Johnson
- ☐ Nelson-Denny Reading Test
- ☐ Other

UNDERGRADUATE STUDENT BODY

Total undergraduate student enrollment: 3,307 Men, 6,160 Women.

Composition of student body (fall 2004):

	Undergraduate	Freshmen
International	1.0	2.7
Black	22.9	20.9
American Indian	0.5	0.3
Asian-American	7.3	6.1
Hispanic	20.0	19.5
White	46.0	47.9
Unreported	2.3	2.6
	100.0%	100.0%

5% are from out of state. Average age of full-time undergraduates is 22. 50% of classes have fewer than 20 students, 50% have between 20 and 50 students.

STUDENT HOUSING

37% of freshmen live in college housing. Housing is guaranteed for all undergraduates. Campus can house 1,310 undergraduates.

EXPENSES

Tuition (2005-06): $4,898 per year (in-state), $7,530 (out-of-state).

Room: $5,746. Board: $2,400.

There is no additional cost for LD program/services.

LD SERVICES

LD program size is not limited.

LD services available to:

☑ Freshmen ☑ Sophomores ☑ Juniors ☑ Seniors

Academic Accommodations

Curriculum		In class	
Foreign language waiver	☐	Early syllabus	☐
Lighter course load	☐	Note takers in class	☑
Math waiver	☐	Priority seating	☐
Other special classes	☑	Tape recorders	☑
Priority registrations	☐	Videotaped classes	☑
Substitution of courses	☐	Text on tape	☐
Exams		**Services**	
Extended time	☐	Diagnostic tests	☑
Oral exams	☑	Learning centers	☑
Take home exams	☐	Proofreaders	☐
Exams on tape or computer	☐	Readers	☑
Untimed exams	☑	Reading Machines/Kurzweil	☐
Other accommodations	☑	Special bookstore section	☐
		Typists	☐

Credit toward degree is not given for remedial courses taken.

Counseling Services

- ☑ Academic
- ☑ Psychological
- ☑ Student Support groups
- ☑ Vocational

Tutoring

Individual tutoring is available.

	Individual	Group
Time management	☑	☐
Organizational skills	☑	☐
Learning strategies	☑	☐
Study skills	☑	☐
Content area	☑	☐
Writing lab	☑	☐
Math lab	☑	☐

UNIQUE LD PROGRAM FEATURES

Peer & mentoring program for learning disabled students.

LD PROGRAM STAFF

There is an advisor/advocate from the LD program available to students.

Monmouth University

West Long Branch, NJ

Address: 400 Cedar Avenue, West Long Branch, NJ, 07764-1898
Admissions telephone: 800 543-9671
Admissions FAX: 732 263-5166
Vice President for Enrollment Management: Lauren Vento Cifelli
Admissions e-mail: admission@monmouth.edu
Web site: http://www.monmouth.edu
SAT Code: 2416 ACT Code: 2571

LD program telephone: 732 571-3460
LD program enrollment: 213, Total campus enrollment: 4,501

GENERAL

Monmouth University is a private, coed, four-year institution. 153-acre campus in West Long Branch (population: 8,258), 60 miles from both New York City and Philadelphia. Served by train; major airport serves Newark (35 miles); bus serves Red Bank (five miles). Public transportation serves campus. Semester system.

LD ADMISSIONS

A personal interview is recommended. Essay is not required.

SECONDARY SCHOOL REQUIREMENTS

Graduation from secondary school required; GED accepted. The following course distribution required: 4 units of English, 3 units of math, 2 units of science, 2 units of history, 5 units of academic electives.

TESTING

SAT Reasoning or ACT required. SAT Subject required.

All enrolled freshmen (fall 2004):

Average SAT I Scores:	Verbal: 525	Math: 535
Average ACT Scores:	Composite: 23	

Child Study Team report is not required. Tests required as part of this documentation:

- ☐ WAIS-IV
- ☐ WISC-IV
- ☐ SATA
- ☐ Woodcock-Johnson
- ☐ Nelson-Denny Reading Test
- ☐ Other

UNDERGRADUATE STUDENT BODY

Total undergraduate student enrollment: 1,770 Men, 2,409 Women.

Composition of student body (fall 2004):

	Undergraduate	Freshmen
International	0.2	0.3
Black	3.8	4.7
American Indian	0.1	0.3
Asian-American	2.0	2.1
Hispanic	5.3	3.9
White	76.8	78.5
Unreported	11.8	10.2
	100.0%	100.0%

6% are from out of state. 8% join a fraternity and 9% join a sorority. Average age of full-time undergraduates is 21. 46% of classes have fewer than 20 students, 54% have between 20 and 50 students.

STUDENT HOUSING

78% of freshmen live in college housing. Freshmen are not required to live on campus. Housing is not guaranteed for all undergraduates. Housing for freshmen is on a first come first served basis. A lottery system is used for upperclassmen to pick rooms. Campus can house 1,742 undergraduates. Single rooms are available for students with medical or special needs. A medical note is required.

EXPENSES

Tuition (2005-06): $20,066 per year.
Room: $4,440. Board: $3,830.

There is no additional cost for LD program/services.

LD SERVICES

LD program size is not limited.

LD services available to:

■ Freshmen ■ Sophomores ■ Juniors ■ Seniors

Academic Accommodations

Curriculum		In class	
Foreign language waiver	☐	Early syllabus	☐
Lighter course load	■	Note takers in class	■
Math waiver	☐	Priority seating	■
Other special classes	☐	Tape recorders	■
Priority registrations	■	Videotaped classes	☐
Substitution of courses	☐	Text on tape	■
Exams		**Services**	
Extended time	■	Diagnostic tests	☐
Oral exams	☐	Learning centers	☐
Take home exams	☐	Proofreaders	☐
Exams on tape or computer	☐	Readers	■
Untimed exams	☐	Reading Machines/Kurzweil	■
Other accommodations	■	Special bookstore section	☐
		Typists	■

Credit toward degree is not given for remedial courses taken.

Counseling Services

- ■ Academic
- ■ Psychological
- ■ Student Support groups
- ☐ Vocational

Tutoring

Individual tutoring is not available.

	Individual	Group
Time management	☐	☐
Organizational skills	☐	☐
Learning strategies	☐	☐
Study skills	☐	☐
Content area	☐	☐
Writing lab	☐	☐
Math lab	☐	☐

UNIQUE LD PROGRAM FEATURES

Diagnostic tests and Child Study Team reports are required for admittance to the LD program.

LD PROGRAM STAFF

Total number of LD Program staff (including director):

Full Time: 3 Part Time: 3

There is an advisor/advocate from the LD program available to students.

Key staff person available to work with LD students: Kelly Korz, Undergraduate Admissions Counselor.

Montclair State University

Montclair, NJ

Address: 1 Normal Avenue, Montclair, NJ, 07043
Admissions telephone: 800 331-9205
Admissions FAX: 973 655-7700
Director of Admissions: Dennis Craig
Admissions e-mail: undergraduate.admissions@montclair.edu
Web site: http://www.montclair.edu
SAT Code: 2520

LD program name: Services for Students with Disabilities
LD program address: Morehead Hall 305
Director: Linda Smith
LD program telephone: 973 655-5431
LD program e-mail: smithli@mail.montclair.edu
LD program enrollment: 207, Total campus enrollment: 11,819

GENERAL

Montclair State University is a public, coed, four-year institution. 200-acre campus in Upper Montclair, part of Montclair (population: 38,977), 10 miles from Newark and 14 miles from New York City. Major airport, bus, and train serve Newark. Public transportation serves campus. Semester system.

LD ADMISSIONS

Students do not complete a separate application and are not simultaneously accepted to the LD program. A member of the LD program does not sit on the admissions committee. High school waivers are accepted for foreign language. A personal interview is not required. Essay is not required. Admissions requirements that may be waived for LD students include foreign language and minimum SAT scores.

For fall 2004, 75 completed self-identified LD applications were received. 40 applications were offered admission, and 38 enrolled.

SECONDARY SCHOOL REQUIREMENTS

Graduation from secondary school required; GED accepted. The following course distribution required: 4 units of English, 3 units of math, 2 units of science, 2 units of foreign language, 2 units of social studies, 3 units of academic electives.

TESTING

SAT Reasoning or ACT required. SAT Subject required.

All enrolled freshmen (fall 2004):

Average SAT I Scores: Verbal: 509 Math: 522

Child Study Team report is not required. A neuropsychological or comprehensive psycho-educational evaluation is required for admission. Must be dated within 36 months of application. Tests required as part of this documentation:

- ■ WAIS-IV
- ■ WISC-IV
- ☐ SATA
- ■ Woodcock-Johnson
- ☐ Nelson-Denny Reading Test
- ☐ Other

UNDERGRADUATE STUDENT BODY

Total undergraduate student enrollment: 3,904 Men, 6,284 Women.

Composition of student body (fall 2004):

	Undergraduate	Freshmen
International	2.0	3.9
Black	11.5	10.3
American Indian	0.3	0.4
Asian-American	6.9	5.5
Hispanic	16.1	15.8
White	60.4	56.2
Unreported	2.8	7.9
	100.0%	100.0%

2% are from out of state. 3% join a fraternity and 5% join a sorority. Average age of full-time undergraduates is 22. 24% of classes have fewer than 20 students, 74% have between 20 and 50 students, 2% have more than 50 students.

STUDENT HOUSING

57% of freshmen live in college housing. Freshmen are not required to live on campus. Housing is guaranteed for all undergraduates. Campus can house 3,357 undergraduates. Single rooms are available for students with medical or special needs. A medical note is required.

EXPENSES

Tuition 2004-05: $5,311 per year (in-state), $8,836 (out-of-state).

There is no additional cost for LD program/services.

LD SERVICES

LD program size is not limited.

LD services available to:

■ Freshmen ■ Sophomores ■ Juniors ■ Seniors

Academic Accommodations

Curriculum		In class	
Foreign language waiver	■	Early syllabus	☐
Lighter course load	■	Note takers in class	■
Math waiver	☐	Priority seating	■
Other special classes	☐	Tape recorders	■
Priority registrations	■	Videotaped classes	☐
Substitution of courses	■	Text on tape	■
Exams		**Services**	
Extended time	■	Diagnostic tests	☐
Oral exams	■	Learning centers	■
Take home exams	☐	Proofreaders	■
Exams on tape or computer	■	Readers	■
Untimed exams	■	Reading Machines/Kurzweil	■
Other accommodations	■	Special bookstore section	☐
		Typists	■

Credit toward degree is not given for remedial courses taken.

Counseling Services

- ■ Academic
- ■ Psychological
- ■ Student Support groups
- ■ Vocational

Tutoring

Individual tutoring is available daily.

Average size of tutoring groups: 1

	Individual	Group
Time management	■	■
Organizational skills	■	■
Learning strategies	■	■
Study skills	■	■
Content area	■	■
Writing lab	■	■
Math lab	■	■

LD PROGRAM STAFF

Total number of LD Program staff (including director):

Full Time: 3 Part Time: 3

There is an advisor/advocate from the LD program available to students. 1 graduate student and 2 peer tutors are available to work with LD students.

Key staff person available to work with LD students: Linda Smith, Director of Services for Students with Disabilities.

LD Program web site: http://www.montclair.edu/wellness

The College of New Jersey

Ewing, NJ

Address: PO Box 7718, 2000 Pennington Road, Ewing, NJ, 08628-0718
Admissions telephone: 800 624-0967
Admissions FAX: 609 637-5174
Director of Admissions: Lisa Angeloni
Admissions e-mail: admiss@vm.tcnj.edu
Web site: http://www.tcnj.edu
SAT Code: 2519 ACT Code: 2614

Coordinator: Terri Yamiolkowski
LD program telephone: 609 771-2571
LD program e-mail: yamiolko@tcnj.edu
Total campus enrollment: 5,918

GENERAL

The College of New Jersey is a public, coed, four-year institution. 289-acre campus in Ewing Township (population: 35,707), six miles from Trenton. Airport, bus, and train serve Trenton/Mercer County; major airport serves Philadelphia (35 miles). Public transportation serves campus. Semester system.

LD ADMISSIONS

A personal interview is not required. Essay is required and may be typed.

SECONDARY SCHOOL REQUIREMENTS

Graduation from secondary school required; GED accepted. The following course distribution required: 4 units of English, 2 units of math, 2 units of science, 2 units of foreign language, 2 units of social studies.

TESTING

SAT Reasoning required; ACT may be substituted. SAT Subject recommended.

All enrolled freshmen (fall 2004):

Average SAT I Scores: Verbal: 622 Math: 639

Child Study Team report is not required. Tests required as part of this documentation:

- ☐ WAIS-IV
- ☐ WISC-IV
- ☐ SATA
- ☐ Woodcock-Johnson
- ☐ Nelson-Denny Reading Test
- ☐ Other

UNDERGRADUATE STUDENT BODY

Total undergraduate student enrollment: 2,448 Men, 3,525 Women.

Composition of student body (fall 2004):

	Undergraduate	Freshmen
International	0.2	0.2
Black	6.3	6.0
American Indian	0.2	0.1
Asian-American	7.0	4.6
Hispanic	8.3	6.6
White	76.4	78.0
Unreported	1.6	4.5
	100.0%	100.0%

5% are from out of state. 3% join a fraternity and 6% join a sorority. Average age of full-time undergraduates is 20. 53% of classes have fewer than 20 students, 46% have between 20 and 50 students, 1% have more than 50 students.

STUDENT HOUSING

96% of freshmen live in college housing. Freshmen are not required to live on campus. Housing is guaranteed for all undergraduates. Campus can house 3,582 undergraduates. Single rooms are available for students with medical or special needs. A medical note is required.

EXPENSES

Tuition (2005-06): $7,051 per year (in-state), $12,314 (out-of-state).
Room: $6,090. Board: $2,717.
There is no additional cost for LD program/services.

LD SERVICES

LD program size is not limited.

LD services available to:

☐ Freshmen ☐ Sophomores ☐ Juniors ☐ Seniors

Academic Accommodations

Curriculum		In class	
Foreign language waiver	☐	Early syllabus	☐
Lighter course load	☑	Note takers in class	☑
Math waiver	☐	Priority seating	☐
Other special classes	☐	Tape recorders	☑
Priority registrations	☐	Videotaped classes	☐
Substitution of courses	☑	Text on tape	☐
Exams		**Services**	
Extended time	☑	Diagnostic tests	☐
Oral exams	☐	Learning centers	☐
Take home exams	☐	Proofreaders	☐
Exams on tape or computer	☑	Readers	☑
Untimed exams	☐	Reading Machines/Kurzweil	☐
Other accommodations	☐	Special bookstore section	☐
		Typists	☐

Credit toward degree is not given for remedial courses taken.

Counseling Services

- ☐ Academic
- ☐ Psychological
- ☐ Student Support groups
- ☐ Vocational

Tutoring

Individual tutoring is available weekly.

Average size of tutoring groups: 5

	Individual	Group
Time management	☐	☐
Organizational skills	☐	☐
Learning strategies	☐	☐
Study skills	☐	☐
Content area	☐	☐
Writing lab	☐	☐
Math lab	☐	☐

UNIQUE LD PROGRAM FEATURES

A comprehensive tutoring center is available to all current students. The college also houses The Adaptive Technology Center for New Jersey Colleges which provides assistive technology loans to students with disabilities.

LD PROGRAM STAFF

Total number of LD Program staff (including director):

Full Time: 1 Part Time: 1

Key staff person available to work with LD students: Terri Yamiolkowski, Coordinator, Office of Differing Abilities Service.

LD Program web site: http://www.tcnj.edu/%7Ewellness/disability/

New Jersey Institute of Technology

Newark, NJ

Address: University Heights, Newark, NJ, 07102-1982
Admissions telephone: 800 925-NJIT
Admissions FAX: 973 596-3461
Director of Admissions: Kathy Kelly
Admissions e-mail: admissions@njit.edu
Web site: http://www.njit.edu
SAT Code: 2513

Associate Director: Phyllis Bolling
LD program telephone: 973 596-3420
LD program e-mail: phyllis.bolling@njit.edu
Total campus enrollment: 5,366

GENERAL

New Jersey Institute of Technology is a public, coed, four-year institution. 45-acre, urban campus in Newark (population: 260,000), 10 miles from New York City; branch campus in Mount Laurel. Served by air, bus, and train; major other airport serves New York City. School operates transportation to train and bus stations. Public transportation serves campus. Semester system.

LD ADMISSIONS

A personal interview is recommended.

SECONDARY SCHOOL REQUIREMENTS

Graduation from secondary school required; GED accepted. The following course distribution required: 4 units of English, 4 units of math, 2 units of science.

TESTING

SAT Reasoning required. SAT Subject recommended.

All enrolled freshmen (fall 2004):

Average SAT I Scores:	Verbal: 544	Math: 608
Average ACT Scores:	Composite:	

Child Study Team report is not required. Tests required as part of this documentation:

- [ ] WAIS-IV
- [ ] WISC-IV
- [ ] SATA
- [ ] Woodcock-Johnson
- [ ] Nelson-Denny Reading Test
- [ ] Other

UNDERGRADUATE STUDENT BODY

Total undergraduate student enrollment: 4,437 Men, 1,261 Women.

Composition of student body (fall 2004):

	Undergraduate	Freshmen
International	4.2	5.9
Black	8.9	10.4
American Indian	0.1	0.2
Asian-American	19.5	22.0
Hispanic	13.1	13.1
White	40.1	35.4
Unreported	14.1	13.0
	100.0%	100.0%

4% are from out of state. 7% join a fraternity and 5% join a sorority. Average age of full-time undergraduates is 22. 43% of classes have fewer than 20 students, 53% have between 20 and 50 students, 4% have more than 50 students.

STUDENT HOUSING

53% of freshmen live in college housing. Freshmen are not required to live on campus. Housing is guaranteed for all undergraduates. Campus can house 1,434 undergraduates.

EXPENSES

There is no additional cost for LD program/services.

LD SERVICES

LD program size is not limited.

LD services available to:

- [x] Freshmen
- [x] Sophomores
- [x] Juniors
- [x] Seniors

Academic Accommodations

Curriculum		In class	
Foreign language waiver	[ ]	Early syllabus	[ ]
Lighter course load	[x]	Note takers in class	[x]
Math waiver	[ ]	Priority seating	[ ]
Other special classes	[ ]	Tape recorders	[x]
Priority registrations	[ ]	Videotaped classes	[ ]
Substitution of courses	[ ]	Text on tape	[ ]
Exams		**Services**	
Extended time	[x]	Diagnostic tests	[ ]
Oral exams	[x]	Learning centers	[ ]
Take home exams	[ ]	Proofreaders	[ ]
Exams on tape or computer	[ ]	Readers	[x]
Untimed exams	[ ]	Reading Machines/Kurzweil	[x]
Other accommodations	[ ]	Special bookstore section	[ ]
		Typists	[ ]

Credit toward degree is not given for remedial courses taken.

Counseling Services

- [ ] Academic
- [ ] Psychological
- [ ] Student Support groups
- [ ] Vocational

Tutoring

	Individual	Group
Time management	[ ]	[ ]
Organizational skills	[ ]	[ ]
Learning strategies	[ ]	[ ]
Study skills	[ ]	[ ]
Content area	[ ]	[ ]
Writing lab	[ ]	[ ]
Math lab	[ ]	[ ]

LD PROGRAM STAFF

Key staff person available to work with LD students: Phyllis Bolling, Associate Director of the Counseling Center.

Princeton University

Princeton, NJ

Address: Princeton, NJ, 08544
Admissions telephone: 609 258-3060
Admissions FAX: 609 258-6743
Dean of Admissions: Janet L Rapelye
Web site: http://www.princeton.edu
SAT Code: 2672

LD program enrollment: 71, Total campus enrollment: 4,801

GENERAL

Princeton University is a private, coed, four-year institution. 600-acre campus in Princeton (population: 16,027), 50 miles from New York City and 45 miles from both Newark and Philadelphia. Served by bus and train; major airports serve Newark and Philadelphia. School operates transportation to New York City and Philadelphia for special events. Public transportation serves campus. Semester system.

LD ADMISSIONS

A personal interview is recommended. Essay is required and may be typed.

SECONDARY SCHOOL REQUIREMENTS

Graduation from secondary school required; GED accepted.

TESTING

SAT Subject recommended.

All enrolled freshmen (fall 2004):

Average SAT I Scores:	Verbal: 730	Math: 740
Average ACT Scores:	Composite:	

Child Study Team report is not required. A neuropsychological or comprehensive psycho-educational evaluation is required for admission. Must be dated within 36 months of application. Tests required as part of this documentation:

☑ WAIS-IV	☐ Woodcock-Johnson
☐ WISC-IV	☐ Nelson-Denny Reading Test
☐ SATA	☑ Other

UNDERGRADUATE STUDENT BODY

Total undergraduate student enrollment: 2,458 Men, 2,286 Women.

Composition of student body (fall 2004):

	Undergraduate	Freshmen
International	8.9	8.4
Black	7.3	8.2
American Indian	0.9	0.7
Asian-American	12.8	13.0
Hispanic	7.6	6.8
White	62.5	62.9
Unreported	0.0	0.0
	100.0%	100.0%

85% are from out of state. Average age of full-time undergraduates is 20. 73% of classes have fewer than 20 students, 16% have between 20 and 50 students, 11% have more than 50 students.

STUDENT HOUSING

100% of freshmen live in college housing. Freshmen are required to live on campus. Housing is guaranteed for all undergraduates. Campus can house 4,535 undergraduates. Single rooms are not available for students with medical or special needs.

EXPENSES

Tuition (2005-06): $31,450 per year.
Room & Board: $8,763.
There is no additional cost for LD program/services

LD SERVICES

LD services available to:

☐ Freshmen ☐ Sophomores ☐ Juniors ☐ Seniors

Academic Accommodations

Curriculum		**In class**	
Foreign language waiver	☐	Early syllabus	☐
Lighter course load	☐	Note takers in class	☐
Math waiver	☐	Priority seating	☐
Other special classes	☐	Tape recorders	☐
Priority registrations	☐	Videotaped classes	☐
Substitution of courses	☐	Text on tape	☐
Exams		**Services**	
Extended time	☐	Diagnostic tests	☐
Oral exams	☐	Learning centers	☐
Take home exams	☐	Proofreaders	☐
Exams on tape or computer	☐	Readers	☐
Untimed exams	☐	Reading Machines/Kurzweil	☐
Other accommodations	☐	Special bookstore section	☐
		Typists	☐

Credit toward degree is not given for remedial courses taken.

Counseling Services

☐ Academic
☐ Psychological
☐ Student Support groups
☐ Vocational

Tutoring

Individual tutoring is available weekly.

	Individual	Group
Time management	☐	☑
Organizational skills	☐	☑
Learning strategies	☐	☑
Study skills	☐	☑
Content area	☐	☑
Writing lab	☐	☑
Math lab	☐	☑

UNIQUE LD PROGRAM FEATURES

Princeton works on a case-by-case basis with individual students who want to request accommodations for a documented learning disability.

LD PROGRAM STAFF

Key staff person available to work with LD students: Maria Flores-Mills, Assistant Dean of Undergraduate Students.

Ramapo College of New Jersey

Mahwah, NJ

Address: 505 Ramapo Valley Road, Mahwah, NJ, 07430-1680
Admissions telephone: 800 9-RAMAPO
Admissions FAX: 201 684-7964
Director of Admissions: Nancy E. Jaeger
Admissions e-mail: admissions@ramapo.edu
Web site: http://www.ramapo.edu
SAT Code: 2884 ACT Code: 2591

LD program name: Office of Specialized Services
Program Assistant: Elizabeth Jocham
LD program e-mail: oss@ramapo.edu
LD program enrollment: 110, Total campus enrollment: 5,278

GENERAL

Ramapo College of New Jersey is a public, coed, four-year institution. 300-acre campus in Mahwah (population: 24,062), 25 miles from Newark and 35 miles from New York City. Served by bus; major airport and train serve Newark. School operates transportation to bus and train terminals periodically. Semester system.

LD ADMISSIONS

Students do not complete a separate application and are not simultaneously accepted to the LD program. A member of the LD program does not sit on the admissions committee. A personal interview is not required. Essay is required and may be typed. After they have been accepted, students with disabilities of all types self-identify with the Office of Specialized Services. The staff facilitates equal access on a case-by-case basis according to documented needs, not by disability designation. Diagnostic tests are not considered during the admissions process to the college; they are only required later by the Office of Specialized Services to establish eligibility and to help determine appropriate academic adjustments.

SECONDARY SCHOOL REQUIREMENTS

Graduation from secondary school required; GED accepted. The following course distribution required: 4 units of English, 3 units of math, 3 units of science, 2 units of foreign language, 4 units of social studies, 2 units of academic electives.

TESTING

SAT Reasoning required. ACT considered if submitted. SAT Subject required.

All enrolled freshmen (fall 2004):
Average SAT I Scores: Verbal: 577 Math: 587

Child Study Team report is not required. A neuropsychological or comprehensive psycho-educational evaluation is required for admission. Must be dated within 12 months of application. Tests required as part of this documentation:

- [x] WAIS-IV
- [ ] WISC-IV
- [ ] SATA
- [x] Woodcock-Johnson
- [ ] Nelson-Denny Reading Test
- [x] Other

UNDERGRADUATE STUDENT BODY

Total undergraduate student enrollment: 1,980 Men, 2,910 Women.

Composition of student body (fall 2004):

	Undergraduate	Freshmen
International	3.2	3.6
Black	5.7	6.6
American Indian	0.1	0.3
Asian-American	4.8	4.1
Hispanic	8.2	8.0
White	78.0	77.4
Unreported	0.0	0.0
	100.0%	100.0%

16% are from out of state. 8% join a fraternity and 5% join a sorority. Average age of full-time undergraduates is 21. 37% of classes have fewer than 20 students, 63% have between 20 and 50 students.

STUDENT HOUSING

89% of freshmen live in college housing. Freshmen are not required to live on campus. Housing is guaranteed for all undergraduates. Three dormitory buildings. The Overlook, a 295 bed, suite style housing complex. Phase IX housing scheduled to open in 2006.

EXPENSES

Tuition (2005-06): $6,091 per year (in-state), $11,008 (out-of-state).
Room: $6,140. Board: $2,624.
There is no additional cost for LD program/services.

LD SERVICES

LD program size is not limited.
LD services available to:

- [x] Freshmen
- [x] Sophomores
- [x] Juniors
- [x] Seniors

Academic Accommodations

Curriculum		In class	
Foreign language waiver	[ ]	Early syllabus	[x]
Lighter course load	[x]	Note takers in class	[x]
Math waiver	[ ]	Priority seating	[x]
Other special classes	[x]	Tape recorders	[x]
Priority registrations	[ ]	Videotaped classes	[ ]
Substitution of courses	[x]	Text on tape	[x]
Exams		**Services**	
Extended time	[x]	Diagnostic tests	[ ]
Oral exams	[ ]	Learning centers	[x]
Take home exams	[ ]	Proofreaders	[ ]
Exams on tape or computer	[x]	Readers	[ ]
Untimed exams	[ ]	Reading Machines/Kurzweil	[x]
Other accommodations	[x]	Special bookstore section	[ ]
		Typists	[ ]

Credit toward degree is not given for remedial courses taken.

Counseling Services

- [x] Academic
- [x] Psychological
- [x] Student Support groups
- [x] Vocational

Tutoring

Individual tutoring is available weekly.
Average size of tutoring groups: 5

	Individual	Group
Time management	[x]	[x]
Organizational skills	[x]	[x]
Learning strategies	[x]	[ ]
Study skills	[x]	[x]
Content area	[x]	[x]
Writing lab	[x]	[ ]
Math lab	[x]	[x]

LD PROGRAM STAFF

Total number of LD Program staff (including director):
Full Time: 5 Part Time: 5

There is an advisor/advocate from the LD program available to students. The advisor/advocate meets with students 2 times per month. 10 peer tutors are available to work with LD students.

Key staff person available to work with LD students: Ramona L. Kopacz, Learning Disabilities Specialist.

LD Program web site: http://www.ramapo.edu

Richard Stockton College of New Jersey

Pomona, NJ

Address: P.O. Box 195, Pomona, NJ, 08240-0195
Admissions telephone: 609 652-4261
Admissions FAX: 609 748-5541
Dean of Enrollment Management: Sal Catalfamo
Admissions e-mail: admissions@stockton.edu
Web site: http://www.stockton.edu
SAT Code: 2889 ACT Code: 2589

Coordinator: Frances H. Bottone
LD program telephone: 609 652-4988
LD program e-mail: frances.bottone@stockton.edu
LD program enrollment: 277, Total campus enrollment: 6,579

GENERAL

Richard Stockton College of New Jersey is a public, coed, four-year institution. 1,600-acre campus in Pomona (population: 4,019), 12 miles from Atlantic City. Major airport serves Philadelphia (50 miles); smaller airport and bus serve Atlantic City; train serves Absecon (eight miles). Public transportation serves campus. Semester system.

LD ADMISSIONS

Students do not complete a separate application and are not simultaneously accepted to the LD program. A member of the LD program does not sit on the admissions committee. A personal interview is not required. Essay is required and may be typed.

SECONDARY SCHOOL REQUIREMENTS

Graduation from secondary school required; GED accepted. The following course distribution required: 4 units of English, 3 units of math, 2 units of science, 2 units of social studies, 5 units of academic electives.

TESTING

SAT Reasoning required; ACT may be substituted. SAT Subject recommended.

All enrolled freshmen (fall 2004):

Average SAT I Scores:	Verbal: 544	Math: 556
Average ACT Scores:	Composite: 25	

Child Study Team report is not required. A neuropsychological or comprehensive psycho-educational evaluation is required for admission. Tests required as part of this documentation:

- [x] WAIS-IV
- [x] WISC-IV
- [x] SATA
- [x] Woodcock-Johnson
- [x] Nelson-Denny Reading Test
- [ ] Other

UNDERGRADUATE STUDENT BODY

Total undergraduate student enrollment: 2,553 Men, 3,585 Women.

Composition of student body (fall 2004):

	Undergraduate	Freshmen
International	0.2	0.7
Black	5.6	7.4
American Indian	0.4	0.5
Asian-American	4.2	3.9
Hispanic	6.2	5.7
White	83.4	81.8
Unreported	0.0	0.0
	100.0%	100.0%

3% are from out of state. 5% join a fraternity and 5% join a sorority. Average age of full-time undergraduates is 22. 33% of classes have fewer than 20 students, 65% have between 20 and 50 students, 2% have more than 50 students.

STUDENT HOUSING

86% of freshmen live in college housing. Freshmen are not required to live on campus. Housing is guaranteed for all undergraduates. Single rooms are available for students with medical or special needs. A medical note is required.

EXPENSES

Tuition (2005-06): $5,250 per year (in-state), $8,520 (out-of-state). Room: $5,370. Board: $2,634.
There is no additional cost for LD program/services.

LD SERVICES

LD program size is not limited.

LD services available to:

- [x] Freshmen
- [x] Sophomores
- [x] Juniors
- [x] Seniors

Academic Accommodations

Curriculum		**In class**	
Foreign language waiver	[ ]	Early syllabus	[ ]
Lighter course load	[x]	Note takers in class	[x]
Math waiver	[ ]	Priority seating	[x]
Other special classes	[ ]	Tape recorders	[x]
Priority registrations	[x]	Videotaped classes	[ ]
Substitution of courses	[x]	Text on tape	[x]
Exams		**Services**	
Extended time	[x]	Diagnostic tests	[ ]
Oral exams	[x]	Learning centers	[ ]
Take home exams	[ ]	Proofreaders	[x]
Exams on tape or computer	[x]	Readers	[x]
Untimed exams	[ ]	Reading Machines/Kurzweil	[x]
Other accommodations	[x]	Special bookstore section	[ ]
		Typists	[x]

Credit toward degree is given for remedial courses taken.

Counseling Services

- [x] Academic
- [x] Psychological
- [ ] Student Support groups
- [x] Vocational

Tutoring

Individual tutoring is not available.

	Individual	Group
Time management	[x]	[ ]
Organizational skills	[x]	[ ]
Learning strategies	[x]	[ ]
Study skills	[x]	[ ]
Content area	[ ]	[ ]
Writing lab	[x]	[ ]
Math lab	[x]	[ ]

UNIQUE LD PROGRAM FEATURES

Stockton's Learning Access Program works with students who have learning, physical and mental disabilities.

LD PROGRAM STAFF

Total number of LD Program staff (including director):

Full Time: 2 Part Time: 2

There is an advisor/advocate from the LD program available to students.

Key staff person available to work with LD students: Frances H. Bottone, Associate Director Counseling and Health Services.

LD Program web site: http://www2/stockton.edu/wellness/LAP.html

Rider University

Lawrenceville, NJ

Address: 2083 Lawrenceville Road, Lawrenceville, NJ, 08648-3099
Admissions telephone: 800 257-9026
Admissions FAX: 609 895-6645
Director of Admissions: Susan C. Christian
Admissions e-mail: admissions@rider.edu
Web site: http://www.rider.edu
SAT Code: 2758 ACT Code: 2590

Director: Dr. Barbara Blandford
LD program telephone: 609 896-5000
LD program e-mail: blandfor@rider.edu
LD program enrollment: 101, Total campus enrollment: 4,268

GENERAL

Rider University is a private, coed, four-year institution. 353-acre, suburban campus in Lawrenceville (population: 4,081), two miles from Trenton and 60 miles from New York City; branch campus in Princeton. Major airport serves Philadelphia (50 miles); smaller airport and train serve Trenton; bus serves Princeton (three miles). Public transportation serves campus. Semester system.

LD ADMISSIONS

A member of the LD program does not sit on the admissions committee. A personal interview is recommended. Essay is required and may be typed.

SECONDARY SCHOOL REQUIREMENTS

Graduation from secondary school required; GED accepted. The following course distribution required: 4 units of English, 2 units of math.

TESTING

SAT Reasoning or ACT required. SAT Subject recommended.

All enrolled freshmen (fall 2004):

Average SAT I Scores:	Verbal: 520	Math: 520
Average ACT Scores:	Composite:	

Child Study Team report is not required. A neuropsychological or comprehensive psycho-educational evaluation is required for admission. Must be dated within 36 months of application. Tests required as part of this documentation:

- ■ WAIS-IV
- ■ WISC-IV
- ☐ SATA
- ■ Woodcock-Johnson
- ■ Nelson-Denny Reading Test
- ■ Other

UNDERGRADUATE STUDENT BODY

Total undergraduate student enrollment: 1,825 Men, 2,551 Women.

Composition of student body (fall 2004):

	Undergraduate	Freshmen
International	1.3	1.3
Black	9.0	8.4
American Indian	0.7	0.2
Asian-American	2.9	3.1
Hispanic	5.1	5.0
White	73.7	74.6
Unreported	7.3	7.4
	100.0%	100.0%

24% are from out of state. 12% join a fraternity and 12% join a sorority. Average age of full-time undergraduates is 20. 51% of classes have fewer than 20 students, 47% have between 20 and 50 students, 2% have more than 50 students.

STUDENT HOUSING

85% of freshmen live in college housing. Freshmen are not required to live on campus. Housing is guaranteed for all undergraduates. Campus can house 2,376 undergraduates. Single rooms are available for students with medical or special needs. A medical note is required.

EXPENSES

Tuition (2005-06): $22,910 per year.
Room: $4,940. Board: $3,900.

There is no additional cost for LD program/services.

LD SERVICES

LD program size is not limited.

LD services available to:

■ Freshmen ■ Sophomores ■ Juniors ■ Seniors

Academic Accommodations

Curriculum		In class	
Foreign language waiver	☐	Early syllabus	☐
Lighter course load	■	Note takers in class	■
Math waiver	☐	Priority seating	■
Other special classes	■	Tape recorders	■
Priority registrations	■	Videotaped classes	☐
Substitution of courses	☐	Text on tape	■
Exams		**Services**	
Extended time	■	Diagnostic tests	■
Oral exams	■	Learning centers	■
Take home exams	☐	Proofreaders	☐
Exams on tape or computer	☐	Readers	■
Untimed exams	☐	Reading Machines/Kurzweil	■
Other accommodations	■	Special bookstore section	☐
		Typists	■

Credit toward degree is not given for remedial courses taken.

Counseling Services

- ■ Academic
- ■ Psychological
- ■ Student Support groups — Meets 5 times per academic year
- ■ Vocational

Tutoring

Individual tutoring is available weekly.

Average size of tutoring groups: 5

	Individual	Group
Time management	■	■
Organizational skills	■	☐
Learning strategies	■	■
Study skills	■	■
Content area	■	■
Writing lab	■	☐
Math lab	■	■

UNIQUE LD PROGRAM FEATURES

Services include screening and referral, supplementary assessment, advice to faculty and staff, and instructional services.

LD PROGRAM STAFF

Total number of LD Program staff (including director):

Full Time: 2 Part Time: 2

There is an advisor/advocate from the LD program available to students. 2 graduate students and 58 peer tutors are available to work with LD students.

Key staff person available to work with LD students: Dr. Barbara Blandford, Director, Services for Students with Disabilities.

Rowan University

Glassboro, NJ

Address: 201 Mullica Hill Road, Glassboro, NJ, 08028
Admissions telephone: 800 447-1165
Admissions FAX: 856 256-4430
Director of Admissions: Marvin Sills
Admissions e-mail: admissions@rowan.edu
Web site: http://www.rowan.edu
SAT Code: 2515 ACT Code: 2560

LD program name: Academic Success Center
Assistant Director: Johanna Velez-Yelen
LD program telephone: 856 256-4260
LD program e-mail: cox@rowan.edu
LD program enrollment: 320, Total campus enrollment: 8,383

GENERAL

Rowan University is a public, coed, four-year institution. 200-acre campus in Glassboro (population: 19,068), 15 miles from Philadelphia; branch campus in Camden. Served by bus; major airport and train serve Philadelphia. Public transportation serves campus. Semester system.

LD ADMISSIONS

Students do not complete a separate application and are not simultaneously accepted to the LD program. A member of the LD program does not sit on the admissions committee. A personal interview is not required. Essay is not required.

For fall 2004, 324 completed self-identified LD applications were received.

SECONDARY SCHOOL REQUIREMENTS

Graduation from secondary school required; GED accepted. The following course distribution required: 4 units of English, 3 units of math, 2 units of science, 2 units of social studies, 5 units of academic electives.

TESTING

SAT Reasoning required; ACT may be substituted. SAT Subject recommended.

All enrolled freshmen (fall 2004):

Average SAT I Scores: Verbal: 541 Math: 556

Child Study Team report is not required. A neuropsychological or comprehensive psycho-educational evaluation is required for admission. Must be dated within 36 months of application. Tests required as part of this documentation:

- ■ WAIS-IV
- ■ WISC-IV
- ☐ SATA
- ■ Woodcock-Johnson
- ■ Nelson-Denny Reading Test
- ■ Other

UNDERGRADUATE STUDENT BODY

Total undergraduate student enrollment: 3,461 Men, 4,696 Women.

Composition of student body (fall 2004):

	Undergraduate	Freshmen
International	0.1	0.0
Black	8.6	9.0
American Indian	0.2	0.3
Asian-American	4.3	3.5
Hispanic	8.2	6.2
White	77.9	79.1
Unreported	0.7	1.9
	100.0%	100.0%

4% are from out of state. 12% join a fraternity and 8% join a sorority. Average age of full-time undergraduates is 22. 43% of classes have fewer than 20 students, 57% have between 20 and 50 students.

STUDENT HOUSING

76% of freshmen live in college housing. Freshmen are required to live on campus. Housing is not guaranteed for all undergraduates. We cannot house all students who want housing. Campus can house 2,899 undergraduates. Single rooms are available for students with medical or special needs. A medical note is required.

EXPENSES

Tuition (2005-06): $6,294 per year (in-state), $12,588 (out-of-state). Room: $5,222. Board: $2,020.

There is no additional cost for LD program/services.

LD SERVICES

LD program size is not limited.

LD services available to:

■ Freshmen ■ Sophomores ■ Juniors ■ Seniors

Academic Accommodations

Curriculum		In class	
Foreign language waiver	☐	Early syllabus	☐
Lighter course load	■	Note takers in class	☐
Math waiver	☐	Priority seating	■
Other special classes	☐	Tape recorders	■
Priority registrations	■	Videotaped classes	☐
Substitution of courses	☐	Text on tape	■
Exams		**Services**	
Extended time	■	Diagnostic tests	☐
Oral exams	■	Learning centers	■
Take home exams	☐	Proofreaders	☐
Exams on tape or computer	☐	Readers	■
Untimed exams	■	Reading Machines/Kurzweil	■
Other accommodations	■	Special bookstore section	☐
		Typists	☐

Credit toward degree is not given for remedial courses taken.

Counseling Services

- ■ Academic — Meets 12 times per academic year
- ■ Psychological
- ■ Student Support groups
- ■ Vocational — Meets 2 times per academic year

Tutoring

Individual tutoring is available weekly.

Average size of tutoring groups: 2

	Individual	Group
Time management	■	■
Organizational skills	■	■
Learning strategies	■	■
Study skills	■	■
Content area	■	■
Writing lab	■	■
Math lab	■	■

LD PROGRAM STAFF

Total number of LD Program staff (including director):

Full Time: 3 Part Time: 3

There is an advisor/advocate from the LD program available to students. The advisor/advocate meets with students 4 times per month. 2 graduate students are available to work with LD students.

Key staff person available to work with LD students: Melissa Cox, Director of Academic Success.

Rutgers University - Camden Campus

Camden, NJ

Address: 406 Penn Street, Camden, NJ, 08102
Admissions telephone: 856 225-6104
Admissions FAX: 856 225-6498
Director of Admissions: Dr. Deborah Bowles
Admissions e-mail: camden@ugadm.rutgers.edu
Web site: http://www.rutgers.edu/
SAT Code: 2765 ACT Code: 2592

Assistant Dean: James Credle
LD program telephone: 973 353-5300
LD program e-mail: credle@andromeda.rutgers.edu
Total campus enrollment: 4,007

GENERAL

Rutgers University - Camden Campus is a public, coed, four-year institution. 25-acre, urban campus in Camden (population: 79,904), across the Delaware River from Philadelphia; branch campuses in New Brunswick and Newark. Served by bus and train; major airport serves Philadelphia. School operates transportation to Philadelphia. Public transportation serves campus. Semester system.

LD ADMISSIONS

A personal interview is recommended. Essay is not required.

SECONDARY SCHOOL REQUIREMENTS

Graduation from secondary school required; GED accepted. The following course distribution required: 4 units of English, 3 units of math, 2 units of science, 2 units of foreign language, 5 units of academic electives.

TESTING

SAT Reasoning or ACT required. SAT Subject required.

All enrolled freshmen (fall 2004):

Average SAT I Scores: Verbal: 554 Math: 570

Child Study Team report is not required. Tests required as part of this documentation:

- ❑ WAIS-IV
- ❑ WISC-IV
- ❑ SATA
- ❑ Woodcock-Johnson
- ❑ Nelson-Denny Reading Test
- ❑ Other

UNDERGRADUATE STUDENT BODY

Total undergraduate student enrollment: 1,489 Men, 2,188 Women.

Composition of student body (fall 2004):

	Undergraduate	Freshmen
International	1.1	0.8
Black	15.1	14.8
American Indian	0.0	0.4
Asian-American	12.1	8.6
Hispanic	6.6	5.8
White	62.3	66.3
Unreported	2.8	3.3
	100.0%	100.0%

3% are from out of state. Average age of full-time undergraduates is 23. 46% of classes have fewer than 20 students, 47% have between 20 and 50 students, 7% have more than 50 students.

STUDENT HOUSING

49% of freshmen live in college housing. Housing is not guaranteed for all undergraduates. Campus can house 520 undergraduates.

EXPENSES

Tuition (2005-06): $7,336 per year (in-state), $14,935 (out-of-state). Room: $5,778. Board: $2,310.

There is no additional cost for LD program/services.

LD SERVICES

LD program size is not limited.

LD services available to:

❑ Freshmen ❑ Sophomores ❑ Juniors ❑ Seniors

Academic Accommodations

Curriculum		In class	
Foreign language waiver	❑	Early syllabus	❑
Lighter course load	■	Note takers in class	❑
Math waiver	❑	Priority seating	❑
Other special classes	❑	Tape recorders	❑
Priority registrations	❑	Videotaped classes	❑
Substitution of courses	❑	Text on tape	❑
Exams		**Services**	
Extended time	■	Diagnostic tests	❑
Oral exams	❑	Learning centers	❑
Take home exams	❑	Proofreaders	❑
Exams on tape or computer	❑	Readers	❑
Untimed exams	❑	Reading Machines/Kurzweil	❑
Other accommodations	❑	Special bookstore section	❑
		Typists	❑

Credit toward degree is not given for remedial courses taken.

Counseling Services

- ❑ Academic
- ❑ Psychological
- ❑ Student Support groups
- ❑ Vocational

Tutoring

	Individual	Group
Time management	❑	❑
Organizational skills	❑	❑
Learning strategies	❑	❑
Study skills	❑	❑
Content area	❑	❑
Writing lab	❑	❑
Math lab	❑	❑

LD PROGRAM STAFF

Key staff person available to work with LD students: Barbara Detterline, Associate Dean.

Rutgers University - Camden College of Arts and Sciences

Camden, NJ

Address: 406 Penn Street, Camden, NJ, 08101
Admissions telephone: 856 225-6104
Admissions FAX: 856 225-6498
Director of Admissions: Deborah Bowles
Admissions e-mail: admissions@asb-ugadm.rutgers.edu
Web site: http://www.rutgers.edu
SAT Code: 2765 ACT Code: 2592

Assistant Dean of Students: William Edwards
LD program telephone: 856 225-6043
Total campus enrollment: 2,813

GENERAL

Rutgers University - Camden College of Arts and Sciences is a public, coed, four-year institution. 25-acre, urban campus in Camden (population: 79,904), across the Delaware River from Philadelphia; branch campuses in New Brunswick and Newark. Served by bus and train; major airport serves Philadelphia. School operates transportation to Philadelphia. Public transportation serves campus. Semester system.

LD ADMISSIONS

Students do not complete a separate application and are not simultaneously accepted to the LD program. A member of the LD program does not sit on the admissions committee. A personal interview is not required. Essay is not required.

SECONDARY SCHOOL REQUIREMENTS

Graduation from secondary school required; GED accepted. The following course distribution required: 4 units of English, 3 units of math, 2 units of science, 2 units of foreign language, 5 units of academic electives.

TESTING

SAT Reasoning or ACT required. SAT Subject required of some applicants. Admissions test requirements for LD students same as for other students.

All enrolled freshmen (fall 2004):

Average SAT I Scores: Verbal: Math:
Average ACT Scores: Composite:

Child Study Team report is not required. A neuropsychological or comprehensive psycho-education evaluation is not required for admission. Tests required as part of this documentation:

- ❑ WAIS-IV
- ❑ WISC-IV
- ❑ SATA
- ❑ Woodcock-Johnson
- ❑ Nelson-Denny Reading Test
- ❑ Other

UNDERGRADUATE STUDENT BODY

Total undergraduate student enrollment: 1,167 Men, 1,646 Women.

Composition of student body (fall 2004):

	Undergraduate	Freshmen
International	0.3	0.8
Black	14.0	14.3
American Indian	0.7	0.5
Asian-American	10.4	8.5
Hispanic	5.7	6.2
White	66.9	65.3
Unreported	2.0	4.4
	100.0%	100.0%

4% are from out of state.

STUDENT HOUSING

Housing is not guaranteed for all undergraduates. Housing available regardless of year, but housing is limited. Single rooms are not available for students with medical or special needs.

EXPENSES

There is no additional cost for LD program/services.

LD SERVICES

LD program size is not limited.

LD services available to:

❑ Freshmen ❑ Sophomores ❑ Juniors ❑ Seniors

Academic Accommodations

Curriculum		In class	
Foreign language waiver	❑	Early syllabus	❑
Lighter course load	■	Note takers in class	❑
Math waiver	❑	Priority seating	❑
Other special classes	❑	Tape recorders	❑
Priority registrations	❑	Videotaped classes	❑
Substitution of courses	❑	Text on tape	❑
Exams		**Services**	
Extended time	❑	Diagnostic tests	❑
Oral exams	❑	Learning centers	❑
Take home exams	❑	Proofreaders	❑
Exams on tape or computer	❑	Readers	❑
Untimed exams	❑	Reading Machines/Kurzweil	❑
Other accommodations	❑	Special bookstore section	❑
		Typists	❑

Credit toward degree is not given for remedial courses taken.

Counseling Services

- ❑ Academic
- ❑ Psychological
- ❑ Student Support groups
- ❑ Vocational

Tutoring

Individual tutoring is not available.

	Individual	Group
Time management	❑	❑
Organizational skills	❑	❑
Learning strategies	❑	❑
Study skills	❑	❑
Content area	❑	❑
Writing lab	❑	❑
Math lab	❑	❑

LD PROGRAM STAFF

There is no advisor/advocate from the LD program available to students.

Key staff person available to work with LD students: Valerie Smith Stephens, Director, Learning Resource Center.

Rutgers University - New Brunswick Campus

Piscataway, NJ

Address: 65 Davidson Road, Room 202, Piscataway, NJ, 08854-8097
Admissions telephone: 732 932-4636
Admissions FAX: 732 445-0237
Associate Director of University Undergraduate Admissions: Diane Harris
Admissions e-mail: admissions@asb-ugadm.rutgers.edu
Web site: http://www.rutgers.edu
SAT Code: 2765 ACT Code: 2592

Director: Cheryl Clarke
LD program telephone: 732 932-1711
LD program e-mail: cclarke@rci.rutgers.edu
Total campus enrollment: 26,813

GENERAL

Rutgers University - New Brunswick Campus is a public, coed, four-year institution. 2,695-acre campus (includes all New Brunswick colleges) in New Brunswick (population: 48,573), 33 miles from New York City; branch campuses in Newark and Camden. Served by bus and train; major airport serves Newark (20 miles). School operates intercollege and community bus service. Public transportation serves campus. Semester system.

LD ADMISSIONS

Essay is not required.

SECONDARY SCHOOL REQUIREMENTS

Graduation from secondary school required; GED accepted. The following course distribution required: 4 units of English, 3 units of math, 2 units of science, 2 units of foreign language, 5 units of academic electives.

TESTING

SAT Reasoning or ACT required. SAT Subject required.

All enrolled freshmen (fall 2004):

Average SAT I Scores:	Verbal: 592	Math: 619
Average ACT Scores:	Composite:	

Child Study Team report is not required. Tests required as part of this documentation:

- ☐ WAIS-IV
- ☐ WISC-IV
- ☐ SATA
- ☐ Woodcock-Johnson
- ☐ Nelson-Denny Reading Test
- ☐ Other

UNDERGRADUATE STUDENT BODY

Total undergraduate student enrollment: 13,193 Men, 15,158 Women.

Composition of student body (fall 2004):

	Undergraduate	Freshmen
International	1.3	2.0
Black	8.8	8.7
American Indian	0.3	0.2
Asian-American	24.8	21.5
Hispanic	9.4	8.3
White	51.8	55.1
Unreported	3.6	4.2
	100.0%	100.0%

8% are from out of state. Average age of full-time undergraduates is 20. 41% of classes have fewer than 20 students, 38% have between 20 and 50 students, 21% have more than 50 students.

STUDENT HOUSING

84% of freshmen live in college housing. Freshmen are not required to live on campus. Housing is guaranteed for all undergraduates. Campus can house 12,637 undergraduates.

EXPENSES

Tuition (2005-06): $5,000-$5,552 (state residents), $10,178-$10,294 (out-of-state).

There is no additional cost for LD program/services.

LD SERVICES

LD program size is not limited.

LD services available to:

☐ Freshmen ☐ Sophomores ☐ Juniors ☐ Seniors

Academic Accommodations

Curriculum		In class	
Foreign language waiver	☐	Early syllabus	☐
Lighter course load	■	Note takers in class	☐
Math waiver	☐	Priority seating	☐
Other special classes	☐	Tape recorders	☐
Priority registrations	☐	Videotaped classes	☐
Substitution of courses	☐	Text on tape	☐
Exams		**Services**	
Extended time	■	Diagnostic tests	☐
Oral exams	☐	Learning centers	☐
Take home exams	☐	Proofreaders	☐
Exams on tape or computer	☐	Readers	☐
Untimed exams	☐	Reading Machines/Kurzweil	☐
Other accommodations	☐	Special bookstore section	☐
		Typists	☐

Credit toward degree is not given for remedial courses taken.

Counseling Services

- ☐ Academic
- ☐ Psychological
- ☐ Student Support groups
- ☐ Vocational

Tutoring

	Individual	Group
Time management	☐	☐
Organizational skills	☐	☐
Learning strategies	☐	☐
Study skills	☐	☐
Content area	☐	☐
Writing lab	☐	☐
Math lab	☐	☐

Rutgers University - Newark Campus

Newark, NJ

Address: 249 University Avenue, Newark, NJ, 07102-1896
Admissions telephone: 973 353-5205
Admissions FAX: 973 353-1440
Director of Admissions - Newark: Bruce Neimeyer
Admissions e-mail: admissions@asb-ugadm.rutgers.edu
Web site: http://rutgers-newark.rutgers.edu
SAT Code: 2765 ACT Code: 2592

Director of Compliance and Student Policy: Brian T. Rose
LD program telephone: 732 932-7312
LD program e-mail: brose@rci.rutgers.edu
Total campus enrollment: 6,608

GENERAL

Rutgers University - Newark Campus is a public, coed, four-year institution. 36-acre, urban campus in Newark (population: 273,546), 10 miles from New York City; branch campuses in New Brunswick and Camden. Served by air, bus, and train. School operates transportation to train station and to other transportation and university locations. Public transportation serves campus. Semester system.

LD ADMISSIONS

A personal interview is not required. Essay is not required.

SECONDARY SCHOOL REQUIREMENTS

Graduation from secondary school required; GED accepted. The following course distribution required: 4 units of English, 3 units of math, 2 units of science, 2 units of foreign language, 5 units of academic electives.

TESTING

SAT Reasoning or ACT required. SAT Subject required.

All enrolled freshmen (fall 2004):

Average SAT I Scores: Verbal: 546 Math: 569

Child Study Team report is not required. Tests required as part of this documentation:

- ☐ WAIS-IV
- ☐ WISC-IV
- ☐ SATA
- ☐ Woodcock-Johnson
- ☐ Nelson-Denny Reading Test
- ☐ Other

UNDERGRADUATE STUDENT BODY

Total undergraduate student enrollment: 2,580 Men, 3,528 Women.

Composition of student body (fall 2004):

	Undergraduate	Freshmen
International	1.4	2.6
Black	13.4	20.2
American Indian	0.4	0.3
Asian-American	27.8	22.1
Hispanic	16.4	17.7
White	34.3	29.5
Unreported	6.3	7.6
	100.0%	100.0%

5% are from out of state. Average age of full-time undergraduates is 22. 40% of classes have fewer than 20 students, 46% have between 20 and 50 students, 14% have more than 50 students.

STUDENT HOUSING

36% of freshmen live in college housing. Freshmen are not required to live on campus. Housing is guaranteed for all undergraduates. Campus can house 878 undergraduates.

EXPENSES

Tuition (2005-06): $7,336 per year (in-state), $14,934 (out-of-state).
Room & Board: $8,984.
There is no additional cost for LD program/services.

LD SERVICES

LD program size is not limited.

LD services available to:

☐ Freshmen ☐ Sophomores ☐ Juniors ☐ Seniors

Academic Accommodations

Curriculum		**In class**	
Foreign language waiver	☐	Early syllabus	☐
Lighter course load	☐	Note takers in class	☐
Math waiver	☐	Priority seating	☐
Other special classes	☐	Tape recorders	☐
Priority registrations	☐	Videotaped classes	☐
Substitution of courses	☐	Text on tape	☐
Exams		**Services**	
Extended time	■	Diagnostic tests	☐
Oral exams	☐	Learning centers	■
Take home exams	☐	Proofreaders	☐
Exams on tape or computer	☐	Readers	☐
Untimed exams	☐	Reading Machines/Kurzweil	☐
Other accommodations	☐	Special bookstore section	☐
		Typists	☐

Credit toward degree is not given for remedial courses taken.

Counseling Services

- ☐ Academic
- ☐ Psychological
- ☐ Student Support groups
- ☐ Vocational

Tutoring

	Individual	Group
Time management	☐	☐
Organizational skills	☐	☐
Learning strategies	☐	☐
Study skills	☐	☐
Content area	☐	☐
Writing lab	☐	☐
Math lab	☐	☐

LD PROGRAM STAFF

Key staff person available to work with LD students: Barbara Detterlein, Assistant Dean.

College of Saint Elizabeth

Morristown, NJ

Address: 2 Convent Road, Morristown, NJ, 07960-6989
Admissions telephone: 800 210-7900
Admissions FAX: 973 290-4710
Dean of Admission: Dean Donna Tartarka
Admissions e-mail: apply@cse.edu
Web site: http://www.cse.edu
SAT Code: 2090 ACT Code: 2546

Director of the Learning Center: Virginia Reiner
LD program telephone: 973 290-4325
LD program e-mail: vreiner@cse.edu
LD program enrollment: 32, Total campus enrollment: 1,327

GENERAL

College of Saint Elizabeth is a private, women's, four-year institution. 200-acre campus in Morristown (population: 18,544), 18 miles from Newark and 35 miles from New York City. Served by train; major airports serve Newark and New York City. Public transportation serves campus. Semester system.

LD ADMISSIONS

Students do not complete a separate application and are simultaneously accepted to the LD program. A member of the LD program does sit on the admissions committee. A personal interview is recommended. Essay is required and may be typed.

SECONDARY SCHOOL REQUIREMENTS

Graduation from secondary school required; GED accepted. The following course distribution required: 3 units of English, 2 units of math, 1 unit of science, 2 units of foreign language, 1 unit of history, 7 units of academic electives.

TESTING

SAT Reasoning required; ACT may be substituted. SAT Subject recommended.

All enrolled freshmen (fall 2004):

Average SAT I Scores: Verbal: 467 Math: 460

Child Study Team report is not required. A neuropsychological or comprehensive psycho-educational evaluation is required for admission. Must be dated within 36 months of application. Tests required as part of this documentation:

- [x] WAIS-IV
- [ ] WISC-IV
- [ ] SATA
- [x] Woodcock-Johnson
- [x] Nelson-Denny Reading Test
- [x] Other

UNDERGRADUATE STUDENT BODY

Total undergraduate student enrollment: 88 Men, 1,163 Women.

Composition of student body (fall 2004):

	Undergraduate	Freshmen
International	4.3	3.0
Black	16.5	16.1
American Indian	0.6	0.1
Asian-American	5.5	5.1
Hispanic	21.3	14.3
White	42.7	53.8
Unreported	9.1	7.6
	100.0%	100.0%

3% are from out of state. Average age of full-time undergraduates is 20. 75% of classes have fewer than 20 students, 25% have between 20 and 50 students.

STUDENT HOUSING

79% of freshmen live in college housing. Freshmen are not required to live on campus. Housing is guaranteed for all undergraduates. Campus can house 321 undergraduates. Single rooms are available for students with medical or special needs. A medical note is not required.

EXPENSES

Tuition (2005-06): $18,640 per year.
Room & Board: $8,975.
There is no additional cost for LD program/services.

LD SERVICES

LD program size is not limited.

LD services available to:

- [x] Freshmen
- [x] Sophomores
- [x] Juniors
- [x] Seniors

Academic Accommodations

Curriculum		In class	
Foreign language waiver	[ ]	Early syllabus	[ ]
Lighter course load	[x]	Note takers in class	[x]
Math waiver	[ ]	Priority seating	[x]
Other special classes	[ ]	Tape recorders	[x]
Priority registrations	[ ]	Videotaped classes	[ ]
Substitution of courses	[ ]	Text on tape	[x]
Exams		**Services**	
Extended time	[x]	Diagnostic tests	[ ]
Oral exams	[x]	Learning centers	[x]
Take home exams	[ ]	Proofreaders	[ ]
Exams on tape or computer	[x]	Readers	[x]
Untimed exams	[x]	Reading Machines/Kurzweil	[ ]
Other accommodations	[ ]	Special bookstore section	[ ]
		Typists	[ ]

Credit toward degree is not given for remedial courses taken.

Counseling Services

- [x] Academic
- [ ] Psychological
- [ ] Student Support groups
- [ ] Vocational

Meets 2 times per academic year

Tutoring

Individual tutoring is available daily.

Average size of tutoring groups: 3

	Individual	Group
Time management	[x]	[x]
Organizational skills	[x]	[x]
Learning strategies	[x]	[x]
Study skills	[x]	[x]
Content area	[x]	[x]
Writing lab	[x]	[x]
Math lab	[x]	[x]

LD PROGRAM STAFF

Total number of LD Program staff (including director):

Full Time: 1 Part Time: 1

There is no advisor/advocate from the LD program available to students. 25 peer tutors are available to work with LD students.

Key staff person available to work with LD students: Virgina Reiner, Director of Academic Skills Center.

Saint Peter's College

Jersey City, NJ

Address: 2641 Kennedy Boulevard, Jersey City, NJ, 07306-5997
Admissions telephone: 888 SPC-9933
Admissions FAX: 201 432-5860
Associate Vice President for Enrollment: Joe Giglio
Admissions e-mail: admissions@spc.edu
Web site: http://www.spc.edu
SAT Code: 2806 ACT Code: 2604

Coordinator of Academic Success Program: Tushar Trivedi
LD program telephone: 201 915-9013
LD program enrollment: 36, Total campus enrollment: 2,374

GENERAL

Saint Peter's College is a private, coed, four-year institution. 15-acre, urban campus in Jersey City (population: 240,055), five miles from both Newark and New York City; branch campus in Englewood Cliffs. Served by bus; major airport and train serve Newark and New York City. School operates transportation to train station and local mall. Public transportation serves campus. Semester system.

LD ADMISSIONS

Students do not complete a separate application and are simultaneously accepted to the LD program. A member of the LD program does not sit on the admissions committee. High school waivers are accepted for math and foreign language. A personal interview is recommended. Essay is required and may be typed.

For fall 2004, 36 completed self-identified LD applications were received. 32 applications were offered admission, and 32 enrolled.

SECONDARY SCHOOL REQUIREMENTS

Graduation from secondary school required; GED accepted. The following course distribution required: 4 units of English, 3 units of math, 2 units of science, 3 units of foreign language, 3 units of social studies, 3 units of history, 3 units of academic electives.

TESTING

SAT Reasoning required; ACT may be substituted. SAT Subject recommended.

All enrolled freshmen (fall 2004):

Average SAT I Scores:	Verbal: 480	Math: 490
Average ACT Scores:	Composite: 20	

Child Study Team report is required if student is classified. A neuropsychological or comprehensive psycho-educational evaluation is required for admission. Must be dated within 24 months of application. Tests required as part of this documentation:

■ WAIS-IV	■ Woodcock-Johnson
■ WISC-IV	☐ Nelson-Denny Reading Test
■ SATA	☐ Other

UNDERGRADUATE STUDENT BODY

Total undergraduate student enrollment: 1,214 Men, 1,548 Women.

Composition of student body (fall 2004):

	Undergraduate	Freshmen
International	3.2	2.6
Black	18.2	15.3
American Indian	0.2	0.3
Asian-American	8.4	5.2
Hispanic	20.6	22.5
White	36.7	18.6
Unreported	12.7	35.5
	100.0%	100.0%

12% are from out of state. Average age of full-time undergraduates is 21. 67% of classes have fewer than 20 students, 33% have between 20 and 50 students.

STUDENT HOUSING

51% of freshmen live in college housing. Freshmen are not required to live on campus. Housing is not guaranteed for all undergraduates. There is an age limit (25 years old) to students allowed to live on campus. Campus can house 730 undergraduates. Single rooms are available for students with medical or special needs. A medical note is required.

EXPENSES

Tuition (2005-06): $20,640 per year.
Room: $5,570. Board: $1,600.
There is no additional cost for LD program/services.

LD SERVICES

LD program size is limited.

LD services available to:

■ Freshmen ■ Sophomores ■ Juniors ■ Seniors

Academic Accommodations

Curriculum		In class	
Foreign language waiver	■	Early syllabus	☐
Lighter course load	☐	Note takers in class	■
Math waiver	■	Priority seating	■
Other special classes	☐	Tape recorders	■
Priority registrations	■	Videotaped classes	☐
Substitution of courses	■	Text on tape	☐
Exams		**Services**	
Extended time	■	Diagnostic tests	■
Oral exams	■	Learning centers	■
Take home exams	■	Proofreaders	■
Exams on tape or computer	■	Readers	■
Untimed exams	■	Reading Machines/Kurzweil	■
Other accommodations	■	Special bookstore section	☐
		Typists	■

Credit toward degree is not given for remedial courses taken.

Counseling Services

■ Academic	Meets 3 times per academic year
■ Psychological	Meets 3 times per academic year
☐ Student Support groups	
☐ Vocational	

Tutoring

Individual tutoring is available weekly.

	Individual	Group
Time management	■	☐
Organizational skills	■	☐
Learning strategies	■	☐
Study skills	■	☐
Content area	■	☐
Writing lab	■	☐
Math lab	■	☐

UNIQUE LD PROGRAM FEATURES

Learning disabled students are dealt with on an individual basis. There is a comprehensive program for learning disabled students. Scheduled faculty training/workshop held in August.

LD PROGRAM STAFF

There is an advisor/advocate from the LD program available to students. The advisor/advocate meets with faculty 2 times per month.

Key staff person available to work with LD students: Tushar Trivedi, Coordinator of Academic Success Program.

Seton Hall University

South Orange, NJ

Address: 400 South Orange Avenue, South Orange, NJ, 07079
Admissions telephone: 800 THE-HALL (out-of-state)
Admissions FAX: 973 275-2040
Associate Provost for Enrollment Management: Sandra Taylor
Admissions e-mail: thehall@shu.edu
Web site: http://www.shu.edu
SAT Code: 2811 ACT Code: 2606

LD program name: Disability Support Services
Director, Disability Support Services: Linda Walter
LD program telephone: 973 313-6003
LD program e-mail: walterli@shu.edu
LD program enrollment: 597, Total campus enrollment: 5,414

GENERAL

Seton Hall University is a private, coed, four-year institution. 58-acre, suburban campus in South Orange (population: 16,964), three miles from Newark and 15 miles from New York City; branch campus in Newark. Served by bus; major airport and train serve Newark. School operates transportation to off-campus apartments. Public transportation serves campus. Semester system.

LD ADMISSIONS

A personal interview is required. Essay is not required.

SECONDARY SCHOOL REQUIREMENTS

Graduation from secondary school required; GED accepted. The following course distribution required: 4 units of English, 3 units of math, 1 unit of science, 2 units of foreign language, 2 units of social studies, 4 units of academic electives.

TESTING

SAT Reasoning or ACT required. SAT Subject required.

All enrolled freshmen (fall 2004):

Average SAT I Scores: Verbal: 547 Math: 550

Child Study Team report is required if student is classified. Tests required as part of this documentation:

- ☐ WAIS-IV
- ☐ WISC-IV
- ☐ SATA
- ☐ Woodcock-Johnson
- ☐ Nelson-Denny Reading Test
- ☐ Other

UNDERGRADUATE STUDENT BODY

Total undergraduate student enrollment: 2,669 Men, 2,796 Women.

Composition of student body (fall 2004):

	Undergraduate	Freshmen
International	0.5	1.1
Black	10.9	11.9
American Indian	0.1	0.1
Asian-American	5.5	7.6
Hispanic	10.3	9.5
White	52.8	52.3
Unreported	19.9	17.5
	100.0%	100.0%

17% are from out of state. 5% join a fraternity and 3% join a sorority. Average age of full-time undergraduates is 20. 49% of classes have fewer than 20 students, 49% have between 20 and 50 students, 2% have more than 50 students.

STUDENT HOUSING

74% of freshmen live in college housing. Freshmen are not required to live on campus. Housing is guaranteed for all undergraduates. Campus can house 2,205 undergraduates. Single rooms are available for students with medical or special needs. A medical note is required.

EXPENSES

Tuition (2005-06): $21,510 per year.

Room: $6,470. Board: $3,692.

There is no additional cost for LD program/services.

LD SERVICES

LD program size is not limited.

LD services available to:

■ Freshmen ■ Sophomores ■ Juniors ■ Seniors

Academic Accommodations

Curriculum		In class	
Foreign language waiver	■	Early syllabus	☐
Lighter course load	■	Note takers in class	☐
Math waiver	■	Priority seating	■
Other special classes	☐	Tape recorders	■
Priority registrations	■	Videotaped classes	☐
Substitution of courses	☐	Text on tape	■
Exams		**Services**	
Extended time	■	Diagnostic tests	■
Oral exams	■	Learning centers	☐
Take home exams	☐	Proofreaders	☐
Exams on tape or computer	☐	Readers	■
Untimed exams	■	Reading Machines/Kurzweil	■
Other accommodations	☐	Special bookstore section	■
		Typists	■

Credit toward degree is not given for remedial courses taken.

Counseling Services

- ☐ Academic
- ☐ Psychological
- ■ Student Support groups
- ☐ Vocational

Tutoring

	Individual	Group
Time management	■	■
Organizational skills	■	■
Learning strategies	■	■
Study skills	■	☐
Content area	■	☐
Writing lab	■	☐
Math lab	■	☐

UNIQUE LD PROGRAM FEATURES

The program for students with disabilities on campus serves students with learning, medical or psychological/psychiatric disabilities as well as students with temporary disabilities (fractures, post surgical, etc). Documentation is required for each of the areas.

LD PROGRAM STAFF

Total number of LD Program staff (including director):

Full Time: 2 Part Time: 2

There is an advisor/advocate from the LD program available to students. 7 graduate students and 5 peer tutors are available to work with LD students.

Key staff person available to work with LD students: Linda Walter, Director, Disability Support Services.

LD Program web site: http://studentaffairs.shu.edu/dss/

Stevens Institute of Technology

Hoboken, NJ

Address: Castle Point on Hudson, Hoboken, NJ, 07030
Admissions telephone: 800 458-5323
Admissions FAX: 201 216-8348
Dean of Undergraduate Admissions: Daniel Gallagher
Admissions e-mail: admissions@stevens.edu
Web site: http://www.stevens.edu
SAT Code: 2819 ACT Code: 2610

Dean of Student Life: Ken Nilsen
LD program telephone: 201 216-5699
LD program e-mail: knilsen@stevens.edu
Total campus enrollment: 1,730

GENERAL

Stevens Institute of Technology is a private, coed, four-year institution. 55-acre campus in Hoboken (population: 38,577), one mile from New York City. Served by bus and train; major airports serve Newark (10 miles) and New York City. Semester system.

LD ADMISSIONS

Students do not complete a separate application and are not simultaneously accepted to the LD program. A member of the LD program does not sit on the admissions committee. A personal interview is required. Essay is required and may be typed.

SECONDARY SCHOOL REQUIREMENTS

Graduation from secondary school required; GED not accepted. The following course distribution required: 4 units of English, 4 units of math, 3 units of science, 2 units of history.

TESTING

SAT Reasoning required; ACT may be substituted. SAT Subject recommended.

All enrolled freshmen (fall 2004):

Average SAT I Scores: Verbal: Math:
Average ACT Scores: Composite:

Child Study Team report is not required. A neuropsychological or comprehensive psycho-education evaluation is not required for admission. Tests required as part of this documentation:

- ☐ WAIS-IV
- ☐ WISC-IV
- ☐ SATA
- ☐ Woodcock-Johnson
- ☐ Nelson-Denny Reading Test
- ☐ Other

UNDERGRADUATE STUDENT BODY

Total undergraduate student enrollment: 1,243 Men, 406 Women.

Composition of student body (fall 2004):

	Undergraduate	Freshmen
International	4.3	5.8
Black	4.3	4.2
American Indian	0.2	0.1
Asian-American	8.0	15.5
Hispanic	10.3	9.4
White	61.0	53.8
Unreported	11.9	11.2
	100.0%	100.0%

35% are from out of state. 34% join a fraternity and 31% join a sorority. Average age of full-time undergraduates is 20. 47% of classes have fewer than 20 students, 45% have between 20 and 50 students, 8% have more than 50 students.

STUDENT HOUSING

85% of freshmen live in college housing. Freshmen are not required to live on campus. Housing is guaranteed for all undergraduates. Campus can house 1,060 undergraduates. Single rooms are available for students with medical or special needs. A medical note is required.

EXPENSES

Tuition (2005-06): $30,240 per year.
Room: $5,200. Board: $5,300.
There is no additional cost for LD program/services.

LD SERVICES

LD program size is not limited.

LD services available to:

☒ Freshmen ☒ Sophomores ☒ Juniors ☒ Seniors

Academic Accommodations

Curriculum		**In class**	
Foreign language waiver	☐	Early syllabus	☐
Lighter course load	☒	Note takers in class	☐
Math waiver	☐	Priority seating	☐
Other special classes	☐	Tape recorders	☐
Priority registrations	☐	Videotaped classes	☐
Substitution of courses	☐	Text on tape	☐
Exams		**Services**	
Extended time	☒	Diagnostic tests	☐
Oral exams	☐	Learning centers	☐
Take home exams	☐	Proofreaders	☐
Exams on tape or computer	☐	Readers	☐
Untimed exams	☒	Reading Machines/Kurzweil	☐
Other accommodations	☐	Special bookstore section	☐
		Typists	☐

Credit toward degree is not given for remedial courses taken.

Counseling Services

- ☒ Academic
- ☐ Psychological
- ☐ Student Support groups
- ☐ Vocational

Tutoring

Individual tutoring is available daily.

Average size of tutoring groups: 1

	Individual	Group
Time management	☐	☒
Organizational skills	☐	☒
Learning strategies	☐	☒
Study skills	☐	☒
Content area	☐	☐
Writing lab	☒	☐
Math lab	☐	☐

LD PROGRAM STAFF

There is an advisor/advocate from the LD program available to students.

Key staff person available to work with LD students: Ken Nilsen, Dean of Student Life.

Thomas Edison State College

Trenton, NJ

Address: 101 W. State Street, Trenton, NJ, 08608-1176
Admissions telephone: 888 442-8372
Admissions FAX: 609 984-8447
Director of Admissions: Renee San Giacomo
Admissions e-mail: admissions@tesc.edu
Web site: http://www.tesc.edu
SAT Code: 682

LD program name: Office for Students with Disabilities
ADA Coordinator: Janice Toliver
LD program telephone: 609 984-1141, extension 3415
LD program e-mail: ada@tesc.edu
LD program enrollment: 9, Total campus enrollment: 10,750

GENERAL

Thomas Edison State College is a public, coed, four-year institution. Two-acre, urban campus in downtown Trenton (population: 85,403), 45 miles from Philadelphia and 76 miles from New York City. Served by bus and train; major airport serves Philadelphia. Public transportation serves campus. Continuous system.

LD ADMISSIONS

A personal interview is not required. Essay is not required. Applicants should be at least 21 years old.

SECONDARY SCHOOL REQUIREMENTS

Graduation from secondary school required; GED accepted.

TESTING

All enrolled freshmen (fall 2004):

Average SAT I Scores: Verbal: Math:
Average ACT Scores: Composite:

Child Study Team report is not required. Tests required as part of this documentation:

☐ WAIS-IV	☐ Woodcock-Johnson
☐ WISC-IV	☐ Nelson-Denny Reading Test
☐ SATA	☐ Other

UNDERGRADUATE STUDENT BODY

Total undergraduate student enrollment: 4,338 Men, 3,814 Women.

Composition of student body (fall 2004):

	Freshmen
International	2.3
Black	11.2
American Indian	1.0
Asian-American	2.0
Hispanic	4.9
White	67.2
Unreported	11.4
	100.0%

42% are from out of state.

EXPENSES

Tuition (2005-06): $3,780 per year (in-state), $5,400 (out-of-state). Comprehensive Plan: $2,750 per year (state residents), $3,950 (out-of-state) for unlimited tests, portfolios, courses. Other plans available.

There is no additional cost for LD program/services.

LD SERVICES

LD program size is not limited.

LD services available to:

■ Freshmen ■ Sophomores ■ Juniors ■ Seniors

Academic Accommodations

Curriculum		**In class**	
Foreign language waiver	☐	Early syllabus	☐
Lighter course load	☐	Note takers in class	☐
Math waiver	☐	Priority seating	☐
Other special classes	☐	Tape recorders	☐
Priority registrations	☐	Videotaped classes	☐
Substitution of courses	■	Text on tape	■
Exams		**Services**	
Extended time	■	Diagnostic tests	☐
Oral exams	☐	Learning centers	☐
Take home exams	☐	Proofreaders	☐
Exams on tape or computer	■	Readers	☐
Untimed exams	☐	Reading Machines/Kurzweil	☐
Other accommodations	■	Special bookstore section	☐
		Typists	☐

Credit toward degree is not given for remedial courses taken.

Counseling Services

■ Academic
☐ Psychological
☐ Student Support groups
☐ Vocational

Tutoring

Individual tutoring is not available.

	Individual	Group
Time management	☐	☐
Organizational skills	☐	☐
Learning strategies	☐	☐
Study skills	☐	☐
Content area	☐	☐
Writing lab	☐	☐
Math lab	☐	☐

UNIQUE LD PROGRAM FEATURES

Documentation is not needed for admission but is needed for disability related services.

LD PROGRAM STAFF

Total number of LD Program staff (including director):

Full Time: 1 Part Time: 1

There is an advisor/advocate from the LD program available to students.

Key staff person available to work with LD students: Janice Toliver, ADA Coordinator.

LD Program web site: www.tesc.edu

Westminster Choir College of Rider University

Princeton, NJ

Address: 101 Walnut Lane, Princeton, NJ, 08540
Admissions telephone: 800 962-4647
Admissions FAX: 609 921-2538
Director of Admissions: Matthew T. Kadlubowski
Admissions e-mail: wccinfo@rider.edu
Web site: http://westminster.rider.edu
SAT Code: 2974 ACT Code: 2619

Director: Dr. Jacqueline Simon
LD program telephone: 609 895-5244

GENERAL

Westminster Choir College of Rider University is a private, coed, four-year institution. 23-acre campus in Princeton (population: 16,027), 50 miles from both New York City and Philadelphia. Served by bus; major airports serve Newark (40 miles) and Philadelphia; train serves Princeton Junction (two miles). School operates transportation to main campus of Rider U. Public transportation serves campus. Semester system.

LD ADMISSIONS

Students do not complete a separate application and are not simultaneously accepted to the LD program. A member of the LD program does not sit on the admissions committee. A personal interview is recommended. Essay is required and may be typed.

SECONDARY SCHOOL REQUIREMENTS

Graduation from secondary school required; GED accepted. The following course distribution required: 4 units of English, 1 unit of math, 2 units of history.

TESTING

SAT Reasoning or ACT required. Admissions test requirements for LD students same as for other students.

All enrolled freshmen (fall 2004):

Average SAT I Scores: Verbal: 551 Math: 528
Average ACT Scores: Composite:

Child Study Team report is not required. A neuropsychological or comprehensive psycho-education evaluation is not required for admission. Tests required as part of this documentation:

- ❑ WAIS-IV
- ❑ WISC-IV
- ❑ SATA
- ❑ Woodcock-Johnson
- ❑ Nelson-Denny Reading Test
- ❑ Other

COMPOSITION OF STUDENT BODY (FALL 2004):

67% are from out of state. Average age of full-time undergraduates is 21.

STUDENT HOUSING

Housing is guaranteed for all undergraduates. Single rooms are not available for students with medical or special needs.

EXPENSES

There is no additional cost for LD program/services.

LD SERVICES

LD program size is not limited.

LD services available to:

❑ Freshmen ❑ Sophomores ❑ Juniors ❑ Seniors

Academic Accommodations

Curriculum		**In class**	
Foreign language waiver	❑	Early syllabus	❑
Lighter course load	■	Note takers in class	❑
Math waiver	❑	Priority seating	❑
Other special classes	❑	Tape recorders	❑
Priority registrations	❑	Videotaped classes	❑
Substitution of courses	❑	Text on tape	❑
Exams		**Services**	
Extended time	❑	Diagnostic tests	❑
Oral exams	❑	Learning centers	❑
Take home exams	❑	Proofreaders	❑
Exams on tape or computer	❑	Readers	❑
Untimed exams	❑	Reading Machines/Kurzweil	❑
Other accommodations	❑	Special bookstore section	❑
		Typists	❑

Credit toward degree is not given for remedial courses taken.

Counseling Services

- ❑ Academic
- ❑ Psychological
- ❑ Student Support groups
- ❑ Vocational

Tutoring

Individual tutoring is not available.

	Individual	Group
Time management	❑	❑
Organizational skills	❑	❑
Learning strategies	❑	❑
Study skills	❑	❑
Content area	❑	❑
Writing lab	❑	❑
Math lab	❑	❑

UNIQUE LD PROGRAM FEATURES

Most LD services available at both campuses; professional consultation offered at Rider U campus only.

LD PROGRAM STAFF

Total number of LD Program staff (including director):

Full Time: 3 Part Time: 3

There is no advisor/advocate from the LD program available to students.

Key staff person available to work with LD students: Barbara Blandford, Director of the Learning Center.

William Paterson University of New Jersey

Wayne, NJ

Address: 300 Pompton Road, Wayne, NJ, 07470
Admissions telephone: 973 720-2125
Admissions FAX: 973 720-2910
Director of Admissions: Jonathan McCoy
Admissions e-mail: admissions@wpunj.edu
Web site: http://www2.wpunj.edu/
SAT Code: 2518 ACT Code: 2584

LD program name: Employment Equity and Diversity
LD program address: Room 101
Coordinator, Disability Services: Jackie Safont
LD program telephone: 973 720-2853
LD program e-mail: disability@wpunj.edu
LD program enrollment: 203, Total campus enrollment: 9,418

GENERAL

William Paterson University of New Jersey is a public, coed, four-year institution. 300-acre campus in Wayne (population: 54,069), 21 miles from Newark. Major airport and train serve Newark; bus serves Paterson (two miles). Public transportation serves campus. Semester system.

SECONDARY SCHOOL REQUIREMENTS

Graduation from secondary school required; GED accepted. The following course distribution required: 4 units of English, 3 units of math, 2 units of science, 2 units of social studies.

TESTING

SAT Reasoning or ACT required.

All enrolled freshmen (fall 2004):

Average SAT I Scores: Verbal: 493 Math: 500
Average ACT Scores: Composite:

Child Study Team report is not required. A neuropsychological or comprehensive psycho-education evaluation is not required for admission. Tests required as part of this documentation:

- [ ] WAIS-IV
- [ ] WISC-IV
- [ ] SATA
- [ ] Woodcock-Johnson
- [ ] Nelson-Denny Reading Test
- [ ] Other

UNDERGRADUATE STUDENT BODY

Total undergraduate student enrollment: 3,504 Men, 4,950 Women.

Composition of student body (fall 2004):

	Undergraduate	Freshmen
International	1.6	1.5
Black	12.9	12.4
American Indian	0.1	0.3
Asian-American	6.8	5.0
Hispanic	18.6	16.2
White	57.1	61.3
Unreported	2.9	3.3
	100.0%	100.0%

3% are from out of state. 2% join a fraternity and 3% join a sorority. Average age of full-time undergraduates is 22. 41% of classes have fewer than 20 students, 58% have between 20 and 50 students, 1% have more than 50 students.

STUDENT HOUSING

42% of freshmen live in college housing. Freshmen are not required to live on campus. Housing is guaranteed for all undergraduates. Campus can house 2,662 undergraduates. Single rooms are available for students with medical or special needs. A medical note is required.

EXPENSES

Tuition (2005-06): $5,358 per year (in-state), $10,474 (out-of-state).
Room: $6,030. Board: $3,030.
There is no additional cost for LD program/services.

LD SERVICES

LD program size is not limited.

LD services available to:

- [x] Freshmen
- [x] Sophomores
- [x] Juniors
- [x] Seniors

Academic Accommodations

Curriculum

- [ ] Foreign language waiver
- [ ] Lighter course load
- [ ] Math waiver
- [ ] Other special classes
- [ ] Priority registrations
- [x] Substitution of courses

Exams

- [x] Extended time
- [x] Oral exams
- [ ] Take home exams
- [x] Exams on tape or computer
- [ ] Untimed exams
- [x] Other accommodations

In class

- [ ] Early syllabus
- [x] Note takers in class
- [ ] Priority seating
- [x] Tape recorders
- [ ] Videotaped classes
- [ ] Text on tape

Services

- [ ] Diagnostic tests
- [ ] Learning centers
- [ ] Proofreaders
- [x] Readers
- [x] Reading Machines/Kurzweil
- [ ] Special bookstore section
- [x] Typists

Credit toward degree is not given for remedial courses taken.

Counseling Services

- [x] Academic
- [ ] Psychological
- [ ] Student Support groups
- [ ] Vocational

Tutoring

Individual tutoring is not available.

	Individual	Group
Time management	[ ]	[ ]
Organizational skills	[ ]	[ ]
Learning strategies	[ ]	[ ]
Study skills	[ ]	[x]
Content area	[ ]	[ ]
Writing lab	[ ]	[x]
Math lab	[ ]	[x]

UNIQUE LD PROGRAM FEATURES

Students usually do not self-disclose disability until after they are already accepted. Students may request services at anytime during their college careers.

LD PROGRAM STAFF

Total number of LD Program staff (including director):

Full Time: 1 Part Time: 1

1 graduate student is available to work with LD students.

Key staff person available to work with LD students: Jackie Safont, Coordinator, Disability Services.

LD Program web site: www.wpunj.edu

Eastern New Mexico University

Portales, NM

Address: Station 2, Portales, NM, 88130
Admissions telephone: 800 367-3668
Admissions FAX: 505 562-2118
Admissions e-mail: admissions.office@enmu.edu
Web site: http://www.enmu.edu
SAT Code: 4299 ACT Code: 2636

Director: Bernita Davis
LD program telephone: 505 562-2280
LD program e-mail: Bernita.Davis@enmu.edu
Total campus enrollment: 3,160

GENERAL

Eastern New Mexico University is a public, coed, four-year institution. 400-acre campus in Portales (population: 11,131), 100 miles from both Amarillo and Lubbock, Tex.; two-year branch campuses in Roswell and Ruidoso. Served by bus; airports serve Amarillo and Lubbock; train serves Albuquerque (230 miles). Semester system.

LD ADMISSIONS

A personal interview is not required. Essay is not required.

SECONDARY SCHOOL REQUIREMENTS

Graduation from secondary school required; GED accepted.

TESTING

SAT Reasoning required. ACT required. SAT Subject recommended.

All enrolled freshmen (fall 2004):

Average SAT I Scores:	Verbal: 456	Math: 464
Average ACT Scores:	Composite: 19	

Child Study Team report is not required. Tests required as part of this documentation:

- [ ] WAIS-IV
- [ ] WISC-IV
- [ ] SATA
- [ ] Woodcock-Johnson
- [ ] Nelson-Denny Reading Test
- [ ] Other

UNDERGRADUATE STUDENT BODY

Total undergraduate student enrollment: 1,216 Men, 1,751 Women.

Composition of student body (fall 2004):

	Undergraduate	Freshmen
International	0.8	0.8
Black	8.0	6.6
American Indian	3.6	2.8
Asian-American	1.0	0.9
Hispanic	28.9	29.4
White	53.8	55.3
Unreported	3.9	4.2
	100.0%	100.0%

19% are from out of state. Average age of full-time undergraduates is 22. 52% of classes have fewer than 20 students, 42% have between 20 and 50 students, 6% have more than 50 students.

STUDENT HOUSING

68% of freshmen live in college housing. Freshmen are required to live on campus. Housing is guaranteed for all undergraduates. Campus can house 1,031 undergraduates.

EXPENSES

Tuition (2005-06): $1,992 per year (in-state), $7,548 (out-of-state).
Room: $2,090. Board: $2,390.

There is no additional cost for LD program/services.

LD SERVICES

LD program size is not limited.

LD services available to:

- [x] Freshmen
- [x] Sophomores
- [x] Juniors
- [x] Seniors

Academic Accommodations

Curriculum		**In class**	
Foreign language waiver	[ ]	Early syllabus	[ ]
Lighter course load	[ ]	Note takers in class	[ ]
Math waiver	[ ]	Priority seating	[ ]
Other special classes	[ ]	Tape recorders	[x]
Priority registrations	[ ]	Videotaped classes	[ ]
Substitution of courses	[ ]	Text on tape	[ ]
Exams		**Services**	
Extended time	[x]	Diagnostic tests	[ ]
Oral exams	[ ]	Learning centers	[ ]
Take home exams	[ ]	Proofreaders	[ ]
Exams on tape or computer	[ ]	Readers	[x]
Untimed exams	[ ]	Reading Machines/Kurzweil	[ ]
Other accommodations	[ ]	Special bookstore section	[ ]
		Typists	[ ]

Credit toward degree is not given for remedial courses taken.

Counseling Services

- [ ] Academic
- [ ] Psychological
- [ ] Student Support groups
- [ ] Vocational

Tutoring

Individual tutoring is available.

	Individual	Group
Time management	[ ]	[ ]
Organizational skills	[ ]	[ ]
Learning strategies	[ ]	[ ]
Study skills	[ ]	[ ]
Content area	[ ]	[ ]
Writing lab	[ ]	[ ]
Math lab	[ ]	[ ]

LD PROGRAM STAFF

Total number of LD Program staff (including director):

Full Time: 3 Part Time: 3

There is an advisor/advocate from the LD program available to students.

Key staff person available to work with LD students: Bernita Davis, Director.

University of New Mexico

Albuquerque, NM

Address: One University Hill NE, Albuquerque, NM, 87131-0001
Admissions telephone: 505 277-2446
Admissions FAX: 505 277-6686
Director of Admissions: Terry Babbitt, Interim
Admissions e-mail: apply@unm.edu
Web site: http://www.unm.edu
SAT Code: 4845 ACT Code: 2650

LD program name: Accessibility Services
LD program address: Mesa Vista, Hall Rm 2021
LD program telephone: 505 277-3506
LD program e-mail: sssub@unm.edu
Total campus enrollment: 18,437

GENERAL

University of New Mexico is a public, coed, four-year institution. 729-acre, urban campus in Albuquerque (population: 448,607); branch campuses in Gallup, Los Alamos, Los Lunas, and Taos and graduate centers in Los Alamos and Santa Fe. Served by air, bus, and train. School operates transportation to parking lots on North Campus and South Campus and to athletic events. Public transportation serves campus. Semester system.

LD ADMISSIONS

A personal interview is not required.

SECONDARY SCHOOL REQUIREMENTS

Graduation from secondary school required; GED accepted. The following course distribution required: 4 units of English, 3 units of math, 2 units of science, 2 units of foreign language, 1 unit of social studies, 1 unit of history.

TESTING

ACT required; SAT Reasoning may be substituted. SAT Subject recommended.

All enrolled freshmen (fall 2004):

Average SAT I Scores:	Verbal: 536	Math: 529
Average ACT Scores:	Composite: 22	

Child Study Team report is not required. Tests required as part of this documentation:

☐ WAIS-IV	☐ Woodcock-Johnson
☐ WISC-IV	☐ Nelson-Denny Reading Test
☐ SATA	☐ Other

UNDERGRADUATE STUDENT BODY

Total undergraduate student enrollment: 7,093 Men, 9,348 Women.

Composition of student body (fall 2004):

	Undergraduate	Freshmen
International	0.4	0.6
Black	3.7	2.9
American Indian	5.9	6.6
Asian-American	3.3	3.3
Hispanic	37.5	34.7
White	43.6	45.9
Unreported	5.6	6.0
	100.0%	100.0%

19% are from out of state. 3% join a fraternity and 3% join a sorority. Average age of full-time undergraduates is 22. 39% of classes have fewer than 20 students, 47% have between 20 and 50 students, 14% have more than 50 students.

STUDENT HOUSING

Freshmen are not required to live on campus. Housing is guaranteed for all undergraduates. Campus can house 2,300 undergraduates.

EXPENSES

Tuition (2005-06): $4,108 per year (in-state), $13,440 (out-of-state).
Room & Board: $6,276.
There is no additional cost for LD program/services.

LD SERVICES

LD program size is not limited.

LD services available to:

☐ Freshmen ☐ Sophomores ☐ Juniors ☐ Seniors

Academic Accommodations

Curriculum		**In class**	
Foreign language waiver	☐	Early syllabus	☐
Lighter course load	☐	Note takers in class	☒
Math waiver	☐	Priority seating	☐
Other special classes	☐	Tape recorders	☒
Priority registrations	☐	Videotaped classes	☒
Substitution of courses	☐	Text on tape	☐
Exams		**Services**	
Extended time	☒	Diagnostic tests	☒
Oral exams	☐	Learning centers	☐
Take home exams	☐	Proofreaders	☐
Exams on tape or computer	☐	Readers	☒
Untimed exams	☒	Reading Machines/Kurzweil	☒
Other accommodations	☐	Special bookstore section	☐
		Typists	☐

Credit toward degree is not given for remedial courses taken.

Counseling Services

☐ Academic
☐ Psychological
☐ Student Support groups
☐ Vocational

Tutoring

Individual tutoring is available.

	Individual	Group
Time management	☐	☐
Organizational skills	☐	☐
Learning strategies	☐	☐
Study skills	☐	☐
Content area	☐	☐
Writing lab	☐	☐
Math lab	☐	☐

UNIQUE LD PROGRAM FEATURES

Services are provided for need-based or with documentation. Case-by-case procedure is used to determine each student's services/accomodations.

LD PROGRAM STAFF

Total number of LD Program staff (including director):

Full Time: 5 Part Time: 5

Key staff person available to work with LD students: Gary Haug, Interim Director.

LD Program web site: http://as.unm.edu

New Mexico Highlands University

Las Vegas, NM

Address: Box 9000, Las Vegas, NM, 87701
Admissions telephone: 505 454-3439
Admissions FAX: 505 454-3552
Director of Admissions: John Coca
Admissions e-mail: admissions@nmhu.edu
Web site: http://www.nmhu.edu
SAT Code: 4532 ACT Code: 2640

LD program name: Disability Services
LD program address: Box 9000, Las Vegas, NM, 87701
Coordinator of Disability Services: Daniel Thomas
LD program telephone: 505 454-3252
LD program e-mail: danielthomas@nmhu.edu
Total campus enrollment: 1,931

GENERAL

New Mexico Highlands University is a public, coed, four-year institution. 175-acre campus in Las Vegas (population: 478,434), 120 miles from Albuquerque. Served by air, bus, and train; major airport serves Albuquerque. Semester system.

LD ADMISSIONS

A personal interview is recommended. Essay is not required.

SECONDARY SCHOOL REQUIREMENTS

Graduation from secondary school required; GED accepted.

TESTING

ACT required.

All enrolled freshmen (fall 2004):

Average SAT I Scores: Verbal: 457 Math: 455
Average ACT Scores: Composite: 18

Child Study Team report is not required. Tests required as part of this documentation:

- ☐ WAIS-IV
- ☐ WISC-IV
- ☐ SATA
- ☐ Woodcock-Johnson
- ☐ Nelson-Denny Reading Test
- ☐ Other

UNDERGRADUATE STUDENT BODY

Total undergraduate student enrollment: 738 Men, 1,156 Women.

Composition of student body (fall 2004):

	Undergraduate	Freshmen
International	0.0	0.5
Black	4.6	4.5
American Indian	13.8	9.3
Asian-American	0.4	0.9
Hispanic	62.0	56.9
White	14.6	22.7
Unreported	4.6	5.2
	100.0%	100.0%

9% are from out of state. Average age of full-time undergraduates is 25. 73% of classes have fewer than 20 students, 26% have between 20 and 50 students, 1% have more than 50 students.

STUDENT HOUSING

Freshmen are not required to live on campus. Housing is guaranteed for all undergraduates. Campus can house 536 undergraduates. Single rooms are available for students with medical or special needs. A medical note is not required.

EXPENSES

Tuition (2005-06): $1,632 per year (in-state), $9,624 (out-of-state).
Room: $1,660. Board: $1,796.
There is no additional cost for LD program/services.

LD SERVICES

LD program size is not limited.

LD services available to:

☐ Freshmen ☐ Sophomores ☐ Juniors ☐ Seniors

Academic Accommodations

Curriculum		In class	
Foreign language waiver	☐	Early syllabus	☐
Lighter course load	■	Note takers in class	■
Math waiver	☐	Priority seating	☐
Other special classes	■	Tape recorders	■
Priority registrations	☐	Videotaped classes	■
Substitution of courses	☐	Text on tape	☐
Exams		**Services**	
Extended time	■	Diagnostic tests	■
Oral exams	■	Learning centers	■
Take home exams	☐	Proofreaders	☐
Exams on tape or computer	☐	Readers	■
Untimed exams	■	Reading Machines/Kurzweil	■
Other accommodations	☐	Special bookstore section	☐
		Typists	☐

Credit toward degree is given for remedial courses taken.

Counseling Services

- ☐ Academic
- ☐ Psychological
- ☐ Student Support groups
- ☐ Vocational

Tutoring

Individual tutoring is available daily.

Average size of tutoring groups: 5

	Individual	Group
Time management	■	■
Organizational skills	■	■
Learning strategies	■	■
Study skills	■	■
Content area	■	■
Writing lab	■	■
Math lab	■	■

LD PROGRAM STAFF

Total number of LD Program staff (including director):

Full Time: 1 Part Time: 1

There is an advisor/advocate from the LD program available to students. The advisor/advocate meets with faculty 1 time per month and student 1 time per month. 2 graduate students are available to work with LD students.

Key staff person available to work with LD students: Daniel Thomas, Coordinator of Disability Services.

New Mexico Institute of Mining and Technology

Socorro, NM

Address: 801 Leroy Place, Socorro, NM, 87801
Admissions telephone: 800 428-TECH
Admissions FAX: 505 835-5989
Director of Admissions: Mike Kloeppel
Admissions e-mail: admission@admin.nmt.edu
Web site: http://www.nmt.edu
SAT Code: 4533 ACT Code: 2642

Coordinator: Elaine DeBrine-Howell
LD program telephone: 505 835-5208
LD program e-mail: edebrine@admin.nmt.edu
Total campus enrollment: 1,341

GENERAL

New Mexico Institute of Mining and Technology is a public, coed, four-year institution. 320-acre main campus in Socorro (population: 8,877), 75 miles from Albuquerque; total campus of about 20,000 acres. Served by bus; major airport and train serve Albuquerque. Semester system.

LD ADMISSIONS

Students do not complete a separate application and are simultaneously accepted to the LD program. A member of the LD program does not sit on the admissions committee. A personal interview is not required. Essay is not required.

SECONDARY SCHOOL REQUIREMENTS

Graduation from secondary school required; GED accepted. The following course distribution required: 4 units of English, 3 units of math, 2 units of science, 2 units of social studies, 1 unit of history, 3 units of academic electives.

TESTING

SAT Subject recommended.

All enrolled freshmen (fall 2004):

Average SAT I Scores: Verbal: 614 Math: 624
Average ACT Scores: Composite: 26

Child Study Team report is not required. A neuropsychological or comprehensive psycho-education evaluation is not required for admission. Tests required as part of this documentation:

- [ ] WAIS-IV
- [ ] WISC-IV
- [ ] SATA
- [ ] Woodcock-Johnson
- [ ] Nelson-Denny Reading Test
- [ ] Other

UNDERGRADUATE STUDENT BODY

Total undergraduate student enrollment: 781 Men, 475 Women.

Composition of student body (fall 2004):

	Undergraduate	Freshmen
International	1.2	3.0
Black	1.9	1.4
American Indian	4.7	3.0
Asian-American	3.1	3.2
Hispanic	25.2	21.3
White	63.9	68.1
Unreported	0.0	0.0
	100.0%	100.0%

17% are from out of state. Average age of full-time undergraduates is 21. 53% of classes have fewer than 20 students, 43% have between 20 and 50 students, 4% have more than 50 students.

STUDENT HOUSING

Freshmen are not required to live on campus. Housing is not guaranteed for all undergraduates. Enrollment is sufficiently large enough that dorm space is not available to all students. Campus can house 644 undergraduates.

EXPENSES

Tuition (2005-06): $3,156 per year (in-state), $9,975 (out-of-state). Room: $2,116. Board: $2,750.
There is no additional cost for LD program/services.

LD SERVICES

LD program size is not limited.

LD services available to:

- [x] Freshmen
- [x] Sophomores
- [x] Juniors
- [x] Seniors

Academic Accommodations

Curriculum		In class	
Foreign language waiver	[ ]	Early syllabus	[ ]
Lighter course load	[x]	Note takers in class	[x]
Math waiver	[ ]	Priority seating	[ ]
Other special classes	[ ]	Tape recorders	[x]
Priority registrations	[ ]	Videotaped classes	[ ]
Substitution of courses	[ ]	Text on tape	[ ]
Exams		**Services**	
Extended time	[x]	Diagnostic tests	[ ]
Oral exams	[x]	Learning centers	[ ]
Take home exams	[ ]	Proofreaders	[ ]
Exams on tape or computer	[ ]	Readers	[x]
Untimed exams	[x]	Reading Machines/Kurzweil	[ ]
Other accommodations	[ ]	Special bookstore section	[ ]
		Typists	[ ]

Credit toward degree is not given for remedial courses taken.

Counseling Services

- [ ] Academic
- [ ] Psychological
- [ ] Student Support groups
- [ ] Vocational

Tutoring

Individual tutoring is available daily.

Average size of tutoring groups: 5

	Individual	Group
Time management	[ ]	[x]
Organizational skills	[ ]	[x]
Learning strategies	[ ]	[x]
Study skills	[ ]	[x]
Content area	[ ]	[x]
Writing lab	[x]	[ ]
Math lab	[x]	[ ]

UNIQUE LD PROGRAM FEATURES

Tech's counseling staff works with disabled students to accommodate their special needs. Services include facilitating modifications of buildings/schedules, coordinating academic accommodations, counseling, assisting with required equipment, and coordinating resources with state and local agencies.

New Mexico State University

Las Cruces, NM

Address: Box 30001, MSC 3004, Las Cruces, NM, 88003-8001
Admissions telephone: 800 662-6678
Admissions FAX: 505 646-6330
Director of Admissions: Angela Mora-Riley
Admissions e-mail: admissions@nmsu.edu
Web site: http://www.nmsu.edu
SAT Code: 4531 ACT Code: 2638

LD program telephone: 505 646-2731
LD program e-mail: mikearm@nmsu.edu
Total campus enrollment: 12,975

GENERAL

New Mexico State University is a public, coed, four-year institution. 900-acre campus in Las Cruces (population: 74,267), 42 miles from El Paso, Tex.; branch campuses in Alamogordo, Carlsbad, Grants, and Las Cruces. Served by bus; major airport and train serve El Paso. School operates transportation on main campus. Public transportation serves campus. Semester system.

LD ADMISSIONS

A personal interview is not required. Essay is not required.

SECONDARY SCHOOL REQUIREMENTS

Graduation from secondary school required; GED accepted. The following course distribution required: 4 units of English, 3 units of math, 2 units of science, 1 unit of foreign language.

TESTING

ACT required; SAT Reasoning may be substituted.

All enrolled freshmen (fall 2004):

Average SAT I Scores: Verbal: Math:
Average ACT Scores: Composite: 21

Child Study Team report is not required. Tests required as part of this documentation:

☐ WAIS-IV ☐ Woodcock-Johnson
☐ WISC-IV ☐ Nelson-Denny Reading Test
☐ SATA ☐ Other

UNDERGRADUATE STUDENT BODY

Total undergraduate student enrollment: 5,810 Men, 6,774 Women.

Composition of student body (fall 2004):

	Undergraduate	Freshmen
International	0.3	0.7
Black	2.8	2.9
American Indian	2.9	3.1
Asian-American	1.7	1.3
Hispanic	43.8	44.9
White	43.1	33.8
Unreported	5.4	13.3
	100.0%	100.0%

19% are from out of state. Average age of full-time undergraduates is 23. 47% of classes have fewer than 20 students, 42% have between 20 and 50 students, 11% have more than 50 students.

STUDENT HOUSING

27% of freshmen live in college housing. Freshmen are not required to live on campus. Housing is guaranteed for all undergraduates. Campus can house 4,000 undergraduates.

EXPENSES

Tuition (2005-06): $2,868 per year (in-state), $12,156 (out-of-state).
Room: $3,014. Board: $2,260.

There is no additional cost for LD program/services.

LD SERVICES

LD program size is not limited.

LD services available to:

☐ Freshmen ☐ Sophomores ☐ Juniors ☐ Seniors

Academic Accommodations

Curriculum		**In class**	
Foreign language waiver	☐	Early syllabus	☐
Lighter course load	☐	Note takers in class	☑
Math waiver	☐	Priority seating	☐
Other special classes	☐	Tape recorders	☑
Priority registrations	☐	Videotaped classes	☐
Substitution of courses	☐	Text on tape	☐
Exams		**Services**	
Extended time	☑	Diagnostic tests	☑
Oral exams	☑	Learning centers	☑
Take home exams	☐	Proofreaders	☐
Exams on tape or computer	☐	Readers	☑
Untimed exams	☑	Reading Machines/Kurzweil	☐
Other accommodations	☐	Special bookstore section	☐
		Typists	☐

Credit toward degree is not given for remedial courses taken.

Counseling Services

☐ Academic
☐ Psychological
☐ Student Support groups
☐ Vocational

Tutoring

	Individual	Group
Time management	☐	☐
Organizational skills	☐	☐
Learning strategies	☐	☐
Study skills	☐	☐
Content area	☐	☐
Writing lab	☐	☐
Math lab	☐	☐

UNIQUE LD PROGRAM FEATURES

Testing services provided at office.

LD PROGRAM STAFF

Total number of LD Program staff (including director):

Full Time: 3 Part Time: 3

Key staff person available to work with LD students: Michael Armendariz, Coordinator, Disabled Student Programs.

College of Santa Fe

Santa Fe, NM

Address: 1600 St. Michael's Drive, Santa Fe, NM, 87505
Admissions telephone: 800 456-2673
Admissions FAX: 505 473-6129

Director of Admissions and Enrollment Management: Mr. Jeff Miller
Admissions e-mail: admissions@csf.edu
Web site: http://www.csf.edu
SAT Code: 4676 ACT Code: 2648

LD program name: Center for Academic Excellence
LD program address: 1600 St. Michael's Drive,
Disabilities Services Coordinator: Ms. Donna Collins
LD program telephone: 505 473-6552
Total campus enrollment: 1,430

GENERAL

College of Santa Fe is a private, coed, four-year institution. 100-acre, suburban campus in Santa Fe (population: 62,203); branch campus in Albuquerque. Served by air and bus; major airport serves Albuquerque (60 miles); train serves Lamy (14 miles). Public transportation serves campus. Semester system.

LD ADMISSIONS

Students do not complete a separate application and are simultaneously accepted to the LD program. A member of the LD program does not sit on the admissions committee. A personal interview is required. Essay is required and may be typed.

SECONDARY SCHOOL REQUIREMENTS

Graduation from secondary school required; GED accepted. The following course distribution required: 4 units of English, 2 units of math, 2 units of science, 2 units of social studies, 6 units of academic electives.

TESTING

SAT Reasoning or ACT required. SAT Subject recommended.

All enrolled freshmen (fall 2004):

Average SAT I Scores:	Verbal: 581	Math: 543
Average ACT Scores:	Composite: 23	

Child Study Team report is not required. A neuropsychological or comprehensive psycho-education evaluation is not required for admission. Tests required as part of this documentation:

- ☐ WAIS-IV
- ☐ WISC-IV
- ☐ SATA
- ☐ Woodcock-Johnson
- ☐ Nelson-Denny Reading Test
- ☐ Other

UNDERGRADUATE STUDENT BODY

Total undergraduate student enrollment: 518 Men, 794 Women.

Composition of student body (fall 2004):

	Undergraduate	Freshmen
International	0.0	0.8
Black	1.3	2.3
American Indian	3.3	3.4
Asian-American	1.3	1.9
Hispanic	14.7	24.8
White	75.4	57.8
Unreported	4.0	9.0
	100.0%	100.0%

60% are from out of state. Average age of full-time undergraduates is 22. 79% of classes have fewer than 20 students, 20% have between 20 and 50 students, 1% have more than 50 students.

STUDENT HOUSING

95% of freshmen live in college housing. Freshmen are required to live on campus. Housing is guaranteed for all undergraduates. Campus can house 499 undergraduates. Single rooms are available for students with medical or special needs. A medical note is not required.

EXPENSES

Tuition (2005-06): $21,530 per year.
Room: $3,204. Board: $3,498.
There is no additional cost for LD program/services.

LD SERVICES

LD program size is not limited.

LD services available to:

■ Freshmen ■ Sophomores ■ Juniors ■ Seniors

Academic Accommodations

Curriculum		In class	
Foreign language waiver	☐	Early syllabus	☐
Lighter course load	■	Note takers in class	■
Math waiver	☐	Priority seating	☐
Other special classes	■	Tape recorders	■
Priority registrations	☐	Videotaped classes	☐
Substitution of courses	☐	Text on tape	☐
Exams		**Services**	
Extended time	■	Diagnostic tests	☐
Oral exams	■	Learning centers	■
Take home exams	☐	Proofreaders	☐
Exams on tape or computer	☐	Readers	■
Untimed exams	■	Reading Machines/Kurzweil	■
Other accommodations	☐	Special bookstore section	☐
		Typists	☐

Credit toward degree is not given for remedial courses taken.

Counseling Services

- ■ Academic
- ■ Psychological
- ■ Student Support groups
- ☐ Vocational

Tutoring

Individual tutoring is available daily.

	Individual	Group
Time management	■	■
Organizational skills	■	■
Learning strategies	■	■
Study skills	■	■
Content area	■	■
Writing lab	■	■
Math lab	■	■

LD PROGRAM STAFF

Total number of LD Program staff (including director):

Full Time: 2 Part Time: 2

There is an advisor/advocate from the LD program available to students. 15 peer tutors are available to work with LD students.

Key staff person available to work with LD students: Ms. Donna Collins, Disabilities Services Coordinator.

College of the Southwest

Hobbs, NM

Address: 6610 Lovington Highway, Hobbs, NM, 88240
Admissions telephone: 800 530-4400
Admissions FAX: 505 392-6006
Director of Admissions: Karen Workentin
Admissions e-mail: Admissions@csw.edu
Web site: http://www.csw.edu
SAT Code: 4116 ACT Code: 2633

LD program name: Office of Special Services
Dean of Admissions: Karen Workentin
LD program telephone: 505 932-6563
LD program e-mail: kworkentin@csw.edu
LD program enrollment: 15, Total campus enrollment: 608

GENERAL

College of the Southwest is a private, coed, four-year institution. 162-acre campus in Hobbs (population: 28,657), 120 miles from Lubbock, Tex.; branch campus in Carlsbad. Served by bus; major airport serves Lubbock; smaller airport serves Odessa, Tex. (95 miles). Public transportation serves campus. Semester system.

LD ADMISSIONS

Students do not complete a separate application and are not simultaneously accepted to the LD program. A member of the LD program does sit on the admissions committee. A personal interview is recommended. Essay is not required.

For fall 2004, 15 completed self-identified LD applications were received.

SECONDARY SCHOOL REQUIREMENTS

Graduation from secondary school required; GED accepted.

TESTING

SAT Subject required.

All enrolled freshmen (fall 2004):

Average SAT I Scores: Verbal: 454 Math: 489
Average ACT Scores: Composite: 19

Child Study Team report is not required. A neuropsychological or comprehensive psycho-educational evaluation is required for admission. Must be dated within 12 months of application. Tests required as part of this documentation:

- ■ WAIS-IV
- ■ WISC-IV
- ☐ SATA
- ■ Woodcock-Johnson
- ☐ Nelson-Denny Reading Test
- ☐ Other

UNDERGRADUATE STUDENT BODY

Total undergraduate student enrollment: 209 Men, 404 Women.

Composition of student body (fall 2004):

	Undergraduate	Freshmen
International	11.1	4.6
Black	4.4	3.0
American Indian	10.0	3.6
Asian-American	0.0	0.5
Hispanic	24.4	30.6
White	46.8	57.0
Unreported	3.3	0.7
	100.0%	100.0%

18% are from out of state. Average age of full-time undergraduates is 24. 83% of classes have fewer than 20 students, 16% have between 20 and 50 students, 1% have more than 50 students.

STUDENT HOUSING

76% of freshmen live in college housing. Freshmen are required to live on campus. Housing is guaranteed for all undergraduates. If there are openings. Campus can house 167 undergraduates. Single rooms are available for students with medical or special needs. A medical note is required.

EXPENSES

Tuition (2005-06): $7,440 per year.
Room: $2,600. Board: $2,400.
There is no additional cost for LD program/services.

LD SERVICES

LD program size is not limited.

LD services available to:

■ Freshmen ■ Sophomores ■ Juniors ■ Seniors

Academic Accommodations

Curriculum		In class	
Foreign language waiver	☐	Early syllabus	■
Lighter course load	■	Note takers in class	■
Math waiver	☐	Priority seating	■
Other special classes	☐	Tape recorders	■
Priority registrations	☐	Videotaped classes	☐
Substitution of courses	☐	Text on tape	■
Exams		**Services**	
Extended time	■	Diagnostic tests	■
Oral exams	■	Learning centers	■
Take home exams	☐	Proofreaders	■
Exams on tape or computer	■	Readers	■
Untimed exams	■	Reading Machines/Kurzweil	☐
Other accommodations	■	Special bookstore section	☐
		Typists	■

Credit toward degree is not given for remedial courses taken.

Counseling Services

- ■ Academic
- ■ Psychological
- ■ Student Support groups
- ■ Vocational

Tutoring

Individual tutoring is available weekly.

Average size of tutoring groups: 5

	Individual	Group
Time management	■	☐
Organizational skills	■	☐
Learning strategies	■	☐
Study skills	☐	☐
Content area	☐	■
Writing lab	☐	■
Math lab	☐	■

LD PROGRAM STAFF

There is an advisor/advocate from the LD program available to students. The advisor/advocate meets with faculty 2 times per month and student 4 times per month.

Key staff person available to work with LD students: Dr. Jo Beth DeSoto, Coordinator.

LD Program web site: jdesoto@csw.edu

Western New Mexico University

Silver City, NM

Address: Box 680, Silver City, NM, 88062
Admissions telephone: 800 872-WNMU
Admissions FAX: 505 538-6127
Admissions e-mail: admstudnt@iron.wnmu.edu
Web site: http://www.wnmu.edu
SAT Code: 4535 ACT Code: 2646

LD program name: Special Needs Program
Special Needs Director: Karen Correa
LD program telephone: 505 538-6138
LD program e-mail: correak2@wnmu.edu
LD program enrollment: 50, Total campus enrollment: 2,367

GENERAL

Western New Mexico University is a public, coed, four-year institution. 80-acre campus in Silver City (population: 10,545). Served by air; major airport serves El Paso, Tex. (150 miles); bus and train serve Deming (50 miles). Public transportation serves campus. Semester system.

LD ADMISSIONS

Students do not complete a separate application and are simultaneously accepted to the LD program. A member of the LD program does not sit on the admissions committee. A personal interview is recommended.

For fall 2004, 50 completed self-identified LD applications were received. 50 applications were offered admission, and 50 enrolled.

SECONDARY SCHOOL REQUIREMENTS

Graduation from secondary school required; GED accepted. The following course distribution required: 4 units of English, 3 units of math, 2 units of science, 2 units of social studies, 1 unit of history.

TESTING

SAT Reasoning or ACT considered if submitted; ACT preferred. SAT Subject recommended.

All enrolled freshmen (fall 2004):

Average SAT I Scores:	Verbal: 469	Math: 465
Average ACT Scores:	Composite: 19	

Child Study Team report is required if student is classified. A neuropsychological or comprehensive psycho-educational evaluation is required for admission. Must be dated within 12 months of application. Tests required as part of this documentation:

- [ ] WAIS-IV
- [ ] WISC-IV
- [ ] SATA
- [ ] Woodcock-Johnson
- [ ] Nelson-Denny Reading Test
- [x] Other

UNDERGRADUATE STUDENT BODY

Total undergraduate student enrollment: 762 Men, 1,174 Women.

Composition of student body (fall 2004):

	Undergraduate	Freshmen
International	4.0	1.3
Black	6.5	7.1
American Indian	3.2	3.0
Asian-American	0.8	0.5
Hispanic	42.8	40.0
White	39.5	37.8
Unreported	3.2	10.3
	100.0%	100.0%

13% are from out of state. Average age of full-time undergraduates is 26. 71% of classes have fewer than 20 students, 28% have between 20 and 50 students, 1% have more than 50 students.

STUDENT HOUSING

Freshmen are required to live on campus. Housing is guaranteed for all undergraduates. Campus can house 427 undergraduates. Single rooms are available for students with medical or special needs. A medical note is not required.

EXPENSES

Tuition (2005-06): $2,064 per year (in-state), $9,624 (out-of-state).

Room: $1,680. Board: $2,990.

There is no additional cost for LD program/services.

LD SERVICES

LD program size is not limited.

LD services available to:

- [x] Freshmen
- [x] Sophomores
- [x] Juniors
- [x] Seniors

Academic Accommodations

Curriculum		In class	
Foreign language waiver	[ ]	Early syllabus	[ ]
Lighter course load	[x]	Note takers in class	[x]
Math waiver	[ ]	Priority seating	[ ]
Other special classes	[ ]	Tape recorders	[x]
Priority registrations	[ ]	Videotaped classes	[ ]
Substitution of courses	[ ]	Text on tape	[ ]
Exams		**Services**	
Extended time	[x]	Diagnostic tests	[ ]
Oral exams	[x]	Learning centers	[x]
Take home exams	[ ]	Proofreaders	[ ]
Exams on tape or computer	[ ]	Readers	[x]
Untimed exams	[ ]	Reading Machines/Kurzweil	[ ]
Other accommodations	[ ]	Special bookstore section	[ ]
		Typists	[ ]

Credit toward degree is not given for remedial courses taken.

Counseling Services

- [x] Academic — Meets 4 times per academic year
- [ ] Psychological
- [ ] Student Support groups
- [ ] Vocational

Tutoring

Individual tutoring is available daily.

Average size of tutoring groups: 3

	Individual	Group
Time management	[x]	[ ]
Organizational skills	[x]	[ ]
Learning strategies	[x]	[ ]
Study skills	[x]	[ ]
Content area	[x]	[x]
Writing lab	[ ]	[ ]
Math lab	[ ]	[ ]

LD PROGRAM STAFF

Total number of LD Program staff (including director):

Full Time: 1 Part Time: 1

There is an advisor/advocate from the LD program available to students. The advisor/advocate meets with faculty 3 times per month and student 10 times per month. 1 graduate student and 7 peer tutors are available to work with LD students.

Key staff person available to work with LD students: Karen Correa, Special Needs Director.

Adelphi University

Garden City, NY

Address: 1 South Avenue, Garden City, NY, 11530
Admissions telephone: 800 ADELPHI
Admissions FAX: 516 877-3039
Director of Admissions: Christine Murphy
Admissions e-mail: admissions@adelphi.edu
Web site: http://www.adelphi.edu
SAT Code: 2003 ACT Code: 2664

LD program name: Learning Disabilities Program
Assistant Dean, LDP: Susan Spencer
LD program telephone: 516 877-3050
LD program e-mail: ldprogram@adelphia.edu
LD program enrollment: 134, Total campus enrollment: 4,425
LD Program web site: http://academics.adelphi.edu/ldprog/

GENERAL

Adelphi University is a private, coed, four-year institution. 75-acre, suburban campus in Garden City (population: 21,672), 20 miles from New York City; branch campuses in Huntington and Manhattan. Served by train; major airports serve New York City; bus serves Hempstead (five miles). Public transportation serves campus. Semester system.

LD ADMISSIONS

Application Deadline: 03/01. Students complete a separate application and are not simultaneously accepted to the LD program. A member of the LD program does not sit on the admissions committee. High school waivers are accepted for foreign language. A personal interview is required. Essay is required and may be typed.

For fall 2004, 89 completed self-identified LD applications were received. 89 applications were offered admission, and 39 enrolled.

SECONDARY SCHOOL REQUIREMENTS

Graduation from secondary school required; GED accepted.

TESTING

SAT Reasoning or ACT required. SAT Subject required.

All enrolled freshmen (fall 2004):

Average SAT I Scores:	Verbal: 548	Math: 558
Average ACT Scores:	Composite: 24	

Child Study Team report is required if student is classified. A neuropsychological or comprehensive psycho-educational evaluation is required for admission. Must be dated within 2 months of application. Tests required as part of this documentation:

- [x] WAIS-IV
- [ ] WISC-IV
- [ ] SATA
- [x] Woodcock-Johnson
- [ ] Nelson-Denny Reading Test
- [ ] Other

UNDERGRADUATE STUDENT BODY

Total undergraduate student enrollment: 982 Men, 2,409 Women.

Composition of student body (fall 2004):

	Undergraduate	Freshmen
International	3.4	2.9
Black	7.9	12.2
American Indian	0.1	0.1
Asian-American	4.9	4.6
Hispanic	7.9	9.1
White	45.6	45.9
Unreported	30.2	25.2
	100.0%	100.0%

10% are from out of state. 3% join a fraternity and 4% join a sorority. Average age of full-time undergraduates is 21. 39% of classes have fewer than 20 students, 59% have between 20 and 50 students, 2% have more than 50 students.

STUDENT HOUSING

43% of freshmen live in college housing. Freshmen are not required to live on campus. Housing is guaranteed for all undergraduates. Campus can house 1,097 undergraduates. Single rooms are not available for students with medical or special needs.

EXPENSES

Tuition (2005-06): $18,620 per year.

Room: $5,990. Board: $3,200.

Additional cost for LD program/services: $2,420 per semester.

LD SERVICES

LD program is limited to %1 students.

LD services available to:

- [x] Freshmen
- [x] Sophomores
- [x] Juniors
- [x] Seniors

Academic Accommodations

Curriculum		In class	
Foreign language waiver	[ ]	Early syllabus	[ ]
Lighter course load	[ ]	Note takers in class	[x]
Math waiver	[ ]	Priority seating	[ ]
Other special classes	[ ]	Tape recorders	[x]
Priority registrations	[x]	Videotaped classes	[ ]
Substitution of courses	[ ]	Text on tape	[ ]
Exams		**Services**	
Extended time	[x]	Diagnostic tests	[x]
Oral exams	[x]	Learning centers	[x]
Take home exams	[ ]	Proofreaders	[ ]
Exams on tape or computer	[ ]	Readers	[x]
Untimed exams	[ ]	Reading Machines/Kurzweil	[x]
Other accommodations	[x]	Special bookstore section	[ ]
		Typists	[x]

Credit toward degree is not given for remedial courses taken.

Counseling Services

[x] Academic	Meets 60 times per academic year
[x] Psychological	Meets 30 times per academic year
[ ] Student Support groups	
[ ] Vocational	

Tutoring

Individual tutoring is available weekly.

	Individual	Group
Time management	[x]	[ ]
Organizational skills	[x]	[ ]
Learning strategies	[x]	[ ]
Study skills	[x]	[ ]
Content area	[ ]	[ ]
Writing lab	[ ]	[ ]
Math lab	[ ]	[ ]

LD PROGRAM STAFF

Total number of LD Program staff (including director):

Full Time: 18 Part Time: 18

There is an advisor/advocate from the LD program available to students. The advisor/advocate meets with students 9 times per month.

Key staff person available to work with LD students: Susan Spencer, Assistant Dean, Learning Disabilities program.

Alfred University

Alfred, NY

Address: 1 Saxon Drive, Alfred, NY, 14802-1205
Admissions telephone: 800 541-9229
Admissions FAX: 607 871-2198
Admissions e-mail: admwww@alfred.edu
Web site: http://www.alfred.edu
SAT Code: 2005 ACT Code: 2666

Director of Special Academic Services: Dr. Terry Taggart
LD program telephone: 607 871-2148
LD program e-mail: taggartmt@alfred.edu
Total campus enrollment: 2,057

GENERAL

Alfred University is a private, coed, four-year institution. 232-acre campus in Alfred (population: 3,954), 75 miles south of Rochester. Served by bus; major airport and train serve Rochester; smaller airport serves Elmira (60 miles). School operates transportation to airports for holiday and semester breaks. Public transportation serves campus. Semester system.

LD ADMISSIONS

A personal interview is recommended. Essay is required and may be typed.

SECONDARY SCHOOL REQUIREMENTS

Graduation from secondary school required; GED accepted. The following course distribution required: 4 units of English, 2 units of math, 2 units of science, 2 units of social studies.

TESTING

SAT Reasoning or ACT required. SAT Subject recommended.

All enrolled freshmen (fall 2004):

Average SAT I Scores: Verbal: 565 Math: 572
Average ACT Scores: Composite: 24

Child Study Team report is not required. Tests required as part of this documentation:

- [ ] WAIS-IV
- [ ] WISC-IV
- [ ] SATA
- [ ] Woodcock-Johnson
- [ ] Nelson-Denny Reading Test
- [ ] Other

UNDERGRADUATE STUDENT BODY

Total undergraduate student enrollment: 994 Men, 1,120 Women.

Composition of student body (fall 2004):

	Undergraduate	Freshmen
International	1.8	1.7
Black	5.7	5.5
American Indian	0.2	0.5
Asian-American	0.8	1.6
Hispanic	3.2	4.1
White	71.8	75.7
Unreported	16.4	10.9
	100.0%	100.0%

31% are from out of state. Average age of full-time undergraduates is 20. 67% of classes have fewer than 20 students, 31% have between 20 and 50 students, 2% have more than 50 students.

STUDENT HOUSING

95% of freshmen live in college housing. Housing is not guaranteed for all undergraduates. Housing is available for freshmen and sophomores. Campus can house 1,357 undergraduates.

EXPENSES

Tuition (2005-06): $20,150 per year. $18,498 per year (entering freshmen), $9,782 (state residents, College of Ceramics), $13,486 (out-of-state, College of Ceramics); tuition varies based on class level.

Room: $5,076. Board: $4,670.

There is no additional cost for LD program/services.

LD SERVICES

LD program size is not limited.

LD services available to:

- [ ] Freshmen
- [ ] Sophomores
- [ ] Juniors
- [ ] Seniors

Academic Accommodations

Curriculum

- [ ] Foreign language waiver
- [x] Lighter course load
- [ ] Math waiver
- [ ] Other special classes
- [ ] Priority registrations
- [ ] Substitution of courses

Exams

- [x] Extended time
- [x] Oral exams
- [ ] Take home exams
- [ ] Exams on tape or computer
- [x] Untimed exams
- [ ] Other accommodations

In class

- [ ] Early syllabus
- [x] Note takers in class
- [ ] Priority seating
- [x] Tape recorders
- [ ] Videotaped classes
- [ ] Text on tape

Services

- [x] Diagnostic tests
- [ ] Learning centers
- [ ] Proofreaders
- [x] Readers
- [ ] Reading Machines/Kurzweil
- [ ] Special bookstore section
- [ ] Typists

Credit toward degree is not given for remedial courses taken.

Counseling Services

- [ ] Academic
- [ ] Psychological
- [ ] Student Support groups
- [ ] Vocational

Tutoring

	Individual	Group
Time management	[ ]	[ ]
Organizational skills	[ ]	[ ]
Learning strategies	[ ]	[ ]
Study skills	[ ]	[ ]
Content area	[ ]	[ ]
Writing lab	[ ]	[ ]
Math lab	[ ]	[ ]

UNIQUE LD PROGRAM FEATURES

Progress of students receiving services from Special Academic Services are monitored.

LD PROGRAM STAFF

Total number of LD Program staff (including director):

Full Time: 1 Part Time: 1

Key staff person available to work with LD students: Terry Taggart, Director of Special Academic Services.

Bard College

Annandale on Hudson, NY

Address: PO Box 5000, Annandale on Hudson, NY, 12504
Admissions telephone: 845 758-7472
Admissions FAX: 845 758-5208
Director of Admissions: Mary Backlund
Admissions e-mail: admission@bard.edu
Web site: http://www.bard.edu
SAT Code: 2037 ACT Code: 2674

LD program name: Academic Resources Center
Dean of Lower College Studies: David Shein
LD program telephone: 845 758-7812
LD program enrollment: 92, Total campus enrollment: 1,544

GENERAL

Bard College is a private, coed, four-year institution. 600-acre campus in Annandale-on-Hudson (population: 2,400), 60 miles from Albany. Major airports serve New York City (95 miles); smaller airports serve Albany and Stewart/Newburgh (60 miles); bus serves Kingston (10 miles); train serves Rhinecliff (six miles). School operates transportation to local towns and to train station. Public transportation serves campus. 4-1-4 system.

LD ADMISSIONS

A personal interview is recommended. Essay is required and may be typed.

SECONDARY SCHOOL REQUIREMENTS

Graduation from secondary school required; GED accepted.

TESTING

SAT Reasoning or ACT considered if submitted.

All enrolled freshmen (fall 2004):

Average SAT I Scores: Verbal: 690 Math: 630

Child Study Team report is not required. Tests required as part of this documentation:

- [ ] WAIS-IV
- [ ] WISC-IV
- [ ] SATA
- [ ] Woodcock-Johnson
- [ ] Nelson-Denny Reading Test
- [ ] Other

UNDERGRADUATE STUDENT BODY

Total undergraduate student enrollment: 592 Men, 751 Women.

Composition of student body (fall 2004):

	Undergraduate	Freshmen
International	6.3	6.0
Black	2.0	2.9
American Indian	0.3	0.5
Asian-American	5.0	5.0
Hispanic	2.8	4.2
White	73.9	71.5
Unreported	9.8	9.9
	100.0%	100.0%

74% are from out of state. Average age of full-time undergraduates is 21. 79% of classes have fewer than 20 students, 21% have between 20 and 50 students.

STUDENT HOUSING

98% of freshmen live in college housing. Freshmen are required to live on campus. Housing is guaranteed for all undergraduates. Campus can house 1,082 undergraduates. Single rooms are available for students with medical or special needs. A medical note is required.

EXPENSES

Tuition (2005-06): $31,850 per year.
Room: $4,670. Board: $4,640.
There is no additional cost for LD program/services.

LD SERVICES

LD program size is not limited.

LD services available to:

- [x] Freshmen
- [x] Sophomores
- [x] Juniors
- [x] Seniors

Academic Accommodations

Curriculum
- [ ] Foreign language waiver
- [x] Lighter course load
- [ ] Math waiver
- [ ] Other special classes
- [ ] Priority registrations
- [ ] Substitution of courses

Exams
- [x] Extended time
- [x] Oral exams
- [x] Take home exams
- [ ] Exams on tape or computer
- [x] Untimed exams
- [ ] Other accommodations

In class
- [ ] Early syllabus
- [ ] Note takers in class
- [ ] Priority seating
- [x] Tape recorders
- [ ] Videotaped classes
- [x] Text on tape

Services
- [ ] Diagnostic tests
- [x] Learning centers
- [ ] Proofreaders
- [ ] Readers
- [x] Reading Machines/Kurzweil
- [ ] Special bookstore section
- [ ] Typists

Credit toward degree is not given for remedial courses taken.

Counseling Services

- [x] Academic
- [x] Psychological
- [x] Student Support groups
- [ ] Vocational

Tutoring

Individual tutoring is available weekly.

Average size of tutoring groups: 1

	Individual	Group
Time management	[x]	[ ]
Organizational skills	[x]	[ ]
Learning strategies	[x]	[ ]
Study skills	[x]	[ ]
Content area	[x]	[ ]
Writing lab	[x]	[ ]
Math lab	[x]	[ ]

LD PROGRAM STAFF

Total number of LD Program staff (including director):

Full Time: 4 Part Time: 4

There is an advisor/advocate from the LD program available to students.

Key staff person available to work with LD students: TBA, Disability Services Coordinator.

LD Program web site: http://inside.bard.edu/academicresources

Barnard College

New York, NY

Address: 3009 Broadway, New York, NY, 10027
Admissions telephone: 212 854-2014
Admissions FAX: 212 854-6220
Dean of Admissions: Jennifer Gill Fondiller
Admissions e-mail: admissions@barnard.edu
Web site: http://www.barnard.edu
SAT Code: 2038 ACT Code: 2718

LD program name: Office of Disability Services
Director, Disability Services: Susan Quinby
LD program telephone: 212 854-4634
LD program e-mail: squinby@barnard.edu
Total campus enrollment: 2,287

GENERAL

Barnard College is a private, women's, four-year institution. Four-acre, urban campus in Manhattan (New York City population: 8,008,278). Served by air, bus, and train. Public transportation serves campus. School operates transportation to Columbia U Health Science Ctr. campus. Semester system.

LD ADMISSIONS

Students do not complete a separate application and are simultaneously accepted to the LD program. A member of the LD program does not sit on the admissions committee. A personal interview is recommended. Essay is required and may be typed.

TESTING

All enrolled freshmen (fall 2004):

Average SAT I Scores:	Verbal: 684	Math: 661
Average ACT Scores:	Composite: 29	

Child Study Team report is not required. A neuropsychological or comprehensive psycho-education evaluation is not required for admission. Tests required as part of this documentation:

- ☐ WAIS-IV
- ☐ WISC-IV
- ☐ SATA
- ☐ Woodcock-Johnson
- ☐ Nelson-Denny Reading Test
- ☐ Other

UNDERGRADUATE STUDENT BODY

Total undergraduate student enrollment: 2,261 Women.

Composition of student body (fall 2004):

	Undergraduate	Freshmen
International	3.3	3.1
Black	4.7	4.9
American Indian	0.4	0.7
Asian-American	16.6	17.2
Hispanic	8.7	7.3
White	66.3	66.8
Unreported	0.0	0.0
	100.0%	100.0%

65% are from out of state. Average age of full-time undergraduates is 20. 68% of classes have fewer than 20 students, 23% have between 20 and 50 students, 9% have more than 50 students.

STUDENT HOUSING

100% of freshmen live in college housing. Freshmen are not required to live on campus. Housing is guaranteed for all undergraduates. Campus can house 2,112 undergraduates.

EXPENSES

Tuition (2005-06): $29,364 per year.
Room: $6,764. Board: $4,152.
There is no additional cost for LD program/services.

LD SERVICES

LD program size is not limited.

LD services available to:

☑ Freshmen ☑ Sophomores ☑ Juniors ☑ Seniors

Academic Accommodations

Curriculum		In class	
Foreign language waiver	☐	Early syllabus	☐
Lighter course load	☑	Note takers in class	☑
Math waiver	☐	Priority seating	☐
Other special classes	☐	Tape recorders	☑
Priority registrations	☐	Videotaped classes	☐
Substitution of courses	☐	Text on tape	☐
Exams		**Services**	
Extended time	☑	Diagnostic tests	☑
Oral exams	☐	Learning centers	☐
Take home exams	☐	Proofreaders	☐
Exams on tape or computer	☐	Readers	☑
Untimed exams	☐	Reading Machines/Kurzweil	☑
Other accommodations	☐	Special bookstore section	☐
		Typists	☐

Credit toward degree is not given for remedial courses taken.

Counseling Services

- ☑ Academic
- ☑ Psychological
- ☑ Student Support groups
- ☐ Vocational

Tutoring

Individual tutoring is available weekly.

	Individual	Group
Time management	☐	☐
Organizational skills	☐	☐
Learning strategies	☐	☐
Study skills	☑	☑
Content area	☐	☐
Writing lab	☑	☑
Math lab	☑	☑

UNIQUE LD PROGRAM FEATURES

Additional time given to complete degree and lighter course load for LD students is determined on a case-by-case basis.

LD PROGRAM STAFF

Total number of LD Program staff (including director):

Full Time: 2 Part Time: 2

There is an advisor/advocate from the LD program available to students.

Key staff person available to work with LD students: Roberta Lupert, LD Specialist.

LD Program web site: http://www.barnard.edu/ods/

Canisius College

Buffalo, NY

Address: 2001 Main Street, Buffalo, NY, 14208-1098
Admissions telephone: 800 843-1517
Admissions FAX: 716 888-3230
Director of Admissions: Jill M. Atkinson
Admissions e-mail: admissions@canisius.edu
Web site: http://www.canisius.edu
SAT Code: 2073 ACT Code: 2690

Director, Disability Support Services: Anne Marie Dobies
LD program telephone: 716 888-3748
LD program e-mail: dobies@canisius.edu
LD program enrollment: 95, Total campus enrollment: 3,519

GENERAL

Canisius College is a private, coed, four-year institution. 32-acre, urban campus in Buffalo (population: 292,648); branch campus in Amherst. Served by air, bus, and train. School operates transportation around campus, to townhouses, and to athletic center. Public transportation serves campus. Semester system.

LD ADMISSIONS

Students do not complete a separate application and are not simultaneously accepted to the LD program. A member of the LD program does not sit on the admissions committee. High school waivers are accepted for math and foreign language. A personal interview is recommended. Essay is not required.

SECONDARY SCHOOL REQUIREMENTS

Graduation from secondary school required; GED accepted. The following course distribution required: 4 units of English, 3 units of math, 1 unit of science, 2 units of foreign language, 2 units of social studies, 4 units of academic electives.

TESTING

SAT Reasoning required; ACT may be substituted. SAT Subject recommended.

All enrolled freshmen (fall 2004):

Average SAT I Scores: Verbal: 549 Math: 555
Average ACT Scores: Composite: 24

Child Study Team report is not required. A neuropsychological or comprehensive psycho-education evaluation is not required for admission. Tests required as part of this documentation:

☐ WAIS-IV
☐ WISC-IV
☐ SATA
☐ Woodcock-Johnson
☐ Nelson-Denny Reading Test
☐ Other

UNDERGRADUATE STUDENT BODY

Total undergraduate student enrollment: 1,595 Men, 1,781 Women.

Composition of student body (fall 2004):

	Undergraduate	Freshmen
International	2.5	2.8
Black	5.6	6.1
American Indian	0.8	0.7
Asian-American	2.4	1.6
Hispanic	2.8	2.2
White	81.9	80.7
Unreported	4.0	5.9
	100.0%	100.0%

9% are from out of state. 1% join a fraternity and 1% join a sorority. Average age of full-time undergraduates is 20. 47% of classes have fewer than 20 students, 52% have between 20 and 50 students, 1% have more than 50 students.

STUDENT HOUSING

61% of freshmen live in college housing. Freshmen are not required to live on campus. Housing is guaranteed for all undergraduates. Campus can house 1,430 undergraduates.

EXPENSES

Tuition (2005-06): $22,370 per year.
Room: $5,250. Board: $3,710.
There is no additional cost for LD program/services.

LD SERVICES

LD program size is not limited.

LD services available to:

■ Freshmen ■ Sophomores ■ Juniors ■ Seniors

Academic Accommodations

Curriculum

Foreign language waiver	☐
Lighter course load	■
Math waiver	☐
Other special classes	☐
Priority registrations	☐
Substitution of courses	☐

Exams

Extended time	■
Oral exams	☐
Take home exams	☐
Exams on tape or computer	☐
Untimed exams	☐
Other accommodations	☐

In class

Early syllabus	☐
Note takers in class	■
Priority seating	☐
Tape recorders	■
Videotaped classes	☐
Text on tape	■

Services

Diagnostic tests	☐
Learning centers	☐
Proofreaders	☐
Readers	■
Reading Machines/Kurzweil	☐
Special bookstore section	☐
Typists	☐

Credit toward degree is not given for remedial courses taken.

Counseling Services

■ Academic
■ Psychological
■ Student Support groups
☐ Vocational

Tutoring

Individual tutoring is available daily.

Average size of tutoring groups: 5

	Individual	Group
Time management	■	☐
Organizational skills	■	☐
Learning strategies	■	☐
Study skills	■	☐
Content area	■	☐
Writing lab	■	■
Math lab	■	■

LD PROGRAM STAFF

Total number of LD Program staff (including director):

Full Time: 1 Part Time: 1

1 graduate student and 30 peer tutors are available to work with LD students.

Key staff person available to work with LD students: Anne Marie Dobies, Director, Disability Support Services.

Cazenovia College

Cazenovia, NY

Address: 22 Sullivan Street, Cazenovia, NY, 13035-1804
Admissions telephone: 800 654-3210
Admissions FAX: 315 655-4860
Dean for Admission, Financial Aid, and Retention: Robert Croot
Admissions e-mail: admission@cazenovia.edu
Web site: http://www.cazenovia.edu
SAT Code: 2078 ACT Code: 2696

LD program name: Office of Special Services
LD program address: Box 5053
LD program contact: Cynthia Pratt
LD program e-mail: cpratt@cazenovia.edu
LD program enrollment: 102, Total campus enrollment: 923

GENERAL

Cazenovia College is a private, coed, four-year institution. 25-acre campus in Cazenovia (population: 6,481), 20 miles from Syracuse; branch campus at Corning Comm Coll. Airport, bus, and train serve Syracuse. School operates transportation to airport and to bus and train stations. Semester system.

LD ADMISSIONS

Application Deadline: 08/15. A member of the LD program does not sit on the admissions committee. A personal interview is recommended. Essay is required and may be typed.

SECONDARY SCHOOL REQUIREMENTS

Graduation from secondary school required; GED accepted. The following course distribution required: 4 units of English, 2 units of math, 2 units of science, 4 units of social studies.

TESTING

SAT Reasoning or ACT recommended. SAT Subject recommended.

All enrolled freshmen (fall 2004):

Average SAT I Scores:	Verbal: 500	Math: 490
Average ACT Scores:	Composite: 21	

Child Study Team report is not required. A neuropsychological or comprehensive psycho-educational evaluation is required for admission. Tests required as part of this documentation:

- ■ WAIS-IV
- ■ WISC-IV
- □ SATA
- ■ Woodcock-Johnson
- □ Nelson-Denny Reading Test
- ■ Other

UNDERGRADUATE STUDENT BODY

Total undergraduate student enrollment: 241 Men, 606 Women.

Composition of student body (fall 2004):

	Undergraduate	Freshmen
International	0.0	0.4
Black	3.7	4.2
American Indian	0.9	1.4
Asian-American	1.4	0.5
Hispanic	2.8	3.2
White	79.3	84.5
Unreported	11.9	5.8
	100.0%	100.0%

15% are from out of state. Average age of full-time undergraduates is 21. 85% of classes have fewer than 20 students, 15% have between 20 and 50 students.

STUDENT HOUSING

90% of freshmen live in college housing. Freshmen are required to live on campus. Housing is guaranteed for all undergraduates. Campus can house 620 undergraduates. Single rooms are available for students with medical or special needs. A medical note is required.

EXPENSES

Tuition (2005-06): $18,940 per year.

Room: $4,200. Board: $3,510.

There is no additional cost for LD program/services.

LD SERVICES

LD program size is not limited.

LD services available to:

■ Freshmen ■ Sophomores ■ Juniors ■ Seniors

Academic Accommodations

Curriculum		In class	
Foreign language waiver	■	Early syllabus	■
Lighter course load	□	Note takers in class	□
Math waiver	□	Priority seating	□
Other special classes	□	Tape recorders	■
Priority registrations	■	Videotaped classes	□
Substitution of courses	□	Text on tape	□
Exams		**Services**	
Extended time	■	Diagnostic tests	□
Oral exams	■	Learning centers	■
Take home exams	□	Proofreaders	■
Exams on tape or computer	□	Readers	■
Untimed exams	□	Reading Machines/Kurzweil	□
Other accommodations	■	Special bookstore section	□
		Typists	□

Credit toward degree is not given for remedial courses taken.

Counseling Services

- □ Academic
- □ Psychological
- □ Student Support groups
- □ Vocational

Tutoring

Individual tutoring is available daily.

Average size of tutoring groups: 4

	Individual	Group
Time management	■	■
Organizational skills	■	■
Learning strategies	■	■
Study skills	■	■
Content area	■	■
Writing lab	□	□
Math lab	□	□

LD PROGRAM STAFF

Total number of LD Program staff (including director):

Full Time: 1 Part Time: 1

There is an advisor/advocate from the LD program available to students. 10 peer tutors are available to work with LD students.

Key staff person available to work with LD students: Cynthia Pratt, Director, Office of Special Services.

City University of New York, Baruch College

New York, NY

Address: 1 Bernard Baruch Way, New York, NY, 10010
Admissions telephone: 646 312-1400
Admissions FAX: 646 312-1362
Director of Undergraduate Admissions: James Murphy
Admissions e-mail: admissions@baruch.cuny.edu
Web site: http://www.baruch.cuny.edu
SAT Code: 2034

Director, Disability Services: Barbara Sirois
LD program telephone: 646 312-4590
LD program e-mail: barbara_sirois@baruch.cuny.edu
Total campus enrollment: 12,734

GENERAL

City University of New York, Baruch College is a public, coed, four-year institution. Urban campus located in New York City (population: 8,008,278). Served by air, bus, and train. Public transportation serves campus. Semester system.

LD ADMISSIONS

A personal interview is not required. Essay is not required. Admissions requirements that may be waived for LD students include Skills Assessment and SAT.

SECONDARY SCHOOL REQUIREMENTS

Graduation from secondary school required; GED accepted. The following course distribution required: 4 units of English, 3 units of math, 2 units of science, 2 units of foreign language, 4 units of social studies.

TESTING

SAT Reasoning required; ACT may be substituted. SAT Subject recommended.

All enrolled freshmen (fall 2004):

Average SAT I Scores: Verbal: 520 Math: 584

Child Study Team report is not required. Tests required as part of this documentation:

- [ ] WAIS-IV
- [ ] WISC-IV
- [ ] SATA
- [ ] Woodcock-Johnson
- [ ] Nelson-Denny Reading Test
- [ ] Other

UNDERGRADUATE STUDENT BODY

Total undergraduate student enrollment: 5,615 Men, 7,471 Women.

Composition of student body (fall 2004):

	Undergraduate	Freshmen
International	4.8	9.9
Black	7.9	13.8
American Indian	0.2	0.1
Asian-American	35.5	26.6
Hispanic	17.6	18.0
White	34.0	31.6
Unreported	0.0	0.0
	100.0%	100.0%

3% are from out of state. 10% join a fraternity and 10% join a sorority. Average age of full-time undergraduates is 22. 25% of classes have fewer than 20 students, 63% have between 20 and 50 students, 12% have more than 50 students.

STUDENT HOUSING

Housing is not guaranteed for all undergraduates. Single rooms are available for students with medical or special needs. A medical note is required.

EXPENSES

Tuition (2005-06): $4,000 per year (in-state), $10,800 (out-of-state).

There is no additional cost for LD program/services.

LD SERVICES

LD program size is not limited.

LD services available to:

- [x] Freshmen
- [x] Sophomores
- [x] Juniors
- [x] Seniors

Academic Accommodations

Curriculum		In class	
Foreign language waiver	[ ]	Early syllabus	[x]
Lighter course load	[x]	Note takers in class	[x]
Math waiver	[ ]	Priority seating	[x]
Other special classes	[ ]	Tape recorders	[x]
Priority registrations	[x]	Videotaped classes	[x]
Substitution of courses	[x]	Text on tape	[x]
Exams		**Services**	
Extended time	[x]	Diagnostic tests	[ ]
Oral exams	[x]	Learning centers	[ ]
Take home exams	[ ]	Proofreaders	[ ]
Exams on tape or computer	[x]	Readers	[x]
Untimed exams	[ ]	Reading Machines/Kurzweil	[x]
Other accommodations	[ ]	Special bookstore section	[ ]
		Typists	[x]

Credit toward degree is not given for remedial courses taken.

Counseling Services

- [ ] Academic
- [ ] Psychological
- [ ] Student Support groups
- [ ] Vocational

Tutoring

Individual tutoring is available weekly.

	Individual	Group
Time management	[ ]	[ ]
Organizational skills	[ ]	[ ]
Learning strategies	[ ]	[ ]
Study skills	[ ]	[ ]
Content area	[x]	[x]
Writing lab	[x]	[x]
Math lab	[x]	[x]

LD PROGRAM STAFF

Total number of LD Program staff (including director):

Full Time: 3 Part Time: 3

There is an advisor/advocate from the LD program available to students. 2 graduate students are available to work with LD students.

Key staff person available to work with LD students: Barbara Sirois, Director, Disability Services.

City University of New York, Brooklyn College

Brooklyn, NY

Address: 2900 Bedford Avenue, Brooklyn, NY, 11210
Admissions telephone: 718 951-5001
Admissions FAX: 719 951-4506
Director of Admissions: Marianne Booufall Tynan
Admissions e-mail: adminqry@brooklyn.cuny.edu
Web site: http://www.brooklyn.cuny.edu
SAT Code: 2046 ACT Code: 20169

Director: Roberta Adelman
LD program telephone: 718 951-5363
LD program e-mail: radelman@brooklyn.cuny.edu
Total campus enrollment: 11,172

GENERAL

City University of New York, Brooklyn College is a public, coed, four-year institution. 26-acre, suburban campus in Brooklyn (New York City population: 8,008,278). Served by air, bus, and train. School provides transportation to subway station. Public transportation serves campus. Semester system.

LD ADMISSIONS

A personal interview is recommended.

SECONDARY SCHOOL REQUIREMENTS

Graduation from secondary school required; GED accepted. The following course distribution required: 4 units of English, 3 units of math, 3 units of science, 3 units of foreign language, 4 units of social studies, 4 units of academic electives.

TESTING

SAT Reasoning required. ACT required.

All enrolled freshmen (fall 2004):

Average SAT I Scores: Verbal: 515 Math: 544

Child Study Team report is not required. Tests required as part of this documentation:

- [ ] WAIS-IV
- [ ] WISC-IV
- [ ] SATA
- [ ] Woodcock-Johnson
- [ ] Nelson-Denny Reading Test
- [ ] Other

UNDERGRADUATE STUDENT BODY

Total undergraduate student enrollment: 3,872 Men, 6,240 Women.

Composition of student body (fall 2004):

	Undergraduate	Freshmen
International	6.5	6.0
Black	18.4	29.0
American Indian	0.3	0.2
Asian-American	16.5	10.4
Hispanic	11.5	11.5
White	46.8	42.9
Unreported	0.0	0.0
	100.0%	100.0%

5% are from out of state. 2% join a fraternity and 2% join a sorority. Average age of full-time undergraduates is 22. 36% of classes have fewer than 20 students, 59% have between 20 and 50 students, 5% have more than 50 students.

STUDENT HOUSING

Housing is not guaranteed for all undergraduates.

EXPENSES

Tuition (2005-06): $4,000 per year (in-state), $8,640 (out-of-state). There is no additional cost for LD program/services.

LD SERVICES

LD program size is not limited.

LD services available to:

- [ ] Freshmen
- [ ] Sophomores
- [ ] Juniors
- [ ] Seniors

Academic Accommodations

Curriculum		In class	
Foreign language waiver	[ ]	Early syllabus	[ ]
Lighter course load	[ ]	Note takers in class	[x]
Math waiver	[ ]	Priority seating	[ ]
Other special classes	[ ]	Tape recorders	[ ]
Priority registrations	[ ]	Videotaped classes	[ ]
Substitution of courses	[ ]	Text on tape	[ ]
Exams		**Services**	
Extended time	[ ]	Diagnostic tests	[ ]
Oral exams	[ ]	Learning centers	[ ]
Take home exams	[ ]	Proofreaders	[ ]
Exams on tape or computer	[ ]	Readers	[x]
Untimed exams	[ ]	Reading Machines/Kurzweil	[x]
Other accommodations	[ ]	Special bookstore section	[ ]
		Typists	[ ]

Credit toward degree is not given for remedial courses taken.

Counseling Services

- [ ] Academic
- [ ] Psychological
- [ ] Student Support groups
- [ ] Vocational

Tutoring

	Individual	Group
Time management	[ ]	[ ]
Organizational skills	[ ]	[ ]
Learning strategies	[ ]	[ ]
Study skills	[ ]	[ ]
Content area	[ ]	[ ]
Writing lab	[ ]	[ ]
Math lab	[ ]	[ ]

LD PROGRAM STAFF

Total number of LD Program staff (including director):

Full Time: 1 Part Time: 1

City University of New York, City College

New York, NY

Address: 160 Convent Avenue, New York, NY, 10031
Admissions telephone: 212 650-6977
Admissions FAX: 212 650-6417
Acting Director of Admissions: Particia Black, Acting
Admissions e-mail: admissions@ccny.cuny.edu
Web site: http://www.ccny.cuny.edu
SAT Code: 2083   ACT Code: 2950

Director of Student Disability Services: Carmeo Rodriguez
LD program telephone: 212 650-5913
LD program e-mail: studentservices@ccny.cuny.edu
Total campus enrollment: 9,117

GENERAL

City University of New York, City College is a public, coed, four-year institution. 35-acre campus in Manhattan (New York City population: 8,008,278); branch campus in New York City. Served by air, bus, and train. School operates transportation to local subway stations. Public transportation serves campus. Semester system.

LD ADMISSIONS

A personal interview is not required. Essay is not required.

SECONDARY SCHOOL REQUIREMENTS

Graduation from secondary school required; GED accepted. The following course distribution required: 4 units of English, 3 units of math, 2 units of science, 3 units of foreign language, 4 units of social studies, 1 unit of academic electives.

TESTING

All enrolled freshmen (fall 2004):

Average SAT I Scores: Verbal: 492 Math: 540

Child Study Team report is not required. A neuropsychological or comprehensive psycho-education evaluation is not required for admission. Tests required as part of this documentation:

- ☐ WAIS-IV
- ☐ WISC-IV
- ☐ SATA
- ☐ Woodcock-Johnson
- ☐ Nelson-Denny Reading Test
- ☐ Other

UNDERGRADUATE STUDENT BODY

Total undergraduate student enrollment: 3,958 Men, 4,109 Women.

Composition of student body (fall 2004):

	Undergraduate	Freshmen
International	13.8	11.8
Black	20.1	27.0
American Indian	0.0	0.2
Asian-American	23.9	16.1
Hispanic	33.5	33.5
White	8.7	11.4
Unreported	0.0	0.0
	100.0%	100.0%

13% are from out of state. 40% of classes have fewer than 20 students, 58% have between 20 and 50 students, 2% have more than 50 students.

STUDENT HOUSING

Housing is not guaranteed for all undergraduates.

EXPENSES

Tuition (2005-06): $4,000 per year (in-state), $10,800 (out-of-state). There is no additional cost for LD program/services.

LD SERVICES

LD program size is not limited.

LD services available to:

☐ Freshmen ☐ Sophomores ☐ Juniors ☐ Seniors

Academic Accommodations

Curriculum		In class	
Foreign language waiver	☐	Early syllabus	☐
Lighter course load	■	Note takers in class	■
Math waiver	☐	Priority seating	☐
Other special classes	☐	Tape recorders	■
Priority registrations	☐	Videotaped classes	☐
Substitution of courses	☐	Text on tape	☐
Exams		**Services**	
Extended time	■	Diagnostic tests	☐
Oral exams	■	Learning centers	■
Take home exams	☐	Proofreaders	☐
Exams on tape or computer	☐	Readers	■
Untimed exams	☐	Reading Machines/Kurzweil	■
Other accommodations	☐	Special bookstore section	☐
		Typists	☐

Credit toward degree is not given for remedial courses taken.

Counseling Services

- ☐ Academic
- ☐ Psychological
- ☐ Student Support groups
- ☐ Vocational

Tutoring

Individual tutoring is not available.

	Individual	Group
Time management	☐	☐
Organizational skills	☐	☐
Learning strategies	☐	☐
Study skills	☐	☐
Content area	☐	☐
Writing lab	☐	☐
Math lab	☐	☐

LD PROGRAM STAFF

Total number of LD Program staff (including director):

Full Time: 2   Part Time: 2

There is no an advisor/advocate from the LD program available to students.

Key staff person available to work with LD students: Carmeo Rodriguez, Director of Student Disability Services.

City University of New York, The College of Staten Island

Staten Island, NY

Address: 2800 Victory Boulevard, Staten Island, NY, 10314
Admissions telephone: 718 982-2010
Admissions FAX: 718 982-2500
Director of Admissions: Mary Beth Reilly
Admissions e-mail: recruitment@mail.csi.cuny.edu
Web site: http://www.csi.cuny.edu
SAT Code: 2778

Director, Disability Services: Margaret Venditti
LD program telephone: 718 982-2513
LD program e-mail: venditti@mail.csi.cuny.edu
LD program enrollment: 112, Total campus enrollment: 11,130

GENERAL

City University of New York, The College of Staten Island is a public, coed, four-year institution. 204-acre, urban campus in Staten Island (New York City population: 8,008,278). Served by air, bus, and train; airport also serves Newark, N.J. (10 miles). Public transportation serves campus. Semester system.

LD ADMISSIONS

Students do not complete a separate application and are not simultaneously accepted to the LD program. A member of the LD program does not sit on the admissions committee. A personal interview is recommended. Essay is not required.

SECONDARY SCHOOL REQUIREMENTS

Graduation from secondary school required; GED accepted. The following course distribution required: 4 units of English, 3 units of math, 2 units of science, 2 units of foreign language, 4 units of social studies.

TESTING

SAT Reasoning required of some applicants. ACT considered if submitted.

All enrolled freshmen (fall 2004):

Average SAT I Scores: Verbal: 514 Math: 523

Child Study Team report is required if student is classified. A neuropsychological or comprehensive psycho-educational evaluation is required for admission. Must be dated within 36 months of application. Tests required as part of this documentation:

- [x] WAIS-IV
- [x] WISC-IV
- [x] SATA
- [x] Woodcock-Johnson
- [x] Nelson-Denny Reading Test
- [ ] Other

UNDERGRADUATE STUDENT BODY

Total undergraduate student enrollment: 4,027 Men, 5,887 Women.

Composition of student body (fall 2004):

	Undergraduate	Freshmen
International	2.6	3.6
Black	12.9	10.8
American Indian	0.1	0.2
Asian-American	9.5	8.3
Hispanic	14.1	11.7
White	60.8	65.4
Unreported	0.0	0.0
	100.0%	100.0%

Average age of full-time undergraduates is 21. 32% of classes have fewer than 20 students, 64% have between 20 and 50 students, 4% have more than 50 students.

EXPENSES

Tuition (2005-06): $4,000 per year (in-state), $8,600 (out-of-state).

There is no additional cost for LD program/services.

LD SERVICES

LD program size is not limited.

LD services available to:

- [x] Freshmen
- [x] Sophomores
- [x] Juniors
- [x] Seniors

Academic Accommodations

Curriculum		In class	
Foreign language waiver	[ ]	Early syllabus	[x]
Lighter course load	[ ]	Note takers in class	[x]
Math waiver	[ ]	Priority seating	[ ]
Other special classes	[ ]	Tape recorders	[x]
Priority registrations	[x]	Videotaped classes	[ ]
Substitution of courses	[ ]	Text on tape	[x]
Exams		**Services**	
Extended time	[x]	Diagnostic tests	[ ]
Oral exams	[x]	Learning centers	[ ]
Take home exams	[ ]	Proofreaders	[ ]
Exams on tape or computer	[x]	Readers	[x]
Untimed exams	[ ]	Reading Machines/Kurzweil	[x]
Other accommodations	[ ]	Special bookstore section	[ ]
		Typists	[ ]

Credit toward degree is not given for remedial courses taken.

Counseling Services

- [x] Academic — Meets 2 times per academic year
- [ ] Psychological
- [ ] Student Support groups
- [ ] Vocational

Tutoring

Individual tutoring is available weekly.

Average size of tutoring groups: 1

	Individual	Group
Time management	[ ]	[ ]
Organizational skills	[ ]	[ ]
Learning strategies	[ ]	[ ]
Study skills	[ ]	[ ]
Content area	[x]	[ ]
Writing lab	[ ]	[ ]
Math lab	[ ]	[ ]

LD PROGRAM STAFF

Total number of LD Program staff (including director):

Full Time: 2 Part Time: 2

There is an advisor/advocate from the LD program available to students. The advisor/advocate meets with students 2 times per month. 2 graduate students and 3 peer tutors are available to work with LD students.

Key staff person available to work with LD students: Karen Gallo, Counselor.

City University of New York, Hunter College

New York, NY

Address: 695 Park Avenue, New York, NY, 10021
Admissions telephone: 212 772-4490
Admissions FAX: 212 650-3472
Director of Admissions: William Zlata
Admissions e-mail: admissions@hunter.cuny.edu
Web site: http://www.hunter.cuny.edu
SAT Code: 2301

LD program name: Office for Access & Accommodations
LD program telephone: 212 772-4857
LD program e-mail: sudi.shayesteh@hunter.cuny.edu
LD program enrollment: 250, Total campus enrollment: 15,361

GENERAL

City University of New York, Hunter College is a public, coed, four-year institution. Main campus of three city blocks in Manhattan (New York City population: 8,008,278); branch campuses at other locations in Manhattan. Served by air, bus, and train. School operates transportation between main campus and Brookdale campus in Manhattan. Public transportation serves campus. Semester system.

LD ADMISSIONS

Students complete a separate application and are not simultaneously accepted to the LD program. A member of the LD program does not sit on the admissions committee. High school waivers are accepted for foreign language. A personal interview is required. Essay is not required.

SECONDARY SCHOOL REQUIREMENTS

Graduation from secondary school required; GED accepted. The following course distribution required: 2 units of English, 2 units of math, 1 unit of science.

TESTING

SAT Reasoning required; ACT may be substituted. SAT Subject recommended.

All enrolled freshmen (fall 2004):

Average SAT I Scores: Verbal: 520 Math: 545

Child Study Team report is not required. A neuropsychological or comprehensive psycho-educational evaluation is required for admission. Must be dated within 60 months of application. Tests required as part of this documentation:

- [x] WAIS-IV
- [x] WISC-IV
- [x] SATA
- [x] Woodcock-Johnson
- [x] Nelson-Denny Reading Test
- [x] Other

UNDERGRADUATE STUDENT BODY

Total undergraduate student enrollment: 4,740 Men, 10,962 Women.

Composition of student body (fall 2004):

	Undergraduate	Freshmen
International	3.9	7.0
Black	14.1	15.8
American Indian	0.3	0.2
Asian-American	24.4	16.6
Hispanic	19.7	21.1
White	37.6	39.3
Unreported	0.0	0.0
	100.0%	100.0%

3% are from out of state. 1% join a fraternity and 1% join a sorority. Average age of full-time undergraduates is 22. 35% of classes have fewer than 20 students, 56% have between 20 and 50 students, 9% have more than 50 students.

STUDENT HOUSING

2% of freshmen live in college housing. Freshmen are not required to live on campus. Housing is not guaranteed for all undergraduates. Campus can house 612 undergraduates. Single rooms are available for students with medical or special needs. A medical note is required.

EXPENSES

Tuition (2005-06): $4,000 per year (in-state), $8,640 (out-of-state).
Room: $3,250.
There is no additional cost for LD program/services.

LD SERVICES

LD program size is not limited.

LD services available to:

- [x] Freshmen
- [x] Sophomores
- [x] Juniors
- [x] Seniors

Academic Accommodations

Curriculum

- Foreign language waiver [x]
- Lighter course load [x]
- Math waiver [ ]
- Other special classes [ ]
- Priority registrations [x]
- Substitution of courses [x]

Exams

- Extended time [x]
- Oral exams [ ]
- Take home exams [ ]
- Exams on tape or computer [x]
- Untimed exams [x]
- Other accommodations [x]

In class

- Early syllabus [ ]
- Note takers in class [x]
- Priority seating [ ]
- Tape recorders [x]
- Videotaped classes [ ]
- Text on tape [x]

Services

- Diagnostic tests [x]
- Learning centers [x]
- Proofreaders [ ]
- Readers [x]
- Reading Machines/Kurzweil [x]
- Special bookstore section [ ]
- Typists [x]

Credit toward degree is not given for remedial courses taken.

Counseling Services

- [x] Academic
- [x] Psychological
- [x] Student Support groups
- [ ] Vocational

Tutoring

Individual tutoring is available.

	Individual	Group
Time management	[x]	[x]
Organizational skills	[x]	[x]
Learning strategies	[x]	[x]
Study skills	[x]	[x]
Content area	[x]	[x]
Writing lab	[x]	[x]
Math lab	[x]	[x]

LD PROGRAM STAFF

Total number of LD Program staff (including director):

Full Time: 3 Part Time: 3

There is an advisor/advocate from the LD program available to students.

Key staff person available to work with LD students: Sudi Shayesteh, Director.

LD Program web site: http://student.services.hunter.cuny.edu

City University of New York, John Jay College of Criminal Justice

New York, NY

Address: 899 10th Avenue, New York, NY, 10019
Admissions telephone: 212 237-8869
Admissions FAX: 212 237-8777
Dean of Admissions and Registration: Sandra Palleja
Admissions e-mail: admiss@jjay.cuny.edu
Web site: http://www.jjay.cuny.edu/
SAT Code: 2115

Director of Services: Matthew McGee
LD program telephone: 212 237-8031
LD program e-mail: mmcgee@jjay.cuny.edu
Total campus enrollment: 12,252

GENERAL

City University of New York, John Jay College of Criminal Justice is a public, coed, four-year institution. Half-acre campus in Manhattan (New York City population: 8,008,278); branch campus at U.S. Military Academy. Served by air, bus, and train. Public transportation serves campus. Semester system.

LD ADMISSIONS

A personal interview is recommended. Essay is not required.

SECONDARY SCHOOL REQUIREMENTS

Graduation from secondary school required; GED accepted. The following course distribution required: 4 units of English, 3 units of math, 2 units of foreign language, 4 units of social studies.

TESTING

SAT Subject recommended.

All enrolled freshmen (fall 2004):

Average SAT I Scores: Verbal: 466 Math: 467

Child Study Team report is not required. Tests required as part of this documentation:

☐ WAIS-IV ☐ Woodcock-Johnson
☐ WISC-IV ☐ Nelson-Denny Reading Test
☐ SATA ☐ Other

UNDERGRADUATE STUDENT BODY

Total undergraduate student enrollment: 4,202 Men, 6,226 Women.

Composition of student body (fall 2004):

	Undergraduate	Freshmen
International	2.8	2.3
Black	23.5	26.9
American Indian	0.2	0.3
Asian-American	6.4	5.8
Hispanic	40.9	36.8
White	26.2	27.9
Unreported	0.0	0.0
	100.0%	100.0%

4% are from out of state. Average age of full-time undergraduates is 22. 21% of classes have fewer than 20 students, 79% have between 20 and 50 students.

STUDENT HOUSING

Housing is not guaranteed for all undergraduates.

EXPENSES

Tuition 2004-05: $4,000 per year (in-state), $8,640 (out-of-state).

There is no additional cost for LD program/services.

LD SERVICES

LD program size is not limited.

LD services available to:

☐ Freshmen ☐ Sophomores ☐ Juniors ☐ Seniors

Academic Accommodations

Curriculum		In class	
Foreign language waiver	☐	Early syllabus	☐
Lighter course load	■	Note takers in class	☐
Math waiver	☐	Priority seating	☐
Other special classes	☐	Tape recorders	■
Priority registrations	☐	Videotaped classes	☐
Substitution of courses	☐	Text on tape	☐
Exams		**Services**	
Extended time	■	Diagnostic tests	■
Oral exams	■	Learning centers	■
Take home exams	☐	Proofreaders	☐
Exams on tape or computer	☐	Readers	☐
Untimed exams	■	Reading Machines/Kurzweil	■
Other accommodations	☐	Special bookstore section	☐
		Typists	☐

Credit toward degree is not given for remedial courses taken.

Counseling Services

☐ Academic
☐ Psychological
☐ Student Support groups
☐ Vocational

Tutoring

Individual tutoring is available daily.

	Individual	Group
Time management	☐	☐
Organizational skills	☐	☐
Learning strategies	☐	☐
Study skills	☐	☐
Content area	☐	☐
Writing lab	☐	☐
Math lab	☐	☐

LD PROGRAM STAFF

Total number of LD Program staff (including director):

Full Time: 2 Part Time: 2

Key staff person available to work with LD students: Matthew McGee, Director of Services.

City University of New York, Lehman College

Bronx, NY

Address: 250 Bedford Park Boulevard W, Bronx, NY, 10468
Admissions telephone: 718 960-8131
Admissions FAX: 718 960-8712
Director of Admissions: Clarence Wilkes
Admissions e-mail: enroll@lehman.cuny.edu
Web site: http://www.lehman.cuny.edu
SAT Code: 2312

Coordinator: Marcos A. Gonzalez
LD program telephone: 718 960-8441
LD program e-mail: marcos@lehman.cuny.edu
Total campus enrollment: 8,108

GENERAL

City University of New York, Lehman College is a public, coed, four-year institution. 37-acre, urban campus in the Bronx (New York City population: 8,008,278). Served by air, bus, and train. Public transportation serves campus. Semester system.

LD ADMISSIONS

A personal interview is required. Essay is required and may be typed.

SECONDARY SCHOOL REQUIREMENTS

Graduation from secondary school required; GED accepted. The following course distribution required: 4 units of English, 2 units of math, 2 units of science, 2 units of foreign language, 1 unit of social studies, 1 unit of history.

TESTING

SAT Reasoning required; ACT may be substituted. SAT Subject recommended.

All enrolled freshmen (fall 2004):

Average SAT I Scores: Verbal: 458 Math: 466

Child Study Team report is not required. Tests required as part of this documentation:

- ☐ WAIS-IV
- ☐ WISC-IV
- ☐ SATA
- ☐ Woodcock-Johnson
- ☐ Nelson-Denny Reading Test
- ☐ Other

UNDERGRADUATE STUDENT BODY

Total undergraduate student enrollment: 1,917 Men, 5,050 Women.

Composition of student body (fall 2004):

	Undergraduate	Freshmen
International	3.9	0.3
Black	23.4	35.0
American Indian	0.1	0.1
Asian-American	5.5	4.4
Hispanic	59.2	49.3
White	7.9	10.9
Unreported	0.0	0.0
	100.0%	100.0%

1% are from out of state. Average age of full-time undergraduates is 24. 41% of classes have fewer than 20 students, 58% have between 20 and 50 students, 1% have more than 50 students.

STUDENT HOUSING

EXPENSES

Tuition (2005-06): $4,000 per year (in-state), $8,640 (out-of-state).
There is no additional cost for LD program/services.

LD SERVICES

LD program size is not limited.

LD services available to:

☐ Freshmen ☐ Sophomores ☐ Juniors ☐ Seniors

Academic Accommodations

Curriculum		In class	
Foreign language waiver	☐	Early syllabus	☐
Lighter course load	☐	Note takers in class	☒
Math waiver	☐	Priority seating	☐
Other special classes	☐	Tape recorders	☒
Priority registrations	☐	Videotaped classes	☐
Substitution of courses	☐	Text on tape	☐
Exams		**Services**	
Extended time	☒	Diagnostic tests	☐
Oral exams	☐	Learning centers	☒
Take home exams	☐	Proofreaders	☐
Exams on tape or computer	☐	Readers	☐
Untimed exams	☒	Reading Machines/Kurzweil	☐
Other accommodations	☐	Special bookstore section	☐
		Typists	☐

Credit toward degree is not given for remedial courses taken.

Counseling Services

- ☐ Academic
- ☐ Psychological
- ☐ Student Support groups
- ☐ Vocational

Tutoring

	Individual	Group
Time management	☐	☐
Organizational skills	☐	☐
Learning strategies	☐	☐
Study skills	☐	☐
Content area	☐	☐
Writing lab	☐	☐
Math lab	☐	☐

LD PROGRAM STAFF

Total number of LD Program staff (including director):

Full Time: 1 Part Time: 1

Key staff person available to work with LD students: Marcos A. Gonzalez, Coordinator.

City University of New York, Medgar Evers College

Brooklyn, NY

Address: 1650 Bedford Avenue, Brooklyn, NY, 11225
Admissions telephone: 718 270-6024
Admissions FAX: 718 270-6198
Acting Director of Enrollment Management: Warren Heusner
Admissions e-mail: enroll@mec.cuny.edu
Web site: http://www.mec.cuny.edu
SAT Code: 2460

Director Differently Abled Student Service: Anthony Phifer
LD program telephone: 718 270-5027
LD program e-mail: aphifer@mec.cuny.edu
Total campus enrollment: 5098

GENERAL

City University of New York, Medgar Evers College is a public, coed, four-year institution. One-acre, urban campus in Brooklyn (New York City population: 8,008,278). Served by air, bus, and train. Public transportation serves campus. Semester system.

LD ADMISSIONS

Essay is not required.

SECONDARY SCHOOL REQUIREMENTS

Graduation from secondary school required; GED accepted.

TESTING

SAT Reasoning considered if submitted. SAT Subject recommended.

All enrolled freshmen (fall 2004):

Average SAT I Scores: Verbal: 379 Math: 386

Child Study Team report is not required. Tests required as part of this documentation:

- ❑ WAIS-IV
- ❑ WISC-IV
- ❑ SATA
- ❑ Woodcock-Johnson
- ❑ Nelson-Denny Reading Test
- ❑ Other

UNDERGRADUATE STUDENT BODY

Total undergraduate student enrollment: 1,017 Men, 3,699 Women.

Composition of student body (fall 2004):

	Undergraduate	Freshmen
International	4.4	4.5
Black	83.8	86.6
American Indian	0.3	0.1
Asian-American	0.8	1.0
Hispanic	7.2	4.6
White	1.0	0.8
Unreported	2.6	2.2
	100.0%	100.0%

3% are from out of state. Average age of full-time undergraduates is 27. 8% of classes have fewer than 20 students, 89% have between 20 and 50 students, 3% have more than 50 students.

STUDENT HOUSING

Housing is not guaranteed for all undergraduates.

EXPENSES

Tuition 2004-05: $4,000 per year (in-state), $8,640 (out-of-state).

There is no additional cost for LD program/services.

LD SERVICES

LD program size is not limited.

LD services available to:

❑ Freshmen ❑ Sophomores ❑ Juniors ❑ Seniors

Academic Accommodations

Curriculum		In class	
Foreign language waiver	❑	Early syllabus	❑
Lighter course load	❑	Note takers in class	❑
Math waiver	❑	Priority seating	❑
Other special classes	❑	Tape recorders	❑
Priority registrations	❑	Videotaped classes	❑
Substitution of courses	❑	Text on tape	❑
Exams		**Services**	
Extended time	❑	Diagnostic tests	❑
Oral exams	❑	Learning centers	❑
Take home exams	❑	Proofreaders	❑
Exams on tape or computer	❑	Readers	❑
Untimed exams	❑	Reading Machines/Kurzweil	❑
Other accommodations	❑	Special bookstore section	❑
		Typists	❑

Credit toward degree is not given for remedial courses taken.

Counseling Services

- ❑ Academic
- ❑ Psychological
- ❑ Student Support groups
- ❑ Vocational

Tutoring

	Individual	Group
Time management	❑	❑
Organizational skills	❑	❑
Learning strategies	❑	❑
Study skills	❑	❑
Content area	❑	❑
Writing lab	❑	❑
Math lab	❑	❑

LD PROGRAM STAFF

Key staff person available to work with LD students: Anthony Phifer, Director, Differently Abled.

City University of New York, New York City Technical College

Brooklyn, NY

Address: 300 Jay Street, Brooklyn, NY, 11201
Admissions telephone: 718 260-5500
Admissions FAX: 718 260-5504
Director of Admissions: Joseph Lento
Admissions e-mail: admissions@citytech.cuny.edu
Web site: http://www.citytech.cuny.edu
SAT Code: 2550

LD program name: Student Support Services
Director, Student Support Services: Faith Fogelman
LD program telephone: 718 260-5143
LD program e-mail: FFogelman@citytech.cuny.edu
LD program enrollment: 301, Total campus enrollment: 11,772

GENERAL

City University of New York, New York City Technical College is a public, coed, four-year institution. Urban campus in Brooklyn (New York City population: 8,008,278). Served by air, bus, and train. Public transportation serves campus. Semester system.

LD ADMISSIONS

Students do not complete a separate application and are not simultaneously accepted to the LD program. A member of the LD program does sit on the admissions committee. High school waivers are accepted for math and foreign language. A personal interview is recommended. Essay is not required.

For fall 2004, 350 completed self-identified LD applications were received. 350 applications were offered admission, and 112 enrolled.

SECONDARY SCHOOL REQUIREMENTS

Graduation from secondary school required; GED accepted. The following course distribution required: 4 units of English, 3 units of math, 2 units of science, 2 units of foreign language, 4 units of social studies.

TESTING

SAT Reasoning or ACT required of some applicants.

All enrolled freshmen (fall 2004):

Average SAT I Scores:	Verbal: 420	Math: 510
Average ACT Scores:	Composite:	

Child Study Team report is not required. A neuropsychological or comprehensive psycho-educational evaluation is required for admission. Must be dated within 6 months of application. Tests required as part of this documentation:

- ■ WAIS-IV
- ■ WISC-IV
- ■ SATA
- ■ Woodcock-Johnson
- ■ Nelson-Denny Reading Test
- ☐ Other

UNDERGRADUATE STUDENT BODY

Total undergraduate student enrollment: 5,546 Men, 5,483 Women.

Composition of student body (fall 2004):

	Undergraduate	Freshmen
International	1.7	2.8
Black	40.5	43.5
American Indian	0.2	0.2
Asian-American	15.1	13.4
Hispanic	30.5	26.6
White	11.9	13.7
Unreported	0.0	0.0
	100.0%	100.0%

Average age of full-time undergraduates is 23. 31% of classes have fewer than 20 students, 69% have between 20 and 50 students.

EXPENSES

Tuition (2005-06): $4,269 per year (in-state), $8,909 (out-of-state).
There is no additional cost for LD program/services.

LD SERVICES

LD program size is not limited.

LD services available to:

■ Freshmen ■ Sophomores ■ Juniors ■ Seniors

Academic Accommodations

Curriculum		In class	
Foreign language waiver	☐	Early syllabus	☐
Lighter course load	■	Note takers in class	■
Math waiver	☐	Priority seating	☐
Other special classes	■	Tape recorders	■
Priority registrations	☐	Videotaped classes	☐
Substitution of courses	☐	Text on tape	☐
Exams		**Services**	
Extended time	■	Diagnostic tests	■
Oral exams	■	Learning centers	■
Take home exams	☐	Proofreaders	☐
Exams on tape or computer	☐	Readers	■
Untimed exams	☐	Reading Machines/Kurzweil	■
Other accommodations	☐	Special bookstore section	☐
		Typists	☐

Credit toward degree is not given for remedial courses taken.

Counseling Services

- ☐ Academic
- ☐ Psychological
- ☐ Student Support groups
- ☐ Vocational

Tutoring

Individual tutoring is available weekly.

Average size of tutoring groups: 5

	Individual	Group
Time management	☐	■
Organizational skills	☐	■
Learning strategies	☐	■
Study skills	☐	■
Content area	☐	■
Writing lab	■	■
Math lab	■	■

LD PROGRAM STAFF

Total number of LD Program staff (including director):

Full Time: 10 Part Time: 10

There is an advisor/advocate from the LD program available to students. The advisor/advocate meets with faculty once per month and students 2 times per month.

Key staff person available to work with LD students: Faith Fogelman, Director, Student Support Services. LD Program web site: http://www.citytech.cuny.edu/students/supportservices/index.shtml

City University of New York, Queens College

Flushing, NY

Address: 65-30 Kissena Boulevard, Flushing, NY, 11367
Admissions telephone: 718 997-5600
Admissions FAX: 718 997-5617
Executive Director of Admissions: Dr. Vincent J. Angrisani
Admissions e-mail: applyto@uapc.cuny.edu
Web site: http://www.qc.edu/
SAT Code: 2750

Learning Disabilities Specialist: John Kiefer
LD program telephone: 718 997-5870
LD program e-mail: jkiefer@qc1.qc.edu
LD program enrollment: 150, Total campus enrollment: 12,628

GENERAL

City University of New York, Queens College is a public, coed, four-year institution. 76-acre, urban campus in Flushing section of Queens (New York City population: 8,008,278); extension center in midtown Manhattan. Served by air, bus, and train. Public transportation serves campus. Semester system.

LD ADMISSIONS

Students do not complete a separate application and are simultaneously accepted to the LD program. A member of the LD program does not sit on the admissions committee. High school waivers are accepted for math and foreign language. A personal interview is not required. Essay is not required.

For fall 2004, 98 completed self-identified LD applications were received. 98 applications were offered admission, and 98 enrolled.

SECONDARY SCHOOL REQUIREMENTS

Graduation from secondary school required; GED accepted. The following course distribution required: 4 units of English, 3 units of math, 2 units of science, 3 units of foreign language, 4 units of social studies.

TESTING

SAT Reasoning required. SAT Subject recommended.

All enrolled freshmen (fall 2004):

Average SAT I Scores: Verbal: 500 Math: 535

Child Study Team report is not required. A neuropsychological or comprehensive psycho-educational evaluation is required for admission. Tests required as part of this documentation:

- [x] WAIS-IV
- [x] WISC-IV
- [ ] SATA
- [x] Woodcock-Johnson
- [x] Nelson-Denny Reading Test
- [ ] Other

UNDERGRADUATE STUDENT BODY

Total undergraduate student enrollment: 4,121 Men, 7,092 Women.

Composition of student body (fall 2004):

	Undergraduate	Freshmen
International	6.2	5.9
Black	8.0	9.9
American Indian	0.2	0.3
Asian-American	20.8	18.9
Hispanic	18.3	16.7
White	46.4	48.5
Unreported	0.0	0.0
	100.0%	100.0%

1% are from out of state. 1% join a fraternity and 1% join a sorority. Average age of full-time undergraduates is 22. 44% of classes have fewer than 20 students, 50% have between 20 and 50 students, 6% have more than 50 students.

STUDENT HOUSING

Housing is not guaranteed for all undergraduates.

EXPENSES

Tuition (2005-06): $4,000 per year (in-state), $10,800 (out-of-state).

There is no additional cost for LD program/services.

LD SERVICES

LD program size is not limited.

LD services available to:

- [x] Freshmen
- [x] Sophomores
- [x] Juniors
- [x] Seniors

Academic Accommodations

Curriculum

- [ ] Foreign language waiver
- [x] Lighter course load
- [ ] Math waiver
- [x] Other special classes
- [ ] Priority registrations
- [ ] Substitution of courses

Exams

- [x] Extended time
- [x] Oral exams
- [ ] Take home exams
- [ ] Exams on tape or computer
- [ ] Untimed exams
- [ ] Other accommodations

In class

- [ ] Early syllabus
- [x] Note takers in class
- [ ] Priority seating
- [x] Tape recorders
- [ ] Videotaped classes
- [ ] Text on tape

Services

- [ ] Diagnostic tests
- [x] Learning centers
- [ ] Proofreaders
- [x] Readers
- [x] Reading Machines/Kurzweil
- [ ] Special bookstore section
- [ ] Typists

Credit toward degree is not given for remedial courses taken.

Counseling Services

- [x] Academic
- [x] Psychological
- [x] Student Support groups
- [ ] Vocational

Tutoring

Individual tutoring is available daily.

Average size of tutoring groups: 3

	Individual	Group
Time management	[x]	[ ]
Organizational skills	[x]	[ ]
Learning strategies	[x]	[ ]
Study skills	[ ]	[x]
Content area	[ ]	[ ]
Writing lab	[ ]	[x]
Math lab	[ ]	[x]

LD PROGRAM STAFF

Total number of LD Program staff (including director):

Full Time: 2 Part Time: 2

There is an advisor/advocate from the LD program available to students. The advisor/advocate meets with faculty once per month and students 2 times per month.

Key staff person available to work with LD students: John Kiefer, Learning Disabilities Specialist.

City University of New York, York College

Jamaica, NY

Address: 94-20 Guy R. Brewer Boulevard, Jamaica, NY, 11451
Admissions telephone: 718 262-2165
Admissions FAX: 718 262-2601
Director of Admissions: Sally Nelson
Admissions e-mail: admissions@york.cuny.edu
Web site: http://www.york.cuny.edu
SAT Code: 2992 ACT Code: 20175

Coordinator for Disability Services: Jeffrey Sliva
LD program telephone: 718 262-2073
LD program e-mail: jsliva@york.cuny.edu
Total campus enrollment: 5,743

GENERAL

City University of New York, York College is a public, coed, four-year institution. 50-acre campus in Jamaica section of Queens (New York City population: 8,008,278). Served by air, bus, and train. Public transportation serves campus. Semester system.

LD ADMISSIONS

Students do not complete a separate application and are not simultaneously accepted to the LD program. A member of the LD program does not sit on the admissions committee. A personal interview is required. Essay is not required.

SECONDARY SCHOOL REQUIREMENTS

Graduation from secondary school required; GED accepted. The following course distribution required: 2 units of English, 2 units of math, 10 units of academic electives.

TESTING

SAT Reasoning required of some applicants. ACT considered if submitted. SAT Reasoning or ACT required of some applicants. SAT Subject recommended.

All enrolled freshmen (fall 2004):

Average SAT I Scores: Verbal: 408 Math: 425

Child Study Team report is not required. A neuropsychological or comprehensive psycho-educational evaluation is required for admission. Tests required as part of this documentation:

- [x] WAIS-IV
- [ ] WISC-IV
- [ ] SATA
- [x] Woodcock-Johnson
- [ ] Nelson-Denny Reading Test
- [ ] Other

UNDERGRADUATE STUDENT BODY

Total undergraduate student enrollment: 1,523 Men, 3,730 Women.

Composition of student body (fall 2004):

	Undergraduate	Freshmen
International	10.3	9.1
Black	50.5	57.8
American Indian	0.3	0.4
Asian-American	11.8	10.5
Hispanic	20.9	15.2
White	6.2	6.9
Unreported	0.0	0.0
	100.0%	100.0%

4% have between 20 and 50 students, 96% have more than 50 students.

STUDENT HOUSING

Single rooms are not available for students with medical or special needs.

EXPENSES

Tuition 2004-05: $4,000 per year.

There is no additional cost for LD program/services.

LD SERVICES

LD program size is not limited.

LD services available to:

- [x] Freshmen
- [x] Sophomores
- [x] Juniors
- [x] Seniors

Academic Accommodations

Curriculum		**In class**	
Foreign language waiver	[ ]	Early syllabus	[ ]
Lighter course load	[x]	Note takers in class	[x]
Math waiver	[ ]	Priority seating	[ ]
Other special classes	[ ]	Tape recorders	[x]
Priority registrations	[ ]	Videotaped classes	[x]
Substitution of courses	[ ]	Text on tape	[ ]
Exams		**Services**	
Extended time	[x]	Diagnostic tests	[ ]
Oral exams	[x]	Learning centers	[ ]
Take home exams	[ ]	Proofreaders	[ ]
Exams on tape or computer	[ ]	Readers	[x]
Untimed exams	[ ]	Reading Machines/Kurzweil	[x]
Other accommodations	[x]	Special bookstore section	[ ]
		Typists	[ ]

Credit toward degree is not given for remedial courses taken.

Counseling Services

- [x] Academic
- [x] Psychological
- [x] Student Support groups
- [x] Vocational

Tutoring

Individual tutoring is available daily.

	Individual	Group
Time management	[ ]	[ ]
Organizational skills	[ ]	[ ]
Learning strategies	[ ]	[ ]
Study skills	[ ]	[ ]
Content area	[ ]	[ ]
Writing lab	[ ]	[ ]
Math lab	[ ]	[ ]

LD PROGRAM STAFF

Total number of LD Program staff (including director):

Full Time: 3 Part Time: 3

There is an advisor/advocate from the LD program available to students.

Key staff person available to work with LD students: Jeffrey Sliva, Coordinator for Disability Services.

Clarkson University

Potsdam, NY

Address: Box 5605, Potsdam, NY, 13699
Admissions telephone: 800 527-6577
Admissions FAX: 315 268-7647
Director of Enrollment Operations: Brian T. Grant
Admissions e-mail: admission@clarkson.edu
Web site: http://www.clarkson.edu
SAT Code: 2084

LD program name: Accommodative Services
Director of Accommodative Services: Helen McLean
LD program telephone: 325 268-7643
LD program e-mail: mcleanhm@clarkson.edu
LD program enrollment: 54, Total campus enrollment: 2,736

GENERAL

Clarkson University is a private, coed, four-year institution. 640-acre campus in Potsdam (population: 15,957), 150 miles from Syracuse. Served by bus; major airport serves Syracuse; smaller airport serves Massena (20 miles); train serves Montreal, Quebec, Canada (150 miles). School operates transportation around campus and to Potsdam and St. Lawrence U and SUNY Coll-Potsdam. Semester system.

LD ADMISSIONS

Students do not complete a separate application and are simultaneously accepted to the LD program. A member of the LD program does not sit on the admissions committee. A personal interview is recommended. Essay is not required.

SECONDARY SCHOOL REQUIREMENTS

Graduation from secondary school required; GED accepted. The following course distribution required: 4 units of English, 3 units of math, 2 units of science.

TESTING

SAT Subject recommended.

All enrolled freshmen (fall 2004):

Average SAT I Scores: Verbal: 574 Math: 617

Child Study Team report is not required. A neuropsychological or comprehensive psycho-educational evaluation is required for admission. Tests required as part of this documentation:

- ■ WAIS-IV
- ■ WISC-IV
- ■ SATA
- ■ Woodcock-Johnson
- ■ Nelson-Denny Reading Test
- ■ Other

UNDERGRADUATE STUDENT BODY

Total undergraduate student enrollment: 1,945 Men, 665 Women.

Composition of student body (fall 2004):

	Undergraduate	Freshmen
International	2.3	2.1
Black	1.7	2.2
American Indian	0.3	0.4
Asian-American	1.4	1.7
Hispanic	1.7	1.8
White	92.7	91.7
Unreported	0.0	0.0
	100.0%	100.0%

24% are from out of state. 15% join a fraternity and 12% join a sorority. Average age of full-time undergraduates is 20. 34% of classes have fewer than 20 students, 42% have between 20 and 50 students, 24% have more than 50 students.

STUDENT HOUSING

90% of freshmen live in college housing. Freshmen are required to live on campus. Housing is guaranteed for all undergraduates. Campus can house 2,179 undergraduates.

EXPENSES

Tuition (2005-06): $25,185 per year.

Room: $4,896. Board: $4,449.

There is no additional cost for LD program/services.

LD SERVICES

LD program size is not limited.

LD services available to:

■ Freshmen ■ Sophomores ■ Juniors ■ Seniors

Academic Accommodations

Curriculum		In class	
Foreign language waiver	☐	Early syllabus	■
Lighter course load	☐	Note takers in class	■
Math waiver	☐	Priority seating	■
Other special classes	☐	Tape recorders	■
Priority registrations	☐	Videotaped classes	■
Substitution of courses	☐	Text on tape	■
Exams		**Services**	
Extended time	■	Diagnostic tests	☐
Oral exams	■	Learning centers	■
Take home exams	☐	Proofreaders	☐
Exams on tape or computer	■	Readers	■
Untimed exams	■	Reading Machines/Kurzweil	■
Other accommodations	☐	Special bookstore section	☐
		Typists	☐

Credit toward degree is not given for remedial courses taken.

Counseling Services

- ■ Academic — Meets 30 times per academic year
- ☐ Psychological
- ☐ Student Support groups
- ☐ Vocational

Tutoring

Individual tutoring is available weekly.

Average size of tutoring groups: 6

	Individual	Group
Time management	■	☐
Organizational skills	■	☐
Learning strategies	■	☐
Study skills	■	☐
Content area	☐	☐
Writing lab	☐	☐
Math lab	☐	■

LD PROGRAM STAFF

Total number of LD Program staff (including director):

Full Time: 3 Part Time: 3

There is an advisor/advocate from the LD program available to students. 60 peer tutors are available to work with LD students.

Key staff person available to work with LD students: Helen McLean, Director of Accommodative Services.

Colgate University

Hamilton, NY

Address: 13 Oak Drive, Hamilton, NY, 13346
Admissions telephone: 315 228-7401
Admissions FAX: 315 228-7544
Dean of Admission: Gary L. Ross
Admissions e-mail: admission@mail.colgate.edu
Web site: http://www.colgate.edu
SAT Code: 2086 ACT Code: 2702

Director: Lynn Waldman
LD program telephone: 315 228-7225
LD program e-mail: lwaldman@mail.colgate.edu
LD program enrollment: 150, Total campus enrollment: 2,824

GENERAL

Colgate University is a private, coed, four-year institution. 550-acre campus in Hamilton (population: 5,733), 38 miles from Syracuse and 25 miles from Utica. Served by bus; major airport serves Syracuse; smaller airport and train serve Utica. Public transportation serves campus. Semester system.

LD ADMISSIONS

A personal interview is not required. Essay is required and may be typed.

SECONDARY SCHOOL REQUIREMENTS

Graduation from secondary school required; GED not accepted. The following course distribution required: 4 units of English, 3 units of math, 3 units of science, 3 units of foreign language, 2 units of social studies, 1 unit of history.

TESTING

SAT Reasoning or ACT required. SAT Subject recommended.

All enrolled freshmen (fall 2004):

Average SAT I Scores: Verbal: 666 Math: 675
Average ACT Scores: Composite: 29

Child Study Team report is not required. Tests required as part of this documentation:

- [ ] WAIS-IV
- [ ] WISC-IV
- [ ] SATA
- [ ] Woodcock-Johnson
- [ ] Nelson-Denny Reading Test
- [ ] Other

UNDERGRADUATE STUDENT BODY

Total undergraduate student enrollment: 1,357 Men, 1,416 Women.

Composition of student body (fall 2004):

	Undergraduate	Freshmen
International	4.2	5.4
Black	5.1	4.4
American Indian	1.0	0.6
Asian-American	6.5	5.6
Hispanic	4.1	3.6
White	69.9	75.3
Unreported	9.2	5.1
	100.0%	100.0%

68% are from out of state. 35% join a fraternity and 32% join a sorority. Average age of full-time undergraduates is 20. 62% of classes have fewer than 20 students, 36% have between 20 and 50 students, 2% have more than 50 students.

STUDENT HOUSING

100% of freshmen live in college housing. Freshmen are required to live on campus. Housing is guaranteed for all undergraduates. Campus can house 2,595 undergraduates. Single rooms are available for students with medical or special needs. A medical note is required.

EXPENSES

Tuition (2005-06): $32,885 per year.

Room: $3,895. Board: $4,170.
There is no additional cost for LD program/services.

LD SERVICES

LD services available to:

- [x] Freshmen
- [x] Sophomores
- [x] Juniors
- [x] Seniors

Academic Accommodations

Curriculum

- [ ] Foreign language waiver
- [x] Lighter course load
- [ ] Math waiver
- [ ] Other special classes
- [ ] Priority registrations
- [ ] Substitution of courses

Exams

- [ ] Extended time
- [ ] Oral exams
- [ ] Take home exams
- [ ] Exams on tape or computer
- [ ] Untimed exams
- [ ] Other accommodations

In class

- [ ] Early syllabus
- [ ] Note takers in class
- [ ] Priority seating
- [ ] Tape recorders
- [ ] Videotaped classes
- [ ] Text on tape

Services

- [ ] Diagnostic tests
- [ ] Learning centers
- [ ] Proofreaders
- [ ] Readers
- [ ] Reading Machines/Kurzweil
- [ ] Special bookstore section
- [ ] Typists

Credit toward degree is not given for remedial courses taken.

Counseling Services

- [x] Academic
- [x] Psychological
- [x] Student Support groups
- [x] Vocational

Tutoring

Individual tutoring is available.

	Individual	Group
Time management	[x]	[x]
Organizational skills	[x]	[x]
Learning strategies	[x]	[x]
Study skills	[x]	[x]
Content area	[x]	[x]
Writing lab	[x]	[x]
Math lab	[x]	[x]

LD PROGRAM STAFF

Total number of LD Program staff (including director):

Full Time: 1 Part Time: 1

There is an advisor/advocate from the LD program available to students.

Key staff person available to work with LD students: Lynn Waldman, Dir. of Acad. Prog. Support and Disability Services.

The College of Saint Rose

Albany, NY

Address: 432 Western Avenue, Albany, NY, 12203-1490
Admissions telephone: 800 637-8556
Admissions FAX: 518 454-2013
Vice President for Admissions and Enrollment Planning: Mary Grondahl
Admissions e-mail: admit@mail.strose.edu
Web site: http://www.strose.edu
SAT Code: 2091   ACT Code: 2714

Coordinator for Special Services: Ginny Rossin
LD program telephone: 518 337-2335
LD program enrollment: 50, Total campus enrollment: 2,958

GENERAL

The College of Saint Rose is a private, coed, four-year institution. 25-acre, urban campus in Albany (population: 95,658), 150 miles from New York City; extension sites in Glens Falls and Herkimer. Served by air and bus; train serves Rensselaer (two miles). School operates transportation to off-campus art building. Public transportation serves campus. Semester system.

LD ADMISSIONS

A personal interview is recommended. Essay is required and may be typed.

SECONDARY SCHOOL REQUIREMENTS

Graduation from secondary school required; GED accepted. The following course distribution required: 4 units of English, 3 units of math, 3 units of science, 3 units of foreign language, 4 units of social studies, 4 units of history.

TESTING

SAT Reasoning or ACT required.

All enrolled freshmen (fall 2004):

Average SAT I Scores: Verbal: 539 Math: 538
Average ACT Scores: Composite: 24

Child Study Team report is not required. Tests required as part of this documentation:

☐ WAIS-IV ☐ Woodcock-Johnson
☐ WISC-IV ☐ Nelson-Denny Reading Test
☐ SATA ☐ Other

UNDERGRADUATE STUDENT BODY

Total undergraduate student enrollment: 786 Men, 2,070 Women.

Composition of student body (fall 2004):

	Undergraduate	Freshmen
International	0.0	0.0
Black	2.5	2.4
American Indian	0.0	0.3
Asian-American	2.0	1.4
Hispanic	5.0	3.1
White	69.0	82.0
Unreported	21.5	10.8
	100.0%	100.0%

4% are from out of state. Average age of full-time undergraduates is 21. 54% of classes have fewer than 20 students, 46% have between 20 and 50 students.

STUDENT HOUSING

Freshmen are not required to live on campus. Housing is not guaranteed for all undergraduates. Housing is generally not available for undergraduate students over the age of 25, married undergraduate students, or graduate students. Campus can house 1,166 undergraduates. Single rooms are not available for students with medical or special needs.

EXPENSES

Tuition (2005-06): $17,368 per year.
Room: $3,684. Board: $4,048.
There is no additional cost for LD program/services.

LD SERVICES

LD program size is not limited.

LD services available to:

☑ Freshmen ☑ Sophomores ☑ Juniors ☑ Seniors

Academic Accommodations

Curriculum		In class	
Foreign language waiver	☐	Early syllabus	☐
Lighter course load	☐	Note takers in class	☑
Math waiver	☐	Priority seating	☑
Other special classes	☐	Tape recorders	☐
Priority registrations	☐	Videotaped classes	☐
Substitution of courses	☐	Text on tape	☑
Exams		**Services**	
Extended time	☑	Diagnostic tests	☐
Oral exams	☑	Learning centers	☑
Take home exams	☐	Proofreaders	☐
Exams on tape or computer	☐	Readers	☐
Untimed exams	☐	Reading Machines/Kurzweil	☑
Other accommodations	☑	Special bookstore section	☐
		Typists	☐

Credit toward degree is not given for remedial courses taken.

Counseling Services

☐ Academic
☐ Psychological
☐ Student Support groups
☐ Vocational

Tutoring

Individual tutoring is available.

	Individual	Group
Time management	☑	☑
Organizational skills	☑	☑
Learning strategies	☑	☑
Study skills	☑	☑
Content area	☑	☑
Writing lab	☑	☑
Math lab	☑	☑

UNIQUE LD PROGRAM FEATURES

There is no separate admissions process for students with disabilities, nor is there a separate Learning Disabled Program to which one can apply. Academic support for students with documented disabilities is coordinated in compliance with the Americans with Disabilities Act. Eligible students requesting services must present appropriate documentation of a disability. Prospective students are encouraged to meet with this office early in the admissions process to obtain a copy of the documentation guidelines and to learn about the services provided. Formal registration with the office is required each semester the student is enrolled in classes.

LD PROGRAM STAFF

Total number of LD Program staff (including director):

Full Time: 3 Part Time: 3

Key staff person available to work with LD students: Ginny Rossin, Coordinator of Special Services.

Columbia University

New York, NY

Address: 2960 Broadway, New York, NY, 10027
Admissions telephone: 212 854-2522
Admissions FAX: 212 854-1209
Admissions Contact: Jessica Marinaccio
Admissions e-mail: ugrad-admiss@columbia.edu
Web site: http://www.columbia.edu

LD program e-mail: disability@columbia.edu
Total campus enrollment: 7,233

GENERAL

Columbia University is a private, coed, four-year institution. Semester system.

TESTING

SAT Subject required.

All enrolled freshmen (fall 2004):

Average SAT I Scores:	Verbal: 702	Math: 715
Average ACT Scores:	Composite: 30	

Child Study Team report is not required. Tests required as part of this documentation:

- ☐ WAIS-IV
- ☐ WISC-IV
- ☐ SATA
- ☐ Woodcock-Johnson
- ☐ Nelson-Denny Reading Test
- ☐ Other

UNDERGRADUATE STUDENT BODY

Total undergraduate student enrollment: 7,233.

Composition of student body (fall 2004):

	Undergraduate	Freshmen
International	6.8	6.8
Black	8.4	7.1
American Indian	0.4	0.3
Asian-American	16.5	15.6
Hispanic	8.0	7.5
White	45.0	47.8
Unreported	14.9	14.9
	100.0%	100.0%

Average age of full-time undergraduates is 20. 69% of classes have fewer than 20 students, 21% have between 20 and 50 students, 10% have more than 50 students.

STUDENT HOUSING

99% of freshmen live in college housing. Freshmen are required to live on campus. Housing is guaranteed for all undergraduates. Campus can house 5,106 undergraduates.

EXPENSES

Tuition 2004-05: $30,260 per year.

Room: $5,290. Board: $3,776.

There is no additional cost for LD program/services.

LD SERVICES

LD program size is not limited.

LD services available to:

☐ Freshmen ☐ Sophomores ☐ Juniors ☐ Seniors

Academic Accommodations

Curriculum		In class	
Foreign language waiver	☐	Early syllabus	☐
Lighter course load	☐	Note takers in class	☒
Math waiver	☐	Priority seating	☐
Other special classes	☐	Tape recorders	☒
Priority registrations	☐	Videotaped classes	☒
Substitution of courses	☐	Text on tape	☐
Exams		**Services**	
Extended time	☒	Diagnostic tests	☐
Oral exams	☐	Learning centers	☐
Take home exams	☐	Proofreaders	☐
Exams on tape or computer	☐	Readers	☒
Untimed exams	☐	Reading Machines/Kurzweil	☒
Other accommodations	☐	Special bookstore section	☐
		Typists	☐

Counseling Services

- ☐ Academic
- ☐ Psychological
- ☐ Student Support groups
- ☐ Vocational

Tutoring

	Individual	Group
Time management	☐	☐
Organizational skills	☐	☐
Learning strategies	☐	☐
Study skills	☐	☐
Content area	☐	☐
Writing lab	☐	☐
Math lab	☐	☐

UNIQUE LD PROGRAM FEATURES

The Office of Disability Services aims to provide individual attention to any student requesting an accommodation. We hope to provide access to Columbia University for all students with disabilities.

LD PROGRAM STAFF

Key staff person available to work with LD students: All Staff can assist with LD Students.

The Cooper Union

New York, NY

Address: 30 Cooper Square, New York, NY, 10003
Admissions telephone: 212 353-4120
Admissions FAX: 212 353-4342
Registrar and Dean of Admissions and Records: Richard Bory
Admissions e-mail: admissions@cooper.edu
Web site: http://www.cooper.edu
SAT Code: 2097 ACT Code: 2724

Dean of Students: Linda Lemiesz
LD program telephone: 212 353-4115
LD program e-mail: lemiesz@cooper.edu
LD program enrollment: 8, Total campus enrollment: 921

GENERAL

The Cooper Union is a private, coed, four-year institution. Urban campus of five buildings in Manhattan (New York City population: 8,008,278). Served by air, bus, and train. Public transportation serves campus. Semester system.

LD ADMISSIONS

Students do not complete a separate application and are not simultaneously accepted to the LD program. A member of the LD program does not sit on the admissions committee. A personal interview is not required. Essay is required and may be typed.

4 applications were offered admission, and 4 enrolled.

SECONDARY SCHOOL REQUIREMENTS

Graduation from secondary school required; GED accepted. The following course distribution required: 4 units of English, 4 units of math, 2 units of science, 2 units of social studies, 5 units of academic electives.

TESTING

SAT Reasoning required; ACT may be substituted.

All enrolled freshmen (fall 2004):

Average SAT I Scores:	Verbal: 680	Math: 710
Average ACT Scores:	Composite:	

Child Study Team report is not required. Tests required as part of this documentation:

- ☐ WAIS-IV
- ☐ WISC-IV
- ☐ SATA
- ☐ Woodcock-Johnson
- ☐ Nelson-Denny Reading Test
- ☐ Other

UNDERGRADUATE STUDENT BODY

Total undergraduate student enrollment: 560 Men, 318 Women.

Composition of student body (fall 2004):

	Undergraduate	Freshmen
International	6.3	8.8
Black	6.3	5.0
American Indian	0.5	0.7
Asian-American	26.1	24.6
Hispanic	7.2	7.5
White	53.6	53.4
Unreported	0.0	0.0
	100.0%	100.0%

44% are from out of state. 5% join a fraternity. Average age of full-time undergraduates is 21. 55% of classes have fewer than 20 students, 44% have between 20 and 50 students, 1% have more than 50 students.

STUDENT HOUSING

89% of freshmen live in college housing. Freshmen are not required to live on campus. Housing is not guaranteed for all undergraduates. Housing is very limited. Campus can house 183 undergraduates. Single rooms are available for students with medical or special needs. A medical note is required.

EXPENSES

Tuition (2005-06): $27,500 per year. All students receive a full-tuition scholarship valued at $25,000.

Room: $9,180.

There is no additional cost for LD program/services.

LD SERVICES

LD program size is not limited.

LD services available to:

☑ Freshmen ☑ Sophomores ☑ Juniors ☑ Seniors

Academic Accommodations

Curriculum		**In class**	
Foreign language waiver	☐	Early syllabus	☐
Lighter course load	☐	Note takers in class	☐
Math waiver	☐	Priority seating	☐
Other special classes	☐	Tape recorders	☐
Priority registrations	☐	Videotaped classes	☐
Substitution of courses	☐	Text on tape	☐
Exams		**Services**	
Extended time	☑	Diagnostic tests	☐
Oral exams	☐	Learning centers	☐
Take home exams	☐	Proofreaders	☐
Exams on tape or computer	☐	Readers	☑
Untimed exams	☑	Reading Machines/Kurzweil	☐
Other accommodations	☐	Special bookstore section	☐
		Typists	☐

Credit toward degree is not given for remedial courses taken.

Counseling Services

- ☐ Academic
- ☐ Psychological
- ☐ Student Support groups
- ☐ Vocational

Tutoring

Individual tutoring is available weekly.

	Individual	Group
Time management	☐	☐
Organizational skills	☐	☐
Learning strategies	☐	☐
Study skills	☐	☐
Content area	☐	☐
Writing lab	☑	☐
Math lab	☐	☐

LD PROGRAM STAFF

There is no advisor/advocate from the LD program available to students.

Key staff person available to work with LD students: Linda Lemiesz, Dean of Students.

Cornell University

Ithaca, NY

Address: 349 Pine Tree Road, Ithaca, NY, 14850
Admissions telephone: 607 255-5241
Admissions FAX: 607 255-0659
Director of Undergraduate Admissions: Jason Locke
Admissions e-mail: admissions@cornell.edu
Web site: http://www.cornell.edu
SAT Code: 2098 ACT Code: 2726

LD program name: Student Disability Services
LD program address: 420 CCC, Ithaca, NY, 14853
Associate Director Student Disability Services: Michele Fish
LD program telephone: 607 254-4545
LD program e-mail: mdf6@cornell.edu
LD program enrollment: 265, Total campus enrollment: 13,625

GENERAL

Cornell University is a private, coed, four-year institution. 745-acre campus in Ithaca (population: 29,287), 60 miles from Syracuse; branch campuses in New York City and abroad in Arecibo, Puerto Rico. Served by air and bus; major airport and train serve Syracuse. School operates transportation to various locations in Tompkins County. Public transportation serves campus. Semester system.

LD ADMISSIONS

Students do not complete a separate application and are not simultaneously accepted to the LD program. A member of the LD program does not sit on the admissions committee. A personal interview is not required. Essay is required and may be typed. Foreign language requirement may be substituted with appropriate disability documentation.

SECONDARY SCHOOL REQUIREMENTS

Graduation from secondary school not required. The following course distribution required: 4 units of English, 3 units of math.

TESTING

SAT Reasoning or ACT required. SAT Subject recommended.

All enrolled freshmen (fall 2004):

Average SAT I Scores: Verbal: 676 Math: 705
Average ACT Scores: Composite: 30

Child Study Team report is not required. A neuropsychological or comprehensive psycho-educational evaluation is required for admission. Tests required as part of this documentation:

- [x] WAIS-IV
- [ ] WISC-IV
- [ ] SATA
- [x] Woodcock-Johnson
- [ ] Nelson-Denny Reading Test
- [ ] Other

UNDERGRADUATE STUDENT BODY

Total undergraduate student enrollment: 7,153 Men, 6,648 Women.

Composition of student body (fall 2004):

	Undergraduate	Freshmen
International	7.0	6.9
Black	4.9	4.7
American Indian	0.6	0.5
Asian-American	17.1	16.3
Hispanic	5.7	5.2
White	55.3	58.0
Unreported	9.4	8.4
	100.0%	100.0%

52% are from out of state. 28% join a fraternity and 22% join a sorority. Average age of full-time undergraduates is 20. 44% of classes have fewer than 20 students, 34% have between 20 and 50 students, 22% have more than 50 students.

STUDENT HOUSING

100% of freshmen live in college housing. Freshmen are not required to live on campus. Housing is not guaranteed for all undergraduates. Cornell guarantees on-campus housing for freshmen, sophmores and transfers. Campus can house 8,153 undergraduates. Single rooms are available for students with medical or special needs. A medical note is required.

EXPENSES

Tuition (2005-06): $31,300 per year.
Room: $6,080. Board: $4,170.

There is no additional cost for LD program/services.

LD SERVICES

LD program size is not limited.

LD services available to:

- [x] Freshmen
- [x] Sophomores
- [x] Juniors
- [x] Seniors

Academic Accommodations

Curriculum		**In class**	
Foreign language waiver	[ ]	Early syllabus	[ ]
Lighter course load	[ ]	Note takers in class	[x]
Math waiver	[ ]	Priority seating	[ ]
Other special classes	[ ]	Tape recorders	[ ]
Priority registrations	[ ]	Videotaped classes	[ ]
Substitution of courses	[ ]	Text on tape	[ ]
Exams		**Services**	
Extended time	[x]	Diagnostic tests	[ ]
Oral exams	[ ]	Learning centers	[x]
Take home exams	[ ]	Proofreaders	[ ]
Exams on tape or computer	[ ]	Readers	[x]
Untimed exams	[ ]	Reading Machines/Kurzweil	[x]
Other accommodations	[ ]	Special bookstore section	[ ]
		Typists	[x]

Credit toward degree is not given for remedial courses taken.

Counseling Services

- [ ] Academic
- [ ] Psychological
- [ ] Student Support groups
- [ ] Vocational

Tutoring

Individual tutoring is available weekly.

	Individual	Group
Time management	[x]	[x]
Organizational skills	[ ]	[x]
Learning strategies	[x]	[x]
Study skills	[x]	[x]
Content area	[x]	[x]
Writing lab	[x]	[x]
Math lab	[x]	[x]

UNIQUE LD PROGRAM FEATURES

Cornell University provides reasonable accommodations and/or services on an individual basis based on current documentation of a disabling condition and interaction with the student.

LD PROGRAM STAFF

Total number of LD Program staff (including director):

Full Time: 4 Part Time: 4

There is no advisor/advocate from the LD program available to students.

Key staff person available to work with LD students: Michele Fish, Associate Director Student Disability Services.

LD Program web site: http://www.CLT.cornell.edu

The Culinary Institute of America

Hyde Park, NY

Address: 1946 Campus Drive, Hyde Park, NY, 12538-1499
Admissions telephone: 800 285-4627
Interim Director of Admissions: Rachel Birchwood
Admissions e-mail: admissions@culinary.edu
Web site: www.ciachef.edu
SAT Code: 3301 ACT Code: 2728

Manager of the Learning Strategies Center: Jennifer Wrage
LD program telephone: 845 451-1287
LD program e-mail: j_wrage@culinary.edu
Total campus enrollment: 2,456

GENERAL

The Culinary Institute of America is a private, coed, four-year institution. 150-acre campus in Hyde Park (population: 20,851), 70 miles from New York City; branch campus in St. Helena, CA. Major airport serves Newark, NJ (70 miles); smaller airport serves Newburgh (21 miles); bus and train serve Poughkeepsie (three miles). Public transportation serves campus. Continuous system.

LD ADMISSIONS

A personal interview is required. Essay is required and may be typed.

SECONDARY SCHOOL REQUIREMENTS

Graduation from secondary school required; GED accepted.

TESTING

All enrolled freshmen (fall 2004):

Average SAT I Scores: Verbal: Math:
Average ACT Scores: Composite:

Child Study Team report is not required. A neuropsychological or comprehensive psycho-education evaluation is not required for admission. Tests required as part of this documentation:

- [ ] WAIS-IV
- [ ] WISC-IV
- [ ] SATA
- [ ] Woodcock-Johnson
- [ ] Nelson-Denny Reading Test
- [ ] Other

UNDERGRADUATE STUDENT BODY

Total undergraduate student enrollment: 1,368 Men, 644 Women.

70% are from out of state. Average age of full-time undergraduates is 23.

STUDENT HOUSING

Freshmen are not required to live on campus. Housing is guaranteed for all undergraduates. Campus can house 1,571 undergraduates. Single rooms are available for students with medical or special needs. A medical note is required.

EXPENSES

Tuition (2005-06): $19,180 per year. $16,940 per year (freshmen and sophomores), $12,180 (juniors and seniors).

Room: $4,280. Board: $2,170.

There is no additional cost for LD program/services.

LD SERVICES

LD program size is not limited.

LD services available to:

- [x] Freshmen
- [x] Sophomores
- [x] Juniors
- [x] Seniors

Academic Accommodations

Curriculum		In class	
Foreign language waiver	[ ]	Early syllabus	[ ]
Lighter course load	[x]	Note takers in class	[x]
Math waiver	[ ]	Priority seating	[x]
Other special classes	[ ]	Tape recorders	[x]
Priority registrations	[x]	Videotaped classes	[ ]
Substitution of courses	[x]	Text on tape	[x]
Exams		**Services**	
Extended time	[x]	Diagnostic tests	[ ]
Oral exams	[x]	Learning centers	[x]
Take home exams	[ ]	Proofreaders	[ ]
Exams on tape or computer	[x]	Readers	[x]
Untimed exams	[ ]	Reading Machines/Kurzweil	[x]
Other accommodations	[x]	Special bookstore section	[ ]
		Typists	[x]

Credit toward degree is not given for remedial courses taken.

Counseling Services

- [ ] Academic
- [ ] Psychological
- [ ] Student Support groups
- [ ] Vocational

Tutoring

Individual tutoring is available daily.

Average size of tutoring groups: 10

	Individual	Group
Time management	[x]	[ ]
Organizational skills	[x]	[ ]
Learning strategies	[x]	[ ]
Study skills	[x]	[ ]
Content area	[x]	[ ]
Writing lab	[x]	[ ]
Math lab	[x]	[ ]

LD PROGRAM STAFF

Total number of LD Program staff (including director):

Full Time: 4 Part Time: 4

There is an advisor/advocate from the LD program available to students. The advisor/advocate meets with students 4 times per month. 25 peer tutors are available to work with LD students.

Key staff person available to work with LD students: Jack Rittel & Mary Dietrich, Disability Support Services.

Daemen College

Amherst, NY

Address: 4380 Main Street, Amherst, NY, 14226-3592
Admissions telephone: 800 462-7652
Admissions FAX: 716 839-8229
Dean of Enrollment Management: Cecil Foster
Admissions e-mail: admissions@daemen.edu
Web site: http://www.daemen.edu
SAT Code: 2762 ACT Code: 2874

Associate Dean of the College: Kathleen C. Boone
LD program telephone: 716 839-8301
LD program e-mail: kboone@daemen.edu
LD program enrollment: 42, Total campus enrollment: 1,594

GENERAL

Daemen College is a private, coed, four-year institution. 35-acre, suburban campus in Amherst (population: 116,510), five miles from Buffalo. Major airport, bus, and train serve Buffalo. School operates transportation to off-campus health clinic. Public transportation serves campus. Semester system.

LD ADMISSIONS

Students do not complete a separate application and are not simultaneously accepted to the LD program. A member of the LD program does not sit on the admissions committee. A personal interview is recommended. Essay is not required. There are no specific admission requirements for LD students however, specific requests from applicants are reviewed on a case-by-case basis.

SECONDARY SCHOOL REQUIREMENTS

Graduation from secondary school required; GED accepted.

TESTING

SAT Reasoning or ACT required. SAT Subject recommended.

All enrolled freshmen (fall 2004):

Average SAT I Scores:	Verbal: 482	Math: 488
Average ACT Scores:	Composite: 21	

Child Study Team report is not required. Tests required as part of this documentation:

- ☐ WAIS-IV
- ☐ WISC-IV
- ☐ SATA
- ☐ Woodcock-Johnson
- ☐ Nelson-Denny Reading Test
- ☐ Other

UNDERGRADUATE STUDENT BODY

Total undergraduate student enrollment: 433 Men, 1,442 Women.

Composition of student body (fall 2004):

	Undergraduate	Freshmen
International	0.0	1.0
Black	23.4	16.1
American Indian	0.4	0.9
Asian-American	1.1	1.5
Hispanic	3.0	2.3
White	72.1	78.2
Unreported	0.0	0.0
	100.0%	100.0%

6% are from out of state. 7% join a fraternity and 3% join a sorority. Average age of full-time undergraduates is 21. 72% of classes have fewer than 20 students, 27% have between 20 and 50 students, 1% have more than 50 students.

STUDENT HOUSING

65% of freshmen live in college housing. Freshmen are required to live on campus. Housing is guaranteed for all undergraduates. Campus can house 614 undergraduates.

EXPENSES

Tuition (2005-06): $16,350 per year.
Room & Board: $7,780.
There is no additional cost for LD program/services.

LD SERVICES

LD program size is not limited.

LD services available to:

■ Freshmen ■ Sophomores ■ Juniors ■ Seniors

Academic Accommodations

Curriculum		**In class**	
Foreign language waiver	☐	Early syllabus	☐
Lighter course load	■	Note takers in class	■
Math waiver	☐	Priority seating	■
Other special classes	☐	Tape recorders	■
Priority registrations	■	Videotaped classes	☐
Substitution of courses	■	Text on tape	■
Exams		**Services**	
Extended time	■	Diagnostic tests	☐
Oral exams	■	Learning centers	■
Take home exams	☐	Proofreaders	☐
Exams on tape or computer	☐	Readers	■
Untimed exams	☐	Reading Machines/Kurzweil	☐
Other accommodations	☐	Special bookstore section	☐
		Typists	■

Credit toward degree is not given for remedial courses taken.

Counseling Services

- ■ Academic
- ■ Psychological
- ☐ Student Support groups
- ☐ Vocational

Tutoring

Individual tutoring is available.

	Individual	Group
Time management	☐	■
Organizational skills	☐	■
Learning strategies	☐	■
Study skills	■	☐
Content area	■	☐
Writing lab	■	☐
Math lab	■	☐

LD PROGRAM STAFF

Total number of LD Program staff (including director):

Full Time: 1 Part Time: 1

Key staff person available to work with LD students: Carol McPhillips, Learning Center Coordinator.

Dominican College of Blauvelt

Orangeburg, NY

Address: 470 Western Highway, Orangeburg, NY, 10962-1210
Admissions telephone: 845 359-3533
Admissions FAX: 845 365-3150
Director of Admissions: Joyce Elbe
Admissions e-mail: admissions@dc.edu
Web site: http://www.dc.edu
SAT Code: 2190 ACT Code: 2730

LD program name: Bridge Program
Coordinator, Bridge Program: Sr. Marianna Minchin
LD program telephone: 845 359-7800
LD program e-mail: christie.cruse@dc.edu
Total campus enrollment: 1,309

GENERAL

Dominican College of Blauvelt is a private, coed, four-year institution. 24-acre campus in Orangeburg (population: 3,388), 17 miles from New York City. Served by bus; major airport serves Newark, N.J. (40 miles); bus and train serve New York City. Public transportation serves campus. Semester system.

LD ADMISSIONS

Students do not complete a separate application and are simultaneously accepted to the LD program. A member of the LD program does not sit on the admissions committee. A personal interview is recommended. Essay is not required.

SECONDARY SCHOOL REQUIREMENTS

Graduation from secondary school required; GED accepted.

TESTING

SAT Reasoning required; ACT may be substituted. SAT Subject recommended.

All enrolled freshmen (fall 2004):

Average SAT I Scores:	Verbal: 445	Math: 446
Average ACT Scores:	Composite:	

Child Study Team report is not required. A neuropsychological or comprehensive psycho-educational evaluation is required for admission. Tests required as part of this documentation:

- ☐ WAIS-IV
- ☐ WISC-IV
- ☐ SATA
- ☐ Woodcock-Johnson
- ☐ Nelson-Denny Reading Test
- ☐ Other

UNDERGRADUATE STUDENT BODY

Total undergraduate student enrollment: 1,309.

Composition of student body (fall 2004):

	Undergraduate	Freshmen
International	0.0	0.0
Black	20.6	16.8
American Indian	0.4	0.2
Asian-American	4.3	5.9
Hispanic	20.2	13.7
White	43.8	53.4
Unreported	10.7	10.0
	100.0%	100.0%

23% are from out of state. Average age of full-time undergraduates is 23. 67% of classes have fewer than 20 students, 33% have between 20 and 50 students.

STUDENT HOUSING

76% of freshmen live in college housing. Freshmen are not required to live on campus. Housing is guaranteed for all undergraduates.

EXPENSES

Tuition (2005-06): $17,240 per year.
Room & Board: $8,720.
There is no additional cost for LD program/services.

LD SERVICES

LD program size is not limited.

LD services available to:

■ Freshmen ☐ Sophomores ☐ Juniors ☐ Seniors

Academic Accommodations

Curriculum		In class	
Foreign language waiver	☐	Early syllabus	☐
Lighter course load	☐	Note takers in class	■
Math waiver	☐	Priority seating	☐
Other special classes	☐	Tape recorders	☐
Priority registrations	☐	Videotaped classes	☐
Substitution of courses	☐	Text on tape	☐
Exams		**Services**	
Extended time	☐	Diagnostic tests	■
Oral exams	☐	Learning centers	■
Take home exams	☐	Proofreaders	☐
Exams on tape or computer	☐	Readers	☐
Untimed exams	☐	Reading Machines/Kurzweil	■
Other accommodations	☐	Special bookstore section	☐
		Typists	■

Credit toward degree is given for remedial courses taken.

Counseling Services

- ■ Academic
- ■ Psychological
- ☐ Student Support groups
- ☐ Vocational

Tutoring

Individual tutoring is available daily.

	Individual	Group
Time management	☐	☐
Organizational skills	☐	☐
Learning strategies	☐	☐
Study skills	☐	☐
Content area	■	☐
Writing lab	■	☐
Math lab	☐	☐

LD PROGRAM STAFF

Total number of LD Program staff (including director):

Full Time: 1 Part Time: 1

There is an advisor/advocate from the LD program available to students.

Key staff person available to work with LD students: Christie Cruse, Director, Bridge Program.

Dowling College

Oakdale Long Island, NY

Address: Idle Hour Boulevard, Oakdale Long Island, NY, 11769
Admissions telephone: 800 DOWLING
Admissions FAX: 631 563-3827
Director of Student Recruitment and Enrollment: Evette Beckett Tuggle
Admissions e-mail: admissions@dowling.edu
Web site: http://www.dowling.edu
SAT Code: 2011 ACT Code: 2665

LD program name: Hauseman Center
LD program telephone: 631 244-3144
LD program e-mail: AlsterE@dowling.edu
LD program enrollment: 139, Total campus enrollment: 3,357

GENERAL

Dowling College is a private, coed, four-year institution. 52-acre campus in Oakdale (population: 8,075), 50 miles from New York City; branch campuses in Brookhaven, Long Island, Manhattan, and corporate locations throughout the region. Served by train; major airport, bus, and train serve New York City; smaller airport serves Ronkonkoma (five miles). School operates transportation to train station. Public transportation serves campus. Semester system.

LD ADMISSIONS

Students do not complete a separate application and are not simultaneously accepted to the LD program. A member of the LD program does not sit on the admissions committee. A personal interview is required. Essay is not required.

For fall 2004, 146 completed self-identified LD applications were received. 146 applications were offered admission, and 140 enrolled.

SECONDARY SCHOOL REQUIREMENTS

Graduation from secondary school required; GED accepted. The following course distribution required: 4 units of English, 3 units of math, 2 units of science, 3 units of social studies.

TESTING

SAT Reasoning or ACT recommended.

All enrolled freshmen (fall 2004):

Average SAT I Scores: Verbal: 470 Math: 480

Child Study Team report is not required. A neuropsychological or comprehensive psycho-educational evaluation is required for admission. Must be dated within 36 months of application. Tests required as part of this documentation:

- [x] WAIS-IV
- [x] WISC-IV
- [ ] SATA
- [x] Woodcock-Johnson
- [x] Nelson-Denny Reading Test
- [ ] Other

UNDERGRADUATE STUDENT BODY

Total undergraduate student enrollment: 1,047 Men, 1,638 Women.

Composition of student body (fall 2004):

	Undergraduate	Freshmen
International	5.8	3.8
Black	16.0	9.9
American Indian	0.6	0.4
Asian-American	2.5	1.9
Hispanic	12.6	10.0
White	53.7	56.4
Unreported	8.8	17.6
	100.0%	100.0%

6% are from out of state. Average age of full-time undergraduates is 23. 61% of classes have fewer than 20 students, 39% have between 20 and 50 students.

STUDENT HOUSING

3% of freshmen live in college housing. Housing is guaranteed for all undergraduates. Single rooms are not available for students with medical or special needs.

EXPENSES

Tuition (2005-06): $17,040 per year.

There is no additional cost for LD program/services.

LD SERVICES

LD program size is not limited.

LD services available to:

- [x] Freshmen
- [x] Sophomores
- [x] Juniors
- [x] Seniors

Academic Accommodations

Curriculum
- [x] Foreign language waiver
- [x] Lighter course load
- [ ] Math waiver
- [ ] Other special classes
- [x] Priority registrations
- [ ] Substitution of courses

Exams
- [x] Extended time
- [ ] Oral exams
- [ ] Take home exams
- [ ] Exams on tape or computer
- [x] Untimed exams
- [x] Other accommodations

In class
- [ ] Early syllabus
- [x] Note takers in class
- [x] Priority seating
- [x] Tape recorders
- [ ] Videotaped classes
- [x] Text on tape

Services
- [ ] Diagnostic tests
- [ ] Learning centers
- [x] Proofreaders
- [x] Readers
- [ ] Reading Machines/Kurzweil
- [ ] Special bookstore section
- [x] Typists

Credit toward degree is given for remedial courses taken.

Counseling Services

- [ ] Academic
- [ ] Psychological
- [ ] Student Support groups
- [ ] Vocational

Tutoring

Individual tutoring is available weekly.

Average size of tutoring groups: 1

	Individual	Group
Time management	[ ]	[ ]
Organizational skills	[ ]	[ ]
Learning strategies	[ ]	[ ]
Study skills	[ ]	[ ]
Content area	[x]	[ ]
Writing lab	[x]	[ ]
Math lab	[x]	[ ]

LD PROGRAM STAFF

There is an advisor/advocate from the LD program available to students.

Key staff person available to work with LD students: Eleanor Alster, Coordinator of Student with Disabilities.

D'Youville College

Buffalo, NY

Address: 1 D'Youville Square, 320 Porter Avenue, Buffalo, NY, 14201-1084
Admissions telephone: 800 777-3921
Admissions FAX: 716 829-7900
Director of Admissions: Ronald H. Dannecker
Admissions e-mail: admiss@dyc.edu
Web site: http://www.dyc.edu
SAT Code: 2197 ACT Code: 2732

Coordinator of Disability Services: Isabelle Vecchio
LD program telephone: 716 829-7728
LD program e-mail: vecchio1@dyc.edu
LD program enrollment: 44, Total campus enrollment: 1,225

GENERAL

D'Youville College is a private, coed, four-year institution. Seven-acre, urban campus in Buffalo (population: 292,648). Served by air, bus, and train. Public transportation serves campus. Semester system.

LD ADMISSIONS

Students do not complete a separate application and are simultaneously accepted to the LD program. A member of the LD program does sit on the admissions committee. High school waivers are accepted for math and foreign language. A personal interview is recommended. Essay is not required.

SECONDARY SCHOOL REQUIREMENTS

Graduation from secondary school required; GED accepted.

TESTING

SAT Reasoning or ACT required. SAT Subject recommended.

All enrolled freshmen (fall 2004):

Average SAT I Scores:	Verbal: 493	Math: 496
Average ACT Scores:	Composite: 23	

Child Study Team report is not required. A neuropsychological or comprehensive psycho-educational evaluation is required for admission. Must be dated within 36 months of application. Tests required as part of this documentation:

- ■ WAIS-IV
- ■ WISC-IV
- ■ SATA
- ■ Woodcock-Johnson
- ■ Nelson-Denny Reading Test
- ☐ Other

UNDERGRADUATE STUDENT BODY

Total undergraduate student enrollment: 242 Men, 719 Women.

Composition of student body (fall 2004):

	Undergraduate	Freshmen
International	0.0	0.1
Black	23.4	21.0
American Indian	0.0	1.1
Asian-American	1.7	3.2
Hispanic	4.8	5.0
White	67.1	65.0
Unreported	3.0	4.6
	100.0%	100.0%

6% are from out of state. Average age of full-time undergraduates is 25. 57% of classes have fewer than 20 students, 43% have between 20 and 50 students.

STUDENT HOUSING

48% of freshmen live in college housing. Freshmen are not required to live on campus. Housing is guaranteed for all undergraduates. Campus can house 483 undergraduates. Single rooms are available for students with medical or special needs. A medical note is required.

EXPENSES

Tuition 2004-05: $14,690 per year.
Room: $3,670. Board: $3,670.

There is no additional cost for LD program/services.

LD SERVICES

LD program size is not limited.

LD services available to:

■ Freshmen ■ Sophomores ■ Juniors ■ Seniors

Academic Accommodations

Curriculum		**In class**	
Foreign language waiver	☐	Early syllabus	☐
Lighter course load	■	Note takers in class	■
Math waiver	☐	Priority seating	☐
Other special classes	☐	Tape recorders	■
Priority registrations	☐	Videotaped classes	■
Substitution of courses	☐	Text on tape	☐
Exams		**Services**	
Extended time	■	Diagnostic tests	☐
Oral exams	■	Learning centers	■
Take home exams	☐	Proofreaders	☐
Exams on tape or computer	☐	Readers	■
Untimed exams	■	Reading Machines/Kurzweil	■
Other accommodations	☐	Special bookstore section	☐
		Typists	☐

Credit toward degree is not given for remedial courses taken.

Counseling Services

- ■ Academic
- ■ Psychological
- ☐ Student Support groups
- ■ Vocational

Tutoring

Individual tutoring is available weekly.

	Individual	Group
Time management	■	☐
Organizational skills	■	☐
Learning strategies	■	☐
Study skills	■	■
Content area	■	■
Writing lab	■	■
Math lab	■	■

UNIQUE LD PROGRAM FEATURES

There is one full-time staff person who works exclusively with disabled students, however, the other Learning Center staff and tutors also work with disabled students.

LD PROGRAM STAFF

Total number of LD Program staff (including director):

Full Time: 1 Part Time: 1

There is no advisor/advocate from the LD program available to students.

Key staff person available to work with LD students: Isabelle Vecchio, Coordinator of Disability Services.

Elmira College

Elmira, NY

Address: 1 Park Place, Elmira, NY, 14901
Admissions telephone: 800 935-6472
Admissions FAX: 607 735-1718
Dean of Admissions: Dean Gary Fallis
Admissions e-mail: admissions@elmira.edu
Web site: http://www.elmira.edu
SAT Code: 2226 ACT Code: 2736

LD program name: Disabilty Services
Director of Educational Services: Carolyn Draht
LD program telephone: 607 735-1922
LD program e-mail: cdraht@elmira.edu
LD program enrollment: 69, Total campus enrollment: 1,558

GENERAL

Elmira College is a private, coed, four-year institution. 42-acre campus in Elmira (population: 30,940), 50 miles from Binghamton. Served by air and bus; larger airport serves Rochester (120 miles). School operates transportation to athletic center. Public transportation serves campus.

LD ADMISSIONS

Students do not complete a separate application and are not simultaneously accepted to the LD program. A member of the LD program does not sit on the admissions committee. A personal interview is recommended. Essay is required and may be typed.

SECONDARY SCHOOL REQUIREMENTS

Graduation from secondary school required; GED accepted. The following course distribution required: 4 units of English, 3 units of math, 3 units of science, 3 units of social studies, 1 unit of history, 2 units of academic electives.

TESTING

SAT Reasoning or ACT required. SAT Subject recommended.

All enrolled freshmen (fall 2004):

Average SAT I Scores: Verbal: 580 Math: 563
Average ACT Scores: Composite: 25

Child Study Team report is not required. A neuropsychological or comprehensive psycho-educational evaluation is required for admission. Tests required as part of this documentation:

- ☑ WAIS-IV
- ☐ WISC-IV
- ☐ SATA
- ☑ Woodcock-Johnson
- ☐ Nelson-Denny Reading Test
- ☑ Other

UNDERGRADUATE STUDENT BODY

Total undergraduate student enrollment: 489 Men, 1,095 Women.

Composition of student body (fall 2004):

	Undergraduate	Freshmen
International	3.1	4.5
Black	0.9	1.5
American Indian	0.0	0.2
Asian-American	0.6	0.5
Hispanic	0.9	0.5
White	81.9	80.0
Unreported	12.6	12.8
	100.0%	100.0%

51% are from out of state. Average age of full-time undergraduates is 20. 71% of classes have fewer than 20 students, 29% have between 20 and 50 students.

STUDENT HOUSING

98% of freshmen live in college housing. Freshmen are required to live on campus. Housing is guaranteed for all undergraduates. Campus can house 1,082 undergraduates. Single rooms are available for students with medical or special needs. A medical note is required.

EXPENSES

Tuition (2005-06): $27,500 per year.
Room: $5,150. Board: $3,550.

There is no additional cost for LD program/services

LD SERVICES

LD program size is not limited.

LD services available to:

☑ Freshmen ☑ Sophomores ☑ Juniors ☑ Seniors

Academic Accommodations

Curriculum		In class	
Foreign language waiver	☐	Early syllabus	☐
Lighter course load	☑	Note takers in class	☑
Math waiver	☐	Priority seating	☐
Other special classes	☐	Tape recorders	☑
Priority registrations	☐	Videotaped classes	☐
Substitution of courses	☐	Text on tape	☑
Exams		**Services**	
Extended time	☑	Diagnostic tests	☐
Oral exams	☑	Learning centers	☐
Take home exams	☐	Proofreaders	☑
Exams on tape or computer	☑	Readers	☑
Untimed exams	☑	Reading Machines/Kurzweil	☑
Other accommodations	☐	Special bookstore section	☐
		Typists	☐

Credit toward degree is not given for remedial courses taken.

Counseling Services

☑	Academic	Meets 260 times per academic year
☑	Psychological	Meets 365 times per academic year
☐	Student Support groups	
☑	Vocational	Meets 260 times per academic year

Tutoring

Individual tutoring is available daily.

Average size of tutoring groups: 4

	Individual	Group
Time management	☑	☐
Organizational skills	☑	☐
Learning strategies	☑	☐
Study skills	☑	☐
Content area	☑	☑
Writing lab	☑	☑
Math lab	☑	☑

LD PROGRAM STAFF

Total number of LD Program staff (including director):

Full Time: 2 Part Time: 2

There is no advisor/advocate from the LD program available to students. 1 graduate student and 30 peer tutors are available to work with LD students.

Key staff person available to work with LD students: Carolyn Draht, Director of Educational Services.

Eugene Lang College of New School University

New York, NY

Address: 66 W. 12th Street, New York, NY, 10011
Admissions telephone: 877 528-3321
Admissions FAX: 212 229-5166
Director of Admissions: Christy Kalan
Admissions e-mail: studentinfo@newschool.edu
Web site: http://www.newschool.edu
SAT Code: 2521 ACT Code: 9384

LD program name: Student Disability Services
LD program address: 65 Fifth Ave #410, New York, NY, 10003
Coordinator: Tava Naiyin Auslan
LD program telephone: 212 229-5626, extension 3135
LD program e-mail: sds@newschool.edu
LD program enrollment: 48, Total campus enrollment: 4,891

GENERAL

Eugene Lang College of New School University is a private, coed, four-year institution. Five-acre, urban campus in the Greenwich Village area of New York City (population: 8,008,278). Served by air, bus, and train. Public transportation serves campus. Semester system.

LD ADMISSIONS

Students complete a separate application and are not simultaneously accepted to the LD program. A member of the LD program does not sit on the admissions committee.

SECONDARY SCHOOL REQUIREMENTS

Graduation from secondary school not required. The following course distribution required: 4 units of English.

TESTING

All enrolled freshmen (fall 2004):

Average SAT I Scores: Verbal: 546 Math: 543
Average ACT Scores: Composite: 23

Child Study Team report is not required. A neuropsychological or comprehensive psycho-educational evaluation is required for admission. Must be dated within 36 months of application. Tests required as part of this documentation:

- ■ WAIS-IV
- ■ WISC-IV
- ■ SATA
- ■ Woodcock-Johnson
- ■ Nelson-Denny Reading Test
- ☐ Other

UNDERGRADUATE STUDENT BODY

Total undergraduate student enrollment: 168 Men, 350 Women.

Composition of student body (fall 2004):

	Undergraduate	Freshmen
International	17.8	21.5
Black	4.9	5.0
American Indian	0.7	0.2
Asian-American	13.8	11.3
Hispanic	7.5	6.6
White	39.2	39.9
Unreported	16.1	15.5
	100.0%	100.0%

79% are from out of state. Average age of full-time undergraduates is 22. 86% of classes have fewer than 20 students, 13% have between 20 and 50 students, 1% have more than 50 students.

STUDENT HOUSING

83% of freshmen live in college housing. Freshmen are not required to live on campus. Housing is not guaranteed for all undergraduates. Demand for housing is greater than supply. Campus can house 1,505 undergraduates.

EXPENSES

Tuition (2005-06): $26,820 per year.
Room: $8,100. Board: $2,710.
There is no additional cost for LD program/services.

LD SERVICES

LD program size is not limited.

LD services available to:

■ Freshmen ■ Sophomores ■ Juniors ■ Seniors

Academic Accommodations

Curriculum		In class	
Foreign language waiver	☐	Early syllabus	■
Lighter course load	■	Note takers in class	■
Math waiver	☐	Priority seating	■
Other special classes	☐	Tape recorders	■
Priority registrations	☐	Videotaped classes	☐
Substitution of courses	☐	Text on tape	■
Exams		**Services**	
Extended time	■	Diagnostic tests	☐
Oral exams	☐	Learning centers	☐
Take home exams	☐	Proofreaders	☐
Exams on tape or computer	■	Readers	■
Untimed exams	☐	Reading Machines/Kurzweil	☐
Other accommodations	■	Special bookstore section	☐
		Typists	☐

Credit toward degree is not given for remedial courses taken.

Counseling Services

- ■ Academic
- ■ Psychological
- ☐ Student Support groups
- ☐ Vocational

Tutoring

Individual tutoring is not available.

	Individual	Group
Time management	■	☐
Organizational skills	■	☐
Learning strategies	■	☐
Study skills	■	☐
Content area	☐	☐
Writing lab	■	☐
Math lab	☐	☐

LD PROGRAM STAFF

Total number of LD Program staff (including director):

Full Time: 2 Part Time: 2

There is an advisor/advocate from the LD program available to students.

Key staff person available to work with LD students: Ms. Tava Naiyin Auslan, Coordinator, Student Disability Services.

LD Program web site: www.newschool.edu

Fashion Institute of Technology

New York, NY

Address: Seventh Avenue at 27th Street, New York, NY, 10001-5992
Admissions telephone: 800 GO-TO-FIT
Admissions FAX: 212 217-7481
Director of Admissions: Dolores Lombardi
Admissions e-mail: fitinfo@fitsuny.edu
Web site: http://www.fitnyc.edu
SAT Code: 2257 ACT Code: 2744

LD program name: FIT-ABLE
Coordinator: Liz Holly Mortensen
LD program telephone: 212 217-8900
LD program e-mail: elizabeth_mortensen@fitnyc.edu
Total campus enrollment: 10,378

GENERAL

Fashion Institute of Technology is a public, coed, four-year institution. Five-acre, urban campus in midtown Manhattan (New York City population: 8,008,278). Served by air, bus, and train; airport also serves Newark, NJ (20 miles). Public transportation serves campus. Semester system.

LD ADMISSIONS

Students do not complete a separate application and are not simultaneously accepted to the LD program. A member of the LD program does not sit on the admissions committee. A personal interview is recommended. Essay is required and may be typed. FIT-ABLE does not waive admissions requirements for any student with a disability. Disclosure at the time of application is not encouraged. If any portion of the application is required in alternate form, such can be provided, as well as assistance in filing the application, at that time.

For fall 2004, 126 completed self-identified LD applications were received.

SECONDARY SCHOOL REQUIREMENTS

Graduation from secondary school required; GED accepted.

TESTING

Child Study Team report is not required. A neuropsychological or comprehensive psycho-educational evaluation is required for admission. Must be dated within 36 months of application. Tests required as part of this documentation:

- [x] WAIS-IV
- [x] WISC-IV
- [ ] SATA
- [x] Woodcock-Johnson
- [ ] Nelson-Denny Reading Test
- [x] Other

UNDERGRADUATE STUDENT BODY

Total undergraduate student enrollment: 1,919 Men, 8,761 Women.

Composition of student body (fall 2004):

	Undergraduate	Freshmen
International	3.2	10.6
Black	6.3	6.8
American Indian	0.1	0.2
Asian-American	7.1	10.3
Hispanic	11.0	9.3
White	54.6	44.6
Unreported	17.7	18.2
	100.0%	100.0%

31% are from out of state. Average age of full-time undergraduates is 22. 36% of classes have fewer than 20 students, 64% have between 20 and 50 students.

STUDENT HOUSING

51% of freshmen live in college housing. Freshmen are not required to live on campus. Housing is not guaranteed for all undergraduates. Students only eligible for 2 consecutive semesters in dorms. Campus can house 1,217 undergraduates. Single rooms are not available for students with medical or special needs.

EXPENSES

Tuition (2005-06): $4,350 per year (in-state), $10,610 (out-of-state).
Room: $4,366. Board: $2,700.
There is no additional cost for LD program/services.

LD SERVICES

LD program size is not limited.
LD services available to:

- [x] Freshmen
- [x] Sophomores
- [x] Juniors
- [x] Seniors

Academic Accommodations

Curriculum		In class	
Foreign language waiver	[ ]	Early syllabus	[x]
Lighter course load	[ ]	Note takers in class	[x]
Math waiver	[ ]	Priority seating	[x]
Other special classes	[ ]	Tape recorders	[x]
Priority registrations	[x]	Videotaped classes	[ ]
Substitution of courses	[x]	Text on tape	[x]
Exams		**Services**	
Extended time	[x]	Diagnostic tests	[ ]
Oral exams	[x]	Learning centers	[x]
Take home exams	[ ]	Proofreaders	[x]
Exams on tape or computer	[x]	Readers	[x]
Untimed exams	[ ]	Reading Machines/Kurzweil	[x]
Other accommodations	[x]	Special bookstore section	[ ]
		Typists	[x]

Credit toward degree is given for remedial courses taken.

Counseling Services

- [x] Academic
- [x] Psychological
- [x] Student Support groups — Meets 6 times per academic year
- [x] Vocational — Meets 6 times per academic year

Tutoring

Individual tutoring is available weekly.

Average size of tutoring groups: 2

	Individual	Group
Time management	[x]	[x]
Organizational skills	[x]	[x]
Learning strategies	[x]	[x]
Study skills	[x]	[x]
Content area	[x]	[x]
Writing lab	[x]	[ ]
Math lab	[ ]	[ ]

UNIQUE LD PROGRAM FEATURES

FIT accepts all students who meet the academic and technical qualifications of their majors.

LD PROGRAM STAFF

Total number of LD Program staff (including director):

Full Time: 1 Part Time: 1

There is an advisor/advocate from the LD program available to students. 10 peer tutors are available to work with LD students.

Key staff person available to work with LD students: Gail Ballard, LD Coordinator.

LD Program web site: www.fitnyc.edu/fitable

Fordham University

New York, NY

Address: 113 West 60th Street, New York, NY, 10023
Admissions telephone: 800 FORDHAM
Admissions FAX: 718 367-9404
Dean of Admission: John Buckley
Admissions e-mail: enroll@fordham.edu
Web site: http://www.fordham.edu
SAT Code: 2259 ACT Code: 2748

LD program name: Office of Disability Services
LD program address: 441 East Fordham Road, Bronx, NY, 10458
Director of Disability Services: Shani Berman
LD program telephone: 718 817-0655
LD program enrollment: 66, Total campus enrollment: 7,394

GENERAL

Fordham University is a private, coed, four-year institution. 85-acre campus at Rose Hill in the Bronx and seven-acre Lincoln Center campus in midtown Manhattan (New York City population: 8,008,278); branch campus in Tarrytown. Served by air, bus, and train. School operates van service between campuses. Public transportation serves campus. Semester system.

LD ADMISSIONS

A member of the LD program does not sit on the admissions committee. A personal interview is recommended. Essay is required and may be typed. Some admissions requirements may be waived on an as-needed basis.

SECONDARY SCHOOL REQUIREMENTS

Graduation from secondary school required; GED accepted. The following course distribution required: 4 units of English, 3 units of math, 3 units of science, 2 units of foreign language, 2 units of social studies, 2 units of history, 6 units of academic electives.

TESTING

SAT Reasoning or ACT required. SAT Subject required.

All enrolled freshmen (fall 2004):

Average SAT I Scores:	Verbal: 596	Math: 589
Average ACT Scores:	Composite: 25	

Child Study Team report is not required. A neuropsychological or comprehensive psycho-educational evaluation is required for admission. Must be dated within 36 months of application. Tests required as part of this documentation:

- [ ] WAIS-IV
- [ ] WISC-IV
- [ ] SATA
- [ ] Woodcock-Johnson
- [ ] Nelson-Denny Reading Test
- [x] Other

UNDERGRADUATE STUDENT BODY

Total undergraduate student enrollment: 2,840 Men, 4,222 Women.

Composition of student body (fall 2004):

	Undergraduate	Freshmen
International	0.7	1.3
Black	4.9	5.5
American Indian	0.3	0.1
Asian-American	6.9	6.0
Hispanic	12.2	11.1
White	58.0	58.2
Unreported	17.0	17.8
	100.0%	100.0%

37% are from out of state. Average age of full-time undergraduates is 20. 53% of classes have fewer than 20 students, 46% have between 20 and 50 students, 1% have more than 50 students.

STUDENT HOUSING

73% of freshmen live in college housing. Freshmen are not required to live on campus. Housing is not guaranteed for all undergraduates. Some students are not accepted with housing by the Office of Admissions; the student must commute to attend. Campus can house 4,010 undergraduates. Single rooms are not available for students with medical or special needs.

EXPENSES

Tuition (2005-06): $27,775 per year.
Room: $7,260. Board: $3,635.

There is no additional cost for LD program/services.

LD SERVICES

LD program size is not limited.

LD services available to:

- [x] Freshmen
- [x] Sophomores
- [x] Juniors
- [x] Seniors

Academic Accommodations

Curriculum		In class	
Foreign language waiver	[ ]	Early syllabus	[ ]
Lighter course load	[x]	Note takers in class	[x]
Math waiver	[ ]	Priority seating	[ ]
Other special classes	[ ]	Tape recorders	[x]
Priority registrations	[ ]	Videotaped classes	[ ]
Substitution of courses	[ ]	Text on tape	[ ]
Exams		**Services**	
Extended time	[x]	Diagnostic tests	[ ]
Oral exams	[ ]	Learning centers	[ ]
Take home exams	[ ]	Proofreaders	[ ]
Exams on tape or computer	[ ]	Readers	[ ]
Untimed exams	[ ]	Reading Machines/Kurzweil	[ ]
Other accommodations	[ ]	Special bookstore section	[ ]
		Typists	[ ]

Credit toward degree is not given for remedial courses taken.

Counseling Services

- [x] Academic
- [x] Psychological
- [ ] Student Support groups
- [x] Vocational

Tutoring

Individual tutoring is available weekly.

	Individual	Group
Time management	[x]	[ ]
Organizational skills	[x]	[ ]
Learning strategies	[ ]	[ ]
Study skills	[x]	[ ]
Content area	[ ]	[ ]
Writing lab	[x]	[ ]
Math lab	[x]	[ ]

UNIQUE LD PROGRAM FEATURES

Although a lighter course load for LD students and additional time given to complete a degree may be given as accommodations, they are granted on a case-by-case basis.

LD PROGRAM STAFF

Total number of LD Program staff (including director):

Full Time: 2 Part Time: 2

There is an advisor/advocate from the LD program available to students. 2 graduate students are available to work with LD students.

Key staff person available to work with LD students: Kristen Macaluso, Coordinator of Disability Services.

Five Towns College

Dix Hills, NY

Address: 305 North Service Road, Dix Hills, NY, 11746-5871
Admissions telephone: 631 424-7000
Admissions FAX: 631 652-2172
Director of Enrollment Services: Jerry Cohen
Admissions e-mail: admissions@ftc.edu
Web site: http://www.ftc.edu
SAT Code: 3142 ACT Code: 2745

Director of Academic Support Service: Susan Barr
LD program telephone: 631 656-2129
LD program e-mail: sbarr@ftc.edu
Total campus enrollment: 1,026

GENERAL

Five Towns College is a private, coed, four-year institution. 35-acre campus in Dix Hills (population: 26,024), 25 miles from New York City. Major airport and train serve New York City; smaller airport serves Islip (20 miles); bus serves Melville (five miles). School operates transportation to affiliated housing. Public transportation serves campus. Semester system.

LD ADMISSIONS

A personal interview is required. Essay is required and may not be typed.

SECONDARY SCHOOL REQUIREMENTS

Graduation from secondary school required; GED accepted. The following course distribution required: 4 units of English, 2 units of math, 2 units of science, 4 units of social studies, 4 units of academic electives.

TESTING

Child Study Team report is required if student is classified. Tests required as part of this documentation:

☐ WAIS-IV	☐ Woodcock-Johnson
☐ WISC-IV	☐ Nelson-Denny Reading Test
☐ SATA	☐ Other

UNDERGRADUATE STUDENT BODY

Total undergraduate student enrollment: 691 Men, 335 Women.

2% are from out of state.

STUDENT HOUSING

Housing is not guaranteed for all undergraduates. Campus can house 270 undergraduates.

EXPENSES

There is no additional cost for LD program/services.

LD SERVICES

LD program size is not limited.

LD services available to:

☐ Freshmen ☐ Sophomores ☐ Juniors ☐ Seniors

Academic Accommodations

Curriculum		**In class**	
Foreign language waiver	☐	Early syllabus	☐
Lighter course load	☐	Note takers in class	☐
Math waiver	☐	Priority seating	☐
Other special classes	☐	Tape recorders	☐
Priority registrations	☐	Videotaped classes	☐
Substitution of courses	☐	Text on tape	☐
Exams		**Services**	
Extended time	■	Diagnostic tests	☐
Oral exams	☐	Learning centers	■
Take home exams	☐	Proofreaders	☐
Exams on tape or computer	☐	Readers	☐
Untimed exams	■	Reading Machines/Kurzweil	☐
Other accommodations	☐	Special bookstore section	☐
		Typists	☐

Credit toward degree is not given for remedial courses taken.

Counseling Services

☐ Academic
☐ Psychological
☐ Student Support groups
☐ Vocational

Tutoring

	Individual	Group
Time management	☐	☐
Organizational skills	☐	☐
Learning strategies	☐	☐
Study skills	☐	☐
Content area	☐	☐
Writing lab	☐	☐
Math lab	☐	☐

UNIQUE LD PROGRAM FEATURES

Requirement for admissions: Must provide copies of current IEP and Psychological report.

LD PROGRAM STAFF

Total number of LD Program staff (including director):

Full Time: 2 Part Time: 2

Hamilton College

Clinton, NY

Address: 198 College Hill Road, Clinton, NY, 13323
Admissions telephone: 800 843-2655
Admissions FAX: 315 859-4457
Dean of Admission and Financial Aid: Monica Inzer
Admissions e-mail: admission@hamilton.edu
Web site: http://www.hamilton.edu
SAT Code: 2286 ACT Code: 2754

Dean of Students: Nancy Thompson
LD program telephone: 315 859-4022
LD program e-mail: nthompso@hamilton.edu
Total campus enrollment: 1,792

GENERAL

Hamilton College is a private, coed, four-year institution. 1,200-acre campus in Clinton (population: 2,209), nine miles from Utica. Airport serves Syracuse (45 miles); smaller airport, bus, and train serve Utica. School operates shuttle to Clinton and local shopping mall. Semester system.

LD ADMISSIONS

A personal interview is not required. Essay is required and may be typed.

SECONDARY SCHOOL REQUIREMENTS

Graduation from secondary school not required.

TESTING

SAT Reasoning or ACT considered if submitted. SAT Subject recommended.

All enrolled freshmen (fall 2004):

Average SAT I Scores: Verbal: 661 Math: 668

Child Study Team report is not required. Tests required as part of this documentation:

- [ ] WAIS-IV
- [ ] WISC-IV
- [ ] SATA
- [ ] Woodcock-Johnson
- [ ] Nelson-Denny Reading Test
- [ ] Other

UNDERGRADUATE STUDENT BODY

Total undergraduate student enrollment: 860 Men, 910 Women.

Composition of student body (fall 2004):

	Undergraduate	Freshmen
International	5.5	4.8
Black	3.7	3.8
American Indian	1.1	0.8
Asian-American	6.6	5.3
Hispanic	5.5	3.6
White	61.4	77.3
Unreported	16.2	4.4
	100.0%	100.0%

59% are from out of state. 34% join a fraternity and 20% join a sorority. Average age of full-time undergraduates is 20. 74% of classes have fewer than 20 students, 25% have between 20 and 50 students, 1% have more than 50 students.

STUDENT HOUSING

100% of freshmen live in college housing. Freshmen are required to live on campus. Housing is guaranteed for all undergraduates. Campus can house 1,756 undergraduates. Single rooms are available for students with medical or special needs.

EXPENSES

Tuition (2005-06): $33,150 per year.
Room: $4,460. Board: $3,850.
There is no additional cost for LD program/services.

LD SERVICES

LD program size is not limited.

LD services available to:

- [x] Freshmen
- [x] Sophomores
- [x] Juniors
- [x] Seniors

Academic Accommodations

Curriculum

- [ ] Foreign language waiver
- [ ] Lighter course load
- [ ] Math waiver
- [ ] Other special classes
- [ ] Priority registrations
- [ ] Substitution of courses

Exams

- [x] Extended time
- [x] Oral exams
- [ ] Take home exams
- [ ] Exams on tape or computer
- [x] Untimed exams
- [ ] Other accommodations

In class

- [ ] Early syllabus
- [ ] Note takers in class
- [ ] Priority seating
- [ ] Tape recorders
- [ ] Videotaped classes
- [ ] Text on tape

Services

- [ ] Diagnostic tests
- [x] Learning centers
- [ ] Proofreaders
- [x] Readers
- [ ] Reading Machines/Kurzweil
- [ ] Special bookstore section
- [ ] Typists

Counseling Services

- [x] Academic
- [x] Psychological
- [ ] Student Support groups
- [ ] Vocational

Tutoring

Individual tutoring is available.

	Individual	Group
Time management	[ ]	[ ]
Organizational skills	[ ]	[ ]
Learning strategies	[ ]	[ ]
Study skills	[ ]	[ ]
Content area	[ ]	[ ]
Writing lab	[x]	[ ]
Math lab	[x]	[ ]

Hartwick College

Oneonta, NY

Address: 1 Hartwick Drive, Oneonta, NY, 13820-4020
Admissions telephone: 607 431-4150
Admissions FAX: 607 431-4154
Dean of Admissions: Patricia Maben
Admissions e-mail: admissions@hartwick.edu
Web site: http://www.hartwick.edu
SAT Code: 2288 ACT Code: 2756

LD program name: Academic Center for Excellence
Assistant Dean for Academic Success: Joan Lambiaso
LD program telephone: 607 431-4435
LD program e-mail: lambiasoj@hartwick.edu
LD program enrollment: 114, Total campus enrollment: 1,479

GENERAL

Hartwick College is a private, coed, four-year institution. 425-acre campus in Oneonta (population: 13,292), 180 miles from New York City and 78 miles from Albany; 900-acre environmental campus at Pine Lake. Served by bus; airport and train serve Albany; other airport serves Binghamton (60 miles). School operates transportation to Pine Lake campus and to airports at holiday breaks. 4-1-4 system.

LD ADMISSIONS

Students do not complete a separate application and are not simultaneously accepted to the LD program. A member of the LD program does not sit on the admissions committee. High school waivers are accepted for math and foreign language. A personal interview is recommended. Essay is required and may be typed.

For fall 2004, 32 completed self-identified LD applications were received.

SECONDARY SCHOOL REQUIREMENTS

Graduation from secondary school required; GED accepted.

TESTING

SAT Reasoning or ACT considered if submitted; SAT Reasoning preferred.

All enrolled freshmen (fall 2004):

Average SAT I Scores: Verbal: 562 Math: 555
Average ACT Scores: Composite: 24

Child Study Team report is not required. A neuropsychological or comprehensive psycho-educational evaluation is required for admission. Must be dated within 12 months of application. Tests required as part of this documentation:

- [x] WAIS-IV
- [x] WISC-IV
- [ ] SATA
- [x] Woodcock-Johnson
- [x] Nelson-Denny Reading Test
- [x] Other

UNDERGRADUATE STUDENT BODY

Total undergraduate student enrollment: 641 Men, 805 Women.

Composition of student body (fall 2004):

	Undergraduate	Freshmen
International	1.5	3.4
Black	6.1	4.9
American Indian	0.5	0.9
Asian-American	2.4	1.3
Hispanic	4.6	3.6
White	62.2	63.2
Unreported	22.7	22.7
	100.0%	100.0%

39% are from out of state. 4% join a fraternity and 7% join a sorority. Average age of full-time undergraduates is 20. 59% of classes have fewer than 20 students, 41% have between 20 and 50 students.

STUDENT HOUSING

99% of freshmen live in college housing. Freshmen are required to live on campus. Housing is guaranteed for all undergraduates. Campus can house 1,204 undergraduates. Single rooms are available for students with medical or special needs. A medical note is required.

EXPENSES

Tuition (2005-06): $26,480 per year.
Room: $3,940. Board: $3,540.
There is no additional cost for LD program/services.

LD SERVICES

LD program size is not limited.

LD services available to:

- [x] Freshmen
- [x] Sophomores
- [x] Juniors
- [x] Seniors

Academic Accommodations

Curriculum		In class	
Foreign language waiver	[ ]	Early syllabus	[ ]
Lighter course load	[x]	Note takers in class	[x]
Math waiver	[ ]	Priority seating	[ ]
Other special classes	[ ]	Tape recorders	[x]
Priority registrations	[ ]	Videotaped classes	[ ]
Substitution of courses	[ ]	Text on tape	[ ]
Exams		**Services**	
Extended time	[x]	Diagnostic tests	[ ]
Oral exams	[ ]	Learning centers	[x]
Take home exams	[ ]	Proofreaders	[ ]
Exams on tape or computer	[ ]	Readers	[x]
Untimed exams	[ ]	Reading Machines/Kurzweil	[ ]
Other accommodations	[ ]	Special bookstore section	[ ]
		Typists	[ ]

Credit toward degree is not given for remedial courses taken.

Counseling Services

[x]	Academic	Meets 35 times per academic year
[ ]	Psychological	
[x]	Student Support groups	Meets 35 times per academic year
[ ]	Vocational	

Tutoring

Individual tutoring is available weekly.

Average size of tutoring groups: 1

	Individual	Group
Time management	[ ]	[x]
Organizational skills	[ ]	[x]
Learning strategies	[ ]	[x]
Study skills	[ ]	[x]
Content area	[ ]	[x]
Writing lab	[ ]	[x]
Math lab	[ ]	[ ]

LD PROGRAM STAFF

Total number of LD Program staff (including director):

Full Time: 1 Part Time: 1

There is an advisor/advocate from the LD program available to students. The advisor/advocate meets with faculty once per month and students 4 times per month. 12 peer tutors are available to work with LD students.

Key staff person available to work with LD students: Patty Jacobsen, Learning Support Specialist.

Hilbert College

Hamburg, NY

Address: 5200 South Park Avenue, Hamburg, NY, 14075-1597
Admissions telephone: 800 649-8003
Admissions FAX: 716 649-0702
Director of Admissions: Harry S. Gong
Admissions e-mail: admissions@hilbert.edu
Web site: http://www.hilbert.edu/
SAT Code: 2334 ACT Code: 2759

Director of Academic Services: Katherine Munroe
LD program telephone: 716 649-7900, extension 395
LD program e-mail: kmunroe@hilbert.edu
Total campus enrollment: 1,107

GENERAL

Hilbert College is a private, coed, four-year institution. 49-acre, suburban campus in Hamburg (population: 56,259), 10 miles from Buffalo. Major airport, bus, and train serve Buffalo. Public transportation serves campus. Semester system.

LD ADMISSIONS

Students do not complete a separate application and are not simultaneously accepted to the LD program. A member of the LD program does not sit on the admissions committee. A personal interview is recommended. Essay is not required.

SECONDARY SCHOOL REQUIREMENTS

Graduation from secondary school required; GED accepted. The following course distribution required: 4 units of English, 2 units of math, 2 units of science, 2 units of social studies, 2 units of history, 4 units of academic electives.

TESTING

ACT considered if submitted. SAT Reasoning recommended; ACT may be substituted. SAT Subject recommended.

All enrolled freshmen (fall 2004):

Average SAT I Scores:	Verbal: 468	Math: 466
Average ACT Scores:	Composite: 19	

Child Study Team report is not required. A neuropsychological or comprehensive psycho-educational evaluation is required for admission. Tests required as part of this documentation:

- [x] WAIS-IV
- [x] WISC-IV
- [ ] SATA
- [x] Woodcock-Johnson
- [ ] Nelson-Denny Reading Test
- [x] Other

UNDERGRADUATE STUDENT BODY

Total undergraduate student enrollment: 355 Men, 609 Women.

Composition of student body (fall 2004):

	Undergraduate	Freshmen
International	4.2	0.2
Black	4.2	4.2
American Indian	2.1	1.3
Asian-American	0.7	0.7
Hispanic	4.2	1.9
White	84.6	87.2
Unreported	0.0	4.5
	100.0%	100.0%

1% are from out of state. Average age of full-time undergraduates is 23. 58% of classes have fewer than 20 students, 42% have between 20 and 50 students.

STUDENT HOUSING

24% of freshmen live in college housing. Freshmen are not required to live on campus. Housing is guaranteed for all undergraduates. Campus can house 166 undergraduates.

EXPENSES

Tuition (2005-06): $14,300 per year.
Room: $2,400. Board: $3,180.
There is no additional cost for LD program/services.

LD SERVICES

LD program size is not limited.

LD services available to:

- [x] Freshmen
- [x] Sophomores
- [x] Juniors
- [x] Seniors

Academic Accommodations

Curriculum		In class	
Foreign language waiver	[ ]	Early syllabus	[ ]
Lighter course load	[x]	Note takers in class	[x]
Math waiver	[ ]	Priority seating	[ ]
Other special classes	[ ]	Tape recorders	[x]
Priority registrations	[ ]	Videotaped classes	[ ]
Substitution of courses	[ ]	Text on tape	[ ]
Exams		**Services**	
Extended time	[x]	Diagnostic tests	[ ]
Oral exams	[x]	Learning centers	[ ]
Take home exams	[ ]	Proofreaders	[ ]
Exams on tape or computer	[x]	Readers	[x]
Untimed exams	[ ]	Reading Machines/Kurzweil	[ ]
Other accommodations	[ ]	Special bookstore section	[ ]
		Typists	[x]

Credit toward degree is not given for remedial courses taken.

Counseling Services

- [x] Academic
- [x] Psychological
- [ ] Student Support groups
- [ ] Vocational

Tutoring

Individual tutoring is available weekly.

Average size of tutoring groups: 3

	Individual	Group
Time management	[x]	[x]
Organizational skills	[x]	[x]
Learning strategies	[x]	[x]
Study skills	[x]	[x]
Content area	[ ]	[ ]
Writing lab	[ ]	[ ]
Math lab	[ ]	[ ]

UNIQUE LD PROGRAM FEATURES

Hilbert does not have a separate program for students with learning disabilities. All students with disabilities who have self-identified and requested academic accommodations receive services through the Department of Academic Services. To be eligible to receive services, students need to provide official documentation supporting their request for services.

LD PROGRAM STAFF

Total number of LD Program staff (including director):

Full Time: 2 Part Time: 2

There is an advisor/advocate from the LD program available to students. 8 peer tutors are available to work with LD students.

Key staff person available to work with LD students: Katherine Munroe, Director of Academic Services.

Hobart and William Smith Colleges

Geneva, NY

Address: 337 Pulteney Street, Geneva, NY, 14456
Admissions telephone: 800 852-2256, 800 245-0100
Admissions FAX: 315 781-3914
Dean of Admissions: Don Emmons
Admissions e-mail: admissions@hws.edu
Web site: http://www.hws.edu
SAT Code: 2294 ACT Code: 2758

LD program name: Center for Teaching and Learning
LD program address: 678 South Main Street
Coordinator of Student Services: Samuel Vann
LD program telephone: 315 781-3351
LD program e-mail: vann@hws.edu
LD program enrollment: 91, Total campus enrollment: 1,839

GENERAL

Hobart and William Smith Colleges is a private, coed, four-year institution. 200-acre campus in Geneva (population: 13,617), 50 miles from both Rochester and Syracuse. Served by bus; airports and train serve Rochester and Syracuse. Public transportation serves campus. Semester system.

LD ADMISSIONS

Students do not complete a separate application and are not simultaneously accepted to the LD program. A member of the LD program does not sit on the admissions committee. High school waivers are accepted for math and foreign language. A personal interview is recommended. Essay is required and may be typed. Foreign Language requirement may be waived.

For fall 2004, 38 completed self-identified LD applications were received. 22 applications were offered admission, and 5 enrolled.

SECONDARY SCHOOL REQUIREMENTS

Graduation from secondary school required; GED accepted. The following course distribution required: 4 units of English, 3 units of math, 3 units of science, 2 units of foreign language, 2 units of social studies, 2 units of history, 2 units of academic electives.

TESTING

SAT Reasoning required; ACT may be substituted. SAT Subject recommended.

All enrolled freshmen (fall 2004):

Average SAT I Scores: Verbal: 585 Math: 590
Average ACT Scores: Composite: 26

Child Study Team report is not required. A neuropsychological or comprehensive psycho-education evaluation is not required for admission. Tests required as part of this documentation:

- [ ] WAIS-IV
- [ ] WISC-IV
- [ ] SATA
- [ ] Woodcock-Johnson
- [ ] Nelson-Denny Reading Test
- [ ] Other

UNDERGRADUATE STUDENT BODY

Total undergraduate student enrollment: 836 Men, 1,056 Women.

Composition of student body (fall 2004):

	Undergraduate	Freshmen
International	1.0	2.1
Black	3.5	3.5
American Indian	0.1	0.1
Asian-American	2.3	1.6
Hispanic	3.1	4.0
White	88.8	87.1
Unreported	1.2	1.6
	100.0%	100.0%

50% are from out of state. 17% join a fraternity. Average age of full-time undergraduates is 20. 65% of classes have fewer than 20 students, 34% have between 20 and 50 students, 1% have more than 50 students.

STUDENT HOUSING

100% of freshmen live in college housing. Freshmen are required to live on campus. Housing is guaranteed for all undergraduates. Campus can house 1,667 undergraduates. Single rooms are available for students with medical or special needs. A medical note is required.

EXPENSES

Tuition (2005-06): $31,850 per year.
Room: $4,431. Board: $3,955.

There is no additional cost for LD program/services.

LD SERVICES

LD program size is not limited.

LD services available to:

- [x] Freshmen
- [x] Sophomores
- [x] Juniors
- [x] Seniors

Academic Accommodations

Curriculum

- Foreign language waiver [x]
- Lighter course load [x]
- Math waiver [ ]
- Other special classes [ ]
- Priority registrations [ ]
- Substitution of courses [ ]

Exams

- Extended time [x]
- Oral exams [x]
- Take home exams [ ]
- Exams on tape or computer [x]
- Untimed exams [x]
- Other accommodations [x]

In class

- Early syllabus [ ]
- Note takers in class [x]
- Priority seating [x]
- Tape recorders [x]
- Videotaped classes [ ]
- Text on tape [x]

Services

- Diagnostic tests [ ]
- Learning centers [x]
- Proofreaders [x]
- Readers [x]
- Reading Machines/Kurzweil [x]
- Special bookstore section [ ]
- Typists [x]

Credit toward degree is not given for remedial courses taken.

Counseling Services

- [x] Academic
- [x] Psychological
- [x] Student Support groups
- [x] Vocational

Tutoring

Individual tutoring is available daily.

Average size of tutoring groups: 4

	Individual	Group
Time management	[x]	[x]
Organizational skills	[x]	[x]
Learning strategies	[x]	[x]
Study skills	[x]	[x]
Content area	[x]	[x]
Writing lab	[x]	[x]
Math lab	[x]	[x]

UNIQUE LD PROGRAM FEATURES

The Center for Teaching and Learning works with faculty on campus through workshops to raise awareness and to teach faculty how to effectively deal with students with disabilities.

LD PROGRAM STAFF

Total number of LD Program staff (including director):

Full Time: 4 Part Time: 4

There is an advisor/advocate from the LD program available to students. The advisor/advocate meets with faculty once per month and students 2 times per month. 30 peer tutors are available to work with LD students.

Key staff person available to work with LD students: Michael Mashewske, Specialist for Services for Students with Disabilities.

LD Program web site: www.hws.edu/academics/enrichment/ctl

Hofstra University

Hempstead, NY

Address: 100 Hofstra University, Hempstead, NY, 11549
Admissions telephone: 800 HOFSTRA
Admissions FAX: 516 463-5100
Vice President for Enrollment Services: Peter Farrell
Admissions e-mail: admitme@hofstra.edu
Web site: http://www.hofstra.edu
SAT Code: 2295 ACT Code: 2760

LD program name: Program for Academic Learning Skills
LD program address: 202 Roosevelt Hall
LD program telephone: 516 463-5761
LD program e-mail: PALS@Hofstra.edu
LD program enrollment: 99, Total campus enrollment: 9,053

GENERAL

Hofstra University is a private, coed, four-year institution. 238-acre campus in Hempstead (population: 755,924), 25 miles from New York City. Served by bus and train; major airports serve New York City. School operates transportation to local supermarket and shopping mall and to bus and train stations. 4-1-4 system.

LD ADMISSIONS

Students do not complete a separate application and are not simultaneously accepted to the LD program. A member of the LD program does sit on the admissions committee. A personal interview is required. Essay is not required.

For fall 2004, 236 completed self-identified LD applications were received. 78 applications were offered admission, and 39 enrolled.

SECONDARY SCHOOL REQUIREMENTS

Graduation from secondary school required; GED accepted. The following course distribution required: 4 units of English, 3 units of math, 3 units of science, 2 units of foreign language, 3 units of social studies.

TESTING

SAT Reasoning required of some applicants; ACT may be substituted. SAT Subject recommended.

All enrolled freshmen (fall 2004):

Average SAT I Scores:	Verbal: 567	Math: 577
Average ACT Scores:	Composite: 24	

Child Study Team report is not required. A neuropsychological or comprehensive psycho-educational evaluation is required for admission. Must be dated within 24 months of application. Tests required as part of this documentation:

- [x] WAIS-IV
- [ ] WISC-IV
- [ ] SATA
- [ ] Woodcock-Johnson
- [ ] Nelson-Denny Reading Test
- [x] Other

UNDERGRADUATE STUDENT BODY

Total undergraduate student enrollment: 4,335 Men, 5,011 Women.

Composition of student body (fall 2004):

	Undergraduate	Freshmen
International	1.3	1.8
Black	8.3	9.6
American Indian	0.2	0.1
Asian-American	4.4	4.2
Hispanic	7.4	8.2
White	64.1	61.7
Unreported	14.3	14.4
	100.0%	100.0%

18% are from out of state. 5% join a fraternity and 6% join a sorority. Average age of full-time undergraduates is 20. 44% of classes have fewer than 20 students, 52% have between 20 and 50 students, 4% have more than 50 students.

STUDENT HOUSING

70% of freshmen live in college housing. Freshmen are not required to live on campus. Housing is guaranteed for all undergraduates. Campus can house 4,200 undergraduates. Single rooms are not available for students with medical or special needs.

EXPENSES

Tuition (2005-06): $22,100 per year.
Room: $6,200. Board: $3,100.
Additional cost for LD program/services: $7,000 (freshman year only).

LD SERVICES

LD program is limited to %1 students.

LD services available to:

- [x] Freshmen
- [x] Sophomores
- [x] Juniors
- [x] Seniors

Academic Accommodations

Curriculum		In class	
Foreign language waiver	[ ]	Early syllabus	[ ]
Lighter course load	[x]	Note takers in class	[ ]
Math waiver	[ ]	Priority seating	[ ]
Other special classes	[ ]	Tape recorders	[ ]
Priority registrations	[ ]	Videotaped classes	[ ]
Substitution of courses	[ ]	Text on tape	[x]
Exams		**Services**	
Extended time	[x]	Diagnostic tests	[ ]
Oral exams	[ ]	Learning centers	[ ]
Take home exams	[ ]	Proofreaders	[ ]
Exams on tape or computer	[ ]	Readers	[ ]
Untimed exams	[ ]	Reading Machines/Kurzweil	[x]
Other accommodations	[ ]	Special bookstore section	[ ]
		Typists	[ ]

Credit toward degree is not given for remedial courses taken.

Counseling Services

- [x] Academic
- [ ] Psychological
- [ ] Student Support groups
- [ ] Vocational

Tutoring

Individual tutoring is available.

	Individual	Group
Time management	[x]	[ ]
Organizational skills	[x]	[ ]
Learning strategies	[x]	[ ]
Study skills	[x]	[ ]
Content area	[ ]	[ ]
Writing lab	[ ]	[ ]
Math lab	[ ]	[ ]

UNIQUE LD PROGRAM FEATURES

For ADD/ADHD, childhoood history of condition required for admission.

LD PROGRAM STAFF

Total number of LD Program staff (including director):

Full Time: 4 Part Time: 4

There is an advisor/advocate from the LD program available to students.

Houghton College

Houghton, NY

Address: 1 Willard Avenue, Houghton, NY, 14744
Admissions telephone: 800 777-2556
Admissions FAX: 585 567-9522
Director of Admissions: Tim Fuller
Admissions e-mail: admission@houghton.edu
Web site: http://www.houghton.edu
SAT Code: 2299 ACT Code: 2766

LD program name: Student Academic Services
Tutoring Coordinator: Eileen Lewis
LD program telephone: 585 567-9239
LD program e-mail: eileen.lewis@houghton.edu
LD program enrollment: 33, Total campus enrollment: 1,468

GENERAL

Houghton College is a private, coed, four-year institution. 1,300-acre campus in Houghton (population: 1,748), 60 miles from Buffalo and 70 miles from Rochester; branch campus in West Seneca. Major airport and bus serve Buffalo; airport and train serve Rochester. School operates transportation to Buffalo and Rochester airports, bus terminals, and train stations. Semester system.

LD ADMISSIONS

Students do not complete a separate application and are not simultaneously accepted to the LD program. A member of the LD program does not sit on the admissions committee. A personal interview is recommended. Essay is required and may be typed.

SECONDARY SCHOOL REQUIREMENTS

Graduation from secondary school required; GED accepted.

TESTING

SAT Reasoning or ACT required.

All enrolled freshmen (fall 2004):

Average SAT I Scores:	Verbal: 591	Math: 579
Average ACT Scores:	Composite: 25	

Child Study Team report is not required. A neuropsychological or comprehensive psycho-educational evaluation is required for admission. Must be dated within 36 months of application. Tests required as part of this documentation:

☑ WAIS-IV	☑ Woodcock-Johnson
☑ WISC-IV	☑ Nelson-Denny Reading Test
☐ SATA	☑ Other

UNDERGRADUATE STUDENT BODY

Total undergraduate student enrollment: 517 Men, 905 Women.

Composition of student body (fall 2004):

	Undergraduate	Freshmen
International	1.8	2.8
Black	2.5	2.3
American Indian	0.0	0.3
Asian-American	3.7	1.8
Hispanic	0.9	1.1
White	85.6	87.7
Unreported	5.5	4.0
	100.0%	100.0%

39% are from out of state. Average age of full-time undergraduates is 22. 61% of classes have fewer than 20 students, 37% have between 20 and 50 students, 2% have more than 50 students.

STUDENT HOUSING

96% of freshmen live in college housing. Freshmen are required to live on campus. Housing is guaranteed for all undergraduates. Campus can house 1,059 undergraduates. Single rooms are available for students with medical or special needs. A medical note is required.

EXPENSES

Tuition (2005-06): $19,420 per year.

Room: $3,300. Board: $3,260.
There is no additional cost for LD program/services.

LD SERVICES

LD program size is not limited.

LD services available to:

☑ Freshmen ☑ Sophomores ☑ Juniors ☑ Seniors

Academic Accommodations

Curriculum		**In class**	
Foreign language waiver	☐	Early syllabus	☐
Lighter course load	☑	Note takers in class	☐
Math waiver	☐	Priority seating	☑
Other special classes	☐	Tape recorders	☑
Priority registrations	☐	Videotaped classes	☑
Substitution of courses	☑	Text on tape	☑
Exams		**Services**	
Extended time	☑	Diagnostic tests	☑
Oral exams	☑	Learning centers	☐
Take home exams	☐	Proofreaders	☐
Exams on tape or computer	☑	Readers	☐
Untimed exams	☐	Reading Machines/Kurzweil	☑
Other accommodations	☐	Special bookstore section	☐
		Typists	☐

Credit toward degree is not given for remedial courses taken.

Counseling Services

☑ Academic	Meets 30 times per academic year
☑ Psychological	Meets 30 times per academic year
☐ Student Support groups	
☐ Vocational	

Tutoring

Individual tutoring is available weekly.

Average size of tutoring groups: 8

	Individual	Group
Time management	☑	☐
Organizational skills	☑	☐
Learning strategies	☑	☐
Study skills	☑	☐
Content area	☑	☐
Writing lab	☑	☐
Math lab	☐	☑

LD PROGRAM STAFF

There is an advisor/advocate from the LD program available to students. The advisor/advocate meets with faculty once per month and students 3 times per month. 35 peer tutors are available to work with LD students.

Key staff person available to work with LD students: Dr. Susan Hice, Director, Student Academic Services.

LD Program web site: www.houghton.edu/orgs/sas/

Iona College

New Rochelle, NY

Address: 715 North Avenue, New Rochelle, NY, 10801
Admissions telephone: 800 231-IONA
Admissions FAX: 914 633-2642
Director of Admissions: Tom Weede
Admissions e-mail: admissions@iona.edu
Web site: http://www.iona.edu/info
SAT Code: 2324 ACT Code: 2770

LD program name: College Assistance Program
Director: Linda Robertello
LD program telephone: 914 633-2159
LD program e-mail: LRobertello@iona.edu
LD program enrollment: 70, Total campus enrollment: 3,425

GENERAL

Iona College is a private, coed, four-year institution. 35-acre, suburban campus in New Rochelle (population: 75,000), 20 miles from New York City; branch campus in Rockland County. Served by train; major airports serve New York City; smaller airport serves Westchester County (12 miles). Public transportation serves campus. Semester system.

LD ADMISSIONS

Application Deadline: 05/01. Students complete a separate application and are simultaneously accepted to the LD program. A member of the LD program does not sit on the admissions committee. High school waivers are accepted for foreign language. A personal interview is required. Essay is required and may be typed. Foreign language requirement may be waived with proper documentation.

For fall 2004, 125 completed self-identified LD applications were received.

SECONDARY SCHOOL REQUIREMENTS

Graduation from secondary school required; GED accepted. The following course distribution required: 4 units of English, 3 units of math, 2 units of science, 2 units of foreign language, 1 unit of social studies, 1 unit of history, 4 units of academic electives.

TESTING

SAT Reasoning required; ACT may be substituted. SAT Subject recommended.

All enrolled freshmen (fall 2004):

Average SAT I Scores:	Verbal: 540	Math: 541
Average ACT Scores:	Composite: 23	

Child Study Team report is required if student is classified. A neuropsychological or comprehensive psycho-educational evaluation is required for admission. Must be dated within 24 months of application. Tests required as part of this documentation:

- [x] WAIS-IV
- [x] WISC-IV
- [x] SATA
- [x] Woodcock-Johnson
- [x] Nelson-Denny Reading Test
- [x] Other

UNDERGRADUATE STUDENT BODY

Total undergraduate student enrollment: 1,618 Men, 1,739 Women.

Composition of student body (fall 2004):

	Undergraduate	Freshmen
International	0.4	1.7
Black	7.2	7.4
American Indian	0.4	0.2
Asian-American	1.1	1.1
Hispanic	11.6	10.7
White	70.8	68.7
Unreported	8.5	10.2
	100.0%	100.0%

16% are from out of state. 2% join a fraternity and 5% join a sorority. Average age of full-time undergraduates is 20. 42% of classes have fewer than 20 students, 58% have between 20 and 50 students.

STUDENT HOUSING

66% of freshmen live in college housing. Housing is not guaranteed for all undergraduates. Housing offers are guaranteed for 2 years. Campus can house 1,028 undergraduates. Single rooms are available for students with medical or special needs. A medical note is required.

EXPENSES

Tuition (2005-06): $20,110 per year.
Room & Board: $9,898.
Additional cost for LD program/services: $1,500.

LD SERVICES

LD program is limited to %1 students.

LD services available to:

- [x] Freshmen
- [x] Sophomores
- [x] Juniors
- [x] Seniors

Academic Accommodations

Curriculum		**In class**	
Foreign language waiver	[ ]	Early syllabus	[ ]
Lighter course load	[x]	Note takers in class	[x]
Math waiver	[ ]	Priority seating	[ ]
Other special classes	[ ]	Tape recorders	[x]
Priority registrations	[ ]	Videotaped classes	[ ]
Substitution of courses	[ ]	Text on tape	[ ]
Exams		**Services**	
Extended time	[x]	Diagnostic tests	[ ]
Oral exams	[x]	Learning centers	[x]
Take home exams	[ ]	Proofreaders	[ ]
Exams on tape or computer	[ ]	Readers	[x]
Untimed exams	[x]	Reading Machines/Kurzweil	[x]
Other accommodations	[ ]	Special bookstore section	[ ]
		Typists	[ ]

Credit toward degree is not given for remedial courses taken.

Counseling Services

- [x] Academic
- [x] Psychological
- [ ] Student Support groups
- [ ] Vocational

Tutoring

Individual tutoring is available weekly.

	Individual	Group
Time management	[x]	[ ]
Organizational skills	[x]	[ ]
Learning strategies	[x]	[ ]
Study skills	[x]	[ ]
Content area	[x]	[ ]
Writing lab	[x]	[ ]
Math lab	[x]	[ ]

LD PROGRAM STAFF

Total number of LD Program staff (including director):

Full Time: 2 Part Time: 2

There is an advisor/advocate from the LD program available to students.

Key staff person available to work with LD students: Linda Robertello, Director of College Assistance Program (CAP).

Ithaca College

Ithaca, NY

Address: 100 Job Hall, Ithaca, NY, 14850-7020
Admissions telephone: 800 429-4274
Admissions FAX: 607 274-1900
Director of Admissions: Paula J. Mitchell
Admissions e-mail: admission@ithaca.edu
Web site: http://www.ithaca.edu
SAT Code: 2325 ACT Code: 2772

LD program name: Academic Support Services for Students with Disabilities
LD program address: 322A Smiddy Hall
Administrative Assistant: Sandy Simkin
LD program telephone: 607 274-1005
LD program e-mail: simkin@ithaca.edu
LD program enrollment: 310, Total campus enrollment: 6,107

GENERAL

Ithaca College is a private, coed, four-year institution. 757-acre campus in Ithaca (population: 29,287), 60 miles from Syracuse; branch campus in Los Angeles and abroad in London, England. Served by air and bus; airport and train serve Syracuse. Public transportation serves campus. Semester system.

LD ADMISSIONS

Application Deadline: 02/01. High school waivers are accepted for foreign language. A personal interview is not required. Essay is not required.

SECONDARY SCHOOL REQUIREMENTS

Graduation from secondary school required; GED accepted. The following course distribution required: 4 units of English, 3 units of math, 3 units of science, 2 units of foreign language, 3 units of social studies, 1 unit of academic electives.

TESTING

SAT Reasoning or ACT required. SAT Subject recommended.

All enrolled freshmen (fall 2004):

Average SAT I Scores: Verbal: 594 Math: 596

Child Study Team report is not required. Tests required as part of this documentation:

- ☐ WAIS-IV
- ☐ WISC-IV
- ☐ SATA
- ☐ Woodcock-Johnson
- ☐ Nelson-Denny Reading Test
- ☐ Other

UNDERGRADUATE STUDENT BODY

Total undergraduate student enrollment: 2,777 Men, 3,432 Women.

Composition of student body (fall 2004):

	Undergraduate	Freshmen
International	3.3	3.3
Black	1.8	2.2
American Indian	0.2	0.3
Asian-American	3.3	2.8
Hispanic	3.4	3.0
White	84.8	86.9
Unreported	3.2	1.5
	100.0%	100.0%

51% are from out of state. 1% join a fraternity and 1% join a sorority. Average age of full-time undergraduates is 19. 61% of classes have fewer than 20 students, 35% have between 20 and 50 students, 4% have more than 50 students.

STUDENT HOUSING

99% of freshmen live in college housing. Freshmen are required to live on campus. Housing is guaranteed for all undergraduates. Campus can house 4,308 undergraduates. Single rooms are available for students with medical or special needs. A medical note is required.

EXPENSES

Tuition (2005-06): $25,194 per year.
Room: $5,120. Board: $4,830.
There is no additional cost for LD program/service

LD SERVICES

LD program size is not limited.

LD services available to:

☑ Freshmen ☑ Sophomores ☑ Juniors ☑ Seniors

Academic Accommodations

Curriculum

- Foreign language waiver ☑
- Lighter course load ☐
- Math waiver ☐
- Other special classes ☐
- Priority registrations ☐
- Substitution of courses ☑

Exams

- Extended time ☑
- Oral exams ☑
- Take home exams ☐
- Exams on tape or computer ☑
- Untimed exams ☑
- Other accommodations ☑

In class

- Early syllabus ☐
- Note takers in class ☑
- Priority seating ☑
- Tape recorders ☑
- Videotaped classes ☐
- Text on tape ☑

Services

- Diagnostic tests ☐
- Learning centers ☐
- Proofreaders ☐
- Readers ☑
- Reading Machines/Kurzweil ☑
- Special bookstore section ☐
- Typists ☑

Credit toward degree is not given for remedial courses taken.

Counseling Services

- ☐ Academic
- ☐ Psychological
- ☐ Student Support groups
- ☐ Vocational

Tutoring

Individual tutoring is not available.

	Individual	Group
Time management	☐	☐
Organizational skills	☐	☐
Learning strategies	☐	☐
Study skills	☐	☐
Content area	☐	☐
Writing lab	☑	☐
Math lab	☑	☐

LD PROGRAM STAFF

Total number of LD Program staff (including director):

Full Time: 2 Part Time: 2

There is an advisor/advocate from the LD program available to students.

Key staff person available to work with LD students: Leslie Schettino, Director of Academic Support Services.

LD Program web site: www.ithaca.edu/acssd

Keuka College

Keuka Park, NY

Address: 141 Central Avenue, Keuka Park, NY, 14478
Admissions telephone: 800 33-KEUKA
Admissions FAX: 315 279-5386
Dean of Admissions and Financial Aid: Claudine Ninestine
Admissions e-mail: admissions@mail.keuka.edu
Web site: http://www.keuka.edu
SAT Code: 2350 ACT Code: 2782

LD program name: Services for Students with Disabilities
Coordinator for Students with Disabilities: Jennifer Robinson
LD program telephone: 315 279-5636
LD program e-mail: jrobins@mail.keuka.edu
LD program enrollment: 72, Total campus enrollment: 1,154

GENERAL

Keuka College is a private, coed, four-year institution. 203-acre campus in Keuka Park (population: 1,000), 50 miles from Rochester. Airport and train serve Rochester; airport also serves Syracuse (60 miles); bus serves Geneva (15 miles). School operates transportation to Penn Yan and selected area shopping malls. 4-1-4 system.

LD ADMISSIONS

Students do not complete a separate application and are not simultaneously accepted to the LD program. A member of the LD program does not sit on the admissions committee. A personal interview is recommended. Essay is required and may be typed.

SECONDARY SCHOOL REQUIREMENTS

Graduation from secondary school required; GED accepted. The following course distribution required: 2 units of English, 3 units of math, 3 units of science, 3 units of foreign language, 3 units of social studies, 2 units of history.

TESTING

SAT Reasoning or ACT required. SAT Subject recommended.

All enrolled freshmen (fall 2004):

Average SAT I Scores:	Verbal: 492	Math: 487
Average ACT Scores:	Composite: 20	

Child Study Team report is not required. A neuropsychological or comprehensive psycho-education evaluation is not required for admission. Tests required as part of this documentation:

- [ ] WAIS-IV
- [ ] WISC-IV
- [ ] SATA
- [ ] Woodcock-Johnson
- [ ] Nelson-Denny Reading Test
- [ ] Other

UNDERGRADUATE STUDENT BODY

Total undergraduate student enrollment: 269 Men, 683 Women.

Composition of student body (fall 2004):

	Undergraduate	Freshmen
International	0.5	0.0
Black	4.9	3.2
American Indian	1.6	0.6
Asian-American	1.2	0.4
Hispanic	2.8	1.2
White	85.0	90.1
Unreported	4.0	4.5
	100.0%	100.0%

9% are from out of state. Average age of full-time undergraduates is 23. 50% of classes have fewer than 20 students, 48% have between 20 and 50 students, 2% have more than 50 students.

STUDENT HOUSING

95% of freshmen live in college housing. Freshmen are required to live on campus. Housing is guaranteed for all undergraduates. Campus can house 740 undergraduates. Single rooms are available for students with medical or special needs. A medical note is not required.

EXPENSES

Tuition (2005-06): $17,800 per year.
Room: $3,990. Board: $3,990.
There is no additional cost for LD program/services.

LD SERVICES

LD program size is not limited.

LD services available to:

- [x] Freshmen
- [x] Sophomores
- [x] Juniors
- [x] Seniors

Academic Accommodations

Curriculum		In class	
Foreign language waiver	[ ]	Early syllabus	[ ]
Lighter course load	[x]	Note takers in class	[x]
Math waiver	[ ]	Priority seating	[ ]
Other special classes	[ ]	Tape recorders	[x]
Priority registrations	[ ]	Videotaped classes	[ ]
Substitution of courses	[ ]	Text on tape	[ ]
Exams		**Services**	
Extended time	[x]	Diagnostic tests	[ ]
Oral exams	[ ]	Learning centers	[x]
Take home exams	[ ]	Proofreaders	[ ]
Exams on tape or computer	[ ]	Readers	[x]
Untimed exams	[ ]	Reading Machines/Kurzweil	[x]
Other accommodations	[ ]	Special bookstore section	[ ]
		Typists	[ ]

Credit toward degree is not given for remedial courses taken.

Counseling Services

- [x] Academic
- [x] Psychological
- [x] Student Support groups
- [x] Vocational

Tutoring

Individual tutoring is available daily.

Average size of tutoring groups: 1

	Individual	Group
Time management	[x]	[ ]
Organizational skills	[x]	[ ]
Learning strategies	[x]	[ ]
Study skills	[x]	[ ]
Content area	[x]	[ ]
Writing lab	[x]	[ ]
Math lab	[x]	[ ]

LD PROGRAM STAFF

Total number of LD Program staff (including director):

Full Time: 3 Part Time: 3

Key staff person available to work with LD students: Jennifer Robinson, Coordinator for Students with Disabilities.

Le Moyne College

Syracuse, NY

Address: 1419 Salt Springs Road, Syracuse, NY, 13214-1399
Admissions telephone: 800 333-4733
Admissions FAX: 315 445-4711
Vice President for Enrollment Management: Dennis J. Nicholson
Admissions e-mail: admission@lemoyne.edu
Web site: http://www.lemoyne.edu
SAT Code: 2366 ACT Code: 2790

Director of Disability Support Services: Roger Purdy
LD program telephone: 315 445-4118
LD program e-mail: purdyrg@lemoyne.edu
LD program enrollment: 96, Total campus enrollment: 2,787

GENERAL

Le Moyne College is a private, coed, four-year institution. 151-acre, suburban campus in Syracuse (population: 147,306). Served by air, bus, and train. Public transportation serves campus. Semester system.

LD ADMISSIONS

A member of the LD program does not sit on the admissions committee. A personal interview is recommended. Essay is required and may be typed. Foreign Language requirement may be substituted dependent on documentation and course of study.

SECONDARY SCHOOL REQUIREMENTS

Graduation from secondary school required; GED accepted. The following course distribution required: 4 units of English, 3 units of math, 3 units of science, 3 units of foreign language, 4 units of social studies.

TESTING

SAT Reasoning or ACT required. SAT Subject recommended.

All enrolled freshmen (fall 2004):

Average SAT I Scores:	Verbal: 540	Math: 560
Average ACT Scores:	Composite: 23	

Child Study Team report is not required. A neuropsychological or comprehensive psycho-educational evaluation is required for admission. Must be dated within 36 months of application. Tests required as part of this documentation:

- ■ WAIS-IV
- ☐ WISC-IV
- ☐ SATA
- ■ Woodcock-Johnson
- ☐ Nelson-Denny Reading Test
- ■ Other

UNDERGRADUATE STUDENT BODY

Total undergraduate student enrollment: 1,007 Men, 1,438 Women.

Composition of student body (fall 2004):

	Undergraduate	Freshmen
International	0.9	0.9
Black	5.5	4.7
American Indian	0.6	0.7
Asian-American	2.7	2.5
Hispanic	3.6	3.3
White	81.2	83.3
Unreported	5.5	4.6
	100.0%	100.0%

5% are from out of state. Average age of full-time undergraduates is 21. 39% of classes have fewer than 20 students, 60% have between 20 and 50 students, 1% have more than 50 students.

STUDENT HOUSING

87% of freshmen live in college housing. Freshmen are required to live on campus. Housing is guaranteed for all undergraduates. Campus can house 1,575 undergraduates. Single rooms are available for students with medical or special needs. A medical note is required.

EXPENSES

Tuition (2005-06): $20,770 per year.
Room: $5,240. Board: $3,050.
There is no additional cost for LD program/services.

LD SERVICES

LD program size is not limited.

LD services available to:

■ Freshmen ■ Sophomores ■ Juniors ■ Seniors

Academic Accommodations

Curriculum		In class	
Foreign language waiver	☐	Early syllabus	☐
Lighter course load	☐	Note takers in class	■
Math waiver	☐	Priority seating	☐
Other special classes	☐	Tape recorders	■
Priority registrations	☐	Videotaped classes	☐
Substitution of courses	☐	Text on tape	■
Exams		**Services**	
Extended time	■	Diagnostic tests	☐
Oral exams	☐	Learning centers	■
Take home exams	☐	Proofreaders	☐
Exams on tape or computer	■	Readers	☐
Untimed exams	☐	Reading Machines/Kurzweil	■
Other accommodations	☐	Special bookstore section	☐
		Typists	☐

Credit toward degree is not given for remedial courses taken.

Counseling Services

- ■ Academic
- ■ Psychological
- ☐ Student Support groups
- ☐ Vocational

Tutoring

Individual tutoring is available weekly.

Average size of tutoring groups: 6

	Individual	Group
Time management	■	■
Organizational skills	■	■
Learning strategies	■	■
Study skills	■	■
Content area	☐	☐
Writing lab	☐	☐
Math lab	☐	☐

UNIQUE LD PROGRAM FEATURES

Services include pre- and post- admission consultation, review of past diagnostic testing, presentation of self-advocacy skills, liason and advocacy measures with faculty and staff, and specialized accommodations as deemed reasonable. Other services provided on a case-by-case basis upon review of documentation.

LD PROGRAM STAFF

Total number of LD Program staff (including director):

Full Time: 1 Part Time: 1

Key staff person available to work with LD students: Roger Purdy, Director of Disability Support Services.

Long Island University, Brooklyn Campus

Brooklyn, NY

Address: 1 University Plaza, Brooklyn, NY, 11201
Admissions telephone: 718 488-1011
Admissions FAX: 718 797-2399
Dean of Admissions: Dean Richard Sunday
Admissions e-mail: admissions@brooklyn.liu.edu
Web site: http://www.brooklyn.liu.edu
SAT Code: 2369

LD program name: Special Educational Services
Director, Special Educational Services: Jeff Lambert
LD program telephone: 718 488-1044
LD program e-mail: jeff.lambert@liu.edu
LD program enrollment: 49, Total campus enrollment: 5,363

GENERAL

Long Island University, Brooklyn Campus is a private, coed, four-year institution. 10-acre, urban campus in Brooklyn (New York City population: 8,008,278); branch campuses in Brentwood, Brookville, and Southampton and in Rockland and Westchester counties. Served by air, bus, and train. Public transportation serves campus. Semester system.

LD ADMISSIONS

Students do not complete a separate application and are simultaneously accepted to the LD program. A member of the LD program does not sit on the admissions committee. High school waivers are accepted for math and foreign language. A personal interview is required. Essay is required and may be typed.

For fall 2004, 14 completed self-identified LD applications were received. 14 applications were offered admission, and 14 enrolled.

SECONDARY SCHOOL REQUIREMENTS

Graduation from secondary school required; GED accepted.

TESTING

SAT Reasoning recommended; ACT may be substituted. SAT Subject recommended.

All enrolled freshmen (fall 2004):

Average SAT I Scores: Verbal: 448 Math: 480

Child Study Team report is not required. A neuropsychological or comprehensive psycho-educational evaluation is required for admission. Must be dated within 60 months of application. Tests required as part of this documentation:

- ■ WAIS-IV
- □ WISC-IV
- ■ SATA
- ■ Woodcock-Johnson
- ■ Nelson-Denny Reading Test
- ■ Other

UNDERGRADUATE STUDENT BODY

Total undergraduate student enrollment: 1,585 Men, 3,924 Women.

Composition of student body (fall 2004):

	Undergraduate	Freshmen
International	0.7	1.8
Black	40.4	42.4
American Indian	0.3	0.2
Asian-American	15.8	14.4
Hispanic	12.3	12.7
White	15.9	20.1
Unreported	14.6	8.4
	100.0%	100.0%

12% are from out of state. 1% join a fraternity and 1% join a sorority. 62% of classes have fewer than 20 students, 35% have between 20 and 50 students, 3% have more than 50 students.

STUDENT HOUSING

Freshmen are not required to live on campus. Housing is guaranteed for all undergraduates. Campus can house 550 undergraduates. Single rooms are not available for students with medical or special needs.

EXPENSES

Tuition (2005-06): $19,152 per year.

Room: $5,600. Board: $3,100.

There is no additional cost for LD program/services.

LD SERVICES

LD program size is not limited.

LD services available to:

■ Freshmen ■ Sophomores ■ Juniors ■ Seniors

Academic Accommodations

Curriculum		In class	
Foreign language waiver	□	Early syllabus	□
Lighter course load	■	Note takers in class	□
Math waiver	□	Priority seating	■
Other special classes	■	Tape recorders	■
Priority registrations	□	Videotaped classes	□
Substitution of courses	■	Text on tape	■
Exams		**Services**	
Extended time	■	Diagnostic tests	□
Oral exams	□	Learning centers	■
Take home exams	□	Proofreaders	□
Exams on tape or computer	■	Readers	■
Untimed exams	■	Reading Machines/Kurzweil	■
Other accommodations	■	Special bookstore section	□
		Typists	■

Credit toward degree is given for remedial courses taken.

Counseling Services

- ■ Academic — Meets 30 times per academic year
- ■ Psychological
- ■ Student Support groups
- ■ Vocational — Meets 4 times per academic year

Tutoring

Individual tutoring is available weekly.

Average size of tutoring groups: 4

	Individual	Group
Time management	■	□
Organizational skills	■	□
Learning strategies	■	□
Study skills	■	■
Content area	■	□
Writing lab	■	□
Math lab	■	□

UNIQUE LD PROGRAM FEATURES

Eligible students are served by our general program of support services for students with disabilities. A variety of individualized accommodations are offered. These may include an extended time allotment for course examinations, counseling to explore time management skills, facilitating student/professor meetings and personal counseling to develop effective learning strategies.

LD PROGRAM STAFF

Total number of LD Program staff (including director):

Full Time: 7 Part Time: 7

There is an advisor/advocate from the LD program available to students. The advisor/advocate meets with faculty once per month and students 4 times per month. Key staff person available to work with LD students: Phyllis Brown-Richardson, Learning Disabilities Specialist.

Long Island University, C.W. Post Campus

Brookville, NY

Address: 720 Northern Boulevard, Brookville, NY, 11548-1300
Admissions telephone: 800 LIU-PLAN
Admissions FAX: 516 299-2137
Executive Director of Admissions and Recruitment: Gary Bergman
Admissions e-mail: enroll@cwpost.liu.edu
Web site: http://www.liu.edu
SAT Code: 2070 ACT Code: 2687

LD program name: ARC
Director, Academic Resource Center: Mathilda Stucke
LD program telephone: 516 299-2937
LD program e-mail: mstucke@liu.edu
Total campus enrollment: 6,417

GENERAL

Long Island University, C.W. Post Campus is a private, coed, four-year institution. 308-acre, suburban campus in Brookville (population: 2,126), 25 miles from New York City; regional branch campuses in Brentwood, Rockland, and Westchester. Major airports, bus, and train serve New York City. School operates transportation to Hicksville train station and local shopping areas. Public transportation serves campus. Semester system.

LD ADMISSIONS

A personal interview is required.

SECONDARY SCHOOL REQUIREMENTS

Graduation from secondary school required; GED accepted. The following course distribution required: 4 units of English, 2 units of math, 3 units of science, 2 units of foreign language, 3 units of social studies, 3 units of academic electives.

TESTING

SAT Reasoning considered if submitted. ACT considered if submitted. SAT Reasoning required of some applicants; ACT may be substituted. SAT Subject recommended.

All enrolled freshmen (fall 2004):

Average SAT I Scores: Verbal: 490 Math: 495

Child Study Team report is required if student is classified. Tests required as part of this documentation:

☐ WAIS-IV
☐ WISC-IV
☐ SATA
☐ Woodcock-Johnson
☐ Nelson-Denny Reading Test
☐ Other

UNDERGRADUATE STUDENT BODY

Total undergraduate student enrollment: 2,705 Men, 3,791 Women.

Composition of student body (fall 2004):

	Undergraduate	Freshmen
International	1.9	2.8
Black	11.9	8.8
American Indian	0.4	0.3
Asian-American	2.5	2.5
Hispanic	9.5	7.1
White	54.9	46.4
Unreported	18.9	32.1
	100.0%	100.0%

9% are from out of state. Average age of full-time undergraduates is 21.

STUDENT HOUSING

45% of freshmen live in college housing. Housing is guaranteed for all undergraduates. Campus can house 1,673 undergraduates.

EXPENSES

Tuition (2005-06): $22,100 per year.
Room: $5,730. Board: $2,970.
Additional cost for LD program/services: $1,600 per semester.

LD SERVICES

LD program size is limited.

LD services available to:

☐ Freshmen ☐ Sophomores ☐ Juniors ☐ Seniors

Academic Accommodations

Curriculum		In class	
Foreign language waiver	☐	Early syllabus	☐
Lighter course load	■	Note takers in class	■
Math waiver	☐	Priority seating	☐
Other special classes	☐	Tape recorders	■
Priority registrations	☐	Videotaped classes	☐
Substitution of courses	☐	Text on tape	☐
Exams		**Services**	
Extended time	■	Diagnostic tests	■
Oral exams	☐	Learning centers	☐
Take home exams	☐	Proofreaders	☐
Exams on tape or computer	☐	Readers	■
Untimed exams	■	Reading Machines/Kurzweil	■
Other accommodations	☐	Special bookstore section	☐
		Typists	☐

Credit toward degree is not given for remedial courses taken.

Counseling Services

☐ Academic
☐ Psychological
☐ Student Support groups
☐ Vocational

Tutoring

	Individual	Group
Time management	☐	☐
Organizational skills	☐	☐
Learning strategies	☐	☐
Study skills	☐	☐
Content area	☐	☐
Writing lab	☐	☐
Math lab	☐	☐

Manhattan College

Riverdale, NY

Address: Manhattan College Parkway, Riverdale, NY, 10471
Admissions telephone: 800 622-9235
Admissions FAX: 718 862-8019
Assistant Vice President for Enrollment Management: William J. Bisset, Jr.
Admissions e-mail: admit@manhattan.edu
Web site: http://www.manhattan.edu
SAT Code: 2395 ACT Code: 2796

ADA Coordinator: Ross Pollack
LD program telephone: 718 862-7101
LD program e-mail: ross.pollack@manhattan.edu
LD program enrollment: 150, Total campus enrollment: 2,909

GENERAL

Manhattan College is a private, coed, four-year institution. 26-acre campus in Riverdale section of the Bronx (New York City population: 8,008,278). Served by air, bus, and train. School operates transportation to Coll. of Mount St. Vincent. Public transportation serves campus. Semester system.

LD ADMISSIONS

Application Deadline: 11/30. Students do not complete a separate application and are not simultaneously accepted to the LD program. A member of the LD program does not sit on the admissions committee. A personal interview is recommended. Essay is not required.

SECONDARY SCHOOL REQUIREMENTS

Graduation from secondary school required; GED accepted. The following course distribution required: 4 units of English, 3 units of math, 2 units of science, 2 units of foreign language, 3 units of social studies, 3 units of history, 2 units of academic electives.

TESTING

SAT Reasoning required; ACT may be substituted. SAT Subject recommended.

All enrolled freshmen (fall 2004):

Average SAT I Scores:	Verbal: 548	Math: 562
Average ACT Scores:	Composite: 30	

Child Study Team report is not required. A neuropsychological or comprehensive psycho-educational evaluation is required for admission. Tests required as part of this documentation:

- [ ] WAIS-IV
- [ ] WISC-IV
- [ ] SATA
- [ ] Woodcock-Johnson
- [ ] Nelson-Denny Reading Test
- [ ] Other

UNDERGRADUATE STUDENT BODY

Total undergraduate student enrollment: 1,353 Men, 1,255 Women.

Composition of student body (fall 2004):

	Undergraduate	Freshmen
International	2.7	2.5
Black	4.6	4.5
American Indian	0.0	0.0
Asian-American	3.2	4.0
Hispanic	5.8	12.4
White	67.4	68.2
Unreported	16.3	8.4
	100.0%	100.0%

22% are from out of state. 47% of classes have fewer than 20 students, 53% have between 20 and 50 students.

STUDENT HOUSING

Freshmen are not required to live on campus. Housing is guaranteed for all undergraduates. Campus can house 1,625 undergraduates.

EXPENSES

Tuition (2005-06): $19,400 per year.

Room & Board: $8,760.

There is no additional cost for LD program/services.

LD SERVICES

LD program size is not limited.

LD services available to:

- [x] Freshmen
- [x] Sophomores
- [x] Juniors
- [x] Seniors

Academic Accommodations

Curriculum		In class	
Foreign language waiver	[ ]	Early syllabus	[ ]
Lighter course load	[x]	Note takers in class	[ ]
Math waiver	[ ]	Priority seating	[ ]
Other special classes	[ ]	Tape recorders	[ ]
Priority registrations	[ ]	Videotaped classes	[ ]
Substitution of courses	[ ]	Text on tape	[ ]
Exams		**Services**	
Extended time	[ ]	Diagnostic tests	[ ]
Oral exams	[ ]	Learning centers	[ ]
Take home exams	[ ]	Proofreaders	[ ]
Exams on tape or computer	[ ]	Readers	[ ]
Untimed exams	[ ]	Reading Machines/Kurzweil	[ ]
Other accommodations	[ ]	Special bookstore section	[ ]
		Typists	[ ]

Credit toward degree is not given for remedial courses taken.

Counseling Services

- [x] Academic
- [x] Psychological
- [x] Student Support groups
- [x] Vocational

Tutoring

	Individual	Group
Time management	[ ]	[ ]
Organizational skills	[ ]	[ ]
Learning strategies	[ ]	[ ]
Study skills	[ ]	[ ]
Content area	[ ]	[ ]
Writing lab	[ ]	[ ]
Math lab	[ ]	[ ]

LD PROGRAM STAFF

Total number of LD Program staff (including director):

Full Time: 1 Part Time: 1

There is an advisor/advocate from the LD program available to students.

Key staff person available to work with LD students: Ross Pollack, ADA Coordinator.

Manhattan School of Music

New York, NY

Address: 120 Claremont Avenue, New York, NY, 10027
Admissions telephone: 212 749-2802, extension 4501
Admissions FAX: 212 749-3025
Director of Admissions: Amy A. Anderson
Admissions e-mail: admission@msmnyc.edu
Web site: http://www.msmnyc.edu
SAT Code: 2396

LD program name: Dean of Students
Dean of Students: Elsa Jean Davidson
LD program telephone: 212 749-2802, extension 4036
LD program e-mail: ejdavidson@msmnyc.edu
Total campus enrollment: 410

GENERAL

Manhattan School of Music is a private, coed, four-year institution. One-acre, urban campus in Manhattan (New York City population: 8,008,278). Served by air, bus, and train; other airport serves Newark, NJ (16 miles). Public transportation serves campus. Semester system.

LD ADMISSIONS

Students do not complete a separate application and are not simultaneously accepted to the LD program. A member of the LD program does not sit on the admissions committee. A personal interview is not required. Essay is required and may be typed.

SECONDARY SCHOOL REQUIREMENTS

Graduation from secondary school required; GED accepted.

TESTING

SAT Subject recommended.

Child Study Team report is not required. A neuropsychological or comprehensive psycho-education evaluation is not required for admission. Tests required as part of this documentation:

- ☐ WAIS-IV
- ☐ WISC-IV
- ☐ SATA
- ☐ Woodcock-Johnson
- ☐ Nelson-Denny Reading Test
- ☐ Other

UNDERGRADUATE STUDENT BODY

Total undergraduate student enrollment: 181 Men, 181 Women.

Composition of student body (fall 2004):

	Undergraduate	Freshmen
International	9.8	20.0
Black	2.9	3.2
American Indian	0.1	0.2
Asian-American	2.9	8.8
Hispanic	2.9	4.4
White	49.0	43.9
Unreported	32.4	19.5
	100.0%	100.0%

65% are from out of state. Average age of full-time undergraduates is 20. 90% of classes have fewer than 20 students, 5% have between 20 and 50 students, 5% have more than 50 students.

STUDENT HOUSING

99% of freshmen live in college housing. Freshmen are required to live on campus. Housing is guaranteed for all undergraduates as long as space is available. Campus can house 256 undergraduates. Single rooms are not available for students with medical or special needs.

EXPENSES

Tuition (2005-06): $26,000 per year.
Room: $8,050. Board: $4,400.

LD SERVICES

LD program size is not limited.

LD services available to:

■ Freshmen ■ Sophomores ■ Juniors ■ Seniors

Academic Accommodations

Curriculum		In class	
Foreign language waiver	☐	Early syllabus	☐
Lighter course load	☐	Note takers in class	☐
Math waiver	☐	Priority seating	☐
Other special classes	☐	Tape recorders	☐
Priority registrations	☐	Videotaped classes	☐
Substitution of courses	☐	Text on tape	☐
Exams		**Services**	
Extended time	☐	Diagnostic tests	☐
Oral exams	☐	Learning centers	☐
Take home exams	☐	Proofreaders	☐
Exams on tape or computer	☐	Readers	☐
Untimed exams	☐	Reading Machines/Kurzweil	☐
Other accommodations	☐	Special bookstore section	☐
		Typists	☐

Credit toward degree is not given for remedial courses taken.

Counseling Services

- ☐ Academic
- ☐ Psychological
- ☐ Student Support groups
- ☐ Vocational

Tutoring

Individual tutoring is available weekly.

Average size of tutoring groups: 1

	Individual	Group
Time management	☐	☐
Organizational skills	☐	☐
Learning strategies	☐	☐
Study skills	☐	☐
Content area	■	☐
Writing lab	☐	☐
Math lab	☐	☐

UNIQUE LD PROGRAM FEATURES

Students with documented LD meet with Deans and the Director of Student Life to determine the best course of action.

LD PROGRAM STAFF

Total number of LD Program staff (including director):

Full Time: 1 Part Time: 1

There is no advisor/advocate from the LD program available to students. 10 peer tutors are available to work with LD students.

Key staff person available to work with LD students: Elsa Jean Davidson, Dean of Students.

Manhattanville College

Purchase, NY

Address: 2900 Purchase Street, Purchase, NY, 10577
Admissions telephone: 800 328-4553
Admissions FAX: 914 694-1732
Director of Admissions: Jose Flores
Admissions e-mail: admissions@mville.edu
Web site: http://www.mville.edu
SAT Code: 2397 ACT Code: 2800

ADA Coordinator: Karen Steinmetz
LD program telephone: 914 323-3186
LD program e-mail: steinmetzk@mville.edu
LD program enrollment: 120, Total campus enrollment: 1,719

GENERAL

Manhattanville College is a private, coed, four-year institution. 100-acre, suburban campus in Purchase (population: 8,000), 25 miles from New York. Served by air; major airport and train serve New York; bus serves White Plains (eight miles). School operates transportation to White Plains. Public transportation serves campus. Semester system.

LD ADMISSIONS

Students do not complete a separate application and are simultaneously accepted to the LD program. A member of the LD program does not sit on the admissions committee. High school waivers are accepted for foreign language. A personal interview is recommended. Essay is not required.

SECONDARY SCHOOL REQUIREMENTS

Graduation from secondary school required; GED accepted. The following course distribution required: 4 units of English, 3 units of math, 2 units of science, 2 units of social studies, 5 units of academic electives.

TESTING

SAT Reasoning required of some applicants. ACT required of some applicants.

All enrolled freshmen (fall 2004):

Average SAT I Scores:	Verbal: 560	Math: 550
Average ACT Scores:	Composite: 24	

Child Study Team report is not required. A neuropsychological or comprehensive psycho-education evaluation is not required for admission. Tests required as part of this documentation:

- [ ] WAIS-IV
- [ ] WISC-IV
- [ ] SATA
- [ ] Woodcock-Johnson
- [ ] Nelson-Denny Reading Test
- [ ] Other

UNDERGRADUATE STUDENT BODY

Total undergraduate student enrollment: 497 Men, 1,081 Women.

Composition of student body (fall 2004):

	Undergraduate	Freshmen
International	7.3	8.0
Black	7.1	5.9
American Indian	0.2	0.3
Asian-American	1.8	2.4
Hispanic	14.6	14.4
White	56.2	54.3
Unreported	12.8	14.7
	100.0%	100.0%

29% are from out of state. Average age of full-time undergraduates is 20. 70% of classes have fewer than 20 students, 29% have between 20 and 50 students, 1% have more than 50 students.

STUDENT HOUSING

85% of freshmen live in college housing. Freshmen are not required to live on campus. Housing is guaranteed for all undergraduates. Campus can house 1,210 undergraduates. Single rooms are available for students with medical or special needs. A medical note is required.

EXPENSES

Tuition 2004-05: $23,620 per year.

Room: $6,020. Board: $4,110.

There is no additional cost for LD program/services.

LD SERVICES

LD program size is not limited.

LD services available to:

- [x] Freshmen
- [x] Sophomores
- [x] Juniors
- [x] Seniors

Academic Accommodations

Curriculum		In class	
Foreign language waiver	[ ]	Early syllabus	[ ]
Lighter course load	[x]	Note takers in class	[x]
Math waiver	[ ]	Priority seating	[ ]
Other special classes	[ ]	Tape recorders	[x]
Priority registrations	[ ]	Videotaped classes	[ ]
Substitution of courses	[ ]	Text on tape	[ ]
Exams		**Services**	
Extended time	[x]	Diagnostic tests	[ ]
Oral exams	[x]	Learning centers	[x]
Take home exams	[ ]	Proofreaders	[ ]
Exams on tape or computer	[ ]	Readers	[x]
Untimed exams	[x]	Reading Machines/Kurzweil	[ ]
Other accommodations	[ ]	Special bookstore section	[ ]
		Typists	[ ]

Credit toward degree is not given for remedial courses taken.

Counseling Services

- [x] Academic
- [x] Psychological
- [x] Student Support groups
- [ ] Vocational

Tutoring

Individual tutoring is available weekly.

Average size of tutoring groups: 1

	Individual	Group
Time management	[x]	[x]
Organizational skills	[x]	[x]
Learning strategies	[x]	[x]
Study skills	[x]	[x]
Content area	[x]	[x]
Writing lab	[x]	[x]
Math lab	[x]	[x]

LD PROGRAM STAFF

Total number of LD Program staff (including director):

Full Time: 4 Part Time: 4

There is an advisor/advocate from the LD program available to students. The advisor/advocate meets with faculty once per month and students once per month.

Key staff person available to work with LD students: Karen Steinmetz, ADA Coordinator.

Marist College

Poughkeepsie, NY

Address: 3399 North Road, Poughkeepsie, NY, 12601
Admissions telephone: 800 436-5483
Admissions FAX: 845 575-3215
Vice President, Admissions and Enrollment Planning: Jay E. Murray
Admissions e-mail: admissions@marist.edu
Web site: http://www.marist.edu
SAT Code: 2400 ACT Code: 2804

LD program name: Learning Disabilities Support Program
LD Program Secretary: Gale Canale
LD program telephone: 845 575-3274
LD program e-mail: Gale.Canale@marist.edu
LD program enrollment: 75, Total campus enrollment: 4,800

GENERAL

Marist College is a private, coed, four-year institution. 150-acre campus in Poughkeepsie (population: 42,777), 75 miles from New York City; branch campuses in Fishkill and Goshen. Served by bus and train; airports serve Newburgh (24 miles) and New York City. School operates transportation to local shopping areas. Public transportation serves campus. Semester system.

LD ADMISSIONS

Application Deadline: 02/15. Students complete a separate application and are simultaneously accepted to the LD program. A member of the LD program does sit on the admissions committee. High school waivers are accepted for foreign language. A personal interview is required. Essay is required and may be typed.

For fall 2004, 150 completed self-identified LD applications were received. 50 applications were offered admission, and 37 enrolled.

SECONDARY SCHOOL REQUIREMENTS

Graduation from secondary school required; GED accepted. The following course distribution required: 4 units of English, 3 units of math, 3 units of science, 2 units of social studies, 1 unit of history, 2 units of academic electives.

TESTING

SAT Reasoning or ACT required. SAT Subject required.

All enrolled freshmen (fall 2004):

Average SAT I Scores:	Verbal: 580	Math: 589
Average ACT Scores:	Composite: 26	

Child Study Team report is required if student is classified. A neuropsychological or comprehensive psycho-educational evaluation is required for admission. Must be dated within 36 months of application. Tests required as part of this documentation:

- [x] WAIS-IV
- [x] WISC-IV
- [ ] SATA
- [x] Woodcock-Johnson
- [x] Nelson-Denny Reading Test
- [x] Other

UNDERGRADUATE STUDENT BODY

Total undergraduate student enrollment: 2,026 Men, 2,687 Women.

Composition of student body (fall 2004):

	Undergraduate	Freshmen
International	0.1	0.2
Black	2.3	3.8
American Indian	0.2	0.2
Asian-American	2.5	2.2
Hispanic	6.4	6.0
White	76.2	78.6
Unreported	12.3	9.0
	100.0%	100.0%

33% are from out of state. 1% join a fraternity and 3% join a sorority. Average age of full-time undergraduates is 21. 50% of classes have fewer than 20 students, 50% have between 20 and 50 students.

STUDENT HOUSING

95% of freshmen live in college housing. Freshmen are not required to live on campus. Housing is guaranteed to freshmen and sophomores only. Campus can house 2,610 undergraduates. Single rooms are available for students with medical or special needs. A medical note is required.

EXPENSES

Tuition (2005-06): $20,712 per year.
Room: $5,964. Board: $3,400.
Additional cost for LD program/services: $1,600 per semester.

LD SERVICES

LD program size is not limited.

LD services available to:

- [x] Freshmen
- [x] Sophomores
- [x] Juniors
- [x] Seniors

Academic Accommodations

Curriculum
- [ ] Foreign language waiver
- [x] Lighter course load
- [ ] Math waiver
- [ ] Other special classes
- [ ] Priority registrations
- [ ] Substitution of courses

Exams
- [x] Extended time
- [x] Oral exams
- [ ] Take home exams
- [x] Exams on tape or computer
- [ ] Untimed exams
- [x] Other accommodations

In class
- [ ] Early syllabus
- [x] Note takers in class
- [ ] Priority seating
- [x] Tape recorders
- [ ] Videotaped classes
- [x] Text on tape

Services
- [ ] Diagnostic tests
- [ ] Learning centers
- [ ] Proofreaders
- [x] Readers
- [x] Reading Machines/Kurzweil
- [ ] Special bookstore section
- [ ] Typists

Credit toward degree is not given for remedial courses taken.

Counseling Services

- [ ] Academic
- [ ] Psychological
- [ ] Student Support groups
- [ ] Vocational

Tutoring

Individual tutoring is available weekly.

	Individual	Group
Time management	[x]	[ ]
Organizational skills	[x]	[ ]
Learning strategies	[x]	[ ]
Study skills	[x]	[ ]
Content area	[ ]	[x]
Writing lab	[x]	[ ]
Math lab	[x]	[ ]

LD PROGRAM STAFF

Total number of LD Program staff (including director):

Full Time: 2 Part Time: 2

There is no advisor/advocate from the LD program available to students.

Key staff person available to work with LD students: Linda Cooper, Director of Special Services.

LD Program web site: www.marist.edu/specserv

Marymount College

Tarrytown, NY

Address: 100 Marymount Avenue, Tarrytown, NY, 10591-3796
Admissions telephone: 800 724-4312
Admissions FAX: 914 332-7442
Director of Admissions: Dorrie Voulgaris
Admissions e-mail: mcenroll@fordham.edu
Web site: http://www.fordham.edu
SAT Code: 2406 ACT Code: 2810

Director of Learning Services: Polly B. Waldman
LD program telephone: 914 332-8310
LD program e-mail: waldman@fordham.edu
LD program enrollment: 20, Total campus enrollment: 1,036

GENERAL

Marymount College is a private, women's, four-year institution. 25-acre campus in Tarrytown (population: 11,090), 25 miles from New York City. Served by train; major airports serve New York City. School operates transportation to local train station. Public transportation serves campus. Semester system.

LD ADMISSIONS

Students do not complete a separate application and are not simultaneously accepted to the LD program. A member of the LD program does not sit on the admissions committee. A personal interview is not required. Essay is not required.

SECONDARY SCHOOL REQUIREMENTS

Graduation from secondary school required; GED accepted. The following course distribution required: 4 units of English, 3 units of math, 2 units of science, 2 units of foreign language, 3 units of social studies, 3 units of history, 2 units of academic electives.

TESTING

SAT Reasoning or ACT required. SAT Subject required.

All enrolled freshmen (fall 2004):

Average SAT I Scores:	Verbal: 507	Math: 483
Average ACT Scores:	Composite: 22	

Child Study Team report is not required. A neuropsychological or comprehensive psycho-educational evaluation is required for admission. Must be dated within 36 months of application. Tests required as part of this documentation:

- ■ WAIS-IV
- ☐ WISC-IV
- ■ SATA
- ■ Woodcock-Johnson
- ☐ Nelson-Denny Reading Test
- ☐ Other

UNDERGRADUATE STUDENT BODY

Total undergraduate student enrollment: 48 Men, 953 Women.

Composition of student body (fall 2004):

	Undergraduate	Freshmen
International	0.0	1.8
Black	18.8	16.6
American Indian	0.4	0.1
Asian-American	3.5	4.6
Hispanic	17.3	13.5
White	42.0	39.3
Unreported	18.0	24.1
	100.0%	100.0%

33% are from out of state. Average age of full-time undergraduates is 22. 60% of classes have fewer than 20 students, 40% have between 20 and 50 students.

STUDENT HOUSING

80% of freshmen live in college housing. Freshmen are not required to live on campus. Housing is guaranteed for all undergraduates. Single rooms are available for students with medical or special needs. A medical note is required.

EXPENSES

Tuition (2005-06): $20,246 per year. $16,680 per year (new students), $16,065 (returning students).

Room: $7,240. Board: $3,076.

There is no additional cost for LD program/services.

LD SERVICES

LD program size is not limited.

LD services available to:

■ Freshmen ■ Sophomores ■ Juniors ■ Seniors

Academic Accommodations

Curriculum		**In class**	
Foreign language waiver	☐	Early syllabus	■
Lighter course load	■	Note takers in class	■
Math waiver	☐	Priority seating	■
Other special classes	☐	Tape recorders	■
Priority registrations	■	Videotaped classes	☐
Substitution of courses	☐	Text on tape	■
Exams		**Services**	
Extended time	■	Diagnostic tests	☐
Oral exams	■	Learning centers	■
Take home exams	■	Proofreaders	☐
Exams on tape or computer	■	Readers	■
Untimed exams	☐	Reading Machines/Kurzweil	■
Other accommodations	☐	Special bookstore section	☐
		Typists	■

Credit toward degree is not given for remedial courses taken.

Counseling Services

- ■ Academic
- ☐ Psychological
- ■ Student Support groups — Meets 8 times per academic year
- ☐ Vocational

Tutoring

Individual tutoring is available weekly.

Average size of tutoring groups: 4

	Individual	Group
Time management	■	☐
Organizational skills	■	☐
Learning strategies	■	☐
Study skills	■	☐
Content area	■	☐
Writing lab	■	☐
Math lab	■	■

UNIQUE LD PROGRAM FEATURES

Students are sent a form for self-disclosure upon receipt of their deposit. Academic and other informal counseling services are available to the student throughout the year by request. Individual faculty members meet with the Director of Learning Services per request as need arises.

LD PROGRAM STAFF

Total number of LD Program staff (including director):

Full Time: 1 Part Time: 1

There is an advisor/advocate from the LD program available to students. 2 graduate students and 30 peer tutors are available to work with LD students.

Key staff person available to work with LD students: Polly B. Waldman, Director of Learning Services.

Marymount Manhattan College

New York, NY

Address: 221 East 71st Street, New York, NY, 10021
Admissions telephone: 800 MARYMOU
Admissions FAX: 212 517-0448
Associate Vice President for Enrollment Services: Thomas G. Friebel
Admissions e-mail: admissions@mmm.edu
Web site: http://www.mmm.edu/
SAT Code: 2405 ACT Code: 2810

LD program name: Access Program
Director, Chair, Division of Sciences: Dr. Ann Jablon
LD program telephone: 212 517-0725
LD program e-mail: ajablon@mmm.edu
LD program enrollment: 30, Total campus enrollment: 2,078

GENERAL

Marymount Manhattan College is a private, coed, four-year institution. One-acre, urban campus in upper east side Manhattan (New York City population: 8,008,278). Served by air, bus, and train. Public transportation serves campus. Semester system.

LD ADMISSIONS

Students do not complete a separate application and are simultaneously accepted to the LD program. A member of the LD program does sit on the admissions committee. High school waivers are accepted for math and foreign language. A personal interview is required. Essay is required and may be typed.

For fall 2004, 40 completed self-identified LD applications were received. 35 applications were offered admission, and 30 enrolled.

SECONDARY SCHOOL REQUIREMENTS

Graduation from secondary school required; GED accepted. The following course distribution required: 4 units of English, 3 units of math, 1 unit of science, 3 units of social studies, 4 units of academic electives.

TESTING

SAT Reasoning or ACT considered if submitted. SAT Subject recommended.

All enrolled freshmen (fall 2004):

Average SAT I Scores:	Verbal: 550	Math: 515
Average ACT Scores:	Composite: 23	

Child Study Team report is not required. A neuropsychological or comprehensive psycho-education evaluation is not required for admission. Tests required as part of this documentation:

- ☐ WAIS-IV
- ☐ WISC-IV
- ☐ SATA
- ☐ Woodcock-Johnson
- ☐ Nelson-Denny Reading Test
- ☐ Other

UNDERGRADUATE STUDENT BODY

Total undergraduate student enrollment: 570 Men, 2,137 Women.

Composition of student body (fall 2004):

	Undergraduate	Freshmen
International	0.9	3.2
Black	12.6	14.6
American Indian	0.4	0.4
Asian-American	4.6	4.3
Hispanic	8.6	12.3
White	72.9	65.2
Unreported	0.0	0.0
	100.0%	100.0%

35% are from out of state. Average age of full-time undergraduates is 21. 75% of classes have fewer than 20 students, 25% have between 20 and 50 students.

STUDENT HOUSING

82% of freshmen live in college housing. Freshmen are not required to live on campus. Housing is limited, preference is given to freshmen. Campus can house 675 undergraduates. Single rooms are available for students with medical or special needs. A medical note is required.

EXPENSES

Tuition (2005-06): $17,686 per year.
Room: $9,520. Board: $2,000-$800.
Additional cost for LD program/services: $4,000 per annum.

LD SERVICES

LD program is limited to %1 students.

LD services available to:

■ Freshmen ■ Sophomores ■ Juniors ■ Seniors

Academic Accommodations

Curriculum		In class	
Foreign language waiver	☐	Early syllabus	☐
Lighter course load	☐	Note takers in class	☐
Math waiver	☐	Priority seating	☐
Other special classes	☐	Tape recorders	■
Priority registrations	☐	Videotaped classes	☐
Substitution of courses	☐	Text on tape	☐
Exams		**Services**	
Extended time	■	Diagnostic tests	■
Oral exams	☐	Learning centers	☐
Take home exams	☐	Proofreaders	☐
Exams on tape or computer	☐	Readers	☐
Untimed exams	☐	Reading Machines/Kurzweil	☐
Other accommodations	☐	Special bookstore section	☐
		Typists	☐

Credit toward degree is not given for remedial courses taken.

Counseling Services

- ■ Academic — Meets 40 times per academic year
- ☐ Psychological
- ☐ Student Support groups
- ☐ Vocational

Tutoring

Individual tutoring is available weekly.

Average size of tutoring groups: 2

	Individual	Group
Time management	☐	■
Organizational skills	☐	■
Learning strategies	☐	■
Study skills	☐	■
Content area	■	☐
Writing lab	☐	■
Math lab	☐	■

LD PROGRAM STAFF

Total number of LD Program staff (including director):

Full Time: 2 Part Time: 2

There is an advisor/advocate from the LD program available to students. The advisor/advocate meets with faculty 4 times per month and students 6 times per month. 3 peer tutors are available to work with LD students.

Key staff person available to work with LD students: Dr. Ann Jablon, Director, Access Program.

Medaille College

Buffalo, NY

Address: 18 Agassiz Circle, Buffalo, NY, 14214
Admissions telephone: 800 292-1582
Admissions FAX: 716 884-0291
Director of Enrollment Management: Steven Klein
Admissions e-mail: sdesing@medaille.edu
Web site: http://www.medaille.edu
SAT Code: 2422 ACT Code: 2822

LD program name: Student Support Services
Disability Specialist: Lisa Morrison
LD program telephone: 716 884-328, extension 1391
LD program e-mail: lmorrison@medaille.edu
LD program enrollment: 40, Total campus enrollment: 1,708

GENERAL

Medaille College is a private, coed, four-year institution. 13-acre, urban campus in Buffalo (population: 292,648); branch campuses in Amherst and Rochester. Served by air, bus, and train; smaller airport serves Niagara Falls (20 miles). Public transportation serves campus. Semester system.

LD ADMISSIONS

Students do not complete a separate application and are simultaneously accepted to the LD program. A member of the LD program does not sit on the admissions committee. A personal interview is required. Essay is required and may be typed.

SECONDARY SCHOOL REQUIREMENTS

Graduation from secondary school required; GED accepted. The following course distribution required: 4 units of English, 2 units of math, 2 units of science, 4 units of social studies.

TESTING

ACT considered if submitted. SAT Reasoning required; ACT may be substituted. SAT Subject recommended.

All enrolled freshmen (fall 2004):

Average SAT I Scores:	Verbal: 470	Math: 480
Average ACT Scores:	Composite: 20	

Child Study Team report is not required. A neuropsychological or comprehensive psycho-educational evaluation is required for admission. Must be dated within 36 months of application. Tests required as part of this documentation:

- ■ WAIS-IV
- ■ WISC-IV
- ☐ SATA
- ■ Woodcock-Johnson
- ☐ Nelson-Denny Reading Test
- ☐ Other

UNDERGRADUATE STUDENT BODY

Total undergraduate student enrollment: 436 Men, 1,076 Women.

Composition of student body (fall 2004):

	Undergraduate	Freshmen
International	0.0	0.4
Black	6.2	17.1
American Indian	0.7	0.6
Asian-American	0.0	0.2
Hispanic	2.9	2.9
White	82.4	70.5
Unreported	7.8	8.3
	100.0%	100.0%

1% are from out of state. Average age of full-time undergraduates is 28. 75% of classes have fewer than 20 students, 25% have between 20 and 50 students.

STUDENT HOUSING

28% of freshmen live in college housing. Freshmen are not required to live on campus. Housing is guaranteed for all undergraduates. Campus can house 500 undergraduates. Single rooms are available for students with medical or special needs. A medical note is required.

EXPENSES

Tuition (2005-06): $15,030 per year.
Room & Board: $7,430.
There is no additional cost for LD program/services.

LD SERVICES

LD program size is not limited.

LD services available to:

■ Freshmen ■ Sophomores ■ Juniors ■ Seniors

Academic Accommodations

Curriculum		In class	
Foreign language waiver	☐	Early syllabus	☐
Lighter course load	■	Note takers in class	■
Math waiver	☐	Priority seating	☐
Other special classes	☐	Tape recorders	■
Priority registrations	☐	Videotaped classes	■
Substitution of courses	■	Text on tape	■
Exams		**Services**	
Extended time	■	Diagnostic tests	☐
Oral exams	☐	Learning centers	■
Take home exams	☐	Proofreaders	☐
Exams on tape or computer	☐	Readers	■
Untimed exams	■	Reading Machines/Kurzweil	■
Other accommodations	☐	Special bookstore section	☐
		Typists	☐

Credit toward degree is not given for remedial courses taken.

Counseling Services

- ■ Academic
- ■ Psychological
- ■ Student Support groups
- ☐ Vocational

Tutoring

Individual tutoring is available daily.

Average size of tutoring groups: 1

	Individual	Group
Time management	■	■
Organizational skills	■	■
Learning strategies	■	■
Study skills	■	■
Content area	■	☐
Writing lab	■	☐
Math lab	■	☐

LD PROGRAM STAFF

Total number of LD Program staff (including director):

Full Time: 1 Part Time: 1

There is an advisor/advocate from the LD program available to students. The advisor/advocate meets with students 2 times per month. 8 peer tutors are available to work with LD students.

Key staff person available to work with LD students: Lisa Morrison, Disability Specialist.

Mercy College

Dobbs Ferry, NY

Address: 555 Broadway, Dobbs Ferry, NY, 10522
Admissions telephone: 800 MERCY-NY
Admissions FAX: 914 674-7382
Admissions e-mail: admissions@mercy.edu
Web site: http://www.mercy.edu
SAT Code: 2409 ACT Code: 2814

LD program name: S.T.A.R.
Associate Dean of Student Affairs: Terry Rich
LD program telephone: 914 674-7416
LD program e-mail: trich@mercy.edu
LD program enrollment: 35, Total campus enrollment: 5,983

GENERAL

Mercy College is a private, coed, four-year institution. 90-acre, suburban campus in Dobbs Ferry (population: 10,622), 20 miles from New York City; branch campuses in the Bronx, Brooklyn, Manhattan, Mt. Vernon, Queens, White Plains, Yonkers, and Yorktown Heights. Served by train; bus serves Yonkers (10 miles); major airports serve New York City and Newark, NJ (25 miles). School provides transportation to branch campuses. Public transportation serves campus. Semester system.

LD ADMISSIONS

Application Deadline: 08/29. Students complete a separate application and are not simultaneously accepted to the LD program. A member of the LD program does not sit on the admissions committee. High school waivers are accepted for foreign language. A personal interview is recommended. Essay is required and may be typed.

For fall 2004, 42 completed self-identified LD applications were received. 35 applications were offered admission, and 35 enrolled.

SECONDARY SCHOOL REQUIREMENTS

Graduation from secondary school required; GED accepted. The following course distribution required: 4 units of English, 4 units of math, 3 units of science, 2 units of foreign language, 2 units of social studies, 3 units of history.

TESTING

SAT Reasoning considered if submitted.

Child Study Team report is required if student is classified. A neuropsychological or comprehensive psycho-educational evaluation is required for admission. Must be dated within 36 months of application. Tests required as part of this documentation:

■ WAIS-IV ■ Woodcock-Johnson
■ WISC-IV ■ Nelson-Denny Reading Test
■ SATA ■ Other

UNDERGRADUATE STUDENT BODY

Total undergraduate student enrollment: 1,997 Men, 4,836 Women.

Composition of student body (fall 2004):

	Undergraduate	Freshmen
International	1.4	1.8
Black	27.9	27.8
American Indian	0.3	0.3
Asian-American	1.7	2.7
Hispanic	35.6	30.2
White	27.0	27.6
Unreported	6.1	9.6
	100.0%	100.0%

3% are from out of state. Average age of full-time undergraduates is 25.

STUDENT HOUSING

Freshmen are not required to live on campus. Housing is not guaranteed for all undergraduates. Campus can house 165 undergraduates. Single rooms are available for students with medical or special needs. A medical note is required.

EXPENSES

Tuition (2005-06): $11,792 per year.
Additional cost for LD program/services: $1,375 per semester.

LD SERVICES

LD program size is not limited.

LD services available to:

■ Freshmen ■ Sophomores ■ Juniors ■ Seniors

Academic Accommodations

Curriculum		In class	
Foreign language waiver	■	Early syllabus	☐
Lighter course load	■	Note takers in class	■
Math waiver	☐	Priority seating	☐
Other special classes	☐	Tape recorders	■
Priority registrations	☐	Videotaped classes	■
Substitution of courses	■	Text on tape	■
Exams		**Services**	
Extended time	■	Diagnostic tests	☐
Oral exams	■	Learning centers	■
Take home exams	☐	Proofreaders	☐
Exams on tape or computer	■	Readers	■
Untimed exams	☐	Reading Machines/Kurzweil	■
Other accommodations	☐	Special bookstore section	☐
		Typists	☐

Credit toward degree is given for remedial courses taken.

Counseling Services

■ Academic — Meets 8 times per academic year
■ Psychological
■ Student Support groups — Meets 5 times per academic year
■ Vocational — Meets 4 times per academic year

Tutoring

Individual tutoring is available daily.

Average size of tutoring groups: 1

	Individual	Group
Time management	■	■
Organizational skills	■	■
Learning strategies	■	■
Study skills	☐	■
Content area	■	☐
Writing lab	☐	■
Math lab	☐	■

LD PROGRAM STAFF

Total number of LD Program staff (including director):

Full Time: 1 Part Time: 1

There is an advisor/advocate from the LD program available to students. The advisor/advocate meets with faculty 2 times per month and students 2 times per month.

Key staff person available to work with LD students: Terry Rich, Associate Dean of Student Affairs.

Molloy College

Rockville Centre, NY

Address: 1000 Hempstead Avenue, P.O. Box 5002, Rockville Centre, NY, 11571
Admissions telephone: 888 4-MOLLOY
Admissions FAX: 516 256-2247
Director of Admissions: Marguerite Lane
Admissions e-mail: admissions@molloy.edu
Web site: http://www.molloy.edu
SAT Code: 2415 ACT Code: 2820

LD program name: DSS/STEEP
Coordinator DSS/STEEP: S. Barbara Nirrengarten
LD program telephone: 516 678-5000, extension 6381
LD program e-mail: bnirrengarten@molloy.edu
LD program enrollment: 35, Total campus enrollment: 2,512

GENERAL

Molloy College is a private, coed, four-year institution. 25-acre, suburban campus in Rockville Centre (population: 24,568), 25 miles from New York City. Major airport, bus, and train serve New York City. Public transportation serves campus. Semester system.

LD ADMISSIONS

Students do not complete a separate application and are simultaneously accepted to the LD program. A member of the LD program does sit on the admissions committee. High school waivers are accepted for foreign language. A personal interview is required. Essay is required and may be typed.

For fall 2004, 38 completed self-identified LD applications were received. 27 applications were offered admission, and 15 enrolled.

SECONDARY SCHOOL REQUIREMENTS

Graduation from secondary school required; GED accepted. The following course distribution required: 4 units of English, 3 units of math, 3 units of science, 3 units of foreign language, 4 units of social studies.

TESTING

SAT Reasoning required; ACT may be substituted. SAT Subject recommended.

All enrolled freshmen (fall 2004):

Average SAT I Scores:	Verbal: 502	Math: 505
Average ACT Scores:	Composite:	

Child Study Team report is required if student is classified. A neuropsychological or comprehensive psycho-educational evaluation is required for admission. Must be dated within 36 months of application. Tests required as part of this documentation:

- [x] WAIS-IV
- [ ] WISC-IV
- [ ] SATA
- [x] Woodcock-Johnson
- [ ] Nelson-Denny Reading Test
- [x] Other

UNDERGRADUATE STUDENT BODY

Total undergraduate student enrollment: 460 Men, 1,550 Women.

Composition of student body (fall 2004):

	Undergraduate	Freshmen
International	0.0	0.1
Black	12.4	18.7
American Indian	0.3	0.2
Asian-American	4.7	5.6
Hispanic	9.0	8.0
White	64.3	63.8
Unreported	9.3	3.6
	100.0%	100.0%

Average age of full-time undergraduates is 23. 69% of classes have fewer than 20 students, 31% have between 20 and 50 students.

EXPENSES

Tuition (2005-06): $15,760 per year.
There is no additional cost for LD program/services.

LD SERVICES

LD program size is not limited.

LD services available to:

- [x] Freshmen
- [x] Sophomores
- [x] Juniors
- [x] Seniors

Academic Accommodations

Curriculum

- [ ] Foreign language waiver
- [x] Lighter course load
- [ ] Math waiver
- [ ] Other special classes
- [ ] Priority registrations
- [ ] Substitution of courses

Exams

- [x] Extended time
- [ ] Oral exams
- [ ] Take home exams
- [x] Exams on tape or computer
- [x] Untimed exams
- [ ] Other accommodations

In class

- [ ] Early syllabus
- [x] Note takers in class
- [ ] Priority seating
- [x] Tape recorders
- [ ] Videotaped classes
- [ ] Text on tape

Services

- [ ] Diagnostic tests
- [ ] Learning centers
- [ ] Proofreaders
- [ ] Readers
- [x] Reading Machines/Kurzweil
- [ ] Special bookstore section
- [ ] Typists

Credit toward degree is not given for remedial courses taken.

Counseling Services

- [x] Academic — Meets 26 times per academic year
- [ ] Psychological
- [x] Student Support groups — Meets 2 times per academic year
- [ ] Vocational

Tutoring

Individual tutoring is available weekly.

Average size of tutoring groups: 2

	Individual	Group
Time management	[x]	[ ]
Organizational skills	[x]	[ ]
Learning strategies	[x]	[ ]
Study skills	[x]	[ ]
Content area	[x]	[ ]
Writing lab	[x]	[ ]
Math lab	[ ]	[ ]

LD PROGRAM STAFF

Total number of LD Program staff (including director):

Full Time: 1 Part Time: 1

There is an advisor/advocate from the LD program available to students. The advisor/advocate meets with students 4 times per month.

Key staff person available to work with LD students: S.Barbara Nirrengarten, Coordinator.

Mount Saint Mary College

Newburgh, NY

Address: 330 Powell Avenue, Newburgh, NY, 12550
Admissions telephone: 888 YES-MSMC
Admissions FAX: 845 562-6762
Director of Admissions: J. Randall Ognibene
Admissions e-mail: mtstmary@msmc.edu
Web site: http://www.msmc.edu
SAT Code: 2423 ACT Code: 2819

Disabilities Specialist: Jacqueline Santiago
LD program telephone: 845 569-3547
LD program e-mail: santiago@msmc.edu
LD program enrollment: 60, Total campus enrollment: 2,099

GENERAL

Mount Saint Mary College is a private, coed, four-year institution. 70-acre, suburban campus in Newburgh (population: 28,259), 60 miles from New York City and 20 miles from Poughkeepsie; branch campus in West Point. Served by air and bus; train serves Poughkeepsie. School operates transportation to various locations. Public transportation serves campus. Semester system.

LD ADMISSIONS

Students do not complete a separate application and are simultaneously accepted to the LD program. A member of the LD program does not sit on the admissions committee. A personal interview is recommended. Essay is not required.

SECONDARY SCHOOL REQUIREMENTS

Graduation from secondary school required; GED accepted.

TESTING

SAT Reasoning or ACT required. SAT Subject recommended.

All enrolled freshmen (fall 2004):

Average SAT I Scores:	Verbal: 514	Math: 511
Average ACT Scores:	Composite: 20	

Child Study Team report is not required. A neuropsychological or comprehensive psycho-educational evaluation is required for admission. Tests required as part of this documentation:

- [x] WAIS-IV
- [ ] WISC-IV
- [x] SATA
- [x] Woodcock-Johnson
- [x] Nelson-Denny Reading Test
- [x] Other

UNDERGRADUATE STUDENT BODY

Total undergraduate student enrollment: 568 Men, 1,347 Women.

Composition of student body (fall 2004):

	Undergraduate	Freshmen
International	0.0	0.0
Black	7.1	10.2
American Indian	0.1	0.2
Asian-American	1.4	2.3
Hispanic	9.0	8.6
White	82.2	78.5
Unreported	0.2	0.2
	100.0%	100.0%

12% are from out of state. Average age of full-time undergraduates is 21. 41% of classes have fewer than 20 students, 59% have between 20 and 50 students.

STUDENT HOUSING

79% of freshmen live in college housing. Freshmen are not required to live on campus. Campus can house 901 undergraduates. Single rooms are available for students with medical or special needs. A medical note is required.

EXPENSES

Tuition (2005-06): $16,410 per year.
Room: $4,680. Board: $3,640.
There is no additional cost for LD program/services.

LD SERVICES

LD program size is not limited.

LD services available to:

- [x] Freshmen
- [x] Sophomores
- [x] Juniors
- [x] Seniors

Academic Accommodations

Curriculum		In class	
Foreign language waiver	[ ]	Early syllabus	[ ]
Lighter course load	[ ]	Note takers in class	[x]
Math waiver	[ ]	Priority seating	[x]
Other special classes	[ ]	Tape recorders	[x]
Priority registrations	[ ]	Videotaped classes	[ ]
Substitution of courses	[ ]	Text on tape	[x]
Exams		**Services**	
Extended time	[x]	Diagnostic tests	[ ]
Oral exams	[ ]	Learning centers	[x]
Take home exams	[ ]	Proofreaders	[ ]
Exams on tape or computer	[x]	Readers	[x]
Untimed exams	[ ]	Reading Machines/Kurzweil	[ ]
Other accommodations	[ ]	Special bookstore section	[ ]
		Typists	[x]

Credit toward degree is not given for remedial courses taken.

Counseling Services

- [x] Academic
- [x] Psychological
- [ ] Student Support groups
- [ ] Vocational

Tutoring

Individual tutoring is available daily.

Average size of tutoring groups: 1

	Individual	Group
Time management	[x]	[ ]
Organizational skills	[x]	[ ]
Learning strategies	[x]	[ ]
Study skills	[x]	[ ]
Content area	[x]	[ ]
Writing lab	[ ]	[x]
Math lab	[ ]	[x]

LD PROGRAM STAFF

There is an advisor/advocate from the LD program available to students. The advisor/advocate meets with faculty once per month and students 2 times per month. 25 peer tutors are available to work with LD students.

Key staff person available to work with LD students: Jacqueline Santiago, Disabilities Specialist.

College of Mount St. Vincent

Riverdale, NY

Address: 6301 Riverdale Avenue, Riverdale, NY, 10471
Admissions telephone: 800 665-CMSV
Admissions FAX: 718 549-7945
Dean of Admissions and Financial Aid: Timothy Nash
Admissions e-mail: admissions.office@mountsaintvincent.edu
Web site: http://www.mountsaintvincent.edu
SAT Code: 2088 ACT Code: 2823

Director of Academic Resources: Peter Knothe
LD program telephone: 718 405-3273
LD program e-mail: peter.knothe@mountsaintvincent.edu
LD program enrollment: 9, Total campus enrollment: 1,393

GENERAL

College of Mount St. Vincent is a private, coed, four-year institution. 70-acre, suburban campus in Riverdale section of the Bronx (New York City population: 8,008,278). Served by major airport, bus, and train. School operates transportation to Manhattan Coll. Public transportation serves campus. Semester system.

LD ADMISSIONS

Students do not complete a separate application and are not simultaneously accepted to the LD program. A member of the LD program does not sit on the admissions committee. A personal interview is recommended. Essay is required and may be typed.

SECONDARY SCHOOL REQUIREMENTS

Graduation from secondary school required; GED accepted. The following course distribution required: 4 units of English, 2 units of math, 2 units of science, 2 units of foreign language, 3 units of social studies, 3 units of academic electives.

TESTING

SAT Subject recommended.

All enrolled freshmen (fall 2004):

Average SAT I Scores: Verbal: 516 Math: 508

Child Study Team report is not required. A neuropsychological or comprehensive psycho-education evaluation is not required for admission. Tests required as part of this documentation:

- [ ] WAIS-IV
- [ ] WISC-IV
- [ ] SATA
- [ ] Woodcock-Johnson
- [ ] Nelson-Denny Reading Test
- [ ] Other

UNDERGRADUATE STUDENT BODY

Total undergraduate student enrollment: 255 Men, 887 Women.

Composition of student body (fall 2004):

	Undergraduate	Freshmen
International	0.3	0.3
Black	8.7	12.5
American Indian	0.6	0.3
Asian-American	9.5	10.6
Hispanic	28.3	30.1
White	49.8	41.6
Unreported	2.8	4.6
	100.0%	100.0%

5% are from out of state. Average age of full-time undergraduates is 20. 49% of classes have fewer than 20 students, 51% have between 20 and 50 students.

STUDENT HOUSING

68% of freshmen live in college housing. Freshmen are not required to live on campus. Housing is guaranteed for all undergraduates. Campus can house 620 undergraduates. Single rooms are available for students with medical or special needs. A medical note is required.

EXPENSES

Tuition (2005-06): $19,950 per year.

Room & Board: $8,250.

There is no additional cost for LD program/services.

LD SERVICES

LD program size is not limited.

LD services available to:

- [x] Freshmen
- [x] Sophomores
- [x] Juniors
- [x] Seniors

Academic Accommodations

Curriculum		In class	
Foreign language waiver	[ ]	Early syllabus	[ ]
Lighter course load	[x]	Note takers in class	[x]
Math waiver	[ ]	Priority seating	[ ]
Other special classes	[ ]	Tape recorders	[ ]
Priority registrations	[ ]	Videotaped classes	[ ]
Substitution of courses	[ ]	Text on tape	[ ]
Exams		**Services**	
Extended time	[x]	Diagnostic tests	[ ]
Oral exams	[ ]	Learning centers	[x]
Take home exams	[ ]	Proofreaders	[ ]
Exams on tape or computer	[ ]	Readers	[x]
Untimed exams	[x]	Reading Machines/Kurzweil	[ ]
Other accommodations	[ ]	Special bookstore section	[ ]
		Typists	[ ]

Credit toward degree is not given for remedial courses taken.

Counseling Services

- [ ] Academic
- [ ] Psychological
- [ ] Student Support groups
- [ ] Vocational

Tutoring

Individual tutoring is available daily.

Average size of tutoring groups: 1

	Individual	Group
Time management	[x]	[x]
Organizational skills	[x]	[x]
Learning strategies	[x]	[x]
Study skills	[x]	[x]
Content area	[x]	[x]
Writing lab	[x]	[x]
Math lab	[x]	[ ]

LD PROGRAM STAFF

Total number of LD Program staff (including director):

Full Time: 2 Part Time: 2

There is an advisor/advocate from the LD program available to students.

Key staff person available to work with LD students: Peter Knothe, Director of Academic Resources.

Nazareth College of Rochester

Rochester, NY

Address: 4245 East Avenue, Rochester, NY, 14618-3790
Admissions telephone: 800 462-3944
Admissions FAX: 585 389-2826
Vice President for Enrollment Management: Thomas DaRin
Admissions e-mail: admissions@naz.edu
Web site: http://www.naz.edu
SAT Code: 2511 ACT Code: 2826

Academic Counselor: Annemarie House
LD program telephone: 585 389-2754
LD program e-mail: ahouse7@naz.edu
LD program enrollment: 77, Total campus enrollment: 2,035

GENERAL

Nazareth College of Rochester is a private, coed, four-year institution. 95-acre, suburban campus in Rochester (population: 219,773). Served by air, bus, and train. Public transportation serves campus. Semester system.

LD ADMISSIONS

Application Deadline: 02/15. Students do not complete a separate application and are simultaneously accepted to the LD program. A member of the LD program does not sit on the admissions committee. A personal interview is recommended. Essay is required and may be typed.

SECONDARY SCHOOL REQUIREMENTS

Graduation from secondary school required; GED accepted. The following course distribution required: 4 units of English, 3 units of math, 3 units of science, 3 units of foreign language, 3 units of social studies.

TESTING

SAT Reasoning or ACT required. SAT Subject recommended.

All enrolled freshmen (fall 2004):

Average SAT I Scores:	Verbal: 570	Math: 570
Average ACT Scores:	Composite: 25	

Child Study Team report is not required. A neuropsychological or comprehensive psycho-educational evaluation is required for admission. Must be dated within 36 months of application. Tests required as part of this documentation:

- [x] WAIS-IV
- [x] WISC-IV
- [ ] SATA
- [x] Woodcock-Johnson
- [ ] Nelson-Denny Reading Test
- [ ] Other

UNDERGRADUATE STUDENT BODY

Total undergraduate student enrollment: 462 Men, 1,436 Women.

Composition of student body (fall 2004):

	Undergraduate	Freshmen
International	0.0	0.1
Black	5.3	4.9
American Indian	1.3	0.5
Asian-American	1.8	2.4
Hispanic	1.6	1.6
White	84.0	85.7
Unreported	6.0	4.8
	100.0%	100.0%

5% are from out of state. Average age of full-time undergraduates is 21. 59% of classes have fewer than 20 students, 41% have between 20 and 50 students.

STUDENT HOUSING

93% of freshmen live in college housing. Freshmen are not required to live on campus. Housing is guaranteed for all undergraduates. Campus can house 1,172 undergraduates. Single rooms are available for students with medical or special needs. A medical note is required.

EXPENSES

Tuition (2005-06): $19,214 per year.

Room & Board: $8,402.

There is no additional cost for LD program/services.

LD SERVICES

LD program size is not limited.

LD services available to:

- [x] Freshmen
- [x] Sophomores
- [x] Juniors
- [x] Seniors

Academic Accommodations

Curriculum

- [ ] Foreign language waiver
- [ ] Lighter course load
- [ ] Math waiver
- [ ] Other special classes
- [ ] Priority registrations
- [ ] Substitution of courses

Exams

- [x] Extended time
- [x] Oral exams
- [ ] Take home exams
- [x] Exams on tape or computer
- [x] Untimed exams
- [ ] Other accommodations

In class

- [x] Early syllabus
- [x] Note takers in class
- [ ] Priority seating
- [x] Tape recorders
- [ ] Videotaped classes
- [x] Text on tape

Services

- [ ] Diagnostic tests
- [ ] Learning centers
- [ ] Proofreaders
- [x] Readers
- [x] Reading Machines/Kurzweil
- [ ] Special bookstore section
- [x] Typists

Credit toward degree is not given for remedial courses taken.

Counseling Services

- [x] Academic
- [ ] Psychological
- [ ] Student Support groups
- [ ] Vocational

Meets 2 times per academic year

Tutoring

Individual tutoring is available weekly.

Average size of tutoring groups: 1

	Individual	Group
Time management	☐	☒
Organizational skills	☐	☒
Learning strategies	☐	☐
Study skills	☐	☒
Content area	☐	☐
Writing lab	☒	☐
Math lab	☐	☒

LD PROGRAM STAFF

There is an advisor/advocate from the LD program available to students. The advisor/advocate meets with faculty once per month. 3 graduate students and 80 peer tutors are available to work with LD students.

Key staff person available to work with LD students: Annemarie House, Academic Counselor for Students with Disabilities.

New York Institute of Technology

Old Westbury, NY

Address: P.O. Box 8000, Old Westbury, NY, 11568-8000
Admissions telephone: 800 345-NYIT
Admissions FAX: 516 686-7613
Dean of Admissions and Financial Aid: Jacquelyn Nealon
Admissions e-mail: admissions@nyit.edu
Web site: http://www.nyit.edu
SAT Code: 2561 ACT Code: 2832

LD program name: Vocational Independence Program
Associate Dean of Student Development: Kate Beckman
LD program telephone: 516 686-1208
LD program e-mail: kbeckman@nyit.edu
LD program enrollment: 113, Total campus enrollment: 6,667

GENERAL

New York Institute of Technology is a private, coed, four-year institution. Two campuses totaling 525 acres in Old Westbury and Central Islip on Long Island (New York City population: 8,008,278); Metropolitan Center in Manhattan. Major airport and train serve New York City; bus serves Hicksville (seven miles). School operates transportation between campuses. Public transportation serves campus. Semester system.

LD ADMISSIONS

A personal interview is recommended. Essay is required and may be typed.

SECONDARY SCHOOL REQUIREMENTS

Graduation from secondary school required; GED accepted. The following course distribution required: 4 units of English, 2 units of math, 1 unit of science, 2 units of social studies, 7 units of academic electives.

TESTING

SAT Reasoning required; ACT may be substituted.

All enrolled freshmen (fall 2004):

Average SAT I Scores: Verbal: 534 Math: 585
Average ACT Scores: Composite: 24

Child Study Team report is not required. Tests required as part of this documentation:

- ☐ WAIS-IV
- ☐ WISC-IV
- ☐ SATA
- ☐ Woodcock-Johnson
- ☐ Nelson-Denny Reading Test
- ☐ Other

UNDERGRADUATE STUDENT BODY

Total undergraduate student enrollment: 3,424 Men, 2,125 Women.

Composition of student body (fall 2004):

	Undergraduate	Freshmen
International	4.3	5.7
Black	12.8	10.2
American Indian	0.2	0.1
Asian-American	11.6	8.4
Hispanic	9.1	8.6
White	36.8	30.9
Unreported	25.2	36.1
	100.0%	100.0%

7% are from out of state. 2% join a fraternity and 1% join a sorority. Average age of full-time undergraduates is 22. 64% of classes have fewer than 20 students, 35% have between 20 and 50 students, 1% have more than 50 students.

STUDENT HOUSING

24% of freshmen live in college housing. Housing is guaranteed for all undergraduates.

EXPENSES

Tuition 2004-05: $17,840 per year.

Room: $4,080. Board: $3,300.

There is no additional cost for LD program/services.

LD SERVICES

LD program size is limited.

LD services available to:

☐ Freshmen ☐ Sophomores ☐ Juniors ☐ Seniors

Academic Accommodations

Curriculum

- Foreign language waiver ☐
- Lighter course load ☐
- Math waiver ☐
- Other special classes ☐
- Priority registrations ☐
- Substitution of courses ☐

Exams

- Extended time ☐
- Oral exams ■
- Take home exams ☐
- Exams on tape or computer ☐
- Untimed exams ■
- Other accommodations ☐

In class

- Early syllabus ☐
- Note takers in class ■
- Priority seating ☐
- Tape recorders ■
- Videotaped classes ☐
- Text on tape ☐

Services

- Diagnostic tests ☐
- Learning centers ■
- Proofreaders ☐
- Readers ■
- Reading Machines/Kurzweil ☐
- Special bookstore section ☐
- Typists ☐

Credit toward degree is not given for remedial courses taken.

Counseling Services

- ☐ Academic
- ☐ Psychological
- ☐ Student Support groups
- ☐ Vocational

Tutoring

	Individual	Group
Time management	☐	☐
Organizational skills	☐	☐
Learning strategies	☐	☐
Study skills	☐	☐
Content area	☐	☐
Writing lab	☐	☐
Math lab	☐	☐

UNIQUE LD PROGRAM FEATURES

LD students earn a certificate, not a degree.

LD PROGRAM STAFF

Key staff person available to work with LD students: James Rein, Dean.

New York School of Interior Design

New York, NY

Address: 170 East 70th Street, New York, NY, 10021-5110
Admissions telephone: 800 33-NYSID, extension 204
Admissions FAX: 212 472-1867
Director of Admissions: David Sprouls
Admissions e-mail: admissions@nysid.edu
Web site: http://www.nysid.edu
SAT Code: 333 ACT Code: 2829

Academic Advisor: Linda Sclafani
LD program telephone: 212 472-1500, extension 303
LD program e-mail: lindas@nysid.edu
Total campus enrollment: 769

GENERAL

New York School of Interior Design is a private, coed, four-year institution. Urban campus on Manhattan's upper east side in New York City (New York City population: 8,008,278). Served by air, bus, and train. Public transportation serves campus. Semester system.

LD ADMISSIONS

A personal interview is not required. Essay is required and may be typed.

SECONDARY SCHOOL REQUIREMENTS

Graduation from secondary school required; GED accepted. The following course distribution required: 4 units of English, 2 units of math, 2 units of science, 2 units of foreign language, 2 units of social studies.

TESTING

SAT Reasoning or ACT required of some applicants. SAT Subject recommended.

Child Study Team report is not required. Tests required as part of this documentation:

☐ WAIS-IV	☐ Woodcock-Johnson
☐ WISC-IV	☐ Nelson-Denny Reading Test
☐ SATA	☐ Other

UNDERGRADUATE STUDENT BODY

Total undergraduate student enrollment: 102 Men, 603 Women.

Composition of student body (fall 2004):

	Freshmen
International	12.0
Black	3.3
American Indian	0.0
Asian-American	10.1
Hispanic	6.6
White	55.4
Unreported	12.6
	100.0%

17% are from out of state. Average age of full-time undergraduates is 32. 89% of classes have fewer than 20 students, 11% have more than 50 students.

EXPENSES

Tuition (2005-06): $17,700 per year.
There is no additional cost for LD program/services.

LD SERVICES

LD program size is not limited.

LD services available to:

■ Freshmen ■ Sophomores ■ Juniors ■ Seniors

Academic Accommodations

Curriculum		**In class**	
Foreign language waiver	☐	Early syllabus	☐
Lighter course load	☐	Note takers in class	☐
Math waiver	☐	Priority seating	☐
Other special classes	☐	Tape recorders	■
Priority registrations	☐	Videotaped classes	■
Substitution of courses	☐	Text on tape	☐
Exams		**Services**	
Extended time	■	Diagnostic tests	☐
Oral exams	■	Learning centers	☐
Take home exams	☐	Proofreaders	☐
Exams on tape or computer	☐	Readers	■
Untimed exams	■	Reading Machines/Kurzweil	☐
Other accommodations	☐	Special bookstore section	☐
		Typists	☐

Credit toward degree is not given for remedial courses taken.

Counseling Services

☐ Academic
☐ Psychological
☐ Student Support groups
☐ Vocational

Tutoring

Individual tutoring is available daily.

Average size of tutoring groups: 1

	Individual	Group
Time management	☐	☐
Organizational skills	☐	☐
Learning strategies	☐	☐
Study skills	☐	☐
Content area	☐	☐
Writing lab	☐	☐
Math lab	☐	☐

LD PROGRAM STAFF

Total number of LD Program staff (including director):

Full Time: 1 Part Time: 1

There is an advisor/advocate from the LD program available to students.

Key staff person available to work with LD students: Linda Sclafani, Academic Advisor.

New York University

New York, NY

Address: 70 Washington Square South, New York, NY, 10012
Admissions telephone: 212 998-4500
Admissions FAX: 212 995-4902
Director of Admissions/Assistant Vice President: Barbara Hall
Admissions e-mail: admissions@nyu.edu
Web site: http://www.nyu.edu
SAT Code: 2562 ACT Code: 2838

LD program name: Moses Ctr for Students with Disabilities
LD program address: 240 Greene Street, 2nd Floor, New York, NY, 10003
Coordinator: Lakshmi Clark
LD program telephone: 212 998-4980
LD program e-mail: lc83@nyu.edu
LD program enrollment: 324, Total campus enrollment: 20,212

GENERAL

New York University is a private, coed, four-year institution. Urban campus in New York City (population: 8,008,278). Served by air, bus, and train. School operates transportation to residence halls, campus facilities, and sports/entertainment complex. Public transportation serves campus. Semester system.

LD ADMISSIONS

A member of the LD program does not sit on the admissions committee. High school waivers are accepted for math and foreign language. A personal interview is required. Essay is required and may be typed.

SECONDARY SCHOOL REQUIREMENTS

Graduation from secondary school required; GED accepted. The following course distribution required: 4 units of English, 3 units of math, 3 units of science, 2 units of foreign language, 4 units of history.

TESTING

SAT Reasoning or ACT required. SAT Subject required.

All enrolled freshmen (fall 2004):

Average SAT I Scores:	Verbal: 658	Math: 660
Average ACT Scores:	Composite: 29	

Child Study Team report is not required. Tests required as part of this documentation:

☐ WAIS-IV ☐ Woodcock-Johnson
☐ WISC-IV ☐ Nelson-Denny Reading Test
☐ SATA ☐ Other

UNDERGRADUATE STUDENT BODY

Total undergraduate student enrollment: 7,616 Men, 11,412 Women.

Composition of student body (fall 2004):

	Undergraduate	Freshmen
International	3.9	3.8
Black	3.7	5.0
American Indian	0.1	0.2
Asian-American	17.9	14.3
Hispanic	7.4	7.0
White	50.7	42.7
Unreported	16.3	27.0
	100.0%	100.0%

69% are from out of state. 5% join a fraternity and 3% join a sorority. Average age of full-time undergraduates is 20. 58% of classes have fewer than 20 students, 30% have between 20 and 50 students, 12% have more than 50 students.

STUDENT HOUSING

88% of freshmen live in college housing. Freshmen are not required to live on campus. Housing is guaranteed for all undergraduates. Campus can house 10,724 undergraduates. Single rooms are available for students with medical or special needs. A medical note is required.

EXPENSES

Tuition (2005-06): $29,890 per year.
Room: $8,010. Board: $3,780.

There is no additional cost for LD program/services.

LD SERVICES

LD program size is not limited.

LD services available to:

■ Freshmen ■ Sophomores ■ Juniors ■ Seniors

Academic Accommodations

Curriculum		In class	
Foreign language waiver	☐	Early syllabus	☐
Lighter course load	■	Note takers in class	■
Math waiver	☐	Priority seating	☐
Other special classes	☐	Tape recorders	■
Priority registrations	☐	Videotaped classes	☐
Substitution of courses	☐	Text on tape	☐
Exams		**Services**	
Extended time	■	Diagnostic tests	☐
Oral exams	☐	Learning centers	■
Take home exams	☐	Proofreaders	☐
Exams on tape or computer	☐	Readers	■
Untimed exams	☐	Reading Machines/Kurzweil	■
Other accommodations	■	Special bookstore section	☐
		Typists	☐

Credit toward degree is not given for remedial courses taken.

Counseling Services

■ Academic
■ Psychological
■ Student Support groups
■ Vocational

Tutoring

Individual tutoring is available.

	Individual	Group
Time management	■	■
Organizational skills	■	■
Learning strategies	■	■
Study skills	■	■
Content area	■	■
Writing lab	■	■
Math lab	■	■

UNIQUE LD PROGRAM FEATURES

Students must meet specific documentation requirements.

LD PROGRAM STAFF

Total number of LD Program staff (including director):

Full Time: 5 Part Time: 5

There is an advisor/advocate from the LD program available to students. 5 graduate students are available to work with LD students.

Key staff person available to work with LD students: Lakshmi Clark, Coordinator.

LD Program web site: www.nyu.edu/csd

Niagara University

Niagara University, NY

Address: Niagara University, NY, 14109
Admissions telephone: 800 462-2111
Admissions FAX: 716 286-8710
Director of Admissions: Michael Konopski
Admissions e-mail: admissions@niagara.edu
Web site: http://www.niagara.edu
SAT Code: 2558 ACT Code: 2842

LD program name: Diane Stoelting
Coordinator-Specialized Support Services: Diane Stoelting
LD program telephone: 716 286-8076
LD program e-mail: ds@niagara.edu
LD program enrollment: 69, Total campus enrollment: 2,825

GENERAL

Niagara University is a private, coed, four-year institution. 160-acre, suburban campus three miles from Niagara Falls (population: 55,593), 20 miles from Buffalo. Served by bus and train; major airport serves Buffalo. Public transportation serves campus. Semester system.

LD ADMISSIONS

Students do not complete a separate application and are not simultaneously accepted to the LD program. A member of the LD program does not sit on the admissions committee. A personal interview is recommended. Essay is not required.

SECONDARY SCHOOL REQUIREMENTS

Graduation from secondary school required; GED accepted. The following course distribution required: 4 units of English, 2 units of math, 2 units of science, 2 units of foreign language, 2 units of social studies, 4 units of academic electives.

TESTING

SAT Reasoning or ACT required. SAT Subject recommended.

All enrolled freshmen (fall 2004):

Average SAT I Scores:	Verbal: 513	Math: 524
Average ACT Scores:	Composite: 22	

Child Study Team report is not required. A neuropsychological or comprehensive psycho-educational evaluation is required for admission. Tests required as part of this documentation:

- [x] WAIS-IV
- [ ] WISC-IV
- [ ] SATA
- [x] Woodcock-Johnson
- [ ] Nelson-Denny Reading Test
- [x] Other

UNDERGRADUATE STUDENT BODY

Total undergraduate student enrollment: 975 Men, 1,485 Women.

Composition of student body (fall 2004):

	Undergraduate	Freshmen
International	2.8	5.1
Black	4.5	4.7
American Indian	0.7	0.8
Asian-American	0.8	0.7
Hispanic	1.2	1.5
White	71.0	77.4
Unreported	19.0	9.8
	100.0%	100.0%

8% are from out of state. Average age of full-time undergraduates is 20. 43% of classes have fewer than 20 students, 57% have between 20 and 50 students.

STUDENT HOUSING

80% of freshmen live in college housing. Freshmen are required to live on campus. Housing is guaranteed for all undergraduates. Campus can house 1,501 undergraduates. Single rooms are available for students with medical or special needs. A medical note is required.

EXPENSES

Tuition (2005-06): $19,000 per year.

Room & Board: $8,450.

There is no additional cost for LD program/services.

LD SERVICES

LD program size is not limited.

LD services available to:

- [x] Freshmen
- [x] Sophomores
- [x] Juniors
- [x] Seniors

Academic Accommodations

Curriculum		In class	
Foreign language waiver	[ ]	Early syllabus	[ ]
Lighter course load	[x]	Note takers in class	[x]
Math waiver	[ ]	Priority seating	[ ]
Other special classes	[ ]	Tape recorders	[x]
Priority registrations	[ ]	Videotaped classes	[ ]
Substitution of courses	[x]	Text on tape	[ ]
Exams		**Services**	
Extended time	[x]	Diagnostic tests	[ ]
Oral exams	[ ]	Learning centers	[x]
Take home exams	[ ]	Proofreaders	[ ]
Exams on tape or computer	[ ]	Readers	[ ]
Untimed exams	[ ]	Reading Machines/Kurzweil	[x]
Other accommodations	[x]	Special bookstore section	[ ]
		Typists	[ ]

Credit toward degree is not given for remedial courses taken.

Counseling Services

- [x] Academic — Meets 12 times per academic year
- [ ] Psychological
- [ ] Student Support groups
- [ ] Vocational

Tutoring

Individual tutoring is available weekly.

Average size of tutoring groups: 4

	Individual	Group
Time management	[x]	[ ]
Organizational skills	[x]	[ ]
Learning strategies	[x]	[ ]
Study skills	[x]	[ ]
Content area	[ ]	[x]
Writing lab	[x]	[ ]
Math lab	[x]	[ ]

LD PROGRAM STAFF

Total number of LD Program staff (including director):

Full Time: 1 Part Time: 1

There is an advisor/advocate from the LD program available to students. The advisor/advocate meets with students 4 times per month. 1 graduate student is available to work with LD students.

Key staff person available to work with LD students: Diane Stoelting, Coodinator Specialized Support Services.

Nyack College

Nyack, NY

Address: 1 South Boulevard, Nyack, NY, 10960-3698
Admissions telephone: 800 33-NYACK
Admissions FAX: 845 358-3047
Director of Admissions: Bethany Ilsley
Admissions e-mail: admissions@nyack.edu
Web site: http://www.nyack.edu
SAT Code: 2560   ACT Code: 2846

Total campus enrollment: 2,056

GENERAL

Nyack College is a private, coed, four-year institution. 64-acre, suburban campus in Nyack (area population: 6,737), 20 miles from New York City; branch campus in Manhattan. Major airports and train serve New York City and Newark, N.J. (30 miles); smaller airport serves White Plains (10 miles); bus serves Nanuet (five miles). School operates transportation to Manhattan campus. Semester system.

LD ADMISSIONS

A personal interview is not required. Essay is required and may be typed.

SECONDARY SCHOOL REQUIREMENTS

Graduation from secondary school required; GED accepted.

TESTING

SAT Reasoning or ACT required of some applicants. SAT Subject recommended.

All enrolled freshmen (fall 2004):

Average SAT I Scores:	Verbal: 467	Math: 455
Average ACT Scores:	Composite: 20	

Child Study Team report is not required. Tests required as part of this documentation:

- ☐ WAIS-IV
- ☐ WISC-IV
- ☐ SATA
- ☐ Woodcock-Johnson
- ☐ Nelson-Denny Reading Test
- ☐ Other

UNDERGRADUATE STUDENT BODY

Total undergraduate student enrollment: 709 Men, 1,015 Women.

Composition of student body (fall 2004):

	Undergraduate	Freshmen
International	6.5	5.1
Black	22.4	35.2
American Indian	0.0	0.0
Asian-American	7.2	5.7
Hispanic	23.1	20.9
White	35.0	29.8
Unreported	5.8	3.3
	100.0%	100.0%

31% are from out of state. 64% of classes have fewer than 20 students, 34% have between 20 and 50 students, 2% have more than 50 students.

STUDENT HOUSING

63% of freshmen live in college housing. Housing is not guaranteed for all undergraduates. Campus can house 748 undergraduates.

EXPENSES

Tuition (2005-06): $14,750 per year.
Room & Board: $7,600.
There is no additional cost for LD program/services.

LD SERVICES

LD services available to:

☐ Freshmen ☐ Sophomores ☐ Juniors ☐ Seniors

Academic Accommodations

Curriculum		In class	
Foreign language waiver	☐	Early syllabus	☐
Lighter course load	■	Note takers in class	■
Math waiver	☐	Priority seating	☐
Other special classes	■	Tape recorders	■
Priority registrations	☐	Videotaped classes	☐
Substitution of courses	☐	Text on tape	☐
Exams		**Services**	
Extended time	■	Diagnostic tests	☐
Oral exams	■	Learning centers	■
Take home exams	☐	Proofreaders	☐
Exams on tape or computer	☐	Readers	■
Untimed exams	■	Reading Machines/Kurzweil	☐
Other accommodations	☐	Special bookstore section	☐
		Typists	☐

Credit toward degree is not given for remedial courses taken.

Counseling Services

- ☐ Academic
- ☐ Psychological
- ☐ Student Support groups
- ☐ Vocational

Tutoring

	Individual	Group
Time management	☐	☐
Organizational skills	☐	☐
Learning strategies	☐	☐
Study skills	☐	☐
Content area	☐	☐
Writing lab	☐	☐
Math lab	☐	☐

LD PROGRAM STAFF

Key staff person available to work with LD students: Elona Collins, Learning Disabilities Coordinator.

Pace University

New York, NY

Address: 1 Pace Plaza, New York, NY, 10038
Admissions telephone: 800 874-7223
Admissions FAX: 212 346-1040
Executive Director of Enrollment Management: Joanna Broda
Admissions e-mail: infoctr@pace.edu
Web site: http://www.pace.edu
SAT Code: 2635 ACT Code: 2852

LD program address: 861 Bedford Road, Pleasantville, NY, 10570
University Compliance Officer: Geoffrey J. Harter
LD program telephone: 914 773-3717
LD program e-mail: gharter@pace.edu
LD program enrollment: 300, Total campus enrollment: 8,668

GENERAL

Pace University is a private, coed, four-year institution. Three-acre, urban campus in New York City (population: 8,008,278) and 200-acre, suburban campus in Pleasantville-Briarcliff, 20 miles from New York City. Airport, bus, and train serve New York City; smaller airport and bus serve White Plains (10 miles from Pleasantville campus). School operates transportation to all campuses and university events. Public transportation serves campus. Semester system.

LD ADMISSIONS

A personal interview is recommended. Essay is not required.

SECONDARY SCHOOL REQUIREMENTS

Graduation from secondary school required; GED accepted. The following course distribution required: 4 units of English, 3 units of math, 2 units of science, 2 units of foreign language, 1 unit of social studies, 2 units of history, 2 units of academic electives.

TESTING

SAT Reasoning or ACT required. SAT Subject recommended.

All enrolled freshmen (fall 2004):

Average SAT I Scores: Verbal: 538 Math: 550
Average ACT Scores: Composite: 21

Child Study Team report is not required. Tests required as part of this documentation:

- [ ] WAIS-IV
- [ ] WISC-IV
- [ ] SATA
- [ ] Woodcock-Johnson
- [ ] Nelson-Denny Reading Test
- [ ] Other

UNDERGRADUATE STUDENT BODY

Total undergraduate student enrollment: 3,585 Men, 5,328 Women.

Composition of student body (fall 2004):

	Undergraduate	Freshmen
International	3.4	4.1
Black	6.6	10.2
American Indian	0.3	0.2
Asian-American	9.1	11.7
Hispanic	11.4	11.7
White	45.8	44.9
Unreported	23.4	17.2
	100.0%	100.0%

11% are from out of state. 5% join a fraternity and 5% join a sorority. Average age of full-time undergraduates is 21. 49% of classes have fewer than 20 students, 50% have between 20 and 50 students, 1% have more than 50 students.

STUDENT HOUSING

59% of freshmen live in college housing. Freshmen are not required to live on campus. Housing is guaranteed for all undergraduates. Campus can house 2,503 undergraduates. Single rooms are available for students with medical or special needs.

EXPENSES

Tuition (2005-06): $22,100 per year.
There is no additional cost for LD program/services.

LD SERVICES

LD program size is not limited.

LD services available to:

- [x] Freshmen
- [x] Sophomores
- [x] Juniors
- [x] Seniors

Academic Accommodations

Curriculum

- [ ] Foreign language waiver
- [ ] Lighter course load
- [ ] Math waiver
- [ ] Other special classes
- [ ] Priority registrations
- [x] Substitution of courses

Exams

- [x] Extended time
- [x] Oral exams
- [x] Take home exams
- [x] Exams on tape or computer
- [x] Untimed exams
- [x] Other accommodations

In class

- [ ] Early syllabus
- [x] Note takers in class
- [ ] Priority seating
- [x] Tape recorders
- [ ] Videotaped classes
- [x] Text on tape

Services

- [ ] Diagnostic tests
- [x] Learning centers
- [ ] Proofreaders
- [x] Readers
- [ ] Reading Machines/Kurzweil
- [ ] Special bookstore section
- [x] Typists

Credit toward degree is not given for remedial courses taken.

Counseling Services

- [x] Academic
- [x] Psychological
- [x] Student Support groups
- [x] Vocational

Tutoring

Individual tutoring is available daily.

	Individual	Group
Time management	[x]	[ ]
Organizational skills	[x]	[ ]
Learning strategies	[ ]	[ ]
Study skills	[x]	[ ]
Content area	[ ]	[ ]
Writing lab	[x]	[ ]
Math lab	[x]	[ ]

LD PROGRAM STAFF

Total number of LD Program staff (including director):

Full Time: 2 Part Time: 2

There is an advisor/advocate from the LD program available to students.

Key staff person available to work with LD students: Geoffrey J. Harter, University Compliance Officer.

Parsons School of Design

New York, NY

Address: 66 Fifth Avenue, New York, NY, 10011
Admissions telephone: 877 528-3321
Admissions FAX: 212 229-5166
Associate Dean for Enrollment Management: Christy Kalan
Admissions e-mail: studentinfo@newschool.edu
Web site: http://www.parsons.edu
SAT Code: 2638 ACT Code: 2854

Managing Director for Student Affairs: Tom McDonald
LD program telephone: 212 229-5472
LD program e-mail: sds@newschool.edu
Total campus enrollment: 2,311

GENERAL

Parsons School of Design is a private, coed, four-year institution. Urban campus in New York City (population: 8,008,278); branch campus abroad in Paris, France. Served by air, bus, and train. Public transportation serves campus. Semester system.

SECONDARY SCHOOL REQUIREMENTS

Graduation from secondary school required; GED accepted.

TESTING

Child Study Team report is not required. Tests required as part of this documentation:

- [ ] WAIS-IV
- [ ] WISC-IV
- [ ] SATA
- [ ] Woodcock-Johnson
- [ ] Nelson-Denny Reading Test
- [ ] Other

UNDERGRADUATE STUDENT BODY

Total undergraduate student enrollment: 587 Men, 1,724 Women.

47% are from out of state.

STUDENT HOUSING

Housing is guaranteed for all undergraduates. Campus can house 1,000 undergraduates.

EXPENSES

Tuition (2005-06): $26,820 per year.

Room: $8,100. Board: $2,710.

There is no additional cost for LD program/services.

LD SERVICES

LD program size is not limited.

LD services available to:

- [ ] Freshmen
- [ ] Sophomores
- [ ] Juniors
- [ ] Seniors

Academic Accommodations

Curriculum		In class	
Foreign language waiver	[ ]	Early syllabus	[ ]
Lighter course load	[x]	Note takers in class	[x]
Math waiver	[ ]	Priority seating	[ ]
Other special classes	[ ]	Tape recorders	[x]
Priority registrations	[ ]	Videotaped classes	[ ]
Substitution of courses	[ ]	Text on tape	[ ]
Exams		**Services**	
Extended time	[x]	Diagnostic tests	[ ]
Oral exams	[ ]	Learning centers	[ ]
Take home exams	[ ]	Proofreaders	[ ]
Exams on tape or computer	[ ]	Readers	[x]
Untimed exams	[ ]	Reading Machines/Kurzweil	[ ]
Other accommodations	[ ]	Special bookstore section	[ ]
		Typists	[ ]

Credit toward degree is not given for remedial courses taken.

Counseling Services

- [ ] Academic
- [ ] Psychological
- [ ] Student Support groups
- [ ] Vocational

Tutoring

	Individual	Group
Time management	[ ]	[ ]
Organizational skills	[ ]	[ ]
Learning strategies	[ ]	[ ]
Study skills	[ ]	[ ]
Content area	[ ]	[ ]
Writing lab	[ ]	[ ]
Math lab	[ ]	[ ]

LD PROGRAM STAFF

Key staff person available to work with LD students: Tom McDonald, Managing Director for Student Affairs.

Polytechnic University

Brooklyn, NY

Address: 6 Metrotech Center, Brooklyn, NY, 11201
Admissions telephone: 800 POLY-TEC
Admissions FAX: 718 260-3446
Dean of University Admissions: Jon Wexler
Admissions e-mail: admitme@poly.edu
Web site: http://www.poly.edu/
SAT Code: 2668 ACT Code: 2860

Director, Student Development: Cheryl McNear
LD program telephone: 718 260-3800
LD program e-mail: cmcnear@poly.edu
LD program enrollment: 11, Total campus enrollment: 1,543

GENERAL

Polytechnic University is a private, coed, four-year institution. 16-acre main campus in downtown Brooklyn (New York City population: 8,008,278); graduate centers in Hawthorne and on Long Island. Served by air, bus, and train. Public transportation serves campus. Semester system.

LD ADMISSIONS

A personal interview is recommended. Essay is required and may be typed.

For fall 2004, 11 completed self-identified LD applications were received. 11 applications were offered admission, and 11 enrolled.

SECONDARY SCHOOL REQUIREMENTS

Graduation from secondary school required; GED accepted. The following course distribution required: 4 units of English, 4 units of math, 4 units of science, 3 units of social studies, 2 units of academic electives.

TESTING

SAT Reasoning required; ACT may be substituted. SAT Subject recommended.

All enrolled freshmen (fall 2004):

Average SAT I Scores: Verbal: 545 Math: 630

Child Study Team report is not required. Tests required as part of this documentation:

- [ ] WAIS-IV
- [ ] WISC-IV
- [ ] SATA
- [ ] Woodcock-Johnson
- [ ] Nelson-Denny Reading Test
- [ ] Other

UNDERGRADUATE STUDENT BODY

Total undergraduate student enrollment: 1,363 Men, 346 Women.

Composition of student body (fall 2004):

	Undergraduate	Freshmen
International	4.6	7.6
Black	10.4	11.1
American Indian	0.0	0.4
Asian-American	30.5	34.9
Hispanic	11.3	9.0
White	31.3	28.8
Unreported	11.9	8.2
	100.0%	100.0%

3% are from out of state. 3% join a fraternity and 4% join a sorority. Average age of full-time undergraduates is 20. 46% of classes have fewer than 20 students, 52% have between 20 and 50 students, 2% have more than 50 students.

STUDENT HOUSING

19% of freshmen live in college housing. Freshmen are not required to live on campus. Housing is guaranteed for all undergraduates. Campus can house 400 undergraduates. Single rooms are available for students with medical or special needs.

EXPENSES

Tuition (2005-06): $27,640 per year.
Room: $6,500. Board: $2,000.
There is no additional cost for LD program/services.

LD SERVICES

LD program size is not limited.

LD services available to:

- [x] Freshmen
- [x] Sophomores
- [x] Juniors
- [x] Seniors

Academic Accommodations

Curriculum

- [ ] Foreign language waiver
- [ ] Lighter course load
- [ ] Math waiver
- [ ] Other special classes
- [ ] Priority registrations
- [ ] Substitution of courses

Exams

- [x] Extended time
- [ ] Oral exams
- [ ] Take home exams
- [ ] Exams on tape or computer
- [x] Untimed exams
- [x] Other accommodations

In class

- [ ] Early syllabus
- [x] Note takers in class
- [ ] Priority seating
- [ ] Tape recorders
- [ ] Videotaped classes
- [ ] Text on tape

Services

- [ ] Diagnostic tests
- [x] Learning centers
- [ ] Proofreaders
- [ ] Readers
- [ ] Reading Machines/Kurzweil
- [ ] Special bookstore section
- [ ] Typists

Credit toward degree is not given for remedial courses taken.

Counseling Services

- [ ] Academic
- [ ] Psychological
- [ ] Student Support groups
- [ ] Vocational

Tutoring

	Individual	Group
Time management	[ ]	[ ]
Organizational skills	[ ]	[ ]
Learning strategies	[ ]	[ ]
Study skills	[ ]	[ ]
Content area	[ ]	[ ]
Writing lab	[ ]	[ ]
Math lab	[ ]	[ ]

LD PROGRAM STAFF

There is no advisor/advocate from the LD program available to students.

Key staff person available to work with LD students: Cheryl McNear, Director, Student Development.

Pratt Institute

Brooklyn, NY

Address: 200 Willoughby Avenue, Brooklyn, NY, 11205
Admissions telephone: 800 331-0834
Admissions FAX: 718 636-3670
Director of Admissions: Heidi Metcalf
Admissions e-mail: admissions@pratt.edu
Web site: http://www.pratt.edu
SAT Code: 2669 ACT Code: 2862

LD program name: Disability Services
Assistant to VP for Student Affairs: Mai L. McDonald
LD program telephone: 718 636-3711
LD program e-mail: mcdonald@pratt.edu
Total campus enrollment: 3,623

GENERAL

Pratt Institute is a private, coed, four-year institution. 25-acre, urban campus in Brooklyn (New York City population: 8,008,278); branch campus in Manhattan; extension center in Utica. Served by air, bus, and train. School operates transportation to several local subway and railway stops. Public transportation serves campus. Semester system.

LD ADMISSIONS

Students do not complete a separate application and are not simultaneously accepted to the LD program. A member of the LD program does not sit on the admissions committee. A personal interview is recommended. Essay is not required.

SECONDARY SCHOOL REQUIREMENTS

Graduation from secondary school required; GED accepted.

TESTING

SAT Reasoning or ACT required. SAT Subject recommended.

Child Study Team report is not required. A neuropsychological or comprehensive psycho-educational evaluation is required for admission. Must be dated within 24 months of application. Tests required as part of this documentation:

- [x] WAIS-IV
- [x] WISC-IV
- [x] SATA
- [x] Woodcock-Johnson
- [x] Nelson-Denny Reading Test
- [ ] Other

UNDERGRADUATE STUDENT BODY

Total undergraduate student enrollment: 1,402 Men, 1,607 Women.

Composition of student body (fall 2004):

	Undergraduate	Freshmen
International	7.1	9.4
Black	9.7	8.0
American Indian	0.7	0.4
Asian-American	11.7	11.9
Hispanic	8.1	7.6
White	62.4	62.6
Unreported	0.3	0.1
	100.0%	100.0%

75% are from out of state. 1% join a fraternity and 1% join a sorority. 86% of classes have fewer than 20 students, 14% have between 20 and 50 students.

STUDENT HOUSING

87% of freshmen live in college housing. Freshmen are not required to live on campus. Housing is guaranteed for all undergraduates. Campus can house 1,476 undergraduates. Single rooms are available for students with medical or special needs. A medical note is required.

EXPENSES

Tuition (2005-06): $26,500 per year.
Room: $5,376. Board: $3,200.
There is no additional cost for LD program/services.

LD SERVICES

LD program size is not limited.

LD services available to:

- [x] Freshmen
- [x] Sophomores
- [x] Juniors
- [x] Seniors

Academic Accommodations

Curriculum

- [ ] Foreign language waiver
- [ ] Lighter course load
- [ ] Math waiver
- [ ] Other special classes
- [ ] Priority registrations
- [ ] Substitution of courses

Exams

- [x] Extended time
- [ ] Oral exams
- [ ] Take home exams
- [ ] Exams on tape or computer
- [ ] Untimed exams
- [x] Other accommodations

In class

- [x] Early syllabus
- [x] Note takers in class
- [ ] Priority seating
- [x] Tape recorders
- [ ] Videotaped classes
- [ ] Text on tape

Services

- [x] Diagnostic tests
- [x] Learning centers
- [ ] Proofreaders
- [ ] Readers
- [ ] Reading Machines/Kurzweil
- [ ] Special bookstore section
- [ ] Typists

Credit toward degree is not given for remedial courses taken.

Counseling Services

- [ ] Academic
- [ ] Psychological
- [ ] Student Support groups
- [ ] Vocational

Tutoring

Individual tutoring is available.

	Individual	Group
Time management	[x]	[ ]
Organizational skills	[ ]	[ ]
Learning strategies	[ ]	[ ]
Study skills	[ ]	[ ]
Content area	[ ]	[ ]
Writing lab	[x]	[ ]
Math lab	[ ]	[ ]

UNIQUE LD PROGRAM FEATURES

Pratt Institute has a Disability Services Program which serves all students with disabilities. Pratt Institute does not have an "LD" program.

LD PROGRAM STAFF

Total number of LD Program staff (including director):

Full Time: 1 Part Time: 1

There is an advisor/advocate from the LD program available to students. 4 peer tutors are available to work with LD students.

Key staff person available to work with LD students: Mai McDonald, Assistant to Vice President for Student Affairs, Disability Services Coordinator.

Rensselaer Polytechnic Institute

Troy, NY

Address: 110 Eighth Street, Troy, NY, 12180-3590
Admissions telephone: 518 276-6216
Admissions FAX: 518 276-4072
Dean of Enrollment Management: Karen Long
Admissions e-mail: admissions@rpi.edu
Web site: http://www.rpi.edu
SAT Code: 2757 ACT Code: 2866

Assistant Dean of Students: Debra Hamilton
LD program telephone: 518 276-2746
LD program e-mail: hamild@rpi.edu
LD program enrollment: 89, Total campus enrollment: 4,929

GENERAL

Rensselaer Polytechnic Institute is a private, coed, four-year institution. 260-acre campus in Troy (population: 49,170), 15 miles from both Albany and Schenectady and 150 miles from New York City; branch campus in Hartford. Airport and bus serve Albany; train serves Rensselaer (10 miles). School operates transportation to area locations and to downtown Albany and Troy. Public transportation serves campus. Semester system.

LD ADMISSIONS

Students do not complete a separate application and are not simultaneously accepted to the LD program. A member of the LD program does not sit on the admissions committee. A personal interview is not required. Essay is required and may be typed. Diagnostic test(s) are required after enrollment, but are not a part of the admissions process.

SECONDARY SCHOOL REQUIREMENTS

Graduation from secondary school required; GED accepted. The following course distribution required: 4 units of English, 4 units of math, 3 units of science, 2 units of social studies.

TESTING

SAT Reasoning or ACT required. SAT Subject recommended.

All enrolled freshmen (fall 2004):

Average SAT I Scores:	Verbal: 633	Math: 687
Average ACT Scores:	Composite: 26	

Child Study Team report is not required. A neuropsychological or comprehensive psycho-educational evaluation is required for admission. Must be dated within 36 months of application. Tests required as part of this documentation:

- ■ WAIS-IV
- ☐ WISC-IV
- ☐ SATA
- ■ Woodcock-Johnson
- ☐ Nelson-Denny Reading Test
- ☐ Other

UNDERGRADUATE STUDENT BODY

Total undergraduate student enrollment: 3,983 Men, 1,289 Women.

Composition of student body (fall 2004):

	Undergraduate	Freshmen
International	2.7	4.2
Black	4.4	4.0
American Indian	0.1	0.4
Asian-American	10.1	11.8
Hispanic	6.1	5.0
White	72.0	70.0
Unreported	4.6	4.6
	100.0%	100.0%

49% are from out of state. 39% join a fraternity and 18% join a sorority. Average age of full-time undergraduates is 20. 42% of classes have fewer than 20 students, 48% have between 20 and 50 students, 10% have more than 50 students.

STUDENT HOUSING

98% of freshmen live in college housing. Freshmen are required to live on campus. Housing is guaranteed for all undergraduates. Campus can house 2,807 undergraduates. Single rooms are available for students with medical or special needs. A medical note is required.

EXPENSES

Tuition (2005-06): $31,000 per year.
Room: $5,290-$5,365. Board: $4,141.
There is no additional cost for LD program/services.

LD SERVICES

LD program size is not limited.

LD services available to:

■ Freshmen ■ Sophomores ■ Juniors ■ Seniors

Academic Accommodations

Curriculum		**In class**	
Foreign language waiver	☐	Early syllabus	☐
Lighter course load	■	Note takers in class	■
Math waiver	☐	Priority seating	☐
Other special classes	☐	Tape recorders	■
Priority registrations	☐	Videotaped classes	☐
Substitution of courses	☐	Text on tape	■
Exams		**Services**	
Extended time	■	Diagnostic tests	☐
Oral exams	☐	Learning centers	■
Take home exams	☐	Proofreaders	☐
Exams on tape or computer	☐	Readers	☐
Untimed exams	☐	Reading Machines/Kurzweil	■
Other accommodations	■	Special bookstore section	☐
		Typists	☐

Credit toward degree is not given for remedial courses taken.

Counseling Services

- ■ Academic
- ■ Psychological
- ☐ Student Support groups
- ■ Vocational

Tutoring

Individual tutoring is available weekly.

	Individual	Group
Time management	■	☐
Organizational skills	■	☐
Learning strategies	■	☐
Study skills	■	■
Content area	■	■
Writing lab	■	☐
Math lab	■	☐

LD PROGRAM STAFF

There is an advisor/advocate from the LD program available to students.

Key staff person available to work with LD students: Debra Hamilton, Assistant Dean of Students, Disablility Services.

LD Program web site: http:///www.rpi.edu/dept/doso/dss

Roberts Wesleyan College

Rochester, NY

Address: 2301 Westside Drive, Rochester, NY, 14624-1997
Admissions telephone: 800 777-4RWC
Admissions FAX: 585 594-6371
Dean of Admissions: Linda Kurtz
Admissions e-mail: admissions@roberts.edu
Web site: http://www.roberts.edu
SAT Code: 2759 ACT Code: 2868

Director: Dr. Jennifer Kehoe
LD program telephone: 585 594-6493
LD program e-mail: Kehoe_Jennifer@Roberts.edu
Total campus enrollment: 1,376

GENERAL

Roberts Wesleyan College is a private, coed, four-year institution. 75-acre, suburban campus in Rochester (population: 219,773), eight miles from downtown. Served by air, bus, and train. Semester system.

LD ADMISSIONS

A personal interview is not required. Essay is required and may be typed.

SECONDARY SCHOOL REQUIREMENTS

Graduation from secondary school required; GED accepted. The following course distribution required: 4 units of English, 2 units of math, 2 units of social studies.

TESTING

SAT Reasoning or ACT required.

Child Study Team report is not required. Tests required as part of this documentation:

- [ ] WAIS-IV
- [ ] WISC-IV
- [ ] SATA
- [ ] Woodcock-Johnson
- [ ] Nelson-Denny Reading Test
- [ ] Other

UNDERGRADUATE STUDENT BODY

Total undergraduate student enrollment: 418 Men, 790 Women.

Composition of student body (fall 2004):

	Undergraduate	Freshmen
International	3.5	3.2
Black	4.7	6.0
American Indian	0.4	0.3
Asian-American	2.7	1.4
Hispanic	1.6	2.5
White	74.7	74.3
Unreported	12.4	12.3
	100.0%	100.0%

15% are from out of state. Average age of full-time undergraduates is 25. 70% of classes have fewer than 20 students, 29% have between 20 and 50 students, 1% have more than 50 students.

STUDENT HOUSING

81% of freshmen live in college housing. Freshmen are required to live on campus. Housing is guaranteed for all undergraduates. Campus can house 840 undergraduates. Single rooms are available for students with medical or special needs. A medical note is not required.

EXPENSES

Tuition (2005-06): $31,000 per year.
Room: $5,290-$5,365. Board: $4,141.
There is no additional cost for LD program/services.

LD SERVICES

LD program size is not limited.

LD services available to:

- [x] Freshmen
- [x] Sophomores
- [x] Juniors
- [x] Seniors

Academic Accommodations

Curriculum		In class	
Foreign language waiver	[ ]	Early syllabus	[ ]
Lighter course load	[x]	Note takers in class	[x]
Math waiver	[ ]	Priority seating	[ ]
Other special classes	[ ]	Tape recorders	[x]
Priority registrations	[ ]	Videotaped classes	[x]
Substitution of courses	[ ]	Text on tape	[ ]
Exams		**Services**	
Extended time	[x]	Diagnostic tests	[ ]
Oral exams	[x]	Learning centers	[x]
Take home exams	[ ]	Proofreaders	[ ]
Exams on tape or computer	[ ]	Readers	[x]
Untimed exams	[x]	Reading Machines/Kurzweil	[x]
Other accommodations	[ ]	Special bookstore section	[ ]
		Typists	[ ]

Credit toward degree is not given for remedial courses taken.

Counseling Services

- [x] Academic
- [x] Psychological
- [x] Student Support groups
- [ ] Vocational

Tutoring

	Individual	Group
Time management	[x]	[x]
Organizational skills	[x]	[x]
Learning strategies	[ ]	[ ]
Study skills	[x]	[x]
Content area	[x]	[x]
Writing lab	[x]	[x]
Math lab	[x]	[x]

LD PROGRAM STAFF

Total number of LD Program staff (including director):

Full Time: 3 Part Time: 3

There is an advisor/advocate from the LD program available to students.

Key staff person available to work with LD students: Dr. Jennifer Kehoe, Director of the Center for Academic Excellence.

University of Rochester

Rochester, NY

Address: Wilson Boulevard, Rochester, NY, 14627
Admissions telephone: 888 822-2256
Admissions FAX: 585 461-4595
Director of Admissions: Gregory MacDonald
Admissions e-mail: admit@admissions.rochester.edu
Web site: http://www.rochester.edu
SAT Code: 2928 ACT Code: 2980

Assistant Dean & Director: Vicki Roth
LD program telephone: 585 275-9049
LD program e-mail: vrth@mail.rochester.edu
Total campus enrollment: 4,535

GENERAL

University of Rochester is a private, coed, four-year institution. 100-acre, suburban campus in Rochester (population: 219,773); separate campus for Eastman School of Music. Served by air, bus, and train. School operates transportation between campuses and to downtown and other nearby areas. Public transportation serves campus. Semester system.

LD ADMISSIONS

A personal interview is not required. Essay is required and may be typed.

SECONDARY SCHOOL REQUIREMENTS

Graduation from secondary school required; GED accepted.

TESTING

SAT Reasoning or ACT required. SAT Subject recommended.

All enrolled freshmen (fall 2004):

Average SAT I Scores:	Verbal: 643	Math: 668
Average ACT Scores:	Composite: 28	

Child Study Team report is not required. Tests required as part of this documentation:

- [ ] WAIS-IV
- [ ] WISC-IV
- [ ] SATA
- [ ] Woodcock-Johnson
- [ ] Nelson-Denny Reading Test
- [ ] Other

UNDERGRADUATE STUDENT BODY

Total undergraduate student enrollment: 2,347 Men, 2,182 Women.

Composition of student body (fall 2004):

	Undergraduate	Freshmen
International	3.4	3.5
Black	3.7	4.3
American Indian	0.3	0.3
Asian-American	8.5	10.6
Hispanic	4.2	4.0
White	67.0	63.7
Unreported	12.9	13.6
	100.0%	100.0%

25% join a fraternity and 20% join a sorority. Average age of full-time undergraduates is 20. 62% of classes have fewer than 20 students, 27% have between 20 and 50 students, 11% have more than 50 students.

STUDENT HOUSING

100% of freshmen live in college housing. Freshmen are required to live on campus. Housing is guaranteed for all undergraduates. Campus can house 3,300 undergraduates.

EXPENSES

Tuition (2005-06): $30,540 per year.
Room: $5,710. Board: $4,128.

There is no additional cost for LD program/services.

LD SERVICES

LD program size is not limited.

LD services available to:

- [ ] Freshmen
- [ ] Sophomores
- [ ] Juniors
- [ ] Seniors

Academic Accommodations

Curriculum		In class	
Foreign language waiver	[ ]	Early syllabus	[ ]
Lighter course load	[x]	Note takers in class	[x]
Math waiver	[ ]	Priority seating	[ ]
Other special classes	[ ]	Tape recorders	[ ]
Priority registrations	[ ]	Videotaped classes	[ ]
Substitution of courses	[ ]	Text on tape	[ ]
Exams		**Services**	
Extended time	[x]	Diagnostic tests	[ ]
Oral exams	[x]	Learning centers	[x]
Take home exams	[ ]	Proofreaders	[ ]
Exams on tape or computer	[ ]	Readers	[x]
Untimed exams	[ ]	Reading Machines/Kurzweil	[x]
Other accommodations	[ ]	Special bookstore section	[ ]
		Typists	[ ]

Credit toward degree is not given for remedial courses taken.

Counseling Services

- [ ] Academic
- [ ] Psychological
- [ ] Student Support groups
- [ ] Vocational

Tutoring

	Individual	Group
Time management	[ ]	[ ]
Organizational skills	[ ]	[ ]
Learning strategies	[ ]	[ ]
Study skills	[ ]	[ ]
Content area	[ ]	[ ]
Writing lab	[ ]	[ ]
Math lab	[ ]	[ ]

LD PROGRAM STAFF

Total number of LD Program staff (including director):

Full Time: 2 Part Time: 2

Key staff person available to work with LD students: Pam Spallacci, Disability Support Coordinator.

Rochester Institute of Technology

Rochester, NY

Address: 1 Lomb Memorial Drive, Rochester, NY, 14623
Admissions telephone: 585 475-6631
Admissions FAX: 585 475-7424
Director of Admissions: Daniel Shelley
Admissions e-mail: admissions@rit.edu
Web site: http://www.rit.edu
SAT Code: 2760 ACT Code: 2870

LD program name: Learning Support Services
LD program address: 2355 Eastman Building
Program Coordinator: Lisa Fraser
LD program telephone: 585 475-5296
Total campus enrollment: 12,304

GENERAL

Rochester Institute of Technology is a private, coed, four-year institution. 1,300-acre, suburban campus in Rochester (population: 219,773), 75 miles from Buffalo and 97 miles from Syracuse; branch campuses abroad in Croatia and the Czech Republic. Served by air, bus, and train. School operates transportation to college-owned apartment complexes and local shopping areas. Public transportation serves campus. Quarter system.

LD ADMISSIONS

Students do not complete a separate application and are not simultaneously accepted to the LD program. A personal interview is recommended. Essay is required and may be typed.

SECONDARY SCHOOL REQUIREMENTS

Graduation from secondary school required; GED accepted. The following course distribution required: 4 units of English, 2 units of math, 2 units of science, 4 units of social studies, 10 units of academic electives.

TESTING

SAT Reasoning or ACT required. SAT Subject recommended.

All enrolled freshmen (fall 2004):

Average SAT I Scores: Verbal: 590 Math: 630
Average ACT Scores: Composite: 27

Child Study Team report is not required. A neuropsychological or comprehensive psycho-educational evaluation is required for admission. Tests required as part of this documentation:

- [ ] WAIS-IV
- [ ] WISC-IV
- [ ] SATA
- [ ] Woodcock-Johnson
- [ ] Nelson-Denny Reading Test
- [ ] Other

UNDERGRADUATE STUDENT BODY

Total undergraduate student enrollment: 8,204 Men, 3,825 Women.

Composition of student body (fall 2004):

	Undergraduate	Freshmen
International	2.9	4.3
Black	3.4	4.6
American Indian	0.4	0.5
Asian-American	6.7	7.0
Hispanic	4.0	3.3
White	74.3	71.2
Unreported	8.3	9.1
	100.0%	100.0%

43% are from out of state. 5% join a fraternity and 5% join a sorority. Average age of full-time undergraduates is 20. 44% of classes have fewer than 20 students, 49% have between 20 and 50 students, 7% have more than 50 students.

STUDENT HOUSING

95% of freshmen live in college housing. Freshmen are required to live on campus. Freshmen are gauranteed campus housing. Sophomores and international students are also given housing priority. Rooms are made available to upperclassmen through a housing lottery system. Apartment housing is plentiful in the areas near campus. Campus can house 6,600 undergraduates. Single rooms are available for students with medical or special needs.

EXPENSES

Tuition (2005-06): $23,247 per year.

Room: $4,863. Board: $3,588.

Additional cost for LD program/services: $440 per quarter.

LD SERVICES

LD program size is not limited.

LD services available to:

- [x] Freshmen
- [x] Sophomores
- [x] Juniors
- [x] Seniors

Academic Accommodations

Curriculum		In class	
Foreign language waiver	[ ]	Early syllabus	[ ]
Lighter course load	[x]	Note takers in class	[x]
Math waiver	[ ]	Priority seating	[ ]
Other special classes	[x]	Tape recorders	[x]
Priority registrations	[x]	Videotaped classes	[ ]
Substitution of courses	[ ]	Text on tape	[ ]
Exams		**Services**	
Extended time	[x]	Diagnostic tests	[x]
Oral exams	[x]	Learning centers	[x]
Take home exams	[ ]	Proofreaders	[ ]
Exams on tape or computer	[ ]	Readers	[x]
Untimed exams	[ ]	Reading Machines/Kurzweil	[x]
Other accommodations	[x]	Special bookstore section	[ ]
		Typists	[ ]

Credit toward degree is not given for remedial courses taken.

Counseling Services

- [x] Academic
- [x] Psychological
- [x] Student Support groups
- [x] Vocational

Tutoring

Individual tutoring is available daily.

	Individual	Group
Time management	[x]	[x]
Organizational skills	[x]	[x]
Learning strategies	[x]	[x]
Study skills	[x]	[x]
Content area	[ ]	[ ]
Writing lab	[x]	[ ]
Math lab	[x]	[ ]

UNIQUE LD PROGRAM FEATURES

Meetings with learning specialists are available for a fee. The fee varies depending on the size and frequency of the meetings.

LD PROGRAM STAFF

Total number of LD Program staff (including director):

Full Time: 20 Part Time: 20

There is an advisor/advocate from the LD program available to students.

Key staff person available to work with LD students: Lisa Fraser, Program Coordinator, Learning Support Services.

LD Program web site: www.rit.edu/~369www/lss.php3

Russell Sage College

Troy, NY

Address: 45 Ferry Street, Troy, NY, 12180-4115
Admissions telephone: 888 837-9724
Admissions FAX: 518 244-6880
Vice President for Enrollment Management: Kathy Rusch
Admissions e-mail: rscadm@sage.edu
Web site: http://www.sage.edu
SAT Code: 2764 ACT Code: 2876

Disabilities Coordinator: Katherine Norman
LD program telephone: 518 244-6874
LD program e-mail: normak@sage.edu
LD program enrollment: 15, Total campus enrollment: 837

GENERAL

Russell Sage College is a private, women's, four-year institution. 14-acre campus in Troy (population: 49,170), 10 miles from both Albany and Schenectady; branch campus in Albany. Airport and bus serve Albany; train serves Rensselaer (12 miles). School operates transportation to Albany campus. Public transportation serves campus. Semester system.

LD ADMISSIONS

Students do not complete a separate application and are not simultaneously accepted to the LD program. A member of the LD program does not sit on the admissions committee. A personal interview is recommended. Essay is required and may be typed.

For fall 2004, 6 completed self-identified LD applications were received. 6 applications were offered admission, and 6 enrolled.

SECONDARY SCHOOL REQUIREMENTS

Graduation from secondary school required; GED accepted. The following course distribution required: 4 units of English, 3 units of math, 3 units of science, 2 units of foreign language, 4 units of social studies.

TESTING

SAT Reasoning or ACT required. SAT Subject recommended.

All enrolled freshmen (fall 2004):

Average SAT I Scores: Verbal: 520 Math: 516
Average ACT Scores: Composite: 23

Child Study Team report is not required. A neuropsychological or comprehensive psycho-educational evaluation is required for admission. Tests required as part of this documentation:

- ■ WAIS-IV
- ■ WISC-IV
- ☐ SATA
- ■ Woodcock-Johnson
- ☐ Nelson-Denny Reading Test
- ☐ Other

UNDERGRADUATE STUDENT BODY

Total undergraduate student enrollment: 797 Women.

Composition of student body (fall 2004):

	Undergraduate	Freshmen
International	0.8	0.4
Black	5.1	4.5
American Indian	0.0	0.0
Asian-American	1.4	1.9
Hispanic	2.9	3.0
White	68.1	76.6
Unreported	21.7	13.6
	100.0%	100.0%

11% are from out of state. Average age of full-time undergraduates is 22.

STUDENT HOUSING

78% of freshmen live in college housing. Freshmen are required to live on campus. Housing is guaranteed for all undergraduates. Campus can house 502 undergraduates. Single rooms are available for students with medical or special needs. A medical note is required.

EXPENSES

Tuition (2005-06): $22,650 per year.
Room: $3,500. Board: $3,890.

There is no additional cost for LD program/services.

LD SERVICES

LD program size is not limited.

LD services available to:

■ Freshmen ■ Sophomores ■ Juniors ■ Seniors

Academic Accommodations

Curriculum		**In class**	
Foreign language waiver	☐	Early syllabus	☐
Lighter course load	■	Note takers in class	■
Math waiver	☐	Priority seating	☐
Other special classes	☐	Tape recorders	■
Priority registrations	☐	Videotaped classes	☐
Substitution of courses	☐	Text on tape	■
Exams		**Services**	
Extended time	■	Diagnostic tests	☐
Oral exams	■	Learning centers	■
Take home exams	☐	Proofreaders	☐
Exams on tape or computer	■	Readers	■
Untimed exams	■	Reading Machines/Kurzweil	☐
Other accommodations	■	Special bookstore section	☐
		Typists	☐

Credit toward degree is not given for remedial courses taken.

Counseling Services

■ Academic	Meets 4 times per academic year
■ Psychological	Meets 12 times per academic year
■ Student Support groups	Meets 10 times per academic year
■ Vocational	Meets 4 times per academic year

Tutoring

Individual tutoring is available weekly.

Average size of tutoring groups: 4

	Individual	Group
Time management	■	■
Organizational skills	■	■
Learning strategies	■	■
Study skills	■	■
Content area	■	■
Writing lab	■	■
Math lab	■	■

LD PROGRAM STAFF

Total number of LD Program staff (including director):

Full Time: 3 Part Time: 3

There is an advisor/advocate from the LD program available to students. The advisor/advocate meets with faculty 4 times per month and students 2 times per month. 2 graduate students and 2 peer tutors are available to work with LD students.

Key staff person available to work with LD students: Katherine Norman, Disabilities Coordinator.

Sage College of Albany

Albany, NY

Address: 140 New Scotland Avenue, Albany, NY, 12208
Admissions telephone: 888 VERYSAGE
Admissions FAX: 518 292-1912
Associate Director of Admissions: Amanda Lanoue
Admissions e-mail: scaadm@sage.edu
Web site: http://www.sage.edu
SAT Code: 2343

LD program name: Learning Success Program
Coordinator: Katherine Norman
LD program telephone: 518 292-8624
LD program e-mail: normak@sage.edu
Total campus enrollment: 1,271

GENERAL

Sage College of Albany is a private, coed, four-year institution. 15-acre campus in Albany (population: 95,658); branch campus in Troy. Served by air and bus; train serves Rensselaer (10 miles). School operates transportation between Albany and Troy campuses. Public transportation serves campus. Semester system.

LD ADMISSIONS

Students do not complete a separate application and are not simultaneously accepted to the LD program. A member of the LD program does not sit on the admissions committee.

SECONDARY SCHOOL REQUIREMENTS

Graduation from secondary school required; GED accepted. The following course distribution required: 4 units of English, 2 units of math, 2 units of science, 2 units of foreign language, 4 units of social studies.

TESTING

SAT Reasoning or ACT required.

Child Study Team report is not required. A neuropsychological or comprehensive psycho-education evaluation is not required for admission. Tests required as part of this documentation:

- ❑ WAIS-IV
- ❑ WISC-IV
- ❑ SATA
- ❑ Woodcock-Johnson
- ❑ Nelson-Denny Reading Test
- ❑ Other

UNDERGRADUATE STUDENT BODY

Total undergraduate student enrollment: 367 Men, 904 Women.

Composition of student body (fall 2004):

	Undergraduate	Freshmen
International	0.0	0.4
Black	8.2	11.7
American Indian	0.1	0.4
Asian-American	1.1	1.3
Hispanic	6.3	2.9
White	73.1	65.6
Unreported	11.2	17.7
	100.0%	100.0%

2% are from out of state. Average age of full-time undergraduates is 21.

STUDENT HOUSING

46% of freshmen live in college housing. Single rooms are not available for students with medical or special needs.

EXPENSES

Tuition 2002-03: $13,750 per year.

Room: $3,150. Board: $3,376.

There are additional costs for LD program/services.

LD SERVICES

LD services available to:

❑ Freshmen ❑ Sophomores ❑ Juniors ❑ Seniors

Academic Accommodations

Curriculum
- Foreign language waiver ❑
- Lighter course load ❑
- Math waiver ❑
- Other special classes ❑
- Priority registrations ❑
- Substitution of courses ❑

Exams
- Extended time ❑
- Oral exams ❑
- Take home exams ❑
- Exams on tape or computer ❑
- Untimed exams ❑
- Other accommodations ❑

In class
- Early syllabus ❑
- Note takers in class ❑
- Priority seating ❑
- Tape recorders ❑
- Videotaped classes ❑
- Text on tape ❑

Services
- Diagnostic tests ❑
- Learning centers ❑
- Proofreaders ❑
- Readers ❑
- Reading Machines/Kurzweil ❑
- Special bookstore section ❑
- Typists ❑

Counseling Services

- ❑ Academic
- ❑ Psychological
- ❑ Student Support groups
- ❑ Vocational

Tutoring

Individual tutoring is not available.

	Individual	Group
Time management	❑	❑
Organizational skills	❑	❑
Learning strategies	❑	❑
Study skills	❑	❑
Content area	❑	❑
Writing lab	❑	❑
Math lab	❑	❑

LD PROGRAM STAFF

There is no advisor/advocate from the LD program available to students.

Sarah Lawrence College

Bronxville, NY

Address: 1 Mead Way, Bronxville, NY, 10708-5999
Admissions telephone: 800 888-2858
Admissions FAX: 914 395-2515
Dean of Enrollment: Thyra L. Briggs
Admissions e-mail: slcadmit@sarahlawrence.edu
Web site: http://www.sarahlawrence.edu
SAT Code: 2810   ACT Code: 2904

Associate Dean of Studies: Beverly Fox
LD program telephone: 914 395-2251
LD program e-mail: bfox@sarahlawrence.edu
Total campus enrollment: 1,260

GENERAL

Sarah Lawrence College is a private, coed, four-year institution. 41-acre, suburban campus in Bronxville (population: 5,843), 15 miles from New York City. Major airport, bus, and train serve New York City; smaller airport serves White Plains (10 miles). Public transportation serves campus. Semester system.

LD ADMISSIONS

A personal interview is recommended. Essay is required and may be typed.

SECONDARY SCHOOL REQUIREMENTS

Graduation from secondary school not required. The following course distribution required: 4 units of English, 2 units of math, 2 units of science, 2 units of foreign language, 2 units of history.

TESTING

All enrolled freshmen (fall 2004):

Average SAT I Scores:	Verbal: 660	Math: 600
Average ACT Scores:	Composite: 27	

Child Study Team report is not required. Tests required as part of this documentation:

- ☐ WAIS-IV
- ☐ WISC-IV
- ☐ SATA
- ☐ Woodcock-Johnson
- ☐ Nelson-Denny Reading Test
- ☐ Other

UNDERGRADUATE STUDENT BODY

Total undergraduate student enrollment: 326 Men, 888 Women.

Composition of student body (fall 2004):

	Undergraduate	Freshmen
International	1.2	1.8
Black	3.6	4.7
American Indian	0.6	0.7
Asian-American	5.2	4.4
Hispanic	4.3	3.0
White	77.5	77.1
Unreported	7.6	8.3
	100.0%	100.0%

78% are from out of state. Average age of full-time undergraduates is 20. 93% of classes have fewer than 20 students, 6% have between 20 and 50 students, 1% have more than 50 students.

STUDENT HOUSING

98% of freshmen live in college housing. Freshmen are required to live on campus. Housing is guaranteed for all undergraduates. Campus can house 984 undergraduates. Single rooms are available for students with medical or special needs. A medical note is required.

EXPENSES

Tuition (2005-06): $33,270 per year.
Room: $7,600. Board: $3,864.
There is no additional cost for LD program/services.

LD SERVICES

LD program size is not limited.

LD services available to:

☐ Freshmen ☐ Sophomores ☐ Juniors ☐ Seniors

Academic Accommodations

Curriculum		In class	
Foreign language waiver	☐	Early syllabus	☐
Lighter course load	☐	Note takers in class	■
Math waiver	☐	Priority seating	☐
Other special classes	☐	Tape recorders	■
Priority registrations	☐	Videotaped classes	☐
Substitution of courses	☐	Text on tape	■
Exams		**Services**	
Extended time	■	Diagnostic tests	☐
Oral exams	☐	Learning centers	☐
Take home exams	☐	Proofreaders	☐
Exams on tape or computer	☐	Readers	■
Untimed exams	☐	Reading Machines/Kurzweil	☐
Other accommodations	☐	Special bookstore section	☐
		Typists	☐

Credit toward degree is not given for remedial courses taken.

Counseling Services

- ☐ Academic
- ☐ Psychological
- ☐ Student Support groups
- ☐ Vocational

Tutoring

Individual tutoring is not available.

	Individual	Group
Time management	☐	☐
Organizational skills	☐	☐
Learning strategies	☐	☐
Study skills	☐	☐
Content area	☐	☐
Writing lab	☐	☐
Math lab	☐	☐

LD PROGRAM STAFF

Key staff person available to work with LD students: Beverly Fox, Associate Dean of Studies.

Siena College

Loudonville, NY

Address: 515 Loudon Road, Loudonville, NY, 12211
Admissions telephone: 888 AT-SIENA
Admissions FAX: 518 783-2436
Director of Admissions: Edward Jones
Admissions e-mail: admit@siena.edu
Web site: http://www.siena.edu
SAT Code: 2814 ACT Code: 2878

Director: Juliet Pellegrini
LD program telephone: 518 783-4239
LD program e-mail: jpellegrini@siena.edu
LD program enrollment: 96, Total campus enrollment: 3,338

GENERAL

Siena College is a private, coed, four-year institution. 155-acre, suburban campus in Loudonville (population: 11,000), two miles from Albany and 150 miles from New York City. Airport and bus serve Albany; train serves Rensselaer (10 miles). Public transportation serves campus. Semester system.

LD ADMISSIONS

Application Deadline: 03/01. Students do not complete a separate application and are not simultaneously accepted to the LD program. A member of the LD program does not sit on the admissions committee. A personal interview is recommended. Essay is required and may be typed.

SECONDARY SCHOOL REQUIREMENTS

Graduation from secondary school required; GED accepted. The following course distribution required: 4 units of English, 3 units of math, 3 units of science, 1 unit of social studies, 2 units of history.

TESTING

SAT Reasoning or ACT required. SAT Subject required.

All enrolled freshmen (fall 2004):

Average SAT I Scores:	Verbal: 554	Math: 569
Average ACT Scores:	Composite: 25	

Child Study Team report is not required. A neuropsychological or comprehensive psycho-educational evaluation is required for admission. Must be dated within 36 months of application. Tests required as part of this documentation:

- [x] WAIS-IV
- [x] WISC-IV
- [x] SATA
- [x] Woodcock-Johnson
- [x] Nelson-Denny Reading Test
- [x] Other

UNDERGRADUATE STUDENT BODY

Total undergraduate student enrollment: 1,564 Men, 1,815 Women.

Composition of student body (fall 2004):

	Undergraduate	Freshmen
International	0.4	0.4
Black	2.2	2.1
American Indian	0.1	0.2
Asian-American	4.1	2.8
Hispanic	2.5	3.2
White	86.2	87.5
Unreported	4.5	3.8
	100.0%	100.0%

15% are from out of state. Average age of full-time undergraduates is 20. 40% of classes have fewer than 20 students, 60% have between 20 and 50 students.

STUDENT HOUSING

93% of freshmen live in college housing. Freshmen are not required to live on campus. Housing is available to all students on a space available basis. Campus can house 2,355 undergraduates. Single rooms are available for students with medical or special needs. A medical note is required.

EXPENSES

Tuition (2005-06): $20,100 per year.

Room: $4,985. Board: $3,000.

There is no additional cost for LD program/services.

LD SERVICES

LD program size is not limited.

LD services available to:

- [x] Freshmen
- [x] Sophomores
- [x] Juniors
- [x] Seniors

Academic Accommodations

Curriculum		In class	
Foreign language waiver	[ ]	Early syllabus	[ ]
Lighter course load	[ ]	Note takers in class	[x]
Math waiver	[ ]	Priority seating	[ ]
Other special classes	[ ]	Tape recorders	[x]
Priority registrations	[x]	Videotaped classes	[ ]
Substitution of courses	[ ]	Text on tape	[x]
Exams		**Services**	
Extended time	[x]	Diagnostic tests	[ ]
Oral exams	[x]	Learning centers	[ ]
Take home exams	[ ]	Proofreaders	[x]
Exams on tape or computer	[x]	Readers	[x]
Untimed exams	[ ]	Reading Machines/Kurzweil	[x]
Other accommodations	[x]	Special bookstore section	[ ]
		Typists	[x]

Credit toward degree is not given for remedial courses taken.

Counseling Services

- [x] Academic
- [x] Psychological
- [ ] Student Support groups
- [ ] Vocational

Tutoring

Individual tutoring is available weekly.

Average size of tutoring groups: 5

	Individual	Group
Time management	[ ]	[ ]
Organizational skills	[ ]	[ ]
Learning strategies	[ ]	[ ]
Study skills	[ ]	[ ]
Content area	[ ]	[ ]
Writing lab	[x]	[ ]
Math lab	[ ]	[ ]

LD PROGRAM STAFF

Total number of LD Program staff (including director):

Full Time: 1 Part Time: 1

There is an advisor/advocate from the LD program available to students.

Key staff person available to work with LD students: Juliet Pellegrini, Director of Services for Students w/ Disabilities.

LD Program web site: www.siena.edu/studentaffairs/disabilities

Skidmore College

Saratoga Springs, NY

Address: 815 North Broadway, Saratoga Springs, NY, 12866
Admissions telephone: 800 867-6007
Admissions FAX: 518 580-5584
Director of Admissions: Mary Lou W. Bates
Admissions e-mail: admissions@skidmore.edu
Web site: http://www.skidmore.edu
SAT Code: 2815 ACT Code: 2906

Disabilities Specialist: Dr. Cynthia Guile
LD program telephone: 518 580-5727
LD program e-mail: cguile@skidmore.edu
Total campus enrollment: 2,637

GENERAL

Skidmore College is a private, coed, four-year institution. 888-acre campus in Saratoga Springs (population: 26,186), 30 miles from Albany. Served by bus and train; airport serves Albany. School operates transportation to various locations in town. Semester system.

LD ADMISSIONS

A personal interview is recommended. Essay is required and may be typed.

SECONDARY SCHOOL REQUIREMENTS

Graduation from secondary school required; GED accepted.

TESTING

SAT Reasoning or ACT required. SAT Subject recommended.

All enrolled freshmen (fall 2004):

Average SAT I Scores: Verbal: 626 Math: 624
Average ACT Scores: Composite: 27

Child Study Team report is not required. Tests required as part of this documentation:

- ☐ WAIS-IV
- ☐ WISC-IV
- ☐ SATA
- ☐ Woodcock-Johnson
- ☐ Nelson-Denny Reading Test
- ☐ Other

UNDERGRADUATE STUDENT BODY

Total undergraduate student enrollment: 999 Men, 1,489 Women.

Composition of student body (fall 2004):

	Undergraduate	Freshmen
International	0.7	1.4
Black	3.1	2.6
American Indian	0.5	0.6
Asian-American	5.3	5.3
Hispanic	3.8	3.5
White	72.5	72.6
Unreported	14.1	14.0
	100.0%	100.0%

71% are from out of state. Average age of full-time undergraduates is 20. 70% of classes have fewer than 20 students, 28% have between 20 and 50 students, 2% have more than 50 students.

STUDENT HOUSING

100% of freshmen live in college housing. Freshmen are required to live on campus. Housing is guaranteed for all undergraduates. Campus can house 1,713 undergraduates.

EXPENSES

Tuition (2005-06): $32,340 per year.
Room & Board: $9,120.

There is no additional cost for LD program/services.

LD SERVICES

LD program size is not limited.

LD services available to:

■ Freshmen ■ Sophomores ■ Juniors ■ Seniors

Academic Accommodations

Curriculum		**In class**	
Foreign language waiver	☐	Early syllabus	☐
Lighter course load	☐	Note takers in class	☐
Math waiver	☐	Priority seating	☐
Other special classes	☐	Tape recorders	☐
Priority registrations	☐	Videotaped classes	☐
Substitution of courses	☐	Text on tape	☐
Exams		**Services**	
Extended time	■	Diagnostic tests	☐
Oral exams	☐	Learning centers	☐
Take home exams	☐	Proofreaders	☐
Exams on tape or computer	☐	Readers	☐
Untimed exams	☐	Reading Machines/Kurzweil	☐
Other accommodations	☐	Special bookstore section	☐
		Typists	☐

Credit toward degree is not given for remedial courses taken.

Counseling Services

- ☐ Academic
- ☐ Psychological
- ☐ Student Support groups
- ☐ Vocational

Tutoring

	Individual	Group
Time management	☐	☐
Organizational skills	☐	☐
Learning strategies	☐	☐
Study skills	☐	☐
Content area	☐	☐
Writing lab	☐	☐
Math lab	☐	☐

LD PROGRAM STAFF

Total number of LD Program staff (including director):

Full Time: 1 Part Time: 1

Key staff person available to work with LD students: Dr. Cynthia Guile, Disabilities Specialist.

St. Bonaventure University

St. Bonaventure, NY

Address: Route 417, St. Bonaventure, NY, 14778
Admissions telephone: 800 462-5050
Admissions FAX: 716 375-4005
Director of Admissions: James M. DiRisio
Admissions e-mail: admissions@sbu.edu
Web site: http://www.sbu.edu
SAT Code: 2793 ACT Code: 2882

Teaching and Learning Center: Nancy Matthews
LD program e-mail: nmatthew@sbu.edu
Total campus enrollment: 2,218

GENERAL

St. Bonaventure University is a private, coed, four-year institution. 600-acre campus in Olean (population: 15,347), 75 miles from Buffalo. Major airport and train serve Buffalo; smaller airport serves Bradford, Pa. (20 miles). School operates transportation to local community, fitness center, and other off-campus locations. Semester system.

LD ADMISSIONS

A personal interview is recommended. Essay is not required.

SECONDARY SCHOOL REQUIREMENTS

Graduation from secondary school required; GED accepted. The following course distribution required: 4 units of English, 3 units of math, 3 units of science, 2 units of foreign language, 4 units of social studies.

TESTING

SAT Reasoning or ACT required. SAT Subject required.

All enrolled freshmen (fall 2004):

Average SAT I Scores:	Verbal: 524	Math: 535
Average ACT Scores:	Composite: 22	

Child Study Team report is not required. Tests required as part of this documentation:

- ☐ WAIS-IV
- ☐ WISC-IV
- ☐ SATA
- ☐ Woodcock-Johnson
- ☐ Nelson-Denny Reading Test
- ☐ Other

UNDERGRADUATE STUDENT BODY

Total undergraduate student enrollment: 1,010 Men, 1,154 Women.

22% are from out of state. 56% of classes have fewer than 20 students, 44% have between 20 and 50 students.

STUDENT HOUSING

Housing is guaranteed for all undergraduates. Campus can house 1,775 undergraduates.

EXPENSES

Tuition (2005-06): $20,610 per year.
Room & Board: $7,335.
There is no additional cost for LD program/services.

LD SERVICES

LD program size is not limited.

LD services available to:

☐ Freshmen ☐ Sophomores ☐ Juniors ☐ Seniors

Academic Accommodations

Curriculum
- Foreign language waiver ☐
- Lighter course load ☐
- Math waiver ☐
- Other special classes ☐
- Priority registrations ☐
- Substitution of courses ☐

Exams
- Extended time ☑
- Oral exams ☐
- Take home exams ☐
- Exams on tape or computer ☐
- Untimed exams ☑
- Other accommodations ☐

In class
- Early syllabus ☐
- Note takers in class ☑
- Priority seating ☐
- Tape recorders ☑
- Videotaped classes ☐
- Text on tape ☐

Services
- Diagnostic tests ☐
- Learning centers ☑
- Proofreaders ☐
- Readers ☑
- Reading Machines/Kurzweil ☐
- Special bookstore section ☐
- Typists ☐

Credit toward degree is not given for remedial courses taken.

Counseling Services

- ☐ Academic
- ☐ Psychological
- ☐ Student Support groups
- ☐ Vocational

Tutoring

	Individual	Group
Time management	☐	☐
Organizational skills	☐	☐
Learning strategies	☐	☐
Study skills	☐	☐
Content area	☐	☐
Writing lab	☐	☐
Math lab	☐	☐

LD PROGRAM STAFF

Key staff person available to work with LD students: Nancy Matthews, Teaching and Learning Center.

St. Francis College

Brooklyn Heights, NY

Address: 180 Remsen Street, Brooklyn Heights, NY, 11201
Admissions telephone: 718 489-5200
Admissions FAX: 718 802-0453
Dean of Admissions: Brother George Larkin, OSF
Admissions e-mail: admissions@stfranciscollege.edu
Web site: http://www.stfranciscollege.edu
SAT Code: 2796 ACT Code: 2882

LD program name: Office of Student Affairs
Dean of Student Affairs: Dr. James C. Adams
LD program telephone: 718 489-5314
LD program e-mail: jadams@stfranciscollege.edu
LD program enrollment: 19, Total campus enrollment: 2,526

GENERAL

St. Francis College is a private, coed, four-year institution. Urban campus in Brooklyn Heights (New York City population: 8,008,278). Served by air, bus, and train. Public transportation serves campus. Semester system.

LD ADMISSIONS

Students do not complete a separate application and are not simultaneously accepted to the LD program. A member of the LD program does not sit on the admissions committee. High school waivers are accepted for math and foreign language. A personal interview is recommended. Essay is required and may be typed.

SECONDARY SCHOOL REQUIREMENTS

Graduation from secondary school required; GED accepted. The following course distribution required: 4 units of English, 2 units of math, 2 units of science, 2 units of foreign language, 4 units of social studies, 2 units of academic electives.

TESTING

SAT Reasoning required. SAT Subject required.

All enrolled freshmen (fall 2004):

Average SAT I Scores: Verbal: 461 Math: 465

Child Study Team report is not required. A neuropsychological or comprehensive psycho-education evaluation is not required for admission. Tests required as part of this documentation:

- ☐ WAIS-IV
- ☐ WISC-IV
- ☐ SATA
- ☐ Woodcock-Johnson
- ☐ Nelson-Denny Reading Test
- ☐ Other

UNDERGRADUATE STUDENT BODY

Total undergraduate student enrollment: 937 Men, 1,399 Women.

Composition of student body (fall 2004):

	Undergraduate	Freshmen
International	5.9	11.1
Black	18.0	19.5
American Indian	0.0	0.1
Asian-American	1.5	2.2
Hispanic	18.0	15.7
White	47.7	46.5
Unreported	8.9	4.9
	100.0%	100.0%

1% are from out of state. 1% join a fraternity and 1% join a sorority. Average age of full-time undergraduates is 21. 45% of classes have fewer than 20 students, 54% have between 20 and 50 students, 1% have more than 50 students.

STUDENT HOUSING

Single rooms are not available for students with medical or special needs.

EXPENSES

Tuition (2005-06): $12,450 per year.
There is no additional cost for LD program/services.

LD SERVICES

LD program size is not limited.

LD services available to:

☑ Freshmen ☑ Sophomores ☑ Juniors ☑ Seniors

Academic Accommodations

Curriculum		In class	
Foreign language waiver	☐	Early syllabus	☐
Lighter course load	☑	Note takers in class	☑
Math waiver	☐	Priority seating	☐
Other special classes	☐	Tape recorders	☐
Priority registrations	☐	Videotaped classes	☐
Substitution of courses	☐	Text on tape	☐
Exams		**Services**	
Extended time	☐	Diagnostic tests	☐
Oral exams	☐	Learning centers	☐
Take home exams	☐	Proofreaders	☐
Exams on tape or computer	☐	Readers	☑
Untimed exams	☐	Reading Machines/Kurzweil	☐
Other accommodations	☐	Special bookstore section	☐
		Typists	☐

Credit toward degree is not given for remedial courses taken.

Counseling Services

- ☐ Academic
- ☐ Psychological
- ☐ Student Support groups
- ☐ Vocational

Tutoring

Individual tutoring is available daily.

	Individual	Group
Time management	☐	☑
Organizational skills	☐	☑
Learning strategies	☐	☑
Study skills	☐	☑
Content area	☑	☐
Writing lab	☑	☐
Math lab	☑	☐

LD PROGRAM STAFF

There is no advisor/advocate from the LD program available to students.

Key staff person available to work with LD students: Mitchell Levenberg, Director of Academic Enhancement Center.

St. John Fisher College

Rochester, NY

Address: 3690 East Avenue, Rochester, NY, 14618
Admissions telephone: 800 444-4640
Admissions FAX: 585 385-8386
Vice President of Enrollment Management: Stacy Ledermann
Admissions e-mail: admissions@sjfc.edu
Web site: http://www.sjfc.edu
SAT Code: 2798 ACT Code: 2886

Coordinator of Disability Services: Christine Hogan
LD program telephone: 585 385-8034
LD program e-mail: chogan@sjfc.edu
LD program enrollment: 85, Total campus enrollment: 2,605

GENERAL

St. John Fisher College is a private, coed, four-year institution. 139-acre, suburban campus in Rochester (population: 219,773), 12 miles from downtown. Served by air, bus, and train. Public transportation serves campus. Semester system.

LD ADMISSIONS

Students do not complete a separate application and are not simultaneously accepted to the LD program. A member of the LD program does not sit on the admissions committee. A personal interview is recommended. Essay is required and may be typed.

SECONDARY SCHOOL REQUIREMENTS

Graduation from secondary school required; GED accepted.

TESTING

SAT Reasoning or ACT required. SAT Subject recommended.

All enrolled freshmen (fall 2004):

Average SAT I Scores:	Verbal: 520	Math: 533
Average ACT Scores:	Composite: 22	

Child Study Team report is not required. A neuropsychological or comprehensive psycho-educational evaluation is required for admission. Must be dated within 36 months of application. Tests required as part of this documentation:

- [x] WAIS-IV
- [ ] WISC-IV
- [x] SATA
- [x] Woodcock-Johnson
- [ ] Nelson-Denny Reading Test
- [ ] Other

UNDERGRADUATE STUDENT BODY

Total undergraduate student enrollment: 947 Men, 1,403 Women.

Composition of student body (fall 2004):

	Undergraduate	Freshmen
International	0.6	0.2
Black	2.8	4.1
American Indian	0.4	0.5
Asian-American	1.3	1.7
Hispanic	3.2	3.0
White	86.8	86.5
Unreported	4.9	4.0
	100.0%	100.0%

3% are from out of state. Average age of full-time undergraduates is 21. 41% of classes have fewer than 20 students, 58% have between 20 and 50 students, 1% have more than 50 students.

STUDENT HOUSING

90% of freshmen live in college housing. Freshmen are not required to live on campus. Housing is guaranteed only for three years, to students who participate in the housing process. Campus can house 1,400 undergraduates. Single rooms are available for students with medical or special needs. A medical note is required.

EXPENSES

Tuition (2005-06): $19,300 per year.

Room: $5,400. Board: $2,900.
There is no additional cost for LD program/services.

LD SERVICES

LD program size is not limited.

LD services available to:

- [x] Freshmen
- [x] Sophomores
- [x] Juniors
- [x] Seniors

Academic Accommodations

Curriculum

- [ ] Foreign language waiver
- [x] Lighter course load
- [ ] Math waiver
- [ ] Other special classes
- [ ] Priority registrations
- [ ] Substitution of courses

Exams

- [x] Extended time
- [ ] Oral exams
- [ ] Take home exams
- [ ] Exams on tape or computer
- [ ] Untimed exams
- [ ] Other accommodations

In class

- [ ] Early syllabus
- [x] Note takers in class
- [ ] Priority seating
- [x] Tape recorders
- [ ] Videotaped classes
- [x] Text on tape

Services

- [ ] Diagnostic tests
- [ ] Learning centers
- [ ] Proofreaders
- [x] Readers
- [ ] Reading Machines/Kurzweil
- [ ] Special bookstore section
- [x] Typists

Credit toward degree is not given for remedial courses taken.

Counseling Services

- [x] Academic
- [x] Psychological
- [ ] Student Support groups
- [x] Vocational

Tutoring

Individual tutoring is available weekly.

Average size of tutoring groups: 1

	Individual	Group
Time management	[ ]	[ ]
Organizational skills	[ ]	[ ]
Learning strategies	[ ]	[ ]
Study skills	[x]	[ ]
Content area	[ ]	[ ]
Writing lab	[x]	[ ]
Math lab	[x]	[ ]

LD PROGRAM STAFF

Total number of LD Program staff (including director):

Full Time: 1 Part Time: 1

There is an advisor/advocate from the LD program available to students.

Key staff person available to work with LD students: Christine Hogan, Coordinator of Disability Services.

St. John's University

Queens, NY

Address: 8000 Utopia Parkway, Queens, NY, 11439
Admissions telephone: 888 978-5646
Admissions FAX: 718 990-5728
Director, Office of Admissions: Matthew Whelan
Admissions e-mail: admissions@stjohns.edu
Web site: http://new.stjohns.edu/
SAT Code: 2799 ACT Code: 2888

LD program name: Student Life
Director of Student Service: Jackie Lochrie
LD program telephone: 718 990-6568
LD program e-mail: lochriej@stjohns.edu
LD program enrollment: 36, Total campus enrollment: 14,848

GENERAL

St. John's University is a private, coed, four-year institution. 96-acre campus in Jamaica section of Queens (New York City population: 8,008,278); branch campuses in Manhattan, Oakdale, and Staten Island and abroad in Rome, Italy (graduate center). Served by air, bus, and train. School operates transportation between campuses. Semester system.

LD ADMISSIONS

A member of the LD program does not sit on the admissions committee. High school waivers are accepted for foreign language. A personal interview is not required. Essay is required and may be typed.

SECONDARY SCHOOL REQUIREMENTS

Graduation from secondary school required; GED accepted. The following course distribution required: 4 units of English.

TESTING

SAT Reasoning or ACT required. SAT Subject recommended.

All enrolled freshmen (fall 2004):

Average SAT I Scores: Verbal: 516 Math: 535

Child Study Team report is not required. A neuropsychological or comprehensive psycho-education evaluation is not required for admission. Tests required as part of this documentation:

- [x] WAIS-IV
- [x] WISC-IV
- [ ] SATA
- [x] Woodcock-Johnson
- [ ] Nelson-Denny Reading Test
- [ ] Other

UNDERGRADUATE STUDENT BODY

Total undergraduate student enrollment: 6,165 Men, 8,320 Women.

Composition of student body (fall 2004):

	Undergraduate	Freshmen
International	2.5	3.3
Black	17.7	16.7
American Indian	0.1	0.2
Asian-American	17.5	15.4
Hispanic	14.6	15.1
White	37.2	41.4
Unreported	10.4	7.9
	100.0%	100.0%

7% are from out of state. 8% join a fraternity and 7% join a sorority. Average age of full-time undergraduates is 20. 36% of classes have fewer than 20 students, 54% have between 20 and 50 students, 10% have more than 50 students.

STUDENT HOUSING

39% of freshmen live in college housing. Freshmen are not required to live on campus. Housing is guaranteed for all undergraduates. Campus can house 2,235 undergraduates. Single rooms are available for students with medical or special needs. A medical note is required.

EXPENSES

Tuition (2005-06): $22,800 per year. $16,900 per year (first-year students). Tuition and fees vary by program and by year of study.

Room: $6,900. Board: $4,100.
There is no additional cost for LD program/services.

LD SERVICES

LD program size is not limited.

LD services available to:

- [x] Freshmen
- [x] Sophomores
- [x] Juniors
- [x] Seniors

Academic Accommodations

Curriculum

- [ ] Foreign language waiver
- [ ] Lighter course load
- [ ] Math waiver
- [ ] Other special classes
- [ ] Priority registrations
- [ ] Substitution of courses

Exams

- [x] Extended time
- [x] Oral exams
- [ ] Take home exams
- [ ] Exams on tape or computer
- [x] Untimed exams
- [ ] Other accommodations

In class

- [ ] Early syllabus
- [ ] Note takers in class
- [ ] Priority seating
- [x] Tape recorders
- [ ] Videotaped classes
- [ ] Text on tape

Services

- [x] Diagnostic tests
- [ ] Learning centers
- [ ] Proofreaders
- [x] Readers
- [ ] Reading Machines/Kurzweil
- [ ] Special bookstore section
- [x] Typists

Credit toward degree is not given for remedial courses taken.

Counseling Services

- [ ] Academic
- [ ] Psychological
- [ ] Student Support groups
- [ ] Vocational

Tutoring

Individual tutoring is available daily.

Average size of tutoring groups: 1

	Individual	Group
Time management	[ ]	[ ]
Organizational skills	[ ]	[ ]
Learning strategies	[ ]	[ ]
Study skills	[ ]	[ ]
Content area	[ ]	[ ]
Writing lab	[ ]	[ ]
Math lab	[ ]	[ ]

LD PROGRAM STAFF

Total number of LD Program staff (including director):

Full Time: 1 Part Time: 1

There is an advisor/advocate from the LD program available to students.

Key staff person available to work with LD students: Jackie Lochrie, Director of Student Service.

LD Program web site: www.stjohns.edu

St. Joseph's College (Brooklyn)

Brooklyn, NY

Address: 245 Clinton Avenue, Brooklyn, NY, 11205-3688
Admissions telephone: 718 636-6868
Admissions FAX: 718 636-8303
Director of Admissions: Theresa La Rocca Meyer
Admissions e-mail: brooklynas@sjcny.edu
Web site: http://www.sjcny.edu
SAT Code: 2802 ACT Code: 2890

Director: Anna Bess Robinson, Ed.D
LD program telephone: 631 447-3318
LD program e-mail: arobinson@sjcny.edu
LD program enrollment: 32, Total campus enrollment: 4,960

GENERAL

St. Joseph's College (Brooklyn) is a private, coed, four-year institution. Two-acre, urban campus in Brooklyn (New York City population: 8,008,278), two miles from Manhattan; branch campus in Patchogue on Long Island. Served by air, bus, and train. Public transportation serves campus. Semester system.

LD ADMISSIONS

A member of the LD program does not sit on the admissions committee. A personal interview is recommended. Essay is not required. Admissions requirements may be waived for LD students on an individual basis.

SECONDARY SCHOOL REQUIREMENTS

Graduation from secondary school required; GED accepted. The following course distribution required: 4 units of English, 3 units of math, 2 units of science, 2 units of foreign language, 4 units of social studies, 1 unit of history, 3 units of academic electives.

TESTING

SAT Reasoning required; ACT may be substituted. SAT Subject required.

All enrolled freshmen (fall 2004):

Average SAT I Scores:	Verbal: 513	Math: 527
Average ACT Scores:	Composite: 21	

Child Study Team report is required if student is classified. A neuropsychological or comprehensive psycho-education evaluation is not required for admission. Tests required as part of this documentation:

- ☐ WAIS-IV
- ☐ WISC-IV
- ☐ SATA
- ☐ Woodcock-Johnson
- ☐ Nelson-Denny Reading Test
- ☐ Other

UNDERGRADUATE STUDENT BODY

Total undergraduate student enrollment: 244 Men, 879 Women.

Composition of student body (fall 2004):

	Undergraduate	Freshmen
International	0.0	0.3
Black	7.4	12.0
American Indian	0.0	0.2
Asian-American	2.5	2.3
Hispanic	8.7	7.1
White	69.1	74.6
Unreported	12.3	3.5
	100.0%	100.0%

5% join a fraternity and 3% join a sorority. Average age of full-time undergraduates is 23. 60% of classes have fewer than 20 students, 40% have between 20 and 50 students.

STUDENT HOUSING

Freshmen are not required to live on campus. Housing is not guaranteed for all undergraduates. Single rooms are not available for students with medical or special needs.

EXPENSES

Tuition (2005-06): $12,424 per year.
There is no additional cost for LD program/services.

LD SERVICES

LD program size is not limited.

LD services available to:

☑ Freshmen ☑ Sophomores ☑ Juniors ☑ Seniors

Academic Accommodations

Curriculum		In class	
Foreign language waiver	☐	Early syllabus	☐
Lighter course load	☑	Note takers in class	☑
Math waiver	☐	Priority seating	☐
Other special classes	☐	Tape recorders	☐
Priority registrations	☐	Videotaped classes	☐
Substitution of courses	☐	Text on tape	☐
Exams		**Services**	
Extended time	☑	Diagnostic tests	☐
Oral exams	☐	Learning centers	☑
Take home exams	☐	Proofreaders	☐
Exams on tape or computer	☐	Readers	☐
Untimed exams	☑	Reading Machines/Kurzweil	☑
Other accommodations	☐	Special bookstore section	☐
		Typists	☐

Credit toward degree is not given for remedial courses taken.

Counseling Services

- ☑ Academic — Meets 2 times per academic year
- ☐ Psychological
- ☐ Student Support groups
- ☐ Vocational

Tutoring

Individual tutoring is available weekly.

Average size of tutoring groups: 1

	Individual	Group
Time management	☑	☐
Organizational skills	☑	☐
Learning strategies	☐	☐
Study skills	☑	☐
Content area	☐	☐
Writing lab	☑	☐
Math lab	☐	☐

LD PROGRAM STAFF

There is an advisor/advocate from the LD program available to students. The advisor/advocate meets with faculty once per month and students once per month. 5 peer tutors are available to work with LD students.

Key staff person available to work with LD students: Anna Bess Robinson, Ed.D, Director of Office of Counseling & Career Services.

St. Lawrence University

Canton, NY

Address: 23 Romoda Drive, Canton, NY, 13617
Admissions telephone: 800 285-1856
Admissions FAX: 315 229-5818
Dean of Admissions and Financial Aid: Teresa Cowdrey
Admissions e-mail: admissions@stlawu.edu
Web site: http://www.stlawu.edu
SAT Code: 2805 ACT Code: 2896

Director: John Meagher
LD program telephone: 315 229-5104
LD program e-mail: jmeagher@stlawu.edu
LD program enrollment: 226, Total campus enrollment: 2,133

GENERAL

St. Lawrence University is a private, coed, four-year institution. 1,000-acre campus in Canton (population: 10,334), 130 miles from Syracuse and 80 miles from Ottawa, Ontario, Canada. Served by bus; major airport serves Ottawa; smaller airport serves Ogdensburg (15 miles); train serves Syracuse. School operates transportation to airports and to Boston, MA, Buffalo, New York City, Rochester, and Syracuse during breaks. Semester system.

LD ADMISSIONS

Students do not complete a separate application and are not simultaneously accepted to the LD program. A member of the LD program does not sit on the admissions committee. High school waivers are accepted for foreign language. A personal interview is recommended. Essay is required and may be typed.

SECONDARY SCHOOL REQUIREMENTS

Graduation from secondary school required; GED accepted.

TESTING

SAT Subject recommended.

All enrolled freshmen (fall 2004):

Average SAT I Scores:	Verbal: 583	Math: 580
Average ACT Scores:	Composite: 25	

Child Study Team report is not required. A neuropsychological or comprehensive psycho-educational evaluation is required for admission. Must be dated within 36 months of application. Tests required as part of this documentation:

- ■ WAIS-IV
- ☐ WISC-IV
- ■ SATA
- ■ Woodcock-Johnson
- ■ Nelson-Denny Reading Test
- ■ Other

UNDERGRADUATE STUDENT BODY

Total undergraduate student enrollment: 928 Men, 1,042 Women.

Composition of student body (fall 2004):

	Undergraduate	Freshmen
International	3.2	3.8
Black	1.8	1.8
American Indian	0.9	0.5
Asian-American	2.1	1.5
Hispanic	2.7	2.7
White	74.0	69.3
Unreported	15.3	20.4
	100.0%	100.0%

46% are from out of state. 12% join a fraternity and 21% join a sorority. Average age of full-time undergraduates is 20. 65% of classes have fewer than 20 students, 34% have between 20 and 50 students, 1% have more than 50 students.

STUDENT HOUSING

100% of freshmen live in college housing. Freshmen are required to live on campus. Housing is guaranteed for all undergraduates. Campus can house 1,929 undergraduates. Single rooms are available for students with medical or special needs. A medical note is required.

EXPENSES

Tuition (2005-06): $31,395 per year.
Room: $4,400. Board: $3,780.
There is no additional cost for LD program/services.

LD SERVICES

LD program size is not limited.

LD services available to:

■ Freshmen ■ Sophomores ■ Juniors ■ Seniors

Academic Accommodations

Curriculum		**In class**	
Foreign language waiver	☐	Early syllabus	☐
Lighter course load	■	Note takers in class	■
Math waiver	☐	Priority seating	■
Other special classes	☐	Tape recorders	■
Priority registrations	■	Videotaped classes	☐
Substitution of courses	☐	Text on tape	■
Exams		**Services**	
Extended time	■	Diagnostic tests	☐
Oral exams	☐	Learning centers	☐
Take home exams	☐	Proofreaders	☐
Exams on tape or computer	■	Readers	■
Untimed exams	■	Reading Machines/Kurzweil	■
Other accommodations	■	Special bookstore section	☐
		Typists	■

Credit toward degree is not given for remedial courses taken.

Counseling Services

- ■ Academic — Meets 2 times per academic year
- ☐ Psychological
- ☐ Student Support groups
- ☐ Vocational

Tutoring

Individual tutoring is available weekly.

Average size of tutoring groups: 1

	Individual	Group
Time management	■	☐
Organizational skills	■	☐
Learning strategies	☐	☐
Study skills	■	☐
Content area	■	☐
Writing lab	■	☐
Math lab	☐	☐

UNIQUE LD PROGRAM FEATURES

St. Lawrence grants "reasonable accommodations" to documented disabled students. Such accommodations, which are the student's responsibility to request, are granted as needed on an individual basis, and are arranged by the student and professor upon consultation with the Director of the Office of Academic Services for Students with Special Needs. Anyone who has a disability is provided counsel on the facilities, equipment, and accommodations available at St. Lawrence.

LD PROGRAM STAFF

Total number of LD Program staff (including director):

Full Time: 1 Part Time: 1

There is an advisor/advocate from the LD program available to students. The advisor/advocate meets with faculty 2 times per month. 65 peer tutors are available to work with LD students.

Key staff person available to work with LD students: John Meagher, Director Academic Services, Students with Special Needs.

LD Program web site: http://stlawu.edu/needs/index.html

St. Thomas Aquinas College

Sparkill, NY

Address: 125 Route 340, Sparkill, NY, 10976
Admissions telephone: 800 999-STAC
Admissions FAX: 845 398-4224
Dean of Enrollment Management: Tracey Howard-Ubelhoer
Admissions e-mail: admissions@stac.edu
Web site: http://www.stac.edu
SAT Code: 2807 ACT Code: 2897

Director of Pathways: Dr. Richard F. Heath
LD program telephone: 845 398-4230
LD program e-mail: rheath@stac.edu
Total campus enrollment: 2,120

GENERAL

St. Thomas Aquinas College is a private, coed, four-year institution. 43-acre, suburban campus in Sparkill (population: 10,000), 16 miles from New York City; branch campus in West Point; additional off-campus centers throughout Rockland County. Major airports serve Newark, N.J. (30 miles) and New York City; bus serves White Plains (10 miles). Public transportation serves campus. Semester system.

LD ADMISSIONS

A personal interview is required. Essay is required and may be typed.

SECONDARY SCHOOL REQUIREMENTS

Graduation from secondary school required; GED accepted. The following course distribution required: 4 units of English, 3 units of math, 3 units of science, 3 units of foreign language, 4 units of social studies, 1 unit of history.

TESTING

SAT Reasoning required; ACT may be substituted. SAT Subject recommended.

All enrolled freshmen (fall 2004):

Average SAT I Scores:	Verbal: 467	Math: 469
Average ACT Scores:	Composite: 18	

Child Study Team report is required if student is classified. Tests required as part of this documentation:

- ☐ WAIS-IV
- ☐ WISC-IV
- ☐ SATA
- ☐ Woodcock-Johnson
- ☐ Nelson-Denny Reading Test
- ☐ Other

UNDERGRADUATE STUDENT BODY

Total undergraduate student enrollment: 2,120.

Composition of student body (fall 2004):

	Undergraduate	Freshmen
International	1.4	1.7
Black	8.0	4.7
American Indian	0.0	0.0
Asian-American	2.0	4.3
Hispanic	18.5	15.7
White	64.4	67.1
Unreported	5.7	6.5
	100.0%	100.0%

40% are from out of state. Average age of full-time undergraduates is 21. 50% of classes have fewer than 20 students, 49% have between 20 and 50 students, 1% have more than 50 students.

STUDENT HOUSING

58% of freshmen live in college housing. Freshmen are not required to live on campus. Housing is guaranteed for all undergraduates. Campus can house 611 undergraduates.

EXPENSES

Tuition (2005-06): $16,200 per year.
Room: $4,780. Board: $4,070.
Additional cost for LD program/services: $3,400 per year.

LD SERVICES

LD program size is limited.

LD services available to:

☐ Freshmen ☐ Sophomores ☐ Juniors ☐ Seniors

Academic Accommodations

Curriculum		In class	
Foreign language waiver	☐	Early syllabus	☐
Lighter course load	☐	Note takers in class	■
Math waiver	☐	Priority seating	☐
Other special classes	■	Tape recorders	■
Priority registrations	☐	Videotaped classes	☐
Substitution of courses	☐	Text on tape	☐
Exams		**Services**	
Extended time	■	Diagnostic tests	■
Oral exams	■	Learning centers	■
Take home exams	☐	Proofreaders	☐
Exams on tape or computer	☐	Readers	☐
Untimed exams	■	Reading Machines/Kurzweil	☐
Other accommodations	☐	Special bookstore section	☐
		Typists	☐

Credit toward degree is not given for remedial courses taken.

Counseling Services

- ☐ Academic
- ☐ Psychological
- ☐ Student Support groups
- ☐ Vocational

Tutoring

	Individual	Group
Time management	☐	☐
Organizational skills	☐	☐
Learning strategies	☐	☐
Study skills	☐	☐
Content area	☐	☐
Writing lab	☐	☐
Math lab	☐	☐

UNIQUE LD PROGRAM FEATURES

Pathways, formerly known as the STAC Exchange, is a structured support program for bright college students with learning disabilities or attention deficit disorders. The student meets with a professional mentor assigned to him or her for regularly scheduled, individual sessions that are tailored to meet specific student needs. Sessions are designed to assist students in compensating for their learning deficits, demonstrating their academic potential, and developing effective learning strategies. Mentors attempt to encourage active learning and inspire confidence in the student's own abilities. Extra mentoring sessions are available and encouraged; study groups are also offered. Incoming Pathways freshmen are also required to attend a four-day summer program prior to their first semester.

LD PROGRAM STAFF

Total number of LD Program staff (including director):

Full Time: 4 Part Time: 4

Key staff person available to work with LD students: Dr. Richard F. Heath, Director of Pathways, Professor of Psychology.

State University of New York at Albany

Albany, NY

Address: 1400 Washington Avenue, Albany, NY, 12222
Admissions telephone: 800 293-7869
Admissions FAX: 518 442-5383
Director of Admissions: Robert Andrea
Admissions e-mail: ugadmissions@albany.edu
Web site: http://www.albany.edu
SAT Code: 2532 ACT Code: 2926

Learning Disabilities Specialist: Carolyn Malloch
LD program telephone: 518 442-5490
LD program e-mail: cmalloch@uamail.albany.edu
LD program enrollment: 201, Total campus enrollment: 11,388

GENERAL

State University of New York at Albany is a public, coed, four-year institution. 560-acre, suburban campus in Albany (population: 95,658), 180 miles from New York City. Served by air and bus; train serves Rensselaer (10 miles); major airport serves New York City. School operates transportation to city center and downtown dormitories. Public transportation serves campus. Semester system.

LD ADMISSIONS

Students do not complete a separate application and are not simultaneously accepted to the LD program. A member of the LD program does not sit on the admissions committee. High school waivers are accepted for math and foreign language. A personal interview is not required. Essay is not required. Students may request special admission status or may be considered for special admission if they appear to have a talent in a particular area.

For fall 2004, 470 completed self-identified LD applications were received. 320 applications were offered admission, and 50 enrolled.

SECONDARY SCHOOL REQUIREMENTS

Graduation from secondary school required; GED accepted. The following course distribution required: 4 units of English, 2 units of math, 2 units of science, 1 unit of foreign language, 3 units of social studies, 2 units of history, 5 units of academic electives.

TESTING

SAT Reasoning required; ACT may be substituted. SAT Subject required.

Child Study Team report is not required. A neuropsychological or comprehensive psycho-educational evaluation is required for admission. Must be dated within 36 months of application. Tests required as part of this documentation:

- [x] WAIS-IV
- [x] WISC-IV
- [x] SATA
- [x] Woodcock-Johnson
- [x] Nelson-Denny Reading Test
- [x] Other

UNDERGRADUATE STUDENT BODY

Total undergraduate student enrollment: 5,943 Men, 5,941 Women.

Composition of student body (fall 2004):

	Undergraduate	Freshmen
International	1.3	1.9
Black	8.0	8.2
American Indian	0.2	0.3
Asian-American	6.9	6.1
Hispanic	8.5	7.4
White	59.3	61.6
Unreported	15.8	14.5
	100.0%	100.0%

4% are from out of state. 2% join a fraternity and 5% join a sorority. Average age of full-time undergraduates is 21. 26% of classes have fewer than 20 students, 51% have between 20 and 50 students, 23% have more than 50 students.

STUDENT HOUSING

98% of freshmen live in college housing. Freshmen are required to live on campus. Upperclassmen who apply for fall semester on-campus housing after March 21 will be assigned rooms based on availability. Campus can house 7,200 undergraduates. Single rooms are available for students with medical or special needs. A medical note is required.

EXPENSES

Tuition (2005-06): $4,350 per year (in-state), $10,610 (out-of-state).
Room: $4,834. Board: $3,216.
There is no additional cost for LD program/services.

LD SERVICES

LD program size is not limited.

LD services available to:

- [x] Freshmen
- [x] Sophomores
- [x] Juniors
- [x] Seniors

Academic Accommodations

Curriculum
- [ ] Foreign language waiver
- [ ] Lighter course load
- [ ] Math waiver
- [ ] Other special classes
- [ ] Priority registrations
- [ ] Substitution of courses

Exams
- [ ] Extended time
- [ ] Oral exams
- [ ] Take home exams
- [ ] Exams on tape or computer
- [ ] Untimed exams
- [ ] Other accommodations

In class
- [ ] Early syllabus
- [ ] Note takers in class
- [ ] Priority seating
- [ ] Tape recorders
- [ ] Videotaped classes
- [ ] Text on tape

Services
- [ ] Diagnostic tests
- [ ] Learning centers
- [ ] Proofreaders
- [ ] Readers
- [ ] Reading Machines/Kurzweil
- [ ] Special bookstore section
- [ ] Typists

Credit toward degree is not given for remedial courses taken.

Counseling Services

- [ ] Academic
- [ ] Psychological
- [ ] Student Support groups
- [ ] Vocational

Tutoring

Individual tutoring is available.

	Individual	Group
Time management	[x]	[ ]
Organizational skills	[x]	[ ]
Learning strategies	[x]	[ ]
Study skills	[x]	[ ]
Content area	[ ]	[ ]
Writing lab	[ ]	[ ]
Math lab	[ ]	[ ]

LD PROGRAM STAFF

Total number of LD Program staff (including director):

Full Time: 1 Part Time: 1

There is an advisor/advocate from the LD program available to students.

Key staff person available to work with LD students: Carolyn Malloch, Learning Disabilities Specialist.

State University of New York at Binghamton

Binghamton, NY

Address: P.O. Box 6000, Binghamton, NY, 13902-6000
Admissions telephone: 607 777-2171
Admissions FAX: 607 777-4445
Director of Admissions: Cheryl Brown
Admissions e-mail: admit@binghamton.edu
Web site: http://www.binghamton.edu
SAT Code: 2535 ACT Code: 2956

LD program name: Services for Students with Disabilities
Director: B. Jean Fairbairn
LD program telephone: 607 777-2686
LD program e-mail: bjfairba@binghamton.edu
LD program enrollment: 63, Total campus enrollment: 11,034

GENERAL

State University of New York at Binghamton is a public, coed, four-year institution. 828-acre campus in Binghamton (population: 47,380), 70 miles from Syracuse. Served by bus; major airport serves Syracuse; smaller airport serves Broome County (seven miles). School operates transportation to local towns. Public transportation serves campus. Semester system.

LD ADMISSIONS

Students do not complete a separate application and are not simultaneously accepted to the LD program. A member of the LD program does not sit on the admissions committee. A personal interview is recommended. Essay is required and may be typed. Admissions requirements are not generally waived. The foreign language general education requirement may be met before admission or at the university. Students with disabilities may request accommodations. Students with language-based difficulties may also petition the University Undergraduate Curriculum Committee for possible course modifications or substitutions of the general education foreign language requirement. Such petitions are reviewed judiciously with the goal of assisting students to meet all general education requirements, including the foreign language requirement, whenever possible.

SECONDARY SCHOOL REQUIREMENTS

Graduation from secondary school required; GED accepted. The following course distribution required: 4 units of English, 3 units of math, 2 units of science, 3 units of foreign language, 2 units of social studies.

TESTING

SAT Reasoning or ACT required. SAT Subject recommended.

All enrolled freshmen (fall 2004):

Average SAT I Scores:	Verbal: 607	Math: 643
Average ACT Scores:	Composite: 26	

Child Study Team report is not required. A neuropsychological or comprehensive psycho-educational evaluation is required for admission. Tests required as part of this documentation:

- [x] WAIS-IV
- [ ] WISC-IV
- [ ] SATA
- [x] Woodcock-Johnson
- [ ] Nelson-Denny Reading Test
- [ ] Other

UNDERGRADUATE STUDENT BODY

Total undergraduate student enrollment: 4,703 Men, 5,464 Women.

Composition of student body (fall 2004):

	Undergraduate	Freshmen
International	3.6	4.0
Black	5.0	4.7
American Indian	0.2	0.2
Asian-American	18.9	16.5
Hispanic	7.1	5.8
White	56.2	52.3
Unreported	9.0	16.5
	100.0%	100.0%

4% are from out of state. 8% join a fraternity and 7% join a sorority. Average age of full-time undergraduates is 20. 40% of classes have fewer than 20 students, 44% have between 20 and 50 students, 16% have more than 50 students.

STUDENT HOUSING

96% of freshmen live in college housing. Freshmen are required to live on campus. Returning students are not guaranteed housing. Campus can house 6,493 undergraduates. Single rooms are available for students with medical or special needs. A medical note is required.

EXPENSES

Tuition (2005-06): $4,350 per year (in-state), $10,610 (out-of-state).
Room: $4,970. Board: $3,182.
There is no additional cost for LD program/services.

LD SERVICES

LD program size is not limited.

LD services available to:

- [x] Freshmen
- [x] Sophomores
- [x] Juniors
- [x] Seniors

Academic Accommodations

Curriculum

- Foreign language waiver [ ]
- Lighter course load [x]
- Math waiver [ ]
- Other special classes [x]
- Priority registrations [ ]
- Substitution of courses [ ]

Exams

- Extended time [x]
- Oral exams [ ]
- Take home exams [ ]
- Exams on tape or computer [x]
- Untimed exams [ ]
- Other accommodations [x]

In class

- Early syllabus [ ]
- Note takers in class [x]
- Priority seating [ ]
- Tape recorders [x]
- Videotaped classes [ ]
- Text on tape [x]

Services

- Diagnostic tests [ ]
- Learning centers [ ]
- Proofreaders [ ]
- Readers [x]
- Reading Machines/Kurzweil [x]
- Special bookstore section [ ]
- Typists [ ]

Credit toward degree is not given for remedial courses taken.

Counseling Services

- [x] Academic — Meets 2 times per academic year
- [x] Psychological — Meets 2 times per academic year
- [ ] Student Support groups
- [ ] Vocational

Tutoring

Individual tutoring is available.

	Individual	Group
Time management	[x]	[ ]
Organizational skills	[x]	[ ]
Learning strategies	[x]	[ ]
Study skills	[x]	[ ]
Content area	[ ]	[ ]
Writing lab	[ ]	[ ]
Math lab	[ ]	[ ]

UNIQUE LD PROGRAM FEATURES

Please see our services for students with disabilities web site at ssd.binghamton.edu

LD PROGRAM STAFF

Total number of LD Program staff (including director):

Full Time: 3 Part Time: 3

There is an advisor/advocate from the LD program available to students.

Key staff person available to work with LD students: Bethany Beecher, Learning Disabilities Specialist.

State University of New York at Buffalo

Buffalo, NY

Address: 3435 Main Street, Buffalo, NY, 14214
Admissions telephone: 800 UB-ADMIT
Admissions FAX: 716 645-6411
Director of Admissions: Patricia Armstrong
Admissions e-mail: ub-admissions@buffalo.edu
Web site: http://www.buffalo.edu
SAT Code: 2925 ACT Code: 2978

LD program name: Office of Disability Services
LD program address: 25 Capen Hall,
Buffalo, NY, 14260-1632
Assistant to the Director: Linda Amabile
LD program telephone: 716 645-2608
LD program enrollment: 156, Total campus enrollment: 17,838

GENERAL

State University of New York at Buffalo is a public, coed, four-year institution. 1,350-acre, urban campus in Buffalo (population: 292,648). Served by air, bus, and train. School operates transportation between north and south campuses. Public transportation serves campus. Semester system.

LD ADMISSIONS

Students do not complete a separate application and are not simultaneously accepted to the LD program. A member of the LD program does not sit on the admissions committee. A personal interview is not required. Essay is not required.

For fall 2004, 334 completed self-identified LD applications were received. 137 applications were offered admission, and 53 enrolled.

SECONDARY SCHOOL REQUIREMENTS

Graduation from secondary school required; GED accepted.

TESTING

SAT Reasoning or ACT required. SAT Subject required.

All enrolled freshmen (fall 2004):

Average SAT I Scores:	Verbal: 556	Math: 584
Average ACT Scores:	Composite: 24	

Child Study Team report is not required. A neuropsychological or comprehensive psycho-educational evaluation is required for admission. Tests required as part of this documentation:

- [ ] WAIS-IV
- [ ] WISC-IV
- [ ] SATA
- [ ] Woodcock-Johnson
- [ ] Nelson-Denny Reading Test
- [ ] Other

UNDERGRADUATE STUDENT BODY

Total undergraduate student enrollment: 9,371 Men, 7,919 Women.

Composition of student body (fall 2004):

	Undergraduate	Freshmen
International	4.6	6.2
Black	6.4	7.0
American Indian	0.4	0.4
Asian-American	7.9	8.6
Hispanic	4.4	3.6
White	67.8	65.0
Unreported	8.5	9.2
	100.0%	100.0%

3% are from out of state. 2% join a fraternity and 1% join a sorority. Average age of full-time undergraduates is 21. 37% of classes have fewer than 20 students, 43% have between 20 and 50 students, 20% have more than 50 students.

STUDENT HOUSING

73% of freshmen live in college housing. Freshmen are not required to live on campus. Housing is guaranteed for all undergraduates. Campus can house 6,673 undergraduates. Single rooms are available for students with medical or special needs. A medical note is required.

EXPENSES

Tuition (2005-06): $4,350 per year (in-state), $11,610 (out-of-state).
Room: $4,336. Board: $2,890.
There is no additional cost for LD program/services.

LD SERVICES

LD program size is not limited.

LD services available to:

[x] Freshmen [x] Sophomores [x] Juniors [x] Seniors

Academic Accommodations

Curriculum		In class	
Foreign language waiver	[ ]	Early syllabus	[ ]
Lighter course load	[x]	Note takers in class	[x]
Math waiver	[ ]	Priority seating	[ ]
Other special classes	[x]	Tape recorders	[x]
Priority registrations	[ ]	Videotaped classes	[ ]
Substitution of courses	[x]	Text on tape	[x]
Exams		**Services**	
Extended time	[x]	Diagnostic tests	[ ]
Oral exams	[x]	Learning centers	[x]
Take home exams	[ ]	Proofreaders	[ ]
Exams on tape or computer	[ ]	Readers	[x]
Untimed exams	[ ]	Reading Machines/Kurzweil	[x]
Other accommodations	[ ]	Special bookstore section	[ ]
		Typists	[ ]

Credit toward degree is given for remedial courses taken.

Counseling Services

- [x] Academic
- [x] Psychological
- [ ] Student Support groups
- [x] Vocational

Tutoring

Individual tutoring is not available.

	Individual	Group
Time management	[x]	[ ]
Organizational skills	[x]	[ ]
Learning strategies	[ ]	[ ]
Study skills	[x]	[ ]
Content area	[ ]	[ ]
Writing lab	[x]	[ ]
Math lab	[x]	[ ]

UNIQUE LD PROGRAM FEATURES

Documentation of a thorough clinical assessment and a professional diagnosis of the disability are required by the Office of Disability Services to qualify for the specialized services and accommodations available to learning disabled students.

LD PROGRAM STAFF

Total number of LD Program staff (including director):

Full Time: 1 Part Time: 1

There is an advisor/advocate from the LD program available to students.

Key staff person available to work with LD students: Randall Borst, Director of Disability Services.

LD Program web site: http://www.student-affairs.buffalo.edu/ods/

State University of New York at Buffalo State College

Buffalo, NY

Address: 1300 Elmwood Avenue, Buffalo, NY, 14222
Admissions telephone: 716 878-4017
Admissions FAX: 716 878-6100
Director of Admissions: Lesa Loritts
Admissions e-mail: admissio@buffalostate.edu
Web site: http://www.buffalostate.edu
SAT Code: 2533 ACT Code: 2930

Coordinator: Marianne Savino
LD program telephone: 716 878-4500
LD program e-mail: savinomr@buffalostate.edu
LD program enrollment: 370, Total campus enrollment: 9,008

GENERAL

State University of New York Buffalo State College is a public, coed, four-year institution. 115-acre, urban campus in Buffalo (population: 292,648). Served by air, bus, and train. Public transportation serves campus. Semester system.

LD ADMISSIONS

Students do not complete a separate application and are simultaneously accepted to the LD program. A member of the LD program does not sit on the admissions committee. A personal interview is not required. Essay is not required. Admissions visit is not required, but a meeting with our office of Disabilities Services is recommended.

SECONDARY SCHOOL REQUIREMENTS

Graduation from secondary school required; GED accepted. The following course distribution required: 2 units of math, 2 units of science.

TESTING

SAT Subject recommended.

All enrolled freshmen (fall 2004):

Average SAT I Scores: Verbal: 499 Math: 504

Child Study Team report is not required. A neuropsychological or comprehensive psycho-educational evaluation is required for admission. Tests required as part of this documentation:

- ■ WAIS-IV
- ■ WISC-IV
- ■ SATA
- ■ Woodcock-Johnson
- ■ Nelson-Denny Reading Test
- ☐ Other

UNDERGRADUATE STUDENT BODY

Total undergraduate student enrollment: 3,866 Men, 5,724 Women.

Composition of student body (fall 2004):

	Undergraduate	Freshmen
International	0.3	0.5
Black	13.9	11.3
American Indian	0.3	0.5
Asian-American	2.5	1.7
Hispanic	4.7	3.6
White	66.1	69.9
Unreported	12.2	12.5
	100.0%	100.0%

1% are from out of state. 1% join a fraternity and 1% join a sorority. Average age of full-time undergraduates is 22. 39% of classes have fewer than 20 students, 51% have between 20 and 50 students, 10% have more than 50 students.

STUDENT HOUSING

49% of freshmen live in college housing. Freshmen are required to live on campus. Housing is guaranteed for all undergraduates. Campus can house 1,776 undergraduates.

EXPENSES

Tuition (2005-06): $4,350 per year (in-state), $10,610 (out-of-state). Room: $3,920. Board: $2,280.
There is no additional cost for LD program/services.

LD SERVICES

LD program size is not limited.

LD services available to:

☐ Freshmen ☐ Sophomores ☐ Juniors ☐ Seniors

Academic Accommodations

Curriculum		**In class**	
Foreign language waiver	☐	Early syllabus	☐
Lighter course load	☐	Note takers in class	■
Math waiver	☐	Priority seating	☐
Other special classes	☐	Tape recorders	■
Priority registrations	☐	Videotaped classes	☐
Substitution of courses	☐	Text on tape	☐
Exams		**Services**	
Extended time	■	Diagnostic tests	☐
Oral exams	■	Learning centers	■
Take home exams	☐	Proofreaders	☐
Exams on tape or computer	☐	Readers	■
Untimed exams	☐	Reading Machines/Kurzweil	■
Other accommodations	☐	Special bookstore section	☐
		Typists	☐

Credit toward degree is not given for remedial courses taken.

Counseling Services

- ☐ Academic
- ☐ Psychological
- ☐ Student Support groups
- ☐ Vocational

Tutoring

	Individual	Group
Time management	☐	☐
Organizational skills	☐	☐
Learning strategies	☐	☐
Study skills	☐	☐
Content area	☐	☐
Writing lab	☐	☐
Math lab	☐	☐

LD PROGRAM STAFF

Total number of LD Program staff (including director):

Full Time: 3 Part Time: 3

Key staff person available to work with LD students: Marianne Savino, Coordinator.

State University of New York at Empire State College

Saratoga Springs, NY

Address: One Union Avenue, Saratoga Springs, NY, 12866
Admissions telephone: 518 587-2100
Admissions FAX: 518 580-0105
Assistant Director of Admissions: Jennifer Riley
Admissions e-mail: admissions@esc.edu
Web site: http://www.esc.edu
SAT Code: 2214

Coordinator: Kelly Hermann
LD program telephone: 518 587-2100, extension 544
LD program e-mail: kelly.hermann@esc.edu
Total campus enrollment: 9,327

GENERAL

State University of New York Empire State College is a public, coed, four-year institution. Coordinating center in Saratoga Springs (population: 26,186), 40 miles from Albany; branch campuses in more than 45 locations throughout New York. Airport serves Albany.

LD ADMISSIONS

A personal interview is not required. Essay is required and may be typed.

SECONDARY SCHOOL REQUIREMENTS

Graduation from secondary school not required.

TESTING

Child Study Team report is not required. Tests required as part of this documentation:

- ❑ WAIS-IV
- ❑ WISC-IV
- ❑ SATA
- ❑ Woodcock-Johnson
- ❑ Nelson-Denny Reading Test
- ❑ Other

UNDERGRADUATE STUDENT BODY

Total undergraduate student enrollment: 3,621 Men, 4,439 Women.

Composition of student body (fall 2004):

	Undergraduate	Freshmen
International	28.3	6.3
Black	9.9	12.3
American Indian	0.4	0.4
Asian-American	0.3	1.2
Hispanic	6.9	6.5
White	48.5	66.1
Unreported	5.7	7.2
	100.0%	100.0%

2% are from out of state. Average age of full-time undergraduates is 35.

EXPENSES

Tuition (2005-06): $4,350 per year (in-state), $10,610 (out-of-state).

There is no additional cost for LD program/services.

LD SERVICES

LD program size is not limited.

LD services available to:

■ Freshmen ■ Sophomores ■ Juniors ■ Seniors

Academic Accommodations

Curriculum		**In class**	
Foreign language waiver	❑	Early syllabus	❑
Lighter course load	❑	Note takers in class	❑
Math waiver	❑	Priority seating	❑
Other special classes	❑	Tape recorders	❑
Priority registrations	❑	Videotaped classes	❑
Substitution of courses	❑	Text on tape	❑
Exams		**Services**	
Extended time	❑	Diagnostic tests	❑
Oral exams	❑	Learning centers	❑
Take home exams	❑	Proofreaders	❑
Exams on tape or computer	❑	Readers	❑
Untimed exams	❑	Reading Machines/Kurzweil	❑
Other accommodations	❑	Special bookstore section	❑
		Typists	❑

Counseling Services

- ❑ Academic
- ❑ Psychological
- ❑ Student Support groups
- ❑ Vocational

Tutoring

	Individual	Group
Time management	❑	❑
Organizational skills	❑	❑
Learning strategies	❑	❑
Study skills	❑	❑
Content area	❑	❑
Writing lab	❑	❑
Math lab	❑	❑

UNIQUE LD PROGRAM FEATURES

Empire State College's educational services are provided statewide through more than 40 locations. Students with disabling conditions who wish to request accommodation are encouraged to discuss their needs with the Center Director. Reasonable accommodations can be arranged directly through the college's regional center or unit location without the need for formal request through the ADA Coordinator at the Saratoga Springs Coordinating Center. When reasonable accommodation is arranged informally, the Center Director should notify the ADA Coordinator about the accommodation.

If the desired accommodation cannot be arranged informally, the Center Director should notify the ADA Coordinator and inform the student about the procedure for formal request of accommodation.

LD PROGRAM STAFF

There is an advisor/advocate from the LD program available to students.

State University of New York at Farmingdale

Farmingdale, NY

Address: 2350 Broadhollow Road, Farmingdale, NY, 11735-1021
Admissions telephone: 631 420-2200
Admissions FAX: 631 420-2633
Assistant Dean for Enrollment Services: Jim Hall
Admissions e-mail: admissions@farmingdale.edu
Web site: http://www.farmingdale.edu
SAT Code: 2526 ACT Code: 2918

Director of Support Services: Malka Edelman
LD program telephone: 631 420-2411
LD program e-mail: malka.edelman@farmingdale.edu
Total campus enrollment: 6,250

GENERAL

State University of New York at Farmingdale is a public, coed, four-year institution. 380-acre campus in Farmingdale (population: 8,399), 35 miles from New York City. Served by train; major airport serves New York City; smaller airport serves Islip (10 miles); bus serves Huntington (two miles). Public transportation serves campus. Semester system.

LD ADMISSIONS

Students do not complete a separate application and are not simultaneously accepted to the LD program. A member of the LD program does not sit on the admissions committee. A personal interview is required.

SECONDARY SCHOOL REQUIREMENTS

Graduation from secondary school required; GED accepted. The following course distribution required: 3 units of English, 2 units of math, 1 unit of science.

TESTING

SAT Reasoning or ACT required. SAT Subject required.

All enrolled freshmen (fall 2004):

Average SAT I Scores: Verbal: 467 Math: 498

Child Study Team report is not required. Tests required as part of this documentation:

- ☐ WAIS-IV
- ☐ WISC-IV
- ☐ SATA
- ☐ Woodcock-Johnson
- ☐ Nelson-Denny Reading Test
- ☐ Other

UNDERGRADUATE STUDENT BODY

Total undergraduate student enrollment: 6,250.

Composition of student body (fall 2004):

	Undergraduate	Freshmen
International	0.4	0.6
Black	12.6	12.2
American Indian	0.4	0.3
Asian-American	4.8	5.4
Hispanic	10.1	9.3
White	56.1	56.2
Unreported	15.6	16.0
	100.0%	100.0%

Average age of full-time undergraduates is 22. 32% of classes have fewer than 20 students, 66% have between 20 and 50 students, 2% have more than 50 students.

STUDENT HOUSING

8% of freshmen live in college housing. Freshmen are not required to live on campus. Housing is guaranteed for all undergraduates. Campus can house 500 undergraduates. Single rooms are not available for students with medical or special needs.

EXPENSES

Tuition (2005-06): $4,350 per year (in-state), $10,610 (out-of-state). There is no additional cost for LD program/services.

LD SERVICES

LD program size is not limited.

LD services available to:

☑ Freshmen ☑ Sophomores ☑ Juniors ☑ Seniors

Academic Accommodations

Curriculum		In class	
Foreign language waiver	☐	Early syllabus	☐
Lighter course load	☐	Note takers in class	☐
Math waiver	☐	Priority seating	☐
Other special classes	☐	Tape recorders	☑
Priority registrations	☐	Videotaped classes	☐
Substitution of courses	☐	Text on tape	☐
Exams		**Services**	
Extended time	☑	Diagnostic tests	☑
Oral exams	☐	Learning centers	☑
Take home exams	☐	Proofreaders	☐
Exams on tape or computer	☐	Readers	☑
Untimed exams	☑	Reading Machines/Kurzweil	☑
Other accommodations	☐	Special bookstore section	☐
		Typists	☐

Credit toward degree is not given for remedial courses taken.

Counseling Services

- ☑ Academic
- ☑ Psychological
- ☐ Student Support groups
- ☐ Vocational

Tutoring

Individual tutoring is not available.

	Individual	Group
Time management	☐	☐
Organizational skills	☐	☐
Learning strategies	☐	☐
Study skills	☐	☐
Content area	☐	☐
Writing lab	☐	☐
Math lab	☐	☐

LD PROGRAM STAFF

Total number of LD Program staff (including director):

Full Time: 1 Part Time: 1

Key staff person available to work with LD students: Malka Edelman, Director of Support Services.

State University of New York at New Paltz

New Paltz, NY

Address: 75 South Manheim Boulevard, Suite 9, New Paltz, NY, 12561-2443
Admissions telephone: 888 639-7589
Admissions FAX: 845 257-3209
Director of Freshmen and International Admission: L. David Eaton
Admissions e-mail: admissions@newpaltz.edu
Web site: http://www.newpaltz.edu
SAT Code: 2541 ACT Code: 2938

Director of Disabled Student Resource Center: Portia Lillo
LD program telephone: 845 257-3020
LD program e-mail: lillop@lan.newpaltz.edu
Total campus enrollment: 6,191

GENERAL

State University of New York New Paltz is a public, coed, four-year institution. 216-acre campus in New Paltz (population: 12,830), 65 miles from Albany. Served by bus; airport serves Newburgh (17 miles); train serves Poughkeepsie (15 miles). Public transportation serves campus. Semester system.

LD ADMISSIONS

A personal interview is not required. Essay is not required.

SECONDARY SCHOOL REQUIREMENTS

Graduation from secondary school required; GED accepted. The following course distribution required: 4 units of English, 3 units of math, 3 units of science, 2 units of foreign language, 3 units of social studies.

TESTING

SAT Reasoning required; ACT may be substituted. SAT Subject recommended.

All enrolled freshmen (fall 2004):

Average SAT I Scores: Verbal: 545 Math: 551

Child Study Team report is not required. Tests required as part of this documentation:

- ☐ WAIS-IV
- ☐ WISC-IV
- ☐ SATA
- ☐ Woodcock-Johnson
- ☐ Nelson-Denny Reading Test
- ☐ Other

UNDERGRADUATE STUDENT BODY

Total undergraduate student enrollment: 2,224 Men, 3,858 Women.

Composition of student body (fall 2004):

	Undergraduate	Freshmen
International	1.1	2.3
Black	7.3	7.3
American Indian	0.0	0.3
Asian-American	4.1	3.7
Hispanic	12.3	9.6
White	59.8	61.1
Unreported	15.4	15.7
	100.0%	100.0%

5% are from out of state. 3% join a fraternity and 2% join a sorority. Average age of full-time undergraduates is 20. 48% of classes have fewer than 20 students, 48% have between 20 and 50 students, 4% have more than 50 students.

STUDENT HOUSING

92% of freshmen live in college housing. Housing is not guaranteed for all undergraduates. Campus can house 2,749 undergraduates.

EXPENSES

Tuition (2005-06): $4,350 per year (in-state), $10,300 (out-of-state).

Room: $4,240. Board: $2,620.

There is no additional cost for LD program/services.

LD SERVICES

LD program size is not limited.

LD services available to:

☐ Freshmen ☐ Sophomores ☐ Juniors ☐ Seniors

Academic Accommodations

Curriculum		**In class**	
Foreign language waiver	☐	Early syllabus	☐
Lighter course load	■	Note takers in class	■
Math waiver	☐	Priority seating	☐
Other special classes	☐	Tape recorders	■
Priority registrations	☐	Videotaped classes	☐
Substitution of courses	☐	Text on tape	☐
Exams		**Services**	
Extended time	■	Diagnostic tests	☐
Oral exams	■	Learning centers	■
Take home exams	☐	Proofreaders	☐
Exams on tape or computer	☐	Readers	■
Untimed exams	☐	Reading Machines/Kurzweil	■
Other accommodations	☐	Special bookstore section	☐
		Typists	☐

Credit toward degree is not given for remedial courses taken.

Counseling Services

- ☐ Academic
- ☐ Psychological
- ☐ Student Support groups
- ☐ Vocational

Tutoring

	Individual	Group
Time management	☐	☐
Organizational skills	☐	☐
Learning strategies	☐	☐
Study skills	☐	☐
Content area	☐	☐
Writing lab	☐	☐
Math lab	☐	☐

LD PROGRAM STAFF

Total number of LD Program staff (including director):

Full Time: 2 Part Time: 2

Key staff person available to work with LD students: Porta Lillo, Director of Disability Resource Center.

State University of New York at Oswego

Oswego, NY

Address: 7060 State Route 104, Oswego, NY, 13126
Admissions telephone: 315 312-2250
Admissions FAX: 315 312-3260
Dean of Admissions: Joseph F. Grant
Admissions e-mail: admiss@oswego.edu
Web site: http://www.oswego.edu
SAT Code: 2543 ACT Code: 2942

Coordinator of Disability Services: Starr Knapp
LD program telephone: 315 312-3358
LD program e-mail: sknapp@oswego.edu
LD program enrollment: 459, Total campus enrollment: 7,059

GENERAL

State University of New York at Oswego is a public, coed, four-year institution. 696-acre campus in Oswego (population: 17,954), 35 miles from Syracuse; branch campus in Phoenix, NY. Served by bus; major airport and train serve Syracuse. School operates campus shuttle. Public transportation serves campus. Semester system.

LD ADMISSIONS

Students do not complete a separate application and are not simultaneously accepted to the LD program. A member of the LD program does not sit on the admissions committee. A personal interview is not required. Essay is not required.

SECONDARY SCHOOL REQUIREMENTS

Graduation from secondary school required; GED accepted. The following course distribution required: 4 units of English, 3 units of math, 3 units of science, 2 units of foreign language, 4 units of social studies.

TESTING

SAT Reasoning or ACT required. SAT Subject recommended.

All enrolled freshmen (fall 2004):

Average SAT I Scores:	Verbal: 543	Math: 546
Average ACT Scores:	Composite: 23	

Child Study Team report is not required. A neuropsychological or comprehensive psycho-education evaluation is not required for admission. Tests required as part of this documentation:

- ☐ WAIS-IV
- ☐ WISC-IV
- ☐ SATA
- ☐ Woodcock-Johnson
- ☐ Nelson-Denny Reading Test
- ☐ Other

UNDERGRADUATE STUDENT BODY

Total undergraduate student enrollment: 3,223 Men, 3,839 Women.

Composition of student body (fall 2004):

	Undergraduate	Freshmen
International	0.6	0.9
Black	5.6	3.9
American Indian	0.4	0.5
Asian-American	2.3	2.0
Hispanic	5.6	3.7
White	85.5	89.0
Unreported	0.0	0.0
	100.0%	100.0%

2% are from out of state. 7% join a fraternity and 6% join a sorority. Average age of full-time undergraduates is 21. 38% of classes have fewer than 20 students, 51% have between 20 and 50 students, 11% have more than 50 students.

STUDENT HOUSING

88% of freshmen live in college housing. Freshmen are required to live on campus. Housing is guaranteed for all undergraduates. Campus can house 3,772 undergraduates. Single rooms are available for students with medical or special needs. A medical note is required.

EXPENSES

Tuition (2005-06): $4,350 per year (in-state), $10,610 (out-of-state). Room: $3,200. Board: $5,090.

There is no additional cost for LD program/services.

LD SERVICES

LD program size is not limited.

LD services available to:

■ Freshmen ■ Sophomores ■ Juniors ■ Seniors

Academic Accommodations

Curriculum		In class	
Foreign language waiver	■	Early syllabus	☐
Lighter course load	■	Note takers in class	■
Math waiver	☐	Priority seating	■
Other special classes	☐	Tape recorders	■
Priority registrations	■	Videotaped classes	☐
Substitution of courses	■	Text on tape	■
Exams		**Services**	
Extended time	■	Diagnostic tests	☐
Oral exams	☐	Learning centers	☐
Take home exams	☐	Proofreaders	■
Exams on tape or computer	■	Readers	■
Untimed exams	☐	Reading Machines/Kurzweil	■
Other accommodations	■	Special bookstore section	☐
		Typists	■

Credit toward degree is not given for remedial courses taken.

Counseling Services

- ■ Academic
- ☐ Psychological
- ☐ Student Support groups
- ■ Vocational

Tutoring

Individual tutoring is available daily.

	Individual	Group
Time management	■	■
Organizational skills	■	■
Learning strategies	■	■
Study skills	■	☐
Content area	■	☐
Writing lab	■	☐
Math lab	■	☐

LD PROGRAM STAFF

Total number of LD Program staff (including director):

Full Time: 1 Part Time: 1

There is an advisor/advocate from the LD program available to students. 2 graduate students are available to work with LD students.

Key staff person available to work with LD students: Starr Knapp, Coordinator of Disability Services.

LD Program web site: www.oswego.edu/dis_svc/

State University of New York at Stony Brook

Stony Brook, NY

Address: Administration Building, Stony Brook, NY, 11794
Admissions telephone: 800 USB-SUNY
Admissions FAX: 631 632-9898
Dean of Admissions and Enrollment Services: Judith Burke-Berhannan
Admissions e-mail: enroll@stonybrook.edu
Web site: http://www.stonybrook.edu
SAT Code: 2548 ACT Code: 2952

LD program name: Disability Support Services
LD program contact: Donna Molloy
LD program telephone: 631 632-6748
Total campus enrollment: 13,858

GENERAL

State University of New York at Stony Brook is a public, coed, four-year institution. 1,100-acre campus in Stony Brook (population: 13,727) on Long Island, 60 miles from New York City. Served by bus and train; major airports serve New York City; smaller airport serves Islip (10 miles). School operates transportation to local shopping areas. Public transportation serves campus. Semester system.

LD ADMISSIONS

A personal interview is not required. Essay is not required.

SECONDARY SCHOOL REQUIREMENTS

Graduation from secondary school required; GED accepted. The following course distribution required: 4 units of English, 3 units of math, 3 units of science, 2 units of foreign language, 4 units of social studies.

TESTING

SAT Reasoning or ACT required. SAT Subject required.

All enrolled freshmen (fall 2004):

Average SAT I Scores: Verbal: 565 Math: 611

Child Study Team report is not required. Tests required as part of this documentation:

- ☐ WAIS-IV
- ☐ WISC-IV
- ☐ SATA
- ☐ Woodcock-Johnson
- ☐ Nelson-Denny Reading Test
- ☐ Other

UNDERGRADUATE STUDENT BODY

Total undergraduate student enrollment: 7,072 Men, 6,574 Women.

Composition of student body (fall 2004):

	Undergraduate	Freshmen
International	4.6	4.6
Black	8.5	9.7
American Indian	0.2	0.2
Asian-American	27.0	23.0
Hispanic	8.1	8.5
White	35.1	36.0
Unreported	16.5	18.0
	100.0%	100.0%

2% are from out of state. 1% join a fraternity and 1% join a sorority. Average age of full-time undergraduates is 21. 36% of classes have fewer than 20 students, 41% have between 20 and 50 students, 23% have more than 50 students.

STUDENT HOUSING

76% of freshmen live in college housing. Freshmen are not required to live on campus. Housing is guaranteed for all undergraduates. Students can live in campus housing for up to 8 semesters. Campus can house 6,358 undergraduates.

EXPENSES

Tuition (2005-06): $4,350 per year (in-state), $10,610 (out-of-state).

Room: $5,120. Board: $3,050.
There is no additional cost for LD program/services.

LD SERVICES

LD program size is not limited.

LD services available to:

■ Freshmen ■ Sophomores ■ Juniors ■ Seniors

Academic Accommodations

Curriculum		**In class**	
Foreign language waiver	☐	Early syllabus	☐
Lighter course load	☐	Note takers in class	■
Math waiver	☐	Priority seating	■
Other special classes	☐	Tape recorders	■
Priority registrations	■	Videotaped classes	☐
Substitution of courses	☐	Text on tape	■
Exams		**Services**	
Extended time	■	Diagnostic tests	☐
Oral exams	☐	Learning centers	☐
Take home exams	☐	Proofreaders	☐
Exams on tape or computer	☐	Readers	■
Untimed exams	☐	Reading Machines/Kurzweil	■
Other accommodations	■	Special bookstore section	☐
		Typists	■

Credit toward degree is not given for remedial courses taken.

Counseling Services

- ☐ Academic
- ☐ Psychological
- ☐ Student Support groups
- ☐ Vocational

Tutoring

Individual tutoring is not available.

	Individual	Group
Time management	☐	■
Organizational skills	☐	■
Learning strategies	☐	■
Study skills	☐	■
Content area	☐	☐
Writing lab	☐	☐
Math lab	☐	☐

LD PROGRAM STAFF

Total number of LD Program staff (including director):

Full Time: 3 Part Time: 3

There is an advisor/advocate from the LD program available to students.

Key staff person available to work with LD students: Donna Molloy, LD Specialist, Associate Director.

State University of New York at Upstate Medical University

Syracuse, NY

Address: 766 Irving Avenue, Syracuse, NY, 13210
Admissions telephone: 800 736-2171
Admissions FAX: 315 464-8867
Director of Admissions: Jennifer Welch
Admissions e-mail: admiss@upstate.edu
Web site: http://www.upstate.edu
SAT Code: 2547 ACT Code: 2981

LD program contact: Donald Midlam
LD program telephone: 315 464-8855
Total campus enrollment: 258

GENERAL

State University of New York Upstate Medical University is a public, coed, four-year institution. 30-acre, urban campus in Syracuse (population: 147,306). Served by air, bus, and train. School operates transportation to campus buildings and parking lots. Public transportation serves campus. Semester system.

LD ADMISSIONS

A personal interview is required. Essay is required and may be typed.

TESTING

SAT Reasoning or ACT considered if submitted.

Child Study Team report is not required. Tests required as part of this documentation:

- ☐ WAIS-IV
- ☐ WISC-IV
- ☐ SATA
- ☐ Woodcock-Johnson
- ☐ Nelson-Denny Reading Test
- ☐ Other

UNDERGRADUATE STUDENT BODY

Total undergraduate student enrollment: 44 Men, 171 Women.

Composition of student body (fall 2004):

	Freshmen
International	3.8
Black	3.3
American Indian	0.4
Asian-American	2.5
Hispanic	1.7
White	88.3
Unreported	0.0
	100.0%

2% are from out of state. Average age of full-time undergraduates is 29.

STUDENT HOUSING

Housing is guaranteed for all undergraduates. Campus can house 270 undergraduates.

EXPENSES

Tuition (2005-06): $4,850 per year (in-state), $11,110 (out-of-state).
Room: $5,280. Board: $2,720.
There is no additional cost for LD program/services.

LD SERVICES

LD program size is not limited.

LD services available to:

☐ Freshmen ☐ Sophomores ☒ Juniors ☒ Seniors

Academic Accommodations

Curriculum

- Foreign language waiver ☐
- Lighter course load ☒
- Math waiver ☐
- Other special classes ☐
- Priority registrations ☐
- Substitution of courses ☐

Exams

- Extended time ☒
- Oral exams ☐
- Take home exams ☐
- Exams on tape or computer ☐
- Untimed exams ☐
- Other accommodations ☐

In class

- Early syllabus ☐
- Note takers in class ☒
- Priority seating ☐
- Tape recorders ☒
- Videotaped classes ☐
- Text on tape ☐

Services

- Diagnostic tests ☐
- Learning centers ☐
- Proofreaders ☐
- Readers ☒
- Reading Machines/Kurzweil ☐
- Special bookstore section ☐
- Typists ☐

Counseling Services

- ☒ Academic
- ☒ Psychological
- ☐ Student Support groups
- ☐ Vocational

Tutoring

	Individual	Group
Time management	☐	☐
Organizational skills	☐	☐
Learning strategies	☐	☐
Study skills	☐	☐
Content area	☐	☐
Writing lab	☐	☐
Math lab	☐	☐

LD PROGRAM STAFF

Key staff person available to work with LD students: Donald Midlam, Associate Dean of Student Services.

State University of New York College of Agriculture and Technology at Cobleskill

Cobleskill, NY

Address: Cobleskill, NY, 12043
Admissions telephone: 800 295-8988
Admissions FAX: 518 255-6769
Director of Admissions: Jim Murray
Admissions e-mail: admissionsoffice@cobleskill.edu
Web site: http://www.cobleskill.edu
SAT Code: 2524 ACT Code: 2914

LD program enrollment: 379, Total campus enrollment: 2,510

GENERAL

State University of New York College of Agriculture and Technology at Cobleskill is a public, coed, four-year institution. 750-acre rural campus in Cobleskill (population: 6,407), 35 miles from Albany and 39 miles from Oneonta. Major airport serves Albany; bus serves Oneonta. Semester system.

LD ADMISSIONS

A personal interview is not required.

SECONDARY SCHOOL REQUIREMENTS

Graduation from secondary school required; GED accepted. The following course distribution required: 4 units of English, 1 unit of math, 1 unit of science, 12 units of academic electives.

TESTING

SAT Reasoning recommended. ACT recommended. SAT Reasoning or ACT required of some applicants.

Child Study Team report is not required. A neuropsychological or comprehensive psycho-educational evaluation is required for admission. Must be dated within 36 months of application. Tests required as part of this documentation:

- [x] WAIS-IV
- [x] WISC-IV
- [ ] SATA
- [x] Woodcock-Johnson
- [ ] Nelson-Denny Reading Test
- [ ] Other

UNDERGRADUATE STUDENT BODY

Total undergraduate student enrollment: 2,510.

Composition of student body (fall 2004):

	Undergraduate	Freshmen
International	2.5	3.4
Black	9.4	5.9
American Indian	0.1	0.4
Asian-American	1.9	1.2
Hispanic	5.4	3.2
White	80.7	85.9
Unreported	0.0	0.0
	100.0%	100.0%

11% are from out of state. Average age of full-time undergraduates is 21.

STUDENT HOUSING

82% of freshmen live in college housing. Freshmen are required to live on campus. Housing is guaranteed for all undergraduates. Campus can house 1,893 undergraduates. Single rooms are available for students with medical or special needs. A medical note is required.

EXPENSES

Tuition 2004-05: $12,615 per year (comprehensive). Tuition varies by program.

There is no additional cost for LD program/services.

LD SERVICES

LD program size is not limited.

LD services available to:

- [x] Freshmen
- [x] Sophomores
- [x] Juniors
- [x] Seniors

Academic Accommodations

Curriculum		**In class**	
Foreign language waiver	[ ]	Early syllabus	[ ]
Lighter course load	[x]	Note takers in class	[ ]
Math waiver	[ ]	Priority seating	[ ]
Other special classes	[ ]	Tape recorders	[ ]
Priority registrations	[ ]	Videotaped classes	[ ]
Substitution of courses	[ ]	Text on tape	[ ]
Exams		**Services**	
Extended time	[ ]	Diagnostic tests	[ ]
Oral exams	[ ]	Learning centers	[x]
Take home exams	[ ]	Proofreaders	[ ]
Exams on tape or computer	[ ]	Readers	[ ]
Untimed exams	[ ]	Reading Machines/Kurzweil	[x]
Other accommodations	[ ]	Special bookstore section	[ ]
		Typists	[ ]

Credit toward degree is not given for remedial courses taken.

Counseling Services

- [ ] Academic
- [ ] Psychological
- [ ] Student Support groups
- [ ] Vocational

Tutoring

Individual tutoring is available daily.

Average size of tutoring groups: 2

	Individual	Group
Time management	[x]	[x]
Organizational skills	[x]	[x]
Learning strategies	[x]	[x]
Study skills	[x]	[x]
Content area	[x]	[x]
Writing lab	[ ]	[ ]
Math lab	[ ]	[ ]

LD PROGRAM STAFF

Total number of LD Program staff (including director):

Full Time: 1 Part Time: 1

35 peer tutors are available to work with LD students.

Key staff person available to work with LD students: Lynn K. Abarno, Coordinator of Disability Support Services.

State University of New York College at Brockport

Brockport, NY

Address: 350 New Campus Drive, Brockport, NY, 14420
Admissions telephone: 585 395-2751
Admissions FAX: 585 395-5452
Director of Undergraduate Admissions: Bernard Valento
Admissions e-mail: admit@brockport.edu
Web site: http://www.brockport.edu
SAT Code: 2537 ACT Code: 2928

LD program name: Office for Students with Disabilities
Coordinator: Maryellen Post
LD program telephone: 585 395-5409
LD program e-mail: osdoffic@brockport.edu
LD program enrollment: 122, Total campus enrollment: 6,980

GENERAL

State University of New York College at Brockport is a public, coed, four-year institution. 435-acre campus in Brockport (population: 8,103), 16 miles from Rochester; branch campuses throughout Rochester. Airport, bus, and train serve Rochester. School operates transportation around campus and Brockport. Semester system.

LD ADMISSIONS

A personal interview is recommended. Essay is not required.

SECONDARY SCHOOL REQUIREMENTS

Graduation from secondary school required; GED accepted. The following course distribution required: 4 units of English, 3 units of math, 3 units of science, 4 units of social studies, 4 units of academic electives.

TESTING

SAT Reasoning or ACT required.

All enrolled freshmen (fall 2004):

Average SAT I Scores:	Verbal: 549	Math: 521
Average ACT Scores:	Composite: 22	

Child Study Team report is not required. A neuropsychological or comprehensive psycho-educational evaluation is required for admission. Must be dated within 36 months of application. Tests required as part of this documentation:

- [x] WAIS-IV
- [ ] WISC-IV
- [ ] SATA
- [x] Woodcock-Johnson
- [x] Nelson-Denny Reading Test
- [ ] Other

UNDERGRADUATE STUDENT BODY

Total undergraduate student enrollment: 2,871 Men, 3,893 Women.

Composition of student body (fall 2004):

	Undergraduate	Freshmen
International	1.6	1.1
Black	2.8	4.7
American Indian	0.3	0.4
Asian-American	1.6	1.0
Hispanic	2.4	2.6
White	80.2	78.7
Unreported	11.1	11.5
	100.0%	100.0%

2% are from out of state. 1% join a fraternity and 1% join a sorority. Average age of full-time undergraduates is 21. 39% of classes have fewer than 20 students, 55% have between 20 and 50 students, 6% have more than 50 students.

STUDENT HOUSING

90% of freshmen live in college housing. Freshmen are required to live on campus. Housing is guaranteed for all undergraduates. Campus can house 2,500 undergraduates. Single rooms are available for students with medical or special needs. A medical note is required.

EXPENSES

Tuition (2005-06): $4,350 per year (in-state), $10,300 (out-of-state).

Room: $4,725. Board: $2,876.
There is no additional cost for LD program/services.

LD SERVICES

LD program size is not limited.

LD services available to:

- [x] Freshmen
- [x] Sophomores
- [x] Juniors
- [x] Seniors

Academic Accommodations

Curriculum

- [ ] Foreign language waiver
- [x] Lighter course load
- [ ] Math waiver
- [ ] Other special classes
- [x] Priority registrations
- [ ] Substitution of courses

Exams

- [x] Extended time
- [ ] Oral exams
- [ ] Take home exams
- [x] Exams on tape or computer
- [ ] Untimed exams
- [x] Other accommodations

In class

- [ ] Early syllabus
- [x] Note takers in class
- [x] Priority seating
- [x] Tape recorders
- [ ] Videotaped classes
- [x] Text on tape

Services

- [ ] Diagnostic tests
- [x] Learning centers
- [ ] Proofreaders
- [ ] Readers
- [x] Reading Machines/Kurzweil
- [ ] Special bookstore section
- [x] Typists

Credit toward degree is not given for remedial courses taken.

Counseling Services

- [x] Academic
- [x] Psychological
- [ ] Student Support groups
- [x] Vocational

Tutoring

Individual tutoring is available weekly.

Average size of tutoring groups: 2

	Individual	Group
Time management	[x]	[x]
Organizational skills	[x]	[x]
Learning strategies	[x]	[x]
Study skills	[x]	[x]
Content area	[x]	[x]
Writing lab	[ ]	[x]
Math lab	[ ]	[x]

LD PROGRAM STAFF

Total number of LD Program staff (including director):

Full Time: 2 Part Time: 2

There is an advisor/advocate from the LD program available to students.

Key staff person available to work with LD students: Maryellen Post, Coordinator, Office for Students with Disabilities.

State University of New York College at Cortland

Cortland, NY

Address: P.O. Box 2000, Cortland, NY, 13045
Admissions telephone: 607 753-4711
Admissions FAX: 607 753-5998
Director of Admissions: Mark Yacavone
Admissions e-mail: admissions@cortland.edu
Web site: http://www.cortland.edu
SAT Code: 2538 ACT Code: 2932

Assistant Coordinator: Ute Gomez
LD program telephone: 607 753-2066
LD program e-mail: gomezu@cortland.edu
Total campus enrollment: 5,796

GENERAL

State University of New York College at Cortland is a public, coed, four-year institution. 191-acre campus in Cortland (population: 18,740), 30 miles from Syracuse and 18 miles from Ithaca. Served by bus; major airport and train serve Syracuse; smaller airport serves Ithaca. School operates transportation to school-owned/operated apartments. Public transportation serves campus. Semester system.

LD ADMISSIONS

A personal interview is recommended. Essay is not required.

SECONDARY SCHOOL REQUIREMENTS

Graduation from secondary school required; GED accepted. The following course distribution required: 4 units of English, 3 units of math, 3 units of science, 3 units of foreign language, 4 units of social studies.

TESTING

SAT Reasoning or ACT required. SAT Subject recommended.

Child Study Team report is not required. Tests required as part of this documentation:

- [ ] WAIS-IV
- [ ] WISC-IV
- [ ] SATA
- [ ] Woodcock-Johnson
- [ ] Nelson-Denny Reading Test
- [ ] Other

UNDERGRADUATE STUDENT BODY

Total undergraduate student enrollment: 2,419 Men, 3,431 Women.

Composition of student body (fall 2004):

	Undergraduate	Freshmen
International	0.0	0.2
Black	3.1	2.6
American Indian	0.3	0.3
Asian-American	2.1	1.2
Hispanic	4.9	3.4
White	82.8	84.3
Unreported	6.8	8.0
	100.0%	100.0%

2% are from out of state. 1% join a fraternity and 4% join a sorority. Average age of full-time undergraduates is 21. 53% of classes have fewer than 20 students, 42% have between 20 and 50 students, 5% have more than 50 students.

STUDENT HOUSING

98% of freshmen live in college housing.

EXPENSES

Tuition (2005-06): $4,350 per year (in-state), $10,610 (out-of-state). Room: $4,460. Board: $3,190.

There is no additional cost for LD program/services.

LD SERVICES

LD program size is not limited.

LD services available to:

- [ ] Freshmen
- [ ] Sophomores
- [ ] Juniors
- [ ] Seniors

Academic Accommodations

Curriculum		In class	
Foreign language waiver	[ ]	Early syllabus	[ ]
Lighter course load	[x]	Note takers in class	[x]
Math waiver	[ ]	Priority seating	[ ]
Other special classes	[ ]	Tape recorders	[x]
Priority registrations	[ ]	Videotaped classes	[ ]
Substitution of courses	[ ]	Text on tape	[ ]
Exams		**Services**	
Extended time	[x]	Diagnostic tests	[ ]
Oral exams	[x]	Learning centers	[x]
Take home exams	[ ]	Proofreaders	[ ]
Exams on tape or computer	[ ]	Readers	[x]
Untimed exams	[x]	Reading Machines/Kurzweil	[x]
Other accommodations	[ ]	Special bookstore section	[ ]
		Typists	[ ]

Credit toward degree is not given for remedial courses taken.

Counseling Services

- [ ] Academic
- [ ] Psychological
- [ ] Student Support groups
- [ ] Vocational

Tutoring

	Individual	Group
Time management	[ ]	[ ]
Organizational skills	[ ]	[ ]
Learning strategies	[ ]	[ ]
Study skills	[ ]	[ ]
Content area	[ ]	[ ]
Writing lab	[ ]	[ ]
Math lab	[ ]	[ ]

LD PROGRAM STAFF

Total number of LD Program staff (including director):

Full Time: 1 Part Time: 1

Key staff person available to work with LD students: Anne Hunt, Coordinator, Student Disability Services.

State University of New York College of Environmental Science and Forestry

Syracuse, NY

Address: 1 Forestry Drive, Syracuse, NY, 13210
Admissions telephone: 800 777-7373
Admissions FAX: 315 470-6933
Director of Admissions: Susan Sanford
Admissions e-mail: esfinfo@esf.edu
Web site: http://www.esf.edu
SAT Code: 2530 ACT Code: 2948

LD program name: Student Counseling
LD program address: 110 Bray Hall
Director: Thomas Slocum
LD program telephone: 315 470-6660
LD program e-mail: toslocum@esf.edu
LD program enrollment: 61, Total campus enrollment: 1,460

GENERAL

State University of New York College of Environmental Science and Forestry is a public, coed, four-year institution. 12-acre, urban campus adjacent to and integrated with Syracuse U in Syracuse (population: 163,860); branch campuses and field stations in Cranberry Lake, Newcomb, Tully, Wanakena, and Warrensburg. Served by air, bus, and train. School operates transportation to south campus of Syracuse U. Public transportation serves campus. Semester system.

LD ADMISSIONS

A personal interview is not required. Essay is not required.

For fall 2004, 41 completed self-identified LD applications were received. 30 applications were offered admission, and 18 enrolled.

SECONDARY SCHOOL REQUIREMENTS

Graduation from secondary school required; GED not accepted. The following course distribution required: 3 units of math, 3 units of science.

TESTING

SAT Reasoning required; ACT may be substituted. SAT Subject recommended.

All enrolled freshmen (fall 2004):

Average SAT I Scores:	Verbal: 562	Math: 574
Average ACT Scores:	Composite: 24	

Child Study Team report is not required. A neuropsychological or comprehensive psycho-education evaluation is not required for admission. Tests required as part of this documentation:

- [ ] WAIS-IV
- [ ] WISC-IV
- [ ] SATA
- [ ] Woodcock-Johnson
- [ ] Nelson-Denny Reading Test
- [ ] Other

UNDERGRADUATE STUDENT BODY

Total undergraduate student enrollment: 725 Men, 466 Women.

Composition of student body (fall 2004):

	Undergraduate	Freshmen
International	0.4	0.9
Black	1.3	1.8
American Indian	0.9	0.5
Asian-American	2.7	1.7
Hispanic	6.6	3.7
White	88.1	91.4
Unreported	0.0	0.0
	100.0%	100.0%

9% are from out of state. Average age of full-time undergraduates is 20. 76% of classes have fewer than 20 students, 17% have between 20 and 50 students, 7% have more than 50 students.

STUDENT HOUSING

95% of freshmen live in college housing. Housing is guaranteed for all undergraduates. Single rooms are available for students with medical or special needs. A medical note is required.

EXPENSES

Tuition (2005-06): $4,350 per year (in-state), $10,610 (out-of-state).

Room: $5,090. Board: $5,090.

There is no additional cost for LD program/services.

LD SERVICES

LD program size is not limited.

LD services available to:

- [x] Freshmen
- [x] Sophomores
- [x] Juniors
- [x] Seniors

Academic Accommodations

Curriculum

- [ ] Foreign language waiver
- [x] Lighter course load
- [ ] Math waiver
- [ ] Other special classes
- [ ] Priority registrations
- [ ] Substitution of courses

Exams

- [x] Extended time
- [x] Oral exams
- [ ] Take home exams
- [ ] Exams on tape or computer
- [ ] Untimed exams
- [x] Other accommodations

In class

- [ ] Early syllabus
- [x] Note takers in class
- [x] Priority seating
- [ ] Tape recorders
- [ ] Videotaped classes
- [ ] Text on tape

Services

- [x] Diagnostic tests
- [ ] Learning centers
- [ ] Proofreaders
- [ ] Readers
- [ ] Reading Machines/Kurzweil
- [ ] Special bookstore section
- [ ] Typists

Credit toward degree is not given for remedial courses taken.

Counseling Services

- [x] Academic
- [x] Psychological
- [ ] Student Support groups
- [x] Vocational

Tutoring

Individual tutoring is available weekly.

Average size of tutoring groups: 2

	Individual	Group
Time management	[ ]	[ ]
Organizational skills	[ ]	[ ]
Learning strategies	[ ]	[ ]
Study skills	[ ]	[ ]
Content area	[ ]	[ ]
Writing lab	[ ]	[ ]
Math lab	[ ]	[ ]

LD PROGRAM STAFF

Total number of LD Program staff (including director):

Full Time: 4 Part Time: 4

There is an advisor/advocate from the LD program available to students. 10 peer tutors are available to work with LD students.

Key staff person available to work with LD students: Thomas Slocum, Director of Student Counseling.

State University of New York College at Fredonia

Fredonia, NY

Address: Fredonia, NY, 14063-1136
Admissions telephone: 800 252-1212
Admissions FAX: 716 673-3249
Director of Admissions: Daniel Tramuta
Admissions e-mail: admissionsinq@fredonia.edu
Web site: http://www.fredonia.edu
SAT Code: 2539   ACT Code: 2934

LD program name: Disability Spport Services for Students
LD program address: Reed Library (4th Floor), Fredonia, NY, 14716
Coordinator: Carolyn Boone
LD program telephone: 716 673-3270
LD program e-mail: Carolyn.Boone@fredonia.edu
LD program enrollment: 44, Total campus enrollment: 4,954

GENERAL

State University of New York College at Fredonia is a public, coed, four-year institution. 266-acre campus in Fredonia (population: 10,706), 45 miles from both Buffalo and Erie, PA. Served by bus; major airport and train serve Buffalo. Public transportation serves campus. Semester system.

LD ADMISSIONS

Students do not complete a separate application and are simultaneously accepted to the LD program. A member of the LD program does not sit on the admissions committee. High school waivers are accepted for foreign language. A personal interview is not required. Essay is not required. Foreign language requirement may be waived.

For fall 2004, 237 completed self-identified LD applications were received. 64 applications were offered admission, and 22 enrolled.

SECONDARY SCHOOL REQUIREMENTS

Graduation from secondary school required; GED accepted. The following course distribution required: 4 units of English, 3 units of math, 3 units of science, 4 units of social studies, 2 units of academic electives.

TESTING

SAT Reasoning or ACT required. SAT Subject recommended.

All enrolled freshmen (fall 2004):

Average SAT I Scores:	Verbal: 554	Math: 560
Average ACT Scores:	Composite: 25	

Child Study Team report is not required. A neuropsychological or comprehensive psycho-educational evaluation is required for admission. Must be dated within 18 months of application. Tests required as part of this documentation:

- ■ WAIS-IV
- ☐ WISC-IV
- ☐ SATA
- ☐ Woodcock-Johnson
- ☐ Nelson-Denny Reading Test
- ☐ Other

UNDERGRADUATE STUDENT BODY

Total undergraduate student enrollment: 1,923 Men, 2,804 Women.

Composition of student body (fall 2004):

	Undergraduate	Freshmen
International	0.7	1.1
Black	1.6	1.1
American Indian	0.4	0.4
Asian-American	1.7	1.3
Hispanic	2.1	2.3
White	92.9	93.4
Unreported	0.6	0.4
	100.0%	100.0%

1% are from out of state. 1% join a fraternity and 1% join a sorority. Average age of full-time undergraduates is 20. 50% of classes have fewer than 20 students, 43% have between 20 and 50 students, 7% have more than 50 students.

STUDENT HOUSING

89% of freshmen live in college housing. Freshmen are required to live on campus. Housing is guaranteed for all undergraduates. Campus can house 2,617 undergraduates. Single rooms are available for students with medical or special needs. A medical note is required.

EXPENSES

Tuition (2005-06): $4,350 per year (in-state), $10,610 (out-of-state). Room: $4,350. Board: $2,980.
There is no additional cost for LD program/services.

LD SERVICES

LD program size is not limited.

LD services available to:

■ Freshmen ■ Sophomores ■ Juniors ■ Seniors

Academic Accommodations

Curriculum		In class	
Foreign language waiver	☐	Early syllabus	☐
Lighter course load	■	Note takers in class	☐
Math waiver	☐	Priority seating	☐
Other special classes	☐	Tape recorders	☐
Priority registrations	☐	Videotaped classes	☐
Substitution of courses	☐	Text on tape	☐
Exams		**Services**	
Extended time	■	Diagnostic tests	☐
Oral exams	☐	Learning centers	■
Take home exams	☐	Proofreaders	☐
Exams on tape or computer	☐	Readers	☐
Untimed exams	☐	Reading Machines/Kurzweil	☐
Other accommodations	☐	Special bookstore section	☐
		Typists	☐

Credit toward degree is not given for remedial courses taken.

Counseling Services

- ■ Academic
- ☐ Psychological
- ☐ Student Support groups
- ☐ Vocational

Meets 2 times per academic year

Tutoring

Individual tutoring is available weekly.

	Individual	Group
Time management	■	☐
Organizational skills	■	☐
Learning strategies	☐	☐
Study skills	☐	☐
Content area	■	■
Writing lab	☐	☐
Math lab	☐	■

UNIQUE LD PROGRAM FEATURES

Accommodations are made on an individualized basis. Not every student with a learning disability will be eligible for every accommodation and other accommodations may be used.

LD PROGRAM STAFF

Total number of LD Program staff (including director):

Full Time: 1   Part Time: 1

There is an advisor/advocate from the LD program available to students. 55 peer tutors are available to work with LD students.

Key staff person available to work with LD students: Carolyn Boone, Coordinator, Disability Support Services for Students.

State University of New York College at Geneseo

Geneseo, NY

Address: 1 College Circle, Geneseo, NY, 14454-1401
Admissions telephone: 585 245-5571
Admissions FAX: 585 245-5550
Director of Admissions: Kristine Shay
Admissions e-mail: admissions@geneseo.edu
Web site: http://www.geneseo.edu
SAT Code: 2540 ACT Code: 2936

Director of Disability Services: Tabitha Buggie-Hunt
LD program telephone: 585 245-5112
LD program e-mail: tbuggieh@geneseo.edu
LD program enrollment: 85, Total campus enrollment: 5,375

GENERAL

State University of New York College at Geneseo is a public, coed, four-year institution. 220-acre campus in Geneseo (population: 9,654), 30 miles from Rochester. Major airport serves Buffalo (70 miles); airport, bus, and train serve Rochester. School operates transportation to Rochester and local malls. Public transportation serves campus. Semester system.

LD ADMISSIONS

High school waivers are accepted for math and foreign language. A personal interview is not required. Essay is not required.

SECONDARY SCHOOL REQUIREMENTS

Graduation from secondary school required; GED accepted.

TESTING

SAT Reasoning or ACT required. SAT Subject recommended.

All enrolled freshmen (fall 2004):

Average SAT I Scores: Verbal: 630 Math: 632
Average ACT Scores: Composite: 27

Child Study Team report is not required. Tests required as part of this documentation:

- ☐ WAIS-IV
- ☐ WISC-IV
- ☐ SATA
- ☐ Woodcock-Johnson
- ☐ Nelson-Denny Reading Test
- ☐ Other

UNDERGRADUATE STUDENT BODY

Total undergraduate student enrollment: 1,884 Men, 3,487 Women.

Composition of student body (fall 2004):

	Undergraduate	Freshmen
International	1.5	2.3
Black	3.1	2.2
American Indian	0.4	0.2
Asian-American	7.4	4.8
Hispanic	3.7	2.6
White	70.8	83.5
Unreported	13.1	4.4
	100.0%	100.0%

2% are from out of state. 10% join a fraternity and 12% join a sorority. Average age of full-time undergraduates is 20. 29% of classes have fewer than 20 students, 63% have between 20 and 50 students, 8% have more than 50 students.

STUDENT HOUSING

100% of freshmen live in college housing. Freshmen are required to live on campus. Housing is guaranteed for all undergraduates. Campus can house 3,026 undergraduates. Single rooms are available for students with medical or special needs. A medical note is required.

EXPENSES

Tuition (2005-06): $4,350 per year (in-state), $10,300 (out-of-state).
Room: $4,600. Board: $3,150-$2,790.

There is no additional cost for LD program/services.

LD SERVICES

LD program size is not limited.

LD services available to:

■ Freshmen ■ Sophomores ■ Juniors ■ Seniors

Academic Accommodations

Curriculum		In class	
Foreign language waiver	☐	Early syllabus	☐
Lighter course load	■	Note takers in class	■
Math waiver	☐	Priority seating	■
Other special classes	☐	Tape recorders	☐
Priority registrations	■	Videotaped classes	☐
Substitution of courses	☐	Text on tape	☐
Exams		**Services**	
Extended time	■	Diagnostic tests	☐
Oral exams	☐	Learning centers	☐
Take home exams	☐	Proofreaders	☐
Exams on tape or computer	■	Readers	■
Untimed exams	☐	Reading Machines/Kurzweil	■
Other accommodations	■	Special bookstore section	☐
		Typists	■

Credit toward degree is not given for remedial courses taken.

Counseling Services

- ■ Academic
- ■ Psychological — Meets 10 times per academic year
- ☐ Student Support groups
- ☐ Vocational

Tutoring

Individual tutoring is not available.

	Individual	Group
Time management	■	■
Organizational skills	■	☐
Learning strategies	☐	☐
Study skills	☐	☐
Content area	☐	☐
Writing lab	■	■
Math lab	■	■

LD PROGRAM STAFF

Total number of LD Program staff (including director):

Full Time: 1 Part Time: 1

There is no advisor/advocate from the LD program available to students.

Key staff person available to work with LD students: Tabitha Buggie-Hunt, Director of Disability Services.

LD Program web site: http://disability.geneseo.edu

State University of New York College at Old Westbury

Old Westbury, NY

Address: 223 Store Hill Road, Old Westbury, NY, 11568
Admissions telephone: 516 876-3073
Admissions FAX: 516 876-3307
Vice President of Enrollment Services: Mary Marquez Bell
Admissions e-mail: enroll@oldwestbury.edu
Web site: http://www.oldwestbury.edu
SAT Code: 2866

LD program address: PO Box 210
Coordinator: William Lupardo
LD program telephone: 516 876-3009
LD program e-mail: lupardow@oldwestbury.edu
LD program enrollment: 60, Total campus enrollment: 3,340

GENERAL

State University of New York College at Old Westbury is a public, coed, four-year institution. 605-acre, suburban campus in Old Westbury (population: 4,228) on Long Island, 17 miles from New York City. Major airport and train serve New York City; bus serves Hicksville (one mile). School operates transportation to Hicksville. Public transportation serves campus. Semester system.

LD ADMISSIONS

A personal interview is recommended. Essay is not required.

SECONDARY SCHOOL REQUIREMENTS

Graduation from secondary school required; GED accepted. The following course distribution required: 4 units of English, 3 units of math, 3 units of science, 2 units of foreign language, 2 units of social studies, 2 units of history, 3 units of academic electives.

TESTING

SAT Reasoning or ACT required. SAT Subject required.

All enrolled freshmen (fall 2004):

Average SAT I Scores:	Verbal: 479	Math: 490
Average ACT Scores:	Composite: 19	

Child Study Team report is not required. Tests required as part of this documentation:

- ☐ WAIS-IV
- ☐ WISC-IV
- ☐ SATA
- ☐ Woodcock-Johnson
- ☐ Nelson-Denny Reading Test
- ☐ Other

UNDERGRADUATE STUDENT BODY

Total undergraduate student enrollment: 1,184 Men, 1,808 Women.

Composition of student body (fall 2004):

	Undergraduate	Freshmen
International	1.0	2.1
Black	35.8	26.2
American Indian	0.3	0.2
Asian-American	7.0	7.5
Hispanic	23.3	15.8
White	22.0	31.5
Unreported	10.6	16.7
	100.0%	100.0%

1% are from out of state. 1% join a fraternity and 1% join a sorority. Average age of full-time undergraduates is 23. 32% of classes have fewer than 20 students, 68% have between 20 and 50 students.

STUDENT HOUSING

69% of freshmen live in college housing. Freshmen are not required to live on campus. Housing is guaranteed for all undergraduates. Campus can house 1,650 undergraduates. Single rooms are available for students with medical or special needs. A medical note is required.

EXPENSES

Tuition (2005-06): $4,350 per year (in-state), $10,300 (out-of-state).

Room: $5,793. Board: $2,290.

There is no additional cost for LD program/services.

LD SERVICES

LD program size is not limited.

LD services available to:

☑ Freshmen ☑ Sophomores ☑ Juniors ☑ Seniors

Academic Accommodations

Curriculum		In class	
Foreign language waiver	☐	Early syllabus	☐
Lighter course load	☑	Note takers in class	☑
Math waiver	☐	Priority seating	☑
Other special classes	☐	Tape recorders	☑
Priority registrations	☐	Videotaped classes	☐
Substitution of courses	☐	Text on tape	☑
Exams		**Services**	
Extended time	☑	Diagnostic tests	☐
Oral exams	☑	Learning centers	☑
Take home exams	☐	Proofreaders	☑
Exams on tape or computer	☑	Readers	☑
Untimed exams	☑	Reading Machines/Kurzweil	☑
Other accommodations	☑	Special bookstore section	☐
		Typists	☑

Credit toward degree is not given for remedial courses taken.

Counseling Services

- ☑ Academic
- ☑ Psychological
- ☑ Student Support groups — Meets 25 times per academic year
- ☑ Vocational

Tutoring

Individual tutoring is available daily.

Average size of tutoring groups: 2

	Individual	Group
Time management	☑	☑
Organizational skills	☑	☑
Learning strategies	☑	☑
Study skills	☑	☑
Content area	☑	☑
Writing lab	☑	☑
Math lab	☑	☑

UNIQUE LD PROGRAM FEATURES

Weekly support groups are available for students with disabilities. Multi-media computer lab available to LD students with adaptive hardware, software and hand-held devices. Video lending library featuring 120+ titles, including regular motion pictures, specific disability information and tutoring and other training videos. Students must provide appropriate documentation when requesting academic accommodations.

LD PROGRAM STAFF

Total number of LD Program staff (including director):

Full Time: 1 Part Time: 1

There is an advisor/advocate from the LD program available to students. 1 graduate student and 5 peer tutors are available to work with LD students.

Key staff person available to work with LD students: William Lupardo, Coordinator, Office of Services for Students with Disabilities. LD Program web site: http://www.oldwestbury.edu/academics/disabilities.cfm

State University of New York College at Oneonta

Oneonta, NY

Address: Ravine Parkway, Oneonta, NY, 13820
Admissions telephone: 800 SUNY-123
Admissions FAX: 607 436-3074
Director of Admissions: Karen A. Brown
Admissions e-mail: admissions@oneonta.edu
Web site: http://www.oneonta.edu
SAT Code: 2542 ACT Code: 2940

LD program name: Student Disability Services
LD program address: Alumni Hall
Coordinator, Student Disability Services: Craig Levins
LD program telephone: 607 436-2137
LD program e-mail: sds@oneonta.edu
LD program enrollment: 224, Total campus enrollment: 5,605

GENERAL

State University of New York College at Oneonta is a public, coed, four-year institution. 250-acre campus in Oneonta (population: 13,292), 75 miles from Albany and 175 miles from New York City. Served by bus; major airport serves Albany; smaller airport serves Binghamton (60 miles); train serves Utica (60 miles). School operates transportation to various points within Oneonta and New York City. Public transportation serves campus. Semester system.

LD ADMISSIONS

Students do not complete a separate application and are not simultaneously accepted to the LD program. A member of the LD program does not sit on the admissions committee. High school waivers are accepted for math and foreign language. A personal interview is recommended. Essay is not required.

SECONDARY SCHOOL REQUIREMENTS

Graduation from secondary school required; GED accepted. The following course distribution required: 4 units of English, 2 units of math, 2 units of science, 2 units of foreign language, 3 units of social studies.

TESTING

SAT Reasoning or ACT required. SAT Subject recommended.

All enrolled freshmen (fall 2004):

Average SAT I Scores:	Verbal: 544	Math: 553
Average ACT Scores:	Composite: 24	

Child Study Team report is not required. A neuropsychological or comprehensive psycho-education evaluation is not required for admission. Tests required as part of this documentation:

- [ ] WAIS-IV
- [ ] WISC-IV
- [ ] SATA
- [ ] Woodcock-Johnson
- [ ] Nelson-Denny Reading Test
- [ ] Other

UNDERGRADUATE STUDENT BODY

Total undergraduate student enrollment: 2,172 Men, 3,286 Women.

Composition of student body (fall 2004):

	Undergraduate	Freshmen
International	1.7	1.3
Black	2.0	2.6
American Indian	0.1	0.1
Asian-American	2.5	1.7
Hispanic	4.8	4.2
White	85.4	83.0
Unreported	3.5	7.1
	100.0%	100.0%

2% are from out of state. 2% join a fraternity and 5% join a sorority. Average age of full-time undergraduates is 20. 42% of classes have fewer than 20 students, 53% have between 20 and 50 students, 5% have more than 50 students.

STUDENT HOUSING

98% of freshmen live in college housing. Freshmen are required to live on campus. Housing is guaranteed for freshmen and sophomores. Campus can house 3,219 undergraduates. Single rooms are available for students with medical or special needs. A medical note is not required.

EXPENSES

Tuition (2005-06): $4,350 per year (in-state), $10,610 (out-of-state).
Room: $4,230. Board: $3,000.
There is no additional cost for LD program/services.

LD SERVICES

LD program size is not limited.

LD services available to:

- [x] Freshmen
- [x] Sophomores
- [x] Juniors
- [x] Seniors

Academic Accommodations

Curriculum		In class	
Foreign language waiver	[ ]	Early syllabus	[ ]
Lighter course load	[x]	Note takers in class	[x]
Math waiver	[ ]	Priority seating	[ ]
Other special classes	[ ]	Tape recorders	[x]
Priority registrations	[ ]	Videotaped classes	[x]
Substitution of courses	[ ]	Text on tape	[x]
Exams		**Services**	
Extended time	[x]	Diagnostic tests	[ ]
Oral exams	[x]	Learning centers	[x]
Take home exams	[ ]	Proofreaders	[ ]
Exams on tape or computer	[x]	Readers	[x]
Untimed exams	[x]	Reading Machines/Kurzweil	[x]
Other accommodations	[ ]	Special bookstore section	[ ]
		Typists	[x]

Credit toward degree is not given for remedial courses taken.

Counseling Services

- [x] Academic
- [x] Psychological
- [x] Student Support groups
- [ ] Vocational

Tutoring

Individual tutoring is available weekly.

Average size of tutoring groups: 4

	Individual	Group
Time management	[x]	[x]
Organizational skills	[ ]	[x]
Learning strategies	[ ]	[x]
Study skills	[x]	[x]
Content area	[x]	[x]
Writing lab	[x]	[ ]
Math lab	[x]	[ ]

LD PROGRAM STAFF

Total number of LD Program staff (including director):

Full Time: 1 Part Time: 1

There is an advisor/advocate from the LD program available to students. The advisor/advocate meets with faculty 5 times per month and students 30 times per month. 15 peer tutors are available to work with LD students.

Key staff person available to work with LD students: Craig Levins, Coordinator, Student Disability Services.

LD Program web site: www.oneonta.edu/development/sds/

State University of New York College at Plattsburgh

Plattsburgh, NY

Address: 101 Broad Street, Plattsburgh, NY, 12901-2697
Admissions telephone: 888 673-0012
Admissions FAX: 518 564-2045
Director of Admissions: Richard J. Higgins
Admissions e-mail: admissions@plattsburgh.edu
Web site: http://www.plattsburgh.edu
SAT Code: 2544 ACT Code: 2944

LD program name: Student Support Services
Director: Dr. Michele Carpentier
LD program telephone: 518 564-2810
LD program e-mail: michele.carpentier@plattsburgh.com
LD program enrollment: 200, Total campus enrollment: 5,275

GENERAL

State University of New York College at Plattsburgh is a public, coed, four-year institution. 300-acre campus in Plattsburgh (population: 18,816), 60 miles from Montreal, Quebec, Canada, and 32 miles from Burlington, VT; branch campuses in Glens Falls, Johnstown, Potsdam, and Watertown. Served by bus and train; major airport serves Burlington. School operates transportation around local area. Public transportation serves campus. Semester system.

LD ADMISSIONS

Students do not complete a separate application and are simultaneously accepted to the LD program. High school waivers are accepted for math and foreign language. A personal interview is recommended. Essay is not required.

For fall 2004, 333 completed self-identified LD applications were received.

SECONDARY SCHOOL REQUIREMENTS

Graduation from secondary school required; GED accepted. The following course distribution required: 4 units of English, 3 units of math, 3 units of science, 3 units of foreign language, 3 units of social studies, 1 unit of history, 1 unit of academic electives.

TESTING

SAT Reasoning considered if submitted. ACT required. SAT Subject recommended.

All enrolled freshmen (fall 2004):

Average SAT I Scores:	Verbal: 518	Math: 527
Average ACT Scores:	Composite: 22	

Child Study Team report is not required. A neuropsychological or comprehensive psycho-educational evaluation is required for admission. Must be dated within 36 months of application. Tests required as part of this documentation:

☐ WAIS-IV	■ Woodcock-Johnson
■ WISC-IV	☐ Nelson-Denny Reading Test
☐ SATA	☐ Other

UNDERGRADUATE STUDENT BODY

Total undergraduate student enrollment: 2,293 Men, 3,089 Women.

Composition of student body (fall 2004):

	Undergraduate	Freshmen
International	4.8	6.1
Black	5.1	5.1
American Indian	0.5	0.4
Asian-American	2.5	2.3
Hispanic	4.2	3.6
White	78.8	74.8
Unreported	4.1	7.7
	100.0%	100.0%

3% are from out of state. Average age of full-time undergraduates is 21. 38% of classes have fewer than 20 students, 56% have between 20 and 50 students, 6% have more than 50 students.

STUDENT HOUSING

89% of freshmen live in college housing. Freshmen are required to live on campus. Housing is guaranteed for all undergraduates. Campus can house 2,879 undergraduates. Single rooms are available for students with medical or special needs. A medical note is required.

EXPENSES

Tuition (2005-06): $4,350 per year (in-state), $10,610 (out-of-state).
Room: $4,400. Board: $2,666.
There is no additional cost for LD program/services.

LD SERVICES

LD program size is not limited.

LD services available to:

■ Freshmen ■ Sophomores ■ Juniors ■ Seniors

Academic Accommodations

Curriculum		**In class**	
Foreign language waiver	☐	Early syllabus	☐
Lighter course load	■	Note takers in class	■
Math waiver	☐	Priority seating	☐
Other special classes	■	Tape recorders	■
Priority registrations	☐	Videotaped classes	☐
Substitution of courses	■	Text on tape	■
Exams		**Services**	
Extended time	■	Diagnostic tests	■
Oral exams	■	Learning centers	■
Take home exams	☐	Proofreaders	☐
Exams on tape or computer	■	Readers	■
Untimed exams	■	Reading Machines/Kurzweil	■
Other accommodations	☐	Special bookstore section	☐
		Typists	☐

Credit toward degree is not given for remedial courses taken.

Counseling Services

■ Academic	Meets 10 times per academic year
■ Psychological	Meets 10 times per academic year
☐ Student Support groups	
☐ Vocational	

Tutoring

Individual tutoring is available weekly.

	Individual	Group
Time management	■	■
Organizational skills	■	■
Learning strategies	■	■
Study skills	■	■
Content area	■	■
Writing lab	■	■
Math lab	■	■

LD PROGRAM STAFF

Total number of LD Program staff (including director):

Full Time: 3 Part Time: 3

2 graduate students and 15 peer tutors are available to work with LD students.

Key staff person available to work with LD students: Cordelia Drake, Counselor of Student Support Services.

State University of New York College at Potsdam

Potsdam, NY

Address: 44 Pierrepont Avenue, Potsdam, NY, 13676
Admissions telephone: 877 768-7326
Admissions FAX: 315 267-2163
Director of Admissions: Thomas Nesbitt
Admissions e-mail: admissions@potsdam.edu
Web site: http://www.potsdam.edu
SAT Code: 2545 ACT Code: 2946

Director, Accommodative Services: Sharon House
LD program telephone: 315 267-3267
LD program e-mail: housese@potsdam.edu
LD program enrollment: 96, Total campus enrollment: 3,539

GENERAL

State University of New York College at Potsdam is a public, coed, four-year institution. 240-acre campus in Potsdam (population: 15,957), 150 miles from Syracuse and 90 miles from Ottawa, Ontario, Canada; Star Lake Campus in Adirondack Park. Served by bus; major airports serve Syracuse and Ottawa; train serves Cornwall, Ontario (30 miles). School operates transportation to Clarkson U and St. Lawrence U. Public transportation serves campus. Semester system.

LD ADMISSIONS

Students do not complete a separate application and are simultaneously accepted to the LD program. A member of the LD program does not sit on the admissions committee. A personal interview is recommended. Essay is not required.

SECONDARY SCHOOL REQUIREMENTS

Graduation from secondary school required; GED accepted. The following course distribution required: 4 units of English, 2 units of math, 2 units of science, 3 units of foreign language, 4 units of social studies.

TESTING

SAT Reasoning or ACT required. SAT Subject recommended.

All enrolled freshmen (fall 2004):

Average SAT I Scores:	Verbal: 536	Math: 534
Average ACT Scores:	Composite: 23	

Child Study Team report is not required. A neuropsychological or comprehensive psycho-educational evaluation is required for admission. Tests required as part of this documentation:

- [x] WAIS-IV
- [ ] WISC-IV
- [ ] SATA
- [ ] Woodcock-Johnson
- [ ] Nelson-Denny Reading Test
- [ ] Other

UNDERGRADUATE STUDENT BODY

Total undergraduate student enrollment: 1,408 Men, 2,067 Women.

Composition of student body (fall 2004):

	Undergraduate	Freshmen
International	1.9	3.1
Black	1.9	1.8
American Indian	1.1	1.9
Asian-American	2.0	1.3
Hispanic	2.5	1.7
White	78.0	78.6
Unreported	12.6	11.6
	100.0%	100.0%

3% are from out of state. 2% join a fraternity and 3% join a sorority. Average age of full-time undergraduates is 22. 58% of classes have fewer than 20 students, 39% have between 20 and 50 students, 3% have more than 50 students.

STUDENT HOUSING

89% of freshmen live in college housing. Freshmen are required to live on campus. Housing is guaranteed for all undergraduates. Campus can house 2,400 undergraduates. Single rooms are available for students with medical or special needs. A medical note is required.

EXPENSES

Tuition (2005-06): $4,350 per year (in-state), $10,610 (out-of-state). Room: $4,420. Board: $3,250.

There is no additional cost for LD program/services.

LD SERVICES

LD program size is not limited.

LD services available to:

- [x] Freshmen
- [x] Sophomores
- [x] Juniors
- [x] Seniors

Academic Accommodations

Curriculum		**In class**	
Foreign language waiver	[ ]	Early syllabus	[ ]
Lighter course load	[ ]	Note takers in class	[x]
Math waiver	[ ]	Priority seating	[ ]
Other special classes	[x]	Tape recorders	[x]
Priority registrations	[ ]	Videotaped classes	[ ]
Substitution of courses	[ ]	Text on tape	[ ]
Exams		**Services**	
Extended time	[x]	Diagnostic tests	[ ]
Oral exams	[x]	Learning centers	[x]
Take home exams	[ ]	Proofreaders	[ ]
Exams on tape or computer	[ ]	Readers	[x]
Untimed exams	[ ]	Reading Machines/Kurzweil	[x]
Other accommodations	[ ]	Special bookstore section	[ ]
		Typists	[ ]

Credit toward degree is not given for remedial courses taken.

Counseling Services

- [ ] Academic
- [ ] Psychological
- [ ] Student Support groups
- [ ] Vocational

Tutoring

Individual tutoring is available weekly.

Average size of tutoring groups: 3

	Individual	Group
Time management	[ ]	[ ]
Organizational skills	[ ]	[ ]
Learning strategies	[ ]	[ ]
Study skills	[ ]	[ ]
Content area	[ ]	[ ]
Writing lab	[x]	[ ]
Math lab	[x]	[ ]

LD PROGRAM STAFF

Total number of LD Program staff (including director):

Full Time: 1 Part Time: 1

There is an advisor/advocate from the LD program available to students.

Key staff person available to work with LD students: Sharon House, Director, Accommodative Services.

State University of New York Institute of Technology at Utica/Rome

Utica, NY

Address: P.O. Box 3050, Utica, NY, 13504-3050
Admissions FAX: 315 792-7837
Director of Admissions: Marybeth Lyons
SAT Code: 755

Director: Mary Brown DePass
LD program telephone: 315 792-7805
LD program e-mail: smb2@sunyit.edu
LD program enrollment: 29, Total campus enrollment: 1,876

GENERAL

State University of New York Institute of Technology at Utica/Rome is a public, coed, graduate institution. 850-acre campus in Utica (population: 60,651), 50 miles from Syracuse. Served by air, bus and train; major airport serves Syracuse. Public transportation serves campus. Semester system.

LD ADMISSIONS

A member of the LD program does not sit on the admissions committee. High school waivers are accepted for foreign language. A personal interview is recommended. Essay is required and may be typed.

SECONDARY SCHOOL REQUIREMENTS

The following course distribution required: 4 units of English, 3 units of math, 3 units of science, 2 units of social studies, 2 units of history.

TESTING

SAT Reasoning or ACT required. SAT Subject recommended.

Child Study Team report is not required. A neuropsychological or comprehensive psycho-education evaluation is not required for admission. Tests required as part of this documentation:

- ☐ WAIS-IV
- ☐ WISC-IV
- ☐ SATA
- ☐ Woodcock-Johnson
- ☐ Nelson-Denny Reading Test
- ☐ Other

UNDERGRADUATE STUDENT BODY

Total undergraduate student enrollment: 1,086 Men, 1,129 Women.

Composition of student body (fall 2004):

	Undergraduate	Freshmen
International	0.0	1.0
Black	8.6	5.8
American Indian	0.1	0.7
Asian-American	1.2	2.7
Hispanic	2.5	2.0
White	82.7	86.3
Unreported	4.9	1.5
	100.0%	100.0%

1% are from out of state.

STUDENT HOUSING

Freshmen are required to live on campus. Housing is guaranteed for all undergraduates. Campus can house 584 undergraduates. Single rooms are available for students with medical or special needs. A medical note is required.

EXPENSES

Tuition (2005-06): $4,350 per year (in-state), $10,610 (out-of-state).
Room: $4,450. Board: $2,840.
There is no additional cost for LD program/services.

LD SERVICES

LD program size is limited.

LD services available to:

■ Freshmen ■ Sophomores ■ Juniors ■ Seniors

Academic Accommodations

Curriculum		In class	
Foreign language waiver	☐	Early syllabus	☐
Lighter course load	■	Note takers in class	■
Math waiver	☐	Priority seating	■
Other special classes	☐	Tape recorders	■
Priority registrations	☐	Videotaped classes	☐
Substitution of courses	☐	Text on tape	■
Exams		**Services**	
Extended time	■	Diagnostic tests	☐
Oral exams	☐	Learning centers	■
Take home exams	☐	Proofreaders	☐
Exams on tape or computer	☐	Readers	☐
Untimed exams	☐	Reading Machines/Kurzweil	■
Other accommodations	☐	Special bookstore section	☐
		Typists	☐

Credit toward degree is not given for remedial courses taken.

Counseling Services

- ■ Academic
- ■ Psychological
- ■ Student Support groups
- ■ Vocational

Meets 2 times per academic year

Tutoring

Individual tutoring is available weekly.

Average size of tutoring groups: 1

	Individual	Group
Time management	■	■
Organizational skills	■	■
Learning strategies	■	■
Study skills	■	■
Content area	■	■
Writing lab	■	■
Math lab	■	■

UNIQUE LD PROGRAM FEATURES

Services are available based upon self disclosure

LD PROGRAM STAFF

Total number of LD Program staff (including director):

Full Time: 1 Part Time: 1

There is an advisor/advocate from the LD program available to students.

Key staff person available to work with LD students: Mary Brown DePass, Director.

LD Program web site: www.sunyit.edu

Syracuse University

Syracuse, NY

Address: 201 Tolley Administration Building, Syracuse, NY, 13244
Admissions telephone: 315 443-3611
Dean of Admissions: Susan E. Donovan, Dean
Admissions e-mail: orange@syr.edu
Web site: http://www.syracuse.edu
SAT Code: 2823 ACT Code: 2968

LD program name: Office of Disability Services
LD program address: 804 University Ave, Room 309
LD program telephone: 315 443-4498
LD program e-mail: odssched@syr.edu
Total campus enrollment: 12,268

GENERAL

Syracuse University is a private, coed, four-year institution. Urban campus of more than 200 acres in Syracuse (population: 147,306). Served by air, bus, and train. School operates transportation between dormitories, apartments, and academic buildings. Public transportation serves campus. Semester system.

LD ADMISSIONS

Students do not complete a separate application and are not simultaneously accepted to the LD program. A member of the LD program does not sit on the admissions committee. A personal interview is recommended. Essay is required and may be typed.

SECONDARY SCHOOL REQUIREMENTS

Graduation from secondary school required; GED accepted. The following course distribution required: 4 units of English, 3 units of math, 3 units of science, 2 units of foreign language, 3 units of social studies, 5 units of academic electives.

TESTING

SAT Reasoning required; ACT may be substituted. SAT Subject required.

Child Study Team report is not required. A neuropsychological or comprehensive psycho-educational evaluation is required for admission. Must be dated within 36 months of application. Tests required as part of this documentation:

■ WAIS-IV	■ Woodcock-Johnson
☐ WISC-IV	■ Nelson-Denny Reading Test
■ SATA	■ Other

UNDERGRADUATE STUDENT BODY

Total undergraduate student enrollment: 4,850 Men, 5,852 Women.

Composition of student body (fall 2004):

	Undergraduate	Freshmen
International	2.9	2.6
Black	5.3	6.1
American Indian	0.1	0.4
Asian-American	6.4	5.5
Hispanic	5.0	4.5
White	71.4	70.5
Unreported	8.9	10.4
	100.0%	100.0%

55% are from out of state. 19% join a fraternity and 20% join a sorority. Average age of full-time undergraduates is 21. 69% of classes have fewer than 20 students, 25% have between 20 and 50 students, 7% have more than 50 students.

STUDENT HOUSING

99% of freshmen live in college housing. Freshmen are required to live on campus. Housing is not guaranteed for all undergraduates. About 73% of undergraduate students live on campus. Campus can house 7,414 undergraduates. Single rooms are available for students with medical or special needs. A medical note is required.

EXPENSES

Tuition (2005-06): $27,210 per year.
Room: $5,620. Board: $4,750.
There is no additional cost for LD program/services.

LD SERVICES

LD program size is not limited.

LD services available to:

■ Freshmen ■ Sophomores ■ Juniors ■ Seniors

Academic Accommodations

Curriculum		**In class**	
Foreign language waiver	☐	Early syllabus	☐
Lighter course load	☐	Note takers in class	■
Math waiver	☐	Priority seating	☐
Other special classes	☐	Tape recorders	■
Priority registrations	☐	Videotaped classes	☐
Substitution of courses	☐	Text on tape	■
Exams		**Services**	
Extended time	■	Diagnostic tests	■
Oral exams	■	Learning centers	■
Take home exams	☐	Proofreaders	☐
Exams on tape or computer	■	Readers	■
Untimed exams	☐	Reading Machines/Kurzweil	■
Other accommodations	■	Special bookstore section	☐
		Typists	☐

Credit toward degree is not given for remedial courses taken.

Counseling Services

■ Academic
■ Psychological
■ Student Support groups
■ Vocational

Tutoring

Individual tutoring is available weekly.

Average size of tutoring groups: 5

	Individual	Group
Time management	■	■
Organizational skills	■	■
Learning strategies	■	■
Study skills	■	■
Content area	■	☐
Writing lab	■	☐
Math lab	■	■

LD PROGRAM STAFF

Total number of LD Program staff (including director):

Full Time: 6 Part Time: 6

There is an advisor/advocate from the LD program available to students.

LD Program web site: www.disabilityservices.syr.edu

Union College

Schenectady, NY

Address: 807 Union Street, Schenectady, NY, 12308
Admissions telephone: 888 843-6688
Admissions FAX: 518 388-6986
Vice President of Admissions and Financial Aid: Dianne Crozier
Admissions e-mail: admissions@union.edu
Web site: http://www.union.edu
SAT Code: 2920 ACT Code: 2970

Director of Student Support Services: Shelly Shinebarger
LD program telephone: 518 388-6116
LD program e-mail: shinebas@union.edu
Total campus enrollment: 2,192

GENERAL

Union College is a private, coed, four-year institution. 100-acre campus in Schenectady (population: 61,821), 15 miles from Albany. Served by bus and train; airport serves Albany. Public transportation serves campus. Trimester system.

LD ADMISSIONS

Application Deadline: 01/15. High school waivers are accepted for foreign language. A personal interview is recommended. Essay is required and may be typed. Foreign language requirement may be waived.

SECONDARY SCHOOL REQUIREMENTS

Graduation from secondary school required; GED accepted. The following course distribution required: 4 units of English, 3 units of math, 2 units of science, 2 units of foreign language, 1 unit of social studies, 1 unit of history.

TESTING

SAT Reasoning or ACT required. SAT Subject recommended.

All enrolled freshmen (fall 2004):

Average SAT I Scores: Verbal: 610 Math: 640
Average ACT Scores: Composite: 27

Child Study Team report is not required. Tests required as part of this documentation:

- ☐ WAIS-IV
- ☐ WISC-IV
- ☐ SATA
- ☐ Woodcock-Johnson
- ☐ Nelson-Denny Reading Test
- ☐ Other

UNDERGRADUATE STUDENT BODY

Total undergraduate student enrollment: 1,100 Men, 1,018 Women.

Composition of student body (fall 2004):

	Undergraduate	Freshmen
International	1.3	1.8
Black	2.7	2.9
American Indian	0.0	0.0
Asian-American	7.1	6.1
Hispanic	4.0	4.2
White	84.7	84.4
Unreported	0.2	0.6
	100.0%	100.0%

53% are from out of state. 29% join a fraternity and 27% join a sorority. Average age of full-time undergraduates is 20. 65% of classes have fewer than 20 students, 34% have between 20 and 50 students, 1% have more than 50 students.

STUDENT HOUSING

99% of freshmen live in college housing. Freshmen are required to live on campus. Housing is not guaranteed for all undergraduates. Seniors who wish to maintain campus residence must participate in spring housing lottery. Campus can house 1,944 undergraduates. Single rooms are available for students with medical or special needs. A medical note is required.

EXPENSES

Tuition (2005-06): $41,595 per year (comprehensive).

There is no additional cost for LD program/services.

LD SERVICES

LD program size is not limited.

LD services available to:

■ Freshmen ■ Sophomores ■ Juniors ■ Seniors

Academic Accommodations

Curriculum		In class	
Foreign language waiver	☐	Early syllabus	☐
Lighter course load	☐	Note takers in class	■
Math waiver	☐	Priority seating	☐
Other special classes	☐	Tape recorders	■
Priority registrations	☐	Videotaped classes	☐
Substitution of courses	☐	Text on tape	■
Exams		**Services**	
Extended time	■	Diagnostic tests	☐
Oral exams	☐	Learning centers	☐
Take home exams	☐	Proofreaders	☐
Exams on tape or computer	☐	Readers	■
Untimed exams	☐	Reading Machines/Kurzweil	■
Other accommodations	■	Special bookstore section	☐
		Typists	☐

Credit toward degree is not given for remedial courses taken.

Counseling Services

- ■ Academic — Meets 5 times per academic year
- ☐ Psychological
- ☐ Student Support groups
- ☐ Vocational

Tutoring

Individual tutoring is available weekly.

Average size of tutoring groups: 1

	Individual	Group
Time management	■	☐
Organizational skills	■	☐
Learning strategies	■	☐
Study skills	■	☐
Content area	☐	☐
Writing lab	■	☐
Math lab	■	☐

LD PROGRAM STAFF

Total number of LD Program staff (including director):

Full Time: 1 Part Time: 1

There is an advisor/advocate from the LD program available to students. The advisor/advocate meets with faculty 2 times per month and students 2 times per month. 16 peer tutors are available to work with LD students.

Key staff person available to work with LD students: Shelly Shinebarger, Director of Student Support Services.

Utica College

Utica, NY

Address: 1600 Burrstone Road, Utica, NY, 13502
Admissions telephone: 800 782-8884
Admissions FAX: 315 792-3003
Vice President for Enrollment Management: Patrick Quinn
Admissions e-mail: admiss@utica.edu
Web site: http://www.utica.edu
SAT Code: 2932 ACT Code: 2973

Coordinator of Learning Services: Kateri Teresa Henkel
LD program telephone: 315 792-3032
LD program e-mail: khenkel@utica.edu
Total campus enrollment: 2,310

GENERAL

Utica College is a private, coed, four-year institution. 138-acre, suburban campus in Utica (population: 60,651), 50 miles from Syracuse. Served by bus and train; major airport serves Syracuse; smaller airport serves Oneida County (10 miles). Public transportation serves campus. Semester system.

LD ADMISSIONS

Students do not complete a separate application and are not simultaneously accepted to the LD program. A member of the LD program does not sit on the admissions committee. A personal interview is recommended. Essay is required and may be typed.

SECONDARY SCHOOL REQUIREMENTS

Graduation from secondary school required; GED accepted. The following course distribution required: 4 units of English, 3 units of math, 3 units of science, 2 units of foreign language, 3 units of social studies, 1 unit of academic electives.

TESTING

SAT Reasoning or ACT required of some applicants. SAT Subject recommended.

All enrolled freshmen (fall 2004):

Average SAT I Scores:	Verbal: 483	Math: 490
Average ACT Scores:	Composite: 20	

Child Study Team report is not required. A neuropsychological or comprehensive psycho-educational evaluation is required for admission. Must be dated within 36 months of application. Tests required as part of this documentation:

- ☐ WAIS-IV
- ☐ WISC-IV
- ☐ SATA
- ☐ Woodcock-Johnson
- ☐ Nelson-Denny Reading Test
- ☐ Other

UNDERGRADUATE STUDENT BODY

Total undergraduate student enrollment: 856 Men, 1,287 Women.

Composition of student body (fall 2004):

	Undergraduate	Freshmen
International	1.2	1.5
Black	12.3	8.4
American Indian	0.5	0.5
Asian-American	2.1	1.8
Hispanic	4.7	3.7
White	59.5	66.2
Unreported	19.7	17.9
	100.0%	100.0%

12% are from out of state. 1% join a fraternity and 1% join a sorority. Average age of full-time undergraduates is 21. 62% of classes have fewer than 20 students, 38% have between 20 and 50 students.

STUDENT HOUSING

77% of freshmen live in college housing. Freshmen are required to live on campus. Housing is not guaranteed for all undergraduates. Housing for graduate students is limited. Campus can house 935 undergraduates. Single rooms are available for students with medical or special needs. A medical note is required.

EXPENSES

Tuition (2005-06): $22,030 per year.
Room: $4,750. Board: $4,306.
There is no additional cost for LD program/services.

LD SERVICES

LD program size is not limited.

LD services available to:

■ Freshmen ■ Sophomores ■ Juniors ■ Seniors

Academic Accommodations

Curriculum		In class	
Foreign language waiver	☐	Early syllabus	☐
Lighter course load	■	Note takers in class	☐
Math waiver	☐	Priority seating	☐
Other special classes	☐	Tape recorders	☐
Priority registrations	☐	Videotaped classes	☐
Substitution of courses	☐	Text on tape	☐
Exams		**Services**	
Extended time	☐	Diagnostic tests	☐
Oral exams	☐	Learning centers	☐
Take home exams	☐	Proofreaders	☐
Exams on tape or computer	☐	Readers	☐
Untimed exams	☐	Reading Machines/Kurzweil	☐
Other accommodations	☐	Special bookstore section	☐
		Typists	☐

Credit toward degree is not given for remedial courses taken.

Counseling Services

- ■ Academic
- ☐ Psychological
- ☐ Student Support groups
- ☐ Vocational

Tutoring

Individual tutoring is available.

	Individual	Group
Time management	■	■
Organizational skills	■	■
Learning strategies	■	■
Study skills	■	■
Content area	■	☐
Writing lab	■	☐
Math lab	■	☐

LD PROGRAM STAFF

Total number of LD Program staff (including director):

Full Time: 1 Part Time: 1

There is an advisor/advocate from the LD program available to students.

Key staff person available to work with LD students: Kateri Teresa Henkel, Coordinator of Learning Services.

Vassar College

Poughkeepsie, NY

Address: 124 Raymond Avenue, Poughkeepsie, NY, 12604
Admissions telephone: 845 437-7300
Admissions FAX: 845 437-7063
Dean of Admissions and Financial Aid: David Borus
Admissions e-mail: admission@vassar.edu
Web site: http://www.vassar.edu
SAT Code: 2956 ACT Code: 2982

LD program address: Box 164
LD program contact: Belinda Guthrie
LD program telephone: 845 437-7584
LD program e-mail: guthrie@vassar.edu
LD program enrollment: 63, Total campus enrollment: 2,475

GENERAL

Vassar College is a private, coed, four-year institution. 1,000-acre campus in Poughkeepsie (population: 42,777), 75 miles north of New York City. Served by bus and train; airport serves Newburgh (30 miles). School operates transportation to local malls. Semester system.

LD ADMISSIONS

Students do not complete a separate application and are simultaneously accepted to the LD program. A member of the LD program does not sit on the admissions committee. High school waivers are accepted for foreign language. A personal interview is not required. Essay is required and may be typed.

SECONDARY SCHOOL REQUIREMENTS

Graduation from secondary school required; GED accepted.

TESTING

SAT Subject recommended.

All enrolled freshmen (fall 2004):

Average SAT I Scores:	Verbal: 696	Math: 676
Average ACT Scores:	Composite: 30	

Child Study Team report is not required. A neuropsychological or comprehensive psycho-educational evaluation is required for admission. Must be dated within 24 months of application. Tests required as part of this documentation:

- ■ WAIS-IV
- ☐ WISC-IV
- ■ SATA
- ■ Woodcock-Johnson
- ■ Nelson-Denny Reading Test
- ☐ Other

UNDERGRADUATE STUDENT BODY

Total undergraduate student enrollment: 945 Men, 1,494 Women.

Composition of student body (fall 2004):

	Undergraduate	Freshmen
International	6.1	5.1
Black	5.7	5.1
American Indian	0.3	0.5
Asian-American	10.7	8.9
Hispanic	6.0	5.2
White	71.2	75.2
Unreported	0.0	0.0
	100.0%	100.0%

60% are from out of state. Average age of full-time undergraduates is 20. 70% of classes have fewer than 20 students, 30% have between 20 and 50 students.

STUDENT HOUSING

99% of freshmen live in college housing. Housing is guaranteed for all undergraduates. Campus can house 2,215 undergraduates. Single rooms are available for students with medical or special needs. A medical note is required.

EXPENSES

Tuition (2005-06): $33,310 per year.
Room: $4,190. Board: $3,710.
There is no additional cost for LD program/services.

LD SERVICES

LD program size is not limited.

LD services available to:

■ Freshmen ■ Sophomores ■ Juniors ■ Seniors

Academic Accommodations

Curriculum		In class	
Foreign language waiver	☐	Early syllabus	■
Lighter course load	■	Note takers in class	■
Math waiver	☐	Priority seating	■
Other special classes	☐	Tape recorders	■
Priority registrations	■	Videotaped classes	☐
Substitution of courses	■	Text on tape	■
Exams		**Services**	
Extended time	■	Diagnostic tests	☐
Oral exams	☐	Learning centers	■
Take home exams	☐	Proofreaders	☐
Exams on tape or computer	■	Readers	■
Untimed exams	☐	Reading Machines/Kurzweil	■
Other accommodations	■	Special bookstore section	☐
		Typists	■

Credit toward degree is not given for remedial courses taken.

Counseling Services

- ■ Academic
- ■ Psychological
- ■ Student Support groups
- ☐ Vocational

Tutoring

Individual tutoring is not available.

	Individual	Group
Time management	■	☐
Organizational skills	■	☐
Learning strategies	■	☐
Study skills	■	☐
Content area	☐	☐
Writing lab	■	☐
Math lab	■	☐

LD PROGRAM STAFF

Total number of LD Program staff (including director):

Full Time: 2 Part Time: 2

There is an advisor/advocate from the LD program available to students.

Key staff person available to work with LD students: Belinda Guthrie, Associate Dean of the College.

Vaughn College of Aeronautics and Technology

Flushing, NY

Address: 86-01 23rd Avenue, Flushing, NY, 11369
Admissions telephone: 800 776-2376, extension 188
Admissions FAX: 718 779-2231
Dean of Admissions: Ernie Shepelsky
Admissions e-mail: admitme@vaughn.edu
Web site: http://www.vaughn.edu
SAT Code: 2001 ACT Code: 2699

LD program name: Academic Support Services
Total campus enrollment: 1,244

GENERAL

Vaughn College of Aeronautics and Technology is a private, coed, four-year institution. Six-acre campus at LaGuardia Airport in the Flushing area of Queens (population: 2,229,379) in New York City. Served by air, bus, and train. Public transportation serves campus. Semester system.

LD ADMISSIONS

SECONDARY SCHOOL REQUIREMENTS

Graduation from secondary school required; GED accepted. The following course distribution required: 4 units of English, 3 units of math, 3 units of science, 2 units of foreign language, 2 units of social studies, 1 unit of history.

TESTING

SAT Reasoning required; ACT may be substituted. SAT Subject recommended.

All enrolled freshmen (fall 2004):

Average SAT I Scores: Verbal: 470 Math: 530

Child Study Team report is not required. Tests required as part of this documentation:

- ☐ WAIS-IV
- ☐ WISC-IV
- ☐ SATA
- ☐ Woodcock-Johnson
- ☐ Nelson-Denny Reading Test
- ☐ Other

UNDERGRADUATE STUDENT BODY

Total undergraduate student enrollment: 1,262 Men, 122 Women.

Composition of student body (fall 2004):

	Undergraduate	Freshmen
International	2.0	3.3
Black	16.9	19.4
American Indian	0.0	0.0
Asian-American	13.4	11.9
Hispanic	45.6	35.4
White	15.0	16.6
Unreported	7.1	13.4
	100.0%	100.0%

6% are from out of state.

STUDENT HOUSING

EXPENSES

Tuition (2005-06): $13,400 per year (in-state), $10,600 (out-of-state). There is no additional cost for LD program/services.

LD SERVICES

LD program size is not limited.

LD services available to:

☐ Freshmen ☐ Sophomores ☐ Juniors ☐ Seniors

Academic Accommodations

Curriculum		In class	
Foreign language waiver	☐	Early syllabus	☐
Lighter course load	■	Note takers in class	☐
Math waiver	☐	Priority seating	☐
Other special classes	☐	Tape recorders	☐
Priority registrations	☐	Videotaped classes	☐
Substitution of courses	☐	Text on tape	☐
Exams		**Services**	
Extended time	■	Diagnostic tests	☐
Oral exams	☐	Learning centers	■
Take home exams	☐	Proofreaders	☐
Exams on tape or computer	☐	Readers	☐
Untimed exams	■	Reading Machines/Kurzweil	☐
Other accommodations	☐	Special bookstore section	☐
		Typists	☐

Credit toward degree is given for remedial courses taken.

Counseling Services

- ☐ Academic
- ☐ Psychological
- ☐ Student Support groups
- ☐ Vocational

Tutoring

Individual tutoring is available weekly.

Average size of tutoring groups: 3

	Individual	Group
Time management	■	■
Organizational skills	■	■
Learning strategies	■	■
Study skills	■	■
Content area	■	■
Writing lab	■	■
Math lab	■	■

LD PROGRAM STAFF

There is an advisor/advocate from the LD program available to students. 5 peer tutors are available to work with LD students.

Key staff person available to work with LD students: Said Lamhaouar, Director.

Villa Maria College of Buffalo

Buffalo, NY

Address: 240 Pine Ridge Road, Buffalo, NY 14225
Admissions telephone: 716 896-0700, extension 1805
Director of Admissions: Kevin Donovan
Admissions e-mail: admissions@villa.edu
Web site: http://www.villa.edu
SAT Code: 2962 ACT Code: 2983

Director Learning Strategies Center: Arlene Sullivan
LD program telephone: 716 896-0700, extension 1860
LD program e-mail: asulli@villa.edu
LD program enrollment: 37, Total campus enrollment: 504

GENERAL

Villa Maria College of Buffalo is a private, coed, two-year institution. Nine-acre campus in Buffalo (population: 300,000). Served by air, bus and train. Public transportation serves campus. Semester system.

LD ADMISSIONS

Students do not complete a separate application and are simultaneously accepted to the LD program. A member of the LD program does not sit on the admissions committee. A personal interview is recommended. Essay is required and may be typed. Foreign language waivers are accepted.

SECONDARY SCHOOL REQUIREMENTS

Graduation from secondary school required; GED accepted.

TESTING

Child Study Team report is not required. A neuropsychological or comprehensive psycho-educational evaluation is required for admission. Tests required as part of this documentation:

- ☐ WAIS-IV
- ☐ WISC-IV
- ☐ SATA
- ☐ Woodcock-Johnson
- ☑ Nelson-Denny Reading Test
- ☐ Other

STUDENT HOUSING

There is no campus housing available.

EXPENSES

Tuition 2004-05:

There is no additional cost for LD program/services.

LD SERVICES

LD program size is not limited.

LD services available to:

☑ Freshmen ☑ Sophomores ☑ Juniors ☑ Seniors

Academic Accommodations

Curriculum		In class	
Foreign language waiver	☑	Early syllabus	☐
Lighter course load	☐	Note takers in class	☑
Math waiver	☐	Priority seating	☐
Other special classes	☐	Tape recorders	☑
Priority registrations	☐	Videotaped classes	☐
Substitution of courses	☑	Text on tape	☑
Exams		**Services**	
Extended time	☑	Diagnostic tests	☐
Oral exams	☑	Learning centers	☑
Take home exams	☐	Proofreaders	☐
Exams on tape or computer	☑	Readers	☑
Untimed exams	☑	Reading Machines/Kurzweil	☐
Other accommodations	☐	Special bookstore section	☐
		Typists	☐

Credit toward degree is not given for remedial courses taken.

Counseling Services

- ☑ Academic
- ☑ Psychological
- ☑ Student Support groups
- ☐ Vocational

Tutoring

Individual tutoring is available daily.

Average size of tutoring groups: 1

	Individual	Group
Time management	☑	☑
Organizational skills	☑	☑
Learning strategies	☑	☑
Study skills	☑	☑
Content area	☑	☑
Writing lab	☑	☑
Math lab	☑	☑

LD PROGRAM STAFF

Total number of LD Program staff (including director):

Part Time: 6-10

There is an advisor/advocate from the LD program available to students.

Key staff person available to work with LD students: Shakova Banks, Coordinator for Students with Disabilities.

Wagner College

Staten Island, NY

Address: 1 Campus Road, Staten Island, NY, 10301
Admissions telephone: 800 221-1010
Admissions FAX: 718 390-3105
Dean of Admissions: Leigh-Ann DePascale
Admissions e-mail: admissions@wagner.edu
Web site: http://www.wagner.edu
SAT Code: 2966 ACT Code: 2984

Assistant Dean of Academic Advisement: Dina Assante
LD program telephone: 718 390-3278
LD program e-mail: dassante@wagner.edu
LD program enrollment: 37, Total campus enrollment: 1,929

GENERAL

Wagner College is a private, coed, four-year institution. 110-acre, suburban campus on Staten Island (New York City population: 8,008,278). Major airports, bus, and train serve New York City; airport also serves Newark, N.J. (15 miles). School operates transportation to ferry and to local mall and movie theaters. Public transportation serves campus. Semester system.

LD ADMISSIONS

A personal interview is recommended. Essay is required and may be typed.

For fall 2004, 95 completed self-identified LD applications were received. 58 applications were offered admission, and 15 enrolled.

SECONDARY SCHOOL REQUIREMENTS

Graduation from secondary school required; GED not accepted. The following course distribution required: 4 units of English, 3 units of math, 2 units of science, 2 units of foreign language, 1 unit of social studies, 3 units of history, 6 units of academic electives.

TESTING

SAT Reasoning or ACT required. SAT Subject recommended.

All enrolled freshmen (fall 2004):

Average SAT I Scores:	Verbal: 556	Math: 556
Average ACT Scores:	Composite: 26	

Child Study Team report is not required. A neuropsychological or comprehensive psycho-education evaluation is not required for admission. Tests required as part of this documentation:

- [ ] WAIS-IV
- [ ] WISC-IV
- [ ] SATA
- [ ] Woodcock-Johnson
- [ ] Nelson-Denny Reading Test
- [ ] Other

UNDERGRADUATE STUDENT BODY

Total undergraduate student enrollment: 697 Men, 971 Women.

Composition of student body (fall 2004):

	Undergraduate	Freshmen
International	0.4	0.2
Black	6.1	5.4
American Indian	0.6	0.3
Asian-American	3.3	2.5
Hispanic	5.3	4.6
White	74.5	78.9
Unreported	9.8	8.1
	100.0%	100.0%

45% are from out of state. 10% join a fraternity and 11% join a sorority. Average age of full-time undergraduates is 20. 62% of classes have fewer than 20 students, 38% have between 20 and 50 students.

STUDENT HOUSING

79% of freshmen live in college housing. Freshmen are not required to live on campus. Housing is guaranteed for all undergraduates. Campus can house 1,420 undergraduates. Single rooms are available for students with medical or special needs. A medical note is required.

EXPENSES

Tuition (2005-06): $25,350 per year.
Room & Board: $7,950.
There is no additional cost for LD program/services.

LD SERVICES

LD program size is not limited.

LD services available to:

- [x] Freshmen
- [x] Sophomores
- [x] Juniors
- [x] Seniors

Academic Accommodations

Curriculum

- [ ] Foreign language waiver
- [x] Lighter course load
- [ ] Math waiver
- [ ] Other special classes
- [ ] Priority registrations
- [ ] Substitution of courses

Exams

- [x] Extended time
- [ ] Oral exams
- [ ] Take home exams
- [ ] Exams on tape or computer
- [x] Untimed exams
- [x] Other accommodations

In class

- [ ] Early syllabus
- [ ] Note takers in class
- [x] Priority seating
- [x] Tape recorders
- [ ] Videotaped classes
- [ ] Text on tape

Services

- [ ] Diagnostic tests
- [x] Learning centers
- [ ] Proofreaders
- [ ] Readers
- [ ] Reading Machines/Kurzweil
- [ ] Special bookstore section
- [ ] Typists

Credit toward degree is not given for remedial courses taken.

Counseling Services

- [x] Academic
- [x] Psychological
- [ ] Student Support groups
- [ ] Vocational

Tutoring

Individual tutoring is available.

	Individual	Group
Time management	[ ]	[ ]
Organizational skills	[ ]	[ ]
Learning strategies	[ ]	[ ]
Study skills	[ ]	[ ]
Content area	[ ]	[ ]
Writing lab	[ ]	[ ]
Math lab	[ ]	[ ]

LD PROGRAM STAFF

Total number of LD Program staff (including director):

Full Time: 1 Part Time: 1

There is an advisor/advocate from the LD program available to students.

Key staff person available to work with LD students: Dina Assante, Assistant Dean of Academic Advisement.

Wells College

Aurora, NY

Address: 170 Main Street, Aurora, NY, 13026
Admissions telephone: 800 952-9355
Admissions FAX: 315 364-3227
Director of Admissions: Susan Raith Sloan
Admissions e-mail: admissions@wells.edu
Web site: http://www.wells.edu
SAT Code: 2971 ACT Code: 2971

Associate Dean: Diane Koester
LD program telephone: 315 364-3241
LD program enrollment: 23, Total campus enrollment: 390

GENERAL

Wells College is a private, women's, four-year institution. 365-acre campus in Aurora (population: 720), 65 miles from Syracuse. Major airport and train serve Syracuse; smaller airport and bus serve Ithaca (30 miles); bus serves Auburn (20 miles). School operates transportation to Ithaca and to Syracuse during holidays. Semester system.

LD ADMISSIONS

A personal interview is recommended. Essay is required and may be typed. Foreign Language requirement may be waived.

SECONDARY SCHOOL REQUIREMENTS

Graduation from secondary school required; GED accepted. The following course distribution required: 4 units of English, 3 units of math, 2 units of science, 1 unit of social studies, 2 units of history, 2 units of academic electives.

TESTING

SAT Reasoning or ACT required. SAT Subject recommended.

All enrolled freshmen (fall 2004):

Average SAT I Scores:	Verbal: 572	Math: 528
Average ACT Scores:	Composite: 24	

Child Study Team report is not required. Tests required as part of this documentation:

- [ ] WAIS-IV
- [ ] WISC-IV
- [ ] SATA
- [ ] Woodcock-Johnson
- [ ] Nelson-Denny Reading Test
- [ ] Other

UNDERGRADUATE STUDENT BODY

Total undergraduate student enrollment: 443 Women.

Composition of student body (fall 2004):

	Undergraduate	Freshmen
International	2.3	2.4
Black	9.2	5.5
American Indian	2.3	1.0
Asian-American	2.3	2.6
Hispanic	6.9	4.5
White	60.9	67.5
Unreported	16.1	16.5
	100.0%	100.0%

24% are from out of state. Average age of full-time undergraduates is 20. 82% of classes have fewer than 20 students, 18% have between 20 and 50 students.

STUDENT HOUSING

99% of freshmen live in college housing. Freshmen are required to live on campus. Housing is guaranteed for all undergraduates. Campus can house 457 undergraduates. Single rooms are available for students with medical or special needs. A medical note is required.

EXPENSES

Tuition (2005-06): $14,840 per year.
Room: $3,640. Board: $3,640.
There is no additional cost for LD program/services.

LD SERVICES

LD program size is not limited.

LD services available to:

- [x] Freshmen
- [x] Sophomores
- [x] Juniors
- [x] Seniors

Academic Accommodations

Curriculum

- [ ] Foreign language waiver
- [x] Lighter course load
- [ ] Math waiver
- [ ] Other special classes
- [ ] Priority registrations
- [ ] Substitution of courses

Exams

- [x] Extended time
- [x] Oral exams
- [ ] Take home exams
- [ ] Exams on tape or computer
- [ ] Untimed exams
- [ ] Other accommodations

In class

- [ ] Early syllabus
- [x] Note takers in class
- [ ] Priority seating
- [x] Tape recorders
- [ ] Videotaped classes
- [ ] Text on tape

Services

- [ ] Diagnostic tests
- [ ] Learning centers
- [ ] Proofreaders
- [ ] Readers
- [ ] Reading Machines/Kurzweil
- [ ] Special bookstore section
- [ ] Typists

Credit toward degree is not given for remedial courses taken.

Counseling Services

- [ ] Academic
- [ ] Psychological
- [ ] Student Support groups
- [ ] Vocational

Tutoring

Individual tutoring is not available.

	Individual	Group
Time management	[ ]	[ ]
Organizational skills	[ ]	[ ]
Learning strategies	[ ]	[ ]
Study skills	[ ]	[ ]
Content area	[ ]	[ ]
Writing lab	[ ]	[ ]
Math lab	[ ]	[ ]

LD PROGRAM STAFF

There is an advisor/advocate from the LD program available to students. 1 peer tutor is available to work with LD students.

Key staff person available to work with LD students: Diane Koester, Associate Dean for Academic and Learning Resources.

Yeshiva University

New York, NY

Address: 500 West 185th Street, New York, NY, 10033
Admissions telephone: 212 960-5277
Admissions FAX: 212 960-0086
Director of Undergraduate Admissions: Michael Kranzler
Admissions e-mail: yuadmit@ymail.yu.edu
Web site: http://www.yu.edu
SAT Code: 2990 ACT Code: 2992

Associate Dean of Students: Dr. Chaim Nissel
LD program telephone: 212 960-5480
LD program e-mail: drnissel@yu.edu
LD program enrollment: 53, Total campus enrollment: 2,803

GENERAL

Yeshiva University is a private, coed, four-year institution. 12-acre Yeshiva Coll. campus in uptown Manhattan (New York City population: 8,008,278); Stern Coll. campus in midtown Manhattan; Syms Sch of Business at both campuses. Served by air, bus, and train. School operates transportation to George Washington Bridge bus station and nearby subway stations. Public transportation serves campuses. Semester system.

LD ADMISSIONS

A personal interview is required. Essay is required and may be typed.

For fall 2004, 24 completed self-identified LD applications were received. 14 applications were offered admission, and 12 enrolled.

SECONDARY SCHOOL REQUIREMENTS

Graduation from secondary school required; GED accepted. The following course distribution required: 4 units of English, 4 units of math, 4 units of science, 4 units of foreign language, 2 units of social studies, 2 units of history.

TESTING

SAT Reasoning or ACT considered if submitted.

All enrolled freshmen (fall 2004):

Average SAT I Scores: Verbal: 628 Math: 632
Average ACT Scores: Composite: 29

Child Study Team report is not required. Tests required as part of this documentation:

- ☐ WAIS-IV
- ☐ WISC-IV
- ☐ SATA
- ☐ Woodcock-Johnson
- ☐ Nelson-Denny Reading Test
- ☐ Other

UNDERGRADUATE STUDENT BODY

Total undergraduate student enrollment: 1,473 Men, 1,226 Women.

Composition of student body (fall 2004):

	Undergraduate	Freshmen
International	0.3	5.0
Black	0.0	0.0
American Indian	0.0	0.0
Asian-American	0.0	0.0
Hispanic	0.0	0.0
White	99.4	93.8
Unreported	0.3	1.2
	100.0%	100.0%

52% are from out of state. Average age of full-time undergraduates is 21. 72% of classes have fewer than 20 students, 27% have between 20 and 50 students, 1% have more than 50 students.

STUDENT HOUSING

87% of freshmen live in college housing. Freshmen are not required to live on campus. Housing is guaranteed for all undergraduates. Campus can house 2,100 undergraduates. Single rooms are available for students with medical or special needs. A medical note is required.

EXPENSES

Tuition (2005-06): $25,600 per year.

Room: $5,690. Board: $2,190.

There is no additional cost for LD program/services.

LD SERVICES

LD program size is not limited.

LD services available to:

☑ Freshmen ☑ Sophomores ☑ Juniors ☑ Seniors

Academic Accommodations

Curriculum		**In class**	
Foreign language waiver	☐	Early syllabus	☐
Lighter course load	☐	Note takers in class	☐
Math waiver	☐	Priority seating	☑
Other special classes	☐	Tape recorders	☑
Priority registrations	☐	Videotaped classes	☐
Substitution of courses	☐	Text on tape	☐
Exams		**Services**	
Extended time	☑	Diagnostic tests	☐
Oral exams	☑	Learning centers	☐
Take home exams	☐	Proofreaders	☐
Exams on tape or computer	☐	Readers	☐
Untimed exams	☑	Reading Machines/Kurzweil	☐
Other accommodations	☑	Special bookstore section	☐
		Typists	☐

Credit toward degree is not given for remedial courses taken.

Counseling Services

- ☐ Academic
- ☐ Psychological
- ☐ Student Support groups
- ☐ Vocational

Tutoring

Individual tutoring is available weekly.

Average size of tutoring groups: 1

	Individual	Group
Time management	☐	☐
Organizational skills	☐	☐
Learning strategies	☐	☐
Study skills	☐	☐
Content area	☐	☐
Writing lab	☐	☐
Math lab	☐	☐

LD PROGRAM STAFF

Total number of LD Program staff (including director):

Full Time: 6 Part Time: 6

There is an advisor/advocate from the LD program available to students. The advisor/advocate meets with faculty once per month and students 2 times per month.

Key staff person available to work with LD students: Dr. Chaim Nissel, Associate Dean of Students.

Appalachian State University

Boone, NC

Address: Boone, NC, 28608
Admissions telephone: 828 262-2120
Admissions FAX: 828 262-3296
Director of Admissions/Enrollment Management: Paul Hiatt
Admissions e-mail: admissions@appstate.edu
Web site: http://www.appstate.edu
SAT Code: 5010 ACT Code: 3062

Coordinator, Office of Disablity Services: Suzanne Wehner
LD program telephone: 828 262-3053
LD program e-mail: wehnerst@appstate.edu
LD program enrollment: 400, Total campus enrollment: 13,146

GENERAL

Appalachian State University is a public, coed, four-year institution. Campuses totalling 1,100 acres in Boone (population: 13,472), 95 miles from Winston-Salem; branch campus in Hickory. Major airports serve Charlotte and Greensboro (both 100 miles); smaller airport and bus serve Hickory; train serves Greensboro. Public transportation serves campus. Semester system.

LD ADMISSIONS

A personal interview is not required. Essay is not required.

SECONDARY SCHOOL REQUIREMENTS

Graduation from secondary school required; GED not accepted. The following course distribution required: 4 units of English, 3 units of math, 3 units of science, 1 unit of social studies, 1 unit of history.

TESTING

SAT Reasoning or ACT required. SAT Subject required.

All enrolled freshmen (fall 2004):

Average SAT I Scores:	Verbal: 559	Math: 564
Average ACT Scores:	Composite: 21	

Child Study Team report is not required. Tests required as part of this documentation:

- [ ] WAIS-IV
- [ ] WISC-IV
- [ ] SATA
- [ ] Woodcock-Johnson
- [ ] Nelson-Denny Reading Test
- [ ] Other

UNDERGRADUATE STUDENT BODY

Total undergraduate student enrollment: 5,755 Men, 5,906 Women.

Composition of student body (fall 2004):

	Undergraduate	Freshmen
International	0.2	0.4
Black	4.0	3.5
American Indian	0.4	0.3
Asian-American	1.6	1.2
Hispanic	2.2	1.4
White	88.9	91.0
Unreported	2.7	2.2
	100.0%	100.0%

17% are from out of state. 3% join a fraternity and 3% join a sorority. Average age of full-time undergraduates is 22. 38% of classes have fewer than 20 students, 56% have between 20 and 50 students, 6% have more than 50 students.

STUDENT HOUSING

98% of freshmen live in college housing. Freshmen are required to live on campus. Housing is not guaranteed for all undergraduates. Only as space is available. Single rooms are available for students with medical or special needs. A medical note is required.

EXPENSES

Tuition (2005-06): $1,821 per year (in-state), $11,563 (out-of-state).

Room: $2,910. Board: $1,748.
There is no additional cost for LD program/services.

LD SERVICES

LD program size is not limited.

LD services available to:

- [x] Freshmen
- [x] Sophomores
- [x] Juniors
- [x] Seniors

Academic Accommodations

Curriculum

- [ ] Foreign language waiver
- [ ] Lighter course load
- [ ] Math waiver
- [x] Other special classes
- [x] Priority registrations
- [x] Substitution of courses

Exams

- [x] Extended time
- [x] Oral exams
- [ ] Take home exams
- [x] Exams on tape or computer
- [x] Untimed exams
- [x] Other accommodations

In class

- [ ] Early syllabus
- [x] Note takers in class
- [x] Priority seating
- [x] Tape recorders
- [ ] Videotaped classes
- [x] Text on tape

Services

- [x] Diagnostic tests
- [x] Learning centers
- [x] Proofreaders
- [x] Readers
- [x] Reading Machines/Kurzweil
- [ ] Special bookstore section
- [x] Typists

Credit toward degree is not given for remedial courses taken.

Counseling Services

- [x] Academic
- [x] Psychological
- [x] Student Support groups
- [x] Vocational

Tutoring

Individual tutoring is available weekly.

Average size of tutoring groups: 3

	Individual	Group
Time management	[x]	[x]
Organizational skills	[x]	[x]
Learning strategies	[x]	[x]
Study skills	[x]	[x]
Content area	[ ]	[ ]
Writing lab	[x]	[x]
Math lab	[x]	[x]

LD PROGRAM STAFF

Total number of LD Program staff (including director):

Full Time: 2 Part Time: 2

There is an advisor/advocate from the LD program available to students.

Key staff person available to work with LD students: Suzanne Wehner, Coordinator, Office of Disablity Services.

Barton College

Wilson, NC

Address: 704-A College Street, PO Box 5000, Wilson, NC, 27893
Admissions telephone: 800 345-4973
Admissions FAX: 252 399-6572
Admissions Director: Amy Denton
Admissions e-mail: enroll@barton.edu
Web site: http://www.barton.edu
SAT Code: 5016 ACT Code: 3066

ADA Compliance Officer: Courtney Manning
LD program telephone: 252 399-6587
LD program e-mail: cmanning@barton.edu
LD program enrollment: 20, Total campus enrollment: 1,231

GENERAL

Barton College is a private, coed, four-year institution. 75-acre campus in Wilson (population: 45,000), 40 miles east of Raleigh. Served by bus and train; major airport serves Raleigh/Durham; smaller airport serves Rocky Mount (10 miles). 4-1-4 system.

LD ADMISSIONS

Students do not complete a separate application and are simultaneously accepted to the LD program. A member of the LD program does not sit on the admissions committee. A personal interview is recommended. Essay is not required.

SECONDARY SCHOOL REQUIREMENTS

Graduation from secondary school required; GED accepted. The following course distribution required: 4 units of English, 3 units of math, 2 units of science, 1 unit of academic electives.

TESTING

SAT Reasoning required; ACT may be substituted. SAT Subject recommended.

All enrolled freshmen (fall 2004):

Average SAT I Scores:	Verbal: 477	Math: 485
Average ACT Scores:	Composite:	

Child Study Team report is not required. A neuropsychological or comprehensive psycho-education evaluation is not required for admission. Tests required as part of this documentation:

- [ ] WAIS-IV
- [ ] WISC-IV
- [ ] SATA
- [ ] Woodcock-Johnson
- [ ] Nelson-Denny Reading Test
- [ ] Other

UNDERGRADUATE STUDENT BODY

Total undergraduate student enrollment: 377 Men, 852 Women.

Composition of student body (fall 2004):

	Undergraduate	Freshmen
International	1.8	2.1
Black	16.8	22.1
American Indian	0.0	0.3
Asian-American	0.4	0.8
Hispanic	2.7	2.1
White	75.6	69.8
Unreported	2.7	2.8
	100.0%	100.0%

19% are from out of state. 17% join a fraternity and 16% join a sorority. Average age of full-time undergraduates is 21. 59% of classes have fewer than 20 students, 41% have between 20 and 50 students.

STUDENT HOUSING

81% of freshmen live in college housing. Freshmen are required to live on campus. Housing is guaranteed for all undergraduates. Campus can house 608 undergraduates. Single rooms are available for students with medical or special needs. A medical note is required.

EXPENSES

Tuition (2005-06): $15,390 per year.
Room & Board: $5,880.
There is no additional cost for LD program/services.

LD SERVICES

LD program size is not limited.

LD services available to:

[x] Freshmen [x] Sophomores [x] Juniors [x] Seniors

Academic Accommodations

Curriculum		In class	
Foreign language waiver	[ ]	Early syllabus	[ ]
Lighter course load	[ ]	Note takers in class	[x]
Math waiver	[ ]	Priority seating	[ ]
Other special classes	[ ]	Tape recorders	[ ]
Priority registrations	[ ]	Videotaped classes	[ ]
Substitution of courses	[ ]	Text on tape	[ ]
Exams		**Services**	
Extended time	[x]	Diagnostic tests	[ ]
Oral exams	[x]	Learning centers	[x]
Take home exams	[ ]	Proofreaders	[ ]
Exams on tape or computer	[x]	Readers	[x]
Untimed exams	[ ]	Reading Machines/Kurzweil	[ ]
Other accommodations	[ ]	Special bookstore section	[ ]
		Typists	[ ]

Credit toward degree is not given for remedial courses taken.

Counseling Services

- [ ] Academic
- [ ] Psychological
- [ ] Student Support groups
- [ ] Vocational

Tutoring

Individual tutoring is available monthly.

	Individual	Group
Time management	[x]	[ ]
Organizational skills	[ ]	[ ]
Learning strategies	[ ]	[ ]
Study skills	[x]	[ ]
Content area	[ ]	[ ]
Writing lab	[x]	[ ]
Math lab	[x]	[ ]

LD PROGRAM STAFF

Total number of LD Program staff (including director):

Full Time: 2 Part Time: 2

There is an advisor/advocate from the LD program available to students.

Key staff person available to work with LD students: Courtney Manning, ADA Compliance Officer.

Belmont Abbey College

Belmont, NC

Address: 100 Belmont-Mount Holly Road, Belmont, NC, 28012
Admissions telephone: 704 825-6665
Admissions FAX: 704 825-6220
Director of Admission: Michel Poll
Admissions e-mail: admissions@bac.edu
Web site: http://www.belmontabbeycollege.edu
SAT Code: 5055 ACT Code: 3070

Academic Dean: Dr. Dean de la Motte
LD program telephone: 704 825-6728
LD program e-mail: deandelamotte@bac.edu
Total campus enrollment: 800

GENERAL

Belmont Abbey College is a private, coed, four-year institution. 650-acre, suburban campus in Belmont (population: 8,705), five miles from Charlotte. Airport and bus serve Charlotte; train serves Gastonia (12 miles). Semester system.

LD ADMISSIONS

A personal interview is recommended. Essay is not required.

SECONDARY SCHOOL REQUIREMENTS

Graduation from secondary school required; GED accepted. The following course distribution required: 4 units of English, 3 units of math, 2 units of science, 2 units of foreign language, 2 units of social studies, 3 units of academic electives.

TESTING

SAT Reasoning required; ACT may be substituted. SAT Subject recommended.

All enrolled freshmen (fall 2004):

Average SAT I Scores: Verbal: 501 Math: 495
Average ACT Scores: Composite: 21

Child Study Team report is not required. Tests required as part of this documentation:

- ❑ WAIS-IV
- ❑ WISC-IV
- ❑ SATA
- ❑ Woodcock-Johnson
- ❑ Nelson-Denny Reading Test
- ❑ Other

UNDERGRADUATE STUDENT BODY

Total undergraduate student enrollment: 381 Men, 492 Women.

Composition of student body (fall 2004):

	Undergraduate	Freshmen
International	4.6	4.2
Black	9.8	12.3
American Indian	0.6	0.3
Asian-American	1.7	1.1
Hispanic	6.3	4.7
White	70.7	72.8
Unreported	6.3	4.6
	100.0%	100.0%

34% are from out of state. 20% join a fraternity and 20% join a sorority. Average age of full-time undergraduates is 26. 87% of classes have fewer than 20 students, 13% have between 20 and 50 students.

STUDENT HOUSING

83% of freshmen live in college housing. Freshmen are required to live on campus. Housing is guaranteed for all undergraduates. Campus can house 617 undergraduates.

EXPENSES

Tuition (2005-06): $15,910 per year.
Room: $4,830. Board: $3,758.

There is no additional cost for LD program/services.

LD SERVICES

LD program size is not limited.

LD services available to:

❑ Freshmen ❑ Sophomores ❑ Juniors ❑ Seniors

Academic Accommodations

Curriculum		In class	
Foreign language waiver	❑	Early syllabus	❑
Lighter course load	❑	Note takers in class	❑
Math waiver	❑	Priority seating	❑
Other special classes	❑	Tape recorders	❑
Priority registrations	❑	Videotaped classes	❑
Substitution of courses	❑	Text on tape	❑
Exams		**Services**	
Extended time	❑	Diagnostic tests	❑
Oral exams	❑	Learning centers	■
Take home exams	❑	Proofreaders	❑
Exams on tape or computer	❑	Readers	❑
Untimed exams	❑	Reading Machines/Kurzweil	❑
Other accommodations	❑	Special bookstore section	❑
		Typists	❑

Credit toward degree is not given for remedial courses taken.

Counseling Services

- ❑ Academic
- ❑ Psychological
- ❑ Student Support groups
- ❑ Vocational

Tutoring

	Individual	Group
Time management	❑	❑
Organizational skills	❑	❑
Learning strategies	❑	❑
Study skills	❑	❑
Content area	❑	❑
Writing lab	❑	❑
Math lab	❑	❑

UNIQUE LD PROGRAM FEATURES

Upon acceptance to the College, students seeking accommodations for learning disabilities must provide a psycho-educational assessment completed by a licensed professional within three years of entering the College. Individual Educational Plans used in high school will not be accepted as substitutes for the assessment.

LD PROGRAM STAFF

Key staff person available to work with LD students: Jennie Latimer, Coordinator of Academic Assistance.

Bennett College

Greensboro, NC

Address: 900 E. Washington Street, Greensboro, NC, 27401
Admissions telephone: 800 413-5323
Admissions FAX: 336 517-2166
Director of Admissions: Ulisa Bowles
Admissions e-mail: admiss@bennett.edu
Web site: http://www.bennett.edu
SAT Code: 5058 ACT Code: 3072

Disability Services Coordinator: Tamara Boynton
LD program telephone: 336 517-1519
LD program e-mail: tboynton@bennett.edu
Total campus enrollment: 504

GENERAL

Bennett College is a private, women's, four-year institution. 55-acre campus in Greensboro (population: 223,891). Served by airport, bus, and train. Public transportation serves campus. Semester system.

LD ADMISSIONS

A personal interview is recommended.

SECONDARY SCHOOL REQUIREMENTS

Graduation from secondary school required; GED accepted. The following course distribution required: 4 units of English, 3 units of math, 2 units of science, 2 units of foreign language, 2 units of social studies, 5 units of academic electives.

TESTING

SAT Reasoning required; ACT may be substituted. SAT Subject recommended.

All enrolled freshmen (fall 2004):

Average SAT I Scores: Verbal: 422 Math: 398

Child Study Team report is not required. Tests required as part of this documentation:

- ☐ WAIS-IV
- ☐ WISC-IV
- ☐ SATA
- ☐ Woodcock-Johnson
- ☐ Nelson-Denny Reading Test
- ☐ Other

UNDERGRADUATE STUDENT BODY

Total undergraduate student enrollment: 619 Women.

Composition of student body (fall 2004):

	Undergraduate	Freshmen
International	0.5	1.5
Black	96.5	95.8
American Indian	1.2	0.0
Asian-American	1.2	0.3
Hispanic	0.6	1.5
White	0.0	0.0
Unreported	0.0	0.9
	100.0%	100.0%

78% are from out of state. Average age of full-time undergraduates is 20. 75% of classes have fewer than 20 students, 25% have between 20 and 50 students.

STUDENT HOUSING

98% of freshmen live in college housing. Freshmen are required to live on campus. Housing is guaranteed for all undergraduates. Campus can house 500 undergraduates. Single rooms are available for students with medical or special needs. A medical note is required.

EXPENSES

Tuition (2005-06): $11,509 per year.
Room: $2,913. Board: $2,937.
There is no additional cost for LD program/services.

LD SERVICES

LD program size is not limited.

LD services available to:

☑ Freshmen ☑ Sophomores ☑ Juniors ☑ Seniors

Academic Accommodations

Curriculum		In class	
Foreign language waiver	☐	Early syllabus	☑
Lighter course load	☑	Note takers in class	☐
Math waiver	☐	Priority seating	☑
Other special classes	☐	Tape recorders	☑
Priority registrations	☑	Videotaped classes	☐
Substitution of courses	☐	Text on tape	☑
Exams		**Services**	
Extended time	☑	Diagnostic tests	☐
Oral exams	☑	Learning centers	☑
Take home exams	☐	Proofreaders	☑
Exams on tape or computer	☑	Readers	☐
Untimed exams	☐	Reading Machines/Kurzweil	☑
Other accommodations	☑	Special bookstore section	☐
		Typists	☐

Credit toward degree is not given for remedial courses taken.

Counseling Services

- ☐ Academic
- ☐ Psychological
- ☐ Student Support groups
- ☐ Vocational

Tutoring

Individual tutoring is available daily.

Average size of tutoring groups: 1

	Individual	Group
Time management	☐	☑
Organizational skills	☐	☑
Learning strategies	☑	☑
Study skills	☑	☑
Content area	☑	☑
Writing lab	☑	☑
Math lab	☑	☑

LD PROGRAM STAFF

Total number of LD Program staff (including director):

Full Time: 1 Part Time: 1

There is an advisor/advocate from the LD program available to students. The advisor/advocate meets with faculty 3 times per month and students 3 times per month. 8 peer tutors are available to work with LD students.

Key staff person available to work with LD students: Tamara Boynton, Disability Services Coordinator.

Brevard College

Brevard, NC

Address: 400 N. Broad Street, Brevard, NC, 28712
Admissions telephone: 800 527-9090
Admissions FAX: 828 884-3790
Dean of Admissions and Financial Aid: Joretta S. Nelson
Admissions e-mail: admissions@brevard.edu
Web site: http://www.brevard.edu
SAT Code: 5067 ACT Code: 3074

LD program name: Office for Students with Special Needs & Disabilities
Director of Academic Support Programs: Shirley E. Arnold
LD program telephone: 828 884-8131
LD program e-mail: arnoldse@brevard.edu
LD program enrollment: 85, Total campus enrollment: 584

GENERAL

Brevard College is a private, coed, four-year institution. 120-acre campus in Brevard (population: 6,789), 35 miles southwest of Asheville. Major airport, bus, and train serve Asheville. Semester system.

LD ADMISSIONS

Students do not complete a separate application and are simultaneously accepted to the LD program. A member of the LD program does not sit on the admissions committee. High school waivers are accepted for math and foreign language. A personal interview is recommended. Essay is required and may be typed. There is no minimum class rank for acceptance. Counseling services (academic and psychological) are offered on an as-needed basis and are available daily. Remedial math and remedial reading are available on placement. Courses may be substituted on a case-by-case basis. For fall 2004, 42 completed self-identified LD applications were received. 42 applications were offered admission, and 35 enrolled.

SECONDARY SCHOOL REQUIREMENTS

Graduation from secondary school required; GED accepted. The following course distribution required: 4 units of English, 3 units of math, 3 units of science, 2 units of foreign language, 4 units of social studies, 1 unit of history, 4 units of academic electives.

TESTING

SAT Reasoning or ACT required. SAT Subject recommended.

All enrolled freshmen (fall 2004):

Average SAT I Scores:	Verbal: 507	Math: 493
Average ACT Scores:	Composite: 19	

Child Study Team report is not required. A neuropsychological or comprehensive psycho-educational evaluation is required for admission. Must be dated within 36 months of application. Tests required as part of this documentation:

- ■ WAIS-IV
- ■ WISC-IV
- ■ SATA
- ■ Woodcock-Johnson
- ■ Nelson-Denny Reading Test
- ■ Other

UNDERGRADUATE STUDENT BODY

Total undergraduate student enrollment: 369 Men, 332 Women.

Composition of student body (fall 2004):

	Undergraduate	Freshmen
International	1.3	1.6
Black	5.1	6.3
American Indian	2.5	1.4
Asian-American	0.6	0.5
Hispanic	1.9	3.0
White	87.3	86.9
Unreported	1.3	0.3
	100.0%	100.0%

53% are from out of state. Average age of full-time undergraduates is 19. 84% of classes have fewer than 20 students, 16% have between 20 and 50 students.

STUDENT HOUSING

92% of freshmen live in college housing. Freshmen are not required to live on campus. Housing is guaranteed for all undergraduates. Campus can house 540 undergraduates. Single rooms are available for students with medical or special needs. A medical note is required.

EXPENSES

Tuition (2005-06): $15,620 per year.

Room: $4,380. Board: $1,600.

There is no additional cost for LD program/services.

LD SERVICES

LD program size is not limited.

LD services available to:

■ Freshmen ■ Sophomores ■ Juniors ■ Seniors

Academic Accommodations

Curriculum		In class	
Foreign language waiver	■	Early syllabus	☐
Lighter course load	■	Note takers in class	■
Math waiver	■	Priority seating	☐
Other special classes	☐	Tape recorders	■
Priority registrations	☐	Videotaped classes	☐
Substitution of courses	■	Text on tape	■
Exams		**Services**	
Extended time	■	Diagnostic tests	☐
Oral exams	■	Learning centers	■
Take home exams	☐	Proofreaders	■
Exams on tape or computer	■	Readers	■
Untimed exams	☐	Reading Machines/Kurzweil	■
Other accommodations	■	Special bookstore section	☐
		Typists	■

Credit toward degree is not given for remedial courses taken.

Counseling Services

- ■ Academic
- ■ Psychological
- ☐ Student Support groups
- ☐ Vocational

Tutoring

Individual tutoring is available daily.

Average size of tutoring groups: 1

	Individual	Group
Time management	■	■
Organizational skills	■	☐
Learning strategies	■	☐
Study skills	■	☐
Content area	■	☐
Writing lab	■	☐
Math lab	■	☐

UNIQUE LD PROGRAM FEATURES

Services are provided at the request of the student. The student must meet with the Director of the Office for Students with Special Needs or Disabilities to (1)request special accommodations and (2)must provide current written documentation that verifies the existence of the disability. The verification of the disability should include a diagnosis, a description of the functional limitations that may affect academic performance, and a recommendation for accommodations. The documentation must contain the signed name of an individual certified and authorized to assess the disability, and who is not related to the student. The Director identifies functional limitations through discussion with the student and the review of documentation. Then a determination can be made about how those limitations could be effectively accommodated.

LD PROGRAM STAFF

There is an advisor/advocate from the LD program available to students. 5 peer tutors are available to work with LD students.

Key staff person available to work with LD students: Susan R. Kuehn

LD Program web site: http://www.brevard.edu/ossnd/index.htm

Campbell University

Buies Creek, NC

Address: P.O. Box 546, Buies Creek, NC, 27506
Admissions telephone: 800 334-4111, extension 1290
Admissions FAX: 910 893-1288
Director of Admissions: Peggy Mason & Allison B. Shell
Admissions e-mail: adm@mailcenter.campbell.edu
Web site: http://www.campbell.edu
SAT Code: 5100 ACT Code: 3076

Assistant Dean of Student Services: John Creech
LD program telephone: 910 893-1901
LD program e-mail: creech@mailcenter.campbell.edu
Total campus enrollment: 2,694

GENERAL

Campbell University is a private, coed, four-year institution. 850-acre campus in Buies Creek (population: 2,215), 30 miles from both Raleigh and Fayetteville; branch campuses in Morrisville, Raleigh, at Camp Lejeune, Ft. Bragg, and Pope Air Force Base, and abroad in Kuala Lumpur, Malaysia. Airport and train serve both Fayetteville and Raleigh-Durham; bus serves Dunn (15 miles). School operates transportation to nearby airports and to bus and train stations. Semester system.

LD ADMISSIONS

A personal interview is recommended. Essay is not required.

SECONDARY SCHOOL REQUIREMENTS

Graduation from secondary school required; GED accepted. The following course distribution required: 4 units of English, 3 units of math, 2 units of science, 2 units of foreign language, 2 units of social studies.

TESTING

SAT Reasoning or ACT required. SAT Subject recommended.

All enrolled freshmen (fall 2004):

Average SAT I Scores: Verbal: 540 Math: 551

Child Study Team report is not required. Tests required as part of this documentation:

- ❑ WAIS-IV
- ❑ WISC-IV
- ❑ SATA
- ❑ Woodcock-Johnson
- ❑ Nelson-Denny Reading Test
- ❑ Other

UNDERGRADUATE STUDENT BODY

Total undergraduate student enrollment: 1,129 Men, 1,324 Women.

Composition of student body (fall 2004):

	Undergraduate	Freshmen
International	3.8	3.3
Black	11.5	9.7
American Indian	0.3	0.6
Asian-American	0.0	0.0
Hispanic	2.7	2.1
White	76.8	79.3
Unreported	4.9	5.0
	100.0%	100.0%

37% are from out of state. Average age of full-time undergraduates is 22. 55% of classes have fewer than 20 students, 34% have between 20 and 50 students, 11% have more than 50 students.

STUDENT HOUSING

90% of freshmen live in college housing. Housing is guaranteed for all undergraduates. Campus can house 1,744 undergraduates.

EXPENSES

Tuition (2005-06): $15,550 per year.

Room: $2,556. Board: $2,785.

There is no additional cost for LD program/services.

LD SERVICES

LD program size is not limited.

LD services available to:

❑ Freshmen ❑ Sophomores ❑ Juniors ❑ Seniors

Academic Accommodations

Curriculum		In class	
Foreign language waiver	❑	Early syllabus	❑
Lighter course load	■	Note takers in class	■
Math waiver	❑	Priority seating	❑
Other special classes	❑	Tape recorders	❑
Priority registrations	❑	Videotaped classes	❑
Substitution of courses	❑	Text on tape	❑
Exams		**Services**	
Extended time	❑	Diagnostic tests	❑
Oral exams	❑	Learning centers	❑
Take home exams	❑	Proofreaders	❑
Exams on tape or computer	❑	Readers	❑
Untimed exams	❑	Reading Machines/Kurzweil	❑
Other accommodations	❑	Special bookstore section	❑
		Typists	❑

Credit toward degree is not given for remedial courses taken.

Counseling Services

- ❑ Academic
- ❑ Psychological
- ❑ Student Support groups
- ❑ Vocational

Tutoring

Individual tutoring is available weekly.

	Individual	Group
Time management	❑	❑
Organizational skills	❑	❑
Learning strategies	❑	❑
Study skills	❑	❑
Content area	❑	❑
Writing lab	❑	❑
Math lab	❑	❑

LD PROGRAM STAFF

Total number of LD Program staff (including director):

Full Time: 1 Part Time: 1

Key staff person available to work with LD students: John Creech, Assistant Dean of Student Services.

Catawba College

Salisbury, NC

Address: 2300 W. Innes Street, Salisbury, NC, 28144
Admissions telephone: 800 228-2922
Admissions FAX: 704 637-4444
Vice President, Dean of Admissions: Dr. Russell Watjen
Admissions e-mail: admission@catawba.edu
Web site: http://www.catawba.edu
SAT Code: 5103 ACT Code: 3080

Director of Academic Resource Center: Emily Gross
LD program telephone: 704 637-4259
LD program e-mail: ekgross@catawba.edu
Total campus enrollment: 1,375

GENERAL

Catawba College is a private, coed, four-year institution. 210-acre suburban campus in Salisbury (population: 26,462), within 50 miles of Charlotte, Greensboro, and Winston-Salem. Served by bus and train; major airport serves Charlotte; smaller airport serves Greensboro. Semester system.

LD ADMISSIONS

A personal interview is recommended. Essay is required and may be typed.

SECONDARY SCHOOL REQUIREMENTS

Graduation from secondary school required; GED accepted. The following course distribution required: 4 units of English, 2 units of math, 2 units of science, 2 units of social studies, 6 units of academic electives.

TESTING

SAT Reasoning required; ACT may be substituted. SAT Subject required.

All enrolled freshmen (fall 2004):

Average SAT I Scores: Verbal: 526 Math: 524
Average ACT Scores: Composite: 21

Child Study Team report is not required. Tests required as part of this documentation:

- ❑ WAIS-IV
- ❑ WISC-IV
- ❑ SATA
- ❑ Woodcock-Johnson
- ❑ Nelson-Denny Reading Test
- ❑ Other

UNDERGRADUATE STUDENT BODY

Total undergraduate student enrollment: 698 Men, 737 Women.

Composition of student body (fall 2004):

	Undergraduate	Freshmen
International	0.7	1.6
Black	10.4	15.2
American Indian	1.2	0.6
Asian-American	1.5	0.7
Hispanic	3.5	1.5
White	81.2	79.5
Unreported	1.5	0.9
	100.0%	100.0%

32% are from out of state. Average age of full-time undergraduates is 23. 59% of classes have fewer than 20 students, 41% have between 20 and 50 students.

STUDENT HOUSING

85% of freshmen live in college housing. Freshmen are required to live on campus. Housing is guaranteed for all undergraduates. Campus can house 756 undergraduates.

EXPENSES

Tuition (2005-06): $18,750 per year.

Room & Board: $6,250.
There is no additional cost for LD program/services.

LD SERVICES

LD program size is not limited.

LD services available to:

❑ Freshmen ❑ Sophomores ❑ Juniors ❑ Seniors

Academic Accommodations

Curriculum		**In class**	
Foreign language waiver	❑	Early syllabus	❑
Lighter course load	❑	Note takers in class	❑
Math waiver	❑	Priority seating	❑
Other special classes	❑	Tape recorders	❑
Priority registrations	❑	Videotaped classes	❑
Substitution of courses	❑	Text on tape	❑
Exams		**Services**	
Extended time	❑	Diagnostic tests	❑
Oral exams	❑	Learning centers	❑
Take home exams	❑	Proofreaders	❑
Exams on tape or computer	❑	Readers	❑
Untimed exams	■	Reading Machines/Kurzweil	❑
Other accommodations	❑	Special bookstore section	❑
		Typists	❑

Credit toward degree is not given for remedial courses taken.

Counseling Services

- ❑ Academic
- ❑ Psychological
- ❑ Student Support groups
- ❑ Vocational

Tutoring

Individual tutoring is available.

	Individual	Group
Time management	❑	❑
Organizational skills	❑	❑
Learning strategies	❑	❑
Study skills	❑	❑
Content area	❑	❑
Writing lab	❑	❑
Math lab	❑	❑

LD PROGRAM STAFF

Total number of LD Program staff (including director):

Full Time: 1 Part Time: 1

Key staff person available to work with LD students: Emily Gross, Director of Academic Resource Center.

Chowan College

Murfreesboro, NC

Address: 200 Jones Drive, Murfreesboro, NC, 27855
Admissions telephone: 252 398-1236
Admissions FAX: 252 398-1190
Vice President for Enrollment Management: Jonathan Wirt
Admissions e-mail: admission@chowan.edu
Web site: http://www.chowan.edu
SAT Code: 5107 ACT Code: 3084

Education Specialist: Charlotte Glaser
LD program telephone: 252 398-3604
LD program e-mail: glasec@chowan.edu
Total campus enrollment: 687

GENERAL

Chowan College is a private, coed, four-year institution. 300-acre campus in Murfreesboro (population: 2,045), 60 miles from Norfolk. Major airport serves Norfolk; bus serves Ahoskie (15 miles); train serves Roanoke Rapids (30 miles). School operates transportation to airport and bus and train stations. Semester system.

SECONDARY SCHOOL REQUIREMENTS

Graduation from secondary school required; GED accepted.

TESTING

SAT Reasoning required; ACT may be substituted. SAT Subject recommended.

All enrolled freshmen (fall 2004):

Average SAT I Scores: Verbal: Math:
Average ACT Scores: Composite:

Child Study Team report is not required. Tests required as part of this documentation:

- ☐ WAIS-IV
- ☐ WISC-IV
- ☐ SATA
- ☐ Woodcock-Johnson
- ☐ Nelson-Denny Reading Test
- ☐ Other

UNDERGRADUATE STUDENT BODY

Total undergraduate student enrollment: 415 Men, 360 Women.

Composition of student body (fall 2004):

	Undergraduate	Freshmen
International	0.0	0.9
Black	30.3	29.2
American Indian	0.0	0.5
Asian-American	0.4	1.2
Hispanic	1.0	2.0
White	58.2	62.1
Unreported	10.1	4.1
	100.0%	100.0%

60% are from out of state. 72% of classes have fewer than 20 students, 28% have between 20 and 50 students.

STUDENT HOUSING

Housing is guaranteed for all undergraduates. Campus can house 1,200 undergraduates.

EXPENSES

Tuition (2005-06): $14,600 per year.
Room: $3,100. Board: $3,500.

LD SERVICES

LD services available to:

☐ Freshmen ☐ Sophomores ☐ Juniors ☐ Seniors

Academic Accommodations

Curriculum		In class	
Foreign language waiver	☐	Early syllabus	☐
Lighter course load	☐	Note takers in class	☐
Math waiver	☐	Priority seating	☐
Other special classes	☐	Tape recorders	■
Priority registrations	☐	Videotaped classes	☐
Substitution of courses	☐	Text on tape	☐
Exams		**Services**	
Extended time	■	Diagnostic tests	☐
Oral exams	■	Learning centers	■
Take home exams	☐	Proofreaders	☐
Exams on tape or computer	☐	Readers	☐
Untimed exams	■	Reading Machines/Kurzweil	☐
Other accommodations	☐	Special bookstore section	☐
		Typists	☐

Credit toward degree is not given for remedial courses taken.

Counseling Services

- ☐ Academic
- ☐ Psychological
- ☐ Student Support groups
- ☐ Vocational

Tutoring

	Individual	Group
Time management	☐	☐
Organizational skills	☐	☐
Learning strategies	☐	☐
Study skills	☐	☐
Content area	☐	☐
Writing lab	☐	☐
Math lab	☐	☐

LD PROGRAM STAFF

Total number of LD Program staff (including director):

Full Time: 1 Part Time: 1

Key staff person available to work with LD students: Charlotte Glaser, Education Specialist.

Davidson College

Davidson, NC

Address: 209 Ridge Road, Davidson, NC, 28035
Admissions telephone: 800 768-0380
Admissions FAX: 704 894-2016
Vice President and Dean of Admission and Financial Aid: Chris Gruber
Admissions e-mail: admission@davidson.edu
Web site: http://www.davidson.edu
SAT Code: 5150 ACT Code: 3086

Assoc. Dean of Student Life: Kathy Bray-Merrell
LD program telephone: 704 894-2225
LD program e-mail: kamerrell@davidson.edu
Total campus enrollment: 1,714

GENERAL

Davidson College is a private, coed, four-year institution. 450-acre campus in Davidson (population: 7,139), 20 miles from Charlotte. Major airport, bus, and train serve Charlotte. School operates transportation to neighboring towns. Public transportation serves campus. Semester system.

SECONDARY SCHOOL REQUIREMENTS

Graduation from secondary school required; GED not accepted. The following course distribution required: 4 units of English, 3 units of math, 2 units of science, 2 units of foreign language.

TESTING

SAT Reasoning or ACT required. SAT Subject required.

All enrolled freshmen (fall 2004):

Average SAT I Scores:	Verbal: 677	Math: 674
Average ACT Scores:	Composite: 29	

Child Study Team report is not required. Tests required as part of this documentation:

- ❑ WAIS-IV
- ❑ WISC-IV
- ❑ SATA
- ❑ Woodcock-Johnson
- ❑ Nelson-Denny Reading Test
- ❑ Other

UNDERGRADUATE STUDENT BODY

Total undergraduate student enrollment: 823 Men, 850 Women.

Composition of student body (fall 2004):

	Undergraduate	Freshmen
International	3.0	3.1
Black	8.0	6.3
American Indian	0.8	0.5
Asian-American	2.4	2.4
Hispanic	4.8	4.2
White	74.7	78.3
Unreported	6.3	5.2
	100.0%	100.0%

81% are from out of state. 40% join a fraternity. Average age of full-time undergraduates is 19. 67% of classes have fewer than 20 students, 33% have between 20 and 50 students.

STUDENT HOUSING

100% of freshmen live in college housing. Freshmen are required to live on campus. Housing is guaranteed for all undergraduates. Campus can house 1,536 undergraduates.

EXPENSES

Tuition (2005-06): $27,653 per year.
Room: $4,308. Board: $3,850.

LD SERVICES

LD services available to:

❑ Freshmen ❑ Sophomores ❑ Juniors ❑ Seniors

Academic Accommodations

Curriculum		In class	
Foreign language waiver	❑	Early syllabus	❑
Lighter course load	■	Note takers in class	■
Math waiver	❑	Priority seating	❑
Other special classes	❑	Tape recorders	■
Priority registrations	❑	Videotaped classes	❑
Substitution of courses	❑	Text on tape	❑
Exams		**Services**	
Extended time	■	Diagnostic tests	■
Oral exams	■	Learning centers	❑
Take home exams	❑	Proofreaders	❑
Exams on tape or computer	❑	Readers	■
Untimed exams	❑	Reading Machines/Kurzweil	❑
Other accommodations	❑	Special bookstore section	❑
		Typists	❑

Counseling Services

- ❑ Academic
- ❑ Psychological
- ❑ Student Support groups
- ❑ Vocational

Tutoring

Individual tutoring is available.

	Individual	Group
Time management	❑	❑
Organizational skills	❑	❑
Learning strategies	❑	❑
Study skills	❑	❑
Content area	❑	❑
Writing lab	❑	❑
Math lab	❑	❑

Duke University

Durham, NC

Address: 2138 Campus Drive, Box 90586, Durham, NC, 27708
Admissions telephone: 919 684-3214
Admissions FAX: 919 681-8941
Director of Undergraduate Admissions: Christoph Guttentag
Admissions e-mail: undergrad-admissions@duke.edu
Web site: http://www.duke.edu/
SAT Code: 5156 ACT Code: 3088

LD program name: Student Disability Access Office
LD program address: 402 Oregon Street, Suite 102
SDAO Director: Emma H. Swain
LD program telephone: 919 668-1267
LD program e-mail: eswain@duke.edu
Total campus enrollment: 6,301

GENERAL

Duke University is a private, coed, four-year institution. 9,350-acre, suburban campus in Durham (population: 187,035), 20 miles from Raleigh; marine lab campus in Beaufort. Served by bus; airport and train serve Raleigh. School operates campus shuttle service. Public transportation serves campus. Semester system.

SECONDARY SCHOOL REQUIREMENTS

Graduation from secondary school required; GED not accepted. The following course distribution required: 4 units of English, 4 units of math, 4 units of science, 4 units of foreign language, 4 units of social studies.

TESTING

SAT Subject required.

All enrolled freshmen (fall 2004):

Average SAT I Scores: Verbal: Math:
Average ACT Scores: Composite:

Child Study Team report is not required. Tests required as part of this documentation:

☐ WAIS-IV ☐ Woodcock-Johnson
☐ WISC-IV ☐ Nelson-Denny Reading Test
☐ SATA ☐ Other

UNDERGRADUATE STUDENT BODY

Total undergraduate student enrollment: 3,129 Men, 2,942 Women.

Composition of student body (fall 2004):

	Undergraduate	Freshmen
International	5.3	4.9
Black	11.4	11.0
American Indian	0.1	0.3
Asian-American	13.2	13.0
Hispanic	5.8	6.9
White	56.6	57.2
Unreported	7.6	6.7
	100.0%	100.0%

85% are from out of state. 29% join a fraternity and 42% join a sorority. 71% of classes have fewer than 20 students, 23% have between 20 and 50 students, 6% have more than 50 students.

STUDENT HOUSING

100% of freshmen live in college housing. Freshmen are required to live on campus. Housing is guaranteed for all undergraduates. Students are required to live on campus for three years - two of those years are freshmen and sophomore year. Campus can house 5,185 undergraduates. Single rooms are available for students with medical or special needs.

EXPENSES

Tuition (2005-06): $31,420 per year.

Room: $4,800. Board: $4,150-$4,030.
There is no additional cost for LD program/services.

LD SERVICES

LD program size is not limited.

LD services available to:

■ Freshmen ■ Sophomores ■ Juniors ■ Seniors

Academic Accommodations

Curriculum		**In class**	
Foreign language waiver	☐	Early syllabus	☐
Lighter course load	☐	Note takers in class	☐
Math waiver	☐	Priority seating	☐
Other special classes	☐	Tape recorders	■
Priority registrations	☐	Videotaped classes	☐
Substitution of courses	☐	Text on tape	☐
Exams		**Services**	
Extended time	■	Diagnostic tests	☐
Oral exams	■	Learning centers	☐
Take home exams	☐	Proofreaders	☐
Exams on tape or computer	■	Readers	☐
Untimed exams	☐	Reading Machines/Kurzweil	☐
Other accommodations	■	Special bookstore section	☐
		Typists	☐

Credit toward degree is not given for remedial courses taken.

Counseling Services

■ Academic
■ Psychological
■ Student Support groups
☐ Vocational

Tutoring

Individual tutoring is available.

	Individual	Group
Time management	☐	☐
Organizational skills	☐	☐
Learning strategies	☐	☐
Study skills	☐	☐
Content area	☐	☐
Writing lab	☐	☐
Math lab	☐	☐

LD PROGRAM STAFF

There is an advisor/advocate from the LD program available to students.

East Carolina University

Greenville, NC

Address: East Fifth Street, Greenville, NC, 27858-4353
Admissions telephone: 252 328-6640
Admissions FAX: 252 328-6945
Director of Admissions: Thomas E. Powell
Admissions e-mail: admis@mail.ecu.edu
Web site: http://www.ecu.edu
SAT Code: 5180   ACT Code: 3094

LD program name: Disability Support Services
LD program address: A-117 Brewster Building
Associate Director: Diane Majewski
LD program telephone: 252 328-6799
LD program e-mail: majewskid@mail.ecu.edu
LD program enrollment: 287, Total campus enrollment: 17,510

GENERAL

East Carolina University is a public, coed, four-year institution. 392-acre main campus and 46-acre medical campus in Greenville (population: 60,476), 90 miles east of Raleigh; 46-acre branch campus in nearby county. Served by airport and bus; major airport serves Raleigh-Durham; train serves Rocky Mount (45 miles). School operates transportation to area housing and shopping. Semester system.

LD ADMISSIONS

A personal interview is not required. Essay is not required.

SECONDARY SCHOOL REQUIREMENTS

Graduation from secondary school required; GED accepted. The following course distribution required: 4 units of English, 4 units of math, 3 units of science, 2 units of foreign language, 2 units of social studies.

TESTING

SAT Reasoning or ACT required. SAT Subject required.

All enrolled freshmen (fall 2004):

Average SAT I Scores:	Verbal: 515	Math: 528
Average ACT Scores:	Composite: 21	

Child Study Team report is not required. Tests required as part of this documentation:

- [ ] WAIS-IV
- [ ] WISC-IV
- [ ] SATA
- [ ] Woodcock-Johnson
- [ ] Nelson-Denny Reading Test
- [ ] Other

UNDERGRADUATE STUDENT BODY

Total undergraduate student enrollment: 6,528 Men, 8,932 Women.

Composition of student body (fall 2004):

	Undergraduate	Freshmen
International	0.5	0.4
Black	14.0	15.2
American Indian	0.7	0.7
Asian-American	2.5	2.2
Hispanic	1.3	1.6
White	79.4	78.8
Unreported	1.6	1.1
	100.0%	100.0%

14% are from out of state. 4% join a fraternity and 4% join a sorority. Average age of full-time undergraduates is 22. 45% of classes have fewer than 20 students, 44% have between 20 and 50 students, 11% have more than 50 students.

STUDENT HOUSING

84% of freshmen live in college housing. Freshmen are not required to live on campus. Housing is guaranteed for all undergraduates. Campus can house 5,303 undergraduates. Single rooms are available for students with medical or special needs.

EXPENSES

Tuition (2005-06): $2,135 per year (in-state), $12,349 (out-of-state).
Room: $3,690. Board: $2,950.

There is no additional cost for LD program/services.

LD SERVICES

LD program size is not limited.

LD services available to:

- [x] Freshmen
- [x] Sophomores
- [x] Juniors
- [x] Seniors

Academic Accommodations

Curriculum
- [ ] Foreign language waiver
- [x] Lighter course load
- [ ] Math waiver
- [ ] Other special classes
- [ ] Priority registrations
- [ ] Substitution of courses

Exams
- [x] Extended time
- [ ] Oral exams
- [ ] Take home exams
- [ ] Exams on tape or computer
- [ ] Untimed exams
- [ ] Other accommodations

In class
- [ ] Early syllabus
- [x] Note takers in class
- [ ] Priority seating
- [x] Tape recorders
- [x] Videotaped classes
- [ ] Text on tape

Services
- [ ] Diagnostic tests
- [ ] Learning centers
- [ ] Proofreaders
- [x] Readers
- [x] Reading Machines/Kurzweil
- [ ] Special bookstore section
- [ ] Typists

Credit toward degree is not given for remedial courses taken.

Counseling Services

- [ ] Academic
- [ ] Psychological
- [ ] Student Support groups
- [ ] Vocational

Tutoring

Individual tutoring is available.

	Individual	Group
Time management	[ ]	[ ]
Organizational skills	[ ]	[ ]
Learning strategies	[ ]	[ ]
Study skills	[ ]	[ ]
Content area	[ ]	[ ]
Writing lab	[ ]	[ ]
Math lab	[ ]	[ ]

UNIQUE LD PROGRAM FEATURES

All services are individualized and determined based on documentation.

LD PROGRAM STAFF

Total number of LD Program staff (including director):

Full Time: 1   Part Time: 1

Key staff person available to work with LD students: Diane Majewski, Associate Director.

LD Program web site: http://www.ecu.edu/studentlife/dss/

Elizabeth City State University

Elizabeth City, NC

Address: 1704 Weeksville Road, Elizabeth City, NC, 27909
Admissions telephone: 800 347-3278
Admissions FAX: 252 335-3537
Director of Admissions: Grady Deese
Admissions e-mail: admissions@mail.ecsu.edu
Web site: http://www.ecsu.edu
SAT Code: 5629 ACT Code: 3095

Assistant to the Chancellor: Attorney H. Bernetta Brown
LD program telephone: 252 335-3596
LD program e-mail: bhbrown@mail.ecsu.edu
LD program enrollment: 12, Total campus enrollment: 2,437

GENERAL

Elizabeth City State University is a public, coed, four-year institution. 114-acre campus in Elizabeth City (population: 17,188). Served by bus; major airports serve Norfolk, VA. (60 miles) and Newport News, VA. (75 miles). Semester system.

LD ADMISSIONS

A personal interview is recommended. Essay is not required.

SECONDARY SCHOOL REQUIREMENTS

Graduation from secondary school required; GED accepted. The following course distribution required: 4 units of English, 3 units of math, 3 units of science, 1 unit of social studies, 1 unit of history, 8 units of academic electives.

TESTING

SAT Reasoning or ACT required. SAT Subject recommended.

All enrolled freshmen (fall 2004):

Average SAT I Scores:	Verbal: 417	Math: 424
Average ACT Scores:	Composite: 16	

Child Study Team report is not required. Tests required as part of this documentation:

- [ ] WAIS-IV
- [ ] WISC-IV
- [ ] SATA
- [ ] Woodcock-Johnson
- [ ] Nelson-Denny Reading Test
- [ ] Other

UNDERGRADUATE STUDENT BODY

Total undergraduate student enrollment: 2,437.

Composition of student body (fall 2004):

	Undergraduate	Freshmen
International	0.0	0.1
Black	83.2	78.7
American Indian	0.0	0.2
Asian-American	0.8	0.7
Hispanic	0.4	0.5
White	14.3	19.1
Unreported	1.3	0.7
	100.0%	100.0%

13% are from out of state. 3% join a fraternity and 2% join a sorority. 58% of classes have fewer than 20 students, 39% have between 20 and 50 students, 3% have more than 50 students.

STUDENT HOUSING

74% of freshmen live in college housing. Freshmen are not required to live on campus. Housing is guaranteed for all undergraduates. Campus can house 1,039 undergraduates.

EXPENSES

Tuition (2005-06): $1,399 per year (in-state), $9,738 (out-of-state).
Room: $2,867. Board: $1,843.

There is no additional cost for LD program/services.

LD SERVICES

LD program size is not limited.

LD services available to:

- [x] Freshmen
- [x] Sophomores
- [x] Juniors
- [x] Seniors

Academic Accommodations

Curriculum		**In class**	
Foreign language waiver	[ ]	Early syllabus	[ ]
Lighter course load	[x]	Note takers in class	[x]
Math waiver	[ ]	Priority seating	[ ]
Other special classes	[ ]	Tape recorders	[x]
Priority registrations	[ ]	Videotaped classes	[ ]
Substitution of courses	[ ]	Text on tape	[ ]
Exams		**Services**	
Extended time	[x]	Diagnostic tests	[ ]
Oral exams	[ ]	Learning centers	[x]
Take home exams	[ ]	Proofreaders	[ ]
Exams on tape or computer	[ ]	Readers	[ ]
Untimed exams	[x]	Reading Machines/Kurzweil	[ ]
Other accommodations	[ ]	Special bookstore section	[ ]
		Typists	[ ]

Credit toward degree is not given for remedial courses taken.

Counseling Services

- [ ] Academic
- [ ] Psychological
- [ ] Student Support groups
- [ ] Vocational

Tutoring

Individual tutoring is available daily.

	Individual	Group
Time management	[ ]	[ ]
Organizational skills	[ ]	[ ]
Learning strategies	[ ]	[ ]
Study skills	[ ]	[ ]
Content area	[ ]	[ ]
Writing lab	[ ]	[ ]
Math lab	[ ]	[ ]

LD PROGRAM STAFF

Total number of LD Program staff (including director):

Full Time: 1 Part Time: 1

There is an advisor/advocate from the LD program available to students. The advisor/advocate meets with students daily.

Key staff person available to work with LD students: Annie A. Hedgebeth, Coordinator.

Elon University

Elon, NC

Address: 2700 Campus Box, Elon, NC, 27244
Admissions telephone: 800 334-8448
Admissions FAX: 336 278-7699
Dean of Admissions and Financial Planning: Susan Klopman
Admissions e-mail: admissions@elon.edu
Web site: http://www.elon.edu
SAT Code: 5183 ACT Code: 3096

Disabilities Service Coordinator: Priscilla Lipe
LD program telephone: 336 278-6500
LD program e-mail: plipe@elon.edu
LD program enrollment: 204, Total campus enrollment: 4,622

GENERAL

Elon University is a private, coed, four-year institution. 502-acre campus in Elon adjacent to Burlington (population: 6,738), 16 miles east of Greensboro. Major airports serve Greensboro and Raleigh (40 miles); bus and train serve Burlington. School operates transportation to Greensboro and Raleigh airports before and after major holidays. 4-1-4 system.

LD ADMISSIONS

A personal interview is not required. Essay is required and may be typed.

SECONDARY SCHOOL REQUIREMENTS

Graduation from secondary school required; GED accepted. The following course distribution required: 4 units of English, 3 units of math, 3 units of science, 2 units of foreign language, 2 units of social studies, 1 unit of history.

TESTING

SAT Reasoning or ACT required. SAT Subject required.

All enrolled freshmen (fall 2004):

Average SAT I Scores:	Verbal: 588	Math: 581
Average ACT Scores:	Composite: 25	

Child Study Team report is required if student is classified. Tests required as part of this documentation:

☐ WAIS-IV ☐ Woodcock-Johnson
☐ WISC-IV ☐ Nelson-Denny Reading Test
☐ SATA ☐ Other

UNDERGRADUATE STUDENT BODY

Total undergraduate student enrollment: 1,624 Men, 2,536 Women.

Composition of student body (fall 2004):

	Undergraduate	Freshmen
International	1.6	1.3
Black	7.7	7.1
American Indian	0.3	0.2
Asian-American	1.1	0.8
Hispanic	1.5	1.1
White	84.4	86.0
Unreported	3.4	3.5
	100.0%	100.0%

72% are from out of state. 25% join a fraternity and 44% join a sorority. Average age of full-time undergraduates is 20. 44% of classes have fewer than 20 students, 56% have between 20 and 50 students.

STUDENT HOUSING

99% of freshmen live in college housing. Freshmen are required to live on campus. Housing is not guaranteed for all undergraduates. Campus housing is available for some juniors and seniors. Campus can house 2,596 undergraduates.

EXPENSES

Tuition (2005-06): $18,699 per year.
Room: $3,112. Board: $3,310.

There is no additional cost for LD program/services.

LD SERVICES

LD program size is not limited.

LD services available to:

☐ Freshmen ☐ Sophomores ☐ Juniors ☐ Seniors

Academic Accommodations

Curriculum		**In class**	
Foreign language waiver	☐	Early syllabus	☐
Lighter course load	■	Note takers in class	■
Math waiver	☐	Priority seating	☐
Other special classes	☐	Tape recorders	☐
Priority registrations	☐	Videotaped classes	☐
Substitution of courses	☐	Text on tape	☐
Exams		**Services**	
Extended time	■	Diagnostic tests	☐
Oral exams	☐	Learning centers	☐
Take home exams	☐	Proofreaders	☐
Exams on tape or computer	☐	Readers	☐
Untimed exams	☐	Reading Machines/Kurzweil	☐
Other accommodations	☐	Special bookstore section	☐
		Typists	☐

Credit toward degree is given for remedial courses taken.

Counseling Services

☐ Academic
☐ Psychological
☐ Student Support groups
☐ Vocational

Tutoring

	Individual	Group
Time management	☐	☐
Organizational skills	☐	☐
Learning strategies	☐	☐
Study skills	☐	☐
Content area	☐	☐
Writing lab	☐	☐
Math lab	☐	☐

UNIQUE LD PROGRAM FEATURES

Applicants do not apply as LD students

LD PROGRAM STAFF

Total number of LD Program staff (including director):

Full Time: 1 Part Time: 1

Key staff person available to work with LD students: Priscilla Lipe, Disabilities Service Coordinator.

Gardner-Webb University

Boiling Springs, NC

Address: P.O. Box 997, Boiling Springs, NC, 28017
Admissions telephone: 800 253-6472
Admissions FAX: 704 406-4488
Dean of Undergraduate Admissions/Enrollment Mgmt: Nathan Alexander
Admissions e-mail: admissions@gardner-webb.edu
Web site: http://www.gardner-webb.edu
SAT Code: 5242 ACT Code: 3102

LD program name: NOEL Program
LD program address: P.O. Box 7274
Director, Noel Programs for the Disabled: Cheryl Potter
LD program telephone: 704 406-4270, extension 4271
LD program e-mail: cpotter@gardner-webb.edu
LD program enrollment: 70, Total campus enrollment: 2,574

GENERAL

Gardner-Webb University is a private, coed, four-year institution. 250-acre campus in Boiling Springs (population: 3,866), 50 miles from Charlotte. Major airport and train serve Charlotte; bus serves Shelby (10 miles). School operates transportation to airport and bus station. Semester system.

LD ADMISSIONS

Students do not complete a separate application and are not simultaneously accepted to the LD program. A member of the LD program does not sit on the admissions committee. A personal interview is recommended. Essay is not required. Admissions requirements that may be waived for LD students include minimun class rank.

SECONDARY SCHOOL REQUIREMENTS

Graduation from secondary school required; GED accepted.

TESTING

SAT Reasoning or ACT recommended. SAT Subject recommended.

All enrolled freshmen (fall 2004):

Average SAT I Scores:	Verbal: 505	Math: 508
Average ACT Scores:	Composite: 21	

Child Study Team report is not required. A neuropsychological or comprehensive psycho-educational evaluation is required for admission. Tests required as part of this documentation:

- [x] WAIS-IV
- [x] WISC-IV
- [x] SATA
- [x] Woodcock-Johnson
- [x] Nelson-Denny Reading Test
- [ ] Other

UNDERGRADUATE STUDENT BODY

Total undergraduate student enrollment: 1,035 Men, 1,988 Women.

Composition of student body (fall 2004):

	Undergraduate	Freshmen
International	0.0	0.0
Black	16.8	16.1
American Indian	2.2	0.6
Asian-American	0.0	0.6
Hispanic	0.6	1.0
White	78.7	79.6
Unreported	1.7	2.1
	100.0%	100.0%

26% are from out of state. Average age of full-time undergraduates is 25. 69% of classes have fewer than 20 students, 31% have between 20 and 50 students.

STUDENT HOUSING

85% of freshmen live in college housing. Freshmen are required to live on campus. Housing is guaranteed for all undergraduates. Campus can house 1,139 undergraduates. Single rooms are available for students with medical or special needs. A medical note is required.

EXPENSES

Tuition (2005-06): $15,960 per year.
Room: $2,840. Board: $2,700.
There is no additional cost for LD program/services.

LD SERVICES

LD program size is not limited.

LD services available to:

- [x] Freshmen
- [x] Sophomores
- [x] Juniors
- [x] Seniors

Academic Accommodations

Curriculum		In class	
Foreign language waiver	[ ]	Early syllabus	[ ]
Lighter course load	[x]	Note takers in class	[x]
Math waiver	[ ]	Priority seating	[x]
Other special classes	[ ]	Tape recorders	[x]
Priority registrations	[x]	Videotaped classes	[ ]
Substitution of courses	[x]	Text on tape	[x]
Exams		**Services**	
Extended time	[x]	Diagnostic tests	[ ]
Oral exams	[x]	Learning centers	[ ]
Take home exams	[ ]	Proofreaders	[ ]
Exams on tape or computer	[x]	Readers	[x]
Untimed exams	[ ]	Reading Machines/Kurzweil	[x]
Other accommodations	[x]	Special bookstore section	[x]
		Typists	[x]

Credit toward degree is given for remedial courses taken.

Counseling Services

- [x] Academic
- [x] Psychological
- [ ] Student Support groups
- [x] Vocational

Meets 4 times per academic year

Tutoring

Individual tutoring is available weekly.

	Individual	Group
Time management	[x]	[x]
Organizational skills	[x]	[x]
Learning strategies	[x]	[x]
Study skills	[x]	[x]
Content area	[x]	[ ]
Writing lab	[x]	[ ]
Math lab	[x]	[ ]

UNIQUE LD PROGRAM FEATURES

When each LD student is determined eligible to receive services through the NOEL program, the student is assigned a specialist. This specialist will work with the student during their entire time at GWU.

LD PROGRAM STAFF

Total number of LD Program staff (including director):

Full Time: 9 Part Time: 9

There is an advisor/advocate from the LD program available to students. The advisor/advocate meets with students 5 times per month.

Key staff person available to work with LD students: Cheryl Potter, Director, Noel Programs for the Disabled.

Greensboro College

Greensboro, NC

Address: 815 W. Market Street, Greensboro, NC, 27401-1875
Admissions telephone: 800 346-8226
Admissions FAX: 336 378-0154
Director of Admissions: Tim Jackson
Admissions e-mail: admissions@gborocollege.edu
Web site: http://www.gborocollege.edu
SAT Code: 5260 ACT Code: 3104

LD program name: Office of Disability Services
Director of Disability Services: Julie Yindra
LD program telephone: 336 272-7102, extension 591
LD program e-mail: jyindra@gborocollege.edu
LD program enrollment: 133, Total campus enrollment: 1,165

GENERAL

Greensboro College is a private, coed, four-year institution. 40-acre, suburban campus in Greensboro (population: 223,891). Served by airport, bus, and train. Public transportation serves campus. Semester system.

LD ADMISSIONS

Students do not complete a separate application and are simultaneously accepted to the LD program. A member of the LD program does not sit on the admissions committee. A personal interview is recommended. Essay is required and may be typed.

SECONDARY SCHOOL REQUIREMENTS

Graduation from secondary school required; GED accepted.

TESTING

SAT Reasoning or ACT required. SAT Subject recommended.

All enrolled freshmen (fall 2004):

Average SAT I Scores: Verbal: 487 Math: 493
Average ACT Scores: Composite: 20

Child Study Team report is not required. A neuropsychological or comprehensive psycho-educational evaluation is required for admission. Must be dated within 36 months of application. Tests required as part of this documentation:

- [x] WAIS-IV
- [x] WISC-IV
- [ ] SATA
- [x] Woodcock-Johnson
- [x] Nelson-Denny Reading Test
- [ ] Other

UNDERGRADUATE STUDENT BODY

Total undergraduate student enrollment: 526 Men, 613 Women.

Composition of student body (fall 2004):

	Undergraduate	Freshmen
International	0.0	0.5
Black	17.3	19.1
American Indian	0.8	0.4
Asian-American	1.2	1.0
Hispanic	2.0	1.0
White	77.9	76.4
Unreported	0.8	1.6
	100.0%	100.0%

42% are from out of state. 2% join a fraternity and 3% join a sorority. Average age of full-time undergraduates is 22. 80% of classes have fewer than 20 students, 20% have between 20 and 50 students.

STUDENT HOUSING

92% of freshmen live in college housing. Freshmen are required to live on campus. Housing is guaranteed for all undergraduates. Campus can house 627 undergraduates. Single rooms are available for students with medical or special needs. A medical note is required.

EXPENSES

Tuition (2005-06): $17,850 per year.
Room: $3,580. Board: $3,340.

There is no additional cost for LD program/services.

LD SERVICES

LD program size is not limited.

LD services available to:

- [x] Freshmen
- [x] Sophomores
- [x] Juniors
- [x] Seniors

Academic Accommodations

Curriculum		In class	
Foreign language waiver	[ ]	Early syllabus	[ ]
Lighter course load	[x]	Note takers in class	[x]
Math waiver	[ ]	Priority seating	[ ]
Other special classes	[ ]	Tape recorders	[x]
Priority registrations	[ ]	Videotaped classes	[ ]
Substitution of courses	[ ]	Text on tape	[x]
Exams		**Services**	
Extended time	[x]	Diagnostic tests	[x]
Oral exams	[x]	Learning centers	[x]
Take home exams	[ ]	Proofreaders	[ ]
Exams on tape or computer	[x]	Readers	[x]
Untimed exams	[x]	Reading Machines/Kurzweil	[x]
Other accommodations	[x]	Special bookstore section	[ ]
		Typists	[x]

Credit toward degree is given for remedial courses taken.

Counseling Services

- [x] Academic
- [x] Psychological
- [ ] Student Support groups
- [x] Vocational

Tutoring

Individual tutoring is available weekly.

Average size of tutoring groups: 1

	Individual	Group
Time management	[ ]	[x]
Organizational skills	[ ]	[x]
Learning strategies	[ ]	[x]
Study skills	[ ]	[x]
Content area	[x]	[ ]
Writing lab	[x]	[ ]
Math lab	[ ]	[ ]

LD PROGRAM STAFF

Total number of LD Program staff (including director):

Full Time: 1 Part Time: 1

There is an advisor/advocate from the LD program available to students. 15 peer tutors are available to work with LD students.

Key staff person available to work with LD students: Julie Yindra, Director of Disability Services.

Guilford College

Greensboro, NC

Address: 5800 West Friendly Avenue, Greensboro, NC, 27410
Admissions telephone: 800 992-7759
Admissions FAX: 336 316-2954
Vice President of Enrollment: Randy Doss
Admissions e-mail: admission@guilford.edu
Web site: http://www.guilford.edu
SAT Code: 5261 ACT Code: 3106

Alternative Learning Specialist: Kim Garner
LD program telephone: 336 316-2451
LD program e-mail: kgarner@guilford.edu
Total campus enrollment: 2,511

GENERAL

Guilford College is a private, coed, four-year institution. 340-acre campus in Greensboro (population: 233,891). Served by airport, bus, and train. Public transportation serves campus. Semester system.

LD ADMISSIONS

Students do not complete a separate application and are not simultaneously accepted to the LD program. A member of the LD program does sit on the admissions committee. High school waivers are accepted for math and foreign language. A personal interview is recommended. Essay is not required. There are no special admission requirements for LD students. Each application is evaluated for admission individually.

SECONDARY SCHOOL REQUIREMENTS

Graduation from secondary school required; GED accepted. The following course distribution required: 4 units of English, 3 units of math, 2 units of science, 2 units of foreign language, 2 units of social studies, 1 unit of history, 2 units of academic electives.

TESTING

SAT Reasoning or ACT required. SAT Subject recommended.

All enrolled freshmen (fall 2004):

Average SAT I Scores:	Verbal: 580	Math: 550
Average ACT Scores:	Composite: 24	

Child Study Team report is not required. A neuropsychological or comprehensive psycho-education evaluation is not required for admission. Tests required as part of this documentation:

- ■ WAIS-IV
- ■ WISC-IV
- ☐ SATA
- ■ Woodcock-Johnson
- ☐ Nelson-Denny Reading Test
- ■ Other

UNDERGRADUATE STUDENT BODY

Total undergraduate student enrollment: 694 Men, 796 Women.

Composition of student body (fall 2004):

	Undergraduate	Freshmen
International	1.1	1.0
Black	13.2	23.8
American Indian	1.9	1.0
Asian-American	0.8	1.5
Hispanic	2.5	1.5
White	75.0	68.5
Unreported	5.5	2.7
	100.0%	100.0%

51% are from out of state. Average age of full-time undergraduates is 20. 58% of classes have fewer than 20 students, 42% have between 20 and 50 students.

STUDENT HOUSING

90% of freshmen live in college housing. Freshmen are required to live on campus. Housing is not guaranteed for all undergraduates. Campus can house 928 undergraduates. Single rooms are available for students with medical or special needs. A medical note is required.

EXPENSES

Tuition (2005-06): $21,310 per year.
Room & Board: $6,530.

There is no additional cost for LD program/services.

LD SERVICES

LD program size is not limited.

LD services available to:

■ Freshmen ■ Sophomores ■ Juniors ■ Seniors

Academic Accommodations

Curriculum		In class	
Foreign language waiver	■	Early syllabus	☐
Lighter course load	■	Note takers in class	■
Math waiver	☐	Priority seating	☐
Other special classes	■	Tape recorders	■
Priority registrations	☐	Videotaped classes	☐
Substitution of courses	■	Text on tape	■
Exams		**Services**	
Extended time	■	Diagnostic tests	☐
Oral exams	■	Learning centers	■
Take home exams	■	Proofreaders	■
Exams on tape or computer	■	Readers	■
Untimed exams	■	Reading Machines/Kurzweil	■
Other accommodations	■	Special bookstore section	☐
		Typists	■

Credit toward degree is not given for remedial courses taken.

Counseling Services

- ☐ Academic
- ☐ Psychological
- ☐ Student Support groups
- ☐ Vocational

Tutoring

Individual tutoring is available weekly.

Average size of tutoring groups: 6

	Individual	Group
Time management	■	☐
Organizational skills	■	☐
Learning strategies	■	■
Study skills	■	☐
Content area	■	☐
Writing lab	☐	☐
Math lab	☐	☐

UNIQUE LD PROGRAM FEATURES

Guilford College only offers LD services, it is not a stand-alone LD program.

LD PROGRAM STAFF

Total number of LD Program staff (including director):

Full Time: 2 Part Time: 2

There is an advisor/advocate from the LD program available to students. 100 peer tutors are available to work with LD students.

Key staff person available to work with LD students: Kim Garner, Alternative Learning Specialist.

High Point University

High Point, NC

Address: 833 Montlieu Avenue, High Point, NC, 27262-3598
Admissions telephone: 800 345-6993
Admissions FAX: 336 888-6382
Dean of Enrollment Management: Jessie McIlrath-Carter
Admissions e-mail: admiss@highpoint.edu
Web site: http://www.highpoint.edu
SAT Code: 5293 ACT Code: 3108

Director of Academic Services: Dr. Kelly A. Norton
LD program telephone: 336 841-9037
LD program e-mail: knorton@highpoint.edu
LD program enrollment: 92, Total campus enrollment: 2,619

GENERAL

High Point University is a private, coed, four-year institution. 81-acre, suburban campus in High Point (population: 85,839), 17 miles from Winston-Salem and 15 miles from Greensboro; branch campus in Winston-Salem. Served by airport, bus, and train; major airport serves Charlotte (75 miles). School operates transportation to airport at breaks. Public transportation serves campus. Semester system.

LD ADMISSIONS

Students do not complete a separate application and are simultaneously accepted to the LD program. A member of the LD program does sit on the admissions committee. High school waivers are accepted for math and foreign language. A personal interview is not required. Essay is not required.

SECONDARY SCHOOL REQUIREMENTS

Graduation from secondary school required; GED accepted. The following course distribution required: 4 units of English, 3 units of math, 2 units of science, 2 units of foreign language, 3 units of social studies.

TESTING

SAT Reasoning required; ACT may be substituted. SAT Subject recommended.

All enrolled freshmen (fall 2004):

Average SAT I Scores:	Verbal: 503	Math: 505
Average ACT Scores:	Composite: 21	

Child Study Team report is not required. A neuropsychological or comprehensive psycho-educational evaluation is required for admission. Must be dated within 36 months of application. Tests required as part of this documentation:

- [x] WAIS-IV
- [x] WISC-IV
- [x] SATA
- [x] Woodcock-Johnson
- [x] Nelson-Denny Reading Test
- [ ] Other

UNDERGRADUATE STUDENT BODY

Total undergraduate student enrollment: 964 Men, 1,626 Women.

Composition of student body (fall 2004):

	Undergraduate	Freshmen
International	0.0	0.1
Black	17.2	23.3
American Indian	0.0	0.3
Asian-American	6.3	2.9
Hispanic	2.6	2.3
White	66.9	67.7
Unreported	7.0	3.4
	100.0%	100.0%

55% are from out of state. 15% join a fraternity and 25% join a sorority. Average age of full-time undergraduates is 21. 72% of classes have fewer than 20 students, 28% have between 20 and 50 students.

STUDENT HOUSING

85% of freshmen live in college housing. Freshmen are required to live on campus. Housing is guaranteed for all undergraduates. Campus can house 1,123 undergraduates. Single rooms are available for students with medical or special needs. A medical note is required.

EXPENSES

Tuition (2005-06): $15,280 per year.
Room: $2,960. Board: $3,990.
There is no additional cost for LD program/services.

LD SERVICES

LD program size is not limited.

LD services available to:

- [x] Freshmen
- [x] Sophomores
- [x] Juniors
- [x] Seniors

Academic Accommodations

Curriculum		In class	
Foreign language waiver	[x]	Early syllabus	[x]
Lighter course load	[x]	Note takers in class	[x]
Math waiver	[x]	Priority seating	[x]
Other special classes	[ ]	Tape recorders	[x]
Priority registrations	[x]	Videotaped classes	[ ]
Substitution of courses	[x]	Text on tape	[x]
Exams		**Services**	
Extended time	[x]	Diagnostic tests	[ ]
Oral exams	[x]	Learning centers	[x]
Take home exams	[ ]	Proofreaders	[x]
Exams on tape or computer	[x]	Readers	[x]
Untimed exams	[ ]	Reading Machines/Kurzweil	[x]
Other accommodations	[x]	Special bookstore section	[ ]
		Typists	[x]

Credit toward degree is given for remedial courses taken.

Counseling Services

- [x] Academic
- [x] Psychological
- [x] Student Support groups
- [x] Vocational

Tutoring

Individual tutoring is available daily.

Average size of tutoring groups: 3

	Individual	Group
Time management	[x]	[x]
Organizational skills	[x]	[x]
Learning strategies	[x]	[x]
Study skills	[x]	[x]
Content area	[x]	[x]
Writing lab	[x]	[x]
Math lab	[x]	[x]

LD PROGRAM STAFF

Total number of LD Program staff (including director):

Full Time: 1 Part Time: 1

There is an advisor/advocate from the LD program available to students. 45 peer tutors are available to work with LD students.

Key staff person available to work with LD students: Dr. Kelly A. Norton, Director of Academic Services.

LD Program web site: http://www.highpoint.edu/academics/asc

Johnson C. Smith University

Charlotte, NC

Address: 100 Beatties Ford Road, Charlotte, NC, 28216
Admissions telephone: 800 782-7303
Admissions FAX: 704 378-1242
Director of Admissions: Jocelyn Biggs
Admissions e-mail: admissions@jcsu.edu
Web site: http://www.jcsu.edu
SAT Code: 5333 ACT Code: 3112

LD program name: Office of Student Support Services
Disability Services Coordinator: James Cuthbertson
LD program telephone: 708 378-1282
LD program e-mail: jcuthbertson@jcsu.edu
LD program enrollment: 26, Total campus enrollment: 1,415

GENERAL

Johnson C. Smith University is a private, coed, four-year institution. 105-acre, urban campus in Charlotte (population: 540,828). Served by air, bus, and train. Public transportation serves campus. Semester system.

LD ADMISSIONS

Students do not complete a separate application and are simultaneously accepted to the LD program. A member of the LD program does not sit on the admissions committee. A personal interview is required. Essay is not required.

SECONDARY SCHOOL REQUIREMENTS

Graduation from secondary school required; GED accepted. The following course distribution required: 4 units of English, 2 units of math, 1 unit of science, 2 units of social studies, 7 units of academic electives.

TESTING

SAT Reasoning required; ACT may be substituted. SAT Subject recommended.

All enrolled freshmen (fall 2004):

Average SAT I Scores: Verbal: 450 Math: 452
Average ACT Scores: Composite: 19

Child Study Team report is required if student is classified. A neuropsychological or comprehensive psycho-education evaluation is not required for admission. Tests required as part of this documentation:

- ☐ WAIS-IV
- ☐ WISC-IV
- ☐ SATA
- ☐ Woodcock-Johnson
- ☐ Nelson-Denny Reading Test
- ☐ Other

UNDERGRADUATE STUDENT BODY

Total undergraduate student enrollment: 724 Men, 977 Women.

Composition of student body (fall 2004):

	Undergraduate	Freshmen
International	0.0	0.0
Black	99.1	99.4
American Indian	0.2	0.1
Asian-American	0.0	0.1
Hispanic	0.2	0.1
White	0.0	0.2
Unreported	0.5	0.1
	100.0%	100.0%

70% are from out of state. 4% join a fraternity and 6% join a sorority. Average age of full-time undergraduates is 21. 44% of classes have fewer than 20 students, 56% have between 20 and 50 students.

STUDENT HOUSING

98% of freshmen live in college housing. Freshmen are required to live on campus. Housing is not guaranteed for all undergraduates. The number of the available housing units is limited. Campus can house 1,127 undergraduates. Single rooms are available for students with medical or special needs. A medical note is required.

EXPENSES

Tuition (2005-06): $12,120 per year.
Room: $3,201. Board: $2,362.
There is no additional cost for LD program/services.

LD SERVICES

LD program size is not limited.

LD services available to:

■ Freshmen ■ Sophomores ■ Juniors ■ Seniors

Academic Accommodations

Curriculum		In class	
Foreign language waiver	☐	Early syllabus	☐
Lighter course load	☐	Note takers in class	■
Math waiver	☐	Priority seating	■
Other special classes	☐	Tape recorders	■
Priority registrations	☐	Videotaped classes	☐
Substitution of courses	☐	Text on tape	☐
Exams		**Services**	
Extended time	■	Diagnostic tests	☐
Oral exams	■	Learning centers	■
Take home exams	☐	Proofreaders	☐
Exams on tape or computer	☐	Readers	■
Untimed exams	■	Reading Machines/Kurzweil	■
Other accommodations	☐	Special bookstore section	☐
		Typists	☐

Credit toward degree is not given for remedial courses taken.

Counseling Services

- ■ Academic
- ■ Psychological
- ■ Student Support groups
- ■ Vocational

Tutoring

Individual tutoring is available daily.

Average size of tutoring groups: 1

	Individual	Group
Time management	■	■
Organizational skills	■	■
Learning strategies	■	■
Study skills	■	■
Content area	■	■
Writing lab	■	■
Math lab	■	■

LD PROGRAM STAFF

Total number of LD Program staff (including director):

Full Time: 4 Part Time: 4

There is an advisor/advocate from the LD program available to students. The advisor/advocate meets with faculty 2 times per month and students 4 times per month. 20 peer tutors are available to work with LD students.

Key staff person available to work with LD students: James Cuthbertson, Disability Services Coordinator.

LD Program web site: http://www.jcsu.edu

Lees-McRae College

Banner Elk, NC

Address: PO Box 128, Banner Elk, NC, 28604
Admissions telephone: 800 280-4562
Admissions FAX: 828 898-8814
Director of Admissions: Walt Crutchfield
Admissions e-mail: admissions@lmc.edu
Web site: http://www.lmc.edu
SAT Code: 5364 ACT Code: 3116

Coordinator of Disability Services: Tamara Tressler-Blewitt
LD program telephone: 800 280-4562, extension 2561
LD program e-mail: tressler-blewitt@lmc.edu
Total campus enrollment: 872

GENERAL

Lees-McRae College is a private, coed, four-year institution. 400-acre, semirural campus in Banner Elk (population: 811), 17 miles from Boone and 50 miles from Johnson City, Tenn. Airport serves Kingsport, Tenn. (45 miles); bus serves Johnson City; train serves Asheville (55 miles). Semester system.

LD ADMISSIONS

A personal interview is not required. Essay is not required.

SECONDARY SCHOOL REQUIREMENTS

Graduation from secondary school required; GED accepted. The following course distribution required: 4 units of English, 3 units of math, 2 units of science, 1 unit of history, 5 units of academic electives.

TESTING

SAT Reasoning or ACT required. SAT Subject recommended.

All enrolled freshmen (fall 2004):

Average SAT I Scores: Verbal: 500 Math: 500
Average ACT Scores: Composite: 21

Child Study Team report is not required. Tests required as part of this documentation:

☐ WAIS-IV ☐ Woodcock-Johnson
☐ WISC-IV ☐ Nelson-Denny Reading Test
☐ SATA ☐ Other

UNDERGRADUATE STUDENT BODY

Total undergraduate student enrollment: 341 Men, 451 Women.

Composition of student body (fall 2004):

	Undergraduate	Freshmen
International	0.0	1.0
Black	6.8	6.0
American Indian	0.0	3.1
Asian-American	0.8	0.6
Hispanic	2.8	2.2
White	87.2	86.1
Unreported	2.4	1.0
	100.0%	100.0%

35% are from out of state. Average age of full-time undergraduates is 23. 75% of classes have fewer than 20 students, 25% have between 20 and 50 students.

STUDENT HOUSING

95% of freshmen live in college housing. Freshmen are required to live on campus. Housing is guaranteed for all undergraduates. Campus can house 596 undergraduates.

EXPENSES

Tuition (2005-06): $16,620 per year.

Room: $2,800. Board: $3,200.
There is no additional cost for LD program/services.

LD SERVICES

LD program size is not limited.

LD services available to:

☐ Freshmen ☐ Sophomores ☐ Juniors ☐ Seniors

Academic Accommodations

Curriculum		**In class**	
Foreign language waiver	☐	Early syllabus	☐
Lighter course load	■	Note takers in class	■
Math waiver	☐	Priority seating	☐
Other special classes	■	Tape recorders	☐
Priority registrations	☐	Videotaped classes	☐
Substitution of courses	☐	Text on tape	☐
Exams		**Services**	
Extended time	■	Diagnostic tests	☐
Oral exams	■	Learning centers	■
Take home exams	☐	Proofreaders	☐
Exams on tape or computer	☐	Readers	■
Untimed exams	■	Reading Machines/Kurzweil	■
Other accommodations	☐	Special bookstore section	☐
		Typists	☐

Credit toward degree is not given for remedial courses taken.

Counseling Services

☐ Academic
☐ Psychological
☐ Student Support groups
☐ Vocational

Tutoring

	Individual	Group
Time management	☐	☐
Organizational skills	☐	☐
Learning strategies	☐	☐
Study skills	☐	☐
Content area	☐	☐
Writing lab	☐	☐
Math lab	☐	☐

LD PROGRAM STAFF

Total number of LD Program staff (including director):

Full Time: 2 Part Time: 2

Key staff person available to work with LD students: Tamara Tressler-Blewitt, Coordinator of Disability Services.

Lenoir-Rhyne College

Hickory, NC

Address: PO Box 7163, Hickory, NC, 28603-7163
Admissions telephone: 800 277-5721
Admissions FAX: 828 328-7378
Director of Admissions and Financial Planning: Rachel A. Nichols
Admissions e-mail: admission@lrc.edu
Web site: http://www.lrc.edu
SAT Code: 5365 ACT Code: 3118

LD program name: Disability Services
LD program address: PO Box 7470
Disabilities Coordinator: Dr. Janette Sims
LD program telephone: 828 328-7296
LD program e-mail: simsj@lrc.edu
Total campus enrollment: 1,407

GENERAL

Lenoir-Rhyne College is a private, coed, four-year institution. 100-acre campus in Hickory (population: 37,222), 50 miles northwest of Charlotte. Served by air; major airport and train serve Charlotte; bus serves Statesville (25 miles). Public transportation serves campus. Semester system.

LD ADMISSIONS

Students do not complete a separate application and are simultaneously accepted to the LD program. A member of the LD program does not sit on the admissions committee. A personal interview is recommended. Essay is not required.

SECONDARY SCHOOL REQUIREMENTS

Graduation from secondary school not required. The following course distribution required: 4 units of English, 3 units of math, 1 unit of science, 2 units of foreign language, 1 unit of history.

TESTING

SAT Reasoning or ACT required. SAT Subject recommended.

All enrolled freshmen (fall 2004):

Average SAT I Scores:	Verbal: 513	Math: 519
Average ACT Scores:	Composite: 21	

Child Study Team report is not required. Tests required as part of this documentation:

- [ ] WAIS-IV
- [ ] WISC-IV
- [ ] SATA
- [ ] Woodcock-Johnson
- [ ] Nelson-Denny Reading Test
- [ ] Other

UNDERGRADUATE STUDENT BODY

Total undergraduate student enrollment: 469 Men, 847 Women.

Composition of student body (fall 2004):

	Undergraduate	Freshmen
International	0.3	0.3
Black	11.8	8.7
American Indian	0.6	0.4
Asian-American	3.1	2.4
Hispanic	0.6	1.0
White	81.4	85.7
Unreported	2.2	1.5
	100.0%	100.0%

26% are from out of state. 23% join a fraternity and 27% join a sorority. Average age of full-time undergraduates is 23. 70% of classes have fewer than 20 students, 29% have between 20 and 50 students, 1% have more than 50 students.

STUDENT HOUSING

88% of freshmen live in college housing. Freshmen are required to live on campus. Housing is guaranteed for all undergraduates. Campus can house 780 undergraduates. Single rooms are available for students with medical or special needs. A medical note is required.

EXPENSES

Tuition (2005-06): $18,130 per year.
Room & Board: $6,680.
There is no additional cost for LD program/services.

LD SERVICES

LD program size is not limited.

LD services available to:

- [x] Freshmen
- [x] Sophomores
- [x] Juniors
- [x] Seniors

Academic Accommodations

Curriculum		In class	
Foreign language waiver	[x]	Early syllabus	[ ]
Lighter course load	[x]	Note takers in class	[x]
Math waiver	[ ]	Priority seating	[ ]
Other special classes	[ ]	Tape recorders	[x]
Priority registrations	[ ]	Videotaped classes	[ ]
Substitution of courses	[ ]	Text on tape	[ ]
Exams		**Services**	
Extended time	[x]	Diagnostic tests	[ ]
Oral exams	[x]	Learning centers	[ ]
Take home exams	[ ]	Proofreaders	[ ]
Exams on tape or computer	[x]	Readers	[x]
Untimed exams	[ ]	Reading Machines/Kurzweil	[x]
Other accommodations	[ ]	Special bookstore section	[ ]
		Typists	[x]

Credit toward degree is not given for remedial courses taken.

Counseling Services

- [x] Academic
- [ ] Psychological
- [ ] Student Support groups
- [ ] Vocational

Tutoring

Individual tutoring is available weekly.

Average size of tutoring groups: 5

	Individual	Group
Time management	[ ]	[x]
Organizational skills	[ ]	[x]
Learning strategies	[ ]	[x]
Study skills	[ ]	[x]
Content area	[ ]	[x]
Writing lab	[x]	[ ]
Math lab	[ ]	[ ]

LD PROGRAM STAFF

Total number of LD Program staff (including director):

Full Time: 2 Part Time: 2

There is an advisor/advocate from the LD program available to students. The advisor/advocate meets with faculty 1 time per month. 10 peer tutors are available to work with LD students.

Key staff person available to work with LD students: Dr. Janette Sims, Disabilities Coordinator.

Livingstone College

Salisbury, NC

Address: 701 W. Monroe Street, Salisbury, NC, 28144
Admissions telephone: 704 216-6001
Admissions FAX: 704 216-6215
Director of Enrollment Management: Anthony Brooks
Admissions e-mail: admissions@livingstone.edu
Web site: http://www.livingstone.edu/
SAT Code: 5367 ACT Code: 24

Director of Empowering Scholars Program: J. Cowan
LD program telephone: 704 216-6065
LD program e-mail: jcowan@livingstone.edu
LD program enrollment: 60, Total campus enrollment: 1,016

GENERAL

Livingstone College is a private, coed, four-year institution. 272-acre campus in Salisbury (population: 26,462), 38 miles from Charlotte. Served by bus and train; major airport serves Charlotte; smaller airport serves Greensboro (60 miles). Public transportation serves campus. Semester system.

LD ADMISSIONS

Students do not complete a separate application and are not simultaneously accepted to the LD program. A member of the LD program does not sit on the admissions committee. A personal interview is required. Essay is not required.

For fall 2004, 23 completed self-identified LD applications were received. 23 applications were offered admission, and 23 enrolled.

SECONDARY SCHOOL REQUIREMENTS

Graduation from secondary school required; GED accepted. The following course distribution required: 4 units of English, 2 units of math, 2 units of science, 2 units of social studies.

TESTING

SAT Reasoning recommended; ACT may be substituted. SAT Subject recommended.

All enrolled freshmen (fall 2004):

Average SAT I Scores:	Verbal: 387	Math: 381
Average ACT Scores:	Composite: 15	

Child Study Team report is not required. A neuropsychological or comprehensive psycho-educational evaluation is required for admission. Must be dated within 12 months of application. Tests required as part of this documentation:

- [ ] WAIS-IV
- [ ] WISC-IV
- [ ] SATA
- [ ] Woodcock-Johnson
- [ ] Nelson-Denny Reading Test
- [x] Other

UNDERGRADUATE STUDENT BODY

Total undergraduate student enrollment: 1,016.

Composition of student body (fall 2004):

	Undergraduate	Freshmen
International	1.5	2.2
Black	95.9	92.8
American Indian	0.4	0.2
Asian-American	0.0	0.0
Hispanic	0.7	0.7
White	0.0	0.8
Unreported	1.5	3.3
	100.0%	100.0%

50% are from out of state. 3% join a fraternity and 2% join a sorority. Average age of full-time undergraduates is 23. 64% of classes have fewer than 20 students, 33% have between 20 and 50 students, 3% have more than 50 students.

STUDENT HOUSING

85% of freshmen live in college housing. Freshmen are required to live on campus. Housing is guaranteed for all undergraduates. Campus can house 721 undergraduates. Single rooms are available for students with medical or special needs. A medical note is required.

EXPENSES

Tuition (2005-06): $10,278 per year.
Room: $2,501. Board: $3,140.
There is no additional cost for LD program/services.

LD SERVICES

LD program size is not limited.

LD services available to:

- [x] Freshmen
- [x] Sophomores
- [x] Juniors
- [x] Seniors

Academic Accommodations

Curriculum

- [ ] Foreign language waiver
- [ ] Lighter course load
- [ ] Math waiver
- [ ] Other special classes
- [ ] Priority registrations
- [ ] Substitution of courses

Exams

- [x] Extended time
- [x] Oral exams
- [ ] Take home exams
- [ ] Exams on tape or computer
- [x] Untimed exams
- [ ] Other accommodations

In class

- [ ] Early syllabus
- [ ] Note takers in class
- [ ] Priority seating
- [x] Tape recorders
- [x] Videotaped classes
- [ ] Text on tape

Services

- [x] Diagnostic tests
- [x] Learning centers
- [ ] Proofreaders
- [x] Readers
- [ ] Reading Machines/Kurzweil
- [ ] Special bookstore section
- [ ] Typists

Credit toward degree is not given for remedial courses taken.

Counseling Services

- [x] Academic
- [ ] Psychological
- [ ] Student Support groups
- [x] Vocational

Tutoring

Individual tutoring is available daily.

Average size of tutoring groups: 3

	Individual	Group
Time management	[x]	[x]
Organizational skills	[x]	[x]
Learning strategies	[x]	[x]
Study skills	[x]	[x]
Content area	[x]	[x]
Writing lab	[x]	[x]
Math lab	[ ]	[ ]

LD PROGRAM STAFF

Total number of LD Program staff (including director):

Full Time: 2 Part Time: 2

There is an advisor/advocate from the LD program available to students. The advisor/advocate meets with faculty 2 times per month and students 20 times per month.

Key staff person available to work with LD students: Judith Cowan, Director of Empowering Scholars Program.

Mars Hill College

Mars Hill, NC

Address: 100 Athletic Street, Mars Hill, NC, 28754
Admissions telephone: 800 543-1514
Admissions FAX: 828 689-1473
Director of Admissions: Chad Holt
Admissions e-mail: admissions@mhc.edu
Web site: http://www.mhc.edu
SAT Code: 5395 ACT Code: 3124

Director of Student Support Services: Barbara McKinney
LD program telephone: 828 689-1464
LD program e-mail: bmckinney@mhc.edu
Total campus enrollment: 1,384

GENERAL

Mars Hill College is a private, coed, four-year institution. 194-acre campus in Mars Hill (population: 1,764), 18 miles north of Asheville and 60 miles from Greenville, S.C. Airport and bus serve Asheville; train serves Greenville. School operates transportation to airport and bus station. Semester system.

SECONDARY SCHOOL REQUIREMENTS

Graduation from secondary school required; GED accepted. The following course distribution required: 4 units of English, 3 units of math, 2 units of science, 2 units of history, 7 units of academic electives.

TESTING

SAT Reasoning recommended. ACT required of some applicants.

All enrolled freshmen (fall 2004):

Average SAT I Scores: Verbal: 492 Math: 506

Child Study Team report is not required. Tests required as part of this documentation:

☐ WAIS-IV	☐ Woodcock-Johnson
☐ WISC-IV	☐ Nelson-Denny Reading Test
☐ SATA	☐ Other

UNDERGRADUATE STUDENT BODY

Total undergraduate student enrollment: 525 Men, 699 Women.

Composition of student body (fall 2004):

	Undergraduate	Freshmen
International	1.7	1.3
Black	16.4	12.4
American Indian	0.6	0.9
Asian-American	1.1	1.0
Hispanic	2.0	1.9
White	78.2	82.2
Unreported	0.0	0.3
	100.0%	100.0%

40% are from out of state. 14% join a fraternity and 12% join a sorority. Average age of full-time undergraduates is 20. 66% of classes have fewer than 20 students, 34% have between 20 and 50 students.

STUDENT HOUSING

70% of freshmen live in college housing. Freshmen are required to live on campus. Housing is guaranteed for all undergraduates. Campus can house 900 undergraduates.

EXPENSES

Tuition (2005-06): $15,252 per year.
Room: $2,900. Board: $3,024.

LD SERVICES

LD program size is not limited.

LD services available to:

☐ Freshmen ☐ Sophomores ☐ Juniors ☐ Seniors

Academic Accommodations

Curriculum		**In class**	
Foreign language waiver	☐	Early syllabus	☐
Lighter course load	☐	Note takers in class	☐
Math waiver	☐	Priority seating	☐
Other special classes	☐	Tape recorders	■
Priority registrations	☐	Videotaped classes	☐
Substitution of courses	☐	Text on tape	☐
Exams		**Services**	
Extended time	■	Diagnostic tests	■
Oral exams	■	Learning centers	☐
Take home exams	☐	Proofreaders	☐
Exams on tape or computer	☐	Readers	■
Untimed exams	☐	Reading Machines/Kurzweil	☐
Other accommodations	☐	Special bookstore section	☐
		Typists	☐

Credit toward degree is not given for remedial courses taken.

Counseling Services

☐ Academic
☐ Psychological
☐ Student Support groups
☐ Vocational

Tutoring

Individual tutoring is available.

	Individual	Group
Time management	☐	☐
Organizational skills	☐	☐
Learning strategies	☐	☐
Study skills	☐	☐
Content area	☐	☐
Writing lab	☐	☐
Math lab	☐	☐

LD PROGRAM STAFF

Total number of LD Program staff (including director):

Full Time: 3 Part Time: 3

Key staff person available to work with LD students: Barbara McKinney, Director of Student Support Services.

Meredith College

Raleigh, NC

Address: 3800 Hillsborough Street, Raleigh, NC, 27607-5298
Admissions telephone: 800 MEREDITH
Admissions FAX: 919 760-2348
Director of Admissions: Heidi L. Fletcher
Admissions e-mail: admissions@meredith.edu
Web site: http://www.meredith.edu
SAT Code: 5410 ACT Code: 3126

LD program name: Disability Services
Assistant Counseling Director: Betty-Shannon Prevatt
LD program telephone: 919 760-8427
LD program e-mail: prevattb@meredith.edu
LD program enrollment: 70, Total campus enrollment: 2,008

GENERAL

Meredith College is a private, women's, four-year institution. 225-acre campus in Raleigh (population: 276,093). Served by air, bus, and train. Public transportation serves campus. Semester system.

LD ADMISSIONS

Students do not complete a separate application and are not simultaneously accepted to the LD program. A member of the LD program does not sit on the admissions committee. A personal interview is recommended. Essay is not required.

SECONDARY SCHOOL REQUIREMENTS

Graduation from secondary school required; GED not accepted. The following course distribution required: 4 units of English, 3 units of math, 3 units of science, 2 units of foreign language, 1 unit of academic electives.

TESTING

SAT Reasoning required; ACT may be substituted. SAT Subject recommended.

All enrolled freshmen (fall 2004):

Average SAT I Scores:	Verbal: 521	Math: 517
Average ACT Scores:	Composite: 21	

Child Study Team report is not required. A neuropsychological or comprehensive psycho-educational evaluation is required for admission. Must be dated within 36 months of application. Tests required as part of this documentation:

■ WAIS-IV	■ Woodcock-Johnson
□ WISC-IV	■ Nelson-Denny Reading Test
■ SATA	□ Other

UNDERGRADUATE STUDENT BODY

Total undergraduate student enrollment: 21 Men, 2,286 Women.

Composition of student body (fall 2004):

	Undergraduate	Freshmen
International	0.5	1.0
Black	10.3	9.4
American Indian	0.2	0.4
Asian-American	2.2	1.7
Hispanic	2.7	2.4
White	78.4	80.6
Unreported	5.7	4.5
	100.0%	100.0%

9% are from out of state. Average age of full-time undergraduates is 21. 73% of classes have fewer than 20 students, 27% have between 20 and 50 students.

STUDENT HOUSING

92% of freshmen live in college housing. Freshmen are required to live on campus. Housing is not guaranteed for all undergraduates. No housing available for graduate students or non-degree-seeking undergraduates. Campus can house 1,120 undergraduates. Single rooms are available for students with medical or special needs. A medical note is required.

EXPENSES

Tuition (2005-06): $19,950 per year.
Room & Board: $5,600.
There is no additional cost for LD program/services.

LD SERVICES

LD program size is not limited.

LD services available to:

■ Freshmen ■ Sophomores ■ Juniors ■ Seniors

Academic Accommodations

Curriculum		**In class**	
Foreign language waiver	□	Early syllabus	□
Lighter course load	■	Note takers in class	■
Math waiver	□	Priority seating	■
Other special classes	□	Tape recorders	□
Priority registrations	■	Videotaped classes	□
Substitution of courses	■	Text on tape	■
Exams		**Services**	
Extended time	■	Diagnostic tests	□
Oral exams	■	Learning centers	■
Take home exams	□	Proofreaders	□
Exams on tape or computer	■	Readers	■
Untimed exams	□	Reading Machines/Kurzweil	■
Other accommodations	■	Special bookstore section	□
		Typists	■

Credit toward degree is not given for remedial courses taken.

Counseling Services

■	Academic	Meets 28 times per academic year
■	Psychological	Meets 14 times per academic year
■	Student Support groups	
■	Vocational	Meets 28 times per academic year

Tutoring

Individual tutoring is available weekly.

	Individual	Group
Time management	■	□
Organizational skills	■	□
Learning strategies	■	□
Study skills	■	□
Content area	□	□
Writing lab	■	□
Math lab	■	□

UNIQUE LD PROGRAM FEATURES

Tutoring and coaching, which focuses on time management, organizational skills, learning strategies, study skills and goal setting.

LD PROGRAM STAFF

Total number of LD Program staff (including director):

Full Time: 3 Part Time: 3

There is an advisor/advocate from the LD program available to students. 2 graduate students are available to work with LD students.

Key staff person available to work with LD students: Betty-Shannon Prevatt, Assistant Counseling Dir./Coord. of Disab. Svc.

LD Program web site: www.meredith.edu/students/counsel/disability

Methodist College

Fayetteville, NC

Address: 5400 Ramsey Street, Fayetteville, NC, 28311-1498
Admissions telephone: 800 488-7110
Admissions FAX: 910 630-7285
Vice President of Enrollment Services: Jamie Legg
Admissions e-mail: admissions@methodist.edu
Web site: http://www.methodist.edu
SAT Code: 5426   ACT Code: 3127

Assistant Dean for Academic Services: Nicolette Campos
LD program telephone: 910 630-7251
LD program e-mail: ncampos@methodist.edu
Total campus enrollment: 2,215

GENERAL

Methodist College is a private, coed, four-year institution. 600-acre campus in Fayetteville (population: 121,015), 60 miles from Raleigh. Served by air, bus, and train; major airport serves Raleigh. School operates transportation to Fayetteville airport, bus, and train stations. Public transportation serves campus. Semester system.

SECONDARY SCHOOL REQUIREMENTS

Graduation from secondary school required; GED accepted. The following course distribution required: 4 units of English, 3 units of math, 3 units of science, 1 unit of social studies, 2 units of history, 4 units of academic electives.

TESTING

SAT Reasoning considered if submitted. ACT considered if submitted. SAT Subject recommended.

All enrolled freshmen (fall 2004):

Average SAT I Scores:	Verbal: 490	Math: 504
Average ACT Scores:	Composite: 21	

Child Study Team report is not required. Tests required as part of this documentation:

- ☐ WAIS-IV
- ☐ WISC-IV
- ☐ SATA
- ☐ Woodcock-Johnson
- ☐ Nelson-Denny Reading Test
- ☐ Other

UNDERGRADUATE STUDENT BODY

Total undergraduate student enrollment: 1,222 Men, 911 Women.

Composition of student body (fall 2004):

	Undergraduate	Freshmen
International	2.1	2.1
Black	19.7	21.1
American Indian	0.4	0.7
Asian-American	2.5	1.8
Hispanic	4.4	5.8
White	64.1	64.0
Unreported	6.8	4.5
	100.0%	100.0%

51% are from out of state. Average age of full-time undergraduates is 23. 71% of classes have fewer than 20 students, 29% have between 20 and 50 students.

STUDENT HOUSING

92% of freshmen live in college housing. Freshmen are required to live on campus. Housing is guaranteed for all undergraduates. Campus can house 880 undergraduates.

EXPENSES

Tuition (2005-06): $17,580 per year.
Room & Board: $6,770.
There is no additional cost for LD program/services.

LD SERVICES

LD services available to:

☐ Freshmen ☐ Sophomores ☐ Juniors ☐ Seniors

Academic Accommodations

Curriculum		**In class**	
Foreign language waiver	☐	Early syllabus	☐
Lighter course load	☐	Note takers in class	☑
Math waiver	☐	Priority seating	☐
Other special classes	☐	Tape recorders	☑
Priority registrations	☐	Videotaped classes	☑
Substitution of courses	☐	Text on tape	☐
Exams		**Services**	
Extended time	☑	Diagnostic tests	☐
Oral exams	☑	Learning centers	☑
Take home exams	☐	Proofreaders	☐
Exams on tape or computer	☐	Readers	☑
Untimed exams	☑	Reading Machines/Kurzweil	☐
Other accommodations	☐	Special bookstore section	☐
		Typists	☐

Credit toward degree is not given for remedial courses taken.

Counseling Services

- ☐ Academic
- ☐ Psychological
- ☐ Student Support groups
- ☐ Vocational

Tutoring

	Individual	Group
Time management	☐	☐
Organizational skills	☐	☐
Learning strategies	☐	☐
Study skills	☐	☐
Content area	☐	☐
Writing lab	☐	☐
Math lab	☐	☐

LD PROGRAM STAFF

Total number of LD Program staff (including director):

Full Time: 3   Part Time: 3

Key staff person available to work with LD students: Nicolette Campos, Assistant Dean for Academic Services.

Mount Olive College

Mount Olive, NC

Address: 634 Henderson Street, Mount Olive, NC, 28365
Admissions telephone: 800 653-0854
Admissions FAX: 919 658-7180
Director of Admissions: Tim Woodard
Admissions e-mail: admissions@moc.edu
Web site: http://www.moc.edu/index.cfm
SAT Code: 5435 ACT Code: 3131

Director of the Learning Center: Jennifer Bancroft
LD program telephone: 919 658-2502
LD program e-mail: jbancroft@moc.edu
Total campus enrollment: 2,582

GENERAL

Mount Olive College is a private, coed, four-year institution. 138-acre campus in Mount Olive (population: 4,567), 60 miles from Raleigh; branch campuses in Durham, Goldsboro, New Bern, and Wilmington. Served by bus; major airport serves Raleigh; smaller airport serves Kinston (40 miles); train serves Wilson (41 miles). Semester system.

LD ADMISSIONS

A personal interview is required. Essay is not required.

SECONDARY SCHOOL REQUIREMENTS

Graduation from secondary school required; GED accepted. The following course distribution required: 4 units of English, 3 units of math, 3 units of science, 3 units of social studies, 3 units of academic electives.

TESTING

SAT Reasoning required; ACT may be substituted. SAT Subject recommended.

Child Study Team report is not required. Tests required as part of this documentation:

- ☐ WAIS-IV
- ☐ WISC-IV
- ☐ SATA
- ☐ Woodcock-Johnson
- ☐ Nelson-Denny Reading Test
- ☐ Other

UNDERGRADUATE STUDENT BODY

Total undergraduate student enrollment: 801 Men, 974 Women.

Composition of student body (fall 2004):

	Undergraduate
International	0.0
Black	26.1
American Indian	0.0
Asian-American	1.1
Hispanic	2.9
White	57.6
Unreported	12.3
	100.0%

13% are from out of state. Average age of full-time undergraduates is 32. 73% of classes have fewer than 20 students, 27% have between 20 and 50 students.

STUDENT HOUSING

27% of freshmen live in college housing. Housing is guaranteed for all undergraduates. Campus can house 306 undergraduates.

EXPENSES

Tuition (2005-06): $11,520 per year.
Room: $2,000. Board: $2,800.

There is no additional cost for LD program/services.

LD SERVICES

LD services available to:

☐ Freshmen ☐ Sophomores ☐ Juniors ☐ Seniors

Academic Accommodations

Curriculum		**In class**	
Foreign language waiver	☐	Early syllabus	☐
Lighter course load	■	Note takers in class	☐
Math waiver	☐	Priority seating	☐
Other special classes	☐	Tape recorders	☐
Priority registrations	☐	Videotaped classes	☐
Substitution of courses	☐	Text on tape	☐
Exams		**Services**	
Extended time	☐	Diagnostic tests	☐
Oral exams	☐	Learning centers	■
Take home exams	☐	Proofreaders	☐
Exams on tape or computer	☐	Readers	☐
Untimed exams	☐	Reading Machines/Kurzweil	☐
Other accommodations	☐	Special bookstore section	☐
		Typists	☐

Credit toward degree is not given for remedial courses taken.

Counseling Services

- ☐ Academic
- ☐ Psychological
- ☐ Student Support groups
- ☐ Vocational

Tutoring

	Individual	Group
Time management	☐	☐
Organizational skills	☐	☐
Learning strategies	☐	☐
Study skills	☐	☐
Content area	☐	☐
Writing lab	☐	☐
Math lab	☐	☐

LD PROGRAM STAFF

Total number of LD Program staff (including director):

Full Time: 1 Part Time: 1

Key staff person available to work with LD students: Jennifer Bancroft, Director of the Learning Center.

University of North Carolina at Asheville

Asheville, NC

Address: 1 University Heights, Asheville, NC, 28804
Admissions telephone: 800 531-9842
Admissions FAX: 828 251-6842
Director of Admissions and Financial Aid: Scot Schaeffer
Admissions e-mail: admissions@unca.edu
Web site: http://www.unca.edu
SAT Code: 5013 ACT Code: 3064

Director: Dr. Heidi Kelley
LD program telephone: 828 251-6980
LD program e-mail: hkelley@unca.edu
LD program enrollment: 100, Total campus enrollment: 3,572

GENERAL

University of North Carolina at Asheville is a public, coed, four-year institution. 265-acre campus in Asheville (population: 68,889), 125 miles from Charlotte. Served by air and bus; major airport serves Charlotte; train serves Greenville (60 miles). Public transportation serves campus. Semester system.

LD ADMISSIONS

Students do not complete a separate application and are not simultaneously accepted to the LD program. A member of the LD program does not sit on the admissions committee. A personal interview is not required. Essay is not required.

SECONDARY SCHOOL REQUIREMENTS

Graduation from secondary school required; GED not accepted. The following course distribution required: 4 units of English, 4 units of math, 3 units of science, 2 units of foreign language, 1 unit of social studies, 1 unit of history.

TESTING

SAT Reasoning or ACT required. SAT Subject required.

All enrolled freshmen (fall 2004):

Average SAT I Scores: Verbal: 593 Math: 576
Average ACT Scores: Composite: 24

Child Study Team report is not required. Tests required as part of this documentation:

- [x] WAIS-IV
- [x] WISC-IV
- [x] SATA
- [x] Woodcock-Johnson
- [x] Nelson-Denny Reading Test
- [x] Other

UNDERGRADUATE STUDENT BODY

Total undergraduate student enrollment: 1,345 Men, 1,866 Women.

Composition of student body (fall 2004):

	Undergraduate	Freshmen
International	0.6	1.1
Black	2.7	2.6
American Indian	0.3	0.3
Asian-American	0.8	1.3
Hispanic	1.8	1.8
White	89.8	90.1
Unreported	4.0	2.8
	100.0%	100.0%

11% are from out of state. 3% join a fraternity and 3% join a sorority. Average age of full-time undergraduates is 21. 51% of classes have fewer than 20 students, 48% have between 20 and 50 students, 1% have more than 50 students.

STUDENT HOUSING

87% of freshmen live in college housing. Freshmen are required to live on campus. Housing is guaranteed for all undergraduates. Campus can house 1,171 undergraduates. Single rooms are available for students with medical or special needs. A medical note is required.

EXPENSES

Tuition 2004-05: $1,897 per year (in-state), $11,097 (out-of-state).

Room: $2,722. Board: $2,590.

There is no additional cost for LD program/services.

LD SERVICES

LD program size is not limited.

LD services available to:

- [x] Freshmen
- [x] Sophomores
- [x] Juniors
- [x] Seniors

Academic Accommodations

Curriculum		In class	
Foreign language waiver	[ ]	Early syllabus	[ ]
Lighter course load	[ ]	Note takers in class	[x]
Math waiver	[ ]	Priority seating	[ ]
Other special classes	[ ]	Tape recorders	[x]
Priority registrations	[ ]	Videotaped classes	[ ]
Substitution of courses	[ ]	Text on tape	[ ]
Exams		**Services**	
Extended time	[x]	Diagnostic tests	[ ]
Oral exams	[x]	Learning centers	[ ]
Take home exams	[ ]	Proofreaders	[ ]
Exams on tape or computer	[ ]	Readers	[x]
Untimed exams	[ ]	Reading Machines/Kurzweil	[x]
Other accommodations	[ ]	Special bookstore section	[ ]
		Typists	[ ]

Credit toward degree is not given for remedial courses taken.

Counseling Services

- [ ] Academic
- [ ] Psychological
- [ ] Student Support groups
- [ ] Vocational

Tutoring

Individual tutoring is available weekly.

Average size of tutoring groups: 1

	Individual	Group
Time management	[ ]	[ ]
Organizational skills	[ ]	[ ]
Learning strategies	[ ]	[ ]
Study skills	[ ]	[ ]
Content area	[ ]	[ ]
Writing lab	[x]	[ ]
Math lab	[x]	[ ]

LD PROGRAM STAFF

Total number of LD Program staff (including director):

Full Time: 1 Part Time: 1

There is an advisor/advocate from the LD program available to students.

Key staff person available to work with LD students: Dr. Heidi Kelley, Director, Liberal Arts Learning and Disability Services.

University of North Carolina at Chapel Hill

Chapel Hill, NC

Address: South Building, CB #9100, Chapel Hill, NC, 27599
Admissions telephone: 919 966-3621
Admissions FAX: 919 962-3045
Director of Undergraduate Admissions: Stephen Farmer
Admissions e-mail: uadm@email.unc.edu
Web site: http://www.unc.edu
SAT Code: 5816 ACT Code: 3162

LD program name: Learning Disability Services
Director, Learning Disability Services: Jane Benson
LD program telephone: 919 962-7227
LD program e-mail: lds@unc.edu
Total campus enrollment: 16,525

GENERAL

University of North Carolina at Chapel Hill is a public, coed, four-year institution. 729-acre campus in Chapel Hill (population: 48,715), eight miles from Durham. Served by bus; major airport serves Raleigh (30 miles); train serves Durham. School operates transportation on campus and to Duke U. Public transportation serves campus. Semester system.

LD ADMISSIONS

A personal interview is not required. Essay is required and may be typed.

SECONDARY SCHOOL REQUIREMENTS

Graduation from secondary school required; GED not accepted. The following course distribution required: 4 units of English, 3 units of math, 3 units of science, 2 units of foreign language, 2 units of social studies, 2 units of academic electives.

TESTING

SAT Reasoning or ACT required. SAT Subject required.

All enrolled freshmen (fall 2004):

Average SAT I Scores:	Verbal: 638	Math: 649
Average ACT Scores:	Composite: 27	

Child Study Team report is not required. Tests required as part of this documentation:

- [ ] WAIS-IV
- [ ] WISC-IV
- [ ] SATA
- [ ] Woodcock-Johnson
- [ ] Nelson-Denny Reading Test
- [ ] Other

UNDERGRADUATE STUDENT BODY

Total undergraduate student enrollment: 6,294 Men, 9,550 Women.

Composition of student body (fall 2004):

	Undergraduate	Freshmen
International	1.2	1.4
Black	11.1	10.9
American Indian	0.9	0.9
Asian-American	7.2	6.2
Hispanic	3.5	2.8
White	72.8	74.2
Unreported	3.3	3.6
	100.0%	100.0%

18% are from out of state. 13% join a fraternity and 15% join a sorority. Average age of full-time undergraduates is 20. 54% of classes have fewer than 20 students, 35% have between 20 and 50 students, 11% have more than 50 students.

STUDENT HOUSING

83% of freshmen live in college housing. Freshmen are not required to live on campus. Housing is guaranteed for all undergraduates. Campus can house 9,636 undergraduates.

EXPENSES

Tuition (2005-06): $3,205 per year (in-state), $17,003 (out-of-state). Room: $3,630. Board: $2,866.
There is no additional cost for LD program/services.

LD SERVICES

LD program size is not limited.

LD services available to:

- [ ] Freshmen
- [ ] Sophomores
- [ ] Juniors
- [ ] Seniors

Academic Accommodations

Curriculum		In class	
Foreign language waiver	[ ]	Early syllabus	[ ]
Lighter course load	[ ]	Note takers in class	[x]
Math waiver	[ ]	Priority seating	[ ]
Other special classes	[ ]	Tape recorders	[x]
Priority registrations	[ ]	Videotaped classes	[ ]
Substitution of courses	[ ]	Text on tape	[ ]
Exams		**Services**	
Extended time	[x]	Diagnostic tests	[ ]
Oral exams	[ ]	Learning centers	[x]
Take home exams	[ ]	Proofreaders	[ ]
Exams on tape or computer	[ ]	Readers	[x]
Untimed exams	[ ]	Reading Machines/Kurzweil	[x]
Other accommodations	[ ]	Special bookstore section	[ ]
		Typists	[ ]

Credit toward degree is not given for remedial courses taken.

Counseling Services

- [ ] Academic
- [ ] Psychological
- [ ] Student Support groups
- [ ] Vocational

Tutoring

	Individual	Group
Time management	[ ]	[ ]
Organizational skills	[ ]	[ ]
Learning strategies	[ ]	[ ]
Study skills	[ ]	[ ]
Content area	[ ]	[ ]
Writing lab	[ ]	[ ]
Math lab	[ ]	[ ]

LD PROGRAM STAFF

Total number of LD Program staff (including director):

Full Time: 3 Part Time: 3

Key staff person available to work with LD students: Jane Benson, Director, Learning Disability Services.

LD Program web site: http://www.unc.edu/depts/lds

University of North Carolina at Charlotte

Charlotte, NC

Address: 9201 University City Boulevard, Charlotte, NC, 28223-0001
Admissions telephone: 704 687-2213
Admissions FAX: 704 687-6483
Director of Admissions: Craig Fulton
Admissions e-mail: unccadm@email.uncc.edu
Web site: http://www.uncc.edu/
SAT Code: 5105 ACT Code: 3163

Director: Jo Ann A. Fernald
LD program telephone: 704 687-4355
LD program e-mail: dissrvcs@email.uncc.edu
LD program enrollment: 85, Total campus enrollment: 15,875

GENERAL

University of North Carolina at Charlotte is a public, coed, four-year institution. 1,000-acre campus in Charlotte (population: 396,000), five miles from downtown area. Served by air, bus, and train. Public transportation serves campus. Semester system.

LD ADMISSIONS

A personal interview is not required. Essay is not required. Admissions requirements that may be waived for LD students include foreign languages.

SECONDARY SCHOOL REQUIREMENTS

Graduation from secondary school required; GED accepted. The following course distribution required: 4 units of English, 3 units of math, 3 units of science, 2 units of foreign language, 2 units of social studies, 2 units of academic electives.

TESTING

SAT Reasoning required; ACT may be substituted. SAT Subject required.

All enrolled freshmen (fall 2004):

Average SAT I Scores: Verbal: 531 Math: 548
Average ACT Scores: Composite: 21

Child Study Team report is not required. Tests required as part of this documentation:

- ☐ WAIS-IV
- ☐ WISC-IV
- ☐ SATA
- ☐ Woodcock-Johnson
- ☐ Nelson-Denny Reading Test
- ☐ Other

UNDERGRADUATE STUDENT BODY

Total undergraduate student enrollment: 6,919 Men, 8,216 Women.

Composition of student body (fall 2004):

	Undergraduate	Freshmen
International	0.8	1.6
Black	10.4	15.1
American Indian	0.5	0.4
Asian-American	5.5	5.2
Hispanic	2.4	2.6
White	80.4	75.1
Unreported	0.0	0.0
	100.0%	100.0%

10% are from out of state. 5% join a fraternity and 4% join a sorority. Average age of full-time undergraduates is 21. 35% of classes have fewer than 20 students, 51% have between 20 and 50 students, 14% have more than 50 students.

STUDENT HOUSING

74% of freshmen live in college housing. Freshmen are not required to live on campus. Housing is guaranteed for all undergraduates. Campus can house 4,234 undergraduates.

EXPENSES

Tuition (2005-06): $2,129 per year (in-state), $12,541 (out-of-state).

Room: $3,954. Board: $2,890.

There is no additional cost for LD program/services.

LD SERVICES

LD program size is not limited.

LD services available to:

☐ Freshmen ☐ Sophomores ☐ Juniors ☐ Seniors

Academic Accommodations

Curriculum		In class	
Foreign language waiver	☐	Early syllabus	☐
Lighter course load	☑	Note takers in class	☑
Math waiver	☐	Priority seating	☐
Other special classes	☐	Tape recorders	☑
Priority registrations	☐	Videotaped classes	☐
Substitution of courses	☐	Text on tape	☐
Exams		**Services**	
Extended time	☑	Diagnostic tests	☐
Oral exams	☑	Learning centers	☑
Take home exams	☐	Proofreaders	☐
Exams on tape or computer	☐	Readers	☐
Untimed exams	☑	Reading Machines/Kurzweil	☑
Other accommodations	☐	Special bookstore section	☐
		Typists	☐

Credit toward degree is not given for remedial courses taken.

Counseling Services

- ☐ Academic
- ☐ Psychological
- ☐ Student Support groups
- ☐ Vocational

Tutoring

	Individual	Group
Time management	☐	☐
Organizational skills	☐	☐
Learning strategies	☐	☐
Study skills	☐	☐
Content area	☐	☐
Writing lab	☐	☐
Math lab	☐	☐

LD PROGRAM STAFF

Total number of LD Program staff (including director):

Full Time: 4 Part Time: 4

Key staff person available to work with LD students: Kelly Grey, Assistant Director.

University of North Carolina at Greensboro

Greensboro, NC

Address: 1000 Spring Garden Street, Greensboro, NC, 27402
Admissions telephone: 336 334-5243
Admissions FAX: 336 334-4180
Director of Admissions: Lise Keller
Admissions e-mail: undergrad_admissions@uncg.edu
Web site: http://www.uncg.edu/
SAT Code: 5913 ACT Code: 3166

Director: Mary E. Culkin
LD program telephone: 336 334-5440
LD program e-mail: ods@uncg.edu
LD program enrollment: 131, Total campus enrollment: 11,441

GENERAL

University of North Carolina at Greensboro is a public, coed, four-year institution. 190-acre campus in Greensboro (population: 223,891), 1-1/2 miles from downtown area. Served by air, bus, and train. Public transportation serves campus. Semester system.

LD ADMISSIONS

Students do not complete a separate application and are not simultaneously accepted to the LD program. A member of the LD program does not sit on the admissions committee. A personal interview is required. Essay is not required.

SECONDARY SCHOOL REQUIREMENTS

Graduation from secondary school required; GED accepted. The following course distribution required: 4 units of English, 3 units of math, 3 units of science, 2 units of foreign language, 1 unit of social studies, 1 unit of history, 1 unit of academic electives.

TESTING

SAT Reasoning required; ACT may be substituted.

All enrolled freshmen (fall 2004):

Average SAT I Scores:	Verbal: 522	Math: 523
Average ACT Scores:	Composite:	

Child Study Team report is not required. A neuropsychological or comprehensive psycho-educational evaluation is required for admission. Tests required as part of this documentation:

■ WAIS-IV	■ Woodcock-Johnson
❑ WISC-IV	❑ Nelson-Denny Reading Test
❑ SATA	❑ Other

UNDERGRADUATE STUDENT BODY

Total undergraduate student enrollment: 3,330 Men, 7,046 Women.

Composition of student body (fall 2004):

	Undergraduate	Freshmen
International	0.4	0.8
Black	19.3	19.3
American Indian	0.5	0.3
Asian-American	3.4	2.9
Hispanic	2.1	2.0
White	70.1	69.4
Unreported	4.2	5.3
	100.0%	100.0%

9% are from out of state. Average age of full-time undergraduates is 21. 38% of classes have fewer than 20 students, 50% have between 20 and 50 students, 12% have more than 50 students.

STUDENT HOUSING

79% of freshmen live in college housing. Freshmen are not required to live on campus. Housing is guaranteed for all undergraduates. Campus can house 4,000 undergraduates.

EXPENSES

Tuition (2005-06): $2,028 per year (in-state), $13,296 (out-of-state).
Room: $3,000. Board: $2,400.
There is no additional cost for LD program/services.

LD SERVICES

LD program size is not limited.

LD services available to:

■ Freshmen ■ Sophomores ■ Juniors ■ Seniors

Academic Accommodations

Curriculum		**In class**	
Foreign language waiver	❑	Early syllabus	■
Lighter course load	❑	Note takers in class	■
Math waiver	❑	Priority seating	❑
Other special classes	❑	Tape recorders	■
Priority registrations	❑	Videotaped classes	❑
Substitution of courses	❑	Text on tape	❑
Exams		**Services**	
Extended time	■	Diagnostic tests	■
Oral exams	■	Learning centers	■
Take home exams	❑	Proofreaders	❑
Exams on tape or computer	❑	Readers	■
Untimed exams	❑	Reading Machines/Kurzweil	❑
Other accommodations	❑	Special bookstore section	❑
		Typists	❑

Credit toward degree is not given for remedial courses taken.

Counseling Services

■ Academic
❑ Psychological
❑ Student Support groups
❑ Vocational

Tutoring

Individual tutoring is available.

	Individual	Group
Time management	■	❑
Organizational skills	■	❑
Learning strategies	■	❑
Study skills	■	❑
Content area	■	❑
Writing lab	■	■
Math lab	■	■

LD PROGRAM STAFF

Total number of LD Program staff (including director):

Full Time: 5 Part Time: 5

There is an advisor/advocate from the LD program available to students.

Key staff person available to work with LD students: Mary E. Culkin, Director.

University of North Carolina at Pembroke

Pembroke, NC

Address: P.O. Box 1510, Pembroke, NC, 28372
Admissions telephone: 800 522-2185
Admissions FAX: 910 521-6497
Vice President for Enrollment Management: Jacqueline Clark
Admissions e-mail: admissions@papa.uncp.edu
Web site: http://www.uncp.edu
SAT Code: 5534 ACT Code: 5534

LD program name: Disability Support Services
Director, Disability Support Services: Mary Helen Walker
LD program telephone: 910 521-6695
LD program e-mail: mary.walker@uncp.edu
LD program enrollment: 226, Total campus enrollment: 4,508

GENERAL

University of North Carolina at Pembroke is a public, coed, four-year institution. 126-acre campus in Pembroke (population: 2,399), 45 miles from Fayetteville; branch campuses in Rockingham and Southern Pines. Airport and train serve Fayetteville; bus serves Lumberton (15 miles). Semester system.

LD ADMISSIONS

Students do not complete a separate application and are not simultaneously accepted to the LD program. A member of the LD program does not sit on the admissions committee.

SECONDARY SCHOOL REQUIREMENTS

Graduation from secondary school required; GED accepted. The following course distribution required: 4 units of English, 3 units of math, 3 units of science, 2 units of foreign language, 1 unit of social studies, 1 unit of history.

TESTING

ACT required. SAT Subject required.

All enrolled freshmen (fall 2004):

Average SAT I Scores:	Verbal: 468	Math: 480
Average ACT Scores:	Composite: 21	

Child Study Team report is not required. A neuropsychological or comprehensive psycho-education evaluation is not required for admission. Tests required as part of this documentation:

- [x] WAIS-IV
- [x] WISC-IV
- [ ] SATA
- [x] Woodcock-Johnson
- [ ] Nelson-Denny Reading Test
- [ ] Other

UNDERGRADUATE STUDENT BODY

Total undergraduate student enrollment: 1,323 Men, 2,183 Women.

Composition of student body (fall 2004):

	Undergraduate	Freshmen
International	0.1	0.8
Black	26.7	23.7
American Indian	19.6	21.7
Asian-American	2.6	1.8
Hispanic	3.0	2.4
White	47.9	49.6
Unreported	0.1	0.0
	100.0%	100.0%

4% are from out of state. 5% join a fraternity and 8% join a sorority. Average age of full-time undergraduates is 23. 48% of classes have fewer than 20 students, 50% have between 20 and 50 students, 2% have more than 50 students.

STUDENT HOUSING

61% of freshmen live in college housing. Freshmen are not required to live on campus. Housing is guaranteed for all undergraduates. Campus can house 1,327 undergraduates. Single rooms are available for students with medical or special needs. A medical note is required.

EXPENSES

Tuition (2005-06): $1,689 per year (in-state), $11,129 (out-of-state). Room: $2,700. Board: $2,190.

LD SERVICES

LD program size is not limited.

LD services available to:

- [x] Freshmen
- [x] Sophomores
- [x] Juniors
- [x] Seniors

Academic Accommodations

Curriculum		In class	
Foreign language waiver	[ ]	Early syllabus	[x]
Lighter course load	[ ]	Note takers in class	[x]
Math waiver	[ ]	Priority seating	[ ]
Other special classes	[ ]	Tape recorders	[x]
Priority registrations	[ ]	Videotaped classes	[ ]
Substitution of courses	[ ]	Text on tape	[x]
Exams		**Services**	
Extended time	[x]	Diagnostic tests	[ ]
Oral exams	[x]	Learning centers	[ ]
Take home exams	[ ]	Proofreaders	[ ]
Exams on tape or computer	[x]	Readers	[x]
Untimed exams	[ ]	Reading Machines/Kurzweil	[ ]
Other accommodations	[x]	Special bookstore section	[ ]
		Typists	[x]

Credit toward degree is not given for remedial courses taken.

Counseling Services

- [x] Academic
- [x] Psychological
- [x] Student Support groups
- [x] Vocational

Tutoring

Individual tutoring is not available.

	Individual	Group
Time management	[x]	[x]
Organizational skills	[x]	[x]
Learning strategies	[x]	[x]
Study skills	[x]	[x]
Content area	[ ]	[ ]
Writing lab	[x]	[x]
Math lab	[x]	[x]

LD PROGRAM STAFF

Total number of LD Program staff (including director):

Full Time: 5 Part Time: 5

There is an advisor/advocate from the LD program available to students. 1 graduate student is available to work with LD students.

Key staff person available to work with LD students: Mary Helen Walker, Director, Disability Support Services.

LD Program web site: http://www.uncp.edu/dss

University of North Carolina at Wilmington

Wilmington, NC

Address: 601 S. College Road, Wilmington, NC, 28403-5963
Admissions telephone: 910 962-3243
Admissions FAX: 910 962-3038
Assistant Vice Chancellor for Admissions: Roxie Shabazz
Admissions e-mail: admissions@uncw.edu
Web site: http://www.uncw.edu
SAT Code: 5907 ACT Code: 3174

LD program name: Student Development Services
Learning Specialist: Christopher Stone
LD program telephone: 910 962-7846
LD program e-mail: stonec@uncw.edu
LD program enrollment: 136, Total campus enrollment: 10,353

GENERAL

University of North Carolina at Wilmington is a public, coed, four-year institution. 661-acre campus in Wilmington (population: 75,838), 125 miles from Raleigh. Served by air and bus; train serves Fayetteville (100 miles). School operates transportation around campus and surrounding area. Public transportation serves campus. Semester system.

LD ADMISSIONS

A personal interview is not required. Essay is not required.

SECONDARY SCHOOL REQUIREMENTS

Graduation from secondary school required; GED accepted. The following course distribution required: 4 units of English, 3 units of math, 3 units of science, 2 units of foreign language, 2 units of social studies, 1 unit of history, 5 units of academic electives.

TESTING

SAT Reasoning required; ACT may be substituted. SAT Subject required.

All enrolled freshmen (fall 2004):

Average SAT I Scores:	Verbal: 558	Math: 568
Average ACT Scores:	Composite: 25	

Child Study Team report is not required. A neuropsychological or comprehensive psycho-educational evaluation is required for admission. Must be dated within 36 months of application. Tests required as part of this documentation:

- [x] WAIS-IV
- [ ] WISC-IV
- [x] SATA
- [x] Woodcock-Johnson
- [x] Nelson-Denny Reading Test
- [x] Other

UNDERGRADUATE STUDENT BODY

Total undergraduate student enrollment: 3,630 Men, 5,508 Women.

Composition of student body (fall 2004):

	Undergraduate	Freshmen
International	0.5	0.6
Black	4.4	4.2
American Indian	0.9	1.0
Asian-American	1.5	1.6
Hispanic	2.1	2.0
White	88.2	89.2
Unreported	2.4	1.4
	100.0%	100.0%

13% are from out of state. 2% join a fraternity and 3% join a sorority. Average age of full-time undergraduates is 21. 24% of classes have fewer than 20 students, 66% have between 20 and 50 students, 10% have more than 50 students.

STUDENT HOUSING

78% of freshmen live in college housing. Freshmen are not required to live on campus. Housing is guaranteed for all undergraduates. Campus can house 2,364 undergraduates.

EXPENSES

Tuition (2005-06): $1,928 per year (in-state), $11,863 (out-of-state).
Room: $3,974. Board: $2,438.
There is no additional cost for LD program/services.

LD SERVICES

LD program size is not limited.

LD services available to:

- [x] Freshmen
- [x] Sophomores
- [x] Juniors
- [x] Seniors

Academic Accommodations

Curriculum		In class	
Foreign language waiver	[ ]	Early syllabus	[ ]
Lighter course load	[ ]	Note takers in class	[x]
Math waiver	[ ]	Priority seating	[ ]
Other special classes	[ ]	Tape recorders	[x]
Priority registrations	[x]	Videotaped classes	[ ]
Substitution of courses	[ ]	Text on tape	[ ]
Exams		**Services**	
Extended time	[x]	Diagnostic tests	[ ]
Oral exams	[x]	Learning centers	[x]
Take home exams	[ ]	Proofreaders	[ ]
Exams on tape or computer	[ ]	Readers	[x]
Untimed exams	[ ]	Reading Machines/Kurzweil	[x]
Other accommodations	[x]	Special bookstore section	[ ]
		Typists	[ ]

Credit toward degree is not given for remedial courses taken.

Counseling Services

- [ ] Academic
- [ ] Psychological
- [ ] Student Support groups
- [ ] Vocational

Tutoring

Individual tutoring is available.

	Individual	Group
Time management	[x]	[ ]
Organizational skills	[x]	[ ]
Learning strategies	[x]	[ ]
Study skills	[x]	[ ]
Content area	[x]	[x]
Writing lab	[x]	[x]
Math lab	[x]	[x]

LD PROGRAM STAFF

Total number of LD Program staff (including director):

Full Time: 3 Part Time: 3

There is an advisor/advocate from the LD program available to students.

Key staff person available to work with LD students: Christopher Stone, Learning Specialist.

North Carolina School of the Arts

Winston-Salem, NC

Address: 1533 S. Main Street, Winston-Salem, NC, 27127-2189
Admissions telephone: 336 770-3291
Admissions FAX: 336 770-3370
Interim Director of Admissions: Sheeler Lawson
Admissions e-mail: admissions@ncarts.edu
Web site: http://www.ncarts.edu
SAT Code: 5512 ACT Code: 3133

Director, Counseling: Christopher Burris
LD program telephone: 336 770-3277
LD program e-mail: Burrisc@ncarts.edu
Total campus enrollment: 790

GENERAL

North Carolina School of the Arts is a public, coed, four-year institution. Urban campus in Winston-Salem (population: 185,776), 20 miles from Greensboro. Served by bus; major airport and train serve Greensboro; airport also serves Charlotte (75 miles). School operates transportation to mall and grocery stores. Public transportation serves campus. Trimester system.

LD ADMISSIONS

A personal interview is required. Essay is not required.

SECONDARY SCHOOL REQUIREMENTS

Graduation from secondary school required; GED accepted. The following course distribution required: 4 units of English, 3 units of math, 3 units of science, 2 units of social studies, 1 unit of history, 4 units of academic electives.

TESTING

Child Study Team report is not required. Tests required as part of this documentation:

- ❑ WAIS-IV
- ❑ WISC-IV
- ❑ SATA
- ❑ Woodcock-Johnson
- ❑ Nelson-Denny Reading Test
- ❑ Other

UNDERGRADUATE STUDENT BODY

Total undergraduate student enrollment: 402 Men, 306 Women.

52% are from out of state.

STUDENT HOUSING

Freshmen are required to live on campus. Housing is guaranteed for all undergraduates.

EXPENSES

Tuition 2004-05: $2,755 per year (in-state), $14,035 (out-of-state).

Room & Board: $5,700.

There is no additional cost for LD program/services.

LD SERVICES

LD program size is not limited.

LD services available to:

❑ Freshmen ❑ Sophomores ❑ Juniors ❑ Seniors

Academic Accommodations

Curriculum		**In class**	
Foreign language waiver	❑	Early syllabus	❑
Lighter course load	❑	Note takers in class	❑
Math waiver	❑	Priority seating	❑
Other special classes	❑	Tape recorders	❑
Priority registrations	❑	Videotaped classes	❑
Substitution of courses	❑	Text on tape	❑
Exams		**Services**	
Extended time	❑	Diagnostic tests	❑
Oral exams	❑	Learning centers	❑
Take home exams	❑	Proofreaders	❑
Exams on tape or computer	❑	Readers	❑
Untimed exams	❑	Reading Machines/Kurzweil	❑
Other accommodations	❑	Special bookstore section	❑
		Typists	❑

Credit toward degree is not given for remedial courses taken.

Counseling Services

- ❑ Academic
- ❑ Psychological
- ❑ Student Support groups
- ❑ Vocational

Tutoring

	Individual	Group
Time management	❑	❑
Organizational skills	❑	❑
Learning strategies	❑	❑
Study skills	❑	❑
Content area	❑	❑
Writing lab	❑	❑
Math lab	❑	❑

LD PROGRAM STAFF

Total number of LD Program staff (including director):

Full Time: 2 Part Time: 2

Key staff person available to work with LD students: Rebecca Somerville.

North Carolina State University

Raleigh, NC

Address: Box 7001, Raleigh, NC, 27695
Admissions telephone: 919 515-2434
Admissions FAX: 919 515-5039
Vice Provost/Director of Admissions: Thomas H. Griffin
Admissions e-mail: undergrad_admissions@ncsu.edu
Web site: http://www.ncsu.edu
SAT Code: 5496   ACT Code: 3164

LD program name: Disability Services for Students
LD program address: Campus Box 7509
Assistant Director: Mark Newmiller
LD program telephone: 919 515-7653
LD program e-mail: mark_newmiller@ncsu.edu
LD program enrollment: 209, Total campus enrollment: 22,754

GENERAL

North Carolina State University is a public, coed, four-year institution. 1,600-acre, urban campus in Raleigh (population: 251,000). Served by air, bus, and train. School operates transportation around campus and to surrounding apartments and neighborhoods. Public transportation serves campus. Semester system.

LD ADMISSIONS

Students do not complete a separate application and are not simultaneously accepted to the LD program. A personal interview is not required. Essay is not required.

SECONDARY SCHOOL REQUIREMENTS

Graduation from secondary school required; GED not accepted. The following course distribution required: 4 units of English, 3 units of math, 3 units of science, 2 units of foreign language, 1 unit of social studies, 1 unit of history, 1 unit of academic electives.

TESTING

SAT Reasoning or ACT required. SAT Subject required.

All enrolled freshmen (fall 2004):

Average SAT I Scores:	Verbal: 580	Math: 613
Average ACT Scores:	Composite: 24	

Child Study Team report is not required. A neuropsychological or comprehensive psycho-educational evaluation is required for admission. Must be dated within 36 months of application. Tests required as part of this documentation:

- ■ WAIS-IV
- ■ WISC-IV
- ■ SATA
- ■ Woodcock-Johnson
- ☐ Nelson-Denny Reading Test
- ■ Other

UNDERGRADUATE STUDENT BODY

Total undergraduate student enrollment: 12,838 Men, 9,152 Women.

Composition of student body (fall 2004):

	Undergraduate	Freshmen
International	0.5	0.8
Black	10.7	10.2
American Indian	0.9	0.7
Asian-American	4.2	5.0
Hispanic	2.4	2.3
White	80.0	80.6
Unreported	1.1	0.4
	100.0%	100.0%

8% are from out of state. 10% join a fraternity and 9% join a sorority. Average age of full-time undergraduates is 21. 34% of classes have fewer than 20 students, 50% have between 20 and 50 students, 16% have more than 50 students.

STUDENT HOUSING

77% of freshmen live in college housing. Freshmen are not required to live on campus. Housing is guaranteed for all undergraduates. Campus can house 7,584 undergraduates. Single rooms are available for students with medical or special needs. A medical note is required.

EXPENSES

Tuition (2005-06): $3,205 per year (in-state), $15,403 (out-of-state).

Room: $4,183. Board: $2,668.
There is no additional cost for LD program/services.

LD SERVICES

LD program size is not limited.

LD services available to:

■ Freshmen ■ Sophomores ■ Juniors ■ Seniors

Academic Accommodations

Curriculum		**In class**	
Foreign language waiver	■	Early syllabus	☐
Lighter course load	■	Note takers in class	■
Math waiver	☐	Priority seating	■
Other special classes	☐	Tape recorders	■
Priority registrations	■	Videotaped classes	☐
Substitution of courses	☐	Text on tape	■
Exams		**Services**	
Extended time	■	Diagnostic tests	☐
Oral exams	☐	Learning centers	☐
Take home exams	☐	Proofreaders	☐
Exams on tape or computer	■	Readers	■
Untimed exams	☐	Reading Machines/Kurzweil	■
Other accommodations	☐	Special bookstore section	☐
		Typists	■

Credit toward degree is not given for remedial courses taken.

Counseling Services

- ☐ Academic
- ☐ Psychological
- ☐ Student Support groups
- ☐ Vocational

Tutoring

Individual tutoring is available daily.

	Individual	Group
Time management	■	■
Organizational skills	■	■
Learning strategies	■	■
Study skills	■	■
Content area	■	■
Writing lab	■	■
Math lab	■	■

UNIQUE LD PROGRAM FEATURES

Tutoring is available through the Undergraduate Tutorial Center for all students. Department of Student Services does not provide tutoring.

LD PROGRAM STAFF

Total number of LD Program staff (including director):

Full Time: 3   Part Time: 3

There is no advisor/advocate from the LD program available to students.

Key staff person available to work with LD students: Mark Newmiller

LD Program web site: www.ncsu.edu/dss

North Carolina Wesleyan College

Rocky Mount, NC

Address: 3400 North Wesleyan Boulevard, Rocky Mount, NC, 27804
Admissions telephone: 800 488-6292
Admissions FAX: 252 985-5295
Director of Admissions: Cecilia Summers
Admissions e-mail: adm@ncwc.edu
Web site: http://www.ncwc.edu
SAT Code: 5501 ACT Code: 3135

LD program name: Student Support Center
Director of Retention: LaRue Chuman
LD program telephone: 252 985-5106
LD program e-mail: lchuman@ncwc.edu
Total campus enrollment: 1,775

GENERAL

North Carolina Wesleyan College is a private, coed, four-year institution. 220-acre campus in Rocky Mount (population: 55,893), 44 miles from Raleigh; branch campuses in Durham, Goldsboro, and Raleigh. Served by air, bus, and train; major airport serves Raleigh/Durham. Public transportation serves campus. Semester system.

LD ADMISSIONS

Students do not complete a separate application and are simultaneously accepted to the LD program. A member of the LD program does not sit on the admissions committee. High school waivers are accepted for foreign language. A personal interview is not required. Essay is not required.

SECONDARY SCHOOL REQUIREMENTS

Graduation from secondary school required; GED not accepted.

TESTING

SAT Reasoning required of some applicants. SAT Reasoning or ACT recommended. SAT Subject required.

All enrolled freshmen (fall 2004):

Average SAT I Scores:	Verbal: 445	Math: 456
Average ACT Scores:	Composite: 17	

Child Study Team report is not required. A neuropsychological or comprehensive psycho-education evaluation is not required for admission. Tests required as part of this documentation:

- [ ] WAIS-IV
- [ ] WISC-IV
- [ ] SATA
- [ ] Woodcock-Johnson
- [ ] Nelson-Denny Reading Test
- [ ] Other

UNDERGRADUATE STUDENT BODY

Total undergraduate student enrollment: 800 Men, 1,086 Women.

Composition of student body (fall 2004):

	Undergraduate	Freshmen
International	0.1	0.2
Black	41.4	41.9
American Indian	1.6	0.8
Asian-American	0.9	0.7
Hispanic	3.7	2.0
White	38.9	46.1
Unreported	13.4	8.3
	100.0%	100.0%

2% join a fraternity and 2% join a sorority. Average age of full-time undergraduates is 24. 68% of classes have fewer than 20 students, 32% have between 20 and 50 students.

STUDENT HOUSING

90% of freshmen live in college housing. Freshmen are required to live on campus. Housing is guaranteed for all undergraduates. Campus can house 674 undergraduates. Single rooms are available for students with medical or special needs. A medical note is not required.

EXPENSES

Tuition (2005-06): $16,000 per year.
Room: $3,000. Board: $3,670.
There is no additional cost for LD program/services.

LD SERVICES

LD program size is not limited.

LD services available to:

- [x] Freshmen
- [x] Sophomores
- [x] Juniors
- [x] Seniors

Academic Accommodations

Curriculum

- [ ] Foreign language waiver
- [x] Lighter course load
- [ ] Math waiver
- [x] Other special classes
- [x] Priority registrations
- [ ] Substitution of courses

Exams

- [x] Extended time
- [x] Oral exams
- [x] Take home exams
- [x] Exams on tape or computer
- [x] Untimed exams
- [x] Other accommodations

In class

- [ ] Early syllabus
- [x] Note takers in class
- [x] Priority seating
- [x] Tape recorders
- [ ] Videotaped classes
- [x] Text on tape

Services

- [x] Diagnostic tests
- [x] Learning centers
- [x] Proofreaders
- [x] Readers
- [ ] Reading Machines/Kurzweil
- [x] Special bookstore section
- [x] Typists

Credit toward degree is not given for remedial courses taken.

Counseling Services

- [x] Academic
- [x] Psychological
- [x] Student Support groups
- [x] Vocational

Tutoring

Individual tutoring is available daily.

Average size of tutoring groups: 2

	Individual	Group
Time management	[ ]	[x]
Organizational skills	[x]	[ ]
Learning strategies	[x]	[ ]
Study skills	[ ]	[x]
Content area	[x]	[ ]
Writing lab	[ ]	[x]
Math lab	[ ]	[x]

LD PROGRAM STAFF

Total number of LD Program staff (including director):

Full Time: 1 Part Time: 1

There is an advisor/advocate from the LD program available to students. 8 peer tutors are available to work with LD students.

Key staff person available to work with LD students: Brad Wingo, Director of the Student Support Center.

LD Program web site: http://www.ncwc.edu/Offices/Student_Support/

Peace College

Raleigh, NC

Address: 15 East Peace Street, Raleigh, NC, 27604-1194
Admissions telephone: 800 PEACE-47
Admissions FAX: 919 508-2306
Dean of Admissions and Financial Aid: Lizzie Wahab
Admissions e-mail: admissions@peace.edu
Web site: http://www.peace.edu
SAT Code: 5533 ACT Code: 3136

LD program name: Disability Services
Director of Educational Services: Marge Terhaar-Yonkers
LD program telephone: 919 508-2007
LD program e-mail: MTerhaar-Yonkers@peace.edu
LD program enrollment: 72, Total campus enrollment: 695

GENERAL

Peace College is a private, women's, four-year institution. 16-acre campus in downtown Raleigh (population: 276,093). Served by air, bus, and train. Semester system.

LD ADMISSIONS

Students do not complete a separate application and are simultaneously accepted to the LD program. A member of the LD program does not sit on the admissions committee. High school waivers are accepted for foreign language. A personal interview is not required. Essay is not required.

For fall 2004, 18 completed self-identified LD applications were received. 18 applications were offered admission, and 18 enrolled.

SECONDARY SCHOOL REQUIREMENTS

Graduation from secondary school required; GED accepted. The following course distribution required: 4 units of English, 3 units of math, 3 units of science, 2 units of foreign language, 1 unit of social studies, 2 units of history.

TESTING

SAT Reasoning considered if submitted. ACT considered if submitted. SAT Subject recommended.

All enrolled freshmen (fall 2004):

Average SAT I Scores:	Verbal: 487	Math: 473
Average ACT Scores:	Composite: 18	

Child Study Team report is not required. A neuropsychological or comprehensive psycho-educational evaluation is required for admission. Must be dated within 42 months of application. Tests required as part of this documentation:

- [x] WAIS-IV
- [x] WISC-IV
- [ ] SATA
- [x] Woodcock-Johnson
- [ ] Nelson-Denny Reading Test
- [ ] Other

UNDERGRADUATE STUDENT BODY

Total undergraduate student enrollment: 634 Women.

Composition of student body (fall 2004):

	Undergraduate	Freshmen
International	0.5	0.8
Black	9.4	12.6
American Indian	0.1	0.7
Asian-American	1.5	1.6
Hispanic	5.4	2.9
White	76.2	77.0
Unreported	6.9	4.4
	100.0%	100.0%

11% are from out of state. Average age of full-time undergraduates is 20. 68% of classes have fewer than 20 students, 32% have between 20 and 50 students.

STUDENT HOUSING

90% of freshmen live in college housing. Freshmen are required to live on campus. Housing is guaranteed for all undergraduates. Campus can house 460 undergraduates. Single rooms are available for students with medical or special needs. A medical note is required.

EXPENSES

Tuition (2005-06): $18,906 per year.

Room & Board: $6,918.
There is no additional cost for LD program/services.

LD SERVICES

LD program size is not limited.

LD services available to:

- [x] Freshmen
- [x] Sophomores
- [x] Juniors
- [x] Seniors

Academic Accommodations

Curriculum		In class	
Foreign language waiver	[x]	Early syllabus	[ ]
Lighter course load	[x]	Note takers in class	[ ]
Math waiver	[ ]	Priority seating	[x]
Other special classes	[ ]	Tape recorders	[x]
Priority registrations	[ ]	Videotaped classes	[ ]
Substitution of courses	[ ]	Text on tape	[ ]
Exams		**Services**	
Extended time	[x]	Diagnostic tests	[ ]
Oral exams	[ ]	Learning centers	[x]
Take home exams	[ ]	Proofreaders	[ ]
Exams on tape or computer	[ ]	Readers	[ ]
Untimed exams	[x]	Reading Machines/Kurzweil	[x]
Other accommodations	[x]	Special bookstore section	[ ]
		Typists	[ ]

Credit toward degree is not given for remedial courses taken.

Counseling Services

- [x] Academic — Meets 28 times per academic year
- [ ] Psychological
- [ ] Student Support groups
- [ ] Vocational

Tutoring

Individual tutoring is available weekly.

Average size of tutoring groups: 5

	Individual	Group
Time management	[x]	[x]
Organizational skills	[x]	[x]
Learning strategies	[x]	[x]
Study skills	[x]	[x]
Content area	[x]	[x]
Writing lab	[x]	[ ]
Math lab	[x]	[ ]

LD PROGRAM STAFF

Total number of LD Program staff (including director):

Full Time: 1 Part Time: 1

There is an advisor/advocate from the LD program available to students. The advisor/advocate meets with faculty 1 time per month and students 4 times per month.

Key staff person available to work with LD students: Marge Terhaar-Yonkers, Director of Educational Services.

Pfeiffer University

Misenheimer, NC

Address: PO Box 960, Misenheimer, NC, 28109
Admissions telephone: 800 338-2060
Admissions FAX: 704 463-1363
Vice President for Marketing and Enrollment: Steve Cumming
Admissions e-mail: admissions@pfeiffer.edu
Web site: http://www.pfeiffer.edu
SAT Code: 5536 ACT Code: 3140

Director of Academic Support Services: Jim Gulledge
LD program telephone: 704 463-1360, extension 2620
LD program e-mail: gulledge@pfeiffer.edu
Total campus enrollment: 1,179

GENERAL

Pfeiffer University is a private, coed, four-year institution. 330-acre campus in Misenheimer (population: 2,000), 16 miles from Salisbury and 35 miles from Charlotte; branch campus in Charlotte. Major airport serves Charlotte; bus and train serve Salisbury. School operates transportation to Charlotte and Salisbury at start and end of semesters and at semester breaks. Semester system.

LD ADMISSIONS

A personal interview is not required. Essay is not required.

SECONDARY SCHOOL REQUIREMENTS

Graduation from secondary school required; GED accepted. The following course distribution required: 4 units of English, 3 units of math, 2 units of science, 2 units of social studies, 2 units of history.

TESTING

SAT Reasoning or ACT required. SAT Subject recommended.

All enrolled freshmen (fall 2004):

Average SAT I Scores: Verbal: 493 Math: 505
Average ACT Scores: Composite: 20

Child Study Team report is not required. Tests required as part of this documentation:

- ☐ WAIS-IV
- ☐ WISC-IV
- ☐ SATA
- ☐ Woodcock-Johnson
- ☐ Nelson-Denny Reading Test
- ☐ Other

UNDERGRADUATE STUDENT BODY

Total undergraduate student enrollment: 425 Men, 560 Women.

Composition of student body (fall 2004):

	Undergraduate	Freshmen
International	2.1	3.2
Black	11.5	20.3
American Indian	1.6	0.7
Asian-American	3.1	1.3
Hispanic	0.6	1.4
White	80.1	71.9
Unreported	1.0	1.2
	100.0%	100.0%

22% are from out of state. Average age of full-time undergraduates is 26. 65% of classes have fewer than 20 students, 35% have between 20 and 50 students.

STUDENT HOUSING

55% of freshmen live in college housing. Freshmen are not required to live on campus. Housing is guaranteed for all undergraduates. Campus can house 717 undergraduates.

EXPENSES

Tuition (2005-06): $15,590 per year.
Room: $3,710. Board: $2,600.
There is no additional cost for LD program/services.

LD SERVICES

LD program size is not limited.

LD services available to:

☐ Freshmen ☐ Sophomores ☐ Juniors ☐ Seniors

Academic Accommodations

Curriculum		In class	
Foreign language waiver	☐	Early syllabus	☐
Lighter course load	■	Note takers in class	■
Math waiver	☐	Priority seating	☐
Other special classes	■	Tape recorders	■
Priority registrations	☐	Videotaped classes	☐
Substitution of courses	☐	Text on tape	☐
Exams		**Services**	
Extended time	■	Diagnostic tests	☐
Oral exams	■	Learning centers	■
Take home exams	☐	Proofreaders	☐
Exams on tape or computer	☐	Readers	■
Untimed exams	☐	Reading Machines/Kurzweil	■
Other accommodations	☐	Special bookstore section	☐
		Typists	☐

Credit toward degree is given for remedial courses taken.

Counseling Services

- ☐ Academic
- ☐ Psychological
- ☐ Student Support groups
- ☐ Vocational

Tutoring

	Individual	Group
Time management	☐	☐
Organizational skills	☐	☐
Learning strategies	☐	☐
Study skills	☐	☐
Content area	☐	☐
Writing lab	☐	☐
Math lab	☐	☐

LD PROGRAM STAFF

Total number of LD Program staff (including director):

Full Time: 2 Part Time: 2

Key staff person available to work with LD students: Jim Gulledge, Director of Academic Support Services.

Queens University of Charlotte

Charlotte, NC

Address: 1900 Selwyn Avenue, Charlotte, NC, 28274
Admissions telephone: 800 849-0202
Admissions FAX: 704 337-2403
Dean of Admissions and Financial Aid: X. William Lee
Admissions e-mail: admissions@queens.edu
Web site: http://www.queens.edu
SAT Code: 5560 ACT Code: 3148

LD program name: Office of Student Disability Services
Coordinator: Sandy Rogelberg
LD program telephone: 704 337-2508
LD program e-mail: rogelbes@queens.edu
Total campus enrollment: 1,601

GENERAL

Queens University of Charlotte is a private, coed, four-year institution. 25-acre, suburban campus in Charlotte (population: 540,828). Served by air, bus, and train. School operates transportation to special events in Charlotte. Public transportation serves campus. Semester system.

LD ADMISSIONS

Students do not complete a separate application and are not simultaneously accepted to the LD program. A member of the LD program does not sit on the admissions committee. A personal interview is recommended. Essay is required and may be typed.

For fall 2004, 50 completed self-identified LD applications were received.

SECONDARY SCHOOL REQUIREMENTS

Graduation from secondary school required; GED accepted. The following course distribution required: 4 units of English, 3 units of math, 2 units of science, 2 units of foreign language, 2 units of social studies.

TESTING

SAT Reasoning or ACT required. SAT Subject recommended.

Child Study Team report is not required. A neuropsychological or comprehensive psycho-educational evaluation is required for admission. Must be dated within 36 months of application. Tests required as part of this documentation:

- ■ WAIS-IV
- ■ WISC-IV
- ■ SATA
- ■ Woodcock-Johnson
- ■ Nelson-Denny Reading Test
- ■ Other

UNDERGRADUATE STUDENT BODY

Total undergraduate student enrollment: 269 Men, 930 Women.

30% join a fraternity and 30% join a sorority. 67% of classes have fewer than 20 students, 33% have between 20 and 50 students.

STUDENT HOUSING

94% of freshmen live in college housing. Housing is guaranteed for all undergraduates. Campus can house 638 undergraduates. Single rooms are available for students with medical or special needs. A medical note is required.

EXPENSES

Tuition (2005-06): $18,028 per year.
Room & Board: $6,500.
There is no additional cost for LD program/services.

LD SERVICES

LD program size is not limited.

LD services available to:

■ Freshmen ■ Sophomores ■ Juniors ■ Seniors

Academic Accommodations

Curriculum		**In class**	
Foreign language waiver	■	Early syllabus	■
Lighter course load	□	Note takers in class	■
Math waiver	■	Priority seating	■
Other special classes	■	Tape recorders	■
Priority registrations	□	Videotaped classes	□
Substitution of courses	■	Text on tape	■
Exams		**Services**	
Extended time	■	Diagnostic tests	□
Oral exams	■	Learning centers	■
Take home exams	■	Proofreaders	□
Exams on tape or computer	■	Readers	■
Untimed exams	■	Reading Machines/Kurzweil	■
Other accommodations	■	Special bookstore section	□
		Typists	■

Credit toward degree is not given for remedial courses taken.

Counseling Services

- ■ Academic
- ■ Psychological
- □ Student Support groups
- □ Vocational

Tutoring

Individual tutoring is available daily.

Average size of tutoring groups: 1

	Individual	Group
Time management	■	□
Organizational skills	■	□
Learning strategies	■	□
Study skills	■	□
Content area	■	□
Writing lab	■	□
Math lab	■	□

LD PROGRAM STAFF

Total number of LD Program staff (including director):

Full Time: 1 Part Time: 1

There is an advisor/advocate from the LD program available to students. The advisor/advocate meets with faculty 4 times per month and students 1 time per month. 13 peer tutors are available to work with LD students.

Key staff person available to work with LD students: Sandy Rogelberg, Coordinator of Student Disability Services.

LD Program web site: rogelbes@queens.edu

Saint Augustine's College

Raleigh, NC

Address: 1315 Oakwood Avenue, Raleigh, NC, 27610-2298
Admissions telephone: 800 948-1126
Admissions FAX: 919 516-5808
Interim Director of Admissions: Byron Bullock
Admissions e-mail: admissions@es.st-aug.edu
Web site: http://www.st-aug.edu
SAT Code: 5596 ACT Code: 3152

Director of the Lower College: Doris Bullock
LD program telephone: 919 516-4394
LD program e-mail: djbullock@st-aug.edu
LD program enrollment: 5, Total campus enrollment: 1,395

GENERAL

Saint Augustine's College is a private, coed, four-year institution. 105-acre campus in Raleigh (population: 276,093). Served by air, bus, and train. Public transportation serves campus. Semester system.

LD ADMISSIONS

Application Deadline: 07/01. Students do not complete a separate application and are not simultaneously accepted to the LD program. A member of the LD program does not sit on the admissions committee. A personal interview is recommended. Essay is not required.

For fall 2004, 10 completed self-identified LD applications were received. 10 applications were offered admission, and 5 enrolled.

SECONDARY SCHOOL REQUIREMENTS

Graduation from secondary school required; GED accepted. The following course distribution required: 4 units of English, 3 units of math, 2 units of science, 2 units of history, 10 units of academic electives.

TESTING

All enrolled freshmen (fall 2004):

Average SAT I Scores:	Verbal: 410	Math: 420
Average ACT Scores:	Composite: 16	

Child Study Team report is not required. A neuropsychological or comprehensive psycho-educational evaluation is required for admission. Must be dated within 12 months of application. Tests required as part of this documentation:

- [x] WAIS-IV
- [x] WISC-IV
- [x] SATA
- [x] Woodcock-Johnson
- [x] Nelson-Denny Reading Test
- [ ] Other

UNDERGRADUATE STUDENT BODY

Total undergraduate student enrollment: 559 Men, 801 Women.

Composition of student body (fall 2004):

	Undergraduate	Freshmen
International	4.3	6.8
Black	93.3	90.6
American Indian	0.0	0.0
Asian-American	0.0	0.0
Hispanic	0.9	1.3
White	0.3	0.4
Unreported	1.2	0.9
	100.0%	100.0%

43% are from out of state. 8% join a fraternity and 12% join a sorority. Average age of full-time undergraduates is 21. 63% of classes have fewer than 20 students, 36% have between 20 and 50 students, 1% have more than 50 students.

STUDENT HOUSING

92% of freshmen live in college housing. Freshmen are required to live on campus. Housing is guaranteed for all undergraduates. Campus can house 1,029 undergraduates. Single rooms are available for students with medical or special needs. A medical note is required.

EXPENSES

Tuition (2005-06): $8,952 per year.
Room & Board: $5,132.
There is no additional cost for LD program/services.

LD SERVICES

LD program is limited to %1 students.

LD services available to:

- [x] Freshmen
- [x] Sophomores
- [x] Juniors
- [x] Seniors

Academic Accommodations

Curriculum		In class	
Foreign language waiver	[ ]	Early syllabus	[ ]
Lighter course load	[x]	Note takers in class	[ ]
Math waiver	[ ]	Priority seating	[ ]
Other special classes	[ ]	Tape recorders	[ ]
Priority registrations	[ ]	Videotaped classes	[ ]
Substitution of courses	[ ]	Text on tape	[ ]
Exams		**Services**	
Extended time	[x]	Diagnostic tests	[x]
Oral exams	[ ]	Learning centers	[x]
Take home exams	[ ]	Proofreaders	[x]
Exams on tape or computer	[ ]	Readers	[ ]
Untimed exams	[x]	Reading Machines/Kurzweil	[ ]
Other accommodations	[ ]	Special bookstore section	[ ]
		Typists	[ ]

Credit toward degree is not given for remedial courses taken.

Counseling Services

- [x] Academic — Meets 3 times per academic year
- [x] Psychological — Meets 10 times per academic year
- [ ] Student Support groups
- [ ] Vocational

Tutoring

Individual tutoring is available twice per month.

Average size of tutoring groups: 10

	Individual	Group
Time management	[x]	[x]
Organizational skills	[x]	[x]
Learning strategies	[x]	[x]
Study skills	[x]	[x]
Content area	[x]	[x]
Writing lab	[x]	[x]
Math lab	[x]	[x]

UNIQUE LD PROGRAM FEATURES

A federally funded TRIO program, Academic Achievers, is available to provide services to students with learning disabilities. Services provided include remedial courses, tutorial services, computer assisted tutorial and peer mentoring.

LD PROGRAM STAFF

There is an advisor/advocate from the LD program available to students. The advisor/advocate meets with faculty 1 time per month and students 2 times per month. 5 peer tutors are available to work with LD students.

Key staff person available to work with LD students: Stanley Elliot, ADA Coordinator.

Salem College

Winston-Salem, NC

Address: P.O. Box 10548, Winston-Salem, NC, 27108
Admissions telephone: 336 721-2621
Admissions FAX: 336 917-5572
Dean of Admissions and Financial Aid: Dana Evans
Admissions e-mail: admissions@salem.edu
Web site: http://www.salem.edu
SAT Code: 5607 ACT Code: 3156

Total campus enrollment: 907

GENERAL

Salem College is a private, women's, four-year institution. 57-acre, urban campus bordering Old Salem, near downtown Winston-Salem (population: 185,776). Served by air and bus; major airport and train serve Greensboro (25 miles). Public transportation serves campus. 4-1-4 system.

LD ADMISSIONS

Students do not complete a separate application and are not simultaneously accepted to the LD program. A member of the LD program does not sit on the admissions committee.

SECONDARY SCHOOL REQUIREMENTS

Graduation from secondary school required; GED accepted.

TESTING

SAT Reasoning or ACT required. SAT Subject recommended.

All enrolled freshmen (fall 2004):

Average SAT I Scores:	Verbal: 561	Math: 540
Average ACT Scores:	Composite: 25	

Child Study Team report is not required. A neuropsychological or comprehensive psycho-educational evaluation is required for admission. Must be dated within 36 months of application. Tests required as part of this documentation:

- [ ] WAIS-IV
- [ ] WISC-IV
- [ ] SATA
- [ ] Woodcock-Johnson
- [ ] Nelson-Denny Reading Test
- [x] Other

UNDERGRADUATE STUDENT BODY

Total undergraduate student enrollment: 30 Men, 896 Women.

Composition of student body (fall 2004):

	Undergraduate	Freshmen
International	12.3	7.0
Black	16.1	19.5
American Indian	0.0	0.2
Asian-American	2.6	1.4
Hispanic	1.9	2.2
White	60.0	66.3
Unreported	7.1	3.4
	100.0%	100.0%

48% are from out of state. Average age of full-time undergraduates is 24. 77% of classes have fewer than 20 students, 23% have between 20 and 50 students.

STUDENT HOUSING

94% of freshmen live in college housing. Freshmen are required to live on campus. Housing is not guaranteed for all undergraduates. Campus housing is available to all traditional students regardless of year. Students in the adult/continuing studies program are not eligible for campus housing. Traditional students are required to live on campus unless residing with family in the area. Campus can house 488 undergraduates.

EXPENSES

Tuition (2005-06): $16,975 per year.
Room & Board: $9,251.
There is no additional cost for LD program/services.

LD SERVICES

LD program size is not limited.

LD services available to:

- [x] Freshmen
- [x] Sophomores
- [x] Juniors
- [x] Seniors

Academic Accommodations

Curriculum		In class	
Foreign language waiver	[ ]	Early syllabus	[ ]
Lighter course load	[x]	Note takers in class	[x]
Math waiver	[ ]	Priority seating	[ ]
Other special classes	[ ]	Tape recorders	[x]
Priority registrations	[ ]	Videotaped classes	[ ]
Substitution of courses	[ ]	Text on tape	[ ]
Exams		**Services**	
Extended time	[x]	Diagnostic tests	[ ]
Oral exams	[ ]	Learning centers	[ ]
Take home exams	[ ]	Proofreaders	[ ]
Exams on tape or computer	[ ]	Readers	[ ]
Untimed exams	[ ]	Reading Machines/Kurzweil	[ ]
Other accommodations	[ ]	Special bookstore section	[ ]
		Typists	[ ]

Credit toward degree is not given for remedial courses taken.

Counseling Services

- [ ] Academic
- [ ] Psychological
- [ ] Student Support groups
- [ ] Vocational

Tutoring

	Individual	Group
Time management	[ ]	[ ]
Organizational skills	[ ]	[ ]
Learning strategies	[ ]	[ ]
Study skills	[ ]	[ ]
Content area	[ ]	[ ]
Writing lab	[ ]	[ ]
Math lab	[ ]	[ ]

Shaw University

Raleigh, NC

Address: 118 East South Street, Raleigh, NC, 27601
Admissions telephone: 800 214-6683
Admissions FAX: 919 546-8271
Director of Admissions: Paul Vandergrift, III
Admissions e-mail: admission@shawu.edu
Web site: http://www.shawuniversity.edu
SAT Code: 5612 ACT Code: 3158

Counselor/Disability Services Specialist: Jerelene Carver
LD program telephone: 919 546-8525
LD program e-mail: jcarver@shawu.edu
LD program enrollment: 50, Total campus enrollment: 2,516

GENERAL

Shaw University is a private, coed, four-year institution. 30-acre campus in Raleigh (population: 276,093). Served by bus and train; major airport serves Morrisville (12 miles). Semester system.

LD ADMISSIONS

Application Deadline: 07/30. Students do not complete a separate application and are simultaneously accepted to the LD program. A member of the LD program does sit on the admissions committee. A personal interview is recommended.

SECONDARY SCHOOL REQUIREMENTS

Graduation from secondary school required; GED accepted. The following course distribution required: 3 units of English, 2 units of math, 2 units of science, 2 units of social studies, 9 units of academic electives.

TESTING

SAT Reasoning or ACT required.

All enrolled freshmen (fall 2004):

Average SAT I Scores:	Verbal: 394	Math: 378
Average ACT Scores:	Composite: 16	

Child Study Team report is not required. A neuropsychological or comprehensive psycho-educational evaluation is required for admission. Must be dated within 36 months of application. Tests required as part of this documentation:

- ■ WAIS-IV
- ■ WISC-IV
- ■ SATA
- ■ Woodcock-Johnson
- ■ Nelson-Denny Reading Test
- □ Other

UNDERGRADUATE STUDENT BODY

Total undergraduate student enrollment: 788 Men, 1,584 Women.

Composition of student body (fall 2004):

	Undergraduate	Freshmen
International	0.2	2.1
Black	94.7	89.3
American Indian	0.0	0.0
Asian-American	0.0	0.0
Hispanic	0.4	0.3
White	2.0	1.6
Unreported	2.7	6.7
	100.0%	100.0%

23% are from out of state. 4% join a fraternity and 5% join a sorority. Average age of full-time undergraduates is 28. 70% of classes have fewer than 20 students, 28% have between 20 and 50 students, 2% have more than 50 students.

STUDENT HOUSING

90% of freshmen live in college housing. Freshmen are not required to live on campus. Housing is guaranteed for all undergraduates. Campus can house 1,292 undergraduates. Single rooms are available for students with medical or special needs. A medical note is required.

EXPENSES

Tuition (2005-06): $7,800 per year.
Room & Board: $6,050.
There is no additional cost for LD program/services.

LD SERVICES

LD program size is not limited.

LD services available to:

■ Freshmen ■ Sophomores ■ Juniors ■ Seniors

Academic Accommodations

Curriculum		In class	
Foreign language waiver	□	Early syllabus	□
Lighter course load	■	Note takers in class	■
Math waiver	□	Priority seating	■
Other special classes	□	Tape recorders	■
Priority registrations	□	Videotaped classes	□
Substitution of courses	□	Text on tape	■
Exams		**Services**	
Extended time	■	Diagnostic tests	■
Oral exams	■	Learning centers	□
Take home exams	□	Proofreaders	□
Exams on tape or computer	■	Readers	□
Untimed exams	■	Reading Machines/Kurzweil	□
Other accommodations	□	Special bookstore section	□
		Typists	□

Credit toward degree is not given for remedial courses taken.

Counseling Services

- ■ Academic
- ■ Psychological
- ■ Student Support groups
- ■ Vocational

Tutoring

Individual tutoring is available daily.

	Individual	Group
Time management	■	■
Organizational skills	■	■
Learning strategies	■	■
Study skills	■	■
Content area	■	■
Writing lab	■	■
Math lab	■	■

LD PROGRAM STAFF

Total number of LD Program staff (including director):

Full Time: 2 Part Time: 2

There is an advisor/advocate from the LD program available to students.

Key staff person available to work with LD students: Jerelene Carver, Counselor/Disability Services Specialist.

St. Andrews Presbyterian College

Laurinburg, NC

Address: 1700 Dogwood Mile, Laurinburg, NC, 28352
Admissions telephone: 800 763-0198
Admissions FAX: 910 277-5087
Vice President for Student Enrollment: Glenn T Batten
Admissions e-mail: admission@sapc.edu
Web site: http://www.sapc.edu
SAT Code: 5214 ACT Code: 3146

LD program name: Disability Services
Director of Disability Services: Dorothy Wells
LD program telephone: 910 277-5331
LD program e-mail: ods@sapc.edu
LD program enrollment: 44, Total campus enrollment: 741

GENERAL

St. Andrews Presbyterian College is a private, coed, four-year institution. 640-acre campus in Laurinburg (population: 15,874), 40 miles from Fayetteville; branch campus in Southern Pines. Served by bus; major airport serves Raleigh/Durham (100 miles); smaller airport serves Fayetteville; train serves Hamlet (15 miles). Public transportation serves campus. Semester system.

LD ADMISSIONS

Students do not complete a separate application and are not simultaneously accepted to the LD program. A member of the LD program does not sit on the admissions committee. High school waivers are accepted for foreign language. A personal interview is not required. Essay is not required.

SECONDARY SCHOOL REQUIREMENTS

Graduation from secondary school required; GED accepted.

TESTING

SAT Reasoning or ACT required. SAT Subject recommended.

All enrolled freshmen (fall 2004):

Average SAT I Scores:	Verbal: 507	Math: 499
Average ACT Scores:	Composite: 21	

Child Study Team report is not required. A neuropsychological or comprehensive psycho-educational evaluation is required for admission. Must be dated within 36 months of application. Tests required as part of this documentation:

- ■ WAIS-IV
- ■ WISC-IV
- ■ SATA
- ■ Woodcock-Johnson
- □ Nelson-Denny Reading Test
- ■ Other

UNDERGRADUATE STUDENT BODY

Total undergraduate student enrollment: 285 Men, 419 Women.

Composition of student body (fall 2004):

	Undergraduate	Freshmen
International	3.4	7.1
Black	9.4	12.1
American Indian	1.5	0.9
Asian-American	0.5	1.1
Hispanic	3.0	1.5
White	82.2	77.3
Unreported	0.0	0.0
	100.0%	100.0%

56% are from out of state. Average age of full-time undergraduates is 20. 76% of classes have fewer than 20 students, 24% have between 20 and 50 students.

STUDENT HOUSING

95% of freshmen live in college housing. Campus can house 700 undergraduates. Single rooms are available for students with medical or special needs. A medical note is required.

EXPENSES

Tuition (2005-06): $15,890 per year.

Room: $2,520. Board: $3,620.

There is no additional cost for LD program/services.

LD SERVICES

LD program size is not limited.

LD services available to:

■ Freshmen ■ Sophomores ■ Juniors ■ Seniors

Academic Accommodations

Curriculum		In class	
Foreign language waiver	■	Early syllabus	□
Lighter course load	■	Note takers in class	■
Math waiver	□	Priority seating	■
Other special classes	□	Tape recorders	■
Priority registrations	□	Videotaped classes	□
Substitution of courses	■	Text on tape	■
Exams		**Services**	
Extended time	■	Diagnostic tests	□
Oral exams	□	Learning centers	■
Take home exams	□	Proofreaders	□
Exams on tape or computer	■	Readers	■
Untimed exams	□	Reading Machines/Kurzweil	■
Other accommodations	■	Special bookstore section	□
		Typists	■

Credit toward degree is not given for remedial courses taken.

Counseling Services

- ■ Academic
- ■ Psychological
- □ Student Support groups
- ■ Vocational

Tutoring

Individual tutoring is available daily.

Average size of tutoring groups: 3

	Individual	Group
Time management	□	■
Organizational skills	□	■
Learning strategies	□	■
Study skills	□	■
Content area	■	■
Writing lab	■	■
Math lab	■	■

UNIQUE LD PROGRAM FEATURES

Tutoring in some subjects is available to all students. Disability Services staff provide note-taking and test proctoring support.

LD PROGRAM STAFF

Total number of LD Program staff (including director):

Full Time: 2 Part Time: 2

There is an advisor/advocate from the LD program available to students. 10 peer tutors are available to work with LD students.

Key staff person available to work with LD students: Dorothy Wells, Director of Disability Services.

LD Program web site: www.sapc.edu/access

Wake Forest University

Winston-Salem, NC

Address: Box 7305, Reynolda Station, Winston-Salem, NC, 27109
Admissions telephone: 336 758-5201
Admissions FAX: 336 758-4324
Director of Admissions: Martha B. Allman
Admissions e-mail: admissions@wfu.edu
Web site: http://www.wfu.edu
SAT Code: 5885 ACT Code: 3168

LD program name: Learning Assistance Center
LD program address: P.O. Box 7283
Director, Learning Assistance Center: Van Westervelt, Ph.D
LD program telephone: 336 758-5929
LD program enrollment: 114, Total campus enrollment: 4,128

GENERAL

Wake Forest University is a private, coed, four-year institution. 340-acre campus in Winston-Salem (population: 185,776); extension campus in Charlotte. Served by air and bus; major airport and train serve Greensboro (30 miles). Public transportation serves campus. Semester system.

LD ADMISSIONS

A personal interview is not required. Essay is required and may be typed.

SECONDARY SCHOOL REQUIREMENTS

Graduation from secondary school required; GED accepted. The following course distribution required: 4 units of English, 3 units of math, 1 unit of science, 2 units of foreign language, 2 units of social studies.

TESTING

SAT Reasoning required. SAT Subject recommended.

Child Study Team report is not required. Tests required as part of this documentation:

- ☐ WAIS-IV
- ☐ WISC-IV
- ☐ SATA
- ☐ Woodcock-Johnson
- ☐ Nelson-Denny Reading Test
- ☐ Other

UNDERGRADUATE STUDENT BODY

Total undergraduate student enrollment: 1,950 Men, 2,042 Women.

Composition of student body (fall 2004):

	Undergraduate	Freshmen
International	1.2	1.2
Black	5.4	6.1
American Indian	0.4	0.3
Asian-American	4.7	3.8
Hispanic	2.9	2.1
White	85.4	86.5
Unreported	0.0	0.0
	100.0%	100.0%

74% are from out of state. 33% join a fraternity and 53% join a sorority. Average age of full-time undergraduates is 20. 58% of classes have fewer than 20 students, 39% have between 20 and 50 students, 3% have more than 50 students.

STUDENT HOUSING

99% of freshmen live in college housing. Freshmen are required to live on campus. Housing is guaranteed for all undergraduates. Campus can house 3,016 undergraduates.

EXPENSES

Tuition (2005-06): $30,110 per year.
Room: $5,200. Board: $3,300.
There is no additional cost for LD program/services.

LD SERVICES

LD program size is not limited.

LD services available to:

■ Freshmen ■ Sophomores ■ Juniors ■ Seniors

Academic Accommodations

Curriculum		In class	
Foreign language waiver	☐	Early syllabus	☐
Lighter course load	■	Note takers in class	☐
Math waiver	☐	Priority seating	☐
Other special classes	☐	Tape recorders	☐
Priority registrations	☐	Videotaped classes	☐
Substitution of courses	☐	Text on tape	☐
Exams		**Services**	
Extended time	■	Diagnostic tests	☐
Oral exams	☐	Learning centers	■
Take home exams	☐	Proofreaders	☐
Exams on tape or computer	☐	Readers	☐
Untimed exams	☐	Reading Machines/Kurzweil	☐
Other accommodations	☐	Special bookstore section	☐
		Typists	☐

Credit toward degree is not given for remedial courses taken.

Counseling Services

- ■ Academic — Meets 30 times per academic year
- ■ Psychological — Meets 15 times per academic year
- ☐ Student Support groups
- ☐ Vocational

Tutoring

Individual tutoring is available weekly.

Average size of tutoring groups: 3

	Individual	Group
Time management	■	☐
Organizational skills	■	☐
Learning strategies	■	☐
Study skills	■	☐
Content area	■	☐
Writing lab	■	☐
Math lab	☐	☐

LD PROGRAM STAFF

Total number of LD Program staff (including director):

Full Time: 2 Part Time: 2

3 graduate students and 100 peer tutors are available to work with LD students.

Key staff person available to work with LD students: Van Westervelt, Ph.D, Director, Learning Assistance Center.

LD Program web site: www.wfu.edu/campuslife/lac

Warren Wilson College

Asheville, NC

Address: PO Box 9000, Asheville, NC, 28815
Admissions telephone: 800 934-3536
Admissions FAX: 828 298-1440
Dean of Admission: Richard Blomgren
Admissions e-mail: admit@warren-wilson.edu
Web site: http://www.warren-wilson.edu
SAT Code: 5886 ACT Code: 3170

LD program name: Academic Support Services
LD program address: CPO 6322
Director of Academic Support Services: Lyn O'Hare
LD program telephone: 828 771-3012
LD program e-mail: lohare@warren-wilson.edu
LD program enrollment: 30, Total campus enrollment: 792

GENERAL

Warren Wilson College is a private, coed, four-year institution. 1,135 acre campus in Asheville (population: 68,889). Served by air and bus; other airport and train serve Greenville, S.C. (60 miles). School operates transportation to Asheville. Semester system.

LD ADMISSIONS

Students do not complete a separate application and are simultaneously accepted to the LD program. A member of the LD program does sit on the admissions committee. A personal interview is recommended.

SECONDARY SCHOOL REQUIREMENTS

Graduation from secondary school required; GED accepted. The following course distribution required: 4 units of English, 3 units of math, 2 units of science, 3 units of history.

TESTING

SAT Reasoning or ACT required. SAT Subject recommended.

All enrolled freshmen (fall 2004):

Average SAT I Scores:	Verbal: 613	Math: 555
Average ACT Scores:	Composite: 24	

Child Study Team report is not required. Tests required as part of this documentation:

☐ WAIS-IV ☐ Woodcock-Johnson
☐ WISC-IV ☐ Nelson-Denny Reading Test
☐ SATA ☐ Other

UNDERGRADUATE STUDENT BODY

Total undergraduate student enrollment: 304 Men, 477 Women.

Composition of student body (fall 2004):

	Undergraduate	Freshmen
International	2.9	3.9
Black	4.8	1.8
American Indian	0.0	0.0
Asian-American	1.4	1.0
Hispanic	2.4	2.1
White	86.1	89.9
Unreported	2.4	1.3
	100.0%	100.0%

80% are from out of state. 90% of classes have fewer than 20 students, 10% have between 20 and 50 students.

STUDENT HOUSING

Housing is guaranteed for all undergraduates. Campus can house 712 undergraduates. Single rooms are available for students with medical or special needs. A medical note is required.

EXPENSES

Tuition (2005-06): $18,616 per year.
Room: $2,733. Board: $2,733.

There is no additional cost for LD program/services.

LD SERVICES

LD program size is not limited.

LD services available to:

☑ Freshmen ☑ Sophomores ☑ Juniors ☑ Seniors

Academic Accommodations

Curriculum		**In class**	
Foreign language waiver	☐	Early syllabus	☑
Lighter course load	☑	Note takers in class	☑
Math waiver	☐	Priority seating	☐
Other special classes	☐	Tape recorders	☐
Priority registrations	☐	Videotaped classes	☐
Substitution of courses	☐	Text on tape	☐
Exams		**Services**	
Extended time	☑	Diagnostic tests	☐
Oral exams	☑	Learning centers	☑
Take home exams	☐	Proofreaders	☐
Exams on tape or computer	☑	Readers	☐
Untimed exams	☑	Reading Machines/Kurzweil	☐
Other accommodations	☐	Special bookstore section	☐
		Typists	☐

Credit toward degree is not given for remedial courses taken.

Counseling Services

☑ Academic
☑ Psychological
☐ Student Support groups
☐ Vocational

Tutoring

Individual tutoring is available weekly.

Average size of tutoring groups: 2

	Individual	Group
Time management	☑	☐
Organizational skills	☑	☐
Learning strategies	☑	☐
Study skills	☑	☐
Content area	☑	☐
Writing lab	☑	☐
Math lab	☑	☐

LD PROGRAM STAFF

Total number of LD Program staff (including director):

Full Time: 1 Part Time: 1

There is an advisor/advocate from the LD program available to students. 7 peer tutors are available to work with LD students.

Key staff person available to work with LD students: Lyn O'Hare, Director of Academic Support Services.

Western Carolina University

Cullowhee, NC

Address: Cullowhee, NC, 28723
Admissions telephone: 877 928-4968
Admissions FAX: 828 227-7319
Director of Admissions: Phil Cauley
Admissions e-mail: admiss@email.wcu.edu
Web site: http://www.wcu.edu
SAT Code: 5897 ACT Code: 3172

LD program name: Student Support Services
Director, Student Support Services: Carol M. Mellen
LD program telephone: 828 227-7127
LD program e-mail: mellen@email.wcu.edu
LD program enrollment: 75, Total campus enrollment: 6,785

GENERAL

Western Carolina University is a public, coed, four-year institution. 265-acre campus in Cullowhee (population: 3,579), 65 miles from Asheville; branch campuses in Asheville and Cherokee. Airport and bus serve Asheville. School operates transportation to Sylva. Semester system.

LD ADMISSIONS

A personal interview is not required. Essay is not required.

SECONDARY SCHOOL REQUIREMENTS

Graduation from secondary school required; GED accepted. The following course distribution required: 4 units of English, 3 units of math, 3 units of science, 2 units of foreign language, 2 units of social studies, 1 unit of history, 5 units of academic electives.

TESTING

SAT Reasoning required; ACT may be substituted. SAT Subject recommended.

All enrolled freshmen (fall 2004):

Average SAT I Scores: Verbal: 510 Math: 517
Average ACT Scores: Composite: 20

Child Study Team report is not required. Tests required as part of this documentation:

- [ ] WAIS-IV
- [ ] WISC-IV
- [ ] SATA
- [ ] Woodcock-Johnson
- [ ] Nelson-Denny Reading Test
- [ ] Other

UNDERGRADUATE STUDENT BODY

Total undergraduate student enrollment: 2,731 Men, 2,934 Women.

Composition of student body (fall 2004):

	Undergraduate	Freshmen
International	0.8	3.1
Black	6.2	5.4
American Indian	1.0	1.7
Asian-American	0.6	0.7
Hispanic	1.2	1.2
White	88.9	86.5
Unreported	1.3	1.4
	100.0%	100.0%

9% are from out of state. 9% join a fraternity and 8% join a sorority. Average age of full-time undergraduates is 20. 35% of classes have fewer than 20 students, 64% have between 20 and 50 students, 1% have more than 50 students.

STUDENT HOUSING

94% of freshmen live in college housing. Freshmen are required to live on campus. Housing is guaranteed for all undergraduates. Campus can house 3,558 undergraduates. Single rooms are available for students with medical or special needs. A medical note is required.

EXPENSES

Tuition (2005-06): $1,651 per year (in-state), $11,087 (out-of-state). Room: $2,428. Board: $2,472.
There is no additional cost for LD program/services.

LD SERVICES

LD program size is not limited.

LD services available to:

- [x] Freshmen
- [x] Sophomores
- [x] Juniors
- [x] Seniors

Academic Accommodations

Curriculum
- Foreign language waiver [ ]
- Lighter course load [ ]
- Math waiver [ ]
- Other special classes [ ]
- Priority registrations [x]
- Substitution of courses [ ]

Exams
- Extended time [x]
- Oral exams [x]
- Take home exams [x]
- Exams on tape or computer [x]
- Untimed exams [ ]
- Other accommodations [x]

In class
- Early syllabus [ ]
- Note takers in class [x]
- Priority seating [x]
- Tape recorders [x]
- Videotaped classes [ ]
- Text on tape [x]

Services
- Diagnostic tests [ ]
- Learning centers [x]
- Proofreaders [x]
- Readers [x]
- Reading Machines/Kurzweil [x]
- Special bookstore section [ ]
- Typists [x]

Credit toward degree is not given for remedial courses taken.

Counseling Services

- [x] Academic
- [x] Psychological
- [ ] Student Support groups
- [ ] Vocational

Tutoring

Individual tutoring is available daily.

	Individual	Group
Time management	[ ]	[x]
Organizational skills	[ ]	[x]
Learning strategies	[ ]	[ ]
Study skills	[ ]	[x]
Content area	[ ]	[ ]
Writing lab	[ ]	[x]
Math lab	[ ]	[x]

LD PROGRAM STAFF

Total number of LD Program staff (including director):

Full Time: 5 Part Time: 5

Key staff person available to work with LD students: Carol M. Mellen, Director, Student Support Services.

Wingate University

Wingate, NC

Address: 220 North Camden Street, Wingate, NC, 28174
Admissions telephone: 800 755-5550
Admissions FAX: 704 233-8110
Dean of Admissions: Rhett Brown
Admissions e-mail: admit@wingate.edu
Web site: http://www.wingate.edu
SAT Code: 5908 ACT Code: 3176

LD program name: Academic Resource Center
LD program address: CB 3068
LD program e-mail: stedje@wingate.edu
LD program enrollment: 84, Total campus enrollment: 1,331

GENERAL

Wingate University is a private, coed, four-year institution. 370-acre, suburban campus in Wingate (population: 2,406), 25 miles from Charlotte; branch campus in Matthews. Major airport and train serve Charlotte; bus serves Monroe (five miles). School operates transportation to airport and bus and train stations prior to holidays and breaks. Semester system.

LD ADMISSIONS

Students do not complete a separate application and are simultaneously accepted to the LD program. A member of the LD program does not sit on the admissions committee. A personal interview is recommended. Essay is required and may be typed.

SECONDARY SCHOOL REQUIREMENTS

Graduation from secondary school required; GED accepted.

TESTING

SAT Reasoning required; ACT may be substituted. SAT Subject recommended.

All enrolled freshmen (fall 2004):

Average SAT I Scores:	Verbal: 507	Math: 517
Average ACT Scores:	Composite: 22	

Child Study Team report is not required. A neuropsychological or comprehensive psycho-educational evaluation is required for admission. Must be dated within 36 months of application. Tests required as part of this documentation:

- [x] WAIS-IV
- [x] WISC-IV
- [ ] SATA
- [x] Woodcock-Johnson
- [ ] Nelson-Denny Reading Test
- [ ] Other

UNDERGRADUATE STUDENT BODY

Total undergraduate student enrollment: 586 Men, 669 Women.

Composition of student body (fall 2004):

	Undergraduate	Freshmen
International	2.2	3.3
Black	8.7	10.6
American Indian	1.4	0.8
Asian-American	1.1	1.1
Hispanic	3.1	1.9
White	82.7	80.3
Unreported	0.8	2.0
	100.0%	100.0%

42% are from out of state. 6% join a fraternity and 10% join a sorority. Average age of full-time undergraduates is 20. 51% of classes have fewer than 20 students, 48% have between 20 and 50 students, 1% have more than 50 students.

STUDENT HOUSING

90% of freshmen live in college housing. Freshmen are required to live on campus. Housing is guaranteed for all undergraduates. Campus can house 1,077 undergraduates. Single rooms are available for students with medical or special needs. A medical note is required.

EXPENSES

Tuition (2005-06): $15,800 per year.
Room & Board: $6,450.

There is no additional cost for LD program/services.

LD SERVICES

LD program size is not limited.

LD services available to:

- [x] Freshmen
- [x] Sophomores
- [x] Juniors
- [x] Seniors

Academic Accommodations

Curriculum		In class	
Foreign language waiver	[ ]	Early syllabus	[ ]
Lighter course load	[x]	Note takers in class	[ ]
Math waiver	[ ]	Priority seating	[ ]
Other special classes	[ ]	Tape recorders	[ ]
Priority registrations	[ ]	Videotaped classes	[ ]
Substitution of courses	[ ]	Text on tape	[ ]
Exams		**Services**	
Extended time	[ ]	Diagnostic tests	[ ]
Oral exams	[ ]	Learning centers	[ ]
Take home exams	[ ]	Proofreaders	[ ]
Exams on tape or computer	[ ]	Readers	[ ]
Untimed exams	[ ]	Reading Machines/Kurzweil	[ ]
Other accommodations	[ ]	Special bookstore section	[ ]
		Typists	[ ]

Credit toward degree is not given for remedial courses taken.

Counseling Services

- [x] Academic
- [x] Psychological
- [ ] Student Support groups
- [ ] Vocational

Tutoring

Individual tutoring is available weekly.

	Individual	Group
Time management	[x]	[x]
Organizational skills	[x]	[x]
Learning strategies	[x]	[x]
Study skills	[x]	[x]
Content area	[x]	[x]
Writing lab	[x]	[ ]
Math lab	[x]	[ ]

UNIQUE LD PROGRAM FEATURES

Services are determined on an individual basis. Students qualify for accommodations based on their diagnostic and educational information. Support Services are centralized and coordinated.

LD PROGRAM STAFF

Total number of LD Program staff (including director):

Full Time: 1 Part Time: 1

There is an advisor/advocate from the LD program available to students.

Key staff person available to work with LD students: Linda Stedje-Larsen

LD Program web site: http://www.wingate.edu/academics/arc/home.htm

Winston-Salem State University

Winston-Salem, NC

Address: 601 Martin Luther King Jr. Drive, Winston-Salem, NC, 27110
Admissions telephone: 336 750-2070
Admissions FAX: 336 750-2079
Director of Admissions: Dr. X. Maurice Allen
Admissions e-mail: admissions@wssu.edu
Web site: http://www.wssu.edu
SAT Code: 5909 ACT Code: 3178

LD program name: Academic Resource Center
Total campus enrollment: 4,568

GENERAL

Winston-Salem State University is a public, coed, four-year institution. 94-acre, suburban campus in Winston-Salem (population: 185,776), 28 miles from Greensboro. Served by bus; major airport and train serve Greensboro. Public transportation serves campus. Semester system.

LD ADMISSIONS

A personal interview is not required. Essay is not required.

SECONDARY SCHOOL REQUIREMENTS

Graduation from secondary school required; GED accepted. The following course distribution required: 4 units of English, 3 units of math, 3 units of science, 2 units of foreign language, 1 unit of social studies, 1 unit of history.

TESTING

ACT considered if submitted. SAT Subject required.

All enrolled freshmen (fall 2004):

Average SAT I Scores: Verbal: 443 Math: 445
Average ACT Scores: Composite:

Child Study Team report is not required. A neuropsychological or comprehensive psycho-education evaluation is not required for admission. Tests required as part of this documentation:

- [ ] WAIS-IV
- [ ] WISC-IV
- [ ] SATA
- [ ] Woodcock-Johnson
- [ ] Nelson-Denny Reading Test
- [ ] Other

UNDERGRADUATE STUDENT BODY

Total undergraduate student enrollment: 939 Men, 2,053 Women.

Composition of student body (fall 2004):

	Undergraduate	Freshmen
International	0.0	0.0
Black	94.0	84.3
American Indian	0.2	0.3
Asian-American	0.6	0.5
Hispanic	1.7	1.0
White	3.4	13.7
Unreported	0.1	0.2
	100.0%	100.0%

7% are from out of state. 5% join a fraternity and 5% join a sorority. Average age of full-time undergraduates is 23. 42% of classes have fewer than 20 students, 57% have between 20 and 50 students, 2% have more than 50 students.

STUDENT HOUSING

82% of freshmen live in college housing. Freshmen are not required to live on campus. Housing is guaranteed for all undergraduates. Campus can house 1,664 undergraduates. Single rooms are available for students with medical or special needs. A medical note is not required.

EXPENSES

Tuition (2005-06): $1,451 per year (in-state), $10,090 (out-of-state).
Room: $3,122. Board: $2,356.
There is no additional cost for LD program/services.

LD SERVICES

LD program size is not limited.

LD services available to:

- [x] Freshmen
- [x] Sophomores
- [x] Juniors
- [x] Seniors

Academic Accommodations

Curriculum

- [ ] Foreign language waiver
- [ ] Lighter course load
- [ ] Math waiver
- [ ] Other special classes
- [ ] Priority registrations
- [ ] Substitution of courses

Exams

- [x] Extended time
- [x] Oral exams
- [ ] Take home exams
- [ ] Exams on tape or computer
- [x] Untimed exams
- [ ] Other accommodations

In class

- [ ] Early syllabus
- [x] Note takers in class
- [ ] Priority seating
- [x] Tape recorders
- [ ] Videotaped classes
- [ ] Text on tape

Services

- [ ] Diagnostic tests
- [x] Learning centers
- [ ] Proofreaders
- [x] Readers
- [x] Reading Machines/Kurzweil
- [ ] Special bookstore section
- [ ] Typists

Credit toward degree is not given for remedial courses taken.

Counseling Services

- [x] Academic
- [x] Psychological
- [ ] Student Support groups
- [ ] Vocational

Tutoring

Individual tutoring is available weekly.

	Individual	Group
Time management	[x]	[ ]
Organizational skills	[ ]	[ ]
Learning strategies	[x]	[ ]
Study skills	[x]	[ ]
Content area	[x]	[ ]
Writing lab	[x]	[ ]
Math lab	[x]	[ ]

LD PROGRAM STAFF

Total number of LD Program staff (including director):

Full Time: 1 Part Time: 1

There is an advisor/advocate from the LD program available to students.

Key staff person available to work with LD students: Myra B. Waddell, Director of Academic Resource Center & Coordinator.

Dickinson State University

Dickinson, ND

Address: 291 Campus Drive, Dickinson, ND, 58601
Admissions telephone: 800 279-4295
Admissions FAX: 701 483-2409
Director of Admissions and Academic Records: Marshall Melbye
Admissions e-mail: dsu.hawks@dsu.nodak.edu
Web site: http://www.dickinsonstate.com
SAT Code: 6477 ACT Code: 3210

LD program name: Student Support Services
Director of Student Support Services: Rick Padilla
LD program telephone: 701 483-2999
LD program e-mail: Richard.Padilla@dickinsonstate.edu
LD program enrollment: 50, Total campus enrollment: 2,479

GENERAL

Dickinson State University is a public, coed, four-year institution. 76-acre campus in Dickinson (population: 16,010), 100 miles from Bismarck. Served by air and bus; train serves Williston (140 miles). Semester system.

LD ADMISSIONS

Students do not complete a separate application and are simultaneously accepted to the LD program. A member of the LD program does not sit on the admissions committee. High school waivers are accepted for math and foreign language. A personal interview is not required. Essay is not required.

For fall 2004, 65 completed self-identified LD applications were received. 65 applications were offered admission, and 50 enrolled.

SECONDARY SCHOOL REQUIREMENTS

Graduation from secondary school required; GED accepted.

TESTING

ACT required.

All enrolled freshmen (fall 2004):

Average SAT I Scores:	Verbal: 476	Math: 483
Average ACT Scores:	Composite: 21	

Child Study Team report is not required. A neuropsychological or comprehensive psycho-educational evaluation is required for admission. Must be dated within 36 months of application. Tests required as part of this documentation:

- [ ] WAIS-IV
- [ ] WISC-IV
- [ ] SATA
- [ ] Woodcock-Johnson
- [ ] Nelson-Denny Reading Test
- [ ] Other

UNDERGRADUATE STUDENT BODY

Total undergraduate student enrollment: 903 Men, 1,198 Women.

Composition of student body (fall 2004):

	Undergraduate	Freshmen
International	4.5	4.0
Black	2.7	1.8
American Indian	3.0	1.0
Asian-American	1.0	0.4
Hispanic	0.7	1.2
White	87.8	87.3
Unreported	0.3	4.3
	100.0%	100.0%

26% are from out of state. 17% of classes have fewer than 20 students, 72% have between 20 and 50 students, 11% have more than 50 students.

STUDENT HOUSING

30% of freshmen live in college housing. Freshmen are required to live on campus. Housing is guaranteed for all undergraduates. Campus can house 592 undergraduates. Single rooms are available for students with medical or special needs. A medical note is required.

EXPENSES

Tuition (2005-06): $4,154 per year (in-state), $9,712 (out-of-state). $2,714 per year (state residents), $3,066 (Minnesota residents), $3,265 (Montana and South Dakota residents), $3,815 (Midwestern Higher Education Commission program and WUE states), $6,392 (other out-of-state).

Room: $1,324. Board: $2,370.
There is no additional cost for LD program/services.

LD SERVICES

LD program size is not limited.

LD services available to:

- [x] Freshmen
- [x] Sophomores
- [x] Juniors
- [x] Seniors

Academic Accommodations

Curriculum		In class	
Foreign language waiver	[ ]	Early syllabus	[ ]
Lighter course load	[x]	Note takers in class	[x]
Math waiver	[ ]	Priority seating	[ ]
Other special classes	[ ]	Tape recorders	[x]
Priority registrations	[ ]	Videotaped classes	[ ]
Substitution of courses	[ ]	Text on tape	[x]
Exams		**Services**	
Extended time	[x]	Diagnostic tests	[ ]
Oral exams	[x]	Learning centers	[x]
Take home exams	[ ]	Proofreaders	[ ]
Exams on tape or computer	[ ]	Readers	[x]
Untimed exams	[x]	Reading Machines/Kurzweil	[ ]
Other accommodations	[ ]	Special bookstore section	[ ]
		Typists	[x]

Credit toward degree is given for remedial courses taken.

Counseling Services

- [x] Academic
- [x] Psychological
- [ ] Student Support groups
- [ ] Vocational

Meets 3 times per academic year

Tutoring

Individual tutoring is available daily.

Average size of tutoring groups: 3

	Individual	Group
Time management	[ ]	[x]
Organizational skills	[ ]	[x]
Learning strategies	[ ]	[x]
Study skills	[x]	[x]
Content area	[x]	[x]
Writing lab	[x]	[x]
Math lab	[x]	[x]

LD PROGRAM STAFF

Total number of LD Program staff (including director):

Full Time: 5 Part Time: 5

There is an advisor/advocate from the LD program available to students. The advisor/advocate meets with faculty 1 time per month. 20 peer tutors are available to work with LD students.

Key staff person available to work with LD students: Rick Padilla, Student Support Services Coordinator.

LD Program web site: www.dsu.nodak.edu/s_support.asp

Jamestown College

Jamestown, ND

Address: 6086 College Lane, Jamestown, ND, 58405
Admissions telephone: 800 336-2554
Admissions FAX: 701 253-4318
Director of Admissions: Judy Erickson
Admissions e-mail: admissions@jc.edu
Web site: http://www.jc.edu
SAT Code: 6318 ACT Code: 3200

LD program enrollment: 5, Total campus enrollment: 1,063

GENERAL

Jamestown College is a private, coed, four-year institution. 107-acre campus in Jamestown (population: 15,527), 100 miles from Fargo and Bismarck. Served by bus; airport serves Fargo. Semester system.

LD ADMISSIONS

A personal interview is not required.

SECONDARY SCHOOL REQUIREMENTS

Graduation from secondary school required; GED accepted.

TESTING

ACT required; SAT Reasoning may be substituted. SAT Subject recommended.

All enrolled freshmen (fall 2004):

Average ACT Scores: Composite: 22

Child Study Team report is not required. Tests required as part of this documentation:

- ☐ WAIS-IV
- ☐ WISC-IV
- ☐ SATA
- ☐ Woodcock-Johnson
- ☐ Nelson-Denny Reading Test
- ☐ Other

UNDERGRADUATE STUDENT BODY

Total undergraduate student enrollment: 496 Men, 641 Women.

Composition of student body (fall 2004):

	Undergraduate	Freshmen
International	3.9	3.2
Black	1.7	1.3
American Indian	0.4	1.3
Asian-American	1.7	1.1
Hispanic	0.4	2.0
White	91.7	90.6
Unreported	0.2	0.5
	100.0%	100.0%

39% are from out of state. Average age of full-time undergraduates is 21. 48% of classes have fewer than 20 students, 49% have between 20 and 50 students, 3% have more than 50 students.

STUDENT HOUSING

95% of freshmen live in college housing. Freshmen are required to live on campus. Housing is guaranteed for all undergraduates. Campus can house 714 undergraduates.

EXPENSES

Tuition (2005-06): $10,000 per year.

Room: $1,760. Board: $2,370.

There is no additional cost for LD program/services.

LD SERVICES

LD program size is not limited.

LD services available to:

☐ Freshmen ☐ Sophomores ☐ Juniors ☐ Seniors

Academic Accommodations

Curriculum		In class	
Foreign language waiver	☐	Early syllabus	☐
Lighter course load	☐	Note takers in class	☑
Math waiver	☐	Priority seating	☐
Other special classes	☐	Tape recorders	☐
Priority registrations	☐	Videotaped classes	☐
Substitution of courses	☐	Text on tape	☐
Exams		**Services**	
Extended time	☑	Diagnostic tests	☐
Oral exams	☑	Learning centers	☑
Take home exams	☐	Proofreaders	☐
Exams on tape or computer	☐	Readers	☑
Untimed exams	☑	Reading Machines/Kurzweil	☐
Other accommodations	☐	Special bookstore section	☐
		Typists	☐

Credit toward degree is given for remedial courses taken.

Counseling Services

- ☐ Academic
- ☐ Psychological
- ☐ Student Support groups
- ☐ Vocational

Tutoring

	Individual	Group
Time management	☐	☐
Organizational skills	☐	☐
Learning strategies	☐	☐
Study skills	☐	☐
Content area	☐	☐
Writing lab	☐	☐
Math lab	☐	☐

LD PROGRAM STAFF

Key staff person available to work with LD students: Myra Watts, Director, Learning and Academic Advising.

University of Mary

Bismarck, ND

Address: 7500 University Drive, Bismarck, ND, 58504
Admissions telephone: 800 288-6279
Admissions FAX: 701 255-7687
Director of Admissions: Dr. Dave Heringer
Admissions e-mail: marauder@umary.edu
Web site: http://www.umary.edu
SAT Code: 6428 ACT Code: 3201

LD program name: Learning Skills Services
Director: Mary Jo Wocken
LD program telephone: 701 355-8264
LD program e-mail: mjwocken@umary.edu
LD program enrollment: 17, Total campus enrollment: 2,227

GENERAL

University of Mary is a private, coed, four-year institution. 107-acre campus in Bismarck (population: 55,532); branch campus in Fargo. Served by air and bus; train serves Minot (112 miles). School operates transportation to downtown Bismarck. Semester system.

LD ADMISSIONS

Students complete a separate application and are not simultaneously accepted to the LD program. A member of the LD program does sit on the admissions committee. A personal interview is recommended. Essay is not required.

For fall 2004, 15 completed self-identified LD applications were received. 6 applications were offered admission, and 6 enrolled.

SECONDARY SCHOOL REQUIREMENTS

Graduation from secondary school required; GED accepted.

TESTING

SAT Reasoning considered if submitted. ACT recommended. SAT Subject recommended.

All enrolled freshmen (fall 2004):

Average ACT Scores: Composite: 22

Child Study Team report is not required. A neuropsychological or comprehensive psycho-educational evaluation is required for admission. Must be dated within 36 months of application. Tests required as part of this documentation:

■	WAIS-IV	■	Woodcock-Johnson
■	WISC-IV	□	Nelson-Denny Reading Test
■	SATA	□	Other

UNDERGRADUATE STUDENT BODY

Total undergraduate student enrollment: 2,227.

Composition of student body (fall 2004):

	Undergraduate	Freshmen
International	1.7	1.8
Black	1.0	1.3
American Indian	1.5	4.9
Asian-American	0.2	0.7
Hispanic	1.9	1.3
White	93.2	89.8
Unreported	0.5	0.2
	100.0%	100.0%

28% are from out of state. Average age of full-time undergraduates is 23. 62% of classes have fewer than 20 students, 32% have between 20 and 50 students, 6% have more than 50 students.

STUDENT HOUSING

87% of freshmen live in college housing. Freshmen are required to live on campus. Housing is guaranteed for all undergraduates. Campus can house 776 undergraduates. Single rooms are available for students with medical or special needs. A medical note is required.

EXPENSES

Tuition (2005-06): $10,600 per year.
Room: $2,200. Board: $2,200.
There is no additional cost for LD program/services.

LD SERVICES

LD program size is not limited.

LD services available to:

■ Freshmen ■ Sophomores ■ Juniors ■ Seniors

Academic Accommodations

Curriculum		In class	
Foreign language waiver	□	Early syllabus	□
Lighter course load	■	Note takers in class	■
Math waiver	□	Priority seating	□
Other special classes	■	Tape recorders	■
Priority registrations	□	Videotaped classes	□
Substitution of courses	□	Text on tape	■
Exams		**Services**	
Extended time	■	Diagnostic tests	□
Oral exams	■	Learning centers	■
Take home exams	□	Proofreaders	■
Exams on tape or computer	□	Readers	■
Untimed exams	■	Reading Machines/Kurzweil	■
Other accommodations	□	Special bookstore section	□
		Typists	□

Credit toward degree is not given for remedial courses taken.

Counseling Services

■ Academic
□ Psychological
□ Student Support groups
□ Vocational

Tutoring

	Individual	Group
Time management	■	□
Organizational skills	■	□
Learning strategies	■	□
Study skills	■	■
Content area	□	□
Writing lab	□	□
Math lab	□	□

LD PROGRAM STAFF

Total number of LD Program staff (including director):

Full Time: 1 Part Time: 1

There is an advisor/advocate from the LD program available to students. 1 peer tutor is available to work with LD students.

Key staff person available to work with LD students: Mary Jo Wocken, Dir. of the Learning Skills Center.

Mayville State University

Mayville, ND

Address: 330 Third Street NE, Mayville, ND, 58257
Admissions telephone: 800 437-4104
Admissions FAX: 701 788-4748
Director of Enrollment Services: Cherine Heckman
Admissions e-mail: admit@mayvillestate.edu
Web site: http://www.mayvillestate.edu
SAT Code: 6478 ACT Code: 3212

LD program name: Academic Support Services
Director of Academic Support Services: Greta Kyllo
LD program telephone: 701 788-4747
LD program e-mail: kyllo@mayvillestate.edu
LD program enrollment: 30, Total campus enrollment: 897

GENERAL

Mayville State University is a public, coed, four-year institution. 60-acre campus in Mayville (population: 1,953), 55 miles from Fargo and 42 miles from Grand Forks. Major airport and train serve Grand Forks; bus serves Hillsboro (16 miles). Semester system.

LD ADMISSIONS

A personal interview is recommended. Essay is not required.

SECONDARY SCHOOL REQUIREMENTS

Graduation from secondary school required; GED accepted. The following course distribution required: 4 units of English, 3 units of math, 3 units of science, 3 units of social studies.

TESTING

ACT required; SAT Reasoning may be substituted. SAT Subject recommended.

All enrolled freshmen (fall 2004):

Average ACT Scores: Composite: 19

Child Study Team report is not required. Tests required as part of this documentation:

- ☐ WAIS-IV
- ☐ WISC-IV
- ☐ SATA
- ☐ Woodcock-Johnson
- ☐ Nelson-Denny Reading Test
- ☐ Other

UNDERGRADUATE STUDENT BODY

Total undergraduate student enrollment: 346 Men, 409 Women.

Composition of student body (fall 2004):

	Undergraduate	Freshmen
International	7.5	4.8
Black	3.2	4.0
American Indian	5.1	4.3
Asian-American	0.3	0.4
Hispanic	1.1	1.4
White	82.8	85.1
Unreported	0.0	0.0
	100.0%	100.0%

27% are from out of state. 49% of classes have fewer than 20 students, 51% have between 20 and 50 students.

STUDENT HOUSING

Freshmen are required to live on campus. Housing is guaranteed for all undergraduates. Campus can house 350 undergraduates. Single rooms are available for students with medical or special needs. A medical note is required.

EXPENSES

Tuition (2005-06): $3,700 per year (in-state), $8,811 (out-of-state).

Room: $1,524. Board: $2,200.
There is no additional cost for LD program/services.

LD SERVICES

LD program size is not limited.

LD services available to:

☑ Freshmen ☑ Sophomores ☑ Juniors ☑ Seniors

Academic Accommodations

Curriculum		In class	
Foreign language waiver	☐	Early syllabus	☐
Lighter course load	☐	Note takers in class	☑
Math waiver	☐	Priority seating	☐
Other special classes	☐	Tape recorders	☑
Priority registrations	☐	Videotaped classes	☐
Substitution of courses	☐	Text on tape	☑
Exams		**Services**	
Extended time	☑	Diagnostic tests	☐
Oral exams	☑	Learning centers	☑
Take home exams	☐	Proofreaders	☐
Exams on tape or computer	☐	Readers	☑
Untimed exams	☑	Reading Machines/Kurzweil	☐
Other accommodations	☐	Special bookstore section	☐
		Typists	☐

Credit toward degree is given for remedial courses taken.

Counseling Services

- ☑ Academic
- ☐ Psychological
- ☐ Student Support groups
- ☐ Vocational

Tutoring

Individual tutoring is available weekly.

	Individual	Group
Time management	☑	☐
Organizational skills	☑	☐
Learning strategies	☑	☐
Study skills	☑	☐
Content area	☑	☐
Writing lab	☐	☐
Math lab	☐	☐

LD PROGRAM STAFF

There is an advisor/advocate from the LD program available to students. 5 peer tutors are available to work with LD students.

Key staff person available to work with LD students: Greta Kyllo, Director of Academic Support Services.

Minot State University

Minot, ND

Address: 500 University Avenue W, Minot, ND, 58707
Admissions telephone: 800 777-0750, extension 3350
Admissions FAX: 701 858-3386
Enrollment Services Representative: Dennis Parisien
Admissions e-mail: askmsu@minotstateu.edu
Web site: http://www.minotstateu.edu
SAT Code: 6479 ACT Code: 3214

Coordinator of Disability Services: Evelyn Klimpel
LD program telephone: 701 858-3372
LD program e-mail: evelyn.klimpel@minotstateu.edu
LD program enrollment: 28, Total campus enrollment: 3,576

GENERAL

Minot State University is a public, coed, four-year institution. 103-acre campus in Minot (population: 36,567), 105 miles from Bismarck. Served by air, bus, and train. Semester system.

LD ADMISSIONS

Students do not complete a separate application and are not simultaneously accepted to the LD program. A member of the LD program does not sit on the admissions committee. A personal interview is not required. Essay is not required.

For fall 2004, 28 completed self-identified LD applications were received.

SECONDARY SCHOOL REQUIREMENTS

Graduation from secondary school required; GED accepted. The following course distribution required: 4 units of English, 3 units of math, 3 units of science, 3 units of social studies.

TESTING

ACT required; SAT Reasoning may be substituted. SAT Subject required.

All enrolled freshmen (fall 2004):

Average ACT Scores: Composite: 22

Child Study Team report is not required. A neuropsychological or comprehensive psycho-educational evaluation is required for admission. Tests required as part of this documentation:

- ☐ WAIS-IV
- ☐ WISC-IV
- ☐ SATA
- ☐ Woodcock-Johnson
- ☐ Nelson-Denny Reading Test
- ☐ Other

UNDERGRADUATE STUDENT BODY

Total undergraduate student enrollment: 1,255 Men, 2,071 Women.

12% are from out of state. 63% of classes have fewer than 20 students, 35% have between 20 and 50 students, 2% have more than 50 students.

STUDENT HOUSING

Freshmen are not required to live on campus. Housing is guaranteed for all undergraduates. Campus can house 643 undergraduates.

EXPENSES

Tuition (2005-06): $3,444 per year (in-state), $9,162 (out-of-state).
Room & Board: $4,460.
There is no additional cost for LD program/services.

LD SERVICES

LD program size is not limited.

LD services available to:

☐ Freshmen ☐ Sophomores ☐ Juniors ☐ Seniors

Academic Accommodations

Curriculum		**In class**	
Foreign language waiver	☐	Early syllabus	☐
Lighter course load	■	Note takers in class	■
Math waiver	☐	Priority seating	■
Other special classes	☐	Tape recorders	■
Priority registrations	■	Videotaped classes	■
Substitution of courses	☐	Text on tape	☐
Exams		**Services**	
Extended time	■	Diagnostic tests	☐
Oral exams	■	Learning centers	■
Take home exams	☐	Proofreaders	■
Exams on tape or computer	■	Readers	■
Untimed exams	■	Reading Machines/Kurzweil	■
Other accommodations	☐	Special bookstore section	☐
		Typists	☐

Credit toward degree is given for remedial courses taken.

Counseling Services

- ☐ Academic
- ☐ Psychological
- ☐ Student Support groups
- ☐ Vocational

Tutoring

Individual tutoring is available daily.

	Individual	Group
Time management	■	☐
Organizational skills	■	☐
Learning strategies	■	☐
Study skills	■	☐
Content area	■	☐
Writing lab	■	☐
Math lab	■	☐

UNIQUE LD PROGRAM FEATURES

Minot State University does not have a service specifically for LD students. LD is just one of the 10 disability categories served at Minot State. The other nine categories served are: orthopedic, visual, hearing, psychological, ADHD/ADD, health related, TBI, speech and other.

LD PROGRAM STAFF

Total number of LD Program staff (including director):

Full Time: 6 Part Time: 6

There is an advisor/advocate from the LD program available to students. The advisor/advocate meets with faculty 3 times per month and student 3 times per month. 3 graduate students are available to work with LD students.

Key staff person available to work with LD students: Evelyn Klimpel, Coordinator of Disability Services.

University of North Dakota

Grand Forks, ND

Address: University Station, Grand Forks, ND, 58202
Admissions telephone: 800 CALL-UND
Admissions FAX: 701 777-2721
Director of Admissions: Heidi Kippenhan
Admissions e-mail: enrollment_services@mail.und.nodak.edu
Web site: http://www.und.edu
SAT Code: 6878 ACT Code: 3218

Director, Disability Support Services: Deb Glennen
LD program telephone: 701 777-3425
LD program e-mail: debglennen@mail.und.nodak.edu
Total campus enrollment: 10,710

GENERAL

University of North Dakota is a public, coed, four-year institution. 570-acre campus in Grand Forks (population: 49,321), 70 miles from Fargo. Served by air, bus, and train. School operates transportation to medical complex and airport. Public transportation serves campus. Semester system.

LD ADMISSIONS

SECONDARY SCHOOL REQUIREMENTS

Graduation from secondary school required; GED accepted. The following course distribution required: 4 units of English, 3 units of math, 3 units of science, 3 units of social studies.

TESTING

ACT required; SAT Reasoning may be substituted. SAT Subject recommended.

All enrolled freshmen (fall 2004):

Average ACT Scores: Composite: 23

Child Study Team report is not required. Tests required as part of this documentation:

- ❑ WAIS-IV
- ❑ WISC-IV
- ❑ SATA
- ❑ Woodcock-Johnson
- ❑ Nelson-Denny Reading Test
- ❑ Other

UNDERGRADUATE STUDENT BODY

Total undergraduate student enrollment: 5,183 Men, 4,602 Women.

Composition of student body (fall 2004):

	Undergraduate	Freshmen
International	2.5	2.3
Black	0.5	0.7
American Indian	1.9	2.8
Asian-American	1.5	1.4
Hispanic	1.0	1.0
White	92.6	91.8
Unreported	0.0	0.0
	100.0%	100.0%

42% are from out of state. 10% join a fraternity and 8% join a sorority. Average age of full-time undergraduates is 21. 36% of classes have fewer than 20 students, 54% have between 20 and 50 students, 10% have more than 50 students.

STUDENT HOUSING

85% of freshmen live in college housing. Freshmen are not required to live on campus. Housing is guaranteed for all undergraduates. Campus can house 3,312 undergraduates.

EXPENSES

Tuition (2005-06): $4,370 per year (in-state), $11,668 (out-of-state). Room & Board: $4,727.

LD SERVICES

LD services available to:

❑ Freshmen ❑ Sophomores ❑ Juniors ❑ Seniors

Academic Accommodations

Curriculum		In class	
Foreign language waiver	❑	Early syllabus	❑
Lighter course load	❑	Note takers in class	❑
Math waiver	❑	Priority seating	❑
Other special classes	❑	Tape recorders	❑
Priority registrations	❑	Videotaped classes	❑
Substitution of courses	❑	Text on tape	❑
Exams		**Services**	
Extended time	❑	Diagnostic tests	❑
Oral exams	❑	Learning centers	❑
Take home exams	❑	Proofreaders	❑
Exams on tape or computer	❑	Readers	❑
Untimed exams	❑	Reading Machines/Kurzweil	❑
Other accommodations	❑	Special bookstore section	❑
		Typists	❑

Counseling Services

- ❑ Academic
- ❑ Psychological
- ❑ Student Support groups
- ❑ Vocational

Tutoring

	Individual	Group
Time management	❑	❑
Organizational skills	❑	❑
Learning strategies	❑	❑
Study skills	❑	❑
Content area	❑	❑
Writing lab	❑	❑
Math lab	❑	❑

UNIQUE LD PROGRAM FEATURES

UND provides reasonable accommodations for all students with disabilities to ensure access to our programs and services.The type of accommodation provided is based on the functional limits of each student's disability.Students with disabilities register with the Disability Support Services office to request and arrange accommodations.

North Dakota State University

Fargo, ND

Address: 1301 12th Avenue N, Fargo, ND, 58105-5454
Admissions telephone: 800 488-NDSU
Admissions FAX: 701 231-8802
Dean for Enrollment Management/Director of Admission: Kate Haugen
Admissions e-mail: NDSU.Admission@ndsu.edu
Web site: http://www.ndsu.edu
SAT Code: 6474 ACT Code: 3202

LD program name: Disablity Services
LD program address: 212 Ceres Hall, P.O. Box 212
Coordinator: Bunnie Johnson-Messelt
LD program telephone: 701 231-7198
LD program e-mail: Bunnie.Johnson-Messelt@ndsu.edu
LD program enrollment: 100, Total campus enrollment: 10,549

GENERAL

North Dakota State University is a public, coed, four-year institution. 258-acre campus in Fargo (population: 90,599). Served by air, bus, and train. Public transportation serves campus. Semester system.

LD ADMISSIONS

Students do not complete a separate application and are not simultaneously accepted to the LD program. A personal interview is not required. Essay is not required. Admissions requirements that may be waived for LD students include standardized test scores or minimum GPA requirement.

SECONDARY SCHOOL REQUIREMENTS

Graduation from secondary school required; GED accepted. The following course distribution required: 4 units of English, 3 units of math, 3 units of science, 3 units of social studies.

TESTING

SAT Subject recommended.

All enrolled freshmen (fall 2004):

Average ACT Scores: Composite: 23

Child Study Team report is not required. Tests required as part of this documentation:

- ☐ WAIS-IV
- ☐ WISC-IV
- ☐ SATA
- ☐ Woodcock-Johnson
- ☐ Nelson-Denny Reading Test
- ☐ Other

UNDERGRADUATE STUDENT BODY

Total undergraduate student enrollment: 5,878 Men, 4,502 Women.

Composition of student body (fall 2004):

	Undergraduate	Freshmen
International	2.9	1.5
Black	1.2	1.3
American Indian	1.0	1.0
Asian-American	1.2	1.2
Hispanic	0.7	0.5
White	93.0	94.5
Unreported	0.0	0.0
	100.0%	100.0%

39% are from out of state. 4% join a fraternity and 2% join a sorority. Average age of full-time undergraduates is 22. 38% of classes have fewer than 20 students, 48% have between 20 and 50 students, 14% have more than 50 students.

STUDENT HOUSING

89% of freshmen live in college housing. Freshmen are required to live on campus. Housing is guaranteed for all undergraduates. Campus can house 3,173 undergraduates. Single rooms are available for students with medical or special needs. A medical note is required.

EXPENSES

Tuition (2005-06): $4,360 per year (in-state), $11,638 (out-of-state). $2,754 per year (state residents), $2,936 (Minnesota, residents), $4,131 (WUE program, Montana and South Dakota, and Manitoba and Saskatchewan, Canada residents), $7,353 (other out-of-state). Some majors have additional fees.

Room: $2,096. Board: $2,684.

There is no additional cost for LD program/services.

LD SERVICES

LD program size is not limited.

LD services available to:

☐ Freshmen ☐ Sophomores ☐ Juniors ☐ Seniors

Academic Accommodations

Curriculum		In class	
Foreign language waiver	☐	Early syllabus	☐
Lighter course load	■	Note takers in class	■
Math waiver	☐	Priority seating	☐
Other special classes	☐	Tape recorders	☐
Priority registrations	☐	Videotaped classes	☐
Substitution of courses	☐	Text on tape	☐
Exams		**Services**	
Extended time	■	Diagnostic tests	☐
Oral exams	■	Learning centers	☐
Take home exams	☐	Proofreaders	☐
Exams on tape or computer	☐	Readers	■
Untimed exams	☐	Reading Machines/Kurzweil	☐
Other accommodations	☐	Special bookstore section	☐
		Typists	☐

Credit toward degree is not given for remedial courses taken.

Counseling Services

- ☐ Academic
- ☐ Psychological
- ☐ Student Support groups
- ☐ Vocational

Tutoring

	Individual	Group
Time management	☐	☐
Organizational skills	☐	☐
Learning strategies	☐	☐
Study skills	☐	☐
Content area	☐	☐
Writing lab	☐	☐
Math lab	☐	☐

LD PROGRAM STAFF

Total number of LD Program staff (including director):

Full Time: 2 Part Time: 2

LD Program web site: http://www.ndsu.edu/counseling/disability.shtml

Valley City State University

Valley City, ND

Address: 101 College Street SW, Valley City, ND, 58072
Admissions telephone: 800 532-8641
Admissions FAX: 701 845-7299
Director of Enrollment Management: Dan Klein
Admissions e-mail: enrollment.services@vcsu.edu
Web site: http://www.vcsu.edu
SAT Code: 6480 ACT Code: 3216

Director of Student Academic Services: Jan Drake
LD program telephone: 701 845-7298
LD program e-mail: jan.drake@vcsu.edu
LD program enrollment: 20, Total campus enrollment: 1,033

GENERAL

Valley City State University is a public, coed, four-year institution. 55-acre campus in Valley City (population: 6,826), 55 miles from Fargo. Served by bus; airport serves Fargo. Semester system.

LD ADMISSIONS

Students do not complete a separate application and are not simultaneously accepted to the LD program. A member of the LD program does not sit on the admissions committee. A personal interview is not required. Essay is not required.

For fall 2004, 14 completed self-identified LD applications were received. 14 applications were offered admission, and 14 enrolled.

SECONDARY SCHOOL REQUIREMENTS

Graduation from secondary school required; GED accepted. The following course distribution required: 4 units of English, 3 units of math, 3 units of science, 3 units of social studies.

TESTING

ACT required; SAT Reasoning may be substituted. SAT Subject recommended.

All enrolled freshmen (fall 2004):

Average SAT I Scores:	Verbal: 471	Math: 491
Average ACT Scores:	Composite: 20	

Child Study Team report is not required. A neuropsychological or comprehensive psycho-education evaluation is not required for admission. Tests required as part of this documentation:

- ☐ WAIS-IV
- ☐ WISC-IV
- ☐ SATA
- ☐ Woodcock-Johnson
- ☐ Nelson-Denny Reading Test
- ☐ Other

UNDERGRADUATE STUDENT BODY

Total undergraduate student enrollment: 430 Men, 575 Women.

Composition of student body (fall 2004):

	Undergraduate	Freshmen
International	9.4	5.2
Black	2.9	2.1
American Indian	0.6	1.9
Asian-American	0.0	0.5
Hispanic	0.6	0.9
White	86.5	89.4
Unreported	0.0	0.0
	100.0%	100.0%

24% are from out of state. 1% join a fraternity and 1% join a sorority. Average age of full-time undergraduates is 21. 68% of classes have fewer than 20 students, 29% have between 20 and 50 students, 3% have more than 50 students.

STUDENT HOUSING

85% of freshmen live in college housing. Freshmen are required to live on campus. Housing is guaranteed for all undergraduates. Campus can house 436 undergraduates. Single rooms are available for students with medical or special needs. A medical note is required.

EXPENSES

Tuition (2005-06): $3,656 per year (in-state), $9,761 (out-of-state).
Room: $2,080. Board: $2,614.
There is no additional cost for LD program/services.

LD SERVICES

LD program size is not limited.

LD services available to:

■ Freshmen ■ Sophomores ■ Juniors ■ Seniors

Academic Accommodations

Curriculum		**In class**	
Foreign language waiver	☐	Early syllabus	☐
Lighter course load	☐	Note takers in class	■
Math waiver	☐	Priority seating	■
Other special classes	☐	Tape recorders	■
Priority registrations	☐	Videotaped classes	☐
Substitution of courses	☐	Text on tape	☐
Exams		**Services**	
Extended time	■	Diagnostic tests	☐
Oral exams	■	Learning centers	☐
Take home exams	☐	Proofreaders	■
Exams on tape or computer	■	Readers	■
Untimed exams	■	Reading Machines/Kurzweil	☐
Other accommodations	☐	Special bookstore section	☐
		Typists	☐

Credit toward degree is given for remedial courses taken.

Counseling Services

- ☐ Academic
- ☐ Psychological
- ☐ Student Support groups
- ☐ Vocational

Tutoring

Individual tutoring is available weekly.

Average size of tutoring groups: 1

	Individual	Group
Time management	☐	■
Organizational skills	☐	■
Learning strategies	■	☐
Study skills	☐	■
Content area	☐	☐
Writing lab	☐	■
Math lab	☐	☐

LD PROGRAM STAFF

Total number of LD Program staff (including director):

Full Time: 1 Part Time: 1

There is an advisor/advocate from the LD program available to students. 26 peer tutors are available to work with LD students.

Key staff person available to work with LD students: Jan Drake, Director of Student Academic Services.

The University of Akron

Akron, OH

Address: 302 Buchtel Common, Akron, OH, 44325
Admissions telephone: 800 655-4884
Admissions FAX: 330 972-7022
Interim Director of Admissions: Diane R. Raybuck
Admissions e-mail: admissions@uakron.edu
Web site: http://www.uakron.edu
SAT Code: 1829 ACT Code: 3338

LD program name: Office of Accessibility
Disability Specialist: Amy Liikala Conwi
LD program telephone: 330 972-7928
LD program e-mail: conwi@uakron.edu
LD program enrollment: 306, Total campus enrollment: 19,242

GENERAL

The University of Akron is a public, coed, four-year institution. 170-acre, urban campus in Akron (population: 217,074), 35 miles from Cleveland; branch campus in Wayne County. Served by air, bus, and train; major airport serves Cleveland. Public transportation serves campus. Semester system.

LD ADMISSIONS

Students do not complete a separate application and are not simultaneously accepted to the LD program. A member of the LD program does not sit on the admissions committee. High school waivers are accepted for math and foreign language. A personal interview is not required. Essay is not required.

SECONDARY SCHOOL REQUIREMENTS

Graduation from secondary school required; GED accepted.

TESTING

All enrolled freshmen (fall 2004):

Average SAT I Scores: Verbal: 501 Math: 509
Average ACT Scores: Composite: 21

Child Study Team report is required if student is classified. A neuropsychological or comprehensive psycho-educational evaluation is required for admission. Tests required as part of this documentation:

- [x] WAIS-IV
- [x] WISC-IV
- [x] SATA
- [x] Woodcock-Johnson
- [x] Nelson-Denny Reading Test
- [x] Other

UNDERGRADUATE STUDENT BODY

Total undergraduate student enrollment: 9,695 Men, 10,485 Women.

Composition of student body (fall 2004):

	Undergraduate	Freshmen
International	0.3	0.8
Black	17.5	14.3
American Indian	0.2	0.4
Asian-American	1.6	1.8
Hispanic	1.1	0.8
White	77.9	78.9
Unreported	1.4	3.0
	100.0%	100.0%

1% are from out of state. 1% join a fraternity and 1% join a sorority. Average age of full-time undergraduates is 22. 45% of classes have fewer than 20 students, 50% have between 20 and 50 students, 5% have more than 50 students.

STUDENT HOUSING

44% of freshmen live in college housing. Freshmen are required to live on campus. Housing is guaranteed for all undergraduates. Campus can house 2,330 undergraduates. Single rooms are available for students with medical or special needs. A medical note is required.

EXPENSES

Tuition (2005-06): $6,810 per year (in-state), $15,536 (out-of-state).
Room: $4,494. Board: $2,822.
There is no additional cost for LD program/services.

LD SERVICES

LD program size is not limited.

LD services available to:

- [x] Freshmen
- [x] Sophomores
- [x] Juniors
- [x] Seniors

Academic Accommodations

Curriculum		In class	
Foreign language waiver	[ ]	Early syllabus	[ ]
Lighter course load	[x]	Note takers in class	[x]
Math waiver	[ ]	Priority seating	[x]
Other special classes	[ ]	Tape recorders	[x]
Priority registrations	[x]	Videotaped classes	[ ]
Substitution of courses	[x]	Text on tape	[x]
Exams		**Services**	
Extended time	[x]	Diagnostic tests	[x]
Oral exams	[x]	Learning centers	[ ]
Take home exams	[ ]	Proofreaders	[ ]
Exams on tape or computer	[x]	Readers	[x]
Untimed exams	[ ]	Reading Machines/Kurzweil	[x]
Other accommodations	[x]	Special bookstore section	[ ]
		Typists	[x]

Credit toward degree is not given for remedial courses taken.

Counseling Services

- [x] Academic
- [x] Psychological
- [x] Student Support groups
- [x] Vocational

Tutoring

Individual tutoring is available daily.

	Individual	Group
Time management	[x]	[x]
Organizational skills	[x]	[x]
Learning strategies	[x]	[x]
Study skills	[x]	[x]
Content area	[x]	[x]
Writing lab	[x]	[x]
Math lab	[x]	[x]

LD PROGRAM STAFF

Total number of LD Program staff (including director):

Full Time: 1 Part Time: 1

There is an advisor/advocate from the LD program available to students.

Key staff person available to work with LD students: Amy Liikala Conwi, Disability Specialist.

LD Program web site: www.uakron.edu/access

Art Academy of Cincinnati

Cincinnati, OH

Address: 1125 St. Gregory Street, Cincinnati, OH, 45202
Admissions telephone: 800 323-5692
Admissions FAX: 513 562-8778
Director of Admissions: Mary Jane Zumwalde
Admissions e-mail: admissions@artacademy.edu
Web site: http://www.artacademy.edu
SAT Code: 1002   ACT Code: 5592

Director/Counselor: Kathy Weimer
LD program telephone: 513 562-6261
LD program e-mail: kweimer@artacademy.edu
Total campus enrollment: 218

GENERAL

Art Academy of Cincinnati is a private, coed, four-year institution. 184-acre campus in Cincinnati (population: 331,285). Served by air, bus, and train. Public transportation serves campus. Semester system.

LD ADMISSIONS

A personal interview is recommended. Essay is required and may be typed.

SECONDARY SCHOOL REQUIREMENTS

Graduation from secondary school required; GED accepted.

TESTING

SAT Reasoning or ACT considered if submitted. SAT Subject recommended.

All enrolled freshmen (fall 2004):

Average SAT I Scores:	Verbal: 533	Math: 444
Average ACT Scores:	Composite: 22	

Child Study Team report is not required. Tests required as part of this documentation:

- [ ] WAIS-IV
- [ ] WISC-IV
- [ ] SATA
- [ ] Woodcock-Johnson
- [ ] Nelson-Denny Reading Test
- [ ] Other

UNDERGRADUATE STUDENT BODY

Total undergraduate student enrollment: 100 Men, 118 Women.

Composition of student body (fall 2004):

	Undergraduate	Freshmen
International	5.2	2.5
Black	0.0	4.4
American Indian	0.0	0.0
Asian-American	1.7	1.3
Hispanic	3.4	0.6
White	89.7	91.2
Unreported	0.0	0.0
	100.0%	100.0%

28% are from out of state. Average age of full-time undergraduates is 21.

EXPENSES

Tuition (2005-06): $18,500 per year.
There is no additional cost for LD program/services.

LD SERVICES

LD program size is not limited.

LD services available to:

- [x] Freshmen
- [x] Sophomores
- [x] Juniors
- [x] Seniors

Academic Accommodations

Curriculum		In class	
Foreign language waiver	[ ]	Early syllabus	[ ]
Lighter course load	[x]	Note takers in class	[x]
Math waiver	[ ]	Priority seating	[ ]
Other special classes	[x]	Tape recorders	[x]
Priority registrations	[ ]	Videotaped classes	[ ]
Substitution of courses	[ ]	Text on tape	[ ]
Exams		**Services**	
Extended time	[x]	Diagnostic tests	[ ]
Oral exams	[ ]	Learning centers	[x]
Take home exams	[ ]	Proofreaders	[ ]
Exams on tape or computer	[ ]	Readers	[ ]
Untimed exams	[x]	Reading Machines/Kurzweil	[ ]
Other accommodations	[ ]	Special bookstore section	[ ]
		Typists	[ ]

Credit toward degree is not given for remedial courses taken.

Counseling Services

- [ ] Academic
- [ ] Psychological
- [ ] Student Support groups
- [ ] Vocational

Tutoring

Individual tutoring is available weekly.

Average size of tutoring groups: 5

	Individual	Group
Time management	[x]	[ ]
Organizational skills	[x]	[ ]
Learning strategies	[x]	[ ]
Study skills	[x]	[x]
Content area	[x]	[ ]
Writing lab	[x]	[x]
Math lab	[ ]	[ ]

LD PROGRAM STAFF

There is an advisor/advocate from the LD program available to students.

Key staff person available to work with LD students: Kathy Weimer, Learning Assistance Center Director/Counselor.

Ashland University

Ashland, OH

Address: 401 College Avenue, Ashland, OH, 44805
Admissions telephone: 800 882-1548
Admissions FAX: 419 289-5999
Director of Admissions: Thomas Mansperger
Admissions e-mail: enrollme@ashland.edu
Web site: http://www.ashland.edu
SAT Code: 1021 ACT Code: 3234

LD program name: ODS/Peer Tutoring
Director, Classroom Support: Susanne Salvo
LD program telephone: 419 289-5904
LD program e-mail: ssalvo@ashland.edu
LD program enrollment: 138, Total campus enrollment: 2,859

GENERAL

Ashland University is a private, coed, four-year institution. 120-acre, suburban campus in Ashland (population: 21,249), 16 miles from Mansfield and 60 miles from Cleveland; branch campuses in Akron, Cleveland, Columbus, Detroit, Elyria, Lorain, Mansfield, Marion, Medina, Milan, Mt. Vernon, Newark, and Stark County. Major airport serves Cleveland; bus serves Mansfield; train serves Elyria (35 miles). School operates transportation to airport at semester breaks. Semester system.

LD ADMISSIONS

Students do not complete a separate application and are not simultaneously accepted to the LD program. A member of the LD program does not sit on the admissions committee. A personal interview is not required. Essay is not required.

SECONDARY SCHOOL REQUIREMENTS

Graduation from secondary school required; GED accepted. The following course distribution required: 3 units of English, 2 units of math, 2 units of science, 3 units of social studies, 1 unit of history.

TESTING

SAT Reasoning considered if submitted. ACT required; SAT Subject recommended.

All enrolled freshmen (fall 2004):

Average SAT I Scores:	Verbal: 518	Math: 516
Average ACT Scores:	Composite: 23	

Child Study Team report is not required. A neuropsychological or comprehensive psycho-educational evaluation is required for admission. Must be dated within 24 months of application. Tests required as part of this documentation:

☑ WAIS-IV	☑ Woodcock-Johnson
☑ WISC-IV	☑ Nelson-Denny Reading Test
☑ SATA	☐ Other

UNDERGRADUATE STUDENT BODY

Total undergraduate student enrollment: 1,193 Men, 1,626 Women.

Composition of student body (fall 2004):

	Undergraduate	Freshmen
International	0.5	1.3
Black	4.7	8.1
American Indian	0.2	0.3
Asian-American	0.5	0.5
Hispanic	2.6	1.6
White	91.5	85.8
Unreported	0.0	2.4
	100.0%	100.0%

9% are from out of state. 9% join a fraternity and 13% join a sorority. Average age of full-time undergraduates is 22. 60% of classes have fewer than 20 students, 40% have between 20 and 50 students.

STUDENT HOUSING

92% of freshmen live in college housing. Freshmen are required to live on campus. Housing is guaranteed for all undergraduates. Campus can house 1,500 undergraduates. Single rooms are available for students with medical or special needs. A medical note is required.

EXPENSES

Tuition (2005-06): $19,314 per year.

Room: $3,928. Board: $3,386.

There is no additional cost for LD program/services.

LD SERVICES

LD program size is not limited.

LD services available to:

☑ Freshmen ☑ Sophomores ☑ Juniors ☑ Seniors

Academic Accommodations

Curriculum		In class	
Foreign language waiver	☐	Early syllabus	☑
Lighter course load	☐	Note takers in class	☑
Math waiver	☐	Priority seating	☐
Other special classes	☐	Tape recorders	☑
Priority registrations	☑	Videotaped classes	☐
Substitution of courses	☐	Text on tape	☑
Exams		**Services**	
Extended time	☑	Diagnostic tests	☐
Oral exams	☑	Learning centers	☑
Take home exams	☐	Proofreaders	☐
Exams on tape or computer	☑	Readers	☑
Untimed exams	☑	Reading Machines/Kurzweil	☑
Other accommodations	☐	Special bookstore section	☐
		Typists	☑

Counseling Services

☑ Academic
☑ Psychological
☐ Student Support groups
☑ Vocational

Tutoring

Individual tutoring is available weekly.

Average size of tutoring groups: 2

	Individual	Group
Time management	☑	☐
Organizational skills	☑	☐
Learning strategies	☑	☐
Study skills	☑	☐
Content area	☑	☐
Writing lab	☑	☐
Math lab	☐	☐

UNIQUE LD PROGRAM FEATURES

Our goal is to facilitate students to become self-advocates within the academic environment and beyond. The professionals in the office guide students in the understanding of their disability and how it impacts learning, empowering students to succeed.

LD PROGRAM STAFF

Total number of LD Program staff (including director):

Full Time: 2 Part Time: 2

There is an advisor/advocate from the LD program available to students.

LD Program web site: www.ashland.edu

Baldwin-Wallace College

Berea, OH

Address: 275 Eastland Road, Berea, OH, 44017
Admissions telephone: 877 BWAPPLY
Admissions FAX: 440 826-3830
Director of Undergraduate Admissions: Susan Dileno
Admissions e-mail: admission@bw.edu
Web site: http://www.bw.edu
SAT Code: 1050 ACT Code: 3236

LD program name: Office of Disability Services
Coordinator, Disability Services: Carol Templeman
LD program telephone: 440 826-2188
LD program e-mail: ctemplem@bw.edu
LD program enrollment: 33, Total campus enrollment: 3,771

GENERAL

Baldwin-Wallace College is a private, coed, four-year institution. 100-acre campus in Berea (population: 18,970), 14 miles southwest of Cleveland. Major airport, bus, and train serve Cleveland. Public transportation serves campus. Semester system.

LD ADMISSIONS

A member of the LD program does not sit on the admissions committee. A personal interview is recommended. Essay is required and may be typed.

SECONDARY SCHOOL REQUIREMENTS

Graduation from secondary school required; GED accepted. The following course distribution required: 4 units of English, 3 units of math, 3 units of science, 2 units of foreign language, 2 units of social studies, 1 unit of history.

TESTING

SAT Reasoning or ACT required. SAT Subject recommended.

All enrolled freshmen (fall 2004):

Average SAT I Scores:	Verbal: 545	Math: 545
Average ACT Scores:	Composite: 24	

Child Study Team report is not required. A neuropsychological or comprehensive psycho-educational evaluation is required for admission. Must be dated within 36 months of application. Tests required as part of this documentation:

- [x] WAIS-IV
- [ ] WISC-IV
- [ ] SATA
- [x] Woodcock-Johnson
- [ ] Nelson-Denny Reading Test
- [ ] Other

UNDERGRADUATE STUDENT BODY

Total undergraduate student enrollment: 1,528 Men, 2,465 Women.

Composition of student body (fall 2004):

	Undergraduate	Freshmen
International	0.4	1.3
Black	3.5	4.5
American Indian	0.1	0.2
Asian-American	3.4	1.8
Hispanic	1.3	1.3
White	84.8	84.7
Unreported	6.5	6.2
	100.0%	100.0%

9% are from out of state. 10% join a fraternity and 31% join a sorority. Average age of full-time undergraduates is 20. 52% of classes have fewer than 20 students, 48% have between 20 and 50 students.

STUDENT HOUSING

81% of freshmen live in college housing. Freshmen are required to live on campus. Housing is guaranteed for all undergraduates. Campus can house 1,857 undergraduates. Single rooms are available for students with medical or special needs. A medical note is required.

EXPENSES

Tuition (2005-06): $20,518 per year.
Room: $3,290. Board: $3,448.
There is no additional cost for LD program/services.

LD SERVICES

LD program size is not limited.

LD services available to:

- [x] Freshmen
- [x] Sophomores
- [x] Juniors
- [ ] Seniors

Academic Accommodations

Curriculum		In class	
Foreign language waiver	[ ]	Early syllabus	[ ]
Lighter course load	[x]	Note takers in class	[x]
Math waiver	[ ]	Priority seating	[ ]
Other special classes	[ ]	Tape recorders	[x]
Priority registrations	[ ]	Videotaped classes	[ ]
Substitution of courses	[ ]	Text on tape	[ ]
Exams		**Services**	
Extended time	[x]	Diagnostic tests	[ ]
Oral exams	[ ]	Learning centers	[x]
Take home exams	[ ]	Proofreaders	[ ]
Exams on tape or computer	[ ]	Readers	[x]
Untimed exams	[ ]	Reading Machines/Kurzweil	[ ]
Other accommodations	[ ]	Special bookstore section	[ ]
		Typists	[ ]

Credit toward degree is not given for remedial courses taken.

Counseling Services

- [x] Academic
- [x] Psychological
- [ ] Student Support groups
- [ ] Vocational

Tutoring

Individual tutoring is available weekly.

Average size of tutoring groups: 1

	Individual	Group
Time management	[x]	[x]
Organizational skills	[x]	[x]
Learning strategies	[x]	[x]
Study skills	[x]	[x]
Content area	[x]	[x]
Writing lab	[x]	[ ]
Math lab	[x]	[x]

LD PROGRAM STAFF

Total number of LD Program staff (including director):

Full Time: 4 Part Time: 4

There is an advisor/advocate from the LD program available to students. 88 peer tutors are available to work with LD students.

Key staff person available to work with LD students: Barbara Coniam, Director of Learning Center.

LD Program web site: www.bw.edu/stulife/judicial/policies/disability

Bluffton University

Bluffton, OH

Address: 1 University Drive, Bluffton, OH, 45817
Admissions telephone: 800 488-3257
Admissions FAX: 419 358-3081
Director of Admissions: Eric Fulcomer
Admissions e-mail: admissions@bluffton.edu
Web site: http://www.bluffton.edu
SAT Code: 1067 ACT Code: 3238

Associate Dean: Sally Weaver Sommer
LD program telephone: 419 358-3322
LD program e-mail: sommers@bluffton.edu
Total campus enrollment: 1,103

GENERAL

Bluffton University is a private, coed, four-year institution. 65-acre campus in Bluffton (population: 3,896), 70 miles from Toledo and 80 miles from Dayton. Major airports serve Dayton and Toledo; bus serves Lima (20 miles); train serves Fostoria (35 miles). Semester system.

LD ADMISSIONS

A personal interview is recommended. Essay is not required.

SECONDARY SCHOOL REQUIREMENTS

Graduation from secondary school required; GED accepted.

TESTING

SAT Reasoning or ACT required. SAT Subject recommended.

All enrolled freshmen (fall 2004):

Average SAT I Scores:	Verbal: 544	Math: 532
Average ACT Scores:	Composite: 22	

Child Study Team report is not required. Tests required as part of this documentation:

- ☐ WAIS-IV
- ☐ WISC-IV
- ☐ SATA
- ☐ Woodcock-Johnson
- ☐ Nelson-Denny Reading Test
- ☐ Other

UNDERGRADUATE STUDENT BODY

Total undergraduate student enrollment: 408 Men, 568 Women.

Composition of student body (fall 2004):

	Undergraduate	Freshmen
International	0.4	1.7
Black	4.1	3.5
American Indian	0.4	0.2
Asian-American	0.8	0.6
Hispanic	1.5	1.4
White	88.7	89.8
Unreported	4.1	2.8
	100.0%	100.0%

21% are from out of state. 44% of classes have fewer than 20 students, 56% have between 20 and 50 students.

STUDENT HOUSING

97% of freshmen live in college housing. Freshmen are required to live on campus. Housing is guaranteed for all undergraduates. Campus can house 828 undergraduates.

EXPENSES

Tuition (2005-06): $19,028 per year.
Room: $3,076. Board: $3,606.

There is no additional cost for LD program/services.

LD SERVICES

LD program size is not limited.

LD services available to:

☐ Freshmen ☐ Sophomores ☐ Juniors ☐ Seniors

Academic Accommodations

Curriculum		**In class**	
Foreign language waiver	☐	Early syllabus	☐
Lighter course load	■	Note takers in class	■
Math waiver	☐	Priority seating	☐
Other special classes	☐	Tape recorders	■
Priority registrations	☐	Videotaped classes	■
Substitution of courses	☐	Text on tape	☐
Exams		**Services**	
Extended time	■	Diagnostic tests	☐
Oral exams	■	Learning centers	■
Take home exams	☐	Proofreaders	☐
Exams on tape or computer	☐	Readers	■
Untimed exams	☐	Reading Machines/Kurzweil	☐
Other accommodations	☐	Special bookstore section	☐
		Typists	☐

Credit toward degree is given for remedial courses taken.

Counseling Services

- ☐ Academic
- ☐ Psychological
- ☐ Student Support groups
- ☐ Vocational

Tutoring

	Individual	Group
Time management	☐	☐
Organizational skills	☐	☐
Learning strategies	☐	☐
Study skills	☐	☐
Content area	☐	☐
Writing lab	☐	☐
Math lab	☐	☐

LD PROGRAM STAFF

Total number of LD Program staff (including director):

Full Time: 1 Part Time: 1

Key staff person available to work with LD students: Jacqui Slinger, Director of Academic & Career Development Services.

Bowling Green State University

Bowling Green, OH

Address: 110 McFall Center, Bowling Green, OH, 43403
Admissions telephone: 419 372-2478
Admissions FAX: 419 372-6955
Director of Admissions: Gary Swegan
Admissions e-mail: admissions@bgnet.bgsu.edu
Web site: http://www.bgsu.edu
SAT Code: 1069 ACT Code: 3240

LD program name: Office of Disability Services
Director, Disability Services: Robert Cunningham, Ph.D.
LD program telephone: 419 372-8495
LD program e-mail: rcunnin@bgnet.bgsu.edu
LD program enrollment: 254, Total campus enrollment: 15,909

GENERAL

Bowling Green State University is a public, coed, four-year institution. 1,230-acre campus in Bowling Green (population: 29,636), 25 miles from Toledo; branch campus in Huron. Served by bus; major airport serves Detroit (60 miles); smaller airport and train serve Toledo. School operates transportation on campus. Semester system.

LD ADMISSIONS

Students do not complete a separate application and are not simultaneously accepted to the LD program. A member of the LD program does not sit on the admissions committee. High school waivers are accepted for math and foreign language. A personal interview is recommended. Essay is not required.

For fall 2004, 30 completed self-identified LD applications were received. 21 applications were offered admission, and 19 enrolled.

SECONDARY SCHOOL REQUIREMENTS

Graduation from secondary school required; GED accepted. The following course distribution required: 4 units of English, 3 units of math, 3 units of science, 2 units of foreign language, 3 units of social studies.

TESTING

ACT required; SAT Reasoning may be substituted. SAT Subject recommended.

All enrolled freshmen (fall 2004):

Average SAT I Scores:	Verbal: 517	Math: 520
Average ACT Scores:	Composite: 22	

Child Study Team report is not required. A neuropsychological or comprehensive psycho-educational evaluation is required for admission. Must be dated within 36 months of application. Tests required as part of this documentation:

- ■ WAIS-IV
- ☐ WISC-IV
- ☐ SATA
- ■ Woodcock-Johnson
- ■ Nelson-Denny Reading Test
- ■ Other

UNDERGRADUATE STUDENT BODY

Total undergraduate student enrollment: 6,933 Men, 8,935 Women.

Composition of student body (fall 2004):

	Undergraduate	Freshmen
International	0.7	0.9
Black	7.9	6.2
American Indian	0.7	0.5
Asian-American	0.9	0.8
Hispanic	3.4	2.8
White	83.4	85.9
Unreported	3.0	2.9
	100.0%	100.0%

6% are from out of state. 8% join a fraternity and 11% join a sorority. Average age of full-time undergraduates is 21. 40% of classes have fewer than 20 students, 54% have between 20 and 50 students, 6% have more than 50 students.

STUDENT HOUSING

92% of freshmen live in college housing. Freshmen are required to live on campus. Housing is guaranteed for all undergraduates. All unmarried freshmen and sophomores must live on campus unless living with parents or guardians within 50 miles. Campus can house 7,286 undergraduates. Single rooms are available for students with medical or special needs. A medical note is required.

EXPENSES

Tuition (2005-06): $7,442 per year (in-state), $14,750 (out-of-state).
Room: $3,978. Board: $2,496.
There is no additional cost for LD program/services.

LD SERVICES

LD program size is not limited.

LD services available to:

■ Freshmen ■ Sophomores ■ Juniors ■ Seniors

Academic Accommodations

Curriculum		**In class**	
Foreign language waiver	☐	Early syllabus	☐
Lighter course load	☐	Note takers in class	■
Math waiver	☐	Priority seating	☐
Other special classes	☐	Tape recorders	■
Priority registrations	■	Videotaped classes	☐
Substitution of courses	■	Text on tape	■
Exams		**Services**	
Extended time	■	Diagnostic tests	☐
Oral exams	■	Learning centers	☐
Take home exams	☐	Proofreaders	☐
Exams on tape or computer	■	Readers	■
Untimed exams	☐	Reading Machines/Kurzweil	■
Other accommodations	■	Special bookstore section	☐
		Typists	☐

Credit toward degree is not given for remedial courses taken.

Counseling Services

- ☐ Academic
- ☐ Psychological
- ■ Student Support groups — Meets 9 times per academic year
- ☐ Vocational

Tutoring

Individual tutoring is not available.

	Individual	Group
Time management	☐	☐
Organizational skills	☐	☐
Learning strategies	☐	☐
Study skills	■	■
Content area	■	■
Writing lab	■	■
Math lab	■	■

UNIQUE LD PROGRAM FEATURES

All services are provided on the basis of documented need to ensure equal access.

LD PROGRAM STAFF

Total number of LD Program staff (including director):

Full Time: 3 Part Time: 3

There is an advisor/advocate from the LD program available to students. 1 graduate students is available to work with LD students.

Key staff person available to work with LD students: Robert Cunningham, Ph.D. Director, Disability Services.

LD Program web site: http://www.bgsu.edu/offices/sa/disability/

Capital University

Columbus, OH

Address: 1 College and Main, Columbus, OH, 43209-2392
Admissions telephone: 866 544-6175
Admissions FAX: 614 236-6926
Director of Admissions: Kimberly V. Ebbrecht
Admissions e-mail: admissions@capital.edu
Web site: http://www.capital.edu
SAT Code: 1099 ACT Code: 3242

LD program name: Disability Services
Disability Consultant: Lydia Block
LD program telephone: 614 236-6284
LD program e-mail: lblock@capital.edu
Total campus enrollment: 2,796

GENERAL

Capital University is a private, coed, four-year institution. 48-acre, suburban campus in Columbus (population: 711,470), four miles from city center; branch campuses in Cleveland and Dayton. Served by air and bus. School operates transportation to law school campus. Public transportation serves campus. Semester system.

LD ADMISSIONS

A personal interview is recommended. Essay is not required.

SECONDARY SCHOOL REQUIREMENTS

Graduation from secondary school required; GED accepted. The following course distribution required: 4 units of English, 3 units of math, 3 units of science, 2 units of foreign language, 3 units of social studies, 1 unit of academic electives.

TESTING

SAT Reasoning or ACT required. SAT Subject recommended.

All enrolled freshmen (fall 2004):

Average SAT I Scores:	Verbal: 541	Math: 540
Average ACT Scores:	Composite: 23	

Child Study Team report is not required. Tests required as part of this documentation:

- [ ] WAIS-IV
- [ ] WISC-IV
- [ ] SATA
- [ ] Woodcock-Johnson
- [ ] Nelson-Denny Reading Test
- [ ] Other

UNDERGRADUATE STUDENT BODY

Total undergraduate student enrollment: 991 Men, 1,717 Women.

Composition of student body (fall 2004):

	Undergraduate	Freshmen
International	1.5	0.7
Black	8.4	12.7
American Indian	0.4	0.3
Asian-American	1.3	1.7
Hispanic	1.5	1.4
White	84.2	77.2
Unreported	2.7	6.0
	100.0%	100.0%

8% are from out of state. 7% join a fraternity and 8% join a sorority. Average age of full-time undergraduates is 23. 81% of classes have fewer than 20 students, 18% have between 20 and 50 students, 1% have more than 50 students.

STUDENT HOUSING

75% of freshmen live in college housing. Housing is not guaranteed for all undergraduates. Only traditional students are housed. Campus can house 1,166 undergraduates. Single rooms are available for students with medical or special needs. A medical note is required.

EXPENSES

Tuition (2005-06): $24,100 per year.

Room: $3,116. Board: $3,228.
There is no additional cost for LD program/services.

LD SERVICES

LD program size is not limited.

LD services available to:

- [x] Freshmen
- [x] Sophomores
- [x] Juniors
- [x] Seniors

Academic Accommodations

Curriculum

- [ ] Foreign language waiver
- [ ] Lighter course load
- [ ] Math waiver
- [ ] Other special classes
- [x] Priority registrations
- [x] Substitution of courses

Exams

- [x] Extended time
- [x] Oral exams
- [ ] Take home exams
- [x] Exams on tape or computer
- [ ] Untimed exams
- [x] Other accommodations

In class

- [x] Early syllabus
- [x] Note takers in class
- [ ] Priority seating
- [x] Tape recorders
- [ ] Videotaped classes
- [x] Text on tape

Services

- [ ] Diagnostic tests
- [x] Learning centers
- [ ] Proofreaders
- [x] Readers
- [ ] Reading Machines/Kurzweil
- [ ] Special bookstore section
- [ ] Typists

Credit toward degree is given for remedial courses taken.

Counseling Services

- [x] Academic
- [ ] Psychological
- [x] Student Support groups
- [ ] Vocational

Tutoring

Individual tutoring is available daily.

Average size of tutoring groups: 2

	Individual	Group
Time management	[x]	[ ]
Organizational skills	[x]	[ ]
Learning strategies	[x]	[ ]
Study skills	[x]	[ ]
Content area	[x]	[x]
Writing lab	[x]	[x]
Math lab	[x]	[x]

LD PROGRAM STAFF

There is an advisor/advocate from the LD program available to students. 43 peer tutors are available to work with LD students.

Key staff person available to work with LD students: Lydia S. Block, Disability Consultant.

Case Western Reserve University

Cleveland, OH

Address: 10900 Euclid Avenue, Cleveland, OH, 44106
Admissions telephone: 216 368-4450
Admissions FAX: 216 368-5111
Dean of Undergraduate Admission: Elizabeth Woyczynski
Admissions e-mail: admission@case.edu
Web site: http://www.case.edu
SAT Code: 1105 ACT Code: 3244

LD program name: Disability Services
Coordinator of Disability Services: Susan Sampson
LD program telephone: 216 368-5230
LD program e-mail: susan.sampson@case.edu
LD program enrollment: 40, Total campus enrollment: 3,516

GENERAL

Case Western Reserve University is a private, coed, four-year institution. 150-acre campus in Cleveland (population: 478,403). Served by air, bus, and train. Public transportation serves campus. Semester system.

LD ADMISSIONS

A personal interview is recommended. Essay is required and may be typed.

SECONDARY SCHOOL REQUIREMENTS

Graduation from secondary school required; GED accepted. The following course distribution required: 4 units of English, 3 units of math, 3 units of science, 2 units of foreign language, 3 units of social studies.

TESTING

SAT Reasoning or ACT required. SAT Subject required.

All enrolled freshmen (fall 2004):

Average SAT I Scores:	Verbal: 638	Math: 671
Average ACT Scores:	Composite: 28	

Child Study Team report is not required. A neuropsychological or comprehensive psycho-educational evaluation is required for admission. Tests required as part of this documentation:

- [x] WAIS-IV
- [ ] WISC-IV
- [ ] SATA
- [x] Woodcock-Johnson
- [x] Nelson-Denny Reading Test
- [x] Other

UNDERGRADUATE STUDENT BODY

Total undergraduate student enrollment: 2,049 Men, 1,332 Women.

Composition of student body (fall 2004):

	Undergraduate	Freshmen
International	3.2	4.4
Black	5.9	5.1
American Indian	0.3	0.4
Asian-American	14.4	15.0
Hispanic	2.3	1.9
White	65.4	68.7
Unreported	8.5	4.5
	100.0%	100.0%

38% are from out of state. 31% join a fraternity and 23% join a sorority. Average age of full-time undergraduates is 20. 56% of classes have fewer than 20 students, 33% have between 20 and 50 students, 11% have more than 50 students.

STUDENT HOUSING

94% of freshmen live in college housing. Freshmen are required to live on campus. Housing is guaranteed for all undergraduates. Single rooms are available for students with medical or special needs. A medical note is required.

EXPENSES

Tuition (2005-06): $28,400 per year.
Room: $5,080. Board: $3,556
There is no additional cost for LD program/services.

LD SERVICES

LD program size is not limited.

LD services available to:

- [x] Freshmen
- [x] Sophomores
- [x] Juniors
- [x] Seniors

Academic Accommodations

Curriculum		In class	
Foreign language waiver	[ ]	Early syllabus	[ ]
Lighter course load	[ ]	Note takers in class	[x]
Math waiver	[ ]	Priority seating	[ ]
Other special classes	[ ]	Tape recorders	[x]
Priority registrations	[ ]	Videotaped classes	[ ]
Substitution of courses	[ ]	Text on tape	[x]
Exams		**Services**	
Extended time	[x]	Diagnostic tests	[x]
Oral exams	[x]	Learning centers	[ ]
Take home exams	[ ]	Proofreaders	[ ]
Exams on tape or computer	[x]	Readers	[x]
Untimed exams	[ ]	Reading Machines/Kurzweil	[x]
Other accommodations	[ ]	Special bookstore section	[ ]
		Typists	[x]

Credit toward degree is not given for remedial courses taken.

Counseling Services

[x]	Academic	Meets 36 times per academic year
[x]	Psychological	Meets 36 times per academic year
[ ]	Student Support groups	
[ ]	Vocational	

Tutoring

Individual tutoring is available weekly.

Average size of tutoring groups: 1

	Individual	Group
Time management	[x]	[ ]
Organizational skills	[x]	[ ]
Learning strategies	[ ]	[ ]
Study skills	[ ]	[ ]
Content area	[x]	[x]
Writing lab	[x]	[ ]
Math lab	[x]	[x]

LD PROGRAM STAFF

Total number of LD Program staff (including director):

Full Time: 1 Part Time: 1

There is an advisor/advocate from the LD program available to students. 1 graduate student and 40 peer tutors are available to work with LD students.

Key staff person available to work with LD students: Susan Sampson, Coordinator of Disability Services.

LD Program web site: http://ess.case.edu/disability

Cedarville University

Cedarville, OH

Address: 251 N. Main Street, Cedarville, OH, 45314
Admissions telephone: 800 233-2784
Admissions FAX: 937 766-7575
Director of Admissions: Roscoe Smith
Admissions e-mail: admissions@cedarville.edu
Web site: http://www.cedarville.edu
SAT Code: 1151 ACT Code: 3245

Director, AAC: Kim Ahlgrim
LD program telephone: 937 766-3845
LD program e-mail: meyermcedarville.edu
LD program enrollment: 17, Total campus enrollment: 3,070

GENERAL

Cedarville University is a private, coed, four-year institution. 400-acre campus in Cedarville (population: 3,828), 20 miles from Dayton and 45 miles from Columbus. Airports serve Dayton and Columbus; bus serves Springfield (15 miles); train serves Hamilton (45 miles). School operates transportation to airport and bus terminal. Semester system.

LD ADMISSIONS

A personal interview is recommended. Essay is not required. Admissions requirements that may be waived for LD students include: any single academic standard may be waived. The Academic Enrichment program and Right Start program are available admission routes for such studies, whether or not a learning disability is present.

SECONDARY SCHOOL REQUIREMENTS

Graduation from secondary school required; GED accepted. The following course distribution required: 4 units of English, 3 units of math, 2 units of foreign language, 3 units of social studies.

TESTING

SAT Subject recommended.

All enrolled freshmen (fall 2004):

Average SAT I Scores: Verbal: 595 Math: 584
Average ACT Scores: Composite: 25

Child Study Team report is not required. Tests required as part of this documentation:

- ☐ WAIS-IV
- ☐ WISC-IV
- ☐ SATA
- ☐ Woodcock-Johnson
- ☐ Nelson-Denny Reading Test
- ☐ Other

UNDERGRADUATE STUDENT BODY

Total undergraduate student enrollment: 1,298 Men, 1,549 Women.

Composition of student body (fall 2004):

	Undergraduate	Freshmen
International	0.4	0.6
Black	1.3	1.6
American Indian	0.3	0.1
Asian-American	1.3	1.2
Hispanic	1.7	1.5
White	95.0	94.8
Unreported	0.0	0.2
	100.0%	100.0%

66% are from out of state. Average age of full-time undergraduates is 20. 58% of classes have fewer than 20 students, 34% have between 20 and 50 students, 8% have more than 50 students.

STUDENT HOUSING

96% of freshmen live in college housing. Freshmen are required to live on campus. Housing is guaranteed for all undergraduates. Campus can house 2,524 undergraduates.

EXPENSES

Tuition (2005-06): $16,050 per year.
Room: $2,684. Board: $2,326.
There is no additional cost for LD program/services.

LD SERVICES

LD program size is not limited.

LD services available to:

☐ Freshmen ☐ Sophomores ☐ Juniors ☐ Seniors

Academic Accommodations

Curriculum		**In class**	
Foreign language waiver	☐	Early syllabus	☐
Lighter course load	■	Note takers in class	■
Math waiver	☐	Priority seating	■
Other special classes	☐	Tape recorders	■
Priority registrations	■	Videotaped classes	☐
Substitution of courses	☐	Text on tape	☐
Exams		**Services**	
Extended time	■	Diagnostic tests	☐
Oral exams	■	Learning centers	☐
Take home exams	☐	Proofreaders	☐
Exams on tape or computer	☐	Readers	■
Untimed exams	■	Reading Machines/Kurzweil	☐
Other accommodations	☐	Special bookstore section	☐
		Typists	☐

Credit toward degree is not given for remedial courses taken.

Counseling Services

- ☐ Academic
- ☐ Psychological
- ☐ Student Support groups
- ☐ Vocational

Tutoring

	Individual	Group
Time management	☐	☐
Organizational skills	☐	☐
Learning strategies	☐	☐
Study skills	☐	☐
Content area	☐	☐
Writing lab	☐	☐
Math lab	☐	☐

LD PROGRAM STAFF

Total number of LD Program staff (including director):

Full Time: 2 Part Time: 2

Key staff person available to work with LD students: Marilyn Meyer, Coordinator of Disability Services.

Cincinnati Christian University

Cincinnati, OH

Address: 2700 Glenway Avenue, Cincinnati, OH, 45204-1799
Admissions telephone: 800 949-4CBC, extension 8141
Director of Undergraduate Admissions: Mrs. Erin Oppy
Admissions e-mail: ccuadmissions@ccuniversity.edu
Web site: http://www.ccuniversity.edu/
SAT Code: 1091 ACT Code: 3248

LD program contact: Cindi Cooper
LD program telephone: 513 244-8420
LD program e-mail: cindi.cooper@CCUniversity.edu
LD program enrollment: 28, Total campus enrollment: 646

GENERAL

Cincinnati Bible College & Seminary is a private, coed, four-year institution. 40-acre campus in Cincinnati (population: 331,285), three miles from downtown. Served by air, bus, and train. Public transportation serves campus. Semester system.

LD ADMISSIONS

Students do not complete a separate application and are simultaneously accepted to the LD program. A personal interview is required. Essay is required and may be typed.

SECONDARY SCHOOL REQUIREMENTS

Graduation from secondary school required; GED accepted.

TESTING

SAT Reasoning considered if submitted. ACT considered if submitted. SAT Subject recommended.

All enrolled freshmen (fall 2004):

Average SAT I Scores:	Verbal: 530	Math: 521
Average ACT Scores:	Composite: 21	

Child Study Team report is required if student is classified. Tests required as part of this documentation:

- [ ] WAIS-IV
- [ ] WISC-IV
- [ ] SATA
- [ ] Woodcock-Johnson
- [ ] Nelson-Denny Reading Test
- [ ] Other

UNDERGRADUATE STUDENT BODY

Total undergraduate student enrollment: 360 Men, 302 Women.

Composition of student body (fall 2004):

	Undergraduate	Freshmen
International	1.2	1.7
Black	4.3	3.9
American Indian	0.0	0.0
Asian-American	0.0	0.0
Hispanic	0.6	0.7
White	92.7	92.0
Unreported	1.2	1.7
	100.0%	100.0%

46% are from out of state. Average age of full-time undergraduates is 22. 53% of classes have fewer than 20 students, 38% have between 20 and 50 students, 9% have more than 50 students.

STUDENT HOUSING

95% of freshmen live in college housing. Freshmen are required to live on campus. Housing is guaranteed for all undergraduates. Campus can house 356 undergraduates. Single rooms are available for students with medical or special needs. A medical note is required.

EXPENSES

Tuition (2005-06): $9,120 per year.
Room & Board: $5,390.

There is no additional cost for LD program/services.

LD SERVICES

LD program size is not limited.

LD services available to:

- [x] Freshmen
- [x] Sophomores
- [x] Juniors
- [x] Seniors

Academic Accommodations

Curriculum		In class	
Foreign language waiver	[ ]	Early syllabus	[x]
Lighter course load	[ ]	Note takers in class	[x]
Math waiver	[ ]	Priority seating	[x]
Other special classes	[x]	Tape recorders	[x]
Priority registrations	[ ]	Videotaped classes	[ ]
Substitution of courses	[x]	Text on tape	[x]
Exams		**Services**	
Extended time	[x]	Diagnostic tests	[ ]
Oral exams	[x]	Learning centers	[x]
Take home exams	[ ]	Proofreaders	[x]
Exams on tape or computer	[ ]	Readers	[x]
Untimed exams	[x]	Reading Machines/Kurzweil	[ ]
Other accommodations	[x]	Special bookstore section	[ ]
		Typists	[x]

Credit toward degree is not given for remedial courses taken.

Counseling Services

- [ ] Academic
- [ ] Psychological
- [ ] Student Support groups
- [ ] Vocational

Tutoring

Individual tutoring is available daily.

Average size of tutoring groups: 4

	Individual	Group
Time management	[x]	[ ]
Organizational skills	[x]	[ ]
Learning strategies	[x]	[ ]
Study skills	[x]	[ ]
Content area	[x]	[x]
Writing lab	[x]	[ ]
Math lab	[ ]	[ ]

LD PROGRAM STAFF

Total number of LD Program staff (including director):

Full Time: 1 Part Time: 1

There is an advisor/advocate from the LD program available to students. 2 peer tutors are available to work with LD students.

Key staff person available to work with LD students: Cindi Cooper, Academic Support Director.

Central State University

Wilberforce, OH

Address: PO Box 1004, Wilberforce, OH, 45384
Admissions telephone: 800 388-2781
Admissions FAX: 937 376-6648
Director of Admissions: Mr. Cleveland James
Admissions e-mail: admissions@csu.ces.edu
Web site: http://www.centralstate.edu
SAT Code: 1107 ACT Code: 3246

LD program name: Counseling Services
Student Support Services: Frank Porter
LD program telephone: 937 376-6649
LD program e-mail: fporter@centralstate.edu
LD program enrollment: 46, Total campus enrollment: 1,812

GENERAL

Central State University is a public, coed, four-year institution. 60-acre campus in Wilberforce (population: 1,579), 18 miles east of Dayton. Airport and bus serve Dayton; train serves Columbus (65 miles). Quarter system.

LD ADMISSIONS

A personal interview is required. Essay is not required. Admissions requirements that may be waived for LD students include: Proficiency Test.

For fall 2004, 21 completed self-identified LD applications were received.

SECONDARY SCHOOL REQUIREMENTS

Graduation from secondary school required; GED accepted. The following course distribution required: 4 units of English, 3 units of math, 3 units of science, 2 units of foreign language, 3 units of social studies.

TESTING

ACT required; SAT Reasoning may be substituted. SAT Subject recommended.

All enrolled freshmen (fall 2004):

Average SAT I Scores:	Verbal: 392	Math: 384
Average ACT Scores:	Composite: 15	

Child Study Team report is not required. Tests required as part of this documentation:

- ☑ WAIS-IV
- ☑ WISC-IV
- ☑ SATA
- ☑ Woodcock-Johnson
- ☑ Nelson-Denny Reading Test
- ☑ Other

UNDERGRADUATE STUDENT BODY

Total undergraduate student enrollment: 611 Men, 709 Women.

Composition of student body (fall 2004):

	Undergraduate	Freshmen
International	0.0	3.4
Black	83.4	82.9
American Indian	0.7	0.0
Asian-American	0.0	0.0
Hispanic	1.2	1.4
White	0.3	0.9
Unreported	14.4	11.4
	100.0%	100.0%

23% are from out of state. 30% join a fraternity and 25% join a sorority. Average age of full-time undergraduates is 21. 59% of classes have fewer than 20 students, 40% have between 20 and 50 students, 1% have more than 50 students.

STUDENT HOUSING

30% of freshmen live in college housing. Freshmen are required to live on campus. Housing is guaranteed for all undergraduates. Campus can house 1,137 undergraduates.

EXPENSES

Tuition (2005-06): $4,994 per year (in-state), $10,814 (out-of-state).

Room: $3,752. Board: $3,230.

There is no additional cost for LD program/services.

LD SERVICES

LD program size is not limited.

LD services available to:

☑ Freshmen ☑ Sophomores ☑ Juniors ☑ Seniors

Academic Accommodations

Curriculum		In class	
Foreign language waiver	☐	Early syllabus	☑
Lighter course load	☑	Note takers in class	☑
Math waiver	☐	Priority seating	☑
Other special classes	☐	Tape recorders	☑
Priority registrations	☐	Videotaped classes	☐
Substitution of courses	☐	Text on tape	☐
Exams		**Services**	
Extended time	☑	Diagnostic tests	☑
Oral exams	☑	Learning centers	☑
Take home exams	☐	Proofreaders	☑
Exams on tape or computer	☐	Readers	☑
Untimed exams	☑	Reading Machines/Kurzweil	☐
Other accommodations	☑	Special bookstore section	☐
		Typists	☐

Credit toward degree is not given for remedial courses taken.

Counseling Services

- ☑ Academic — Meets 10 times per academic year
- ☐ Psychological
- ☐ Student Support groups
- ☐ Vocational

Tutoring

Individual tutoring is available weekly.

Average size of tutoring groups: 3

	Individual	Group
Time management	☑	☑
Organizational skills	☑	☑
Learning strategies	☑	☑
Study skills	☑	☑
Content area	☑	☑
Writing lab	☑	☑
Math lab	☐	☐

UNIQUE LD PROGRAM FEATURES

Students are required to self-disclose information about their disability upon entering college. Many times it is the parent who contacts the Office of Disability Services to give the student's name. This initiates the ODS staff searching for the students to get them registered for services. Information regarding Disability Services is provided to all faculty and this information is included on all class syllabi. Often, students are referred by faculty who observe the student having great difficulty keeping up in the class. The Office of Disability Services makes regular referrals to the Bureau of Vocation and Rehabilitation Services. Staff attend annual training conferences provided by AHEAD (Association in Higher Education and Disability) and SOCHE (Southwestern Ohio Council For Higher Education)

LD PROGRAM STAFF

Total number of LD Program staff (including director):

Full Time: 5 Part Time: 5

There is an advisor/advocate from the LD program available to students. The advisor/advocate meets with faculty 1 time per month and students 4 times per month. 6 peer tutors are available to work with LD students.

Key staff person available to work with LD students: Mr. Frank Porter and Ms. Erma Yow, Office of Disability Services.

Cleveland Institute of Art

Cleveland, OH

Address: 11141 E. Boulevard, Cleveland, OH, 44106
Admissions telephone: 800 223-4700
Admissions FAX: 216 754-3634
Director of Admissions: Catherine Redhead
Admissions e-mail: admiss@gate.cia.edu
Web site: http://www.cia.edu
SAT Code: 1152 ACT Code: 3243

Director, Academic and International Services: Todd Emery
LD program telephone: 216 421-7463
LD program e-mail: temery@gate.cia.edu
Total campus enrollment: 602

GENERAL

Cleveland Institute of Art is a private, coed, four-year institution. Urban campus of three buildings in Cleveland (population: 478,403). Served by air, bus, and train. Public transportation serves campus. Semester system.

SECONDARY SCHOOL REQUIREMENTS

Graduation from secondary school required; GED accepted.

TESTING

SAT Reasoning or ACT required. SAT Subject recommended.

All enrolled freshmen (fall 2004):

Average SAT I Scores:	Verbal: 574	Math: 532
Average ACT Scores:	Composite: 22	

Child Study Team report is not required. Tests required as part of this documentation:

- [ ] WAIS-IV
- [ ] WISC-IV
- [ ] SATA
- [ ] Woodcock-Johnson
- [ ] Nelson-Denny Reading Test
- [ ] Other

UNDERGRADUATE STUDENT BODY

Total undergraduate student enrollment: 602.

Composition of student body (fall 2004):

	Undergraduate	Freshmen
International	1.0	1.7
Black	9.4	4.7
American Indian	0.0	0.2
Asian-American	3.1	2.4
Hispanic	1.0	2.4
White	85.5	87.9
Unreported	0.0	0.7
	100.0%	100.0%

30% are from out of state. Average age of full-time undergraduates is 22. 84% of classes have fewer than 20 students, 16% have between 20 and 50 students.

STUDENT HOUSING

70% of freshmen live in college housing. Freshmen are required to live on campus. Housing is not guaranteed for all undergraduates. More students than beds. Campus can house 128 undergraduates.

EXPENSES

Tuition (2005-06): $25,870 per year.

Room: $5,120. Board: $3,606.

There is no additional cost for LD program/services.

LD SERVICES

LD program size is not limited.

LD services available to:

- [ ] Freshmen
- [ ] Sophomores
- [ ] Juniors
- [ ] Seniors

Academic Accommodations

Curriculum		In class	
Foreign language waiver	[ ]	Early syllabus	[ ]
Lighter course load	[x]	Note takers in class	[x]
Math waiver	[ ]	Priority seating	[ ]
Other special classes	[ ]	Tape recorders	[ ]
Priority registrations	[ ]	Videotaped classes	[ ]
Substitution of courses	[ ]	Text on tape	[ ]
Exams		**Services**	
Extended time	[x]	Diagnostic tests	[ ]
Oral exams	[x]	Learning centers	[ ]
Take home exams	[ ]	Proofreaders	[ ]
Exams on tape or computer	[ ]	Readers	[ ]
Untimed exams	[x]	Reading Machines/Kurzweil	[ ]
Other accommodations	[ ]	Special bookstore section	[ ]
		Typists	[ ]

Credit toward degree is given for remedial courses taken.

Counseling Services

- [ ] Academic
- [ ] Psychological
- [ ] Student Support groups
- [ ] Vocational

Tutoring

	Individual	Group
Time management	[ ]	[ ]
Organizational skills	[ ]	[ ]
Learning strategies	[ ]	[ ]
Study skills	[ ]	[ ]
Content area	[ ]	[ ]
Writing lab	[ ]	[ ]
Math lab	[ ]	[ ]

LD PROGRAM STAFF

Key staff person available to work with LD students: Todd Emery, Director, Academic and International Services.

Cleveland Institute of Music

Cleveland, OH

Address: 11021 East Boulevard, Cleveland, OH, 44106
Admissions telephone: 216 795-3107
Admissions FAX: 216 791-1530
Director of Admission: William Fay
Admissions e-mail: cimadmission@cwru.edu
Web site: http://www.cim.edu/
SAT Code: 1124 ACT Code: 3250

Total campus enrollment: 228

GENERAL

Cleveland Institute of Music is a private, coed, four-year institution. 500-acre campus in the University Circle district of Cleveland (population: 478,403), five miles from downtown. Served by air, bus, and train. School operates transportation around campus. Public transportation serves campus. Semester system.

SECONDARY SCHOOL REQUIREMENTS

Graduation from secondary school required; GED accepted.

TESTING

All enrolled freshmen (fall 2004):

Average SAT I Scores: Verbal: n/a Math: n/a
Average ACT Scores: Composite: n/a

Child Study Team report is not required. Tests required as part of this documentation:

- [ ] WAIS-IV
- [ ] WISC-IV
- [ ] SATA
- [ ] Woodcock-Johnson
- [ ] Nelson-Denny Reading Test
- [ ] Other

UNDERGRADUATE STUDENT BODY

Total undergraduate student enrollment: 104 Men, 119 Women.

Composition of student body (fall 2004):

	Undergraduate	Freshmen
International	13.6	11.0
Black	2.3	0.9
American Indian	2.3	0.4
Asian-American	9.1	7.9
Hispanic	2.3	3.1
White	70.4	76.7
Unreported	0.0	0.0
	100.0%	100.0%

83% are from out of state.

STUDENT HOUSING

Freshmen are required to live on campus. Housing is not guaranteed for all undergraduates. Campus housing limited to freshmen and sophomore students. Campus can house 100 undergraduates. Single rooms are available for students with medical or special needs. A medical note is required.

EXPENSES

Tuition (2005-06): $25,870 per year.
Room: $5,120. Board: $3,606.
There is no additional cost for LD program/services.

LD SERVICES

LD program size is not limited.

LD services available to:

- [x] Freshmen
- [x] Sophomores
- [x] Juniors
- [x] Seniors

Academic Accommodations

Curriculum

- [ ] Foreign language waiver
- [ ] Lighter course load
- [ ] Math waiver
- [ ] Other special classes
- [ ] Priority registrations
- [ ] Substitution of courses

Exams

- [x] Extended time
- [ ] Oral exams
- [ ] Take home exams
- [ ] Exams on tape or computer
- [x] Untimed exams
- [x] Other accommodations

In class

- [ ] Early syllabus
- [x] Note takers in class
- [ ] Priority seating
- [x] Tape recorders
- [ ] Videotaped classes
- [ ] Text on tape

Services

- [x] Diagnostic tests
- [x] Learning centers
- [ ] Proofreaders
- [x] Readers
- [ ] Reading Machines/Kurzweil
- [ ] Special bookstore section
- [ ] Typists

Credit toward degree is not given for remedial courses taken.

Counseling Services

- [ ] Academic
- [ ] Psychological
- [ ] Student Support groups
- [ ] Vocational

Tutoring

Individual tutoring is available weekly.

Average size of tutoring groups: 1

	Individual	Group
Time management	[x]	[ ]
Organizational skills	[x]	[ ]
Learning strategies	[x]	[ ]
Study skills	[ ]	[x]
Content area	[ ]	[ ]
Writing lab	[ ]	[x]
Math lab	[ ]	[ ]

LD PROGRAM STAFF

Total number of LD Program staff (including director):

Full Time: 2 Part Time: 2

Cleveland State University

Cleveland, OH

Address: 1983 E. 24th Street, Cleveland, OH, 44115
Admissions telephone: 888 CSU-OHIO
Vice Provost for Enrollment Management: Jill Jeppe-Oakley
Admissions e-mail: admissions@csuohio.edu
Web site: http://www.csuohio.edu
SAT Code: 1221 ACT Code: 3270

LD program name: Disabilities Services
Coordinator: Mr. Gerald Gillinov
LD program telephone: 216 687-2015
LD program e-mail: g.gillinov@csuohio.edu
LD program enrollment: 61, Total campus enrollment: 9,842

GENERAL

Cleveland State University is a public, coed, four-year institution. 82-acre campus in Cleveland (population: 478,403). Served by air, bus, and train. Public transportation serves campus. Semester system.

LD ADMISSIONS

Students do not complete a separate application and are simultaneously accepted to the LD program. A member of the LD program does not sit on the admissions committee. A personal interview is recommended. Essay is not required.

For fall 2004, 38 completed self-identified LD applications were received. 33 applications were offered admission, and 33 enrolled.

SECONDARY SCHOOL REQUIREMENTS

Graduation from secondary school required; GED accepted.

TESTING

SAT Reasoning or ACT required.

All enrolled freshmen (fall 2004):

Average SAT I Scores:	Verbal: 479	Math: 484
Average ACT Scores:	Composite: 19	

Child Study Team report is required if student is classified. A neuropsychological or comprehensive psycho-educational evaluation is required for admission. Must be dated within 36 months of application. Tests required as part of this documentation:

■ WAIS-IV ■ Woodcock-Johnson
■ WISC-IV ■ Nelson-Denny Reading Test
■ SATA □ Other

UNDERGRADUATE STUDENT BODY

Total undergraduate student enrollment: 6,688 Men, 8,718 Women.

Composition of student body (fall 2004):

	Undergraduate	Freshmen
International	1.7	2.0
Black	25.6	20.7
American Indian	0.1	0.2
Asian-American	2.7	2.6
Hispanic	3.5	2.8
White	56.0	63.0
Unreported	10.4	8.7
	100.0%	100.0%

3% are from out of state. 7% join a fraternity and 7% join a sorority. Average age of full-time undergraduates is 24. 41% of classes have fewer than 20 students, 49% have between 20 and 50 students, 10% have more than 50 students.

STUDENT HOUSING

19% of freshmen live in college housing. Freshmen are not required to live on campus. Housing is guaranteed for all undergraduates. Campus can house 550 undergraduates. Single rooms are available for students with medical or special needs. A medical note is required.

EXPENSES

Tuition 2004-05: $6,420 per year (in-state), $12,636 (out-of-state).

Room & Board: $6,392.

There is no additional cost for LD program/services.

LD SERVICES

LD program size is not limited.

LD services available to:

■ Freshmen ■ Sophomores ■ Juniors ■ Seniors

Academic Accommodations

Curriculum		In class	
Foreign language waiver	□	Early syllabus	■
Lighter course load	■	Note takers in class	■
Math waiver	□	Priority seating	■
Other special classes	□	Tape recorders	■
Priority registrations	■	Videotaped classes	□
Substitution of courses	■	Text on tape	■
Exams		**Services**	
Extended time	■	Diagnostic tests	□
Oral exams	■	Learning centers	□
Take home exams	□	Proofreaders	■
Exams on tape or computer	■	Readers	■
Untimed exams	□	Reading Machines/Kurzweil	■
Other accommodations	□	Special bookstore section	□
		Typists	■

Credit toward degree is not given for remedial courses taken.

Counseling Services

■ Academic — Meets 10 times per academic year
□ Psychological
□ Student Support groups
■ Vocational

Tutoring

Individual tutoring is available daily.

	Individual	Group
Time management	□	■
Organizational skills	□	■
Learning strategies	□	■
Study skills	□	■
Content area	■	□
Writing lab	■	□
Math lab	■	□

LD PROGRAM STAFF

Total number of LD Program staff (including director):

Full Time: 2 Part Time: 2

There is an advisor/advocate from the LD program available to students. 1 graduate students and 10 peer tutors are available to work with LD students.

Key staff person available to work with LD students: Mr. Gerald Gillinov, Coordinator, Services for Persons w/ Disabilities.

The College of Wooster

Wooster, OH

Address: 1189 Beall Avenue, Wooster, OH, 44691
Admissions telephone: 800-877-9905
Admissions FAX: 330 263-2621
Director of Admissions: Ric Martinez
Admissions e-mail: admissions@wooster.edu
Web site: http://www.wooster.edu/
SAT Code: 1134 ACT Code: 3260

Director of the Learning Center: Pamela Rose
LD program telephone: 330 263-2595
LD program e-mail: prose@wooster.edu
Total campus enrollment: 1,827

GENERAL

The College of Wooster is a private, coed, four-year institution. 240-acre campus in Wooster (population: 24,811), 55 miles from Cleveland. Served by bus; major airport serves Cleveland; smaller airport serves Akron (25 miles); train serves Canton (35 miles). School operates transportation to Akron and Cleveland and to airports. Semester system.

LD ADMISSIONS

A personal interview is recommended. Essay is required and may be typed. Admissions requirements that may be waived for LD students include foreign language.

SECONDARY SCHOOL REQUIREMENTS

Graduation from secondary school required; GED accepted. The following course distribution required: 4 units of English, 3 units of math, 3 units of science, 2 units of foreign language, 3 units of social studies, 2 units of academic electives.

TESTING

SAT Reasoning or ACT required. SAT Subject recommended.

All enrolled freshmen (fall 2004):

Average SAT I Scores:	Verbal: 606	Math: 598
Average ACT Scores:	Composite: 26	

Child Study Team report is not required. Tests required as part of this documentation:

- ☐ WAIS-IV
- ☐ WISC-IV
- ☐ SATA
- ☐ Woodcock-Johnson
- ☐ Nelson-Denny Reading Test
- ☐ Other

UNDERGRADUATE STUDENT BODY

Total undergraduate student enrollment: 861 Men, 962 Women.

Composition of student body (fall 2004):

	Undergraduate	Freshmen
International	5.5	6.5
Black	4.4	4.6
American Indian	0.0	0.3
Asian-American	0.8	1.2
Hispanic	1.9	1.5
White	76.1	76.4
Unreported	11.3	9.5
	100.0%	100.0%

43% are from out of state. 8% join a fraternity and 12% join a sorority. Average age of full-time undergraduates is 20. 70% of classes have fewer than 20 students, 29% have between 20 and 50 students, 1% have more than 50 students.

STUDENT HOUSING

99% of freshmen live in college housing. Freshmen are required to live on campus. Housing is guaranteed for all undergraduates. Campus can house 1,881 undergraduates.

EXPENSES

Tuition (2005-06): $28,005 per year.
Room: $3,210. Board: $3,850.
There is no additional cost for LD program/services.

LD SERVICES

LD program size is not limited.

LD services available to:

☐ Freshmen ☐ Sophomores ☐ Juniors ☐ Seniors

Academic Accommodations

Curriculum		**In class**	
Foreign language waiver	☐	Early syllabus	☐
Lighter course load	☐	Note takers in class	☐
Math waiver	☐	Priority seating	☐
Other special classes	☐	Tape recorders	■
Priority registrations	☐	Videotaped classes	☐
Substitution of courses	☐	Text on tape	☐
Exams		**Services**	
Extended time	☐	Diagnostic tests	☐
Oral exams	■	Learning centers	■
Take home exams	☐	Proofreaders	☐
Exams on tape or computer	☐	Readers	■
Untimed exams	■	Reading Machines/Kurzweil	☐
Other accommodations	☐	Special bookstore section	☐
		Typists	☐

Credit toward degree is not given for remedial courses taken.

Counseling Services

- ☐ Academic
- ☐ Psychological
- ☐ Student Support groups
- ☐ Vocational

Tutoring

	Individual	Group
Time management	☐	☐
Organizational skills	☐	☐
Learning strategies	☐	☐
Study skills	☐	☐
Content area	☐	☐
Writing lab	☐	☐
Math lab	☐	☐

LD PROGRAM STAFF

Total number of LD Program staff (including director):

Full Time: 2 Part Time: 2

Key staff person available to work with LD students: Pamela Rose, Director of the Learning Center.

Columbus College of Art and Design

Columbus, OH

Address: 107 N. Ninth Street, Columbus, OH, 43215
Admissions telephone: 614 222-3261
Admissions FAX: 614 232-8344
Director of Admissions: Thomas E. Green
Admissions e-mail: admissions@ccad.edu
Web site: http://www.ccad.edu
SAT Code: 1085 ACT Code: 3281

Director of Advisement: Roderick Jungbauer
LD program telephone: 614 222-3292
LD program e-mail: rjungbauer@ccad.edu
LD program enrollment: 61, Total campus enrollment: 1,562

GENERAL

Columbus College of Art and Design is a private, coed, four-year institution. 17-acre, urban campus in Columbus (population: 711,470). Served by air and bus; train serves Bucyrus (50 miles). Public transportation serves campus. Semester system.

LD ADMISSIONS

Students do not complete a separate application and are not simultaneously accepted to the LD program. A member of the LD program does not sit on the admissions committee. A personal interview is recommended. Essay is required and may be typed.

SECONDARY SCHOOL REQUIREMENTS

Graduation from secondary school required; GED accepted.

TESTING

SAT Reasoning or ACT required.

All enrolled freshmen (fall 2004):

Average SAT I Scores:	Verbal: 510	Math: 488
Average ACT Scores:	Composite: 20	

Child Study Team report is not required. A neuropsychological or comprehensive psycho-education evaluation is not required for admission. Tests required as part of this documentation:

- ☐ WAIS-IV
- ☐ WISC-IV
- ☐ SATA
- ☐ Woodcock-Johnson
- ☐ Nelson-Denny Reading Test
- ☐ Other

UNDERGRADUATE STUDENT BODY

Total undergraduate student enrollment: 844 Men, 893 Women.

Composition of student body (fall 2004):

	Undergraduate	Freshmen
International	3.0	4.9
Black	9.4	7.9
American Indian	0.0	0.3
Asian-American	1.3	3.4
Hispanic	0.9	2.7
White	75.6	74.0
Unreported	9.8	6.8
	100.0%	100.0%

10% are from out of state. Average age of full-time undergraduates is 21. 57% of classes have fewer than 20 students, 43% have between 20 and 50 students.

STUDENT HOUSING

66% of freshmen live in college housing. Freshmen are required to live on campus. Housing is not guaranteed for all undergraduates. Freshmen are given housing priority; if room available upperclassmen can be housed. Campus can house 312 undergraduates. Single rooms are not available for students with medical or special needs.

EXPENSES

Tuition (2005-06): $19,728 per year.
Room & Board: $6,450.

There is no additional cost for LD program/services.

LD SERVICES

LD program size is not limited.

LD services available to:

■ Freshmen ■ Sophomores ■ Juniors ■ Seniors

Academic Accommodations

Curriculum		**In class**	
Foreign language waiver	☐	Early syllabus	☐
Lighter course load	■	Note takers in class	■
Math waiver	☐	Priority seating	☐
Other special classes	☐	Tape recorders	■
Priority registrations	■	Videotaped classes	☐
Substitution of courses	☐	Text on tape	☐
Exams		**Services**	
Extended time	■	Diagnostic tests	☐
Oral exams	■	Learning centers	■
Take home exams	☐	Proofreaders	☐
Exams on tape or computer	■	Readers	■
Untimed exams	☐	Reading Machines/Kurzweil	■
Other accommodations	☐	Special bookstore section	☐
		Typists	☐

Credit toward degree is not given for remedial courses taken.

Counseling Services

- ■ Academic
- ■ Psychological
- ☐ Student Support groups
- ☐ Vocational

Tutoring

Individual tutoring is available weekly.

Average size of tutoring groups: 1

	Individual	Group
Time management	☐	☐
Organizational skills	☐	☐
Learning strategies	■	☐
Study skills	■	☐
Content area	☐	☐
Writing lab	■	☐
Math lab	☐	☐

LD PROGRAM STAFF

Total number of LD Program staff (including director):

Full Time: 1 Part Time: 1

There is an advisor/advocate from the LD program available to students. The advisor/advocate meets with faculty 1 time per month and students 1 time per month.

Key staff person available to work with LD students: Roderick Jungbauer, Director of Advisement/Disability Services.

University of Dayton

Dayton, OH

Address: 300 College Park, Dayton, OH, 45469
Admissions telephone: 800 837-7433
Admissions FAX: 937 229-4729
Director of Admissions: Robert F. Durkle
Admissions e-mail: admission@udayton.edu
Web site: http://www.udayton.edu
SAT Code: 1834 ACT Code: 3342

LD program name: LEAD: Disability Services
Assistant Coordinator: Dude Coudret
LD program telephone: 937 229-2066
LD program e-mail: Dude.Coudret@notes.udayton.edu
LD program enrollment: 600, Total campus enrollment: 7,158

GENERAL

University of Dayton is a private, coed, four-year institution. 110-acre, urban campus in Dayton (population: 166,179). Served by air and bus; train serves Cincinnati (60 miles). Public transportation serves campus. Semester system.

LD ADMISSIONS

High school waivers are accepted for math and foreign language. A personal interview is recommended. Essay is required and may be typed.

For fall 2004, 150 completed self-identified LD applications were received. 150 applications were offered admission, and 150 enrolled.

SECONDARY SCHOOL REQUIREMENTS

Graduation from secondary school required; GED accepted.

TESTING

SAT Reasoning or ACT required. SAT Subject recommended.

All enrolled freshmen (fall 2004):

Average SAT I Scores:	Verbal: 568	Math: 583
Average ACT Scores:	Composite: 25	

Child Study Team report is not required. A neuropsychological or comprehensive psycho-education evaluation is not required for admission. Tests required as part of this documentation:

- [ ] WAIS-IV
- [ ] WISC-IV
- [ ] SATA
- [ ] Woodcock-Johnson
- [ ] Nelson-Denny Reading Test
- [ ] Other

UNDERGRADUATE STUDENT BODY

Total undergraduate student enrollment: 3,513 Men, 3,654 Women.

Composition of student body (fall 2004):

	Undergraduate	Freshmen
International	0.4	0.6
Black	3.3	4.4
American Indian	0.3	0.2
Asian-American	0.7	1.2
Hispanic	2.5	2.5
White	87.1	86.0
Unreported	5.7	5.1
	100.0%	100.0%

35% are from out of state. 15% join a fraternity and 19% join a sorority. Average age of full-time undergraduates is 20. 34% of classes have fewer than 20 students, 62% have between 20 and 50 students, 4% have more than 50 students.

STUDENT HOUSING

94% of freshmen live in college housing. Freshmen are required to live on campus. Housing is guaranteed for all undergraduates. Campus can house 5,890 undergraduates. Single rooms are available for students with medical or special needs. A medical note is required.

EXPENSES

Tuition (2005-06): $21,246 per year (in-state), $21,245 (out-of-state).
Room: $4,000. Board: $2,780.
There is no additional cost for LD program/services.

LD SERVICES

LD program size is not limited.

LD services available to:

- [x] Freshmen
- [x] Sophomores
- [x] Juniors
- [x] Seniors

Academic Accommodations

Curriculum		In class	
Foreign language waiver	[ ]	Early syllabus	[x]
Lighter course load	[x]	Note takers in class	[x]
Math waiver	[ ]	Priority seating	[x]
Other special classes	[x]	Tape recorders	[x]
Priority registrations	[x]	Videotaped classes	[ ]
Substitution of courses	[x]	Text on tape	[x]
Exams		**Services**	
Extended time	[x]	Diagnostic tests	[ ]
Oral exams	[x]	Learning centers	[x]
Take home exams	[ ]	Proofreaders	[x]
Exams on tape or computer	[x]	Readers	[x]
Untimed exams	[ ]	Reading Machines/Kurzweil	[x]
Other accommodations	[x]	Special bookstore section	[ ]
		Typists	[x]

Credit toward degree is not given for remedial courses taken.

Counseling Services

- [x] Academic — Meets 3 times per academic year
- [ ] Psychological
- [ ] Student Support groups
- [ ] Vocational

Tutoring

Individual tutoring is available weekly.

Average size of tutoring groups: 5

	Individual	Group
Time management	[x]	[x]
Organizational skills	[x]	[x]
Learning strategies	[x]	[x]
Study skills	[x]	[x]
Content area	[x]	[x]
Writing lab	[x]	[x]
Math lab	[x]	[x]

UNIQUE LD PROGRAM FEATURES

While we offer reasonable accommodations for students with learning disabilities, we do not offer a specific formal program. Reasonable accommodations are made on the basis of need.

LD PROGRAM STAFF

Total number of LD Program staff (including director):

Full Time: 9 Part Time: 9

There is not an advisor/advocate from the LD program available to students. 1 graduate student and 20 peer tutors are available to work with LD students.

Key staff person available to work with LD students: Brenda Cooper, Coordinator.

LD Program web site: http://academic.udayton.edu/osd/

Denison University

Granville, OH

Address: 1 Main Street, Granville, OH, 43023
Admissions telephone: 800 336-4766
Admissions FAX: 740 587-6306
Director of Admissions: Perry Robinson
Admissions e-mail: admissions@denison.edu
Web site: http://www.denison.edu
SAT Code: 1164 ACT Code: 3266

LD program name: Academic Support Services
LD program address: 104 Doane Hall, Granville, OH, 43023
Associate Dean/Director: Jennifer Grube Vestal
LD program telephone: 740 587-6666
LD program e-mail: vestal@denison.edu
LD program enrollment: 168, Total campus enrollment: 2,229

GENERAL

Denison University is a private, coed, four-year institution. 1,200-acre campus in Granville (population: 3,167), 28 miles from Columbus. Airport and bus serve Columbus; smaller airport serves Newark (10 miles). School operates transportation to Columbus airport. Semester system.

LD ADMISSIONS

Students do not complete a separate application and are simultaneously accepted to the LD program. A member of the LD program does not sit on the admissions committee. A personal interview is recommended. Essay is required and may be typed. LD documentation is required if student wishes to register and receive accommodations at Denison.

SECONDARY SCHOOL REQUIREMENTS

Graduation from secondary school required; GED accepted. The following course distribution required: 4 units of English, 4 units of math, 4 units of science, 3 units of foreign language, 2 units of social studies, 1 unit of history, 1 unit of academic electives.

TESTING

SAT Reasoning or ACT required. SAT Subject required.

All enrolled freshmen (fall 2004):

Average SAT I Scores:	Verbal: 621	Math: 618
Average ACT Scores:	Composite: 27	

Child Study Team report is not required. A neuropsychological or comprehensive psycho-education evaluation is not required for admission. Tests required as part of this documentation:

- ☐ WAIS-IV
- ☐ WISC-IV
- ☐ SATA
- ☐ Woodcock-Johnson
- ☐ Nelson-Denny Reading Test
- ☐ Other

UNDERGRADUATE STUDENT BODY

Total undergraduate student enrollment: 904 Men, 1,203 Women.

Composition of student body (fall 2004):

	Undergraduate	Freshmen
International	3.6	4.7
Black	5.7	5.2
American Indian	0.2	0.2
Asian-American	3.7	2.7
Hispanic	2.4	2.7
White	83.1	83.1
Unreported	1.3	1.4
	100.0%	100.0%

54% are from out of state. 21% join a fraternity and 40% join a sorority. Average age of full-time undergraduates is 20. 67% of classes have fewer than 20 students, 33% have between 20 and 50 students.

STUDENT HOUSING

100% of freshmen live in college housing. Freshmen are required to live on campus. Housing is guaranteed for all undergraduates. Campus can house 2,142 undergraduates. Single rooms are available for students with medical or special needs. A medical note is required.

EXPENSES

Tuition (2005-06): $28,170 per year.
Room: $4,470. Board: $3,650.
There is no additional cost for LD program/services.

LD SERVICES

LD program size is not limited.

LD services available to:

■ Freshmen ■ Sophomores ■ Juniors ■ Seniors

Academic Accommodations

Curriculum		In class	
Foreign language waiver	☐	Early syllabus	☐
Lighter course load	■	Note takers in class	■
Math waiver	☐	Priority seating	■
Other special classes	☐	Tape recorders	■
Priority registrations	☐	Videotaped classes	☐
Substitution of courses	☐	Text on tape	■
Exams		**Services**	
Extended time	■	Diagnostic tests	☐
Oral exams	☐	Learning centers	■
Take home exams	☐	Proofreaders	☐
Exams on tape or computer	☐	Readers	■
Untimed exams	☐	Reading Machines/Kurzweil	☐
Other accommodations	☐	Special bookstore section	☐
		Typists	☐

Credit toward degree is not given for remedial courses taken.

Counseling Services

- ■ Academic — Meets 2 times per academic year
- ☐ Psychological
- ☐ Student Support groups
- ☐ Vocational

Tutoring

Individual tutoring is available weekly.

	Individual	Group
Time management	■	☐
Organizational skills	■	☐
Learning strategies	■	☐
Study skills	■	■
Content area	■	■
Writing lab	■	☐
Math lab	☐	☐

UNIQUE LD PROGRAM FEATURES

Services and reasonable accommodations are based on documentation of a disability. Said documentation should be sent to Admissions once deposit is paid.

LD PROGRAM STAFF

Total number of LD Program staff (including director):

Full Time: 2 Part Time: 2

There is an advisor/advocate from the LD program available to students.

Key staff person available to work with LD students: Jennifer Grube Vestal, Associate Dean of Students/Director of Academic Support & Enrichment.

LD Program web site: www.denison.edu/acad-support/disabilities/

The University of Findlay

Findlay, OH

Address: 1000 N. Main Street, Findlay, OH, 45840
Admissions telephone: 800 548-0932
Admissions FAX: 419 434-4898
Director of Undergraduate Admissions: Randall Langston
Admissions e-mail: admissions@findlay.edu
Web site: http://www.findlay.edu
SAT Code: 1223 ACT Code: 3272

LD program name: Office of Disability Services
Director of Disability Services: Lori Colchagoff
LD program telephone: 419 434-5532
LD program e-mail: lcolchagoff@findlay.edu
LD program enrollment: 29, Total campus enrollment: 3,460

GENERAL

The University of Findlay is a private, coed, four-year institution. 190-acre campus in Findlay (population: 38,967), 45 miles from Toledo. Major airports serve Toledo and Columbus (95 miles); bus serves North Baltimore (10 miles); train serves Fostoria (15 miles). School operates transportation to equine farms. Semester system.

LD ADMISSIONS

Students do not complete a separate application and are simultaneously accepted to the LD program. A member of the LD program does not sit on the admissions committee. A personal interview is recommended. Essay is not required.

For fall 2004, 22 completed self-identified LD applications were received. 22 applications were offered admission, and 13 enrolled.

SECONDARY SCHOOL REQUIREMENTS

Graduation from secondary school required; GED accepted.

TESTING

ACT required; SAT Reasoning may be substituted. SAT Subject recommended.

All enrolled freshmen (fall 2004):

Average SAT I Scores:	Verbal: 518	Math: 513
Average ACT Scores:	Composite: 22	

Child Study Team report is not required. A neuropsychological or comprehensive psycho-education evaluation is not required for admission. Tests required as part of this documentation:

- [ ] WAIS-IV
- [ ] WISC-IV
- [ ] SATA
- [ ] Woodcock-Johnson
- [ ] Nelson-Denny Reading Test
- [ ] Other

UNDERGRADUATE STUDENT BODY

Total undergraduate student enrollment: 1,464 Men, 1,917 Women.

Composition of student body (fall 2004):

	Undergraduate	Freshmen
International	5.2	3.4
Black	2.3	3.4
American Indian	0.1	0.4
Asian-American	0.2	1.3
Hispanic	0.8	1.5
White	47.3	74.4
Unreported	44.1	15.6
	100.0%	100.0%

15% are from out of state. 4% join a fraternity and 3% join a sorority. Average age of full-time undergraduates is 22. 61% of classes have fewer than 20 students, 37% have between 20 and 50 students, 2% have more than 50 students.

STUDENT HOUSING

76% of freshmen live in college housing. Freshmen are required to live on campus. Housing is guaranteed for all undergraduates. Campus can house 1,215 undergraduates. Single rooms are available for students with medical or special needs. A medical note is required.

EXPENSES

Tuition (2005-06): $20,796 per year. Additional $2,820 fee for equestrian studies program and $970 fee for pre-veterinary medicine program.

Room: $3,756. Board: $3,736.
There is no additional cost for LD program/services.

LD SERVICES

LD program size is not limited.

LD services available to:

- [x] Freshmen
- [x] Sophomores
- [x] Juniors
- [x] Seniors

Academic Accommodations

Curriculum

- [ ] Foreign language waiver
- [ ] Lighter course load
- [ ] Math waiver
- [ ] Other special classes
- [x] Priority registrations
- [ ] Substitution of courses

Exams

- [x] Extended time
- [x] Oral exams
- [ ] Take home exams
- [ ] Exams on tape or computer
- [x] Untimed exams
- [x] Other accommodations

In class

- [ ] Early syllabus
- [x] Note takers in class
- [ ] Priority seating
- [x] Tape recorders
- [ ] Videotaped classes
- [ ] Text on tape

Services

- [ ] Diagnostic tests
- [ ] Learning centers
- [x] Proofreaders
- [x] Readers
- [x] Reading Machines/Kurzweil
- [ ] Special bookstore section
- [x] Typists

Credit toward degree is not given for remedial courses taken.

Counseling Services

- [ ] Academic
- [ ] Psychological
- [ ] Student Support groups
- [ ] Vocational

Tutoring

Individual tutoring is available daily.

Average size of tutoring groups: 1

	Individual	Group
Time management	[x]	[x]
Organizational skills	[x]	[x]
Learning strategies	[x]	[x]
Study skills	[x]	[x]
Content area	[x]	[x]
Writing lab	[x]	[ ]
Math lab	[x]	[x]

LD PROGRAM STAFF

Total number of LD Program staff (including director):

Full Time: 1 Part Time: 1

There is an advisor/advocate from the LD program available to students. The advisor/advocate meets with faculty 2 times per month and students 2 times per month. 1 graduate student and 25 peer tutors are available to work with LD students.

Key staff person available to work with LD students: Lori Colchagoff, Director of Disability Services.

Franciscan University of Steubenville

Steubenville, OH

Address: 1235 University Boulevard, Steubenville, OH, 43952-1763
Admissions telephone: 800 783-6220
Admissions FAX: 740 284-5456
Director of Admissions: Margaret Weber
Admissions e-mail: admissions@franciscan.edu
Web site: http://www.franciscan.edu
SAT Code: 1133 ACT Code: 3258

Director Student Academic Support Services: Rose Kline
LD program telephone: 740 283-6245, extension 2112
LD program e-mail: rkline@franciscan.edu
Total campus enrollment: 1,913

GENERAL

Franciscan University of Steubenville is a private, coed, four-year institution. 124-acre campus in Steubenville (population: 19,015), 42 miles from Pittsburgh; branch campus abroad in Gaming, Austria. Served by bus; major airport and train serve Pittsburgh. Public transportation serves campus. Semester system.

LD ADMISSIONS

Application Deadline: 05/01. Students do not complete a separate application and are not simultaneously accepted to the LD program. A member of the LD program does sit on the admissions committee. A personal interview is recommended. Essay is required and may be typed. LD students must meet same admissions requirements of other students. Identification of a disability is in no way considered in admission decisions.

SECONDARY SCHOOL REQUIREMENTS

Graduation from secondary school required; GED accepted.

TESTING

SAT Reasoning or ACT required. SAT Subject recommended.

All enrolled freshmen (fall 2004):

Average SAT I Scores:	Verbal: 593	Math: 565
Average ACT Scores:	Composite: 24	

Child Study Team report is not required. A neuropsychological or comprehensive psycho-educational evaluation is required for admission. Tests required as part of this documentation:

- [x] WAIS-IV
- [x] WISC-IV
- [x] SATA
- [x] Woodcock-Johnson
- [x] Nelson-Denny Reading Test
- [ ] Other

UNDERGRADUATE STUDENT BODY

Total undergraduate student enrollment: 704 Men, 1,029 Women.

Composition of student body (fall 2004):

	Undergraduate	Freshmen
International	0.0	0.9
Black	1.1	0.7
American Indian	0.0	0.2
Asian-American	1.1	1.6
Hispanic	0.8	3.7
White	90.9	86.1
Unreported	6.1	6.8
	100.0%	100.0%

78% are from out of state. Average age of full-time undergraduates is 21. 48% of classes have fewer than 20 students, 50% have between 20 and 50 students, 2% have more than 50 students.

STUDENT HOUSING

83% of freshmen live in college housing. Freshmen are required to live on campus. Housing is not guaranteed for all undergraduates. Campus housing is assigned to new students over 21 years of age on an as available basis Campus can house 1,072 undergraduates. Single rooms are available for students with medical or special needs. A medical note is required.

EXPENSES

Tuition (2005-06): $16,070 per year.
Room: $2,950. Board: $2,550.
There is no additional cost for LD program/services.

LD SERVICES

LD program size is not limited.

LD services available to:

- [x] Freshmen
- [x] Sophomores
- [x] Juniors
- [x] Seniors

Academic Accommodations

Curriculum		In class	
Foreign language waiver	[ ]	Early syllabus	[ ]
Lighter course load	[x]	Note takers in class	[x]
Math waiver	[ ]	Priority seating	[ ]
Other special classes	[ ]	Tape recorders	[x]
Priority registrations	[x]	Videotaped classes	[ ]
Substitution of courses	[ ]	Text on tape	[ ]
Exams		**Services**	
Extended time	[x]	Diagnostic tests	[ ]
Oral exams	[x]	Learning centers	[ ]
Take home exams	[ ]	Proofreaders	[ ]
Exams on tape or computer	[ ]	Readers	[x]
Untimed exams	[x]	Reading Machines/Kurzweil	[x]
Other accommodations	[ ]	Special bookstore section	[ ]
		Typists	[ ]

Credit toward degree is not given for remedial courses taken.

Counseling Services

- [x] Academic
- [ ] Psychological
- [ ] Student Support groups
- [ ] Vocational

Tutoring

Individual tutoring is available daily.

Average size of tutoring groups: 1

	Individual	Group
Time management	[x]	[ ]
Organizational skills	[x]	[ ]
Learning strategies	[x]	[ ]
Study skills	[x]	[ ]
Content area	[x]	[ ]
Writing lab	[x]	[ ]
Math lab	[ ]	[ ]

UNIQUE LD PROGRAM FEATURES

The goals of our program include self-advocacy and independent learning. We strive to meet the individual accommodation needs of each student. New assistive technology includes screen reader software, voice to text and text to voice software, and enlarged text capabilities. Fransiscan University has a 70% graduation rate of students with disabilities.

LD PROGRAM STAFF

Total number of LD Program staff (including director):

Full Time: 2 Part Time: 2

There is an advisor/advocate from the LD program available to students.

Key staff person available to work with LD students: Rose Kline, Director Student Academic Support Services.

Heidelberg College

Tiffin, OH

Address: 310 E. Market Street, Tiffin, OH, 44883
Admissions telephone: 800 HEIDELBERG
Admissions FAX: 419 448-2334
Vice President for Enrollment: Lindsay Sooy
Admissions e-mail: adminfo@heidelberg.edu
Web site: http://www.heidelberg.edu
SAT Code: 1292 ACT Code: 3278

Director of the Learning Center: William Miller
LD program telephone: 419 448-2301
LD program e-mail: wmiller@heidelberg.edu
Total campus enrollment: 1,131

GENERAL

Heidelberg College is a private, coed, four-year institution. 110-acre campus in Tiffin (population: 18,135), 45 miles from Toledo; branch campus in Maumee. Major airports serve Columbus (80 miles) and Cleveland (95 miles); smaller airport serves Toledo; bus serves Findlay (20 miles); train serves Fostoria (20 miles). School operates transportation to airports in Cleveland and Columbus. Semester system.

LD ADMISSIONS

Application Deadline: 08/01. Students do not complete a separate application and are not simultaneously accepted to the LD program. A member of the LD program does not sit on the admissions committee. A personal interview is recommended. Essay is not required.

SECONDARY SCHOOL REQUIREMENTS

Graduation from secondary school required; GED accepted.

TESTING

SAT Reasoning or ACT required. SAT Subject recommended.

All enrolled freshmen (fall 2004):

Average SAT I Scores:	Verbal: 507	Math: 504
Average ACT Scores:	Composite: 21	

Child Study Team report is required if student is classified. A neuropsychological or comprehensive psycho-educational evaluation is required for admission. Must be dated within 12 months of application. Tests required as part of this documentation:

- ☑ WAIS-IV
- ☑ WISC-IV
- ☐ SATA
- ☑ Woodcock-Johnson
- ☑ Nelson-Denny Reading Test
- ☐ Other

UNDERGRADUATE STUDENT BODY

Total undergraduate student enrollment: 589 Men, 711 Women.

Composition of student body (fall 2004):

	Undergraduate	Freshmen
International	2.0	2.2
Black	6.2	4.5
American Indian	0.3	0.1
Asian-American	0.0	0.2
Hispanic	0.8	0.8
White	89.3	91.3
Unreported	1.4	0.9
	100.0%	100.0%

7% are from out of state. 20% join a fraternity and 20% join a sorority. 57% of classes have fewer than 20 students, 41% have between 20 and 50 students, 2% have more than 50 students.

STUDENT HOUSING

95% of freshmen live in college housing. Freshmen are required to live on campus. Housing is guaranteed for all undergraduates. Campus can house 840 undergraduates. Single rooms are available for students with medical or special needs. A medical note is required.

EXPENSES

Tuition (2005-06): $15,740 per year.
Room: $3,296. Board: $3,812.
There is no additional cost for LD program/services.

LD SERVICES

LD program size is not limited.

LD services available to:

☑ Freshmen ☑ Sophomores ☑ Juniors ☑ Seniors

Academic Accommodations

Curriculum		In class	
Foreign language waiver	☐	Early syllabus	☐
Lighter course load	☐	Note takers in class	☑
Math waiver	☐	Priority seating	☐
Other special classes	☑	Tape recorders	☑
Priority registrations	☐	Videotaped classes	☐
Substitution of courses	☐	Text on tape	☐
Exams		**Services**	
Extended time	☑	Diagnostic tests	☐
Oral exams	☑	Learning centers	☑
Take home exams	☐	Proofreaders	☐
Exams on tape or computer	☐	Readers	☑
Untimed exams	☑	Reading Machines/Kurzweil	☐
Other accommodations	☐	Special bookstore section	☐
		Typists	☐

Credit toward degree is given for remedial courses taken.

Counseling Services

- ☐ Academic
- ☐ Psychological
- ☐ Student Support groups
- ☐ Vocational

Tutoring

Individual tutoring is available weekly.

	Individual	Group
Time management	☑	☐
Organizational skills	☑	☐
Learning strategies	☑	☐
Study skills	☑	☐
Content area	☐	☑
Writing lab	☐	☐
Math lab	☐	☐

LD PROGRAM STAFF

Total number of LD Program staff (including director):

There is no advisor/advocate from the LD program available to students. 24 peer tutors are available to work with LD students.

Key staff person available to work with LD students: William Miller, Director of the Learning Center.

Hiram College

Hiram, OH

Address: PO Box 67, Hiram, OH, 44234
Admissions telephone: 800 362-5280
Admissions FAX: 330 569-5944
Director of Admission: James Barrett
Admissions e-mail: admission@hiram.edu
Web site: http://www.hiram.edu
SAT Code: 1297 ACT Code: 3280

Director of Counseling: Lynn Taylor, Ph.D.
LD program telephone: 330 569-5952
LD program e-mail: taylorlb@hiram.edu
Total campus enrollment: 1,108

GENERAL

Hiram College is a private, coed, four-year institution. 110-acre campus in Hiram (population: 1,242), 35 miles from Cleveland. Major airport, bus, and train serve Cleveland; smaller airport serves Akron (20 miles). School operates transportation to surrounding towns and cities.

LD ADMISSIONS

A personal interview is recommended. Essay is required and may be typed.

SECONDARY SCHOOL REQUIREMENTS

Graduation from secondary school required; GED accepted. The following course distribution required: 4 units of English, 3 units of math, 3 units of science, 2 units of foreign language, 3 units of social studies, 1 unit of history, 2 units of academic electives.

TESTING

SAT Reasoning or ACT required. SAT Subject recommended.

All enrolled freshmen (fall 2004):

Average SAT I Scores:	Verbal: 570	Math: 544
Average ACT Scores:	Composite: 24	

Child Study Team report is not required. Tests required as part of this documentation:

- ☐ WAIS-IV
- ☐ WISC-IV
- ☐ SATA
- ☐ Woodcock-Johnson
- ☐ Nelson-Denny Reading Test
- ☐ Other

UNDERGRADUATE STUDENT BODY

Total undergraduate student enrollment: 408 Men, 463 Women.

Composition of student body (fall 2004):

	Undergraduate	Freshmen
International	5.5	3.0
Black	9.2	10.6
American Indian	0.5	0.2
Asian-American	2.8	1.4
Hispanic	0.5	1.4
White	70.0	80.5
Unreported	11.5	2.9
	100.0%	100.0%

17% are from out of state. Average age of full-time undergraduates is 19. 88% of classes have fewer than 20 students, 12% have between 20 and 50 students.

STUDENT HOUSING

Housing is guaranteed for all undergraduates. Campus can house 850 undergraduates.

EXPENSES

Tuition 2004-05: $21,970 per year.

Room: $3,485. Board: $3,790-$4,020.

There is no additional cost for LD program/services.

LD SERVICES

LD program size is not limited.

LD services available to:

☐ Freshmen ☐ Sophomores ☐ Juniors ☐ Seniors

Academic Accommodations

Curriculum		**In class**	
Foreign language waiver	☐	Early syllabus	☐
Lighter course load	☐	Note takers in class	■
Math waiver	☐	Priority seating	☐
Other special classes	☐	Tape recorders	■
Priority registrations	☐	Videotaped classes	☐
Substitution of courses	☐	Text on tape	☐
Exams		**Services**	
Extended time	■	Diagnostic tests	☐
Oral exams	■	Learning centers	☐
Take home exams	☐	Proofreaders	☐
Exams on tape or computer	☐	Readers	■
Untimed exams	☐	Reading Machines/Kurzweil	☐
Other accommodations	☐	Special bookstore section	☐
		Typists	☐

Credit toward degree is not given for remedial courses taken.

Counseling Services

- ☐ Academic
- ☐ Psychological
- ☐ Student Support groups
- ☐ Vocational

Tutoring

	Individual	Group
Time management	☐	☐
Organizational skills	☐	☐
Learning strategies	☐	☐
Study skills	☐	☐
Content area	☐	☐
Writing lab	☐	☐
Math lab	☐	☐

LD PROGRAM STAFF

Total number of LD Program staff (including director):

Key staff person available to work with LD students: Lynn Taylor, Ph.D., Director of Counseling.

John Carroll University

University Heights, OH

Address: 20700 N. Park Boulevard, University Heights, OH, 44118
Admissions telephone: 216 397-4294
Admissions FAX: 216 397-4981
Director of Admissions: Thomas P. Fanning
Admissions e-mail: admission@jcu.edu
Web site: http://www.jcu.edu
SAT Code: 1342 ACT Code: 3282

LD program name: Services for Students with Disabilities
Coordinator: Kate Yurick
LD program telephone: 216 397-4967
LD program enrollment: 240, Total campus enrollment: 3,350

GENERAL

John Carroll University is a private, coed, four-year institution. 60-acre, suburban campus in Cleveland (population: 478,403). Served by air, bus, and train. Public transportation serves campus. Semester system.

LD ADMISSIONS

Students do not complete a separate application and are not simultaneously accepted to the LD program. A member of the LD program does not sit on the admissions committee. A personal interview is not required. Essay is not required.

SECONDARY SCHOOL REQUIREMENTS

Graduation from secondary school required; GED accepted. The following course distribution required: 4 units of English, 3 units of math, 2 units of science, 2 units of foreign language, 2 units of social studies, 3 units of academic electives.

TESTING

SAT Reasoning or ACT required. SAT Subject recommended.

All enrolled freshmen (fall 2004):

Average SAT I Scores:	Verbal: 577	Math: 579
Average ACT Scores:	Composite: 23	

Child Study Team report is not required. A neuropsychological or comprehensive psycho-educational evaluation is required for admission. Must be dated within 36 months of application. Tests required as part of this documentation:

☐ WAIS-IV ☐ Woodcock-Johnson
☐ WISC-IV ☐ Nelson-Denny Reading Test
☐ SATA ■ Other

UNDERGRADUATE STUDENT BODY

Total undergraduate student enrollment: 1,634 Men, 1,891 Women.

Composition of student body (fall 2004):

	Undergraduate	Freshmen
International	0.0	0.0
Black	3.5	3.7
American Indian	0.0	0.1
Asian-American	2.2	2.3
Hispanic	2.7	2.8
White	87.4	87.6
Unreported	4.2	3.5
	100.0%	100.0%

27% are from out of state. 9% join a fraternity and 13% join a sorority. Average age of full-time undergraduates is 20. 50% of classes have fewer than 20 students, 50% have between 20 and 50 students.

STUDENT HOUSING

86% of freshmen live in college housing. Freshmen are not required to live on campus. Housing is guaranteed for all undergraduates. Campus can house 1,964 undergraduates. Single rooms are available for students with medical or special needs. A medical note is required.

EXPENSES

Tuition (2005-06): $23,380 per year.
Room: $4,064. Board: $3,462.
There is no additional cost for LD program/services

LD SERVICES

LD program size is not limited.

LD services available to:

■ Freshmen ■ Sophomores ■ Juniors ■ Seniors

Academic Accommodations

Curriculum		In class	
Foreign language waiver	☐	Early syllabus	☐
Lighter course load	■	Note takers in class	■
Math waiver	☐	Priority seating	☐
Other special classes	☐	Tape recorders	☐
Priority registrations	☐	Videotaped classes	☐
Substitution of courses	☐	Text on tape	☐
Exams		**Services**	
Extended time	■	Diagnostic tests	☐
Oral exams	■	Learning centers	☐
Take home exams	☐	Proofreaders	☐
Exams on tape or computer	☐	Readers	■
Untimed exams	☐	Reading Machines/Kurzweil	■
Other accommodations	☐	Special bookstore section	☐
		Typists	☐

Credit toward degree is not given for remedial courses taken.

Counseling Services

■ Academic
■ Psychological — Meets 12 times per academic year
☐ Student Support groups
☐ Vocational

Tutoring

Individual tutoring is not available.

	Individual	Group
Time management	■	☐
Organizational skills	■	☐
Learning strategies	■	☐
Study skills	☐	☐
Content area	☐	☐
Writing lab	☐	☐
Math lab	☐	☐

LD PROGRAM STAFF

Total number of LD Program staff (including director):

Full Time: 1 Part Time: 1

There is an advisor/advocate from the LD program available to students.

Key staff person available to work with LD students: Kate Yurick, Coordinator, Services for Students with Disabilities.

LD Program web site: www.jcu.edu/student1/disabilities

Kent State University

Kent, OH

Address: PO Box 5190, Kent, OH, 44242-0001
Admissions telephone: 800 988-KENT
Admissions FAX: 330 672-2499
Director of Admissions: Nancy Dellavecchia
Admissions e-mail: KENTADM@Admissions.Kent.edu
Web site: http://www.kent.edu
SAT Code: 1367 ACT Code: 3284

LD program name: Student Disability Services
Director, Student Disability Services: Anne Jannarone
LD program telephone: 330 672-3391
LD program e-mail: ajannaro@kent.edu
LD program enrollment: 489, Total campus enrollment: 19,060

GENERAL

Kent State University is a public, coed, four-year institution. 1,200-acre campus in Kent (population: 27,906), 10 miles from Akron; branch campuses in Ashtabula, East Liverpool, Geauga, Salem, Stark County, Trumbull County, and Tuscarawas County. Served by bus; major airport and train serve Cleveland (40 miles). School operates transportation on campus, in Kent, and to Akron, Cleveland, Ravenna, and Stow. Semester system.

LD ADMISSIONS

Students do not complete a separate application and are simultaneously accepted to the LD program. A member of the LD program does not sit on the admissions committee. High school waivers are accepted for foreign language. A personal interview is required. Essay is not required.

SECONDARY SCHOOL REQUIREMENTS

Graduation from secondary school required; GED accepted.

TESTING

SAT Reasoning or ACT required. SAT Subject recommended.

All enrolled freshmen (fall 2004):

Average SAT I Scores:	Verbal: 510	Math: 508
Average ACT Scores:	Composite: 21	

Child Study Team report is required if student is classified. A neuropsychological or comprehensive psycho-educational evaluation is required for admission. Must be dated within 60 months of application. Tests required as part of this documentation:

- ■ WAIS-IV
- ☐ WISC-IV
- ☐ SATA
- ■ Woodcock-Johnson
- ☐ Nelson-Denny Reading Test
- ☐ Other

UNDERGRADUATE STUDENT BODY

Total undergraduate student enrollment: 7,405 Men, 10,977 Women.

Composition of student body (fall 2004):

	Undergraduate	Freshmen
International	0.6	0.8
Black	8.8	8.0
American Indian	0.4	0.4
Asian-American	1.9	1.4
Hispanic	1.1	1.1
White	84.6	85.9
Unreported	2.6	2.4
	100.0%	100.0%

7% are from out of state. 1% join a fraternity and 1% join a sorority. Average age of full-time undergraduates is 21. 49% of classes have fewer than 20 students, 43% have between 20 and 50 students, 8% have more than 50 students.

STUDENT HOUSING

78% of freshmen live in college housing. Freshmen are required to live on campus. Housing is guaranteed for all undergraduates. Campus can house 6,731 undergraduates. Single rooms are available for students with medical or special needs. A medical note is required.

EXPENSES

Tuition (2005-06): $7,954 per year (in-state), $15,386 (out-of-state). $10,748 per year (state residents, comprehensive), $16,236 (out-of-state, comprehensive).

Room: $4,050. Board: $2,600.

There is no additional cost for LD program/services.

LD SERVICES

LD program size is not limited.

LD services available to:

■ Freshmen ■ Sophomores ■ Juniors ■ Seniors

Academic Accommodations

Curriculum		**In class**	
Foreign language waiver	☐	Early syllabus	■
Lighter course load	■	Note takers in class	■
Math waiver	☐	Priority seating	■
Other special classes	☐	Tape recorders	■
Priority registrations	■	Videotaped classes	☐
Substitution of courses	■	Text on tape	■
Exams		**Services**	
Extended time	■	Diagnostic tests	☐
Oral exams	■	Learning centers	■
Take home exams	☐	Proofreaders	☐
Exams on tape or computer	■	Readers	■
Untimed exams	☐	Reading Machines/Kurzweil	☐
Other accommodations	■	Special bookstore section	☐
		Typists	■

Credit toward degree is not given for remedial courses taken.

Counseling Services

- ■ Academic
- ■ Psychological
- ■ Student Support groups
- ☐ Vocational

Tutoring

Individual tutoring is available weekly.

Average size of tutoring groups: 2

	Individual	Group
Time management	■	☐
Organizational skills	■	☐
Learning strategies	■	☐
Study skills	■	■
Content area	■	■
Writing lab	■	■
Math lab	■	■

LD PROGRAM STAFF

Total number of LD Program staff (including director):

Full Time: 7 Part Time: 7

There is an advisor/advocate from the LD program available to students. The advisor/advocate meets with faculty once per month. 4 graduate students and 80 peer tutors are available to work with LD students.

Key staff person available to work with LD students: Anne Jannarone, Director, Student Disability Services.

LD Program web site: www.kent.edu/sds

Kenyon College

Gambier, OH

Address: Ransom Hall, Gambier, OH, 43022-9623
Admissions telephone: 800 848-2468
Admissions FAX: 740 427-5770
Acting Dean of Admissions and Financial Aid: Jennifer Britz
Admissions e-mail: admissions@kenyon.edu
Web site: http://www.kenyon.edu
SAT Code: 1370 ACT Code: 3286

LD program name: Office of Disability Services
Coordinator of Disability Services: Erin F. Salva
LD program telephone: 740 427-5453
LD program e-mail: salvae@kenyon.edu
Total campus enrollment: 1,634

GENERAL

Kenyon College is a private, coed, four-year institution. 1,000-acre campus in Gambier (population: 1,871), 50 miles from Columbus. Major airport and bus serve Columbus; train serves Cleveland (115 miles). School operates transportation to Mt. Vernon and Columbus. Semester system.

LD ADMISSIONS

Application Deadline: 01/15. High school waivers are accepted for foreign language. A personal interview is recommended. Essay is required and may be typed.

SECONDARY SCHOOL REQUIREMENTS

Graduation from secondary school required; GED accepted. The following course distribution required: 4 units of English, 3 units of math, 3 units of science, 3 units of foreign language, 1 unit of social studies, 1 unit of history, 3 units of academic electives.

TESTING

SAT Reasoning or ACT required. SAT Subject recommended.

All enrolled freshmen (fall 2004):

Average SAT I Scores:	Verbal: 673	Math: 648
Average ACT Scores:	Composite: 29	

Child Study Team report is not required. A neuropsychological or comprehensive psycho-education evaluation is not required for admission. Tests required as part of this documentation:

- ☑ WAIS-IV
- ☑ WISC-IV
- ☑ SATA
- ☑ Woodcock-Johnson
- ☑ Nelson-Denny Reading Test
- ☑ Other

UNDERGRADUATE STUDENT BODY

Total undergraduate student enrollment: 714 Men, 873 Women.

Composition of student body (fall 2004):

	Undergraduate	Freshmen
International	2.8	2.6
Black	3.4	3.4
American Indian	0.9	0.3
Asian-American	3.8	3.4
Hispanic	3.4	2.5
White	80.4	83.3
Unreported	5.3	4.5
	100.0%	100.0%

75% are from out of state. 27% join a fraternity and 9% join a sorority. Average age of full-time undergraduates is 20. 70% of classes have fewer than 20 students, 29% have between 20 and 50 students, 1% have more than 50 students.

STUDENT HOUSING

100% of freshmen live in college housing. Freshmen are required to live on campus. Housing is guaranteed for all undergraduates. Campus can house 1,597 undergraduates.

EXPENSES

Tuition (2005-06): $32,980 per year.
Room: $2,620. Board: $2,950.
There is no additional cost for LD program/services.

LD SERVICES

LD program size is not limited.

LD services available to:

☑ Freshmen ☑ Sophomores ☑ Juniors ☑ Seniors

Academic Accommodations

Curriculum		In class	
Foreign language waiver	☐	Early syllabus	☑
Lighter course load	☐	Note takers in class	☑
Math waiver	☐	Priority seating	☐
Other special classes	☐	Tape recorders	☑
Priority registrations	☑	Videotaped classes	☑
Substitution of courses	☑	Text on tape	☑
Exams		**Services**	
Extended time	☑	Diagnostic tests	☐
Oral exams	☑	Learning centers	☐
Take home exams	☐	Proofreaders	☐
Exams on tape or computer	☑	Readers	☑
Untimed exams	☑	Reading Machines/Kurzweil	☑
Other accommodations	☐	Special bookstore section	☐
		Typists	☐

Counseling Services

- ☐ Academic
- ☐ Psychological
- ☐ Student Support groups
- ☐ Vocational

Tutoring

Individual tutoring is available weekly.

Average size of tutoring groups: 4

	Individual	Group
Time management	☑	☐
Organizational skills	☑	☐
Learning strategies	☑	☐
Study skills	☑	☐
Content area	☐	☐
Writing lab	☐	☑
Math lab	☐	☑

UNIQUE LD PROGRAM FEATURES

LD students are not required to self-identify during the admissions process. Tutoring (which is available to all students, not just LD students) sometimes involves an extra cost. The hourly rate for peer tutoring runs from $7 to $10, while professional-tutoring charges average $25-$30.

LD PROGRAM STAFF

Total number of LD Program staff (including director):

Full Time: 1 Part Time: 1

There is an advisor/advocate from the LD program available to students. The advisor/advocate meets with students 3 times per month.

Key staff person available to work with LD students: Erin F. Salva, Coordinator of Disability Services.

Lake Erie College

Painesville, OH

Address: 391 W. Washington Street, Painesville, OH, 44077
Admissions telephone: 800 916-0904
Admissions FAX: 440 375-7005
Dean of Admissions and Financial Aid: Jennifer Calhoun
Admissions e-mail: admissions@lec.edu
Web site: http://www.lec.edu
SAT Code: 1391 ACT Code: 3288

LD program name: Learning Center
Learning Center Director: Linda Casalina
LD program telephone: 440 375-7131
LD program e-mail: lcasalina@lec.edu
LD program enrollment: 64, Total campus enrollment: 760

GENERAL

Lake Erie College is a private, coed, four-year institution. 57-acre campus in Painesville (population: 17,503), 28 miles from Cleveland. Major airport, bus, and train serve Cleveland. School operates transportation to equestrian center. Public transportation serves campus. Semester system.

LD ADMISSIONS

Students do not complete a separate application and are simultaneously accepted to the LD program. A member of the LD program does sit on the admissions committee. High school waivers are accepted for math and foreign language. A personal interview is recommended. Essay is not required. Admissions requirements that may be waived for LD students include: ASSET test if ACT/SAT scores are considered low. MFE recommended.

For fall 2004, 18 completed self-identified LD applications were received. 18 applications were offered admission, and 18 enrolled.

SECONDARY SCHOOL REQUIREMENTS

Graduation from secondary school required; GED accepted.

TESTING

SAT Reasoning or ACT required. SAT Subject recommended.

All enrolled freshmen (fall 2004):

Average SAT I Scores:	Verbal: 519	Math: 509
Average ACT Scores:	Composite: 21	

Child Study Team report is not required. A neuropsychological or comprehensive psycho-educational evaluation is required for admission. Must be dated within 36 months of application. Tests required as part of this documentation:

- ■ WAIS-IV
- ■ WISC-IV
- ■ SATA
- ■ Woodcock-Johnson
- ■ Nelson-Denny Reading Test
- ☐ Other

UNDERGRADUATE STUDENT BODY

Total undergraduate student enrollment: 760.

Composition of student body (fall 2004):

	Undergraduate	Freshmen
International	1.4	0.8
Black	8.6	7.8
American Indian	0.0	0.0
Asian-American	1.4	0.3
Hispanic	2.9	1.7
White	81.4	84.0
Unreported	4.3	5.4
	100.0%	100.0%

15% are from out of state. 4% join a sorority. Average age of full-time undergraduates is 22. 84% of classes have fewer than 20 students, 16% have between 20 and 50 students.

STUDENT HOUSING

79% of freshmen live in college housing. Freshmen are required to live on campus. Housing is guaranteed for all undergraduates. Campus can house 290 undergraduates. Single rooms are available for students with medical or special needs. A medical note is required.

EXPENSES

Tuition (2005-06): $20,500 per year.
Room: $3,310. Board: $3,024.
There is no additional cost for LD program/services.

LD SERVICES

LD program size is not limited.

LD services available to:

■ Freshmen ■ Sophomores ■ Juniors ■ Seniors

Academic Accommodations

Curriculum		In class	
Foreign language waiver	☐	Early syllabus	■
Lighter course load	■	Note takers in class	■
Math waiver	☐	Priority seating	☐
Other special classes	■	Tape recorders	■
Priority registrations	☐	Videotaped classes	☐
Substitution of courses	☐	Text on tape	■
Exams		**Services**	
Extended time	■	Diagnostic tests	☐
Oral exams	■	Learning centers	■
Take home exams	☐	Proofreaders	■
Exams on tape or computer	■	Readers	■
Untimed exams	■	Reading Machines/Kurzweil	■
Other accommodations	☐	Special bookstore section	☐
		Typists	■

Credit toward degree is not given for remedial courses taken.

Counseling Services

■ Academic	Meets 2 times per academic year
☐ Psychological	
■ Student Support groups	Meets 2 times per academic year
☐ Vocational	

Tutoring

Individual tutoring is available weekly.

Average size of tutoring groups: 1

	Individual	Group
Time management	■	■
Organizational skills	■	■
Learning strategies	■	■
Study skills	■	■
Content area	■	■
Writing lab	■	■
Math lab	■	☐

LD PROGRAM STAFF

Total number of LD Program staff (including director):

Full Time: 1 Part Time: 1

There is an advisor/advocate from the LD program available to students. The advisor/advocate meets with faculty 1 time per month and students 1 time per month. 4 graduate students and 11 peer tutors are available to work with LD students.

Key staff person available to work with LD students: Linda Casalina, Learning Center Director.

Lourdes College

Sylvania, OH

Address: 6832 Convent Boulevard, Sylvania, OH, 43560-2898
Admissions telephone: 800 878-3210, extension 1299
Admissions FAX: 419 882-3987
Director of Admissions: Amy Mergen
Admissions e-mail: lcadmits@lourdes.edu
Web site: http://www.lourdes.edu
SAT Code: 1427 ACT Code: 3598

LD program name: Lourdes College Disability Services
Assistant Director, Disability Services: Christine Miller
LD program telephone: 419 824-3523
LD program e-mail: mcmiller@lourdes.edu
LD program enrollment: 19, Total campus enrollment: 1,390

GENERAL

Lourdes College is a private, coed, four-year institution. 89-acre, suburban campus in Sylvania (population: 18,670), one mile from Toledo; branch campus in Sandusky. Airport, bus, and train serve Toledo. Public transportation serves campus. Semester system.

LD ADMISSIONS

Students do not complete a separate application and are simultaneously accepted to the LD program. A member of the LD program does not sit on the admissions committee. A personal interview is required. Essay is not required.

For fall 2004, 8 completed self-identified LD applications were received. 8 applications were offered admission, and 6 enrolled.

SECONDARY SCHOOL REQUIREMENTS

Graduation from secondary school required; GED accepted. The following course distribution required: 4 units of English, 3 units of math.

TESTING

All enrolled freshmen (fall 2004):

Average SAT I Scores:	Verbal: 470	Math: 495
Average ACT Scores:	Composite: 20	

Child Study Team report is not required. A neuropsychological or comprehensive psycho-educational evaluation is required for admission. Must be dated within 48 months of application. Tests required as part of this documentation:

- ■ WAIS-IV
- ☐ WISC-IV
- ■ SATA
- ■ Woodcock-Johnson
- ■ Nelson-Denny Reading Test
- ■ Other

UNDERGRADUATE STUDENT BODY

Total undergraduate student enrollment: 231 Men, 988 Women.

Composition of student body (fall 2004):

	Undergraduate	Freshmen
International	0.0	0.0
Black	12.5	15.3
American Indian	0.0	0.9
Asian-American	0.0	0.3
Hispanic	1.0	2.3
White	76.9	70.4
Unreported	9.6	10.8
	100.0%	100.0%

7% are from out of state. Average age of full-time undergraduates is 27. 72% of classes have fewer than 20 students, 28% have between 20 and 50 students.

EXPENSES

Tuition (2005-06): $11,070 per year.
There is no additional cost for LD program/services.

LD SERVICES

LD program size is not limited.

LD services available to:

■ Freshmen ■ Sophomores ■ Juniors ■ Seniors

Academic Accommodations

Curriculum		**In class**	
Foreign language waiver	☐	Early syllabus	☐
Lighter course load	■	Note takers in class	■
Math waiver	☐	Priority seating	■
Other special classes	☐	Tape recorders	■
Priority registrations	☐	Videotaped classes	☐
Substitution of courses	☐	Text on tape	■
Exams		**Services**	
Extended time	■	Diagnostic tests	☐
Oral exams	■	Learning centers	■
Take home exams	☐	Proofreaders	■
Exams on tape or computer	■	Readers	■
Untimed exams	■	Reading Machines/Kurzweil	☐
Other accommodations	■	Special bookstore section	☐
		Typists	☐

Credit toward degree is not given for remedial courses taken.

Counseling Services

- ■ Academic
- ■ Psychological
- ☐ Student Support groups
- ☐ Vocational

Tutoring

Individual tutoring is available weekly.

Average size of tutoring groups: 2

	Individual	Group
Time management	☐	■
Organizational skills	☐	■
Learning strategies	☐	■
Study skills	☐	■
Content area	☐	■
Writing lab	■	☐
Math lab	■	☐

LD PROGRAM STAFF

There is an advisor/advocate from the LD program available to students. 22 peer tutors are available to work with LD students.

Key staff person available to work with LD students: Kim Grieve, Director, Disability Services.

LD Program web site: www.lourdes.edu/disability_services.htm

Malone College

Canton, OH

Address: 515 25th Street NW, Canton, OH, 44709
Admissions telephone: 800 521-1146
Admissions FAX: 330 471-8149
Vice President for Enrollment Management: John A. Chopka
Admissions e-mail: admissions@malone.edu
Web site: http://www.malone.edu
SAT Code: 1439 ACT Code: 3289

Director of Student Retention and Disability Support Services.: Patty Little
LD program telephone: 330 471-8359
LD program e-mail: plittle@malone.edu
LD program enrollment: 18, Total campus enrollment: 1,936

GENERAL

Malone College is a private, coed, four-year institution. 78-acre campus in Canton (population: 80,806), 20 miles south of Akron. Served by bus; major airports serve Akron and Cleveland (56 miles). Public transportation serves campus. Semester system.

LD ADMISSIONS

Students do not complete a separate application and are simultaneously accepted to the LD program. A member of the LD program does not sit on the admissions committee. A personal interview is recommended. Essay is required and may be typed.

For fall 2004, 25 completed self-identified LD applications were received. 21 applications were offered admission, and 20 enrolled.

SECONDARY SCHOOL REQUIREMENTS

Graduation from secondary school required; GED accepted. The following course distribution required: 4 units of English, 3 units of math, 3 units of science, 2 units of foreign language, 2 units of social studies, 1 unit of history, 2 units of academic electives.

TESTING

ACT required; SAT Reasoning may be substituted. SAT Subject recommended.

All enrolled freshmen (fall 2004):

Average SAT I Scores: Verbal: 539 Math: 524
Average ACT Scores: Composite: 22

Child Study Team report is required if student is classified. A neuropsychological or comprehensive psycho-educational evaluation is required for admission. Must be dated within 24 months of application. Tests required as part of this documentation:

- [x] WAIS-IV
- [x] WISC-IV
- [ ] SATA
- [x] Woodcock-Johnson
- [ ] Nelson-Denny Reading Test
- [ ] Other

UNDERGRADUATE STUDENT BODY

Total undergraduate student enrollment: 760 Men, 1,140 Women.

Composition of student body (fall 2004):

	Undergraduate	Freshmen
International	1.7	0.9
Black	2.7	5.8
American Indian	0.0	0.0
Asian-American	0.7	0.5
Hispanic	0.7	0.6
White	94.2	91.7
Unreported	0.0	0.5
	100.0%	100.0%

9% are from out of state. Average age of full-time undergraduates is 23. 57% of classes have fewer than 20 students, 42% have between 20 and 50 students, 1% have more than 50 students.

STUDENT HOUSING

83% of freshmen live in college housing. Freshmen are required to live on campus. Housing is guaranteed for all undergraduates. Campus can house 961 undergraduates.

EXPENSES

Tuition (2005-06): $16,530 per year. Tuition is different for adult degree-completion programs.

Room: $3,250. Board: $3,000.

There is no additional cost for LD program/services.

LD SERVICES

LD program size is not limited.

LD services available to:

- [x] Freshmen
- [x] Sophomores
- [x] Juniors
- [x] Seniors

Academic Accommodations

Curriculum		In class	
Foreign language waiver	[ ]	Early syllabus	[ ]
Lighter course load	[ ]	Note takers in class	[x]
Math waiver	[ ]	Priority seating	[ ]
Other special classes	[ ]	Tape recorders	[x]
Priority registrations	[ ]	Videotaped classes	[ ]
Substitution of courses	[ ]	Text on tape	[x]
Exams		**Services**	
Extended time	[x]	Diagnostic tests	[ ]
Oral exams	[x]	Learning centers	[ ]
Take home exams	[ ]	Proofreaders	[ ]
Exams on tape or computer	[x]	Readers	[x]
Untimed exams	[ ]	Reading Machines/Kurzweil	[ ]
Other accommodations	[ ]	Special bookstore section	[ ]
		Typists	[x]

Credit toward degree is given for remedial courses taken.

Counseling Services

- [x] Academic
- [x] Psychological
- [ ] Student Support groups
- [x] Vocational

Tutoring

Individual tutoring is available weekly.

Average size of tutoring groups: 2

	Individual	Group
Time management	[ ]	[ ]
Organizational skills	[ ]	[ ]
Learning strategies	[ ]	[ ]
Study skills	[x]	[x]
Content area	[ ]	[ ]
Writing lab	[x]	[ ]
Math lab	[x]	[ ]

UNIQUE LD PROGRAM FEATURES

The minimum GPA accepted is 2.5 on a 4.0 scale. Counseling services offered as requested by student rather than a fixed number of times per academic year.

LD PROGRAM STAFF

There is an advisor/advocate from the LD program available to students. The advisor/advocate meets with students 1 time per month. 30 peer tutors are available to work with LD students.

Key staff person available to work with LD students: Patty Little, Director of Student Retention and Disability Support Services.

Marietta College

Marietta, OH

Address: 215 Fifth Street, Marietta, OH, 45750
Admissions telephone: 800 331-7896
Admissions FAX: 740 376-8888
Director of Admission: Ms. Marke M. Vickers
Admissions e-mail: admit@marietta.edu
Web site: http://www.marietta.edu
SAT Code: 1444 ACT Code: 3290

LD program name: Academic Resource Center
Director: Debra Higgins
LD program telephone: 740 376-4700
LD program e-mail: mbe001@marietta.edu
LD program enrollment: 55, Total campus enrollment: 1,351

GENERAL

Marietta College is a private, coed, four-year institution. 120-acre campus in Marietta (population: 14,515), 115 miles from Columbus. Served by bus; airport serves Parkersburg, WV (10 miles); major airport serves Columbus; train serves Charleston, WV (90 miles). School operates transportation to shopping malls and airport. Semester system.

LD ADMISSIONS

A member of the LD program does not sit on the admissions committee. A personal interview is recommended. Essay is required and may be typed.

SECONDARY SCHOOL REQUIREMENTS

Graduation from secondary school required; GED accepted. The following course distribution required: 4 units of English, 3 units of math, 2 units of science, 2 units of foreign language, 2 units of social studies, 3 units of academic electives.

TESTING

SAT Reasoning or ACT required. SAT Subject recommended.

All enrolled freshmen (fall 2004):

Average SAT I Scores:	Verbal: 543	Math: 537
Average ACT Scores:	Composite: 23	

Child Study Team report is not required. A neuropsychological or comprehensive psycho-educational evaluation is required for admission. Tests required as part of this documentation:

■ WAIS-IV ■ Woodcock-Johnson
■ WISC-IV ■ Nelson-Denny Reading Test
■ SATA ■ Other

UNDERGRADUATE STUDENT BODY

Total undergraduate student enrollment: 598 Men, 607 Women.

Composition of student body (fall 2004):

	Undergraduate	Freshmen
International	2.7	3.6
Black	3.4	2.7
American Indian	0.0	0.4
Asian-American	1.4	1.3
Hispanic	1.1	1.0
White	83.2	85.2
Unreported	8.2	5.8
	100.0%	100.0%

50% are from out of state. 20% join a fraternity and 30% join a sorority. Average age of full-time undergraduates is 20. 61% of classes have fewer than 20 students, 39% have between 20 and 50 students.

STUDENT HOUSING

98% of freshmen live in college housing. Freshmen are required to live on campus. Housing is guaranteed for all undergraduates. Campus can house 1,081 undergraduates. Single rooms are available for students with medical or special needs. A medical note is required.

EXPENSES

Tuition (2005-06): $22,070 per year.
Room: $3,446. Board: $3,000.
There is no additional cost for LD program/services.

LD SERVICES

LD program size is not limited.

LD services available to:

■ Freshmen ■ Sophomores ■ Juniors ■ Seniors

Academic Accommodations

Curriculum		**In class**	
Foreign language waiver	☐	Early syllabus	☐
Lighter course load	☐	Note takers in class	■
Math waiver	☐	Priority seating	☐
Other special classes	☐	Tape recorders	■
Priority registrations	☐	Videotaped classes	☐
Substitution of courses	☐	Text on tape	■
Exams		**Services**	
Extended time	■	Diagnostic tests	☐
Oral exams	■	Learning centers	■
Take home exams	☐	Proofreaders	☐
Exams on tape or computer	■	Readers	■
Untimed exams	☐	Reading Machines/Kurzweil	■
Other accommodations	■	Special bookstore section	☐
		Typists	☐

Credit toward degree is not given for remedial courses taken.

Counseling Services

■ Academic
☐ Psychological
☐ Student Support groups
☐ Vocational

Tutoring

Individual tutoring is available daily.

Average size of tutoring groups: 3

	Individual	Group
Time management	■	☐
Organizational skills	■	☐
Learning strategies	■	☐
Study skills	■	☐
Content area	■	☐
Writing lab	■	☐
Math lab	■	☐

UNIQUE LD PROGRAM FEATURES

Recent documentation, guidelines, criteria requirements available for specific disabilities.

LD PROGRAM STAFF

Total number of LD Program staff (including director):

Full Time: 1 Part Time: 1

There is an advisor/advocate from the LD program available to students.

Key staff person available to work with LD students: Mary Bea Eaton, Disability Specialist.

LD Program web site: www.marietta.edu/~arc

Miami University

Oxford, OH

Address: 501 E. High Street, Oxford, OH, 45056
Admissions telephone: 513 529-2531
Admissions FAX: 513 529-1550
Director of Admissions: Michael Mills
Admissions e-mail: admission@muohio.edu
Web site: http://www.muohio.edu
SAT Code: 1463 ACT Code: 3294

LD program name: Rinella Learning Center
Asst Dean of Students: Dr. Linda Dixon
LD program telephone: 513 529-8741
LD program e-mail: dixonlj@muohio.edu
Total campus enrollment: 15,059

GENERAL

Miami University is a public, coed, four-year institution. Campus of more than 2,000 acres in Oxford (population: 21,943), 35 miles from Cincinnati; branch campuses in Hamilton and Middletown. Served by bus; major airport serves Cincinnati; train serves Hamilton (20 miles). School operates transportation in local area. Public transportation serves campus. Semester system.

LD ADMISSIONS

Students do not complete a separate application and are not simultaneously accepted to the LD program. A member of the LD program does not sit on the admissions committee. A personal interview is not required. Essay is required and may be typed. Admissions requirements that may be waived for LD students include: no admission requirements are waived; however, some are fulfilled by course substitution depending on disability type.

SECONDARY SCHOOL REQUIREMENTS

Graduation from secondary school required; GED accepted. The following course distribution required: 4 units of English, 3 units of math, 3 units of science, 2 units of foreign language, 3 units of social studies.

TESTING

SAT Reasoning or ACT required. SAT Subject required.

All enrolled freshmen (fall 2004):

Average SAT I Scores:	Verbal: 601	Math: 619
Average ACT Scores:	Composite: 27	

Child Study Team report is not required. A neuropsychological or comprehensive psycho-educational evaluation is required for admission. Tests required as part of this documentation:

- [x] WAIS-IV
- [ ] WISC-IV
- [ ] SATA
- [x] Woodcock-Johnson
- [x] Nelson-Denny Reading Test
- [ ] Other

UNDERGRADUATE STUDENT BODY

Total undergraduate student enrollment: 6,853 Men, 8,300 Women.

Composition of student body (fall 2004):

	Undergraduate	Freshmen
International	0.0	0.4
Black	3.3	3.4
American Indian	0.5	0.5
Asian-American	3.6	3.0
Hispanic	2.3	1.7
White	83.8	86.7
Unreported	6.5	4.3
	100.0%	100.0%

27% are from out of state. 22% join a fraternity and 27% join a sorority. Average age of full-time undergraduates is 20. 37% of classes have fewer than 20 students, 54% have between 20 and 50 students, 9% have more than 50 students.

STUDENT HOUSING

99% of freshmen live in college housing. Freshmen are required to live on campus. Housing is guaranteed for all undergraduates. Campus can house 7,100 undergraduates.

EXPENSES

Tuition (2005-06): $19,877 per year (in-state), $19,897 (out-of-state).
Room: $3,860. Board: $3,750.
There is no additional cost for LD program/services.

LD SERVICES

LD program size is not limited.

LD services available to:

- [x] Freshmen
- [x] Sophomores
- [x] Juniors
- [x] Seniors

Academic Accommodations

Curriculum

- [ ] Foreign language waiver
- [x] Lighter course load
- [ ] Math waiver
- [ ] Other special classes
- [ ] Priority registrations
- [ ] Substitution of courses

Exams

- [x] Extended time
- [x] Oral exams
- [ ] Take home exams
- [ ] Exams on tape or computer
- [x] Untimed exams
- [ ] Other accommodations

In class

- [ ] Early syllabus
- [ ] Note takers in class
- [ ] Priority seating
- [x] Tape recorders
- [ ] Videotaped classes
- [ ] Text on tape

Services

- [ ] Diagnostic tests
- [x] Learning centers
- [ ] Proofreaders
- [x] Readers
- [x] Reading Machines/Kurzweil
- [ ] Special bookstore section
- [ ] Typists

Credit toward degree is not given for remedial courses taken.

Counseling Services

- [ ] Academic
- [ ] Psychological
- [ ] Student Support groups
- [ ] Vocational

Tutoring

Individual tutoring is available.

	Individual	Group
Time management	[x]	[x]
Organizational skills	[x]	[x]
Learning strategies	[x]	[x]
Study skills	[x]	[x]
Content area	[x]	[x]
Writing lab	[x]	[x]
Math lab	[x]	[x]

LD PROGRAM STAFF

Total number of LD Program staff (including director):

Full Time: 1 Part Time: 1

There is an advisor/advocate from the LD program available to students.

Key staff person available to work with LD students: Doug Green, Assistant Director, Learning Disabilities.

College of Mount St. Joseph

Cincinnati, OH

Address: 5701 Delhi Road, Cincinnati, OH, 45233
Admissions telephone: 800 654-9314
Admissions FAX: 513 244-4629
Director of Admissions: Peggy Minnich
Admissions e-mail: admission@mail.msj.edu
Web site: http://www.msj.edu
SAT Code: 1129 ACT Code: 3254

LD program name: Project EXCEL
Director, Project EXCEL: Jane Pohlman, M.Ed.
LD program telephone: 513 244-4623
LD program e-mail: jane_pohlman@mail.msj.edu
LD program enrollment: 117, Total campus enrollment: 1,858

GENERAL

College of Mount St. Joseph is a private, coed, four-year institution. 75-acre campus in Cincinnati (population: 331,285), seven miles from downtown. Served by air, bus, and train. Public transportation serves campus. Semester system.

LD ADMISSIONS

Students complete a separate application and are simultaneously accepted to the LD program. A member of the LD program does not sit on the admissions committee. A personal interview is required. Essay is not required. Students applying to EXCEL must submit scores for either the SAT or the ACT. There is no exact minimum score. There must be reasonable evidence that the student can successfully meet the College's academic requirements.

For fall 2004, 44 completed self-identified LD applications were received. 41 applications were offered admission, and 39 enrolled.

SECONDARY SCHOOL REQUIREMENTS

Graduation from secondary school required; GED accepted. The following course distribution required: 4 units of English, 2 units of math, 2 units of science, 2 units of foreign language, 1 unit of social studies, 1 unit of history.

TESTING

SAT Reasoning or ACT required. SAT Subject recommended.

All enrolled freshmen (fall 2004):

Average SAT I Scores: Verbal: 500 Math: 510
Average ACT Scores: Composite: 21

Child Study Team report is not required. A neuropsychological or comprehensive psycho-educational evaluation is required for admission. Must be dated within 48 months of application. Tests required as part of this documentation:

- ■ WAIS-IV
- ☐ WISC-IV
- ■ SATA
- ■ Woodcock-Johnson
- ■ Nelson-Denny Reading Test
- ☐ Other

UNDERGRADUATE STUDENT BODY

Total undergraduate student enrollment: 595 Men, 1,476 Women.

Composition of student body (fall 2004):

	Undergraduate	Freshmen
International	0.0	0.1
Black	9.2	9.2
American Indian	0.0	0.2
Asian-American	0.3	0.5
Hispanic	0.6	0.6
White	86.6	84.2
Unreported	3.3	5.2
	100.0%	100.0%

15% are from out of state. Average age of full-time undergraduates is 21. 60% of classes have fewer than 20 students, 40% have between 20 and 50 students.

STUDENT HOUSING

57% of freshmen live in college housing. Freshmen are required to live on campus. Housing is guaranteed for all undergraduates. Campus can house 488 undergraduates. Single rooms are available for students with medical or special needs. A medical note is not required.

EXPENSES

Tuition (2005-06): $18,400 per year.
Room: $3,000. Board: $3,070.
Additional cost for LD program/services: $1,530 per semester.

LD SERVICES

LD program size is not limited.

LD services available to:

■ Freshmen ■ Sophomores ■ Juniors ■ Seniors

Academic Accommodations

Curriculum

- Foreign language waiver ☐
- Lighter course load ■
- Math waiver ☐
- Other special classes ☐
- Priority registrations ☐
- Substitution of courses ☐

Exams

- Extended time ■
- Oral exams ☐
- Take home exams ☐
- Exams on tape or computer ☐
- Untimed exams ☐
- Other accommodations ☐

In class

- Early syllabus ☐
- Note takers in class ■
- Priority seating ☐
- Tape recorders ☐
- Videotaped classes ☐
- Text on tape ☐

Services

- Diagnostic tests ☐
- Learning centers ■
- Proofreaders ☐
- Readers ■
- Reading Machines/Kurzweil ☐
- Special bookstore section ☐
- Typists ☐

Credit toward degree is given for remedial courses taken.

Counseling Services

- ■ Academic — Meets 32 times per academic year
- ■ Psychological
- ☐ Student Support groups
- ☐ Vocational

Tutoring

Individual tutoring is available weekly.

Average size of tutoring groups: 1

	Individual	Group
Time management	■	☐
Organizational skills	■	☐
Learning strategies	■	☐
Study skills	■	☐
Content area	■	☐
Writing lab	■	☐
Math lab	■	☐

UNIQUE LD PROGRAM FEATURES

Project EXCEL is a comprehensive academic support program for students with specific learning disabilities who are enrolled in the traditional academic curriculum at the College of Mount St. Joseph. Students can be admitted to the College through Project EXCEL. Academic performance issues which exist concomitant with a diagnosed Attention Deficit Disorder (ADD/ADHD) will be considered in the review of a student's diagnostic profile.

LD PROGRAM STAFF

Total number of LD Program staff (including director):

Full Time: 5 Part Time: 5

There is an advisor/advocate from the LD program available to students.

Key staff person available to work with LD students: Jane Pohlman, M.Ed., Director, Project EXCEL.

LD Program web site: http://www.msj.edu/academics/services/excel

Mount Union College

Alliance, OH

Address: 1972 Clark Avenue, Alliance, OH, 44601
Admissions telephone: 800 334-6682
Admissions FAX: 330 823-5097
Director of Admissions: Amy Tomko (VP Enroll. Serv.)
Admissions e-mail: admissn@muc.edu
Web site: http://www.muc.edu
SAT Code: 1492 ACT Code: 3298

LD program name: Disability Support Services
Director, Disability Support Services: Karen A. Saracusa
LD program telephone: 330 823-7372
LD program e-mail: saracuka@muc.edu
LD program enrollment: 37, Total campus enrollment: 2,333

GENERAL

Mount Union College is a private, coed, four-year institution. 115-acre campus in Alliance (population: 23,253), 24 miles from Canton and 78 miles from Cleveland. Served by bus and train; major airport serves Cleveland. Public transportation serves campus. Semester system.

SECONDARY SCHOOL REQUIREMENTS

Graduation from secondary school required; GED accepted.

TESTING

ACT required; SAT Reasoning may be substituted. SAT Subject recommended.

All enrolled freshmen (fall 2004):

Average SAT I Scores:	Verbal: 518	Math: 538
Average ACT Scores:	Composite: 22	

Child Study Team report is not required. Tests required as part of this documentation:

☐ WAIS-IV ☐ Woodcock-Johnson
☐ WISC-IV ☐ Nelson-Denny Reading Test
☐ SATA ☐ Other

UNDERGRADUATE STUDENT BODY

Total undergraduate student enrollment: 996 Men, 1,372 Women.

Composition of student body (fall 2004):

	Undergraduate	Freshmen
International	0.9	1.3
Black	3.8	3.7
American Indian	0.2	0.2
Asian-American	0.4	0.3
Hispanic	1.3	0.7
White	88.8	90.9
Unreported	4.6	2.9
	100.0%	100.0%

10% are from out of state. 20% join a fraternity and 22% join a sorority. Average age of full-time undergraduates is 20. 54% of classes have fewer than 20 students, 45% have between 20 and 50 students, 1% have more than 50 students.

STUDENT HOUSING

93% of freshmen live in college housing. Freshmen are required to live on campus. Housing is guaranteed for all undergraduates. Campus can house 1,385 undergraduates. Single rooms are available for students with medical or special needs. A medical note is required.

EXPENSES

Tuition (2005-06): $19,600 per year.
Room & Board: $5,990.
There is no additional cost for LD program/services.

LD SERVICES

LD program size is not limited.

LD services available to:

☑ Freshmen ☑ Sophomores ☑ Juniors ☑ Seniors

Academic Accommodations

Curriculum		In class	
Foreign language waiver	☐	Early syllabus	☐
Lighter course load	☐	Note takers in class	☑
Math waiver	☐	Priority seating	☐
Other special classes	☐	Tape recorders	☑
Priority registrations	☐	Videotaped classes	☐
Substitution of courses	☑	Text on tape	☑
Exams		**Services**	
Extended time	☑	Diagnostic tests	☐
Oral exams	☑	Learning centers	☑
Take home exams	☐	Proofreaders	☐
Exams on tape or computer	☑	Readers	☑
Untimed exams	☐	Reading Machines/Kurzweil	☑
Other accommodations	☑	Special bookstore section	☐
		Typists	☐

Credit toward degree is not given for remedial courses taken.

Counseling Services

☐ Academic
☐ Psychological
☐ Student Support groups
☐ Vocational

Tutoring

Individual tutoring is available daily.

Average size of tutoring groups: 5

	Individual	Group
Time management	☑	☐
Organizational skills	☑	☐
Learning strategies	☑	☐
Study skills	☑	☐
Content area	☑	☑
Writing lab	☑	☑
Math lab	☑	☑

LD PROGRAM STAFF

Total number of LD Program staff (including director):

Full Time: 1 Part Time: 1

There is an advisor/advocate from the LD program available to students. The advisor/advocate meets with faculty 20 times per month and student 2 times per month.

Key staff person available to work with LD students: Karen A. Saracusa, Director, Disability Support Services.

Mount Vernon Nazarene University

Mount Vernon, OH

Address: 800 Martinsburg Road, Mount Vernon, OH, 43050
Admissions telephone: 866 462-6868
Admissions FAX: 740 393-0511
Director of Admissions: Tim Eades
Admissions e-mail: admissions@mvnu.edu
Web site: http://www.mvnu.edu
SAT Code: 1531 ACT Code: 3372

LD program name: Disability Services
Director of Academic Support: Dr. Carol Matthews
LD program telephone: 740 392-6868, extension 4536
LD program e-mail: carol.matthews@mvnu.edu
LD program enrollment: 52, Total campus enrollment: 2,166

GENERAL

Mount Vernon Nazarene University is a private, coed, four-year institution. 401-acre campus in Mount Vernon (population: 14,375), 45 miles from Columbus; branch campuses in Columbus, Lima, and Newark. Served by air; major airport, bus, and train serve Columbus. Public transportation serves campus. 4-1-4 system.

LD ADMISSIONS

Students do not complete a separate application and are not simultaneously accepted to the LD program. A member of the LD program does sit on the admissions committee. A personal interview is not required. Essay is required and may be typed.

SECONDARY SCHOOL REQUIREMENTS

Graduation from secondary school required; GED accepted. The following course distribution required: 4 units of English, 3 units of math, 2 units of science, 3 units of social studies, 8 units of academic electives.

TESTING

SAT Reasoning or ACT required.

All enrolled freshmen (fall 2004):

Average SAT I Scores:	Verbal: 527	Math: 514
Average ACT Scores:	Composite: 23	

Child Study Team report is not required. A neuropsychological or comprehensive psycho-educational evaluation is required for admission. Tests required as part of this documentation:

- [x] WAIS-IV
- [x] WISC-IV
- [ ] SATA
- [x] Woodcock-Johnson
- [ ] Nelson-Denny Reading Test
- [ ] Other

UNDERGRADUATE STUDENT BODY

Total undergraduate student enrollment: 925 Men, 1,181 Women.

Composition of student body (fall 2004):

	Undergraduate	Freshmen
International	1.3	0.4
Black	0.0	3.3
American Indian	0.3	0.2
Asian-American	0.7	0.6
Hispanic	1.3	0.7
White	96.4	93.0
Unreported	0.0	1.8
	100.0%	100.0%

12% are from out of state. Average age of full-time undergraduates is 26. 58% of classes have fewer than 20 students, 37% have between 20 and 50 students, 5% have more than 50 students.

STUDENT HOUSING

93% of freshmen live in college housing. Freshmen are required to live on campus. Housing is guaranteed for all undergraduates. Campus can house 1,070 undergraduates. Single rooms are available for students with medical or special needs. A medical note is required.

EXPENSES

Tuition (2005-06): $15,384 per year.
Room: $2,718. Board: $2,206.
There is no additional cost for LD program/services.

LD SERVICES

LD program size is not limited.

LD services available to:

- [x] Freshmen
- [x] Sophomores
- [x] Juniors
- [x] Seniors

Academic Accommodations

Curriculum

- [ ] Foreign language waiver
- [ ] Lighter course load
- [ ] Math waiver
- [ ] Other special classes
- [ ] Priority registrations
- [ ] Substitution of courses

Exams

- [x] Extended time
- [x] Oral exams
- [ ] Take home exams
- [ ] Exams on tape or computer
- [ ] Untimed exams
- [ ] Other accommodations

In class

- [ ] Early syllabus
- [x] Note takers in class
- [ ] Priority seating
- [x] Tape recorders
- [ ] Videotaped classes
- [ ] Text on tape

Services

- [ ] Diagnostic tests
- [ ] Learning centers
- [ ] Proofreaders
- [ ] Readers
- [ ] Reading Machines/Kurzweil
- [ ] Special bookstore section
- [ ] Typists

Counseling Services

- [ ] Academic
- [ ] Psychological
- [ ] Student Support groups
- [ ] Vocational

Tutoring

Individual tutoring is not available.

	Individual	Group
Time management	[ ]	[ ]
Organizational skills	[ ]	[ ]
Learning strategies	[ ]	[ ]
Study skills	[ ]	[ ]
Content area	[ ]	[ ]
Writing lab	[ ]	[ ]
Math lab	[ ]	[ ]

LD PROGRAM STAFF

There is an advisor/advocate from the LD program available to students.

Key staff person available to work with LD students: Dr. Carol Matthews, Director of Academic Support.

Muskingum College

New Concord, OH

Address: 163 Stormont Street, New Concord, OH, 43762
Admissions telephone: 800 752-6082
Admissions FAX: 740 826-8100
Director of Admission: Beth DaLonzo
Admissions e-mail: adminfo@muskingum.edu
Web site: http://www.muskingum.edu
SAT Code: 1496 ACT Code: 3300

LD program name: PLUS Program
Director of Admission: Beth DaLonzo
LD program telephone: 740 826-8137
LD program e-mail: bdalonzo@muskingum.edu
LD program enrollment: 168, Total campus enrollment: 1,663

GENERAL

Muskingum College is a private, coed, four-year institution. 215-acre campus in New Concord (population: 2,651), 70 miles east of Columbus and 125 miles south of Cleveland. Major airport serves Columbus; bus serves Cambridge (nine miles); train serves Canton (88 miles). Semester system.

LD ADMISSIONS

Application Deadline: 08/01. Students complete a separate application and are simultaneously accepted to the LD program. A member of the LD program does sit on the admissions committee. High school waivers are accepted for math and foreign language. A personal interview is required. Essay is not required.

For fall 2004, 237 completed self-identified LD applications were received. 130 applications were offered admission, and 69 enrolled.

SECONDARY SCHOOL REQUIREMENTS

Graduation from secondary school required; GED accepted. The following course distribution required: 4 units of English, 2 units of math, 2 units of science, 2 units of foreign language, 1 unit of social studies, 2 units of history.

TESTING

SAT Reasoning or ACT required. SAT Subject recommended.

All enrolled freshmen (fall 2004):

Average SAT I Scores:	Verbal: 517	Math: 524
Average ACT Scores:	Composite: 22	

Child Study Team report is not required. A neuropsychological or comprehensive psycho-educational evaluation is required for admission. Must be dated within 36 months of application. Tests required as part of this documentation:

■ WAIS-IV ■ Woodcock-Johnson
■ WISC-IV ☐ Nelson-Denny Reading Test
☐ SATA ☐ Other

UNDERGRADUATE STUDENT BODY

Total undergraduate student enrollment: 788 Men, 856 Women.

Composition of student body (fall 2004):

	Undergraduate	Freshmen
International	2.2	2.2
Black	4.7	3.5
American Indian	0.2	0.2
Asian-American	0.6	0.7
Hispanic	0.6	0.6
White	91.7	91.5
Unreported	0.0	1.3
	100.0%	100.0%

13% are from out of state. 20% join a fraternity and 25% join a sorority. Average age of full-time undergraduates is 20. 61% of classes have fewer than 20 students, 39% have between 20 and 50 students.

STUDENT HOUSING

93% of freshmen live in college housing. Freshmen are required to live on campus. Housing is not guaranteed for all undergraduates. Housing typically available for unmarried undergraduate students with following exception: students 25 years of age or older cannot live in college housing without approval of dean of students. Campus can house 1,200 undergraduates. Single rooms are not available for students with medical or special needs.

EXPENSES

Tuition (2005-06): $15,700 per year.
Room: $3,260. Board: $3,260.
Additional cost for LD program/services: $5,300.

LD SERVICES

LD program size is not limited.

LD services available to:

■ Freshmen ■ Sophomores ■ Juniors ■ Seniors

Academic Accommodations

Curriculum		In class	
Foreign language waiver	☐	Early syllabus	☐
Lighter course load	■	Note takers in class	■
Math waiver	☐	Priority seating	☐
Other special classes	☐	Tape recorders	■
Priority registrations	☐	Videotaped classes	☐
Substitution of courses	☐	Text on tape	■
Exams		**Services**	
Extended time	■	Diagnostic tests	☐
Oral exams	■	Learning centers	■
Take home exams	☐	Proofreaders	■
Exams on tape or computer	☐	Readers	■
Untimed exams	■	Reading Machines/Kurzweil	■
Other accommodations	☐	Special bookstore section	■
		Typists	■

Credit toward degree is not given for remedial courses taken.

Counseling Services

■ Academic — Meets many times per academic year
■ Psychological
☐ Student Support groups
☐ Vocational

Tutoring

Individual tutoring is available daily.

Average size of tutoring groups: 1

	Individual	Group
Time management	■	■
Organizational skills	■	■
Learning strategies	■	■
Study skills	■	■
Content area	■	☐
Writing lab	☐	☐
Math lab	☐	☐

UNIQUE LD PROGRAM FEATURES

Degree requirements for LD students are the same as those for all students.

LD PROGRAM STAFF

Total number of LD Program staff (including director):

Full Time: 20 Part Time: 20

There is an advisor/advocate from the LD program available to students.

Key staff person available to work with LD students: Eileen Henry, Director, Center for the Advancement of Learning.

LD Program web site: http://www.muskingum.edu/home/cal/plus.html

Notre Dame College of Ohio

Cleveland, OH

Address: 4545 College Road, Cleveland, OH, 44121
Admissions telephone: 800 NDC-1680, extension 355
Admissions FAX: 216 373-5278
Director of Admissions: David Armstrong, Esq.
Admissions e-mail: admissions@ndc.edu
Web site: http://www.notredamecollege.edu
SAT Code: 1566 ACT Code: 3302

Dean of Student Development: Patricia O'Toole
LD program telephone: 216 373-5335
LD program e-mail: potoole@ndc.edu
Total campus enrollment: 999

GENERAL

Notre Dame College of Ohio is a private, coed, four-year institution. 53-acre campus in South Euclid (population: 23,537), 15 miles from Cleveland. Served by air, bus, and train. Public transportation serves campus. Semester system.

LD ADMISSIONS

A personal interview is not required. Essay is not required.

SECONDARY SCHOOL REQUIREMENTS

Graduation from secondary school required; GED accepted. The following course distribution required: 4 units of English, 3 units of math, 3 units of science, 2 units of foreign language, 3 units of social studies.

TESTING

SAT Reasoning required; ACT may be substituted. SAT Subject recommended.

All enrolled freshmen (fall 2004):

Average SAT I Scores:	Verbal: 482	Math: 469
Average ACT Scores:	Composite: 19	

Child Study Team report is not required. Tests required as part of this documentation:

- [ ] WAIS-IV
- [ ] WISC-IV
- [ ] SATA
- [ ] Woodcock-Johnson
- [ ] Nelson-Denny Reading Test
- [ ] Other

UNDERGRADUATE STUDENT BODY

Total undergraduate student enrollment: 706 Women.

Composition of student body (fall 2004):

	Undergraduate	Freshmen
International	7.5	6.3
Black	21.8	24.7
American Indian	0.0	0.0
Asian-American	1.7	0.9
Hispanic	2.3	1.7
White	62.7	61.0
Unreported	4.0	5.4
	100.0%	100.0%

6% are from out of state. Average age of full-time undergraduates is 21. 61% of classes have fewer than 20 students, 39% have between 20 and 50 students.

STUDENT HOUSING

Freshmen are required to live on campus. Housing is not guaranteed for all undergraduates. Housing is limited to traditional-aged students. Campus can house 336 undergraduates. Single rooms are available for students with medical or special needs. A medical note is required.

EXPENSES

Tuition (2005-06): $18,670 per year.
Room: $3,300. Board: $3,378
There is no additional cost for LD program/services.

LD SERVICES

LD program size is not limited.

LD services available to:

- [ ] Freshmen
- [ ] Sophomores
- [ ] Juniors
- [ ] Seniors

Academic Accommodations

Curriculum		In class	
Foreign language waiver	[ ]	Early syllabus	[ ]
Lighter course load	[ ]	Note takers in class	[ ]
Math waiver	[ ]	Priority seating	[ ]
Other special classes	[ ]	Tape recorders	[x]
Priority registrations	[ ]	Videotaped classes	[ ]
Substitution of courses	[ ]	Text on tape	[ ]
Exams		**Services**	
Extended time	[x]	Diagnostic tests	[ ]
Oral exams	[x]	Learning centers	[x]
Take home exams	[ ]	Proofreaders	[ ]
Exams on tape or computer	[ ]	Readers	[ ]
Untimed exams	[ ]	Reading Machines/Kurzweil	[ ]
Other accommodations	[ ]	Special bookstore section	[ ]
		Typists	[ ]

Credit toward degree is not given for remedial courses taken.

Counseling Services

- [ ] Academic
- [ ] Psychological
- [ ] Student Support groups
- [ ] Vocational

Tutoring

Individual tutoring is available daily.

Average size of tutoring groups: 1

	Individual	Group
Time management	[ ]	[ ]
Organizational skills	[ ]	[ ]
Learning strategies	[ ]	[ ]
Study skills	[ ]	[ ]
Content area	[ ]	[ ]
Writing lab	[ ]	[ ]
Math lab	[ ]	[ ]

LD PROGRAM STAFF

Key staff person available to work with LD students: Jeanne Christian, Director of the Learning Center.

Oberlin College

Oberlin, OH

Address: 173 W. Lorain Street, Oberlin, OH, 44074
Admissions telephone: 800 622-6243
Admissions FAX: 440 775-6905
Dean of Admissions: Debra Chermonte
Admissions e-mail: college.admissions@oberlin.edu
Web site: http://www.oberlin.edu
SAT Code: 1587 ACT Code: 3304

LD program name: Student Academic Services
LD program address: Peters Hall 118,
50 North Professor Street, Oberlin, OH, 44074-1091
Coordinator: Jane Boomer
LD program telephone: 440 775-8467
LD program e-mail: jane.boomer@oberlin.edu
LD program enrollment: 311, Total campus enrollment: 2,807

GENERAL

Oberlin College is a private, coed, four-year institution. 440-acre campus in Oberlin (population: 8,195), 34 miles from Cleveland. Served by air; major airport serves Cleveland; bus and train serve Elyria (10 miles). School operates transportation to Cleveland every third Saturday. Public transportation serves campus. 4-1-4 system.

LD ADMISSIONS

A personal interview is recommended. Essay is required and may be typed. Admissions for LD students is the same as for all other students.

SECONDARY SCHOOL REQUIREMENTS

Graduation from secondary school required; GED accepted. The following course distribution required: 4 units of English, 4 units of math, 3 units of science, 3 units of foreign language, 3 units of social studies.

TESTING

SAT Reasoning or ACT required. SAT Subject required.

All enrolled freshmen (fall 2004):

Average SAT I Scores:	Verbal: 680	Math: 657
Average ACT Scores:	Composite: 28	

Child Study Team report is not required. Tests required as part of this documentation:

- [ ] WAIS-IV
- [ ] WISC-IV
- [ ] SATA
- [ ] Woodcock-Johnson
- [ ] Nelson-Denny Reading Test
- [ ] Other

UNDERGRADUATE STUDENT BODY

Total undergraduate student enrollment: 1,212 Men, 1,628 Women.

Composition of student body (fall 2004):

	Undergraduate	Freshmen
International	4.2	6.3
Black	5.0	6.1
American Indian	1.1	0.9
Asian-American	9.3	7.6
Hispanic	4.7	4.9
White	75.7	74.1
Unreported	0.0	0.1
	100.0%	100.0%

89% are from out of state. Average age of full-time undergraduates is 20. 69% of classes have fewer than 20 students, 28% have between 20 and 50 students, 3% have more than 50 students.

STUDENT HOUSING

100% of freshmen live in college housing. Freshmen are required to live on campus. Housing is guaranteed for all undergraduates. Campus can house 2,324 undergraduates. Single rooms are available for students with medical or special needs. A medical note is required.

EXPENSES

Tuition (2005-06): $32,524 per year.
Room: $4,300. Board: $3,880.

There is no additional cost for LD program/services.

LD SERVICES

LD program size is not limited.

LD services available to:

- [x] Freshmen
- [x] Sophomores
- [x] Juniors
- [x] Seniors

Academic Accommodations

Curriculum
- [ ] Foreign language waiver
- [x] Lighter course load
- [ ] Math waiver
- [ ] Other special classes
- [x] Priority registrations
- [ ] Substitution of courses

Exams
- [x] Extended time
- [x] Oral exams
- [ ] Take home exams
- [x] Exams on tape or computer
- [x] Untimed exams
- [x] Other accommodations

In class
- [ ] Early syllabus
- [x] Note takers in class
- [ ] Priority seating
- [x] Tape recorders
- [x] Videotaped classes
- [x] Text on tape

Services
- [ ] Diagnostic tests
- [ ] Learning centers
- [ ] Proofreaders
- [x] Readers
- [x] Reading Machines/Kurzweil
- [ ] Special bookstore section
- [x] Typists

Credit toward degree is not given for remedial courses taken.

Counseling Services

- [x] Academic
- [x] Psychological
- [x] Student Support groups
- [x] Vocational

Tutoring

Individual tutoring is available weekly.

Average size of tutoring groups: 1

	Individual	Group
Time management	[x]	[ ]
Organizational skills	[x]	[ ]
Learning strategies	[x]	[ ]
Study skills	[x]	[ ]
Content area	[x]	[ ]
Writing lab	[x]	[ ]
Math lab	[ ]	[x]

LD PROGRAM STAFF

Total number of LD Program staff (including director):

Full Time: 2 Part Time: 2

There is an advisor/advocate from the LD program available to students. The advisor/advocate meets with faculty 4 times per month. 50 peer tutors are available to work with LD students.

Key staff person available to work with LD students: Jane Boomer, Coordinator of Services for Students w/Disabilities.

LD Program web site: www.oberlin.edu/learning

Ohio Dominican University

Columbus, OH

Address: 1216 Sunbury Road, Columbus, OH, 43219
Admissions telephone: 800 955-OHIO
Admissions FAX: 614 251-0156
Vice President for Enrollment Management and Marketing: Kevin Brown
Admissions e-mail: admissions@ohiodominican.edu
Web site: http://www.ohiodominican.edu
SAT Code: 1131 ACT Code: 3256

Director of Student Resources: David B. Erwin
LD program telephone: 614 251-4593
LD program e-mail: erwind@ohiodominican.edu
Total campus enrollment: 2,545

GENERAL

Ohio Dominican University is a private, coed, four-year institution. 62-acre, urban campus in Columbus (population: 711,470), four miles from downtown area. Served by air, bus, and train. Semester system.

SECONDARY SCHOOL REQUIREMENTS

Graduation from secondary school required; GED accepted. The following course distribution required: 4 units of English, 3 units of math, 3 units of science, 3 units of foreign language, 3 units of social studies.

TESTING

SAT Subject recommended.

All enrolled freshmen (fall 2004):

Average SAT I Scores: Verbal: Math:
Average ACT Scores: Composite: 22

Child Study Team report is not required. Tests required as part of this documentation:

- ❑ WAIS-IV
- ❑ WISC-IV
- ❑ SATA
- ❑ Woodcock-Johnson
- ❑ Nelson-Denny Reading Test
- ❑ Other

UNDERGRADUATE STUDENT BODY

Total undergraduate student enrollment: 687 Men, 1,510 Women.

Composition of student body (fall 2004):

	Undergraduate	Freshmen
International	0.5	0.7
Black	13.5	24.1
American Indian	0.0	0.3
Asian-American	1.2	1.1
Hispanic	0.7	1.2
White	84.1	72.3
Unreported	0.0	0.3
	100.0%	100.0%

1% are from out of state. Average age of full-time undergraduates is 24. 48% of classes have fewer than 20 students, 52% have between 20 and 50 students.

STUDENT HOUSING

77% of freshmen live in college housing. Housing is not guaranteed for all undergraduates. Campus can house 800 undergraduates.

EXPENSES

Tuition (2005-06): $19,500 per year (in-state).

Room & Board: $6,500.
There is no additional cost for LD program/services.

LD SERVICES

LD services available to:

❑ Freshmen ❑ Sophomores ❑ Juniors ❑ Seniors

Academic Accommodations

Curriculum		**In class**	
Foreign language waiver	❑	Early syllabus	❑
Lighter course load	❑	Note takers in class	❑
Math waiver	❑	Priority seating	❑
Other special classes	❑	Tape recorders	❑
Priority registrations	❑	Videotaped classes	❑
Substitution of courses	❑	Text on tape	❑
Exams		**Services**	
Extended time	❑	Diagnostic tests	❑
Oral exams	❑	Learning centers	❑
Take home exams	❑	Proofreaders	❑
Exams on tape or computer	❑	Readers	❑
Untimed exams	❑	Reading Machines/Kurzweil	❑
Other accommodations	❑	Special bookstore section	❑
		Typists	❑

Counseling Services

- ❑ Academic
- ❑ Psychological
- ❑ Student Support groups
- ❑ Vocational

Tutoring

	Individual	Group
Time management	❑	❑
Organizational skills	❑	❑
Learning strategies	❑	❑
Study skills	❑	❑
Content area	❑	❑
Writing lab	❑	❑
Math lab	❑	❑

LD PROGRAM STAFF

Key staff person available to work with LD students: David B. Erwin, Director of Student Resources.

Ohio Northern University

Ada, OH

Address: 525 S. Main Street, Ada, OH, 45810
Admissions telephone: 888 408-4ONU
Admissions FAX: 419 772-2313
Vice President, Dean of Admissions and Financial Aid: Jeff Dittman
Admissions e-mail: admissions-ug@onu.edu
Web site: http://www.onu.edu
SAT Code: 1591 ACT Code: 3310

Associate Vice President: Dr. Roger Goldberg
LD program telephone: 419 772-2032
LD program e-mail: r-goldberg@onu.edu
Total campus enrollment: 2,607

GENERAL

Ohio Northern University is a private, coed, four-year institution. 260-acre campus in Ada (population: 5,582), 80 miles from Columbus. Major airport serves Columbus; bus serves Lima (15 miles); train serves Fostoria (45 miles). Quarter system.

LD ADMISSIONS

Application Deadline: 08/15. A personal interview is recommended. Essay is not required.

SECONDARY SCHOOL REQUIREMENTS

Graduation from secondary school required; GED accepted. The following course distribution required: 4 units of English, 2 units of math, 2 units of science, 2 units of social studies, 2 units of history, 4 units of academic electives.

TESTING

ACT required; SAT Reasoning may be substituted. SAT Subject recommended.

All enrolled freshmen (fall 2004):

Average SAT I Scores:	Verbal: 568	Math: 594
Average ACT Scores:	Composite: 26	

Child Study Team report is not required. Tests required as part of this documentation:

- ☐ WAIS-IV
- ☐ WISC-IV
- ☐ SATA
- ☐ Woodcock-Johnson
- ☐ Nelson-Denny Reading Test
- ☐ Other

UNDERGRADUATE STUDENT BODY

Total undergraduate student enrollment: 1,221 Men, 1,160 Women.

Composition of student body (fall 2004):

	Undergraduate	Freshmen
International	0.4	0.5
Black	1.2	1.1
American Indian	0.3	0.2
Asian-American	0.8	0.9
Hispanic	0.7	0.7
White	96.6	96.6
Unreported	0.0	0.0
	100.0%	100.0%

14% are from out of state. 20% join a fraternity and 21% join a sorority. Average age of full-time undergraduates is 20. 55% of classes have fewer than 20 students, 41% have between 20 and 50 students, 4% have more than 50 students.

STUDENT HOUSING

97% of freshmen live in college housing. Freshmen are required to live on campus. Housing is guaranteed for all undergraduates. Campus can house 1,910 undergraduates. Single rooms are available for students with medical or special needs. A medical note is required.

EXPENSES

Tuition (2005-06): $26,835 per year. $23,310 per year (arts and sciences and business programs), $24,900 (engineering programs), $26,199 (pharmacy programs).
Room: $3,360. Board: $3,360.
There is no additional cost for LD program/services.

LD SERVICES

LD program size is not limited.

LD services available to:

■ Freshmen ■ Sophomores ■ Juniors ■ Seniors

Academic Accommodations

Curriculum		In class	
Foreign language waiver	☐	Early syllabus	☐
Lighter course load	■	Note takers in class	■
Math waiver	☐	Priority seating	☐
Other special classes	■	Tape recorders	■
Priority registrations	☐	Videotaped classes	☐
Substitution of courses	☐	Text on tape	☐
Exams		**Services**	
Extended time	■	Diagnostic tests	☐
Oral exams	■	Learning centers	☐
Take home exams	☐	Proofreaders	☐
Exams on tape or computer	☐	Readers	■
Untimed exams	■	Reading Machines/Kurzweil	☐
Other accommodations	☐	Special bookstore section	☐
		Typists	☐

Credit toward degree is not given for remedial courses taken.

Counseling Services

- ■ Academic
- ■ Psychological
- ☐ Student Support groups
- ☐ Vocational

Tutoring

Individual tutoring is available daily.

	Individual	Group
Time management	■	■
Organizational skills	■	■
Learning strategies	■	☐
Study skills	■	■
Content area	☐	☐
Writing lab	■	☐
Math lab	☐	☐

Ohio University

Athens, OH

Address: Athens, OH, 45701
Admissions telephone: 740 593-4100
Admissions FAX: 740 593-0560
Director of Admissions: Jean Lewis, Interim Director
Admissions e-mail: admissions@ohio.edu
Web site: http://www.ohio.edu
SAT Code: 1593 ACT Code: 3314

LD program name: Katherine Fahay
Director/Disability Services: Katherine Fahey
LD program telephone: 740 593-2620
LD program e-mail: fahey@ohio.edu
Total campus enrollment: 16,950

GENERAL

Ohio University is a public, coed, four-year institution. 1,700-acre campus in Athens (population: 21,342), 75 miles from Columbus; branch campuses in Chillicothe, Ironton, Lancaster, St. Clairsville, and Zanesville. Major airport serves Columbus; other airport serves Parkersburg, WV (50 miles); train serves Huntington, WV (83 miles). Public transportation serves campus. Quarter system.

LD ADMISSIONS

Students do not complete a separate application and are not simultaneously accepted to the LD program. A member of the LD program does not sit on the admissions committee. A personal interview is not required. Essay is not required.

SECONDARY SCHOOL REQUIREMENTS

Graduation from secondary school required; GED accepted. The following course distribution required: 4 units of English, 3 units of math, 3 units of science, 2 units of foreign language, 3 units of social studies.

TESTING

ACT required; SAT Reasoning may be substituted. SAT Subject required.

All enrolled freshmen (fall 2004):

Average SAT I Scores:	Verbal: 550	Math: 550
Average ACT Scores:	Composite: 23	

Child Study Team report is required if student is classified. A neuropsychological or comprehensive psycho-educational evaluation is required for admission. Tests required as part of this documentation:

- ■ WAIS-IV
- ☐ WISC-IV
- ☐ SATA
- ■ Woodcock-Johnson
- ☐ Nelson-Denny Reading Test
- ☐ Other

UNDERGRADUATE STUDENT BODY

Total undergraduate student enrollment: 7,755 Men, 9,423 Women.

Composition of student body (fall 2004):

	Undergraduate	Freshmen
International	0.4	1.5
Black	3.4	3.1
American Indian	0.2	0.2
Asian-American	0.9	0.8
Hispanic	1.5	1.2
White	93.6	93.2
Unreported	0.0	0.0
	100.0%	100.0%

10% are from out of state. 12% join a fraternity and 13% join a sorority. Average age of full-time undergraduates is 21. 45% of classes have fewer than 20 students, 45% have between 20 and 50 students, 10% have more than 50 students.

STUDENT HOUSING

96% of freshmen live in college housing. Freshmen are required to live on campus. Housing is guaranteed for all undergraduates. Campus can house 7,649 undergraduates. Single rooms are available for students with medical or special needs. A medical note is required.

EXPENSES

Tuition (2005-06): $6,687 per year (in-state), $15,651 (out-of-state). Room: $3,855. Board: $3,831.
There is no additional cost for LD program/services.

LD SERVICES

LD program size is not limited.

LD services available to:

■ Freshmen ■ Sophomores ■ Juniors ■ Seniors

Academic Accommodations

Curriculum		**In class**	
Foreign language waiver	☐	Early syllabus	☐
Lighter course load	☐	Note takers in class	☐
Math waiver	☐	Priority seating	☐
Other special classes	☐	Tape recorders	☐
Priority registrations	■	Videotaped classes	☐
Substitution of courses	☐	Text on tape	☐
Exams		**Services**	
Extended time	■	Diagnostic tests	☐
Oral exams	☐	Learning centers	☐
Take home exams	☐	Proofreaders	☐
Exams on tape or computer	☐	Readers	☐
Untimed exams	☐	Reading Machines/Kurzweil	■
Other accommodations	☐	Special bookstore section	☐
		Typists	☐

Credit toward degree is not given for remedial courses taken.

Counseling Services

- ☐ Academic
- ■ Psychological — Meets 13 times per academic year
- ☐ Student Support groups
- ☐ Vocational

Tutoring

Individual tutoring is available weekly.

	Individual	Group
Time management	☐	☐
Organizational skills	☐	☐
Learning strategies	☐	■
Study skills	☐	☐
Content area	☐	☐
Writing lab	■	☐
Math lab	☐	■

LD PROGRAM STAFF

Total number of LD Program staff (including director):

Full Time: 1 Part Time: 1

There is an advisor/advocate from the LD program available to students.

Key staff person available to work with LD students: Katherine Fahey, Director Disability Services.

Ohio Wesleyan University

Delaware, OH

Address: 61 S. Sandusky Street, Delaware, OH, 43015
Admissions telephone: 800 922-8953
Admissions FAX: 740 368-3314
Vice President of Admission and Financial Aid: Carol Wheatley
Admissions e-mail: owuadmit@owu.edu
Web site: http://web.owu.edu
SAT Code: 1594 ACT Code: 3316

LD program name: Office of Learning Disability Service
Associate Dean of Academic Affairs: Blake Michael
LD program telephone: 740 368-3275
LD program e-mail: acadvocp@owu.edu
LD program enrollment: 254, Total campus enrollment: 1,944

GENERAL

Ohio Wesleyan University is a private, coed, four-year institution. 200-acre campus in Delaware (population: 25,243), 20 miles from Columbus. Served by bus; major airport serves Columbus. School operates transportation to Columbus. Public transportation serves campus. Semester system.

LD ADMISSIONS

A personal interview is recommended. Essay is required and may be typed. Admissions requirements that may be waived for LD students varies. Consideration is done on a case-by-case basis.

SECONDARY SCHOOL REQUIREMENTS

Graduation from secondary school required; GED accepted. The following course distribution required: 4 units of English, 3 units of math, 3 units of science, 3 units of foreign language, 3 units of social studies.

TESTING

SAT Reasoning or ACT required. SAT Subject recommended.

All enrolled freshmen (fall 2004):

Average SAT I Scores:	Verbal: 606	Math: 604
Average ACT Scores:	Composite: 27	

Child Study Team report is not required. Tests required as part of this documentation:

- ☐ WAIS-IV
- ☐ WISC-IV
- ☐ SATA
- ☐ Woodcock-Johnson
- ☐ Nelson-Denny Reading Test
- ☐ Other

UNDERGRADUATE STUDENT BODY

Total undergraduate student enrollment: 904 Men, 982 Women.

Composition of student body (fall 2004):

	Undergraduate	Freshmen
International	7.3	9.5
Black	4.1	4.2
American Indian	0.0	0.1
Asian-American	1.4	1.6
Hispanic	2.0	1.5
White	83.4	81.6
Unreported	1.8	1.5
	100.0%	100.0%

47% are from out of state. 40% join a fraternity and 28% join a sorority. Average age of full-time undergraduates is 20. 58% of classes have fewer than 20 students, 42% have between 20 and 50 students.

STUDENT HOUSING

97% of freshmen live in college housing. Freshmen are required to live on campus. Housing is guaranteed for all undergraduates. Campus can house 1,695 undergraduates. Single rooms are available for students with medical or special needs. A medical note is required.

EXPENSES

Tuition (2005-06): $27,920 per year.

Room: $3,750. Board: $3,800.

There is no additional cost for LD program/services.

LD SERVICES

LD program size is not limited.

LD services available to:

■ Freshmen ■ Sophomores ■ Juniors ■ Seniors

Academic Accommodations

Curriculum		In class	
Foreign language waiver	■	Early syllabus	☐
Lighter course load	■	Note takers in class	■
Math waiver	☐	Priority seating	☐
Other special classes	■	Tape recorders	■
Priority registrations	☐	Videotaped classes	☐
Substitution of courses	☐	Text on tape	☐
Exams		**Services**	
Extended time	■	Diagnostic tests	☐
Oral exams	■	Learning centers	■
Take home exams	☐	Proofreaders	☐
Exams on tape or computer	☐	Readers	☐
Untimed exams	☐	Reading Machines/Kurzweil	☐
Other accommodations	☐	Special bookstore section	☐
		Typists	☐

Credit toward degree is not given for remedial courses taken.

Counseling Services

- ■ Academic
- ■ Psychological
- ■ Student Support groups
- ■ Vocational

Tutoring

Individual tutoring is available.

	Individual	Group
Time management	■	■
Organizational skills	■	■
Learning strategies	■	■
Study skills	■	■
Content area	☐	☐
Writing lab	■	☐
Math lab	■	☐

LD PROGRAM STAFF

Total number of LD Program staff (including director):

Full Time: 1 Part Time: 1

There is an advisor/advocate from the LD program available to students.

Key staff person available to work with LD students: Kara Kapustar, Learning Disabilities Instructional Aide.

Otterbein College

Westerville, OH

Address: One Otterbein College, Westerville, OH, 43081
Admissions telephone: 800 488-8144
Admissions FAX: 614 823-1200
Director of Admission: Cass Johnson
Admissions e-mail: UOtterB@Otterbein.edu
Web site: http://www.otterbein.edu
SAT Code: 1597 ACT Code: 3318

LD program name: Academic Support Center
Director of Academic Support: Ellen Kasulis
LD program telephone: 614 823-1362
LD program enrollment: 88, Total campus enrollment: 2,756

GENERAL

Otterbein College is a private, coed, four-year institution. 140-acre, suburban campus in Westerville (population: 35,318), 12 miles from Columbus. Served by bus; major airport serves Columbus; train serves Sandusky (91 miles). School operates transportation to off-campus college-sponsored functions. Public transportation serves campus. Quarter system.

LD ADMISSIONS

Students do not complete a separate application and are simultaneously accepted to the LD program. A member of the LD program does sit on the admissions committee. High school waivers are accepted for foreign language. A personal interview is not required. Essay is not required.

For fall 2004, 29 completed self-identified LD applications were received. 25 applications were offered admission, and 22 enrolled.

SECONDARY SCHOOL REQUIREMENTS

Graduation from secondary school required; GED accepted. The following course distribution required: 4 units of English, 3 units of math, 3 units of science, 2 units of foreign language, 3 units of social studies, 2 units of history.

TESTING

SAT Reasoning or ACT required. SAT Subject recommended.

All enrolled freshmen (fall 2004):

Average SAT I Scores:	Verbal: 574	Math: 561
Average ACT Scores:	Composite: 23	

Child Study Team report is not required. A neuropsychological or comprehensive psycho-educational evaluation is required for admission. Must be dated within 48 months of application. Tests required as part of this documentation:

- [x] WAIS-IV
- [x] WISC-IV
- [x] SATA
- [x] Woodcock-Johnson
- [ ] Nelson-Denny Reading Test
- [ ] Other

UNDERGRADUATE STUDENT BODY

Total undergraduate student enrollment: 891 Men, 1,660 Women.

Composition of student body (fall 2004):

	Undergraduate	Freshmen
International	0.6	1.3
Black	6.6	6.2
American Indian	0.0	0.0
Asian-American	0.9	0.9
Hispanic	1.5	1.1
White	88.9	89.0
Unreported	1.5	1.5
	100.0%	100.0%

11% are from out of state. 63% of classes have fewer than 20 students, 34% have between 20 and 50 students, 3% have more than 50 students.

STUDENT HOUSING

Freshmen are required to live on campus. Housing is guaranteed for all undergraduates. Campus can house 1,178 undergraduates.

EXPENSES

Tuition (2005-06): $22,518 per year.

Room: $2,994. Board: $3,474.

There is no additional cost for LD program/services.

LD SERVICES

LD program size is not limited.

LD services available to:

- [x] Freshmen
- [x] Sophomores
- [x] Juniors
- [x] Seniors

Academic Accommodations

Curriculum		In class	
Foreign language waiver	[ ]	Early syllabus	[ ]
Lighter course load	[ ]	Note takers in class	[x]
Math waiver	[ ]	Priority seating	[ ]
Other special classes	[ ]	Tape recorders	[x]
Priority registrations	[x]	Videotaped classes	[ ]
Substitution of courses	[ ]	Text on tape	[ ]
Exams		**Services**	
Extended time	[x]	Diagnostic tests	[ ]
Oral exams	[ ]	Learning centers	[x]
Take home exams	[ ]	Proofreaders	[ ]
Exams on tape or computer	[ ]	Readers	[ ]
Untimed exams	[ ]	Reading Machines/Kurzweil	[ ]
Other accommodations	[ ]	Special bookstore section	[ ]
		Typists	[ ]

Credit toward degree is given for remedial courses taken.

Counseling Services

- [x] Academic
- [x] Psychological
- [ ] Student Support groups
- [x] Vocational

Tutoring

Individual tutoring is available daily.

	Individual	Group
Time management	[x]	[x]
Organizational skills	[x]	[x]
Learning strategies	[x]	[x]
Study skills	[x]	[x]
Content area	[x]	[x]
Writing lab	[x]	[ ]
Math lab	[x]	[ ]

LD PROGRAM STAFF

There is an advisor/advocate from the LD program available to students.

Key staff person available to work with LD students: Ellen Kasulis, Director of Academic Support.

University of Rio Grande

Rio Grande, OH

Address: PO Box 500, Rio Grande, OH, 45674
Admissions telephone: 800 288-2746 (in-state, KY, PA, WV only)
Admissions FAX: 740 245-7260
Executive Director of Admissions: Dr. Barry Dorsey
Admissions e-mail: admissions@rio.edu
Web site: http://www.rio.edu
SAT Code: 1663 ACT Code: 3324

LD program name: Accessibility
Counselor/Coordinator: Marshall Kimmel
LD program telephone: 740 245-7339
LD program e-mail: mkimmel@rio.edu
LD program enrollment: 168, Total campus enrollment: 2,267

GENERAL

University of Rio Grande is a private, coed, four-year institution. 68-acre campus in Rio Grande (population: 915), 12 miles from Gallipolis and 100 miles from Columbus. Major airport serves Columbus; smaller airport serves Charleston, WV (65 miles); bus serves Chillicothe (50 miles); train serves Huntington, WV (60 miles). Semester system.

LD ADMISSIONS

Students do not complete a separate application and are not simultaneously accepted to the LD program. A member of the LD program does not sit on the admissions committee. A personal interview is required. Essay is not required.

SECONDARY SCHOOL REQUIREMENTS

Graduation from secondary school required; GED accepted.

TESTING

All enrolled Freshmen (fall 2004):

Average SAT I Scores: Verbal: Math:
Average ACT Scores: Composite: 19

Child Study Team report is not required. A neuropsychological or comprehensive psycho-educational evaluation is required for admission. Must be dated within 36 months of application. Tests required as part of this documentation:

- ■ WAIS-IV
- ■ WISC-IV
- ■ SATA
- ■ Woodcock-Johnson
- ■ Nelson-Denny Reading Test
- ☐ Other

UNDERGRADUATE STUDENT BODY

Total undergraduate student enrollment: 792 Men, 1,140 Women.

Composition of student body (fall 2004):

	Undergraduate	Freshmen
International	0.5	1.2
Black	3.9	3.2
American Indian	0.0	0.2
Asian-American	0.7	0.4
Hispanic	0.2	0.4
White	70.6	69.8
Unreported	24.1	24.8
	100.0%	100.0%

78% are from out of state. 1% join a fraternity and 1% join a sorority. Average age of full-time undergraduates is 25. 65% of classes have fewer than 20 students, 34% have between 20 and 50 students, 1% have more than 50 students.

STUDENT HOUSING

28% of freshmen live in college housing. Housing is guaranteed for all undergraduates. Campus can house 600 undergraduates. Single rooms are available for students with medical or special needs. A medical note is required.

EXPENSES

Tuition (2005-06): $11,820 per year (in-state), $13,050 (out-of-state). $2,183-$8,235 per year (state residents, in-district), $2,610-$8,421 (state residents, out-of-district), $5,664 (West Virginia residents), $9,090 (other out-of-state). (Tuition varies by class level.)
Room & Board: $6,024-$5,542.
There is no additional cost for LD program/services.

LD SERVICES

LD program size is not limited.

LD services available to:

■ Freshmen ■ Sophomores ■ Juniors ■ Seniors

Academic Accommodations

Curriculum		**In class**	
Foreign language waiver	☐	Early syllabus	☐
Lighter course load	■	Note takers in class	■
Math waiver	☐	Priority seating	☐
Other special classes	■	Tape recorders	■
Priority registrations	☐	Videotaped classes	☐
Substitution of courses	■	Text on tape	■
Exams		**Services**	
Extended time	■	Diagnostic tests	☐
Oral exams	■	Learning centers	■
Take home exams	☐	Proofreaders	☐
Exams on tape or computer	■	Readers	■
Untimed exams	■	Reading Machines/Kurzweil	☐
Other accommodations	■	Special bookstore section	☐
		Typists	☐

Credit toward degree is given for remedial courses taken.

Counseling Services

- ■ Academic
- ■ Psychological
- ■ Student Support groups
- ■ Vocational

Tutoring

Individual tutoring is available daily.

	Individual	Group
Time management	■	■
Organizational skills	■	■
Learning strategies	■	■
Study skills	■	■
Content area	■	■
Writing lab	■	■
Math lab	■	■

LD PROGRAM STAFF

Total number of LD Program staff (including director):

Full Time: 3 Part Time: 3

There is an advisor/advocate from the LD program available to students. 10 peer tutors are available to work with LD students.

Key staff person available to work with LD students: Marshall Kimmel, Counselor/Coordinator.

LD Program web site: http://www.rio.edu/StudentLife/Accessibility.htm

Shawnee State University

Portsmouth, OH

Address: 940 Second Street, Portsmouth, OH, 45662
Admissions telephone: 800 959-2778
Admissions FAX: 740 351-3111
Director of Admissions and Retention: Bob Trusz
Admissions e-mail: To_SSU@shawnee.edu
Web site: http://www.shawnee.edu
SAT Code: 1790 ACT Code: 3336

LD program name: Disability Svcs/Student Success Center
Disability Services Coordinator: Scott Douthat
LD program telephone: 740 351-3276
LD program e-mail: sdouthat@shawnee.edu
Total campus enrollment: 3,798

GENERAL

Shawnee State University is a public, coed, four-year institution. 50-acre campus in Portsmouth (population: 20,909), 65 miles from Huntington, WV. Served by bus; airport serves Huntington; larger airports serve Columbus and Cincinnati (both 100 miles); train serves South Shore, Ky (three miles). Quarter system.

LD ADMISSIONS

Students do not complete a separate application and are not simultaneously accepted to the LD program. A personal interview is recommended. Essay is not required.

SECONDARY SCHOOL REQUIREMENTS

Graduation from secondary school required; GED accepted.

TESTING

All enrolled freshmen (fall 2004):

Average SAT I Scores: Verbal: Math:
Average ACT Scores: Composite: 19

Child Study Team report is not required. Tests required as part of this documentation:

☐	WAIS-IV	☐	Woodcock-Johnson
☐	WISC-IV	☐	Nelson-Denny Reading Test
☐	SATA	☐	Other

UNDERGRADUATE STUDENT BODY

Total undergraduate student enrollment: 1,271 Men, 2,093 Women.

Composition of student body (fall 2004):

	Undergraduate	Freshmen
International	1.9	0.7
Black	2.1	2.6
American Indian	1.1	0.9
Asian-American	0.1	0.1
Hispanic	0.8	0.5
White	84.9	87.3
Unreported	9.1	7.9
	100.0%	100.0%

9% are from out of state. 5% join a fraternity and 3% join a sorority. Average age of full-time undergraduates is 23. 51% of classes have fewer than 20 students, 46% have between 20 and 50 students, 3% have more than 50 students.

STUDENT HOUSING

24% of freshmen live in college housing. Freshmen are required to live on campus. Housing is not guaranteed for all undergraduates. Campus can house 296 undergraduates.

EXPENSES

Tuition (2005-06): $4,896 per year (in-state), $8,784 (out-of-state).
Room: $4,419. Board: $2,319.
There is no additional cost for LD program/services.

LD SERVICES

LD program size is not limited.

LD services available to:

■ Freshmen ■ Sophomores ■ Juniors ■ Seniors

Academic Accommodations

Curriculum		**In class**	
Foreign language waiver	☐	Early syllabus	☐
Lighter course load	■	Note takers in class	■
Math waiver	☐	Priority seating	☐
Other special classes	■	Tape recorders	■
Priority registrations	☐	Videotaped classes	☐
Substitution of courses	☐	Text on tape	☐
Exams		**Services**	
Extended time	☐	Diagnostic tests	☐
Oral exams	■	Learning centers	■
Take home exams	☐	Proofreaders	☐
Exams on tape or computer	☐	Readers	■
Untimed exams	■	Reading Machines/Kurzweil	■
Other accommodations	☐	Special bookstore section	☐
		Typists	☐

Credit toward degree is not given for remedial courses taken.

Counseling Services

■ Academic
■ Psychological
■ Student Support groups
■ Vocational

Tutoring

Individual tutoring is available.

	Individual	Group
Time management	☐	☐
Organizational skills	☐	☐
Learning strategies	☐	☐
Study skills	☐	☐
Content area	☐	☐
Writing lab	☐	☐
Math lab	☐	☐

LD PROGRAM STAFF

Total number of LD Program staff (including director):

Full Time: 1 Part Time: 1

Key staff person available to work with LD students: Scott Douthat, Disability Services Coordinator.

The Ohio State University - Columbus

Columbus, OH

Address: 190 N. Oval Mall, Columbus, OH, 43210
Admissions telephone: 614 292-3980
Admissions FAX: 614 292-4818
Director: Mabel G. Freeman
Admissions e-mail: askabuckeye@osu.edu
Web site: http://www.osu.edu
SAT Code: 1592   ACT Code: 3312

LD program name: Office of Disability Services
LD program address: 150 Pomerene Hall,
1760 Neil Avenue, Columbus, OH, 43210-1297
Assistant Director: Lois Burke
LD program telephone: 614 292-3307
LD program e-mail: burke.4@osu.edu
LD program enrollment: 312, Total campus enrollment: 37,509

GENERAL

The Ohio State University - Columbus is a public, coed, four-year institution. 3,390-acre campus in Columbus (population: 711,470); branch campuses in Lima, Mansfield, Marion, Newark, and Wooster. Served by air and bus; train serves Cincinnati (100 miles). School operates transportation on campus and to some nearby neighborhoods. Public transportation serves campus. Quarter system.

LD ADMISSIONS

Students do not complete a separate application and are not simultaneously accepted to the LD program. A member of the LD program does not sit on the admissions committee. A personal interview is not required. Essay is required and may be typed. Admissions requirements are not waived for students with learning disabilities.

For fall 2004, 220 completed self-identified LD applications were received. 110 applications were offered admission, and 48 enrolled.

SECONDARY SCHOOL REQUIREMENTS

Graduation from secondary school required; GED accepted. The following course distribution required: 4 units of English, 3 units of math, 2 units of science, 2 units of foreign language, 2 units of social studies, 1 unit of academic electives.

TESTING

SAT Reasoning or ACT required. SAT Subject required.

All enrolled freshmen (fall 2004):

Average SAT I Scores: Verbal: 581 Math: 604
Average ACT Scores: Composite: 26

Child Study Team report is required if student is classified. A neuropsychological or comprehensive psycho-educational evaluation is required for admission. Must be dated within 36 months of application. Tests required as part of this documentation:

- [x] WAIS-IV
- [x] WISC-IV
- [x] SATA
- [x] Woodcock-Johnson
- [x] Nelson-Denny Reading Test
- [ ] Other

UNDERGRADUATE STUDENT BODY

Total undergraduate student enrollment: 18,630 Men, 17,419 Women.

Composition of student body (fall 2004):

	Undergraduate	Freshmen
International	1.7	3.3
Black	6.7	7.7
American Indian	0.3	0.4
Asian-American	5.7	5.5
Hispanic	2.8	2.4
White	81.5	78.8
Unreported	1.3	1.9
	100.0%	100.0%

11% are from out of state. 6% join a fraternity and 7% join a sorority. Average age of full-time undergraduates is 21. 43% of classes have fewer than 20 students, 40% have between 20 and 50 students, 17% have more than 50 students.

STUDENT HOUSING

90% of freshmen live in college housing. Freshmen are required to live on campus. Housing is guaranteed for all undergraduates. Campus can house 9,526 undergraduates. Housing for students can be given on a case-by-case basis when requested. Additional support for housing requests provided based on disability needs when documentation is provided and the student is eligible for support services/ accommodations from this office.

EXPENSES

Tuition (2005-06): $7,479 per year (in-state), $18,066 (out-of-state).
Room & Board: $7,275.
There is no additional cost for LD program/services

LD SERVICES

LD program size is not limited.

LD services available to:

- [x] Freshmen
- [x] Sophomores
- [x] Juniors
- [x] Seniors

Academic Accommodations

Curriculum		In class	
Foreign language waiver	[ ]	Early syllabus	[ ]
Lighter course load	[ ]	Note takers in class	[ ]
Math waiver	[ ]	Priority seating	[ ]
Other special classes	[ ]	Tape recorders	[ ]
Priority registrations	[x]	Videotaped classes	[ ]
Substitution of courses	[ ]	Text on tape	[ ]
Exams		**Services**	
Extended time	[x]	Diagnostic tests	[ ]
Oral exams	[ ]	Learning centers	[ ]
Take home exams	[ ]	Proofreaders	[ ]
Exams on tape or computer	[ ]	Readers	[ ]
Untimed exams	[ ]	Reading Machines/Kurzweil	[ ]
Other accommodations	[ ]	Special bookstore section	[ ]
		Typists	[ ]

Credit toward degree is not given for remedial courses taken.

Counseling Services

- [ ] Academic
- [ ] Psychological
- [ ] Student Support groups
- [ ] Vocational

Tutoring

	Individual	Group
Time management	[ ]	[ ]
Organizational skills	[ ]	[ ]
Learning strategies	[ ]	[ ]
Study skills	[ ]	[ ]
Content area	[ ]	[ ]
Writing lab	[ ]	[ ]
Math lab	[ ]	[ ]

UNIQUE LD PROGRAM FEATURES

Reasonable accommodations, auxiliary aids and support services are individualized and based upon disability documentation, functional limitations, and a collaborative assessment of needs. There are other staff members to assist students in accessing exam accommodations, getting printed materials in alternative format, and learning how to use adapted equipment.

LD PROGRAM STAFF

Total number of LD Program staff (including director):

Full Time: 8   Part Time: 8

Key staff person available to work with LD students: Lois Burke, Assistant Director.

LD Program web site: www.ods.ohio-state.edu

The University of Toledo

Toledo, OH

Address: 2801 W. Bancroft, Toledo, OH, 43606
Admissions telephone: 800 5-TOLEDO
Admissions FAX: 419 530-5872
Interim Director of Undergraduate Admissions: Martino Harmon
Admissions e-mail: enroll@utnet.utoledo.edu
Web site: http://www.utoledo.edu
SAT Code: 1845 ACT Code: 3344

Learning Disabilities Specialist: Mary Ann Stibbe
LD program telephone: 419 530-4981
LD program e-mail: mary.stibbe@utoledo.edu
Total campus enrollment: 16,366

GENERAL

The University of Toledo is a public, coed, four-year institution. 407-acre, suburban campus in Toledo (population: 313,619); branch campuses in Maumee, Oregon, Sylvania, and downtown Toledo. Served by air, bus, and train. School operates transportation to apartments and University Comm and Tech Coll. Public transportation serves downtown campus. Semester system.

LD ADMISSIONS

A personal interview is required. Essay is not required.

SECONDARY SCHOOL REQUIREMENTS

Graduation from secondary school required; GED accepted. The following course distribution required: 4 units of English, 3 units of math, 3 units of science, 3 units of social studies.

TESTING

ACT required; SAT Reasoning may be substituted. SAT Subject required.

All enrolled freshmen (fall 2004):

Average SAT I Scores:	Verbal: 509	Math: 519
Average ACT Scores:	Composite: 21	

Child Study Team report is not required. Tests required as part of this documentation:

- ☐ WAIS-IV
- ☐ WISC-IV
- ☐ SATA
- ☐ Woodcock-Johnson
- ☐ Nelson-Denny Reading Test
- ☐ Other

UNDERGRADUATE STUDENT BODY

Total undergraduate student enrollment: 7,602 Men, 8,348 Women.

Composition of student body (fall 2004):

	Undergraduate	Freshmen
International	0.4	1.5
Black	15.1	12.1
American Indian	0.2	0.2
Asian-American	1.5	1.7
Hispanic	2.0	2.4
White	76.1	76.8
Unreported	4.7	5.3
	100.0%	100.0%

9% are from out of state. 42% of classes have fewer than 20 students, 49% have between 20 and 50 students, 9% have more than 50 students.

STUDENT HOUSING

Freshmen are not required to live on campus. Housing is guaranteed for all undergraduates. Campus can house 3,490 undergraduates.

EXPENSES

Tuition (2005-06): $6,430 per year (in-state), $15,241 (out-of-state).

Room: $5,106. Board: $2,700.
There is no additional cost for LD program/services.

LD SERVICES

LD program size is not limited.

LD services available to:

☐ Freshmen ☐ Sophomores ☐ Juniors ☐ Seniors

Academic Accommodations

Curriculum		In class	
Foreign language waiver	☐	Early syllabus	☐
Lighter course load	■	Note takers in class	■
Math waiver	☐	Priority seating	☐
Other special classes	☐	Tape recorders	■
Priority registrations	☐	Videotaped classes	■
Substitution of courses	☐	Text on tape	☐
Exams		**Services**	
Extended time	■	Diagnostic tests	☐
Oral exams	■	Learning centers	■
Take home exams	☐	Proofreaders	☐
Exams on tape or computer	☐	Readers	■
Untimed exams	■	Reading Machines/Kurzweil	■
Other accommodations	☐	Special bookstore section	☐
		Typists	☐

Credit toward degree is not given for remedial courses taken.

Counseling Services

- ☐ Academic
- ☐ Psychological
- ☐ Student Support groups
- ☐ Vocational

Tutoring

	Individual	Group
Time management	☐	☐
Organizational skills	☐	☐
Learning strategies	☐	☐
Study skills	☐	☐
Content area	☐	☐
Writing lab	☐	☐
Math lab	☐	☐

LD PROGRAM STAFF

Total number of LD Program staff (including director):

Full Time: 2 Part Time: 2

Key staff person available to work with LD students: Mary Ann Stibbe, Learning Disabilities Specialist.

Union Institute & University

Cincinnati, OH

Address: 440 E. McMillan Street, Cincinnati, OH, 45206
Admissions telephone: 800 486-3116
Admissions FAX: 513 861-3218
Admissions Director: Emily Harbold
Admissions e-mail: admissions@tui.edu
Web site: http://www.tui.edu
SAT Code: 732

Director, Learner Support Network: Anne Connor
LD program e-mail: anne.connor@tui.edu
Total campus enrollment: 652

GENERAL

Union Institute & University is a private, coed, four-year institution. Urban campus in Cincinnati (population: 331,285); branch campuses in Miami, Fla., and in Los Angeles, Sacramento, and San Diego. Served by air, bus, and train. Public transportation serves campus. Semester system.

TESTING

All enrolled freshmen (fall 2004):

Average SAT I Scores: Verbal: Math:

Average ACT Scores: Composite:

Child Study Team report is not required. Tests required as part of this documentation:

- ☐ WAIS-IV
- ☐ WISC-IV
- ☐ SATA
- ☐ Woodcock-Johnson
- ☐ Nelson-Denny Reading Test
- ☐ Other

UNDERGRADUATE STUDENT BODY

Total undergraduate student enrollment: 222 Men, 430 Women.

8% are from out of state.

EXPENSES

Tuition (2005-06): $9,720 per year.

There is no additional cost for LD program/services.

LD SERVICES

LD program size is not limited.

LD services available to:

☐ Freshmen ☐ Sophomores ☐ Juniors ☐ Seniors

Academic Accommodations

Curriculum		**In class**	
Foreign language waiver	☐	Early syllabus	☐
Lighter course load	☐	Note takers in class	☐
Math waiver	☐	Priority seating	☐
Other special classes	■	Tape recorders	■
Priority registrations	☐	Videotaped classes	☐
Substitution of courses	☐	Text on tape	☐
Exams		**Services**	
Extended time	■	Diagnostic tests	■
Oral exams	■	Learning centers	■
Take home exams	☐	Proofreaders	☐
Exams on tape or computer	☐	Readers	■
Untimed exams	■	Reading Machines/Kurzweil	☐
Other accommodations	☐	Special bookstore section	☐
		Typists	☐

Credit toward degree is not given for remedial courses taken.

Counseling Services

- ☐ Academic
- ☐ Psychological
- ☐ Student Support groups
- ☐ Vocational

Tutoring

	Individual	Group
Time management	☐	☐
Organizational skills	☐	☐
Learning strategies	☐	☐
Study skills	☐	☐
Content area	☐	☐
Writing lab	☐	☐
Math lab	☐	☐

LD PROGRAM STAFF

Total number of LD Program staff (including director):

Full Time: 2 Part Time: 2

Key staff person available to work with LD students: Anne Connor, Director, Learner Support Network.

Urbana University

Urbana, OH

Address: 579 College Way, Urbana, OH, 43078
Admissions telephone: 800 7URBANA (in-state)
Admissions FAX: 937 484-1389
Vice President for Enrollment and Student Services: Mrs. Melissa Tolle
Admissions e-mail: admiss@urbana.edu
Web site: http://www.urbana.edu
SAT Code: 1847 ACT Code: 3346

Dean of Students: Paula Brown
LD program telephone: 317 484-1378
LD program e-mail: pbrown@urbana.edu
Total campus enrollment: 1,432

GENERAL

Urbana University is a private, coed, four-year institution. 128-acre campus in Urbana (population: 11,613), 40 miles from Dayton; branch campuses in Bellefontaine, Dayton, and Piqua. Major airports serve Dayton and Columbus (50 miles); bus serves Springfield (12 miles). Semester system.

LD ADMISSIONS

A personal interview is recommended. Essay is required and may be typed.

SECONDARY SCHOOL REQUIREMENTS

Graduation from secondary school required; GED accepted. The following course distribution required: 4 units of English, 2 units of math, 2 units of science, 2 units of social studies.

TESTING

All enrolled freshmen (fall 2004):

Average SAT I Scores: Verbal: Math:
Average ACT Scores: Composite:

Child Study Team report is not required. Tests required as part of this documentation:

- [ ] WAIS-IV
- [ ] WISC-IV
- [ ] SATA
- [ ] Woodcock-Johnson
- [ ] Nelson-Denny Reading Test
- [ ] Other

UNDERGRADUATE STUDENT BODY

Total undergraduate student enrollment: 625 Men, 807 Women.

2% are from out of state.

STUDENT HOUSING

Housing is guaranteed for all undergraduates. Campus can house 450 undergraduates.

EXPENSES

Tuition (2005-06): $15,050 per year.
Room:$2,030. Board: $3,660.
There is no additional cost for LD program/services.

LD SERVICES

LD program size is not limited.

LD services available to:

[ ] Freshmen [ ] Sophomores [ ] Juniors [ ] Seniors

Academic Accommodations

Curriculum		**In class**	
Foreign language waiver	[ ]	Early syllabus	[ ]
Lighter course load	[x]	Note takers in class	[x]
Math waiver	[ ]	Priority seating	[ ]
Other special classes	[ ]	Tape recorders	[x]
Priority registrations	[ ]	Videotaped classes	[ ]
Substitution of courses	[ ]	Text on tape	[ ]
Exams		**Services**	
Extended time	[x]	Diagnostic tests	[ ]
Oral exams	[x]	Learning centers	[ ]
Take home exams	[ ]	Proofreaders	[ ]
Exams on tape or computer	[ ]	Readers	[x]
Untimed exams	[x]	Reading Machines/Kurzweil	[ ]
Other accommodations	[ ]	Special bookstore section	[ ]
		Typists	[ ]

Credit toward degree is given for remedial courses taken.

Counseling Services

- [ ] Academic
- [ ] Psychological
- [ ] Student Support groups
- [ ] Vocational

Tutoring

	Individual	Group
Time management	[ ]	[ ]
Organizational skills	[ ]	[ ]
Learning strategies	[ ]	[ ]
Study skills	[ ]	[ ]
Content area	[ ]	[ ]
Writing lab	[ ]	[ ]
Math lab	[ ]	[ ]

LD PROGRAM STAFF

Key staff person available to work with LD students: Paula Brown, Dean of Students.

Ursuline College

Pepper Pike, OH

Address: 2550 Lander Road, Pepper Pike, OH, 44124
Admissions telephone: 888 URSULINE
Admissions FAX: 440 684-6138
Director of Admission: Sarah Sundermeier
Admissions e-mail: admission@ursuline.edu
Web site: http://www.ursuline.edu
SAT Code: 1848 ACT Code: 3449

LD program name: FOCUS
Director: Eileen Kohut
LD program telephone: 440 684-8123
LD program e-mail: ekohut@ursuline.edu
LD program enrollment: 27, Total campus enrollment: 1,139

GENERAL

Ursuline College is a private, women's, four-year institution. 115-acre, suburban campus in Pepper Pike (population: 6,040), 12 miles from Cleveland. Major airport, bus, and train serve Cleveland; smaller airport serves Richmond Heights (10 miles). Public transportation serves campus. Semester system.

LD ADMISSIONS

Students do not complete a separate application and are not simultaneously accepted to the LD program. A member of the LD program does sit on the admissions committee. A personal interview is recommended. Essay is required and may be typed.

SECONDARY SCHOOL REQUIREMENTS

Graduation from secondary school required; GED accepted. The following course distribution required: 4 units of English, 3 units of math, 3 units of science, 2 units of foreign language, 3 units of social studies.

TESTING

SAT Reasoning or ACT required.

All enrolled freshmen (fall 2004):

Average SAT I Scores:	Verbal: 494	Math: 470
Average ACT Scores:	Composite: 20	

Child Study Team report is not required. A neuropsychological or comprehensive psycho-education evaluation is not required for admission. Tests required as part of this documentation:

- [ ] WAIS-IV
- [ ] WISC-IV
- [ ] SATA
- [ ] Woodcock-Johnson
- [ ] Nelson-Denny Reading Test
- [ ] Other

UNDERGRADUATE STUDENT BODY

Total undergraduate student enrollment: 78 Men, 941 Women.

Composition of student body (fall 2004):

	Undergraduate	Freshmen
International	0.0	0.8
Black	22.8	24.5
American Indian	0.0	0.3
Asian-American	0.0	0.5
Hispanic	3.3	1.9
White	73.1	70.7
Unreported	0.8	1.3
	100.0%	100.0%

1% are from out of state. Average age of full-time undergraduates is 25. 86% of classes have fewer than 20 students, 14% have between 20 and 50 students.

STUDENT HOUSING

59% of freshmen live in college housing. Freshmen are not required to live on campus. Housing is not guaranteed for all undergraduates. Available for full time students only, until capacity is achieved. Campus can house 184 undergraduates. Single rooms are not available for students with medical or special needs.

EXPENSES

Tuition (2005-06): $18,900 per year.
Room & Board: $6,366.

Additional cost for LD program/services: $1,350.

LD SERVICES

LD program is limited to 1% of students.

LD services available to:

- [x] Freshmen
- [x] Sophomores
- [x] Juniors
- [x] Seniors

Academic Accommodations

Curriculum		In class	
Foreign language waiver	[ ]	Early syllabus	[ ]
Lighter course load	[x]	Note takers in class	[x]
Math waiver	[ ]	Priority seating	[ ]
Other special classes	[x]	Tape recorders	[x]
Priority registrations	[ ]	Videotaped classes	[ ]
Substitution of courses	[ ]	Text on tape	[ ]
Exams		**Services**	
Extended time	[x]	Diagnostic tests	[x]
Oral exams	[x]	Learning centers	[x]
Take home exams	[ ]	Proofreaders	[x]
Exams on tape or computer	[ ]	Readers	[x]
Untimed exams	[x]	Reading Machines/Kurzweil	[x]
Other accommodations	[ ]	Special bookstore section	[ ]
		Typists	[ ]

Credit toward degree is not given for remedial courses taken.

Counseling Services

- [x] Academic
- [ ] Psychological
- [ ] Student Support groups
- [x] Vocational

Tutoring

Individual tutoring is available daily.

Average size of tutoring groups: 4

	Individual	Group
Time management	[x]	[x]
Organizational skills	[x]	[x]
Learning strategies	[x]	[x]
Study skills	[x]	[x]
Content area	[x]	[x]
Writing lab	[ ]	[ ]
Math lab	[ ]	[ ]

UNIQUE LD PROGRAM FEATURES

LD program service charges apply only to those students in the FOCUS program. Other accademic support services for students with learning disabilities are free.

LD PROGRAM STAFF

Total number of LD Program staff (including director):

Full Time: 3 Part Time: 3

There is an advisor/advocate from the LD program available to students.

Key staff person available to work with LD students: Annette Gromada, Learning Disabilities Specialist.

Walsh University

North Canton, OH

Address: 2020 E. Maple Street, North Canton, OH, 44720
Admissions telephone: 800 362-9846
Admissions FAX: 330 490-7165
Dean of Enrollment Management: Brett Freshour
Admissions e-mail: admissions@walsh.edu
Web site: http://www.walsh.edu
SAT Code: 1926 ACT Code: 3349

Director of Counseling: Frances Morrow
LD program telephone: 330 490-7312
LD program e-mail: fmorrow@walsh.edu
LD program enrollment: 35, Total campus enrollment: 1,694

GENERAL

Walsh University is a private, coed, four-year institution. 100-acre campus in North Canton (population: 16,369), 60 miles from Cleveland. Served by bus and train; airport serves Akron (20 miles). Public transportation serves campus. Semester system.

LD ADMISSIONS

Students do not complete a separate application and are simultaneously accepted to the LD program. A member of the LD program does not sit on the admissions committee. A personal interview is recommended. Essay is not required.

SECONDARY SCHOOL REQUIREMENTS

Graduation from secondary school required; GED accepted.

TESTING

SAT Reasoning or ACT required. SAT Subject recommended.

All enrolled freshmen (fall 2004):

Average SAT I Scores:	Verbal: 504	Math: 512
Average ACT Scores:	Composite: 21	

Child Study Team report is not required. A neuropsychological or comprehensive psycho-education evaluation is not required for admission. Tests required as part of this documentation:

- [ ] WAIS-IV
- [ ] WISC-IV
- [ ] SATA
- [ ] Woodcock-Johnson
- [ ] Nelson-Denny Reading Test
- [ ] Other

UNDERGRADUATE STUDENT BODY

Total undergraduate student enrollment: 565 Men, 839 Women.

Composition of student body (fall 2004):

	Undergraduate	Freshmen
International	0.9	1.8
Black	6.8	5.9
American Indian	0.3	0.5
Asian-American	0.0	0.3
Hispanic	1.5	0.8
White	88.4	80.0
Unreported	2.1	10.7
	100.0%	100.0%

2% are from out of state. Average age of full-time undergraduates is 21. 62% of classes have fewer than 20 students, 38% have between 20 and 50 students.

STUDENT HOUSING

75% of freshmen live in college housing. Freshmen are required to live on campus. Housing is guaranteed for all undergraduates. Campus can house 728 undergraduates. Single rooms are available for students with medical or special needs. A medical note is required.

EXPENSES

Tuition (2005-06): $16,000 per year.
Room: $3,600. Board: $3,300.

There is no additional cost for LD program/services.

LD SERVICES

LD program size is not limited.

LD services available to:

- [x] Freshmen
- [x] Sophomores
- [x] Juniors
- [x] Seniors

Academic Accommodations

Curriculum		In class	
Foreign language waiver	[ ]	Early syllabus	[ ]
Lighter course load	[x]	Note takers in class	[ ]
Math waiver	[ ]	Priority seating	[x]
Other special classes	[x]	Tape recorders	[x]
Priority registrations	[ ]	Videotaped classes	[ ]
Substitution of courses	[x]	Text on tape	[ ]
Exams		**Services**	
Extended time	[x]	Diagnostic tests	[x]
Oral exams	[x]	Learning centers	[x]
Take home exams	[ ]	Proofreaders	[ ]
Exams on tape or computer	[x]	Readers	[x]
Untimed exams	[x]	Reading Machines/Kurzweil	[ ]
Other accommodations	[ ]	Special bookstore section	[x]
		Typists	[x]

Credit toward degree is given for remedial courses taken.

Counseling Services

[x]	Academic	Meets 5 times per academic year
[x]	Psychological	Meets 5 times per academic year
[ ]	Student Support groups	
[x]	Vocational	Meets 5 times per academic year

Tutoring

Individual tutoring is available weekly.

Average size of tutoring groups: 2

	Individual	Group
Time management	[ ]	[x]
Organizational skills	[ ]	[x]
Learning strategies	[ ]	[x]
Study skills	[ ]	[x]
Content area	[x]	[x]
Writing lab	[x]	[ ]
Math lab	[x]	[ ]

LD PROGRAM STAFF

Total number of LD Program staff (including director):

Full Time: 2 Part Time: 2

There is an advisor/advocate from the LD program available to students. The advisor/advocate meets with students 2 times per month. 20 peer tutors are available to work with LD students.

Key staff person available to work with LD students: Ryan Sweet, Director of Learning Resource Center.

Wilmington College

Wilmington, OH

Address: Pyle Center Box 1327, Wilmington, OH, 45177
Admissions telephone: 937 382-6661
Admissions FAX: 937 383-8542
Vice President for Enrollment Management: Tina Garland
Admissions e-mail: admission@wilmington.edu
Web site: http://www.wilmington.edu
SAT Code: 1909 ACT Code: 3362

Director: Dennis R. Smith, Ph.D.
LD program telephone: 937 382-666, extension 1430
LD program e-mail: dennis_smith@wilmington.edu
Total campus enrollment: 1,701

GENERAL

Wilmington College is a private, coed, four-year institution. 65-acre campus in Wilmington (population: 11,921), 30 miles from Dayton; branch campuses in Eastgate and Sharonville. Airport serves Dayton. Semester system.

LD ADMISSIONS

A personal interview is required. Essay is not required. All Admissions requirements may be waived for LD students depending on the student and the situation.

SECONDARY SCHOOL REQUIREMENTS

Graduation from secondary school required; GED accepted. The following course distribution required: 4 units of English, 2 units of math, 2 units of science, 2 units of social studies.

TESTING

SAT Reasoning considered if submitted.

All enrolled freshmen (fall 2004):

Average ACT Scores: Composite: 21

Child Study Team report is not required. Tests required as part of this documentation:

☐ WAIS-IV
☐ WISC-IV
☐ SATA
☐ Woodcock-Johnson
☐ Nelson-Denny Reading Test
☐ Other

UNDERGRADUATE STUDENT BODY

Total undergraduate student enrollment: 576 Men, 696 Women.

Composition of student body (fall 2004):

	Undergraduate	Freshmen
International	0.6	0.5
Black	9.9	8.0
American Indian	0.9	0.2
Asian-American	0.9	0.3
Hispanic	0.3	0.9
White	76.0	69.1
Unreported	11.4	21.0
	100.0%	100.0%

18% are from out of state. 15% join a fraternity and 15% join a sorority. Average age of full-time undergraduates is 19. 55% of classes have fewer than 20 students, 45% have between 20 and 50 students.

STUDENT HOUSING

79% of freshmen live in college housing. Housing is guaranteed for all undergraduates. Campus can house 842 undergraduates.

EXPENSES

Tuition (2005-06): $19,206 per year.
Room & Board: $7,054.

There is no additional cost for LD program/services.

LD SERVICES

LD program size is not limited.

LD services available to:

☐ Freshmen ☐ Sophomores ☐ Juniors ☐ Seniors

Academic Accommodations

Curriculum		**In class**	
Foreign language waiver	☐	Early syllabus	☐
Lighter course load	☐	Note takers in class	■
Math waiver	☐	Priority seating	☐
Other special classes	■	Tape recorders	■
Priority registrations	☐	Videotaped classes	☐
Substitution of courses	☐	Text on tape	☐
Exams		**Services**	
Extended time	■	Diagnostic tests	■
Oral exams	■	Learning centers	■
Take home exams	☐	Proofreaders	☐
Exams on tape or computer	☐	Readers	■
Untimed exams	■	Reading Machines/Kurzweil	☐
Other accommodations	☐	Special bookstore section	☐
		Typists	☐

Credit toward degree is not given for remedial courses taken.

Counseling Services

☐ Academic
☐ Psychological
☐ Student Support groups
☐ Vocational

Tutoring

	Individual	Group
Time management	☐	☐
Organizational skills	☐	☐
Learning strategies	☐	☐
Study skills	☐	☐
Content area	☐	☐
Writing lab	☐	☐
Math lab	☐	☐

LD PROGRAM STAFF

Total number of LD Program staff (including director):

Full Time: 3 Part Time: 3

Key staff person available to work with LD students: Dennis R. Smith, Ph.D., Director, Academic Resource Center.

Wittenberg University

Springfield, OH

Address: PO Box 720, Springfield, OH, 45501
Admissions telephone: 800 677-7558, extension 6314
Admissions FAX: 937 327-6379
Dean of Admissions: Evan Lipp
Admissions e-mail: admission@wittenberg.edu
Web site: http://www.wittenberg.edu
SAT Code: 1922 ACT Code: 3364

Administrative Assistant: Lynne Banion
LD program telephone: 937 327-7924
LD program e-mail: lbanion@wittenberg.edu
LD program enrollment: 88, Total campus enrollment: 2,164

GENERAL

Wittenberg University is a private, coed, four-year institution. 71-acre campus in Springfield (population: 65,358), 25 miles from Dayton. Served by bus; major airport serves Dayton and Columbus (40 miles). School operates transportation to airport on certain occasions. Public transportation serves campus. Semester system.

LD ADMISSIONS

Students do not complete a separate application and are simultaneously accepted to the LD program. A member of the LD program does not sit on the admissions committee. A personal interview is required. Essay is required and may be typed. LD Applications are handled on a case-by-case basis.

SECONDARY SCHOOL REQUIREMENTS

Graduation from secondary school required; GED not accepted. The following course distribution required: 4 units of English, 3 units of math, 3 units of science, 2 units of foreign language, 2 units of history.

TESTING

SAT Reasoning or ACT required. SAT Subject recommended.

All enrolled freshmen (fall 2004):

Average SAT I Scores:	Verbal: 568	Math: 566
Average ACT Scores:	Composite: 24	

Child Study Team report is required if student is classified. A neuropsychological or comprehensive psycho-educational evaluation is required for admission. Must be dated within 36 months of application. Tests required as part of this documentation:

- [x] WAIS-IV
- [ ] WISC-IV
- [ ] SATA
- [x] Woodcock-Johnson
- [ ] Nelson-Denny Reading Test
- [ ] Other

UNDERGRADUATE STUDENT BODY

Total undergraduate student enrollment: 922 Men, 1,186 Women.

Composition of student body (fall 2004):

	Undergraduate	Freshmen
International	0.0	0.5
Black	5.2	6.4
American Indian	0.7	0.4
Asian-American	1.7	1.6
Hispanic	1.9	1.2
White	77.8	81.4
Unreported	12.7	8.5
	100.0%	100.0%

42% are from out of state. 16% join a fraternity and 29% join a sorority. Average age of full-time undergraduates is 20. 58% of classes have fewer than 20 students, 41% have between 20 and 50 students, 1% have more than 50 students.

STUDENT HOUSING

96% of freshmen live in college housing. Freshmen are required to live on campus. Housing is guaranteed for all undergraduates. Campus can house 2,067 undergraduates. Single rooms are available for students with medical or special needs. A medical note is required.

EXPENSES

Tuition (2005-06): $27,342 per year.
Room: $3,660. Board: $3,394.
There is no additional cost for LD program/services.

LD SERVICES

LD program size is not limited.

LD services available to:

- [x] Freshmen
- [x] Sophomores
- [x] Juniors
- [x] Seniors

Academic Accommodations

Curriculum		In class	
Foreign language waiver	[ ]	Early syllabus	[ ]
Lighter course load	[ ]	Note takers in class	[ ]
Math waiver	[ ]	Priority seating	[ ]
Other special classes	[ ]	Tape recorders	[ ]
Priority registrations	[ ]	Videotaped classes	[ ]
Substitution of courses	[ ]	Text on tape	[ ]
Exams		**Services**	
Extended time	[x]	Diagnostic tests	[ ]
Oral exams	[ ]	Learning centers	[ ]
Take home exams	[ ]	Proofreaders	[ ]
Exams on tape or computer	[ ]	Readers	[ ]
Untimed exams	[ ]	Reading Machines/Kurzweil	[ ]
Other accommodations	[ ]	Special bookstore section	[ ]
		Typists	[ ]

Credit toward degree is not given for remedial courses taken.

Counseling Services

- [x] Academic — Meets 2 times per academic year
- [ ] Psychological
- [ ] Student Support groups
- [ ] Vocational

Tutoring

Individual tutoring is available weekly.

	Individual	Group
Time management	[ ]	[ ]
Organizational skills	[ ]	[ ]
Learning strategies	[ ]	[ ]
Study skills	[ ]	[ ]
Content area	[ ]	[ ]
Writing lab	[x]	[x]
Math lab	[x]	[x]

LD PROGRAM STAFF

Total number of LD Program staff (including director):

Full Time: 1 Part Time: 1

There is an advisor/advocate from the LD program available to students. The advisor/advocate meets with faculty 1 time per month and students 5 times per month. 65 peer tutors are available to work with LD students.

Key staff person available to work with LD students: Lisa Rhine, Assistant Provost for Academic Services.

Wright State University

Dayton, OH

Address: 3640 Colonel Glenn Highway, Dayton, OH, 45435
Admissions telephone: 800 247-1770
Admissions FAX: 937 775-5795
Director of Admissions: Cathy Davis
Admissions e-mail: admissions@wright.edu
Web site: http://www.wright.edu
SAT Code: 1179 ACT Code: 3295

Academic Support Specialist: Cassandra Mitchell
LD program telephone: 937 775-5680
LD program e-mail: cassandra.mitchell@wright.edu
Total campus enrollment: 12,128

GENERAL

Wright State University is a public, coed, four-year institution. 557-acre, suburban campus in Dayton (population: 166,179); branch campus in Celina. Served by air and bus. Public transportation serves campus. Quarter system.

LD ADMISSIONS

A personal interview is required. Essay is required and may be typed.

SECONDARY SCHOOL REQUIREMENTS

Graduation from secondary school required; GED accepted. The following course distribution required: 4 units of English, 3 units of math, 3 units of science, 2 units of foreign language, 3 units of social studies.

TESTING

ACT required; SAT Reasoning may be substituted. SAT Subject recommended.

All enrolled freshmen (fall 2004):

Average SAT I Scores:	Verbal: 503	Math: 502
Average ACT Scores:	Composite: 21	

Child Study Team report is required if student is classified. Tests required as part of this documentation:

☐ WAIS-IV ☐ Woodcock-Johnson
☐ WISC-IV ☐ Nelson-Denny Reading Test
☐ SATA ☐ Other

UNDERGRADUATE STUDENT BODY

Total undergraduate student enrollment: 5,321 Men, 6,899 Women.

Composition of student body (fall 2004):

	Undergraduate	Freshmen
International	0.7	1.0
Black	17.6	12.3
American Indian	0.4	0.4
Asian-American	2.4	2.0
Hispanic	0.9	1.1
White	72.7	77.6
Unreported	5.3	5.6
	100.0%	100.0%

3% are from out of state. 2% join a fraternity and 2% join a sorority. 39% of classes have fewer than 20 students, 54% have between 20 and 50 students, 7% have more than 50 students.

STUDENT HOUSING

62% of freshmen live in college housing. Freshmen are not required to live on campus. Housing is guaranteed for all undergraduates.

EXPENSES

Tuition (2005-06): $6,864 per year (in-state), $13,239 (out-of-state).

Room & Board: $6,751.
Additional cost for LD program/services: $0 per based on services.

LD SERVICES

LD program size is not limited.

LD services available to:

☐ Freshmen ☐ Sophomores ☐ Juniors ☐ Seniors

Academic Accommodations

Curriculum		In class	
Foreign language waiver	☐	Early syllabus	☐
Lighter course load	■	Note takers in class	■
Math waiver	☐	Priority seating	☐
Other special classes	■	Tape recorders	■
Priority registrations	☐	Videotaped classes	☐
Substitution of courses	☐	Text on tape	☐
Exams		**Services**	
Extended time	■	Diagnostic tests	■
Oral exams	☐	Learning centers	■
Take home exams	☐	Proofreaders	☐
Exams on tape or computer	☐	Readers	■
Untimed exams	■	Reading Machines/Kurzweil	■
Other accommodations	☐	Special bookstore section	☐
		Typists	☐

Credit toward degree is not given for remedial courses taken.

Counseling Services

☐ Academic
☐ Psychological
☐ Student Support groups
☐ Vocational

Tutoring

	Individual	Group
Time management	☐	☐
Organizational skills	☐	☐
Learning strategies	☐	☐
Study skills	☐	☐
Content area	☐	☐
Writing lab	☐	☐
Math lab	☐	☐

LD PROGRAM STAFF

Total number of LD Program staff (including director):

Full Time: 8 Part Time: 8

Key staff person available to work with LD students: Cassandra Mitchell, Academic Support Specialist.

Youngstown State University

Youngstown, OH

Address: 1 University Plaza, Youngstown, OH, 44555
Admissions telephone: 877 468-6978
Admissions FAX: 330 941-3674
Director of Undergraduate Admissions: Sue Davis
Admissions e-mail: enroll@ysu.edu
Web site: http://www.ysu.edu
SAT Code: 1975 ACT Code: 3368

LD program name: Disability Services
Coordinator: Jain Savage
LD program telephone: 330 941-1372
LD program e-mail: jasavage@ysu.edu
LD program enrollment: 64, Total campus enrollment: 11,796

GENERAL

Youngstown State University is a public, coed, four-year institution. 150-acre, urban campus in Youngstown (population: 82,026), 60 miles from both Cleveland and Pittsburgh. Served by air, bus, and train; major airports serve Cleveland and Pittsburgh. Public transportation serves campus. Semester system.

LD ADMISSIONS

Students do not complete a separate application and are not simultaneously accepted to the LD program. A member of the LD program does not sit on the admissions committee. A personal interview is required. Essay is not required.

64 applications were offered admission, and 64 enrolled.

SECONDARY SCHOOL REQUIREMENTS

Graduation from secondary school required; GED accepted.

TESTING

SAT Reasoning or ACT required. SAT Subject recommended.

All enrolled freshmen (fall 2004):

Average SAT I Scores:	Verbal: 491	Math: 492
Average ACT Scores:	Composite: 20	

Child Study Team report is required if student is classified. A neuropsychological or comprehensive psycho-educational evaluation is required for admission. Must be dated within 36 months of application. Tests required as part of this documentation:

- ■ WAIS-IV
- ■ WISC-IV
- ■ SATA
- ■ Woodcock-Johnson
- ■ Nelson-Denny Reading Test
- □ Other

UNDERGRADUATE STUDENT BODY

Total undergraduate student enrollment: 5,182 Men, 5,854 Women.

Composition of student body (fall 2004):

	Undergraduate	Freshmen
International	0.5	0.5
Black	13.4	11.3
American Indian	0.6	0.4
Asian-American	0.9	0.9
Hispanic	1.8	1.9
White	75.6	78.3
Unreported	7.2	6.7
	100.0%	100.0%

9% are from out of state. 4% join a fraternity and 3% join a sorority. Average age of full-time undergraduates is 22. 40% of classes have fewer than 20 students, 53% have between 20 and 50 students, 7% have more than 50 students.

STUDENT HOUSING

20% of freshmen live in college housing. Freshmen are not required to live on campus. Housing is guaranteed for all undergraduates. Campus can house 1,300 undergraduates. Single rooms are available for students with medical or special needs. A medical note is not required.

EXPENSES

Tuition (2005-06): $6,163 per year (in-state), $11,371 (out-of-state).
Room & Board: $6,280.
There is no additional cost for LD program/services.

LD SERVICES

LD program size is not limited.

LD services available to:

■ Freshmen ■ Sophomores ■ Juniors ■ Seniors

Academic Accommodations

Curriculum		**In class**	
Foreign language waiver	□	Early syllabus	□
Lighter course load	□	Note takers in class	■
Math waiver	□	Priority seating	□
Other special classes	□	Tape recorders	■
Priority registrations	■	Videotaped classes	□
Substitution of courses	■	Text on tape	■
Exams		**Services**	
Extended time	■	Diagnostic tests	□
Oral exams	□	Learning centers	□
Take home exams	□	Proofreaders	□
Exams on tape or computer	■	Readers	■
Untimed exams	■	Reading Machines/Kurzweil	■
Other accommodations	■	Special bookstore section	□
		Typists	■

Credit toward degree is not given for remedial courses taken.

Counseling Services

- ■ Academic
- ■ Psychological
- □ Student Support groups
- ■ Vocational

Tutoring

Individual tutoring is available.

	Individual	Group
Time management	□	□
Organizational skills	□	□
Learning strategies	□	□
Study skills	■	□
Content area	□	□
Writing lab	■	□
Math lab	■	□

LD PROGRAM STAFF

Total number of LD Program staff (including director):

Full Time: 2 Part Time: 2

There is not an advisor/advocate from the LD program available to students.

Key staff person available to work with LD students: Jain Savage, Coordinator.

Xavier University

Cincinnati, OH

Address: 3800 Victory Parkway, Cincinnati, OH, 45207
Admissions telephone: 800 344-4698, extension 3301
Admissions FAX: 513 745-4319
Dean of Admissions: Marc Camille
Admissions e-mail: xuadmit@xavier.edu
Web site: http://www.xavier.edu
SAT Code: 1965 ACT Code: 3366

LD program name: Learning Assistance Center
LD program address: ML 2612, Cincinnati, OH, 45207
Director of Learning Assistance Center: Ann Dinan
LD program telephone: 513 745-3283
LD program e-mail: xulac@xavier.edu
Total campus enrollment: 3,943

GENERAL

Xavier University is a private, coed, four-year institution. 130-acre, suburban campus in Cincinnati (population: 331,285). Served by air, bus, and train. School operates shuttle service within a two-mile radius of campus. Public transportation serves campus. Semester system.

LD ADMISSIONS

Students do not complete a separate application and are simultaneously accepted to the LD program. A member of the LD program does not sit on the admissions committee. A personal interview is not required. Essay is required and may be typed.

SECONDARY SCHOOL REQUIREMENTS

Graduation from secondary school required; GED accepted.

TESTING

SAT Reasoning or ACT required. SAT Subject recommended.

All enrolled freshmen (fall 2004):

Average SAT I Scores: Verbal: 583 Math: 588
Average ACT Scores: Composite: 26

Child Study Team report is not required. A neuropsychological or comprehensive psycho-educational evaluation is required for admission. Tests required as part of this documentation:

- ☒ WAIS-IV
- ☒ WISC-IV
- ☒ SATA
- ☒ Woodcock-Johnson
- ☒ Nelson-Denny Reading Test
- ☐ Other

UNDERGRADUATE STUDENT BODY

Total undergraduate student enrollment: 1,675 Men, 2,331 Women.

Composition of student body (fall 2004):

	Undergraduate	Freshmen
International	0.7	1.1
Black	9.6	10.2
American Indian	0.5	0.2
Asian-American	3.2	2.0
Hispanic	3.4	2.1
White	82.6	83.9
Unreported	0.0	0.5
	100.0%	100.0%

65% are from out of state. Average age of full-time undergraduates is 21. 49% of classes have fewer than 20 students, 50% have between 20 and 50 students, 1% have more than 50 students.

STUDENT HOUSING

89% of freshmen live in college housing. Freshmen are required to live on campus. Housing is guaranteed for all undergraduates. Priority goes to first year and sophomore students. Others are not guaranteed housing. Campus can house 1,812 undergraduates. Single rooms are available for students with medical or special needs. A medical note is required.

EXPENSES

Tuition (2005-06): $21,850 per year.
Room: $4,530. Board: $3,530.
There is no additional cost for LD program/services.

LD SERVICES

LD program size is not limited.

LD services available to:

☒ Freshmen ☒ Sophomores ☒ Juniors ☒ Seniors

Academic Accommodations

Curriculum		In class	
Foreign language waiver	☒	Early syllabus	☐
Lighter course load	☐	Note takers in class	☒
Math waiver	☒	Priority seating	☒
Other special classes	☐	Tape recorders	☒
Priority registrations	☒	Videotaped classes	☒
Substitution of courses	☒	Text on tape	☐
Exams		**Services**	
Extended time	☒	Diagnostic tests	☒
Oral exams	☒	Learning centers	☒
Take home exams	☐	Proofreaders	☐
Exams on tape or computer	☒	Readers	☒
Untimed exams	☐	Reading Machines/Kurzweil	☐
Other accommodations	☐	Special bookstore section	☐
		Typists	☒

Credit toward degree is not given for remedial courses taken.

Counseling Services

- ☐ Academic
- ☐ Psychological
- ☐ Student Support groups
- ☐ Vocational

Tutoring

Individual tutoring is available daily.

	Individual	Group
Time management	☒	☒
Organizational skills	☒	☒
Learning strategies	☒	☒
Study skills	☒	☒
Content area	☒	☒
Writing lab	☒	☐
Math lab	☒	☐

UNIQUE LD PROGRAM FEATURES

A coaching program has been added that is offered to all students including LD students.

LD PROGRAM STAFF

Total number of LD Program staff (including director):

Full Time: 3 Part Time: 3

31 peer tutors are available to work with LD students.

Key staff person available to work with LD students: Ann Dinan, Ph.D., Director of Learning Assistance Center.

LD Program web site: http://www.xu.edu/lac/

Cameron University

Lawton, OK

Address: 2800 W. Gore Boulevard, Lawton, OK, 73505-6377
Admissions telephone: 888 454-7600
Admissions FAX: 580 581-5514
Director of Admissions: Zoe Durant
Admissions e-mail: admissions@cameron.edu
Web site: http://www.cameron.edu
SAT Code: 6080 ACT Code: 3386

LD program name: Office of Student Development
Total campus enrollment: 5,482

GENERAL

Cameron University is a public, coed, four-year institution. 369-acre campus in Lawton (population: 92,757), 90 miles from Oklahoma City; branch campuses in Altus and Duncan. Served by air and bus; major airport serves Oklahoma City. Semester system.

LD ADMISSIONS

A personal interview is not required. Essay is not required.

SECONDARY SCHOOL REQUIREMENTS

Graduation from secondary school required; GED accepted. The following course distribution required: 4 units of English, 3 units of math, 2 units of science, 2 units of history, 3 units of academic electives.

TESTING

ACT required; SAT Reasoning may be substituted. SAT Subject recommended.

All enrolled freshmen (fall 2004):

Average SAT I Scores: Verbal: Math:
Average ACT Scores: Composite: 20

Child Study Team report is not required. Tests required as part of this documentation:

- ❑ WAIS-IV
- ❑ WISC-IV
- ❑ SATA
- ❑ Woodcock-Johnson
- ❑ Nelson-Denny Reading Test
- ❑ Other

UNDERGRADUATE STUDENT BODY

Total undergraduate student enrollment: 1,904 Men, 2,610 Women.

Composition of student body (fall 2004):

	Undergraduate	Freshmen
International	0.4	0.6
Black	19.1	19.3
American Indian	8.0	7.4
Asian-American	2.9	3.1
Hispanic	9.7	8.7
White	59.9	60.9
Unreported	0.0	0.0
	100.0%	100.0%

7% are from out of state. 4% join a fraternity and 6% join a sorority. Average age of full-time undergraduates is 25. 53% of classes have fewer than 20 students, 44% have between 20 and 50 students, 3% have more than 50 students.

STUDENT HOUSING

6% of freshmen live in college housing. Freshmen are not required to live on campus. Housing is not guaranteed for all undergraduates. Campus can house 512 undergraduates. Single rooms are available for students with medical or special needs. A medical note is required.

EXPENSES

Tuition (2005-06): $3,240 per year (in-state), $7,860 (out-of-state). Room & Board: $3,972.

LD SERVICES

LD services available to:

■ Freshmen ■ Sophomores ■ Juniors ■ Seniors

Academic Accommodations

Curriculum		**In class**	
Foreign language waiver	❑	Early syllabus	❑
Lighter course load	❑	Note takers in class	❑
Math waiver	❑	Priority seating	❑
Other special classes	❑	Tape recorders	❑
Priority registrations	❑	Videotaped classes	❑
Substitution of courses	❑	Text on tape	❑
Exams		**Services**	
Extended time	❑	Diagnostic tests	❑
Oral exams	❑	Learning centers	❑
Take home exams	❑	Proofreaders	❑
Exams on tape or computer	❑	Readers	❑
Untimed exams	❑	Reading Machines/Kurzweil	❑
Other accommodations	❑	Special bookstore section	❑
		Typists	❑

Credit toward degree is not given for remedial courses taken.

Counseling Services

- ❑ Academic
- ❑ Psychological
- ❑ Student Support groups
- ❑ Vocational

Tutoring

Individual tutoring is not available.

	Individual	Group
Time management	❑	❑
Organizational skills	❑	❑
Learning strategies	❑	❑
Study skills	❑	❑
Content area	❑	❑
Writing lab	❑	❑
Math lab	❑	❑

LD PROGRAM STAFF

Total number of LD Program staff (including director):

Full Time: 2 Part Time: 2

Key staff person available to work with LD students: Jennifer Holland, Director, Student Development.

LD Program web site: www.cameron.edu/student_development

University of Central Oklahoma

Edmond, OK

Address: 100 North University Drive, Edmond, OK, 73034
Admissions telephone: 405 974-2338
Admissions FAX: 405 341-4964
Director of Admissions: Linda Lofton
Admissions e-mail: admituco@ucok.edu
Web site: http://www.ucok.edu
SAT Code: 6091 ACT Code: 3390

LD program name: Disability Support Services
LD program address: 100 North University Dr, Box 144,
Assistant Director: Kimberly Fields
LD program telephone: 405 974-2549
LD program e-mail: kfields1@ucok.edu
Total campus enrollment: 14,135

GENERAL

University of Central Oklahoma is a public, coed, four-year institution. 200-acre, suburban campus in Edmond (population: 68,315), 10 miles from Oklahoma City. Served by bus; major airport serves Oklahoma City. Public transportation serves campus. Semester system.

LD ADMISSIONS

Students do not complete a separate application and are not simultaneously accepted to the LD program. A member of the LD program does not sit on the admissions committee. A personal interview is not required.

SECONDARY SCHOOL REQUIREMENTS

Graduation from secondary school required; GED accepted. The following course distribution required: 4 units of English, 3 units of math, 2 units of science, 1 unit of social studies, 2 units of history, 3 units of academic electives.

TESTING

ACT required; SAT Reasoning may be substituted.

All enrolled freshmen (fall 2004):

Average SAT I Scores: Verbal: Math:
Average ACT Scores: Composite: 21

Child Study Team report is not required. A neuropsychological or comprehensive psycho-educational evaluation is required for admission. Tests required as part of this documentation:

- [x] WAIS-IV
- [ ] WISC-IV
- [ ] SATA
- [x] Woodcock-Johnson
- [x] Nelson-Denny Reading Test
- [x] Other

UNDERGRADUATE STUDENT BODY

Total undergraduate student enrollment: 5,133 Men, 7,155 Women.

Composition of student body (fall 2004):

	Undergraduate	Freshmen
International	5.4	8.5
Black	10.1	8.9
American Indian	5.9	5.5
Asian-American	2.6	3.0
Hispanic	4.2	3.0
White	68.6	67.1
Unreported	3.2	4.0
	100.0%	100.0%

2% are from out of state. Average age of full-time undergraduates is 22. 30% of classes have fewer than 20 students, 66% have between 20 and 50 students, 4% have more than 50 students.

STUDENT HOUSING

Freshmen are not required to live on campus. Housing is guaranteed for all undergraduates. Campus can house 1,650 undergraduates.

EXPENSES

Tuition (2005-06): $2,175 per year (in-state), $6,750 (out-of-state). Tuition varies by class level.
Room: $2,006. Board: $2,200.
There is no additional cost for LD program/services.

LD SERVICES

LD program size is not limited.

LD services available to:

- [x] Freshmen
- [x] Sophomores
- [x] Juniors
- [x] Seniors

Academic Accommodations

Curriculum		In class	
Foreign language waiver	☐	Early syllabus	☐
Lighter course load	☐	Note takers in class	☒
Math waiver	☐	Priority seating	☐
Other special classes	☐	Tape recorders	☐
Priority registrations	☒	Videotaped classes	☐
Substitution of courses	☐	Text on tape	☒
Exams		**Services**	
Extended time	☒	Diagnostic tests	☐
Oral exams	☐	Learning centers	☐
Take home exams	☐	Proofreaders	☐
Exams on tape or computer	☐	Readers	☐
Untimed exams	☐	Reading Machines/Kurzweil	☐
Other accommodations	☒	Special bookstore section	☐
		Typists	☐

Credit toward degree is not given for remedial courses taken.

Counseling Services

- [ ] Academic
- [ ] Psychological
- [ ] Student Support groups
- [ ] Vocational

Tutoring

Individual tutoring is available.

	Individual	Group
Time management	☐	☐
Organizational skills	☐	☐
Learning strategies	☐	☐
Study skills	☐	☐
Content area	☐	☐
Writing lab	☐	☐
Math lab	☐	☐

LD PROGRAM STAFF

Key staff person available to work with LD students: Kimberly Fields, Disability Support Services Assistant Director.

LD Program web site: http://bronze.ucok.edu/disability_support/index.htm

East Central University

Ada, OK

Address: 14th Street and Francis Avenue, Ada, OK, 74820
Admissions telephone: 580 310-5239
Admissions FAX: 580 310-5432
Director of Admissions: Pamela Armstrong
Admissions e-mail: parmstro@mailclerk.ecok.edu
Web site: http://www.ecok.edu
SAT Code: 6186 ACT Code: 3394

LD program name: Student Support Services
LD program address: 1100 East 14th Street
Director of Student Support Services: Dwain West
LD program telephone: 580 310-5300
LD program e-mail: dwest@mailclerk.ecok.edu
LD program enrollment: 26, Total campus enrollment: 3,846

GENERAL

East Central University is a public, coed, four-year institution. 130-acre campus in Ada (population: 15,691), 90 miles from Oklahoma City; branch campuses in Ardmore and McAlester. Served by air; major airport and bus serve Oklahoma City; train serves Pauls Valley (33 miles). Semester system.

LD ADMISSIONS

Students do not complete a separate application and are simultaneously accepted to the LD program. A member of the LD program does sit on the admissions committee. A personal interview is not required. Essay is not required.

For fall 2004, 26 completed self-identified LD applications were received.

SECONDARY SCHOOL REQUIREMENTS

Graduation from secondary school required; GED accepted. The following course distribution required: 4 units of English, 3 units of math, 2 units of science, 1 unit of social studies, 2 units of history, 3 units of academic electives.

TESTING

SAT Reasoning or ACT considered if submitted; ACT preferred.

All enrolled freshmen (fall 2004):

Composite: 21

Child Study Team report is not required. A neuropsychological or comprehensive psycho-education evaluation is not required for admission. Tests required as part of this documentation:

- ☐ WAIS-IV
- ☐ WISC-IV
- ☐ SATA
- ☐ Woodcock-Johnson
- ☐ Nelson-Denny Reading Test
- ☐ Other

UNDERGRADUATE STUDENT BODY

Total undergraduate student enrollment: 1,395 Men, 2,028 Women.

Composition of student body (fall 2004):

	Undergraduate	Freshmen
International	0.0	0.0
Black	4.4	4.9
American Indian	18.7	19.6
Asian-American	0.6	0.9
Hispanic	3.6	2.5
White	72.7	72.1
Unreported	0.0	0.0
	100.0%	100.0%

3% are from out of state.

STUDENT HOUSING

Freshmen are not required to live on campus. Housing is guaranteed for all undergraduates. Campus can house 1,064 undergraduates. Single rooms are available for students with medical or special needs. A medical note is required.

EXPENSES

Tuition (2005-06): $2,253 per year (in-state), $6,886 (out-of-state). Tuition is higher for upper-division courses.

Room: $1,070. Board: $1,930.
There is no additional cost for LD program/services.

LD SERVICES

LD program size is not limited.

LD services available to:

■ Freshmen ■ Sophomores ■ Juniors ■ Seniors

Academic Accommodations

Curriculum		In class	
Foreign language waiver	☐	Early syllabus	■
Lighter course load	☐	Note takers in class	■
Math waiver	☐	Priority seating	■
Other special classes	☐	Tape recorders	■
Priority registrations	■	Videotaped classes	■
Substitution of courses	☐	Text on tape	■
Exams		**Services**	
Extended time	■	Diagnostic tests	☐
Oral exams	■	Learning centers	■
Take home exams	☐	Proofreaders	■
Exams on tape or computer	■	Readers	■
Untimed exams	☐	Reading Machines/Kurzweil	☐
Other accommodations	■	Special bookstore section	☐
		Typists	■

Credit toward degree is not given for remedial courses taken.

Counseling Services

■	Academic	Meets 4 times per academic year
☐	Psychological	
☐	Student Support groups	
■	Vocational	Meets 1 time per academic year

Tutoring

Individual tutoring is available daily.

Average size of tutoring groups: 4

	Individual	Group
Time management	■	☐
Organizational skills	■	☐
Learning strategies	■	☐
Study skills	■	☐
Content area	■	☐
Writing lab	■	☐
Math lab	■	☐

LD PROGRAM STAFF

Total number of LD Program staff (including director):

Full Time: 7 Part Time: 7

There is an advisor/advocate from the LD program available to students. The advisor/advocate meets with faculty several times per month and student 3 times per month. 10 peer tutors are available to work with LD students.

Key staff person available to work with LD students: Dwain West, Director of Student Support Services.

Northeastern State University

Tahlequah, OK

Address: 600 N. Grand, Tahlequah, OK, 74464
Admissions telephone: 918 458-2200
Admissions FAX: 918 458-2342
Director of Admissions: Dawn Cain
Admissions e-mail: nsuinfo@nsuok.edu
Web site: http://www.nsuok.edu
SAT Code: 6485 ACT Code: 3408

LD program name: Student Affairs
Administrative Asst to Dean of Student Affairs: Donna Agee
LD program telephone: 918 456-5511, extension 2120
LD program e-mail: ageedm@nsuok.edu
LD program enrollment: 181, Total campus enrollment: 8,543

GENERAL

Northeastern State University is a public, coed, four-year institution. 160-acre campus in Tahlequah (population: 14,458), 30 miles from Muskogee; branch campuses in Muskogee, Potlau, and Tulsa. Airport serves Tulsa (60 miles); bus serves Muskogee. School operates transportation on campus. Semester system.

LD ADMISSIONS

Students do not complete a separate application and are not simultaneously accepted to the LD program. A member of the LD program does not sit on the admissions committee. A personal interview is required. Essay is not required.

For fall 2004, 183 completed self-identified LD applications were received.

SECONDARY SCHOOL REQUIREMENTS

Graduation from secondary school required; GED accepted. The following course distribution required: 4 units of English, 3 units of math, 2 units of science, 2 units of history.

TESTING

ACT required.

All enrolled freshmen (fall 2004):

Average SAT I Scores: Verbal: Math:
Average ACT Scores: Composite: 20

Child Study Team report is not required. A neuropsychological or comprehensive psycho-educational evaluation is required for admission. Must be dated within 36 months of application. Tests required as part of this documentation:

- [x] WAIS-IV
- [x] WISC-IV
- [x] SATA
- [x] Woodcock-Johnson
- [x] Nelson-Denny Reading Test
- [ ] Other

UNDERGRADUATE STUDENT BODY

Total undergraduate student enrollment: 2,920 Men, 4,295 Women.

Composition of student body (fall 2004):

	Undergraduate	Freshmen
International	4.1	2.4
Black	6.9	5.8
American Indian	34.9	29.2
Asian-American	0.6	0.7
Hispanic	1.8	1.5
White	51.6	60.3
Unreported	0.1	0.1
	100.0%	100.0%

2% are from out of state. 1% join a fraternity and 1% join a sorority. Average age of full-time undergraduates is 20. 39% of classes have fewer than 20 students, 54% have between 20 and 50 students, 7% have more than 50 students.

STUDENT HOUSING

90% of freshmen live in college housing. Freshmen are required to live on campus. Housing is guaranteed for all undergraduates. Campus can house 1,988 undergraduates. Single rooms are available for students with medical or special needs. A medical note is required.

EXPENSES

Tuition (2005-06): $2,295 per year (in-state), $7,065 (out-of-state).

Room: $1,536. Board: $1,544.
Additional cost for LD program/services: $20 per credit hour for remedial.

LD SERVICES

LD program size is not limited.

LD services available to:

- [x] Freshmen
- [x] Sophomores
- [x] Juniors
- [x] Seniors

Academic Accommodations

Curriculum		In class	
Foreign language waiver	[ ]	Early syllabus	[ ]
Lighter course load	[x]	Note takers in class	[x]
Math waiver	[ ]	Priority seating	[ ]
Other special classes	[ ]	Tape recorders	[x]
Priority registrations	[ ]	Videotaped classes	[ ]
Substitution of courses	[ ]	Text on tape	[ ]
Exams		**Services**	
Extended time	[x]	Diagnostic tests	[ ]
Oral exams	[x]	Learning centers	[ ]
Take home exams	[ ]	Proofreaders	[ ]
Exams on tape or computer	[ ]	Readers	[x]
Untimed exams	[x]	Reading Machines/Kurzweil	[ ]
Other accommodations	[ ]	Special bookstore section	[ ]
		Typists	[ ]

Credit toward degree is not given for remedial courses taken.

Counseling Services

- [x] Academic
- [x] Psychological
- [ ] Student Support groups
- [ ] Vocational

Tutoring

Individual tutoring is available daily.

Average size of tutoring groups: 1

	Individual	Group
Time management	[ ]	[ ]
Organizational skills	[ ]	[ ]
Learning strategies	[ ]	[ ]
Study skills	[ ]	[ ]
Content area	[ ]	[x]
Writing lab	[ ]	[ ]
Math lab	[ ]	[x]

LD PROGRAM STAFF

Total number of LD Program staff (including director):

Full Time: 5 Part Time: 5

There is an advisor/advocate from the LD program available to students. 1 graduate student and 10 peer tutors are available to work with LD students.

Key staff person available to work with LD students: Dr. Ron Cambiano, Dean of Student Affairs.

LD Program web site: www.nsuok.edu/studentaffairs/disabled.html

University of Oklahoma

Norman, OK

Address: 660 Parrington Oval, Norman, OK, 73019-0390
Admissions telephone: 800 234-6868
Admissions FAX: 405 325-7124
Director of Admissions: Pat Lynch
Admissions e-mail: admrec@ou.edu
Web site: http://www.ou.edu
SAT Code: 6879 ACT Code: 6879

Director of Judicial and Disability Services: Suzette Dyer
LD program telephone: 405 325-3852
LD program e-mail: ods@ou.edu
LD program enrollment: 247, Total campus enrollment: 21,103

GENERAL

University of Oklahoma is a public, coed, four-year institution. 3,200-acre campus in Norman (population: 95,694), 20 miles from Oklahoma City; branch campuses in Oklahoma City and Tulsa. Major airport, bus, and train serve Oklahoma City. School operates transportation to various locations in Norman. Public transportation serves campus. Semester system.

LD ADMISSIONS

Students do not complete a separate application and are not simultaneously accepted to the LD program. A member of the LD program does not sit on the admissions committee. A personal interview is required. Essay is not required.

SECONDARY SCHOOL REQUIREMENTS

Graduation from secondary school required; GED accepted. The following course distribution required: 4 units of English, 3 units of math, 2 units of science, 2 units of social studies, 1 unit of history, 3 units of academic electives.

TESTING

SAT Reasoning or ACT required. SAT Subject recommended.

All enrolled freshmen (fall 2004):

Average SAT I Scores:	Verbal: 589	Math: 597
Average ACT Scores:	Composite: 26	

Child Study Team report is not required. A neuropsychological or comprehensive psycho-educational evaluation is required for admission. Tests required as part of this documentation:

- [ ] WAIS-IV
- [ ] WISC-IV
- [ ] SATA
- [x] Woodcock-Johnson
- [ ] Nelson-Denny Reading Test
- [ ] Other

UNDERGRADUATE STUDENT BODY

Total undergraduate student enrollment: 9,616 Men, 9,614 Women.

Composition of student body (fall 2004):

	Undergraduate	Freshmen
International	1.1	2.3
Black	4.8	5.4
American Indian	7.3	7.6
Asian-American	5.0	5.2
Hispanic	3.3	3.8
White	78.5	75.7
Unreported	0.0	0.0
	100.0%	100.0%

18% are from out of state. 16% join a fraternity and 25% join a sorority. 42% of classes have fewer than 20 students, 47% have between 20 and 50 students, 11% have more than 50 students.

STUDENT HOUSING

Freshmen are required to live on campus. Housing is guaranteed for all undergraduates. Campus can house 5,500 undergraduates. Single rooms are available for students with medical or special needs. A medical note is required.

EXPENSES

Tuition (2005-06): $2,862 per year (in-state), $10,755 (out-of-state).
Board: $5,902.
There is no additional cost for LD program/services.

LD SERVICES

LD program size is not limited.

LD services available to:

- [x] Freshmen
- [x] Sophomores
- [x] Juniors
- [x] Seniors

Academic Accommodations

Curriculum		In class	
Foreign language waiver	[ ]	Early syllabus	[ ]
Lighter course load	[x]	Note takers in class	[x]
Math waiver	[ ]	Priority seating	[ ]
Other special classes	[ ]	Tape recorders	[x]
Priority registrations	[x]	Videotaped classes	[ ]
Substitution of courses	[x]	Text on tape	[x]
Exams		**Services**	
Extended time	[x]	Diagnostic tests	[x]
Oral exams	[ ]	Learning centers	[ ]
Take home exams	[ ]	Proofreaders	[ ]
Exams on tape or computer	[x]	Readers	[x]
Untimed exams	[ ]	Reading Machines/Kurzweil	[x]
Other accommodations	[ ]	Special bookstore section	[ ]
		Typists	[x]

Credit toward degree is not given for remedial courses taken.

Counseling Services

- [x] Academic
- [x] Psychological
- [x] Student Support groups
- [x] Vocational

Tutoring

Individual tutoring is available.

	Individual	Group
Time management	[x]	[x]
Organizational skills	[x]	[x]
Learning strategies	[x]	[x]
Study skills	[x]	[x]
Content area	[x]	[x]
Writing lab	[x]	[x]
Math lab	[x]	[x]

UNIQUE LD PROGRAM FEATURES

OU does not have an LD program, only support services.

LD PROGRAM STAFF

Total number of LD Program staff (including director):

Full Time: 1 Part Time: 1

There is an advisor/advocate from the LD program available to students. 4 graduate students are available to work with LD students.

Key staff person available to work with LD students: Suzette Dyer, Director.

Oklahoma Baptist University

Shawnee, OK

Address: 500 W. University, Shawnee, OK, 74804
Admissions telephone: 800 654-3285
Admissions FAX: 405 878-2046
Dean of Admission: Trent Argo
Admissions e-mail: admissions@okbu.edu
Web site: http://www.okbu.edu
SAT Code: 6541 ACT Code: 3414

LD program name: Disability Services
Director of Student Services: Mr. Canaan Crane
LD program telephone: 405 878-2416
LD program e-mail: canaan.crane@okbu.edu
LD program enrollment: 38, Total campus enrollment: 1,676

GENERAL

Oklahoma Baptist University is a private, coed, four-year institution. 125-acre campus in Shawnee (population: 28,692), 35 miles from Oklahoma City. Served by air and bus; major airport serves Oklahoma City. 4-1-4 system.

LD ADMISSIONS

Students do not complete a separate application and are not simultaneously accepted to the LD program. A member of the LD program does not sit on the admissions committee. A personal interview is required. Essay is not required.

SECONDARY SCHOOL REQUIREMENTS

Graduation from secondary school required; GED accepted.

TESTING

SAT Reasoning considered if submitted. ACT considered if submitted. SAT Subject recommended.

All enrolled freshmen (fall 2004):

Average SAT I Scores:	Verbal: 561	Math: 580
Average ACT Scores:	Composite: 24	

Child Study Team report is not required. A neuropsychological or comprehensive psycho-educational evaluation is required for admission. Must be dated within 24 months of application. Tests required as part of this documentation:

- [x] WAIS-IV
- [x] WISC-IV
- [ ] SATA
- [x] Woodcock-Johnson
- [x] Nelson-Denny Reading Test
- [ ] Other

UNDERGRADUATE STUDENT BODY

Total undergraduate student enrollment: 834 Men, 1,077 Women.

Composition of student body (fall 2004):

	Undergraduate	Freshmen
International	2.4	2.8
Black	2.4	1.6
American Indian	6.2	4.4
Asian-American	2.2	1.2
Hispanic	2.4	2.1
White	82.0	86.5
Unreported	2.4	1.3
	100.0%	100.0%

38% are from out of state. 5% join a fraternity and 5% join a sorority. Average age of full-time undergraduates is 20. 66% of classes have fewer than 20 students. 32% have between 20 and 50 students. 02% have more than 50 students.

STUDENT HOUSING

98% of freshmen live in college housing. Freshmen are required to live on campus. Housing is guaranteed for all undergraduates. Campus can house 1,304 undergraduates. Single rooms are available for students with medical or special needs. A medical note is required.

EXPENSES

Tuition (2005-06): $12,924 per year.

Room: $1,840. Board: $2,300.
There is no additional cost for LD program/services.

LD SERVICES

LD program size is not limited.

LD services available to:

- [x] Freshmen
- [x] Sophomores
- [x] Juniors
- [x] Seniors

Academic Accommodations

Curriculum		**In class**	
Foreign language waiver	[ ]	Early syllabus	[x]
Lighter course load	[x]	Note takers in class	[x]
Math waiver	[ ]	Priority seating	[x]
Other special classes	[x]	Tape recorders	[x]
Priority registrations	[x]	Videotaped classes	[ ]
Substitution of courses	[x]	Text on tape	[x]
Exams		**Services**	
Extended time	[x]	Diagnostic tests	[ ]
Oral exams	[x]	Learning centers	[ ]
Take home exams	[x]	Proofreaders	[ ]
Exams on tape or computer	[x]	Readers	[x]
Untimed exams	[x]	Reading Machines/Kurzweil	[x]
Other accommodations	[x]	Special bookstore section	[ ]
		Typists	[x]

Credit toward degree is given for remedial courses taken.

Counseling Services

- [x] Academic
- [x] Psychological
- [ ] Student Support groups
- [x] Vocational

Meets 3 times per academic year

Tutoring

Individual tutoring is available weekly.

Average size of tutoring groups: 5

	Individual	Group
Time management	[x]	[x]
Organizational skills	[x]	[x]
Learning strategies	[x]	[x]
Study skills	[x]	[x]
Content area	[x]	[ ]
Writing lab	[x]	[x]
Math lab	[x]	[ ]

LD PROGRAM STAFF

Total number of LD Program staff (including director):

Full Time: 1 Part Time: 1

There is an advisor/advocate from the LD program available to students. The advisor/advocate meets with faculty 1 time per month and student 2 times per month.

Key staff person available to work with LD students: Mr. Canaan Crane, Director of Student Services.

Oklahoma Christian University

Oklahoma City, OK

Address: Box 11000, Oklahoma City, OK, 73136-1100
Admissions telephone: 405 425-5050
Admissions FAX: 405 425-5069
Director of Admissions: Risa Forrester
Admissions e-mail: info@oc.edu
Web site: http://www.oc.edu/
SAT Code: 6086 ACT Code: 3415

LD program name: Disability Support Services
Coordinator of ADA/504 Services: Amy Janzen
LD program telephone: 405 425-5907
LD program e-mail: amy.janzen@oc.edu
LD program enrollment: 40, Total campus enrollment: 1,748

GENERAL

Oklahoma Christian University is a private, coed, four-year institution. 200-acre, urban campus in Oklahoma City (population: 506,132); branch campus in Portland, Oreg. Served by air, bus, and train. Semester system.

LD ADMISSIONS

Application Deadline: 09/01. Students do not complete a separate application and are not simultaneously accepted to the LD program. A member of the LD program does not sit on the admissions committee. A personal interview is recommended. Essay is not required.

For fall 2004, 18 completed self-identified LD applications were received. 18 applications were offered admission, and 17 enrolled.

SECONDARY SCHOOL REQUIREMENTS

Graduation from secondary school required; GED accepted. The following course distribution required: 4 units of English, 3 units of math, 2 units of science, 1 unit of social studies, 2 units of history, 3 units of academic electives.

TESTING

SAT Reasoning or ACT considered if submitted; ACT preferred. SAT Subject required.

All enrolled freshmen (fall 2004):

Average SAT I Scores:	Verbal: 547	Math: 525
Average ACT Scores:	Composite: 23	

Child Study Team report is not required. A neuropsychological or comprehensive psycho-educational evaluation is required for admission. Must be dated within 24 months of application. Tests required as part of this documentation:

- [x] WAIS-IV
- [ ] WISC-IV
- [x] SATA
- [x] Woodcock-Johnson
- [x] Nelson-Denny Reading Test
- [ ] Other

UNDERGRADUATE STUDENT BODY

Total undergraduate student enrollment: 883 Men, 851 Women.

Composition of student body (fall 2004):

	Undergraduate	Freshmen
International	0.0	0.0
Black	6.6	7.2
American Indian	2.8	2.0
Asian-American	1.2	1.3
Hispanic	3.7	2.8
White	84.5	84.6
Unreported	1.2	2.1
	100.0%	100.0%

53% are from out of state. 30% join a fraternity and 31% join a sorority. Average age of full-time undergraduates is 21. 60% of classes have fewer than 20 students, 34% have between 20 and 50 students, 6% have more than 50 students.

STUDENT HOUSING

90% of freshmen live in college housing. Freshmen are required to live on campus. Housing is guaranteed for all undergraduates. Campus can house 1,375 undergraduates. Single rooms are available for students with medical or special needs. A medical note is required.

EXPENSES

Tuition (2005-06): $12,486 per year.
Room & Board: $5,060.
There is no additional cost for LD program/services

LD SERVICES

LD program size is not limited.

LD services available to:

[x] Freshmen [x] Sophomores [x] Juniors [x] Seniors

Academic Accommodations

Curriculum		In class	
Foreign language waiver	[ ]	Early syllabus	[ ]
Lighter course load	[ ]	Note takers in class	[x]
Math waiver	[ ]	Priority seating	[x]
Other special classes	[ ]	Tape recorders	[x]
Priority registrations	[ ]	Videotaped classes	[ ]
Substitution of courses	[ ]	Text on tape	[ ]
Exams		**Services**	
Extended time	[x]	Diagnostic tests	[ ]
Oral exams	[x]	Learning centers	[ ]
Take home exams	[ ]	Proofreaders	[ ]
Exams on tape or computer	[x]	Readers	[x]
Untimed exams	[x]	Reading Machines/Kurzweil	[ ]
Other accommodations	[ ]	Special bookstore section	[ ]
		Typists	[ ]

Credit toward degree is not given for remedial courses taken.

Counseling Services

- [x] Academic
- [x] Psychological
- [ ] Student Support groups
- [ ] Vocational

Tutoring

Individual tutoring is available daily.

Average size of tutoring groups: 1

	Individual	Group
Time management	[ ]	[x]
Organizational skills	[ ]	[x]
Learning strategies	[ ]	[x]
Study skills	[ ]	[x]
Content area	[x]	[ ]
Writing lab	[x]	[ ]
Math lab	[x]	[ ]

LD PROGRAM STAFF

Total number of LD Program staff (including director):

There is an advisor/advocate from the LD program available to students. The advisor/advocate meets with faculty 1 time per month and student 1 time per month.

Key staff person available to work with LD students: Amy Janzen, Coordinator of ADA/504 Services.

Oklahoma City University

Oklahoma City, OK

Address: 2501 N. Blackwelder, Oklahoma City, OK, 73106-1493
Admissions telephone: 405 521-5050
Admissions FAX: 405 521-5916
Director of Admissions: Shery Boyles
Admissions e-mail: uadmissions@okcu.edu
Web site: http://www.okcu.edu
SAT Code: 6543 ACT Code: 3416

LD program name: Student Health Services
Director of Student Health Services: Brenda Johnston
LD program telephone: 405 208-5991
LD program e-mail: bjohnston@okcu.edu
Total campus enrollment: 1,869

GENERAL

Oklahoma City University is a private, coed, four-year institution. 68-acre campus in Oklahoma City (population: 506,132). Served by air, bus, and train. Semester system.

LD ADMISSIONS

Students complete a separate application and are not simultaneously accepted to the LD program. A member of the LD program does not sit on the admissions committee. A personal interview is not required. Essay is required and may be typed.

SECONDARY SCHOOL REQUIREMENTS

Graduation from secondary school required; GED accepted. The following course distribution required: 4 units of English, 3 units of math, 3 units of science, 2 units of foreign language, 3 units of social studies, 3 units of history.

TESTING

SAT Reasoning or ACT required. SAT Subject recommended.

All enrolled freshmen (fall 2004):

Average SAT I Scores:	Verbal: 567	Math: 560
Average ACT Scores:	Composite: 24	

Child Study Team report is not required. A neuropsychological or comprehensive psycho-educational evaluation is required for admission. Tests required as part of this documentation:

- ■ WAIS-IV
- ■ WISC-IV
- ☐ SATA
- ☐ Woodcock-Johnson
- ■ Nelson-Denny Reading Test
- ■ Other

UNDERGRADUATE STUDENT BODY

Total undergraduate student enrollment: 771 Men, 1,090 Women.

Composition of student body (fall 2004):

	Undergraduate	Freshmen
International	4.9	21.8
Black	9.0	7.0
American Indian	4.6	3.4
Asian-American	5.6	2.3
Hispanic	5.6	3.6
White	69.7	57.5
Unreported	0.6	4.4
	100.0%	100.0%

30% are from out of state. 13% join a fraternity and 20% join a sorority. Average age of full-time undergraduates is 22. 80% of classes have fewer than 20 students, 19% have between 20 and 50 students.

STUDENT HOUSING

82% of freshmen live in college housing. Freshmen are required to live on campus. Housing is guaranteed for all undergraduates. Campus can house 1,051 undergraduates. Single rooms are available for students with medical or special needs.

EXPENSES

Tuition (2005-06): $16,700 per year.
Room: $3,050. Board: $3,200.
There is no additional cost for LD program/services.

LD SERVICES

LD program size is not limited.

LD services available to:

■ Freshmen ■ Sophomores ■ Juniors ■ Seniors

Academic Accommodations

Curriculum		**In class**	
Foreign language waiver	■	Early syllabus	☐
Lighter course load	☐	Note takers in class	☐
Math waiver	☐	Priority seating	■
Other special classes	☐	Tape recorders	☐
Priority registrations	☐	Videotaped classes	☐
Substitution of courses	■	Text on tape	■
Exams		**Services**	
Extended time	■	Diagnostic tests	☐
Oral exams	■	Learning centers	■
Take home exams	☐	Proofreaders	■
Exams on tape or computer	☐	Readers	■
Untimed exams	☐	Reading Machines/Kurzweil	☐
Other accommodations	■	Special bookstore section	☐
		Typists	☐

Credit toward degree is not given for remedial courses taken.

Counseling Services

- ☐ Academic
- ☐ Psychological
- ☐ Student Support groups
- ☐ Vocational

Tutoring

Individual tutoring is available.

Average size of tutoring groups: 1

	Individual	Group
Time management	☐	☐
Organizational skills	☐	☐
Learning strategies	■	☐
Study skills	■	☐
Content area	☐	☐
Writing lab	■	☐
Math lab	☐	☐

LD PROGRAM STAFF

There is an advisor/advocate from the LD program available to students.

Key staff person available to work with LD students: Brenda Johnston, Director of Student Health Services.

Oklahoma Wesleyan University

Bartlesville, OK

Address: 2201 Silver Lake Road, Bartlesville, OK, 74006
Admissions telephone: 800 GO-TO-BWC
Admissions FAX: 918 335-6229
Enrollment Director: Jim Weidman
Admissions e-mail: admissions@okwu.edu
Web site: http://www.okwu.edu
SAT Code: 6135 ACT Code: 3387

Director, Learning Center: Ruth Ann Colaw
LD program telephone: 918 335-6209
LD program e-mail: racolaw@okwu.edu
Total campus enrollment: 1,040

GENERAL

Oklahoma Wesleyan University is a private, coed, four-year institution. 27-acre campus in Bartlesville (population: 34,748), 45 miles from Tulsa. Served by bus; major airport and train serve Tulsa. Semester system.

LD ADMISSIONS

Application Deadline: 08/15. A personal interview is not required. Essay is not required.

SECONDARY SCHOOL REQUIREMENTS

Graduation from secondary school not required. The following course distribution required: 4 units of English, 2 units of math, 1 unit of science, 2 units of history, 6 units of academic electives.

TESTING

SAT Reasoning or ACT required. SAT Subject recommended.

All enrolled freshmen (fall 2004):

Average SAT I Scores: Verbal: 528 Math: 507
Average ACT Scores: Composite: 21

Child Study Team report is not required. Tests required as part of this documentation:

- ☐ WAIS-IV
- ☐ WISC-IV
- ☐ SATA
- ☐ Woodcock-Johnson
- ☐ Nelson-Denny Reading Test
- ☐ Other

UNDERGRADUATE STUDENT BODY

Total undergraduate student enrollment: 1,040.

Composition of student body (fall 2004):

	Undergraduate	Freshmen
International	1.6	1.8
Black	4.8	4.2
American Indian	2.4	7.1
Asian-American	1.6	0.7
Hispanic	1.6	1.6
White	84.8	80.5
Unreported	3.2	4.1
	100.0%	100.0%

42% are from out of state. Average age of full-time undergraduates is 25. 87% of classes have fewer than 20 students, 13% have between 20 and 50 students.

STUDENT HOUSING

Freshmen are required to live on campus. Housing is guaranteed for all undergraduates. Campus can house 292 undergraduates.

EXPENSES

Tuition (2005-06): $12,900 per year.
Room: $2,650. Board: $2,550.

There is no additional cost for LD program/services.

LD SERVICES

LD program size is not limited.

LD services available to:

☐ Freshmen ☐ Sophomores ☐ Juniors ☐ Seniors

Academic Accommodations

Curriculum		**In class**	
Foreign language waiver	☐	Early syllabus	☐
Lighter course load	■	Note takers in class	☐
Math waiver	☐	Priority seating	☐
Other special classes	☐	Tape recorders	■
Priority registrations	☐	Videotaped classes	■
Substitution of courses	☐	Text on tape	☐
Exams		**Services**	
Extended time	■	Diagnostic tests	☐
Oral exams	■	Learning centers	■
Take home exams	☐	Proofreaders	☐
Exams on tape or computer	☐	Readers	■
Untimed exams	■	Reading Machines/Kurzweil	☐
Other accommodations	☐	Special bookstore section	☐
		Typists	☐

Credit toward degree is not given for remedial courses taken.

Counseling Services

- ☐ Academic
- ☐ Psychological
- ☐ Student Support groups
- ☐ Vocational

Tutoring

	Individual	Group
Time management	☐	☐
Organizational skills	☐	☐
Learning strategies	☐	☐
Study skills	☐	☐
Content area	☐	☐
Writing lab	☐	☐
Math lab	☐	☐

LD PROGRAM STAFF

Total number of LD Program staff (including director):

Full Time: 1 Part Time: 1

Key staff person available to work with LD students: Ruth Ann Colaw, Director, Learning Center.

Oral Roberts University

Tulsa, OK

Address: 7777 S. Lewis Avenue, Tulsa, OK, 74171
Admissions telephone: 800 678-8876
Admissions FAX: 918 495-6222
Director of Admissions: Chris Belcher
Admissions e-mail: admissions@oru.edu
Web site: http://www.oru.edu
SAT Code: 6552 ACT Code: 3427

Director, Student Resources: Don Roberson
LD program telephone: 918 495-7018
LD program e-mail: droberson@oru.edu
Total campus enrollment: 3,776

GENERAL

Oral Roberts University is a private, coed, four-year institution. 500-acre, suburban campus in Tulsa (population: 393,049). Served by air and bus. School operates shuttle service. Public transportation serves campus. Semester system.

LD ADMISSIONS

A personal interview is required. Essay is not required.

SECONDARY SCHOOL REQUIREMENTS

Graduation from secondary school required; GED accepted. The following course distribution required: 4 units of English, 2 units of math, 1 unit of science, 2 units of foreign language, 2 units of social studies.

TESTING

SAT Reasoning or ACT required. SAT Subject recommended.

All enrolled freshmen (fall 2004):

Average SAT I Scores:	Verbal: 542	Math: 527
Average ACT Scores:	Composite: 23	

Child Study Team report is not required. Tests required as part of this documentation:

☐ WAIS-IV ☐ Woodcock-Johnson
☐ WISC-IV ☐ Nelson-Denny Reading Test
☐ SATA ☐ Other

UNDERGRADUATE STUDENT BODY

Total undergraduate student enrollment: 1,289 Men, 1,798 Women.

Composition of student body (fall 2004):

	Undergraduate	Freshmen
International	6.8	5.1
Black	21.4	15.5
American Indian	2.3	1.7
Asian-American	3.2	2.2
Hispanic	9.8	5.8
White	51.4	63.8
Unreported	5.1	5.9
	100.0%	100.0%

64% are from out of state. Average age of full-time undergraduates is 22. 58% of classes have fewer than 20 students, 37% have between 20 and 50 students, 5% have more than 50 students.

STUDENT HOUSING

69% of freshmen live in college housing. Housing is guaranteed for all undergraduates. Campus can house 2,745 undergraduates.

EXPENSES

Tuition (2005-06): $15,400 per year.
Room: $3,280. Board: $3,490.

There is no additional cost for LD program/services.

LD SERVICES

LD program size is not limited.

LD services available to:

☐ Freshmen ☐ Sophomores ☐ Juniors ☐ Seniors

Academic Accommodations

Curriculum		In class	
Foreign language waiver	☐	Early syllabus	☐
Lighter course load	☐	Note takers in class	■
Math waiver	☐	Priority seating	☐
Other special classes	☐	Tape recorders	■
Priority registrations	☐	Videotaped classes	☐
Substitution of courses	☐	Text on tape	☐
Exams		**Services**	
Extended time	■	Diagnostic tests	■
Oral exams	■	Learning centers	■
Take home exams	☐	Proofreaders	☐
Exams on tape or computer	☐	Readers	■
Untimed exams	☐	Reading Machines/Kurzweil	■
Other accommodations	☐	Special bookstore section	■
		Typists	☐

Credit toward degree is not given for remedial courses taken.

Counseling Services

☐ Academic
☐ Psychological
☐ Student Support groups
☐ Vocational

Tutoring

	Individual	Group
Time management	☐	☐
Organizational skills	☐	☐
Learning strategies	☐	☐
Study skills	☐	☐
Content area	☐	☐
Writing lab	☐	☐
Math lab	☐	☐

LD PROGRAM STAFF

Total number of LD Program staff (including director):

Full Time: 1 Part Time: 1

Key staff person available to work with LD students: Don Roberson, Dir. Student Resources.

Southeastern Oklahoma State University

Durant, OK

Address: 1405 N. Fourth, PMB 4225, Durant, OK, 74701-0609
Admissions telephone: 800 435-1327
Admissions FAX: 580 745-7502
Director of Enrollment Management: Kyle Stafford
Admissions e-mail: admissions@sosu.edu
Web site: http://www.sosu.edu
SAT Code: 6657 ACT Code: 3438

LD program name: Student Support Services
LD program address: 1405 N. 4th PMB Box 4112
Coordinator for Disability Services: Susan Dodson
LD program telephone: 580 745-2394
LD program e-mail: sdodson@sosu.edu
LD program enrollment: 25, Total campus enrollment: 3,659

GENERAL

Southeastern Oklahoma State University is a public, coed, four-year institution. 173-acre campus in Durant (population: 13,549), 90 miles from Dallas. Served by air and bus; major airport and train serve Dallas. Semester system.

LD ADMISSIONS

Students do not complete a separate application and are not simultaneously accepted to the LD program. A member of the LD program does not sit on the admissions committee. A personal interview is not required. Essay is not required.

SECONDARY SCHOOL REQUIREMENTS

Graduation from secondary school required; GED accepted. The following course distribution required: 4 units of English, 3 units of math, 2 units of science, 2 units of history, 3 units of academic electives.

TESTING

ACT required of some applicants. SAT Reasoning or ACT considered if submitted; ACT preferred. SAT Subject recommended.

All enrolled freshmen (fall 2004):

Average SAT I Scores:	Verbal: n/a	Math: n/a
Average ACT Scores:	Composite: 20	

Child Study Team report is not required. A neuropsychological or comprehensive psycho-education evaluation is not required for admission. Tests required as part of this documentation:

- ☐ WAIS-IV
- ☐ WISC-IV
- ☐ SATA
- ☐ Woodcock-Johnson
- ☐ Nelson-Denny Reading Test
- ☐ Other

UNDERGRADUATE STUDENT BODY

Total undergraduate student enrollment: 1,704 Men, 1,935 Women.

Composition of student body (fall 2004):

	Undergraduate	Freshmen
International	0.6	1.5
Black	4.3	4.8
American Indian	33.9	29.2
Asian-American	0.6	0.5
Hispanic	2.1	1.9
White	58.5	62.1
Unreported	0.0	0.0
	100.0%	100.0%

22% are from out of state. 1% join a fraternity and 2% join a sorority. Average age of full-time undergraduates is 23. 40% of classes have fewer than 20 students, 58% have between 20 and 50 students, 2% have more than 50 students.

STUDENT HOUSING

27% of freshmen live in college housing. Freshmen are not required to live on campus. Housing is guaranteed for all undergraduates. Campus can house 632 undergraduates. Single rooms are available for students with medical or special needs. A medical note is required.

EXPENSES

Tuition (2005-06): (Tuition varies by year.)
There is no additional cost for LD program/services.

LD SERVICES

LD program size is not limited.

LD services available to:

☑ Freshmen ☑ Sophomores ☑ Juniors ☑ Seniors

Academic Accommodations

Curriculum		**In class**	
Foreign language waiver	☐	Early syllabus	☐
Lighter course load	☐	Note takers in class	☑
Math waiver	☐	Priority seating	☐
Other special classes	☑	Tape recorders	☑
Priority registrations	☐	Videotaped classes	☐
Substitution of courses	☐	Text on tape	☐
Exams		**Services**	
Extended time	☑	Diagnostic tests	☑
Oral exams	☐	Learning centers	☑
Take home exams	☐	Proofreaders	☐
Exams on tape or computer	☐	Readers	☑
Untimed exams	☐	Reading Machines/Kurzweil	☑
Other accommodations	☑	Special bookstore section	☐
		Typists	☐

Credit toward degree is not given for remedial courses taken.

Counseling Services

- ☑ Academic
- ☑ Psychological
- ☐ Student Support groups
- ☐ Vocational

Tutoring

Individual tutoring is available daily.

Average size of tutoring groups: 5

	Individual	Group
Time management	☐	☑
Organizational skills	☐	☑
Learning strategies	☑	☑
Study skills	☐	☑
Content area	☑	☑
Writing lab	☑	☑
Math lab	☑	☑

LD PROGRAM STAFF

Total number of LD Program staff (including director):

Full Time: 3 Part Time: 3

There is not an advisor/advocate from the LD program available to students.

Key staff person available to work with LD students: Susan Dodson, Coordinator for Disability Services.

LD Program web site: www.sosu.edu/sss

Southern Nazarene University

Bethany, OK

Address: 6729 N.W. 39th Expressway, Bethany, OK, 73008
Admissions telephone: 800 648-9899
Admissions FAX: 405 491-6320
Director of Admissions: Larry Hess
Admissions e-mail: admissions@snu.edu
Web site: http://www.snu.edu
SAT Code: 6036 ACT Code: 3384

Director, Academic Center: Loral Henck
LD program telephone: 405 491-6694
LD program e-mail: LHenck@snu.edu
LD program enrollment: 22, Total campus enrollment: 1,767

GENERAL

Southern Nazarene University is a private, coed, four-year institution. 40-acre, suburban campus in Bethany (population: 20,307), one mile from Oklahoma City; branch campus in Tulsa. Airport, bus, and train serve Oklahoma City. Semester system.

LD ADMISSIONS

Students do not complete a separate application and are simultaneously accepted to the LD program. A member of the LD program does not sit on the admissions committee. High school waivers are accepted for math and foreign language. A personal interview is required. Essay is not required.

For fall 2004, 51 completed self-identified LD applications were received. 51 applications were offered admission, and 51 enrolled.

SECONDARY SCHOOL REQUIREMENTS

Graduation from secondary school required; GED accepted.

TESTING

SAT Reasoning considered if submitted. ACT recommended. SAT Subject recommended.

All enrolled freshmen (fall 2004):

Average ACT Scores: Composite: 22

Child Study Team report is required if student is classified. A neuropsychological or comprehensive psycho-educational evaluation is required for admission. Tests required as part of this documentation:

- [x] WAIS-IV
- [x] WISC-IV
- [x] SATA
- [x] Woodcock-Johnson
- [x] Nelson-Denny Reading Test
- [x] Other

UNDERGRADUATE STUDENT BODY

Total undergraduate student enrollment: 1,767.

Composition of student body (fall 2004):

	Undergraduate	Freshmen
International	0.3	0.2
Black	6.6	8.7
American Indian	1.6	3.0
Asian-American	1.6	1.8
Hispanic	6.2	3.7
White	83.7	81.5
Unreported	0.0	1.1
	100.0%	100.0%

31% are from out of state. 0.54% of classes have fewer than 20 students. 43% have between 20 and 50 students. 3% have more than 50 students.

STUDENT HOUSING

Freshmen are not required to live on campus. Housing is guaranteed for all undergraduates. Campus can house 1,012 undergraduates. Single rooms are available for students with medical or special needs. A medical note is required.

EXPENSES

Tuition (2005-06): $12,870 per year.

Room: $2,458. Board: $2,808.

There is no additional cost for LD program/services.

LD SERVICES

LD program size is not limited.

LD services available to:

- [x] Freshmen
- [x] Sophomores
- [x] Juniors
- [x] Seniors

Academic Accommodations

Curriculum		In class	
Foreign language waiver	[ ]	Early syllabus	[ ]
Lighter course load	[x]	Note takers in class	[x]
Math waiver	[ ]	Priority seating	[ ]
Other special classes	[ ]	Tape recorders	[x]
Priority registrations	[ ]	Videotaped classes	[ ]
Substitution of courses	[ ]	Text on tape	[ ]
Exams		**Services**	
Extended time	[x]	Diagnostic tests	[ ]
Oral exams	[x]	Learning centers	[x]
Take home exams	[ ]	Proofreaders	[ ]
Exams on tape or computer	[ ]	Readers	[x]
Untimed exams	[ ]	Reading Machines/Kurzweil	[x]
Other accommodations	[ ]	Special bookstore section	[ ]
		Typists	[ ]

Credit toward degree is not given for remedial courses taken.

Counseling Services

- [x] Academic
- [x] Psychological
- [x] Student Support groups
- [x] Vocational

Tutoring

Individual tutoring is available daily.

	Individual	Group
Time management	[x]	[x]
Organizational skills	[x]	[x]
Learning strategies	[x]	[x]
Study skills	[x]	[x]
Content area	[x]	[x]
Writing lab	[x]	[x]
Math lab	[x]	[x]

LD PROGRAM STAFF

Total number of LD Program staff (including director):

Full Time: 1 Part Time: 1

There is an advisor/advocate from the LD program available to students. 1 graduate student and 12 peer tutors are available to work with LD students.

Key staff person available to work with LD students: Jeannette Hanson, Disability Support.

St. Gregory's University

Shawnee, OK

Address: 1900 W. MacArthur Street, Shawnee, OK, 74804
Admissions telephone: 888 STGREGS
Admissions FAX: 405 878-5198
Director of Admissions: Michael Deegan
Admissions e-mail: admissions@stgregorys.edu
Web site: http://www.stgregorys.edu
SAT Code: 6621 ACT Code: 3432

LD program name: Partners in Learning (PIL)
Director, Partners in Learning Program: Melody Harrington
LD program telephone: 405 878-5310
LD program e-mail: maharrington@stgregorys.edu
LD program enrollment: 14, Total campus enrollment: 782

GENERAL

St. Gregory's University is a private, coed, four-year institution. 1,000-acre, suburban campus in Shawnee (population: 28,692), 32 miles from Oklahoma City. Served by bus; major airport and bus serve Oklahoma City. Semester system.

LD ADMISSIONS

Application Deadline: 08/15. Students complete a separate application and are not simultaneously accepted to the LD program. A member of the LD program does sit on the admissions committee. High school waivers are accepted for math and foreign language. A personal interview is required. Essay is not required. Students must meet 2 of 3 admissions criteria:

1. 2.75 High School GPA on 4.0 Scale
2. 21 ACT Composite or 990 SAT Composite
3. Ranked in top half of graduating class

LD students may be admitted conditionally if they only meet 1 of 3 criteria.

For fall 2004, 30 completed self-identified LD applications were received. 25 applications were offered admission, and 12 enrolled.

SECONDARY SCHOOL REQUIREMENTS

Graduation from secondary school required; GED accepted. The following course distribution required: 4 units of English, 3 units of math, 2 units of science, 2 units of history.

TESTING

ACT required; SAT Reasoning may be substituted.

All enrolled freshmen (fall 2004):

Average SAT I Scores: Verbal: Math:
Average ACT Scores: Composite:

Child Study Team report is not required. A neuropsychological or comprehensive psycho-educational evaluation is required for admission. Must be dated within 24 months of application. Tests required as part of this documentation:

■ WAIS-IV ■ Woodcock-Johnson
■ WISC-IV ■ Nelson-Denny Reading Test
■ SATA ■ Other

UNDERGRADUATE STUDENT BODY

Total undergraduate student enrollment: 348 Men, 404 Women.

Composition of student body (fall 2004):

	Undergraduate	Freshmen
International	9.0	9.4
Black	9.9	5.8
American Indian	17.1	12.2
Asian-American	0.9	1.5
Hispanic	9.9	8.2
White	53.2	61.4
Unreported	0.0	1.5
	100.0%	100.0%

14% are from out of state.

STUDENT HOUSING

Housing is guaranteed for all undergraduates. Campus can house 442 undergraduates. Single rooms are available for students with medical or special needs. A medical note is not required.

EXPENSES

Tuition (2005-06): $11,800 per year.

Room: $3,000. Board: $2,320.

Additional cost for LD program/services: $7,000 per year.

LD SERVICES

LD program is limited to 1% students.

LD services available to:

■ Freshmen ■ Sophomores ■ Juniors ■ Seniors

Academic Accommodations

Curriculum		**In class**	
Foreign language waiver	☐	Early syllabus	■
Lighter course load	■	Note takers in class	■
Math waiver	☐	Priority seating	■
Other special classes	☐	Tape recorders	■
Priority registrations	☐	Videotaped classes	■
Substitution of courses	☐	Text on tape	■
Exams		**Services**	
Extended time	■	Diagnostic tests	☐
Oral exams	■	Learning centers	■
Take home exams	☐	Proofreaders	■
Exams on tape or computer	■	Readers	■
Untimed exams	■	Reading Machines/Kurzweil	■
Other accommodations	■	Special bookstore section	☐
		Typists	■

Credit toward degree is not given for remedial courses taken.

Counseling Services

■ Academic — Meets 4 times per academic year
☐ Psychological
☐ Student Support groups
☐ Vocational

Tutoring

Individual tutoring is available daily.

Average size of tutoring groups: 2

	Individual	Group
Time management	■	■
Organizational skills	■	■
Learning strategies	■	■
Study skills	■	■
Content area	■	■
Writing lab	■	■
Math lab	■	■

LD PROGRAM STAFF

Total number of LD Program staff (including director):

Full Time: 2 Part Time: 2

There is an advisor/advocate from the LD program available to students. The advisor/advocate meets with faculty 2 times per month and student 4 times per month. 1 graduate student and 20 peer tutors are available to work with LD students.

Key staff person available to work with LD students: Melody Harrington, Director, Partners in Learning Program.

University of Tulsa

Tulsa, OK

Address: 600 S. College Avenue, Tulsa, OK, 74104
Admissions telephone: 800 331-3050
Admissions FAX: 918 631-5003
Dean of Admissions: John C. Corso
Admissions e-mail: admission@utulsa.edu
Web site: http://www.utulsa.edu
SAT Code: 6883 ACT Code: 3444

LD program name: Center for Student Academic Support
Coordinator of Support Services: Ruby Wile
LD program telephone: 918 631-2331
LD program e-mail: ruby-wile@utulsa.edu
LD program enrollment: 62, Total campus enrollment: 2,756

GENERAL

University of Tulsa is a private, coed, four-year institution. 200-acre, urban campus in Tulsa (metropolitan population: 393,049). Served by air and bus. Public transportation serves campus. Semester system.

LD ADMISSIONS

Students do not complete a separate application and are not simultaneously accepted to the LD program. A member of the LD program does not sit on the admissions committee. A personal interview is recommended. Essay is required and may be typed.

77 applications were offered admission, and 77 enrolled.

SECONDARY SCHOOL REQUIREMENTS

Graduation from secondary school required; GED accepted.

TESTING

SAT Reasoning or ACT required. SAT Subject recommended.

All enrolled freshmen (fall 2004):

Average SAT I Scores:	Verbal: 610	Math: 610
Average ACT Scores:	Composite: 26	

Child Study Team report is not required. A neuropsychological or comprehensive psycho-educational evaluation is required for admission. Tests required as part of this documentation:

■ WAIS-IV	■ Woodcock-Johnson
■ WISC-IV	☐ Nelson-Denny Reading Test
☐ SATA	☐ Other

UNDERGRADUATE STUDENT BODY

Total undergraduate student enrollment: 1,322 Men, 1,447 Women.

Composition of student body (fall 2004):

	Undergraduate	Freshmen
International	5.9	9.4
Black	6.5	7.3
American Indian	2.9	5.0
Asian-American	2.1	1.9
Hispanic	3.1	3.3
White	71.1	65.5
Unreported	8.4	7.6
	100.0%	100.0%

23% are from out of state. 21% join a fraternity and 23% join a sorority. Average age of full-time undergraduates is 21. 62% of classes have fewer than 20 students, 37% have between 20 and 50 students, 1% have more than 50 students.

STUDENT HOUSING

83% of freshmen live in college housing. Freshmen are required to live on campus. Housing is guaranteed for all undergraduates. Campus can house 1,951 undergraduates. Single rooms are available for students with medical or special needs. A medical note is required.

EXPENSES

Tuition (2005-06): $18,780 per year.

Room: $3,540. Board: $2,948.
There is no additional cost for LD program/services.

LD SERVICES

LD program size is not limited.

LD services available to:

■ Freshmen ■ Sophomores ■ Juniors ■ Seniors

Academic Accommodations

Curriculum		In class	
Foreign language waiver	■	Early syllabus	☐
Lighter course load	■	Note takers in class	■
Math waiver	■	Priority seating	■
Other special classes	☐	Tape recorders	■
Priority registrations	■	Videotaped classes	☐
Substitution of courses	■	Text on tape	☐
Exams		**Services**	
Extended time	■	Diagnostic tests	☐
Oral exams	☐	Learning centers	■
Take home exams	☐	Proofreaders	☐
Exams on tape or computer	■	Readers	■
Untimed exams	■	Reading Machines/Kurzweil	■
Other accommodations	☐	Special bookstore section	☐
		Typists	☐

Credit toward degree is not given for remedial courses taken.

Counseling Services

■ Academic
■ Psychological
■ Student Support groups
■ Vocational

Tutoring

Individual tutoring is available weekly.

Average size of tutoring groups: 1

	Individual	Group
Time management	■	■
Organizational skills	■	■
Learning strategies	■	■
Study skills	■	■
Content area	■	☐
Writing lab	■	☐
Math lab	■	■

LD PROGRAM STAFF

Total number of LD Program staff (including director):

Full Time: 2 Part Time: 2

There is an advisor/advocate from the LD program available to students. 9 graduate students and 70 peer tutors are available to work with LD students.

Key staff person available to work with LD students: Dr. Jane Corso, Director, Student Academic Support Center.

Concordia University

Portland, OR

Address: 2811 N.E. Holman Street, Portland, OR, 97211
Admissions telephone: 800 321-9371
Admissions FAX: 503 280-8531
Vice President for Enrollment and Student Services: Bobi Swan
Admissions e-mail: admissions@cu-portland.edu
Web site: http://www.cu-portland.edu
SAT Code: 4079 ACT Code: 3458

LD program name: Student Services
Dir. Counseling and Learning Services: Terry McGlassen
LD program telephone: 503 493-6545
LD program e-mail: tmcglassen@cu-portland.edu
LD program enrollment: 10, Total campus enrollment: 883

GENERAL

Concordia University is a private, coed, four-year institution. 13-acre campus in Portland (population: 529,121). Served by air, bus, and train. Public transportation serves campus. Semester system.

LD ADMISSIONS

Application Deadline: 07/01. Students do not complete a separate application and are simultaneously accepted to the LD program. A member of the LD program does not sit on the admissions committee. A personal interview is not required. Essay is not required.

For fall 2004, 10 completed self-identified LD applications were received. 10 applications were offered admission, and 10 enrolled.

SECONDARY SCHOOL REQUIREMENTS

Graduation from secondary school required; GED accepted.

TESTING

SAT Reasoning or ACT required. SAT Subject recommended.

All enrolled freshmen (fall 2004):

Average SAT I Scores:	Verbal: 496	Math: 507
Average ACT Scores:	Composite: 21	

Child Study Team report is not required. A neuropsychological or comprehensive psycho-educational evaluation is required for admission. Must be dated within 24 months of application. Tests required as part of this documentation:

- ■ WAIS-IV
- ■ WISC-IV
- ■ SATA
- ■ Woodcock-Johnson
- ■ Nelson-Denny Reading Test
- ☐ Other

UNDERGRADUATE STUDENT BODY

Total undergraduate student enrollment: 335 Men, 575 Women.

Composition of student body (fall 2004):

	Undergraduate	Freshmen
International	3.2	1.7
Black	3.2	4.7
American Indian	1.6	1.3
Asian-American	9.7	3.7
Hispanic	6.5	2.5
White	70.2	74.5
Unreported	5.6	11.6
	100.0%	100.0%

41% are from out of state. Average age of full-time undergraduates is 24. 78% of classes have fewer than 20 students, 21% have between 20 and 50 students, 1% have more than 50 students.

STUDENT HOUSING

86% of freshmen live in college housing. Freshmen are required to live on campus. Housing is guaranteed for all undergraduates. Campus can house 430 undergraduates. Single rooms are available for students with medical or special needs. A medical note is required.

EXPENSES

Tuition (2005-06): $18,900 per year.
Room: $2,700. Board: $3,000.
There is no additional cost for LD program/services.

LD SERVICES

LD program size is not limited.

LD services available to:

■ Freshmen ■ Sophomores ■ Juniors ■ Seniors

Academic Accommodations

Curriculum		In class	
Foreign language waiver	☐	Early syllabus	■
Lighter course load	■	Note takers in class	■
Math waiver	☐	Priority seating	■
Other special classes	☐	Tape recorders	■
Priority registrations	■	Videotaped classes	■
Substitution of courses	☐	Text on tape	■
Exams		**Services**	
Extended time	■	Diagnostic tests	☐
Oral exams	■	Learning centers	■
Take home exams	☐	Proofreaders	■
Exams on tape or computer	■	Readers	■
Untimed exams	■	Reading Machines/Kurzweil	■
Other accommodations	■	Special bookstore section	☐
		Typists	■

Credit toward degree is not given for remedial courses taken.

Counseling Services

- ■ Academic — Meets 4 times per academic year
- ■ Psychological
- ☐ Student Support groups
- ☐ Vocational

Tutoring

Individual tutoring is available daily.

Average size of tutoring groups: 1

	Individual	Group
Time management	■	☐
Organizational skills	■	☐
Learning strategies	■	☐
Study skills	■	☐
Content area	■	☐
Writing lab	■	☐
Math lab	■	■

LD PROGRAM STAFF

Total number of LD Program staff (including director):

Full Time: 1 Part Time: 1

There is an advisor/advocate from the LD program available to students. The advisor/advocate meets with faculty 3 times per month and students 1 time per month. 20 peer tutors are available to work with LD students.

Key staff person available to work with LD students: Terry McGlassen, Director.

Corban College

Salem, OR

Address: 5000 Deer Park Drive SE, Salem, OR, 97301
Admissions telephone: 800 845-3005
Admissions FAX: 503 585-4316
Director of Admissions: Marty Ziesemer
Admissions e-mail: admissions@corban.edu
Web site: http://www.corban.edu
SAT Code: 4956 ACT Code: 477

LD program name: Learning Disability Program
Director of Career and Academic Services: Daren Milionis
LD program telephone: 503 375-7012
LD program e-mail: dmilionis@wbc.edu
LD program enrollment: 10, Total campus enrollment: 735

GENERAL

Corban College is a private, coed, four-year institution. 100-acre, suburban campus in Salem (population: 136,924), 45 miles from Portland. Served by bus and train; major airport serves Portland. Semester system.

LD ADMISSIONS

Application Deadline: 08/01. Students do not complete a separate application and are simultaneously accepted to the LD program. A member of the LD program does sit on the admissions committee. A personal interview is recommended. Essay is required and may be typed.

For fall 2004, 3 completed self-identified LD applications were received. 3 applications were offered admission, and 3 enrolled.

SECONDARY SCHOOL REQUIREMENTS

Graduation from secondary school required; GED accepted. The following course distribution required: 4 units of English, 3 units of math, 2 units of science, 1 unit of foreign language, 3 units of social studies.

TESTING

SAT Reasoning required; ACT may be substituted. SAT Subject required.

All enrolled freshmen (fall 2004):

Average SAT I Scores:	Verbal: 552	Math: 538
Average ACT Scores:	Composite: 22	

A neuropsychological or comprehensive psycho-educational evaluation is required for admission. Must be dated within 36 months of application. Tests required as part of this documentation:

- ■ WAIS-IV
- ■ WISC-IV
- ☐ SATA
- ■ Woodcock-Johnson
- ☐ Nelson-Denny Reading Test
- ☐ Other

UNDERGRADUATE STUDENT BODY

Total undergraduate student enrollment: 291 Men, 405 Women.

Composition of student body (fall 2004):

	Undergraduate	Freshmen
International	0.6	0.3
Black	0.6	0.6
American Indian	3.6	1.8
Asian-American	1.8	2.4
Hispanic	2.4	2.7
White	89.2	90.5
Unreported	1.8	1.7
	100.0%	100.0%

34% are from out of state. Average age of full-time undergraduates is 23. 62% of classes have fewer than 20 students, 35% have between 20 and 50 students, 3% have more than 50 students.

STUDENT HOUSING

100% of freshmen live in college housing. Freshmen are required to live on campus. Housing is guaranteed for all undergraduates. Campus can house 420 undergraduates. Single rooms are available for students with medical or special needs. A medical note is required.

EXPENSES

Tuition (2005-06): $17,834 per year.
Room: $3,244. Board: $3,190.
There is no additional cost for LD program/services.

LD SERVICES

LD program size is not limited.

LD services available to:

■ Freshmen ■ Sophomores ■ Juniors ■ Seniors

Academic Accommodations

Curriculum		In class	
Foreign language waiver	☐	Early syllabus	☐
Lighter course load	■	Note takers in class	■
Math waiver	☐	Priority seating	■
Other special classes	☐	Tape recorders	■
Priority registrations	☐	Videotaped classes	☐
Substitution of courses	■	Text on tape	■
Exams		**Services**	
Extended time	■	Diagnostic tests	☐
Oral exams	■	Learning centers	■
Take home exams	☐	Proofreaders	■
Exams on tape or computer	■	Readers	■
Untimed exams	■	Reading Machines/Kurzweil	☐
Other accommodations	☐	Special bookstore section	☐
		Typists	☐

Credit toward degree is not given for remedial courses taken.

Counseling Services

■ Academic	Meets 3 times per academic year
■ Psychological	Meets 3 times per academic year
☐ Student Support groups	
☐ Vocational	

Tutoring

Individual tutoring is available daily.

Average size of tutoring groups: 1

	Individual	Group
Time management	■	☐
Organizational skills	☐	☐
Learning strategies	■	☐
Study skills	■	☐
Content area	☐	☐
Writing lab	☐	☐
Math lab	☐	☐

LD PROGRAM STAFF

There is an advisor/advocate from the LD program available to students. The advisor/advocate meets with faculty 2 times per month and students 1 time per month. 12 peer tutors are available to work with LD students.

Key staff person available to work with LD students: Daren Milionis, Director of Career and Academic Services.

Eastern Oregon University

La Grande, OR

Address: 1 University Boulevard, La Grande, OR, 97850
Admissions telephone: 800 452-8639
Admissions FAX: 541 962-3418
Director of Admissions: Sherri Edvalson
Admissions e-mail: admissions@eou.edu
Web site: http://www.eou.edu
SAT Code: 4300 ACT Code: 3460

Disability Services Coordinator: Pat Arnson
LD program telephone: 541 962-3081
LD program e-mail: parnson@eou.edu
Total campus enrollment: 3,069

GENERAL

Eastern Oregon University is a public, coed, four-year institution. 121-acre campus in LaGrande (population: 12,327), 261 miles from Portland; branch centers in Baker, Burns, Enterprise, John Day, Ontario, and Pendleton. Served by bus; major airport serves Portland; smaller airport serves Pendleton (50 miles). Quarter system.

LD ADMISSIONS

A personal interview is not required. Essay is not required.

SECONDARY SCHOOL REQUIREMENTS

Graduation from secondary school required; GED accepted. The following course distribution required: 4 units of English, 3 units of math, 2 units of science, 2 units of foreign language, 3 units of social studies.

TESTING

SAT Reasoning required; ACT may be substituted.

All enrolled freshmen (fall 2004):

Average SAT I Scores: Verbal: 495 Math: 500
Average ACT Scores: Composite: 20

Child Study Team report is not required. Tests required as part of this documentation:

- ☐ WAIS-IV
- ☐ WISC-IV
- ☐ SATA
- ☐ Woodcock-Johnson
- ☐ Nelson-Denny Reading Test
- ☐ Other

UNDERGRADUATE STUDENT BODY

Total undergraduate student enrollment: 1,194 Men, 1,626 Women.

Composition of student body (fall 2004):

	Undergraduate	Freshmen
International	2.0	2.6
Black	2.6	1.9
American Indian	2.0	1.8
Asian-American	2.0	3.3
Hispanic	2.3	2.9
White	84.2	80.5
Unreported	4.9	7.0
	100.0%	100.0%

30% are from out of state. Average age of full-time undergraduates is 24. 48% of classes have fewer than 20 students, 43% have between 20 and 50 students, 9% have more than 50 students.

STUDENT HOUSING

68% of freshmen live in college housing. Freshmen are required to live on campus. Housing is guaranteed for all undergraduates. Priority given to continuing students, early admits, and new students based on date of application. Campus can house 548 undergraduates.

EXPENSES

Tuition (2005-06): $4,551 per year.

Room: $4,200. Board: $3,000.

There is no additional cost for LD program/services.

LD SERVICES

LD program size is not limited.

LD services available to:

☐ Freshmen ☐ Sophomores ☐ Juniors ☐ Seniors

Academic Accommodations

Curriculum		In class	
Foreign language waiver	☐	Early syllabus	☐
Lighter course load	■	Note takers in class	■
Math waiver	☐	Priority seating	☐
Other special classes	☐	Tape recorders	■
Priority registrations	☐	Videotaped classes	■
Substitution of courses	☐	Text on tape	☐
Exams		**Services**	
Extended time	■	Diagnostic tests	☐
Oral exams	■	Learning centers	■
Take home exams	☐	Proofreaders	☐
Exams on tape or computer	☐	Readers	■
Untimed exams	■	Reading Machines/Kurzweil	■
Other accommodations	☐	Special bookstore section	☐
		Typists	☐

Credit toward degree is not given for remedial courses taken.

Counseling Services

- ☐ Academic
- ☐ Psychological
- ☐ Student Support groups
- ☐ Vocational

Tutoring

	Individual	Group
Time management	☐	☐
Organizational skills	☐	☐
Learning strategies	☐	☐
Study skills	☐	☐
Content area	☐	☐
Writing lab	☐	☐
Math lab	☐	☐

LD PROGRAM STAFF

Total number of LD Program staff (including director):

Full Time: 2 Part Time: 2

Key staff person available to work with LD students: Pat Arnson, Disability Services Coordinator.

George Fox University

Newberg, OR

Address: 414 N. Meridian Street, Newberg, OR, 97132
Admissions telephone: 800 765-4369
Admissions FAX: 503 554-3110
Director of Undergraduate Admissions: Dale Seipp
Admissions e-mail: admissions@georgefox.edu
Web site: http://www.georgefox.edu
SAT Code: 4325 ACT Code: 3462

LD program name: Disability Services
Director: Rick Muthiah
LD program telephone: 503 554-2314
LD program e-mail: rmuthiah@georgefox.edu
LD program enrollment: 25, Total campus enrollment: 1,713

GENERAL

George Fox University is a private, coed, four-year institution. 75-acre campus in Newberg (population: 18,064), 23 miles from Portland; branch campuses in Boise, Eugene, Portland, and Salem. Served by bus; major airport and train serve Portland. Semester system.

LD ADMISSIONS

Students complete a separate application and are not simultaneously accepted to the LD program. A member of the LD program does not sit on the admissions committee. A personal interview is not required. Essay is required and may be typed. No documentation is needed for admission to the instiution, but documentation is required to request LD services. Students do not complete a separate application for admission to the institution other than the standard application. Students requesting servcies for a disability are required to complete a service request form and submit documentation.

SECONDARY SCHOOL REQUIREMENTS

Graduation from secondary school required; GED accepted.

TESTING

SAT Reasoning or ACT required. SAT Subject recommended.

All enrolled freshmen (fall 2004):

Average SAT I Scores:	Verbal: 538	Math: 531
Average ACT Scores:	Composite: 23	

Child Study Team report is not required. A neuropsychological or comprehensive psycho-educational evaluation is required for admission. Must be dated within 36 months of application. Tests required as part of this documentation:

- [x] WAIS-IV
- [x] WISC-IV
- [x] SATA
- [x] Woodcock-Johnson
- [x] Nelson-Denny Reading Test
- [ ] Other

UNDERGRADUATE STUDENT BODY

Total undergraduate student enrollment: 690 Men, 975 Women.

Composition of student body (fall 2004):

	Undergraduate	Freshmen
International	0.8	2.1
Black	1.0	0.7
American Indian	1.5	1.4
Asian-American	5.8	3.8
Hispanic	2.5	3.1
White	82.8	84.7
Unreported	5.6	4.2
	100.0%	100.0%

39% are from out of state. Average age of full-time undergraduates is 20. 63% of classes have fewer than 20 students, 36% have between 20 and 50 students, 1% have more than 50 students.

STUDENT HOUSING

98% of freshmen live in college housing. Freshmen are required to live on campus. Housing is not guaranteed for all undergraduates. Must be under 23 years old or request an exception to policy. Campus can house 1,035 undergraduates. Single rooms are available for students with medical or special needs. A medical note is required.

EXPENSES

Tuition (2005-06): $21,400 per year.
Room: $3,770. Board: $3,010.
There is no additional cost for LD program/services.

LD SERVICES

LD program size is not limited.

LD services available to:

- [x] Freshmen
- [x] Sophomores
- [x] Juniors
- [x] Seniors

Academic Accommodations

Curriculum		In class	
Foreign language waiver	[ ]	Early syllabus	[ ]
Lighter course load	[ ]	Note takers in class	[x]
Math waiver	[ ]	Priority seating	[x]
Other special classes	[x]	Tape recorders	[x]
Priority registrations	[ ]	Videotaped classes	[ ]
Substitution of courses	[ ]	Text on tape	[ ]
Exams		**Services**	
Extended time	[x]	Diagnostic tests	[ ]
Oral exams	[x]	Learning centers	[x]
Take home exams	[ ]	Proofreaders	[ ]
Exams on tape or computer	[ ]	Readers	[x]
Untimed exams	[x]	Reading Machines/Kurzweil	[ ]
Other accommodations	[x]	Special bookstore section	[ ]
		Typists	[ ]

Credit toward degree is given for remedial courses taken.

Counseling Services

- [ ] Academic
- [ ] Psychological
- [ ] Student Support groups
- [ ] Vocational

Tutoring

Individual tutoring is available weekly.

	Individual	Group
Time management	[x]	[ ]
Organizational skills	[x]	[ ]
Learning strategies	[x]	[ ]
Study skills	[x]	[ ]
Content area	[x]	[ ]
Writing lab	[x]	[ ]
Math lab	[x]	[x]

LD PROGRAM STAFF

Total number of LD Program staff (including director):

Full Time: 1 Part Time: 1

There is an advisor/advocate from the LD program available to students. 1 graduate student and 7 peer tutors are available to work with LD students.

Key staff person available to work with LD students: Rick Muthiah, Director of Academic Resource Center and Disabilities.

LD Program web site: ds.georgefox.edu

Lewis & Clark College

Portland, OR

Address: 0615 S.W. Palatine Hill Road, Portland, OR, 97219-7899
Admissions telephone: 800 444-4111
Admissions FAX: 503 768-7055
Dean of Admissions: Michael B. Sexton
Admissions e-mail: admissions@lclark.edu
Web site: http://www.lclark.edu
SAT Code: 4384 ACT Code: 3464

LD program name: Student Support Services
Coordinator: Ms. Dale Holloway
LD program telephone: 503 768-7175
LD program e-mail: holloway@lclark.edu
LD program enrollment: 135, Total campus enrollment: 1,872

GENERAL

Lewis & Clark College is a private, coed, four-year institution. 134-acre, suburban campus in Portland (population: 529,121). Served by air, bus, and train. School operates transportation to transit station and downtown. Public transportation serves campus. Semester system.

LD ADMISSIONS

Students do not complete a separate application and are simultaneously accepted to the LD program. A member of the LD program does not sit on the admissions committee. A personal interview is not required. Essay is required and may be typed. Admissions requirements that may be waived for LD students include: foreign language requirement may be replaced with international studies courses.

SECONDARY SCHOOL REQUIREMENTS

Graduation from secondary school required; GED accepted.

TESTING

SAT Reasoning or ACT required of some applicants. SAT Subject recommended.

All enrolled freshmen (fall 2004):

Average SAT I Scores: Verbal: Math:
Average ACT Scores: Composite:

Child Study Team report is not required. A neuropsychological or comprehensive psycho-educational evaluation is required for admission. Must be dated within 24 months of application. Tests required as part of this documentation:

- ■ WAIS-IV
- ■ WISC-IV
- ■ SATA
- ■ Woodcock-Johnson
- ■ Nelson-Denny Reading Test
- ☐ Other

UNDERGRADUATE STUDENT BODY

Total undergraduate student enrollment: 679 Men, 1,001 Women.

Composition of student body (fall 2004):

	Undergraduate	Freshmen
International	2.8	3.7
Black	1.3	1.0
American Indian	0.7	1.3
Asian-American	5.4	5.4
Hispanic	5.2	3.6
White	67.8	67.4
Unreported	16.8	17.6
	100.0%	100.0%

77% are from out of state. Average age of full-time undergraduates is 20. 61% of classes have fewer than 20 students, 38% have between 20 and 50 students, 1% have more than 50 students.

STUDENT HOUSING

98% of freshmen live in college housing. Freshmen are required to live on campus. Housing is guaranteed for all undergraduates. Campus can house 1,156 undergraduates. Single rooms are available for students with medical or special needs. A medical note is required.

EXPENSES

Tuition (2005-06): $27,494 per year.
Room: $3,974. Board: $3,674.
There is no additional cost for LD program/services.

LD SERVICES

LD program size is not limited.

LD services available to:

■ Freshmen ■ Sophomores ■ Juniors ■ Seniors

Academic Accommodations

Curriculum		In class	
Foreign language waiver	☐	Early syllabus	☐
Lighter course load	■	Note takers in class	■
Math waiver	☐	Priority seating	☐
Other special classes	☐	Tape recorders	■
Priority registrations	☐	Videotaped classes	☐
Substitution of courses	■	Text on tape	■
Exams		**Services**	
Extended time	■	Diagnostic tests	■
Oral exams	☐	Learning centers	☐
Take home exams	☐	Proofreaders	■
Exams on tape or computer	■	Readers	■
Untimed exams	☐	Reading Machines/Kurzweil	☐
Other accommodations	■	Special bookstore section	☐
		Typists	■

Credit toward degree is not given for remedial courses taken.

Counseling Services

- ■ Academic
- ■ Psychological
- ■ Student Support groups
- ■ Vocational

Tutoring

Individual tutoring is available weekly.

	Individual	Group
Time management	■	☐
Organizational skills	■	☐
Learning strategies	■	☐
Study skills	■	☐
Content area	■	☐
Writing lab	■	☐
Math lab	■	☐

UNIQUE LD PROGRAM FEATURES

Peer tutors for LD students can come from a student government-run program that is open to all students or they can be located by Student Support Services by contacting professors for recommendations. There is no specific pool of tutors designated for LD students.

LD PROGRAM STAFF

Total number of LD Program staff (including director):

Full Time: 1 Part Time: 1

There is an advisor/advocate from the LD program available to students.

Key staff person available to work with LD students: Ms. Dale Holloway, Coordinator of Student Support Services.

LD Program web site: http://www.lclark.edu/dept/access/

Linfield College

McMinnville, OR

Address: 900 S.E. Baker Street, McMinnville, OR, 97128-6894
Admissions telephone: 800 640-2287
Admissions FAX: 503 883-2472
Director of Admissions: Lisa Knodle-Bragiel
Admissions e-mail: admission@linfield.edu
Web site: http://www.linfield.edu
SAT Code: 4387 ACT Code: 3466

LD program name: Learning Support Services
Director of Learning Support Services: Dr. Judith Haynes
LD program telephone: 503 883-2444
LD program e-mail: jhaynes@linfield.edu
LD program enrollment: 150, Total campus enrollment: 1,656

GENERAL

Linfield College is a private, coed, four-year institution. 193-acre campus in McMinnville (population: 26,499), 38 miles from Portland; branch campus (School of Nursing) in Portland. Major airport serves Portland; air, bus, and train serve Salem (22 miles). Public transportation serves campus. 4-1-4 system.

LD ADMISSIONS

Students do not complete a separate application and are simultaneously accepted to the LD program. A member of the LD program does sit on the admissions committee. A personal interview is recommended. Essay is required and may be typed.

For fall 2004, 40 completed self-identified LD applications were received. 34 applications were offered admission, and 10 enrolled.

SECONDARY SCHOOL REQUIREMENTS

Graduation from secondary school required; GED accepted.

TESTING

SAT Reasoning or ACT required. SAT Subject recommended.

All enrolled freshmen (fall 2004):

Average SAT I Scores:	Verbal: 557	Math: 566
Average ACT Scores:	Composite: 25	

Child Study Team report is not required. A neuropsychological or comprehensive psycho-education evaluation is not required for admission. Tests required as part of this documentation:

- [ ] WAIS-IV
- [ ] WISC-IV
- [ ] SATA
- [ ] Woodcock-Johnson
- [ ] Nelson-Denny Reading Test
- [ ] Other

UNDERGRADUATE STUDENT BODY

Total undergraduate student enrollment: 714 Men, 888 Women.

Composition of student body (fall 2004):

	Undergraduate	Freshmen
International	1.6	2.1
Black	0.9	1.4
American Indian	1.4	1.4
Asian-American	7.9	6.8
Hispanic	2.1	2.1
White	77.1	80.5
Unreported	9.0	5.7
	100.0%	100.0%

43% are from out of state. 22% join a fraternity and 28% join a sorority. Average age of full-time undergraduates is 21. 65% of classes have fewer than 20 students, 34% have between 20 and 50 students, 1% have more than 50 students.

STUDENT HOUSING

96% of freshmen live in college housing. Freshmen are required to live on campus. Housing is guaranteed for all undergraduates. Campus can house 1,283 undergraduates. Single rooms are available for students with medical or special needs. A medical note is required.

EXPENSES

Tuition (2005-06): $22,790 per year.
Room: $3,540. Board: $3,070.
There is no additional cost for LD program/services.

LD SERVICES

LD program size is not limited.

LD services available to:

- [x] Freshmen
- [x] Sophomores
- [x] Juniors
- [x] Seniors

Academic Accommodations

Curriculum
- [ ] Foreign language waiver
- [x] Lighter course load
- [ ] Math waiver
- [ ] Other special classes
- [x] Priority registrations
- [x] Substitution of courses

Exams
- [x] Extended time
- [x] Oral exams
- [ ] Take home exams
- [x] Exams on tape or computer
- [x] Untimed exams
- [x] Other accommodations

In class
- [ ] Early syllabus
- [x] Note takers in class
- [x] Priority seating
- [x] Tape recorders
- [x] Videotaped classes
- [x] Text on tape

Services
- [ ] Diagnostic tests
- [x] Learning centers
- [x] Proofreaders
- [x] Readers
- [x] Reading Machines/Kurzweil
- [ ] Special bookstore section
- [x] Typists

Credit toward degree is not given for remedial courses taken.

Counseling Services

- [x] Academic
- [x] Psychological
- [x] Student Support groups
- [x] Vocational

Tutoring

Individual tutoring is available daily.

Average size of tutoring groups: 5

	Individual	Group
Time management	[x]	[x]
Organizational skills	[x]	[x]
Learning strategies	[x]	[x]
Study skills	[x]	[x]
Content area	[x]	[x]
Writing lab	[x]	[x]
Math lab	[x]	[x]

UNIQUE LD PROGRAM FEATURES

Though some services require a documented disability, many services are offered to all the students in the Linfield community. Student progress may be monitored. We customize programs to fit each student's needs.

LD PROGRAM STAFF

Total number of LD Program staff (including director):

Full Time: 2 Part Time: 2

There is an advisor/advocate from the LD program available to students. The advisor/advocate meets with students 4 times per month. 85 peer tutors are available to work with LD students.

Key staff person available to work with LD students: Dr. Judith Haynes, Director of Learning Support Services.

LD Program web site: http://www.linfield.edu/learning_support/index.html

Marylhurst University

Marylhurst, OR

Address: PO Box 261, Marylhurst, OR, 97036-0261
Admissions telephone: 800 634-9982, extension 6268
Admissions FAX: 503 635-6585
Dean of Admissions and Enrollment Relations: John French
Admissions e-mail: admissions@marylhurst.edu
Web site: http://www.marylhurst.edu
SAT Code: 440 ACT Code: 3470

LD program name: Disability and Student Services
Coordinator: Ruth McKenna
LD program telephone: 503 636-8141, extension 3344
LD program e-mail: rmckenna@marylhurst.edu
Total campus enrollment: 847

GENERAL

Marylhurst University is a private, coed, four-year institution. 47-acre campus in Marylhurst (population: 23,000), 11 miles from Portland. Major airport, bus, and train serve Portland. Public transportation serves campus. Quarter system.

LD ADMISSIONS

A personal interview is not required. Essay is not required.

SECONDARY SCHOOL REQUIREMENTS

Graduation from secondary school required; GED accepted.

TESTING

SAT Reasoning or ACT required of some applicants. SAT Subject recommended.

All enrolled freshmen (fall 2004):

Average SAT I Scores: Verbal: 575 Math: 495
Average ACT Scores: Composite: 20

Child Study Team report is not required. A neuropsychological or comprehensive psycho-educational evaluation is required for admission. Must be dated within 36 months of application. Tests required as part of this documentation:

☑	WAIS-IV	☑	Woodcock-Johnson
☑	WISC-IV	☐	Nelson-Denny Reading Test
☐	SATA	☐	Other

UNDERGRADUATE STUDENT BODY

Total undergraduate student enrollment: 150 Men, 522 Women.

Composition of student body (fall 2004):

	Undergraduate	Freshmen
International	0.0	2.2
Black	0.0	1.1
American Indian	0.0	0.7
Asian-American	0.0	0.8
Hispanic	0.0	0.8
White	30.0	24.2
Unreported	70.0	70.2
	100.0%	100.0%

14% are from out of state. Average age of full-time undergraduates is 29. 95% of classes have fewer than 20 students, 5% have between 20 and 50 students.

STUDENT HOUSING

Freshmen are not required to live on campus. Housing is guaranteed for all undergraduates. Campus can house 40 undergraduates.

EXPENSES

Tuition (2005-06): $13,860 per year (in-state), $14,985 (out-of-state).

There is no additional cost for LD program/services.

LD SERVICES

LD program size is not limited.

LD services available to:

☑ Freshmen ☑ Sophomores ☑ Juniors ☑ Seniors

Academic Accommodations

Curriculum		**In class**	
Foreign language waiver	☐	Early syllabus	☑
Lighter course load	☑	Note takers in class	☑
Math waiver	☐	Priority seating	☑
Other special classes	☐	Tape recorders	☑
Priority registrations	☑	Videotaped classes	☐
Substitution of courses	☑	Text on tape	☑
Exams		**Services**	
Extended time	☑	Diagnostic tests	☐
Oral exams	☑	Learning centers	☐
Take home exams	☑	Proofreaders	☑
Exams on tape or computer	☑	Readers	☑
Untimed exams	☑	Reading Machines/Kurzweil	☐
Other accommodations	☑	Special bookstore section	☐
		Typists	☑

Credit toward degree is not given for remedial courses taken.

Counseling Services

☑	Academic	Meets 3 times per academic year
☑	Psychological	Meets once per academic year
☐	Student Support groups	
☑	Vocational	Meets once per academic year

Tutoring

Individual tutoring is available weekly.

Average size of tutoring groups: 1

	Individual	Group
Time management	☐	☐
Organizational skills	☐	☐
Learning strategies	☐	☐
Study skills	☐	☐
Content area	☐	☐
Writing lab	☐	☑
Math lab	☐	☐

LD PROGRAM STAFF

There is an advisor/advocate from the LD program available to students. The advisor/advocate meets with faculty 2 times per month and student once per month.

Key staff person available to work with LD students: Ruth McKenna, Coordinator of Disability and Student Services.

Northwest Christian College

Eugene, OR

Address: 828 E. 11th Avenue, Eugene, OR, 97401
Admissions telephone: 877 463-6622
Admissions FAX: 541 684-7317
Dean of Admissions and Financial Aid: Cheryl Brelsford
Admissions e-mail: admissions@nwcc.edu
Web site: http://www.nwcc.edu
SAT Code: 4543 ACT Code: 3478

Disability Officer: Anne Maggs
LD program e-mail: annemaggs@nwcc.edu
Total campus enrollment: 393

GENERAL

Northwest Christian College is a private, coed, four-year institution. Eight-acre, urban campus in Eugene (population: 137,893), 110 miles from Portland. Served by air, bus, and train. Public transportation serves campus. Semester system.

LD ADMISSIONS

Students do not complete a separate application and are not simultaneously accepted to the LD program. A member of the LD program does not sit on the admissions committee. A personal interview is required. Essay is required and may be typed.

SECONDARY SCHOOL REQUIREMENTS

Graduation from secondary school required; GED accepted. The following course distribution required: 4 units of English, 3 units of math, 2 units of science, 2 units of foreign language, 2 units of social studies, 1 unit of history.

TESTING

SAT Reasoning or ACT required. SAT Subject recommended.

All enrolled freshmen (fall 2004):

Average SAT I Scores:	Verbal: 503	Math: 486
Average ACT Scores:	Composite: 20	

Child Study Team report is not required. A neuropsychological or comprehensive psycho-educational evaluation is required for admission. Tests required as part of this documentation:

- [ ] WAIS-IV
- [ ] WISC-IV
- [ ] SATA
- [ ] Woodcock-Johnson
- [ ] Nelson-Denny Reading Test
- [ ] Other

UNDERGRADUATE STUDENT BODY

Total undergraduate student enrollment: 159 Men, 259 Women.

Composition of student body (fall 2004):

	Undergraduate	Freshmen
International	0.0	0.3
Black	1.9	1.0
American Indian	0.0	0.3
Asian-American	3.8	1.8
Hispanic	0.0	1.6
White	84.7	84.4
Unreported	9.6	10.6
	100.0%	100.0%

14% are from out of state. Average age of full-time undergraduates is 24. 87% of classes have fewer than 20 students, 12% have between 20 and 50 students, 1% have more than 50 students.

STUDENT HOUSING

79% of freshmen live in college housing. Freshmen are required to live on campus. Housing is guaranteed for all undergraduates. Campus can house 119 undergraduates. Single rooms are available for students with medical or special needs. A medical note is required.

EXPENSES

Tuition (2005-06): $18,210 per year.

Room: $2,512. Board: $3,406.

There is no additional cost for LD program/services.

LD SERVICES

LD program size is not limited.

LD services available to:

- [x] Freshmen
- [x] Sophomores
- [x] Juniors
- [x] Seniors

Academic Accommodations

Curriculum		In class	
Foreign language waiver	[ ]	Early syllabus	[ ]
Lighter course load	[x]	Note takers in class	[ ]
Math waiver	[ ]	Priority seating	[ ]
Other special classes	[ ]	Tape recorders	[x]
Priority registrations	[ ]	Videotaped classes	[x]
Substitution of courses	[ ]	Text on tape	[ ]
Exams		**Services**	
Extended time	[x]	Diagnostic tests	[ ]
Oral exams	[x]	Learning centers	[ ]
Take home exams	[ ]	Proofreaders	[ ]
Exams on tape or computer	[ ]	Readers	[ ]
Untimed exams	[ ]	Reading Machines/Kurzweil	[ ]
Other accommodations	[ ]	Special bookstore section	[ ]
		Typists	[ ]

Credit toward degree is not given for remedial courses taken.

Counseling Services

- [x] Academic
- [ ] Psychological
- [ ] Student Support groups
- [ ] Vocational

Tutoring

Individual tutoring is available daily.

Average size of tutoring groups: 1

	Individual	Group
Time management	[x]	[ ]
Organizational skills	[ ]	[ ]
Learning strategies	[x]	[ ]
Study skills	[x]	[ ]
Content area	[ ]	[ ]
Writing lab	[x]	[ ]
Math lab	[x]	[ ]

LD PROGRAM STAFF

Total number of LD Program staff (including director):

There is an advisor/advocate from the LD program available to students.

Key staff person available to work with LD students: Anne Maggs, Disability Officer.

LD Program web site: http://www.nwcc.edu/studentlife/

University of Oregon

Eugene, OR

Address: 1217 University of Oregon, Eugene, OR, 97403-1217
Admissions telephone: 800 232-3825
Admissions FAX: 541 346-5815
Director of Admissions: Martha Pitts
Admissions e-mail: uoadmit@uoregon.edu
Web site: http://www.uoregon.edu
SAT Code: 4846 ACT Code: 3498

LD program name: Disability Services
Director, Disability Services: Steve Pickett
LD program telephone: 541 346-1155
LD program e-mail: spickett@uoregon.edu
Total campus enrollment: 16,350

GENERAL

University of Oregon is a public, coed, four-year institution. 280-acre main campus in Eugene (population: 137,893), 114 miles from Portland. Served by air, bus, and train; major airport serves Portland. Public transportation serves campus. Quarter system.

LD ADMISSIONS

Students do not complete a separate application and are not simultaneously accepted to the LD program. A member of the LD program does sit on the admissions committee. High school waivers are accepted for math and foreign language. A personal interview is not required. Essay is not required. Some admission requirements such as GPA, SAT scores, and class standing can be more flexible in the DRC process.

SECONDARY SCHOOL REQUIREMENTS

Graduation from secondary school required; GED accepted. The following course distribution required: 4 units of English, 3 units of math, 2 units of science, 2 units of foreign language, 3 units of social studies.

TESTING

SAT Reasoning or ACT required. SAT Subject required.

All enrolled freshmen (fall 2004):

Average SAT I Scores:	Verbal: 555	Math: 559
Average ACT Scores:	Composite:	

Child Study Team report is not required. A neuropsychological or comprehensive psycho-educational evaluation is required for admission. Must be dated within 36 months of application. Tests required as part of this documentation:

- ■ WAIS-IV
- ■ WISC-IV
- ■ SATA
- ■ Woodcock-Johnson
- ☐ Nelson-Denny Reading Test
- ■ Other

UNDERGRADUATE STUDENT BODY

Total undergraduate student enrollment: 6,600 Men, 7,476 Women.

Composition of student body (fall 2004):

	Undergraduate	Freshmen
International	2.3	4.4
Black	1.7	1.8
American Indian	1.0	1.1
Asian-American	7.4	6.1
Hispanic	3.4	3.0
White	78.4	75.9
Unreported	5.8	7.7
	100.0%	100.0%

24% are from out of state. 8% join a fraternity and 10% join a sorority. Average age of full-time undergraduates is 21. 40% of classes have fewer than 20 students, 45% have between 20 and 50 students, 15% have more than 50 students.

STUDENT HOUSING

63% of freshmen live in college housing. Freshmen are not required to live on campus. Housing is guaranteed for all undergraduates.

EXPENSES

There is no additional cost for LD program/services.

LD SERVICES

LD program size is not limited.

LD services available to:

■ Freshmen ■ Sophomores ■ Juniors ■ Seniors

Academic Accommodations

Curriculum		**In class**	
Foreign language waiver	☐	Early syllabus	■
Lighter course load	■	Note takers in class	■
Math waiver	☐	Priority seating	■
Other special classes	☐	Tape recorders	■
Priority registrations	■	Videotaped classes	☐
Substitution of courses	☐	Text on tape	■
Exams		**Services**	
Extended time	■	Diagnostic tests	■
Oral exams	■	Learning centers	■
Take home exams	☐	Proofreaders	☐
Exams on tape or computer	■	Readers	■
Untimed exams	■	Reading Machines/Kurzweil	■
Other accommodations	■	Special bookstore section	☐
		Typists	■

Credit toward degree is not given for remedial courses taken.

Counseling Services

- ■ Academic
- ■ Psychological
- ■ Student Support groups
- ☐ Vocational

Tutoring

Individual tutoring is available weekly.

	Individual	Group
Time management	■	■
Organizational skills	■	■
Learning strategies	■	■
Study skills	■	■
Content area	☐	☐
Writing lab	■	☐
Math lab	■	☐

UNIQUE LD PROGRAM FEATURES

ds.uoregon.edu

LD PROGRAM STAFF

Total number of LD Program staff (including director):

Full Time: 4 Part Time: 4

There is an advisor/advocate from the LD program available to students.

Key staff person available to work with LD students: Molly Sirois, Counselor.

LD Program web site: ds.uoregon.edu

Oregon Institute of Technology

Klamath Falls, OR

Address: 3201 Campus Drive, Klamath Falls, OR, 97601
Admissions telephone: 541 885-1155
Admissions FAX: 541 885-1115
Director of Admissions: Palmer Muntz
Admissions e-mail: oit@oit.edu
Web site: http://www.oit.edu
SAT Code: 4587 ACT Code: 3484

Director: Ron McCutcheon
LD program telephone: 541 885-1031
LD program e-mail: mccutchr@oit.edu
Total campus enrollment: 3,366

GENERAL

Oregon Institute of Technology is a public, coed, four-year institution. 173-acre campus in Klamath Falls (population: 19,462), 81 miles to Medford. Served by air, bus, and train; major airport serves Portland (280 miles). Public transportation serves campus. Quarter system.

LD ADMISSIONS

A personal interview is not required. Essay is not required. All applicants may request SAT/ACT waiver but must complete later in enrollment. Minimum GPA may be revised downward by Admissions Committee.

SECONDARY SCHOOL REQUIREMENTS

Graduation from secondary school required; GED accepted. The following course distribution required: 4 units of English, 3 units of math, 2 units of science, 2 units of foreign language, 3 units of social studies.

TESTING

SAT Reasoning or ACT required. SAT Subject recommended.

All enrolled freshmen (fall 2004):

Average SAT I Scores:	Verbal: 538	Math: 517
Average ACT Scores:	Composite: 23	

Child Study Team report is not required. Tests required as part of this documentation:

- [ ] WAIS-IV
- [ ] WISC-IV
- [ ] SATA
- [ ] Woodcock-Johnson
- [ ] Nelson-Denny Reading Test
- [ ] Other

UNDERGRADUATE STUDENT BODY

Total undergraduate student enrollment: 1,699 Men, 1,387 Women.

Composition of student body (fall 2004):

	Undergraduate	Freshmen
International	0.3	0.8
Black	0.3	1.1
American Indian	2.5	1.8
Asian-American	3.5	5.1
Hispanic	6.6	3.9
White	84.3	81.1
Unreported	2.5	6.2
	100.0%	100.0%

16% are from out of state. Average age of full-time undergraduates is 25. 56% of classes have fewer than 20 students, 41% have between 20 and 50 students, 3% have more than 50 students.

STUDENT HOUSING

54% of freshmen live in college housing. Freshmen are not required to live on campus. Housing is guaranteed for all undergraduates. Campus can house 500 undergraduates.

EXPENSES

Tuition (2005-06): $3,849 per year (in-state), $13,950 (out-of-state).
Room & Board: $5,935-$5,935.

There is no additional cost for LD program/services.

LD SERVICES

LD program size is not limited.

LD services available to:

- [ ] Freshmen
- [ ] Sophomores
- [ ] Juniors
- [ ] Seniors

Academic Accommodations

Curriculum

- [ ] Foreign language waiver
- [x] Lighter course load
- [ ] Math waiver
- [ ] Other special classes
- [ ] Priority registrations
- [ ] Substitution of courses

Exams

- [x] Extended time
- [x] Oral exams
- [ ] Take home exams
- [ ] Exams on tape or computer
- [ ] Untimed exams
- [ ] Other accommodations

In class

- [ ] Early syllabus
- [x] Note takers in class
- [ ] Priority seating
- [x] Tape recorders
- [ ] Videotaped classes
- [ ] Text on tape

Services

- [ ] Diagnostic tests
- [x] Learning centers
- [ ] Proofreaders
- [x] Readers
- [x] Reading Machines/Kurzweil
- [ ] Special bookstore section
- [ ] Typists

Credit toward degree is not given for remedial courses taken.

Counseling Services

- [ ] Academic
- [ ] Psychological
- [ ] Student Support groups
- [ ] Vocational

Tutoring

	Individual	Group
Time management	[ ]	[ ]
Organizational skills	[ ]	[ ]
Learning strategies	[ ]	[ ]
Study skills	[ ]	[ ]
Content area	[ ]	[ ]
Writing lab	[ ]	[ ]
Math lab	[ ]	[ ]

UNIQUE LD PROGRAM FEATURES

May apply to OIT's Student Support Services program if other eligibility requirements are met.

LD PROGRAM STAFF

Total number of LD Program staff (including director):

Key staff person available to work with LD students: Ron McCutcheon, Director, Campus Access & Equal Opportunity.

Oregon State University

Corvallis, OR

Address: 104 Kerr Administration Building, Corvallis, OR, 97331
Admissions telephone: 800 291-4192
Admissions FAX: 541 737-2482
Director of Admissions: Michele Sandlin
Admissions e-mail: osuadmit@oregonstate.edu
Web site: http://oregonstate.edu
SAT Code: 4586

LD program enrollment: 304, Total campus enrollment: 15,713

GENERAL

Oregon State University is a public, coed, four-year institution. 422-acre campus in Corvallis (population: 49,321), 85 miles from Portland. Served by bus; airport serves Eugene (35 miles); train serves Albany (10 miles). Public transportation serves campus. Quarter system.

LD ADMISSIONS

Students do not complete a separate application and are not simultaneously accepted to the LD program. A member of the LD program does not sit on the admissions committee. A personal interview is recommended. Essay is required and may be typed. Admissions requirements that may be waived for LD students include foreign language- but will be required to complete 2 terms of sign language at OSU.

For fall 2004, 146 completed self-identified LD applications were received.

SECONDARY SCHOOL REQUIREMENTS

Graduation from secondary school required; GED accepted. The following course distribution required: 4 units of English, 3 units of math, 2 units of science, 2 units of foreign language, 3 units of social studies.

TESTING

SAT Subject required.

All enrolled freshmen (fall 2004):

Average SAT I Scores:	Verbal: 532	Math: 548
Average ACT Scores:	Composite: 23	

Child Study Team report is not required. A neuropsychological or comprehensive psycho-educational evaluation is required for admission. Must be dated within 24 months of application. Tests required as part of this documentation:

- [x] WAIS-IV
- [ ] WISC-IV
- [ ] SATA
- [x] Woodcock-Johnson
- [x] Nelson-Denny Reading Test
- [ ] Other

UNDERGRADUATE STUDENT BODY

Total undergraduate student enrollment: 7,927 Men, 6,950 Women.

Composition of student body (fall 2004):

	Undergraduate	Freshmen
International	0.6	1.5
Black	1.3	1.4
American Indian	1.4	1.2
Asian-American	8.4	8.2
Hispanic	3.8	3.5
White	78.3	78.4
Unreported	6.2	5.8
	100.0%	100.0%

12% are from out of state. 13% join a fraternity and 12% join a sorority. Average age of full-time undergraduates is 21. 38% of classes have fewer than 20 students, 44% have between 20 and 50 students, 18% have more than 50 students.

STUDENT HOUSING

76% of freshmen live in college housing. Freshmen are not required to live on campus. Housing is guaranteed for all undergraduates. Campus can house 4,363 undergraduates. Single rooms are available for students with medical or special needs. A medical note is required.

EXPENSES

There is no additional cost for LD program/services.

LD SERVICES

LD program size is not limited.

LD services available to:

- [x] Freshmen
- [x] Sophomores
- [x] Juniors
- [x] Seniors

Academic Accommodations

Curriculum

- [ ] Foreign language waiver
- [x] Lighter course load
- [ ] Math waiver
- [ ] Other special classes
- [ ] Priority registrations
- [ ] Substitution of courses

Exams

- [x] Extended time
- [x] Oral exams
- [ ] Take home exams
- [ ] Exams on tape or computer
- [ ] Untimed exams
- [ ] Other accommodations

In class

- [ ] Early syllabus
- [x] Note takers in class
- [ ] Priority seating
- [x] Tape recorders
- [ ] Videotaped classes
- [ ] Text on tape

Services

- [ ] Diagnostic tests
- [x] Learning centers
- [ ] Proofreaders
- [ ] Readers
- [x] Reading Machines/Kurzweil
- [ ] Special bookstore section
- [ ] Typists

Credit toward degree is not given for remedial courses taken.

Counseling Services

- [ ] Academic
- [ ] Psychological
- [ ] Student Support groups
- [ ] Vocational

Tutoring

Individual tutoring is not available.

	Individual	Group
Time management	[ ]	[ ]
Organizational skills	[ ]	[ ]
Learning strategies	[ ]	[ ]
Study skills	[ ]	[ ]
Content area	[ ]	[ ]
Writing lab	[ ]	[ ]
Math lab	[ ]	[ ]

LD PROGRAM STAFF

Total number of LD Program staff (including director):

Full Time: 3 Part Time: 3

There is an advisor/advocate from the LD program available to students.

Key staff person available to work with LD students: Tracy Bentley-Townlin, Ph.D., Director of Services for Students with Disabilities.

LD Program web site: http://ssd.oregonstate.edu

Pacific University

Forest Grove, OR

Address: 2043 College Way, Forest Grove, OR, 97116
Admissions telephone: 800 677-6712
Admissions FAX: 503 352-2975
Executive Director of Admissions: Erin Healey
Admissions e-mail: admissions@pacificu.edu
Web site: http://www.pacificu.edu
SAT Code: 4601 ACT Code: 3488

LD program telephone: 503 352-2107
LD program e-mail: gehringe@pacificu.edu
LD program enrollment: 37, Total campus enrollment: 1,232

GENERAL

Pacific University is a private, coed, four-year institution. 55-acre campus in Forest Grove (population: 17,708), 25 miles from Portland; branch campuses in Eugene and Portland. Airport, bus, and train serve Portland. School operates transportation to Portland for special events. Public transportation serves campus. 4-1-4 system.

LD ADMISSIONS

A personal interview is recommended. Essay is required and may be typed.

SECONDARY SCHOOL REQUIREMENTS

Graduation from secondary school required; GED accepted.

TESTING

SAT Reasoning or ACT required. SAT Subject recommended.

All enrolled freshmen (fall 2004):

Average SAT I Scores:	Verbal: 550	Math: 550
Average ACT Scores:	Composite: 24	

Child Study Team report is not required. Tests required as part of this documentation:

- [ ] WAIS-IV
- [ ] WISC-IV
- [ ] SATA
- [ ] Woodcock-Johnson
- [ ] Nelson-Denny Reading Test
- [ ] Other

UNDERGRADUATE STUDENT BODY

Total undergraduate student enrollment: 430 Men, 739 Women.

Composition of student body (fall 2004):

	Undergraduate	Freshmen
International	0.3	0.2
Black	1.0	0.9
American Indian	1.7	1.0
Asian-American	25.9	19.8
Hispanic	3.1	3.0
White	62.6	69.1
Unreported	5.4	6.0
	100.0%	100.0%

55% are from out of state. 10% join a fraternity and 8% join a sorority. Average age of full-time undergraduates is 21. 62% of classes have fewer than 20 students, 35% have between 20 and 50 students, 3% have more than 50 students.

STUDENT HOUSING

98% of freshmen live in college housing. Freshmen are required to live on campus. Housing is not guaranteed for all undergraduates. Cannot accommodate all juniors and seniors in residence halls. Campus can house 755 undergraduates. Single rooms are available for students with medical or special needs. A medical note is required.

EXPENSES

Tuition (2005-06): $20,908 per year.

Room: $2,928. Board: $3,124.

There is no additional cost for LD program/services.

LD SERVICES

LD program size is not limited.

LD services available to:

- [x] Freshmen
- [x] Sophomores
- [x] Juniors
- [x] Seniors

Academic Accommodations

Curriculum		In class	
Foreign language waiver	[ ]	Early syllabus	[ ]
Lighter course load	[x]	Note takers in class	[x]
Math waiver	[ ]	Priority seating	[ ]
Other special classes	[ ]	Tape recorders	[x]
Priority registrations	[ ]	Videotaped classes	[ ]
Substitution of courses	[ ]	Text on tape	[x]
Exams		**Services**	
Extended time	[x]	Diagnostic tests	[ ]
Oral exams	[x]	Learning centers	[ ]
Take home exams	[ ]	Proofreaders	[ ]
Exams on tape or computer	[x]	Readers	[x]
Untimed exams	[x]	Reading Machines/Kurzweil	[ ]
Other accommodations	[ ]	Special bookstore section	[ ]
		Typists	[x]

Credit toward degree is not given for remedial courses taken.

Counseling Services

- [ ] Academic
- [ ] Psychological
- [ ] Student Support groups
- [ ] Vocational

Tutoring

Individual tutoring is available.

	Individual	Group
Time management	[ ]	[ ]
Organizational skills	[ ]	[ ]
Learning strategies	[ ]	[ ]
Study skills	[ ]	[ ]
Content area	[x]	[ ]
Writing lab	[x]	[ ]
Math lab	[x]	[ ]

LD PROGRAM STAFF

Total number of LD Program staff (including director):

Full Time: 1 Part Time: 1

There is an advisor/advocate from the LD program available to students.

Key staff person available to work with LD students: Edna K. Gehring, M.S., Learning Support Services.

University of Portland

Portland, OR

Address: 5000 N. Willamette Boulevard, Portland, OR, 97203
Admissions telephone: 888 627-5601
Admissions FAX: 503 943-7315
Dean of Admissions: James Lyons, Dean
Admissions e-mail: admissio@up.edu
Web site: http://www.up.edu
SAT Code: 4847 ACT Code: 3500

Coordinator: Melanie Gangle
LD program telephone: 503 943-7134
LD program e-mail: gangle@up.edu
LD program enrollment: 66, Total campus enrollment: 2,829

GENERAL

University of Portland is a private, coed, four-year institution. 125-acre, suburban campus in Portland (population: 529,121), four miles from city center. Served by air, bus, and train. Public transportation serves campus. Semester system.

LD ADMISSIONS

Students do not complete a separate application and are not simultaneously accepted to the LD program. A member of the LD program does not sit on the admissions committee. A personal interview is recommended. Essay is required and may be typed.

SECONDARY SCHOOL REQUIREMENTS

Graduation from secondary school required; GED accepted. The following course distribution required: 2 units of English, 2 units of math, 2 units of social studies, 2 units of history, 7 units of academic electives.

TESTING

SAT Reasoning or ACT required. SAT Subject required.

All enrolled freshmen (fall 2004):

Average SAT I Scores: Verbal: 587 Math: 588
Average ACT Scores: Composite:

Child Study Team report is not required. A neuropsychological or comprehensive psycho-educational evaluation is required for admission. Must be dated within 60 months of application. Tests required as part of this documentation:

- ■ WAIS-IV
- ■ WISC-IV
- ☐ SATA
- ■ Woodcock-Johnson
- ■ Nelson-Denny Reading Test
- ☐ Other

UNDERGRADUATE STUDENT BODY

Total undergraduate student enrollment: 1,087 Men, 1,425 Women.

Composition of student body (fall 2004):

	Undergraduate	Freshmen
International	0.5	1.6
Black	2.0	1.6
American Indian	0.8	0.6
Asian-American	9.6	9.4
Hispanic	3.9	3.9
White	75.6	78.9
Unreported	7.6	4.0
	100.0%	100.0%

49% are from out of state. Average age of full-time undergraduates is 21. 34% of classes have fewer than 20 students, 63% have between 20 and 50 students, 3% have more than 50 students.

STUDENT HOUSING

91% of freshmen live in college housing. Freshmen are not required to live on campus. Housing is not guaranteed for all undergraduates, not enough rooms available for everyone. Campus can house 907 undergraduates. Single rooms are available for students with medical or special needs. A medical note is required.

EXPENSES

Tuition (2005-06): $24,580 per year.
Room: $3,700. Board: $3,700.
There is no additional cost for LD program/services.

LD SERVICES

LD program size is not limited.

LD services available to:

■ Freshmen ■ Sophomores ■ Juniors ■ Seniors

Academic Accommodations

Curriculum		**In class**	
Foreign language waiver	☐	Early syllabus	☐
Lighter course load	■	Note takers in class	■
Math waiver	☐	Priority seating	☐
Other special classes	☐	Tape recorders	☐
Priority registrations	☐	Videotaped classes	☐
Substitution of courses	☐	Text on tape	☐
Exams		**Services**	
Extended time	■	Diagnostic tests	☐
Oral exams	☐	Learning centers	☐
Take home exams	☐	Proofreaders	☐
Exams on tape or computer	☐	Readers	■
Untimed exams	☐	Reading Machines/Kurzweil	■
Other accommodations	☐	Special bookstore section	☐
		Typists	☐

Credit toward degree is not given for remedial courses taken.

Counseling Services

- ■ Academic
- ■ Psychological
- ☐ Student Support groups
- ☐ Vocational

Tutoring

Individual tutoring is not available.

	Individual	Group
Time management	■	☐
Organizational skills	■	☐
Learning strategies	■	☐
Study skills	■	☐
Content area	☐	☐
Writing lab	■	■
Math lab	■	■

LD PROGRAM STAFF

Total number of LD Program staff (including director):

Full Time: 1 Part Time: 1

There is an advisor/advocate from the LD program available to students.

Key staff person available to work with LD students: Melanie Gangle, Coordinator, Office for Students with Disabilities.

Southern Oregon University

Ashland, OR

Address: 1250 Siskiyou Boulevard, Ashland, OR, 97520
Admissions telephone: 800 482-7672 (in-state)
Admissions FAX: 541 552-6614
Director of Admissions: Mara Affre
Admissions e-mail: admissions@sou.edu
Web site: http://www.sou.edu
SAT Code: 4702 ACT Code: 3496

Director, Disability Services for Students: Margaret Dibb
LD program telephone: 541 552-6213
LD program e-mail: dibbm@sou.edu
Total campus enrollment: 4,672

GENERAL

Southern Oregon University is a public, coed, four-year institution. 175-acre campus in Ashland (population: 19,522), 10 miles from Medford; branch campus in Medford. Served by bus; airport serves Medford; train serves Klamath Falls (70 miles). Public transportation serves campus. Quarter system.

LD ADMISSIONS

Students do not complete a separate application and are not simultaneously accepted to the LD program. A member of the LD program does not sit on the admissions committee. High school waivers are accepted for math and foreign language. A personal interview is not required. Essay is required and may be typed. Admissions requirements that may be waived for LD students include: substitutions of coursework in foreign language and math requirements may be made on an individual basis, based on current documentation of specific disability.

SECONDARY SCHOOL REQUIREMENTS

Graduation from secondary school required; GED accepted. The following course distribution required: 4 units of English, 3 units of math, 2 units of science, 2 units of foreign language, 3 units of social studies.

TESTING

SAT Reasoning or ACT required. SAT Subject recommended.

All enrolled freshmen (fall 2004):

Average SAT I Scores:	Verbal: 525	Math: 511
Average ACT Scores:	Composite: 23	

Child Study Team report is not required. A neuropsychological or comprehensive psycho-educational evaluation is required for admission. Tests required as part of this documentation:

- ☐ WAIS-IV
- ☐ WISC-IV
- ☐ SATA
- ☐ Woodcock-Johnson
- ☐ Nelson-Denny Reading Test
- ☐ Other

UNDERGRADUATE STUDENT BODY

Total undergraduate student enrollment: 2,132 Men, 2,758 Women.

Composition of student body (fall 2004):

	Undergraduate	Freshmen
International	0.7	2.3
Black	2.5	1.5
American Indian	2.5	2.3
Asian-American	4.5	3.7
Hispanic	4.7	4.0
White	80.1	79.2
Unreported	5.0	7.0
	100.0%	100.0%

Average age of full-time undergraduates is 22. 46% of classes have fewer than 20 students, 48% have between 20 and 50 students, 6% have more than 50 students.

STUDENT HOUSING

69% of freshmen live in college housing. Freshmen are required to live on campus. Housing is guaranteed for all undergraduates. Campus can house 1,100 undergraduates. Single rooms are available for students with medical or special needs.

EXPENSES

Tuition (2005-06): $3,789 per year (in-state), $15,219 (out-of-state).
Room: $4,354. Board: $2,900.
There is no additional cost for LD program/services.

LD SERVICES

LD program size is not limited.

LD services available to:

☑ Freshmen ☑ Sophomores ☑ Juniors ☑ Seniors

Academic Accommodations

Curriculum		In class	
Foreign language waiver	☐	Early syllabus	☐
Lighter course load	☑	Note takers in class	☑
Math waiver	☐	Priority seating	☐
Other special classes	☑	Tape recorders	☑
Priority registrations	☐	Videotaped classes	☐
Substitution of courses	☐	Text on tape	☐
Exams		**Services**	
Extended time	☑	Diagnostic tests	☐
Oral exams	☑	Learning centers	☑
Take home exams	☐	Proofreaders	☐
Exams on tape or computer	☐	Readers	☑
Untimed exams	☐	Reading Machines/Kurzweil	☑
Other accommodations	☐	Special bookstore section	☐
		Typists	☐

Credit toward degree is not given for remedial courses taken.

Counseling Services

- ☑ Academic
- ☑ Psychological
- ☑ Student Support groups
- ☑ Vocational

Tutoring

Individual tutoring is available.

	Individual	Group
Time management	☑	☑
Organizational skills	☑	☑
Learning strategies	☑	☑
Study skills	☑	☑
Content area	☑	☑
Writing lab	☑	☑
Math lab	☑	☑

UNIQUE LD PROGRAM FEATURES

Students with disabilities who do not meet university admission requirements are invited to participate in the special admissions process, and to coordinate this with DSS. Support services available from both DSS and TRIO programs.

LD PROGRAM STAFF

Total number of LD Program staff (including director):

Full Time: 5 Part Time: 5

Key staff person available to work with LD students: Margaret Dibb, Director, Disability services.

Warner Pacific College

Portland, OR

Address: 2219 S.E. 68th Avenue, Portland, OR, 97215
Admissions telephone: 800 582-7885, extension 1020
Admissions FAX: 503 517-1352
Senior Vice President: Shannon Mackey
Admissions e-mail: admissions@warnerpacific.edu
Web site: http://www.warnerpacific.edu
SAT Code: 4595 ACT Code: 3486

Total campus enrollment: 503

GENERAL

Warner Pacific College is a private, coed, four-year institution. 15-acre, suburban campus in Portland (population: 529,121). Served by air, bus, and train. Public transportation serves campus. Semester system.

LD ADMISSIONS

A personal interview is recommended. Essay is required and may be typed.

SECONDARY SCHOOL REQUIREMENTS

Graduation from secondary school required; GED accepted.

TESTING

SAT Reasoning required; ACT may be substituted. SAT Subject recommended.

All enrolled freshmen (fall 2004):

Average SAT I Scores:	Verbal: 511	Math: 492
Average ACT Scores:	Composite: 19	

Child Study Team report is not required. Tests required as part of this documentation:

- [ ] WAIS-IV
- [ ] WISC-IV
- [ ] SATA
- [ ] Woodcock-Johnson
- [ ] Nelson-Denny Reading Test
- [ ] Other

UNDERGRADUATE STUDENT BODY

Total undergraduate student enrollment: 217 Men, 417 Women.

Composition of student body (fall 2004):

	Undergraduate	Freshmen
International	3.5	1.8
Black	7.0	3.6
American Indian	0.0	1.2
Asian-American	1.2	2.7
Hispanic	4.7	2.1
White	77.8	79.0
Unreported	5.8	9.6
	100.0%	100.0%

27% are from out of state. 69% of classes have fewer than 20 students, 30% have between 20 and 50 students, 1% have more than 50 students.

STUDENT HOUSING

Freshmen are required to live on campus. Housing is guaranteed for all undergraduates. Campus can house 289 undergraduates.

EXPENSES

Tuition (2005-06): $18,640 per year.
Room & Board: $5,360-$5,360.

There is no additional cost for LD program/services.

LD SERVICES

LD program size is not limited.

LD services available to:

- [ ] Freshmen
- [ ] Sophomores
- [ ] Juniors
- [ ] Seniors

Academic Accommodations

Curriculum		In class	
Foreign language waiver	[ ]	Early syllabus	[ ]
Lighter course load	[ ]	Note takers in class	[ ]
Math waiver	[ ]	Priority seating	[ ]
Other special classes	[x]	Tape recorders	[ ]
Priority registrations	[ ]	Videotaped classes	[ ]
Substitution of courses	[ ]	Text on tape	[ ]
Exams		**Services**	
Extended time	[x]	Diagnostic tests	[ ]
Oral exams	[ ]	Learning centers	[x]
Take home exams	[ ]	Proofreaders	[ ]
Exams on tape or computer	[ ]	Readers	[x]
Untimed exams	[ ]	Reading Machines/Kurzweil	[ ]
Other accommodations	[ ]	Special bookstore section	[ ]
		Typists	[ ]

Credit toward degree is given for remedial courses taken.

Counseling Services

- [ ] Academic
- [ ] Psychological
- [ ] Student Support groups
- [ ] Vocational

Tutoring

	Individual	Group
Time management	[ ]	[ ]
Organizational skills	[ ]	[ ]
Learning strategies	[ ]	[ ]
Study skills	[ ]	[ ]
Content area	[ ]	[ ]
Writing lab	[ ]	[ ]
Math lab	[ ]	[ ]

LD PROGRAM STAFF

Total number of LD Program staff (including director):

Key staff person available to work with LD students: Rod Johanson, Director of Academic Support Services.

Willamette University

Salem, OR

Address: 900 State Street, Salem, OR, 97301
Admissions telephone: 877 LIB-ARTS
Admissions FAX: 503 375-5363
Vice President for Enrollment: Dr. Robin Brown, VP Enrollment
Admissions e-mail: LIBARTS@willamette.edu
Web site: http://www.willamette.edu
SAT Code: 4954 ACT Code: 3504

Director of Disability & Learning Services: JoAnne Hill
LD program telephone: 503 370-6471
LD program e-mail: jhill@willamette.edu
Total campus enrollment: 1,977

GENERAL

Willamette University is a private, coed, four-year institution. 72-acre campus in Salem (population: 163,924), 45 miles from Portland. Served by air, bus, and train; major airport serves Portland. Public transportation serves campus. Semester system.

LD ADMISSIONS

A personal interview is recommended. Essay is required and may be typed. Applicants are not asked for any information concerning disabilities and are asked not to provide any disability information on their applications. If applicants provide any disability information, that information is forwarded to our Disability Services office and is not used in applicant screening.

SECONDARY SCHOOL REQUIREMENTS

Graduation from secondary school required; GED accepted.

TESTING

SAT Reasoning or ACT required. SAT Subject required.

All enrolled freshmen (fall 2004):

Average SAT I Scores:	Verbal: 620	Math: 630
Average ACT Scores:	Composite: 27	

Child Study Team report is not required. Tests required as part of this documentation:

- [ ] WAIS-IV
- [ ] WISC-IV
- [ ] SATA
- [ ] Woodcock-Johnson
- [ ] Nelson-Denny Reading Test
- [ ] Other

UNDERGRADUATE STUDENT BODY

Total undergraduate student enrollment: 781 Men, 992 Women.

Composition of student body (fall 2004):

	Undergraduate	Freshmen
International	0.0	0.3
Black	0.8	1.7
American Indian	0.6	1.0
Asian-American	4.9	6.4
Hispanic	3.9	4.7
White	61.8	61.4
Unreported	28.0	24.5
	100.0%	100.0%

60% are from out of state. 30% join a fraternity and 29% join a sorority. Average age of full-time undergraduates is 20. 66% of classes have fewer than 20 students, 34% have between 20 and 50 students.

STUDENT HOUSING

97% of freshmen live in college housing. Freshmen are required to live on campus. Housing is guaranteed for all undergraduates. Campus can house 1,342 undergraduates.

EXPENSES

Tuition (2005-06): $28,250 per year.
Room & Board: $7,000

There is no additional cost for LD program/services.

LD SERVICES

LD program size is not limited.

LD services available to:

- [x] Freshmen
- [x] Sophomores
- [x] Juniors
- [x] Seniors

Academic Accommodations

Curriculum		**In class**	
Foreign language waiver	[ ]	Early syllabus	[ ]
Lighter course load	[x]	Note takers in class	[x]
Math waiver	[ ]	Priority seating	[ ]
Other special classes	[ ]	Tape recorders	[x]
Priority registrations	[ ]	Videotaped classes	[ ]
Substitution of courses	[ ]	Text on tape	[ ]
Exams		**Services**	
Extended time	[x]	Diagnostic tests	[ ]
Oral exams	[ ]	Learning centers	[ ]
Take home exams	[ ]	Proofreaders	[ ]
Exams on tape or computer	[ ]	Readers	[ ]
Untimed exams	[ ]	Reading Machines/Kurzweil	[ ]
Other accommodations	[ ]	Special bookstore section	[ ]
		Typists	[ ]

Counseling Services

- [ ] Academic
- [ ] Psychological
- [ ] Student Support groups
- [ ] Vocational

Tutoring

Individual tutoring is available weekly.

	Individual	Group
Time management	[ ]	[ ]
Organizational skills	[ ]	[ ]
Learning strategies	[ ]	[ ]
Study skills	[ ]	[ ]
Content area	[ ]	[ ]
Writing lab	[ ]	[ ]
Math lab	[ ]	[ ]

UNIQUE LD PROGRAM FEATURES

Willamette University is moving toward a universal accessibility model. What is good for a student with a disability is often good for all students. There are a total of 82 students registered. The ADHD count is not included in the LD number. All students with disabilities are serviced through the same office.

LD PROGRAM STAFF

Total number of LD Program staff (including director):

Full Time: 2 Part Time: 2

Key staff person available to work with LD students: JoAnne Hill, Director of Disability & Learning Services.

Albright College

Reading, PA

Address: P.O. Box 15234, 13th and Bern Streets, Reading, PA, 19612-5234
Admissions telephone: 800 252-1856
Admissions FAX: 610 921-7294
Vice President for Enrollment Management: Gregory E. Eichhorn
Admissions e-mail: admission@alb.edu
Web site: http://www.albright.edu
SAT Code: 2004 ACT Code: 3518

Assistant Academic Dean/Director: Tiffenia D. Archie, Ph.D
LD program telephone: 610 921-7662
LD program e-mail: tarchie@alb.edu
LD program enrollment: 38, Total campus enrollment: 2,165

GENERAL

Albright College is a private, coed, four-year institution. 110-acre, suburban campus in Reading (population: 81,207), 45 miles from Philadelphia. Served by air and bus; major airport and train serve Philadelphia. School operates transportation to hospitals and school-sponsored special events. Public transportation serves campus. 4-1-4 system.

LD ADMISSIONS

Students do not complete a separate application and are simultaneously accepted to the LD program. A member of the LD program does sit on the admissions committee. High school waivers are accepted for foreign language. A personal interview is recommended. Essay is required and may be typed.

SECONDARY SCHOOL REQUIREMENTS

Graduation from secondary school required; GED accepted. The following course distribution required: 4 units of English, 2 units of math, 3 units of science, 2 units of foreign language, 2 units of social studies, 1 unit of history, 2 units of academic electives.

TESTING

SAT Reasoning or ACT required.

All enrolled freshmen (fall 2004):

Average SAT I Scores: Verbal: 519 Math: 511

Child Study Team report is not required. A neuropsychological or comprehensive psycho-educational evaluation is required for admission. Must be dated within 36 months of application. Tests required as part of this documentation:

- [x] WAIS-IV
- [ ] WISC-IV
- [ ] SATA
- [x] Woodcock-Johnson
- [x] Nelson-Denny Reading Test
- [x] Other

UNDERGRADUATE STUDENT BODY

Total undergraduate student enrollment: 772 Men, 1,037 Women.

Composition of student body (fall 2004):

	Undergraduate	Freshmen
International	4.3	3.8
Black	11.5	9.0
American Indian	0.4	0.4
Asian-American	2.8	2.2
Hispanic	4.0	4.1
White	77.0	78.0
Unreported	0.0	2.5
	100.0%	100.0%

27% are from out of state. 25% join a fraternity and 30% join a sorority. Average age of full-time undergraduates is 20. 65% of classes have fewer than 20 students, 34% have between 20 and 50 students, 1% have more than 50 students.

STUDENT HOUSING

91% of freshmen live in college housing. Freshmen are required to live on campus. Housing is guaranteed for all undergraduates. Campus can house 1,105 undergraduates. Single rooms are available for students with medical or special needs. A medical note is required.

EXPENSES

Tuition (2005-06): $25,232 per year.
Room: $4,489. Board: $3,397.
There is no additional cost for LD program/services.

LD SERVICES

LD program size is not limited.

LD services available to:

- [x] Freshmen
- [x] Sophomores
- [x] Juniors
- [x] Seniors

Academic Accommodations

Curriculum

- [ ] Foreign language waiver
- [x] Lighter course load
- [ ] Math waiver
- [ ] Other special classes
- [x] Priority registrations
- [ ] Substitution of courses

Exams

- [x] Extended time
- [x] Oral exams
- [ ] Take home exams
- [x] Exams on tape or computer
- [x] Untimed exams
- [ ] Other accommodations

In class

- [ ] Early syllabus
- [x] Note takers in class
- [ ] Priority seating
- [x] Tape recorders
- [ ] Videotaped classes
- [x] Text on tape

Services

- [ ] Diagnostic tests
- [x] Learning centers
- [ ] Proofreaders
- [x] Readers
- [ ] Reading Machines/Kurzweil
- [ ] Special bookstore section
- [ ] Typists

Credit toward degree is not given for remedial courses taken.

Counseling Services

- [ ] Academic
- [ ] Psychological
- [ ] Student Support groups
- [ ] Vocational

Tutoring

Individual tutoring is available weekly.

Average size of tutoring groups: 8

	Individual	Group
Time management	[x]	[ ]
Organizational skills	[x]	[ ]
Learning strategies	[x]	[ ]
Study skills	[x]	[ ]
Content area	[ ]	[ ]
Writing lab	[x]	[ ]
Math lab	[ ]	[ ]

LD PROGRAM STAFF

Total number of LD Program staff (including director):

Full Time: 1 Part Time: 1

There is an advisor/advocate from the LD program available to students.

Key staff person available to work with LD students: Tiffenia D. Archie, Ph.D., Assistant Academic Dean/Director of Academic Support

Allegheny College

Meadville, PA

Address: 520 North Main Street, Meadville, PA, 16335
Admissions telephone: 800 521-5293
Admissions FAX: 814 337-0431
Dean of Admissions and Enrollment Management: W. Scott Friedhoff
Admissions e-mail: admissions@allegheny.edu
Web site: http://www.allegheny.edu
SAT Code: 2006 ACT Code: 3520

Director of Student Support Services: Nancy Sheridan
LD program telephone: 814 332-2898
LD program e-mail: nancy.sheridan@allegheny.edu
LD program enrollment: 60, Total campus enrollment: 1,955

GENERAL

Allegheny College is a private, coed, four-year institution. 254-acre campus in Meadville (population: 13,685), 90 miles from both Pittsburgh and Cleveland. Served by bus; major airport serves Pittsburgh; smaller airport and train serve Erie (35 miles). School operates transportation to Erie and Pittsburgh airports at school breaks. Public transportation serves campus. Semester system.

LD ADMISSIONS

A member of the LD program does not sit on the admissions committee. A personal interview is recommended. Essay is required and may be typed. Recommended secondary school units may be waived.

SECONDARY SCHOOL REQUIREMENTS

Graduation from secondary school required; GED accepted. The following course distribution required: 4 units of English, 3 units of math, 3 units of science, 2 units of foreign language, 3 units of social studies, 1 unit of academic electives.

TESTING

SAT Reasoning or ACT required. SAT Subject recommended.

All enrolled freshmen (fall 2004):

Average SAT I Scores:	Verbal: 605	Math: 608
Average ACT Scores:	Composite: 26	

Child Study Team report is not required. Tests required as part of this documentation:

- [ ] WAIS-IV
- [ ] WISC-IV
- [ ] SATA
- [ ] Woodcock-Johnson
- [ ] Nelson-Denny Reading Test
- [ ] Other

UNDERGRADUATE STUDENT BODY

Total undergraduate student enrollment: 890 Men, 989 Women.

Composition of student body (fall 2004):

	Undergraduate	Freshmen
International	1.1	0.9
Black	1.2	1.5
American Indian	0.0	0.3
Asian-American	3.4	2.9
Hispanic	0.9	1.2
White	93.4	93.2
Unreported	0.0	0.0
	100.0%	100.0%

33% are from out of state. 26% join a fraternity and 28% join a sorority. Average age of full-time undergraduates is 20. 61% of classes have fewer than 20 students, 37% have between 20 and 50 students, 2% have more than 50 students.

STUDENT HOUSING

99% of freshmen live in college housing. Freshmen are required to live on campus. Housing is guaranteed for all undergraduates. Campus can house 1,438 undergraduates. Single rooms are available for students with medical or special needs. A medical note is required.

EXPENSES

Tuition (2005-06): $26,650 per year.

Room: $3,340. Board: $3,210.
There is no additional cost for LD program/services.

LD SERVICES

LD program size is not limited.

LD services available to:

- [x] Freshmen
- [x] Sophomores
- [x] Juniors
- [x] Seniors

Academic Accommodations

Curriculum
- [ ] Foreign language waiver
- [x] Lighter course load
- [ ] Math waiver
- [ ] Other special classes
- [x] Priority registrations
- [ ] Substitution of courses

Exams
- [x] Extended time
- [x] Oral exams
- [ ] Take home exams
- [x] Exams on tape or computer
- [ ] Untimed exams
- [ ] Other accommodations

In class
- [ ] Early syllabus
- [x] Note takers in class
- [x] Priority seating
- [x] Tape recorders
- [ ] Videotaped classes
- [x] Text on tape

Services
- [ ] Diagnostic tests
- [x] Learning centers
- [ ] Proofreaders
- [x] Readers
- [ ] Reading Machines/Kurzweil
- [ ] Special bookstore section
- [x] Typists

Credit toward degree is not given for remedial courses taken.

Counseling Services

- [x] Academic
- [x] Psychological
- [ ] Student Support groups
- [ ] Vocational

Tutoring

Individual tutoring is available daily.

	Individual	Group
Time management	[x]	[x]
Organizational skills	[x]	[ ]
Learning strategies	[x]	[ ]
Study skills	[x]	[x]
Content area	[x]	[ ]
Writing lab	[ ]	[ ]
Math lab	[ ]	[ ]

UNIQUE LD PROGRAM FEATURES

Allegheny strives to meet each individual's needs.

LD PROGRAM STAFF

Total number of LD Program staff (including director):

Full Time: 1 Part Time: 1

There is an advisor/advocate from the LD program available to students.

Key staff person available to work with LD students: Nancy Sheridan, Director of Student Support Services.

Alvernia College

Reading, PA

Address: 400 St. Bernardine Street, Reading, PA, 19607-1799
Admissions telephone: 888 258-3764
Admissions FAX: 610 796-8336
Assistant Dean of Enrollment Management: Catherine Emery
Admissions e-mail: admissions@alvernia.edu
Web site: http://www.alvernia.edu
SAT Code: 2431 ACT Code: 3521

Total campus enrollment: 2,016

GENERAL

Alvernia College is a private, coed, four-year institution. 85-acre campus in Reading (population: 81,207), 50 miles from Philadelphia. Served by air and bus; major airport and train serve Philadelphia. Public transportation serves campus. Semester system.

SECONDARY SCHOOL REQUIREMENTS

Graduation from secondary school required; GED accepted. The following course distribution required: 4 units of English, 2 units of math, 2 units of science, 2 units of foreign language, 2 units of social studies, 4 units of academic electives.

TESTING

SAT Reasoning or ACT considered if submitted; SAT Reasoning preferred.

Child Study Team report is not required. Tests required as part of this documentation:

- ☐ WAIS-IV
- ☐ WISC-IV
- ☐ SATA
- ☐ Woodcock-Johnson
- ☐ Nelson-Denny Reading Test
- ☐ Other

UNDERGRADUATE STUDENT BODY

Total undergraduate student enrollment: 533 Men, 1,049 Women.

Composition of student body (fall 2004):

	Undergraduate	Freshmen
International	0.6	0.9
Black	8.6	14.8
American Indian	0.1	0.5
Asian-American	1.2	1.2
Hispanic	6.8	3.4
White	73.5	76.4
Unreported	9.2	2.8
	100.0%	100.0%

8% are from out of state. Average age of full-time undergraduates is 23. 58% of classes have fewer than 20 students, 41% have between 20 and 50 students, 1% have more than 50 students.

STUDENT HOUSING

71% of freshmen live in college housing. Housing is guaranteed for all undergraduates. Campus can house 530 undergraduates.

EXPENSES

Tuition (2005-06): $18,900 per year.
Room: $3,477. Board: $3,822.

LD SERVICES

LD program size is not limited.

LD services available to:

☐ Freshmen ☐ Sophomores ☐ Juniors ☐ Seniors

Academic Accommodations

Curriculum		**In class**	
Foreign language waiver	☐	Early syllabus	☐
Lighter course load	☐	Note takers in class	■
Math waiver	☐	Priority seating	☐
Other special classes	☐	Tape recorders	■
Priority registrations	☐	Videotaped classes	☐
Substitution of courses	☐	Text on tape	☐
Exams		**Services**	
Extended time	■	Diagnostic tests	☐
Oral exams	■	Learning centers	■
Take home exams	☐	Proofreaders	☐
Exams on tape or computer	☐	Readers	☐
Untimed exams	☐	Reading Machines/Kurzweil	☐
Other accommodations	☐	Special bookstore section	☐
		Typists	☐

Credit toward degree is not given for remedial courses taken.

Counseling Services

- ☐ Academic
- ☐ Psychological
- ☐ Student Support groups
- ☐ Vocational

Tutoring

	Individual	Group
Time management	☐	☐
Organizational skills	☐	☐
Learning strategies	☐	☐
Study skills	☐	☐
Content area	☐	☐
Writing lab	☐	☐
Math lab	☐	☐

LD PROGRAM STAFF

Key staff person available to work with LD students: Wanda Copeland, Director of Academic Advancement.

Arcadia University

Glenside, PA

Address: 450 South Easton Road, Glenside, PA, 19038-3295
Admissions telephone: 877 272-2342
Admissions FAX: 215 881-8767
Vice President for Enrollment Management: Mark Lapreziosa
Admissions e-mail: admiss@arcadia.edu
Web site: http://www.arcadia.edu
SAT Code: 2039 ACT Code: 3524

Director, Education Enhancement Center: Linda Pizzi
LD program telephone: 215 572-4086
LD program e-mail: pizzi@arcadia.edu
LD program enrollment: 47, Total campus enrollment: 1,918

GENERAL

Arcadia University is a private, coed, four-year institution. 55-acre, suburban campus in Glenside (population: 7,914), 20 miles from Philadelphia. Served by train; major airport and bus serve Philadelphia. Semester system.

LD ADMISSIONS

A personal interview is recommended. Essay is not required.

SECONDARY SCHOOL REQUIREMENTS

Graduation from secondary school required; GED accepted. The following course distribution required: 4 units of English, 3 units of math, 3 units of science, 3 units of foreign language, 4 units of social studies, 3 units of academic electives.

TESTING

SAT Reasoning required; ACT may be substituted. SAT Subject recommended.

All enrolled freshmen (fall 2004):

Average SAT I Scores:	Verbal: 554	Math: 533
Average ACT Scores:	Composite: 24	

Child Study Team report is not required. A neuropsychological or comprehensive psycho-educational evaluation is required for admission. Must be dated within 36 months of application. Tests required as part of this documentation:

- [x] WAIS-IV
- [x] WISC-IV
- [ ] SATA
- [x] Woodcock-Johnson
- [ ] Nelson-Denny Reading Test
- [ ] Other

UNDERGRADUATE STUDENT BODY

Total undergraduate student enrollment: 454 Men, 1,195 Women.

Composition of student body (fall 2004):

	Undergraduate	Freshmen
International	0.1	0.9
Black	8.2	9.1
American Indian	0.4	0.2
Asian-American	3.0	2.7
Hispanic	2.6	2.3
White	80.7	80.7
Unreported	5.0	4.1
	100.0%	100.0%

28% are from out of state. Average age of full-time undergraduates is 20. 69% of classes have fewer than 20 students, 30% have between 20 and 50 students, 1% have more than 50 students.

STUDENT HOUSING

85% of freshmen live in college housing. Freshmen are not required to live on campus. Housing is guaranteed for all undergraduates. Campus can house 1,066 undergraduates. Single rooms are available for students with medical or special needs. A medical note is required.

EXPENSES

Tuition (2005-06): $23,990 per year.

Room: $6,380. Board: $2,920.
There is no additional cost for LD program/services.

LD SERVICES

LD program size is not limited.

LD services available to:

- [x] Freshmen
- [x] Sophomores
- [x] Juniors
- [x] Seniors

Academic Accommodations

Curriculum		**In class**	
Foreign language waiver	[ ]	Early syllabus	[ ]
Lighter course load	[x]	Note takers in class	[x]
Math waiver	[ ]	Priority seating	[x]
Other special classes	[x]	Tape recorders	[x]
Priority registrations	[ ]	Videotaped classes	[ ]
Substitution of courses	[x]	Text on tape	[x]
Exams		**Services**	
Extended time	[x]	Diagnostic tests	[ ]
Oral exams	[ ]	Learning centers	[x]
Take home exams	[ ]	Proofreaders	[ ]
Exams on tape or computer	[x]	Readers	[ ]
Untimed exams	[ ]	Reading Machines/Kurzweil	[x]
Other accommodations	[ ]	Special bookstore section	[ ]
		Typists	[ ]

Credit toward degree is given for remedial courses taken.

Counseling Services

- [x] Academic
- [ ] Psychological
- [ ] Student Support groups
- [ ] Vocational

Tutoring

Individual tutoring is available daily.

Average size of tutoring groups: 1

	Individual	Group
Time management	[x]	[ ]
Organizational skills	[x]	[ ]
Learning strategies	[x]	[ ]
Study skills	[x]	[ ]
Content area	[x]	[ ]
Writing lab	[x]	[ ]
Math lab	[x]	[ ]

LD PROGRAM STAFF

Total number of LD Program staff (including director):

Full Time: 1 Part Time: 1

There is no advisor/advocate from the LD program available to students. 60 peer tutors are available to work with LD students.

Key staff person available to work with LD students: Andrea Coren, Learning Disabilities Specialist.

The University of the Arts

Philadelphia, PA

Address: 320 South Broad Street, Philadelphia, PA, 19102
Admissions telephone: 800 616-ARTS
Admissions FAX: 215 717-6045
Director of Admissions: Barbara Elliott
Admissions e-mail: admissions@uarts.edu
Web site: http://www.uarts.edu
SAT Code: 2664 ACT Code: 3664

Learning Skills Specialist: Neila Douglas
LD program telephone: 215 875-2254
LD program e-mail: ndouglas@uarts.edu
Total campus enrollment: 2,026

GENERAL

The University of the Arts is a private, coed, four-year institution. 18-acre, urban campus in Philadelphia (population: 1,517,550). Served by air, bus, and train. School operates transportation to immediate area around campus in the evening. Public transportation serves campus. Semester system.

LD ADMISSIONS

A personal interview is recommended.

SECONDARY SCHOOL REQUIREMENTS

Graduation from secondary school required; GED accepted. The following course distribution required: 4 units of English.

TESTING

ACT considered if submitted.

All enrolled freshmen (fall 2004):

Average SAT I Scores:	Verbal: 537	Math: 506
Average ACT Scores:	Composite: 21	

Child Study Team report is not required. Tests required as part of this documentation:

- ☐ WAIS-IV
- ☐ WISC-IV
- ☐ SATA
- ☐ Woodcock-Johnson
- ☐ Nelson-Denny Reading Test
- ☐ Other

UNDERGRADUATE STUDENT BODY

Total undergraduate student enrollment: 895 Men, 1,043 Women.

Composition of student body (fall 2004):

	Undergraduate	Freshmen
International	2.0	2.3
Black	12.1	9.4
American Indian	0.0	0.2
Asian-American	2.6	3.4
Hispanic	3.8	4.1
White	65.8	68.8
Unreported	13.7	11.8
	100.0%	100.0%

51% are from out of state. Average age of full-time undergraduates is 20. 77% of classes have fewer than 20 students, 23% have between 20 and 50 students.

STUDENT HOUSING

80% of freshmen live in college housing. Freshmen are not required to live on campus. Housing is not guaranteed for all undergraduates. Campus can house 690 undergraduates.

EXPENSES

Tuition 2004-05: $22,060 per year.

Room: $5,800. Board: $2,000.

There is no additional cost for LD program/services.

LD SERVICES

LD program size is not limited.

LD services available to:

☐ Freshmen ☐ Sophomores ☐ Juniors ☐ Seniors

Academic Accommodations

Curriculum		In class	
Foreign language waiver	☐	Early syllabus	☐
Lighter course load	■	Note takers in class	■
Math waiver	☐	Priority seating	☐
Other special classes	☐	Tape recorders	■
Priority registrations	☐	Videotaped classes	☐
Substitution of courses	☐	Text on tape	☐
Exams		**Services**	
Extended time	■	Diagnostic tests	☐
Oral exams	☐	Learning centers	☐
Take home exams	☐	Proofreaders	☐
Exams on tape or computer	☐	Readers	■
Untimed exams	☐	Reading Machines/Kurzweil	☐
Other accommodations	☐	Special bookstore section	☐
		Typists	☐

Credit toward degree is not given for remedial courses taken.

Counseling Services

- ☐ Academic
- ☐ Psychological
- ☐ Student Support groups
- ☐ Vocational

Tutoring

Individual tutoring is available.

	Individual	Group
Time management	☐	☐
Organizational skills	☐	☐
Learning strategies	☐	☐
Study skills	☐	☐
Content area	☐	☐
Writing lab	☐	☐
Math lab	☐	☐

LD PROGRAM STAFF

Total number of LD Program staff (including director):

Full Time: 1 Part Time: 1

There is an advisor/advocate from the LD program available to students.

Bloomsburg University of Pennsylvania

Bloomsburg, PA

Address: 400 East Second Street, Bloomsburg, PA, 17815
Admissions telephone: 570 389-4316
Admissions FAX: 570 389-4741
Director of Admissions and Records: Christopher Keller
Admissions e-mail: buadmiss@bloomu.edu
Web site: http://www.bloomu.edu
SAT Code: 2646 ACT Code: 3692

Director, Accommodative Services: Peter B. Walters
LD program telephone: 570 389-4491
LD program e-mail: pwalters@bloomu.edu
Total campus enrollment: 7,524

GENERAL

Bloomsburg University of Pennsylvania is a public, coed, four-year institution. 282-acre campus in Bloomsburg (population: 12,375), 80 miles from Harrisburg. Served by bus; airport serves Wilkes-Barre/Scranton (40 miles). School operates transportation to upper campus and Bloomsburg. Semester system.

LD ADMISSIONS

A personal interview is recommended. Essay is not required.

SECONDARY SCHOOL REQUIREMENTS

Graduation from secondary school required; GED accepted. The following course distribution required: 4 units of English, 3 units of math, 2 units of science, 2 units of social studies, 2 units of history.

TESTING

SAT Reasoning or ACT required. SAT Subject recommended.

All enrolled freshmen (fall 2004):

Average SAT I Scores: Verbal: 501 Math: 512

Child Study Team report is not required. Tests required as part of this documentation:

- [ ] WAIS-IV
- [ ] WISC-IV
- [ ] SATA
- [ ] Woodcock-Johnson
- [ ] Nelson-Denny Reading Test
- [ ] Other

UNDERGRADUATE STUDENT BODY

Total undergraduate student enrollment: 2,827 Men, 4,395 Women.

Composition of student body (fall 2004):

	Undergraduate	Freshmen
International	0.3	0.5
Black	7.9	4.9
American Indian	0.0	0.1
Asian-American	0.9	1.0
Hispanic	2.8	1.7
White	84.6	89.7
Unreported	3.5	2.1
	100.0%	100.0%

10% are from out of state. 4% join a fraternity and 6% join a sorority. Average age of full-time undergraduates is 20. 25% of classes have fewer than 20 students, 68% have between 20 and 50 students, 7% have more than 50 students.

STUDENT HOUSING

90% of freshmen live in college housing. Freshmen are required to live on campus. Housing is guaranteed for all undergraduates. Campus can house 3,076 undergraduates.

EXPENSES

Tuition (2005-06): $5,031 per year (in-state), $12,454 (out-of-state).
Room: $3,126. Board: $2,250.
There is no additional cost for LD program/services.

LD SERVICES

LD program size is not limited.

LD services available to:

- [ ] Freshmen
- [ ] Sophomores
- [ ] Juniors
- [ ] Seniors

Academic Accommodations

Curriculum		**In class**	
Foreign language waiver	[ ]	Early syllabus	[ ]
Lighter course load	[x]	Note takers in class	[x]
Math waiver	[ ]	Priority seating	[ ]
Other special classes	[x]	Tape recorders	[x]
Priority registrations	[ ]	Videotaped classes	[ ]
Substitution of courses	[ ]	Text on tape	[ ]
Exams		**Services**	
Extended time	[x]	Diagnostic tests	[ ]
Oral exams	[x]	Learning centers	[ ]
Take home exams	[ ]	Proofreaders	[ ]
Exams on tape or computer	[ ]	Readers	[x]
Untimed exams	[ ]	Reading Machines/Kurzweil	[x]
Other accommodations	[ ]	Special bookstore section	[ ]
		Typists	[ ]

Credit toward degree is not given for remedial courses taken.

Counseling Services

- [ ] Academic
- [ ] Psychological
- [ ] Student Support groups
- [ ] Vocational

Tutoring

	Individual	Group
Time management	[ ]	[ ]
Organizational skills	[ ]	[ ]
Learning strategies	[ ]	[ ]
Study skills	[ ]	[ ]
Content area	[ ]	[ ]
Writing lab	[ ]	[ ]
Math lab	[ ]	[ ]

UNIQUE LD PROGRAM FEATURES

University tutoring is available to all students. Tutoring is not provided on the basis of disability. Lighter course load for LD students, but a minimum of 24 credits needs to be earned in an academic year for financial aid.

LD PROGRAM STAFF

Total number of LD Program staff (including director):

Full Time: 1 Part Time: 1

Key staff person available to work with LD students: Peter B. Walters, Director, Accommodative Services.

Bryn Athyn College of the New Church

Bryn Athyn, PA

Address: 2895 College Drive, P.O. Box 717, Bryn Athyn, PA, 19009
Admissions telephone: 215 938-2511
Admissions FAX: 502 267-2658
Director of Admissions: Marcy Latta
Admissions e-mail: marcy.latta@brynathyn.edu
Web site: http://www.brynathyn.edu
SAT Code: 2002 ACT Code: 3727

Total campus enrollment: 153

GENERAL

Bryn Athyn College of the New Church is a private, coed, four-year institution. 170-acre, suburban campus in Bryn Athyn (population: 1,351), 15 miles from central Philadelphia. Major airport serves Philadelphia; bus serves Willow Grove (four miles); train serves Huntingdon Valley (one mile). Trimester system.

LD ADMISSIONS

A personal interview is required. Essay is required and may be typed.

SECONDARY SCHOOL REQUIREMENTS

Graduation from secondary school required; GED accepted. The following course distribution required: 4 units of English, 3 units of math, 3 units of science, 2 units of foreign language.

TESTING

SAT Reasoning or ACT required. SAT Subject required.

All enrolled freshmen (fall 2004):

Average SAT I Scores:	Verbal: 564	Math: 536
Average ACT Scores:	Composite: 26	

Child Study Team report is required if student is classified. Tests required as part of this documentation:

- [ ] WAIS-IV
- [ ] WISC-IV
- [ ] SATA
- [ ] Woodcock-Johnson
- [ ] Nelson-Denny Reading Test
- [ ] Other

UNDERGRADUATE STUDENT BODY

Total undergraduate student enrollment: 51 Men, 87 Women.

Composition of student body (fall 2004):

	Undergraduate	Freshmen
International	11.9	13.4
Black	0.0	0.0
American Indian	0.0	0.0
Asian-American	0.0	1.4
Hispanic	0.0	1.4
White	86.4	83.1
Unreported	1.7	0.7
	100.0%	100.0%

26% are from out of state. Average age of full-time undergraduates is 22. 92% of classes have fewer than 20 students, 8% have between 20 and 50 students.

STUDENT HOUSING

62% of freshmen live in college housing. Freshmen are not required to live on campus. Housing is guaranteed for all undergraduates. Campus can house 98 undergraduates. Single rooms are not available for students with medical or special needs.

EXPENSES

Tuition (2005-06): $8,096 per year.
Room & Board: $5,360-$5,360.
Additional cost for LD program/services: $10 per hour.

LD SERVICES

LD services available to:

- [x] Freshmen
- [x] Sophomores
- [x] Juniors
- [x] Seniors

Academic Accommodations

Curriculum		In class	
Foreign language waiver	[ ]	Early syllabus	[ ]
Lighter course load	[x]	Note takers in class	[ ]
Math waiver	[ ]	Priority seating	[ ]
Other special classes	[ ]	Tape recorders	[x]
Priority registrations	[ ]	Videotaped classes	[ ]
Substitution of courses	[ ]	Text on tape	[ ]
Exams		**Services**	
Extended time	[x]	Diagnostic tests	[ ]
Oral exams	[x]	Learning centers	[ ]
Take home exams	[ ]	Proofreaders	[ ]
Exams on tape or computer	[ ]	Readers	[ ]
Untimed exams	[x]	Reading Machines/Kurzweil	[ ]
Other accommodations	[ ]	Special bookstore section	[ ]
		Typists	[ ]

Credit toward degree is given for remedial courses taken.

Counseling Services

- [ ] Academic
- [x] Psychological
- [ ] Student Support groups
- [ ] Vocational

Tutoring

Individual tutoring is available weekly.

	Individual	Group
Time management	[ ]	[ ]
Organizational skills	[ ]	[ ]
Learning strategies	[ ]	[ ]
Study skills	[ ]	[ ]
Content area	[ ]	[ ]
Writing lab	[x]	[ ]
Math lab	[ ]	[ ]

LD PROGRAM STAFF

There is no advisor/advocate from the LD program available to students.

Key staff person available to work with LD students: Edith Van Zyverden, Academic Support Coordinator.

Bryn Mawr College

Bryn Mawr, PA

Address: 101 North Merion Avenue, Bryn Mawr, PA, 19010
Admissions telephone: 800 BMC-1885
Admissions FAX: 610 526-7471
Director of Admissions: Jennifer Rickard
Admissions e-mail: admissions@brynmawr.edu
Web site: http://www.brynmawr.edu
SAT Code: 2049 ACT Code: 3526

Accessibility Coordinator: Stephanie Bell
LD program telephone: 610 526-7351
LD program e-mail: sbell@brynmawr.edu
Total campus enrollment: 1,327

GENERAL

Bryn Mawr College is a private, women's, four-year institution. 135-acre, suburban campus in Bryn Mawr (population: 4,382), 11 miles from Philadelphia. Major airport, bus, and train serve Philadelphia. School operates transportation to Haverford Coll and Swarthmore Coll and to Philadelphia on weekends. Public transportation serves campus. Semester system.

SECONDARY SCHOOL REQUIREMENTS

Graduation from secondary school required; GED accepted. The following course distribution required: 2 units of academic electives.

TESTING

SAT Subject recommended.

All enrolled freshmen (fall 2004):

Average SAT I Scores: Verbal: 668 Math: 645
Average ACT Scores: Composite: 28

Child Study Team report is not required. Tests required as part of this documentation:

- ❑ WAIS-IV
- ❑ WISC-IV
- ❑ SATA
- ❑ Woodcock-Johnson
- ❑ Nelson-Denny Reading Test
- ❑ Other

UNDERGRADUATE STUDENT BODY

Total undergraduate student enrollment: 14 Men, 1,319 Women.

Composition of student body (fall 2004):

	Undergraduate	Freshmen
International	8.7	8.0
Black	5.0	4.7
American Indian	0.0	0.1
Asian-American	12.3	10.5
Hispanic	3.4	3.4
White	42.1	45.3
Unreported	28.5	28.0
	100.0%	100.0%

80% are from out of state. Average age of full-time undergraduates is 20. 69% of classes have fewer than 20 students, 27% have between 20 and 50 students, 4% have more than 50 students.

STUDENT HOUSING

100% of freshmen live in college housing. Freshmen are required to live on campus. Housing is guaranteed for all undergraduates. Campus can house 1,200 undergraduates.

EXPENSES

Tuition (2005-06): $29,570 per year.
Room: $5,740. Board: $4,350.

LD SERVICES

LD program size is not limited.

LD services available to:

❑ Freshmen ❑ Sophomores ❑ Juniors ❑ Seniors

Academic Accommodations

Curriculum		In class	
Foreign language waiver	❑	Early syllabus	❑
Lighter course load	❑	Note takers in class	❑
Math waiver	❑	Priority seating	❑
Other special classes	❑	Tape recorders	❑
Priority registrations	❑	Videotaped classes	❑
Substitution of courses	❑	Text on tape	❑
Exams		**Services**	
Extended time	❑	Diagnostic tests	❑
Oral exams	❑	Learning centers	❑
Take home exams	❑	Proofreaders	❑
Exams on tape or computer	❑	Readers	❑
Untimed exams	❑	Reading Machines/Kurzweil	❑
Other accommodations	❑	Special bookstore section	❑
		Typists	❑

Counseling Services

- ❑ Academic
- ❑ Psychological
- ❑ Student Support groups
- ❑ Vocational

Tutoring

	Individual	Group
Time management	❑	❑
Organizational skills	❑	❑
Learning strategies	❑	❑
Study skills	❑	❑
Content area	❑	❑
Writing lab	❑	❑
Math lab	❑	❑

UNIQUE LD PROGRAM FEATURES

Accommodations are provided on a case-by-case basis when appropriate. Please contact Accessibility Services.

LD PROGRAM STAFF

Key staff person available to work with LD students: Stephanie Bell, Accessibility Coordinator, Disability Services

Bucknell University

Lewisburg, PA

Address: Lewisburg, PA, 17837
Admissions telephone: 570 577-1101
Admissions FAX: 570 577-3538
Dean of Admissions: Mark D. Davies
Admissions e-mail: admissions@bucknell.edu
Web site: http://www.bucknell.edu
SAT Code: 2050 ACT Code: 3528

Associate Dean of Arts and Sciences: Elaine Garrett
LD program telephone: 570 577-1301
LD program e-mail: garrett@bucknell.edu
LD program enrollment: 54, Total campus enrollment: 3,454

GENERAL

Bucknell University is a private, coed, four-year institution. 393-acre campus in Lewisburg (population: 5,620), 75 miles from Harrisburg. Airport and train serve Harrisburg. School operates transportation to airports and bus and train stations at scheduled vacation periods. Semester system.

LD ADMISSIONS

Application Deadline: 01/01. A personal interview is recommended. Essay is required and may be typed.

For fall 2004, 63 completed self-identified LD applications were received. 10 applications were offered admission, and 8 enrolled.

SECONDARY SCHOOL REQUIREMENTS

Graduation from secondary school required; GED accepted. The following course distribution required: 4 units of English, 3 units of math, 2 units of science, 2 units of foreign language, 2 units of social studies, 2 units of history, 1 unit of academic electives.

TESTING

SAT Reasoning required; ACT may be substituted. SAT Subject required.

All enrolled freshmen (fall 2004):

Average SAT I Scores:	Verbal: 636	Math: 666
Average ACT Scores:	Composite: 29	

Child Study Team report is not required. A neuropsychological or comprehensive psycho-educational evaluation is required for admission. Must be dated within 24 months of application. Tests required as part of this documentation:

- ☐ WAIS-IV
- ☐ WISC-IV
- ☐ SATA
- ☐ Woodcock-Johnson
- ☐ Nelson-Denny Reading Test
- ☐ Other

UNDERGRADUATE STUDENT BODY

Total undergraduate student enrollment: 1,761 Men, 1,669 Women.

Composition of student body (fall 2004):

	Undergraduate	Freshmen
International	3.3	2.6
Black	2.6	2.6
American Indian	0.6	0.5
Asian-American	7.4	5.9
Hispanic	2.4	2.3
White	80.9	84.2
Unreported	2.8	1.9
	100.0%	100.0%

67% are from out of state. 35% join a fraternity and 38% join a sorority. Average age of full-time undergraduates is 20. 54% of classes have fewer than 20 students, 44% have between 20 and 50 students, 2% have more than 50 students.

STUDENT HOUSING

100% of freshmen live in college housing. Freshmen are required to live on campus. Housing is guaranteed for all undergraduates. Campus can house 2,720 undergraduates. Single rooms are available for students with medical or special needs. A medical note is required.

EXPENSES

Tuition (2005-06): $32,592 per year.

Room: $3,670. Board: $3,202.
There is no additional cost for LD program/services.

LD SERVICES

LD program size is not limited.

LD services available to:

☑ Freshmen ☑ Sophomores ☑ Juniors ☑ Seniors

Academic Accommodations

Curriculum		**In class**	
Foreign language waiver	☐	Early syllabus	☐
Lighter course load	☐	Note takers in class	☐
Math waiver	☐	Priority seating	☐
Other special classes	☐	Tape recorders	☑
Priority registrations	☐	Videotaped classes	☐
Substitution of courses	☐	Text on tape	☐
Exams		**Services**	
Extended time	☑	Diagnostic tests	☐
Oral exams	☑	Learning centers	☐
Take home exams	☐	Proofreaders	☐
Exams on tape or computer	☐	Readers	☐
Untimed exams	☐	Reading Machines/Kurzweil	☑
Other accommodations	☐	Special bookstore section	☐
		Typists	☐

Credit toward degree is not given for remedial courses taken.

Counseling Services

- ☑ Academic
- ☑ Psychological
- ☐ Student Support groups
- ☑ Vocational

Tutoring

Individual tutoring is available weekly.

Average size of tutoring groups: 1

	Individual	Group
Time management	☑	☐
Organizational skills	☑	☐
Learning strategies	☑	☐
Study skills	☑	☐
Content area	☐	☐
Writing lab	☑	☐
Math lab	☑	☐

UNIQUE LD PROGRAM FEATURES

Bucknell does not have an LD program nor any staff who work exclusively with LD students. We provide reasonable accommodations as needed to students who provide documentation of a Learning Disability.

LD PROGRAM STAFF

There is no advisor/advocate from the LD program available to students.

Key staff person available to work with LD students: Elaine Garrett, Associate Dean of Arts and Sciences

LD Program web site: www.bucknell.edu/DisabilityServices

Cabrini College

Radnor, PA

Address: 610 King of Prussia Road, Radnor, PA, 19087-3698
Admissions telephone: 800 848-1003
Admissions FAX: 610 903-8508
Director of Admissions: Mark Osborn
Admissions e-mail: admit@cabrini.edu
Web site: http://www.cabrini.edu
SAT Code: 2071 ACT Code: 3532

LD program name: Disability Support Services
Coordinator of Disability Support Services: Anne Abbuhl
LD program telephone: 610 902-8572
LD program e-mail: ama722@cabrini.edu
LD program enrollment: 130, Total campus enrollment: 1,649

GENERAL

Cabrini College is a private, coed, four-year institution. 112-acre, suburban campus in Radnor (population: 30,878), 15 miles from Philadelphia. Major airport and train serve Philadelphia; bus serves King of Prussia (five miles). School operates transportation to train station, off-campus housing, King of Prussia, Philadelphia (weekends only), Wayne, and Villanova U. Semester system.

LD ADMISSIONS

A member of the LD program does not sit on the admissions committee. A personal interview is recommended. Essay is not required.

For fall 2004, 21 completed self-identified LD applications were received. 18 applications were offered admission, and 11 enrolled.

SECONDARY SCHOOL REQUIREMENTS

Graduation from secondary school required; GED accepted. The following course distribution required: 4 units of English, 3 units of math, 3 units of science, 2 units of foreign language, 3 units of social studies, 3 units of history, 2 units of academic electives.

TESTING

SAT Reasoning or ACT required. SAT Subject recommended.

All enrolled freshmen (fall 2004):

Average SAT I Scores:	Verbal: 487	Math: 476
Average ACT Scores:	Composite:	

Child Study Team report is not required. A neuropsychological or comprehensive psycho-educational evaluation is required for admission. Must be dated within 36 months of application. Tests required as part of this documentation:

- [x] WAIS-IV
- [x] WISC-IV
- [ ] SATA
- [x] Woodcock-Johnson
- [ ] Nelson-Denny Reading Test
- [ ] Other

UNDERGRADUATE STUDENT BODY

Total undergraduate student enrollment: 583 Men, 1,056 Women.

Composition of student body (fall 2004):

	Undergraduate	Freshmen
International	0.8	1.2
Black	8.2	6.6
American Indian	0.0	0.1
Asian-American	2.1	1.8
Hispanic	3.1	2.0
White	78.1	80.5
Unreported	7.7	7.8
	100.0%	100.0%

27% are from out of state. Average age of full-time undergraduates is 21. 62% of classes have fewer than 20 students, 38% have between 20 and 50 students.

STUDENT HOUSING

84% of freshmen live in college housing. Freshmen are not required to live on campus. Priority is given to undergraduates but housing is not guaranteed. Campus can house 927 undergraduates. Single rooms are available for students with medical or special needs. A medical note is required.

EXPENSES

Tuition (2005-06): $23,200 per year.
Room & Board: $9,340-$9,340.

There is no additional cost for LD program/services.

LD SERVICES

LD program size is not limited.

LD services available to:

- [x] Freshmen
- [x] Sophomores
- [x] Juniors
- [x] Seniors

Academic Accommodations

Curriculum
- [ ] Foreign language waiver
- [x] Lighter course load
- [ ] Math waiver
- [ ] Other special classes
- [ ] Priority registrations
- [ ] Substitution of courses

Exams
- [ ] Extended time
- [ ] Oral exams
- [ ] Take home exams
- [ ] Exams on tape or computer
- [ ] Untimed exams
- [ ] Other accommodations

In class
- [ ] Early syllabus
- [x] Note takers in class
- [ ] Priority seating
- [x] Tape recorders
- [ ] Videotaped classes
- [ ] Text on tape

Services
- [ ] Diagnostic tests
- [x] Learning centers
- [ ] Proofreaders
- [ ] Readers
- [ ] Reading Machines/Kurzweil
- [ ] Special bookstore section
- [ ] Typists

Credit toward degree is not given for remedial courses taken.

Counseling Services

- [ ] Academic
- [ ] Psychological
- [ ] Student Support groups
- [ ] Vocational

Tutoring

Individual tutoring is available daily.

Average size of tutoring groups: 3

	Individual	Group
Time management	[x]	[x]
Organizational skills	[x]	[x]
Learning strategies	[x]	[x]
Study skills	[x]	[x]
Content area	[x]	[x]
Writing lab	[x]	[x]
Math lab	[x]	[x]

UNIQUE LD PROGRAM FEATURES

Documentation of LD or ADD must be current and include an assessment of cognitive functioning, information processing, and academic achievement. Reasonable accommodations are determined on an individual basis.

LD PROGRAM STAFF

Total number of LD Program staff (including director):

Full Time: 1 Part Time: 1

There is an advisor/advocate from the LD program available to students.

Key staff person available to work with LD students: Anne Abbuhl, Coordinator of Disability Support Services.

California University of Pennsylvania

California, PA

Address: 250 University Avenue, Box 94, California, PA, 15419
Admissions telephone: 724 938-4404
Admissions FAX: 724 938-4564
Dean of Admissions: William Edmonds
Admissions e-mail: inquiry@cup.edu
Web site: http://www.cup.edu
SAT Code: 2647 ACT Code: 3694

LD program name: Office for Students With Disabilities
Director: Cheryl L. Bilitski
LD program telephone: 724 938-5781
LD program e-mail: osdmail@cup.edu
LD program enrollment: 82, Total campus enrollment: 5,455

GENERAL

California University of Pennsylvania is a public, coed, four-year institution. 148-acre campus in California (population: 5,274), 45 miles from Pittsburgh; branch campus in Southpointe. Major airport serves Pittsburgh; train serves Connelsville (30 miles). Public transportation serves campus. Semester system.

LD ADMISSIONS

Students complete a separate application and are not simultaneously accepted to the LD program. A member of the LD program does not sit on the admissions committee. A personal interview is recommended. Essay is not required.

SECONDARY SCHOOL REQUIREMENTS

Graduation from secondary school required; GED accepted. The following course distribution required: 4 units of English, 3 units of math, 1 unit of science, 2 units of social studies, 2 units of history, 6 units of academic electives.

TESTING

SAT Reasoning required. ACT considered if submitted. SAT Subject recommended.

All enrolled freshmen (fall 2004):

Average SAT I Scores: Verbal: 492 Math: 496
Average ACT Scores: Composite:

Child Study Team report is not required. A neuropsychological or comprehensive psycho-educational evaluation is required for admission. Must be dated within 36 months of application. Tests required as part of this documentation:

- ■ WAIS-IV
- ☐ WISC-IV
- ☐ SATA
- ■ Woodcock-Johnson
- ☐ Nelson-Denny Reading Test
- ☐ Other

UNDERGRADUATE STUDENT BODY

Total undergraduate student enrollment: 2,380 Men, 2,696 Women.

Composition of student body (fall 2004):

	Undergraduate	Freshmen
International	0.4	0.7
Black	5.5	5.2
American Indian	0.4	0.2
Asian-American	0.2	0.3
Hispanic	1.2	0.5
White	84.1	70.4
Unreported	8.2	22.7
	100.0%	100.0%

5% are from out of state. 10% join a fraternity and 10% join a sorority. Average age of full-time undergraduates is 21. 35% of classes have fewer than 20 students, 54% have between 20 and 50 students, 11% have more than 50 students.

STUDENT HOUSING

68% of freshmen live in college housing. Freshmen are required to live on campus. Housing is guaranteed for all undergraduates. Campus can house 1,671 undergraduates. Single rooms are available for students with medical or special needs. A medical note is required.

EXPENSES

Tuition (2005-06): $5,031 per year (in-state), $7,454 (out-of-state).
Room: $5,140. Board: $2,768.
There is no additional cost for LD program/services.

LD SERVICES

LD program size is not limited.

LD services available to:

■ Freshmen ■ Sophomores ■ Juniors ■ Seniors

Academic Accommodations

Curriculum		In class	
Foreign language waiver	☐	Early syllabus	☐
Lighter course load	■	Note takers in class	☐
Math waiver	☐	Priority seating	☐
Other special classes	☐	Tape recorders	☐
Priority registrations	☐	Videotaped classes	☐
Substitution of courses	☐	Text on tape	☐
Exams		**Services**	
Extended time	☐	Diagnostic tests	☐
Oral exams	☐	Learning centers	☐
Take home exams	☐	Proofreaders	☐
Exams on tape or computer	☐	Readers	☐
Untimed exams	☐	Reading Machines/Kurzweil	☐
Other accommodations	☐	Special bookstore section	☐
		Typists	☐

Credit toward degree is not given for remedial courses taken.

Counseling Services

- ■ Academic
- ■ Psychological
- ■ Student Support groups
- ■ Vocational

Tutoring

Individual tutoring is not available.

	Individual	Group
Time management	☐	☐
Organizational skills	☐	☐
Learning strategies	☐	☐
Study skills	☐	☐
Content area	☐	☐
Writing lab	☐	☐
Math lab	☐	☐

LD PROGRAM STAFF

Total number of LD Program staff (including director):

Full Time: 1 Part Time: 1

There is an advisor/advocate from the LD program available to students. Four graduate students are available to work with LD students.

Key staff person available to work with LD students: Cheryl L. Bilitski, Director, Office for Students with Disabilities.

LD Program web site: www.sai.cup.edu/osd

Carlow University

Pittsburgh, PA

Address: 3333 Fifth Avenue, Pittsburgh, PA, 15213-3165
Admissions telephone: 800 333-2275
Admissions FAX: 412 578-6668
Director of Admissions: Christine Devine
Admissions e-mail: admissions@carlow.edu
Web site: http://www.carlow.edu
SAT Code: 2421 ACT Code: 3638

LD program name: Disabilities Services
LD program address: 3333 Fifth Avenue, Pittsburgh, PA, 15213
Director of Disability Services: Joan A. House
LD program telephone: 412 578-6257
LD program e-mail: houseja@carlow.edu
LD program enrollment: 20, Total campus enrollment: 1,664

GENERAL

Carlow College is a private, coed, four-year institution. 14-acre campus in Pittsburgh (population: 334,563), 10 minutes from downtown; remote locations in Beaver, Cranberry, downtown Pittsburgh, and Greensburg. Served by air, bus, and train. Public transportation serves campus. Semester system.

LD ADMISSIONS

Students do not complete a separate application and are not simultaneously accepted to the LD program. A member of the LD program does not sit on the admissions committee. A personal interview is recommended. Essay is recommended.

For fall 2004, 3 completed self-identified LD applications were received. 3 applications were offered admission, and 3 enrolled.

SECONDARY SCHOOL REQUIREMENTS

Graduation from secondary school required; GED accepted. The following course distribution required: 4 units of English, 3 units of math, 3 units of science, 2 units of social studies, 2 units of history, 4 units of academic electives.

TESTING

SAT Reasoning required; ACT may be substituted. SAT Subject recommended.

All enrolled freshmen (fall 2004):

Average SAT I Scores:	Verbal: 518	Math: 496
Average ACT Scores:	Composite: 21	

Child Study Team report is not required. A neuropsychological or comprehensive psycho-educational evaluation is required for admission. Must be dated within 36 months of application. Tests required as part of this documentation:

- ☑ WAIS-IV
- ☑ WISC-IV
- ☑ SATA
- ☑ Woodcock-Johnson
- ☑ Nelson-Denny Reading Test
- ☐ Other

UNDERGRADUATE STUDENT BODY

Total undergraduate student enrollment: 100 Men, 1,523 Women.

Composition of student body (fall 2004):

	Undergraduate	Freshmen
International	0.4	0.5
Black	10.1	22.1
American Indian	0.4	0.7
Asian-American	0.1	1.0
Hispanic	0.8	0.4
White	79.8	68.0
Unreported	8.4	7.3
	100.0%	100.0%

4% are from out of state. Average age of full-time undergraduates is 24. 88% of classes have fewer than 20 students, 12% have between 20 and 50 students.

STUDENT HOUSING

65% of freshmen live in college housing. Freshmen are not required to live on campus. Housing is guaranteed for all undergraduates. Campus can house 360 undergraduates. Single rooms are available for students with medical or special needs. A medical note is required.

EXPENSES

Tuition (2005-06): $16,754 per year.
Room: $3,510. Board: $3,360.
There is no additional cost for LD program/services.

LD SERVICES

LD program size is not limited.

LD services available to:

☑ Freshmen ☑ Sophomores ☑ Juniors ☑ Seniors

Academic Accommodations

Curriculum		In class	
Foreign language waiver	☐	Early syllabus	☐
Lighter course load	☑	Note takers in class	☑
Math waiver	☐	Priority seating	☑
Other special classes	☐	Tape recorders	☑
Priority registrations	☐	Videotaped classes	☑
Substitution of courses	☐	Text on tape	☑
Exams		**Services**	
Extended time	☑	Diagnostic tests	☐
Oral exams	☑	Learning centers	☑
Take home exams	☐	Proofreaders	☐
Exams on tape or computer	☑	Readers	☑
Untimed exams	☐	Reading Machines/Kurzweil	☐
Other accommodations	☐	Special bookstore section	☐
		Typists	☑

Counseling Services

- ☐ Academic
- ☐ Psychological
- ☐ Student Support groups
- ☐ Vocational

Tutoring

Individual tutoring is available weekly.

Average size of tutoring groups: 5

	Individual	Group
Time management	☑	☑
Organizational skills	☑	☑
Learning strategies	☑	☑
Study skills	☑	☑
Content area	☑	☑
Writing lab	☑	☑
Math lab	☑	☑

LD PROGRAM STAFF

Total number of LD Program staff (including director):

Full Time: 1 Part Time: 1

There is an advisor/advocate from the LD program available to students. One graduate student is available to work with LD students.

Key staff person available to work with LD students: Joan A. House, Director of Disability Services.

Carnegie Mellon University

Pittsburgh, PA

Address: 5000 Forbes Avenue, Pittsburgh, PA, 15213
Admissions telephone: 412 268-2082
Admissions FAX: 412 268-7838
Director of Admissions: Michael Steidel
Admissions e-mail: undergraduate-admissions@andrew.cmu.edu
Web site: http://www.cmu.edu
SAT Code: 2074 ACT Code: 3534

Manager, Disability Resources: Larry Powell
LD program telephone: 412 268-7472
LD program e-mail: lpowell@andrew.cmu.edu
LD program enrollment: 120, Total campus enrollment: 5,529

GENERAL

Carnegie Mellon University is a private, coed, four-year institution. 103-acre, suburban campus in Pittsburgh (population: 334,563). Served by air, bus, and train. School operates shuttle bus within limited area. Public transportation serves campus. Semester system.

LD ADMISSIONS

Application Deadline: 01/01. Students do not complete a separate application and are not simultaneously accepted to the LD program. A member of the LD program does not sit on the admissions committee. A personal interview is recommended. Essay is required and may be typed.

For fall 2004, 25 completed self-identified LD applications were received.

SECONDARY SCHOOL REQUIREMENTS

Graduation from secondary school required; GED accepted. The following course distribution required: 4 units of English, 4 units of math, 3 units of science, 2 units of foreign language, 3 units of academic electives.

TESTING

SAT Reasoning or ACT required. SAT Subject recommended.

All enrolled freshmen (fall 2004):

Average SAT I Scores:	Verbal: 657	Math: 718
Average ACT Scores:	Composite: 30	

Child Study Team report is not required. Tests required as part of this documentation:

- [ ] WAIS-IV
- [ ] WISC-IV
- [ ] SATA
- [ ] Woodcock-Johnson
- [ ] Nelson-Denny Reading Test
- [ ] Other

UNDERGRADUATE STUDENT BODY

Total undergraduate student enrollment: 3,308 Men, 1,916 Women.

Composition of student body (fall 2004):

	Undergraduate	Freshmen
International	10.9	12.2
Black	5.3	5.3
American Indian	0.7	0.5
Asian-American	23.8	23.4
Hispanic	5.3	5.2
White	41.1	42.3
Unreported	12.9	11.1
	100.0%	100.0%

69% are from out of state. 14% join a fraternity and 11% join a sorority. Average age of full-time undergraduates is 20. 67% of classes have fewer than 20 students, 24% have between 20 and 50 students, 9% have more than 50 students.

STUDENT HOUSING

98% of freshmen live in college housing. Freshmen are required to live on campus. Housing is guaranteed for all undergraduates. Campus can house 3,943 undergraduates. Single rooms are available for students with medical or special needs. A medical note is required.

EXPENSES

Tuition (2005-06): $31,650 per year. $25,670 per year (first-year students), $23,820 (all others).
Room: $5,182. Board: $3,734-$3,424.
There is no additional cost for LD program/services.

LD SERVICES

LD program size is not limited.

LD services available to:

- [x] Freshmen
- [x] Sophomores
- [x] Juniors
- [x] Seniors

Academic Accommodations

Curriculum		In class	
Foreign language waiver	[ ]	Early syllabus	[ ]
Lighter course load	[ ]	Note takers in class	[x]
Math waiver	[ ]	Priority seating	[x]
Other special classes	[ ]	Tape recorders	[x]
Priority registrations	[ ]	Videotaped classes	[ ]
Substitution of courses	[ ]	Text on tape	[x]
Exams		**Services**	
Extended time	[x]	Diagnostic tests	[ ]
Oral exams	[x]	Learning centers	[x]
Take home exams	[ ]	Proofreaders	[x]
Exams on tape or computer	[x]	Readers	[ ]
Untimed exams	[ ]	Reading Machines/Kurzweil	[ ]
Other accommodations	[ ]	Special bookstore section	[ ]
		Typists	[ ]

Credit toward degree is not given for remedial courses taken.

Counseling Services

- [x] Academic
- [x] Psychological
- [x] Student Support groups
- [x] Vocational

Tutoring

Individual tutoring is available weekly.

	Individual	Group
Time management	[x]	[ ]
Organizational skills	[x]	[ ]
Learning strategies	[x]	[ ]
Study skills	[x]	[ ]
Content area	[x]	[ ]
Writing lab	[x]	[ ]
Math lab	[x]	[ ]

LD PROGRAM STAFF

Total number of LD Program staff (including director):

Full Time: 3 Part Time: 3

There is an advisor/advocate from the LD program available to students.

Key staff person available to work with LD students: Larry Powell, Manager of Disability Resources.

Cedar Crest College

Allentown, PA

Address: 100 College Drive, Allentown, PA, 18104-6196
Admissions telephone: 800 360-1222
Admissions FAX: 610 606-4647
Vice President for Enrollment and Advancement: Judith Neyhart
Admissions e-mail: cccadmis@cedarcrest.edu
Web site: http://www.cedarcrest.edu
SAT Code: 2079 ACT Code: 3536

LD program telephone: 610 606-4628
LD program e-mail: chrspindler@cedarcrest.edu
LD program enrollment: 21, Total campus enrollment: 1,784

GENERAL

Cedar Crest College is a private, women's, four-year institution. 84-acre campus in Allentown (population: 106,632), 65 miles from Philadelphia and 90 miles from New York City. Served by air and bus; major airport and train serve Philadelphia. Public transportation serves campus. Semester system.

LD ADMISSIONS

A personal interview is recommended. Essay is required and may be typed.

SECONDARY SCHOOL REQUIREMENTS

Graduation from secondary school required; GED accepted. The following course distribution required: 4 units of English, 3 units of math, 2 units of science, 2 units of foreign language, 3 units of social studies.

TESTING

SAT Reasoning required; ACT may be substituted. SAT Subject recommended.

All enrolled freshmen (fall 2004):

Average SAT I Scores:	Verbal: 544	Math: 532
Average ACT Scores:	Composite: 23	

Child Study Team report is not required. Tests required as part of this documentation:

- [ ] WAIS-IV
- [ ] WISC-IV
- [ ] SATA
- [ ] Woodcock-Johnson
- [ ] Nelson-Denny Reading Test
- [ ] Other

UNDERGRADUATE STUDENT BODY

Total undergraduate student enrollment: 80 Men, 1,513 Women.

Composition of student body (fall 2004):

	Undergraduate	Freshmen
International	0.0	0.2
Black	5.6	5.5
American Indian	0.0	0.2
Asian-American	1.6	2.7
Hispanic	4.1	5.2
White	88.1	85.3
Unreported	0.6	0.9
	100.0%	100.0%

18% are from out of state. Average age of full-time undergraduates is 22. 72% of classes have fewer than 20 students, 25% have between 20 and 50 students, 3% have more than 50 students.

STUDENT HOUSING

87% of freshmen live in college housing. Freshmen are required to live on campus. Housing is guaranteed for all undergraduates. Campus can house 560 undergraduates.

EXPENSES

Tuition (2005-06): $22,712 per year.
Room: $4,240. Board: $3,663.
There is no additional cost for LD program/services.

LD SERVICES

LD program size is not limited.

LD services available to:

- [x] Freshmen
- [x] Sophomores
- [x] Juniors
- [x] Seniors

Academic Accommodations

Curriculum		In class	
Foreign language waiver	[ ]	Early syllabus	[ ]
Lighter course load	[ ]	Note takers in class	[x]
Math waiver	[ ]	Priority seating	[ ]
Other special classes	[x]	Tape recorders	[x]
Priority registrations	[ ]	Videotaped classes	[ ]
Substitution of courses	[ ]	Text on tape	[ ]
Exams		**Services**	
Extended time	[x]	Diagnostic tests	[ ]
Oral exams	[ ]	Learning centers	[x]
Take home exams	[ ]	Proofreaders	[ ]
Exams on tape or computer	[ ]	Readers	[ ]
Untimed exams	[ ]	Reading Machines/Kurzweil	[ ]
Other accommodations	[ ]	Special bookstore section	[ ]
		Typists	[ ]

Credit toward degree is not given for remedial courses taken.

Counseling Services

- [ ] Academic
- [ ] Psychological
- [ ] Student Support groups
- [ ] Vocational

Tutoring

	Individual	Group
Time management	[ ]	[ ]
Organizational skills	[ ]	[ ]
Learning strategies	[ ]	[ ]
Study skills	[ ]	[ ]
Content area	[ ]	[ ]
Writing lab	[ ]	[ ]
Math lab	[ ]	[ ]

LD PROGRAM STAFF

Total number of LD Program staff (including director):

Full Time: 1 Part Time: 1

Key staff person available to work with LD students: Christine Spindler, Director of Academic Services.

Chatham College

Pittsburgh, PA

Address: Woodland Road, Pittsburgh, PA, 15232
Admissions telephone: 800 837-1290
Admissions FAX: 412 365-1609
Vice President of Enrollment Management: Alan McIvor
Admissions e-mail: admissions@chatham.edu
Web site: http://www.chatham.edu
SAT Code: 2081 ACT Code: 3538

Assistant Dean, PACE Center: Janet K. James
LD program telephone: 412 365-1611
LD program e-mail: james@chatham.edu
Total campus enrollment: 665

GENERAL

Chatham College is a private, women's, four-year institution. 32-acre, urban campus in Pittsburgh (population: 334,563), six miles from downtown; branch campus in Wexford. Served by air, bus, and train. School operates transportation to libraries, cultural centers, and nearby colleges. Public transportation serves campus. 4-1-4 system.

LD ADMISSIONS

A personal interview is recommended. Essay is required and may be typed.

SECONDARY SCHOOL REQUIREMENTS

Graduation from secondary school required; GED accepted. The following course distribution required: 4 units of English, 2 units of math, 2 units of science.

TESTING

SAT Reasoning or ACT required. SAT Subject recommended.

All enrolled freshmen (fall 2004):

Average SAT I Scores:	Verbal: 562	Math: 523
Average ACT Scores:	Composite: 23	

Child Study Team report is not required. A neuropsychological or comprehensive psycho-education evaluation is not required for admission. Tests required as part of this documentation:

- [ ] WAIS-IV
- [ ] WISC-IV
- [ ] SATA
- [ ] Woodcock-Johnson
- [ ] Nelson-Denny Reading Test
- [ ] Other

UNDERGRADUATE STUDENT BODY

Total undergraduate student enrollment: 1 Men, 588 Women.

Composition of student body (fall 2004):

	Undergraduate	Freshmen
International	8.8	6.3
Black	11.0	11.6
American Indian	1.1	0.2
Asian-American	2.2	1.9
Hispanic	5.5	2.8
White	58.2	69.1
Unreported	13.2	8.1
	100.0%	100.0%

23% are from out of state. Average age of full-time undergraduates is 21. 79% of classes have fewer than 20 students, 20% have between 20 and 50 students, 1% have more than 50 students.

STUDENT HOUSING

90% of freshmen live in college housing. Freshmen are not required to live on campus. Housing is guaranteed for all undergraduates. Campus can house 406 undergraduates. Single rooms are available for students with medical or special needs.

EXPENSES

Tuition (2005-06): $22,870 per year.
Room: $3,880. Board: $3,530.

There is no additional cost for LD program/services.

LD SERVICES

LD program size is not limited.

LD services available to:

- [x] Freshmen
- [x] Sophomores
- [x] Juniors
- [x] Seniors

Academic Accommodations

Curriculum		In class	
Foreign language waiver	[ ]	Early syllabus	[x]
Lighter course load	[x]	Note takers in class	[x]
Math waiver	[ ]	Priority seating	[x]
Other special classes	[ ]	Tape recorders	[x]
Priority registrations	[ ]	Videotaped classes	[ ]
Substitution of courses	[ ]	Text on tape	[x]
Exams		**Services**	
Extended time	[x]	Diagnostic tests	[ ]
Oral exams	[x]	Learning centers	[x]
Take home exams	[ ]	Proofreaders	[x]
Exams on tape or computer	[x]	Readers	[x]
Untimed exams	[ ]	Reading Machines/Kurzweil	[x]
Other accommodations	[x]	Special bookstore section	[ ]
		Typists	[ ]

Credit toward degree is not given for remedial courses taken.

Counseling Services

- [x] Academic
- [x] Psychological — Meets 12 times per academic year
- [ ] Student Support groups
- [ ] Vocational

Tutoring

Individual tutoring is available monthly.

Average size of tutoring groups: 3

	Individual	Group
Time management	[x]	[x]
Organizational skills	[x]	[x]
Learning strategies	[x]	[x]
Study skills	[x]	[x]
Content area	[x]	[x]
Writing lab	[x]	[x]
Math lab	[x]	[x]

LD PROGRAM STAFF

Total number of LD Program staff (including director):

Full Time: 3 Part Time: 3

There is an advisor/advocate from the LD program available to students.

Key staff person available to work with LD students: Janet K. James, Assistant Dean, PACE Center.

LD Program web site: james@chatham.edu

Chestnut Hill College

Philadelphia, PA

Address: 9601 Germantown Avenue, Philadelphia, PA, 19118-2693
Admissions telephone: 800 248-0052 (out-of-state)
Admissions FAX: 215 248-7082
Associate Director of Admissions: Jodie King, M.S.
Admissions e-mail: chcapply@chc.edu
Web site: http://www.chc.edu
SAT Code: 2082 ACT Code: 3540

Associate Dean for Academic Advising: Catharine Fee
LD program telephone: 215 249-7199
LD program e-mail: cathafee@chc.edu
Total campus enrollment: 1,002

GENERAL

Chestnut Hill College is a private, women's, four-year institution. 45-acre, suburban campus in Philadelphia (population: 1,517,550). Served by air, bus, and train. School operates transportation for Campus Ministry, sports, and other activities. Public transportation serves campus. Semester system.

LD ADMISSIONS

A personal interview is recommended. Essay is required and may be typed.

SECONDARY SCHOOL REQUIREMENTS

Graduation from secondary school required; GED accepted.

TESTING

SAT Reasoning or ACT recommended. SAT Subject recommended.

All enrolled freshmen (fall 2004):

Average SAT I Scores: Verbal: 497 Math: 478
Average ACT Scores: Composite: 19

Child Study Team report is not required. Tests required as part of this documentation:

☐ WAIS-IV	☐ Woodcock-Johnson
☐ WISC-IV	☐ Nelson-Denny Reading Test
☐ SATA	☐ Other

UNDERGRADUATE STUDENT BODY

Total undergraduate student enrollment: 125 Men, 797 Women.

Composition of student body (fall 2004):

	Undergraduate	Freshmen
International	0.5	1.5
Black	27.4	35.5
American Indian	0.6	0.5
Asian-American	3.0	2.2
Hispanic	8.6	5.8
White	58.4	52.4
Unreported	1.5	2.1
	100.0%	100.0%

20% are from out of state. Average age of full-time undergraduates is 20. 90% of classes have fewer than 20 students, 10% have between 20 and 50 students.

STUDENT HOUSING

75% of freshmen live in college housing. Freshmen are not required to live on campus. Housing is not guaranteed for all undergraduates. Campus can house 352 undergraduates. Single rooms are available for students with medical or special needs. A medical note is not required.

EXPENSES

Tuition (2005-06): $20,500 per year.
Room & Board: $7,700

There is no additional cost for LD program/services.

LD SERVICES

LD program size is not limited.

LD services available to:

☑ Freshmen ☑ Sophomores ☑ Juniors ☑ Seniors

Academic Accommodations

Curriculum		**In class**	
Foreign language waiver	☐	Early syllabus	☐
Lighter course load	☑	Note takers in class	☐
Math waiver	☐	Priority seating	☐
Other special classes	☐	Tape recorders	☐
Priority registrations	☐	Videotaped classes	☐
Substitution of courses	☐	Text on tape	☐
Exams		**Services**	
Extended time	☑	Diagnostic tests	☐
Oral exams	☑	Learning centers	☐
Take home exams	☐	Proofreaders	☐
Exams on tape or computer	☐	Readers	☑
Untimed exams	☑	Reading Machines/Kurzweil	☐
Other accommodations	☐	Special bookstore section	☐
		Typists	☐

Credit toward degree is not given for remedial courses taken.

Counseling Services

☐ Academic
☐ Psychological
☐ Student Support groups
☐ Vocational

Tutoring

Individual tutoring is not available.

	Individual	Group
Time management	☐	☐
Organizational skills	☐	☐
Learning strategies	☑	☐
Study skills	☑	☐
Content area	☐	☐
Writing lab	☑	☐
Math lab	☑	☐

LD PROGRAM STAFF

Total number of LD Program staff (including director):

Full Time: 1 Part Time: 1

There is no advisor/advocate from the LD program available to students.

Key staff person available to work with LD students: Barbara Bradley, Director of the Learning Resource Center

Cheyney University of Pennsylvania

Cheyney, PA

Address: 1837 University Circle, Cheyney, PA, 19319
Admissions telephone: 800 CHEYNEY
Admissions FAX: 610 399-2099
Director of Admission: Ms. Gemma Stemley
Admissions e-mail: admissions@cheyney.edu
Web site: http://www.cheyney.edu
SAT Code: 2648 ACT Code: 3696

LD program contact: Etta Baldwin
LD program telephone: 610 399-2319
LD program e-mail: ebaldwin@cheyney.edu
Total campus enrollment: 1,376

GENERAL

Cheyney University of Pennsylvania is a public, coed, four-year institution. 275-acre, semirural campus in Cheyney (population: less than 1,000), 18 miles from Philadelphia; branch campus in Philadelphia. Major airport serves Philadelphia; train serves Elwyn (10 miles); bus serves Chester (10 miles). Public transportation serves campus. Semester system.

LD ADMISSIONS

Essay is not required.

SECONDARY SCHOOL REQUIREMENTS

Graduation from secondary school required; GED accepted. The following course distribution required: 4 units of English, 3 units of math, 2 units of science, 2 units of foreign language, 2 units of history.

TESTING

All enrolled freshmen (fall 2004):

Average SAT I Scores: Verbal: 379 Math: 378
Average ACT Scores: Composite: 15

Child Study Team report is not required. Tests required as part of this documentation:

- ❑ WAIS-IV
- ❑ WISC-IV
- ❑ SATA
- ❑ Woodcock-Johnson
- ❑ Nelson-Denny Reading Test
- ❑ Other

UNDERGRADUATE STUDENT BODY

Total undergraduate student enrollment: 1,376.

Composition of student body (fall 2004):

	Undergraduate	Freshmen
International	0.3	0.6
Black	95.0	93.8
American Indian	0.0	0.0
Asian-American	0.0	0.1
Hispanic	0.2	0.6
White	0.0	0.6
Unreported	4.5	4.3
	100.0%	100.0%

18% are from out of state. Average age of full-time undergraduates is 21.

STUDENT HOUSING

96% of freshmen live in college housing. Freshmen are not required to live on campus. Housing is guaranteed for all undergraduates. Campus can house 1,100 undergraduates. Single rooms are available for students with medical or special needs. A medical note is not required.

EXPENSES

Tuition (2005-06): $4,016 per year (in-state), $9,036 (residents of Delaware, Maryland, New Jersey, New York, and Washington, D.C.), $10,040 (other out-of-state).

LD SERVICES

LD services available to:

■ Freshmen ■ Sophomores ■ Juniors ■ Seniors

Academic Accommodations

Curriculum

- Foreign language waiver ❑
- Lighter course load ❑
- Math waiver ❑
- Other special classes ❑
- Priority registrations ❑
- Substitution of courses ❑

Exams

- Extended time ❑
- Oral exams ❑
- Take home exams ❑
- Exams on tape or computer ❑
- Untimed exams ❑
- Other accommodations ❑

In class

- Early syllabus ❑
- Note takers in class ❑
- Priority seating ❑
- Tape recorders ❑
- Videotaped classes ❑
- Text on tape ❑

Services

- Diagnostic tests ❑
- Learning centers ❑
- Proofreaders ❑
- Readers ❑
- Reading Machines/Kurzweil ❑
- Special bookstore section ❑
- Typists ❑

Counseling Services

- ■ Academic
- ❑ Psychological
- ❑ Student Support groups
- ❑ Vocational

Tutoring

Individual tutoring is available.

	Individual	Group
Time management	❑	❑
Organizational skills	❑	❑
Learning strategies	❑	❑
Study skills	❑	❑
Content area	❑	❑
Writing lab	❑	❑
Math lab	❑	❑

LD PROGRAM STAFF

Key staff person available to work with LD students: Etta Baldwin

Clarion University of Pennsylvania

Clarion, PA

Address: 840 Wood Street, Clarion, PA, 16214
Admissions telephone: 800 672-7171
Admissions FAX: 814 393-2030
Dean of Enrollment Management: William Bailey
Admissions e-mail: admissions@clarion.edu
Web site: http://www.clarion.edu
SAT Code: 2649 ACT Code: 3698

Coordinator, Disability Support Services: Jennifer May
LD program telephone: 814 393-2095
LD program e-mail: jmay@clarion.edu
Total campus enrollment: 5,855

GENERAL

Clarion University of Pennsylvania is a public, coed, four-year institution. 99-acre campus in Clarion (population: 6,185), 90 miles from Pittsburgh; branch campus in Oil City. Airport, bus, and train serve Pittsburgh; smaller airport serves Franklin (30 miles). Semester system.

SECONDARY SCHOOL REQUIREMENTS

Graduation from secondary school required; GED accepted. The following course distribution required: 4 units of English, 2 units of math, 3 units of science, 4 units of social studies.

TESTING

SAT Reasoning or ACT required.

Child Study Team report is not required. Tests required as part of this documentation:

- ☐ WAIS-IV
- ☐ WISC-IV
- ☐ SATA
- ☐ Woodcock-Johnson
- ☐ Nelson-Denny Reading Test
- ☐ Other

UNDERGRADUATE STUDENT BODY

Total undergraduate student enrollment: 2,221 Men, 3,591 Women.

Composition of student body (fall 2004):

	Undergraduate	Freshmen
International	0.2	0.9
Black	5.0	5.3
American Indian	0.0	0.3
Asian-American	1.2	0.7
Hispanic	1.2	0.9
White	87.0	90.2
Unreported	5.4	1.7
	100.0%	100.0%

4% are from out of state.

STUDENT HOUSING

Housing is guaranteed for all undergraduates.

EXPENSES

Tuition (2005-06): $4,810 per year (in-state), $9,620 (out-of-state).
Room: $0-$3,194. Board: $0-$1,622.
There is no additional cost for LD program/services.

LD SERVICES

LD program size is not limited.

LD services available to:

☐ Freshmen ☐ Sophomores ☐ Juniors ☐ Seniors

Academic Accommodations

Curriculum		In class	
Foreign language waiver	☐	Early syllabus	☐
Lighter course load	☐	Note takers in class	■
Math waiver	☐	Priority seating	☐
Other special classes	☐	Tape recorders	■
Priority registrations	☐	Videotaped classes	☐
Substitution of courses	☐	Text on tape	☐
Exams		**Services**	
Extended time	■	Diagnostic tests	☐
Oral exams	■	Learning centers	■
Take home exams	☐	Proofreaders	☐
Exams on tape or computer	☐	Readers	■
Untimed exams	■	Reading Machines/Kurzweil	■
Other accommodations	☐	Special bookstore section	☐
		Typists	☐

Credit toward degree is not given for remedial courses taken.

Counseling Services

- ☐ Academic
- ☐ Psychological
- ☐ Student Support groups
- ☐ Vocational

Tutoring

	Individual	Group
Time management	☐	☐
Organizational skills	☐	☐
Learning strategies	☐	☐
Study skills	☐	☐
Content area	☐	☐
Writing lab	☐	☐
Math lab	☐	☐

LD PROGRAM STAFF

Total number of LD Program staff (including director):

Full Time: 1 Part Time: 1

Key staff person available to work with LD students: Jennifer May, Coordinator, Disability Support Services.

College Misericordia

Dallas, PA

Address: 301 Lake Street, Dallas, PA, 18612-1098
Admissions telephone: 866 262-6363
Admissions FAX: 570 675-2441
Executive Director of Admissions and Financial Aid: Jane Dessoye
Admissions e-mail: admiss@misericordia.edu
Web site: http://www.misericordia.edu
SAT Code: 2087 ACT Code: 3539

LD program name: Alternative Learners Project
LD program telephone: 570 674-6400
LD program e-mail: admiss@misericordia.edu
LD program enrollment: 55, Total campus enrollment: 2,071

GENERAL

College Misericordia is a private, coed, four-year institution. 125-acre, suburban campus in Dallas (population: 8,179), nine miles from Wilkes-Barre. Airport serves Avoca (22 miles). Public transportation serves campus. Semester system.

LD ADMISSIONS

Students do not complete a separate application and are simultaneously accepted to the LD program. A member of the LD program does sit on the admissions committee. A personal interview is required. Essay is not required.

For fall 2004, 45 completed self-identified LD applications were received. 20 applications were offered admission, and 12 enrolled.

SECONDARY SCHOOL REQUIREMENTS

Graduation from secondary school required; GED accepted. The following course distribution required: 4 units of English, 4 units of math, 4 units of science, 4 units of social studies.

TESTING

SAT Reasoning required; ACT may be substituted. SAT Subject recommended.

All enrolled freshmen (fall 2004):

Average SAT I Scores: Verbal: 499 Math: 502
Average ACT Scores: Composite: 23

Child Study Team report is not required. A neuropsychological or comprehensive psycho-educational evaluation is required for admission. Tests required as part of this documentation:

- ■ WAIS-IV
- ☐ WISC-IV
- ☐ SATA
- ☐ Woodcock-Johnson
- ☐ Nelson-Denny Reading Test
- ☐ Other

UNDERGRADUATE STUDENT BODY

Total undergraduate student enrollment: 452 Men, 1,274 Women.

Composition of student body (fall 2004):

	Undergraduate	Freshmen
International	0.1	0.2
Black	1.2	1.5
American Indian	0.6	0.3
Asian-American	0.9	0.9
Hispanic	2.2	1.4
White	95.0	95.7
Unreported	0.0	0.0
	100.0%	100.0%

14% are from out of state. Average age of full-time undergraduates is 21. 62% of classes have fewer than 20 students, 37% have between 20 and 50 students, 1% have more than 50 students.

STUDENT HOUSING

78% of freshmen live in college housing. Freshmen are not required to live on campus. Housing is guaranteed for all undergraduates. Campus can house 700 undergraduates. Single rooms are available for students with medical or special needs. A medical note is required.

EXPENSES

Tuition (2005-06): $18,700 per year.

Room: $4,730. Board: $3,520.

Additional cost for LD program/services: $500 per semester.

LD SERVICES

LD program size is not limited.

LD services available to:

■ Freshmen ■ Sophomores ■ Juniors ■ Seniors

Academic Accommodations

Curriculum		**In class**	
Foreign language waiver	☐	Early syllabus	☐
Lighter course load	■	Note takers in class	■
Math waiver	☐	Priority seating	☐
Other special classes	☐	Tape recorders	■
Priority registrations	☐	Videotaped classes	☐
Substitution of courses	☐	Text on tape	■
Exams		**Services**	
Extended time	■	Diagnostic tests	☐
Oral exams	■	Learning centers	■
Take home exams	☐	Proofreaders	■
Exams on tape or computer	■	Readers	■
Untimed exams	■	Reading Machines/Kurzweil	■
Other accommodations	■	Special bookstore section	☐
		Typists	■

Credit toward degree is not given for remedial courses taken.

Counseling Services

- ■ Academic — Meets 30 times per academic year
- ☐ Psychological
- ☐ Student Support groups
- ☐ Vocational

Tutoring: Individual tutoring is not available.

	Individual	Group
Time management	■	■
Organizational skills	■	■
Learning strategies	■	■
Study skills	■	■
Content area	■	■
Writing lab	☐	■
Math lab	☐	■

UNIQUE LD PROGRAM FEATURES

Services include learning strategies, and accommodations. Prior to each semester, a written Program of Accommodation is established for each student. Each student is assigned a Program Coordinator, an ALP staff member who coordinates the delivery of the Program of Accommodations. As students progress, they become more personally responsible for dealing with faculty members.

LD PROGRAM STAFF

Total number of LD Program staff (including director):

Full Time: 4; Part Time: 4

There is an advisor/advocate from the LD program available to students. The advisor/advocate meets with students four times per month. Key staff person available to work with LD students: Dr. Joseph Rogan, ALP Director.

LD Program web site: www.misericordia.edu

Delaware Valley College

Doylestown, PA

Address: 700 East Butler Avenue, Doylestown, PA, 18901
Admissions telephone: 800 2-DELVAL
Admissions FAX: 215 230-2968
Director of Admissions: Stephen Zenko
Admissions e-mail: admitme@devalcol.edu
Web site: http://www.devalcol.edu
SAT Code: 2510   ACT Code: 3510

Total campus enrollment: 1,897

GENERAL

Delaware Valley College is a private, coed, four-year institution. 600-acre campus in Doylestown (population: 17,619), 20 miles from Philadelphia. Served by bus and train; major airport serves Philadelphia. Public transportation serves campus. Semester system.

LD ADMISSIONS

A personal interview is recommended.

SECONDARY SCHOOL REQUIREMENTS

Graduation from secondary school required; GED accepted. The following course distribution required: 3 units of English, 2 units of math, 2 units of science, 2 units of social studies, 6 units of academic electives.

TESTING

SAT Reasoning required; ACT may be substituted.

All enrolled freshmen (fall 2004):

Average SAT I Scores:	Verbal: 505	Math: 506
Average ACT Scores:	Composite: 21	

Child Study Team report is not required. Tests required as part of this documentation:

☐ WAIS-IV ☐ Woodcock-Johnson
☐ WISC-IV ☐ Nelson-Denny Reading Test
☐ SATA ☐ Other

UNDERGRADUATE STUDENT BODY

Total undergraduate student enrollment: 908 Men, 1,012 Women.

Composition of student body (fall 2004):

	Undergraduate	Freshmen
International	1.1	0.6
Black	4.0	3.9
American Indian	0.5	0.3
Asian-American	0.4	0.5
Hispanic	1.3	1.3
White	86.0	80.8
Unreported	6.7	12.6
	100.0%	100.0%

40% are from out of state. 4% join a fraternity and 5% join a sorority. Average age of full-time undergraduates is 21. 56% of classes have fewer than 20 students, 41% have between 20 and 50 students, 3% have more than 50 students.

STUDENT HOUSING

89% of freshmen live in college housing. Housing is not guaranteed for all undergraduates and graduate students. Campus can house 969 undergraduates. Single rooms are not available for students with medical or special needs.

EXPENSES

Tuition (2005-06): $20,644 per year.

Room: $3,686. Board: $4,444.
There is no additional cost for LD program/services.

LD SERVICES

LD program size is not limited.

LD services available to:

☐ Freshmen ☐ Sophomores ☐ Juniors ☐ Seniors

Academic Accommodations

Curriculum		**In class**	
Foreign language waiver	☐	Early syllabus	☐
Lighter course load	■	Note takers in class	■
Math waiver	☐	Priority seating	☐
Other special classes	☐	Tape recorders	☐
Priority registrations	☐	Videotaped classes	☐
Substitution of courses	☐	Text on tape	☐
Exams		**Services**	
Extended time	■	Diagnostic tests	☐
Oral exams	☐	Learning centers	☐
Take home exams	☐	Proofreaders	☐
Exams on tape or computer	☐	Readers	☐
Untimed exams	☐	Reading Machines/Kurzweil	■
Other accommodations	☐	Special bookstore section	☐
		Typists	☐

Credit toward degree is not given for remedial courses taken.

Counseling Services

☐ Academic
☐ Psychological
☐ Student Support groups
☐ Vocational

Tutoring

Individual tutoring is available daily.

Average size of tutoring groups: 1

	Individual	Group
Time management	■	■
Organizational skills	☐	■
Learning strategies	■	■
Study skills	■	■
Content area	☐	■
Writing lab	☐	■
Math lab	■	■

LD PROGRAM STAFF

Total number of LD Program staff (including director):

Full Time: 1   Part Time: 1

Key staff person available to work with LD students: Sharon Malka, Learning Support Specialist.

DeSales University

Center Valley, PA

Address: 2755 Station Avenue, Center Valley, PA, 18034-9568
Admissions telephone: 877 4-DESALES
Admissions FAX: 610 282-0131
Dean of Enrollment Management: Peter Rautzhan
Admissions e-mail: admiss@desales.edu
Web site: http://www.desales.edu
SAT Code: 2021 ACT Code: 3525

LD program name: Academic Resource Center
Director: Dr. Rosalind Edman
LD program telephone: 610 282-1100, extension 1293
LD program e-mail: rosalind.edman@desales.edu
LD program enrollment: 54, Total campus enrollment: 2,175

GENERAL

DeSales University is a private, coed, four-year institution. 400-acre campus in Center Valley (population: 3,000), seven miles from Allentown and 50 miles from Philadelphia; off-campus sites in Easton, Landsdale, and Harrisburg (for adult and graduate programs). Major airport serves Philadelphia; smaller airport serves Allentown; bus serves Coopersburg (one mile). School operates transportation to local mall and to cultural and social activities. Semester system.

LD ADMISSIONS

Students do not complete a separate application and are not simultaneously accepted to the LD program. A member of the LD program does not sit on the admissions committee. A personal interview is not required. Essay is not required.

SECONDARY SCHOOL REQUIREMENTS

Graduation from secondary school required; GED accepted. The following course distribution required: 4 units of English, 3 units of math, 2 units of science, 2 units of foreign language, 2 units of social studies, 1 unit of history, 6 units of academic electives.

TESTING

SAT Reasoning required; ACT may be substituted.

All enrolled freshmen (fall 2004):

Average SAT I Scores: Verbal: 553 Math: 544

Child Study Team report is not required. A neuropsychological or comprehensive psycho-education evaluation is not required for admission. Tests required as part of this documentation:

- ☐ WAIS-IV
- ☐ WISC-IV
- ☐ SATA
- ☐ Woodcock-Johnson
- ☐ Nelson-Denny Reading Test
- ☐ Other

UNDERGRADUATE STUDENT BODY

Total undergraduate student enrollment: 906 Men, 1,107 Women.

Composition of student body (fall 2004):

	Undergraduate	Freshmen
International	0.0	0.1
Black	0.3	0.6
American Indian	0.3	0.3
Asian-American	1.1	0.6
Hispanic	0.8	1.1
White	70.3	42.4
Unreported	27.2	54.9
	100.0%	100.0%

17% are from out of state. Average age of full-time undergraduates is 25. 43% of classes have fewer than 20 students, 55% have between 20 and 50 students, 2% have more than 50 students.

STUDENT HOUSING

87% of freshmen live in college housing. Freshmen are not required to live on campus. Housing is guaranteed for all undergraduates. Campus can house 833 undergraduates. Single rooms are available for students with medical or special needs. A medical note is required.

EXPENSES

Tuition (2005-06): $20,000 per year.
Room: $3,900. Board: $3,980.
There is no additional cost for LD program/services.

LD SERVICES

LD program size is not limited.

LD services available to:

☒ Freshmen ☒ Sophomores ☒ Juniors ☒ Seniors

Academic Accommodations

Curriculum		In class	
Foreign language waiver	☐	Early syllabus	☐
Lighter course load	☒	Note takers in class	☒
Math waiver	☐	Priority seating	☐
Other special classes	☐	Tape recorders	☒
Priority registrations	☐	Videotaped classes	☐
Substitution of courses	☐	Text on tape	☒
Exams		**Services**	
Extended time	☒	Diagnostic tests	☐
Oral exams	☒	Learning centers	☒
Take home exams	☐	Proofreaders	☐
Exams on tape or computer	☒	Readers	☒
Untimed exams	☒	Reading Machines/Kurzweil	☒
Other accommodations	☐	Special bookstore section	☐
		Typists	☒

Credit toward degree is given for remedial courses taken.

Counseling Services

- ☒ Academic
- ☒ Psychological
- ☐ Student Support groups
- ☒ Vocational

Tutoring

Individual tutoring is available weekly.

Average size of tutoring groups: 3

	Individual	Group
Time management	☒	☐
Organizational skills	☒	☐
Learning strategies	☒	☐
Study skills	☒	☐
Content area	☒	☐
Writing lab	☒	☐
Math lab	☐	☒

LD PROGRAM STAFF

Total number of LD Program staff (including director):

Full Time: 2 Part Time: 2

There is an advisor/advocate from the LD program available to students.

Key staff person available to work with LD students: Renee Grammes, Reading/Study Skills Specialist.

LD Program web site: www.desales.edu

Dickinson College

Carlisle, PA

Address: P.O. Box 1773, Carlisle, PA, 17013-2896
Admissions telephone: 800 644-1773
Admissions FAX: 717 245-1442
Director of Admissions: Christopher Seth Allen
Admissions e-mail: admit@dickinson.edu
Web site: http://www.dickinson.edu
SAT Code: 2186 ACT Code: 3550

Associate Dean of Admissions: Cathy Davenport
LD program telephone: 717 245-1231
LD program e-mail: davenpor@dickinson.edu
LD program enrollment: 130, Total campus enrollment: 2,321

GENERAL

Dickinson College is a private, coed, four-year institution. 115-acre campus in Carlisle (population: 17,970), 18 miles from Harrisburg. Served by bus; airport and train serve Harrisburg. School operates transportation to airport and train station during busy times. Public transportation serves campus. Semester system.

LD ADMISSIONS

Students do not complete a separate application and are simultaneously accepted to the LD program. A member of the LD program does not sit on the admissions committee. High school waivers are accepted for math and foreign language. A personal interview is recommended. Essay is required and may be typed. Some courses may be substituted to meet admission requirements.

For fall 2004, 74 completed self-identified LD applications were received. 23 applications were offered admission, and 9 enrolled.

SECONDARY SCHOOL REQUIREMENTS

Graduation from secondary school required; GED accepted. The following course distribution required: 4 units of English, 3 units of math, 3 units of science, 2 units of foreign language, 2 units of social studies, 2 units of academic electives.

TESTING

SAT Reasoning or ACT recommended. SAT Subject recommended.

All enrolled freshmen (fall 2004):

Average SAT I Scores: Verbal: 640 Math: 634
Average ACT Scores: Composite: 28

Child Study Team report is not required. A neuropsychological or comprehensive psycho-education evaluation is not required for admission. Tests required as part of this documentation:

☐ WAIS-IV ☐ Woodcock-Johnson
☐ WISC-IV ☐ Nelson-Denny Reading Test
☐ SATA ☐ Other

UNDERGRADUATE STUDENT BODY

Total undergraduate student enrollment: 917 Men, 1,291 Women.

Composition of student body (fall 2004):

	Undergraduate	Freshmen
International	4.8	3.1
Black	5.4	3.9
American Indian	0.0	0.4
Asian-American	4.6	3.6
Hispanic	4.5	2.9
White	80.7	86.1
Unreported	0.0	0.0
	100.0%	100.0%

59% are from out of state. 17% join a fraternity and 26% join a sorority. Average age of full-time undergraduates is 20. 64% of classes have fewer than 20 students, 35% have between 20 and 50 students, 1% have more than 50 students.

STUDENT HOUSING

100% of freshmen live in college housing. Freshmen are required to live on campus. Housing is guaranteed for all undergraduates. Campus can house 1,897 undergraduates. Single rooms are available for students with medical or special needs. A medical note is required.

EXPENSES

Tuition (2005-06): $31,800 per year.

Room: $4,150. Board: $3,900.

There is no additional cost for LD program/services.

LD SERVICES

LD program size is not limited.

LD services available to:

☑ Freshmen ☑ Sophomores ☑ Juniors ☑ Seniors

Academic Accommodations

Curriculum		In class	
Foreign language waiver	☐	Early syllabus	☐
Lighter course load	☑	Note takers in class	☑
Math waiver	☐	Priority seating	☐
Other special classes	☐	Tape recorders	☑
Priority registrations	☐	Videotaped classes	☐
Substitution of courses	☐	Text on tape	☐
Exams		**Services**	
Extended time	☐	Diagnostic tests	☐
Oral exams	☑	Learning centers	☐
Take home exams	☐	Proofreaders	☐
Exams on tape or computer	☐	Readers	☑
Untimed exams	☑	Reading Machines/Kurzweil	☐
Other accommodations	☐	Special bookstore section	☐
		Typists	☐

Credit toward degree is not given for remedial courses taken.

Counseling Services

☑ Academic — Meets 28 times per academic year
☐ Psychological
☐ Student Support groups
☐ Vocational

Tutoring

Individual tutoring is available weekly.

Average size of tutoring groups: 1

	Individual	Group
Time management	☑	☑
Organizational skills	☑	☑
Learning strategies	☑	☑
Study skills	☑	☑
Content area	☑	☑
Writing lab	☑	☑
Math lab	☑	☑

UNIQUE LD PROGRAM FEATURES

College attemps to provide for specific needs of individuals.

LD PROGRAM STAFF

Total number of LD Program staff (including director):

Full Time: 1 Part Time: 1

There is an advisor/advocate from the LD program available to students. 28 peer tutors are available to work with LD students.

Key staff person available to work with LD students: Keith Jervis, Coordinator, Learning Support Counseling.

Drexel University

Philadelphia, PA

Address: 3141 Chestnut Street, Philadelphia, PA, 19104-2875
Admissions telephone: 800 2-DREXEL
Admissions FAX: 215 895-5939
Dean of Enrollment: Joan McDonald
Admissions e-mail: enroll@drexel.edu
Web site: http://www.drexel.edu
SAT Code: 2194 ACT Code: 3556

Director, Disability Services: Robin Stokes
LD program telephone: 215 895-1401
LD program e-mail: ras28@drexel.edu
Total campus enrollment: 11,960

GENERAL

Drexel University is a private, coed, four-year institution. 38-acre, urban campus in Philadelphia (population: 1,517,550); branch campus in Wilmington, DE. Served by air, bus, and train. School operates transportation around campus. Public transportation serves campus. Quarter system.

LD ADMISSIONS

A personal interview is recommended. Essay is not required.

SECONDARY SCHOOL REQUIREMENTS

Graduation from secondary school required; GED accepted. The following course distribution required: 3 units of math, 1 unit of science.

TESTING

SAT Reasoning required; ACT may be substituted. SAT Subject recommended.

All enrolled freshmen (fall 2004):

Average SAT I Scores: Verbal: 589 Math: 619

Child Study Team report is not required. Tests required as part of this documentation:

☐ WAIS-IV	☐ Woodcock-Johnson
☐ WISC-IV	☐ Nelson-Denny Reading Test
☐ SATA	☐ Other

UNDERGRADUATE STUDENT BODY

Total undergraduate student enrollment: 6,817 Men, 4,202 Women.

Composition of student body (fall 2004):

	Undergraduate	Freshmen
International	6.3	5.7
Black	4.7	9.9
American Indian	0.2	0.2
Asian-American	12.0	12.0
Hispanic	2.6	2.6
White	72.3	63.2
Unreported	1.9	6.4
	100.0%	100.0%

40% are from out of state. 6% join a fraternity and 6% join a sorority. Average age of full-time undergraduates is 21. 52% of classes have fewer than 20 students, 40% have between 20 and 50 students, 8% have more than 50 students.

STUDENT HOUSING

82% of freshmen live in college housing. Freshmen are required to live on campus. Housing is guaranteed for all undergraduates. Campus can house 2,604 undergraduates.

EXPENSES

Tuition (2005-06): $22,700 per year. Tuition varies by program.
Room: $6,255-$7,215. Board: $4,260.
There is no additional cost for LD program/services.

LD SERVICES

LD program size is not limited.

LD services available to:

☐ Freshmen ☐ Sophomores ☐ Juniors ☐ Seniors

Academic Accommodations

Curriculum		**In class**	
Foreign language waiver	☐	Early syllabus	☐
Lighter course load	■	Note takers in class	■
Math waiver	☐	Priority seating	☐
Other special classes	☐	Tape recorders	■
Priority registrations	☐	Videotaped classes	☐
Substitution of courses	☐	Text on tape	☐
Exams		**Services**	
Extended time	■	Diagnostic tests	☐
Oral exams	■	Learning centers	■
Take home exams	☐	Proofreaders	☐
Exams on tape or computer	☐	Readers	☐
Untimed exams	☐	Reading Machines/Kurzweil	■
Other accommodations	☐	Special bookstore section	☐
		Typists	☐

Credit toward degree is not given for remedial courses taken.

Counseling Services

☐ Academic
☐ Psychological
☐ Student Support groups
☐ Vocational

Tutoring

	Individual	Group
Time management	☐	☐
Organizational skills	☐	☐
Learning strategies	☐	☐
Study skills	☐	☐
Content area	☐	☐
Writing lab	☐	☐
Math lab	☐	☐

LD PROGRAM STAFF

Key staff person available to work with LD students: Dr. Cathy Schmidt, LD Coordinator.

Duquesne University

Pittsburgh, PA

Address: 600 Forbes Avenue, Pittsburgh, PA, 15282
Admissions telephone: 800 456-0590
Admissions FAX: 412 396-5644
Dean of Admissions: Paul-James Cukanna
Admissions e-mail: admissions@duq.edu
Web site: http://www.duq.edu
SAT Code: 2196 ACT Code: 3560

Director: Dr. Frederick Lorensen
LD program telephone: 412 396-6657
LD program e-mail: lorensen@duq.edu
LD program enrollment: 50, Total campus enrollment: 5,584

GENERAL

Duquesne University is a private, coed, four-year institution. 43-acre, urban campus in Pittsburgh (population: 334,563); extension campus in Harrisburg. Served by air, bus, and train. Public transportation serves campus. Semester system.

LD ADMISSIONS

A personal interview is recommended. Essay is required and may be typed.

SECONDARY SCHOOL REQUIREMENTS

Graduation from secondary school required; GED accepted. The following course distribution required: 4 units of English, 2 units of math, 2 units of science, 2 units of foreign language, 2 units of social studies, 4 units of academic electives.

TESTING

SAT Reasoning or ACT required. SAT Subject required.

All enrolled freshmen (fall 2004):

Average SAT I Scores: Verbal: 557 Math: 562
Average ACT Scores: Composite: 24

Child Study Team report is not required. Tests required as part of this documentation:

- ☐ WAIS-IV
- ☐ WISC-IV
- ☐ SATA
- ☐ Woodcock-Johnson
- ☐ Nelson-Denny Reading Test
- ☐ Other

UNDERGRADUATE STUDENT BODY

Total undergraduate student enrollment: 2,274 Men, 3,130 Women.

Composition of student body (fall 2004):

	Undergraduate	Freshmen
International	1.4	2.2
Black	3.0	4.1
American Indian	0.0	0.1
Asian-American	1.9	1.4
Hispanic	1.5	1.4
White	83.8	81.8
Unreported	8.4	9.0
	100.0%	100.0%

18% are from out of state. 16% join a fraternity and 14% join a sorority. Average age of full-time undergraduates is 21. 42% of classes have fewer than 20 students, 50% have between 20 and 50 students, 8% have more than 50 students.

STUDENT HOUSING

87% of freshmen live in college housing. Freshmen are not required to live on campus. Housing is guaranteed for all undergraduates. Campus can house 3,571 undergraduates. Single rooms are available for students with medical or special needs. A medical note is required.

EXPENSES

Tuition (2005-06): $19,721 per year.
Room: $4,394. Board: $3,660.
There is no additional cost for LD program/services.

LD SERVICES

LD program size is limited.

LD services available to:

☑ Freshmen ☑ Sophomores ☑ Juniors ☑ Seniors

Academic Accommodations

Curriculum		**In class**	
Foreign language waiver	☐	Early syllabus	☐
Lighter course load	☑	Note takers in class	☑
Math waiver	☐	Priority seating	☐
Other special classes	☐	Tape recorders	☑
Priority registrations	☑	Videotaped classes	☐
Substitution of courses	☐	Text on tape	☐
Exams		**Services**	
Extended time	☑	Diagnostic tests	☐
Oral exams	☑	Learning centers	☑
Take home exams	☐	Proofreaders	☐
Exams on tape or computer	☐	Readers	☑
Untimed exams	☐	Reading Machines/Kurzweil	☐
Other accommodations	☐	Special bookstore section	☐
		Typists	☐

Credit toward degree is not given for remedial courses taken.

Counseling Services

- ☑ Academic
- ☑ Psychological
- ☐ Student Support groups
- ☐ Vocational

Tutoring

Individual tutoring is available weekly.

	Individual	Group
Time management	☑	☐
Organizational skills	☑	☐
Learning strategies	☑	☐
Study skills	☑	☐
Content area	☑	☐
Writing lab	☑	☐
Math lab	☑	☐

LD PROGRAM STAFF

Total number of LD Program staff (including director):

Full Time: 2 Part Time: 2

Key staff person available to work with LD students: Dr. Frederick Lorensen, Director of Freshmen Development & Special Student Services

East Stroudsburg University of Pennsylvania

East Stroudsburg, PA

Address: 200 Prospect Street, East Stroudsburg, PA, 18301-2999
Admissions telephone: 570 422-3542
Admissions FAX: 570 422-3933
Director of Admissions: Alan T. Chesterton
Admissions e-mail: undergrads@po-box.esu.edu
Web site: http://www.esu.edu
SAT Code: 2650

Assistive Technology Specialist: Adrian Wehmeyer
LD program telephone: 570 422-3954
LD program e-mail: awehmeyer@po-box.esu.edu
Total campus enrollment: 5,409

GENERAL

East Stroudsburg University of Pennsylvania is a public, coed, four-year institution. 213-acre campus in East Stroudsburg (population: 9,888), 40 miles from Allentown and 75 miles from New York City. Served by bus; major airport serves Newark, NJ. (70 miles); smaller airport serves Allentown. School operates transportation to special events and club activities. Public transportation serves campus. Semester system.

LD ADMISSIONS

A personal interview is recommended. Essay is not required.

SECONDARY SCHOOL REQUIREMENTS

Graduation from secondary school required; GED accepted.

TESTING

SAT Reasoning or ACT required. SAT Subject recommended.

All enrolled freshmen (fall 2004):

Average SAT I Scores: Verbal: 492 Math: 493

Child Study Team report is not required. Tests required as part of this documentation:

- ☐ WAIS-IV
- ☐ WISC-IV
- ☐ SATA
- ☐ Woodcock-Johnson
- ☐ Nelson-Denny Reading Test
- ☐ Other

UNDERGRADUATE STUDENT BODY

Total undergraduate student enrollment: 2,087 Men, 2,880 Women.

Composition of student body (fall 2004):

	Undergraduate	Freshmen
International	0.2	0.4
Black	3.2	3.7
American Indian	0.2	0.3
Asian-American	0.8	1.1
Hispanic	4.9	3.8
White	90.7	90.7
Unreported	0.0	0.0
	100.0%	100.0%

19% are from out of state. 6% join a fraternity and 6% join a sorority. Average age of full-time undergraduates is 21. 29% of classes have fewer than 20 students, 68% have between 20 and 50 students, 3% have more than 50 students.

STUDENT HOUSING

82% of freshmen live in college housing. Freshmen are not required to live on campus. Housing is guaranteed for all undergraduates. Campus can house 2,233 undergraduates.

EXPENSES

Tuition (2005-06): $4,810 per year (in-state), $12,026 (out-of-state).
Room: $2,864. Board: $1,642.
There is no additional cost for LD program/services.

LD SERVICES

LD program size is not limited.

LD services available to:

☐ Freshmen ☐ Sophomores ☐ Juniors ☐ Seniors

Academic Accommodations

Curriculum		In class	
Foreign language waiver	☐	Early syllabus	☐
Lighter course load	☑	Note takers in class	☑
Math waiver	☐	Priority seating	☐
Other special classes	☐	Tape recorders	☑
Priority registrations	☐	Videotaped classes	☐
Substitution of courses	☐	Text on tape	☐
Exams		**Services**	
Extended time	☑	Diagnostic tests	☐
Oral exams	☑	Learning centers	☐
Take home exams	☐	Proofreaders	☐
Exams on tape or computer	☐	Readers	☑
Untimed exams	☐	Reading Machines/Kurzweil	☑
Other accommodations	☐	Special bookstore section	☐
		Typists	☐

Credit toward degree is not given for remedial courses taken.

Counseling Services

- ☐ Academic
- ☐ Psychological
- ☐ Student Support groups
- ☐ Vocational

Tutoring

	Individual	Group
Time management	☐	☐
Organizational skills	☐	☐
Learning strategies	☐	☐
Study skills	☐	☐
Content area	☐	☐
Writing lab	☐	☐
Math lab	☐	☐

UNIQUE LD PROGRAM FEATURES

The Office of Disability Services provides intensive advising to eligible students with disabilities in order to assist them in developing compensatory strategies and obtaining equal access to educational programs. Mandatory freshmen seminar series and C.A.T.S. (College Achievement Training Seminars) are research-based and are designed to facilitate student adjustment to the university, development of self-advocacy and self-efficacy skills, and enhancement of study strategies.

LD PROGRAM STAFF

Total number of LD Program staff (including director):

Full Time: 1 Part Time: 1

Key staff person available to work with LD students: Edith F. Miller, Ed.D., Professor/Disability Services Director

Eastern University

St. Davids, PA

Address: 1300 Eagle Road, St. Davids, PA, 19087-3696
Admissions telephone: 800 452-0996
Admissions FAX: 610 341-1723
Director of Enrollment Management: David Urban
Admissions e-mail: ugadm@eastern.edu
Web site: http://www.eastern.edu
SAT Code: 2220 ACT Code: 3562

LD program name: Cushing Center for Counseling and Academic Support
LD program telephone: (610) 341-5837
Total campus enrollment: 2,249

GENERAL

Eastern University is a private, coed, four-year institution. 107-acre, suburban campus in St. Davids (population: 1,500), 19 miles from Philadelphia. Served by bus and train; major airport serves Philadelphia. School operates transportation to churches on Sundays. Public transportation serves campus. Semester system.

LD ADMISSIONS

Specific accommodations are determined after admission on an individual basis.

SECONDARY SCHOOL REQUIREMENTS

Graduation from secondary school required; GED accepted.

TESTING

SAT Reasoning required; ACT may be substituted. SAT Subject recommended.

All enrolled freshmen (fall 2004):

Average SAT I Scores: Verbal: 555 Math: 534
Average ACT Scores: Composite: 22

Child Study Team report is not required. Tests required as part of this documentation:

- ❑ WAIS-IV
- ❑ WISC-IV
- ❑ SATA
- ❑ Woodcock-Johnson
- ❑ Nelson-Denny Reading Test
- ❑ Other

UNDERGRADUATE STUDENT BODY

Total undergraduate student enrollment: 643 Men, 1,259 Women.

Composition of student body (fall 2004):

	Undergraduate	Freshmen
International	0.5	1.5
Black	9.0	13.4
American Indian	0.5	0.5
Asian-American	0.9	1.3
Hispanic	2.4	5.1
White	85.3	74.4
Unreported	1.4	3.8
	100.0%	100.0%

40% are from out of state.

STUDENT HOUSING

94% of freshmen live in college housing. Housing is guaranteed for all undergraduates. Campus can house 1,069 undergraduates.

EXPENSES

Tuition (2005-06): $18,830 per year. Tuition varies by program.
Room: $4,280. Board: $3,560.
There is no additional cost for LD program/services.

LD SERVICES

LD services available to:

❑ Freshmen ❑ Sophomores ❑ Juniors ❑ Seniors

Academic Accommodations

Curriculum		In class	
Foreign language waiver	❑	Early syllabus	❑
Lighter course load	❑	Note takers in class	❑
Math waiver	❑	Priority seating	❑
Other special classes	❑	Tape recorders	❑
Priority registrations	❑	Videotaped classes	❑
Substitution of courses	❑	Text on tape	❑
Exams		**Services**	
Extended time	❑	Diagnostic tests	❑
Oral exams	❑	Learning centers	■
Take home exams	❑	Proofreaders	❑
Exams on tape or computer	❑	Readers	❑
Untimed exams	❑	Reading Machines/Kurzweil	❑
Other accommodations	❑	Special bookstore section	❑
		Typists	❑

Counseling Services

- ❑ Academic
- ❑ Psychological
- ❑ Student Support groups
- ❑ Vocational

Tutoring

	Individual	Group
Time management	❑	❑
Organizational skills	❑	❑
Learning strategies	❑	❑
Study skills	❑	❑
Content area	❑	❑
Writing lab	❑	❑
Math lab	❑	❑

Edinboro University of Pennsylvania

Edinboro, PA

Address: Edinboro, PA, 16444
Admissions telephone: 888 846-2676
Admissions FAX: 814 732-2420
Associate Vice President for Enrollment Mgmt. and Retention: Terrence Carlin
Admissions e-mail: eup_admissions@edinboro.edu
Web site: http://webs.edinboro.edu/home
SAT Code: 2651 ACT Code: 3702

LD program name: Office for Students with Disabilities
LD program address: Crawford Center, 200 Glasgow Rd.
Learning Disabilities Coordinator: Janet Jenkins
LD program telephone: 814 732-1393
LD program e-mail: jjenkins@edinboro.edu
LD program enrollment: 300, Total campus enrollment: 6,735

GENERAL

Edinboro University of Pennsylvania is a public, coed, four-year institution. 585-acre campus in Edinboro (population: 6,950), 18 miles from Erie; branch campuses in Erie and Millcreek Township. Airport, bus, and train serve Erie; major airport serves Pittsburgh (100 miles). School operates transportation to branch campus in Millcreek Township. Public transportation serves campus. Semester system.

LD ADMISSIONS

Students do not complete a separate application and are not simultaneously accepted to the LD program. A member of the LD program does not sit on the admissions committee. A personal interview is recommended. Essay is not required. Application fee may be waived.

SECONDARY SCHOOL REQUIREMENTS

Graduation from secondary school required; GED accepted. The following course distribution required: 4 units of English, 3 units of math, 3 units of science, 2 units of foreign language, 3 units of social studies, 4 units of academic electives.

TESTING

SAT Reasoning or ACT required. SAT Subject recommended.

All enrolled freshmen (fall 2004):

Average SAT I Scores:	Verbal: 481	Math: 466
Average ACT Scores:	Composite: 19	

Child Study Team report is not required. A neuropsychological or comprehensive psycho-educational evaluation is required for admission. Must be dated within 36 months of application. Tests required as part of this documentation:

- ■ WAIS-IV
- ■ WISC-IV
- ☐ SATA
- ■ Woodcock-Johnson
- ■ Nelson-Denny Reading Test
- ☐ Other

UNDERGRADUATE STUDENT BODY

Total undergraduate student enrollment: 2,860 Men, 3,824 Women.

Composition of student body (fall 2004):

	Undergraduate	Freshmen
International	0.9	2.4
Black	10.2	7.5
American Indian	0.2	0.3
Asian-American	0.9	0.7
Hispanic	1.7	1.1
White	86.1	88.0
Unreported	0.0	0.0
	100.0%	100.0%

10% are from out of state. 2% join a fraternity and 2% join a sorority. Average age of full-time undergraduates is 22. 29% of classes have fewer than 20 students, 64% have between 20 and 50 students, 7% have more than 50 students.

STUDENT HOUSING

75% of freshmen live in college housing. Freshmen are required to live on campus. Housing is guaranteed for all undergraduates. Campus can house 2,400 undergraduates. Single rooms are available for students with medical or special needs. A medical note is required.

EXPENSES

Tuition (2005-06): $4,906 per year (in-state), $9,814 (out-of-state).

Room: $3,400. Board: $2,118.
Additional cost for LD program/services: $876.

LD SERVICES

LD program size is not limited.

LD services available to:

■ Freshmen ■ Sophomores ■ Juniors ■ Seniors

Academic Accommodations

Curriculum		In class	
Foreign language waiver	☐	Early syllabus	☐
Lighter course load	■	Note takers in class	■
Math waiver	☐	Priority seating	☐
Other special classes	☐	Tape recorders	■
Priority registrations	■	Videotaped classes	☐
Substitution of courses	☐	Text on tape	■
Exams		**Services**	
Extended time	■	Diagnostic tests	☐
Oral exams	☐	Learning centers	☐
Take home exams	☐	Proofreaders	☐
Exams on tape or computer	☐	Readers	■
Untimed exams	☐	Reading Machines/Kurzweil	☐
Other accommodations	☐	Special bookstore section	☐
		Typists	☐

Credit toward degree is not given for remedial courses taken.

Counseling Services

- ■ Academic
- ■ Psychological
- ■ Student Support groups
- ■ Vocational

Tutoring

Individual tutoring is available daily.

	Individual	Group
Time management	■	■
Organizational skills	■	■
Learning strategies	■	■
Study skills	■	■
Content area	■	■
Writing lab	■	■
Math lab	■	■

LD PROGRAM STAFF

Total number of LD Program staff (including director):

Full Time: 2 Part Time: 2

There is an advisor/advocate from the LD program available to students. The advisor/advocate meets with students two times per month. One graduate student and 70 peer tutors are available to work with LD students.

Key staff person available to work with LD students: Kathleen Strosser, Assistant Director, Office for Students with Disabilities

LD Program web site: www.edinboro.edu

Elizabethtown College

Elizabethtown, PA

Address: 1 Alpha Drive, Elizabethtown, PA, 17022-2298
Admissions telephone: 717 361-1400
Admissions FAX: 717 361-1365
Dean of Admissions and Enrollment Management: W. Kent Barnds
Admissions e-mail: admissions@etown.edu
Web site: http://www.etown.edu
SAT Code: 2225 ACT Code: 3568

LD program name: Disability Services
Director of Learning Services: Shirley Deichert
LD program telephone: 717 361-1227
LD program e-mail: deichesa@etown.edu
LD program enrollment: 90, Total campus enrollment: 2,113

GENERAL

Elizabethtown College is a private, coed, four-year institution. 185-acre campus in Elizabethtown (population: 11,887), 90 miles from both Philadelphia and Baltimore; 20 miles from both Harrisburg and Lancaster. Served by train; airport and bus serve Harrisburg; bus serves Lancaster. School operates transportation to train station. Semester system.

LD ADMISSIONS

A personal interview is recommended. The Admissions Office sends all new students a "Disability Identification" form, which should be returned by June 1 prior to enrollment for the fall semester and by December 20 prior to enrollment for the spring semester. Based on submitted documentation, the Disability Review Board provides students with appropriate accommodations, within the framework of the Americans with Disabilities Act. The Board endeavors to make every effort to reasonably accommodate disabilities. The Director of Disability Services then meets with each student to inform him/her of the accommodations to be provided.

SECONDARY SCHOOL REQUIREMENTS

Graduation from secondary school required; GED accepted. The following course distribution required: 4 units of English, 3 units of math, 2 units of science, 2 units of foreign language, 2 units of social studies, 2 units of history.

TESTING

SAT Reasoning or ACT required. SAT Subject recommended.

All enrolled freshmen (fall 2004):

Average SAT I Scores:	Verbal: 570	Math: 575
Average ACT Scores:	Composite: 24	

Child Study Team report is not required. Tests required as part of this documentation:

- ☐ WAIS-IV
- ☐ WISC-IV
- ☐ SATA
- ☐ Woodcock-Johnson
- ☐ Nelson-Denny Reading Test
- ☐ Other

UNDERGRADUATE STUDENT BODY

Total undergraduate student enrollment: 715 Men, 1,186 Women.

Composition of student body (fall 2004):

	Undergraduate	Freshmen
International	1.7	2.8
Black	0.9	1.0
American Indian	0.2	0.3
Asian-American	2.0	1.8
Hispanic	0.6	1.2
White	94.6	92.9
Unreported	0.0	0.0
	100.0%	100.0%

27% are from out of state. Average age of full-time undergraduates is 20. 73% of classes have fewer than 20 students, 27% have between 20 and 50 students.

STUDENT HOUSING

96% of freshmen live in college housing. Freshmen are required to live on campus. Housing is not guaranteed for all undergraduates. Housing is not offered beyond the eighth semester. Campus can house 1,484 undergraduates. Single rooms are available for students with medical or special needs. A medical note is not required.

EXPENSES

Tuition (2005-06): $25,200 per year.
Room: $3,450. Board: $3,450.
There is no additional cost for LD program/services.

LD SERVICES

LD program size is not limited.

LD services available to:

☑ Freshmen ☑ Sophomores ☑ Juniors ☑ Seniors

Academic Accommodations

Curriculum		In class	
Foreign language waiver	☐	Early syllabus	☑
Lighter course load	☑	Note takers in class	☑
Math waiver	☐	Priority seating	☑
Other special classes	☐	Tape recorders	☑
Priority registrations	☑	Videotaped classes	☑
Substitution of courses	☑	Text on tape	☑
Exams		**Services**	
Extended time	☑	Diagnostic tests	☐
Oral exams	☑	Learning centers	☑
Take home exams	☐	Proofreaders	☑
Exams on tape or computer	☑	Readers	☑
Untimed exams	☐	Reading Machines/Kurzweil	☑
Other accommodations	☐	Special bookstore section	☐
		Typists	☐

Credit toward degree is not given for remedial courses taken.

Counseling Services

- ☑ Academic
- ☑ Psychological
- ☑ Student Support groups
- ☑ Vocational

Tutoring

Individual tutoring is available daily.

Average size of tutoring groups: 1

	Individual	Group
Time management	☑	☐
Organizational skills	☑	☐
Learning strategies	☑	☐
Study skills	☑	☐
Content area	☑	☐
Writing lab	☑	☐
Math lab	☑	☑

LD PROGRAM STAFF

Total number of LD Program staff (including director):

Full Time: 1 Part Time: 1

There is an advisor/advocate from the LD program available to students. 150 peer tutors are available to work with LD students.

Key staff person available to work with LD students: Shirley Deichert, Director of Learning and Disability Services.

LD Program web site: www.etown.edu/disability

Franklin & Marshall College

Lancaster, PA

Address: P.O. Box 3003, Lancaster, PA, 17604
Admissions telephone: 717 291-3953
Admissions FAX: 717 291-4389
Director of Admission: Dennis Trotter
Admissions e-mail: admission@fandm.edu
Web site: http://www.fandm.edu
SAT Code: 2261 ACT Code: 3574

Director of Counseling Services: Dr. Kenneth John
LD program telephone: 717 291-4083
LD program e-mail: ken.john@fandm.edu
Total campus enrollment: 1,972

GENERAL

Franklin & Marshall College is a private, coed, four-year institution. 125-acre campus in Lancaster (population: 56,348), 30 miles from Harrisburg and 60 miles from Philadelphia. Served by bus and train; major airport serves Philadelphia; smaller airport serves Harrisburg. Public transportation serves campus. Semester system.

LD ADMISSIONS

A personal interview is recommended. Essay is required and may be typed.

SECONDARY SCHOOL REQUIREMENTS

Graduation from secondary school required; GED accepted. The following course distribution required: 4 units of English, 3 units of math, 2 units of science, 2 units of foreign language, 1 unit of social studies, 2 units of history.

TESTING

SAT Reasoning or ACT required. SAT Subject recommended.

All enrolled freshmen (fall 2004):

Average SAT I Scores: Verbal: 623 Math: 636

Child Study Team report is not required. Tests required as part of this documentation:

- ❑ WAIS-IV
- ❑ WISC-IV
- ❑ SATA
- ❑ Woodcock-Johnson
- ❑ Nelson-Denny Reading Test
- ❑ Other

UNDERGRADUATE STUDENT BODY

Total undergraduate student enrollment: 945 Men, 942 Women.

Composition of student body (fall 2004):

	Undergraduate	Freshmen
International	5.1	8.1
Black	3.0	2.4
American Indian	0.2	0.1
Asian-American	4.5	4.2
Hispanic	3.2	2.9
White	79.5	77.3
Unreported	4.5	5.0
	100.0%	100.0%

64% are from out of state. 35% join a fraternity and 20% join a sorority. Average age of full-time undergraduates is 20. 50% of classes have fewer than 20 students, 49% have between 20 and 50 students, 1% have more than 50 students.

STUDENT HOUSING

100% of freshmen live in college housing. Freshmen are required to live on campus. Housing is guaranteed for all undergraduates. Campus can house 1,275 undergraduates.

EXPENSES

Tuition (2005-06): $32,480 per year.
Room: $5,250. Board: $2,810.
There is no additional cost for LD program/services.

LD SERVICES

LD services available to:

❑ Freshmen ❑ Sophomores ❑ Juniors ❑ Seniors

Academic Accommodations

Curriculum		**In class**	
Foreign language waiver	❑	Early syllabus	❑
Lighter course load	❑	Note takers in class	❑
Math waiver	❑	Priority seating	❑
Other special classes	❑	Tape recorders	❑
Priority registrations	❑	Videotaped classes	❑
Substitution of courses	❑	Text on tape	❑
Exams		**Services**	
Extended time	❑	Diagnostic tests	❑
Oral exams	❑	Learning centers	❑
Take home exams	❑	Proofreaders	❑
Exams on tape or computer	❑	Readers	❑
Untimed exams	❑	Reading Machines/Kurzweil	❑
Other accommodations	❑	Special bookstore section	❑
		Typists	❑

Credit toward degree is not given for remedial courses taken.

Counseling Services

- ❑ Academic
- ❑ Psychological
- ❑ Student Support groups
- ❑ Vocational

Tutoring

	Individual	Group
Time management	❑	❑
Organizational skills	❑	❑
Learning strategies	❑	❑
Study skills	❑	❑
Content area	❑	❑
Writing lab	❑	❑
Math lab	❑	❑

LD PROGRAM STAFF

Total number of LD Program staff (including director):

Full Time: 1 Part Time: 1

Key staff person available to work with LD students: Dr. Kenneth John, Director of Counseling Services

Gannon University

Erie, PA

Address: 109 University Square, Erie, PA, 16541
Admissions telephone: 800 GANNON-U
Admissions FAX: 814 871-5803
Director of Admissions: Christopher Tremblay
Admissions e-mail: admissions@gannon.edu
Web site: http://www.gannon.edu
SAT Code: 2270 ACT Code: 3576

Director: St. Joyce Lowrey
LD program telephone: 814 871-5326
LD program e-mail: lowrey001@gannon.edu
Total campus enrollment: 2,430

GENERAL

Gannon University is a private, coed, four-year institution. 13-acre, urban campus in Erie (population: 103,717), 90 miles from both Buffalo and Cleveland, and 120 miles from Pittsburgh. Served by air, bus, and train. Public transportation serves campus. Semester system.

LD ADMISSIONS

Students do not complete a separate application and are simultaneously accepted to the LD program. A member of the LD program does sit on the admissions committee. A personal interview is recommended. Essay is required and may be typed. Some admission requirements may be waived.

For fall 2004, 61 completed self-identified LD applications were received. 23 applications were offered admission, and 9 enrolled.

SECONDARY SCHOOL REQUIREMENTS

Graduation from secondary school required; GED accepted. The following course distribution required: 4 units of English, 4 units of math, 2 units of science.

TESTING

SAT Reasoning required; ACT may be substituted. SAT Subject recommended.

All enrolled freshmen (fall 2004):

Average SAT I Scores:	Verbal: 527	Math: 533
Average ACT Scores:	Composite: 22	

Child Study Team report is not required. A neuropsychological or comprehensive psycho-educational evaluation is required for admission. Tests required as part of this documentation:

■ WAIS-IV	□ Woodcock-Johnson
■ WISC-IV	□ Nelson-Denny Reading Test
□ SATA	□ Other

UNDERGRADUATE STUDENT BODY

Total undergraduate student enrollment: 1,031 Men, 1,459 Women.

Composition of student body (fall 2004):

	Undergraduate	Freshmen
International	1.1	1.3
Black	4.4	4.8
American Indian	0.2	0.3
Asian-American	1.3	1.2
Hispanic	1.1	0.9
White	87.0	89.6
Unreported	4.9	1.9
	100.0%	100.0%

22% are from out of state. Average age of full-time undergraduates is 20. 57% of classes have fewer than 20 students, 43% have between 20 and 50 students.

STUDENT HOUSING

74% of freshmen live in college housing. Freshmen are required to live on campus. Housing is guaranteed for all undergraduates. Campus can house 1,169 undergraduates. Single rooms are available for students with medical or special needs. A medical note is required.

EXPENSES

Tuition (2005-06): $18,220 per year. $15,330 per year (business, education, humanities, and science programs); $16,270 (computer science, engineering, and health science programs).

Room: $4,020. Board: $3,390.
Additional cost for LD program/services: $300 per semester.

LD SERVICES

LD services available to:

■ Freshmen ■ Sophomores ■ Juniors ■ Seniors

Academic Accommodations

Curriculum		**In class**	
Foreign language waiver	□	Early syllabus	□
Lighter course load	□	Note takers in class	□
Math waiver	□	Priority seating	□
Other special classes	■	Tape recorders	■
Priority registrations	□	Videotaped classes	□
Substitution of courses	■	Text on tape	■
Exams		**Services**	
Extended time	■	Diagnostic tests	□
Oral exams	■	Learning centers	■
Take home exams	□	Proofreaders	□
Exams on tape or computer	□	Readers	■
Untimed exams	□	Reading Machines/Kurzweil	■
Other accommodations	□	Special bookstore section	□
		Typists	■

Credit toward degree is not given for remedial courses taken.

Counseling Services

□ Academic
□ Psychological
□ Student Support groups
□ Vocational

Tutoring

Individual tutoring is available weekly.

Average size of tutoring groups: 1

	Individual	Group
Time management	■	■
Organizational skills	□	■
Learning strategies	□	■
Study skills	□	■
Content area	□	□
Writing lab	□	□
Math lab	□	□

LD PROGRAM STAFF

Total number of LD Program staff (including director):

Full Time: 3 Part Time: 3

There is an advisor/advocate from the LD program available to students. One graduate student and two peer tutors are available to work with LD students.

Key staff person available to work with LD students: Cheryl Guy, Educational Specialist

LD Program web site: http://www.gannon.edu/resource/psld/index.ihtml

Geneva College

Beaver Falls, PA

Address: 3200 College Avenue, Beaver Falls, PA, 15010
Admissions telephone: 800 847-8255
Admissions FAX: 724 847-6776
Associate Vice President for Enrollment Management: David Layton
Admissions e-mail: admissions@geneva.edu
Web site: http://www.geneva.edu
SAT Code: 2273 ACT Code: 3578

LD program name: ACCESS
Director of Student Services: Nancy Smith
LD program telephone: 724 847-5005
LD program e-mail: nismith@geneva.edu
LD program enrollment: 80, Total campus enrollment: 1,809

GENERAL

Geneva College is a private, coed, four-year institution. 55-acre campus in Beaver Falls (population: 9,920), 35 miles from Pittsburgh. Major airport, bus, and train serve Pittsburgh. School operates transportation to airport for holidays. Public transportation serves campus. Semester system.

LD ADMISSIONS

Students do not complete a separate application and are simultaneously accepted to the LD program. A member of the LD program does not sit on the admissions committee. High school waivers are accepted for foreign language. A personal interview is required.

SECONDARY SCHOOL REQUIREMENTS

Graduation from secondary school required; GED accepted. The following course distribution required: 4 units of English, 2 units of math, 1 unit of science, 2 units of foreign language, 3 units of social studies, 4 units of academic electives.

TESTING

SAT Subject recommended.

All enrolled freshmen (fall 2004):

Average SAT I Scores:	Verbal: 551	Math: 534
Average ACT Scores:	Composite: 23	

Child Study Team report is not required. A neuropsychological or comprehensive psycho-educational evaluation is required for admission. Must be dated within 36 months of application. Tests required as part of this documentation:

- [ ] WAIS-IV
- [ ] WISC-IV
- [ ] SATA
- [ ] Woodcock-Johnson
- [ ] Nelson-Denny Reading Test
- [x] Other

UNDERGRADUATE STUDENT BODY

Total undergraduate student enrollment: 760 Men, 1,069 Women.

Composition of student body (fall 2004):

	Undergraduate	Freshmen
International	1.3	1.2
Black	4.0	8.9
American Indian	0.3	0.3
Asian-American	1.5	0.8
Hispanic	1.3	0.9
White	91.1	87.0
Unreported	0.5	0.9
	100.0%	100.0%

26% are from out of state. Average age of full-time undergraduates is 23. 62% of classes have fewer than 20 students, 37% have between 20 and 50 students, 1% have more than 50 students.

STUDENT HOUSING

82% of freshmen live in college housing. Freshmen are required to live on campus. Housing is guaranteed for all undergraduates. Campus can house 1,000 undergraduates. Single rooms are available for students with medical or special needs. A medical note is required.

EXPENSES

Tuition (2005-06): $16,910 per year.

Room: $3,530. Board: $3,240.
There is no additional cost for LD program/services.

LD SERVICES

LD program size is not limited.

LD services available to:

- [x] Freshmen
- [x] Sophomores
- [x] Juniors
- [x] Seniors

Academic Accommodations

Curriculum		In class	
Foreign language waiver	[ ]	Early syllabus	[ ]
Lighter course load	[x]	Note takers in class	[x]
Math waiver	[ ]	Priority seating	[ ]
Other special classes	[ ]	Tape recorders	[ ]
Priority registrations	[ ]	Videotaped classes	[x]
Substitution of courses	[ ]	Text on tape	[ ]
Exams		**Services**	
Extended time	[x]	Diagnostic tests	[x]
Oral exams	[ ]	Learning centers	[ ]
Take home exams	[ ]	Proofreaders	[x]
Exams on tape or computer	[ ]	Readers	[x]
Untimed exams	[ ]	Reading Machines/Kurzweil	[x]
Other accommodations	[x]	Special bookstore section	[ ]
		Typists	[ ]

Credit toward degree is not given for remedial courses taken.

Counseling Services

- [x] Academic
- [x] Psychological
- [ ] Student Support groups
- [ ] Vocational

Tutoring

Individual tutoring is available daily.

Average size of tutoring groups: 3

	Individual	Group
Time management	[x]	[ ]
Organizational skills	[ ]	[ ]
Learning strategies	[ ]	[ ]
Study skills	[x]	[ ]
Content area	[ ]	[ ]
Writing lab	[x]	[ ]
Math lab	[ ]	[ ]

LD PROGRAM STAFF

Total number of LD Program staff (including director):

Full Time: 1 Part Time: 1

There is an advisor/advocate from the LD program available to students. 50 peer tutors are available to work with LD students.

Key staff person available to work with LD students: Nancy Smith, Director of Student Services

Gettysburg College

Gettysburg, PA

Address: 300 North Washington Street, Gettysburg, PA, 17325
Admissions telephone: 800 431-0803
Admissions FAX: 717 337-6145
Director of Admissions: Gail Sweezey
Admissions e-mail: admiss@gettysburg.edu
Web site: http://www.gettysburg.edu
SAT Code: 2275 ACT Code: 3580

Dean of Academic Advising: Gail Ann Rickert
LD program telephone: 717 337-6579
LD program e-mail: grickert@gettysburg.edu
Total campus enrollment: 2,466

GENERAL

Gettysburg College is a private, coed, four-year institution. 200-acre campus in Gettysburg (population: 7,490), 36 miles from Harrisburg, 55 miles from Baltimore MD, and 80 miles from Washington, DC. Major airport serves Baltimore MD; smaller airport, bus, and train serve Harrisburg. School operates transportation to all nearby transportation centers. Semester system.

LD ADMISSIONS

A personal interview is recommended. Essay is required and may be typed.

SECONDARY SCHOOL REQUIREMENTS

Graduation from secondary school required; GED accepted. The following course distribution required: 3 units of English, 3 units of math, 3 units of science, 3 units of foreign language, 3 units of social studies, 3 units of history, 4 units of academic electives.

TESTING

SAT Reasoning or ACT required. SAT Subject recommended.

All enrolled freshmen (fall 2004):

Average SAT I Scores: Verbal: 636 Math: 635
Average ACT Scores: Composite: 29

Child Study Team report is not required. Tests required as part of this documentation:

- [ ] WAIS-IV
- [ ] WISC-IV
- [ ] SATA
- [ ] Woodcock-Johnson
- [ ] Nelson-Denny Reading Test
- [ ] Other

UNDERGRADUATE STUDENT BODY

Total undergraduate student enrollment: 1,091 Men, 1,167 Women.

Composition of student body (fall 2004):

	Undergraduate	Freshmen
International	1.0	1.7
Black	3.1	3.4
American Indian	0.1	0.0
Asian-American	2.0	1.2
Hispanic	1.7	1.6
White	92.1	92.1
Unreported	0.0	0.0
	100.0%	100.0%

72% are from out of state. 40% join a fraternity and 26% join a sorority. Average age of full-time undergraduates is 20. 68% of classes have fewer than 20 students, 32% have between 20 and 50 students.

STUDENT HOUSING

100% of freshmen live in college housing. Freshmen are required to live on campus. Housing is guaranteed for all undergraduates. Campus can house 2,211 undergraduates.

EXPENSES

Tuition (2005-06): $31,790 per year.
Room: $4,134. Board: $3,660.
There is no additional cost for LD program/services.

LD SERVICES

LD services available to:

- [ ] Freshmen
- [ ] Sophomores
- [ ] Juniors
- [ ] Seniors

Academic Accommodations

Curriculum

- [ ] Foreign language waiver
- [ ] Lighter course load
- [ ] Math waiver
- [ ] Other special classes
- [ ] Priority registrations
- [ ] Substitution of courses

Exams

- [x] Extended time
- [ ] Oral exams
- [ ] Take home exams
- [ ] Exams on tape or computer
- [ ] Untimed exams
- [ ] Other accommodations

In class

- [ ] Early syllabus
- [ ] Note takers in class
- [ ] Priority seating
- [x] Tape recorders
- [ ] Videotaped classes
- [ ] Text on tape

Services

- [ ] Diagnostic tests
- [ ] Learning centers
- [ ] Proofreaders
- [ ] Readers
- [ ] Reading Machines/Kurzweil
- [ ] Special bookstore section
- [ ] Typists

Credit toward degree is not given for remedial courses taken.

Counseling Services

- [ ] Academic
- [ ] Psychological
- [ ] Student Support groups
- [ ] Vocational

Tutoring

Individual tutoring is available.

	Individual	Group
Time management	[ ]	[ ]
Organizational skills	[ ]	[ ]
Learning strategies	[ ]	[ ]
Study skills	[ ]	[ ]
Content area	[ ]	[ ]
Writing lab	[ ]	[ ]
Math lab	[ ]	[ ]

UNIQUE LD PROGRAM FEATURES

All arrangements for LD students are made on an individual basis.

LD PROGRAM STAFF

Key staff person available to work with LD students: Gail Ann Rickert, Dean of Academic Advising

Grove City College

Grove City, PA

Address: 100 Campus Drive, Grove City, PA, 16127
Admissions telephone: 724 458-2100
Admissions FAX: 724 458-3395
Director of Admissions: Jeffrey C. Mincey
Admissions e-mail: admissions@gcc.edu
Web site: http://www.gcc.edu
SAT Code: 2277 ACT Code: 3582

Total campus enrollment: 2,318

GENERAL

Grove City College is a private, coed, four-year institution. 150-acre campus in Grove City (population: 8,024), 60 miles from Pittsburgh. Served by bus; major airport serves Pittsburgh. Semester system.

LD ADMISSIONS

Application Deadline: 02/01. A member of the LD program does not sit on the admissions committee. A personal interview is recommended. Essay is required and may be typed.

SECONDARY SCHOOL REQUIREMENTS

Graduation from secondary school required; GED accepted.

TESTING

SAT Reasoning or ACT required. SAT Subject required.

All enrolled freshmen (fall 2004):

Average SAT I Scores:	Verbal: 635	Math: 636
Average ACT Scores:	Composite: 28	

Child Study Team report is not required. A neuropsychological or comprehensive psycho-education evaluation is not required for admission. Tests required as part of this documentation:

- ☐ WAIS-IV
- ☐ WISC-IV
- ☐ SATA
- ☐ Woodcock-Johnson
- ☐ Nelson-Denny Reading Test
- ☐ Other

UNDERGRADUATE STUDENT BODY

Total undergraduate student enrollment: 1,157 Men, 1,174 Women.

Composition of student body (fall 2004):

	Undergraduate	Freshmen
International	0.5	0.9
Black	0.3	0.2
American Indian	0.2	0.1
Asian-American	2.1	1.8
Hispanic	0.8	0.4
White	94.9	96.0
Unreported	1.2	0.6
	100.0%	100.0%

46% are from out of state. 15% join a fraternity and 19% join a sorority. Average age of full-time undergraduates is 20. 36% of classes have fewer than 20 students, 53% have between 20 and 50 students, 11% have more than 50 students.

STUDENT HOUSING

90% of freshmen live in college housing. Freshmen are required to live on campus. Housing is not guaranteed for all undergraduates. If a student is over 25 they must live off campus.

EXPENSES

Tuition (2005-06): $10,440 per year. $7,870 per year (B.A. programs), $8,214 (B.S. programs), $8,424 (B.S.Mech.Eng. and B.S.Elec.Eng. programs).
Room & Board: $5,344.
There is no additional cost for LD program/services.

LD SERVICES

LD program size is not limited.

LD services available to:

☐ Freshmen ☐ Sophomores ☐ Juniors ☐ Seniors

Academic Accommodations

Curriculum		**In class**	
Foreign language waiver	☐	Early syllabus	☐
Lighter course load	☒	Note takers in class	☐
Math waiver	☐	Priority seating	☐
Other special classes	☐	Tape recorders	☒
Priority registrations	☐	Videotaped classes	☐
Substitution of courses	☐	Text on tape	☐
Exams		**Services**	
Extended time	☐	Diagnostic tests	☐
Oral exams	☐	Learning centers	☐
Take home exams	☐	Proofreaders	☐
Exams on tape or computer	☐	Readers	☐
Untimed exams	☐	Reading Machines/Kurzweil	☐
Other accommodations	☐	Special bookstore section	☐
		Typists	☐

Credit toward degree is not given for remedial courses taken.

Counseling Services

- ☐ Academic
- ☐ Psychological
- ☐ Student Support groups
- ☐ Vocational

Tutoring

Individual tutoring is available.

	Individual	Group
Time management	☐	☐
Organizational skills	☐	☐
Learning strategies	☐	☐
Study skills	☐	☐
Content area	☐	☐
Writing lab	☐	☐
Math lab	☐	☐

LD PROGRAM STAFF

There is no advisor/advocate from the LD program available to students.

Gwynedd-Mercy College

Gwynedd Valley, PA

Address: 1325 Sumneytown Pike, P.O. Box 901, Gwynedd Valley, PA, 19437-0901
Admissions telephone: 800 DIAL-GMC (in-state)
Admissions FAX: 215 641-5556
Vice President, Enrollment Management: James Abbuhl
Admissions e-mail: admissions@gmc.edu
Web site: http://www.gmc.edu
SAT Code: 2278 ACT Code: 3583

Director of Counseling Services: Stephanie Fratantaro
LD program telephone: 215 641-5571
LD program e-mail: fratantaro.s@gmc.edu
Total campus enrollment: 2,160

GENERAL

Gwynedd-Mercy College is a private, coed, four-year institution. 170-acre, suburban campus in Gwynedd Valley, one mile from Spring House (population 3,290) and 20 miles from Philadelphia. Major airport, bus, and train serve Philadelphia; smaller airport and bus serve Willow Grove (12 miles). School operates transportation to bus and train stations. Public transportation serves campus. Semester system.

SECONDARY SCHOOL REQUIREMENTS

Graduation from secondary school required; GED accepted. The following course distribution required: 4 units of English, 3 units of math, 3 units of science, 1 unit of history.

TESTING

SAT Reasoning required. ACT considered if submitted.

All enrolled freshmen (fall 2004):

Average SAT I Scores: Verbal: 500 Math: 495

Child Study Team report is not required. Tests required as part of this documentation:

- ☐ WAIS-IV
- ☐ WISC-IV
- ☐ SATA
- ☐ Woodcock-Johnson
- ☐ Nelson-Denny Reading Test
- ☐ Other

UNDERGRADUATE STUDENT BODY

Total undergraduate student enrollment: 514 Men, 1,436 Women.

Composition of student body (fall 2004):

	Undergraduate	Freshmen
International	0.0	2.1
Black	2.8	13.3
American Indian	0.0	0.1
Asian-American	1.9	3.1
Hispanic	0.5	1.6
White	94.8	79.8
Unreported	0.0	0.0
	100.0%	100.0%

4% are from out of state. Average age of full-time undergraduates is 22. 63% of classes have fewer than 20 students, 34% have between 20 and 50 students, 3% have more than 50 students.

STUDENT HOUSING

59% of freshmen live in college housing. Freshmen are not required to live on campus. Undergraduates are given priority but housing is not guaranteed. Campus can house 350 undergraduates.

EXPENSES

Tuition (2005-06): $17,580 per year. $15,600 per year, $16,600 for allied health and nursing programs.
Room & Board: $0-$7,720.

There is no additional cost for LD program/services.

LD SERVICES

LD program size is not limited.

LD services available to:

☑ Freshmen ☑ Sophomores ☑ Juniors ☑ Seniors

Academic Accommodations

Curriculum		**In class**	
Foreign language waiver	☐	Early syllabus	☐
Lighter course load	☑	Note takers in class	☐
Math waiver	☐	Priority seating	☐
Other special classes	☐	Tape recorders	☑
Priority registrations	☐	Videotaped classes	☐
Substitution of courses	☐	Text on tape	☐
Exams		**Services**	
Extended time	☑	Diagnostic tests	☐
Oral exams	☑	Learning centers	☑
Take home exams	☐	Proofreaders	☐
Exams on tape or computer	☐	Readers	☑
Untimed exams	☑	Reading Machines/Kurzweil	☑
Other accommodations	☐	Special bookstore section	☐
		Typists	☐

Credit toward degree is not given for remedial courses taken.

Counseling Services

- ☐ Academic
- ☐ Psychological
- ☐ Student Support groups
- ☐ Vocational

Tutoring

Individual tutoring is available daily.

	Individual	Group
Time management	☐	☑
Organizational skills	☐	☑
Learning strategies	☐	☑
Study skills	☐	☑
Content area	☐	☐
Writing lab	☐	☑
Math lab	☐	☑

LD PROGRAM STAFF

Total number of LD Program staff (including director):

Full Time: 3 Part Time: 3

Key staff person available to work with LD students: Stephanie Fratantaro, Director of Counseling Services

Haverford College

Haverford, PA

Address: 370 West Lancaster Avenue, Haverford, PA, 19041-1392
Admissions telephone: 610 896-1350
Admissions FAX: 610 896-1338
Director of Admission: Greg Kannerstein
Admissions e-mail: admitme@haverford.edu
Web site: http://www.haverford.edu
SAT Code: 2289 ACT Code: 3590

LD program name: Office of Disabilities Services
Director, Counseling & Coordinator, Disabilities: Rick Webb
LD program telephone: 610 896-1290
LD program e-mail: rwebb@haverford.edu
LD program enrollment: 40, Total campus enrollment: 1,172

GENERAL

Haverford College is a private, coed, four-year institution. 200-acre, suburban campus in Haverford (population: 48,498), 10 miles from downtown Philadelphia. Major airport, bus, and train serve Philadelphia. School operates transportation to Bryn Mawr Coll and Swarthmore Coll. Public transportation serves campus. Semester system.

LD ADMISSIONS

Application Deadline: 01/15. A personal interview is recommended. Essay is required and may be typed. Admission requirements are not waived but each student's performance is evaluated.

For fall 2004, 51 completed self-identified LD applications were received. 9 applications were offered admission, and 7 enrolled.

SECONDARY SCHOOL REQUIREMENTS

Graduation from secondary school required; GED accepted. The following course distribution required: 4 units of English, 3 units of math, 1 unit of science, 3 units of foreign language, 1 unit of social studies.

TESTING

SAT Reasoning or ACT required. SAT Subject recommended.

All enrolled freshmen (fall 2004):

Average SAT I Scores: Verbal: 690 Math: 680

Child Study Team report is not required. Tests required as part of this documentation:

- [x] WAIS-IV
- [ ] WISC-IV
- [ ] SATA
- [x] Woodcock-Johnson
- [x] Nelson-Denny Reading Test
- [x] Other

UNDERGRADUATE STUDENT BODY

Total undergraduate student enrollment: 546 Men, 592 Women.

Composition of student body (fall 2004):

	Undergraduate	Freshmen
International	4.2	3.2
Black	9.1	5.7
American Indian	0.0	0.6
Asian-American	10.0	13.5
Hispanic	8.2	6.4
White	68.5	70.6
Unreported	0.0	0.0
	100.0%	100.0%

79% are from out of state. Average age of full-time undergraduates is 21. 71% of classes have fewer than 20 students, 27% have between 20 and 50 students, 2% have more than 50 students.

STUDENT HOUSING

100% of freshmen live in college housing. Freshmen are required to live on campus. Housing is guaranteed for all undergraduates. Campus can house 1,172 undergraduates. Single rooms are available for students with medical or special needs. A medical note is required.

EXPENSES

Tuition (2005-06): $31,466 per year.

Room: $5,540. Board: $4,300.

There is no additional cost for LD program/services.

LD SERVICES

LD program size is not limited.

LD services available to:

- [x] Freshmen
- [x] Sophomores
- [x] Juniors
- [x] Seniors

Academic Accommodations

Curriculum		In class	
Foreign language waiver	[ ]	Early syllabus	[ ]
Lighter course load	[x]	Note takers in class	[ ]
Math waiver	[ ]	Priority seating	[ ]
Other special classes	[ ]	Tape recorders	[ ]
Priority registrations	[ ]	Videotaped classes	[ ]
Substitution of courses	[ ]	Text on tape	[ ]
Exams		**Services**	
Extended time	[ ]	Diagnostic tests	[ ]
Oral exams	[ ]	Learning centers	[ ]
Take home exams	[ ]	Proofreaders	[ ]
Exams on tape or computer	[ ]	Readers	[ ]
Untimed exams	[ ]	Reading Machines/Kurzweil	[ ]
Other accommodations	[ ]	Special bookstore section	[ ]
		Typists	[ ]

Credit toward degree is not given for remedial courses taken.

Counseling Services

- [x] Academic
- [x] Psychological
- [ ] Student Support groups
- [ ] Vocational

Tutoring

	Individual	Group
Time management	[x]	[ ]
Organizational skills	[x]	[ ]
Learning strategies	[x]	[ ]
Study skills	[x]	[ ]
Content area	[x]	[ ]
Writing lab	[x]	[ ]
Math lab	[x]	[ ]

UNIQUE LD PROGRAM FEATURES

All accommodations are determined on an individual basis.

LD PROGRAM STAFF

There is no advisor/advocate from the LD program available to students.

Key staff person available to work with LD students: Rick Webb, Coordinator, Disabilities Services

LD Program web site: www.haverford.edu/ods/ODS.htm

Holy Family University

Philadelphia, PA

Address: 9701 Frankford Avenue, Philadelphia, PA, 19114-2094
Admissions telephone: 800 637-1191
Admissions FAX: 215 281-1022
Director of Admissions: Lauren McDermott
Admissions e-mail: undergra@holyfamily.edu
Web site: http://www.holyfamily.edu
SAT Code: 2297 ACT Code: 3592

Director: Diana R. Piperata, Ph.D.
LD program telephone: 215 637-7700, extension 3232
LD program e-mail: dpiperata@holyfamily.edu
LD program enrollment: 64, Total campus enrollment: 2,073

GENERAL

Holy Family University is a private, coed, four-year institution. 47-acre, suburban campus in Philadelphia (population: 1,517,550), 12 miles from downtown; additional campus in Newtown. Served by air, bus, and train. Public transportation serves campus. Semester system.

LD ADMISSIONS

Application Deadline: 08/01. Students do not complete a separate application and are not simultaneously accepted to the LD program. A member of the LD program does not sit on the admissions committee. A personal interview is recommended. Essay is required and may not be typed.

For fall 2004, 4 completed self-identified LD applications were received. 4 applications were offered admission, and 3 enrolled.

SECONDARY SCHOOL REQUIREMENTS

Graduation from secondary school required; GED accepted. The following course distribution required: 4 units of English, 3 units of math, 2 units of science, 2 units of history, 3 units of academic electives.

TESTING

SAT Reasoning or ACT required. SAT Subject recommended.

All enrolled freshmen (fall 2004):

Average SAT I Scores:	Verbal: 492	Math: 484
Average ACT Scores:	Composite:	

Child Study Team report is not required. A neuropsychological or comprehensive psycho-educational evaluation is required for admission. Must be dated within 36 months of application. Tests required as part of this documentation:

- [x] WAIS-IV
- [x] WISC-IV
- [x] SATA
- [x] Woodcock-Johnson
- [x] Nelson-Denny Reading Test
- [x] Other

UNDERGRADUATE STUDENT BODY

Total undergraduate student enrollment: 425 Men, 1,424 Women.

Composition of student body (fall 2004):

	Undergraduate	Freshmen
International	0.7	2.6
Black	4.9	3.1
American Indian	0.3	0.3
Asian-American	3.6	2.5
Hispanic	1.6	1.8
White	87.9	86.0
Unreported	1.0	3.7
	100.0%	100.0%

10% are from out of state. Average age of full-time undergraduates is 20.

STUDENT HOUSING

8% of freshmen live in college housing. Housing is not guaranteed for all undergraduates. Single rooms are available for students with medical or special needs. A medical note is required.

EXPENSES

Tuition (2005-06): $17,240 per year.
Room: $4,700. Board: $3,300.
There is no additional cost for LD program/services.

LD SERVICES

LD program size is not limited.

LD services available to:

- [x] Freshmen
- [x] Sophomores
- [x] Juniors
- [x] Seniors

Academic Accommodations

Curriculum		In class	
Foreign language waiver	[ ]	Early syllabus	[ ]
Lighter course load	[ ]	Note takers in class	[x]
Math waiver	[ ]	Priority seating	[x]
Other special classes	[x]	Tape recorders	[x]
Priority registrations	[ ]	Videotaped classes	[ ]
Substitution of courses	[ ]	Text on tape	[x]
Exams		**Services**	
Extended time	[x]	Diagnostic tests	[ ]
Oral exams	[x]	Learning centers	[x]
Take home exams	[x]	Proofreaders	[x]
Exams on tape or computer	[ ]	Readers	[x]
Untimed exams	[ ]	Reading Machines/Kurzweil	[x]
Other accommodations	[x]	Special bookstore section	[ ]
		Typists	[x]

Credit toward degree is given for remedial courses taken.

Counseling Services

- [x] Academic
- [x] Psychological
- [x] Student Support groups
- [x] Vocational

Tutoring

Individual tutoring is available daily.

	Individual	Group
Time management	[x]	[x]
Organizational skills	[x]	[x]
Learning strategies	[x]	[x]
Study skills	[x]	[x]
Content area	[x]	[x]
Writing lab	[x]	[x]
Math lab	[x]	[x]

LD PROGRAM STAFF

Total number of LD Program staff (including director):

Full Time: 1 Part Time: 1

There is an advisor/advocate from the LD program available to students. 12 peer tutors are available to work with LD students.

Key staff person available to work with LD students: Zoe Gingold, Coordinator of Disability Services

Immaculata University

Immaculata, PA

Address: 1145 King Road, Immaculata, PA, 19345-0702
Admissions telephone: 877 IC TODAY
Admissions FAX: 610 640-1083
Dean of Enrollment Management: Michael Walden
Admissions e-mail: admiss@immaculata.edu
Web site: http://www.immaculata.edu
SAT Code: 2320   ACT Code: 3596

LD program address: 1T Faculty Center,
Dean: Dr. Janet Kane
LD program telephone: 610 647-4400, extension 3019
LD program e-mail: jkane@immaculata.edu
LD program enrollment: 11, Total campus enrollment: 2,850

GENERAL

Immaculata University is a private, women's, four-year institution. 375-acre, suburban campus in Immaculata (population: 10,000), 20 miles from Philadelphia. Major airport serves Philadelphia; bus and train serve Paoli (five miles). School operates transportation to other schools, train station, and shopping malls. Public transportation serves campus. Semester system.

LD ADMISSIONS

Students do not complete a separate application and are not simultaneously accepted to the LD program. A member of the LD program does not sit on the admissions committee. High school waivers are accepted for math and foreign language. A personal interview is recommended. Essay is not required.

SECONDARY SCHOOL REQUIREMENTS

Graduation from secondary school required; GED accepted. The following course distribution required: 4 units of English, 2 units of math, 2 units of science, 2 units of foreign language, 2 units of social studies, 4 units of academic electives.

TESTING

SAT Reasoning required; ACT may be substituted. SAT Subject recommended.

All enrolled freshmen (fall 2004):

Average SAT I Scores: Verbal: 481   Math: 502

Child Study Team report is not required. A neuropsychological or comprehensive psycho-educational evaluation is required for admission. Must be dated within 24 months of application. Tests required as part of this documentation:

- ■ WAIS-IV
- ■ WISC-IV
- ☐ SATA
- ■ Woodcock-Johnson
- ☐ Nelson-Denny Reading Test
- ■ Other

UNDERGRADUATE STUDENT BODY

Total undergraduate student enrollment: 353 Men, 2,224 Women.

Composition of student body (fall 2004):

	Undergraduate	Freshmen
International	0.7	1.2
Black	13.9	7.1
American Indian	0.0	0.1
Asian-American	4.2	1.2
Hispanic	4.9	1.6
White	71.4	87.1
Unreported	4.9	1.7
	100.0%	100.0%

18% are from out of state. 21% join a sorority. Average age of full-time undergraduates is 23. 83% of classes have fewer than 20 students, 17% have between 20 and 50 students.

STUDENT HOUSING

84% of freshmen live in college housing. Freshmen are not required to live on campus. Housing is guaranteed for all undergraduates. Campus can house 484 undergraduates. Single rooms are available for students with medical or special needs. A medical note is required.

EXPENSES

Tuition (2005-06): $19,500 per year.
Room: $4,750. Board: $4,100.
There is no additional cost for LD program/services.

LD SERVICES

LD program size is not limited.

LD services available to:

■ Freshmen   ■ Sophomores   ■ Juniors   ■ Seniors

Academic Accommodations

Curriculum		In class	
Foreign language waiver	■	Early syllabus	☐
Lighter course load	■	Note takers in class	■
Math waiver	☐	Priority seating	■
Other special classes	☐	Tape recorders	■
Priority registrations	☐	Videotaped classes	☐
Substitution of courses	■	Text on tape	☐
Exams		**Services**	
Extended time	■	Diagnostic tests	■
Oral exams	☐	Learning centers	■
Take home exams	■	Proofreaders	■
Exams on tape or computer	☐	Readers	☐
Untimed exams	■	Reading Machines/Kurzweil	☐
Other accommodations	■	Special bookstore section	☐
		Typists	☐

Credit toward degree is not given for remedial courses taken.

Counseling Services

- ■ Academic
- ■ Psychological
- ☐ Student Support groups
- ■ Vocational

Tutoring

Individual tutoring is available weekly.

Average size of tutoring groups: 1

	Individual	Group
Time management	☐	■
Organizational skills	☐	■
Learning strategies	☐	☐
Study skills	☐	■
Content area	■	☐
Writing lab	■	☐
Math lab	■	☐

LD PROGRAM STAFF

Total number of LD Program staff (including director):

Full Time: 1   Part Time: 1

There is an advisor/advocate from the LD program available to students.

Key staff person available to work with LD students: Dr. Janet Kane, Dean

Indiana University of Pennsylvania

Indiana, PA

Address: 1011 South Drive, Indiana, PA, 15705
Admissions telephone: 800 442-6830
Admissions FAX: 724 357-6281
Dean of Admissions: Dr. Rhonda Luckey
Admissions e-mail: admissions-inquiry@iup.edu
Web site: http://www.iup.edu
SAT Code: 2652 ACT Code: 3704

Director, Advising and Testing Center: Dr. Catherine Dugan
LD program telephone: 724 357-4067
LD program e-mail: cmdugan@iup.edu
Total campus enrollment: 12,163

GENERAL

Indiana University of Pennsylvania is a public, coed, four-year institution. 350-acre, suburban campus in Indiana (population: 14,895), 50 miles from Pittsburgh; branch campuses in Armstrong, Harrisburg, Monroeville, and Punxsutawney. Served by bus; major airport serves Pittsburgh; train serves Latrobe (20 miles). Public transportation serves campus. Semester system.

SECONDARY SCHOOL REQUIREMENTS

Graduation from secondary school required; GED accepted.

TESTING

SAT Reasoning required; ACT may be substituted. SAT Subject recommended.

All enrolled freshmen (fall 2004):

Average SAT I Scores: Verbal: 527 Math: 519

Child Study Team report is not required. Tests required as part of this documentation:

- ❑ WAIS-IV
- ❑ WISC-IV
- ❑ SATA
- ❑ Woodcock-Johnson
- ❑ Nelson-Denny Reading Test
- ❑ Other

UNDERGRADUATE STUDENT BODY

Total undergraduate student enrollment: 5,234 Men, 6,529 Women.

Composition of student body (fall 2004):

	Undergraduate	Freshmen
International	0.8	1.9
Black	7.0	6.1
American Indian	0.2	0.2
Asian-American	1.2	1.0
Hispanic	0.9	0.9
White	80.0	81.1
Unreported	9.9	8.8
	100.0%	100.0%

3% are from out of state. 10% join a fraternity and 11% join a sorority. Average age of full-time undergraduates is 20. 28% of classes have fewer than 20 students, 59% have between 20 and 50 students, 13% have more than 50 students.

STUDENT HOUSING

81% of freshmen live in college housing. Freshmen are required to live on campus. Housing is guaranteed for all undergraduates. Campus can house 3,993 undergraduates.

EXPENSES Tuition (2005-06): $5,031 per year (in-state), $12,454 (out-of-state). $4,016 per year (state residents), $6,024 (Ohio and West Virginia residents), $10,040 (other out-of-state).Room: $3,028. Board: $1,960.There is no additional cost for LD program/services.

LD SERVICES

LD program size is not limited.

LD services available to:

❑ Freshmen ❑ Sophomores ❑ Juniors ❑ Seniors

Academic Accommodations

Curriculum		In class	
Foreign language waiver	❑	Early syllabus	❑
Lighter course load	❑	Note takers in class	■
Math waiver	❑	Priority seating	❑
Other special classes	❑	Tape recorders	■
Priority registrations	❑	Videotaped classes	❑
Substitution of courses	❑	Text on tape	❑
Exams		**Services**	
Extended time	❑	Diagnostic tests	❑
Oral exams	■	Learning centers	■
Take home exams	❑	Proofreaders	❑
Exams on tape or computer	❑	Readers	■
Untimed exams	■	Reading Machines/Kurzweil	■
Other accommodations	❑	Special bookstore section	❑
		Typists	❑

Credit toward degree is not given for remedial courses taken.

Counseling Services

- ❑ Academic
- ❑ Psychological
- ❑ Student Support groups
- ❑ Vocational

Tutoring

	Individual	Group
Time management	❑	❑
Organizational skills	❑	❑
Learning strategies	❑	❑
Study skills	❑	❑
Content area	❑	❑
Writing lab	❑	❑
Math lab	❑	❑

LD PROGRAM STAFF

Total number of LD Program staff (including director):

Full Time: 5 Part Time: 5

Key staff person available to work with LD students: Dr. Catherine Dugan, Director, Advising and Testing Center.

Juniata College

Huntingdon, PA

Address: 1700 Moore Street, Huntingdon, PA, 16652
Admissions telephone: 877 JUNIATA
Admissions FAX: 814 641-3100
Dean of Enrollment: Terri Bollman-Dalansky
Admissions e-mail: admissions@juniata.edu
Web site: http://www.juniata.edu
SAT Code: 2341 ACT Code: 3600

Director, Academic Support Services: Sarah M. Clarkson
LD program telephone: 814 641-3161
LD program e-mail: clarkss@juniata.edu
Total campus enrollment: 1,427

GENERAL

Juniata College is a private, coed, four-year institution. 110-acre campus in Huntingdon (population: 6,918), 30 miles from both Altoona and State College, plus 316-acre nature preserve, 665-acre environmental field station in Marklesburg. Served by train; airport and bus serve State College; smaller airport serves Altoona. School operates transportation to State College. Semester system.

LD ADMISSIONS

Application Deadline: 03/15. Students do not complete a separate application and are not simultaneously accepted to the LD program. A personal interview is recommended. Essay is required and may be typed. Each applicant who identifies as an LD candidate is interviewed by the appropriate personnel and counseled regarding their potential for success.

SECONDARY SCHOOL REQUIREMENTS

Graduation from secondary school required; GED accepted. The following course distribution required: 4 units of English, 3 units of math, 3 units of science, 2 units of foreign language, 1 unit of social studies, 3 units of history.

TESTING

SAT Reasoning or ACT recommended. SAT Subject recommended.

All enrolled freshmen (fall 2004):

Average SAT I Scores: Verbal: 580 Math: 582

Child Study Team report is not required. Tests required as part of this documentation:

- ☐ WAIS-IV
- ☐ WISC-IV
- ☐ SATA
- ☐ Woodcock-Johnson
- ☐ Nelson-Denny Reading Test
- ☐ Other

UNDERGRADUATE STUDENT BODY

Total undergraduate student enrollment: 547 Men, 755 Women.

Composition of student body (fall 2004):

	Undergraduate	Freshmen
International	0.8	4.1
Black	1.0	1.5
American Indian	0.8	0.4
Asian-American	2.3	1.5
Hispanic	1.8	1.2
White	92.3	90.7
Unreported	1.0	0.6
	100.0%	100.0%

24% are from out of state. Average age of full-time undergraduates is 20. 66% of classes have fewer than 20 students, 31% have between 20 and 50 students, 3% have more than 50 students.

STUDENT HOUSING

96% of freshmen live in college housing. Freshmen are required to live on campus. Housing is guaranteed for all undergraduates. Campus can house 1,175 undergraduates. Single rooms are not available for students with medical or special needs.

EXPENSES

Tuition (2005-06): $25,260 per year.
Room: $3,800. Board: $3,440.

There is no additional cost for LD program/services.

LD SERVICES

LD program size is not limited.

LD services available to:

☑ Freshmen ☑ Sophomores ☑ Juniors ☑ Seniors

Academic Accommodations

Curriculum		**In class**	
Foreign language waiver	☐	Early syllabus	☐
Lighter course load	☑	Note takers in class	☐
Math waiver	☐	Priority seating	☐
Other special classes	☐	Tape recorders	☐
Priority registrations	☐	Videotaped classes	☐
Substitution of courses	☐	Text on tape	☐
Exams		**Services**	
Extended time	☑	Diagnostic tests	☐
Oral exams	☐	Learning centers	☐
Take home exams	☐	Proofreaders	☐
Exams on tape or computer	☐	Readers	☐
Untimed exams	☑	Reading Machines/Kurzweil	☐
Other accommodations	☐	Special bookstore section	☐
		Typists	☐

Credit toward degree is not given for remedial courses taken.

Counseling Services

- ☑ Academic
- ☑ Psychological
- ☐ Student Support groups
- ☐ Vocational

Tutoring

Individual tutoring is available daily.

	Individual	Group
Time management	☐	☐
Organizational skills	☐	☐
Learning strategies	☐	☐
Study skills	☑	☑
Content area	☐	☐
Writing lab	☑	☐
Math lab	☐	☐

UNIQUE LD PROGRAM FEATURES

Juniata does not have a formal "program" for learning-disabled students; it provides limited support services on an as-needed basis. Services are provided during working hours only.

LD PROGRAM STAFF

Total number of LD Program staff (including director):

Full Time: 1 Part Time: 1

There is an advisor/advocate from the LD program available to students.

Key staff person available to work with LD students: Sarah M. Clarkson, Director, Academic Support Services.

King's College

Wilkes-Barre, PA

Address: 133 North River Street, Wilkes-Barre, PA, 18711
Admissions telephone: 888 546-4772
Admissions FAX: 570 208-5971
Director of Admissions: Michelle Lawrence-Schmude
Admissions e-mail: admissions@kings.edu
Web site: http://www.kings.edu
SAT Code: 2353 ACT Code: 3604

LD program name: First Year Academic Studies Program
Director, Academic Skills Program: Jacintha Burke
LD program telephone: 570 208-5800
LD program e-mail: jaburke@kings.edu
LD program enrollment: 58, Total campus enrollment: 2,060

GENERAL

King's College is a private, coed, four-year institution. 48-acre campus in Wilkes-Barre (population: 43,123), 100 miles from Philadelphia. Served by bus; major airport serves Philadelphia, smaller airport serves Avoca (10 miles). Public transportation serves campus. Semester system.

LD ADMISSIONS

Application Deadline: 04/01. Students complete a separate application and are simultaneously accepted to the LD program. A member of the LD program does not sit on the admissions committee. High school waivers are accepted for foreign language. A personal interview is required. Essay is required and may be typed. Foreign language requirement may be waived.

For fall 2004, 30 completed self-identified LD applications were received. 15 applications were offered admission, and 8 enrolled.

SECONDARY SCHOOL REQUIREMENTS

Graduation from secondary school required; GED accepted. The following course distribution required: 4 units of English, 3 units of math, 3 units of science, 2 units of foreign language, 3 units of social studies, 1 unit of history.

TESTING

SAT Reasoning or ACT required.

All enrolled freshmen (fall 2004):

Average SAT I Scores: Verbal: 524 Math: 524

Child Study Team report is required if student is classified. A neuropsychological or comprehensive psycho-educational evaluation is required for admission. Must be dated within 24 months of application. Tests required as part of this documentation:

- [x] WAIS-IV
- [x] WISC-IV
- [ ] SATA
- [x] Woodcock-Johnson
- [ ] Nelson-Denny Reading Test
- [x] Other

UNDERGRADUATE STUDENT BODY

Total undergraduate student enrollment: 991 Men, 1,077 Women.

Composition of student body (fall 2004):

	Undergraduate	Freshmen
International	0.3	0.5
Black	2.4	1.8
American Indian	0.0	0.1
Asian-American	0.4	0.5
Hispanic	2.0	1.5
White	84.0	87.2
Unreported	10.9	8.4
	100.0%	100.0%

25% are from out of state. Average age of full-time undergraduates is 20. 56% of classes have fewer than 20 students, 44% have between 20 and 50 students.

STUDENT HOUSING

69% of freshmen live in college housing. Freshmen are required to live on campus. Housing is guaranteed for all undergraduates. Campus can house 866 undergraduates. Single rooms are available for students with medical or special needs. A medical note is required.

EXPENSES

Tuition (2005-06): $20,320 per year.
Room: $3,980. Board: $4,610.
Additional cost for LD program/services: $2,400 per semester, first year.

LD SERVICES

LD program size is limited.

LD services available to:

- [x] Freshmen
- [x] Sophomores
- [x] Juniors
- [x] Seniors

Academic Accommodations

Curriculum

- Foreign language waiver [ ]
- Lighter course load [x]
- Math waiver [ ]
- Other special classes [ ]
- Priority registrations [ ]
- Substitution of courses [ ]

Exams

- Extended time [x]
- Oral exams [x]
- Take home exams [ ]
- Exams on tape or computer [ ]
- Untimed exams [x]
- Other accommodations [ ]

In class

- Early syllabus [ ]
- Note takers in class [x]
- Priority seating [x]
- Tape recorders [x]
- Videotaped classes [ ]
- Text on tape [ ]

Services

- Diagnostic tests [ ]
- Learning centers [x]
- Proofreaders [ ]
- Readers [ ]
- Reading Machines/Kurzweil [x]
- Special bookstore section [ ]
- Typists [ ]

Credit toward degree is given for remedial courses taken.

Counseling Services

- [x] Academic — Meets 50 times per academic year
- [ ] Psychological
- [ ] Student Support groups
- [ ] Vocational

Tutoring

Individual tutoring is available daily.

Average size of tutoring groups: 4

	Individual	Group
Time management	[x]	[x]
Organizational skills	[x]	[x]
Learning strategies	[x]	[x]
Study skills	[x]	[x]
Content area	[x]	[ ]
Writing lab	[x]	[ ]
Math lab	[x]	[ ]

LD PROGRAM STAFF

Total number of LD Program staff (including director):

Full Time: 2 Part Time: 2

There is an advisor/advocate from the LD program available to students. The advisor/advocate meets with faculty four times per month and students 12 times per month.

Kutztown University of Pennsylvania

Kutztown, PA

Address: 15200 Kutztown Road, Kutztown, PA, 19530-0730
Admissions telephone: 877 628-1915
Admissions FAX: 610 683-1375
Director of Admissions: Dr. William Stahler
Admissions e-mail: admission@kutztown.edu
Web site: http://www.kutztown.edu
SAT Code: 2653 ACT Code: 3706

Coordinator of Disability Services - ADA: Patricia Richter
LD program telephone: 610 683-4108
LD program e-mail: richter@kutztown.edu
Total campus enrollment: 8,527

GENERAL

Kutztown University of Pennsylvania is a public, coed, four-year institution. 326-acre campus in Kutztown (population: 5,067), 20 miles from both Allentown and Reading and 90 miles from Philadelphia. Served by bus; airport serves Allentown and Reading; train serves Philadelphia. Public transportation serves campus. Semester system.

LD ADMISSIONS

A personal interview is not required. Essay is not required.

SECONDARY SCHOOL REQUIREMENTS

Graduation from secondary school required; GED accepted.

TESTING

SAT Reasoning required; ACT may be substituted. SAT Subject recommended.

All enrolled freshmen (fall 2004):

Average SAT I Scores: Verbal: 500 Math: 499

Child Study Team report is not required. Tests required as part of this documentation:

- ☐ WAIS-IV
- ☐ WISC-IV
- ☐ SATA
- ☐ Woodcock-Johnson
- ☐ Nelson-Denny Reading Test
- ☐ Other

UNDERGRADUATE STUDENT BODY

Total undergraduate student enrollment: 2,925 Men, 4,368 Women.

Composition of student body (fall 2004):

	Undergraduate	Freshmen
International	0.2	0.8
Black	9.6	6.4
American Indian	0.3	0.2
Asian-American	1.2	1.0
Hispanic	4.1	3.3
White	82.6	86.6
Unreported	2.0	1.7
	100.0%	100.0%

9% are from out of state. 4% join a fraternity and 4% join a sorority. Average age of full-time undergraduates is 21. 26% of classes have fewer than 20 students, 65% have between 20 and 50 students, 9% have more than 50 students.

STUDENT HOUSING

88% of freshmen live in college housing. Housing is not guaranteed for all undergraduates. Campus can house 3,500 undergraduates. Single rooms are available for students with medical or special needs. A medical note is required.

EXPENSES

Tuition (2005-06): $4,910 per year (in-state), $12,176 (out-of-state). Room: $3,950. Board: $1,980.
There is no additional cost for LD program/services.

LD SERVICES

LD program size is not limited.

LD services available to:

☐ Freshmen ☐ Sophomores ☐ Juniors ☐ Seniors

Academic Accommodations

Curriculum		In class	
Foreign language waiver	☐	Early syllabus	☐
Lighter course load	■	Note takers in class	■
Math waiver	☐	Priority seating	☐
Other special classes	☐	Tape recorders	☐
Priority registrations	☐	Videotaped classes	☐
Substitution of courses	☐	Text on tape	☐
Exams		**Services**	
Extended time	■	Diagnostic tests	☐
Oral exams	■	Learning centers	■
Take home exams	☐	Proofreaders	☐
Exams on tape or computer	☐	Readers	■
Untimed exams	☐	Reading Machines/Kurzweil	☐
Other accommodations	☐	Special bookstore section	☐
		Typists	☐

Credit toward degree is not given for remedial courses taken.

Counseling Services

- ☐ Academic
- ☐ Psychological
- ☐ Student Support groups
- ☐ Vocational

Tutoring

Individual tutoring is available daily.

Average size of tutoring groups: 2

	Individual	Group
Time management	■	☐
Organizational skills	■	☐
Learning strategies	■	☐
Study skills	■	☐
Content area	■	☐
Writing lab	☐	☐
Math lab	☐	■

LD PROGRAM STAFF

Total number of LD Program staff (including director):

Full Time: 2 Part Time: 2

Key staff person available to work with LD students: Patricia Richter, Coordinator of Disability Services - ADA.

LaRoche College

Pittsburgh, PA

Address: 9000 Babcock Boulevard, Pittsburgh, PA, 15237
Admissions telephone: 800 838-4LRC
Admissions FAX: 412 536-1048
Director of Admissions and Enrollment Management: Thomas B. Hassett
Admissions e-mail: admissions@laroche.edu
Web site: http://www.laroche.edu
SAT Code: 2379 ACT Code: 3607

Assistant Dean/Advisor: R. Lance Shaeffer
LD program telephone: 412 536-1295
LD program e-mail: shaeffl1@laroche.edu
LD program enrollment: 49, Total campus enrollment: 1,484

GENERAL

LaRoche College is a private, coed, four-year institution. 80-acre, suburban campus in Pittsburgh (population: 334,563). Served by air, bus, and train. Public transportation serves campus. Semester system.

LD ADMISSIONS

Students do not complete a separate application and are simultaneously accepted to the LD program. A personal interview is recommended. Essay is required and may be typed.

For fall 2004, 10 completed self-identified LD applications were received. 10 applications were offered admission, and 10 enrolled.

SECONDARY SCHOOL REQUIREMENTS

Graduation from secondary school required; GED accepted. The following course distribution required: 4 units of English, 3 units of math, 3 units of science, 3 units of social studies, 3 units of history.

TESTING

SAT Reasoning or ACT required. SAT Subject recommended.

All enrolled freshmen (fall 2004):

Average SAT I Scores:	Verbal: 460	Math: 460
Average ACT Scores:	Composite: 19	

Child Study Team report is required if student is classified. Tests required as part of this documentation:

- [ ] WAIS-IV
- [ ] WISC-IV
- [ ] SATA
- [ ] Woodcock-Johnson
- [ ] Nelson-Denny Reading Test
- [ ] Other

UNDERGRADUATE STUDENT BODY

Total undergraduate student enrollment: 640 Men, 1,021 Women.

Composition of student body (fall 2004):

	Undergraduate	Freshmen
International	2.3	9.2
Black	6.9	4.2
American Indian	2.3	1.0
Asian-American	0.9	0.8
Hispanic	0.9	0.7
White	84.8	83.6
Unreported	1.9	0.5
	100.0%	100.0%

6% are from out of state. Average age of full-time undergraduates is 22. 81% of classes have fewer than 20 students, 19% have between 20 and 50 students.

STUDENT HOUSING

75% of freshmen live in college housing. Freshmen are not required to live on campus. Housing is guaranteed for all undergraduates. Campus can house 627 undergraduates.

EXPENSES

Tuition (2005-06): $16,780 per year.
Room: $4,600. Board: $2,744.
There is no additional cost for LD program/services.

LD SERVICES

LD program size is not limited.

LD services available to:

- [x] Freshmen
- [x] Sophomores
- [x] Juniors
- [x] Seniors

Academic Accommodations

Curriculum		In class	
Foreign language waiver	[ ]	Early syllabus	[ ]
Lighter course load	[x]	Note takers in class	[x]
Math waiver	[ ]	Priority seating	[ ]
Other special classes	[ ]	Tape recorders	[x]
Priority registrations	[ ]	Videotaped classes	[x]
Substitution of courses	[ ]	Text on tape	[ ]
Exams		**Services**	
Extended time	[x]	Diagnostic tests	[ ]
Oral exams	[x]	Learning centers	[x]
Take home exams	[ ]	Proofreaders	[ ]
Exams on tape or computer	[ ]	Readers	[x]
Untimed exams	[x]	Reading Machines/Kurzweil	[ ]
Other accommodations	[ ]	Special bookstore section	[ ]
		Typists	[ ]

Credit toward degree is not given for remedial courses taken.

Counseling Services

- [ ] Academic
- [ ] Psychological
- [ ] Student Support groups
- [ ] Vocational

Tutoring

Individual tutoring is available.

	Individual	Group
Time management	[ ]	[ ]
Organizational skills	[ ]	[ ]
Learning strategies	[ ]	[ ]
Study skills	[ ]	[ ]
Content area	[ ]	[ ]
Writing lab	[ ]	[ ]
Math lab	[ ]	[ ]

LD PROGRAM STAFF

Total number of LD Program staff (including director):

Full Time: 3 Part Time: 3

Key staff person available to work with LD students: R. Lance Shaeffer, Assistant Dean for Academic Enrichment & Project Achieve/ACT 101.

LaSalle University

Philadelphia, PA

Address: 1900 West Olney Avenue, Philadelphia, PA, 19141-1199
Admissions telephone: 800 328-1910
Admissions FAX: 215 951-1656
Dean of Admission and Financial Aid: Robert Voss
Admissions e-mail: admiss@lasalle.edu
Web site: http://www.lasalle.edu
SAT Code: 2363 ACT Code: 3608

Affirmative Action Officer: Rose Lee Pauline
LD program telephone: 215 951-1014
Total campus enrollment: 4,341

GENERAL

LaSalle University is a private, coed, four-year institution. 100-acre, urban campus in Philadelphia (population: 1,517,550); branch campus in Bucks County. Served by air, bus, and train. School operates transportation to other areas of Philadelphia. Public transportation serves campus. Semester system.

LD ADMISSIONS

A personal interview is recommended. Essay is required and may be typed.

SECONDARY SCHOOL REQUIREMENTS

Graduation from secondary school required; GED accepted. The following course distribution required: 4 units of English, 3 units of math, 1 unit of science, 2 units of foreign language, 1 unit of history, 5 units of academic electives.

TESTING

SAT Reasoning required; ACT may be substituted. SAT Subject recommended.

All enrolled freshmen (fall 2004):

Average SAT I Scores:	Verbal: 538	Math: 533
Average ACT Scores:	Composite: 23	

Child Study Team report is not required. Tests required as part of this documentation:

- ☐ WAIS-IV
- ☐ WISC-IV
- ☐ SATA
- ☐ Woodcock-Johnson
- ☐ Nelson-Denny Reading Test
- ☐ Other

UNDERGRADUATE STUDENT BODY

Total undergraduate student enrollment: 1,666 Men, 2,239 Women.

Composition of student body (fall 2004):

	Undergraduate	Freshmen
International	0.7	0.8
Black	7.9	14.4
American Indian	0.4	0.2
Asian-American	3.7	3.4
Hispanic	9.4	6.6
White	69.2	68.8
Unreported	8.7	5.8
	100.0%	100.0%

34% are from out of state. 7% join a fraternity and 10% join a sorority. Average age of full-time undergraduates is 21. 45% of classes have fewer than 20 students, 55% have between 20 and 50 students.

STUDENT HOUSING

82% of freshmen live in college housing. Freshmen are not required to live on campus. Housing is guaranteed for all undergraduates. Campus can house 2,172 undergraduates.

EXPENSES

Tuition (2005-06): $25,880 per year.
Room: $4,920. Board: $4,930.
There is no additional cost for LD program/services.

LD SERVICES

LD program size is not limited.

LD services available to:

☐ Freshmen ☐ Sophomores ☐ Juniors ☐ Seniors

Academic Accommodations

Curriculum		In class	
Foreign language waiver	☐	Early syllabus	☐
Lighter course load	■	Note takers in class	■
Math waiver	☐	Priority seating	☐
Other special classes	☐	Tape recorders	■
Priority registrations	☐	Videotaped classes	☐
Substitution of courses	☐	Text on tape	☐
Exams		**Services**	
Extended time	■	Diagnostic tests	☐
Oral exams	☐	Learning centers	☐
Take home exams	☐	Proofreaders	☐
Exams on tape or computer	☐	Readers	☐
Untimed exams	■	Reading Machines/Kurzweil	☐
Other accommodations	☐	Special bookstore section	☐
		Typists	☐

Credit toward degree is not given for remedial courses taken.

Counseling Services

- ☐ Academic
- ☐ Psychological
- ☐ Student Support groups
- ☐ Vocational

Tutoring

	Individual	Group
Time management	☐	☐
Organizational skills	☐	☐
Learning strategies	☐	☐
Study skills	☐	☐
Content area	☐	☐
Writing lab	☐	☐
Math lab	☐	☐

LD PROGRAM STAFF

Total number of LD Program staff (including director):

Full Time: 5 Part Time: 5

Lebanon Valley College of Pennsylvania

Annville, PA

Address: 101 North College Avenue, Annville, PA, 17003
Admissions telephone: 866 LVC-4ADM
Admissions FAX: 717 867-6026
Dean of Admission and Financial Aid: Susan Sarisky
Admissions e-mail: admission@lvc.edu
Web site: http://www.lvc.edu
SAT Code: 2364 ACT Code: 3610

LD program name: Office of Disability Services
Coordinator, Disability Services: Yvonne Foster
LD program telephone: 717 867-6158
LD program e-mail: foster@lvc.edu
LD program enrollment: 105, Total campus enrollment: 1,738

GENERAL

Lebanon Valley College of Pennsylvania is a private, coed, four-year institution. 250-acre campus in Annville (population: 4,518), 21 miles from Harrisburg and 85 miles from Philadelphia; branch campuses in Camp Hill, Lancaster, and York. Served by bus; major airport serves Philadelphia; airport and train serve Harrisburg. Public transportation serves campus. Semester system.

LD ADMISSIONS

Students do not complete a separate application and are simultaneously accepted to the LD program. A member of the LD program does not sit on the admissions committee. A personal interview is recommended. Essay is not required.

For fall 2004, 50 completed self-identified LD applications were received. 38 applications were offered admission, and 28 enrolled.

SECONDARY SCHOOL REQUIREMENTS

Graduation from secondary school required; GED accepted. The following course distribution required: 4 units of English, 2 units of math, 1 unit of science, 2 units of foreign language, 1 unit of social studies.

TESTING

SAT Reasoning required; ACT may be substituted. SAT Subject required.

All enrolled freshmen (fall 2004):

Average SAT I Scores: Verbal: 552 Math: 561
Average ACT Scores: Composite:

Child Study Team report is not required. A neuropsychological or comprehensive psycho-educational evaluation is required for admission. Must be dated within 36 months of application. Tests required as part of this documentation:

- [x] WAIS-IV
- [x] WISC-IV
- [ ] SATA
- [x] Woodcock-Johnson
- [x] Nelson-Denny Reading Test
- [ ] Other

UNDERGRADUATE STUDENT BODY

Total undergraduate student enrollment: 772 Men, 1,148 Women.

Composition of student body (fall 2004):

	Undergraduate	Freshmen
International	0.5	0.4
Black	1.4	1.6
American Indian	0.3	0.2
Asian-American	3.1	1.6
Hispanic	2.4	1.4
White	88.2	91.0
Unreported	4.1	3.8
	100.0%	100.0%

10% join a fraternity and 12% join a sorority. Average age of full-time undergraduates is 20. 57% of classes have fewer than 20 students, 42% have between 20 and 50 students, 1% have more than 50 students.

STUDENT HOUSING

87% of freshmen live in college housing. Freshmen are required to live on campus. Housing is not guaranteed for all undergraduates. Housing is provided for eight semesters. Campus can house 1,151 undergraduates. Single rooms are available for students with medical or special needs. A medical note is required.

EXPENSES

Tuition (2005-06): $24,210 per year.
Room: $3,340. Board: $3,500.
There is no additional cost for LD program/services.

LD SERVICES

LD program size is not limited.

LD services available to:

- [x] Freshmen
- [x] Sophomores
- [x] Juniors
- [x] Seniors

Academic Accommodations

Curriculum		In class	
Foreign language waiver	[ ]	Early syllabus	[x]
Lighter course load	[x]	Note takers in class	[x]
Math waiver	[ ]	Priority seating	[x]
Other special classes	[ ]	Tape recorders	[x]
Priority registrations	[x]	Videotaped classes	[x]
Substitution of courses	[ ]	Text on tape	[ ]
Exams		**Services**	
Extended time	[x]	Diagnostic tests	[x]
Oral exams	[x]	Learning centers	[x]
Take home exams	[ ]	Proofreaders	[x]
Exams on tape or computer	[x]	Readers	[x]
Untimed exams	[ ]	Reading Machines/Kurzweil	[x]
Other accommodations	[x]	Special bookstore section	[ ]
		Typists	[ ]

Credit toward degree is not given for remedial courses taken.

Counseling Services

- [x] Academic
- [x] Psychological
- [ ] Student Support groups
- [x] Vocational

Tutoring

Individual tutoring is available daily.

Average size of tutoring groups: 1

	Individual	Group
Time management	[x]	[ ]
Organizational skills	[x]	[ ]
Learning strategies	[x]	[ ]
Study skills	[x]	[ ]
Content area	[x]	[ ]
Writing lab	[x]	[ ]
Math lab	[x]	[ ]

LD PROGRAM STAFF

Total number of LD Program staff (including director):

Full Time: 1 Part Time: 1

There is an advisor/advocate from the LD program available to students.

Key staff person available to work with LD students: Yvonne Foster, Coordinator, Disability Services.

LD Program web site: www.lvc.edu/disability-services

Lehigh University

Bethlehem, PA

Address: 27 Memorial Drive West, Bethlehem, PA, 18015
Admissions telephone: 610 758-3100
Admissions FAX: 610 758-4361
Interim Dean of Admissions and Financial Aid: Eric Kaplan
Admissions e-mail: admissions@lehigh.edu
Web site: http://www.lehigh.edu
SAT Code: 2365 ACT Code: 3612

LD program name: Academic Support Services
LD program address: UC 212, 29 Trembley Dr
Assistant Dean: Cheryl A. Ashcroft
LD program telephone: 610 758-4152
LD program e-mail: caa4@lehigh.edu
LD program enrollment: 189, Total campus enrollment: 4,577

GENERAL

Lehigh University is a private, coed, four-year institution. 1,600-acre campus (main campus plus two others) in Bethlehem (population: 71,329), 55 miles from Philadelphia. Served by bus; airport serves Newark, NJ. (45 miles); smaller airport serves Lehigh Valley (six miles); train serves Philadelphia. School operates transportation to locations around campus. Public transportation serves campus. Semester system.

LD ADMISSIONS

Students do not complete a separate application and are not simultaneously accepted to the LD program. A member of the LD program does not sit on the admissions committee. High school waivers are accepted for foreign language. A personal interview is recommended. Essay is required and may be typed.

SECONDARY SCHOOL REQUIREMENTS

Graduation from secondary school required; GED accepted. The following course distribution required: 4 units of English, 3 units of math, 2 units of science, 2 units of foreign language, 2 units of social studies, 3 units of academic electives.

TESTING

SAT Reasoning or ACT required. SAT Subject recommended.

All enrolled freshmen (fall 2004):

Average SAT I Scores: Verbal: 632 Math: 672

Child Study Team report is not required. A neuropsychological or comprehensive psycho-educational evaluation is required for admission. Must be dated within 36 months of application. Tests required as part of this documentation:

- [x] WAIS-IV
- [ ] WISC-IV
- [x] SATA
- [x] Woodcock-Johnson
- [x] Nelson-Denny Reading Test
- [ ] Other

UNDERGRADUATE STUDENT BODY

Total undergraduate student enrollment: 2,750 Men, 1,900 Women.

Composition of student body (fall 2004):

	Undergraduate	Freshmen
International	2.1	2.7
Black	2.5	2.9
American Indian	0.0	0.3
Asian-American	6.0	6.0
Hispanic	2.8	2.3
White	79.8	77.8
Unreported	6.8	8.0
	100.0%	100.0%

69% are from out of state. 33% join a fraternity and 39% join a sorority. Average age of full-time undergraduates is 20. 62% of classes have fewer than 20 students, 32% have between 20 and 50 students, 6% have more than 50 students.

STUDENT HOUSING

Freshmen are required to live on campus. Housing is guaranteed for all undergraduates. Campus can house 3,426 undergraduates. Single rooms are available for students with medical or special needs. A medical note is required.

EXPENSES

Tuition (2005-06): $31,180 per year.

Room: $4,890. Board: $3,670.
There is no additional cost for LD program/services.

LD SERVICES

LD program size is not limited.

LD services available to:

- [x] Freshmen
- [x] Sophomores
- [x] Juniors
- [x] Seniors

Academic Accommodations

Curriculum

- [ ] Foreign language waiver
- [x] Lighter course load
- [ ] Math waiver
- [ ] Other special classes
- [ ] Priority registrations
- [ ] Substitution of courses

Exams

- [ ] Extended time
- [ ] Oral exams
- [ ] Take home exams
- [ ] Exams on tape or computer
- [ ] Untimed exams
- [ ] Other accommodations

In class

- [ ] Early syllabus
- [ ] Note takers in class
- [ ] Priority seating
- [ ] Tape recorders
- [ ] Videotaped classes
- [ ] Text on tape

Services

- [ ] Diagnostic tests
- [x] Learning centers
- [ ] Proofreaders
- [ ] Readers
- [x] Reading Machines/Kurzweil
- [ ] Special bookstore section
- [ ] Typists

Credit toward degree is not given for remedial courses taken.

Counseling Services

- [x] Academic
- [x] Psychological
- [ ] Student Support groups
- [x] Vocational

Tutoring

Individual tutoring is available weekly.

Average size of tutoring groups: 6

	Individual	Group
Time management	[ ]	[ ]
Organizational skills	[ ]	[ ]
Learning strategies	[ ]	[ ]
Study skills	[ ]	[ ]
Content area	[ ]	[ ]
Writing lab	[ ]	[ ]
Math lab	[ ]	[ ]

LD PROGRAM STAFF

Total number of LD Program staff (including director):

Full Time: 2 Part Time: 2

There is an advisor/advocate from the LD program available to students. Four graduate students and 25 peer tutors are available to work with LD students.

Key staff person available to work with LD students: Cheryl A. Ashcroft, Assistant Dean/Academic Support Services.

LD Program web site: www.lehigh.edu/disabilities

Lincoln University

Lincoln University, PA

Address: P.O. Box 179, Lincoln University, PA, 19352
Admissions telephone: 800 790-0191
Admissions FAX: 610 932-1209
Director of Admissions: Michael Taylor
Admissions e-mail: admiss@lu.lincoln.edu
Web site: http://www.lincoln.edu
SAT Code: 2367 ACT Code: 3614

Director, Academic Advising Center: Nancy A. Kenner
LD program telephone: 610 932-8300, extension 3624
LD program e-mail: kenner@lu.lincoln.edu
Total campus enrollment: 1,523

GENERAL

Lincoln University is a public, coed, four-year institution. 422-acre campus in Lincoln University (population: 5,000), 45 miles from Philadelphia and 55 miles from Baltimore, MD. Major airport serves Philadelphia; bus and train serve Wilmington, DE. (25 miles). Semester system.

LD ADMISSIONS

A personal interview is not required. Essay is required and may be typed.

SECONDARY SCHOOL REQUIREMENTS

Graduation from secondary school required; GED not accepted. The following course distribution required: 4 units of English, 3 units of math, 3 units of science, 3 units of social studies, 5 units of academic electives.

TESTING

SAT Reasoning or ACT required. SAT Subject recommended.

All enrolled freshmen (fall 2004):

Average SAT I Scores: Verbal: 420 Math: 414

Child Study Team report is not required. Tests required as part of this documentation:

- ☐ WAIS-IV
- ☐ WISC-IV
- ☐ SATA
- ☐ Woodcock-Johnson
- ☐ Nelson-Denny Reading Test
- ☐ Other

UNDERGRADUATE STUDENT BODY

Total undergraduate student enrollment: 577 Men, 861 Women.

Composition of student body (fall 2004):

	Undergraduate	Freshmen
International	3.6	8.1
Black	95.5	90.6
American Indian	0.0	0.1
Asian-American	0.0	0.0
Hispanic	0.4	0.3
White	0.5	0.9
Unreported	0.0	0.0
	100.0%	100.0%

53% are from out of state. 3% join a fraternity and 8% join a sorority. Average age of full-time undergraduates is 21. 44% of classes have fewer than 20 students, 54% have between 20 and 50 students, 2% have more than 50 students.

STUDENT HOUSING

99% of freshmen live in college housing. Freshmen are required to live on campus. Housing is guaranteed for all undergraduates. Campus can house 1,400 undergraduates.

EXPENSES

Tuition (2005-06): $5,782 per year (in-state), $10,022 (out-of-state).
Room: $3,692. Board: $3,100.
There is no additional cost for LD program/services.

LD SERVICES

LD program size is not limited.

LD services available to:

☐ Freshmen ☐ Sophomores ☐ Juniors ☐ Seniors

Academic Accommodations

Curriculum		In class	
Foreign language waiver	☐	Early syllabus	☐
Lighter course load	■	Note takers in class	☐
Math waiver	☐	Priority seating	☐
Other special classes	☐	Tape recorders	■
Priority registrations	☐	Videotaped classes	■
Substitution of courses	☐	Text on tape	☐
Exams		**Services**	
Extended time	■	Diagnostic tests	☐
Oral exams	■	Learning centers	■
Take home exams	☐	Proofreaders	☐
Exams on tape or computer	☐	Readers	■
Untimed exams	■	Reading Machines/Kurzweil	☐
Other accommodations	☐	Special bookstore section	☐
		Typists	☐

Credit toward degree is not given for remedial courses taken.

Counseling Services

- ☐ Academic
- ☐ Psychological
- ☐ Student Support groups
- ☐ Vocational

Tutoring

	Individual	Group
Time management	☐	☐
Organizational skills	☐	☐
Learning strategies	☐	☐
Study skills	☐	☐
Content area	☐	☐
Writing lab	☐	☐
Math lab	☐	☐

LD PROGRAM STAFF

Total number of LD Program staff (including director):

Full Time: 1 Part Time: 1

Key staff person available to work with LD students: Dr. Ayo Gooden, Director, Act 101/T.I.M.E. Program.

Lock Haven University of Pennsylvania

Lock Haven, PA

Address: 401 North Fairview Street, Lock Haven, PA, 17745
Admissions telephone: 800 332-8900 (in-state), 800 233-8978 (out-of-state)
Admissions FAX: 570 893-2201
Director of Admission: Stephen Lee
Admissions e-mail: admissions@lhup.edu
Web site: http://www.lhup.edu
SAT Code: 2654 ACT Code: 3708

Director: Dr. Reynol Junco
LD program telephone: 570 893-2926
LD program e-mail: rjunco@lhup.edu
Total campus enrollment: 4,875

GENERAL

Lock Haven University of Pennsylvania is a public, coed, four-year institution. 165-acre campus in Lock Haven (population: 9,149), 30 miles from Williamsport and 125 miles from Harrisburg; branch campus in Clearfield. Major airport serves Pittsburgh (180 miles); bus serves Williamsport; train serves State College (45 miles). Semester system.

LD ADMISSIONS

A personal interview is not required. Essay is not required.

SECONDARY SCHOOL REQUIREMENTS

Graduation from secondary school required; GED accepted. The following course distribution required: 4 units of English, 3 units of math, 3 units of science, 2 units of social studies, 2 units of history.

TESTING

SAT Reasoning or ACT required. SAT Subject recommended.

All enrolled freshmen (fall 2004):

Average SAT I Scores:	Verbal: 487	Math: 493
Average ACT Scores:	Composite: 20	

Child Study Team report is not required. Tests required as part of this documentation:

- ☐ WAIS-IV
- ☐ WISC-IV
- ☐ SATA
- ☐ Woodcock-Johnson
- ☐ Nelson-Denny Reading Test
- ☐ Other

UNDERGRADUATE STUDENT BODY

Total undergraduate student enrollment: 1,681 Men, 2,400 Women.

Composition of student body (fall 2004):

	Undergraduate	Freshmen
International	0.6	1.2
Black	4.7	3.8
American Indian	0.2	0.3
Asian-American	0.7	0.8
Hispanic	3.1	1.6
White	89.2	91.2
Unreported	1.5	1.1
	100.0%	100.0%

9% are from out of state. 5% join a fraternity and 4% join a sorority. Average age of full-time undergraduates is 21. 30% of classes have fewer than 20 students, 66% have between 20 and 50 students, 4% have more than 50 students.

STUDENT HOUSING

78% of freshmen live in college housing. Freshmen are required to live on campus. Housing is not guaranteed for all undergraduates. Campus housing is available for all unmarried students regardless of year but not all students can be accommodated because of space issues. Campus can house 1,764 undergraduates.

EXPENSES

Tuition (2005-06):
There is no additional cost for LD program/services.

LD SERVICES

LD program size is not limited.

LD services available to:

☐ Freshmen ☐ Sophomores ☐ Juniors ☐ Seniors

Academic Accommodations

Curriculum		In class	
Foreign language waiver	☐	Early syllabus	☐
Lighter course load	☐	Note takers in class	■
Math waiver	☐	Priority seating	☐
Other special classes	☐	Tape recorders	■
Priority registrations	☐	Videotaped classes	☐
Substitution of courses	☐	Text on tape	☐
Exams		**Services**	
Extended time	■	Diagnostic tests	☐
Oral exams	☐	Learning centers	☐
Take home exams	☐	Proofreaders	☐
Exams on tape or computer	☐	Readers	■
Untimed exams	☐	Reading Machines/Kurzweil	■
Other accommodations	☐	Special bookstore section	☐
		Typists	☐

Credit toward degree is not given for remedial courses taken.

Counseling Services

- ☐ Academic
- ☐ Psychological
- ☐ Student Support groups
- ☐ Vocational

Tutoring

	Individual	Group
Time management	☐	☐
Organizational skills	☐	☐
Learning strategies	☐	☐
Study skills	☐	☐
Content area	☐	☐
Writing lab	☐	☐
Math lab	☐	☐

LD PROGRAM STAFF

Key staff person available to work with LD students: Dr. Reynol Junco, Director, Office of Disability Services for Students.

Lycoming College

Williamsport, PA

Address: 700 College Place, Williamsport, PA, 17701
Admissions telephone: 800 345-3920
Admissions FAX: 570 321-4317
Dean of Admissions and Financial Aid: James D. Spencer
Admissions e-mail: admissions@lycoming.edu
Web site: http://www.lycoming.edu
SAT Code: 2372 ACT Code: 3622

LD program name: Academic Resource Center
Director, Academic Resource Center: Daniel J. Hartsock
LD program telephone: 570 321-4294
LD program e-mail: hartsock@lycoming.edu
LD program enrollment: 29, Total campus enrollment: 1,505

GENERAL

Lycoming College is a private, coed, four-year institution. 35-acre campus in Williamsport (population: 30,706), 90 miles from Harrisburg. Served by air and bus; major airport serves Philadelphia (160 miles); train serves Harrisburg. Public transportation serves campus. Semester system.

LD ADMISSIONS

A personal interview is recommended. Essay is required and may be typed.

SECONDARY SCHOOL REQUIREMENTS

Graduation from secondary school required; GED accepted. The following course distribution required: 4 units of English, 3 units of math, 2 units of science, 2 units of foreign language, 4 units of social studies, 3 units of history, 2 units of academic electives.

TESTING

SAT Reasoning or ACT required. SAT Subject recommended.

All enrolled freshmen (fall 2004):

Average SAT I Scores:	Verbal: 540	Math: 530
Average ACT Scores:	Composite: 23	

Child Study Team report is not required. Tests required as part of this documentation:

☐ WAIS-IV ☐ Woodcock-Johnson
☐ WISC-IV ☐ Nelson-Denny Reading Test
☐ SATA ☐ Other

UNDERGRADUATE STUDENT BODY

Total undergraduate student enrollment: 649 Men, 780 Women.

Composition of student body (fall 2004):

	Undergraduate	Freshmen
International	1.0	0.8
Black	2.2	2.2
American Indian	0.6	0.4
Asian-American	1.0	0.8
Hispanic	1.2	0.6
White	94.0	95.2
Unreported	0.0	0.0
	100.0%	100.0%

21% are from out of state. 20% join a fraternity and 25% join a sorority. Average age of full-time undergraduates is 20. 60% of classes have fewer than 20 students, 37% have between 20 and 50 students, 3% have more than 50 students.

STUDENT HOUSING

85% of freshmen live in college housing. Freshmen are required to live on campus. Housing is guaranteed for all undergraduates. Campus can house 1,245 undergraduates. Single rooms are available for students with medical or special needs. A medical note is required.

EXPENSES

Tuition (2005-06): $23,680 per year.
Room: $3,356. Board: $3,186.

There is no additional cost for LD program/services.

LD SERVICES

LD program size is not limited.

LD services available to:

☒ Freshmen ☒ Sophomores ☒ Juniors ☒ Seniors

Academic Accommodations

Curriculum		**In class**	
Foreign language waiver	☐	Early syllabus	☐
Lighter course load	☒	Note takers in class	☒
Math waiver	☐	Priority seating	☐
Other special classes	☒	Tape recorders	☒
Priority registrations	☐	Videotaped classes	☒
Substitution of courses	☐	Text on tape	☐
Exams		**Services**	
Extended time	☒	Diagnostic tests	☐
Oral exams	☒	Learning centers	☒
Take home exams	☐	Proofreaders	☐
Exams on tape or computer	☐	Readers	☒
Untimed exams	☒	Reading Machines/Kurzweil	☒
Other accommodations	☐	Special bookstore section	☐
		Typists	☐

Credit toward degree is given for remedial courses taken.

Counseling Services

☐ Academic
☐ Psychological
☐ Student Support groups
☐ Vocational

Tutoring

Individual tutoring is available weekly.

Average size of tutoring groups: 1

	Individual	Group
Time management	☒	☒
Organizational skills	☒	☐
Learning strategies	☒	☒
Study skills	☒	☒
Content area	☒	☐
Writing lab	☒	☐
Math lab	☐	☐

LD PROGRAM STAFF

Total number of LD Program staff (including director):

Full Time: 1 Part Time: 1

There is an advisor/advocate from the LD program available to students.

Key staff person available to work with LD students: Daniel J. Hartsock, Director, Academic Resource Center.

LD Program web site: http://www.lycoming.edu/arc/

Mansfield University of Pennsylvania

Mansfield, PA

Address: Alumni Hall, Mansfield, PA, 16933
Admissions telephone: 800 577-6826
Admissions FAX: 570 662-4121
Director of Admissions: Brian D. Barden
Admissions e-mail: admissns@mansfield.edu
Web site: http://www.mansfield.edu
SAT Code: 2655 ACT Code: 3710

Chairperson, Academic & Human Dev.: Dr. William Chabala
LD program telephone: 570 662-4798
LD program e-mail: wchabala@mansfield.edu
LD program enrollment: 35, Total campus enrollment: 3,127

GENERAL

Mansfield University of Pennsylvania is a public, coed, four-year institution. 205-acre campus in Mansfield (population: 3,411), 50 miles from Williamsport and 30 miles from Elmira, N.Y. Served by bus; airport serves Corning, NY. (45 miles). School operates transportation to area locations and shopping center. Public transportation serves campus. Semester system.

LD ADMISSIONS

Students do not complete a separate application and are simultaneously accepted to the LD program. A member of the LD program does sit on the admissions committee. A personal interview is recommended. Essay is not required.

For fall 2004, 15 completed self-identified LD applications were received. 10 applications were offered admission, and 6 enrolled.

SECONDARY SCHOOL REQUIREMENTS

Graduation from secondary school required; GED accepted. The following course distribution required: 4 units of English, 3 units of math, 2 units of science, 4 units of social studies, 6 units of academic electives.

TESTING

SAT Reasoning or ACT required. SAT Subject recommended.

All enrolled freshmen (fall 2004):

Average SAT I Scores:	Verbal: 489	Math: 499
Average ACT Scores:	Composite: 20	

Child Study Team report is required if student is classified. A neuropsychological or comprehensive psycho-education evaluation is not required for admission. Tests required as part of this documentation:

- ☐ WAIS-IV
- ☐ WISC-IV
- ☐ SATA
- ☐ Woodcock-Johnson
- ☐ Nelson-Denny Reading Test
- ☐ Other

UNDERGRADUATE STUDENT BODY

Total undergraduate student enrollment: 1,174 Men, 1,716 Women.

Composition of student body (fall 2004):

	Undergraduate	Freshmen
International	0.0	0.9
Black	10.5	6.2
American Indian	1.0	1.0
Asian-American	0.7	0.6
Hispanic	2.0	1.2
White	82.8	88.5
Unreported	3.0	1.6
	100.0%	100.0%

17% are from out of state. 5% join a fraternity and 5% join a sorority. Average age of full-time undergraduates is 22. 43% of classes have fewer than 20 students, 50% have between 20 and 50 students, 7% have more than 50 students.

STUDENT HOUSING

79% of freshmen live in college housing. Freshmen are required to live on campus. Housing is guaranteed for all undergraduates. Campus can house 1,800 undergraduates. Single rooms are available for students with medical or special needs. A medical note is required.

EXPENSES

Tuition (2005-06): $5,050 per year (in-state), $12,627 (out-of-state). Room: $3,692. Board: $1,988.
There is no additional cost for LD program/services.

LD SERVICES

LD program size is not limited.

LD services available to:

■ Freshmen ■ Sophomores ■ Juniors ■ Seniors

Academic Accommodations

Curriculum		In class	
Foreign language waiver	☐	Early syllabus	☐
Lighter course load	■	Note takers in class	■
Math waiver	☐	Priority seating	☐
Other special classes	☐	Tape recorders	■
Priority registrations	☐	Videotaped classes	☐
Substitution of courses	☐	Text on tape	☐
Exams		**Services**	
Extended time	■	Diagnostic tests	■
Oral exams	☐	Learning centers	■
Take home exams	☐	Proofreaders	☐
Exams on tape or computer	☐	Readers	☐
Untimed exams	☐	Reading Machines/Kurzweil	☐
Other accommodations	■	Special bookstore section	☐
		Typists	☐

Credit toward degree is not given for remedial courses taken.

Counseling Services

- ■ Academic
- ■ Psychological
- ☐ Student Support groups
- ☐ Vocational

Tutoring

Individual tutoring is available daily.

Average size of tutoring groups: 1

	Individual	Group
Time management	■	■
Organizational skills	■	■
Learning strategies	■	☐
Study skills	■	☐
Content area	■	☐
Writing lab	■	☐
Math lab	■	☐

LD PROGRAM STAFF

Total number of LD Program staff (including director):

Full Time: 1 Part Time: 1

There is an advisor/advocate from the LD program available to students.

Key staff person available to work with LD students: Dr. William Chabala, Chairperson, Academic & Human Development

Marywood University

Scranton, PA

Address: 2300 Adams Avenue, Scranton, PA, 18509-1598
Admissions telephone: 800 348-6234
Admissions FAX: 570 961-4763
Director of Admissions: Robert W. Reese
Admissions e-mail: ugadm@marywood.edu
Web site: http://www.marywood.edu
SAT Code: 2407 ACT Code: 3626

LD program name: Disability Services
Coordinator of Disability Services: Christopher Moy
LD program telephone: 570 340-6045
LD program e-mail: moy@marywood.edu
Total campus enrollment: 1,811

GENERAL

Marywood University is a private, coed, four-year institution. 115-acre, suburban campus in Scranton (population: 76,415), 115 miles north of Philadelphia and 120 miles west of New York City, NY. Served by bus; airport serves Avoca (10 miles). School operates transportation to downtown Scranton and the U of Scranton. Public transportation serves campus. Semester system.

LD ADMISSIONS

A personal interview is recommended. Essay is not required. Admissions requirements that may be waived for LD students include foreign language and math.

SECONDARY SCHOOL REQUIREMENTS

Graduation from secondary school required; GED accepted. The following course distribution required: 4 units of English, 2 units of math, 1 unit of science, 3 units of social studies, 6 units of academic electives.

TESTING

SAT Reasoning required; ACT may be substituted. SAT Subject recommended.

All enrolled freshmen (fall 2004):

Average SAT I Scores:	Verbal:524	Math:503
Average ACT Scores:	Composite:21	

Child Study Team report is not required. Tests required as part of this documentation:

- [ ] WAIS-IV
- [ ] WISC-IV
- [ ] SATA
- [ ] Woodcock-Johnson
- [ ] Nelson-Denny Reading Test
- [ ] Other

UNDERGRADUATE STUDENT BODY

Total undergraduate student enrollment: 463 Men, 1,205 Women.

Composition of student body (fall 2004):

	Undergraduate	Freshmen
International	1.2	1.3
Black	3.2	2.1
American Indian	0.6	0.3
Asian-American	1.2	1.0
Hispanic	1.5	2.2
White	87.9	88.5
Unreported	4.4	4.6
	100.0%	100.0%

20% are from out of state. Average age of full-time undergraduates is 21. 64% of classes have fewer than 20 students, 36% have between 20 and 50 students.

STUDENT HOUSING

62% of freshmen live in college housing. Freshmen are required to live on campus. Housing is guaranteed for all undergraduates. Campus can house 629 undergraduates. Single rooms are available for students with medical or special needs.

EXPENSES

Tuition (2005-06): $20,700 per year.

Room: $5,152. Board: $3,948.

There is no additional cost for LD program/services.

LD SERVICES

LD program size is not limited.

LD services available to:

- [x] Freshmen
- [x] Sophomores
- [x] Juniors
- [x] Seniors

Academic Accommodations

Curriculum		In class	
Foreign language waiver	[ ]	Early syllabus	[ ]
Lighter course load	[x]	Note takers in class	[x]
Math waiver	[ ]	Priority seating	[ ]
Other special classes	[ ]	Tape recorders	[x]
Priority registrations	[ ]	Videotaped classes	[ ]
Substitution of courses	[ ]	Text on tape	[ ]
Exams		**Services**	
Extended time	[x]	Diagnostic tests	[x]
Oral exams	[x]	Learning centers	[x]
Take home exams	[ ]	Proofreaders	[ ]
Exams on tape or computer	[ ]	Readers	[x]
Untimed exams	[x]	Reading Machines/Kurzweil	[x]
Other accommodations	[ ]	Special bookstore section	[ ]
		Typists	[ ]

Credit toward degree is not given for remedial courses taken.

Counseling Services

- [x] Academic
- [x] Psychological
- [ ] Student Support groups
- [ ] Vocational

Tutoring

Individual tutoring is available.

Average size of tutoring groups: 1

	Individual	Group
Time management	[ ]	[ ]
Organizational skills	[ ]	[ ]
Learning strategies	[ ]	[ ]
Study skills	[ ]	[ ]
Content area	[ ]	[ ]
Writing lab	[ ]	[ ]
Math lab	[ ]	[ ]

LD PROGRAM STAFF

Total number of LD Program staff (including director):

Full Time: 1 Part Time: 1

There is an advisor/advocate from the LD program available to students.

Key staff person available to work with LD students: Christopher Moy, Coordinator of Disability Services.

Mercyhurst College

Erie, PA

Address: 501 East 38th Street, Erie, PA, 16546
Admissions telephone: 814 824-2202
Admissions FAX: 814 824-2071
Director of Admissions: J.P.Cooney
Admissions e-mail: jcooney@mercyhurst.edu
Web site: http://www.mercyhurst.edu
SAT Code: 2410 ACT Code: 3629

LD program name: Learning Differences Program
Director, Learning Differences Program: Dianne Rogers
LD program telephone: 814 824-2450
LD program e-mail: drogers@mercyhurst.edu
LD program enrollment: 79, Total campus enrollment: 3,807

GENERAL

Mercyhurst College is a private, coed, four-year institution. 88-acre, suburban campus in Erie (population: 103,717), 100 miles from Buffalo, Cleveland, and Pittsburgh; branch campus in North East. Served by bus and train; airport serves Buffalo. Trimester system.

LD ADMISSIONS

Application Deadline: 03/15. Students do not complete a separate application and are simultaneously accepted to the LD program. A member of the LD program does sit on the admissions committee. High school waivers are accepted for foreign language. A personal interview is recommended. Essay is not required.

For fall 2004, 90 completed self-identified LD applications were received. 61 applications were offered admission, and 24 enrolled.

SECONDARY SCHOOL REQUIREMENTS

Graduation from secondary school required; GED accepted. The following course distribution required: 4 units of English, 3 units of math, 2 units of science, 2 units of foreign language, 5 units of social studies.

TESTING

SAT Reasoning or ACT required. SAT Subject recommended.

All enrolled freshmen (fall 2004):

Average SAT I Scores:	Verbal: 545	Math: 545
Average ACT Scores:	Composite: 22	

Child Study Team report is required if student is classified. A neuropsychological or comprehensive psycho-educational evaluation is required for admission. Must be dated within 36 months of application. Tests required as part of this documentation:

- ■ WAIS-IV
- ■ WISC-IV
- □ SATA
- ■ Woodcock-Johnson
- □ Nelson-Denny Reading Test
- ■ Other

UNDERGRADUATE STUDENT BODY

Total undergraduate student enrollment: 1,204 Men, 1,957 Women.

Composition of student body (fall 2004):

	Undergraduate	Freshmen
International	3.9	3.7
Black	3.1	2.9
American Indian	0.2	0.3
Asian-American	0.5	0.5
Hispanic	2.0	1.3
White	78.3	82.6
Unreported	12.0	8.7
	100.0%	100.0%

51% are from out of state. 51% of classes have fewer than 20 students, 48% have between 20 and 50 students, 1% have more than 50 students.

STUDENT HOUSING

83% of freshmen live in college housing. Freshmen are required to live on campus. Housing is guaranteed for all undergraduates. Campus can house 2,066 undergraduates. Single rooms are not available for students with medical or special needs.

EXPENSES

Tuition (2005-06): $17,760 per year.
Room: $3,576. Board: $3,498.
Additional cost for LD program/services: $1,500 per academic year.

LD SERVICES

LD program is limited to %1 students.

LD services available to:

■ Freshmen ■ Sophomores ■ Juniors ■ Seniors

Academic Accommodations

Curriculum		In class	
Foreign language waiver	□	Early syllabus	□
Lighter course load	■	Note takers in class	■
Math waiver	□	Priority seating	□
Other special classes	□	Tape recorders	■
Priority registrations	■	Videotaped classes	□
Substitution of courses	□	Text on tape	■
Exams		**Services**	
Extended time	■	Diagnostic tests	□
Oral exams	■	Learning centers	■
Take home exams	□	Proofreaders	■
Exams on tape or computer	■	Readers	■
Untimed exams	■	Reading Machines/Kurzweil	■
Other accommodations	□	Special bookstore section	□
		Typists	■

Credit toward degree is not given for remedial courses taken.

Counseling Services

- ■ Academic — Meets 30 times per academic year
- □ Psychological
- □ Student Support groups
- ■ Vocational — Meets 2 times per academic year

Tutoring

Individual tutoring is available daily.

Average size of tutoring groups: 3

	Individual	Group
Time management	■	■
Organizational skills	■	■
Learning strategies	■	■
Study skills	■	■
Content area	□	■
Writing lab	■	□
Math lab	■	□

LD PROGRAM STAFF

Total number of LD Program staff (including director):

Full Time: 1 Part Time: 1

There is no advisor/advocate from the LD program available to students.

Key staff person available to work with LD students: Dianne Rogers, Director, Learning Differences Program

Messiah College

Grantham, PA

Address: 1 College Avenue, Grantham, PA, 17027-0800
Admissions telephone: 800 233-4220
Admissions FAX: 717 796-5374
Dean for Enrollment Management: William G. Strausbaugh
Admissions e-mail: admiss@messiah.edu
Web site: http://www.messiah.edu
SAT Code: 2411 ACT Code: 3630

LD program name: Disability Services
LD program address: P.O. Box 3019
Director of Disability Services: Keith W. Drahn
LD program telephone: 717 766-2511, extension 7258
LD program e-mail: KDrahn@messiah.edu
LD program enrollment: 25, Total campus enrollment: 2,917

GENERAL

Messiah College is a private, coed, four-year institution. 400-acre campus in Grantham (population: 5,000), 10 miles from Harrisburg; branch campus in Philadelphia. Airport and train serve Harrisburg. Semester system.

LD ADMISSIONS

A personal interview is recommended.

SECONDARY SCHOOL REQUIREMENTS

Graduation from secondary school required; GED accepted. The following course distribution required: 4 units of English, 2 units of math, 2 units of science, 2 units of foreign language, 2 units of social studies, 4 units of academic electives.

TESTING

SAT Reasoning or ACT required of some applicants. SAT Subject recommended.

All enrolled freshmen (fall 2004):

Average SAT I Scores:	Verbal: 602	Math: 589
Average ACT Scores:	Composite: 26	

Child Study Team report is required if student is classified. Tests required as part of this documentation:

- ☐ WAIS-IV
- ☐ WISC-IV
- ☐ SATA
- ☐ Woodcock-Johnson
- ☐ Nelson-Denny Reading Test
- ☐ Other

UNDERGRADUATE STUDENT BODY

Total undergraduate student enrollment: 1,109 Men, 1,749 Women.

Composition of student body (fall 2004):

	Undergraduate	Freshmen
International	2.5	2.5
Black	2.7	2.7
American Indian	0.3	0.1
Asian-American	1.3	1.6
Hispanic	2.0	2.0
White	90.0	90.1
Unreported	1.2	1.0
	100.0%	100.0%

48% are from out of state. Average age of full-time undergraduates is 20. 42% of classes have fewer than 20 students, 54% have between 20 and 50 students, 4% have more than 50 students.

STUDENT HOUSING

99% of freshmen live in college housing. Housing is guaranteed for all undergraduates. Campus can house 2,369 undergraduates.

EXPENSES

Tuition (2005-06): $21,420 per year.
Room: $3,540. Board: $3,260.
There is no additional cost for LD program/services.

LD SERVICES

LD program size is not limited.

LD services available to:

☑ Freshmen ☑ Sophomores ☑ Juniors ☑ Seniors

Academic Accommodations

Curriculum		In class	
Foreign language waiver	☐	Early syllabus	☐
Lighter course load	☑	Note takers in class	☑
Math waiver	☐	Priority seating	☐
Other special classes	☐	Tape recorders	☑
Priority registrations	☐	Videotaped classes	☐
Substitution of courses	☐	Text on tape	☐
Exams		**Services**	
Extended time	☑	Diagnostic tests	☐
Oral exams	☑	Learning centers	☑
Take home exams	☐	Proofreaders	☐
Exams on tape or computer	☐	Readers	☑
Untimed exams	☑	Reading Machines/Kurzweil	☑
Other accommodations	☐	Special bookstore section	☐
		Typists	☐

Credit toward degree is not given for remedial courses taken.

Counseling Services

- ☐ Academic
- ☐ Psychological
- ☐ Student Support groups
- ☐ Vocational

Tutoring

	Individual	Group
Time management	☐	☐
Organizational skills	☐	☐
Learning strategies	☐	☐
Study skills	☐	☐
Content area	☐	☐
Writing lab	☐	☐
Math lab	☐	☐

LD PROGRAM STAFF

Key staff person available to work with LD students: Keith W. Drahn, Director of Disability Services

LD Program web site: http://www.messiah.edu/offices/disability/

Millersville University of Pennsylvania

Millersville, PA

Address: P.O. Box 1002, Millersville, PA, 17551-0302
Admissions telephone: 800 MU-ADMIT
Admissions FAX: 717 871-2147
Director of Admissions: Douglas Zander
Admissions e-mail: Admissions@millersville.edu
Web site: http://www.millersville.edu
SAT Code: 2656 ACT Code: 3712

LD program name: Learning Services
Director of Learning Services: Sherlynn Bessick
LD program telephone: 717 872-3178
LD program e-mail: Sherlynn.Bessick@millersville.edu
LD program enrollment: 185, Total campus enrollment: 6,991

GENERAL

Millersville University of Pennsylvania is a public, coed, four-year institution. 220-acre campus in Millersville (population: 7,774), five miles from Lancaster. Major airport serves Baltimore, MD (90 miles); smaller airport serves Harrisburg (40 miles); bus and train serve Lancaster. School operates transportation on campus, to student apartment complexes, and to local shopping center on weekends. Public transportation serves campus. 4-1-4 system.

LD ADMISSIONS

Students do not complete a separate application and are not simultaneously accepted to the LD program. A member of the LD program does not sit on the admissions committee. A personal interview is recommended. Essay is not required.

SECONDARY SCHOOL REQUIREMENTS

Graduation from secondary school required; GED accepted. The following course distribution required: 4 units of English, 3 units of math, 3 units of science, 3 units of social studies, 2 units of history.

TESTING

SAT Reasoning or ACT required. SAT Subject recommended.

All enrolled freshmen (fall 2004):

Average SAT I Scores: Verbal: 522 Math: 528

Child Study Team report is not required. A neuropsychological or comprehensive psycho-educational evaluation is required for admission. Must be dated within 36 months of application. Tests required as part of this documentation:

- ☑ WAIS-IV
- ☑ WISC-IV
- ☑ SATA
- ☑ Woodcock-Johnson
- ☑ Nelson-Denny Reading Test
- ☑ Other

UNDERGRADUATE STUDENT BODY

Total undergraduate student enrollment: 2,749 Men, 3,848 Women.

Composition of student body (fall 2004):

	Undergraduate	Freshmen
International	0.0	0.0
Black	9.1	5.8
American Indian	0.4	0.2
Asian-American	1.7	1.9
Hispanic	3.8	3.0
White	72.3	85.2
Unreported	12.7	3.9
	100.0%	100.0%

4% are from out of state. 3% join a fraternity and 4% join a sorority. Average age of full-time undergraduates is 20. 22% of classes have fewer than 20 students, 73% have between 20 and 50 students, 5% have more than 50 students.

STUDENT HOUSING

98% of freshmen live in college housing. Freshmen are required to live on campus. Housing is guaranteed for all undergraduates. Campus can house 2,524 undergraduates. Single rooms are available for students with medical or special needs. A medical note is required.

EXPENSES

Tuition (2005-06): $5,032 per year (in-state), $12,454 (out-of-state).

Room: $3,474. Board: $2,404.
There is no additional cost for LD program/services.

LD SERVICES

LD program size is not limited.

LD services available to:

☑ Freshmen ☑ Sophomores ☑ Juniors ☑ Seniors

Academic Accommodations

Curriculum		In class	
Foreign language waiver	☐	Early syllabus	☐
Lighter course load	☑	Note takers in class	☑
Math waiver	☐	Priority seating	☐
Other special classes	☐	Tape recorders	☑
Priority registrations	☐	Videotaped classes	☐
Substitution of courses	☐	Text on tape	☐
Exams		**Services**	
Extended time	☑	Diagnostic tests	☑
Oral exams	☑	Learning centers	☑
Take home exams	☐	Proofreaders	☐
Exams on tape or computer	☐	Readers	☑
Untimed exams	☑	Reading Machines/Kurzweil	☑
Other accommodations	☑	Special bookstore section	☐
		Typists	☐

Credit toward degree is not given for remedial courses taken.

Counseling Services

- ☑ Academic
- ☑ Psychological
- ☑ Student Support groups
- ☑ Vocational

Tutoring

Individual tutoring is available daily.

Average size of tutoring groups: 4

	Individual	Group
Time management	☑	☑
Organizational skills	☑	☑
Learning strategies	☑	☑
Study skills	☑	☑
Content area	☑	☑
Writing lab	☑	☑
Math lab	☑	☑

LD PROGRAM STAFF

Total number of LD Program staff (including director):

Full Time: 2 Part Time: 2

There is an advisor/advocate from the LD program available to students. Four graduate students and 250 peer tutors are available to work with LD students.

Key staff person available to work with LD students: Sherlynn Bessick, Director of Learning Services

LD Program web site: http://www.millersville.edu/~aspls/learningserv.html

Moore College of Art and Design

Philadelphia, PA

Address: 20th Street and the Parkway, Philadelphia, PA, 19103
Admissions telephone: 800 523-2025
Admissions FAX: 215 568-3547
Director of Admissions: Heeseung Lee
Admissions e-mail: admiss@moore.edu
Web site: http://www.moore.edu
SAT Code: 2417 ACT Code: 3632

LD program name: Disability Committee
Associate Dean of Educational Support: Claudine Thomas
LD program telephone: 215 965-4061
LD program e-mail: cthomas@moore.edu
Total campus enrollment: 501

GENERAL

Moore College of Art and Design is a private, women's, four-year institution. 1-1/2-acre, urban campus in Philadelphia (population: 1,517,550). Served by air, bus, and train. Public transportation serves campus. Semester system.

LD ADMISSIONS

Students do not complete a separate application and are not simultaneously accepted to the LD program. A member of the LD program does not sit on the admissions committee. A personal interview is required. Essay is not required.

SECONDARY SCHOOL REQUIREMENTS

Graduation from secondary school required; GED accepted.

TESTING

SAT Reasoning recommended. ACT considered if submitted.

All enrolled freshmen (fall 2004):

Average SAT I Scores: Verbal: 512 Math: 506
Average ACT Scores: Composite: 19

Child Study Team report is not required. A neuropsychological or comprehensive psycho-education evaluation is not required for admission. Tests required as part of this documentation:

- [ ] WAIS-IV
- [ ] WISC-IV
- [ ] SATA
- [ ] Woodcock-Johnson
- [ ] Nelson-Denny Reading Test
- [ ] Other

UNDERGRADUATE STUDENT BODY

Total undergraduate student enrollment: 501.

Composition of student body (fall 2004):

	Freshmen
International	2.3
Black	7.0
American Indian	0.0
Asian-American	5.3
Hispanic	3.2
White	77.5
Unreported	4.7
	100.0

32% are from out of state. Average age of full-time undergraduates is 22. 84% of classes have fewer than 20 students, 16% have between 20 and 50 students.

STUDENT HOUSING

Freshmen are not required to live on campus. Housing is guaranteed for all undergraduates. Single rooms are not available for students with medical or special needs.

EXPENSES

Tuition (2005-06): $22,091 per year.
Room: $5,227. Board: $3,427.
There is no additional cost for LD program/services.

LD SERVICES

LD program size is not limited.

LD services available to:

[x] Freshmen [x] Sophomores [x] Juniors [x] Seniors

Academic Accommodations

Curriculum		**In class**	
Foreign language waiver	[ ]	Early syllabus	[ ]
Lighter course load	[ ]	Note takers in class	[ ]
Math waiver	[ ]	Priority seating	[ ]
Other special classes	[ ]	Tape recorders	[x]
Priority registrations	[ ]	Videotaped classes	[ ]
Substitution of courses	[ ]	Text on tape	[ ]
Exams		**Services**	
Extended time	[x]	Diagnostic tests	[ ]
Oral exams	[ ]	Learning centers	[x]
Take home exams	[ ]	Proofreaders	[ ]
Exams on tape or computer	[ ]	Readers	[ ]
Untimed exams	[x]	Reading Machines/Kurzweil	[ ]
Other accommodations	[ ]	Special bookstore section	[ ]
		Typists	[ ]

Credit toward degree is not given for remedial courses taken.

Counseling Services

- [x] Academic — Meets 2 times per academic year
- [ ] Psychological
- [ ] Student Support groups
- [ ] Vocational

Tutoring

Individual tutoring is available weekly.

Average size of tutoring groups: 1

	Individual	Group
Time management	[x]	[x]
Organizational skills	[x]	[ ]
Learning strategies	[ ]	[x]
Study skills	[x]	[ ]
Content area	[ ]	[ ]
Writing lab	[x]	[ ]
Math lab	[ ]	[ ]

LD PROGRAM STAFF

Total number of LD Program staff (including director):

Full Time: 3 Part Time: 3

There is an advisor/advocate from the LD program available to students. The advisor/advocate meets with faculty two times per month and student three times per month. Four peer tutors are available to work with LD students.

Key staff people available to work with LD students: Claudine Thomas, Associate Dean and Joan Stevens, Dean of Students

Moravian College

Bethlehem, PA

Address: 1200 Main Street, Bethlehem, PA, 18018
Admissions telephone: 800 441-3191
Admissions FAX: 610 861-3956
Director of Admission: James P. Mackin
Admissions e-mail: admissions@moravian.edu
Web site: http://www.moravian.edu
SAT Code: 2418 ACT Code: 3634

LD program name: Moravian College Learning Services
Director of Learning Services: Laurie M. Roth
LD program telephone: 610 861-1510
LD program e-mail: melmr01@moravian.edu
LD program enrollment: 35, Total campus enrollment: 1,816

GENERAL

Moravian College is a private, coed, four-year institution. 60-acre campus in Bethlehem (population: 71,329), 55 miles from Philadelphia. Served by bus; airport serves Lehigh Valley; other airport and train serve Philadelphia. School operates transportation between Church Street and Main Street campuses. Public transportation serves campus. Semester system.

LD ADMISSIONS

There is no separate admission process and no separate curriculum or academic program for students with learning disabilities. A personal interview is recommended. Essay is required and may be typed.

SECONDARY SCHOOL REQUIREMENTS

Graduation from secondary school required; GED accepted. The following course distribution required: 4 units of English, 3 units of math, 2 units of science, 2 units of foreign language, 4 units of social studies.

TESTING

SAT Reasoning required; ACT may be substituted. SAT Subject required.

Child Study Team report is not required. Tests required as part of this documentation:

- [ ] WAIS-IV
- [ ] WISC-IV
- [ ] SATA
- [ ] Woodcock-Johnson
- [ ] Nelson-Denny Reading Test
- [ ] Other

UNDERGRADUATE STUDENT BODY

Total undergraduate student enrollment: 688 Men, 1,035 Women.

Composition of student body (fall 2004):

	Undergraduate	Freshmen
International	0.8	1.4
Black	1.8	2.0
American Indian	0.3	0.1
Asian-American	1.6	2.0
Hispanic	2.9	3.4
White	91.0	90.5
Unreported	1.6	0.6
	100.0%	100.0%

37% are from out of state. 14% join a fraternity and 22% join a sorority. 63% of classes have fewer than 20 students, 37% have between 20 and 50 students.

STUDENT HOUSING

90% of freshmen live in college housing. Housing is guaranteed for all undergraduates. Students must live in college housing unless they live at home with a parent or guardian, or they receive authorization from the college to live off-campus. Campus can house 1,057 undergraduates. Single rooms are available for students with medical or special needs. A medical note is required.

EXPENSES

Tuition (2005-06): $24,813 per year.
Room: $4,230. Board: $3,300.
There is no additional cost for LD program/services.

LD SERVICES

LD program size is not limited.

LD services available to:

- [x] Freshmen
- [x] Sophomores
- [x] Juniors
- [x] Seniors

Academic Accommodations

Curriculum		In class	
Foreign language waiver	[ ]	Early syllabus	[ ]
Lighter course load	[x]	Note takers in class	[x]
Math waiver	[ ]	Priority seating	[ ]
Other special classes	[ ]	Tape recorders	[x]
Priority registrations	[ ]	Videotaped classes	[ ]
Substitution of courses	[ ]	Text on tape	[ ]
Exams		**Services**	
Extended time	[x]	Diagnostic tests	[ ]
Oral exams	[x]	Learning centers	[x]
Take home exams	[ ]	Proofreaders	[ ]
Exams on tape or computer	[x]	Readers	[x]
Untimed exams	[ ]	Reading Machines/Kurzweil	[ ]
Other accommodations	[x]	Special bookstore section	[ ]
		Typists	[ ]

Credit toward degree is not given for remedial courses taken.

Counseling Services

- [ ] Academic
- [ ] Psychological
- [ ] Student Support groups
- [ ] Vocational

Tutoring

Individual tutoring is available weekly.

Average size of tutoring groups: 1

	Individual	Group
Time management	[x]	[x]
Organizational skills	[x]	[x]
Learning strategies	[x]	[x]
Study skills	[x]	[x]
Content area	[x]	[x]
Writing lab	[x]	[x]
Math lab	[ ]	[x]

UNIQUE LD PROGRAM FEATURES

It is the responsibility of the student to request services and provide appropriate documentation. The Office of Learning Services provides services and accommocations for learning disabled students. The Counseling Center provides services and accommodations for all other disabilities.

LD PROGRAM STAFF

Total number of LD Program staff (including director):

Full Time: 1 Part Time: 1

There is an advisor/advocate from the LD program available to students.

Key staff person available to work with LD students: Laurie M. Roth, Director of Learning Services

Mount Aloysius College

Cresson, PA

Address: 7373 Admiral Peary Highway, Cresson, PA, 16630
Admissions telephone: 888 823-2220
Admissions FAX: 814 886-6441
Dean of Enrollment Management: Francis C. Crouse Jr.
Admissions e-mail: admissions@mtaloy.edu
Web site: http://www.mtaloy.edu
SAT Code: 2420 ACT Code: 3635

Dean of Students Affairs: Dane Foust
LD program telephone: 814 886-6472
LD program e-mail: Dfoust@mtaloy.edu
Total campus enrollment: 1,451

GENERAL

Mount Aloysius College is a private, coed, four-year institution. 75-acre campus in Cresson (population: 4,055), 12 miles from Altoona and 90 miles from Pittsburgh. Served by bus; airport serves Pittsburgh; smaller airport serves Johnstown (20 miles); train serves Altoona. Semester system.

LD ADMISSIONS

A personal interview is required. Essay is not required.

SECONDARY SCHOOL REQUIREMENTS

Graduation from secondary school required; GED accepted. The following course distribution required: 4 units of English, 3 units of math, 3 units of science, 3 units of social studies, 3 units of academic electives.

TESTING

SAT Reasoning or ACT required. SAT Subject recommended.

All enrolled freshmen (fall 2004):

Average SAT I Scores: Verbal: 457 Math: 457
Average ACT Scores: Composite: 17

Child Study Team report is not required. Tests required as part of this documentation:

- ☐ WAIS-IV
- ☐ WISC-IV
- ☐ SATA
- ☐ Woodcock-Johnson
- ☐ Nelson-Denny Reading Test
- ☐ Other

UNDERGRADUATE STUDENT BODY

Total undergraduate student enrollment: 285 Men, 868 Women.

Composition of student body (fall 2004):

	Undergraduate	Freshmen
International	7.2	2.0
Black	1.8	1.4
American Indian	0.7	0.4
Asian-American	0.1	0.1
Hispanic	0.7	0.6
White	79.4	84.1
Unreported	10.1	11.4
	100.0%	100.0%

2% are from out of state. Average age of full-time undergraduates is 25. 72% of classes have fewer than 20 students, 28% have between 20 and 50 students.

STUDENT HOUSING

39% of freshmen live in college housing. Housing is not guaranteed for all undergraduates. Campus can house 200 undergraduates.

EXPENSES

Tuition (2005-06): $14,220 per year. $12,460 per year for liberal arts programs, $14,360 for health studies programs.

Room: $3,130. Board: $3,060.
There is no additional cost for LD program/services.

LD SERVICES

LD program size is not limited.

LD services available to:

☐ Freshmen ☐ Sophomores ☐ Juniors ☐ Seniors

Academic Accommodations

Curriculum		**In class**	
Foreign language waiver	☐	Early syllabus	☐
Lighter course load	■	Note takers in class	■
Math waiver	☐	Priority seating	☐
Other special classes	☐	Tape recorders	■
Priority registrations	☐	Videotaped classes	☐
Substitution of courses	☐	Text on tape	☐
Exams		**Services**	
Extended time	■	Diagnostic tests	☐
Oral exams	■	Learning centers	■
Take home exams	☐	Proofreaders	☐
Exams on tape or computer	☐	Readers	■
Untimed exams	☐	Reading Machines/Kurzweil	☐
Other accommodations	☐	Special bookstore section	■
		Typists	☐

Credit toward degree is not given for remedial courses taken.

Counseling Services

- ☐ Academic
- ☐ Psychological
- ☐ Student Support groups
- ☐ Vocational

Tutoring

	Individual	Group
Time management	☐	☐
Organizational skills	☐	☐
Learning strategies	☐	☐
Study skills	☐	☐
Content area	☐	☐
Writing lab	☐	☐
Math lab	☐	☐

LD PROGRAM STAFF

Total number of LD Program staff (including director):

Full Time: 3 Part Time: 3

Key staff person available to work with LD students: Dane Foust, Dean of Students Affairs.

Muhlenberg College

Allentown, PA

Address: 2400 West Chew Street, Allentown, PA, 18104
Admissions telephone: 484 664-3200
Admissions FAX: 484 664-3234
Dean of Admission & Financial Aid: Christopher Hooker-Haring
Admissions e-mail: admissions@muhlenberg.edu
Web site: http://www.muhlenberg.edu
SAT Code: 2424 ACT Code: 3640

Director of Academic Support Services: Wendy Cole
LD program telephone: 484 664-3433
LD program e-mail: cole@muhlenberg.edu
Total campus enrollment: 2,446

GENERAL

Muhlenberg College is a private, coed, four-year institution. 75-acre, suburban campus in Allentown (population: 106,632), 60 miles from Philadelphia and 90 miles from New York City, NY. Served by bus; airport and train serve Philadelphia; smaller airport serves Bethlehem (10 miles). School operates transportation to Philadelphia and New York City, NY. Public transportation serves campus. Semester system.

LD ADMISSIONS

A personal interview is recommended. Essay is required and may be typed.

SECONDARY SCHOOL REQUIREMENTS

Graduation from secondary school required; GED accepted. The following course distribution required: 4 units of English, 3 units of math, 2 units of science, 2 units of foreign language, 2 units of history, 1 unit of academic electives.

TESTING

SAT Reasoning or ACT required of some applicants. SAT Subject recommended.

All enrolled freshmen (fall 2004):

Average SAT I Scores: Verbal: 608 Math: 612

Child Study Team report is not required. Tests required as part of this documentation:

- [ ] WAIS-IV
- [ ] WISC-IV
- [ ] SATA
- [ ] Woodcock-Johnson
- [ ] Nelson-Denny Reading Test
- [ ] Other

UNDERGRADUATE STUDENT BODY

Total undergraduate student enrollment: 889 Men, 1,231 Women.

Composition of student body (fall 2004):

	Undergraduate	Freshmen
International	0.2	0.5
Black	1.4	2.1
American Indian	0.5	0.2
Asian-American	3.2	2.4
Hispanic	3.2	3.6
White	91.4	91.0
Unreported	0.1	0.2
	100.0%	100.0%

66% are from out of state. 19% join a fraternity and 20% join a sorority. Average age of full-time undergraduates is 19. 57% of classes have fewer than 20 students, 41% have between 20 and 50 students, 2% have more than 50 students.

STUDENT HOUSING

99% of freshmen live in college housing. Freshmen are required to live on campus. Housing is guaranteed for all undergraduates. Campus can house 1,855 undergraduates.

EXPENSES

Tuition (2005-06): $28,510 per year.

Room: $4,070. Board: $3,200.
There is no additional cost for LD program/services.

LD SERVICES

LD program size is not limited.

LD services available to:

- [ ] Freshmen
- [ ] Sophomores
- [ ] Juniors
- [ ] Seniors

Academic Accommodations

Curriculum		In class	
Foreign language waiver	[ ]	Early syllabus	[ ]
Lighter course load	[x]	Note takers in class	[x]
Math waiver	[ ]	Priority seating	[ ]
Other special classes	[ ]	Tape recorders	[x]
Priority registrations	[ ]	Videotaped classes	[ ]
Substitution of courses	[ ]	Text on tape	[ ]
Exams		**Services**	
Extended time	[x]	Diagnostic tests	[ ]
Oral exams	[x]	Learning centers	[x]
Take home exams	[ ]	Proofreaders	[ ]
Exams on tape or computer	[ ]	Readers	[x]
Untimed exams	[ ]	Reading Machines/Kurzweil	[x]
Other accommodations	[ ]	Special bookstore section	[ ]
		Typists	[ ]

Credit toward degree is not given for remedial courses taken.

Counseling Services

- [ ] Academic
- [ ] Psychological
- [ ] Student Support groups
- [ ] Vocational

Tutoring

Individual tutoring is available weekly.

Average size of tutoring groups: 1

	Individual	Group
Time management	[ ]	[ ]
Organizational skills	[ ]	[ ]
Learning strategies	[ ]	[ ]
Study skills	[ ]	[ ]
Content area	[ ]	[ ]
Writing lab	[ ]	[ ]
Math lab	[ ]	[ ]

LD PROGRAM STAFF

Total number of LD Program staff (including director):

Full Time: 2 Part Time: 2

Key staff person available to work with LD students: Wendy Cole, Director of Academic Support Services

Neumann College

Aston, PA

Address: 1 Neumann Drive, Aston, PA, 19014-1298
Admissions telephone: 800 963-8626
Admissions FAX: 610 558-5652
Admissions e-mail: neumann@neumann.edu
Web site: http://www.neumann.edu
SAT Code: 2628   ACT Code: 3649

Disability Services Coordinator: James Kain
LD program telephone: 610 361-5349
LD program e-mail: jkain@neumann.edu
LD program enrollment: 7, Total campus enrollment: 2,197

GENERAL

Neumann College is a private, coed, four-year institution. 37-acre, suburban campus in Aston (population: 16,203), 19 miles from Philadelphia. Served by bus; major airport and train serve Philadelphia. Public transportation serves campus. Semester system.

LD ADMISSIONS

A personal interview is recommended. Essay is not required.

For fall 2004, 10 completed self-identified LD applications were received. 9 applications were offered admission, and 7 enrolled.

SECONDARY SCHOOL REQUIREMENTS

Graduation from secondary school required; GED accepted. The following course distribution required: 4 units of English, 2 units of math, 2 units of science, 2 units of foreign language, 2 units of social studies, 4 units of academic electives.

TESTING

SAT Reasoning or ACT required. SAT Subject recommended.

All enrolled freshmen (fall 2004):

Average SAT I Scores: Verbal: 442   Math: 435

Child Study Team report is not required. Tests required as part of this documentation:

- ☐ WAIS-IV
- ☐ WISC-IV
- ☐ SATA
- ☐ Woodcock-Johnson
- ☐ Nelson-Denny Reading Test
- ☐ Other

UNDERGRADUATE STUDENT BODY

Total undergraduate student enrollment: 611 Men, 1,130 Women.

Composition of student body (fall 2004):

	Undergraduate	Freshmen
International	1.7	0.6
Black	10.8	12.7
American Indian	0.2	0.2
Asian-American	2.4	1.3
Hispanic	2.4	1.3
White	68.0	73.6
Unreported	14.5	10.3
	100.0%	100.0%

24% are from out of state. Average age of full-time undergraduates is 20. 46% of classes have fewer than 20 students, 54% have between 20 and 50 students.

STUDENT HOUSING

72% of freshmen live in college housing. Housing is guaranteed for all undergraduates. Campus can house 760 undergraduates.

EXPENSES

Tuition (2005-06): $17,300 per year.

Room: $4,796. Board: $3,280.

Additional cost for LD program/services: $0 per .

LD SERVICES

LD program size is not limited.

LD services available to:

☐ Freshmen   ☐ Sophomores   ☐ Juniors   ☐ Seniors

Academic Accommodations

Curriculum		**In class**	
Foreign language waiver	☐	Early syllabus	☐
Lighter course load	☒	Note takers in class	☒
Math waiver	☐	Priority seating	☐
Other special classes	☐	Tape recorders	☒
Priority registrations	☐	Videotaped classes	☐
Substitution of courses	☐	Text on tape	☐
Exams		**Services**	
Extended time	☒	Diagnostic tests	☐
Oral exams	☒	Learning centers	☒
Take home exams	☐	Proofreaders	☐
Exams on tape or computer	☐	Readers	☒
Untimed exams	☐	Reading Machines/Kurzweil	☐
Other accommodations	☐	Special bookstore section	☐
		Typists	☐

Credit toward degree is given for remedial courses taken.

Counseling Services

- ☐ Academic
- ☐ Psychological
- ☐ Student Support groups
- ☐ Vocational

Tutoring

	Individual	Group
Time management	☐	☐
Organizational skills	☐	☐
Learning strategies	☐	☐
Study skills	☐	☐
Content area	☐	☐
Writing lab	☐	☐
Math lab	☐	☐

LD PROGRAM STAFF

Total number of LD Program staff (including director):

Full Time: 1   Part Time: 1

Key staff person available to work with LD students: James Kain, Disability Services Coordinator.

University of Pennsylvania

Philadelphia, PA

Address: 3451 Walnut Street, Philadelphia, PA, 19104
Admissions telephone: 215 898-7507
Admissions FAX: 215 898-9670
Dean of Admissions: Willis J. Stetson, Jr.
Admissions e-mail: info@admissions.ugao.upenn.edu
Web site: http://www.upenn.edu
SAT Code: 2926 ACT Code: 3668

LD program name: Student Disabilities Services
LD program address: Weingarten Center
Director: Myrna Cohen, Ph.D.
LD program telephone: 215 573-9235
LD program e-mail: cohenm@pobox.upenn.edu
LD program enrollment: 172, Total campus enrollment: 9,719

GENERAL

University of Pennsylvania is a private, coed, four-year institution. 260-acre, urban campus in Philadelphia (population: 1,517,550). Served by air, bus, and train. School operates transportation throughout campus and to local off-campus areas. Public transportation serves campus. Semester system.

LD ADMISSIONS

Students do not complete a separate application and are simultaneously accepted to the LD program. A member of the LD program does not sit on the admissions committee. A personal interview is not required. Essay is required and may be typed.

SECONDARY SCHOOL REQUIREMENTS

Graduation from secondary school required; GED accepted.

TESTING

SAT Reasoning or ACT considered if submitted. SAT Subject recommended.

All enrolled freshmen (fall 2004):

Average SAT I Scores: Verbal: 694 Math: 718
Average ACT Scores: Composite: 30

Child Study Team report is not required. A neuropsychological or comprehensive psycho-educational evaluation is required for admission. Must be dated within 36 months of application. Tests required as part of this documentation:

- [x] WAIS-IV
- [x] WISC-IV
- [x] SATA
- [x] Woodcock-Johnson
- [x] Nelson-Denny Reading Test
- [ ] Other

UNDERGRADUATE STUDENT BODY

Total undergraduate student enrollment: 5,015 Men, 4,715 Women.

Composition of student body (fall 2004):

	Undergraduate	Freshmen
International	10.3	9.0
Black	7.0	6.3
American Indian	0.2	0.3
Asian-American	18.4	17.9
Hispanic	5.2	5.5
White	46.1	49.0
Unreported	12.8	12.0
	100.0%	100.0%

81% are from out of state. 24% join a fraternity and 18% join a sorority. Average age of full-time undergraduates is 19. 75% of classes have fewer than 20 students, 18% have between 20 and 50 students, 7% have more than 50 students.

STUDENT HOUSING

99% of freshmen live in college housing. Freshmen are not required to live on campus. Housing is guaranteed for all undergraduates. Campus can house 7,205 undergraduates. Single rooms are available for students with medical or special needs. A medical note is required.

EXPENSES

Tuition (2005-06): $29,030 per year.

Room: $5,730. Board: $3,672.
There is no additional cost for LD program/services.

LD SERVICES

LD program size is not limited.

LD services available to:

- [x] Freshmen
- [x] Sophomores
- [x] Juniors
- [x] Seniors

Academic Accommodations

Curriculum		In class	
Foreign language waiver	[ ]	Early syllabus	[ ]
Lighter course load	[ ]	Note takers in class	[x]
Math waiver	[ ]	Priority seating	[x]
Other special classes	[ ]	Tape recorders	[x]
Priority registrations	[ ]	Videotaped classes	[ ]
Substitution of courses	[ ]	Text on tape	[x]
Exams		**Services**	
Extended time	[x]	Diagnostic tests	[ ]
Oral exams	[x]	Learning centers	[x]
Take home exams	[ ]	Proofreaders	[ ]
Exams on tape or computer	[x]	Readers	[x]
Untimed exams	[ ]	Reading Machines/Kurzweil	[x]
Other accommodations	[ ]	Special bookstore section	[ ]
		Typists	[x]

Credit toward degree is not given for remedial courses taken.

Counseling Services

- [x] Academic
- [x] Psychological
- [x] Student Support groups
- [ ] Vocational

Tutoring

Individual tutoring is available weekly.

	Individual	Group
Time management	[x]	[x]
Organizational skills	[x]	[x]
Learning strategies	[x]	[x]
Study skills	[x]	[x]
Content area	[x]	[x]
Writing lab	[x]	[x]
Math lab	[x]	[x]

LD PROGRAM STAFF

Total number of LD Program staff (including director):

Full Time: 4 Part Time: 4

There is an advisor/advocate from the LD program available to students. Four graduate students are available to work with LD students.

Key staff person available to work with LD students: Myrna Cohen, Ph.D., Director, Weingarten Learning Resource Center.

LD Program web site: www.vpul.upenn.edu/lrc/sds/index.html

Philadelphia University

Philadelphia, PA

Address: School House Lane and Henry Avenue, Philadelphia, PA, 19144
Admissions telephone: 800 951-7287
Admissions FAX: 215 951-2907
Director of Admissions: Christine Greb
Admissions e-mail: admissions@philau.edu
Web site: http://www.philau.edu
SAT Code: 2666 ACT Code: 3668

LD program name: Disability Services Office
Assistant Dean of Academic Affairs: James A. Savoie
LD program telephone: 215 951-2705
LD program e-mail: savoiej@philau.edu
Total campus enrollment: 2,706

GENERAL

Philadelphia University is a private, coed, four-year institution. 100-acre, suburban campus in Philadelphia (population: 1,517,550), seven miles from downtown; branch campus in Bucks County. Served by air, bus, and train. Public transportation serves campus. Semester system.

SECONDARY SCHOOL REQUIREMENTS

Graduation from secondary school required; GED accepted. The following course distribution required: 4 units of English, 3 units of math, 3 units of science, 2 units of social studies, 1 unit of history, 2 units of academic electives.

TESTING

SAT Reasoning or ACT required. SAT Subject required.

All enrolled freshmen (fall 2004):

Average SAT I Scores: Verbal: 523 Math: 535

Child Study Team report is not required. Tests required as part of this documentation:

- ☐ WAIS-IV
- ☐ WISC-IV
- ☐ SATA
- ☐ Woodcock-Johnson
- ☐ Nelson-Denny Reading Test
- ☐ Other

UNDERGRADUATE STUDENT BODY

Total undergraduate student enrollment: 928 Men, 1,828 Women.

Composition of student body (fall 2004):

	Undergraduate	Freshmen
International	1.9	2.5
Black	8.2	9.2
American Indian	0.3	0.1
Asian-American	4.3	4.3
Hispanic	2.1	2.7
White	73.5	78.0
Unreported	9.7	3.2
	100.0%	100.0%

38% are from out of state. 1% join a fraternity and 1% join a sorority. Average age of full-time undergraduates is 20. 63% of classes have fewer than 20 students, 37% have between 20 and 50 students.

STUDENT HOUSING

Freshmen are not required to live on campus. Housing available for all freshmen; upperclass housing available by lottery system. Campus can house 1,215 undergraduates. Single rooms are available for students with medical or special needs. A medical note is required.

EXPENSES

Tuition (2005-06): $22,070 per year.
Room: $3,910. Board: $4,026.
There is no additional cost for LD program/services.

LD SERVICES

LD program size is not limited.

LD services available to:

■ Freshmen ■ Sophomores ■ Juniors ■ Seniors

Academic Accommodations

Curriculum		In class	
Foreign language waiver	☐	Early syllabus	☐
Lighter course load	■	Note takers in class	■
Math waiver	☐	Priority seating	☐
Other special classes	☐	Tape recorders	■
Priority registrations	■	Videotaped classes	■
Substitution of courses	☐	Text on tape	■
Exams		**Services**	
Extended time	■	Diagnostic tests	☐
Oral exams	■	Learning centers	■
Take home exams	☐	Proofreaders	☐
Exams on tape or computer	■	Readers	■
Untimed exams	☐	Reading Machines/Kurzweil	■
Other accommodations	■	Special bookstore section	☐
		Typists	■

Credit toward degree is not given for remedial courses taken.

Counseling Services

- ■ Academic
- ■ Psychological
- ☐ Student Support groups
- ■ Vocational

Tutoring

Individual tutoring is available.

Average size of tutoring groups: 1

	Individual	Group
Time management	■	☐
Organizational skills	■	☐
Learning strategies	■	☐
Study skills	■	☐
Content area	■	☐
Writing lab	■	☐
Math lab	■	☐

LD PROGRAM STAFF

There is an advisor/advocate from the LD program available to students.

Key staff person available to work with LD students: Amy Schwab, Coordinator Student Disability Services.

LD Program web site: www.PhilaU.edu/disabilityservices

Peirce College

Philadelphia, PA

Address: 1420 Pine Street, Philadelphia, PA, 19102
Admissions telephone: 877 670-9190
Admissions FAX: 215 670-9366
Senior Enrollment Representative: Nadine Maher
Admissions e-mail: info@peirce.edu
Web site: http://www.peirce.edu
SAT Code: 2674 ACT Code: 3659

LD program name: Walker Center for Academic Excellence
LD program address: 2nd floor, Alumni Hall
Assistant Dean, Student Support Services: Rita Toliver
LD program telephone: 888 467-3472, extension 9265
LD program e-mail: rjtoliver@peirce.edu
LD program enrollment: 3, Total campus enrollment: 1,892

GENERAL

Peirce College is a private, coed, four-year institution. One-acre, urban campus in Philadelphia (population: 1,517,550). Served by air, bus, and train. Public transportation serves campus. Continuous system.

LD ADMISSIONS

Students do not complete a separate application and are not simultaneously accepted to the LD program. A member of the LD program does sit on the admissions committee. A personal interview is not required. Essay is not required.

SECONDARY SCHOOL REQUIREMENTS

Graduation from secondary school required; GED accepted.

TESTING

Child Study Team report is not required. A neuropsychological or comprehensive psycho-educational evaluation is required for admission. Must be dated within 1 months of application. Tests required as part of this documentation:

- ■ WAIS-IV
- □ WISC-IV
- □ SATA
- ■ Woodcock-Johnson
- □ Nelson-Denny Reading Test
- □ Other

UNDERGRADUATE STUDENT BODY

Total undergraduate student enrollment: 1,892.

Composition of student body (fall 2004):

	Undergraduate	Freshmen
International	3.4	2.5
Black	40.5	49.2
American Indian	0.0	0.4
Asian-American	1.0	1.5
Hispanic	6.3	4.5
White	29.5	29.6
Unreported	19.3	12.3
	100.0%	100.0%

Average age of full-time undergraduates is 32. 71% of classes have fewer than 20 students, 28% have between 20 and 50 students, 1% have more than 50 students.

STUDENT HOUSING

Freshmen are not required to live on campus. Housing is not guaranteed for all undergraduates.

EXPENSES

Tuition (2005-06):
There is no additional cost for LD program/services.

LD SERVICES

LD program size is not limited.

LD services available to:

■ Freshmen ■ Sophomores ■ Juniors ■ Seniors

Academic Accommodations

Curriculum		In class	
Foreign language waiver	□	Early syllabus	■
Lighter course load	■	Note takers in class	■
Math waiver	□	Priority seating	■
Other special classes	□	Tape recorders	■
Priority registrations	□	Videotaped classes	□
Substitution of courses	□	Text on tape	■
Exams		**Services**	
Extended time	■	Diagnostic tests	■
Oral exams	■	Learning centers	■
Take home exams	□	Proofreaders	■
Exams on tape or computer	■	Readers	■
Untimed exams	■	Reading Machines/Kurzweil	□
Other accommodations	□	Special bookstore section	□
		Typists	■

Credit toward degree is not given for remedial courses taken.

Counseling Services

- ■ Academic
- □ Psychological
- □ Student Support groups
- □ Vocational

Tutoring

Individual tutoring is available weekly.

Average size of tutoring groups: 4

	Individual	Group
Time management	■	■
Organizational skills	■	■
Learning strategies	■	■
Study skills	■	■
Content area	■	□
Writing lab	■	□
Math lab	□	□

LD PROGRAM STAFF

Total number of LD Program staff (including director):

Full Time: 2 Part Time: 2

There is an advisor/advocate from the LD program available to students. The advisor/advocate meets with faculty and students one time per month.

Key staff person available to work with LD students: Christina Santos, SSS Counselor/Administrator.

Pennsylvania College of Technology

Williamsport, PA

Address: 1 College Avenue, Williamsport, PA, 17701
Admissions telephone: 800 367-9222
Admissions FAX: 570 321-5551
Director of Admissions: Chester Schuman
Admissions e-mail: admissions@pct.edu
Web site: http://www.pct.edu
SAT Code: 2989

Director: Sharon Waters
LD program telephone: 570 326-3761
LD program e-mail: swaters@pct.edu
Total campus enrollment: 6,358

GENERAL

Pennsylvania College of Technology is a public, coed, four-year institution. 928-acre, suburban campus in Williamsport (population: 30,706), 70 miles from Wilkes-Barre; branch campus in Wellsboro; aviation center in Montoursville; earth science center in Montgomery. Served by bus; major airport serves Wilkes-Barre. Public transportation serves campus. Semester system.

LD ADMISSIONS

A personal interview is not required. Essay is not required.

SECONDARY SCHOOL REQUIREMENTS

Graduation from secondary school required; GED accepted.

TESTING

Child Study Team report is not required. Tests required as part of this documentation:

- ☐ WAIS-IV
- ☐ WISC-IV
- ☐ SATA
- ☐ Woodcock-Johnson
- ☐ Nelson-Denny Reading Test
- ☐ Other

UNDERGRADUATE STUDENT BODY

Total undergraduate student enrollment: 3,633 Men, 1,905 Women.

Composition of student body (fall 2004):

	Undergraduate	Freshmen
International	0.2	0.4
Black	3.5	3.0
American Indian	0.2	0.4
Asian-American	0.9	1.1
Hispanic	1.4	1.0
White	93.8	94.1
Unreported	0.0	0.0
	100.0%	100.0%

6% are from out of state. Average age of full-time undergraduates is 21. 55% of classes have fewer than 20 students, 45% have between 20 and 50 students.

STUDENT HOUSING

Freshmen are not required to live on campus. Housing is guaranteed for all undergraduates. Campus can house 1,442 undergraduates.

EXPENSES

Tuition (2005-06): $8,580 per year (in-state), $11,160 (out-of-state).

Room: $4,200. Board: $1,400.
There is no additional cost for LD program/services.

LD SERVICES

LD services available to:

☐ Freshmen ☐ Sophomores ☐ Juniors ☐ Seniors

Academic Accommodations

Curriculum		In class	
Foreign language waiver	☐	Early syllabus	☐
Lighter course load	☐	Note takers in class	☒
Math waiver	☐	Priority seating	☐
Other special classes	☒	Tape recorders	☒
Priority registrations	☐	Videotaped classes	☐
Substitution of courses	☐	Text on tape	☐
Exams		**Services**	
Extended time	☐	Diagnostic tests	☐
Oral exams	☐	Learning centers	☒
Take home exams	☐	Proofreaders	☐
Exams on tape or computer	☐	Readers	☒
Untimed exams	☐	Reading Machines/Kurzweil	☐
Other accommodations	☐	Special bookstore section	☐
		Typists	☐

Credit toward degree is not given for remedial courses taken.

Counseling Services

- ☐ Academic
- ☐ Psychological
- ☐ Student Support groups
- ☐ Vocational

Tutoring

	Individual	Group
Time management	☐	☐
Organizational skills	☐	☐
Learning strategies	☐	☐
Study skills	☐	☐
Content area	☐	☐
Writing lab	☐	☐
Math lab	☐	☐

LD PROGRAM STAFF

Key staff person available to work with LD students: Sharon Waters, Director, Career/Academic Support and Counsel

Pennsylvania State University - Altoona

Altoona, PA

Address: 3000 Ivyside Park, Altoona, PA, 16601-3760
Admissions telephone: 800 848-9843
Admissions FAX: 814 949-5564
Admissions Officer: Fredina Ingold
Admissions e-mail: aaadmit@psu.edu
Web site: http://www.psu.edu
SAT Code: 2660

Director, Disability Services: Bill Welsh
LD program telephone: 814 863-1807
LD program e-mail: wjw9@psu.edu
Total campus enrollment: 3,813

GENERAL

Pennsylvania State University - Altoona is a public, coed, four-year institution. 92-acre campus in Altoona (population: 49,523), 95 miles from Pittsburgh. Semester system.

LD ADMISSIONS

Students do not complete a separate application and are not simultaneously accepted to the LD program. A member of the LD program does not sit on the admissions committee. A personal interview is not required. Essay is not required.

SECONDARY SCHOOL REQUIREMENTS

Graduation from secondary school required; GED accepted. The following course distribution required: 4 units of English, 3 units of math, 3 units of science, 2 units of foreign language, 3 units of social studies.

TESTING

SAT Reasoning or ACT required.

Child Study Team report is not required. A neuropsychological or comprehensive psycho-education evaluation is not required for admission. Tests required as part of this documentation:

- ❑ WAIS-IV
- ❑ WISC-IV
- ❑ SATA
- ❑ Woodcock-Johnson
- ❑ Nelson-Denny Reading Test
- ❑ Other

UNDERGRADUATE STUDENT BODY

Total undergraduate student enrollment: 1,920 Men, 1,893 Women.

Composition of student body (fall 2004):

	Undergraduate	Freshmen
International	1.2	0.8
Black	6.9	5.3
American Indian	0.1	0.1
Asian-American	2.6	1.9
Hispanic	2.2	2.1
White	87.0	89.8
Unreported	0.0	0.0
	100.0%	100.0%

12% are from out of state. 4% join a fraternity and 3% join a sorority. Average age of full-time undergraduates is 21.

STUDENT HOUSING

Single rooms are not available for students with medical or special needs.

EXPENSES

Tuition 2001-02: $6,936 per year (state residents, lower division), $7,288 (state residents, upper division), $10,774 (out-of-state, lower division), $11,132 (out-of-state, upper division).

Room: $2,682. Board: $2,628.
There is no additional cost for LD program/services.

LD SERVICES

LD program size is not limited.

LD services available to:

❑ Freshmen ❑ Sophomores ❑ Juniors ❑ Seniors

Academic Accommodations

Curriculum		**In class**	
Foreign language waiver	❑	Early syllabus	❑
Lighter course load	❑	Note takers in class	❑
Math waiver	❑	Priority seating	❑
Other special classes	❑	Tape recorders	❑
Priority registrations	❑	Videotaped classes	❑
Substitution of courses	❑	Text on tape	❑
Exams		**Services**	
Extended time	❑	Diagnostic tests	❑
Oral exams	❑	Learning centers	❑
Take home exams	❑	Proofreaders	❑
Exams on tape or computer	❑	Readers	❑
Untimed exams	❑	Reading Machines/Kurzweil	❑
Other accommodations	❑	Special bookstore section	❑
		Typists	❑

Credit toward degree is not given for remedial courses taken.

Counseling Services

- ❑ Academic
- ❑ Psychological
- ❑ Student Support groups
- ❑ Vocational

Tutoring

Individual tutoring is not available.

	Individual	Group
Time management	❑	❑
Organizational skills	❑	❑
Learning strategies	❑	❑
Study skills	❑	❑
Content area	❑	❑
Writing lab	❑	❑
Math lab	❑	❑

LD PROGRAM STAFF

There is no advisor/advocate from the LD program available to students.

Key staff person available to work with LD students: Bill Welsh, Director, Disability Services

Pennsylvania State University - Berks

Reading, PA

Address: P.O. Box 7009, Reading, PA, 19610-6009
Admissions telephone: 610 396-6060
Admissions FAX: 610 396-6077
Admissions Officer: John Gemmell
Web site: http://www.psu.edu
SAT Code: 2660

Director, Disability Services: Bill Welsh
LD program telephone: 814 863-1807
LD program e-mail: wjw9@psu.edu
Total campus enrollment: 2,316

GENERAL

Pennsylvania State University - Berks is a public, coed, four-year institution. 240-acre campus in Reading (population: 81,207). Served by air. Semester system.

LD ADMISSIONS

Students do not complete a separate application and are not simultaneously accepted to the LD program. A member of the LD program does not sit on the admissions committee. A personal interview is not required. Essay is not required.

SECONDARY SCHOOL REQUIREMENTS

Graduation from secondary school required; GED accepted. The following course distribution required: 4 units of English, 3 units of math, 3 units of science, 2 units of foreign language, 3 units of social studies.

TESTING

SAT Reasoning or ACT required.

Child Study Team report is not required. A neuropsychological or comprehensive psycho-education evaluation is not required for admission. Tests required as part of this documentation:

- ❑ WAIS-IV
- ❑ WISC-IV
- ❑ SATA
- ❑ Woodcock-Johnson
- ❑ Nelson-Denny Reading Test
- ❑ Other

UNDERGRADUATE STUDENT BODY

Total undergraduate student enrollment: 1,390 Men, 926 Women.

Composition of student body (fall 2004):

	Undergraduate	Freshmen
International	0.6	0.4
Black	6.1	6.2
American Indian	0.0	0.2
Asian-American	4.4	4.2
Hispanic	3.3	2.8
White	85.6	86.2
Unreported	0.0	0.0
	100.0%	100.0%

8% are from out of state. Average age of full-time undergraduates is 20.

STUDENT HOUSING

Single rooms are not available for students with medical or special needs.

EXPENSES

Tuition 2001-02: $6,936 per year (state residents, lower division), $7,288 (state residents, upper division), $10,774 (out-of-state, lower division), $11,132 (out-of-state, upper division).
Room: $2,682. Board: $2,628.

There is no additional cost for LD program/services.

LD SERVICES

LD program size is not limited.

LD services available to:

❑ Freshmen ❑ Sophomores ❑ Juniors ❑ Seniors

Academic Accommodations

Curriculum		In class	
Foreign language waiver	❑	Early syllabus	❑
Lighter course load	❑	Note takers in class	❑
Math waiver	❑	Priority seating	❑
Other special classes	❑	Tape recorders	❑
Priority registrations	❑	Videotaped classes	❑
Substitution of courses	❑	Text on tape	❑
Exams		**Services**	
Extended time	❑	Diagnostic tests	❑
Oral exams	❑	Learning centers	❑
Take home exams	❑	Proofreaders	❑
Exams on tape or computer	❑	Readers	❑
Untimed exams	❑	Reading Machines/Kurzweil	❑
Other accommodations	❑	Special bookstore section	❑
		Typists	❑

Credit toward degree is not given for remedial courses taken.

Counseling Services

- ❑ Academic
- ❑ Psychological
- ❑ Student Support groups
- ❑ Vocational

Tutoring

Individual tutoring is not available.

	Individual	Group
Time management	❑	❑
Organizational skills	❑	❑
Learning strategies	❑	❑
Study skills	❑	❑
Content area	❑	❑
Writing lab	❑	❑
Math lab	❑	❑

LD PROGRAM STAFF

There is not an advisor/advocate from the LD program available to students.

Key staff person available to work with LD students: Bill Welsh, Director, Disability Services

Pennsylvania State University, Erie, The Behrend College

Erie, PA

Address: 5091 Station Road, Erie, PA, 16563
Admissions telephone: 866 374-3378
Admissions FAX: 814 898-6044
Director of Admissions and Financial Aid: Mary-Ellen Madigan
Admissions e-mail: behrend.admissions@psu.edu
Web site: http://www.pserie.psu.edu/
SAT Code: 2660 ACT Code: 3656

LD program name: Services for Students with Disabilities
Director of Educational Equity Programs: Andres Herrera
LD program telephone: 814 898-6111
LD program e-mail: aah10@psu.edu
LD program enrollment: 57, Total campus enrollment: 3,440

GENERAL

Pennsylvania State University, Erie, The Behrend College is a public, coed, four-year institution. 731-acre campus in Erie (population: 103,717), 127 miles from Pittsburgh. Served by air, bus, and train. Public transportation serves campus. Semester system.

LD ADMISSIONS

Students do not complete a separate application and are simultaneously accepted to the LD program. A member of the LD program does not sit on the admissions committee. A personal interview is not required. Essay is not required.

For fall 2004, 15 completed self-identified LD applications were received. 15 applications were offered admission, and 15 enrolled.

SECONDARY SCHOOL REQUIREMENTS

Graduation from secondary school required; GED accepted. The following course distribution required: 4 units of English, 3 units of math, 3 units of science, 2 units of foreign language, 3 units of social studies.

TESTING

SAT Reasoning or ACT required. SAT Subject recommended.

All enrolled freshmen (fall 2004):

Average SAT I Scores: Verbal: 517 Math: 540

Child Study Team report is not required. A neuropsychological or comprehensive psycho-educational evaluation is required for admission. Must be dated within 36 months of application. Tests required as part of this documentation:

- ■ WAIS-IV
- ■ WISC-IV
- ■ SATA
- ■ Woodcock-Johnson
- ■ Nelson-Denny Reading Test
- ■ Other

UNDERGRADUATE STUDENT BODY

Total undergraduate student enrollment: 2,235 Men, 1,315 Women.

Composition of student body (fall 2004):

	Undergraduate	Freshmen
International	1.3	1.4
Black	3.2	3.1
American Indian	0.1	0.1
Asian-American	1.9	2.2
Hispanic	2.1	1.6
White	91.4	91.6
Unreported	0.0	0.0
	100.0%	100.0%

7% are from out of state. 4% join a fraternity and 48% join a sorority. Average age of full-time undergraduates is 20. 34% of classes have fewer than 20 students, 61% have between 20 and 50 students, 5% have more than 50 students.

STUDENT HOUSING

80% of freshmen live in college housing. Freshmen are not required to live on campus. Housing is guaranteed for all undergraduates. Campus can house 1,687 undergraduates.

EXPENSES

Tuition (2005-06): $7,054 per year (state residents, lower division), $7,410 (state residents, upper division), $13,534 (out-of-state, lower division), $13,676 (out-of-state, upper division).

There is no additional cost for LD program/services.

LD SERVICES

LD program size is not limited.

LD services available to:

■ Freshmen ■ Sophomores ■ Juniors ■ Seniors

Academic Accommodations

Curriculum		In class	
Foreign language waiver	■	Early syllabus	☐
Lighter course load	☐	Note takers in class	■
Math waiver	☐	Priority seating	■
Other special classes	☐	Tape recorders	■
Priority registrations	■	Videotaped classes	☐
Substitution of courses	☐	Text on tape	■
Exams		**Services**	
Extended time	■	Diagnostic tests	☐
Oral exams	■	Learning centers	■
Take home exams	☐	Proofreaders	☐
Exams on tape or computer	■	Readers	■
Untimed exams	■	Reading Machines/Kurzweil	■
Other accommodations	■	Special bookstore section	☐
		Typists	■

Credit toward degree is not given for remedial courses taken.

Counseling Services

- ■ Academic
- ■ Psychological
- ■ Student Support groups
- ■ Vocational

Tutoring

Individual tutoring is available daily.

Average size of tutoring groups: 2

	Individual	Group
Time management	■	■
Organizational skills	■	■
Learning strategies	■	■
Study skills	■	■
Content area	■	■
Writing lab	■	■
Math lab	■	■

LD PROGRAM STAFF

Total number of LD Program staff (including director):

Full Time: 1 Part Time: 1

There is an advisor/advocate from the LD program available to students. The advisor/advocate meets with faculty two times per month and students four times per month. 60 peer tutors are available to work with LD students.

Key staff person available to work with LD students: Andres Herrera, Director of Educational Equity Programs.

LD Program web site: http://pennstatebehrend.psu.edu/student/Educational%20Equities/DISABILITY.htm

Pennsylvania State University - Lehigh Valley

Fogelsville, PA

Address: 8380 Mohr Lane, Fogelsville, PA, 18051-9999
Admissions telephone: 610 285-5035
Admissions FAX: 610 285-5220
Admissions Officer: Judith Cary
Admissions e-mail: admission-lv@psu.edu
Web site: http://www.psu.edu
SAT Code: 2660

Director, Disability Services: Bill Welsh
LD program telephone: 816 863-1807
LD program e-mail: wjw9@psu.edu
Total campus enrollment: 685

GENERAL

Pennsylvania State University - Lehigh Valley is a public, coed, four-year institution. Campus in Fogelsville (population: 900), 10 miles from Allentown. Airport serves Allentown. Semester system.

LD ADMISSIONS

Students do not complete a separate application and are not simultaneously accepted to the LD program. A member of the LD program does not sit on the admissions committee. A personal interview is not required. Essay is not required.

SECONDARY SCHOOL REQUIREMENTS

Graduation from secondary school required; GED accepted. The following course distribution required: 4 units of English, 3 units of math, 3 units of science, 2 units of foreign language, 3 units of social studies.

TESTING

SAT Reasoning or ACT required.

All enrolled freshmen (fall 2004):

Average SAT I Scores: Verbal: Math:
Average ACT Scores: Composite:

Child Study Team report is not required. A neuropsychological or comprehensive psycho-education evaluation is not required for admission. Tests required as part of this documentation:

- ☐ WAIS-IV
- ☐ WISC-IV
- ☐ SATA
- ☐ Woodcock-Johnson
- ☐ Nelson-Denny Reading Test
- ☐ Other

UNDERGRADUATE STUDENT BODY

Total undergraduate student enrollment: 426 Men, 259 Women.

Composition of student body (fall 2004):

	Undergraduate	Freshmen
International	1.1	0.9
Black	0.5	1.3
American Indian	0.0	0.0
Asian-American	10.1	9.3
Hispanic	3.7	4.5
White	84.6	84.0
Unreported	0.0	0.0
	100.0%	100.0%

3% are from out of state. Average age of full-time undergraduates is 22.

STUDENT HOUSING

Single rooms are not available for students with medical or special needs.

EXPENSES

Tuition 2001-02: $6,832 per year (state residents, lower division), $7,288 (state residents, upper division), $10,574 (out-of-state, lower division), $11,132 (out-of-state, upper division).

There is no additional cost for LD program/services.

LD SERVICES

LD program size is not limited.

LD services available to:

☐ Freshmen ☐ Sophomores ☐ Juniors ☐ Seniors

Academic Accommodations

Curriculum		**In class**	
Foreign language waiver	☐	Early syllabus	☐
Lighter course load	☐	Note takers in class	☐
Math waiver	☐	Priority seating	☐
Other special classes	☐	Tape recorders	☐
Priority registrations	☐	Videotaped classes	☐
Substitution of courses	☐	Text on tape	☐
Exams		**Services**	
Extended time	☐	Diagnostic tests	☐
Oral exams	☐	Learning centers	☐
Take home exams	☐	Proofreaders	☐
Exams on tape or computer	☐	Readers	☐
Untimed exams	☐	Reading Machines/Kurzweil	☐
Other accommodations	☐	Special bookstore section	☐
		Typists	☐

Credit toward degree is not given for remedial courses taken.

Counseling Services

- ☐ Academic
- ☐ Psychological
- ☐ Student Support groups
- ☐ Vocational

Tutoring

Individual tutoring is not available.

	Individual	Group
Time management	☐	☐
Organizational skills	☐	☐
Learning strategies	☐	☐
Study skills	☐	☐
Content area	☐	☐
Writing lab	☐	☐
Math lab	☐	☐

LD PROGRAM STAFF

There is no advisor/advocate from the LD program available to students.

Key staff person available to work with LD students: Bill Welsh, Director, Disability Services

Pennsylvania State University - Schuylkill

Schuylkill Haven, PA

Address: 200 University Drive, Schuylkill Haven, PA, 17972-2208
Admissions telephone: 570 385-6242
Admissions FAX: 570 385-3672
Admissions Officer: Jerry Bowman
Admissions e-mail: jxb25@psu.edu
Web site: http://www.psu.edu
SAT Code: 2660

Director, Disability Services: Bill Welsh
LD program telephone: 814 863-1807
LD program e-mail: wjw9@psu.edu
Total campus enrollment: 1,052

GENERAL

Pennsylvania State University - Schuylkill is a public, coed, four-year institution. 14-acre campus in Schuylhill Haven (population: 5,548), 34 miles from both Allentown and Harrisburg. Airport serves Harrisburg. Semester system.

LD ADMISSIONS

Students do not complete a separate application and are not simultaneously accepted to the LD program. A member of the LD program does not sit on the admissions committee. A personal interview is not required. Essay is not required. Admissions test requirements for LD students same as for other students.

SECONDARY SCHOOL REQUIREMENTS

Graduation from secondary school required; GED accepted. The following course distribution required: 4 units of English, 3 units of math, 3 units of science, 2 units of foreign language, 3 units of social studies.

TESTING

SAT Reasoning or ACT required.

Child Study Team report is not required. A neuropsychological or comprehensive psycho-education evaluation is not required for admission. Tests required as part of this documentation:

- ❑ WAIS-IV
- ❑ WISC-IV
- ❑ SATA
- ❑ Woodcock-Johnson
- ❑ Nelson-Denny Reading Test
- ❑ Other

UNDERGRADUATE STUDENT BODY

Total undergraduate student enrollment: 457 Men, 595 Women.

Composition of student body (fall 2004):

	Undergraduate	Freshmen
International	0.0	0.1
Black	12.8	12.8
American Indian	0.0	0.1
Asian-American	6.4	3.9
Hispanic	2.5	2.7
White	78.3	80.4
Unreported	0.0	0.0
	100.0%	100.0%

11% are from out of state. Average age of full-time undergraduates is 22.

STUDENT HOUSING

Single rooms are not available for students with medical or special needs.

EXPENSES

Tuition 2001-02: $6,832 per year (state residents, lower division), $7,288 (state residents, upper division), $10,574 (out-of-state, lower division), $11,132 (out-of-state, upper division).

Room: $3,700.
There is no additional cost for LD program/services.

LD SERVICES

LD program size is not limited.

LD services available to:

❑ Freshmen ❑ Sophomores ❑ Juniors ❑ Seniors

Academic Accommodations

Curriculum		**In class**	
Foreign language waiver	❑	Early syllabus	❑
Lighter course load	❑	Note takers in class	❑
Math waiver	❑	Priority seating	❑
Other special classes	❑	Tape recorders	❑
Priority registrations	❑	Videotaped classes	❑
Substitution of courses	❑	Text on tape	❑
Exams		**Services**	
Extended time	❑	Diagnostic tests	❑
Oral exams	❑	Learning centers	❑
Take home exams	❑	Proofreaders	❑
Exams on tape or computer	❑	Readers	❑
Untimed exams	❑	Reading Machines/Kurzweil	❑
Other accommodations	❑	Special bookstore section	❑
		Typists	❑

Credit toward degree is not given for remedial courses taken.

Counseling Services

- ❑ Academic
- ❑ Psychological
- ❑ Student Support groups
- ❑ Vocational

Tutoring

Individual tutoring is not available.

	Individual	Group
Time management	❑	❑
Organizational skills	❑	❑
Learning strategies	❑	❑
Study skills	❑	❑
Content area	❑	❑
Writing lab	❑	❑
Math lab	❑	❑

LD PROGRAM STAFF

There is no advisor/advocate from the LD program available to students.

Key staff person available to work with LD students: Bill Welsh, Director, Disability Services.

Pennsylvania State University - University Park

University Park, PA

Address: University Park Campus, University Park, PA, 16802
Admissions telephone: 814 865-5471
Admissions FAX: 814 863-7590
Vice Provost: Randall Deike
Web site: http://www.psu.edu
SAT Code: 2660 ACT Code: 3656

Director, Disability Services: William J. Welsh
LD program telephone: 814 863-1807
Total campus enrollment: 34,824

GENERAL

Pennsylvania State University - University Park is a public, coed, four-year institution. 6,138-acre main campus at University Park near State College (population: 38,420), 90 miles northwest of Harrisburg; branch campuses in 23 locations. Served by air and bus; major airport serves Harrisburg; train serves Lewistown (35 miles). Public transportation serves campus. Semester system.

LD ADMISSIONS

A personal interview is required. Essay is not required.

SECONDARY SCHOOL REQUIREMENTS

Graduation from secondary school required; GED accepted. The following course distribution required: 4 units of English, 3 units of math, 3 units of science, 2 units of foreign language, 3 units of social studies.

TESTING

SAT Reasoning or ACT required. SAT Subject recommended.

All enrolled freshmen (fall 2004):

Average SAT I Scores: Verbal: 590 Math: 618

Child Study Team report is not required. A neuropsychological or comprehensive psycho-educational evaluation is required for admission. Tests required as part of this documentation:

- ■ WAIS-IV
- ☐ WISC-IV
- ☐ SATA
- ■ Woodcock-Johnson
- ☐ Nelson-Denny Reading Test
- ■ Other

UNDERGRADUATE STUDENT BODY

Total undergraduate student enrollment: 18,418 Men, 16,121 Women.

Composition of student body (fall 2004):

	Undergraduate	Freshmen
International	2.0	2.3
Black	4.4	4.1
American Indian	0.1	0.2
Asian-American	5.8	5.7
Hispanic	3.7	3.2
White	84.0	84.5
Unreported	0.0	0.0
	100.0%	100.0%

23% are from out of state. 13% join a fraternity and 10% join a sorority. Average age of full-time undergraduates is 20. 30% of classes have fewer than 20 students, 51% have between 20 and 50 students, 19% have more than 50 students.

STUDENT HOUSING

92% of freshmen live in college housing. Freshmen are required to live on campus. Housing is guaranteed for all undergraduates. Campus can house 12,719 undergraduates. Single rooms are available for students with medical or special needs. A medical note is required.

EXPENSES

Tuition (2005-06): $7,054 per year (state residents, lower division), $7,410 (state residents, upper division), $15,180 (out-of-state, lower division), $15,544 (out-of-state, upper division).

There is no additional cost for LD program/services.

LD SERVICES

LD program size is not limited.

LD services available to:

■ Freshmen ■ Sophomores ■ Juniors ■ Seniors

Academic Accommodations

Curriculum		In class	
Foreign language waiver	☐	Early syllabus	☐
Lighter course load	■	Note takers in class	■
Math waiver	☐	Priority seating	■
Other special classes	☐	Tape recorders	■
Priority registrations	■	Videotaped classes	☐
Substitution of courses	☐	Text on tape	☐
Exams		**Services**	
Extended time	■	Diagnostic tests	☐
Oral exams	☐	Learning centers	■
Take home exams	☐	Proofreaders	☐
Exams on tape or computer	■	Readers	■
Untimed exams	☐	Reading Machines/Kurzweil	■
Other accommodations	■	Special bookstore section	☐
		Typists	■

Credit toward degree is given for remedial courses taken.

Counseling Services

- ☐ Academic
- ☐ Psychological
- ☐ Student Support groups
- ☐ Vocational

Tutoring

	Individual	Group
Time management	☐	☐
Organizational skills	☐	☐
Learning strategies	☐	☐
Study skills	☐	☐
Content area	☐	☐
Writing lab	☐	☐
Math lab	☐	☐

LD PROGRAM STAFF

Total number of LD Program staff (including director):

Full Time: 4 Part Time: 4

There is no advisor/advocate from the LD program available to students.

Key staff person available to work with LD students: William J. Welsh, Director, Disability Services

Philadelphia Biblical University

Langhorne, PA

Address: 200 Manor Avenue, Langhorne, PA, 19047-2990
Admissions telephone: 800 366-0049
Admissions FAX: 215 702-4248
Director of Admissions: Lisa Yoder
Admissions e-mail: admissions@pbu.edu
Web site: http://www.pbu.edu
SAT Code: 2661 ACT Code: 3658

Coordinator, Disability Services: Jean Minto
LD program e-mail: jminto@pbu.edu
LD program enrollment: 31, Total campus enrollment: 1,022

GENERAL

Philadelphia Biblical University is a private, coed, four-year institution. 105-acre, suburban campus in Langhorne (population: 1,981), four miles from Philadelphia; branch campuses in Liberty Corner, NJ; Cable, WI; abroad in Kandern, Germany; and Bankok, Thailand. Served by train; major airport serves Philadelphia (31 miles); bus serves Bristol (three miles). School operates transportation to student apartments. Public transportation serves campus. Semester system.

LD ADMISSIONS

A personal interview is recommended.

SECONDARY SCHOOL REQUIREMENTS

Graduation from secondary school required; GED accepted.

TESTING

SAT Reasoning or ACT required. SAT Subject recommended.

All enrolled freshmen (fall 2004):

Average SAT I Scores:	Verbal: 543	Math: 519
Average ACT Scores:	Composite: 22	

Child Study Team report is not required. Tests required as part of this documentation:

☐ WAIS-IV ☐ Woodcock-Johnson
☐ WISC-IV ☐ Nelson-Denny Reading Test
☐ SATA ☐ Other

UNDERGRADUATE STUDENT BODY

Total undergraduate student enrollment: 479 Men, 581 Women.

Composition of student body (fall 2004):

	Undergraduate	Freshmen
International	2.2	2.0
Black	6.5	10.8
American Indian	0.0	0.2
Asian-American	1.6	2.1
Hispanic	2.2	2.4
White	87.5	82.3
Unreported	0.0	0.2
	100.0%	100.0%

53% are from out of state. Average age of full-time undergraduates is 23. 57% of classes have fewer than 20 students, 40% have between 20 and 50 students, 2% have more than 50 students.

STUDENT HOUSING

88% of freshmen live in college housing. Housing is guaranteed for all undergraduates. Campus can house 487 undergraduates.

EXPENSES

Tuition (2005-06): $14,180 per year.
Room: $3,100. Board: $3,000.
There is no additional cost for LD program/services.

LD SERVICES

LD program size is not limited.

LD services available to:

☐ Freshmen ☐ Sophomores ☐ Juniors ☐ Seniors

Academic Accommodations

Curriculum		In class	
Foreign language waiver	☐	Early syllabus	☐
Lighter course load	■	Note takers in class	■
Math waiver	☐	Priority seating	☐
Other special classes	☐	Tape recorders	■
Priority registrations	☐	Videotaped classes	☐
Substitution of courses	☐	Text on tape	☐
Exams		**Services**	
Extended time	☐	Diagnostic tests	☐
Oral exams	■	Learning centers	■
Take home exams	☐	Proofreaders	☐
Exams on tape or computer	☐	Readers	■
Untimed exams	■	Reading Machines/Kurzweil	☐
Other accommodations	■	Special bookstore section	☐
		Typists	☐

Counseling Services

☐ Academic
☐ Psychological
☐ Student Support groups
☐ Vocational

Tutoring

Individual tutoring is available.

	Individual	Group
Time management	☐	☐
Organizational skills	☐	☐
Learning strategies	☐	☐
Study skills	☐	☐
Content area	☐	☐
Writing lab	☐	☐
Math lab	☐	☐

LD PROGRAM STAFF

There is an advisor/advocate from the LD program available to students.

University of Pittsburgh at Bradford

Bradford, PA

Address: 300 Campus Drive, Bradford, PA, 16701
Admissions telephone: 800 872-1787
Admissions FAX: 814 362-7578
Director of Admissions: Alexander P. Nazemetz
Web site: http://www.upb.pitt.edu
SAT Code: 2935 ACT Code: 3731

Learning Development Specialist: Kara Kennedy
LD program telephone: 814 362-7609
LD program e-mail: kjk3@exchange.upb.pitt.edu
LD program enrollment: 15, Total campus enrollment: 1,460

GENERAL

University of Pittsburgh at Bradford is a public, coed, four-year institution. 125-acre campus in Bradford (population: 9,175), 80 miles from Buffalo, NY. Served by air and bus; major airport serves Buffalo, NY; train serves Erie (90 miles). Public transportation serves campus. Semester system.

LD ADMISSIONS

A personal interview is recommended. Essay is not required.

SECONDARY SCHOOL REQUIREMENTS

Graduation from secondary school required; GED accepted. The following course distribution required: 4 units of English, 2 units of math, 1 unit of science, 2 units of foreign language, 1 unit of history, 5 units of academic electives.

TESTING

SAT Reasoning required; ACT may be substituted. SAT Subject recommended.

All enrolled freshmen (fall 2004):

Average SAT I Scores:	Verbal: 502	Math: 506
Average ACT Scores:	Composite: 20	

Child Study Team report is not required. Tests required as part of this documentation:

- ☐ WAIS-IV
- ☐ WISC-IV
- ☐ SATA
- ☐ Woodcock-Johnson
- ☐ Nelson-Denny Reading Test
- ☐ Other

UNDERGRADUATE STUDENT BODY

Total undergraduate student enrollment: 569 Men, 896 Women.

Composition of student body (fall 2004):

	Undergraduate	Freshmen
International	0.0	0.1
Black	7.3	3.2
American Indian	0.0	0.4
Asian-American	1.3	1.0
Hispanic	1.3	1.0
White	86.0	89.8
Unreported	4.1	4.5
	100.0%	100.0%

6% are from out of state. 8% join a fraternity and 8% join a sorority. Average age of full-time undergraduates is 22. 60% of classes have fewer than 20 students, 39% have between 20 and 50 students, 1% have more than 50 students.

STUDENT HOUSING

69% of freshmen live in college housing. Freshmen are required to live on campus. Housing is guaranteed for all undergraduates. Campus can house 554 undergraduates.

EXPENSES

Tuition (2005-06): $9,676 per year (in-state), $19,570 (out-of-state). Tuition varies by program.
Room: $3,900. Board: $2,820.
There is no additional cost for LD program/services.

LD SERVICES

LD program size is not limited.

LD services available to:

☐ Freshmen ☐ Sophomores ☐ Juniors ☐ Seniors

Academic Accommodations

Curriculum		In class	
Foreign language waiver	☐	Early syllabus	☐
Lighter course load	☐	Note takers in class	■
Math waiver	☐	Priority seating	☐
Other special classes	☐	Tape recorders	☐
Priority registrations	☐	Videotaped classes	☐
Substitution of courses	☐	Text on tape	☐
Exams		**Services**	
Extended time	■	Diagnostic tests	☐
Oral exams	☐	Learning centers	■
Take home exams	☐	Proofreaders	☐
Exams on tape or computer	☐	Readers	■
Untimed exams	☐	Reading Machines/Kurzweil	☐
Other accommodations	☐	Special bookstore section	☐
		Typists	☐

Credit toward degree is not given for remedial courses taken.

Counseling Services

- ☐ Academic
- ☐ Psychological
- ☐ Student Support groups
- ☐ Vocational

Tutoring

	Individual	Group
Time management	☐	☐
Organizational skills	☐	☐
Learning strategies	☐	☐
Study skills	☐	☐
Content area	☐	☐
Writing lab	☐	☐
Math lab	☐	☐

LD PROGRAM STAFF

Total number of LD Program staff (including director):

Full Time: 2 Part Time: 2

Key staff person available to work with LD students: Kara Kennedy, Learning Development Specialist.

University of Pittsburgh at Greensburg

Greensburg, PA

Address: 1150 Mt. Pleasant Road, Greensburg, PA, 15601
Admissions telephone: 724 836-9880
Admissions FAX: 724 836-7160
Director of Admissions and Financial Aid: Brandi S. Darr
Admissions e-mail: upgadmit@pitt.edu
Web site: http://www.upg.pitt.edu/
SAT Code: 2936 ACT Code: 3733

LD program name: Learning Resource Center
Director Learning Resources Center: Lou Ann Sears
LD program telephone: 724 836-7098
LD program e-mail: 1053@pitt.edu
LD program enrollment: 10, Total campus enrollment: 1,860

GENERAL

University of Pittsburgh, Greensburg is a public, coed, four-year institution. 205-acre campus in Greensburg (population: 15,889), 30 miles from Pittsburgh. Served by bus and train; major airport serves Pittsburgh. School operates transportation to Oakland campus and to bus and train stations. Semester system.

LD ADMISSIONS

A personal interview is required. Essay is not required.

SECONDARY SCHOOL REQUIREMENTS

Graduation from secondary school required; GED accepted. The following course distribution required: 4 units of English, 2 units of math, 1 unit of science, 2 units of social studies, 2 units of history, 3 units of academic electives.

TESTING

SAT Reasoning required; ACT may be substituted. SAT Subject required.

All enrolled freshmen (fall 2004):

Average SAT I Scores: Verbal: 525 Math: 533

Child Study Team report is not required. A neuropsychological or comprehensive psycho-educational evaluation is required for admission. Tests required as part of this documentation:

- ☒ WAIS-IV
- ☐ WISC-IV
- ☒ SATA
- ☒ Woodcock-Johnson
- ☒ Nelson-Denny Reading Test
- ☐ Other

UNDERGRADUATE STUDENT BODY

Total undergraduate student enrollment: 798 Men, 1,025 Women.

Composition of student body (fall 2004):

	Undergraduate	Freshmen
International	0.2	0.2
Black	3.0	2.3
American Indian	0.2	0.2
Asian-American	3.2	1.7
Hispanic	0.3	0.3
White	93.1	95.3
Unreported	0.0	0.0
	100.0%	100.0%

2% are from out of state. Average age of full-time undergraduates is 21. 40% of classes have fewer than 20 students, 53% have between 20 and 50 students, 7% have more than 50 students.

STUDENT HOUSING

60% of freshmen live in college housing. Freshmen are not required to live on campus. Housing is guaranteed for all undergraduates. Campus can house 653 undergraduates. Single rooms are available for students with medical or special needs. A medical note is required.

EXPENSES

Tuition (2005-06): $9,330 per year (in-state), $19,200 (out-of-state). Tuition varies by program.
Room & Board: $6,960.

There is no additional cost for LD program/services.

LD SERVICES

LD program size is not limited.

LD services available to:

☒ Freshmen ☒ Sophomores ☒ Juniors ☒ Seniors

Academic Accommodations

Curriculum		In class	
Foreign language waiver	☒	Early syllabus	☒
Lighter course load	☒	Note takers in class	☒
Math waiver	☐	Priority seating	☒
Other special classes	☐	Tape recorders	☒
Priority registrations	☒	Videotaped classes	☐
Substitution of courses	☐	Text on tape	☒
Exams		**Services**	
Extended time	☒	Diagnostic tests	☐
Oral exams	☐	Learning centers	☒
Take home exams	☐	Proofreaders	☐
Exams on tape or computer	☒	Readers	☒
Untimed exams	☐	Reading Machines/Kurzweil	☒
Other accommodations	☒	Special bookstore section	☐
		Typists	☒

Credit toward degree is not given for remedial courses taken.

Counseling Services

- ☒ Academic
- ☒ Psychological
- ☒ Student Support groups
- ☒ Vocational

Tutoring

Individual tutoring is available weekly.

Average size of tutoring groups: 1

	Individual	Group
Time management	☒	☐
Organizational skills	☒	☐
Learning strategies	☒	☐
Study skills	☒	☐
Content area	☒	☐
Writing lab	☒	☐
Math lab	☒	☐

LD PROGRAM STAFF

Total number of LD Program staff (including director):

Full Time: 1 Part Time: 1

There is an advisor/advocate from the LD program available to students. 25 peer tutors are available to work with LD students.

Key staff person available to work with LD students: Lou Ann Sears, Director Learning Resource Center

University of Pittsburgh at Johnstown

Johnstown, PA

Address: 450 Schoolhouse Road, Johnstown, PA, 15904
Admissions telephone: 800 765-4875
Admissions FAX: 814 269-7044
Director of Admissions: James F. Gyure
Admissions e-mail: upjadmit@pitt.edu
Web site: http://www.upj.pitt.edu
SAT Code: 2934

Disability Services: Theresa Horner, LPC
LD program telephone: 814 269-7109
LD program e-mail: thorner@pitt.edu
Total campus enrollment: 3,209

GENERAL

University of Pittsburgh at Johnstown is a public, coed, four-year institution. 650-acre campus near Johnstown (population: 23,906), 70 miles from Pittsburgh. Served by air, bus, and train; major airport serves Pittsburgh. Public transportation serves campus. Semester system.

LD ADMISSIONS

Students do not complete a separate application and are not simultaneously accepted to the LD program. A member of the LD program does not sit on the admissions committee. A personal interview is not required. Essay is not required.

SECONDARY SCHOOL REQUIREMENTS

Graduation from secondary school required; GED accepted. The following course distribution required: 4 units of English, 2 units of math, 2 units of science, 2 units of foreign language, 4 units of social studies.

TESTING

SAT Reasoning or ACT required. SAT Subject required.

All enrolled freshmen (fall 2004):

Average SAT I Scores:	Verbal: 513	Math: 521
Average ACT Scores:	Composite: 21	

Child Study Team report is not required. A neuropsychological or comprehensive psycho-educational evaluation is required for admission. Tests required as part of this documentation:

- ☐ WAIS-IV
- ☐ WISC-IV
- ☐ SATA
- ☐ Woodcock-Johnson
- ☐ Nelson-Denny Reading Test
- ☐ Other

UNDERGRADUATE STUDENT BODY

Total undergraduate student enrollment: 1,450 Men, 1,646 Women.

Composition of student body (fall 2004):

	Undergraduate	Freshmen
International	0.0	0.0
Black	1.5	1.1
American Indian	0.0	0.1
Asian-American	1.0	1.0
Hispanic	0.7	0.5
White	95.2	95.8
Unreported	1.6	1.5
	100.0%	100.0%

3% join a fraternity and 2% join a sorority. Average age of full-time undergraduates is 18. 24% of classes have fewer than 20 students, 70% have between 20 and 50 students, 6% have more than 50 students.

STUDENT HOUSING

81% of freshmen live in college housing. Freshmen are not required to live on campus. Housing is guaranteed for all undergraduates. Campus can house 1,720 undergraduates. Single rooms are available for students with medical or special needs. A medical note is required.

EXPENSES

Tuition (2005-06): $9,888 per year (in-state), $19,776 (out-of-state). Tuition varies by program.
Room: $3,700. Board: $2,340.
There is no additional cost for LD program/services.

LD SERVICES

LD program size is not limited.

LD services available to:

☑ Freshmen ☑ Sophomores ☑ Juniors ☑ Seniors

Academic Accommodations

Curriculum		In class	
Foreign language waiver	☐	Early syllabus	☐
Lighter course load	☑	Note takers in class	☑
Math waiver	☐	Priority seating	☐
Other special classes	☐	Tape recorders	☑
Priority registrations	☐	Videotaped classes	☐
Substitution of courses	☐	Text on tape	☐
Exams		**Services**	
Extended time	☑	Diagnostic tests	☑
Oral exams	☑	Learning centers	☑
Take home exams	☐	Proofreaders	☐
Exams on tape or computer	☐	Readers	☑
Untimed exams	☑	Reading Machines/Kurzweil	☑
Other accommodations	☐	Special bookstore section	☐
		Typists	☐

Credit toward degree is given for remedial courses taken.

Counseling Services

- ☐ Academic
- ☐ Psychological
- ☐ Student Support groups
- ☐ Vocational

Tutoring

Individual tutoring is available.

	Individual	Group
Time management	☐	☐
Organizational skills	☐	☐
Learning strategies	☐	☐
Study skills	☐	☐
Content area	☐	☐
Writing lab	☐	☐
Math lab	☐	☐

LD PROGRAM STAFF

Total number of LD Program staff (including director):

Full Time: 2 Part Time: 2

Key staff person available to work with LD students: Theresa Horner, LPC, Disability Services

University of Pittsburgh at Pittsburgh Campus

Pittsburgh, PA

Address: 4200 Fifth Avenue, Pittsburgh, PA, 15260
Admissions telephone: 412 624-7488
Admissions FAX: 412 648-8815
Director, Office of Admissions and Financial Aid: Dr. Betsy A. Porter
Admissions e-mail: oafa@pitt.edu
Web site: http://www.pitt.edu/
SAT Code: 2927 ACT Code: 3734

Director: Lynnett Van Slyke
LD program telephone: 412 648-7890
LD program e-mail: vanslyke@pitt.edu
LD program enrollment: 180, Total campus enrollment: 17,181

GENERAL

University of Pittsburgh, Pittsburgh Campus is a public, coed, four-year institution. 132-acre, urban campus in Pittsburgh (population: 370,000); branch campuses in Bradford, Greensburg, Johnstown, and Titusville. Served by air, bus, and train. School operates campus shuttle. Public transportation serves campus; students may ride free throughout county. Semester system.

LD ADMISSIONS

A personal interview is not required. Essay is not required.

SECONDARY SCHOOL REQUIREMENTS

Graduation from secondary school required; GED accepted. The following course distribution required: 4 units of English, 3 units of math, 3 units of science, 1 unit of social studies, 4 units of academic electives.

TESTING

SAT Reasoning or ACT required. SAT Subject required.

All enrolled freshmen (fall 2004):

Average SAT I Scores: Verbal: 610 Math: 621
Average ACT Scores: Composite: 26

Child Study Team report is not required. Tests required as part of this documentation:

- [ ] WAIS-IV
- [ ] WISC-IV
- [ ] SATA
- [ ] Woodcock-Johnson
- [ ] Nelson-Denny Reading Test
- [ ] Other

UNDERGRADUATE STUDENT BODY

Total undergraduate student enrollment: 8,405 Men, 9,393 Women.

Composition of student body (fall 2004):

	Undergraduate	Freshmen
International	0.4	0.7
Black	9.7	9.4
American Indian	0.3	0.2
Asian-American	4.3	3.9
Hispanic	1.2	1.1
White	80.4	81.7
Unreported	3.7	3.0
	100.0%	100.0%

13% are from out of state. 8% join a fraternity and 7% join a sorority. Average age of full-time undergraduates is 21. 42% of classes have fewer than 20 students, 42% have between 20 and 50 students, 16% have more than 50 students.

STUDENT HOUSING

94% of freshmen live in college housing. Freshmen are not required to live on campus. Housing is guaranteed for three years to all first year, fall term freshmen admitted through the Office of Admissions and Financial Aid whose tuition deposit is received by May 1. Each spring, eligible students living on campus have the opportunity to select their accommodations for the following academic year through an online lottery. Full-time students who have lived on campus during their first year with a housing guarantee, are guaranteed housing for their second and third years if they continue to satisfy all housing application and deadline requirements each year. Campus can house 6,200 undergraduates.

EXPENSES

Tuition (2005-06): $10,736 per year (in-state), $20,084 (out-of-state). Tuition varies by program.

Room: $4,510. Board: $2,920.

There is no additional cost for LD program/services.

LD SERVICES

LD program size is not limited.

LD services available to:

- [x] Freshmen
- [x] Sophomores
- [x] Juniors
- [x] Seniors

Academic Accommodations

Curriculum		In class	
Foreign language waiver	[ ]	Early syllabus	[ ]
Lighter course load	[x]	Note takers in class	[ ]
Math waiver	[ ]	Priority seating	[ ]
Other special classes	[ ]	Tape recorders	[x]
Priority registrations	[ ]	Videotaped classes	[ ]
Substitution of courses	[ ]	Text on tape	[x]
Exams		**Services**	
Extended time	[x]	Diagnostic tests	[ ]
Oral exams	[ ]	Learning centers	[x]
Take home exams	[ ]	Proofreaders	[ ]
Exams on tape or computer	[x]	Readers	[x]
Untimed exams	[ ]	Reading Machines/Kurzweil	[x]
Other accommodations	[x]	Special bookstore section	[ ]
		Typists	[ ]

Counseling Services

- [ ] Academic
- [ ] Psychological
- [ ] Student Support groups
- [ ] Vocational

Tutoring

	Individual	Group
Time management	[x]	[ ]
Organizational skills	[x]	[ ]
Learning strategies	[x]	[ ]
Study skills	[ ]	[ ]
Content area	[ ]	[ ]
Writing lab	[ ]	[ ]
Math lab	[ ]	[ ]

LD PROGRAM STAFF

Total number of LD Program staff (including director):

Full Time: 3 Part Time: 3

Key staff person available to work with LD students: Leigh Culley, Coordinator of Services

Point Park University

Pittsburgh, PA

Address: 201 Wood Street, Pittsburgh, PA, 15222
Admissions telephone: 800 321-0129
Admissions FAX: 412 391-3902
Dean of Full-Time Enrollment: Joell Minford
Admissions e-mail: enroll@pointpark.edu
Web site: http://www.pointpark.edu
SAT Code: 2676 ACT Code: 3530

LD program name: Program for Academic Success
Director, Program for Academic Success: Patricia Boykin
LD program telephone: 412 392-4738
LD program e-mail: pboykin@pointpark.edu
LD program enrollment: 8, Total campus enrollment: 2,844

GENERAL

Point Park College is a private, coed, four-year institution. Urban campus of three high-rise buildings in Pittsburgh (population: 370,000). Served by air, bus, and train. Public transportation serves campus. Semester system.

LD ADMISSIONS

Students do not complete a separate application and are not simultaneously accepted to the LD program. A member of the LD program does not sit on the admissions committee. A personal interview is not required. Essay is not required.

SECONDARY SCHOOL REQUIREMENTS

Graduation from secondary school required; GED accepted.

TESTING

SAT Reasoning or ACT required.

All enrolled freshmen (fall 2004):

Average SAT I Scores:	Verbal: 527	Math: 498
Average ACT Scores:	Composite: 22	

Child Study Team report is not required. A neuropsychological or comprehensive psycho-educational evaluation is required for admission. Must be dated within 36 months of application. Tests required as part of this documentation:

- ■ WAIS-IV
- □ WISC-IV
- □ SATA
- ■ Woodcock-Johnson
- □ Nelson-Denny Reading Test
- □ Other

UNDERGRADUATE STUDENT BODY

Total undergraduate student enrollment: 1,188 Men, 1,456 Women.

Composition of student body (fall 2004):

	Undergraduate	Freshmen
International	1.0	1.0
Black	10.9	16.9
American Indian	0.3	0.3
Asian-American	0.8	0.6
Hispanic	2.3	1.3
White	84.2	76.6
Unreported	0.5	3.3
	100.0%	100.0%

15% are from out of state. Average age of full-time undergraduates is 23. 77% of classes have fewer than 20 students, 23% have between 20 and 50 students.

STUDENT HOUSING

69% of freshmen live in college housing. Freshmen are not required to live on campus. Housing is guaranteed for all undergraduates. Campus can house 592 undergraduates. Single rooms are not available for students with medical or special needs.

EXPENSES

Tuition (2005-06): $16,280 per year. $13,226 per year, $13,982 for applied arts, dance, film/video production, and theatre programs.

Room & Board: $7,420.
There is no additional cost for LD program/services.

LD SERVICES

LD program size is not limited.

LD services available to:

■ Freshmen ■ Sophomores ■ Juniors ■ Seniors

Academic Accommodations

Curriculum		In class	
Foreign language waiver	□	Early syllabus	□
Lighter course load	■	Note takers in class	■
Math waiver	□	Priority seating	■
Other special classes	□	Tape recorders	■
Priority registrations	□	Videotaped classes	□
Substitution of courses	□	Text on tape	□
Exams		**Services**	
Extended time	■	Diagnostic tests	□
Oral exams	■	Learning centers	□
Take home exams	□	Proofreaders	□
Exams on tape or computer	■	Readers	■
Untimed exams	□	Reading Machines/Kurzweil	□
Other accommodations	■	Special bookstore section	□
		Typists	□

Credit toward degree is not given for remedial courses taken.

Counseling Services

- ■ Academic
- □ Psychological
- □ Student Support groups
- ■ Vocational

Tutoring

Individual tutoring is available weekly.

	Individual	Group
Time management	■	□
Organizational skills	■	□
Learning strategies	■	□
Study skills	■	□
Content area	■	□
Writing lab	■	□
Math lab	□	□

LD PROGRAM STAFF

Total number of LD Program staff (including director):

Full Time: 4 Part Time: 4

There is an advisor/advocate from the LD program available to students.

Key staff person available to work with LD students: Patricia Boykin, Director, Program for Academic Success

Robert Morris University

Moon Township, PA

Address: 6001 University Boulevard, Moon Township, PA, 15108-1189
Admissions telephone: 800 762-0097
Admissions FAX: 412 299-2425
Dean of Enrollment Services: Marianne Budziszewski
Admissions e-mail: enrollmentoffice@rmu.edu
Web site: http://www.rmu.edu
SAT Code: 2769 ACT Code: 3674

Director, Center for Student Success: Cassandra L. Oden
LD program telephone: 412 262-8349
LD program e-mail: oden@rmu.edu
LD program enrollment: 37, Total campus enrollment: 3,861

GENERAL

Robert Morris University is a private, coed, four-year institution. 230-acre, suburban campus in Moon Township (population: 22,290), 17 miles from Pittsburgh; additional campus in Pittsburgh. Major airport, bus, and train serve Pittsburgh. School operates transportation to branch campus. Public transportation serves campus. Semester system.

LD ADMISSIONS

Students do not complete a separate application and are not simultaneously accepted to the LD program. A member of the LD program does not sit on the admissions committee. A personal interview is recommended. Essay is not required.

For fall 2004, 89 completed self-identified LD applications were received. 89 applications were offered admission, and 42 enrolled.

SECONDARY SCHOOL REQUIREMENTS

Graduation from secondary school required; GED accepted. The following course distribution required: 4 units of English, 3 units of math, 2 units of science, 4 units of social studies, 3 units of academic electives.

TESTING

SAT Reasoning required; ACT may be substituted. SAT Subject recommended.

All enrolled freshmen (fall 2004):

Average SAT I Scores:	Verbal: 501	Math: 513
Average ACT Scores:	Composite: 20	

Child Study Team report is required if student is classified. A neuropsychological or comprehensive psycho-educational evaluation is required for admission. Must be dated within 36 months of application. Tests required as part of this documentation:

- ☑ WAIS-IV
- ☑ WISC-IV
- ☐ SATA
- ☐ Woodcock-Johnson
- ☐ Nelson-Denny Reading Test
- ☐ Other

UNDERGRADUATE STUDENT BODY

Total undergraduate student enrollment: 1,950 Men, 1,863 Women.

Composition of student body (fall 2004):

	Undergraduate	Freshmen
International	2.5	1.8
Black	7.4	7.5
American Indian	0.3	0.3
Asian-American	0.9	0.6
Hispanic	0.9	1.0
White	88.0	88.6
Unreported	0.0	0.2
	100.0%	100.0%

8% are from out of state. 5% join a fraternity and 4% join a sorority. Average age of full-time undergraduates is 21. 50% of classes have fewer than 20 students, 50% have between 20 and 50 students.

STUDENT HOUSING

80% of freshmen live in college housing. Freshmen are not required to live on campus. Housing is not guaranteed for all undergraduates. Campus can house 1,190 undergraduates. Single rooms are available for students with medical or special needs. A medical note is required.

EXPENSES

Tuition (2005-06): $15,152 per year.
Room: $4,650. Board: $3,020.
There is no additional cost for LD program/services.

LD SERVICES

LD program size is not limited.

LD services available to:

☑ Freshmen ☑ Sophomores ☑ Juniors ☑ Seniors

Academic Accommodations

Curriculum		In class	
Foreign language waiver	☐	Early syllabus	☐
Lighter course load	☐	Note takers in class	☐
Math waiver	☐	Priority seating	☑
Other special classes	☐	Tape recorders	☑
Priority registrations	☑	Videotaped classes	☐
Substitution of courses	☐	Text on tape	☐
Exams		**Services**	
Extended time	☑	Diagnostic tests	☐
Oral exams	☑	Learning centers	☑
Take home exams	☐	Proofreaders	☐
Exams on tape or computer	☑	Readers	☑
Untimed exams	☐	Reading Machines/Kurzweil	☑
Other accommodations	☑	Special bookstore section	☐
		Typists	☐

Credit toward degree is not given for remedial courses taken.

Counseling Services

- ☑ Academic
- ☑ Psychological
- ☐ Student Support groups
- ☐ Vocational

Tutoring

Individual tutoring is available daily.

Average size of tutoring groups: 2

	Individual	Group
Time management	☑	☑
Organizational skills	☑	☑
Learning strategies	☑	☑
Study skills	☑	☑
Content area	☑	☐
Writing lab	☑	☑
Math lab	☑	☑

LD PROGRAM STAFF

Total number of LD Program staff (including director):

Full Time: 4 Part Time: 4

There is not an advisor/advocate from the LD program available to students. Two graduate students and 25 peer tutors are available to work with LD students.

Key staff person available to work with LD students: Cassandra L. Oden, Director, Center for Student Success

Rosemont College

Rosemont, PA

Address: 1400 Montgomery Avenue, Rosemont, PA, 19010-1699
Admissions telephone: 800 331-0708
Admissions FAX: 610 520-4399
Director of Admissions: Rennie H. Andrews
Admissions e-mail: admissions@rosemont.edu
Web site: http://www.rosemont.edu
SAT Code: 2763 ACT Code: 3676

VP Student Affairs / Dean of Students: Marilyn Moller
LD program telephone: 610 527-0200
LD program e-mail: mmoller@rosemont.edu
Total campus enrollment: 666

GENERAL

Rosemont College is a private, women's, four-year institution. 56-acre, suburban campus in Rosemont (population: 4,500), 11 miles from Philadelphia. Airport, bus, and train serve Philadelphia. School operates transportation to Villanova U. Public transportation serves campus. Semester system.

LD ADMISSIONS

A personal interview is recommended.

SECONDARY SCHOOL REQUIREMENTS

Graduation from secondary school required; GED accepted. The following course distribution required: 4 units of English, 2 units of math, 2 units of science, 2 units of foreign language, 2 units of social studies, 2 units of history, 2 units of academic electives.

TESTING

SAT Reasoning required; ACT may be substituted. SAT Subject recommended.

All enrolled freshmen (fall 2004):

Average SAT I Scores: Verbal: 551 Math: 519

Child Study Team report is not required. Tests required as part of this documentation:

- [ ] WAIS-IV
- [ ] WISC-IV
- [ ] SATA
- [ ] Woodcock-Johnson
- [ ] Nelson-Denny Reading Test
- [ ] Other

UNDERGRADUATE STUDENT BODY

Total undergraduate student enrollment: 108 Men, 845 Women.

Composition of student body (fall 2004):

	Undergraduate	Freshmen
International	0.9	2.3
Black	38.5	29.4
American Indian	0.0	0.0
Asian-American	6.4	5.9
Hispanic	10.1	5.7
White	44.0	47.5
Unreported	0.1	9.2
	100.0%	100.0%

44% are from out of state. Average age of full-time undergraduates is 21. 91% of classes have fewer than 20 students, 9% have between 20 and 50 students.

STUDENT HOUSING

90% of freshmen live in college housing. Freshmen are required to live on campus. Housing is guaranteed for all undergraduates. Campus can house 420 undergraduates. Single rooms are available for students with medical or special needs. A medical note is required.

EXPENSES

Tuition (2005-06): $19,450 per year.

Room: $4,400. Board: $4,400.

There is no additional cost for LD program/services.

LD SERVICES

LD program size is not limited.

LD services available to:

- [x] Freshmen
- [x] Sophomores
- [x] Juniors
- [x] Seniors

Academic Accommodations

Curriculum

- [ ] Foreign language waiver
- [x] Lighter course load
- [ ] Math waiver
- [ ] Other special classes
- [ ] Priority registrations
- [ ] Substitution of courses

Exams

- [x] Extended time
- [x] Oral exams
- [ ] Take home exams
- [ ] Exams on tape or computer
- [x] Untimed exams
- [ ] Other accommodations

In class

- [ ] Early syllabus
- [x] Note takers in class
- [ ] Priority seating
- [x] Tape recorders
- [ ] Videotaped classes
- [ ] Text on tape

Services

- [x] Diagnostic tests
- [x] Learning centers
- [ ] Proofreaders
- [x] Readers
- [ ] Reading Machines/Kurzweil
- [ ] Special bookstore section
- [ ] Typists

Credit toward degree is not given for remedial courses taken.

Counseling Services

- [x] Academic
- [ ] Psychological
- [ ] Student Support groups
- [ ] Vocational

Tutoring

	Individual	Group
Time management	[x]	[x]
Organizational skills	[x]	[x]
Learning strategies	[x]	[x]
Study skills	[x]	[x]
Content area	[x]	[x]
Writing lab	[x]	[x]
Math lab	[x]	[x]

LD PROGRAM STAFF

Total number of LD Program staff (including director):

Full Time: 1 Part Time: 1

10 peer tutors are available to work with LD students.

Key staff person available to work with LD students: Marilyn Moller, Vice President Student Affairs/Dean of Students.

Saint Francis University

Loretto, PA

Address: P.O. Box 600, Loretto, PA, 15940
Admissions telephone: 800 457-6300
Admissions FAX: 814 472-3335
Dean of Enrollment Management: Erin McCloskey
Admissions e-mail: admissions@francis.edu
Web site: http://www.francis.edu/
SAT Code: 2797 ACT Code: 3682

LD program name: Academic Center for Enrichment
LD program address: 200 Schwab Hall, Loretto, PA, 15931
Director: Denise Kovach
LD program telephone: 814 472-3176
LD program e-mail: dkovach@francis.edu
LD program enrollment: 45, Total campus enrollment: 1,332

GENERAL

Saint Francis University is a private, coed, four-year institution. 600-acre campus in Loretto (population: 1,190), 20 miles from Altoona and 85 miles from Pittsburgh. Major airport serves Pittsburgh; smaller airport and train serve Altoona; bus serves Ebensburg (five miles). Semester system.

LD ADMISSIONS

Students do not complete a separate application and are simultaneously accepted to the LD program. A member of the LD program does not sit on the admissions committee. High school waivers are accepted for math and foreign language. A personal interview is recommended.

SECONDARY SCHOOL REQUIREMENTS

Graduation from secondary school required; GED accepted. The following course distribution required: 4 units of English, 2 units of math, 1 unit of science, 2 units of social studies, 7 units of academic electives.

TESTING

SAT Reasoning or ACT required.

All enrolled freshmen (fall 2004):

Average SAT I Scores:	Verbal: 516	Math: 527
Average ACT Scores:	Composite: 22	

Child Study Team report is not required. A neuropsychological or comprehensive psycho-educational evaluation is required for admission. Must be dated within 36 months of application. Tests required as part of this documentation:

- ■ WAIS-IV
- ☐ WISC-IV
- ☐ SATA
- ■ Woodcock-Johnson
- ☐ Nelson-Denny Reading Test
- ☐ Other

UNDERGRADUATE STUDENT BODY

Total undergraduate student enrollment: 1,332.

Composition of student body (fall 2004):

	Undergraduate	Freshmen
International	0.1	0.6
Black	4.9	6.3
American Indian	0.3	0.2
Asian-American	1.5	0.6
Hispanic	0.9	0.9
White	87.1	84.7
Unreported	5.2	6.7
	100.0%	100.0%

20% are from out of state. 8% join a sorority. Average age of full-time undergraduates is 20. 50% of classes have fewer than 20 students, 47% have between 20 and 50 students, 3% have more than 50 students.

STUDENT HOUSING

Freshmen are required to live on campus. Housing is guaranteed for all undergraduates. Campus can house 966 undergraduates. Single rooms are available for students with medical or special needs. A medical note is required.

EXPENSES

Tuition (2005-06): $20,360 per year.

Room: $3,672. Board: $3,896.
There is no additional cost for LD program/services.

LD SERVICES

LD program size is not limited.

LD services available to:

■ Freshmen ■ Sophomores ■ Juniors ■ Seniors

Academic Accommodations

Curriculum		**In class**	
Foreign language waiver	■	Early syllabus	☐
Lighter course load	■	Note takers in class	■
Math waiver	■	Priority seating	■
Other special classes	☐	Tape recorders	■
Priority registrations	■	Videotaped classes	☐
Substitution of courses	■	Text on tape	■
Exams		**Services**	
Extended time	■	Diagnostic tests	☐
Oral exams	■	Learning centers	■
Take home exams	☐	Proofreaders	☐
Exams on tape or computer	■	Readers	■
Untimed exams	■	Reading Machines/Kurzweil	■
Other accommodations	☐	Special bookstore section	☐
		Typists	■

Credit toward degree is given for remedial courses taken.

Counseling Services

- ■ Academic
- ■ Psychological
- ☐ Student Support groups
- ■ Vocational

Tutoring

Individual tutoring is available daily.

Average size of tutoring groups: 1

	Individual	Group
Time management	■	■
Organizational skills	■	■
Learning strategies	■	■
Study skills	■	■
Content area	■	■
Writing lab	■	☐
Math lab	☐	☐

LD PROGRAM STAFF

Total number of LD Program staff (including director):

Full Time: 3 Part Time: 3

There is no advisor/advocate from the LD program available to students. 25 peer tutors are available to work with LD students.

Key staff person available to work with LD students: Denise Kovach, Director.

Saint Joseph's University

Philadelphia, PA

Address: 5600 City Avenue, Philadelphia, PA, 19131
Admissions telephone: 888 BEAHAWK
Admissions FAX: 610 660-1314
Director of Admissions: Susan Kassab
Admissions e-mail: admit@sju.edu
Web site: http://www.sju.edu
SAT Code: 2801 ACT Code: 3684

Asst. Coordinator: Vana Miller
LD program telephone: 610 660-1620
LD program e-mail: vmiller@sju.edu
LD program enrollment: 119, Total campus enrollment: 4,978

GENERAL

Saint Joseph's University is a private, coed, four-year institution. 60-acre, suburban campus in Philadelphia (population: 1,517,550), five miles from city center. Served by air, bus, and train. School operates transportation to campus residence halls. Public transportation serves campus. Semester system.

LD ADMISSIONS

Students do not complete a separate application and are simultaneously accepted to the LD program. A member of the LD program does not sit on the admissions committee. High school waivers are accepted for foreign language. A personal interview is not required. Essay is required and may be typed.

SECONDARY SCHOOL REQUIREMENTS

Graduation from secondary school required; GED not accepted. The following course distribution required: 4 units of English, 3 units of math, 2 units of science, 2 units of foreign language, 1 unit of history, 2 units of academic electives.

TESTING

SAT Reasoning required; ACT may be substituted. SAT Subject recommended.

All enrolled freshmen (fall 2004):

Average SAT I Scores:	Verbal: 569	Math: 574
Average ACT Scores:	Composite: 27	

Child Study Team report is not required. A neuropsychological or comprehensive psycho-educational evaluation is required for admission. Must be dated within 36 months of application. Tests required as part of this documentation:

- [x] WAIS-IV
- [x] WISC-IV
- [ ] SATA
- [x] Woodcock-Johnson
- [x] Nelson-Denny Reading Test
- [x] Other

UNDERGRADUATE STUDENT BODY

Total undergraduate student enrollment: 2,126 Men, 2,464 Women.

Composition of student body (fall 2004):

	Undergraduate	Freshmen
International	1.2	1.2
Black	2.0	7.2
American Indian	0.2	0.1
Asian-American	1.2	2.4
Hispanic	1.6	2.5
White	84.3	80.1
Unreported	9.5	6.5
	100.0%	100.0%

49% are from out of state. 8% join a fraternity and 13% join a sorority. Average age of full-time undergraduates is 20. 38% of classes have fewer than 20 students, 60% have between 20 and 50 students, 2% have more than 50 students.

STUDENT HOUSING

95% of freshmen live in college housing. Freshmen are required to live on campus. Campus housing is only guaranteed for freshmen and sophomores. Campus can house 2,421 undergraduates. Single rooms are available for students with medical or special needs. A medical note is required.

EXPENSES

Tuition (2005-06): $27,320 per year.
Room: $6,363. Board: $3,610.
There is no additional cost for LD program/services.

LD SERVICES

LD program size is not limited.

LD services available to:

- [x] Freshmen
- [x] Sophomores
- [x] Juniors
- [x] Seniors

Academic Accommodations

Curriculum		In class	
Foreign language waiver	[x]	Early syllabus	[x]
Lighter course load	[x]	Note takers in class	[x]
Math waiver	[ ]	Priority seating	[ ]
Other special classes	[ ]	Tape recorders	[x]
Priority registrations	[ ]	Videotaped classes	[ ]
Substitution of courses	[ ]	Text on tape	[x]
Exams		**Services**	
Extended time	[x]	Diagnostic tests	[ ]
Oral exams	[x]	Learning centers	[x]
Take home exams	[ ]	Proofreaders	[ ]
Exams on tape or computer	[x]	Readers	[x]
Untimed exams	[ ]	Reading Machines/Kurzweil	[ ]
Other accommodations	[ ]	Special bookstore section	[ ]
		Typists	[x]

Credit toward degree is not given for remedial courses taken.

Counseling Services

[x]	Academic	Meets 10 times per academic year
[ ]	Psychological	
[ ]	Student Support groups	
[x]	Vocational	Meets 2 times per academic year

Tutoring

Individual tutoring is available weekly.

	Individual	Group
Time management	[ ]	[x]
Organizational skills	[x]	[x]
Learning strategies	[ ]	[x]
Study skills	[x]	[x]
Content area	[ ]	[ ]
Writing lab	[x]	[ ]
Math lab	[ ]	[ ]

LD PROGRAM STAFF

Total number of LD Program staff (including director):

Full Time: 1 Part Time: 1

There is an advisor/advocate from the LD program available to students.

Key staff person available to work with LD students: Jim Scott, Coordinator

Saint Vincent College

Latrobe, PA

Address: 300 Fraser Purchase Road, Latrobe, PA, 15650-2690
Admissions telephone: 800 782-5549
Admissions FAX: 724 532-5069
Director of Admissions: David Collins
Admissions e-mail: admission@stvincent.edu
Web site: http://www.stvincent.edu
SAT Code: 2808 ACT Code: 3686

LD program name: Academic Affairs
Associate Director of Academic Affairs: Sandy Quinlivan
LD program telephone: 724 805-2371
LD program e-mail: sandy.quinlivan@email.stvincent.edu
LD program enrollment: 23, Total campus enrollment: 1,409

GENERAL

Saint Vincent College is a private, coed, four-year institution. 200-acre campus in Latrobe (population: 8,994), 35 miles from Pittsburgh. Served by air and train; major airport serves Pittsburgh; bus serves Greensburg (eight miles). Public transportation serves campus. Semester system.

LD ADMISSIONS

A personal interview is recommended. Essay is required and may be typed.

SECONDARY SCHOOL REQUIREMENTS

Graduation from secondary school required; GED accepted. The following course distribution required: 4 units of English, 3 units of math, 1 unit of science, 3 units of social studies, 5 units of academic electives.

TESTING

SAT Reasoning required; ACT may be substituted. SAT Subject recommended.

All enrolled freshmen (fall 2004):

Average SAT I Scores:	Verbal: 550	Math: 556
Average ACT Scores:	Composite: 23	

Child Study Team report is not required. Tests required as part of this documentation:

- ☐ WAIS-IV
- ☐ WISC-IV
- ☐ SATA
- ☐ Woodcock-Johnson
- ☐ Nelson-Denny Reading Test
- ☐ Other

UNDERGRADUATE STUDENT BODY

Total undergraduate student enrollment: 623 Men, 599 Women.

Composition of student body (fall 2004):

	Undergraduate	Freshmen
International	3.0	2.1
Black	1.8	2.0
American Indian	0.4	0.2
Asian-American	0.3	0.8
Hispanic	0.6	0.8
White	85.2	91.4
Unreported	8.7	2.7
	100.0%	100.0%

12% are from out of state. Average age of full-time undergraduates is 20. 51% of classes have fewer than 20 students, 49% have between 20 and 50 students.

STUDENT HOUSING

91% of freshmen live in college housing. Freshmen are required to live on campus. Housing is not guaranteed for all undergraduates, however, we try to accommodate as many as possible. Campus can house 1,074 undergraduates. Single rooms are available for students with medical or special needs. A medical note is required.

EXPENSES

Tuition (2005-06): $21,104 per year.

Room: $3,798-$3,500. Board: $3,374.
There is no additional cost for LD program/services.

LD SERVICES

LD program size is not limited.

LD services available to:

☒ Freshmen ☒ Sophomores ☒ Juniors ☒ Seniors

Academic Accommodations

Curriculum		**In class**	
Foreign language waiver	☐	Early syllabus	☐
Lighter course load	☒	Note takers in class	☒
Math waiver	☐	Priority seating	☒
Other special classes	☐	Tape recorders	☒
Priority registrations	☒	Videotaped classes	☐
Substitution of courses	☐	Text on tape	☐
Exams		**Services**	
Extended time	☒	Diagnostic tests	☐
Oral exams	☒	Learning centers	☒
Take home exams	☐	Proofreaders	☒
Exams on tape or computer	☐	Readers	☒
Untimed exams	☒	Reading Machines/Kurzweil	☒
Other accommodations	☒	Special bookstore section	☐
		Typists	☒

Credit toward degree is not given for remedial courses taken.

Counseling Services

☒	Academic	Meets 8 times per academic year
☒	Psychological	Meets 8 times per academic year
☒	Student Support groups	Meets 8 times per academic year
☒	Vocational	Meets 8 times per academic year

Tutoring

Individual tutoring is available weekly.

Average size of tutoring groups: 2

	Individual	Group
Time management	☒	☒
Organizational skills	☒	☒
Learning strategies	☒	☒
Study skills	☒	☒
Content area	☒	☒
Writing lab	☒	☒
Math lab	☐	☐

LD PROGRAM STAFF

There is an advisor/advocate from the LD program available to students. The advisor/advocate meets with students once per month. 50 peer tutors are available to work with LD students.

Key staff person available to work with LD students: Sandy Quinlivan, Associate Director of Academic Affairs

University of Scranton

Scranton, PA

Address: 800 Linden Street, Scranton, PA, 18510-4694
Admissions telephone: 888 SCRANTON
Admissions FAX: 570 941-5928
Director of Admissions: Joseph Roback
Admissions e-mail: admissions@scranton.edu
Web site: http://www.scranton.edu
SAT Code: 2929 ACT Code: 3736

LD program name: Learning and Teaching Excellence Ctr
Equity and Diversity Officer: JoAnn Usry
LD program telephone: 570 941-6645
LD program e-mail: usryj2@uofs.edu
LD program enrollment: 180, Total campus enrollment: 4,045

GENERAL

University of Scranton is a private, coed, four-year institution. 50-acre, urban campus in Scranton (population: 76,415), 125 miles from both New York City and Philadelphia. Served by bus; airport serves Avoca (five miles). School operates transportation to Marywood U. Public transportation serves campus. Semester system.

LD ADMISSIONS

Students do not complete a separate application and are not simultaneously accepted to the LD program. A member of the LD program does not sit on the admissions committee.

SECONDARY SCHOOL REQUIREMENTS

Graduation from secondary school required; GED accepted. The following course distribution required: 4 units of English, 3 units of math, 1 unit of science, 2 units of foreign language, 2 units of social studies.

TESTING

SAT Reasoning or ACT required. SAT Subject recommended.

All enrolled freshmen (fall 2004):

Average SAT I Scores:	Verbal: 559	Math: 562
Average ACT Scores:	Composite: 24	

Child Study Team report is not required. A neuropsychological or comprehensive psycho-education evaluation is not required for admission. Tests required as part of this documentation:

- [ ] WAIS-IV
- [ ] WISC-IV
- [ ] SATA
- [ ] Woodcock-Johnson
- [ ] Nelson-Denny Reading Test
- [ ] Other

UNDERGRADUATE STUDENT BODY

Total undergraduate student enrollment: 1,738 Men, 2,322 Women.

Composition of student body (fall 2004):

	Undergraduate	Freshmen
International	0.4	0.5
Black	1.2	1.5
American Indian	0.3	0.2
Asian-American	2.6	2.4
Hispanic	6.1	4.0
White	79.7	83.4
Unreported	9.7	8.0
	100.0%	100.0%

48% are from out of state. Average age of full-time undergraduates is 21. 47% of classes have fewer than 20 students, 53% have between 20 and 50 students.

STUDENT HOUSING

84% of freshmen live in college housing. Freshmen are required to live on campus. Housing is guaranteed for all undergraduates. Campus can house 2,004 undergraduates. Single rooms are available for students with medical or special needs. A medical note is required.

EXPENSES

Tuition (2005-06): $23,750 per year. $19,330 per year, $21,530 for physical therapy program.

Room: $5,786. Board: $4,118.
There is no additional cost for LD program/services.

LD SERVICES

LD program size is not limited.

LD services available to:

- [x] Freshmen
- [x] Sophomores
- [x] Juniors
- [x] Seniors

Academic Accommodations

Curriculum		**In class**	
Foreign language waiver	[ ]	Early syllabus	[ ]
Lighter course load	[ ]	Note takers in class	[ ]
Math waiver	[ ]	Priority seating	[x]
Other special classes	[ ]	Tape recorders	[x]
Priority registrations	[x]	Videotaped classes	[ ]
Substitution of courses	[ ]	Text on tape	[x]
Exams		**Services**	
Extended time	[x]	Diagnostic tests	[x]
Oral exams	[x]	Learning centers	[x]
Take home exams	[ ]	Proofreaders	[x]
Exams on tape or computer	[x]	Readers	[ ]
Untimed exams	[x]	Reading Machines/Kurzweil	[x]
Other accommodations	[x]	Special bookstore section	[ ]
		Typists	[ ]

Credit toward degree is not given for remedial courses taken.

Counseling Services

- [x] Academic
- [x] Psychological
- [x] Student Support groups
- [ ] Vocational

Tutoring

Individual tutoring is available weekly.

Average size of tutoring groups: 3

	Individual	Group
Time management	[x]	[x]
Organizational skills	[x]	[x]
Learning strategies	[x]	[x]
Study skills	[x]	[x]
Content area	[x]	[x]
Writing lab	[x]	[ ]
Math lab	[x]	[x]

LD PROGRAM STAFF

Total number of LD Program staff (including director):

Full Time: 3 Part Time: 3

There is no advisor/advocate from the LD program available to students. One graduate student and 100 peer tutors are available to work with LD students.

Key staff person available to work with LD students: Jim Muniz.

LD Program web site: http://academic.scranton.edu/department/ctle/services.html

Seton Hill University

Greensburg, PA

Address: Seton Hill Drive, Greensburg, PA, 15601
Admissions telephone: 800 826-6234
Admissions FAX: 724 830-1294
Director of Admissions and Adult Student Services: Dr. Mary Kay Cooper
Admissions e-mail: admit@setonhill.edu
Web site: http://www.setonhill.edu
SAT Code: 2812 ACT Code: 3688

LD program name: Office of Disability Services
LD program address: Box 228 K, Greensburg, PA, 15601
Director: Terri Bassi
LD program telephone: 724 838-4295
LD program e-mail: bassi@setonhill.edu
LD program enrollment: 49, Total campus enrollment: 1,347

GENERAL

Seton Hill University is a private, coed, four-year institution. 200-acre campus in Greensburg (population: 15,889), 35 miles east of Pittsburgh. Served by bus and train; major airport serves Pittsburgh; smaller airport serves Latrobe (10 miles). School operates transportation to local malls and St. Vincent Coll. Semester system.

LD ADMISSIONS

Students do not complete a separate application and are not simultaneously accepted to the LD program. A member of the LD program does not sit on the admissions committee. A personal interview is recommended. Essay is not required.

SECONDARY SCHOOL REQUIREMENTS

Graduation from secondary school required; GED accepted. The following course distribution required: 4 units of English, 2 units of math, 1 unit of science, 2 units of social studies, 4 units of academic electives.

TESTING

SAT Reasoning or ACT recommended. SAT Subject recommended.

Child Study Team report is not required. A neuropsychological or comprehensive psycho-education evaluation is not required for admission. Tests required as part of this documentation:

- ☐ WAIS-IV
- ☐ WISC-IV
- ☐ SATA
- ☐ Woodcock-Johnson
- ☐ Nelson-Denny Reading Test
- ☐ Other

UNDERGRADUATE STUDENT BODY

Total undergraduate student enrollment: 203 Men, 925 Women.

Composition of student body (fall 2004):

	Undergraduate	Freshmen
International	0.7	1.9
Black	10.1	6.2
American Indian	0.4	0.3
Asian-American	1.0	1.4
Hispanic	2.7	1.1
White	83.8	88.1
Unreported	1.3	1.0
	100.0%	100.0%

17% are from out of state. Average age of full-time undergraduates is 21. 68% of classes have fewer than 20 students, 32% have between 20 and 50 students.

STUDENT HOUSING

81% of freshmen live in college housing. Freshmen are not required to live on campus. Housing is guaranteed for all undergraduates. Campus can house 600 undergraduates. Single rooms are available for students with medical or special needs. A medical note is required.

EXPENSES

Tuition (2005-06): $21,870 per year.
Room & Board: $6,820.
There is no additional cost for LD program/services.

LD SERVICES

LD program size is not limited.

LD services available to:

■ Freshmen ■ Sophomores ■ Juniors ■ Seniors

Academic Accommodations

Curriculum		In class	
Foreign language waiver	☐	Early syllabus	■
Lighter course load	☐	Note takers in class	■
Math waiver	☐	Priority seating	■
Other special classes	☐	Tape recorders	■
Priority registrations	☐	Videotaped classes	☐
Substitution of courses	■	Text on tape	■
Exams		**Services**	
Extended time	■	Diagnostic tests	☐
Oral exams	■	Learning centers	☐
Take home exams	☐	Proofreaders	■
Exams on tape or computer	■	Readers	■
Untimed exams	■	Reading Machines/Kurzweil	■
Other accommodations	■	Special bookstore section	☐
		Typists	■

Credit toward degree is given for remedial courses taken.

Counseling Services

- ■ Academic
- ■ Psychological
- ■ Student Support groups
- ☐ Vocational

Tutoring

Individual tutoring is available weekly.

Average size of tutoring groups: 3

	Individual	Group
Time management	■	■
Organizational skills	■	■
Learning strategies	■	■
Study skills	■	■
Content area	■	■
Writing lab	■	■
Math lab	☐	☐

LD PROGRAM STAFF

There is an advisor/advocate from the LD program available to students.

Key staff person available to work with LD students: Terri Bassi, Director of Counseling, Disability, and Health Services

Shippensburg University of Pennsylvania

Shippensburg, PA

Address: 1871 Old Main Drive, Shippensburg, PA, 17257-2299
Admissions telephone: 800 822-8028
Admissions FAX: 717 477-4016
Dean of Undergraduate and Graduate Admissions: Joseph Cretella
Admissions e-mail: admiss@ship.edu
Web site: http://www.ship.edu
SAT Code: 2657 ACT Code: 3714

Assistant Director: Paula Madey
LD program telephone: 717 477-1161
LD program e-mail: pdmade@wharf.ship.edu
Total campus enrollment: 6,579

GENERAL

Shippensburg University of Pennsylvania is a public, coed, four-year institution. 200-acre campus in Shippensburg (population: 5,586), 50 miles from Harrisburg. Served by bus; major airport and train serve Harrisburg. School operates transportation to local mall and around campus and town. Public transportation serves campus. Semester system.

LD ADMISSIONS

Students do not complete a separate application and are not simultaneously accepted to the LD program. A member of the LD program does not sit on the admissions committee. A personal interview is recommended. Essay is not required.

SECONDARY SCHOOL REQUIREMENTS

Graduation from secondary school required; GED accepted.

TESTING

SAT Reasoning or ACT required. SAT Subject recommended.

All enrolled freshmen (fall 2004):

Average SAT I Scores: Verbal: 520 Math: 527

Child Study Team report is not required. A neuropsychological or comprehensive psycho-education evaluation is not required for admission. Tests required as part of this documentation:

- [ ] WAIS-IV
- [ ] WISC-IV
- [ ] SATA
- [ ] Woodcock-Johnson
- [ ] Nelson-Denny Reading Test
- [ ] Other

UNDERGRADUATE STUDENT BODY

Total undergraduate student enrollment: 2,852 Men, 3,386 Women.

Composition of student body (fall 2004):

	Undergraduate	Freshmen
International	0.3	0.3
Black	5.9	4.4
American Indian	0.3	0.3
Asian-American	1.8	1.4
Hispanic	1.1	1.4
White	85.0	88.8
Unreported	5.6	3.4
	100.0%	100.0%

6% are from out of state. 7% join a fraternity and 9% join a sorority. Average age of full-time undergraduates is 21. 23% of classes have fewer than 20 students, 77% have between 20 and 50 students.

STUDENT HOUSING

91% of freshmen live in college housing. Freshmen are required to live on campus. Housing is guaranteed for all undergraduates. Graduate housing is only available in the summer. Campus can house 2,646 undergraduates.

EXPENSES

Tuition (2005-06): $5,031 per year (in-state), $12,454 (out-of-state).

Room: $3,290. Board: $2,156.

There is no additional cost for LD program/services.

LD SERVICES

LD program size is not limited.

LD services available to:

- [x] Freshmen
- [x] Sophomores
- [x] Juniors
- [x] Seniors

Academic Accommodations

Curriculum		In class	
Foreign language waiver	[ ]	Early syllabus	[ ]
Lighter course load	[x]	Note takers in class	[x]
Math waiver	[ ]	Priority seating	[ ]
Other special classes	[ ]	Tape recorders	[x]
Priority registrations	[ ]	Videotaped classes	[ ]
Substitution of courses	[ ]	Text on tape	[ ]
Exams		**Services**	
Extended time	[x]	Diagnostic tests	[ ]
Oral exams	[x]	Learning centers	[x]
Take home exams	[ ]	Proofreaders	[ ]
Exams on tape or computer	[ ]	Readers	[x]
Untimed exams	[ ]	Reading Machines/Kurzweil	[x]
Other accommodations	[ ]	Special bookstore section	[ ]
		Typists	[ ]

Credit toward degree is not given for remedial courses taken.

Counseling Services

- [ ] Academic
- [ ] Psychological
- [ ] Student Support groups
- [ ] Vocational

Tutoring

Individual tutoring is available.

	Individual	Group
Time management	[ ]	[ ]
Organizational skills	[ ]	[ ]
Learning strategies	[ ]	[ ]
Study skills	[ ]	[ ]
Content area	[ ]	[ ]
Writing lab	[ ]	[ ]
Math lab	[ ]	[ ]

LD PROGRAM STAFF

Total number of LD Program staff (including director):

Full Time: 1 Part Time: 1

There is an advisor/advocate from the LD program available to students.

Key staff people available to work with LD students: Nanette Hatzes and Paula Madey

Slippery Rock University of Pennsylvania

Slippery Rock, PA

Address: 1 Morrow Way, Slippery Rock, PA, 16057-1383
Admissions telephone: 800 SRU-9111
Admissions FAX: 724 738-2913
Coordinator of Freshmen Admissions: Mimi Conner
Admissions e-mail: asktherock@sru.edu
Web site: http://www.sru.edu
SAT Code: 2658 ACT Code: 3716

LD program name: Office for Students with Disabilities
LD program address: 122 Bailey Library
Director, Office for Students with Disabilities: Linda M. Smith
LD program telephone: 724 738-2203
LD program e-mail: linda.smith@sru.edu
LD program enrollment: 328, Total campus enrollment: 7,202

GENERAL

Slippery Rock University of Pennsylvania is a public, coed, four-year institution. 600-acre campus in Slippery Rock (population: 3,068), 50 miles from Pittsburgh. Major airport, bus, and train serve Pittsburgh. School operates transportation around campus and through local community. Semester system.

LD ADMISSIONS

Students do not complete a separate application and are simultaneously accepted to the LD program.

SECONDARY SCHOOL REQUIREMENTS

Graduation from secondary school required; GED accepted.

TESTING

SAT Reasoning or ACT required. SAT Subject recommended.

All enrolled freshmen (fall 2004):

Average SAT I Scores:	Verbal:491	Math:492
Average ACT Scores:	Composite:20	

Child Study Team report is not required. Tests required as part of this documentation:

- [ ] WAIS-IV
- [ ] WISC-IV
- [ ] SATA
- [ ] Woodcock-Johnson
- [ ] Nelson-Denny Reading Test
- [ ] Other

UNDERGRADUATE STUDENT BODY

Total undergraduate student enrollment: 2,734 Men, 3,766 Women.

Composition of student body (fall 2004):

	Undergraduate	Freshmen
International	0.8	1.4
Black	6.0	4.3
American Indian	0.3	0.3
Asian-American	0.7	0.7
Hispanic	0.9	0.9
White	90.3	89.4
Unreported	1.0	3.0
	100.0%	100.0%

4% are from out of state. 4% join a fraternity and 6% join a sorority. Average age of full-time undergraduates is 21. 25% of classes have fewer than 20 students, 63% have between 20 and 50 students, 12% have more than 50 students.

STUDENT HOUSING

94% of freshmen live in college housing. Freshmen are required to live on campus. Housing is guaranteed for all undergraduates. Campus can house 2,808 undergraduates. Single rooms are available for students with medical or special needs. A medical note is required.

EXPENSES

There is no additional cost for LD program/services.

LD SERVICES

LD program size is not limited.

LD services available to:

- [x] Freshmen
- [x] Sophomores
- [x] Juniors
- [x] Seniors

Academic Accommodations

Curriculum		In class	
Foreign language waiver	[ ]	Early syllabus	[ ]
Lighter course load	[ ]	Note takers in class	[x]
Math waiver	[ ]	Priority seating	[x]
Other special classes	[ ]	Tape recorders	[x]
Priority registrations	[x]	Videotaped classes	[ ]
Substitution of courses	[ ]	Text on tape	[x]
Exams		**Services**	
Extended time	[x]	Diagnostic tests	[ ]
Oral exams	[x]	Learning centers	[ ]
Take home exams	[ ]	Proofreaders	[ ]
Exams on tape or computer	[ ]	Readers	[x]
Untimed exams	[x]	Reading Machines/Kurzweil	[x]
Other accommodations	[ ]	Special bookstore section	[ ]
		Typists	[ ]

Credit toward degree is not given for remedial courses taken.

Counseling Services

- [ ] Academic
- [ ] Psychological
- [ ] Student Support groups
- [ ] Vocational

Tutoring

Individual tutoring is available.

	Individual	Group
Time management	[ ]	[ ]
Organizational skills	[ ]	[ ]
Learning strategies	[ ]	[ ]
Study skills	[ ]	[ ]
Content area	[ ]	[ ]
Writing lab	[ ]	[ ]
Math lab	[ ]	[ ]

UNIQUE LD PROGRAM FEATURES

Students with disabilities are admitted on the same criteria as all students. After students are admitted to the university they must provide documentation of their disability and request accommodations.

LD PROGRAM STAFF

Total number of LD Program staff (including director):

Full Time: 1 Part Time: 1

One graduate student is available to work with LD students.

Key staff person available to work with LD students: Linda M. Smith, Director, Office for Students with Disabilities.

Susquehanna University

Selinsgrove, PA

Address: 514 University Avenue, Selinsgrove, PA, 17870
Admissions telephone: 800 326-9672
Admissions FAX: 570 372-2722
Director of Admissions: Chris Markle
Admissions e-mail: suadmiss@susqu.edu
Web site: http://www.susqu.edu
SAT Code: 2820 ACT Code: 3720

Associate Dean: Dr. Kathy Bradley
LD program telephone: 570 372-4751
LD program e-mail: bradley@susqu.edu
Total campus enrollment: 2,071

GENERAL

Susquehanna University is a private, coed, four-year institution. 210-acre campus in Selinsgrove (population: 5,383), 50 miles north of Harrisburg. Airport and train serve Harrisburg; bus serves Sunbury (10 miles). School operates transportation to New York City, NY; Washington, DC; nearby colleges; and airport on request. Public transportation serves campus. Semester system.

LD ADMISSIONS

A personal interview is recommended. Essay is required and may be typed.

SECONDARY SCHOOL REQUIREMENTS

Graduation from secondary school required; GED accepted. The following course distribution required: 4 units of English, 3 units of math, 3 units of science, 2 units of foreign language, 1 unit of social studies, 1 unit of history, 2 units of academic electives.

TESTING

SAT Reasoning recommended; ACT may be substituted. SAT Subject recommended.

Child Study Team report is not required. Tests required as part of this documentation:

- ☐ WAIS-IV
- ☐ WISC-IV
- ☐ SATA
- ☐ Woodcock-Johnson
- ☐ Nelson-Denny Reading Test
- ☐ Other

UNDERGRADUATE STUDENT BODY

Total undergraduate student enrollment: 752 Men, 1,020 Women.

Composition of student body (fall 2004):

	Undergraduate	Freshmen
International	0.6	0.6
Black	2.2	2.2
American Indian	0.1	0.2
Asian-American	1.1	1.6
Hispanic	2.2	1.8
White	92.3	92.7
Unreported	1.5	0.9
	100.0%	100.0%

37% are from out of state. 21% join a fraternity and 24% join a sorority. Average age of full-time undergraduates is 20. 46% of classes have fewer than 20 students, 54% have between 20 and 50 students.

STUDENT HOUSING

98% of freshmen live in college housing. Freshmen are required to live on campus. Housing is guaranteed for all undergraduates. Campus can house 1,388 undergraduates.

EXPENSES

Tuition (2005-06): $25,950 per year.
Room: $3,800. Board: $3,400.
There is no additional cost for LD program/services.

LD SERVICES

LD services available to:

☐ Freshmen ☐ Sophomores ☐ Juniors ☐ Seniors

Academic Accommodations

Curriculum		**In class**	
Foreign language waiver	☐	Early syllabus	☐
Lighter course load	☐	Note takers in class	■
Math waiver	☐	Priority seating	☐
Other special classes	☐	Tape recorders	■
Priority registrations	☐	Videotaped classes	☐
Substitution of courses	☐	Text on tape	☐
Exams		**Services**	
Extended time	■	Diagnostic tests	■
Oral exams	☐	Learning centers	■
Take home exams	☐	Proofreaders	☐
Exams on tape or computer	☐	Readers	☐
Untimed exams	■	Reading Machines/Kurzweil	■
Other accommodations	☐	Special bookstore section	☐
		Typists	☐

Counseling Services

- ☐ Academic
- ☐ Psychological
- ☐ Student Support groups
- ☐ Vocational

Tutoring

	Individual	Group
Time management	☐	☐
Organizational skills	☐	☐
Learning strategies	☐	☐
Study skills	☐	☐
Content area	☐	☐
Writing lab	☐	☐
Math lab	☐	☐

Swarthmore College

Swarthmore, PA

Address: 500 College Avenue, Swarthmore, PA, 19081
Admissions telephone: 800 667-3110
Admissions FAX: 610 328-8580
Dean of Admissions and Financial Aid: James L. Bock
Admissions e-mail: admissions@swarthmore.edu
Web site: http://www.swarthmore.edu
SAT Code: 2821 ACT Code: 3722

LD program name: Disability Services
LD program contact: Admissions Office
LD program telephone: 610 328-3800
LD program e-mail: admissions@swarthmore.edu
LD program enrollment: 16, Total campus enrollment: 1,474

GENERAL

Swarthmore College is a private, coed, four-year institution. 357-acre, suburban campus in Swarthmore (population: 6,170), 11 miles from Philadelphia. Major airport, bus, and train serve Philadelphia. School operates transportation to airport before and after breaks. Public transportation serves campus. Semester system.

LD ADMISSIONS

A personal interview is recommended. Essay is required and may be typed. Some requirements may be waived on an individual basis.

SECONDARY SCHOOL REQUIREMENTS

Graduation from secondary school not required.

TESTING

SAT Subject required.

All enrolled freshmen (fall 2004):

Average SAT I Scores: Verbal: 719 Math: 711

Child Study Team report is not required. Tests required as part of this documentation:

- [ ] WAIS-IV
- [ ] WISC-IV
- [ ] SATA
- [ ] Woodcock-Johnson
- [ ] Nelson-Denny Reading Test
- [ ] Other

UNDERGRADUATE STUDENT BODY

Total undergraduate student enrollment: 690 Men, 777 Women.

Composition of student body (fall 2004):

	Undergraduate	Freshmen
International	5.7	5.7
Black	6.8	6.4
American Indian	1.1	0.9
Asian-American	16.4	16.0
Hispanic	9.6	8.6
White	41.3	49.7
Unreported	19.1	12.7
	100.0%	100.0%

82% are from out of state. 7% join a fraternity. Average age of full-time undergraduates is 20. 74% of classes have fewer than 20 students, 24% have between 20 and 50 students, 2% have more than 50 students.

STUDENT HOUSING

100% of freshmen live in college housing. Freshmen are required to live on campus. Housing is guaranteed for all undergraduates. Campus can house 1,344 undergraduates. Single rooms are available for students with medical or special needs.

EXPENSES

Tuition (2005-06): $31,196 per year.
Room: $5,006. Board: $4,758.
Additional cost for LD program/services: $0 per .

LD SERVICES

LD program size is not limited.

LD services available to:

- [x] Freshmen
- [x] Sophomores
- [x] Juniors
- [x] Seniors

Academic Accommodations

Curriculum		In class	
Foreign language waiver	[ ]	Early syllabus	[x]
Lighter course load	[x]	Note takers in class	[x]
Math waiver	[ ]	Priority seating	[ ]
Other special classes	[ ]	Tape recorders	[x]
Priority registrations	[ ]	Videotaped classes	[x]
Substitution of courses	[ ]	Text on tape	[ ]
Exams		**Services**	
Extended time	[x]	Diagnostic tests	[x]
Oral exams	[x]	Learning centers	[ ]
Take home exams	[ ]	Proofreaders	[ ]
Exams on tape or computer	[x]	Readers	[x]
Untimed exams	[x]	Reading Machines/Kurzweil	[x]
Other accommodations	[ ]	Special bookstore section	[ ]
		Typists	[ ]

Counseling Services

- [x] Academic
- [x] Psychological
- [ ] Student Support groups
- [ ] Vocational

Tutoring

	Individual	Group
Time management	[ ]	[ ]
Organizational skills	[ ]	[ ]
Learning strategies	[ ]	[ ]
Study skills	[ ]	[ ]
Content area	[ ]	[ ]
Writing lab	[ ]	[ ]
Math lab	[ ]	[ ]

UNIQUE LD PROGRAM FEATURES

Students are accommodated case-by-case, with appropriate documentation.

LD PROGRAM STAFF

There is an advisor/advocate from the LD program available to students.

Key staff person available to work with LD students: Myrt Westphal, Assistant Dean

Temple University

Philadelphia, PA

Address: 1801 North Broad Street, Philadelphia, PA, 19122-6096
Admissions telephone: 888 340-2222
Admissions FAX: 215 204-5694
Acting Director of Admissions: Dr. Timm Rinehart
Admissions e-mail: tuadm@temple.edu
Web site: http://www.temple.edu
SAT Code: 2906 ACT Code: 3724

LD program name: Disability Resources and Services
LD program address: 1301 C. B. Moore Ave (004-00)
LD program telephone: 215 204-1280
LD program e-mail: dorothy.cebula@temple.edu
LD program enrollment: 455, Total campus enrollment: 23,429

GENERAL

Temple University is a public, coed, four-year institution. 105-acre main campus in Philadelphia (population: 1,517,550); branch campuses in Ambler, Center City, and Tyler. Served by air, bus, and train. School operates transportation between campuses. Semester system.

LD ADMISSIONS

Students do not complete a separate application and are simultaneously accepted to the LD program. A member of the LD program does not sit on the admissions committee. High school waivers are accepted for math and foreign language. A personal interview is not required. Essay is required and may be typed.

SECONDARY SCHOOL REQUIREMENTS

Graduation from secondary school required; GED accepted. The following course distribution required: 4 units of English, 3 units of math, 2 units of science, 2 units of foreign language, 2 units of social studies, 1 unit of history, 1 unit of academic electives.

TESTING

SAT Reasoning or ACT required. SAT Subject recommended.

All enrolled freshmen (fall 2004):

Average SAT I Scores:	Verbal: 541	Math: 547
Average ACT Scores:	Composite: 22	

Child Study Team report is not required. A neuropsychological or comprehensive psycho-educational evaluation is required for admission. Tests required as part of this documentation:

■ WAIS-IV	■ Woodcock-Johnson
□ WISC-IV	■ Nelson-Denny Reading Test
■ SATA	□ Other

UNDERGRADUATE STUDENT BODY

Total undergraduate student enrollment: 8,188 Men, 11,418 Women.

Composition of student body (fall 2004):

	Undergraduate	Freshmen
International	1.8	3.4
Black	17.1	19.9
American Indian	0.2	0.2
Asian-American	9.9	8.4
Hispanic	3.3	3.3
White	60.4	56.9
Unreported	7.3	7.9
	100.0%	100.0%

22% are from out of state. 1% join a fraternity and 1% join a sorority. Average age of full-time undergraduates is 21. 38% of classes have fewer than 20 students, 54% have between 20 and 50 students, 8% have more than 50 students.

STUDENT HOUSING

72% of freshmen live in college housing. Freshmen are not required to live on campus. Priority is given to incoming undergraduates and then to continuing students. Housing for upperclassmen is available if space allows. Campus can house 4,447 undergraduates. Single rooms are available for students with medical or special needs. A medical note is required.

EXPENSES

Tuition (2005-06): $9,140 per year (in-state), $16,736 (out-of-state). Tuition varies by program.

Room: $5,058. Board: $2,708.

There is no additional cost for LD program/services.

LD SERVICES

LD program size is not limited.

LD services available to:

■ Freshmen ■ Sophomores ■ Juniors ■ Seniors

Academic Accommodations

Curriculum		In class	
Foreign language waiver	□	Early syllabus	□
Lighter course load	□	Note takers in class	■
Math waiver	□	Priority seating	□
Other special classes	■	Tape recorders	■
Priority registrations	□	Videotaped classes	■
Substitution of courses	□	Text on tape	□
Exams		**Services**	
Extended time	■	Diagnostic tests	■
Oral exams	■	Learning centers	■
Take home exams	□	Proofreaders	□
Exams on tape or computer	□	Readers	■
Untimed exams	■	Reading Machines/Kurzweil	■
Other accommodations	□	Special bookstore section	□
		Typists	□

Credit toward degree is not given for remedial courses taken.

Counseling Services

□ Academic
□ Psychological
□ Student Support groups
□ Vocational

Tutoring

	Individual	Group
Time management	□	□
Organizational skills	□	□
Learning strategies	□	□
Study skills	□	□
Content area	□	□
Writing lab	□	□
Math lab	□	□

LD PROGRAM STAFF

Total number of LD Program staff (including director):

Full Time: 3 Part Time: 3

There is an advisor/advocate from the LD program available to students.

Key staff person available to work with LD students: Dorothy Cebula, Director

Temple University at Ambler Campus

Ambler, PA

Address: 580 Meetinghouse Road, Ambler, PA, 19002
Admissions telephone: 215 283-1252
Assistant Dean: Kevin Freese
Web site: http://www.temple.edu/ambler
SAT Code: 2906 ACT Code: 3724

Director: Dorothy M. Cebula, Ph.D.
LD program telephone: 215 204-1280
LD program e-mail: hellodrs@astro.ocis.temple.edu
LD program enrollment: 32, Total campus enrollment: 2,172

GENERAL

Temple University, Ambler Campus is a public, coed, four-year institution. 186-acre campus in Ambler (population: 6,426), 27 miles from Philadelphia; branch campus in Ft. Washington. Major airport, bus, and train serve Philadelphia. School operates transportation between campuses and to local areas. Semester system.

LD ADMISSIONS

Students do not complete a separate application and are not simultaneously accepted to the LD program. A member of the LD program does not sit on the admissions committee. A personal interview is not required. Essay is not required.

SECONDARY SCHOOL REQUIREMENTS

Graduation from secondary school required; GED accepted. The following course distribution required: 4 units of English, 3 units of math, 2 units of science, 2 units of foreign language, 2 units of social studies, 1 unit of history, 1 unit of academic electives.

TESTING

SAT Reasoning required.

Child Study Team report is not required. A neuropsychological or comprehensive psycho-education evaluation is not required for admission. Tests required as part of this documentation:

- ❑ WAIS-IV
- ❑ WISC-IV
- ❑ SATA
- ❑ Woodcock-Johnson
- ❑ Nelson-Denny Reading Test
- ❑ Other

UNDERGRADUATE STUDENT BODY

Total undergraduate student enrollment: 846 Men, 1,326 Women.

Composition of student body (fall 2004):

	Undergraduate	Freshmen
International	0.9	1.3
Black	13.0	10.5
American Indian	0.1	0.3
Asian-American	2.3	2.9
Hispanic	2.3	2.1
White	74.4	76.7
Unreported	7.0	6.2
	100.0%	100.0%

31% are from out of state. 1% join a fraternity and 1% join a sorority. Average age of full-time undergraduates is 21.

STUDENT HOUSING

Housing is guaranteed for all undergraduates. Single rooms are not available for students with medical or special needs.

EXPENSES

Tuition 2001-02: $6,974 per year (in-state), $12,712 (out-of-state). Tuition varies by program.
Room: $4,338. Board: $1,964-$2,462.
There is no additional cost for LD program/services.

LD SERVICES

LD program size is not limited.

LD services available to:

❑ Freshmen ❑ Sophomores ❑ Juniors ❑ Seniors

Academic Accommodations

Curriculum		In class	
Foreign language waiver	❑	Early syllabus	❑
Lighter course load	❑	Note takers in class	❑
Math waiver	❑	Priority seating	❑
Other special classes	❑	Tape recorders	❑
Priority registrations	❑	Videotaped classes	❑
Substitution of courses	❑	Text on tape	❑
Exams		**Services**	
Extended time	❑	Diagnostic tests	❑
Oral exams	❑	Learning centers	❑
Take home exams	❑	Proofreaders	❑
Exams on tape or computer	❑	Readers	❑
Untimed exams	❑	Reading Machines/Kurzweil	❑
Other accommodations	❑	Special bookstore section	❑
		Typists	❑

Credit toward degree is not given for remedial courses taken.

Counseling Services

- ❑ Academic
- ❑ Psychological
- ❑ Student Support groups
- ❑ Vocational

Tutoring

Individual tutoring is not available.

	Individual	Group
Time management	❑	❑
Organizational skills	❑	❑
Learning strategies	❑	❑
Study skills	❑	❑
Content area	❑	❑
Writing lab	❑	❑
Math lab	❑	❑

LD PROGRAM STAFF

There is no advisor/advocate from the LD program available to students.

Thiel College

Greenville, PA

Address: 75 College Avenue, Greenville, PA, 16125
Admissions telephone: 800 248-4435
Admissions FAX: 724 589-2013
Director of Admissions: Jeff Baylor
Admissions e-mail: admission@thiel.edu
Web site: http://www.thiel.edu
SAT Code: 2910 ACT Code: 3730

LD program name: Office of Special Needs
Coordinator, Office of Special Needs: Susan Cowan
LD program telephone: 724 589-2063
LD program e-mail: scowan@thiel.edu
LD program enrollment: 41, Total campus enrollment: 1,245

GENERAL

Thiel College is a private, coed, four-year institution. 135-acre campus in Greenville (population: 6,380), 80 miles from Pittsburgh and 75 miles from Cleveland. Major airport and train serve Pittsburgh; smaller airport serves Youngstown, Ohio (20 miles); bus serves Mercer (15 miles). Semester system.

LD ADMISSIONS

Students do not complete a separate application and are not simultaneously accepted to the LD program. A member of the LD program does not sit on the admissions committee. A personal interview is not required. Essay is not required.

30 applications were offered admission, and 25 enrolled.

SECONDARY SCHOOL REQUIREMENTS

Graduation from secondary school required; GED accepted. The following course distribution required: 4 units of English, 2 units of math, 2 units of science, 2 units of foreign language, 3 units of social studies.

TESTING

SAT Reasoning or ACT recommended. SAT Subject required.

All enrolled freshmen (fall 2004):

Average SAT I Scores:	Verbal: 479	Math: 475
Average ACT Scores:	Composite: 20	

Child Study Team report is not required. A neuropsychological or comprehensive psycho-educational evaluation is required for admission. Must be dated within 46 months of application. Tests required as part of this documentation:

- ■ WAIS-IV
- ☐ WISC-IV
- ■ SATA
- ■ Woodcock-Johnson
- ■ Nelson-Denny Reading Test
- ☐ Other

UNDERGRADUATE STUDENT BODY

Total undergraduate student enrollment: 592 Men, 597 Women.

Composition of student body (fall 2004):

	Undergraduate	Freshmen
International	3.3	5.1
Black	4.9	6.3
American Indian	0.0	0.2
Asian-American	0.8	0.6
Hispanic	0.8	0.6
White	79.6	75.0
Unreported	10.6	12.2
	100.0%	100.0%

21% are from out of state. 12% join a fraternity and 22% join a sorority. Average age of full-time undergraduates is 20. 57% of classes have fewer than 20 students, 40% have between 20 and 50 students, 3% have more than 50 students.

STUDENT HOUSING

98% of freshmen live in college housing. Freshmen are required to live on campus. Housing is guaranteed for all undergraduates. Campus can house 1,192 undergraduates. Single rooms are available for students with medical or special needs. A medical note is required.

EXPENSES

Tuition (2005-06): $16,200 per year.
Room: $3,566. Board: $3,424.
There is no additional cost for LD program/services.

LD SERVICES

LD program size is not limited.

LD services available to:

■ Freshmen ■ Sophomores ■ Juniors ■ Seniors

Academic Accommodations

Curriculum		In class	
Foreign language waiver	■	Early syllabus	☐
Lighter course load	☐	Note takers in class	■
Math waiver	☐	Priority seating	■
Other special classes	☐	Tape recorders	■
Priority registrations	☐	Videotaped classes	■
Substitution of courses	☐	Text on tape	☐
Exams		**Services**	
Extended time	■	Diagnostic tests	☐
Oral exams	■	Learning centers	■
Take home exams	☐	Proofreaders	■
Exams on tape or computer	■	Readers	■
Untimed exams	■	Reading Machines/Kurzweil	☐
Other accommodations	☐	Special bookstore section	☐
		Typists	☐

Credit toward degree is given for remedial courses taken.

Counseling Services

- ■ Academic
- ☐ Psychological
- ☐ Student Support groups
- ☐ Vocational

Tutoring

Individual tutoring is available weekly.

Average size of tutoring groups: 1

	Individual	Group
Time management	☐	☐
Organizational skills	☐	☐
Learning strategies	☐	☐
Study skills	☐	☐
Content area	☐	☐
Writing lab	■	☐
Math lab	☐	☐

LD PROGRAM STAFF

There is no advisor/advocate from the LD program available to students.

Key staff person available to work with LD students: Susan Cowan, Coordinator, Office Of Special Needs

Thomas Jefferson University, College of Health Professions

Philadelphia, PA

Address: 130 South Ninth Street, Philadelphia, PA, 19107
Admissions telephone: 877 533-3247
Acting Director of Admissions and Enrollment Management: Karen Jacobs
SAT Code: 2903

LD program name: Office of Student Affairs
Assistant Dean and Director: William Thygeson
LD program telephone: 215 503-8189
LD program e-mail: William.Thygeson@jefferson.edu
LD program enrollment: 3, Total campus enrollment: 908

GENERAL

Thomas Jefferson University, College of Health Professions is a private, coed, graduate institution. 13-acre, urban campus in Philadelphia (population: 1,517,550). Served by air, bus, and train. Public transportation serves campus. Semester system.

LD ADMISSIONS

A personal interview is not required. Essay is not required.

TESTING

Child Study Team report is not required. Tests required as part of this documentation:

- ☑ WAIS-IV
- ☐ WISC-IV
- ☑ SATA
- ☑ Woodcock-Johnson
- ☑ Nelson-Denny Reading Test
- ☑ Other

UNDERGRADUATE STUDENT BODY

Total undergraduate student enrollment: 143 Men, 695 Women.

Composition of student body (fall 2004):

	Undergraduate	Freshmen
International	0.9	1.9
Black	20.9	10.2
American Indian	0.9	0.5
Asian-American	0.8	7.0
Hispanic	3.5	2.3
White	60.0	65.1
Unreported	13.0	13.0
	100.0%	100.0%

50% are from out of state. Average age of full-time undergraduates is 28. 60% of classes have fewer than 20 students, 27% have between 20 and 50 students, 13% have more than 50 students.

STUDENT HOUSING

Freshmen are not required to live on campus. Housing is guaranteed for all undergraduates. Campus can house 615 undergraduates. Single rooms are available for students with medical or special needs. A medical note is not required.

EXPENSES

Tuition (2005-06): $21,975 per year.

LD SERVICES

LD program size is not limited.

LD services available to:

☐ Freshmen ☐ Sophomores ☑ Juniors ☑ Seniors

Academic Accommodations

Curriculum		In class	
Foreign language waiver	☐	Early syllabus	☐
Lighter course load	☑	Note takers in class	☑
Math waiver	☐	Priority seating	☑
Other special classes	☐	Tape recorders	☑
Priority registrations	☐	Videotaped classes	☐
Substitution of courses	☐	Text on tape	☐
Exams		**Services**	
Extended time	☑	Diagnostic tests	☐
Oral exams	☑	Learning centers	☐
Take home exams	☐	Proofreaders	☐
Exams on tape or computer	☑	Readers	☑
Untimed exams	☑	Reading Machines/Kurzweil	☐
Other accommodations	☑	Special bookstore section	☐
		Typists	☐

Credit toward degree is not given for remedial courses taken.

Counseling Services

- ☑ Academic
- ☑ Psychological
- ☐ Student Support groups
- ☐ Vocational

Tutoring

Individual tutoring is available daily.

Average size of tutoring groups: 1

	Individual	Group
Time management	☑	☑
Organizational skills	☑	☑
Learning strategies	☑	☑
Study skills	☑	☑
Content area	☐	☐
Writing lab	☑	☐
Math lab	☐	☐

UNIQUE LD PROGRAM FEATURES

LD Services are provided on a case-by-case basis depending upon documented disability.

LD PROGRAM STAFF

There is an advisor/advocate from the LD program available to students.

Key staff person available to work with LD students: William Thygeson, Assistant Dean and Director of Student Affairs

Ursinus College

Collegeville, PA

Address: Box 1000, Collegeville, PA, 19426
Admissions telephone: 610 409-3200
Admissions FAX: 610 409-3662
Director of Admissions: Paul Cramer
Admissions e-mail: Admissions@Ursinus.edu
Web site: http://www.ursinus.edu
SAT Code: 2931 ACT Code: 3738

Director of Admissions: Paul Cramer
LD program telephone: 610 409-3200
LD program enrollment: 35, Total campus enrollment: 1,499

GENERAL

Ursinus College is a private, coed, four-year institution. 165-acre, suburban campus in Collegeville (population: 8,032), 25 miles from Philadelphia. Served by bus; major airport serves Philadelphia; train serves Norristown (15 miles). School operates transportation to Valley Forge. Public transportation serves campus. Semester system.

LD ADMISSIONS

Application Deadline: 02/15. A personal interview is recommended. Essay is required and may be typed.

For fall 2004, 43 completed self-identified LD applications were received. 29 applications were offered admission, and 8 enrolled.

SECONDARY SCHOOL REQUIREMENTS

Graduation from secondary school required; GED not accepted. The following course distribution required: 4 units of English, 3 units of math, 1 unit of science, 2 units of foreign language, 1 unit of social studies, 5 units of academic electives.

TESTING

SAT Reasoning or ACT required of some applicants. SAT Subject recommended.

All enrolled freshmen (fall 2004):

Average SAT I Scores:	Verbal: 605	Math: 609
Average ACT Scores:	Composite: 26	

Child Study Team report is not required. A neuropsychological or comprehensive psycho-educational evaluation is required for admission. Must be dated within 24 months of application. Tests required as part of this documentation:

- [ ] WAIS-IV
- [x] WISC-IV
- [ ] SATA
- [ ] Woodcock-Johnson
- [ ] Nelson-Denny Reading Test
- [ ] Other

UNDERGRADUATE STUDENT BODY

Total undergraduate student enrollment: 569 Men, 755 Women.

Composition of student body (fall 2004):

	Undergraduate	Freshmen
International	2.3	1.6
Black	5.1	6.6
American Indian	0.0	0.4
Asian-American	4.3	4.0
Hispanic	2.8	2.8
White	77.6	79.1
Unreported	7.9	5.5
	100.0%	100.0%

37% are from out of state. 17% join a fraternity and 28% join a sorority. Average age of full-time undergraduates is 20. 78% of classes have fewer than 20 students, 21% have between 20 and 50 students, 1% have more than 50 students.

STUDENT HOUSING

98% of freshmen live in college housing. Freshmen are not required to live on campus. Housing is guaranteed for all undergraduates. Campus can house 1,388 undergraduates. Single rooms are available for students with medical or special needs. A medical note is required.

EXPENSES

Tuition (2005-06): $31,450 per year.
Room & Board: $7,350
Additional cost for LD program/services: $0 per depends on service.

LD SERVICES

LD program size is not limited.

LD services available to:

- [x] Freshmen
- [x] Sophomores
- [x] Juniors
- [x] Seniors

Academic Accommodations

Curriculum		In class	
Foreign language waiver	[ ]	Early syllabus	[ ]
Lighter course load	[x]	Note takers in class	[x]
Math waiver	[ ]	Priority seating	[ ]
Other special classes	[ ]	Tape recorders	[x]
Priority registrations	[ ]	Videotaped classes	[ ]
Substitution of courses	[ ]	Text on tape	[ ]
Exams		**Services**	
Extended time	[x]	Diagnostic tests	[ ]
Oral exams	[ ]	Learning centers	[ ]
Take home exams	[ ]	Proofreaders	[ ]
Exams on tape or computer	[ ]	Readers	[x]
Untimed exams	[ ]	Reading Machines/Kurzweil	[ ]
Other accommodations	[ ]	Special bookstore section	[ ]
		Typists	[ ]

Credit toward degree is not given for remedial courses taken.

Counseling Services

- [ ] Academic
- [ ] Psychological
- [ ] Student Support groups
- [ ] Vocational

Tutoring

Individual tutoring is available weekly.

	Individual	Group
Time management	[ ]	[ ]
Organizational skills	[ ]	[ ]
Learning strategies	[ ]	[ ]
Study skills	[x]	[ ]
Content area	[x]	[x]
Writing lab	[x]	[x]
Math lab	[x]	[x]

UNIQUE LD PROGRAM FEATURES

Counseling services offered to LD students are the same as those offered to all students.

LD PROGRAM STAFF

There is no advisor/advocate from the LD program available to students.

Key staff person available to work with LD students: Edward Gildea, Coordinator, Freshmen Advising

Villanova University

Villanova, PA

Address: 800 Lancaster Avenue, Villanova, PA, 19085
Admissions telephone: 610 519-4000
Admissions FAX: 610 519-6450
Director of University Admission: Michael M. Gaynor
Admissions e-mail: gotovu@villanova.edu
Web site: http://www.villanova.edu
SAT Code: 2959 ACT Code: 3744

LD program name: Learning Support Services
Director, Learning Support Services: Nancy Mott
LD program telephone: 610 519-5636
LD program e-mail: nancy.mott@villanova.edu
LD program enrollment: 207, Total campus enrollment: 7,290

GENERAL

Villanova University is a private, coed, four-year institution. 252-acre campus in Villanova (population: 5,900), 12 miles west of Philadelphia. Major airport, train, and bus serve Philadelphia. School operates transportation to Rosemont Coll and around local area. Public transportation serves campus. Semester system.

LD ADMISSIONS

Students do not complete a separate application and are not simultaneously accepted to the LD program. A member of the LD program does not sit on the admissions committee. A personal interview is not required. Essay is required and may be typed.

SECONDARY SCHOOL REQUIREMENTS

Graduation from secondary school required; GED accepted. The following course distribution required: 4 units of English, 4 units of math, 4 units of science, 2 units of foreign language, 2 units of academic electives.

TESTING

SAT Reasoning or ACT required. SAT Subject required.

All enrolled freshmen (fall 2004):

Average SAT I Scores:	Verbal: 620	Math: 640
Average ACT Scores:	Composite: 27	

Child Study Team report is not required. A neuropsychological or comprehensive psycho-educational evaluation is required for admission. Must be dated within 48 months of application. Tests required as part of this documentation:

■ WAIS-IV
□ WISC-IV
■ SATA
■ Woodcock-Johnson
■ Nelson-Denny Reading Test
■ Other

UNDERGRADUATE STUDENT BODY

Total undergraduate student enrollment: 3,616 Men, 3,698 Women.

Composition of student body (fall 2004):

	Undergraduate	Freshmen
International	1.4	2.2
Black	3.5	3.4
American Indian	0.2	0.2
Asian-American	6.3	5.6
Hispanic	5.4	5.0
White	81.0	81.7
Unreported	2.2	1.8
	100.0%	100.0%

68% are from out of state. 12% join a fraternity and 33% join a sorority. Average age of full-time undergraduates is 21. 41% of classes have fewer than 20 students, 54% have between 20 and 50 students, 5% have more than 50 students.

STUDENT HOUSING

97% of freshmen live in college housing. Freshmen are not required to live on campus. Housing is not guaranteed for all undergraduates. Campus can house 4,365 undergraduates. Single rooms are available for students with medical or special needs. A medical note is required.

EXPENSES

Tuition (2005-06): $29,094 per year. $23,312 per year for most programs.
Room: $4,910. Board: $4,400.
There is no additional cost for LD program/services.

LD SERVICES

LD program size is not limited.

LD services available to:

■ Freshmen ■ Sophomores ■ Juniors ■ Seniors

Academic Accommodations

Curriculum		In class	
Foreign language waiver	□	Early syllabus	□
Lighter course load	■	Note takers in class	■
Math waiver	□	Priority seating	■
Other special classes	□	Tape recorders	■
Priority registrations	□	Videotaped classes	□
Substitution of courses	□	Text on tape	■
Exams		**Services**	
Extended time	■	Diagnostic tests	□
Oral exams	■	Learning centers	■
Take home exams	□	Proofreaders	□
Exams on tape or computer	□	Readers	■
Untimed exams	■	Reading Machines/Kurzweil	■
Other accommodations	■	Special bookstore section	□
		Typists	□

Credit toward degree is not given for remedial courses taken.

Counseling Services

■ Academic
■ Psychological
■ Student Support groups
□ Vocational

Tutoring

Individual tutoring is available weekly.

Average size of tutoring groups: 1

	Individual	Group
Time management	■	■
Organizational skills	■	■
Learning strategies	■	□
Study skills	■	■
Content area	■	□
Writing lab	■	□
Math lab	■	□

UNIQUE LD PROGRAM FEATURES

Students need for accommodation is evaluated on a case by case basis.

LD PROGRAM STAFF

Total number of LD Program staff (including director):

Full Time: 1 Part Time: 1

There is an advisor/advocate from the LD program available to students. One graduate student and 25 peer tutors are available to work with LD students.

Key staff person available to work with LD students: Nancy Mott, Director, Learning Support Services

LD Program web site: learningsupportservices.villanova.edu

Washington & Jefferson College

Washington, PA

Address: 60 South Lincoln Street, Washington, PA, 15301
Admissions telephone: 888 WAN-DJAY
Admissions FAX: 724 223-6534
Dean of Enrollment: Alton Newell
Admissions e-mail: admission@washjeff.edu
Web site: http://www.washjeff.edu
SAT Code: 2967 ACT Code: 3746

LD program name: Center for Learning & Teaching
Associate Director: Catherine Sherman, M.Ed.
LD program telephone: 724 250-3533
LD program e-mail: csherman@washjeff.edu
Total campus enrollment: 1,355

GENERAL

Washington & Jefferson College is a private, coed, four-year institution. 52-acre campus in Washington (population: 15,268), 27 miles southwest of Pittsburgh. Served by air; major airport, bus, and train serve Pittsburgh. 4-1-4 system.

LD ADMISSIONS

Students do not complete a separate application and are not simultaneously accepted to the LD program. A member of the LD program does not sit on the admissions committee. High school waivers are accepted for foreign language. A personal interview is recommended. Essay is required and may be typed.

SECONDARY SCHOOL REQUIREMENTS

Graduation from secondary school required; GED accepted. The following course distribution required: 3 units of English, 3 units of math, 1 unit of science, 2 units of foreign language, 6 units of academic electives.

TESTING

SAT Reasoning or ACT required. SAT Subject recommended.

All enrolled freshmen (fall 2004):

Average SAT I Scores:	Verbal: 565	Math: 577
Average ACT Scores:	Composite: 25	

Child Study Team report is not required. A neuropsychological or comprehensive psycho-educational evaluation is required for admission. Must be dated within 36 months of application. Tests required as part of this documentation:

- [x] WAIS-IV
- [x] WISC-IV
- [ ] SATA
- [x] Woodcock-Johnson
- [ ] Nelson-Denny Reading Test
- [x] Other

UNDERGRADUATE STUDENT BODY

Total undergraduate student enrollment: 631 Men, 609 Women.

Composition of student body (fall 2004):

	Undergraduate	Freshmen
International	0.0	0.0
Black	2.4	2.4
American Indian	0.2	0.1
Asian-American	1.9	1.3
Hispanic	1.1	1.0
White	92.3	86.8
Unreported	2.1	8.4
	100.0%	100.0%

19% are from out of state. 47% join a fraternity and 44% join a sorority. Average age of full-time undergraduates is 19. 64% of classes have fewer than 20 students, 35% have between 20 and 50 students, 1% have more than 50 students.

STUDENT HOUSING

96% of freshmen live in college housing. Freshmen are required to live on campus. Housing is guaranteed for all undergraduates. Campus can house 1,155 undergraduates. Single rooms are available for students with medical or special needs. A medical note is required.

EXPENSES

Tuition (2005-06): $25,930 per year.
Room: $4,150. Board: $3,010.
There is no additional cost for LD program/services.

LD SERVICES

LD program size is not limited.

LD services available to:

- [x] Freshmen
- [x] Sophomores
- [x] Juniors
- [x] Seniors

Academic Accommodations

Curriculum		In class	
Foreign language waiver	[ ]	Early syllabus	[ ]
Lighter course load	[ ]	Note takers in class	[x]
Math waiver	[ ]	Priority seating	[x]
Other special classes	[ ]	Tape recorders	[x]
Priority registrations	[ ]	Videotaped classes	[ ]
Substitution of courses	[ ]	Text on tape	[x]
Exams		**Services**	
Extended time	[x]	Diagnostic tests	[ ]
Oral exams	[x]	Learning centers	[x]
Take home exams	[ ]	Proofreaders	[ ]
Exams on tape or computer	[ ]	Readers	[x]
Untimed exams	[x]	Reading Machines/Kurzweil	[ ]
Other accommodations	[x]	Special bookstore section	[ ]
		Typists	[ ]

Credit toward degree is not given for remedial courses taken.

Counseling Services

- [x] Academic
- [x] Psychological
- [ ] Student Support groups
- [ ] Vocational

Tutoring

Individual tutoring is available daily.

	Individual	Group
Time management	[x]	[ ]
Organizational skills	[x]	[ ]
Learning strategies	[x]	[ ]
Study skills	[x]	[ ]
Content area	[ ]	[ ]
Writing lab	[x]	[ ]
Math lab	[x]	[ ]

LD PROGRAM STAFF

Total number of LD Program staff (including director):

Full Time: 1 Part Time: 1

There is an advisor/advocate from the LD program available to students.

Key staff person available to work with LD students: Catherine Sherman, M.Ed., Associate Director, Center for Learning & Teaching

LD Program web site: www.washjeff.edu/CLT

Waynesburg College

Waynesburg, PA

Address: 51 West College Street, Waynesburg, PA, 15370
Admissions telephone: 800 225-7393
Admissions FAX: 724 627-8124
Director of Admissions: Robin L. King
Admissions e-mail: admissions@waynesburg.edu
Web site: http://www.waynesburg.edu/
SAT Code: 2969 ACT Code: 3748

Director: Thomas Helmick
LD program telephone: 724 852-3400
LD program e-mail: thelmick@waynesburg.edu
LD program enrollment: 35, Total campus enrollment: 1,634

GENERAL

Waynesburg College is a private, coed, four-year institution. 30-acre campus in Waynesburg (population: 4,184), 50 miles from Pittsburgh. Major airport, bus, and train serve Pittsburgh; smaller airport serves Morgantown, W.Va. (30 miles). School operates transportation to Pittsburgh airport before breaks. Semester system.

LD ADMISSIONS

Students do not complete a separate application and are not simultaneously accepted to the LD program. A member of the LD program does not sit on the admissions committee. A personal interview is recommended. Essay is not required.

For fall 2004, 24 completed self-identified LD applications were received. 24 applications were offered admission, and 20 enrolled.

SECONDARY SCHOOL REQUIREMENTS

Graduation from secondary school required; GED accepted. The following course distribution required: 4 units of English, 3 units of math, 2 units of science, 2 units of social studies, 5 units of academic electives.

TESTING

SAT Reasoning or ACT required. SAT Subject required.

Child Study Team report is not required. A neuropsychological or comprehensive psycho-educational evaluation is required for admission. Must be dated within 24 months of application. Tests required as part of this documentation:

- [x] WAIS-IV
- [x] WISC-IV
- [x] SATA
- [x] Woodcock-Johnson
- [x] Nelson-Denny Reading Test
- [ ] Other

UNDERGRADUATE STUDENT BODY

Total undergraduate student enrollment: 647 Men, 812 Women.

Composition of student body (fall 2004):

	Undergraduate	Freshmen
International	0.1	0.1
Black	4.1	3.9
American Indian	0.5	0.2
Asian-American	0.0	0.0
Hispanic	0.8	0.4
White	90.7	91.9
Unreported	3.8	3.5
	100.0%	100.0%

17% are from out of state. Average age of full-time undergraduates is 21. 59% of classes have fewer than 20 students, 41% have between 20 and 50 students.

STUDENT HOUSING

81% of freshmen live in college housing. Freshmen are required to live on campus. Housing is guaranteed for all undergraduates. Campus can house 744 undergraduates. Single rooms are not available for students with medical or special needs.

EXPENSES

Tuition (2005-06): $14,810 per year.
Room: $3,100. Board: $2,980.
There is no additional cost for LD program/services.

LD SERVICES

LD program size is not limited.

LD services available to:

- [x] Freshmen
- [x] Sophomores
- [x] Juniors
- [x] Seniors

Academic Accommodations

Curriculum		In class	
Foreign language waiver	[ ]	Early syllabus	[ ]
Lighter course load	[ ]	Note takers in class	[ ]
Math waiver	[ ]	Priority seating	[x]
Other special classes	[ ]	Tape recorders	[x]
Priority registrations	[ ]	Videotaped classes	[ ]
Substitution of courses	[ ]	Text on tape	[ ]
Exams		**Services**	
Extended time	[x]	Diagnostic tests	[ ]
Oral exams	[x]	Learning centers	[x]
Take home exams	[ ]	Proofreaders	[ ]
Exams on tape or computer	[ ]	Readers	[x]
Untimed exams	[ ]	Reading Machines/Kurzweil	[ ]
Other accommodations	[ ]	Special bookstore section	[ ]
		Typists	[x]

Credit toward degree is given for remedial courses taken.

Counseling Services

- [x] Academic
- [ ] Psychological
- [ ] Student Support groups
- [ ] Vocational

Tutoring

Individual tutoring is available daily.

	Individual	Group
Time management	[ ]	[ ]
Organizational skills	[x]	[ ]
Learning strategies	[x]	[ ]
Study skills	[ ]	[ ]
Content area	[ ]	[ ]
Writing lab	[ ]	[ ]
Math lab	[ ]	[ ]

LD PROGRAM STAFF

Total number of LD Program staff (including director):

Full Time: 4 Part Time: 4

There is no advisor/advocate from the LD program available to students.

Key staff person available to work with LD students: Thomas Helmick, Director, Human Resources & Disabilities Services

West Chester University of Pennsylvania

West Chester, PA

Address: West Chester, PA, 19383
Admissions telephone: 877 315-2165
Admissions FAX: 610 436-2907
Director of Admissions: Marsha L. Haug
Admissions e-mail: ugadmiss@wcupa.edu
Web site: http://www.wcupa.edu
SAT Code: 2659

LD program address: Lawrence Center, Room 105
Assistant Dir. Student Support Services: Kim Jackson
LD program telephone: 610 436-2775
LD program e-mail: kjackson2@wcupa.edu
LD program enrollment: 300, Total campus enrollment: 10,644

GENERAL

West Chester University of Pennsylvania is a public, coed, four-year institution. 388-acre, suburban campus in West Chester (population: 17,862), 25 miles from Philadelphia. Served by bus; major airport serves Philadelphia; train serves Paoli (20 miles). School operates transportation to south section of campus. Semester system.

LD ADMISSIONS

Students do not complete a separate application and are not simultaneously accepted to the LD program. A member of the LD program does not sit on the admissions committee. A personal interview is not required. Essay is required and may be typed.

For fall 2004, 266 completed self-identified LD applications were received. 133 applications were offered admission, and 124 enrolled.

SECONDARY SCHOOL REQUIREMENTS

Graduation from secondary school required; GED accepted. The following course distribution required: 4 units of English, 3 units of math, 2 units of science, 4 units of history, 3 units of academic electives.

TESTING

SAT Reasoning required; ACT may be substituted. SAT Subject recommended.

All enrolled freshmen (fall 2004):

Average SAT I Scores: Verbal: 529 Math: 532

Child Study Team report is not required. A neuropsychological or comprehensive psycho-educational evaluation is required for admission. Must be dated within 60 months of application. Tests required as part of this documentation:

- [x] WAIS-IV
- [x] WISC-IV
- [x] SATA
- [x] Woodcock-Johnson
- [x] Nelson-Denny Reading Test
- [x] Other

UNDERGRADUATE STUDENT BODY

Total undergraduate student enrollment: 4,097 Men, 6,123 Women.

Composition of student body (fall 2004):

	Undergraduate	Freshmen
International	0.1	0.4
Black	8.9	8.3
American Indian	0.2	0.3
Asian-American	1.8	1.9
Hispanic	3.1	2.4
White	85.7	86.3
Unreported	0.2	0.4
	100.0%	100.0%

11% are from out of state. 8% join a fraternity and 8% join a sorority. Average age of full-time undergraduates is 21. 30% of classes have fewer than 20 students, 66% have between 20 and 50 students, 4% have more than 50 students.

STUDENT HOUSING

91% of freshmen live in college housing. Freshmen are not required to live on campus. Housing is guaranteed for all undergraduates. Campus can house 3,928 undergraduates. Single rooms are available for students with medical or special needs. A medical note is required.

EXPENSES

Tuition (2005-06): $5,031 per year (in-state), $12,454 (out-of-state).
Room: $4,140. Board: $2,068.

There is no additional cost for LD program/services.

LD SERVICES

LD program size is not limited. LD services available to:

- [x] Freshmen
- [x] Sophomores
- [x] Juniors
- [x] Seniors

Academic Accommodations

Curriculum

- [ ] Foreign language waiver
- [x] Lighter course load
- [ ] Math waiver
- [ ] Other special classes
- [ ] Priority registrations
- [ ] Substitution of courses

Exams

- [x] Extended time
- [x] Oral exams
- [ ] Take home exams
- [ ] Exams on tape or computer
- [ ] Untimed exams
- [ ] Other accommodations

In class

- [ ] Early syllabus
- [x] Note takers in class
- [ ] Priority seating
- [x] Tape recorders
- [ ] Videotaped classes
- [ ] Text on tape

Services

- [ ] Diagnostic tests
- [x] Learning centers
- [ ] Proofreaders
- [x] Readers
- [x] Reading Machines/Kurzweil
- [ ] Special bookstore section
- [ ] Typists

Credit toward degree is not given for remedial courses taken.

Counseling Services

- [ ] Academic
- [ ] Psychological
- [ ] Student Support groups
- [ ] Vocational

Tutoring

Individual tutoring is available weekly.

Average size of tutoring groups: 3

	Individual	Group
Time management	[x]	[ ]
Organizational skills	[x]	[ ]
Learning strategies	[x]	[ ]
Study skills	[x]	[ ]
Content area	[ ]	[ ]
Writing lab	[x]	[ ]
Math lab	[ ]	[x]

UNIQUE LD PROGRAM FEATURES

Advocacy with faculty for classroom accommodations and substitution of courses for foreign language is provided. A liaison with governmental agencies and private practitioners for provision of services is available through the Office of Services for Students with Disabilities.

LD PROGRAM STAFF

Total number of LD Program staff (including director):

Full Time: 3 Part Time: 3

There is an advisor/advocate from the LD program available to students. The advisor/advocate meets with students four times per month. Six graduate students are available to work with LD students. Key staff person available to work with LD students: Dr. Martin Patwell, Director of Services for Students w/Disabilities.

LD Program web site: www.wcupa.edu/_academics/cae.sds

Westminster College

New Wilmington, PA

Address: South Market Street, New Wilmington, PA, 16172
Admissions telephone: 800 942-8033
Admissions FAX: 724 946-6171
Dean of Admissions: Douglas Swartz
Admissions e-mail: admis@westminster.edu
Web site: http://www.westminster.edu
SAT Code: 2975 ACT Code: 3752

LD program name: Office of Disability Support Services
LD program address: 208 Thompson-Clark Hall
Dean, Student Affairs: Dr. Neal Edman
LD program telephone: 724 946-7110
LD program e-mail: nedman@westminster.edu
LD program enrollment: 53, Total campus enrollment: 1,616

GENERAL

Westminster College is a private, coed, four-year institution. 300-acre campus in New Wilmington (population: 2,452), 60 miles from Pittsburgh. Served by bus; airport and train serve Youngstown, OH (25 miles). Semester system.

LD ADMISSIONS

Students do not complete a separate application and are not simultaneously accepted to the LD program. A member of the LD program does not sit on the admissions committee. A personal interview is recommended. Essay is required and may be typed. Reasonable accommodations will be made if a student cannot meet admission requirements.

For fall 2004, 4 completed self-identified LD applications were received. 3 applications were offered admission, and 6 enrolled.

SECONDARY SCHOOL REQUIREMENTS

Graduation from secondary school required; GED accepted. The following course distribution required: 4 units of English, 3 units of math, 2 units of science, 2 units of foreign language, 2 units of social studies, 1 unit of history, 3 units of academic electives.

TESTING

SAT Reasoning or ACT required.

All enrolled freshmen (fall 2004):

Average SAT I Scores:	Verbal: 541	Math: 540
Average ACT Scores:	Composite: 23	

Child Study Team report is not required. A neuropsychological or comprehensive psycho-education evaluation is not required for admission. Tests required as part of this documentation:

- ☐ WAIS-IV
- ☐ WISC-IV
- ☐ SATA
- ☐ Woodcock-Johnson
- ☐ Nelson-Denny Reading Test
- ☐ Other

UNDERGRADUATE STUDENT BODY

Total undergraduate student enrollment: 555 Men, 901 Women.

Composition of student body (fall 2004):

	Undergraduate	Freshmen
International	0.0	0.0
Black	3.4	1.9
American Indian	0.3	0.0
Asian-American	0.0	0.5
Hispanic	0.3	0.7
White	71.2	73.2
Unreported	24.8	23.7
	100.0%	100.0%

20% are from out of state. 45% join a fraternity and 42% join a sorority. Average age of full-time undergraduates is 20. 65% of classes have fewer than 20 students, 35% have between 20 and 50 students.

STUDENT HOUSING

97% of freshmen live in college housing. Housing is guaranteed for all undergraduates. Campus can house 1,100 undergraduates. Single rooms are available for students with medical or special needs. A medical note is required.

EXPENSES

Tuition (2005-06): $21,700 per year.
Room: $3,500. Board: $3,100.
There is no additional cost for LD program/services.

LD SERVICES

LD program size is not limited.

LD services available to:

■ Freshmen ■ Sophomores ■ Juniors ■ Seniors

Academic Accommodations

Curriculum		In class	
Foreign language waiver	■	Early syllabus	☐
Lighter course load	☐	Note takers in class	■
Math waiver	■	Priority seating	■
Other special classes	☐	Tape recorders	■
Priority registrations	☐	Videotaped classes	■
Substitution of courses	■	Text on tape	☐
Exams		**Services**	
Extended time	■	Diagnostic tests	☐
Oral exams	■	Learning centers	■
Take home exams	☐	Proofreaders	☐
Exams on tape or computer	■	Readers	■
Untimed exams	■	Reading Machines/Kurzweil	■
Other accommodations	☐	Special bookstore section	☐
		Typists	☐

Credit toward degree is not given for remedial courses taken.

Counseling Services

- ■ Academic
- ■ Psychological
- ☐ Student Support groups
- ■ Vocational

Tutoring

Individual tutoring is available weekly.

Average size of tutoring groups: 1

	Individual	Group
Time management	■	☐
Organizational skills	■	☐
Learning strategies	■	☐
Study skills	■	☐
Content area	■	☐
Writing lab	☐	☐
Math lab	☐	☐

LD PROGRAM STAFF

Total number of LD Program staff (including director):

Full Time: 1 Part Time: 1

There is an advisor/advocate from the LD program available to students. 35 peer tutors are available to work with LD students.

Key staff person available to work with LD students: Bonnie Yvonne A. VanBruggen, Director

Widener University

Chester, PA

Address: 1 University Place, Chester, PA, 19013
Admissions telephone: 800 870-6481
Admissions FAX: 610 499-4676
Admissions e-mail: admissions.office@widener.edu
Web site: http://www.widener.edu
SAT Code: 2642 ACT Code: 3652

Director, Enable: Rebecca Corsey, Psy.D.
LD program telephone: 610 499-4179
LD program e-mail: Rebecca.A.Corsey@widener.edu
Total campus enrollment: 2,501

GENERAL

Widener University is a private, coed, four-year institution. 105-acre, suburban main campus in Chester (population: 36,854), 10 miles from Philadelphia; branch campuses in Harrisburg and in Wilmington, Del. Served by train; major airport serves Philadelphia. School operates shuttle bus on campus. Public transportation serves campus. Semester system.

LD ADMISSIONS

Students do not complete a separate application and are not simultaneously accepted to the LD program. A member of the LD program does not sit on the admissions committee. High school waivers are accepted for foreign language. A personal interview is recommended. Essay is required and may be typed. If a portion of a student's application is not an accurate representation of the student's skills or academic readiness because of the impact of a specific learning disability, the student may request a consultation with Admissions staff and the Director of Enable to discuss this portion of the application.

SECONDARY SCHOOL REQUIREMENTS

Graduation from secondary school required; GED not accepted. The following course distribution required: 4 units of English, 3 units of math, 3 units of science, 2 units of foreign language, 4 units of social studies, 3 units of academic electives.

TESTING

SAT Reasoning required; ACT may be substituted. SAT Subject recommended.

All enrolled freshmen (fall 2004):

Average SAT I Scores: Verbal: 500 Math: 490
Average ACT Scores: Composite: 21

Child Study Team report is not required. A neuropsychological or comprehensive psycho-educational evaluation is required for admission. Tests required as part of this documentation:

- ■ WAIS-IV
- ■ WISC-IV
- ☐ SATA
- ■ Woodcock-Johnson
- ☐ Nelson-Denny Reading Test
- ☐ Other

UNDERGRADUATE STUDENT BODY

Total undergraduate student enrollment: 1,233 Men, 1,002 Women.

Composition of student body (fall 2004):

	Undergraduate	Freshmen
International	0.7	1.5
Black	14.0	12.0
American Indian	0.4	0.2
Asian-American	1.9	2.2
Hispanic	3.2	1.9
White	71.7	73.5
Unreported	8.1	8.7
	100.0%	100.0%

37% are from out of state. 56% of classes have fewer than 20 students, 44% have between 20 and 50 students.

STUDENT HOUSING

61% of freshmen live in college housing. Freshmen are not required to live on campus. Housing is limited to undergraduate students. Campus can house 1,455 undergraduates. Single rooms are available for students with medical or special needs. A medical note is required.

EXPENSES

Tuition (2005-06): $24,620 per year.
Room & Board: $8,520
There is no additional cost for LD program/services.

LD SERVICES

LD program size is not limited.

LD services available to:

■ Freshmen ■ Sophomores ■ Juniors ■ Seniors

Academic Accommodations

Curriculum		**In class**	
Foreign language waiver	■	Early syllabus	☐
Lighter course load	■	Note takers in class	■
Math waiver	☐	Priority seating	☐
Other special classes	☐	Tape recorders	■
Priority registrations	☐	Videotaped classes	☐
Substitution of courses	☐	Text on tape	■
Exams		**Services**	
Extended time	■	Diagnostic tests	■
Oral exams	■	Learning centers	■
Take home exams	☐	Proofreaders	■
Exams on tape or computer	■	Readers	■
Untimed exams	■	Reading Machines/Kurzweil	■
Other accommodations	☐	Special bookstore section	☐
		Typists	☐

Credit toward degree is not given for remedial courses taken.

Counseling Services

- ■ Academic
- ■ Psychological
- ☐ Student Support groups
- ☐ Vocational

Tutoring

Individual tutoring is available daily.

Average size of tutoring groups: 1

	Individual	Group
Time management	■	☐
Organizational skills	■	☐
Learning strategies	■	☐
Study skills	■	☐
Content area	☐	☐
Writing lab	■	☐
Math lab	■	☐

LD PROGRAM STAFF

Total number of LD Program staff (including director):

Full Time: 2 Part Time: 2

There is an advisor/advocate from the LD program available to students.

Key staff person available to work with LD students: Rebecca Corsey, Psy.D., Director, Enable

LD Program web site: http://www.widener.edu/?pageId=490

Wilkes University

Wilkes-Barre, PA

Address: 84 West South Street, Wilkes-Barre, PA, 18766
Admissions telephone: 800 WILKES-U
Admissions FAX: 570 408-4904
Dean of Student Enrollment: Michael Frantz
Admissions e-mail: admissions@wilkes.edu
Web site: http://www.wilkes.edu
SAT Code: 2977 ACT Code: 3756

LD program name: University College
LD program address: Conyngham Hall,
Executive Director: Thomas S. Thomas
LD program telephone: 570 408-4154
LD program e-mail: thomast@wilkes.edu
LD program enrollment: 45, Total campus enrollment: 2,108

GENERAL

Wilkes University is a private, coed, four-year institution. 25-acre campus in Wilkes-Barre (population: 43,123), 120 miles from both New York City and Philadelphia. Served by air and bus. Public transportation serves campus. Semester system.

LD ADMISSIONS

Students do not complete a separate application and are not simultaneously accepted to the LD program. A member of the LD program does not sit on the admissions committee. High school waivers are accepted for foreign language. A personal interview is recommended. Essay is not required.

SECONDARY SCHOOL REQUIREMENTS

Graduation from secondary school required; GED accepted.

TESTING

SAT Reasoning required; ACT may be substituted. SAT Subject recommended.

All enrolled freshmen (fall 2004):

Average SAT I Scores: Verbal: 526 Math: 537

Child Study Team report is not required. A neuropsychological or comprehensive psycho-educational evaluation is required for admission. Must be dated within 36 months of application. Tests required as part of this documentation:

- [x] WAIS-IV
- [x] WISC-IV
- [ ] SATA
- [x] Woodcock-Johnson
- [ ] Nelson-Denny Reading Test
- [ ] Other

UNDERGRADUATE STUDENT BODY

Total undergraduate student enrollment: 883 Men, 888 Women.

Composition of student body (fall 2004):

	Undergraduate	Freshmen
International	0.0	0.2
Black	2.9	2.0
American Indian	0.4	0.2
Asian-American	3.0	2.2
Hispanic	1.6	1.6
White	92.1	93.7
Unreported	0.0	0.1
	100.0%	100.0%

13% are from out of state. Average age of full-time undergraduates is 20. 51% of classes have fewer than 20 students, 47% have between 20 and 50 students, 2% have more than 50 students.

STUDENT HOUSING

68% of freshmen live in college housing. Freshmen are not required to live on campus. Housing is guaranteed for all undergraduates. Campus can house 872 undergraduates. Single rooms are available for students with medical or special needs. A medical note is required.

EXPENSES

Tuition (2005-06): $20,592 per year.
Room: $5,600. Board: $3,640.

There is no additional cost for LD program/services.

LD SERVICES

LD program size is not limited.

LD services available to:

- [x] Freshmen
- [x] Sophomores
- [x] Juniors
- [x] Seniors

Academic Accommodations

Curriculum		In class	
Foreign language waiver	[ ]	Early syllabus	[x]
Lighter course load	[ ]	Note takers in class	[x]
Math waiver	[ ]	Priority seating	[x]
Other special classes	[ ]	Tape recorders	[x]
Priority registrations	[x]	Videotaped classes	[ ]
Substitution of courses	[ ]	Text on tape	[x]
Exams		**Services**	
Extended time	[x]	Diagnostic tests	[x]
Oral exams	[x]	Learning centers	[x]
Take home exams	[ ]	Proofreaders	[ ]
Exams on tape or computer	[x]	Readers	[x]
Untimed exams	[x]	Reading Machines/Kurzweil	[x]
Other accommodations	[x]	Special bookstore section	[ ]
		Typists	[ ]

Credit toward degree is given for remedial courses taken.

Counseling Services

- [x] Academic — Meets 28 times per academic year
- [ ] Psychological
- [ ] Student Support groups
- [ ] Vocational

Tutoring

Individual tutoring is available weekly.

Average size of tutoring groups: 1

	Individual	Group
Time management	[x]	[x]
Organizational skills	[x]	[x]
Learning strategies	[x]	[x]
Study skills	[x]	[x]
Content area	[x]	[x]
Writing lab	[x]	[ ]
Math lab	[x]	[ ]

LD PROGRAM STAFF

Total number of LD Program staff (including director):

Full Time: 2 Part Time: 2

There is an advisor/advocate from the LD program available to students. The advisor/advocate meets with students four times per month.

Key staff person available to work with LD students: Thomas S. Thomas, Director, Learning Center.

Wilson College

Chambersburg, PA

Address: 1015 Philadelphia Avenue, Chambersburg, PA, 17201
Admissions telephone: 800 421-8402
Admissions FAX: 717 262-2546
Dean of Enrollment: Kathleen H. Berard
Admissions e-mail: admissions@wilson.edu
Web site: http://www.wilson.edu
SAT Code: 2979 ACT Code: 3758

LD program name: Learning Resource Center
Director: Kate Kramer-Jefferson
LD program telephone: 717 264-4141, extension 3351
LD program e-mail: kkramer-jefferson@wilson.edu
LD program enrollment: 37, Total campus enrollment: 776

GENERAL

Wilson College is a private, women's, four-year institution. 262-acre campus in Chambersburg (population: 17,862), 55 miles from Harrisburg and 76 miles from Baltimore, MD. Served by bus; airport and train serve Harrisburg; major airport serves Baltimore, MD. School operates transportation to airport for school breaks and a weekly shuttle. 4-1-4 system.

LD ADMISSIONS

Students do not complete a separate application and are not simultaneously accepted to the LD program. A member of the LD program does not sit on the admissions committee. High school waivers are accepted for math and foreign language. A personal interview is recommended. Essay is required and may be typed.

SECONDARY SCHOOL REQUIREMENTS

Graduation from secondary school required; GED accepted.

TESTING

SAT Reasoning required; ACT may be substituted. SAT Subject recommended.

All enrolled freshmen (fall 2004):

Average SAT I Scores:	Verbal: 514	Math: 473
Average ACT Scores:	Composite: 21	

Child Study Team report is not required. A neuropsychological or comprehensive psycho-education evaluation is not required for admission. Tests required as part of this documentation:

- [ ] WAIS-IV
- [ ] WISC-IV
- [ ] SATA
- [ ] Woodcock-Johnson
- [ ] Nelson-Denny Reading Test
- [ ] Other

UNDERGRADUATE STUDENT BODY

Total undergraduate student enrollment: 92 Men, 618 Women.

Composition of student body (fall 2004):

	Undergraduate	Freshmen
International	5.6	4.4
Black	1.4	3.6
American Indian	0.0	0.3
Asian-American	0.0	0.6
Hispanic	1.4	2.5
White	88.8	87.1
Unreported	2.8	1.5
	100.0%	100.0%

27% are from out of state. Average age of full-time undergraduates is 20. 84% of classes have fewer than 20 students, 16% have between 20 and 50 students.

STUDENT HOUSING

86% of freshmen live in college housing. Freshmen are required to live on campus. Housing is guaranteed for all undergraduates. Campus can house 406 undergraduates. Single rooms are available for students with medical or special needs. A medical note is required.

EXPENSES

Tuition (2005-06): $19,570 per year. Tuition varies by program.
Room: $3,920. Board: $3,690.
There is no additional cost for LD program/services.

LD SERVICES

LD program size is not limited.

LD services available to:

- [x] Freshmen
- [x] Sophomores
- [x] Juniors
- [x] Seniors

Academic Accommodations

Curriculum		In class	
Foreign language waiver	[x]	Early syllabus	[ ]
Lighter course load	[x]	Note takers in class	[x]
Math waiver	[x]	Priority seating	[x]
Other special classes	[ ]	Tape recorders	[x]
Priority registrations	[ ]	Videotaped classes	[ ]
Substitution of courses	[x]	Text on tape	[x]
Exams		**Services**	
Extended time	[x]	Diagnostic tests	[ ]
Oral exams	[x]	Learning centers	[x]
Take home exams	[x]	Proofreaders	[ ]
Exams on tape or computer	[x]	Readers	[x]
Untimed exams	[ ]	Reading Machines/Kurzweil	[ ]
Other accommodations	[x]	Special bookstore section	[ ]
		Typists	[x]

Credit toward degree is not given for remedial courses taken.

Counseling Services

- [x] Academic
- [x] Psychological
- [ ] Student Support groups
- [ ] Vocational

Tutoring

Individual tutoring is available weekly.

Average size of tutoring groups: 1

	Individual	Group
Time management	[x]	[ ]
Organizational skills	[x]	[ ]
Learning strategies	[x]	[ ]
Study skills	[x]	[ ]
Content area	[x]	[ ]
Writing lab	[x]	[ ]
Math lab	[x]	[ ]

UNIQUE LD PROGRAM FEATURES

Frequent meetings with students are strongly encouraged throughout the academic year, however, two meetings per semester are required.

LD PROGRAM STAFF

Total number of LD Program staff (including director):

Full Time: 1 Part Time: 1

There is an advisor/advocate from the LD program available to students. 20 peer tutors are available to work with LD students.

Key staff person available to work with LD students: Kate Kramer-Jefferson, Director

LD Program web site: http://www.wilson.edu/library/LRC/disability.htm

York College of Pennsylvania

York, PA

Address: Country Club Road, York, PA, 17405-7199
Admissions telephone: 800 455-8018
Admissions FAX: 717 849-1607
Director of Admissions: Nancy Spataro
Admissions e-mail: admissions@ycp.edu
Web site: http://www.ycp.edu
SAT Code: 2991 ACT Code: 3762

Coordinator of Academic Advising: Dr. Carol Bair
LD program telephone: 717 815-1531
LD program e-mail: cbair@ycp.edu
LD program enrollment: 78, Total campus enrollment: 5,379

GENERAL

York College of Pennsylvania is a private, coed, four-year institution. 118-acre, suburban campus in York (population: 40,862), 88 miles from Philadelphia and 45 miles from Baltimore; branch campus in Hanover. Served by air and bus; major airport serves Harrisburg (25 miles); train serves Lancaster (25 miles). Public transportation serves campus. Semester system.

LD ADMISSIONS

Students do not complete a separate application and are not simultaneously accepted to the LD program. A member of the LD program does not sit on the admissions committee. A personal interview is required. Essay is required and may be typed.

For fall 2004, 37 completed self-identified LD applications were received. 32 applications were offered admission, and 23 enrolled.

SECONDARY SCHOOL REQUIREMENTS

Graduation from secondary school required; GED accepted. The following course distribution required: 4 units of English, 3 units of math, 3 units of science, 2 units of foreign language, 3 units of social studies.

TESTING

SAT Reasoning or ACT required. SAT Subject required.

All enrolled freshmen (fall 2004):

Average SAT I Scores:	Verbal: 552	Math: 543
Average ACT Scores:	Composite: 24	

Child Study Team report is not required. A neuropsychological or comprehensive psycho-educational evaluation is required for admission. Must be dated within 36 months of application. Tests required as part of this documentation:

- [x] WAIS-IV
- [x] WISC-IV
- [ ] SATA
- [x] Woodcock-Johnson
- [x] Nelson-Denny Reading Test
- [x] Other

UNDERGRADUATE STUDENT BODY

Total undergraduate student enrollment: 2,068 Men, 3,051 Women.

Composition of student body (fall 2004):

	Undergraduate	Freshmen
International	0.0	0.0
Black	1.4	1.6
American Indian	0.3	0.2
Asian-American	1.8	1.5
Hispanic	0.9	1.6
White	91.5	93.1
Unreported	4.1	2.0
	100.0%	100.0%

45% are from out of state. 10% join a fraternity and 10% join a sorority. Average age of full-time undergraduates is 21. 31% of classes have fewer than 20 students, 68% have between 20 and 50 students, 1% have more than 50 students.

STUDENT HOUSING

72% of freshmen live in college housing. Freshmen are required to live on campus. Housing is guaranteed for all undergraduates. Campus can house 1,872 undergraduates. Single rooms are available for students with medical or special needs. A medical note is required.

EXPENSES

Tuition (2005-06): $9,350 per year.
Room: $3,625. Board: $2,875.
There is no additional cost for LD program/services.

LD SERVICES

LD program size is not limited.

LD services available to:

- [x] Freshmen
- [x] Sophomores
- [x] Juniors
- [x] Seniors

Academic Accommodations

Curriculum		In class	
Foreign language waiver	[ ]	Early syllabus	[ ]
Lighter course load	[ ]	Note takers in class	[ ]
Math waiver	[ ]	Priority seating	[ ]
Other special classes	[ ]	Tape recorders	[ ]
Priority registrations	[ ]	Videotaped classes	[ ]
Substitution of courses	[ ]	Text on tape	[ ]
Exams		**Services**	
Extended time	[x]	Diagnostic tests	[ ]
Oral exams	[ ]	Learning centers	[x]
Take home exams	[ ]	Proofreaders	[ ]
Exams on tape or computer	[ ]	Readers	[ ]
Untimed exams	[ ]	Reading Machines/Kurzweil	[ ]
Other accommodations	[ ]	Special bookstore section	[ ]
		Typists	[ ]

Credit toward degree is not given for remedial courses taken.

Counseling Services

- [x] Academic
- [ ] Psychological
- [ ] Student Support groups
- [ ] Vocational

Tutoring

Average size of tutoring groups: 1

	Individual	Group
Time management	[x]	[x]
Organizational skills	[ ]	[ ]
Learning strategies	[x]	[x]
Study skills	[x]	[x]
Content area	[x]	[x]
Writing lab	[x]	[x]
Math lab	[x]	[x]

LD PROGRAM STAFF

Total number of LD Program staff (including director):

Full Time: 1 Part Time: 1

There is an advisor/advocate from the LD program available to students.

Key staff person available to work with LD students: Dr. Carol Bair, Coordinator of Academic Advising

Conservatory of Music of Puerto Rico

Hato Rey, PR

Address: 350 Rafael Lamar Street, Hato Rey, PR, 00918-2199
Admissions FAX: 787 758-8268
Director of Admissions: Eutimia Santiago
SAT Code: 1115

LD program name: Counseling / Student Affairs Office
LD program address: Rafael Lamar # 350
Dean of Students Affair: Mike Rajaballey
LD program e-mail: pruibal@cmpr.gobierno.pr
LD program enrollment: 1, Total campus enrollment: 298

GENERAL

Conservatory of Music of Puerto Rico is a public, coed, four-year institution. Six-acre campus in Hato Rey, near San Juan (population: 421,958). Airport in Isla Verde (Carolina). Public transportation serves campus. Semester system.

LD ADMISSIONS

Application Deadline: 03/31. Students do not complete a separate application and are simultaneously accepted to the LD program. A member of the LD program does not sit on the admissions committee. A personal interview is required. Essay is required and may be typed.

SECONDARY SCHOOL REQUIREMENTS

Graduation from secondary school required; GED accepted. The following course distribution required: 3 units of English, 3 units of math, 3 units of science, 1 unit of social studies, 2 units of history, 3 units of academic electives.

TESTING

Child Study Team report is not required. Tests required as part of this documentation:

- ☐ WAIS-IV
- ☐ WISC-IV
- ☐ SATA
- ☐ Woodcock-Johnson
- ☐ Nelson-Denny Reading Test
- ☐ Other

UNDERGRADUATE STUDENT BODY

Total undergraduate student enrollment: 298.

Composition of student body (fall 2004):

	Undergraduate	Freshman
International	0.0	0.0
Black	0.0	0.0
American Indian	0.0	0.0
Asian-American	0.0	0.0
Hispanic	100.0	100.0
White	0.0	0.0
Unreported	0.0	0.0
	100.0%	100.0%

Average age of full-time undergraduates is 23. 98% of classes have fewer than 20 students, 2% have between 20 and 50 students.

STUDENT HOUSING

Freshman are not required to live on campus. Housing is not guaranteed for all undergraduates. Single rooms are not available for students with medical or special needs.

EXPENSES

Tuition (2005-06): (Tuition is higher for international students.)

There is no additional cost for LD program/services.

LD SERVICES

LD program size is not limited.

LD services available to:

■ Freshmen ■ Sophomores ■ Juniors ■ Seniors

Academic Accommodations

Curriculum		In class	
Foreign language waiver	☐	Early syllabus	☐
Lighter course load	☐	Note takers in class	■
Math waiver	☐	Priority seating	■
Other special classes	■	Tape recorders	■
Priority registrations	■	Videotaped classes	☐
Substitution of courses	☐	Texts on tape	■
Exams		**Services**	
Extended time	■	Diagnostic tests	☐
Oral exams	■	Learning centers	■
Take home exams	☐	Proofreaders	☐
Exams on tape or computer	☐	Readers	■
Untimed exams	■	Reading Machines/Kurzweil	■
Other accommodations	■	Special bookstore section	☐
		Typists	☐

Credit toward degree is not given for remedial courses taken.

Counseling Services

- ■ Academic
- ☐ Psychological
- ■ Student Support groups
- ☐ Vocational

Tutoring

Individual tutoring is available weekly.

Average size of tutoring groups: 3

	Individual	Group
Time management	■	☐
Organizational skills	■	☐
Learning strategies	■	☐
Study skills	■	☐
Content area	■	☐
Writing lab	☐	☐
Math lab	☐	☐

LD PROGRAM STAFF

Total number of LD Program staff (including director):

Full Time: 5 Part Time: 5

There is an advisor/advocate from the LD program available to students. 3 peer tutors are available to work with LD students.

Key staff person available to work with LD students: Pilar Ruibal, Counselor.

Inter American University of Puerto Rico

San German, PR

Address: P.O. Box 5100, San German, PR, 00683-9801
Admissions FAX: 787 892-6350
Admissions Contact: Mildred Camacho
SAT Code: 946
LD program e-mail: raquel-cruz@sg.inter.edu
LD program enrollment: 10, Total campus enrollment: 5,050

GENERAL

Inter American University of Puerto Rico is a private, coed, four-year institution. 260-acre campus in San German (population: 12,033), 14 miles from Mayaguez and 104 miles from San Juan. Major airport serves Carolina (104 miles); smaller airport serves Mayaguez. Public transportation serves campus. Semester system.

LD ADMISSIONS

Students do not complete a separate application and are simultaneously accepted to the LD program. A member of the LD program does not sit on the admissions committee. High school waivers are accepted for foreign language requirement. A personal interview is recommended. Essay is not required.

SECONDARY SCHOOL REQUIREMENTS

Graduation from secondary school required; GED accepted.

TESTING

All enrolled freshman (fall 2004):

Average SAT I Scores: Verbal: Math:
Average ACT Scores: Composite:

Child Study Team report is not required. A neuropsychological or comprehensive psycho-education evaluation is not required for admission. Tests required as part of this documentation:

- [ ] WAIS-IV
- [ ] WISC-IV
- [ ] SATA
- [ ] Woodcock-Johnson
- [ ] Nelson-Denny Reading Test
- [ ] Other

UNDERGRADUATE STUDENT BODY

Total undergraduate student enrollment: 2,237 Men, 2,568 Women.

Composition of student body (fall 2004):

	Undergraduate	Freshman
International	0.0	0.0
Black	0.0	0.0
American Indian	0.0	0.0
Asian-American	0.0	0.0
Hispanic	100.0	100.0
White	0.0	0.0
Unreported	0.0	0.0
	100.0%	100.0%

31% of classes have fewer than 20 students, 69% have between 20 and 50 students.

STUDENT HOUSING

Freshman are not required to live on campus. Housing is guaranteed for all undergraduates. Single rooms are available for students with medical or special needs. A medical note is not required.

EXPENSES

Tuition (2005-06): $4,200 per year.
Room: $900. Board: $1,500.
There is no additional cost for LD program/services.

LD SERVICES

LD program size is not limited.

LD services available to:

- [x] Freshmen
- [x] Sophomores
- [x] Juniors
- [x] Seniors

Academic Accommodations

Curriculum		In class	
Foreign language waiver	[ ]	Early syllabus	[ ]
Lighter course load	[ ]	Note takers in class	[x]
Math waiver	[ ]	Priority seating	[ ]
Other special classes	[ ]	Tape recorders	[x]
Priority registrations	[ ]	Videotaped classes	[ ]
Substitution of courses	[x]	Texts on tape	[ ]
Exams		**Services**	
Extended time	[x]	Diagnostic tests	[ ]
Oral exams	[x]	Learning centers	[ ]
Take home exams	[x]	Proofreaders	[x]
Exams on tape or computer	[x]	Readers	[x]
Untimed exams	[ ]	Reading Machines/Kurzweil	[ ]
Other accommodations	[x]	Special bookstore section	[ ]
		Typists	[ ]

Credit toward degree is not given for remedial courses taken.

Counseling Services

- [x] Academic
- [x] Psychological
- [x] Student Support groups
- [x] Vocational

Tutoring

Individual tutoring is available weekly.

Average size of tutoring groups: 1

	Individual	Group
Time management	[x]	[x]
Organizational skills	[ ]	[x]
Learning strategies	[x]	[x]
Study skills	[x]	[x]
Content area	[ ]	[ ]
Writing lab	[ ]	[ ]
Math lab	[ ]	[ ]

LD PROGRAM STAFF

Total number of LD Program staff (including director):

Full Time: 1 Part Time: 1

There is an advisor/advocate from the LD program available to students.

Key staff person available to work with LD students: Raquel Cruz Hance, Coordinator of the Office of Services to Students.

Pontifical Catholic University of Puerto Rico

Ponce, PR

Address: 2250 Las Americas Avenue, Suite 563, Ponce, PR, 00717-0777
Admissions telephone: 800 981-5040
Admissions FAX: 787 651-2044
Director of Admissions: Ana O. Bonilla
Admissions e-mail: abonilla@email.pucpr.edu
Web site: http://www.pucpr.edu
SAT Code: 910

LD program name: OSPI
Director: Wanda Soto
LD program e-mail: wsoto@email.pucpr.edu
LD program enrollment: 263, Total campus enrollment: 5,517

GENERAL

Pontifical Catholic University of Puerto Rico is a private, coed, four-year institution. 120-acre, urban campus in Ponce (population: 155,038), 35 miles from San Juan; branch campuses in Arecibo, Guayama, and Mayaguez. Served by air; major airport serves San Juan. School operates transportation to all parts of Puerto Rico. Public transportation serves campus. Semester system.

LD ADMISSIONS

Application Deadline: 06/15. Students do not complete a separate application and are not simultaneously accepted to the LD program. A personal interview is required. Essay is not required.

For fall 2004, 263 completed self-identified LD applications were received. 263 applications were offered admission, and 263 enrolled.

SECONDARY SCHOOL REQUIREMENTS

Graduation from secondary school required; GED accepted. The following course distribution required: 2 units of English, 2 units of math, 2 units of science, 2 units of foreign language, 2 units of social studies, 2 units of history, 6 units of academic electives.

TESTING

SAT Subject recommended.

All enrolled freshman (fall 2004):

Average SAT I Scores: Verbal: Math:
Average ACT Scores: Composite:

Child Study Team report is not required. A neuropsychological or comprehensive psycho-educational evaluation is required for admission. Must be dated within 6 months of application. Tests required as part of this documentation:

- [x] WAIS-IV
- [ ] WISC-IV
- [ ] SATA
- [x] Woodcock-Johnson
- [ ] Nelson-Denny Reading Test
- [x] Other

UNDERGRADUATE STUDENT BODY

Total undergraduate student enrollment: 1,953 Men, 3,577 Women.

Composition of student body (fall 2004):

	Undergraduate	Freshman
International	0.0	0.0
Black	0.0	0.0
American Indian	0.0	0.0
Asian-American	0.0	0.0
Hispanic	100.0	100.0
White	0.0	0.0
Unreported	0.0	0.0
	100.0%	100.0%

43% of classes have fewer than 20 students, 57% have between 20 and 50 students.

STUDENT HOUSING

1% of freshman live in college housing. Freshman are not required to live on campus. Housing is guaranteed for all undergraduates. Campus can house 178 undergraduates. Single rooms are not available for students with medical or special needs.

EXPENSES

There is no additional cost for LD program/services.

LD SERVICES

LD program size is not limited.

LD services available to:

- [x] Freshmen
- [x] Sophomores
- [x] Juniors
- [x] Seniors

Academic Accommodations

Curriculum

- [ ] Foreign language waiver
- [ ] Lighter course load
- [ ] Math waiver
- [x] Other special classes
- [ ] Priority registrations
- [ ] Substitution of courses

Exams

- [x] Extended time
- [x] Oral exams
- [x] Take home exams
- [ ] Exams on tape or computer
- [ ] Untimed exams
- [x] Other accommodations

In class

- [ ] Early syllabus
- [x] Note takers in class
- [x] Priority seating
- [x] Tape recorders
- [ ] Videotaped classes
- [ ] Texts on tape

Services

- [ ] Diagnostic tests
- [x] Learning centers
- [ ] Proofreaders
- [x] Readers
- [ ] Reading Machines/Kurzweil
- [ ] Special bookstore section
- [ ] Typists

Credit toward degree is not given for remedial courses taken.

Counseling Services

- [x] Academic — Meets 2 times per academic year
- [x] Psychological — Meets 6 times per academic year
- [x] Student Support groups — Meets 6 times per academic year
- [ ] Vocational

Tutoring

Individual tutoring is available daily.

Average size of tutoring groups: 6

	Individual	Group
Time management	[ ]	[ ]
Organizational skills	[x]	[ ]
Learning strategies	[x]	[ ]
Study skills	[x]	[ ]
Content area	[ ]	[ ]
Writing lab	[x]	[ ]
Math lab	[x]	[ ]

LD PROGRAM STAFF

Total number of LD Program staff (including director):

Full Time: 2 Part Time: 2

There is an advisor/advocate from the LD program available to students. The advisor/advocate meets with faculty 2 times per month and students 6 times per month. 1 graduate student and 17 peer tutors are available to work with LD students.

Key staff person available to work with LD students: Ana Gaud, Certified Assistive Technology Specialist.

University of Puerto Rico at Humacao

Humacao, PR

Address: 100 Road 908 HUC Station, Humacao, PR, 00791-4300
Admissions FAX: 787 850-9428
Director of Admissions: Inara Ferrer
SAT Code: 874

Director and Counselor: Prof. Carmen Sepulveda
LD program telephone: 787 850-9383
LD program e-mail: c_sepulveda@webmail.uprh.edu
LD program enrollment: 19, Total campus enrollment: 4,462

GENERAL

University of Puerto Rico at Humacao is a public, coed, four-year institution. 62-acre campus in Humacao (population: 20,682), 35 miles from San Juan. Airport serves Carolina (28 miles). Public transportation serves campus. Semester system.

LD ADMISSIONS

Students do not complete a separate application and are not simultaneously accepted to the LD program. A member of the LD program does not sit on the admissions committee.

SECONDARY SCHOOL REQUIREMENTS

Graduation from secondary school required; GED accepted.

TESTING

All enrolled freshman (fall 2004):

Average SAT I Scores: Verbal: 524 Math: 536

Child Study Team report is not required. A neuropsychological or comprehensive psycho-educational evaluation is required for admission. Tests required as part of this documentation:

- ☐ WAIS-IV
- ☐ WISC-IV
- ☐ SATA
- ☐ Woodcock-Johnson
- ☐ Nelson-Denny Reading Test
- ☐ Other

UNDERGRADUATE STUDENT BODY

Total undergraduate student enrollment: 1,273 Men, 3,203 Women.

Composition of student body (fall 2004):

	Undergraduate	Freshman
International	0.1	0.1
Black	0.0	0.0
American Indian	0.0	0.0
Asian-American	0.0	0.1
Hispanic	99.5	99.6
White	0.0	0.1
Unreported	0.4	0.1
	100.0%	100.0%

2% join a fraternity. Average age of full-time undergraduates is 20.

EXPENSES

Tuition (2005-06): $1,245 per year (Puerto Rican residents); $3,340 per year (nonresidents); mainland U.S. residents pay home state's nonresident tuition.

There is no additional cost for LD program/services.

LD SERVICES

LD program size is not limited.

LD services available to:

■ Freshmen ■ Sophomores ■ Juniors ■ Seniors

Academic Accommodations

Curriculum

- Foreign language waiver ☐
- Lighter course load ☐
- Math waiver ☐
- Other special classes ■
- Priority registrations ■
- Substitution of courses ☐

Exams

- Extended time ■
- Oral exams ■
- Take home exams ☐
- Exams on tape or computer ☐
- Untimed exams ☐
- Other accommodations ■

In class

- Early syllabus ☐
- Note takers in class ■
- Priority seating ■
- Tape recorders ■
- Videotaped classes ☐
- Texts on tape ■

Services

- Diagnostic tests ☐
- Learning centers ☐
- Proofreaders ☐
- Readers ■
- Reading Machines/Kurzweil ■
- Special bookstore section ☐
- Typists ☐

Counseling Services

- ■ Academic
- ☐ Psychological
- ■ Student Support groups
- ■ Vocational

Tutoring

Individual tutoring is available weekly.

Average size of tutoring groups: 2

	Individual	Group
Time management	■	■
Organizational skills	■	■
Learning strategies	■	■
Study skills	■	■
Content area	☐	☐
Writing lab	☐	☐
Math lab	☐	☐

UNIQUE LD PROGRAM FEATURES

SERPI is the Spanish abbreviation for the Office of Services for Students with Disabilities. It offers services to all students with disabilities. The program identifies the services and access needs of these individuals with disabilities at our campus, while developing activities that promote the adaptation of our students to the university experience. The program also works to inform and advise the university community on the compliance of the state and federal requirement laws that protect individuals with disabilities. The program strives to increase and strengthen its services, focusing on retention, so these students may complete their desired academic degree.

LD PROGRAM STAFF

Total number of LD Program staff (including director):

Full Time: 3 Part Time: 3

27 peer tutors are available to work with LD students.

Key staff person available to work with LD students: Prof. Carmen Sepulveda, Director and Counselor.

LD Program web site: www.uprh.edu/serpi/

University of Puerto Rico at Mayaguez

Mayaguez, PR

Address: P.O. Box 9000, Mayaguez, PR, 00681-9000
Admissions FAX: 787 834-5265
Director of Admissions: Mrs. Norma Torres
Admissions e-mail: admisiones@uprm.edu
Web site: http://www.uprm.edu
SAT Code: 912

LD program name: Students with Disabilities Services
LD program address: Box. 9035
Associate Dean of Students: Teresita Cruz
LD program e-mail: tcruz@uprm.edu
LD program enrollment: 25, Total campus enrollment: 11,032

GENERAL

University of Puerto Rico at Mayaguez is a public, coed, four-year institution. 520-acre, urban campus in Mayaguez (population: 78,647), 100 miles from San Juan. Served by air; major airport serves San Juan. Public transportation serves campus. Semester system.

LD ADMISSIONS

A personal interview is required. Essay is not required.

For fall 2004, 19 completed self-identified LD applications were received. 8 applications were offered admission, and 8 enrolled.

SECONDARY SCHOOL REQUIREMENTS

Graduation from secondary school required; GED accepted. The following course distribution required: 4 units of English, 2 units of math, 4 units of science, 4 units of foreign language, 4 units of social studies, 2 units of history, 4 units of academic electives.

TESTING

All enrolled freshman (fall 2004):

Average SAT I Scores: Verbal: 582 Math: 628
Average ACT Scores: Composite:

Child Study Team report is not required. A neuropsychological or comprehensive psycho-educational evaluation is required for admission. Must be dated within 36 months of application. Tests required as part of this documentation:

- [x] WAIS-IV
- [x] WISC-IV
- [ ] SATA
- [x] Woodcock-Johnson
- [ ] Nelson-Denny Reading Test
- [ ] Other

UNDERGRADUATE STUDENT BODY

Total undergraduate student enrollment: 5,649 Men, 5,702 Women.

Composition of student body (fall 2004):

	Undergraduate	Freshman
International	0.0	0.0
Black	0.0	0.0
American Indian	0.0	0.0
Asian-American	0.0	0.0
Hispanic	100.0	100.0
White	0.0	0.0
Unreported	0.0	0.0
	100.0%	100.0%

29% of classes have fewer than 20 students, 67% have between 20 and 50 students, 4% have more than 50 students.

STUDENT HOUSING

No campus housing available.

EXPENSES

Tuition (2005-06): $1,245 per year (Puerto Rican residents), $2,400 (nonresidents).
There is no additional cost for LD program/services.

LD SERVICES

LD program size is not limited.

LD services available to:

- [x] Freshmen
- [x] Sophomores
- [x] Juniors
- [x] Seniors

Academic Accommodations

Curriculum

- [ ] Foreign language waiver
- [ ] Lighter course load
- [ ] Math waiver
- [ ] Other special classes
- [x] Priority registrations
- [ ] Substitution of courses

Exams

- [x] Extended time
- [x] Oral exams
- [ ] Take home exams
- [ ] Exams on tape or computer
- [ ] Untimed exams
- [ ] Other accommodations

In class

- [ ] Early syllabus
- [x] Note takers in class
- [x] Priority seating
- [ ] Tape recorders
- [ ] Videotaped classes
- [ ] Texts on tape

Services

- [ ] Diagnostic tests
- [ ] Learning centers
- [ ] Proofreaders
- [ ] Readers
- [ ] Reading Machines/Kurzweil
- [ ] Special bookstore section
- [ ] Typists

Credit toward degree is not given for remedial courses taken.

Counseling Services

- [x] Academic
- [x] Psychological
- [ ] Student Support groups
- [x] Vocational

Tutoring

Individual tutoring is not available.

	Individual	Group
Time management	[ ]	[x]
Organizational skills	[ ]	[x]
Learning strategies	[ ]	[x]
Study skills	[ ]	[x]
Content area	[ ]	[ ]
Writing lab	[ ]	[ ]
Math lab	[ ]	[ ]

LD PROGRAM STAFF

There is no advisor/advocate from the LD program available to students.

Key staff person available to work with LD students: Teresita Cruz, Associate Dean of Students.

Brown University

Providence, RI

Address: Box 1920, Providence, RI, 02912
Admissions telephone: 401 863-2378
Admissions FAX: 401 863-9300
Director of Admission: Michael Goldberger
Admissions e-mail: admission_undergraduate@brown.edu
Web site: http://www.brown.edu
SAT Code: 3094

LD program name: Disability Support Services
LD program address: Providence, RI, 02912
Coordinator Disability Support Services: Catherine Axe
LD program telephone: 401 863-9588
LD program e-mail: dss@brown.edu
LD program enrollment: 113, Total campus enrollment: 6,014

GENERAL

Brown University is a private, coed, four-year institution. 140-acre campus in Providence (population: 173,618), 45 miles from Boston. Served by bus and train; major airport serves Boston; smaller airport serves Warwick (10 miles). School operates transportation around campus. Public transportation serves campus. Semester system.

LD ADMISSIONS

Students do not complete a separate application and are not simultaneously accepted to the LD program. A member of the LD program does not sit on the admissions committee. High school waivers are accepted for math and foreign language. A personal interview is not required. Essay is required and may be typed.

SECONDARY SCHOOL REQUIREMENTS

Graduation from secondary school required; GED not accepted. The following course distribution required: 4 units of English, 3 units of math, 3 units of science, 3 units of foreign language, 2 units of history, 1 unit of academic electives.

TESTING

SAT Subject required.

All enrolled freshmen (fall 2004):

Average SAT I Scores:	Verbal: 700	Math: 700
Average ACT Scores:	Composite: 30	

Child Study Team report is not required. A neuropsychological or comprehensive psycho-educational evaluation is required for admission. Must be dated within 36 months of application. Tests required as part of this documentation:

- ☑ WAIS-IV
- ☐ WISC-IV
- ☑ SATA
- ☑ Woodcock-Johnson
- ☑ Nelson-Denny Reading Test
- ☐ Other

UNDERGRADUATE STUDENT BODY

Total undergraduate student enrollment: 2,812 Men, 3,217 Women.

Composition of student body (fall 2004):

	Undergraduate	Freshmen
International	5.9	6.2
Black	6.9	6.5
American Indian	0.8	0.6
Asian-American	13.9	13.5
Hispanic	8.0	7.0
White	54.0	51.3
Unreported	10.5	14.9
	100.0%	100.0%

96% are from out of state. 5% join a fraternity and 1% join a sorority. Average age of full-time undergraduates is 20. 65% of classes have fewer than 20 students, 23% have between 20 and 50 students, 12% have more than 50 students.

STUDENT HOUSING

100% of freshmen live in college housing. Freshmen are required to live on campus. Housing is guaranteed for all undergraduates. Campus can house 4,643 undergraduates. Single rooms are available for students with medical or special needs. A medical note is required.

EXPENSES

Tuition (2005-06): $32,264 per year.
Room: $5,498. Board: $3,298.
There is no additional cost for LD program/services.

LD SERVICES

LD program size is not limited.

LD services available to:

☑ Freshmen ☑ Sophomores ☑ Juniors ☑ Seniors

Academic Accommodations

Curriculum		In class	
Foreign language waiver	☐	Early syllabus	☑
Lighter course load	☑	Note takers in class	☑
Math waiver	☐	Priority seating	☑
Other special classes	☐	Tape recorders	☑
Priority registrations	☐	Videotaped classes	☐
Substitution of courses	☐	Text on tape	☑
Exams		**Services**	
Extended time	☑	Diagnostic tests	☐
Oral exams	☐	Learning centers	☑
Take home exams	☐	Proofreaders	☐
Exams on tape or computer	☑	Readers	☑
Untimed exams	☐	Reading Machines/Kurzweil	☑
Other accommodations	☑	Special bookstore section	☐
		Typists	☐

Credit toward degree is not given for remedial courses taken.

Counseling Services

- ☑ Academic
- ☑ Psychological — Meets 5 times per academic year
- ☑ Student Support groups
- ☐ Vocational

Tutoring

Individual tutoring is available weekly.

Average size of tutoring groups: 1

	Individual	Group
Time management	☑	☑
Organizational skills	☑	☑
Learning strategies	☑	☑
Study skills	☑	☑
Content area	☑	☐
Writing lab	☑	☑
Math lab	☑	☑

LD PROGRAM STAFF

Total number of LD Program staff (including director):

Full Time: 1 Part Time: 1

There is an advisor/advocate from the LD program available to students.

Key staff person available to work with LD students: Catherine Axe, Coordinator, Disability Services.

LD Program web site: www.brown.edu/dss

Bryant University

Smithfield, RI

Address: 1150 Douglas Pike, Smithfield, RI, 02917
Admissions telephone: 800 622-7001
Admissions FAX: 401 232-6741
Director of Admission: Cynthia L. Bonn
Admissions e-mail: admission@bryant.edu
Web site: http://www.bryant.edu
SAT Code: 3095 ACT Code: 3802

LD program name: Academic Center for Excellence
Director: Laurie L. Hazard, Ed.D.
LD program telephone: 401 232-6746
LD program e-mail: lhazard@bryant.edu
LD program enrollment: 100, Total campus enrollment: 3,047

GENERAL

Bryant University is a private, coed, four-year institution. 392-acre, suburban campus in Smithfield (population: 20,613), 12 miles from Providence. Airport, bus, and train serve Providence; larger airport serves Boston (54 miles). Public transportation serves campus. Semester system.

LD ADMISSIONS

A personal interview is recommended. Essay is required and may be typed. Admissions requirements that may be waived for LD students include foreign language requirement. Note: Bryant does not have a LD program.

For fall 2004, 132 completed self-identified LD applications were received. 56 applications were offered admission, and 17 enrolled.

SECONDARY SCHOOL REQUIREMENTS

Graduation from secondary school required; GED accepted. The following course distribution required: 4 units of English, 4 units of math, 3 units of science, 2 units of foreign language, 2 units of history.

TESTING

SAT Reasoning or ACT required. SAT Subject required.

All enrolled freshmen (fall 2004):

Average SAT I Scores: Verbal: 535 Math: 569
Average ACT Scores: Composite: 24

Child Study Team report is not required. Tests required as part of this documentation:

- [ ] WAIS-IV
- [ ] WISC-IV
- [ ] SATA
- [ ] Woodcock-Johnson
- [ ] Nelson-Denny Reading Test
- [ ] Other

UNDERGRADUATE STUDENT BODY

Total undergraduate student enrollment: 1,821 Men, 1,186 Women.

Composition of student body (fall 2004):

	Undergraduate	Freshmen
International	1.4	1.8
Black	3.2	3.1
American Indian	0.3	0.3
Asian-American	3.5	2.5
Hispanic	3.4	3.3
White	83.5	84.0
Unreported	4.7	5.0
	100.0%	100.0%

73% are from out of state. 11% join a fraternity and 7% join a sorority. Average age of full-time undergraduates is 20. 17% of classes have fewer than 20 students, 83% have between 20 and 50 students.

STUDENT HOUSING

96% of freshmen live in college housing. Freshmen are not required to live on campus. Housing is guaranteed for all undergraduates. Campus can house 2,484 undergraduates. Single rooms are not available for students with medical or special needs.

EXPENSES

Tuition (2005-06): $24,762 per year. $20,988 per year (freshmen, includes laptop computer usage fee), $19,776 (returning students).

Room: $5,550. Board: $4,018.
There is no additional cost for LD program/services.

LD SERVICES

LD program size is not limited.

LD services available to:

- [x] Freshmen
- [x] Sophomores
- [x] Juniors
- [x] Seniors

Academic Accommodations

Curriculum		In class	
Foreign language waiver	[ ]	Early syllabus	[ ]
Lighter course load	[ ]	Note takers in class	[ ]
Math waiver	[ ]	Priority seating	[ ]
Other special classes	[ ]	Tape recorders	[x]
Priority registrations	[ ]	Videotaped classes	[ ]
Substitution of courses	[ ]	Text on tape	[ ]
Exams		**Services**	
Extended time	[x]	Diagnostic tests	[ ]
Oral exams	[ ]	Learning centers	[x]
Take home exams	[ ]	Proofreaders	[ ]
Exams on tape or computer	[ ]	Readers	[ ]
Untimed exams	[ ]	Reading Machines/Kurzweil	[ ]
Other accommodations	[ ]	Special bookstore section	[ ]
		Typists	[ ]

Credit toward degree is not given for remedial courses taken.

Counseling Services

- [x] Academic
- [ ] Psychological
- [ ] Student Support groups
- [ ] Vocational

Tutoring

Individual tutoring is available weekly.

	Individual	Group
Time management	[ ]	[ ]
Organizational skills	[ ]	[ ]
Learning strategies	[ ]	[ ]
Study skills	[ ]	[ ]
Content area	[ ]	[ ]
Writing lab	[ ]	[ ]
Math lab	[ ]	[ ]

UNIQUE LD PROGRAM FEATURES

Do not have an LD program.

LD PROGRAM STAFF

Total number of LD Program staff (including director):

Full Time: 1 Part Time: 1

There is not an advisor/advocate from the LD program available to students.

Key staff person available to work with LD students: Sally Riconscente, Assistant Director/LD Services.

Johnson & Wales University

Providence, RI

Address: 8 Abbott Park Place, Providence, RI, 02903-3703
Admissions telephone: 800 342-5598
Admissions FAX: 401 598-2948
Dean of Admissions: Maureen Dumas
Admissions e-mail: admissions@jwu.edu
Web site: http://www.jwu.edu
SAT Code: 3465 ACT Code: 3804

Director, Center for Academic Support: Meryl Berstein
LD program telephone: 401 598-4689
LD program e-mail: mberstein@jwu.edu
Total campus enrollment: 9,246

GENERAL

Johnson & Wales University is a private, coed, four-year institution. 69-acre campus in Providence (population: 173,618); branch campuses in Charleston, S.C., Norfolk, Va., North Miami, Fla., Vail, Colo., and Worcester, Mass., and abroad in Gothenburg, Sweden. Served by bus and train; major airport serves Boston (50 miles); airport serves Warwick (11 miles). School operates transportation around campus. Public transportation serves campus. Quarter system.

LD ADMISSIONS

A personal interview is not required. Essay is not required.

SECONDARY SCHOOL REQUIREMENTS

Graduation from secondary school required; GED accepted.

TESTING

SAT Reasoning required of some applicants; ACT may be substituted. SAT Subject recommended.

All enrolled freshmen (fall 2004):

Average SAT I Scores: Verbal: Math:
Average ACT Scores: Composite:

Child Study Team report is not required. Tests required as part of this documentation:

☐ WAIS-IV ☐ Woodcock-Johnson
☐ WISC-IV ☐ Nelson-Denny Reading Test
☐ SATA ☐ Other

UNDERGRADUATE STUDENT BODY

Total undergraduate student enrollment: 9,246.

Composition of student body (fall 2004):

	Undergraduate	Freshmen
International	4.7	4.7
Black	9.2	10.6
American Indian	0.4	0.2
Asian-American	2.8	2.9
Hispanic	6.0	6.2
White	62.0	69.9
Unreported	14.9	5.5
	100.0%	100.0%

Average age of full-time undergraduates is 20. 29% of classes have fewer than 20 students, 70% have between 20 and 50 students.

STUDENT HOUSING

100% of freshmen live in college housing. Housing is guaranteed for all undergraduates. We recommend anyone over 23 live off campus.

EXPENSES

Tuition (2005-06): $19,200 per year. $14,562 per year (College of Business), $15,246 (technology programs), $15,393 (hospitality programs), $17,652 (equine programs and College of Culinary Arts).

Room & Board: $7,545-$7,545.
There is no additional cost for LD program/services.

LD SERVICES

LD program size is not limited.

LD services available to:

☐ Freshmen ☐ Sophomores ☐ Juniors ☐ Seniors

Academic Accommodations

Curriculum		**In class**	
Foreign language waiver	☐	Early syllabus	☐
Lighter course load	☐	Note takers in class	■
Math waiver	☐	Priority seating	☐
Other special classes	■	Tape recorders	■
Priority registrations	☐	Videotaped classes	☐
Substitution of courses	☐	Text on tape	☐
Exams		**Services**	
Extended time	■	Diagnostic tests	☐
Oral exams	■	Learning centers	■
Take home exams	☐	Proofreaders	☐
Exams on tape or computer	☐	Readers	■
Untimed exams	■	Reading Machines/Kurzweil	■
Other accommodations	☐	Special bookstore section	☐
		Typists	☐

Credit toward degree is not given for remedial courses taken.

Counseling Services

☐ Academic
☐ Psychological
☐ Student Support groups
☐ Vocational

Tutoring

	Individual	Group
Time management	☐	☐
Organizational skills	☐	☐
Learning strategies	☐	☐
Study skills	☐	☐
Content area	☐	☐
Writing lab	☐	☐
Math lab	☐	☐

LD PROGRAM STAFF

Total number of LD Program staff (including director):

Full Time: 5 Part Time: 5

Key staff person available to work with LD students: Meryl Berstein, Director, Center for Academic Support.

Providence College

Providence, RI

Address: 549 River Avenue, Providence, RI, 02918
Admissions telephone: 401 865-2535
Admissions FAX: 401 865-2826
Dean of Enrollment Management: Christopher P. Lydon
Admissions e-mail: pcadmiss@providence.edu
Web site: http://www.providence.edu
SAT Code: 3693 ACT Code: 3806

Disability Support Services Coordinator:
Nicole Kudarauskas
LD program telephone: 401 865-1121
LD program e-mail: nkudarau@providence.edu
Total campus enrollment: 4,488

GENERAL

Providence College is a private, coed, four-year institution. 105-acre, suburban campus in Providence (population: 173,618), 35 miles from Newport and 50 miles from Boston. Served by bus and train; airport serves Warwick (10 miles). School operates transportation within local neighborhood and to nearby public transportation terminals. Public transportation serves campus. Semester system.

LD ADMISSIONS

Students do not complete a separate application and are simultaneously accepted to the LD program. A member of the LD program does not sit on the admissions committee. A personal interview is not required. Essay is required and may be typed.

SECONDARY SCHOOL REQUIREMENTS

Graduation from secondary school required; GED not accepted. The following course distribution required: 4 units of English, 4 units of math, 3 units of science, 3 units of foreign language, 2 units of social studies, 2 units of history.

TESTING

SAT Reasoning or ACT required. SAT Subject required.

All enrolled freshmen (fall 2004):

Average SAT I Scores:	Verbal: 597	Math: 604
Average ACT Scores:	Composite: 25	

Child Study Team report is not required. A neuropsychological or comprehensive psycho-education evaluation is not required for admission. Tests required as part of this documentation:

- ☐ WAIS-IV
- ☐ WISC-IV
- ☐ SATA
- ☐ Woodcock-Johnson
- ☐ Nelson-Denny Reading Test
- ☐ Other

UNDERGRADUATE STUDENT BODY

Total undergraduate student enrollment: 1,866 Men, 2,523 Women.

Composition of student body (fall 2004):

	Undergraduate	Freshmen
International	1.0	0.9
Black	2.0	1.6
American Indian	0.0	0.1
Asian-American	1.9	1.6
Hispanic	2.2	2.4
White	83.4	81.8
Unreported	9.5	11.6
	100.0%	100.0%

75% are from out of state. Average age of full-time undergraduates is 20. 50% of classes have fewer than 20 students, 47% have between 20 and 50 students, 3% have more than 50 students.

STUDENT HOUSING

97% of freshmen live in college housing. Freshmen are required to live on campus. Housing is guaranteed for all undergraduates. Campus can house 3,074 undergraduates. Single rooms are available for students with medical or special needs. A medical note is required.

EXPENSES

Tuition (2005-06): $24,800 per year.
Room: $4,970. Board: $4,300.
There is no additional cost for LD program/services.

LD SERVICES

LD program size is not limited.

LD services available to:

■ Freshmen ■ Sophomores ■ Juniors ■ Seniors

Academic Accommodations

Curriculum		In class	
Foreign language waiver	☐	Early syllabus	☐
Lighter course load	■	Note takers in class	■
Math waiver	☐	Priority seating	☐
Other special classes	☐	Tape recorders	■
Priority registrations	■	Videotaped classes	☐
Substitution of courses	☐	Text on tape	■
Exams		**Services**	
Extended time	■	Diagnostic tests	☐
Oral exams	■	Learning centers	■
Take home exams	☐	Proofreaders	☐
Exams on tape or computer	■	Readers	■
Untimed exams	■	Reading Machines/Kurzweil	☐
Other accommodations	■	Special bookstore section	☐
		Typists	■

Credit toward degree is not given for remedial courses taken.

Counseling Services

- ■ Academic
- ■ Psychological
- ☐ Student Support groups
- ☐ Vocational

Tutoring

Individual tutoring is available daily.

Average size of tutoring groups: 1

	Individual	Group
Time management	■	■
Organizational skills	■	■
Learning strategies	■	■
Study skills	■	■
Content area	☐	☐
Writing lab	■	■
Math lab	☐	☐

LD PROGRAM STAFF

Total number of LD Program staff (including director):

Full Time: 2 Part Time: 2

There is an advisor/advocate from the LD program available to students. 3 graduate students are available to work with LD students.

Key staff person available to work with LD students: Nicole Kudarauskas, Disability Support Services Coordinator.

University of Rhode Island

Kingston, RI

Address: Kingston, RI, 02881-0806
Admissions telephone: 401 874-7100
Admissions FAX: 401 874-5523
Dean of Admissions: David G. Taggart
Admissions e-mail: uriadmit@uri.edu
Web site: http://www.uri.edu
SAT Code: 3919 ACT Code: 3818

LD program name: Disability Services for Students
LD program address: 330 Memorial Union
Assistant Director, Disability Services: Pamela Rohland
LD program telephone: 401 874-2098
LD program e-mail: rohland@uri.edu
LD program enrollment: 127, Total campus enrollment: 11,397

GENERAL

University of Rhode Island is a public, coed, four-year institution. 1,200-acre campus in Kingston (population: 5,446), 30 miles from Providence; branch campuses on Narragansett Bay and in Providence, and West Greenwich. Served by bus; major airport serves Boston (50 miles); smaller airport and train serve Providence. School operates transportation to parking areas. Public transportation serves campus. Semester system.

LD ADMISSIONS

Students do not complete a separate application and are simultaneously accepted to the LD program. A member of the LD program does sit on the admissions committee. High school waivers are accepted for foreign language. A personal interview is not required. Essay is not required. Admissions requirements that may be waived for LD students include foreign language 2 year requirement

SECONDARY SCHOOL REQUIREMENTS

Graduation from secondary school required; GED accepted. The following course distribution required: 4 units of English, 3 units of math, 2 units of science, 2 units of foreign language, 2 units of social studies, 5 units of academic electives.

TESTING

SAT Reasoning or ACT required. SAT Subject recommended.

All enrolled freshmen (fall 2004):

Average SAT I Scores:	Verbal: 554	Math: 566
Average ACT Scores:	Composite: n/a	

Child Study Team report is not required. A neuropsychological or comprehensive psycho-educational evaluation is required for admission. Must be dated within 36 months of application. Tests required as part of this documentation:

- [x] WAIS-IV
- [x] WISC-IV
- [ ] SATA
- [x] Woodcock-Johnson
- [x] Nelson-Denny Reading Test
- [ ] Other

UNDERGRADUATE STUDENT BODY

Total undergraduate student enrollment: 4,622 Men, 5,957 Women.

Composition of student body (fall 2004):

	Undergraduate	Freshmen
International	0.4	0.3
Black	4.1	4.3
American Indian	0.1	0.3
Asian-American	2.2	2.7
Hispanic	4.2	4.2
White	72.7	76.2
Unreported	16.3	12.0
	100.0%	100.0%

38% are from out of state. 9% join a fraternity and 10% join a sorority. Average age of full-time undergraduates is 21. 35% of classes have fewer than 20 students, 57% have between 20 and 50 students, 8% have more than 50 students.

STUDENT HOUSING

95% of freshmen live in college housing. Freshmen are not required to live on campus. Housing is not guaranteed for all undergraduates. On-campus housing is guaranteed to first-year students only. Campus can house 5,041 undergraduates. Single rooms are available for students with medical or special needs. A medical note is required.

EXPENSES

Tuition (2005-06): $5,258 per year (in-state), $17,900 (out-of-state).
Room: $4,620. Board: $3,494.
There is no additional cost for LD program/services.

LD SERVICES

LD program size is not limited.

LD services available to:

- [x] Freshmen
- [x] Sophomores
- [x] Juniors
- [x] Seniors

Academic Accommodations

Curriculum

- [ ] Foreign language waiver
- [x] Lighter course load
- [ ] Math waiver
- [ ] Other special classes
- [x] Priority registrations
- [x] Substitution of courses

Exams

- [x] Extended time
- [x] Oral exams
- [ ] Take home exams
- [x] Exams on tape or computer
- [ ] Untimed exams
- [x] Other accommodations

In class

- [ ] Early syllabus
- [x] Note takers in class
- [ ] Priority seating
- [x] Tape recorders
- [ ] Videotaped classes
- [x] Text on tape

Services

- [ ] Diagnostic tests
- [x] Learning centers
- [ ] Proofreaders
- [x] Readers
- [x] Reading Machines/Kurzweil
- [x] Special bookstore section
- [x] Typists

Credit toward degree is not given for remedial courses taken.

Counseling Services

- [x] Academic
- [ ] Psychological
- [ ] Student Support groups
- [ ] Vocational

Meets 2 times per academic year

Tutoring

Individual tutoring is not available.

	Individual	Group
Time management	[x]	[x]
Organizational skills	[x]	[x]
Learning strategies	[x]	[x]
Study skills	[x]	[x]
Content area	[x]	[x]
Writing lab	[x]	[x]
Math lab	[x]	[x]

LD PROGRAM STAFF

Total number of LD Program staff (including director):

Full Time: 2 Part Time: 2

There is an advisor/advocate from the LD program available to students. The advisor/advocate meets with faculty 2 times per month and student 3 times per month.

Key staff person available to work with LD students: Pamela Rohland, Asst. Director, Disability Services for Students.

LD Program web site: www.uri.edu/disability_services

Rhode Island School of Design

Providence, RI

Address: 2 College Street, Providence, RI, 02903
Admissions telephone: 401 454-6300
Admissions FAX: 401 454-6309
Director of Admissions: Edward Newhall
Admissions e-mail: admissions@risd.edu
Web site: http://www.risd.edu
SAT Code: 3726 ACT Code: 3812

LD program e-mail: rmcmahon@risd.edu
LD program enrollment: 71, Total campus enrollment: 1,882

GENERAL

Rhode Island School of Design is a private, coed, four-year institution. 13-acre, urban campus in Providence (population: 173,618), 50 miles from Boston. Served by bus and train; major airport serves Boston; smaller airport serves Warwick (12 miles). School operates transportation to airport. Public transportation serves campus. 4-1-4 system.

LD ADMISSIONS

A personal interview is not required.

SECONDARY SCHOOL REQUIREMENTS

Graduation from secondary school required; GED accepted.

TESTING

SAT Reasoning required; ACT may be substituted. SAT Subject recommended.

All enrolled freshmen (fall 2004):

Average SAT I Scores:	Verbal: 595	Math: 608
Average ACT Scores:	Composite:	

Child Study Team report is not required. Tests required as part of this documentation:

- ☐ WAIS-IV
- ☐ WISC-IV
- ☐ SATA
- ☐ Woodcock-Johnson
- ☐ Nelson-Denny Reading Test
- ☐ Other

UNDERGRADUATE STUDENT BODY

Total undergraduate student enrollment: 721 Men, 1,108 Women.

Composition of student body (fall 2004):

	Undergraduate	Freshmen
International	12.8	11.3
Black	2.0	2.4
American Indian	0.5	0.5
Asian-American	13.8	13.6
Hispanic	5.0	5.3
White	40.0	53.6
Unreported	25.9	13.3
	100.0%	100.0%

92% are from out of state. Average age of full-time undergraduates is 19. 77% of classes have fewer than 20 students, 22% have between 20 and 50 students, 1% have more than 50 students.

STUDENT HOUSING

100% of freshmen live in college housing. Freshmen are required to live on campus. Housing is not guaranteed for all undergraduates. Demand exceeds supply. Campus can house 790 undergraduates.

EXPENSES

Tuition (2005-06): $29,410 per year.

Room: $4,780. Board: $3,575.

There is no additional cost for LD program/services.

LD SERVICES

LD program size is not limited.

LD services available to:

■ Freshmen ■ Sophomores ■ Juniors ■ Seniors

Academic Accommodations

Curriculum		**In class**	
Foreign language waiver	☐	Early syllabus	☐
Lighter course load	■	Note takers in class	■
Math waiver	☐	Priority seating	■
Other special classes	☐	Tape recorders	☐
Priority registrations	☐	Videotaped classes	☐
Substitution of courses	☐	Text on tape	☐
Exams		**Services**	
Extended time	■	Diagnostic tests	☐
Oral exams	■	Learning centers	☐
Take home exams	☐	Proofreaders	☐
Exams on tape or computer	☐	Readers	■
Untimed exams	■	Reading Machines/Kurzweil	■
Other accommodations	☐	Special bookstore section	☐
		Typists	☐

Credit toward degree is not given for remedial courses taken.

Counseling Services

- ■ Academic
- ■ Psychological
- ☐ Student Support groups
- ☐ Vocational

Tutoring

Individual tutoring is available weekly.

	Individual	Group
Time management	☐	☐
Organizational skills	☐	☐
Learning strategies	☐	☐
Study skills	☐	☐
Content area	■	■
Writing lab	■	■
Math lab	☐	☐

LD PROGRAM STAFF

Total number of LD Program staff (including director):

There is an advisor/advocate from the LD program available to students.

Key staff person available to work with LD students: Roberta McMahon, Director, Student Development & Counseling Service.

Roger Williams University

Bristol, RI

Address: 1 Old Ferry Road, Bristol, RI, 02809
Admissions telephone: 800 458-7144
Admissions FAX: 401 254-3557
Dean of Enrollment Management: Michelle L. Beauregard
Admissions e-mail: admit@rwu.edu
Web site: http://www.rwu.edu
SAT Code: 3729 ACT Code: 3814

Coordinator for Disability Support Services: Lisa Bauer
LD program telephone: 401 254-3736
LD program e-mail: lbauer@rwu.edu
Total campus enrollment: 4,190

GENERAL

Roger Williams University is a private, coed, four-year institution. 140-acre campus in Bristol (population: 22,469), 20 miles from Providence; branch campus in Providence. Airport, bus, and train serve Providence; major airport serves Boston (75 miles). School operates transportation to downtown malls and to bus and train stations. Public transportation serves campus. Semester system.

LD ADMISSIONS

A personal interview is recommended. Essay is required and may be typed.

SECONDARY SCHOOL REQUIREMENTS

Graduation from secondary school required; GED accepted. The following course distribution required: 4 units of English, 3 units of math, 3 units of science, 3 units of social studies, 2 units of history.

TESTING

SAT Reasoning or ACT required. SAT Subject recommended.

All enrolled freshmen (fall 2004):

Average SAT I Scores:	Verbal: 533	Math: 540
Average ACT Scores:	Composite: 24	

Child Study Team report is not required. Tests required as part of this documentation:

- ☐ WAIS-IV
- ☐ WISC-IV
- ☐ SATA
- ☐ Woodcock-Johnson
- ☐ Nelson-Denny Reading Test
- ☐ Other

UNDERGRADUATE STUDENT BODY

Total undergraduate student enrollment: 1,957 Men, 2,074 Women.

Composition of student body (fall 2004):

	Undergraduate	Freshmen
International	1.3	1.5
Black	0.3	1.3
American Indian	0.2	0.2
Asian-American	1.6	1.6
Hispanic	1.7	2.1
White	80.9	81.3
Unreported	14.0	12.0
	100.0%	100.0%

80% are from out of state. Average age of full-time undergraduates is 20. 39% of classes have fewer than 20 students, 61% have between 20 and 50 students.

STUDENT HOUSING

97% of freshmen live in college housing. Freshmen are required to live on campus. Housing is guaranteed for all undergraduates. Campus can house 2,656 undergraduates.

EXPENSES

Tuition (2005-06): $23,290 per year (in-state), $1,265 (out-of-state).

Room: $5,100-$5,304. Board: $5,304-$4,730.
There is no additional cost for LD program/services.

LD SERVICES

LD program size is not limited.

LD services available to:

■ Freshmen ■ Sophomores ■ Juniors ■ Seniors

Academic Accommodations

Curriculum		In class	
Foreign language waiver	☐	Early syllabus	☐
Lighter course load	■	Note takers in class	■
Math waiver	☐	Priority seating	☐
Other special classes	☐	Tape recorders	■
Priority registrations	☐	Videotaped classes	☐
Substitution of courses	☐	Text on tape	☐
Exams		**Services**	
Extended time	■	Diagnostic tests	☐
Oral exams	☐	Learning centers	■
Take home exams	☐	Proofreaders	☐
Exams on tape or computer	☐	Readers	■
Untimed exams	☐	Reading Machines/Kurzweil	☐
Other accommodations	☐	Special bookstore section	☐
		Typists	☐

Counseling Services

- ☐ Academic
- ☐ Psychological
- ☐ Student Support groups
- ☐ Vocational

Tutoring

Individual tutoring is available daily.

	Individual	Group
Time management	■	☐
Organizational skills	■	☐
Learning strategies	■	☐
Study skills	■	☐
Content area	☐	☐
Writing lab	■	☐
Math lab	■	☐

LD PROGRAM STAFF

Total number of LD Program staff (including director):

Full Time: 2 Part Time: 2

There is an advisor/advocate from the LD program available to students.

Key staff person available to work with LD students: Laura B. Choiniere, Director, CAD/Learning Specialist.

Salve Regina University

Newport, RI

Address: 100 Ochre Point Avenue, Newport, RI, 02840-4192
Admissions telephone: 888 GO-SALVE
Admissions FAX: 401 848-2823
Vice President of Enrollment Services: Ms. Colleen Emerson
Admissions e-mail: sruadmis@salve.edu
Web site: http://www.salve.edu
SAT Code: 3759 ACT Code: 3816

LD program name: Disability Services
LD program address: Academic Development Center
Director, Disability Services: Kathryn Rok
LD program telephone: 401 341-3150
LD program e-mail: rokk@salve.edu
Total campus enrollment: 2,069

GENERAL

Salve Regina University is a private, coed, four-year institution. 65-acre campus in Newport (population: 26,475), 35 miles from Providence; branch campus in Riverside. Served by bus; airport serves Warwick (28 miles); smaller airport serves Middletown (five miles); train serves Kingston (15 miles). School operates transportation to downtown Newport and Middletown. Public transportation serves campus. Semester system.

LD ADMISSIONS

Students do not complete a separate application and are simultaneously accepted to the LD program. A member of the LD program does not sit on the admissions committee. A personal interview is not required. Essay is required and may be typed. Admissions requirements that may be waived for LD students include None.

SECONDARY SCHOOL REQUIREMENTS

Graduation from secondary school required; GED accepted. The following course distribution required: 4 units of English, 3 units of math, 2 units of science, 2 units of foreign language, 1 unit of social studies, 4 units of academic electives.

TESTING

SAT Reasoning or ACT required. SAT Subject recommended.

All enrolled freshmen (fall 2004):

Average SAT I Scores:	Verbal: 539	Math: 540
Average ACT Scores:	Composite: 24	

Child Study Team report is not required. A neuropsychological or comprehensive psycho-education evaluation is not required for admission. Tests required as part of this documentation:

- ☐ WAIS-IV
- ☐ WISC-IV
- ☐ SATA
- ☐ Woodcock-Johnson
- ☐ Nelson-Denny Reading Test
- ☐ Other

UNDERGRADUATE STUDENT BODY

Total undergraduate student enrollment: 573 Men, 1,262 Women.

Composition of student body (fall 2004):

	Undergraduate	Freshmen
International	1.1	1.1
Black	1.4	1.4
American Indian	0.5	0.4
Asian-American	2.0	1.6
Hispanic	3.0	2.2
White	84.7	84.3
Unreported	7.3	9.0
	100.0%	100.0%

79% are from out of state. Average age of full-time undergraduates is 20. 53% of classes have fewer than 20 students, 47% have between 20 and 50 students.

STUDENT HOUSING

96% of freshmen live in college housing. Freshmen are required to live on campus. Housing is guaranteed for all undergraduates. Campus can house 1,200 undergraduates. Single rooms are not available for students with medical or special needs.

EXPENSES

Tuition (2005-06): $23,500 per year.
Room & Board: $9,500.
There is no additional cost for LD program/services.

LD SERVICES

LD program size is not limited.

LD services available to:

☐ Freshmen ☐ Sophomores ☐ Juniors ☐ Seniors

Academic Accommodations

Curriculum		In class	
Foreign language waiver	☐	Early syllabus	☐
Lighter course load	■	Note takers in class	■
Math waiver	☐	Priority seating	☐
Other special classes	☐	Tape recorders	■
Priority registrations	☐	Videotaped classes	■
Substitution of courses	☐	Text on tape	☐
Exams		**Services**	
Extended time	■	Diagnostic tests	☐
Oral exams	■	Learning centers	■
Take home exams	☐	Proofreaders	☐
Exams on tape or computer	☐	Readers	■
Untimed exams	■	Reading Machines/Kurzweil	■
Other accommodations	■	Special bookstore section	☐
		Typists	☐

Credit toward degree is not given for remedial courses taken.

Counseling Services

- ☐ Academic
- ☐ Psychological
- ☐ Student Support groups
- ☐ Vocational

Tutoring

Individual tutoring is available.

	Individual	Group
Time management	■	■
Organizational skills	■	■
Learning strategies	■	■
Study skills	■	■
Content area	■	■
Writing lab	■	■
Math lab	■	■

LD PROGRAM STAFF

Total number of LD Program staff (including director):

Full Time: 2 Part Time: 2

There is an advisor/advocate from the LD program available to students. 50 peer tutors are available to work with LD students.

Key staff person available to work with LD students: Kathryn Rok, Director, Disability Services.

LD Program web site: http://www.salve.edu/offices/acdevel/index.cfm

Anderson College

Anderson, SC

Address: 316 Boulevard, Anderson, SC, 29621
Admissions telephone: 864 231-5607
Admissions FAX: 864 231-2033
Director of Admissions: Pam Bryant
Admissions e-mail: admissions@ac.edu
Web site: http://www.ac.edu
SAT Code: 5008 ACT Code: 3832

Director of Academic Services: Linda Carlson
LD program telephone: 864 231-2026
LD program e-mail: lcarlson@ac.edu
LD program enrollment: 18, Total campus enrollment: 1,666

GENERAL

Anderson College is a private, coed, four-year institution. 32-acre, suburban campus in Anderson (population: 25,514), 20 miles from Greenville. Served by bus; major airport serves Greenville; train serves Clemson (15 miles). Semester system.

LD ADMISSIONS

Students do not complete a separate application and are simultaneously accepted to the LD program. A personal interview is not required. Essay is not required.

For fall 2004, 8 completed self-identified LD applications were received. 8 applications were offered admission, and 8 enrolled.

SECONDARY SCHOOL REQUIREMENTS

Graduation from secondary school required; GED accepted. The following course distribution required: 4 units of English, 3 units of math, 3 units of science, 2 units of foreign language, 2 units of social studies, 2 units of history, 4 units of academic electives.

TESTING

SAT Reasoning required; ACT may be substituted. SAT Subject recommended.

All enrolled freshmen (fall 2004):

Average SAT I Scores:	Verbal: 504	Math: 506
Average ACT Scores:	Composite: 20	

Child Study Team report is not required. Tests required as part of this documentation:

- ☐ WAIS-IV
- ☐ WISC-IV
- ☐ SATA
- ☐ Woodcock-Johnson
- ☐ Nelson-Denny Reading Test
- ☐ Other

UNDERGRADUATE STUDENT BODY

Total undergraduate student enrollment: 458 Men, 628 Women.

Composition of student body (fall 2004):

	Undergraduate	Freshmen
International	1.2	1.5
Black	8.3	11.8
American Indian	0.3	0.3
Asian-American	1.5	0.9
Hispanic	2.1	1.3
White	86.6	82.6
Unreported	0.0	1.6
	100.0%	100.0%

25% are from out of state. Average age of full-time undergraduates is 23. 46% of classes have fewer than 20 students, 54% have between 20 and 50 students.

STUDENT HOUSING

87% of freshmen live in college housing. Freshmen are required to live on campus. Housing is guaranteed for all undergraduates. Campus can house 879 undergraduates. Single rooms are available for students with medical or special needs. A medical note is not required.

EXPENSES

Tuition (2005-06): $14,100 per year.
Room: $3,050. Board: $3,000.
There is no additional cost for LD program/services.

LD SERVICES

LD program size is not limited.

LD services available to:

☐ Freshmen ☐ Sophomores ☐ Juniors ☐ Seniors

Academic Accommodations

Curriculum		In class	
Foreign language waiver	☐	Early syllabus	☐
Lighter course load	☒	Note takers in class	☒
Math waiver	☐	Priority seating	☐
Other special classes	☐	Tape recorders	☒
Priority registrations	☐	Videotaped classes	☐
Substitution of courses	☐	Text on tape	☐
Exams		**Services**	
Extended time	☒	Diagnostic tests	☐
Oral exams	☒	Learning centers	☐
Take home exams	☐	Proofreaders	☐
Exams on tape or computer	☐	Readers	☒
Untimed exams	☐	Reading Machines/Kurzweil	☐
Other accommodations	☐	Special bookstore section	☐
		Typists	☐

Credit toward degree is not given for remedial courses taken.

Counseling Services

- ☐ Academic
- ☐ Psychological
- ☐ Student Support groups
- ☐ Vocational

Tutoring

Individual tutoring is available.

	Individual	Group
Time management	☐	☐
Organizational skills	☐	☐
Learning strategies	☐	☐
Study skills	☐	☐
Content area	☐	☐
Writing lab	☐	☐
Math lab	☐	☐

LD PROGRAM STAFF

Total number of LD Program staff (including director):

Full Time: 1 Part Time: 1

Key staff person available to work with LD students: Linda Carlson, Director of Academic Services.

Charleston Southern University

Charleston, SC

Address: PO Box 118087, 9200 University Boulevard, Charleston, SC, 29423
Admissions telephone: 800 947-7474
Admissions FAX: 843 863-7070
Director of Enrollment Services: Cheryl Burton
Admissions e-mail: enroll@csuniv.edu
Web site: http://www.csuniv.edu
SAT Code: 5079 ACT Code: 3833

Director of DIsability Services/Counseling: Mr. Bob Ratliff
LD program telephone: 843 863-7212
LD program e-mail: rratliff@csuniv.edu
Total campus enrollment: 2,482

GENERAL

Charleston Southern University is a private, coed, four-year institution. 500-acre campus in Charleston (population: 96,650), 10 miles from downtown. Served by airport, bus, and train.

LD ADMISSIONS

A personal interview is recommended. Essay is required and may be typed.

SECONDARY SCHOOL REQUIREMENTS

Graduation from secondary school required; GED accepted. The following course distribution required: 4 units of English, 3 units of math, 3 units of science, 3 units of history, 3 units of academic electives.

TESTING

SAT Reasoning required; ACT may be substituted. SAT Subject recommended.

All enrolled freshmen (fall 2004):

Average SAT I Scores:	Verbal: 530	Math: 525
Average ACT Scores:	Composite: 22	

Child Study Team report is not required. Tests required as part of this documentation:

- ❑ WAIS-IV
- ❑ WISC-IV
- ❑ SATA
- ❑ Woodcock-Johnson
- ❑ Nelson-Denny Reading Test
- ❑ Other

UNDERGRADUATE STUDENT BODY

Total undergraduate student enrollment: 947 Men, 1,497 Women.

Composition of student body (fall 2004):

	Undergraduate	Freshmen
International	1.4	1.9
Black	29.0	27.1
American Indian	0.6	0.6
Asian-American	1.5	1.9
Hispanic	2.7	1.0
White	53.4	54.8
Unreported	11.4	12.7
	100.0%	100.0%

24% are from out of state. 3% join a fraternity and 3% join a sorority. 53% of classes have fewer than 20 students, 44% have between 20 and 50 students, 3% have more than 50 students.

STUDENT HOUSING

74% of freshmen live in college housing. Housing is not guaranteed for all undergraduates. Campus can house 1,254 undergraduates.

EXPENSES

Tuition (2005-06): $15,980 per year.
Room & Board: $6,142

There is no additional cost for LD program/services.

LD SERVICES

LD program size is not limited.

LD services available to:

❑ Freshmen ❑ Sophomores ❑ Juniors ❑ Seniors

Academic Accommodations

Curriculum		In class	
Foreign language waiver	❑	Early syllabus	❑
Lighter course load	❑	Note takers in class	■
Math waiver	❑	Priority seating	❑
Other special classes	❑	Tape recorders	■
Priority registrations	❑	Videotaped classes	❑
Substitution of courses	❑	Text on tape	❑
Exams		**Services**	
Extended time	■	Diagnostic tests	❑
Oral exams	■	Learning centers	■
Take home exams	❑	Proofreaders	❑
Exams on tape or computer	❑	Readers	■
Untimed exams	❑	Reading Machines/Kurzweil	❑
Other accommodations	❑	Special bookstore section	❑
		Typists	❑

Credit toward degree is not given for remedial courses taken.

Counseling Services

- ❑ Academic
- ❑ Psychological
- ❑ Student Support groups
- ❑ Vocational

Tutoring

	Individual	Group
Time management	❑	❑
Organizational skills	❑	❑
Learning strategies	❑	❑
Study skills	❑	❑
Content area	❑	❑
Writing lab	❑	❑
Math lab	❑	❑

LD PROGRAM STAFF

Total number of LD Program staff (including director):

Full Time: 2 Part Time: 2

Key staff person available to work with LD students: Mr. Bob Ratliff, Director of Disability Services/Counseling.

Clemson University

Clemson, SC

Address: 105 Sikes Hall, Clemson, SC, 29634
Admissions telephone: 864 656-2287
Admissions FAX: 864 656-2464
Director of Admissions: Robert S. Barkley
Admissions e-mail: cuadmissions@clemson.edu
Web site: http://www.clemson.edu
SAT Code: 5111 ACT Code: 3842

Interpreter for Student Disability Services: Barbara Boggs
LD program telephone: 864 656-0516
LD program e-mail: bboggs@clemson.edu
Total campus enrollment: 13,936

GENERAL

Clemson University is a public, coed, four-year institution. 1,400-acre campus in Clemson (population: 11,939), 55 miles from Greenville-Spartanburg. Served by bus and train; major airport serves Greenville-Spartanburg; smaller airport serves Oconee/Seneca (five miles). School operates transportation on campus and in local area. Public transportation serves campus. Semester system.

LD ADMISSIONS

A member of the LD program does not sit on the admissions committee. A personal interview is not required. Essay is not required.

SECONDARY SCHOOL REQUIREMENTS

Graduation from secondary school required; GED accepted. The following course distribution required: 4 units of English, 3 units of math, 3 units of science, 3 units of foreign language, 3 units of social studies, 1 unit of history, 2 units of academic electives.

TESTING

SAT Reasoning required; ACT may be substituted. SAT Subject required.

All enrolled freshmen (fall 2004):

Average SAT I Scores: Verbal: 589 Math: 615
Average ACT Scores: Composite: 26

Child Study Team report is not required. Tests required as part of this documentation:

- [ ] WAIS-IV
- [ ] WISC-IV
- [ ] SATA
- [ ] Woodcock-Johnson
- [ ] Nelson-Denny Reading Test
- [ ] Other

UNDERGRADUATE STUDENT BODY

Total undergraduate student enrollment: 7,641 Men, 6,334 Women.

Composition of student body (fall 2004):

	Undergraduate	Freshmen
International	0.4	0.5
Black	6.4	6.9
American Indian	0.3	0.2
Asian-American	2.2	1.8
Hispanic	1.4	1.0
White	82.1	82.0
Unreported	7.2	7.6
	100.0%	100.0%

30% are from out of state. 17% join a fraternity and 31% join a sorority. Average age of full-time undergraduates is 21. 27% of classes have fewer than 20 students, 62% have between 20 and 50 students, 11% have more than 50 students.

STUDENT HOUSING

98% of freshmen live in college housing. Freshmen are required to live on campus. Housing is guaranteed for all undergraduates. As space permits. Campus can house 6,500 undergraduates.

EXPENSES

There is no additional cost for LD program/services.

LD SERVICES

LD program size is not limited.

LD services available to:

- [x] Freshmen
- [x] Sophomores
- [x] Juniors
- [x] Seniors

Academic Accommodations

Curriculum

- Foreign language waiver [ ]
- Lighter course load [x]
- Math waiver [ ]
- Other special classes [ ]
- Priority registrations [ ]
- Substitution of courses [ ]

Exams

- Extended time [x]
- Oral exams [x]
- Take home exams [ ]
- Exams on tape or computer [ ]
- Untimed exams [x]
- Other accommodations [ ]

In class

- Early syllabus [ ]
- Note takers in class [x]
- Priority seating [ ]
- Tape recorders [x]
- Videotaped classes [ ]
- Text on tape [ ]

Services

- Diagnostic tests [x]
- Learning centers [x]
- Proofreaders [ ]
- Readers [x]
- Reading Machines/Kurzweil [ ]
- Special bookstore section [ ]
- Typists [ ]

Credit toward degree is not given for remedial courses taken.

Counseling Services

- [x] Academic
- [ ] Psychological
- [ ] Student Support groups
- [ ] Vocational

Tutoring

Individual tutoring is available.

	Individual	Group
Time management	[ ]	[ ]
Organizational skills	[ ]	[ ]
Learning strategies	[ ]	[ ]
Study skills	[ ]	[ ]
Content area	[ ]	[ ]
Writing lab	[ ]	[ ]
Math lab	[ ]	[ ]

UNIQUE LD PROGRAM FEATURES

Clemson University does not have a program. We are a compliance university who provides academic accommodations and support services aimed to "level the playing field". We provide equal access, but cannot guarantee the student's success.

LD PROGRAM STAFF

Total number of LD Program staff (including director):

Full Time: 2 Part Time: 2

Key staff person available to work with LD students: Barbara Boggs, Interpreter for Student Disability Svcs.

Coastal Carolina University

Conway, SC

Address: PO Box 261954, Conway, SC, 29528-6054
Admissions telephone: 800 277-7000
Admissions FAX: 843 349-2127
Associate Vice President of Enrollment Services: Judy W. Vogt
Admissions e-mail: admissions@coastal.edu
Web site: http://www.coastal.edu
SAT Code: 5837 ACT Code: 3843

Coordinator: Vonna Gengo
LD program telephone: 843 349-2307
LD program e-mail: vgengo@coastal.edu
Total campus enrollment: 6,020

GENERAL

Coastal Carolina University is a public, coed, four-year institution. 244-acre campus in Conway (population: 11,788), nine miles from Myrtle Beach and 100 miles from Charleston; branch campuses in Georgetown and Myrtle Beach. Served by bus; major airport serves Myrtle Beach; train serves Florence (50 miles). Public transportation serves campus. Semester system.

LD ADMISSIONS

A personal interview is required. Essay is not required.

SECONDARY SCHOOL REQUIREMENTS

Graduation from secondary school required; GED accepted. The following course distribution required: 4 units of English, 3 units of math, 3 units of science, 2 units of foreign language, 2 units of social studies, 1 unit of history, 4 units of academic electives.

TESTING

SAT Reasoning or ACT required. SAT Subject recommended.

All enrolled freshmen (fall 2004):

Average SAT I Scores:	Verbal: 513	Math: 528
Average ACT Scores:	Composite: 21	

Child Study Team report is not required. Tests required as part of this documentation:

- [ ] WAIS-IV
- [ ] WISC-IV
- [ ] SATA
- [ ] Woodcock-Johnson
- [ ] Nelson-Denny Reading Test
- [ ] Other

UNDERGRADUATE STUDENT BODY

Total undergraduate student enrollment: 2,089 Men, 2,682 Women.

Composition of student body (fall 2004):

	Undergraduate	Freshmen
International	1.0	2.5
Black	10.1	11.4
American Indian	0.4	0.3
Asian-American	1.1	0.9
Hispanic	1.7	1.5
White	84.5	83.0
Unreported	1.2	0.4
	100.0%	100.0%

41% are from out of state. 7% join a fraternity and 6% join a sorority. Average age of full-time undergraduates is 21. 36% of classes have fewer than 20 students, 56% have between 20 and 50 students, 8% have more than 50 students.

STUDENT HOUSING

77% of freshmen live in college housing. Freshmen are not required to live on campus. Housing is guaranteed for all undergraduates. Campus can house 2,250 undergraduates.

EXPENSES

Tuition (2005-06): $6,860 per year (in-state), $15,100 (out-of-state). There is no additional cost for LD program/services.

LD SERVICES

LD program size is not limited.

LD services available to:

- [x] Freshmen
- [x] Sophomores
- [x] Juniors
- [x] Seniors

Academic Accommodations

Curriculum		In class	
Foreign language waiver	[ ]	Early syllabus	[ ]
Lighter course load	[x]	Note takers in class	[x]
Math waiver	[ ]	Priority seating	[ ]
Other special classes	[x]	Tape recorders	[x]
Priority registrations	[ ]	Videotaped classes	[x]
Substitution of courses	[ ]	Text on tape	[ ]
Exams		**Services**	
Extended time	[x]	Diagnostic tests	[ ]
Oral exams	[x]	Learning centers	[x]
Take home exams	[ ]	Proofreaders	[ ]
Exams on tape or computer	[ ]	Readers	[x]
Untimed exams	[x]	Reading Machines/Kurzweil	[x]
Other accommodations	[ ]	Special bookstore section	[ ]
		Typists	[ ]

Credit toward degree is not given for remedial courses taken.

Counseling Services

- [ ] Academic
- [ ] Psychological
- [ ] Student Support groups
- [ ] Vocational

Tutoring

	Individual	Group
Time management	[ ]	[ ]
Organizational skills	[ ]	[ ]
Learning strategies	[ ]	[ ]
Study skills	[ ]	[ ]
Content area	[ ]	[ ]
Writing lab	[ ]	[ ]
Math lab	[ ]	[ ]

UNIQUE LD PROGRAM FEATURES

All students who register are requested to participate in a coaching relationship with the counselor. Academic plan is developed and followed. Weekly meeting with the student throughout the first semester. Meeting includes time management, organization, specific areas of weakness(i.e. reading, math, writing), tutoring, and study group.

LD PROGRAM STAFF

Total number of LD Program staff (including director):

Full Time: 1 Part Time: 1

10 peer tutors are available to work with LD students.

Key staff person available to work with LD students: Vonna Gengo, Coordinator, Student Disability Services/Counselor.

Coker College

Hartsville, SC

Address: 300 E. College Avenue, Hartsville, SC, 29550
Admissions telephone: 843 383-8050
Admissions FAX: 843 383-8056
Director of Admissions and Student Financial Aid: Mrs. Perry Wilson
Admissions e-mail: admissions@coker.edu
Web site: http://www.coker.edu
SAT Code: 5112 ACT Code: 3844

LD program name: Registrar
LD program address: 300 E. College Ave.,
Vice President: Dr. Steve Terry
LD program telephone: 843 383-8035
LD program e-mail: sterry@coker.edu
Total campus enrollment: 527

GENERAL

Coker College is a private, coed, four-year institution. 15-acre, main campus in Hartsville (population: 7,556), 70 miles from Columbia and 30 miles from Florence; branch campuses in Columbia and Fort Jackson. Major airport serves Charlotte, N.C. (85 miles); smaller airports serve Columbia and Florence; bus serves Bishopville (15 miles); train serves Florence. Semester system.

LD ADMISSIONS

Application Deadline: 07/01. Students do not complete a separate application and are simultaneously accepted to the LD program. A member of the LD program does not sit on the admissions committee. A personal interview is recommended. Essay is not required. An essay is not required for admissions. However, an essay is required to obtain support services once a student is enrolled.

SECONDARY SCHOOL REQUIREMENTS

Graduation from secondary school required; GED accepted. The following course distribution required: 4 units of English, 3 units of math, 3 units of science, 2 units of foreign language, 3 units of social studies.

TESTING

SAT Reasoning or ACT required. SAT Subject recommended.

All enrolled freshmen (fall 2004):

Average SAT I Scores:	Verbal: 505	Math: 519
Average ACT Scores:	Composite: 21	

Child Study Team report is not required. A neuropsychological or comprehensive psycho-educational evaluation is required for admission. Must be dated within 12 months of application. Tests required as part of this documentation:

- [ ] WAIS-IV
- [ ] WISC-IV
- [ ] SATA
- [ ] Woodcock-Johnson
- [ ] Nelson-Denny Reading Test
- [x] Other

UNDERGRADUATE STUDENT BODY

Total undergraduate student enrollment: 167 Men, 282 Women.

Composition of student body (fall 2004):

	Undergraduate	Freshmen
International	0.7	1.7
Black	16.9	24.3
American Indian	0.0	0.4
Asian-American	0.7	0.6
Hispanic	1.5	1.5
White	80.2	71.5
Unreported	0.0	0.0
	100.0%	100.0%

20% are from out of state. Average age of full-time undergraduates is 21. 77% of classes have fewer than 20 students, 23% have between 20 and 50 students.

STUDENT HOUSING

85% of freshmen live in college housing. Freshmen are required to live on campus. Housing is guaranteed for all undergraduates. Campus can house 364 undergraduates. Single rooms are available for students with medical or special needs. A medical note is not required.

EXPENSES

Tuition (2005-06): $16,968 per year.
Room: $2,986. Board: $2,690.
There is no additional cost for LD program/services.

LD SERVICES

LD program size is not limited.

LD services available to:

- [x] Freshmen
- [x] Sophomores
- [x] Juniors
- [x] Seniors

Academic Accommodations

Curriculum

- [ ] Foreign language waiver
- [x] Lighter course load
- [ ] Math waiver
- [ ] Other special classes
- [ ] Priority registrations
- [ ] Substitution of courses

Exams

- [x] Extended time
- [x] Oral exams
- [x] Take home exams
- [ ] Exams on tape or computer
- [x] Untimed exams
- [ ] Other accommodations

In class

- [ ] Early syllabus
- [ ] Note takers in class
- [ ] Priority seating
- [x] Tape recorders
- [ ] Videotaped classes
- [ ] Text on tape

Services

- [ ] Diagnostic tests
- [ ] Learning centers
- [ ] Proofreaders
- [ ] Readers
- [ ] Reading Machines/Kurzweil
- [ ] Special bookstore section
- [ ] Typists

Credit toward degree is not given for remedial courses taken.

Counseling Services

- [x] Academic
- [x] Psychological
- [ ] Student Support groups
- [ ] Vocational

Tutoring

Individual tutoring is available daily.

Average size of tutoring groups: 4

	Individual	Group
Time management	[ ]	[x]
Organizational skills	[ ]	[x]
Learning strategies	[ ]	[x]
Study skills	[ ]	[x]
Content area	[ ]	[ ]
Writing lab	[x]	[ ]
Math lab	[x]	[ ]

LD PROGRAM STAFF

There is an advisor/advocate from the LD program available to students.

Key staff person available to work with LD students: Open, Advising Coordinator.

College of Charleston

Charleston, SC

Address: 66 George Street, Charleston, SC, 29424-0001
Admissions telephone: 843 953-5670
Admissions FAX: 843 953-6322
Dean of Admissions and Continuing Education: Suzette Stille
Admissions e-mail: admissions@cofc.edu
Web site: http://www.cofc.edu
SAT Code: 5113 ACT Code: 3846

LD program name: Center for Disability Services
Director, Center for Disability Services: Bobbie Lindstrom
LD program telephone: 843 953-1431
LD program e-mail: lindstromb@cofc.edu
LD program enrollment: 670, Total campus enrollment: 9,866

GENERAL

College of Charleston is a public, coed, four-year institution. 52-acre, urban campus in Charleston (population: 96,650); branch campus in North Charleston. Major airport, bus, and train serve North Charleston (12 miles). Public transportation serves campus. Semester system.

LD ADMISSIONS

Students do not complete a separate application and are not simultaneously accepted to the LD program. A member of the LD program does not sit on the admissions committee. A personal interview is not required. Essay is required and may be typed.

SECONDARY SCHOOL REQUIREMENTS

Graduation from secondary school required; GED accepted. The following course distribution required: 4 units of English, 3 units of math, 3 units of science, 2 units of foreign language, 3 units of social studies, 4 units of academic electives.

TESTING

SAT Reasoning or ACT required. SAT Subject recommended.

All enrolled freshmen (fall 2004):

Average SAT I Scores:	Verbal: 607	Math: 601
Average ACT Scores:	Composite: 24	

Child Study Team report is not required. A neuropsychological or comprehensive psycho-educational evaluation is required for admission. Tests required as part of this documentation:

- [x] WAIS-IV
- [ ] WISC-IV
- [ ] SATA
- [x] Woodcock-Johnson
- [ ] Nelson-Denny Reading Test
- [ ] Other

UNDERGRADUATE STUDENT BODY

Total undergraduate student enrollment: 3,635 Men, 6,299 Women.

Composition of student body (fall 2004):

	Undergraduate	Freshmen
International	1.2	1.7
Black	5.2	7.9
American Indian	0.4	0.4
Asian-American	1.4	1.5
Hispanic	1.9	1.5
White	84.3	83.5
Unreported	5.6	3.5
	100.0%	100.0%

32% are from out of state. 13% join a fraternity and 15% join a sorority. Average age of full-time undergraduates is 21. 33% of classes have fewer than 20 students, 63% have between 20 and 50 students, 4% have more than 50 students.

STUDENT HOUSING

87% of freshmen live in college housing. Freshmen are not required to live on campus. Housing is guaranteed for all undergraduates. Campus can house 2,862 undergraduates.

EXPENSES

Tuition (2005-06): $6,668 per year (in-state), $15,342 (out-of-state).

Room: $4,768. Board: $2,180.
There is no additional cost for LD program/services.

LD SERVICES

LD program size is not limited.

LD services available to:

- [x] Freshmen
- [x] Sophomores
- [x] Juniors
- [x] Seniors

Academic Accommodations

Curriculum		In class	
Foreign language waiver	[ ]	Early syllabus	[ ]
Lighter course load	[x]	Note takers in class	[ ]
Math waiver	[ ]	Priority seating	[ ]
Other special classes	[ ]	Tape recorders	[x]
Priority registrations	[x]	Videotaped classes	[ ]
Substitution of courses	[x]	Text on tape	[x]
Exams		**Services**	
Extended time	[x]	Diagnostic tests	[x]
Oral exams	[ ]	Learning centers	[x]
Take home exams	[ ]	Proofreaders	[ ]
Exams on tape or computer	[ ]	Readers	[ ]
Untimed exams	[ ]	Reading Machines/Kurzweil	[x]
Other accommodations	[ ]	Special bookstore section	[ ]
		Typists	[ ]

Credit toward degree is not given for remedial courses taken.

Counseling Services

- [x] Academic
- [x] Psychological
- [x] Student Support groups
- [ ] Vocational

Tutoring

	Individual	Group
Time management	[x]	[ ]
Organizational skills	[x]	[ ]
Learning strategies	[x]	[ ]
Study skills	[x]	[ ]
Content area	[x]	[ ]
Writing lab	[ ]	[x]
Math lab	[ ]	[x]

LD PROGRAM STAFF

Total number of LD Program staff (including director):

Full Time: 2 Part Time: 2

There is an advisor/advocate from the LD program available to students. The advisor/advocate meets with student 2 times per month.

Key staff person available to work with LD students: Ann Lacy, Coordinator of SNAP Services.

LD Program web site: www.cofc.edu/~cds

Columbia International University

Columbia, SC

Address: 7435 Monticello Road, Columbia, SC, 29203
Admissions telephone: 800 777-2227, extension 13024
Director of Admissions: John D. Basie
SAT Code: 5116 ACT Code: 3848

LD program name: Academic Services
Bible College Administrative Assistant: Amanda Thomas
LD program telephone: 803 754-4100, extension 3640
LD program e-mail: athomas@ciu.edu
LD program enrollment: 31, Total campus enrollment: 594

GENERAL

Columbia International University is a private, coed, four-year institution. 400-acre campus in Columbia (population: 116,278), eight miles from downtown; branch campus abroad in Korntal, Germany. Served by airport, bus, and train; major airport serves Charlotte, NC. (75 miles). Semester system.

LD ADMISSIONS

Students do not complete a separate application and are not simultaneously accepted to the LD program. A member of the LD program does not sit on the admissions committee. High school waivers are accepted for math and foreign language. A personal interview is not required. Essay is required and may be typed.

SECONDARY SCHOOL REQUIREMENTS

Graduation from secondary school required; GED accepted. The following course distribution required: 4 units of English.

TESTING

SAT Reasoning required of some applicants; ACT may be substituted. SAT Subject recommended.

All enrolled freshmen (fall 2004):

Average SAT I Scores: Verbal: 564 Math: 541
Average ACT Scores: Composite: 23

Child Study Team report is not required. A neuropsychological or comprehensive psycho-educational evaluation is required for admission. Must be dated within 120 months of application. Tests required as part of this documentation:

- [x] WAIS-IV
- [x] WISC-IV
- [x] SATA
- [x] Woodcock-Johnson
- [x] Nelson-Denny Reading Test
- [x] Other

UNDERGRADUATE STUDENT BODY

Total undergraduate student enrollment: 290 Men, 352 Women.

Composition of student body (fall 2004):

	Undergraduate	Freshmen
International	2.2	2.6
Black	0.0	1.4
American Indian	0.0	0.2
Asian-American	1.1	0.7
Hispanic	1.1	1.0
White	79.1	81.6
Unreported	16.5	12.5
	100.0%	100.0%

60% are from out of state. Average age of full-time undergraduates is 22. 54% of classes have fewer than 20 students, 35% have between 20 and 50 students, 11% have more than 50 students.

STUDENT HOUSING

91% of freshmen live in college housing. Freshmen are required to live on campus. Housing is guaranteed for all undergraduates. Campus can house 475 undergraduates. Single rooms are available for students with medical or special needs. A medical note is required.

EXPENSES

Tuition (2005-06): $13,206 per year.

Room & Board: $5,542
There is no additional cost for LD program/services.

LD SERVICES

LD program size is not limited.

LD services available to:

- [x] Freshmen
- [x] Sophomores
- [x] Juniors
- [x] Seniors

Academic Accommodations

Curriculum		In class	
Foreign language waiver	[ ]	Early syllabus	[ ]
Lighter course load	[x]	Note takers in class	[x]
Math waiver	[ ]	Priority seating	[ ]
Other special classes	[ ]	Tape recorders	[x]
Priority registrations	[ ]	Videotaped classes	[ ]
Substitution of courses	[ ]	Text on tape	[x]
Exams		**Services**	
Extended time	[x]	Diagnostic tests	[x]
Oral exams	[x]	Learning centers	[ ]
Take home exams	[ ]	Proofreaders	[x]
Exams on tape or computer	[ ]	Readers	[x]
Untimed exams	[x]	Reading Machines/Kurzweil	[x]
Other accommodations	[ ]	Special bookstore section	[ ]
		Typists	[x]

Credit toward degree is not given for remedial courses taken.

Counseling Services

- [x] Academic
- [ ] Psychological
- [ ] Student Support groups
- [ ] Vocational

Tutoring

Individual tutoring is available daily.

Average size of tutoring groups: 1

	Individual	Group
Time management	[x]	[x]
Organizational skills	[x]	[x]
Learning strategies	[ ]	[x]
Study skills	[ ]	[x]
Content area	[ ]	[ ]
Writing lab	[ ]	[ ]
Math lab	[ ]	[ ]

LD PROGRAM STAFF

Total number of LD Program staff (including director):

Full Time: 1 Part Time: 1

There is an advisor/advocate from the LD program available to students. The advisor/advocate meets with faculty 1 times per month and student 4 times per month. 1 graduate students and 2 peer tutors are available to work with LD students.

Key staff person available to work with LD students: Robert W. Ferris, Acting Director, Academic Services.

Converse College

Spartanburg, SC

Address: 580 E. Main Street, Spartanburg, SC, 29302
Admissions telephone: 864 596-9040
Admissions FAX: 864 596-9225
Interim Director of Admissions: John White
Admissions e-mail: info@converse.edu
Web site: http://www.converse.edu
SAT Code: 5121 ACT Code: 3852

Total campus enrollment: 756

GENERAL

Converse College is a private, women's, four-year institution. 70-acre campus in Spartanburg (population: 39,673), in the Piedmont section of South Carolina. Served by bus and train; major airport serves Charlotte, NC. (70 miles); smaller airport serves Greenville (12 miles). 4-1-4 system.

LD ADMISSIONS

A personal interview is recommended. Essay is required and may be typed.

SECONDARY SCHOOL REQUIREMENTS

Graduation from secondary school required; GED accepted. The following course distribution required: 4 units of English, 3 units of math, 2 units of science, 2 units of foreign language, 1 unit of history, 6 units of academic electives.

TESTING

SAT Reasoning recommended. ACT recommended. SAT Subject recommended.

All enrolled freshmen (fall 2004):

Average SAT I Scores: Verbal:558 Math: 540
Average ACT Scores: Composite: 23

Child Study Team report is not required. Tests required as part of this documentation:

- ☐ WAIS-IV
- ☐ WISC-IV
- ☐ SATA
- ☐ Woodcock-Johnson
- ☐ Nelson-Denny Reading Test
- ☐ Other

UNDERGRADUATE STUDENT BODY

Total undergraduate student enrollment: 732 Women.

Composition of student body (fall 2004):

	Undergraduate	Freshmen
International	4.1	2.6
Black	10.2	10.4
American Indian	0.5	0.4
Asian-American	1.0	0.4
Hispanic	2.0	1.1
White	80.7	69.9
Unreported	1.5	15.2
	100.0%	100.0%

24% are from out of state. Average age of full-time undergraduates is 21. 79% of classes have fewer than 20 students, 21% have between 20 and 50 students.

STUDENT HOUSING

90% of freshmen live in college housing. Freshmen are required to live on campus. Housing is guaranteed for all undergraduates.

EXPENSES

Tuition (2005-06): $21,176 per year.
Room & Board: $6,460

LD SERVICES

LD program size is not limited.

LD services available to:

☐ Freshmen ☐ Sophomores ☐ Juniors ☐ Seniors

Academic Accommodations

Curriculum		**In class**	
Foreign language waiver	☐	Early syllabus	☐
Lighter course load	☐	Note takers in class	☐
Math waiver	☐	Priority seating	☐
Other special classes	☐	Tape recorders	■
Priority registrations	☐	Videotaped classes	☐
Substitution of courses	☐	Text on tape	☐
Exams		**Services**	
Extended time	■	Diagnostic tests	☐
Oral exams	■	Learning centers	☐
Take home exams	☐	Proofreaders	☐
Exams on tape or computer	☐	Readers	■
Untimed exams	■	Reading Machines/Kurzweil	☐
Other accommodations	☐	Special bookstore section	☐
		Typists	☐

Credit toward degree is not given for remedial courses taken.

Counseling Services

- ☐ Academic
- ☐ Psychological
- ☐ Student Support groups
- ☐ Vocational

Tutoring

	Individual	Group
Time management	☐	☐
Organizational skills	☐	☐
Learning strategies	☐	☐
Study skills	☐	☐
Content area	☐	☐
Writing lab	☐	☐
Math lab	☐	☐

LD PROGRAM STAFF

Key staff person available to work with LD students: Dr. Kathleen Miller, Director of Academic Support.

Erskine College

Due West, SC

Address: 2 Washington Street, Due West, SC, 29639
Admissions telephone: 800 241-8721
Admissions FAX: 864 379-2167
Director of Admissions: Bart Walker
Admissions e-mail: admissions@erskine.edu
Web site: http://www.erskine.edu
SAT Code: 5188 ACT Code: 3854

Dean of Students: Robyn Agnew
LD program telephone: 864 379-8701
LD program e-mail: ragnew@erskine.edu
Total campus enrollment: 617

GENERAL

Erskine College is a private, coed, four-year institution. 85-acre campus in Due West (population: 1,209), 25 miles from Greenwood. Major airport, bus, and train serve Greenwood. School operates transportation to airport and bus terminals. 4-1-4 system.

LD ADMISSIONS

A personal interview is required. Essay is not required.

SECONDARY SCHOOL REQUIREMENTS

Graduation from secondary school required; GED accepted.

TESTING

SAT Reasoning required; ACT may be substituted. SAT Subject required.

All enrolled freshmen (fall 2004):

Average SAT I Scores: Verbal: 563 Math: 564
Average ACT Scores: Composite: 23

Child Study Team report is not required. Tests required as part of this documentation:

☐ WAIS-IV ☐ Woodcock-Johnson
☐ WISC-IV ☐ Nelson-Denny Reading Test
☐ SATA ☐ Other

UNDERGRADUATE STUDENT BODY

Total undergraduate student enrollment: 234 Men, 354 Women.

Composition of student body (fall 2004):

	Undergraduate	Freshmen
International	1.1	2.1
Black	6.1	6.8
American Indian	0.0	0.2
Asian-American	0.0	0.5
Hispanic	1.7	1.0
White	89.4	86.1
Unreported	1.7	3.3
	100.0%	100.0%

21% are from out of state. 14% join a fraternity and 25% join a sorority. Average age of full-time undergraduates is 20. 66% of classes have fewer than 20 students, 34% have between 20 and 50 students.

STUDENT HOUSING

98% of freshmen live in college housing. Freshmen are required to live on campus. Housing is guaranteed for all undergraduates. Campus can house 644 undergraduates.

EXPENSES

Tuition (2005-06): $17,700 per year.

Room: $3,126. Board: $3,300.
There is no additional cost for LD program/services.

LD SERVICES

LD program size is not limited.

LD services available to:

☐ Freshmen ☐ Sophomores ☐ Juniors ☐ Seniors

Academic Accommodations

Curriculum		**In class**	
Foreign language waiver	☐	Early syllabus	☐
Lighter course load	☐	Note takers in class	☐
Math waiver	☐	Priority seating	☐
Other special classes	☐	Tape recorders	■
Priority registrations	☐	Videotaped classes	☐
Substitution of courses	☐	Text on tape	☐
Exams		**Services**	
Extended time	■	Diagnostic tests	☐
Oral exams	☐	Learning centers	☐
Take home exams	☐	Proofreaders	☐
Exams on tape or computer	☐	Readers	☐
Untimed exams	■	Reading Machines/Kurzweil	☐
Other accommodations	☐	Special bookstore section	☐
		Typists	☐

Credit toward degree is not given for remedial courses taken.

Counseling Services

☐ Academic
☐ Psychological
☐ Student Support groups
☐ Vocational

Tutoring

	Individual	Group
Time management	☐	☐
Organizational skills	☐	☐
Learning strategies	☐	☐
Study skills	☐	☐
Content area	☐	☐
Writing lab	☐	☐
Math lab	☐	☐

LD PROGRAM STAFF

Key staff person available to work with LD students: Robyn Agnew, Dean of Students.

Francis Marion University

Florence, SC

Address: PO Box 100547, Florence, SC, 29501
Admissions telephone: 800 368-7551
Admissions FAX: 843 661-4635
Director of Admissions: Drucilla Russell
Admissions e-mail: admission@fmarion.edu
Web site: http://www.fmarion.edu
SAT Code: 5442 ACT Code: 3856

Director of Counseling and Testing Center:
Rebecca Lawson
LD program telephone: 843 673-9707
LD program e-mail: rlaswon@fmarion.edu
Total campus enrollment: 3,227

GENERAL

Francis Marion University is a public, coed, four-year institution. 309-acre, rural campus in Florence (population: 30,248), 80 miles from Columbia. Served by airport, bus, and train; major airport serves Charlotte, NC (100 miles). Public transportation serves campus. Semester system.

LD ADMISSIONS

Students do not complete a separate application and are not simultaneously accepted to the LD program. A member of the LD program does not sit on the admissions committee. A personal interview is not required. Essay is not required.

SECONDARY SCHOOL REQUIREMENTS

Graduation from secondary school required; GED accepted. The following course distribution required: 4 units of English, 3 units of math, 3 units of science, 2 units of foreign language, 2 units of social studies, 1 unit of history, 4 units of academic electives.

TESTING

SAT Reasoning considered if submitted. ACT considered if submitted.

All enrolled freshmen (fall 2004):

Average SAT I Scores:	Verbal: 472	Math: 476
Average ACT Scores:	Composite: 19	

Child Study Team report is not required. A neuropsychological or comprehensive psycho-educational evaluation is required for admission. Must be dated within 36 months of application. Tests required as part of this documentation:

- [x] WAIS-IV
- [x] WISC-IV
- [ ] SATA
- [ ] Woodcock-Johnson
- [ ] Nelson-Denny Reading Test
- [x] Other

UNDERGRADUATE STUDENT BODY

Total undergraduate student enrollment: 1,103 Men, 1,692 Women.

Composition of student body (fall 2004):

	Undergraduate	Freshmen
International	0.9	1.1
Black	40.3	39.5
American Indian	0.7	0.6
Asian-American	1.1	1.1
Hispanic	2.4	1.1
White	53.1	53.6
Unreported	1.5	3.0
	100.0%	100.0%

6% are from out of state. 3% join a fraternity and 5% join a sorority. Average age of full-time undergraduates is 21. 47% of classes have fewer than 20 students, 50% have between 20 and 50 students, 3% have more than 50 students.

STUDENT HOUSING

64% of freshmen live in college housing. Freshmen are not required to live on campus. Housing is guaranteed for all undergraduates. Campus can house 1,381 undergraduates. Single rooms are not available for students with medical or special needs.

EXPENSES

Tuition (2005-06): $5,849 per year (in-state), $11,698 (out-of-state). Room: $2,760. Board: $2,370.

There is no additional cost for LD program/services.

LD SERVICES

LD program size is not limited.

LD services available to:

- [x] Freshmen
- [x] Sophomores
- [x] Juniors
- [x] Seniors

Academic Accommodations

Curriculum		**In class**	
Foreign language waiver	[ ]	Early syllabus	[ ]
Lighter course load	[x]	Note takers in class	[x]
Math waiver	[ ]	Priority seating	[ ]
Other special classes	[ ]	Tape recorders	[x]
Priority registrations	[ ]	Videotaped classes	[ ]
Substitution of courses	[ ]	Text on tape	[ ]
Exams		**Services**	
Extended time	[x]	Diagnostic tests	[ ]
Oral exams	[x]	Learning centers	[ ]
Take home exams	[ ]	Proofreaders	[ ]
Exams on tape or computer	[ ]	Readers	[x]
Untimed exams	[ ]	Reading Machines/Kurzweil	[ ]
Other accommodations	[ ]	Special bookstore section	[ ]
		Typists	[ ]

Credit toward degree is not given for remedial courses taken.

Counseling Services

- [ ] Academic
- [ ] Psychological
- [ ] Student Support groups
- [ ] Vocational

Tutoring

Individual tutoring is not available.

	Individual	Group
Time management	[ ]	[ ]
Organizational skills	[ ]	[ ]
Learning strategies	[ ]	[ ]
Study skills	[ ]	[ ]
Content area	[x]	[ ]
Writing lab	[x]	[ ]
Math lab	[x]	[ ]

LD PROGRAM STAFF

Total number of LD Program staff (including director):

Full Time: 1 Part Time: 1

There is an advisor/advocate from the LD program available to students. The advisor/advocate meets with faculty 1 times per month and student 2 times per month.

Key staff person available to work with LD students: Rebecca Lawson, Director of Counseling and Testing Center.

Furman University

Greenville, SC

Address: 3300 Poinsett Highway, Greenville, SC, 29613
Admissions telephone: 864 294-2034
Admissions FAX: 864 294-3127
Director of Admissions: Woody O'Cain
Admissions e-mail: admissions@furman.edu
Web site: http://www.furman.edu/
SAT Code: 5222 ACT Code: 3858

Director, Disability Services: Ms. Donna Taylor
LD program telephone: 864 294-2322
LD program e-mail: donna.taylor@furman.edu
LD program enrollment: 145, Total campus enrollment: 2,807

GENERAL

Furman University is a private, coed, four-year institution. 750-acre campus five miles north of Greenville (population: 56,002). Served by airport, bus, and train. School operates transportation downtown and to airports.

LD ADMISSIONS

A personal interview is recommended. Essay is required and may be typed.

SECONDARY SCHOOL REQUIREMENTS

Graduation from secondary school required; GED accepted. The following course distribution required: 4 units of English, 3 units of math, 2 units of science, 2 units of foreign language, 3 units of social studies.

TESTING

SAT Reasoning or ACT required. SAT Subject required.

All enrolled freshmen (fall 2004):

Average SAT I Scores: Verbal: 635 Math: 639
Average ACT Scores: Composite: 27

Child Study Team report is not required. Tests required as part of this documentation:

- [ ] WAIS-IV
- [ ] WISC-IV
- [ ] SATA
- [ ] Woodcock-Johnson
- [ ] Nelson-Denny Reading Test
- [ ] Other

UNDERGRADUATE STUDENT BODY

Total undergraduate student enrollment: 1,230 Men, 1,537 Women.

Composition of student body (fall 2004):

	Undergraduate	Freshmen
International	1.1	1.0
Black	5.5	6.2
American Indian	0.1	0.1
Asian-American	1.5	1.9
Hispanic	1.2	1.0
White	86.6	85.8
Unreported	4.0	4.0
	100.0%	100.0%

70% are from out of state. 35% join a fraternity and 40% join a sorority. Average age of full-time undergraduates is 20. 55% of classes have fewer than 20 students, 45% have between 20 and 50 students.

STUDENT HOUSING

98% of freshmen live in college housing. Freshmen are required to live on campus. Housing is guaranteed for all undergraduates. Campus can house 2,425 undergraduates. Single rooms are not available for students with medical or special needs.

EXPENSES

Tuition (2005-06): $25,888 per year.
Room: $3,712. Board: $3,200.

There is no additional cost for LD program/services.

LD SERVICES

LD program size is not limited.

LD services available to:

- [x] Freshmen
- [x] Sophomores
- [x] Juniors
- [x] Seniors

Academic Accommodations

Curriculum		In class	
Foreign language waiver	[ ]	Early syllabus	[ ]
Lighter course load	[x]	Note takers in class	[x]
Math waiver	[ ]	Priority seating	[ ]
Other special classes	[ ]	Tape recorders	[x]
Priority registrations	[ ]	Videotaped classes	[ ]
Substitution of courses	[ ]	Text on tape	[ ]
Exams		**Services**	
Extended time	[x]	Diagnostic tests	[ ]
Oral exams	[x]	Learning centers	[ ]
Take home exams	[ ]	Proofreaders	[ ]
Exams on tape or computer	[ ]	Readers	[x]
Untimed exams	[ ]	Reading Machines/Kurzweil	[ ]
Other accommodations	[ ]	Special bookstore section	[ ]
		Typists	[ ]

Credit toward degree is not given for remedial courses taken.

Counseling Services

- [x] Academic
- [x] Psychological
- [ ] Student Support groups
- [ ] Vocational

Tutoring

Individual tutoring is not available.

	Individual	Group
Time management	[ ]	[ ]
Organizational skills	[ ]	[ ]
Learning strategies	[ ]	[ ]
Study skills	[ ]	[ ]
Content area	[ ]	[ ]
Writing lab	[ ]	[ ]
Math lab	[ ]	[ ]

LD PROGRAM STAFF

Total number of LD Program staff (including director):

Full Time: 1 Part Time: 1

There is not an advisor/advocate from the LD program available to students.

Key staff person available to work with LD students: Ms. Donna Taylor, Director, Disability Services.

Lander University

Greenwood, SC

Address: 320 Stanley Avenue, Greenwood, SC, 29649-2099
Admissions telephone: 888 4-LANDER
Admissions FAX: 864 388-8125
Director of Admissions: Jonathan T. Reece
Admissions e-mail: admissions@lander.edu
Web site: http://www.lander.edu
SAT Code: 5363 ACT Code: 3860

LD program name: Office of Student Disability Services
Advisor to students with disabilities: Mr. Lafayette Harrison
LD program telephone: 864 388-8814
LD program e-mail: lharriso@lander.edu
LD program enrollment: 115, Total campus enrollment: 2,733

GENERAL

Lander University is a public, coed, four-year institution. 100-acre campus in Greenwood (population: 22,071), 75 miles from Columbia; branch campus in Greenville. Served by bus; major airport and train serve Greenville (60 miles). Semester system.

LD ADMISSIONS

Students do not complete a separate application and are simultaneously accepted to the LD program. A member of the LD program does not sit on the admissions committee. A personal interview is required. Essay is not required.

SECONDARY SCHOOL REQUIREMENTS

Graduation from secondary school required; GED accepted. The following course distribution required: 4 units of English, 4 units of math, 3 units of science, 2 units of foreign language, 2 units of social studies, 1 unit of history, 2 units of academic electives.

TESTING

SAT Reasoning or ACT required. SAT Subject recommended.

All enrolled freshmen (fall 2004):

Average SAT I Scores:	Verbal: 483	Math: 491
Average ACT Scores:	Composite: 20	

Child Study Team report is not required. A neuropsychological or comprehensive psycho-educational evaluation is required for admission. Must be dated within 36 months of application. Tests required as part of this documentation:

- [x] WAIS-IV
- [x] WISC-IV
- [x] SATA
- [x] Woodcock-Johnson
- [x] Nelson-Denny Reading Test
- [ ] Other

UNDERGRADUATE STUDENT BODY

Total undergraduate student enrollment: 902 Men, 1,534 Women.

Composition of student body (fall 2004):

	Undergraduate	Freshmen
International	1.7	1.5
Black	23.7	22.4
American Indian	0.0	0.1
Asian-American	0.8	0.5
Hispanic	1.1	1.4
White	72.7	74.1
Unreported	0.0	0.0
	100.0%	100.0%

3% are from out of state. 12% join a fraternity and 12% join a sorority. Average age of full-time undergraduates is 22. 39% of classes have fewer than 20 students, 57% have between 20 and 50 students, 4% have more than 50 students.

STUDENT HOUSING

80% of freshmen live in college housing. Freshmen are not required to live on campus. Housing is guaranteed for all undergraduates. Campus can house 1,032 undergraduates. Single rooms are available for students with medical or special needs. A medical note is required.

EXPENSES

There is no additional cost for LD program/services.

LD SERVICES

LD program size is not limited.

LD services available to:

- [x] Freshmen
- [x] Sophomores
- [x] Juniors
- [x] Seniors

Academic Accommodations

Curriculum		In class	
Foreign language waiver	[ ]	Early syllabus	[x]
Lighter course load	[x]	Note takers in class	[x]
Math waiver	[ ]	Priority seating	[x]
Other special classes	[ ]	Tape recorders	[x]
Priority registrations	[x]	Videotaped classes	[ ]
Substitution of courses	[x]	Text on tape	[x]
Exams		**Services**	
Extended time	[x]	Diagnostic tests	[ ]
Oral exams	[x]	Learning centers	[x]
Take home exams	[x]	Proofreaders	[x]
Exams on tape or computer	[x]	Readers	[x]
Untimed exams	[x]	Reading Machines/Kurzweil	[x]
Other accommodations	[x]	Special bookstore section	[ ]
		Typists	[x]

Credit toward degree is not given for remedial courses taken.

Counseling Services

- [x] Academic — Meets 2 times per academic year
- [ ] Psychological
- [ ] Student Support groups
- [ ] Vocational

Tutoring

Individual tutoring is available daily.

Average size of tutoring groups: 4

	Individual	Group
Time management	[x]	[x]
Organizational skills	[x]	[x]
Learning strategies	[x]	[x]
Study skills	[x]	[x]
Content area	[x]	[x]
Writing lab	[x]	[x]
Math lab	[x]	[x]

UNIQUE LD PROGRAM FEATURES

All self-identified LD students are provided the services required and requested by the student.

Advisor/advocate meets with faculty on an as needed basis.

LD PROGRAM STAFF

Total number of LD Program staff (including director):

Full Time: 1 Part Time: 1

There is an advisor/advocate from the LD program available to students. 30 peer tutors are available to work with LD students.

Key staff person available to work with LD students: Mr. Lafayette Harrison, Advisor to students with disabilities.

Limestone College

Gaffney, SC

Address: 1115 College Drive, Gaffney, SC, 29340-3799
Admissions telephone: 800 795-7151, extension 554; FAX: 864 487-8706
Vice President for Enrollment Services: Chris Phenicie
Admissions e-mail: admiss@limestone.edu
Web site: http://www.limestone.edu
SAT Code: 5366 ACT Code: 3862

LD program name: Program for Alternative Learning Styles
Director of PALS Program: Karen Kearse
LD program telephone: 864 488-8337
LD program e-mail: kkearse@limestone.edu
LD program enrollment: 26, Total campus enrollment: 3,024

GENERAL

Limestone College is a private, coed, four-year institution. 115-acre campus in Gaffney (population: 12,968), 20 miles from Spartanburg and 45 miles from Charlotte, N.C.; 12 evening session sites in South Carolina. Airports serve Charlotte and Greenville-Spartanburg (45 miles); bus and train serve Spartanburg. Semester system.

LD ADMISSIONS

Application Deadline: 08/20. Students do not complete a separate application and are not simultaneously accepted to the LD program. A member of the LD program does sit on the admissions committee. High school waivers are accepted for foreign language. A personal interview is required. Essay is not required.

SECONDARY SCHOOL REQUIREMENTS

Graduation from secondary school required; GED accepted. The following course distribution required: 4 units of English, 3 units of math, 2 units of science, 3 units of social studies.

TESTING

SAT Reasoning or ACT required. SAT Subject required.

All enrolled freshmen (fall 2004):

Average SAT I Scores: Verbal: 485 Math: 489
Average ACT Scores: Composite: 19

Child Study Team report is not required. A neuropsychological or comprehensive psycho-educational evaluation is required for admission. Must be dated within 36 months of application. Tests required as part of this documentation:

■ WAIS-IV
□ WISC-IV
□ SATA
■ Woodcock-Johnson
□ Nelson-Denny Reading Test
□ Other

UNDERGRADUATE STUDENT BODY

Total undergraduate student enrollment: 256 Men, 260 Women.

Composition of student body (fall 2004):

	Undergraduate	Freshmen
International	0.3	0.9
Black	36.4	45.6
American Indian	0.6	0.3
Asian-American	0.9	0.6
Hispanic	2.0	1.8
White	59.8	50.6
Unreported	0.0	0.2
	100.0%	100.0%

37% are from out of state. 2% join a fraternity and 2% join a sorority. Average age of full-time undergraduates is 21. 67% of classes have fewer than 20 students, 33% have between 20 and 50 students.

STUDENT HOUSING

Freshmen are required to live on campus. Housing is guaranteed for all undergraduates. Campus can house 345 undergraduates. Single rooms are available for students with medical or special needs. A medical note is required.

EXPENSES

Tuition (2005-06): $14,040 per year.

Room & Board: $5,800

Additional cost for LD program/services: $1,500 per semester, first year.

LD SERVICES

LD program size is not limited. LD services available to:

■ Freshmen ■ Sophomores ■ Juniors ■ Seniors

Academic Accommodations

Curriculum

Foreign language waiver	□
Lighter course load	■
Math waiver	□
Other special classes	■
Priority registrations	□
Substitution of courses	□

Exams

Extended time	■
Oral exams	■
Take home exams	■
Exams on tape or computer	□
Untimed exams	■
Other accommodations	■

In class

Early syllabus	□
Note takers in class	■
Priority seating	□
Tape recorders	□
Videotaped classes	□
Text on tape	■

Services

Diagnostic tests	□
Learning centers	■
Proofreaders	■
Readers	■
Reading Machines/Kurzweil	□
Special bookstore section	□
Typists	□

Credit toward degree is not given for remedial courses taken.

Counseling Services

■	Academic	Meets 28 times per academic year
■	Psychological	Meets 28 times per academic year
■	Student Support groups	Meets 14 times per academic year
■	Vocational	Meets 14 times per academic year

Tutoring

Individual tutoring is available daily.

Average size of tutoring groups: 13

	Individual	Group
Time management	■	□
Organizational skills	■	□
Learning strategies	■	□
Study skills	■	■
Content area	■	□
Writing lab	■	□
Math lab	□	■

UNIQUE LD PROGRAM FEATURES

The PALS course of study has been developed for students with certified learning disabilities who might otherwise not achieve success at the college level. Two major goals are to provide students with academic support and provide them with instruction in appropriate college survival skills. Participants will receive group instruction in time management, study skills, notetaking, and organization. Individual attention will be provided in the event students require more intensive intervention. In addition, the program director will maintain contact with faculty and provide support for faculty members with those students enrolled in their classes.

LD PROGRAM STAFF

Total number of LD Program staff (including director):

Full Time: 1 Part Time: 1

There is an advisor/advocate from the LD program available to students. The advisor/advocate meets with faculty 1 times per month and student 4 times per month. 26 peer tutors are available to work with LD students.

Key staff person available to work with LD students: Karen Kearse, Director of PALS Program.

LD Program web site: http://www1.limestone.edu/prospect/pals.htm

Newberry College

Newberry, SC

Address: 2100 College Street, Newberry, SC, 29108
Admissions telephone: 800 845-4955, extension 5127
Admissions FAX: 803 321-5138
Director of Admissions: John Casey
Admissions e-mail: admissions@newberry.edu
Web site: http://www.newberry.edu/
SAT Code: 5493 ACT Code: 3870

LD program name: Disability Services
Director of the Academic Skills Center: Marilyn Cooper
LD program telephone: 803 321-5187
LD program e-mail: dtaylor@newberry.edu
LD program enrollment: 20, Total campus enrollment: 789

GENERAL

Newberry College is a private, coed, four-year institution. 60-acre campus in Newberry (population: 10,580), 35 miles from Columbia. Served by bus; major airport, bus, and train serve Columbia. Semester system.

LD ADMISSIONS

A member of the LD program does sit on the admissions committee. A personal interview is required. Essay is not required.

SECONDARY SCHOOL REQUIREMENTS

Graduation from secondary school required; GED accepted. The following course distribution required: 4 units of English, 3 units of math, 2 units of science, 2 units of foreign language, 2 units of social studies, 1 unit of history, 1 unit of academic electives.

TESTING

ACT considered if submitted.

All enrolled freshmen (fall 2004):

Average SAT I Scores: Verbal: 542 Math: 475
Average ACT Scores: Composite: 19

Child Study Team report is required if student is classified. A neuropsychological or comprehensive psycho-educational evaluation is required for admission. Must be dated within 36 months of application. Tests required as part of this documentation:

- [x] WAIS-IV
- [x] WISC-IV
- [ ] SATA
- [x] Woodcock-Johnson
- [ ] Nelson-Denny Reading Test
- [ ] Other

UNDERGRADUATE STUDENT BODY

Total undergraduate student enrollment: 387 Men, 325 Women.

Composition of student body (fall 2004):

	Undergraduate	Freshmen
International	3.0	2.3
Black	28.1	26.0
American Indian	1.3	0.8
Asian-American	0.0	0.1
Hispanic	1.7	1.0
White	65.9	69.8
Unreported	0.0	0.0
	100.0%	100.0%

11% are from out of state. 36% join a fraternity and 25% join a sorority. Average age of full-time undergraduates is 19. 61% of classes have fewer than 20 students, 39% have between 20 and 50 students.

STUDENT HOUSING

92% of freshmen live in college housing. Freshmen are required to live on campus. Housing is guaranteed for all undergraduates. Campus can house 623 undergraduates. Single rooms are available for students with medical or special needs. A medical note is required.

EXPENSES

Tuition (2005-06): $18,170 per year.
Room & Board: $6,320.
Additional cost for LD program/services: $31 per student.

LD SERVICES

LD program size is not limited.

LD services available to:

- [x] Freshmen
- [x] Sophomores
- [x] Juniors
- [x] Seniors

Academic Accommodations

Curriculum		In class	
Foreign language waiver	[ ]	Early syllabus	[ ]
Lighter course load	[ ]	Note takers in class	[x]
Math waiver	[ ]	Priority seating	[x]
Other special classes	[ ]	Tape recorders	[ ]
Priority registrations	[ ]	Videotaped classes	[ ]
Substitution of courses	[ ]	Text on tape	[ ]
Exams		**Services**	
Extended time	[x]	Diagnostic tests	[ ]
Oral exams	[x]	Learning centers	[x]
Take home exams	[ ]	Proofreaders	[x]
Exams on tape or computer	[ ]	Readers	[ ]
Untimed exams	[x]	Reading Machines/Kurzweil	[ ]
Other accommodations	[ ]	Special bookstore section	[ ]
		Typists	[ ]

Credit toward degree is given for remedial courses taken.

Counseling Services

- [ ] Academic
- [ ] Psychological
- [ ] Student Support groups
- [ ] Vocational

Tutoring

Individual tutoring is available daily.

	Individual	Group
Time management	[x]	[x]
Organizational skills	[x]	[x]
Learning strategies	[x]	[x]
Study skills	[x]	[x]
Content area	[x]	[ ]
Writing lab	[x]	[x]
Math lab	[x]	[x]

LD PROGRAM STAFF

Total number of LD Program staff (including director):

There is an advisor/advocate from the LD program available to students. The advisor/advocate meets with faculty 20 times per month and student 3 times per month. 35 peer tutors are available to work with LD students.

Key staff person available to work with LD students: Marilyn Cooper, Director of the Academic Skills Center.

North Greenville College

Tigerville, SC

Address: PO Box 1892, Tigerville, SC, 29688
Admissions telephone: 800 468-6642
Admissions FAX: 864 977-7177
Executive Director of Admissions and Financial Aid: Rev. Charles Freeman
Admissions e-mail: admissions@ngc.edu
Web site: http://www.ngc.edu
SAT Code: 5498

Learning Disabilities Liason: Nancy A. Isgett
LD program telephone: 864 977-7129
LD program e-mail: nisgett@ngc.edu
Total campus enrollment: 1,764

GENERAL

North Greenville College is a private, coed, four-year institution. Rural campus in Tigerville, 18 miles north of Greenville (population: 56,006). Airport and bus serve Greenville. Semester system.

LD ADMISSIONS

A personal interview is recommended. Essay is not required.

SECONDARY SCHOOL REQUIREMENTS

Graduation from secondary school required; GED accepted. The following course distribution required: 4 units of English, 2 units of math, 2 units of science, 2 units of foreign language, 1 unit of social studies, 1 unit of history, 2 units of academic electives.

TESTING

SAT Subject recommended.

All enrolled freshmen (fall 2004):

Average SAT I Scores: Verbal: 516 Math: 508
Average ACT Scores: Composite: 20

Child Study Team report is not required. Tests required as part of this documentation:

- ☐ WAIS-IV
- ☐ WISC-IV
- ☐ SATA
- ☐ Woodcock-Johnson
- ☐ Nelson-Denny Reading Test
- ☐ Other

UNDERGRADUATE STUDENT BODY

Total undergraduate student enrollment: 721 Men, 659 Women.

Composition of student body (fall 2004):

	Undergraduate	Freshmen
International	0.6	4.2
Black	8.6	23.4
American Indian	0.2	0.8
Asian-American	0.4	1.1
Hispanic	1.3	1.9
White	88.3	67.7
Unreported	0.6	0.9
	100.0%	100.0%

16% are from out of state.

STUDENT HOUSING

Housing is guaranteed for all undergraduates. Campus can house 1,200 undergraduates.

EXPENSES

There is no additional cost for LD program/services.

LD SERVICES

LD program size is not limited.

LD services available to:

☐ Freshmen ☐ Sophomores ☐ Juniors ☐ Seniors

Academic Accommodations

Curriculum		In class	
Foreign language waiver	☐	Early syllabus	☐
Lighter course load	■	Note takers in class	■
Math waiver	☐	Priority seating	☐
Other special classes	☐	Tape recorders	☐
Priority registrations	☐	Videotaped classes	☐
Substitution of courses	☐	Text on tape	☐
Exams		**Services**	
Extended time	■	Diagnostic tests	☐
Oral exams	■	Learning centers	☐
Take home exams	☐	Proofreaders	☐
Exams on tape or computer	☐	Readers	☐
Untimed exams	■	Reading Machines/Kurzweil	☐
Other accommodations	☐	Special bookstore section	☐
		Typists	☐

Credit toward degree is not given for remedial courses taken.

Counseling Services

- ☐ Academic
- ☐ Psychological
- ☐ Student Support groups
- ☐ Vocational

Tutoring

	Individual	Group
Time management	☐	☐
Organizational skills	☐	☐
Learning strategies	☐	☐
Study skills	☐	☐
Content area	☐	☐
Writing lab	☐	☐
Math lab	☐	☐

LD PROGRAM STAFF

Total number of LD Program staff (including director):

Full Time: 1 Part Time: 1

Key staff person available to work with LD students: Nancy A. Isgett, Learning Disabilities Liason.

Presbyterian College

Clinton, SC

Address: 503 S. Broad Street, Clinton, SC, 29325
Admissions telephone: 864 833-8230
Admissions FAX: 864 833-8195
Vice President for Enrollment/Dean of Admissions: Richard Dana Paul
Admissions e-mail: admissions@presby.edu
Web site: http://www.presby.edu
SAT Code: 5540 ACT Code: 3874

Vice President: Dr. J. David Gillespie
LD program telephone: 864 833-8233
LD program e-mail: dgillesp@presby.edu
LD program enrollment: 104, Total campus enrollment: 1,187

GENERAL

Presbyterian College is a private, coed, four-year institution. 240-acre campus in Clinton (population: 8,091), 35 miles from Greenville. Major airport and bus serve Greenville-Spartanburg. Semester system.

LD ADMISSIONS

A personal interview is recommended. Essay is required and may be typed.

SECONDARY SCHOOL REQUIREMENTS

Graduation from secondary school required; GED accepted. The following course distribution required: 4 units of English, 3 units of math, 2 units of science, 2 units of foreign language, 2 units of history, 2 units of academic electives.

TESTING

SAT Subject required.

All enrolled freshmen (fall 2004):

Average SAT I Scores:	Verbal: 562	Math: 571
Average ACT Scores:	Composite: 24	

Child Study Team report is not required. Tests required as part of this documentation:

- ☐ WAIS-IV
- ☐ WISC-IV
- ☐ SATA
- ☐ Woodcock-Johnson
- ☐ Nelson-Denny Reading Test
- ☐ Other

UNDERGRADUATE STUDENT BODY

Total undergraduate student enrollment: 572 Men, 663 Women.

Composition of student body (fall 2004):

	Undergraduate	Freshmen
International	0.0	0.0
Black	4.7	4.6
American Indian	0.3	0.1
Asian-American	0.9	0.9
Hispanic	1.2	1.3
White	91.2	91.5
Unreported	1.7	1.6
	100.0%	100.0%

40% are from out of state. 43% join a fraternity and 38% join a sorority. Average age of full-time undergraduates is 20. 63% of classes have fewer than 20 students, 36% have between 20 and 50 students.

STUDENT HOUSING

99% of freshmen live in college housing. Freshmen are required to live on campus. Housing is guaranteed for all undergraduates. Campus can house 1,147 undergraduates.

EXPENSES

Tuition (2005-06): $21,222 per year.

Room: $3,340. Board: $3,460.

There is no additional cost for LD program/services.

LD SERVICES

LD program size is not limited.

LD services available to:

■ Freshmen ■ Sophomores ■ Juniors ■ Seniors

Academic Accommodations

Curriculum		**In class**	
Foreign language waiver	☐	Early syllabus	☐
Lighter course load	■	Note takers in class	☐
Math waiver	☐	Priority seating	☐
Other special classes	☐	Tape recorders	■
Priority registrations	☐	Videotaped classes	☐
Substitution of courses	☐	Text on tape	☐
Exams		**Services**	
Extended time	■	Diagnostic tests	■
Oral exams	■	Learning centers	■
Take home exams	☐	Proofreaders	☐
Exams on tape or computer	☐	Readers	☐
Untimed exams	☐	Reading Machines/Kurzweil	☐
Other accommodations	☐	Special bookstore section	☐
		Typists	☐

Credit toward degree is given for remedial courses taken.

Counseling Services

- ☐ Academic
- ☐ Psychological
- ☐ Student Support groups
- ☐ Vocational

Tutoring

	Individual	Group
Time management	☐	☐
Organizational skills	☐	☐
Learning strategies	☐	☐
Study skills	☐	☐
Content area	☐	☐
Writing lab	☐	☐
Math lab	☐	☐

LD PROGRAM STAFF

Total number of LD Program staff (including director):

Key staff person available to work with LD students: Mrs. Susan Carbonneau, Administrative Assistant, Academic Afairs.

University of South Carolina - Aiken

Aiken, SC

Address: 471 University Parkway, Aiken, SC, 29801
Admissions telephone: 888 969-8722
Admissions FAX: 803 641-3727
Dean of Enrollment Planning: Mr. Andrew Hendrix
Admissions e-mail: admit@sc.edu
Web site: http://www.usca.edu
SAT Code: 5840 ACT Code: 3879

LD program name: Office of Disability Services
Director of Disability Services: Kay Benitez
LD program telephone: 803 641-3609
LD program e-mail: kayb@usca.edu
LD program enrollment: 107, Total campus enrollment: 3,268

GENERAL

University of South Carolina Aiken is a public, coed, four-year institution. 354-acre campus in Aiken (population: 25,337), 15 miles from Augusta, Ga., and 55 miles from Columbia. Served by bus; airport serves Augusta; train serves Denmark (30 miles). Semester system.

LD ADMISSIONS

Students do not complete a separate application and are not simultaneously accepted to the LD program. A member of the LD program does not sit on the admissions committee. High school waivers are accepted for foreign language. A personal interview is recommended. Essay is not required. Admissions requirements for LD students are the same criteria as any other applicant.

For fall 2004, 68 completed self-identified LD applications were received. 42 applications were offered admission, and 42 enrolled.

SECONDARY SCHOOL REQUIREMENTS

Graduation from secondary school not required. The following course distribution required: 4 units of English, 4 units of math, 3 units of science, 2 units of foreign language, 2 units of social studies, 1 unit of history, 4 units of academic electives.

TESTING

SAT Reasoning required; ACT may be substituted. SAT Subject recommended.

All enrolled freshmen (fall 2004):

Average SAT I Scores:	Verbal: 492	Math: 502
Average ACT Scores:	Composite: 19	

Child Study Team report is not required. A neuropsychological or comprehensive psycho-educational evaluation is required for admission. Must be dated within 36 months of application. Tests required as part of this documentation:

- [x] WAIS-IV
- [x] WISC-IV
- [x] SATA
- [x] Woodcock-Johnson
- [x] Nelson-Denny Reading Test
- [ ] Other

UNDERGRADUATE STUDENT BODY

Total undergraduate student enrollment: 1,058 Men, 2,032 Women.

Composition of student body (fall 2004):

	Undergraduate	Freshmen
International	1.5	1.8
Black	28.5	25.1
American Indian	0.3	0.3
Asian-American	0.6	0.8
Hispanic	1.9	1.6
White	62.7	66.6
Unreported	4.5	3.8
	100.0%	100.0%

16% are from out of state. Average age of full-time undergraduates is 22. 51% of classes have fewer than 20 students, 49% have between 20 and 50 students.

STUDENT HOUSING

Freshmen are not required to live on campus. Housing is guaranteed for all undergraduates. Campus can house 680 undergraduates. Single rooms are available for students with medical or special needs. A medical note is required.

EXPENSES

Tuition (2005-06): $5,910 per year (in-state), $12,003 (out-of-state). Room: $3,000. Board: $1,650.
There is no additional cost for LD program/services.

LD SERVICES

LD program size is not limited.

LD services available to:

- [x] Freshmen
- [x] Sophomores
- [x] Juniors
- [x] Seniors

Academic Accommodations

Curriculum		**In class**	
Foreign language waiver	[x]	Early syllabus	[ ]
Lighter course load	[x]	Note takers in class	[x]
Math waiver	[x]	Priority seating	[x]
Other special classes	[ ]	Tape recorders	[x]
Priority registrations	[x]	Videotaped classes	[x]
Substitution of courses	[x]	Text on tape	[x]
Exams		**Services**	
Extended time	[x]	Diagnostic tests	[ ]
Oral exams	[x]	Learning centers	[x]
Take home exams	[ ]	Proofreaders	[x]
Exams on tape or computer	[x]	Readers	[x]
Untimed exams	[ ]	Reading Machines/Kurzweil	[x]
Other accommodations	[x]	Special bookstore section	[ ]
		Typists	[x]

Credit toward degree is not given for remedial courses taken.

Counseling Services

[x]	Academic	Meets 6 times per academic year
[x]	Psychological	Meets 10 times per academic year
[x]	Student Support groups	Meets 30 times per academic year
[x]	Vocational	Meets 2 times per academic year

Tutoring

Individual tutoring is available weekly.

Average size of tutoring groups: 1

	Individual	Group
Time management	[ ]	[x]
Organizational skills	[ ]	[x]
Learning strategies	[ ]	[x]
Study skills	[ ]	[x]
Content area	[x]	[x]
Writing lab	[x]	[x]
Math lab	[x]	[x]

LD PROGRAM STAFF

Total number of LD Program staff (including director):

Full Time: 1 Part Time: 1

There is not an advisor/advocate from the LD program available to students. 1 graduate students and 4 peer tutors are available to work with LD students.

Key staff person available to work with LD students: Kay Benitez, Director of Disability Services and Assistive Tech.

LD Program web site: http://www.usca.edu/ds/

University of South Carolina - Columbia

Columbia, SC

Address: Columbia, SC, 29208
Admissions telephone: 800 868-5872
Admissions FAX: 803 777-0101
Director of Undergraduate Admissions: R. Scott Verzyl
Admissions e-mail: admissions-ugrad@sc.edu
Web site: http://www.sc.edu
SAT Code: 5818 ACT Code: 3880

Director, Student Disability: Deborah C. Haynes
LD program telephone: 803 777-6142
LD program e-mail: debbieh@gwm.sc.edu
LD program enrollment: 327, Total campus enrollment: 17,689

GENERAL

University of South Carolina (Columbia) is a public, coed, four-year institution. 351-acre, urban campus in Columbia (population: 116,278); branch campuses in Allendale, Beaufort, Lancaster, Sumter, and Union. Served by air, bus, and train. School operates transportation to parking areas. Public transportation serves campus. Semester system.

LD ADMISSIONS

A personal interview is recommended. Essay is not required. Admissions requirements that may be waived for LD students include petition for waiver or substitution of the 20 academic units required for admission

SECONDARY SCHOOL REQUIREMENTS

Graduation from secondary school required; GED accepted. The following course distribution required: 4 units of English, 3 units of math, 3 units of science, 2 units of foreign language, 2 units of social studies, 1 unit of history, 4 units of academic electives.

TESTING

SAT Reasoning or ACT required. SAT Subject required.

All enrolled freshmen (fall 2004):

Average SAT I Scores: Verbal: 569 Math: 582
Average ACT Scores: Composite: 24

Child Study Team report is not required. Tests required as part of this documentation:

- ☐ WAIS-IV
- ☐ WISC-IV
- ☐ SATA
- ☐ Woodcock-Johnson
- ☐ Nelson-Denny Reading Test
- ☐ Other

UNDERGRADUATE STUDENT BODY

Total undergraduate student enrollment: 7,091 Men, 8,415 Women.

Composition of student body (fall 2004):

	Undergraduate	Freshmen
International	0.6	1.2
Black	11.3	14.7
American Indian	0.4	0.3
Asian-American	2.9	2.8
Hispanic	2.0	1.7
White	69.6	70.6
Unreported	13.2	8.7
	100.0%	100.0%

13% are from out of state. 14% join a fraternity and 15% join a sorority. Average age of full-time undergraduates is 21. 43% of classes have fewer than 20 students, 46% have between 20 and 50 students, 11% have more than 50 students.

STUDENT HOUSING

90% of freshmen live in college housing. Housing is not guaranteed for all undergraduates. Guaranteed on-campus housing for freshmen Campus can house 6,937 undergraduates.

EXPENSES

Tuition (2005-06): $6,914 per year (in-state), $18,556 (out-of-state). Tuition is higher for health professions programs.

Room & Board: $6,080

There is no additional cost for LD program/services.

LD SERVICES

LD program size is not limited.

LD services available to:

☐ Freshmen ☐ Sophomores ☐ Juniors ☐ Seniors

Academic Accommodations

Curriculum		In class	
Foreign language waiver	☐	Early syllabus	☐
Lighter course load	■	Note takers in class	■
Math waiver	☐	Priority seating	☐
Other special classes	☐	Tape recorders	■
Priority registrations	☐	Videotaped classes	☐
Substitution of courses	☐	Text on tape	☐
Exams		**Services**	
Extended time	■	Diagnostic tests	☐
Oral exams	☐	Learning centers	☐
Take home exams	☐	Proofreaders	☐
Exams on tape or computer	☐	Readers	■
Untimed exams	■	Reading Machines/Kurzweil	■
Other accommodations	☐	Special bookstore section	☐
		Typists	☐

Credit toward degree is not given for remedial courses taken.

Counseling Services

- ☐ Academic
- ☐ Psychological
- ☐ Student Support groups
- ☐ Vocational

Tutoring

	Individual	Group
Time management	☐	☐
Organizational skills	☐	☐
Learning strategies	☐	☐
Study skills	☐	☐
Content area	☐	☐
Writing lab	☐	☐
Math lab	☐	☐

UNIQUE LD PROGRAM FEATURES

LD PROGRAM STAFF

Total number of LD Program staff (including director):

Full Time: 2 Part Time: 2

Key staff person available to work with LD students: Deborah C. Haynes, Director, Student Disability.

University of South Carolina - Upstate

Spartanburg, SC

Address: 800 University Way, Spartanburg, SC, 29303
Admissions telephone: 800 277-8727
Admissions FAX: 864 503-5727
Director of Admissions: Ms. Donette Stewart
Admissions e-mail: admissions@uscupstate.edu
Web site: http://www.uscupstate.edu/
SAT Code: 5850 ACT Code: 3889

LD program name: Office of Disability Services
Assistant Director of Student Development: Jim Gorske
LD program telephone: 864 503-5199
LD program e-mail: jgorske@uscupstate.edu
LD program enrollment: 20, Total campus enrollment: 4,277

GENERAL

University of South Carolina - Upstate is a public, coed, four-year institution. 298-acre campus in Spartanburg (population: 39,673), 95 miles from Columbia and 70 miles from Charlotte, N.C.; branch campus in Greenville. Served by air, bus, and train. Public transportation serves campus. Semester system.

LD ADMISSIONS

Application Deadline: 08/15. Students do not complete a separate application and are not simultaneously accepted to the LD program. A member of the LD program does not sit on the admissions committee. High school waivers are accepted for foreign language. A personal interview is recommended. Essay is not required.

SECONDARY SCHOOL REQUIREMENTS

Graduation from secondary school required; GED accepted. The following course distribution required: 4 units of English, 3 units of math, 3 units of science, 2 units of foreign language, 2 units of social studies, 1 unit of history, 4 units of academic electives.

TESTING

SAT Reasoning or ACT required. SAT Subject recommended.

All enrolled freshmen (fall 2004):

Average SAT I Scores:	Verbal: 502	Math: 510
Average ACT Scores:	Composite: 21	

Child Study Team report is not required. A neuropsychological or comprehensive psycho-education evaluation is not required for admission. Tests required as part of this documentation:

- [ ] WAIS-IV
- [ ] WISC-IV
- [ ] SATA
- [ ] Woodcock-Johnson
- [ ] Nelson-Denny Reading Test
- [ ] Other

UNDERGRADUATE STUDENT BODY

Total undergraduate student enrollment: 1,397 Men, 2,502 Women.

Composition of student body (fall 2004):

	Undergraduate	Freshmen
International	1.9	1.8
Black	26.6	25.5
American Indian	0.3	0.3
Asian-American	2.2	2.7
Hispanic	1.1	2.5
White	63.4	64.1
Unreported	4.5	3.1
	100.0%	100.0%

5% are from out of state. 3% join a fraternity. Average age of full-time undergraduates is 23. 51% of classes have fewer than 20 students, 48% have between 20 and 50 students, 1% have more than 50 students.

STUDENT HOUSING

50% of freshmen live in college housing. Freshmen are not required to live on campus. Housing is guaranteed for all undergraduates. Campus can house 744 undergraduates. Single rooms are available for students with medical or special needs. A medical note is required.

EXPENSES

Tuition (2005-06): $6,436 per year (in-state), $13,274 (out-of-state).
Room: $3,200. Board: $2,040.
There is no additional cost for LD program/services.

LD SERVICES

LD program size is not limited.

LD services available to:

- [x] Freshmen
- [x] Sophomores
- [x] Juniors
- [x] Seniors

Academic Accommodations

Curriculum		In class	
Foreign language waiver	[ ]	Early syllabus	[ ]
Lighter course load	[ ]	Note takers in class	[x]
Math waiver	[ ]	Priority seating	[x]
Other special classes	[ ]	Tape recorders	[x]
Priority registrations	[x]	Videotaped classes	[ ]
Substitution of courses	[x]	Text on tape	[x]
Exams		**Services**	
Extended time	[x]	Diagnostic tests	[ ]
Oral exams	[ ]	Learning centers	[x]
Take home exams	[ ]	Proofreaders	[x]
Exams on tape or computer	[x]	Readers	[ ]
Untimed exams	[ ]	Reading Machines/Kurzweil	[x]
Other accommodations	[x]	Special bookstore section	[ ]
		Typists	[ ]

Credit toward degree is not given for remedial courses taken.

Counseling Services

- [x] Academic
- [ ] Psychological
- [ ] Student Support groups
- [ ] Vocational

Tutoring

Individual tutoring is available weekly.

	Individual	Group
Time management	[x]	[x]
Organizational skills	[x]	[x]
Learning strategies	[x]	[ ]
Study skills	[x]	[x]
Content area	[x]	[ ]
Writing lab	[x]	[ ]
Math lab	[x]	[ ]

LD PROGRAM STAFF

Total number of LD Program staff (including director):

Full Time: 1 Part Time: 1

There is an advisor/advocate from the LD program available to students. 5 peer tutors are available to work with LD students.

Key staff person available to work with LD students: Jim Gorske, Assistant Director of Student Development.

Southern Wesleyan University

Central, SC

Address: PO Box 1020, SWU, Wesleyan Drive, Central, SC, 29630
Admissions telephone: 800 282-8798
Admissions FAX: 864 644-5972
Director of Admissions: Chad Peters
Admissions e-mail: admissions@swu.edu
Web site: http://www.swu.edu
SAT Code: 5896 ACT Code: 3837

Director: Carol Sinnamon
LD program telephone: 804 644-5133
LD program e-mail: csinnamon@swu.edu
Total campus enrollment: 2,047

GENERAL

Southern Wesleyan University is a private, coed, four-year institution. 210-acre campus in Central (population: 3,522), 20 miles from Greenville; branch campuses in Charleston, Columbia, Greenville, Greenwood, and North Augusta. Airport and bus serve Greenville; major airport serves Atlanta (120 miles); train serves Clemson (five miles). School operates transportation to Atlanta, Clemson, and Greenville. Semester system.

LD ADMISSIONS

A personal interview is recommended.

SECONDARY SCHOOL REQUIREMENTS

Graduation from secondary school required; GED accepted. The following course distribution required: 4 units of English, 2 units of math, 2 units of science, 2 units of social studies.

TESTING

SAT Reasoning or ACT required. SAT Subject recommended.

All enrolled freshmen (fall 2004):

Average SAT I Scores: Verbal: 508 Math: 510
Average ACT Scores: Composite: 20

Child Study Team report is not required. Tests required as part of this documentation:

- ❑ WAIS-IV
- ❑ WISC-IV
- ❑ SATA
- ❑ Woodcock-Johnson
- ❑ Nelson-Denny Reading Test
- ❑ Other

UNDERGRADUATE STUDENT BODY

Total undergraduate student enrollment: 740 Men, 1,256 Women.

Composition of student body (fall 2004):

	Undergraduate	Freshmen
International	0.0	0.4
Black	9.8	34.5
American Indian	0.0	0.6
Asian-American	0.8	0.3
Hispanic	3.3	1.6
White	85.3	59.0
Unreported	0.8	3.6
	100.0%	100.0%

13% are from out of state. Average age of full-time undergraduates is 34. 88% of classes have fewer than 20 students, 12% have between 20 and 50 students.

STUDENT HOUSING

84% of freshmen live in college housing. Freshmen are required to live on campus. Housing is guaranteed for all undergraduates. Campus can house 362 undergraduates.

EXPENSES

Tuition (2005-06): $15,000 per year.
Room & Board: $5,450

There is no additional cost for LD program/services.

LD SERVICES

LD program size is not limited.

LD services available to:

❑ Freshmen ❑ Sophomores ❑ Juniors ❑ Seniors

Academic Accommodations

Curriculum		**In class**	
Foreign language waiver	❑	Early syllabus	❑
Lighter course load	❑	Note takers in class	■
Math waiver	❑	Priority seating	❑
Other special classes	❑	Tape recorders	❑
Priority registrations	❑	Videotaped classes	❑
Substitution of courses	❑	Text on tape	❑
Exams		**Services**	
Extended time	■	Diagnostic tests	❑
Oral exams	❑	Learning centers	■
Take home exams	❑	Proofreaders	❑
Exams on tape or computer	❑	Readers	❑
Untimed exams	❑	Reading Machines/Kurzweil	❑
Other accommodations	❑	Special bookstore section	❑
		Typists	❑

Credit toward degree is not given for remedial courses taken.

Counseling Services

- ❑ Academic
- ❑ Psychological
- ❑ Student Support groups
- ❑ Vocational

Tutoring

	Individual	Group
Time management	❑	❑
Organizational skills	❑	❑
Learning strategies	❑	❑
Study skills	❑	❑
Content area	❑	❑
Writing lab	❑	❑
Math lab	❑	❑

UNIQUE LD PROGRAM FEATURES

We consult with the student and staff each semester to provide services through individualized plans offering support and encouraging independence

LD PROGRAM STAFF

Total number of LD Program staff (including director):

Full Time: 1 Part Time: 1

The Citadel

Charleston, SC

Address: 171 Moultrie Street, Charleston, SC, 29409
Admissions telephone: 843 953-5230
Admissions FAX: 843 953-7036
Director of Admissions: Lt. Col. John W. Powell, Jr.
Admissions e-mail: admissions@citadel.edu
Web site: http://www.citadel.edu
SAT Code: 5108   ACT Code: 3838

LD program name: Access Svcs, Instruction and Support
Director, OASIS: Dr. Barbara Zaremba
LD program telephone: 843 953-1820
LD program e-mail: zarembab@citadel.edu
Total campus enrollment: 2,177

GENERAL

The Citadel is a public, coed, four-year institution. 100-acre, urban campus in Charleston (population: 96,650). Served by airport, bus, and train. Public transportation serves campus. Semester system.

LD ADMISSIONS

Students do not complete a separate application and are not simultaneously accepted to the LD program. A member of the LD program does not sit on the admissions committee. A personal interview is not required. Essay is not required.

SECONDARY SCHOOL REQUIREMENTS

Graduation from secondary school required; GED accepted. The following course distribution required: 4 units of English, 3 units of math, 3 units of science, 2 units of foreign language, 2 units of social studies, 1 unit of history, 4 units of academic electives.

TESTING

SAT Reasoning required; ACT may be substituted. SAT Subject recommended.

All enrolled freshmen (fall 2004):

Average SAT I Scores:	Verbal: 538	Math: 539
Average ACT Scores:	Composite: 22	

Child Study Team report is not required. A neuropsychological or comprehensive psycho-educational evaluation is required for admission. Tests required as part of this documentation:

- [x] WAIS-IV
- [ ] WISC-IV
- [ ] SATA
- [x] Woodcock-Johnson
- [ ] Nelson-Denny Reading Test
- [ ] Other

UNDERGRADUATE STUDENT BODY

Total undergraduate student enrollment: 1,970 Men, 130 Women.

Composition of student body (fall 2004):

	Undergraduate	Freshmen
International	1.4	2.1
Black	7.2	7.7
American Indian	0.0	0.1
Asian-American	2.5	2.6
Hispanic	5.4	4.2
White	82.8	83.1
Unreported	0.7	0.2
	100.0%	100.0%

52% are from out of state. Average age of full-time undergraduates is 20. 43% of classes have fewer than 20 students, 54% have between 20 and 50 students, 3% have more than 50 students.

STUDENT HOUSING

100% of freshmen live in college housing. Freshmen are required to live on campus. Housing is guaranteed for all undergraduates. Campus can house 1,913 undergraduates. Single rooms are not available for students with medical or special needs.

EXPENSES

Tuition (2005-06): $13,806 per year (comprehensive, state residents), $20,481 (comprehensive, out-of-state) for freshmen. $10,546 per year (comprehensive, state residents), $21,221 (comprehensive, out-of-state) for upperclassmen.

There is no additional cost for LD program/services.

LD SERVICES

LD program size is not limited.

LD services available to:

- [x] Freshmen
- [x] Sophomores
- [x] Juniors
- [x] Seniors

Academic Accommodations

Curriculum		**In class**	
Foreign language waiver	[ ]	Early syllabus	[x]
Lighter course load	[ ]	Note takers in class	[x]
Math waiver	[ ]	Priority seating	[ ]
Other special classes	[ ]	Tape recorders	[x]
Priority registrations	[x]	Videotaped classes	[ ]
Substitution of courses	[x]	Text on tape	[x]
Exams		**Services**	
Extended time	[x]	Diagnostic tests	[ ]
Oral exams	[x]	Learning centers	[x]
Take home exams	[ ]	Proofreaders	[x]
Exams on tape or computer	[x]	Readers	[x]
Untimed exams	[x]	Reading Machines/Kurzweil	[ ]
Other accommodations	[x]	Special bookstore section	[ ]
		Typists	[x]

Credit toward degree is not given for remedial courses taken.

Counseling Services

- [x] Academic
- [ ] Psychological
- [x] Student Support groups
- [ ] Vocational

Tutoring

Individual tutoring is available weekly.

	Individual	Group
Time management	[x]	[ ]
Organizational skills	[x]	[ ]
Learning strategies	[x]	[ ]
Study skills	[x]	[ ]
Content area	[x]	[ ]
Writing lab	[x]	[x]
Math lab	[x]	[x]

LD PROGRAM STAFF

Total number of LD Program staff (including director):

Full Time: 2   Part Time: 2

There is an advisor/advocate from the LD program available to students.

Key staff person available to work with LD students: Dr. Barbara Zaremba, Director, OASIS.

LD Program web site: http://www3.citadel.edu/oasis/

Winthrop University

Rock Hill, SC

Address: 701 Oakland Avenue, Rock Hill, SC, 29733
Admissions telephone: 803 323-2191
Admissions FAX: 803 323-2137
Director of Admissions: Debi Barber
Admissions e-mail: admissions@winthrop.edu
Web site: http://www.winthrop.edu
SAT Code: 5910 ACT Code: 3884

Counselor for Students with Disabilities: Gena Smith
LD program telephone: 803 323-2233
LD program e-mail: smithg@winthrop.edu
Total campus enrollment: 5,213

GENERAL

Winthrop University is a public, coed, four-year institution. 418-acre campus in Rock Hill (population: 49,765), 20 miles from Charlotte, N.C. Major airport, bus, and train serve Charlotte. Semester system.

SECONDARY SCHOOL REQUIREMENTS

Graduation from secondary school required; GED accepted. The following course distribution required: 4 units of English, 3 units of math, 3 units of science, 2 units of foreign language, 2 units of social studies, 1 unit of history, 4 units of academic electives.

TESTING

SAT Reasoning or ACT required.

All enrolled freshmen (fall 2004):

Average SAT I Scores:	Verbal: 536	Math: 532
Average ACT Scores:	Composite: 21	

Child Study Team report is not required. Tests required as part of this documentation:

- [ ] WAIS-IV
- [ ] WISC-IV
- [ ] SATA
- [ ] Woodcock-Johnson
- [ ] Nelson-Denny Reading Test
- [ ] Other

UNDERGRADUATE STUDENT BODY

Total undergraduate student enrollment: 1,485 Men, 3,353 Women.

Composition of student body (fall 2004):

	Undergraduate	Freshmen
International	1.6	1.7
Black	28.1	27.6
American Indian	0.5	0.4
Asian-American	1.1	1.0
Hispanic	1.4	1.3
White	67.3	68.0
Unreported	0.0	0.0
	100.0%	100.0%

11% are from out of state. 12% join a fraternity and 14% join a sorority. Average age of full-time undergraduates is 21. 41% of classes have fewer than 20 students, 55% have between 20 and 50 students, 4% have more than 50 students.

STUDENT HOUSING

86% of freshmen live in college housing. Freshmen are required to live on campus. Housing is guaranteed for all undergraduates. Campus can house 2,559 undergraduates.

EXPENSES

Tuition (2005-06): $8,756 per year (in-state), $16,150 (out-of-state).
Room: $3,420. Board: $1,932.

There is no additional cost for LD program/services.

LD SERVICES

LD program size is not limited.

LD services available to:

- [ ] Freshmen
- [ ] Sophomores
- [ ] Juniors
- [ ] Seniors

Academic Accommodations

Curriculum		In class	
Foreign language waiver	[ ]	Early syllabus	[ ]
Lighter course load	[ ]	Note takers in class	[x]
Math waiver	[ ]	Priority seating	[ ]
Other special classes	[ ]	Tape recorders	[x]
Priority registrations	[ ]	Videotaped classes	[ ]
Substitution of courses	[ ]	Text on tape	[ ]
Exams		**Services**	
Extended time	[x]	Diagnostic tests	[ ]
Oral exams	[x]	Learning centers	[ ]
Take home exams	[ ]	Proofreaders	[ ]
Exams on tape or computer	[ ]	Readers	[x]
Untimed exams	[ ]	Reading Machines/Kurzweil	[ ]
Other accommodations	[ ]	Special bookstore section	[ ]
		Typists	[ ]

Credit toward degree is not given for remedial courses taken.

Counseling Services

- [ ] Academic
- [ ] Psychological
- [ ] Student Support groups
- [ ] Vocational

Tutoring

	Individual	Group
Time management	[ ]	[ ]
Organizational skills	[ ]	[ ]
Learning strategies	[ ]	[ ]
Study skills	[ ]	[ ]
Content area	[ ]	[ ]
Writing lab	[ ]	[ ]
Math lab	[ ]	[ ]

LD PROGRAM STAFF

Total number of LD Program staff (including director):

Full Time: 1 Part Time: 1

Key staff person available to work with LD students: Gena Smith, Counselor for Students with Disabilities.

Wofford College

Spartanburg, SC

Address: 429 N. Church Street, Spartanburg, SC, 29303-3663
Admissions telephone: 864 597-4130
Admissions FAX: 864 597-4147
Director of Admissions: Brand R. Stille
Admissions e-mail: admissions@wofford.edu
Web site: http://www.wofford.edu
SAT Code: 5912 ACT Code: 3886

Associate Dean of Students: Elizabeth D. Wallace
LD program telephone: 864 597-4371
LD program e-mail: wallaceedEwofford.edu
Total campus enrollment: 1,161

GENERAL

Wofford College is a private, coed, four-year institution. 140-acre campus in Spartanburg (population: 39,673), 65 miles from Charlotte, N.C. Served by air, bus, and train; major airport serves Charlotte. School operates transportation to airport by arrangement. Public transportation serves campus. 4-1-4 system.

LD ADMISSIONS

A personal interview is recommended. Essay is required and may be typed.

SECONDARY SCHOOL REQUIREMENTS

Graduation from secondary school required; GED accepted.

TESTING

SAT Reasoning or ACT required. SAT Subject required.

All enrolled freshmen (fall 2004):

Average SAT I Scores:	Verbal: 616	Math: 631
Average ACT Scores:	Composite: 25	

Child Study Team report is not required. Tests required as part of this documentation:

- ☐ WAIS-IV
- ☐ WISC-IV
- ☐ SATA
- ☐ Woodcock-Johnson
- ☐ Nelson-Denny Reading Test
- ☐ Other

UNDERGRADUATE STUDENT BODY

Total undergraduate student enrollment: 578 Men, 529 Women.

Composition of student body (fall 2004):

	Undergraduate	Freshmen
International	0.6	0.4
Black	4.0	7.1
American Indian	0.3	0.1
Asian-American	2.8	2.2
Hispanic	0.9	0.9
White	90.5	88.6
Unreported	0.9	0.7
	100.0%	100.0%

33% are from out of state. 50% join a fraternity and 60% join a sorority. Average age of full-time undergraduates is 20. 72% of classes have fewer than 20 students, 27% have between 20 and 50 students, 1% have more than 50 students.

STUDENT HOUSING

98% of freshmen live in college housing. Freshmen are required to live on campus. Housing is guaranteed for all undergraduates. Campus can house 1,066 undergraduates. Single rooms are available for students with medical or special needs. A medical note is required.

EXPENSES

Tuition (2005-06): $24,130 per year.
Room & Board: $6,805

LD SERVICES

LD program size is not limited.

LD services available to:

☐ Freshmen ☐ Sophomores ☐ Juniors ☐ Seniors

Academic Accommodations

Curriculum		**In class**	
Foreign language waiver	☐	Early syllabus	☐
Lighter course load	■	Note takers in class	☐
Math waiver	☐	Priority seating	☐
Other special classes	☐	Tape recorders	■
Priority registrations	☐	Videotaped classes	☐
Substitution of courses	☐	Text on tape	☐
Exams		**Services**	
Extended time	■	Diagnostic tests	☐
Oral exams	☐	Learning centers	☐
Take home exams	☐	Proofreaders	☐
Exams on tape or computer	☐	Readers	☐
Untimed exams	☐	Reading Machines/Kurzweil	☐
Other accommodations	☐	Special bookstore section	☐
		Typists	☐

Counseling Services

- ☐ Academic
- ☐ Psychological
- ☐ Student Support groups
- ☐ Vocational

Tutoring

	Individual	Group
Time management	☐	☐
Organizational skills	☐	☐
Learning strategies	☐	☐
Study skills	☐	☐
Content area	☐	☐
Writing lab	☐	☐
Math lab	☐	☐

LD PROGRAM STAFF

Total number of LD Program staff (including director):

Full Time: 2 Part Time: 2

Key staff person available to work with LD students: Elizabeth D. Wallace, Associate Dean of Students.

Augustana College

Sioux Falls, SD

Address: 2001 S. Summit Avenue, Sioux Falls, SD, 57197
Admissions telephone: 800 727-2844
Admissions FAX: 605 274-5518
Vice President for Enrollment: Nancy Davidson
Admissions e-mail: admission@augie.edu
Web site: http://www.augie.edu
SAT Code: 1025 ACT Code: 3902

LD program name: Academic Resource Services
LD program address: 2001 South Summit Avenue,
Academic Resource Services Director: Susan Bies
LD program telephone: 605 274-5503
LD program e-mail: susan_Bies@augie.edu
Total campus enrollment: 1,770

GENERAL

Augustana College is a private, coed, four-year institution. 100-acre campus in Sioux Falls (population: 123,975), 160 miles from Omaha. Served by air and bus. Public transportation serves campus. 4-1-4 system.

LD ADMISSIONS

Students do not complete a separate application and are not simultaneously accepted to the LD program. A member of the LD program does sit on the admissions committee. A personal interview is recommended. Essay is not required.

SECONDARY SCHOOL REQUIREMENTS

Graduation from secondary school required; GED accepted.

TESTING

SAT Reasoning or ACT required. SAT Subject recommended.

All enrolled freshmen (fall 2004):

Average SAT I Scores:	Verbal: 620	Math: 630
Average ACT Scores:	Composite: 25	

Child Study Team report is not required. A neuropsychological or comprehensive psycho-education evaluation is not required for admission. Tests required as part of this documentation:

- ☐ WAIS-IV
- ☐ WISC-IV
- ☐ SATA
- ☐ Woodcock-Johnson
- ☐ Nelson-Denny Reading Test
- ☐ Other

UNDERGRADUATE STUDENT BODY

Total undergraduate student enrollment: 617 Men, 1,157 Women.

Composition of student body (fall 2004):

	Undergraduate	Freshmen
International	0.7	1.8
Black	1.0	1.2
American Indian	0.5	0.5
Asian-American	0.7	0.6
Hispanic	0.2	0.4
White	96.4	95.4
Unreported	0.5	0.1
	100.0%	100.0%

49% are from out of state. Average age of full-time undergraduates is 20. 43% of classes have fewer than 20 students, 55% have between 20 and 50 students, 2% have more than 50 students.

STUDENT HOUSING

98% of freshmen live in college housing. Freshmen are required to live on campus. Housing is guaranteed for all undergraduates. Campus can house 1,300 undergraduates. Single rooms are available for students with medical or special needs. A medical note is required.

EXPENSES

Tuition (2005-06): $18,634 per year.
Room: $2,678. Board: $2,656.

There is no additional cost for LD program/services.

LD SERVICES

LD program size is not limited.

LD services available to:

☑ Freshmen ☑ Sophomores ☑ Juniors ☑ Seniors

Academic Accommodations

Curriculum		In class	
Foreign language waiver	☐	Early syllabus	☐
Lighter course load	☐	Note takers in class	☑
Math waiver	☐	Priority seating	☐
Other special classes	☐	Tape recorders	☑
Priority registrations	☐	Videotaped classes	☑
Substitution of courses	☐	Text on tape	☐
Exams		**Services**	
Extended time	☑	Diagnostic tests	☐
Oral exams	☑	Learning centers	☑
Take home exams	☐	Proofreaders	☐
Exams on tape or computer	☐	Readers	☑
Untimed exams	☑	Reading Machines/Kurzweil	☐
Other accommodations	☑	Special bookstore section	☐
		Typists	☐

Credit toward degree is not given for remedial courses taken.

Counseling Services

- ☑ Academic
- ☑ Psychological
- ☐ Student Support groups
- ☐ Vocational

Tutoring

Individual tutoring is available daily.

	Individual	Group
Time management	☐	☐
Organizational skills	☐	☐
Learning strategies	☐	☐
Study skills	☐	☐
Content area	☐	☐
Writing lab	☑	☑
Math lab	☐	☐

LD PROGRAM STAFF

Total number of LD Program staff (including director):

Full Time: 1 Part Time: 1

There is an advisor/advocate from the LD program available to students.

Key staff person available to work with LD students: Susan Bies, Academic Resource Services Director.

LD Program web site: http://www.augie.edu/student_serv/disability.html

Dakota State University

Madison, SD

Address: 820 N. Washington Avenue, Madison, SD, 57042
Admissions telephone: 888 DSU-9988
Admissions FAX: 605 256-5020
Director of Admission: Amy Crissinger
Admissions e-mail: dsuinfo@dsu.edu
Web site: http://www.dsu.edu
SAT Code: 6247 ACT Code: 3910

LD program name: Disability Services
Associate Professor: Robert Jackson
LD program telephone: 605 256-5823
LD program e-mail: robert.jackson@dsu.edu
LD program enrollment: 35, Total campus enrollment: 2,065

GENERAL

Dakota State University is a public, coed, four-year institution. 40-acre campus in Madison (population: 6,540), 50 miles from Sioux Falls; branch campus in Sioux Falls. Airport, bus, and train serve Sioux Falls. Semester system.

LD ADMISSIONS

Students do not complete a separate application and are not simultaneously accepted to the LD program. A member of the LD program does sit on the admissions committee. A personal interview is not required. Essay is not required.

For fall 2004, 37 completed self-identified LD applications were received. 36 applications were offered admission, and 36 enrolled.

SECONDARY SCHOOL REQUIREMENTS

Graduation from secondary school required; GED accepted.

TESTING

SAT Reasoning or ACT required.

All enrolled freshmen (fall 2004):

Average SAT I Scores:	Verbal:	Math:
Average ACT Scores:	Composite: 21	

Child Study Team report is not required. A neuropsychological or comprehensive psycho-educational evaluation is required for admission. Must be dated within 24 months of application. Tests required as part of this documentation:

- [x] WAIS-IV
- [ ] WISC-IV
- [ ] SATA
- [x] Woodcock-Johnson
- [x] Nelson-Denny Reading Test
- [ ] Other

UNDERGRADUATE STUDENT BODY

Total undergraduate student enrollment: 941 Men, 902 Women.

Composition of student body (fall 2004):

	Undergraduate	Freshmen
International	1.8	0.9
Black	1.5	1.2
American Indian	0.0	1.0
Asian-American	1.1	0.9
Hispanic	1.5	0.7
White	90.1	90.2
Unreported	4.0	5.1
	100.0%	100.0%

16% are from out of state. Average age of full-time undergraduates is 23. 48% of classes have fewer than 20 students, 49% have between 20 and 50 students, 3% have more than 50 students.

STUDENT HOUSING

Housing is guaranteed for all undergraduates. Campus can house 692 undergraduates. Single rooms are available for students with medical or special needs. A medical note is required.

EXPENSES

Tuition (2005-06): $2,290 per year (in-state), $7,278 (out-of-state).
Room: $1,815. Board: $1,911.
There is no additional cost for LD program/services.

LD SERVICES

LD program size is not limited.

LD services available to:

- [x] Freshmen
- [x] Sophomores
- [x] Juniors
- [x] Seniors

Academic Accommodations

Curriculum		In class	
Foreign language waiver	[ ]	Early syllabus	[x]
Lighter course load	[ ]	Note takers in class	[x]
Math waiver	[ ]	Priority seating	[x]
Other special classes	[x]	Tape recorders	[x]
Priority registrations	[ ]	Videotaped classes	[x]
Substitution of courses	[ ]	Text on tape	[x]
Exams		**Services**	
Extended time	[x]	Diagnostic tests	[ ]
Oral exams	[x]	Learning centers	[x]
Take home exams	[ ]	Proofreaders	[ ]
Exams on tape or computer	[x]	Readers	[x]
Untimed exams	[x]	Reading Machines/Kurzweil	[x]
Other accommodations	[ ]	Special bookstore section	[x]
		Typists	[ ]

Credit toward degree is not given for remedial courses taken.

Counseling Services

- [x] Academic — Meets 8 times per academic year
- [ ] Psychological
- [ ] Student Support groups
- [ ] Vocational

Tutoring

Individual tutoring is available daily.

Average size of tutoring groups: 6

	Individual	Group
Time management	[x]	[x]
Organizational skills	[x]	[x]
Learning strategies	[x]	[x]
Study skills	[x]	[x]
Content area	[x]	[x]
Writing lab	[x]	[ ]
Math lab	[ ]	[ ]

UNIQUE LD PROGRAM FEATURES

DSU provides services as needed. Instructors are informed of needs and make necessary accommodations for the students.

LD PROGRAM STAFF

Total number of LD Program staff (including director):

Full Time: 3 Part Time: 3

There is an advisor/advocate from the LD program available to students. The advisor/advocate meets with faculty 4 times per month and student 2 times per month. 15 peer tutors are available to work with LD students.

Key staff person available to work with LD students: Robert Jackson, Associate Professor.

LD Program web site: www.departments.dsu.edu/disability_services/

Dakota Wesleyan University

Mitchell, SD

Address: 1200 W. University Avenue, Mitchell, SD, 57301
Admissions telephone: 800 333-8506
Admissions FAX: 605 995-2699
Director of Admissions Operations and Outreach Programming: Laura Miller
Admissions e-mail: admissions@dwu.edu
Web site: http://www.dwu.edu
SAT Code: 6155 ACT Code: 3906

Director of Student Support Services: Amy Novak
LD program telephone: 605 995-2902
LD program e-mail: amnovak@dwu.edu
Total campus enrollment: 738

GENERAL

Dakota Wesleyan University is a private, coed, four-year institution. 40-acre campus in Mitchell (population: 14,558), 71 miles from Sioux Falls. Served by air and bus; larger airport and train serve Sioux Falls. Semester system.

LD ADMISSIONS

A personal interview is not required. Essay is not required.

SECONDARY SCHOOL REQUIREMENTS

Graduation from secondary school required; GED accepted.

TESTING

SAT Reasoning or ACT required. SAT Subject recommended.

All enrolled freshmen (fall 2004):

Average SAT I Scores:	Verbal:	Math:
Average ACT Scores:	Composite: 21	

Child Study Team report is not required. Tests required as part of this documentation:

- ☐ WAIS-IV
- ☐ WISC-IV
- ☐ SATA
- ☐ Woodcock-Johnson
- ☐ Nelson-Denny Reading Test
- ☐ Other

UNDERGRADUATE STUDENT BODY

Total undergraduate student enrollment: 274 Men, 413 Women.

Composition of student body (fall 2004):

	Undergraduate	Freshmen
International	0.0	1.3
Black	3.0	4.7
American Indian	4.4	2.6
Asian-American	0.7	1.3
Hispanic	0.7	1.4
White	91.2	88.7
Unreported	0.0	0.0
	100.0%	100.0%

28% are from out of state. Average age of full-time undergraduates is 24. 74% of classes have fewer than 20 students, 25% have between 20 and 50 students, 1% have more than 50 students.

STUDENT HOUSING

90% of freshmen live in college housing. Freshmen are required to live on campus. Housing is guaranteed for all undergraduates. Campus can house 386 undergraduates.

EXPENSES

Tuition (2005-06): $15,600 per year.
Room: $2,033. Board: $2,711.

There is no additional cost for LD program/services.

LD SERVICES

LD program size is limited.

LD services available to:

☐ Freshmen ☐ Sophomores ☐ Juniors ☐ Seniors

Academic Accommodations

Curriculum		**In class**	
Foreign language waiver	☐	Early syllabus	☐
Lighter course load	■	Note takers in class	☐
Math waiver	☐	Priority seating	☐
Other special classes	☐	Tape recorders	■
Priority registrations	☐	Videotaped classes	■
Substitution of courses	☐	Text on tape	☐
Exams		**Services**	
Extended time	■	Diagnostic tests	■
Oral exams	■	Learning centers	■
Take home exams	☐	Proofreaders	☐
Exams on tape or computer	☐	Readers	■
Untimed exams	■	Reading Machines/Kurzweil	■
Other accommodations	☐	Special bookstore section	☐
		Typists	☐

Credit toward degree is given for remedial courses taken.

Counseling Services

- ☐ Academic
- ☐ Psychological
- ☐ Student Support groups
- ☐ Vocational

Tutoring

	Individual	Group
Time management	☐	☐
Organizational skills	☐	☐
Learning strategies	☐	☐
Study skills	☐	☐
Content area	☐	☐
Writing lab	☐	☐
Math lab	☐	☐

LD PROGRAM STAFF

Total number of LD Program staff (including director):

Full Time: 3 Part Time: 3

Key staff person available to work with LD students: Amy Novak, Director of Student Support Services.

Mount Marty College

Yankton, SD

Address: 1105 W. Eighth Street, Yankton, SD, 57078
Admissions telephone: 800 658-4552
Admissions FAX: 605 668-1607
Director of Admissions: Brandi Tschumper
Admissions e-mail: mmcadmit@mtmc.edu
Web site: http://www.mtmc.edu
SAT Code: 6416 ACT Code: 3914

Academic Dean: James Foster
LD program telephone: 605 668-1584
LD program e-mail: jfoster@mtmc.edu
Total campus enrollment: 1,075

GENERAL

Mount Marty College is a private, coed, four-year institution. 80-acre campus in Yankton (population: 13,528), 60 miles from Sioux City, Iowa; branch campuses in Sioux Falls and Watertown. Served by air; major airport serves Sioux Falls (80 miles). Public transportation serves campus. Semester system.

LD ADMISSIONS

Students do not complete a separate application and are simultaneously accepted to the LD program. A member of the LD program does sit on the admissions committee. A personal interview is not required. Essay is not required.

SECONDARY SCHOOL REQUIREMENTS

Graduation from secondary school required; GED accepted.

TESTING

ACT required; SAT Reasoning may be substituted.

All enrolled freshmen (fall 2004):

Average SAT I Scores:	Verbal:	Math:
Average ACT Scores:	Composite: 22	

Child Study Team report is not required. A neuropsychological or comprehensive psycho-educational evaluation is required for admission. Must be dated within 6 months of application. Tests required as part of this documentation:

- [x] WAIS-IV
- [x] WISC-IV
- [x] SATA
- [x] Woodcock-Johnson
- [x] Nelson-Denny Reading Test
- [ ] Other

UNDERGRADUATE STUDENT BODY

Total undergraduate student enrollment: 352 Men, 717 Women.

Composition of student body (fall 2004):

	Undergraduate	Freshmen
International	0.6	0.7
Black	3.1	2.2
American Indian	0.6	2.0
Asian-American	0.6	1.4
Hispanic	4.9	1.3
White	90.2	91.7
Unreported	0.0	0.7
	100.0%	100.0%

35% are from out of state. Average age of full-time undergraduates is 21. 70% of classes have fewer than 20 students, 29% have between 20 and 50 students.

STUDENT HOUSING

98% of freshmen live in college housing. Freshmen are not required to live on campus. Housing is guaranteed for all undergraduates. Campus can house 356 undergraduates. Single rooms are not available for students with medical or special needs.

EXPENSES

Tuition (2005-06): $14,050 per year.

Room & Board: $4,860.

There is no additional cost for LD program/services.

LD SERVICES

LD program size is not limited.

LD services available to:

- [x] Freshmen
- [x] Sophomores
- [x] Juniors
- [x] Seniors

Academic Accommodations

Curriculum		In class	
Foreign language waiver	[ ]	Early syllabus	[ ]
Lighter course load	[x]	Note takers in class	[x]
Math waiver	[ ]	Priority seating	[ ]
Other special classes	[ ]	Tape recorders	[x]
Priority registrations	[ ]	Videotaped classes	[ ]
Substitution of courses	[ ]	Text on tape	[ ]
Exams		**Services**	
Extended time	[x]	Diagnostic tests	[ ]
Oral exams	[x]	Learning centers	[x]
Take home exams	[ ]	Proofreaders	[ ]
Exams on tape or computer	[ ]	Readers	[x]
Untimed exams	[x]	Reading Machines/Kurzweil	[ ]
Other accommodations	[ ]	Special bookstore section	[ ]
		Typists	[ ]

Credit toward degree is not given for remedial courses taken.

Counseling Services

- [x] Academic
- [x] Psychological
- [ ] Student Support groups
- [ ] Vocational

Tutoring

Individual tutoring is available daily.

Average size of tutoring groups: 2

	Individual	Group
Time management	[x]	[x]
Organizational skills	[x]	[x]
Learning strategies	[x]	[x]
Study skills	[x]	[x]
Content area	[x]	[x]
Writing lab	[x]	[x]
Math lab	[x]	[x]

LD PROGRAM STAFF

Total number of LD Program staff (including director):

Full Time: 1 Part Time: 1

There is an advisor/advocate from the LD program available to students. The advisor/advocate meets with faculty once per month and students 2 times per month. 16 peer tutors are available to work with LD students.

Key staff person available to work with LD students: Jan Hausmann, Director of Learning Center.

Northern State University

Aberdeen, SD

Address: 1200 S. Jay Street, Aberdeen, SD, 57401-7198
Admissions telephone: 800 678-5330
Admissions FAX: 605 626-2587
Director of Admissions: Brandt Munsen
Admissions e-mail: admissions@northern.edu
Web site: http://www.northern.edu
SAT Code: 6487 ACT Code: 3916

LD program name: NSU Services
Director of Disability Services: Karen Gerety
LD program telephone: 605 626-2371
LD program e-mail: geretyk@northern.edu
LD program enrollment: 28, Total campus enrollment: 2,218

GENERAL

Northern State University is a public, coed, four-year institution. 72-acre campus in Aberdeen (population: 24,658), 200 miles from Sioux Falls. Served by air and bus; larger airport serves Sioux Falls; train serves Fargo, NorthDakota (180 miles). Semester system.

LD ADMISSIONS

Application Deadline: 09/01. Students do not complete a separate application and are simultaneously accepted to the LD program. A member of the LD program does not sit on the admissions committee. A personal interview is not required. Essay is not required.

For fall 2004, 10 completed self-identified LD applications were received. All of these applications were offered admission, and all enrolled.

SECONDARY SCHOOL REQUIREMENTS

Graduation from secondary school required; GED accepted. The following course distribution required: 4 units of English, 3 units of math, 3 units of science, 3 units of social studies.

TESTING

ACT recommended.

All enrolled freshmen (fall 2004):

Average SAT I Scores:	Verbal:	Math:
Average ACT Scores:	Composite: 21	

Child Study Team report is not required. A neuropsychological or comprehensive psycho-education evaluation is not required for admission. Tests required as part of this documentation:

- ☐ WAIS-IV
- ☐ WISC-IV
- ☐ SATA
- ☐ Woodcock-Johnson
- ☐ Nelson-Denny Reading Test
- ☐ Other

UNDERGRADUATE STUDENT BODY

Total undergraduate student enrollment: 1,104 Men, 1,545 Women. 14% are from out of state. 44% of classes have fewer than 20 students, 52% have between 20 and 50 students, 4% have more than 50 students.

STUDENT HOUSING

70% of freshmen live in college housing. Freshmen are required to live on campus. Housing is guaranteed for all undergraduates. Campus can house 889 undergraduates. Single rooms are available for students with medical or special needs. A medical note is not required.

EXPENSES

Tuition (2005-06): $2,291 per year (in-state), $7,278 (out-of-state).
Room: $2,024. Board: $1,957.
There is no additional cost for LD program/services.

LD SERVICES

LD program size is not limited.

LD services available to:

☒ Freshmen ☒ Sophomores ☒ Juniors ☒ Seniors

Academic Accommodations

Curriculum		**In class**	
Foreign language waiver	☐	Early syllabus	☐
Lighter course load	☒	Note takers in class	☒
Math waiver	☐	Priority seating	☐
Other special classes	☐	Tape recorders	☒
Priority registrations	☐	Videotaped classes	☐
Substitution of courses	☐	Text on tape	☐
Exams		**Services**	
Extended time	☒	Diagnostic tests	☒
Oral exams	☒	Learning centers	☐
Take home exams	☐	Proofreaders	☐
Exams on tape or computer	☐	Readers	☒
Untimed exams	☒	Reading Machines/Kurzweil	☐
Other accommodations	☐	Special bookstore section	☐
		Typists	☐

Credit toward degree is not given for remedial courses taken.

Counseling Services

- ☒ Academic
- ☒ Psychological
- ☒ Student Support groups
- ☒ Vocational

Tutoring

Individual tutoring is available weekly.

	Individual	Group
Time management	☒	☒
Organizational skills	☒	☒
Learning strategies	☒	☒
Study skills	☒	☒
Content area	☒	☒
Writing lab	☒	☒
Math lab	☒	☒

LD PROGRAM STAFF

Total number of LD Program staff (including director):

Full Time: 1 Part Time: 1

There is an advisor/advocate from the LD program available to students. The advisor/advocate meets with faculty 4 times per month and students 12 times per month. 4 graduate students and 12 peer tutors are available to work with LD students.

Key staff person available to work with LD students: Karen Gerety, Director of Disability Services.

LD Program web site: www.northern.edu

University of Sioux Falls

Sioux Falls, SD

Address: 1101 W. 22nd Street, Sioux Falls, SD, 57105
Admissions telephone: 800 888-1047
Admissions FAX: 605 331-6615
Associate Vice President for Enrollment and Marketing: Greg A. Fritz
Admissions e-mail: admissions@usiouxfalls.edu
Web site: http://www.usiouxfalls.edu
SAT Code: 6651 ACT Code: 3920

LD program name: Disability Services/ADA
Coordinator: Libby Larson
LD program telephone: 605 331-6790
LD program e-mail: libby.larson@usiouxfalls.edu
LD program enrollment: 28, Total campus enrollment: 1,304

GENERAL

University of Sioux Falls is a private, coed, four-year institution. 23-acre, suburban campus in Sioux Falls (population: 123,975), 180 miles from Omaha. Served by air and bus; other airport and train serve Omaha. Public transportation serves campus. 4-1-4 system.

LD ADMISSIONS

Students do not complete a separate application and are simultaneously accepted to the LD program. A member of the LD program does not sit on the admissions committee. A personal interview is recommended. Essay is not required.

For fall 2004, 28 completed self-identified LD applications were received. 15 applications were offered admission, and 15 enrolled.

SECONDARY SCHOOL REQUIREMENTS

Graduation from secondary school required; GED accepted.

TESTING

ACT required. SAT Subject recommended.

All enrolled freshmen (fall 2004):

Average SAT I Scores:	Verbal:	Math:
Average ACT Scores:	Composite: 22	

Child Study Team report is not required. A neuropsychological or comprehensive psycho-educational evaluation is required for admission. Must be dated within 36 months of application. Tests required as part of this documentation:

■ WAIS-IV	■ Woodcock-Johnson
■ WISC-IV	■ Nelson-Denny Reading Test
■ SATA	☐ Other

UNDERGRADUATE STUDENT BODY

Total undergraduate student enrollment: 514 Men, 608 Women.

Composition of student body (fall 2004):

	Undergraduate	Freshmen
International	0.0	0.5
Black	1.2	2.5
American Indian	0.4	0.5
Asian-American	0.4	0.6
Hispanic	0.8	0.8
White	96.5	94.8
Unreported	0.8	0.3
	100.0%	100.0%

31% are from out of state. Average age of full-time undergraduates is 23. 59% of classes have fewer than 20 students, 39% have between 20 and 50 students, 2% have more than 50 students.

STUDENT HOUSING

90% of freshmen live in college housing. Freshmen are required to live on campus. Housing is guaranteed for all undergraduates. Campus can house 468 undergraduates. Single rooms are available for students with medical or special needs. A medical note is required.

EXPENSES

Tuition (2005-06): $15,900 per year.
Room & Board: $4,900.
There is no additional cost for LD program/services.

LD SERVICES

LD program size is not limited.

LD services available to:

■ Freshmen ■ Sophomores ■ Juniors ■ Seniors

Academic Accommodations

Curriculum		In class	
Foreign language waiver	☐	Early syllabus	☐
Lighter course load	☐	Note takers in class	■
Math waiver	☐	Priority seating	■
Other special classes	☐	Tape recorders	■
Priority registrations	☐	Videotaped classes	☐
Substitution of courses	☐	Text on tape	■
Exams		**Services**	
Extended time	■	Diagnostic tests	☐
Oral exams	■	Learning centers	■
Take home exams	☐	Proofreaders	■
Exams on tape or computer	■	Readers	■
Untimed exams	■	Reading Machines/Kurzweil	☐
Other accommodations	☐	Special bookstore section	■
		Typists	☐

Credit toward degree is given for remedial courses taken.

Counseling Services

■ Academic
■ Psychological
■ Student Support groups
☐ Vocational

Tutoring

Individual tutoring is not available.

	Individual	Group
Time management	☐	■
Organizational skills	☐	■
Learning strategies	☐	■
Study skills	☐	■
Content area	☐	■
Writing lab	☐	■
Math lab	☐	■

LD PROGRAM STAFF

There is an advisor/advocate from the LD program available to students. The advisor/advocate meets with faculty once per month and student 2 times per month. 9 peer tutors are available to work with LD students.

Key staff person available to work with LD students: Libby Larson, Disability Services Coordinator/ADA Coordinator.

LD Program web site: http://www.usiouxfalls.edu/stuserv/disabilities.htm

South Dakota School of Mines and Technology

Rapid City, SD

Address: 501 E. St. Joseph Street, Rapid City, SD, 57701
Admissions telephone: 800 544-8162
Admissions FAX: 605 394-1268
Director of Admissions: Joseph B. Mueller
Admissions e-mail: admissions@sdsmt.edu
Web site: http://www.sdsmt.edu
SAT Code: 6652 ACT Code: 3922

Director: Jolie McCoy
LD program telephone: 605 394-1924
LD program e-mail: jolie.mccoy@sdsmt.edu
Total campus enrollment: 2,042

GENERAL

South Dakota School of Mines and Technology is a public, coed, four-year institution. 120-acre campus in Rapid City (population: 59,607), 350 miles from Denver. Served by air and bus; major airport and train serve Denver. Semester system.

SECONDARY SCHOOL REQUIREMENTS

Graduation from secondary school required; GED accepted. The following course distribution required: 4 units of English, 3 units of math, 6 units of science, 3 units of social studies.

TESTING

ACT required; SAT Reasoning may be substituted.

All enrolled freshmen (fall 2004):

Average SAT I Scores:	Verbal: 585	Math: 593
Average ACT Scores:	Composite: 24	

Child Study Team report is not required. Tests required as part of this documentation:

☐ WAIS-IV ☐ Woodcock-Johnson
☐ WISC-IV ☐ Nelson-Denny Reading Test
☐ SATA ☐ Other

UNDERGRADUATE STUDENT BODY

Total undergraduate student enrollment: 1,413 Men, 662 Women.

Composition of student body (fall 2004):

	Undergraduate	Freshmen
International	0.6	1.7
Black	0.0	0.3
American Indian	3.0	3.0
Asian-American	1.4	1.4
Hispanic	1.7	1.1
White	83.1	84.5
Unreported	10.2	8.0
	100.0%	100.0%

25% are from out of state. 21% join a fraternity and 22% join a sorority. Average age of full-time undergraduates is 22. 33% of classes have fewer than 20 students, 58% have between 20 and 50 students, 9% have more than 50 students.

STUDENT HOUSING

62% of freshmen live in college housing. Freshmen are required to live on campus. Housing is guaranteed for all undergraduates. Campus can house 570 undergraduates.

EXPENSES

Tuition (2005-06): $2,291 per year (in-state), $7,278 (out-of-state). $1,872 per year (state residents), $2,064 (Minnesota residents), $2,808 (WUE and Iowa and Nebraska residents), $5,955 (residents of other states).

Room: $1,830. Board: $2,073.

There is no additional cost for LD program/services.

LD SERVICES

LD program size is not limited.

LD services available to:

☐ Freshmen ☐ Sophomores ☐ Juniors ☐ Seniors

Academic Accommodations

Curriculum		**In class**	
Foreign language waiver	☐	Early syllabus	☐
Lighter course load	☐	Note takers in class	☐
Math waiver	☐	Priority seating	☐
Other special classes	☐	Tape recorders	☐
Priority registrations	☐	Videotaped classes	☐
Substitution of courses	☐	Text on tape	☐
Exams		**Services**	
Extended time	☐	Diagnostic tests	☐
Oral exams	☐	Learning centers	■
Take home exams	☐	Proofreaders	☐
Exams on tape or computer	☐	Readers	☐
Untimed exams	☐	Reading Machines/Kurzweil	■
Other accommodations	☐	Special bookstore section	☐
		Typists	☐

Counseling Services

☐ Academic
☐ Psychological
☐ Student Support groups
☐ Vocational

Tutoring

	Individual	Group
Time management	☐	☐
Organizational skills	☐	☐
Learning strategies	☐	☐
Study skills	☐	☐
Content area	☐	☐
Writing lab	☐	☐
Math lab	☐	☐

UNIQUE LD PROGRAM FEATURES

Professional counseling and student ADA services are offered free of charge to all students. Students with disabilities who are seeking accommodations should contact the university counselor. The Assistive Technologies Lab, is equipped with state-of-the-art computers, scanners, and software to facilitate learning for students with ADA certified disabilities such as visual or auditory impairments, dyslexia, ambulatory impairments, etc. Students wishing to use the Assistive Technologies Lab must be ADA certified through the campus counselor and ADA coordinator. The office is open during most daytime and some evening hours.

LD PROGRAM STAFF

Key staff person available to work with LD students: Jolie McCoy, Director, Counseling and Student ADA Services.

South Dakota State University

Brookings, SD

Address: Box 2201, Brookings, SD, 57007
Admissions telephone: 800 952-3541
Admissions FAX: 605 688-6891
Director of High School Relations: Tracy Welsh
Admissions e-mail: SDSU_Admissions@sdstate.edu
Web site: http://www3.sdstate.edu
SAT Code: 6653 ACT Code: 3924

LD program name: Disability Services
LD program address: Box 510 WH 110,
Coordinator: Nancy Hartenhoff-Crooks
LD program telephone: 605 688-4504
LD program e-mail: nancy.crooks@sdstate.edu
LD program enrollment: 51, Total campus enrollment: 9,572

GENERAL

South Dakota State University is a public, coed, four-year institution. 272-acre campus in Brookings (population: 18,504), 50 miles from Sioux Falls. Branch campuses in Pierre, Rapid City, and Sioux Falls. Served by air and bus; major airport serves Minneapolis-St. Paul (180 miles); smaller airport serves Sioux Falls. Semester system.

LD ADMISSIONS

A personal interview is not required. Essay is not required.

SECONDARY SCHOOL REQUIREMENTS

Graduation from secondary school required; GED accepted. The following course distribution required: 4 units of English, 3 units of math, 3 units of science, 3 units of social studies.

TESTING

SAT Reasoning considered if submitted. ACT required.

All enrolled freshmen (fall 2004):

Average SAT I Scores:	Verbal:	Math:
Average ACT Scores:	Composite: 23	

Child Study Team report is not required. Tests required as part of this documentation:

- ☐ WAIS-IV
- ☐ WISC-IV
- ☐ SATA
- ☐ Woodcock-Johnson
- ☐ Nelson-Denny Reading Test
- ☐ Other

UNDERGRADUATE STUDENT BODY

Total undergraduate student enrollment: 3,713 Men, 4,080 Women.

Composition of student body (fall 2004):

	Undergraduate	Freshmen
International	0.0	0.2
Black	1.0	0.7
American Indian	1.8	1.4
Asian-American	1.0	0.8
Hispanic	0.6	0.6
White	90.5	91.7
Unreported	5.2	4.6
	100.0%	100.0%

26% are from out of state. 4% join a fraternity and 2% join a sorority. Average age of full-time undergraduates is 22. 35% of classes have fewer than 20 students, 52% have between 20 and 50 students, 13% have more than 50 students.

STUDENT HOUSING

97% of freshmen live in college housing. Freshmen are required to live on campus. Housing is not guaranteed for all undergraduates. We would not have enough room if all wanted to stay in the residence halls. Upperclassmen who are more than 2 years past high school graduation are eligible to live off campus and most choose to do so. Campus can house 3,399 undergraduates. Single rooms are available for students with medical or special needs. A medical note is not required.

EXPENSES

Tuition (2005-06): $2,291 per year (in-state), $7,278 (out-of-state).
Room: $2,113. Board: $2,656.
There is no additional cost for LD program/services.

LD SERVICES

LD program size is not limited.

LD services available to:

☑ Freshmen ☑ Sophomores ☑ Juniors ☑ Seniors

Academic Accommodations

Curriculum		**In class**	
Foreign language waiver	☐	Early syllabus	☐
Lighter course load	☑	Note takers in class	☑
Math waiver	☐	Priority seating	☑
Other special classes	☐	Tape recorders	☑
Priority registrations	☐	Videotaped classes	☑
Substitution of courses	☐	Text on tape	☑
Exams		**Services**	
Extended time	☑	Diagnostic tests	☑
Oral exams	☑	Learning centers	☐
Take home exams	☐	Proofreaders	☐
Exams on tape or computer	☑	Readers	☑
Untimed exams	☑	Reading Machines/Kurzweil	☑
Other accommodations	☑	Special bookstore section	☐
		Typists	☑

Credit toward degree is not given for remedial courses taken.

Counseling Services

- ☑ Academic
- ☑ Psychological
- ☐ Student Support groups
- ☐ Vocational

Tutoring

Individual tutoring is available.

	Individual	Group
Time management	☑	☑
Organizational skills	☑	☑
Learning strategies	☑	☑
Study skills	☑	☑
Content area	☑	☑
Writing lab	☑	☑
Math lab	☑	☑

UNIQUE LD PROGRAM FEATURES

Requirements for admissions to the univeristy are the same for all students and LD documentation is not required or wanted until admissions is established to avoid discrimination issues.

LD PROGRAM STAFF

Total number of LD Program staff (including director):

Full Time: 2 Part Time: 2

There is an advisor/advocate from the LD program available to students.

Key staff person available to work with LD students: Nancy Hartenhoff-Crooks, Coordinator of Disability Services.

LD Program web site: http://www3.sdstate.edu/StudentLife/DisabilityServices/

University of South Dakota at Vermillion

Vermillion, SD

Address: 414 E. Clark Street, Vermillion, SD, 57069
Admissions Telephone: 605 677-5434
Admissions FAX: 605 677-6323
Director of Admissions: Michelle Lavallee
Admissions E-mail: admiss@usd.edu
Web Site: http://www.usd.edu
SAT Code: 6881 ACT Code: 3928

Director of Disability Services: Dr. Elaine Pearson
LD Program telephone: 605 677-6389
LD Program e-mail: epearson@usd.edu
Total Campus Enrollment: 6,024

GENERAL

University of South Dakota at Vermillion is a public, coed, four-year institution. 216-acre campus in Vermillion (population: 9,765), 41 miles from Sioux City, Iowa; branch campuses in Pierre, Rapid City, Sioux Falls, Watertown, and Yankton. Airport and bus serve Sioux City; larger airport and train serve Omaha (145 miles). Semester system.

LD ADMISSIONS

A personal interview is not required. Essay is not required. Accomodations are made on an individual basis regarding test scores, high school rank and minimum GPA. Admissions and the LD program work together on admission criteria for students depending on each student's disability.

SECONDARY SCHOOL REQUIREMENTS

Graduation from secondary school required; GED accepted. The following course distribution required: 4 units of English, 3 units of math, 3 units of science, 3 units of social studies.

TESTING

ACT required; SAT Reasoning may be substituted. SAT Subject recommended.

All enrolled freshmen (fall 2004):

Average SAT I Scores:	Verbal: 552	Math: 550
Average ACT Scores:	Composite: 23	

Child Study Team report is not required. Tests required as part of this documentation:

- [ ] WAIS-IV
- [ ] WISC-IV
- [ ] SATA
- [ ] Woodcock-Johnson
- [ ] Nelson-Denny Reading Test
- [ ] Other

UNDERGRADUATE STUDENT BODY

Total undergraduate student enrollment: 2,190 Men; 3,173 Women.

Composition of student body (fall 2004):

	Undergraduate	Freshmen
International	1.1	1.4
Black	1.0	0.8
American-Indian	2.1	2.1
Asian-American	1.5	0.7
Hispanic	0.8	1.0
White	88.2	88.3
Unreported	5.3	5.7
	100.0%	100.0%

22% are from out of state. 22% join a fraternity and 14% join a sorority. Average age of full-time undergraduates is 21. 52% of classes have fewer than 20 students, 43% have between 20 and 50 students, 6% have more than 50 students.

STUDENT HOUSING

Housing is guaranteed for all undergraduates. Campus can house 2,082 undergraduates.

EXPENSES

Tuition (2005-06): $2,291 per year (in-state), $7,278 (out-of-state). $1,997 per year (state residents), $2,995 (residents of adjacent states), $6,352 (other out-of-state).

Room: $2,253-$1,937. Board: $1,986-$1,804.

There is no additional cost for LD program/services.

LD SERVICES

LD program size is not limited.

LD services available to:

- [x] Freshmen
- [x] Sophomores
- [x] Juniors
- [x] Seniors

Academic Accommodations

Curriculum		In class	
Foreign language waiver	[ ]	Early syllabus	[ ]
Lighter course load	[x]	Note takers in class	[x]
Math waiver	[ ]	Priority seating	[ ]
Other special classes	[x]	Tape recorders	[x]
Priority registration	[ ]	Videotaped classes	[ ]
Substitution of courses	[ ]	Text on tape	[ ]
Exams		**Services**	
Extended time	[x]	Diagnostic tests	[x]
Oral exams	[x]	Learning centers	[x]
Take home exams	[ ]	Proofreaders	[ ]
Exams on tape or computer	[ ]	Readers	[x]
Untimed exams	[x]	Reading Machines/Kurzweil	[x]
Other accommodations	[ ]	Special bookstore section	[ ]
		Typists	[ ]

Credit toward degree is not given for remedial courses taken.

Counseling Services

- [ ] Academic
- [ ] Psychological
- [ ] Student support groups
- [ ] Vocational

Tutoring

Individual tutoring is available.

	Individual	Group
Time management	[ ]	[ ]
Organizational skills	[ ]	[ ]
Learning strategies	[ ]	[ ]
Study skills	[ ]	[ ]
Content area	[ ]	[ ]
Writing lab	[ ]	[ ]
Math lab	[ ]	[ ]

UNIQUE LD PROGRAM FEATURES

The school has a proactive, monitoring program that allows students to interact with faculty and staff on an individual basis.

LD PROGRAM STAFF

Total number of LD Program staff (including director):

Full Time: 3 Part Time: 3

There is an advisor/advocate from the LD program available to students.

Key staff person available to work with LD students: Dr. Elaine Pearson, Director of Disability Services.

Austin Peay State University

Clarksville, TN

Address: PO Box 4675, Clarksville, TN, 37044
Admissions telephone: 800 844-2778 (out-of-state)
Admissions FAX: 931 221-6168
Director of Admissions: Scott McDonald
Admissions e-mail: admissions@apsu01.apsu.edu
Web site: http://www.apsu.edu
SAT Code: 1028 ACT Code: 3944

LD program name: Office of Disability Services
LD program address: PO Box 4578
Assistant Director: Bryon Kluesner
LD program telephone: 931 221-6230
LD program e-mail: kluesnerb@apsu.edu
LD program enrollment: 34, Total campus enrollment: 8,108

GENERAL

Austin Peay State University is a public, coed, four-year institution. 210-acre campus in Clarksville (population: 103,455), 45 miles northwest of Nashville; branch campus in Ft. Campbell, KY. Served by bus; airport serves Nashville. Public transportation serves campus. Semester system.

LD ADMISSIONS

Students do not complete a separate application and are not simultaneously accepted to the LD program. A personal interview is required. Essay is not required.

SECONDARY SCHOOL REQUIREMENTS

Graduation from secondary school required; GED accepted. The following course distribution required: 4 units of English, 3 units of math, 2 units of science, 2 units of foreign language, 1 unit of social studies, 1 unit of history.

TESTING

SAT Reasoning considered if submitted. ACT considered if submitted. SAT Subject recommended.

All enrolled freshmen (fall 2004):

Average SAT I Scores:	Verbal: 538	Math: 512
Average ACT Scores:	Composite: 21	

Child Study Team report is not required. A neuropsychological or comprehensive psycho-educational evaluation is required for admission. Must be dated within 36 months of application. Tests required as part of this documentation:

- [x] WAIS-IV
- [ ] WISC-IV
- [ ] SATA
- [x] Woodcock-Johnson
- [ ] Nelson-Denny Reading Test
- [ ] Other

UNDERGRADUATE STUDENT BODY

Total undergraduate student enrollment: 2,729 Men, 3,929 Women.

Composition of student body (fall 2004):

	Undergraduate	Freshmen
International	0.3	0.3
Black	16.3	18.9
American Indian	0.6	0.6
Asian-American	2.7	2.5
Hispanic	4.5	5.3
White	66.4	63.6
Unreported	9.2	8.8
	100.0%	100.0%

3% are from out of state. 6% join a fraternity and 5% join a sorority. Average age of full-time undergraduates is 25. 39% of classes have fewer than 20 students, 57% have between 20 and 50 students, 4% have more than 50 students.

STUDENT HOUSING

32% of freshmen live in college housing. Housing is guaranteed for all undergraduates. Campus can house 1,500 undergraduates. Single rooms are available for students with medical or special needs. A medical note is required.

EXPENSES

Tuition (2005-06): $3,352 per year (in-state), $11,840 (out-of-state). Room: $2,600. Board: $1,696.
There is no additional cost for LD program/services.

LD SERVICES

LD program size is not limited.

LD services available to:

- [x] Freshmen
- [x] Sophomores
- [x] Juniors
- [x] Seniors

Academic Accommodations

Curriculum		In class	
Foreign language waiver	[ ]	Early syllabus	[ ]
Lighter course load	[x]	Note takers in class	[x]
Math waiver	[ ]	Priority seating	[x]
Other special classes	[ ]	Tape recorders	[x]
Priority registrations	[x]	Videotaped classes	[x]
Substitution of courses	[ ]	Text on tape	[x]
Exams		**Services**	
Extended time	[x]	Diagnostic tests	[ ]
Oral exams	[x]	Learning centers	[x]
Take home exams	[ ]	Proofreaders	[ ]
Exams on tape or computer	[x]	Readers	[x]
Untimed exams	[ ]	Reading Machines/Kurzweil	[x]
Other accommodations	[x]	Special bookstore section	[ ]
		Typists	[x]

Credit toward degree is not given for remedial courses taken.

Counseling Services

- [x] Academic
- [x] Psychological
- [x] Student Support groups
- [ ] Vocational

Tutoring

Individual tutoring is available.

	Individual	Group
Time management	[ ]	[ ]
Organizational skills	[ ]	[ ]
Learning strategies	[x]	[x]
Study skills	[x]	[x]
Content area	[ ]	[ ]
Writing lab	[x]	[x]
Math lab	[x]	[x]

LD PROGRAM STAFF

Total number of LD Program staff (including director):

Full Time: 3 Part Time: 3

There is an advisor/advocate from the LD program available to students. 2 graduate students are available to work with LD students.

Key staff person available to work with LD students: Beulah C. Oldham, Director, Office of Disability Services.

LD Program web site: http://www.apsu.edu/disability/

Belmont University

Nashville, TN

Address: 1900 Belmont Boulevard, Nashville, TN, 37212
Admissions telephone: 615 460-6785
Admissions FAX: 615 460-5434
Dean of Admissions: Kathryn H. Baugher
Admissions e-mail: buadmission@mail.belmont.edu
Web site: http://www.belmont.edu
SAT Code: 1058 ACT Code: 3946

LD program name: Counseling & Disability Services
Director: Tammye Tanksley
LD program telephone: 615 460-6875
LD program e-mail: tanksleyt@mail.belmont.edu
LD program enrollment: 25, Total campus enrollment: 3,317

GENERAL

Belmont University is a private, coed, four-year institution. 55-acre campus in Nashville (population: 545,524). Served by airport, bus, and train. Public transportation serves campus. Semester system.

LD ADMISSIONS

Application Deadline: 05/01. Students do not complete a separate application and are not simultaneously accepted to the LD program. A member of the LD program does not sit on the admissions committee. A personal interview is not required. Essay is required and may be typed. No admissions requirements waived.

SECONDARY SCHOOL REQUIREMENTS

Graduation from secondary school required; GED accepted. The following course distribution required: 4 units of English, 3 units of math, 2 units of science, 2 units of foreign language, 2 units of social studies, 5 units of academic electives.

TESTING

SAT Reasoning or ACT required.

All enrolled freshmen (fall 2004):

Average SAT I Scores:	Verbal: 579	Math: 574
Average ACT Scores:	Composite: 25	

Child Study Team report is not required. A neuropsychological or comprehensive psycho-education evaluation is not required for admission. Tests required as part of this documentation:

- [x] WAIS-IV
- [x] WISC-IV
- [ ] SATA
- [x] Woodcock-Johnson
- [ ] Nelson-Denny Reading Test
- [ ] Other

UNDERGRADUATE STUDENT BODY

Total undergraduate student enrollment: 1,038 Men, 1,579 Women.

Composition of student body (fall 2004):

	Undergraduate	Freshmen
International	1.0	1.0
Black	2.3	3.5
American Indian	0.4	0.4
Asian-American	1.8	1.5
Hispanic	2.3	2.0
White	91.0	89.5
Unreported	1.2	2.1
	100.0%	100.0%

59% are from out of state. 3% join a fraternity and 3% join a sorority. Average age of full-time undergraduates is 21. 49% of classes have fewer than 20 students, 51% have between 20 and 50 students.

STUDENT HOUSING

98% of freshmen live in college housing. Freshmen are required to live on campus. Housing is not guaranteed for all undergraduates. Housing shortage for underclassmen precludes uppercalssmen from living in campus housing. Campus can house 1,750 undergraduates. Single rooms are available for students with medical or special needs. A medical note is required.

EXPENSES

Tuition (2005-06): $16,360 per year.
Room: $3,005-$5,180. Board: $3,350.
There is no additional cost for LD program/services.

LD SERVICES

LD program size is not limited.

LD services available to:

[x] Freshmen [x] Sophomores [x] Juniors [x] Seniors

Academic Accommodations

Curriculum		**In class**	
Foreign language waiver	[ ]	Early syllabus	[ ]
Lighter course load	[x]	Note takers in class	[x]
Math waiver	[ ]	Priority seating	[x]
Other special classes	[ ]	Tape recorders	[x]
Priority registrations	[ ]	Videotaped classes	[ ]
Substitution of courses	[ ]	Text on tape	[ ]
Exams		**Services**	
Extended time	[x]	Diagnostic tests	[ ]
Oral exams	[x]	Learning centers	[ ]
Take home exams	[ ]	Proofreaders	[ ]
Exams on tape or computer	[x]	Readers	[x]
Untimed exams	[x]	Reading Machines/Kurzweil	[ ]
Other accommodations	[x]	Special bookstore section	[ ]
		Typists	[ ]

Credit toward degree is not given for remedial courses taken.

Counseling Services

- [x] Academic
- [x] Psychological
- [ ] Student Support groups
- [x] Vocational

Tutoring

Individual tutoring is not available.

	Individual	Group
Time management	[ ]	[ ]
Organizational skills	[ ]	[ ]
Learning strategies	[ ]	[ ]
Study skills	[ ]	[ ]
Content area	[ ]	[ ]
Writing lab	[x]	[ ]
Math lab	[x]	[ ]

LD PROGRAM STAFF

Total number of LD Program staff (including director):

Full Time: 1 Part Time: 1

There is an advisor/advocate from the LD program available to students.

Key staff person available to work with LD students: Tammye Tanksley, Director of Counseling/Developmental Support.

Bethel College

McKenzie, TN

Address: 325 Cherry Street, McKenzie, TN, 38201
Admissions telephone: 731 352-4030
Admissions FAX: 731 352-4069
Director of Admissions: Tina Hodges
Admissions e-mail: admissions@bethel-college.edu
Web site: http://www.bethel-college.edu
SAT Code: 1063 ACT Code: 3948

Director of Retention: Sandy Louden
LD program telephone: 731 352-4095
LD program e-mail: loudens@bethel-college.edu
Total campus enrollment: 1,115

GENERAL

Bethel College is a private, coed, four-year institution. 100-acre campus in McKenzie (population: 5,295), 120 miles from Memphis. Major airports serve Memphis and Nashville (135 miles); bus serves Jackson (40 miles); train serves Memphis. Semester system.

LD ADMISSIONS

A personal interview is recommended. Essay is not required. Potential students may contact Director of Admissions to discuss individual needs.

SECONDARY SCHOOL REQUIREMENTS

Graduation from secondary school required; GED accepted. The following course distribution required: 4 units of English, 2 units of math, 2 units of science.

TESTING

SAT Reasoning or ACT required. SAT Subject recommended.

All enrolled freshmen (fall 2004):

Average SAT I Scores: Verbal: Math:
Average ACT Scores: Composite:

Child Study Team report is not required. Tests required as part of this documentation:

- ☐ WAIS-IV
- ☐ WISC-IV
- ☐ SATA
- ☐ Woodcock-Johnson
- ☐ Nelson-Denny Reading Test
- ☐ Other

UNDERGRADUATE STUDENT BODY

Total undergraduate student enrollment: 385 Men, 391 Women.

21% are from out of state.

STUDENT HOUSING

Housing is guaranteed for all undergraduates. Campus can house 324 undergraduates.

EXPENSES

Tuition (2005-06):
There is no additional cost for LD program/services.

LD SERVICES

LD program size is not limited.

LD services available to:

☐ Freshmen ☐ Sophomores ☐ Juniors ☐ Seniors

Academic Accommodations

Curriculum		**In class**	
Foreign language waiver	☐	Early syllabus	☐
Lighter course load	☐	Note takers in class	☐
Math waiver	☐	Priority seating	☐
Other special classes	☐	Tape recorders	■
Priority registrations	☐	Videotaped classes	☐
Substitution of courses	☐	Text on tape	☐
Exams		**Services**	
Extended time	☐	Diagnostic tests	☐
Oral exams	☐	Learning centers	☐
Take home exams	☐	Proofreaders	☐
Exams on tape or computer	☐	Readers	☐
Untimed exams	■	Reading Machines/Kurzweil	☐
Other accommodations	☐	Special bookstore section	☐
		Typists	☐

Credit toward degree is not given for remedial courses taken.

Counseling Services

- ☐ Academic
- ☐ Psychological
- ☐ Student Support groups
- ☐ Vocational

Tutoring

	Individual	Group
Time management	☐	☐
Organizational skills	☐	☐
Learning strategies	☐	☐
Study skills	☐	☐
Content area	☐	☐
Writing lab	☐	☐
Math lab	☐	☐

UNIQUE LD PROGRAM FEATURES

Our strength lies in our small size, one that encourages student unity and personal interaction. By nurturing individual students and providing quality education, Bethel College helps students achieve their dreams.

LD PROGRAM STAFF

Total number of LD Program staff (including director):

Full Time: 1 Part Time: 1

Key staff person available to work with LD students: Sandy Louden, Director of Retention.

Bryan College

Dayton, TN

Address: PO Box 7000, Dayton, TN, 37321-7000
Admissions telephone: 800 277-9522
Admissions FAX: 423 775-7199
Director of Admissions: Michael Sapienza
Admissions e-mail: admissions@bryan.edu
Web site: http://www.bryan.edu
SAT Code: 1908 ACT Code: 4038

ADA Coordinator: Liz Moseley
LD program telephone: 423 775-7225
LD program e-mail: elizabeth.moseley@bryan.edu
LD program enrollment: 7, Total campus enrollment: 647

GENERAL

Bryan College is a private, coed, four-year institution. 100-acre, rural campus in Dayton (population: 6,180), 40 miles from Chattanooga. Major airport serves Atlanta, GA (150 miles); smaller airport and bus serve Chattanooga. Semester system.

LD ADMISSIONS

Students do not complete a separate application and are simultaneously accepted to the LD program. A personal interview is recommended. Essay is required and may be typed. Admissions requirements that may be waived for LD students are determined on individual basis.

SECONDARY SCHOOL REQUIREMENTS

Graduation from secondary school required; GED accepted.

TESTING

ACT required; SAT Reasoning may be substituted. SAT Subject recommended.

All enrolled freshmen (fall 2004):

Average SAT I Scores:	Verbal: 592	Math: 557
Average ACT Scores:	Composite: 23	

Child Study Team report is not required. Tests required as part of this documentation:

- ☐ WAIS-IV
- ☐ WISC-IV
- ☐ SATA
- ☐ Woodcock-Johnson
- ☐ Nelson-Denny Reading Test
- ☐ Other

UNDERGRADUATE STUDENT BODY

Total undergraduate student enrollment: 647.

Composition of student body (fall 2004):

	Undergraduate	Freshmen
International	0.8	1.4
Black	3.0	4.1
American Indian	0.0	0.0
Asian-American	0.8	0.5
Hispanic	3.0	1.6
White	92.4	92.4
Unreported	0.0	0.0
	100.0%	100.0%

60% are from out of state. 68% of classes have fewer than 20 students, 31% have between 20 and 50 students, 1% have more than 50 students.

STUDENT HOUSING

92% of freshmen live in college housing. Freshmen are required to live on campus. Housing is guaranteed for all undergraduates. Campus can house 524 undergraduates. Single rooms are available for students with medical or special needs. A medical note is required.

EXPENSES

Tuition (2005-06): $14,700 per year.
Room: $3,000. Board: $1,470.
There is no additional cost for LD program/services.

LD SERVICES

LD program size is not limited.

LD services available to:

■ Freshmen ■ Sophomores ■ Juniors ■ Seniors

Academic Accommodations

Curriculum		**In class**	
Foreign language waiver	☐	Early syllabus	☐
Lighter course load	■	Note takers in class	■
Math waiver	☐	Priority seating	☐
Other special classes	☐	Tape recorders	■
Priority registrations	☐	Videotaped classes	☐
Substitution of courses	■	Text on tape	■
Exams		**Services**	
Extended time	■	Diagnostic tests	☐
Oral exams	■	Learning centers	■
Take home exams	■	Proofreaders	☐
Exams on tape or computer	☐	Readers	■
Untimed exams	■	Reading Machines/Kurzweil	☐
Other accommodations	☐	Special bookstore section	☐
		Typists	■

Credit toward degree is not given for remedial courses taken.

Counseling Services

- ■ Academic
- ■ Psychological
- ☐ Student Support groups
- ☐ Vocational

Tutoring

Individual tutoring is available weekly.

Average size of tutoring groups: 1

	Individual	Group
Time management	■	☐
Organizational skills	■	☐
Learning strategies	■	☐
Study skills	☐	☐
Content area	■	☐
Writing lab	■	☐
Math lab	☐	☐

LD PROGRAM STAFF

Total number of LD Program staff (including director):

There is an advisor/advocate from the LD program available to students.

Key staff person available to work with LD students: Liz Moseley, ADA Coordinator.

Christian Brothers University

Memphis, TN

Address: 650 East Parkway S, Memphis, TN, 38104
Admissions telephone: 800 288-7576
Admissions FAX: 901 321-3202
Dean of Admissions: Tracey Dysart
Admissions e-mail: admissions@cbu.edu
Web site: http://www.cbu.edu
SAT Code: 1121 ACT Code: 3952

Director of Student Disability Services: Karen Conway
LD program telephone: 901 321-3536
LD program e-mail: kconway@cbu.edu
LD program enrollment: 30, Total campus enrollment: 1,572

GENERAL

Christian Brothers University is a private, coed, four-year institution. 70-acre campus in Memphis (population: 650,100). Served by airport, bus, and train. Public transportation serves campus. Semester system.

LD ADMISSIONS

Students do not complete a separate application and are not simultaneously accepted to the LD program. A member of the LD program does not sit on the admissions committee. A personal interview is required. Essay is not required.

For fall 2004, 40 completed self-identified LD applications were received. All of the applications were offered admission, and all enrolled.

SECONDARY SCHOOL REQUIREMENTS

Graduation from secondary school required; GED accepted. The following course distribution required: 4 units of English, 3 units of math.

TESTING

SAT Reasoning or ACT required. SAT Subject recommended.

All enrolled freshmen (fall 2004):

Average SAT I Scores:	Verbal: 551	Math: 562
Average ACT Scores:	Composite: 24	

Child Study Team report is not required. A neuropsychological or comprehensive psycho-education evaluation is not required for admission. Tests required as part of this documentation:

- [ ] WAIS-IV
- [ ] WISC-IV
- [ ] SATA
- [ ] Woodcock-Johnson
- [ ] Nelson-Denny Reading Test
- [ ] Other

UNDERGRADUATE STUDENT BODY

Total undergraduate student enrollment: 741 Men, 918 Women.

Composition of student body (fall 2004):

	Undergraduate	Freshmen
International	2.6	2.3
Black	29.7	36.5
American Indian	0.0	0.0
Asian-American	4.5	5.2
Hispanic	3.0	2.1
White	53.8	50.0
Unreported	6.4	3.9
	100.0%	100.0%

26% are from out of state. 23% join a fraternity and 22% join a sorority. Average age of full-time undergraduates is 21. 68% of classes have fewer than 20 students, 32% have between 20 and 50 students.

STUDENT HOUSING

60% of freshmen live in college housing. Freshmen are required to live on campus. Housing is guaranteed for all undergraduates. Campus can house 576 undergraduates. Single rooms are available for students with medical or special needs. A medical note is required.

EXPENSES

Tuition (2005-06): $18,630 per year.

Room: $2,480. Board: $3,020.
There is no additional cost for LD program/services.

LD SERVICES

LD program size is not limited.

LD services available to:

- [x] Freshmen
- [x] Sophomores
- [x] Juniors
- [x] Seniors

Academic Accommodations

Curriculum		In class	
Foreign language waiver	[ ]	Early syllabus	[ ]
Lighter course load	[ ]	Note takers in class	[x]
Math waiver	[ ]	Priority seating	[ ]
Other special classes	[ ]	Tape recorders	[x]
Priority registrations	[ ]	Videotaped classes	[ ]
Substitution of courses	[ ]	Text on tape	[ ]
Exams		**Services**	
Extended time	[x]	Diagnostic tests	[ ]
Oral exams	[x]	Learning centers	[ ]
Take home exams	[ ]	Proofreaders	[ ]
Exams on tape or computer	[ ]	Readers	[x]
Untimed exams	[x]	Reading Machines/Kurzweil	[ ]
Other accommodations	[ ]	Special bookstore section	[ ]
		Typists	[ ]

Credit toward degree is not given for remedial courses taken.

Counseling Services

- [ ] Academic
- [ ] Psychological
- [ ] Student Support groups
- [ ] Vocational

Tutoring

Individual tutoring is available.

Average size of tutoring groups: 1

	Individual	Group
Time management	[ ]	[x]
Organizational skills	[ ]	[x]
Learning strategies	[x]	[ ]
Study skills	[ ]	[x]
Content area	[ ]	[ ]
Writing lab	[ ]	[x]
Math lab	[ ]	[x]

LD PROGRAM STAFF

Total number of LD Program staff (including director):

Full Time: 2 Part Time: 2

There is an advisor/advocate from the LD program available to students.

Key staff person available to work with LD students: Karen Conway, Director of Student Disability Services.

Crichton College

Memphis, TN

Address: 255 N. Highland, Memphis, TN, 38111-1375
Admissions telephone: 901 320-9797
Admissions FAX: 901 320-9791
Vice President for Admissions and Enrollment Management: Mr. David Wilson
Admissions e-mail: info@crichton.edu
Web site: http://www.crichton.edu
SAT Code: 1782 ACT Code: 3995

Vice President of Academic Affairs: Dr. Robert Wharton
LD program telephone: 901 320-9700
LD program e-mail: rbwharton@crichton.edu
Total campus enrollment: 974

GENERAL

Crichton College is a private, coed, four-year institution. Seven-acre campus in Memphis (population: 650,100). Served by airport, bus, and train. School operates transportation to housing. Public transportation serves campus. Semester system.

LD ADMISSIONS

A personal interview is recommended. Essay is required and may be typed.

SECONDARY SCHOOL REQUIREMENTS

Graduation from secondary school required; GED accepted. The following course distribution required: 3 units of English, 3 units of math, 2 units of science, 3 units of foreign language, 3 units of social studies.

TESTING

ACT required; SAT Reasoning may be substituted. SAT Subject recommended.

All enrolled freshmen (fall 2004):

Average SAT I Scores:	Verbal:	Math:
Average ACT Scores:	Composite: 23	

Child Study Team report is not required. Tests required as part of this documentation:

❑ WAIS-IV	❑ Woodcock-Johnson
❑ WISC-IV	❑ Nelson-Denny Reading Test
❑ SATA	❑ Other

UNDERGRADUATE STUDENT BODY

Total undergraduate student enrollment: 473 Men, 570 Women.

Composition of student body (fall 2004):

	Undergraduate	Freshmen
International	1.1	0.5
Black	37.2	52.0
American Indian	0.0	0.1
Asian-American	0.0	0.2
Hispanic	2.1	0.9
White	26.6	31.3
Unreported	33.0	15.0
	100.0%	100.0%

14% are from out of state. Average age of full-time undergraduates is 34. 79% of classes have fewer than 20 students, 18% have between 20 and 50 students, 3% have more than 50 students.

STUDENT HOUSING

Housing is guaranteed for all undergraduates.

EXPENSES

Tuition (2005-06): $9,960 per year.
Room: $3,600. Board: $2,244.

There is no additional cost for LD program/services.

LD SERVICES

LD program size is not limited.

LD services available to:

❑ Freshmen ❑ Sophomores ❑ Juniors ❑ Seniors

Academic Accommodations

Curriculum		**In class**	
Foreign language waiver	❑	Early syllabus	❑
Lighter course load	❑	Note takers in class	■
Math waiver	❑	Priority seating	❑
Other special classes	❑	Tape recorders	■
Priority registrations	❑	Videotaped classes	■
Substitution of courses	❑	Text on tape	❑
Exams		**Services**	
Extended time	■	Diagnostic tests	■
Oral exams	■	Learning centers	❑
Take home exams	❑	Proofreaders	❑
Exams on tape or computer	❑	Readers	■
Untimed exams	■	Reading Machines/Kurzweil	❑
Other accommodations	❑	Special bookstore section	❑
		Typists	❑

Credit toward degree is not given for remedial courses taken.

Counseling Services

❑ Academic
❑ Psychological
❑ Student Support groups
❑ Vocational

Tutoring

	Individual	Group
Time management	❑	❑
Organizational skills	❑	❑
Learning strategies	❑	❑
Study skills	❑	❑
Content area	❑	❑
Writing lab	❑	❑
Math lab	❑	❑

LD PROGRAM STAFF

Total number of LD Program staff (including director):

Full Time: 28 Part Time: 28

Key staff person available to work with LD students: Dr. Robert Wharton, Vice President of Academic Affairs.

Cumberland University

Lebanon, TN

Address: 1 Cumberland Square, Lebanon, TN, 37087-3408
Admissions telephone: 800 467-0562
Admissions FAX: 615 444-2569
Director of Admissions: Ms. Melinda Y. Bone
Admissions e-mail: admissions@cumberland.edu
Web site: http://www.cumberland.edu
SAT Code: 1146 ACT Code: 3954

Vice President for Enrollment Management: Melinda Bone
LD program telephone: 615 444-2562, extension 1225
LD program e-mail: mbone@cumberland.edu
Total campus enrollment: 908

GENERAL

Cumberland University is a private, coed, four-year institution. 40-acre, urban campus in Lebanon (population: 20,235), 25 miles from Nashville. Served by bus; airport serves Nashville. Semester system.

LD ADMISSIONS

A personal interview is required. Essay is not required.

SECONDARY SCHOOL REQUIREMENTS

Graduation from secondary school required; GED accepted. The following course distribution required: 4 units of English, 3 units of math, 3 units of science, 2 units of foreign language, 2 units of social studies, 1 unit of history, 12 units of academic electives.

TESTING

ACT required; SAT Reasoning may be substituted.

All enrolled freshmen (fall 2004):

Average SAT I Scores: Verbal: Math:
Average ACT Scores: Composite:

Child Study Team report is not required. Tests required as part of this documentation:

- [ ] WAIS-IV
- [ ] WISC-IV
- [ ] SATA
- [ ] Woodcock-Johnson
- [ ] Nelson-Denny Reading Test
- [ ] Other

UNDERGRADUATE STUDENT BODY

Total undergraduate student enrollment: 434 Men, 474 Women.

11% are from out of state.

STUDENT HOUSING

Housing is guaranteed for all undergraduates. Campus can house 416 undergraduates.

EXPENSES

Tuition (2005-06): $13,344 per year.
Room: $1,970. Board: $2,750.
There is no additional cost for LD program/services.

LD SERVICES

LD program size is not limited.

LD services available to:

- [ ] Freshmen
- [ ] Sophomores
- [ ] Juniors
- [ ] Seniors

Academic Accommodations

Curriculum		**In class**	
Foreign language waiver	☐	Early syllabus	☐
Lighter course load	☐	Note takers in class	☐
Math waiver	☐	Priority seating	☐
Other special classes	☐	Tape recorders	■
Priority registrations	☐	Videotaped classes	☐
Substitution of courses	☐	Text on tape	☐
Exams		**Services**	
Extended time	■	Diagnostic tests	☐
Oral exams	■	Learning centers	■
Take home exams	☐	Proofreaders	☐
Exams on tape or computer	☐	Readers	■
Untimed exams	■	Reading Machines/Kurzweil	■
Other accommodations	☐	Special bookstore section	☐
		Typists	☐

Credit toward degree is given for remedial courses taken.

Counseling Services

- [ ] Academic
- [ ] Psychological
- [ ] Student Support groups
- [ ] Vocational

Tutoring

	Individual	Group
Time management	☐	☐
Organizational skills	☐	☐
Learning strategies	☐	☐
Study skills	☐	☐
Content area	☐	☐
Writing lab	☐	☐
Math lab	☐	☐

LD PROGRAM STAFF

Key staff person available to work with LD students: Charles Collier, Director: Student Disabilities Service Office.

East Tennessee State University

Johnson City, TN

Address: 807 University Parkway, Johnson City, TN, 37614-0000
Admissions telephone: 800 462-3878
Admissions FAX: 423 439-4630
Director of Admissions: Mike Pitts
Admissions e-mail: go2etsu@etsu.edu
Web site: http://www.etsu.edu
SAT Code: 1198 ACT Code: 3958

Director, Disability Services: Linda O. Gibson
LD program telephone: 423 439-8346
LD program e-mail: gibsonl@etsu.edu
Total campus enrollment: 9,672

GENERAL

East Tennessee State University is a public, coed, four-year institution. 360-acre campus in Johnson City (population: 55,469), 20 miles from Bristol; branch campuses in Bristol, Greeneville, and Kingsport. Served by airport and bus; major airport serves Knoxville (90 miles); train serves Roanoke, VA. (150 miles). School operates transportation to local parking areas. Public transportation serves campus. Semester system.

LD ADMISSIONS

A personal interview is not required. Essay is not required. Required secondary school courses in specific area of disability may be waived.

SECONDARY SCHOOL REQUIREMENTS

Graduation from secondary school required; GED accepted. The following course distribution required: 4 units of English, 3 units of math, 2 units of science, 2 units of foreign language, 1 unit of social studies, 1 unit of history.

TESTING

ACT required; SAT Reasoning may be substituted. SAT Subject recommended.

All enrolled freshmen (fall 2004):

Average SAT I Scores: Verbal: 513 Math: 503
Average ACT Scores: Composite: 22

Child Study Team report is not required. Tests required as part of this documentation:

- ❑ WAIS-IV
- ❑ WISC-IV
- ❑ SATA
- ❑ Woodcock-Johnson
- ❑ Nelson-Denny Reading Test
- ❑ Other

UNDERGRADUATE STUDENT BODY

Total undergraduate student enrollment: 3,885 Men, 5,240 Women.

Composition of student body (fall 2004):

	Undergraduate	Freshmen
International	1.3	1.3
Black	4.4	4.0
American Indian	0.5	0.4
Asian-American	1.0	1.1
Hispanic	1.2	1.0
White	88.8	90.5
Unreported	2.8	1.7
	100.0%	100.0%

9% are from out of state. 7% join a fraternity and 6% join a sorority. Average age of full-time undergraduates is 23. 41% of classes have fewer than 20 students, 51% have between 20 and 50 students, 8% have more than 50 students.

STUDENT HOUSING

48% of freshmen live in college housing. Freshmen are not required to live on campus. Housing is guaranteed for all undergraduates. Campus can house 2,540 undergraduates.

EXPENSES

Tuition (2005-06): $3,587 per year (in-state), $9,082 (out-of-state).
Room: $2,259. Board: $2,738.
There is no additional cost for LD program/services.

LD SERVICES

LD program size is not limited.

LD services available to:

❑ Freshmen ❑ Sophomores ❑ Juniors ❑ Seniors

Academic Accommodations

Curriculum		In class	
Foreign language waiver	❑	Early syllabus	❑
Lighter course load	■	Note takers in class	■
Math waiver	❑	Priority seating	❑
Other special classes	❑	Tape recorders	❑
Priority registrations	❑	Videotaped classes	❑
Substitution of courses	❑	Text on tape	❑
Exams		**Services**	
Extended time	❑	Diagnostic tests	❑
Oral exams	■	Learning centers	❑
Take home exams	❑	Proofreaders	❑
Exams on tape or computer	❑	Readers	❑
Untimed exams	■	Reading Machines/Kurzweil	❑
Other accommodations	❑	Special bookstore section	❑
		Typists	❑

Credit toward degree is given for remedial courses taken.

Counseling Services

- ❑ Academic
- ❑ Psychological
- ❑ Student Support groups
- ❑ Vocational

Tutoring

	Individual	Group
Time management	❑	❑
Organizational skills	❑	❑
Learning strategies	❑	❑
Study skills	❑	❑
Content area	❑	❑
Writing lab	❑	❑
Math lab	❑	❑

LD PROGRAM STAFF

Total number of LD Program staff (including director):

Full Time: 5 Part Time: 5

Key staff person available to work with LD students: Linda O. Gibson, Director, Disability Services.

King College

Bristol, TN

Address: 1350 King College Road, Bristol, TN, 37620
Admissions telephone: 800 362-0014
Admissions FAX: 423 652-4727
Associate Vice President for Enrollment Management: Melinda Clark
Admissions e-mail: admissions@king.edu
Web site: http://www.king.edu
SAT Code: 1371 ACT Code: 3970

LD program name: Learning Resource Center
Learning Specialist: Lisa Yokshas
LD program telephone: 423 652-4303
LD program e-mail: ljyoksha@king.edu
LD program enrollment: 7, Total campus enrollment: 744

GENERAL

King College is a private, coed, four-year institution. 135-acre, suburban campus in Bristol (population: 24,821), 100 miles from Knoxville. Served by bus; airport serves Blountville (20 miles). School operates transportation to airport. Semester system.

LD ADMISSIONS

Students do not complete a separate application and are simultaneously accepted to the LD program. A member of the LD program does sit on the admissions committee. A personal interview is not required. Essay is not required.

SECONDARY SCHOOL REQUIREMENTS

Graduation from secondary school required; GED accepted. The following course distribution required: 4 units of English, 3 units of math, 1 unit of science, 2 units of foreign language, 2 units of social studies, 2 units of history, 4 units of academic electives.

TESTING

SAT Reasoning or ACT required. SAT Subject recommended.

All enrolled freshmen (fall 2004):

Average SAT I Scores:	Verbal: 540	Math: 519
Average ACT Scores:	Composite: 23	

Child Study Team report is not required. A neuropsychological or comprehensive psycho-educational evaluation is required for admission. Must be dated within 60 months of application. Tests required as part of this documentation:

- ☑ WAIS-IV
- ☐ WISC-IV
- ☑ SATA
- ☑ Woodcock-Johnson
- ☑ Nelson-Denny Reading Test
- ☐ Other

UNDERGRADUATE STUDENT BODY

Total undergraduate student enrollment: 276 Men, 379 Women.

Composition of student body (fall 2004):

	Undergraduate	Freshmen
International	1.2	4.2
Black	1.7	1.0
American Indian	0.0	0.3
Asian-American	1.2	0.9
Hispanic	1.7	1.5
White	78.5	72.2
Unreported	15.7	19.9
	100.0%	100.0%

50% are from out of state. Average age of full-time undergraduates is 23. 77% of classes have fewer than 20 students, 23% have between 20 and 50 students.

STUDENT HOUSING

82% of freshmen live in college housing. Freshmen are required to live on campus. Housing is guaranteed for all undergraduates. Campus can house 485 undergraduates.

EXPENSES

Tuition (2005-06): $16,626 per year.

Room: $2,850. Board: $2,870.

There is no additional cost for LD program/services.

LD SERVICES

LD program size is not limited.

LD services available to:

☑ Freshmen ☑ Sophomores ☑ Juniors ☑ Seniors

Academic Accommodations

Curriculum		**In class**	
Foreign language waiver	☐	Early syllabus	☐
Lighter course load	☑	Note takers in class	☑
Math waiver	☐	Priority seating	☐
Other special classes	☑	Tape recorders	☑
Priority registrations	☐	Videotaped classes	☐
Substitution of courses	☐	Text on tape	☐
Exams		**Services**	
Extended time	☑	Diagnostic tests	☐
Oral exams	☑	Learning centers	☑
Take home exams	☐	Proofreaders	☐
Exams on tape or computer	☐	Readers	☐
Untimed exams	☑	Reading Machines/Kurzweil	☐
Other accommodations	☐	Special bookstore section	☐
		Typists	☐

Credit toward degree is given for remedial courses taken.

Counseling Services

- ☑ Academic
- ☑ Psychological
- ☐ Student Support groups
- ☐ Vocational

Tutoring

Individual tutoring is available daily.

Average size of tutoring groups: 2

	Individual	Group
Time management	☑	☑
Organizational skills	☑	☑
Learning strategies	☑	☑
Study skills	☑	☑
Content area	☑	☑
Writing lab	☑	☑
Math lab	☑	☑

UNIQUE LD PROGRAM FEATURES

Educational consultation with professors and advisors. Preferential placement for first year students, academic counseling and time management available.

LD PROGRAM STAFF

Total number of LD Program staff (including director):

Full Time: 1 Part Time: 1

There is an advisor/advocate from the LD program available to students. 11 peer tutors are available to work with LD students.

Key staff person available to work with LD students: Lisa Yokshas, Learning Specialist.

Lambuth University

Jackson, TN

Address: 705 Lambuth Boulevard, Jackson, TN, 38301
Admissions telephone: 800 LAMBUTH, extension 3223
Admissions FAX: 731 425-3496
Director of Admissions: Lisa Warmath
Admissions e-mail: admit@lambuth.edu
Web site: http://www.lambuth.edu
SAT Code: 1394 ACT Code: 3974

Director of Student Disabilities Services: Donna Overstreet
LD program telephone: 731 425-3297
LD program e-mail: overstre@lambuth.edu
LD program enrollment: 7, Total campus enrollment: 806

GENERAL

Lambuth University is a private, coed, four-year institution. 50-acre campus in Jackson (population: 59,643), 80 miles northeast of Memphis. Served by bus; airport and train serve Memphis and Nashville (120 miles). Public transportation serves campus. Semester system.

LD ADMISSIONS

Students do not complete a separate application and are simultaneously accepted to the LD program. A member of the LD program does sit on the admissions committee. A personal interview is recommended. Essay is required and may be typed. All students, regardless of disability, must meet the same admission requirements.

SECONDARY SCHOOL REQUIREMENTS

Graduation from secondary school required; GED accepted.

TESTING

ACT required; SAT Reasoning may be substituted. SAT Subject recommended.

All enrolled freshmen (fall 2004):

Average SAT I Scores:	Verbal: 530	Math: 510
Average ACT Scores:	Composite: 22	

Child Study Team report is not required. A neuropsychological or comprehensive psycho-educational evaluation is required for admission. Must be dated within 36 months of application. Tests required as part of this documentation:

■ WAIS-IV ■ Woodcock-Johnson
■ WISC-IV ■ Nelson-Denny Reading Test
■ SATA ☐ Other

UNDERGRADUATE STUDENT BODY

Total undergraduate student enrollment: 382 Men, 521 Women.

Composition of student body (fall 2004):

	Undergraduate	Freshmen
International	0.5	2.1
Black	11.5	17.4
American Indian	0.0	0.3
Asian-American	1.4	0.7
Hispanic	2.3	2.5
White	83.4	76.5
Unreported	0.9	0.5
	100.0%	100.0%

20% are from out of state. 30% join a fraternity and 29% join a sorority. Average age of full-time undergraduates is 22. 72% of classes have fewer than 20 students, 27% have between 20 and 50 students.

STUDENT HOUSING

84% of freshmen live in college housing. Freshmen are required to live on campus. Housing is guaranteed for all undergraduates. Campus can house 628 undergraduates. Single rooms are available for students with medical or special needs. A medical note is not required.

EXPENSES

Tuition (2005-06): $15,000 per year.
Room: $3,000. Board: $3,300.
There is no additional cost for LD program/services.

LD SERVICES

LD program size is not limited.

LD services available to:

■ Freshmen ■ Sophomores ■ Juniors ■ Seniors

Academic Accommodations

Curriculum		In class	
Foreign language waiver	☐	Early syllabus	☐
Lighter course load	☐	Note takers in class	☐
Math waiver	☐	Priority seating	☐
Other special classes	☐	Tape recorders	■
Priority registrations	☐	Videotaped classes	☐
Substitution of courses	☐	Text on tape	☐
Exams		**Services**	
Extended time	■	Diagnostic tests	■
Oral exams	■	Learning centers	■
Take home exams	☐	Proofreaders	☐
Exams on tape or computer	☐	Readers	☐
Untimed exams	■	Reading Machines/Kurzweil	☐
Other accommodations	☐	Special bookstore section	☐
		Typists	☐

Credit toward degree is not given for remedial courses taken.

Counseling Services

■ Academic
■ Psychological
■ Student Support groups
☐ Vocational

Tutoring

Individual tutoring is available weekly.

	Individual	Group
Time management	■	■
Organizational skills	■	■
Learning strategies	■	■
Study skills	■	■
Content area	■	■
Writing lab	■	☐
Math lab	■	■

UNIQUE LD PROGRAM FEATURES

Accommodations for class presentation, evaluation, and access will be determined on a case-by-case basis once the student has disclosed a disability and appropriate documentation supporting the request for accommodations has been provided to the University.

The students and their advocate meet on an as needed basis.

LD PROGRAM STAFF

There is an advisor/advocate from the LD program available to students. 5 peer tutors are available to work with LD students.

Key staff person available to work with LD students: Donna Overstreet, Director of Student Disabilities Services.

Lee University

Cleveland, TN

Address: PO Box 3450, Cleveland, TN, 37320
Admissions telephone: 800 533-9930
Admissions FAX: 423 614-8533
Vice President for Enrollment Management: Phil Cook
Admissions e-mail: admissions@leeuniversity.edu
Web site: http://www.leeuniversity.edu
SAT Code: 1401 ACT Code: 3978

LD program name: Academic Support Program
LD program address: 1120 N. Ocoee St,
Director: Gayle Gallaher, Ph.D.
LD program telephone: 423 614-8181
LD program e-mail: ggallaher@leeuniversity.edu
LD program enrollment: 105, Total campus enrollment: 3,571

GENERAL

Lee University is a private, coed, four-year institution. 60-acre campus in Cleveland (population: 37,192), 30 miles from Chattanooga; branch campus in Charlotte, N.C. Served by bus; airport and train serve Chattanooga; major airport serves Atlanta (110 miles). Semester system.

LD ADMISSIONS

Students do not complete a separate application and are simultaneously accepted to the LD program. A member of the LD program does not sit on the admissions committee. A personal interview is required. Essay is not required.

For fall 2004, 22 completed self-identified LD applications were received. 14 applications were offered admission, and 11 enrolled.

SECONDARY SCHOOL REQUIREMENTS

Graduation from secondary school required; GED accepted. The following course distribution required: 4 units of English, 3 units of math, 2 units of science, 1 unit of foreign language, 2 units of social studies, 1 unit of history.

TESTING

SAT Reasoning recommended. ACT recommended. SAT Subject recommended.

All enrolled freshmen (fall 2004):

Average SAT I Scores:	Verbal: 536	Math: 517
Average ACT Scores:	Composite: 23	

Child Study Team report is not required. A neuropsychological or comprehensive psycho-educational evaluation is required for admission. Tests required as part of this documentation:

- ■ WAIS-IV
- ■ WISC-IV
- ■ SATA
- ■ Woodcock-Johnson
- ☐ Nelson-Denny Reading Test
- ■ Other

UNDERGRADUATE STUDENT BODY

Total undergraduate student enrollment: 1,379 Men, 1,776 Women.

Composition of student body (fall 2004):

	Undergraduate	Freshmen
International	2.9	4.2
Black	3.1	4.9
American Indian	0.3	0.5
Asian-American	1.2	0.8
Hispanic	2.9	2.8
White	85.8	82.1
Unreported	3.8	4.7
	100.0%	100.0%

Average age of full-time undergraduates is 22. 48% of classes have fewer than 20 students, 43% have between 20 and 50 students, 9% have more than 50 students.

STUDENT HOUSING

74% of freshmen live in college housing. Freshmen are required to live on campus. Housing is guaranteed for all undergraduates. Campus can house 1,807 undergraduates. Single rooms are available for students with medical or special needs. A medical note is required.

EXPENSES

Tuition (2005-06): $9,400 per year.
Room: $2,680. Board: $2,490.
There is no additional cost for LD program/services.

LD SERVICES

LD program size is not limited.

LD services available to:

☐ Freshmen ☐ Sophomores ☐ Juniors ☐ Seniors

Academic Accommodations

Curriculum		**In class**	
Foreign language waiver	☐	Early syllabus	☐
Lighter course load	■	Note takers in class	■
Math waiver	☐	Priority seating	☐
Other special classes	☐	Tape recorders	■
Priority registrations	☐	Videotaped classes	■
Substitution of courses	☐	Text on tape	☐
Exams		**Services**	
Extended time	■	Diagnostic tests	☐
Oral exams	■	Learning centers	■
Take home exams	☐	Proofreaders	☐
Exams on tape or computer	☐	Readers	■
Untimed exams	■	Reading Machines/Kurzweil	■
Other accommodations	■	Special bookstore section	☐
		Typists	■

Credit toward degree is given for remedial courses taken.

Counseling Services

- ■ Academic
- ■ Psychological
- ☐ Student Support groups
- ■ Vocational

Tutoring

Individual tutoring is available.

Average size of tutoring groups: 1

	Individual	Group
Time management	■	☐
Organizational skills	■	☐
Learning strategies	■	☐
Study skills	■	☐
Content area	■	■
Writing lab	■	■
Math lab	■	■

LD PROGRAM STAFF

Total number of LD Program staff (including director):

Full Time: 2 Part Time: 2

There is an advisor/advocate from the LD program available to students.

Key staff person available to work with LD students: Gayle Gallaher, Ph.D., Director of Academic Support Programs.

LD Program web site: www.leeuniversity.edu

Lipscomb University

Nashville, TN

Address: 3901 Granny White Pike, Nashville, TN, 37204-3951
Admissions telephone: 877 582-4766
Admissions FAX: 615 269-1804
Director of Admissions: Ricky Holaway
Admissions e-mail: admissions@lipscomb.edu
Web site: http://www.lipscomb.edu
SAT Code: 1161 ACT Code: 3956

LD program name: Disability Services
LD program address: 3901 Granny White Pike,
Director of Disability Services: Ashley Dumas
LD program telephone: 615 279-5737
LD program e-mail: ashley.dumas@lipscomb.edu
Total campus enrollment: 2,315

GENERAL

Lipscomb University is a private, coed, four-year institution. 65-acre campus in Nashville (population: 545,524). Served by air and bus. Public transportation serves campus. Semester system.

LD ADMISSIONS

A personal interview is required. Essay is not required.

SECONDARY SCHOOL REQUIREMENTS

Graduation from secondary school required; GED accepted. The following course distribution required: 4 units of English, 2 units of math, 2 units of science, 2 units of foreign language, 2 units of social studies, 2 units of history, 2 units of academic electives.

TESTING

ACT required; SAT Reasoning may be substituted. SAT Subject recommended.

All enrolled freshmen (fall 2004):

Average SAT I Scores:	Verbal: 556	Math: 550
Average ACT Scores:	Composite: 24	

Child Study Team report is not required. Tests required as part of this documentation:

- ☐ WAIS-IV
- ☐ WISC-IV
- ☐ SATA
- ☐ Woodcock-Johnson
- ☐ Nelson-Denny Reading Test
- ☐ Other

UNDERGRADUATE STUDENT BODY

Total undergraduate student enrollment: 1,004 Men, 1,303 Women.

Composition of student body (fall 2004):

	Undergraduate	Freshmen
International	1.5	1.2
Black	5.2	4.7
American Indian	0.2	0.2
Asian-American	1.0	1.5
Hispanic	0.8	1.4
White	76.6	79.7
Unreported	14.7	11.3
	100.0%	100.0%

35% are from out of state. Average age of full-time undergraduates is 21. 50% of classes have fewer than 20 students, 44% have between 20 and 50 students, 6% have more than 50 students.

STUDENT HOUSING

Freshmen are required to live on campus. Housing is guaranteed for all undergraduates. Single rooms are available for students with medical or special needs. A medical note is required.

EXPENSES

Tuition (2005-06): $13,928 per year.
Room & Board: $6,410.
There is no additional cost for LD program/services.

LD SERVICES

LD program size is not limited.

LD services available to:

■ Freshmen ■ Sophomores ■ Juniors ■ Seniors

Academic Accommodations

Curriculum		In class	
Foreign language waiver	■	Early syllabus	☐
Lighter course load	■	Note takers in class	■
Math waiver	■	Priority seating	■
Other special classes	☐	Tape recorders	■
Priority registrations	■	Videotaped classes	☐
Substitution of courses	■	Text on tape	■
Exams		**Services**	
Extended time	■	Diagnostic tests	■
Oral exams	■	Learning centers	☐
Take home exams	☐	Proofreaders	☐
Exams on tape or computer	■	Readers	■
Untimed exams	■	Reading Machines/Kurzweil	■
Other accommodations	■	Special bookstore section	☐
		Typists	■

Credit toward degree is not given for remedial courses taken.

Counseling Services

- ■ Academic
- ■ Psychological
- ☐ Student Support groups
- ■ Vocational

Tutoring

Individual tutoring is not available.

	Individual	Group
Time management	■	☐
Organizational skills	■	☐
Learning strategies	■	☐
Study skills	■	☐
Content area	☐	■
Writing lab	☐	■
Math lab	☐	■

LD PROGRAM STAFF

Total number of LD Program staff (including director):

Full Time: 1 Part Time: 1

There is an advisor/advocate from the LD program available to students.

Key staff person available to work with LD students: Ashley Dumas, Director of Disability Services.

Martin Methodist College

Pulaski, TN

Address: 433 W. Madison Street, Pulaski, TN, 38478
Admissions telephone: 931 363-9804
Admissions FAX: 931 363-9803
Vice President for Enrollment: Robby Shelton
Admissions e-mail: admit@martinmethodist.edu
Web site: http://www.martinmethodist.edu
SAT Code: 1449 ACT Code: 3986

LD program name: Student Support Services
Director, Student Support Services: David Chisholm
LD program telephone: 931 424-7334
LD program e-mail: dchisholm@martinmethodist.edu
Total campus enrollment: 705

GENERAL

Martin Methodist College is a private, coed, four-year institution. 11-acre campus in Pulaski (population: 7,871), 70 miles southwest of Nashville and 50 miles northwest of Huntsville, Ala. Served by bus; major airports serve Huntsville and Nashville. Semester system.

LD ADMISSIONS

Application Deadline: 08/01. Students do not complete a separate application and are simultaneously accepted to the LD program. A member of the LD program does not sit on the admissions committee. A personal interview is recommended. Essay is not required.

SECONDARY SCHOOL REQUIREMENTS

Graduation from secondary school not required. The following course distribution required: 4 units of English, 2 units of math, 1 unit of science, 1 unit of social studies, 1 unit of history, 6 units of academic electives.

TESTING

ACT required; SAT Reasoning may be substituted. SAT Subject required.

All enrolled freshmen (fall 2004):

Average SAT I Scores:	Verbal:	Math:
Average ACT Scores:	Composite: 20	

Child Study Team report is not required. Tests required as part of this documentation:

- [ ] WAIS-IV
- [ ] WISC-IV
- [ ] SATA
- [ ] Woodcock-Johnson
- [ ] Nelson-Denny Reading Test
- [ ] Other

UNDERGRADUATE STUDENT BODY

Total undergraduate student enrollment: 219 Men, 363 Women.

Composition of student body (fall 2004):

	Undergraduate	Freshmen
International	15.6	8.8
Black	12.8	11.8
American Indian	0.0	0.6
Asian-American	0.6	0.2
Hispanic	1.1	0.6
White	68.2	77.6
Unreported	1.7	0.4
	100.0%	100.0%

24% are from out of state. 72% of classes have fewer than 20 students, 27% have between 20 and 50 students, 1% have more than 50 students.

STUDENT HOUSING

30% of freshmen live in college housing. Freshmen are required to live on campus. Housing is guaranteed for all undergraduates. Campus can house 386 undergraduates. Single rooms are available for students with medical or special needs. A medical note is not required.

EXPENSES

Tuition (2005-06): $14,070 per year.
Room: $3,000. Board: $2,200.

There is no additional cost for LD program/services.

LD SERVICES

LD program size is limited.

LD services available to:

- [x] Freshmen
- [x] Sophomores
- [x] Juniors
- [x] Seniors

Academic Accommodations

Curriculum		In class	
Foreign language waiver	[ ]	Early syllabus	[ ]
Lighter course load	[x]	Note takers in class	[x]
Math waiver	[ ]	Priority seating	[ ]
Other special classes	[ ]	Tape recorders	[x]
Priority registrations	[ ]	Videotaped classes	[ ]
Substitution of courses	[ ]	Text on tape	[ ]
Exams		**Services**	
Extended time	[x]	Diagnostic tests	[x]
Oral exams	[ ]	Learning centers	[x]
Take home exams	[ ]	Proofreaders	[ ]
Exams on tape or computer	[ ]	Readers	[ ]
Untimed exams	[x]	Reading Machines/Kurzweil	[ ]
Other accommodations	[ ]	Special bookstore section	[ ]
		Typists	[ ]

Credit toward degree is not given for remedial courses taken.

Counseling Services

- [ ] Academic
- [ ] Psychological
- [ ] Student Support groups
- [ ] Vocational

Tutoring

Individual tutoring is available weekly.

Average size of tutoring groups: 4

	Individual	Group
Time management	[x]	[x]
Organizational skills	[ ]	[x]
Learning strategies	[ ]	[x]
Study skills	[x]	[ ]
Content area	[x]	[ ]
Writing lab	[x]	[ ]
Math lab	[x]	[ ]

LD PROGRAM STAFF

Total number of LD Program staff (including director):

Full Time: 3 Part Time: 3

There is no advisor/advocate from the LD program available to students. 10 peer tutors are available to work with LD students.

Key staff person available to work with LD students: Gordon Thayer, Staff Manager, Student Support Services.

Maryville College

Maryville, TN

Address: 502 E. Lamar Alexander Parkway, Maryville, TN, 37804-5907
Admissions telephone: 800 597-2687
Admissions FAX: 865 981-8005
Vice President of Admissions and Enrollment: Ned Willard
Admissions e-mail: admissions@maryvillecollege.edu
Web site: http://www.maryvillecollege.edu
SAT Code: 1454 ACT Code: 3988

LD program name: Learning Center
Director of Learning Services: Ms. Lori Hunter
LD program telephone: 865 981-8124
LD program e-mail: lori.hunter@maryvillecollege.edu
LD program enrollment: 32, Total campus enrollment: 1,080

GENERAL

Maryville College is a private, coed, four-year institution. 350-acre campus in Maryville (population: 23,120), 15 miles from Knoxville. Airport and bus serve Knoxville. 4-1-4 system.

LD ADMISSIONS

A personal interview is recommended. Essay is not required.

SECONDARY SCHOOL REQUIREMENTS

Graduation from secondary school required; GED accepted. The following course distribution required: 4 units of English, 3 units of math, 2 units of science, 2 units of foreign language, 2 units of social studies, 1 unit of academic electives.

TESTING

SAT Reasoning or ACT required. SAT Subject recommended.

All enrolled freshmen (fall 2004):

Average SAT I Scores:	Verbal: 563	Math: 541
Average ACT Scores:	Composite: 24	

Child Study Team report is not required. Tests required as part of this documentation:

- [ ] WAIS-IV
- [ ] WISC-IV
- [ ] SATA
- [ ] Woodcock-Johnson
- [ ] Nelson-Denny Reading Test
- [ ] Other

UNDERGRADUATE STUDENT BODY

Total undergraduate student enrollment: 432 Men, 594 Women.

Composition of student body (fall 2004):

	Undergraduate	Freshmen
International	0.3	4.0
Black	4.1	5.5
American Indian	0.3	0.5
Asian-American	1.6	1.2
Hispanic	1.3	1.1
White	92.1	87.4
Unreported	0.3	0.3
	100.0%	100.0%

28% are from out of state. Average age of full-time undergraduates is 21. 62% of classes have fewer than 20 students, 38% have between 20 and 50 students.

STUDENT HOUSING

85% of freshmen live in college housing. Housing is guaranteed for all undergraduates. Campus can house 777 undergraduates. Single rooms are available for students with medical or special needs. A medical note is required.

EXPENSES

Tuition (2005-06): $21,624 per year.
Room: $3,500. Board: $3,500.
There is no additional cost for LD program/services.

LD SERVICES

LD program size is not limited.

LD services available to:

- [x] Freshmen
- [x] Sophomores
- [x] Juniors
- [x] Seniors

Academic Accommodations

Curriculum		In class	
Foreign language waiver	[ ]	Early syllabus	[ ]
Lighter course load	[x]	Note takers in class	[x]
Math waiver	[ ]	Priority seating	[x]
Other special classes	[ ]	Tape recorders	[x]
Priority registrations	[ ]	Videotaped classes	[ ]
Substitution of courses	[ ]	Text on tape	[x]
Exams		**Services**	
Extended time	[x]	Diagnostic tests	[ ]
Oral exams	[x]	Learning centers	[x]
Take home exams	[ ]	Proofreaders	[ ]
Exams on tape or computer	[x]	Readers	[x]
Untimed exams	[x]	Reading Machines/Kurzweil	[x]
Other accommodations	[ ]	Special bookstore section	[ ]
		Typists	[x]

Credit toward degree is not given for remedial courses taken.

Counseling Services

[x]	Academic	Meets 28 times per academic year
[ ]	Psychological	
[x]	Student Support groups	Meets 28 times per academic year
[ ]	Vocational	

Tutoring

Individual tutoring is available daily.

Average size of tutoring groups: 3

	Individual	Group
Time management	[x]	[x]
Organizational skills	[x]	[x]
Learning strategies	[x]	[x]
Study skills	[x]	[x]
Content area	[x]	[x]
Writing lab	[x]	[x]
Math lab	[x]	[x]

LD PROGRAM STAFF

Total number of LD Program staff (including director):

Full Time: 2 Part Time: 2

There is an advisor/advocate from the LD program available to students. The advisor/advocate meets with faculty 1 time per month and students 2 times per month. 30 peer tutors are available to work with LD students.

Key staff person available to work with LD students: Ms. Lori Hunter, Director of Learning Services.

The University of Memphis

Memphis, TN

Address: Memphis, TN, 38152
Admissions telephone: 901 678-2111
Admissions FAX: 901 678-3053
Director of Admissions: David Wallace
Admissions e-mail: recruitment@memphis.edu
Web site: http://www.memphis.edu
SAT Code: 1459 ACT Code: 3992

LD program name: Student Disability Services
LD program address: 110 Wilder Tower,
Director, Student Disability Services: Susan TePaske
LD program telephone: 901 678-2880
LD program e-mail: stepaske@memphis.edu
LD program enrollment: 469, Total campus enrollment: 15,928

GENERAL

The University of Memphis is a public, coed, four-year institution. 1,178-acre, suburban campus in Memphis (population: 650,100). Served by air, bus, and train. Semester system.

LD ADMISSIONS

Students do not complete a separate application and are not simultaneously accepted to the LD program. A member of the LD program does not sit on the admissions committee. A personal interview is not required. Essay is not required.

SECONDARY SCHOOL REQUIREMENTS

Graduation from secondary school required; GED accepted. The following course distribution required: 4 units of English, 3 units of math, 2 units of science, 2 units of foreign language, 2 units of social studies, 1 unit of history.

TESTING

SAT Reasoning or ACT required. SAT Subject recommended.

All enrolled freshmen (fall 2004):

Average SAT I Scores:	Verbal: 536	Math: 523
Average ACT Scores:	Composite: 21	

Child Study Team report is not required. A neuropsychological or comprehensive psycho-educational evaluation is required for admission. Must be dated within 36 months of application. Tests required as part of this documentation:

- ■ WAIS-IV
- ☐ WISC-IV
- ☐ SATA
- ■ Woodcock-Johnson
- ☐ Nelson-Denny Reading Test
- ■ Other

UNDERGRADUATE STUDENT BODY

Total undergraduate student enrollment: 6,455 Men, 9,157 Women.

Composition of student body (fall 2004):

	Undergraduate	Freshmen
International	2.0	2.1
Black	39.4	38.1
American Indian	0.1	0.3
Asian-American	2.9	2.1
Hispanic	1.9	1.4
White	53.2	55.7
Unreported	0.5	0.3
	100.0%	100.0%

9% are from out of state. 7% join a fraternity and 5% join a sorority. Average age of full-time undergraduates is 22. 36% of classes have fewer than 20 students, 53% have between 20 and 50 students, 11% have more than 50 students.

STUDENT HOUSING

27% of freshmen live in college housing. Freshmen are not required to live on campus. Housing is guaranteed for all undergraduates. Campus can house 2,482 undergraduates. Single rooms are available for students with medical or special needs. A medical note is required.

EXPENSES

Tuition (2005-06): $4,902 per year (in-state), $14,748 (out-of-state).

Room: $1,930. Board: $3,119.

There is no additional cost for LD program/services.

LD SERVICES

LD program size is not limited.

LD services available to:

■ Freshmen ■ Sophomores ■ Juniors ■ Seniors

Academic Accommodations

Curriculum		In class	
Foreign language waiver	■	Early syllabus	☐
Lighter course load	■	Note takers in class	■
Math waiver	☐	Priority seating	■
Other special classes	☐	Tape recorders	■
Priority registrations	■	Videotaped classes	☐
Substitution of courses	■	Text on tape	☐
Exams		**Services**	
Extended time	■	Diagnostic tests	■
Oral exams	☐	Learning centers	■
Take home exams	☐	Proofreaders	■
Exams on tape or computer	■	Readers	■
Untimed exams	■	Reading Machines/Kurzweil	■
Other accommodations	■	Special bookstore section	☐
		Typists	☐

Credit toward degree is not given for remedial courses taken.

Counseling Services

- ■ Academic
- ■ Psychological
- ■ Student Support groups
- ■ Vocational

Tutoring

Individual tutoring is available weekly.

	Individual	Group
Time management	■	☐
Organizational skills	■	☐
Learning strategies	■	☐
Study skills	■	☐
Content area	■	☐
Writing lab	■	☐
Math lab	■	☐

UNIQUE LD PROGRAM FEATURES

The LD/ADHD Program at The University of Memphis promotes development and independence of students with LD and ADHD through early intervention and education about disability-related functional limitations. Through counseling and coaching students learn appropriate techniques and accommodations to compensate for functional limitations and move toward academic success.

LD PROGRAM STAFF

Total number of LD Program staff (including director):

Full Time: 3 Part Time: 3

There is an advisor/advocate from the LD program available to students. The advisor/advocate meets with student 4 times per month. 3 graduate students are available to work with LD students.

Key staff person available to work with LD students: Susan TePaske, Director, Student Disability Services. LD Program web site: http://www.people.memphis.edu/~sds

Middle Tennessee State University

Murfreesboro, TN

Address: 1301 E. Main Street, CAB Room 205, Murfreesboro, TN, 37132
Admissions telephone: 800 331-6878
Admissions FAX: 615 898-5478
Director of Admissions: Lynn Palmer
Admissions e-mail: admissions@mtsu.edu
Web site: http://www.mtsu.edu
SAT Code: 1466 ACT Code: 3994

LD program name: Disabled Student Services
LD program address: P.O. Box 7
LD program telephone: 615 898-2783
LD program e-mail: acagle@mtsu.edu
Total campus enrollment: 20,288

GENERAL

Middle Tennessee State University is a public, coed, four-year institution. 500-acre campus in Murfreesboro (population: 68,816), 30 miles from Nashville. Served by bus; major airport serves Nashville. Public transportation serves campus. School operates transportation to local shopping areas. Semester system.

LD ADMISSIONS

Students do not complete a separate application and are simultaneously accepted to the LD program. A member of the LD program does not sit on the admissions committee. High school waivers are accepted for math and foreign language. A personal interview is not required. Essay is not required. Admissions requirements that may be waived for LD students depends on documentation

SECONDARY SCHOOL REQUIREMENTS

Graduation from secondary school required; GED accepted. The following course distribution required: 4 units of English, 3 units of math, 2 units of science, 2 units of foreign language, 1 unit of social studies, 1 unit of history.

TESTING

SAT Reasoning or ACT required. SAT Subject recommended.

All enrolled freshmen (fall 2004):

Average SAT I Scores:	Verbal: 534	Math: 527
Average ACT Scores:	Composite: 22	

Child Study Team report is not required. A neuropsychological or comprehensive psycho-educational evaluation is required for admission. Tests required as part of this documentation:

- ■ WAIS-IV
- ■ WISC-IV
- ■ SATA
- ■ Woodcock-Johnson
- ■ Nelson-Denny Reading Test
- ☐ Other

UNDERGRADUATE STUDENT BODY

Total undergraduate student enrollment: 8,404 Men, 9,726 Women.

Composition of student body (fall 2004):

	Undergraduate	Freshmen
International	0.0	0.0
Black	11.8	12.0
American Indian	0.3	0.4
Asian-American	2.4	2.5
Hispanic	2.2	1.9
White	82.8	82.8
Unreported	0.5	0.4
	100.0%	100.0%

8% are from out of state. 6% join a fraternity and 8% join a sorority. Average age of full-time undergraduates is 21. 36% of classes have fewer than 20 students, 59% have between 20 and 50 students, 5% have more than 50 students.

STUDENT HOUSING

47% of freshmen live in college housing. Freshmen are not required to live on campus. Housing is guaranteed for all undergraduates. Campus can house 3,362 undergraduates. Single rooms are available for students with medical or special needs. A medical note is required.

EXPENSES

Tuition (2005-06): $1,904 per year (in-state), $6,798 (out-of-state).
Room: $2,680. Board: $1,042.
There is no additional cost for LD program/services.

LD SERVICES

LD program size is not limited.

LD services available to:

■ Freshmen ■ Sophomores ■ Juniors ■ Seniors

Academic Accommodations

Curriculum		**In class**	
Foreign language waiver	■	Early syllabus	☐
Lighter course load	☐	Note takers in class	■
Math waiver	☐	Priority seating	■
Other special classes	☐	Tape recorders	■
Priority registrations	☐	Videotaped classes	☐
Substitution of courses	■	Text on tape	■
Exams		**Services**	
Extended time	■	Diagnostic tests	☐
Oral exams	■	Learning centers	■
Take home exams	☐	Proofreaders	■
Exams on tape or computer	■	Readers	■
Untimed exams	☐	Reading Machines/Kurzweil	■
Other accommodations	■	Special bookstore section	☐
		Typists	■

Credit toward degree is not given for remedial courses taken.

Counseling Services

- ■ Academic
- ■ Psychological
- ■ Student Support groups
- ■ Vocational

Tutoring

Individual tutoring is available weekly.

Average size of tutoring groups: 1

	Individual	Group
Time management	■	☐
Organizational skills	■	☐
Learning strategies	■	☐
Study skills	■	☐
Content area	■	☐
Writing lab	☐	■
Math lab	☐	■

LD PROGRAM STAFF

Total number of LD Program staff (including director):

Full Time: 4 Part Time: 4

There is an advisor/advocate from the LD program available to students. 10 peer tutors are available to work with LD students.

Key staff person available to work with LD students: Janet Norman, Assistant Director of Disabled Student Services.

LD Program web site: www.mtsu.edu/~dssemail/

Milligan College

Milligan College, TN

Address: PO Box 500, Milligan College, TN, 37682
Admissions telephone: 800 262-8337
Admissions FAX: 423 461-8982
Vice President for Enrollment Management: Tracy Brinn
Admissions e-mail: admissions@milligan.edu
Web site: http://www.milligan.edu
SAT Code: 1469 ACT Code: 3996

Vice President: Mark Matson
LD program telephone: 423 461-8720
LD program e-mail: mmatson@milligan.edu
LD program enrollment: 9, Total campus enrollment: 753

GENERAL

Milligan College is a private, coed, four-year institution. 145-acre campus in Milligan College, three miles from Johnson City (population: 55,469). Airport serves Blountville (20 miles); major airport serves Knoxville (100 miles); bus serves Johnson City; train serves both Nashville and Greenville, S.C. (180 miles). Semester system.

LD ADMISSIONS

Application Deadline: 08/01. Students do not complete a separate application and are simultaneously accepted to the LD program. A member of the LD program does not sit on the admissions committee. A personal interview is not required. Essay is required and may be typed.

SECONDARY SCHOOL REQUIREMENTS

Graduation from secondary school required; GED accepted.

TESTING

SAT Reasoning or ACT required. SAT Subject recommended.

All enrolled freshmen (fall 2004):

Average SAT I Scores:	Verbal:537	Math: 544
Average ACT Scores:	Composite: 23	

Child Study Team report is not required. A neuropsychological or comprehensive psycho-educational evaluation is required for admission. Must be dated within 36 months of application. Tests required as part of this documentation:

☑ WAIS-IV	☐ Woodcock-Johnson
☑ WISC-IV	☐ Nelson-Denny Reading Test
☐ SATA	☐ Other

UNDERGRADUATE STUDENT BODY

Total undergraduate student enrollment: 319 Men, 470 Women.

Composition of student body (fall 2004):

	Undergraduate	Freshmen
International	3.1	2.5
Black	3.1	2.1
American Indian	0.0	0.1
Asian-American	1.0	0.8
Hispanic	2.6	1.1
White	90.2	93.4
Unreported	0.0	0.0
	100.0%	100.0%

59% are from out of state. Average age of full-time undergraduates is 21. 72% of classes have fewer than 20 students, 26% have between 20 and 50 students, 2% have more than 50 students.

STUDENT HOUSING

92% of freshmen live in college housing. Freshmen are required to live on campus. Housing is guaranteed for all undergraduates. Campus can house 534 undergraduates.

EXPENSES

Tuition (2005-06): $16,730 per year.

Room: $2,350. Board: $2,400.

There is no additional cost for LD program/services.

LD SERVICES

LD program size is not limited.

LD services available to:

☑ Freshmen ☑ Sophomores ☑ Juniors ☑ Seniors

Academic Accommodations

Curriculum		In class	
Foreign language waiver	☐	Early syllabus	☑
Lighter course load	☑	Note takers in class	☐
Math waiver	☐	Priority seating	☐
Other special classes	☐	Tape recorders	☐
Priority registrations	☐	Videotaped classes	☐
Substitution of courses	☐	Text on tape	☐
Exams		**Services**	
Extended time	☑	Diagnostic tests	☐
Oral exams	☐	Learning centers	☑
Take home exams	☐	Proofreaders	☐
Exams on tape or computer	☐	Readers	☐
Untimed exams	☐	Reading Machines/Kurzweil	☐
Other accommodations	☑	Special bookstore section	☐
		Typists	☐

Credit toward degree is not given for remedial courses taken.

Counseling Services

☑ Academic
☐ Psychological
☐ Student Support groups
☐ Vocational

Tutoring

Individual tutoring is available weekly.

	Individual	Group
Time management	☐	☐
Organizational skills	☐	☐
Learning strategies	☐	☐
Study skills	☐	☐
Content area	☐	☐
Writing lab	☐	☐
Math lab	☐	☐

LD PROGRAM STAFF

Total number of LD Program staff (including director):

Full Time: 1 Part Time: 1

There is an advisor/advocate from the LD program available to students.

Key staff person available to work with LD students: Traci Smith, Director of Student Success.

Rhodes College

Memphis, TN

Address: 2000 N. Parkway, Memphis, TN, 38112
Admissions telephone: 800 844-5969
Admissions FAX: 901 843-3631
Dean of Admissions and Financial Aid: David J. Wottle
Admissions e-mail: adminfo@rhodes.edu
Web site: http://www.rhodes.edu
SAT Code: 1730 ACT Code: 4008

Coordinator: Melissa Butler McCowen
LD program telephone: 901 843-3994
LD program e-mail: mbutler@rhodes.edu
LD program enrollment: 33, Total campus enrollment: 1,615

GENERAL

Rhodes College is a private, coed, four-year institution. 100-acre, urban campus in Memphis (population: 650,100). Served by air, bus, and train. Semester system.

LD ADMISSIONS

Students do not complete a separate application and are not simultaneously accepted to the LD program. A member of the LD program does not sit on the admissions committee. A personal interview is recommended.

SECONDARY SCHOOL REQUIREMENTS

Graduation from secondary school required; GED accepted. The following course distribution required: 4 units of English, 3 units of math, 2 units of science, 2 units of foreign language, 2 units of social studies, 2 units of history, 3 units of academic electives.

TESTING

SAT Subject recommended.

All enrolled freshmen (fall 2004):

Average SAT I Scores:	Verbal: 646	Math: 636
Average ACT Scores:	Composite: 28	

Child Study Team report is not required. A neuropsychological or comprehensive psycho-educational evaluation is required for admission. Tests required as part of this documentation:

- ■ WAIS-IV
- ■ WISC-IV
- ■ SATA
- ■ Woodcock-Johnson
- ■ Nelson-Denny Reading Test
- ☐ Other

UNDERGRADUATE STUDENT BODY

Total undergraduate student enrollment: 663 Men, 872 Women.

Composition of student body (fall 2004):

	Undergraduate	Freshmen
International	1.5	0.9
Black	2.5	4.4
American Indian	0.2	0.3
Asian-American	3.0	3.4
Hispanic	0.8	1.3
White	86.9	86.5
Unreported	5.1	3.2
	100.0%	100.0%

73% are from out of state. 49% join a fraternity and 53% join a sorority. Average age of full-time undergraduates is 20. 68% of classes have fewer than 20 students, 31% have between 20 and 50 students, 1% have more than 50 students.

STUDENT HOUSING

96% of freshmen live in college housing. Freshmen are required to live on campus. Housing is not guaranteed for all undergraduates. The College can accommodate 75% of the student body on campus and can generally accommodate students who desire campus housing. Campus can house 1,220 undergraduates. Single rooms are not available for students with medical or special needs.

EXPENSES

Tuition (2005-06): $27,564 per year.
Room & Board: $6,904
There is no additional cost for LD program/services.

LD SERVICES

LD program size is not limited.

LD services available to:

■ Freshmen ■ Sophomores ■ Juniors ■ Seniors

Academic Accommodations

Curriculum		In class	
Foreign language waiver	☐	Early syllabus	☐
Lighter course load	■	Note takers in class	■
Math waiver	☐	Priority seating	■
Other special classes	☐	Tape recorders	■
Priority registrations	☐	Videotaped classes	☐
Substitution of courses	☐	Text on tape	■
Exams		**Services**	
Extended time	■	Diagnostic tests	☐
Oral exams	☐	Learning centers	☐
Take home exams	☐	Proofreaders	☐
Exams on tape or computer	☐	Readers	☐
Untimed exams	☐	Reading Machines/Kurzweil	■
Other accommodations	☐	Special bookstore section	☐
		Typists	☐

Credit toward degree is not given for remedial courses taken.

Counseling Services

- ☐ Academic
- ■ Psychological
- ☐ Student Support groups
- ■ Vocational

Tutoring

Individual tutoring is not available.

	Individual	Group
Time management	■	☐
Organizational skills	■	☐
Learning strategies	☐	■
Study skills	☐	■
Content area	☐	■
Writing lab	■	☐
Math lab	☐	■

LD PROGRAM STAFF

Total number of LD Program staff (including director):

Full Time: 1 Part Time: 1

There is an advisor/advocate from the LD program available to students.

Key staff person available to work with LD students: Melissa Butler McCowen, Coordinator of Disability and Career Services.

Southern Adventist University

Collegedale, TN

Address: PO Box 370, Collegedale, TN, 37315
Admissions telephone: 800 768-8437
Admissions FAX: 423 236-1844
Admissions Contact: Marc Grundy
Admissions e-mail: admissions@southern.edu
Web site: http://www.southern.edu
SAT Code: 1727 ACT Code: 4006

LD program name: Center for Learning Success
LD program telephone: 423 236-2577
LD program enrollment: 40, Total campus enrollment: 2,238

GENERAL

Southern Adventist University is a private, coed, four-year institution. 1,000-acre campus in Collegedale (population: 948), 18 miles from Chattanooga; branch campuses in Orlando and abroad in Bolivia, India, and South Africa. Airport and bus serve Chattanooga; train serves Atlanta (120 miles). Semester system.

LD ADMISSIONS

A member of the LD program does not sit on the admissions committee. A personal interview is required. Essay is not required. Some courses may be substituted.

SECONDARY SCHOOL REQUIREMENTS

Graduation from secondary school required; GED accepted. The following course distribution required: 3 units of English, 2 units of math, 2 units of science, 1 unit of social studies, 2 units of history, 7 units of academic electives.

TESTING

SAT Subject recommended.

All enrolled freshmen (fall 2004):

Average SAT I Scores: Verbal: Math:
Average ACT Scores: Composite: 23

Child Study Team report is not required. A neuropsychological or comprehensive psycho-educational evaluation is required for admission. Must be dated within 12 months of application. Tests required as part of this documentation:

- [x] WAIS-IV
- [ ] WISC-IV
- [x] SATA
- [x] Woodcock-Johnson
- [x] Nelson-Denny Reading Test
- [x] Other

UNDERGRADUATE STUDENT BODY

Total undergraduate student enrollment: 948 Men, 1,150 Women.

Composition of student body (fall 2004):

	Undergraduate	Freshmen
International	6.2	4.9
Black	11.0	9.8
American Indian	0.2	0.4
Asian-American	6.0	5.2
Hispanic	10.4	10.9
White	66.2	68.8
Unreported	0.0	0.0
	100.0%	100.0%

78% are from out of state. Average age of full-time undergraduates is 20. 57% of classes have fewer than 20 students, 37% have between 20 and 50 students, 6% have more than 50 students.

STUDENT HOUSING

89% of freshmen live in college housing. Freshmen are required to live on campus. Housing is guaranteed for all undergraduates. Campus can house 1,543 undergraduates. Single rooms are available for students with medical or special needs. A medical note is required.

EXPENSES

Tuition (2005-06): $13,580 per year.
Room: $2,480.
There is no additional cost for LD program/services.

LD SERVICES

LD program size is not limited.

LD services available to:

- [x] Freshmen
- [x] Sophomores
- [x] Juniors
- [x] Seniors

Academic Accommodations

Curriculum

- [ ] Foreign language waiver
- [x] Lighter course load
- [ ] Math waiver
- [ ] Other special classes
- [ ] Priority registrations
- [x] Substitution of courses

Exams

- [x] Extended time
- [x] Oral exams
- [ ] Take home exams
- [x] Exams on tape or computer
- [ ] Untimed exams
- [x] Other accommodations

In class

- [ ] Early syllabus
- [x] Note takers in class
- [x] Priority seating
- [x] Tape recorders
- [ ] Videotaped classes
- [x] Text on tape

Services

- [x] Diagnostic tests
- [x] Learning centers
- [ ] Proofreaders
- [x] Readers
- [x] Reading Machines/Kurzweil
- [ ] Special bookstore section
- [x] Typists

Credit toward degree is not given for remedial courses taken.

Counseling Services

- [x] Academic — Meets 10 times per academic year
- [x] Psychological
- [ ] Student Support groups
- [x] Vocational

Tutoring

Individual tutoring is available weekly.

Average size of tutoring groups: 1

	Individual	Group
Time management	[x]	[x]
Organizational skills	[x]	[x]
Learning strategies	[x]	[x]
Study skills	[x]	[x]
Content area	[x]	[ ]
Writing lab	[ ]	[ ]
Math lab	[ ]	[ ]

LD PROGRAM STAFF

Total number of LD Program staff (including director):

Full Time: 3 Part Time: 3

There is no advisor/advocate from the LD program available to students. 20 peer tutors are available to work with LD students.

Key staff person available to work with LD students: Eldon Roberts, Disability Services Coordinator.

LD Program web site: cls.southern.edu

University of Tennessee

Knoxville, TN

Address: 800 Andy Holt Tower, Knoxville, TN, 37996
Admissions telephone: 865 974-2184
Admissions FAX: 865 974-6341
Dean of Admissions and Records: Nancy T. McGlasson
Admissions e-mail: admissions@tennessee.edu
Web site: http://www.tennessee.edu
SAT Code: 1843   ACT Code: 4026

Coordinator: LaRosia Carrington
LD program telephone: 865 974-6087
LD program e-mail: ods@utk.edu
Total campus enrollment: 19,634

GENERAL

University of Tennessee is a public, coed, four-year institution. 533-acre, suburban campus in Knoxville (population: 173,890). Served by air and bus. School operates transportation to agricultural campus. Public transportation serves campus. Semester system.

LD ADMISSIONS

A personal interview is required. Essay is not required.

SECONDARY SCHOOL REQUIREMENTS

Graduation from secondary school required; GED accepted. The following course distribution required: 4 units of English, 3 units of math, 2 units of science, 2 units of foreign language, 1 unit of social studies, 1 unit of history.

TESTING

ACT required; SAT Reasoning may be substituted.

All enrolled freshmen (fall 2004):

Average SAT I Scores:	Verbal: 556	Math: 557
Average ACT Scores:	Composite: 25	

Child Study Team report is not required. Tests required as part of this documentation:

☐ WAIS-IV	☐ Woodcock-Johnson
☐ WISC-IV	☐ Nelson-Denny Reading Test
☐ SATA	☐ Other

UNDERGRADUATE STUDENT BODY

Total undergraduate student enrollment: 9,718 Men, 10,291 Women.

Composition of student body (fall 2004):

	Undergraduate	Freshmen
International	0.6	0.9
Black	10.6	8.0
American Indian	0.4	0.4
Asian-American	2.9	2.6
Hispanic	1.5	1.3
White	83.5	86.1
Unreported	0.5	0.7
	100.0%	100.0%

14% are from out of state. 15% join a fraternity and 20% join a sorority. Average age of full-time undergraduates is 21. 37% of classes have fewer than 20 students, 56% have between 20 and 50 students, 7% have more than 50 students.

STUDENT HOUSING

91% of freshmen live in college housing. Freshmen are required to live on campus. Housing is not guaranteed for all undergraduates. Housing is available on a first-come, first-serve basis. Campus can house 3,593 undergraduates. Single rooms are available for students with medical or special needs. A medical note is required.

EXPENSES

Tuition (2005-06): Tuition is higher for engineering courses.
There is no additional cost for LD program/services.

LD SERVICES

LD program size is not limited.

LD services available to:

☐ Freshmen ☐ Sophomores ☐ Juniors ☐ Seniors

Academic Accommodations

Curriculum		**In class**	
Foreign language waiver	☐	Early syllabus	☐
Lighter course load	☐	Note takers in class	■
Math waiver	☐	Priority seating	☐
Other special classes	☐	Tape recorders	■
Priority registrations	☐	Videotaped classes	☐
Substitution of courses	☐	Text on tape	☐
Exams		**Services**	
Extended time	■	Diagnostic tests	■
Oral exams	■	Learning centers	☐
Take home exams	☐	Proofreaders	☐
Exams on tape or computer	☐	Readers	■
Untimed exams	☐	Reading Machines/Kurzweil	■
Other accommodations	☐	Special bookstore section	☐
		Typists	☐

Counseling Services

☐ Academic
☐ Psychological
☐ Student Support groups
☐ Vocational

Tutoring

	Individual	Group
Time management	☐	☐
Organizational skills	☐	☐
Learning strategies	☐	☐
Study skills	☐	☐
Content area	☐	☐
Writing lab	☐	☐
Math lab	☐	☐

LD PROGRAM STAFF

Total number of LD Program staff (including director):

Full Time: 2   Part Time: 2

Key staff person available to work with LD students: Shannon Crabtree, Learning Disabilities Coordinator.

University of Tennessee at Chattanooga

Chattanooga, TN

Address: 615 McCallie Avenue, Chattanooga, TN, 37403
Admissions telephone: 800 UTC-MOCS
Admissions FAX: 423 425-4157
Director of Admissions/Recruitment: Yancy Freeman
Admissions e-mail: yancy-freeman@utc.edu
Web site: http://www.utc.edu
SAT Code: 1831 ACT Code: 4022

LD program name: Office for Students with Disabilities
LD program address: Dept 2953
Manager: Michelle Rigler
LD program telephone: 423 425-4006
LD program e-mail: Michelle-Rigler@utc.edu
LD program enrollment: 175, Total campus enrollment: 7,405

GENERAL

University of Tennessee at Chattanooga is a public, coed, four-year institution. 117-acre, urban campus in Chattanooga (population: 155,554). Served by air and bus; major airport serves Atlanta (120 miles). Public transportation serves campus. Semester system.

LD ADMISSIONS

Students do not complete a separate application and are not simultaneously accepted to the LD program. A member of the LD program does not sit on the admissions committee. A personal interview is required. Essay is not required. Students must be otherwise qualified for admission and are evaluated in the same manner as other applicants.

SECONDARY SCHOOL REQUIREMENTS

Graduation from secondary school required; GED accepted. The following course distribution required: 4 units of English, 3 units of math, 2 units of science, 2 units of foreign language, 2 units of social studies, 1 unit of history.

TESTING

SAT Reasoning or ACT required. SAT Subject recommended.

All enrolled freshmen (fall 2004):

Average SAT I Scores:	Verbal:	Math:
Average ACT Scores:	Composite: 21	

Child Study Team report is not required. A neuropsychological or comprehensive psycho-educational evaluation is required for admission. Must be dated within 36 months of application. Tests required as part of this documentation:

- ■ WAIS-IV
- ■ WISC-IV
- ☐ SATA
- ■ Woodcock-Johnson
- ☐ Nelson-Denny Reading Test
- ☐ Other

UNDERGRADUATE STUDENT BODY

Total undergraduate student enrollment: 2,999 Men, 4,106 Women.

Composition of student body (fall 2004):

	Undergraduate	Freshmen
International	0.0	0.0
Black	26.9	22.2
American Indian	0.3	0.3
Asian-American	2.3	2.4
Hispanic	0.8	1.0
White	69.7	74.1
Unreported	0.0	0.0
	100.0%	100.0%

7% are from out of state. 9% join a fraternity and 10% join a sorority. Average age of full-time undergraduates is 22. 37% of classes have fewer than 20 students, 59% have between 20 and 50 students, 4% have more than 50 students.

STUDENT HOUSING

Freshmen are required to live on campus. Housing is guaranteed for all undergraduates. Campus can house 2,975 undergraduates. Single rooms are available for students with medical or special needs. A medical note is required.

EXPENSES

There is no additional cost for LD program/services.

LD SERVICES

LD program size is not limited.

LD services available to:

■ Freshmen ■ Sophomores ■ Juniors ■ Seniors

Academic Accommodations

Curriculum		In class	
Foreign language waiver	☐	Early syllabus	☐
Lighter course load	■	Note takers in class	☐
Math waiver	☐	Priority seating	☐
Other special classes	☐	Tape recorders	☐
Priority registrations	☐	Videotaped classes	☐
Substitution of courses	☐	Text on tape	☐
Exams		**Services**	
Extended time	■	Diagnostic tests	☐
Oral exams	■	Learning centers	☐
Take home exams	☐	Proofreaders	☐
Exams on tape or computer	☐	Readers	■
Untimed exams	■	Reading Machines/Kurzweil	☐
Other accommodations	☐	Special bookstore section	☐
		Typists	☐

Credit toward degree is not given for remedial courses taken.

Counseling Services

- ■ Academic
- ■ Psychological
- ■ Student Support groups
- ■ Vocational

Tutoring

Individual tutoring is available daily.

	Individual	Group
Time management	☐	☐
Organizational skills	☐	☐
Learning strategies	☐	☐
Study skills	☐	☐
Content area	☐	☐
Writing lab	■	☐
Math lab	■	☐

LD PROGRAM STAFF

Total number of LD Program staff (including director):

Full Time: 4 Part Time: 4

There is an advisor/advocate from the LD program available to students. 20 peer tutors are available to work with LD students.

Key staff person available to work with LD students: Michelle Rigler, Manager.

University of Tennessee at Martin

Martin, TN

Address: University Street, Martin, TN, 38238
Admissions telephone: 800 829-UTM1
Admissions FAX: 731 881-7029
Director of Admissions: Judy Rayburn
Admissions e-mail: admitme@utm.edu
Web site: http://www.utm.edu
SAT Code: 1844 ACT Code: 4032

LD program name: PACE
LD program address: 210 Clement Hall, Martin
Coordinator: Stephanie Mueller
LD program telephone: 731 881-7744
LD program e-mail: smueller@utm.edu
LD program enrollment: 18, Total campus enrollment: 5,667

GENERAL

University of Tennessee at Martin is a public, coed, four-year institution. 250-acre campus in Martin (population: 10,515), 50 miles north of Jackson; extension sites in Jackson, Lexington, Nashville, Oak Ridge, Paris, Ripley, Savannah, Selmer, Tiptonville, Union City, and Waverly. Served by bus; major airports serve Memphis (125 miles) and Nashville (150 miles); train serves Dyersburg (50 miles) and Fulton (10 miles). Semester system.

LD ADMISSIONS

Students do not complete a separate application and are simultaneously accepted to the LD program. A member of the LD program does not sit on the admissions committee. A personal interview is required. Essay is required and may not be typed.

For fall 2004, 18 completed self-identified LD applications were received. All of the applications were offered admission, and all enrolled.

SECONDARY SCHOOL REQUIREMENTS

Graduation from secondary school required; GED accepted. The following course distribution required: 4 units of English, 3 units of math, 2 units of science, 2 units of foreign language, 2 units of history.

TESTING

SAT Subject recommended.

All enrolled freshmen (fall 2004):

Average SAT I Scores: Verbal: Math:
Average ACT Scores: Composite: 22

Child Study Team report is not required. A neuropsychological or comprehensive psycho-education evaluation is not required for admission. Tests required as part of this documentation:

☐ WAIS-IV ☐ Woodcock-Johnson
☐ WISC-IV ☐ Nelson-Denny Reading Test
☐ SATA ☐ Other

UNDERGRADUATE STUDENT BODY

Total undergraduate student enrollment: 2,402 Men, 3,076 Women.

Composition of student body (fall 2004):

	Undergraduate	Freshmen
International	1.2	2.2
Black	13.5	15.8
American Indian	0.3	0.4
Asian-American	0.2	0.5
Hispanic	0.9	1.0
White	83.9	80.1
Unreported	0.0	0.0
	100.0%	100.0%

8% are from out of state. 8% join a fraternity and 5% join a sorority. Average age of full-time undergraduates is 22. 51% of classes have fewer than 20 students, 41% have between 20 and 50 students, 8% have more than 50 students.

STUDENT HOUSING

71% of freshmen live in college housing. Freshmen are required to live on campus. Housing is guaranteed for all undergraduates. Campus can house 2,000 undergraduates. Single rooms are available for students with medical or special needs. A medical note is required.

EXPENSES

Tuition (2005-06): $3,582 per year (in-state), $12,248 (out-of-state). Room: $3,106. Board: $2,044.
There is no additional cost for LD program/services.

LD SERVICES

LD program size is not limited.

LD services available to:

☑ Freshmen ☑ Sophomores ☑ Juniors ☑ Seniors

Academic Accommodations

Curriculum		**In class**	
Foreign language waiver	☐	Early syllabus	☐
Lighter course load	☐	Note takers in class	☑
Math waiver	☐	Priority seating	☐
Other special classes	☐	Tape recorders	☑
Priority registrations	☐	Videotaped classes	☐
Substitution of courses	☐	Text on tape	☑
Exams		**Services**	
Extended time	☑	Diagnostic tests	☐
Oral exams	☑	Learning centers	☑
Take home exams	☐	Proofreaders	☐
Exams on tape or computer	☑	Readers	☑
Untimed exams	☑	Reading Machines/Kurzweil	☑
Other accommodations	☑	Special bookstore section	☐
		Typists	☑

Credit toward degree is not given for remedial courses taken.

Counseling Services

☑ Academic
☐ Psychological
☐ Student Support groups
☐ Vocational

Tutoring

Individual tutoring is available daily.

Average size of tutoring groups: 6

	Individual	Group
Time management	☑	☐
Organizational skills	☑	☐
Learning strategies	☑	☐
Study skills	☑	☐
Content area	☑	☐
Writing lab	☑	☐
Math lab	☑	☐

LD PROGRAM STAFF

Total number of LD Program staff (including director):

Full Time: 2 Part Time: 2

There is an advisor/advocate from the LD program available to students. 3 graduate students and 6 peer tutors are available to work with LD students.

Key staff person available to work with LD students: Sharon Robertson, Assistant Director, Student Success Center.

Tennessee Technological University

Cookeville, TN

Address: Campus Box 5006 USPS 077-460, Cookeville, TN, 38505
Admissions telephone: 800 255-8881
Admissions FAX: 931 372-6250
Associate Vice President: Rebecca Tolbert
Admissions e-mail: admissions@tntech.edu
Web site: http://www.tntech.edu
SAT Code: 1804 ACT Code: 4012

LD program name: Disability Services
LD program address: P.O. Box 5091, TTU,
Director, Disability Services: Sammie Young
LD program telephone: 931 372-6119
LD program e-mail: syoung@tntech.edu
LD program enrollment: 36, Total campus enrollment: 7,224

GENERAL

Tennessee Technological University is a public, coed, four-year institution. 235-acre campus in Cookeville (population: 23,923), 78 miles from Nashville. Served by bus; major airport serves Nashville. Semester system.

LD ADMISSIONS

Students do not complete a separate application and are not simultaneously accepted to the LD program. A member of the LD program does not sit on the admissions committee. A personal interview is not required. Essay is not required.

For fall 2004, 31 completed self-identified LD applications were received.

SECONDARY SCHOOL REQUIREMENTS

Graduation from secondary school required; GED accepted. The following course distribution required: 4 units of English, 3 units of math, 2 units of science, 2 units of foreign language, 1 unit of social studies, 1 unit of history.

TESTING

SAT Reasoning considered if submitted. ACT recommended. SAT Reasoning may be substituted. SAT Subject recommended.

All enrolled freshmen (fall 2004):

Average SAT I Scores:	Verbal: 551	Math: 566
Average ACT Scores:	Composite: 23	

Child Study Team report is not required. A neuropsychological or comprehensive psycho-educational evaluation is required for admission. Must be dated within 36 months of application. Tests required as part of this documentation:

- [x] WAIS-IV
- [x] WISC-IV
- [ ] SATA
- [x] Woodcock-Johnson
- [ ] Nelson-Denny Reading Test
- [ ] Other

UNDERGRADUATE STUDENT BODY

Total undergraduate student enrollment: 3,854 Men, 3,245 Women.

Composition of student body (fall 2004):

	Undergraduate	Freshmen
International	0.4	0.6
Black	4.2	4.0
American Indian	0.1	0.3
Asian-American	0.6	1.2
Hispanic	0.5	0.9
White	85.2	88.1
Unreported	9.0	4.9
	100.0%	100.0%

5% are from out of state. 12% join a fraternity and 9% join a sorority. Average age of full-time undergraduates is 22. 48% of classes have fewer than 20 students, 45% have between 20 and 50 students, 7% have more than 50 students.

STUDENT HOUSING

85% of freshmen live in college housing. Freshmen are required to live on campus. Housing is guaranteed for all undergraduates. Campus can house 2,616 undergraduates. Single rooms are available for students with medical or special needs. A medical note is required.

EXPENSES

Tuition (2005-06): $4,300 per year (in-state), $8,910 (out-of-state).
Room: $2,675. Board: $3,600.
There is no additional cost for LD program/services.

LD SERVICES

LD program size is not limited.

LD services available to:

- [x] Freshmen
- [x] Sophomores
- [x] Juniors
- [x] Seniors

Academic Accommodations

Curriculum		**In class**	
Foreign language waiver	[ ]	Early syllabus	[ ]
Lighter course load	[ ]	Note takers in class	[x]
Math waiver	[ ]	Priority seating	[ ]
Other special classes	[ ]	Tape recorders	[x]
Priority registrations	[ ]	Videotaped classes	[x]
Substitution of courses	[ ]	Text on tape	[ ]
Exams		**Services**	
Extended time	[x]	Diagnostic tests	[ ]
Oral exams	[x]	Learning centers	[ ]
Take home exams	[ ]	Proofreaders	[ ]
Exams on tape or computer	[x]	Readers	[x]
Untimed exams	[ ]	Reading Machines/Kurzweil	[x]
Other accommodations	[ ]	Special bookstore section	[ ]
		Typists	[ ]

Credit toward degree is not given for remedial courses taken.

Counseling Services

- [ ] Academic
- [ ] Psychological
- [ ] Student Support groups
- [ ] Vocational

Tutoring

Individual tutoring is not available.

	Individual	Group
Time management	[ ]	[ ]
Organizational skills	[ ]	[ ]
Learning strategies	[ ]	[ ]
Study skills	[ ]	[ ]
Content area	[ ]	[ ]
Writing lab	[ ]	[x]
Math lab	[ ]	[x]

LD PROGRAM STAFF

Total number of LD Program staff (including director):

Full Time: 2 Part Time: 2

1 graduate student is available to work with LD students.

Key staff person available to work with LD students: Ted Hennis, Coordinator, Learning Disability Services.

LD Program web site: tntech.edu/disability/

Tennessee Wesleyan College

Athens, TN

Address: PO Box 40, Athens, TN, 37371-0040
Admissions telephone: 800 PICK-TWC
Admissions FAX: 423 745-9335
Director of Admissions: Ruthie Cawood
Admissions e-mail: admissions@twcnet.edu
Web site: http://www.twcnet.edu
SAT Code: 1805 ACT Code: 4014

Assistant Professor/Director: Catherine Emanuel
LD program telephone: 423 746-5305
LD program e-mail: cemanuel@twcnet.edu
Total campus enrollment: 815

GENERAL

Tennessee Wesleyan College is a private, coed, four-year institution. 40-acre, urban campus in Athens (population: 13,220), 50 miles from both Chattanooga and Knoxville; branch campuses in Chattanooga and Knoxville. Served by bus; major airport and train serve Knoxville. Semester system.

LD ADMISSIONS

A personal interview is recommended. Essay is required and may be typed. Admissions requirements that may be waived for LD students include, limits waived on testing or special circumstances.

SECONDARY SCHOOL REQUIREMENTS

Graduation from secondary school required; GED accepted.

TESTING

SAT Reasoning considered if submitted. ACT considered if submitted. SAT Subject recommended.

All enrolled freshmen (fall 2004):

Average SAT I Scores:	Verbal: 512	Math: 521
Average ACT Scores:	Composite: 20	

Child Study Team report is required if student is classified. Tests required as part of this documentation:

- [ ] WAIS-IV
- [ ] WISC-IV
- [ ] SATA
- [ ] Woodcock-Johnson
- [ ] Nelson-Denny Reading Test
- [ ] Other

UNDERGRADUATE STUDENT BODY

Total undergraduate student enrollment: 291 Men, 495 Women.

Composition of student body (fall 2004):

	Undergraduate	Freshmen
International	0.0	3.2
Black	3.0	2.1
American Indian	0.0	0.2
Asian-American	0.6	0.6
Hispanic	1.2	1.6
White	75.9	75.7
Unreported	19.3	16.6
	100.0%	100.0%

8% are from out of state. 4% join a sorority. Average age of full-time undergraduates is 22. 63% of classes have fewer than 20 students, 36% have between 20 and 50 students, 1% have more than 50 students.

STUDENT HOUSING

12% of freshmen live in college housing. Freshmen are not required to live on campus. Housing is guaranteed for all undergraduates. Campus can house 286 undergraduates.

EXPENSES

Tuition (2005-06): $13,000 per year.
Room & Board: $5,100.
There is no additional cost for LD program/services.

LD SERVICES

LD program size is not limited.

LD services available to:

- [ ] Freshmen
- [ ] Sophomores
- [ ] Juniors
- [ ] Seniors

Academic Accommodations

Curriculum		**In class**	
Foreign language waiver	[ ]	Early syllabus	[ ]
Lighter course load	[x]	Note takers in class	[x]
Math waiver	[ ]	Priority seating	[ ]
Other special classes	[ ]	Tape recorders	[x]
Priority registrations	[ ]	Videotaped classes	[ ]
Substitution of courses	[ ]	Text on tape	[ ]
Exams		**Services**	
Extended time	[x]	Diagnostic tests	[ ]
Oral exams	[x]	Learning centers	[x]
Take home exams	[ ]	Proofreaders	[ ]
Exams on tape or computer	[ ]	Readers	[x]
Untimed exams	[x]	Reading Machines/Kurzweil	[ ]
Other accommodations	[ ]	Special bookstore section	[ ]
		Typists	[ ]

Credit toward degree is not given for remedial courses taken.

Counseling Services

- [ ] Academic
- [ ] Psychological
- [ ] Student Support groups
- [ ] Vocational

Tutoring

	Individual	Group
Time management	[ ]	[ ]
Organizational skills	[ ]	[ ]
Learning strategies	[ ]	[ ]
Study skills	[ ]	[ ]
Content area	[ ]	[ ]
Writing lab	[ ]	[ ]
Math lab	[ ]	[ ]

LD PROGRAM STAFF

Total number of LD Program staff (including director):

Key staff person available to work with LD students: Catherine Emanuel, Asst. Professor and Director of the Learning Center.

Trevecca Nazarene University

Nashville, TN

Address: 333 Murfreesboro Road, Nashville, TN, 37210
Admissions telephone: 888 210-4TNU
Admissions FAX: 615 248-7406
Dean of Enrollment Services: Jan Forman
Admissions e-mail: admissions_und@trevecca.edu
Web site: http://www.trevecca.edu
SAT Code: 1809 ACT Code: 4016

Coordinator of Disability Services: Amy Murphy
LD program telephone: 615 248-1346
LD program e-mail: academic_support@trevecca.edu
LD program enrollment: 12, Total campus enrollment: 1,241

GENERAL

Trevecca Nazarene University is a private, coed, four-year institution. 65-acre campus in Nashville (population: 545,524). Served by air, bus, and train. Semester system.

LD ADMISSIONS

Students do not complete a separate application and are not simultaneously accepted to the LD program. A member of the LD program does not sit on the admissions committee. A personal interview is not required. Essay is not required.

For fall 2004, 2 completed self-identified LD applications were received. All applications were offered admission, and all enrolled.

SECONDARY SCHOOL REQUIREMENTS

Graduation from secondary school required; GED accepted.

TESTING

ACT required; SAT Reasoning may be substituted.

All enrolled freshmen (fall 2004):

Average SAT I Scores:	Verbal: 550	Math: 527
Average ACT Scores:	Composite: 22	

Child Study Team report is not required. A neuropsychological or comprehensive psycho-educational evaluation is required for admission. Must be dated within 36 months of application. Tests required as part of this documentation:

- [x] WAIS-IV
- [ ] WISC-IV
- [x] SATA
- [x] Woodcock-Johnson
- [x] Nelson-Denny Reading Test
- [x] Other

UNDERGRADUATE STUDENT BODY

Total undergraduate student enrollment: 523 Men, 636 Women.

Composition of student body (fall 2004):

	Undergraduate	Freshmen
International	3.0	1.9
Black	3.8	7.1
American Indian	0.4	0.1
Asian-American	0.8	0.9
Hispanic	1.7	2.1
White	87.8	80.7
Unreported	2.5	7.2
	100.0%	100.0%

41% are from out of state. 54% of classes have fewer than 20 students, 43% have between 20 and 50 students, 3% have more than 50 students.

STUDENT HOUSING

87% of freshmen live in college housing. Housing is guaranteed for all undergraduates.

EXPENSES

Tuition (2005-06): $13,432 per year.

Room: $2,780. Board: $3,382.

There is no additional cost for LD program/services.

LD SERVICES

LD program size is not limited.

LD services available to:

- [x] Freshmen
- [x] Sophomores
- [x] Juniors
- [x] Seniors

Academic Accommodations

Curriculum

- [ ] Foreign language waiver
- [ ] Lighter course load
- [ ] Math waiver
- [ ] Other special classes
- [ ] Priority registrations
- [ ] Substitution of courses

Exams

- [x] Extended time
- [x] Oral exams
- [ ] Take home exams
- [ ] Exams on tape or computer
- [ ] Untimed exams
- [x] Other accommodations

In class

- [ ] Early syllabus
- [x] Note takers in class
- [ ] Priority seating
- [x] Tape recorders
- [ ] Videotaped classes
- [x] Text on tape

Services

- [ ] Diagnostic tests
- [x] Learning centers
- [ ] Proofreaders
- [ ] Readers
- [x] Reading Machines/Kurzweil
- [ ] Special bookstore section
- [ ] Typists

Credit toward degree is not given for remedial courses taken.

Counseling Services

- [ ] Academic
- [ ] Psychological
- [ ] Student Support groups
- [ ] Vocational

Tutoring

Individual tutoring is available weekly.

	Individual	Group
Time management	[x]	[x]
Organizational skills	[x]	[x]
Learning strategies	[x]	[x]
Study skills	[x]	[x]
Content area	[x]	[x]
Writing lab	[x]	[x]
Math lab	[x]	[x]

LD PROGRAM STAFF

Total number of LD Program staff (including director):

Full Time: 1 Part Time: 1

There is an advisor/advocate from the LD program available to students.

Key staff person available to work with LD students: Amy Murphy, Coordinator of Disability Services.

Tusculum College

Greeneville, TN

Address: PO Box 5035, Greeneville, TN, 37743
Admissions telephone: 800 729-0256, extension 312
Admissions FAX: 423 638-7166
Vice President for Enrollment Services: George Wolf
Admissions e-mail: admissions@tusculum.edu
Web site: http://www.tusculum.edu
SAT Code: 1812 ACT Code: 4018

LD program name: Learning Center
LD program address: 9 Shiloh Road Box 5025
Director: Lori Mccallister
LD program telephone: 423 636-7300
LD program e-mail: lmccalli@tusculum.edu
LD program enrollment: 12, Total campus enrollment: 2,053

GENERAL

Tusculum College is a private, coed, four-year institution. 142-acre campus in Tusculum (population: 2,004), 35 miles west of Johnson City and 80 miles east of Knoxville; branch campus in Knoxville. Served by bus; major airport and train serve Knoxville; smaller airport serves Blountville/Tri-Cities (40 miles). Semester system.

LD ADMISSIONS

Students do not complete a separate application and are not simultaneously accepted to the LD program. A member of the LD program does not sit on the admissions committee. A personal interview is recommended. Essay is required and may be typed.

For fall 2004, 5 completed self-identified LD applications were received. All applications were offered admission, and all enrolled.

SECONDARY SCHOOL REQUIREMENTS

Graduation from secondary school required; GED accepted. The following course distribution required: 4 units of English, 3 units of math, 2 units of science, 3 units of social studies.

TESTING

SAT Reasoning or ACT required. SAT Subject recommended.

All enrolled freshmen (fall 2004):

Average SAT I Scores:	Verbal: 470	Math: 490
Average ACT Scores:	Composite: 20	

Child Study Team report is not required. A neuropsychological or comprehensive psycho-educational evaluation is required for admission. Must be dated within 36 months of application. Tests required as part of this documentation:

- [x] WAIS-IV
- [x] WISC-IV
- [ ] SATA
- [x] Woodcock-Johnson
- [ ] Nelson-Denny Reading Test
- [ ] Other

UNDERGRADUATE STUDENT BODY

Total undergraduate student enrollment: 731 Men, 826 Women.

Composition of student body (fall 2004):

	Undergraduate	Freshmen
International	6.4	2.9
Black	22.4	13.2
American Indian	0.3	0.2
Asian-American	0.3	0.6
Hispanic	0.6	1.0
White	68.3	80.4
Unreported	1.7	1.7
	100.0%	100.0%

19% are from out of state. 3% join a fraternity and 3% join a sorority. Average age of full-time undergraduates is 23.

STUDENT HOUSING

80% of freshmen live in college housing. Freshmen are required to live on campus. Housing is not guaranteed for all undergraduates. Large adult program is not included. Campus can house 630 undergraduates. Single rooms are available for students with medical or special needs. A medical note is required.

EXPENSES

Tuition (2005-06): $15,100 per year.
Room & Board: $6,230-$5,950.
There is no additional cost for LD program/services.

LD SERVICES

LD program size is not limited.

LD services available to:

- [x] Freshmen
- [x] Sophomores
- [x] Juniors
- [x] Seniors

Academic Accommodations

Curriculum		In class	
Foreign language waiver	[ ]	Early syllabus	[ ]
Lighter course load	[ ]	Note takers in class	[x]
Math waiver	[ ]	Priority seating	[ ]
Other special classes	[ ]	Tape recorders	[x]
Priority registrations	[ ]	Videotaped classes	[x]
Substitution of courses	[ ]	Text on tape	[ ]
Exams		**Services**	
Extended time	[x]	Diagnostic tests	[ ]
Oral exams	[x]	Learning centers	[x]
Take home exams	[ ]	Proofreaders	[ ]
Exams on tape or computer	[ ]	Readers	[x]
Untimed exams	[ ]	Reading Machines/Kurzweil	[x]
Other accommodations	[ ]	Special bookstore section	[ ]
		Typists	[ ]

Credit toward degree is not given for remedial courses taken.

Counseling Services

- [x] Academic
- [x] Psychological
- [ ] Student Support groups
- [ ] Vocational

Tutoring

Individual tutoring is available daily.

Average size of tutoring groups: 3

	Individual	Group
Time management	[x]	[x]
Organizational skills	[x]	[x]
Learning strategies	[x]	[x]
Study skills	[x]	[x]
Content area	[x]	[x]
Writing lab	[x]	[x]
Math lab	[x]	[x]

LD PROGRAM STAFF

Total number of LD Program staff (including director):

Full Time: 2 Part Time: 2

The advisor/advocate meets with faculty 5 times per month and students 10 times per month. 25 peer tutors are available to work with LD students.

Key staff person available to work with LD students: Lori McCallister, Director, Tusculum College Learning Center.

LD Program web site: http://www.tusculum.ed/learning/

Union University

Jackson, TN

Address: 1050 Union University Drive, Jackson, TN, 38305
Admissions telephone: 800 338-6466
Admissions FAX: 731 661-5017
Director of Admissions/Assistant to Provost: Rich Grimm
Admissions e-mail: info@uu.edu
Web site: http://www.uu.edu
SAT Code: 1826 ACT Code: 4020

LD program name: Counseling Services
LD program address: 1050 Union University Drive
Director of Counseling Services: Dr. Paul Deschenes
LD program telephone: 731 661-5322
LD program e-mail: pdeschen@uu.edu
LD program enrollment: 24, Total campus enrollment: 2,074

GENERAL

Union University is a private, coed, four-year institution. 290-acre campus in Jackson (population: 88,000), 80 miles from Memphis; branch campus in Germantown. Served by air and bus; major airport serves Memphis; train serves Dyersburg (45 miles). Public transportation serves campus. 4-1-4 system.

LD ADMISSIONS

Application Deadline: 06/01. A personal interview is recommended. Essay is not required.

For fall 2004, 3 completed self-identified LD applications were received. All of these applications were offered admission, and 2 enrolled.

SECONDARY SCHOOL REQUIREMENTS

Graduation from secondary school required; GED accepted. The following course distribution required: 4 units of English, 3 units of math, 3 units of science, 1 unit of foreign language, 2 units of social studies, 1 unit of history, 1 unit of academic electives.

TESTING

SAT Reasoning or ACT required. SAT Subject recommended.

All enrolled freshmen (fall 2004):

Average SAT I Scores:	Verbal: 589	Math: 563
Average ACT Scores:	Composite: 24	

Child Study Team report is not required. A neuropsychological or comprehensive psycho-educational evaluation is required for admission. Must be dated within 36 months of application. Tests required as part of this documentation:

☑ WAIS-IV	☑ Woodcock-Johnson
☐ WISC-IV	☑ Nelson-Denny Reading Test
☐ SATA	☑ Other

UNDERGRADUATE STUDENT BODY

Total undergraduate student enrollment: 801 Men, 1,164 Women.

Composition of student body (fall 2004):

	Undergraduate	Freshmen
International	2.3	2.3
Black	3.2	8.2
American Indian	0.5	0.1
Asian-American	1.1	0.9
Hispanic	1.1	0.8
White	91.1	86.4
Unreported	0.7	1.3
	100.0%	100.0%

31% are from out of state. 9% join a fraternity and 11% join a sorority. 66% of classes have fewer than 20 students, 33% have between 20 and 50 students, 1% have more than 50 students.

STUDENT HOUSING

89% of freshmen live in college housing. Freshmen are required to live on campus. Housing is guaranteed for all undergraduates. Campus can house 1,193 undergraduates. Single rooms are available for students with medical or special needs. A medical note is required.

EXPENSES

Tuition (2005-06): $15,900 per year.
Room: $3,290. Board: $2,480.

LD SERVICES

LD program size is not limited.

LD services available to:

☑ Freshmen ☑ Sophomores ☑ Juniors ☑ Seniors

Academic Accommodations

Curriculum		**In class**	
Foreign language waiver	☐	Early syllabus	☑
Lighter course load	☑	Note takers in class	☑
Math waiver	☐	Priority seating	☑
Other special classes	☑	Tape recorders	☑
Priority registrations	☐	Videotaped classes	☐
Substitution of courses	☐	Text on tape	☐
Exams		**Services**	
Extended time	☑	Diagnostic tests	☑
Oral exams	☑	Learning centers	☑
Take home exams	☐	Proofreaders	☐
Exams on tape or computer	☐	Readers	☐
Untimed exams	☑	Reading Machines/Kurzweil	☐
Other accommodations	☐	Special bookstore section	☐
		Typists	☐

Credit toward degree is not given for remedial courses taken.

Counseling Services

☑ Academic
☑ Psychological
☐ Student Support groups
☑ Vocational

Tutoring

Individual tutoring is available.

Average size of tutoring groups: 1

	Individual	Group
Time management	☑	☐
Organizational skills	☑	☐
Learning strategies	☑	☐
Study skills	☑	☑
Content area	☑	☐
Writing lab	☑	☐
Math lab	☑	☑

LD PROGRAM STAFF

Total number of LD Program staff (including director):

Full Time: 1 Part Time: 1

There is an advisor/advocate from the LD program available to students. 15 peer tutors are available to work with LD students.

Key staff person available to work with LD students: Dr. Paul Deschenes, Director of Counseling Services. LD Program web site: http://www.uu.edu/studentservices/counseling

Vanderbilt University

Nashville, TN

Address: Nashville, TN, 37240
Admissions telephone: 800 288-0432
Admissions FAX: 615 343-7765
Dean of Admissions: William M. Shain, Dean
Admissions e-mail: admissions@vanderbilt.edu
Web site: http://www.vanderbilt.edu
SAT Code: 1871 ACT Code: 4036

LD program name: Opportunity Development Center
LD program address: Box 351809 Station B,
LD program enrollment: 280, Total campus enrollment: 6,272

GENERAL

Vanderbilt University is a private, coed, four-year institution. 330-acre, urban campus in Nashville (population: 545,524). Served by air and bus; train serves Dyersburg (168 miles). School operates campus shuttle system. Public transportation serves campus. Semester system.

LD ADMISSIONS

Students do not complete a separate application and are not simultaneously accepted to the LD program. A member of the LD program does not sit on the admissions committee. A personal interview is not required. Essay is required and may be typed.

SECONDARY SCHOOL REQUIREMENTS

Graduation from secondary school not required. The following course distribution required: 4 units of English, 3 units of math, 2 units of science, 2 units of foreign language, 2 units of social studies, 2 units of history.

TESTING

SAT Reasoning or ACT required. SAT Subject required.

All enrolled freshmen (fall 2004):

Average SAT I Scores: Verbal: Math:
Average ACT Scores: Composite:

Child Study Team report is not required. A neuropsychological or comprehensive psycho-educational evaluation is required for admission. Must be dated within 36 months of application. Tests required as part of this documentation:

- ■ WAIS-IV
- ■ WISC-IV
- ■ SATA
- ■ Woodcock-Johnson
- ■ Nelson-Denny Reading Test
- ☐ Other

UNDERGRADUATE STUDENT BODY

Total undergraduate student enrollment: 2,930 Men, 3,147 Women.

Composition of student body (fall 2004):

	Undergraduate	Freshmen
International	2.4	2.3
Black	8.7	7.4
American Indian	0.2	0.2
Asian-American	6.7	5.9
Hispanic	5.2	4.5
White	69.2	72.6
Unreported	7.6	7.1
	100.0%	100.0%

80% are from out of state. 34% join a fraternity and 50% join a sorority. Average age of full-time undergraduates is 19. 67% of classes have fewer than 20 students, 27% have between 20 and 50 students, 6% have more than 50 students.

STUDENT HOUSING

99% of freshmen live in college housing. Freshmen are required to live on campus. Housing is not guaranteed for all undergraduates. Current undergraduate enrollment exceeds residence hall capacity. Therefore, approximately 17% of undergraduates are authorized to live off campus each year. Campus can house 4,869 undergraduates. Single rooms are available for students with medical or special needs. A medical note is required.

EXPENSES

Tuition (2005-06): $30,920 per year.
Room & Board: $10,286.
There is no additional cost for LD program/services.

LD SERVICES

LD program size is not limited.

LD services available to:

■ Freshmen ■ Sophomores ■ Juniors ■ Seniors

Academic Accommodations

Curriculum		In class	
Foreign language waiver	■	Early syllabus	☐
Lighter course load	■	Note takers in class	■
Math waiver	☐	Priority seating	■
Other special classes	☐	Tape recorders	■
Priority registrations	☐	Videotaped classes	☐
Substitution of courses	■	Text on tape	■
Exams		**Services**	
Extended time	■	Diagnostic tests	■
Oral exams	■	Learning centers	■
Take home exams	☐	Proofreaders	■
Exams on tape or computer	■	Readers	■
Untimed exams	☐	Reading Machines/Kurzweil	☐
Other accommodations	■	Special bookstore section	☐
		Typists	■

Credit toward degree is given for remedial courses taken.

Counseling Services

- ■ Academic
- ■ Psychological
- ☐ Student Support groups
- ☐ Vocational

Tutoring

Individual tutoring is available daily.

Average size of tutoring groups: 3

	Individual	Group
Time management	■	■
Organizational skills	■	■
Learning strategies	■	■
Study skills	■	■
Content area	■	■
Writing lab	■	■
Math lab	☐	■

LD PROGRAM STAFF

Total number of LD Program staff (including director):

Full Time: 3 Part Time: 3

There is an advisor/advocate from the LD program available to students.

Key staff person available to work with LD students: Sara Ezell, Assistant Director for Disability Programs.

Abilene Christian University

Abilene, TX

Address: ACU Box 29100, Abilene, TX, 79699-9000
Admissions telephone: 800 460-6228, extension 2650
Admissions FAX: 325 674-2130
Director of Enrollment Management: Robert Heil
Admissions e-mail: info@admissions.acu.edu
Web site: http://www.acu.edu
SAT Code: 6001 ACT Code: 4050

LD program name: Alpha Academic Services
LD program address: ACU Box 29204
Director, Alpha Academic Services: Gloria Bradshaw
LD program telephone: 325 674-2667
LD program e-mail: bradshawg@acu.edu
LD program enrollment: 112, Total campus enrollment: 4,209

GENERAL

Abilene Christian University is a private, coed, four-year institution. 208-acre, suburban campus in Abilene (population: 115,930), 180 miles from Dallas-Fort Worth. Served by air and bus; major airport and train serve Dallas-Fort Worth. Public transportation serves campus. Semester system.

LD ADMISSIONS

Application Deadline: 08/15. Students complete a separate application and are not simultaneously accepted to the LD program. A personal interview is required. Essay is required and may not be typed.

For fall 2004, 30 completed self-identified LD applications were received. 22 applications were offered admission, and 19 enrolled.

SECONDARY SCHOOL REQUIREMENTS

Graduation from secondary school required; GED accepted. The following course distribution required: 4 units of English, 3 units of math, 3 units of science, 2 units of foreign language.

TESTING

SAT Reasoning required; ACT may be substituted. SAT Subject recommended.

All enrolled freshmen (fall 2004):

Average SAT I Scores:	Verbal: 558	Math: 556
Average ACT Scores:	Composite: 24	

Child Study Team report is required if student is classified. A neuropsychological or comprehensive psycho-educational evaluation is required for admission. Must be dated within 36 months of application. Tests required as part of this documentation:

- [x] WAIS-IV
- [ ] WISC-IV
- [ ] SATA
- [x] Woodcock-Johnson
- [ ] Nelson-Denny Reading Test
- [ ] Other

UNDERGRADUATE STUDENT BODY

Total undergraduate student enrollment: 1,911 Men, 2,323 Women.

Composition of student body (fall 2004):

	Undergraduate	Freshmen
International	4.0	4.1
Black	6.9	6.8
American Indian	0.8	0.5
Asian-American	1.1	1.1
Hispanic	7.2	6.7
White	79.5	79.3
Unreported	0.5	1.5
	100.0%	100.0%

20% are from out of state. 8% join a fraternity and 12% join a sorority. Average age of full-time undergraduates is 20. 43% of classes have fewer than 20 students, 48% have between 20 and 50 students, 9% have more than 50 students.

STUDENT HOUSING

95% of freshmen live in college housing. Freshmen are required to live on campus. Housing is guaranteed for all undergraduates. Campus can house 1,892 undergraduates. Single rooms are available for students with medical or special needs. A medical note is required.

EXPENSES

Tuition (2005-06): $14,610 per year.
Room: $2,750. Board: $2,920.

There is no additional cost for LD program/services.

LD SERVICES

LD program size is not limited.

LD services available to:

- [x] Freshmen
- [x] Sophomores
- [ ] Juniors
- [x] Seniors

Academic Accommodations

Curriculum		In class	
Foreign language waiver	[ ]	Early syllabus	[ ]
Lighter course load	[ ]	Note takers in class	[x]
Math waiver	[ ]	Priority seating	[ ]
Other special classes	[ ]	Tape recorders	[x]
Priority registrations	[ ]	Videotaped classes	[ ]
Substitution of courses	[ ]	Text on tape	[ ]
Exams		**Services**	
Extended time	[x]	Diagnostic tests	[x]
Oral exams	[x]	Learning centers	[ ]
Take home exams	[ ]	Proofreaders	[ ]
Exams on tape or computer	[x]	Readers	[x]
Untimed exams	[ ]	Reading Machines/Kurzweil	[ ]
Other accommodations	[ ]	Special bookstore section	[ ]
		Typists	[ ]

Credit toward degree is not given for remedial courses taken.

Counseling Services

- [x] Academic
- [x] Psychological
- [ ] Student Support groups
- [ ] Vocational

Tutoring

Individual tutoring is available weekly.

Average size of tutoring groups: 3

	Individual	Group
Time management	[x]	[ ]
Organizational skills	[x]	[ ]
Learning strategies	[x]	[ ]
Study skills	[x]	[ ]
Content area	[ ]	[x]
Writing lab	[x]	[ ]
Math lab	[ ]	[x]

UNIQUE LD PROGRAM FEATURES

Program also serves first-generation, low-income students.

LD PROGRAM STAFF

Total number of LD Program staff (including director):

Full Time: 5 Part Time: 5

There is an advisor/advocate from the LD program available to students. The advisor/advocate meets with students once per month. 1 graduate student and 10 peer tutors are available to work with LD students.

Key staff person available to work with LD students: Gloria Bradshaw, Director, Alpha Academic Services.

LD Program web site: www.acu.edu/academics/trio/alpha.html

Angelo State University

San Angelo, TX

Address: 2601 W. Avenue N, San Angelo, TX, 76909
Admissions telephone: 800 946-8627
Admissions FAX: 325 942-2078
Director of Admissions and Retention:
Admissions e-mail: admissions@angelo.edu
Web site: http://www.angelo.edu
SAT Code: 6644 ACT Code: 4164

Associate Dean for Student Services: Mr. Nolen Mears
LD program telephone: 325 942-2191
LD program e-mail: nolen.mears@angelo.edu
Total campus enrollment: 5,712

GENERAL

Angelo State University is a public, coed, four-year institution. 268-acre campus in San Angelo (population: 88,439), 200 miles from Austin; branch campus at Goodfellow Air Force Base. Served by air and bus. Public transportation serves campus. Semester system.

LD ADMISSIONS

A personal interview is required. Essay is not required.

SECONDARY SCHOOL REQUIREMENTS

Graduation from secondary school required; GED accepted. The following course distribution required: 4 units of English, 3 units of math, 3 units of science, 2 units of foreign language, 3 units of social studies.

TESTING

SAT Reasoning or ACT required. SAT Subject recommended.

All enrolled freshmen (fall 2004):

Average SAT I Scores:	Verbal: 485	Math: 491
Average ACT Scores:	Composite: 20	

Child Study Team report is not required. Tests required as part of this documentation:

☐ WAIS-IV ☐ Woodcock-Johnson
☐ WISC-IV ☐ Nelson-Denny Reading Test
☐ SATA ☐ Other

UNDERGRADUATE STUDENT BODY

Total undergraduate student enrollment: 2,580 Men, 3,249 Women.

Composition of student body (fall 2004):

	Undergraduate	Freshmen
International	0.1	1.3
Black	6.0	6.0
American Indian	0.5	0.3
Asian-American	1.0	1.2
Hispanic	24.0	22.8
White	68.4	68.4
Unreported	0.0	0.0
	100.0%	100.0%

2% are from out of state. 3% join a fraternity and 4% join a sorority. Average age of full-time undergraduates is 23. 21% of classes have fewer than 20 students, 68% have between 20 and 50 students, 11% have more than 50 students.

STUDENT HOUSING

54% of freshmen live in college housing. Housing is guaranteed for all undergraduates. Campus can house 1,506 undergraduates.

EXPENSES

Tuition (2005-06): $4,234 per year (in-state), $12,514 (out-of-state).
Room & Board: $4,544
There is no additional cost for LD program/services.

LD SERVICES

LD program size is not limited.

LD services available to:

☐ Freshmen ☐ Sophomores ☐ Juniors ☐ Seniors

Academic Accommodations

Curriculum		In class	
Foreign language waiver	☐	Early syllabus	☐
Lighter course load	☐	Note takers in class	■
Math waiver	☐	Priority seating	☐
Other special classes	☐	Tape recorders	■
Priority registrations	☐	Videotaped classes	☐
Substitution of courses	☐	Text on tape	☐
Exams		**Services**	
Extended time	■	Diagnostic tests	■
Oral exams	■	Learning centers	■
Take home exams	☐	Proofreaders	☐
Exams on tape or computer	☐	Readers	☐
Untimed exams	☐	Reading Machines/Kurzweil	☐
Other accommodations	☐	Special bookstore section	☐
		Typists	☐

Credit toward degree is not given for remedial courses taken.

Counseling Services

☐ Academic
☐ Psychological
☐ Student Support groups
☐ Vocational

Tutoring

	Individual	Group
Time management	☐	☐
Organizational skills	☐	☐
Learning strategies	☐	☐
Study skills	☐	☐
Content area	☐	☐
Writing lab	☐	☐
Math lab	☐	☐

LD PROGRAM STAFF

Total number of LD Program staff (including director):

Full Time: 1 Part Time: 1

Key staff person available to work with LD students: Mr. Nolen Mears, Associate Dean for Student Services.

Austin College

Sherman, TX

Address: 900 N. Grand Avenue, Sherman, TX, 75090-4400
Admissions telephone: 800 442-5363
Admissions FAX: 903 813-3198
Vice President for Institutional Enrollment: Nan Davis
Admissions e-mail: admission@austincollege.edu
Web site: http://www.austincollege.edu
SAT Code: 6016 ACT Code: 4058

Director Academic Skills Center: Laura Marquez
LD program telephone: 903 813-2454
LD program e-mail: lmarquez@austincollege.edu
LD program enrollment: 30, Total campus enrollment: 1,288

GENERAL

Austin College is a private, coed, four-year institution. 70-acre campus in Sherman (population: 35,082), 60 miles from Dallas. Served by bus; major airports and train serve Dallas. 4-1-4 system.

LD ADMISSIONS

A personal interview is recommended. Essay is required and may be typed.

SECONDARY SCHOOL REQUIREMENTS

Graduation from secondary school required; GED accepted. The following course distribution required: 4 units of English, 3 units of math, 3 units of science, 2 units of foreign language, 2 units of social studies, 1 unit of academic electives.

TESTING

SAT Reasoning or ACT required. SAT Subject required.

All enrolled freshmen (fall 2004):

Average SAT I Scores:	Verbal: 622	Math: 621
Average ACT Scores:	Composite: 26	

Child Study Team report is not required. Tests required as part of this documentation:

- ☐ WAIS-IV
- ☐ WISC-IV
- ☐ SATA
- ☐ Woodcock-Johnson
- ☐ Nelson-Denny Reading Test
- ☐ Other

UNDERGRADUATE STUDENT BODY

Total undergraduate student enrollment: 542 Men, 685 Women.

Composition of student body (fall 2004):

	Undergraduate	Freshmen
International	0.8	2.0
Black	2.4	4.1
American Indian	0.5	0.9
Asian-American	9.5	9.8
Hispanic	10.3	8.4
White	76.5	74.8
Unreported	0.0	0.0
	100.0%	100.0%

8% are from out of state. 30% join a fraternity and 30% join a sorority. Average age of full-time undergraduates is 20. 54% of classes have fewer than 20 students, 45% have between 20 and 50 students, 1% have more than 50 students.

STUDENT HOUSING

95% of freshmen live in college housing. Freshmen are required to live on campus. Housing is guaranteed for all undergraduates. Campus can house 951 undergraduates. Single rooms are available for students with medical or special needs. A medical note is required.

EXPENSES

Tuition (2005-06): $20,310 per year.
Room: $3,385. Board: $3,991.
There is no additional cost for LD program/services.

LD SERVICES

LD program size is not limited.

LD services available to:

☑ Freshmen ☑ Sophomores ☑ Juniors ☑ Seniors

Academic Accommodations

Curriculum		In class	
Foreign language waiver	☐	Early syllabus	☐
Lighter course load	☐	Note takers in class	☑
Math waiver	☐	Priority seating	☐
Other special classes	☐	Tape recorders	☑
Priority registrations	☐	Videotaped classes	☐
Substitution of courses	☐	Text on tape	☑
Exams		**Services**	
Extended time	☑	Diagnostic tests	☐
Oral exams	☐	Learning centers	☑
Take home exams	☐	Proofreaders	☐
Exams on tape or computer	☑	Readers	☐
Untimed exams	☐	Reading Machines/Kurzweil	☑
Other accommodations	☐	Special bookstore section	☐
		Typists	☐

Credit toward degree is not given for remedial courses taken.

Counseling Services

- ☑ Academic
- ☐ Psychological
- ☐ Student Support groups
- ☐ Vocational

Tutoring

Individual tutoring is available weekly.

	Individual	Group
Time management	☑	☑
Organizational skills	☑	☑
Learning strategies	☑	☑
Study skills	☑	☑
Content area	☑	☑
Writing lab	☑	☑
Math lab	☑	☑

LD PROGRAM STAFF

Total number of LD Program staff (including director):

Full Time: 1 Part Time: 1

There is an advisor/advocate from the LD program available to students.

Key staff person available to work with LD students: Laura Marquez, Director Academic Skills Center.

Baylor University

Waco, TX

Address: 1 Bear Place, Waco, TX, 76798
Admissions telephone: 800 BAYLOR U
Director of Admissions: Stephanie Willis
Admissions e-mail: Admissions@Baylor.edu
Web site: http://www.baylor.edu
SAT Code: 6032 ACT Code: 4062

LD program name: Office of Access/Learning Accommodation
LD program address: 1 Bear Place #97204
Director: Dr. Sheila Graham Smith
LD program telephone: 254 710-3605
LD program e-mail: www.baylor.edu/OALA
LD program enrollment: 325, Total campus enrollment: 11,580

GENERAL

Baylor University is a private, coed, four-year institution. 432-acre, suburban campus in Waco (population: 113,726), 90 miles from Dallas-Fort Worth, 105 miles from Austin; branch campus in Dallas. Served by air and bus; train serves McGregor (20 miles). Public transportation serves campus. Semester system.

LD ADMISSIONS

Students do not complete a separate application and are not simultaneously accepted to the LD program. A member of the LD program does not sit on the admissions committee. A personal interview is required. Essay is not required.

For fall 2004, 50 completed self-identified LD applications were received.

SECONDARY SCHOOL REQUIREMENTS

Graduation from secondary school required; GED accepted. The following course distribution required: 4 units of English, 3 units of math, 2 units of science, 2 units of foreign language, 1 unit of social studies, 1 unit of history, 3 units of academic electives.

TESTING

SAT Reasoning or ACT required. SAT Subject required.

All enrolled freshmen (fall 2004):

Average SAT I Scores: Verbal: 589 Math: 601
Average ACT Scores: Composite: 25

Child Study Team report is not required. A neuropsychological or comprehensive psycho-educational evaluation is required for admission. Must be dated within 36 months of application. Tests required as part of this documentation:

- [x] WAIS-IV
- [x] WISC-IV
- [ ] SATA
- [x] Woodcock-Johnson
- [ ] Nelson-Denny Reading Test
- [ ] Other

UNDERGRADUATE STUDENT BODY

Total undergraduate student enrollment: 5,146 Men, 7,044 Women.

Composition of student body (fall 2004):

	Undergraduate	Freshmen
International	1.1	1.4
Black	8.3	7.1
American Indian	0.6	0.6
Asian-American	7.8	6.1
Hispanic	10.4	8.5
White	69.5	74.1
Unreported	2.3	2.2
	100.0%	100.0%

17% are from out of state. 13% join a fraternity and 17% join a sorority. Average age of full-time undergraduates is 21. 35% of classes have fewer than 20 students, 55% have between 20 and 50 students, 10% have more than 50 students.

STUDENT HOUSING

98% of freshmen live in college housing. Freshmen are required to live on campus. Housing is guaranteed for all undergraduates. Campus can house 4,200 undergraduates. Single rooms are available for students with medical or special needs. A medical note is required.

EXPENSES

Tuition (2005-06): $19,050 per year.
Room: $3,346. Board: $3,428.
There is no additional cost for LD program/services.

LD SERVICES

LD program size is not limited.

LD services available to:

- [x] Freshmen
- [x] Sophomores
- [x] Juniors
- [x] Seniors

Academic Accommodations

Curriculum		**In class**	
Foreign language waiver	[ ]	Early syllabus	[ ]
Lighter course load	[x]	Note takers in class	[x]
Math waiver	[ ]	Priority seating	[x]
Other special classes	[ ]	Tape recorders	[x]
Priority registrations	[ ]	Videotaped classes	[ ]
Substitution of courses	[ ]	Text on tape	[ ]
Exams		**Services**	
Extended time	[x]	Diagnostic tests	[ ]
Oral exams	[x]	Learning centers	[ ]
Take home exams	[ ]	Proofreaders	[x]
Exams on tape or computer	[ ]	Readers	[x]
Untimed exams	[ ]	Reading Machines/Kurzweil	[x]
Other accommodations	[x]	Special bookstore section	[ ]
		Typists	[ ]

Credit toward degree is not given for remedial courses taken.

Counseling Services

- [ ] Academic
- [ ] Psychological
- [ ] Student Support groups
- [ ] Vocational

Tutoring

Individual tutoring is available daily.

	Individual	Group
Time management	[x]	[ ]
Organizational skills	[x]	[ ]
Learning strategies	[x]	[ ]
Study skills	[x]	[ ]
Content area	[ ]	[ ]
Writing lab	[ ]	[ ]
Math lab	[ ]	[ ]

LD PROGRAM STAFF

Total number of LD Program staff (including director):

Full Time: 3 Part Time: 3

There is an advisor/advocate from the LD program available to students. The advisor/advocate meets with students 4 times per month. 2 graduate students and 5 peer tutors are available to work with LD students.

Key staff person available to work with LD students: Dr. Sheila Graham Smith, Director of Access & Learning Accommodations.

LD Program web site: www.baylor.edu/oala

Dallas Baptist University

Dallas, TX

Address: 3000 Mountain Creek Parkway, Dallas, TX, 75211-9299
Admissions telephone: 800 460-1328
Director of Undergraduate Admissions: Anita L. Douris
Admissions e-mail: admiss@dbu.edu
Web site: http://www.dbu.edu
SAT Code: 6159 ACT Code: 4080

LD program name: Disabled Student Services
Assoc. V.P for Student Affrs., Dean of Students: Mark Hale
LD program telephone: 214 333-5101
LD program e-mail: markh@dbu.edu
LD program enrollment: 50, Total campus enrollment: 3,541

GENERAL

Dallas Baptist University is a private, coed, four-year institution. 293-acre, urban campus in Dallas (population: 1,188,580), 13 miles from downtown area; branch campuses in Arlington, Fort Worth, and North Dallas. Served by air, bus, and train. 4-1-4 system.

LD ADMISSIONS

Students do not complete a separate application and are not simultaneously accepted to the LD program. A member of the LD program does not sit on the admissions committee. A personal interview is recommended. Essay is required and may be typed.

SECONDARY SCHOOL REQUIREMENTS

Graduation from secondary school required; GED accepted.

TESTING

SAT Reasoning or ACT required. SAT Subject required.

All enrolled freshmen (fall 2004):

Average SAT I Scores:	Verbal: 562	Math: 538
Average ACT Scores:	Composite: 23	

Child Study Team report is not required. A neuropsychological or comprehensive psycho-education evaluation is not required for admission. Tests required as part of this documentation:

- [x] WAIS-IV
- [x] WISC-IV
- [x] SATA
- [x] Woodcock-Johnson
- [x] Nelson-Denny Reading Test
- [ ] Other

UNDERGRADUATE STUDENT BODY

Total undergraduate student enrollment: 1,286 Men, 2,054 Women.

Composition of student body (fall 2004):

	Undergraduate	Freshmen
International	0.0	6.7
Black	3.4	19.0
American Indian	1.5	1.5
Asian-American	1.2	1.6
Hispanic	8.0	8.6
White	85.8	55.0
Unreported	0.0	7.6
	100.0%	100.0%

7% are from out of state. Average age of full-time undergraduates is 23. 55% of classes have fewer than 20 students, 41% have between 20 and 50 students, 4% have more than 50 students.

STUDENT HOUSING

91% of freshmen live in college housing. Freshmen are not required to live on campus. Housing is guaranteed for all undergraduates. Campus can house 1,287 undergraduates. Single rooms are available for students with medical or special needs. A medical note is required.

EXPENSES

Tuition (2005 06): $12,270 per year.
Room: $1,900. Board: $2,870.
There is no additional cost for LD program/services.

LD SERVICES

LD program size is not limited.

LD services available to:

- [x] Freshmen
- [x] Sophomores
- [x] Juniors
- [x] Seniors

Academic Accommodations

Curriculum

- [ ] Foreign language waiver
- [ ] Lighter course load
- [ ] Math waiver
- [ ] Other special classes
- [ ] Priority registrations
- [ ] Substitution of courses

Exams

- [x] Extended time
- [x] Oral exams
- [ ] Take home exams
- [ ] Exams on tape or computer
- [x] Untimed exams
- [ ] Other accommodations

In class

- [ ] Early syllabus
- [x] Note takers in class
- [x] Priority seating
- [x] Tape recorders
- [x] Videotaped classes
- [x] Text on tape

Services

- [ ] Diagnostic tests
- [x] Learning centers
- [ ] Proofreaders
- [x] Readers
- [x] Reading Machines/Kurzweil
- [ ] Special bookstore section
- [x] Typists

Credit toward degree is not given for remedial courses taken.

Counseling Services

- [x] Academic
- [x] Psychological
- [ ] Student Support groups
- [x] Vocational

Tutoring

Individual tutoring is available weekly.

Average size of tutoring groups: 1

	Individual	Group
Time management	[ ]	[x]
Organizational skills	[ ]	[x]
Learning strategies	[ ]	[x]
Study skills	[ ]	[x]
Content area	[ ]	[x]
Writing lab	[x]	[x]
Math lab	[x]	[x]

LD PROGRAM STAFF

Total number of LD Program staff (including director):

Full Time: 1 Part Time: 1

There is an advisor/advocate from the LD program available to students.

Key staff person available to work with LD students: Mark Hale, Associate Vice President for Student Affairs, Dean of Students.

East Texas Baptist University

Marshall, TX

Address: 1209 N. Grove, Marshall, TX, 75670
Admissions telephone: 800 804-ETBU
Dean of Admissions and Marketing: Vince Blankenship
Admissions e-mail: admissions@etbu.edu
Web site: http://www.etbu.edu
SAT Code: 6187 ACT Code: 4086

LD program name: Advising and Career Development
Director of Advising: Bob Flannery
LD program telephone: 903 923-2079
LD program e-mail: bflannery@etbu.edu
LD program enrollment: 21, Total campus enrollment: 1,412

GENERAL

East Texas Baptist University is a private, coed, four-year institution. 200-acre campus in Marshall (population: 23,935), 20 miles from Longview and 35 miles from Shreveport, La. Served by bus and train; major airports serve Shreveport. 4-4-1 system.

LD ADMISSIONS

Application Deadline: 08/18. Students do not complete a separate application and are simultaneously accepted to the LD program. A personal interview is not required. Essay is not required.

SECONDARY SCHOOL REQUIREMENTS

Graduation from secondary school required; GED accepted.

TESTING

ACT required; SAT Reasoning may be substituted. SAT Subject recommended.

All enrolled freshmen (fall 2004):

Average SAT I Scores: Verbal: 499 Math: 519
Average ACT Scores: Composite: 21

Child Study Team report is not required. A neuropsychological or comprehensive psycho-educational evaluation is required for admission. Must be dated within 24 months of application. Tests required as part of this documentation:

☐ WAIS-IV ☐ Woodcock-Johnson
☐ WISC-IV ☐ Nelson-Denny Reading Test
☐ SATA ☐ Other

UNDERGRADUATE STUDENT BODY

Total undergraduate student enrollment: 705 Men, 804 Women.

Composition of student body (fall 2004):

	Undergraduate	Freshmen
International	0.0	0.7
Black	22.4	15.6
American Indian	0.0	0.6
Asian-American	0.3	0.3
Hispanic	4.0	3.6
White	73.3	78.9
Unreported	0.0	0.2
	100.0%	100.0%

9% are from out of state. 15% join a fraternity and 15% join a sorority. Average age of full-time undergraduates is 21. 53% of classes have fewer than 20 students, 45% have between 20 and 50 students, 2% have more than 50 students.

STUDENT HOUSING

95% of freshmen live in college housing. Freshmen are required to live on campus. Housing is guaranteed for all undergraduates. Campus can house 1,096 undergraduates. Single rooms are available for students with medical or special needs. A medical note is required.

EXPENSES

Tuition (2005-06): $12,840 per year.

Room: $1,600. Board: $2,273.

There is no additional cost for LD program/services.

LD SERVICES

LD program size is not limited.

LD services available to:

☑ Freshmen ☑ Sophomores ☑ Juniors ☑ Seniors

Academic Accommodations

Curriculum		In class	
Foreign language waiver	☐	Early syllabus	☐
Lighter course load	☐	Note takers in class	☐
Math waiver	☐	Priority seating	☐
Other special classes	☐	Tape recorders	☐
Priority registrations	☐	Videotaped classes	☐
Substitution of courses	☐	Text on tape	☐
Exams		**Services**	
Extended time	☑	Diagnostic tests	☐
Oral exams	☐	Learning centers	☐
Take home exams	☐	Proofreaders	☐
Exams on tape or computer	☐	Readers	☐
Untimed exams	☐	Reading Machines/Kurzweil	☐
Other accommodations	☐	Special bookstore section	☐
		Typists	☐

Credit toward degree is not given for remedial courses taken.

Counseling Services

☑ Academic — Meets 2 times per academic year
☑ Psychological
☐ Student Support groups
☐ Vocational

Tutoring

Individual tutoring is available daily.

	Individual	Group
Time management	☐	☐
Organizational skills	☐	☐
Learning strategies	☐	☐
Study skills	☐	☐
Content area	☐	☐
Writing lab	☐	☐
Math lab	☐	☐

LD PROGRAM STAFF

Total number of LD Program staff (including director):

Full Time: 1 Part Time: 1

There is an advisor/advocate from the LD program available to students.

Key staff person available to work with LD students: Bob Flannery, Director of Advising.

LD Program web site: www.etbu.edu/advising

Hardin-Simmons University

Abilene, TX

Address: 2200 Hickory, Abilene, TX, 79698-1000
Admissions telephone: 800 568-2692
Admissions FAX: 325 671-2115
Associate Vice President for Enrollment Services: Dr. Shane Davidson
Admissions e-mail: enroll@hsutx.edu
Web site: http://www.hsutx.edu/
SAT Code: 6268 ACT Code: 4096

LD program name: Students with Disabilities
LD program address: Box16158
Coordinator, Students with Disabilities: Becky Casey
LD program telephone: 325 670-5842
LD program e-mail: bcasey@hsutx.edu
LD program enrollment: 30, Total campus enrollment: 1,942

GENERAL

Hardin-Simmons University is a private, coed, four-year institution. 100-acre, urban campus in Abilene (population: 115,930). Served by air and bus; major airport serves Dallas/Ft. Worth (150 miles); train serves Ft. Worth. Public transportation serves campus. Semester system.

LD ADMISSIONS

Students complete a separate application and are not simultaneously accepted to the LD program. A member of the LD program does not sit on the admissions committee. A personal interview is not required. Essay is not required.

For fall 2004, 60 completed self-identified LD applications were received.

SECONDARY SCHOOL REQUIREMENTS

Graduation from secondary school required; GED accepted. The following course distribution required: 3 units of English, 2 units of math, 2 units of science, 2 units of social studies, 7 units of academic electives.

TESTING

SAT Reasoning or ACT required. SAT Subject required.

All enrolled freshmen (fall 2004):

Average SAT I Scores:	Verbal: 511	Math: 514
Average ACT Scores:	Composite: 21	

Child Study Team report is not required. A neuropsychological or comprehensive psycho-educational evaluation is required for admission. Must be dated within 36 months of application. Tests required as part of this documentation:

- [x] WAIS-IV
- [x] WISC-IV
- [ ] SATA
- [x] Woodcock-Johnson
- [ ] Nelson-Denny Reading Test
- [x] Other

UNDERGRADUATE STUDENT BODY

Total undergraduate student enrollment: 891 Men, 1,011 Women.

Composition of student body (fall 2004):

	Undergraduate	Freshmen
International	0.0	0.0
Black	5.9	4.8
American Indian	1.2	0.6
Asian-American	1.3	1.1
Hispanic	8.9	8.7
White	77.8	81.7
Unreported	4.9	3.1
	100.0%	100.0%

6% are from out of state. 11% join a fraternity and 11% join a sorority. Average age of full-time undergraduates is 21. 59% of classes have fewer than 20 students, 40% have between 20 and 50 students, 1% have more than 50 students.

STUDENT HOUSING

87% of freshmen live in college housing. Freshmen are required to live on campus. Housing is guaranteed for all undergraduates. Campus can house 1,117 undergraduates. Single rooms are available for students with medical or special needs. A medical note is required.

EXPENSES

Tuition (2005-06): $13,650 per year. Tuition is different for nursing program. Room: $2,148. Board: $2,067.

There is no additional cost for LD program/services.

LD SERVICES

LD program size is not limited.

LD services available to:

- [x] Freshmen
- [x] Sophomores
- [x] Juniors
- [x] Seniors

Academic Accommodations

Curriculum		In class	
Foreign language waiver	[ ]	Early syllabus	[ ]
Lighter course load	[x]	Note takers in class	[x]
Math waiver	[ ]	Priority seating	[ ]
Other special classes	[ ]	Tape recorders	[x]
Priority registrations	[ ]	Videotaped classes	[ ]
Substitution of courses	[ ]	Text on tape	[ ]
Exams		**Services**	
Extended time	[x]	Diagnostic tests	[ ]
Oral exams	[x]	Learning centers	[ ]
Take home exams	[ ]	Proofreaders	[ ]
Exams on tape or computer	[x]	Readers	[x]
Untimed exams	[x]	Reading Machines/Kurzweil	[ ]
Other accommodations	[ ]	Special bookstore section	[ ]
		Typists	[ ]

Credit toward degree is given for remedial courses taken.

Counseling Services

- [x] Academic — Meets 2 times per academic year
- [ ] Psychological
- [ ] Student Support groups
- [ ] Vocational

Tutoring

Individual tutoring is available daily.

Average size of tutoring groups: 1

	Individual	Group
Time management	[x]	[ ]
Organizational skills	[x]	[ ]
Learning strategies	[x]	[ ]
Study skills	[x]	[ ]
Content area	[x]	[ ]
Writing lab	[x]	[ ]
Math lab	[x]	[ ]

LD PROGRAM STAFF

There is an advisor/advocate from the LD program available to students. The advisor/advocate meets with faculty once per month and students once per month. 10 peer tutors are available to work with LD students.

Key staff person available to work with LD students: Becky Casey, Coordinator, Students with Disabilities.

LD Program web site:
http://www.hsutx.edu/academics/advising/osd/index.html

Houston Baptist University

Houston, TX

Address: 7502 Fondren Road, Houston, TX, 77074-3298
Admissions FAX: 281 649-3217
Director of Admissions/Asssistant V.P. for Enrollment Services: David Melton
Admissions e-mail: unadm@hbu.edu
Web site: http://www.hbu.edu
SAT Code: 6282 ACT Code: 4101

Professor: Dr. Verna Peterson, Licensed Psychologist
LD program e-mail: vpeterson@hbu.edu
LD program enrollment: 9, Total campus enrollment: 1,815

GENERAL

Houston Baptist University is a private, coed, four-year institution. 100-acre, urban campus in Houston (population: 1,953,431). Served by air and bus. Public transportation serves campus. Quarter system.

LD ADMISSIONS

A personal interview is recommended. Essay is required and may be typed.

SECONDARY SCHOOL REQUIREMENTS

Graduation from secondary school required; GED accepted. The following course distribution required: 4 units of English, 3 units of math, 3 units of science, 2 units of foreign language, 2 units of social studies, 2 units of history, 2 units of academic electives.

TESTING

SAT Reasoning or ACT required. SAT Subject recommended.

All enrolled freshmen (fall 2004):

Average SAT I Scores: Verbal: 540 Math: 541
Average ACT Scores: Composite: 22

Child Study Team report is not required. Tests required as part of this documentation:

- [ ] WAIS-IV
- [ ] WISC-IV
- [ ] SATA
- [ ] Woodcock-Johnson
- [ ] Nelson-Denny Reading Test
- [ ] Other

UNDERGRADUATE STUDENT BODY

Total undergraduate student enrollment: 597 Men, 1,356 Women.

Composition of student body (fall 2004):

	Undergraduate	Freshmen
International	5.5	6.4
Black	14.0	19.7
American Indian	2.2	0.8
Asian-American	19.1	12.4
Hispanic	11.4	14.8
White	47.8	45.8
Unreported	0.0	0.1
	100.0%	100.0%

6% are from out of state. 11% join a fraternity and 1% join a sorority. Average age of full-time undergraduates is 22. 55% of classes have fewer than 20 students, 44% have between 20 and 50 students, 1% have more than 50 students.

STUDENT HOUSING

39% of freshmen live in college housing. Freshmen are required to live on campus. Housing is guaranteed for all undergraduates. Campus can house 718 undergraduates. Single rooms are available for students with medical or special needs. A medical note is required.

EXPENSES

Tuition (2005-06): $13,950 per year.

Room & Board: $4,710

There is no additional cost for LD program/services.

LD SERVICES

LD program size is not limited.

LD services available to:

- [x] Freshmen
- [x] Sophomores
- [x] Juniors
- [x] Seniors

Academic Accommodations

Curriculum

- [ ] Foreign language waiver
- [x] Lighter course load
- [ ] Math waiver
- [ ] Other special classes
- [ ] Priority registrations
- [ ] Substitution of courses

Exams

- [x] Extended time
- [x] Oral exams
- [ ] Take home exams
- [ ] Exams on tape or computer
- [x] Untimed exams
- [ ] Other accommodations

In class

- [ ] Early syllabus
- [ ] Note takers in class
- [ ] Priority seating
- [ ] Tape recorders
- [ ] Videotaped classes
- [ ] Text on tape

Services

- [x] Diagnostic tests
- [x] Learning centers
- [ ] Proofreaders
- [ ] Readers
- [ ] Reading Machines/Kurzweil
- [ ] Special bookstore section
- [ ] Typists

Credit toward degree is not given for remedial courses taken.

Counseling Services

- [x] Academic
- [x] Psychological
- [ ] Student Support groups
- [ ] Vocational

Tutoring

	Individual	Group
Time management	[ ]	[ ]
Organizational skills	[ ]	[ ]
Learning strategies	[ ]	[ ]
Study skills	[ ]	[ ]
Content area	[ ]	[ ]
Writing lab	[ ]	[ ]
Math lab	[ ]	[ ]

LD PROGRAM STAFF

Total number of LD Program staff (including director):

Full Time: 1 Part Time: 1

There is an advisor/advocate from the LD program available to students.

Key staff person available to work with LD students: Dr. Verna Peterson, Licensed Psychologist.

University of Houston

Houston, TX

Address: 212 E. Cullen Building, Houston, TX, 77204
Admissions telephone: 713 743-1010
Associate Vice President of Enrollment Services: Susanna Finnell
Admissions e-mail: admissions@uh.edu
Web site: http://www.uh.edu
SAT Code: 6870 ACT Code: 4236

LD program name: Justin Dart, Jr Center
LD program address: CSD Building, Room 100
Director: Cheryl Amoruso
LD program telephone: 713 743-5400
LD program e-mail: camoruso@uh.edu
LD program enrollment: 312, Total campus enrollment: 27,312

GENERAL

University of Houston is a public, coed, four-year institution. 551-acre, urban campus in Houston (population: 1,953,631), three miles from downtown; branch campuses at Cinco Ranch and in North Houston and Ft. Bend. Served by air, bus, and train. School operates transportation to airport. Public transportation serves campus. Semester system.

LD ADMISSIONS

Students do not complete a separate application and are simultaneously accepted to the LD program. A member of the LD program does not sit on the admissions committee. A personal interview is required. Essay is not required.

SECONDARY SCHOOL REQUIREMENTS

Graduation from secondary school required; GED accepted. The following course distribution required: 4 units of English, 3 units of math, 2 units of science, 2 units of social studies, 2 units of history.

TESTING

SAT Reasoning or ACT required. SAT Subject required.

All enrolled freshmen (fall 2004):

Average SAT I Scores:	Verbal: 518	Math: 544
Average ACT Scores:	Composite: 21	

Child Study Team report is not required. A neuropsychological or comprehensive psycho-educational evaluation is required for admission. Must be dated within 36 months of application. Tests required as part of this documentation:

- ■ WAIS-IV
- ☐ WISC-IV
- ☐ SATA
- ■ Woodcock-Johnson
- ☐ Nelson-Denny Reading Test
- ☐ Other

UNDERGRADUATE STUDENT BODY

Total undergraduate student enrollment: 11,940 Men, 13,290 Women.

Composition of student body (fall 2004):

	Undergraduate	Freshmen
International	4.2	4.9
Black	18.4	14.8
American Indian	0.4	0.4
Asian-American	25.4	20.8
Hispanic	19.6	20.9
White	31.0	36.6
Unreported	1.0	1.6
	100.0%	100.0%

2% are from out of state. 4% join a fraternity and 3% join a sorority. Average age of full-time undergraduates is 22. 28% of classes have fewer than 20 students, 51% have between 20 and 50 students, 21% have more than 50 students.

STUDENT HOUSING

25% of freshmen live in college housing. Freshmen are not required to live on campus. Housing is guaranteed for all undergraduates. Campus can house 4,060 undergraduates. Single rooms are available for students with medical or special needs. A medical note is required.

EXPENSES

Tuition (2005-06): $6,625 per year (in-state), $14,253 (out-of-state).

Room & Board: $6,628

There is no additional cost for LD program/services.

LD SERVICES

LD program size is not limited.

LD services available to:

■ Freshmen ■ Sophomores ■ Juniors ■ Seniors

Academic Accommodations

Curriculum		**In class**	
Foreign language waiver	☐	Early syllabus	☐
Lighter course load	■	Note takers in class	■
Math waiver	☐	Priority seating	☐
Other special classes	☐	Tape recorders	■
Priority registrations	☐	Videotaped classes	■
Substitution of courses	☐	Text on tape	☐
Exams		**Services**	
Extended time	■	Diagnostic tests	■
Oral exams	■	Learning centers	■
Take home exams	☐	Proofreaders	☐
Exams on tape or computer	☐	Readers	■
Untimed exams	☐	Reading Machines/Kurzweil	■
Other accommodations	☐	Special bookstore section	☐
		Typists	☐

Credit toward degree is not given for remedial courses taken.

Counseling Services

- ■ Academic
- ■ Psychological
- ■ Student Support groups
- ■ Vocational

Tutoring

Individual tutoring is available daily.

	Individual	Group
Time management	■	■
Organizational skills	■	■
Learning strategies	■	■
Study skills	■	■
Content area	■	■
Writing lab	■	■
Math lab	■	■

UNIQUE LD PROGRAM FEATURES

The Center for Students with Disabilities (CSD) provides numerous academic support services to individuals with any type of learning disability, health impairment, physical limitation or psychiatric disorder. Our goal is to help ensure that qualified students with disabilities at the University of Houston are able to successfully compete with non-disabled students. CSD services are confidential. CSD student information is shared only with the student's written permission to do so. Student CSD records are not a part of their permanent student record. We work closely with other departments on campus to provide a wide range of services, including accommodations, tutoring, counseling, job placement and academic advising. CSD also serves as a resource center, and refers students to other community organizations and agencies as appropriate.

LD PROGRAM STAFF

Total number of LD Program staff (including director):

Full Time: 6 Part Time: 6

There is an advisor/advocate from the LD program available to students.

Key staff person available to work with LD students: Scott Crain, Counselor.

University of Houston - Downtown

Houston, TX

Address: 1 Main Street, Houston, TX, 77002
Admissions telephone: 713 221-8522
Dean of Student Affairs: Carmen Holland
Admissions e-mail: uhdadmit@uhd.edu
Web site: http://www.uhd.edu
SAT Code: 6922 ACT Code: 4170

LD program name: Disability Services
Director, Disabled Student Services: Duraese Hall
LD program telephone: 713 226-5227
LD program e-mail: Halld@uhd.edu
Total campus enrollment: 11,261

GENERAL

University of Houston - Downtown is a public, coed, four-year institution. Urban campus in Houston (population: 1,953,631). Served by air, bus, and train. School operates transportation to parking lots. Public transportation serves campus. Semester system.

SECONDARY SCHOOL REQUIREMENTS

Graduation from secondary school required; GED accepted.

TESTING

All enrolled freshmen (fall 2004):

Child Study Team report is not required. Tests required as part of this documentation:

- [ ] WAIS-IV
- [ ] WISC-IV
- [ ] SATA
- [ ] Woodcock-Johnson
- [ ] Nelson-Denny Reading Test
- [ ] Other

UNDERGRADUATE STUDENT BODY

Total undergraduate student enrollment: 3,679 Men, 5,253 Women.

Composition of student body (fall 2004):

	Undergraduate	Freshmen
International	5.0	4.4
Black	24.3	26.2
American Indian	0.3	0.3
Asian-American	8.9	9.9
Hispanic	51.1	35.6
White	10.4	23.6
Unreported	0.0	0.0
	100.0%	100.0%

1% are from out of state. Average age of full-time undergraduates is 24. 24% of classes have fewer than 20 students, 73% have between 20 and 50 students, 3% have more than 50 students.

EXPENSES

Tuition (2005-06): $3,375 per year (in-state), $11,655 (out-of-state).

There is no additional cost for LD program/services.

LD SERVICES

LD program size is not limited.

LD services available to:

- [x] Freshmen
- [x] Sophomores
- [x] Juniors
- [x] Seniors

Academic Accommodations

Curriculum

- [x] Foreign language waiver
- [x] Lighter course load
- [ ] Math waiver
- [ ] Other special classes
- [x] Priority registrations
- [ ] Substitution of courses

Exams

- [x] Extended time
- [ ] Oral exams
- [ ] Take home exams
- [x] Exams on tape or computer
- [ ] Untimed exams
- [x] Other accommodations

In class

- [ ] Early syllabus
- [ ] Note takers in class
- [x] Priority seating
- [ ] Tape recorders
- [ ] Videotaped classes
- [ ] Text on tape

Services

- [x] Diagnostic tests
- [x] Learning centers
- [ ] Proofreaders
- [ ] Readers
- [x] Reading Machines/Kurzweil
- [ ] Special bookstore section
- [ ] Typists

Credit toward degree is not given for remedial courses taken.

Counseling Services

- [x] Academic
- [ ] Psychological
- [ ] Student Support groups
- [x] Vocational

Tutoring

Individual tutoring is available weekly.

	Individual	Group
Time management	[ ]	[ ]
Organizational skills	[ ]	[ ]
Learning strategies	[ ]	[ ]
Study skills	[ ]	[ ]
Content area	[ ]	[ ]
Writing lab	[ ]	[ ]
Math lab	[ ]	[ ]

LD PROGRAM STAFF

There is an advisor/advocate from the LD program available to students.

Key staff person available to work with LD students: Duraese Hall, Director, Disabled Student Services.

LD Program web site:
http://www.uhd.edu/academic/colleges/university/disabled

Howard Payne University

Brownwood, TX

Address: 1000 Fisk Avenue, Brownwood, TX, 76801
Admissions telephone: 800 880-4478
Director of Admissions: Cheryl Mangrum
Admissions e-mail: enroll@hputx.edu
Web site: http://www.hputx.edu
SAT Code: 6278 ACT Code: 4102

LD program name: Center for Academic/Personal Success
Director of Academic Success Programs: Amy Dodson
LD program telephone: 325 649-8618
LD program e-mail: adodson@hputx.edu
Total campus enrollment: 1,319

GENERAL

Howard Payne University is a private, coed, four-year institution. 30-acre campus in Brownwood (population: 18,813), 78 miles from Abilene and 140 miles from Austin; branch campuses in Benbrook, Corpus Christi, El Paso, Granbury, Harlingen, Midland, and San Angelo. Served by air and bus; major airport and train serve Dallas (150 miles). Semester system.

LD ADMISSIONS

Essay is not required.

SECONDARY SCHOOL REQUIREMENTS

Graduation from secondary school required; GED accepted.

TESTING

SAT Reasoning or ACT required.

All enrolled freshmen (fall 2004):

Average SAT I Scores: Verbal: 500 Math: 497
Average ACT Scores: Composite: 21

Child Study Team report is not required. Tests required as part of this documentation:

- [ ] WAIS-IV
- [ ] WISC-IV
- [ ] SATA
- [ ] Woodcock-Johnson
- [ ] Nelson-Denny Reading Test
- [ ] Other

UNDERGRADUATE STUDENT BODY

Total undergraduate student enrollment: 781 Men, 745 Women.

Composition of student body (fall 2004):

	Undergraduate	Freshmen
International	0.0	0.6
Black	14.2	8.1
American Indian	1.3	1.1
Asian-American	0.3	1.1
Hispanic	8.9	12.4
White	73.0	75.2
Unreported	2.3	1.5
	100.0%	100.0%

2% are from out of state. 11% join a fraternity and 11% join a sorority. Average age of full-time undergraduates is 21. 78% of classes have fewer than 20 students, 22% have between 20 and 50 students.

STUDENT HOUSING

91% of freshmen live in college housing. Freshmen are required to live on campus. Housing is not guaranteed for all undergraduates. Juniors and seniors may live on campus if space is available. Campus can house 770 undergraduates. Single rooms are available for students with medical or special needs. A medical note is required.

EXPENSES

Tuition (2005-06): $12,000 per year.
Room & Board: $4,615
There is no additional cost for LD program/services.

LD SERVICES

LD program size is not limited.

LD services available to:

- [x] Freshmen
- [x] Sophomores
- [x] Juniors
- [x] Seniors

Academic Accommodations

Curriculum

- [ ] Foreign language waiver
- [ ] Lighter course load
- [ ] Math waiver
- [ ] Other special classes
- [ ] Priority registrations
- [ ] Substitution of courses

Exams

- [x] Extended time
- [x] Oral exams
- [ ] Take home exams
- [x] Exams on tape or computer
- [x] Untimed exams
- [x] Other accommodations

In class

- [ ] Early syllabus
- [x] Note takers in class
- [x] Priority seating
- [x] Tape recorders
- [ ] Videotaped classes
- [ ] Text on tape

Services

- [ ] Diagnostic tests
- [x] Learning centers
- [x] Proofreaders
- [ ] Readers
- [ ] Reading Machines/Kurzweil
- [ ] Special bookstore section
- [ ] Typists

Credit toward degree is given for remedial courses taken.

Counseling Services

- [x] Academic
- [x] Psychological
- [ ] Student Support groups
- [ ] Vocational

Tutoring

Individual tutoring is available daily.

Average size of tutoring groups: 1

	Individual	Group
Time management	[x]	[ ]
Organizational skills	[x]	[ ]
Learning strategies	[x]	[ ]
Study skills	[x]	[ ]
Content area	[x]	[ ]
Writing lab	[x]	[ ]
Math lab	[x]	[ ]

LD PROGRAM STAFF

Total number of LD Program staff (including director):

Full Time: 1 Part Time: 1

There is an advisor/advocate from the LD program available to students. The advisor/advocate meets with faculty once per month and students once per month. 15 peer tutors are available to work with LD students.

Key staff person available to work with LD students: Amy Dodson, Director of Academic Success Programs.

LD Program web site: www.hputx.edu

University of the Incarnate Word

San Antonio, TX

Address: 4301 Broadway, San Antonio, TX, 78209-6397
Admissions telephone: 800 749-9673
Dean of Enrollment Services: Andrea Cyterski-Acosta
Admissions e-mail: admis@universe.uiwtx.edu
Web site: http://www.uiw.edu
SAT Code: 6303 ACT Code: 4106

LD program name: Student Disability Services
Academic Counselor, SDS: Ada Soto
LD program telephone: 210 805-5813
LD program e-mail: soto@universe.uiwtx.edu
LD program enrollment: 100, Total campus enrollment: 4,022

GENERAL

University of the Incarnate Word is a private, coed, four-year institution. 57-acre, urban campus in San Antonio (population: 1,144,646). Served by air, bus, and train. Public transportation serves campus. Semester system.

LD ADMISSIONS

Students do not complete a separate application and are not simultaneously accepted to the LD program. A member of the LD program does not sit on the admissions committee. A personal interview is not required. Essay is not required.

SECONDARY SCHOOL REQUIREMENTS

Graduation from secondary school required; GED accepted. The following course distribution required: 4 units of English, 3 units of math, 3 units of science, 2 units of foreign language, 3 units of social studies.

TESTING

SAT Reasoning or ACT required. SAT Subject recommended.

All enrolled freshmen (fall 2004):

Average SAT I Scores: Verbal: 484 Math: 472
Average ACT Scores: Composite: 19

Child Study Team report is not required. A neuropsychological or comprehensive psycho-educational evaluation is required for admission. Must be dated within 36 months of application. Tests required as part of this documentation:

- ☑ WAIS-IV
- ☑ WISC-IV
- ☑ SATA
- ☑ Woodcock-Johnson
- ☑ Nelson-Denny Reading Test
- ☐ Other

UNDERGRADUATE STUDENT BODY

Total undergraduate student enrollment: 1,183 Men, 2,336 Women.

Composition of student body (fall 2004):

	Undergraduate	Freshmen
International	1.0	3.8
Black	6.8	7.1
American Indian	0.4	0.6
Asian-American	1.9	1.5
Hispanic	64.4	54.4
White	21.8	24.6
Unreported	3.7	8.0
	100.0%	100.0%

1% are from out of state. 2% join a fraternity and 2% join a sorority. Average age of full-time undergraduates is 22. 54% of classes have fewer than 20 students, 45% have between 20 and 50 students, 1% have more than 50 students.

STUDENT HOUSING

48% of freshmen live in college housing. Freshmen are not required to live on campus. Housing is guaranteed for all undergraduates. Campus can house 800 undergraduates. Single rooms are available for students with medical or special needs. A medical note is required.

EXPENSES

Tuition (2005-06): $16,500 per year.
Room: $3,750. Board: $2,484.
There is no additional cost for LD program/services.

LD SERVICES

LD program size is not limited.

LD services available to:

☑ Freshmen ☑ Sophomores ☑ Juniors ☑ Seniors

Academic Accommodations

Curriculum

- Foreign language waiver ☐
- Lighter course load ☑
- Math waiver ☐
- Other special classes ☐
- Priority registrations ☑
- Substitution of courses ☑

Exams

- Extended time ☑
- Oral exams ☑
- Take home exams ☐
- Exams on tape or computer ☑
- Untimed exams ☑
- Other accommodations ☑

In class

- Early syllabus ☑
- Note takers in class ☑
- Priority seating ☑
- Tape recorders ☑
- Videotaped classes ☑
- Text on tape ☑

Services

- Diagnostic tests ☐
- Learning centers ☑
- Proofreaders ☐
- Readers ☑
- Reading Machines/Kurzweil ☑
- Special bookstore section ☐
- Typists ☑

Credit toward degree is not given for remedial courses taken.

Counseling Services

- ☑ Academic
- ☑ Psychological
- ☐ Student Support groups
- ☐ Vocational

Meets 4 times per academic year

Tutoring

Individual tutoring is available daily.

Average size of tutoring groups: 1

	Individual	Group
Time management	☑	☑
Organizational skills	☑	☑
Learning strategies	☑	☑
Study skills	☑	☑
Content area	☑	☑
Writing lab	☑	☑
Math lab	☑	☑

LD PROGRAM STAFF

Total number of LD Program staff (including director):

Full Time: 2 Part Time: 2

There is an advisor/advocate from the LD program available to students. 2 graduate students and 3 peer tutors are available to work with LD students.

Key staff person available to work with LD students: Dr. Rhonda Rapp, Director, SDS.

LD Program web site: http://www.uiw.edu/sds/

Jarvis Christian College

Hawkins, TX

Address: PO Box 1470, Hawkins, TX, 75765-1470
Admissions telephone: 903 769-5730
Registrar: Dr. Mary McKinney-Jones
Admissions e-mail: Recruitment@jarvis.edu
Web site: http://www.jarvis.edu
SAT Code: 6319 ACT Code: 4110

LD program name: Student Support Services
LD program address: PO Box 1470
Director - Student Support Services: Lorene Holmes
LD program telephone: 903 769-5738
LD program e-mail: lorene_holmes@jarvis.edu
Total campus enrollment: 538

GENERAL

Jarvis Christian College is a private, coed, four-year institution. 250-acre campus in Hawkins (population: 1,331), 100 miles from Dallas. Major airport serves Dallas; smaller airport and bus serve Tyler (21 miles); train serves Mineola (18 miles). School operates transportation to Tyler and Longview. Semester system.

LD ADMISSIONS

Students do not complete a separate application and are simultaneously accepted to the LD program. A member of the LD program does sit on the admissions committee. High school waivers are accepted for foreign language. A personal interview is recommended. Essay is not required.

SECONDARY SCHOOL REQUIREMENTS

Graduation from secondary school required; GED accepted. The following course distribution required: 3 units of English, 2 units of math, 1 unit of science, 3 units of social studies, 7 units of academic electives.

TESTING

SAT Reasoning or ACT considered if submitted; ACT preferred.

All enrolled freshmen (fall 2004):

Average SAT I Scores:	Verbal: 395	Math: 390
Average ACT Scores:	Composite: 15	

Child Study Team report is not required. A neuropsychological or comprehensive psycho-education evaluation is not required for admission. Tests required as part of this documentation:

- [ ] WAIS-IV
- [ ] WISC-IV
- [ ] SATA
- [ ] Woodcock-Johnson
- [ ] Nelson-Denny Reading Test
- [ ] Other

UNDERGRADUATE STUDENT BODY

Total undergraduate student enrollment: 241 Men, 334 Women.

Composition of student body (fall 2004):

	Undergraduate	Freshmen
International	0.0	0.9
Black	100.0	97.9
American Indian	0.0	0.0
Asian-American	0.0	0.0
Hispanic	0.0	0.6
White	0.0	0.6
Unreported	0.0	0.0
	100.0%	100.0%

10% are from out of state. Average age of full-time undergraduates is 20. 57% of classes have fewer than 20 students, 42% have between 20 and 50 students, 1% have more than 50 students.

STUDENT HOUSING

96% of freshmen live in college housing. Freshmen are not required to live on campus. Housing is guaranteed for all undergraduates. Campus can house 750 undergraduates. Single rooms are available for students with medical or special needs. A medical note is required.

EXPENSES

Tuition (2005-06): $6,280 per year.

Room: $2,056. Board: $2,100.

There is no additional cost for LD program/services.

LD SERVICES

LD program size is not limited.

LD services available to:

- [x] Freshmen
- [x] Sophomores
- [x] Juniors
- [x] Seniors

Academic Accommodations

Curriculum

- [ ] Foreign language waiver
- [x] Lighter course load
- [ ] Math waiver
- [ ] Other special classes
- [ ] Priority registrations
- [ ] Substitution of courses

Exams

- [x] Extended time
- [x] Oral exams
- [ ] Take home exams
- [ ] Exams on tape or computer
- [ ] Untimed exams
- [ ] Other accommodations

In class

- [ ] Early syllabus
- [ ] Note takers in class
- [ ] Priority seating
- [x] Tape recorders
- [x] Videotaped classes
- [ ] Text on tape

Services

- [x] Diagnostic tests
- [ ] Learning centers
- [ ] Proofreaders
- [ ] Readers
- [ ] Reading Machines/Kurzweil
- [ ] Special bookstore section
- [ ] Typists

Credit toward degree is not given for remedial courses taken.

Counseling Services

- [x] Academic — Meets 2 times per academic year
- [x] Psychological — Meets once per academic year
- [x] Student Support groups — Meets once per academic year
- [x] Vocational — Meets once per academic year

Tutoring

Individual tutoring is available weekly.

Average size of tutoring groups: 3

	Individual	Group
Time management	[x]	[x]
Organizational skills	[x]	[x]
Learning strategies	[x]	[x]
Study skills	[x]	[x]
Content area	[x]	[x]
Writing lab	[x]	[x]
Math lab	[x]	[x]

LD PROGRAM STAFF

Total number of LD Program staff (including director):

Full Time: 5 Part Time: 5

There is no advisor/advocate from the LD program available to students. 5 peer tutors are available to work with LD students.

Key staff person available to work with LD students: Rouseal Wortham, Counseling Director.

LD Program web site: Student Support Services@Jarvis.edu

Lamar University

Beaumont, TX

Address: Lamar Station, Box 10001, Beaumont, TX, 77710
Admissions telephone: 409 880-8888
Director of Academic Services: James Rush
Admissions e-mail: admissions@hal.lamar.edu
Web site: http://www.lamar.edu
SAT Code: 6360 ACT Code: 4114

LD program name: Services For Students With Disabilities
LD program address: PO Box 10087
Coordinator: Callie Trahan, LMSW
LD program telephone: 409 880-8026
LD program e-mail: callie.trahan@lamar.edu
LD program enrollment: 53, Total campus enrollment: 9,726

GENERAL

Lamar University is a public, coed, four-year institution. 200-acre campus in Beaumont (population: 113,866), 90 miles from Houston; branch campuses in Orange and Port Arthur. Served by air, bus, and train; major airport serves Houston. Public transportation serves campus. Semester system.

LD ADMISSIONS

Students do not complete a separate application and are not simultaneously accepted to the LD program. A member of the LD program does not sit on the admissions committee. A personal interview is required. Essay is not required.

SECONDARY SCHOOL REQUIREMENTS

Graduation from secondary school required; GED accepted. The following course distribution required: 4 units of English, 3 units of math, 2 units of science, 3 units of social studies, 3 units of academic electives.

TESTING

All enrolled freshmen (fall 2004):

Average SAT I Scores: Verbal: 465 Math: 463
Average ACT Scores: Composite: 17

Child Study Team report is not required. A neuropsychological or comprehensive psycho-education evaluation is not required for admission. Tests required as part of this documentation:

- ■ WAIS-IV
- ■ WISC-IV
- ☐ SATA
- ■ Woodcock-Johnson
- ☐ Nelson-Denny Reading Test
- ☐ Other

UNDERGRADUATE STUDENT BODY

Total undergraduate student enrollment: 3,244 Men, 4,782 Women.

Composition of student body (fall 2004):

	Undergraduate	Freshmen
International	0.5	0.7
Black	33.2	24.2
American Indian	0.4	0.6
Asian-American	2.2	3.0
Hispanic	5.9	5.3
White	52.1	63.9
Unreported	5.7	2.3
	100.0%	100.0%

2% are from out of state. 1% join a fraternity and 2% join a sorority. Average age of full-time undergraduates is 22. 28% of classes have fewer than 20 students, 60% have between 20 and 50 students, 12% have more than 50 students.

STUDENT HOUSING

1% of freshmen live in college housing. Freshmen are required to live on campus. Housing is guaranteed for all undergraduates. Campus can house 1,500 undergraduates. Single rooms are not available for students with medical or special needs.

EXPENSES

Tuition (2005-06): $3,450 per year (in-state), $11,730 (out-of-state).

Room: $3,600. Board: $1,810.

There is no additional cost for LD program/services.

LD SERVICES

LD program size is not limited.

LD services available to:

■ Freshmen ■ Sophomores ■ Juniors ■ Seniors

Academic Accommodations

Curriculum		**In class**	
Foreign language waiver	☐	Early syllabus	☐
Lighter course load	☐	Note takers in class	■
Math waiver	☐	Priority seating	☐
Other special classes	☐	Tape recorders	■
Priority registrations	☐	Videotaped classes	☐
Substitution of courses	■	Text on tape	■
Exams		**Services**	
Extended time	■	Diagnostic tests	☐
Oral exams	■	Learning centers	☐
Take home exams	☐	Proofreaders	☐
Exams on tape or computer	■	Readers	■
Untimed exams	☐	Reading Machines/Kurzweil	☐
Other accommodations	☐	Special bookstore section	☐
		Typists	☐

Credit toward degree is not given for remedial courses taken.

Counseling Services

- ■ Academic
- ■ Psychological
- ■ Student Support groups
- ■ Vocational

Tutoring

Individual tutoring is not available.

	Individual	Group
Time management	☐	■
Organizational skills	☐	■
Learning strategies	☐	■
Study skills	☐	■
Content area	☐	■
Writing lab	☐	■
Math lab	☐	■

UNIQUE LD PROGRAM FEATURES

The office of Services for Students with Disabilities offers a variety of services designed to assist students with any type of disability in becoming full participating members of the university community. Some of the services provided include academic accommodations, assistive technology, sign language, note takers, physical access, and priority registration. Documentation of disability is required to receive services. Students with disabilities should notify the coordinator of SFSWD prior to registration in any university program. A meeting with the student and coordinator will be arranged in order to determine the assignment of academic adjustments/accommodations. No questions as to disability status are asked on applications to Lamar University.

LD PROGRAM STAFF

Total number of LD Program staff (including director):

Full Time: 2 Part Time: 2

There is an advisor/advocate from the LD program available to students.

Key staff person available to work with LD students: Callie Trahan, LMSW, Coordinator.

LD Program web site: http://dept.lamar.edu/sfwd

LeTourneau University

Longview, TX

Address: PO Box 7001, Longview, TX, 75607-7001
Admissions telephone: 800 759-8811
Admissions FAX: 903 233-3411
Director of Admissions: James Townsend
Admissions e-mail: admissions@letu.edu
Web site: http://www.letu.edu
SAT Code: 6365 ACT Code: 4120

LD program name: Student Services
LD program address: PO Box 7001
Dean of Student Services: William Franklin, Ph. D.
LD program telephone: 903 233-4460
LD program e-mail: BillFranklin@letu.edu
Total campus enrollment: 3,388

GENERAL

LeTourneau University is a private, coed, four-year institution. 162-acre campus in Longview (population: 73,344), 60 miles from Shreveport, La., and 120 miles from Dallas; branch centers in Austin, Dallas, Houston, and Tyler. Served by air, bus and train; major airport serves Dallas. Semester system.

LD ADMISSIONS

A personal interview is required.

SECONDARY SCHOOL REQUIREMENTS

Graduation from secondary school required; GED accepted. The following course distribution required: 4 units of English, 3 units of math, 3 units of science, 2 units of social studies, 1 unit of history.

TESTING

SAT Reasoning or ACT required. SAT Subject required.

All enrolled freshmen (fall 2004):

Average SAT I Scores: Verbal: 577 Math: 590
Average ACT Scores: Composite: 25

Child Study Team report is not required. Tests required as part of this documentation:

- ❑ WAIS-IV
- ❑ WISC-IV
- ❑ SATA
- ❑ Woodcock-Johnson
- ❑ Nelson-Denny Reading Test
- ❑ Other

UNDERGRADUATE STUDENT BODY

Total undergraduate student enrollment: 1,415 Men, 1,392 Women.

Composition of student body (fall 2004):

	Undergraduate	Freshmen
International	1.8	0.8
Black	5.5	22.0
American Indian	0.3	0.4
Asian-American	1.5	1.3
Hispanic	4.0	8.5
White	83.2	64.9
Unreported	3.7	2.1
	100.0%	100.0%

50% are from out of state. Average age of full-time undergraduates is 21. 79% of classes have fewer than 20 students, 20% have between 20 and 50 students, 1% have more than 50 students.

STUDENT HOUSING

87% of freshmen live in college housing. Freshmen are required to live on campus. Housing is guaranteed for all undergraduates. Campus can house 981 undergraduates.

EXPENSES

Tuition (2005-06): $15,710 per year.
Room & Board: $6,286

LD SERVICES

LD services available to:

❑ Freshmen ❑ Sophomores ❑ Juniors ❑ Seniors

Academic Accommodations

Curriculum		**In class**	
Foreign language waiver	❑	Early syllabus	❑
Lighter course load	■	Note takers in class	❑
Math waiver	❑	Priority seating	❑
Other special classes	❑	Tape recorders	❑
Priority registrations	❑	Videotaped classes	❑
Substitution of courses	❑	Text on tape	❑
Exams		**Services**	
Extended time	❑	Diagnostic tests	❑
Oral exams	❑	Learning centers	❑
Take home exams	❑	Proofreaders	❑
Exams on tape or computer	❑	Readers	❑
Untimed exams	❑	Reading Machines/Kurzweil	❑
Other accommodations	❑	Special bookstore section	❑
		Typists	❑

Credit toward degree is not given for remedial courses taken.

Counseling Services

- ❑ Academic
- ❑ Psychological
- ❑ Student Support groups
- ❑ Vocational

Tutoring

	Individual	Group
Time management	❑	❑
Organizational skills	❑	❑
Learning strategies	❑	❑
Study skills	❑	❑
Content area	❑	❑
Writing lab	❑	❑
Math lab	❑	❑

LD PROGRAM STAFF

Key staff person available to work with LD students: William Franklin, Ph. D., Dean of Student Services.

Lubbock Christian University

Lubbock, TX

Address: 5601 19th Street, Lubbock, TX, 79407
Admissions telephone: 800 933-7601
Admissions FAX: 806 720-7162
Vice President of Enrollment Management: Matt Paden
Admissions e-mail: admissions@lcu.edu
Web site: http://www.lcu.edu
SAT Code: 6378 ACT Code: 4123

LD program name: LCU Academic Support
Coordinator of Disability Services: Dana Turner
LD program telephone: 806 720-7486
LD program e-mail: dana.turner@lcu.edu
LD program enrollment: 46, Total campus enrollment: 1,778

GENERAL

Lubbock Christian University is a private, coed, four-year institution. 120-acre, urban campus in Lubbock (population: 199,564); branch campus in Midland. Served by air and bus. Public transportation serves campus. Semester system.

LD ADMISSIONS

Students do not complete a separate application and are not simultaneously accepted to the LD program. A member of the LD program does not sit on the admissions committee. A personal interview is required. Essay is not required.

SECONDARY SCHOOL REQUIREMENTS

Graduation from secondary school required; GED accepted.

TESTING

SAT Reasoning or ACT required. SAT Subject recommended.

All enrolled freshmen (fall 2004):

Average SAT I Scores:	Verbal: 513	Math: 500
Average ACT Scores:	Composite: 21	

Child Study Team report is not required. A neuropsychological or comprehensive psycho-educational evaluation is required for admission. Must be dated within 36 months of application. Tests required as part of this documentation:

☑ WAIS-IV	☑ Woodcock-Johnson
☑ WISC-IV	☑ Nelson-Denny Reading Test
☑ SATA	☑ Other

UNDERGRADUATE STUDENT BODY

Total undergraduate student enrollment: 734 Men, 967 Women.

Composition of student body (fall 2004):

	Undergraduate	Freshmen
International	0.4	0.1
Black	5.6	5.9
American Indian	0.4	0.5
Asian-American	0.7	0.6
Hispanic	10.0	14.1
White	83.0	78.8
Unreported	0.0	0.0
	100.0%	100.0%

13% are from out of state. 21% join a fraternity and 22% join a sorority. Average age of full-time undergraduates is 23. 57% of classes have fewer than 20 students, 42% have between 20 and 50 students, 1% have more than 50 students.

STUDENT HOUSING

74% of freshmen live in college housing. Freshmen are required to live on campus. Housing is guaranteed for all undergraduates. Campus can house 612 undergraduates. Single rooms are available for students with medical or special needs. A medical note is required.

EXPENSES

Tuition (2005-06): $11,644 per year.
Room: $2,000. Board: $2,250.

There is no additional cost for LD program/services.

LD SERVICES

LD program size is not limited.

LD services available to:

☑ Freshmen ☑ Sophomores ☑ Juniors ☑ Seniors

Academic Accommodations

Curriculum		In class	
Foreign language waiver	☐	Early syllabus	☐
Lighter course load	☑	Note takers in class	☑
Math waiver	☐	Priority seating	☑
Other special classes	☐	Tape recorders	☑
Priority registrations	☑	Videotaped classes	☐
Substitution of courses	☐	Text on tape	☐
Exams		**Services**	
Extended time	☑	Diagnostic tests	☐
Oral exams	☑	Learning centers	☑
Take home exams	☐	Proofreaders	☑
Exams on tape or computer	☑	Readers	☑
Untimed exams	☑	Reading Machines/Kurzweil	☑
Other accommodations	☑	Special bookstore section	☐
		Typists	☐

Credit toward degree is given for remedial courses taken.

Counseling Services

☑ Academic	Meets 2 times per academic year
☑ Psychological	Meets 2 times per academic year
☐ Student Support groups	
☑ Vocational	Meets 2 times per academic year

Tutoring

Individual tutoring is available.

Average size of tutoring groups: 1

	Individual	Group
Time management	☐	☐
Organizational skills	☐	☐
Learning strategies	☐	☐
Study skills	☐	☐
Content area	☐	☐
Writing lab	☐	☐
Math lab	☐	☑

LD PROGRAM STAFF

Total number of LD Program staff (including director):

Full Time: 2 Part Time: 2

There is an advisor/advocate from the LD program available to students. The advisor/advocate meets with students once per month. 45 peer tutors are available to work with LD students.

Key staff person available to work with LD students: Dana Turner, Coordinator of Disability Services.

LD Program web site:
http://www.lcu.edu/LCU/cstudent/academicsupport/disability.htm

University of Mary Hardin-Baylor

Belton, TX

Address: 900 College Street, UMHB Box 8425, Belton, TX, 76513
Admissions telephone: 800 727-8642
Admissions FAX: 254 295-5049
Vice President for Enrollment Management: Robbin Steen
Admissions e-mail: admission@umhb.edu
Web site: http://www.umhb.edu
SAT Code: 6396 ACT Code: 4128

Director of Counseling and Testing: Nate Williams
LD program telephone: 254 295-4696
LD program e-mail: nwilliams@umhb.edu
LD program enrollment: 50, Total campus enrollment: 2,582

GENERAL

University of Mary Hardin-Baylor is a private, coed, four-year institution. 100-acre campus in Belton (population: 14,623), 60 miles from Austin. Served by bus; major airport serves Austin; smaller airport serves Killeen (20 miles); train serves Temple (10 miles). Semester system.

LD ADMISSIONS

Application Deadline: 08/24. Students do not complete a separate application and are simultaneously accepted to the LD program. A member of the LD program does not sit on the admissions committee. A personal interview is recommended. Essay is not required.

SECONDARY SCHOOL REQUIREMENTS

Graduation from secondary school required; GED accepted. The following course distribution required: 4 units of English, 3 units of math, 2 units of social studies.

TESTING

ACT required; SAT Reasoning may be substituted. SAT Subject recommended.

All enrolled freshmen (fall 2004):

Average SAT I Scores: Verbal: 535 Math: 536
Average ACT Scores: Composite: 22

Child Study Team report is not required. A neuropsychological or comprehensive psycho-education evaluation is not required for admission. Tests required as part of this documentation:

☐ WAIS-IV
☐ WISC-IV
☐ SATA
☐ Woodcock-Johnson
☐ Nelson-Denny Reading Test
☐ Other

UNDERGRADUATE STUDENT BODY

Total undergraduate student enrollment: 879 Men, 1,558 Women.

Composition of student body (fall 2004):

	Undergraduate	Freshmen
International	0.0	0.6
Black	7.8	10.5
American Indian	0.6	0.5
Asian-American	1.7	1.4
Hispanic	9.7	10.8
White	80.2	76.2
Unreported	0.0	0.0
	100.0%	100.0%

2% are from out of state. Average age of full-time undergraduates is 23. 49% of classes have fewer than 20 students, 48% have between 20 and 50 students, 3% have more than 50 students.

STUDENT HOUSING

90% of freshmen live in college housing. Freshmen are required to live on campus. Housing is not guaranteed for all undergraduates. Housing is guaranteed as long as space permits. Campus can house 1,071 undergraduates. Single rooms are available for students with medical or special needs. A medical note is required.

EXPENSES

Tuition (2005-06): $12,600 per year.
Room: $2,000. Board: $2,000.
There is no additional cost for LD program/services.

LD SERVICES

LD program size is not limited.

LD services available to:

■ Freshmen ■ Sophomores ■ Juniors ■ Seniors

Academic Accommodations

Curriculum		**In class**	
Foreign language waiver	☐	Early syllabus	☐
Lighter course load	☐	Note takers in class	■
Math waiver	☐	Priority seating	☐
Other special classes	■	Tape recorders	■
Priority registrations	☐	Videotaped classes	☐
Substitution of courses	☐	Text on tape	☐
Exams		**Services**	
Extended time	■	Diagnostic tests	■
Oral exams	■	Learning centers	■
Take home exams	☐	Proofreaders	☐
Exams on tape or computer	☐	Readers	■
Untimed exams	■	Reading Machines/Kurzweil	☐
Other accommodations	☐	Special bookstore section	☐
		Typists	☐

Credit toward degree is not given for remedial courses taken.

Counseling Services

☐ Academic
☐ Psychological
☐ Student Support groups
☐ Vocational

Tutoring

Individual tutoring is available.

Average size of tutoring groups: 1

	Individual	Group
Time management	☐	☐
Organizational skills	☐	☐
Learning strategies	☐	☐
Study skills	☐	☐
Content area	☐	☐
Writing lab	☐	☐
Math lab	☐	☐

LD PROGRAM STAFF

Total number of LD Program staff (including director):

Full Time: 6 Part Time: 6

There is an advisor/advocate from the LD program available to students.

Key staff person available to work with LD students: Nate Williams, Director of Counseling and Testing.

McMurry University

Abilene, TX

Admissions telephone: 800 460-2392
Vice President for Enrollment Management/Student Relations: Scott Smiley
Admissions e-mail: admissions@mcm.edu
Web site: http://www.mcm.edu
SAT Code: 6402 ACT Code: 4130

LD program address: McMurry Station, Box 657
Disability Services Coordinator: James Greer, MA, LMFT
LD program telephone: 325 793-4880
LD program e-mail: greerj@mcmurryadm.mcm.edu
LD program enrollment: 36, Total campus enrollment: 1,386

GENERAL

McMurry University is a private, coed, four-year institution. 41-acre, suburban campus in Abilene (population: 115,930), 155 miles from Dallas. Served by air and bus; major airport serves Dallas-Fort Worth. Public transportation serves campus. Semester system.

LD ADMISSIONS

Students do not complete a separate application and are not simultaneously accepted to the LD program. A member of the LD program does not sit on the admissions committee. A personal interview is required. Essay is not required.

SECONDARY SCHOOL REQUIREMENTS

Graduation from secondary school required; GED accepted. The following course distribution required: 4 units of English, 3 units of math, 2 units of science, 3 units of social studies.

TESTING

SAT Reasoning or ACT required. SAT Subject recommended.

All enrolled freshmen (fall 2004):

Average SAT I Scores: Verbal: 495 Math: 500
Average ACT Scores: Composite: 21

Child Study Team report is not required. A neuropsychological or comprehensive psycho-educational evaluation is required for admission. Must be dated within 36 months of application. Tests required as part of this documentation:

- [x] WAIS-IV
- [x] WISC-IV
- [x] SATA
- [x] Woodcock-Johnson
- [x] Nelson-Denny Reading Test
- [ ] Other

UNDERGRADUATE STUDENT BODY

Total undergraduate student enrollment: 674 Men, 704 Women.

Composition of student body (fall 2004):

	Undergraduate	Freshmen
International	1.4	1.0
Black	9.6	8.6
American Indian	0.4	0.9
Asian-American	1.1	1.0
Hispanic	18.4	13.2
White	68.0	72.8
Unreported	1.1	2.5
	100.0%	100.0%

5% are from out of state. 15% join a fraternity and 20% join a sorority. Average age of full-time undergraduates is 21. 63% of classes have fewer than 20 students, 36% have between 20 and 50 students, 1% have more than 50 students.

STUDENT HOUSING

82% of freshmen live in college housing. Freshmen are required to live on campus. Housing is guaranteed for all undergraduates. Campus can house 667 undergraduates. Single rooms are available for students with medical or special needs. A medical note is required.

EXPENSES

Tuition (2005-06): $14,300 per year.
Room: $2,898. Board: $2,945.
There is no additional cost for LD program/services.

LD SERVICES

LD program size is not limited.

LD services available to:

- [x] Freshmen
- [x] Sophomores
- [x] Juniors
- [x] Seniors

Academic Accommodations

Curriculum

- [ ] Foreign language waiver
- [ ] Lighter course load
- [ ] Math waiver
- [ ] Other special classes
- [ ] Priority registrations
- [x] Substitution of courses

Exams

- [x] Extended time
- [x] Oral exams
- [ ] Take home exams
- [ ] Exams on tape or computer
- [ ] Untimed exams
- [x] Other accommodations

In class

- [ ] Early syllabus
- [x] Note takers in class
- [x] Priority seating
- [ ] Tape recorders
- [ ] Videotaped classes
- [ ] Text on tape

Services

- [ ] Diagnostic tests
- [x] Learning centers
- [x] Proofreaders
- [x] Readers
- [ ] Reading Machines/Kurzweil
- [ ] Special bookstore section
- [ ] Typists

Credit toward degree is not given for remedial courses taken.

Counseling Services

- [x] Academic
- [x] Psychological
- [ ] Student Support groups
- [x] Vocational

Tutoring

Individual tutoring is available daily.

	Individual	Group
Time management	[ ]	[ ]
Organizational skills	[ ]	[ ]
Learning strategies	[x]	[ ]
Study skills	[x]	[ ]
Content area	[ ]	[ ]
Writing lab	[ ]	[ ]
Math lab	[ ]	[ ]

LD PROGRAM STAFF

Total number of LD Program staff (including director):

Full Time: 2 Part Time: 2

There is an advisor/advocate from the LD program available to students. 13 peer tutors are available to work with LD students.

Key staff person available to work with LD students: James Greer, MA, LMFT, Disability Services Coordinator.

LD Program web site: http://www.mcm.edu/students/disability/index.htm

Midwestern State University

Wichita Falls, TX

Address: 3410 Taft Boulevard, Wichita Falls, TX, 76308-2099
Admissions telephone: 800 842-1922
Director of Admissions: Barbara Merkle
Admissions e-mail: admissions@mwsu.edu
Web site: http://www.mwsu.edu
SAT Code: 6408 ACT Code: 4132

LD program name: Counseling & Disability Service
LD program address: 3410 Taft Boulevard
Dir. Counseling & Disability Services: Degra Higginbotham
LD program telephone: 940 397-4618
LD program e-mail: debra.higginbotham@mwsu.edu
LD program enrollment: 121, Total campus enrollment: 5,606

GENERAL

Midwestern State University is a public, coed, four-year institution. 175-acre main campus in Wichita Falls (population: 104,197), 130 miles from Dallas. Served by air and bus; major airport and train serve Dallas. Public transportation serves campus. Semester system.

LD ADMISSIONS

Students do not complete a separate application and are not simultaneously accepted to the LD program. A member of the LD program does not sit on the admissions committee. A personal interview is required. Essay is not required. Each student is expected to meet the academic/test requirements of all students.

SECONDARY SCHOOL REQUIREMENTS

Graduation from secondary school required; GED accepted. The following course distribution required: 4 units of English, 3 units of math, 2 units of science, 6 units of academic electives.

TESTING

SAT Reasoning or ACT required. SAT Subject required.

All enrolled freshmen (fall 2004):

Average SAT I Scores:	Verbal: 481	Math: 489
Average ACT Scores:	Composite: 20	

Child Study Team report is not required. A neuropsychological or comprehensive psycho-educational evaluation is required for admission. Must be dated within 36 months of application. Tests required as part of this documentation:

- [x] WAIS-IV
- [ ] WISC-IV
- [x] SATA
- [x] Woodcock-Johnson
- [ ] Nelson-Denny Reading Test
- [x] Other

UNDERGRADUATE STUDENT BODY

Total undergraduate student enrollment: 2,269 Men, 3,019 Women.

Composition of student body (fall 2004):

	Undergraduate	Freshmen
International	1.2	5.0
Black	16.4	11.5
American Indian	1.2	1.2
Asian-American	4.9	3.0
Hispanic	10.0	8.7
White	63.7	69.1
Unreported	2.6	1.5
	100.0%	100.0%

7% are from out of state. 10% join a fraternity and 10% join a sorority. Average age of full-time undergraduates is 30. 35% of classes have fewer than 20 students, 54% have between 20 and 50 students, 11% have more than 50 students.

STUDENT HOUSING

35% of freshmen live in college housing. Freshmen are required to live on campus. Housing is guaranteed for all undergraduates. First-come, first-serve basis. Waiting list available. Campus can house 891 undergraduates. Single rooms are not available for students with medical or special needs.

EXPENSES

Tuition (2005-06): $1,500 per year (in-state), $9,780 (out-of-state).

Room: $2,580. Board: $2,500.
There is no additional cost for LD program/services.

LD SERVICES

LD program size is not limited.

LD services available to:

- [x] Freshmen
- [x] Sophomores
- [x] Juniors
- [x] Seniors

Academic Accommodations

Curriculum		**In class**	
Foreign language waiver	[ ]	Early syllabus	[ ]
Lighter course load	[ ]	Note takers in class	[x]
Math waiver	[ ]	Priority seating	[x]
Other special classes	[ ]	Tape recorders	[x]
Priority registrations	[ ]	Videotaped classes	[ ]
Substitution of courses	[ ]	Text on tape	[ ]
Exams		**Services**	
Extended time	[x]	Diagnostic tests	[ ]
Oral exams	[x]	Learning centers	[x]
Take home exams	[ ]	Proofreaders	[ ]
Exams on tape or computer	[x]	Readers	[x]
Untimed exams	[x]	Reading Machines/Kurzweil	[x]
Other accommodations	[x]	Special bookstore section	[ ]
		Typists	[x]

Credit toward degree is given for remedial courses taken.

Counseling Services

- [x] Academic
- [x] Psychological
- [ ] Student Support groups
- [ ] Vocational

Tutoring

Individual tutoring is available.

	Individual	Group
Time management	[ ]	[ ]
Organizational skills	[ ]	[ ]
Learning strategies	[ ]	[ ]
Study skills	[ ]	[ ]
Content area	[ ]	[ ]
Writing lab	[ ]	[ ]
Math lab	[ ]	[ ]

UNIQUE LD PROGRAM FEATURES

As per law, MSU does not base admissions or take into consideration disability for entrance requirements.

LD PROGRAM STAFF

Total number of LD Program staff (including director):

Full Time: 2 Part Time: 2

There is an advisor/advocate from the LD program available to students.

Key staff person available to work with LD students: Debra Higginbotham, Director, Counseling & Disability Services.

LD Program web site: http://students.mwsu.edu/disability/index.asp

University of North Texas

Denton, TX

Address: PO Box 311277, Denton, TX, 76203
Admissions telephone: 800 UNT-8211
Admissions FAX: 940 565-2408
Director of Admissions and School Relations: Marcilla Collinsworth
Admissions e-mail: undergrad@unt.edu
Web site: http://www.unt.edu
SAT Code: 6481 ACT Code: 4136

LD program name: Office of Disability & Accommodations
LD program address: PO Box 310770
Assistant Director, Disability Accommodations: Jane Jones
LD program telephone: 940 565-4323
LD program e-mail: Janej@unt.edu
LD program enrollment: 414, Total campus enrollment: 24,274

GENERAL

University of North Texas is a public, coed, four-year institution. 500-acre campus in Denton (population: 70,000), 30 miles from Dallas. Served by bus; major airport and train serve Dallas-Fort Worth. School operates transportation to some areas of campus and around Denton. Public transportation serves campus. Semester system.

LD ADMISSIONS

Students do not complete a separate application and are not simultaneously accepted to the LD program. A member of the LD program does not sit on the admissions committee. A personal interview is not required. Essay is not required. Students can request a consultation with an Admissions Officer to review requirements that may be waived.

SECONDARY SCHOOL REQUIREMENTS

Graduation from secondary school required; GED accepted. The following course distribution required: 4 units of English, 4 units of math, 3 units of science, 3 units of foreign language, 4 units of social studies, 3 units of academic electives.

TESTING

SAT Reasoning or ACT required.

All enrolled freshmen (fall 2004):

Average SAT I Scores: Verbal: 545 Math: 545
Average ACT Scores: Composite: 23

Child Study Team report is not required. A neuropsychological or comprehensive psycho-educational evaluation is required for admission. Must be dated within 60 months of application. Tests required as part of this documentation:

- ■ WAIS-IV
- ■ WISC-IV
- ■ SATA
- ■ Woodcock-Johnson
- ■ Nelson-Denny Reading Test
- ■ Other

UNDERGRADUATE STUDENT BODY

Total undergraduate student enrollment: 9,684 Men, 11,991 Women.

Composition of student body (fall 2004):

	Undergraduate	Freshmen
International	2.2	3.3
Black	13.0	11.7
American Indian	0.8	0.8
Asian-American	2.8	4.4
Hispanic	11.5	10.4
White	69.3	68.0
Unreported	0.4	1.4
	100.0%	100.0%

10% are from out of state. 5% join a fraternity and 4% join a sorority. Average age of full-time undergraduates is 20. 35% of classes have fewer than 20 students, 49% have between 20 and 50 students, 16% have more than 50 students.

STUDENT HOUSING

92% of freshmen live in college housing. Freshmen are required to live on campus. Housing is guaranteed for all undergraduates. Campus can house 5,588 undergraduates. Single rooms are available for students with medical or special needs. A medical note is required.

EXPENSES

Tuition (2005-06): $3,930 per year (in-state), $12,210 (out-of-state).
Room & Board: $5,350
There is no additional cost for LD program/services.

LD SERVICES

LD program size is not limited.

LD services available to:

■ Freshmen ■ Sophomores ■ Juniors ■ Seniors

Academic Accommodations

Curriculum		**In class**	
Foreign language waiver	□	Early syllabus	□
Lighter course load	□	Note takers in class	■
Math waiver	□	Priority seating	■
Other special classes	□	Tape recorders	■
Priority registrations	□	Videotaped classes	□
Substitution of courses	□	Text on tape	□
Exams		**Services**	
Extended time	■	Diagnostic tests	■
Oral exams	■	Learning centers	■
Take home exams	□	Proofreaders	□
Exams on tape or computer	■	Readers	■
Untimed exams	■	Reading Machines/Kurzweil	■
Other accommodations	□	Special bookstore section	□
		Typists	■

Credit toward degree is not given for remedial courses taken.

Counseling Services

- ■ Academic
- ■ Psychological
- ■ Student Support groups
- ■ Vocational

Tutoring

Individual tutoring is available weekly.

Average size of tutoring groups: 3

	Individual	Group
Time management	■	■
Organizational skills	■	■
Learning strategies	■	■
Study skills	■	□
Content area	□	□
Writing lab	■	□
Math lab	■	□

LD PROGRAM STAFF

Total number of LD Program staff (including director):

Full Time: 3 Part Time: 3

There is an advisor/advocate from the LD program available to students. The advisor/advocate meets with faculty 4 times per month. 2 graduate students are available to work with LD students.

Key staff person available to work with LD students: Jane Jones, CRC, Assistant Director, Disability Accommodations.

Northwood University - Texas Campus

Cedar Hill, TX

Address: 1114 West FM 1382, Cedar Hill, TX, 75104
Admissions telephone: 800 927-9663
Director of Admissions: Sylvia Correa
Admissions e-mail: txadmit@northwood.edu
Web site: http://www.northwood.edu
SAT Code: 6499 ACT Code: 4135

LD program name: Academic Counseling
LD program telephone: 972 293-5465
LD program e-mail: rojas@northwood.edu
LD program enrollment: 10, Total campus enrollment: 1,139

GENERAL

Northwood University - Texas Campus is a private, coed, four-year institution. 360-acre campus in Cedar Hill (population: 32,092), 10 miles from Dallas; branch campuses and educational facilities in Midland, Mich., and West Palm Beach, Fla. Served by air, bus, and train; major airport serves Irving (20 miles). Quarter system.

LD ADMISSIONS

Application Deadline: 08/01. Students do not complete a separate application and are simultaneously accepted to the LD program. A member of the LD program does not sit on the admissions committee. A personal interview is recommended. Essay is required and may be typed. No requirements are waived for LD students. They must apply for admission and submit official secondary school transcripts and SAT Reasoning/ACT scores prior to being reviewed for admission. If they feel their LD should be considered when reviewing the application, they must supply appropriate documentation regarding their LD. Students must then meet with the Academic Counselor to determine what modifications can/will be made for the student prior to enrollment.

For fall 2004, 5 completed self-identified LD applications were received. 4 applications were offered admission, and 2 enrolled.

SECONDARY SCHOOL REQUIREMENTS

Graduation from secondary school required; GED accepted.

TESTING

SAT Reasoning or ACT required. SAT Subject recommended.

All enrolled freshmen (fall 2004):

Average SAT I Scores:	Verbal: 472	Math: 474
Average ACT Scores:	Composite: 20	

Child Study Team report is not required. A neuropsychological or comprehensive psycho-educational evaluation is required for admission. Must be dated within 36 months of application. Tests required as part of this documentation:

- [x] WAIS-IV
- [x] WISC-IV
- [x] SATA
- [x] Woodcock-Johnson
- [x] Nelson-Denny Reading Test
- [ ] Other

UNDERGRADUATE STUDENT BODY

Total undergraduate student enrollment: 477 Men, 637 Women.

Composition of student body (fall 2004):

	Undergraduate	Freshmen
International	0.0	3.4
Black	20.8	21.5
American Indian	0.0	0.2
Asian-American	4.7	2.7
Hispanic	29.5	26.5
White	45.0	44.4
Unreported	0.0	1.3
	100.0%	100.0%

10% are from out of state. Average age of full-time undergraduates is 20. 54% of classes have fewer than 20 students, 45% have between 20 and 50 students, 1% have more than 50 students.

STUDENT HOUSING

48% of freshmen live in college housing. Freshmen are required to live on campus. Housing is guaranteed for all undergraduates. Campus can house 248 undergraduates. Single rooms are available for students with medical or special needs. A medical note is required.

EXPENSES

Tuition (2005-06): $14,625 per year.
Room: $3,405. Board: $2,985.
There is no additional cost for LD program/services.

LD SERVICES

LD program size is not limited.

LD services available to:

- [x] Freshmen
- [x] Sophomores
- [x] Juniors
- [x] Seniors

Academic Accommodations

Curriculum		In class	
Foreign language waiver	[ ]	Early syllabus	[ ]
Lighter course load	[ ]	Note takers in class	[x]
Math waiver	[ ]	Priority seating	[x]
Other special classes	[ ]	Tape recorders	[x]
Priority registrations	[ ]	Videotaped classes	[ ]
Substitution of courses	[ ]	Text on tape	[ ]
Exams		**Services**	
Extended time	[x]	Diagnostic tests	[ ]
Oral exams	[x]	Learning centers	[ ]
Take home exams	[x]	Proofreaders	[ ]
Exams on tape or computer	[ ]	Readers	[ ]
Untimed exams	[x]	Reading Machines/Kurzweil	[ ]
Other accommodations	[x]	Special bookstore section	[ ]
		Typists	[ ]

Credit toward degree is not given for remedial courses taken.

Counseling Services

- [x] Academic
- [ ] Psychological
- [ ] Student Support groups
- [ ] Vocational

Tutoring

Individual tutoring is available daily.

	Individual	Group
Time management	[ ]	[ ]
Organizational skills	[ ]	[ ]
Learning strategies	[ ]	[ ]
Study skills	[ ]	[ ]
Content area	[ ]	[ ]
Writing lab	[ ]	[x]
Math lab	[ ]	[x]

LD PROGRAM STAFF

There is an advisor/advocate from the LD program available to students. 2 peer tutors are available to work with LD students.

Key staff person available to work with LD students: Rene Rojas, Academic Counselor.

Our Lady of the Lake University

San Antonio, TX

Address: 411 S. W. 24th Street, San Antonio, TX, 78207-4689
Admissions telephone: 800 436-6558
Acting Director of Admissions: Michael Boatner
Admissions e-mail: admission@lake.ollusa.edu
Web site: http://www.ollusa.edu
SAT Code: 6550 ACT Code: 4140

LD program name: Center for Academic Achievement
Assistant Director: Theresa Gately
LD program e-mail: gatet@lake.ollusa.edu
LD program enrollment: 19, Total campus enrollment: 1,931

GENERAL

Our Lady of the Lake University is a private, coed, four-year institution. 72-acre campus in San Antonio (population: 1,144,646). Served by air, bus, and train. Public transportation serves campus. Semester system.

LD ADMISSIONS

Students do not complete a separate application and are simultaneously accepted to the LD program. A member of the LD program does not sit on the admissions committee. A personal interview is recommended. Essay is not required.

SECONDARY SCHOOL REQUIREMENTS

Graduation from secondary school required; GED accepted. The following course distribution required: 4 units of English, 3 units of math, 2 units of science, 3 units of social studies, 2 units of academic electives.

TESTING

SAT Reasoning or ACT required.

All enrolled freshmen (fall 2004):

Average SAT I Scores:	Verbal: 488	Math: 479
Average ACT Scores:	Composite: 20	

Child Study Team report is not required. A neuropsychological or comprehensive psycho-educational evaluation is required for admission. Must be dated within 36 months of application. Tests required as part of this documentation:

- [x] WAIS-IV
- [x] WISC-IV
- [ ] SATA
- [x] Woodcock-Johnson
- [ ] Nelson-Denny Reading Test
- [ ] Other

UNDERGRADUATE STUDENT BODY

Total undergraduate student enrollment: 474 Men, 1,722 Women.

Composition of student body (fall 2004):

	Undergraduate	Freshmen
International	0.0	0.3
Black	3.2	7.2
American Indian	0.5	0.4
Asian-American	1.4	0.9
Hispanic	76.4	67.0
White	12.6	14.0
Unreported	5.9	10.2
	100.0%	100.0%

1% are from out of state. Average age of full-time undergraduates is 23. 72% of classes have fewer than 20 students, 27% have between 20 and 50 students, 1% have more than 50 students.

STUDENT HOUSING

Freshmen are not required to live on campus. Housing is guaranteed for all undergraduates. Campus can house 639 undergraduates. Single rooms are available for students with medical or special needs. A medical note is required.

EXPENSES

Tuition (2005-06): $17,048 per year.

Room: $3,226. Board: $2,158.
There is no additional cost for LD program/services.

LD SERVICES

LD program size is not limited.

LD services available to:

- [x] Freshmen
- [x] Sophomores
- [x] Juniors
- [x] Seniors

Academic Accommodations

Curriculum		In class	
Foreign language waiver	[ ]	Early syllabus	[x]
Lighter course load	[ ]	Note takers in class	[ ]
Math waiver	[ ]	Priority seating	[x]
Other special classes	[ ]	Tape recorders	[x]
Priority registrations	[ ]	Videotaped classes	[ ]
Substitution of courses	[x]	Text on tape	[x]
Exams		**Services**	
Extended time	[x]	Diagnostic tests	[ ]
Oral exams	[x]	Learning centers	[x]
Take home exams	[ ]	Proofreaders	[ ]
Exams on tape or computer	[ ]	Readers	[x]
Untimed exams	[ ]	Reading Machines/Kurzweil	[ ]
Other accommodations	[x]	Special bookstore section	[ ]
		Typists	[x]

Credit toward degree is not given for remedial courses taken.

Counseling Services

- [ ] Academic
- [x] Psychological
- [ ] Student Support groups
- [ ] Vocational

Tutoring

Individual tutoring is available daily.

Average size of tutoring groups: 2

	Individual	Group
Time management	[ ]	[ ]
Organizational skills	[ ]	[x]
Learning strategies	[ ]	[x]
Study skills	[ ]	[x]
Content area	[ ]	[ ]
Writing lab	[ ]	[ ]
Math lab	[ ]	[ ]

LD PROGRAM STAFF

Total number of LD Program staff (including director):

Full Time: 2 Part Time: 2

There is an advisor/advocate from the LD program available to students. 12 peer tutors are available to work with LD students.

Key staff person available to work with LD students: Maria L. Gonzales, Director.

LD Program web site: http://www.ollusa.edu/_services/caa/

Prairie View A&M University

Prairie View, TX

Address: PO Box 188, Prairie View, TX, 77446
Admissions telephone: 800 787-7826
Admissions FAX: 936 857-2699
Director of Undergraduate Admissions: Mary Gooch
Admissions e-mail: admissions@pvamu.edu
Web site: http://www.pvamu.edu
SAT Code: 6580 ACT Code: 4202

Program Coordinator for Disability Students: Belinda Lewis
LD program telephone: 936 854-2610
LD program e-mail: belinda_lewis@pvamu.edu
Total campus enrollment: 6,324

GENERAL

Prairie View A&M University is a public, coed, four-year institution. 1,440-acre campus in Prairie View (population: 4,410), 45 miles from Houston. Served by bus; major airport and train serve Houston. Semester system.

LD ADMISSIONS

A personal interview is not required. Essay is not required.

SECONDARY SCHOOL REQUIREMENTS

Graduation from secondary school required; GED accepted. The following course distribution required: 4 units of English, 3 units of math, 3 units of science, 2 units of social studies, 4 units of academic electives.

TESTING

SAT Reasoning or ACT required. SAT Subject recommended.

All enrolled freshmen (fall 2004):

Average SAT I Scores: Verbal: 470 Math: 474
Average ACT Scores: Composite: 19

Child Study Team report is not required. Tests required as part of this documentation:

- ☐ WAIS-IV
- ☐ WISC-IV
- ☐ SATA
- ☐ Woodcock-Johnson
- ☐ Nelson-Denny Reading Test
- ☐ Other

UNDERGRADUATE STUDENT BODY

Total undergraduate student enrollment: 2,367 Men, 3,020 Women.

Composition of student body (fall 2004):

	Undergraduate	Freshmen
International	0.6	1.4
Black	94.8	91.6
American Indian	0.1	0.1
Asian-American	0.3	0.9
Hispanic	3.1	2.9
White	1.1	3.1
Unreported	0.0	0.0
	100.0%	100.0%

6% are from out of state. 1% join a fraternity and 1% join a sorority. Average age of full-time undergraduates is 24.

STUDENT HOUSING

75% of freshmen live in college housing. Freshmen are required to live on campus. Housing is not guaranteed for all undergraduates. The university does not have enough on-campus housing to accommodate all of its enrolled undergraduate students. Campus can house 3,291 undergraduates.

EXPENSES

Tuition (2005-06): $1,500 per year (in-state), $9,780 (out-of-state).

There is no additional cost for LD program/services.

LD SERVICES

LD program size is not limited.

LD services available to:

☐ Freshmen ☐ Sophomores ☐ Juniors ☐ Seniors

Academic Accommodations

Curriculum		**In class**	
Foreign language waiver	☐	Early syllabus	☐
Lighter course load	☐	Note takers in class	☐
Math waiver	☐	Priority seating	☐
Other special classes	☐	Tape recorders	■
Priority registrations	☐	Videotaped classes	☐
Substitution of courses	☐	Text on tape	☐
Exams		**Services**	
Extended time	■	Diagnostic tests	☐
Oral exams	☐	Learning centers	■
Take home exams	☐	Proofreaders	☐
Exams on tape or computer	☐	Readers	☐
Untimed exams	■	Reading Machines/Kurzweil	☐
Other accommodations	☐	Special bookstore section	☐
		Typists	☐

Credit toward degree is not given for remedial courses taken.

Counseling Services

- ☐ Academic
- ☐ Psychological
- ☐ Student Support groups
- ☐ Vocational

Tutoring

	Individual	Group
Time management	☐	☐
Organizational skills	☐	☐
Learning strategies	☐	☐
Study skills	☐	☐
Content area	☐	☐
Writing lab	☐	☐
Math lab	☐	☐

LD PROGRAM STAFF

Total number of LD Program staff (including director):

Full Time: 2 Part Time: 2

Key staff person available to work with LD students: Belinda Lewis, Program Coordinator for Disability Students.

Rice University

Houston, TX

Address: PO Box 1892, Houston, TX, 77251-1892
Admissions telephone: 800 527-OWLS
Admissions FAX: 713 348-5952
Director of Admissions: Julie M. Browning
Web site: http://www.rice.edu
SAT Code: 6609 ACT Code: 4152

LD program name: Disability Support Services
LD program address: 6100 Main Street MS 529
Director, Disability Support Services: Jean Ashmore
LD program telephone: 713 348-5841
LD program e-mail: adarice@rice.edu
LD program enrollment: 17, Total campus enrollment: 3,025

GENERAL

Rice University is a private, coed, four-year institution. 300-acre, urban campus in Houston (population: 1,953,631). Served by air and bus. School operates transportation around campus. Public transportation serves campus. Semester system.

LD ADMISSIONS

A personal interview is recommended. Essay is required and may be typed. Requirements for LD students are the same as all applicants.

SECONDARY SCHOOL REQUIREMENTS

Graduation from secondary school not required. The following course distribution required: 4 units of English, 3 units of math, 2 units of science, 2 units of foreign language, 2 units of social studies, 3 units of academic electives.

TESTING

SAT Reasoning or ACT required. SAT Subject required.

Child Study Team report is not required. A neuropsychological or comprehensive psycho-educational evaluation is required for admission. Must be dated within 12 months of application. Tests required as part of this documentation:

- [x] WAIS-IV
- [ ] WISC-IV
- [x] SATA
- [x] Woodcock-Johnson
- [ ] Nelson-Denny Reading Test
- [ ] Other

UNDERGRADUATE STUDENT BODY

Total undergraduate student enrollment: 3,025.

Composition of student body (fall 2004):

	Undergraduate	Freshmen
International	2.9	2.7
Black	7.0	6.8
American Indian	0.4	0.5
Asian-American	15.2	15.1
Hispanic	11.6	11.2
White	57.4	55.4
Unreported	5.5	8.3
	100.0%	100.0%

50% are from out of state. Average age of full-time undergraduates is 19. 60% of classes have fewer than 20 students, 30% have between 20 and 50 students, 10% have more than 50 students.

STUDENT HOUSING

96% of freshmen live in college housing. Freshmen are not required to live on campus. Housing is not guaranteed for all undergraduates. Guaranteed for freshmen. Depending on demand, most students live at least 3 of their 4 years on campus. Campus can house 2,078 undergraduates. Single rooms are available for students with medical or special needs. A medical note is required.

EXPENSES

Tuition (2005-06): $23,310 per year.

Room: $5,700. Board: $3,280.

There is no additional cost for LD program/services.

LD SERVICES

LD program size is not limited.

LD services available to:

- [x] Freshmen
- [x] Sophomores
- [x] Juniors
- [x] Seniors

Academic Accommodations

Curriculum		In class	
Foreign language waiver	[ ]	Early syllabus	[x]
Lighter course load	[ ]	Note takers in class	[x]
Math waiver	[ ]	Priority seating	[x]
Other special classes	[ ]	Tape recorders	[x]
Priority registrations	[ ]	Videotaped classes	[ ]
Substitution of courses	[ ]	Text on tape	[x]
Exams		**Services**	
Extended time	[x]	Diagnostic tests	[ ]
Oral exams	[ ]	Learning centers	[ ]
Take home exams	[x]	Proofreaders	[ ]
Exams on tape or computer	[x]	Readers	[ ]
Untimed exams	[ ]	Reading Machines/Kurzweil	[x]
Other accommodations	[x]	Special bookstore section	[ ]
		Typists	[x]

Credit toward degree is not given for remedial courses taken.

Counseling Services

- [x] Academic — Meets 6 times per academic year
- [x] Psychological — Meets 12 times per academic year
- [ ] Student Support groups
- [ ] Vocational

Tutoring

Individual tutoring is available weekly.

	Individual	Group
Time management	[x]	[ ]
Organizational skills	[x]	[ ]
Learning strategies	[ ]	[ ]
Study skills	[ ]	[ ]
Content area	[ ]	[ ]
Writing lab	[x]	[ ]
Math lab	[ ]	[ ]

UNIQUE LD PROGRAM FEATURES

The Rice University Disability Support Services office supports all students with disabilities, including those with Learning Disabilities. Services are individualized. Common accommodations are extended time testing, distraction-reduced testing, alternative format books, and note taking. Rice University has programs to assist students in the development of writing skills; these programs are open to all students and are not specifically designed for students with Learning Disabilities.

LD PROGRAM STAFF

Total number of LD Program staff (including director):

Full Time: 1 Part Time: 1

Key staff person available to work with LD students: Jean Ashmore, Director, Disability Support Services.

LD Program web site: www.dss.rice.edu

St. Edward's University

Austin, TX

Address: 3001 S. Congress Avenue, Austin, TX, 78704
Admissions telephone: 800 555-0164
Admissions FAX: 512 464-8877
Director of Admissions: Tracy Manier
Admissions e-mail: seu.admit@admin.stedwards.edu
Web site: http://www.stedwards.edu
SAT Code: 6619   ACT Code: 4156

LD program name: Student Disability Services
Student Disability Services Director: Lorrain Perea
LD program telephone: 512 448-8557
LD program e-mail: lorrainp@admin.stedwards.edu
LD program enrollment: 55, Total campus enrollment: 3,731

GENERAL

St. Edward's University is a private, coed, four-year institution. 160-acre, urban campus in Austin (population: 656,562). Served by air, bus, and train. Public transportation serves campus. Semester system.

LD ADMISSIONS

Application Deadline: 06/01. Students do not complete a separate application and are simultaneously accepted to the LD program. A member of the LD program does sit on the admissions committee. High school waivers are accepted for math and foreign language. A personal interview is recommended. Essay is required and may be typed.

SECONDARY SCHOOL REQUIREMENTS

Graduation from secondary school required; GED accepted. The following course distribution required: 4 units of English, 3 units of math, 2 units of science, 2 units of foreign language, 1 unit of social studies, 2 units of history.

TESTING

SAT Reasoning or ACT required. SAT Subject required.

All enrolled freshmen (fall 2004):

Average SAT I Scores:	Verbal: 561	Math: 552
Average ACT Scores:	Composite: 24	

Child Study Team report is not required. A neuropsychological or comprehensive psycho-educational evaluation is required for admission. Must be dated within 36 months of application. Tests required as part of this documentation:

■ WAIS-IV	■ Woodcock-Johnson
☐ WISC-IV	■ Nelson-Denny Reading Test
☐ SATA	■ Other

UNDERGRADUATE STUDENT BODY

Total undergraduate student enrollment: 1,460 Men, 1,909 Women.

Composition of student body (fall 2004):

	Undergraduate	Freshmen
International	0.5	2.5
Black	3.5	5.3
American Indian	1.0	0.7
Asian-American	2.0	2.4
Hispanic	33.0	29.8
White	55.5	54.9
Unreported	4.5	4.4
	100.0%	100.0%

5% are from out of state. Average age of full-time undergraduates is 20. 51% of classes have fewer than 20 students, 49% have between 20 and 50 students.

STUDENT HOUSING

88% of freshmen live in college housing. Freshmen are required to live on campus. Housing is guaranteed for all undergraduates. Campus can house 1,056 undergraduates. Single rooms are available for students with medical or special needs. A medical note is required.

EXPENSES

Tuition (2005-06): $17,320 per year.
Room: $3,640. Board: $2,900.

There is no additional cost for LD program/services.

LD SERVICES

LD program size is not limited.

LD services available to:

■ Freshmen ■ Sophomores ■ Juniors ■ Seniors

Academic Accommodations

Curriculum		**In class**	
Foreign language waiver	☐	Early syllabus	☐
Lighter course load	■	Note takers in class	☐
Math waiver	☐	Priority seating	☐
Other special classes	■	Tape recorders	☐
Priority registrations	☐	Videotaped classes	☐
Substitution of courses	☐	Text on tape	☐
Exams		**Services**	
Extended time	■	Diagnostic tests	☐
Oral exams	■	Learning centers	■
Take home exams	☐	Proofreaders	☐
Exams on tape or computer	☐	Readers	■
Untimed exams	☐	Reading Machines/Kurzweil	☐
Other accommodations	☐	Special bookstore section	☐
		Typists	■

Credit toward degree is not given for remedial courses taken.

Counseling Services

■ Academic	Meets 2 times per academic year
■ Psychological	Meets 3 times per academic year
■ Student Support groups	Meets 4 times per academic year
■ Vocational	Meets 2 times per academic year

Tutoring

Individual tutoring is available daily.

Average size of tutoring groups: 1

	Individual	Group
Time management	☐	☐
Organizational skills	☐	☐
Learning strategies	☐	☐
Study skills	☐	☐
Content area	☐	☐
Writing lab	☐	☐
Math lab	☐	☐

UNIQUE LD PROGRAM FEATURES

On-going academic counseling. Our program serves all students with disabilities--medical, psychiatric, and learning, and those with dual diagnoses.

LD PROGRAM STAFF

Total number of LD Program staff (including director):

Full Time: 2   Part Time: 2

There is an advisor/advocate from the LD program available to students.

Key staff person available to work with LD students: Lorrain Perea, Student Disability Services Director.

St. Mary's University of San Antonio

San Antonio, TX

Address: 1 Camino Santa Maria, San Antonio, TX, 78228
Admissions telephone: 800 FOR-STMU
Admissions FAX: 210 431-6742
Director of Admissions: Maria Ramos-Smalling
Admissions e-mail: uadm@stmarytx.edu
Web site: http://www.stmarytx.edu
SAT Code: 6637 ACT Code: 4158

Dean of Students: Karen Johnson
LD program telephone: 210 436-3714
Total campus enrollment: 2,531

GENERAL

St. Mary's University of San Antonio is a private, coed, four-year institution. 135-acre campus in San Antonio (population: 1,144,646). Served by air, bus, and train. Public transportation serves campus. Semester system.

LD ADMISSIONS

A personal interview is recommended. Essay is required and may be typed.

SECONDARY SCHOOL REQUIREMENTS

Graduation from secondary school required; GED accepted. The following course distribution required: 4 units of English, 3 units of math, 3 units of science, 2 units of foreign language, 3 units of social studies, 1 unit of academic electives.

TESTING

SAT Reasoning or ACT required. SAT Subject required.

All enrolled freshmen (fall 2004):

Average SAT I Scores:	Verbal: 535	Math: 540
Average ACT Scores:	Composite: 22	

Child Study Team report is not required. Tests required as part of this documentation:

- ☐ WAIS-IV
- ☐ WISC-IV
- ☐ SATA
- ☐ Woodcock-Johnson
- ☐ Nelson-Denny Reading Test
- ☐ Other

UNDERGRADUATE STUDENT BODY

Total undergraduate student enrollment: 1,073 Men, 1,540 Women.

Composition of student body (fall 2004):

	Undergraduate	Freshmen
International	3.9	4.7
Black	2.6	3.4
American Indian	0.0	0.2
Asian-American	3.9	2.6
Hispanic	69.7	68.1
White	20.0	20.4
Unreported	0.0	0.6
	100.0%	100.0%

7% are from out of state. 13% join a fraternity and 13% join a sorority. Average age of full-time undergraduates is 20. 33% of classes have fewer than 20 students, 67% have between 20 and 50 students.

STUDENT HOUSING

72% of freshmen live in college housing. Freshmen are not required to live on campus. Housing is guaranteed for all undergraduates. Campus can house 1,213 undergraduates.

EXPENSES

Tuition (2005-06): $18,274 per year. $13,726 per year (sophomores, juniors, and seniors), $15,016 (freshmen).
Room: $3,916. Board: $2,772.
There is no additional cost for LD program/services.

LD SERVICES

LD program size is not limited.

LD services available to:

☐ Freshmen ☐ Sophomores ☐ Juniors ☐ Seniors

Academic Accommodations

Curriculum		In class	
Foreign language waiver	☐	Early syllabus	☐
Lighter course load	☐	Note takers in class	☐
Math waiver	☐	Priority seating	☐
Other special classes	☐	Tape recorders	☐
Priority registrations	☐	Videotaped classes	☐
Substitution of courses	☐	Text on tape	☐
Exams		**Services**	
Extended time	■	Diagnostic tests	■
Oral exams	■	Learning centers	■
Take home exams	☐	Proofreaders	☐
Exams on tape or computer	☐	Readers	☐
Untimed exams	☐	Reading Machines/Kurzweil	☐
Other accommodations	☐	Special bookstore section	☐
		Typists	☐

Credit toward degree is not given for remedial courses taken.

Counseling Services

- ☐ Academic
- ☐ Psychological
- ☐ Student Support groups
- ☐ Vocational

Tutoring

	Individual	Group
Time management	☐	☐
Organizational skills	☐	☐
Learning strategies	☐	☐
Study skills	☐	☐
Content area	☐	☐
Writing lab	☐	☐
Math lab	☐	☐

LD PROGRAM STAFF

Key staff person available to work with LD students: Dr. Kurt Weber, Staff Psychologist.

University of St. Thomas

Houston, TX

Address: 3800 Montrose Boulevard, Houston, TX, 77006-4696
Admissions telephone: 800 856-8565
Admissions FAX: 713 525-3558
Assistant Director of Admissions: Mr. Eduardo Prieto, Dean
Admissions e-mail: admissions@stthom.edu
Web site: http://www.stthom.edu
SAT Code: 6880 ACT Code: 4238

LD program name: Counseling Services
Director of Counseling Services: Dr. Rose Signorello
LD program telephone: 713 525-3162
LD program e-mail: signorr@stthom.edu
LD program enrollment: 26, Total campus enrollment: 1,910

GENERAL

University of St. Thomas is a private, coed, four-year institution. 21-acre, urban campus in Houston (population: 1,953,631). Served by air, bus, and train. Public transportation serves campus. Semester system.

LD ADMISSIONS

A personal interview is not required. Essay is not required.

SECONDARY SCHOOL REQUIREMENTS

Graduation from secondary school required; GED accepted. The following course distribution required: 4 units of English, 3 units of math, 3 units of science, 2 units of foreign language, 2 units of social studies, 1 unit of history, 3 units of academic electives.

TESTING

SAT Reasoning or ACT required. SAT Subject required.

All enrolled freshmen (fall 2004):

Average SAT I Scores: Verbal: 579 Math: 572
Average ACT Scores: Composite: 25

Child Study Team report is not required. Tests required as part of this documentation:

- ☐ WAIS-IV
- ☐ WISC-IV
- ☐ SATA
- ☐ Woodcock-Johnson
- ☐ Nelson-Denny Reading Test
- ☐ Other

UNDERGRADUATE STUDENT BODY

Total undergraduate student enrollment: 652 Men, 1,199 Women.

Composition of student body (fall 2004):

	Undergraduate	Freshmen
International	1.3	3.4
Black	4.6	5.4
American Indian	1.3	0.6
Asian-American	12.5	12.4
Hispanic	33.0	29.5
White	39.4	39.9
Unreported	7.9	8.8
	100.0%	100.0%

3% are from out of state. Average age of full-time undergraduates is 21. 52% of classes have fewer than 20 students, 48% have between 20 and 50 students.

STUDENT HOUSING

45% of freshmen live in college housing. Freshmen are not required to live on campus. Housing is not guaranteed for all undergraduates. Housing is limited. Campus can house 383 undergraduates.

EXPENSES

Tuition (2005-06): $16,950 per year.
Room: $4,000. Board: $3,300.

There is no additional cost for LD program/services.

LD SERVICES

LD program size is not limited.

LD services available to:

■ Freshmen ■ Sophomores ■ Juniors ■ Seniors

Academic Accommodations

Curriculum		**In class**	
Foreign language waiver	☐	Early syllabus	■
Lighter course load	■	Note takers in class	■
Math waiver	☐	Priority seating	■
Other special classes	■	Tape recorders	■
Priority registrations	■	Videotaped classes	☐
Substitution of courses	☐	Text on tape	☐
Exams		**Services**	
Extended time	■	Diagnostic tests	☐
Oral exams	■	Learning centers	■
Take home exams	☐	Proofreaders	☐
Exams on tape or computer	■	Readers	☐
Untimed exams	☐	Reading Machines/Kurzweil	☐
Other accommodations	■	Special bookstore section	☐
		Typists	☐

Credit toward degree is not given for remedial courses taken.

Counseling Services

- ■ Academic
- ■ Psychological
- ■ Student Support groups
- ☐ Vocational

Tutoring

Individual tutoring is available daily.

	Individual	Group
Time management	■	■
Organizational skills	■	■
Learning strategies	■	■
Study skills	■	■
Content area	☐	☐
Writing lab	☐	☐
Math lab	☐	☐

LD PROGRAM STAFF

Total number of LD Program staff (including director):

Full Time: 1 Part Time: 1

There is an advisor/advocate from the LD program available to students.

Key staff person available to work with LD students: Dr. Rose Signorello, Director of Counseling Services.

LD Program web site: http://www.stthom.edu/counseling

Sam Houston State University

Huntsville, TX

Address: 1803 Avenue I, Huntsville, TX, 77341
Admissions telephone: 936 294-1828
Admissions FAX: 936 294-3758
Director of Admissions: Joey Chandler
Admissions e-mail: admissions@shsu.edu
Web site: http://www.shsu.edu
SAT Code: 6643 ACT Code: 4162

LD program name: Counseling Center
LD program address: Box 2059
Director: Dr. William Metcalfe
LD program telephone: 936 294-1720
LD program e-mail: metcalfe@shsu.edu
Total campus enrollment: 12,297

GENERAL

Sam Houston State University is a public, coed, four-year institution. 2,143-acre campus in Huntsville (population: 35,078), 72 miles from Houston. Served by bus; major airport serves Houston; train serves College Station (54 miles). Public transportation serves campus. Semester system.

LD ADMISSIONS

Students complete a separate application and are simultaneously accepted to the LD program.

SECONDARY SCHOOL REQUIREMENTS

Graduation from secondary school required; GED accepted. The following course distribution required: 4 units of English, 3 units of math, 2 units of science, 3 units of social studies, 1 unit of academic electives.

TESTING

SAT Reasoning or ACT required. SAT Subject recommended.

All enrolled freshmen (fall 2004):

Average SAT I Scores:	Verbal: 508	Math: 504
Average ACT Scores:	Composite: 21	

Child Study Team report is not required. Tests required as part of this documentation:

- [ ] WAIS-IV
- [ ] WISC-IV
- [ ] SATA
- [ ] Woodcock-Johnson
- [ ] Nelson-Denny Reading Test
- [ ] Other

UNDERGRADUATE STUDENT BODY

Total undergraduate student enrollment: 4,871 Men, 6,402 Women.

Composition of student body (fall 2004):

	Undergraduate	Freshmen
International	0.9	0.8
Black	17.9	14.9
American Indian	0.7	0.7
Asian-American	1.0	1.0
Hispanic	13.7	10.6
White	65.8	72.0
Unreported	0.0	0.0
	100.0%	100.0%

1% are from out of state. Average age of full-time undergraduates is 21. 19% of classes have fewer than 20 students, 63% have between 20 and 50 students, 18% have more than 50 students.

STUDENT HOUSING

83% of freshmen live in college housing. Freshmen are required to live on campus. Housing is guaranteed for all undergraduates. Campus can house 3,500 undergraduates. Single rooms are available for students with medical or special needs. A medical note is required.

EXPENSES

Tuition (2005-06): $3,300 per year (in-state), $10,980 (out-of-state). Room: $2,224. Board: $2,176.

LD SERVICES

LD program size is not limited.

LD services available to:

- [x] Freshmen
- [x] Sophomores
- [x] Juniors
- [x] Seniors

Academic Accommodations

Curriculum

- [ ] Foreign language waiver
- [ ] Lighter course load
- [ ] Math waiver
- [ ] Other special classes
- [ ] Priority registrations
- [ ] Substitution of courses

Exams

- [x] Extended time
- [x] Oral exams
- [ ] Take home exams
- [x] Exams on tape or computer
- [ ] Untimed exams
- [ ] Other accommodations

In class

- [ ] Early syllabus
- [x] Note takers in class
- [ ] Priority seating
- [x] Tape recorders
- [ ] Videotaped classes
- [x] Text on tape

Services

- [ ] Diagnostic tests
- [x] Learning centers
- [ ] Proofreaders
- [ ] Readers
- [x] Reading Machines/Kurzweil
- [ ] Special bookstore section
- [ ] Typists

Credit toward degree is not given for remedial courses taken.

Counseling Services

- [ ] Academic
- [ ] Psychological
- [ ] Student Support groups
- [ ] Vocational

Tutoring

Individual tutoring is available daily.

	Individual	Group
Time management	☐	☐
Organizational skills	☐	☐
Learning strategies	☐	☐
Study skills	☐	☐
Content area	☐	☐
Writing lab	☐	☐
Math lab	☐	☐

LD PROGRAM STAFF

Total number of LD Program staff (including director):

Full Time: 1 Part Time: 1

There is an advisor/advocate from the LD program available to students.

Key staff person available to work with LD students: Dr. William Metcalfe, Director.

LD Program web site: http://www.shsu.edu/~counsel/index.html

Schreiner University

Kerrville, TX

Address: 2100 Memorial Boulevard, Kerrville, TX, 78028
Admissions telephone: 800 343-4919
Admissions FAX: 830 792-7226
Acting Dean of Admissions and Financial Aid: Sandra Speed
Admissions e-mail: admissions@schreiner.edu
Web site: http://www.schreiner.edu
SAT Code: 6647

LD program name: Learning Support Services
LD program contact: Admission Office
LD program telephone: 800 343-4919
LD program e-mail: admission@schreiner.edu
LD program enrollment: 66, Total campus enrollment: 793

GENERAL

Schreiner University is a private, coed, four-year institution. 175-acre campus in Kerrville (population: 20,425), 50 miles from San Antonio. Served by bus; major airport and train serve San Antonio. Semester system.

LD ADMISSIONS

Application Deadline: 04/01. Students do not complete a separate application and are simultaneously accepted to the LD program. A member of the LD program does sit on the admissions committee. High school waivers are accepted for math and foreign language. A personal interview is required. Essay is required and may not be typed.

For fall 2004, 83 completed self-identified LD applications were received. 22 applications were offered admission, and 18 enrolled.

SECONDARY SCHOOL REQUIREMENTS

Graduation from secondary school required; GED accepted.

TESTING

SAT Reasoning or ACT required. SAT Subject required.

All enrolled freshmen (fall 2004):

Average SAT I Scores:	Verbal: 500	Math: 503
Average ACT Scores:	Composite: 21	

Child Study Team report is not required. A neuropsychological or comprehensive psycho-educational evaluation is required for admission. Must be dated within 12 months of application. Tests required as part of this documentation:

- [x] WAIS-IV
- [ ] WISC-IV
- [x] SATA
- [x] Woodcock-Johnson
- [x] Nelson-Denny Reading Test
- [x] Other

UNDERGRADUATE STUDENT BODY

Total undergraduate student enrollment: 302 Men, 489 Women.

Composition of student body (fall 2004):

	Undergraduate	Freshmen
International	0.9	0.8
Black	2.4	3.0
American Indian	0.5	1.0
Asian-American	2.4	0.9
Hispanic	19.0	17.2
White	74.8	77.1
Unreported	0.0	0.0
	100.0%	100.0%

1% are from out of state. 17% join a fraternity and 10% join a sorority. Average age of full-time undergraduates is 23. 58% of classes have fewer than 20 students, 42% have between 20 and 50 students.

STUDENT HOUSING

76% of freshmen live in college housing. Freshmen are required to live on campus. Housing is guaranteed for all undergraduates. Campus can house 440 undergraduates. Single rooms are available for students with medical or special needs. A medical note is required.

EXPENSES

Tuition (2005-06): $14,742 per year.
Room & Board: $7,332
Additional cost for LD program/services: $3,150 per first semester.

LD SERVICES

LD program is limited to a certain number of students.

LD services available to:

- [x] Freshmen
- [x] Sophomores
- [x] Juniors
- [x] Seniors

Academic Accommodations

Curriculum		In class	
Foreign language waiver	[ ]	Early syllabus	[ ]
Lighter course load	[x]	Note takers in class	[x]
Math waiver	[ ]	Priority seating	[ ]
Other special classes	[ ]	Tape recorders	[x]
Priority registrations	[ ]	Videotaped classes	[ ]
Substitution of courses	[ ]	Text on tape	[x]
Exams		**Services**	
Extended time	[x]	Diagnostic tests	[ ]
Oral exams	[x]	Learning centers	[ ]
Take home exams	[ ]	Proofreaders	[ ]
Exams on tape or computer	[ ]	Readers	[x]
Untimed exams	[ ]	Reading Machines/Kurzweil	[x]
Other accommodations	[x]	Special bookstore section	[ ]
		Typists	[ ]

Credit toward degree is not given for remedial courses taken.

Counseling Services

- [x] Academic — Meets 14 times per academic year
- [ ] Psychological
- [ ] Student Support groups
- [ ] Vocational

Tutoring

Individual tutoring is available daily.

Average size of tutoring groups: 2

	Individual	Group
Time management	[x]	[ ]
Organizational skills	[x]	[ ]
Learning strategies	[x]	[ ]
Study skills	[x]	[ ]
Content area	[x]	[ ]
Writing lab	[ ]	[ ]
Math lab	[ ]	[ ]

UNIQUE LD PROGRAM FEATURES

New freshmen in the program are enrolled in a special section of a required freshmen seminar class that is taught by the Director and focuses on issues of special concern to the success of LD college students.

LD PROGRAM STAFF

Total number of LD Program staff (including director):

Full Time: 4 Part Time: 4

There is an advisor/advocate from the LD program available to students.

Key staff person available to work with LD students: Dr. Jude Gallik, Director.

LD Program web site: http://www.schreiner.edu/academics/lss.html

Southern Methodist University

Dallas, TX

Address: PO Box 750181, Dallas, TX, 75275-0181
Admissions telephone: 800 323-0672
Admissions FAX: 214 768-0103
Director of Admission and Enrollment Management: Ron W. Moss
Admissions e-mail: enrol_serv@mail.smu.edu
Web site: http://www.smu.edu
SAT Code: 6660 ACT Code: 4171

LD program name: Services for Students with Disabilities
Learning Disabilities Specialist: Alexa Ray
LD program telephone: 214 768-1918
LD program e-mail: alexar@smu.edu
LD program enrollment: 290, Total campus enrollment: 6,208

GENERAL

Southern Methodist University is a private, coed, four-year institution. 170-acre, suburban campus, five miles from downtown Dallas (population: 1,188,580); branch campuses in Galveston, Houston, Plano, and Richardson and in Taos, N.Mex. Served by air, bus, and train. Public transportation serves campus. Semester system.

LD ADMISSIONS

Students complete a separate application and are not simultaneously accepted to the LD program. A member of the LD program does not sit on the admissions committee. A personal interview is not required. Essay is not required. No requirements are waived, but substitutions for the entrance requirement of two years of a foreign language are sometimes accepted with appropriate documentation of a language-based learning disability.

SECONDARY SCHOOL REQUIREMENTS

Graduation from secondary school required; GED not accepted. The following course distribution required: 4 units of English, 3 units of math, 3 units of science, 2 units of foreign language, 1 unit of social studies, 2 units of history.

TESTING

SAT Reasoning or ACT required. SAT Subject recommended.

All enrolled freshmen (fall 2004):

Average SAT I Scores:	Verbal: 600	Math: 606
Average ACT Scores:	Composite: 26	

Child Study Team report is not required. A neuropsychological or comprehensive psycho-educational evaluation is required for admission. Must be dated within 36 months of application. Tests required as part of this documentation:

☑ WAIS-IV	☑ Woodcock-Johnson
☐ WISC-IV	☑ Nelson-Denny Reading Test
☑ SATA	☐ Other

UNDERGRADUATE STUDENT BODY

Total undergraduate student enrollment: 2,667 Men, 3,169 Women.

Composition of student body (fall 2004):

	Undergraduate	Freshmen
International	3.5	4.4
Black	4.6	5.3
American Indian	0.5	0.5
Asian-American	5.8	6.1
Hispanic	8.2	8.8
White	77.4	74.9
Unreported	0.0	0.0
	100.0%	100.0%

35% are from out of state. 29% join a fraternity and 35% join a sorority. Average age of full-time undergraduates is 20. 50% of classes have fewer than 20 students, 39% have between 20 and 50 students, 11% have more than 50 students.

STUDENT HOUSING

94% of freshmen live in college housing. Freshmen are required to live on campus. Housing is not guaranteed for all undergraduates. Single rooms are available for students with medical or special needs.

EXPENSES

Tuition (2005-06): $23,846 per year.

Room: $5,507. Board: $3,800.

There is no additional cost for LD program/services.

LD SERVICES

LD program size is not limited.

LD services available to:

☑ Freshmen ☑ Sophomores ☑ Juniors ☑ Seniors

Academic Accommodations

Curriculum		**In class**	
Foreign language waiver	☐	Early syllabus	☐
Lighter course load	☐	Note takers in class	☑
Math waiver	☐	Priority seating	☐
Other special classes	☐	Tape recorders	☑
Priority registrations	☑	Videotaped classes	☐
Substitution of courses	☑	Text on tape	☑
Exams		**Services**	
Extended time	☑	Diagnostic tests	☑
Oral exams	☑	Learning centers	☑
Take home exams	☐	Proofreaders	☐
Exams on tape or computer	☑	Readers	☑
Untimed exams	☐	Reading Machines/Kurzweil	☑
Other accommodations	☐	Special bookstore section	☐
		Typists	☑

Counseling Services

☐ Academic
☐ Psychological
☑ Student Support groups — Meets 8 times per academic year
☐ Vocational

Tutoring

Individual tutoring is available.

	Individual	Group
Time management	☑	☑
Organizational skills	☑	☑
Learning strategies	☑	☑
Study skills	☑	☑
Content area	☐	☐
Writing lab	☐	☐
Math lab	☐	☐

UNIQUE LD PROGRAM FEATURES

SMU does offer academic counseling and coaching for undergraduate students with LD/ADHD on an individual basis.

LD PROGRAM STAFF

Total number of LD Program staff (including director):

Full Time: 2 Part Time: 2

There is an advisor/advocate from the LD program available to students.

Key staff person available to work with LD students: Rebecca Marin, Coordinator.

LD Program web site: http://www.smu.edu/studentlife/OSSD_Facts.asp

Southwestern University

Georgetown, TX

Address: PO Box 770, Georgetown, TX, 78627-0770
Admissions telephone: 800 252-3166
Admissions FAX: 512 863-9601
Vice President for Enrollment Management: Thomas Oliver
Admissions e-mail: admission@southwestern.edu
Web site: http://www.southwestern.edu
SAT Code: 6674 ACT Code: 4186

LD program name: Academic Services
LD program address: 1001 E. University
Academic Services Coordinator: Deborah McCarthy
LD program telephone: 512 863-1536
LD program e-mail: mccarthd@southwestern.edu
LD program enrollment: 70, Total campus enrollment: 1,276

GENERAL

Southwestern University is a private, coed, four-year institution. 700-acre campus in Georgetown (population: 28,339), 26 miles from Austin. Major airport and train serve Austin; bus serves Round Rock (12 miles). Semester system.

LD ADMISSIONS

A member of the LD program does not sit on the admissions committee. A personal interview is recommended. Essay is required and may be typed.

SECONDARY SCHOOL REQUIREMENTS

Graduation from secondary school required; GED accepted. The following course distribution required: 4 units of English, 4 units of math, 3 units of science, 2 units of foreign language, 3 units of social studies, 3 units of history.

TESTING

SAT Reasoning required; ACT may be substituted. SAT Subject recommended.

All enrolled freshmen (fall 2004):

Average SAT I Scores: Verbal: 632 Math: 622
Average ACT Scores: Composite: 27

Child Study Team report is not required. A neuropsychological or comprehensive psycho-educational evaluation is required for admission. Must be dated within 36 months of application. Tests required as part of this documentation:

- ■ WAIS-IV
- ■ WISC-IV
- ☐ SATA
- ■ Woodcock-Johnson
- ■ Nelson-Denny Reading Test
- ■ Other

UNDERGRADUATE STUDENT BODY

Total undergraduate student enrollment: 573 Men, 747 Women.

Composition of student body (fall 2004):

	Undergraduate	Freshmen
International	0.8	0.7
Black	2.2	3.6
American Indian	1.1	0.9
Asian-American	4.6	4.4
Hispanic	12.6	12.8
White	77.3	76.2
Unreported	1.4	1.4
	100.0%	100.0%

8% are from out of state. 30% join a fraternity and 30% join a sorority. Average age of full-time undergraduates is 20. 76% of classes have fewer than 20 students, 24% have between 20 and 50 students.

STUDENT HOUSING

100% of freshmen live in college housing. Freshmen are required to live on campus. Housing is not guaranteed for all undergraduates. Although we only have a one-year housing requirement, 82-83% of students live on campus. Normally, all students desiring on-campus housing receive it. Campus can house 1,012 undergraduates. Single rooms are available for students with medical or special needs. A medical note is required.

EXPENSES

Tuition (2005-06): $21,900 per year.
Room: $3,570-$4,000. Board: $3,640.
There is no additional cost for LD program/services.

LD SERVICES

LD program size is not limited.

LD services available to:

■ Freshmen ■ Sophomores ■ Juniors ■ Seniors

Academic Accommodations

Curriculum		In class	
Foreign language waiver	■	Early syllabus	☐
Lighter course load	■	Note takers in class	■
Math waiver	☐	Priority seating	■
Other special classes	☐	Tape recorders	■
Priority registrations	■	Videotaped classes	☐
Substitution of courses	☐	Text on tape	☐
Exams		**Services**	
Extended time	■	Diagnostic tests	☐
Oral exams	■	Learning centers	■
Take home exams	☐	Proofreaders	☐
Exams on tape or computer	■	Readers	■
Untimed exams	☐	Reading Machines/Kurzweil	☐
Other accommodations	■	Special bookstore section	☐
		Typists	■

Credit toward degree is not given for remedial courses taken.

Counseling Services

- ■ Academic
- ■ Psychological
- ■ Student Support groups
- ■ Vocational

Tutoring

Individual tutoring is available weekly.

Average size of tutoring groups: 4

	Individual	Group
Time management	■	☐
Organizational skills	■	☐
Learning strategies	■	☐
Study skills	■	☐
Content area	■	☐
Writing lab	☐	■
Math lab	☐	■

UNIQUE LD PROGRAM FEATURES

Accommodations provided on an individual basis. Course substitutions for foreign language requirement are rare but there is a review process in place for these requests.

LD PROGRAM STAFF

Total number of LD Program staff (including director):

Full Time: 1 Part Time: 1

There is an advisor/advocate from the LD program available to students. The advisor/advocate meets with students 3 times per month. 5 peer tutors are available to work with LD students.

Key staff person available to work with LD students: Deborah McCarthy, Academic Services Coordinator.

Stephen F. Austin State University

Nacogdoches, TX

Address: SFA Station 13051, Nacogdoches, TX, 75962
Admissions telephone: 800 731-2902
Admissions FAX: 936 468-3849
Director of Admissions: Monique Cossich
Admissions e-mail: admissions@sfasu.edu
Web site: http://www.sfasu.edu
SAT Code: 6682 ACT Code: 4188

LD program name: Disability Services
LD program address: PO Box 6130, SFA Station
Director of Disability Services: Chuck Lopez
LD program telephone: 936 468-3004
LD program e-mail: clopez@sfasu.edu
Total campus enrollment: 9,568

GENERAL

Stephen F. Austin State University is a public, coed, four-year institution. 430-acre campus in Nacogdoches (population: 29,914), 140 miles from Houston. Served by bus; major airport serves Houston. Public transportation serves campus. Semester system.

LD ADMISSIONS

A member of the LD program does not sit on the admissions committee. A personal interview is recommended. Essay is not required.

SECONDARY SCHOOL REQUIREMENTS

Graduation from secondary school required; GED accepted. The following course distribution required: 4 units of English, 3 units of math, 3 units of science, 2 units of foreign language.

TESTING

SAT Reasoning or ACT required. SAT Subject recommended.

All enrolled freshmen (fall 2004):

Average SAT I Scores: Verbal: 501 Math: 498
Average ACT Scores: Composite: 21

Child Study Team report is not required. A neuropsychological or comprehensive psycho-educational evaluation is required for admission. Must be dated within 36 months of application. Tests required as part of this documentation:

- ■ WAIS-IV
- ☐ WISC-IV
- ☐ SATA
- ■ Woodcock-Johnson
- ☐ Nelson-Denny Reading Test
- ☐ Other

UNDERGRADUATE STUDENT BODY

Total undergraduate student enrollment: 4,316 Men, 5,967 Women.

Composition of student body (fall 2004):

	Undergraduate	Freshmen
International	0.0	0.5
Black	15.4	16.0
American Indian	1.3	0.8
Asian-American	1.7	1.1
Hispanic	8.5	7.4
White	72.7	74.0
Unreported	0.4	0.2
	100.0%	100.0%

2% are from out of state. 13% join a fraternity and 9% join a sorority. Average age of full-time undergraduates is 21. 29% of classes have fewer than 20 students, 62% have between 20 and 50 students, 9% have more than 50 students.

STUDENT HOUSING

86% of freshmen live in college housing. Freshmen are required to live on campus. Housing is guaranteed for all undergraduates. Campus can house 4,308 undergraduates. Single rooms are not available for students with medical or special needs.

EXPENSES

Tuition (2005-06): $1,500 per year (in-state), $9,780 (out-of-state).
Room: $3,002. Board: $2,457.
There is no additional cost for LD program/services.

LD SERVICES

LD program size is not limited.

LD services available to:

■ Freshmen ■ Sophomores ■ Juniors ■ Seniors

Academic Accommodations

Curriculum		In class	
Foreign language waiver	☐	Early syllabus	☐
Lighter course load	■	Note takers in class	■
Math waiver	☐	Priority seating	☐
Other special classes	■	Tape recorders	■
Priority registrations	☐	Videotaped classes	☐
Substitution of courses	☐	Text on tape	☐
Exams		**Services**	
Extended time	■	Diagnostic tests	■
Oral exams	■	Learning centers	■
Take home exams	☐	Proofreaders	☐
Exams on tape or computer	☐	Readers	■
Untimed exams	☐	Reading Machines/Kurzweil	■
Other accommodations	☐	Special bookstore section	☐
		Typists	☐

Credit toward degree is not given for remedial courses taken.

Counseling Services

- ☐ Academic
- ☐ Psychological
- ☐ Student Support groups
- ☐ Vocational

Tutoring

Individual tutoring is available weekly.

	Individual	Group
Time management	■	■
Organizational skills	■	■
Learning strategies	■	■
Study skills	■	■
Content area	■	■
Writing lab	■	■
Math lab	■	■

LD PROGRAM STAFF

Total number of LD Program staff (including director):

Full Time: 3 Part Time: 3

There is no advisor/advocate from the LD program available to students.

Key staff person available to work with LD students: Chuck Lopez, Director of Disability Services.

Tarleton State University

Stephenville, TX

Address: Box T 0001, Tarleton Station, Stephenville, TX, 76402
Admissions telephone: 800 687-8236
Admissions FAX: 254 968-9951
Director of Admissions: Ms. Cindy Hess
Admissions e-mail: uadm@tarleton.edu
Web site: http://www.tarleton.edu
SAT Code: 6817 ACT Code: 4204

LD program name: Teaching and Learning Center
LD program address: Box T-0700
Interim Director/Instructor: Ms. Phyllis Guthrie
LD program telephone: 254 968-9477
LD program e-mail: guthrie@tarleton.edu
LD program enrollment: 85, Total campus enrollment: 7,451

GENERAL

Tarleton State University is a public, coed, four-year institution. 125-acre campus in Stephenville (population: 35,082), 60 miles from Fort Worth; branch campuses at Fort Hood and in Granbury and Killeen. Served by bus; major airport serves Dallas-Fort Worth; train serves Cleburne (60 miles). School operates transportation on campus. Semester system.

LD ADMISSIONS

Students do not complete a separate application and are not simultaneously accepted to the LD program. A member of the LD program does not sit on the admissions committee. A personal interview is required. Essay is not required.

SECONDARY SCHOOL REQUIREMENTS

Graduation from secondary school not required. The following course distribution required: 4 units of English, 3 units of math, 2 units of science, 2 units of social studies, 1 unit of history, 2 units of academic electives.

TESTING

SAT Reasoning or ACT required. SAT Subject recommended.

All enrolled freshmen (fall 2004):

Average SAT I Scores:	Verbal: 484	Math: 487
Average ACT Scores:	Composite: 20	

Child Study Team report is not required. A neuropsychological or comprehensive psycho-education evaluation is not required for admission. Tests required as part of this documentation:

- [x] WAIS-IV
- [x] WISC-IV
- [ ] SATA
- [x] Woodcock-Johnson
- [x] Nelson-Denny Reading Test
- [ ] Other

UNDERGRADUATE STUDENT BODY

Total undergraduate student enrollment: 3,088 Men, 3,627 Women.

Composition of student body (fall 2004):

	Undergraduate	Freshmen
International	0.1	0.7
Black	3.0	8.6
American Indian	0.5	1.1
Asian-American	0.3	1.0
Hispanic	7.0	7.9
White	88.8	80.6
Unreported	0.3	0.1
	100.0%	100.0%

4% are from out of state. 3% join a fraternity and 2% join a sorority. Average age of full-time undergraduates is 22. 37% of classes have fewer than 20 students, 54% have between 20 and 50 students, 9% have more than 50 students.

STUDENT HOUSING

65% of freshmen live in college housing. Freshmen are required to live on campus. Housing is guaranteed for all undergraduates. Campus can house 1,450 undergraduates. Single rooms are available for students with medical or special needs. A medical note is required.

EXPENSES

Tuition (2005-06): $3,300 per year (in-state), $11,500 (out-of-state).
Room: $3,710. Board: $2,544.
There is no additional cost for LD program/services.

LD SERVICES

LD program size is not limited.

LD services available to:

- [x] Freshmen
- [x] Sophomores
- [x] Juniors
- [x] Seniors

Academic Accommodations

Curriculum

- [ ] Foreign language waiver
- [x] Lighter course load
- [ ] Math waiver
- [ ] Other special classes
- [ ] Priority registrations
- [ ] Substitution of courses

Exams

- [x] Extended time
- [x] Oral exams
- [ ] Take home exams
- [x] Exams on tape or computer
- [ ] Untimed exams
- [x] Other accommodations

In class

- [x] Early syllabus
- [ ] Note takers in class
- [ ] Priority seating
- [x] Tape recorders
- [ ] Videotaped classes
- [ ] Text on tape

Services

- [ ] Diagnostic tests
- [x] Learning centers
- [ ] Proofreaders
- [ ] Readers
- [ ] Reading Machines/Kurzweil
- [ ] Special bookstore section
- [ ] Typists

Credit toward degree is not given for remedial courses taken.

Counseling Services

- [x] Academic
- [ ] Psychological
- [ ] Student Support groups
- [ ] Vocational

Meets 2 times per academic year

Tutoring

Individual tutoring is not available.

	Individual	Group
Time management	[ ]	[x]
Organizational skills	[ ]	[ ]
Learning strategies	[ ]	[x]
Study skills	[ ]	[x]
Content area	[ ]	[ ]
Writing lab	[ ]	[x]
Math lab	[ ]	[ ]

LD PROGRAM STAFF

There is an advisor/advocate from the LD program available to students. The advisor/advocate meets with faculty once per month and students once per month. 1 graduate student and 2 peer tutors are available to work with LD students.

Key staff person available to work with LD students: Kayla Wood, Instructor and Coordinator.

Texas A&M International University

Laredo, TX

Address: 5201 University Boulevard, Laredo, TX, 78041-1900
Admissions telephone: 956 326-2200
Admissions FAX: 956 326-2199
Director of Admissions: Rosie Espinoza
Admissions e-mail: enroll@tamiu.edu
Web site: http://www.tamiu.edu
SAT Code: 359 ACT Code: 4215

Director, Student Counseling Services:
Dr. Terence Hannigan
LD program telephone: 956 326-2230
LD program e-mail: thannigan@tamiu.edu
Total campus enrollment: 3,330

GENERAL

Texas A&M International University is a public, coed, four-year institution. 300-acre, suburban campus in Laredo (population: 176,576), 154 miles from San Antonio. Served by air and bus; major airport and train serve San Antonio. Public transportation serves campus. Semester system.

LD ADMISSIONS

Application Deadline: 07/01. Students do not complete a separate application and are not simultaneously accepted to the LD program. A member of the LD program does not sit on the admissions committee. A personal interview is recommended. Essay is not required.

For fall 2004, 13 completed self-identified LD applications were received.

SECONDARY SCHOOL REQUIREMENTS

Graduation from secondary school required; GED accepted. The following course distribution required: 4 units of English, 3 units of math, 2 units of science, 3 units of social studies.

TESTING

SAT Reasoning or ACT required. SAT Subject recommended.

All enrolled freshmen (fall 2004):

Average SAT I Scores: Verbal: 444 Math: 451
Average ACT Scores: Composite: 18

Child Study Team report is not required. A neuropsychological or comprehensive psycho-educational evaluation is required for admission. Must be dated within 60 months of application. Tests required as part of this documentation:

- ■ WAIS-IV
- ■ WISC-IV
- ☐ SATA
- ■ Woodcock-Johnson
- ☐ Nelson-Denny Reading Test
- ☐ Other

UNDERGRADUATE STUDENT BODY

Total undergraduate student enrollment: 937 Men, 1,672 Women.

Composition of student body (fall 2004):

	Undergraduate	Freshmen
International	4.4	3.7
Black	0.0	0.6
American Indian	0.0	0.1
Asian-American	0.8	0.5
Hispanic	91.7	92.4
White	2.9	2.5
Unreported	0.2	0.2
	100.0%	100.0%

6% are from out of state. Average age of full-time undergraduates is 22. 51% of classes have fewer than 20 students, 42% have between 20 and 50 students, 7% have more than 50 students.

STUDENT HOUSING

1% of freshmen live in college housing. Freshmen are not required to live on campus. Housing is not guaranteed for all undergraduates. Limited number of applicable housing units available. Campus can house 684 undergraduates. Single rooms are available for students with medical or special needs. A medical note is required.

EXPENSES

Tuition (2005-06): $3,150 per year (in-state), $11,430 (out-of-state).
Room: $4,290. Board: $2,100.
There is no additional cost for LD program/services.

LD SERVICES

LD program size is not limited.

LD services available to:

☐ Freshmen ☐ Sophomores ☐ Juniors ☐ Seniors

Academic Accommodations

Curriculum		In class	
Foreign language waiver	☐	Early syllabus	☐
Lighter course load	■	Note takers in class	■
Math waiver	☐	Priority seating	■
Other special classes	■	Tape recorders	■
Priority registrations	☐	Videotaped classes	■
Substitution of courses	☐	Text on tape	☐
Exams		**Services**	
Extended time	■	Diagnostic tests	☐
Oral exams	■	Learning centers	☐
Take home exams	☐	Proofreaders	☐
Exams on tape or computer	☐	Readers	■
Untimed exams	■	Reading Machines/Kurzweil	■
Other accommodations	☐	Special bookstore section	☐
		Typists	☐

Credit toward degree is not given for remedial courses taken.

Counseling Services

- ■ Academic
- ■ Psychological
- ☐ Student Support groups
- ☐ Vocational

Tutoring

Individual tutoring is available daily.

	Individual	Group
Time management	☐	☐
Organizational skills	☐	☐
Learning strategies	☐	☐
Study skills	☐	☐
Content area	☐	☐
Writing lab	☐	☐
Math lab	☐	☐

LD PROGRAM STAFF

Total number of LD Program staff (including director):

Full Time: 1 Part Time: 1

There is an advisor/advocate from the LD program available to students. The advisor/advocate meets with students once per month.

Key staff person available to work with LD students: Ruby Gonzalez, Disabilities Services Coordinator.

Texas A&M University - College Station

College Station, TX

Address: College Station, TX, 77843
Admissions telephone: 979 845-3741
Admissions FAX: 979 847-8737
Director of Admissions: Dr. Kenneth Poenisch
Admissions e-mail: admissions@tamu.edu
Web site: http://www.tamu.edu
SAT Code: 6003 ACT Code: 4198

LD program name: Disability Services
LD program address: 1257 TAMU
Director: Anne Reber
LD program telephone: 979 845-1637
LD program e-mail: a-reber@tamu.edu
LD program enrollment: 770, Total campus enrollment: 35,732

GENERAL

Texas A&M University - College Station is a public, coed, four-year institution. 5,200-acre campus in College Station (population: 67,890), 90 miles from Houston; branch campus in Galveston. Served by air; bus serves Bryan (five miles); major airport and train serve Houston. School operates transportation from campus to student apartments and parking lots. Public transportation serves campus. Semester system.

LD ADMISSIONS

Students complete a separate application and are not simultaneously accepted to the LD program. A member of the LD program does not sit on the admissions committee. A personal interview is not required. Essay is required and may be typed. No admissions requirements are waived for LD students.

SECONDARY SCHOOL REQUIREMENTS

Graduation from secondary school required; GED accepted. The following course distribution required: 4 units of English, 4 units of math, 3 units of science, 2 units of foreign language, 2 units of social studies, 1 unit of history.

TESTING

SAT Reasoning or ACT required. SAT Subject required.

All enrolled freshmen (fall 2004):

Average SAT I Scores:	Verbal: 578	Math: 605
Average ACT Scores:	Composite: 25	

Child Study Team report is not required. A neuropsychological or comprehensive psycho-educational evaluation is required for admission. Must be dated within 36 months of application. Tests required as part of this documentation:

- [x] WAIS-IV
- [ ] WISC-IV
- [ ] SATA
- [x] Woodcock-Johnson
- [x] Nelson-Denny Reading Test
- [x] Other

UNDERGRADUATE STUDENT BODY

Total undergraduate student enrollment: 18,753 Men, 17,850 Women.

Composition of student body (fall 2004):

	Undergraduate	Freshmen
International	0.6	1.4
Black	3.0	2.3
American Indian	0.5	0.5
Asian-American	3.8	3.3
Hispanic	12.2	10.1
White	79.8	81.8
Unreported	0.1	0.6
	100.0%	100.0%

4% are from out of state. 3% join a fraternity and 6% join a sorority. Average age of full-time undergraduates is 21. 19% of classes have fewer than 20 students, 57% have between 20 and 50 students, 24% have more than 50 students.

STUDENT HOUSING

69% of freshmen live in college housing. Freshmen are not required to live on campus. Housing is not guaranteed for all undergraduates. Limited number of dorm rooms available-majority of undergraduates live off-campus. Campus can house 10,103 undergraduates. Single rooms are available for students with medical or special needs. A medical note is required.

EXPENSES

There is no additional cost for LD program/services.

LD SERVICES

LD program size is not limited.

LD services available to:

- [x] Freshmen
- [x] Sophomores
- [x] Juniors
- [x] Seniors

Academic Accommodations

Curriculum		In class	
Foreign language waiver	[ ]	Early syllabus	[ ]
Lighter course load	[x]	Note takers in class	[x]
Math waiver	[ ]	Priority seating	[x]
Other special classes	[ ]	Tape recorders	[x]
Priority registrations	[x]	Videotaped classes	[ ]
Substitution of courses	[ ]	Text on tape	[x]
Exams		**Services**	
Extended time	[x]	Diagnostic tests	[x]
Oral exams	[ ]	Learning centers	[ ]
Take home exams	[ ]	Proofreaders	[ ]
Exams on tape or computer	[ ]	Readers	[ ]
Untimed exams	[x]	Reading Machines/Kurzweil	[x]
Other accommodations	[ ]	Special bookstore section	[ ]
		Typists	[ ]

Credit toward degree is not given for remedial courses taken.

Counseling Services

[x]	Academic	Meets 3 times per academic year
[ ]	Psychological	
[x]	Student Support groups	Meets 12 times per academic year
[ ]	Vocational	

Tutoring

Individual tutoring is not available.

	Individual	Group
Time management	[x]	[x]
Organizational skills	[x]	[x]
Learning strategies	[x]	[x]
Study skills	[x]	[x]
Content area	[ ]	[ ]
Writing lab	[x]	[ ]
Math lab	[x]	[x]

LD PROGRAM STAFF

Total number of LD Program staff (including director):

Full Time: 5 Part Time: 5

There is an advisor/advocate from the LD program available to students. The advisor/advocate meets with students once per month. 2 graduate students are available to work with LD students.

Key staff person available to work with LD students: Disability Services, All Accommodations Counselors.

LD Program web site: http://studentlife.tamu.edu/ssd/

Texas A&M University - Corpus Christi

Corpus Christi, TX

Address: 6300 Ocean Drive, Corpus Christi, TX, 78412-5503
Admissions telephone: 800 482-6822
Admissions FAX: 361 825-5887
Director of Admissions: Margaret Dechant
Admissions e-mail: admiss@falcon.tamucc.edu
Web site: http://www.tamucc.edu
SAT Code: 366 ACT Code: 4045

LD program name: Services for Students with Disabilities
LD program address: 6300 Ocean Dr, Unit# 5717,
Director of Disability Services: Rachel A. Fox
LD program telephone: 361 825-5816
LD program e-mail: exam.services@mail.tamucc.edu
LD program enrollment: 17, Total campus enrollment: 6,581

GENERAL

Texas A&M University - Corpus Christi is a public, coed, four-year institution. 240-acre, suburban campus in Corpus Christi (population: 277,454). Served by air and bus; larger airport and train serve San Antonio (150 miles). Public transportation serves campus. Semester system.

LD ADMISSIONS

Students do not complete a separate application and are not simultaneously accepted to the LD program. A member of the LD program does not sit on the admissions committee. A personal interview is not required. Essay is not required.

For fall 2004, 17 completed self-identified LD applications were received.

SECONDARY SCHOOL REQUIREMENTS

Graduation from secondary school required; GED accepted. The following course distribution required: 4 units of English, 3 units of math, 3 units of science, 2 units of foreign language, 3 units of social studies.

TESTING

SAT Reasoning or ACT required.

Child Study Team report is not required. A neuropsychological or comprehensive psycho-educational evaluation is required for admission. Tests required as part of this documentation:

- [x] WAIS-IV
- [x] WISC-IV
- [ ] SATA
- [x] Woodcock-Johnson
- [ ] Nelson-Denny Reading Test
- [x] Other

UNDERGRADUATE STUDENT BODY

Total undergraduate student enrollment: 2,423 Men, 3,543 Women.

Composition of student body (fall 2004):

	Undergraduate	Freshmen
International	0.3	0.8
Black	3.1	2.9
American Indian	0.7	0.6
Asian-American	2.2	2.0
Hispanic	41.5	36.9
White	52.2	56.8
Unreported	0.0	0.0
	100.0%	100.0%

2% are from out of state. Average age of full-time undergraduates is 23. 28% of classes have fewer than 20 students, 54% have between 20 and 50 students, 18% have more than 50 students.

STUDENT HOUSING

Freshmen are not required to live on campus. Housing is guaranteed for all undergraduates. Campus can house 1,384 undergraduates. Single rooms are available for students with medical or special needs. A medical note is required.

EXPENSES

There is no additional cost for LD program/services.

LD SERVICES

LD program size is not limited.

LD services available to:

- [x] Freshmen
- [x] Sophomores
- [x] Juniors
- [x] Seniors

Academic Accommodations

Curriculum		In class	
Foreign language waiver	[ ]	Early syllabus	[ ]
Lighter course load	[ ]	Note takers in class	[x]
Math waiver	[ ]	Priority seating	[ ]
Other special classes	[ ]	Tape recorders	[x]
Priority registrations	[ ]	Videotaped classes	[x]
Substitution of courses	[x]	Text on tape	[x]
Exams		**Services**	
Extended time	[x]	Diagnostic tests	[ ]
Oral exams	[x]	Learning centers	[x]
Take home exams	[ ]	Proofreaders	[ ]
Exams on tape or computer	[x]	Readers	[x]
Untimed exams	[ ]	Reading Machines/Kurzweil	[ ]
Other accommodations	[ ]	Special bookstore section	[ ]
		Typists	[ ]

Credit toward degree is not given for remedial courses taken.

Counseling Services

- [ ] Academic
- [ ] Psychological
- [ ] Student Support groups
- [ ] Vocational

Tutoring

Individual tutoring is not available.

	Individual	Group
Time management	[x]	[ ]
Organizational skills	[x]	[ ]
Learning strategies	[x]	[ ]
Study skills	[x]	[ ]
Content area	[ ]	[ ]
Writing lab	[ ]	[ ]
Math lab	[ ]	[x]

LD PROGRAM STAFF

Total number of LD Program staff (including director):

Full Time: 3 Part Time: 3

There is an advisor/advocate from the LD program available to students. The advisor/advocate meets with student 25 times per month. 1 peer tutor is available to work with LD students.

Texas A&M University - Galveston

Galveston, TX

Address: PO Box 1675, Galveston, TX, 77553-1675
Admissions telephone: 877 322-4443
Admissions FAX: 409 740-4731
Director of Admissions: Cheryl Moon
Admissions e-mail: seaaggie@tamug.edu
Web site: http://www.tamug.edu
SAT Code: 6835 ACT Code: 6592

Director for Student Counseling: Dr. Bob Sindylek
LD program telephone: 409 740-4587
LD program e-mail: sindyler@tamug.edu
LD program enrollment: 40, Total campus enrollment: 1,577

GENERAL

Texas A&M University at Galveston is a public, coed, four-year institution. 150-acre campus in Galveston (population: 57,247), 40 miles from Houston. Served by bus; major airports serve Houston. Public transportation serves campus. Semester system.

LD ADMISSIONS

Students do not complete a separate application and are simultaneously accepted to the LD program. A member of the LD program does not sit on the admissions committee. A personal interview is required.

SECONDARY SCHOOL REQUIREMENTS

Graduation from secondary school required; GED accepted. The following course distribution required: 4 units of English, 3 units of math, 3 units of science.

TESTING

SAT Reasoning or ACT required. SAT Subject recommended.

All enrolled freshmen (fall 2004):

Average SAT I Scores: Verbal: 556 Math: 563
Average ACT Scores: Composite: 23

Child Study Team report is not required. A neuropsychological or comprehensive psycho-education evaluation is not required for admission. Tests required as part of this documentation:

- ☐ WAIS-IV
- ☐ WISC-IV
- ☐ SATA
- ☐ Woodcock-Johnson
- ☐ Nelson-Denny Reading Test
- ☐ Other

UNDERGRADUATE STUDENT BODY

Total undergraduate student enrollment: 668 Men, 698 Women.

Composition of student body (fall 2004):

	Undergraduate	Freshmen
International	0.8	0.9
Black	2.1	2.7
American Indian	0.8	1.0
Asian-American	0.8	1.4
Hispanic	9.3	8.9
White	85.1	84.5
Unreported	1.1	0.6
	100.0%	100.0%

24% are from out of state. Average age of full-time undergraduates is 20. 67% of classes have fewer than 20 students, 27% have between 20 and 50 students, 6% have more than 50 students.

STUDENT HOUSING

75% of freshmen live in college housing. Freshmen are required to live on campus. Housing is guaranteed for all undergraduates. Campus can house 650 undergraduates.

EXPENSES

Tuition (2005-06): $4,110 per year (in-state), $12,390 (out-of-state).

Room: $1,958. Board: $2,912.
There is no additional cost for LD program/services.

LD SERVICES

LD program size is not limited.

LD services available to:

■ Freshmen ■ Sophomores ■ Juniors ■ Seniors

Academic Accommodations

Curriculum		In class	
Foreign language waiver	☐	Early syllabus	☐
Lighter course load	■	Note takers in class	■
Math waiver	☐	Priority seating	☐
Other special classes	☐	Tape recorders	■
Priority registrations	☐	Videotaped classes	■
Substitution of courses	☐	Text on tape	☐
Exams		**Services**	
Extended time	■	Diagnostic tests	☐
Oral exams	■	Learning centers	☐
Take home exams	☐	Proofreaders	☐
Exams on tape or computer	☐	Readers	☐
Untimed exams	☐	Reading Machines/Kurzweil	☐
Other accommodations	☐	Special bookstore section	☐
		Typists	☐

Credit toward degree is not given for remedial courses taken.

Counseling Services

- ☐ Academic
- ☐ Psychological
- ☐ Student Support groups
- ☐ Vocational

Tutoring

Individual tutoring is available daily.

Average size of tutoring groups: 20

	Individual	Group
Time management	☐	☐
Organizational skills	☐	☐
Learning strategies	☐	☐
Study skills	☐	☐
Content area	☐	■
Writing lab	☐	■
Math lab	☐	■

LD PROGRAM STAFF

Total number of LD Program staff (including director):

Full Time: 4 Part Time: 4

There is not an advisor/advocate from the LD program available to students.

Key staff person available to work with LD students: Dr. Bob Sindylek, Director for Student Counseling.

Texas A&M University - Kingsville

Kingsville, TX

Address: MSC 105, Kingsville, TX, 78363
Admissions telephone: 800 687-6000
Admissions FAX: 361 593-2195
Director of Admission: Dr. Maggie Williams
Admissions e-mail: kapam00@tamuk.edu
Web site: http://www.tamuk.edu
SAT Code: 6822 ACT Code: 4212

Assistant Coordinator/Counselor: Esperanza Cavazos
Total campus enrollment: 5,645

GENERAL

Texas A&M University - Kingsville is a public, coed, four-year institution. 250-acre campus in Kingsville (population: 25,575), 40 miles from Corpus Christi. Served by bus; airport serves Corpus Christi; larger airport and train serve San Antonio (150 miles). Semester system.

LD ADMISSIONS

A personal interview is not required. Essay is not required.

SECONDARY SCHOOL REQUIREMENTS

Graduation from secondary school required; GED accepted.

TESTING

SAT Reasoning or ACT required.

All enrolled freshmen (fall 2004):

Average SAT I Scores:	Verbal: 454	Math: 468
Average ACT Scores:	Composite: 18	

Child Study Team report is not required. Tests required as part of this documentation:

☐ WAIS-IV	☐ Woodcock-Johnson
☐ WISC-IV	☐ Nelson-Denny Reading Test
☐ SATA	☐ Other

UNDERGRADUATE STUDENT BODY

Total undergraduate student enrollment: 2,535 Men, 2,474 Women.

Composition of student body (fall 2004):

	Undergraduate	Freshmen
International	0.8	1.2
Black	7.1	6.0
American Indian	0.2	0.3
Asian-American	0.9	0.9
Hispanic	68.2	65.6
White	21.7	25.4
Unreported	1.1	0.6
	100.0%	100.0%

2% are from out of state. 1% join a fraternity and 1% join a sorority. Average age of full-time undergraduates is 22. 38% of classes have fewer than 20 students, 60% have between 20 and 50 students, 2% have more than 50 students.

STUDENT HOUSING

60% of freshmen live in college housing. Freshmen are required to live on campus. Housing is guaranteed for all undergraduates. Campus can house 1,858 undergraduates.

EXPENSES

Tuition (2005-06): $3,300 per year (in-state), $11,580 (out-of-state).
Room & Board: $4,672-$4,672.
There is no additional cost for LD program/services.

There is no additional cost for LD program/services.

LD SERVICES

LD program size is not limited.

LD services available to:

☒ Freshmen ☒ Sophomores ☒ Juniors ☒ Seniors

Academic Accommodations

Curriculum		In class	
Foreign language waiver	☐	Early syllabus	☐
Lighter course load	☐	Note takers in class	☒
Math waiver	☐	Priority seating	☐
Other special classes	☒	Tape recorders	☒
Priority registrations	☐	Videotaped classes	☒
Substitution of courses	☐	Text on tape	☐
Exams		**Services**	
Extended time	☒	Diagnostic tests	☐
Oral exams	☒	Learning centers	☒
Take home exams	☐	Proofreaders	☐
Exams on tape or computer	☐	Readers	☒
Untimed exams	☐	Reading Machines/Kurzweil	☒
Other accommodations	☐	Special bookstore section	☐
		Typists	☐

Credit toward degree is not given for remedial courses taken.

Counseling Services

☒ Academic
☒ Psychological
☐ Student Support groups
☐ Vocational

Tutoring

Individual tutoring is available.

	Individual	Group
Time management	☐	☐
Organizational skills	☐	☐
Learning strategies	☐	☐
Study skills	☐	☐
Content area	☒	☒
Writing lab	☒	☒
Math lab	☒	☒

LD PROGRAM STAFF

Total number of LD Program staff (including director):

Full Time: 1 Part Time: 1

There is an advisor/advocate from the LD program available to students.

Key staff person available to work with LD students: Esperanza Cavazos, Assistant Coordinator/Counselor.

Texas Christian University

Fort Worth, TX

Address: 2800 S. University Drive, Fort Worth, TX, 76129
Admissions telephone: 800 TCU-FROG
Admissions FAX: 817 257-7268
Dean of Admissions: Raymond A. Brown, Dean
Admissions e-mail: frogmail@tcu.edu
Web site: http://www.tcu.edu
SAT Code: 6820 ACT Code: 4206

LD program name: Center for Academic Services
LD program address: TCU Box 297710
Director, Center for Academic Services: Marsha Ramsey
LD program telephone: 817 257-7486
LD program e-mail: m.ramsey@tcu.edu
LD program enrollment: 182, Total campus enrollment: 7,154

GENERAL

Texas Christian University is a private, coed, four-year institution. 300-acre, suburban campus in Fort Worth (population: 534,694). Served by air, bus, and train; major airport serves Irving (25 miles). Public transportation serves campus. Semester system.

LD ADMISSIONS

Students do not complete a separate application and are not simultaneously accepted to the LD program. A member of the LD program does not sit on the admissions committee. A personal interview is not required. Essay is required and may be typed. Requirements for LD students are the same as for other students

SECONDARY SCHOOL REQUIREMENTS

Graduation from secondary school required; GED not accepted. The following course distribution required: 4 units of English, 3 units of math, 3 units of science, 2 units of foreign language, 3 units of social studies, 2 units of academic electives.

TESTING

SAT Reasoning or ACT required. SAT Subject recommended.

Child Study Team report is not required. A neuropsychological or comprehensive psycho-educational evaluation is required for admission. Must be dated within 36 months of application. Tests required as part of this documentation:

- [x] WAIS-IV
- [x] WISC-IV
- [ ] SATA
- [x] Woodcock-Johnson
- [x] Nelson-Denny Reading Test
- [x] Other

UNDERGRADUATE STUDENT BODY

Total undergraduate student enrollment: 2,927 Men, 3,958 Women.

Composition of student body (fall 2004):

	Undergraduate	Freshmen
International	2.3	3.8
Black	4.0	5.1
American Indian	0.4	0.5
Asian-American	2.6	2.1
Hispanic	5.7	6.4
White	82.1	78.5
Unreported	2.9	3.6
	100.0%	100.0%

22% are from out of state. 34% join a fraternity and 36% join a sorority. Average age of full-time undergraduates is 21. 50% of classes have fewer than 20 students, 42% have between 20 and 50 students, 8% have more than 50 students.

STUDENT HOUSING

95% of freshmen live in college housing. Freshmen are required to live on campus. Housing is guaranteed for all undergraduates. Campus can house 3,215 undergraduates. Single rooms are available for students with medical or special needs. A medical note is required.

EXPENSES

Tuition (2005-06): $21,280 per year (in-state), $21,320 (out-of-state). Room: $4,180. Board: $2,800.
There is no additional cost for LD program/services.

LD SERVICES

LD program size is not limited.

LD services available to:

- [x] Freshmen
- [x] Sophomores
- [x] Juniors
- [x] Seniors

Academic Accommodations

Curriculum		In class	
Foreign language waiver	[ ]	Early syllabus	[ ]
Lighter course load	[ ]	Note takers in class	[ ]
Math waiver	[ ]	Priority seating	[ ]
Other special classes	[ ]	Tape recorders	[ ]
Priority registrations	[ ]	Videotaped classes	[ ]
Substitution of courses	[ ]	Text on tape	[ ]
Exams		**Services**	
Extended time	[ ]	Diagnostic tests	[ ]
Oral exams	[ ]	Learning centers	[ ]
Take home exams	[ ]	Proofreaders	[ ]
Exams on tape or computer	[ ]	Readers	[ ]
Untimed exams	[ ]	Reading Machines/Kurzweil	[ ]
Other accommodations	[ ]	Special bookstore section	[ ]
		Typists	[ ]

Credit toward degree is not given for remedial courses taken.

Counseling Services

- [ ] Academic
- [ ] Psychological
- [ ] Student Support groups
- [ ] Vocational

Tutoring

Individual tutoring is not available.

	Individual	Group
Time management	[x]	[x]
Organizational skills	[x]	[x]
Learning strategies	[x]	[x]
Study skills	[x]	[x]
Content area	[ ]	[ ]
Writing lab	[x]	[x]
Math lab	[x]	[x]

LD PROGRAM STAFF

There is an advisor/advocate from the LD program available to students.

Key staff person available to work with LD students: Marsha Ramsey, Director, Center for Academic Services.

Texas Lutheran University

Seguin, TX

Address: 1000 W. Court, Seguin, TX, 78155-5999
Admissions telephone: 800 771-8521
Admissions FAX: 830 372-8096
Vice President for Enrollment Services: E. Norman Jones
Admissions e-mail: admissions@tlu.edu
Web site: http://www.tlu.edu
SAT Code: 6823 ACT Code: 4214

A.D.A. Coordinator: Terry A. Weers
LD program telephone: 830 372-8009
LD program e-mail: tweers@tlu.edu
LD program enrollment: 30, Total campus enrollment: 1,414

GENERAL

Texas Lutheran University is a private, coed, four-year institution. 160-acre campus in Seguin (population: 25,000), 35 miles from San Antonio. Served by bus; major airport and train serve San Antonio. Semester system.

LD ADMISSIONS

Students do not complete a separate application and are not simultaneously accepted to the LD program. A member of the LD program does not sit on the admissions committee. A personal interview is not required. Essay is required and may be typed. LD students generally meet the same requirements as other students.

For fall 2004, 7 completed self-identified LD applications were received. 7 applications were offered admission, and 7 enrolled.

SECONDARY SCHOOL REQUIREMENTS

Graduation from secondary school required; GED accepted.

TESTING

SAT Reasoning or ACT required. SAT Subject recommended.

All enrolled freshmen (fall 2004):

Average SAT I Scores:	Verbal: 510	Math: 530
Average ACT Scores:	Composite: 22	

Child Study Team report is not required. A neuropsychological or comprehensive psycho-educational evaluation is required for admission. Must be dated within 36 months of application. Tests required as part of this documentation:

- ■ WAIS-IV
- ☐ WISC-IV
- ☐ SATA
- ■ Woodcock-Johnson
- ☐ Nelson-Denny Reading Test
- ☐ Other

UNDERGRADUATE STUDENT BODY

Total undergraduate student enrollment: 681 Men, 792 Women.

Composition of student body (fall 2004):

	Undergraduate	Freshmen
International	0.8	1.3
Black	11.5	7.6
American Indian	0.5	0.4
Asian-American	1.3	1.3
Hispanic	16.5	16.7
White	68.4	71.0
Unreported	1.0	1.7
	100.0%	100.0%

6% are from out of state. 48% of classes have fewer than 20 students, 52% have between 20 and 50 students.

STUDENT HOUSING

Freshmen are required to live on campus. Housing is guaranteed for all undergraduates. Campus can house 991 undergraduates. Single rooms are available for students with medical or special needs. A medical note is required.

EXPENSES

Tuition (2005-06): $17,600 per year.

Room: $2,460. Board: $2,900.

There is no additional cost for LD program/services.

LD SERVICES

LD program size is not limited.

LD services available to:

■ Freshmen ■ Sophomores ■ Juniors ■ Seniors

Academic Accommodations

Curriculum		**In class**	
Foreign language waiver	☐	Early syllabus	☐
Lighter course load	☐	Note takers in class	■
Math waiver	☐	Priority seating	■
Other special classes	☐	Tape recorders	■
Priority registrations	■	Videotaped classes	☐
Substitution of courses	☐	Text on tape	☐
Exams		**Services**	
Extended time	■	Diagnostic tests	☐
Oral exams	■	Learning centers	☐
Take home exams	☐	Proofreaders	☐
Exams on tape or computer	☐	Readers	☐
Untimed exams	☐	Reading Machines/Kurzweil	☐
Other accommodations	■	Special bookstore section	☐
		Typists	☐

Credit toward degree is not given for remedial courses taken.

Counseling Services

- ■ Academic — Meets 4 times per academic year
- ■ Psychological
- ☐ Student Support groups
- ☐ Vocational

Tutoring

Individual tutoring is available weekly.

Average size of tutoring groups: 12

	Individual	Group
Time management	■	■
Organizational skills	■	■
Learning strategies	■	■
Study skills	■	■
Content area	■	■
Writing lab	■	☐
Math lab	■	■

LD PROGRAM STAFF

Total number of LD Program staff (including director):

Full Time: 1 Part Time: 1

There is an advisor/advocate from the LD program available to students. The advisor/advocate meets with students once per month. 1 graduate student and 29 peer tutors are available to work with LD students.

Key staff person available to work with LD students: Terry A. Weers, A.D.A. Coordinator.

Texas State University - San Marcos

San Marcos, TX

Address: 601 University Drive, San Marcos, TX, 78666
Admissions telephone: 512 245-2364
Admissions FAX: 512 245-8044
Director of Admissions: Christy Kangas
Admissions e-mail: admissions@txstate.edu
Web site: http://www.txstate.edu
SAT Code: 6667 ACT Code: 4178

Director of Office of Disability Services: Tina Schultze
LD program telephone: 512 245-3451
LD program e-mail: ts12@txstate.edu
LD program enrollment: 657, Total campus enrollment: 22,402

GENERAL

Texas State University - San Marcos is a public, coed, four-year institution. 427-acre campus in San Marcos (population: 34,733), 50 miles from San Antonio and 30 miles from Austin; branch campus in North Austin. Served by bus and train; major airports serve San Antonio and Austin. School operates transportation to local apartment complexes and to Austin. Semester system.

LD ADMISSIONS

Students do not complete a separate application and are not simultaneously accepted to the LD program. A personal interview is required. Essay is not required.

SECONDARY SCHOOL REQUIREMENTS

Graduation from secondary school required; GED accepted. The following course distribution required: 4 units of English, 3 units of math, 3 units of science, 2 units of foreign language, 4 units of social studies, 4 units of academic electives.

TESTING

SAT Reasoning recommended. ACT recommended. SAT Subject required.

All enrolled freshmen (fall 2004):

Average SAT I Scores: Verbal: 529 Math: 534
Average ACT Scores: Composite: 22

Child Study Team report is not required. A neuropsychological or comprehensive psycho-educational evaluation is required for admission. Must be dated within 60 months of application. Tests required as part of this documentation:

- [ ] WAIS-IV
- [ ] WISC-IV
- [ ] SATA
- [ ] Woodcock-Johnson
- [ ] Nelson-Denny Reading Test
- [x] Other

UNDERGRADUATE STUDENT BODY

Total undergraduate student enrollment: 9,072 Men, 11,107 Women.

Composition of student body (fall 2004):

	Undergraduate	Freshmen
International	0.8	1.0
Black	4.3	4.9
American Indian	0.7	0.7
Asian-American	1.4	1.9
Hispanic	18.6	19.2
White	74.0	71.3
Unreported	0.2	1.0
	100.0%	100.0%

1% are from out of state. 5% join a fraternity and 5% join a sorority. Average age of full-time undergraduates is 22. 17% of classes have fewer than 20 students, 63% have between 20 and 50 students, 20% have more than 50 students.

STUDENT HOUSING

88% of freshmen live in college housing. Freshmen are required to live on campus. Housing is not guaranteed for all undergraduates. Upper level students are provided for on a first come first serve basis. Campus can house 6,022 undergraduates. Single rooms are available for students with medical or special needs.

EXPENSES

Tuition (2005-06): $3,780 per year (in-state), $12,060 (out-of-state).
Room: $3,524. Board: $2,086.
There is no additional cost for LD program/services.

LD SERVICES

LD program size is not limited.

LD services available to:

- [x] Freshmen
- [x] Sophomores
- [x] Juniors
- [x] Seniors

Academic Accommodations

Curriculum		In class	
Foreign language waiver	[ ]	Early syllabus	[ ]
Lighter course load	[x]	Note takers in class	[x]
Math waiver	[ ]	Priority seating	[ ]
Other special classes	[ ]	Tape recorders	[x]
Priority registrations	[ ]	Videotaped classes	[ ]
Substitution of courses	[ ]	Text on tape	[ ]
Exams		**Services**	
Extended time	[x]	Diagnostic tests	[x]
Oral exams	[x]	Learning centers	[x]
Take home exams	[ ]	Proofreaders	[ ]
Exams on tape or computer	[ ]	Readers	[x]
Untimed exams	[x]	Reading Machines/Kurzweil	[x]
Other accommodations	[ ]	Special bookstore section	[ ]
		Typists	[ ]

Credit toward degree is not given for remedial courses taken.

Counseling Services

- [ ] Academic
- [ ] Psychological
- [ ] Student Support groups
- [ ] Vocational

Tutoring

Individual tutoring is available weekly.

	Individual	Group
Time management	[x]	[ ]
Organizational skills	[x]	[x]
Learning strategies	[x]	[ ]
Study skills	[x]	[x]
Content area	[x]	[ ]
Writing lab	[x]	[ ]
Math lab	[x]	[ ]

LD PROGRAM STAFF

Total number of LD Program staff (including director):

Full Time: 2 Part Time: 2

There is an advisor/advocate from the LD program available to students.

Key staff person available to work with LD students: TBA, Cognitive Disabilities Specialist.

LD Program web site:
http://www.ods.txstate.edu/learningdisabilityguideline.htm

Texas Tech University

Lubbock, TX

Address: Box 42013, Lubbock, TX, 79409
Admissions telephone: 806 742-1480
Admissions FAX: 806 742-0062
Interim Director of Admissions and School Relations: Djuana Young
Admissions e-mail: admissions@ttu.edu
Web site: http://www.ttu.edu
SAT Code: 6827 ACT Code: 4220

LD program name: TECHniques
LD program address: Box 42182
Assistant Director: Leann Elkins
LD program telephone: 806 742-1822
LD program e-mail: leann.elkins@ttu.edu
LD program enrollment: 716, Total campus enrollment: 23,329

GENERAL

Texas Tech University is a public, coed, four-year institution. 1,839-acre campus in Lubbock (population: 199,564); branch campuses in Amarillo and Junction. Served by air and bus. School operates transportation around campus and to nearby off-campus residential areas. Public transportation serves campus. Semester system.

LD ADMISSIONS

Application Deadline: 06/01. Students complete a separate application and are not simultaneously accepted to the LD program. A member of the LD program does not sit on the admissions committee. A personal interview is required. Essay is required and may be typed. No admissions requirements may be waived for LD students.

SECONDARY SCHOOL REQUIREMENTS

Graduation from secondary school required; GED not accepted. The following course distribution required: 4 units of English, 3 units of math, 2 units of science, 2 units of foreign language.

TESTING

SAT Reasoning or ACT required. SAT Subject recommended.

All enrolled freshmen (fall 2004):

Average SAT I Scores: Verbal: 552 Math: 573
Average ACT Scores: Composite: 24

Child Study Team report is not required. A neuropsychological or comprehensive psycho-educational evaluation is required for admission. Tests required as part of this documentation:

- [x] WAIS-IV
- [ ] WISC-IV
- [ ] SATA
- [x] Woodcock-Johnson
- [ ] Nelson-Denny Reading Test
- [ ] Other

UNDERGRADUATE STUDENT BODY

Total undergraduate student enrollment: 11,414 Men, 9,855 Women.

Composition of student body (fall 2004):

	Undergraduate	Freshmen
International	1.7	1.0
Black	3.3	3.1
American Indian	0.7	0.7
Asian-American	2.9	2.3
Hispanic	10.3	11.2
White	80.9	81.4
Unreported	0.2	0.3
	100.0%	100.0%

6% are from out of state. 14% join a fraternity and 19% join a sorority. Average age of full-time undergraduates is 21. 22% of classes have fewer than 20 students, 56% have between 20 and 50 students, 22% have more than 50 students.

STUDENT HOUSING

87% of freshmen live in college housing. Freshmen are required to live on campus. Housing is guaranteed for all undergraduates. Campus can house 6,354 undergraduates. Single rooms are not available for students with medical or special needs.

EXPENSES

Tuition (2005-06): $3,870 per year (in-state), $12,150 (out-of-state).
Room: $3,663. Board: $3,212.
Additional cost for LD program/services: $1,250 per semester.

LD SERVICES

LD program is limited to 1 of students.

LD services available to:

- [x] Freshmen
- [x] Sophomores
- [x] Juniors
- [ ] Seniors

Academic Accommodations

Curriculum		**In class**	
Foreign language waiver	[ ]	Early syllabus	[ ]
Lighter course load	[ ]	Note takers in class	[x]
Math waiver	[ ]	Priority seating	[x]
Other special classes	[ ]	Tape recorders	[x]
Priority registrations	[ ]	Videotaped classes	[ ]
Substitution of courses	[x]	Text on tape	[x]
Exams		**Services**	
Extended time	[x]	Diagnostic tests	[ ]
Oral exams	[ ]	Learning centers	[x]
Take home exams	[x]	Proofreaders	[ ]
Exams on tape or computer	[ ]	Readers	[x]
Untimed exams	[x]	Reading Machines/Kurzweil	[ ]
Other accommodations	[ ]	Special bookstore section	[ ]
		Typists	[x]

Credit toward degree is not given for remedial courses taken.

Counseling Services

- [ ] Academic
- [ ] Psychological
- [ ] Student Support groups
- [ ] Vocational

Tutoring

Individual tutoring is available daily.

	Individual	Group
Time management	[x]	[x]
Organizational skills	[x]	[x]
Learning strategies	[x]	[x]
Study skills	[x]	[x]
Content area	[x]	[ ]
Writing lab	[x]	[ ]
Math lab	[x]	[ ]

LD PROGRAM STAFF

Total number of LD Program staff (including director):

Full Time: 6 Part Time: 6

There is an advisor/advocate from the LD program available to students.

Key staff person available to work with LD students: Frank V. Silvas, Director.

LD Program web site: www.techniques.ttu.edu

University of Texas at Arlington

Arlington, TX

Address: 701 S. Nedderman Drive, Arlington, TX, 76019-0111
Admissions telephone: 817 272-6287
Admissions FAX: 817 272-3435
Interim Director of Admissions: Hans Gatterdam
Admissions e-mail: admissions@uta.edu
Web site: http://www.uta.edu
SAT Code: 6013 ACT Code: 4200

LD program name: Office for Students with Disabilities
LD program address: Box 19355, Arlington, TX, 76016
Director/Dean of Students OSD: Dianne Hengst, Psy. D.
LD program telephone: 817 272-3364
LD program e-mail: dianne@uta.edu
LD program enrollment: 100, Total campus enrollment: 19,114

GENERAL

University of Texas at Arlington is a public, coed, four-year institution. 390-acre, urban campus in Arlington (population: 332,969), 13 miles from Fort Worth and 23 miles from Dallas. Served by bus; major airport and train serve Dallas-Fort Worth. School operates transportation around campus. 4-1-4-1 system.

LD ADMISSIONS

Students do not complete a separate application and are not simultaneously accepted to the LD program. A member of the LD program does not sit on the admissions committee. A personal interview is not required. Essay is not required.

SECONDARY SCHOOL REQUIREMENTS

Graduation from secondary school required; GED accepted. The following course distribution required: 4 units of English, 3 units of math, 3 units of science, 2 units of foreign language, 3 units of social studies, 5 units of academic electives.

TESTING

SAT Reasoning or ACT required. SAT Subject required.

All enrolled freshmen (fall 2004):

Average SAT I Scores:	Verbal: 526	Math: 540
Average ACT Scores:	Composite: 22	

Child Study Team report is not required. A neuropsychological or comprehensive psycho-educational evaluation is required for admission. Must be dated within 5 months of application. Tests required as part of this documentation:

- [x] WAIS-IV
- [x] WISC-IV
- [x] SATA
- [x] Woodcock-Johnson
- [x] Nelson-Denny Reading Test
- [ ] Other

UNDERGRADUATE STUDENT BODY

Total undergraduate student enrollment: 7,620 Men, 8,710 Women.

Composition of student body (fall 2004):

	Undergraduate	Freshmen
International	2.1	5.4
Black	12.6	14.0
American Indian	0.5	0.8
Asian-American	13.7	11.9
Hispanic	13.6	12.5
White	57.5	55.4
Unreported	0.0	0.0
	100.0%	100.0%

3% are from out of state. 5% join a fraternity and 4% join a sorority. Average age of full-time undergraduates is 22. 28% of classes have fewer than 20 students, 48% have between 20 and 50 students, 24% have more than 50 students.

STUDENT HOUSING

41% of freshmen live in college housing. Freshmen are not required to live on campus. Housing is guaranteed for all undergraduates. Campus can house 3,352 undergraduates. Single rooms are available for students with medical or special needs. A medical note is required.

EXPENSES

There is no additional cost for LD program/services.

LD SERVICES

LD program size is not limited.

LD services available to:

- [x] Freshmen
- [x] Sophomores
- [x] Juniors
- [x] Seniors

Academic Accommodations

Curriculum		In class	
Foreign language waiver	[ ]	Early syllabus	[ ]
Lighter course load	[ ]	Note takers in class	[x]
Math waiver	[ ]	Priority seating	[x]
Other special classes	[ ]	Tape recorders	[x]
Priority registrations	[ ]	Videotaped classes	[ ]
Substitution of courses	[x]	Text on tape	[ ]
Exams		**Services**	
Extended time	[x]	Diagnostic tests	[ ]
Oral exams	[ ]	Learning centers	[ ]
Take home exams	[ ]	Proofreaders	[ ]
Exams on tape or computer	[ ]	Readers	[x]
Untimed exams	[ ]	Reading Machines/Kurzweil	[x]
Other accommodations	[x]	Special bookstore section	[ ]
		Typists	[x]

Credit toward degree is not given for remedial courses taken.

Counseling Services

- [x] Academic
- [x] Psychological
- [ ] Student Support groups
- [ ] Vocational

Tutoring

Individual tutoring is available.

	Individual	Group
Time management	[ ]	[x]
Organizational skills	[ ]	[x]
Learning strategies	[ ]	[x]
Study skills	[ ]	[x]
Content area	[ ]	[ ]
Writing lab	[ ]	[x]
Math lab	[ ]	[x]

LD PROGRAM STAFF

Total number of LD Program staff (including director):

Full Time: 1 Part Time: 1

There is an advisor/advocate from the LD program available to students. The advisor/advocate meets with students once per month.

Key staff person available to work with LD students: Dianne Hengst, Psy. D., Director, Office for Students with Disabilities and Dean of Students.

LD Program web site: www.uta.edu/disability

University of Texas at Austin

Austin, TX

Address: Main Building, Room 7, Austin, TX, 78712-1111
Admissions telephone: 512 475-7440
Admissions FAX: 512 475-7475
Director of Admissions: Bruce Walker
Admissions e-mail: askadmit@uts.cc.utexas.edu
Web site: http://www.utexas.edu
SAT Code: 6882 ACT Code: 4240

LD program address: 1 University Station A5800
Student Affairs Administrator: Krista Schutz-Hampton
LD program telephone: 512 471-6259
LD program e-mail: khampton@mail.utexas.edu
Total campus enrollment: 37,377

GENERAL

University of Texas at Austin is a public, coed, four-year institution. 360-acre, urban campus in Austin (population: 656,562); branch campuses in Arlington, Brownsville, Dallas, Edinburg, El Paso, Odessa, and San Antonio. Served by air, bus, and train; smaller airport serves San Antonio (65 miles). School operates transportation around the city. Public transportation serves campus. Semester system.

LD ADMISSIONS

Students do not complete a separate application and are not simultaneously accepted to the LD program. A member of the LD program does not sit on the admissions committee. A personal interview is required. Essay is required and may be typed. Admissions requirements that may be waived for LD students varies by individual case.

SECONDARY SCHOOL REQUIREMENTS

Graduation from secondary school required; GED accepted. The following course distribution required: 4 units of English, 3 units of math, 2 units of science, 2 units of foreign language, 3 units of social studies, 2 units of academic electives.

TESTING

SAT Reasoning or ACT required. SAT Subject required.

All enrolled freshmen (fall 2004):

Average SAT I Scores: Verbal: 603 Math: 627
Average ACT Scores: Composite: 26

Child Study Team report is not required. A neuropsychological or comprehensive psycho-educational evaluation is required for admission. Must be dated within 36 months of application. Tests required as part of this documentation:

- ☐ WAIS-IV
- ☐ WISC-IV
- ☐ SATA
- ☒ Woodcock-Johnson
- ☒ Nelson-Denny Reading Test
- ☒ Other

UNDERGRADUATE STUDENT BODY

Total undergraduate student enrollment: 19,096 Men, 19,513 Women.

Composition of student body (fall 2004):

	Undergraduate	Freshmen
International	2.5	3.4
Black	4.5	3.8
American Indian	0.4	0.4
Asian-American	17.9	17.2
Hispanic	16.9	15.2
White	57.5	59.6
Unreported	0.3	0.4
	100.0%	100.0%

5% are from out of state. 9% join a fraternity and 12% join a sorority. Average age of full-time undergraduates is 21. 34% of classes have fewer than 20 students, 42% have between 20 and 50 students, 24% have more than 50 students.

STUDENT HOUSING

54% of freshmen live in college housing. Freshmen are not required to live on campus. Housing is not guaranteed for all undergraduates. Dorm and apartment housing space is limited, but is open to everyone. A certain limited number of spaces (our Living Learning Centers) are reserved for freshmen only. Campus can house 7,413 undergraduates. Single rooms are available for students with medical or special needs. A medical note is required.

EXPENSES

There is no additional cost for LD program/services.

LD SERVICES

LD program size is not limited.

LD services available to:

☒ Freshmen ☒ Sophomores ☒ Juniors ☒ Seniors

Academic Accommodations

Curriculum		In class	
Foreign language waiver	☐	Early syllabus	☐
Lighter course load	☒	Note takers in class	☐
Math waiver	☐	Priority seating	☐
Other special classes	☐	Tape recorders	☐
Priority registrations	☒	Videotaped classes	☐
Substitution of courses	☐	Text on tape	☐
Exams		**Services**	
Extended time	☒	Diagnostic tests	☐
Oral exams	☐	Learning centers	☒
Take home exams	☐	Proofreaders	☐
Exams on tape or computer	☐	Readers	☐
Untimed exams	☐	Reading Machines/Kurzweil	☐
Other accommodations	☐	Special bookstore section	☐
		Typists	☐

Credit toward degree is not given for remedial courses taken.

Counseling Services

- ☐ Academic
- ☐ Psychological
- ☐ Student Support groups
- ☐ Vocational

Tutoring

Individual tutoring is available.

	Individual	Group
Time management	☐	☒
Organizational skills	☐	☒
Learning strategies	☐	☒
Study skills	☐	☒
Content area	☐	☒
Writing lab	☐	☒
Math lab	☐	☒

UNIQUE LD PROGRAM FEATURES

Services are determined on an individual basis, based on appropriate documentation.

LD PROGRAM STAFF

Total number of LD Program staff (including director):

Full Time: 3 Part Time: 3

There is an advisor/advocate from the LD program available to students.

Key staff person available to work with LD students: Krista Schutz-Hampton or Alyssa Joseph-West, Student Affairs Administrators.

LD Program web site: http://deanofstudents.utexas.edu/ssd

University of Texas at El Paso

El Paso, TX

Address: 500 W. University Avenue, El Paso, TX, 79968
Admissions telephone: 915 747-5890
Admissions FAX: 915 747-8893
Director of Admissions: Tammie Aragon-Campos
Admissions e-mail: futureminer@utep.edu
Web site: http://www.utep.edu
SAT Code: 6829 ACT Code: 4223

Director: Susan Lopez
LD program telephone: 915 747-5148
LD program e-mail: slopez@utep.edu
Total campus enrollment: 15,592

GENERAL

University of Texas at El Paso is a public, coed, four-year institution. 330-acre campus in El Paso (population: 563,662). Served by air, bus, and train. Public transportation serves campus. Semester system.

LD ADMISSIONS

A personal interview is required. Essay is not required.

SECONDARY SCHOOL REQUIREMENTS

Graduation from secondary school required; GED accepted.

TESTING

SAT Reasoning or ACT required of some applicants.

All enrolled freshmen (fall 2004):

Average SAT I Scores:	Verbal: 454	Math: 461
Average ACT Scores:	Composite: 19	

Child Study Team report is not required. Tests required as part of this documentation:

- [ ] WAIS-IV
- [ ] WISC-IV
- [ ] SATA
- [ ] Woodcock-Johnson
- [ ] Nelson-Denny Reading Test
- [ ] Other

UNDERGRADUATE STUDENT BODY

Total undergraduate student enrollment: 6,221 Men, 7,421 Women.

Composition of student body (fall 2004):

	Undergraduate	Freshmen
International	9.5	10.5
Black	2.7	2.5
American Indian	0.1	0.2
Asian-American	0.9	1.1
Hispanic	76.6	74.9
White	8.3	10.2
Unreported	1.9	0.6
	100.0%	100.0%

3% are from out of state. Average age of full-time undergraduates is 22. 31% of classes have fewer than 20 students, 56% have between 20 and 50 students, 13% have more than 50 students.

STUDENT HOUSING

Freshmen are not required to live on campus. Housing is guaranteed for all undergraduates. Campus can house 428 undergraduates.

EXPENSES

Tuition (2005-06): $3,930 per year (in-state), $12,210 (out-of-state).
Room: $4,095.

There is no additional cost for LD program/services.

LD SERVICES

LD program size is not limited.

LD services available to:

- [ ] Freshmen
- [ ] Sophomores
- [ ] Juniors
- [ ] Seniors

Academic Accommodations

Curriculum		In class	
Foreign language waiver	[ ]	Early syllabus	[ ]
Lighter course load	[x]	Note takers in class	[x]
Math waiver	[ ]	Priority seating	[ ]
Other special classes	[ ]	Tape recorders	[x]
Priority registrations	[ ]	Videotaped classes	[ ]
Substitution of courses	[ ]	Text on tape	[ ]
Exams		**Services**	
Extended time	[x]	Diagnostic tests	[x]
Oral exams	[x]	Learning centers	[ ]
Take home exams	[ ]	Proofreaders	[ ]
Exams on tape or computer	[ ]	Readers	[x]
Untimed exams	[ ]	Reading Machines/Kurzweil	[x]
Other accommodations	[ ]	Special bookstore section	[ ]
		Typists	[ ]

Credit toward degree is not given for remedial courses taken.

Counseling Services

- [ ] Academic
- [ ] Psychological
- [ ] Student Support groups
- [ ] Vocational

Tutoring

	Individual	Group
Time management	[ ]	[ ]
Organizational skills	[ ]	[ ]
Learning strategies	[ ]	[ ]
Study skills	[ ]	[ ]
Content area	[ ]	[ ]
Writing lab	[ ]	[ ]
Math lab	[ ]	[ ]

LD PROGRAM STAFF

Total number of LD Program staff (including director):

Full Time: 2 Part Time: 2

Key staff person available to work with LD students: Susan Lopez, Director.

University of Texas at Dallas

Richardson, TX

Address: 800 W. Campbell Road, Richardson, TX, 75080
Admissions telephone: 800 889-2443
Admissions FAX: 972 883-6803
Director of Admissions: Sue Sherbet
Admissions e-mail: admissions-status@utdallas.edu
Web site: http://www.utdallas.edu
SAT Code: 6897 ACT Code: 4243

LD program name: Disability Services
LD program address: P.O. Box 830688, SU22
Coordinator: Kerry Tate
LD program telephone: 972 883-2098
LD program e-mail: ktate@utdallas.edu
LD program enrollment: 52, Total campus enrollment: 9,070

GENERAL

University of Texas at Dallas is a public, coed, four-year institution. 455-acre, suburban campus in Richardson (population: 91,802), 18 miles from Dallas; branch campus in Dallas. Major airport, bus, and train serve Dallas. Public transportation serves campus. Semester system.

LD ADMISSIONS

Students do not complete a separate application and are not simultaneously accepted to the LD program. A member of the LD program does not sit on the admissions committee. A personal interview is not required. Essay is required and may be typed.

For fall 2004, 62 completed self-identified LD applications were received.

SECONDARY SCHOOL REQUIREMENTS

Graduation from secondary school required; GED accepted. The following course distribution required: 4 units of English, 4 units of math, 3 units of science, 2 units of foreign language, 3 units of social studies, 2 units of academic electives.

TESTING

SAT Reasoning required; ACT may be substituted. SAT Subject required.

All enrolled freshmen (fall 2004):

Average SAT I Scores:	Verbal: 610	Math: 635
Average ACT Scores:	Composite: 27	

Child Study Team report is not required. A neuropsychological or comprehensive psycho-educational evaluation is required for admission. Must be dated within 48 months of application. Tests required as part of this documentation:

- ■ WAIS-IV
- ☐ WISC-IV
- ☐ SATA
- ■ Woodcock-Johnson
- ■ Nelson-Denny Reading Test
- ■ Other

UNDERGRADUATE STUDENT BODY

Total undergraduate student enrollment: 3,893 Men, 3,598 Women.

Composition of student body (fall 2004):

	Undergraduate	Freshmen
International	3.7	5.3
Black	5.6	6.8
American Indian	0.6	0.7
Asian-American	20.4	19.1
Hispanic	8.7	9.7
White	60.1	57.7
Unreported	0.8	0.6
	100.0%	100.0%

10% are from out of state. 5% join a fraternity and 3% join a sorority. Average age of full-time undergraduates is 22. 29% of classes have fewer than 20 students, 44% have between 20 and 50 students, 26% have more than 50 students.

STUDENT HOUSING

73% of freshmen live in college housing. Freshmen are not required to live on campus. Housing is guaranteed for all undergraduates. Campus can house 3,722 undergraduates. Single rooms are available for students with medical or special needs. A medical note is required.

EXPENSES

Tuition (2005-06): $6,832 per year (in-state), $15,112 (out-of-state).
Room: $3,700. Board: $2,575.
There is no additional cost for LD program/services.

LD SERVICES

LD program size is not limited.

LD services available to:

■ Freshmen ■ Sophomores ■ Juniors ■ Seniors

Academic Accommodations

Curriculum		In class	
Foreign language waiver	☐	Early syllabus	☐
Lighter course load	■	Note takers in class	■
Math waiver	☐	Priority seating	☐
Other special classes	■	Tape recorders	■
Priority registrations	☐	Videotaped classes	☐
Substitution of courses	☐	Text on tape	☐
Exams		**Services**	
Extended time	■	Diagnostic tests	☐
Oral exams	■	Learning centers	☐
Take home exams	☐	Proofreaders	☐
Exams on tape or computer	■	Readers	■
Untimed exams	☐	Reading Machines/Kurzweil	■
Other accommodations	■	Special bookstore section	☐
		Typists	☐

Credit toward degree is not given for remedial courses taken.

Counseling Services

- ■ Academic — Meets 4 times per academic year
- ☐ Psychological
- ☐ Student Support groups
- ☐ Vocational

Tutoring

Individual tutoring is available weekly.

Average size of tutoring groups: 3

	Individual	Group
Time management	☐	☐
Organizational skills	☐	☐
Learning strategies	■	■
Study skills	☐	☐
Content area	☐	☐
Writing lab	■	■
Math lab	■	■

LD PROGRAM STAFF

Total number of LD Program staff (including director):

Full Time: 1 Part Time: 1

There is no advisor/advocate from the LD program available to students.

Key staff person available to work with LD students: Kerry Tate, Coordinator.

LD Program web site: http://www.utdallas.edu/student/slife/hcsvc.html

University of Texas - Pan American

Edinburg, TX

Address: 1201 W. University Drive, Edinburg, TX, 78541-2999
Admissions telephone: 956 381-2206
Admissions FAX: 956 381-2212
Registrar and Director of Admissions: William Morris
Admissions e-mail: admissions@panam.edu
Web site: http://www.utpa.edu
SAT Code: 6570 ACT Code: 4142

LD program address: 1201 W. University Drive, EH 1.101
Director of Student Health Services: Glenn R. Gray
LD program telephone: 956 316-7005
LD program e-mail: grayr@utpa.edu
Total campus enrollment: 14,788

GENERAL

University of Texas - Pan American is a public, coed, four-year institution. 200-acre campus in Edinburg (population: 48,465), 150 miles from Corpus Christi. Served by bus. Public transportation serves campus. Semester system.

LD ADMISSIONS

Students complete a separate application and are not simultaneously accepted to the LD program. A member of the LD program does not sit on the admissions committee. A personal interview is not required. Essay is not required.

For fall 2004, 138 completed self-identified LD applications were received.

SECONDARY SCHOOL REQUIREMENTS

Graduation from secondary school required; GED accepted. The following course distribution required: 4 units of English, 3 units of math, 3 units of science, 2 units of foreign language, 4 units of social studies, 3 units of academic electives.

TESTING

ACT required; SAT Reasoning may be substituted. SAT Subject recommended.

All enrolled freshmen (fall 2004):

Average SAT I Scores: Verbal: Math:
Average ACT Scores: Composite: 18

Child Study Team report is not required. A neuropsychological or comprehensive psycho-educational evaluation is required for admission. Must be dated within 36 months of application. Tests required as part of this documentation:

■ WAIS-IV
■ WISC-IV
■ SATA
■ Woodcock-Johnson
■ Nelson-Denny Reading Test
☐ Other

UNDERGRADUATE STUDENT BODY

Total undergraduate student enrollment: 4,955 Men, 7,016 Women.

Composition of student body (fall 2004):

	Undergraduate	Freshmen
International	5.1	2.8
Black	0.2	0.2
American Indian	0.0	0.1
Asian-American	1.3	1.1
Hispanic	89.6	88.7
White	3.8	5.0
Unreported	0.0	2.1
	100.0%	100.0%

1% join a fraternity and 1% join a sorority. Average age of full-time undergraduates is 22. 17% of classes have fewer than 20 students, 65% have between 20 and 50 students, 18% have more than 50 students.

STUDENT HOUSING

Freshmen are not required to live on campus. Housing is guaranteed for all undergraduates. Campus can house 592 undergraduates.

EXPENSES

Tuition (2005-06): $2,564 per year (in-state), $11,564 (out-of-state).
Room: $2,406. Board: $1,827.
There is no additional cost for LD program/services.

LD SERVICES

LD program size is not limited.

LD services available to:

■ Freshmen ■ Sophomores ■ Juniors ■ Seniors

Academic Accommodations

Curriculum
Foreign language waiver ☐
Lighter course load ☐
Math waiver ☐
Other special classes ☐
Priority registrations ■
Substitution of courses ■

Exams
Extended time ■
Oral exams ■
Take home exams ☐
Exams on tape or computer ■
Untimed exams ■
Other accommodations ■

In class
Early syllabus ■
Note takers in class ■
Priority seating ■
Tape recorders ■
Videotaped classes ■
Text on tape ☐

Services
Diagnostic tests ■
Learning centers ■
Proofreaders ☐
Readers ■
Reading Machines/Kurzweil ■
Special bookstore section ☐
Typists ■

Credit toward degree is not given for remedial courses taken.

Counseling Services

☐ Academic
☐ Psychological
☐ Student Support groups
☐ Vocational

Tutoring

Individual tutoring is not available.

	Individual	Group
Time management	☐	☐
Organizational skills	☐	☐
Learning strategies	☐	☐
Study skills	☐	☐
Content area	☐	☐
Writing lab	☐	☐
Math lab	☐	☐

LD PROGRAM STAFF

Total number of LD Program staff (including director):

Full Time: 4 Part Time: 4

There is no advisor/advocate from the LD program available to students. 3 graduate students are available to work with LD students.

Key staff person available to work with LD students: Esperanza Cavazos, Associate Director.

University of Texas of the Permian Basin

Odessa, TX

Address: 4901 E. University Boulevard, Odessa, TX, 79762-0001
Admissions telephone: 432 552-2605
Admissions FAX: 432 552-3605
Director of Admissions: Vickie Gomez, M.A.
Admissions e-mail: admissions@utpb.edu
Web site: http://www.utpb.edu
SAT Code: 448 ACT Code: 4225

LD program name: PASS Office
Director of PASS Office: Efren D. Castro, Ed.D.
LD program telephone: 432 552-2630
LD program e-mail: castro_e@utpb.edu
LD program enrollment: 20, Total campus enrollment: 2,585

GENERAL

University of Texas of the Permian Basin is a public, coed, four-year institution. 600-acre, urban campus in Odessa (population: 90,943), 138 miles from Lubbock. Served by bus; airport serves Midland (10 miles). Semester system.

LD ADMISSIONS

Students do not complete a separate application and are not simultaneously accepted to the LD program. A member of the LD program does sit on the admissions committee. A personal interview is not required. Essay is not required. Admissions requirements for LD students are the same as requirements for all students, including conditional or provisional admissions. Contact Admissions Office for information. LD services are provided by application after student is admitted to the school.

For fall 2004, 20 completed self-identified LD applications were received. 20 applications were offered admission, and 20 enrolled.

SECONDARY SCHOOL REQUIREMENTS

Graduation from secondary school not required. The following course distribution required: 4 units of English, 3 units of math, 2 units of science, 2 units of foreign language, 2 units of social studies, 1 unit of history, 6 units of academic electives.

TESTING

SAT Reasoning or ACT required. SAT Subject recommended.

All enrolled freshmen (fall 2004):

Average SAT I Scores:	Verbal: 500	Math: 499
Average ACT Scores:	Composite: 22	

Child Study Team report is not required. A neuropsychological or comprehensive psycho-educational evaluation is required for admission. Must be dated within 36 months of application. Tests required as part of this documentation:

- ☑ WAIS-IV
- ☑ WISC-IV
- ☐ SATA
- ☑ Woodcock-Johnson
- ☑ Nelson-Denny Reading Test
- ☑ Other

UNDERGRADUATE STUDENT BODY

Total undergraduate student enrollment: 552 Men, 1,027 Women.

Composition of student body (fall 2004):

	Undergraduate	Freshmen
International	0.8	0.3
Black	3.8	4.5
American Indian	0.4	0.5
Asian-American	2.3	0.7
Hispanic	35.6	36.5
White	57.1	57.0
Unreported	0.0	0.5
	100.0%	100.0%

3% are from out of state. 1% join a fraternity. Average age of full-time undergraduates is 24. 44% of classes have fewer than 20 students, 47% have between 20 and 50 students, 9% have more than 50 students.

STUDENT HOUSING

40% of freshmen live in college housing. Freshmen are not required to live on campus. Housing is guaranteed for all undergraduates. Campus can house 422 undergraduates. Single rooms are available for students with medical or special needs. A medical note is required.

EXPENSES

Tuition (2005-06): $3,270 per year (in-state), $11,340 (out-of-state).

Room: $2,036. Board: $2,042.

There is no additional cost for LD program/services.

LD SERVICES

LD program size is not limited.

LD services available to:

☑ Freshmen ☑ Sophomores ☑ Juniors ☑ Seniors

Academic Accommodations

Curriculum		In class	
Foreign language waiver	☑	Early syllabus	☑
Lighter course load	☑	Note takers in class	☑
Math waiver	☑	Priority seating	☑
Other special classes	☐	Tape recorders	☑
Priority registrations	☑	Videotaped classes	☑
Substitution of courses	☑	Text on tape	☑
Exams		**Services**	
Extended time	☑	Diagnostic tests	☑
Oral exams	☑	Learning centers	☑
Take home exams	☑	Proofreaders	☑
Exams on tape or computer	☑	Readers	☑
Untimed exams	☑	Reading Machines/Kurzweil	☑
Other accommodations	☑	Special bookstore section	☑
		Typists	☑

Credit toward degree is not given for remedial courses taken.

Counseling Services

- ☑ Academic
- ☑ Psychological
- ☑ Student Support groups
- ☑ Vocational

Tutoring

Individual tutoring is available weekly.

Average size of tutoring groups: 3

	Individual	Group
Time management	☑	☑
Organizational skills	☑	☑
Learning strategies	☑	☑
Study skills	☑	☑
Content area	☑	☑
Writing lab	☑	☑
Math lab	☑	☑

LD PROGRAM STAFF

Total number of LD Program staff (including director):

Full Time: 2 Part Time: 2

There is an advisor/advocate from the LD program available to students. The advisor/advocate meets with faculty once per month and students once per month. 20 graduate students and 30 peer tutors are available to work with LD students.

Key staff person available to work with LD students: Efren D. Castro, Ed.D., Director of PASS Office.

LD Program web site: www.utpb.edu

University of Texas at San Antonio

San Antonio, TX

Address: 6900 N. Loop 1604 W, San Antonio, TX, 78249
Admissions telephone: 800 669-0919
Admissions FAX: 210 458-2001
Interim Director of Admissions and Registrar: George Norton
Admissions e-mail: prospects@utsa.edu
Web site: http://www.utsa.edu
SAT Code: 6919 ACT Code: 4239

Director, Disability Services: Lorraine Harrison
LD program telephone: 210 458-4157
LD program e-mail: LHarrison@utsa.edu
Total campus enrollment: 22,537

GENERAL

University of Texas at San Antonio is a public, coed, four-year institution. 600-acre, suburban campus in San Antonio (population: 1,144,646); additional downtown center. Served by air, bus, and train. School operates transportation to apartments on and near campus and to downtown center. Public transportation serves campus. Semester system.

LD ADMISSIONS

A personal interview is not required. Essay is not required.

SECONDARY SCHOOL REQUIREMENTS

Graduation from secondary school required; GED accepted.

TESTING

SAT Reasoning or ACT required. SAT Subject required.

All enrolled freshmen (fall 2004):

Average SAT I Scores: Verbal: 488 Math: 496
Average ACT Scores: Composite: 20

Child Study Team report is not required. Tests required as part of this documentation:

- ☐ WAIS-IV
- ☐ WISC-IV
- ☐ SATA
- ☐ Woodcock-Johnson
- ☐ Nelson-Denny Reading Test
- ☐ Other

UNDERGRADUATE STUDENT BODY

Total undergraduate student enrollment: 7,167 Men, 8,859 Women.

Composition of student body (fall 2004):

	Undergraduate	Freshmen
International	1.8	2.0
Black	7.3	6.5
American Indian	0.6	0.5
Asian-American	5.3	4.9
Hispanic	41.5	46.4
White	43.5	39.7
Unreported	0.0	0.0
	100.0%	100.0%

4% are from out of state. Average age of full-time undergraduates is 22.

STUDENT HOUSING

2% of freshmen live in college housing. Freshmen are not required to live on campus. Housing is not guaranteed for all undergraduates. Campus can house 1,002 undergraduates.

EXPENSES

Tuition (2005-06): $3,968 per year (in-state), $12,248 (out-of-state). Room: $4,595. Board: $1,210.

There is no additional cost for LD program/services.

LD SERVICES

LD program size is not limited.

LD services available to:

☐ Freshmen ☐ Sophomores ☐ Juniors ☐ Seniors

Academic Accommodations

Curriculum		**In class**	
Foreign language waiver	☐	Early syllabus	☐
Lighter course load	■	Note takers in class	■
Math waiver	☐	Priority seating	☐
Other special classes	☐	Tape recorders	■
Priority registrations	☐	Videotaped classes	☐
Substitution of courses	☐	Text on tape	☐
Exams		**Services**	
Extended time	☐	Diagnostic tests	☐
Oral exams	☐	Learning centers	☐
Take home exams	☐	Proofreaders	☐
Exams on tape or computer	☐	Readers	■
Untimed exams	☐	Reading Machines/Kurzweil	■
Other accommodations	☐	Special bookstore section	☐
		Typists	☐

Credit toward degree is not given for remedial courses taken.

Counseling Services

- ☐ Academic
- ☐ Psychological
- ☐ Student Support groups
- ☐ Vocational

Tutoring

	Individual	Group
Time management	☐	☐
Organizational skills	☐	☐
Learning strategies	☐	☐
Study skills	☐	☐
Content area	☐	☐
Writing lab	☐	☐
Math lab	☐	☐

LD PROGRAM STAFF

Total number of LD Program staff (including director):

Full Time: 2 Part Time: 2

Key staff person available to work with LD students: Lorraine Harrison, Director, Disability Services.

University of Texas at Tyler

Tyler, TX

Address: 3900 University Boulevard, Tyler, TX, 75799
Admissions telephone: 800 UT-TYLER
Admissions FAX: 903 566-7068
Dean of Enrollment Management: James Hutto
Admissions e-mail: admissions@mail.uttyl.edu
Web site: http://www.uttyler.edu
SAT Code: 389 ACT Code: 4231

LD program address: 3900 University Boulevard
Director: Ida MacDonald, M.A., LPC
LD program telephone: 903 566-7079
LD program e-mail: Ida_MacDonald@uttyler.edu
LD program enrollment: 13, Total campus enrollment: 4,086

GENERAL

University of Texas at Tyler is a public, coed, four-year institution. 200-acre, suburban campus in Tyler (population: 83,650), 90 miles from Dallas. Served by air and bus; major airport serves Dallas; train serves Longview (45 miles). Public transportation serves campus. Semester system.

LD ADMISSIONS

Students do not complete a separate application and are not simultaneously accepted to the LD program. A member of the LD program does not sit on the admissions committee. A personal interview is required. Essay is not required.

For fall 2004, 15 completed self-identified LD applications were received.

SECONDARY SCHOOL REQUIREMENTS

Graduation from secondary school required; GED accepted. The following course distribution required: 4 units of English, 3 units of math, 3 units of science, 2 units of foreign language, 3 units of social studies.

TESTING

SAT Reasoning or ACT required. SAT Subject recommended.

All enrolled freshmen (fall 2004):

Average SAT I Scores: Verbal: 527 Math: 541
Average ACT Scores: Composite: 23

Child Study Team report is not required. A neuropsychological or comprehensive psycho-educational evaluation is required for admission. Must be dated within 36 months of application. Tests required as part of this documentation:

- ■ WAIS-IV
- ☐ WISC-IV
- ☐ SATA
- ■ Woodcock-Johnson
- ■ Nelson-Denny Reading Test
- ☐ Other

UNDERGRADUATE STUDENT BODY

Total undergraduate student enrollment: 944 Men, 1,758 Women.

Composition of student body (fall 2004):

	Undergraduate	Freshmen
International	0.2	1.4
Black	6.2	9.7
American Indian	1.8	1.0
Asian-American	2.8	1.8
Hispanic	4.4	5.4
White	82.4	78.8
Unreported	2.2	1.9
	100.0%	100.0%

1% are from out of state. Average age of full-time undergraduates is 23. 48% of classes have fewer than 20 students, 44% have between 20 and 50 students, 8% have more than 50 students.

STUDENT HOUSING

48% of freshmen live in college housing. Freshmen are not required to live on campus. Housing is not guaranteed for all undergraduates. Campus can house 584 undergraduates.

EXPENSES

Tuition (2005-06): $3,450 per year (in-state), $11,730 (out-of-state).
Room & Board: $7,010.
There is no additional cost for LD program/services.

LD SERVICES

LD program size is not limited.

LD services available to:

■ Freshmen ■ Sophomores ■ Juniors ■ Seniors

Academic Accommodations

Curriculum		In class	
Foreign language waiver	☐	Early syllabus	☐
Lighter course load	☐	Note takers in class	■
Math waiver	☐	Priority seating	■
Other special classes	☐	Tape recorders	■
Priority registrations	☐	Videotaped classes	■
Substitution of courses	■	Text on tape	☐
Exams		**Services**	
Extended time	■	Diagnostic tests	☐
Oral exams	■	Learning centers	☐
Take home exams	☐	Proofreaders	☐
Exams on tape or computer	■	Readers	■
Untimed exams	☐	Reading Machines/Kurzweil	■
Other accommodations	■	Special bookstore section	☐
		Typists	■

Credit toward degree is not given for remedial courses taken.

Counseling Services

- ☐ Academic
- ■ Psychological
- ☐ Student Support groups
- ■ Vocational

Tutoring

Individual tutoring is not available.

	Individual	Group
Time management	■	☐
Organizational skills	■	☐
Learning strategies	■	☐
Study skills	■	☐
Content area	☐	☐
Writing lab	☐	☐
Math lab	☐	☐

LD PROGRAM STAFF

There is an advisor/advocate from the LD program available to students.

Key staff person available to work with LD students: Ida MacDonald, M.A., LPC, Director, Student Services.

Texas Wesleyan University

Fort Worth, TX

Address: 1201 Wesleyan, Fort Worth, TX, 76105-1536
Admissions telephone: 800 580-8980
Admissions FAX: 817 531-4425
Interim Provost: Pati Alexander, Vice President of Enrollment
Admissions e-mail: freshmen@txwesleyan.edu
Web site: http://www.txwesleyan.edu
SAT Code: 6828 ACT Code: 4222

Director of Counseling: Mike Ellison
LD program telephone: 817 531-4444
LD program e-mail: mellison@txwes.edu
Total campus enrollment: 1,491

GENERAL

Texas Wesleyan University is a private, coed, four-year institution. 74-acre, urban campus in Fort Worth (population: 534,694). Served by air and bus; airport serves Dallas (35 miles). Public transportation serves campus. Semester system.

LD ADMISSIONS

A personal interview is recommended. Essay is required and may be typed.

SECONDARY SCHOOL REQUIREMENTS

Graduation from secondary school required; GED accepted.

TESTING

Child Study Team report is not required. Tests required as part of this documentation:

- ❑ WAIS-IV
- ❑ WISC-IV
- ❑ SATA
- ❑ Woodcock-Johnson
- ❑ Nelson-Denny Reading Test
- ❑ Other

UNDERGRADUATE STUDENT BODY

Total undergraduate student enrollment: 601 Men, 1,113 Women.

Composition of student body (fall 2004):

	Undergraduate	Freshmen
International	2.5	0.5
Black	22.0	18.9
American Indian	1.9	0.5
Asian-American	1.9	1.1
Hispanic	18.2	20.5
White	46.0	43.9
Unreported	7.5	14.6
	100.0%	100.0%

1% are from out of state. 60% of classes have fewer than 20 students, 40% have between 20 and 50 students.

STUDENT HOUSING

Housing is guaranteed for all undergraduates. Campus can house 250 undergraduates.

EXPENSES

Tuition (2005-06): $12,950 per year. Tuition varies by program.
Room: $3,750. Board: $1,255.
There is no additional cost for LD program/services.

LD SERVICES

LD program size is not limited.

LD services available to:

❑ Freshmen ❑ Sophomores ❑ Juniors ❑ Seniors

Academic Accommodations

Curriculum		**In class**	
Foreign language waiver	❑	Early syllabus	❑
Lighter course load	■	Note takers in class	❑
Math waiver	❑	Priority seating	❑
Other special classes	❑	Tape recorders	❑
Priority registrations	❑	Videotaped classes	❑
Substitution of courses	❑	Text on tape	❑
Exams		**Services**	
Extended time	❑	Diagnostic tests	❑
Oral exams	❑	Learning centers	❑
Take home exams	❑	Proofreaders	❑
Exams on tape or computer	❑	Readers	❑
Untimed exams	❑	Reading Machines/Kurzweil	❑
Other accommodations	❑	Special bookstore section	❑
		Typists	❑

Credit toward degree is given for remedial courses taken.

Counseling Services

- ❑ Academic
- ❑ Psychological
- ❑ Student Support groups
- ❑ Vocational

Tutoring

	Individual	Group
Time management	❑	❑
Organizational skills	❑	❑
Learning strategies	❑	❑
Study skills	❑	❑
Content area	❑	❑
Writing lab	❑	❑
Math lab	❑	❑

LD PROGRAM STAFF

Total number of LD Program staff (including director):

Full Time: 1 Part Time: 1

Key staff person available to work with LD students: Joseph Scott Methin, Counselor.

Texas Woman's University

Denton, TX

Address: Box 425619, Denton, TX, 76204-5587
Admissions telephone: 888 948-9984
Admissions FAX: 940 898-3081
Director of Admissions: Erma Nieto
Admissions e-mail: admissions@twu.edu
Web site: http://www.twu.edu
SAT Code: 6826 ACT Code: 4224

Director, Disability Support Services: JoAnn Nunnelly
LD program telephone: 940 898-3835
LD program e-mail: JNunnelly@twu.edu
Total campus enrollment: 5,826

GENERAL

Texas Woman's University is a public, coed, four-year institution. 270-acre campus in Denton (population: 80,537), 35 miles from Dallas-Ft. Worth; branch campuses in Dallas and Houston. Served by bus; major airport and train serve Dallas-Fort Worth. Public transportation serves campus. Semester system.

SECONDARY SCHOOL REQUIREMENTS

Graduation from secondary school required; GED accepted. The following course distribution required: 4 units of English, 3 units of math, 2 units of science, 2 units of social studies, 11 units of academic electives.

TESTING

SAT Reasoning or ACT required of some applicants. SAT Subject recommended.

All enrolled freshmen (fall 2004):

Average SAT I Scores: Verbal: 489 Math: 478
Average ACT Scores: Composite: 20

Child Study Team report is not required. Tests required as part of this documentation:

- ❑ WAIS-IV
- ❑ WISC-IV
- ❑ SATA
- ❑ Woodcock-Johnson
- ❑ Nelson-Denny Reading Test
- ❑ Other

UNDERGRADUATE STUDENT BODY

Total undergraduate student enrollment: 250 Men, 4,155 Women.

Composition of student body (fall 2004):

	Undergraduate	Freshmen
International	1.4	2.9
Black	25.4	21.6
American Indian	0.6	0.9
Asian-American	7.5	4.8
Hispanic	19.8	13.0
White	45.3	56.7
Unreported	0.0	0.1
	100.0%	100.0%

2% are from out of state. 6% join a sorority. Average age of full-time undergraduates is 25. 47% of classes have fewer than 20 students, 46% have between 20 and 50 students, 7% have more than 50 students.

STUDENT HOUSING

70% of freshmen live in college housing. Freshmen are required to live on campus. Housing is guaranteed for all undergraduates. Campus can house 1,437 undergraduates. Single rooms are available for students with medical or special needs.

EXPENSES

Tuition (2005-06): $3,630 per year (in-state), $10,170 (out-of-state). Room: $2,804. Board: $2,551.

There is no additional cost for LD program/services.

LD SERVICES

LD program size is not limited.

LD services available to:

❑ Freshmen ❑ Sophomores ❑ Juniors ❑ Seniors

Academic Accommodations

Curriculum		**In class**	
Foreign language waiver	❑	Early syllabus	❑
Lighter course load	■	Note takers in class	■
Math waiver	❑	Priority seating	❑
Other special classes	❑	Tape recorders	■
Priority registrations	❑	Videotaped classes	❑
Substitution of courses	❑	Text on tape	❑
Exams		**Services**	
Extended time	■	Diagnostic tests	❑
Oral exams	■	Learning centers	■
Take home exams	❑	Proofreaders	❑
Exams on tape or computer	❑	Readers	■
Untimed exams	❑	Reading Machines/Kurzweil	❑
Other accommodations	❑	Special bookstore section	❑
		Typists	❑

Credit toward degree is not given for remedial courses taken.

Counseling Services

- ❑ Academic
- ❑ Psychological
- ❑ Student Support groups
- ❑ Vocational

Tutoring

	Individual	Group
Time management	❑	❑
Organizational skills	❑	❑
Learning strategies	❑	❑
Study skills	❑	❑
Content area	❑	❑
Writing lab	❑	❑
Math lab	❑	❑

LD PROGRAM STAFF

Key staff person available to work with LD students: JoAnn Nunnelly, Director, Disability Support Services.

West Texas A&M University

Canyon, TX

Address: 2501 Fourth Avenue, Canyon, TX, 79016-0001
Admissions telephone: 800 99-WTAMU
Admissions FAX: 806 651-5285
Director of Admissions: Lila Vars
Admissions e-mail: admissions@mail.wtamu.edu
Web site: http://www.wtamu.edu
SAT Code: 6938 ACT Code: 4250

LD program name: Student Disability Services
LD program address: Box 60923
Counselor: Eric Lathrop
LD program telephone: 806 651-2335
LD program e-mail: elathrop@mail.wtamu.edu
LD program enrollment: 105, Total campus enrollment: 5,822

GENERAL

West Texas A&M University is a public, coed, four-year institution. 135-acre campus in Canyon (population: 12,875), 12 miles from Amarillo. Served by bus; airport serves Amarillo. Semester system.

LD ADMISSIONS

A member of the LD program does not sit on the admissions committee. A personal interview is required. Essay is not required. No admissions requirements may be waived for LD students.

For fall 2004, 86 completed self-identified LD applications were received. 25 applications were offered admission, and 25 enrolled.

SECONDARY SCHOOL REQUIREMENTS

Graduation from secondary school required; GED accepted. The following course distribution required: 4 units of English, 3 units of math, 3 units of science.

TESTING

SAT Reasoning or ACT required. SAT Subject recommended.

All enrolled freshmen (fall 2004):

Average SAT I Scores: Verbal: 503 Math: 507
Average ACT Scores: Composite: 21

Child Study Team report is not required. A neuropsychological or comprehensive psycho-educational evaluation is required for admission. Tests required as part of this documentation:

- ☑ WAIS-IV
- ☑ WISC-IV
- ☐ SATA
- ☑ Woodcock-Johnson
- ☐ Nelson-Denny Reading Test
- ☐ Other

UNDERGRADUATE STUDENT BODY

Total undergraduate student enrollment: 2,369 Men, 3,026 Women.

Composition of student body (fall 2004):

	Undergraduate	Freshmen
International	0.5	1.8
Black	3.8	4.4
American Indian	1.0	1.0
Asian-American	1.5	1.4
Hispanic	18.6	13.9
White	74.6	77.5
Unreported	0.0	0.0
	100.0%	100.0%

8% are from out of state. 4% join a fraternity and 4% join a sorority. Average age of full-time undergraduates is 22. 34% of classes have fewer than 20 students, 57% have between 20 and 50 students, 9% have more than 50 students.

STUDENT HOUSING

Freshmen are required to live on campus. Housing is guaranteed for all undergraduates. Campus can house 1,500 undergraduates. Single rooms are not available for students with medical or special needs.

EXPENSES

Tuition (2005-06): $2,760 per year (in-state), $11,040 (out-of-state).
There is no additional cost for LD program/services.

LD SERVICES

LD program size is not limited.

LD services available to:

☑ Freshmen ☑ Sophomores ☑ Juniors ☑ Seniors

Academic Accommodations

Curriculum		In class	
Foreign language waiver	☐	Early syllabus	☐
Lighter course load	☑	Note takers in class	☑
Math waiver	☐	Priority seating	☐
Other special classes	☐	Tape recorders	☑
Priority registrations	☐	Videotaped classes	☐
Substitution of courses	☐	Text on tape	☐
Exams		**Services**	
Extended time	☑	Diagnostic tests	☐
Oral exams	☑	Learning centers	☐
Take home exams	☐	Proofreaders	☐
Exams on tape or computer	☐	Readers	☑
Untimed exams	☑	Reading Machines/Kurzweil	☑
Other accommodations	☐	Special bookstore section	☑
		Typists	☐

Credit toward degree is not given for remedial courses taken.

Counseling Services

- ☑ Academic
- ☑ Psychological — Meets 10 times per academic year
- ☑ Student Support groups
- ☐ Vocational

Tutoring

Individual tutoring is available weekly.

Average size of tutoring groups: 1

	Individual	Group
Time management	☑	☐
Organizational skills	☑	☐
Learning strategies	☑	☐
Study skills	☑	☐
Content area	☑	☐
Writing lab	☑	☐
Math lab	☑	☐

LD PROGRAM STAFF

Total number of LD Program staff (including director):

Full Time: 3 Part Time: 3

There is an advisor/advocate from the LD program available to students. 20 peer tutors are available to work with LD students.

Key staff person available to work with LD students: Eric Lathrop, Counselor.

LD Program web site:
http://www.wtamu.edu/administrative/ss/ls/ds/index.htm

Wiley College

Marshall, TX

Address: 711 Wiley Avenue, Marshall, TX, 75670
Admissions telephone: 800 658-6889
Admissions FAX: 903 927-3366
Director of Admissions and Recruitment: Ms.Lalita Estes
Admissions e-mail: admissions@wileyc.edu
Web site: http://www.wileyc.edu
SAT Code: 6940

Associate Vice President: Dr. Robert Watkins
LD program telephone: 903 927-3220
LD program e-mail: rwatkins@wileyc.edu
Total campus enrollment: 622

GENERAL

Wiley College is a private, coed, four-year institution. 63-acre campus in Marshall (population: 23,935), 38 miles from Shreveport, La., and 150 miles from Dallas. Served by bus and train; major airport serves Shreveport. Semester system.

LD ADMISSIONS

A personal interview is not required. Essay is not required. School has open admissions policy.

SECONDARY SCHOOL REQUIREMENTS

Graduation from secondary school required; GED accepted. The following course distribution required: 4 units of English, 2 units of math, 2 units of science, 2 units of social studies, 6 units of academic electives.

TESTING

Child Study Team report is not required. Tests required as part of this documentation:

- ❑ WAIS-IV
- ❑ WISC-IV
- ❑ SATA
- ❑ Woodcock-Johnson
- ❑ Nelson-Denny Reading Test
- ❑ Other

UNDERGRADUATE STUDENT BODY

Total undergraduate student enrollment: 242 Men, 380 Women.

51% are from out of state.

STUDENT HOUSING

Housing is guaranteed for all undergraduates. Campus can house 386 undergraduates.

EXPENSES

There is no additional cost for LD program/services.

LD SERVICES

LD program size is not limited.

LD services available to:

❑ Freshmen ❑ Sophomores ❑ Juniors ❑ Seniors

Academic Accommodations

Curriculum		In class	
Foreign language waiver	❑	Early syllabus	❑
Lighter course load	■	Note takers in class	❑
Math waiver	❑	Priority seating	❑
Other special classes	❑	Tape recorders	❑
Priority registrations	❑	Videotaped classes	❑
Substitution of courses	❑	Text on tape	❑
Exams		**Services**	
Extended time	❑	Diagnostic tests	■
Oral exams	❑	Learning centers	■
Take home exams	❑	Proofreaders	❑
Exams on tape or computer	❑	Readers	❑
Untimed exams	❑	Reading Machines/Kurzweil	❑
Other accommodations	❑	Special bookstore section	❑
		Typists	❑

Credit toward degree is not given for remedial courses taken.

Counseling Services

- ❑ Academic
- ❑ Psychological
- ❑ Student Support groups
- ❑ Vocational

Tutoring

	Individual	Group
Time management	❑	❑
Organizational skills	❑	❑
Learning strategies	❑	❑
Study skills	❑	❑
Content area	❑	❑
Writing lab	❑	❑
Math lab	❑	❑

LD PROGRAM STAFF

Total number of LD Program staff (including director):

Full Time: 4 Part Time: 4

Key staff person available to work with LD students: Dr. Robert Watkins, Associate Vice President & Chair, Division of Education & Special/General Studies.

Richmond, The American International University in London

London, UK

Address: Queens Road, Richmond Upon Thames, London, UK,
Admissions telephone: 617 450-5617
Admissions FAX: 617 450-5601
Director, U.S. Admissions: Brian E. Davis
Admissions e-mail: enroll@richmond.ac.uk
Web site: http://www.richmond.ac.uk
SAT Code: 823 ACT Code: 5244

Vice President for Student Affairs: Dr. John O'Connell
LD program e-mail: oconnej@richmond.ac.uk
Total campus enrollment: 904

GENERAL

Richmond, The American International University in London is a private, coed, four-year institution. Five-acre Richmond Hill campus (housing freshmen and sophomores) on the Thames River seven miles from London (population: 7,500,000), and Kensington campus (housing juniors and seniors) in center of London; branch campus abroad in Florence, Italy. Airport, bus, and train serve London. School operates transportation between campuses. Public transportation serves campus. Semester system.

LD ADMISSIONS

A personal interview is recommended. Essay is required and may be typed.

SECONDARY SCHOOL REQUIREMENTS

Graduation from secondary school required; GED accepted. The following course distribution required: 4 units of English, 3 units of math, 3 units of science, 2 units of foreign language, 3 units of social studies.

TESTING

Child Study Team report is not required. Tests required as part of this documentation:

- ☐ WAIS-IV
- ☐ WISC-IV
- ☐ SATA
- ☐ Woodcock-Johnson
- ☐ Nelson-Denny Reading Test
- ☐ Other

UNDERGRADUATE STUDENT BODY

Total undergraduate student enrollment: 396 Men, 508 Women.

STUDENT HOUSING

Housing is guaranteed for all undergraduates. Campus can house 500 undergraduates.

EXPENSES

There is no additional cost for LD program/services.

LD SERVICES

LD program size is not limited.

LD services available to:

☐ Freshmen ☐ Sophomores ☐ Juniors ☐ Seniors

Academic Accommodations

Curriculum		In class	
Foreign language waiver	☐	Early syllabus	☐
Lighter course load	☐	Note takers in class	☐
Math waiver	☐	Priority seating	☐
Other special classes	■	Tape recorders	■
Priority registrations	☐	Videotaped classes	☐
Substitution of courses	☐	Text on tape	☐
Exams		**Services**	
Extended time	■	Diagnostic tests	☐
Oral exams	■	Learning centers	☐
Take home exams	☐	Proofreaders	☐
Exams on tape or computer	☐	Readers	☐
Untimed exams	■	Reading Machines/Kurzweil	☐
Other accommodations	☐	Special bookstore section	☐
		Typists	☐

Credit toward degree is not given for remedial courses taken.

Counseling Services

- ☐ Academic
- ☐ Psychological
- ☐ Student Support groups
- ☐ Vocational

Tutoring

	Individual	Group
Time management	☐	☐
Organizational skills	☐	☐
Learning strategies	☐	☐
Study skills	☐	☐
Content area	☐	☐
Writing lab	☐	☐
Math lab	☐	☐

LD PROGRAM STAFF

Total number of LD Program staff (including director):

Full Time: 2 Part Time: 2

Key staff person available to work with LD students: Dr. John O'Connell, Vice President for Student Affairs.

Brigham Young University

Provo, UT

Address: A-209 ASB, Provo, UT, 84602
Admissions telephone: 801 422-2507
Admissions FAX: 801 422-0005
Director of Admissions: Tom Gourle
Admissions e-mail: admissions@byu.edu
Web site: http://www.byu.edu
SAT Code: 4019 ACT Code: 4266

LD program name: University Accessibility Center
LD program address: 1520 WSC, Provo, UT, 84602
Coordinator: John M. Call
LD program telephone: 801 422-7065
LD program e-mail: john_call@byu.edu
LD program enrollment: 225, Total campus enrollment: 30,847

GENERAL

Brigham Young University is a private, coed, four-year institution. 638-acre campus in Provo (population: 105,166), 45 miles from Salt Lake City. Served by air and bus; major airport and train serve Salt Lake City. Public transportation serves campus. Semester system.

LD ADMISSIONS

Students do not complete a separate application and are simultaneously accepted to the LD program. A member of the LD program does not sit on the admissions committee. A personal interview is not required. Essay is required and may be typed.

SECONDARY SCHOOL REQUIREMENTS

Graduation from secondary school required; GED accepted. The following course distribution required: 4 units of English, 3 units of math, 2 units of science, 2 units of foreign language, 2 units of history.

TESTING

ACT required of some applicants; SAT Reasoning may be substituted.

All enrolled freshmen (fall 2004):

Average SAT I Scores: Verbal: 606 Math: 615
Average ACT Scores: Composite: 27

Child Study Team report is not required. A neuropsychological or comprehensive psycho-educational evaluation is required for admission. Must be dated within 48 months of application. Tests required as part of this documentation:

- ■ WAIS-IV
- ☐ WISC-IV
- ☐ SATA
- ■ Woodcock-Johnson
- ☐ Nelson-Denny Reading Test
- ☐ Other

UNDERGRADUATE STUDENT BODY

Total undergraduate student enrollment: 14,715 Men, 15,100 Women.

Composition of student body (fall 2004):

	Undergraduate	Freshmen
International	1.9	4.1
Black	0.5	0.4
American Indian	0.7	0.7
Asian-American	3.8	3.0
Hispanic	3.3	3.3
White	74.1	82.2
Unreported	15.7	6.3
	100.0%	100.0%

70% are from out of state. Average age of full-time undergraduates is 21. 39% of classes have fewer than 20 students, 49% have between 20 and 50 students, 12% have more than 50 students.

STUDENT HOUSING

80% of freshmen live in college housing. Freshmen are not required to live on campus. Housing is not guaranteed for all undergraduates. Campus housing is available to any unmarried student, but there is not enough housing to accommodate all unmarried students; student housing is provided on a first-come, first-served basis. Campus can house 7,812 undergraduates. Single rooms are not available for students with medical or special needs.

EXPENSES

Tuition (2005-06): $3,410 per year. $3,060 per year (Latter-Day Saints members), $4,590 (non-members).

Room & Board: $5,570

There is no additional cost for LD program/services.

LD SERVICES

LD program size is not limited.

LD services available to:

■ Freshmen ■ Sophomores ■ Juniors ■ Seniors

Academic Accommodations

Curriculum		In class	
Foreign language waiver	☐	Early syllabus	☐
Lighter course load	■	Note takers in class	■
Math waiver	☐	Priority seating	☐
Other special classes	☐	Tape recorders	■
Priority registrations	■	Videotaped classes	☐
Substitution of courses	■	Text on tape	■
Exams		**Services**	
Extended time	■	Diagnostic tests	■
Oral exams	■	Learning centers	■
Take home exams	☐	Proofreaders	■
Exams on tape or computer	■	Readers	■
Untimed exams	☐	Reading Machines/Kurzweil	■
Other accommodations	■	Special bookstore section	☐
		Typists	■

Counseling Services

- ■ Academic
- ■ Psychological
- ■ Student Support groups
- ■ Vocational

Tutoring

Individual tutoring is not available.

	Individual	Group
Time management	■	■
Organizational skills	■	■
Learning strategies	■	■
Study skills	■	■
Content area	☐	☐
Writing lab	☐	■
Math lab	☐	■

LD PROGRAM STAFF

Total number of LD Program staff (including director):

Full Time: 3 Part Time: 3

There is an advisor/advocate from the LD program available to students. 4 graduate students are available to work with LD students.

Key staff person available to work with LD students: John M. Call, Coord., Academic Accommodations and Technology.

LD Program web site: www.byu.edu/uac

University of Utah

Salt Lake City, UT

Address: 201 S. Presidents Circle, Salt Lake City, UT, 84112
Admissions telephone: 801 581-7281
Admissions FAX: 801 585-7864
Director of Admissions: John Boswell
Admissions e-mail: Admissions@sa.utah.edu
Web site: http://www.utah.edu
SAT Code: 4853 ACT Code: 4274

LD program name: Center for Disability Services
LD program address: 162 Union
Director: Joe Pete Wilson
LD program telephone: 801 581-5020
LD program e-mail: JoePete@sa.utah.edu
LD program enrollment: 220, Total campus enrollment: 22,775

GENERAL

University of Utah is a public, coed, four-year institution. 1,500-acre campus in Salt Lake City (population: 181,743); branch campuses in Bountiful, Cedar Park, Park City, and Sandy. Served by air, bus, and train. School operates transportation around campus and research park. Public transportation serves campus. Semester system.

LD ADMISSIONS

Students do not complete a separate application and are simultaneously accepted to the LD program. A member of the LD program does not sit on the admissions committee. High school waivers are accepted for foreign language. A personal interview is recommended. Essay is not required. Foreign language may be waived for admissions purposes, but may still be required for degree completion.

For fall 2004, 35 completed self-identified LD applications were received. 15 applications were offered admission, and 12 enrolled.

SECONDARY SCHOOL REQUIREMENTS

Graduation from secondary school required; GED accepted. The following course distribution required: 4 units of English, 2 units of math, 2 units of science, 2 units of foreign language, 1 unit of history, 4 units of academic electives.

TESTING

ACT required; SAT Reasoning may be substituted. SAT Subject recommended.

All enrolled freshmen (fall 2004):

Average SAT I Scores:	Verbal:	Math:
Average ACT Scores:	Composite: 24	

Child Study Team report is not required. A neuropsychological or comprehensive psycho-educational evaluation is required for admission. Must be dated within 36 months of application. Tests required as part of this documentation:

- [x] WAIS-IV
- [x] WISC-IV
- [ ] SATA
- [x] Woodcock-Johnson
- [x] Nelson-Denny Reading Test
- [x] Other

UNDERGRADUATE STUDENT BODY

Total undergraduate student enrollment: 12,038 Men, 10,196 Women.

Composition of student body (fall 2004):

	Undergraduate	Freshmen
International	1.4	2.3
Black	0.5	0.6
American Indian	0.7	0.7
Asian-American	7.0	4.7
Hispanic	4.9	4.0
White	78.9	81.4
Unreported	6.6	6.3
	100.0%	100.0%

7% are from out of state. 1% join a fraternity and 2% join a sorority. Average age of full-time undergraduates is 23. 42% of classes have fewer than 20 students, 38% have between 20 and 50 students, 20% have more than 50 students.

STUDENT HOUSING

29% of freshmen live in college housing. Freshmen are not required to live on campus. Housing is guaranteed for all undergraduates. Campus can house 2,035 undergraduates. Single rooms are available for students with medical or special needs. A medical note is required.

EXPENSES

Tuition (2005-06): $3,629 per year (in-state), $12,702 (out-of-state).
Room: $2,193. Board: $2,475.
There is no additional cost for LD program/services.

LD SERVICES

LD program size is not limited.

LD services available to:

- [x] Freshmen
- [x] Sophomores
- [x] Juniors
- [x] Seniors

Academic Accommodations

Curriculum

- [ ] Foreign language waiver
- [x] Lighter course load
- [ ] Math waiver
- [ ] Other special classes
- [x] Priority registrations
- [x] Substitution of courses

Exams

- [x] Extended time
- [x] Oral exams
- [ ] Take home exams
- [x] Exams on tape or computer
- [ ] Untimed exams
- [x] Other accommodations

In class

- [ ] Early syllabus
- [x] Note takers in class
- [x] Priority seating
- [x] Tape recorders
- [ ] Videotaped classes
- [x] Text on tape

Services

- [ ] Diagnostic tests
- [ ] Learning centers
- [ ] Proofreaders
- [x] Readers
- [x] Reading Machines/Kurzweil
- [ ] Special bookstore section
- [ ] Typists

Credit toward degree is not given for remedial courses taken.

Counseling Services

- [x] Academic — Meets 8 times per academic year
- [x] Psychological — Meets 8 times per academic year
- [x] Student Support groups — Meets 8 times per academic year
- [ ] Vocational

Tutoring

Individual tutoring is available weekly.

Average size of tutoring groups: 3

	Individual	Group
Time management	[x]	[x]
Organizational skills	[x]	[x]
Learning strategies	[x]	[x]
Study skills	[x]	[x]
Content area	[x]	[ ]
Writing lab	[x]	[ ]
Math lab	[ ]	[ ]

UNIQUE LD PROGRAM FEATURES

Course load based on individual need or severity of diagnosis.

LD PROGRAM STAFF

Total number of LD Program staff (including director):

Full Time: 8 Part Time: 8

There is an advisor/advocate from the LD program available to students. The advisor/advocate meets with faculty 4 times per month and students 4 times per month.

LD Program web site: http://disability.utah.edu

Utah State University

Logan, UT

Address: Old Main Hill, Logan, UT, 84322
Admissions telephone: 435 797-1079
Admissions FAX: 435 797-3708
Associate Vice President, Student Services: Jimmy Moore
Admissions e-mail: admit@cc.usu.edu
Web site: http://www.usu.edu
SAT Code: 4857 ACT Code: 4276

LD Program Name: Director, Diane Craig Hardman
LD program telephone: 435 797-2444
LD program e-mail: dhardman@cc.usu.edu
Total campus enrollment: 13,585

GENERAL

Utah State University is a public, coed, four-year institution. 88-acre campus in Logan (population: 42,670), 90 miles from Salt Lake City; branch campuses in Brigham City, Moab, Ogden, Roosevelt, Tooele, and Vernal. Served by bus; major airport serves Salt Lake City; train serves Cache Junction (10 miles). School operates transportation around campus. Public transportation serves campus. Semester system.

LD ADMISSIONS

A personal interview is required. Essay is not required. Admission requirements are not waived.

SECONDARY SCHOOL REQUIREMENTS

Graduation from secondary school required; GED accepted. The following course distribution required: 4 units of English, 3 units of math, 3 units of science, 1 unit of history, 4 units of academic electives.

TESTING

ACT required; SAT Reasoning may be substituted. SAT Subject recommended.

All enrolled freshmen (fall 2004):

Average SAT I Scores:	Verbal: 547	Math: 559
Average ACT Scores:	Composite: 24	

Child Study Team report is not required. Tests required as part of this documentation:

- ❑ WAIS-IV
- ❑ WISC-IV
- ❑ SATA
- ❑ Woodcock-Johnson
- ❑ Nelson-Denny Reading Test
- ❑ Other

UNDERGRADUATE STUDENT BODY

Total undergraduate student enrollment: 9,323 Men, 9,972 Women.

Composition of student body (fall 2004):

	Undergraduate	Freshmen
International	0.8	2.3
Black	0.5	0.6
American Indian	0.5	0.4
Asian-American	1.8	1.4
Hispanic	3.1	2.2
White	92.0	91.0
Unreported	1.3	2.1
	100.0%	100.0%

31% are from out of state. 2% join a fraternity and 2% join a sorority. Average age of full-time undergraduates is 22. 41% of classes have fewer than 20 students, 46% have between 20 and 50 students, 13% have more than 50 students.

STUDENT HOUSING

Freshmen are not required to live on campus. Housing is guaranteed for all undergraduates. Campus can house 3,200 undergraduates.

EXPENSES

Tuition (2005-06): $3,128 per year (in-state), $10,072 (out-of-state). Room: $1,550. Board: $2,780.
There is no additional cost for LD program/services.

LD SERVICES

LD program size is not limited.

LD services available to:

❑ Freshmen ❑ Sophomores ❑ Juniors ❑ Seniors

Academic Accommodations

Curriculum		In class	
Foreign language waiver	❑	Early syllabus	❑
Lighter course load	■	Note takers in class	■
Math waiver	❑	Priority seating	❑
Other special classes	❑	Tape recorders	■
Priority registrations	❑	Videotaped classes	❑
Substitution of courses	❑	Text on tape	❑
Exams		**Services**	
Extended time	■	Diagnostic tests	❑
Oral exams	❑	Learning centers	❑
Take home exams	❑	Proofreaders	❑
Exams on tape or computer	❑	Readers	■
Untimed exams	❑	Reading Machines/Kurzweil	■
Other accommodations	❑	Special bookstore section	❑
		Typists	❑

Credit toward degree is not given for remedial courses taken.

Counseling Services

- ❑ Academic
- ❑ Psychological
- ❑ Student Support groups
- ❑ Vocational

Tutoring

	Individual	Group
Time management	❑	❑
Organizational skills	❑	❑
Learning strategies	❑	❑
Study skills	❑	❑
Content area	❑	❑
Writing lab	❑	❑
Math lab	❑	❑

UNIQUE LD PROGRAM FEATURES

Extensive remedial/coaching not provided at USU.

LD PROGRAM STAFF

Total number of LD Program staff (including director):

Full Time: 3 Part Time: 3

Key staff person available to work with LD students: Diane Craig Hardman, Director, Disability Resource Center.

Utah Valley State College

Orem, UT

Address: 800 W. University Parkway, Orem, UT, 84058-5999
Admissions telephone: 801 863-8466
Admissions FAX: 801 225-4677
Director of Admissions: Liz Childs
Admissions e-mail: info@uvsc.edu
Web site: http://www.uvsc.edu
SAT Code: 4870

LD program name: Accessibility Services
Accessibility Services Director: Kimberly Beck
LD program telephone: 801 863-8747
LD program e-mail: beckki@uvsc.edu
LD program enrollment: 382, Total campus enrollment: 24,149

GENERAL

Utah Valley State College is a public, coed, four-year institution. 185-acre campus in Orem (population: 84,324), five miles from Provo. Served by air and bus; major airport serves Salt Lake City (33 miles). Semester system.

LD ADMISSIONS

Students complete a separate application and are not simultaneously accepted to the LD program. A personal interview is not required. Essay is not required.

For fall 2004, 402 completed self-identified LD applications were received. 402 applications were offered admission, and 382 enrolled.

SECONDARY SCHOOL REQUIREMENTS

Graduation from secondary school required; GED accepted.

TESTING

SAT Reasoning or ACT required of some applicants. SAT Subject recommended.

All enrolled freshmen (fall 2004):

Average SAT I Scores:	Verbal: 492	Math: 494
Average ACT Scores:	Composite: 20	

Child Study Team report is not required. A neuropsychological or comprehensive psycho-educational evaluation is required for admission. Must be dated within 36 months of application. Tests required as part of this documentation:

- ☐ WAIS-IV
- ☐ WISC-IV
- ☐ SATA
- ☐ Woodcock-Johnson
- ☐ Nelson-Denny Reading Test
- ☑ Other

UNDERGRADUATE STUDENT BODY

Total undergraduate student enrollment: 12,621 Men, 9,988 Women.

Composition of student body (fall 2004):

	Undergraduate	Freshmen
International	4.4	2.7
Black	0.5	0.4
American Indian	1.1	1.0
Asian-American	2.2	1.7
Hispanic	3.5	3.3
White	84.0	87.4
Unreported	4.3	3.5
	100.0%	100.0%

9% are from out of state. Average age of full-time undergraduates is 23. 40% of classes have fewer than 20 students, 55% have between 20 and 50 students, 5% have more than 50 students.

STUDENT HOUSING

Housing is not guaranteed for all undergraduates. Only off campus, non-college-affiliated, -operated, -owned, housing is available. Single rooms are not available for students with medical or special needs.

EXPENSES

Tuition (2005-06): $2,562 per year (in-state), $8,966 (out-of-state). $1,542 per year (state residents, lower division), $1,782 (state residents, upper division), $5,582 (out-of-state, lower division), $6,456 (out-of-state, upper division).

There is no additional cost for LD program/services.

LD SERVICES

LD program size is not limited.

LD services available to:

☑ Freshmen ☑ Sophomores ☑ Juniors ☑ Seniors

Academic Accommodations

Curriculum		In class	
Foreign language waiver	☐	Early syllabus	☐
Lighter course load	☑	Note takers in class	☑
Math waiver	☐	Priority seating	☐
Other special classes	☑	Tape recorders	☑
Priority registrations	☐	Videotaped classes	☐
Substitution of courses	☐	Text on tape	☐
Exams		**Services**	
Extended time	☑	Diagnostic tests	☑
Oral exams	☑	Learning centers	☐
Take home exams	☐	Proofreaders	☐
Exams on tape or computer	☐	Readers	☑
Untimed exams	☑	Reading Machines/Kurzweil	☐
Other accommodations	☑	Special bookstore section	☐
		Typists	☐

Credit toward degree is not given for remedial courses taken.

Counseling Services

- ☑ Academic
- ☑ Psychological
- ☑ Student Support groups
- ☑ Vocational

Tutoring

Individual tutoring is available daily.

Average size of tutoring groups: 1

	Individual	Group
Time management	☑	☑
Organizational skills	☑	☑
Learning strategies	☑	☑
Study skills	☑	☑
Content area	☑	☑
Writing lab	☑	☑
Math lab	☑	☑

LD PROGRAM STAFF

Total number of LD Program staff (including director):

Full Time: 9 Part Time: 9

There is an advisor/advocate from the LD program available to students. 21 peer tutors are available to work with LD students.

Key staff person available to work with LD students: Kimberly Beck, Accessibility Services Director.

LD Program web site: http://www.uvsc.edu/asd/

Southern Utah University

Cedar City, UT

Address: 351 W. Center Street, Cedar City, UT, 84720
Admissions telephone: 435 586-7740
Admissions FAX: 435 865-8223
Director of Admissions: Stephen Allen
Admissions e-mail: adminfo@suu.edu
Web site: http://www.suu.edu
SAT Code: 4092 ACT Code: 4271

Coordinator/Student Disabilities Service: Carmen Alldredge
LD program telephone: 435 865-8022
LD program e-mail: alldredge@suu.edu
Total campus enrollment: 6,381

GENERAL

Southern Utah University is a public, coed, four-year institution. 133-acre campus in Cedar City (population: 20,527), 160 miles from Las Vegas; branch campus in St. George. Served by bus; major airport serves Las Vegas; train serves Milford (50 miles). Semester system.

LD ADMISSIONS

A personal interview is required. Essay is not required.

SECONDARY SCHOOL REQUIREMENTS

Graduation from secondary school required; GED accepted.

TESTING

All enrolled freshmen (fall 2004):

Average SAT I Scores: Verbal: Math:
Average ACT Scores: Composite:

Child Study Team report is not required. Tests required as part of this documentation:

- ☐ WAIS-IV
- ☐ WISC-IV
- ☐ SATA
- ☐ Woodcock-Johnson
- ☐ Nelson-Denny Reading Test
- ☐ Other

UNDERGRADUATE STUDENT BODY

Total undergraduate student enrollment: 2,601 Men, 3,283 Women.

Composition of student body (fall 2004):

	Undergraduate	Freshmen
International	0.0	0.6
Black	0.8	0.7
American Indian	2.0	1.5
Asian-American	3.1	2.1
Hispanic	3.0	2.1
White	87.8	90.3
Unreported	3.3	2.7
	100.0%	100.0%

17% are from out of state. 3% join a fraternity and 3% join a sorority. Average age of full-time undergraduates is 22. 57% of classes have fewer than 20 students, 38% have between 20 and 50 students, 5% have more than 50 students.

STUDENT HOUSING

41% of freshmen live in college housing. Housing is guaranteed for all undergraduates.

EXPENSES

Tuition (2005-06): $2,834 per year (in-state), $9,354 (out-of-state).
Room: $1,590. Board: $2,564.

There is no additional cost for LD program/services.

LD SERVICES

LD program size is not limited.

LD services available to:

☐ Freshmen ☐ Sophomores ☐ Juniors ☐ Seniors

Academic Accommodations

Curriculum		In class	
Foreign language waiver	☐	Early syllabus	☐
Lighter course load	☑	Note takers in class	☑
Math waiver	☐	Priority seating	☐
Other special classes	☐	Tape recorders	☑
Priority registrations	☐	Videotaped classes	☐
Substitution of courses	☐	Text on tape	☐
Exams		**Services**	
Extended time	☑	Diagnostic tests	☑
Oral exams	☑	Learning centers	☑
Take home exams	☐	Proofreaders	☐
Exams on tape or computer	☐	Readers	☑
Untimed exams	☐	Reading Machines/Kurzweil	☐
Other accommodations	☐	Special bookstore section	☐
		Typists	☐

Credit toward degree is not given for remedial courses taken.

Counseling Services

- ☐ Academic
- ☐ Psychological
- ☐ Student Support groups
- ☐ Vocational

Tutoring

	Individual	Group
Time management	☐	☐
Organizational skills	☐	☐
Learning strategies	☐	☐
Study skills	☐	☐
Content area	☐	☐
Writing lab	☐	☐
Math lab	☐	☐

LD PROGRAM STAFF

Total number of LD Program staff (including director):

Full Time: 1 Part Time: 1

Key staff person available to work with LD students: Carmen Alldredge, Coordinator/Student Disabilities Service.

Weber State University

Ogden, UT

Address: 1103 University Circle, Ogden, UT, 84408-1103
Admissions telephone: 801 626-6744
Admissions FAX: 801 626-6747
Director of Admissions: Christopher C. Rivera
Admissions e-mail: admissions@weber.edu
Web site: http://weber.edu
SAT Code: 4941   ACT Code: 4282

LD program name: Services for Students with Disabilities
Director/Services for Students with Disabilities: Jeff Morris
LD program telephone: 801 626-6413
LD program e-mail: jmorris2@weber.edu
LD program enrollment: 217, Total campus enrollment: 18,113

GENERAL

Weber State University is a public, coed, four-year institution. 526-acre, urban campus in Ogden (population: 77,226), 35 miles from Salt Lake City. Served by air, bus, and train; major airport serves Salt Lake City. School operates transportation to parking lot. Public transportation serves campus. Semester system.

LD ADMISSIONS

Students do not complete a separate application and are not simultaneously accepted to the LD program. A member of the LD program does not sit on the admissions committee. A personal interview is not required. Essay is not required.

For fall 2004, 62 completed self-identified LD applications were received. 62 applications were offered admission, and 62 enrolled.

SECONDARY SCHOOL REQUIREMENTS

Graduation from secondary school required; GED accepted.

TESTING

All enrolled freshmen (fall 2004):

Average SAT I Scores:	Verbal:	Math:
Average ACT Scores:	Composite: 22	

Child Study Team report is not required. A neuropsychological or comprehensive psycho-educational evaluation is required for admission. Tests required as part of this documentation:

- ☐ WAIS-IV
- ☐ WISC-IV
- ☐ SATA
- ☐ Woodcock-Johnson
- ☐ Nelson-Denny Reading Test
- ☑ Other

UNDERGRADUATE STUDENT BODY

Total undergraduate student enrollment: 8,135 Men, 8,482 Women.

Composition of student body (fall 2004):

	Undergraduate	Freshmen
International	1.0	0.9
Black	0.5	0.7
American Indian	0.2	0.5
Asian-American	0.9	1.4
Hispanic	4.7	3.6
White	37.8	60.7
Unreported	54.9	32.2
	100.0%	100.0%

6% are from out of state. 1% join a fraternity and 1% join a sorority. Average age of full-time undergraduates is 25. 37% of classes have fewer than 20 students, 54% have between 20 and 50 students, 9% have more than 50 students.

STUDENT HOUSING

3% of freshmen live in college housing. Freshmen are not required to live on campus. Housing is guaranteed for all undergraduates. Campus can house 644 undergraduates. Single rooms are available for students with medical or special needs.

EXPENSES

Tuition (2005-06): $2,573 per year (in-state), $9,008 (out-of-state). Room: $3,200. Board: $3,200.

There is no additional cost for LD program/services.

LD SERVICES

LD program size is not limited.

LD services available to:

☑ Freshmen ☑ Sophomores ☑ Juniors ☑ Seniors

Academic Accommodations

Curriculum		In class	
Foreign language waiver	☐	Early syllabus	☐
Lighter course load	☑	Note takers in class	☑
Math waiver	☐	Priority seating	☐
Other special classes	☐	Tape recorders	☐
Priority registrations	☐	Videotaped classes	☐
Substitution of courses	☐	Text on tape	☐
Exams		**Services**	
Extended time	☑	Diagnostic tests	☐
Oral exams	☑	Learning centers	☐
Take home exams	☐	Proofreaders	☐
Exams on tape or computer	☐	Readers	☑
Untimed exams	☑	Reading Machines/Kurzweil	☑
Other accommodations	☐	Special bookstore section	☐
		Typists	☐

Credit toward degree is not given for remedial courses taken.

Counseling Services

- ☐ Academic
- ☐ Psychological
- ☐ Student Support groups
- ☐ Vocational

Tutoring

Individual tutoring is available weekly.

Average size of tutoring groups: 1

	Individual	Group
Time management	☐	☐
Organizational skills	☐	☐
Learning strategies	☐	☐
Study skills	☐	☐
Content area	☑	☑
Writing lab	☐	☐
Math lab	☑	☑

LD PROGRAM STAFF

Total number of LD Program staff (including director):

Full Time: 5   Part Time: 5

There is no advisor/advocate from the LD program available to students. 10 peer tutors are available to work with LD students.

Jeff Morris, Director/Services for Students with Disabilities.

LD Program web site: http://department.weber.edu/ssd/

Westminster College

Salt Lake City, UT

Address: 1840 S. 1300 E, Salt Lake City, UT, 84105-3697
Admissions telephone: 800 748-4753
Admissions FAX: 801 832-3101
Director of Admissions: Joel Bauman
Admissions e-mail: admission@westminstercollege.edu
Web site: http://www.westminstercollege.edu
SAT Code: 4948 ACT Code: 4284

LD program name: START Center
Associate Director of Start Center: Ginny Dewitt
LD program telephone: 801 832-2281
LD program e-mail: gdewitt@westminstercollege.edu
LD program enrollment: 24, Total campus enrollment: 1,896

GENERAL

Westminster College is a private, coed, four-year institution. 27-acre campus in Salt Lake City (population: 181,743). Served by air, bus, and train. Public transportation serves campus. 4-1-4 system.

LD ADMISSIONS

Students do not complete a separate application and are simultaneously accepted to the LD program. A member of the LD program does not sit on the admissions committee. A personal interview is recommended. Essay is not required.

For fall 2004, 5 completed self-identified LD applications were received. 5 applications were offered admission, and 5 enrolled.

SECONDARY SCHOOL REQUIREMENTS

Graduation from secondary school required; GED accepted. The following course distribution required: 4 units of English, 2 units of math, 3 units of science, 2 units of foreign language, 2 units of social studies, 1 unit of history, 2 units of academic electives.

TESTING

SAT Reasoning or ACT required. SAT Subject recommended.

All enrolled freshmen (fall 2004):

Average SAT I Scores:	Verbal: 564	Math: 549
Average ACT Scores:	Composite: 24	

Child Study Team report is not required. A neuropsychological or comprehensive psycho-educational evaluation is required for admission. Must be dated within 36 months of application. Tests required as part of this documentation:

- [x] WAIS-IV
- [ ] WISC-IV
- [x] SATA
- [x] Woodcock-Johnson
- [x] Nelson-Denny Reading Test
- [x] Other

UNDERGRADUATE STUDENT BODY

Total undergraduate student enrollment: 819 Men, 1,160 Women.

Composition of student body (fall 2004):

	Undergraduate	Freshmen
International	1.3	2.4
Black	0.9	0.7
American Indian	0.6	0.8
Asian-American	3.1	3.4
Hispanic	4.4	4.4
White	81.3	84.8
Unreported	8.4	3.5
	100.0%	100.0%

8% are from out of state. Average age of full-time undergraduates is 23. 68% of classes have fewer than 20 students, 32% have between 20 and 50 students.

STUDENT HOUSING

55% of freshmen live in college housing. Freshmen are required to live on campus. Housing is guaranteed for all undergraduates. Campus can house 500 undergraduates. Single rooms are available for students with medical or special needs. A medical note is required.

EXPENSES

Tuition (2005-06): $19,440 per year.
Room & Board: $5,932
There is no additional cost for LD program/services.

LD SERVICES

LD program size is not limited.

LD services available to:

- [x] Freshmen
- [x] Sophomores
- [x] Juniors
- [x] Seniors

Academic Accommodations

Curriculum

- [ ] Foreign language waiver
- [ ] Lighter course load
- [ ] Math waiver
- [ ] Other special classes
- [x] Priority registrations
- [ ] Substitution of courses

Exams

- [x] Extended time
- [ ] Oral exams
- [ ] Take home exams
- [ ] Exams on tape or computer
- [x] Untimed exams
- [x] Other accommodations

In class

- [ ] Early syllabus
- [x] Note takers in class
- [ ] Priority seating
- [x] Tape recorders
- [ ] Videotaped classes
- [x] Text on tape

Services

- [ ] Diagnostic tests
- [ ] Learning centers
- [ ] Proofreaders
- [x] Readers
- [ ] Reading Machines/Kurzweil
- [ ] Special bookstore section
- [x] Typists

Credit toward degree is not given for remedial courses taken.

Counseling Services

- [x] Academic
- [ ] Psychological
- [ ] Student Support groups
- [ ] Vocational

Meets 3 times per academic year

Tutoring

Individual tutoring is available.

	Individual	Group
Time management	☐	☐
Organizational skills	☐	☐
Learning strategies	☒	☐
Study skills	☐	☐
Content area	☐	☐
Writing lab	☒	☐
Math lab	☒	☐

LD PROGRAM STAFF

Total number of LD Program staff (including director):

Full Time: 1 Part Time: 1

There is no advisor/advocate from the LD program available to students.

Key staff person available to work with LD students: Ginny Dewitt, Associate Director of Start Center.

LD Program web site: http://www.westminstercollege.edu/start_center/

Bennington College

Bennington, VT

Address: 1 College Drive, Bennington, VT, 05201
Admissions telephone: 800 833-6845
Admissions FAX: 802 440-4320
Director of Admissions and the First Year: Ken Himmelman
Admissions e-mail: admissions@bennington.edu
Web site: http://www.bennington.edu
SAT Code: 3080 ACT Code: 4296

LD program name: Wendy Hirsch, LD Program
Dean of Studies: Wendy Hirsch
LD program telephone: 802 440-4400
LD program e-mail: whirsch@bennington.edu
LD program enrollment: 12, Total campus enrollment: 671

GENERAL

Bennington College is a private, coed, four-year institution. 550-acre campus in Bennington (population: 9,168), 42 miles from Albany, N.Y. Served by air and bus; major airport and train serve Albany. School operates transportation into Bennington. Semester system.

LD ADMISSIONS

Students do not complete a separate application and are not simultaneously accepted to the LD program. A member of the LD program does not sit on the admissions committee. High school waivers are accepted for math and foreign language. A personal interview is required. Essay is required and may be typed.

SECONDARY SCHOOL REQUIREMENTS

Graduation from secondary school required; GED accepted.

TESTING

SAT Reasoning considered if submitted. ACT considered if submitted. SAT Subject recommended.

All enrolled freshmen (fall 2004):

Average SAT I Scores:	Verbal: 640	Math: 560
Average ACT Scores:	Composite: 25	

Child Study Team report is not required. A neuropsychological or comprehensive psycho-educational evaluation is required for admission. Must be dated within 36 months of application. Tests required as part of this documentation:

- ■ WAIS-IV
- ■ WISC-IV
- ■ SATA
- ■ Woodcock-Johnson
- ■ Nelson-Denny Reading Test
- ☐ Other

UNDERGRADUATE STUDENT BODY

Total undergraduate student enrollment: 183 Men, 405 Women.

Composition of student body (fall 2004):

	Undergraduate	Freshmen
International	1.0	4.0
Black	2.0	1.6
American Indian	0.0	0.1
Asian-American	4.0	1.8
Hispanic	3.5	3.3
White	83.5	86.1
Unreported	6.0	3.1
	100.0%	100.0%

95% are from out of state. Average age of full-time undergraduates is 20. 80% of classes have fewer than 20 students, 20% have between 20 and 50 students.

STUDENT HOUSING

100% of freshmen live in college housing. Freshmen are required to live on campus. Housing is guaranteed for all undergraduates. Campus can house 600 undergraduates. Single rooms are available for students with medical or special needs. A medical note is required.

EXPENSES

Tuition (2005-06): $32,700 per year.

Room: $4,460. Board: $3,860.
There is no additional cost for LD program/services.

LD SERVICES

LD program size is not limited.

LD services available to:

■ Freshmen ■ Sophomores ■ Juniors ■ Seniors

Academic Accommodations

Curriculum		In class	
Foreign language waiver	☐	Early syllabus	■
Lighter course load	■	Note takers in class	■
Math waiver	☐	Priority seating	■
Other special classes	☐	Tape recorders	☐
Priority registrations	■	Videotaped classes	☐
Substitution of courses	■	Text on tape	☐
Exams		**Services**	
Extended time	■	Diagnostic tests	■
Oral exams	■	Learning centers	☐
Take home exams	☐	Proofreaders	☐
Exams on tape or computer	■	Readers	■
Untimed exams	■	Reading Machines/Kurzweil	☐
Other accommodations	☐	Special bookstore section	☐
		Typists	☐

Credit toward degree is not given for remedial courses taken.

Counseling Services

- ■ Academic
- ■ Psychological
- ☐ Student Support groups
- ☐ Vocational

Tutoring

Individual tutoring is available weekly.

Average size of tutoring groups: 2

	Individual	Group
Time management	■	■
Organizational skills	■	■
Learning strategies	☐	☐
Study skills	■	☐
Content area	■	■
Writing lab	■	☐
Math lab	☐	■

LD PROGRAM STAFF

Total number of LD Program staff (including director):

Full Time: 2 Part Time: 2

There is an advisor/advocate from the LD program available to students. 10 peer tutors are available to work with LD students.

Key staff person available to work with LD students: Wendy Hirsch, Dean of Studies.

Burlington College

Burlington, VT

Address: 95 N. Avenue, Burlington, VT, 05401
Admissions telephone: 802 862-9616, extension 104
Admissions FAX: 802 660-4431
Director of Admissions and Public Relations: Cathleen Sullivan
Admissions e-mail: admissions@burlcol.edu
Web site: http://www.burlcol.edu
SAT Code: 1119

LD program name: Student Services
Dean of Student Services: Michael Watson Ph.D.
LD program telephone: 802 862-9616, extension 124
LD program e-mail: mwatson@burlcol.edu
LD program enrollment: 6, Total campus enrollment: 194

GENERAL

Burlington College is a private, coed, four-year institution. One-acre campus in Burlington (population: 38,889); branch campus in Newport. Served by air and bus; train serves Essex Junction (15 miles). Public transportation serves campus. Semester system.

LD ADMISSIONS

Students do not complete a separate application and are not simultaneously accepted to the LD program. A member of the LD program does not sit on the admissions committee. High school waivers are accepted for math and foreign language. A personal interview is recommended. Essay is required and may be typed.

For fall 2004, 2 completed self-identified LD applications were received. 2 applications were offered admission, and 2 enrolled.

SECONDARY SCHOOL REQUIREMENTS

Graduation from secondary school required; GED accepted.

TESTING

All enrolled freshmen (fall 2004):

Average SAT I Scores: Verbal: Math:
Average ACT Scores: Composite:

Child Study Team report is not required. A neuropsychological or comprehensive psycho-educational evaluation is required for admission. Must be dated within 48 months of application. Tests required as part of this documentation:

- [x] WAIS-IV
- [x] WISC-IV
- [x] SATA
- [x] Woodcock-Johnson
- [x] Nelson-Denny Reading Test
- [ ] Other

UNDERGRADUATE STUDENT BODY

Total undergraduate student enrollment: 98 Men, 169 Women.

Composition of student body (fall 2004):

	Undergraduate	Freshmen
International	0.0	0.0
Black	4.0	1.6
American Indian	4.0	2.7
Asian-American	0.0	0.5
Hispanic	4.0	4.3
White	60.0	63.8
Unreported	28.0	27.1
	100.0%	100.0%

46% are from out of state. Average age of full-time undergraduates is 30. 1% of classes have fewer than 20 students.

STUDENT HOUSING

Freshmen are not required to live on campus. Housing is not guaranteed for all undergraduates. Housing capabilities for 12 students as the majority of students are commuters. There are no resources to help students find housing in town if necessary. Many of students are older and have homes. There is always housing available, but it is not necessary for the student body. Campus can house 12 undergraduates. Single rooms are available for students with medical or special needs. A medical note is not required.

EXPENSES

Tuition (2005-06): $14,670 per year.
There is no additional cost for LD program/services.

LD SERVICES

LD program size is not limited.

LD services available to:

- [x] Freshmen
- [x] Sophomores
- [x] Juniors
- [x] Seniors

Academic Accommodations

Curriculum		In class	
Foreign language waiver	[ ]	Early syllabus	[ ]
Lighter course load	[x]	Note takers in class	[ ]
Math waiver	[ ]	Priority seating	[ ]
Other special classes	[ ]	Tape recorders	[x]
Priority registrations	[ ]	Videotaped classes	[ ]
Substitution of courses	[x]	Text on tape	[ ]
Exams		**Services**	
Extended time	[ ]	Diagnostic tests	[ ]
Oral exams	[x]	Learning centers	[ ]
Take home exams	[ ]	Proofreaders	[x]
Exams on tape or computer	[ ]	Readers	[ ]
Untimed exams	[ ]	Reading Machines/Kurzweil	[ ]
Other accommodations	[ ]	Special bookstore section	[ ]
		Typists	[ ]

Credit toward degree is not given for remedial courses taken.

Counseling Services

- [x] Academic
- [x] Psychological
- [ ] Student Support groups
- [x] Vocational

Tutoring

Individual tutoring is available weekly.

Average size of tutoring groups: 2

	Individual	Group
Time management	[x]	[ ]
Organizational skills	[x]	[ ]
Learning strategies	[x]	[ ]
Study skills	[x]	[ ]
Content area	[x]	[ ]
Writing lab	[x]	[ ]
Math lab	[x]	[ ]

LD PROGRAM STAFF

Total number of LD Program staff (including director):

There is an advisor/advocate from the LD program available to students. The advisor/advocate meets with faculty 4 times per month and student 4 times per month.

Key staff person available to work with LD students: Michael Watson Ph.D., Dean of Student Services.

Castleton State College

Castleton, VT

Address: Castleton, VT, 05735
Admissions telephone: 800 639-8521
Admissions FAX: 802 468-1476
Dean of Enrollment: Maurice Quimet
Admissions e-mail: info@castleton.edu
Web site: http://www.castleton.edu
SAT Code: 3765 ACT Code: 4314

Learning Specialist: Miriam St. George
LD program telephone: 802 468-1428
LD program e-mail: miriam.stgeorge@castleton.edu
Total campus enrollment: 1,796

GENERAL

Castleton State College is a public, coed, four-year institution. 160-acre campus in Castleton (population: 4,367), 12 miles from Rutland. Airport, bus, and train serve Rutland; other airport serves Albany, N.Y. (70 miles). Semester system.

LD ADMISSIONS

A personal interview is recommended.

SECONDARY SCHOOL REQUIREMENTS

Graduation from secondary school required; GED accepted. The following course distribution required: 4 units of English, 3 units of math, 2 units of science, 3 units of social studies.

TESTING

SAT Reasoning required; ACT may be substituted. SAT Subject recommended.

All enrolled freshmen (fall 2004):

Average SAT I Scores:	Verbal: 480	Math: 475
Average ACT Scores:	Composite: 19	

Child Study Team report is not required. Tests required as part of this documentation:

- ☐ WAIS-IV
- ☐ WISC-IV
- ☐ SATA
- ☐ Woodcock-Johnson
- ☐ Nelson-Denny Reading Test
- ☐ Other

UNDERGRADUATE STUDENT BODY

Total undergraduate student enrollment: 606 Men, 936 Women.

Composition of student body (fall 2004):

	Undergraduate	Freshmen
International	0.5	0.1
Black	0.0	0.5
American Indian	0.5	0.5
Asian-American	0.9	1.0
Hispanic	0.7	0.7
White	93.5	91.6
Unreported	3.9	5.6
	100.0%	100.0%

35% are from out of state. Average age of full-time undergraduates is 21. 74% of classes have fewer than 20 students, 25% have between 20 and 50 students, 1% have more than 50 students.

STUDENT HOUSING

80% of freshmen live in college housing. Freshmen are required to live on campus. Housing is guaranteed for all undergraduates. Campus can house 850 undergraduates.

EXPENSES

Tuition (2005-06): $6,312 per year (in-state), $13,632 (out-of-state). $4,404 per year (state residents), $6,624 (New England Regional Student Program), $10,320 (other out-of-state).

Room & Board: $6,674

There is no additional cost for LD program/services.

LD SERVICES

LD program size is not limited.

LD services available to:

☐ Freshmen ☐ Sophomores ☐ Juniors ☐ Seniors

Academic Accommodations

Curriculum		**In class**	
Foreign language waiver	☐	Early syllabus	☐
Lighter course load	☐	Note takers in class	■
Math waiver	☐	Priority seating	☐
Other special classes	☐	Tape recorders	■
Priority registrations	☐	Videotaped classes	☐
Substitution of courses	☐	Text on tape	☐
Exams		**Services**	
Extended time	■	Diagnostic tests	☐
Oral exams	■	Learning centers	■
Take home exams	☐	Proofreaders	☐
Exams on tape or computer	☐	Readers	■
Untimed exams	☐	Reading Machines/Kurzweil	■
Other accommodations	☐	Special bookstore section	☐
		Typists	☐

Credit toward degree is given for remedial courses taken.

Counseling Services

- ☐ Academic
- ☐ Psychological
- ☐ Student Support groups
- ☐ Vocational

Tutoring

	Individual	Group
Time management	☐	☐
Organizational skills	☐	☐
Learning strategies	☐	☐
Study skills	☐	☐
Content area	☐	☐
Writing lab	☐	☐
Math lab	☐	☐

LD PROGRAM STAFF

Total number of LD Program staff (including director):

Full Time: 1 Part Time: 1

Key staff person available to work with LD students: Miriam St. George, Learning Specialist.

Champlain College

Burlington, VT

Address: 163 S. Willard Street, Burlington, VT, 05401
Admissions telephone: 800 570-5858
Admissions FAX: 802 860-2767
Director of Admissions: Josephine H. Churchill
Admissions e-mail: admission@champlain.edu
Web site: http://www.champlain.edu
SAT Code: 3291 ACT Code: 4298

Counselor/Coordinator. Support for Students with Disabilities: Allyson Krings M.S., LPCLD
LD program telephone: 802 651-5961
LD program e-mail: krings@champlain.edu
Total campus enrollment: 2,491

GENERAL

Champlain College is a private, coed, four-year institution. 19-acre campus in Burlington (population: 38,889). Served by air and bus; train serves Essex Junction (eight miles). School operates transportation to off-campus parking facility. Public transportation serves campus. Semester system.

LD ADMISSIONS

Students do not complete a separate application and are simultaneously accepted to the LD program. A member of the LD program does not sit on the admissions committee. A personal interview is recommended. Essay is required and may be typed.

SECONDARY SCHOOL REQUIREMENTS

Graduation from secondary school required; GED accepted. The following course distribution required: 4 units of English, 3 units of math, 3 units of science, 1 unit of social studies, 3 units of history, 4 units of academic electives.

TESTING

SAT Reasoning or ACT required. SAT Subject recommended.

All enrolled freshmen (fall 2004):

Average SAT I Scores: Verbal: 508 Math: 513
Average ACT Scores: Composite: 21

Child Study Team report is not required. Tests required as part of this documentation:

- [ ] WAIS-IV
- [ ] WISC-IV
- [ ] SATA
- [ ] Woodcock-Johnson
- [ ] Nelson-Denny Reading Test
- [ ] Other

UNDERGRADUATE STUDENT BODY

Total undergraduate student enrollment: 1,172 Men, 1,351 Women.

Composition of student body (fall 2004):

	Undergraduate	Freshmen
International	0.5	0.4
Black	0.2	0.8
American Indian	1.2	0.9
Asian-American	0.5	1.6
Hispanic	0.5	1.1
White	97.1	95.2
Unreported	0.0	0.0
	100.0%	100.0%

42% are from out of state. Average age of full-time undergraduates is 20. 38% of classes have fewer than 20 students. 62% have between 20 and 50 students.

STUDENT HOUSING

90% of freshmen live in college housing. Freshmen are not required to live on campus. Housing is guaranteed for all undergraduates. Campus can house 750 undergraduates.

EXPENSES

Tuition (2005-06): $14,660 per year.
Room: $5,855. Board: $3,840.
There is no additional cost for LD program/services.

LD SERVICES

LD program size is not limited.

LD services available to:

- [ ] Freshmen
- [ ] Sophomores
- [ ] Juniors
- [ ] Seniors

Academic Accommodations

Curriculum		In class	
Foreign language waiver	[ ]	Early syllabus	[ ]
Lighter course load	[ ]	Note takers in class	[x]
Math waiver	[ ]	Priority seating	[x]
Other special classes	[ ]	Tape recorders	[ ]
Priority registrations	[ ]	Videotaped classes	[ ]
Substitution of courses	[ ]	Text on tape	[ ]
Exams		**Services**	
Extended time	[x]	Diagnostic tests	[ ]
Oral exams	[ ]	Learning centers	[ ]
Take home exams	[ ]	Proofreaders	[ ]
Exams on tape or computer	[ ]	Readers	[ ]
Untimed exams	[x]	Reading Machines/Kurzweil	[ ]
Other accommodations	[ ]	Special bookstore section	[ ]
		Typists	[ ]

Credit toward degree is not given for remedial courses taken.

Counseling Services

- [ ] Academic
- [ ] Psychological
- [ ] Student Support groups
- [ ] Vocational

Tutoring

	Individual	Group
Time management	[ ]	[ ]
Organizational skills	[ ]	[ ]
Learning strategies	[ ]	[ ]
Study skills	[ ]	[ ]
Content area	[ ]	[ ]
Writing lab	[ ]	[ ]
Math lab	[ ]	[ ]

LD PROGRAM STAFF

Total number of LD Program staff (including director):

Key staff person available to work with LD students: Allyson Krings M.S., LPC, Counselor/Coord. Support for Students with Disabil.

College of St. Joseph

Rutland, VT

Address: 71 Clement Road, Rutland, VT, 05701
Admissions telephone: 802 773-5900, extension 3206
Admissions FAX: 802 776-5258
Dean of Admissions: Patricia Ryan
Admissions e-mail: admissions@csj.edu
Web site: http://www.csj.edu
SAT Code: 3297

LD program name: Project Success
Director of Project Success: Charlotte Gillam
LD program telephone: 802 776-5239
LD program e-mail: cgillam@csj.edu
LD program enrollment: 69, Total campus enrollment: 266

GENERAL

College of St. Joseph is a private, coed, four-year institution. 90-acre campus in Rutland (population: 17,292), 70 miles from Burlington and 85 miles from Albany, NY. Served by bus and train; airports serve Boston (170 miles) and Albany. Public transportation serves campus. Semester system.

LD ADMISSIONS

Students do not complete a separate application and are simultaneously accepted to the LD program. A member of the LD program does not sit on the admissions committee. A personal interview is recommended. Essay is required and may be typed.

For fall 2004, 19 completed self-identified LD applications were received. 16 applications were offered admission, and 16 enrolled.

SECONDARY SCHOOL REQUIREMENTS

Graduation from secondary school required; GED accepted. The following course distribution required: 4 units of English, 3 units of math, 2 units of science, 2 units of social studies, 1 unit of history, 6 units of academic electives.

TESTING

SAT Reasoning required; ACT may be substituted.

All enrolled freshmen (fall 2004):

Average SAT I Scores:	Verbal: 465	Math: 445
Average ACT Scores:	Composite:	

Child Study Team report is not required. A neuropsychological or comprehensive psycho-educational evaluation is required for admission. Tests required as part of this documentation:

☑ WAIS-IV	☑ Woodcock-Johnson
☑ WISC-IV	☐ Nelson-Denny Reading Test
☐ SATA	☐ Other

UNDERGRADUATE STUDENT BODY

Total undergraduate student enrollment: 126 Men, 245 Women.

Composition of student body (fall 2004):

	Undergraduate	Freshmen
International	0.0	0.0
Black	15.8	5.3
American Indian	0.0	0.0
Asian-American	0.0	0.0
Hispanic	0.0	0.0
White	84.2	94.7
Unreported	0.0	0.0
	100.0%	100.0%

48% are from out of state. Average age of full-time undergraduates is 20. 91% of classes have fewer than 20 students, 9% have between 20 and 50 students.

STUDENT HOUSING

55% of freshmen live in college housing. Freshmen are required to live on campus. Housing is guaranteed for all undergraduates. Campus can house 170 undergraduates. Single rooms are available for students with medical or special needs. A medical note is not required.

EXPENSES

Tuition (2005-06): $13,800 per year.
Room & Board: $6,850.
There is no additional cost for LD program/services.

LD SERVICES

LD program size is not limited.

LD services available to:

☑ Freshmen ☑ Sophomores ☑ Juniors ☑ Seniors

Academic Accommodations

Curriculum		In class	
Foreign language waiver	☐	Early syllabus	☐
Lighter course load	☑	Note takers in class	☑
Math waiver	☐	Priority seating	☑
Other special classes	☐	Tape recorders	☑
Priority registrations	☐	Videotaped classes	☐
Substitution of courses	☐	Text on tape	☐
Exams		**Services**	
Extended time	☑	Diagnostic tests	☐
Oral exams	☑	Learning centers	☑
Take home exams	☐	Proofreaders	☑
Exams on tape or computer	☐	Readers	☐
Untimed exams	☑	Reading Machines/Kurzweil	☐
Other accommodations	☐	Special bookstore section	☐
		Typists	☐

Credit toward degree is not given for remedial courses taken.

Counseling Services

☐ Academic
☐ Psychological
☐ Student Support groups
☐ Vocational

Tutoring

Individual tutoring is available daily.

Average size of tutoring groups: 6

	Individual	Group
Time management	☑	☐
Organizational skills	☑	☐
Learning strategies	☑	☐
Study skills	☑	☑
Content area	☐	☐
Writing lab	☑	☑
Math lab	☑	☑

UNIQUE LD PROGRAM FEATURES

It should be noted that Project Success provides services for all students at the College, even if they are not documented LD students. Non-LD students are provided support through tutoring and proofreading of papers.

LD PROGRAM STAFF

Total number of LD Program staff (including director):

Full Time: 1 Part Time: 1

There is an advisor/advocate from the LD program available to students. The advisor/advocate meets with faculty 1 time per month. 3 peer tutors are available to work with LD students.

Key staff person available to work with LD students: Charlotte Gillam, Director of Project Success.

Green Mountain College

Poultney, VT

Address: 1 College Circle, Poultney, VT, 05764-1199
Admissions telephone: 800 776-6675
Admissions FAX: 802 287-8099
Dean of Enrollment Services: Joel Wincowski
Admissions e-mail: admiss@greenmtn.edu
Web site: http://www.greenmtn.edu
SAT Code: 3418   ACT Code: 4302

DIrector, Calhoun Learning Center: Nancy Ruby
LD program telephone: 802 287-8287
LD program e-mail: rubyn@greenmtn.edu
Total campus enrollment: 659

GENERAL

Green Mountain College is a private, coed, four-year institution. 155-acre campus in Poultney (population: 3,633), 20 miles from Rutland. Major airport serves Albany, NY (70 miles); bus serves Rutland; train serves Whitehall, NY (10 miles). Semester system.

LD ADMISSIONS

A personal interview is recommended. Essay is required and may be typed.

SECONDARY SCHOOL REQUIREMENTS

Graduation from secondary school required; GED accepted. The following course distribution required: 4 units of English, 3 units of math, 2 units of science, 1 unit of social studies, 2 units of history, 6 units of academic electives.

TESTING

SAT Reasoning or ACT required.

All enrolled freshmen (fall 2004):

Average SAT I Scores: Verbal: Math:
Average ACT Scores: Composite:

Child Study Team report is not required. Tests required as part of this documentation:

- [ ] WAIS-IV
- [ ] WISC-IV
- [ ] SATA
- [ ] Woodcock-Johnson
- [ ] Nelson-Denny Reading Test
- [ ] Other

UNDERGRADUATE STUDENT BODY

Total undergraduate student enrollment: 351 Men, 308 Women.

92% are from out of state.

STUDENT HOUSING

Housing is guaranteed for all undergraduates. Campus can house 607 undergraduates.

EXPENSES

Tuition (2005-06): $21,604 per year (in-state), $21,600 (out-of-state).
Room: $4,700. Board: $2,990.
There is no additional cost for LD program/services.

LD SERVICES

LD program size is not limited.

LD services available to:

- [ ] Freshmen
- [ ] Sophomores
- [ ] Juniors
- [ ] Seniors

Academic Accommodations

Curriculum		**In class**	
Foreign language waiver	[ ]	Early syllabus	[ ]
Lighter course load	[x]	Note takers in class	[x]
Math waiver	[ ]	Priority seating	[ ]
Other special classes	[x]	Tape recorders	[x]
Priority registrations	[ ]	Videotaped classes	[ ]
Substitution of courses	[ ]	Text on tape	[ ]
Exams		**Services**	
Extended time	[x]	Diagnostic tests	[x]
Oral exams	[x]	Learning centers	[x]
Take home exams	[ ]	Proofreaders	[ ]
Exams on tape or computer	[ ]	Readers	[x]
Untimed exams	[x]	Reading Machines/Kurzweil	[x]
Other accommodations	[ ]	Special bookstore section	[x]
		Typists	[ ]

Credit toward degree is not given for remedial courses taken.

Counseling Services

- [ ] Academic
- [ ] Psychological
- [ ] Student Support groups
- [ ] Vocational

Tutoring

	Individual	Group
Time management	[ ]	[ ]
Organizational skills	[ ]	[ ]
Learning strategies	[ ]	[ ]
Study skills	[ ]	[ ]
Content area	[ ]	[ ]
Writing lab	[ ]	[ ]
Math lab	[ ]	[ ]

LD PROGRAM STAFF

Total number of LD Program staff (including director):

Full Time: 2   Part Time: 2

Key staff person available to work with LD students: Nancy Ruby, Director, Calhoun Learning Center.

Johnson State College

Johnson, VT

Address: 337 College Hill, Johnson, VT, 05656-9405
Admissions telephone: 800 635-2356
Admissions FAX: 802 635-1230
Associate Dean of Enrollment Services: Penny P. Howrigan
Admissions e-mail: jscapply@jsc.vsc.edu
Web site: http://www.johnsonstatecollege.com
SAT Code: 3766 ACT Code: 4316

Director of Academic Support Services: Katherine Veilleux
LD program telephone: 802 635-1259
LD program e-mail: Katherine.Veilleux@jsc.vsc.edu
Total campus enrollment: 1,441

GENERAL

Johnson State College is a public, coed, four-year institution. 350-acre campus in Johnson (population: 3,272), 45 miles from Burlington and 100 miles from Montreal, Quebec, Canada. Major airport and bus serve Burlington; train serves Waterbury (30miles). School operates transportation to Burlington and ski area. Semester system.

LD ADMISSIONS

A personal interview is recommended. Essay is required and may be typed.

SECONDARY SCHOOL REQUIREMENTS

Graduation from secondary school required; GED accepted. The following course distribution required: 4 units of English, 3 units of math, 3 units of science, 3 units of social studies.

TESTING

SAT Reasoning required. ACT recommended. SAT Subject required.

All enrolled freshmen (fall 2004):

Average SAT I Scores: Verbal: 450 Math: 450
Average ACT Scores: Composite: 23

Child Study Team report is not required. Tests required as part of this documentation:

- ☐ WAIS-IV
- ☐ WISC-IV
- ☐ SATA
- ☐ Woodcock-Johnson
- ☐ Nelson-Denny Reading Test
- ☐ Other

UNDERGRADUATE STUDENT BODY

Total undergraduate student enrollment: 584 Men, 777 Women.

Composition of student body (fall 2004):

	Undergraduate	Freshmen
International	0.0	0.0
Black	2.8	0.7
American Indian	1.6	1.1
Asian-American	0.3	0.5
Hispanic	0.6	1.5
White	86.9	87.5
Unreported	7.8	8.7
	100.0%	100.0%

39% are from out of state.

STUDENT HOUSING

Housing is guaranteed for all undergraduates.

EXPENSES

Tuition (2005-06): $6,312 per year (in-state), $13,632 (out-of-state). Room: $3,974. Board: $2,700.

There is no additional cost for LD program/services.

LD SERVICES

LD program size is not limited.

LD services available to:

☐ Freshmen ☐ Sophomores ☐ Juniors ☐ Seniors

Academic Accommodations

Curriculum		In class	
Foreign language waiver	☐	Early syllabus	☐
Lighter course load	☐	Note takers in class	■
Math waiver	☐	Priority seating	☐
Other special classes	☐	Tape recorders	■
Priority registrations	☐	Videotaped classes	☐
Substitution of courses	☐	Text on tape	☐
Exams		**Services**	
Extended time	■	Diagnostic tests	☐
Oral exams	■	Learning centers	■
Take home exams	☐	Proofreaders	☐
Exams on tape or computer	☐	Readers	■
Untimed exams	☐	Reading Machines/Kurzweil	■
Other accommodations	☐	Special bookstore section	☐
		Typists	☐

Credit toward degree is given for remedial courses taken.

Counseling Services

- ☐ Academic
- ☐ Psychological
- ☐ Student Support groups
- ☐ Vocational

Tutoring

	Individual	Group
Time management	☐	☐
Organizational skills	☐	☐
Learning strategies	☐	☐
Study skills	☐	☐
Content area	☐	☐
Writing lab	☐	☐
Math lab	☐	☐

LD PROGRAM STAFF

Total number of LD Program staff (including director):

Full Time: 8 Part Time: 8

Key staff person available to work with LD students: Katherine Veilleux, Director of Acdemic Support Services.

Landmark College

Putney, VT

Address: 1 River Road South, Putney VT, 05346
Admissions telephone: 802 387-6718
Admissions FAX: 802 387-6868
Dean of Admissions: Dale Herold
Admissions e-mail: admissions@landmark.edu
Web site: http://www.landmark.edu

Assistant Director of Admissions: Rachel Beran
LD program telephone: 802 387-6718
LD program e-mail: rberan@landmark.edu
LD program enrollment: 390, Total campus enrollment: 397

GENERAL

Landmark College is a private, coed, two-year institution. 125-acre campus in Putney (population: 1,100), 8 miles from Brattleboro. Major airport serves Hartford, CT (80 miles); bus and train serve Brattleboro. Semester system.

LD ADMISSIONS

Application deadline is rolling. Students do not complete a separate application and are simultaneously accepted to the LD program. A member of the LD program does sit on the admissions committee. High school waivers are accepted for foreign language and mathematics. A personal interview is required. Essay is required and may be typed.

SECONDARY SCHOOL REQUIREMENTS

Graduation from secondary school required; GED accepted.

TESTING

Child Study Team report is not required. A neuropsychological or comprehensive psycho-educational evaluation is required for admission. Must be dated within 36 months of application. Tests required as part of this documentation:

■	WAIS-IV	■	Woodcock-Johnson
■	WISC-IV	■	Nelson-Denny Reading Test
□	SATA	□	Other

STUDENT HOUSING

Single rooms are available for students with specific disabilities. A medical note is required.

LD SERVICES

LD program size is limited.

LD services available to:

■ Freshmen ■ Sophomores ■ Juniors ■ Seniors

Academic Accommodations

Curriculum		**In class**	
Foreign language waiver	□	Early syllabus	□
Lighter course load	■	Note takers in class	□
Math waiver	□	Priority seating	□
Other special classes	□	Tape recorders	■
Priority registrations	□	Videotaped classes	□
Substitution of courses	□	Text on tape	■
Exams		**Services**	
Extended time	■	Diagnostic tests	□
Oral exams	■	Learning centers	■
Take home exams	□	Proofreaders	■
Exams on tape or computer	■	Readers	□
Untimed exams	■	Reading Machines/Kurzweil	■
Other accommodations	■	Special bookstore section	■
		Typists	□

Credit toward degree is not given for remedial courses taken.

Counseling Services

■ Academic
□ Psychological
□ Student Support groups
□ Vocational

Tutoring

Individual tutoring is available daily.

	Individual	Group
Time management	■	■
Organizational skills	■	■
Learning strategies	■	■
Study skills	■	■
Content area	■	■
Writing lab	■	■
Math lab	■	■

LD PROGRAM STAFF

There is an advisor/advocate from the LD program available to faculty and students. The advisor/advocate meets with faculty as needed and with students four times per month.

Key staff person available to work with LD students: John Kipp, Academic Dean

Lyndon State College

Lyndonville, VT

Address: PO Box 919, Lyndonville, VT, 05851
Admissions telephone: 800 225-1998 (in New England)
Admissions FAX: 802 626-6335
Director of Admissions: Michelle McCaffrey
Admissions e-mail: admissions@lyndonstate.edu
Web site: http://www.lyndonstate.edu
SAT Code: 3767 ACT Code: 4318

LD program name: Project EXCEL
Learning Specialist: Mary Etter
LD program telephone: 802 626-6210
LD program e-mail: mary.etter@lyndonstate.edu
Total campus enrollment: 1, 304

GENERAL

Lyndon State College is a public, coed, four-year institution. 175-acre campus in Lyndonville (population: 1,227), 85 miles from Burlington. Served by bus; airport serves Burlington; train serves Montpelier (45 miles). School operates transportation to Lyndonville and St. Johnsbury. Public transportation serves campus. Semester system.

LD ADMISSIONS

Students do not complete a separate application and are simultaneously accepted to the LD program. A member of the LD program does not sit on the admissions committee. A personal interview is recommended. Essay is not required.

SECONDARY SCHOOL REQUIREMENTS

Graduation from secondary school required; GED accepted. The following course distribution required: 4 units of English, 3 units of math, 2 units of science, 2 units of foreign language, 2 units of social studies, 2 units of history.

TESTING

SAT Reasoning or ACT considered if submitted; SAT Reasoning preferred. SAT Subject recommended.

All enrolled freshmen (fall 2004):

Average SAT I Scores:	Verbal: 457	Math: 444
Average ACT Scores:	Composite:	

Child Study Team report is not required. Tests required as part of this documentation:

- ☐ WAIS-IV
- ☐ WISC-IV
- ☐ SATA
- ☐ Woodcock-Johnson
- ☐ Nelson-Denny Reading Test
- ☐ Other

UNDERGRADUATE STUDENT BODY

Total undergraduate student enrollment: 643 Men, 545 Women.

48% are from out of state. Average age of full-time undergraduates is 22.

STUDENT HOUSING

65% of freshmen live in college housing. Freshmen are required to live on campus. There are annual limits on the number of upperclassmen allowed in the residence halls. Campus can house 600 undergraduates. Single rooms are available for students with medical or special needs. A medical note is required.

EXPENSES

There is no additional cost for LD program/services.

LD SERVICES

LD program size is not limited.

LD services available to:

■ Freshmen ■ Sophomores ■ Juniors ■ Seniors

Academic Accommodations

Curriculum		In class	
Foreign language waiver	☐	Early syllabus	☐
Lighter course load	■	Note takers in class	■
Math waiver	☐	Priority seating	☐
Other special classes	☐	Tape recorders	■
Priority registrations	☐	Videotaped classes	☐
Substitution of courses	☐	Text on tape	☐
Exams		**Services**	
Extended time	■	Diagnostic tests	☐
Oral exams	■	Learning centers	■
Take home exams	☐	Proofreaders	☐
Exams on tape or computer	☐	Readers	■
Untimed exams	■	Reading Machines/Kurzweil	■
Other accommodations	☐	Special bookstore section	☐
		Typists	☐

Credit toward degree is not given for remedial courses taken.

Counseling Services

- ☐ Academic
- ☐ Psychological
- ☐ Student Support groups
- ☐ Vocational

Tutoring

Individual tutoring is available daily.

	Individual	Group
Time management	☐	■
Organizational skills	☐	■
Learning strategies	☐	☐
Study skills	■	☐
Content area	☐	☐
Writing lab	■	☐
Math lab	■	☐

LD PROGRAM STAFF

Total number of LD Program staff (including director):

Full Time: 1 Part Time: 1

Key staff person available to work with LD students: Mary Etter, Learning Specialist.

Marlboro College

Marlboro, VT

Address: PO Box A, 2582 South Road, Marlboro, VT, 05344-0300
Admissions telephone: 800 343-0049
Admissions FAX: 802 451-7555
Vice President, Enrollment: Alan E. Young
Admissions e-mail: admissions@marlboro.edu
Web site: http://www.marlboro.edu
SAT Code: 3509 ACT Code: 4304

Director of Academic Advising: Catherine O'Callaghan
LD program telephone: 802 258-9235
LD program e-mail: cocallag@marlboro.edu
Total campus enrollment: 357

GENERAL

Marlboro College is a private, coed, four-year institution. 366-acre campus in Marlboro (population: 978), nine miles from Brattleboro and 60 miles from Springfield, Mass. Major airport serves Hartford (90 miles). School operates transportation to Brattleboro. Semester system.

LD ADMISSIONS

A personal interview is required. Essay is required and may be typed.

SECONDARY SCHOOL REQUIREMENTS

Graduation from secondary school required; GED accepted. The following course distribution required: 4 units of English, 3 units of math, 3 units of science, 3 units of foreign language, 1 unit of social studies, 2 units of history, 5 units of academic electives.

TESTING

SAT Reasoning required; ACT may be substituted. SAT Subject recommended.

All enrolled freshmen (fall 2004):

Average SAT I Scores: Verbal: 640 Math: 550
Average ACT Scores: Composite: 26

Child Study Team report is not required. Tests required as part of this documentation:

- ☐ WAIS-IV
- ☐ WISC-IV
- ☐ SATA
- ☐ Woodcock-Johnson
- ☐ Nelson-Denny Reading Test
- ☐ Other

UNDERGRADUATE STUDENT BODY

Total undergraduate student enrollment: 142 Men, 189 Women.

Composition of student body (fall 2004):

	Undergraduate	Freshmen
International	1.0	1.2
Black	3.0	0.8
American Indian	1.0	0.4
Asian-American	1.0	0.4
Hispanic	3.0	0.8
White	76.1	92.5
Unreported	14.9	3.9
	100.0%	100.0%

89% are from out of state. Average age of full-time undergraduates is 19. 88% of classes have fewer than 20 students, 12% have between 20 and 50 students.

STUDENT HOUSING

100% of freshmen live in college housing. Freshmen are required to live on campus. Housing is not guaranteed for all undergraduates. Housing is awarded based on number of earned credits. Campus can house 270 undergraduates.

EXPENSES

Tuition (2005-06): $26,940 per year.
Room: $4,540. Board: $3,650.
There is no additional cost for LD program/services.

LD SERVICES

LD services available to:

■ Freshmen ■ Sophomores ■ Juniors ■ Seniors

Academic Accommodations

Curriculum		**In class**	
Foreign language waiver	☐	Early syllabus	☐
Lighter course load	☐	Note takers in class	☐
Math waiver	☐	Priority seating	☐
Other special classes	☐	Tape recorders	☐
Priority registrations	☐	Videotaped classes	☐
Substitution of courses	☐	Text on tape	☐
Exams		**Services**	
Extended time	■	Diagnostic tests	☐
Oral exams	☐	Learning centers	■
Take home exams	☐	Proofreaders	☐
Exams on tape or computer	☐	Readers	☐
Untimed exams	■	Reading Machines/Kurzweil	☐
Other accommodations	☐	Special bookstore section	☐
		Typists	☐

Credit toward degree is not given for remedial courses taken.

Counseling Services

- ☐ Academic
- ☐ Psychological
- ☐ Student Support groups
- ☐ Vocational

Tutoring

	Individual	Group
Time management	☐	☐
Organizational skills	☐	☐
Learning strategies	☐	☐
Study skills	☐	☐
Content area	☐	☐
Writing lab	☐	☐
Math lab	☐	☐

LD PROGRAM STAFF

Total number of LD Program staff (including director):

Full Time: 1 Part Time: 1

Key staff person available to work with LD students: Jeremy Holch, Director of Academic Support Services.

Middlebury College

Middlebury, VT

Address: Middlebury, VT, 05753
Admissions telephone: 802 443-3000
Admissions FAX: 802 443-2056
Director of Admissions: John E. Hanson
Admissions e-mail: admissions@middlebury.edu
Web site: http://www.middlebury.edu
SAT Code: 3526 ACT Code: 4306

ADA Coordinator: Jodi E. Litchfield
LD program telephone: 802 443-5936
LD program e-mail: litchfie@middlebury.edu
Total campus enrollment: 2,357

GENERAL

Middlebury College is a private, coed, four-year institution. 350-acre campus in Middlebury (population: 8,183), 35 miles from Burlington; additional mountain campus. Served by bus; airports serve Burlington and Manchester (140 miles); train serves Essex Junction (35 miles). Public transportation serves campus. 4-1-4 system.

SECONDARY SCHOOL REQUIREMENTS

Graduation from secondary school is not required.

TESTING

ACT required. SAT Subject recommended.

All enrolled freshmen (fall 2004):

Average SAT I Scores: Verbal: 720 Math: 720
Average ACT Scores: Composite: 30

Child Study Team report is not required. Tests required as part of this documentation:

- ☐ WAIS-IV
- ☐ WISC-IV
- ☐ SATA
- ☐ Woodcock-Johnson
- ☐ Nelson-Denny Reading Test
- ☐ Other

UNDERGRADUATE STUDENT BODY

Total undergraduate student enrollment: 1,118 Men, 1,189 Women.

Composition of student body (fall 2004):

	Undergraduate	Freshmen
International	9.5	8.1
Black	3.1	2.7
American Indian	0.3	0.5
Asian-American	6.2	7.3
Hispanic	5.5	5.0
White	68.5	70.2
Unreported	6.9	6.2
	100.0%	100.0%

93% are from out of state. Average age of full-time undergraduates is 20. 68% of classes have fewer than 20 students, 27% have between 20 and 50 students, 5% have more than 50 students.

STUDENT HOUSING

100% of freshmen live in college housing. Freshmen are required to live on campus. Housing is guaranteed for all undergraduates. Campus can house 2,350 undergraduates.

EXPENSES

Tuition (2005-06): $42,120 per year (comprehensive).
There is no additional cost for LD program/services.

LD SERVICES

LD program size is not limited.

LD services available to:

☐ Freshmen ☐ Sophomores ☐ Juniors ☐ Seniors

Academic Accommodations

Curriculum		In class	
Foreign language waiver	☐	Early syllabus	☐
Lighter course load	■	Note takers in class	■
Math waiver	☐	Priority seating	☐
Other special classes	☐	Tape recorders	■
Priority registrations	☐	Videotaped classes	☐
Substitution of courses	☐	Text on tape	☐
Exams		**Services**	
Extended time	■	Diagnostic tests	■
Oral exams	■	Learning centers	■
Take home exams	☐	Proofreaders	☐
Exams on tape or computer	☐	Readers	■
Untimed exams	☐	Reading Machines/Kurzweil	■
Other accommodations	☐	Special bookstore section	☐
		Typists	☐

Counseling Services

- ☐ Academic
- ☐ Psychological
- ☐ Student Support groups
- ☐ Vocational

Tutoring

	Individual	Group
Time management	☐	☐
Organizational skills	☐	☐
Learning strategies	☐	☐
Study skills	☐	☐
Content area	☐	☐
Writing lab	☐	☐
Math lab	☐	☐

UNIQUE LD PROGRAM FEATURES

No specific program for LD, but office exists to meet their needs; requirements for these students are the same as for all students. 128 students who identied with the ADA office; 64 of which identify as having a learning disability.

LD PROGRAM STAFF

Total number of LD Program staff (including director):

Full Time: 1 Part Time: 1

Key staff person available to work with LD students: Jodi E. Litchfield, ADA Coordinator.

Norwich University

Northfield, VT

Address: 158 Harmon Drive, Northfield, VT, 05663
Admissions telephone: 800 468-6679
Admissions FAX: 802 485-2032
Dean of Admissions and Marketing: Karen McGrath
Admissions e-mail: nuadm@norwich.edu
Web site: http://www.norwich.edu
SAT Code: 3669 ACT Code: 4308

Director of Learning Support Center: Paula Gills
LD program telephone: 802 485-2132
LD program e-mail: gills@norwich.edu
LD program enrollment: 60, Total campus enrollment: 1,951

GENERAL

Norwich University is a private, coed, four-year institution. 1,125-acre campus in Northfield (population: 5,791), 50 miles from Burlington. Airport serves Burlington; bus and train serve Montpelier (12 miles). Semester system.

LD ADMISSIONS

Students do not complete a separate application and are not simultaneously accepted to the LD program. A member of the LD program does not sit on the admissions committee. A personal interview is recommended. Essay is not required.

SECONDARY SCHOOL REQUIREMENTS

Graduation from secondary school required; GED accepted. The following course distribution required: 3 units of history.

TESTING

SAT Reasoning or ACT required. SAT Subject recommended.

All enrolled freshmen (fall 2004):

Average SAT I Scores: Verbal: 528 Math: 528
Average ACT Scores: Composite: 22

Child Study Team report is not required. A neuropsychological or comprehensive psycho-education evaluation is not required for admission. Tests required as part of this documentation:

- ☐ WAIS-IV
- ☐ WISC-IV
- ☐ SATA
- ☐ Woodcock-Johnson
- ☐ Nelson-Denny Reading Test
- ☐ Other

UNDERGRADUATE STUDENT BODY

Total undergraduate student enrollment: 1,951.

Composition of student body (fall 2004):

	Undergraduate	Freshmen
International	2.3	2.3
Black	2.6	3.4
American Indian	0.2	0.2
Asian-American	2.3	1.9
Hispanic	3.6	4.0
White	81.1	79.6
Unreported	7.9	8.6
	100.0%	100.0%

76% are from out of state. Average age of full-time undergraduates is 21. 57% of classes have fewer than 20 students, 42% have between 20 and 50 students, 1% have more than 50 students.

STUDENT HOUSING

99% of freshmen live in college housing. Freshmen are required to live on campus. Housing is not guaranteed for all undergraduates. Some juniors and seniors who are not in the Corps of Cadets may be asked or required to live off-campus. Campus can house 1,593 undergraduates.

EXPENSES

Tuition (2005-06): $20,024 per year.

Room & Board: $7,374.

There is no additional cost for LD program/services.

LD SERVICES

LD program size is not limited.

LD services available to:

■ Freshmen ■ Sophomores ■ Juniors ■ Seniors

Academic Accommodations

Curriculum		**In class**	
Foreign language waiver	☐	Early syllabus	☐
Lighter course load	☐	Note takers in class	☐
Math waiver	☐	Priority seating	☐
Other special classes	☐	Tape recorders	☐
Priority registrations	■	Videotaped classes	☐
Substitution of courses	☐	Text on tape	■
Exams		**Services**	
Extended time	■	Diagnostic tests	☐
Oral exams	■	Learning centers	■
Take home exams	☐	Proofreaders	☐
Exams on tape or computer	☐	Readers	■
Untimed exams	☐	Reading Machines/Kurzweil	☐
Other accommodations	■	Special bookstore section	☐
		Typists	☐

Credit toward degree is not given for remedial courses taken.

Counseling Services

- ☐ Academic
- ☐ Psychological
- ☐ Student Support groups
- ☐ Vocational

Tutoring

Individual tutoring is available weekly.

	Individual	Group
Time management	■	☐
Organizational skills	■	☐
Learning strategies	■	☐
Study skills	■	☐
Content area	■	☐
Writing lab	☐	☐
Math lab	■	☐

LD PROGRAM STAFF

Total number of LD Program staff (including director):

Full Time: 3 Part Time: 3

There is not an advisor/advocate from the LD program available to students. 30 peer tutors are available to work with LD students.

Key staff person available to work with LD students: Paula Gills, Director of Learning Support Center.

Saint Michael's College

Colchester, VT

Address: 1 Winooski Park, Colchester, VT, 05439
Admissions telephone: 800 762-8000
Admissions FAX: 802 654-2906
Vice President for Admission and Enrollment Management: Jacqueline Murphy
Admissions e-mail: admission@smcvt.edu
Web site: http://www.smcvt.edu
SAT Code: 3757 ACT Code: 4312

Associate Dean of the College: Dr. William Wilson
LD program telephone: 802 654-2347
LD program e-mail: wwilson@smcvt.edu
LD program enrollment: 192, Total campus enrollment: 1,983

GENERAL

Saint Michael's College is a private, coed, four-year institution. 480-acre campus in Colchester (population: 16,986), three miles from Burlington and 90 miles from Montreal, Quebec, Canada. Airport and bus serve Burlington; major airport serves Montreal; train serves Essex Junction (three miles). School operates transportation to north side of campus. Public transportation serves campus. Semester system.

LD ADMISSIONS

A personal interview is recommended. Essay is required and may be typed.

For fall 2004, 121 completed self-identified LD applications were received. 60 applications were offered admission, and 27 enrolled.

SECONDARY SCHOOL REQUIREMENTS

Graduation from secondary school required; GED accepted. The following course distribution required: 4 units of English, 3 units of math, 3 units of science, 3 units of foreign language, 3 units of social studies.

TESTING

SAT Reasoning required; ACT may be substituted. SAT Subject required.

All enrolled freshmen (fall 2004):

Average SAT I Scores: Verbal: 563 Math: 561
Average ACT Scores: Composite:

Child Study Team report is not required. A neuropsychological or comprehensive psycho-educational evaluation is required for admission. Must be dated within 36 months of application. Tests required as part of this documentation:

- [x] WAIS-IV
- [x] WISC-IV
- [ ] SATA
- [x] Woodcock-Johnson
- [x] Nelson-Denny Reading Test
- [x] Other

UNDERGRADUATE STUDENT BODY

Total undergraduate student enrollment: 917 Men, 1,104 Women.

Composition of student body (fall 2004):

	Undergraduate	Freshmen
International	0.8	2.2
Black	0.2	1.5
American Indian	0.2	0.1
Asian-American	1.5	1.1
Hispanic	1.2	1.1
White	96.1	94.0
Unreported	0.0	0.0
	100.0%	100.0%

77% are from out of state. Average age of full-time undergraduates is 20. 60% of classes have fewer than 20 students, 39% have between 20 and 50 students, 1% have more than 50 students.

STUDENT HOUSING

99% of freshmen live in college housing. Freshmen are required to live on campus. Housing is guaranteed for all undergraduates. Campus can house 1,900 undergraduates. Single rooms are available for students with medical or special needs. A medical note is required.

EXPENSES

Tuition (2005-06): $26,550 per year.
Room & Board: $6,560.
There is no additional cost for LD program/services.

LD SERVICES

LD program size is not limited.

LD services available to:

- [x] Freshmen
- [x] Sophomores
- [x] Juniors
- [x] Seniors

Academic Accommodations

Curriculum
- [ ] Foreign language waiver
- [x] Lighter course load
- [ ] Math waiver
- [ ] Other special classes
- [ ] Priority registrations
- [ ] Substitution of courses

Exams
- [x] Extended time
- [ ] Oral exams
- [ ] Take home exams
- [ ] Exams on tape or computer
- [ ] Untimed exams
- [ ] Other accommodations

In class
- [ ] Early syllabus
- [x] Note takers in class
- [ ] Priority seating
- [x] Tape recorders
- [ ] Videotaped classes
- [ ] Text on tape

Services
- [ ] Diagnostic tests
- [x] Learning centers
- [ ] Proofreaders
- [x] Readers
- [ ] Reading Machines/Kurzweil
- [ ] Special bookstore section
- [ ] Typists

Credit toward degree is not given for remedial courses taken.

Counseling Services

- [x] Academic
- [x] Psychological
- [x] Student Support groups
- [x] Vocational

Tutoring

Individual tutoring is available weekly.

Average size of tutoring groups: 4

	Individual	Group
Time management	[x]	[x]
Organizational skills	[x]	[x]
Learning strategies	[x]	[x]
Study skills	[x]	[x]
Content area	[x]	[ ]
Writing lab	[x]	[ ]
Math lab	[x]	[x]

LD PROGRAM STAFF

Total number of LD Program staff (including director):

Full Time: 1 Part Time: 1

There is an advisor/advocate from the LD program available to students.

Key staff person available to work with LD students: Antonia Messuri, LD Coordinator.

University of Vermont

Burlington, VT

Address: South Prospect Street, Burlington, VT, 05405-0160
Admissions telephone: 802 656-3370
Admissions FAX: 802 656-8611
Director of Admissions and Financial Aid: Donald M. Honeman
Admissions e-mail: admissions@uvm.edu
Web site: http://www.uvm.edu
SAT Code: 3920 ACT Code: 4322

LD program name: ACCESS
LD program address: A-170 Living-Learning Center,
Assistant Director, ACCESS: Margaret Ottinger
LD program telephone: 802 656-7853
LD program e-mail: Margaret.Ottinger@uvm.edu
LD program enrollment: 150, Total campus enrollment: 9,235

GENERAL

University of Vermont is a public, coed, four-year institution. 425-acre campus in Burlington (population: 38,889), 80 miles from Montreal, Quebec, Canada, and 230 miles from Boston. Served by air and bus; train serves Essex Junction (seven miles). School operates transportation around campus and to downtown Burlington. Public transportation serves campus. Semester system.

LD ADMISSIONS

Students do not complete a separate application and are not simultaneously accepted to the LD program. A member of the LD program does not sit on the admissions committee. High school waivers are accepted for foreign language. A personal interview is not required. Essay is not required. Admissions requirements that may be waived for LD students include foreign language requirement

For fall 2004, 100 completed self-identified LD applications were received.

SECONDARY SCHOOL REQUIREMENTS

Graduation from secondary school required; GED accepted. The following course distribution required: 4 units of English, 3 units of math, 2 units of science, 2 units of foreign language, 3 units of social studies.

TESTING

SAT Reasoning or ACT required. SAT Subject required.

All enrolled freshmen (fall 2004):

Average SAT I Scores:	Verbal: 577	Math: 578
Average ACT Scores:	Composite: 25	

Child Study Team report is not required. A neuropsychological or comprehensive psycho-educational evaluation is required for admission. Must be dated within 36 months of application. Tests required as part of this documentation:

- ■ WAIS-IV
- ■ WISC-IV
- ■ SATA
- ■ Woodcock-Johnson
- ■ Nelson-Denny Reading Test
- ■ Other

UNDERGRADUATE STUDENT BODY

Total undergraduate student enrollment: 3,752 Men, 4,840 Women.

Composition of student body (fall 2004):

	Undergraduate	Freshmen
International	0.6	0.7
Black	1.0	1.1
American Indian	0.1	0.2
Asian-American	2.1	1.8
Hispanic	2.4	1.9
White	91.8	92.8
Unreported	2.0	1.5
	100.0%	100.0%

61% are from out of state. 7% join a fraternity and 6% join a sorority. Average age of full-time undergraduates is 20. 49% of classes have fewer than 20 students, 42% have between 20 and 50 students, 9% have more than 50 students.

STUDENT HOUSING

98% of freshmen live in college housing. Freshmen are required to live on campus. Housing guaranteed to undergraduates as long as they live continuously on campus. Students who move off-campus must place their names on a waiting list should they wish to return to campus housing. Campus can house 4,337 undergraduates. Single rooms are available for students with medical or special needs. A medical note is required.

EXPENSES

Tuition (2005-06): $9,452 per year (in-state), $23,638 (out-of-state).
Room: $4,936. Board: $2,396.
There is no additional cost for LD program/services.

LD SERVICES

LD program size is not limited.

LD services available to:

■ Freshmen ■ Sophomores ■ Juniors ■ Seniors

Academic Accommodations

Curriculum		In class	
Foreign language waiver	☐	Early syllabus	☐
Lighter course load	■	Note takers in class	■
Math waiver	☐	Priority seating	☐
Other special classes	■	Tape recorders	■
Priority registrations	■	Videotaped classes	☐
Substitution of courses	☐	Text on tape	■
Exams		**Services**	
Extended time	■	Diagnostic tests	☐
Oral exams	☐	Learning centers	■
Take home exams	☐	Proofreaders	☐
Exams on tape or computer	■	Readers	■
Untimed exams	☐	Reading Machines/Kurzweil	■
Other accommodations	■	Special bookstore section	☐
		Typists	☐

Credit toward degree is not given for remedial courses taken.

Counseling Services

- ■ Academic
- ☐ Psychological
- ☐ Student Support groups
- ☐ Vocational

Tutoring

Individual tutoring is available weekly.

	Individual	Group
Time management	■	■
Organizational skills	■	■
Learning strategies	■	■
Study skills	■	■
Content area	■	■
Writing lab	■	☐
Math lab	■	☐

LD PROGRAM STAFF

Total number of LD Program staff (including director):

Full Time: 7 Part Time: 7

There is an advisor/advocate from the LD program available to students.

Key staff person available to work with LD students: Margaret Ottinger, Asst Dir, Academic Support Programs/ACCESS.

LD Program web site: www.uvm.edu/access

Vermont Technical College

Randolph Center, VT

Address: One Main Street, Randolph Center, VT, 05061
Admissions telephone: 800 442-8821
Admissions FAX: 802 728-1390
Director of Admissions: Dwight Cross
Admissions e-mail: admissions@vtc.edu
Web site: http://www.vtc.edu
SAT Code: 3941 ACT Code: 4323

Learning Specialist: Robin Goodall
LD program telephone: 802 728-1278
LD program e-mail: rgoodall@vtc.edu
Total campus enrollment: 1,332

GENERAL

Vermont Technical College is a public, coed, four-year institution. 544-acre, rural campus in Randolph (population: 4,853), 50 miles from Burlington; branch campuses in Bennington, Brattleboro, and Colchester. Served by bus and train; major airport serves Burlington; smaller airport serves West Lebanon (35 miles). Semester system.

LD ADMISSIONS

A personal interview is recommended. Essay is not required.

SECONDARY SCHOOL REQUIREMENTS

Graduation from secondary school required; GED accepted. The following course distribution required: 4 units of English, 3 units of math, 2 units of science, 2 units of social studies, 2 units of history, 2 units of academic electives.

TESTING

SAT Reasoning required; ACT may be substituted.

All enrolled freshmen (fall 2004):

Average SAT I Scores: Verbal: 480 Math: 510
Average ACT Scores: Composite:

Child Study Team report is not required. Tests required as part of this documentation:

- ☐ WAIS-IV
- ☐ WISC-IV
- ☐ SATA
- ☐ Woodcock-Johnson
- ☐ Nelson-Denny Reading Test
- ☐ Other

UNDERGRADUATE STUDENT BODY

Total undergraduate student enrollment: 880 Men, 392 Women.

Composition of student body (fall 2004):

	Undergraduate	Freshmen
International	0.0	0.0
Black	0.0	1.2
American Indian	0.0	0.7
Asian-American	3.3	2.4
Hispanic	2.1	1.1
White	94.6	92.5
Unreported	0.0	2.1
	100.0%	100.0%

20% are from out of state. Average age of full-time undergraduates is 27. 68% of classes have fewer than 20 students, 32% have between 20 and 50 students.

STUDENT HOUSING

75% of freshmen live in college housing. Freshmen are required to live on campus. Housing is guaranteed for all undergraduates.

EXPENSES

Tuition (2005-06): $11,544 per year (in-state), $14,640 (out-of-state).

Room: $3,974. Board: $2,700.
There is no additional cost for LD program/services.

LD SERVICES

LD program size is not limited.

LD services available to:

☐ Freshmen ☐ Sophomores ☐ Juniors ☐ Seniors

Academic Accommodations

Curriculum		**In class**	
Foreign language waiver	☐	Early syllabus	☐
Lighter course load	☒	Note takers in class	☒
Math waiver	☐	Priority seating	☐
Other special classes	☐	Tape recorders	☒
Priority registrations	☐	Videotaped classes	☐
Substitution of courses	☐	Text on tape	☐
Exams		**Services**	
Extended time	☒	Diagnostic tests	☒
Oral exams	☒	Learning centers	☒
Take home exams	☐	Proofreaders	☐
Exams on tape or computer	☐	Readers	☒
Untimed exams	☒	Reading Machines/Kurzweil	☒
Other accommodations	☐	Special bookstore section	☐
		Typists	☐

Credit toward degree is not given for remedial courses taken.

Counseling Services

- ☐ Academic
- ☐ Psychological
- ☐ Student Support groups
- ☐ Vocational

Tutoring

	Individual	Group
Time management	☐	☐
Organizational skills	☐	☐
Learning strategies	☐	☐
Study skills	☐	☐
Content area	☐	☐
Writing lab	☐	☐
Math lab	☐	☐

LD PROGRAM STAFF

Total number of LD Program staff (including director):

Full Time: 4 Part Time: 4

Key staff person available to work with LD students: Robin Goodall, Learning Specialist.

Averett University

Danville, VA

Address: 420 W. Main Street, Danville, VA, 24541
Admissions telephone: 800 283-7388
Admissions FAX: 434 797-2784
Vice President of Enrollment Management: Kathie Tune
Admissions e-mail: admit@averett.edu
Web site: http://www.averett.edu
SAT Code: 5017 ACT Code: 4338

LD program enrollment: 30, Total campus enrollment: 2,071

GENERAL

Averett University is a private, coed, four-year institution. 25-acre campus in Danville (population: 48,411), 45 miles from Greensboro, NC.; branch/satellite campuses in over 20 locations throughout Virginia. Served by airport, bus, and train; major airport serves Greensboro. School operates transportation to athletic complex, aviation facilities, and equestrian center. Public transportation serves campus. Semester system.

LD ADMISSIONS

Application Deadline: 09/01. Students do not complete a separate application and are simultaneously accepted to the LD program. A member of the LD program does not sit on the admissions committee. High school waivers are accepted for foreign language. A personal interview is recommended. Essay is required and may be typed. Minimum SAT I score requirement may be waived

For fall 2004, 6 completed self-identified LD applications were received. 3 applications were offered admission, and 2 enrolled.

SECONDARY SCHOOL REQUIREMENTS

Graduation from secondary school required; GED accepted. The following course distribution required: 4 units of English, 3 units of math, 2 units of science, 3 units of social studies, 3 units of history.

TESTING

SAT Reasoning considered if submitted. ACT considered if submitted. SAT Reasoning or ACT required of some applicants. SAT Subject recommended.

All enrolled freshmen (fall 2004):

Average SAT I Scores:	Verbal: 481	Math: 490
Average ACT Scores:	Composite: 19	

Child Study Team report is not required. A neuropsychological or comprehensive psycho-education evaluation is not required for admission. Tests required as part of this documentation:

- [ ] WAIS-IV
- [ ] WISC-IV
- [ ] SATA
- [ ] Woodcock-Johnson
- [ ] Nelson-Denny Reading Test
- [ ] Other

UNDERGRADUATE STUDENT BODY

Total undergraduate student enrollment: 686 Men, 1,077 Women.

Composition of student body (fall 2004):

	Undergraduate	Freshmen
International	1.9	1.4
Black	25.0	31.9
American Indian	0.9	0.7
Asian-American	1.4	1.4
Hispanic	2.8	1.8
White	68.0	62.8
Unreported	0.0	0.0
	100.0%	100.0%

15% are from out of state. 5% join a fraternity and 4% join a sorority. Average age of full-time undergraduates is 21. 86% of classes have fewer than 20 students, 14% have between 20 and 50 students.

STUDENT HOUSING

83% of freshmen live in college housing. Freshmen are required to live on campus. Housing is guaranteed for all undergraduates. Campus can house 521 undergraduates. Single rooms are available for students with medical or special needs. A medical note is required.

EXPENSES

Tuition (2005-06): $18,040 per year.
Room: $4,860. Board: $1,700.
There is no additional cost for LD program/services.

LD SERVICES

LD program size is not limited.

LD services available to:

- [x] Freshmen
- [x] Sophomores
- [x] Juniors
- [x] Seniors

Academic Accommodations

Curriculum		In class	
Foreign language waiver	[x]	Early syllabus	[x]
Lighter course load	[x]	Note takers in class	[x]
Math waiver	[ ]	Priority seating	[x]
Other special classes	[ ]	Tape recorders	[x]
Priority registrations	[ ]	Videotaped classes	[ ]
Substitution of courses	[x]	Text on tape	[x]
Exams		**Services**	
Extended time	[x]	Diagnostic tests	[x]
Oral exams	[x]	Learning centers	[x]
Take home exams	[x]	Proofreaders	[x]
Exams on tape or computer	[x]	Readers	[x]
Untimed exams	[x]	Reading Machines/Kurzweil	[x]
Other accommodations	[ ]	Special bookstore section	[x]
		Typists	[ ]

Credit toward degree is not given for remedial courses taken.

Counseling Services

- [x] Academic
- [x] Psychological
- [ ] Student Support groups
- [x] Vocational

Tutoring

Individual tutoring is available weekly.

Average size of tutoring groups: 1

	Individual	Group
Time management	[x]	[ ]
Organizational skills	[x]	[ ]
Learning strategies	[x]	[ ]
Study skills	[x]	[ ]
Content area	[x]	[ ]
Writing lab	[x]	[x]
Math lab	[x]	[ ]

LD PROGRAM STAFF

There is an advisor/advocate from the LD program available to students. 12 peer tutors are available to work with LD students.

Bluefield College

Bluefield, VA

Address: 3000 College Drive, Bluefield, VA, 24605
Admissions telephone: 800 872-0175
Admissions FAX: 276 326-4288
Director of Admissions: Tim Havens
Admissions e-mail: admissions@mail.bluefield.edu
Web site: http://www.bluefield.edu
SAT Code: 5063 ACT Code: 4340

Dir of Services for Students with Disabilities: Oscar Gomez
LD program telephone: 276 326-4277
LD program e-mail: ogomez@bluefield.edu
LD program enrollment: 12, Total campus enrollment: 814

GENERAL

Bluefield College is a private, coed, four-year institution. 85-acre campus in Bluefield (population: 5,078), 90 miles from Roanoke. Served by bus; major airport serves Roanoke; train serves Hinton, WV. (45 miles). Public transportation serves campus. Semester system.

LD ADMISSIONS

Students do not complete a separate application and are not simultaneously accepted to the LD program. A member of the LD program does not sit on the admissions committee. A personal interview is recommended. Essay is not required.

SECONDARY SCHOOL REQUIREMENTS

Graduation from secondary school required; GED accepted. The following course distribution required: 4 units of English, 3 units of math, 3 units of science, 3 units of social studies, 6 units of academic electives.

TESTING

SAT Reasoning required; ACT may be substituted. SAT Subject recommended.

All enrolled freshmen (fall 2004):

Average SAT I Scores:	Verbal: 470	Math: 460
Average ACT Scores:	Composite: 19	

Child Study Team report is required if student is classified. A neuropsychological or comprehensive psycho-education evaluation is not required for admission. Tests required as part of this documentation:

☐ WAIS-IV	☐ Woodcock-Johnson
☐ WISC-IV	☐ Nelson-Denny Reading Test
☐ SATA	☐ Other

UNDERGRADUATE STUDENT BODY

Total undergraduate student enrollment: 814.

Composition of student body (fall 2004):

	Undergraduate	Freshmen
International	3.4	0.7
Black	6.7	16.1
American Indian	0.0	0.1
Asian-American	0.8	0.6
Hispanic	0.0	0.9
White	89.1	81.6
Unreported	0.0	0.0
	100.0%	100.0%

16% are from out of state. 10% join a fraternity and 11% join a sorority. Average age of full-time undergraduates is 28. 85% of classes have fewer than 20 students, 15% have between 20 and 50 students.

STUDENT HOUSING

71% of freshmen live in college housing. Freshmen are required to live on campus. Housing is guaranteed for all undergraduates. Campus can house 240 undergraduates.

EXPENSES

Tuition (2005-06): $10,860 per year.

Room: $2,280. Board: $3,425.
There is no additional cost for LD program/services.

LD SERVICES

LD program size is not limited.

LD services available to:

■ Freshmen ■ Sophomores ■ Juniors ■ Seniors

Academic Accommodations

Curriculum		**In class**	
Foreign language waiver	☐	Early syllabus	☐
Lighter course load	☐	Note takers in class	■
Math waiver	☐	Priority seating	☐
Other special classes	☐	Tape recorders	■
Priority registrations	☐	Videotaped classes	☐
Substitution of courses	☐	Text on tape	☐
Exams		**Services**	
Extended time	■	Diagnostic tests	☐
Oral exams	■	Learning centers	☐
Take home exams	☐	Proofreaders	☐
Exams on tape or computer	☐	Readers	☐
Untimed exams	■	Reading Machines/Kurzweil	☐
Other accommodations	☐	Special bookstore section	☐
		Typists	☐

Credit toward degree is not given for remedial courses taken.

Counseling Services

☐ Academic
☐ Psychological
☐ Student Support groups
☐ Vocational

Tutoring

Individual tutoring is available weekly.

Average size of tutoring groups: 1

	Individual	Group
Time management	■	☐
Organizational skills	■	☐
Learning strategies	■	☐
Study skills	■	☐
Content area	■	☐
Writing lab	■	☐
Math lab	■	☐

LD PROGRAM STAFF

Total number of LD Program staff (including director):

Full Time: 2 Part Time: 2

There is no advisor/advocate from the LD program available to students.

Key staff person available to work with LD students: Oscar Gomez, Director of Services for Students with Disabilities.

Bridgewater College

Bridgewater, VA

Address: 402 E. College Street, Bridgewater, VA, 22812-1599
Admissions telephone: 800 759-8328
Admissions FAX: 540 828-5481
Director of Enrollment Operations: Linda F. Stout
Admissions e-mail: admissions@bridgewater.edu
Web site: http://www.bridgewater.edu
SAT Code: 5069 ACT Code: 4342

Vice President/Dean for Academic Affairs:
Dr. Arthur C. Hessler
LD program telephone: 540 828-5608
LD program e-mail: ahessler@bridgewater.edu
Total campus enrollment: 1,532

GENERAL

Bridgewater College is a private, coed, four-year institution. 190-acre campus in Bridgewater (population: 5,203), 110 miles from Roanoke and 130 miles from Washington, DC. Major airport serves Washington, DC; smaller airport and train serve Staunton (20 miles); bus serves Harrisonburg (five miles). 4-1-4 system.

LD ADMISSIONS

A personal interview is recommended. Essay is required and may be typed.

SECONDARY SCHOOL REQUIREMENTS

Graduation from secondary school required; GED accepted. The following course distribution required: 4 units of English, 3 units of math, 2 units of science, 2 units of foreign language, 4 units of academic electives.

TESTING

SAT Reasoning required; ACT may be substituted.

All enrolled freshmen (fall 2004):

Average SAT I Scores:	Verbal: 517	Math: 519
Average ACT Scores:	Composite: 21	

Child Study Team report is not required. Tests required as part of this documentation:

☐ WAIS-IV ☐ Woodcock-Johnson
☐ WISC-IV ☐ Nelson-Denny Reading Test
☐ SATA ☐ Other

UNDERGRADUATE STUDENT BODY

Total undergraduate student enrollment: 548 Men, 712 Women.

Composition of student body (fall 2004):

	Undergraduate	Freshmen
International	0.2	0.6
Black	8.0	7.9
American Indian	0.4	0.3
Asian-American	0.7	0.9
Hispanic	1.1	1.1
White	89.6	89.2
Unreported	0.0	0.0
	100.0%	100.0%

23% are from out of state. Average age of full-time undergraduates is 20. 56% of classes have fewer than 20 students, 43% have between 20 and 50 students, 1% have more than 50 students.

STUDENT HOUSING

93% of freshmen live in college housing. Freshmen are required to live on campus. Housing is guaranteed for all undergraduates. Campus can house 1,308 undergraduates. Single rooms are available for students with medical or special needs. A medical note is required.

EXPENSES

Tuition (2005-06): $18,990 per year.
Room: $4,465. Board: $4,335.
There is no additional cost for LD program/services.

LD SERVICES

LD services available to:

☐ Freshmen ☐ Sophomores ☐ Juniors ☐ Seniors

Academic Accommodations

Curriculum		**In class**	
Foreign language waiver	■	Early syllabus	☐
Lighter course load	■	Note takers in class	■
Math waiver	■	Priority seating	■
Other special classes	☐	Tape recorders	■
Priority registrations	☐	Videotaped classes	☐
Substitution of courses	■	Text on tape	■
Exams		**Services**	
Extended time	■	Diagnostic tests	☐
Oral exams	☐	Learning centers	☐
Take home exams	☐	Proofreaders	☐
Exams on tape or computer	☐	Readers	■
Untimed exams	■	Reading Machines/Kurzweil	☐
Other accommodations	☐	Special bookstore section	■
		Typists	☐

Credit toward degree is not given for remedial courses taken.

Counseling Services

■ Academic
■ Psychological
■ Student Support groups
☐ Vocational

Tutoring

Individual tutoring is available daily.

Average size of tutoring groups: 3

	Individual	Group
Time management	■	■
Organizational skills	■	■
Learning strategies	■	☐
Study skills	■	■
Content area	■	■
Writing lab	☐	■
Math lab	☐	■

LD PROGRAM STAFF

Total number of LD Program staff (including director):

Full Time: 1 Part Time: 1

There is an advisor/advocate from the LD program available to students.

Key staff person available to work with LD students: Dr. Raymond W. Studwell, Director of Academic Support Services.

Christopher Newport University

Newport News, VA

Address: 1 University Place, Newport News, VA, 23606
Admissions telephone: 800 333-4268
Admissions FAX: 757 594-7333
Director of Admissions: Patricia Cavender
Admissions e-mail: admit@cnu.edu
Web site: http://www.cnu.edu
SAT Code: 5128 ACT Code: 4345

LD program enrollment: 190, Total campus enrollment: 4,540

GENERAL

Christopher Newport University is a public, coed, four-year institution. 150-acre campus in Newport News (population: 180,150). Served by airport and train; bus serves Fort Eustis (10 miles). Public transportation serves campus. Semester system.

LD ADMISSIONS

Students do not complete a separate application and are not simultaneously accepted to the LD program. A member of the LD program does not sit on the admissions committee.

SECONDARY SCHOOL REQUIREMENTS

Graduation from secondary school required; GED accepted. The following course distribution required: 4 units of English, 4 units of math, 3 units of science, 3 units of foreign language, 3 units of social studies, 3 units of history.

TESTING

SAT Reasoning recommended. ACT considered if submitted. SAT Subject recommended.

All enrolled freshmen (fall 2004):

Average SAT I Scores:	Verbal: 565	Math: 557
Average ACT Scores:	Composite: 23	

Child Study Team report is not required. A neuropsychological or comprehensive psycho-education evaluation is not required for admission. Tests required as part of this documentation:

- [ ] WAIS-IV
- [ ] WISC-IV
- [ ] SATA
- [ ] Woodcock-Johnson
- [ ] Nelson-Denny Reading Test
- [ ] Other

UNDERGRADUATE STUDENT BODY

Total undergraduate student enrollment: 1,998 Men, 3,160 Women.

Composition of student body (fall 2004):

	Undergraduate	Freshmen
International	0.1	0.1
Black	5.2	8.9
American Indian	0.4	0.6
Asian-American	3.2	2.9
Hispanic	3.1	2.5
White	85.4	83.2
Unreported	2.6	1.8
	100.0%	100.0%

2% are from out of state. 7% join a fraternity and 14% join a sorority. Average age of full-time undergraduates is 20. 35% of classes have fewer than 20 students, 60% have between 20 and 50 students, 5% have more than 50 students.

STUDENT HOUSING

92% of freshmen live in college housing. Freshmen are required to live on campus. Housing is guaranteed for all undergraduates. Campus can house 2,422 undergraduates.

EXPENSES

Tuition (2005-06): $3,442 per year (in-state), $10,464 (out-of-state). Room: $5,000. Board: $2,500.
There is no additional cost for LD program/services.

LD SERVICES

LD program size is not limited.

LD services available to:

- [ ] Freshmen
- [ ] Sophomores
- [ ] Juniors
- [ ] Seniors

Academic Accommodations

Curriculum		**In class**	
Foreign language waiver	[ ]	Early syllabus	[ ]
Lighter course load	[ ]	Note takers in class	[ ]
Math waiver	[ ]	Priority seating	[ ]
Other special classes	[ ]	Tape recorders	[x]
Priority registrations	[ ]	Videotaped classes	[ ]
Substitution of courses	[ ]	Text on tape	[ ]
Exams		**Services**	
Extended time	[x]	Diagnostic tests	[ ]
Oral exams	[x]	Learning centers	[ ]
Take home exams	[ ]	Proofreaders	[ ]
Exams on tape or computer	[ ]	Readers	[ ]
Untimed exams	[ ]	Reading Machines/Kurzweil	[x]
Other accommodations	[ ]	Special bookstore section	[ ]
		Typists	[ ]

Credit toward degree is not given for remedial courses taken.

Counseling Services

- [ ] Academic
- [ ] Psychological
- [ ] Student Support groups
- [ ] Vocational

Tutoring

Individual tutoring is not available.

	Individual	Group
Time management	[ ]	[ ]
Organizational skills	[ ]	[ ]
Learning strategies	[ ]	[ ]
Study skills	[ ]	[ ]
Content area	[ ]	[ ]
Writing lab	[ ]	[ ]
Math lab	[ ]	[ ]

UNIQUE LD PROGRAM FEATURES

Christopher Newport University offers disability student services. The University does not have a specific LD program.

LD PROGRAM STAFF

Total number of LD Program staff (including director):

Full Time: 1 Part Time: 1

Key staff person available to work with LD students: Deborah Witt, Coordinator, Disabilities Support Services.

Eastern Mennonite University

Harrisonburg, VA

Address: 1200 Park Road, Harrisonburg, VA, 22802-2462
Admissions telephone: 800 368-2665
Admissions FAX: 540 432-4444
Director of Admissions: Stephanie Shafer
Admissions e-mail: admiss@emu.edu
Web site: http://www.emu.edu
SAT Code: 5181 ACT Code: 4348

LD program name: Student Disability Support Services
Coordinator: Joyce C. Hedrick
LD program telephone: 540 432-4233
LD program e-mail: hedrickj@emu.edu
LD program enrollment: 62, Total campus enrollment: 1,029

GENERAL

Eastern Mennonite University is a private, coed, four-year institution. 93-acre campus in Harrisonburg (population: 1,228), 60 miles from Charlottesville; branch campus in Lancaster, PA. Served by bus; major airport serves Washington, DC. (100 miles); smaller airport serves Weyers Cave (15 miles); train serves Staunton (20 miles). Public transportation serves campus. Semester system.

LD ADMISSIONS

Students do not complete a separate application and are simultaneously accepted to the LD program. A member of the LD program does not sit on the admissions committee. A personal interview is recommended. Essay is not required.

SECONDARY SCHOOL REQUIREMENTS

Graduation from secondary school required; GED accepted. The following course distribution required: 4 units of English, 3 units of math, 3 units of science, 2 units of foreign language, 3 units of social studies, 6 units of academic electives.

TESTING

SAT Reasoning or ACT required. SAT Subject recommended.

All enrolled freshmen (fall 2004):

Average SAT I Scores:	Verbal: 527	Math: 522
Average ACT Scores:	Composite: 23	

Child Study Team report is not required. A neuropsychological or comprehensive psycho-educational evaluation is required for admission. Must be dated within 36 months of application. Tests required as part of this documentation:

- ■ WAIS-IV
- ☐ WISC-IV
- ■ SATA
- ■ Woodcock-Johnson
- ■ Nelson-Denny Reading Test
- ■ Other

UNDERGRADUATE STUDENT BODY

Total undergraduate student enrollment: 413 Men, 607 Women.

Composition of student body (fall 2004):

	Undergraduate	Freshmen
International	1.9	3.9
Black	9.6	6.3
American Indian	0.0	0.0
Asian-American	3.8	2.3
Hispanic	6.7	2.5
White	72.7	82.8
Unreported	5.3	2.2
	100.0%	100.0%

59% are from out of state. Average age of full-time undergraduates is 21. 64% of classes have fewer than 20 students, 33% have between 20 and 50 students, 3% have more than 50 students.

STUDENT HOUSING

94% of freshmen live in college housing. Freshmen are required to live on campus. Housing is guaranteed for all undergraduates. Campus can house 828 undergraduates. Single rooms are available for students with medical or special needs. A medical note is required.

EXPENSES

Tuition (2005-06): $19,500 per year.

Room & Board: $5,950.

There is no additional cost for LD program/services.

LD SERVICES

LD program size is not limited.

LD services available to:

■ Freshmen ■ Sophomores ■ Juniors ■ Seniors

Academic Accommodations

Curriculum		In class	
Foreign language waiver	☐	Early syllabus	■
Lighter course load	■	Note takers in class	■
Math waiver	☐	Priority seating	■
Other special classes	■	Tape recorders	■
Priority registrations	■	Videotaped classes	■
Substitution of courses	■	Text on tape	■
Exams		**Services**	
Extended time	■	Diagnostic tests	■
Oral exams	■	Learning centers	■
Take home exams	■	Proofreaders	■
Exams on tape or computer	■	Readers	■
Untimed exams	■	Reading Machines/Kurzweil	■
Other accommodations	■	Special bookstore section	☐
		Typists	■

Credit toward degree is given for remedial courses taken.

Counseling Services

- ■ Academic
- ■ Psychological — Meets 26 times per academic year
- ■ Student Support groups
- ■ Vocational

Tutoring

Individual tutoring is available daily.

Average size of tutoring groups: 2

	Individual	Group
Time management	■	■
Organizational skills	■	■
Learning strategies	■	■
Study skills	■	■
Content area	■	■
Writing lab	■	■
Math lab	■	■

UNIQUE LD PROGRAM FEATURES

Services are very user-friendly. We work closely with faculty who are very supportive.

LD PROGRAM STAFF

Total number of LD Program staff (including director):

There is an advisor/advocate from the LD program available to students. The advisor/advocate meets with faculty 8 times per month and students 3 times per month. 1 graduate student and 28 peer tutors are available to work with LD students.

Key staff person available to work with LD students: Joyce C. Hedrick, Coordinator, Student Disability Support Services.

LD Program web site: http://www.emu.edu/academicsupport/

Emory & Henry College

Emory, VA

Address: PO Box 947, Emory, VA, 24327
Admissions telephone: 800 848-5493
Admissions FAX: 276 944-6935
Dean of Admissions and Financial Aid: Liz Daniels
Admissions e-mail: ehadmiss@ehc.edu
Web site: http://www.ehc.edu
SAT Code: 5185 ACT Code: 4350

LD program name: Powell Resource Center
Director of Academic Support Services: Lisa Honeycutt
LD program telephone: 276 944-6145
LD program e-mail: lhoneycutt@ehc.edu
LD program enrollment: 70, Total campus enrollment: 930

GENERAL

Emory & Henry College is a private, coed, four-year institution. 163-acre campus in Emory (Emory-Meadow View population: 2,266), 35 miles from the Tri-Cities, VA and TN. Major airports serve Roanoke and Knoxville TN (both 125 miles); smaller airport serves the Tri-Cities; bus serves Abingdon (10 miles). Semester system.

LD ADMISSIONS

A member of the LD program does not sit on the admissions committee. A personal interview is not required. Essay is not required.

SECONDARY SCHOOL REQUIREMENTS

Graduation from secondary school required; GED accepted. The following course distribution required: 4 units of English, 3 units of math, 2 units of science, 2 units of foreign language, 2 units of social studies.

TESTING

SAT Reasoning or ACT required. SAT Subject recommended.

All enrolled freshmen (fall 2004):

Average SAT I Scores:	Verbal: 532	Math: 515
Average ACT Scores:	Composite: 23	

Child Study Team report is not required. Tests required as part of this documentation:

- ☐ WAIS-IV
- ☐ WISC-IV
- ☐ SATA
- ☐ Woodcock-Johnson
- ☐ Nelson-Denny Reading Test
- ☐ Other

UNDERGRADUATE STUDENT BODY

Total undergraduate student enrollment: 471 Men, 518 Women.

Composition of student body (fall 2004):

	Undergraduate	Freshmen
International	0.4	0.3
Black	5.6	4.2
American Indian	0.0	0.3
Asian-American	1.5	1.4
Hispanic	0.7	1.0
White	90.3	92.0
Unreported	1.5	0.8
	100.0%	100.0%

26% are from out of state. 13% join a fraternity and 22% join a sorority. Average age of full-time undergraduates is 20. 67% of classes have fewer than 20 students, 33% have between 20 and 50 students.

STUDENT HOUSING

88% of freshmen live in college housing. Freshmen are required to live on campus. Housing is guaranteed for all undergraduates. Campus can house 692 undergraduates.

EXPENSES

Tuition (2005-06): $19,530 per year.

Room: $3,500. Board: $3,540.

There is no additional cost for LD program/services.

LD SERVICES

LD program size is not limited.

LD services available to:

■ Freshmen ■ Sophomores ■ Juniors ■ Seniors

Academic Accommodations

Curriculum		In class	
Foreign language waiver	☐	Early syllabus	☐
Lighter course load	☐	Note takers in class	■
Math waiver	☐	Priority seating	☐
Other special classes	☐	Tape recorders	■
Priority registrations	☐	Videotaped classes	☐
Substitution of courses	☐	Text on tape	☐
Exams		**Services**	
Extended time	■	Diagnostic tests	☐
Oral exams	☐	Learning centers	☐
Take home exams	☐	Proofreaders	☐
Exams on tape or computer	☐	Readers	■
Untimed exams	☐	Reading Machines/Kurzweil	■
Other accommodations	☐	Special bookstore section	☐
		Typists	☐

Credit toward degree is not given for remedial courses taken.

Counseling Services

- ☐ Academic
- ☐ Psychological
- ☐ Student Support groups
- ☐ Vocational

Tutoring

Individual tutoring is available daily.

Average size of tutoring groups: 3

	Individual	Group
Time management	■	■
Organizational skills	■	■
Learning strategies	■	■
Study skills	■	■
Content area	■	■
Writing lab	■	■
Math lab	■	■

UNIQUE LD PROGRAM FEATURES

Students with diagnosed disabilities who wish to have accommodations made for the disability must send the most recent copy of the psycho-educational testing report to the Director of Academic Support Services. The report should not be more than three years old. The student must then meet with the Director of Academic Support to discuss specific accommodations. After reviewing the documentation, reasonable accommodations will be made on a case-by-case basis.

LD PROGRAM STAFF

Total number of LD Program staff (including director):

Full Time: 1 Part Time: 1

20 peer tutors are available to work with LD students.

Key staff person available to work with LD students: Lisa Honeycutt, Director of Academic Support Services.

LD Program web site: www.ehc.edu/learn/support.html

Ferrum College

Ferrum, VA

Address: 215 Ferrum Mountain Road, Ferrum, VA, 24088
Admissions telephone: 800 868-9797
Admissions FAX: 540 365-4266
Director of Admissions: Gilda Q. Woods
Admissions e-mail: admissions@ferrum.edu
Web site: http://www.ferrum.edu
SAT Code: 5213 ACT Code: 4352

Assistant Professor of Teacher Education: Nancy Beach
LD program telephone: 540 365-4262
LD program e-mail: nbeach@ferrum.edu
Total campus enrollment: 941

GENERAL

Ferrum College is a private, coed, four-year institution. 720-acre campus in Ferrum (population: 1,313), 30 miles from Roanoke. Major airport and bus serve Roanoke; train serves Lynchburg (75 miles). Semester system.

LD ADMISSIONS

A personal interview is not required. Essay is not required.

SECONDARY SCHOOL REQUIREMENTS

Graduation from secondary school required; GED accepted.

TESTING

SAT Reasoning required; ACT may be substituted.

All enrolled freshmen (fall 2004):

Average SAT I Scores: Verbal: 455 Math: 445
Average ACT Scores: Composite: 18

Child Study Team report is not required. Tests required as part of this documentation:

- [ ] WAIS-IV
- [ ] WISC-IV
- [ ] SATA
- [ ] Woodcock-Johnson
- [ ] Nelson-Denny Reading Test
- [ ] Other

UNDERGRADUATE STUDENT BODY

Total undergraduate student enrollment: 530 Men, 390 Women.

Composition of student body (fall 2004):

	Undergraduate	Freshmen
International	0.6	1.2
Black	22.8	19.2
American Indian	0.0	0.0
Asian-American	0.0	0.2
Hispanic	2.5	1.7
White	63.5	67.3
Unreported	10.6	10.4
	100.0%	100.0%

14% are from out of state. Average age of full-time undergraduates is 21. 67% of classes have fewer than 20 students, 33% have between 20 and 50 students.

STUDENT HOUSING

94% of freshmen live in college housing. Freshmen are required to live on campus. Housing is guaranteed for all undergraduates. Campus can house 850 undergraduates.

EXPENSES

Tuition (2005-06): $17,990 per year.
Room & Board: $6,100.
There is no additional cost for LD program/services.

LD SERVICES

LD program size is not limited.

LD services available to:

- [x] Freshmen
- [x] Sophomores
- [x] Juniors
- [x] Seniors

Academic Accommodations

Curriculum

- [ ] Foreign language waiver
- [ ] Lighter course load
- [ ] Math waiver
- [ ] Other special classes
- [ ] Priority registrations
- [ ] Substitution of courses

Exams

- [x] Extended time
- [ ] Oral exams
- [ ] Take home exams
- [ ] Exams on tape or computer
- [x] Untimed exams
- [ ] Other accommodations

In class

- [ ] Early syllabus
- [ ] Note takers in class
- [ ] Priority seating
- [x] Tape recorders
- [x] Videotaped classes
- [ ] Text on tape

Services

- [ ] Diagnostic tests
- [x] Learning centers
- [ ] Proofreaders
- [ ] Readers
- [ ] Reading Machines/Kurzweil
- [ ] Special bookstore section
- [ ] Typists

Credit toward degree is not given for remedial courses taken.

Counseling Services

- [x] Academic
- [ ] Psychological
- [ ] Student Support groups
- [ ] Vocational

Tutoring

Individual tutoring is available daily.

Average size of tutoring groups: 1

	Individual	Group
Time management	[ ]	[ ]
Organizational skills	[ ]	[ ]
Learning strategies	[ ]	[ ]
Study skills	[ ]	[ ]
Content area	[ ]	[ ]
Writing lab	[ ]	[ ]
Math lab	[ ]	[ ]

LD PROGRAM STAFF

Total number of LD Program staff (including director):

Full Time: 1 Part Time: 1

There is an advisor/advocate from the LD program available to students.

Key staff person available to work with LD students: Nancy Beach, Assistant Professor of Teacher Education.

George Mason University

Fairfax, VA

Address: 4400 University Drive, Fairfax, VA, 22030
Admissions telephone: 703 993-2400
Admissions FAX: 703 993-2392
Dean of Admissions: Andrew Flagel
Admissions e-mail: admissions@gmu.edu
Web site: http://www.gmu.edu
SAT Code: 5827 ACT Code: 4357

LD program name: Disability Resource Center
Director: Deborah Wyne
LD program telephone: 703 993-2474
LD program e-mail: dwyne@gmu.edu
LD program enrollment: 1,125,Total campus enrollment: 17,408

GENERAL

George Mason University is a public, coed, four-year institution. 677-acre, suburban main campus in Fairfax (population: 21,498), 18 miles from Washington, DC; branch campuses in Arlington and Prince William County. Served by bus; major airports and train serve Washington, DC. School operates transportation to the city, public metro station, and between campuses. Public transportation serves campus. Semester system.

LD ADMISSIONS

Students do not complete a separate application and are not simultaneously accepted to the LD program. A member of the LD program does not sit on the admissions committee. A personal interview is recommended.

SECONDARY SCHOOL REQUIREMENTS

Graduation from secondary school required; GED accepted. The following course distribution required: 4 units of English, 3 units of math, 3 units of science, 2 units of foreign language, 3 units of social studies, 3 units of academic electives.

TESTING

SAT Reasoning or ACT required. SAT Subject recommended.

All enrolled freshmen (fall 2004):

Average SAT I Scores:	Verbal: 548	Math: 555
Average ACT Scores:	Composite: 22	

Child Study Team report is not required. A neuropsychological or comprehensive psycho-educational evaluation is required for admission. Must be dated within 36 months of application. Tests required as part of this documentation:

- ■ WAIS-IV
- ■ WISC-IV
- ☐ SATA
- ■ Woodcock-Johnson
- ■ Nelson-Denny Reading Test
- ☐ Other

UNDERGRADUATE STUDENT BODY

Total undergraduate student enrollment: 6,934 Men, 8,868 Women.

Composition of student body (fall 2004):

	Undergraduate	Freshmen
International	3.4	4.2
Black	7.6	8.1
American Indian	0.3	0.4
Asian-American	15.9	16.4
Hispanic	6.3	7.3
White	50.8	51.6
Unreported	15.7	12.0
	100.0%	100.0%

10% are from out of state. 5% join a fraternity and 5% join a sorority. Average age of full-time undergraduates is 21. 32% of classes have fewer than 20 students, 54% have between 20 and 50 students, 14% have more than 50 students.

STUDENT HOUSING

61% of freshmen live in college housing. Freshmen are not required to live on campus. Housing is not guaranteed for all undergraduates. Demand for housing exceeds supply. New construction in progress and more planned. Campus can house 3,972 undergraduates. Single rooms are available for students with medical or special needs. A medical note is required.

EXPENSES

Tuition (2005-06): $4,356 per year (in-state), $15,636 (out-of-state).
Room: $3,700. Board: $2,780.
There is no additional cost for LD program/services.

LD SERVICES

LD program size is not limited.

LD services available to:

■ Freshmen ■ Sophomores ■ Juniors ■ Seniors

Academic Accommodations

Curriculum		**In class**	
Foreign language waiver	■	Early syllabus	☐
Lighter course load	■	Note takers in class	■
Math waiver	■	Priority seating	■
Other special classes	☐	Tape recorders	■
Priority registrations	■	Videotaped classes	☐
Substitution of courses	■	Text on tape	☐
Exams		**Services**	
Extended time	■	Diagnostic tests	☐
Oral exams	■	Learning centers	■
Take home exams	☐	Proofreaders	☐
Exams on tape or computer	■	Readers	■
Untimed exams	■	Reading Machines/Kurzweil	■
Other accommodations	■	Special bookstore section	☐
		Typists	■

Credit toward degree is not given for remedial courses taken.

Counseling Services

- ■ Academic
- ■ Psychological
- ■ Student Support groups
- ☐ Vocational

Tutoring

Individual tutoring is available.

	Individual	Group
Time management	☐	☐
Organizational skills	☐	☐
Learning strategies	☐	☐
Study skills	☐	☐
Content area	☐	☐
Writing lab	☐	☐
Math lab	☐	☐

LD PROGRAM STAFF

Total number of LD Program staff (including director):

Full Time: 2 Part Time: 2

There is an advisor/advocate from the LD program available to students.

Key staff person available to work with LD students: Deborah Wyne, Director.

Hampden-Sydney College

Hampden-Sydney, VA

Address: PO Box 667, Hampden-Sydney, VA, 23943
Admissions telephone: 800 755-0733
Admissions FAX: 434 223-6346
Dean of Admissions: Anita H. Garland
Admissions e-mail: hsapp@hsc.edu
Web site: http://www.hsc.edu
SAT Code: 5291   ACT Code: 4356

Associate Dean for Academic Support: Elizabeth Ford
LD program telephone: 434 223-6286
Total campus enrollment: 1,082

GENERAL

Hampden-Sydney College is a private, men's, four-year institution. 600-acre campus in Hampden-Sydney (population: 1,264), 65 miles from Richmond. Major airport serves Lynchburg (60 miles); bus serves Farmville (six miles); airport and train serve Richmond. Semester system.

LD ADMISSIONS

A personal interview is recommended. Essay is required and may be typed. Occasionally foreign language requirement from high school may be waived (not guaranteed).

SECONDARY SCHOOL REQUIREMENTS

Graduation from secondary school required; GED accepted. The following course distribution required: 4 units of English, 3 units of math, 2 units of science, 2 units of foreign language, 1 unit of social studies, 1 unit of history, 3 units of academic electives.

TESTING

SAT Reasoning or ACT required. SAT Subject required.

All enrolled freshmen (fall 2004):

Average SAT I Scores: Verbal: 570 Math: 570
Average ACT Scores: Composite: 24

Child Study Team report is not required. Tests required as part of this documentation:

- [ ] WAIS-IV
- [ ] WISC-IV
- [ ] SATA
- [ ] Woodcock-Johnson
- [ ] Nelson-Denny Reading Test
- [ ] Other

UNDERGRADUATE STUDENT BODY

Total undergraduate student enrollment: 1,024 Men, 2 Women.

Composition of student body (fall 2004):

	Undergraduate	Freshmen
International	0.3	1.4
Black	5.9	3.5
American Indian	0.0	0.7
Asian-American	0.6	1.1
Hispanic	2.2	1.4
White	90.1	91.1
Unreported	0.9	0.8
	100.0%	100.0%

37% are from out of state. 34% join a fraternity. Average age of full-time undergraduates is 20. 69% of classes have fewer than 20 students, 31% have between 20 and 50 students.

STUDENT HOUSING

100% of freshmen live in college housing. Freshmen are required to live on campus. Housing is guaranteed for all undergraduates. Campus can house 1,030 undergraduates.

EXPENSES

Tuition (2005-06): $21,878 per year.
Room: $3,116. Board: $4,254.
There is no additional cost for LD program/services.

LD SERVICES

LD program size is not limited.

LD services available to:

- [ ] Freshmen
- [ ] Sophomores
- [ ] Juniors
- [ ] Seniors

Academic Accommodations

Curriculum

- [ ] Foreign language waiver
- [x] Lighter course load
- [ ] Math waiver
- [ ] Other special classes
- [ ] Priority registrations
- [ ] Substitution of courses

Exams

- [x] Extended time
- [x] Oral exams
- [ ] Take home exams
- [ ] Exams on tape or computer
- [ ] Untimed exams
- [ ] Other accommodations

In class

- [ ] Early syllabus
- [x] Note takers in class
- [ ] Priority seating
- [x] Tape recorders
- [x] Videotaped classes
- [ ] Text on tape

Services

- [ ] Diagnostic tests
- [ ] Learning centers
- [ ] Proofreaders
- [ ] Readers
- [x] Reading Machines/Kurzweil
- [ ] Special bookstore section
- [ ] Typists

Credit toward degree is not given for remedial courses taken.

Counseling Services

- [ ] Academic
- [ ] Psychological
- [ ] Student Support groups
- [ ] Vocational

Tutoring

	Individual	Group
Time management	[ ]	[ ]
Organizational skills	[ ]	[ ]
Learning strategies	[ ]	[ ]
Study skills	[ ]	[ ]
Content area	[ ]	[ ]
Writing lab	[ ]	[ ]
Math lab	[ ]	[ ]

LD PROGRAM STAFF

Total number of LD Program staff (including director):

Full Time: 2   Part Time: 2

Key staff person available to work with LD students: Elizabeth Ford, Associate Dean for Academic Support.

Hampton University

Hampton, VA

Address: Tyler Street, Hampton, VA, 23668
Admissions telephone: 800 624-3328
Admissions FAX: 757 727-5095
Director of Admissions: Ms. Angela Boyd
Admissions e-mail: admissions@hamptonu.edu
Web site: http://www.hamptonu.edu
SAT Code: 5292 ACT Code: 4358

Director of Testing: Janice Halima Rashada
LD program telephone: 757 727-5493
LD program e-mail: janice.rashada@hamptonu.edu
LD program enrollment: 20, Total campus enrollment: 5,317

GENERAL

Hampton University is a private, coed, four-year institution. 314-acre, urban campus in Hampton (population: 146,437), 10 miles from Norfolk and 60 miles from Richmond; branch campus in Roanoke. Served by bus; airport and train serve Newport News (10 miles); larger airport serves Norfolk. School operates transportation to distant dorm locations. Public transportation serves campus. Semester system.

LD ADMISSIONS

A personal interview is not required. Essay is required and may be typed. All students must meet same requirements for admission.

For fall 2004, 35 completed self-identified LD applications were received.

SECONDARY SCHOOL REQUIREMENTS

Graduation from secondary school required; GED accepted. The following course distribution required: 4 units of English, 3 units of math, 2 units of science, 2 units of social studies, 6 units of academic electives.

TESTING

SAT Reasoning or ACT required.

All enrolled freshmen (fall 2004):

Average SAT I Scores:	Verbal: 540	Math: 520
Average ACT Scores:	Composite: 19	

Child Study Team report is not required. A neuropsychological or comprehensive psycho-educational evaluation is required for admission. Must be dated within 36 months of application. Tests required as part of this documentation:

- [ ] WAIS-IV
- [ ] WISC-IV
- [ ] SATA
- [ ] Woodcock-Johnson
- [ ] Nelson-Denny Reading Test
- [x] Other

UNDERGRADUATE STUDENT BODY

Total undergraduate student enrollment: 1,904 Men, 3,049 Women.

70% are from out of state. 5% join a fraternity and 4% join a sorority. Average age of full-time undergraduates is 20.

STUDENT HOUSING

71% of freshmen live in college housing. Freshmen are required to live on campus. Housing is not guaranteed for all undergraduates. All unmarried students are eligible, but amount of housing insufficient to accommodate. Campus can house 3,080 undergraduates. Single rooms are available for students with medical or special needs. A medical note is required.

EXPENSES

Tuition (2005-06): $12,722 per year.
Room & Board: $0-$6,746.
There is no additional cost for LD program/services.

LD SERVICES

LD program size is not limited.

LD services available to:

- [x] Freshmen
- [x] Sophomores
- [x] Juniors
- [ ] Seniors

Academic Accommodations

Curriculum		In class	
Foreign language waiver	[ ]	Early syllabus	[ ]
Lighter course load	[x]	Note takers in class	[x]
Math waiver	[ ]	Priority seating	[ ]
Other special classes	[ ]	Tape recorders	[x]
Priority registrations	[ ]	Videotaped classes	[ ]
Substitution of courses	[ ]	Text on tape	[ ]
Exams		**Services**	
Extended time	[x]	Diagnostic tests	[ ]
Oral exams	[x]	Learning centers	[ ]
Take home exams	[ ]	Proofreaders	[ ]
Exams on tape or computer	[ ]	Readers	[x]
Untimed exams	[x]	Reading Machines/Kurzweil	[ ]
Other accommodations	[ ]	Special bookstore section	[ ]
		Typists	[ ]

Credit toward degree is not given for remedial courses taken.

Counseling Services

- [x] Academic — Meets 2 times per academic year
- [ ] Psychological
- [ ] Student Support groups
- [ ] Vocational

Tutoring

Individual tutoring is available.

	Individual	Group
Time management	[ ]	[ ]
Organizational skills	[ ]	[ ]
Learning strategies	[ ]	[ ]
Study skills	[ ]	[ ]
Content area	[ ]	[ ]
Writing lab	[ ]	[ ]
Math lab	[ ]	[ ]

LD PROGRAM STAFF

Total number of LD Program staff (including director):

Full Time: 2 Part Time: 2

There is an advisor/advocate from the LD program available to students. The advisor/advocate meets with faculty 4 times per month and students 4 times per month.

Key staff person available to work with LD students: Mrs. Janice Halima Rashada, Director of Testing and 504 Compliance Officer.

Hollins University

Roanoke, VA

Address: PO Box 9707, Roanoke, VA, 24020
Admissions telephone: 800 456-9595
Admissions FAX: 540 362-6218
Dean of Admissions: Celia McCormick, Dean
Admissions e-mail: huadm@hollins.edu
Web site: http://www.hollins.edu
SAT Code: 5294 ACT Code: 4360

LD program name: Academic Services
Dean of Academic Services: Alison Ridley
LD program e-mail: aridley@hollins.edu
LD program enrollment: 37, Total campus enrollment: 819

GENERAL

Hollins University is a private, women's, four-year institution. 475-acre campus in Roanoke (population: 94,911), six miles from downtown district. Served by airport and bus; train serves Lynchburg (40 miles). School operates transportation downtown. 4-1-4 system.

LD ADMISSIONS

Students do not complete a separate application and are simultaneously accepted to the LD program. A member of the LD program does not sit on the admissions committee. A personal interview is required. Essay is required and may be typed. A student requesting accommodation and support services needs to provide a diagnostic report which clearly identifies a learning disability based on testing and evaluation.

SECONDARY SCHOOL REQUIREMENTS

Graduation from secondary school required; GED accepted. The following course distribution required: 4 units of English, 3 units of math, 3 units of science, 3 units of foreign language, 3 units of social studies.

TESTING

SAT Reasoning or ACT required. SAT Subject recommended.

All enrolled freshmen (fall 2004):

Average SAT I Scores: Verbal: 607 Math: 552
Average ACT Scores: Composite: 25

Child Study Team report is not required. A neuropsychological or comprehensive psycho-educational evaluation is required for admission. Must be dated within 48 months of application. Tests required as part of this documentation:

- [ ] WAIS-IV
- [ ] WISC-IV
- [ ] SATA
- [ ] Woodcock-Johnson
- [ ] Nelson-Denny Reading Test
- [ ] Other

UNDERGRADUATE STUDENT BODY

Total undergraduate student enrollment: 818 Women.

Composition of student body (fall 2004):

	Undergraduate	Freshmen
International	2.2	2.4
Black	9.2	8.8
American Indian	0.5	0.7
Asian-American	2.2	1.6
Hispanic	2.2	1.9
White	83.7	84.6
Unreported	0.0	0.0
	100.0%	100.0%

58% are from out of state. Average age of full-time undergraduates is 22. 82% of classes have fewer than 20 students, 18% have between 20 and 50 students.

STUDENT HOUSING

99% of freshmen live in college housing. Freshmen are required to live on campus. Housing is guaranteed for all undergraduates. Campus can house 925 undergraduates. Single rooms are available for students with medical or special needs. A medical note is required.

EXPENSES

Tuition (2005-06): $22,470 per year.
Room: $4,880. Board: $3,280.
There is no additional cost for LD program/services.

LD SERVICES

LD program size is not limited.

LD services available to:

- [x] Freshmen
- [x] Sophomores
- [x] Juniors
- [x] Seniors

Academic Accommodations

Curriculum
- [x] Foreign language waiver
- [x] Lighter course load
- [ ] Math waiver
- [ ] Other special classes
- [ ] Priority registrations
- [x] Substitution of courses

Exams
- [x] Extended time
- [x] Oral exams
- [x] Take home exams
- [x] Exams on tape or computer
- [x] Untimed exams
- [x] Other accommodations

In class
- [ ] Early syllabus
- [x] Note takers in class
- [ ] Priority seating
- [x] Tape recorders
- [ ] Videotaped classes
- [x] Text on tape

Services
- [ ] Diagnostic tests
- [x] Learning centers
- [ ] Proofreaders
- [ ] Readers
- [x] Reading Machines/Kurzweil
- [ ] Special bookstore section
- [x] Typists

Credit toward degree is not given for remedial courses taken.

Counseling Services

- [x] Academic — Meets 26 times per academic year
- [x] Psychological — Meets 6 times per academic year
- [ ] Student Support groups
- [ ] Vocational

Tutoring

Individual tutoring is available weekly.

Average size of tutoring groups: 1

	Individual	Group
Time management	[ ]	[x]
Organizational skills	[ ]	[x]
Learning strategies	[ ]	[x]
Study skills	[ ]	[x]
Content area	[x]	[ ]
Writing lab	[x]	[ ]
Math lab	[x]	[ ]

UNIQUE LD PROGRAM FEATURES

We evaluate LD needs on a case-by-case basis. Documentation is required.

LD PROGRAM STAFF

Total number of LD Program staff (including director):

Full Time: 1 Part Time: 1

There is an advisor/advocate from the LD program available to students. The advisor/advocate meets with student 4 times per month. 14 peer tutors are available to work with LD students.

Key staff person available to work with LD students: Alison Ridley, Dean of Academic Services.

James Madison University

Harrisonburg, VA

Address: 800 S. Main Street, Harrisonburg, VA, 22807
Admissions telephone: 540 568-5681; FAX: 540 568-3332
Director of Admissions: Michael D. Walsh
Admissions e-mail: admissions@jmu.edu
Web site: http://www.jmu.edu
SAT Code: 5392 ACT Code: 4370

LD program name: Office of Disability Services
LD program address: MSC 1009, Wilson Hall 107,
Learning Strategies Coordinator: Melinda Burchard
LD program telephone: 540 568-6705
LD program e-mail: burchams@jmu.edu
LD program enrollment: 147, Total campus enrollment: 14,954

GENERAL

James Madison University is a public, coed, four-year institution. 605-acre campus in Harrisonburg (population: 40,468), 70 miles from both Lexington and Winchester and 123 miles from both Washington, DC and Richmond. Served by bus; major airport serves Washington, DC; smaller airport serves Weyers Cave (15 miles); train serves Staunton (25 miles). Public transportation serves campus. Semester system.

LD ADMISSIONS

Students do not complete a separate application and are not simultaneously accepted to the LD program. A member of the LD program does not sit on the admissions committee. High school waivers are accepted for math and foreign language. A personal interview is not required. Essay is required and may be typed. Students must meet the same requirements as all students.

26 applications were offered admission, and 24 enrolled.

SECONDARY SCHOOL REQUIREMENTS

Graduation from secondary school required; GED accepted. The following course distribution required: 4 units of English, 4 units of math, 3 units of science, 3 units of foreign language, 1 unit of social studies, 3 units of history.

TESTING

SAT Reasoning required; ACT may be substituted. SAT Subject recommended.

All enrolled freshmen (fall 2004):

Average SAT I Scores: Verbal: 579 Math: 583
Average ACT Scores: Composite:

Child Study Team report is required if student is classified. A neuropsychological or comprehensive psycho-educational evaluation is required for admission. Tests required as part of this documentation:

- ■ WAIS-IV
- ■ WISC-IV
- ■ SATA
- ■ Woodcock-Johnson
- ■ Nelson-Denny Reading Test
- ■ Other

UNDERGRADUATE STUDENT BODY

Total undergraduate student enrollment: 6,061 Men, 8,529 Women.

Composition of student body (fall 2004):

	Undergraduate	Freshmen
International	0.7	0.8
Black	1.9	2.9
American Indian	0.2	0.2
Asian-American	4.7	4.9
Hispanic	1.7	1.9
White	84.8	85.0
Unreported	6.0	4.3
	100.0%	100.0%

29% are from out of state. 9% join a fraternity and 14% join a sorority. Average age of full-time undergraduates is 20. 30% of classes have fewer than 20 students, 56% have between 20 and 50 students, 14% have more than 50 students.

STUDENT HOUSING

99% of freshmen live in college housing. Freshmen are required to live on campus. Housing is not guaranteed for all undergraduates. Residence Hall units are limited. Campus can house 5,474 undergraduates. Single rooms are available for students with medical or special needs. A medical note is required.

EXPENSES

Tuition (2005-06):

There is no additional cost for LD program/services.

LD SERVICES

LD program size is not limited. LD services available to:

■ Freshmen ■ Sophomores ■ Juniors ■ Seniors

Academic Accommodations

Curriculum		In class	
Foreign language waiver	☐	Early syllabus	☐
Lighter course load	■	Note takers in class	■
Math waiver	☐	Priority seating	☐
Other special classes	■	Tape recorders	■
Priority registrations	■	Videotaped classes	☐
Substitution of courses	☐	Text on tape	■
Exams		**Services**	
Extended time	■	Diagnostic tests	■
Oral exams	■	Learning centers	■
Take home exams	☐	Proofreaders	☐
Exams on tape or computer	■	Readers	■
Untimed exams	☐	Reading Machines/Kurzweil	■
Other accommodations	■	Special bookstore section	☐
		Typists	■

Credit toward degree is not given for remedial courses taken.

Counseling Services

■	Academic	Meets 32 times per academic year
■	Psychological	Meets 14 times per academic year
■	Student Support groups	Meets 32 times per academic year
■	Vocational	Meets 32 times per academic year

Tutoring

Individual tutoring is not available.

	Individual	Group
Time management	■	■
Organizational skills	■	■
Learning strategies	■	■
Study skills	■	■
Content area	■	■
Writing lab	■	■
Math lab	■	■

UNIQUE LD PROGRAM FEATURES

The Office of Disability Services offers four services for students with learning disabilities and other disabilities impacting learning. Students may opt to participate in individualized Learning Strategies Instruction. Students may opt to take a three-credit course on learning strategies. Strategic Learning for College Success. Learning Leaders, a one-credit course in which the JMU student mentors an elementary student with a similar disability. Any student with a disability may participate in workshops on Self-Advocacy which teaches about post-secondary rights and the communication of accommodation needs. In addition, Disability Services collaborates with various learning resource centers to effectively serve students with diverse needs.

LD PROGRAM STAFF

Total number of LD Program staff (including director):

Full Time: 3 Part Time: 3

There is an advisor/advocate from the LD program available to students. 1 graduate students are available to work with LD students.

Key staff person available to work with LD students: Melinda Burchard, Learning Strategies Coordinator.

Liberty University

Lynchburg, VA

Address: 1971 University Boulevard, Lynchburg, VA, 24502-2269
Admissions telephone: 800 543-5317, extension 2
Admissions FAX: 800 542-2311
Executive Director for Enrollment Management: Richard Plyter
Admissions e-mail: admissions@liberty.edu
Web site: http://www.liberty.edu
SAT Code: 5385 ACT Code: 4364

LD/ADHD Advisor: Connie Hansen
LD program telephone: 434 582-2279
LD program e-mail: cbhansen@liberty.edu
Total campus enrollment: 8,697

GENERAL

Liberty University is a private, coed, four-year institution. 160-acre campus in Lynchburg (population: 65,269), 50 miles from Roanoke. Served by air, bus, and train; larger airport serves Richmond (120 miles). Public transportation serves campus. Semester system.

LD ADMISSIONS

A personal interview is not required. Essay is not required.

SECONDARY SCHOOL REQUIREMENTS

Graduation from secondary school required; GED accepted. The following course distribution required: 4 units of English, 3 units of math, 2 units of science, 2 units of foreign language, 2 units of social studies, 2 units of academic electives.

TESTING

SAT Reasoning required; ACT may be substituted. SAT Subject recommended.

All enrolled freshmen (fall 2004):

Average SAT I Scores:	Verbal: 514	Math: 500
Average ACT Scores:	Composite: 22	

Child Study Team report is not required. Tests required as part of this documentation:

☐ WAIS-IV	☐ Woodcock-Johnson
☐ WISC-IV	☐ Nelson-Denny Reading Test
☐ SATA	☐ Other

UNDERGRADUATE STUDENT BODY

Total undergraduate student enrollment: 2,639 Men, 2,752 Women.

Composition of student body (fall 2004):

	Undergraduate	Freshmen
International	4.5	3.8
Black	11.3	10.9
American Indian	0.9	0.8
Asian-American	2.0	1.6
Hispanic	2.7	2.9
White	76.1	76.4
Unreported	2.5	3.6
	100.0%	100.0%

62% are from out of state. Average age of full-time undergraduates is 22. 28% of classes have fewer than 20 students, 61% have between 20 and 50 students, 11% have more than 50 students.

STUDENT HOUSING

89% of freshmen live in college housing. Housing is not guaranteed for all undergraduates. Can not live on campus after the age of 29 Campus can house 5,332 undergraduates.

EXPENSES

Tuition (2005-06): $13,700 per year.

Room & Board: $5,400

There is no additional cost for LD program/services.

LD SERVICES

LD program size is not limited.

LD services available to:

☐ Freshmen ☐ Sophomores ☐ Juniors ☐ Seniors

Academic Accommodations

Curriculum		**In class**	
Foreign language waiver	☐	Early syllabus	☐
Lighter course load	☐	Note takers in class	☐
Math waiver	☐	Priority seating	☐
Other special classes	☐	Tape recorders	☐
Priority registrations	☐	Videotaped classes	☐
Substitution of courses	☐	Text on tape	☐
Exams		**Services**	
Extended time	■	Diagnostic tests	☐
Oral exams	■	Learning centers	■
Take home exams	☐	Proofreaders	☐
Exams on tape or computer	☐	Readers	☐
Untimed exams	☐	Reading Machines/Kurzweil	☐
Other accommodations	☐	Special bookstore section	☐
		Typists	☐

Credit toward degree is given for remedial courses taken.

Counseling Services

☐ Academic
☐ Psychological
☐ Student Support groups
☐ Vocational

Tutoring

	Individual	Group
Time management	☐	☐
Organizational skills	☐	☐
Learning strategies	☐	☐
Study skills	☐	☐
Content area	☐	☐
Writing lab	☐	☐
Math lab	☐	☐

LD PROGRAM STAFF

Total number of LD Program staff (including director):

Full Time: 3 Part Time: 3

Key staff person available to work with LD students: Denny McHaney, Coordinator of Disability Academic Support.

Longwood University

Farmville, VA

Address: 201 High Street, Farmville, VA, 23909
Admissions telephone: 800 281-4677
Admissions FAX: 434 395-2332
Director of Admissions and Enrollment Management: Robert Chonko
Admissions e-mail: admit@longwood.edu
Web site: http://www.longwood.edu
SAT Code: 5368 ACT Code: 4366

LD program name: The Office of Disability Support Services
Director, Disability Support Services: Susan Rood
LD program telephone: 434 395-2391
LD program e-mail: roodse@longwood.edu
LD program enrollment: 128, Total campus enrollment: 3,739

GENERAL

Longwood University is a public, coed, four-year institution. 160-acre campus in Farmville (population: 6,845), 60 miles from Richmond; branch campus in South Boston/Halifax County. Served by bus; major airport and train serve Richmond; smaller airport serves Lynchburg (60 miles). Public transportation serves campus. Semester system.

LD ADMISSIONS

Students do not complete a separate application and are not simultaneously accepted to the LD program. A member of the LD program does not sit on the admissions committee. High school waivers are accepted for foreign language. A personal interview is not required. Essay is required and may be typed.

SECONDARY SCHOOL REQUIREMENTS

Graduation from secondary school required; GED accepted. The following course distribution required: 4 units of English, 3 units of math, 3 units of science, 2 units of foreign language, 1 unit of social studies, 2 units of history, 3 units of academic electives.

TESTING

SAT Reasoning required; ACT may be substituted. SAT Subject recommended.

All enrolled freshmen (fall 2004):

Average SAT I Scores:	Verbal: 544	Math: 532
Average ACT Scores:	Composite:	

Child Study Team report is not required. A neuropsychological or comprehensive psycho-education evaluation is not required for admission. Tests required as part of this documentation:

- [ ] WAIS-IV
- [ ] WISC-IV
- [ ] SATA
- [ ] Woodcock-Johnson
- [ ] Nelson-Denny Reading Test
- [ ] Other

UNDERGRADUATE STUDENT BODY

Total undergraduate student enrollment: 1,225 Men, 2,335 Women.

Composition of student body (fall 2004):

	Undergraduate	Freshmen
International	0.4	0.5
Black	5.8	6.5
American Indian	0.4	0.4
Asian-American	1.9	2.0
Hispanic	1.6	1.5
White	89.9	89.1
Unreported	0.0	0.0
	100.0%	100.0%

10% are from out of state. 12% join a fraternity and 17% join a sorority. Average age of full-time undergraduates is 18. 37% of classes have fewer than 20 students, 59% have between 20 and 50 students, 4% have more than 50 students.

STUDENT HOUSING

97% of freshmen live in college housing. Freshmen are required to live on campus. Housing is not guaranteed for all undergraduates. Some juniors and all seniors may apply to live off-campus. Campus can house 2,466 undergraduates. Single rooms are available for students with medical or special needs. A medical note is required.

EXPENSES

Tuition (2005-06): $3,586 per year (in-state), $10,270 (out-of-state).
Room: $3,288. Board: $2,298.
There is no additional cost for LD program/services.

LD SERVICES

LD program size is not limited.

LD services available to:

- [x] Freshmen
- [x] Sophomores
- [x] Juniors
- [x] Seniors

Academic Accommodations

Curriculum		In class	
Foreign language waiver	[x]	Early syllabus	[ ]
Lighter course load	[x]	Note takers in class	[x]
Math waiver	[ ]	Priority seating	[ ]
Other special classes	[ ]	Tape recorders	[x]
Priority registrations	[x]	Videotaped classes	[ ]
Substitution of courses	[x]	Text on tape	[ ]
Exams		**Services**	
Extended time	[x]	Diagnostic tests	[ ]
Oral exams	[x]	Learning centers	[x]
Take home exams	[ ]	Proofreaders	[ ]
Exams on tape or computer	[x]	Readers	[x]
Untimed exams	[x]	Reading Machines/Kurzweil	[x]
Other accommodations	[x]	Special bookstore section	[ ]
		Typists	[x]

Credit toward degree is not given for remedial courses taken.

Counseling Services

- [ ] Academic
- [ ] Psychological
- [ ] Student Support groups
- [ ] Vocational

Tutoring

Individual tutoring is available daily.

Average size of tutoring groups: 5

	Individual	Group
Time management	[x]	[x]
Organizational skills	[x]	[x]
Learning strategies	[x]	[x]
Study skills	[x]	[x]
Content area	[x]	[x]
Writing lab	[x]	[x]
Math lab	[x]	[x]

LD PROGRAM STAFF

Total number of LD Program staff (including director):

Full Time: 2 Part Time: 2

There is an advisor/advocate from the LD program available to students. The advisor/advocate meets with faculty 2 times per month and students 4 times per month. 2 graduate students and 17 peer tutors are available to work with LD students.

Key staff person available to work with LD students: Susan Rood, Director, Disability Support Services.

LD Program web site: www.longwood.edu/disability

Lynchburg College

Lynchburg, VA

Address: 1501 Lakeside Drive, Lynchburg, VA, 24501
Admissions telephone: 800 426-8101, extension 8300
Admissions FAX: 434 544-8653
Vice President for Enrollment Management: Sharon Walters-Bower
Admissions e-mail: admissions@lynchburg.edu
Web site: http://www.lynchburg.edu
SAT Code: 5372

LD program name: Support Services
Support Services Coordinator: Shawn Arnold
LD program telephone: 434 544-8687
LD program e-mail: arnold_sm@lynchburg.edu
LD program enrollment: 183, Total campus enrollment: 1,934

GENERAL

Lynchburg College is a private, coed, four-year institution. 214-acre, suburban campus in Lynchburg (population: 65,269), 120 miles west of Richmond; 470-acre nature study center in Bedford County. Served by air, bus, and train; major airport serves Roanoke (60 miles). Public transportation serves campus. Semester system.

LD ADMISSIONS

Students do not complete a separate application and are simultaneously accepted to the LD program. A member of the LD program does not sit on the admissions committee. A personal interview is recommended. Essay is not required.

For fall 2004, 86 completed self-identified LD applications were received. 86 applications were offered admission, and 79 enrolled.

SECONDARY SCHOOL REQUIREMENTS

Graduation from secondary school required; GED accepted. The following course distribution required: 4 units of English, 3 units of math, 4 units of science, 2 units of foreign language, 2 units of social studies, 2 units of history.

TESTING

SAT Reasoning or ACT required. SAT Subject recommended.

All enrolled freshmen (fall 2004):

Average SAT I Scores:	Verbal: 494	Math: 492
Average ACT Scores:	Composite: 21	

Child Study Team report is not required. A neuropsychological or comprehensive psycho-educational evaluation is required for admission. Must be dated within 72 months of application. Tests required as part of this documentation:

- [x] WAIS-IV
- [ ] WISC-IV
- [x] SATA
- [x] Woodcock-Johnson
- [x] Nelson-Denny Reading Test
- [ ] Other

UNDERGRADUATE STUDENT BODY

Total undergraduate student enrollment: 660 Men, 1,061 Women.

Composition of student body (fall 2004):

	Undergraduate	Freshmen
International	0.2	0.7
Black	8.8	8.1
American Indian	0.5	0.6
Asian-American	1.9	1.6
Hispanic	2.1	2.6
White	80.9	82.1
Unreported	5.6	4.3
	100.0%	100.0%

44% are from out of state. 8% join a fraternity and 10% join a sorority. Average age of full-time undergraduates is 21. 53% of classes have fewer than 20 students, 47% have between 20 and 50 students.

STUDENT HOUSING

93% of freshmen live in college housing. Freshmen are required to live on campus. Housing is guaranteed for all undergraduates. Campus can house 1,512 undergraduates. Single rooms are available for students with medical or special needs.

EXPENSES

Tuition (2005-06): $23,700 per year.
Room: $3,200. Board: $3,200.
There is no additional cost for LD program/services.

LD SERVICES

LD program size is not limited.

LD services available to:

- [x] Freshmen
- [x] Sophomores
- [x] Juniors
- [x] Seniors

Academic Accommodations

Curriculum		In class	
Foreign language waiver	[ ]	Early syllabus	[ ]
Lighter course load	[ ]	Note takers in class	[x]
Math waiver	[ ]	Priority seating	[x]
Other special classes	[ ]	Tape recorders	[x]
Priority registrations	[ ]	Videotaped classes	[ ]
Substitution of courses	[x]	Text on tape	[x]
Exams		**Services**	
Extended time	[x]	Diagnostic tests	[ ]
Oral exams	[x]	Learning centers	[x]
Take home exams	[ ]	Proofreaders	[ ]
Exams on tape or computer	[x]	Readers	[x]
Untimed exams	[x]	Reading Machines/Kurzweil	[ ]
Other accommodations	[x]	Special bookstore section	[ ]
		Typists	[x]

Credit toward degree is not given for remedial courses taken.

Counseling Services

- [x] Academic — Meets 6 times per academic year
- [ ] Psychological
- [ ] Student Support groups
- [ ] Vocational

Tutoring

Individual tutoring is not available.

Average size of tutoring groups: 6

	Individual	Group
Time management	[x]	[x]
Organizational skills	[x]	[x]
Learning strategies	[x]	[x]
Study skills	[x]	[x]
Content area	[ ]	[ ]
Writing lab	[ ]	[x]
Math lab	[ ]	[x]

LD PROGRAM STAFF

Total number of LD Program staff (including director):

Full Time: 2 Part Time: 2

There is an advisor/advocate from the LD program available to students. The advisor/advocate meets with faculty 1 time per month and students 4 times per month. 60 peer tutors are available to work with LD students.

Key staff person available to work with LD students: Shawn Arnold, Support Services Coordinator.

Mary Baldwin College

Staunton, VA

Address: New and Frederick Streets, Staunton, VA, 24401
Admissions telephone: 800 468-2262
Admissions FAX: 540 887-7279
Dean of Admissions and Financial Aid: Lisa Branson
Admissions e-mail: admit@mbc.edu
Web site: http://www.mbc.edu
SAT Code: 5397 ACT Code: 4374

Director Learning Skills Center: Beverly Askegaard
LD program telephone: 540 887-7250
LD program e-mail: baskegaa@mbc.edu
LD program enrollment: 35, Total campus enrollment: 1,524

GENERAL

Mary Baldwin College is a private, women's, four-year institution. 54-acre campus in Staunton (population: 23,853); branch campuses for adult degree program in Charlottesville, Richmond, Roanoke, and Weyers Cave. Served by train; major airport serves Roanoke (75 miles); smaller airports serve Charlottesville (40 miles) and Weyers Cave (15 miles); bus serves Verona (six miles).

LD ADMISSIONS

A member of the LD program does sit on the admissions committee. A personal interview is not required. Essay is not required.

SECONDARY SCHOOL REQUIREMENTS

Graduation from secondary school required; GED accepted. The following course distribution required: 4 units of English, 3 units of math, 2 units of science, 2 units of foreign language, 3 units of social studies.

TESTING

SAT Subject recommended.

All enrolled freshmen (fall 2004):

Average SAT I Scores:	Verbal: 526	Math: 498
Average ACT Scores:	Composite: 20	

Child Study Team report is not required. A neuropsychological or comprehensive psycho-educational evaluation is required for admission. Tests required as part of this documentation:

- [ ] WAIS-IV
- [ ] WISC-IV
- [ ] SATA
- [ ] Woodcock-Johnson
- [ ] Nelson-Denny Reading Test
- [x] Other

UNDERGRADUATE STUDENT BODY

Total undergraduate student enrollment: 67 Men, 1,321 Women.

Composition of student body (fall 2004):

	Undergraduate	Freshmen
International	2.7	0.8
Black	24.2	15.6
American Indian	0.8	0.4
Asian-American	3.1	1.7
Hispanic	3.9	2.4
White	64.9	78.8
Unreported	0.4	0.3
	100.0%	100.0%

38% are from out of state. Average age of full-time undergraduates is 21. 66% of classes have fewer than 20 students, 34% have between 20 and 50 students.

STUDENT HOUSING

88% of freshmen live in college housing. Freshmen are not required to live on campus. Housing is guaranteed for all undergraduates. Campus can house 742 undergraduates.

EXPENSES

Tuition (2005-06): $20,405 per year.

Room: $3,738. Board: $2,122.

There is no additional cost for LD program/services.

LD SERVICES

LD program size is not limited.

LD services available to:

- [x] Freshmen
- [x] Sophomores
- [x] Juniors
- [x] Seniors

Academic Accommodations

Curriculum		In class	
Foreign language waiver	[ ]	Early syllabus	[ ]
Lighter course load	[ ]	Note takers in class	[x]
Math waiver	[ ]	Priority seating	[ ]
Other special classes	[ ]	Tape recorders	[x]
Priority registrations	[ ]	Videotaped classes	[x]
Substitution of courses	[x]	Text on tape	[ ]
Exams		**Services**	
Extended time	[x]	Diagnostic tests	[ ]
Oral exams	[x]	Learning centers	[x]
Take home exams	[ ]	Proofreaders	[ ]
Exams on tape or computer	[ ]	Readers	[x]
Untimed exams	[x]	Reading Machines/Kurzweil	[ ]
Other accommodations	[ ]	Special bookstore section	[ ]
		Typists	[ ]

Credit toward degree is not given for remedial courses taken.

Counseling Services

- [ ] Academic
- [ ] Psychological
- [ ] Student Support groups
- [ ] Vocational

Tutoring

Individual tutoring is available daily.

Average size of tutoring groups: 1

	Individual	Group
Time management	[x]	[ ]
Organizational skills	[x]	[ ]
Learning strategies	[x]	[ ]
Study skills	[x]	[ ]
Content area	[x]	[ ]
Writing lab	[x]	[ ]
Math lab	[x]	[ ]

LD PROGRAM STAFF

Total number of LD Program staff (including director):

Full Time: 1 Part Time: 1

There is not an advisor/advocate from the LD program available to students.

Key staff person available to work with LD students: Beverly Askegaard, Director Learning Skills Center.

University of Mary Washington

Fredericksburg, VA

Address: 1301 College Avenue, Fredericksburg, VA, 22401
Admissions telephone: 800 468-5614
Admissions FAX: 540 654-1857
Vice President for Admissions and Financial Aid: Dr. Martin Wilder
Admissions e-mail: admit@umw.edu
Web site: http://www.umw.edu
SAT Code: 5398 ACT Code: 4414

LD program name: Office of Disability Services
Director of Disability Services: Stephanie Smith
LD program telephone: 540 654-1266
LD program e-mail: ssmith@umw.edu
LD program enrollment: 59, Total campus enrollment: 4,130

GENERAL

University of Mary Washington is a public, coed, four-year institution. 176-acre campus in Fredericksburg (population: 19,279), 50 miles from both Richmond and Washington, D.C. Served by bus and train; major airport serves Washington, D.C. School operates campus escort service. Public transportation serves campus. Semester system.

LD ADMISSIONS

Students do not complete a separate application and are not simultaneously accepted to the LD program. A member of the LD program does not sit on the admissions committee. A personal interview is required.

SECONDARY SCHOOL REQUIREMENTS

Graduation from secondary school required; GED accepted. The following course distribution required: 4 units of English, 3 units of math, 3 units of science, 2 units of social studies, 2 units of history.

TESTING

SAT Subject recommended.

All enrolled freshmen (fall 2004):

Average SAT I Scores:	Verbal: 628	Math: 602
Average ACT Scores:	Composite: 27	

Child Study Team report is not required. A neuropsychological or comprehensive psycho-educational evaluation is required for admission. Must be dated within 36 months of application. Tests required as part of this documentation:

- ■ WAIS-IV
- ☐ WISC-IV
- ■ SATA
- ■ Woodcock-Johnson
- ■ Nelson-Denny Reading Test
- ☐ Other

UNDERGRADUATE STUDENT BODY

Total undergraduate student enrollment: 1,361 Men, 2,812 Women.

Composition of student body (fall 2004):

	Undergraduate	Freshmen
International	0.3	0.8
Black	1.6	4.2
American Indian	0.1	0.4
Asian-American	5.4	4.6
Hispanic	2.9	3.6
White	89.7	86.4
Unreported	0.0	0.0
	100.0%	100.0%

35% are from out of state. Average age of full-time undergraduates is 20. 44% of classes have fewer than 20 students, 55% have between 20 and 50 students, 1% have more than 50 students.

STUDENT HOUSING

97% of freshmen live in college housing. Freshmen are required to live on campus. Housing is not guaranteed for all undergraduates. BLS students are not eligible for campus housing unless special permission has been given by the Dean of Student Life or his/her designee. Campus can house 2,575 undergraduates. Single rooms are available for students with medical or special needs. A medical note is required.

EXPENSES

Tuition (2005-06): $2,806 per year (in-state), $11,948 (out-of-state).
Room: $3,484. Board: $2,518.
There is no additional cost for LD program/services.

LD SERVICES

LD program size is not limited.

LD services available to:

■ Freshmen ■ Sophomores ■ Juniors ■ Seniors

Academic Accommodations

Curriculum		**In class**	
Foreign language waiver	☐	Early syllabus	☐
Lighter course load	■	Note takers in class	■
Math waiver	☐	Priority seating	☐
Other special classes	☐	Tape recorders	■
Priority registrations	☐	Videotaped classes	☐
Substitution of courses	■	Text on tape	■
Exams		**Services**	
Extended time	■	Diagnostic tests	☐
Oral exams	■	Learning centers	☐
Take home exams	☐	Proofreaders	☐
Exams on tape or computer	■	Readers	☐
Untimed exams	☐	Reading Machines/Kurzweil	■
Other accommodations	■	Special bookstore section	☐
		Typists	■

Credit toward degree is not given for remedial courses taken.

Counseling Services

- ☐ Academic
- ☐ Psychological
- ☐ Student Support groups
- ☐ Vocational

Tutoring

Individual tutoring is available weekly.

Average size of tutoring groups: 1

	Individual	Group
Time management	■	■
Organizational skills	■	■
Learning strategies	■	■
Study skills	■	■
Content area	■	☐
Writing lab	■	☐
Math lab	☐	☐

LD PROGRAM STAFF

Total number of LD Program staff (including director):

Full Time: 1 Part Time: 1

There is no advisor/advocate from the LD program available to students. 20 peer tutors are available to work with LD students.

Key staff person available to work with LD students: Stephanie Smith, Director of Disability Services.

Marymount University

Arlington, VA

Address: 2807 N. Glebe Road, Arlington, VA, 22207
Admissions telephone: 800 548-7638
Admissions FAX: 703 522-0349
Vice President for Enrollment Management: Chris E. Domes
Admissions e-mail: admissions@marymount.edu
Web site: http://www.marymount.edu
SAT Code: 5405 ACT Code: 4378

LD program name: Disability Support Services
LD program telephone: 703 284-1605
LD program e-mail: kelly.desenti@marymount.edu
LD program enrollment: 34, Total campus enrollment: 2,227

GENERAL

Marymount University is a private, coed, four-year institution. 21-acre campus in Arlington (population: 189,453), five miles from Washington, D.C.; branch campuses in Ballston and Sterling. Airport, bus, and train serve Washington, D.C. School operates transportation to metro station. Public transportation serves campus. Semester system.

LD ADMISSIONS

A member of the LD program does not sit on the admissions committee. A personal interview is not required. Essay is not required.

SECONDARY SCHOOL REQUIREMENTS

Graduation from secondary school required; GED accepted.

TESTING

SAT Reasoning or ACT required.

All enrolled freshmen (fall 2004):

Average SAT I Scores: Verbal: 511 Math: 496
Average ACT Scores: Composite: 21

Child Study Team report is not required. A neuropsychological or comprehensive psycho-educational evaluation is required for admission. Must be dated within 36 months of application. Tests required as part of this documentation:

- ☑ WAIS-IV
- ☐ WISC-IV
- ☑ SATA
- ☑ Woodcock-Johnson
- ☑ Nelson-Denny Reading Test
- ☐ Other

UNDERGRADUATE STUDENT BODY

Total undergraduate student enrollment: 582 Men, 1,459 Women.

Composition of student body (fall 2004):

	Undergraduate	Freshmen
International	4.0	8.4
Black	12.6	15.9
American Indian	0.0	0.2
Asian-American	9.0	7.9
Hispanic	10.7	10.3
White	53.3	46.5
Unreported	10.4	10.8
	100.0%	100.0%

38% are from out of state. Average age of full-time undergraduates is 22. 48% of classes have fewer than 20 students, 51% have between 20 and 50 students, 1% have more than 50 students.

STUDENT HOUSING

70% of freshmen live in college housing. Freshmen are required to live on campus. Housing is not guaranteed for all undergraduates. Priority given to freshmen and sophomores under 21. Campus can house 716 undergraduates. Single rooms are available for students with medical or special needs. A medical note is required.

EXPENSES

Tuition (2005-06): $17,970 per year.
Room & Board: $7,820

There is no additional cost for LD program/services.

LD SERVICES

LD program size is not limited.

LD services available to:

☑ Freshmen ☑ Sophomores ☑ Juniors ☑ Seniors

Academic Accommodations

Curriculum		In class	
Foreign language waiver	☐	Early syllabus	☐
Lighter course load	☑	Note takers in class	☑
Math waiver	☐	Priority seating	☐
Other special classes	☐	Tape recorders	☑
Priority registrations	☐	Videotaped classes	☐
Substitution of courses	☐	Text on tape	☑
Exams		**Services**	
Extended time	☑	Diagnostic tests	☐
Oral exams	☑	Learning centers	☑
Take home exams	☐	Proofreaders	☐
Exams on tape or computer	☐	Readers	☑
Untimed exams	☐	Reading Machines/Kurzweil	☐
Other accommodations	☑	Special bookstore section	☐
		Typists	☑

Credit toward degree is not given for remedial courses taken.

Counseling Services

- ☑ Academic — Meets 20 times per academic year
- ☑ Psychological — Meets 12 times per academic year
- ☐ Student Support groups
- ☐ Vocational

Tutoring

Individual tutoring is available daily.

	Individual	Group
Time management	☑	☐
Organizational skills	☑	☐
Learning strategies	☑	☐
Study skills	☐	☐
Content area	☐	☐
Writing lab	☐	☐
Math lab	☐	☐

LD PROGRAM STAFF

Total number of LD Program staff (including director):

Full Time: 1 Part Time: 1

There is an advisor/advocate from the LD program available to students.

Key staff person available to work with LD students: Kelly L. DeSenti, Assistant Director CCCS, Coordinator DSS.

LD Program web site: http://www.marymount.edu/ssa/disabili/

Norfolk State University

Norfolk, VA

Address: 700 Park Avenue, Norfolk, VA, 23504
Admissions telephone: 757 823-8396
Admissions FAX: 757 823-2078
Director of Admissions: Michelle Marable
Admissions e-mail: admissions@nsu.edu
Web site: http://www.nsu.edu
SAT Code: 5864 ACT Code: 4425

LD program address: 700 Park Ave, Norfolk, VA, 23504
Coordinator/Disability Services: Mariane Shepherd
LD program telephone: 757 823-2014
LD program e-mail: mshepherd@nsu.edu
Total campus enrollment: 5,393

GENERAL

Norfolk State University is a public, coed, four-year institution. 134-acre, urban campus in Norfolk (population: 234,403); branch campuses in Portsmouth and Virginia Beach. Served by air and bus; train serves Newport News (23 miles). School operates campus shuttle. Public transportation serves campus. Semester system.

LD ADMISSIONS

Application Deadline: 05/31. Students do not complete a separate application and are not simultaneously accepted to the LD program. A personal interview is required. Essay is not required.

SECONDARY SCHOOL REQUIREMENTS

Graduation from secondary school required; GED accepted. The following course distribution required: 4 units of English, 3 units of math, 3 units of science, 3 units of history, 9 units of academic electives.

TESTING

SAT Reasoning or ACT required. SAT Subject recommended.

All enrolled freshmen (fall 2004):

Average SAT I Scores:	Verbal: 440	Math: 450
Average ACT Scores:	Composite: 18	

Child Study Team report is required if student is classified. Tests required as part of this documentation:

- [ ] WAIS-IV
- [ ] WISC-IV
- [ ] SATA
- [ ] Woodcock-Johnson
- [ ] Nelson-Denny Reading Test
- [ ] Other

UNDERGRADUATE STUDENT BODY

Total undergraduate student enrollment: 2,201 Men, 3,762 Women.

Composition of student body (fall 2004):

	Undergraduate	Freshmen
International	0.7	0.8
Black	88.1	88.7
American Indian	0.2	0.2
Asian-American	0.6	0.9
Hispanic	2.3	1.6
White	3.5	4.6
Unreported	4.6	3.2
	100.0%	100.0%

32% are from out of state. 10% join a fraternity and 10% join a sorority. Average age of full-time undergraduates is 21. 61% of classes have fewer than 20 students, 36% have between 20 and 50 students, 3% have more than 50 students.

STUDENT HOUSING

71% of freshmen live in college housing. Freshmen are not required to live on campus. Housing is guaranteed for all undergraduates. Campus can house 1,944 undergraduates. Single rooms are available for students with medical or special needs. A medical note is required.

EXPENSES

Tuition (2005-06): $2,115 per year (in-state), $11,925 (out-of-state).
Room & Board: $6,474

There is no additional cost for LD program/services.

LD SERVICES

LD program size is not limited.

LD services available to:

- [x] Freshmen
- [x] Sophomores
- [x] Juniors
- [x] Seniors

Academic Accommodations

Curriculum		In class	
Foreign language waiver	[ ]	Early syllabus	[ ]
Lighter course load	[ ]	Note takers in class	[x]
Math waiver	[ ]	Priority seating	[ ]
Other special classes	[ ]	Tape recorders	[x]
Priority registrations	[ ]	Videotaped classes	[x]
Substitution of courses	[ ]	Text on tape	[ ]
Exams		**Services**	
Extended time	[x]	Diagnostic tests	[x]
Oral exams	[x]	Learning centers	[x]
Take home exams	[ ]	Proofreaders	[ ]
Exams on tape or computer	[ ]	Readers	[x]
Untimed exams	[x]	Reading Machines/Kurzweil	[x]
Other accommodations	[ ]	Special bookstore section	[ ]
		Typists	[ ]

Credit toward degree is not given for remedial courses taken.

Counseling Services

- [ ] Academic
- [ ] Psychological
- [ ] Student Support groups
- [ ] Vocational

Tutoring

Individual tutoring is available daily.

Average size of tutoring groups: 1

	Individual	Group
Time management	[ ]	[ ]
Organizational skills	[ ]	[ ]
Learning strategies	[ ]	[x]
Study skills	[ ]	[x]
Content area	[ ]	[ ]
Writing lab	[ ]	[ ]
Math lab	[ ]	[ ]

LD PROGRAM STAFF

Total number of LD Program staff (including director):

Full Time: 3 Part Time: 3

There is an advisor/advocate from the LD program available to students. The advisor/advocate meets with faculty 5 times per month and students 50 times per month. 2 peer tutors are available to work with LD students.

Key staff person available to work with LD students: Mariane Shepherd, Coordinator/Disability Services.

LD Program web site: http://www.nsu.edu/disabilityservices/

Old Dominion University

Norfolk, VA

Address: 5115 Hampton Boulevard, Norfolk, VA, 23529
Admissions telephone: 800 348-7926
Admissions FAX: 757 683-3255
Director of Admissions: Alice McAdory
Admissions e-mail: admit@odu.edu
Web site: http://www.odu.edu
SAT Code: 5126 ACT Code: 5126

LD program name: Disability Services
Director of Disability Services: Sheryn Milton
LD program telephone: 757 683-4655
LD program e-mail: smilton@odu.edu
LD program enrollment: 182, Total campus enrollment: 14,417

GENERAL

Old Dominion University is a public, coed, four-year institution. 157-acre campus in Norfolk (population: 234,403); branch campuses in Hampton, Portsmouth, and Virginia Beach, on U.S. Navy ships at sea, and at more than 40 distance education sites in Indiana, North Carolina, and Virginia. Served by air and bus; train serves Newport News (25 miles). School operates transportation to local malls and Norfolk St. U. Public transportation serves campus. Semester system.

LD ADMISSIONS

Students complete a separate application and are not simultaneously accepted to the LD program. A member of the LD program does not sit on the admissions committee. A personal interview is required. Essay is not required.

SECONDARY SCHOOL REQUIREMENTS

Graduation from secondary school required; GED accepted. The following course distribution required: 4 units of English, 3 units of math, 3 units of science, 3 units of foreign language, 3 units of history, 1 unit of academic electives.

TESTING

SAT Reasoning required; ACT may be substituted. SAT Subject recommended.

All enrolled freshmen (fall 2004):

Average SAT I Scores:	Verbal: 529	Math: 528
Average ACT Scores:	Composite: 21	

Child Study Team report is not required. A neuropsychological or comprehensive psycho-educational evaluation is required for admission. Must be dated within 36 months of application. Tests required as part of this documentation:

- [x] WAIS-IV
- [x] WISC-IV
- [ ] SATA
- [x] Woodcock-Johnson
- [ ] Nelson-Denny Reading Test
- [x] Other

UNDERGRADUATE STUDENT BODY

Total undergraduate student enrollment: 5,586 Men, 7,512 Women.

Composition of student body (fall 2004):

	Undergraduate	Freshmen
International	2.0	2.1
Black	25.7	22.9
American Indian	0.6	0.7
Asian-American	6.6	6.1
Hispanic	3.7	3.4
White	56.8	60.6
Unreported	4.6	4.2
	100.0%	100.0%

8% are from out of state. 5% join a fraternity and 3% join a sorority. Average age of full-time undergraduates is 22. 36% of classes have fewer than 20 students, 54% have between 20 and 50 students, 10% have more than 50 students.

STUDENT HOUSING

60% of freshmen live in college housing. Freshmen are not required to live on campus. Housing is guaranteed for all undergraduates. Campus can house 3,342 undergraduates. Single rooms are available for students with medical or special needs. A medical note is required.

EXPENSES

Tuition (2005-06): $5,100 per year (in-state), $14,520 (out-of-state).
Room: $3,342. Board: $2,460.
There is no additional cost for LD program/services.

LD SERVICES

LD program size is not limited.

LD services available to:

- [x] Freshmen
- [x] Sophomores
- [x] Juniors
- [x] Seniors

Academic Accommodations

Curriculum		In class	
Foreign language waiver	[ ]	Early syllabus	[ ]
Lighter course load	[x]	Note takers in class	[x]
Math waiver	[ ]	Priority seating	[x]
Other special classes	[x]	Tape recorders	[x]
Priority registrations	[x]	Videotaped classes	[ ]
Substitution of courses	[x]	Text on tape	[ ]
Exams		**Services**	
Extended time	[x]	Diagnostic tests	[ ]
Oral exams	[ ]	Learning centers	[ ]
Take home exams	[ ]	Proofreaders	[ ]
Exams on tape or computer	[x]	Readers	[x]
Untimed exams	[ ]	Reading Machines/Kurzweil	[ ]
Other accommodations	[x]	Special bookstore section	[ ]
		Typists	[x]

Credit toward degree is not given for remedial courses taken.

Counseling Services

- [x] Academic — Meets 2 times per academic year
- [ ] Psychological
- [x] Student Support groups — Meets 9 times per academic year
- [ ] Vocational

Tutoring

Individual tutoring is not available.

	Individual	Group
Time management	[x]	[x]
Organizational skills	[x]	[x]
Learning strategies	[x]	[x]
Study skills	[x]	[x]
Content area	[ ]	[ ]
Writing lab	[ ]	[ ]
Math lab	[ ]	[ ]

UNIQUE LD PROGRAM FEATURES

Disability Services strives to coordinate services using a developmental model that will enable students with disabilities to act as independently as possible in a supportive atmosphere that promotes self-reliance.

LD PROGRAM STAFF

Total number of LD Program staff (including director):

Full Time: 3 Part Time: 3

There is an advisor/advocate from the LD program available to students. 1 graduate student is available to work with LD students.

Key staff person available to work with LD students: Cathy Canady, Learning Coordinator, Disability Services.

LD Program web site: http://studentservices.odu.edu/disabilityservices

Radford University

Radford, VA

Address: PO Box 6890, RU Station, Radford, VA, 24142
Admissions telephone: 800 890-4265
Admissions FAX: 540 831-5138
Director of Admissions: David W. Kraus
Admissions e-mail: ruadmiss@radford.edu
Web site: http://www.radford.edu
SAT Code: 5565 ACT Code: 4422

Associate Vice President for Student Affairs: Dr. Ken Lott
LD program telephone: 540 831-6348
LD program e-mail: klott@radford.edu
LD program enrollment: 222, Total campus enrollment: 8,356

GENERAL

Radford University is a public, coed, four-year institution. 177-acre campus in Radford (population: 15,859), 45 miles west of Roanoke; branch campuses in Abingdon and Roanoke. Airport and bus serve Roanoke; train serves Lynchburg (100 miles). School operates transportation to northern and eastern Virginia. Semester system.

LD ADMISSIONS

Students do not complete a separate application and are not simultaneously accepted to the LD program. A member of the LD program does not sit on the admissions committee. A personal interview is required. Essay is not required.

SECONDARY SCHOOL REQUIREMENTS

Graduation from secondary school required; GED accepted.

TESTING

SAT Subject recommended.

All enrolled freshmen (fall 2004):

Average SAT I Scores: Verbal: 498 Math: 495
Average ACT Scores: Composite:

Child Study Team report is required if student is classified. A neuropsychological or comprehensive psycho-educational evaluation is required for admission. Must be dated within 60 months of application. Tests required as part of this documentation:

- ■ WAIS-IV
- ☐ WISC-IV
- ☐ SATA
- ■ Woodcock-Johnson
- ■ Nelson-Denny Reading Test
- ☐ Other

UNDERGRADUATE STUDENT BODY

Total undergraduate student enrollment: 3,236 Men, 4,825 Women.

Composition of student body (fall 2004):

	Undergraduate	Freshmen
International	0.1	0.7
Black	6.2	5.8
American Indian	0.1	0.2
Asian-American	2.9	2.1
Hispanic	3.0	2.3
White	87.7	88.9
Unreported	0.0	0.0
	100.0%	100.0%

12% are from out of state. 8% join a fraternity and 12% join a sorority. Average age of full-time undergraduates is 20. 34% of classes have fewer than 20 students, 61% have between 20 and 50 students, 5% have more than 50 students.

STUDENT HOUSING

94% of freshmen live in college housing. Freshmen are required to live on campus. Housing is guaranteed for all undergraduates. Campus can house 3,365 undergraduates. Single rooms are available for students with medical or special needs. A medical note is required.

EXPENSES

Tuition (2005-06): $3,235 per year (in-state), $10,473 (out-of-state).
Room: $3,300. Board: $2,820.
There is no additional cost for LD program/services.

LD SERVICES

LD program size is not limited.

LD services available to:

■ Freshmen ■ Sophomores ■ Juniors ■ Seniors

Academic Accommodations

Curriculum		In class	
Foreign language waiver	☐	Early syllabus	☐
Lighter course load	☐	Note takers in class	■
Math waiver	☐	Priority seating	■
Other special classes	☐	Tape recorders	■
Priority registrations	■	Videotaped classes	☐
Substitution of courses	☐	Text on tape	■
Exams		**Services**	
Extended time	■	Diagnostic tests	☐
Oral exams	■	Learning centers	■
Take home exams	☐	Proofreaders	■
Exams on tape or computer	■	Readers	■
Untimed exams	☐	Reading Machines/Kurzweil	■
Other accommodations	■	Special bookstore section	☐
		Typists	■

Credit toward degree is not given for remedial courses taken.

Counseling Services

- ☐ Academic
- ■ Psychological — Meets 6 times per academic year
- ☐ Student Support groups
- ☐ Vocational

Tutoring

Individual tutoring is available daily.

	Individual	Group
Time management	■	☐
Organizational skills	■	☐
Learning strategies	■	☐
Study skills	■	☐
Content area	■	☐
Writing lab	■	☐
Math lab	■	☐

LD PROGRAM STAFF

Total number of LD Program staff (including director):

Full Time: 1 Part Time: 1

There is an advisor/advocate from the LD program available to students. 3 peer tutors are available to work with LD students.

Key staff person available to work with LD students: Joann Stephens-Forrest, Coordinator.

Randolph-Macon College

Ashland, VA

Address: PO Box 5005, Ashland, VA, 23005-5505
Admissions telephone: 800 888-1762
Admissions FAX: 804 752-4707
Dean of Admissions: John C. Conkright
Admissions e-mail: admissions@rmc.edu
Web site: http://www.rmc.edu
SAT Code: 5566 ACT Code: 4386

LD program name: Higgins Academic Center
Director of Disability Support Services: Jack Trammell
LD program telephone: 804 752-7343
LD program e-mail: jtrammel@rmc.edu
LD program enrollment: 70, Total campus enrollment: 1,127

GENERAL

Randolph-Macon College is a private, coed, four-year institution. 110-acre, suburban campus in Ashland (population: 6,619), 15 miles north of Richmond and 90 miles south of Washington, D.C. Served by train; airport and bus serve Richmond. School operates transportation to Richmond. 4-1-4 system.

LD ADMISSIONS

Students do not complete a separate application and are not simultaneously accepted to the LD program. A member of the LD program does sit on the admissions committee. High school waivers are accepted for foreign language. A personal interview is recommended. Essay is required and may be typed. Students with a documented learning disability that specifies difficulty with foreign languages may be allowed to substitute other classes for the foreign language requirement.

For fall 2004, 15 completed self-identified LD applications were received. 10 applications were offered admission, and 10 enrolled.

SECONDARY SCHOOL REQUIREMENTS

Graduation from secondary school required; GED accepted. The following course distribution required: 4 units of English, 3 units of math, 3 units of science, 2 units of foreign language, 1 unit of social studies, 2 units of history, 1 unit of academic electives.

TESTING

SAT Reasoning required; ACT may be substituted. SAT Subject required.

All enrolled freshmen (fall 2004):

Average SAT I Scores: Verbal: 561 Math: 553
Average ACT Scores: Composite:

Child Study Team report is not required. A neuropsychological or comprehensive psycho-educational evaluation is required for admission. Must be dated within 36 months of application. Tests required as part of this documentation:

- [x] WAIS-IV
- [ ] WISC-IV
- [ ] SATA
- [x] Woodcock-Johnson
- [ ] Nelson-Denny Reading Test
- [ ] Other

UNDERGRADUATE STUDENT BODY

Total undergraduate student enrollment: 583 Men, 567 Women.

Composition of student body (fall 2004):

	Undergraduate	Freshmen
International	1.5	1.1
Black	4.9	5.5
American Indian	0.3	0.2
Asian-American	2.2	1.4
Hispanic	1.5	1.4
White	89.6	90.4
Unreported	0.0	0.0
	100.0%	100.0%

40% are from out of state. 33% join a fraternity and 33% join a sorority. Average age of full-time undergraduates is 20. 71% of classes have fewer than 20 students, 29% have between 20 and 50 students.

STUDENT HOUSING

95% of freshmen live in college housing. Freshmen are required to live on campus. Housing is guaranteed for all undergraduates. Campus can house 930 undergraduates. Single rooms are available for students with medical or special needs. A medical note is required.

EXPENSES

Tuition (2005-06): $23,310 per year.
Room: $3,955. Board: $3,305.
There is no additional cost for LD program/services.

LD SERVICES

LD program size is not limited.

LD services available to:

- [x] Freshmen
- [x] Sophomores
- [x] Juniors
- [x] Seniors

Academic Accommodations

Curriculum		In class	
Foreign language waiver	[ ]	Early syllabus	[ ]
Lighter course load	[ ]	Note takers in class	[x]
Math waiver	[ ]	Priority seating	[ ]
Other special classes	[ ]	Tape recorders	[x]
Priority registrations	[ ]	Videotaped classes	[ ]
Substitution of courses	[x]	Text on tape	[x]
Exams		**Services**	
Extended time	[x]	Diagnostic tests	[ ]
Oral exams	[ ]	Learning centers	[x]
Take home exams	[ ]	Proofreaders	[ ]
Exams on tape or computer	[x]	Readers	[ ]
Untimed exams	[x]	Reading Machines/Kurzweil	[x]
Other accommodations	[ ]	Special bookstore section	[ ]
		Typists	[ ]

Credit toward degree is not given for remedial courses taken.

Counseling Services

- [x] Academic
- [x] Psychological
- [ ] Student Support groups
- [ ] Vocational

Meets 2 times per academic year

Tutoring

Individual tutoring is available daily.

Average size of tutoring groups: 2

	Individual	Group
Time management	[x]	[ ]
Organizational skills	[x]	[ ]
Learning strategies	[x]	[ ]
Study skills	[x]	[ ]
Content area	[x]	[ ]
Writing lab	[x]	[ ]
Math lab	[x]	[ ]

LD PROGRAM STAFF

Total number of LD Program staff (including director):

Full Time: 2 Part Time: 2

There is an advisor/advocate from the LD program available to students. The advisor/advocate meets with faculty 2 times per month and students 1 time per month. 45 peer tutors are available to work with LD students.

Key staff person available to work with LD students: Jack Trammell, Director of Disability Support Services.

Randolph-Macon Woman's College

Lynchburg, VA

Address: 2500 Rivermont Avenue, Lynchburg, VA, 24503-1526
Admissions telephone: 800 745-7692
Admissions FAX: 434 947-8996
Director of Admissions: Patricia N. LeDonne
Admissions e-mail: admissions@rmwc.edu
Web site: http://www.rmwc.edu
SAT Code: 5567 ACT Code: 4388

Director: Tina Barnes
LD program telephone: 434 947-8132
LD program e-mail: tbarnes@rmwc.edu
LD program enrollment: 9, Total campus enrollment: 732

GENERAL

Randolph-Macon Woman's College is a private, women's, four-year institution. 100-acre campus in Lynchburg (population: 65,269), 150 miles southwest of Washington, D.C. Served by air, bus, and train. School operates transportation to athletic events/facilities, nature preserves, shopping malls, and special academic and social programs. Public transportation serves campus. Semester system.

LD ADMISSIONS

Students do not complete a separate application and are simultaneously accepted to the LD program. A member of the LD program does sit on the admissions committee. A personal interview is recommended. Essay is required and may be typed. While requirements are not waived, specific circumstances may be taken into consideration if the student requests.

SECONDARY SCHOOL REQUIREMENTS

Graduation from secondary school required; GED accepted. The following course distribution required: 4 units of English, 3 units of math, 2 units of science, 2 units of foreign language, 2 units of history, 1 unit of academic electives.

TESTING

SAT Reasoning or ACT required. SAT Subject recommended.

All enrolled freshmen (fall 2004):

Average SAT I Scores:	Verbal: 603	Math: 564
Average ACT Scores:	Composite: 24	

Child Study Team report is not required. Tests required as part of this documentation:

- ☐ WAIS-IV
- ☐ WISC-IV
- ☐ SATA
- ☐ Woodcock-Johnson
- ☐ Nelson-Denny Reading Test
- ■ Other

UNDERGRADUATE STUDENT BODY

Total undergraduate student enrollment: 2 Men, 719 Women.

Composition of student body (fall 2004):

	Undergraduate	Freshmen
International	8.2	8.4
Black	8.2	8.5
American Indian	0.5	0.4
Asian-American	3.9	3.1
Hispanic	7.7	4.3
White	69.1	73.3
Unreported	2.4	2.0
	100.0%	100.0%

50% are from out of state. Average age of full-time undergraduates is 20. 82% of classes have fewer than 20 students, 18% have between 20 and 50 students.

STUDENT HOUSING

96% of freshmen live in college housing. Freshmen are required to live on campus. Housing is guaranteed for all undergraduates. Campus can house 650 undergraduates. Single rooms are available for students with medical or special needs. A medical note is required.

EXPENSES

Tuition (2005-06): $22,550 per year.

Room & Board: $8,610

There is no additional cost for LD program/services.

LD SERVICES

LD program size is not limited.

LD services available to:

■ Freshmen ■ Sophomores ■ Juniors ■ Seniors

Academic Accommodations

Curriculum		In class	
Foreign language waiver	☐	Early syllabus	☐
Lighter course load	☐	Note takers in class	■
Math waiver	☐	Priority seating	■
Other special classes	☐	Tape recorders	■
Priority registrations	■	Videotaped classes	☐
Substitution of courses	☐	Text on tape	■
Exams		**Services**	
Extended time	■	Diagnostic tests	☐
Oral exams	■	Learning centers	■
Take home exams	■	Proofreaders	☐
Exams on tape or computer	■	Readers	■
Untimed exams	☐	Reading Machines/Kurzweil	■
Other accommodations	■	Special bookstore section	☐
		Typists	■

Credit toward degree is not given for remedial courses taken.

Counseling Services

- ■ Academic
- ■ Psychological
- ☐ Student Support groups
- ■ Vocational

Tutoring

Individual tutoring is available weekly.

Average size of tutoring groups: 1

	Individual	Group
Time management	■	☐
Organizational skills	■	☐
Learning strategies	■	☐
Study skills	■	☐
Content area	■	☐
Writing lab	■	☐
Math lab	■	☐

UNIQUE LD PROGRAM FEATURES

The College does not have specific programs for students with disabilities. It has an office of Disability Services where documentation is received, reviewed, and maintained and where specific, reasonable, appropriate accommodations are determined and assigned to students with documented disabilities.

LD PROGRAM STAFF

Total number of LD Program staff (including director):

Full Time: 1 Part Time: 1

There is an advisor/advocate from the LD program available to students. 5 peer tutors are available to work with LD students.

Key staff person available to work with LD students: Tina Barnes, Director of the Learning Resources Center & Disability Services.

University of Richmond

Univ. of Richmond, VA

Address: 28 Westhampton Way, Univ. of Richmond, VA, 23173
Admissions telephone: 800 700-1662
Admissions FAX: 804 287-6003
Dean of Admission: Pamela W. Spence
Admissions e-mail: admissions@richmond.edu
Web site: http://www.richmond.edu
SAT Code: 5569 ACT Code: 4410

Staff Psychologist: Mary M. Churchill, Ph.D.
LD program telephone: 804 289-8119
LD program e-mail: mchurchi@richmond.edu
Total campus enrollment: 2,976

GENERAL

University of Richmond is a private, coed, four-year institution. 350-acre, suburban campus, six miles from center of Richmond (population: 197,790). Served by air, bus, and train. Public transportation serves campus. Semester system.

LD ADMISSIONS

No requirements are waived for LD students.

SECONDARY SCHOOL REQUIREMENTS

Graduation from secondary school required; GED accepted. The following course distribution required: 4 units of English, 3 units of math, 2 units of science, 2 units of foreign language, 2 units of history.

TESTING

SAT Reasoning or ACT required. SAT Subject required.

All enrolled freshmen (fall 2004):

Average SAT I Scores: Verbal: 653 Math: 664
Average ACT Scores: Composite: 28

Child Study Team report is not required. Tests required as part of this documentation:

- ❑ WAIS-IV
- ❑ WISC-IV
- ❑ SATA
- ❑ Woodcock-Johnson
- ❑ Nelson-Denny Reading Test
- ❑ Other

UNDERGRADUATE STUDENT BODY

Total undergraduate student enrollment: 1,455 Men, 1,566 Women.

Composition of student body (fall 2004):

	Undergraduate	Freshmen
International	0.0	1.3
Black	5.0	4.6
American Indian	0.0	0.1
Asian-American	3.9	3.8
Hispanic	2.6	1.8
White	88.0	84.5
Unreported	0.5	3.9
	100.0%	100.0%

85% are from out of state. 45% join a fraternity and 45% join a sorority. Average age of full-time undergraduates is 20. 59% of classes have fewer than 20 students, 40% have between 20 and 50 students, 1% have more than 50 students.

STUDENT HOUSING

99% of freshmen live in college housing. Freshmen are not required to live on campus. Housing is not guaranteed for all undergraduates. Campus housing is available for all undergraduate students who are enrolled full-time (12 hours). Campus can house 2,686 undergraduates.

EXPENSES

Tuition (2005-06): $34,850 per year.

Room: $2,582. Board: $3,078.

LD SERVICES

LD services available to:

❑ Freshmen ❑ Sophomores ❑ Juniors ❑ Seniors

Academic Accommodations

Curriculum		**In class**	
Foreign language waiver	❑	Early syllabus	❑
Lighter course load	❑	Note takers in class	❑
Math waiver	❑	Priority seating	❑
Other special classes	❑	Tape recorders	❑
Priority registrations	❑	Videotaped classes	❑
Substitution of courses	❑	Text on tape	❑
Exams		**Services**	
Extended time	❑	Diagnostic tests	❑
Oral exams	❑	Learning centers	❑
Take home exams	❑	Proofreaders	❑
Exams on tape or computer	❑	Readers	❑
Untimed exams	❑	Reading Machines/Kurzweil	❑
Other accommodations	❑	Special bookstore section	❑
		Typists	❑

Counseling Services

- ❑ Academic
- ❑ Psychological
- ❑ Student Support groups
- ❑ Vocational

Tutoring

	Individual	Group
Time management	❑	❑
Organizational skills	❑	❑
Learning strategies	❑	❑
Study skills	❑	❑
Content area	❑	❑
Writing lab	❑	❑
Math lab	❑	❑

UNIQUE LD PROGRAM FEATURES

Broad range of assistance, designed in coordination with each individual's request. Learning disability accommodations proceed through the counseling center, with a board licensed, Ph.D. psychologist. Physical disabilities are channeled through the Vice President for Student Affairs. These usually involve physical adaptation of facilities and related concerns. Every student requesting accommodations is seen individually and worked with one-on-one.

LD PROGRAM STAFF

Key staff person available to work with LD students: Mary M. Churchill, Ph.D., Staff Psychologist.

Roanoke College

Salem, VA

Address: 221 College Lane, Salem, VA, 24153-3794
Admissions telephone: 800 388-2276
Admissions FAX: 540 375-2267
Dean for Admissions and Financial Aid: Michael C. Maxey
Admissions e-mail: admissions@roanoke.edu
Web site: http://www.roanoke.edu
SAT Code: 5571 ACT Code: 4392

Total campus enrollment: 1,850

GENERAL

Roanoke College is a private, coed, four-year institution. 68-acre, suburban campus in Salem (population: 24,747), five miles west of Roanoke. Major airport and bus serve Roanoke; train serves Lynchburg (40 miles). Semester system.

LD ADMISSIONS

A personal interview is recommended. Essay is not required.

SECONDARY SCHOOL REQUIREMENTS

Graduation from secondary school required; GED accepted. The following course distribution required: 4 units of English, 3 units of math, 2 units of science, 2 units of social studies, 5 units of academic electives.

TESTING

SAT Reasoning or ACT required. SAT Subject recommended.

All enrolled freshmen (fall 2004):

Average SAT I Scores: Verbal: 560 Math: 550
Average ACT Scores: Composite:

Child Study Team report is not required. Tests required as part of this documentation:

- ☐ WAIS-IV
- ☐ WISC-IV
- ☐ SATA
- ☐ Woodcock-Johnson
- ☐ Nelson-Denny Reading Test
- ☐ Other

UNDERGRADUATE STUDENT BODY

Total undergraduate student enrollment: 689 Men, 1,101 Women.

Composition of student body (fall 2004):

	Undergraduate	Freshmen
International	0.8	1.2
Black	5.0	3.9
American Indian	0.0	0.6
Asian-American	2.3	1.9
Hispanic	1.9	2.0
White	78.6	82.5
Unreported	11.4	8.0
	100.0%	100.0%

42% are from out of state. 16% join a fraternity and 24% join a sorority. Average age of full-time undergraduates is 20. 59% of classes have fewer than 20 students, 41% have between 20 and 50 students.

STUDENT HOUSING

90% of freshmen live in college housing. Housing is not guaranteed for all undergraduates. Housing is guaranteed for freshmen. Campus can house 1,170 undergraduates.

EXPENSES

Tuition (2005-06): $22,848 per year.
Room: $3,526. Board: $3,769.
There is no additional cost for LD program/services.

LD SERVICES

LD program size is not limited.

LD services available to:

☒ Freshmen ☒ Sophomores ☒ Juniors ☒ Seniors

Academic Accommodations

Curriculum		In class	
Foreign language waiver	☐	Early syllabus	☐
Lighter course load	☐	Note takers in class	☒
Math waiver	☐	Priority seating	☐
Other special classes	☐	Tape recorders	☒
Priority registrations	☐	Videotaped classes	☐
Substitution of courses	☐	Text on tape	☐
Exams		**Services**	
Extended time	☒	Diagnostic tests	☐
Oral exams	☒	Learning centers	☒
Take home exams	☐	Proofreaders	☐
Exams on tape or computer	☐	Readers	☐
Untimed exams	☒	Reading Machines/Kurzweil	☐
Other accommodations	☐	Special bookstore section	☐
		Typists	☐

Credit toward degree is not given for remedial courses taken.

Counseling Services

- ☐ Academic
- ☐ Psychological
- ☐ Student Support groups
- ☐ Vocational

Tutoring

Individual tutoring is available.

	Individual	Group
Time management	☐	☐
Organizational skills	☐	☐
Learning strategies	☐	☐
Study skills	☐	☐
Content area	☐	☐
Writing lab	☐	☐
Math lab	☐	☐

LD PROGRAM STAFF

There is an advisor/advocate from the LD program available to students.

Key staff person available to work with LD students: Gregory S. Wells, Academic Services Advisor.

Saint Paul's College

Lawrenceville, VA

Address: 115 College Drive, Lawrenceville, VA, 23868
Admissions telephone: 800 678-7071
Admissions FAX: 434 848-6407
Director of Admissions and Recruitment: Mrs. Rosemary Lewise
Admissions e-mail: admissions@saintpauls.edu
Web site: http://www.saintpauls.edu
SAT Code: 5604 ACT Code: 4394

LD program address: 115 College Drive, Lawrenceville, VA, 23868
Director of Student Support Services: Ms. Shawn Briggs
LD program telephone: 434 848-6442
LD program e-mail: sbriggs@saintpauls.edu
LD program enrollment: 12, Total campus enrollment: 627

GENERAL

Saint Paul's College is a private, coed, four-year institution. 75-acre campus in Lawrenceville (population:1,275), approximately 75 miles south of Richmond. Major airport serves Richmond; bus serves South Hill (17 miles); train serves Petersburg (50 miles). School operates transportation to airport and bus station. Semester system.

LD ADMISSIONS

Students do not complete a separate application and are simultaneously accepted to the LD program. A member of the LD program does not sit on the admissions committee. High school waivers are accepted for math and foreign language. A personal interview is required. Essay is required and may be typed.

For fall 2004, 12 completed self-identified LD applications were received. 12 applications were offered admission, and 12 enrolled.

SECONDARY SCHOOL REQUIREMENTS

Graduation from secondary school required; GED accepted. The following course distribution required: 4 units of English, 2 units of math, 2 units of science.

TESTING

SAT Reasoning required; ACT may be substituted. SAT Subject recommended.

All enrolled freshmen (fall 2004):

Average SAT I Scores: Verbal: Math:
Average ACT Scores: Composite:

Child Study Team report is required if student is classified. A neuropsychological or comprehensive psycho-educational evaluation is required for admission. Tests required as part of this documentation:

- ☐ WAIS-IV
- ☐ WISC-IV
- ☐ SATA
- ☐ Woodcock-Johnson
- ☐ Nelson-Denny Reading Test
- ■ Other

UNDERGRADUATE STUDENT BODY

Total undergraduate student enrollment: 201 Men, 349 Women.

Composition of student body (fall 2004):

	Undergraduate	Freshmen
International	0.4	1.0
Black	99.6	96.6
American Indian	0.0	0.0
Asian-American	0.0	0.3
Hispanic	0.0	0.0
White	0.0	2.1
Unreported	0.0	0.0
	100.0%	100.0%

10% are from out of state. 73% of classes have fewer than 20 students, 15% have between 20 and 50 students, 12% have more than 50 students.

STUDENT HOUSING

Freshmen are not required to live on campus. Housing is guaranteed for all undergraduates. Campus can house 400 undergraduates.

EXPENSES

Tuition (2005-06): $9,600 per year.
Room: $2,550. Board: $2,980.
There is no additional cost for LD program/services.

LD SERVICES

LD program size is not limited.

LD services available to:

■ Freshmen ■ Sophomores ■ Juniors ■ Seniors

Academic Accommodations

Curriculum		**In class**	
Foreign language waiver	☐	Early syllabus	☐
Lighter course load	■	Note takers in class	■
Math waiver	☐	Priority seating	☐
Other special classes	☐	Tape recorders	■
Priority registrations	☐	Videotaped classes	☐
Substitution of courses	☐	Text on tape	☐
Exams		**Services**	
Extended time	■	Diagnostic tests	■
Oral exams	☐	Learning centers	■
Take home exams	■	Proofreaders	■
Exams on tape or computer	☐	Readers	☐
Untimed exams	■	Reading Machines/Kurzweil	☐
Other accommodations	■	Special bookstore section	☐
		Typists	☐

Credit toward degree is not given for remedial courses taken.

Counseling Services

- ■ Academic
- ■ Psychological
- ■ Student Support groups
- ■ Vocational

Tutoring

Individual tutoring is available daily.

Average size of tutoring groups: 1

	Individual	Group
Time management	■	■
Organizational skills	■	■
Learning strategies	■	■
Study skills	■	■
Content area	☐	☐
Writing lab	☐	☐
Math lab	■	■

UNIQUE LD PROGRAM FEATURES

Student Support Services is a federally funded program that targets three groups of students: those who come from low income families, those who are the first generation college students in their families, and those who came to the College with an officially identified learning disability.

LD PROGRAM STAFF

Total number of LD Program staff (including director):

Full Time: 3 Part Time: 3

There is an advisor/advocate from the LD program available to students. The advisor/advocate meets with faculty 1 time per month and students 4 times per month. 15 peer tutors are available to work with LD students.

Key staff person available to work with LD students: Rev. Joy D. Carrington, Educational Counselor.

Shenandoah University

Winchester, VA

Address: 1460 University Drive, Winchester, VA, 22601
Admissions telephone: 800 432-2266
Admissions FAX: 540 665-4627
Director of Admissions: David Anthony
Admissions e-mail: admit@su.edu
Web site: http://www.su.edu
SAT Code: 5613 ACT Code: 5613

LD program name: Academic Support Services
Director, Academic Support Services: Judy Landes
LD program telephone: 540 665-4928
LD program e-mail: jlandes@su.edu
Total campus enrollment: 1538

GENERAL

Shenandoah University is a private, coed, four-year institution. 100-acre campus in Winchester (population: 23,585), 72 miles from Washington, D.C.; branch campus in Leesburg. Served by bus; major airport serves Washington, D.C.; smaller airport serves Hagerstown, Md., (45 miles); train serves Martinsburg, W.Va. (25 miles). Public transportation serves campus. Semester system.

LD ADMISSIONS

A personal interview is not required. Essay is not required.

SECONDARY SCHOOL REQUIREMENTS

Graduation from secondary school required; GED accepted. The following course distribution required: 4 units of English, 3 units of math, 2 units of science, 2 units of foreign language, 2 units of academic electives.

TESTING

SAT Reasoning or ACT required. SAT Subject required.

All enrolled freshmen (fall 2004):

Average SAT I Scores:	Verbal: 517	Math: 508
Average ACT Scores:	Composite: 24	

Child Study Team report is not required. Tests required as part of this documentation:

- [ ] WAIS-IV
- [ ] WISC-IV
- [ ] SATA
- [ ] Woodcock-Johnson
- [ ] Nelson-Denny Reading Test
- [ ] Other

UNDERGRADUATE STUDENT BODY

Total undergraduate student enrollment: 590 Men, 771 Women.

Composition of student body (fall 2004):

	Undergraduate	Freshmen
International	5.5	4.8
Black	1.2	3.8
American Indian	0.0	0.1
Asian-American	0.3	1.1
Hispanic	0.3	0.8
White	92.7	89.4
Unreported	0.0	0.0
	100.0%	100.0%

37% are from out of state. Average age of full-time undergraduates is 22. 69% of classes have fewer than 20 students, 30% have between 20 and 50 students, 1% have more than 50 students.

STUDENT HOUSING

90% of freshmen live in college housing. Freshmen are required to live on campus. Housing is guaranteed for all undergraduates. Campus can house 654 undergraduates. Single rooms are available for students with medical or special needs. A medical note is required.

EXPENSES

Tuition (2005-06): $19,900 per year.
Room & Board: $7,550

There is no additional cost for LD program/services.

LD SERVICES

LD program size is not limited.

LD services available to:

- [x] Freshmen
- [x] Sophomores
- [x] Juniors
- [x] Seniors

Academic Accommodations

Curriculum

- [x] Foreign language waiver
- [x] Lighter course load
- [x] Math waiver
- [x] Other special classes
- [x] Priority registrations
- [x] Substitution of courses

Exams

- [x] Extended time
- [x] Oral exams
- [x] Take home exams
- [x] Exams on tape or computer
- [ ] Untimed exams
- [x] Other accommodations

In class

- [x] Early syllabus
- [x] Note takers in class
- [x] Priority seating
- [x] Tape recorders
- [x] Videotaped classes
- [x] Text on tape

Services

- [ ] Diagnostic tests
- [x] Learning centers
- [ ] Proofreaders
- [x] Readers
- [x] Reading Machines/Kurzweil
- [ ] Special bookstore section
- [x] Typists

Credit toward degree is not given for remedial courses taken.

Counseling Services

- [x] Academic
- [x] Psychological
- [x] Student Support groups
- [x] Vocational

Tutoring

Individual tutoring is available weekly.

Average size of tutoring groups: 1

	Individual	Group
Time management	[x]	[x]
Organizational skills	[x]	[x]
Learning strategies	[x]	[x]
Study skills	[x]	[x]
Content area	[ ]	[ ]
Writing lab	[x]	[x]
Math lab	[x]	[x]

LD PROGRAM STAFF

Total number of LD Program staff (including director):

Full Time: 2 Part Time: 2

There is an advisor/advocate from the LD program available to students. The advisor/advocate meets with faculty 1 time per month and students 3 times per month. 113 peer tutors are available to work with LD students.

Key staff person available to work with LD students: Judy Landes, Director, Academic Support Services.

LD Program web site: www.su.edu/studaffs/disability/index.asp

Sweet Briar College

Sweet Briar, VA

Address: 134 Chapel Road, Sweet Briar, VA, 24595
Admissions telephone: 800 381-6142
Admissions FAX: 434 381-6152
Director of Admissions: Ken Huus
Admissions e-mail: admissions@sbc.edu
Web site: http://www.sbc.edu
SAT Code: 5634 ACT Code: 4406

LD program name: Academic Advising
LD program address: P.O. Box D, Sweet Briar, VA, 24595
Academic Resource Center: Dr. Sandy Duis
LD program telephone: 434 381-6406
LD program e-mail: sduis@sbc.edu
LD program enrollment: 84, Total campus enrollment: 728

GENERAL

Sweet Briar College is a private, women's, four-year institution. 3,300-acre campus in Sweet Briar (population: 2,251), 12 miles from Lynchburg. Served by bus; major airports serve Richmond (120 miles) and Washington, D.C. (160 miles); train serves Lynchburg. School operates transportation to neighboring cities and to special events. Semester system.

LD ADMISSIONS

A member of the LD program does sit on the admissions committee. High school waivers are accepted for math and foreign language. A personal interview is recommended. Essay is required and may be typed. Sweet Briar does not discriminate on the basis of disability in the admissions process. If an applicant believes that an accommodated admission review is warranted, the applicant must initiate the process (by law, the Admissions Office cannot address a disability unless the applicant is self-identified). The applicant must submit a written request for an accommodated admissions review to the Dean of Admissions and enclose with that request the appropriate documentation. The request will be evaluated by the Dean of the College or the Associate Dean of Academic Affairs, who will forward a recommendation to the Dean of Admissions for inclusion in the admissions review process.

SECONDARY SCHOOL REQUIREMENTS

Graduation from secondary school required; GED accepted. The following course distribution required: 4 units of English, 3 units of math, 3 units of science, 2 units of foreign language, 3 units of social studies.

TESTING

SAT Reasoning or ACT required. SAT Subject required.

All enrolled freshmen (fall 2004):

Average SAT I Scores:	Verbal: 586	Math: 548
Average ACT Scores:	Composite: 24	

Child Study Team report is not required. A neuropsychological or comprehensive psycho-educational evaluation is required for admission. Must be dated within 60 months of application. Tests required as part of this documentation:

- ■ WAIS-IV
- ☐ WISC-IV
- ☐ SATA
- ■ Woodcock-Johnson
- ☐ Nelson-Denny Reading Test
- ■ Other

UNDERGRADUATE STUDENT BODY

Total undergraduate student enrollment: 28 Men, 710 Women.

Composition of student body (fall 2004):

	Undergraduate	Freshmen
International	1.2	3.3
Black	1.2	2.2
American Indian	1.2	0.4
Asian-American	2.9	2.2
Hispanic	2.9	2.4
White	83.0	85.3
Unreported	7.6	4.2
	100.0%	100.0%

60% are from out of state. Average age of full-time undergraduates is 20. 90% of classes have fewer than 20 students, 10% have between 20 and 50 students.

STUDENT HOUSING

95% of freshmen live in college housing. Freshmen are required to live on campus. Housing is guaranteed for all undergraduates. Campus can house 551 undergraduates. Single rooms are available for students with medical or special needs. A medical note is required.

EXPENSES

Tuition (2005-06): $22,230 per year.
Room: $3,630. Board: $5,400.
There is no additional cost for LD program/services.

LD SERVICES

LD program size is not limited.

LD services available to:

■ Freshmen ■ Sophomores ■ Juniors ■ Seniors

Academic Accommodations

Curriculum		In class	
Foreign language waiver	☐	Early syllabus	☐
Lighter course load	☐	Note takers in class	☐
Math waiver	☐	Priority seating	☐
Other special classes	☐	Tape recorders	☐
Priority registrations	☐	Videotaped classes	☐
Substitution of courses	☐	Text on tape	☐
Exams		**Services**	
Extended time	■	Diagnostic tests	☐
Oral exams	☐	Learning centers	■
Take home exams	☐	Proofreaders	☐
Exams on tape or computer	☐	Readers	☐
Untimed exams	☐	Reading Machines/Kurzweil	☐
Other accommodations	☐	Special bookstore section	☐
		Typists	☐

Credit toward degree is not given for remedial courses taken.

Counseling Services

- ■ Academic
- ■ Psychological — Meets 8 times per academic year
- ■ Student Support groups
- ☐ Vocational

Tutoring

Individual tutoring is available weekly.

	Individual	Group
Time management	■	☐
Organizational skills	■	☐
Learning strategies	■	☐
Study skills	■	☐
Content area	■	☐
Writing lab	■	☐
Math lab	☐	☐

LD PROGRAM STAFF

Total number of LD Program staff (including director):

Full Time: 1 Part Time: 1

There is an advisor/advocate from the LD program available to students.

Key staff person available to work with LD students: Dr. Alix Ingber, Director of Academic Advising.

The College of William and Mary in Virginia

Williamsburg, VA

Address: PO Box 8795, Williamsburg, VA, 23187-8795
Admissions telephone: 757 221-4223
Admissions FAX: 757 221-1242
Associate Provost for Enrollment: Karen Cottrell
Admissions e-mail: admiss@wm.edu
Web site: http://www.wm.edu
SAT Code: 5115 ACT Code: 4344

LD program telephone: 757 221-2510
Total campus enrollment: 5,642

GENERAL

The College of William and Mary in Virginia is a public, coed, four-year institution. 1,200-acre campus in Williamsburg (population: 11,998), 15 miles from Newport News and 50 miles from Richmond; branch campus for marine science at Gloucester Point on the York River. Served by bus and train; airport serves Newport News. School operates transportation on campus and to surrounding apartments and shopping centers. Public transportation serves campus. Semester system.

LD ADMISSIONS

A personal interview is not required. Essay is required and may be typed.

SECONDARY SCHOOL REQUIREMENTS

Graduation from secondary school is not required.

TESTING

SAT Reasoning or ACT required. SAT Subject recommended.

All enrolled freshmen (fall 2004):

Average SAT I Scores:	Verbal: 674	Math: 661
Average ACT Scores:	Composite: 29	

Child Study Team report is not required. Tests required as part of this documentation:

- ☐ WAIS-IV
- ☐ WISC-IV
- ☐ SATA
- ☐ Woodcock-Johnson
- ☐ Nelson-Denny Reading Test
- ☐ Other

UNDERGRADUATE STUDENT BODY

Total undergraduate student enrollment: 2,433 Men, 3,171 Women.

Composition of student body (fall 2004):

	Undergraduate	Freshmen
International	1.8	1.8
Black	6.5	5.9
American Indian	0.7	0.5
Asian-American	6.5	6.6
Hispanic	5.5	4.3
White	67.1	67.1
Unreported	11.9	13.9
	100.0%	100.0%

35% are from out of state. 33% join a fraternity and 34% join a sorority. Average age of full-time undergraduates is 20. 47% of classes have fewer than 20 students, 46% have between 20 and 50 students, 7% have more than 50 students.

STUDENT HOUSING

100% of freshmen live in college housing. Freshmen are required to live on campus. Housing is guaranteed for all undergraduates. Campus can house 4,206 undergraduates. Single rooms are not available for students with medical or special needs.

EXPENSES

Tuition (2005-06): $4,730 per year (in-state), $20,000 (out-of-state). Room: $3,856. Board: $2,561.

There is no additional cost for LD program/services.

LD SERVICES

LD program size is not limited.

LD services available to:

☑ Freshmen ☑ Sophomores ☑ Juniors ☑ Seniors

Academic Accommodations

Curriculum		In class	
Foreign language waiver	☐	Early syllabus	☐
Lighter course load	☐	Note takers in class	☑
Math waiver	☐	Priority seating	☐
Other special classes	☐	Tape recorders	☑
Priority registrations	☐	Videotaped classes	☐
Substitution of courses	☐	Text on tape	☐
Exams		**Services**	
Extended time	☑	Diagnostic tests	☑
Oral exams	☐	Learning centers	☐
Take home exams	☐	Proofreaders	☐
Exams on tape or computer	☐	Readers	☑
Untimed exams	☐	Reading Machines/Kurzweil	☐
Other accommodations	☐	Special bookstore section	☐
		Typists	☐

Credit toward degree is not given for remedial courses taken.

Counseling Services

- ☐ Academic
- ☐ Psychological
- ☐ Student Support groups
- ☐ Vocational

Tutoring

	Individual	Group
Time management	☐	☐
Organizational skills	☐	☐
Learning strategies	☐	☐
Study skills	☐	☐
Content area	☐	☐
Writing lab	☐	☐
Math lab	☐	☐

UNIQUE LD PROGRAM FEATURES

We do not offer a special LD program but resources are available to all students with disabilities.

LD PROGRAM STAFF

Key staff person available to work with LD students: Lisa Colligan, Assistant Dean of Students.

University of Virginia

Charlottesville, VA

Address: Peabody Hall, Charlottesville, VA, 22904
Admissions telephone: 434 982-3200
Admissions FAX: 434 924-3587
Dean of Admission: John A. Blackburn
Admissions e-mail: undergrad-admission@virginia.edu
Web site: http://www.virginia.edu
SAT Code: 5820 ACT Code: 4412

Total campus enrollment: 14,129

GENERAL

University of Virginia is a public, coed, four-year institution. 1,151-acre campus in Charlottesville (population: 45,049), 70 miles from Richmond. Served by air, bus, and train; major airport serves Richmond. School operates transportation to off-campus living areas. Public transportation serves campus. Semester system.

LD ADMISSIONS

SECONDARY SCHOOL REQUIREMENTS

Graduation from secondary school required; GED accepted. The following course distribution required: 4 units of English, 4 units of math, 2 units of science, 2 units of foreign language, 1 unit of social studies.

TESTING

SAT Subject recommended.

All enrolled freshmen (fall 2004):

Average SAT I Scores:	Verbal: 659	Math: 671
Average ACT Scores:	Composite: 28	

Child Study Team report is not required. Tests required as part of this documentation:

- [ ] WAIS-IV
- [ ] WISC-IV
- [ ] SATA
- [ ] Woodcock-Johnson
- [ ] Nelson-Denny Reading Test
- [ ] Other

UNDERGRADUATE STUDENT BODY

Total undergraduate student enrollment: 14,129.

Composition of student body (fall 2004):

	Undergraduate	Freshmen
International	5.2	4.6
Black	9.3	8.7
American Indian	0.2	0.2
Asian-American	10.8	10.5
Hispanic	4.5	3.2
White	62.8	67.1
Unreported	7.2	5.7
	100.0%	100.0%

29% are from out of state. 30% join a fraternity and 30% join a sorority. Average age of full-time undergraduates is 20. 49% of classes have fewer than 20 students, 35% have between 20 and 50 students, 16% have more than 50 students.

STUDENT HOUSING

100% of freshmen live in college housing. Freshmen are required to live on campus. Housing is guaranteed for all undergraduates. Campus can house 6,200 undergraduates.

EXPENSES

Tuition (2005-06): $5,602 per year (in-state), $22,522 (out-of-state). Room: $3,289. Board: $3,100.

LD SERVICES

LD program size is not limited.

LD services available to:

- [x] Freshmen
- [x] Sophomores
- [x] Juniors
- [x] Seniors

Academic Accommodations

Curriculum

- [ ] Foreign language waiver
- [ ] Lighter course load
- [ ] Math waiver
- [ ] Other special classes
- [ ] Priority registrations
- [ ] Substitution of courses

Exams

- [x] Extended time
- [x] Oral exams
- [ ] Take home exams
- [ ] Exams on tape or computer
- [x] Untimed exams
- [ ] Other accommodations

In class

- [ ] Early syllabus
- [x] Note takers in class
- [ ] Priority seating
- [x] Tape recorders
- [ ] Videotaped classes
- [ ] Text on tape

Services

- [x] Diagnostic tests
- [x] Learning centers
- [ ] Proofreaders
- [x] Readers
- [ ] Reading Machines/Kurzweil
- [ ] Special bookstore section
- [ ] Typists

Counseling Services

- [ ] Academic
- [ ] Psychological
- [ ] Student Support groups
- [ ] Vocational

Tutoring

	Individual	Group
Time management	[ ]	[ ]
Organizational skills	[ ]	[ ]
Learning strategies	[ ]	[ ]
Study skills	[ ]	[ ]
Content area	[ ]	[ ]
Writing lab	[ ]	[ ]
Math lab	[ ]	[ ]

University of Virginia's College at Wise

Wise, VA

Address: 1 College Avenue, Wise, VA, 24293
Admissions telephone: 888 282-9324
Admissions FAX: 276 328-0251
Director of Admissions and Financial Aid: Russell D. Necessary
Admissions e-mail: admissions@uvawise.edu
Web site: http://www.uvawise.edu
SAT Code: 5124

ADA Coordinator: Narda Porter
LD program telephone: 276 328-0177
LD program e-mail: n_porter@uvawise.edu
LD program enrollment: 34, Total campus enrollment: 1,836

GENERAL

University of Virginia's College at Wise is a public, coed, four-year institution. 367-acre campus in Wise (population: 3,255), 60 miles from Kingsport, Tenn.; branch campus in Abingdon. Airport serves Blountville, Tenn. (60 miles); bus serves Abingdon (50 miles). Semester system.

LD ADMISSIONS

Students complete a separate application and are not simultaneously accepted to the LD program. A member of the LD program does not sit on the admissions committee. A personal interview is recommended. Essay is not required. Students with special situations may supply additional supports or information to be considered for admission if they fall below a 2.3 GPA.

For fall 2004, 39 completed self-identified LD applications were received.

SECONDARY SCHOOL REQUIREMENTS

Graduation from secondary school required; GED accepted. The following course distribution required: 4 units of English, 3 units of math, 2 units of science, 2 units of foreign language, 1 unit of social studies, 1 unit of history, 5 units of academic electives.

TESTING

SAT Reasoning or ACT required.

All enrolled freshmen (fall 2004):

Average SAT I Scores:	Verbal: 494	Math: 481
Average ACT Scores:	Composite: 19	

Child Study Team report is not required. A neuropsychological or comprehensive psycho-educational evaluation is required for admission. Tests required as part of this documentation:

- [x] WAIS-IV
- [x] WISC-IV
- [x] SATA
- [x] Woodcock-Johnson
- [x] Nelson-Denny Reading Test
- [x] Other

UNDERGRADUATE STUDENT BODY

Total undergraduate student enrollment: 630 Men, 817 Women.

Composition of student body (fall 2004):

	Undergraduate	Freshmen
International	0.0	0.3
Black	7.0	5.3
American Indian	0.3	0.2
Asian-American	1.1	1.2
Hispanic	1.6	1.2
White	90.0	91.8
Unreported	0.0	0.0
	100.0%	100.0%

6% are from out of state. 7% join a fraternity and 8% join a sorority. Average age of full-time undergraduates is 23. 53% of classes have fewer than 20 students, 45% have between 20 and 50 students, 2% have more than 50 students.

STUDENT HOUSING

63% of freshmen live in college housing. Freshmen are not required to live on campus. Housing is guaranteed for all undergraduates. Campus can house 550 undergraduates.

EXPENSES

Tuition (2005-06): $2,984 per year (in-state), $13,062 (out-of-state).

Room: $3,253. Board: $2,712.

There is no additional cost for LD program/services.

LD SERVICES

LD program size is not limited.

LD services available to:

- [x] Freshmen
- [x] Sophomores
- [x] Juniors
- [x] Seniors

Academic Accommodations

Curriculum		In class	
Foreign language waiver	[ ]	Early syllabus	[ ]
Lighter course load	[x]	Note takers in class	[x]
Math waiver	[ ]	Priority seating	[x]
Other special classes	[ ]	Tape recorders	[x]
Priority registrations	[x]	Videotaped classes	[x]
Substitution of courses	[x]	Text on tape	[x]
Exams		**Services**	
Extended time	[x]	Diagnostic tests	[ ]
Oral exams	[ ]	Learning centers	[x]
Take home exams	[ ]	Proofreaders	[x]
Exams on tape or computer	[x]	Readers	[x]
Untimed exams	[ ]	Reading Machines/Kurzweil	[x]
Other accommodations	[x]	Special bookstore section	[ ]
		Typists	[x]

Credit toward degree is not given for remedial courses taken.

Counseling Services

- [x] Academic
- [x] Psychological
- [x] Student Support groups
- [x] Vocational

Tutoring

Individual tutoring is available daily.

Average size of tutoring groups: 1

	Individual	Group
Time management	[x]	[x]
Organizational skills	[x]	[x]
Learning strategies	[x]	[x]
Study skills	[x]	[x]
Content area	[x]	[x]
Writing lab	[x]	[x]
Math lab	[ ]	[ ]

UNIQUE LD PROGRAM FEATURES

Disability Services at U Va-Wise serve all students with disabilities on campus, not just students with learning disabilities. LD students are served out of Disability Services. In addition, the college admissions process is separate and distinct from the Disability Services intake process. If students identify during the admissions process, that documentation is sent to the Disability Services office and kept confidential until such time as the student is admitted or not. The College, therefore, does not necessarily know how many students with disabilities apply and are admitted to the college. Disability services keeps records only on those students who have provided appropriate documentation and are being served by the office.

LD PROGRAM STAFF

Total number of LD Program staff (including director):

Full Time: 1 Part Time: 1

There is an advisor/advocate from the LD program available to students. 30 peer tutors are available to work with LD students.

Key staff person available to work with LD students: Narda Porter, ADA Coordinator.

Virginia Commonwealth University

Richmond, VA

Address: Box 842527, Richmond, VA, 23284
Admissions telephone: 800 841-3638
Admissions FAX: 804 828-1899
Director of Admissions: Delores Taylor
Admissions e-mail: ugrad@vcu.edu
Web site: http://www.vcu.edu
SAT Code: 5570

Coordinator, Disability Support Services: Joyce Knight
LD program telephone: 804 828-1139
LD program e-mail: jbknight@vcu.edu
Total campus enrollment: 19,180

GENERAL

Virginia Commonwealth University is a public, coed, four-year institution. Two urban campuses totalling 130 acres in Richmond (population: 197,790). Served by air, bus, and train; major airport serves Washington, D.C. (100 miles). School operates transportation between campuses and to downtown area. Public transportation serves campus. Semester system.

LD ADMISSIONS

A personal interview is recommended. Essay is not required. Disability maybe taken into consideration on an individual basis for meeting minimum academic requirements.

SECONDARY SCHOOL REQUIREMENTS

Graduation from secondary school required; GED accepted. The following course distribution required: 4 units of English, 3 units of math, 2 units of science, 3 units of history, 7 units of academic electives.

TESTING

SAT Reasoning required; ACT may be substituted. SAT Subject recommended.

All enrolled freshmen (fall 2004):

Average SAT I Scores:	Verbal: 539	Math: 526
Average ACT Scores:	Composite: 21	

Child Study Team report is not required. Tests required as part of this documentation:

- ☐ WAIS-IV
- ☐ WISC-IV
- ☐ SATA
- ☐ Woodcock-Johnson
- ☐ Nelson-Denny Reading Test
- ☐ Other

UNDERGRADUATE STUDENT BODY

Total undergraduate student enrollment: 7,071 Men, 10,077 Women.

Composition of student body (fall 2004):

	Undergraduate	Freshmen
International	2.0	1.5
Black	20.4	20.4
American Indian	0.3	0.6
Asian-American	10.7	9.2
Hispanic	3.6	3.1
White	57.3	60.4
Unreported	5.7	4.8
	100.0%	100.0%

5% are from out of state. 2% join a fraternity and 3% join a sorority. 44% of classes have fewer than 20 students, 45% have between 20 and 50 students, 11% have more than 50 students.

STUDENT HOUSING

66% of freshmen live in college housing. Freshmen are not required to live on campus. Housing is not guaranteed for all undergraduates. Limited campus housing is available for upperclassmen. Campus can house 3,172 undergraduates.

EXPENSES

Tuition (2005-06): $3,969 per year (in-state), $15,904 (out-of-state). Room: $4,102. Board: $2,940.

There is no additional cost for LD program/services.

LD SERVICES

LD program size is not limited.

LD services available to:

☑ Freshmen ☑ Sophomores ☑ Juniors ☑ Seniors

Academic Accommodations

Curriculum		**In class**	
Foreign language waiver	☐	Early syllabus	☐
Lighter course load	☐	Note takers in class	☑
Math waiver	☐	Priority seating	☐
Other special classes	☐	Tape recorders	☑
Priority registrations	☐	Videotaped classes	☐
Substitution of courses	☐	Text on tape	☐
Exams		**Services**	
Extended time	☑	Diagnostic tests	☐
Oral exams	☑	Learning centers	☐
Take home exams	☐	Proofreaders	☐
Exams on tape or computer	☐	Readers	☑
Untimed exams	☐	Reading Machines/Kurzweil	☑
Other accommodations	☐	Special bookstore section	☐
		Typists	☐

Credit toward degree is not given for remedial courses taken.

Counseling Services

- ☐ Academic
- ☐ Psychological
- ☐ Student Support groups
- ☐ Vocational

Tutoring

	Individual	Group
Time management	☐	☐
Organizational skills	☐	☐
Learning strategies	☐	☐
Study skills	☐	☐
Content area	☐	☐
Writing lab	☐	☐
Math lab	☐	☐

LD PROGRAM STAFF

Total number of LD Program staff (including director):

Full Time: 1 Part Time: 1

Key staff person available to work with LD students: Joyce Knight, Coordinator, Disability Support Services.

Virginia Intermont College

Bristol, VA

Address: 1013 Moore Street, Bristol, VA, 24201
Admissions telephone: 800 451-1VIC
Admissions FAX: 276 466-7855
Vice President of Admissions: Craig Wesley
Admissions e-mail: viadmit@vic.edu
Web site: http://www.vic.edu
SAT Code: 5857 ACT Code: 4416

LD program name: Student Support Services
School Psychologist/LD Specialist: Barbara Holbrook
LD program telephone: 276 466-7906
LD program e-mail: bholbrook@vic.edu
LD program enrollment: 23, Total campus enrollment: 1,152

GENERAL

Virginia Intermont College is a private, coed, four-year institution. 25-acre campus in Bristol (population: 17,367), 110 miles from Roanoke; branch campuses in Big Stone Gap, Marion, Pennington Gap, and Richlands. Served by bus; airport serves Tri-Cities (25 miles). Public transportation serves campus. Semester system.

LD ADMISSIONS

Students do not complete a separate application and are simultaneously accepted to the LD program. A member of the LD program does not sit on the admissions committee. A personal interview is not required. Essay is not required.

For fall 2004, 9 completed self-identified LD applications were received. 9 applications were offered admission, and 9 enrolled.

SECONDARY SCHOOL REQUIREMENTS

Graduation from secondary school required; GED accepted. The following course distribution required: 4 units of English, 2 units of math, 1 unit of science, 2 units of social studies, 6 units of academic electives.

TESTING

SAT Reasoning required; ACT may be substituted. SAT Subject recommended.

All enrolled freshmen (fall 2004):

Average SAT I Scores:	Verbal: 490	Math: 480
Average ACT Scores:	Composite: 20	

Child Study Team report is not required. A neuropsychological or comprehensive psycho-educational evaluation is required for admission. Must be dated within 36 months of application. Tests required as part of this documentation:

- [x] WAIS-IV
- [ ] WISC-IV
- [ ] SATA
- [x] Woodcock-Johnson
- [ ] Nelson-Denny Reading Test
- [ ] Other

UNDERGRADUATE STUDENT BODY

Total undergraduate student enrollment: 232 Men, 686 Women.

36% are from out of state. Average age of full-time undergraduates is 35. 82% of classes have fewer than 20 students, 18% have between 20 and 50 students.

STUDENT HOUSING

75% of freshmen live in college housing. Freshmen are required to live on campus. Housing is guaranteed for all undergraduates. Campus can house 475 undergraduates. Single rooms are available for students with medical or special needs. A medical note is required.

EXPENSES

Tuition (2005-06): $15,500 per year.
Room: $2,750. Board: $3,000.
There is no additional cost for LD program/services.

LD SERVICES

LD program size is not limited.

LD services available to:

- [x] Freshmen
- [x] Sophomores
- [x] Juniors
- [x] Seniors

Academic Accommodations

Curriculum

- [ ] Foreign language waiver
- [x] Lighter course load
- [ ] Math waiver
- [x] Other special classes
- [ ] Priority registrations
- [ ] Substitution of courses

Exams

- [x] Extended time
- [x] Oral exams
- [ ] Take home exams
- [x] Exams on tape or computer
- [x] Untimed exams
- [ ] Other accommodations

In class

- [ ] Early syllabus
- [x] Note takers in class
- [ ] Priority seating
- [x] Tape recorders
- [ ] Videotaped classes
- [x] Text on tape

Services

- [x] Diagnostic tests
- [x] Learning centers
- [x] Proofreaders
- [x] Readers
- [ ] Reading Machines/Kurzweil
- [ ] Special bookstore section
- [x] Typists

Credit toward degree is not given for remedial courses taken.

Counseling Services

- [x] Academic
- [x] Psychological
- [x] Student Support groups
- [ ] Vocational

Tutoring

Individual tutoring is available twice per month.

Average size of tutoring groups: 3

	Individual	Group
Time management	[x]	[ ]
Organizational skills	[x]	[ ]
Learning strategies	[x]	[ ]
Study skills	[x]	[x]
Content area	[x]	[x]
Writing lab	[x]	[ ]
Math lab	[x]	[ ]

LD PROGRAM STAFF

Total number of LD Program staff (including director):

Full Time: 3 Part Time: 3

There is an advisor/advocate from the LD program available to students.

Key staff person available to work with LD students: Barbara Holbrook, School Psychologist / LD Specialist.

LD Program web site: www.vic.edu

Virginia Military Institute

Lexington, VA

Address: VMI Parade, Lexington, VA, 24450-0304
Admissions telephone: 800 767-4207
Admissions FAX: 540 464-7746
Director of Admissions: Col. Vern Beitzel
Admissions e-mail: admissions@vmi.edu
Web site: http://www.vmi.edu
SAT Code: 5858 ACT Code: 4418

LD program address: 215 Carroll Hall, Lexington, VA, 24450
Disabilities Coordinator: Lenna Ojure
LD program telephone: 540 464-7765
LD program e-mail: ojure@vmi.edu
LD program enrollment: 6, Total campus enrollment: 1,362

GENERAL

Virginia Military Institute is a public, coed, four-year institution. 134-acre campus in Lexington (population: 6,867), 55 miles from Roanoke and 70 miles from Charlottesville. Airports serve Roanoke and Charlottesville; bus serves Buena Vista (six miles); train serves Charlottesville. Semester system.

LD ADMISSIONS

Students do not complete a separate application and are not simultaneously accepted to the LD program. A member of the LD program does not sit on the admissions committee.

For fall 2004, 6 completed self-identified LD applications were received.

SECONDARY SCHOOL REQUIREMENTS

Graduation from secondary school required; GED not accepted. The following course distribution required: 4 units of English, 3 units of math, 3 units of science, 3 units of foreign language.

TESTING

SAT Reasoning or ACT required. SAT Subject recommended.

All enrolled freshmen (fall 2004):

Average SAT I Scores:	Verbal: 579	Math: 586
Average ACT Scores:	Composite: 25	

Child Study Team report is not required. A neuropsychological or comprehensive psycho-educational evaluation is required for admission. Must be dated within 12 months of application. Tests required as part of this documentation:

- [x] WAIS-IV
- [ ] WISC-IV
- [ ] SATA
- [x] Woodcock-Johnson
- [x] Nelson-Denny Reading Test
- [ ] Other

UNDERGRADUATE STUDENT BODY

Total undergraduate student enrollment: 1,250 Men, 61 Women.

Composition of student body (fall 2004):

	Undergraduate	Freshmen
International	1.7	2.3
Black	4.7	5.3
American Indian	0.3	0.4
Asian-American	3.6	3.0
Hispanic	3.0	2.6
White	86.7	86.3
Unreported	0.0	0.1
	100.0%	100.0%

47% are from out of state. Average age of full-time undergraduates is 20. 71% of classes have fewer than 20 students, 29% have between 20 and 50 students.

STUDENT HOUSING

100% of freshmen live in college housing. Freshmen are required to live on campus. Housing is guaranteed for all undergraduates. Campus can house 1,440 undergraduates.

EXPENSES

Tuition (2005-06): $4,382 per year (in-state), $18,581 (out-of-state). Room: $1,766. Board: $3,949.
There is no additional cost for LD program/services.

LD SERVICES

LD program size is not limited.

LD services available to:

- [x] Freshmen
- [x] Sophomores
- [x] Juniors
- [x] Seniors

Academic Accommodations

Curriculum

- [x] Foreign language waiver
- [ ] Lighter course load
- [ ] Math waiver
- [ ] Other special classes
- [x] Priority registrations
- [x] Substitution of courses

Exams

- [x] Extended time
- [ ] Oral exams
- [ ] Take home exams
- [ ] Exams on tape or computer
- [ ] Untimed exams
- [x] Other accommodations

In class

- [x] Early syllabus
- [x] Note takers in class
- [x] Priority seating
- [x] Tape recorders
- [ ] Videotaped classes
- [x] Text on tape

Services

- [ ] Diagnostic tests
- [x] Learning centers
- [x] Proofreaders
- [ ] Readers
- [x] Reading Machines/Kurzweil
- [ ] Special bookstore section
- [ ] Typists

Credit toward degree is not given for remedial courses taken.

Counseling Services

- [x] Academic
- [x] Psychological
- [x] Student Support groups
- [x] Vocational

Tutoring

Individual tutoring is available weekly.

Average size of tutoring groups: 1

	Individual	Group
Time management	[x]	[x]
Organizational skills	[x]	[x]
Learning strategies	[x]	[x]
Study skills	[x]	[x]
Content area	[x]	[x]
Writing lab	[x]	[x]
Math lab	[x]	[x]

LD PROGRAM STAFF

Total number of LD Program staff (including director):

Full Time: 1 Part Time: 1

There is an advisor/advocate from the LD program available to students. 10 peer tutors are available to work with LD students.

Key staff person available to work with LD students: Lenna Ojure, Learning Specialist, Disabilities Coordinator.

Virginia Polytechnic Institute and State University

Blacksburg, VA

Address: Blacksburg, VA, 24061
Admissions telephone: 540 231-6267
Admissions FAX: 540 231-3242
Director of Admissions: Norinne Bailey Spencer
Admissions e-mail: vtadmiss@vt.edu
Web site: http://www.vt.edu
SAT Code: 5859 ACT Code: 4420

LD program name: Services for Students with Disabilities
Director: Dr. Susan Angle
LD program telephone: 540 231-3788
LD program e-mail: spangle@vt.edu
LD program enrollment: 185, Total campus enrollment: 21,330

GENERAL

Virginia Polytechnic Institute and State University is a public, coed, four-year institution. 2,600-acre campus in Blacksburg (population: 39,573), 38 miles west of Roanoke. Major airport serves Roanoke; bus serves Christianburg (eight miles); train serves Clifton Forge/Roanoke (38 miles). Public transportation serves campus. Semester system.

LD ADMISSIONS

Students do not complete a separate application and are not simultaneously accepted to the LD program. A member of the LD program does not sit on the admissions committee. A personal interview is not required. Essay is not required.

SECONDARY SCHOOL REQUIREMENTS

Graduation from secondary school required; GED accepted. The following course distribution required: 4 units of English, 3 units of math, 2 units of science, 1 unit of social studies, 1 unit of history, 3 units of academic electives.

TESTING

SAT Reasoning or ACT required. SAT Subject recommended.

All enrolled freshmen (fall 2004):

Average SAT I Scores: Verbal: 587 Math: 612
Average ACT Scores: Composite: 25

Child Study Team report is not required. A neuropsychological or comprehensive psycho-education evaluation is not required for admission. Tests required as part of this documentation:

- [ ] WAIS-IV
- [ ] WISC-IV
- [ ] SATA
- [ ] Woodcock-Johnson
- [ ] Nelson-Denny Reading Test
- [ ] Other

UNDERGRADUATE STUDENT BODY

Total undergraduate student enrollment: 12,742 Men, 8,790 Women.

Composition of student body (fall 2004):

	Undergraduate	Freshmen
International	2.0	2.6
Black	3.5	5.6
American Indian	0.3	0.2
Asian-American	6.8	6.9
Hispanic	1.8	2.1
White	73.5	75.5
Unreported	12.1	7.1
	100.0%	100.0%

27% are from out of state. Average age of full-time undergraduates is 20. 22% of classes have fewer than 20 students, 56% have between 20 and 50 students, 22% have more than 50 students.

STUDENT HOUSING

98% of freshmen live in college housing. Freshmen are required to live on campus. Housing is not guaranteed for all undergraduates. On-campus housing is guaranteed for freshmen. Returning students are allocated housing using a lottery system. In the past several years, housing has been offered to 85 percent or more of the returning students asking to return to on-campus housing options. Campus can house 8,775 undergraduates. Single rooms are available for students with medical or special needs. A medical note is required.

EXPENSES

Tuition (2005-06): $4,959 per year (in-state), $16,298 (out-of-state).
Room & Board: $6,776

There is no additional cost for LD program/services.

LD SERVICES

LD program size is not limited.

LD services available to:

- [x] Freshmen
- [x] Sophomores
- [x] Juniors
- [x] Seniors

Academic Accommodations

Curriculum

- [ ] Foreign language waiver
- [x] Lighter course load
- [ ] Math waiver
- [ ] Other special classes
- [x] Priority registrations
- [x] Substitution of courses

Exams

- [x] Extended time
- [x] Oral exams
- [ ] Take home exams
- [x] Exams on tape or computer
- [ ] Untimed exams
- [x] Other accommodations

In class

- [ ] Early syllabus
- [x] Note takers in class
- [x] Priority seating
- [x] Tape recorders
- [ ] Videotaped classes
- [x] Text on tape

Services

- [ ] Diagnostic tests
- [x] Learning centers
- [ ] Proofreaders
- [x] Readers
- [x] Reading Machines/Kurzweil
- [ ] Special bookstore section
- [ ] Typists

Credit toward degree is not given for remedial courses taken.

Counseling Services

- [ ] Academic
- [ ] Psychological
- [ ] Student Support groups
- [ ] Vocational

Tutoring

Individual tutoring is available weekly.

	Individual	Group
Time management	[x]	[x]
Organizational skills	[x]	[x]
Learning strategies	[x]	[x]
Study skills	[x]	[x]
Content area	[x]	[x]
Writing lab	[x]	[x]
Math lab	[x]	[x]

UNIQUE LD PROGRAM FEATURES

Virginia Tech's Services for Students with Disabilities Office provides academic accommodations to over 500 students each semester who have presented qualified documentation of a disability. Disabilities may range from learning disabilities, attention deficit disorders, mobility, psychiatric, vision, medical, and hearing loss to traumatic brain injuries. There is no charge for services but the student must self-identify/disclose to the office in order to be eligible for accommodations in the classroom or residents halls.

LD PROGRAM STAFF

Total number of LD Program staff (including director):

Full Time: 4 Part Time: 4

There is an advisor/advocate from the LD program available to students.

Key staff person available to work with LD students: Dr. Susan Angle, Director.

LD Program web site: www.ssd.vt.edu

Virginia State University

Petersburg, VA

Address: 1 Hayden Street, Petersburg, VA, 23806
Admissions telephone: 800 871-7611
Admissions FAX: 804 524-5055
Director of Admissions: Irene Logan (Interim)
Admissions e-mail: admiss@vsu.edu
Web site: http://www.vsu.edu
SAT Code: 5860 ACT Code: 4424

Coordinator of Students with Disability Program: Rosezelia Roy
LD program telephone: 804 524-5061
LD program e-mail: rroy@vsu.edu
Total campus enrollment: 4,173

GENERAL

Virginia State University is a public, coed, four-year institution. 236-acre campus in Petersburg (population: 33,740), 35 miles from Richmond. Served by bus and train; airport serves Richmond. Public transportation serves campus. Semester system.

LD ADMISSIONS

A personal interview is not required. Essay is required and may be typed.

SECONDARY SCHOOL REQUIREMENTS

Graduation from secondary school required; GED accepted. The following course distribution required: 4 units of English, 3 units of math, 2 units of science, 2 units of social studies.

TESTING

SAT Reasoning required; ACT may be substituted. SAT Subject recommended.

All enrolled freshmen (fall 2004):

Average SAT I Scores:	Verbal: 424	Math: 417
Average ACT Scores:	Composite: 18	

Child Study Team report is not required. Tests required as part of this documentation:

☐ WAIS-IV	☐ Woodcock-Johnson
☐ WISC-IV	☐ Nelson-Denny Reading Test
☐ SATA	☐ Other

UNDERGRADUATE STUDENT BODY

Total undergraduate student enrollment: 1,491 Men, 2,008 Women.

Composition of student body (fall 2004):

	Undergraduate	Freshmen
International	0.0	0.0
Black	97.6	96.5
American Indian	0.0	0.2
Asian-American	0.4	0.3
Hispanic	1.3	0.8
White	0.7	2.1
Unreported	0.0	0.1
	100.0%	100.0%

35% are from out of state. 5% join a fraternity and 8% join a sorority. Average age of full-time undergraduates is 21. 41% of classes have fewer than 20 students, 54% have between 20 and 50 students, 5% have more than 50 students.

STUDENT HOUSING

93% of freshmen live in college housing. Freshmen are required to live on campus. Housing is guaranteed for all undergraduates. Campus can house 2,008 undergraduates.

EXPENSES

Tuition (2005-06): $2,317 per year (in state), $9,668 (out-of-state). Room: $3,760. Board: $2,724.

There is no additional cost for LD program/services.

LD SERVICES

LD program size is not limited.

LD services available to:

☐ Freshmen ☐ Sophomores ☐ Juniors ☐ Seniors

Academic Accommodations

Curriculum		In class	
Foreign language waiver	☐	Early syllabus	☐
Lighter course load	■	Note takers in class	☐
Math waiver	☐	Priority seating	☐
Other special classes	☐	Tape recorders	■
Priority registrations	☐	Videotaped classes	☐
Substitution of courses	☐	Text on tape	☐
Exams		**Services**	
Extended time	■	Diagnostic tests	☐
Oral exams	■	Learning centers	■
Take home exams	☐	Proofreaders	☐
Exams on tape or computer	☐	Readers	■
Untimed exams	■	Reading Machines/Kurzweil	☐
Other accommodations	☐	Special bookstore section	■
		Typists	☐

Credit toward degree is not given for remedial courses taken.

Counseling Services

☐ Academic
☐ Psychological
☐ Student Support groups
☐ Vocational

Tutoring

	Individual	Group
Time management	☐	☐
Organizational skills	☐	☐
Learning strategies	☐	☐
Study skills	☐	☐
Content area	☐	☐
Writing lab	☐	☐
Math lab	☐	☐

LD PROGRAM STAFF

Total number of LD Program staff (including director):

Full Time: 3 Part Time: 3

Key staff person available to work with LD students: Rosezelia W. Roy, Coordinator of Students with Disability Program.

Virginia Union University

Richmond, VA

Address: 1500 N. Lombardy Street, Richmond, VA, 23220
Admissions telephone: 800 368-3227
Admissions FAX: 804 329-8477
Director of Admissions: Gil M. Powell
Admissions e-mail: admissions@vuu.edu
Web site: http://www.vuu.edu/
SAT Code: 5862 ACT Code: 4428

LD program name: Academic Empowerment
Administrative Assistant: Darius Beecham
LD program telephone: 804 342-3885
LD program e-mail: ljackson@vuu.edu
Total campus enrollment: 1,400

GENERAL

Virginia Union University is a private, coed, four-year institution. 82-acre campus in Richmond (population: 197,790), 100 miles from Washington, D.C. Served by air, bus, and train. Public transportation serves campus. Semester system.

LD ADMISSIONS

A personal interview is not required. Essay is not required.

SECONDARY SCHOOL REQUIREMENTS

Graduation from secondary school required; GED accepted. The following course distribution required: 4 units of English, 3 units of math, 2 units of science, 2 units of foreign language, 1 unit of social studies, 1 unit of history, 3 units of academic electives.

TESTING

SAT Reasoning required; ACT may be substituted.

All enrolled freshmen (fall 2004):

Average SAT I Scores: Verbal: 378 Math: 365
Average ACT Scores: Composite: 15

Child Study Team report is not required. Tests required as part of this documentation:

- ❑ WAIS-IV
- ❑ WISC-IV
- ❑ SATA
- ❑ Woodcock-Johnson
- ❑ Nelson-Denny Reading Test
- ❑ Other

UNDERGRADUATE STUDENT BODY

Total undergraduate student enrollment: 1,400.

Composition of student body (fall 2004):

	Undergraduate	Freshmen
International	0.0	0.0
Black	92.2	97.7
American Indian	0.0	0.0
Asian-American	0.2	0.2
Hispanic	1.4	0.3
White	0.9	0.9
Unreported	5.3	0.9
	100.0%	100.0%

44% are from out of state.

STUDENT HOUSING

Freshmen are not required to live on campus. Housing is not guaranteed for all undergraduates. Campus can house 641 undergraduates.

EXPENSES

Tuition (2005-06): $11,600 per year.
Room: $2,662. Board: $3,000.

There is no additional cost for LD program/services.

LD SERVICES

LD program size is not limited.

LD services available to:

❑ Freshmen ❑ Sophomores ❑ Juniors ❑ Seniors

Academic Accommodations

Curriculum		**In class**	
Foreign language waiver	❑	Early syllabus	❑
Lighter course load	❑	Note takers in class	❑
Math waiver	❑	Priority seating	❑
Other special classes	❑	Tape recorders	❑
Priority registrations	❑	Videotaped classes	❑
Substitution of courses	❑	Text on tape	❑
Exams		**Services**	
Extended time	❑	Diagnostic tests	❑
Oral exams	❑	Learning centers	■
Take home exams	❑	Proofreaders	❑
Exams on tape or computer	❑	Readers	❑
Untimed exams	❑	Reading Machines/Kurzweil	■
Other accommodations	❑	Special bookstore section	❑
		Typists	❑

Credit toward degree is not given for remedial courses taken.

Counseling Services

- ❑ Academic
- ❑ Psychological
- ❑ Student Support groups
- ❑ Vocational

Tutoring

	Individual	Group
Time management	❑	❑
Organizational skills	❑	❑
Learning strategies	❑	❑
Study skills	❑	❑
Content area	❑	❑
Writing lab	❑	❑
Math lab	❑	❑

LD PROGRAM STAFF

Total number of LD Program staff (including director):

Full Time: 3 Part Time: 3

Key staff person available to work with LD students: Linda Jackson, Director, Academic Empowerment.

Virginia Wesleyan College

Norfolk, VA

Address: 1584 Wesleyan Drive, Norfolk, VA, 23502-5599
Admissions telephone: 800 737-8684
Admissions FAX: 757 461-5238
Vice President for Enrollment Mgmt./Dean of Admissions: Richard T. Hinshaw
Admissions e-mail: admissions@vwc.edu
Web site: http://www.vwc.edu
SAT Code: 5867 ACT Code: 4429

LD program name: Learning Center
Coordinator, Disabilities Services: Fayne C. Pearson
LD program telephone: 757 455-3246
LD program e-mail: fpearson@vwc.edu
LD program enrollment: 50, Total campus enrollment: 1,442

GENERAL

Virginia Wesleyan College is a private, coed, four-year institution. 300-acre, suburban campus in Norfolk/Virginia Beach (area population: 659,659), 10 miles from downtown area. Served by air and bus; airport and train serve Newport News (20 miles). School transportation to airport, recreational and shopping areas, and health care facilities. Public transportation serves campus. 4-1-4 system.

LD ADMISSIONS

Students do not complete a separate application and are simultaneously accepted to the LD program. A member of the LD program does not sit on the admissions committee. A personal interview is recommended. Essay is required and may be typed.

For fall 2004, 80 completed self-identified LD applications were received. 40 applications were offered admission, and 35 enrolled.

SECONDARY SCHOOL REQUIREMENTS

Graduation from secondary school required; GED accepted. The following course distribution required: 4 units of English, 3 units of math, 2 units of science, 1 unit of history.

TESTING

SAT Reasoning or ACT required. SAT Subject recommended.

All enrolled freshmen (fall 2004):

Average SAT I Scores:	Verbal: 504	Math: 498
Average ACT Scores:	Composite: 20	

Child Study Team report is not required. A neuropsychological or comprehensive psycho-educational evaluation is required for admission. Must be dated within 36 months of application. Tests required as part of this documentation:

- ■ WAIS-IV
- ☐ WISC-IV
- ■ SATA
- ■ Woodcock-Johnson
- ☐ Nelson-Denny Reading Test
- ■ Other

UNDERGRADUATE STUDENT BODY

Total undergraduate student enrollment: 444 Men, 964 Women.

Composition of student body (fall 2004):

	Undergraduate	Freshmen
International	0.6	0.7
Black	12.9	13.7
American Indian	0.3	0.7
Asian-American	1.5	1.7
Hispanic	2.5	3.4
White	78.2	78.5
Unreported	4.0	1.3
	100.0%	100.0%

21% are from out of state. 10% join a fraternity and 15% join a sorority. Average age of full-time undergraduates is 21. 79% of classes have fewer than 20 students, 21% have between 20 and 50 students.

STUDENT HOUSING

78% of freshmen live in college housing. Freshmen are required to live on campus. Housing is guaranteed for all undergraduates. Campus can house 550 undergraduates.

EXPENSES

Tuition (2005-06): $21,573 per year.
Room & Board: $6,700
There is no additional cost for LD program/services.

LD SERVICES

LD program size is not limited.

LD services available to:

■ Freshmen ■ Sophomores ■ Juniors ■ Seniors

Academic Accommodations

Curriculum		In class	
Foreign language waiver	■	Early syllabus	☐
Lighter course load	■	Note takers in class	■
Math waiver	■	Priority seating	■
Other special classes	☐	Tape recorders	■
Priority registrations	■	Videotaped classes	☐
Substitution of courses	■	Text on tape	■
Exams		**Services**	
Extended time	■	Diagnostic tests	☐
Oral exams	■	Learning centers	■
Take home exams	☐	Proofreaders	■
Exams on tape or computer	☐	Readers	■
Untimed exams	■	Reading Machines/Kurzweil	☐
Other accommodations	■	Special bookstore section	☐
		Typists	■

Credit toward degree is given for remedial courses taken.

Counseling Services

- ■ Academic — Meets 4 times per academic year
- ☐ Psychological
- ☐ Student Support groups
- ☐ Vocational

Tutoring

Individual tutoring is available daily.

Average size of tutoring groups: 2

	Individual	Group
Time management	■	■
Organizational skills	■	■
Learning strategies	■	■
Study skills	■	■
Content area	■	☐
Writing lab	■	☐
Math lab	■	☐

LD PROGRAM STAFF

Total number of LD Program staff (including director):

Full Time: 2 Part Time: 2

There is an advisor/advocate from the LD program available to students.

Key staff person available to work with LD students: Fayne C. Pearson, Coordinator, Learning Center/Disabilities Services.

LD Program web site: http://www.vwc.edu/academics/lrc/

Washington and Lee University

Lexington, VA

Address: Lexington, VA, 24450-0303
Admissions telephone: 540 463-8710
Admissions FAX: 540 458-8062
Dean of Admissions and Financial Aid: William M. Hartog III
Admissions e-mail: admissions@wlu.edu
Web site: http://www.wlu.edu
SAT Code: 5887 ACT Code: 4430

LD program address: Washington Hall
Associate Dean of the College: Dr. George Bent
LD program telephone: 540 458-8748
LD program e-mail: bentg@wlu.edu
LD program enrollment: 56, Total campus enrollment: 1,760

GENERAL

Washington and Lee University is a private, coed, four-year institution. 300-acre campus in Lexington (population: 6,867), 50 miles from both Roanoke and Lynchburg. Served by bus; airport serves Roanoke; train serves Staunton (30 miles).

LD ADMISSIONS

Students do not complete a separate application and are not simultaneously accepted to the LD program. A member of the LD program does sit on the admissions committee. A personal interview is recommended. Essay is required and may be typed. Course-requirement waivers will be considered on a case-by-case basis.

SECONDARY SCHOOL REQUIREMENTS

Graduation from secondary school required; GED not accepted. The following course distribution required: 4 units of English, 3 units of math, 1 unit of science, 2 units of foreign language, 1 unit of social studies, 1 unit of history, 4 units of academic electives.

TESTING

SAT Reasoning or ACT required. SAT Subject recommended.

All enrolled freshmen (fall 2004):

Average SAT I Scores:	Verbal: 686	Math: 692
Average ACT Scores:	Composite: 30	

Child Study Team report is not required. Tests required as part of this documentation:

- ☐ WAIS-IV
- ☐ WISC-IV
- ☐ SATA
- ☐ Woodcock-Johnson
- ☐ Nelson-Denny Reading Test
- ☐ Other

UNDERGRADUATE STUDENT BODY

Total undergraduate student enrollment: 961 Men, 807 Women.

Composition of student body (fall 2004):

	Undergraduate	Freshmen
International	2.4	3.9
Black	3.3	4.0
American Indian	0.7	0.3
Asian-American	5.0	3.2
Hispanic	1.5	1.0
White	86.7	87.2
Unreported	0.4	0.4
	100.0%	100.0%

87% are from out of state. 79% join a fraternity and 74% join a sorority. Average age of full-time undergraduates is 20. 66% of classes have fewer than 20 students, 33% have between 20 and 50 students, 1% have more than 50 students.

STUDENT HOUSING

100% of freshmen live in college housing. Housing is guaranteed for all undergraduates. Freshmen and sophomores are required to live on campus. Limited campus housing is also available for upperclass students, many of whom prefer off-campus housing. Campus can house 1,280 undergraduates. Single rooms are available for students with medical or special needs. A medical note is required.

EXPENSES

Tuition (2005-06): $27,960 per year.
Room: $3,425. Board: $3,800.
There is no additional cost for LD program/services.

LD SERVICES

LD program size is not limited.

LD services available to:

☒ Freshmen ☒ Sophomores ☒ Juniors ☒ Seniors

Academic Accommodations

Curriculum		In class	
Foreign language waiver	☒	Early syllabus	☐
Lighter course load	☐	Note takers in class	☒
Math waiver	☐	Priority seating	☐
Other special classes	☐	Tape recorders	☒
Priority registrations	☐	Videotaped classes	☐
Substitution of courses	☒	Text on tape	☒
Exams		**Services**	
Extended time	☒	Diagnostic tests	☐
Oral exams	☐	Learning centers	☐
Take home exams	☐	Proofreaders	☐
Exams on tape or computer	☐	Readers	☐
Untimed exams	☒	Reading Machines/Kurzweil	☒
Other accommodations	☐	Special bookstore section	☐
		Typists	☐

Credit toward degree is not given for remedial courses taken.

Counseling Services

- ☒ Academic
- ☐ Psychological
- ☐ Student Support groups
- ☐ Vocational

Tutoring

Individual tutoring is available weekly.

Average size of tutoring groups: 1

	Individual	Group
Time management	☒	☐
Organizational skills	☒	☐
Learning strategies	☒	☐
Study skills	☒	☐
Content area	☒	☐
Writing lab	☒	☐
Math lab	☒	☐

LD PROGRAM STAFF

Total number of LD Program staff (including director):

Full Time: 2 Part Time: 2

There is an advisor/advocate from the LD program available to students. 75 peer tutors are available to work with LD students.

Key staff person available to work with LD students: Dr. George Bent, Associate Dean of the College.

Central Washington University

Ellensburg, WA

Address: 400 E. University Way, Ellensburg, WA, 98926-7501
Admissions telephone: 866 298-4968
Admissions FAX: 509 963-3022
Director of Admissions: Michael Reilly
Admissions e-mail: cwuadmis@cwu.edu
Web site: http://www.cwu.edu
SAT Code: 4044 ACT Code: 4444

LD program name: Disability Support Services
Director, Disability Support Services: Robert Campbell
LD program telephone: 509 963-2171
LD program e-mail: campbelr@cwu.edu
Total campus enrollment: 9,340

GENERAL

Central Washington University is a public, coed, four-year institution. 350-acre campus in Ellensburg (population: 15,414), 110 miles from Seattle; branch campuses in Lakewood, Lynnwood, Moses Lake, SeaTac, Wenatchee, and Yakima. Served by bus; major airport serves Seattle; smaller airport and train serve Yakima (38 miles). Quarter system.

LD ADMISSIONS

Students do not complete a separate application and are not simultaneously accepted to the LD program. A member of the LD program does not sit on the admissions committee. A personal interview is not required. Essay is not required.

SECONDARY SCHOOL REQUIREMENTS

Graduation from secondary school required; GED accepted. The following course distribution required: 4 units of English, 3 units of math, 2 units of science, 2 units of foreign language, 3 units of social studies.

TESTING

SAT Reasoning or ACT required. SAT Subject recommended.

All enrolled freshmen (fall 2004):

Average SAT I Scores:	Verbal: 500	Math: 497
Average ACT Scores:	Composite: 20	

Child Study Team report is not required. A neuropsychological or comprehensive psycho-educational evaluation is required for admission. Tests required as part of this documentation:

- [x] WAIS-IV
- [ ] WISC-IV
- [ ] SATA
- [x] Woodcock-Johnson
- [x] Nelson-Denny Reading Test
- [ ] Other

UNDERGRADUATE STUDENT BODY

Total undergraduate student enrollment: 3,872 Men, 4,434 Women.

Composition of student body (fall 2004):

	Undergraduate	Freshmen
International	0.3	1.5
Black	2.0	2.0
American Indian	1.4	1.8
Asian-American	4.4	5.3
Hispanic	7.7	6.0
White	81.3	78.7
Unreported	2.9	4.7
	100.0%	100.0%

4% are from out of state. Average age of full-time undergraduates is 23. 36% of classes have fewer than 20 students, 59% have between 20 and 50 students, 5% have more than 50 students.

STUDENT HOUSING

97% of freshmen live in college housing. Freshmen are required to live on campus. Housing is not guaranteed for all undergraduates. Campus can house 3,134 undergraduates.

EXPENSES

Tuition 2004-05: $3,909 per year (in-state), $11,457 (out-of-state).

Room & Board: $5,861.

There is no additional cost for LD program/services.

LD SERVICES

LD program size is not limited.

LD services available to:

- [x] Freshmen
- [x] Sophomores
- [x] Juniors
- [x] Seniors

Academic Accommodations

Curriculum		In class	
Foreign language waiver	[ ]	Early syllabus	[ ]
Lighter course load	[x]	Note takers in class	[x]
Math waiver	[ ]	Priority seating	[ ]
Other special classes	[x]	Tape recorders	[x]
Priority registrations	[ ]	Videotaped classes	[ ]
Substitution of courses	[ ]	Texts on tape	[ ]
Exams		**Services**	
Extended time	[x]	Diagnostic tests	[ ]
Oral exams	[x]	Learning centers	[ ]
Take home exams	[ ]	Proofreaders	[ ]
Exams on tape or computer	[x]	Readers	[x]
Untimed exams	[ ]	Reading Machines/Kurzweil	[x]
Other accommodations	[x]	Special bookstore section	[ ]
		Typists	[ ]

Credit toward degree is not given for remedial courses taken.

Counseling Services

- [ ] Academic
- [x] Psychological
- [x] Student Support groups
- [x] Vocational

Tutoring

	Individual	Group
Time management	[ ]	[ ]
Organizational skills	[ ]	[ ]
Learning strategies	[ ]	[ ]
Study skills	[ ]	[ ]
Content area	[ ]	[ ]
Writing lab	[ ]	[ ]
Math lab	[ ]	[ ]

UNIQUE LD PROGRAM FEATURES

There are 3 full time staff available to work with LD students in the Disability Support Services Office and each professor works with students as needed.

LD PROGRAM STAFF

Total number of LD Program staff (including director):

Full Time: 3 Part Time: 3

There is an advisor/advocate from the LD program available to students.

Key staff person available to work with LD students: Robert Campbell, Director, Disability Support Services.

City University

Bellevue, WA

Address: 11900 N.E. First Street, Bellevue, WA, 98005
Admissions telephone: 800 426-5596
Admissions FAX: 425 709-5361
Vice President of Admissions/Student Services: Melissa Mecham
Admissions e-mail: info@cityu.edu
Web site: http://www.cityu.edu

Disability Resource Coordinator: Esther Hunt
LD program telephone: 800 426-5596
LD program e-mail: ehunt@cityu.edu
Total campus enrollment: 4,678

GENERAL

City University is a private, coed, four-year institution. Two-acre, main campus and administrative offices in Bellevue (population: 109,569); distance learning centers in Bremerton, Everett, Renton, Seattle, Spokane, Tacoma, the Tri-Cities (Kennewick, Pasco, and Richland), Vancouver, and Yakima, in San Jose, California, and abroad in Vancouver, Canada, Bratislava and Trencin Slovakia. Served by air, bus, and train. Public transportation serves campus and all distance learning centers. Quarter system.

LD ADMISSIONS

Students do not complete a separate application and are not simultaneously accepted to the LD program. A member of the LD program does not sit on the admissions committee. A personal interview is not required. Essay is not required.

SECONDARY SCHOOL REQUIREMENTS

Graduation from secondary school required; GED accepted.

TESTING

All enrolled freshmen (fall 2004):

Average SAT I Scores: Verbal: Math:
Average ACT Scores: Composite:

Child Study Team report is not required. A neuropsychological or comprehensive psycho-education evaluation is not required for admission. Tests required as part of this documentation:

- [ ] WAIS-IV
- [ ] WISC-IV
- [ ] SATA
- [ ] Woodcock-Johnson
- [ ] Nelson-Denny Reading Test
- [ ] Other

UNDERGRADUATE STUDENT BODY

Total undergraduate student enrollment: 2,042 Men, 2,057 Women.

Composition of student body (fall 2004):

	Undergraduate	Freshmen
International	0.0	5.3
Black	2.2	5.0
American Indian	2.2	1.3
Asian-American	4.3	5.7
Hispanic	2.2	3.1
White	80.4	65.1
Unreported	8.7	14.5
	100.0%	100.0%

13% are from out of state. Average age of full-time undergraduates is 29.

EXPENSES

There is no additional cost for LD program/services.

LD SERVICES

LD program size is not limited.

LD services available to:

- [ ] Freshmen
- [ ] Sophomores
- [x] Juniors
- [x] Seniors

Academic Accommodations

Curriculum

- [ ] Foreign language waiver
- [ ] Lighter course load
- [ ] Math waiver
- [ ] Other special classes
- [ ] Priority registrations
- [ ] Substitution of courses

Exams

- [x] Extended time
- [x] Oral exams
- [x] Take home exams
- [x] Exams on tape or computer
- [x] Untimed exams
- [ ] Other accommodations

In class

- [ ] Early syllabus
- [x] Note takers in class
- [x] Priority seating
- [x] Tape recorders
- [x] Videotaped classes
- [x] Texts on tape

Services

- [ ] Diagnostic tests
- [ ] Learning centers
- [ ] Proofreaders
- [ ] Readers
- [ ] Reading Machines/Kurzweil
- [ ] Special bookstore section
- [x] Typists

Credit toward degree is not given for remedial courses taken.

Counseling Services

- [x] Academic
- [ ] Psychological
- [ ] Student Support groups
- [ ] Vocational

Tutoring

Individual tutoring is not available.

	Individual	Group
Time management	[ ]	[ ]
Organizational skills	[ ]	[ ]
Learning strategies	[ ]	[ ]
Study skills	[ ]	[ ]
Content area	[ ]	[ ]
Writing lab	[ ]	[ ]
Math lab	[ ]	[ ]

LD PROGRAM STAFF

There is an advisor/advocate from the LD program available to students.

Cornish College of the Arts

Seattle, WA

Address: 1000 Lenora Street, Seattle, WA, 98121
Admissions telephone: 800 726-ARTS
Admissions FAX: 206 720-1011
Associate Dean of Enrollment Services: Eric Pedersen
Admissions e-mail: admissions@cornish.edu
Web site: http://www.cornish.edu
SAT Code: 58 ACT Code: 4501

LD program name: Student Affairs
Director of Student Affairs: George Luis Sedano
LD program telephone: 206 726-5111
LD program e-mail: gsedano@cornish.edu
LD program enrollment: 15, Total campus enrollment: 728

GENERAL

Cornish College of the Arts is a private, coed, four-year institution. Four-acre, urban campus in Seattle (population: 563,374). Served by air, bus, and train. Public transportation serves campus. Semester system.

LD ADMISSIONS

Students do not complete a separate application and are not simultaneously accepted to the LD program. A member of the LD program does not sit on the admissions committee. A personal interview is recommended. Essay is required and may be typed.

SECONDARY SCHOOL REQUIREMENTS

Graduation from secondary school required; GED accepted.

TESTING

All enrolled freshmen (fall 2004):

Child Study Team report is not required. A neuropsychological or comprehensive psycho-educational evaluation is required for admission. Must be dated within 36 months of application. Tests required as part of this documentation:

- ■ WAIS-IV
- ■ WISC-IV
- ■ SATA
- ■ Woodcock-Johnson
- ■ Nelson-Denny Reading Test
- ☐ Other

UNDERGRADUATE STUDENT BODY

Total undergraduate student enrollment: 244 Men, 406 Women.

Composition of student body (fall 2004):

	Undergraduate	Freshmen
International	0.7	3.7
Black	3.5	3.0
American Indian	2.8	1.6
Asian-American	5.0	5.4
Hispanic	2.8	4.0
White	65.3	61.7
Unreported	19.9	20.6
	100.0%	100.0%

48% are from out of state. Average age of full-time undergraduates is 22. 86% of classes have fewer than 20 students, 14% have between 20 and 50 students.

STUDENT HOUSING

Housing is not guaranteed for all undergraduates.

EXPENSES

Tuition 2004-05: $19,600 per year.

There is no additional cost for LD program/services.

LD SERVICES

LD program size is not limited.

LD services available to:

■ Freshmen ■ Sophomores ■ Juniors ■ Seniors

Academic Accommodations

Curriculum

Foreign language waiver	☐
Lighter course load	■
Math waiver	☐
Other special classes	☐
Priority registrations	☐
Substitution of courses	☐

Exams

Extended time	■
Oral exams	■
Take home exams	☐
Exams on tape or computer	■
Untimed exams	☐
Other accommodations	■

In class

Early syllabus	■
Note takers in class	■
Priority seating	☐
Tape recorders	■
Videotaped classes	☐
Texts on tape	■

Services

Diagnostic tests	☐
Learning centers	☐
Proofreaders	☐
Readers	■
Reading Machines/Kurzweil	☐
Special bookstore section	☐
Typists	☐

Credit toward degree is not given for remedial courses taken.

Counseling Services

- ■ Academic
- ■ Psychological
- ☐ Student Support groups
- ☐ Vocational

Tutoring

Individual tutoring is not available.

	Individual	Group
Time management	☐	☐
Organizational skills	☐	☐
Learning strategies	☐	☐
Study skills	☐	☐
Content area	☐	☐
Writing lab	■	☐
Math lab	☐	☐

LD PROGRAM STAFF

Total number of LD Program staff (including director):

Full Time: 2 Part Time : 2

There is an advisor/advocate from the LD program available to students. The advisor/advocate meets with faculty once per month and student once per month.

Key staff person available to work with LD students: George Luis Sedano, Director of Student Affairs.

LD Program web site: www.cornish.edu/studentaffairs

Eastern Washington University

Cheney, WA

Address: 526 Fifth Street, Cheney, WA, 99004
Admissions telephone: 888 740-1914
Admissions FAX: 509 359-6692
Director of Admissions: Michelle Whittingham
Admissions e-mail: admissions@mail.ewu.edu
Web site: http://www.ewu.edu
SAT Code: 4301 ACT Code: 4454

LD program name: Disability Support Services
Director - Disability Support Services: Kevin Hills
LD program telephone: 509 359-4706
LD program e-mail: khills@mail.ewu.edu
Total campus enrollment: 9,390

GENERAL

Eastern Washington University is a public, coed, four-year institution. 335-acre, suburban campus in Cheney (population: 8,832), 17 miles from Spokane; two branch centers in Spokane. Served by bus; airport and train serve Spokane. Public transportation serves campus. Quarter system.

LD ADMISSIONS

A member of the LD program does sit on the admissions committee. A personal interview is required. Essay is not required.

SECONDARY SCHOOL REQUIREMENTS

Graduation from secondary school required; GED accepted. The following course distribution required: 4 units of English, 3 units of math, 2 units of science, 2 units of foreign language, 3 units of social studies, 1 unit of academic electives.

TESTING

SAT Reasoning or ACT required. SAT Subject required.

All enrolled freshmen (fall 2004):

Average SAT I Scores: Verbal: 494 Math: 502
Average ACT Scores: Composite: 21

Child Study Team report is not required. Tests required as part of this documentation:

- [ ] WAIS-IV
- [ ] WISC-IV
- [ ] SATA
- [ ] Woodcock-Johnson
- [ ] Nelson-Denny Reading Test
- [ ] Other

UNDERGRADUATE STUDENT BODY

Total undergraduate student enrollment: 3,408 Men, 4,550 Women.

Composition of student body (fall 2004):

	Undergraduate	Freshmen
International	0.7	1.4
Black	4.1	2.6
American Indian	2.2	2.0
Asian-American	5.3	3.7
Hispanic	7.9	5.6
White	75.6	69.5
Unreported	4.2	15.2
	100.0%	100.0%

9% are from out of state. Average age of full-time undergraduates is 22. 24% of classes have fewer than 20 students, 63% have between 20 and 50 students, 13% have more than 50 students.

STUDENT HOUSING

70% of freshmen live in college housing. Freshmen are not required to live on campus. Housing is guaranteed for all undergraduates. Campus can house 2,150 undergraduates. Single rooms are available for students with medical or special needs. A medical note is required.

EXPENSES

Tuition 2004-05: $3,822 per year (in-state), $13,299 (out-of-state).

Room & Board: $5,460.

There is no additional cost for LD program/services.

LD SERVICES

LD program size is not limited.

LD services available to:

- [x] Freshmen
- [x] Sophomores
- [x] Juniors
- [x] Seniors

Academic Accommodations

Curriculum

- [ ] Foreign language waiver
- [x] Lighter course load
- [ ] Math waiver
- [x] Other special classes
- [ ] Priority registrations
- [ ] Substitution of courses

Exams

- [x] Extended time
- [x] Oral exams
- [ ] Take home exams
- [x] Exams on tape or computer
- [x] Untimed exams
- [x] Other accommodations

In class

- [x] Early syllabus
- [x] Note takers in class
- [ ] Priority seating
- [x] Tape recorders
- [ ] Videotaped classes
- [ ] Texts on tape

Services

- [ ] Diagnostic tests
- [x] Learning centers
- [ ] Proofreaders
- [x] Readers
- [x] Reading Machines/Kurzweil
- [ ] Special bookstore section
- [ ] Typists

Credit toward degree is not given for remedial courses taken.

Counseling Services

- [x] Academic
- [x] Psychological
- [x] Student Support groups
- [ ] Vocational

Tutoring

Individual tutoring is available weekly.

	Individual	Group
Time management	[x]	[x]
Organizational skills	[x]	[x]
Learning strategies	[x]	[x]
Study skills	[x]	[x]
Content area	[x]	[x]
Writing lab	[x]	[x]
Math lab	[x]	[x]

UNIQUE LD PROGRAM FEATURES

Disability Support Services works with students on an individual basis. All services can be made available depending upon individual need. Need is determined through comprehensive written documentation from an appropriate professional service provider and from Disability Support Services interviews with students.

LD PROGRAM STAFF

Total number of LD Program staff (including director):

Full Time: 2 Part Time: 2

There is an advisor/advocate from the LD program available to students.

Key staff person available to work with LD students: Kevin Hills, Director - Disability Support Services.

LD Program web site: http://www.ewu.edu/x2336.xml

Gonzaga University

Spokane, WA

Address: 502 E. Boone Avenue, Spokane, WA, 99258-0001
Admissions telephone: 800 322-2584
Admissions FAX: 509 323-5780
Dean of Admission: Julie McCulloh
Admissions e-mail: mcculloh@gu.gonzaga.edu
Web site: http://www.gonzaga.edu
SAT Code: 4330 ACT Code: 4458

Assistant Director, Disability Support Services: Angela Merritt
LD program telephone: 509 323-4091
LD program e-mail: merritt@gonzaga.edu
LD program enrollment: 65, Total campus enrollment: 4,110

GENERAL

Gonzaga University is a private, coed, four-year institution. 108-acre, urban campus in Spokane (population: 195,629); branch campus abroad in Florence, Italy. Served by air, bus, and train. Public transportation serves campus. Semester system.

LD ADMISSIONS

Application Deadline: 02/01. Students do not complete a separate application and are not simultaneously accepted to the LD program. A member of the LD program does sit on the admissions committee. High school waivers are accepted for foreign language. A personal interview is recommended. Essay is required and may be typed. No admissions requirements are waived for LD students.

For fall 2004, 40 completed self-identified LD applications were received. 40 applications were offered admission, and 25 enrolled.

SECONDARY SCHOOL REQUIREMENTS

Graduation from secondary school required; GED accepted. The following course distribution required: 4 units of English, 3 units of math, 3 units of science, 2 units of foreign language, 2 units of social studies, 2 units of history, 3 units of academic electives.

TESTING

SAT Reasoning or ACT required. SAT Subject recommended.

All enrolled freshmen (fall 2004):

Average SAT I Scores:	Verbal: 586	Math: 589
Average ACT Scores:	Composite: 26	

Child Study Team report is not required. A neuropsychological or comprehensive psycho-educational evaluation is required for admission. Must be dated within 18 months of application. Tests required as part of this documentation:

- [x] WAIS-IV
- [ ] WISC-IV
- [ ] SATA
- [x] Woodcock-Johnson
- [x] Nelson-Denny Reading Test
- [x] Other

UNDERGRADUATE STUDENT BODY

Total undergraduate student enrollment: 1,262 Men, 1,485 Women.

Composition of student body (fall 2004):

	Undergraduate	Freshmen
International	0.5	1.3
Black	1.2	1.2
American Indian	0.7	1.0
Asian-American	6.1	5.5
Hispanic	4.4	3.4
White	78.7	79.4
Unreported	8.4	8.2
	100.0%	100.0%

49% are from out of state. Average age of full-time undergraduates is 20. 41% of classes have fewer than 20 students, 57% have between 20 and 50 students, 2% have more than 50 students.

STUDENT HOUSING

99% of freshmen live in college housing. Freshmen are required to live on campus. Housing is not guaranteed for all undergraduates. Guaranteed housing for first and second year students. Campus can house 2,200 undergraduates. Single rooms are available for students with medical or special needs. A medical note is required.

EXPENSES

Tuition 2004-05: $21,730 per year.

Room: $3,240. Board: $3,190.

There is no additional cost for LD program/services.

LD SERVICES

LD program size is not limited.

LD services available to:

[x] Freshmen [x] Sophomores [x] Juniors [x] Seniors

Academic Accommodations

Curriculum		In class	
Foreign language waiver	[ ]	Early syllabus	[ ]
Lighter course load	[ ]	Note takers in class	[x]
Math waiver	[ ]	Priority seating	[x]
Other special classes	[ ]	Tape recorders	[x]
Priority registrations	[x]	Videotaped classes	[ ]
Substitution of courses	[ ]	Texts on tape	[x]
Exams		**Services**	
Extended time	[x]	Diagnostic tests	[ ]
Oral exams	[x]	Learning centers	[ ]
Take home exams	[ ]	Proofreaders	[ ]
Exams on tape or computer	[x]	Readers	[x]
Untimed exams	[ ]	Reading Machines/Kurzweil	[x]
Other accommodations	[ ]	Special bookstore section	[ ]
		Typists	[ ]

Credit toward degree is not given for remedial courses taken.

Counseling Services

[x]	Academic	Meets 4 times per academic year
[x]	Psychological	Meets 16 times per academic year
[x]	Student Support groups	Meets 16 times per academic year
[ ]	Vocational	

Tutoring

Individual tutoring is not available.

	Individual	Group
Time management	[x]	[ ]
Organizational skills	[x]	[ ]
Learning strategies	[x]	[ ]
Study skills	[x]	[ ]
Content area	[ ]	[ ]
Writing lab	[x]	[ ]
Math lab	[x]	[ ]

LD PROGRAM STAFF

Total number of LD Program staff (including director):

Full Time: 3 Part Time: 3

There is an advisor/advocate from the LD program available to students.

Key staff person available to work with LD students: Kathryne Shearer, Director, Disability Support Services.

Henry Cogswell College

Everett, WA

Address: 3002 Colby Avenue, Everett, WA, 98201
Admissions telephone: 425 258-3351
Admissions FAX: 425 257-0405
Director of Admissions: Jane Buckman
Admissions e-mail: admissions@henrycogswell.edu
Web site: http://www.henrycogswell.edu
SAT Code: 584   ACT Code: 4483

Dean of Enrollment: Jane Buckman
LD program telephone: 4252583351116
LD program e-mail: j.buckman@henrycogswell.edu
LD program enrollment: 5, Total campus enrollment: 229

GENERAL

Henry Cogswell College is a private, coed, four-year institution. One-acre, urban campus in Everett (population: 91,488), 26 miles from Seattle. Served by bus and train; major airport serves Seattle. Public transportation serves campus. Trimester system.

LD ADMISSIONS

A personal interview is recommended. Essay is required and may be typed.

For fall 2004, 5 completed self-identified LD applications were received. 5 applications were offered admission, and 5 enrolled.

SECONDARY SCHOOL REQUIREMENTS

Graduation from secondary school required; GED accepted. The following course distribution required: 4 units of English, 2 units of math, 2 units of science, 3 units of social studies, 2 units of academic electives.

TESTING

SAT Reasoning or ACT required of some applicants. SAT Subject recommended.

Child Study Team report is not required. Tests required as part of this documentation:

- ☐ WAIS-IV
- ☐ WISC-IV
- ☐ SATA
- ☐ Woodcock-Johnson
- ☐ Nelson-Denny Reading Test
- ☐ Other

UNDERGRADUATE STUDENT BODY

Total undergraduate student enrollment: 205 Men, 53 Women.

Composition of student body (fall 2004):

	Undergraduate	Freshmen
International	0.0	0.0
Black	8.3	1.3
American Indian	0.0	0.4
Asian-American	11.1	8.3
Hispanic	2.8	3.9
White	66.7	74.3
Unreported	11.1	11.8
	100.0%	100.0%

3% are from out of state. Average age of full-time undergraduates is 24. 92% of classes have fewer than 20 students, 8% have between 20 and 50 students.

EXPENSES

Tuition 2004-05: $15,840 per year.

There is no additional cost for LD program/services.

LD SERVICES

LD program size is not limited.

LD services available to:

☐ Freshmen ☐ Sophomores ☐ Juniors ☐ Seniors

Academic Accommodations

Curriculum		**In class**	
Foreign language waiver	☐	Early syllabus	☐
Lighter course load	☐	Note takers in class	☐
Math waiver	☐	Priority seating	☐
Other special classes	☐	Tape recorders	☐
Priority registrations	☐	Videotaped classes	☐
Substitution of courses	☐	Texts on tape	☐
Exams		**Services**	
Extended time	☐	Diagnostic tests	☐
Oral exams	☐	Learning centers	☐
Take home exams	☐	Proofreaders	☐
Exams on tape or computer	☐	Readers	☐
Untimed exams	☐	Reading Machines/Kurzweil	☐
Other accommodations	☐	Special bookstore section	☐
		Typists	☐

Credit toward degree is not given for remedial courses taken.

Counseling Services

- ☐ Academic
- ☐ Psychological
- ☐ Student Support groups
- ☐ Vocational

Tutoring

Individual tutoring is available weekly.

Average size of tutoring groups: 1

	Individual	Group
Time management	☐	☐
Organizational skills	☐	☐
Learning strategies	☐	☐
Study skills	■	☐
Content area	■	☐
Writing lab	■	☐
Math lab	■	☐

LD PROGRAM STAFF

Total number of LD Program staff (including director):

Full Time: 1   Part Time: 1

There is an advisor/advocate from the LD program available to students. The advisor/advocate meets with faculty once per month and student once per month. 3 peer tutors are available to work with LD students.

Key staff person available to work with LD students: Jane Buckman, Dean of Enrollment.

Heritage College

Toppenish, WA

Address: 3240 Fort Road, Toppenish, WA, 98948
Admissions telephone: 509 865-8508
Admissions FAX: 509 865-8659
Director of Admissions: Leticia Garcia
Admissions e-mail: 3w_Admissions@heritage.edu
Web site: http://www.heritage.edu
SAT Code: 4344

LD program name: Student Life Department
Director of Student Life: Dana Firestone
LD program telephone: 509 865-8500
LD program e-mail: firestone_d@heritage.edu
LD program enrollment: 3, Total campus enrollment: 810

GENERAL

Heritage College is a private, coed, four-year institution. 12-acre campus in Toppenish (population: 8,946); branch campus in Omak. Served by bus; major airport serves Seattle (160 miles); smaller airport serves Yakima (20 miles). Public transportation serves campus. Semester system.

LD ADMISSIONS

A personal interview is required. Essay is not required.

SECONDARY SCHOOL REQUIREMENTS

Graduation from secondary school required; GED accepted.

TESTING

Child Study Team report is not required. Tests required as part of this documentation:

- ☐ WAIS-IV
- ☐ WISC-IV
- ☐ SATA
- ☐ Woodcock-Johnson
- ☐ Nelson-Denny Reading Test
- ☐ Other

UNDERGRADUATE STUDENT BODY

Total undergraduate student enrollment: 165 Men, 483 Women.

Composition of student body (fall 2004):

	Undergraduate	Freshmen
International	0.0	0.0
Black	0.0	0.9
American Indian	17.8	11.7
Asian-American	0.8	1.2
Hispanic	71.2	54.2
White	10.2	32.0
Unreported	0.0	0.0
	100.0%	100.0%

Average age of full-time undergraduates is 28. 80% of classes have fewer than 20 students, 20% have between 20 and 50 students.

EXPENSES

Tuition 2004-05: $8,850 per year (in-state), $10,950 (out-of-state).

There is no additional cost for LD program/services.

LD SERVICES

LD program size is not limited.

LD services available to:

■ Freshmen ■ Sophomores ■ Juniors ■ Seniors

Academic Accommodations

Curriculum		**In class**	
Foreign language waiver	☐	Early syllabus	■
Lighter course load	☐	Note takers in class	■
Math waiver	☐	Priority seating	■
Other special classes	☐	Tape recorders	■
Priority registrations	☐	Videotaped classes	☐
Substitution of courses	☐	Texts on tape	■
Exams		**Services**	
Extended time	■	Diagnostic tests	☐
Oral exams	■	Learning centers	■
Take home exams	☐	Proofreaders	☐
Exams on tape or computer	■	Readers	■
Untimed exams	■	Reading Machines/Kurzweil	■
Other accommodations	■	Special bookstore section	☐
		Typists	■

Credit toward degree is not given for remedial courses taken.

Counseling Services

- ■ Academic
- ■ Psychological
- ■ Student Support groups
- ■ Vocational

Tutoring

Individual tutoring is available daily.

Average size of tutoring groups: 1

	Individual	Group
Time management	■	☐
Organizational skills	■	☐
Learning strategies	■	☐
Study skills	■	☐
Content area	■	☐
Writing lab	■	☐
Math lab	■	☐

UNIQUE LD PROGRAM FEATURES

LD program is individually tailored to meet each student's needs. Similar service is provided to students with other disabilities.

LD PROGRAM STAFF

Total number of LD Program staff (including director):

Full Time: 2 Part Time: 2

There is an advisor/advocate from the LD program available to students. The advisor/advocate meets with faculty 2 times per month and students 2 times per month. 3 peer tutors are available to work with LD students.

Key staff person available to work with LD students: Dana Firestone, Director of Student Life.

Northwest University

Kirkland, WA

Address: 5520 108th Avenue, NE, Kirkland, WA, 98083
Admissions telephone: 800 6-NWEST-1
Admissions FAX: 425 827-0148
Associate Vice President of Enrollment: Rose K. Smith
Admissions e-mail: admissions@northwestu.edu
Web site: http://www.northwestu.edu
SAT Code: 4541 ACT Code: 4466

LD program name: Student Success
LD program address: PO box 579, Kirkland, WA, 98083-0579
Director for Student Success: Amy Jones
LD program telephone: 425 889-7823
LD program e-mail: amy.jones@northwestu.edu
LD program enrollment: 12, Total campus enrollment: 1,068

GENERAL

Northwest University is a private, coed, four-year institution. 65-acre, suburban campus in Kirkland (population: 45,054), 10 miles from Seattle. Major airport, bus, and train serve Seattle. Public transportation serves campus. Semester system.

LD ADMISSIONS

Students do not complete a separate application and are simultaneously accepted to the LD program. A member of the LD program does not sit on the admissions committee. A personal interview is not required. Essay is required and may be typed. No admissions requirements are waived for LD students.

SECONDARY SCHOOL REQUIREMENTS

Graduation from secondary school required; GED accepted.

TESTING

SAT Reasoning or ACT required.

All enrolled freshmen (fall 2004):

Average SAT I Scores:	Verbal: 510	Math: 540
Average ACT Scores:	Composite: 22	

Child Study Team report is not required. A neuropsychological or comprehensive psycho-educational evaluation is required for admission. Tests required as part of this documentation:

- [x] WAIS-IV
- [x] WISC-IV
- [x] SATA
- [x] Woodcock-Johnson
- [x] Nelson-Denny Reading Test
- [x] Other

UNDERGRADUATE STUDENT BODY

Total undergraduate student enrollment: 420 Men, 626 Women.

Composition of student body (fall 2004):

	Undergraduate	Freshmen
International	0.0	0.7
Black	2.3	2.8
American Indian	0.0	0.5
Asian-American	5.3	5.8
Hispanic	1.5	4.0
White	87.9	82.1
Unreported	3.0	4.1
	100.0%	100.0%

21% are from out of state.

STUDENT HOUSING

Housing is guaranteed for all undergraduates. Campus can house 655 undergraduates. Single rooms are available for students with medical or special needs. A medical note is required.

EXPENSES

Tuition 2004-05: $14,200 per year.

Room & Board: $6,450.

There is no additional cost for LD program/services.

LD SERVICES

LD program size is not limited.

LD services available to:

- [x] Freshmen
- [x] Sophomores
- [x] Juniors
- [x] Seniors

Academic Accommodations

Curriculum

- [ ] Foreign language waiver
- [x] Lighter course load
- [ ] Math waiver
- [ ] Other special classes
- [x] Priority registrations
- [ ] Substitution of courses

Exams

- [x] Extended time
- [x] Oral exams
- [ ] Take home exams
- [x] Exams on tape or computer
- [x] Untimed exams
- [x] Other accommodations

In class

- [x] Early syllabus
- [ ] Note takers in class
- [x] Priority seating
- [x] Tape recorders
- [ ] Videotaped classes
- [ ] Texts on tape

Services

- [ ] Diagnostic tests
- [x] Learning centers
- [x] Proofreaders
- [x] Readers
- [ ] Reading Machines/Kurzweil
- [ ] Special bookstore section
- [x] Typists

Credit toward degree is not given for remedial courses taken.

Counseling Services

- [x] Academic
- [x] Psychological
- [ ] Student Support groups
- [ ] Vocational

Tutoring

Individual tutoring is available daily.

Average size of tutoring groups: 7

	Individual	Group
Time management	[x]	[x]
Organizational skills	[x]	[x]
Learning strategies	[x]	[x]
Study skills	[x]	[x]
Content area	[x]	[x]
Writing lab	[x]	[ ]
Math lab	[ ]	[x]

UNIQUE LD PROGRAM FEATURES

We work with each student individually to workout an accommodation plan.

LD PROGRAM STAFF

Total number of LD Program staff (including director):

Full Time: 1 Part Time: 1

There is an advisor/advocate from the LD program available to students. The advisor/advocate meets with faculty once per month and student once per month. 2 peer tutors are available to work with LD students.

Key staff person available to work with LD students: Amy Jones, Director for Student Success.

Pacific Lutheran University

Tacoma, WA

Address: 12180 Park Street S., Tacoma, WA, 98447
Admissions telephone: 800 274-6758
Admissions FAX: 253 536-5136
Admissions e-mail: admissions@plu.edu
Web site: http://www.plu.edu
SAT Code: 4597 ACT Code: 4470

Director of Services for Students with Disabilities: Alene Minetti
LD program telephone: 253 535-7206
Total campus enrollment: 3,324

GENERAL

Pacific Lutheran University is a private, coed, four-year institution. 126-acre, suburban campus in Tacoma (population: 193,556), 30 miles from Seattle. Served by bus and train; major airport serves Seattle. Public transportation serves campus. 4-1-4 system.

LD ADMISSIONS

A personal interview is recommended. Essay is required and may be typed.

SECONDARY SCHOOL REQUIREMENTS

Graduation from secondary school required; GED accepted. The following course distribution required: 4 units of English, 2 units of math, 2 units of science, 2 units of foreign language, 2 units of social studies, 3 units of academic electives.

TESTING

SAT Reasoning or ACT required. SAT Subject recommended.

All enrolled freshmen (fall 2004):

Average SAT I Scores: Verbal: 560 Math: 554
Average ACT Scores: Composite: 25

Child Study Team report is not required. Tests required as part of this documentation:

- ☐ WAIS-IV
- ☐ WISC-IV
- ☐ SATA
- ☐ Woodcock-Johnson
- ☐ Nelson-Denny Reading Test
- ☐ Other

UNDERGRADUATE STUDENT BODY

Total undergraduate student enrollment: 1,223 Men, 1,922 Women.

Composition of student body (fall 2004):

	Undergraduate	Freshmen
International	1.9	5.4
Black	1.3	2.0
American Indian	0.6	0.6
Asian-American	4.9	5.4
Hispanic	3.4	2.3
White	75.8	76.1
Unreported	12.1	8.4
	100.0%	100.0%

26% are from out of state. Average age of full-time undergraduates is 21. 47% of classes have fewer than 20 students, 50% have between 20 and 50 students, 3% have more than 50 students.

STUDENT HOUSING

86% of freshmen live in college housing. Freshmen are not required to live on campus. Housing is guaranteed for all undergraduates. Campus can house 1,650 undergraduates. Single rooms are available for students with medical or special needs. A medical note is required.

EXPENSES

Tuition 2004-05: $20,790 per year.

Room: $3,150. Board: $3,260.

There is no additional cost for LD program/services.

LD SERVICES

LD services available to:

■ Freshmen ■ Sophomores ■ Juniors ■ Seniors

Academic Accommodations

Curriculum		In class	
Foreign language waiver	☐	Early syllabus	☐
Lighter course load	☐	Note takers in class	■
Math waiver	☐	Priority seating	☐
Other special classes	■	Tape recorders	■
Priority registrations	☐	Videotaped classes	■
Substitution of courses	☐	Texts on tape	☐
Exams		**Services**	
Extended time	■	Diagnostic tests	☐
Oral exams	■	Learning centers	■
Take home exams	☐	Proofreaders	☐
Exams on tape or computer	☐	Readers	■
Untimed exams	■	Reading Machines/Kurzweil	■
Other accommodations	☐	Special bookstore section	☐
		Typists	☐

Credit toward degree is not given for remedial courses taken.

Counseling Services

- ☐ Academic
- ☐ Psychological
- ☐ Student Support groups
- ☐ Vocational

Tutoring

Individual tutoring is available daily.

	Individual	Group
Time management	■	☐
Organizational skills	■	☐
Learning strategies	■	☐
Study skills	■	☐
Content area	■	☐
Writing lab	■	☐
Math lab	■	☐

LD PROGRAM STAFF

Total number of LD Program staff (including director):

Full Time: 1 Part Time: 1

There is an advisor/advocate from the LD program available to students.

Key staff person available to work with LD students: Alene Minetti, Director of Services for Students with Disabilities.

University of Puget Sound

Tacoma, WA

Address: 1500 N. Warner Street, Tacoma, WA, 98416
Admissions telephone: 800 396-7191
Admissions FAX: 253 879-3993
Vice President for Enrollment: George Mills
Admissions e-mail: admission@ups.edu
Web site: http://www.ups.edu
SAT Code: 4067 ACT Code: 4450

LD program name: Center for Writing and Learning
Coordinator Disability Services: Ivey West
LD program telephone: 253 879-2692
LD program e-mail: iwest@ups.edu

GENERAL

University of Puget Sound is a private, coed, four-year institution. 97-acre campus in Tacoma (population: 193,556), 35 miles from Seattle. Served by air, bus, and train. School operates transportation to airport for entering freshmen. Public transportation serves campus. Semester system.

LD ADMISSIONS

Students do not complete a separate application and are not simultaneously accepted to the LD program. A member of the LD program does not sit on the admissions committee. High school waivers are accepted for foreign language. A personal interview is recommended. Essay is required and may be typed.

SECONDARY SCHOOL REQUIREMENTS

Graduation from secondary school required; GED accepted.

TESTING

SAT Reasoning required; ACT may be substituted. SAT Subject recommended.

All enrolled freshmen (fall 2004):

Average SAT I Scores:	Verbal: 631	Math: 621
Average ACT Scores:	Composite: 27	

Child Study Team report is not required. A neuropsychological or comprehensive psycho-education evaluation is not required for admission. Tests required as part of this documentation:

- [ ] WAIS-IV
- [ ] WISC-IV
- [ ] SATA
- [ ] Woodcock-Johnson
- [ ] Nelson-Denny Reading Test
- [ ] Other

UNDERGRADUATE STUDENT BODY

Total undergraduate student enrollment: 1,026 Men, 1,593 Women.

Composition of student body (fall 2004):

	Undergraduate	Freshmen
International	0.0	0.5
Black	1.2	2.1
American Indian	1.3	1.2
Asian-American	7.7	8.4
Hispanic	3.4	3.0
White	76.6	76.5
Unreported	9.8	8.3
	100.0%	100.0%

68% are from out of state. 22% join a fraternity and 23% join a sorority. Average age of full-time undergraduates is 20. 53% of classes have fewer than 20 students, 47% have between 20 and 50 students.

STUDENT HOUSING

98% of freshmen live in college housing. Freshmen are not required to live on campus. Housing is guaranteed for all undergraduates. Campus can house 1,639 undergraduates. Single rooms are available for students with medical or special needs. A medical note is required.

EXPENSES

Tuition 2004-05: $26,700 per year.

Room: $3,680. Board: $3,050.

There is no additional cost for LD program/services.

LD SERVICES

LD program size is not limited.

LD services available to:

- [x] Freshmen
- [x] Sophomores
- [x] Juniors
- [x] Seniors

Academic Accommodations

Curriculum		In class	
Foreign language waiver	[x]	Early syllabus	[ ]
Lighter course load	[x]	Note takers in class	[x]
Math waiver	[ ]	Priority seating	[ ]
Other special classes	[ ]	Tape recorders	[x]
Priority registrations	[ ]	Videotaped classes	[ ]
Substitution of courses	[ ]	Texts on tape	[x]
Exams		**Services**	
Extended time	[x]	Diagnostic tests	[ ]
Oral exams	[ ]	Learning centers	[x]
Take home exams	[ ]	Proofreaders	[x]
Exams on tape or computer	[x]	Readers	[ ]
Untimed exams	[ ]	Reading Machines/Kurzweil	[x]
Other accommodations	[ ]	Special bookstore section	[ ]
		Typists	[x]

Credit toward degree is not given for remedial courses taken.

Counseling Services

- [ ] Academic
- [ ] Psychological
- [ ] Student Support groups
- [ ] Vocational

Tutoring

Individual tutoring is available weekly.

Average size of tutoring groups: 1

	Individual	Group
Time management	[x]	[x]
Organizational skills	[x]	[x]
Learning strategies	[x]	[x]
Study skills	[x]	[x]
Content area	[x]	[ ]
Writing lab	[x]	[ ]
Math lab	[x]	[ ]

LD PROGRAM STAFF

Total number of LD Program staff (including director):

Full Time: 1 Part Time: 1

There is an advisor/advocate from the LD program available to students. 30 peer tutors are available to work with LD students.

Key staff person available to work with LD students: Ivey West, Coordinator, Disability Services.

LD Program web site: ups.edu/CWL/disabilities_home.htm

Saint Martin's College

Lacey, WA

Address: 5300 Pacific Avenue SE, Lacey, WA, 98503
Admissions telephone: 800 368-8803
Admissions FAX: 360 412-6189
Director of Marketing and Enrollment Management: Todd Abbott
Admissions e-mail: admissions@stmartin.edu
Web site: http://www.stmartin.edu
SAT Code: 4674 ACT Code: 4474

LD program name: Disability Support Services
Director of Disability Services: Karen McSwain
LD program telephone: 360 438-4580
LD program e-mail: kmcswain@stmartin.edu
Total campus enrollment: 1,251

GENERAL

Saint Martin's College is a private, coed, four-year institution. 303-acre, suburban campus in Lacey (population: 31,226), 60 miles from Seattle; branch campuses at Ft. Lewis and McChord Air Force Base. Served by train; major airport serves Seattle; bus serves Olympia (five miles). Public transportation serves campus. Semester system.

LD ADMISSIONS

A personal interview is not required. Essay is required and may be typed. Admissions requirements that may be waived for LD students include SAT Reasoning scores and secondary school class GPA.

SECONDARY SCHOOL REQUIREMENTS

Graduation from secondary school required; GED accepted.

TESTING

SAT Reasoning or ACT required. SAT Subject required.

All enrolled freshmen (fall 2004):

Average SAT I Scores:	Verbal: 504	Math: 510
Average ACT Scores:	Composite: 20	

Child Study Team report is not required. A neuropsychological or comprehensive psycho-educational evaluation is required for admission. Tests required as part of this documentation:

- ☑ WAIS-IV
- ☐ WISC-IV
- ☐ SATA
- ☑ Woodcock-Johnson
- ☐ Nelson-Denny Reading Test
- ☑ Other

UNDERGRADUATE STUDENT BODY

Total undergraduate student enrollment: 559 Men, 642 Women.

Composition of student body (fall 2004):

	Undergraduate	Freshmen
International	0.0	3.9
Black	7.9	9.1
American Indian	3.2	1.7
Asian-American	10.3	9.0
Hispanic	12.7	6.1
White	62.7	63.0
Unreported	3.2	7.2
	100.0%	100.0%

8% are from out of state. Average age of full-time undergraduates is 26. 77% of classes have fewer than 20 students, 23% have between 20 and 50 students.

STUDENT HOUSING

82% of freshmen live in college housing. Freshmen are required to live on campus. Housing is guaranteed for all undergraduates. Campus can house 336 undergraduates. Single rooms are available for students with medical or special needs. A medical note is required.

EXPENSES

Tuition 2004-05: $18,660 per year.

Room: $2,420. Board: $3,300.

There is no additional cost for LD program/services.

LD SERVICES

LD program size is not limited.

LD services available to:

☑ Freshmen ☑ Sophomores ☑ Juniors ☑ Seniors

Academic Accommodations

Curriculum		In class	
Foreign language waiver	☑	Early syllabus	☐
Lighter course load	☑	Note takers in class	☑
Math waiver	☑	Priority seating	☐
Other special classes	☐	Tape recorders	☑
Priority registrations	☐	Videotaped classes	☐
Substitution of courses	☑	Texts on tape	☑
Exams		**Services**	
Extended time	☑	Diagnostic tests	☐
Oral exams	☑	Learning centers	☑
Take home exams	☐	Proofreaders	☐
Exams on tape or computer	☑	Readers	☑
Untimed exams	☑	Reading Machines/Kurzweil	☐
Other accommodations	☑	Special bookstore section	☐
		Typists	☑

Credit toward degree is not given for remedial courses taken.

Counseling Services

- ☐ Academic
- ☐ Psychological
- ☐ Student Support groups
- ☐ Vocational

Tutoring

Individual tutoring is available weekly.

Average size of tutoring groups: 2

	Individual	Group
Time management	☑	☐
Organizational skills	☑	☐
Learning strategies	☑	☐
Study skills	☑	☐
Content area	☐	☐
Writing lab	☐	☐
Math lab	☐	☐

LD PROGRAM STAFF

Total number of LD Program staff (including director):

Full Time: 2 Part Time: 2

There is an advisor/advocate from the LD program available to students. 8 peer tutors are available to work with LD students.

Key staff person available to work with LD students: Karen McSwain, Director of Disability Services.

Seattle University

Seattle, WA

Address: 901 12th Avenue, Seattle, WA, 98122-4340
Admissions telephone: 800 426-7123
Admissions FAX: 206 296-5656
Dean of Admissions: Michael McKeon
Admissions e-mail: admissions@seattleu.edu
Web site: http://www.seattleu.edu
SAT Code: 4695 ACT Code: 4478

LD program name: Disabilities Services
Disabilities Specialist: Richard Okamoto
LD program telephone: 206 296-5740
LD program e-mail: lc@seattleu.edu
Total campus enrollment: 3,911

GENERAL

Seattle University is a private, coed, four-year institution. 46-acre, urban campus in Seattle (population: 563,374); branch campus in Bellevue. Served by air, bus, and train. Public transportation serves campus. Quarter system.

SECONDARY SCHOOL REQUIREMENTS

Graduation from secondary school required; GED accepted. The following course distribution required: 4 units of English, 3 units of math, 2 units of science, 2 units of foreign language, 3 units of social studies, 2 units of academic electives.

TESTING

SAT Subject recommended.

All enrolled freshmen (fall 2004):

Average SAT I Scores: Verbal: 572 Math: 570
Average ACT Scores: Composite: 24

Child Study Team report is not required. Tests required as part of this documentation:

- [ ] WAIS-IV
- [ ] WISC-IV
- [ ] SATA
- [ ] Woodcock-Johnson
- [ ] Nelson-Denny Reading Test
- [ ] Other

UNDERGRADUATE STUDENT BODY

Total undergraduate student enrollment: 1,298 Men, 2,054 Women.

Composition of student body (fall 2004):

	Undergraduate	Freshmen
International	2.1	8.8
Black	4.7	5.0
American Indian	1.9	1.5
Asian-American	21.6	21.6
Hispanic	7.9	7.2
White	56.1	50.5
Unreported	5.7	5.4
	100.0%	100.0%

17% are from out of state. Average age of full-time undergraduates is 22. 50% of classes have fewer than 20 students, 49% have between 20 and 50 students, 1% have more than 50 students.

STUDENT HOUSING

87% of freshmen live in college housing. Freshmen are required to live on campus. Housing is guaranteed for all undergraduates. Campus can house 1,600 undergraduates.

EXPENSES

Tuition 2004-05: $21,285 per year (in-state), $21,185 (out-of-state).

Room: $4,653. Board: $2,385.

There is no additional cost for LD program/services.

LD SERVICES

LD program size is not limited.

LD services available to:

- [x] Freshmen
- [x] Sophomores
- [x] Juniors
- [x] Seniors

Academic Accommodations

Curriculum

- [ ] Foreign language waiver
- [x] Lighter course load
- [ ] Math waiver
- [ ] Other special classes
- [ ] Priority registrations
- [ ] Substitution of courses

Exams

- [x] Extended time
- [x] Oral exams
- [ ] Take home exams
- [ ] Exams on tape or computer
- [ ] Untimed exams
- [ ] Other accommodations

In class

- [ ] Early syllabus
- [x] Note takers in class
- [ ] Priority seating
- [x] Tape recorders
- [ ] Videotaped classes
- [ ] Texts on tape

Services

- [ ] Diagnostic tests
- [x] Learning centers
- [ ] Proofreaders
- [x] Readers
- [x] Reading Machines/Kurzweil
- [ ] Special bookstore section
- [ ] Typists

Counseling Services

- [x] Academic
- [x] Psychological
- [ ] Student Support groups
- [ ] Vocational

Tutoring

Individual tutoring is available.

	Individual	Group
Time management	[ ]	[ ]
Organizational skills	[ ]	[ ]
Learning strategies	[x]	[x]
Study skills	[x]	[x]
Content area	[ ]	[ ]
Writing lab	[x]	[x]
Math lab	[x]	[x]

LD PROGRAM STAFF

Total number of LD Program staff (including director):

Full Time: 1 Part Time: 1

Key staff person available to work with LD students: Richard Okamoto, Disabilities Specialist.

The Evergreen State College

Olympia, WA

Address: 2700 Evergreen Parkway NW, Olympia, WA, 98505
Admissions telephone: 360 867-6170
Admissions FAX: 360 867-6576
Director of Admissions: Doug Scrima
Admissions e-mail: admissions@evergreen.edu
Web site: http://www.evergreen.edu
SAT Code: 4292 ACT Code: 4457

Director, Access Services: Linda Pickering
LD program telephone: 360 867-6348
LD program e-mail: pickeril@evergreen.edu
Total campus enrollment: 4,138

GENERAL

The Evergreen State College is a public, coed, four-year institution. 1,000-acre campus in Olympia (population: 42,514), 70 miles from Seattle; branch campus in Tacoma. Served by bus; major airport serves Seattle; train serves Lacey (10 miles). Public transportation serves campus. Quarter system.

LD ADMISSIONS

Students do not complete a separate application and are not simultaneously accepted to the LD program. A member of the LD program does not sit on the admissions committee. A personal interview is not required. Essay is not required.

SECONDARY SCHOOL REQUIREMENTS

Graduation from secondary school required; GED accepted. The following course distribution required: 4 units of English, 3 units of math, 2 units of science, 2 units of foreign language, 3 units of social studies, 1 unit of academic electives.

TESTING

SAT Reasoning or ACT required. SAT Subject recommended.

All enrolled freshmen (fall 2004):

Average SAT I Scores:	Verbal: 587	Math: 539
Average ACT Scores:	Composite: 23	

Child Study Team report is not required. A neuropsychological or comprehensive psycho-education evaluation is not required for admission. Tests required as part of this documentation:

- [x] WAIS-IV
- [ ] WISC-IV
- [ ] SATA
- [x] Woodcock-Johnson
- [ ] Nelson-Denny Reading Test
- [x] Other

UNDERGRADUATE STUDENT BODY

Total undergraduate student enrollment: 1,670 Men, 2,331 Women.

Composition of student body (fall 2004):

	Undergraduate	Freshmen
International	0.0	0.2
Black	4.0	5.2
American Indian	2.3	4.2
Asian-American	5.2	4.5
Hispanic	5.0	4.5
White	69.5	65.6
Unreported	14.0	15.8
	100.0%	100.0%

24% are from out of state. Average age of full-time undergraduates is 25. 40% of classes have fewer than 20 students, 49% have between 20 and 50 students, 11% have more than 50 students.

STUDENT HOUSING

79% of freshmen live in college housing. Freshmen are not required to live on campus. Housing is not guaranteed for all undergraduates. Guaranteed on-campus housing for freshmen, then other students as space allows. Campus can house 935 undergraduates. Single rooms are available for students with medical or special needs. A medical note is not required.

EXPENSES

Tuition 2004-05: $3,907 per year (in-state), $14,532 (out-of-state).

Room: $3,760. Board: $2,024.

There is no additional cost for LD program/services.

LD SERVICES

LD program size is not limited.

LD services available to:

- [x] Freshmen
- [x] Sophomores
- [x] Juniors
- [x] Seniors

Academic Accommodations

Curriculum		In class	
Foreign language waiver	[ ]	Early syllabus	[ ]
Lighter course load	[ ]	Note takers in class	[x]
Math waiver	[ ]	Priority seating	[ ]
Other special classes	[ ]	Tape recorders	[x]
Priority registrations	[ ]	Videotaped classes	[ ]
Substitution of courses	[ ]	Texts on tape	[x]
Exams		**Services**	
Extended time	[x]	Diagnostic tests	[x]
Oral exams	[ ]	Learning centers	[ ]
Take home exams	[ ]	Proofreaders	[ ]
Exams on tape or computer	[ ]	Readers	[ ]
Untimed exams	[ ]	Reading Machines/Kurzweil	[ ]
Other accommodations	[x]	Special bookstore section	[ ]
		Typists	[ ]

Credit toward degree is not given for remedial courses taken.

Counseling Services

- [x] Academic
- [x] Psychological
- [ ] Student Support groups
- [ ] Vocational

Tutoring

Individual tutoring is available daily.

Average size of tutoring groups: 1

	Individual	Group
Time management	[x]	[x]
Organizational skills	[x]	[x]
Learning strategies	[x]	[x]
Study skills	[x]	[x]
Content area	[x]	[x]
Writing lab	[x]	[x]
Math lab	[x]	[x]

UNIQUE LD PROGRAM FEATURES

Depending on the nature of your disability and how it impacts your educational experience, services and accommodations provided on an individually determined basis, may include: accessible facilities, alternative testing, accessible parking, sign language interpreters/CART, note takers, priority registration, adaptive equipment/assistive technology, books on tape, tutorial assistance from KEY Student Services and the Learning Resource Center, counseling referrals, and peer support and advocacy.

LD PROGRAM STAFF

Total number of LD Program staff (including director):

Full Time: 2 Part Time: 2

There is an advisor/advocate from the LD program available to students. 30 peer tutors are available to work with LD students.

Key staff person available to work with LD students: Linda Pickering, Director, Access Services.

Walla Walla College

College Place, WA

Address: 204 S. College Avenue, College Place, WA, 99324-1198
Admissions telephone: 800 541-8900
Admissions FAX: 509 527-2397
Director of Admissions: Dallas Weis
Admissions e-mail: info@wwc.edu
Web site: http://www.wwc.edu
SAT Code: 4940 ACT Code: 4486

Disability Support Services Coordinator: Sue Huett, M.Ed
LD program telephone: 509 527-2366
LD program e-mail: huetsu@wwc.edu
Total campus enrollment: 1,718

GENERAL

Walla Walla College is a private, coed, four-year institution. 77-acre campus in College Place (population: 7,818), 45 miles from the Tri-Cities (Kennewick, Pasco, and Richland); branch campus in Portland, Oregon. Airport and bus serve Walla Walla (five miles); train serves Pasco. School operates transportation to Walla Walla and the Tri-Cities. Quarter system.

LD ADMISSIONS

A personal interview is not required. Essay is not required. Admissions requirements that may be waived for LD students include low ACT/SAT Reasoning scores and low secondary school class GPA.

SECONDARY SCHOOL REQUIREMENTS

Graduation from secondary school required; GED accepted. The following course distribution required: 4 units of English, 3 units of math, 1 unit of science, 2 units of history.

TESTING

ACT required; SAT Reasoning may be substituted. SAT Subject recommended.

Child Study Team report is not required. Tests required as part of this documentation:

☐ WAIS-IV ☐ Woodcock-Johnson
☐ WISC-IV ☐ Nelson-Denny Reading Test
☐ SATA ☐ Other

UNDERGRADUATE STUDENT BODY

Total undergraduate student enrollment: 812 Men, 768 Women.

Composition of student body (fall 2004):

	Undergraduate	Freshmen
International	0.3	0.0
Black	3.6	2.8
American Indian	0.6	0.4
Asian-American	3.9	4.7
Hispanic	7.5	6.4
White	78.8	80.4
Unreported	5.3	5.3
	100.0%	100.0%

58% are from out of state. Average age of full-time undergraduates is 22. 64% of classes have fewer than 20 students, 33% have between 20 and 50 students, 3% have more than 50 students.

STUDENT HOUSING

88% of freshmen live in college housing. Housing is guaranteed for all undergraduates.

EXPENSES

Tuition 2004-05: $17,655 per year.

Room: $2,355. Board: $2,370.

There is no additional cost for LD program/services.

LD SERVICES

LD program size is not limited.

LD services available to:

☐ Freshmen ☐ Sophomores ☐ Juniors ☐ Seniors

Academic Accommodations

Curriculum		**In class**	
Foreign language waiver	☐	Early syllabus	☐
Lighter course load	■	Note takers in class	■
Math waiver	☐	Priority seating	☐
Other special classes	☐	Tape recorders	■
Priority registrations	☐	Videotaped classes	☐
Substitution of courses	☐	Texts on tape	☐
Exams		**Services**	
Extended time	■	Diagnostic tests	☐
Oral exams	■	Learning centers	■
Take home exams	☐	Proofreaders	☐
Exams on tape or computer	☐	Readers	■
Untimed exams	☐	Reading Machines/Kurzweil	☐
Other accommodations	☐	Special bookstore section	☐
		Typists	☐

Credit toward degree is not given for remedial courses taken.

Counseling Services

☐ Academic
☐ Psychological
☐ Student Support groups
☐ Vocational

Tutoring

	Individual	Group
Time management	☐	☐
Organizational skills	☐	☐
Learning strategies	☐	☐
Study skills	☐	☐
Content area	☐	☐
Writing lab	☐	☐
Math lab	☐	☐

LD PROGRAM STAFF

Total number of LD Program staff (including director):

Full Time: 1 Part Time: 1

University of Washington

Seattle, WA

Address: Seattle, WA, 98195
Admissions telephone: 206 543-9686
Admissions FAX: 206 685-3655
Director of Admissions and Records: W.W. Washburn
Admissions e-mail: askuwadm@u.washington.edu
Web site: http://www.washington.edu
SAT Code: 4854 ACT Code: 4484

LD program name: Disabled Student Services
Director: Dyane Hanes
LD program telephone: 206 543-8925
LD program enrollment: 175, Total campus enrollment: 27,732

GENERAL

University of Washington is a public, coed, four-year institution. 703-acre, suburban campus in Seattle (population: 563,374); branch campuses in Bothell and Tacoma. Served by air, bus, and train. School operates transportation to medical centers. Public transportation serves campus. Quarter system.

LD ADMISSIONS

Students do not complete a separate application and are not simultaneously accepted to the LD program. A member of the LD program does not sit on the admissions committee. High school waivers are accepted for foreign language. A personal interview is required. Essay is required and may be typed. Some admissions requirements may be substituted for LD students.

SECONDARY SCHOOL REQUIREMENTS

Graduation from secondary school not required. The following course distribution required: 4 units of English, 3 units of math, 2 units of science, 2 units of foreign language, 3 units of social studies.

TESTING

SAT Reasoning or ACT required. SAT Subject required.

All enrolled freshmen (fall 2004):

Average SAT I Scores:	Verbal: 579	Math: 604
Average ACT Scores:	Composite: 25	

Child Study Team report is not required. A neuropsychological or comprehensive psycho-educational evaluation is required for admission. Tests required as part of this documentation:

- ■ WAIS-IV
- ☐ WISC-IV
- ☐ SATA
- ■ Woodcock-Johnson
- ■ Nelson-Denny Reading Test
- ■ Other

UNDERGRADUATE STUDENT BODY

Total undergraduate student enrollment: 13,064 Men, 13,796 Women.

Composition of student body (fall 2004):

	Undergraduate	Freshmen
International	2.4	3.5
Black	3.0	2.8
American Indian	1.3	1.1
Asian-American	29.2	24.5
Hispanic	4.6	3.5
White	54.0	52.3
Unreported	5.5	12.3
	100.0%	100.0%

12% are from out of state. 12% join a fraternity and 11% join a sorority. Average age of full-time undergraduates is 21. 37% of classes have fewer than 20 students, 46% have between 20 and 50 students, 17% have more than 50 students.

STUDENT HOUSING

55% of freshmen live in college housing. Freshmen are not required to live on campus. Housing is not guaranteed for all undergraduates. Housing is limited. Units are assigned on a priority basis. Campus can house 6,618 undergraduates. Single rooms are available for students with medical or special needs. A medical note is required.

EXPENSES

Tuition 2004-05: $4,770 per year (in-state), $17,400 (out-of-state). (Tuition varies by program.)

Room: $3,564. Board: $4,590.

There is no additional cost for LD program/services.

LD SERVICES

LD program size is not limited.

LD services available to:

■ Freshmen ■ Sophomores ■ Juniors ■ Seniors

Academic Accommodations

Curriculum		**In class**	
Foreign language waiver	☐	Early syllabus	☐
Lighter course load	■	Note takers in class	☐
Math waiver	☐	Priority seating	☐
Other special classes	■	Tape recorders	■
Priority registrations	☐	Videotaped classes	☐
Substitution of courses	☐	Texts on tape	☐
Exams		**Services**	
Extended time	■	Diagnostic tests	☐
Oral exams	■	Learning centers	■
Take home exams	☐	Proofreaders	☐
Exams on tape or computer	☐	Readers	■
Untimed exams	☐	Reading Machines/Kurzweil	■
Other accommodations	☐	Special bookstore section	☐
		Typists	☐

Credit toward degree is not given for remedial courses taken.

Counseling Services

- ■ Academic
- ■ Psychological
- ■ Student Support groups
- ■ Vocational

Tutoring

Individual tutoring is available.

	Individual	Group
Time management	■	■
Organizational skills	■	■
Learning strategies	■	■
Study skills	■	■
Content area	■	■
Writing lab	■	■
Math lab	■	■

LD PROGRAM STAFF

Total number of LD Program staff (including director):

Full Time: 4 Part Time: 4

There is an advisor/advocate from the LD program available to students.

Key staff person available to work with LD students: Dyane Hanes, Director.

Washington State University

Pullman, WA

Address: French Administration Building, Pullman, WA, 99164
Admissions telephone: 888 468-6978
Admissions FAX: 509 335-4902
Director of Admissions: Ms. Wendy Peterson
Admissions e-mail: admiss2@wsu.edu
Web site: http://www.wsu.edu
SAT Code: 4705 ACT Code: 4482

LD program name: Disability Resource Center
LD program address: PO Box 644122,
Director: Susan Schaeffer
LD program telephone: 509 335-1566
LD program e-mail: schaeff@wsu.edu
LD program enrollment: 664, Total campus enrollment: 19,281

GENERAL

Washington State University is a public, coed, four-year institution. 620-acre campus in Pullman (population: 24,675), 80 miles from Spokane; branch campuses in Spokane, the Tri-Cities (Kennewick, Pasco, and Richland), and Vancouver. Served by air and bus; major airport and train serve Spokane. Public transportation serves campus. Semester system.

LD ADMISSIONS

Students do not complete a separate application and are not simultaneously accepted to the LD program. A member of the LD program does not sit on the admissions committee. A personal interview is required. Essay is not required.

For fall 2004, 210 completed self-identified LD applications were received.

SECONDARY SCHOOL REQUIREMENTS

Graduation from secondary school required; GED accepted. The following course distribution required: 4 units of English, 3 units of math, 2 units of science, 2 units of foreign language, 2 units of social studies, 1 unit of history, 1 unit of academic electives.

TESTING

SAT Reasoning or ACT required. SAT Subject required.

All enrolled freshmen (fall 2004):

Average SAT I Scores:	Verbal: 527	Math: 545
Average ACT Scores:	Composite: 22	

Child Study Team report is not required. A neuropsychological or comprehensive psycho-educational evaluation is required for admission. Tests required as part of this documentation:

- [x] WAIS-IV
- [x] WISC-IV
- [ ] SATA
- [x] Woodcock-Johnson
- [ ] Nelson-Denny Reading Test
- [ ] Other

UNDERGRADUATE STUDENT BODY

Total undergraduate student enrollment: 8,388 Men, 9,088 Women.

Composition of student body (fall 2004):

	Undergraduate	Freshmen
International	1.0	3.2
Black	2.7	2.7
American Indian	1.1	1.3
Asian-American	6.4	5.6
Hispanic	4.2	4.0
White	78.8	75.7
Unreported	5.8	7.5
	100.0%	100.0%

10% are from out of state. 14% join a fraternity and 16% join a sorority. Average age of full-time undergraduates is 22. 41% of classes have fewer than 20 students, 41% have between 20 and 50 students, 18% have more than 50 students.

STUDENT HOUSING

89% of freshmen live in college housing. Freshmen are required to live on campus. Housing is not guaranteed for all undergraduates. School provides assistance in locating off-campus housing if on-campus housing is not available. Campus can house 8,412 undergraduates. Single rooms are available for students with medical or special needs. A medical note is required.

EXPENSES

Tuition 2004-05: $4,745 per year (in-state), $13,163 (out-of-state).

Room: $3,150. Board: $3,196.

There is no additional cost for LD program/services.

LD SERVICES

LD program size is not limited.

LD services available to:

- [x] Freshmen
- [x] Sophomores
- [x] Juniors
- [x] Seniors

Academic Accommodations

Curriculum

- [x] Foreign language waiver
- [ ] Lighter course load
- [ ] Math waiver
- [ ] Other special classes
- [x] Priority registrations
- [ ] Substitution of courses

Exams

- [x] Extended time
- [x] Oral exams
- [ ] Take home exams
- [x] Exams on tape or computer
- [ ] Untimed exams
- [ ] Other accommodations

In class

- [ ] Early syllabus
- [x] Note takers in class
- [x] Priority seating
- [x] Tape recorders
- [x] Videotaped classes
- [x] Texts on tape

Services

- [x] Diagnostic tests
- [x] Learning centers
- [ ] Proofreaders
- [x] Readers
- [x] Reading Machines/Kurzweil
- [ ] Special bookstore section
- [x] Typists

Credit toward degree is not given for remedial courses taken.

Counseling Services

[x]	Academic	Meets 3 times per academic year
[x]	Psychological	Meets 6 times per academic year
[x]	Student Support groups	Meets 6 times per academic year
[x]	Vocational	Meets 2 times per academic year

Tutoring

Individual tutoring is not available.

	Individual	Group
Time management	[ ]	[ ]
Organizational skills	[ ]	[ ]
Learning strategies	[ ]	[ ]
Study skills	[ ]	[ ]
Content area	[ ]	[ ]
Writing lab	[ ]	[ ]
Math lab	[ ]	[ ]

LD PROGRAM STAFF

Total number of LD Program staff (including director):

Full Time: 5 Part Time: 5

There is an advisor/advocate from the LD program available to students. The advisor/advocate meets with faculty 10 times per month.

Key staff person available to work with LD students: Jeanne Carter, Disability Specialist.

LD Program web site: www.wsu.edu/DRC

Western Washington University

Bellingham, WA

Address: 516 High Street, Bellingham, WA, 98225
Admissions telephone: 360 650-3440
Admissions FAX: 360 650-7369
Director of Admissions: Karen G. Copetas
Admissions e-mail: admit@cc.wwu.edu
Web site: http://www.wwu.edu
SAT Code: 4947 ACT Code: 4490

LD program name: Disability Resources for Students
Director: David Brunnemer
LD program telephone: 360 650-3083
LD program e-mail: David.Brunnemer@wwu.edu
LD program enrollment: 198, Total campus enrollment: 12,862

GENERAL

Western Washington University is a public, coed, four-year institution. 195-acre campus in Bellingham (population: 67,171), 60 miles from Vancouver, British Columbia, Canada, and 90 miles from Seattle; branch campuses in Bremerton, Everett, Oak Harbor, Port Angeles, and Seattle. Served by air, bus, and train; major airport serves Seattle. Public transportation serves campus. Quarter system.

LD ADMISSIONS

Students do not complete a separate application and are not simultaneously accepted to the LD program. A member of the LD program does not sit on the admissions committee. High school waivers are accepted for foreign language. A personal interview is not required. Essay is not required.

SECONDARY SCHOOL REQUIREMENTS

Graduation from secondary school required; GED accepted. The following course distribution required: 4 units of English, 3 units of math, 2 units of science, 2 units of foreign language, 3 units of social studies, 1 unit of academic electives.

TESTING

SAT Reasoning or ACT required. SAT Subject recommended.

All enrolled freshmen (fall 2004):

Average SAT I Scores: Verbal: 560 Math: 560
Average ACT Scores: Composite: 24

Child Study Team report is not required. A neuropsychological or comprehensive psycho-education evaluation is not required for admission. Tests required as part of this documentation:

- [ ] WAIS-IV
- [ ] WISC-IV
- [ ] SATA
- [ ] Woodcock-Johnson
- [ ] Nelson-Denny Reading Test
- [ ] Other

UNDERGRADUATE STUDENT BODY

Total undergraduate student enrollment: 5,147 Men, 6,500 Women.

Composition of student body (fall 2004):

	Undergraduate	Freshmen
International	0.0	0.8
Black	2.5	2.1
American Indian	1.8	2.2
Asian-American	9.0	7.7
Hispanic	3.4	3.3
White	79.2	79.0
Unreported	4.1	4.9
	100.0%	100.0%

7% are from out of state. Average age of full-time undergraduates is 21. 48% of classes have fewer than 20 students, 40% have between 20 and 50 students, 12% have more than 50 students.

STUDENT HOUSING

92% of freshmen live in college housing. Freshmen are not required to live on campus. Housing is not guaranteed for all undergraduates. Campus can house 3,844 undergraduates. Single rooms are available for students with medical or special needs. A medical note is required.

EXPENSES

Tuition 2004-05: $3,894 per year (in-state), $13,281 (out-of-state).

Room & Board: $6,273.

There is no additional cost for LD program/services.

LD SERVICES

LD program size is not limited.

LD services available to:

- [x] Freshmen
- [x] Sophomores
- [x] Juniors
- [x] Seniors

Academic Accommodations

Curriculum		In class	
Foreign language waiver	[ ]	Early syllabus	[x]
Lighter course load	[x]	Note takers in class	[x]
Math waiver	[ ]	Priority seating	[ ]
Other special classes	[ ]	Tape recorders	[x]
Priority registrations	[x]	Videotaped classes	[ ]
Substitution of courses	[x]	Texts on tape	[x]
Exams		**Services**	
Extended time	[x]	Diagnostic tests	[ ]
Oral exams	[x]	Learning centers	[ ]
Take home exams	[x]	Proofreaders	[x]
Exams on tape or computer	[x]	Readers	[x]
Untimed exams	[ ]	Reading Machines/Kurzweil	[x]
Other accommodations	[x]	Special bookstore section	[ ]
		Typists	[x]

Credit toward degree is not given for remedial courses taken.

Counseling Services

- [x] Academic — Meets 4 times per academic year
- [x] Psychological — Meets 2 times per academic year
- [ ] Student Support groups
- [ ] Vocational

Tutoring

Individual tutoring is available daily.

Average size of tutoring groups: 3

	Individual	Group
Time management	[x]	[x]
Organizational skills	[x]	[x]
Learning strategies	[x]	[x]
Study skills	[x]	[x]
Content area	[x]	[x]
Writing lab	[x]	[x]
Math lab	[x]	[x]

LD PROGRAM STAFF

Total number of LD Program staff (including director):

Full Time: 1 Part Time: 1

There is an advisor/advocate from the LD program available to students. The advisor/advocate meets with faculty 3 times per month and student 3 times per month. 1 graduate student and 16 peer tutors are available to work with LD students.

Key staff person available to work with LD students: David Brunnemer, Director.

LD Program web site: www.wwu.edu/depts/drs/index.htm

Whitman College

Walla Walla, WA

Address: 345 Boyer Avenue, Walla Walla, WA, 99362-2083
Admissions telephone: 877 462-9448
Admissions FAX: 509 527-4967
Dean of Admission and Financial Aid: J. Antonio Cabasco
Admissions e-mail: admission@whitman.edu
Web site: http://www.whitman.edu
SAT Code: 4951 ACT Code: 4492

LD program name: Academic Resource Center
Director of Academic Resource Center: Clare Carson
LD program telephone: 509 527-5213
LD program e-mail: carsonc@whitman.edu
LD program enrollment: 120, Total campus enrollment: 1,481

GENERAL

Whitman College is a private, coed, four-year institution. 117-acre campus in Walla Walla (population: 29,686), 170 miles from Spokane. Served by air and bus; other airport and train serve Pasco (45 miles). Public transportation serves campus. Semester system.

LD ADMISSIONS

Students do not complete a separate application and are not simultaneously accepted to the LD program. A member of the LD program does not sit on the admissions committee. A personal interview is required. Essay is required and may be typed.

SECONDARY SCHOOL REQUIREMENTS

Graduation from secondary school required; GED accepted. The following course distribution required: 4 units of English, 4 units of math, 3 units of science, 2 units of foreign language, 2 units of social studies, 2 units of history.

TESTING

SAT Reasoning or ACT required. SAT Subject required.

All enrolled freshmen (fall 2004):

Average SAT I Scores:	Verbal: 670	Math: 660
Average ACT Scores:	Composite: 30	

Child Study Team report is not required. A neuropsychological or comprehensive psycho-education evaluation is not required for admission. Tests required as part of this documentation:

- [x] WAIS-IV
- [x] WISC-IV
- [x] SATA
- [x] Woodcock-Johnson
- [x] Nelson-Denny Reading Test
- [ ] Other

UNDERGRADUATE STUDENT BODY

Total undergraduate student enrollment: 639 Men, 800 Women.

Composition of student body (fall 2004):

	Undergraduate	Freshmen
International	3.4	2.9
Black	2.1	2.0
American Indian	1.6	1.2
Asian-American	9.9	8.7
Hispanic	2.3	3.0
White	67.2	69.5
Unreported	13.5	12.7
	100.0%	100.0%

56% are from out of state. 34% join a fraternity and 32% join a sorority. Average age of full-time undergraduates is 20. 70% of classes have fewer than 20 students, 29% have between 20 and 50 students, 1% have more than 50 students.

STUDENT HOUSING

100% of freshmen live in college housing. Freshmen are required to live on campus. Housing is guaranteed for all undergraduates. Campus can house 1,034 undergraduates. Single rooms are available for students with medical or special needs. A medical note is not required.

EXPENSES

Tuition 2004-05: $26,870 per year.

Room: $3,300. Board: $3,880.

There is no additional cost for LD program/services.

LD SERVICES

LD program size is not limited.

LD services available to:

- [x] Freshmen
- [x] Sophomores
- [x] Juniors
- [x] Seniors

Academic Accommodations

Curriculum

- [ ] Foreign language waiver
- [ ] Lighter course load
- [ ] Math waiver
- [ ] Other special classes
- [ ] Priority registrations
- [ ] Substitution of courses

Exams

- [x] Extended time
- [x] Oral exams
- [ ] Take home exams
- [x] Exams on tape or computer
- [x] Untimed exams
- [ ] Other accommodations

In class

- [ ] Early syllabus
- [x] Note takers in class
- [ ] Priority seating
- [x] Tape recorders
- [ ] Videotaped classes
- [x] Texts on tape

Services

- [ ] Diagnostic tests
- [ ] Learning centers
- [ ] Proofreaders
- [x] Readers
- [x] Reading Machines/Kurzweil
- [ ] Special bookstore section
- [x] Typists

Counseling Services

- [x] Academic
- [ ] Psychological
- [x] Student Support groups
- [ ] Vocational

Tutoring

Individual tutoring is available daily.

Average size of tutoring groups: 2

	Individual	Group
Time management	[x]	[x]
Organizational skills	[x]	[x]
Learning strategies	[x]	[x]
Study skills	[x]	[x]
Content area	[x]	[x]
Writing lab	[x]	[x]
Math lab	[x]	[x]

LD PROGRAM STAFF

Total number of LD Program staff (including director):

Full Time: 2 Part Time: 2

There is an advisor/advocate from the LD program available to students.

Key staff person available to work with LD students: Clare Carson, Director of Academic Resource Center.

LD Program web site: http://www.whitman.edu/academic_resources/

Whitworth College

Spokane, WA

Address: 300 W. Hawthorne, Spokane, WA, 99251
Admissions telephone: 800 533-4668
Admissions FAX: 509 777-3758
Dean of Enrollment: Fred Pfursich
Admissions e-mail: admissions@whitworth.edu
Web site: http://www.whitworth.edu
SAT Code: 4953 ACT Code: 4494

Assistant Director: Andrew Pyrc
LD program telephone: 509 777-4534
LD program e-mail: apyrc@whitworth.edu
Total campus enrollment: 2,136

GENERAL

Whitworth College is a private, coed, four-year institution. 200-acre, suburban campus in Spokane (population: 195,629). Served by air, bus, and train. Public transportation serves campus. 4-1-4 system.

LD ADMISSIONS

A personal interview is required. Essay is required and may be typed.

SECONDARY SCHOOL REQUIREMENTS

Graduation from secondary school required; GED accepted.

TESTING

SAT Reasoning or ACT required. SAT Subject recommended.

All enrolled freshmen (fall 2004):

Average SAT I Scores: Verbal: 585 Math: 579
Average ACT Scores: Composite: 25

Child Study Team report is not required. A neuropsychological or comprehensive psycho-educational evaluation is required for admission. Must be dated within 36 months of application. Tests required as part of this documentation:

☑ WAIS-IV	☑ Woodcock-Johnson
☐ WISC-IV	☐ Nelson-Denny Reading Test
☐ SATA	☐ Other

UNDERGRADUATE STUDENT BODY

Total undergraduate student enrollment: 720 Men, 1,176 Women.

Composition of student body (fall 2004):

	Undergraduate	Freshmen
International	0.4	1.1
Black	2.3	2.1
American Indian	1.7	1.1
Asian-American	4.5	4.9
Hispanic	2.1	2.3
White	86.5	86.2
Unreported	2.5	2.3
	100.0%	100.0%

40% are from out of state. 58% of classes have fewer than 20 students, 39% have between 20 and 50 students, 3% have more than 50 students.

STUDENT HOUSING

83% of freshmen live in college housing. Freshmen are required to live on campus. Housing is not guaranteed for all undergraduates. We do not have sufficient housing to accommodate all of our undergraduate students. Freshmen and sophomores are required to live on campus. Juniors and seniors have first priority for Boppell Hall and the Theme Houses. Campus can house 1,119 undergraduates. Single rooms are available for students with medical or special needs. A medical note is required.

EXPENSES

Tuition 2004-05: $20,980 per year.

Room & Board: $6,500.

There is no additional cost for LD program/services.

LD SERVICES

LD program size is not limited.

LD services available to:

☑ Freshmen ☑ Sophomores ☑ Juniors ☑ Seniors

Academic Accommodations

Curriculum		**In class**	
Foreign language waiver	☐	Early syllabus	☐
Lighter course load	☑	Note takers in class	☑
Math waiver	☐	Priority seating	☑
Other special classes	☐	Tape recorders	☑
Priority registrations	☐	Videotaped classes	☑
Substitution of courses	☑	Texts on tape	☑
Exams		**Services**	
Extended time	☑	Diagnostic tests	☐
Oral exams	☐	Learning centers	☐
Take home exams	☐	Proofreaders	☐
Exams on tape or computer	☑	Readers	☑
Untimed exams	☑	Reading Machines/Kurzweil	☐
Other accommodations	☑	Special bookstore section	☐
		Typists	☐

Credit toward degree is not given for remedial courses taken.

Counseling Services

☐ Academic
☐ Psychological
☐ Student Support groups
☐ Vocational

Tutoring

Individual tutoring is available.

	Individual	Group
Time management	☑	☐
Organizational skills	☑	☐
Learning strategies	☑	☐
Study skills	☑	☐
Content area	☐	☑
Writing lab	☐	☑
Math lab	☐	☑

UNIQUE LD PROGRAM FEATURES

Academic support and accommodations are provided on an individual basis. Students are not categorized or distinguished from the rest of the applicant pool because of a disability. However, a student wishing to receive academic accommodations must disclose and provide appropriate documentation in a timely manner to be eligible to receive services.

LD PROGRAM STAFF

Total number of LD Program staff (including director):

Full Time: 1 Part Time: 1

There is an advisor/advocate from the LD program available to students.

Key staff person available to work with LD students: Andrew Pyrc, Assistant Director.

Alderson-Broaddus College

Philippi, WV

Address: College Hill, Philippi, WV, 26416
Admissions telephone: 800 263-1549
Admissions FAX: 304 457-6239
Director of Admissions: Kim Klaus
Admissions e-mail: admissions@ab.edu
Web site: http://www.ab.edu
SAT Code: 5005 ACT Code: 4508

LD program name: 504 Program
LD program address: Campus Box 2155, Philippi, WV, 26416
Coord./Learning Resource Center Director: Della Colantone
LD program telephone: 304 457-6274
LD program e-mail: colantonedm@mail.ab.edu
LD program enrollment: 16, Total campus enrollment: 689

GENERAL

Alderson-Broaddus College is a private, coed, four-year institution. 170-acre campus in Philippi (population: 2,870), 120 miles south of Pittsburgh. Major airport serves Pittsburgh; smaller airport serves Bridgeport (25 miles); bus and train serve Clarksburg (25 miles). Semester system.

LD ADMISSIONS

Application Deadline: 08/01. Students do not complete a separate application and are simultaneously accepted to the LD program. A member of the LD program does not sit on the admissions committee. A personal interview is recommended. Essay is not required.

For fall 2004, 2 completed self-identified LD applications were received. 2 applications were offered admission, and 2 enrolled.

SECONDARY SCHOOL REQUIREMENTS

Graduation from secondary school required; GED accepted. The following course distribution required: 4 units of English, 3 units of math, 1 unit of foreign language, 2 units of social studies.

TESTING

SAT Reasoning considered if submitted. ACT required. SAT Subject recommended.

All enrolled freshmen (fall 2004):

Average SAT I Scores:	Verbal: 520	Math: 499
Average ACT Scores:	Composite: 21	

Child Study Team report is not required. A neuropsychological or comprehensive psycho-educational evaluation is required for admission. Must be dated within 60 months of application. Tests required as part of this documentation:

- ■ WAIS-IV
- ☐ WISC-IV
- ☐ SATA
- ☐ Woodcock-Johnson
- ☐ Nelson-Denny Reading Test
- ☐ Other

UNDERGRADUATE STUDENT BODY

Total undergraduate student enrollment: 263 Men, 422 Women.

Composition of student body (fall 2004):

	Undergraduate	Freshmen
International	2.0	1.3
Black	4.7	2.8
American Indian	0.0	0.1
Asian-American	0.7	1.0
Hispanic	1.3	0.7
White	83.3	83.9
Unreported	8.0	10.0
	100.0%	100.0%

30% are from out of state. 1% join a fraternity and 4% join a sorority. Average age of full-time undergraduates is 23. 67% of classes have fewer than 20 students, 30% have between 20 and 50 students, 3% have more than 50 students.

STUDENT HOUSING

42% of freshmen live in college housing. Freshmen are required to live on campus. Housing is guaranteed for all undergraduates. Campus can house 544 undergraduates. Single rooms are available for students with medical or special needs. A medical note is required.

EXPENSES

Tuition (2005-06): $17,970 per year.
Room: $2,828. Board: $2,980.
There is no additional cost for LD program/services.

LD SERVICES

LD program size is not limited.

LD services available to:

■ Freshmen ■ Sophomores ■ Juniors ■ Seniors

Academic Accommodations

Curriculum		In class	
Foreign language waiver	☐	Early syllabus	■
Lighter course load	☐	Note takers in class	■
Math waiver	☐	Priority seating	■
Other special classes	☐	Tape recorders	■
Priority registrations	☐	Videotaped classes	☐
Substitution of courses	☐	Text on tape	☐
Exams		**Services**	
Extended time	■	Diagnostic tests	☐
Oral exams	■	Learning centers	■
Take home exams	☐	Proofreaders	■
Exams on tape or computer	■	Readers	■
Untimed exams	■	Reading Machines/Kurzweil	☐
Other accommodations	■	Special bookstore section	☐
		Typists	■

Credit toward degree is given for remedial courses taken.

Counseling Services

■	Academic	Meets 5 times per academic year
■	Psychological	Meets 5 times per academic year
☐	Student Support groups	
☐	Vocational	

Tutoring

Individual tutoring is available daily.

	Individual	Group
Time management	■	■
Organizational skills	■	■
Learning strategies	■	■
Study skills	■	■
Content area	■	☐
Writing lab	■	☐
Math lab	■	☐

LD PROGRAM STAFF

Total number of LD Program staff (including director):

Full Time: 1 Part Time: 1

There is an advisor/advocate from the LD program available to students. The advisor/advocate meets with faculty 1 time per month and students 1 time per month. 17 peer tutors are available to work with LD students.

Key staff person available to work with LD students: Della Colantone, 504 Coordinator/Learning Resource Center Director.

Bethany College

Bethany, WV

Address: PO Box 419, Bethany, WV, 26032
Admissions telephone: 800 922-7611
Admissions FAX: 304 829-7142
Vice President for Enrollment Management and Marketing: Wray Blair
Admissions e-mail: admission@bethanywv.edu
Web site: http://www.bethanywv.edu
SAT Code: 5060 ACT Code: 4512

LD program name: Special Advising
LD program address: PO Box 417, Bethany, WV, 26032
Director, Academic Svcs./Special Advising: Rebecca Pauls
LD program telephone: 304 829-7400
LD program e-mail: rpauls@bethanywv.edu
LD program enrollment: 20, Total campus enrollment: 857

GENERAL

Bethany College is a private, coed, four-year institution. 400-acre campus in Bethany (population: 985), 15 miles from Wheeling. Major airport and train serve Pittsburgh, PA (45 miles); bus serves Wheeling. School operates transportation to Wheeling and Pittsburgh, PA. 4-1-4 system.

LD ADMISSIONS

Students do not complete a separate application and are simultaneously accepted to the LD program. A member of the LD program does not sit on the admissions committee. A personal interview is required. Essay is required and may be typed.

For fall 2004, 2 completed self-identified LD applications were received. 2 applications were offered admission, and 1 enrolled.

SECONDARY SCHOOL REQUIREMENTS

Graduation from secondary school required; GED accepted. The following course distribution required: 4 units of English, 3 units of math, 3 units of science, 2 units of foreign language, 3 units of social studies.

TESTING

SAT Reasoning recommended. ACT recommended. SAT Subject recommended.

All enrolled freshmen (fall 2004):

Average SAT I Scores:	Verbal: 505	Math: 496
Average ACT Scores:	Composite: 22	

Child Study Team report is not required. A neuropsychological or comprehensive psycho-educational evaluation is required for admission. Must be dated within 36 months of application. Tests required as part of this documentation:

- ☑ WAIS-IV
- ☐ WISC-IV
- ☐ SATA
- ☑ Woodcock-Johnson
- ☐ Nelson-Denny Reading Test
- ☐ Other

UNDERGRADUATE STUDENT BODY

Total undergraduate student enrollment: 425 Men, 349 Women.

Composition of student body (fall 2004):

	Undergraduate	Freshmen
International	3.8	2.7
Black	2.8	1.7
American Indian	0.5	0.3
Asian-American	0.0	0.6
Hispanic	0.9	0.9
White	92.0	93.8
Unreported	0.0	0.0
	100.0%	100.0%

74% are from out of state. 39% join a fraternity and 49% join a sorority. Average age of full-time undergraduates is 21. 69% of classes have fewer than 20 students, 28% have between 20 and 50 students, 3% have more than 50 students.

STUDENT HOUSING

97% of freshmen live in college housing. Freshmen are not required to live on campus. Housing is guaranteed for all undergraduates. Campus can house 876 undergraduates. Single rooms are available for students with medical or special needs. A medical note is required.

EXPENSES

Tuition (2005-06): $14,370 per year.
Room: $3,550. Board: $3,475.
Additional cost for LD program/services: $2,500

LD SERVICES

LD program is limited to %1 students.

LD services available to:

☑ Freshmen ☑ Sophomores ☑ Juniors ☑ Seniors

Academic Accommodations

Curriculum		In class	
Foreign language waiver	☐	Early syllabus	☐
Lighter course load	☐	Note takers in class	☑
Math waiver	☐	Priority seating	☐
Other special classes	☑	Tape recorders	☑
Priority registrations	☐	Videotaped classes	☐
Substitution of courses	☐	Text on tape	☐
Exams		**Services**	
Extended time	☑	Diagnostic tests	☐
Oral exams	☑	Learning centers	☑
Take home exams	☐	Proofreaders	☐
Exams on tape or computer	☐	Readers	☑
Untimed exams	☑	Reading Machines/Kurzweil	☐
Other accommodations	☐	Special bookstore section	☐
		Typists	☐

Credit toward degree is given for remedial courses taken.

Counseling Services

- ☑ Academic
- ☐ Psychological
- ☐ Student Support groups
- ☑ Vocational

Meets 2 times per academic year

Tutoring

Individual tutoring is available weekly.

Average size of tutoring groups: 3

	Individual	Group
Time management	☑	☐
Organizational skills	☑	☐
Learning strategies	☑	☐
Study skills	☑	☐
Content area	☐	☐
Writing lab	☐	☐
Math lab	☐	☐

LD PROGRAM STAFF

Total number of LD Program staff (including director):

Full Time: 2 Part Time: 2

There is an advisor/advocate from the LD program available to students. The advisor/advocate meets with student 12 times per month.

Key staff person available to work with LD students: Rebecca Pauls, Director, Academic Services and Special Advising.

Bluefield State College

Bluefield, WV

Address: 219 Rock Street, Bluefield, WV, 24701
Admissions telephone: 304 327-4065
Admissions FAX: 304 325-7747
Director of Enrollment Management: John C. Cardwell
Admissions e-mail: bscadmit@bluefieldstate.edu
Web site: http://www.bluefieldstate.edu
SAT Code: 5064 ACT Code: 4514

Director of Student Support Services: Carolyn Kirby
LD program telephone: 304 327-4098
LD program e-mail: cturner@bluefieldstate.edu
LD program enrollment: 4, Total campus enrollment: 3,506

GENERAL

Bluefield State College is a public, coed, four-year institution. 45-acre campus, one mile from Bluefield (population: 11,451), 90 miles from Charleston; branch campuses in Beckley, Lewisburg, and Welch. Served by bus; airport serves Roanoke, VA. (96 miles); train serves Hinton (25 miles). Semester system.

LD ADMISSIONS

Application Deadline: 08/15. Students do not complete a separate application and are not simultaneously accepted to the LD program. A member of the LD program does not sit on the admissions committee. High school waivers are accepted for foreign language. A personal interview is recommended. Essay is not required.

For fall 2004, 4 completed self-identified LD applications were received. 4 applications were offered admission, and 4 enrolled.

SECONDARY SCHOOL REQUIREMENTS

Graduation from secondary school required; GED accepted. The following course distribution required: 4 units of English, 3 units of math, 3 units of science, 3 units of social studies, 1 unit of history, 1 unit of academic electives.

TESTING

ACT required; SAT Reasoning may be substituted. SAT Subject recommended.

All enrolled freshmen (fall 2004):

Average SAT I Scores:	Verbal: 459	Math: 434
Average ACT Scores:	Composite: 19	

Child Study Team report is not required. A neuropsychological or comprehensive psycho-educational evaluation is required for admission. Must be dated within 24 months of application. Tests required as part of this documentation:

- [x] WAIS-IV
- [x] WISC-IV
- [ ] SATA
- [ ] Woodcock-Johnson
- [x] Nelson-Denny Reading Test
- [ ] Other

UNDERGRADUATE STUDENT BODY

Total undergraduate student enrollment: 1,063 Men, 1,585 Women.

Composition of student body (fall 2004):

	Undergraduate	Freshmen
International	0.0	0.9
Black	7.7	9.9
American Indian	0.2	0.4
Asian-American	0.0	0.3
Hispanic	0.5	0.5
White	91.6	88.0
Unreported	0.0	0.0
	100.0%	100.0%

6% are from out of state. 2% join a fraternity and 2% join a sorority. Average age of full-time undergraduates is 26. 58% of classes have fewer than 20 students, 41% have between 20 and 50 students, 1% have more than 50 students.

EXPENSES

Tuition (2005-06): $3,410 per year (in-state), $7,014 (out-of-state).

There is no additional cost for LD program/services.

LD SERVICES

LD program size is not limited.

LD services available to:

- [x] Freshmen
- [x] Sophomores
- [x] Juniors
- [x] Seniors

Academic Accommodations

Curriculum		**In class**	
Foreign language waiver	[ ]	Early syllabus	[ ]
Lighter course load	[x]	Note takers in class	[x]
Math waiver	[ ]	Priority seating	[ ]
Other special classes	[ ]	Tape recorders	[x]
Priority registrations	[ ]	Videotaped classes	[ ]
Substitution of courses	[ ]	Text on tape	[ ]
Exams		**Services**	
Extended time	[x]	Diagnostic tests	[ ]
Oral exams	[x]	Learning centers	[ ]
Take home exams	[ ]	Proofreaders	[ ]
Exams on tape or computer	[ ]	Readers	[x]
Untimed exams	[x]	Reading Machines/Kurzweil	[x]
Other accommodations	[ ]	Special bookstore section	[ ]
		Typists	[ ]

Credit toward degree is not given for remedial courses taken.

Counseling Services

- [x] Academic — Meets 3 times per academic year
- [ ] Psychological
- [ ] Student Support groups
- [ ] Vocational

Tutoring

Individual tutoring is available weekly.

Average size of tutoring groups: 2

	Individual	Group
Time management	[ ]	[x]
Organizational skills	[ ]	[x]
Learning strategies	[ ]	[x]
Study skills	[ ]	[x]
Content area	[ ]	[ ]
Writing lab	[ ]	[x]
Math lab	[ ]	[ ]

LD PROGRAM STAFF

Total number of LD Program staff (including director):

Full Time: 2 Part Time: 2

There is an advisor/advocate from the LD program available to students. The advisor/advocate meets with faculty 1 time per month and students 1 time per month. 25 peer tutors are available to work with LD students.

Key staff person available to work with LD students: Carolyn Kirby, Director of Student Support Services.

University of Charleston

Charleston, WV

Address: 2300 MacCorkle Avenue SE, Charleston, WV, 25304
Admissions telephone: 800 995-4682
Admissions FAX: 304 357-4781
Director of Admissions: Thomas Hoiles
Admissions e-mail: admissions@ucwv.edu
Web site: http://www.ucwv.edu
SAT Code: 5419 ACT Code: 4528

LD program name: Learning Support Services
Director, Learning Support Services: Catherine Moore
LD program telephone: 304 357-4931
LD program e-mail: catherinemoore@ucwv.edu
LD program enrollment: 15, Total campus enrollment: 901

GENERAL

University of Charleston is a private, coed, four-year institution. 40-acre campus in Charleston (population: 53,421). Served by airport, bus, and train. School operates transportation within Charleston. Public transportation serves campus. Semester system.

LD ADMISSIONS

Students complete a separate application and are not simultaneously accepted to the LD program. A member of the LD program does not sit on the admissions committee. High school waivers are accepted for math and foreign language. A personal interview is recommended. Essay is not required.

SECONDARY SCHOOL REQUIREMENTS

Graduation from secondary school required; GED accepted.

TESTING

SAT Reasoning or ACT considered if submitted. SAT Subject recommended.

All enrolled freshmen (fall 2004):

Average SAT I Scores:	Verbal: 501	Math: 517
Average ACT Scores:	Composite: 23	

Child Study Team report is not required. A neuropsychological or comprehensive psycho-educational evaluation is required for admission. Must be dated within 24 months of application. Tests required as part of this documentation:

- [x] WAIS-IV
- [x] WISC-IV
- [x] SATA
- [x] Woodcock-Johnson
- [ ] Nelson-Denny Reading Test
- [ ] Other

UNDERGRADUATE STUDENT BODY

Total undergraduate student enrollment: 340 Men, 751 Women.

Composition of student body (fall 2004):

	Undergraduate	Freshmen
International	2.1	3.7
Black	2.7	6.5
American Indian	0.0	0.1
Asian-American	0.5	0.1
Hispanic	1.6	1.2
White	50.9	51.8
Unreported	42.2	36.6
	100.0%	100.0%

16% are from out of state. 73% of classes have fewer than 20 students, 26% have between 20 and 50 students, 2% have more than 50 students.

STUDENT HOUSING

55% of freshmen live in college housing. Housing is guaranteed for all undergraduates. Campus can house 490 undergraduates. Single rooms are available for students with medical or special needs. A medical note is required.

EXPENSES

Tuition (2005-06): $20,200 per year.
Room: $4,060. Board: $3,340.
There is no additional cost for LD program/services.

LD SERVICES

LD program size is not limited.

LD services available to:

- [x] Freshmen
- [x] Sophomores
- [x] Juniors
- [x] Seniors

Academic Accommodations

Curriculum		In class	
Foreign language waiver	[x]	Early syllabus	[ ]
Lighter course load	[x]	Note takers in class	[x]
Math waiver	[x]	Priority seating	[x]
Other special classes	[x]	Tape recorders	[x]
Priority registrations	[ ]	Videotaped classes	[ ]
Substitution of courses	[ ]	Text on tape	[x]
Exams		**Services**	
Extended time	[x]	Diagnostic tests	[ ]
Oral exams	[x]	Learning centers	[x]
Take home exams	[ ]	Proofreaders	[ ]
Exams on tape or computer	[x]	Readers	[x]
Untimed exams	[x]	Reading Machines/Kurzweil	[x]
Other accommodations	[ ]	Special bookstore section	[ ]
		Typists	[ ]

Credit toward degree is not given for remedial courses taken.

Counseling Services

- [x] Academic — Meets 30 times per academic year
- [ ] Psychological
- [ ] Student Support groups
- [ ] Vocational

Tutoring

Individual tutoring is available daily.

Average size of tutoring groups: 3

	Individual	Group
Time management	[x]	[x]
Organizational skills	[x]	[x]
Learning strategies	[ ]	[ ]
Study skills	[x]	[x]
Content area	[ ]	[ ]
Writing lab	[ ]	[ ]
Math lab	[x]	[x]

LD PROGRAM STAFF

Total number of LD Program staff (including director):

Full Time: 2 Part Time: 2

There is not an advisor/advocate from the LD program available to students.

Key staff person available to work with LD students: Catherine Moore, Director, Learning Support Services.

Concord College

Athens, WV

Address: Vermillion Street, Athens, WV, 24712
Admissions telephone: 888 384-5249
Admissions FAX: 304 384-9044
Associate Director of Admissions: Michael Curry
Admissions e-mail: admissions@concord.edu
Web site: http://www.concord.edu
SAT Code: 5120 ACT Code: 4516

LD program name: Office of Disability Services
LD program address: Campus Box 86, PO Box 1000
Disability Services Coordinator: Nancy Ellison
LD program telephone: (304) 384-6086
LD program e-mail: ods@concord.edu
LD program enrollment: 40, Total campus enrollment: 2,919

GENERAL

Concord College is a public, coed, four-year institution. 100-acre campus in Athens (population: 1,102), 80 miles from Charleston; branch campus in Beckley. Major airports serve Charleston and Roanoke, VA. (90 miles); smaller airport serves Bluefield (18 miles); bus serves Princeton (five miles); train serves Hinton (25 miles). Semester system.

LD ADMISSIONS

Students do not complete a separate application and are simultaneously accepted to the LD program. A member of the LD program does not sit on the admissions committee. A personal interview is not required. Essay is not required.

For fall 2004, 12 completed self-identified LD applications were received. 12 applications were offered admission, and 9 enrolled.

SECONDARY SCHOOL REQUIREMENTS

Graduation from secondary school required; GED accepted. The following course distribution required: 4 units of English, 2 units of math, 2 units of science, 2 units of social studies, 1 unit of history.

TESTING

SAT Subject recommended.

All enrolled freshmen (fall 2004):

Average SAT I Scores:	Verbal: 502	Math: 484
Average ACT Scores:	Composite: 20	

Child Study Team report is not required. A neuropsychological or comprehensive psycho-educational evaluation is required for admission. Must be dated within 36 months of application. Tests required as part of this documentation:

☐ WAIS-IV ☐ Woodcock-Johnson
☐ WISC-IV ☐ Nelson-Denny Reading Test
☐ SATA ☐ Other

UNDERGRADUATE STUDENT BODY

Total undergraduate student enrollment: 1,313 Men, 1,742 Women.

Composition of student body (fall 2004):

	Undergraduate	Freshmen
International	0.0	0.0
Black	7.2	4.8
American Indian	0.0	0.1
Asian-American	1.7	1.2
Hispanic	0.0	0.4
White	91.1	93.5
Unreported	0.0	0.0
	100.0%	100.0%

11% are from out of state. Average age of full-time undergraduates is 22. 57% of classes have fewer than 20 students, 39% have between 20 and 50 students, 4% have more than 50 students.

STUDENT HOUSING

60% of freshmen live in college housing. Freshmen are required to live on campus. Housing is guaranteed for all undergraduates. Campus can house 1,150 undergraduates. Single rooms are available for students with medical or special needs. A medical note is not required.

EXPENSES

Tuition (2005-06): $250 per year (in-state), $800 (out-of-state).
Room: $2,966. Board: $2,830.
There is no additional cost for LD program/services.

LD SERVICES

LD program size is not limited.

LD services available to:

☑ Freshmen ☑ Sophomores ☑ Juniors ☑ Seniors

Academic Accommodations

Curriculum		**In class**	
Foreign language waiver	☐	Early syllabus	☐
Lighter course load	☑	Note takers in class	☑
Math waiver	☐	Priority seating	☐
Other special classes	☐	Tape recorders	☑
Priority registrations	☐	Videotaped classes	☐
Substitution of courses	☐	Text on tape	☑
Exams		**Services**	
Extended time	☑	Diagnostic tests	☐
Oral exams	☑	Learning centers	☐
Take home exams	☐	Proofreaders	☐
Exams on tape or computer	☐	Readers	☑
Untimed exams	☑	Reading Machines/Kurzweil	☐
Other accommodations	☑	Special bookstore section	☐
		Typists	☐

Credit toward degree is not given for remedial courses taken.

Counseling Services

☐ Academic
☐ Psychological
☐ Student Support groups
☐ Vocational

Tutoring

Individual tutoring is available weekly.

Average size of tutoring groups: 2

	Individual	Group
Time management	☐	☐
Organizational skills	☐	☐
Learning strategies	☐	☐
Study skills	☐	☐
Content area	☐	☐
Writing lab	☐	☐
Math lab	☐	☐

LD PROGRAM STAFF

Total number of LD Program staff (including director):

Full Time: 1 Part Time: 1

There is an advisor/advocate from the LD program available to students. The advisor/advocate meets with faculty 1 time per month and students 3 times per month. 35 peer tutors are available to work with LD students.

Key staff person available to work with LD students: Nancy Ellison, Disability Services Coordinator.

Davis and Elkins College

Elkins, WV

Address: 100 Campus Drive, Elkins, WV, 26241
Admissions telephone: 304 637-1230
Admissions FAX: 304 637-1800
Director of Admissions: Renee Heckel
Admissions e-mail: admiss@davisandelkins.edu
Web site: http://www.davisandelkins.edu
SAT Code: 5151 ACT Code: 4518

LD program name: Supported Learning Program
Director, CAPS Center: Ken McCoy
LD program telephone: 304 637-1290
LD program e-mail: klm@davisandelkins.edu
LD program enrollment: 39, Total campus enrollment: 625

GENERAL

Davis and Elkins College is a private, coed, four-year institution. 170-acre campus in Elkins (population: 7,032), 105 miles east of Charleston and 130 miles south of Pittsburgh. Served by airport; major airports serve Pittsburgh and Washington, DC. (150 miles); bus serves Weston (24 miles). School operates transportation to Clarksburg, downtown Elkins, and airport and bus terminals. 4-1-4 system.

LD ADMISSIONS

Application Deadline: 08/20. Students complete a separate application and are not simultaneously accepted to the LD program. A member of the LD program does not sit on the admissions committee. High school waivers are accepted for foreign language. A personal interview is recommended. Essay is required and may be typed.

For fall 2004, 35 completed self-identified LD applications were received. 26 applications were offered admission, and 12 enrolled.

SECONDARY SCHOOL REQUIREMENTS

Graduation from secondary school required; GED accepted. The following course distribution required: 4 units of English, 3 units of math, 3 units of science, 1 unit of foreign language, 3 units of social studies.

TESTING

SAT Reasoning or ACT required. SAT Subject recommended.

All enrolled freshmen (fall 2004):

Average SAT I Scores: Verbal: 505 Math: 491
Average ACT Scores: Composite: 20

Child Study Team report is not required. A neuropsychological or comprehensive psycho-educational evaluation is required for admission. Must be dated within 36 months of application. Tests required as part of this documentation:

- [x] WAIS-IV
- [x] WISC-IV
- [x] SATA
- [x] Woodcock-Johnson
- [x] Nelson-Denny Reading Test
- [x] Other

UNDERGRADUATE STUDENT BODY

Total undergraduate student enrollment: 260 Men, 408 Women.

Composition of student body (fall 2004):

	Undergraduate	Freshmen
International	0.0	0.0
Black	3.2	4.4
American Indian	0.0	0.8
Asian-American	0.8	2.6
Hispanic	3.2	1.9
White	88.0	81.4
Unreported	4.8	8.9
	100.0%	100.0%

39% are from out of state. 12% join a fraternity and 8% join a sorority. Average age of full-time undergraduates is 23. 82% of classes have fewer than 20 students, 18% have between 20 and 50 students.

STUDENT HOUSING

96% of freshmen live in college housing. Freshmen are required to live on campus. Housing is guaranteed for all undergraduates. Campus can house 572 undergraduates. Single rooms are available for students with medical or special needs. A medical note is required.

EXPENSES

Tuition (2005-06): $16,312 per year.

Room & Board: $6,105
Additional cost for LD program/services: $2,700 per year.

LD SERVICES

LD program is limited to %1 students.

LD services available to:

- [x] Freshmen
- [x] Sophomores
- [x] Juniors
- [x] Seniors

Academic Accommodations

Curriculum		**In class**	
Foreign language waiver	[ ]	Early syllabus	[ ]
Lighter course load	[x]	Note takers in class	[x]
Math waiver	[ ]	Priority seating	[ ]
Other special classes	[ ]	Tape recorders	[x]
Priority registrations	[ ]	Videotaped classes	[ ]
Substitution of courses	[ ]	Text on tape	[x]
Exams		**Services**	
Extended time	[x]	Diagnostic tests	[ ]
Oral exams	[x]	Learning centers	[x]
Take home exams	[ ]	Proofreaders	[ ]
Exams on tape or computer	[x]	Readers	[x]
Untimed exams	[x]	Reading Machines/Kurzweil	[x]
Other accommodations	[ ]	Special bookstore section	[ ]
		Typists	[x]

Credit toward degree is not given for remedial courses taken.

Counseling Services

- [x] Academic — Meets 30 times per academic year
- [ ] Psychological
- [ ] Student Support groups
- [ ] Vocational

Tutoring

Individual tutoring is available weekly.

Average size of tutoring groups: 1

	Individual	Group
Time management	[x]	[x]
Organizational skills	[x]	[x]
Learning strategies	[x]	[ ]
Study skills	[x]	[x]
Content area	[x]	[ ]
Writing lab	[ ]	[x]
Math lab	[ ]	[x]

LD PROGRAM STAFF

Total number of LD Program staff (including director):

Full Time: 2 Part Time: 2

There is an advisor/advocate from the LD program available to students. The advisor/advocate meets with faculty 4 times per month and students 4 times per month. 3 peer tutors are available to work with LD students.

Key staff person available to work with LD students: Mary Ellen Schubert, Instructor.

LD Program web site: www.davisandelkins.edu

Fairmont State University

Fairmont, WV

Address: 1201 Locust Avenue, Fairmont, WV, 26554
Admissions telephone: 304 367-4892
Admissions FAX: 304 367-4789
Director of Admissions: Steve Leadman
Admissions e-mail: admit@fairmontstate.edu
Web site: http://www.fairmontstate.edu
SAT Code: 5211 ACT Code: 4520

ADA Coordinator: Andrea Pammer
LD program telephone: 304 367-4686
LD program e-mail: apammer@fairmontstate.edu
Total campus enrollment: 4,026

GENERAL

Fairmont State University is a public, coed, four-year institution. 89-acre campus in Fairmont (population: 19,097), 90 miles from Pittsburgh; branch campus in Clarksburg. Served by bus; major airport serves Pittsburgh; smaller airports serve Bridgeport (20 miles) and Morgantown (20 miles); train serves Connellsville, PA. (50 miles). Public transportation serves campus. Semester system.

LD ADMISSIONS

A personal interview is required. Essay is not required.

SECONDARY SCHOOL REQUIREMENTS

Graduation from secondary school required; GED accepted. The following course distribution required: 4 units of English, 3 units of math, 3 units of science, 3 units of social studies.

TESTING

SAT Reasoning or ACT required.

All enrolled freshmen (fall 2004):

Average SAT I Scores: Verbal: Math:
Average ACT Scores: Composite:

Child Study Team report is not required. Tests required as part of this documentation:

☐ WAIS-IV ☐ Woodcock-Johnson
☐ WISC-IV ☐ Nelson-Denny Reading Test
☐ SATA ☐ Other

UNDERGRADUATE STUDENT BODY

Total undergraduate student enrollment: 2,864 Men, 3,632 Women.

Composition of student body (fall 2004):

	Undergraduate	Freshmen
International	0.0	0.0
Black	2.6	1.2
American Indian	0.0	0.0
Asian-American	0.0	0.1
Hispanic	0.0	0.4
White	97.4	92.5
Unreported	0.0	5.8
	100.0%	100.0%

6% are from out of state.

STUDENT HOUSING

Freshmen are required to live on campus. Housing is not guaranteed for all undergraduates. Campus can house 670 undergraduates.

EXPENSES

Tuition (2005-06): $2,000 per year (in-state), $5,306 (out-of-state).
Room: $2,860. Board: $2,804.
There is no additional cost for LD program/services.

LD SERVICES

LD program size is not limited.

LD services available to:

☐ Freshmen ☐ Sophomores ☐ Juniors ☐ Seniors

Academic Accommodations

Curriculum		**In class**	
Foreign language waiver	☐	Early syllabus	☐
Lighter course load	☐	Note takers in class	■
Math waiver	☐	Priority seating	☐
Other special classes	☐	Tape recorders	☐
Priority registrations	☐	Videotaped classes	☐
Substitution of courses	☐	Text on tape	☐
Exams		**Services**	
Extended time	■	Diagnostic tests	☐
Oral exams	■	Learning centers	■
Take home exams	☐	Proofreaders	☐
Exams on tape or computer	☐	Readers	■
Untimed exams	■	Reading Machines/Kurzweil	■
Other accommodations	☐	Special bookstore section	☐
		Typists	☐

Credit toward degree is not given for remedial courses taken.

Counseling Services

☐ Academic
☐ Psychological
☐ Student Support groups
☐ Vocational

Tutoring

	Individual	Group
Time management	☐	☐
Organizational skills	☐	☐
Learning strategies	☐	☐
Study skills	☐	☐
Content area	☐	☐
Writing lab	☐	☐
Math lab	☐	☐

Glenville State College

Glenville, WV

Address: 200 High Street, Glenville, WV, 26351
Admissions telephone: 800 924-2010
Admissions FAX: 304 462-8619
Vice President for Enrollment Services: Michelle Wicks
Admissions e-mail: admissions@glenville.edu
Web site: http://www.glenville.edu
SAT Code: 5254 ACT Code: 4522

LD program name: Academic Support
Coordinator, Academic Support: Daniel Reed
LD program telephone: 304 462-7361, extension 7105
LD program e-mail: Daniel.Reed@glenville.edu
LD program enrollment: 13, Total campus enrollment: 1,319

GENERAL

Glenville State College is a public, coed, four-year institution. 347-acre campus in Glenville (population: 1,544), 100 miles from Charleston; branch campus in Summersville; extension centers in Spencer and Weston. Major airport and train serve Charleston; smaller airport and bus serve Clarksburg (65 miles). Semester system.

LD ADMISSIONS

Students do not complete a separate application and are not simultaneously accepted to the LD program. A member of the LD program does not sit on the admissions committee. A personal interview is required. Essay is not required.

For fall 2004, 13 completed self-identified LD applications were received. 13 applications were offered admission, and 13 enrolled.

SECONDARY SCHOOL REQUIREMENTS

Graduation from secondary school required; GED accepted. The following course distribution required: 4 units of English, 3 units of math, 3 units of science, 3 units of social studies.

TESTING

ACT required; SAT Reasoning may be substituted. SAT Subject required.

All enrolled freshmen (fall 2004):

Average SAT I Scores:	Verbal: 422	Math: 438
Average ACT Scores:	Composite: 19	

Child Study Team report is not required. A neuropsychological or comprehensive psycho-educational evaluation is required for admission. Must be dated within 24 months of application. Tests required as part of this documentation:

- [x] WAIS-IV
- [x] WISC-IV
- [ ] SATA
- [x] Woodcock-Johnson
- [ ] Nelson-Denny Reading Test
- [x] Other

UNDERGRADUATE STUDENT BODY

Total undergraduate student enrollment: 880 Men, 1,264 Women.

6% are from out of state. 2% join a fraternity and 2% join a sorority. Average age of full-time undergraduates is 23. 46% of classes have fewer than 20 students, 49% have between 20 and 50 students, 5% have more than 50 students.

STUDENT HOUSING

70% of freshmen live in college housing. Freshmen are required to live on campus. Housing is guaranteed for all undergraduates. Campus can house 596 undergraduates. Single rooms are available for students with medical or special needs. A medical note is required.

EXPENSES

Tuition (2005-06): $3,628 per year (in-state), $8,640 (out-of-state). Room: $2,550. Board: $2,650.

There is no additional cost for LD program/services.

LD SERVICES

LD program size is not limited.

LD services available to:

- [x] Freshmen
- [x] Sophomores
- [x] Juniors
- [x] Seniors

Academic Accommodations

Curriculum		**In class**	
Foreign language waiver	[ ]	Early syllabus	[ ]
Lighter course load	[ ]	Note takers in class	[x]
Math waiver	[ ]	Priority seating	[x]
Other special classes	[ ]	Tape recorders	[x]
Priority registrations	[ ]	Videotaped classes	[ ]
Substitution of courses	[ ]	Text on tape	[x]
Exams		**Services**	
Extended time	[x]	Diagnostic tests	[ ]
Oral exams	[x]	Learning centers	[x]
Take home exams	[ ]	Proofreaders	[x]
Exams on tape or computer	[ ]	Readers	[x]
Untimed exams	[ ]	Reading Machines/Kurzweil	[x]
Other accommodations	[ ]	Special bookstore section	[ ]
		Typists	[ ]

Credit toward degree is not given for remedial courses taken.

Counseling Services

- [x] Academic
- [ ] Psychological
- [ ] Student Support groups
- [x] Vocational

Tutoring

Individual tutoring is available daily.

	Individual	Group
Time management	[ ]	[ ]
Organizational skills	[ ]	[ ]
Learning strategies	[ ]	[ ]
Study skills	[ ]	[ ]
Content area	[x]	[ ]
Writing lab	[x]	[ ]
Math lab	[x]	[ ]

LD PROGRAM STAFF

Total number of LD Program staff (including director):

Full Time: 4 Part Time: 4

There is an advisor/advocate from the LD program available to students. 8 peer tutors are available to work with LD students.

Key staff person available to work with LD students: Daniel Reed, Coordinator, Academic Support.

Marshall University

Huntington, WV

Address: 1 John Marshall Drive, Huntington, WV, 25755
Admissions telephone: 800 642-3499
Admissions FAX: 304 696-3135
Interim Director of Admissions: Craig S. Grooms
Admissions e-mail: admissions@marshall.edu
Web site: http://www.marshall.edu
SAT Code: 5396 ACT Code: 4526

LD program name: H.E.L.P.
Office Manager: Diana Porter
LD program telephone: 304 696-6252
LD program e-mail: porterd@marshall.edu
LD program enrollment: 187, Total campus enrollment: 9,859

GENERAL

Marshall University is a public, coed, four-year institution. 70-acre campus in Huntington (population: 51,475), 50 miles from Charleston. Served by air, bus, and train; larger airport serves Charleston. Public transportation serves campus. Semester system.

LD ADMISSIONS

Students complete a separate application and are not simultaneously accepted to the LD program. A member of the LD program does not sit on the admissions committee. High school waivers are accepted for math and foreign language. A personal interview is required. Essay is required and may not be typed.

For fall 2004, 75 completed self-identified LD applications were received. 45 applications were offered admission, and 40 enrolled.

SECONDARY SCHOOL REQUIREMENTS

Graduation from secondary school required; GED accepted. The following course distribution required: 4 units of English, 3 units of math, 3 units of science, 3 units of social studies.

TESTING

ACT required; SAT Reasoning may be substituted. SAT Subject recommended.

All enrolled freshmen (fall 2004):

Average SAT I Scores: Verbal: Math:
Average ACT Scores: Composite: 22

Child Study Team report is not required. A neuropsychological or comprehensive psycho-educational evaluation is required for admission. Must be dated within 36 months of application. Tests required as part of this documentation:

- ☑ WAIS-IV
- ☑ WISC-IV
- ☑ SATA
- ☑ Woodcock-Johnson
- ☑ Nelson-Denny Reading Test
- ☑ Other

UNDERGRADUATE STUDENT BODY

Total undergraduate student enrollment: 4,332 Men, 5,321 Women.

Composition of student body (fall 2004):

	Undergraduate	Freshmen
International	0.5	0.9
Black	5.8	4.9
American Indian	0.2	0.3
Asian-American	1.0	0.9
Hispanic	1.3	0.8
White	88.9	88.0
Unreported	2.3	4.2
	100.0%	100.0%

16% are from out of state. Average age of full-time undergraduates is 21. 35% of classes have fewer than 20 students, 60% have between 20 and 50 students, 4% have more than 50 students.

STUDENT HOUSING

Freshmen are required to live on campus. Housing is not guaranteed for all undergraduates. Limited campus housing. Campus can house 1,816 undergraduates.

EXPENSES

Tuition (2005-06): $3,932 per year (in-state), $10,634 (out-of-state). $2,724 per year (state residents), $5,008 (residents of out-of-state counties bordering West Virginia), $7,294 (other out-of-state).

Room: $3,156. Board: $2,776.
Additional cost for LD program/services: $275 per sem hr (in-state).

LD SERVICES

LD program size is limited.

LD services available to:

☑ Freshmen ☑ Sophomores ☑ Juniors ☑ Seniors

Academic Accommodations

Curriculum		In class	
Foreign language waiver	☐	Early syllabus	☐
Lighter course load	☐	Note takers in class	☑
Math waiver	☐	Priority seating	☐
Other special classes	☐	Tape recorders	☑
Priority registrations	☐	Videotaped classes	☐
Substitution of courses	☐	Text on tape	☐
Exams		**Services**	
Extended time	☐	Diagnostic tests	☑
Oral exams	☑	Learning centers	☑
Take home exams	☐	Proofreaders	☐
Exams on tape or computer	☐	Readers	☑
Untimed exams	☑	Reading Machines/Kurzweil	☐
Other accommodations	☐	Special bookstore section	☐
		Typists	☐

Credit toward degree is not given for remedial courses taken.

Counseling Services

- ☑ Academic
- ☐ Psychological
- ☐ Student Support groups
- ☐ Vocational

Tutoring

Individual tutoring is available daily.

Average size of tutoring groups: 1

	Individual	Group
Time management	☑	☐
Organizational skills	☑	☐
Learning strategies	☑	☐
Study skills	☑	☐
Content area	☑	☐
Writing lab	☑	☐
Math lab	☑	☐

LD PROGRAM STAFF

Total number of LD Program staff (including director):

Full Time: 12 Part Time: 12

There is an advisor/advocate from the LD program available to students. 45 graduate students are available to work with LD students.

Key staff person available to work with LD students: Dr. Barbara Guyer, Director, HELP Program.

Mountain State University

Beckley, WV

Address: 609 S. Kanawha Street, Beckley, WV, 25802
Admissions telephone: 800 766-6067
Admissions FAX: 304 253-3463
Coordinator of Admissions: Miranda Winters
Admissions e-mail: gomsu@mountainstate.edu
Web site: http://www.mountainstate.edu
SAT Code: 5054 ACT Code: 4510

LD program name: Testing and Tutoring Center
LD program address: P.O.Box 9003, Beckley, WV, 25802
Dean of Students: Reginald Garcon
LD program telephone: 800 766-6067, extension 1434
LD program e-mail: rgarcon@mountainstate.edu
LD program enrollment: 4, Total campus enrollment: 3,742

GENERAL

Mountain State University is a private, coed, four-year institution. Four-acre campus in Beckley (population: 17,254), 60 miles from Charleston. Served by air and bus; major airport and train serve Charleston; train serves Prince (20 miles). Semester system.

LD ADMISSIONS

Application Deadline: 08/26. Students do not complete a separate application and are simultaneously accepted to the LD program. A member of the LD program does sit on the admissions committee. High school waivers are accepted for math and foreign language. A personal interview is recommended. Essay is not required.

For fall 2004, 4 completed self-identified LD applications were received. 4 applications were offered admission, and 4 enrolled.

SECONDARY SCHOOL REQUIREMENTS

Graduation from secondary school required; GED accepted. The following course distribution required: 4 units of English, 2 units of math, 2 units of science, 3 units of social studies.

TESTING

SAT Reasoning or ACT required of some applicants. SAT Subject recommended.

All enrolled freshmen (fall 2004):

Average SAT I Scores:	Verbal: 495	Math: 490
Average ACT Scores:	Composite: 19	

Child Study Team report is not required. A neuropsychological or comprehensive psycho-education evaluation is not required for admission. Tests required as part of this documentation:

- ❑ WAIS-IV
- ❑ WISC-IV
- ❑ SATA
- ❑ Woodcock-Johnson
- ❑ Nelson-Denny Reading Test
- ❑ Other

UNDERGRADUATE STUDENT BODY

Total undergraduate student enrollment: 853 Men, 1,569 Women.

Composition of student body (fall 2004):

	Undergraduate	Freshmen
International	1.8	2.4
Black	11.1	9.7
American Indian	1.3	1.0
Asian-American	0.8	0.8
Hispanic	1.5	2.0
White	83.2	83.8
Unreported	0.3	0.3
	100.0%	100.0%

12% are from out of state. Average age of full-time undergraduates is 30. 58% of classes have fewer than 20 students, 41% have between 20 and 50 students, 1% have more than 50 students.

STUDENT HOUSING

11% of freshmen live in college housing. Freshmen are required to live on campus. Housing is guaranteed for all undergraduates. Campus can house 206 undergraduates. Single rooms are available for students with medical or special needs. A medical note is required.

EXPENSES

Tuition (2005-06): $5,700 per year. Tuition varies for upper-division health science programs.

Room: $2,810. Board: $2,630.
There is no additional cost for LD program/services.

LD SERVICES

LD program size is not limited.

LD services available to:

■ Freshmen ■ Sophomores ■ Juniors ■ Seniors

Academic Accommodations

Curriculum		In class	
Foreign language waiver	❑	Early syllabus	❑
Lighter course load	❑	Note takers in class	■
Math waiver	❑	Priority seating	❑
Other special classes	❑	Tape recorders	■
Priority registrations	❑	Videotaped classes	■
Substitution of courses	❑	Text on tape	❑
Exams		**Services**	
Extended time	■	Diagnostic tests	■
Oral exams	■	Learning centers	■
Take home exams	❑	Proofreaders	❑
Exams on tape or computer	❑	Readers	■
Untimed exams	■	Reading Machines/Kurzweil	■
Other accommodations	❑	Special bookstore section	❑
		Typists	❑

Credit toward degree is given for remedial courses taken.

Counseling Services

- ■ Academic — Meets 3 times per academic year
- ❑ Psychological
- ❑ Student Support groups
- ❑ Vocational

Tutoring

Individual tutoring is available weekly.

Average size of tutoring groups: 1

	Individual	Group
Time management	■	❑
Organizational skills	■	❑
Learning strategies	■	❑
Study skills	■	❑
Content area	■	❑
Writing lab	■	❑
Math lab	■	❑

LD PROGRAM STAFF

Total number of LD Program staff (including director):

Full Time: 3 Part Time: 3

There is an advisor/advocate from the LD program available to students. The advisor/advocate meets with faculty 1 time per month and students 1 time per month. 3 graduate students and 3 peer tutors are available to work with LD students.

Key staff person available to work with LD students: Dr. Rhonda Shepherd, Director of Testing & Tutoring Center.

Ohio Valley U

Vienna, WV

Address: 1 Campus View Drive, Vienna, WV, 26105-8000
Admissions telephone: 877 446-8668
Admissions FAX: 304 865-6001
Vice President for Enrollment: Rob Dudley
Admissions e-mail: admissions@ovc.edu
Web site: http://www.ovc.edu
SAT Code: 5519 ACT Code: 4548

LD program name: K. L. Muller
Director of Student Enrichment: Kalema L. Muller
LD program telephone: 304 865-6082
LD program e-mail: klmuller@ovc.edu
LD program enrollment: 8, Total campus enrollment: 520

GENERAL

Ohio Valley U is a private, coed, four-year institution. 270-acre campus in Vienna (population: 10,861). Served by air and bus; major airport serves Columbus, Ohio (95 miles); train serves Charleston (90 miles). School operates transportation around campus. Semester system.

LD ADMISSIONS

Students do not complete a separate application and are simultaneously accepted to the LD program. A member of the LD program does sit on the admissions committee. A personal interview is recommended. Essay is not required. Admissions requirements that may be waived for LD students include ACT scores greater than or equal to 18.

For fall 2004, 8 completed self-identified LD applications were received. 8 applications were offered admission, and 8 enrolled.

SECONDARY SCHOOL REQUIREMENTS

Graduation from secondary school required; GED accepted.

TESTING

ACT required; SAT Reasoning may be substituted. SAT Subject recommended.

All enrolled freshmen (fall 2004):

Average SAT I Scores:	Verbal: 540	Math: 500
Average ACT Scores:	Composite: 20	

Child Study Team report is required if student is classified. A neuropsychological or comprehensive psycho-educational evaluation is required for admission. Must be dated within 24 months of application. Tests required as part of this documentation:

- ■ WAIS-IV
- ■ WISC-IV
- ■ SATA
- ■ Woodcock-Johnson
- ■ Nelson-Denny Reading Test
- ☐ Other

UNDERGRADUATE STUDENT BODY

Total undergraduate student enrollment: 211 Men, 242 Women.

Composition of student body (fall 2004):

	Undergraduate	Freshmen
International	2.1	6.0
Black	5.3	3.6
American Indian	1.1	0.8
Asian-American	0.0	0.4
Hispanic	1.1	0.6
White	89.3	88.2
Unreported	1.1	0.4
	100.0%	100.0%

58% are from out of state. 50% join a fraternity and 50% join a sorority. Average age of full-time undergraduates is 21. 71% of classes have fewer than 20 students, 29% have between 20 and 50 students.

STUDENT HOUSING

91% of freshmen live in college housing. Freshmen are required to live on campus. Housing is guaranteed for all undergraduates. Campus can house 325 undergraduates. Single rooms are available for students with medical or special needs. A medical note is required.

EXPENSES

Tuition (2005-06): $11,700 per year.
Room: $3,080. Board: $2,800.
There is no additional cost for LD program/services.

LD SERVICES

LD program size is not limited.

LD services available to:

■ Freshmen ■ Sophomores ■ Juniors ■ Seniors

Academic Accommodations

Curriculum		In class	
Foreign language waiver	☐	Early syllabus	☐
Lighter course load	■	Note takers in class	☐
Math waiver	☐	Priority seating	■
Other special classes	☐	Tape recorders	■
Priority registrations	☐	Videotaped classes	☐
Substitution of courses	☐	Text on tape	☐
Exams		**Services**	
Extended time	■	Diagnostic tests	☐
Oral exams	■	Learning centers	☐
Take home exams	☐	Proofreaders	☐
Exams on tape or computer	☐	Readers	■
Untimed exams	■	Reading Machines/Kurzweil	☐
Other accommodations	■	Special bookstore section	☐
		Typists	☐

Credit toward degree is given for remedial courses taken.

Counseling Services

- ■ Academic
- ■ Psychological
- ■ Student Support groups
- ■ Vocational

Tutoring

Individual tutoring is available daily.

Average size of tutoring groups: 1

	Individual	Group
Time management	■	☐
Organizational skills	■	☐
Learning strategies	■	☐
Study skills	■	☐
Content area	■	☐
Writing lab	■	☐
Math lab	■	☐

LD PROGRAM STAFF

Total number of LD Program staff (including director):

Full Time: 1 Part Time: 1

There is an advisor/advocate from the LD program available to students. The advisor/advocate meets with students 2 times per month.

Key staff person available to work with LD students: Kalema L. Muller, Director of Student Enrichment.

Shepherd University

Shepherdstown, WV

Address: PO Box 3210, Shepherdstown, WV, 25443-3210
Admissions telephone: 800 344-5231
Admissions FAX: 304 876-5165
Director of Admissions: Ms. Kimberly Scranage
Admissions e-mail: admoff@shepherd.edu
Web site: http://www.shepherd.edu
SAT Code: 5615 ACT Code: 4532

LD program name: Disability Support Services
LD program address: Shepherdstown, wv, 25443
Dir. of Multicultural Student Affairs: Thomas C. Segar
LD program telephone: 304 876-5453
LD program e-mail: tsegar@shepherd.edu
LD program enrollment: 60, Total campus enrollment: 5,141

GENERAL

Shepherd University is a public, coed, four-year institution. 320-acre campus in Shepherdstown (population: 803), 65 miles from Washington, D.C.; branch campus in Petersburg. Major airport serves Washington, D.C.; smaller airport and bus serve Hagerstown, Md. (16 miles); train serves Harpers Ferry (eight miles). School provides transportation around campus. Public transportation serves campus. Semester system.

LD ADMISSIONS

Students do not complete a separate application and are simultaneously accepted to the LD program. A member of the LD program does not sit on the admissions committee. A personal interview is recommended.

For fall 2004, 11 completed self-identified LD applications were received. 9 applications were offered admission, and 9 enrolled.

SECONDARY SCHOOL REQUIREMENTS

Graduation from secondary school required; GED accepted. The following course distribution required: 4 units of English, 3 units of math, 3 units of science, 3 units of social studies, 1 unit of history, 7 units of academic electives.

TESTING

ACT required; SAT Reasoning may be substituted. SAT Subject recommended.

All enrolled freshmen (fall 2004):

Average SAT I Scores: Verbal: 518 Math: 501
Average ACT Scores: Composite: 21

Child Study Team report is not required. A neuropsychological or comprehensive psycho-educational evaluation is required for admission. Must be dated within 60 months of application. Tests required as part of this documentation:

- ■ WAIS-IV
- ■ WISC-IV
- ■ SATA
- ■ Woodcock-Johnson
- ■ Nelson-Denny Reading Test
- ☐ Other

UNDERGRADUATE STUDENT BODY

Total undergraduate student enrollment: 1,771 Men, 2,620 Women.

Composition of student body (fall 2004):

	Undergraduate	Freshmen
International	0.4	0.8
Black	5.1	5.4
American Indian	0.1	0.5
Asian-American	1.1	1.3
Hispanic	2.4	1.8
White	90.9	90.1
Unreported	0.0	0.1
	100.0%	100.0%

33% are from out of state. 4% join a fraternity and 2% join a sorority. Average age of full-time undergraduates is 23. 56% of classes have fewer than 20 students, 43% have between 20 and 50 students, 1% have more than 50 students.

STUDENT HOUSING

52% of freshmen live in college housing. Freshmen are required to live on campus. Housing is guaranteed for all undergraduates. Campus can house 1,019 undergraduates.

EXPENSES

Tuition (2005-06): $4,046 per year (in-state), $10,618 (out-of-state).

Room & Board: $6,020.
There is no additional cost for LD program/services.

LD SERVICES

LD program size is not limited.

LD services available to:

■ Freshmen ■ Sophomores ■ Juniors ■ Seniors

Academic Accommodations

Curriculum		In class	
Foreign language waiver	☐	Early syllabus	☐
Lighter course load	■	Note takers in class	■
Math waiver	☐	Priority seating	■
Other special classes	☐	Tape recorders	■
Priority registrations	■	Videotaped classes	☐
Substitution of courses	☐	Text on tape	■
Exams		**Services**	
Extended time	■	Diagnostic tests	☐
Oral exams	■	Learning centers	☐
Take home exams	☐	Proofreaders	☐
Exams on tape or computer	☐	Readers	■
Untimed exams	■	Reading Machines/Kurzweil	☐
Other accommodations	☐	Special bookstore section	☐
		Typists	☐

Credit toward degree is not given for remedial courses taken.

Counseling Services

- ☐ Academic
- ☐ Psychological
- ☐ Student Support groups
- ☐ Vocational

Tutoring

	Individual	Group
Time management	■	☐
Organizational skills	■	☐
Learning strategies	■	☐
Study skills	■	☐
Content area	■	☐
Writing lab	■	☐
Math lab	☐	☐

UNIQUE LD PROGRAM FEATURES

Accommodations are given on a case-by-case basis with appropriate documentation from a licensed professional.

LD PROGRAM STAFF

Total number of LD Program staff (including director):

Full Time: 1 Part Time: 1

There is an advisor/advocate from the LD program available to students.

Key staff person available to work with LD students: Thomas C. Segar, Dir. of Multicultural Student Affairs / Dir. of ADA.

LD Program web site: www.shepherd.edu/mcssweb/disabilities

West Liberty State College

West Liberty, WV

Address: Route 88, PO Box 295, West Liberty, WV, 26074-0295
Admissions telephone: 800-732-6204
Admissions FAX: 304 336-8403
Interim Director of Admissions: Ms. Brenda King
Admissions e-mail: wladmsn1@wlsc.edu
Web site: http://www.wlsc.edu
SAT Code: 5901 ACT Code: 4534

Student Enrichment Coordinator: Michele Straub
LD program telephone: 304 336-8216
LD program e-mail: mstraub@wlsc.edu
LD program enrollment: 14, Total campus enrollment: 2,374

GENERAL

West Liberty State College is a public, coed, four-year institution. 290-acre campus in West Liberty (population: 1,220), 10 miles from Wheeling; extended campus locations in Weirton and Wheeling. Major airport and train serve Pittsburgh (50 miles); bus serves Wheeling. Semester system.

LD ADMISSIONS

A personal interview is required. Admissions requirements that may be waived for LD students include ACT/SAT minimum score if all other requirements are met.

For fall 2004, 14 completed self-identified LD applications were received. 14 applications were offered admission, and 14 enrolled.

SECONDARY SCHOOL REQUIREMENTS

Graduation from secondary school required; GED accepted. The following course distribution required: 4 units of English, 2 units of math, 2 units of science, 2 units of social studies, 1 unit of history.

TESTING

ACT required; SAT Reasoning may be substituted. SAT Subject required.

All enrolled freshmen (fall 2004):

Average SAT I Scores:	Verbal: 446	Math: 441
Average ACT Scores:	Composite: 19	

Child Study Team report is not required. A neuropsychological or comprehensive psycho-educational evaluation is required for admission. Must be dated within 60 months of application. Tests required as part of this documentation:

- [x] WAIS-IV
- [ ] WISC-IV
- [ ] SATA
- [x] Woodcock-Johnson
- [ ] Nelson-Denny Reading Test
- [ ] Other

UNDERGRADUATE STUDENT BODY

Total undergraduate student enrollment: 1,172 Men, 1,461 Women.

Composition of student body (fall 2004):

	Undergraduate	Freshmen
International	0.4	0.5
Black	4.3	3.2
American Indian	0.2	0.1
Asian-American	0.4	0.2
Hispanic	0.2	0.6
White	93.9	95.2
Unreported	0.6	0.2
	100.0%	100.0%

28% are from out of state. Average age of full-time undergraduates is 21. 54% of classes have fewer than 20 students, 43% have between 20 and 50 students, 3% have more than 50 students.

STUDENT HOUSING

80% of freshmen live in college housing. Freshmen are not required to live on campus. Housing is guaranteed for all undergraduates. Campus can house 1,427 undergraduates. Single rooms are available for students with medical or special needs. A medical note is required.

EXPENSES

Tuition (2005-06): $3,686 per year (in-state), $9,054 (out-of-state).
Room & Board: $5,456.
There is no additional cost for LD program/services.

LD SERVICES

LD program size is not limited.

LD services available to:

- [x] Freshmen
- [x] Sophomores
- [x] Juniors
- [x] Seniors

Academic Accommodations

Curriculum		**In class**	
Foreign language waiver	[ ]	Early syllabus	[x]
Lighter course load	[ ]	Note takers in class	[x]
Math waiver	[ ]	Priority seating	[x]
Other special classes	[ ]	Tape recorders	[x]
Priority registrations	[x]	Videotaped classes	[ ]
Substitution of courses	[ ]	Text on tape	[x]
Exams		**Services**	
Extended time	[x]	Diagnostic tests	[ ]
Oral exams	[x]	Learning centers	[x]
Take home exams	[ ]	Proofreaders	[x]
Exams on tape or computer	[x]	Readers	[x]
Untimed exams	[x]	Reading Machines/Kurzweil	[ ]
Other accommodations	[ ]	Special bookstore section	[ ]
		Typists	[ ]

Credit toward degree is not given for remedial courses taken.

Counseling Services

- [x] Academic
- [x] Psychological
- [ ] Student Support groups
- [ ] Vocational

Tutoring

Individual tutoring is available weekly.

Average size of tutoring groups: 1

	Individual	Group
Time management	[x]	[x]
Organizational skills	[x]	[x]
Learning strategies	[ ]	[ ]
Study skills	[x]	[x]
Content area	[ ]	[ ]
Writing lab	[ ]	[ ]
Math lab	[x]	[x]

LD PROGRAM STAFF

Total number of LD Program staff (including director):

Full Time: 1 Part Time: 1

There is no advisor/advocate from the LD program available to students. 20 peer tutors are available to work with LD students.

Key staff person available to work with LD students: Michele Straub, Student Enrichment Coordinator.

West Virginia University

Morgantown, WV

Address: PO Box 6201, Morgantown, WV, 26506-6201
Admissions telephone: 800 344-9881
Admissions FAX: 304 293-3080
Director of Admissions: Mr. Cheng Khoo
Admissions e-mail: wvuadmissions@arc.wvu.edu
Web site: http://www.wvu.edu
SAT Code: 5904   ACT Code: 4540

Exceutive Director of Social Justice: Jennifer McIntosh
LD program telephone: 304 293-5496
LD program e-mail: jennifer.mcintosh@mail.wvu.edu
LD program enrollment: 600, Total campus enrollment: 18,653

GENERAL

West Virginia University is a public, coed, four-year institution. Two campuses totaling 913 acres in Morgantown and Evansdale (Morgantown population: 26,809), 75 miles from Pittsburgh; regional campuses in Institute, Keyser, and Montgomery; six regional learning centers throughout the state. Served by air and bus; major airport serves Pittsburgh; train serves Connellsville. School operates transportation to areas in Morgantown. Public transportation serves campus. Semester system.

LD ADMISSIONS

Students do not complete a separate application and are not simultaneously accepted to the LD program. A member of the LD program does not sit on the admissions committee. A personal interview is not required. Essay is not required.

SECONDARY SCHOOL REQUIREMENTS

Graduation from secondary school required; GED accepted. The following course distribution required: 4 units of English, 3 units of math, 3 units of science, 3 units of social studies.

TESTING

SAT Reasoning or ACT required. SAT Subject required.

All enrolled freshmen (fall 2004):

Average SAT I Scores:	Verbal: 529	Math: 543
Average ACT Scores:	Composite: 23	

Child Study Team report is not required. A neuropsychological or comprehensive psycho-educational evaluation is required for admission. Must be dated within 2 months of application. Tests required as part of this documentation:

☑ WAIS-IV	☑ Woodcock-Johnson
☐ WISC-IV	☐ Nelson-Denny Reading Test
☐ SATA	☑ Other

UNDERGRADUATE STUDENT BODY

Total undergraduate student enrollment: 8,633 Men, 7,488 Women.

Composition of student body (fall 2004):

	Undergraduate	Freshmen
International	0.8	1.7
Black	2.8	3.7
American Indian	0.4	0.3
Asian-American	1.8	1.8
Hispanic	1.4	1.5
White	91.9	90.0
Unreported	0.9	1.0
	100.0%	100.0%

38% are from out of state. 5% join a fraternity and 5% join a sorority. Average age of full-time undergraduates is 21. 33% of classes have fewer than 20 students, 50% have between 20 and 50 students, 17% have more than 50 students.

STUDENT HOUSING

83% of freshmen live in college housing. Freshmen are required to live on campus. Housing is not guaranteed for all undergraduates. Campus can house 5,250 undergraduates. Single rooms are available for students with medical or special needs. A medical note is not required.

EXPENSES

Tuition (2005-06): $4,164 per year (in-state), $12,874 (out-of-state). Tuition is higher for business/economics, engineering/mineral resources, and health sciences programs.

Room & Board: $6,144.

There is no additional cost for LD program/services.

LD SERVICES

LD program size is not limited.

LD services available to:

☑ Freshmen ☑ Sophomores ☑ Juniors ☑ Seniors

Academic Accommodations

Curriculum		In class	
Foreign language waiver	☐	Early syllabus	☐
Lighter course load	☑	Note takers in class	☑
Math waiver	☐	Priority seating	☐
Other special classes	☐	Tape recorders	☑
Priority registrations	☐	Videotaped classes	☐
Substitution of courses	☐	Text on tape	☐
Exams		**Services**	
Extended time	☑	Diagnostic tests	☑
Oral exams	☑	Learning centers	☑
Take home exams	☐	Proofreaders	☐
Exams on tape or computer	☐	Readers	☐
Untimed exams	☑	Reading Machines/Kurzweil	☑
Other accommodations	☐	Special bookstore section	☐
		Typists	☑

Credit toward degree is not given for remedial courses taken.

Counseling Services

☐ Academic
☑ Psychological — Meets 24 times per academic year
☐ Student Support groups
☑ Vocational

Tutoring

Individual tutoring is available.

	Individual	Group
Time management	☐	☑
Organizational skills	☐	☑
Learning strategies	☐	☑
Study skills	☐	☑
Content area	☐	☑
Writing lab	☑	☐
Math lab	☑	☐

LD PROGRAM STAFF

Total number of LD Program staff (including director):

Full Time: 3   Part Time: 3

There is an advisor from the LD program available to students. 1 graduate student is available to work with LD students.

Key staff person available to work with LD students: Richard Strasburger, Ed.D., Disability Counselor.

West Virginia University at Parkersburg

Parkersburg, WV

Address: 300 Campus Drive, Parkersburg, WV, 26101-9577
Admissions telephone: 304 424-8220
Admissions FAX: 304 424-8332
Registrar: Cecelia Malhotra
Admissions e-mail: wvupinfo@wvup.edu
Web site: http://www.wvup.edu
SAT Code: 5932 ACT Code: 4542

Learning Center: Janice McCune
LD program telephone: 304 424-8278
LD program e-mail: Janice.McCune@mail.wvu.edu
LD program enrollment: 14, Total campus enrollment: 3,722

GENERAL

West Virginia University at Parkersburg is a public, coed, four-year institution. 125-acre campus in Parkersburg (population: 33,099), 75 miles from Charleston; branch campus in Ripley. Served by air and bus; major airport serves Columbus, Ohio (110 miles). Public transportation serves campus. Semester system.

LD ADMISSIONS

Students do not complete a separate application and are not simultaneously accepted to the LD program. A personal interview is not required. Essay is not required.

For fall 2004, 14 completed self-identified LD applications were received. 14 applications were offered admission, and 14 enrolled.

SECONDARY SCHOOL REQUIREMENTS

Graduation from secondary school required; GED accepted.

TESTING

All enrolled freshmen (fall 2004):

Average SAT I Scores: Verbal: Math:
Average ACT Scores: Composite:

Child Study Team report is not required. A neuropsychological or comprehensive psycho-educational evaluation is required for admission. Tests required as part of this documentation:

- [x] WAIS-IV
- [ ] WISC-IV
- [ ] SATA
- [ ] Woodcock-Johnson
- [ ] Nelson-Denny Reading Test
- [ ] Other

UNDERGRADUATE STUDENT BODY

Total undergraduate student enrollment: 1,255 Men, 2,036 Women.

Composition of student body (fall 2004):

	Undergraduate	Freshmen
International	0.0	0.0
Black	0.4	0.5
American Indian	0.0	0.2
Asian-American	0.2	0.4
Hispanic	0.1	0.2
White	99.3	98.6
Unreported	0.0	0.0
	100.0%	100.0%

4% are from out of state. Average age of full-time undergraduates is 25. 57% of classes have fewer than 20 students, 41% have between 20 and 50 students, 2% have more than 50 students.

STUDENT HOUSING

Housing is not guaranteed for all undergraduates. No housing available to any students. Single rooms are not available for students with medical or special needs.

EXPENSES

Tuition (2005-06): $1,668 per year (in-state), $5,772 (out-of-state).

There is no additional cost for LD program/services.

LD SERVICES

LD program size is not limited.

LD services available to:

- [x] Freshmen
- [x] Sophomores
- [x] Juniors
- [x] Seniors

Academic Accommodations

Curriculum		**In class**	
Foreign language waiver	[ ]	Early syllabus	[ ]
Lighter course load	[ ]	Note takers in class	[ ]
Math waiver	[ ]	Priority seating	[ ]
Other special classes	[ ]	Tape recorders	[x]
Priority registrations	[ ]	Videotaped classes	[ ]
Substitution of courses	[ ]	Text on tape	[ ]
Exams		**Services**	
Extended time	[x]	Diagnostic tests	[x]
Oral exams	[x]	Learning centers	[x]
Take home exams	[ ]	Proofreaders	[ ]
Exams on tape or computer	[ ]	Readers	[ ]
Untimed exams	[ ]	Reading Machines/Kurzweil	[x]
Other accommodations	[ ]	Special bookstore section	[ ]
		Typists	[ ]

Credit toward degree is not given for remedial courses taken.

Counseling Services

- [ ] Academic
- [ ] Psychological
- [ ] Student Support groups
- [ ] Vocational

Tutoring

Individual tutoring is available daily.

Average size of tutoring groups: 1

	Individual	Group
Time management	[x]	[ ]
Organizational skills	[x]	[ ]
Learning strategies	[x]	[ ]
Study skills	[x]	[ ]
Content area	[x]	[ ]
Writing lab	[x]	[ ]
Math lab	[x]	[ ]

LD PROGRAM STAFF

Total number of LD Program staff (including director):

Full Time: 2 Part Time: 2

There is no advisor/advocate from the LD program available to students. 25 peer tutors are available to work with LD students.

Key staff person available to work with LD students: Janice McCune, Leaning Center.

West Virginia Wesleyan College

Buckhannon, WV

Address: 59 College Avenue, Buckhannon, WV, 26201
Admissions telephone: 800 722-9933
Admissions FAX: 304 473-8108
Director of Admission and Financial Aid: Robert Skinner
Admissions e-mail: admissions@wvwc.edu
Web site: http://www.wvwc.edu
SAT Code: 5905 ACT Code: 4544

LD program name: Lindamood Bell Program
Director of Student Academic Support Services: Shawn Kuba
LD program telephone: 304 473-8560
LD program e-mail: Kuba_S@wvwc.edu
Total campus enrollment: 1,486

GENERAL

West Virginia Wesleyan College is a private, coed, four-year institution. 80-acre campus in Buckhannon (population: 5,725), 30 miles from Clarksburg and 135 miles from Pittsburgh. Major airport serves Pittsburgh; smaller airport and bus serve Clarksburg. School operates transportation to Clarksburg airport at student breaks. Semester system.

LD ADMISSIONS

A personal interview is recommended.

SECONDARY SCHOOL REQUIREMENTS

Graduation from secondary school required; GED accepted. The following course distribution required: 4 units of English, 3 units of math, 3 units of science, 2 units of foreign language, 2 units of social studies, 2 units of history.

TESTING

SAT Reasoning or ACT required. SAT Subject required.

All enrolled freshmen (fall 2004):

Average SAT I Scores:	Verbal: 513	Math: 517
Average ACT Scores:	Composite: 23	

Child Study Team report is not required. Tests required as part of this documentation:

- ☐ WAIS-IV
- ☐ WISC-IV
- ☐ SATA
- ☐ Woodcock-Johnson
- ☐ Nelson-Denny Reading Test
- ☐ Other

UNDERGRADUATE STUDENT BODY

Total undergraduate student enrollment: 700 Men, 837 Women.

47% are from out of state. 28% join a fraternity and 28% join a sorority. Average age of full-time undergraduates is 20. 55% of classes have fewer than 20 students, 44% have between 20 and 50 students, 1% have more than 50 students.

STUDENT HOUSING

95% of freshmen live in college housing. Freshmen are required to live on campus. Housing is guaranteed for all undergraduates. Campus can house 1,333 undergraduates.

EXPENSES

Tuition (2005-06): $20,250 per year.
Room & Board: $5,550.

LD SERVICES

LD program size is not limited.

LD services available to:

☐ Freshmen ☐ Sophomores ☐ Juniors ☐ Seniors

Academic Accommodations

Curriculum		**In class**	
Foreign language waiver	☐	Early syllabus	☐
Lighter course load	☐	Note takers in class	■
Math waiver	☐	Priority seating	☐
Other special classes	■	Tape recorders	■
Priority registrations	☐	Videotaped classes	☐
Substitution of courses	☐	Text on tape	☐
Exams		**Services**	
Extended time	■	Diagnostic tests	■
Oral exams	■	Learning centers	■
Take home exams	☐	Proofreaders	☐
Exams on tape or computer	☐	Readers	■
Untimed exams	■	Reading Machines/Kurzweil	■
Other accommodations	☐	Special bookstore section	☐
		Typists	☐

Credit toward degree is not given for remedial courses taken.

Counseling Services

- ☐ Academic
- ☐ Psychological
- ☐ Student Support groups
- ☐ Vocational

Tutoring

	Individual	Group
Time management	☐	☐
Organizational skills	☐	☐
Learning strategies	☐	☐
Study skills	☐	☐
Content area	☐	☐
Writing lab	☐	☐
Math lab	☐	☐

LD PROGRAM STAFF

Key staff person available to work with LD students: Shawn Kuba, Director of Student Academic Support Services.

Wheeling Jesuit University

Wheeling, WV

Address: 316 Washington Avenue, Wheeling, WV, 26003
Admissions telephone: 800 624-6992
Admissions FAX: 304 243-2397
Director of Admissions: Carol Descak
Admissions e-mail: admiss@wju.edu
Web site: http://www.wju.edu
SAT Code: 5906 ACT Code: 4546

LD program name: Disability Services
Director of Academic Resource Center: Kathy Tagg, M.A.
LD program telephone: 304 243-2427
LD program e-mail: ktagg@wju.edu
LD program enrollment: 39, Total campus enrollment: 1,232

GENERAL

Wheeling Jesuit University is a private, coed, four-year institution. 70-acre, suburban campus in Wheeling (population: 31,419), 60 miles from Pittsburgh. Served by bus; major airport and train serve Pittsburgh. School operates transportation around local community. Public transportation serves campus. Semester system.

LD ADMISSIONS

Students do not complete a separate application and are simultaneously accepted to the LD program. A member of the LD program does not sit on the admissions committee. A personal interview is recommended. Essay is not required.

SECONDARY SCHOOL REQUIREMENTS

Graduation from secondary school required; GED accepted. The following course distribution required: 4 units of English, 2 units of math, 1 unit of science, 2 units of social studies, 6 units of academic electives.

TESTING

SAT Reasoning or ACT required. SAT Subject recommended.

All enrolled freshmen (fall 2004):

Average SAT I Scores:	Verbal: 526	Math: 526
Average ACT Scores:	Composite: 22	

Child Study Team report is not required. A neuropsychological or comprehensive psycho-educational evaluation is required for admission. Tests required as part of this documentation:

- ☐ WAIS-IV
- ☐ WISC-IV
- ☐ SATA
- ■ Woodcock-Johnson
- ☐ Nelson-Denny Reading Test
- ☐ Other

UNDERGRADUATE STUDENT BODY

Total undergraduate student enrollment: 505 Men, 744 Women.

Composition of student body (fall 2004):

	Undergraduate	Freshmen
International	2.1	3.1
Black	2.1	2.2
American Indian	0.7	0.2
Asian-American	2.4	1.2
Hispanic	2.4	1.7
White	86.1	82.6
Unreported	4.2	9.0
	100.0%	100.0%

64% are from out of state. Average age of full-time undergraduates is 21. 59% of classes have fewer than 20 students, 41% have between 20 and 50 students.

STUDENT HOUSING

85% of freshmen live in college housing. Freshmen are required to live on campus. Housing is guaranteed for all undergraduates. Campus can house 1,000 undergraduates. Single rooms are available for students with medical or special needs. A medical note is required.

EXPENSES

Tuition (2005-06): $21,000 per year.
Room: $3,060. Board: $3,550.
There is no additional cost for LD program/services.

LD SERVICES

LD program size is not limited.

LD services available to:

■ Freshmen ■ Sophomores ■ Juniors ■ Seniors

Academic Accommodations

Curriculum		In class	
Foreign language waiver	■	Early syllabus	☐
Lighter course load	■	Note takers in class	■
Math waiver	☐	Priority seating	☐
Other special classes	☐	Tape recorders	☐
Priority registrations	☐	Videotaped classes	☐
Substitution of courses	☐	Text on tape	☐
Exams		**Services**	
Extended time	■	Diagnostic tests	☐
Oral exams	■	Learning centers	■
Take home exams	☐	Proofreaders	■
Exams on tape or computer	☐	Readers	■
Untimed exams	■	Reading Machines/Kurzweil	☐
Other accommodations	☐	Special bookstore section	☐
		Typists	☐

Credit toward degree is not given for remedial courses taken.

Counseling Services

- ■ Academic
- ■ Psychological
- ☐ Student Support groups
- ■ Vocational

Tutoring

Individual tutoring is available daily.

Average size of tutoring groups: 1

	Individual	Group
Time management	■	☐
Organizational skills	■	☐
Learning strategies	■	☐
Study skills	■	☐
Content area	■	■
Writing lab	■	☐
Math lab	■	☐

LD PROGRAM STAFF

Total number of LD Program staff (including director):

Full Time: 1 Part Time: 1

There is an advisor/advocate from the LD program available to students. The advisor/advocate meets with faculty 1 time per month and students 4 times per month. 28 peer tutors are available to work with LD students.

Key staff person available to work with LD students: Kathy Tagg, M.A., Director of Academic Resource Center.

LD Program web site: www.wju.edu/arc/ld.asp

Alverno College

Milwaukee, WI

Address: 3400 S. 43rd Street, PO Box 343922, Milwaukee, WI, 53234-3922
Admissions telephone: 800 933-3401
Admissions FAX: 414 382-6354
Director of Admissions: Mary Kay Farrell
Admissions e-mail: admissions@alverno.edu
Web site: http://www.alverno.edu
SAT Code: 1012 ACT Code: 4558

Coordinator for Disability Services: Colleen Barnett
LD program telephone: 414 382-6026
LD program e-mail: Colleen.Barnett@alverno.edu
LD program enrollment: 45, Total campus enrollment: 2,053

GENERAL

Alverno College is a private, women's, four-year institution. 40-acre, urban campus in Milwaukee (population: 596,974). Served by air, bus, and train. Public transportation serves campus. Semester system.

LD ADMISSIONS

A personal interview is not required. Essay is not required. Admissions requirements for applicants with LD are same as admissions for all applicants.

SECONDARY SCHOOL REQUIREMENTS

Graduation from secondary school required; GED accepted.

TESTING

SAT Reasoning or ACT considered if submitted; ACT preferred.

All enrolled freshmen (fall 2004):

Average SAT I Scores:	Verbal:	Math:
Average ACT Scores:	Composite: 19	

Child Study Team report is not required. Tests required as part of this documentation:

☐ WAIS-IV	☐ Woodcock-Johnson
☐ WISC-IV	☐ Nelson-Denny Reading Test
☐ SATA	☐ Other

UNDERGRADUATE STUDENT BODY

Total undergraduate student enrollment: 23 Men, 1,756 Women.

Composition of student body (fall 2004):

	Undergraduate	Freshmen
International	0.4	0.6
Black	20.2	22.8
American Indian	1.1	1.4
Asian-American	5.1	4.2
Hispanic	16.6	11.2
White	56.6	59.8
Unreported	0.0	0.0
	100.0%	100.0%

3% are from out of state. 1% join a sorority. Average age of full-time undergraduates is 24. 67% of classes have fewer than 20 students, 33% have between 20 and 50 students.

STUDENT HOUSING

27% of freshmen live in college housing. Freshmen are required to live on campus. Housing is guaranteed for all undergraduates. Campus can house 200 undergraduates.

EXPENSES

Tuition (2005-06): $15,168 per year.
Room: $2,100. Board: $4,110.

There is no additional cost for LD program/services.

LD SERVICES

LD program size is not limited.

LD services available to:

☐ Freshmen ☐ Sophomores ☐ Juniors ☐ Seniors

Academic Accommodations

Curriculum		**In class**	
Foreign language waiver	☐	Early syllabus	☐
Lighter course load	■	Note takers in class	■
Math waiver	☐	Priority seating	☐
Other special classes	☐	Tape recorders	■
Priority registrations	☐	Videotaped classes	☐
Substitution of courses	☐	Texts on tape	☐
Exams		**Services**	
Extended time	■	Diagnostic tests	☐
Oral exams	☐	Learning centers	■
Take home exams	☐	Proofreaders	☐
Exams on tape or computer	☐	Readers	☐
Untimed exams	☐	Reading Machines/Kurzweil	■
Other accommodations	☐	Special bookstore section	☐
		Typists	☐

Credit toward degree is not given for remedial courses taken.

Counseling Services

☐ Academic
☐ Psychological
☐ Student Support groups
☐ Vocational

Tutoring

	Individual	Group
Time management	☐	☐
Organizational skills	☐	☐
Learning strategies	☐	☐
Study skills	☐	☐
Content area	☐	☐
Writing lab	☐	☐
Math lab	☐	☐

LD PROGRAM STAFF

Total number of LD Program staff (including director):

Full Time: 1 Part Time: 1

Key staff person available to work with LD students: Colleen Barnett, Coordinator for Disability Services.

Bellin College of Nursing

Green Bay, WI

Address: 725 South Webster Avenue, Green Bay, WI, 54305
Admissions telephone: 800 236-8707
Admissions FAX: 920 433-7416
Director of Admissions: Penny Croghan
SAT Code: 1046 ACT Code: 4563

Vice President: Teresa Halcsik
LD program telephone: 920 433-3465
LD program e-mail: thalcsik@bcon.edu
Total campus enrollment: 217

GENERAL

Bellin College of Nursing is a private, coed, four-year institution. Suburban campus in Green Bay (population: 102,313). Served by air and bus; airport and train serve Milwaukee (120 miles). Public transportation serves campus. Semester system.

SECONDARY SCHOOL REQUIREMENTS

Graduation from secondary school required; GED accepted. The following course distribution required: 4 units of English, 3 units of math, 3 units of science, 3 units of social studies.

TESTING

SAT Reasoning or ACT required. SAT Subject recommended.

All enrolled freshmen (fall 2004):

Average ACT Scores: Composite: 23

Child Study Team report is not required. Tests required as part of this documentation:

- ❑ WAIS-IV
- ❑ WISC-IV
- ❑ SATA
- ❑ Woodcock-Johnson
- ❑ Nelson-Denny Reading Test
- ❑ Other

UNDERGRADUATE STUDENT BODY

Total undergraduate student enrollment: 217.

Composition of student body (fall 2004):

	Undergraduate	Freshmen
International	0.0	0.0
Black	0.0	0.0
American Indian	0.0	1.1
Asian-American	0.0	2.2
Hispanic	0.0	1.1
White	100.0	95.6
Unreported	0.0	0.0
	100.0%	100.0%

3% are from out of state.

EXPENSES

Tuition (2005-06): $13,559 per year.

LD SERVICES

LD program size is not limited.

LD services available to:

■ Freshmen ■ Sophomores ■ Juniors ■ Seniors

Academic Accommodations

Curriculum		In class	
Foreign language waiver	❑	Early syllabus	❑
Lighter course load	❑	Note takers in class	❑
Math waiver	❑	Priority seating	❑
Other special classes	❑	Tape recorders	■
Priority registrations	❑	Videotaped classes	❑
Substitution of courses	❑	Texts on tape	❑
Exams		**Services**	
Extended time	■	Diagnostic tests	❑
Oral exams	❑	Learning centers	❑
Take home exams	❑	Proofreaders	❑
Exams on tape or computer	❑	Readers	❑
Untimed exams	■	Reading Machines/Kurzweil	❑
Other accommodations	❑	Special bookstore section	❑
		Typists	❑

Credit toward degree is not given for remedial courses taken.

Counseling Services

- ❑ Academic
- ❑ Psychological
- ❑ Student Support groups
- ❑ Vocational

Tutoring

Individual tutoring is available weekly.

Average size of tutoring groups: 1

	Individual	Group
Time management	❑	❑
Organizational skills	❑	❑
Learning strategies	❑	❑
Study skills	❑	❑
Content area	❑	❑
Writing lab	❑	❑
Math lab	❑	❑

LD PROGRAM STAFF

There is no advisor/advocate from the LD program available to students.

Key staff person available to work with LD students: Teresa Halcsik, Vice President.

Beloit College

Beloit, WI

Address: 700 College Avenue, Beloit, WI, 53511
Admissions telephone: 800 356-0751
Admissions FAX: 608 363-2075
Vice President for Enrollment Services: Jim Zielinski
Admissions e-mail: admiss@beloit.edu
Web site: http://www.beloit.edu
SAT Code: 1059 ACT Code: 4564

LD program name: Learning Support Services Center
Director of Learning Support Services Center: Diane Arnzen
LD program telephone: 608 363-2572
LD program e-mail: arnzend@beloit.edu
LD program enrollment: 79, Total campus enrollment: 1,389

GENERAL

Beloit College is a private, coed, four-year institution. 40-acre campus in Beloit (population: 35,775), 70 miles from Milwaukee and 90 miles from Chicago. Served by bus; major airport and train serve Chicago; airport serves Milwaukee. School operates shuttle bus service. Semester system.

LD ADMISSIONS

Students complete a separate application and are not simultaneously accepted to the LD program. A member of the LD program does not sit on the admissions committee. High school waivers are accepted for math and foreign language. A personal interview is recommended. Essay is required and may be typed.

SECONDARY SCHOOL REQUIREMENTS

Graduation from secondary school required; GED accepted.

TESTING

SAT Reasoning or ACT required. SAT Subject recommended.

All enrolled freshmen (fall 2004):

Average SAT I Scores: Verbal: 650 Math: 610
Average ACT Scores: Composite: 27

Child Study Team report is not required. A neuropsychological or comprehensive psycho-educational evaluation is required for admission. Must be dated within 36 months of application. Tests required as part of this documentation:

- ■ WAIS-IV
- ❑ WISC-IV
- ❑ SATA
- ■ Woodcock-Johnson
- ■ Nelson-Denny Reading Test
- ❑ Other

UNDERGRADUATE STUDENT BODY

Total undergraduate student enrollment: 518 Men, 755 Women.

Composition of student body (fall 2004):

	Undergraduate	Freshmen
International	3.4	5.4
Black	2.5	2.7
American Indian	0.9	0.5
Asian-American	3.4	3.2
Hispanic	1.5	2.5
White	88.3	85.2
Unreported	0.0	0.5
	100.0%	100.0%

80% are from out of state. 15% join a fraternity and 5% join a sorority. Average age of full-time undergraduates is 20. 73% of classes have fewer than 20 students, 27% have between 20 and 50 students.

STUDENT HOUSING

100% of freshmen live in college housing. Freshmen are required to live on campus. Housing is guaranteed for all undergraduates. Campus can house 1,080 undergraduates.

EXPENSES

Tuition (2005-06): $26,664 per year.
Room & Board: $5,924
There is no additional cost for LD program/services.

LD SERVICES

LD program size is not limited.

LD services available to:

■ Freshmen ■ Sophomores ■ Juniors ■ Seniors

Academic Accommodations

Curriculum		In class	
Foreign language waiver	❑	Early syllabus	❑
Lighter course load	❑	Note takers in class	■
Math waiver	❑	Priority seating	❑
Other special classes	❑	Tape recorders	■
Priority registrations	❑	Videotaped classes	❑
Substitution of courses	❑	Texts on tape	■
Exams		**Services**	
Extended time	■	Diagnostic tests	❑
Oral exams	■	Learning centers	■
Take home exams	❑	Proofreaders	❑
Exams on tape or computer	■	Readers	■
Untimed exams	❑	Reading Machines/Kurzweil	■
Other accommodations	■	Special bookstore section	❑
		Typists	■

Credit toward degree is not given for remedial courses taken.

Counseling Services

- ❑ Academic
- ❑ Psychological
- ❑ Student Support groups
- ❑ Vocational

Tutoring

Individual tutoring is available daily.

Average size of tutoring groups: 2

	Individual	Group
Time management	■	■
Organizational skills	■	■
Learning strategies	■	■
Study skills	■	■
Content area	❑	❑
Writing lab	■	❑
Math lab	■	❑

UNIQUE LD PROGRAM FEATURES

Focused on student self-advocacy.

LD PROGRAM STAFF

Total number of LD Program staff (including director):

Full Time: 2 Part Time: 2

There is an advisor/advocate from the LD program available to students. 80 peer tutors are available to work with LD students.

Key staff person available to work with LD students: Diane Arnzen, Director of Learning Support Services Center.

LD Program web site: www.beloit.edu/~dss

Carroll College

Waukesha, WI

Address: 100 N. East Avenue, Waukesha, WI, 53186
Admissions telephone: 800 CARROLL
Admissions FAX: 262 524-7139
Vice President of Enrollment: James V Wiseman
Admissions e-mail: cc.info@ccadmin.cc.edu
Web site: http://www.cc.edu
SAT Code: 1101 ACT Code: 4570

Disability Services Coordinator: Andrea Broman
LD program telephone: 262 524-7335
LD program e-mail: abroman@cc.edu
LD program enrollment: 14, Total campus enrollment: 2,763

GENERAL

Carroll College is a private, coed, four-year institution. 52-acre campus in Waukesha (population: 64,825), 15 miles from Milwaukee; branch campus in Milwaukee. Served by bus; major airport and train serve Milwaukee. Public transportation serves campus. Semester system.

SECONDARY SCHOOL REQUIREMENTS

Graduation from secondary school required; GED accepted.

TESTING

ACT required; SAT Reasoning may be substituted. SAT Subject recommended.

All enrolled freshmen (fall 2004):

Average ACT Scores: Composite: 23

Child Study Team report is not required. Tests required as part of this documentation:

- [ ] WAIS-IV
- [ ] WISC-IV
- [ ] SATA
- [ ] Woodcock-Johnson
- [ ] Nelson-Denny Reading Test
- [ ] Other

UNDERGRADUATE STUDENT BODY

Total undergraduate student enrollment: 891 Men, 1,789 Women.

Composition of student body (fall 2004):

	Undergraduate
International	1.0
Black	1.6
American Indian	0.5
Asian-American	1.9
Hispanic	2.4
White	87.8
Unreported	4.8
	100.0%

22% are from out of state. 6% join a fraternity and 6% join a sorority. Average age of full-time undergraduates is 20. 53% of classes have fewer than 20 students, 43% have between 20 and 50 students, 4% have more than 50 students.

STUDENT HOUSING

Freshmen are required to live on campus. Housing is guaranteed for all undergraduates. Campus can house 1,202 undergraduates. Single rooms are available for students with medical or special needs. A medical note is required.

EXPENSES

Tuition (2005-06): $18,650 per year.
Room: $3,150. Board: $2,660.

There is no additional cost for LD program/services.

LD SERVICES

LD program size is not limited.

LD services available to:

- [x] Freshmen
- [x] Sophomores
- [x] Juniors
- [x] Seniors

Academic Accommodations

Curriculum		In class	
Foreign language waiver	[x]	Early syllabus	[ ]
Lighter course load	[x]	Note takers in class	[x]
Math waiver	[x]	Priority seating	[ ]
Other special classes	[ ]	Tape recorders	[ ]
Priority registrations	[ ]	Videotaped classes	[ ]
Substitution of courses	[x]	Texts on tape	[ ]
Exams		**Services**	
Extended time	[x]	Diagnostic tests	[ ]
Oral exams	[x]	Learning centers	[x]
Take home exams	[ ]	Proofreaders	[x]
Exams on tape or computer	[ ]	Readers	[ ]
Untimed exams	[ ]	Reading Machines/Kurzweil	[ ]
Other accommodations	[ ]	Special bookstore section	[ ]
		Typists	[ ]

Credit toward degree is not given for remedial courses taken.

Counseling Services

- [x] Academic
- [ ] Psychological
- [ ] Student Support groups
- [ ] Vocational

Tutoring

Individual tutoring is available weekly.

	Individual	Group
Time management	[x]	[ ]
Organizational skills	[x]	[ ]
Learning strategies	[x]	[ ]
Study skills	[x]	[ ]
Content area	[x]	[ ]
Writing lab	[x]	[ ]
Math lab	[x]	[x]

LD PROGRAM STAFF

There is an advisor/advocate from the LD program available to students.

Key staff person available to work with LD students: Andrea Broman, Disability Services Coordinator.

Carthage College

Kenosha, WI

Address: 2001 Alford Park Drive, Kenosha, WI, 53140
Admissions telephone: 800 351-4058
Admissions FAX: 262 551-5762
Vice President for Enrollment: Brenda Poggendorf
Admissions e-mail: admissions@carthage.edu
Web site: http://www.carthage.edu
SAT Code: 1103 ACT Code: 4571

Learning Specialist: Diane Schowalter
LD program telephone: 262 551-5802
LD program e-mail: dschowalter1@carthage.edu
Total campus enrollment: 2,560

GENERAL

Carthage College is a private, coed, four-year institution. 83-acre campus in Kenosha (population: 90,352), 30 miles from Milwaukee and 60 miles from Chicago. Served by bus and train; major airports serve Milwaukee and Chicago. Public transportation serves campus. 4-1-4 system.

LD ADMISSIONS

A personal interview is recommended. Essay is not required.

SECONDARY SCHOOL REQUIREMENTS

Graduation from secondary school required; GED accepted.

TESTING

ACT required; SAT Reasoning may be substituted. SAT Subject recommended.

All enrolled freshmen (fall 2004):

Average SAT I Scores: Verbal: 537 Math: 552
Average ACT Scores: Composite: 24

Child Study Team report is not required. Tests required as part of this documentation:

- ☐ WAIS-IV
- ☐ WISC-IV
- ☐ SATA
- ☐ Woodcock-Johnson
- ☐ Nelson-Denny Reading Test
- ☐ Other

UNDERGRADUATE STUDENT BODY

Total undergraduate student enrollment: 1,008 Men, 1,252 Women.

Composition of student body (fall 2004):

	Undergraduate	Freshmen
International	0.3	0.6
Black	3.8	4.9
American Indian	0.3	0.5
Asian-American	2.4	1.3
Hispanic	4.3	4.2
White	81.1	81.3
Unreported	7.8	7.2
	100.0%	100.0%

52% are from out of state. 8% join a fraternity and 13% join a sorority. Average age of full-time undergraduates is 20. 53% of classes have fewer than 20 students, 47% have between 20 and 50 students.

STUDENT HOUSING

87% of freshmen live in college housing. Freshmen are not required to live on campus. Housing is not guaranteed for all undergraduates. Housing only available for students 24 years of age or younger. Campus can house 1,402 undergraduates. Single rooms are available for students with medical or special needs. A medical note is required.

EXPENSES

Tuition (2005-06): $22,500 per year.

Room & Board: $6,500

There is no additional cost for LD program/services.

LD SERVICES

LD program size is not limited.

LD services available to:

■ Freshmen ■ Sophomores ■ Juniors ■ Seniors

Academic Accommodations

Curriculum		In class	
Foreign language waiver	☐	Early syllabus	☐
Lighter course load	☐	Note takers in class	■
Math waiver	☐	Priority seating	☐
Other special classes	☐	Tape recorders	☐
Priority registrations	☐	Videotaped classes	☐
Substitution of courses	☐	Texts on tape	☐
Exams		**Services**	
Extended time	■	Diagnostic tests	■
Oral exams	■	Learning centers	☐
Take home exams	☐	Proofreaders	☐
Exams on tape or computer	☐	Readers	■
Untimed exams	■	Reading Machines/Kurzweil	■
Other accommodations	☐	Special bookstore section	☐
		Typists	☐

Credit toward degree is not given for remedial courses taken.

Counseling Services

- ■ Academic
- ■ Psychological
- ■ Student Support groups
- ☐ Vocational

Tutoring

Individual tutoring is available weekly.

	Individual	Group
Time management	■	■
Organizational skills	■	■
Learning strategies	■	■
Study skills	■	■
Content area	■	■
Writing lab	■	■
Math lab	■	■

LD PROGRAM STAFF

There is an advisor/advocate from the LD program available to students.

Key staff person available to work with LD students: Diane Schowalter, Learning Specialist.

Edgewood College

Madison, WI

Address: 1000 Edgewood College Drive, Madison, WI, 53711-1997
Admissions telephone: 800 444-4861
Admissions FAX: 608 663-3291
Dean of Admissions and Financial Aid: Scott Flanagan
Admissions e-mail: admissions@edgewood.edu
Web site: http://www.edgewood.edu
SAT Code: 1202 ACT Code: 4582

Disabilities Services Coordinator: Elizabeth Watson
LD program telephone: 608 663-8347
LD program e-mail: ewatson@edgewood.edu
Total campus enrollment: 1,960

GENERAL

Edgewood College is a private, coed, four-year institution. 55-acre, suburban campus in Madison (population: 208,054). Served by air and bus; major airport serves Milwaukee (70 miles); train serves Columbus (30 miles). Public transportation serves campus. 4-1-4 system.

LD ADMISSIONS

A personal interview is not required. Essay is not required. No admissions requirements are waived for LD students.

SECONDARY SCHOOL REQUIREMENTS

Graduation from secondary school required; GED accepted. The following course distribution required: 4 units of English, 2 units of math, 2 units of science, 2 units of social studies, 1 unit of history.

TESTING

All enrolled freshmen (fall 2004):

Child Study Team report is not required. Tests required as part of this documentation:

☐ WAIS-IV ☐ Woodcock-Johnson
☐ WISC-IV ☐ Nelson-Denny Reading Test
☐ SATA ☐ Other

UNDERGRADUATE STUDENT BODY

Total undergraduate student enrollment: 427 Men, 1,108 Women.

Composition of student body (fall 2004):

	Undergraduate	Freshmen
International	1.0	1.8
Black	1.0	2.2
American Indian	0.3	0.4
Asian-American	2.3	1.6
Hispanic	2.0	1.6
White	90.8	70.5
Unreported	2.6	21.9
	100.0%	100.0%

7% are from out of state. Average age of full-time undergraduates is 21. 69% of classes have fewer than 20 students, 31% have between 20 and 50 students.

STUDENT HOUSING

71% of freshmen live in college housing. Housing is guaranteed for all undergraduates. Campus can house 360 undergraduates.

EXPENSES

Tuition (2005-06): $17,000 per year.
Board: $2,900.
There is no additional cost for LD program/services.

LD SERVICES

LD program size is not limited.

LD services available to:

☐ Freshmen ☐ Sophomores ☐ Juniors ☐ Seniors

Academic Accommodations

Curriculum		**In class**	
Foreign language waiver	☐	Early syllabus	☐
Lighter course load	■	Note takers in class	■
Math waiver	☐	Priority seating	☐
Other special classes	☐	Tape recorders	■
Priority registrations	☐	Videotaped classes	☐
Substitution of courses	☐	Texts on tape	☐
Exams		**Services**	
Extended time	■	Diagnostic tests	☐
Oral exams	■	Learning centers	■
Take home exams	☐	Proofreaders	☐
Exams on tape or computer	☐	Readers	■
Untimed exams	☐	Reading Machines/Kurzweil	■
Other accommodations	☐	Special bookstore section	☐
		Typists	☐

Credit toward degree is not given for remedial courses taken.

Counseling Services

☐ Academic
☐ Psychological
☐ Student Support groups
☐ Vocational

Tutoring

	Individual	Group
Time management	☐	☐
Organizational skills	☐	☐
Learning strategies	☐	☐
Study skills	☐	☐
Content area	☐	☐
Writing lab	☐	☐
Math lab	☐	☐

LD PROGRAM STAFF

Total number of LD Program staff (including director):

Full Time: 4 Part Time: 4

Key staff person available to work with LD students: Elizabeth Watson, Disabilities Services Coordinator.

Lakeland College

Plymouth, WI

Address: W3711 South Drive, Plymouth, WI, 53073
Admissions telephone: 800 242-3347
Admissions FAX: 920 565-1206
Director of Admissions: Nate Dehne
Admissions e-mail: admissions@lakeland.edu
Web site: http://www.lakeland.edu
SAT Code: 1393 ACT Code: 4592

Total campus enrollment: 3,443

GENERAL

Lakeland College is a private, coed, four-year institution. 240-acre campus in Sheboygan (population: 50,792), 50 miles from Milwaukee. Served by air and bus; major airport and train serve Milwaukee. School operates transportation around Sheboygan. Semester system.

LD ADMISSIONS

A personal interview is recommended. Essay is required and may be typed.

SECONDARY SCHOOL REQUIREMENTS

Graduation from secondary school required; GED accepted.

TESTING

SAT Subject recommended.

All enrolled freshmen (fall 2004):

Average ACT Scores: Composite: 20

Child Study Team report is not required. Tests required as part of this documentation:

- [ ] WAIS-IV
- [ ] WISC-IV
- [ ] SATA
- [ ] Woodcock-Johnson
- [ ] Nelson-Denny Reading Test
- [ ] Other

UNDERGRADUATE STUDENT BODY

Total undergraduate student enrollment: 1,343 Men, 2,001 Women.

Composition of student body (fall 2004):

	Undergraduate	Freshmen
International	5.6	4.7
Black	10.3	6.0
American Indian	0.9	0.6
Asian-American	3.3	2.5
Hispanic	2.3	1.9
White	72.0	74.2
Unreported	5.6	10.1
	100.0%	100.0%

16% are from out of state. 69% of classes have fewer than 20 students, 31% have between 20 and 50 students.

STUDENT HOUSING

Housing is guaranteed for all undergraduates. Campus can house 488 undergraduates.

EXPENSES

Tuition (2005-06): $15,100 per year.
Room: $2,745. Board: $2,890.
There is no additional cost for LD program/services.

LD SERVICES

LD program size is not limited.

LD services available to:

- [x] Freshmen
- [x] Sophomores
- [x] Juniors
- [x] Seniors

Academic Accommodations

Curriculum

- [ ] Foreign language waiver
- [x] Lighter course load
- [ ] Math waiver
- [ ] Other special classes
- [ ] Priority registrations
- [ ] Substitution of courses

Exams

- [x] Extended time
- [x] Oral exams
- [ ] Take home exams
- [ ] Exams on tape or computer
- [x] Untimed exams
- [ ] Other accommodations

In class

- [ ] Early syllabus
- [x] Note takers in class
- [ ] Priority seating
- [x] Tape recorders
- [ ] Videotaped classes
- [ ] Texts on tape

Services

- [ ] Diagnostic tests
- [x] Learning centers
- [ ] Proofreaders
- [x] Readers
- [x] Reading Machines/Kurzweil
- [ ] Special bookstore section
- [ ] Typists

Credit toward degree is given for remedial courses taken.

Counseling Services

- [ ] Academic
- [ ] Psychological
- [ ] Student Support groups
- [ ] Vocational

Tutoring

Individual tutoring is available.

	Individual	Group
Time management	[ ]	[ ]
Organizational skills	[ ]	[ ]
Learning strategies	[ ]	[ ]
Study skills	[ ]	[ ]
Content area	[ ]	[ ]
Writing lab	[ ]	[ ]
Math lab	[ ]	[ ]

LD PROGRAM STAFF

Total number of LD Program staff (including director):

Full Time: 1 Part Time: 1

Key staff person available to work with LD students: Paul White, Director of the Hayssen Academic Resource Center.

Lawrence University

Appleton, WI

Address: PO Box 599, Appleton, WI, 54912
Admissions telephone: 800 227-0982
Admissions FAX: 920 832-6782
Dean of Admissions and Financial Aid: Ken Anselment
Admissions e-mail: excel@lawrence.edu
Web site: http://www.lawrence.edu
SAT Code: 1398 ACT Code: 4596

LD program name: Student Academic Services
Dean of Student Academic Services: Martha K. Hemwall
LD program telephone: 920 832-6530
LD program e-mail: geoffrey.c.gajewski@lawrence.edu
LD program enrollment: 22, Total campus enrollment: 1,380

GENERAL

Lawrence University is a private, coed, four-year institution. 84-acre campus in Appleton (population: 68,000), 38 miles from Green Bay. Served by air and bus; major airport and train serve Milwaukee (100 miles). Public transportation serves campus. Trimester system.

LD ADMISSIONS

A personal interview is not required. Essay is required and may be typed.

SECONDARY SCHOOL REQUIREMENTS

Graduation from secondary school required; GED not accepted.

TESTING

SAT Reasoning or ACT considered if submitted. SAT Subject recommended.

All enrolled freshmen (fall 2004):

Average SAT I Scores:	Verbal: 643	Math: 637
Average ACT Scores:	Composite: 28	

Child Study Team report is not required. Tests required as part of this documentation:

- [ ] WAIS-IV
- [ ] WISC-IV
- [ ] SATA
- [ ] Woodcock-Johnson
- [ ] Nelson-Denny Reading Test
- [ ] Other

UNDERGRADUATE STUDENT BODY

Total undergraduate student enrollment: 606 Men, 717 Women.

Composition of student body (fall 2004):

	Undergraduate	Freshmen
International	9.4	9.2
Black	1.1	1.9
American Indian	0.0	0.1
Asian-American	3.1	2.6
Hispanic	1.7	3.1
White	77.0	73.7
Unreported	7.7	9.4
	100.0%	100.0%

58% are from out of state. 24% join a fraternity and 11% join a sorority. Average age of full-time undergraduates is 20. 70% of classes have fewer than 20 students, 28% have between 20 and 50 students, 2% have more than 50 students.

STUDENT HOUSING

99% of freshmen live in college housing. Freshmen are required to live on campus. Housing is guaranteed for all undergraduates. All students are required to live in campus housing unless they (a) are more than five years out of high school, (b) are married, and/or (c) have children. Campus can house 1,349 undergraduates. Single rooms are available for students with medical or special needs. A medical note is required.

EXPENSES

Tuition (2005-06): $27,714 per year.
Room: $2,769. Board: $3,265.
There is no additional cost for LD program/services.

LD SERVICES

LD program size is not limited.

LD services available to:

- [x] Freshmen
- [x] Sophomores
- [x] Juniors
- [x] Seniors

Academic Accommodations

Curriculum		In class	
Foreign language waiver	[x]	Early syllabus	[ ]
Lighter course load	[x]	Note takers in class	[x]
Math waiver	[x]	Priority seating	[ ]
Other special classes	[ ]	Tape recorders	[x]
Priority registrations	[ ]	Videotaped classes	[ ]
Substitution of courses	[ ]	Texts on tape	[ ]
Exams		**Services**	
Extended time	[x]	Diagnostic tests	[ ]
Oral exams	[x]	Learning centers	[x]
Take home exams	[ ]	Proofreaders	[ ]
Exams on tape or computer	[ ]	Readers	[x]
Untimed exams	[x]	Reading Machines/Kurzweil	[ ]
Other accommodations	[x]	Special bookstore section	[ ]
		Typists	[x]

Credit toward degree is not given for remedial courses taken.

Counseling Services

- [x] Academic
- [x] Psychological
- [ ] Student Support groups
- [ ] Vocational

Tutoring

Individual tutoring is available daily.

Average size of tutoring groups: 1

	Individual	Group
Time management	[x]	[ ]
Organizational skills	[x]	[ ]
Learning strategies	[x]	[ ]
Study skills	[x]	[ ]
Content area	[x]	[ ]
Writing lab	[x]	[ ]
Math lab	[x]	[ ]

UNIQUE LD PROGRAM FEATURES

Lawrence does not have a formal program, but offers a full array of services to students with learning differences. Accommodations are determined through meetings and discussions with the dean, faculty advisor and individual student.

LD PROGRAM STAFF

Total number of LD Program staff (including director):

Full Time: 2 Part Time: 2

There is an advisor/advocate from the LD program available to students. 80 peer tutors are available to work with LD students.

Key staff person available to work with LD students: Geoffrey Gajewski, Associate Dean of Student Academic Services.

LD Program web site: http://www.lawrence.edu/dept/student_acad/

Marian College of Fond du Lac

Fond du Lac, WI

Address: 45 S. National Avenue, Fond du Lac, WI, 54935
Admissions telephone: 800 2-MARIAN
Admissions FAX: 920 923-8755
Dean of Admission and Assistant Vice President of Enrollment: Eric Peterson
Admissions e-mail: admissions@mariancollege.edu
Web site: http://www.mariancollege.edu
SAT Code: 1443 ACT Code: 4606

Coordinator of Disability Services: Wendy Yurk
LD program telephone: 920 923-7162
LD program e-mail: wyurk@mariancollege.edu
Total campus enrollment: 1,999

GENERAL

Marian College of Fond du Lac is a private, coed, four-year institution. 97-acre campus in Fond du Lac (population: 42,203), 60 miles from Milwaukee; branch campuses in Milwaukee and Appleton. Served by bus; major airport and train serve Milwaukee; smaller airport serves Oshkosh (23 miles). Public transportation serves campus. Semester system.

LD ADMISSIONS

A personal interview is recommended. Essay is not required. Diagnosis of specific learning disability and supporting documentation required for services.

SECONDARY SCHOOL REQUIREMENTS

Graduation from secondary school required; GED accepted. The following course distribution required: 4 units of English, 2 units of math, 1 unit of science, 1 unit of history.

TESTING

ACT required; SAT Reasoning may be substituted. SAT Subject recommended.

All enrolled freshmen (fall 2004):

Average ACT Scores: Composite: 20

Child Study Team report is required if student is classified. Tests required as part of this documentation:

- ☐ WAIS-IV
- ☐ WISC-IV
- ☐ SATA
- ☐ Woodcock-Johnson
- ☐ Nelson-Denny Reading Test
- ☐ Other

UNDERGRADUATE STUDENT BODY

Total undergraduate student enrollment: 509 Men, 1,120 Women.

Composition of student body (fall 2004):

	Undergraduate	Freshmen
International	0.7	0.9
Black	7.4	5.0
American Indian	0.7	0.9
Asian-American	1.5	0.8
Hispanic	3.3	1.7
White	84.2	87.9
Unreported	2.2	2.8
	100.0%	100.0%

15% are from out of state. 13% join a fraternity and 11% join a sorority. Average age of full-time undergraduates is 22. 70% of classes have fewer than 20 students, 30% have between 20 and 50 students.

STUDENT HOUSING

74% of freshmen live in college housing. Freshmen are required to live on campus. Housing is guaranteed for all undergraduates. Campus can house 445 undergraduates.

EXPENSES

Tuition (2005-06): $16,380 per year.
Room: $3,350. Board: $1,720.
There is no additional cost for LD program/services.

LD SERVICES

LD program size is not limited.

LD services available to:

☑ Freshmen ☑ Sophomores ☑ Juniors ☑ Seniors

Academic Accommodations

Curriculum		**In class**	
Foreign language waiver	☐	Early syllabus	☐
Lighter course load	☐	Note takers in class	☑
Math waiver	☐	Priority seating	☐
Other special classes	☑	Tape recorders	☑
Priority registrations	☐	Videotaped classes	☐
Substitution of courses	☐	Texts on tape	☐
Exams		**Services**	
Extended time	☑	Diagnostic tests	☐
Oral exams	☑	Learning centers	☑
Take home exams	☐	Proofreaders	☐
Exams on tape or computer	☐	Readers	☑
Untimed exams	☐	Reading Machines/Kurzweil	☑
Other accommodations	☐	Special bookstore section	☐
		Typists	☐

Credit toward degree is not given for remedial courses taken.

Counseling Services

- ☐ Academic
- ☐ Psychological
- ☐ Student Support groups
- ☐ Vocational

Tutoring

	Individual	Group
Time management	☐	☐
Organizational skills	☐	☐
Learning strategies	☐	☐
Study skills	☐	☐
Content area	☐	☐
Writing lab	☐	☐
Math lab	☐	☐

LD PROGRAM STAFF

Key staff person available to work with LD students: Wendy Yurk, Coordinator of Disability Services.

Marquette University

Milwaukee, WI

Address: PO Box 1881, Milwaukee, WI, 53201-1881
Admissions telephone: 800 222-6544
Admissions FAX: 414 288-3764
Dean of Undergraduate Admissions: Robert (Roby) Blust
Admissions e-mail: admissions@marquette.edu
Web site: http://www.marquette.edu
SAT Code: 1448 ACT Code: 4610

Coordinator, Office of Disability Services: Patricia Almon
LD program telephone: 414 288-1645
LD program e-mail: patricia.almon@marquette.edu
LD program enrollment: 90, Total campus enrollment: 7,923

GENERAL

Marquette University is a private, coed, four-year institution. 80-acre, urban campus in Milwaukee (population: 596,974); branch campuses in Kenosha and Waukesha. Served by air, bus, and train. School operates transportation on campus and in local area. Public transportation serves campus. Semester system.

LD ADMISSIONS

A personal interview is not required. Essay is not required. Course waivers will be determined on a case-by-case basis after the student has been accepted.

SECONDARY SCHOOL REQUIREMENTS

Graduation from secondary school required; GED accepted. The following course distribution required: 4 units of English, 2 units of math, 2 units of science, 2 units of foreign language, 2 units of social studies, 2 units of academic electives.

TESTING

SAT Reasoning or ACT required. SAT Subject recommended.

All enrolled freshmen (fall 2004):

Average SAT I Scores:	Verbal: 587	Math: 591
Average ACT Scores:	Composite: 26	

Child Study Team report is not required. Tests required as part of this documentation:

☐ WAIS-IV ☐ Woodcock-Johnson
☐ WISC-IV ☐ Nelson-Denny Reading Test
☐ SATA ☐ Other

UNDERGRADUATE STUDENT BODY

Total undergraduate student enrollment: 3,340 Men, 4,159 Women.

Composition of student body (fall 2004):

	Undergraduate	Freshmen
International	2.6	2.0
Black	3.3	4.6
American Indian	0.4	0.3
Asian-American	3.9	4.1
Hispanic	4.0	4.1
White	85.7	84.6
Unreported	0.1	0.3
	100.0%	100.0%

52% are from out of state. 5% join a fraternity and 9% join a sorority. Average age of full-time undergraduates is 20. 36% of classes have fewer than 20 students, 53% have between 20 and 50 students, 11% have more than 50 students.

STUDENT HOUSING

93% of freshmen live in college housing. Freshmen are required to live on campus. Housing is guaranteed for all undergraduates. Campus can house 4,738 undergraduates. Single rooms are available for students with medical or special needs. A medical note is required.

EXPENSES

Tuition (2005-06): $22,950 per year.

Room: $4,850. Board: $2,870.

There is no additional cost for LD program/services.

LD SERVICES

LD program size is not limited.

LD services available to:

■ Freshmen ■ Sophomores ■ Juniors ■ Seniors

Academic Accommodations

Curriculum		**In class**	
Foreign language waiver	■	Early syllabus	☐
Lighter course load	■	Note takers in class	■
Math waiver	☐	Priority seating	☐
Other special classes	☐	Tape recorders	■
Priority registrations	■	Videotaped classes	☐
Substitution of courses	■	Texts on tape	■
Exams		**Services**	
Extended time	■	Diagnostic tests	■
Oral exams	■	Learning centers	☐
Take home exams	☐	Proofreaders	☐
Exams on tape or computer	■	Readers	☐
Untimed exams	☐	Reading Machines/Kurzweil	■
Other accommodations	☐	Special bookstore section	☐
		Typists	☐

Credit toward degree is not given for remedial courses taken.

Counseling Services

■ Academic — Meets 4 times per academic year
■ Psychological — Meets 10 times per academic year
☐ Student Support groups
☐ Vocational

Tutoring

Individual tutoring is not available.

Average size of tutoring groups: 6

	Individual	Group
Time management	■	☐
Organizational skills	■	☐
Learning strategies	■	☐
Study skills	■	☐
Content area	☐	■
Writing lab	■	☐
Math lab	☐	☐

UNIQUE LD PROGRAM FEATURES

Marquette has no specific LD program. Marquette's Office of Disability Services is responsible for providing appropriate accommodations for all students with disabilities who qualify for admission to the University.

LD PROGRAM STAFF

Total number of LD Program staff (including director):

Full Time: 1 Part Time: 1

There is no advisor/advocate from the LD program available to students. 2 graduate students and 37 peer tutors are available to work with LD students.

Key staff person available to work with LD students: Patricia Almon, Coordinator, Office of Disability Services.

Milwaukee Institute of Art and Design

Milwaukee, WI

Address: 273 E. Erie Street, Milwaukee, WI, 53202
Admissions telephone: 888 749-MIAD
Admissions FAX: 414 291-8077
Director of Admissions Counseling: Mark Fetherston
Admissions e-mail: admissions@miad.edu
Web site: http://www.miad.edu
SAT Code: 1506 ACT Code: 4701

Total campus enrollment: 636

GENERAL

Milwaukee Institute of Art and Design is a private, coed, four-year institution. 295,000 square-foot, urban campus in Milwaukee (population: 596,974). Served by air, bus, and train. Public transportation serves campus. Semester system.

SECONDARY SCHOOL REQUIREMENTS

Graduation from secondary school required; GED accepted.

TESTING

All enrolled freshmen (fall 2004):

Child Study Team report is not required. Tests required as part of this documentation:

- ❑ WAIS-IV
- ❑ WISC-IV
- ❑ SATA
- ❑ Woodcock-Johnson
- ❑ Nelson-Denny Reading Test
- ❑ Other

UNDERGRADUATE STUDENT BODY

Total undergraduate student enrollment: 323 Men, 327 Women.

Composition of student body (fall 2004):

	Undergraduate	Freshmen
International	1.4	4.4
Black	3.5	3.5
American Indian	0.0	0.6
Asian-American	1.4	3.3
Hispanic	7.7	6.8
White	86.0	81.4
Unreported	0.0	0.0
	100.0%	100.0%

28% are from out of state. Average age of full-time undergraduates is 22. 86% of classes have fewer than 20 students, 14% have between 20 and 50 students.

STUDENT HOUSING

69% of freshmen live in college housing. Housing is guaranteed for all undergraduates. Campus can house 150 undergraduates.

EXPENSES

Tuition (2005-06): $22,200 per year.
Room & Board: $6,800
There is no additional cost for LD program/services.

LD SERVICES

LD program size is not limited.

LD services available to:

❑ Freshmen ❑ Sophomores ❑ Juniors ❑ Seniors

Academic Accommodations

Curriculum		In class	
Foreign language waiver	❑	Early syllabus	❑
Lighter course load	❑	Note takers in class	❑
Math waiver	❑	Priority seating	❑
Other special classes	❑	Tape recorders	❑
Priority registrations	❑	Videotaped classes	❑
Substitution of courses	❑	Texts on tape	❑
Exams		**Services**	
Extended time	■	Diagnostic tests	❑
Oral exams	■	Learning centers	■
Take home exams	❑	Proofreaders	❑
Exams on tape or computer	❑	Readers	❑
Untimed exams	❑	Reading Machines/Kurzweil	❑
Other accommodations	❑	Special bookstore section	❑
		Typists	❑

Credit toward degree is not given for remedial courses taken.

Counseling Services

- ❑ Academic
- ❑ Psychological
- ❑ Student Support groups
- ❑ Vocational

Tutoring

	Individual	Group
Time management	❑	❑
Organizational skills	❑	❑
Learning strategies	❑	❑
Study skills	❑	❑
Content area	❑	❑
Writing lab	❑	❑
Math lab	❑	❑

LD PROGRAM STAFF

Key staff person available to work with LD students: Jennifer Crandall, Exec. Director of Academic Resources.

Milwaukee School of Engineering

Milwaukee, WI

Address: 1025 N. Broadway, Milwaukee, WI, 53202-3109
Admissions telephone: 800 332-6763
Admissions FAX: 414 277-7475
Dean of Enrollment Management: Mr. Paul Borens
Admissions e-mail: explore@msoe.edu
Web site: http://www.msoe.edu
SAT Code: 1476 ACT Code: 4616

Coordinator of Services for Students with Disabilities: Ms. Christine Bergan
LD program telephone: 414 277-7281
LD program e-mail: bergan@msoe.edu
LD program enrollment: 31, Total campus enrollment: 2,363

GENERAL

Milwaukee School of Engineering is a private, coed, four-year institution. 14-acre, urban campus in Milwaukee (population: 596,974). Served by air, bus, and train. School operates transportation within a three-mile radius of campus and to airport and bus and train stations. Public transportation serves campus. Quarter system.

LD ADMISSIONS

Students do not complete a separate application and are not simultaneously accepted to the LD program. A member of the LD program does not sit on the admissions committee. A personal interview is not required. Essay is not required.

SECONDARY SCHOOL REQUIREMENTS

Graduation from secondary school required; GED accepted. The following course distribution required: 4 units of English, 4 units of math, 2 units of science.

TESTING

SAT Reasoning or ACT required. SAT Subject recommended.

All enrolled freshmen (fall 2004):

Average SAT I Scores:	Verbal: 585	Math: 623
Average ACT Scores:	Composite: 25	

Child Study Team report is not required. A neuropsychological or comprehensive psycho-education evaluation is not required for admission. Tests required as part of this documentation:

- ☐ WAIS-IV
- ☐ WISC-IV
- ☐ SATA
- ☐ Woodcock-Johnson
- ☐ Nelson-Denny Reading Test
- ☐ Other

UNDERGRADUATE STUDENT BODY

Total undergraduate student enrollment: 1,900 Men, 346 Women.

Composition of student body (fall 2004):

	Undergraduate	Freshmen
International	0.9	2.2
Black	4.2	2.9
American Indian	0.9	0.6
Asian-American	2.9	3.0
Hispanic	2.4	2.3
White	73.4	81.1
Unreported	15.3	7.9
	100.0%	100.0%

25% are from out of state. 9% join a fraternity and 13% join a sorority. Average age of full-time undergraduates is 22. 45% of classes have fewer than 20 students, 55% have between 20 and 50 students.

STUDENT HOUSING

83% of freshmen live in college housing. Freshmen are required to live on campus. Housing is guaranteed for all undergraduates. Single rooms are available for students with medical or special needs. A medical note is not required.

EXPENSES

Tuition (2005-06): $23,955 per year.
Room: $3,780. Board: $2,112.
There is no additional cost for LD program/services.

LD SERVICES

LD program size is not limited.

LD services available to:

■ Freshmen ■ Sophomores ■ Juniors ■ Seniors

Academic Accommodations

Curriculum		In class	
Foreign language waiver	☐	Early syllabus	■
Lighter course load	☐	Note takers in class	■
Math waiver	☐	Priority seating	■
Other special classes	☐	Tape recorders	■
Priority registrations	■	Videotaped classes	☐
Substitution of courses	☐	Texts on tape	■
Exams		**Services**	
Extended time	■	Diagnostic tests	■
Oral exams	■	Learning centers	■
Take home exams	■	Proofreaders	■
Exams on tape or computer	■	Readers	■
Untimed exams	■	Reading Machines/Kurzweil	☐
Other accommodations	■	Special bookstore section	☐
		Typists	■

Credit toward degree is given for remedial courses taken.

Counseling Services

■	Academic	Meets 30 times per academic year
■	Psychological	Meets 15 times per academic year
☐	Student Support groups	
☐	Vocational	

Tutoring

Individual tutoring is available daily.

Average size of tutoring groups: 5

	Individual	Group
Time management	■	■
Organizational skills	■	■
Learning strategies	■	■
Study skills	■	■
Content area	■	■
Writing lab	■	■
Math lab	■	■

UNIQUE LD PROGRAM FEATURES

Services/facilities for the physically disabled include wheelchair accessibility. Services and/or facilities available for the visually impaired, hearing impaired, and for those with speech or communication disorders.

LD PROGRAM STAFF

Total number of LD Program staff (including director):

Full Time: 4 Part Time: 4

There is an advisor/advocate from the LD program available to students. The advisor/advocate meets with faculty 10 times per month and students 20 times per month. 5 peer tutors are available to work with LD students.

Mount Mary College

Milwaukee, WI

Address: 2900 N. Menomonee River Parkway, Milwaukee, WI, 53222
Admissions telephone: 800 321-6265
Admissions FAX: 414 256-0180
Admissions e-mail: admiss@mtmary.edu
Web site: http://www.mtmary.edu
SAT Code: 1490 ACT Code: 4620

LD program name: Office of Disability Services
Director of Academic Services: Marci Ocker
LD program telephone: 4142584810324
LD program e-mail: ockerm@mtmary.edu
Total campus enrollment: 1,404

GENERAL

Mount Mary College is a private, women's, four-year institution. 80-acre, suburban campus in Milwaukee (population: 596,974). Served by air, bus, and train. Public transportation serves campus. Semester system.

LD ADMISSIONS

Students do not complete a separate application and are not simultaneously accepted to the LD program. A member of the LD program does not sit on the admissions committee. A personal interview is required. Essay is not required.

SECONDARY SCHOOL REQUIREMENTS

Graduation from secondary school required; GED accepted. The following course distribution required: 4 units of English, 2 units of math, 2 units of science, 2 units of social studies, 2 units of history, 2 units of academic electives.

TESTING

SAT Reasoning or ACT required. SAT Subject recommended.

All enrolled freshmen (fall 2004):

Average SAT I Scores:	Verbal: 465	Math: 507
Average ACT Scores:	Composite: 20	

Child Study Team report is not required. A neuropsychological or comprehensive psycho-educational evaluation is required for admission. Must be dated within 12 months of application. Tests required as part of this documentation:

- [ ] WAIS-IV
- [ ] WISC-IV
- [ ] SATA
- [ ] Woodcock-Johnson
- [ ] Nelson-Denny Reading Test
- [x] Other

UNDERGRADUATE STUDENT BODY

Total undergraduate student enrollment: 41 Men, 1,039 Women.

Composition of student body (fall 2004):

	Undergraduate	Freshmen
International	2.2	0.7
Black	23.2	16.2
American Indian	2.9	1.0
Asian-American	2.2	3.4
Hispanic	8.7	4.5
White	60.8	71.9
Unreported	0.0	2.3
	100.0%	100.0%

5% are from out of state. Average age of full-time undergraduates is 24. 86% of classes have fewer than 20 students, 13% have between 20 and 50 students, 1% have more than 50 students.

STUDENT HOUSING

35% of freshmen live in college housing. Freshmen are required to live on campus. Housing is guaranteed for all undergraduates. Campus can house 200 undergraduates. Single rooms are available for students with medical or special needs. A medical note is not required.

EXPENSES

Tuition (2005-06): $16,925 per year.
Room & Board: $5,700
There is no additional cost for LD program/services.

LD SERVICES

LD program size is not limited.

LD services available to:

- [x] Freshmen
- [x] Sophomores
- [x] Juniors
- [x] Seniors

Academic Accommodations

Curriculum		In class	
Foreign language waiver	[ ]	Early syllabus	[ ]
Lighter course load	[ ]	Note takers in class	[x]
Math waiver	[ ]	Priority seating	[ ]
Other special classes	[x]	Tape recorders	[x]
Priority registrations	[ ]	Videotaped classes	[ ]
Substitution of courses	[ ]	Texts on tape	[x]
Exams		**Services**	
Extended time	[x]	Diagnostic tests	[ ]
Oral exams	[x]	Learning centers	[x]
Take home exams	[x]	Proofreaders	[x]
Exams on tape or computer	[x]	Readers	[x]
Untimed exams	[x]	Reading Machines/Kurzweil	[x]
Other accommodations	[x]	Special bookstore section	[ ]
		Typists	[ ]

Credit toward degree is not given for remedial courses taken.

Counseling Services

- [x] Academic
- [ ] Psychological
- [ ] Student Support groups
- [ ] Vocational

Tutoring

Individual tutoring is available daily.

	Individual	Group
Time management	[x]	[ ]
Organizational skills	[x]	[ ]
Learning strategies	[x]	[ ]
Study skills	[x]	[ ]
Content area	[x]	[ ]
Writing lab	[x]	[ ]
Math lab	[x]	[ ]

LD PROGRAM STAFF

Total number of LD Program staff (including director):

Full Time: 2 Part Time: 2

There is an advisor/advocate from the LD program available to students.

Key staff person available to work with LD students: Marci Ocker, Director of Disability Services.

Northland College

Ashland, WI

Address: 1411 Ellis Avenue, Ashland, WI, 54806
Admissions telephone: 800 753-1840
Admissions FAX: 715 682-1258
Director of Admission: Jason Turley
Admissions e-mail: admit@northland.edu
Web site: http://www.northland.edu
SAT Code: 1561 ACT Code: 4624

LD program name: Campus Health Center
Campus Nurse: Judi Holevatz
LD program telephone: 715 682-1230
LD program e-mail: jholevatz@northland.edu
Total campus enrollment: 719

GENERAL

Northland College is a private, coed, four-year institution. 130-acre campus in Ashland (population: 8,620), 75 miles from Duluth, Minn. Served by bus; airports serve Ironwood, Mich. (45 miles) and Duluth. Public transportation serves campus. 4-1-4 system.

LD ADMISSIONS

A personal interview is recommended. Essay is required and may be typed.

SECONDARY SCHOOL REQUIREMENTS

Graduation from secondary school required; GED accepted. The following course distribution required: 3 units of English, 3 units of math, 3 units of science, 3 units of social studies, 3 units of history, 3 units of academic electives.

TESTING

SAT Reasoning or ACT required. SAT Subject recommended.

All enrolled freshmen (fall 2004):

Average SAT I Scores:	Verbal: 550	Math: 540
Average ACT Scores:	Composite: 24	

Child Study Team report is not required. Tests required as part of this documentation:

- ☐ WAIS-IV
- ☐ WISC-IV
- ☐ SATA
- ☐ Woodcock-Johnson
- ☐ Nelson-Denny Reading Test
- ☐ Other

UNDERGRADUATE STUDENT BODY

Total undergraduate student enrollment: 338 Men, 463 Women.

Composition of student body (fall 2004):

	Undergraduate	Freshmen
International	1.6	2.4
Black	1.6	1.4
American Indian	3.2	2.8
Asian-American	1.6	0.8
Hispanic	0.8	1.8
White	87.3	87.9
Unreported	4.0	2.9
	100.0%	100.0%

76% are from out of state. Average age of full-time undergraduates is 22. 71% of classes have fewer than 20 students, 29% have between 20 and 50 students.

STUDENT HOUSING

99% of freshmen live in college housing. Freshmen are required to live on campus. Housing is guaranteed for all undergraduates. Campus can house 560 undergraduates. Single rooms are available for students with medical or special needs. A medical note is required.

EXPENSES

Tuition (2005-06): $19,135 per year.
Room: $2,270. Board: $3,340.
There is no additional cost for LD program/services.

LD SERVICES

LD program size is not limited.

LD services available to:

☐ Freshmen ☐ Sophomores ☐ Juniors ☐ Seniors

Academic Accommodations

Curriculum		**In class**	
Foreign language waiver	☐	Early syllabus	■
Lighter course load	☐	Note takers in class	■
Math waiver	☐	Priority seating	☐
Other special classes	☐	Tape recorders	■
Priority registrations	☐	Videotaped classes	☐
Substitution of courses	☐	Texts on tape	☐
Exams		**Services**	
Extended time	■	Diagnostic tests	☐
Oral exams	■	Learning centers	☐
Take home exams	☐	Proofreaders	■
Exams on tape or computer	☐	Readers	■
Untimed exams	☐	Reading Machines/Kurzweil	☐
Other accommodations	☐	Special bookstore section	☐
		Typists	■

Credit toward degree is given for remedial courses taken.

Counseling Services

- ☐ Academic
- ☐ Psychological
- ☐ Student Support groups
- ☐ Vocational

Tutoring

Individual tutoring is available daily.

Average size of tutoring groups: 2

	Individual	Group
Time management	■	☐
Organizational skills	■	☐
Learning strategies	■	☐
Study skills	■	☐
Content area	■	☐
Writing lab	☐	☐
Math lab	■	☐

UNIQUE LD PROGRAM FEATURES

Each individual student and their need is considered on campus. The LD program, however, is minimal.

LD PROGRAM STAFF

Total number of LD Program staff (including director):

Full Time: 1 Part Time: 1

There is an advisor/advocate from the LD program available to students. The advisor/advocate meets with faculty once per month and students once per month.

Key staff person available to work with LD students: Judi Holevatz, Campus Nurse.

Ripon College

Ripon, WI

Address: 300 Seward Street, Ripon, WI, 54971-0248
Admissions telephone: 800 94-RIPON
Admissions FAX: 920 748-8335
Vice President and Dean of Admission and Financial Aid: Brooke Konopacki
Admissions e-mail: adminfo@ripon.edu
Web site: http://www.ripon.edu
SAT Code: 1664   ACT Code: 4336

LD program name: Student Support Services
Director, Student Support Services: Dan Krhin
LD program telephone: 920 748-8107
LD program e-mail: krhind@ripon.edu
LD program enrollment: 21, Total campus enrollment: 927

GENERAL

Ripon College is a private, coed, four-year institution. 250-acre campus in Ripon (population: 6,828), 80 miles from Milwaukee. Major airport serves Milwaukee; smaller airports serve Appleton (40 miles) and Oshkosh (18 miles); bus serves Fond du Lac (20 miles). School operates transportation to Appleton, Milwaukee, and Oshkosh. Semester system.

LD ADMISSIONS

Students do not complete a separate application and are simultaneously accepted to the LD program. A member of the LD program does not sit on the admissions committee. High school waivers are accepted for foreign language. A personal interview is recommended. Essay is required and may be typed. Admissions requirements may be waived for LD students on a case-by-case basis.

For fall 2004, 20 completed self-identified LD applications were received.

SECONDARY SCHOOL REQUIREMENTS

Graduation from secondary school required; GED accepted. The following course distribution required: 4 units of English, 2 units of math, 2 units of science, 2 units of social studies.

TESTING

SAT Reasoning or ACT required. SAT Subject recommended.

All enrolled freshmen (fall 2004):

Average SAT I Scores:	Verbal: 550	Math: 535
Average ACT Scores:	Composite: 23	

Child Study Team report is not required. A neuropsychological or comprehensive psycho-educational evaluation is required for admission. Must be dated within 48 months of application. Tests required as part of this documentation:

☐ WAIS-IV	■ Woodcock-Johnson
☐ WISC-IV	☐ Nelson-Denny Reading Test
☐ SATA	■ Other

UNDERGRADUATE STUDENT BODY

Total undergraduate student enrollment: 423 Men, 478 Women.

Composition of student body (fall 2004):

	Undergraduate	Freshmen
International	1.0	1.5
Black	4.5	2.5
American Indian	2.0	1.0
Asian-American	3.0	2.1
Hispanic	1.0	3.1
White	81.6	86.3
Unreported	6.9	3.5
	100.0%	100.0%

34% are from out of state. 35% join a fraternity and 23% join a sorority. Average age of full-time undergraduates is 20. 62% of classes have fewer than 20 students, 36% have between 20 and 50 students, 2% have more than 50 students.

STUDENT HOUSING

99% of freshmen live in college housing. Freshmen are required to live on campus. Housing is guaranteed for all undergraduates. Campus can house 944 undergraduates. Single rooms are available for students with medical or special needs. A medical note is required.

EXPENSES

Tuition (2005-06): $21,310 per year.

Room: $2,680. Board: $2,930.
There is no additional cost for LD program/services.

LD SERVICES

LD program size is not limited.

LD services available to:

■ Freshmen   ■ Sophomores   ■ Juniors   ■ Seniors

Academic Accommodations

Curriculum		**In class**	
Foreign language waiver	☐	Early syllabus	☐
Lighter course load	☐	Note takers in class	■
Math waiver	☐	Priority seating	☐
Other special classes	☐	Tape recorders	■
Priority registrations	☐	Videotaped classes	☐
Substitution of courses	☐	Texts on tape	■
Exams		**Services**	
Extended time	■	Diagnostic tests	☐
Oral exams	■	Learning centers	☐
Take home exams	☐	Proofreaders	■
Exams on tape or computer	■	Readers	■
Untimed exams	■	Reading Machines/Kurzweil	☐
Other accommodations	☐	Special bookstore section	☐
		Typists	☐

Credit toward degree is not given for remedial courses taken.

Counseling Services

■ Academic	Meets 3 times per academic year
☐ Psychological	
☐ Student Support groups	
■ Vocational	Meets 2 times per academic year

Tutoring

Individual tutoring is available weekly.

Average size of tutoring groups: 1

	Individual	Group
Time management	■	☐
Organizational skills	■	☐
Learning strategies	■	☐
Study skills	■	☐
Content area	■	☐
Writing lab	■	☐
Math lab	☐	☐

UNIQUE LD PROGRAM FEATURES

Proactive and motivated support staff.

LD PROGRAM STAFF

Total number of LD Program staff (including director):

Full Time: 3   Part Time: 3

There is an advisor/advocate from the LD program available to students. The advisor/advocate meets with students 3 times per month. 20 peer tutors are available to work with LD students.

Key staff person available to work with LD students: Dan Krhin, Director, Student Support Services.

St. Norbert College

De Pere, WI

Address: 100 Grant Street, De Pere, WI, 54115-2099
Admissions telephone: 800 236-4878
Admissions FAX: 920 403-4072
Dean of Admission and Enrollment Management: Dan Meyer
Admissions e-mail: admit@snc.edu
Web site: http://www.snc.edu
SAT Code: 1706 ACT Code: 4644

Director of Academic Support Services:
Karen Goode-Bartholomew
LD program telephone: 920 403-1326
LD program e-mail: karen.goode-bartholomew@snc.edu
LD program enrollment: 39, Total campus enrollment: 2,020

GENERAL

St. Norbert College is a private, coed, four-year institution. 87-acre, suburban campus in DePere (population: 20,559), five miles from Green Bay. Airport and bus serve Green Bay. Public transportation serves campus. Semester system.

LD ADMISSIONS

High school waivers are accepted for foreign language. A personal interview is not required. Essay is required and may be typed.

SECONDARY SCHOOL REQUIREMENTS

Graduation from secondary school required; GED accepted.

TESTING

SAT Reasoning or ACT required. SAT Subject recommended.

All enrolled freshmen (fall 2004):

Average ACT Scores: Composite: 24

Child Study Team report is not required. Tests required as part of this documentation:

- [ ] WAIS-IV
- [ ] WISC-IV
- [ ] SATA
- [ ] Woodcock-Johnson
- [ ] Nelson-Denny Reading Test
- [ ] Other

UNDERGRADUATE STUDENT BODY

Total undergraduate student enrollment: 878 Men, 1,181 Women.

Composition of student body (fall 2004):

	Undergraduate	Freshmen
International	2.1	2.3
Black	1.5	0.9
American Indian	1.1	1.0
Asian-American	1.7	1.3
Hispanic	1.9	1.5
White	85.6	90.4
Unreported	6.1	2.6
	100.0%	100.0%

28% are from out of state. 7% join a fraternity and 10% join a sorority. Average age of full-time undergraduates is 21. 52% of classes have fewer than 20 students, 48% have between 20 and 50 students.

STUDENT HOUSING

96% of freshmen live in college housing. Freshmen are required to live on campus. Housing is guaranteed for all undergraduates. Campus can house 1,525 undergraduates. Single rooms are available for students with medical or special needs. A medical note is required.

EXPENSES

Tuition (2005-06): $22,209 per year.
Room: $3,212. Board: $2,856.
There is no additional cost for LD program/services.

LD SERVICES

LD program size is not limited.

LD services available to:

- [x] Freshmen
- [x] Sophomores
- [x] Juniors
- [x] Seniors

Academic Accommodations

Curriculum

- [ ] Foreign language waiver
- [x] Lighter course load
- [ ] Math waiver
- [ ] Other special classes
- [x] Priority registrations
- [x] Substitution of courses

Exams

- [x] Extended time
- [ ] Oral exams
- [ ] Take home exams
- [ ] Exams on tape or computer
- [ ] Untimed exams
- [x] Other accommodations

In class

- [ ] Early syllabus
- [x] Note takers in class
- [x] Priority seating
- [x] Tape recorders
- [ ] Videotaped classes
- [x] Texts on tape

Services

- [ ] Diagnostic tests
- [x] Learning centers
- [ ] Proofreaders
- [x] Readers
- [ ] Reading Machines/Kurzweil
- [ ] Special bookstore section
- [x] Typists

Credit toward degree is given for remedial courses taken.

Counseling Services

- [x] Academic
- [x] Psychological
- [ ] Student Support groups
- [x] Vocational

Tutoring

Individual tutoring is available weekly.

Average size of tutoring groups: 3

	Individual	Group
Time management	[x]	[x]
Organizational skills	[x]	[x]
Learning strategies	[x]	[x]
Study skills	[x]	[x]
Content area	[x]	[x]
Writing lab	[x]	[x]
Math lab	[x]	[x]

LD PROGRAM STAFF

Total number of LD Program staff (including director):

Full Time: 2 Part Time: 2

50 peer tutors are available to work with LD students.

Key staff person available to work with LD students: Karen Goode-Bartholomew, Director of Academic Support Services.

Silver Lake College

Manitowoc, WI

Address: 2406 S. Alverno Road, Manitowoc, WI, 54220
Admissions telephone: 800 236-4752, extension 175
Admissions FAX: 920 684-7082
Vice President and Dean of Students: Jan Algozine
Admissions e-mail: admslc@silver.sl.edu
Web site: http://www.sl.edu
SAT Code: 1300 ACT Code: 4586

Vice-President and Academic Dean: George Grinde
LD program telephone: 920 686-6125
LD program e-mail: ggrinde@silver.sl.edu
Total campus enrollment: 756

GENERAL

Silver Lake College is a private, coed, four-year institution. 30-acre campus in Manitowoc (population: 34,053), 38 miles from Green Bay and 75 miles from Milwaukee; branch campuses in Appleton, Fond du Lac, Green Bay, Madison, Marinette, Milwaukee, Rhinelander, and Wausau. Served by bus; airport serves Green Bay. School operates transportation to off-campus student housing. Semester system.

LD ADMISSIONS

A personal interview is required.

SECONDARY SCHOOL REQUIREMENTS

Graduation from secondary school required; GED accepted. The following course distribution required: 3 units of English, 2 units of math, 1 unit of science, 1 unit of social studies, 1 unit of history, 7 units of academic electives.

TESTING

ACT required of some applicants.

All enrolled freshmen (fall 2004):

Average ACT Scores: Composite: 20

Child Study Team report is not required. Tests required as part of this documentation:

- ☐ WAIS-IV
- ☐ WISC-IV
- ☐ SATA
- ☐ Woodcock-Johnson
- ☐ Nelson-Denny Reading Test
- ☐ Other

UNDERGRADUATE STUDENT BODY

Total undergraduate student enrollment: 183 Men, 480 Women.

Composition of student body (fall 2004):

	Undergraduate	Freshmen
International	3.6	0.2
Black	0.0	0.4
American Indian	0.0	4.8
Asian-American	0.0	1.0
Hispanic	0.0	0.6
White	96.4	93.0
Unreported	0.0	0.0
	100.0%	100.0%

2% are from out of state. Average age of full-time undergraduates is 27. 93% of classes have fewer than 20 students, 7% have between 20 and 50 students.

STUDENT HOUSING

67% of freshmen live in college housing. Housing is guaranteed for all undergraduates.

EXPENSES

Tuition (2005-06): $16,000 per year.

Room: $4,250. Board: $1,800.
There is no additional cost for LD program/services.

LD SERVICES

LD program size is not limited.

LD services available to:

☐ Freshmen ☐ Sophomores ☐ Juniors ☐ Seniors

Academic Accommodations

Curriculum		**In class**	
Foreign language waiver	☐	Early syllabus	☐
Lighter course load	☑	Note takers in class	☑
Math waiver	☐	Priority seating	☐
Other special classes	☐	Tape recorders	☐
Priority registrations	☐	Videotaped classes	☐
Substitution of courses	☐	Texts on tape	☐
Exams		**Services**	
Extended time	☐	Diagnostic tests	☐
Oral exams	☑	Learning centers	☐
Take home exams	☐	Proofreaders	☐
Exams on tape or computer	☐	Readers	☑
Untimed exams	☐	Reading Machines/Kurzweil	☐
Other accommodations	☐	Special bookstore section	☐
		Typists	☐

Credit toward degree is not given for remedial courses taken.

Counseling Services

- ☐ Academic
- ☐ Psychological
- ☐ Student Support groups
- ☐ Vocational

Tutoring

	Individual	Group
Time management	☐	☐
Organizational skills	☐	☐
Learning strategies	☐	☐
Study skills	☐	☐
Content area	☐	☐
Writing lab	☐	☐
Math lab	☐	☐

LD PROGRAM STAFF

Total number of LD Program staff (including director):

Full Time: 1 Part Time: 1

Key staff person available to work with LD students: Carol O'Rourke, Director of Learning Resource Center.

Viterbo University

La Crosse, WI

Address: 900 Viterbo Drive, La Crosse, WI, 54601
Admissions telephone: 800 VITERBO
Admissions FAX: 608 796-3020
Vice President of Enrollment: Roland Nelson
Admissions e-mail: admission@viterbo.edu
Web site: http://www.viterbo.edu
SAT Code: 1878 ACT Code: 4662

LD program name: Learning Center
ADA Coordinator: Wayne Wojciechowski
LD program telephone: 608 796-3085
LD program e-mail: wawojciechowski@viterbo.edu
LD program enrollment: 42, Total campus enrollment: 1,922

GENERAL

Viterbo University is a private, coed, four-year institution. 21-acre campus in LaCrosse (population: 51,818), 150 miles from Minneapolis-St. Paul. Served by air, bus, and train; major airport serves Minneapolis-St. Paul. School operates transportation to outdoor athletic complex. Public transportation serves campus. Semester system.

LD ADMISSIONS

Application Deadline: 12/15. Students do not complete a separate application and are simultaneously accepted to the LD program. A member of the LD program does sit on the admissions committee. A personal interview is recommended. Essay is not required. Admissions requirements that may be waived for LD students include low secondary school class rank and low ACT scores.

For fall 2004, 10 completed self-identified LD applications were received. 10 applications were offered admission, and 10 enrolled.

SECONDARY SCHOOL REQUIREMENTS

Graduation from secondary school required; GED accepted. The following course distribution required: 3 units of English, 2 units of math, 2 units of science, 2 units of social studies, 5 units of academic electives.

SAT Reasoning or ACT considered if submitted; ACT preferred.

All enrolled freshmen (fall 2004):

Average ACT Scores: Composite: 22

Child Study Team report is not required. A neuropsychological or comprehensive psycho-educational evaluation is required for admission. Must be dated within 36 months of application. Tests required as part of this documentation:

- ■ WAIS-IV
- ■ WISC-IV
- ■ SATA
- ■ Woodcock-Johnson
- ■ Nelson-Denny Reading Test
- □ Other

UNDERGRADUATE STUDENT BODY

Total undergraduate student enrollment: 448 Men, 1,266 Women.

Composition of student body (fall 2004):

	Undergraduate	Freshmen
International	2.2	1.3
Black	1.3	1.2
American Indian	0.3	0.3
Asian-American	1.3	1.6
Hispanic	0.6	1.0
White	92.1	92.0
Unreported	2.2	2.6
	100.0%	100.0%

24% are from out of state. Average age of full-time undergraduates is 22. 63% of classes have fewer than 20 students, 35% have between 20 and 50 students, 2% have more than 50 students.

STUDENT HOUSING

79% of freshmen live in college housing. Freshmen are required to live on campus. Housing is guaranteed for all undergraduates. Campus can house 561 undergraduates. Single rooms are not available for students with medical or special needs.

EXPENSES

Tuition (2005-06): $16,240 per year.

Room: $2,340. Board: $3,090.

There is no additional cost for LD program/services.

LD SERVICES

LD program size is not limited.

LD services available to:

■ Freshmen ■ Sophomores ■ Juniors ■ Seniors

Academic Accommodations

Curriculum		In class	
Foreign language waiver	■	Early syllabus	■
Lighter course load	■	Note takers in class	■
Math waiver	□	Priority seating	■
Other special classes	■	Tape recorders	■
Priority registrations	■	Videotaped classes	□
Substitution of courses	■	Texts on tape	■
Exams		**Services**	
Extended time	■	Diagnostic tests	□
Oral exams	■	Learning centers	■
Take home exams	□	Proofreaders	■
Exams on tape or computer	■	Readers	■
Untimed exams	■	Reading Machines/Kurzweil	■
Other accommodations	■	Special bookstore section	□
		Typists	■

Credit toward degree is not given for remedial courses taken.

Counseling Services

- ■ Academic
- ■ Psychological
- □ Student Support groups
- ■ Vocational

Tutoring

Individual tutoring is available weekly.

Average size of tutoring groups: 2

	Individual	Group
Time management	■	■
Organizational skills	■	■
Learning strategies	■	■
Study skills	■	■
Content area	■	■
Writing lab	■	■
Math lab	■	■

UNIQUE LD PROGRAM FEATURES

All services are provided as specified in appropriate documentation. Counseling and academic services are provided as frequently as requested by student or staff.

LD PROGRAM STAFF

Total number of LD Program staff (including director):

Full Time: 6 Part Time: 6

There is an advisor/advocate from the LD program available to students. The advisor/advocate meets with faculty once per month and student once per month. 80 peer tutors are available to work with LD students.

Key staff person available to work with LD students: Jane Eddy, Director of the Learning Center.

LD Program web site: www.viterbo.edu/academics/as/learningcenter/index/htm

Wisconsin Lutheran College

Milwaukee, WI

Address: 8800 W. Bluemound Road, Milwaukee, WI, 53226
Admissions telephone: 888 WIS-LUTH
Admissions FAX: 414 443-8514
Director of Admissions: Craig Swiontek
Admissions e-mail: admissions@wlc.edu
Web site: http://www.wlc.edu
SAT Code: 1513 ACT Code: 4699

Director of Student Support and Special Projects: Karen Sitz
LD program telephone: 414 443-8797
LD program e-mail: karen_sitz@wlc.edu
Total campus enrollment: 697

GENERAL
Wisconsin Lutheran College is a private, coed, four-year institution. 19-acre, residential campus in Milwaukee (population: 596,974). Served by air, bus, and train. Public transportation serves campus. Semester system.

LD ADMISSIONS
Essay is not required. Admissions requirements that may be waived for LD students are decided on a case-by-case basis.

SECONDARY SCHOOL REQUIREMENTS
Graduation from secondary school required; GED accepted. The following course distribution required: 4 units of English, 3 units of math, 2 units of science, 2 units of foreign language, 2 units of history, 3 units of academic electives.

TESTING
ACT required; SAT Reasoning may be substituted. SAT Subject recommended.

All enrolled freshmen (fall 2004):

Average ACT Scores: Composite: 24

Child Study Team report is not required. Tests required as part of this documentation:

- [ ] WAIS-IV
- [ ] WISC-IV
- [ ] SATA
- [ ] Woodcock-Johnson
- [ ] Nelson-Denny Reading Test
- [ ] Other

UNDERGRADUATE STUDENT BODY
Total undergraduate student enrollment: 268 Men, 448 Women.

Composition of student body (fall 2004):

	Undergraduate	Freshmen
International	1.1	1.3
Black	1.1	1.2
American Indian	0.0	0.0
Asian-American	0.0	0.4
Hispanic	3.8	1.7
White	92.9	94.8
Unreported	1.1	0.6
	100.0%	100.0%

21% are from out of state. 63% of classes have fewer than 20 students, 37% have between 20 and 50 students.

STUDENT HOUSING
Freshmen are required to live on campus. Housing is guaranteed for all undergraduates. Campus can house 600 undergraduates.

EXPENSES
Tuition (2005-06): $17,340 per year.
Room: $3,180-$2,920. Board: $2,860-$2,710.

There is no additional cost for LD program/services.

LD SERVICES
LD program size is not limited.

LD services available to:

- [ ] Freshmen
- [ ] Sophomores
- [ ] Juniors
- [ ] Seniors

Academic Accommodations

Curriculum		In class	
Foreign language waiver	[ ]	Early syllabus	[ ]
Lighter course load	[ ]	Note takers in class	[x]
Math waiver	[ ]	Priority seating	[ ]
Other special classes	[ ]	Tape recorders	[x]
Priority registrations	[ ]	Videotaped classes	[x]
Substitution of courses	[ ]	Texts on tape	[ ]
Exams		**Services**	
Extended time	[x]	Diagnostic tests	[ ]
Oral exams	[ ]	Learning centers	[x]
Take home exams	[ ]	Proofreaders	[ ]
Exams on tape or computer	[ ]	Readers	[ ]
Untimed exams	[x]	Reading Machines/Kurzweil	[ ]
Other accommodations	[ ]	Special bookstore section	[ ]
		Typists	[ ]

Credit toward degree is not given for remedial courses taken.

Counseling Services

- [ ] Academic
- [ ] Psychological
- [ ] Student Support groups
- [ ] Vocational

Tutoring

	Individual	Group
Time management	[ ]	[ ]
Organizational skills	[ ]	[ ]
Learning strategies	[ ]	[ ]
Study skills	[ ]	[ ]
Content area	[ ]	[ ]
Writing lab	[ ]	[ ]
Math lab	[ ]	[ ]

UNIQUE LD PROGRAM FEATURES
Services are provided on an as-needed case-by-case basis.

LD PROGRAM STAFF
Key staff person available to work with LD students: Karen Sitz, Director of Student Support and Special Projects.

University of Wisconsin - Eau Claire

Eau Claire, WI

Address: 105 Garfield Avenue, Eau Claire, WI, 54701
Admissions telephone: 715 836-5415
Admissions FAX: 715 836-2409
Director of Admissions: Kristina Anderson
Admissions e-mail: admissions@uwec.edu
Web site: http://www.uwec.edu
SAT Code: 1913 ACT Code: 4670

Director: Elizabeth Hicks
LD program telephone: 715 836-4542
LD program e-mail: hicksea@uwec.edu
Total campus enrollment: 10,034

GENERAL

University of Wisconsin - Eau Claire is a public, coed, four-year institution. 333-acre campus in Eau Claire (population: 61,704), 90 miles from Minneapolis-St. Paul. Served by air and bus; major airport serves Minneapolis-St. Paul; train serves Tomah (70 miles). Public transportation serves campus. Semester system.

LD ADMISSIONS

A personal interview is not required. Essay is not required.

SECONDARY SCHOOL REQUIREMENTS

Graduation from secondary school required; GED accepted. The following course distribution required: 4 units of English, 3 units of math, 3 units of science, 2 units of foreign language, 3 units of social studies, 2 units of academic electives.

TESTING

ACT required; SAT Reasoning may be substituted. SAT Subject recommended.

All enrolled freshmen (fall 2004):

Average SAT I Scores:	Verbal: 560	Math: 568
Average ACT Scores:	Composite: 24	

Child Study Team report is not required. Tests required as part of this documentation:

☐ WAIS-IV
☐ WISC-IV
☐ SATA
☐ Woodcock-Johnson
☐ Nelson-Denny Reading Test
☐ Other

UNDERGRADUATE STUDENT BODY

Total undergraduate student enrollment: 4,132 Men, 6,086 Women.

Composition of student body (fall 2004):

	Undergraduate	Freshmen
International	0.5	1.2
Black	0.3	0.5
American Indian	0.4	0.6
Asian-American	2.3	2.7
Hispanic	1.0	0.9
White	94.3	93.4
Unreported	1.2	0.7
	100.0%	100.0%

22% are from out of state. 1% join a fraternity and 1% join a sorority. Average age of full-time undergraduates is 21. 29% of classes have fewer than 20 students, 59% have between 20 and 50 students, 12% have more than 50 students.

STUDENT HOUSING

92% of freshmen live in college housing. Freshmen are required to live on campus. Housing is not guaranteed for all undergraduates. Campus can house 3,924 undergraduates.

EXPENSES

Tuition (2005-06): $5,226 per year (in-state), $15,492 (out-of-state).
Room & Board: $4,266
There is no additional cost for LD program/services.

LD SERVICES

LD program size is not limited.

LD services available to:

☐ Freshmen ☐ Sophomores ☐ Juniors ☐ Seniors

Academic Accommodations

Curriculum		**In class**	
Foreign language waiver	☐	Early syllabus	☐
Lighter course load	■	Note takers in class	■
Math waiver	☐	Priority seating	☐
Other special classes	☐	Tape recorders	■
Priority registrations	☐	Videotaped classes	☐
Substitution of courses	☐	Texts on tape	☐
Exams		**Services**	
Extended time	■	Diagnostic tests	☐
Oral exams	■	Learning centers	■
Take home exams	☐	Proofreaders	☐
Exams on tape or computer	☐	Readers	■
Untimed exams	■	Reading Machines/Kurzweil	■
Other accommodations	☐	Special bookstore section	☐
		Typists	☐

Credit toward degree is not given for remedial courses taken.

Counseling Services

☐ Academic
☐ Psychological
☐ Student Support groups
☐ Vocational

Tutoring

	Individual	Group
Time management	☐	☐
Organizational skills	☐	☐
Learning strategies	☐	☐
Study skills	☐	☐
Content area	☐	☐
Writing lab	☐	☐
Math lab	☐	☐

LD PROGRAM STAFF

Total number of LD Program staff (including director):

Full Time: 1 Part Time: 1

Key staff person available to work with LD students: Elizabeth Hicks, Director.

University of Wisconsin - Green Bay

Green Bay, WI

Address: 2420 Nicolet Drive, Green Bay, WI, 54311
Admissions telephone: 888 367-8942
Admissions FAX: 920 465-5754
Interim Admissions Director: Pam Harvey-Jacobs
Admissions e-mail: uwgb@uwgb.edu
Web site: http://www.uwgb.edu
SAT Code: 1859 ACT Code: 4688

LD program name: Disability Services
Coordinator of Disability Services: Lynn Niemi
LD program telephone: 920 465-2849
LD program e-mail: niemil@uwgb.edu
Total campus enrollment: 5,489

GENERAL

University of Wisconsin - Green Bay is a public, coed, four-year institution. 700-acre, semi-rural campus in Green Bay (population: 102,313). Served by air and bus; major airport and train serve Milwaukee (115 miles). Public transportation serves campus. Semester system.

LD ADMISSIONS

The school has an individualized admission process designed to assess each applicant's likelihood of succeeding in the curriculum.

SECONDARY SCHOOL REQUIREMENTS

Graduation from secondary school required; GED accepted. The following course distribution required: 4 units of English, 3 units of math, 3 units of science, 3 units of social studies, 2 units of academic electives.

TESTING

ACT required; SAT Reasoning may be substituted. SAT Subject recommended.

All enrolled freshmen (fall 2004):

Average ACT Scores: Composite: 23

Child Study Team report is not required. Tests required as part of this documentation:

☐	WAIS-IV	☐	Woodcock-Johnson
☐	WISC-IV	☐	Nelson-Denny Reading Test
☐	SATA	☐	Other

UNDERGRADUATE STUDENT BODY

Total undergraduate student enrollment: 1,814 Men, 3,569 Women.

Composition of student body (fall 2004):

	Undergraduate	Freshmen
International	0.4	0.7
Black	1.1	0.8
American Indian	1.0	1.4
Asian-American	3.5	2.6
Hispanic	1.1	1.0
White	92.0	91.5
Unreported	0.9	2.0
	100.0%	100.0%

5% are from out of state. 1% join a fraternity and 1% join a sorority. Average age of full-time undergraduates is 21. 27% of classes have fewer than 20 students, 57% have between 20 and 50 students, 16% have more than 50 students.

STUDENT HOUSING

75% of freshmen live in college housing. Freshmen are not required to live on campus. Housing is guaranteed for all undergraduates. Campus can house 1,920 undergraduates. Single rooms are available for students with medical or special needs. A medical note is not required.

EXPENSES

Tuition (2005-06): $4,300 per year (in-state), $14,200 (out-of-state).

Room: $2,620. Board: $1,780.

There is no additional cost for LD program/services.

LD SERVICES

LD program size is not limited.

LD services available to:

■ Freshmen ■ Sophomores ■ Juniors ■ Seniors

Academic Accommodations

Curriculum		**In class**	
Foreign language waiver	☐	Early syllabus	☐
Lighter course load	■	Note takers in class	■
Math waiver	☐	Priority seating	■
Other special classes	☐	Tape recorders	■
Priority registrations	■	Videotaped classes	☐
Substitution of courses	☐	Texts on tape	■
Exams		**Services**	
Extended time	■	Diagnostic tests	☐
Oral exams	☐	Learning centers	☐
Take home exams	☐	Proofreaders	☐
Exams on tape or computer	☐	Readers	■
Untimed exams	■	Reading Machines/Kurzweil	☐
Other accommodations	☐	Special bookstore section	☐
		Typists	■

Credit toward degree is not given for remedial courses taken.

Counseling Services

☐ Academic
☐ Psychological
☐ Student Support groups
☐ Vocational

Tutoring

Individual tutoring is available.

	Individual	Group
Time management	☐	☐
Organizational skills	☐	☐
Learning strategies	☐	☐
Study skills	■	☐
Content area	☐	☐
Writing lab	■	☐
Math lab	■	☐

LD PROGRAM STAFF

There is an advisor/advocate from the LD program available to students.

Key staff person available to work with LD students: Lynn Niemi, Coordinator of Disability Services.

LD Program web site: http://www.uwgb.edu/esms/ds.htm

University of Wisconsin - LaCrosse

La Crosse, WI

Address: 1725 State Street, La Crosse, WI, 54601
Admissions telephone: 608 785-8939
Admissions FAX: 608 785-8940
Director of Admissions: Kathryn Keifer
Admissions e-mail: admissions@uwlax.edu
Web site: http://www.uwlax.edu
SAT Code: 1914 ACT Code: 4672

Director: June Reinert
LD program telephone: 608 785-6900
LD program e-mail: reinert.june@uwlax.edu
LD program enrollment: 58, Total campus enrollment: 7,844

GENERAL

University of Wisconsin - LaCrosse is a public, coed, four-year institution. 121-acre campus in LaCrosse (population: 51,818), 150 miles from both Madison and Minneapolis-St. Paul. Served by air, bus, and train; major airport serves Minneapolis-St. Paul. Public transportation serves campus. Semester system.

LD ADMISSIONS

A personal interview is recommended. Essay is not required. Admissions requirements that may be waived for LD students include ACT 20 or above Class rank 30%.

SECONDARY SCHOOL REQUIREMENTS

Graduation from secondary school required; GED accepted. The following course distribution required: 4 units of English, 3 units of math, 3 units of science, 3 units of social studies, 4 units of academic electives.

TESTING

ACT required; SAT Reasoning may be substituted. SAT Subject recommended.

All enrolled freshmen (fall 2004):

Average SAT I Scores: Verbal: 558 Math: 580
Average ACT Scores: Composite: 25

Child Study Team report is not required. Tests required as part of this documentation:

■ WAIS-IV
☐ WISC-IV
☐ SATA
■ Woodcock-Johnson
☐ Nelson-Denny Reading Test
☐ Other

UNDERGRADUATE STUDENT BODY

Total undergraduate student enrollment: 3,541 Men, 4,945 Women.

Composition of student body (fall 2004):

	Undergraduate	Freshmen
International	0.6	0.7
Black	0.9	0.8
American Indian	0.2	0.6
Asian-American	3.7	2.9
Hispanic	1.4	1.5
White	91.6	92.8
Unreported	1.6	0.7
	100.0%	100.0%

17% are from out of state. 1% join a fraternity and 1% join a sorority. Average age of full-time undergraduates is 21. 39% of classes have fewer than 20 students, 54% have between 20 and 50 students, 7% have more than 50 students.

STUDENT HOUSING

90% of freshmen live in college housing. Freshmen are not required to live on campus. Housing is guaranteed for all undergraduates. No student is restricted from applying for housing and housing decisions are not based on marital status or year in school, however, not all students can be guaranteed housing due to capacity limitations. Single rooms are not available for students with medical or special needs.

EXPENSES

Tuition (2005-06): $5,229 per year (in-state), $15,223 (out-of-state). Minnesota residents are charged in-state tuition for most programs.

Room: $2,680. Board: $2,101.

There is no additional cost for LD program/services.

LD SERVICES

LD program size is not limited.

LD services available to:

■ Freshmen ■ Sophomores ■ Juniors ■ Seniors

Academic Accommodations

Curriculum
Foreign language waiver ☐
Lighter course load ☐
Math waiver ☐
Other special classes ☐
Priority registrations ■
Substitution of courses ☐

Exams
Extended time ■
Oral exams ■
Take home exams ☐
Exams on tape or computer ☐
Untimed exams ☐
Other accommodations ■

In class
Early syllabus ☐
Note takers in class ■
Priority seating ☐
Tape recorders ■
Videotaped classes ☐
Texts on tape ■

Services
Diagnostic tests ☐
Learning centers ☐
Proofreaders ☐
Readers ■
Reading Machines/Kurzweil ■
Special bookstore section ☐
Typists ☐

Credit toward degree is not given for remedial courses taken.

Counseling Services

☐ Academic
☐ Psychological
☐ Student Support groups
☐ Vocational

Tutoring

	Individual	Group
Time management	■	■
Organizational skills	☐	☐
Learning strategies	■	■
Study skills	■	■
Content area	☐	☐
Writing lab	■	☐
Math lab	■	☐

LD PROGRAM STAFF

Total number of LD Program staff (including director):

Full Time: 1 Part Time: 1

Key staff person available to work with LD students: June Reinert, Director, Disability Resource Services.

University of Wisconsin - Madison

Madison, WI

Address: 500 Lincoln Drive, Madison, WI, 53706
Admissions telephone: 608 262-3961
Admissions FAX: 608 262-7706
Director of Admissions: Robert A. Seltzer
Admissions e-mail: onwisconsin@admissions.wisc.edu
Web site: http://www.wisc.edu
SAT Code: 1846 ACT Code: 4656

Director, McBurney Disability Resource Center: J. Trey Duffy
LD program telephone: 608 263-5174
LD program e-mail: jtduffy@wisc.edu
Total campus enrollment: 29,766

GENERAL

University of Wisconsin - Madison is a public, coed, four-year institution. 1,000-acre campus in Madison (population: 208,054). Served by air and bus; major airports serve Milwaukee (80 miles) and Chicago (120 miles); train serves Columbus (30 miles). School operates transportation on campus and in local area. Public transportation serves campus. Semester system.

LD ADMISSIONS

A personal interview is not required. Essay is required and may be typed. Some admissions requirements that may be waived for LD students.

SECONDARY SCHOOL REQUIREMENTS

Graduation from secondary school required; GED accepted. The following course distribution required: 4 units of English, 3 units of math, 3 units of science, 2 units of foreign language, 3 units of social studies, 2 units of academic electives.

TESTING

SAT Reasoning or ACT required. SAT Subject required.

All enrolled freshmen (fall 2004):

Average SAT I Scores: Verbal: 611 Math: 649
Average ACT Scores: Composite: 28

Child Study Team report is not required. Tests required as part of this documentation:

- ❑ WAIS-IV
- ❑ WISC-IV
- ❑ SATA
- ❑ Woodcock-Johnson
- ❑ Nelson-Denny Reading Test
- ❑ Other

UNDERGRADUATE STUDENT BODY

Total undergraduate student enrollment: 29,766.

Composition of student body (fall 2004):

	Undergraduate	Freshmen
International	2.5	3.4
Black	2.7	2.4
American Indian	0.8	0.6
Asian-American	5.9	5.1
Hispanic	3.3	2.6
White	81.9	84.0
Unreported	2.9	1.9
	100.0%	100.0%

38% are from out of state. 9% join a fraternity and 8% join a sorority. Average age of full-time undergraduates is 20. 43% of classes have fewer than 20 students, 39% have between 20 and 50 students, 18% have more than 50 students.

STUDENT HOUSING

79% of freshmen live in college housing. Freshmen are not required to live on campus. Housing is not guaranteed for all undergraduates. There are more undergraduate students than there are residence hall spaces. Priority is given to in-state students first. Off-campus housing options are plentiful. Campus can house 6,700 undergraduates. Single rooms are available for students with medical or special needs. A medical note is required.

EXPENSES

Tuition (2005-06): $6,220 per year (in-state), $21,060 (out-of-state).
Room: $3,170. Board: $3,330.
There is no additional cost for LD program/services.

LD SERVICES

LD services available to:

❑ Freshmen ❑ Sophomores ❑ Juniors ❑ Seniors

Academic Accommodations

Curriculum		In class	
Foreign language waiver	❑	Early syllabus	❑
Lighter course load	■	Note takers in class	■
Math waiver	❑	Priority seating	■
Other special classes	❑	Tape recorders	❑
Priority registrations	■	Videotaped classes	❑
Substitution of courses	■	Texts on tape	■
Exams		**Services**	
Extended time	■	Diagnostic tests	❑
Oral exams	■	Learning centers	■
Take home exams	❑	Proofreaders	❑
Exams on tape or computer	❑	Readers	■
Untimed exams	■	Reading Machines/Kurzweil	❑
Other accommodations	■	Special bookstore section	❑
		Typists	❑

Credit toward degree is not given for remedial courses taken.

Counseling Services

- ❑ Academic
- ❑ Psychological
- ❑ Student Support groups
- ❑ Vocational

Tutoring

	Individual	Group
Time management	❑	❑
Organizational skills	❑	❑
Learning strategies	❑	❑
Study skills	❑	❑
Content area	❑	❑
Writing lab	❑	❑
Math lab	❑	❑

LD PROGRAM STAFF

There is an advisor/advocate from the LD program available to students.

Key staff person available to work with LD students: Cathy Treuba, Learning Disabilities Services Coordinator.

University of Wisconsin - Milwaukee

Milwaukee, WI

Address: PO Box 413, Milwaukee, WI, 53201
Admissions telephone: 414 229-3800
Admissions FAX: 414 229-6940
Director of Enrollment Services: Beth Weckmueller
Admissions e-mail: uwmlook@des.uwm.edu
Web site: http://www.uwm.edu
SAT Code: 1473 ACT Code: 4658

LD program name: Student Accessibility Center
Learning Disabilities Program Manager: Laurie Petersen
LD program telephone: 414 229-6239
LD program e-mail: lauriep@uwm.edu
LD program enrollment: 250, Total campus enrollment: 22,307

GENERAL

University of Wisconsin - Milwaukee is a public, coed, four-year institution. 93-acre, suburban campus in Milwaukee (population: 596,974). Served by air, bus, and train. School operates transportation to designated parking lots and throughout the city. Semester system.

LD ADMISSIONS

Students do not complete a separate application and are simultaneously accepted to the LD program. A member of the LD program does not sit on the admissions committee. A personal interview is required. Essay is not required. Admissions requirements that may be waived for LD students are determined by an alternative admission process available through the Academic Opportunity Center.

SECONDARY SCHOOL REQUIREMENTS

Graduation from secondary school required; GED accepted. The following course distribution required: 4 units of English, 3 units of math, 3 units of science, 3 units of social studies, 4 units of academic electives.

TESTING

ACT required; SAT Reasoning may be substituted. SAT Subject recommended.

All enrolled freshmen (fall 2004):

Average SAT I Scores:	Verbal: 550	Math: 549
Average ACT Scores:	Composite: 22	

Child Study Team report is required if student is classified. A neuropsychological or comprehensive psycho-educational evaluation is required for admission. Must be dated within 36 months of application. Tests required as part of this documentation:

- [x] WAIS-IV
- [ ] WISC-IV
- [ ] SATA
- [x] Woodcock-Johnson
- [ ] Nelson-Denny Reading Test
- [ ] Other

UNDERGRADUATE STUDENT BODY

Total undergraduate student enrollment: 8,916 Men, 11,043 Women.

Composition of student body (fall 2004):

	Undergraduate	Freshmen
International	0.2	0.6
Black	7.1	7.2
American Indian	0.8	0.7
Asian-American	5.1	4.6
Hispanic	3.5	3.8
White	83.3	83.1
Unreported	0.0	0.0
	100.0%	100.0%

3% are from out of state. 1% join a fraternity and 1% join a sorority. Average age of full-time undergraduates is 22. 36% of classes have fewer than 20 students, 50% have between 20 and 50 students, 14% have more than 50 students.

STUDENT HOUSING

35% of freshmen live in college housing. Freshmen are not required to live on campus. Housing is not guaranteed for all undergraduates. Limited space available to juniors and seniors; not available to all students requesting on-campus housing. Campus can house 2,700 undergraduates. Single rooms are available for students with medical or special needs. A medical note is required.

EXPENSES

Tuition (2005-06): $6,246 per year (in-state), $18,998 (out-of-state).
Room: $3,370. Board: $2,760.
There is no additional cost for LD program/services.

LD SERVICES

LD program size is not limited.

LD services available to:

- [x] Freshmen
- [x] Sophomores
- [x] Juniors
- [x] Seniors

Academic Accommodations

Curriculum		In class	
Foreign language waiver	[ ]	Early syllabus	[ ]
Lighter course load	[x]	Note takers in class	[x]
Math waiver	[ ]	Priority seating	[ ]
Other special classes	[ ]	Tape recorders	[x]
Priority registrations	[ ]	Videotaped classes	[ ]
Substitution of courses	[ ]	Texts on tape	[ ]
Exams		**Services**	
Extended time	[x]	Diagnostic tests	[x]
Oral exams	[x]	Learning centers	[x]
Take home exams	[ ]	Proofreaders	[ ]
Exams on tape or computer	[x]	Readers	[x]
Untimed exams	[ ]	Reading Machines/Kurzweil	[x]
Other accommodations	[ ]	Special bookstore section	[ ]
		Typists	[ ]

Credit toward degree is not given for remedial courses taken.

Counseling Services

- [x] Academic — Meets 12 times per academic year
- [ ] Psychological
- [ ] Student Support groups
- [ ] Vocational

Tutoring

Individual tutoring is available weekly.

Average size of tutoring groups: 5

	Individual	Group
Time management	[x]	[ ]
Organizational skills	[x]	[ ]
Learning strategies	[x]	[ ]
Study skills	[x]	[ ]
Content area	[x]	[x]
Writing lab	[x]	[x]
Math lab	[x]	[x]

LD PROGRAM STAFF

Total number of LD Program staff (including director):

Full Time: 2 Part Time: 2

There is an advisor/advocate from the LD program available to students.

Key staff person available to work with LD students: Laurie Petersen, Learning Disabilities Program Manager.

LD Program web site: www.sac.uwm.edu

University of Wisconsin - Oshkosh

Oshkosh, WI

Address: 800 Algoma Boulevard, Oshkosh, WI, 54901
Admissions telephone: 920 424-0202
Admissions FAX: 920 424-1098
Director of Admissions: Jill M. Endries
Admissions e-mail: oshadmuw@uwosh.edu
Web site: http://www.uwosh.edu
SAT Code: 1916 ACT Code: 4674

Head of Project Success: William Kitz
LD program telephone: 920 424-1033
LD program e-mail: kitz@uwosh.edu
Total campus enrollment: 9,812

GENERAL

University of Wisconsin Oshkosh is a public, coed, four-year institution. 165-acre campus in Oshkosh (population: 62,916), 90 miles from Milwaukee. Served by bus; major airport and train serve Milwaukee; other airport serves Appleton (20 miles). Public transportation serves campus. Semester system.

LD ADMISSIONS

A personal interview is recommended.

SECONDARY SCHOOL REQUIREMENTS

Graduation from secondary school required; GED accepted. The following course distribution required: 4 units of English, 3 units of math, 3 units of science, 3 units of social studies, 1 unit of history, 4 units of academic electives.

TESTING

ACT required; SAT Reasoning may be substituted.

All enrolled freshmen (fall 2004):

Average ACT Scores: Composite: 23

Child Study Team report is not required. Tests required as part of this documentation:

- ☐ WAIS-IV
- ☐ WISC-IV
- ☐ SATA
- ☐ Woodcock-Johnson
- ☐ Nelson-Denny Reading Test
- ☐ Other

UNDERGRADUATE STUDENT BODY

Total undergraduate student enrollment: 3,842 Men, 5,572 Women.

Composition of student body (fall 2004):

	Undergraduate	Freshmen
International	0.7	0.9
Black	0.8	0.9
American Indian	0.8	0.8
Asian-American	3.5	2.4
Hispanic	1.3	1.1
White	92.3	93.1
Unreported	0.6	0.8
	100.0%	100.0%

3% are from out of state. Average age of full-time undergraduates is 22. 27% of classes have fewer than 20 students, 61% have between 20 and 50 students, 12% have more than 50 students.

STUDENT HOUSING

Freshmen are required to live on campus. Housing is guaranteed for all undergraduates. Campus can house 3,638 undergraduates.

EXPENSES

Tuition (2005-06): $4,910 per year (in-state), $15,760 (out-of-state).

Room & Board: $5,444

There is no additional cost for LD program/services.

LD SERVICES

LD program size is not limited.

LD services available to:

☐ Freshmen ☐ Sophomores ☐ Juniors ☐ Seniors

Academic Accommodations

Curriculum		**In class**	
Foreign language waiver	☐	Early syllabus	☐
Lighter course load	☑	Note takers in class	☑
Math waiver	☐	Priority seating	☐
Other special classes	☐	Tape recorders	☑
Priority registrations	☐	Videotaped classes	☑
Substitution of courses	☐	Texts on tape	☐
Exams		**Services**	
Extended time	☑	Diagnostic tests	☐
Oral exams	☑	Learning centers	☑
Take home exams	☐	Proofreaders	☐
Exams on tape or computer	☐	Readers	☑
Untimed exams	☐	Reading Machines/Kurzweil	☐
Other accommodations	☐	Special bookstore section	☐
		Typists	☐

Credit toward degree is not given for remedial courses taken.

Counseling Services

- ☐ Academic
- ☐ Psychological
- ☐ Student Support groups
- ☐ Vocational

Tutoring

	Individual	Group
Time management	☐	☐
Organizational skills	☐	☐
Learning strategies	☐	☐
Study skills	☐	☐
Content area	☐	☐
Writing lab	☐	☐
Math lab	☐	☐

LD PROGRAM STAFF

Key staff person available to work with LD students: Dr. William Kitz, Professor of Education.

University of Wisconsin - Parkside

Kenosha, WI

Address: 900 Wood Road, Kenosha, WI, 53141-2000
Admissions telephone: 877 633-3897
Admissions FAX: 262 595-2008
Director of Admissions: Matthew Jensen
Admissions e-mail: admissions@uwp.edu
Web site: http://www.uwp.edu
SAT Code: 1860 ACT Code: 4690

Coordinator of Disability Services: Renee Sartin Kirby
LD program telephone: 262 595-2610
LD program e-mail: renee.kirby@uwp.edu
Total campus enrollment: 4,965

GENERAL

University of Wisconsin - Parkside is a public, coed, four-year institution. 751-acre, suburban campus in Kenosha (population: 90,352), 30 miles from Milwaukee. Served by bus and train; major airport serves Milwaukee. Public transportation serves campus. Semester system.

LD ADMISSIONS

A personal interview is not required. Essay is not required. Students do not self-identify on application.

SECONDARY SCHOOL REQUIREMENTS

Graduation from secondary school required; GED accepted. The following course distribution required: 4 units of English, 3 units of math, 3 units of science, 3 units of social studies, 4 units of academic electives.

TESTING

ACT required of some applicants; SAT Reasoning may be substituted. SAT Subject recommended.

All enrolled freshmen (fall 2004):

Child Study Team report is not required. Tests required as part of this documentation:

- ☐ WAIS-IV
- ☐ WISC-IV
- ☐ SATA
- ☐ Woodcock-Johnson
- ☐ Nelson-Denny Reading Test
- ☐ Other

UNDERGRADUATE STUDENT BODY

Total undergraduate student enrollment: 2,009 Men, 2,925 Women.

Composition of student body (fall 2004):

	Undergraduate	Freshmen
International	0.2	1.1
Black	13.6	9.7
American Indian	0.7	0.5
Asian-American	2.8	2.8
Hispanic	7.1	6.5
White	75.2	79.3
Unreported	0.4	0.1
	100.0%	100.0%

10% are from out of state. 44% of classes have fewer than 20 students, 47% have between 20 and 50 students, 9% have more than 50 students.

STUDENT HOUSING

Housing is guaranteed for all undergraduates. Campus can house 765 undergraduates.

EXPENSES

Tuition (2005-06):

There is no additional cost for LD program/services.

LD SERVICES

LD program size is not limited.

LD services available to:

☐ Freshmen ☐ Sophomores ☐ Juniors ☐ Seniors

Academic Accommodations

Curriculum		**In class**	
Foreign language waiver	☐	Early syllabus	☐
Lighter course load	☐	Note takers in class	■
Math waiver	☐	Priority seating	☐
Other special classes	☐	Tape recorders	☐
Priority registrations	☐	Videotaped classes	☐
Substitution of courses	☐	Texts on tape	☐
Exams		**Services**	
Extended time	■	Diagnostic tests	☐
Oral exams	☐	Learning centers	■
Take home exams	☐	Proofreaders	☐
Exams on tape or computer	☐	Readers	☐
Untimed exams	■	Reading Machines/Kurzweil	■
Other accommodations	☐	Special bookstore section	☐
		Typists	☐

Credit toward degree is not given for remedial courses taken.

Counseling Services

- ☐ Academic
- ☐ Psychological
- ☐ Student Support groups
- ☐ Vocational

Tutoring

	Individual	Group
Time management	☐	☐
Organizational skills	☐	☐
Learning strategies	☐	☐
Study skills	☐	☐
Content area	☐	☐
Writing lab	☐	☐
Math lab	☐	☐

LD PROGRAM STAFF

Total number of LD Program staff (including director):

Full Time: 1 Part Time: 1

Key staff person available to work with LD students: Renee Sartin Kirby, Coordinator of Disability Services.

University of Wisconsin - Platteville

Platteville, WI

Address: 1 University Plaza, Platteville, WI, 53818
Admissions telephone: 800 362-5515
Admissions FAX: 608 342-1122
Dean of Enrollment Management Services: Angela Udelhoven
Admissions e-mail: admit@uwplatt.edu
Web site: http://www.uwplatt.edu
SAT Code: 1917 ACT Code: 4676

LD program name: Services for Students with Disabilities
Director, Svcs. for Students with Disabilities: Rebecca Peters
LD program telephone: 608 342-1818
LD program e-mail: petersre@uwplatt.edu
Total campus enrollment: 5,607

GENERAL

University of Wisconsin - Platteville is a public, coed, four-year institution. 400-acre campus in Platteville (population: 9,989), 25 miles from Dubuque, Iowa. Major airport serves Madison (75 miles); smaller airport and train serve Dubuque. Semester system.

SECONDARY SCHOOL REQUIREMENTS

Graduation from secondary school required; GED accepted. The following course distribution required: 4 units of English, 3 units of math, 3 units of science, 3 units of social studies, 4 units of academic electives.

TESTING

ACT required.

All enrolled freshmen (fall 2004):

Average ACT Scores: Composite: 23

Child Study Team report is not required. Tests required as part of this documentation:

- [ ] WAIS-IV
- [ ] WISC-IV
- [ ] SATA
- [ ] Woodcock-Johnson
- [ ] Nelson-Denny Reading Test
- [ ] Other

UNDERGRADUATE STUDENT BODY

Total undergraduate student enrollment: 3,157 Men, 1,997 Women.

Composition of student body (fall 2004):

	Undergraduate	Freshmen
International	0.2	0.5
Black	0.9	1.0
American Indian	0.4	0.3
Asian-American	0.9	1.1
Hispanic	1.0	0.8
White	94.8	95.3
Unreported	1.8	1.0
	100.0%	100.0%

9% are from out of state. Average age of full-time undergraduates is 21. 49% of classes have fewer than 20 students, 46% have between 20 and 50 students, 5% have more than 50 students.

STUDENT HOUSING

92% of freshmen live in college housing. Freshmen are required to live on campus. Housing is not guaranteed for all undergraduates. Campus housing is only guaranteed for freshmen and sophomores. Campus can house 2,311 undergraduates. Single rooms are available for students with medical or special needs. A medical note is required.

EXPENSES

Tuition (2005-06): $3,500 per year (in-state), $13,546 (out-of-state).

There is no additional cost for LD program/services.

LD SERVICES

LD services available to:

[x] Freshmen [x] Sophomores [x] Juniors [x] Seniors

Academic Accommodations

Curriculum		**In class**	
Foreign language waiver	[ ]	Early syllabus	[x]
Lighter course load	[x]	Note takers in class	[x]
Math waiver	[ ]	Priority seating	[ ]
Other special classes	[ ]	Tape recorders	[x]
Priority registrations	[ ]	Videotaped classes	[ ]
Substitution of courses	[ ]	Texts on tape	[x]
Exams		**Services**	
Extended time	[x]	Diagnostic tests	[ ]
Oral exams	[x]	Learning centers	[x]
Take home exams	[ ]	Proofreaders	[x]
Exams on tape or computer	[x]	Readers	[x]
Untimed exams	[x]	Reading Machines/Kurzweil	[ ]
Other accommodations	[x]	Special bookstore section	[ ]
		Typists	[x]

Credit toward degree is not given for remedial courses taken.

Counseling Services

- [x] Academic
- [x] Psychological
- [x] Student Support groups
- [x] Vocational

Tutoring

Individual tutoring is available weekly.

Average size of tutoring groups: 1

	Individual	Group
Time management	[x]	[ ]
Organizational skills	[x]	[ ]
Learning strategies	[x]	[ ]
Study skills	[x]	[ ]
Content area	[x]	[ ]
Writing lab	[x]	[ ]
Math lab	[x]	[ ]

LD PROGRAM STAFF

Total number of LD Program staff (including director):

Full Time: 2 Part Time: 2

There is an advisor/advocate from the LD program available to students. The advisor/advocate meets with faculty 25 times per month and students 2 times per month. 1 graduate student and 25 peer tutors are available to work with LD students.

Key staff person available to work with LD students: Rebecca Peters, Director, Services for Students with Disabilities.

University of Wisconsin - River Falls

River Falls, WI

Address: 410 S. Third Street, River Falls, WI, 54022
Admissions telephone: 715 425-3500
Admissions FAX: 715 425-0676
Director of Admissions: Dr. Alan Tuchtenhagen
Admissions e-mail: admit@uwrf.edu
Web site: http://www.uwrf.edu
SAT Code: 1918 ACT Code: 4678

Disability Services Coordinator: Mark Johnson
LD program telephone: 715 425-3531
LD program e-mail: mark.r.johnson@uwrf.edu
Total campus enrollment: 5,504

GENERAL

University of Wisconsin - River Falls is a public, coed, four-year institution. 225-acre campus in River Falls (population: 12,560), 30 miles from Minneapolis-St. Paul. Major airport and train serve Minneapolis-St. Paul; smaller airport serves New Richmond (20 miles); bus serves Hudson (10 miles). Semester system.

SECONDARY SCHOOL REQUIREMENTS

Graduation from secondary school required; GED accepted. The following course distribution required: 4 units of English, 3 units of math, 3 units of science, 3 units of social studies, 4 units of academic electives.

TESTING

SAT Reasoning considered if submitted. ACT required.

All enrolled freshmen (fall 2004):

Average ACT Scores: Composite: 22

Child Study Team report is not required. Tests required as part of this documentation:

- [ ] WAIS-IV
- [ ] WISC-IV
- [ ] SATA
- [ ] Woodcock-Johnson
- [ ] Nelson-Denny Reading Test
- [ ] Other

UNDERGRADUATE STUDENT BODY

Total undergraduate student enrollment: 2,362 Men, 3,698 Women.

Composition of student body (fall 2004):

	Undergraduate	Freshmen
International	0.2	1.0
Black	1.4	1.2
American Indian	0.4	0.6
Asian-American	4.4	2.9
Hispanic	1.8	1.3
White	91.8	93.0
Unreported	0.0	0.0
	100.0%	100.0%

36% are from out of state. 5% join a fraternity and 5% join a sorority. Average age of full-time undergraduates is 22.

STUDENT HOUSING

95% of freshmen live in college housing. Freshmen are required to live on campus. Housing is guaranteed for all undergraduates. Campus can house 2,200 undergraduates. Single rooms are available for students with medical or special needs. A medical note is not required.

EXPENSES

Tuition (2005-06): $3,384 per year (state residents), $3,694 (Minnesota residents), $11,440 (other out-of-state).

There is no additional cost for LD program/services.

LD SERVICES

LD program size is not limited.

LD services available to:

- [x] Freshmen
- [x] Sophomores
- [x] Juniors
- [x] Seniors

Academic Accommodations

Curriculum		In class	
Foreign language waiver	[ ]	Early syllabus	[ ]
Lighter course load	[x]	Note takers in class	[x]
Math waiver	[ ]	Priority seating	[ ]
Other special classes	[ ]	Tape recorders	[ ]
Priority registrations	[ ]	Videotaped classes	[ ]
Substitution of courses	[ ]	Texts on tape	[ ]
Exams		**Services**	
Extended time	[x]	Diagnostic tests	[ ]
Oral exams	[x]	Learning centers	[ ]
Take home exams	[ ]	Proofreaders	[ ]
Exams on tape or computer	[ ]	Readers	[x]
Untimed exams	[ ]	Reading Machines/Kurzweil	[ ]
Other accommodations	[ ]	Special bookstore section	[ ]
		Typists	[ ]

Credit toward degree is not given for remedial courses taken.

Counseling Services

- [ ] Academic
- [ ] Psychological
- [ ] Student Support groups
- [ ] Vocational

Tutoring

Individual tutoring is available.

	Individual	Group
Time management	[x]	[x]
Organizational skills	[x]	[x]
Learning strategies	[x]	[x]
Study skills	[x]	[x]
Content area	[x]	[x]
Writing lab	[x]	[x]
Math lab	[x]	[x]

LD PROGRAM STAFF

Total number of LD Program staff (including director):

Full Time: 1 Part Time: 1

There is an advisor/advocate from the LD program available to students.

Key staff person available to work with LD students: Mark Johnson, Disability Services Coordinator.

University of Wisconsin - Stevens Point

Stevens Point, WI

Address: 2100 Main Street, Stevens Point, WI, 54481
Admissions telephone: 715 346-2441
Admissions FAX: 715 346-3296
Director of Admissions: Catherine Glennon
Admissions e-mail: admiss@uwsp.edu
Web site: http://www.uwsp.edu
SAT Code: 1919 ACT Code: 4680

LD program name: Office of Disability Services
Director of Disability Services: Jim Joque
LD program telephone: 715 346-3365
LD program e-mail: jjoque@uwsp.edu
LD program enrollment: 87, Total campus enrollment: 8,467

GENERAL

University of Wisconsin - Stevens Point is a public, coed, four-year institution. 335-acre campus in Stevens Point (population: 24,551), 165 miles from Milwaukee; collaborative campuses in Marshfield and Wausau. Served by bus; major airport serves Milwaukee; smaller airport serves Mosinee (15 miles); train serves Portage (60 miles). Public transportation serves campus. Semester system.

LD ADMISSIONS

Students complete a separate application and are simultaneously accepted to the LD program. A member of the LD program does not sit on the admissions committee. A personal interview is recommended. Essay is not required.

SECONDARY SCHOOL REQUIREMENTS

Graduation from secondary school required; GED accepted. The following course distribution required: 4 units of English, 3 units of math, 3 units of science, 3 units of social studies.

TESTING

ACT required; SAT Reasoning may be substituted. SAT Subject recommended.

All enrolled freshmen (fall 2004):

Average SAT I Scores:	Verbal: 536	Math: 526
Average ACT Scores:	Composite: 23	

Child Study Team report is not required. A neuropsychological or comprehensive psycho-educational evaluation is required for admission. Tests required as part of this documentation:

- ☑ WAIS-IV
- ☑ WISC-IV
- ☑ SATA
- ☑ Woodcock-Johnson
- ☑ Nelson-Denny Reading Test
- ☐ Other

UNDERGRADUATE STUDENT BODY

Total undergraduate student enrollment: 3,701 Men, 4,811 Women.

Composition of student body (fall 2004):

	Undergraduate	Freshmen
International	1.1	1.5
Black	1.2	1.0
American Indian	0.7	0.8
Asian-American	1.8	2.2
Hispanic	1.2	1.0
White	94.0	93.5
Unreported	0.0	0.0
	100.0%	100.0%

7% are from out of state. 1% join a fraternity and 1% join a sorority. Average age of full-time undergraduates is 22. 31% of classes have fewer than 20 students, 55% have between 20 and 50 students, 14% have more than 50 students.

STUDENT HOUSING

90% of freshmen live in college housing. Freshmen are required to live on campus. Housing is guaranteed for all undergraduates. Campus can house 3,316 undergraduates. Single rooms are available for students with medical or special needs. A medical note is required.

EXPENSES

Tuition (2005-06): $5,064 per year (in-state), $15,813 (out-of-state).

Room: $2,498. Board: $1,864.
There is no additional cost for LD program/services.

LD SERVICES

LD program size is not limited.

LD services available to:

☑ Freshmen ☑ Sophomores ☑ Juniors ☑ Seniors

Academic Accommodations

Curriculum		In class	
Foreign language waiver	☐	Early syllabus	☐
Lighter course load	☑	Note takers in class	☑
Math waiver	☐	Priority seating	☑
Other special classes	☑	Tape recorders	☐
Priority registrations	☑	Videotaped classes	☐
Substitution of courses	☐	Texts on tape	☑
Exams		**Services**	
Extended time	☑	Diagnostic tests	☐
Oral exams	☑	Learning centers	☑
Take home exams	☐	Proofreaders	☐
Exams on tape or computer	☑	Readers	☑
Untimed exams	☐	Reading Machines/Kurzweil	☑
Other accommodations	☑	Special bookstore section	☐
		Typists	☑

Credit toward degree is not given for remedial courses taken.

Counseling Services

- ☑ Academic
- ☑ Psychological
- ☐ Student Support groups
- ☑ Vocational

Meets 2 times per academic year

Tutoring

Individual tutoring is available daily.

Average size of tutoring groups: 4

	Individual	Group
Time management	☐	☐
Organizational skills	☐	☐
Learning strategies	☐	☐
Study skills	☐	☑
Content area	☑	☑
Writing lab	☑	☐
Math lab	☐	☑

LD PROGRAM STAFF

Total number of LD Program staff (including director):

Full Time: 1 Part Time: 1

There is an advisor/advocate from the LD program available to students. The advisor/advocate meets with students once per month. 20 peer tutors are available to work with LD students.

Key staff person available to work with LD students: Jim Joque, Director of Disability Services.

LD Program web site: http://www.uwsp.edu/special/disability

University of Wisconsin - Stout

Menomonie, WI

Address: 1 Clock Tower Plaza, Menomonie, WI, 54751
Admissions telephone: 800 447-8688
Admissions FAX: 715 232-1667
Director of Admissions: Cindy Gilberts
Admissions e-mail: admissions@uwstout.edu
Web site: http://www.uwstout.edu
SAT Code: 1740 ACT Code: 4652

LD program name: Disability Services
LD program address: 206 Bowman Hall,
LD program telephone: 715 232-2995
LD program e-mail: shefchikd@uwstout.edu
LD program enrollment: 168, Total campus enrollment: 6,972

GENERAL

University of Wisconsin - Stout is a public, coed, four-year institution. 110-acre campus in Menomonie (population: 14,937), 50 miles from Minneapolis-St. Paul. Served by bus; major airport serves Minneapolis-St. Paul; smaller airport serves Eau Claire (30 miles). 4-1-4 system.

LD ADMISSIONS

Students do not complete a separate application and are not simultaneously accepted to the LD program. A member of the LD program does sit on the admissions committee. High school waivers are accepted for foreign language requirement. A personal interview is not required. Essay is not required.

SECONDARY SCHOOL REQUIREMENTS

Graduation from secondary school required; GED accepted. The following course distribution required: 4 units of English, 3 units of math, 3 units of science, 3 units of social studies, 4 units of academic electives.

TESTING

All enrolled freshmen (fall 2004):

Average ACT Scores: Composite: 21

Child Study Team report is not required. A neuropsychological or comprehensive psycho-educational evaluation is required for admission. Must be dated within 36 months of application. Tests required as part of this documentation:

- [x] WAIS-IV
- [x] WISC-IV
- [ ] SATA
- [x] Woodcock-Johnson
- [x] Nelson-Denny Reading Test
- [x] Other

UNDERGRADUATE STUDENT BODY

Total undergraduate student enrollment: 3,774 Men, 3,484 Women.

Composition of student body (fall 2004):

	Undergraduate	Freshmen
International	1.2	0.6
Black	1.3	1.1
American Indian	0.6	0.4
Asian-American	3.2	2.2
Hispanic	0.9	0.7
White	92.1	94.3
Unreported	0.7	0.7
	100.0%	100.0%

28% are from out of state. 2% join a fraternity and 3% join a sorority. Average age of full-time undergraduates is 21. 30% of classes have fewer than 20 students, 65% have between 20 and 50 students, 5% have more than 50 students.

STUDENT HOUSING

92% of freshmen live in college housing. Freshmen are required to live on campus. Housing is guaranteed for all undergraduates. Campus can house 2,936 undergraduates. Single rooms are available for students with medical or special needs. A medical note is required.

EXPENSES

Tuition (2005-06): $4,745 per year (in-state), $15,078 (out-of-state). Room: $2,820. Board: $1,758.

There is no additional cost for LD program/services.

LD SERVICES

LD program size is not limited.

LD services available to:

- [x] Freshmen
- [x] Sophomores
- [x] Juniors
- [x] Seniors

Academic Accommodations

Curriculum

- [ ] Foreign language waiver
- [x] Lighter course load
- [ ] Math waiver
- [x] Other special classes
- [x] Priority registrations
- [ ] Substitution of courses

Exams

- [x] Extended time
- [ ] Oral exams
- [ ] Take home exams
- [x] Exams on tape or computer
- [x] Untimed exams
- [x] Other accommodations

In class

- [ ] Early syllabus
- [x] Note takers in class
- [x] Priority seating
- [x] Tape recorders
- [ ] Videotaped classes
- [x] Texts on tape

Services

- [x] Diagnostic tests
- [ ] Learning centers
- [ ] Proofreaders
- [x] Readers
- [x] Reading Machines/Kurzweil
- [ ] Special bookstore section
- [x] Typists

Credit toward degree is not given for remedial courses taken.

Counseling Services

- [x] Academic — Meets 24 times per academic year
- [ ] Psychological
- [ ] Student Support groups
- [ ] Vocational

Tutoring

Individual tutoring is not available.

	Individual	Group
Time management	[x]	[ ]
Organizational skills	[x]	[ ]
Learning strategies	[x]	[x]
Study skills	[x]	[ ]
Content area	[ ]	[ ]
Writing lab	[x]	[ ]
Math lab	[x]	[ ]

LD PROGRAM STAFF

Total number of LD Program staff (including director):

Full Time: 2 Part Time: 2

There is an advisor/advocate from the LD program available to students.

Key staff person available to work with LD students: Debra Shefchik, Director Disability Services.

University of Wisconsin - Superior

Superior, WI

Address: Belknap and Catlin, PO Box 2000, Superior, WI, 54880-4500
Admissions telephone: 715 394-8230
Admissions FAX: 715 394-8407
Director of Admissions: Jim Miller
Admissions e-mail: admissions@uwsuper.edu
Web site: http://www.uwsuper.edu
SAT Code: 1920 ACT Code: 4682

Director of Career and Advising Center: Mary Lee Vance
LD program telephone: 715 394-8580
LD program e-mail: mvance@uwsuper.edu
Total campus enrollment: 2,548

GENERAL

University of Wisconsin - Superior is a public, coed, four-year institution. 230-acre campus in Superior (population: 27,368), adjacent to Duluth, Minn. Served by bus; airport serves Duluth; train serves Minneapolis (150 miles). Public transportation serves campus. Semester system.

LD ADMISSIONS

A personal interview is recommended. Essay is not required.

SECONDARY SCHOOL REQUIREMENTS

Graduation from secondary school required; GED accepted. The following course distribution required: 4 units of English, 3 units of math, 3 units of science, 3 units of social studies, 4 units of academic electives.

TESTING

ACT required; SAT Reasoning may be substituted. SAT Subject recommended.

All enrolled freshmen (fall 2004):

Average SAT I Scores: Verbal: 611 Math: 564
Average ACT Scores: Composite: 22

Child Study Team report is not required. Tests required as part of this documentation:

- ☐ WAIS-IV
- ☐ WISC-IV
- ☐ SATA
- ☐ Woodcock-Johnson
- ☐ Nelson-Denny Reading Test
- ☐ Other

UNDERGRADUATE STUDENT BODY

Total undergraduate student enrollment: 976 Men, 1,370 Women.

Composition of student body (fall 2004):

	Undergraduate	Freshmen
International	3.6	6.0
Black	2.1	1.3
American Indian	1.8	2.7
Asian-American	0.6	0.9
Hispanic	0.3	0.7
White	89.8	87.8
Unreported	1.8	0.6
	100.0%	100.0%

47% are from out of state. Average age of full-time undergraduates is 23. 50% of classes have fewer than 20 students, 39% have between 20 and 50 students, 11% have more than 50 students.

STUDENT HOUSING

55% of freshmen live in college housing. Freshmen are required to live on campus. Housing is guaranteed for all undergraduates. Campus can house 720 undergraduates.

EXPENSES

There is no additional cost for LD program/services.

LD SERVICES

LD program size is not limited.

LD services available to:

☐ Freshmen ☐ Sophomores ☐ Juniors ☐ Seniors

Academic Accommodations

Curriculum		In class	
Foreign language waiver	☐	Early syllabus	☐
Lighter course load	☐	Note takers in class	■
Math waiver	☐	Priority seating	☐
Other special classes	■	Tape recorders	■
Priority registrations	☐	Videotaped classes	☐
Substitution of courses	☐	Texts on tape	☐
Exams		**Services**	
Extended time	■	Diagnostic tests	☐
Oral exams	■	Learning centers	■
Take home exams	☐	Proofreaders	☐
Exams on tape or computer	☐	Readers	■
Untimed exams	■	Reading Machines/Kurzweil	■
Other accommodations	☐	Special bookstore section	☐
		Typists	☐

Credit toward degree is not given for remedial courses taken.

Counseling Services

- ☐ Academic
- ☐ Psychological
- ☐ Student Support groups
- ☐ Vocational

Tutoring

	Individual	Group
Time management	☐	☐
Organizational skills	☐	☐
Learning strategies	☐	☐
Study skills	☐	☐
Content area	☐	☐
Writing lab	☐	☐
Math lab	☐	☐

UNIQUE LD PROGRAM FEATURES

We have a program for students who do not meet our admission criteria that is open to all students. The Access Program operates in conjunction with Wisconsin Indianhead Technical College allowing students to take 6 credits in a personal atmosphere. They prove academic ability on the WITC campus then transfer to UW-Superior with a head start. They also may stay on the WITC campus if they prefer. This the third successful year of this program.

LD PROGRAM STAFF

Key staff person available to work with LD students: Mary Lee Vance, Director of Career and Advising Center.

University of Wisconsin - Whitewater

Whitewater, WI

Address: 800 W. Main Street, Whitewater, WI, 53190
Admissions telephone: 262 472-1440
Admissions FAX: 262 472-1515
Executive Director of Admissions: Steve McKellips
Admissions e-mail: uwwadmit@mail.uww.edu
Web site: http://www.uww.edu
SAT Code: 1921 ACT Code: 4684

LD program name: Project Assist
Director: Nancy Amacher
LD program telephone: 262 472-4788
LD program e-mail: amachern@uww.edu
Total campus enrollment: 9,533

GENERAL

University of Wisconsin - Whitewater is a public, coed, four-year institution. 400-acre campus in Whitewater (population: 13,437), 45 miles from Milwaukee. Major airport and train serve Milwaukee; bus serves Janesville (20 miles). Semester system.

LD ADMISSIONS

A personal interview is not required. Essay is not required. Most students with LD are admitted to the school meeting the same requirements as all other students. Their admission is not a separate process. Once denied, however, a student with a disability can request an admission exception in which they provide documentation regarding their disability. Typically, a personal interview is done with disability staff. If an exception is granted, a commitment to participate in the Project ASSIST program is required for one year, including the successful completion of the month-long summer transition program, prior to the start of their first semester. All other students with LD, as well as those with other types of disabilities can receive the typical legally mandated services such as note taking, testing accommodations and alternative-media based on their documented disability needs. Specialized transportation, work experience, job placement and assistive technology are all available for a fee. Attendant care services are available by three area care providers.

SECONDARY SCHOOL REQUIREMENTS

Graduation from secondary school required; GED accepted. The following course distribution required: 4 units of English, 3 units of math, 3 units of science, 2 units of foreign language, 3 units of social studies, 4 units of academic electives.

TESTING

SAT Reasoning recommended. ACT recommended. SAT Subject recommended.

All enrolled freshmen (fall 2004):

Average SAT I Scores: Verbal: Math:
Average ACT Scores: Composite: 22

Child Study Team report is not required. Tests required as part of this documentation:

- [ ] WAIS-IV
- [ ] WISC-IV
- [ ] SATA
- [ ] Woodcock-Johnson
- [ ] Nelson-Denny Reading Test
- [ ] Other

UNDERGRADUATE STUDENT BODY

Total undergraduate student enrollment: 4,402 Men, 4,949 Women.

Composition of student body (fall 2004):

	Undergraduate	Freshmen
International	0.3	0.5
Black	8.1	4.4
American Indian	0.6	0.5
Asian-American	3.5	2.6
Hispanic	3.1	2.5
White	84.4	89.5
Unreported	0.0	0.0
	100.0%	100.0%

6% are from out of state. Average age of full-time undergraduates is 21. 35% of classes have fewer than 20 students, 60% have between 20 and 50 students, 5% have more than 50 students.

STUDENT HOUSING

90% of freshmen live in college housing. Freshmen are required to live on campus. Housing is guaranteed for all undergraduates. Campus can house 4,000 undergraduates.

EXPENSES

Tuition (2005-06): $4,280 per year (in-state), $16,010 (out-of-state).
Room: $1,220. Board: $840.
Additional cost for LD program/services: $950 per semester.

LD SERVICES

LD program size is not limited.

LD services available to:

- [ ] Freshmen
- [ ] Sophomores
- [ ] Juniors
- [ ] Seniors

Academic Accommodations

Curriculum		**In class**	
Foreign language waiver	[ ]	Early syllabus	[ ]
Lighter course load	[x]	Note takers in class	[x]
Math waiver	[ ]	Priority seating	[ ]
Other special classes	[x]	Tape recorders	[x]
Priority registrations	[ ]	Videotaped classes	[ ]
Substitution of courses	[ ]	Texts on tape	[ ]
Exams		**Services**	
Extended time	[x]	Diagnostic tests	[ ]
Oral exams	[ ]	Learning centers	[x]
Take home exams	[ ]	Proofreaders	[ ]
Exams on tape or computer	[ ]	Readers	[x]
Untimed exams	[x]	Reading Machines/Kurzweil	[x]
Other accommodations	[ ]	Special bookstore section	[ ]
		Typists	[ ]

Credit toward degree is not given for remedial courses taken.

Counseling Services

- [ ] Academic
- [ ] Psychological
- [ ] Student Support groups
- [ ] Vocational

Tutoring

	Individual	Group
Time management	[ ]	[ ]
Organizational skills	[ ]	[ ]
Learning strategies	[ ]	[ ]
Study skills	[ ]	[ ]
Content area	[ ]	[ ]
Writing lab	[ ]	[ ]
Math lab	[ ]	[ ]

LD PROGRAM STAFF

Total number of LD Program staff (including director):

Full Time: 4 Part Time: 4

Key staff person available to work with LD students: Jamie Leurquin, Assistant Director.

University of Wisconsin - Baraboo/Sauk County

Baraboo, WI

Address: 1006 Connie Road, Baraboo, WI 53913
Admissions telephone: 608 356-8351
Admissions FAX: 608 356-0752
Assistant Director Student Services/Financial Aid: Tom Martin
Admissions e-mail: boouinfo@uwc.edu
Web site: http://www.baraboo-sauk.uwc.edu
SAT Code: 1996 ACT Code: 4157

LD program address: 780 Regent Street, Madison, WI 53708
Director of Academic Success programs: Chris Logterman
LD program telephone: 608 356-8351, extension 219
LD program e-mail: clogterm@uwc.edu
LD program enrollment: 12, Total campus enrollment: 561

GENERAL

University of Wisconsin - Baraboo/Sauk County is a public, coed, two-year institution. 68-acre campus in Baraboo (population: 11,000), 45 miles from Madison. Major airport serves Madison; bus and train serve Wisconsin Dells (15 miles). Semester system.

LD ADMISSIONS

Application deadline is 09/01. A personal interview is recommended. Essay is not required. Students do not complete a separate application process and are not simultaneously accepted. A member of the LD program does not sit on the admissions committee.

SECONDARY SCHOOL REQUIREMENTS

Graduation from secondary school required; GED accepted. Minimum class rank accepted is upper 75%.

TESTING

Child Study Team report is not required. Tests required as part of this documentation:

- ☐ WAIS-IV
- ☐ WISC-IV
- ☐ SATA
- ☐ Woodcock-Johnson
- ☐ Nelson-Denny Reading Test
- ☐ Other

STUDENT HOUSING

Housing is not available.

EXPENSES

Tuition (2005-06): $4,910 per year (in-state), $15,760 (out-of-state).

Room & Board: $5,444

There is no additional cost for LD program/services.

LD SERVICES

LD program size is not limited.

LD services available to:

■ Freshmen ■ Sophomores ■ Juniors ■ Seniors

Academic Accommodations

Curriculum		In class	
Foreign language waiver	☐	Early syllabus	☐
Lighter course load	■	Note takers in class	■
Math waiver	☐	Priority seating	■
Other special classes	☐	Tape recorders	☐
Priority registrations	☐	Videotaped classes	☐
Substitution of courses	☐	Texts on tape	■
Exams		**Services**	
Extended time	■	Diagnostic tests	☐
Oral exams	■	Learning centers	☐
Take home exams	☐	Proofreaders	☐
Exams on tape or computer	■	Readers	■
Untimed exams	☐	Reading Machines/Kurzweil	■
Other accommodations	■	Special bookstore section	☐
		Typists	■

Credit toward degree is not given for remedial courses taken.

Counseling Services

- ☐ Academic
- ☐ Psychological
- ☐ Student Support groups
- ☐ Vocational

Tutoring

Individual tutoring is available weekly.

Average size of tutoring groups is 1-5.

	Individual	Group
Time management	■	■
Organizational skills	■	■
Learning strategies	☐	☐
Study skills	■	■
Content area	☐	☐
Writing lab	■	☐
Math lab	■	■

LD PROGRAM STAFF

Total number of LD Program staff (including director):

There is an advisor/advocate from the LD program and 4 peer tutors available to students.

Key staff person available to work with LD students: Brian Schultz, Coordinator of Services for Students with Disabilities.

University of Wyoming

Laramie, WY

Address: 1000 E. University Avenue, Laramie, WY, 82071
Admissions telephone: 800 342-5996
Admissions FAX: 307 766-4042
Associate Vice Pres. of Enrollment and Director of Admissions: Sara Axelson
Admissions e-mail: Why-wyo@uwyo.edu
Web site: http://www.uwyo.edu
SAT Code: 4855 ACT Code: 5006

LD program name: Disability Support Services
Director, University Disability Support Services: Chris Primus
LD program telephone: 307 766-6189
LD program e-mail: udss@uwyo.edu
LD program enrollment: 95 Total campus enrollment: 9,589

GENERAL

University of Wyoming is a public, coed, four-year institution. 785-acre campus in Laramie (population: 27,204), 125 miles from Denver; branch campus in Casper. Served by air and bus; major airport serves Denver. School operates transportation to university apartments. Semester system.

LD ADMISSIONS

Students do not complete a separate application and are not simultaneously accepted to the LD program. A personal interview is not required. Essay is not required. Any student who knows they may not meet at least conditional admissions standards and who feel that extenuating circumstances may have affected their meeting that criteria, may ask Admissions to take a closer look at their application. Applicants should include a letter explaining those extenuating circumstances and what steps they anticipate taking in college that will contibute to their success.

SECONDARY SCHOOL REQUIREMENTS

Graduation from secondary school required. The following course distribution required: 4 units of English, 3 units of math, 3 units of science. GED accepted.

TESTING

SAT Reasoning or ACT required of some applicants. SAT Subject recommended.

All enrolled freshmen (fall 2004):

Average SAT I Scores:	Verbal: 535	Math: 544
Average ACT Scores:	Composite: 23	

Child Study Team report is not required. A neuropsychological or comprehensive psycho-education evaluation is not required for admission. Tests required as part of this documentation:

- [ ] WAIS-IV
- [ ] WISC-IV
- [ ] SATA
- [ ] Woodcock-Johnson
- [ ] Nelson-Denny Reading Test
- [ ] Other

UNDERGRADUATE STUDENT BODY

Total undergraduate student enrollment: 4,169 Men, 4,760 Women.

Composition of student body (fall 2004):

	Undergraduate	Freshmen
International	0.6	1.1
Black	1.1	1.1
American Indian	1.0	1.0
Asian-American	1.3	1.1
Hispanic	3.6	3.5
White	86.8	86.8
Unreported	5.6	5.4
	100.0%	100.0%

25% are from out of state. 7% join a fraternity and 5% join a sorority. Average age of full-time undergraduates is 22. 40% of classes have fewer than 20 students, 49% have between 20 and 50 students, 11% have more than 50 students.

STUDENT HOUSING

71% of freshmen live in college housing. Freshmen are required to live on campus. Housing is guaranteed for all undergraduates. Campus can house 2,689 undergraduates. Single rooms are not available for students with medical or special needs.

EXPENSES

Tuition (2005-06): $2,760 per year (in-state), $9,150 (out-of-state).

Room: $2,709. Board: $3,531.

There is no additional cost for LD program/services.

LD SERVICES

LD program size is not limited.

LD services available to:

- [x] Freshmen
- [x] Sophomores
- [x] Juniors
- [x] Seniors

Academic Accommodations

Curriculum		In class	
Foreign language waiver	[ ]	Early syllabus	[x]
Lighter course load	[x]	Note takers in class	[x]
Math waiver	[ ]	Priority seating	[ ]
Other special classes	[x]	Tape recorders	[x]
Priority registrations	[x]	Videotaped classes	[ ]
Substitution of courses	[x]	Text on tape	[x]
Exams		**Services**	
Extended time	[x]	Diagnostic tests	[ ]
Oral exams	[ ]	Learning centers	[x]
Take home exams	[ ]	Proofreaders	[ ]
Exams on tape or computer	[x]	Readers	[x]
Untimed exams	[ ]	Reading Machines/Kurzweil	[x]
Other accommodations	[x]	Special bookstore section	[ ]
		Typists	[ ]

Credit toward degree is not given for remedial courses taken.

Counseling Services

- [x] Academic
- [x] Psychological
- [x] Student Support groups
- [x] Vocational

Tutoring

Individual tutoring is available.

	Individual	Group
Time management	[x]	[x]
Organizational skills	[x]	[x]
Learning strategies	[ ]	[ ]
Study skills	[x]	[x]
Content area	[x]	[x]
Writing lab	[x]	[x]
Math lab	[x]	[x]

UNIQUE LD PROGRAM FEATURES

Admissions does not inquire about disabling conditions in their application process.

LD PROGRAM STAFF

Total number of LD Program staff (including director):

Full Time: 4 Part Time: 4

There is an advisor/advocate from the LD program available to students. 5 peer tutors are available to work with LD students.

Key staff person available to work with LD students: Chris Primus, Director, University Disability Support Services.

LD Program web site: http://uwadmnweb.uwyo.edu/UDSS/

Sheridan College

Sheridan, WY

Address: P.O. Box 1500, Sheridan, WY 82801
Admissions telephone: 307 674-6446, extension 2002
Admissions FAX: 307 674-7205
Director of Admissions: Zane Garstad
Admissions e-mail: zgarstad@sheridan.edu
Web site: http://www.sheridan.edu
SAT Code: 4536 ACT Code: 5002

LD program name: Academic Advising/Disability Svcs.
Student Advisor/Disabilities Coordinator: Lisa Wallace
LD program enrollment: 19 Total campus enrollment: 2,761

GENERAL

Sheridan College is a public, coed, two-year institution. 124-acre campus in Sheridan (population: 16,000). Served by air. Semester system.

LD ADMISSIONS

Students do not complete a separate application and are simultaneously accepted to the LD program. A member of the LD program does not sit on the admissions committee. A personal interview is required. Essay is not required.

SECONDARY SCHOOL REQUIREMENTS

Graduation from secondary school required, GED is accepted.

TESTING

Child Study Team report is not required. A neuropsychological or comprehensive psycho-education evaluation is required for admission. Must be dated within 36 months of the application. Tests required as part of this documentation:

- [x] WAIS-IV
- [x] WISC-IV
- [x] SATA
- [x] Woodcock-Johnson
- [x] Nelson-Denny Reading Test
- [ ] Other

STUDENT HOUSING

Single rooms are available to students with specific disabilities.

Medical note is required.

EXPENSES

Tuition 2005-06: $1,368 per year (state residents), $4,104 (out-of-state). There is no additional cost for LD program/services.

LD SERVICES

LD program size is not limited.

LD services available to:

- [x] Freshmen
- [x] Sophomores
- [x] Juniors
- [x] Seniors

Academic Accommodations

Curriculum

- [x] Foreign language waiver
- [x] Lighter course load
- [x] Math waiver
- [ ] Other special classes
- [ ] Priority registrations
- [x] Substitution of courses

Exams

- [x] Extended time
- [x] Oral exams
- [ ] Take home exams
- [x] Exams on tape or computer
- [ ] Untimed exams
- [ ] Other accommodations

In class

- [ ] Early syllabus
- [x] Note takers in class
- [x] Priority seating
- [x] Tape recorders
- [ ] Videotaped classes
- [x] Text on tape

Services

- [ ] Diagnostic tests
- [x] Learning centers
- [ ] Proofreaders
- [x] Readers
- [ ] Reading Machines/Kurzweil
- [ ] Special bookstore section
- [x] Typists

Credit toward degree is not given for remedial courses taken.

Counseling Services

- [x] Academic
- [ ] Psychological
- [ ] Student Support groups
- [ ] Vocational

Tutoring

Individual tutoring is available daily.

Average size of tutoring group is 5.

	Individual	Group
Time management	[x]	[ ]
Organizational skills	[x]	[ ]
Learning strategies	[x]	[ ]
Study skills	[x]	[ ]
Content area	[x]	[x]
Writing lab	[x]	[ ]
Math lab	[x]	[ ]

LD PROGRAM STAFF

Total number of LD Program staff (including director):

Full Time: 1 Part Time: 2

There is an advisor/advocate from the LD program available to students. 10 peer tutors are available to work with LD students.

Key staff person available to work with LD students: Lisa Wallace, Student Advisor/Disability Services

Central Wyoming College

Riverton, WY

Address: 2660 Peck Avenue, Riverton WI, 82501
Admissions telephone: 800 865-0193
Admissions FAX: 307 855-2092
Admissions Officer: Tami Shultz
Admissions e-mail: tshultz@cwc.edu
Web site: http://www.cwc.edu
SAT Code: 4115 ACT Code: 4999

Director, Student Support Services: Marilu Duncan
LD program telephone: 307 855-2227
LD program e-mail: mduncan@cwc.edu
LD program enrollment: 71, Total campus enrollment: 1,732

GENERAL

Central Wyoming College is a public, coed, two-year institution. 120-acre campus in Riverton (population: 9,200). Served by air. Bus serves Shoshoni (28 miles). Public transportation serves campus. Semester system.

LD ADMISSIONS

No application deadline. Students do not complete a separate application and are not simultaneously accepted to the LD program. A member of the LD program does not sit on the admissions committee. A personal interview is required. Essay is not required.

SECONDARY SCHOOL REQUIREMENTS

Graduation from secondary school required, GED is accepted.

TESTING

Child Study Team report is required. A neuropsychological or comprehensive psycho-education evaluation is required for admission. Must be dated within 60 months of the application. Tests required as part of this documentation:

- [x] WAIS-IV
- [x] WISC-IV
- [ ] SATA
- [x] Woodcock-Johnson
- [ ] Nelson-Denny Reading Test
- [ ] Other

STUDENT HOUSING

Single rooms are available to students with specific disabilities.

EXPENSES

Tuition 2005-06: There is no additional cost for LD program/services.

LD SERVICES

LD program size is not limited.

LD services available to:

- [x] Freshmen
- [x] Sophomores
- [x] Juniors
- [x] Seniors

Academic Accommodations

Curriculum		In class	
Foreign language waiver	[ ]	Early syllabus	[ ]
Lighter course load	[ ]	Note takers in class	[x]
Math waiver	[ ]	Priority seating	[x]
Other special classes	[ ]	Tape recorders	[x]
Priority registrations	[ ]	Videotaped classes	[ ]
Substitution of courses	[ ]	Text on tape	[x]
Exams		**Services**	
Extended time	[x]	Diagnostic tests	[x]
Oral exams	[x]	Learning centers	[x]
Take home exams	[ ]	Proofreaders	[x]
Exams on tape or computer	[x]	Readers	[x]
Untimed exams	[ ]	Reading Machines/Kurzweil	[x]
Other accommodations	[x]	Special bookstore section	[ ]
		Typists	[x]

Credit toward degree is not given for remedial courses taken.

Counseling Services

- [x] Academic
- [x] Psychological
- [ ] Student Support groups
- [x] Vocational

Tutoring

Individual tutoring is available daily.

Average size of tutoring group is 5.

	Individual	Group
Time management	[x]	[x]
Organizational skills	[x]	[x]
Learning strategies	[x]	[x]
Study skills	[x]	[x]
Content area	[x]	[x]
Writing lab	[ ]	[ ]
Math lab	[ ]	[ ]

LD PROGRAM STAFF

Total number of LD Program staff (including director):

Part Time: 1

There is an advisor/advocate from the LD program available to faculty and students. The advisor/advocate from the LD program meets with faculty and students one to two times per month. 15 peer tutors are available to work with LD students.

Key staff person available to work with LD students: Elaine Patterson, Disabilities Diagnostitician

LD program web site: http://www.cwc.edu/student_services/

Academic Accommodations Index

Academic Accommodations Index

	Curriculum						In Class						Exams						Services						
	Foreign Language Waiver	Lighter Course Load	Math Waiver	Other Special Classes	Priority Registration	Substition of Courses	Early Syllabus	Note Takers in Class	Priority Seating	Tape Recorders	Videotaped Classes	Text on Tape	Extended Time	Oral Exams	Take Home Exams	Exams on Tape or PC	Untimed Exams	Other Accommodations	Diagnostic Tests	Learning Centers	Proofreaders	Readers	Reading Machines	Special Bookstore Section	Typists
Alabama																									
Alabama St U		✓						✓		✓			✓	✓			✓			✓					
Alabama, U of		✓			✓	✓		✓	✓			✓	✓	✓		✓		✓		✓			✓		✓
Alabama, U of, Birmingham					✓		✓	✓	✓	✓		✓	✓	✓		✓		✓				✓	✓		
Alabama, U of, Huntsville		✓					✓	✓	✓	✓	✓	✓	✓	✓			✓	✓				✓	✓		✓
Auburn U		✓			✓					✓			✓										✓		
Auburn U Montgomery		✓						✓		✓	✓		✓	✓			✓			✓		✓	✓		
Birmingham-Southern Coll									✓	✓			✓	✓			✓	✓							
Evergreen Valley Coll		✓		✓	✓			✓		✓		✓	✓	✓		✓		✓	✓				✓		
Faulkner U	✓	✓	✓		✓	✓	✓	✓	✓	✓		✓	✓	✓		✓	✓	✓		✓		✓	✓		✓
Huntingdon Coll		✓						✓					✓	✓		✓	✓	✓				✓			
Jacksonville St U				✓	✓		✓	✓	✓	✓			✓	✓		✓	✓	✓		✓		✓	✓		
Judson Coll										✓			✓	✓			✓								
Miles Coll																									
Mobile, U of										✓			✓			✓	✓			✓					
Montevallo, U of		✓			✓			✓	✓	✓		✓	✓			✓						✓			
North Alabama, U of								✓		✓			✓	✓			✓			✓		✓			
Orange Coast Coll				✓	✓			✓		✓		✓	✓	✓		✓				✓		✓			
Santa Barbara City Coll		✓			✓							✓	✓			✓		✓	✓	✓			✓		
Samford U					✓	✓	✓	✓	✓	✓	✓	✓	✓	✓		✓	✓	✓		✓		✓	✓		✓
South Alabama, U of		✓						✓		✓			✓	✓			✓		✓	✓		✓	✓		
Spring Hill Coll	✓								✓	✓			✓			✓		✓				✓			

Stillman Coll						✓			✓	✓			✓	✓	✓	✓	✓					✓	✓		
Troy St U		✓						✓	✓	✓		✓	✓	✓							✓	✓			
Troy St U Dothan		✓								✓			✓	✓			✓		✓			✓	✓		
Tuskegee U																			✓	✓					
West Alabama, U of		✓						✓		✓			✓	✓			✓		✓	✓		✓			
Alaska																									
Alaska Pacific U		✓						✓		✓							✓								
Alaska, U of, Anchorage		✓			✓	✓	✓	✓		✓		✓	✓	✓		✓		✓		✓		✓	✓		
Alaska, U of, Fairbanks								✓		✓			✓	✓			✓		✓		✓	✓	✓		
Arizona																									
Arizona St U		✓																							
Arizona St U West		✓			✓	✓	✓	✓	✓	✓		✓	✓	✓		✓		✓		✓		✓	✓		✓
Arizona, U of		✓						✓					✓							✓			✓		
Embry-Riddle Aeronautical U		✓						✓		✓							✓						✓		
Northern Arizona U													✓												
Phoenix, U of																									
Prescott Coll								✓		✓			✓									✓			
Arkansas																									
Arkansas St U								✓		✓			✓									✓			
Arkansas Tech U								✓		✓			✓	✓			✓	✓				✓	✓		
Arkansas, U of				✓	✓			✓	✓	✓			✓	✓		✓			✓	✓		✓	✓		✓
Arkansas, U of, Little Rock		✓						✓					✓	✓								✓	✓		
Central Arkansas, U of					✓			✓	✓	✓		✓	✓									✓			✓
Harding U		✓		✓	✓			✓	✓	✓		✓	✓	✓							✓	✓	✓		
Henderson St U								✓		✓		✓				✓	✓								✓
Hendrix Coll					✓					✓		✓	✓					✓							
John Brown U								✓		✓		✓	✓	✓		✓		✓				✓			✓
Lyon Coll										✓			✓	✓	✓		✓	✓				✓			
Ouachita Baptist U				✓				✓		✓	✓		✓	✓								✓	✓		

	Curriculum						In Class						Exams						Services						
	Foreign Language Waiver	Lighter Course Load	Math Waiver	Other Special Classes	Priority Registration	Substition of Courses	Early Syllabus	Note Takers in Class	Priority Seating	Tape Recorders	Videotaped Classes	Text on Tape	Extended Time	Oral Exams	Take Home Exams	Exams on Tape or PC	Untimed Exams	Other Accommodations	Diagnostic Tests	Learning Centers	Proofreaders	Readers	Reading Machines	Special Bookstore Section	Typists
Ozarks, U of the		✓		✓	✓			✓		✓		✓	✓	✓					✓	✓	✓	✓	✓		✓
Southern Arkansas U								✓		✓			✓							✓		✓			
Williams Baptist Coll		✓		✓				✓	✓	✓		✓	✓	✓		✓	✓			✓		✓	✓		
California																									
Alliant International U		✓			✓		✓	✓	✓	✓	✓	✓	✓	✓	✓	✓	✓	✓			✓	✓	✓		✓
Art Ctr Coll of Design													✓												
Azusa Pacific U								✓					✓							✓					
Biola U	✓		✓		✓		✓	✓	✓	✓		✓	✓			✓		✓	✓		✓	✓	✓		✓
California Baptist U		✓			✓			✓	✓	✓		✓	✓	✓				✓		✓		✓			✓
California Coll of Arts & Crafts		✓						✓		✓			✓				✓								
California Inst of Tech		✓						✓		✓			✓	✓			✓		✓			✓			
California Inst of the Arts																									
California Lutheran U					✓		✓	✓	✓	✓			✓	✓		✓	✓	✓		✓		✓			
California Polytech St U								✓		✓		✓	✓			✓								✓	
California St Polytech U					✓			✓		✓			✓	✓						✓			✓		
California St U, Bakersfield								✓		✓	✓		✓	✓			✓		✓			✓	✓		
California St U, Chico		✓			✓			✓	✓	✓		✓	✓	✓		✓	✓	✓	✓	✓		✓	✓		✓
California St U, East Bay								✓		✓			✓	✓						✓		✓			
California St U, Fullerton								✓		✓			✓					✓	✓	✓		✓			
California St U, Long Beach		✓						✓		✓			✓	✓			✓		✓	✓		✓	✓		
California St U, Los Angeles		✓			✓	✓		✓		✓		✓	✓	✓		✓		✓	✓			✓			✓
California St U, Monterey Bay		✓			✓			✓					✓					✓		✓			✓		
California St U, Sacramento						✓		✓		✓								✓	✓	✓		✓			

Cal St U, San Bernardino				✓	✓	✓		✓	✓	✓		✓	✓	✓		✓		✓	✓	✓	✓	✓	✓		✓
California St U, Stanislaus		✓						✓		✓			✓									✓	✓		
California, U of, Davis								✓		✓			✓	✓						✓		✓	✓		
California, U of, Irvine		✓			✓			✓		✓		✓	✓									✓	✓		
California, U of, Los Angeles		✓			✓			✓		✓		✓	✓					✓	✓			✓	✓		
California, U of, Riverside																									
California, U of, San Diego					✓			✓	✓	✓		✓	✓	✓		✓	✓	✓	✓	✓	✓	✓	✓	✓	✓
California, U of, Santa Cruz		✓						✓		✓	✓		✓	✓						✓		✓	✓		
Chapman U		✓			✓			✓		✓			✓	✓						✓		✓			
Charles R Drew U					✓		✓	✓	✓	✓	✓		✓	✓	✓	✓			✓	✓	✓	✓			✓
Claremont McKenna Coll	✓					✓		✓		✓			✓				✓								
Concordia U													✓	✓			✓			✓					
Dominican U of California		✓			✓			✓	✓	✓		✓	✓			✓		✓				✓			✓
Fresno Pacific U								✓		✓		✓	✓	✓	✓			✓		✓		✓			✓
Harvey Mudd Coll		✓								✓			✓				✓								
Holy Names U		✓				✓		✓		✓	✓	✓	✓	✓				✓		✓		✓	✓		
Humboldt St U								✓		✓			✓							✓		✓	✓		
Humphreys Coll			✓						✓				✓							✓					
Judaism, U of		✓						✓		✓			✓	✓			✓					✓			
LaVerne, U of	✓		✓		✓	✓	✓	✓	✓	✓		✓	✓	✓		✓	✓	✓		✓		✓	✓		✓
Life Pacific Coll		✓						✓	✓	✓			✓	✓	✓		✓	✓							
Loyola Marymount U		✓		✓	✓			✓	✓	✓		✓	✓	✓				✓		✓		✓	✓		
Master's Coll & Sem													✓												
Menlo Coll	✓	✓	✓	✓		✓		✓		✓			✓			✓		✓		✓					✓
Mills Coll		✓						✓		✓			✓									✓	✓		
Mt St. Mary's Coll													✓					✓		✓					
National U								✓		✓	✓		✓				✓		✓			✓	✓		
Notre Dame de Namur U	✓	✓				✓	✓	✓	✓	✓		✓	✓	✓	✓	✓	✓	✓	✓	✓	✓	✓			✓
Occidental Coll		✓								✓			✓			✓				✓					

	Curriculum						In Class						Exams						Services						
	Foreign Language Waiver	Lighter Course Load	Math Waiver	Other Special Classes	Priority Registration	Substition of Courses	Early Syllabus	Note Takers in Class	Priority Seating	Tape Recorders	Videotaped Classes	Text on Tape	Extended Time	Oral Exams	Take Home Exams	Exams on Tape or PC	Untimed Exams	Other Accommodations	Diagnostic Tests	Learning Centers	Proofreaders	Readers	Reading Machines	Special Bookstore Section	Typists
Pacific Oaks Coll								✓																	
Pacific Union Coll		✓				✓		✓	✓	✓		✓	✓	✓		✓		✓	✓	✓	✓	✓	✓		✓
Pacific, U of the		✓											✓							✓			✓		
Patten U		✓						✓		✓	✓		✓	✓	✓	✓	✓			✓	✓	✓			
Pepperdine U					✓			✓	✓	✓			✓	✓					✓			✓	✓		
Pitzer Coll		✓						✓		✓			✓									✓	✓		
Point Loma Nazarene U	✓	✓					✓	✓		✓		✓	✓	✓			✓				✓				
Pomona Coll		✓						✓		✓			✓	✓								✓			
Redlands, U of	✓	✓	✓			✓		✓		✓		✓	✓	✓			✓	✓				✓			✓
San Diego St U				✓									✓							✓					
San Diego, U of		✓						✓		✓			✓										✓		
San Francisco Art Inst								✓		✓										✓					
San Francisco St U				✓				✓																	
San Francisco, U of		✓		✓				✓		✓	✓		✓				✓		✓	✓		✓	✓		
San Jose St U		✓						✓		✓			✓	✓					✓	✓		✓	✓		
Santa Clara U		✓			✓	✓	✓	✓	✓	✓		✓	✓					✓				✓	✓		
Scripps Coll		✓	✓		✓	✓	✓		✓	✓			✓		✓	✓	✓					✓			✓
Simpson U					✓		✓	✓	✓				✓	✓			✓	✓				✓			✓
Sonoma St U				✓	✓			✓		✓		✓	✓			✓		✓		✓		✓	✓		
Southern California, U of		✓						✓		✓	✓		✓									✓	✓		
St. Mary's Coll	✓	✓	✓		✓	✓	✓	✓		✓			✓	✓		✓	✓	✓				✓	✓		✓
Stanford U		✓				✓		✓		✓		✓	✓	✓	✓	✓		✓	✓	✓		✓	✓		✓
Vanguard U of Southern Cal								✓					✓	✓			✓								

Westmont Coll		✓			✓			✓		✓		✓	✓	✓		✓	✓	✓				✓			✓
Whittier Coll		✓				✓		✓		✓		✓	✓	✓						✓		✓	✓		✓
Woodbury U					✓			✓		✓		✓	✓				✓	✓		✓					
Canada																									
Alberta, U of								✓	✓			✓	✓	✓		✓		✓	✓			✓	✓		✓
Calgary, U of																									
Dalhousie U								✓	✓	✓		✓	✓	✓				✓		✓		✓	✓		✓
McGill U		✓						✓		✓		✓	✓	✓		✓					✓	✓	✓		✓
NSCAD U								✓		✓			✓	✓		✓	✓		✓		✓	✓			✓
Prince Edward Island, U of																									
Simon Fraser U		✓						✓		✓			✓	✓						✓		✓	✓		
Victoria, U of	✓	✓	✓				✓	✓	✓	✓	✓	✓	✓	✓	✓	✓				✓		✓	✓		✓
York U		✓		✓			✓	✓				✓	✓	✓		✓		✓	✓	✓	✓				✓
Colorado																									
Colorado Christian U				✓						✓										✓					
Colorado Coll						✓	✓	✓	✓	✓		✓	✓			✓		✓		✓		✓			
Colorado Sch of Mines								✓	✓				✓												
Colorado St U		✓			✓	✓		✓		✓		✓	✓			✓		✓	✓			✓	✓		
Colorado St U, Pueblo								✓		✓			✓									✓			
Colorado, U of, Boulder								✓				✓	✓			✓			✓	✓	✓	✓	✓		
Colorado, U of, Co Springs		✓		✓				✓	✓	✓	✓		✓	✓				✓	✓	✓		✓	✓		✓
Colorado, U of, Denver								✓					✓	✓					✓			✓	✓		
Denver, U of		✓			✓	✓	✓	✓		✓	✓	✓	✓	✓	✓	✓			✓	✓		✓	✓		✓
Fort Lewis Coll								✓		✓			✓	✓								✓			
Mesa St Coll		✓						✓		✓			✓	✓						✓			✓		
Metropolitan St Coll of Denver													✓	✓						✓	✓	✓			
Northern Colorado, U of								✓		✓			✓					✓				✓			
Regis U		✓						✓		✓		✓	✓	✓		✓				✓		✓	✓		
Western St Coll		✓											✓						✓						

	Curriculum						In Class						Exams						Services						
	Foreign Language Waiver	Lighter Course Load	Math Waiver	Other Special Classes	Priority Registration	Substition of Courses	Early Syllabus	Note Takers in Class	Priority Seating	Tape Recorders	Videotaped Classes	Text on Tape	Extended Time	Oral Exams	Take Home Exams	Exams on Tape or PC	Untimed Exams	Other Accommodations	Diagnostic Tests	Learning Centers	Proofreaders	Readers	Reading Machines	Special Bookstore Section	Typists
Connecticut																									
Albertus Magnus Coll		✓								✓			✓				✓			✓					
Bridgeport, U of		✓															✓			✓					
Central Connecticut St U								✓		✓			✓	✓						✓		✓	✓		
Connecticut Coll		✓						✓					✓			✓		✓							
Connecticut, U of		✓			✓	✓		✓		✓		✓	✓	✓		✓	✓					✓	✓		
Eastern Connecticut St U		✓			✓	✓	✓	✓	✓	✓		✓	✓	✓		✓		✓		✓	✓	✓	✓		✓
Fairfield U		✓						✓		✓			✓	✓								✓	✓		
Hartford, U of								✓		✓			✓							✓		✓			
Mitchell Coll		✓			✓	✓	✓	✓		✓		✓	✓	✓		✓	✓	✓		✓			✓		✓
New Haven, U of		✓						✓	✓	✓		✓	✓			✓		✓	✓	✓	✓	✓	✓		✓
Quinnipiac U																				✓					
Sacred Heart U		✓				✓		✓		✓			✓	✓			✓	✓		✓		✓	✓		✓
Southern Connecticut St U		✓		✓				✓		✓			✓									✓	✓		
St. Joseph Coll		✓			✓	✓	✓	✓	✓	✓		✓	✓	✓	✓	✓	✓	✓		✓	✓	✓			
Teikyo Post U	✓	✓				✓							✓				✓	✓		✓					
Trinity Coll								✓	✓	✓		✓	✓	✓		✓		✓				✓			✓
Wesleyan U					✓		✓	✓				✓	✓			✓									
Yale U																									
Delaware																									
Delaware St U		✓						✓		✓			✓	✓			✓			✓		✓			
Delaware, U of																									
Wesley Coll		✓						✓		✓			✓				✓								

District of Columbia																									
American U		✓			✓			✓					✓					✓		✓		✓			
Catholic U of America	✓	✓			✓	✓	✓	✓	✓	✓	✓	✓	✓	✓	✓	✓	✓	✓		✓		✓	✓		✓
Corcoran Coll of Art & Design													✓							✓					
District of Columbia, U of the				✓				✓		✓			✓	✓			✓		✓	✓		✓	✓		
Gallaudet U		✓		✓				✓	✓	✓		✓	✓		✓	✓	✓		✓	✓		✓	✓		
George Washington U		✓			✓	✓		✓	✓	✓		✓	✓			✓	✓	✓			✓	✓	✓		
Georgetown U		✓			✓			✓		✓			✓									✓			
Howard U								✓	✓	✓		✓	✓			✓		✓				✓	✓		✓
Trinity U								✓		✓		✓	✓									✓			
Florida																									
Baptist Coll		✓						✓		✓			✓	✓			✓					✓			
Barry U		✓		✓				✓		✓			✓	✓						✓		✓	✓		
Central Florida, U of								✓		✓	✓		✓						✓			✓	✓		
Clearwater Christian Coll		✓								✓	✓		✓	✓			✓					✓			
Eckerd Coll																									
Edward Waters Coll		✓						✓		✓			✓	✓			✓					✓			
Embry-Riddle Aeronautical U		✓						✓		✓							✓						✓		
Flagler Coll		✓			✓			✓					✓	✓				✓					✓		
Florida A&M U	✓	✓	✓	✓		✓				✓			✓			✓				✓	✓	✓	✓		
Florida Atlantic U		✓								✓													✓		
Florida Gulf Coast U		✓			✓	✓	✓	✓	✓	✓		✓	✓			✓	✓	✓	✓	✓		✓	✓		✓
Florida Inst of Tech								✓		✓			✓				✓		✓	✓					
Florida International U		✓		✓				✓		✓	✓		✓	✓			✓		✓	✓		✓	✓		
Florida Memorial Coll		✓											✓						✓	✓					
Florida St U	✓	✓	✓			✓	✓	✓		✓		✓	✓	✓			✓		✓			✓	✓	✓	
Florida, U of		✓						✓		✓			✓						✓			✓	✓		
Jacksonville U		✓		✓		✓		✓	✓	✓	✓	✓	✓	✓			✓	✓		✓		✓	✓	✓	
Lynn U				✓						✓			✓	✓			✓			✓		✓	✓		

	Curriculum						In Class						Exams						Services						
	Foreign Language Waiver	Lighter Course Load	Math Waiver	Other Special Classes	Priority Registration	Substition of Courses	Early Syllabus	Note Takers in Class	Priority Seating	Tape Recorders	Videotaped Classes	Text on Tape	Extended Time	Oral Exams	Take Home Exams	Exams on Tape or PC	Untimed Exams	Other Accommodations	Diagnostic Tests	Learning Centers	Proofreaders	Readers	Reading Machines	Special Bookstore Section	Typists
Miami International U		✓					✓	✓	✓				✓	✓	✓	✓	✓		✓	✓				✓	
Miami, U of										✓			✓							✓		✓			
New Coll of Florida							✓	✓	✓	✓			✓	✓								✓			✓
North Florida, U of								✓		✓			✓	✓			✓			✓		✓	✓		
Northwood U																									
Nova Southeastern U		✓						✓		✓			✓	✓					✓	✓		✓	✓		
Ringling Sch of Art & Design								✓		✓		✓	✓							✓			✓		
Rollins Coll		✓						✓		✓			✓				✓			✓		✓	✓		
South Florida, U of		✓						✓		✓			✓	✓								✓	✓		
Southeastern Coll Assem God		✓						✓		✓		✓	✓	✓			✓	✓	✓	✓	✓	✓	✓		
St. Leo U		✓						✓		✓			✓	✓						✓		✓	✓		
St. Thomas U								✓		✓			✓				✓			✓	✓				
Stetson U		✓						✓		✓			✓	✓						✓		✓			
Tampa, U of		✓						✓					✓							✓					
Trinity Baptist Coll		✓											✓	✓			✓		✓						
Warner Southern Coll													✓	✓						✓	✓	✓	✓		
West Florida, U of		✓						✓					✓							✓		✓	✓		
Georgia																									
Agnes Scott Coll		✓						✓		✓			✓	✓			✓					✓	✓		
Armstrong Atlantic St U				✓				✓		✓			✓						✓	✓		✓	✓		
Art Inst of Atlanta								✓					✓	✓											
Atlanta Coll of Art								✓					✓	✓			✓								
Augusta St U		✓			✓	✓		✓	✓	✓		✓	✓	✓		✓		✓	✓	✓	✓	✓	✓		✓

Berry Coll					✓			✓	✓	✓			✓	✓		✓						✓			✓
Brenau U		✓		✓	✓			✓	✓	✓		✓	✓	✓			✓		✓	✓	✓	✓	✓		
Brewton-Parker Coll								✓					✓							✓		✓			
Clark Atlanta U		✓								✓			✓				✓					✓			
Clayton Coll & St U		✓			✓			✓	✓	✓		✓	✓			✓		✓				✓	✓		
Columbus St U								✓		✓	✓		✓	✓			✓		✓	✓		✓	✓		
Covenant Coll		✓											✓						✓						
Emmanuel Coll																									
Emory U		✓		✓				✓					✓	✓								✓			
Fort Valley St U		✓						✓		✓				✓			✓			✓		✓	✓		
Georgia Coll & St U		✓			✓					✓			✓	✓			✓		✓			✓			
Georgia Inst of Tech	✓	✓			✓			✓	✓	✓	✓	✓	✓	✓		✓		✓	✓	✓		✓			✓
Georgia Southern U	✓	✓		✓	✓	✓		✓	✓	✓		✓	✓	✓		✓		✓	✓	✓	✓	✓	✓		✓
Georgia St U		✓			✓	✓		✓	✓			✓	✓	✓		✓		✓	✓				✓		
Georgia, U of		✓			✓			✓		✓		✓	✓	✓					✓	✓		✓	✓		✓
Kennesaw St U					✓				✓	✓		✓	✓	✓		✓			✓				✓		
LaGrange Coll		✓						✓		✓			✓	✓			✓					✓			
Life U					✓			✓		✓	✓		✓	✓				✓							
Mercer U	✓	✓			✓	✓			✓	✓		✓	✓							✓					
Morehouse Coll	✓	✓	✓			✓		✓	✓	✓			✓	✓			✓	✓	✓	✓		✓		✓	✓
North Georgia Coll & St U					✓	✓		✓	✓	✓			✓			✓	✓		✓			✓	✓		✓
Paine Coll																									
Piedmont Coll		✓								✓				✓			✓			✓					
Reinhardt Coll		✓			✓			✓	✓	✓		✓	✓	✓				✓		✓	✓	✓			
Savannah Coll of Art & Design								✓		✓												✓			
Shorter Coll																									
South U		✓							✓	✓			✓	✓		✓	✓	✓		✓					
Spelman Coll					✓	✓		✓	✓	✓		✓	✓	✓				✓		✓		✓			
Toccoa Falls Coll								✓	✓				✓	✓			✓	✓		✓		✓			✓

	Curriculum						In Class						Exams						Services						
	Foreign Language Waiver	Lighter Course Load	Math Waiver	Other Special Classes	Priority Registration	Substition of Courses	Early Syllabus	Note Takers in Class	Priority Seating	Tape Recorders	Videotaped Classes	Text on Tape	Extended Time	Oral Exams	Take Home Exams	Exams on Tape or PC	Untimed Exams	Other Accommodations	Diagnostic Tests	Learning Centers	Proofreaders	Readers	Reading Machines	Special Bookstore Section	Typists
Truett-McCornell Coll								✓	✓	✓		✓	✓	✓		✓	✓	✓		✓		✓	✓	✓	
Valdosta St U		✓			✓	✓		✓	✓	✓		✓	✓			✓		✓				✓	✓		✓
Wesleyan Coll								✓	✓				✓							✓					
West Georgia, U of	✓				✓			✓		✓			✓	✓			✓					✓	✓		
Hawaii																									
Brigham Young U, Hawaii					✓			✓		✓	✓		✓	✓			✓		✓	✓		✓	✓		
Chaminade U of Honolulu		✓																							
Hawaii Pacific U	✓				✓	✓			✓	✓		✓	✓	✓	✓	✓	✓	✓		✓	✓	✓			✓
Hawaii, U of, Hilo				✓				✓		✓	✓		✓	✓						✓		✓	✓		
Hawaii, U of, Manoa		✓			✓	✓	✓	✓		✓		✓	✓			✓			✓		✓	✓	✓		✓
Idaho																									
Albertson Coll		✓						✓		✓			✓	✓	✓		✓	✓		✓		✓			
Boise St U										✓				✓					✓	✓					
Idaho St U	✓		✓		✓			✓		✓			✓	✓		✓	✓	✓	✓	✓		✓	✓		✓
Idaho, U of		✓						✓		✓	✓		✓	✓						✓		✓	✓		
Lewis-Clark St Coll		✓								✓		✓	✓					✓		✓	✓	✓	✓		
Northwest Nazarene U		✓		✓	✓		✓	✓	✓	✓		✓	✓	✓		✓	✓	✓		✓	✓	✓			✓
Illinois																									
Augustana Coll																									
Aurora U		✓				✓	✓	✓	✓	✓		✓	✓	✓		✓		✓		✓	✓	✓	✓		
Benedictine U		✓				✓	✓	✓	✓	✓	✓	✓	✓	✓	✓	✓	✓	✓		✓	✓	✓	✓		✓
Blackburn Coll						✓	✓	✓	✓	✓	✓	✓	✓	✓			✓			✓	✓	✓	✓		✓
Bradley U		✓								✓	✓		✓				✓			✓					

Chicago St U		✓			✓	✓	✓	✓	✓	✓		✓	✓	✓		✓		✓	✓	✓		✓	✓		✓
Chicago, U of																									
Columbia Coll Chicago								✓					✓												
Concordia U, River Forest																									
DePaul U	✓	✓			✓					✓		✓	✓			✓	✓		✓			✓			
Eastern Illinois U		✓		✓	✓	✓		✓	✓	✓		✓	✓	✓		✓		✓		✓		✓	✓		
Elmhurst Coll																									
Eureka Coll		✓																		✓					
Governors St U		✓					✓	✓		✓		✓	✓	✓			✓	✓		✓					
Greenville Coll		✓											✓												
Illinois Coll	✓	✓	✓		✓	✓	✓	✓	✓	✓			✓	✓			✓	✓	✓			✓			
Illinois Inst of Tech		✓						✓		✓	✓		✓	✓			✓			✓		✓			
Illinois St U								✓					✓			✓		✓	✓	✓		✓	✓		✓
Illinois Wesleyan U		✓				✓				✓			✓	✓											
Illinois, U of, Chicago								✓		✓			✓	✓						✓		✓	✓		
Illinois, U of, Springfield					✓	✓	✓	✓	✓	✓		✓	✓	✓		✓		✓		✓	✓	✓			✓
Illinois, U of, Urbana-Champ		✓		✓	✓		✓	✓	✓	✓		✓	✓	✓	✓	✓	✓	✓	✓	✓	✓	✓	✓	✓	✓
Knox Coll		✓						✓		✓			✓	✓			✓			✓		✓			
Lake Forest Coll								✓		✓		✓	✓	✓	✓		✓			✓		✓	✓		✓
Lewis U								✓					✓	✓			✓								
Loyola U, Chicago	✓		✓			✓	✓	✓		✓		✓	✓	✓		✓				✓		✓	✓		✓
MacMurray Coll		✓						✓						✓			✓			✓		✓			
McKendree Coll		✓	✓						✓	✓		✓	✓	✓	✓	✓	✓			✓			✓		
Millikin U		✓		✓				✓		✓			✓	✓			✓			✓		✓			
Monmouth Coll								✓	✓	✓			✓	✓			✓	✓		✓		✓			✓
Moraine Valley Comm Coll				✓	✓		✓	✓	✓	✓		✓	✓	✓		✓		✓	✓	✓		✓			
National-Louis U				✓						✓	✓			✓					✓	✓		✓	✓		
North Central Coll		✓						✓	✓	✓		✓	✓	✓		✓	✓	✓	✓	✓		✓	✓		✓
North Park U		✓				✓		✓		✓		✓	✓	✓	✓	✓	✓	✓		✓					

	Curriculum						In Class						Exams						Services						
	Foreign Language Waiver	Lighter Course Load	Math Waiver	Other Special Classes	Priority Registration	Substition of Courses	Early Syllabus	Note Takers in Class	Priority Seating	Tape Recorders	Videotaped Classes	Text on Tape	Extended Time	Oral Exams	Take Home Exams	Exams on Tape or PC	Untimed Exams	Other Accommodations	Diagnostic Tests	Learning Centers	Proofreaders	Readers	Reading Machines	Special Bookstore Section	Typists
Northeastern Illinois U								✓		✓			✓	✓			✓					✓	✓		
Northern Illinois U		✓			✓			✓	✓	✓		✓	✓	✓		✓				✓		✓	✓		
Northwestern U		✓			✓	✓		✓	✓	✓		✓	✓	✓		✓		✓	✓		✓	✓	✓		✓
Olivet Nazarene U		✓						✓	✓	✓			✓	✓		✓	✓	✓	✓	✓		✓	✓		
Quincy U		✓						✓		✓			✓	✓			✓			✓		✓	✓		
Robert Morris Coll		✓						✓		✓		✓	✓	✓				✓		✓		✓			
Rockford Coll		✓			✓		✓	✓	✓	✓		✓	✓	✓		✓	✓	✓	✓	✓	✓	✓	✓	✓	✓
Roosevelt U		✓						✓					✓				✓		✓	✓					
St. Anthony Coll of Nursing		✓								✓			✓									✓			
St. Francis Medical Ctr Coll													✓					✓							
St. Francis, U of								✓	✓	✓		✓	✓	✓			✓	✓		✓		✓			
St. Xavier U								✓		✓		✓	✓	✓		✓				✓					✓
Sch of the Art Inst of Chicago		✓			✓			✓		✓		✓	✓	✓			✓	✓		✓		✓			
Southern Illinois U Carbondale		✓		✓		✓		✓		✓	✓	✓	✓	✓					✓	✓		✓	✓		
Southern Ill U Edwardsville		✓		✓	✓	✓	✓	✓	✓	✓			✓	✓		✓	✓		✓	✓	✓	✓	✓		✓
Trinity Christian Coll								✓		✓		✓	✓	✓			✓			✓		✓			✓
Trinity International U																									
Waubonsee Comm Coll						✓	✓	✓		✓		✓	✓	✓	✓	✓	✓			✓	✓	✓	✓		✓
Western Illinois U										✓			✓	✓								✓			
Wheaton Coll																									
Indiana																									
Anderson U	✓	✓		✓				✓		✓			✓	✓		✓	✓			✓	✓	✓			✓
Ball St U		✓						✓		✓			✓	✓						✓		✓	✓		

Bethel Coll													✓	✓			✓			✓					
Butler U		✓			✓	✓		✓	✓	✓		✓	✓			✓		✓		✓		✓	✓		✓
Calumet Coll of St. Joseph								✓		✓		✓	✓	✓			✓			✓	✓	✓			
DePauw U		✓			✓		✓	✓	✓	✓		✓	✓	✓		✓	✓	✓	✓	✓		✓	✓		✓
Earlham Coll																									
Evansville, U of								✓	✓	✓		✓	✓					✓			✓				
Franklin Coll		✓		✓	✓			✓		✓	✓	✓	✓	✓		✓	✓			✓		✓			
Goshen Coll							✓	✓		✓			✓			✓	✓			✓		✓	✓	✓	
Grace Coll & Sem		✓						✓		✓			✓	✓		✓	✓	✓		✓	✓	✓	✓		
Hanover Coll								✓		✓			✓				✓								
Huntington Coll					✓			✓	✓			✓	✓	✓		✓				✓	✓	✓			✓
Indiana St U		✓						✓					✓	✓						✓		✓			
Indiana U Bloomington		✓			✓	✓		✓	✓	✓		✓	✓	✓		✓		✓				✓	✓		✓
Indiana U East		✓						✓		✓				✓			✓		✓	✓		✓	✓		
Indiana U Kokomo		✓						✓						✓			✓		✓	✓		✓			
Indiana U Northwest		✓																	✓	✓					
Indiana U South Bend		✓																	✓	✓					
Indiana U Southeast		✓		✓				✓						✓			✓						✓	✓	
In U-Purdue U Fort Wayne										✓								✓				✓	✓		
In U-Purdue U Indianapolis		✓						✓		✓	✓			✓			✓		✓	✓		✓	✓		
Indiana Wesleyan U								✓		✓	✓		✓	✓			✓					✓	✓		
Indianapolis, U of		✓		✓		✓			✓	✓		✓	✓	✓			✓	✓	✓	✓	✓	✓	✓		
Ivy Tech St Coll, Southwest							✓	✓				✓	✓	✓		✓		✓		✓			✓		
Manchester Coll		✓						✓		✓			✓	✓			✓			✓		✓			
Marian Coll		✓		✓				✓		✓			✓				✓		✓	✓		✓			
Notre Dame, U of								✓		✓	✓	✓	✓	✓			✓		✓	✓		✓	✓		
Purdue U					✓	✓		✓	✓	✓		✓	✓	✓		✓		✓	✓	✓		✓	✓		✓
Purdue U, Calumet						✓		✓	✓	✓		✓	✓	✓		✓						✓	✓		✓
Purdue U, North Central		✓				✓		✓		✓		✓	✓	✓		✓		✓		✓		✓			✓

	Curriculum						In Class						Exams						Services						
	Foreign Language Waiver	Lighter Course Load	Math Waiver	Other Special Classes	Priority Registration	Substition of Courses	Early Syllabus	Note Takers in Class	Priority Seating	Tape Recorders	Videotaped Classes	Text on Tape	Extended Time	Oral Exams	Take Home Exams	Exams on Tape or PC	Untimed Exams	Other Accommodations	Diagnostic Tests	Learning Centers	Proofreaders	Readers	Reading Machines	Special Bookstore Section	Typists
Rose-Hulman Inst of Tech								✓		✓			✓				✓			✓					
Southern Indiana, U of					✓	✓		✓	✓			✓	✓	✓		✓		✓		✓		✓			✓
St. Francis, U of	✓	✓				✓			✓	✓			✓	✓		✓	✓	✓		✓	✓	✓	✓		✓
St. Joseph's Coll		✓		✓						✓			✓	✓			✓								
St. Mary-of-the-Woods Coll	✓			✓		✓		✓		✓			✓	✓		✓	✓	✓		✓		✓			
Taylor U					✓	✓		✓		✓		✓	✓	✓		✓		✓		✓		✓	✓		
Valparaiso U				✓	✓			✓	✓	✓	✓		✓	✓	✓	✓	✓	✓				✓	✓		
Wabash Coll										✓			✓				✓			✓					
Iowa																									
Briar Cliff U		✓			✓			✓		✓			✓	✓				✓					✓		
Buena Vista U										✓										✓					
Central Coll		✓				✓		✓		✓	✓	✓	✓	✓		✓	✓		✓	✓		✓	✓		
Clarke Coll		✓											✓	✓			✓			✓		✓			
Coe Coll		✓						✓		✓		✓	✓	✓			✓	✓		✓	✓				✓
Cornell Coll							✓		✓	✓		✓	✓	✓			✓	✓		✓					
Dordt Coll	✓	✓				✓	✓	✓	✓	✓		✓	✓	✓		✓	✓	✓		✓	✓	✓			
Drake U		✓						✓	✓	✓		✓	✓			✓		✓				✓	✓		✓
Dubuque, U of		✓		✓				✓		✓			✓	✓			✓			✓				✓	
Faith Baptist Bible Coll		✓											✓												
Graceland U		✓						✓		✓			✓	✓			✓		✓	✓		✓			
Grand View Coll		✓						✓		✓	✓		✓	✓			✓			✓		✓	✓		
Grinnell Coll		✓						✓		✓			✓	✓			✓					✓			
Hawkeye Comm Coll		✓			✓	✓		✓	✓	✓		✓	✓	✓				✓		✓	✓	✓	✓		✓

Iowa St U	✓	✓			✓	✓	✓	✓	✓	✓	✓	✓	✓			✓		✓		✓		✓	✓		
Iowa Wesleyan Coll				✓				✓		✓			✓	✓			✓	✓	✓	✓	✓	✓	✓		✓
Iowa, U of					✓			✓	✓	✓		✓	✓			✓		✓				✓	✓		✓
Loras Coll		✓		✓				✓		✓			✓				✓			✓			✓		
Luther Coll	✓		✓		✓	✓		✓		✓		✓	✓	✓				✓		✓					✓
Morningside Coll	✓					✓		✓	✓	✓		✓	✓	✓		✓	✓		✓	✓	✓	✓	✓		
Mt Mercy Coll		✓			✓			✓	✓	✓	✓		✓	✓		✓		✓		✓	✓	✓	✓		✓
Northern Iowa, U of					✓	✓		✓	✓	✓		✓	✓			✓		✓				✓	✓		✓
Northwestern Coll, Iowa								✓		✓			✓	✓	✓	✓	✓			✓	✓				✓
Simpson Coll		✓						✓		✓			✓	✓			✓			✓		✓			
St. Ambrose U										✓			✓	✓			✓	✓	✓	✓					
Waldorf Coll		✓		✓				✓		✓		✓	✓	✓			✓	✓		✓		✓			
Wartburg Coll										✓			✓	✓								✓			
William Penn U		✓						✓		✓			✓				✓								
Kansas																									
Baker U		✓						✓	✓	✓			✓	✓		✓				✓		✓			✓
Benedictine Coll	✓		✓					✓		✓			✓	✓			✓			✓		✓			✓
Bethany Coll				✓				✓		✓			✓	✓			✓		✓	✓		✓			
Bethel Coll		✓						✓		✓	✓		✓	✓			✓			✓		✓			
Central Christian Coll		✓		✓				✓					✓	✓			✓					✓			
Emporia St U	✓	✓	✓		✓	✓	✓	✓	✓	✓		✓	✓	✓		✓		✓	✓			✓	✓		✓
Friends U				✓				✓		✓	✓	✓	✓	✓		✓	✓			✓		✓	✓		✓
Kansas St U		✓			✓	✓		✓				✓	✓	✓		✓		✓			✓	✓	✓		
Kansas, U of					✓			✓	✓	✓		✓	✓	✓		✓		✓	✓	✓		✓			✓
Manhattan Christian Coll		✓						✓	✓				✓	✓			✓					✓			
McPherson Coll								✓					✓	✓						✓			✓		
MidAmerica Nazarene U							✓	✓	✓	✓	✓	✓	✓	✓		✓	✓		✓	✓		✓			
Newman U								✓		✓			✓	✓			✓			✓		✓	✓		
Pittsburg St U								✓		✓			✓	✓			✓	✓	✓	✓		✓			

	Curriculum						In Class						Exams						Services						
	Foreign Language Waiver	Lighter Course Load	Math Waiver	Other Special Classes	Priority Registration	Substition of Courses	Early Syllabus	Note Takers in Class	Priority Seating	Tape Recorders	Videotaped Classes	Text on Tape	Extended Time	Oral Exams	Take Home Exams	Exams on Tape or PC	Untimed Exams	Other Accommodations	Diagnostic Tests	Learning Centers	Proofreaders	Readers	Reading Machines	Special Bookstore Section	Typists
St. Mary, U of		✓								✓			✓				✓			✓					
Sterling Coll		✓						✓		✓			✓	✓			✓		✓	✓	✓	✓			
Tabor Coll		✓		✓				✓		✓			✓	✓			✓			✓	✓	✓			
Washburn U		✓						✓		✓			✓	✓				✓		✓		✓	✓		
Wichita St U								✓		✓	✓		✓	✓			✓		✓			✓	✓		
Kentucky																									
Bellarmine U								✓		✓	✓		✓	✓			✓	✓	✓	✓		✓			✓
Berea Coll		✓						✓	✓	✓			✓					✓	✓	✓					
Centre Coll		✓		✓	✓			✓	✓	✓	✓	✓	✓	✓		✓	✓	✓		✓	✓	✓			✓
Cumberlands College																									
Eastern Kentucky U				✓				✓		✓			✓	✓					✓	✓		✓	✓		
Georgetown Coll								✓					✓				✓					✓			
Kentucky Christian U								✓					✓	✓			✓			✓		✓			
Kentucky Wesleyan Coll								✓												✓					
Kentucky, U of					✓	✓				✓		✓	✓	✓		✓		✓	✓			✓	✓		✓
Lindsey Wilson Coll		✓						✓	✓	✓			✓	✓			✓			✓		✓	✓		
Louisville, U of								✓		✓			✓	✓								✓	✓		
Mid-Continent Coll		✓						✓		✓	✓		✓	✓			✓					✓			
Midway Coll									✓	✓		✓	✓	✓	✓		✓	✓							
Morehead St U		✓						✓		✓			✓					✓					✓		
Murray St U		✓		✓				✓		✓		✓	✓	✓			✓		✓	✓		✓	✓	✓	
Northern Kentucky U				✓	✓				✓	✓			✓			✓				✓		✓	✓		
Pikeville Coll													✓	✓			✓					✓			

Spalding U		✓		✓				✓		✓			✓	✓			✓		✓	✓					
Thomas More Coll		✓		✓				✓	✓	✓		✓	✓	✓	✓	✓	✓			✓	✓	✓			
Transylvania U							✓	✓	✓				✓				✓								✓
Western Kentucky U					✓			✓	✓	✓	✓	✓	✓	✓					✓	✓	✓	✓	✓		
Louisiana																									
Centenary Coll of Louisiana								✓	✓	✓		✓	✓	✓			✓			✓		✓	✓		
Dillard U					✓			✓	✓	✓			✓	✓	✓		✓	✓		✓	✓	✓			
Grambling St U		✓																	✓						
Louisiana Coll								✓		✓		✓	✓	✓		✓	✓	✓		✓		✓			✓
Louisiana St U & A&M Coll				✓	✓			✓		✓		✓	✓	✓		✓						✓			
Louisiana, U of, Lafayette				✓				✓		✓			✓	✓			✓		✓	✓		✓	✓		
Louisiana, U of, Monroe																									
Loyola U New Orleans	✓	✓	✓			✓		✓	✓	✓		✓	✓			✓				✓	✓	✓	✓		✓
McNeese St U				✓				✓					✓	✓						✓		✓	✓		
New Orleans, U of																									
Nicholls St U		✓						✓		✓			✓	✓			✓			✓					
Our Lady of Holy Cross Coll								✓		✓			✓	✓			✓					✓			
Southeastern Louisiana U					✓	✓	✓	✓		✓			✓	✓		✓		✓			✓		✓		✓
Southern U & A&M Coll					✓			✓	✓	✓		✓	✓	✓		✓		✓		✓		✓			
Tulane U						✓		✓	✓	✓		✓	✓	✓		✓	✓	✓	✓	✓	✓	✓	✓		✓
Maine																									
Bates Coll								✓		✓			✓	✓			✓					✓			
Bowdoin Coll								✓		✓			✓	✓						✓		✓	✓		
Colby Coll		✓						✓		✓			✓									✓	✓		
College of the Atlantic		✓		✓				✓		✓			✓		✓		✓	✓			✓				
Husson Coll		✓						✓		✓			✓				✓						✓		
Maine Coll of Art								✓		✓			✓	✓			✓			✓		✓			
Maine Maritime Acad								✓	✓	✓	✓	✓	✓	✓		✓	✓	✓				✓			
Maine, U of, Augusta		✓						✓					✓												

	Curriculum						In Class						Exams						Services						
	Foreign Language Waiver	Lighter Course Load	Math Waiver	Other Special Classes	Priority Registration	Substition of Courses	Early Syllabus	Note Takers in Class	Priority Seating	Tape Recorders	Videotaped Classes	Text on Tape	Extended Time	Oral Exams	Take Home Exams	Exams on Tape or PC	Untimed Exams	Other Accommodations	Diagnostic Tests	Learning Centers	Proofreaders	Readers	Reading Machines	Special Bookstore Section	Typists
Maine, U of, Farmington		✓						✓	✓	✓		✓	✓					✓		✓					✓
Maine, U of, Fort Kent		✓								✓	✓		✓	✓			✓					✓			
Maine, U of, Machias		✓						✓	✓	✓		✓	✓				✓	✓		✓		✓	✓		✓
Maine, U of, Orono		✓						✓					✓	✓				✓				✓			
Maine, U of, Presque Isle		✓						✓		✓	✓		✓	✓								✓			
New England, U of		✓			✓			✓	✓			✓	✓			✓				✓		✓	✓		
Southern Maine, U of			✓	✓		✓	✓	✓		✓		✓	✓			✓	✓	✓		✓	✓	✓	✓		✓
St. Joseph's Coll								✓		✓			✓	✓								✓	✓		
Thomas Coll		✓			✓			✓	✓	✓		✓	✓	✓		✓				✓					✓
Unity Coll								✓					✓							✓		✓			
Maryland																									
Baltimore, U of							✓	✓		✓	✓	✓	✓	✓		✓				✓		✓	✓		✓
Capitol Coll		✓					✓	✓	✓	✓	✓	✓	✓	✓		✓		✓			✓				✓
Columbia Union Coll		✓											✓				✓			✓					
Coppin St U													✓				✓								
Frostburg St U								✓		✓			✓				✓					✓			
Goucher Coll		✓						✓		✓			✓							✓			✓		
Hood Coll		✓		✓		✓		✓	✓	✓			✓	✓	✓	✓	✓	✓					✓		✓
Johns Hopkins U		✓			✓	✓		✓	✓	✓		✓	✓	✓		✓	✓	✓				✓	✓		✓
Loyola Coll		✓						✓		✓			✓	✓								✓	✓		
Maryland, U of, Baltimore					✓	✓		✓	✓	✓	✓		✓	✓		✓	✓	✓		✓		✓			✓
Maryland, U of, College Park		✓			✓	✓	✓	✓	✓	✓			✓	✓	✓	✓				✓	✓	✓	✓		✓
Maryland, U of, Eastern Shore								✓		✓			✓				✓								

Maryland, U of, University Coll		✓						✓		✓				✓			✓					✓			
McDaniel Coll						✓		✓		✓		✓	✓							✓		✓	✓		
Morgan St U		✓		✓	✓			✓	✓	✓			✓	✓				✓		✓		✓			
Mt St. Mary's U		✓				✓		✓		✓		✓	✓	✓		✓				✓	✓	✓	✓		✓
Notre Dame of Md, Coll of	✓	✓				✓	✓		✓	✓		✓	✓	✓		✓	✓	✓			✓				
Salisbury U		✓						✓					✓	✓								✓			
St. Mary's Coll		✓			✓	✓		✓	✓	✓		✓	✓	✓			✓	✓			✓				
Villa Julie Coll	✓				✓	✓	✓	✓	✓	✓			✓	✓	✓		✓	✓		✓	✓	✓	✓		✓
Washington Coll										✓			✓												
Massachusetts																									
American International Coll		✓						✓		✓			✓	✓			✓		✓	✓		✓	✓		
Amherst Coll								✓		✓			✓									✓			
Art Inst of Boston, Lesley U		✓		✓				✓		✓			✓	✓						✓		✓	✓		
Assumption Coll					✓			✓	✓	✓			✓	✓			✓			✓			✓		
Babson Coll		✓						✓		✓			✓										✓		
Bay Path Coll		✓						✓	✓	✓		✓	✓				✓	✓		✓					✓
Becker Coll								✓		✓			✓	✓						✓					
Bentley Coll	✓	✓			✓	✓	✓	✓	✓	✓			✓	✓		✓		✓		✓	✓	✓	✓		✓
Berklee Coll of Music													✓				✓			✓		✓			
Boston Architectural Ctr		✓						✓	✓	✓	✓		✓	✓		✓	✓	✓		✓	✓	✓			
Boston Coll		✓			✓	✓		✓		✓		✓	✓			✓		✓		✓		✓	✓		
Boston U		✓						✓		✓			✓	✓				✓		✓		✓	✓		
Brandeis U						✓		✓		✓		✓	✓			✓		✓					✓		
Bridgewater St Coll		✓						✓		✓			✓	✓			✓			✓		✓			
Clark U		✓										✓	✓	✓								✓			
College of the Holy Cross													✓							✓					
Curry Coll		✓		✓				✓		✓		✓	✓	✓		✓	✓	✓	✓	✓		✓	✓		
Dean Coll		✓		✓				✓		✓			✓	✓			✓			✓		✓	✓		
Eastern Nazarene Coll		✓						✓		✓			✓	✓			✓		✓	✓			✓		

	Curriculum						In Class						Exams						Services						
	Foreign Language Waiver	Lighter Course Load	Math Waiver	Other Special Classes	Priority Registration	Substition of Courses	Early Syllabus	Note Takers in Class	Priority Seating	Tape Recorders	Videotaped Classes	Text on Tape	Extended Time	Oral Exams	Take Home Exams	Exams on Tape or PC	Untimed Exams	Other Accommodations	Diagnostic Tests	Learning Centers	Proofreaders	Readers	Reading Machines	Special Bookstore Section	Typists
Elms Coll																									
Emerson Coll		✓						✓		✓		✓	✓	✓		✓				✓	✓		✓		✓
Emmanuel Coll		✓		✓				✓		✓			✓	✓						✓		✓			
Endicott Coll		✓						✓	✓	✓		✓	✓	✓	✓		✓			✓	✓	✓			
Fitchburg St Coll		✓						✓		✓			✓	✓											
Framingham St Coll		✓																		✓					
Gordon Coll		✓																		✓					
Hampshire Coll		✓						✓		✓			✓									✓	✓		
Harvard U										✓	✓		✓				✓					✓			
Lasell Coll		✓						✓		✓			✓	✓			✓			✓		✓	✓		
Lesley U		✓		✓				✓		✓			✓	✓			✓			✓		✓	✓		
Massachusetts Coll of Lib Arts		✓						✓		✓			✓	✓			✓		✓	✓		✓			
Mass Coll of Pharmacy								✓										✓		✓					
Massachusetts Inst of Tech								✓		✓			✓									✓	✓		
Massachusetts Maritime Acad										✓			✓							✓					
Massachusetts, U of, Amherst		✓		✓			✓	✓	✓	✓		✓	✓	✓		✓	✓	✓			✓	✓	✓		✓
Massachusetts, U of, Boston		✓						✓		✓			✓	✓								✓	✓		
Mass, U of, Dartmouth		✓						✓		✓		✓	✓	✓			✓	✓		✓		✓	✓		
Massachusetts, U of, Lowell	✓	✓			✓			✓	✓	✓			✓	✓	✓	✓	✓	✓		✓	✓	✓			✓
Merrimack Coll		✓						✓		✓			✓	✓						✓		✓			
Montserrat Coll of Art		✓								✓			✓	✓						✓			✓		
Mt Holyoke Coll		✓				✓	✓	✓	✓	✓		✓	✓	✓		✓		✓	✓		✓	✓			✓
Mt Ida Coll		✓						✓					✓				✓			✓					

Mt Wachusett Comm Coll		✓				✓	✓	✓		✓		✓	✓	✓		✓		✓		✓		✓	✓		✓
Nichols Coll		✓											✓				✓			✓			✓		
Northeastern U		✓				✓		✓		✓	✓	✓	✓	✓				✓	✓	✓		✓	✓		
Pine Manor Coll		✓						✓					✓	✓			✓	✓		✓		✓			
Regis Coll		✓	✓					✓		✓			✓	✓			✓	✓		✓		✓			
Simmons Coll	✓					✓		✓		✓			✓	✓			✓	✓		✓		✓	✓		
Smith Coll								✓		✓		✓	✓			✓	✓	✓				✓	✓		✓
Springfield Coll		✓						✓		✓			✓				✓					✓	✓		
Stonehill Coll		✓						✓		✓		✓	✓						✓	✓		✓	✓	✓	
Suffolk U		✓			✓	✓		✓	✓	✓		✓	✓	✓			✓	✓		✓		✓	✓		✓
Tufts U								✓		✓			✓	✓						✓		✓			
Wellesley Coll								✓		✓			✓							✓					
Wentworth Inst of Tech								✓		✓			✓	✓			✓			✓		✓			
Western New England Coll		✓						✓		✓			✓							✓		✓	✓		
Wheaton Coll		✓						✓		✓			✓	✓						✓		✓	✓		
Wheelock Coll		✓						✓					✓	✓						✓		✓	✓		
Williams Coll								✓		✓			✓												
Worcester Polytech Inst		✓						✓		✓			✓	✓						✓		✓	✓		
Worcester St Coll	✓	✓			✓			✓	✓	✓			✓	✓		✓	✓			✓	✓	✓	✓		
Mexico																									
Monterrey Inst, Veracruz													✓												
Monterrey Inst, Juarez City											✓			✓											
Monterrey Inst, Leon											✓		✓												
Monterrey Inst, Mazatlan																									
Monterrey Inst, Monterrey								✓			✓		✓	✓											
Monterrey Inst, Obregon City													✓												
Monterrey Inst, U System											✓		✓												
Michigan																									
Adrian Coll				✓				✓		✓			✓	✓			✓	✓	✓	✓		✓	✓		

	Curriculum						In Class						Exams						Services						
	Foreign Language Waiver	Lighter Course Load	Math Waiver	Other Special Classes	Priority Registration	Substition of Courses	Early Syllabus	Note Takers in Class	Priority Seating	Tape Recorders	Videotaped Classes	Text on Tape	Extended Time	Oral Exams	Take Home Exams	Exams on Tape or PC	Untimed Exams	Other Accommodations	Diagnostic Tests	Learning Centers	Proofreaders	Readers	Reading Machines	Special Bookstore Section	Typists
Albion Coll		✓						✓	✓	✓	✓	✓	✓	✓		✓	✓	✓		✓	✓	✓	✓		✓
Alma Coll						✓		✓	✓	✓		✓	✓	✓			✓		✓			✓	✓		
Andrews U		✓		✓				✓		✓	✓		✓	✓			✓		✓	✓		✓	✓		
Aquinas Coll	✓	✓	✓	✓	✓	✓		✓		✓		✓	✓	✓		✓				✓		✓			✓
Calvin Coll		✓			✓			✓		✓		✓	✓			✓		✓				✓			
Central Michigan U			✓					✓	✓	✓			✓	✓			✓					✓	✓		✓
Concordia U	✓	✓				✓							✓	✓			✓	✓		✓					
Cornerstone U				✓				✓		✓	✓		✓	✓			✓		✓	✓		✓			
Creative Studies, Coll for		✓						✓		✓				✓			✓		✓	✓		✓			
Davenport U								✓		✓										✓			✓		
Eastern Michigan U		✓			✓	✓	✓	✓	✓	✓		✓	✓			✓		✓	✓	✓		✓	✓		
Ferris St U		✓		✓				✓		✓		✓	✓							✓		✓	✓		✓
Grand Valley St U		✓						✓		✓	✓		✓				✓					✓	✓		
Hillsdale Coll		✓											✓							✓					
Hope Coll		✓			✓	✓		✓		✓		✓	✓	✓		✓	✓			✓		✓	✓		✓
Kalamazoo Coll										✓			✓						✓	✓					
Kettering U								✓		✓			✓						✓			✓	✓		
Lawrence Tech U		✓						✓	✓	✓		✓	✓	✓			✓	✓		✓		✓	✓		✓
Madonna U		✓				✓	✓	✓	✓	✓		✓	✓	✓	✓	✓		✓	✓	✓	✓	✓	✓		✓
Michigan St U		✓			✓														✓						
Michigan Tech U		✓		✓				✓		✓			✓	✓			✓			✓		✓	✓		
Michigan, U of, Ann Arbor		✓						✓		✓	✓		✓	✓			✓		✓				✓		
Michigan, U of, Dearborn	✓	✓	✓		✓			✓	✓	✓		✓	✓	✓		✓						✓	✓		✓

Michigan, U of, Flint								✓					✓												
Northern Michigan U								✓					✓							✓		✓			
Northwood U, Midland		✓			✓								✓	✓			✓			✓	✓		✓		
Oakland U		✓			✓			✓	✓	✓	✓	✓	✓			✓			✓	✓		✓	✓		✓
Olivet Coll		✓					✓	✓	✓	✓			✓	✓			✓				✓	✓			
Reformed Bible Coll		✓						✓		✓		✓	✓	✓				✓	✓	✓		✓			✓
Rochester Coll		✓						✓	✓	✓		✓	✓	✓			✓				✓		✓		
Saginaw Valley St U		✓								✓			✓	✓		✓						✓	✓		
Spring Arbor U		✓						✓		✓			✓	✓			✓			✓		✓			
Walsh Coll of Accountancy								✓		✓			✓												
Wayne St U		✓						✓		✓		✓	✓			✓	✓		✓	✓			✓		
Western Michigan U		✓			✓	✓			✓	✓		✓	✓			✓		✓		✓		✓	✓		
Minnesota																									
Augsburg Coll								✓		✓		✓	✓	✓				✓		✓		✓	✓		✓
Bemidji St U		✓			✓	✓	✓	✓	✓	✓		✓	✓	✓		✓		✓			✓	✓	✓		✓
Bethel U		✓			✓	✓	✓	✓	✓	✓		✓	✓	✓		✓		✓		✓		✓	✓		✓
Carleton Coll	✓					✓	✓	✓		✓		✓	✓			✓		✓	✓	✓			✓		
Concordia Coll		✓			✓			✓	✓	✓		✓	✓			✓				✓	✓	✓	✓		✓
Concordia U, St. Paul								✓		✓	✓		✓	✓			✓			✓		✓	✓		
Crown Coll		✓			✓			✓	✓	✓			✓	✓			✓	✓		✓	✓	✓			
Gustavus Adolphus Coll								✓		✓			✓	✓						✓		✓	✓		
Hamline U					✓		✓	✓	✓	✓		✓	✓	✓		✓	✓	✓		✓		✓	✓		✓
Macalester Coll		✓						✓		✓			✓	✓			✓			✓	✓	✓	✓		
Minneapolis Coll of Art								✓		✓			✓							✓		✓			
Minnesota St U, Mankato	✓	✓	✓					✓		✓			✓	✓		✓				✓		✓	✓		
Minnesota, U of, Crookston		✓			✓			✓	✓	✓			✓	✓		✓	✓	✓		✓		✓	✓		
Minnesota, U of, Duluth		✓						✓		✓			✓						✓	✓		✓	✓		
Minnesota, U of, Morris		✓		✓	✓		✓	✓	✓	✓	✓	✓	✓	✓		✓	✓	✓		✓	✓	✓	✓		✓
Minnesota, U of, Twin Cities				✓	✓	✓	✓	✓		✓	✓	✓		✓		✓						✓	✓		

	Curriculum						In Class						Exams						Services						
	Foreign Language Waiver	Lighter Course Load	Math Waiver	Other Special Classes	Priority Registration	Substition of Courses	Early Syllabus	Note Takers in Class	Priority Seating	Tape Recorders	Videotaped Classes	Text on Tape	Extended Time	Oral Exams	Take Home Exams	Exams on Tape or PC	Untimed Exams	Other Accommodations	Diagnostic Tests	Learning Centers	Proofreaders	Readers	Reading Machines	Special Bookstore Section	Typists
North Central U				✓						✓			✓							✓					
Northwestern Coll, Minnesota		✓		✓	✓		✓	✓		✓		✓	✓	✓		✓	✓	✓		✓		✓	✓		✓
Oak Hills Christian Coll																									
Southwest Minnesota St U		✓		✓				✓		✓			✓	✓			✓		✓	✓		✓			
St. Benedict, Coll of													✓				✓						✓		
St. Catherine, Coll of		✓						✓		✓			✓	✓			✓		✓	✓		✓	✓		
St. Cloud St U		✓						✓					✓	✓						✓		✓			
St. John's U													✓				✓						✓		
St. Mary's U						✓		✓		✓		✓	✓	✓		✓		✓		✓		✓	✓		✓
St. Olaf Coll		✓						✓		✓		✓	✓	✓		✓						✓			✓
St. Scholastica, Coll of					✓	✓		✓		✓		✓	✓			✓					✓	✓	✓		✓
St. Thomas, U of	✓		✓			✓	✓	✓		✓		✓	✓	✓		✓		✓		✓	✓	✓	✓		✓
Winona St U		✓			✓			✓	✓			✓	✓	✓		✓		✓		✓			✓		
Mississippi																									
Belhaven Coll		✓															✓								
Blue Mountain Coll		✓						✓		✓			✓	✓			✓			✓		✓			
Jackson St U		✓		✓				✓		✓			✓	✓					✓	✓		✓	✓	✓	
Millsaps Coll		✓		✓				✓	✓	✓			✓	✓			✓			✓		✓			
Mississippi Coll								✓		✓			✓	✓								✓			
Mississippi St U		✓			✓	✓		✓	✓	✓		✓	✓	✓		✓				✓		✓	✓		
Mississippi U for Women								✓	✓	✓			✓	✓						✓		✓			
Mississippi, U of																									
Rust Coll		✓																	✓						

Southern Mississippi, U of		✓		✓		✓	✓	✓	✓	✓	✓	✓	✓	✓		✓	✓	✓	✓	✓	✓	✓	✓	✓	✓
William Carey Coll								✓		✓			✓	✓			✓		✓				✓		
Missouri																									
Avila U		✓		✓				✓		✓			✓	✓						✓		✓			
Central Methodist U		✓											✓							✓		✓			
Central Missouri St U	✓	✓	✓	✓	✓	✓		✓	✓	✓	✓	✓	✓	✓		✓		✓		✓	✓	✓	✓	✓	✓
Columbia Coll		✓											✓												
Culver-Stockton Coll		✓						✓		✓	✓		✓	✓			✓			✓		✓			
Drury U		✓		✓	✓			✓	✓	✓		✓	✓	✓			✓					✓			
Evangel U										✓			✓	✓		✓	✓	✓	✓	✓		✓			
Fontbonne U				✓				✓		✓			✓	✓			✓			✓		✓	✓	✓	
Hannibal-LaGrange Coll								✓	✓				✓	✓			✓								
Harris-Stowe St Coll								✓		✓			✓							✓		✓			
Jewish Hospital Coll of Nurs		✓								✓			✓	✓			✓		✓						
Kansas City Art Inst		✓						✓		✓		✓	✓	✓			✓	✓		✓		✓			
Lincoln U										✓			✓									✓			
Lindenwood U		✓						✓					✓	✓			✓					✓	✓		
Maryville U of St. Louis		✓						✓		✓			✓	✓			✓			✓		✓			
Missouri Southern St U					✓	✓		✓	✓	✓		✓	✓	✓		✓		✓		✓		✓			✓
Missouri, U of, Columbia		✓						✓		✓			✓	✓			✓	✓	✓	✓		✓	✓		✓
Missouri, U of, Kansas City		✓						✓	✓	✓		✓	✓						✓	✓		✓	✓		✓
Missouri, U of, Rolla		✓						✓		✓			✓	✓						✓		✓	✓		
Missouri, U of, St. Louis		✓						✓	✓	✓		✓	✓			✓						✓	✓		
Northwest Missouri St U		✓								✓			✓							✓		✓	✓		
Ozarks, Coll of the		✓				✓		✓		✓		✓	✓			✓		✓							
Park U				✓		✓		✓		✓	✓	✓	✓	✓	✓	✓	✓	✓		✓	✓	✓	✓		✓
Southeast Missouri St U								✓		✓		✓	✓	✓			✓	✓		✓		✓	✓		
Southwest Baptist U		✓					✓		✓	✓	✓	✓	✓	✓		✓	✓	✓		✓	✓	✓			
Southwest Missouri St U		✓						✓					✓	✓			✓		✓	✓		✓			

	Curriculum						In Class						Exams						Services						
	Foreign Language Waiver	Lighter Course Load	Math Waiver	Other Special Classes	Priority Registration	Substition of Courses	Early Syllabus	Note Takers in Class	Priority Seating	Tape Recorders	Videotaped Classes	Text on Tape	Extended Time	Oral Exams	Take Home Exams	Exams on Tape or PC	Untimed Exams	Other Accommodations	Diagnostic Tests	Learning Centers	Proofreaders	Readers	Reading Machines	Special Bookstore Section	Typists
St. Louis U				✓	✓	✓		✓	✓	✓		✓	✓			✓		✓	✓		✓	✓	✓		
Stephens Coll																				✓					
Truman St U		✓			✓		✓	✓	✓				✓	✓		✓		✓				✓	✓		✓
Washington U in St. Louis		✓						✓		✓		✓	✓					✓		✓		✓			✓
Webster U		✓						✓	✓	✓		✓	✓	✓		✓	✓			✓	✓	✓	✓		✓
Westminster Coll		✓		✓				✓		✓		✓	✓	✓		✓	✓	✓		✓	✓	✓	✓		✓
William Jewell Coll								✓		✓			✓				✓								
William Woods U								✓		✓		✓	✓	✓		✓	✓	✓				✓			
Montana																									
Carroll Coll		✓						✓					✓	✓						✓		✓			
Great Falls, U of								✓		✓	✓	✓	✓	✓		✓	✓	✓	✓	✓		✓	✓		
Montana St U, Billings					✓			✓	✓	✓		✓	✓	✓		✓		✓		✓		✓	✓		✓
Montana St U, Bozeman		✓			✓			✓	✓	✓		✓	✓	✓		✓		✓		✓		✓	✓		
Montana Tech		✓								✓			✓	✓						✓					
Montana, U of		✓			✓	✓		✓	✓	✓		✓	✓	✓		✓		✓			✓	✓	✓		✓
Montana, U of, Western					✓			✓		✓	✓	✓	✓	✓		✓	✓			✓		✓	✓		✓
Rocky Mountain Coll		✓		✓				✓		✓			✓				✓					✓			
Nebraska																									
Bellevue U						✓	✓	✓	✓	✓	✓	✓	✓	✓	✓	✓		✓	✓		✓	✓	✓		✓
Concordia U		✓						✓		✓	✓		✓					✓		✓	✓	✓	✓		
Creighton U		✓						✓		✓			✓	✓					✓			✓	✓		
Dana Coll										✓			✓				✓		✓	✓	✓				
Doane Coll		✓						✓		✓			✓							✓					

Grace U		✓						✓									✓					✓			
Hastings Coll	✓	✓						✓					✓	✓		✓	✓	✓		✓	✓	✓			
Midland Lutheran Coll								✓		✓	✓		✓	✓					✓	✓		✓			
Nebraska Methodist Coll									✓	✓	✓	✓	✓	✓	✓	✓	✓	✓		✓	✓	✓			
Nebraska Wesleyan U								✓		✓	✓		✓	✓			✓					✓			
Nebraska, U of, Kearney																									
Nebraska, U of, Lincoln		✓			✓	✓		✓	✓	✓		✓	✓	✓		✓		✓				✓	✓		✓
Nebraska, U of, Medical Ctr		✓							✓	✓		✓	✓												
Nebraska, U of, Omaha				✓	✓	✓		✓	✓	✓	✓	✓	✓	✓								✓	✓		✓
Peru St Coll								✓	✓	✓	✓	✓	✓	✓				✓		✓		✓			✓
St. Mary, Coll of		✓						✓		✓			✓	✓				✓	✓	✓	✓	✓			
Union Coll		✓						✓		✓	✓	✓	✓	✓		✓	✓	✓	✓	✓		✓	✓		✓
Wayne St Coll								✓		✓			✓						✓	✓		✓	✓		
York Coll	✓	✓					✓	✓	✓	✓		✓	✓	✓		✓	✓	✓	✓	✓	✓	✓			
Nevada																									
Nevada, U of, Las Vegas				✓	✓	✓		✓	✓	✓		✓	✓	✓				✓		✓		✓	✓		✓
Nevada, U of, Reno		✓		✓		✓		✓	✓	✓		✓	✓	✓		✓			✓	✓		✓	✓		✓
Sierra Nevada Coll		✓						✓						✓			✓								
Truckee Meadows Comm Coll		✓		✓	✓	✓		✓	✓			✓	✓	✓		✓		✓				✓			
New Hampshire																									
Colby-Sawyer Coll		✓								✓			✓							✓					
Dartmouth Coll	✓	✓						✓	✓	✓		✓	✓		✓	✓				✓		✓			
Franklin Pierce Coll		✓						✓	✓				✓				✓				✓	✓			
Keene St Coll		✓						✓		✓			✓	✓			✓					✓	✓		
New England Coll		✓	✓			✓		✓		✓			✓	✓		✓	✓	✓		✓	✓				
New Hampshire Tech Coll																									
New Hampshire, U of		✓			✓			✓	✓	✓		✓	✓	✓		✓		✓				✓	✓		✓
Plymouth St U								✓				✓	✓	✓			✓					✓			
Rivier Coll										✓			✓	✓			✓								

	Curriculum						In Class						Exams						Services						
	Foreign Language Waiver	Lighter Course Load	Math Waiver	Other Special Classes	Priority Registration	Substition of Courses	Early Syllabus	Note Takers in Class	Priority Seating	Tape Recorders	Videotaped Classes	Text on Tape	Extended Time	Oral Exams	Take Home Exams	Exams on Tape or PC	Untimed Exams	Other Accommodations	Diagnostic Tests	Learning Centers	Proofreaders	Readers	Reading Machines	Special Bookstore Section	Typists
Southern New Hampshire U		✓			✓		✓	✓	✓	✓		✓	✓	✓		✓	✓			✓		✓	✓		✓
St. Anselm Coll		✓							✓	✓		✓	✓			✓	✓	✓		✓					
New Jersey																									
Bloomfield Coll		✓								✓		✓	✓			✓			✓	✓		✓	✓		✓
Caldwell Coll		✓		✓				✓		✓			✓	✓			✓			✓		✓	✓		
Centenary Coll		✓						✓		✓			✓	✓			✓			✓		✓	✓		
Drew U		✓						✓		✓		✓	✓												
Fairleigh Dickinson U		✓		✓						✓			✓	✓					✓	✓			✓		
Georgian Court U		✓						✓		✓				✓			✓	✓	✓	✓		✓			
Kean U				✓				✓		✓	✓			✓			✓	✓	✓	✓		✓			
Monmouth U		✓			✓			✓	✓	✓		✓	✓					✓				✓	✓		✓
Montclair St U	✓	✓			✓	✓		✓	✓	✓		✓	✓	✓		✓	✓	✓		✓	✓	✓	✓		✓
New Jersey Inst of Tech		✓						✓		✓			✓	✓								✓	✓		
New Jersey, Coll of		✓				✓		✓		✓			✓			✓						✓			
Princeton U																									
Ramapo Coll, New Jersey		✓		✓		✓	✓	✓	✓	✓		✓	✓			✓		✓		✓			✓		
Richard Stockton Coll		✓			✓	✓		✓	✓	✓		✓	✓	✓		✓		✓			✓	✓	✓		✓
Rider U		✓		✓	✓			✓	✓	✓		✓	✓	✓				✓	✓	✓		✓	✓		✓
Rowan U		✓			✓				✓	✓		✓	✓	✓			✓	✓		✓		✓	✓		
Rutgers U, Camden		✓											✓												
Rutgers U, Coll of Arts & Sci		✓																							
Rutgers U, New Brunswick		✓											✓												
Rutgers U, Newark													✓							✓					

Seton Hall U	✓	✓	✓		✓				✓	✓		✓	✓	✓			✓		✓			✓	✓	✓	✓
St. Elizabeth, Coll of		✓						✓	✓	✓		✓	✓	✓		✓	✓			✓		✓			
St. Peter's Coll	✓		✓		✓	✓		✓	✓	✓			✓	✓	✓	✓	✓	✓	✓	✓	✓	✓	✓		✓
Stevens Inst of Tech		✓											✓				✓								
Thomas Edison St Coll						✓						✓	✓			✓		✓							
Westminster Choir Coll, Rider		✓																							
William Paterson U						✓		✓		✓			✓	✓		✓		✓				✓	✓		✓
New Mexico																									
Eastern New Mexico U										✓			✓									✓			
New Mexico Highlands U		✓		✓				✓		✓	✓		✓	✓			✓		✓	✓		✓	✓		
New Mexico Inst of Mining		✓						✓		✓			✓	✓			✓					✓			
New Mexico St U								✓		✓			✓	✓			✓		✓	✓		✓			
New Mexico, U of								✓		✓	✓		✓				✓		✓			✓	✓		
Santa Fe, Coll of		✓		✓				✓		✓			✓	✓			✓			✓		✓	✓		
Southwest, Coll of the		✓					✓	✓	✓	✓		✓	✓	✓		✓	✓	✓	✓	✓	✓	✓			✓
Western New Mexico U		✓						✓		✓			✓	✓						✓		✓			
New York																									
Adelphi U					✓			✓		✓			✓	✓				✓	✓	✓		✓	✓		✓
Alfred U		✓						✓		✓			✓	✓			✓		✓			✓			
Bard Coll		✓								✓		✓	✓	✓	✓		✓			✓			✓		
Barnard Coll		✓						✓		✓			✓						✓			✓	✓		
Canisius Coll		✓						✓		✓		✓	✓									✓			
Cazenovia Coll	✓				✓		✓			✓			✓	✓				✓		✓	✓	✓			
Clarkson U							✓	✓	✓	✓	✓	✓	✓	✓		✓	✓			✓		✓	✓		
Colgate U		✓																							
Columbia U								✓		✓	✓		✓									✓	✓		
Cooper Union													✓				✓					✓			
Cornell U								✓					✓							✓		✓	✓		✓
Culinary Inst of America		✓			✓	✓		✓	✓	✓		✓	✓	✓		✓		✓		✓		✓	✓		✓

	Curriculum						In Class						Exams						Services						
	Foreign Language Waiver	Lighter Course Load	Math Waiver	Other Special Classes	Priority Registration	Substition of Courses	Early Syllabus	Note Takers in Class	Priority Seating	Tape Recorders	Videotaped Classes	Text on Tape	Extended Time	Oral Exams	Take Home Exams	Exams on Tape or PC	Untimed Exams	Other Accommodations	Diagnostic Tests	Learning Centers	Proofreaders	Readers	Reading Machines	Special Bookstore Section	Typists
CUNY, Baruch Coll		✓			✓	✓	✓	✓	✓	✓	✓	✓	✓	✓		✓						✓	✓		✓
CUNY, Brooklyn Coll								✓														✓	✓		
CUNY, City Coll		✓						✓		✓			✓	✓						✓		✓	✓		
CUNY, Coll of Staten Island					✓		✓	✓		✓		✓	✓	✓		✓						✓	✓		
CUNY, Hunter Coll	✓	✓			✓	✓		✓		✓		✓	✓			✓	✓	✓	✓	✓		✓	✓		✓
CUNY, John Jay Coll		✓								✓			✓	✓			✓		✓	✓			✓		
CUNY, Lehman Coll								✓		✓			✓				✓			✓					
CUNY, Medgar Evers Coll																									
CUNY, NYC Tech Coll		✓		✓				✓		✓			✓	✓					✓	✓		✓	✓		
CUNY, Queens Coll		✓		✓				✓		✓			✓	✓						✓		✓	✓		
CUNY, York Coll		✓						✓		✓	✓		✓	✓				✓				✓	✓		
D'Youville Coll		✓						✓		✓	✓		✓	✓			✓			✓		✓	✓		
Daemen Coll		✓			✓	✓		✓	✓	✓		✓	✓	✓						✓		✓			✓
Dominican Coll of Blauvelt								✓											✓	✓			✓		✓
Dowling Coll	✓	✓			✓			✓	✓	✓		✓	✓				✓	✓			✓	✓			✓
Elmira Coll		✓						✓		✓		✓	✓	✓		✓	✓				✓	✓	✓		
Eugene Lang Coll of New Sch		✓					✓	✓	✓	✓		✓	✓			✓		✓				✓			
Fashion Inst of Tech					✓	✓	✓	✓	✓	✓		✓	✓	✓		✓		✓		✓	✓	✓	✓		✓
Five Towns Coll													✓				✓			✓					
Fordham U		✓						✓		✓			✓												
Hamilton Coll													✓	✓			✓			✓		✓			
Hartwick Coll		✓						✓		✓			✓							✓		✓			
Hilbert Coll		✓						✓		✓			✓	✓		✓						✓			✓

Hobart & William Smith Coll	✓	✓						✓	✓	✓		✓	✓	✓		✓	✓	✓		✓	✓	✓	✓		✓
Hofstra U		✓										✓	✓										✓		
Houghton Coll		✓				✓			✓	✓	✓	✓	✓	✓		✓			✓				✓		
Iona Coll		✓						✓		✓			✓	✓			✓			✓		✓	✓		
Ithaca Coll	✓					✓		✓	✓	✓		✓	✓	✓		✓	✓	✓				✓	✓		✓
Keuka Coll		✓						✓		✓			✓							✓		✓	✓		
LeMoyne Coll								✓		✓		✓	✓			✓				✓			✓		
Long Island U, Brooklyn		✓		✓		✓			✓	✓		✓	✓			✓	✓	✓		✓		✓	✓		✓
Long Island U, CW Post		✓						✓		✓			✓				✓		✓			✓	✓		
Manhattan Coll		✓																							
Manhattan Sch of Music																									
Manhattanville Coll		✓						✓		✓			✓	✓			✓			✓		✓			
Marist Coll		✓						✓		✓		✓	✓	✓		✓		✓				✓	✓		
Marymount Coll		✓			✓		✓	✓	✓	✓		✓	✓	✓	✓	✓				✓		✓	✓		✓
Marymount Manhattan Coll										✓			✓						✓						
Medaille Coll		✓				✓		✓		✓	✓	✓	✓				✓			✓		✓	✓		
Mercy Coll	✓	✓				✓		✓		✓	✓	✓	✓	✓		✓				✓		✓	✓		
Molloy Coll		✓						✓		✓			✓			✓	✓						✓		
Mt St. Mary Coll								✓	✓	✓		✓	✓			✓				✓		✓			✓
Mt St. Vincent, Coll of		✓						✓					✓				✓			✓		✓			
Nazareth Coll of Rochester							✓	✓		✓		✓	✓	✓		✓	✓					✓	✓		✓
New York Inst of Tech								✓		✓				✓			✓			✓		✓			
NY Sch of Interior Design										✓	✓		✓	✓			✓					✓			
New York U		✓						✓		✓			✓					✓		✓		✓	✓		
Niagara U		✓				✓		✓		✓			✓					✓		✓			✓		
Nyack Coll		✓		✓				✓		✓			✓	✓			✓			✓		✓			
Pace U						✓		✓		✓		✓	✓	✓	✓	✓	✓	✓		✓		✓			✓
Parsons Sch of Design		✓						✓		✓			✓									✓			
Polytechnic U								✓					✓				✓	✓		✓					

	Curriculum						In Class						Exams						Services						
	Foreign Language Waiver	Lighter Course Load	Math Waiver	Other Special Classes	Priority Registration	Substition of Courses	Early Syllabus	Note Takers in Class	Priority Seating	Tape Recorders	Videotaped Classes	Text on Tape	Extended Time	Oral Exams	Take Home Exams	Exams on Tape or PC	Untimed Exams	Other Accommodations	Diagnostic Tests	Learning Centers	Proofreaders	Readers	Reading Machines	Special Bookstore Section	Typists
Pratt Inst							✓	✓		✓			✓					✓	✓	✓					
Rensselaer Polytech Inst		✓						✓		✓		✓	✓					✓		✓			✓		
Roberts Wesleyan Coll		✓						✓		✓	✓		✓	✓			✓			✓		✓	✓		
Rochester Inst of Tech		✓		✓	✓			✓		✓			✓	✓				✓	✓	✓		✓	✓		
Rochester, U of		✓						✓					✓	✓						✓		✓	✓		
Russell Sage Coll		✓						✓		✓		✓	✓	✓		✓	✓	✓		✓		✓			
Sage Coll of Albany																									
Sarah Lawrence Coll								✓		✓		✓	✓									✓			
Siena Coll					✓			✓		✓		✓	✓	✓		✓		✓			✓	✓	✓		✓
Skidmore Coll													✓												
St. Bonaventure U								✓		✓			✓				✓			✓		✓			
St. Francis Coll		✓						✓														✓			
St. John Fisher Coll		✓						✓		✓		✓	✓									✓			✓
St. John's U										✓			✓	✓			✓		✓			✓			✓
St. Joseph's Coll, Brooklyn		✓						✓					✓				✓			✓			✓		
St. Lawrence U		✓			✓			✓	✓	✓		✓	✓			✓	✓	✓				✓	✓		✓
St. Thomas Aquinas Coll				✓				✓		✓			✓	✓			✓		✓	✓					
SUNY at Albany																									
SUNY at Binghamton		✓		✓				✓		✓		✓	✓			✓		✓				✓	✓		
SUNY at Buffalo		✓		✓		✓		✓		✓		✓	✓	✓						✓		✓	✓		
SUNY at Farmingdale										✓			✓				✓		✓	✓		✓	✓		
SUNY at New Paltz		✓						✓		✓			✓	✓						✓		✓	✓		
SUNY at Oswego	✓	✓			✓	✓		✓	✓	✓		✓	✓			✓		✓			✓	✓	✓		✓

SUNY at Stony Brook					✓			✓	✓	✓		✓	✓					✓				✓	✓		✓
SUNY Cobleskill		✓																		✓			✓		
SUNY Coll at Brockport		✓			✓			✓	✓	✓		✓	✓			✓		✓		✓			✓		✓
SUNY Coll at Cortland		✓						✓		✓			✓	✓			✓			✓		✓	✓		
SUNY Coll at Fredonia		✓											✓							✓					
SUNY Coll at Geneseo		✓			✓			✓	✓				✓			✓		✓				✓	✓		✓
SUNY Coll at Old Westbury		✓						✓	✓	✓		✓	✓	✓		✓	✓	✓		✓	✓	✓	✓		✓
SUNY Coll at Oneonta		✓						✓		✓	✓	✓	✓	✓		✓	✓			✓		✓	✓		✓
SUNY Coll at Plattsburgh		✓		✓		✓		✓		✓		✓	✓	✓		✓	✓		✓	✓		✓	✓		
SUNY Coll at Potsdam				✓				✓		✓			✓	✓						✓		✓	✓		
SUNY Coll of Environment		✓						✓	✓				✓	✓				✓	✓						
SUNY Inst of Tech at Utica		✓						✓	✓	✓		✓	✓							✓			✓		
SUNY Upstate Medical U		✓						✓		✓			✓									✓			
SUNY, Buffalo St Coll								✓		✓			✓	✓						✓		✓	✓		
SUNY, Empire St Coll																									
Syracuse U								✓		✓		✓	✓	✓		✓		✓	✓	✓		✓	✓		
Union Coll								✓		✓		✓	✓					✓				✓	✓		
Utica Coll		✓																							
Vassar Coll		✓			✓	✓	✓	✓	✓	✓		✓	✓			✓		✓		✓		✓	✓		✓
Vaughn Coll of Aeronautics		✓											✓				✓			✓					
Villa Maria Coll at Buffalo	✓					✓		✓		✓		✓	✓	✓		✓	✓			✓		✓			
Wagner Coll		✓							✓	✓			✓				✓	✓		✓					
Wells Coll		✓						✓		✓			✓	✓											
Yeshiva U									✓	✓			✓	✓			✓	✓							
North Carolina																									
Appalachian St U				✓	✓	✓		✓	✓	✓		✓	✓	✓		✓	✓	✓	✓	✓	✓	✓	✓		✓
Barton Coll								✓					✓	✓		✓				✓		✓			
Belmont Abbey Coll																				✓					
Bennett Coll		✓			✓		✓		✓	✓		✓	✓	✓		✓		✓		✓	✓		✓		

	Curriculum						In Class						Exams						Services						
	Foreign Language Waiver	Lighter Course Load	Math Waiver	Other Special Classes	Priority Registration	Substition of Courses	Early Syllabus	Note Takers in Class	Priority Seating	Tape Recorders	Videotaped Classes	Text on Tape	Extended Time	Oral Exams	Take Home Exams	Exams on Tape or PC	Untimed Exams	Other Accommodations	Diagnostic Tests	Learning Centers	Proofreaders	Readers	Reading Machines	Special Bookstore Section	Typists
Brevard Coll	✓	✓	✓			✓		✓		✓		✓	✓	✓		✓		✓		✓	✓	✓	✓		✓
Campbell U		✓						✓																	
Catawba Coll																	✓								
Chowan Coll										✓			✓	✓			✓			✓					
Davidson Coll		✓						✓		✓			✓	✓					✓			✓			
Duke U										✓			✓	✓		✓		✓							
East Carolina U		✓						✓		✓	✓		✓									✓	✓		
Elizabeth City St U		✓						✓		✓			✓				✓			✓					
Elon U		✓						✓					✓												
Gardner-Webb U		✓			✓	✓		✓	✓	✓		✓	✓	✓		✓		✓				✓	✓	✓	✓
Greensboro Coll		✓						✓		✓		✓	✓	✓		✓	✓	✓	✓	✓		✓	✓		✓
Guilford Coll	✓	✓		✓		✓		✓		✓		✓	✓	✓	✓	✓	✓	✓		✓	✓	✓	✓		✓
High Point U	✓	✓	✓		✓	✓	✓	✓	✓	✓		✓	✓	✓		✓		✓		✓	✓	✓	✓		✓
Johnson C Smith U								✓	✓	✓			✓	✓			✓			✓		✓	✓		
Lees-McRae Coll		✓		✓				✓					✓	✓			✓			✓		✓	✓		
Lenoir-Rhyne Coll	✓	✓						✓		✓			✓	✓		✓						✓	✓		✓
Livingstone Coll										✓	✓		✓	✓			✓		✓	✓		✓			
Mars Hill Coll										✓			✓	✓					✓			✓			
Meredith Coll		✓			✓	✓		✓	✓			✓	✓	✓		✓		✓		✓		✓	✓		✓
Methodist Coll								✓		✓	✓		✓	✓			✓			✓		✓			
Mt Olive Coll		✓																		✓					
North Carolina Sch of the Arts																									
North Carolina St U	✓	✓			✓			✓	✓	✓		✓	✓			✓						✓	✓		✓

North Carolina Wesleyan Coll		✓		✓	✓			✓	✓	✓		✓	✓	✓	✓	✓	✓	✓	✓	✓	✓	✓		✓	✓
North Carolina, U of, Asheville								✓		✓			✓	✓								✓	✓		
NC, U of, Chapel Hill								✓		✓			✓							✓		✓	✓		
North Carolina, U of, Charlotte		✓						✓		✓			✓	✓			✓			✓			✓		
NC, U of, Greensboro							✓	✓		✓			✓	✓					✓	✓		✓			
NC, U of, Pembroke							✓	✓		✓		✓	✓	✓		✓		✓				✓			✓
NC, U of, Wilmington					✓			✓		✓			✓	✓				✓		✓		✓	✓		
Peace Coll	✓	✓							✓	✓			✓				✓	✓		✓			✓		
Pfeiffer U		✓		✓				✓		✓			✓	✓						✓		✓	✓		
Queens U of Charlotte	✓		✓	✓		✓	✓	✓	✓	✓		✓	✓	✓	✓	✓	✓	✓		✓		✓	✓		✓
Salem Coll		✓						✓		✓			✓												
Shaw U		✓						✓	✓	✓		✓	✓	✓		✓	✓		✓						
St. Andrews Presbyterian Coll	✓	✓				✓		✓	✓	✓		✓	✓			✓		✓		✓		✓	✓		✓
St. Augustine's Coll		✓											✓				✓		✓	✓	✓				
Wake Forest U		✓											✓							✓					
Warren Wilson Coll		✓					✓	✓					✓	✓		✓	✓			✓					
Western Carolina U					✓			✓	✓	✓		✓	✓	✓	✓	✓		✓		✓	✓	✓	✓		✓
Wingate U		✓																							
Winston-Salem St U								✓		✓			✓	✓			✓			✓		✓	✓		
North Dakota																									
Dickinson St U		✓						✓		✓		✓	✓	✓			✓			✓		✓			✓
Jamestown Coll								✓					✓	✓			✓			✓		✓			
Mary, U of		✓		✓				✓		✓		✓	✓	✓			✓			✓	✓	✓	✓		
Mayville St U								✓		✓		✓	✓	✓			✓			✓		✓			
Minot St U		✓			✓			✓	✓	✓	✓		✓	✓		✓	✓			✓	✓	✓	✓		
North Dakota St U		✓						✓					✓	✓								✓			
North Dakota, U of																									
Valley City St U								✓	✓	✓			✓	✓		✓	✓				✓	✓			

	Curriculum						In Class						Exams						Services						
	Foreign Language Waiver	Lighter Course Load	Math Waiver	Other Special Classes	Priority Registration	Substition of Courses	Early Syllabus	Note Takers in Class	Priority Seating	Tape Recorders	Videotaped Classes	Text on Tape	Extended Time	Oral Exams	Take Home Exams	Exams on Tape or PC	Untimed Exams	Other Accommodations	Diagnostic Tests	Learning Centers	Proofreaders	Readers	Reading Machines	Special Bookstore Section	Typists
Ohio																									
Akron, U of		✓			✓	✓		✓	✓	✓		✓	✓	✓		✓		✓	✓			✓	✓		✓
Art Acad of Cincinnati		✓		✓				✓		✓			✓				✓			✓					
Ashland U					✓		✓	✓		✓		✓	✓	✓		✓	✓			✓		✓	✓		✓
Baldwin-Wallace Coll		✓						✓		✓			✓							✓		✓			
Bluffton U		✓						✓		✓	✓		✓	✓						✓		✓			
Bowling Green St U					✓	✓		✓		✓		✓	✓	✓		✓		✓				✓	✓		
Capital U					✓	✓	✓	✓		✓		✓	✓	✓		✓		✓		✓		✓			
Case Western Reserve U								✓		✓		✓	✓	✓		✓			✓			✓	✓		✓
Cedarville U		✓			✓			✓	✓	✓			✓	✓			✓					✓			
Central St U		✓					✓	✓	✓	✓			✓	✓			✓	✓	✓	✓	✓	✓			
Cincinnati Christian U				✓		✓	✓	✓	✓	✓		✓	✓	✓			✓	✓		✓	✓	✓			✓
Cleveland Inst of Art		✓						✓					✓	✓			✓								
Cleveland Inst of Music								✓		✓			✓				✓	✓	✓	✓		✓			
Cleveland St U		✓			✓	✓	✓	✓	✓	✓		✓	✓	✓		✓					✓	✓	✓		✓
Columbus Coll of Art & Design		✓			✓			✓		✓			✓	✓		✓				✓		✓	✓		
Dayton, U of		✓		✓	✓	✓	✓	✓	✓	✓		✓	✓	✓		✓		✓		✓	✓	✓	✓		✓
Denison U		✓						✓	✓	✓		✓	✓							✓		✓			
Findlay, U of					✓			✓		✓			✓	✓			✓	✓			✓	✓	✓		✓
Franciscan U of Steubenville		✓			✓			✓		✓			✓	✓			✓					✓	✓		
Heidelberg Coll				✓				✓		✓			✓	✓			✓			✓		✓			
Hiram Coll								✓		✓			✓	✓								✓			
John Carroll U		✓						✓					✓	✓								✓	✓		

Kent St U		✔			✔	✔	✔	✔	✔	✔		✔	✔	✔		✔		✔		✔		✔			✔
Kenyon Coll					✔	✔	✔	✔		✔	✔	✔	✔	✔		✔	✔					✔	✔		
Lake Erie Coll		✔		✔			✔	✔		✔		✔	✔	✔		✔	✔			✔	✔	✔	✔		✔
Lourdes Coll		✔						✔	✔	✔		✔	✔	✔		✔	✔	✔		✔	✔	✔			
Malone Coll								✔		✔		✔	✔	✔		✔						✔			✔
Marietta Coll								✔		✔		✔	✔	✔		✔		✔		✔		✔	✔		
Miami U		✔								✔			✔	✔			✔			✔		✔	✔		
Mt St. Joseph, Coll of		✔						✔					✔							✔		✔			
Mt Union Coll						✔		✔		✔		✔	✔	✔		✔		✔		✔		✔	✔		
Mt Vernon Nazarene U								✔		✔			✔	✔											
Muskingum Coll		✔						✔		✔		✔	✔	✔			✔			✔	✔	✔	✔		✔
Notre Dame Coll										✔			✔	✔						✔					
Oberlin Coll		✔			✔			✔		✔	✔	✔	✔	✔		✔	✔	✔				✔	✔		✔
Ohio Dominican Univ																									
Ohio Northern U		✔		✔				✔		✔			✔	✔			✔					✔			
Ohio St U, Columbus					✔								✔												
Ohio U					✔								✔										✔		
Ohio Wesleyan U	✔	✔		✔				✔		✔			✔	✔						✔					
Otterbein Coll					✔			✔		✔			✔							✔					
Rio Grande, U of		✔		✔		✔		✔		✔		✔	✔	✔		✔	✔	✔		✔		✔			
Shawnee St U		✔		✔				✔		✔				✔			✔			✔		✔	✔		
Toledo, U of		✔						✔		✔	✔		✔	✔			✔			✔		✔	✔		
Union Inst & U				✔						✔			✔	✔			✔		✔	✔		✔			
Urbana U		✔						✔		✔			✔	✔			✔					✔			
Ursuline Coll		✔		✔				✔		✔			✔	✔			✔		✔	✔	✔	✔	✔		
Walsh U		✔		✔		✔			✔	✔			✔	✔		✔	✔		✔	✔		✔		✔	✔
Wilmington Coll				✔				✔		✔			✔	✔			✔		✔	✔		✔			
Wittenberg U													✔												
Wooster, Coll of										✔				✔			✔			✔		✔			

	Curriculum						In Class						Exams						Services						
	Foreign Language Waiver	Lighter Course Load	Math Waiver	Other Special Classes	Priority Registration	Substition of Courses	Early Syllabus	Note Takers in Class	Priority Seating	Tape Recorders	Videotaped Classes	Text on Tape	Extended Time	Oral Exams	Take Home Exams	Exams on Tape or PC	Untimed Exams	Other Accommodations	Diagnostic Tests	Learning Centers	Proofreaders	Readers	Reading Machines	Special Bookstore Section	Typists
Wright St U		✓		✓				✓		✓			✓				✓		✓	✓		✓	✓		
Xavier U	✓		✓		✓	✓		✓	✓	✓	✓		✓	✓		✓			✓	✓		✓			✓
Youngstown St U					✓	✓		✓		✓		✓	✓			✓	✓	✓				✓	✓		✓
Oklahoma																									
Cameron U																									
Central Oklahoma, U of					✓			✓				✓	✓					✓							
East Central U					✓		✓	✓	✓	✓	✓	✓	✓	✓		✓		✓		✓	✓	✓			✓
Northeastern St U		✓						✓		✓			✓	✓			✓					✓			
Northwestern Oklahoma St U																									
Oklahoma Baptist U		✓		✓	✓	✓	✓	✓	✓	✓		✓	✓	✓	✓	✓	✓	✓				✓	✓		✓
Oklahoma Christian U								✓	✓	✓			✓	✓		✓	✓					✓			
Oklahoma City U	✓					✓			✓			✓	✓	✓				✓		✓	✓	✓			
Oklahoma Wesleyan U		✓								✓	✓		✓	✓			✓			✓		✓			
Oklahoma, U of		✓			✓	✓		✓		✓		✓	✓			✓			✓			✓	✓		✓
Oral Roberts U								✓		✓			✓	✓					✓	✓		✓	✓	✓	
Southeastern Oklahoma St U				✓				✓		✓			✓					✓	✓	✓		✓	✓		
Southern Nazarene U		✓						✓		✓			✓	✓						✓		✓	✓		
St. Gregory's U		✓					✓	✓	✓	✓	✓	✓	✓	✓		✓	✓	✓		✓	✓	✓	✓		✓
Tulsa, U of	✓	✓	✓		✓	✓		✓	✓	✓			✓			✓	✓			✓		✓	✓		
Oregon																									
Concordia U		✓			✓		✓	✓	✓	✓	✓	✓	✓	✓		✓	✓	✓		✓	✓	✓	✓		✓
Corban Coll		✓				✓		✓	✓	✓		✓	✓	✓		✓	✓			✓	✓	✓			
Eastern Oregon U		✓						✓		✓	✓		✓	✓			✓			✓		✓	✓		

George Fox U				✓				✓	✓	✓			✓	✓			✓	✓		✓		✓			
Lewis & Clark Coll		✓				✓		✓		✓		✓	✓			✓		✓	✓		✓	✓			✓
Linfield Coll		✓			✓	✓		✓	✓	✓	✓	✓	✓	✓		✓	✓	✓		✓	✓	✓	✓		✓
Marylhurst U		✓			✓	✓	✓	✓	✓	✓		✓	✓	✓	✓	✓	✓	✓			✓	✓			✓
Northwest Christian Coll		✓								✓	✓		✓	✓											
Oregon Inst of Tech		✓						✓		✓			✓	✓						✓		✓	✓		
Oregon St U		✓						✓		✓			✓	✓						✓			✓		
Oregon, U of		✓			✓		✓	✓	✓	✓		✓	✓	✓		✓	✓	✓	✓	✓		✓	✓		✓
Pacific U		✓						✓		✓		✓	✓	✓		✓	✓					✓			✓
Portland, U of		✓						✓					✓									✓	✓		
Southern Oregon U		✓		✓				✓		✓			✓	✓						✓		✓	✓		
Warner Pacific Coll				✓									✓							✓		✓			
Willamette U		✓						✓		✓			✓												
Pennsylvania																									
Albright Coll		✓			✓			✓		✓		✓	✓	✓		✓	✓			✓		✓			
Allegheny Coll		✓			✓			✓	✓	✓		✓	✓	✓		✓				✓		✓			✓
Alvernia Coll								✓		✓			✓	✓						✓					
Arcadia U		✓		✓		✓		✓	✓	✓		✓	✓			✓				✓			✓		
Arts, U of the		✓						✓		✓			✓									✓			
Bloomsburg U, Pennsylvania		✓		✓				✓		✓			✓	✓								✓	✓		
Bryn Athyn Coll, New Church		✓								✓			✓	✓			✓								
Bryn Mawr Coll																									
Bucknell U										✓			✓	✓									✓		
Cabrini Coll		✓						✓		✓										✓					
California U of Pennsylvania		✓																							
Carlow U		✓						✓	✓	✓	✓	✓	✓	✓		✓				✓		✓			✓
Carnegie Mellon U								✓	✓	✓		✓	✓	✓		✓				✓	✓				
Cedar Crest Coll				✓				✓		✓			✓							✓					
Chatham Coll		✓					✓	✓	✓	✓		✓	✓	✓		✓		✓		✓	✓	✓	✓		

	Curriculum						In Class						Exams						Services						
	Foreign Language Waiver	Lighter Course Load	Math Waiver	Other Special Classes	Priority Registration	Substition of Courses	Early Syllabus	Note Takers in Class	Priority Seating	Tape Recorders	Videotaped Classes	Text on Tape	Extended Time	Oral Exams	Take Home Exams	Exams on Tape or PC	Untimed Exams	Other Accommodations	Diagnostic Tests	Learning Centers	Proofreaders	Readers	Reading Machines	Special Bookstore Section	Typists
Chestnut Hill Coll		✓											✓	✓			✓					✓			
Cheyney U of Pennsylvania																									
Clarion U of Pennsylvania								✓		✓			✓	✓			✓			✓		✓	✓		
College Misericordia		✓						✓		✓		✓	✓	✓		✓	✓	✓		✓	✓	✓	✓		✓
Delaware Valley Coll		✓						✓					✓										✓		
DeSales U		✓						✓		✓		✓	✓	✓		✓	✓			✓		✓	✓		✓
Dickinson Coll		✓						✓		✓				✓			✓					✓			
Drexel U		✓						✓		✓			✓	✓						✓			✓		
Duquesne U		✓			✓			✓		✓			✓	✓						✓		✓			
East Stroudsburg U		✓						✓		✓			✓	✓								✓	✓		
Eastern U																				✓					
Edinboro U		✓			✓			✓		✓		✓	✓									✓			
Elizabethtown Coll		✓			✓	✓	✓	✓	✓	✓	✓	✓	✓	✓		✓				✓	✓	✓	✓		
Franklin & Marshall Coll																									
Gannon U				✓		✓				✓		✓	✓	✓						✓		✓	✓		✓
Geneva Coll		✓						✓			✓		✓					✓	✓		✓	✓	✓		
Gettysburg Coll										✓			✓												
Grove City Coll		✓								✓															
Gwynedd-Mercy Coll		✓								✓			✓	✓			✓			✓		✓	✓		
Haverford Coll		✓																							
Holy Family U				✓				✓	✓	✓		✓	✓	✓	✓			✓		✓	✓	✓	✓		✓
Immaculata U	✓	✓				✓		✓	✓	✓			✓		✓		✓	✓	✓	✓	✓				
Indiana U								✓		✓				✓			✓			✓		✓	✓		

Juniata Coll		✓											✓				✓								
King's Coll		✓						✓	✓	✓			✓	✓			✓			✓			✓		
Kutztown U		✓						✓					✓	✓						✓		✓			
LaRoche Coll		✓						✓		✓	✓		✓	✓			✓			✓		✓			
LaSalle U		✓						✓		✓			✓				✓								
Lebanon Valley Coll		✓			✓		✓	✓	✓	✓	✓		✓	✓		✓		✓	✓	✓	✓	✓	✓		
Lehigh U		✓																		✓			✓		
Lincoln U		✓								✓	✓		✓	✓			✓			✓		✓			
Lock Haven U								✓		✓			✓									✓	✓		
Lycoming Coll		✓		✓				✓		✓	✓		✓	✓			✓			✓		✓	✓		
Mansfield U of Pennsylvania		✓						✓		✓			✓					✓	✓	✓					
Marywood U		✓						✓		✓			✓	✓			✓		✓	✓		✓	✓		
Mercyhurst Coll		✓			✓			✓		✓		✓	✓	✓		✓	✓			✓	✓	✓	✓		✓
Messiah Coll		✓						✓		✓			✓	✓			✓			✓		✓	✓		
Millersville U		✓						✓		✓			✓	✓			✓	✓	✓	✓		✓	✓		
Moore Coll of Art & Design										✓			✓				✓			✓					
Moravian Coll		✓						✓		✓			✓	✓		✓		✓		✓		✓			
Mount Aloysius Coll		✓						✓		✓			✓	✓						✓		✓		✓	
Muhlenberg Coll		✓						✓		✓			✓	✓						✓		✓	✓		
Neumann Coll		✓						✓		✓			✓	✓						✓		✓			
Peirce Coll		✓					✓	✓	✓	✓		✓	✓	✓		✓	✓		✓	✓	✓	✓			✓
Pennsylvania Coll of Tech				✓				✓		✓										✓		✓			
Penn St U at Erie, Behrend	✓				✓			✓	✓	✓		✓	✓	✓		✓	✓	✓		✓		✓	✓		✓
Pennsylvania St U, Altoona																									
Pennsylvania St U, Berks																									
Penn St U, Lehigh Valley																									
Pennsylvania St U, Schuylkill																									
Pennsylvania St U, U Park		✓			✓			✓	✓	✓			✓			✓		✓		✓		✓	✓		✓
Pennsylvania, U of								✓	✓	✓		✓	✓	✓		✓				✓		✓	✓		✓

	Curriculum						In Class						Exams						Services						
	Foreign Language Waiver	Lighter Course Load	Math Waiver	Other Special Classes	Priority Registration	Substition of Courses	Early Syllabus	Note Takers in Class	Priority Seating	Tape Recorders	Videotaped Classes	Text on Tape	Extended Time	Oral Exams	Take Home Exams	Exams on Tape or PC	Untimed Exams	Other Accommodations	Diagnostic Tests	Learning Centers	Proofreaders	Readers	Reading Machines	Special Bookstore Section	Typists
Philadelphia Biblical U		✓						✓		✓				✓			✓	✓		✓		✓			
Philadelphia U		✓			✓			✓		✓	✓	✓	✓	✓		✓		✓		✓		✓	✓		✓
Pittsburgh, U of, Bradford								✓					✓							✓		✓			
Pittsburgh, U of, Greensburg	✓	✓			✓		✓	✓	✓	✓		✓	✓			✓		✓		✓		✓	✓		✓
Pittsburgh, U of, Johnstown		✓						✓		✓			✓	✓			✓		✓	✓		✓	✓		
Pittsburgh, U of, Pittsburgh		✓								✓		✓	✓			✓		✓		✓		✓	✓		
Point Park U		✓						✓	✓	✓			✓	✓		✓		✓				✓			
Robert Morris U					✓				✓	✓			✓	✓		✓		✓		✓		✓	✓		
Rosemont Coll		✓						✓		✓			✓	✓			✓		✓	✓		✓			
Scranton, U of					✓				✓	✓		✓	✓	✓		✓	✓	✓	✓	✓	✓		✓		
Seton Hill U						✓	✓	✓	✓	✓		✓	✓	✓		✓	✓	✓			✓	✓	✓		✓
Shippensburg U of Penn		✓						✓		✓			✓	✓						✓		✓	✓		
Slippery Rock U of Penn					✓			✓	✓	✓		✓	✓	✓			✓					✓	✓		
St. Francis U	✓	✓	✓		✓	✓		✓	✓	✓		✓	✓	✓		✓	✓			✓		✓	✓		✓
St. Joseph's U	✓	✓					✓	✓		✓		✓	✓	✓		✓				✓		✓			✓
St. Vincent Coll		✓			✓			✓	✓	✓			✓	✓			✓	✓		✓	✓	✓	✓		✓
Susquehanna U								✓		✓			✓				✓		✓	✓			✓		
Swarthmore Coll		✓					✓	✓		✓	✓		✓	✓		✓	✓		✓			✓	✓		
Temple U				✓				✓		✓	✓		✓	✓			✓		✓	✓		✓	✓		
Temple U, Ambler																									
Thiel Coll	✓							✓	✓	✓	✓		✓	✓		✓	✓			✓	✓	✓			
Thomas Jefferson U		✓						✓	✓	✓			✓	✓		✓	✓	✓				✓			
Ursinus Coll		✓						✓		✓			✓									✓			

Villanova U		✓						✓	✓	✓		✓	✓	✓			✓	✓		✓		✓	✓		
Washington & Jefferson Coll								✓	✓	✓		✓	✓	✓			✓	✓		✓		✓			
Waynesburg Coll									✓	✓			✓	✓						✓		✓			✓
West Chester U		✓						✓		✓			✓	✓						✓		✓	✓		
Westminster Coll	✓		✓			✓		✓	✓	✓	✓		✓	✓		✓	✓			✓		✓	✓		
Widener U	✓	✓						✓		✓		✓	✓	✓		✓	✓		✓	✓	✓	✓	✓		
Wilkes U					✓		✓	✓	✓	✓		✓	✓	✓		✓	✓	✓	✓	✓		✓	✓		
Wilson Coll	✓	✓	✓			✓		✓	✓	✓		✓	✓	✓	✓	✓		✓		✓		✓			✓
York Coll of Pennsylvania													✓							✓					
Puerto Rico																									
Conservatory of Music				✓	✓			✓	✓	✓		✓	✓	✓			✓	✓		✓		✓	✓		
Inter American U						✓		✓		✓			✓	✓	✓	✓		✓			✓	✓			
Pontifical Catholic U				✓				✓	✓	✓			✓	✓	✓			✓		✓		✓			
Puerto Rico, U of, Humacao				✓	✓			✓	✓	✓		✓	✓	✓				✓				✓	✓		
Puerto Rico, U of, Mayaguez					✓			✓	✓				✓	✓											
Rhode Island																									
Brown U		✓					✓	✓	✓	✓		✓	✓			✓		✓		✓		✓	✓		
Bryant U										✓			✓							✓					
Johnson & Wales U				✓				✓		✓			✓	✓			✓			✓		✓	✓		
Providence Coll		✓			✓			✓		✓		✓	✓	✓		✓	✓	✓		✓		✓			✓
Rhode Island Sch of Design		✓						✓	✓				✓	✓			✓					✓	✓		
Rhode Island, U of		✓			✓	✓		✓		✓		✓	✓	✓		✓		✓		✓		✓	✓	✓	✓
Roger Williams U		✓						✓		✓			✓							✓		✓			
Salve Regina U		✓						✓		✓	✓		✓	✓			✓	✓		✓		✓	✓		
South Carolina																									
Anderson Coll		✓						✓		✓			✓	✓								✓			
Charleston Southern U								✓		✓			✓	✓						✓		✓			
Charleston, College of		✓			✓	✓				✓		✓	✓						✓	✓			✓		
Clemson U		✓						✓		✓			✓	✓			✓		✓	✓		✓			

	Curriculum						In Class						Exams						Services						
	Foreign Language Waiver	Lighter Course Load	Math Waiver	Other Special Classes	Priority Registration	Substition of Courses	Early Syllabus	Note Takers in Class	Priority Seating	Tape Recorders	Videotaped Classes	Text on Tape	Extended Time	Oral Exams	Take Home Exams	Exams on Tape or PC	Untimed Exams	Other Accommodations	Diagnostic Tests	Learning Centers	Proofreaders	Readers	Reading Machines	Special Bookstore Section	Typists
Coastal Carolina U		✓		✓				✓		✓	✓		✓	✓			✓			✓		✓	✓		
Coker Coll		✓								✓			✓	✓	✓		✓								
Columbia International U		✓						✓		✓		✓	✓	✓			✓		✓		✓	✓	✓		✓
Converse Coll										✓			✓	✓			✓					✓			
Erskine Coll										✓			✓				✓								
Francis Maricn U		✓						✓		✓			✓	✓								✓			
Furman U		✓						✓		✓			✓	✓								✓			
Lander U		✓			✓	✓	✓	✓	✓	✓		✓	✓	✓	✓	✓	✓	✓		✓	✓	✓	✓		✓
Limestone Coll		✓		✓				✓				✓	✓	✓	✓		✓	✓		✓	✓	✓			
Newberry Coll								✓	✓				✓	✓			✓			✓	✓				
North Greenville Coll		✓						✓					✓	✓			✓								
Presbyterian Coll		✓								✓			✓	✓					✓	✓					
South Carolina, U of, Aiken	✓	✓	✓		✓	✓		✓	✓	✓	✓	✓	✓	✓		✓		✓		✓	✓	✓	✓		✓
South Carolina, U, Columbia		✓						✓		✓			✓				✓					✓	✓		
South Carolina, U of, Upstate					✓	✓		✓	✓	✓		✓	✓			✓		✓		✓	✓		✓		
Southern Wesleyan U								✓					✓							✓					
The Citadel					✓	✓	✓	✓		✓		✓	✓	✓		✓	✓	✓		✓	✓	✓			✓
Winthrop U								✓		✓			✓	✓								✓			
Wofford Coll		✓								✓			✓												
South Dakota																									
Augustana Coll								✓		✓	✓		✓	✓			✓	✓		✓		✓			
Dakota St U				✓			✓	✓	✓	✓	✓	✓	✓	✓		✓	✓			✓		✓	✓	✓	
Dakota Wesleyan U		✓								✓	✓		✓	✓			✓		✓	✓		✓	✓		

Mt Marty Coll		✓						✓		✓			✓	✓			✓			✓		✓			
Northern St U		✓						✓		✓			✓	✓			✓		✓			✓			
Sioux Falls, U of								✓	✓	✓		✓	✓	✓		✓	✓			✓	✓	✓		✓	
South Dakota Sch of Mines																				✓			✓		
South Dakota St U		✓						✓	✓	✓	✓	✓	✓	✓		✓	✓	✓	✓			✓	✓		✓
South Dakota, U of, Vermillion		✓		✓				✓		✓			✓	✓			✓		✓	✓		✓	✓		
Tennessee																									
Austin Peay St U		✓			✓			✓	✓	✓	✓	✓	✓	✓		✓		✓		✓		✓	✓		✓
Belmont U		✓						✓	✓	✓			✓	✓		✓	✓	✓				✓			
Bethel Coll										✓							✓								
Bryan Coll		✓				✓		✓		✓		✓	✓	✓	✓		✓			✓		✓			✓
Christian Brothers U								✓		✓			✓	✓			✓					✓			
Crichton Coll								✓		✓	✓		✓	✓			✓		✓			✓			
Cumberland U										✓			✓	✓			✓			✓		✓	✓		
East Tennessee St U		✓						✓						✓			✓								
King Coll		✓		✓				✓		✓			✓	✓			✓			✓					
Lambuth U										✓			✓	✓			✓		✓	✓					
Lee U		✓						✓		✓	✓		✓	✓			✓	✓		✓		✓	✓		✓
Lipscomb U	✓	✓	✓		✓	✓		✓	✓	✓		✓	✓	✓		✓	✓	✓	✓			✓	✓		✓
Martin Methodist Coll		✓						✓		✓			✓				✓		✓	✓					
Maryville Coll		✓						✓	✓	✓		✓	✓	✓		✓	✓			✓		✓	✓		✓
Memphis, U of	✓	✓			✓	✓		✓	✓	✓			✓			✓	✓	✓	✓	✓	✓	✓	✓		
Middle Tennessee St U	✓					✓		✓	✓	✓		✓	✓	✓		✓		✓		✓	✓	✓	✓		✓
Milligan Coll		✓					✓						✓					✓		✓					
Rhodes Coll		✓						✓	✓	✓		✓	✓										✓		
Southern Adventist U		✓				✓		✓	✓	✓		✓	✓	✓		✓		✓	✓	✓		✓	✓		✓
Tallahassee Comm Coll		✓	✓	✓	✓	✓		✓	✓	✓		✓	✓	✓		✓	✓			✓		✓	✓		✓
Tennessee Tech U								✓		✓	✓		✓	✓		✓						✓	✓		
Tennessee Wesleyan Coll		✓						✓		✓			✓	✓			✓			✓		✓			

	Curriculum						In Class						Exams						Services						
	Foreign Language Waiver	Lighter Course Load	Math Waiver	Other Special Classes	Priority Registration	Substition of Courses	Early Syllabus	Note Takers in Class	Priority Seating	Tape Recorders	Videotaped Classes	Text on Tape	Extended Time	Oral Exams	Take Home Exams	Exams on Tape or PC	Untimed Exams	Other Accommodations	Diagnostic Tests	Learning Centers	Proofreaders	Readers	Reading Machines	Special Bookstore Section	Typists
Tennessee, U of								✓		✓			✓	✓					✓			✓	✓		
Tennessee, U of, Chattanooga		✓											✓	✓			✓					✓			
Tennessee, U of, Martin								✓		✓		✓	✓	✓		✓	✓	✓		✓		✓	✓		✓
Trevecca Nazarene U								✓		✓		✓	✓	✓				✓		✓			✓		
Tusculum Coll								✓		✓	✓		✓	✓						✓		✓	✓		
Union U		✓		✓			✓	✓	✓	✓			✓	✓			✓		✓	✓					
Vanderbilt U	✓	✓				✓		✓	✓	✓		✓	✓	✓		✓		✓	✓	✓	✓	✓			✓
Texas																									
Abilene Christian U								✓		✓			✓	✓		✓			✓			✓			
Angelo St U								✓		✓			✓	✓					✓	✓					
Austin Coll								✓		✓		✓	✓			✓				✓			✓		
Baylor U		✓						✓	✓	✓			✓	✓				✓			✓	✓	✓		
Dallas Baptist U								✓	✓	✓	✓	✓	✓	✓			✓			✓		✓	✓		✓
East Texas Baptist U													✓												
Hardin-Simmons U		✓						✓		✓			✓	✓		✓	✓					✓			
Houston Baptist U		✓											✓	✓			✓		✓	✓					
Houston, U of		✓						✓		✓	✓		✓	✓					✓	✓		✓	✓		
Houston, U of, Downtown	✓	✓			✓				✓				✓			✓		✓	✓	✓			✓		
Howard Payne U								✓	✓	✓			✓	✓		✓	✓	✓		✓	✓				
Incarnate Word, U of the		✓			✓	✓	✓	✓	✓	✓	✓	✓	✓	✓		✓	✓	✓		✓		✓	✓		✓
Jarvis Christian Coll		✓								✓	✓		✓	✓					✓						
Lamar U						✓		✓		✓		✓	✓	✓		✓						✓			
LeTourneau U		✓																							

Lubbock Christian U		✓			✓			✓	✓	✓			✓	✓		✓	✓	✓		✓	✓	✓	✓		
Mary Hardin-Baylor, U of				✓				✓		✓			✓	✓			✓		✓	✓		✓			
McMurry U						✓		✓	✓				✓	✓				✓		✓	✓	✓			
Midwestern St U								✓	✓	✓			✓	✓		✓	✓	✓		✓		✓	✓		✓
North Texas, U of								✓	✓	✓			✓	✓		✓	✓		✓	✓		✓	✓		✓
Northwood U								✓	✓	✓			✓	✓	✓		✓	✓							
Our Lady of the Lake U						✓	✓		✓	✓		✓	✓	✓				✓		✓		✓			✓
Prairie View A&M U										✓			✓				✓			✓					
Rice U							✓	✓	✓	✓		✓	✓		✓	✓		✓					✓		✓
Sam Houston St U								✓		✓		✓	✓	✓		✓				✓			✓		
Schreiner U		✓						✓		✓		✓	✓	✓				✓				✓	✓		
Southern Methodist U					✓	✓		✓		✓		✓	✓	✓		✓			✓	✓		✓	✓		✓
Southwestern U	✓	✓			✓			✓	✓	✓			✓	✓		✓		✓		✓		✓			✓
St. Edward's U		✓		✓									✓	✓						✓		✓			✓
St. Mary's U of San Antonio													✓	✓					✓	✓					
St. Thomas, U of		✓		✓	✓		✓	✓	✓	✓			✓	✓		✓		✓		✓					
Stephen F Austin St U		✓		✓				✓		✓			✓	✓					✓	✓		✓	✓		
Tarleton St U		✓					✓			✓			✓	✓		✓		✓		✓					
Texas A&M International U		✓		✓				✓	✓	✓	✓		✓	✓			✓					✓	✓		
Texas A&M U at Galveston		✓						✓		✓	✓		✓	✓											
Texas A&M U, College Station		✓			✓			✓	✓	✓		✓	✓				✓		✓				✓		
Texas A&M U, Corpus Christi						✓		✓		✓	✓	✓	✓	✓		✓				✓		✓			
Texas A&M U, Kingsville				✓				✓		✓	✓		✓	✓						✓		✓	✓		
Texas Christian U																									
Texas Lutheran U					✓			✓	✓	✓			✓	✓				✓							
Texas St U, San Marcos		✓						✓		✓			✓	✓			✓		✓	✓		✓	✓		
Texas Tech U						✓		✓	✓	✓		✓	✓		✓		✓			✓		✓			✓
Texas Wesleyan U		✓																							
Texas Woman's U		✓						✓		✓			✓	✓						✓		✓			

	Curriculum						In Class						Exams						Services						
	Foreign Language Waiver	Lighter Course Load	Math Waiver	Other Special Classes	Priority Registration	Substition of Courses	Early Syllabus	Note Takers in Class	Priority Seating	Tape Recorders	Videotaped Classes	Text on Tape	Extended Time	Oral Exams	Take Home Exams	Exams on Tape or PC	Untimed Exams	Other Accommodations	Diagnostic Tests	Learning Centers	Proofreaders	Readers	Reading Machines	Special Bookstore Section	Typists
Texas, U of, Arlington						✓		✓	✓	✓			✓					✓				✓	✓		✓
Texas, U of, Austin		✓			✓								✓							✓					
Texas, U of, Dallas		✓		✓				✓		✓			✓	✓		✓		✓				✓	✓		
Texas, U of, El Paso		✓						✓		✓			✓	✓					✓			✓	✓		
Texas, U of, Pan American					✓	✓	✓	✓	✓	✓	✓		✓	✓		✓	✓	✓	✓	✓		✓	✓		✓
Texas, U of, Permian Basin	✓	✓	✓		✓	✓	✓	✓	✓	✓	✓	✓	✓	✓	✓	✓	✓	✓	✓	✓	✓	✓	✓	✓	✓
Texas, U of, San Antonio		✓						✓		✓												✓	✓		
Texas, U of, Tyler						✓		✓	✓	✓	✓		✓	✓		✓		✓				✓	✓		✓
West Texas A&M U		✓						✓		✓			✓	✓			✓					✓	✓	✓	
Wiley Coll		✓																	✓	✓					
United Kingdom																									
American Inter U in London				✓						✓			✓	✓			✓								
Utah																									
Brigham Young U		✓			✓	✓		✓		✓		✓	✓	✓		✓		✓	✓	✓	✓	✓	✓		✓
Southern Utah U		✓						✓		✓			✓	✓					✓	✓		✓			
Utah St U		✓						✓		✓			✓									✓	✓		
Utah Valley St Coll		✓		✓				✓		✓			✓	✓			✓	✓	✓			✓			
Utah, U of		✓			✓	✓		✓	✓	✓		✓	✓	✓		✓		✓				✓	✓		
Weber St U		✓						✓					✓	✓			✓					✓	✓		
Westminster Coll					✓			✓		✓		✓	✓				✓	✓				✓			✓
Vermont																									
Bennington Coll		✓			✓	✓	✓	✓	✓				✓	✓		✓	✓		✓			✓			
Burlington Coll		✓				✓				✓				✓							✓				

Castleton St Coll								✓		✓			✓	✓						✓		✓	✓		
Champlain Coll								✓	✓				✓				✓								
Green Mountain Coll		✓		✓				✓		✓			✓	✓			✓		✓	✓		✓	✓	✓	
Johnson St Coll								✓		✓			✓	✓						✓		✓	✓		
Landmark Coll	✓	✓	✓	✓	✓	✓	✓	✓	✓	✓	✓	✓	✓	✓	✓	✓	✓	✓	✓	✓	✓	✓	✓	✓	✓
Lyndon St Coll		✓						✓		✓			✓	✓			✓			✓		✓	✓		
Marlboro Coll													✓				✓			✓					
Middlebury Coll		✓						✓		✓			✓	✓					✓	✓		✓	✓		
Norwich U					✓							✓	✓	✓				✓		✓		✓			
St. Joseph, Coll of		✓						✓	✓	✓			✓	✓			✓			✓	✓				
St. Michael's Coll		✓						✓		✓			✓							✓		✓			
Vermont Tech Coll		✓						✓		✓			✓	✓			✓		✓	✓		✓	✓		
Vermont, U of		✓		✓	✓			✓		✓		✓	✓			✓		✓		✓		✓	✓		
Virginia																									
Averett U	✓	✓				✓	✓	✓	✓	✓		✓	✓	✓	✓	✓	✓		✓	✓	✓	✓	✓		
Bluefield Coll								✓		✓			✓	✓			✓								
Bridgewater Coll	✓	✓	✓			✓		✓	✓	✓		✓	✓				✓					✓		✓	
Christopher Newport U										✓			✓	✓									✓		
Eastern Mennonite U		✓		✓	✓	✓	✓	✓	✓	✓	✓	✓	✓	✓	✓	✓	✓	✓	✓	✓	✓	✓	✓		✓
Emory & Henry Coll								✓		✓			✓									✓	✓		
Ferrum Coll										✓	✓		✓				✓			✓					
George Mason U	✓	✓	✓		✓	✓		✓	✓	✓			✓	✓		✓	✓	✓		✓		✓	✓		✓
Hampden-Sydney Coll		✓						✓		✓	✓		✓	✓									✓		
Hampton U		✓						✓		✓			✓	✓			✓					✓			
Hollins U	✓	✓				✓		✓		✓		✓	✓	✓	✓	✓	✓	✓		✓			✓		✓
James Madison U		✓		✓	✓			✓		✓		✓	✓	✓		✓		✓	✓	✓		✓	✓		✓
Liberty U													✓	✓						✓					
Longwood U	✓	✓			✓	✓		✓		✓			✓	✓		✓	✓	✓		✓		✓	✓		✓
Lynchburg Coll						✓		✓	✓	✓		✓	✓	✓		✓	✓	✓		✓		✓			✓

	Curriculum						In Class						Exams						Services						
	Foreign Language Waiver	Lighter Course Load	Math Waiver	Other Special Classes	Priority Registration	Substition of Courses	Early Syllabus	Note Takers in Class	Priority Seating	Tape Recorders	Videotaped Classes	Text on Tape	Extended Time	Oral Exams	Take Home Exams	Exams on Tape or PC	Untimed Exams	Other Accommodations	Diagnostic Tests	Learning Centers	Proofreaders	Readers	Reading Machines	Special Bookstore Section	Typists
Mary Baldwin Coll						✓		✓		✓	✓		✓	✓			✓			✓		✓			
Mary Washington, U of		✓				✓		✓		✓		✓	✓	✓		✓		✓					✓		✓
Marymount U		✓						✓		✓		✓	✓	✓				✓		✓		✓			✓
Norfolk St U								✓		✓	✓		✓	✓			✓		✓	✓		✓	✓		
Old Dominion U		✓		✓	✓	✓		✓	✓	✓			✓			✓		✓				✓			✓
Radford U					✓			✓	✓	✓		✓	✓	✓		✓		✓		✓	✓	✓	✓		✓
Randolph-Macon Coll						✓		✓		✓		✓	✓			✓	✓			✓			✓		
Randolph-Macon Woman Coll					✓			✓	✓	✓		✓	✓	✓	✓	✓		✓		✓		✓	✓		✓
Richmond, U of																									
Roanoke Coll								✓		✓			✓	✓			✓			✓					
Shenandoah U	✓	✓	✓	✓	✓	✓	✓	✓	✓	✓	✓	✓	✓	✓	✓	✓		✓		✓		✓	✓		✓
St. Paul's Coll		✓						✓		✓			✓		✓		✓	✓	✓	✓	✓				
Sweet Briar Coll													✓							✓					
Virginia Commonwealth U								✓		✓			✓	✓								✓	✓		
Virginia Intermont Coll		✓		✓				✓		✓		✓	✓	✓		✓	✓		✓	✓	✓	✓			✓
Virginia Military Inst	✓				✓	✓	✓	✓	✓	✓		✓	✓					✓		✓	✓		✓		
Virginia Polytech Inst & St U		✓			✓	✓		✓	✓	✓		✓	✓	✓		✓		✓		✓		✓	✓		
Virginia St U		✓								✓			✓	✓			✓			✓		✓		✓	
Virginia Union U																				✓			✓		
Virginia Wesleyan Coll	✓	✓	✓		✓	✓		✓	✓	✓		✓	✓	✓			✓	✓		✓	✓	✓			✓
Virginia, U of								✓		✓			✓	✓			✓		✓	✓		✓			
Virginia, U of, Coll at Wise		✓			✓	✓		✓	✓	✓	✓	✓	✓			✓		✓		✓	✓	✓	✓		✓
Washington & Lee U	✓					✓		✓		✓		✓	✓				✓						✓		

William & Mary, Coll of								✓		✓			✓						✓			✓			
Washington																									
Central Washington U		✓		✓				✓		✓			✓	✓		✓		✓				✓	✓		
City U								✓	✓	✓	✓	✓	✓	✓	✓	✓	✓								✓
Cornish Coll of the Arts		✓					✓	✓		✓		✓	✓	✓		✓		✓				✓			
Eastern Washington U		✓		✓			✓	✓		✓			✓	✓		✓	✓	✓		✓		✓	✓		
Gonzaga U					✓			✓	✓	✓		✓	✓	✓		✓						✓	✓		
Henry Cogswell Coll																									
Heritage Coll							✓	✓	✓	✓		✓	✓	✓		✓	✓	✓		✓		✓	✓		✓
Northwest U		✓			✓		✓		✓	✓			✓	✓		✓	✓	✓		✓	✓	✓			✓
Pacific Lutheran U				✓				✓		✓	✓		✓	✓			✓			✓		✓	✓		
Puget Sound, U of	✓	✓						✓		✓		✓	✓			✓				✓	✓		✓		✓
Seattle U		✓						✓		✓			✓	✓						✓		✓	✓		
St. Martin's Coll	✓	✓	✓			✓		✓		✓		✓	✓	✓		✓	✓	✓		✓		✓			✓
The Evergreen St Coll								✓		✓		✓	✓					✓	✓						
Walla Walla Coll		✓						✓		✓			✓	✓						✓		✓			
Washington St U	✓				✓			✓	✓	✓	✓	✓	✓	✓		✓			✓	✓		✓	✓		✓
Washington, U of		✓		✓						✓			✓	✓						✓		✓	✓		
Western Washington U		✓			✓	✓	✓	✓		✓		✓	✓	✓	✓	✓		✓			✓	✓	✓		✓
Whitman Coll								✓		✓		✓	✓	✓		✓	✓					✓	✓		✓
Whitworth Coll		✓				✓		✓	✓	✓	✓	✓	✓			✓	✓	✓				✓			
West Virginia																									
Alderson-Broaddus Coll							✓	✓	✓	✓			✓	✓		✓	✓	✓		✓	✓	✓			✓
Bethany Coll				✓				✓		✓			✓	✓			✓			✓		✓			
Bluefield St Coll		✓						✓		✓			✓	✓			✓					✓	✓		
Charleston, U of	✓	✓	✓	✓				✓	✓	✓		✓	✓	✓		✓	✓			✓		✓	✓		
Concord Coll		✓						✓		✓		✓	✓	✓			✓	✓				✓			
Davis & Elkins Coll		✓						✓		✓		✓	✓	✓		✓	✓			✓		✓	✓		✓
Fairmont St U								✓					✓	✓			✓			✓		✓	✓		

	Curriculum						In Class						Exams						Services						
	Foreign Language Waiver	Lighter Course Load	Math Waiver	Other Special Classes	Priority Registration	Substition of Courses	Early Syllabus	Note Takers in Class	Priority Seating	Tape Recorders	Videotaped Classes	Text on Tape	Extended Time	Oral Exams	Take Home Exams	Exams on Tape or PC	Untimed Exams	Other Accommodations	Diagnostic Tests	Learning Centers	Proofreaders	Readers	Reading Machines	Special Bookstore Section	Typists
Glenville St Coll								✓	✓	✓		✓	✓	✓						✓	✓	✓	✓		
Marshall U								✓		✓				✓			✓		✓	✓		✓			
Mountain St U								✓		✓	✓		✓	✓			✓		✓	✓		✓	✓		
Ohio Valley U		✓							✓	✓			✓	✓			✓	✓				✓			
Shepherd U		✓			✓			✓	✓	✓		✓	✓	✓			✓					✓			
West Liberty St Coll					✓		✓	✓	✓	✓		✓	✓	✓		✓	✓			✓	✓	✓			
West Virginia U		✓						✓		✓			✓	✓			✓		✓	✓			✓		✓
West Virginia U, Parkersburg										✓			✓	✓					✓	✓			✓		
West Virginia Wesleyan Coll				✓				✓		✓			✓	✓			✓		✓	✓		✓	✓		
Wheeling Jesuit U	✓	✓						✓					✓	✓			✓			✓	✓	✓			
Wisconsin																									
Alverno Coll		✓						✓		✓			✓							✓			✓		
Bellin Coll of Nursing										✓			✓				✓								
Beloit Coll								✓		✓		✓	✓	✓		✓		✓		✓		✓	✓		✓
Carroll Coll	✓	✓	✓			✓		✓					✓	✓						✓	✓				
Carthage Coll								✓					✓	✓			✓		✓			✓	✓		
Edgewood Coll		✓						✓		✓			✓	✓						✓		✓	✓		
Lakeland Coll		✓						✓		✓			✓	✓			✓			✓		✓	✓		
Lawrence U	✓	✓	✓					✓		✓			✓	✓			✓	✓		✓		✓			✓
Marian Coll of Fond du Lac				✓				✓		✓			✓	✓						✓		✓	✓		
Marquette U	✓	✓			✓	✓		✓		✓		✓	✓	✓		✓			✓				✓		
Milwaukee Inst Art & Design													✓	✓						✓					
Milwaukee Sch of Engineering					✓		✓	✓	✓	✓		✓	✓	✓	✓	✓	✓	✓	✓	✓	✓	✓			✓

Mt Mary Coll				✓				✓		✓		✓	✓	✓	✓	✓	✓	✓		✓	✓	✓	✓		
Northland Coll							✓	✓		✓			✓	✓							✓	✓			✓
Ripon Coll								✓		✓		✓	✓	✓		✓	✓				✓	✓			
Silver Lake Coll		✓						✓						✓								✓			
St. Norbert Coll		✓			✓	✓		✓	✓	✓		✓	✓					✓		✓		✓			✓
Viterbo U	✓	✓		✓	✓	✓	✓	✓	✓	✓		✓	✓	✓		✓	✓	✓		✓	✓	✓	✓		✓
Wisconsin Lutheran Coll								✓		✓	✓		✓				✓			✓					
Wisconsin, U of, Baraboo		✓						✓	✓			✓	✓	✓		✓		✓				✓	✓		✓
Wisconsin, U of, Eau Claire		✓						✓		✓			✓	✓			✓			✓		✓	✓		
Wisconsin, U of, Green Bay		✓			✓			✓	✓	✓		✓	✓				✓					✓			✓
Wisconsin, U of, LaCrosse					✓			✓		✓		✓	✓	✓				✓				✓	✓		
Wisconsin, U of, Madison		✓			✓	✓		✓	✓			✓	✓	✓			✓	✓		✓		✓			
Wisconsin, U of, Milwaukee		✓						✓		✓			✓	✓		✓			✓	✓		✓	✓		
Wisconsin, U of, Oshkosh		✓						✓		✓	✓		✓	✓						✓		✓			
Wisconsin, U of, Parkside								✓					✓				✓			✓			✓		
Wisconsin, U of, Platteville		✓					✓	✓		✓		✓	✓	✓		✓	✓	✓		✓	✓	✓			✓
Wisconsin, U of, River Falls		✓						✓					✓	✓								✓			
Wisconsin, U, Stevens Point		✓		✓	✓			✓	✓			✓	✓	✓		✓		✓		✓		✓	✓		✓
Wisconsin, U of, Stout		✓		✓	✓			✓	✓	✓		✓	✓			✓	✓	✓	✓			✓	✓		✓
Wisconsin, U of, Superior				✓				✓		✓			✓	✓			✓			✓		✓	✓		
Wisconsin, U of, Whitewater		✓		✓				✓		✓			✓				✓			✓		✓	✓		
Wyoming																									
Central Wyoming Coll							✓	✓	✓		✓	✓	✓		✓		✓	✓	✓	✓	✓	✓	✓		✓
Sheridan Coll	✓	✓	✓			✓		✓	✓	✓		✓	✓	✓		✓				✓		✓			✓
Wyoming, U of		✓		✓	✓	✓	✓	✓		✓		✓	✓			✓		✓		✓		✓	✓		

Service Levels

Colleges with Programs

Adelphi U, NY
American International Coll, MA
American U, DC
Art Insts International Minnesota, MN
Brenau U, GA
California State U - Bakersfield, CA
California State U - Los Angeles, CA
Centenary Coll, NJ
Coll of Mount St. Joseph, OH
Concordia Coll, NY
Curry Coll, MA
Davis and Elkins Coll, WV
Dean Coll, MA
Denver, U of, CO
DePaul U, IL
Eastern Kentucky U, KY
Fairleigh Dickinson U, NJ
Fort Valley State U, GA
Gannon U, PA
Gardner-Webb U, NC
Governors State U, IL
Graceland U, IA
Hofstra U, NY
Indianapolis, U of, IN
Inter American U, PR
Iona Coll, NY
Johnson State Coll, VT
King's Coll, PA
Landmark Coll, VT
Limestone Coll, SC
Long Island U - C.W. Post Campus, NY
Loras Coll, IA
Louisiana Coll, LA
Lynn U, FL
Marian Coll, IN
Marist Coll, NY
Mars Hill Coll, NC
Marshall U, WV
Mary Washington, U of, VA
Marymount Manhattan Coll, NY
Mercy Coll, NY
Mercyhurst Coll, PA
Misericordia, Coll, PA
Mitchell Coll, CT
Morningside Coll, IA
Mount Ida Coll, MA
Muskingum Coll, OH
New Jersey City U, NJ
New York Inst of Tech, NY
Ozarks, U of the, AR
Pontifical Catholic, PR
Prairie View A&M U, TX
Puerto Rico, U of, Rio Piedras, PR
Queens U of Charlotte, NC
Reinhardt Coll, GA
Rowan U, NJ
Sage Coll of Albany, NY
Schreiner U, TX
South Florida, U of, FL
Southern Oregon U, OR
Southwest Missouri State U, MO
St. Gregory's U, OK
St. Peter's Coll, NJ
St. Thomas Aquinas Coll, NY
Tennessee, U of, Martin, TN
Texas A&M International U, TX
U of North Carolina - Chapel Hill, NC
U of San Francisco, CA
U of Toledo, OH
Ursuline Coll, OH
West Virginia Wesleyan Coll, WV
Westminster Coll, MO
Wichita State U, KS
York U, CN

Abilene Christian U, TX
Adrian Coll, MI
Agnes Scott Coll, GA
Alabama State U, AL
Alabama, U of, Birmingham, AL
Alaska, U of, Anchorage, AK
Albertson Coll, ID
Albion Coll, MI
Albright Coll, PA
Alderson-Broaddus Coll, WV
Alfred U, NY
Allegheny Coll, PA
Alliant International U, CA
Alma Coll, MI
Alverno Coll, WI
Amherst Coll, MA
Anderson Coll, SC
Anderson U, IN
Andrews U, MI
Appalachian State U, NC
Aquinas Coll, MI
Arcadia U, PA
Arizona State U West, AZ
Arkansas State U, AR
Arkansas Tech U, AR
Arkansas, U of, AR
Arkansas, U of, Little Rock, AR
Art Academy of Cincinnati, OH
Art Center Coll of Design, CA
Art Inst of Atlanta, GA
Art Inst of Phoenix, AZ
Ashland U, OH
Athabasca U, CN
Atlantic, Coll of the, ME
Auburn U, AL
Auburn U - Montgomery, AL
Augsburg Coll, MN
Augusta State U, GA
Augustana Coll, SD
Augustana Coll, IL
Aurora U, IL
Austin Coll, TX
Austin Peay State U, TN
Avila U, MO
Babson Coll, MA
Baker U, KS
Baldwin-Wallace Coll, OH
Ball State U, IN
Baptist Coll of Florida, FL
Bard Coll, NY
Barnard Coll, NY
Barry U, FL
Bay Path Coll, MA
Baylor U, TX
Bellevue U, NE
Bellin Coll of Nursing, WI
Belmont U, TN
Beloit Coll, WI
Bemidji State U, MN
Benedictine Coll, KS
Benedictine U, IL
Bennington Coll, VT
Bentley Coll, MA
Berea Coll, KY
Berklee Coll of Music, MA
Berry Coll, GA
Bethany Coll, WV
Bethel Coll, KS
Bethel Coll, IN
Bethel U, MN
Bloomfield Coll, NJ
Bloomsburg U of Pennsylvania, PA
Blue Mountain Coll, MS
Bluefield Coll, VA
Bluefield State Coll, WV
Bluffton U, OH
Boston Architectural Center, MA
Boston Coll, MA
Boston U, MA
Bowdoin Coll, ME
Bowling Green State U, OH
Bradley U, IL
Brandeis U, MA
Brevard Coll, NC
Brewton-Parker Coll, GA
Briar Cliff U, IA
Bridgewater State Coll, MA
Brigham Young U - Provo, UT
Brown U, RI
Bryan Coll, TN
Bryant U, RI
Bryn Mawr Coll, PA
Buena Vista U, IA
Burlington Coll, VT
Butler U, IN
Cabrini Coll, PA
Caldwell Coll, NJ
California Baptist U, CA
California Inst of Tech, CA
California Inst of the Arts, CA
Cal Polytech State U - San Luis Obispo, CA
California State Polytech U - Pomona, CA
California State U - Chico, CA
California State U - East Bay, CA
California State U - Fresno, CA
California State U - Fullerton, CA
California State U - Monterey Bay, CA
California State U - Sacramento, CA
California State U - San Bernardino, CA
California State U - Stanislaus, CA
California, U of, Santa Cruz, CA
Calvin Coll, MI
Cameron U, OK
Canisius Coll, NY
Carleton Coll, MN
Carlow U, PA
Carnegie Mellon U, PA
Carthage Coll, WI
Case Western Reserve U, OH
Catholic U of America, DC
Cazenovia Coll, NY
Central Christian Coll, KS
Central Coll, IA
Central Connecticut State U, CT
Central Michigan U, MI
Central Washington U, WA
Centre Coll, KY
Chapman U, CA
Chatham Coll, PA
Chicago State U, IL
Christian Brothers U, TN
Claremont McKenna Coll, CA
Clarion U of Pennsylvania, PA
Clarkson Coll, NE
Clayton Coll and State U, GA
Clearwater Christian Coll, FL
Clemson U, SC
Cleveland Inst of Music, OH
Coastal Carolina U, SC
Coe Coll, IA
Colgate U, NY
Coll of Charleston, SC
Coll of Mount St. Vincent, NY
Coll of New Jersey, NJ
Coll of St. Elizabeth, NJ
Coll of St. Rose, NY
Coll of the Ozarks, MO
Coll of William and Mary, VA
Coll of Wooster, OH
Colorado Coll, CO
Colorado School of Mines, CO
Colorado State U, CO
Columbia Coll, IL
Columbia Coll of Nursing, WI
Columbia International U, SC
Columbia U, NY
Columbus Coll of Art and Design, OH
Columbus State U, GA
Concord U, WV
Concordia Coll - Moorhead, MN
Concordia U, NE
Concordia U, MI
Concordia U - St. Paul, MN
Connecticut Coll, CT
Connecticut, U of, CT
Cornell U, NY
Cornerstone U, MI
Cornish Coll of the Arts, WA
Creighton U, NE
Culinary Inst of America, NY
Culver-Stockton Coll, MO
CUNY, Baruch Coll, NY
CUNY, John Jay Coll of Criminal Justice, NY
CUNY - Coll of Staten Island, NY
CUNY - Lehman Coll, NY
CUNY - Medgar Evers Coll, NY
CUNY - Queens Coll, NY
CUNY - York Coll, NY
Dakota State U, SD
Dakota Wesleyan U, SD
Dalhousie U, CN
Dallas Baptist U, TX
Dalton State Coll, GA
Dana Coll, NE
Dartmouth Coll, NH
Dayton, U of, OH
Delaware Valley Coll, PA
Denison U, OH
DePauw U, IN
DeVry U - Metro D.C., VA
Dickinson Coll, PA
Dickinson State U, ND
Dillard U, LA
Dominican U, IL
Dominican U of California, CA
Dordt Coll, IA
Drake U, IA
Drury U, MO

Colleges with Services

Duquesne U, PA
East Carolina U, NC
East Stroudsburg U of Pennsylvania, PA
East Tennessee State U, TN
East Texas Baptist U, TX
Eastern Connecticut State U, CT
Eastern Illinois U, IL
Eastern Mennonite U, VA
Eastern Washington U, WA
Eckerd Coll, FL
Edgewood Coll, WI
Edinboro U of Pennsylvania, PA
Elizabeth City State U, NC
Elizabethtown Coll, PA
Elmhurst Coll, IL
Elmira Coll, NY
Emerson Coll, MA
Emmanuel Coll, MA
Emory and Henry Coll, VA
Emory U, GA
Emporia State U, KS
Endicott Coll, MA
Eureka Coll, IL
Evergreen State Coll, WA
Fashion Inst of Tech, NY
Faulkner U, AL
Ferris State U, MI
Ferrum Coll, VA
Findlay, U of, OH
Fitchburg State Coll, MA
Flagler Coll, FL
Florida Atlantic U, FL
Florida Gulf Coast U, FL
Florida State U, FL
Florida, U of, FL
Fontbonne U, MO
Fordham U, NY
Fort Lewis Coll, CO
Francis Marion U, SC
Franciscan U of Steubenville, OH
Franklin and Marshall Coll, PA
Franklin Coll, IN
Franklin Coll Switzerland, SW
Franklin Pierce Coll, NH
Fresno Pacific U, CA
Friends U, KS
Frostburg State U, MD
Furman U, SC
Gallaudet U, DC
Geneva Coll, PA
George Washington U, DC
Georgetown Coll, KY
Georgetown U, DC
Georgia Coll and State U, GA
Georgia Inst of Tech, GA
Georgia Southern U, GA
Georgia State U, GA
Georgia, U of, GA
Georgian Court U, NJ
Glenville State Coll, WV
Gonzaga U, WA
Gordon Coll, MA
Goshen Coll, IN
Goucher Coll, MD
Grace Coll and Seminary, IN
Grand View Coll, IA
Great Falls, U of, MT
Green Mountain Coll, VT
Greensboro Coll, NC
Grinnell Coll, IA
Gwynedd-Mercy Coll, PA
Hamilton Coll, NY
Hamline U, MN
Hampshire Coll, MA
Harding U, AR
Hardin-Simmons U, TX
Harris-Stowe State Coll, MO
Hartwick Coll, NY
Harvey Mudd Coll, CA
Hastings Coll, NE
Haverford Coll, PA
Hawaii, U of, Manoa, HI
Hebrew Coll, MA
Heidelberg Coll, OH
Henderson State U, AR
Heritage U, WA
High Point U, NC
Hobart and William Smith Colls, NY
Hollins U, VA
Holy Cross, Coll of the, MA
Holy Family U, PA
Holy Names U, CA
Hood Coll, MD
Houghton Coll, NY
Houston Baptist U, TX
Humboldt State U, CA
Huntingdon Coll, AL
Huntington U, IN
Idaho State U, ID
Idaho, U of, ID
Illinois Coll, IL
Illinois Inst of Tech, IL
Illinois State U, IL
Illinois Wesleyan U, IL
Illinois, U of, Springfield, IL
Illinois, U of, Urbana-Champaign, IL
Immaculata U, PA
Indiana U Bloomington, IN
Indiana U of Pennsylvania, PA
Indiana U-Purdue U - Fort Wayne, IN
Iowa, U of, IA
Ithaca Coll, NY
Jacksonville State U, AL
Jacksonville U, FL
James Madison U, VA
Jamestown Coll, ND
Jefferson Coll of Health Professions, PA
John Brown U, AR
John Carroll U, OH
Johns Hopkins U, MD
Johnson & Wales U, CO
Johnson C. Smith U, NC
Juniata Coll, PA
Kalamazoo Coll, MI
Kansas State U, KS
Kean U, NJ
Keene State Coll, NH
Kennesaw State U, GA
Kent State U, OH
Kentucky Christian U, KY
Kentucky Wesleyan Coll, KY
Kettering U, MI
Keystone Coll, PA
King Coll, TN
Knox Coll, IL
Kutztown U of Pennsylvania, PA
La Roche Coll, PA
La Salle U, PA
Lake Erie Coll, OH
Lamar U, TX
Lambuth U, TN
Lander U, SC
Lawrence U, WI
Lebanon Valley Coll, PA
Lee U, TN
Lees-McRae Coll, NC
Lehigh U, PA
LeMoyne Coll, NY
Lenoir-Rhyne Coll, NC
Lewis and Clark Coll, OR
Lewis U, IL
Liberty U, VA
Life U, GA
Lindsey Wilson Coll, KY
Linfield Coll, OR
Lipscomb U, TN
Long Island U - Brooklyn, NY
Louisiana State U in Shreveport, LA
Louisiana State U - Baton Rouge, LA
Louisiana, U of, Lafayette, LA
Lourdes Coll, OH
Loyola Coll in Maryland, MD
Loyola U Chicago, IL
Loyola U New Orleans, LA
Lubbock Christian U, TX
Luther Coll, IA
Lycoming Coll, PA
Lyndon State Coll, VT
Macalester Coll, MN
MacMurray Coll, IL
Madonna U, MI
Maine Maritime Academy, ME
Maine, U of, Farmington, ME
Maine, U of, Machias, ME
Malone Coll, OH
Manchester Coll, IN
Manhattanville Coll, NY
Marian Coll of Fond du Lac, WI
Marietta Coll, OH
Marquette U, WI
Mary, U of, ND
Maryland, U of, Baltimore County, MD
Maryland, U of, Coll Park, MD
Marylhurst U, OR
Marymount U, VA
Maryville Coll, TN
Maryville U of St. Louis, MO
Marywood U, PA
Massachusetts Coll of Art, MA
Massachusetts Coll of Liberal Arts, MA
Massachusetts Inst of Tech, MA
Massachusetts, U of, Amherst, MA
Master's Coll and Seminary, CA
McDaniel Coll, MD
McGill U, CN
McKendree Coll, IL
McMurry U, TX
Medaille Coll, NY

Menlo Coll, CA
Mercer U, GA
Meredith Coll, NC
Mesa State Coll, CO
Messiah Coll, PA
Methodist Coll, NC
Metropolitan State Coll of Denver, CO
Miami U - Oxford, OH
Michigan State U, MI
Michigan Technological U, MI
Michigan, U of, Dearborn, MI
Michigan, U of, Flint, MI
Middle Tennessee State U, TN
Middlebury Coll, VT
Midwestern State U, TX
Millersville U of Pennsylvania, PA
Millikin U, IL
Mills Coll, CA
Millsaps Coll, MS
Milwaukee Inst of Art and Design, WI
Milwaukee School of Engineering, WI
Minneapolis Coll of Art and Design, MN
Minnesota State U - Mankato, MN
Minnesota State U - Moorhead, MN
Minot State U, ND
Mississippi Coll, MS
Mississippi State U, MS
Mississippi U for Women, MS
Missouri Southern State U, MO
Missouri, U of, Kansas City, MO
Molloy Coll, NY
Monmouth Coll, IL
Montana State U - Billings, MT
Montana State U - Bozeman, MT
Montclair State U, NJ
Montevallo, U of, AL
Montserrat Coll of Art, MA
Moore Coll of Art and Design, PA
Moravian Coll, PA
Morehouse Coll, GA
Morgan State U, MD
Mount Holyoke Coll, MA
Mount Mercy Coll, IA
Mount St. Mary Coll, NY
Mount St. Mary's Coll, CA
Mount St. Mary's U, MD
Mount Vernon Nazarene U, OH
Muhlenberg Coll, PA
Murray State U, KY
National U, CA
Nazareth Coll of Rochester, NY
Nebraska Wesleyan U, NE
Nebraska, U of, Omaha, NE
Neumann Coll, PA
Nevada, U of, Las Vegas, NV
New Coll of Florida, FL
New England Coll, NH
New Haven, U of, CT
New Jersey Inst of Tech, NJ
New School U, NY
New York U, NY
Niagara U, NY
Nicholls State U, LA
Nichols Coll, MA
Norfolk State U, VA
North Alabama, U of, AL
North Carolina State U - Raleigh, NC
North Carolina Wesleyan Coll, NC
North Carolina, U of, Asheville, NC
North Carolina, U of, Greensboro, NC
North Central Coll, IL
North Dakota State U, ND
North Georgia Coll and State U, GA
North Greenville Coll, SC
North Park U, IL
Northeastern Illinois U, IL
Northeastern State U, OK
Northern Arizona U, AZ
Northern Colorado, U of, CO
Northern Illinois U, IL
Northern Iowa, U of, IA
Northern Kentucky U, KY
Northern State U, SD
Northwest Christian Coll, OR
Northwest Missouri State U, MO
Northwest Nazarene U, ID
Northwest U, WA
Northwestern Coll (Minnesota), MN
Northwestern State U of Louisiana, LA
Northwestern U, IL
Northwood U, MI
Northwood U - Florida Campus, FL
Northwood U - Texas Campus, TX
Norwich U, VT
Notre Dame Coll of Ohio, OH
Notre Dame de Namur U, CA
Notre Dame of Maryland, Coll of, MD
Nova Scotia Coll of Art and Design, CN
Nyack Coll, NY
Oakland U, MI
Oberlin Coll, OH
Occidental Coll, CA
Ohio State U - Columbus, OH
Ohio Valley Coll, WV
Ohio Wesleyan U, OH
Oklahoma Christian U, OK
Oklahoma City U, OK
Old Dominion U, VA
Olivet Coll, MI
Olivet Nazarene U, IL
Oral Roberts U, OK
Oregon Inst of Tech, OR
Oregon State U, OR
Otterbein Coll, OH
Ouachita Baptist U, AR
Our Lady of the Lake U, TX
Pace U, NY
Pacific Union Coll, CA
Pacific U, OR
Park U, MO
Parsons School of Design, NY
Paul Smith's Coll, NY
Peace Coll, NC
Peirce Coll, PA
Pennsylvania State U - Altoona, PA
Pennsylvania State U - Berks, PA
Pennsylvania State U - Lehigh Valley, PA
Pennsylvania State U, U Park, PA
Pennsylvania State - Erie, The Behrend Coll, PA
Peru State Coll, NE
Pfeiffer U, NC
Philadelphia U, PA
Pine Manor Coll, MA
Pittsburg State U, KS
Pittsburgh, U of, Greensburg, PA
Pitzer Coll, CA
Point Loma Nazarene U, CA
Point Park U, PA
Pomona Coll, CA
Portland, U of, OR
Post U, CT
Pratt Inst, NY
Presbyterian Coll, SC
Prescott Coll, AZ
Princeton U, NJ
Providence Coll, RI
Purdue U, IN
Purdue U - North Central, IN
Quincy U, IL
Quinnipiac U, CT
Radford U, VA
Ramapo Coll of New Jersey, NJ
Randolph-Macon Coll, VA
Randolph-Macon Woman's Coll, VA
Redlands, U of, CA
Reformed Bible Coll, MI
Regis Coll, MA
Rensselaer Polytechnic Inst, NY
Rhode Island Coll, RI
Rhodes Coll, TN
Rice U, TX
Richard Stockton Coll of New Jersey, NJ
Richmond, The American International U in London, UK
Rider U, NJ
Roanoke Coll, VA
Robert Morris U, PA
Rochester Coll, MI
Rochester Inst of Tech, NY
Rockford Coll, IL
Rocky Mountain Coll, MT
Roger Williams U, RI
Rollins Coll, FL
Rose-Hulman Inst of Tech, IN
Russell Sage Coll, NY
Rutgers U - Camden Coll of Arts and Sciences, NJ
Sacred Heart U, CT
Saginaw Valley State U, MI
Samford U, AL
San Diego State U, CA
Santa Clara U, CA
Santa Fe, Coll of, NM
Savannah Coll of Art and Design, GA
School of the Art Inst of Chicago, IL
Scripps Coll, CA
Seattle U, WA
Seton Hall U, NJ
Seton Hill U, PA
Shaw U, NC
Shawnee State U, OH
Shenandoah U, VA
Shepherd U, WV
Shippensburg U of Pennsylvania, PA
Siena Coll, NY
Simmons Coll, MA
Simon Fraser U, CN

Colleges with Services

Simpson Coll, IA
Simpson U, CA
Skidmore Coll, NY
Smith Coll, MA
Sonoma State U, CA
South Alabama, U of, AL
South Dakota School of Mines & Tech, SD
Southeast Missouri State U, MO
SE Coll of the Assemblies of God, FL
Southeastern Louisiana U, LA
Southern California, U of, CA
Southern Christian U, AL
Southern Connecticut State U, CT
Southern Illinois U - Carbondale, IL
Southern Illinois U - Edwardsville, IL
Southern Maine, U of, ME
Southern Methodist U, TX
Southern Nazarene U, OK
Southern New Hampshire U, NH
Southern U and A&M Coll, LA
Southwest Baptist U, MO
Southwest Minnesota State U, MN
Southwest, Coll of the, NM
Southwestern Oklahoma State U, OK
Southwestern U, TX
Spalding U, KY
Spelman Coll, GA
Spring Arbor U, MI
Springfield Coll, MA
St. Ambrose U, IA
St. Andrews Presbyterian Coll, NC
St. Augustine's Coll, NC
St. Benedict, Coll of, MN
St. Catherine, Coll of, MN
St. Edward's U, TX
St. Francis U, PA
St. Francis, U of, IL
St. Francis, U of, IN
St. John's U, NY
St. John's U, MN
St. Joseph Coll, CT
St. Joseph's Coll, ME
St. Joseph's Coll, IN
St. Joseph's U, PA
St. Lawrence U, NY
St. Leo U, FL
St. Louis U, MO
St. Martin's Coll, WA
St. Mary, Coll of, NE
St. Mary-of-the-Woods Coll, IN
St. Mary's Coll, IN
St. Mary's Coll of California, CA
St. Mary's Coll of Maryland, MD
St. Mary's U of Minnesota, MN
St. Mary's U of San Antonio, TX
St. Michael's Coll, VT
St. Norbert Coll, WI
St. Olaf Coll, MN
St. Paul's Coll, VA
St. Scholastica, The Coll of, MN
St. Thomas, U of, MN
St. Vincent Coll, PA
St. Xavier U, IL
Stanford U, CA
Stephen F. Austin State U, TX
Sterling Coll, KS

Stetson U, FL
Stonehill Coll, MA
Suffolk U, MA
SUNY at Binghamton, NY
SUNY at Buffalo, NY
SUNY at New Paltz, NY
SUNY Coll at Old Westbury, NY
SUNY Coll at Oneonta, NY
SUNY Coll of A&T - Cobleskill, NY
SUNY Coll of Arts/Sciences - Geneseo, NY
SUNY Coll - Brockport, NY
SUNY Coll - Cortland, NY
SUNY Coll - Potsdam, NY
SUNY Inst of Tech at Utica/Rome, NY
SUNY Upstate Medical U, NY
SUNY, Empire State Coll, NY
SUNY - Albany, NY
SUNY - Buffalo State Coll, NY
SUNY - Fredonia, NY
SUNY - Oswego, NY
SUNY - Plattsburgh, NY
Swarthmore Coll, PA
Sweet Briar Coll, VA
Syracuse U, NY
Tabor Coll, KS
Tampa, U of, FL
Taylor U, IN
Temple U, PA
Temple U, Ambler Campus, PA
Tennessee Wesleyan Coll, TN
Texas A&M U - Coll Station, TX
Texas A&M U - Corpus Christi, TX
Texas A&M U - Galveston, TX
Texas A&M U - Kingsville, TX
Texas A&M U - Texarkana, TX
Texas Christian U, TX
Texas Lutheran U, TX
Texas State U - San Marcos, TX
Texas, U of, the Permian Basin, TX
Texas, U of, Tyler, TX
The Citadel, SC
Thomas More Coll, KY
Tiffin U, OH
Trevecca Nazarene U, TN
Trinity Baptist Coll, FL
Trinity Christian Coll, IL
Trinity Coll, CT
Trinity U, DC
Troy State U Dothan, AL
Troy State U - Troy, AL
Truman State U, MO
Tufts U, MA
Tulane U, LA
Tusculum Coll, TN
Tuskegee U, AL
Union Coll, NY
Union Coll, NE
Union Inst and U, OH
Union U, TN
Unity Coll, ME
U of Akron, OH
U of Alabama, AL
U of Alabama - Huntsville, AL
U of Alaska - Fairbanks, AK
U of Baltimore, MD
U of Bridgeport, CT

U of California - Irvine, CA
U of California - Los Angeles, CA
U of California - Riverside, CA
U of California - San Diego, CA
U of Central Arkansas, AR
U of Central Florida, FL
U of Central Oklahoma, OK
U of Colorado - Boulder, CO
U of Colorado - Colorado Springs, CO
U of Delaware, DE
U of Dubuque, IA
U of Evansville, IN
U of Houston, TX
U of Illinois - Chicago, IL
U of Kansas, KS
U of Kentucky, KY
U of La Verne, CA
U of Maine - Augusta, ME
U of Maine - Orono, ME
U of Maine - Presque Isle, ME
U of Massachusetts - Boston, MA
U of Massachusetts - Dartmouth, MA
U of Massachusetts - Lowell, MA
U of Memphis, TN
U of Miami, FL
U of Michigan - Ann Arbor, MI
U of Minnesota - Crookston, MN
U of Minnesota - Duluth, MN
U of Minnesota - Morris, MN
U of Minnesota - Twin Cities, MN
U of Mississippi, MS
U of Missouri - Columbia, MO
U of Missouri - Rolla, MO
U of Missouri - St. Louis, MO
U of Montana, MT
U of New England, ME
U of New Hampshire, NH
U of North Carolina - Charlotte, NC
U of North Carolina - Wilmington, NC
U of North Dakota, ND
U of North Florida, FL
U of North Texas, TX
U of Notre Dame, IN
U of Oregon, OR
U of Pennsylvania, PA
U of Pittsburgh, PA
U of Pittsburgh - Bradford, PA
U of Pittsburgh - Johnstown, PA
U of Prince Edward Island, CN
U of Puget Sound, WA
U of Rhode Island, RI
U of Rio Grande, OH
U of Rochester, NY
U of Science and Arts of Oklahoma, OK
U of Scranton, PA
U of Sioux Falls, SD
U of South Carolina - Aiken, SC
U of South Carolina - Columbia, SC
U of Southern Indiana, IN
U of Southern Mississippi, MS
U of Tennessee, TN
U of Tennessee - Chattanooga, TN
U of Texas - Arlington, TX
U of Texas - Austin, TX
U of Texas - Dallas, TX
U of Texas - Pan American, TX

U of the District of Columbia, DC
U of the Incarnate Word, TX
U of the Pacific, CA
U of Tulsa, OK
U of Utah, UT
U of Vermont, VT
U of Victoria, CN
U of West Alabama, AL
U of West Florida, FL
U of West Georgia, GA
U of Wisconsin - Green Bay, WI
U of Wisconsin - La Crosse, WI
U of Wisconsin - Madison, WI
U of Wisconsin - Stout, WI
U of Wisconsin - Superior, WI
U of Wisconsin - Whitewater, WI
U of Wyoming, WY
Utah Valley State Coll, UT
Utica Coll, NY
Valdosta State U, GA
Valley City State U, ND
Valparaiso U, IN
Vanderbilt U, TN
Vanguard U of Southern California, CA
Vassar Coll, NY
Vermont Technical Coll, VT
Villa Julie Coll, MD
Villanova U, PA
Virginia Intermont Coll, VA
Virginia Military Inst, VA
Virginia Polytech Inst and State U, VA
Virginia Wesleyan Coll, VA
Virginia, U of, VA
Virginia, U of, Wise, VA
Viterbo U, WI
Wake Forest U, NC
Waldorf Coll, IA
Walla Walla Coll, WA
Walsh U, OH
Warren Wilson Coll, NC
Washburn U, KS
Washington and Jefferson Coll, PA
Washington and Lee U, VA
Washington Coll, MD
Washington State U, WA
Washington U in St. Louis, MO
Washington, U of, WA
Wayne State Coll, NE
Wayne State U, MI
Waynesburg Coll, PA
Webster U, MO
Wellesley Coll, MA
Wells Coll, NY
Wentworth Inst of Tech, MA
Wesley Coll, DE
Wesleyan Coll, GA
Wesleyan U, CT
West Chester U of Pennsylvania, PA
West Liberty State Coll, WV
West Texas A&M U, TX
West Virginia U at Parkersburg, WV
Western Carolina U, NC
Western Kentucky U, KY
Western Michigan U, MI
Western New England Coll, MA
Western Oregon U, OR
Western Washington U, WA
Westminster Choir Coll of Rider U, NJ
Westminster Coll, PA
Westminster Coll, UT
Westmont Coll, CA
Wheaton Coll, MA
Wheaton Coll, IL
Wheeling Jesuit U, WV
Whitman Coll, WA
Whittier Coll, CA
Whitworth Coll, WA
Widener U, PA
Willamette U, OR
William Carey Coll, MS
William Jewell Coll, MO
William Paterson U of New Jersey, NJ
William Penn U, IA
William Woods U, MO
Williams Baptist Coll, AR
Williams Coll, MA
Wilmington Coll, OH
Wilson Coll, PA
Wingate U, NC
Winona State U, MN
Winston-Salem State U, NC
Winthrop U, SC
Wittenberg U, OH
Wofford Coll, SC
Woodbury U, CA
Worcester Polytechnic Inst, MA
Worcester State Coll, MA
Xavier U, OH
Yale U, CT
York Coll of Pennsylvania, PA
Youngstown State U, OH

Colleges with Accommodations

Acadia U, CN
Adams State Coll, CO
Advancing Tech, U of, AZ
Alabama A&M U, AL
Alaska Bible Coll, AK
Alaska Pacific U, AK
Alaska, U of, Southeast, AK
Albany Coll of Pharmacy of Union U, NY
Albany State U, GA
Alberta, U of, CN
Albertus Magnus Coll, CT
Alcorn State U, MS
Alice Lloyd Coll, KY
Allen Coll, IA
Allen U, SC
Alvernia Coll, PA
Amberton U, TX
American Baptist Coll, TN
American Coll of Greece, GR
American Indian Arts, Inst of, NM
American Indian Coll, Assemblies of God, AZ
American InterContinental U - Buckhead, GA
American Intercontinental U - Dubai, ARE
American InterContinental U - FL
American InterContinental U - Houston, TX
American Intercontinental U - London, EN
American InterContinental U - Dunwoody, GA
American InterContinental U - LA, CA
American Military U, VA
American U in Bulgaria, BU
American U of Paris, FR
American U of Puerto Rico, PR
Angelo State U, TX
Anna Maria Coll, MA
Antillean Adventist U, PR
Antioch Coll, OH
Appalachian Bible Coll, WV
Aquinas Coll, TN
Arizona State U, AZ
Arizona State U East, AZ
Arkansas Baptist Coll, AR
Arkansas, U of, Fort Smith, AR
Arlington Baptist Coll, TX
Armstrong Atlantic State U, GA
Armstrong U, CA
Art Inst of Boston at Lesley U, MA
Art Inst of California - San Diego, CA
Art Inst of California - San Francisco, CA
Art Inst of Colorado, CO
Art Inst of Dallas, TX
Art Inst of Fort Lauderdale, FL
Art Inst of Las Vegas, NV
Art Inst of LA - Orange County, CA
Art Inst of Pittsburgh, PA
Art Inst of Portland, OR
Art Inst of Washington, VA
Art U, Academy of, CA
Asbury Coll, KY
Ashford U, IA
Assumption Coll, MA
Athens State U, AL
Atlanta Christian Coll, GA
Atlanta Coll of Art, GA
Atlantic Union Coll, MA
Averett U, VA
Azusa Pacific U, CA

Bacone Coll, OK
Baker Coll of Auburn Hills, MI
Baker Coll of Cadillac, MI
Baker Coll of Clinton Township, MI
Baker Coll of Flint, MI
Baker Coll of Jackson, MI
Baker Coll of Muskegon, MI
Baker Coll of Owosso, MI
Baker Coll of Port Huron, MI
Baltimore Hebrew U, MD
Baptist Bible Coll, MO
Baptist Bible Coll and Seminary, PA
Baptist Coll of Health Sciences, TN
Barber Scotia Coll, NC
Barclay Coll, KS
Barton Coll, NC
Bastyr U, WA
Bates Coll, ME
Beacon Coll, FL
Becker Coll, MA
Belhaven Coll, MS
Bellarmine U, KY
Belmont Abbey Coll, NC
Benedict Coll, SC
Benjamin Franklin Inst of Tech, MA
Bennett Coll, NC
Berkeley Coll, NY
Berkeley Coll - New Jersey, NJ
Beth Medrash Govoha, NJ
Bethany Coll, KS
Bethany Coll, CA
Bethany Lutheran Coll, MN
Bethel Coll, TN
Bethune-Cookman Coll, FL
Beulah Heights Bible Coll, GA
BI Norwegian School of Management, NL
Biola U, CA
Birmingham-Southern Coll, AL
Black Hills State U, SD
Blackburn Coll, IL
Blessing-Rieman Coll of Nursing, IL
Boise Bible Coll, ID
Boise State U, ID
Boricua Coll, NY
Boston Conservatory, MA
Bowie State U, MD
Brescia U, KY
Bridgewater Coll, VA
Brigham Young U - Hawaii, HI
Brigham Young U - Idaho, ID
British Columbia, U of, CN
Brock U, CN
Brooks Inst of Photography, CA
Bryn Athyn Coll of the New Church, PA
Bucknell U, PA
Cabarrus Coll of Health Sciences, NC
Calgary, U of, CN
California Coll of the Arts and Crafts, CA
California Lutheran U, CA
California Maritime Academy, CA
California State U - Dominguez Hills, CA
California State U - Long Beach, CA
California State U - Northridge, CA
California State U - San Marcos, CA
California U of Pennsylvania, PA
California, U of, Berkeley, CA

California, U of, Davis, CA
California, U of, Santa Barbara, CA
Calumet Coll of St. Joseph, IN
Calvary Bible Coll and Theological Seminary, MO
Cambridge Coll, MA
Campbell U, NC
Campbellsville U, KY
Capital U, OH
Capitol Coll, MD
Cardinal Stritch U, WI
Caribbean U, PR
Carleton U, CN
Carroll Coll, MT
Carroll Coll, WI
Carson-Newman Coll, TN
Castleton State Coll, VT
Catawba Coll, NC
Cedar Crest Coll, PA
Cedarville U, OH
Centenary Coll of Louisiana, LA
Central Baptist Coll, AR
Central Bible Coll, MO
Central Christian Coll of the Bible, MO
Central de Bayamon, Universidad, PR
Central Methodist U, MO
Central Missouri State U, MO
Central State U, OH
Chadron State Coll, NE
Chaminade U of Honolulu, HI
Champlain Coll, VT
Charles R. Drew U of Medicine and Science, CA
Charleston Southern U, SC
Charter Oak State Coll, CT
Chester Coll of New England, NH
Chestnut Hill Coll, PA
Cheyney U of Pennsylvania, PA
Chowan Coll, NC
Christendom Coll, VA
Christian Heritage Coll, CA
Christopher Newport U, VA
Cincinnati Christian U, OH
Cincinnati Coll of Mortuary Science, OH
Cincinnati, U of, OH
Circleville Bible Coll, OH
City U, WA
Claflin U, SC
Clark Atlanta U, GA
Clark U, MA
Clarke Coll, IA
Clarkson U, NY
Clear Creek Baptist Bible Coll, KY
Cleary U, MI
Cleveland Chiropractic Coll, MO
Cleveland Inst of Art, OH
Cleveland State U, OH
Cogswell Polytechnical Coll, CA
Coker Coll, SC
Colby Coll, ME
Colby-Sawyer Coll, NH
Colegio Biblico Pentecostal, PR
Coleman Coll, CA
Coll for Creative Studies, MI
Coll of New Rochelle, NY
Coll of St. Joseph, VT

Coll of St. Thomas More, TX
Colorado Christian U, CO
Colorado State U - Pueblo, CO
Colorado Technical U, CO
Colorado, U of, Denver and Health Sciences Center, CO
Columbia Coll, MO
Columbia Coll, SC
Columbia Coll - Hollywood, CA
Columbia Union Coll, MD
Conception Seminary Coll, MO
Concordia Coll, AL
Concordia U, CN
Concordia U, OR
Concordia U, CA
Concordia U Wisconsin, WI
Concordia U - Austin, TX
Concordia U - River Forest, IL
Conservatory of Music of Puerto Rico, PR
Converse Coll, SC
Cooper Union, The, NY
Coppin State U, MD
Corban Coll, OR
Corcoran Coll of Art and Design, DC
Cornell Coll, IA
Covenant Coll, GA
Cox Coll of Nursing & Health Sciences, MO
Crichton Coll, TN
Crossroads Coll, MN
Crown Coll, MN
Cumberland U, TN
Cumberlands, U of the, KY
CUNY, City Coll, NY
CUNY - Brooklyn Coll, NY
CUNY - Hunter Coll, NY
CUNY - New York City Coll of Tech, NY
Curtis Inst of Music, PA
Daemen Coll, NY
Dallas Christian Coll, TX
Dallas, U of, TX
Daniel Webster Coll, NH
Davenport U, MI
Davidson Coll, NC
Davis Coll, NY
Deaconess Coll of Nursing, MO
Defiance Coll, OH
Delaware State U, DE
Delta State U, MS
DeSales U, PA
Design Inst of San Diego, CA
Detroit Mercy, U of, MI
DeVry Inst of Tech - Calgary, CN
DeVry Inst of Tech - New York, NY
DeVry Inst of Tech - New York, NY
DeVry U - South Florida, FL
DeVry U - Decatur, GA
DeVry U - Houston, TX
DeVry U - Orlando, FL
DeVry U - Philadelphia, PA
DeVry U Center - Bethesda, MD
DeVry U Center - Charlotte, NC
DeVry U Center - Edina, MN
DeVry U Center - Henderson, NV
DeVry U Center - Indianapolis, IN
DeVry U Center - Merrillville, IN
DeVry U Center - Milwaukee, WI
DeVry U Center - Portland, OR
DeVry U - Addison, IL
DeVry U - Alpharetta, GA
DeVry U - Chicago, IL
DeVry U - Columbus, OH
DeVry U - Denver, CO
DeVry U - Fremont, CA
DeVry U - Irving, TX
DeVry U - Long Beach, CA
DeVry U - Missouri, MO
DeVry U - North Brunswick, NJ
DeVry U - Phoenix, AZ
DeVry U - Pomona, CA
DeVry U - Seattle, WA
DeVry U - Tinley Park, IL
DeVry U - West Hills, CA
Divine Word Coll, IA
Dixie State Coll of Utah, UT
Doane Coll, NE
Dominican Coll of Blauvelt, NY
Dowling Coll, NY
Drew U, NJ
Drexel U, PA
Duke U, NC
D'Youville Coll, NY
Earlham Coll, IN
East Central U, OK
Eastern Michigan U, MI
Eastern Nazarene Coll, MA
Eastern New Mexico U, NM
Eastern Oregon U, OR
Eastern U, PA
East-West U, IL
Edward Waters Coll, FL
Elms Coll, MA
Elon U, NC
Embry Riddle Aeronautical U, FL
Embry Riddle Aeronautical U - Prescott, AZ
Emmanuel Coll, GA
Emmaus Bible Coll, IA
Erskine Coll, SC
Este, Universidad del, PR
Eugene Bible Coll, OR
Evangel U, MO
Excelsior Coll, NY
Fairfield U, CT
Fairmont State U, WV
Faith Baptist Bible Coll and Theological Seminary, IA
Fayetteville State U, NC
Felician Coll, NJ
Finlandia U, MI
Fisk U, TN
Five Towns Coll, NY
Florida A&M U, FL
Florida Christian Coll, FL
Florida Coll, FL
Florida Inst of Tech, FL
Florida International U, FL
Florida Memorial Coll, FL
Florida Metropolitan U - Brandon, FL
Florida Metropolitan U - Jacksonville, FL
Florida Metropolitan U - Lakeland, FL
Florida Metropolitan U - Melbourne, FL
Florida Metropolitan U - North Orlando, FL
Florida Metropolitan U - Pinellas, FL
Florida Metropolitan U - South Orlando, FL
Florida Metropolitan U - Tampa, FL
Florida Metropolitan U - Fort Lauderdale, FL
Florida Southern Coll, FL
Fort Hays State U, KS
Framingham State Coll, MA
Frank Lloyd Wright Sch of Architecture, AZ
Franklin U, OH
Free Will Baptist Bible Coll, TN
Freed-Hardeman U, TN
George Fox U, OR
George Mason U, VA
Georgia Southwestern State U, GA
Gettysburg Coll, PA
Goddard Coll, VT
God's Bible School and Coll, OH
Golden Gate U, CA
Goldey Beacom Coll, DE
Grace Bible Coll, MI
Grace U, NE
Grambling State U, LA
Grand Canyon U, AZ
Grand Valley State U, MI
Granite State Coll, NH
Gratz Coll, PA
Great Basin Coll, NV
Great Lakes Christian Coll, MI
Greenville Coll, IL
Grove City Coll, PA
Guam, U of, GU
Guelph, U of, CN
Guilford Coll, NC
Gustavus Adolphus Coll, MN
Hampden-Sydney Coll, VA
Hampton U, VA
Hannibal-LaGrange Coll, MO
Hanover Coll, IN
Harrington Coll of Design, IL
Hartford, U of, CT
Harvard U, MA
Haskell Indian Nations U, KS
Hawaii Pacific U, HI
Hawaii, U of, Hilo, HI
Hawaii, U of, West Oahu, HI
Hellenic Coll, MA
Hendrix Coll, AR
Henry Cogswell Coll, WA
Heritage Christian U, AL
Hilbert Coll, NY
Hillsdale Coll, MI
Hiram Coll, OH
Holy Apostles Coll and Seminary, CT
Hope Coll, MI
Hope International U, CA
Houston, U of, Clear Lake, TX
Houston, U of, Downtown, TX
Houston, U of, Victoria, TX
Howard Payne U, TX
Howard U, DC
Humphreys Coll, CA
Huron U USA in London, UK
Husson Coll, ME
Huston-Tillotson U, TX
Illinois Inst of Art at Chicago, IL
Illinois Inst of Art at Schaumburg, IL
Indiana Inst of Tech, IN

Colleges with Accommodations

Indiana State U, IN
Indiana U East, IN
Indiana U Northwest, IN
Indiana U Southeast, IN
Indiana U - Kokomo, IN
Indiana U-Purdue U - Indianapolis, IN
Indiana U - South Bend, IN
Indiana Wesleyan U, IN
Inst of Computer Tech, CA
Inter American U - Arecibo, PR
Inter American U - Barranquitas, PR
Inter American U - Guayama, PR
Inter American U - Aguadilla, PR
Inter American U - Bayamon, PR
Inter American U - Fajardo, PR
Inter American U - Metro Campus, PR
Inter American U - Ponce, PR
Interior Designers Inst, CA
International Academy of Design & Tech, IL
International Academy of Design & Tech, FL
International Coll, FL
International Coll of the Cayman Islands, CI
Iowa State U, IA
Iowa Wesleyan Coll, IA
Jackson State U, MS
Jarvis Christian Coll, TX
John F. Kennedy U, CA
John Wesley Coll, NC
Johnson & Wales U at Charlotte, NC
Johnson & Wales U at North Miami, FL
Johnson and Wales U, RI
Johnson Bible Coll, TN
Jones Coll, FL
Judaism, U of, CA
Judson Coll, IL
Judson Coll, AL
Juilliard School, NY
Kansas City Art Inst, MO
Kansas Wesleyan U, KS
Kendall Coll, IL
Kentucky Mountain Bible Coll, KY
Kentucky State U, KY
Kenyon Coll, OH
Keuka Coll, NY
King's Coll, NY
Knoxville Coll, TN
La Sierra U, CA
Laboratory Inst of Merchandising, NY
Lafayette Coll, PA
LaGrange Coll, GA
Laguna Coll of Art and Design, CA
Lake Forest Coll, IL
Lake Superior State U, MI
Lakeland Coll, WI
Lakeview Coll of Nursing, IL
Lancaster Bible Coll, PA
Lane Coll, TN
Langston U, OK
Lasell Coll, MA
Laura and Alvin Siegal Coll of Judaic Studies, OH
Lawrence Technological U, MI
LeMoyne-Owen Coll, TN
Lesley U, MA
LeTourneau U, TX
Lewis-Clark State Coll, ID

Life Pacific Coll, CA
Lincoln Christian Coll and Seminary, IL
Lincoln Memorial U, TN
Lincoln U, MO
Lincoln U, CA
Lincoln U, PA
Lindenwood U, MO
Livingstone Coll, NC
Lock Haven U of Pennsylvania, PA
Loma Linda U, CA
Longwood U, VA
Longy School of Music, MA
Louisiana State U Health Sciences Center, LA
Louisiana Tech U, LA
Louisiana, U of, Monroe, LA
Loyola Marymount U, CA
Lyme Academy Coll of Fine Arts, CT
Lynchburg Coll, VA
Lyon Coll, AR
Magnolia Bible Coll, MS
Maharishi U of Management, IA
Maine Coll of Art, ME
Manhattan Christian Coll, KS
Manhattan Coll, NY
Manhattan School of Music, NY
Mannes Coll of Music, NY
Mansfield U of Pennsylvania, PA
Maranatha Baptist Bible Coll, WI
Marlboro Coll, VT
Martin Luther Coll, MN
Martin Methodist Coll, TN
Martin U, IN
Mary Baldwin Coll, VA
Mary Hardin-Baylor, U of, TX
Marygrove Coll, MI
Maryland Inst Coll of Art, MD
Maryland, U of, Baltimore, MD
Maryland, U of, Eastern Shore, MD
Marymount Coll, NY
Massachusetts Coll of Pharmacy and Health Sciences, MA
Massachusetts Maritime Academy, MA
Mayville State U, ND
McNeese State U, LA
McPherson Coll, KS
Medcenter One Coll of Nursing, ND
MedCentral Coll of Nursing, OH
Medical Coll of Georgia, GA
Medical U of South Carolina, SC
Memorial U of Newfoundland, CN
Memphis Coll of Art, TN
Mercy Coll of Health Sciences, IA
Merrimack Coll, MA
Metropolitan Coll of New York, NY
Metropolitan State U, MN
Metropolitana, Universidad, PR
Miami International U of Art & Design, FL
Mid-America Christian U, OK
MidAmerica Nazarene U, KS
Mid-Continent U, KY
Midland Lutheran Coll, NE
Midway Coll, KY
Midwestern U, IL
Miles Coll, AL
Milligan Coll, TN

Mississippi Valley State U, MS
Mississippi, U of, Medical Center, MS
Missouri Baptist U, MO
Missouri Tech, MO
Missouri Valley Coll, MO
Missouri Western State Coll, MO
Mobile, U of, AL
Monmouth U, NJ
Montana State U - Northern, MT
Montana Tech of the U of Montana, MT
Montana, U of, Western, MT
Monterrey Inst of Tech and Higher Ed
Montreat Coll, NC
Moody Bible Inst, IL
Morehead State U, KY
Morris Brown Coll, GA
Morris Coll, SC
Morrison U, NV
Mount Aloysius Coll, PA
Mount Carmel Coll of Nursing, OH
Mount Marty Coll, SD
Mount Mary Coll, WI
Mount Olive Coll, NC
Mount Union Coll, OH
Mountain State U, WV
Mt. Sierra Coll, CA
Multnomah Bible Coll, OR
Museum of Fine Arts, School of the, MA
Myers U, OH
NAES Coll, IL
Naropa U, CO
National American U, SD
National Hispanic U, CA
National-Louis U, IL
Nazarene Bible Coll, CO
Nebraska Christian Coll, NE
Nebraska Methodist Coll, NE
Nebraska, U of, Lincoln, NE
Nebraska, U of, Medical Center, NE
Ner Israel Rabbinical Coll, MD
Nevada, U of, Reno, NV
New Coll of California, CA
New England Conservatory of Music, MA
New England Inst of Art, MA
New Hampshire, U of, at Manchester, NH
New Mexico Highlands U, NM
New Mexico Inst of Mining and Tech, NM
New Mexico State U, NM
New York School of Interior Design, NY
Newberry Coll, SC
Newbury Coll, MA
Newman U, KS
Newschool of Architecture, CA
North Carolina A&T State U, NC
North Carolina Central U, NC
North Carolina School of the Arts, NC
North Central U, MN
Northeastern U, MA
Northern Michigan U, MI
Northland Coll, WI
Northwest Coll of Art, WA
Northwestern Coll (Iowa), IA
Northwestern Oklahoma State U, OK
Northwestern Polytechnic U, CA
Nova Southeastern U, FL
Oak Hills Christian Coll, MN

Oakland City U, IN
Oakwood Coll, AL
Oglala Lakota Coll, SD
Oglethorpe U, GA
Ohio Dominican U, OH
Ohio Northern U, OH
Ohio State U - Lima, OH
Ohio State U - Mansfield, OH
Ohio State U - Marion, OH
Ohio State U - Newark, OH
Ohio U, OH
Oklahoma Baptist U, OK
Oklahoma Panhandle State U, OK
Oklahoma State U, OK
Oklahoma Wesleyan U, OK
Oklahoma, U of, Health Sciences Ctr, OK
O'More Coll of Design, TN
Oregon Coll of Art and Craft, OR
Oregon Health and Sciences U, OR
Otis Coll of Art and Design, CA
Ottawa U, KS
Ottawa, U of, CN
Our Lady of Holy Cross Coll, LA
Our Lady of the Lake Coll, LA
Ozark Christian Coll, MO
Pacific Lutheran U, WA
Pacific Northwest Coll of Art, OR
Pacific Oaks Coll, CA
Pacific States U, CA
Paier Coll of Art, CT
Paine Coll, GA
Palm Beach Atlantic U, FL
Palmer Coll of Chiropractic, IA
Patten U, CA
Paul Quinn Coll, TX
Pennsylvania Coll of Tech, PA
Pennsylvania State U - Schuylkill, PA
Pennsylvania State U - Abington, PA
Pennsylvania State U - Harrisburg, PA
Pepperdine U, CA
Philadelphia Biblical U, PA
Philander Smith Coll, AR
Phoenix, U of, AZ
Piedmont Baptist Coll, NC
Piedmont Coll, GA
Pikeville Coll, KY
Platt Coll, CO
Plymouth State U, NH
Polytechnic U, NY
Pontifical Coll Josephinum, OH
Portland State U, OR
Potomac Coll, DC
Presentation Coll, SD
Principia Coll, IL
Puerto Rico, U of, Arecibo, PR
Puerto Rico, U of, Bayamon U Coll, PR
Puerto Rico, U of, Cayey U Coll, PR
Puerto Rico, U of, Mayaguez, PR
Puerto Rico, U of, Medical Sciences Campus, PR
Puerto Rico, U of, Ponce, PR
Puget Sound Christian Coll, WA
Purdue U - Calumet, IN
Rabbinical Coll of America, NJ
Reed Coll, OR
Regent U, VA
Regent's Coll, UK
Regis U, CO
Research Coll of Nursing, MO
Rhode Island School of Design, RI
Richmond, U of, VA
Ringling School of Art and Design, FL
Ripon Coll, WI
Ritsumeikan Asia Pacific U, JP
Rivier Coll, NH
Roanoke Bible Coll, NC
Robert Morris Coll, IL
Roberts Wesleyan Coll, NY
Rockhurst U, MO
Rocky Mountain Coll of Art & Design, CO
Roosevelt U, IL
Rosemont Coll, PA
Rush U, IL
Rust Coll, MS
Rutgers - Camden, NJ
Rutgers - New Brunswick, NJ
Rutgers - Newark, NJ
Ryerson U, CN
Sacred Heart Major Seminary, MI
Sacred Heart, U of the, PR
Salem Coll, NC
Salem International U, WV
Salem State Coll, MA
Salisbury U, MD
Salish Kootenai Coll, MT
Salve Regina U, RI
Sam Houston State U, TX
Samuel Merritt Coll, CA
San Francisco Art Inst, CA
San Francisco Conserv of Music, CA
San Francisco State U, CA
San Jose State U, CA
Sarah Lawrence Coll, NY
Savannah State U, GA
Schiller International U, FL
Seattle Pacific U, WA
Sewanee - U of the South, TN
Shasta Bible Coll, CA
Sheldon Jackson Coll, AK
Shimer Coll, IL
Shorter Coll, GA
Si Tanka U, SD
Siena Heights U, MI
Sierra Nevada Coll, NV
Silver Lake Coll, WI
Simon's Rock Coll of Bard, MA
Sinte Gleska U, SD
Slippery Rock U of Pennsylvania, PA
Sojourner-Douglass Coll, MD
South Carolina State U, SC
South Dakota State U, SD
South U (Florida), FL
South U (Georgia), GA
Southeastern Baptist Coll, MS
Southeastern Baptist Theological Seminary, NC
Southeastern Bible Coll, AL
Southeastern Oklahoma State U, OK
Southeastern U, DC
Southern Adventist U, TN
Southern Arkansas U, AR
Southern CA Inst of Architecture, CA
Southern Polytechnic State U, GA
Southern U at New Orleans, LA
Southern Utah U, UT
Southern Vermont Coll, VT
Southern Wesleyan U, SC
Southwestern Adventist U, TX
Southwestern Assemblies of God U, TX
Southwestern Christian Coll, TX
Southwestern Christian U, OK
Southwestern Coll, KS
Southwestern Coll, AZ
Spring Hill Coll, AL
St. Anselm Coll, NH
St. Anthony Coll of Nursing, IL
St. Bonaventure U, NY
St. Cloud State U, MN
St. Francis Coll, NY
St. John Fisher Coll, NY
St. John Vianney Coll Seminary, FL
St. John's Coll, NM
St. John's Coll, MD
St. John's Coll, IL
St. John's Seminary, MA
St. John's Seminary Coll, CA
St. Joseph Seminary Coll, LA
St. Joseph's Coll New York - Brooklyn, NY
St. Joseph's Coll - Suffolk, NY
St. Louis Christian Coll, MO
St. Louis Coll of Pharmacy, MO
St. Luke's Coll, MO
St. Mary, U of, KS
St. Thomas U, FL
St. Thomas, U of, TX
Stephens Coll, MO
Sterling Coll, VT
Stevens Inst of Tech, NJ
Stevens-Henager Coll - Provo, UT
Stevens-Henager Coll - Salt Lake City, UT
Stevens-Henager Coll - Ogden, UT
Stillman Coll, AL
Strayer U, DC
Sul Ross State U, TX
Sullivan U, KY
SUNY Coll of Environmental Science and Forestry, NY
SUNY Coll of Tech at Alfred, NY
SUNY Downstate Medical Center, NY
SUNY Maritime Coll, NY
SUNY Purchase Coll, NY
SUNY - Farmingdale, NY
SUNY - Stony Brook, NY
Susquehanna U, PA
Talladega Coll, AL
Talmudic U of Florida, FL
Talmudical Academy of New Jersey, NJ
Tarleton State U, TX
Taylor U - Fort Wayne, IN
Teikyo Loretto Heights U, CO
Tennessee State U, TN
Tennessee Technological U, TN
Tennessee Temple U, TN
Texas A&M U - Commerce, TX
Texas Chiropractic Coll, TX
Texas Coll, TX
Texas Southern U, TX
Texas Tech U, TX

Colleges with Accommodations

Texas Wesleyan U, TX
Texas Woman's U, TX
Texas, U of, Brownsville and Texas Southmost Coll, TX
Texas, U of, El Paso, TX
The American U - Cairo, EG
The Art Inst of Tampa, FL
The Criswell Coll, TX
The U of Winnipeg, CN
Thiel Coll, PA
Thomas Aquinas Coll, CA
Thomas Coll, ME
Thomas Edison State Coll, NJ
Thomas More Coll of Liberal Arts, NH
Thomas U, GA
Tilburg U, NS
Toccoa Falls Coll, GA
Toronto, U of, CN
Tougaloo Coll, MS
Touro Coll, NY
Towson U, MD
Transylvania U, KY
Trent U, CN
Trinity Bible Coll, ND
Trinity Coll of Florida, FL
Trinity International U, FL
Trinity International U, IL
Trinity Lutheran Coll, WA
Trinity U, TX
Trinity Western U, CN
Tri-State U, IN
Troy State U - Montgomery, AL
Truett McConnell Coll, GA
Turabo, Universidad del, PR
Union Coll, KY
United States Air Force Academy, CO
United States Coast Guard Academy, CT
United States Merchant Marine Acad, NY
United States Military Academy, NY
United States Naval Academy, MD
Universidad Politecnica, PR
U of Arizona, AZ
U of Arkansas - Monticello, AR
U of Arkansas - Pine Bluff, AR
U of Charleston, WV
U of Chicago, IL
U of Kansas Medical Center, KS
U of Louisville, KY
U of Maine - Fort Kent, ME
U of Maryland - U Coll, MD
U of Nebraska - Kearney, NE
U of New Brunswick, CN
U of New Mexico, NM
U of New Orleans, LA
U of North Carolina - Pembroke, NC
U of Oklahoma, OK
U of Puerto Rico - Humacao, PR
U of Regina, CN
U of San Diego, CA
U of Saskatchewan, CN
U of South Carolina - Upstate, SC
U of South Dakota, SD
U of Texas - San Antonio, TX
U of the Arts, PA
U of the Sciences in Philadelphia, PA
U of Windsor, CN
U of Wisconsin - Eau Claire, WI
U of Wisconsin - Milwaukee, WI
U of Wisconsin - Oshkosh, WI
U of Wisconsin - Parkside, WI
Upper Iowa U, IA
Urbana U, OH
Ursinus Coll, PA
Utah State U, UT
Valley Forge Christian Coll, PA
VanderCook Coll of Music, IL
Vaughn Coll of Aeronautics and Tech, NY
Vennard Coll, IA
Virgin Islands, U of the, VI
Virginia Commonwealth U, VA
Virginia State U, VA
Virginia Union U, VA
Visual Arts, Coll of, MN
Visual Arts, School of, NY
Voorhees Coll, SC
Wabash Coll, IN
Wagner Coll, NY
Warner Pacific Coll, OR
Warner Southern Coll, FL
Wartburg Coll, IA
Washington Bible Coll, MD
Waterloo, U of, CN
Wayland Baptist U, TX
Webb Inst, NY
Webber International U, FL
Weber State U, UT
Wesley Coll, MS
West Los Angeles, U of, CA
West Suburban Coll of Nursing, IL
West Virginia State U, WV
West Virginia U, WV
West Virginia U Inst of Tech, WV
Western Connecticut State U, CT
Western Illinois U, IL
Western International U, AZ
Western New Mexico U, NM
Western Ontario, U of, CN
Western State Coll of Colorado, CO
Westfield State Coll, MA
Wheelock Coll, MA
Wilberforce U, OH
Wiley Coll, TX
Wilkes U, PA
William Jessup U, CA
Wilmington Coll, DE
Winona State U - Rochester Center, MN
Wisconsin Lutheran Coll, WI
Wisconsin, U of, Platteville, WI
Wisconsin, U of, River Falls, WI
Wisconsin, U of, Stevens Point, WI
Wright State U, OH
Xavier U of Louisiana, LA
Yeshiva Beth Yehuda - Yeshiva Gedolah of Greater Detroit, MI
Yeshiva Ohr Elchonon-Chabad/West Coast Talmud Seminary, CA
Yeshiva U, NY
York Coll, NE